THE ENCYCLOPEDIA *of* HOLLYWOOD FILM ACTORS

ABOUT THE AUTHOR

BARRY MONUSH is the Associate Editor of *Screen World*
and a researcher at the Museum of Television and Radio
in New York City. He also contributes to the the film magazine
Scarlet Street. His favorite film of all time is *Sunset Boulevard*.

SCREEN WORLD PRESENTS

THE ENCYCLOPEDIA *of* HOLLYWOOD FILM ACTORS

FROM THE SILENT ERA TO 1965

BARRY MONUSH

APPLAUSE
THEATRE & CINEMA BOOKS

Screen World Presents: The Encyclopedia of Hollywood Film Actors
From the Silent Era to 1965
by Barry Monush
Copyright © 2003 by Barry Monush

ISBN: 1-55783-551-9

Library of Congress Cataloging-in-Publication Data
Screen World Presents the Encyclopedia of Hollywood Film Actors
    / edited by Barry Monush.
    p. cm.
ISBN: 1-55783-551-9 (v. 1)
1. Motion picture actors and actresses—
    United States—Biography—Dictionaries.
1. Monush, Barry.

PN 1998.2.S38 2002
791.43'028'092273 – dc21
                    2002152728

British Library Cataloging in Publication Data
A catalogue record for this book is available from the British Library

APPLAUSE THEATRE & CINEMA BOOKS
151 West 46th Street, 8th floor
New York, NY 10036
Phone: 212-575-9265
Fax: 646-562-5852
Email: info@applausepub.com

SALES AND DISTRIBUTION:
USA
HAL LEONARD CORPORATION
7777 West Bluemound Road
P.O. Box 13819
Milwaukee, WI 53213
Phone: 414-774-3630
Fax: 414-774-3259
Email: halinfo@halleonard.com
Internet: www.halleonard.com

UK
COMBINED BOOK SERVICES LTD
Units 1/K, Paddock Wood Distribution Centre
Paddock Wood, Tonbridge, Kent TN12 6UU
United Kingdom
Phone: (44) 01892 837171
Fax: (44) 01892 837272

Printed in Canada

TABLE OF CONTENTS

Introduction by Jeffrey Lyons   vii
Preface   ix
The Encyclopedia of Hollywood Film Actors   1
Bibliography   818

To Tom,
who makes going to *any* movie—good, bad, or indifferent—
an absolute pleasure.

INTRODUCTION

Early in his career, future Oscar winner Nicolas Cage was costarring in *Peggy Sue Got Married*, and was experimenting on camera with an unusual voice. A bit perturbed, so the story goes, his costar and title player Kathleen Turner gave him some valuable advice: "Film lasts forever," she cautioned. "Be careful what you do." Good advice. Film is indeed forever, and so is this comprehensive gathering of life stories and careers of many of the screen's immortals and supporting players. It's all here, as never before.

The secret of any good interview is research. You never can have too many sources. And I've never seen any better than *Screen World Presents: The Encyclopedia of Hollywood Film Actor*s. Anyone can assemble biographical sketches of actors and actresses, toss them together, and call it an Encyclopedia. The trick is conveying a sense of why each star listed deserves a place in film history; to be sure, some have been the subject of many biographies. But others, like Royal Dano, a fine but forgotten 1950s character actor, or the luminous Madge Evans, one of the bright stars of her era, might otherwise be forgotten. The book includes the early television credits of Sir Stanley Baker, a now nearly forgotten British tough guy who

was a friend of Sirs Sean Connery and Michael Caine in their pre-stardom years. The book is a treasure trove of research about actors few people remember like Eric Blore, Charles Butterworth, and William Haines.

Open any page and you will learn a fascinating tidbit. Early in her career, for example, Betty Grable was billed as "Frances Dean," and Margaret Hamilton, who terrorized generations of children as the Wicked Witch in *The Wizard of Oz*, ran a nursery school and taught kindergarten before she became an actress. This amazing compilation contains a hard-to-find listing of Robert Benchley's witty short films, and describes Al Jolson, perhaps the best all-around performer of the 20th century, as having an "overly ripe personality." The accompanying photographs are the type which used to appear in wallets and picture frames at Woolworth's, and no doubt come from studio files, conveying the glamour those stars enjoyed in their heyday.

Just as *Screen World* and its companion volume *Theater World*, this is a starting point for research, or simply to wander through the lives of some of the greatest movie stars of all time. Enjoy!

Jeffrey Lyons

Jeffrey Lyons, the film and theater critic for New York's WNBC-TV and the film critic for KNBC Los Angeles, also hosts "The Lyons Den," a nationally syndicated radio showbusiness report. A son of the late Broadway columnist Leonard Lyons, he's reviewed nearly 10,000 movies since 1970, wrote 101 Great Movies for Kids, *and with his brother, co-authored two baseball trivia books,* Out of Left Field *and* Curveballs and Screwballs. *His godmother, Madge Evans, is profiled on page 223.*

PREFACE

A Word or Two About Movie Stars

It is a common assumption that many people go to movies because of the stars in them. I know I do. Although there are plenty of directors whose work I find worth checking out on a regular basis and various genres or topics that intrigue me, I know that certain actors can get me to see even the most unappetizing of projects. This is an accomplishment. And it is even more of an accomplishment to come away from a bad film with your admiration for a performer unblemished. I believe that the best actors *can* do wonders with bad material and I never cease to marvel at how dedicated or devoted so many of them are to giving their all, even in hopeless circumstances.

Of course, all of life is change, hence the mind-boggling number of performers who have come and gone since the inception of motion pictures — some making so indelible a mark that their names have become a part of show business folklore, while others are remembered by close relatives, if at all. This, of course, does not always have to do with talent, for some incredibly gifted people were never given their proper due or chance to show just how impressive they could be. And there are just as many cases where people became famous stars despite the lack of anything akin to a great range or awesome depth of performance. Instead, they had that "something extra" that James Mason tried to explain to Judy Garland in *A Star Is Born*, a God-given spark that could not be taught by experts or created by the Hollywood dream factory, but simply bestowed upon them at birth. How fortunate for us that these particular people chose the correct profession in which to express themselves.

Although the advantages of being a movie star are obvious, passing into that higher realm of notoriety can have its downside as well. For one thing, a performer can never predict when the audience has had enough of them, whether that second or third chance for reinvention or rebirth will come along, or if they've exhausted whatever it is they have to offer. Audiences are fickle and shockingly disloyal. Chances are moviegoers like a star because they expect to see them in a certain type of role and have little desire to watch them stretch beyond that pigeonhole. Of course, it's unlikely that most actors went into the profession to play one part and one part only. Instead the aim (apart from receiving complimentary drinks from adoring fans) was to amass as varied a list of credits and roles as possible. This does not always go down well with the critical masses. But just as it is all too common that audiences *don't* want a performer to stray too far away from that which makes the viewer comfortable, they are just as likely to sense a sameness, an unwillingness or inability to grow, and a stale sense of repetition with those playing it too safe and familiar. Just as quickly they move on to the next big thing, until that "big thing" proves too small in their eyes. It is a no-win situation.

I am, therefore, amazed and impressed by how long certain actors were and are able to sustain their careers. In a business eager to move on to the fresh and new, it is remarkable how several performers were able to keep interest in their services alive over several decades. I have a certain level of respect even for actors for whom I have little or no fondness; to get anywhere beyond the auditioning stage is achievement enough; to get a substantial part in a film is even more impressive; to keep your name before the public for even so much as a five-year period should not be underestimated.

Everyone brings some degree of baggage to each and every movie they see, and actors seem to take the worst beating. This has much to do with their prominence in the media. Interviews, press releases, and think pieces lead us to believe that we know these people or have certain perceptions about them. This can be distracting when watching a movie, in so much as it is often hard to look past the actor and see the character. If you'll notice, critics tend to be a lot more impressed by independent or foreign movies that feature performers they've never heard of before. In contrast, a known actor often finds him or herself being reviewed in connection to previous roles or their private life. We have all heard people say that they will *not* go see someone's movie because of something they read about that actor's personal life, which, of course, should in no way effect what we are seeing on screen. I have even heard people reject an actor on the basis that they had the audacity to change their hairstyle; again, a no-win situation.

But the stars keep on coming and we are still interested in them. I have often heard it said that we like them because they mirror ourselves, or because they represent a larger-than-life version of what we would like to be. Someone once theorized to me that they are "our heroes" and I suppose to some degree he was right. This is why it is probably better *not* to know them outside of the images we see on the screen. It is not too far-fetched to say all of us have a tendency to forget that these people deal in the business of illusions. We assume that they are exactly like certain characters they are playing, so that when presented in person with the real thing, we can be severely disappointed. I myself have met my share of actors up close and have been shocked to see how serious most of them are (in a profession that seems like so much fun to we outsiders), how insecure many can be, how critical or disinterested they are of work that does not involve themselves, how unenlightened so many are about the work that has gone on before them, and how many strike me as borderline nuts. And yet I love them just the same and cannot help but find them fascinating.

A Foreword of Sorts

This first volume of *Screen World Presents: The Encyclopedia of Hollywood Film Actors, From the Silent Era to 1965* covers approximately the first fifty years of the star system (1915-1965). Although the mostly forgotten Florence Lawrence is often cited as the first performer whose name was used to sell a movie, I would credit the true origin of lasting film stardom to Charlie Chaplin, Mary Pickford, and Lillian Gish (the only American-born actor of this group). All of these actors came to prominence in the years 1912-1916, Ms. Gish being featured in what is frequently declared as the first truly important full-length motion picture, *The Birth of a Nation*, in 1915. If we jump fifty years from that point we find Ms. Lawrence long out of the picture and dead, having committed suicide in 1938, after ending up in bit roles; Ms. Pickford rich and happily retired in Beverly Hills; Mr. Chaplin, living in exile, having reached a near folkloric level of immortality and just on the verge of creating his last film; and Ms. Gish, a real trouper in her 70s, still seeking and receiving work. We also see the last remains of the studio star system, which pretty much fell apart during the 1960s.

Other than the 1920s, which started silent and ended with sound, there is probably no other decade of film that changed so thoroughly and excitingly as did the 1960s. For that reason it is my own personal favorite period for motion pictures. Where else can you find a ten-year span that started off with a film like *Please Don't Eat the Daisies* and finished with *Midnight Cowboy*; two pictures as far apart as can be in style and approach, and yet both fine examples of what they were setting out to accomplish? Although hundreds of actors, famous and not, continued to work as movies made this change, it is not inaccurate to suggest that many stars who were prominent as the 1960s dawned were dropping out of fashion by the latter half of the decade. *Daisies*'s star Doris Day was finished with films by 1969, leaving behind a Hollywood that no longer deemed her relevant. Likewise, an actor like *Midnight Cowboy*'s Dustin Hoffman would probably have seemed out of place or failed to make an impact at the start of the very decade that would make him famous.

Of course, the late 1960s also brought the demise of the production code and the beginning of the ratings system.

Once the movies were told they could get away with pretty much whatever they pleased, a certain degree of honesty and realism that had been denied by restrictions and limitations was now possible. As a result certain performers who looked right at home in glossier studio product were now glaringly out of place. It all seemed to happen overnight.

I have therefore tried to include in this volume as many performers who became prominent "motion picture" names before or in the year 1965. This, of course, is problematic with some people who were certainly in films prior to the "cut-off" date but hadn't exactly made a major impact in the medium until afterwards. If a star that was around before 1965 is missing from this volume, chances are you'll find them in volume two.

Choosing who to include and who to leave out of this project was often a difficult process. There are certain people whose inclusion in any reference on motion pictures is inarguable. They are all here, I hope. In other cases I have used personal judgment, because some, although they might not have as many credits as others, are extremely engaging performers who have lit up the screen no matter how little exposure they've received there. All actors who have received Academy Awards are included. Of course, we all have our opinions on which ones have been deserved and not deserved, but winning this trophy is something that cannot be dismissed. Because of it, these Oscar winners have earned their place in history and should be remembered.

A capsule description of the performer's career (some longer than others, according to importance) is followed by a list of film appearances, as complete as I know it to be. When I have included actors who are known principally for their work in foreign movies, I've narrowed their film list down to only their motion pictures that played in the United States. I've listed short subjects only for performers who were prominent in this area. As anyone who has compiled such a text knows, it is a nightmare to try to verify the existence of certain credits or an actor's appearance in them. Often a project was announced for someone and then cancelled or re-cast, only to have the credit remain on the actor's résumé or in reference books. In other instances a movie underwent several title changes or variations depending on where it was released. As a result, sometimes a filmography will accidentally include *multiple* titles for the same movie, with each one treated as if it is different picture altogether. The age of video and cable television has also brought forth further confusion as to where or when, if at all, a movie premiered. In many cases a movie intended for theatrical release went directly to videocassette, while others have shown up in the dead of night on cable television's graveyard shift, only to wind up with theatrical premieres after the fact. Therefore, deciding on which ones are movies and which are telefilms can be a headache and, often, a dead end. I have tried to split up the motion picture work from the television work, although in some instances this is still questionable. Likewise, many a foreign film has played here as a theatrical release, only to be revealed as a television presentation in its country of origin. I have tried to treat things according to how they were presented in the United States. This, too, is far from a certain thing.

For television credits I have tried to include specials (which encompass dramatic anthology series episodes, since these are not officially telefilms; therefore a production of *Playhouse 90* in which someone appeared is listed as "sp" for special), mini-series, and television movies, as well as series on which they were regular cast members. Guest spots on variety shows, talk shows, or series have not been included due to the fact that such a list would be uncontrollable.

Theatre credits included are only those reflecting the work the person did in New York, on or off Broadway, the latter indicated by (ob) following the title.

I tried to include real names and places and dates of birth with as much accuracy as possible, and, in some instances, where the person grew up and what college or university they attended. Of course, in many cases, a performer has beefed up certain statistics or information that has been passed on from generation to generation only to have some of it revealed as being bogus. (For example Greer Garson and MGM perpetrated a myth that stuck around for decades, that the star was born in Ireland, when in fact her place of birth was London, England.) I welcome any corrections on erroneous information.

Key to Abbreviations:

To save space, the following abbreviations can be found:

(nUSr)   no United States release; this has been hard to verify, but I have tried to indicate in as many instances as possible when a film was not given an official theatrical run in the United States.
(dtv)   direct-to-video
(dtc)   direct-to-cable
(sp)   a television special, or, in several cases, an episode of an anthology series that does not qualify as a movie, and therefore is treated like a special here.
(ms)   miniseries
(dir.)   director
(prod.) producer
(wr.)   writer
(ed)   educated at

I'd Like to Thank...

A very special and important thanks goes to John Willis, without whom this project would not be possible, in more ways than one. Many thanks to Walter Willison as well, who welcomed me into the *Screen World* family many years ago. And of course, I am also indebted to Glenn Young at Applause Books for giving this book the go-ahead and for Matthew Callan, John Cerullo, Greg Collins, Paul Sugarman, Michelle Thompson, Gabrielle Morgan, Carol Flannery, Signe Bergstrom, Mark Glubke, and the rest of the staff at Hal Leonard/Applause for their contributions in banging it all into shape.

In addition to the aforementioned John Willis and the late Daniel Blum, I would like to thank several people who were helpful in obtaining the photos used in this book. These include Gene Massimo, Kimberly Scherling, Richard Valley, Tom Amorosi, and Larry Billman. And thanks to the various studios and production companies, those that have endured and those that have come and gone over the years, including AFD, Allied Artists, American International Pictures, Artisan, Artistic License, Avco Embassy, Cannon, Castle Hill, Cinema 5, Cinerama, Columbia, Continental, DeLaurentiis Entertainment Group, DreamWorks, Eagle-Lion Classics, Fine Line, Goldwyn, Gramercy, The Ladd Company, Lions Gate, Lippert, Lorimar, MGM, Miramax, Monogram, National General Pictures, New Line, New Yorker, Orion, PRC, Paramount, RKO, Republic, Savoy, Sony, Strand, Taurus, Tri-Star, 20th Century-Fox, United Artists, Universal, Walt Disney, and Warner Bros.

There is no possible way for me to have done such a book without a very special thanks to every person with whom I have ever sat in a theatre or auditorium and watched a movie. In addition to my mother, my father, my sister Michelle, and my brother Bryan, as well as other family members and relatives — Hilda, Donna, Olga, Craig — I would like to thank my absolute favorite companion in everything, Tom Lynch, as well as Tom Amorosi, Bendix Anderson, Dominick Balletta, Benjamin Barrett, Rich Burgeios, Thomas Buxereau, David Christopher, Dennis Christopher, Richard D'Attile, Donna Cleary Deutchman, Larry Deutchman, Brian Durnin, Jeremy Freedman, Barry Frishman, Rich Hampton, Jim Hollifield, Greg Howard, Scott Kincel, Paul Larkins, Lois Lynch, Lori Lynch, Joe Lyttle, John McIntyre, John Metcalf, Rob Milite, David Munro, Joe Ondre, David Pickens, April Polites, Julie Riefler, Michael Richard, Malcolm Robinson, Frank Rosato, Greg Rossi, Scott Schecter, George Scherling, Kimberly Scherling, Nick Setteducato, Robert Setteducato, Robert Sleeman, John Stachneiwicz, Walt Stern, Sheldon Stone, Lynn Culp Sulpy, Doug Sulpy, John Thomas, Tom Thomas, Richard Valley, Robin Verspril, Scott Verspril, Karl Vetter, Robert Vetter, Jon Webster, Mark Weinberg, Steven West, Ilene Wilets, David Zeliff, and all those other wonderful people out there in the dark whose names presently escape me.

BARRY MONUSH

A

BUD ABBOTT

(William Alexander Abbott) Born: Asbury Park, NJ, October 2, 1895. Died: April 24, 1974.

& LOU COSTELLO

(Louis Francis Cristillo) Born: Paterson, NJ, March 6, 1906. Died: March 3, 1959.

Bud Abbott and Lou Costello were the most popular comedy team of the 1940s. Their carefully formulated exchanges feautured straight man Abbott leading a fidgety Costello through an increasingly frustrating minefield of physical and verbal obstacles. Their movies were unapologetically designed to shoehorn these routines into a showcase for Costello's deft pratfalls, while Abbott dutifully fed his colorful sidekick the set-up lines.

The team first came together in 1935 when they were both on the vaudeville bill at the Eltinge Theatre in New York City. Prior to this, Abbott had worked as a box-office manager and producer, and as a straight man for comic Harry Evanson. Costello had done extra and stunt work for the movies before ending up as a burlesque comedian, teaming with straight man Joe Lyons. Abbott and Costello's success onstage landed them regular radio work on *The Kate Smith Hour* in 1938, and on Broadway in the revue *Streets of Paris*. This resulted in a 1940 contract with Universal Pictures where they would stay for 15 years, with occasional sidetrips to other studios, notably MGM, who had wanted them in the first place.

Initially thrown into the supporting cast of a minor musical comedy, *One Night in the Tropics*, they stole the show (at one point incorporating their most enduring routine, "Who's On First?" into the proceedings) and clearly proved themselves worthy of their own vehicles. Their first starring assignment, *Buck Privates*, was a safe bet (comedians set loose in the army) and the money rolled in. It set the tone for what was to follow: find an appropriate, or rather inappropriate, backdrop for the team to run wild, pepper it with songs, gags, girls, and maybe a chase scene. More importantly there were plenty of old routines which they'd done together onstage and radio, so these were sprinkled throughout their movies, with little regard to whether they had much to do with anything else that was happening in the film. Therefore, movie audiences got to experience such favorites as "7x13=28" (*In the Navy*), "The Susquehanna Hat Company" (*In Society*) and "My Bonnie" (*Naughty Nineties*), not to mention a reprise of "Who's On First?" which popped up in its definitive incarnation in *The Naughty Nineties*, a mere five years after they'd first filmed it. The odd couple was sent to cause havoc at a haunted house (*Hold That Ghost*), a mansion (*In Society*), the South Seas (*Pardon My Sarong*), a ski resort (*Hit the Ice*) and a dude ranch (*Ride 'em Cowboy*) with predictable, but sometimes undeniably amusing, results. During all this they scurried over to MGM for *Rio Rita*, with Kathryn Grayson sharing screen time; *Lost in a Harem*; and *Abbott and Costello in Hollywood*, none of which looked all that different from their Universal attractions, outside of Metro's glossier sheen.

Abbott and Costello Meet Frankenstein, which teamed the duo with not only the Frankenstein Monster but Dracula and the Wolf Man, made sure there were chills among the chuckles. It not only became their biggest hit and most highly-regarded effort, but proved to be the model for future combinations of horror and humor. Their off-beat fantasy *The Time of Their Lives*, in which they basically did not act off each other as a team, contained some of their best work, whereas a previous attempt to split them up, *Little Giant*, featuring Abbott in a dual role, was coldly received. By the end of the 1940s their popularity was beginning to wane and ideas seemed to be running dry. Their films in the 1950s often had a cheaper, half-hearted feel and, taking a cue from the Frankenstein film, usually had them meeting some such fantasy figure as The Invisible Man or The Mummy, reaching a career nadir by encountering Dr. Jekyll and Mr. Hyde. Over at Warners, they were thrown into two especially juvenile excursions, *Jack and the Beanstalk* and *Abbott and Costello Meet Captain Kidd*, which were noteworthy because they were the team's only pictures in color. They broke up shortly after their last pairing, *Dance With Me, Henry*, in 1956, both of them looking tired and too old for this sort of nonsense. Lou appeared in one solo effort, *The 30-Foot Bride of Candy Rock*, released shortly after his death. Abbott remained mostly inactive, though he supplied the voice of his animated self for a series of Abbott and Costello cartoons, made for television in 1966. By that time, frequent telecasts of their films had made them favorites once again, though to many critics their appeal remained a mystery.

Screen: Abbott and Costello: 1940: One Night in the Tropics; 1941: Buck Privates; In the Navy; Hold That Ghost; Keep 'em Flying; 1942: Ride 'em Cowboy; Rio Rita; Pardon My Sarong; Who Done It?; 1943: It Ain't Hay; Hit the Ice; 1944: In Society; Lost in a Harem; 1945: Here Come the Co-Eds; The Naughty Nineties; Abbott and Costello in Hollywood; 1946: Little Giant; The Time of Their Lives; 1947: Buck Privates Come Home; The Wistful Widow of Wagon Gap; 1948: The Noose Hangs High; Abbott and Costello Meet Frankenstein; Mexican Hayride; 1949: Africa Screams; Abbott and Costello Meet the Killer — Boris Karloff; 1950: Abbott and Costello in the Foreign Legion; 1951: Abbott and Costello Meet the Invisible Man; Comin' Round the Mountain; 1952: Jack and the Beanstalk; Lost in Alaska; Abbott and Costello Meet Captain Kidd; 1953: Abbott and Costello Go to Mars; Abbott and Costello Meet Dr. Jekyll & Mr. Hyde; 1955: Abbott and Costello Meet the Keystone Cops; Abbott and Costello Meet the Mummy; 1956: Dance With Me, Henry.
Costello: 1959: The 30-Foot Bride of Candy Rock.
NY Stage: Abbott and Costello: 1939: Streets of Paris.
Select TV: Abbott and Costello: 1951–54: The Colgate Comedy Hour (series); 1952–53: The Abbott and Costello Show (series).
Abbott: 1961: The Joke's on Me (sp); 1966: The Abbott and Costello Show (series; voice).
Costello: 1958: Blaze of Glory (sp).

WALTER ABEL

Born: St. Paul, MN, June 6, 1898. ed: AADA.
Died: March 26, 1987.

Mustachioed character actor Walter Abel worked as both an actor and stage manager with various touring companies before establishing himself on Broadway. He made his talking picture debut on a high note, starring in the 1930 film version of *Liliom*, long before it was turned into *Carousel*. Five years later his movie career proper was launched after securing a contract with RKO. For them he played D'Artagnan in one of the lesser versions of *The Three Musketeers*; an amnesiac who may have committed murder in *Two in the Dark*; a corporate executive accused of killing his boss in *The Witness Chair*; and a widowed father contemplating re-marriage in *Second Wife*. It was clear from these early efforts that Abel lacked star quality, so he was almost immediately relegated to supporting mode. In 1938 he made his first movie for Paramount, *Men With Wings*, as a reporter and airplane enthusiast, and it was for that company that he would do most of his work during the next decade, often playing bosses and fathers in varying states of exasperation. There were standout appearances in *Arise, My Love*, as an editor; *Holiday Inn*, as a frantic manager; *The Affairs of Susan*, as one of Joan Fontaine's stable of lovers; and, in a more serious vein, the Marine commander in *Wake Island*. His later, more sporadic movie career included roles as a cavalry officer in *The Indian Fighter*; Montgomery Clift's dad in *Raintree County*; and the boss who goes flying out the window in the thriller *Mirage*.
Screen: 1918: Out of a Clear Sky; 1920: The North Wind's Malice; 1930: Liliom; 1935: The Three Musketeers; 1936: Two in the Dark; The Lady Consents; The Witness Chair; Second Wife; Fury; We Went to College; 1937: Green Light; Portia on Trial; Wise Girl; 1938: Law of the Underworld; Racket Busters; Men With Wings; 1939: King of the Turf; 1940: Dance, Girl, Dance; Arise, My Love; Who Killed Aunt Maggie?; Michael Shayne: Private Detective; Miracle on Main Street; 1941: Hold Back the Dawn; Skylark; Glamour Boy; 1942: Holiday Inn; Beyond the Blue Horizon; Wake Island; Star Spangled Rhythm; 1943: Fired Wife; So Proudly We Hail!; 1944: An American Romance; Follow the Boys; The Hitler Gang (narrator); Mr. Skeffington; 1945: The Affairs of Susan; Kiss and Tell; Duffy's Tavern; 1946: 13 Rue Madeleine; The Kid From Brooklyn; Dream Girl; 1948: That Lady in Ermine; 1953: So This Is Love; Island in the Sky; 1954: Night People; 1955: The Indian Fighter; 1956: The Steel Jungle; 1957: Raintree County; Bernardine; 1958: Handle With Care; 1965: Mirage; Quick, Let's Get Married/The Confession/7 Different Ways (nUSr); 1973: Silent Night, Bloody Night; 1985: Grace Quigley.
NY Stage: 1919: Forbidden; 1922: Back to Methuselah; 1923: A Square Peg; 1924: Spoole Sonata; Fashion; The Crime in the Whistler Room; S.S. Glencairn (and 1928 revival); 1925: Beyond; Michael Auclair; Love for Love; The Enemy; 1926: The Hangman's House; 1927: The House of Women; 1928: Skidding; 1929: The Sea Gull; First Mortgage; 1930: At the Bottom; 1931: I Love an Actress; 1932: Mourning Becomes Electra; When Ladies Meet; 1933: Divine Grudge; The Drums Begin; 1934: Wife Insurance; Invitation to a Murder; 1936: The Wingless Victory; 1945: The Mermaids Singing; 1947: Parlor Story; 1949: The Biggest Thief in Town; 1950: The Wisteria Trees; 1952: The Long Watch; 1958: The Pleasure of His Company; 1962: Night Life; 1967: The Ninety-Day Mistress; 1974: Saturday Sunday Monday; 1975: Trelawny of the Wells.
Select TV: 1950: Hedda Gabler (sp); Uncle Vanya (sp); 1951: Ruggles of Red Gap (sp); 1953: There's No Place Like Home (sp); 1954: Twelve Angry Men (sp); 1956: Sincerely Willis Wayde (sp); 1959: Suspicion (series); 1960: The Enchanted (sp); 1966: And Baby Makes Five (sp); 1974: Man Without a Country.

EDIE ADAMS

(Edith Elizabeth Enke) Born: Kingston, PA, April 15, 1927. ed: Juilliard School of Music, Columbia School of Drama.

Adept at musicals, comedies, and dramas, Edie Adams may have lacked a singular, shimmering talent but she did her job with an engaging professionalism. The winner of such contests as Miss US TV (!), Adams was hired to sing on Ernie Kovacs's variety series, *Ernie in Kovacsland*, in 1951. After appearing together in the offbeat comedian's follow-up series, the two were married in 1955. Subsequently she found fame on Broadway, billed as Edith Adams, winning a Theatre World Award for *Wonderful Town* and a Tony Award, in 1956, for playing Daisy Mae in the musical *Li'l Abner*. When she was ready for films she made an impressive debut, as Fred MacMurray's vengeful secretary, in the Oscar-winning *The Apartment*. Thereafter, she played off such comedy pros as Bob Hope (*Call Me Bwana*), Sid Caesar (*It's a Mad Mad Mad Mad World*), and Jack Lemmon (*Under the Yum Yum Tree*), and had a showy bit as a stripper (with the intriguing name Barbara of Seville) in *Love With the Proper Stranger*. Following Kovacs's death in an auto accident in 1962, Adams had her own short-lived variety series, *The Edie Adams Show* (1963–64). She showed up as one of Rex Harrison's greedy mistresses, a fading film star, in the ensemble piece *The Honey Pot*, but once the 1960s came to a close her movie roles were few. In a 1984 television biopic of Kovacs she played Mae West, while Melody Anderson portrayed Adams.
Screen: 1960: The Apartment; 1961: Lover Come Back; 1963: Call Me Bwana; It's a Mad Mad Mad Mad World; Under the Yum Yum Tree; Love With the Proper Stranger; 1964: The Best Man; 1966: Made in Paris; The Oscar; 1967: The Honey Pot; 1978: Up in Smoke; 1979: Racquet (dtv/dtc); 1980: The Happy Hooker Goes Hollywood; 1982: Boxoffice.

NY Stage: 1953: Wonderful Town; 1956: Li'l Abner.

Select TV: 1951: Ernie in Kovacsland (series); 1952–53: The Ernie Kovacs Show (series); 1956: The Ernie Kovacs Show (series); 1957: Cinderella (sp); 1958: The Chevy Show (series); 1960–61: Take a Good Look; 1961: The Spiral Staircase (sp); 1963–64: The Edie Adams Show/Here's Edie (series); 1972: Evil Roy Slade; 1976: The Return of Joe Forrester/Cop on the Beat; 1978: Superdome; 1979: Fast Friends; The Seekers; 1980: Make Me an Offer; Portrait of an Escort; A Cry for Love; 1984: Ernie Kovacs: Between the Laughter; 1987: Adventures Beyond Belief/Neat and Tidy; Shooting Stars; 1989: Jake Spanner: Private Eye; 1993: Armistead Maupin's Tales of the City (ms).

JULIE ADAMS

(BETTY MAY ADAMS) BORN: WATERLOO, IA, OCTOBER 17, 1926.

A former secretary, this extremely attractive brunette with the animated eyes first appeared in movies as "Betty," then "Julia" and, finally, Julie Adams. After some early work in live television she signed with Lippert Pictures in 1949. That second-string studio decided she looked most at home on the range, so she found herself dressing up several "B" westerns, her first being The Dalton Gang. In 1951 Universal brought her on board and kept her saddle-bound in oaters like Horizons West and The Stand at Apache River. Adams was also given parts in "A" movies like Bright Victory, as Arthur Kennedy's girl who can't cope with his blindness, and Bend of the River, which, although still a western, starred James Stewart. Her lasting claim to fame, however, came when she was chosen to play the scientific researcher who is carried off in her bathing suit by The Creature From the Black Lagoon. Showcase roles failed to materialize and she was cast to be pleasant opposite such male stars as Donald O'Connor (Francis Joins the WACs), Charlton Heston (The Private War of Major Benson), and Jeff Chandler (Away All Boats). In 1957, after appearing as Richard Egan's wife in one of her better features for the company, Slaughter on Tenth Avenue, she and the studio parted company. Things hardly improved, though, and, ironically, her time with Universal would be the period for which she would be best remembered. In later years she was a regular on several television series, including Yancy Derringer, The Jimmy Stewart Show, Code Red, and two daytime serials, General Hospital and Capitol. Still looking sensational, she showed up in Dennis Hopper's 1971 weirdie The Last Movie, as an older women who attracts Hopper's dubious attention.

Screen: AS BETTY ADAMS: 1949: Red, Hot and Blue; Hostile Country; The Dalton Gang; 1950: Colorado Ranger; Crooked River; Marshal of Heldorado; For Heaven's Sake; Fast on the Draw/Sudden Death; West of the Brazos.

AS JULIA ADAMS: 1951: The Hollywood Story; Bright Victory; Finders Keepers; The Treasure of Lost Canyon; 1952: Bend of the River; Horizons West; The Lawless Breed; 1953: Mississippi Gambler; The Man From the Alamo; Wings of the Hawk; 1954: The Stand at Apache River;

AS JULIE ADAMS: 1954: Francis Joins the WACs; The Creature From the Black Lagoon; 1955: Six Bridges to Cross; The Looters; One Desire; 1956: The Private War of Major Benson; Away All Boats; 1957: Slaughter on Tenth Avenue; Four Girls in Town; 1958: Slim Carter; Tarawa Beachhead; 1959: Gunfight at Dodge City; 1960: Raymie; 1962: The Underwater City; 1965: Tickle Me; 1967: The Valley of Mystery; 1971: The Last Movie; 1974: McQ; 1975: The Killer Inside; The Wild McCulloughs; Psychic Killer; 1980: Goodbye Franklin High; The Fifth Floor; 1988: Black Roses (dtv).

Select TV: 1958–59: Yancy Derringer (series); 1969–70: General Hospital (series); 1971: The Trackers; 1971–72: The Jimmy Stewart Show (series); 1973: Go Ask Alice; 1981: Code Red; 1981–82: Code Red (series); 1980: Capitol (series); 1991: Backtrack; 1993: Conviction: The Kitty Dodds Story.

NICK ADAMS

(NICHOLAS ADAMSHOCK) BORN: NANTICOKE, PA, JULY 10, 1931. ED: ST. PETER'S COL. DIED: FEBRUARY 7, 1968.

Nick Adams was one of the many young actors who exemplified the restless youth of the 1950s, but his best role was that of the nebbishy private Ben Whitledge in the comedy hit No Time for Sergeants. Prior to that he had been seen in in many supporting roles, including parts in three of the biggest films of 1955: Mister Roberts, as a sailor; Rebel Without a Cause, as one of the rebellious teens; and Picnic, as Bomber, the paperboy. He was part of a wagon train better left unassisted by Richard Widmark in The Last Wagon, and was the impressionable lad who gets caught in the feud between brother John Derek and his nemesis Cage Clarke in Fury at Showdown. Next came No Time for Sergeants, a huge success for which co-star Andy Griffith got all the glory. Rather than waiting for the movies to make him a leading man, he gained his stardom in back-to-back television series, The Rebel and Saints and Sinners. Shortly after the cancellation of the latter he was one of The Interns, falling in love with a terminally ill patient, and did a credible Polish accent in Hell Is for Heroes. In 1963 he picked up a well-deserved supporting Oscar nomination for Twilight of Honor, a part that required him to give two interpretations of his character in conflicting flashbacks, as he tried to clear his name of murder. It was all downhill from there. Before his untimely death from a drug overdose, Adams had descended to performing in a cheapjack look at the life of Young Dillinger, and the Japanese monster flicks Frankenstein Conquers the World and Monster Zero.

Screen: 1952: Somebody Loves Me; 1955: Mister Roberts; Strange Lady in Town; I Died a Thousand Times; Rebel Without a Cause; Picnic; 1956: The Last Wagon; A Strange Adventure; Our Miss Brooks; 1957: Fury at Showdown; 1958: Sing, Boy, Sing; No Time for Sergeants; Teacher's Pet; 1959: The FBI Story; Pillow Talk; 1962: The Interns; Hell Is for Heroes; 1963: The Hook; Twilight of Honor; 1964: The Young Lovers; 1965: Young Dillinger; Die Monster Die; 1966: Don't Worry, We'll Think of a Title; Frankenstein Conquers the World; Monster Zero/Godzilla vs. Monster Zero; 1967: The Killing Bottle; 1968: Fever Heat; Mission Mars.

Select TV: 1957: The Troublemakers (sp); 1959–60: The Rebel (series); 1962: Savage Sunday (sp); 1962–63: Saints and Sinners (series); 1967: Willie and the Yank/Mosby's Marauders.

JOHN AGAR

BORN: CHICAGO, IL, JANUARY 31, 1921. DIED: APRIL 7, 2002.

Occasionally a performer becomes living proof that carving out a career in the movie business is not all struggle and rejection. John Agar was just such a sterling example. An ex-army sergeant, Agar's career began when John Ford gave him a small role in Fort Apache, which starred Shirley Temple. (The two married in 1946 but divorced three years later.) Although he had precious little acting experience, Hollywood was sufficiently impressed with his looks to give him further employment. After one more with the wife, *Adventure in Baltimore*, he showed up in a pair of John Wayne movies: *She Wore a Yellow Ribbon*, as a cavalry lieutenant; and *Sands of Iwo Jima*, where he had his most noteworthy role, as the private whose hatred for drill sergeant Wayne transforms into respect. Both were prestigious hits in 1949 and represented the novice actor's apogee in film. Never a star attraction, and severely limited in range, he was quickly relegated to "B" movies, ranging from *Man of Conflict* (a father and son drama with Edward Arnold) to *Bait* (in which he lusted after married Cleo Moore.) He slid even further from his auspicious beginnings, but found a particular place in the hearts of horror fans in such genre fare as *The Mole People*; *The Brain From Planet Arous* (in which both he and his dog were possessed by evil brains!), and *Attack of the Puppet People*. He also stayed busy in a succession of second-string westerns, including *Star in the Dust* and *Frontier Gun*. In the 1970s he retired from showbiz to sell insurance and to open an amusement park inspired by his involvment in the remake of *King Kong*, but he was occasionally coaxed back to movies for walk-ons and bit parts.

Screen: 1948: Fort Apache; 1949: Adventure in Baltimore; I Married a Communist/The Woman on Pier 13; Sands of Iwo Jima; She Wore a Yellow Ribbon; 1950: Breakthrough; 1951: Along the Great Divide; The Magic Carpet; 1952: Woman of the North Country; 1953: Man of Conflict; 1954: The Rocket Man; The Golden Mistress; Bait; Shield for Murder; 1955: Revenge of the Creature; The Lonesome Trail; Tarantula; Hold Back Tomorrow; 1956: Star in the Dust; The Mole People; 1957: Flesh and the Spur; Joe Butterfly; Ride a Violent Mile; The Brain From Planet Arous; Daughter of Dr. Jekyll; 1958: Attack of the Puppet People; Frontier Gun; Jet Attack; 1959: Invisible Invaders; 1960: Raymie; 1961: Lisette; The Hand of Death; Journey to the 7th Planet; 1963: The Young and the Brave; Cavalry Command; Of Love and Desire; 1964: Law of the Lawless; Stage to Thunder Rock; 1965: Young Fury; 1966: Johnny Reno; Women of the Prehistoric Planet; Waco; Zontar the Thing From Venus; 1967: The St. Valentine's Day Massacre; Curse of the Swamp Creature; Night Fright; 1968: Hell Raiders; 1969: The Undefeated; 1970: Chisum; 1971: Big Jake; 1976: King Kong; 1977: How's Your Love Life?; 1981: Mr. No Legs (nUSr); 1989: Miracle Mile; 1990: Nightbreed.

Select TV: 1953: The Old Man's Bride (sp); 1954: The Farnsworth Case (sp); Little War in San Dede (sp); 1957: Thousand Dollar Gun (sp); 1959: Destination Space (sp); 1990: The Perfect Bride.

BRIAN AHERNE

BORN: WORCESTERSHIRE, ENGLAND, MAY 2, 1902. ED: MALVERN COL., UNIV. OF LONDON, DIED: FEBRUARY 10, 1986.

A British attraction of the stage while in his 20s, Brian Aherne later crossed the Atlantic to become a Hollywood regular during the 1930s and 1940s. Despite his thorough professionalism and competence, he lacked pulling power with audiences, seldom being the reason anyone attended his films. A child actor at eight years old, then an architecture student in college, Aherne returned to acting at 20, appearing in a handful of British silents. A starring role in the 1931 Broadway production of *The Barretts of Wimpole Street* brought interest from Hollywood, although he was not asked to repeat his work in the movie adapation. Instead, he went over to Paramount to play a sculptor who carves Marlene Dietrich's statue and then abandons her, in the moldy melodrama *Song of Songs*. His workloaded became sufficient for him to make a comfortable living in the U.S., usually opposite stronger leading ladies. In *What Every Woman Knows*, he adopted a Scottish accent as Helen Hayes's dim politician husband; in *Sylvia Scarlet*, he was an artist with an eye on boyish Katharine Hepburn; in *Merrily We Live*, he was hired on as Constance Bennett's family chauffeur in a screwball variation of *My Man Godfrey*; and in *Skylark*, he tried to coax Claudette Colbert away from husband Ray Milland. Although he was not box-office magic, Aherne did rate an occasional showcase, such as *The Great Garrick*, playing an arrogant actor, and *Captain Fury*, as an Irishman fighting evil land baron George Zucco in 19th century Australia.

He received an Oscar nomination, for Best Supporting Actor, for his finely understated playing of the doomed Emperor Maximilian in the bio epic *Juarez*. From 1939 to 1945 he was married to actress Joan Fontaine, but they never appeared on screen together. (Ironically, she appeared in the remake of one of Aherne's British films, *The Constant Nymph*.) He had one of his best parts, as the garrulous editor who falls for Rosalind Russell in the charming comedy *My Sister Eileen*; took a dual role, playing a drunken millionaire and Puerto Rican planter, in the "B" *The Man Who Lost Himself*; teamed with Loretta Young, as a mystery author out to solve a real murder, in *A Night to Remember*; and was back with Russell, as a reporter, in a minor offering called *What a Woman!* In his 50s he began to concentrate on character roles, playing an attorney prosecuting priest Montgomery Clift in *I Confess*; the captain of the ill-fated *Titanic*; a man of the cloth in *The Swan*; and Joan Crawford's love interest in *The Best of Everything*. He had retired quietly from the screen by the late 1960s. In addition to his autobiography, *A Proper Job* (1969), he penned a biography of fellow thespian and friend George Sanders, called *A Dreadful Man* (1980).

Screen: 1924: The Eleventh Commandment; 1925: King of the Castle; The Squire of Long Hadley; 1926: Safety First; 1927: A Woman Redeemed; 1928: Shooting Stars; 1929: Underground; 1930: The W Plan; 1931: Madame Guillotine; 1933: I Was a Spy; The Constant Nymph; Song of Songs; 1934: What Every Woman Knows; The Fountain; 1935: I Live My Life; Sylvia Scarlet; 1936: Beloved Enemy; 1937: The Great Garrick; 1938: Merrily We Live; 1939: Captain Fury; Juarez; 1940: Hired Wife; The Lady in Question; My Son, My Son; Vigil in the Night; 1941: Skylark; The Man Who Lost Himself; Smilin' Through; 1942: My Sister Eileen; 1943: A Night to Remember; Forever and a Day; First Comes Courage; What a Woman!; 1946: The Locket; 1948: Smart Woman; Angel on the Amazon; 1953: I Confess; Titanic; 1954: Prince Valiant; A Bullet Is Waiting; 1956: The Swan; 1959: The Best of Everything; 1961: Susan Slade; 1963: Lancelot and Guinevere/Sword of Lancelot; 1965: The Cavern; 1967: Rosie!

NY Stage: 1927: Silver Cord; 1928: She Stoops to Conquer (and 1949); 1931: The Barretts of Wimpole Street; Lucrece; 1934: Romeo and Juliet; 1936: St. Joan; 1937: Othello; 1945: The Barretts of Wimpole Street; (revival); The French Touch; 1951: The Constant Wife; 1953: Escapade; 1954: Quadrille; 1960: Dear Liar.

Select TV: 1950: Dear Brutus (sp); 1951: A Well-Remembered Voice (sp); The Buccaneer (sp); 1953: Two for Tea (sp); 1955: The Old Flame (sp); The Martyr (sp); 1956: Pursuit of a Princess (sp); 1963: The Waltz King (sp).

CLAUDE AKINS

BORN: NELSON, GA, MAY 25, 1918. DIED: JANUARY 27, 1994.

A gruff, burly actor, Claude Akins came to films after making a brief living as a salesman. His experience in stock theatre prepared him for the variety of his early film roles. As a supporting character he shuttled between military movies (*From Here to Eternity*, as a bullying sergeant; *The Caine Mutiny*, as the colorfully-named crewman, Horrible), westerns (*Johnny Concho*, *The Lonely Man*, etc.), and gangster flicks (*Down Three Dark Streets*, *Shield for Murder*). He often played hard and unsympathetic men or even out-and-out villains. He was highly visible as a detective in the mostly-black company of *Porgy and Bess*, and was atypically cast as a fire-and-brimstone preacher in *Inherit the Wind*. As with many character players, it was television that brought him wider exposure, and he took more sympathetic leading roles on the series *B.J. and the Bear* and its spinoff, *Lobo*.

Screen: 1953: From Here to Eternity; 1954: Bitter Creek; The Caine Mutiny; Witness to Murder; The Raid; The Human Jungle; Down Three Dark Streets; The Adventures of Hajji Baba; Shield for Murder; 1955: The Sea Chase; Man with a Gun; 1956: Battle Stations; The Proud and Profane; Johnny Concho; The Burning Hills; The Sharkfighters; 1957: Hot Summer Night; The Kettles on Old MacDonald's Farm; The Lonely Man; Joe Dakota; 1958: The Defiant Ones; Onionhead; 1959: Rio Bravo; Don't Give Up the Ship; Porgy and Bess; Yellowstone Kelly; Hound-Dog Man; 1960: Comanche Station; Inherit the Wind; 1961: Claudelle Inglish; 1962: Merrill's Marauders; 1963: Black Gold; 1964: A Distant Trumpet; The Killers; 1966: Ride Beyond Vengeance; Return of the Seven; Incident at Phantom Hill; 1967: First to Fight; Waterhole #3; 1968: The Devil's Brigade; 1969: The Great Bank Robbery; 1970: Flap; 1971: A Man Called Sledge; 1972: Skyjacked; 1973: Battle for the Planet of the Apes; 1975: Timber Tramps; 1977: Tentacles; 1986: Pushed Too Far; Monster in the Closet; 1987: The Curse; 1992: Falling From Grace.

Select TV: 1971: The Night Stalker; Lock, Stock and Barrel; River of Mystery; 1973: The Norliss Tapes; 1974: Death Squad; 1975: In Tandem; Medical Story; Eric; 1974–76: Movin' On (series); 1977: The Rhinemann Exchange (ms); Yesterday's Child; Killer on Board; Nashville 99 (series); Tarantulas: The Deadly Cargo; 1978: Little Mo; 1979: B.J. and the Bear (series); Murder in Music City; Ebony, Ivory and Jade; The Concrete Cowboys; 1979–81: Lobo/The Misadventures of Sheriff Lobo (series); 1983: Desperate Intruder; 1984: Legmen (series); Celebrity; 1986: Dream West (ms); Manhunt for Claude Dallas; 1987: If It's Tuesday It Still Must Be Belgium; 1989: Mothers, Daughters and Lovers; 1991: The Gambler Returns: The Luck of the Draw; Incident at Victoria Falls; 1992: Grass Roots; 1993: Seasons of the Heart; 1994: The Search.

EDDIE ALBERT

(EDWARD ALBERT HEIMBERGER) BORN: ROCK ISLAND, IL, APRIL 22, 1908. ED: UNIV. OF MN.

An easygoing actor with a comfortable manner, Eddie Albert was a busy character performer whose flair for comedy was matched by his ability to pull off a strong dramatic part. Getting his start on radio in a show called *The Honeymooners*, Albert was brought to Hollywood in 1938 to repeat his role as one of the cadets in the film version of the hit Broadway comedy *Brother Rat*. (There was also a sequel, *Brother Rat and a Baby*.) At Warner Bros. he was given the lead in the disjointed adaptation of *On Your Toes*. (This would mark one of two instances where Albert — who could sing — appeared in a musical but was not allowed to warble a single note; the other was *Oklahoma!*) He won top-billing in the comedy *An Angel From Texas*, as an innocent getting conned into backing a show; tamed lions in *The Wagons Roll at Night*; and played it straight assisting Edward G. Robinson in the creation of the famous news service

in *A Dispatch from Reuters*. He had little to work with at Universal in a standard wartime tribute, *Eagle Squadron*, or at RKO in *Ladies' Day*, a romantic comedy that paired him with the bombastic Lupe Velez. Following naval service during World War II, he married actress Margo in 1945; had his own radio program *The Eddie Albert Show*; and was Susan Hayward's pianist buddy in *Smash Up — The Story of a Woman*. He also returned to Broadway, where he introduced "Let's Take an Old-Fashioned Walk," in Irving Berlin's *Miss Liberty*.

During the 1950s, he moved comfortably between television and motion pictures. One of his best dramatic parts was as the salesman in love with Jennifer Jones in William Wyler's *Carrie*. In 1953, Wyler again effectively utilized Albert's casual charm as Gregory Peck's photographer sidekick in *Roman Holiday*, a role that garnered Albert his first Oscar nomination. In startling contrast, he played the cowardly officer in Robert Aldrich's potent war drama *Attack*. There were good buddy roles in movies like *The Sun Also Rises* and *The Joker Is Wild*, and two that featured his wife: *I'll Cry Tomorrow*, which depicted them as recovering alcoholics, and *Who's Got the Action?*, which was Margo's last film appearance. In England, Albert got top-billing in a minor espionage thriller, *Orders to Kill*, and also headed the cast list of a children's fantasy, *Two Little Bears*, as a dad who is surprised to find that his kids have turned into cubs overnight. Soon after giving a fine performance as a suicidal military patient in *Captain Newman, M.D.*, he won television stardom in the dopey sitcom *Green Acres*, which capitalized on his adept comic timing. When the show went off the air he returned to the movies to further prove his abilities as a character actor. His superb rendition of Cybil Shepherd's unfriendly father in *The Heartbreak Kid* nabbed him his second nomination from the Academy, and he followed this with a sharp turn as the nasty prison warden in the hit Burt Reynolds comedy-drama, *The Longest Yard*. Disney gave him one last star part, in their hit fantasy *Escape to Witch Mountain*, where he helped two orphans with psychic powers. His marriage to Margo lasted until her death in 1985. Their son is actor Edward Albert.

Screen: 1938: Brother Rat; 1939: On Your Toes; Four Wives; 1940: Brother Rat and Baby; An Angel From Texas; My Love Came Back; A Dispatch From Reuters; 1941: Four Mothers; The Wagons Roll at Night; Thieves Fall Out; The Great Mr. Nobody; Out of the Fog; 1942: Treat 'em Rough; Eagle Squadron; 1943: Ladies' Day; Lady Bodyguard; Bombardier; 1945: Strange Voyage; 1946: Rendezvous With Annie; The Perfect Marriage; 1947: Smash Up — The Story of a Woman; Time Out of Mind; Hit Parade of 1947; 1948: The Dude Goes West; You Gotta Stay Happy; Every Girl Should Be Married; 1950: The Fuller Brush Girl; 1951: U.S.S. Teakettle/You're in the Navy Now; Meet Me After the Show; 1952: Actors and Sin; Carrie; 1953: Roman Holiday; 1955: The Girl Rush; Oklahoma!; I'll Cry Tomorrow; 1956: Attack; The Teahouse of the August Moon; 1957: The Sun Also Rises; The Joker Is Wild; 1958: Orders to Kill; The Gun Runners; The Roots of Heaven; 1959: Beloved Infidel; 1961: The Young Doctors; The Two Little Bears; 1962: Madison Avenue; The Longest Day; Who's Got the Action?; 1963: Miracle of the White Stallions; Captain Newman, M.D.; 1966: The Party's Over (filmed 1963); 7 Women; 1972: The Heartbreak Kid; 1974: The Take; McQ; The Longest Yard; 1975: Escape to Witch Mountain; The Devil's Rain; Hustle; Whiffs; 1976: Birch Interval; Moving Violation; 1979: The Concorde — Airport '79; Blood Barrier (dtc); 1980: Foolin' Around; How to Beat the High Cost of Living; 1981: Yesterday/This Time Forever/Scoring (dtc); Take This Job and Shove It; 1982: Yes, Giorgio; 1983: The Act/Bless 'em All (dtv); 1984: Dreamscape; 1985: Stitches; Head Office;

1987: Turnaround (dtv); **1989:** The Big Picture; **1992:** Brenda Starr (filmed 1987).

NY Stage: 1936: Brother Rat; **1937:** Room Service; **1938:** The Boys From Syracuse; **1949:** Miss Liberty; **1953:** The Seven Year Itch; **1958:** Say Darling; **1960:** The Music Man; **1973:** No Hard Feelings; **1983:** You Can't Take it With You.

Select TV: 1952: Leave It to Larry (series); Enchanted Evening (sp); **1953:** Nothing But the Best (series); 1984 (sp); Tin Wedding (sp); **1954:** Saturday Night Revue (series); I'm a Fool (sp); **1955:** A Connecticut Yankee (sp); Into the Night (sp); The Chocolate Soldier (sp); Johnny Belinda (sp); **1956:** Rise and Walk (sp); **1957:** Pattern for Death (sp); **1959:** The Dingaling Girl (sp); Lazarus Walks Again (sp); The Silver Whistle (sp); **1961:** Louise and the Horseless Buggy (sp); Famous (sp); The Spiral Staircase (sp); **1965–71:** Green Acres (series); **1971:** See the Man Run; **1972:** Fireball Forward; **1973:** The Borrowers (sp); **1974:** Benjamin Franklin; The Ambassador (sp); **1975:** Switch; Promise Him Anything...; **1975–78:** Switch (series); **1978:** Crash/Crash of Flight 401; Evening in Byzantium (ms); The Word (ms); **1980:** Trouble in High Timber Country; Beulah Land (ms); **1981:** The Oklahoma City Dolls; Peter and Paul (ms); Goliath Awaits (ms); **1982:** Rooster; **1983:** The Demon Murder Case; **1984:** Burning Rage; **1986:** Dress Gray (ms); **1987:** Mercy or Murder?; **1988:** War and Remembrance (ms); **1990:** Return to Green Acres; **1991:** The Girl From Mars; **1995:** The Barefoot Executive.

FRANK ALBERTSON

BORN: FERGUS FALLS, MN, FEBRUARY 2, 1909.
DIED: FEBRUARY 29, 1964.

A former extra and prop boy during the silent era, Frank Albertson was signed to a Fox contract in 1928. His all-American boy quality served him well as he appeared in leads or secondary roles in such films as *The Brat*, as a disillusioned rich boy; *A Connecticut Yankee*, as a prisoner in love with princess Maureen O'Sullivan; and *Big Business Girl*, as a bandleader stuck on Loretta Young. He gradually moved into character parts, and among his better known roles are the oldest Miller son in MGM's adaptation of *Ah, Wilderness!*; Katharine Hepburn's longsuffering brother who endures her put-on social airs and graces in *Alice Adams*; the naïve playwright caught up in the Marx Brothers' shenanigans in *Room Service*; Donna Reed's suitor with the "Hee-Haw!" catchphrase in *It's a Wonderful Life*; and the lecherous millionaire who gives Janet Leigh the money that sets the plot rolling in *Psycho*. During the 1940s he could still be seen headlining some "B" melodramas, including *Citadel of Crime*, involving moonshiners; *The Man From Headquarters*, as a reporter accused of murder; *City of Silent Men*, as an ex-con trying to go straight; *Mystery Broadcast*, a whodunnit set in a radio studio; *Rosie the Riveter*, a Republic cash-in on the popular factory worker icon of World War II; and *Ginger*, a boy and his pooch story.

Screen: 1928: Prep and Pep; The Farmer's Daughter; **1929:** Salute; Words and Music; Blue Skies; **1930:** Son of the Gods; The Big Party; Happy Days; Born Reckless; Men Without Women; So This Is London; Wild Company; Just Imagine; Spring Is Here; **1931:** A Connecticut Yankee; The Brat; Big Business Girl; Traveling Husbands; Way Back Home; **1932:** Huddle; Cohens and Kellys in Hollywood; Air Mail; Racing Youth; **1933:** Ever in My Heart; Ann Carver's Profession; Midshipman Jack; King for a Night; Billion Dollar Scandal; Dangerous Crossroads; The Cohens and Kellys in Trouble; Rainbow Over Broadway; **1934:** The Last Gentleman; Hollywood Hoodlum; The Life of Vergie Winters; Enter Madame; Bachelor of Arts; **1935:** Doubting

Thomas; Alice Adams; Waterfront Lady; Ah, Wilderness!; Personal Maid's Secret; Kind Lady; East of Java; **1936:** The Farmer in the Dell; Fury; The Plainsman; **1937:** Navy Blue and Gold; **1938:** Hold That Kiss; Spring Madness; The Shining Hour; Mother Carey's Chickens; Fugitives for a Night; Room Service; **1939:** Bachelor Mother; **1940:** The Ghost Comes Home; Framed; Dr. Christian Meets the Women; When the Daltons Rode; Behind the News; **1941:** Ellery Queen's Penthouse Mystery; Man Made Monster; Father Steps Out; Flying Cadets; Citadel of Crime; Burma Convoy; Louisiana Purchase; **1942:** Wake Island; Underground Agent; Junior G-Men of the Air; The Man From Headquarters; Shepherd of the Ozarks; City of Silent Men; Silent Witness; **1943:** Keep 'em Slugging; Here Comes Elmer; Mystery Broadcast; O My Darling Clementine; **1944:** And the Angels Sing; Rosie the Riveter; **1945:** I Love a Soldier; Arson Squad; How Do-o-o-o You Do?; **1946:** Gay Blades; They Made Me a Killer; Ginger; It's a Wonderful Life; **1947:** The Hucksters; Killer Dill; **1948:** Shed No Tears; **1950:** Nightfall; **1957:** The Enemy Below; **1958:** The Last Hurrah; **1960:** Psycho; **1961:** Girl on the Run; **1962:** Don't Knock the Twist; **1963:** Papa's Delicate Condition; Bye Bye Birdie; Johnny Cool.

NY Stage: 1936: Brother Rat; **1941:** The More The Merrier; The Walrus and the Carpenter; **1949:** Mr. Adam; **1951:** Seventeen; **1953:** Late Love.

Select TV: 1949: It Pays to Advertise (sp); **1952:** The Trial of Steven Kent (sp); **1954:** Stir Mugs.

JACK ALBERTSON

BORN: MALDEN, MA, JUNE 16, 1907.
DIED: NOVEMBER 25, 1981.

One of Hollywood's apparent late bloomers, Jack Albertson had, in fact, been around for years, performing in vaudeville, playing small roles in films, and hosting one of television's first variety offerings, *Broadway Jamboree*, back in 1948. One of his earliest movie roles found him saving the day when he forwarded Kris Kringle's mail to the county courthouse in the classic *Miracle on 34th Street*. He continued to provide stellar support, often for comic effect, in movies like *Teacher's Pet*, *The Shaggy Dog*, *Lover Come Back*, and *Son of Flubber*. He won a Tony Award in 1964 for his poignant portrayal of the emotionally distant father in *The Subject Was Roses*, and he compounded his triumph by receiving the Oscar in 1968 for his reprise in the film version. His new-found stardom landed him a singing role as the hero's grandfather in *Willy Wonka and the Chocolate Factory*, and he was one of the survivors of the capsized ocean liner in the smash hit *The Poseidon Adventure*. His film success was solidified by his highly-rated television series, *Chico and the Man*, which won him his second Emmy Award in 1976. (His first had been for guesting on the *Cher* variety show in 1975.) His sister was character actress Mabel Albertson (1901–82).

Screen: 1940: Strike Up the Band; **1947:** Miracle on 34th Street; **1954:** Top Banana; **1955:** Bring Your Smile Along; **1956:** Over-Exposed; The Harder They Fall; The Unguarded Moment; The Eddy Duchin Story; **1957:** You Can't Run Away From It; Don't Go Near the Water; Man of a Thousand Faces; Monkey on My Back; **1958:** Teacher's Pet; **1959:** Never Steal Anything Small; The Shaggy Dog; **1961:** Man-Trap; Lover Come Back; Period of Adjustment; The George Raft Story; **1962:** Who's Got the Action?; Days of Wine and Roses; Convicts 4; **1963:** Son of Flubber; **1964:** Kissin' Cousins; The Patsy; Roustabout; A Tiger Walks; **1965:** How to Murder Your Wife; **1967:** The Flim Flam Man; **1968:** How to Save a Marriage (And Ruin Your Life); The Subject Was Roses; **1969:**

Changes; Justine; **1970:** Squeeze Flower (nUSr); Rabbit Run; **1971:** Willy Wonka and the Chocolate Factory; The Late Liz; **1972:** Pickup on 101/Where the Eagle Flies; The Poseidon Adventure; **1981:** The Fox and the Hound (voice); Dead and Buried.

NY Stage: 1941: Meet the People; 1945: A Lady Says Yes; 1947: The Cradle Will Rock; 1949: High Button Shoes; 1950: Tickets Please; 1951: Top Banana; 1964: The Subject Was Roses; 1972: The Sunshine Boys.

Select TV: 1948: Broadway Jamboree (series); 1958–59: The Thin Man (series); 1962: Room for One More (series); 1962–63: Ensign O'Toole (series); 1969: The Monk; 1970: A Clear and Present Danger; 1971: Once Upon a Dead Man; Congratulations It's a Boy!; Lock, Stock and Barrel; 1971–72: Dr. Simon Locke (series); 1973: Montserrat (sp); 1974–78: Chico and the Man (series); 1978: The Comedy Company; 1978–79: Grandpa Goes to Washington (series); 1979: Valentine; 1980: Marriage Is Alive and Well; 1981: Charlie and the Great Balloon Chase; 1982: My Body My Child; Terror at Alcatraz.

LOLA ALBRIGHT
BORN: AKRON, OH, JULY 20, 1925.

Lola Albright went from radio station stenographer, via modeling, to playing a string of bit parts at MGM (she can be seen as a hat model in *Easter Parade*, for example). In 1949 she made her first impression, as one of Kirk Douglas's conquests, in *Champion*, after which she appeared in a succession of leads in "B" productions for Columbia, including *Bodyhold*, about a wrestling plumber; *Beauty on Parade*, being encouraged by mother Ruth Warrick to choose career over marriage; and a decent thriller, *The Killer That Stalked New York*. A pair of low-budget Wayne Morris vehicles for Monogram, *Sierra Passage* and *Arctic Flight*, seemed to indicate that she wasn't making progress. She was one of the many attractive dolls drifting through Frank Sinatra's bachelor pad in *The Tender Trap*, and she provided the screams for an odd sci-fi movie, *The Monolith Monsters*, in which a town was terrorized by killer stones. It was television that brought her her biggest audience, playing Craig Stevens's girlfriend in the hit detective series *Peter Gunn*. Back on the big screen, Albright won some good notices as a stripper in *A Cold Wind in August* and for her superb turn as Tuesday Weld's mom in *Lord Love a Duck*, but after 1968 her work was done exclusively for the small screen. From 1952 to 1958 she was married to actor Jack Carson, with whom she had co-starred in *The Good Humor Man*.

Screen: 1948: The Pirate; Easter Parade; Julia Misbehaves; 1949: The Girl From Jones Beach; Tulsa; Champion; 1950: Bodyhold; Beauty on Parade; When You're Smiling; The Good Humor Man; The Killer That Stalked New York; Sierra Passage; 1952: Arctic Flight; 1953: The Silver Whip; 1954: Treasure of Ruby Hills; 1955: The Tender Trap; The Magnificent Matador; 1957: The Monolith Monsters; Pawnee; Oregon Passage; 1958: Seven Guns to Mesa; 1961: A Cold Wind in August; 1962: Kid Galahad; 1964: Joy House/The Love Cage; 1966: Lord Love a Duck; 1967: The Way West; 1968: Where Were You When the Lights Went Out?; The Money Jungle; The Impossible Years.

Select TV: 1958–61: Peter Gunn (series); 1961: Famous (sp); 1965–66: Peyton Place (series); 1967: How I Spent My Summer Vacation; 1968: The Helicopter Spies; 1977: Delta County USA; Terraces.

ROBERT ALDA
(ALPHONSO GIUSEPPE GIOVANNI ROBERTO D'ABRUZZO) BORN: NEW YORK, NY, FEBRUARY 26, 1914. DIED: MAY 3, 1986.

A handful of great breaks for dark, slick-looking Robert Alda was followed by many lean years where the work was nothing more than a paycheck. A singer in vaudeville, as a member of Charie O'Hearn and His Millionaires, he later moved into radio, where his assignments included his own show *Alda and Henry*. With no genuine acting experience, he broke into films in a big way when he was chosen by Warner Bros. to play George Gershwin in their lavish bio tribute *Rhapsody in Blue*, though the clichéd storyline left Alda little to do except display a rather blank personality amidst a lot of great music. He stayed on at Warners for a few more films including *Cinderella Jones*, which was actually shot before the Gershwin picture; the horror film *The Beast With Five Fingers*, taking a backseat to Peter Lorre; *Cloak and Dagger*, as an Italian partisan; and the popular Ann Sheridan melodrama *Nora Prentiss*. He failed to become a big attraction, however, so he took off for Broadway, where he achieved the greatest success of his career, playing gambler Skye Masterson in the original 1950 production of *Guys and Dolls*, winning the Tony Award. He spent most of the 1950s emceeing television quiz shows and appeared in one widely-seen picture, *Imitation of Life*, as a sleazy agent hitting on Lana Turner, before moving to Italy where he acted in many European productions that never reached U.S. shores. In later years he guested on several television series, including his son Alan Alda's show, *M*A*S*H*.

Screen: 1945: Rhapsody in Blue; 1946: Cinderella Jones; Cloak and Dagger; The Beast With Five Fingers; The Man I Love; 1947: Nora Prentiss; 1948: April Showers; 1949: Homicide; 1950: Hollywood Varieties; Tarzan and the Slave Girl; 1951: Mr. Universe; Two Gals and a Guy; 1958: Beautiful But Dangerous (Europe: 1955); 1959: Imitation of Life; A Soldier and a Half (nUSr); A Che Sorvono Questi (nUSr); 1960: Musketeers of the Sea (nUSr); 1961: Force of Impulse; 1962: The Devil's Hand (nUSr); 1963: Cleopatra's Daughter (nUSr); Revenge of the Barbarians (nUSr); Toto and Peppino Divided in Berlin (nUSr); 1967: Schizo/All Woman (nUSr); 1969: The Girl Who Knew Too Much; 1973: Seven Steps From Murder (nUSr); The Serpent; 1976: I Will I Will…For Now; Bittersweet Love; Won Ton Ton, the Dog Who Saved Hollywood; House of Exorcism/Lisa and the Devil; 1977: Cagliostro (Europe: 1974); 1978: Every Girl Should Have One; 1979: Holiday Hookers/Love by Appointment; 1982: The Squeeze/The Rip-Off (Europe: 1978).

NY Stage: 1950: Guys and Dolls; 1956: Harbor Lights; 1964: What Makes Sammy Run?; 1969: My Daughter Your Son; 1970: The Front Page.

Select TV: 1950: By Popular Demand (series); 1953: Personality Parade (series); What's Your Bid? (series); 1954–55: Secret File USA (series); 1956: Can Do (series); 1958: Assignment Abroad (sp); The Gentleman From Seventh Avenue (sp); 1966–67: Love of Life (series); 1975: Last Hours Before Morning; 1978: Perfect Gentlemen; Fame; 1979: Supertrain (series); 1981: Code Red.

ROSS ALEXANDER
BORN: BROOKLYN, NY, JULY 27, 1907. DIED: JANUARY 2, 1937.

Lanky, enthusiastic, and possessing a heavily-emphasized Brooklyn accent, Ross Alexander studied acting in Rochester, NY, before making his Broadway bow while still a teen. During a run of theatre work, he made his movie debut at Paramount's Astoria studio, playing Claudette Colbert's suitor in *The Wiser Sex*. He was signed up by Warner Bros. and contributed to the ensemble drama *Gentleman Are Born*, marrying Jean Muir amid the hardships of the Depression, and *Flirtation Walk*, where he added a shot of adrenaline to this stodgy musical. He graduated to some star parts in secondary releases, including *Maybe It's Love*, facing a troubled relationship with Gloria Stuart; *Brides Are Like That*, again involved in a problematic marriage, this time with Anita Louise; *Boulder Dam*, as a fugitive mechanic who accidentally kills his boss; *Hot Money*, as an unscrupulous promoter; and *Here Comes Carter*, as a movie publicist. The studio continued to hand him second lead material in "A" productions like *Captain Blood*, *A Midsummer Night's Dream* (as Demetrius), and the musical *Ready, Willing and Able*. His likeable personality was not enough to break him into the front rank of stars and he tragically shot himself at the age of 29.

Screen: 1932: The Wiser Sex; 1934: Social Register; Gentlemen Are Born; Flirtation Walk; 1935: Maybe It's Love; Going Highbrow; We're in the Money; Shipmates Forever; A Midsummer Night's Dream; Captain Blood; 1936: Boulder Dam; Brides Are Like That; I Married a Doctor; Hot Money; China Clipper; Here Comes Carter/Loudspeaker Lowdown; 1937: Ready, Willing and Able.

NY Stage: 1926: The Ladder; 1929: Let Us Be Gay; 1930: After Tomorrow; That's Gratitude; 1932: The Stork Is Dead; Honeymoon; 1933: The Party's Over; Under Glass; 1934: The Wooden Slipper; No Questions Asked.

LOUISE ALLBRITTON
BORN: OKLAHOMA CITY, OK, JULY 3, 1920.
ED: UNIV. OF OK, PASADENA PLAYHOUSE.
DIED: FEBRUARY 16, 1979.

A tall, classy blonde, Louise Allbritton spent most of her movie career at Universal in the 1940s, but her starring roles and leads were almost always in "B" pictures. She studied acting at the Pasadena Playhouse, which led to a part at Columbia as one of the *Parachute Nurse*(s). In 1942 she was signed by Universal where she took a back seat to the action in *Danger in the Pacific*, as the fiancée of scientist Don Terry, and to Abbott and Costello in *Who Done It?*, as the producer of a radio mystery program. The following year she scored her first top-billed part, as a working woman trying to conceal her marriage, in the forgettable *Fired Wife*. She continued to show a pleasing knack for humor in such light fare as *Her Primitive Man*, taken on a headhunting expedition by author Robert Paige; *San Diego, I Love You*, raising her younger brothers during wartime; and *The Men in Her Diary*, filing for divorce after reading her husband's secretary's diary. Her stay with Universal ended in a supporting part in an "A" feature, *The Egg and I*, trying to steal Fred MacMurray from Claudette Colbert, a plot point not found in the original novel. After some freelance assignments, she ended her U.S. movie career at Columbia, playing a dance hall proprietress in the Randolph Scott western *The Doolins of Oklahoma*. After her marriage to news correspondent Charles Collingwood she moved to New York, confining her acting to television, from which she retired in the early 1960s.

Screen: 1942: Parachute Nurse, Not a Ladies Man, Danger in the Pacific, Who Done It?, Pittsburgh; 1943: It Comes Up Love, Good Morning Judge, Fired Wife, Son of Dracula; 1944: Follow the Boys, This Is the Life, Her Primitive Man, San Diego, I Love You, Bowery to Broadway; 1945: The Men in Her Diary, That

Night With You; 1946: Tangier; 1947: The Egg and I; 1948: Sitting Pretty; Walk a Crooked Mile; Don't Trust Your Husband; 1949: The Doolins of Oklahoma; 1964: Felicia (nUSr)

Select TV: 1950: The Rockingham Tea Set (sp); The Stage Door (series); The Champion (sp); The Other Woman (sp); 1952: I've Got a Secret (series); The Darkroom (sp); 1954–55: Concerning Miss Marlowe (series).

FRED ALLEN
(JOHN SULLIVAN) BORN: CAMBRIDGE, MA, MAY 31, 1894. ED: BOSTON UNIV. DIED: MARCH 17, 1956.

This inimitable baggy-eyed comedian, one of the legendary stars in radio's heyday, began in vaudeville, where he often teamed with his wife, Portland Hoffa. The two were soon heard over the nation's airwaves, where Allen became famous for his mock radio "feud" with fellow comedian Jack Benny, which spilled over to the mildly received feature film *Love Thy Neighbor*. Prior to that he added some much-needed zip to two of 20th Century-Fox's hodgepodge musicals that dotted the cinematic landscape of the 1930s: in *Thanks a Million*, he was a theatrical manager trying to spice up Dick Powell's political campaign, and in *Sally, Irene and Mary*, he played the wisecracking agent of three manicurists aiming for Broadway stardom. His one true cinematic starring role was in the hilarious *It's in the Bag*, as a flea-circus owner trying to track down a chair with money sewn into its seat. Despite moments of sublime inspiration, it did not result in any follow-up vehicles. Instead, he ended up back at Fox for roles in two multi-episode films, *We're Not Married!*, paired with Ginger Rogers, as two bickering radio stars; and *O. Henry's Full House*, a disappointing teaming with the equally sardonic Oscar Levant in the "Ransom of Red Chief" segment. Unlike Jack Benny, Allen's transition to television was not a successful one. He authored two autobiographies: *Treadmill to Oblivion* (1954) and *Much Ado About Me* (1956).

Screen: 1935: Thanks a Million; 1938: Sally, Irene and Mary; 1940: Love Thy Neighbor; 1945: It's in the Bag; 1952: We're Not Married!; O. Henry's Full House.

NY Stage: 1922: The Passing Show of 1922; 1924: Vogues of 1924; 1929: Polly; The Little Show; 1930: Three's A Crowd.

Select TV: 1950: Colgate Comedy Hour (series); 1951–52: Chesterfield Sound Off Time (series); 1953–54: Judge for Yourself (series); 1954–56: What's My Line? (series).

STEVE ALLEN
BORN: NEW YORK, NY, DECEMBER 26, 1921.
ED: AZ ST. UNIV. DIED: OCTOBER 30, 2000.

Clever, bespectacled Steve Allen was a jack of all trades: radio performer, songwriter (most notably "This Could Be the Start of Something"), author, pianist, occasional actor, game show emcee and, most significantly, host of both the original *Tonight Show* (1954–57), the forerunner of all late-night talk entertainments, and his own primetime variety series *The Steve Allen Show* (1956–61). He came to the small screen via work as a disc jockey and talk show host on local L.A. radio stations. A man of seemingly effortless wit, he restricted most of his movie appearances to guest spots, usually playing himself. However, his resemblance to the great big-band clarinetist landed him the lead in *The Benny Goodman Story*. While he didn't display any awesome thespian talent, the film proved moderately popular at the box office, riding on the successful coat-tails of the previous year's

The Glenn Miller Story. There was also a bizarre Albert Zugsmith mishmash called *College Confidential*, which found Allen playing a sociology professor studying teen sex habits. Attempts at Broadway fared even less well, with short-runs as an actor (*The Pink Elephant*) and composer-lyricist (*Sophie*, in 1963). He was married to actress Jayne Meadows from 1954 until his death. His countless publications include the autobiography *Hi-Ho Steverino! — My Adventures in the Wonderful Wacky World of Television* (1992).

Screen: 1949: Down Memory Lane; 1950: I'll Get By; 1955: The Benny Goodman Story; 1959: The Big Circus; 1960: College Confidential; 1966: Don't Worry, We'll Think of a Title; 1967: Warning Shot; 1968: Where Were You When the Lights Went Out?; 1969: The Comic; 1975: The Sunshine Boys; 1980: Heart Beat; 1983: The Funny Farm; 1987: Amazon Women on the Moon; 1989: Great Balls of Fire!; 1992: The Player; 1994: The St. Tammany Miracle (dtv); 1995: Casino; 1998: Off the Menu: The Last Day's of Chasen's; Lenny Bruce: Swear to Tell the Truth.

NY Stage: 1953: The Pink Elephant; 1995: The Mikado.

Select TV: 1950–52: The Steve Allen Show (series); 1951–52: Songs for Sale (series); 1953: Talent Patrol (series); 1953–54: What's My Line? (series); 1954–57: Tonight (series); 1956–61: The Steve Allen Show (series); 1962–64: The Steve Allen Show (series); 1964–67: I've Got a Secret (series); 1967: The Steve Allen Comedy Hour (series); 1967–68: The Steve Allen Show (series); 1968: Now You See It, Now You Don't; 1972–73: I've Got a Secret (series); 1976: Rich Man, Poor Man (ms); Steve Allen's Laugh-Back (series); 1977–81: Meeting of Minds (series); 1979: Stone; 1980: The Gossip Columnist; 1980–81: The Steve Allen Comedy Hour (series); 1984: The Ratings Game; 1985: Life's Most Embarrassing Moments (series); Alice in Wonderland (and songs).

SARA ALLGOOD

BORN: DUBLIN, IRELAND, OCTOBER 31, 1883.
DIED: SEPTEMBER 13, 1950.

Short, rotund, apple-cheeked and extremely Irish, Sara Allgood joined Dublin's Abbey Players in 1904, but it was nearly 40 years before she was asked to come to Hollywood. Once there she immediately made an impression as the strong and loving matriarch of the Welsh coal mining family in *How Green Was My Valley.* The role won her an Oscar nomination and led to a career as a busy character player. The majority of her work was at 20th Century-Fox, where she performed in *Roxie Hart,* as a prison matron, and *Jane Eyre,* as a kindly housekeeper, to name but two of her assignments. Prior to her American debut she had appeared in many British films, most notably repeating her acclaimed stage role in Alfred Hitchcock's 1930 film version of *Juno and the Paycock.* She also caused a *Storm in a Teacup,* as the simple villager whose refusal to pay for a dog license causes a bureaucratic uproar.

Screen: 1918: Just Peggy; 1929: Blackmail; 1930: Juno and the Paycock; 1932: The World the Flesh the Devil; 1933: The Fortunate Fool; 1934: Lilly of Killarney/Bride of the Lake; 1935: Riders to the Sea; The Passing of the Third Floor Back; Lazybones; Peg of Old Drury; 1936: It's Love Again; Pot Luck; Sabotage/A Woman Alone; Southern Roses; 1937: Storm in a Teacup; The Sky's the Limit; 1938: Kathleen Mavourneen; The Londonderry Air; 1939: On the Night of the Fire; 1941: That Hamilton Woman; Dr. Jekyll and Mr. Hyde; How Green Was My Valley; Lydia; 1942: Roxie Hart; This Above All; It Happened in Flatbush; The War Against Mrs. Hadley; Life Begins at Eight-Thirty; 1943: Forever and a Day; City Without Men; 1944: The

Lodger; Jane Eyre; Between Two Worlds; 1945: The Keys of the Kingdom; The Strange Affair of Uncle Harry; Kitty; 1946: The Spiral Staircase; Cluny Brown; 1947: The Fabulous Dorseys; Ivy; Mother Wore Tights; Mourning Becomes Electra; My Wild Irish Rose; 1948: The Girl From Manhattan; One Touch of Venus; The Man From Texas; The Accused; 1949: Challenge to Lassie; 1950: Cheaper by the Dozen; Sierra.

NY Stage: 1911 AND 1913: Irish Players in Repertory; 1927: The Plough and the Stars; Juno and the Paycock; 1937: Storm Over Patsy; 1938: Shadow and Substance; 1940: Juno and the Paycock (revival); At the Stroke of Eight.

JUNE ALLYSON

(ELLA GEISMAN) BORN: BRONX, NY, OCTOBER 7, 1917.

In the days when studios wanted their leading ladies to be wholesome and sweet, June Allyson fit the bill to perfection. Perky and eager, with a scratchy speaking voice and an ultra-happy smile, she found that her limited talents did not carry comfortably into middle age. A professional dancer in her teens, she worked in a few Vitaphone shorts before landing roles in the Broadway musicals *Sing Out the News, Panama Hattie,* and *Best Foot Forward.* The last of these led to a contract at MGM, where she repeated her role in a film version, the highlight of which had co-stars Gloria DeHaven and Nancy Walker joining her for a snappy number called "The Three Bs." She had a show-stopping bit singing "Treat Me Rough" to Mickey Rooney at the beginning of *Girl Crazy,* but then disappeared for the rest of the film. The studio was eager to launch her as an exciting new attraction, and her girl-next-door qualities were emphasized in musicals, comedies, and — less successfully — dramas for the next 11 years. Her first real lead was in the pleasantly inoffensive wartime musical, *Two Girls and a Sailor,* playing sister to Gloria DeHaven. Audience response to her chemistry with her other co-star, Van Johnson, led to a succession of films pairing the two: *High Barbaree, The Bride Goes Wild, Too Young to Kiss,* and *Remains to Be Seen.* The results of their efforts, however, are unlikely to get them elected to the Hall of Fame for all-time great movie partnerships. There were other popular musicals, such as *Two Sisters From Boston,* with Kathryn Grayson as the other sibling, and *Good News,* where brainy college girl Allyson tutored football star Peter Lawford. The latter included her fetching renditions of "The French Lesson" and "The Best Things in Life Are Free" and is probably the most enjoyable film she did at MGM.

Allyson played older sister to Margaret O'Brien in the Joe Pasternak musical *Music for Millions,* a tearful cornucopia of classical numbers, while another attempt to find her a suitable on-screen partner resulted in two featherweight comedies with Robert Walker: *Her Highness and the Bellboy,* and *The Sailor Takes a Wife.* There were two more musical highlights: *Till the Clouds Roll By,* warbling "Cleopatterer" to Ray McDonald, and *Words and Music,* singing "Thou Swell," but she looked lost amidst all the swashbuckling in the 1948 version of *The Three Musketeers,* as Constance, and received some of her worst notices ever as Claudette Colbert's troublemaking daughter in the melodramatic *The Secret Heart.* Allyson, apparently, did not keep good company with nasty characters. Likewise, her interpretation of Jo March in the 1949 version of *Little Women* paled in comparison to Katharine Hepburn's performance from the previous decade. In 1949 she found herself nicely teamed with James Stewart in the sentimental baseball biopic, *The Stratton*

Story, the first of three money-making properties in which she played his devoted wife. This was followed five years later by *The Glenn Miller Story*, her own personal favorite of her films, and one of Universal's all time hits. Paramount's tedious Air Force flick, *Strategic Air Command*, came a year after that.

Her last MGM offerings were very minor assignments. She starred with husband Dick Powell in *The Reformer and the Redhead* (though the black-and-white photography meant you had to trust the title in terms of her hair color), and *Right Cross*, where Ricardo Montalban had the best role. There was also *Battle Circus*, in which she was unsuitably co-starred with Humphrey Bogart. Bidding goodbye to Metro in 1954 with a fine ensemble piece, *Executive Suite*, she freelanced doing an against-type performance as Jose Ferrer's shrewish wife in *The Shrike*. It was a game attempt to break the routine, but she was little more than competent. Undaunted by her cool reception for *Little Women*, she unwisely remade three more classics from the 1930s and, again, proved a poor replacement for the originals: *The Opposite Sex* (Norma Shearer, in *The Women*), *You Can't Run Away From It* (Claudette Colbert, in *It Happened One Night*), and *My Man Godfrey* (Carole Lombard). As the 1960s arrived her wholesome quality seemed at odds with the times and she confined herself mainly to television. Her return to the movies in 1972, however, was in a startlingly uncharacteristic role, as a lesbian murder suspect in the thriller *They Only Kill Their Masters*.

Following their appearance together in the 1944 musical *Meet the People*, Allyson and Powell married the following year and remained happily wed until his death from cancer in 1963. (He had served as her director for *You Can't Run Away From It*.) From 1959 to 1961 Allyson hosted the dramatic television anthology *The DuPont Show With June Allyson*, and returned to Broadway as part of the replacement cast of *40 Carats* in 1970.

Screen: 1943: Best Foot Forward; Girl Crazy; Thousands Cheer; 1944: Meet the People; Two Girls and a Sailor; Music for Millions; 1945: Her Highness and the Bellboy; The Sailor Takes a Wife; 1946: Two Sisters From Boston; Till the Clouds Roll By; The Secret Heart; 1947: High Barbaree; Good News; 1948: The Bride Goes Wild; The Three Musketeers; Words and Music; 1949: Little Women; The Stratton Story; 1950: The Reformer and the Redhead; Right Cross; 1951: Too Young to Kiss; 1952: The Girl in White; 1953: Battle Circus; Remains to Be Seen; 1954: The Glenn Miller Story; Executive Suite; Woman's World; 1955: Strategic Air Command; The McConnell Story; The Shrike; 1956: The Opposite Sex; You Can't Run Away From It; 1957: Interlude; My Man Godfrey; 1959: A Stranger in My Arms; 1972: They Only Kill Their Masters; 1978: Blackout; 1994: That's Entertainment! III.

NY Stage: 1938: Sing Out the News; 1939: Very Warm for May; 1940: Higher and Higher; Panama Hattie; 1941: Best Foot Forward; 1970: 40 Carats.

Select TV: 1959–61: The DuPont Show With June Allyson (series); 1962: A Time to Die (sp); Special Assignment (sp); 1963: The Third Side of the Coin (sp); 1971: See the Man Run; 1972: The Twentieth Century Follies (sp); 1973: Letters From Three Lovers; 1977: Curse of the Black Widow; 1978: Three on a Date; Vega$; 1982: The Kid With the Broken Halo.

DON AMECHE

(DOMINIC FELIX AMICI). BORN: KENOSHA, WI, MAY 31, 1908. DIED: DECEMBER 6, 1993.

One of the most unpretentious leading men in film history, Don Ameche's technical efficiency and accessible personality managed to prolong his career long after his more revered contemporaries had called it quits. After a stint in vaudeville he

landed the lead in a Broadway play, *Jerry for Short*, and used his deep voice and precise enunciation to establish himself as a frequent radio performer in the early 1930s. This led to a contract with 20th Century-Fox in 1936 and the studio started him out with a bang, playing the twin sons of Jean Hersholt in *The Sins of Man*. His follow-up, the studio's first all-Technicolor feature, *Ramona*, found him improbably cast as a love-sick Indian. More fittingly, Ameche's light, debonair qualities were put to good romantic use in *Ladies in Love*, where he was paired with Janet Gaynor. Also in the cast was the up-and-coming Fox contract player Tyrone Power, who would act alongside Ameche on several occasions and become a good friend off screen. Ameche was chosen as leading man for skater Sonja Henie's movie debut, *One in a Million*, where his talents did much to compensate for her inexperience. *Love Is News* was the first in which he wore his trademark moustache, while the popular musical, *You Can't Have Everything*, was his maiden outing with Alice Faye.

With Faye and Power he found himself in two of the big offerings of 1938: *In Old Chicago*, as the good O'Leary brother, who rises to mayor and perishes in the fire; and *Alexander's Ragtime Band*, singing "Easter Parade" in this wall-to-wall extravaganza of Irving Berlin tunes. He was also a singing D'Artagnan in a spurious rendition of *The Three Musketeers* (who were portrayed by the Ritz Brothers), before going over to Paramount, where he gave one of his best performances, as a Parisian taxi-driver who proves a match for temperamental Claudette Colbert in Ernst Lubitsch's *Midnight*. Back at Fox, he played one of his most famous, or infamous, roles, the titular inventor of the telephone in *The Story of Alexander Graham Bell*, which led to an endless series of wisecracks at Ameche's expense. The film was a reasonably entertaining biopic, though it didn't ring too loudly at the box office. Ameche did have a hit with *Hollywood Cavalcade*, a soap opera glimpse of Hollywood history in which, as a director, Ameche was supported by a cast of genuine silent movie comedians. He returned to bio-land for *Swanee River*, playing Stephen Foster, and *Lillian Russell* (with Alice Faye again), as that singer's husband. He was wasted in a series of typically drab Fox musicals of the 1940s: *Down Argentine Way*; *That Night in Rio*, which at least gave him an opportunity to play dual roles, as a nightclub entertainer and a banker; and *Moon Over Miami*. He, therefore, had no qualms about going to Paramount to partner Mary Martin in the comedy *Kiss the Boys Goodbye*; to MGM for *The Feminine Touch*, as a professor whose book on jealousy arouses that emotion in wife Rosalind Russell; and to Columbia for the 1943 film version of *Something to Shout About*, which allowed him to sing "You'd Be So Nice to Come Home To."

Fox reinstated themselves in his good graces by casting him as a rogue who looks back on his supposedly naughty life in another charming Lubitsch concoction, *Heaven Can Wait*, a huge box-office success and the actor's own favorite of his films. This was followed by a very serious role, as an Iowa druggist grieving over the loss of his son in the war in *Happy Land* (not to be confused by any means with the Sonja Henie ice-skating epic he'd done five years earlier, called *Happy Landing*). After the war story *Wing and a Prayer*, he ended his association with Fox and freelanced for the remainder of the 1940s. Two vehicles with Colbert, *Guest Wife* and *Sleep My Love*, added little luster to a dimming film career, so he returned to his fruitful radio roots, where he and Frances Langford had great success portraying a constantly sniping couple, *The Bickersons*. He briefly turned to television before his triumph on Broadway in the Cole Porter musical *Silk Stockings*, introducing "All of You" among others. From this came some supporting parts in films, including *A Fever in the Blood*, *Picture Mommy Dead*, and the Disney comedy *The Boatniks*. In

1983, he was called out of semi-retirement to replace an ailing Ray Milland in the comedy *Trading Places*. As one of the scheming millionaire brothers (Ralph Bellamy was the other), he reminded audiences of his deft comic touch and found himself in demand all over again. For his charming bit as a senior citizen rejuvenated by an alien force in the sci-fi hit *Cocoon*, he won a very popular Academy Award as Best Supporting Actor of 1985. There was the inevitable inferior sequel, followed by another good performance as a simple Italian shoeshiner posing as a gangster, in the otherwise flimsy *Things Change*. Audiences were afforded one final glimpse of him, as a grandpa in *Corrina, Corrina*, released several months after his death.

Screen: 1936: Sins of Man; Ramona; Ladies in Love; One in a Million; 1937: Love Is News; Fifty Roads to Town; You Can't Have Everything; Love Under Fire; 1938: In Old Chicago; Happy Landing; Alexander's Ragtime Band; Josette; Gateway; 1939: The Three Musketeers; Midnight; The Story of Alexander Graham Bell; Hollywood Cavalcade; Swanee River; 1940: Lillian Russell; Four Sons; Down Argentine Way; 1941: That Night in Rio; Moon Over Miami; Kiss the Boys Goodbye; The Feminine Touch; Confirm or Deny; 1942: The Magnificent Dope; Girl Trouble; 1943: Something to Shout About; Heaven Can Wait; Happy Land; 1944: Greenwich Village; Wing and a Prayer; 1945: It's in the Bag; Guest Wife; 1946: So Goes My Love; 1947: That's My Man; 1948: Sleep My Love; 1949: Slightly French; 1954: Phantom Caravan; 1955: Fire One; 1961: A Fever in the Blood; 1966: Rings Around the World; Picture Mommy Dead; 1970: Suppose They Gave a War and Nobody Came; The Boatniks; 1983: Trading Places; 1985: Cocoon; 1987: Harry and the Hendersons; 1988: Coming to America; Things Change; Cocoon: The Return; 1990: Odd Ball Hall; 1991: Oscar; 1992: Folks!; 1993: Homeward Bound: The Incredible Journey (voice); 1994: Corrina, Corrina.

NY Stage: 1929: Jerry for Short; 1955: Silk Stockings; 1957: Holiday for Lovers; 1958: Goldilocks; 1961: 13 Daughters; 1967: Henry Sweet Henry; 1989: Our Town.

Select TV: 1950: Take a Chance (series); 1950–51: Holiday Hotel/Don Ameche's Musical Playhouse (series); 1953: Coke Time With Eddie Fisher (series); 1956: High Button Shoes (sp); 1957: Your Every Wish (sp); Junior Miss (sp); 1958: Albert Anastasia (sp); 1961–65: International Showtime (series); 1968: Shadow Over Elveron; 1972: Gidget Gets Married; 1986: A Masterpiece of Murder; 1987: Pals; 1991: Our Shining Moment; 1992: Sunstroke.

LEON AMES

(LEON WAYCOFF) BORN: PORTLAND, IN, JANUARY 20, 1902. DIED: OCTOBER 12, 1993.

One of the movies' great father figures, Leon Ames lent his authoritarian presence to an exhaustive résumé of films during Hollywood's golden era. Joining the Charles K. Champlin Theatre Company as a stage manager, he drifted into acting, eventually playing the lead in *Tomorrow and Tomorrow*, in Los Angeles. This led to his first significant film assignment, in 1932, as the hero of Universal's *Murders in the Rue Morgue*, using his real name. Three years later he changed his name to Ames, starting with the RKO release *Strangers All*. During this period he obtained work in some fairly minor pictures including the leads in some Grand National "B's" like *Cipher Bureau* and *Panama Patrol*. It took a return to the stage to revitalize interest in Ames and MGM put him under contract in 1943 for what would prove to be his most fertile period. He started out

in his first year at the studio with his memorable role of the father whose decision to move his family to New York causes an uproar, in the classic musical *Meet Me in St. Louis*. There were the requisite 1940s military roles in *Thirty Seconds Over Tokyo, They Were Expendable*, and *Battleground*, followed by a flight into fancy as a mysterious man in *Yolanda and the Thief*. A good part as the prosecuting attorney in *The Postman Always Rings Twice* preceded a return to fatherhood with *Little Women*. After leaving Metro he was Doris Day's dad in a nostalgic Warners outing, *On Moonlight Bay*, a role he returned to in the sequel, *By the Light of the Silvery Moon*. For two years he played the most famous patriarch of them all, Clarence Day, in the television adaptation of *Life With Father*, which he reprised onstage. His name was so synonymous with paternity that it came as no surprise when he was asked to star in the small screen version of *Father of the Bride*. There were sporadic periods of retirement but he could still be seen performing into his 80s, ending his screen career by playing Kathleen Turner's grandfather in *Peggy Sue Got Married*. He was one of the founders of the Screen Actors Guild, in 1933.

Screen: AS LEON WAYCOFF: 1931: Quick Millions; 1932: Murders in the Rue Morgue; 13 Women; The Famous Ferguson Case; State's Attorney; A Successful Calamity; Silver Dollar; That's My Boy; Stowaway; Cannonball Express; Uptown New York; 1933: Parachute Jumper; Alimony Madness; The Man Who Dared; Forgotten; Ship of Wanted Men; 1934: The Count of Monte Cristo; I'll Tell the World; Now I'll Tell; The Crosby Case; 1935: Reckless; Rescue Squad.

AS LEON AMES: 1935: Strangers All; Mutiny Ahead; Get That Man; 1937: Dangerously Yours; Death in the Air; Murder in Greenwich Village; Charlie Chan on Broadway; 45 Fathers; 1938: International Settlement; Bluebeard's Eighth Wife; Walking Down Broadway; The Spy Ring; Island in the Sky; Come on Leathernecks; The Mysterious Mr. Moto; Strange Faces; Cipher Bureau; Suez; Secrets of a Nurse; 1939: Risky Business; I Was a Convict; Pack Up Your Troubles; Mr. Moto in Danger Island; Blackwell's Island; Panama Patrol; Man of Conquest; Fugitive at Large; Code of the Streets; Legion of Lost Flyers; Calling All Marines; Thunder Afloat; Marshal of Mesa City; 1940: East Side Kids; 1941: No Greater Sin; Ellery Queen and the Murder Ring; 1943: Crime Doctor; The Iron Major; 1944: Thirty Seconds Over Tokyo; Between Two Women; The Thin Man Goes Home; Meet Me in St. Louis; 1945: Son of Lassie; Week-end at the Waldorf; Anchors Aweigh; They Were Expendable; Yolanda and the Thief; 1946: The Postman Always Rings Twice; Lady in the Lake; No Leave, No Love; The Great Morgan; The Show-Off; The Cockeyed Miracle; 1947: Undercover Maisie; Song of the Thin Man; Merton of the Movies; 1948: Alias a Gentleman; On an Island With You; A Date With Judy; The Velvet Touch; 1949: Little Women; Any Number Can Play; Scene of the Crime; Battleground; Ambush; 1950: The Big Hangover; Dial 1119; Watch the Birdie; The Skipper Surprised His Wife; The Happy Years; Crisis; 1951: Cattle Driver; On Moonlight Bay; It's a Big Country; 1952: Angel Face; 1953: By the Light of the Silvery Moon; Let's Do It Again; Sabre Jet; 1957: Peyton Place; 1960: From the Terrace; 1961: The Absent Minded Professor; 1963: Son of Flubber; 1964: The Misadventures of Merlin Jones; 1965: The Monkey's Uncle; 1970: On a Clear Day You Can See Forever; Tora! Tora! Tora!; 1972: Hammersmith Is Out; Cool Breeze; 1973: Brother of the Wind (narrator); 1975: The Meal/Deadly Encounter; Timber Tramps; 1977: Claws; 1979: Just You and Me, Kid; 1983: Testament; 1986: Jake Speed; Peggy Sue Got Married.

NY Stage: 1936: Bright Honor; 1937: A House in the Country; Thirsty Soil; 1940: The Male Animal; 1941: The Land Is Bright; 1942: Guest in the House; Little Darling; The Russian People;

1943: Slightly Married; 1958: Winesburg, Ohio; Howie; 1967: Life With Father.

Select TV: 1953–55: Life With Father (series); 1955: Ah, Wilderness!; 1956: Frontier Judge (series); 1957: Adam Had Four Sons (sp); 1958: Tongues of Angels (sp); The Odd Ball (sp); 1959: The Raider (sp); 1961: The Assassin (sp); 1961–62: Father of the Bride (series); 1963–65: Mr. Ed (series); 1976: Sherlock Holmes in New York.

EDDIE "ROCHESTER" ANDERSON

BORN: OAKLAND, CA, SEPTEMBER 18, 1905.
DIED: FEBRUARY 28, 1977.

Eddie Anderson became famous for playing a character that bordered on the stereotypical black, but what saved Rochester from being offensive was a sassy delivery that made you feel he was far smarter than his show business boss, Jack Benny. A former member of a touring revue group, Anderson had already acted some small film roles when he was asked to do a one shot deal on Benny's radio show. His raspy-voiced character was so well received that he became a regular. Benny's long-suffering manservant, Rochester, was born. Anderson continued his movie career, including appearances as Rochester in some hurriedly produced spin-offs with Benny: *Man About Town*, *Buck Benny Rides Again*, *Love Thy Neighbor*, and *The Meanest Man in the World*. He also appeared in supporting roles in two Oscar-winners for Best Picture: *You Can't Take It With You*, as Donald, the loyal servant to the wacky Vanderhof family, and *Gone With the Wind*, in heavy makeup as the elderly Uncle Peter. There was no escaping the fact that he was on hand to enact the usual bug-eyed nervous Negro in the haunted house comedy *Topper Returns*, but he did at least get a lead over at MGM in the acceptable adaptation of the stage musical *Cabin in the Sky*, though he was hardly an admirable representative of the black race, playing Ethel Waters's layabout husband, Little Joe. When Benny brought his show over to television in 1950, Anderson stayed on for the series's long run, which finally ended in 1965, making it a 28-year career as part of Benny's stock company. Anderson was last seen on the big screen as a cab driver in the all-star romp *It's a Mad Mad Mad Mad World*, contributing to a sight gag involving a statue of Abraham Lincoln.

Screen: 1932: Hat Check Girl; What Price Hollywood?; 1935: Transient Lady; Behold My Wife; 1936: Two in a Crowd; The Music Goes Round; Star for a Night; The Green Pastures; Rainbow on the River; Three Men on a Horse; Show Boat; 1937: Melody for Two; Love Is News; Bill Cracks Down; Reported Missing; On Such a Night; White Bondage; Over the Goal; One Mile From Heaven; 1938: Kentucky; Restless Living; You Can't Take It With You; Gold Diggers in Paris; Jezebel; Thanks for the Memory; Going Places; Exposed; Strange Faces; 1939: Honolulu; You Can't Cheat an Honest Man; Man About Town; Gone With the Wind; 1940: Buck Benny Rides Again; Love Thy Neighbor; 1941: Topper Returns; Birth of the Blues; Kiss the Boys Goodbye; 1942: Tales of Manhattan; Star Spangled Rhythm; 1943: The Meanest Man in the World; Cabin in the Sky; What's Buzzin', Cousin?; 1944: Broadway Rhythm; 1945: Brewster's Millions; I Love a Bandleader; The Sailor Takes a Wife; 1946: The Show-Off; 1963: It's a Mad Mad Mad Mad World.

Select TV: 1957: The Green Pastures (sp); 1950–65: The Jack Benny Show (series); 1963: Last of the Private Eyes (sp); 1970–73: The Harlem Globetrotters (series; voice).

JUDITH ANDERSON

(FRANCES MARGARET ANDERSON)
BORN: ADELAIDE, AUSTRALIA, FEBRUARY 10, 1898.
DIED: JANUARY 3, 1992.

One of the theatre's great names, Judith Anderson's film legacy was confined mostly to supporting roles, often playing cold, imperious, or sinister women. She was in her teens when she made her stage debut, in Sydney, in 1915's *A Royal Divorce*. Several years later she made her Broadway bow, in *Peter Weston*. Among her triumphs in New York were *Strange Interlude*, *The Old Maid*, *Macbeth* (playing Lady Macbeth, twice on Broadway: 1937, 1941, and then twice on television in 1955 and 1961, winning Emmy Awards on both occasions), and *Medea*, for which she won the Tony Award. On screen she debuted in what would be her only romantic lead, opposite George Bancroft in the crime drama *Blood Money*. It was back to the stage until Alfred Hitchcock cast her in what would turn out to be her most famous movie role, in the 1940 Best Picture Oscar winner, *Rebecca*. For her depiction of the cruel and mysterious housekeeper, Mrs. Danvers, whom she played with deliciously dangerous lesbian undertones, she received an Oscar nomination. Her threatening, aloof aura would be put to maximum effect in Hollywood in *Lady Scarface*, top-billed as a tough Chicago gangleader; *Laura*, as Gene Tierney's unscrupulous aunt; and *The Furies*, where she so displeased Barbara Stanwyck that she had a pair of scissors hurled into her eye. Despite her magisterial presence, Anderson had no restrictions when it came to choosing her roles. They ranged from classy parts like Big Mama in the 1958 film version of *Cat on a Hot Tin Roof*, to the scheming servant killed off by Anne Baxter in *The Ten Commandments*, to the cruel stepmother in the Jerry Lewis gender-switch comedy *Cinderfella*, to an old Indian woman in *A Man Called Horse*. In 1971 she caused a stir when she chose to play the title role in *Hamlet* at the age of 73. Created a Dame in 1960, she spent her later years living comfortably in Santa Barbara while appearing on a daytime serial of the same name.

Screen: 1933: Blood Money; 1940: Rebecca; Forty Little Mothers; 1941: Free and Easy; Lady Scarface; 1942: All Through the Night; Kings Row; 1943: Edge of Darkness; Stage Door Canteen; 1944: Laura; 1945: And Then There Were None; 1946: Diary of a Chambermaid; The Strange Love of Martha Ivers; Specter of the Rose; 1947: Pursued; The Red House; Tycoon; 1950: The Furies; 1953: Salome; 1956: The Ten Commandments; 1958: Cat on a Hot Tin Roof; 1960: Cinderfella; 1961: Don't Bother to Knock/Why Bother to Knock? (nUSr); 1970: A Man Called Horse; 1974: Inn of the Damned; 1982: Star Trek III: The Search for Spock; 1986: Impure Thoughts (narrator; dtv).

NY Stage: 1923: Peter Weston; 1924: Cobra; 1925: The Dove; 1927: Behold the Bridegroom; 1928: Anna; 1931: As You Desire Me; 1932: Mourning Becomes Electra; Firebird; 1933: Conquest; The Mask and the Face; The Drums Begin; 1934: Come of Age; Divided by Three; 1935: The Old Maid; 1936: Hamlet; 1937: Macbeth; 1939: Family Portrait; 1941: Macbeth; 1942: The Three Sisters; 1947: Medea; 1950: The Tower Beyond Tragedy; 1952: Come of Age; John Brown's Body; 1953: In the Summer House; 1958: Comes a Day; 1966: Elizabeth the Queen; 1971: Hamlet; 1982: Medea.

Select TV: 1951: The Silver Cord (sp); 1954: Macbeth (sp); Christmas Story (sp); 1955: Louise (sp); Virtue (sp); 1956: Caesar and Cleopatra (sp); The Cradle Song (sp); 1957: The Clouded Image (sp); 1958: The Bridge of San Luis Rey (sp); 1959: The Second Happiest Day (sp); 1959: Medea (sp); The Moon and Sixpence (sp); 1960: To the Sound of Trumpets (sp); The Cradle

Song (sp); Macbeth (sp); **1968:** Elizabeth the Queen (sp); **1969:** The File on Devlin (sp); **1973:** The Borrowers (sp); **1974:** The Underground Man; **1982:** Medea (sp); **1984–87:** Santa Barbara (series).

URSULA ANDRESS

BORN: BERN, SWITZERLAND, MARCH 19, 1936.

Lynx-eyed, vivacious Ursula Andress was the nearest thing to a cartoonist's version of a sex symbol. In the 1960s she complied with her image in a series of roles that bore little resemblance to reality. Debuting as a teenager in Italian films with *Le Avventure di Giacomo Casanova/Sins of Casanova*, she later achieved worldwide stardom with a memorable first appearance in the inaugural James Bond adventure, *Dr. No*, rising like Aphrodite from the foam, clad in a skintight, waterlogged bikini. In no time she was Elvis's leading lady in one of his lookalike pop vehicles, *Fun in Acapulco*, as a bullfighter, and was ogled by Frank Sinatra and Dean Martin in the jokey western *4 for Texas*. She was repeatedly cast for her shapely figure and stunning looks, and it was certainly difficult to take her very seriously, judging from the roles she took. Consider the dreadful Hammer remake of *She*, where she was a well-preserved 200-year old ruler; or the fact that she literally parachuted into the plot of *What's New, Pussycat?*; that she killed someone with her lethal brassiere in *The Tenth Victim*; or that, in the unbridled Bond spoof *Casino Royale*, she wiped out Peter Sellers and a parade of Scotsmen with her bagpipes. Her heyday subsided and she wallowed in a string of international productions, including a jungle adventure, *The Southern Star*, and the Charles Bronson western *Red Sun*. Many others never surfaced on U.S. shores, although drive-in denizens of the 1970s and 1980s might have caught her in such gems as *The Loves and Times of Scaramouche* and *The Sensuous Nurse*, in which she was hired to kill a man with excessive sex! From 1957 to 1966 she was married to actor John Derek (with whom she appeared in *Once Before I Die*) and later had a child with actor Harry Hamlin, who had appeared with her in the kitschy fantasy *Clash of the Titans*.

Screen (US releases only): 1963: Dr. No; Fun in Acapulco; 4 for Texas; **1965:** Nightmare in the Sun; She; What's New, Pussycat?; The Tenth Victim; **1966:** Up to His Ears; The Blue Max; **1967:** Once Before I Die; Casino Royale; **1968:** Anyone Can Play; **1969:** The Southern Star; **1970:** Perfect Friday; **1972:** Red Sun; **1975:** Loaded Guns; **1976:** Stateline Motel; The Loves and Times of Scaramouche; **1979:** Slave of the Cannibal God; The Sensuous Nurse (filmed 1976); The Fifth Musketeer; **1980:** Safari Express; Tigers in Lipstick/Wild Beds (dtv); **1981:** Clash of the Titans.

Select TV: 1986: Peter the Great (ms); **1988:** Man Against the Mob/The Chinatown Murders; **1993:** Curse of the Golden Rose III; **1994:** Golden Rose IV.

DANA ANDREWS

(CARVER DANA ANDREWS) BORN: COLLINS, MI, JANUARY 1, 1909. ED: SAM HOUSTON ST. TEACHERS COL. DIED: DECEMBER 17, 1992.

A number of major films of the 1940s happen to feature Dana Andrews, thereby making him a notable figure of that period. But it would be wrong to call him irreplaceable and indeed there were times when his solid virility could be rather wooden. Overall he was a reliable, if uninspired actor who was, on occasion,

capable of rising impressively to the occasion. He studied acting at the Pasadena Playhouse while working as an L.A. gas station attendant, making his professional stage debut in 1935 in *Cymbeline*. A few years later a talent scout from Goldwyn Studios spotted and signed him, and Fox had enough faith in him to buy half his contract. He shuttled back and forth between them from 1940 to 1951, initially performing supporting roles, showing up as cavalry soldiers in both *Lucky Cisco Kid* and *Kit Carson*. He was eventually entrusted with one of the leads in the adaptation of the Broadway smash *Tobacco Road*, but this watered down film rendition did not repeat the stage success. That same year, 1941, he was ideally cast as the villain bemused by Gary Cooper's timidity in the irresistible comedy *Ball of Fire*, after which Fox rewarded him with his first top-billing, in the title role of *Berlin Correspondent*, a "B" movie. The film that raised his stock in the business was William Wellman's brilliant anti-lynching western, *The Ox-Bow Incident*. He was heartbreakingly good as the rancher falsely accused of murder who begins to realize that all the pleading in the world will not save him from a group of single-minded vigilantes.

He joined the ensemble of Goldwyn's Russian-flavored war film, *The North Star*; helped support Danny Kaye, as a G.I., in the comedian's movie debut, *Up in Arms*; and was the obsessed detective in *Laura*, playing it very cool amid the showier supporting characters. He was a less-than-thrilling romantic prospect for Jeanne Crain in the musical *State Fair*; showed his smarmier side as the press agent who marries Alice Faye for her money in *Fallen Angel*; and then excelled as the platoon sergeant ordered to capture a farmhouse in Italy in a superior war film, *A Walk in the Sun*. It did less well than the tedious western *Canyon Passage*, a Universal Technicolor opus stolen by Hoagy Carmichael. Goldwyn's *The Best Years of Our Lives* was one of the great triumphs of the 1940s, a huge moneymaker and a Best Picture Oscar-winner. The gritty story was enhanced by fine performances all around, including Andrews's work as a WWII vet who comes home to a sluttish wife and a demeaning job, and finds solace in the arms of Teresa Wright. *Boomerang!* was one of the many fascinating semi-documentary dramas of the postwar era, and *Night Song* challenged him with a character who was blind. The era was now deep into film noir and Andrews's slightly-worn handsome looks and penchant for a clipped, cynical line made him ideal for this kind of harsh material. His films in that genre include *The Iron Curtain*, hunting Reds; *Where the Sidewalk Ends*, as a cop who accidentally kills a suspect; and *While the City Sleeps*, as a world-weary television reporter solving a crime.

Both of his studios ended their arrangements with him in 1951. Goldwyn said goodbye with *I Want You*, often referred to as a poor-man's *Best Years…*, and Fox bid adieu with the war film *The Frogmen*, in which he took second billing to 20th Century's newer attraction, Richard Widmark. The 1950s brought very little in the way of excitement. *Elephant Walk* found him behaving more sensibly than either Elizabeth Taylor or Peter Finch in a jungle love triangle; *Spring Reunion* cast him as Betty Hutton's last leading man; *Night of the Demon* was a made-in-Britain horror thriller that became a cult favorite; and *Zero Hour*, later stumbled into posterity as the movie that inspired the spoof *Airplane!* As his roles diminished and the budgets got smaller, Andrews turned to Broadway, replacing Henry Fonda in *Two for the Seesaw*. During the 1960s and 1970s Andrews was a regular supporting player in the inevitable authoritarian and military roles (*In Harm's Way*, *Battle of the Bulge*, etc.). He also had some final star parts in *Madison Avenue*; *Crack in the World*, as a scientist accidentally causing the near-destruction of the Earth; the drive-in fave *Hot Rods to Hell*, as a vacationing dad whose family is terrorized by motorcyclists; and the Nazis-on-ice thriller *The Frozen Dead*. He took time out from the big screen to appear on the daytime serial *Bright Promise*, and to serve as president of the Screen Actors Guild (1964–66). His younger brother is actor Steve Forrest.

Screen: 1940: The Westerner; Lucky Cisco Kid; Sailor's Lady; Kit Carson; 1941: Tobacco Road; Belle Starr; Ball of Fire; 1942: Swamp Water; Berlin Correspondent; 1943: Crash Dive; The Ox-Bow Incident; The North Star/Armored Attack; 1944: The Purple Heart; Wing and a Prayer; Up in Arms; Laura; 1945: State Fair; Fallen Angel; A Walk in the Sun; 1946: Canyon Passage; The Best Years of Our Lives; 1947: Boomerang!; Night Song; Daisy Kenyon; 1948: The Iron Curtain; Deep Waters; No Minor Vices; 1949: Britannia Mews/Forbidden Street; Sword in the Desert; My Foolish Heart; 1950: Where the Sidewalk Ends; Edge of Doom; 1951: Sealed Cargo; The Frogmen; I Want You; 1952: Assignment Paris; 1954: Elephant Walk; Duel in the Jungle; Three Hours to Kill; 1955: Smoke Signal; Strange Lady in Town; 1956: Comanche; While the City Sleeps; Beyond a Reasonable Doubt; 1957: Spring Reunion; Night of the Demon/Curse of the Demon; Zero Hour; 1958: Enchanted Island; The Fearmakers; 1960: The Crowded Sky; 1962: Madison Avenue; 1965: Crack in the World; The Satan Bug; In Harm's Way; Brainstorm; Town Tamer; The Loved One; Battle of the Bulge; Spy in Your Eye; 1966: Johnny Reno; 1967: Hot Rods to Hell; The Frozen Dead; 1968: The Cobra; Il Diamante Che Nessuno Voleva Rubare/No Diamonds for Ursula (nUSr); The Devil's Brigade; 1973: Innocent Bystanders; 1974: Airport 1975; 1975: Take a Hard Ride; 1976: The Last Tycoon; 1978: Good Guys Wear Black; Born Again; 1979: The Pilot; 1984: Prince Jack.

NY Stage: 1958: Two for the Seesaw; 1962: The Captains and the Kings.

Select TV: 1958: The Right Hand Man (sp); 1960: Alas Babylon (sp); The Playoff (sp); 1962: Mutiny (sp); 1964: A Wind of Hurricane Force (sp); 1969–72: Bright Promise (series); 1971: The Failing of Raymond; 1975: A Shadow in the Streets; The First 36 Hours of Dr. Durant; 1977: The Last Hurrah; 1979: Ike (ms).

HARRY ANDREWS
BORN: TONBRIDGE, KENT, ENGLAND, NOVEMBER 10, 1911. ED: WREKIN COL. DIED: MARCH 6, 1989.

A stern and rugged British character actor with ears as distinctive as Bing Crosby's, Harry Andrews spent nearly 20 years in live theatre before making his movie debut in the 1952 film *The Red Beret*. Over the next 30 years his lantern-jawed face was a familiar addition to many international productions, usually in historical (John de Stogumber in *Saint Joan*, and the apostle Peter in the religious epic *Barabbas*) or military dramas (including *A Hill in Korea*, and *The Hill*, the latter offering perhaps his greatest showcase, as the pigheaded martinet in charge of a prison camp). His craggy, weathered appearance made him one of the most authentic-looking whalers in director John Huston's impressive filming of *Moby Dick*. Outside of these genres he was an Amish dad searching for his daughter in sinful New York in *The Night They Raided Minsky's*; Dr. Sorin in the 1968 adaptation of Chekhov's *The Sea Gull*; the aging homosexual with designs on Peter McEnery in the film adaptation of Joe Orton's *Entertaining Mr. Sloane*; and a drama critic who has his heart cut out in retaliation for a bad review in *Theatre of Blood*.

Screen: 1952: The Red Beret/Paratrooper; 1954: The Black Knight; 1955: The Man Who Loved Redheads; Helen of Troy; 1956: A Hill in Korea/Hell in Korea; Alexander the Great; Moby Dick; 1957: Saint Joan; 1958: I Accuse!; Ice Cold in Alex/Desert

Atttack; 1959: The Devil's Disciple; Solomon and Sheba; A Touch of Larceny; 1960: In the Nick; Circle of Deception; 1962: The Best of Enemies; Barabbas; Lisa;/The Inspector; Reach for Glory; 1963: Nine Hours to Rama; 55 Days at Peking; 1964: Nothing But the Best; 633 Squadron; 1965: The Hill; Sands of the Kalahari; Underworld Informers; The Agony and the Ecstasy; The Truth About Spring; 1966: The Girl-Getters/The System; Modesty Blaise; 1967: The Deadly Affair; The Jokers; The Night of the Generals; The Long Duel; I'll Never Forget What's 'isname; 1968: A Dandy in Aspic; Danger Route; The Charge of the Light Brigade; The Night They Raided Minsky's; The Sea Gull; 1969: Play Dirty; Battle of Britain; A Nice Girl Like Me. The Southern Star; 1970: Brotherly Love/Country Dance; Too Late the Hero; Entertaining Mr. Sloane; 1971: Wuthering Heights; Nicholas and Alexandra; 1972: Burke and Hare; Night Child/What the Peeper Saw; The Nightcomers; I Want What I Want; The Ruling Class; Man of La Mancha; 1973: Theatre of Blood; The Last Days of Man on Earth/The Final Programme; The Mackintosh Man; 1974: The Internecine Project; 1975: Man at the Top; 1976: Sky Riders; The Blue Bird; The Passover Plot; 1977: Equus; 1978: Crossed Swords/The Prince and the Pauper; The Big Sleep; The Medusa Touch; Death on the Nile; Watership Down (voice); Superman; 1980: Hawk the Slayer; 1986: Mesmerized/Shocked.

NY Stage: 1936: Hamlet; 1946: Henry IV Part 1; Henry IV Part 2; Oedipus; 1951: Caesar and Cleopatra; Antony and Cleopatra.

Select TV: 1969: Destiny of a Spy; 1972: An Affair of Honor; 1974: The Story of Jacob and Joseph; 1975: Edward the King; 1976: Clayhanger (series) 1979: S.O.S. Titanic; 1980: Never Never Land (sp); The Curse of King Tut's Tomb; 1982: A.J. Wentworth; BA (series); The Seven Dials Mystery; 1988: Cause Celebre; Inside Story; Jack the Ripper.

JULIE ANDREWS
(JULIA ELIZABETH WELLS) BORN: WALTON-ON-THAMES, SURREY, ENGLAND, OCTOBER 1, 1935.

Julie Andrews is simply one of the great singers of her age, which would have carried her only so far, since the Hollywood musical genre was slipping away as she arrived on the scene. Fortunately she also possessed a comforting personality, without a trace of treacle, a sly sense of comic timing, and an accomplished dramatic sensibility. Even in those few periods when she seemed to have fallen out of fashion she remained one of those rare stars who never lost their luster or mystique. Her parents were musical hall entertainers, and Andrews made her professional London stage debut as a 12-year-old, singing in the 1947 revue *Starlight Roof*. Her work on radio and in pantomimes drew attention to her extraordinary vocal range and she was snatched up for the New York stage to make her Broadway bow in *The Boy Friend* in 1954. Over the next 14 years she seemed incapable of making a mistake, excelling in one medium after another. Her performance as Eliza Doolittle in the classic 1956 Lerner and Loewe musical *My Fair Lady* was a sensation, as was her follow-up, *Camelot*, as Guenevere. Television audiences had seen Andrews in the acclaimed Rodgers and Hammerstein musical *Cinderella* and in a taped Carnegie Hall concert with Carol Burnett, but she was long overdue for her big screen debut. When she finally accepted an offer from Walt Disney she'd been on the consciousness of the American public for a full 10 years.

Passed over for the 1964 film version of *My Fair Lady* in favor of the better-known Audrey Hepburn, she more than compensated by winning the Academy Award that same year for her debut role in Disney's phenomenally popular musical fantasy *Mary Poppins*. As the magical nanny whose stony reserve hides a loving heart, Andrews projected the wholesome image to which she would be forever linked, despite the fact that within a few months she was successfully essaying a more mature part in the anti-war comedy *The Americanization of Emily*. By the following year, when her second musical vehicle, *The Sound of Music*, broke all box-office records to become the highest-grossing movie in history, Andrews had become a household name. Her glowing performance as the novice who becomes governess and singing teacher to a household of children has enthralled audiences for decades, and she rightfully earned her second Oscar nomination. Within the space of a year she had found two signature roles. Although she took a backseat to Paul Newman in Alfred Hitchcock's Cold War thriller *Torn Curtain*, and to Max von Sydow in the historical saga *Hawaii*, her name on the marquee was instrumental in bringing in the crowds for both films. Her comedic flair was very much in evidence in the deft satire of the Roaring Twenties, *Thoroughly Modern Millie*, a purposefully campy affair that became one of the greatest money-makers ever released by Universal Studios.

From these endless highs came the inevitable plunge into disfavor. The mood of the country in the late 1960s was not conducive to her sort of showcase and her G-rated image was seen as a relic from another time. *Star!*, a three-hour biopic of legendary entertainer Gertrude Lawrence, provided a superb showcase for the varied talents of Andrews, who worked harder at this than on any of her other films, but it laid such an egg at the box office that it was hastily recut, retitled *Those Were the Happy Times*, and unjustly branded with a bad reputation. When a second expensive vehicle, *Darling Lili*, flopped it was clear that her time in the spotlight was waning. She married the director of *Darling Lili*, Blake Edwards, and did a well-liked Emmy Award–winning variety series that was cancelled after a year. She confined herself to television specials and seemed immured to the film scene until she resurfaced in her husband's 1979 hit, *"10"*. Her role as Dudley Moore's girlfriend may have been secondary to the corn-braided Bo Derek, but she proved that something special had been missing from the movies while she'd been away.

Suddenly, she was back with a vengeance, as Edwards rolled out two comedies to help quash the goody-goody image with which she'd been saddled. The first, *S.O.B.*, was a mordant farce skewering the movie industry, and it got a lot of press because Andrews bared her breasts, but its brilliant moments got lost amidst the coarseness. *Victor/Victoria*, however, proved to be one of the crowning achievements of both her career and her husband's. In a hilarious Shakespearean gender switch, Andrews impersonated a man making a living at impersonating a woman. It deservedly brought her a third Oscar nomination. Two more films with Edwards were more restrained: *The Man Who Loved Women*, as Burt Reynolds's psychiatrist, and *That's Life*, in which she beautifully played a thinly-disguised version of herself, a famed singer caring for her insecure husband. After a soft sitcom failed she finally returned to Broadway for a repeat of *Victor/Victoria*, which proved an instant sell-out at the box office. When she alone from the production was singled out for a Tony nomination, she made a small stir by turning down the honor. Like everything else she did, it was done with tact and taste, and no one thought any less of her for it. When, in the late 1990s, it was announced that her vocal chords had been damaged in a botched operation, the world reacted as if it had been deprived of one of its most serene voices and one of the last links to a more civilized sort of show business. Back working for Disney, she impersonated royalty in the surprisingly popular *The Princess Diaries*, where her presence gave this G-rated comedy what little charm it had. Under the name Julie Edwards, she authored the children's books *Mandy* and *The Last of the Really Great Whanghoodles*, and under her own name penned *Little Bo*, as well as several *Dumpy the Dump Truck* stories.

Screen: 1964: Mary Poppins; The Americanization of Emily; 1965: The Sound of Music; 1966: Hawaii; Torn Curtain; 1967: The Singing Princess (voice); Thoroughly Modern Millie; 1968: Star!/Those Were the Happy Times; 1970: Darling Lili; 1974: The Tamarind Seed; 1979: "10"; 1980: Little Miss Marker; 1981: S.O.B.; 1982: Victor/Victoria; 1983: The Man Who Loved Women; 1986: That's Life; Duet for One; 1992: A Fine Romance; 2001: The Princess Diaries.

NY Stage: 1954: The Boyfriend; 1956: My Fair Lady; 1960: Camelot; 1993: Putting It Together (ob); 1995: Victor/Victoria.

Select TV: 1956: High Tor (sp); 1957: Cinderella (sp); 1962: Julie and Carol at Carnegie Hall (sp); 1965: The Julie Andrews Show (sp); 1969: An Evening With Julie Andrews and Harry Belafonte (sp); 1971: Julie and Carol at Lincoln Center (sp); 1972–73: The Julie Andrews Hour (series); 1973: Julie on Sesame Street (sp); Julie's Christmas Special (sp); 1974: Julie and Dick in Covent Garden (sp); Julie and Jackie: How Sweet It Is (sp); 1975: Julie: My Favorite Things (sp); One to One (sp); 1978: Julie Andrews: One Step Into Spring (sp); 1980: Julie Andrews' Invitation to the Dance (sp); 1987: Julie Andrews: The Sound of Christmas (sp); 1989: Julie and Carol: Together Again (sp); 1990: Julie Andrews…in Concert (sp); 1991: Our Sons; 1992: Julie (series); 1999: One Special Night; 2000: Relative Values (theatrical in UK); 2001: On Golden Pond (sp).

THE ANDREWS SISTERS

BORN: MINNEAPOLIS, MN.
LaVerne: BORN: JULY 6, 1915.
DIED: MAY 8, 1967.
Maxene: BORN: JANUARY 3, 1916.
DIED: OCTOBER 21, 1995.
Patty: BORN: FEBRUARY 16, 1920.

The inimitable sound of the Andrews Sisters instantly conjures up images of the American homefront during World War II. The singing trio had begun performing in vaudeville as youngsters, joined up with various bands, and finally broke into the big time in 1937 with their recording of "Bei Mir Bist Du Schoen." During the early 1940s their vocal harmonies epitomized the sound of an era with such song hits as "Apple Blossom Time," "Hold Tight," and "Rum and Coca Cola." Universal signed them to a contract but, because they didn't exactly fit Hollywood's idea of "attractive," they were initially used for specialty numbers. They backed up the Ritz Brothers in *Argentine Nights* and Abbott and Costello on three occasions, most notably in *Buck Privates*, where they introduced one of their greatest numbers, "Boogie Woogie Bugle Boy." The cheaply-produced *Give Out, Sisters* finally made them the stars of their own vehicle, posing them as old maids and having them sing "The Pennsylvania Polka." Universal gave them more flimsy assignments: *Always a Bridesmaid*, in which they started a lonelyhearts club; *Moonlight and Cactus*, about a ranch run by women; and ending in 1945 with *Her Lucky Night*, which had them spoofing the vogue for polkas by singing "The Polka Polka." After leaving Universal they continued to be heard on radio and did some concert engagements until Patty decided to go solo. Despite the growing animosity between the sisters they still made some appearances together up until LaVerne's death in 1967. In 1974 Patti and Maxene reteamed for their Broadway debuts in the hit musical *Over Here!*, a roaring success which did nothing to decrease the hostility between the two women.

Screen: ANDREWS SISTERS: **1940:** Argentine Nights; **1941:** Buck Privates; In the Navy; Hold That Ghost; **1942:** Give Out, Sisters; Private Buckaroo; What's Cookin'?; **1943:** Always a Bridesmaid; How's About It?; Swingtime Johnny; **1944:** Follow the Boys; Hollywood Canteen; Moonlight and Cactus; **1945:** Her Lucky Night; **1946:** Make Mine Music (voices); **1947:** Road to Rio; **1948:** Melody Time (voices). PATTY: **1970:** The Phynx; **1980:** The Gong Show Movie.

NY Stage: PATTY AND MAXENE: **1974:** Over Here!

PIER ANGELI

(ANNA MARIA PIERANGELI). BORN: CAGLIARI, SARDINIA, ITALY, JUNE 19, 1932. RAISED IN ROME. DIED: SEPTEMBER 10, 1971.

Frail, tiny, and undeniably lovely, this Italian actress came to prominence in 1950s Hollywood following a pair of films (under her real name) in her native country, *Domani e Troppo Tardi*, in 1949, and *Domani e un Altro Giorno*, in 1951. There was much publicity from MGM when she won the role of the war bride in *Teresa*, and her reviews were encouraging. There followed a series of assignments for whenever the studio needed a European girl to play opposite some saleable leading man: *The Light Touch*, with Stewart Granger; *The Devil Makes Three*, with Gene Kelly; and *The Story of Three Loves*, in an episode with Kirk Douglas. None of these really took off but they looked like gold alongside her loan-out to Warner Bros., *The Silver Chalice*, one of the great dogs of the 1950s. Her co-star was Paul Newman and the pair made up for it back at her home lot with the fine boxing pic, *Somebody Up There Likes Me*. Angeli was also very sweet as the object of Danny Kaye's affections in *Merry Andrews*, which came after the critically-lambasted *The Vintage*. Around this time, she was possibly better known to readers of fan magazines as the wife (1954–58) of singer Vic Damone. In 1960 she took off to Europe for the British *The Angry Silence*, doing a good job as Richard Attenborough's wife, before participating in an unpopular Biblical spectacle, *Sodom and Gomorrah*, as Lot's wife. Towards the end of her career she appeared in all kinds of European films, often using her real name. Most of those efforts remain unreleased in America. In 1971, not yet 40, the actress took an overdose of barbiturates. Her twin sister, actress Marisa Pavan, came to U.S. film around the same time that Angeli did and earned an Oscar nomination for *The Rose Tattoo*.

Screen (US releases only): **1951:** Teresa; The Light Touch; **1952:** The Devil Makes Three; **1953:** The Story of Three Loves; Sombrero; **1954:** The Flame and the Flesh; The Silver Chalice; **1956:** Port Afrique; Somebody Up There Likes Me; Meet Me in Las Vegas; **1957:** The Vintage; **1958:** Merry Andrew; **1960:** S.O.S. Pacific; The Angry Silence; **1962:** White Slave Ship; **1963:** Sodom and Gomorrah; **1965:** The Battle of the Bulge; **1966:** Spy in Your Eye; **1970:** Every Bastard a King; **1971:** Love Me — Love My Wife; Octaman.

EVELYN ANKERS

BORN: VALPARAISO, CHILE, AUGUST 17, 1918. ED: RADA. DIED: AUGUST 28, 1985.

Another of Universal studio's second-string "B" stars, Evelyn Ankers was the daughter of a British mining engineer (which accounted for her being born in Chile), who trained for the acting profession upon returning to England, eventually attending RADA. She had already made her debut in a small part in the U.K. film *The Bells of St. Mary's* in 1936, and did a few more British pictures before coming to Broadway to play one of the *Ladies in Retirement* in 1941. This resulted in a contract with Universal studios where she soon gained a reputation as the perfect startled heroine in a series of horror movies, including her most famous film *The Wolf Man*; *The Ghost of Frankenstein*; the circus-set *Captive Wild Woman* (which was Acquanetta, not Ankers), and its even cheaper sequel, *Jungle Woman*; *The Mad Ghoul* (she was a singer, warbling "I Dreamt I Dwelt in Marble Halls"); and *Son of Dracula*, taking a backseat in this instance to Louise Allbritton, who got to marry the count after all. For a break she got to be on the side of evil in *Weird Woman* (one of the studio's "Inner Sanctum" mysteries), trying to destroy newlyweds Lon Chaney, Jr. and Anne Gwynne. After leaving Universal (her last there was *The Frozen Ghost*, another "Inner Sanctum" entry with Chaney) she remained at the sub-"A" level for movies like PRC's *Queen of Burlesque*; RKO's first Lex Barker loincloth offering, *Tarzan's Magic Fountain*; Eagle Lion's *Parole Inc.*; and Columbia's *The Texan and Calamity Jane*, sharing the title roles with James Ellison. Clearly her career had trickled off. During the early 1950s she did some television appearances, but was content to let her husband, Richard Denning (whom she had married in 1942), do the acting. Eventually the couple settled on the island of Maui, where Evelyn quietly retired.

Screen: **1936:** Land Without Music/Forbidden Music; Rembrandt; **1937:** The Bells of St. Mary's; Fire Over England; Knight Without Armour; Wings of the Morning; **1938:** Murder in the Family; The Claydon Treasure Mystery; Over the Moon; Villiers Diamond; Second Thoughts; **1941:** Hold That Ghost; Hit the Road; Bachelor Daddy/Sandy Steps Out; Burma Convoy; The Wolf Man; **1942:** The Ghost of Frankenstein; North to the Klondike; Eagle Squadron; Pierre of the Plains; Sherlock Holmes and the Voice of Terror; The Great Impersonation; **1943:** Keep 'em Slugging; The Mad Ghoul; You're a Lucky Fellow Mr. Smith; All By Myself; Hers to Hold; Captive Wild Woman; Son of Dracula; His Butler's Sister; **1944:** Follow the Boys; Ladies Courageous; Pardon My Rhythm; Invisible Man's Revenge; Jungle Woman; The Pearl of Death; Weird Woman; Bowery to Broadway; **1945:** The Fatal Witness; The Frozen Ghost; **1946:** Queen of Burlesque; The French Key; Black Beauty; Flight to Nowhere; **1947:** Spoilers of the North; Last of the Redmen; The Lone Wolf in London; **1949:** Tarzan's Magic Fountain; Parole Inc.; **1950:** The Texan Meets Calamity Jane; **1960:** No Greater Love.

NY Stage: **1941:** Ladies in Retirement.

ANN-MARGRET

(ANN-MARGRET OLSSON)
BORN: VALSJOBYN, SWEDEN, APRIL 28, 1941. RAISED IN WILMETTE, IL.

Initially dismissed by some as nothing more than a cartoonish sex kitten, Ann-Margret certainly emphasized that aspect of her personality on many occasions, slinking, tossing about her mane of red hair and all but purring to express her sexual appetite. In time she confounded the skeptics by tapping into her vulnerable side, becoming an actress of genuine depth and ability. And, hell, she was still sexy too. Her family moved to the United States in 1946, where she was raised in Wilmette, Illinois. After making her professional debut at 16 on Ted Mack's *Original Amateur Hour*, she danced in Las Vegas, where she was spotted by comedian George Burns. Appearances on television (including *The Jack Benny*

Show) led to her debut for director Frank Capra in his last film, *Pocketful of Miracles*, as the naïve daughter raised in comfort, who doesn't realize her mother, Bette Davis, is a street vagrant. The next one, a gaudy musical re-do of Fox's venerable *State Fair*, was the first to focus on Ann-Margret as a sexual tigress, pairing her up with Pat Boone, of all people. Superstardom came with her third assignment, the zippy film version of the stage hit *Bye Bye Birdie*, where she made musical history with her explosive opening rendition of the title song, a sequence added to the movie as an afterthought. Janet Leigh and Dick Van Dyke, billed above her, were not pleased at how much emphasis was given over to their younger co-star in the ads and publicity.

The director of *Birdie*, George Sidney, cast her opposite Elvis Presley in what would turn out to be the pop idol's most entertaining movie, *Viva Las Vegas*, and it marked the only time one of his co-stars gave him a run for his money in the musical numbers. Sidney let Ann-Margaret down with the idiotic *The Swinger*, which required her, at one point, to slosh about in paint, and her reputation for sexy over-acting was confirmed by the ghastly *Kitten With a Whip*, as a hellraising delinquent who blackmails politician John Forsythe. She was miscast in the Claire Trevor role in the remake of *Stagecoach*, and then went back to being just another busty babe in the Matt Helm adventure *Murderers' Row*, and the biker flick *C.C. and Company*. In between she did herself no good whatsoever by making several movies in Europe including *The Tiger and the Pussycat*, the Tiger being Vittorio Gassman. Everything changed, however, when she took on the supporting role of an emotionally unstable fading beauty who has the misfortune to hook up with misogynist Jack Nicholson in *Carnal Knowledge*, and suprised everyone with her gutsy performance. She received an Oscar nomination in the supporting category but it didn't exactly fuel up her movie career. Instead, she got more attention around this time when she was nearly killed in a fall while rehearsing for her Vegas act in 1972.

There was another career peak when she threw herself full force into the role of the mother partially responsible for her son Roger Daltrey's multiple afflictions, in the outrageous rock opera *Tommy*, at one point rolling about an all-white room in a flood of beans, chocolate and champagne. For it she scored another Oscar nomination. After that she revealed her abilities at comedy in *Joseph Andrews*, as an 18th century seductress with the most unsubtle name of Lady Booby, and *The Last Remake of Beau Geste*, but still kept getting stuck in rotten movies like *The Villain*, as the comic book western heroine, and *Looking to Get Out*, about a bunch of losers in Vegas. Better by default was *I Ought to Be in Pictures*, where she was quietly effective as Walter Matthau's practical girlfriend. There were better prospects on television where she got good notices for such telefilms as *Who Will Love My Children?* and the remake of *A Streetcar Named Desire*. Back on the big screen she found herself going through hell as Roy Scheider's wife in *52 Pick-Up*; played the younger woman Gene Hackman turns to when he walks out on his family in *Twice in a Lifetime*; then turned in another subtle performance, as Alan Alda's blossoming ex in *A New Life*. Since there weren't many opportunities for her to sing on screen by the 1990s, it was good to see her do so in Disney's *Newsies*, though the part seemed superfluous to the story. None of these did well financially, but *Grumpy Old Men* certainly did, and although it wasn't a particularly good movie, it was nice to see her being fought over by Jack Lemmon and Walter Matthau, being genuinely worthy of the attention. It did not mean, however, that she also rated industry respect, her role in *Any Given Sunday*, as Cameron Diaz's alcoholic mom, being trimmed considerably, and her part in *The Limey* having been chopped out altogether. In 1967 she married former actor Roger Smith who became her manager. In 1994 she published her autobiography, *Ann-Margret: My Story*.

Screen: 1961: Pocketful of Miracles; 1962: State Fair; 1963: Bye Bye Birdie; 1964: Viva Las Vegas; Kitten With a Whip; The Pleasure Seekers; 1965: Bus Riley's Back in Town; Once a Thief; The Cincinnati Kid; 1966: Made in Paris; The Swinger; Stagecoach; Murderers' Row; 1967: The Prophet (nUSr); The Tiger and the Pussycat; 1968: Rebus; Criminal Affair (nUSr); 1970: C.C. and Company; R.P.M.; 1971: Carnal Knowledge; 1973: The Train Robbers; The Outside Man; 1975: Tommy; 1976: The Twist/Folies Bourgeoises; 1977: The Last Remake of Beau Geste; Joseph Andrews; 1978: The Cheap Detective; Magic; 1979: The Villain; 1980: Middle Age Crazy; 1982: I Ought to Be in Pictures; Lookin' to Get Out; 1983: The Return of the Soldier (filmed 1981); 1985: Twice in a Lifetime; 1986: 52 Pick-Up; 1988: A Tiger's Tale; A New Life; 1992: Newsies; 1993: Grumpy Old Men; 1995: Grumpier Old Men; 1999: Any Given Sunday; 2002: A Woman's a Helluva Thing (dtv); Interstate 60 (dtv).

Select TV: 1968: The Ann-Margret Show (sp); 1969: Ann-Margret: From Hollywood With Love (sp); 1971: Dames at Sea (sp); 1975: Ann-Margret Olsson (sp); 1976: Ann-Margret Smith (sp); 1977: Rhinestone Cowgirl (sp); 1978: Cinderella at the Palace (sp); 1983: Who Will Love My Children?; 1984: A Streetcar Named Desire; 1987: The Two Mrs. Grenvilles; 1991: Our Sons; 1993: Queen (ms); 1994: Nobody's Children; Scarlett (ms); Following Her Heart; 1996: Seduced by Madness: The Diane Borchardt Story; Blue Rodeo; 1998: Four Corners (series); Life of the Party: The Pamela Harriman Story; 1999: Happy Face Murders; 2000: Perfect Murder, Perfect Town; The 10th Kingdom (ms); 2001: The Last Producer; Blonde.

ROSCOE "FATTY" ABRUCKLE

BORN: SMITH CENTER, KS, MARCH 24, 1887.
RAISED IN SANTA ANA, CA. DIED: JUNE 29, 1933.

The unfortunate subject of Hollywood's first career-ruining scandal, much of Roscoe Arbuckle's work as one of silent film's most beloved and inventive comedians has been left to speculation due to the limited availability of many of his efforts. His style was well-orchestrated mayhem, with props flying about and bodies tumbling to and fro, at a seemingly non-stop pace. It all worked very well for short subjects, and once it came time to advance into features, the rotund comic slowly began to show a flair for a more fully sustained sense of character comedy, until that came crashing to a halt. A vaudevillian while still a teenager, he first appeared before a camera as early as 1909, acting in some one-reelers for the Polyscope Company. Joining Mack Sennett's company in 1913 (where, among other things, he was seen as one of the Keystone Cops), Arbuckle got his break when he was teamed for a series of shorts with Mabel Normand, starting with "The Waiter's Picnic," becoming popular enough to be referred to in the titles of many of these under his none-too-flattering "stage name," including "Fatty's Day Off," "Fatty at San Diego," and "Fatty's Flirtations." The comic really came into his own with his knock-about two-reelers made for Joseph Schenck, starting in 1917, including "The Butcher Boy," which introduced the great Buster Keaton to movie audiences. Serving frequently as his own director and producer, Arbuckle's wild, anything-goes approach often made for a breathless 20 minutes. With his transfer to Famous Players-Lasky in 1920, he moved into features, starting with a western, *The Round-Up*, and continuing through further box-office hits like *Brewster's Millions* and *The Traveling Salesman*. The following year he was accused of raping and bringing on the death of party girl Virginia Rappe during a wild gathering in San Francisco. Despite his acquittal, there were boycotts of his movies (his final two Paramount features, *Freight Prepaid* and *Leap Year*, were both shelved) and he was deemed unhirable. A broken man, he returned to vaudeville and directing, using the pseudonymn William B. Goodrich. He managed to star in a handful of Vitaphone short subjects in 1933, the year of his death of a heart attack at the age of 46.

Screen (shorts): 1910: The Sanitarium/The Clinic; 1913: The Gangsters; Passions; He Had Three; Help! Help! Hydrophobia!; The Waiters' Picnic; A Bandit; For the Love of Mabel; The Tell Tale Light; A Noise From the Deep; Love and Courage; The Riot; Mabel's New Hero; Fatty's Day Off; Mabel's Dramatic Debut; The Gypsy Queen; Mother's Boy; The Faithful Taxicab; A Quiet Little Wedding; Fatty at San Diego; Fatty Joins the Force; The Woman Haters; Fatty's Flirtations; He Would a-Hunting Go; 1914: A Misplaced Foot; The Under Sheriff; A Flirt's Mistake; In the Clutches of a Gang; Rebecca's Wedding Day; A Film Johnnie; Tango Tangles; A Rival Demon; His Favorite Pastime; Barnyard Flirtations; Chicken Chaser; A Suspended Ordeal; The Water Dog; The Alarm; The Knockout; Fatty and Minnie-Hee-Haw; Our Country Cousin; Fatty and the Heiress; Fatty's Finish; The Sky Pirate; Caught in a Fire; The Baggage Smasher; Those Happy Days; That Minstrel Man; Those Country Kids; Fatty's Gift; The Masquerade; A Brand New Hero; The Rounders; Fatty's Debut; Fatty Again; Killing Horace; Their Ups and Downs; Zip the Dodger; An Incompetent Hero; Lovers' Post Office; The Sea Nymphs; Fatty's Jonah Day; Fatty's Wine Party; 1915: Leading Lizzie Astray; Among the Mourners; Shotguns That Kick; Fatty's Magic Party; Mabel and Fatty's Wash Day; Rum and Wallpaper; Mabel and Fatty's Simple Life; Fatty and Mabel at the San Diego Exposition; Mabel Fatty and the Law; Fatty's New Role; Colored Villainy; Fatty and Mabel's Married Life; Fatty's Reckless Fling; Fatty's Chance Acquaintance; Love in Armour; Fatty's Faithful Fido; That Little Band of Gold; When Love Took Wings; Mabel and Fatty Viewing the World's Fair at San Francisco; Miss Fatty's Seaside Lovers; The Little Teacher; Fatty's Plucky Pup; Fatty's Tin Type Tangle; Fickle Fatty's Fall; 1916: The Vintage Scandal; Fatty and the Broadway Stars; Fatty and Mabel Adrift; He Did and He Didn't; The Bright Lights; The Other Man; His Wife's Mistakes; The Waiters' Ball; A Creampuff Romance; Rebecca's Wedding Day; 1917: The Butcher Boy; Rough House; His Wedding Night; Fatty at Coney Island; A Country Hero; Oh! Doctor; Out West; 1918: The Bell Boy; Goodnight Nurse; Moonshine; The Cook; The Sheriff; Camping Out; 1919: A Desert Hero; Backstage; The Garage; The Hayseed; The Pullman Porter; Love; The Bank Clerk; 1933: How've You Bean?; Buzzin' Around; Close Relations; Tomallio; In the Dough.

Screen (features): 1920: The Round-Up; The Life of the Party; 1921: Brewster's Millions; The Dollar-a-Year Man; The Traveling Salesman; Crazy to Marry; Gasoline Gus; Freight Prepaid (nUSr); Leap Year (nUSr); 1923: Hollywood.

EVE ARDEN
(EUNICE QUEDENS) BORN: MILL VALLEY, CA, APRIL 30, 1908. DIED: NOVEMBER 12, 1990.

With full, questioning lips, and eyebrows ready to arch at a moment's notice, Eve Arden basically played slight variations on the same type: the wisecracking best friend, but she played it to such perfection that her name in the credits of any film was a reason to rejoice. She began by acting with a San Francisco stock company and taking bit parts in films under her real name, including *Dancing Lady*, as a phony Southern belle. Her participation in a revue at the Pasadena Playhouse, *Lo and Behold*, now using the name Eve Arden, led to appearances in two Ziegfeld Follies shows on Broadway and, once again, Hollywood beckoned, officially "debuting" her in 1937, in the supporting cast of a low-budget Universal comedy *Oh Doctor!*, as part of a team of crooks. For the next 15 years she never seemed to stop working, mainly in comedies or in comical roles, with occasional side trips back to the stage. Her second 1937 release, *Stage Door*, really set the tone for the Arden people would come to cherish, playing a sassy aspiring actress, lulling about the female-filled boarding house, often with a cat draped about her neck, tossing off acidic observations on whatever the other ladies had to say, making even the lesser lines sound good. Pretty much forgotten during this period was a rare foray into seriousness, *Small Town Czar*, as the girlfriend of criminal Barton MacLane, a story told by Ed Sullivan of all people.

Returning from two appearances on Broadway, Arden really entered into her own during the 1940s, including *Slightly Honorable*, which was a comedy, even though she ended up with a knife in her back; *Comrade X*, just one of many instances when she was relegated to supporting a lesser talent, in this case Hedy Lamarr; the first unfaithful version of *No, No, Nanette* (and then, a decade later, its unofficial "remake," *Two for Tea*); *Ziegfeld Girl*, where even she, James Stewart, and Judy Garland couldn't raise it above the clichés; and her first genuine star-billing role, in a Warners "B," *She Couldn't Say No*, though most of the story really focused on elderly Clem Bevans. Bopping around from studio to studio, she was a dance hall hostess in *Manpower*, at Warners; did what she could with a poor Red Skelton MGM offering *Whistling in the Dark*; repeated her stage role in Paramount's adaptation of *Let's Face It*, where she at least got to sing the only Cole Porter they bothered to keep, "Let's Not Talk About Love;" and played the classy magazine editor in Columbia's very popular Technicolor musical *Cover Girl*. In 1944 she signed her very first exclusive contract, with Warners, in order to secure the role of the Russian guerilla in the adaptation of the Broadway hit *The Doughgirls*, though the film did not repeat its previous success. However, her being on the Warners lot led to her being cast as the tart-tongued waitress, dispensing very Arden-like observations in one of the top movies of the 1940s, *Mildred Pierce*. In addition to handing her one of the all-time quotable lines ("Alligators have the right idea, they eat their young."), it brought her her only Oscar nomination. Also at Warners she was French in *Night and Day*; Ann Sheridan's nasty sister-in-law in *The Unfaithful*, and had another meaty part, as Eleanor Parker's stylish, frank, and meddlesome friend, in *The Voice of the Turtle*, from the long-running Broadway comedy.

There wasn't much left of the adaptation of the musical hit *One Touch of Venus*, so one was ever grateful to have Arden in there trying, and she herself did get to sing something called "Waiting at the Church" in the Donald O'Connor vehicle *Curtain Call at Cactus Creek*. She finally made it to the front ranks, playing a school teacher in the highly popular radio show, *Our Miss Brooks*, in 1948; its subsequent television incarnation (for which she got an Emmy Award in 1953) and a drab movie spin-off, released by Warners, in 1956. Following its run she was back doing supporting stints in two major releases, where there were slightly more serious shadings to her work, in *Anatomy of a Murder*, as James Stewart's legal assistant, and *The Dark at the Top of the Stairs*, as Dorothy McGuire's set-in-her-ways sister whose life isn't as rosy as it seems. There was a fairly long period away from the large screen save for another salvage job in one of those idiotic AIP teen movies, *Sergeant Deadhead*. During that time she showed up in another sitcom, *The Mothers-in-Law*, which firmly re-established television as her place of employment in her advancing years. In 1978 a whole new generation was won over by her bone dry delivery when she played the high school principal in the blockbuster musical *Grease*, followed by a sequel, and a few more unworthy films that didn't diminish that fact that she almost never came away from the wreckage looking bad. She published her autobiography, *Three Phases of Eve*, in 1985.

Screen: AS EUNICE QUEDENS: 1929: Song of Love; 1933: Dancing Lady.

AS EVE ARDEN: 1937: Oh Doctor!; Stage Door; 1938: Coconut Grove; Having Wonderful Time; Letter of Introduction; 1939: Women in the Wind; Big Town Czar; The Forgotten Woman; Eternally Yours; At the Circus; 1940: A Child Is Born; Slightly Honorable; Comrade X; No, No, Nanette; She Couldn't Say No; 1941: That Uncertain Feeling; Ziegfeld Girl; She Knew All the Answers; San Antonio Rose; Manpower; Whistling in the Dark; The Last of the Duanes; Sing for Your Supper; Obliging Young Lady; Bedtime Story; 1943: Hit Parade of 1943; Let's Face It; 1944: Cover Girl; The Doughgirls; 1945: Earl Carroll Vanities; Pan-Americana; Patrick the Great; Mildred Pierce; 1946: My Reputation; The Kid From Brooklyn; Night and Day; 1947: Song of Scheherazade; The Arnelo Affair; The Unfaithful; The Voice of the Turtle/One for the Book; 1948: One Touch of Venus; Whiplash; 1949: The Lady Takes a Sailor; My Dream Is Yours; 1950: Paid in Full; Curtain Call at Cactus Creek; Tea for Two; Three Husbands; 1951: Goodbye, My Fancy; 1952: We're Not Married!; 1953: The Lady Wants Mink; 1956: Our Miss Brooks; 1959: Anatomy of a Murder; 1960: The Dark at the Top of the Stairs; 1965: Sergeant Deadhead; 1975: The Strongest Man in the World; 1978: Grease; 1981: Under the Rainbow; 1982: Pandemonium; Grease 2.

NY Stage: 1934: Ziegfeld Follies of 1934; 1935: Parade; 1936: Ziegfeld Follies of 1936; 1939: Very Warm for May; 1940: Two for the Show; 1942: Let's Face It.

Select TV: 1951: Julie (sp); 1952–56: Our Miss Brooks (series); 1957–58: The Eve Arden Show (series); 1967–69: The Mothers-in-Law (series); 1969: In Name Only; 1972: A Very Missing Person; All My Darling Daughters; 1978: A Guide for the Married Woman; 1980: The Dream Merchants (ms); 1983: Alice in Wonderland (sp); 1984: Faerie Tale Theatre: Cinderella (sp).

RICHARD ARLEN

(CORNELIUS RICHARD VAN MATTIMORE) BORN: CHARLOTTESVILLE, VA, SEPTEMBER 1, 1899. ED: UNIV. OF PA. DIED: MARCH 28, 1976.

Your standard slick-haired, rugged, solidly-built Hollywood he-man, Richard Arlen was one of the busiest names of them all, but his work is barely taken into consideration by most, simply because he spent so much time in "B's" and second features. A former pilot with the Royal Canadian Flying Corps, Arlen entered films working in the Paramount studios labs. This led to doing extra work, using the last half of his real name, Van Mattimore. It was under this name that he played his first real role, in an independent quickie called *Vengeance of the Deep*. Finally Paramount decided to put him under contract and gave him some secondary parts and romantic leads in *Behind the Front*, as Wallace Beery's son, and *Padlocked*, opposite Lois Moran. His wartime flying experience was instrumental in him being chosen for the role that

brought him stardom, the young World War I flyer David Armstrong, in the first movie to win the Best Picture Oscar, *Wings*, a gigantic hit in its day and a rare silent that continued to play well over the years. He found himself in some other major releases of the silence-to-sound period, including *The Four Feathers*, as the soldier who must prove himself after being branded a coward; *Thunderbolt*, as a bank clerk framed by gangster George Bancroft; and *The Virginian*, as the friend of Gary Cooper who turns to cattle rustling, thereby leading to his hanging. He remained at the studio until 1935, showing up in everything from the South Seas adventure *The Sea God* to the soap opera *Wayward* to the horror classic *Island of Lost Souls* to the sprightly comedy *Three-Cornered Moon*. Certainly his oddest role was as the Chesire Cat in the studio's eccentric attempt to film *Alice in Wonderland*, a part he got, no doubt, because of his cunning smile.

Arlen himself knew that if there was one genre he came off best in it was westerns, so he made a slew of them, riding the range in such titles as *Under the Tonto Rim* and *The Light of Western Stars*. After leaving the company that had been so good to him for so long, he freelanced in a lot of second-string stuff, popping up as a soldier returning from the dead in *Three Live Ghosts*, a millionaire clergyman in *The Calling of Dan Matthews*, and a fur trapper in *Call of the Yukon*, among others. In 1939 he joined Universal's "B" unit, starring in a string of action quickies with Andy Devine as his sidekick, including *Mutiny on the Blackhawk*, *Legion of Lost Flyers*, and *Black Diamonds*, and ending in 1941 with *Men of the Timberland*. He stayed in "B's" when he moved over to the Pine-Thomas unit that was distributed through his old alma mater, Paramount, appearing in such action-related programmers as *Wildcat*, *Wrecking Crew*, and *Alaska Highway*. So identified was he with second string material by this point that it was surprising to see him pop up in an "A" movie like the Betty Grable musical *When My Baby Smiles at Me*, as her suitor. Keeping busy into his 60s, he could be found in most of the low budget A.C. Lyles westerns of the 1960s, like *Young Fury*, *Apache Uprising*, and *Red Tomahawk*, all of which only further emphasized the long-established image of Arlen as a tight-lipped, stoic actor whose playing was low-keyed to say the least. Apparently the association with Paramount was something from which he would never escape, for these quickies were also released by that studio. From 1927 to 1945 he was married to actress Jobyna Ralston, who had appeared with him in *Wings*.

Screen: AS VAN MATTIMORE: 1923: Vengeance of the Deep.

AS RICHARD ARLEN: 1925: In the Name of Love; The Coast of Folly; 1926: The Enchanted Hill; Behind the Front; Padlocked; 1927: Rolled Stockings; The Blood Ship; Figures Don't Lie; Wings; Sally in Our Alley; She's a Sheik; 1928: Under the Tonto Rim; Feel My Pulse; Ladies of the Mob; Beggars of Life; Manhattan Cocktail; 1929: The Man I Love; The Four Feathers; Thunderbolt; Dangerous Curves; The Virginian; 1930: Dangerous Paradise; Burning Up; The Light of Western Stars; Paramount on Parade; The Border Legion; The Sea God; The Santa Fe Trail; Only Saps Work; 1931: The Conquering Horde; Gun Smoke; The Lawyer's Secret; The Secret Call; Caught; Touchdown; 1932: Wayward; Sky Bride; Guilty as Hell; Tiger Shark; The All-American; 1933: Island of Lost Souls; Song of the Eagle; College Humor; Three-Cornered Moon; Golden Harvest; Alice in Wonderland; Hell and High Water; 1934: Come on Marines; She Made Her Bed; Ready for Love; 1935: Helldorado; Let 'em Have It; Three Live Ghosts; 1936: The Calling of Dan Matthews; The Mine With the Iron Door; Secret Valley; 1937: Silent Barriers; Artists & Models; Murder in Greenwich Village/Park Avenue Girl; 1938: No Time to Marry; Call of the

Yukon; Straight, Place and Show; **1939:** Missing Daughters; Mutiny on the Blackhawk; Tropic Fury; Legion of Lost Flyers; **1940:** Man From Montreal; Danger on Wheels; Hot Steel; The Leather Pushers; Black Diamonds; The Devil's Pipeline; **1941:** Lucky Devils; A Dangerous Game; Mutiny in the Arctic; Men of the Timberland; Power Dive; Raiders of the Desert; Forced Landing; Flying Blind; **1942:** Torpedo Boat; Wildcat; Wrecking Crew; **1943:** Alaska Highway; Submarine Alert; Minesweeper; Aerial Gunner; **1944:** Timber Queen; The Lady and the Monster; Storm Over Lisbon; That's My Baby; The Big Bonanza; **1945:** The Phantom Speaks; Identity Unknown; **1946:** Accomplice; The French Key; **1947:** Buffalo Bill Rides Again; **1948:** The Return of Wildfire; When My Baby Smiles at Me; Speed to Spare; **1949:** Grand Canyon; **1950:** Kansas Raiders; **1951:** Silver City; Flaming Feather; **1952:** Hurricane Smith; The Blazing Forest; **1953:** Sabre Jet; **1955:** Devil's Harbor/Devil's Point; **1956:** Hidden Guns; The Mountain; **1958:** Blonde Blackmailer/Stolen Time; **1959:** Warlock; **1960:** Raymie; **1961:** The Last Time I Saw Archie; **1963:** The Young and the Brave; The Shepherd of the Hills; The Crawling Hand; Cavalry Command; Thunder Mountain; **1964:** Law of the Lawless; The Best Man; **1965:** Young Fury; Black Spurs; The Bounty Killer; Town Tamer; The Human Duplicators; **1966:** Apache Uprising; Johnny Reno; Waco; To the Shore of Hell; **1967:** Road to Nashville; Red Tomahawk; Fort Utah; Hostile Guns; **1968:** Rogue's Gallery; Buckskin; **1970:** Sex and the College Girl (filmed 1964); **1976:** Won Ton Ton, the Dog Who Saved Hollywood; **1977:** A Whale of a Tale.

NY Stage: 1945: Too Hot for Maneuvers.

Select TV: 1957: Deep Water (sp); Child of Trouble (sp).

GEORGE ARLISS

(GEORGE AUGUSTUS ANDREWS) BORN: LONDON, ENGLAND, APRIL 10, 1868. DIED: FEBRUARY 5, 1946.

A very commanding, florid, aristocratic British performer with a long, bony face often given a highly theatrical emphasis by a monocle, George Arliss became a screen star at 60, adding great dashes of color to the early days of talkies. In time he came to represent the sort of balcony-playing that actors were taught to stay away from though, in truth, there is still something quite entertaining about his enthusiasm and eagerness to please when seen today. He made his London stage debut in 1890, in *Across Her Path*, came to the U.S. in 1901, and spent the next 20 years becoming a major star of the New York theatre in such plays as *The Devil*, *Alexander Hamilton*, and *Old English*. Much of his early movie work was made to preserve certain stage triumphs on film, including *Disraeli*, in 1921, and *The Green Goddess*, in 1923. With the arrival of talking films it was agreed on by Warner Bros. that movie audiences should get a chance to hear as well as see these Arliss roles, so he remade *Disraeli* for them in 1929. It turned out to be a surprise box-office hit, earning him an Academy Award. If indeed Arliss had a tendency to slop it on a bit too thick at times, his performance is certainly the breath of life in what is a stage-bound and barely interesting story of the British Prime Minster and his attempts to purchase of the Suez Canal. There was an additional nomination during that same period, 1929–30, with the new version of *The Green Goddess*, in which he was an improbably sinister Rajah with a hatred for the British.

Delighted by his success, the studio presented *Old English*, from another of his Broadway triumphs; and *The Millionaire*, which he'd previously done as *The Ruling Passion*, a more light-hearted affair than most, in which he was a tycoon so bored with retirement that he decides to operate a gas station to feel like one

of the regular folk. Back to the historical, he brushed off another old stage property, *Alexander Hamilton*, one he himself had co-written, mixing history with a bit of hanky panky with a married woman (June Collyer). After this, he did another remake of a silent he'd done, *The Man Who Played God*, which became one of his most popular films, as a pianist who realizes he is losing his hearing. He left Warners, after making *Voltaire*, to join the newly-established 20th Century Pictures, shortly before it joined forces with Fox, for another big hit, *The House of Rothschild*, in a dual role, hammy as the dying father but scoring most proficiently as the crafty son. It was interesting to see Hollywood tackle the subject of anti-Semitism so fervently in 1934 and the film is probably the least-dated of the Arliss vehicles. After starring as *Cardinal Richelieu*, he left Hollywood, making the remainder of his movies in Britain. Among these were *The Guv'nor*, in which he tried to stretch by playing a hobo; *His Lordship*, which found him in a dual role; and his last, *Dr. Syn*, as a heroic nightrider of the 19th century. By this time his popularity had passed to a point that most of these weren't even booked to play in the U.S. and he retired from acting in 1937 to care for his wife and frequent co-star, Florence Montgomery Arliss, who was going blind. There were two autobiographies: *Up the Years From Bloomsbury* (1927) and *My Ten Years at the Studios* (1940).

Screen: 1921: The Devil; Disraeli; **1922:** The Ruling Passion; The Man Who Played God; **1923:** The Green Goddess; **1924:** Twenty Dollars a Week; **1929:** Disraeli; **1930:** The Green Goddess; Old English; **1931:** The Millionaire; Alexander Hamilton; **1932:** The Man Who Played God; A Successful Calamity; **1933:** The King's Vacation; The Working Man; Voltaire; **1934:** The House of Rothschild; The Last Gentleman; **1935:** The Iron Duke; Cardinal Richelieu; The Guv'nor/Mister Hobo; Transatlantic Tunnel/The Tunnel; **1936:** East Meets West; **1937:** Man of Affairs/His Lordship; Dr. Syn.

NY Stage: 1901: Mrs. Patrick Campbell Repertory; **1902:** Magda; Darling of the Gods; **1904:** Becky Sharp; Hedda Gabler; Leah Kleschna; **1905:** The Eyes of the Heart; The Rose; **1906:** The New York Idea; **1907:** Rosmersholm; **1908:** The Devil; **1909:** Septimus; **1911:** Disraeli; **1916:** Paganini; **1917:** The Professor's Love Story; Disrael (revival); Hamilton (and co-writer); **1918:** Out There; **1920:** Poldekin; **1921:** The Green Goddess; **1924:** Old English; **1928:** The Merchant of Venice.

LOUIS ARMSTRONG

BORN: NEW ORLEANS, LA, AUGUST 4, 1901. DIED: JULY 6, 1971.

The one and only "Satchmo," master trumpeter and unique song stylist without peer, Louis Armstrong, with his unmistakable raspy voice, ingratiating smile and ever-present handkerchief, was one of the world's great jazz musicians. He also became one of the most welcome movie performers, though nearly all of his appearances found him playing himself in guest spots or specialty numbers. No matter, it is often Louis Armstrong with a personality bursting with affection and life, that you remember long after the rest of the film has been forgotten. For over 30 years he could be found stealing the show, whether cutting up with the irresistible curio "Skeleton in the Closet" in *Pennies From Heaven*; leading a parade in the Mae West vehicle *Every Day's a Holiday*; introducing the Oscar-nominated "Jeepers Creepers" in *Going Places*; being joined by such fellow jazz giants as Benny Goodman, Tommy Dorsey, and Lionel Hampton for *A Song Is Born*; dueting playfully with Bing Crosby on "Now You Has Jazz" in *High Society*, a remake of *The*

Philadelphia Story, appropriately set during the Newport Jazz Festival to accommodate Satchmo; memorably joining Danny Kaye for a medley in *The Five Pennies*; or reprising his hit single of the title tune in a duet with Barbra Streisand in *Hello, Dolly!* For both *Paris Blues* and *A Man Called Adam*, although he was still there with his trumpet, he was actually called on to play dramatic characters rather than himself and did so quite well indeed.

Screen: 1930: Ex-Flame; 1936: Pennies From Heaven; 1937: Every Day's a Holiday; Artists & Models; 1938: Dr. Rhythm; Going Places; 1941: Birth of the Blues; 1943: Cabin in the Sky; 1944: Jam Session; Atlantic City; 1945: Pillow to Post; 1947: New Orleans; 1948: A Song is Born; 1951: The Strip; Here Comes the Groom; 1952: Glory Alley; 1954: The Glenn Miller Story; 1956: High Society; 1957: Satchmo the Great; 1959: The Beat Generation; The Five Pennies; 1960: Jazz on a Summer's Day; 1961: Paris Blues; 1965: When the Boys Meet the Girls; 1966: A Man Called Adam; 1969: Hello, Dolly!

Select TV: 1956: The Lord Don't Play Favorites (sp).

ROBERT ARMSTRONG

(DONALD ROBERT SMITH) BORN: SAGINAW, MI, NOVEMBER 20, 1890. ED: UNIV. OF MI. DIED: APRIL 20, 1973.

The movies' greatest ape wrangler, grim-faced Robert Armstrong's film immortality comes from having to act opposite a barrage of special effects. A former law student, he lost interest in the legal profession and began creating and appearing in sketches in vaudeville. A role in the Broadway play *Is Zat So?*, as a prizefighter, brought him to Hollywood on a permanent basis where he started off under contract to Pathe playing — surprise! — a prizefighter in *The Main Event*. He was typecast in tough guy parts, playing a sailor in *A Girl in Every Port*; a gangster in *Celebrity*; another boxer, albeit a comical one, in *Be Yourself* (which allowed him to sing with Fanny Brice at one point); and the title role in *The Racketeer*. RKO signed him up and he graduated to fight manager for *Iron Man*, then was hunted down by Lesley Banks in *The Most Dangerous Game*, which was produced by Merian C. Cooper. It was that same producer who cast him as the fast-talking showman Carl Denham in the classic fantasy *King Kong*, sweeping his shipmates into an unforgettable adventure and uttering one of the cinema's memorable closing lines: "It was beauty killed the beast." Later that year he reprised the character in an inferior sequel, *Son of Kong*, and played a very loose variation of Denham 16 years later in a jokier Cooper ape opus, *Mighty Joe Young*. Between those two the better part of his career was spent supporting bigger stars in such movies as *G Men*, as James Cagney's disagreeable justice department superior; *The Ex-Mrs. Bradford*, as a bookmaker William Powell suspects of murder; and another with Cagney, *Blood on the Sun*, as an Asian. Otherwise he could be found in countless second features like *Flirting with Danger*, as an explosives expert; *Little Big Shot*, as a con artist; *Without Orders*, as a pilot with girl trouble; and some Universal serials.

Screen: 1927: The Main Event; 1928: The Leopard Lady; A Girl in Every Port; Square Crooks; The Cop; Celebrity; The Baby Cyclone; Show Folks; Ned McCobb's Daughter; 1929: Shady Lady; The Leatherneck; The Woman From Hell; Big News; Oh Yeah!; The Racketeer; 1930: Big Money; Be Yourself; Danger Lights; Dumbbells in Ermine; Paid; 1931: Easy Money; The Tip-Off; Suicide Fleet; Iron Man; Ex-Bad Boy; 1932: Panama Flo; The Lost Squadron; Is My Face Red?; Hold 'em Jail; The Most Dangerous Game; Penguin Pool Murder; Radio Patrol; 1933: Blind Adventure; Billion Dollar Scandal; King Kong; I Love That Man; Fast Workers; Above the Clouds; Son of Kong; 1934: Search for Beauty; Palooka; The Hell Cat; She Made Her Bed; Manhattan Love Song; Kansas City Princess; Flirting With Danger; 1935: The Mystery Man; Sweet Music; G Men; Gigolette; Remember Last Night?; Little Big Shot; 1936: Dangerous Waters; The Ex-Mrs. Bradford; Public Enemy's Wife; All American Chump; Without Orders; 1937: The Three Legionnaires; It Can't Last Forever; Nobody's Baby; The Girl Said No; She Loved a Fireman; 1938: There Goes My Heart; The Night Hawk; 1939: The Flying Irishman; Unmarried; Man of Conquest; Winter Carnival; Flight at Midnight; Call a Messenger; 1940: Framed; Forgotten Girls; Enemy Agent; San Francisco Docks; The Bride Wore Crutches; Behind the News; Meet the Fleet; 1941: Mr. Dynamite; Citadel of Crime; Dive Bomber; San Francisco Docks; Sky Raiders (serial); 1942: My Favorite Spy; Baby Face Morgan; Let's Get Tough; It Happened in Flatbush; Gang Busters (serial); 1943: Around the World; The Kansan; Adventures of the Flying Cadets (serial); Wings Over the Pacific; The Mad Ghoul; 1944: The Navy Way; Action in Arabia; Mr. Winkle Goes to War; Belle of the Yukon; 1945: Gangs of the Waterfront; Blood on the Sun; The Falcon in San Francisco; The Royal Mounted Rides Again (serial); Arson Squad; 1946: Gay Blades; Criminal Court; Flight to Nowhere; G.I. War Brides; Blonde Alibi; Decoy; 1947: The Fall Guy; The Fugitive; Exposed; The Sea of Grass; 1948: Return of the Bad Men; The Paleface; 1949: The Lucky Stiff; Crime Doctor's Diary; The Streets of San Francisco; Mighty Joe Young; Captain China; Sons of New Mexico; 1950: Destination Big House; 1952: The Pace That Thrills; 1955: Las Vegas Shakedown; Double Jeopardy; 1956: The Peacemaker; 1957: The Crooked Circle; 1963: Johnny Cool; 1964: For Those Who Think Young.

NY Stage: 1919: Boys Will Be Boys; 1920: Honey Girl; 1925: Is Zat So?; 1926: Sure Fire; 1944: Sleep No More.

JAMES ARNESS

(JAMES AURNESS) BORN: MINNEAPOLIS, MN, MAY 26, 1923. ED: BELOIT COL.

The older brother of actor Peter Graves, stolid, tree-sized James Arness drifted into acting in the late 1940s, after serving in World War II. Using his real name, he made his film debut as one of Loretta Young's brawling Swedish brothers in *The Farmer's Daughter*. He kept busy in a series of second leads; had one of the star roles in a campy quickie, *Two Lost Worlds*, battling dinosaurs on an uncharted island; and mostly kept his mouth shut and face under make-up for the job that would give him lasting sci-fi cult status, the title role in the gripping, atmospheric *The Thing from Another World*. He became a familiar figure in minor adventure films and westerns like *Stars in My Crown* (which not only billed him as James Arness for the first time but found his future *Gunsmoke* co-star, Amanda Blake, among its cast), *Cavalry Scout*, and *Horizons West*, and gave support to John Wayne in *Big Jim McLain*, cast as his fellow-agent, tracking down evil commies in Hawaii; *Island in the Sky*; *Hondo*; and *The Sea Chase*. There was another important role in a superior sci-fi picture, *Them!*, this time cast as the hero, fighting a horde of giant ants living in the Los Angeles reservoirs. His show business immortality, however, came from his starring role on the longest running dramatic series in television history, *Gunsmoke* (1955–75), playing the taciturn, heroic marshal Matt Dillon. The year after the show commenced Arness got to carry his own western, *Gun the Man Down*, swearing revenge on the guys who deserted him during a bank robbery, but it was strictly treated as programmer material. Aside from a gag appearance in Bob Hope's *Alias Jesse James*, he would never again be seen on the big screen. After *Gunsmoke*'s long run, there were two more series, *How the West Was Won* and *McClain's Law*, as well as several *Gunsmoke* reunion movies.

Screen: AS JAMES AURNESS: 1947: The Farmer's Daughter; Roses Are Red; 1949: Battleground; 1950: Sierra; Two Lost Worlds; Wyoming Mail; Wagon Master.

AS JAMES ARNESS: 1950: Stars in My Crown; 1951: Cavalry Scout; Iron Man; The People Against O'Hara; Belle La Grand; The Thing from Another World; 1952: The Girl in White; Carbine Williams; Horizons West; Big Jim McLain; Hellgate; 1953: Lone Hand; Veils of Bagdad; Island in the Sky; Hondo; 1954: Her Twelve Men; Them!; 1955: Many Rivers to Cross; The Sea Chase; Flame of the Islands; 1956: The First Traveling Saleslady; Gun the Man Down; 1959: Alias Jesse James.

Select TV: 1954: The Chase (sp); 1955–75: Gunsmoke (series); 1976: The Macahans; 1977: How the West Was Won (ms); 1978–79: How the West Was Won (series); 1981–82: McClain's Law (series); 1987: The Alamo: 13 Days to Glory; 1987: Gunsmoke: Return to Dodge; 1988: Red River; 1990: Gunsmoke: The Last Apache; 1992: Gunsmoke: To the Last Man; 1993: Gunsmoke: The Last Ride (and exec. prod.); 1994: Gunsmoke: One Man's Justice.

EDWARD ARNOLD

(GUENTHER EDWARD ARNOLD SCHNEIDER)
BORN: NEW YORK, NY, FEBRUARY 18, 1890.
DIED: APRIL 26, 1956.

Burly, deep-voiced character player Edward Arnold, with his intimidating glare and condescending laugh, was so omnipresent and so imposing a personality that he is as well remember by cinema devotees as many of the stars of his day. Making his professional debut as a teen actor with the Ben Greet Players, then acting with Maxine Elliott's company, he ended up at the Essany Film Company in Chicago, appearing in many short subjects between some feature assignments. There followed a distinguished Broadway stage career, starting with *The Storm*, in 1919, and concluding with the 1932 production of *Whistling in the Dark*, which earned him a contract with Universal Pictures. His first role there was as the bad guy betrayed by hero Lew Ayres in a programmer *Okay America*, and the movie industry decided then and there that it had found a sublimely convincing villain. Among his rotters of this period were an Egyptian pasha trying to get Myrna Loy in his clutches in *The Barbarian*; a gangster who pulls strings to have the murder he committed pinned on bellhop Eric Linden in *Afraid to Talk*; and Emperor Valerius in the Eddie Cantor comedy *Roman Scandals*. He himself was done wrong in *Unknown Blonde*, top-billed as a divorce lawyer. On the side of the law he was a police official in *Secret of the Blue Room*, *Hide-Out*, and the 1935 version of *Crime and Punishment*, taunting murderer Peter Lorre. There was a sympathetic part as the likable drunk whom Joan Crawford marries and helps rehabilitate in *Sadie McKee*, after which he found a role he could really make his own, the turn-of-the-century symbol of wealth and dapper attire, *Diamond Jim* (Brady), a character he would later reprise in *Lillian Russell*.

There was such demand for Arnold in the mid-1930s that he was temporarily thought of as star material, as in *Come and Get It*, among his meatiest performances, as a logger who rises to paper-mill tycoon; *Meet Nero Wolfe*, making him the first actor to portray Rex Stout's corpulent detective; *John Meade's Woman*, making more money off the lumber industry, while breaking

Francine Lattimore's heart; and *The Toast of New York*, once again rising to the top of his game, as real-life financier Jim Fisk, an obvious attempt to repeat the Diamond Jim formula. There was no doubt that Arnold was the perfect Hollywood image of a millionaire fat cat, with his confident, persuasive air and effortless way of physically and intellectually dominating a scene. He played this kind of character for humor quite successfully in *Easy Living*, tossing his wife's mink out the window during an argument and setting the plot in motion. Around this point, Frank Capra invited him to join his stock company and brilliantly utilized his unsympathetic qualities, casting him as James Stewart's humorless, industrialist dad who doesn't want his son getting tangled up with Jean Arthur's family of eccentrics in *You Can't Take It With You*; and a pair of power-hungry political bosses, in *Mr. Smith Goes to Washington*, trying to destroy the naïve Stewart; and *Meet John Doe*, seemingly benign, with his wire-rimmed spectacles and measured speech pattern, but seething with evil. These last two rank among Arnold's greatest performances.

Staying rich, he was a munitions tycoon dumped by Norma Shearer in *Idiot's Delight*, and ended up in prison convicted of embezzlement, in *Johnny Apollo*. There was another great showy part, in *All That Money Can Buy*, as Daniel Webster, speaking against the Devil himself, Walter Huston, in defense of American ideals; and then the central role in *Eyes in the Night*, as a blind detective in this "B" effort that received a good enough response to warrant a follow-up, *The Hidden Eye*. Arnold spent most of the 1940s contracted to MGM, where he was the wicked Grand Vizier in *Kismet*, a congressman in *Command Decision*, an annoying lawyer in *Ziegfeld Follies*, and Pawnee Bill in *Annie Get Your Gun*. Over at Paramount, he had one of his best comical roles as Joan Caulfield's suffering dad in *Dear Ruth*, a part he would reprise in two sequels. He was still fairly busy during the 1950s, as straight man to Jerry Lewis in *Living It Up*; playing a crooked lawyer in *The City That Never Sleeps*; and a blackmailing lobbyist in a "B" movie for Columbia, *Miami Expose*, during the making of which he died from a cerebral hemorrhage. His memoirs, *Lorenzo Goes to Hollywood* (the name referring to his first theatrical assignment, in *The Merchant of Venice*), were published in 1940.

Screen (features): 1916: Vultures of Society; The Return of Eve; The Primitive Strain; 1917: The Slacker's Heart; 1919: Phil-for-Short; A Broadway Saint; 1920: The Cost; 1932: Okay America; Three on a Match; Afraid to Talk; I Am a Fugitive From a Chain Gang; 1933: Rasputin and the Empress; Whistling in the Dark; The White Sister; The Barbarian; Jennie Gerhardt; Her Bodyguard; Secret of the Blue Room; Lawyer Man; I'm No Angel; Roman Scandals; 1934: Madame Spy; Sadie McKee; Thirty Day Princess; Unknown Blonde; Hide-Out; Million Dollar Ransom; The President Vanishes; Wednesday's Child; 1935: Biography of a Bachelor Girl; Cardinal Richelieu; The Glass Key; Diamond Jim; Crime and Punishment; Remember Last Night?; 1936: Sutter's Gold; Meet Nero Wolfe; Come and Get It; 1937: John Meade's Woman; Easy Living; The Toast of New York; Blossoms on Broadway; 1938: The Crowd Roars; You Can't Take It With You; 1939: Let Freedom Ring; Idiot's Delight; Man About Town; Mr. Smith Goes to Washington; 1940: Slightly Honorable; The Earl of Chicago; Johnny Apollo; Lillian Russell; 1941: The Penalty; The Lady From Cheyenne; Meet John Doe; Nothing But the Truth; Unholy Partners; Design for Scandal; All That Money Can Buy/The Devil and Daniel Webster; 1942: Johnny Eager; The War Against Mrs. Hadley; Eyes in the Night; 1943: The Youngest Profession; 1944: Standing Room Only; Janie; Kismet; Mrs. Parkington; Main Street After Dark; 1945: Week-end at the Waldorf; The Hidden Eye; 1946: Ziegfeld Follies; Janie Gets Married; Three Wise Fools; No Leave, No

Love; The Mighty McGurk; My Brother Talks to Horses; **1947:** Dear Ruth; The Hucksters; **1948:** Three Daring Daughters; Big City; Wallflower; Command Decision; **1949:** John Loves Mary; Take Me Out to the Ball Game; Big Jack; Dear Wife; **1950:** The Yellow Cab Man; Annie Get Your Gun; The Skipper Surprised His Wife; **1951:** Dear Brat; **1952:** Belles on the Their Toes; **1953:** The City That Never Sleeps; Man of Conflict; **1954:** Living It Up; **1956:** The Houston Story; The Ambassador's Daughter; Miami Expose.

NY Stage: **1919:** The Storm; **1920:** Beyond the Horizon; **1923:** Mad Honeymoon; The Nervous Wreck; **1924:** Her Way Out; **1925:** Easy Come, Easy Go; **1927:** Julie; **1928:** The Grey Fox; **1929:** Conflict; **1931:** Miracle at Verdun; The Third Little Show; **1932:** Whistling in the Dark.

Select TV: **1950:** Our Town (sp); **1952:** Junior (sp); **1953:** Lost and Found (sp); Since the Day (sp); **1954:** Walking John Stopped Here (sp); The Tryst (sp); Twelve Angry Men (sp); Edward Arnold Theatre (series); **1955:** Twelve to Eternity (sp); **1956:** The Victim (sp).

JEAN ARTHUR

(GLADYS GEORGIANNA GREENE) BORN: NEW YORK, NY, OCTOBER 17, 1900. DIED: JUNE 19, 1991.

A former model who toiled in small roles for years before gaining recognition for her fetching comic style in some of the 1930s brightest comedies, Jean Arthur was one of the screen's warmest personalities. She was signed by Fox in 1923, where she was first employed in a small part in a John Ford film, *Cameo Kirby*, followed by roles in mostly "B" westerns with titles like *The Drug Store Cowboy*, *The Hurricane Horseman*, and *Twisted Triggers*. Having made no impact whatsoever, she then drifted over to Paramount during the transition from silents to talkies, appearing in films like *The Saturday Night Kid*, battling sister Clara Bow for the same man; *The Greene Murder Case*, responsible for the killing of a millionaire in this Philo Vance mystery; and *Street of Chance*, as the sister-in-law of gambler William Powell. Nothing of her work during this period seemed to hint at the heights she would reach, as she was just another ingénue, playing girlfriends, sisters, and delicate little things, filling the roles as needed. Feeling inadequate, she took a break from the movies to learn her craft onstage, appearing mainly in stock. When she returned she may have felt more assured, but the movies she wound up in weren't anything to crow about, including the extremely budget-conscious *Get That Venus*, as a shopkeeper's daughter; and *Whirlpool*, as a reporter, for Columbia. Because of the latter Columbia put her under contract, casting her in the drama *The Defense Rests*, trying to expose corrupt lawyer Jack Holt but falling for him instead, and *The Most Precious Thing in Life*, one of those icky soap operas of the time about self-sacrificing mothers and the children they watch from afar.

In 1935, with more than a decade of credits behind her, the critics and public finally began to take note, starting with a rare John Ford comedy, *The Whole Town's Talking*, falling in love with fellow clerk Edward G. Robinson, who just happens to look like a noted gangster. The studio gave her top-billing for *Party Wire*, a romance with Victor Jory, of all people, and *Public Menace*, as a ship's manicurist who helps reporter George Murphy. She was then paired her with Herbert Marshall for *If You Could Only Cook*, a screwball comedy in which they became servants for gangster Leo Carrillo. Over at Universal she took on an interesting assignment, playing both women in the life of Edward Arnold in *Diamond Jim*, Jane Mathews and Emma Perry, while at Paramount

she was a very game Calamity Jane, taunting and loving Gary Cooper's Wild Bill Hickok in *The Plainsman*. Back alongside William Powell, for *The Ex-Mrs. Bradford*, she suggested an ideal sleuthing partner should Myrna Loy have decided to back out of the *Thin Man* series. She then achieved her cinematic peak in three Frank Capra hits. The first was *Mr. Deeds Goes to Town*, in which she gave probably her best performance, as the cynical newspaper reporter intent on making a fool of Gary Cooper who instead falls in love with his innocence and charm. She then led the colorful ensemble in the 1938 Best Picture Oscar-winner *You Can't Take It With You*, as the one sane member of the unconventional household, while in *Mr. Smith Goes to Washington*, her role was pretty similar to her *Deeds* one, only this time she was a secretary and James Stewart the one she falls for. It was another performance of impeccable skill and the 1930s could suddenly add another emeplary name to its roster.

There were dramas like *Only Angels Have Wings*, which teamed her memorably with Cary Grant, and the big budget western *Arizona*, playing opposite William Holden, who was 18 years her junior, but it was clear that comedy was her forte. In that genre she also made *History Is Made at Night*, a piece with serious overtones, as a socialite in love with waiter Charles Boyer; *Easy Living*, as a stenographer on the receiving end of a fur coat flung out the window by millionaire Edward Arnold; *The Devil and Miss Jones*, as a shopgirl who doesn't realize her fellow-worker (Charles Coburn) is really her boss; and another one with Grant, the semi-serious *The Talk of the Town*, only this time things were made even brighter by having Ronald Colman on hand as well. The last was directed by George Stevens, who used her again for the topical comedy *The More the Merrier*, about overcrowded wartime Washington, DC in 1943. Though it was hardly her finest hour in the spotlight, it was nice to see her finally get an Oscar nomination, if only to acknowledge all the stellar work she'd done to date. The Columbia contract came to a close in 1944 with *The Impatient Years*, about a couple trying to adjust to the separation the war has forced upon them and for the first time in a long time it seemed that even Arthur's notices were less than rapturous. By the late 1940s she seemed to have lost interest in films, though her last two assignments were among her best: Billy Wilder's expert satire *A Foreign Affair*, as a mousey Congresswoman who loosens up while checking on morale in postwar Berlin; and one more with Stevens, the classic western, *Shane*, as a gentle homesteader. Thereafter her few credits were onstage, including a lesser-known musical version of *Peter Pan*, and two from which she bailed out before their Broadway openings, *Saint Joan* and *The Freaking Out of Stephanie Blake*. There were scattered jobs on television, too, Arthur last showing up in her own short-lived series in 1966. Her limited availability to audiences during these years may have kept her from gaining a whole new legion of fans, but those wise enough to tune into to her best work from her golden era were never less than amply rewarded by her skills.

Screen: **1923:** Cameo Kirby; The Temple of Venus; **1924:** Fast and Fearless; Biff-Bang Buddy; Bringin' Home the Bacon; Thundering Romance; Travelin' Fast; **1925:** The Drug Store Cowboy; Seven Chances; The Fighting Smile; Tearin' Loose; A Man of Nerve; **1926:** Thundering Through; The Roaring Rider; Double Daring; Lightning Bill; The Hurricane Horseman; The Fighting Cheat; The Cowboy Cop; Twisted Triggers; The College Boob; The Block Signal; **1927:** Husband Hunters; The Broken Gate; Horse Shoes; Flying Luck; Winners of the Wilderness; Born to Battle; The Poor Nut; The Masked Menace (serial); **1928:** Wallflowers; Easy Come, Easy Go; Warming Up; Brotherly Love; **1929:** Sins of the Fathers; The Canary Murder Case; Stairs of Sand; The Mysterious Dr. Fu Manchu; The Greene Murder Case;

The Saturday Night Kid; Half Way to Heaven; **1930:** Street of Chance; Young Eagles; Paramount on Parade; The Return of Dr. Fu Manchu; The Silver Horde; Danger Lights; **1931:** The Gang Buster; The Lawyer's Secret; The Virtuous Husband; Ex-Bad Boy; **1933:** Get That Venus; The Past of Mary Holmes; **1934:** Whirlpool; The Defense Rests; The Most Precious Thing in Life; **1935:** The Whole Town's Talking; Public Hero No. 1; Party Wire; Diamond Jim; The Public Menace; If You Could Only Cook; **1936:** Mr. Deeds Goes to Town; The Ex-Mrs. Bradford; Adventure in Manhattan; The Plainsman; More Than a Secretary; **1937:** History Is Made at Night; Easy Living; **1938:** You Can't Take It With You; **1939:** Only Angels Have Wings; Mr. Smith Goes to Washington; **1940:** Too Many Husbands; Arizona; **1941:** The Devil and Miss Jones; **1942:** The Talk of the Town; **1943:** The More the Merrier; A Lady Takes a Chance; **1944:** The Impatient Years; **1948:** A Foreign Affair; **1953:** Shane.
NY Stage: 1932: Foreign Affairs; 1932: The Man Who Reclaimed His Head; 1933: $25 an Hour; The Curtain Rises; 1934: The Bride of Torozko; 1950: Peter Pan.
Select TV: 1966: The Jean Arthur Show (series).

PEGGY ASHCROFT

(Edith Margaret Emily Ashcroft) Born: Croydon, England, December 22, 1907. Died: June 14, 1991.

One of England's foremost stage actresses, Peggy Ashcroft's movie fame came late in life, thanks to an Oscar. She made her London theatre debut in *Dear Brutus* in 1926, and followed that with several West End triumphs over the next 47 years including *The Heiress*, *Hedda Gabler*, *The Deep Blue Sea*, *Happy Days*, and many Shakespearean roles. When enticed she would appear sporadically over the years on film, playing small parts in prestigious offerings like Hitchcock's *The 39 Steps*, as the woman who lends Robert Donat an overcoat that saves his life; *The Nun's Story*, as the Mother Superior presiding over the Belgian convent in which Audrey Hepburn comes to take her vows; and *Sunday Bloody Sunday*, as Glenda Jackson's mother. It was not until she retired from the stage that she made a lasting impression on American audiences with her Academy Award-winning performance (at age 77) as the level-headed traveler, Mrs. Moore, in David Lean's long-winded epic *A Passage to India*, easily the most satisfying thing in the film. Around that same time she was also widely seen in another epic set in India, the mini-series *The Jewel in the Crown*. Of course there were few motion picture opportunities to an actress of her years even if she did have an Oscar on her résumé. Her only other film appearance of note after her win was in *Madame Sousatzka*, as one of the eccentrics sharing the crumbling apartment building with Shirley MacLaine. She was created a Dame in 1956, along with Sybil Thorndike the youngest woman to receive that honor.
Screen: 1933: The Wandering Jew/A People Eternal; 1935: The 39 Steps; 1936: Rhodes of Africa/Rhodes; 1941: Quiet Wedding; 1959: The Nun's Story; 1967: Tell Me Lies; 1968: Secret Ceremony; 1969: Three Into Two Won't Go; 1971: Sunday Bloody Sunday; 1973: The Pedestrian; 1977: Joseph Andrews; 1980: Hullabaloo Over George and Bonnie's Pictures (television in UK); 1984: A Passage to India; 1988: When the Wind Blows (voice); Madame Sousatzka; 1990: She's Been Away.
NY Stage: 1937: High Tor; 1948: Edward, My Son.
Select TV: 1959: Shadow of Hearts (sp); 1966: War of the Roses (ms); 1967: Days in the Trees (sp); 1971: The Cherry

Orchard (sp); **1980:** Caught on a Train (sp); Cream in My Coffee (sp); **1985:** The Jewel in the Crown (ms).

FRED ASTAIRE

(Frederick Austerlitz) Born: Omaha, NE, May 10, 1899. Died: June 22, 1987.

Fred Astaire was the best thing that ever happened to the movies. Charming, witty, unique, a masterful interpreter of song, and the epitome of a lost world of grace and finesse, the screen's finest dancer began in vaudeville as a child, performing with his older sister Adele. When he was only 18 the team made their New York stage debut in *Over the Top*. Over the next 14 years they became two of the most cherished performers on the Broadway and London stage, where they starred in such hits as *Lady Be Good*, *Funny Face*, and *The Band Wagon*. When Adele retired to marry, Fred went solo for one more stage success, *Gay Divorce*, in 1932. Soon afterwards Hollywood came calling and the timing could not have been better. The screen musical had been stumbling to find both its proper footing and voice, and Astaire signed a contract with RKO just in time to help set things on a new and exciting course. Almost overnight the screen musical found its greatest star. He debuted over at MGM, in 1933, in a supporting part (as himself, actually) in *Dancing Lady*, showing up late in the film for two numbers with perhaps the least graceful partner he'd ever have, Joan Crawford. He ended that year in a bigger role, paired off with Ginger Rogers in RKO's box-office hit *Flying Down to Rio*, where they easily stole the show from the far-less ingratiating stars, Dolores Del Rio and Gene Raymond, dancing to "The Carioca." The studio found box-office gold as the duo teamed in eight additional efforts during the 1930s, a series of snappy films that defined the musical escapism of the era with their art deco settings, sophisticated scores, fluffy plots, and a stock company of wry supporting players. More importantly, Astaire demanded lengthy rehearsal periods for the numbers, forever wiping away memories of the clodhoppers who often stomped their way through the early talkies, and giving each number a seemingly effortless grace and professionalism. Also instrumental to the flow of the number was his insistence on his full body being in the frame, rather than quick cuts to the feet, or angles that shot the dancer from the knees up. His dances with Rogers would further the story and act like moments of romance, told through body movement.

The Astaire-Rogers duets would come to rank among the seminal moments of cinema history, as they introduced countless standards such as "Cheek to Cheek" (*Top Hat*); "Let's Face the Music and Dance" (*Follow the Fleet*), one of the most melancholy and haunting of all their numbers; "Pick Yourself Up" (*Swing Time*); and "Let's Call the Whole Thing Off" (*Shall We Dance*), which required the team to perform on rollerskates. Both *The Gay Divorcee* (the retitled-for-the-censors version of Astaire's stage hit) and *Top Hat* were considered good enough to nominate for Best Picture Oscars and those two, along with *Roberta* (where they took billing below Irene Dunne), *Follow the Fleet*, *Swing Time*, and *Shall We Dance* were among the most popular money-makers of their day. Through these films Astaire got to sing two songs that would go on to win Oscars, the show-stopping and then-record length "The Continental" (*The Gay Divorcee*) and "The Way You Look Tonight" (*Swing Time*). There was a break in this batch for Astaire with *A Damsel in Distress*, which put him opposite an actress who couldn't dance, Joan Fontaine, and gave him a pair of comics who could, Burns and Allen, the latter with pleasing results, including a "Fun House" number that earned an Oscar for

Astaire's most frequent co-choreographer and alter ego, Hermes Pan. The Astaire-Rogers pairing finally started to lose some steam with *Carefree* (which, at one point, included a Technicolor sequence), and came to a halt in 1939 with the biopic *The Story of Vernon and Irene Castle*. A decade later they came together one last time, most successfully, for *The Barkleys of Broadway*, which even had them reprise one of their greatest numbers, "They Can't Take That Away from Me," from *Shall We Dance*.

Unlike Rogers, Astaire had no intention of giving up musicals, despite the fact that he was a most assured and pleasing actor, never extending himself beyond his capabilities as Ginger so often would do. To launch his solo career, he went to the studio that would become synonymous with the best that Hollywood had to offer in terms of the song-and-dance genre, MGM. He found himself opposite Eleanor Powell, who wasn't much of an actress but matched him step for step in a dynamite tap finale set to Cole Porter's "Begin the Beguine." An independent, *Second Chorus*, marked one of the lower points of a career consisting of an unusually high percentage of peaks. Fortunately, this was followed by a pair of felicitous double teamings, first with Rita Hayworth (no one else ever *looked* so good dancing opposite Astaire) in the military-themed *You'll Never Get Rich* and *You Were Never Lovelier*; and then with Bing Crosby in *Holiday Inn* and *Blue Skies*. Shortly before filming the latter, he signed a contract and became an official part of MGM during its musical heyday. While there he appeared in four different segments (more than any of the other players) of the all-star *Ziegfeld Follies*, including an historical duet with Gene Kelly for "The Babbit and the Bromide;" teamed with Judy Garland for one of his finest comical numbers, "A Couple of Swells," from the enormously popular *Easter Parade*; found yet another of his best partners in Vera-Ellen, notably in the underrated *The Belle of New York*; and appeared in his most sparkling vehicle of all, Vincente Minnelli's rapturous and witty *The Band Wagon*. In that one he let loose with a number at an arcade, clowned hilariously in a baby bonnet for "Triplets," and created sparks in his exciting "Girl Hunt Ballet" with sexy Cyd Charisse.

His many dazzling solos during his post-Rogers period included his drunken expression of defeat in "One for My Baby" (from *The Sky's the Limit*); a marvelous display of physical dexterity as he did some fancy moves with a rubber ball in *Broadway Melody of 1940*; a playful audition for an unimpressed Adolphe Menjou in *You Were Never Lovelier*; a joyous turn with a hat rack and a now-legendary dance on the ceiling in *Royal Wedding*; a literally explosive tour de force with a collection of fireworks in *Holiday Inn*; an awesome demonstration of how to play a piano keyboard with your feet in *Let's Dance*; and a touch of movie magic that allowed him to dance with multiple images of himself in the song he should have introduced, "Puttin' on the Ritz," a Harry Richmond hit that was reprised for *Blue Skies*. Although he threatened to retire in 1947, he was easily coaxed back in front of the cameras to replace Gene Kelly in *Easter Parade*, a most fortunate turn of events because there was still a great need for all he had to offer. Taking a break from MGM in 1955, he was in a popular success with Leslie Caron, *Daddy Long Legs* (introducing another in his long list of hit songs, "Something's Got to Give"), although they were not physically ideal next to one another. Next came another classic pairing, this time with Audrey Hepburn, in the effervescent *Funny Face*, which had little to do with Astaire's previous stage triumph of the same name except for some of the same songs. In 1957 he did one last one for MGM, temporarily bidding goodbye to the musical film with *Silk Stockings*, giving a nod to the oncoming change in the pop scene with the number "The Ritz Roll and Rock." With television an increasingly powerful

presence, he moved over in that direction and conquered that medium as well, with a series of variety specials that helped revolutionize that format as he'd done in movies 25 years earlier. He and the specials won raves and awards by the carload (Astaire himself received Emmy Awards as a performer for *An Evening With Fred Astaire* and *Astaire Time*).

As he turned 60, he figured it was time to concentrate almost exclusively on straight acting, starting with a subtly effective turn as a scientist with a penchant for race cars in *On the Beach*, a haunting look at the end of the world and a surprise box-office hit. There was a lead as Debbie Reynolds's irresistibly irresponsible dad in *The Pleasure of His Company*, a role that seemed tailor-made for him, although it had started as a stage play; and a secondary part as Jack Lemmon's boss in *The Notorious Landlady*. He worked far less in the 1960s than one would have wished. However, since this was the decade when musicals came back into vogue, he got to do one last lead in this genre in *Finian's Rainbow*, where he proved that not an ounce of his talent and charm had evaporated over the years. He nabbed his only Oscar nomination, playing a con man in one of the all-star disaster pictures of the 1970s, *The Towering Inferno*; won another Emmy Award for the television movie *A Family Upside Down*; and could still be seen knocking off some fancy steps with Gene Kelly in the documentary *That's Entertainment, Part 2*, when he was age 76 no less. There were some unworthy, barely distributed items like *Midas Run*, as a con man masterminding a heist; *The Amazing Dobermans*, as a religious fanatic training the title dogs; and, worst of all, *Purple Taxi*, a foreign-financed effort that made little sense to the few who managed to see it. Somehow he came away from all of these unscathed. His last dramatic assignment was at least in an "A" production, *Ghost Story*, acting alongside some other elderly gentlemen like Melvyn Douglas and Douglas Fairbanks, Jr., all of them haunted by a dirty deed they'd done in the past. In addition to a special Academy Award, given in 1950, he received the American Film Institute Life Achievement Award, in 1981. There are not, however, enough awards to do justice to an artist whose contribution to the cinema is immeasurable. He leant his name to a chain of dance instruction studios and published his autobiography, *Steps in Time*, in 1959.

Screen: 1933: Dancing Lady; Flying Down to Rio; 1934: The Gay Divorcee; 1935: Roberta (and choreography); Top Hat; 1936: Follow the Fleet; Swing Time; 1937: Shall We Dance; A Damsel in Distress; 1938: Carefree; 1939: The Story of Vernon and Irene Castle; 1940: Broadway Melody of 1940; Second Chorus; 1941: You'll Never Get Rich; 1942: Holiday Inn; You Were Never Lovelier; 1943: The Sky's the Limit (and choreography); 1945: Yolanda and the Thief; 1946: Ziegfeld Follies; Blue Skies; 1948: Easter Parade; 1949: The Barkleys of Broadway; 1950: Three Little Words; Let's Dance; 1951: Royal Wedding; 1952: The Belle of New York; 1953: The Band Wagon; 1955: Daddy Long Legs (and co-choreography); 1957: Funny Face (and co-choreography); Silk Stockings; 1959: On the Beach; 1961: The Pleasure of His Company; 1962: The Notorious Landlady; 1968: Finian's Rainbow; 1969: Midas Run; 1974: That's Entertainment!; The Towering Inferno; 1976: That's Entertainment, Part 2; The Amazing Dobermans; 1980: Purple Taxi (Europe: 1977); 1981: Ghost Story; 1985: George Stevens: A Filmmaker's Journey.

NY Stage: 1917: Over the Top; 1918: The Passing Show of 1918; 1919: Apple Blossoms; 1921: The Love Letter; 1922: For Goodness Sake; The Bunch and Judy; 1924: Lady be Good; 1927: Funny Face; 1930: Smiles; 1931: The Band Wagon; 1932: Gay Divorce.

Select TV: 1957: Imp on a Cobweb Leash (sp); 1958: An Evening With Fred Astaire (sp); 1959: Man on a Bicycle (sp); Another Evening With Fred Astaire (sp); 1960: Astaire Time (sp);

1961–63: Alcoa Premiere Theatre (series); 1964: Think Pretty (sp); 1968: The Fred Astaire Show (sp); 1969–70: It Takes a Thief (series); 1970: The Over-the-Hill Gang Rides Again; Santa Claus Is Coming to Town (sp; voice); 1972: Jack Lemmon in 'S Wonderful 'S Marvelous 'S Gershwin (sp); Make Mine Red, White and Blue (sp); 1974: Fred Astaire Salutes the Fox Musical (sp); 1977: The Easter Bunny is Coming to Town (sp; voice); 1978: A Family Upside Down; 1979: The Man in the Santa Claus Suit.

NILS ASTHER
BORN: MALMO, SWEDEN, JANUARY 17, 1897.
DIED: OCTOBER 13, 1981.

Following an 11-year period of working in both the Swedish and German cinema, suave Nils Asther came to Hollywood towards the end of the silent era. There he became an adequate leading man starting with a comical take on *Uncle Tom's Cabin* (!), entitled *Topsy and Eva*, as the estate owner who takes pity on Little Eva. This was followed by the hit melodrama *Sorrell and Son*, as the offspring of H.B. Warner; *Laugh, Clown, Laugh*, as the nobleman who wins the love of Loretta Young, much to the displeasure of Lon Chaney; and the famed Joan Crawford flapper epic *Our Dancing Daughters*, as a socialite. There were also two highly-regarded romantic teamings with Greta Garbo: *Wild Orchids*, as a prince, and *The Single Standard*, as a most unlikely former prizefighter. With the transition to sound, his accent put him in a less-desirable light, and he became an all-purpose foreigner in movies like *Letty Lytton*, as an evil South American who tries to poison Joan Crawford; and *Storm at Daybreak*, carrying on with Kay Francis behind her husband's back. Perhaps his most notable role was in Frank Capra's atypical *The Bitter Tea of General Yen*, in 1933, as the warlord who falls in love with Barbara Stanwyck. Shortly afterwards, he decided to leave Hollywood and resume his career in England, where his movies included melodramas like *Abdul the Damned* and *The Marriage of Corbal*. Returning to the states during World War II, he signed with Paramount Pictures, working mostly for their "B" unit, with one standout role, as the scientist searching for a rejuvenation formula in *The Man in Half Moon Street*. After *The Man From Tangiers*, in 1950, he never made another Engish-language film. Instead, he dabbled in stage and television before heading back to Sweden, where he made a handful of features, the last being *Gudrun* in 1963.

Screen (US/UK releases only): 1927: Topsy and Eva; Sorrell and Son; 1928: When Fleet Meets Fleet; The Blue Danube; Adventure Mad; Laugh, Clown, Laugh; The Cossacks; Adrienne Lecouvreur; Loves of an Actress; The Cardboard Lover; Our Dancing Daughters; 1929: Dream of Love; Wild Orchids; The Hollywood Revue of 1929; The Single Standard; 1930: The Wrath of the Seas; King of Jazz; The Sea Bat; 1931: But the Flesh Is Weak; 1932: Letty Lynton; The Washington Masquerade; 1933: If I Were Free; The Bitter Tea of General Yen; Storm at Daybreak; The Right to Romance; 1934: By Candlelight; Madame Spy; The Crime Doctor; The Love Captive; Love Time; 1935: Abdul the Damned; 1936: The Marriage of Corbal/The Prisoner of Corbal; Guilty Melody; 1937: Make Up; 1938: Tea Leaves in the Wind; 1940: The Man Who Lost Himself; 1941: Forced Landing; Flying Blind; Dr. Kildare's Wedding Day; The Night Before the Divorce; The Night of January 16th; 1942: Sweater Girl; Night Monster; 1943: Submarine Alert; Mystery Broadcast; 1944: Alaska; The Hour Before the Dawn; The Man in Half Moon Street; 1945: Bluebeard; Love, Honor and Goodbye; Son of Lassie; Jealousy; 1948: The Feathered Serpent; 1953: That Man From Tangier.
NY Stage: 1953: The Strong are Lonely.

JOHN ASTIN
BORN: BALTIMORE, MD, MARCH 30, 1930.
ED: WASHINGTON DRAMA SCH., JOHN HOPKINS UNIV.

A character actor specializing in comical roles, John Astin, with the wickedly toothy smile, made his professional debut in an Off Broadway production of *The Threepenny Opera*. In films he made his mark by playing nerdy types: in *West Side Story*, as a social director at the gym dance; and *That Touch of Mink*, as a poor dolt with designs on Doris Day. Turning to television he found his niche playing the weird and leering Gomez in the cult television show *The Addams Family*, the part for which he would be best known. Shortly afterwards, he landed his most extensive screen role, as the lecherous father of innocent sex kitten Ewa Aulin in the all-star romp *Candy*, which brought him much attention among students of odd cinema. Other roles would include a hyper Mexican officer helping Peter Ustinov recapture the Alamo in *Viva Max!*; an executive drop-out in *Get to Know Your Rabbit*; a lecherous game show host in *National Lampoon's European Vacation*; a college dean in *Teen Wolf Too*; and (almost unrecognizable) a horny ghost in *The Frighteners*. On television, in addition to acting, he dabbled in directing as well, with the movies *Operation Petticoat* (which later became another series of his) and *Rossetti and Ryan: Men Who Love Women*. He is the father of actors Sean Astin and Mackenzie Astin from his marriage (1973–82) to actress Patty Duke, with whom he appeared in the telefilm *Two on a Bench*.
Screen: 1958: The Pusher; 1961: West Side Story; 1962: That Touch of Mink; 1963: Move Over, Darling; The Wheeler Dealers; 1967: The Spirit Is Willing; 1968: Candy; 1969: Viva Max!; 1971: Bunny O'Hare; 1972: Get to Know Your Rabbit; Every Little Crook and Nanny; 1973: The Brothers O'Toole; 1977: Freaky Friday; 1985: National Lampoon's European Vacation; 1987: Body Slam; Teen Wolf Too; 1988: Return of the Killer Tomatoes; 1990: Gremlins 2: The New Batch; Night Life (dtv); Killer Tomatoes Strike Back (dtv); 1991: Killer Tomatoes Eat France (dtv); 1992: Stepmonster (dtv); 1994: The Silence of the Hams (dtv); 1996: The Frighteners; 2001: Betaville (nUSr).
NY Stage: 1955: The Threepenny Opera; 1956: Major Barbara; 1958: Ulysses in Nighttown; The Power and the Glory; 1959: Tall Story.
Select TV: 1962–63: I'm Dickens…He's Fenster (series); 1964–66: The Addams Family (series); 1967: The Pruitts of Southampton (series); 1969: The Experiment (sp); 1971: Two on a Bench; 1972: Evil Roy Slade; 1973–75: The Addams Family (voice); 1974: Skyway to Death; Only With Married Men; 1975: The Dream Makers; 1977: Operation Petticoat (and dir.); 1977–78: Operation Petticoat (series); 1979: Halloween With the Addams Family (sp); 1985–86: Mary (series); 1987: Adventures Beyond Belief/Neat and Tidy; 1993: Huck and the King of Hearts; 1995: Harrison Bergeron; 1998: The New Addams Family (series).

MARY ASTOR
(LUCILE LANGEHANKE) BORN: QUINCY, IL, MAY 3, 1906. DIED: SEPTEMBER 25, 1987.

The wide range of Mary Astor took her, with total conviction, from bitchy vixens to sensible mothers, sweethearts to dangerous femme fatales. Although one often thinks of her as appearing in other star's movies, she is very much one of the outstanding players of Hollywood's prime decades. Guided by a determined stage father, first into piano lessons (which, fittingly, would play a part in her Oscar winning role) and then modeling, Astor broke in to films in 1921, acting in a handful of two-reelers (including "The Beggar Maid" and "The Bashful Suitor") and doing small parts for Famous Players-Lasky in New York. Her feature debut came in 1922 in *John Smith*, and, still working for Lasky, she traveled west the following year where her name was changed to Mary Astor in order to groom her for stardom. In support she did *The Marriage Maker* and then was promoted to the lead for *The Fighting Coward*, as a Mississippi belle. At 18, she won her first really significant role, opposite John Barrymore in *Beau Brummel*, as Lady Alvanley in this profitable moneymaker for Warner Bros. She spent the remainder of the silent era under contract to First National, where she did a whole batch of movies she would later dismiss as "trash," including *Enticement*, as a flapper after socialite Clive Brook; *The Pace That Thrills*, as the wealthy girlfriend of racer Ben Lyon; and *The Sea Tiger*, as a Spaniard. Of course her two most notable parts of this period were done elsewhere: *Don Juan*, again with Barrymore (with whom she was supposedly having an affair at the time), at Warners, and the sound-alike *Don Q — Son of Zorro*, at United Artists, her services having been personally requested by the picture's star, Douglas Fairbanks.

There was a brief stay at the Fox Studios, on the cusp of the sound era, which she then officially entered via Paramount with *Ladies Love Brutes*, on the verge of divorcing Fredric March while stirring up romance with George Bancroft. More important was her role in the first adaptation of the stage hit *Holiday*, as Ann Harding's ambitious sister. RKO signed her up for a batch of films that kept her pretty much in the same busy but unremarkable position she'd been in for close to a decade. These ranged from *White Shoulders* — where she was saved from poverty by Jack Holt, only to leave him for wicked Ricardo Cortez — to *The Lost Squadron*, married to crazed movie director Erich von Stroheim. Eventually some good parts in some worthwhile, major productions helped raise her status, including *Red Dust*, as the timid wife who gets the hots for Clark Gable, and, best of all, *Dodsworth*, as the gentle lady who rescues Walter Houston from his floundering marriage. In between she earned her keep, first working for Warners (*The World Changes*, *The Kennel Murder Case*, *I Am a Thief*, etc.), freelancing, and then signing up for a quick shift on the Columbia lot (*Trapped by Television*, *No Time to Marry*, etc.). Far more fame came outside her day job via a custody battle with her second husband, in which her personal, and very revealing, diaries were made public. Despite the resulting scandal, or because of it, she was soon featured in some important pictures of the late 1930s, including *The Prisoner of Zenda*, as Antoinette, mistress to the King; *The Hurricane*, as Raymond Massey's understanding wife whose compassion encourages Jon Hall to save her life when the big storm hits; and *Midnight*, which found her at her most enjoyably bitchy, paired for the last time with John Barrymore.

It was frustrating to see her asked to play second best to Carole Landis in *Turnabout*, and curious to see her playing the wife of Mormon founder *Brigham Young — Frontiersman*. But her peak year was right around the corner when 1941 arrived, doing two big ones for Warners: *The Great Lie*, a florid Bette Davis melodrama with Astor in her Academy Award-winning turn as the pianist carrying George Brent's baby; and then, unforgettably, as the cool and dangerous Brigid O'Shaughnessy, who fails to con Humphrey Bogart while bodies drop around her in the classic *The Maltese Falcon*. The latter assured her a place in screen history as one of the great scheming femme fatales and it was

followed by her very funny performance as the millionairess craving Joel McCrea in Preston Sturges's screwball *The Palm Beach Story*. She signed up with MGM, who pictured her as a motherly sort, and she played her most famous of these roles in one of the pinnacles of the movie musical, *Meet Me in St. Louis*, where her brood included Judy Garland and Margaret O'Brien. She was Elizabeth Taylor's mom both in *Cynthia* and *Little Women*, and had a standout role as a whore past her prime in *Act of Violence*. From the early 1950s onward she worked sporadically, including a Broadway short run in *The Starcross Story*, and television adaptations of *Sunset Boulevard* and *The Women*. On screen she played more moms, having now turned 50, including those of Robert Wagner (*A Kiss Before Dying*) and John Saxon (*This Happy Feeling*) which were more convincing than the thought of her having sired Cornel Wilde (*The Devil's Hairpin*) or June Allyson (*A Stranger in My Arms*). The critical consensus was that Astor was the only reason for Fox having filmed *Return to Peyton Place*, but soon after her supporting role in the Bette Davis gothic thriller *Hush...Hush, Sweet Charlotte*, she retired. There were two autobiographies: *My Story* (1959) and *A Life on Film* (1971).

Screen: 1922: John Smith; The Man Who Played God; 1923: Second Fiddle; Success; The Bright Shawl; The Rapids; Puritan Passions; The Marriage Maker; Hollywood; Woman Proof; 1924: The Fighting Coward; Beau Brummel; The Fighting American; Unguarded Woman; The Price of a Party; Inez From Hollywood; 1925: Oh Doctor; Enticement; Playing With Souls; Don Q — Son of Zorro; The Pace That Thrills; The Scarlet Saint; 1926: The Wise Guy; Don Juan; Forever After; High Steppers; 1927: The Rough Riders; The Sea Tiger; Sunset Derby; Rose of the Golden West; Two Arabian Knights; No Place to Go; 1928: Sailors' Wives; Dressed to Kill; Heart to Heart; Three-Ring Marriage; Dry Martini; 1929: Romance of the Underworld; New Year's Eve; Woman From Hell; 1930: Ladies Love Brutes; The Runaway Bride; Holiday; 1931: The Lash; The Royal Bed; Behind Office Doors; Sin Ship; Other Men's Women; White Shoulders; Smart Woman; 1932: Men of Chance; The Lost Squadron; A Successful Calamity; Those We Love; Red Dust; 1933: The Little Giant; Jennie Gerhardt; The World Changes; The Kennel Murder Case; Convention City; 1934: Easy to Love; Upperworld; Return of the Terror; The Man With Two Faces; The Case of the Howling Dog; 1935: I Am a Thief; Red Hot Tires; Straight From the Heart; Dinky; Page Miss Glory; Man of Iron; 1936: The Murder of Dr. Harrigan; And So They Were Married; Trapped by Television; Dodsworth; Lady From Nowhere; 1937: The Prisoner of Zenda; The Hurricane; 1938: Paradise for Three; No Time to Marry; There's Always a Woman; Woman Against Woman; Listen, Darling; 1939: Midnight; 1940: Turnabout; Brigham Young-Frontiersman; 1941: The Great Lie; The Maltese Falcon; 1942: Across the Pacific; In This Our Life; The Palm Beach Story; 1943: Young Ideas; Thousands Cheer; 1944: Blonde Fever; Meet Me in St. Louis; 1946: Claudia and David; 1947: Cynthia; Fiesta; Desert Fury; Cass Timberlane; 1949: Act of Violence; Little Women; Any Number Can Play; 1956: A Kiss Before Dying; The Power and the Prize; 1957: The Devil's Hairpin; 1958: This Happy Feeling; 1959: A Stranger in My Arms; 1961: Return to Peyton Place; 1964: Youngblood Hawke; Hush...Hush, Sweet Charlotte.
NY Stage: 1945: Many Happy Returns; 1954: The Starcross Story.
Select TV: 1954: Jack Sparling (sp); The Philadelphia Story (sp); 1955: The Thief (sp); The Hickory Limb (sp); The Women (sp); Dinner at Eight (sp); 1956: Farewell Appearance (sp); You Me and the Gatepost (sp); The Catamaran (sp); Sunset Boulevard (sp); 1957: The Man Who Played God (sp); Mr. and Mrs. McAdam (sp); The Troublemakers (sp); 1958: The Lonely Stage (sp); 1958: The Littlest Enemy (sp); The Return of Ansel Gibbs

(sp); **1959:** Diary of a Nurse (sp); The Philadelphia Story (sp); **1960:** The Women of Hadley (sp); Revolt in Hadley (sp); Journey to the Day (sp).

RICHARD ATTENBOROUGH
BORN: CAMBRIDGE, ENGLAND, AUGUST 29, 1923. ED: RADA.

One of the British cinema's renaissance men, Richard Attenborough was still a teen attending the Royal Academy of Dramatic Arts when he landed his first film role, in Noël Coward's patriotic war drama *In Which We Serve*. He was still active more than 50 years later, having moved into producing and directing over the years with varying degrees of success. His first impact as a performer was made in the London theatre, playing the paranoid teenage gangster in *Brighton Rock*, a role he would recreate with very satisfying results in the 1947 movie version. His baby-face kept him in youthful roles with *London Belongs to Me*, as a lad accused of murder; *The Guinea Pig*, sent from elementary to public school with hellish results; and *Boys in Brown*, as a bad boy shipped off to reform school. None of these succeeded in making him a star attraction, so he drifted back and forth between stage and some very minor screen credits. His most noteworthy achievement in the early 1950s found him among the original cast of Agatha Christie's *The Mousetrap*, which would go on to become the longest running play in history. He found himself back on screen in a popular military comedy, *Private's Progress*, as a crafty slacker taking green recruit Ian Carmichael under his wing. This was the first Attenborough movie in some time to get some sort of showing the United States, as did *Dunkirk*, a war movie that MGM helped finance. He found himself a tour de force part in a small movie, *The Man Upstairs*, as an unstable fellow whom the police try to stop from killing himself; in support as a POW in *Danger Within*; and playing an unscrupulous businessman in *I'm All Right, Jack*, probably the most famous of the comedies from the Boulting Brothers, for whom Attenborough had been under contract for many years.

It was with the highly praised drama *The Angry Silence*, a socially conscious piece about a factory strike and the outsider who suffers when he refuses to participate, that his status finally grew in the international market, having served as producer as well as star. Bryan Forbes was one of the other producers and together they formed their own company, Beaver, which made such notable movies as *Whistle Down the Wind*, *The League of Gentlemen*, *The L-Shaped Room*, and *Séance on a Wet Afternoon*. Attenborough was in the second one, as one of the participants in a robbery, and the fourth, giving one of his best performances, as the timid and pathetic husband of Kim Stanley, talked into kidnapping a child. For the latter, and a war movie, *Guns at Batasi*, in which his was a strict sergeant-major, he received the British Film Award. Before and after these he finally got himself into the American side of filmmaking, being seen in two high profile Steve McQueen hits: *The Great Escape*, as the prisoner who masterminds the breakout; and *The Sand Pebbles*, as a sailor who falls for a Chinese woman. Also for U.S. producers, he was the navigator responsible for stranding his fellow passengers in the desert in *The Flight of the Phoenix*, and had a delightful song and dance bit as a circus showman in the musical *Doctor Dolittle*. Back in England he had leads in some comedies: *The Bliss of Mr. Blossom*, as a brassiere manufacturer oblivious to his wife's love being in the attic; *Only When I Larf*, as a con artist; *A Severed Head*, as a psychiatrist carrying on with married patient Lee Remick; and *Loot*, as the nit-witted inspector in this black farce

from the famed Joe Orton play. On a far more serious note, he played the real-life serial killer John Christie in *10 Rillington Place*.

He made his first stab at directing with the offbeat all-star revue *Oh! What a Lovely War*, a strange hybrid of song and social commentary that did not repeat the success it had had onstage. Although he still took some supporting roles in the 1970s, in time he decided to concentrate less on acting and more on directing, coming to associate himself with large scale historical epics, reaching his critical peak with his dream project, a biography of *Gandhi*. Not only was this the most financially successful of his efforts in this field, it also won him Academy Awards for Best Director and Picture. Although he was often criticized for being too in love with the old fashioned spectacle, he managed to win over some of his non-supporters with the gentle romance *Shadlowlands*, perhaps his best work behind the camera. In 1993 he ended a 13 year acting hiatus by appearing in the smash hit *Jurassic Park*, all bushy-bearded and grandfatherly as the dinosaur park's creator. He then proved to be the only reason for the remake of *Miracle on 34th Street*, reprising Edmund Gwenn's role as a good-hearted fellow who really believes he is Kris Kringle. Later he appeared fleetingly as the English Ambassador at the end of the full-length *Hamlet* and as a court advisor in *Elizabeth*. Attenborough's wife is former actress Sheila Sim, his younger brother producer David Attenborough. First knighted in 1976, he later had the title of Baron bestowed upon him. His complete list of directorial credits are *Oh! What a Lovely War* (and prod.; 1969), *Young Winston* (1972), *A Bridge Too Far* (1977), *Magic* (1978), *Gandhi* (and prod.; 1982), *A Chorus Line* (1985), *Cry Freedom* (and prod.; 1987), *Chaplin* (and prod.; 1992), *Shadowlands* (and prod.; 1993), *In Love and War* (and prod.; 1996), and *Grey Owl* (and prod.; 1999), which became one of the most expensive movies to go directly to video.

Screen: **1942:** In Which We Serve; **1943:** Schweik's New Adventures; **1944:** The Hundred Pound Window; **1945:** Journey Together; **1946:** A Matter of Life and Death/Stairway to Heaven; School for Secrets/Secret Flight; **1947:** The Man Within/The Smugglers; Dancing With Crime; Brighton Rock/Young Scarface; **1948:** London Belongs to Me/Dulcimer Street; **1949:** The Guinea Pig; The Lost People; **1950:** Boys in Brown; Morning Departure/Operation Disaster; **1951:** Hell Is Sold Out; The Magic Box; **1952:** Gift Horse/Glory at Sea; Father's Doing Fine; **1954:** Eight O'Clock Walk; **1955:** The Ship That Died of Shame/PT Raiders; **1956:** Private's Progress; The Baby and the Battleship; **1957:** Brothers in Law; The Scamp; **1958:** Dunkirk; Sea of Sand/Desert Patrol; The Man Upstairs; **1959:** Danger Within/Breakout; I'm All Right, Jack; Jet Storm; S.O.S. Pacific; **1960:** The Angry Silence (and co-prod.); The League of Gentlemen; **1962:** Only Two Can Play; All Night Long; The Dock Brief/Trial and Error; **1963:** The Great Escape; **1964:** Séance on a Wet Afternoon (and co-prod.); The Third Secret; Guns at Batasi; **1965:** The Flight of the Phoenix; **1966:** The Sand Pebbles; **1967:** Doctor Dolittle; **1968:** The Bliss of Mrs. Blossom; Only When I Larf; **1970:** The Magic Christian; The Last Grenade; **1971:** A Severed Head; 10 Rillington Place; **1972:** Loot; **1975:** Ten Little Indians; Brannigan; Rosebud; Conduct Unbecoming; **1977:** The Chess Players; **1980:** The Human Factor; **1993:** Jurassic Park; **1994:** Miracle on 34th Street; **1996:** Wavelength/E=MC^2 (dtv); Hamlet; **1997:** The Lost World: Jurassic Park; **1998:** Elizabeth.

Select TV: **1970:** David Copperfield; **2000:** Joseph and the Amazing Technicolor Dreamcoat (sp); The Railway Children; Jack and the Beanstalk; The Real Story; **2001:** Puchoon.

LIONEL ATWILL

BORN: CROYDON, SURREY, ENGLAND,
MARCH 1, 1885. DIED: APRIL 22, 1946.

An elegant, deeply despicable screen villain for close to 15 years, Lionel Atwill aroused suspicion in even his sympathetic roles. A stage performer in England from the age of 20, he appeared in a handful of silent features while distinguishing himself in both British and American plays, such as *The Grand Duke* and *The Outsider*. He came to Hollywood in 1932 to debut as a murder suspect in *Silent Witness*, a role he'd done onstage. This was not one of his nasty characters, but with his first foray into the horror genre, as a weird, club-footed scientist in *Doctor X*, he soon became established as one of the movies' smoothest scoundrels. This film had been made in very poor color for Warners, as was one of his best-known features, *Mystery of the Wax Museum*, as the wheelchair-bound artist whose wax figures conceal human remains. In *Murders in the Zoo* he sewed someone's lips shut, and in *The Vampire Bat*, he was a doctor with a penchant for draining the blood from his victims. For cheapo Monogram pictures he starred as a wealthy deaf-mute suspected of murder in *The Sphinx*, then moved up to a somewhat larger budget with *The Solitaire Man*, as a police inspector who might be a jewel thief. On a much less malevolent note, he lost his legs in an accident in *Beggars in Ermine*; attempted to seduce Irene Dunne in the 1934 version of *The Age of Innocence*; lusted after Marlene Dietrich in one of her dreariest melodramas, *The Song of Songs*; and actually won her heart at the fade-out in *The Devil Is a Woman*.

It was back to horror for *Mark of the Vampire*, investigating bloody murders at a castle, before buckling some swashes in *Captain Blood*, coming in second place to the superior sneering of Basil Rathbone. In *The Great Garrick* he had a colorful role as playwright Beaumarchais; appeared as a Viennese baron in *The Great Waltz*; hid behind a beard as the family physician in *The Hound of the Baskervilles*; popped up as De Rochefort in Fox's Ritz Brothers-version of *The Three Musketeers*; and tried to keep Edward Arnold out of prison in *Johnny Apollo*. In 1939 he made his most memorable foray into the horror genre with *Son of Frankenstein*, as the virtuous police chief with the fake arm. He stayed with the series for *Ghost of Frankenstein*, *Frankenstein Meets the Wolf Man*, *House of Frankenstein*, and *House of Dracula*, playing a different character in each film. By the 1940s most of his pictures were severely low budget and his reputation was somewhat tarnished when he was brought to trial for corrupting a minor. He was cleared of the charges but a year later was charged with perjury. He died while making the serial *Lost City of the Jungle* and a double was required to finish his role.

Screen: 1918: Eve's Daughter; For Sale; 1919: The Marriage Price; 1921: The Highest Bidder; Indiscretion; The Vampire Bat; 1932: The Silent Witness; Doctor X; 1933: Vampire Bat; The Secret of Madame Blanche; Mystery of the Wax Museum; Murders in the Zoo; The Sphinx; The Song of Songs; Solitaire Man; Secret of the Blue Room; 1934: Beggars in Ermine; Nana; Stamboul Quest; One More River; The Age of Innocence; The Firebird; The Man Who Reclaimed His Head; 1935: Mark of the Vampire; The Devil is a Woman; Murder Man; Rendezvous; Captain Blood; 1936: Lady of Secrets; Absolute Quiet; Till We Meet Again; 1937: The High Command; The Road Back; Last Train From Madrid; Lancer Spy; The Wrong Road; The Great Garrick; 1938: Three Comrades; The Great Waltz; 1939: The Three Musketeers; Son of Frankenstein; The Hound of the Baskervilles; The Gorilla; The Sun Never Sets; Mr. Moto Takes a Vacation; The Secret of Dr. Kildare; Balalaika; 1940: The Mad Empress; Charlie Chan in Panama; Johnny Apollo; Charlie Chan's Murder Cruise; The Girl in 313; Boom Town; The Great Profile; 1941: Man Made Monster; 1942: Junior G-Men of the Air (serial); Ghost of Frankenstein; The Strange Case of Dr. Rx; Pardon My Sarong; To Be or Not to Be; Cairo; Night Monster; Sherlock Holmes and the Secret Weapon; The Mad Doctor of Market Street; 1943: Captain America (serial); Frankenstein Meets the Wolf Man; House of Frankenstein; 1944: Raiders of Ghost City (serial); Lady in the Death House; Secrets of Scotland Yard; 1945: Fog Island; Crime Inc.; House of Dracula; 1946: Genius at Work; Lost City of the Jungle (serial).

NY Stage: 1917: The Lodger; Eve's Daughter; L'elevation; 1918: The Indestructible Wife; The Wild Duck; Hedda Gabler; A Doll's House; Another Man's Shoes; Tiger! Tiger!; 1921: Deburau; The Grand Duke; 1923: The Comedian; The Heart of Cellini; 1924: The Outsider; 1925: Caesar and Cleopatra; 1926: Beau Gallant; Slaves All; 1927: The Thief; The King Can Do No Wrong; 1928: Napoleon; 1929: Fioretta; Stripped; 1931: The Silent Witness.

MISCHA AUER

(MISCHA OUNSKOWSKY) BORN: ST. PETERSBURG, RUSSIA, NOVEMBER 17, 1905. DIED: MARCH 5, 1967.

Pop-eyed and mournful-looking, Mischa Auer specialized in playing sinister foreigners in his early career, but soon graduated to the comical performances for which he is best remembered today. The grandson of violinist Leopold Auer, Mischa came to the U.S. to escape the Russian Revolution, settling in New York City. Stage work in *Morals* and *Dope* led to a part in the film *Something Always Happens*. Throughout the early 1930s he could be found playing a Hindu spy in *Inside the Lines*; more secret agents in *Murder at Dawn*, *Mata Hari*, *After Tonight*, and *Sons o' Guns*; more Hindus in *Clive of India* and *Lives of a Bengal Lancer*; a murderer who is strangled by his pet ape in *The Monster Walks*; and the assassin who shot Archduke Ferdinand in *Storm at Daybreak*. His career blossomed in the late 1930s with his two most famous roles: his delicious Oscar-nominated turn as the gorilla-imitating protégé of Alice Brady in *My Man Godfrey*; and the ballet impresario with a blunt opinion of Ann Miller's dancing abilities ("Confidentially, she stinks!") in the 1938 Oscar-winner for Best Picture, *You Can't Take It With You*. Universal signed him up as a supporting player and, depending on one's tolerance for his manic energy, he was ingratiating or infuriating in a trio of Deanna Durbin films (*Three Smart Girls*; *One Hundred Men and a Girl*, as a likeable musician; and *Spring Parade*); the hit western, *Destry Rides Again*, in which he was married to Una Merkel; and three Baby Sandy comedies (*East Side of Heaven*, *Unexpected Father*, and *Sandy Is a Lady*). Following World War II, he returned to Europe where he continued to work in films, including Orson Welles's *Mr. Arkadin*, as the owner of a flea circus.

Screen: 1928: Something Always Happens; 1929: Marquis Preferred; The Studio Murder Mystery; The Mighty; 1930: The Benson Murder Case; Paramount on Parade; Inside the Lines; Just Imagine; 1931: No Limit; The Unholy Garden; Delicious; King of the Wild (serial); The Yellow Ticket; Command Performance; Working Girls; Drums of Jeopardy; Women Love Once; The Lady From Nowhere; The Spy; Mata Hari; 1932: The Midnight Patrol; Arsene Lupin; Call Her Savage; Sinister Hands; Drifting Souls; The Last of the Mohicans; The Monster Walks; Beauty Parlor; Murder at Dawn; No Greater Love; Scarlet Dawn; The

Unwritten Law; Western Code; The Intruder; Rasputin and the Empress; **1933:** Infernal Machine; Sucker Money; Corruption; Tarzan the Fearless; After Tonight; Cradle Song; Clear All Wires; Girl Without a Room; Dangerously Yours; The Flaming Signal; Gabriel Over the White House; Storm at Daybreak; The Woman Condemned; **1934:** The Crosby Case; Student Tour; Viva Villa; Wharf Angel; Bulldog Drummond Strikes Back; Stamboul Quest; Beyond the Laws; **1935:** Condemned to Live; The Adventures of Rex and Rinty (serial); Lives of a Bengal Lancer; The Crusades; Clive of India; Anna Karenina; Mystery Woman; Murder in the Fleet; I Dream Too Much; We're Only Human; **1936:** Here Comes Trouble; Tough Guy; The House of a Thousand Candles; One Rainy Afternoon; The Gay Desperado; Sons O' Guns; The Princess Comes Across; Three Smart Girls; My Man Godfrey; Winterset; **1937:** That Girl From Paris; We Have Our Moments; One Hundred Men and a Girl; Top of the Town; Merry-Go-Round of 1938; Prescription for Romance; Pick a Star; Marry the Girl; Vogues of 1938; It's All Yours; **1938:** The Rage of Paris; Service De Luxe; Little Tough Guys in Society; Sweethearts; You Can't Take It With You; **1939:** East Side of Heaven; Destry Rides Again; Unexpected Father; **1940:** Alias the Deacon; Sandy Is a Lady; Margie; Spring Parade; Seven Sinners; Trail of the Vigilantes; Public Deb. No. 1; **1941:** The Flame of New Orleans; Cracked Nuts; Hold That Ghost; Sing Another Chorus; Moonlight in Hawaii; Hellzapoppin; **1942:** Don't Get Personal; Twin Beds; **1943:** Around the World; **1944:** Lady in the Dark; Up in Mabel's Room; **1945:** A Royal Scandal; Brewster's Millions; And Then There Were None; **1946:** Sentimental Journey; She Wrote the Book; **1947:** For You I Die; **1948:** Sofia; **1950:** Fame and the Devil; **1952:** The Sky Is Red; Song of Paris/Bachelor in Paris; **1954:** Escalier de Service (nUSr); **1955:** Frou-Frou; **1956:** Mannequins de Paris (nUSr); La Polka des Monottes (nUSr); Please Mr. Balzac (nUSr); **1957:** The Monte Carlo Story; Le Tombeur (nUSr); **1958:** Mam'zelle Pigalle/That Naughty Girl (nUSr); The Foxiest Girl in Paris; Tabarin (nUSr); Sacrée Jeunesse (nUSr); **1959:** Future Vedettes/School for Love (nUSr); **1960:** A Dog, a Mouse and a Sputnik; **1962:** Mr. Arkadin/Confidential Report (filmed 1955); We Joined the Navy; **1963:** Ladies First; Dynamite Girl; **1964:** Whatever Happened to Baby Toto? (nUSr); Queste Pazze Pazze Pazze Donne (nUSr); **1966:** The Christmas That Almost Wasn't; Per Amore…Per Magia (nUSr); Arrivederci Baby.

NY Stage: 1925: Morals; 1926: Dope; 1942: The Lady Comes Across; 1946: Lovely Me; 1964: The Merry Widow.

Select TV: 1960: Ninotchka (sp).

JEAN-PIERRE AUMONT

(JEAN-PIERRE PHILIPPE SALOMONS) BORN: PARIS, FRANCE, JANUARY 5, 1909. ED: PARIS CONSERVATORY. DIED: JANUARY 30, 2001.

Although he never reached the upper echelons of stardom, Jean-Pierre Aumont was a reliable performer during the course of his 60 years in film. He debuted in the 1931 French production *Echec et Mat/Checkmate*, and was still on hand for an appearance in a Jeanne Moreau vehicle, *The Proprietor*, in 1996. Following service with the Free French forces during World War II, he came to America for his Broadway debut in *Rose Burke* (1942), and his Hollywood bow in 1943, for MGM's *Assignment in Brittany*, posing as a Nazi leader in league with the French underground. Similarly, he rallied French POWs against Nazi Peter Lorre in *The Cross of Lorraine*, thereby making him a one-man propaganda machine for the French allies. Once the war was over he went to RKO for Ginger Rogers's last vehicle there, *Heartbeat*, where she

was supposed to pick his pocket but ended up marrying him instead. Hard of the heels of that failure he played composer Rimsky-Korsakov in Universal's *Song of Scheherezade* before appearing in one of that studio's infamously dopey Technicolor extravaganzas, *Siren of Atlantis*, which introduced him to his wife, Maria Montez. (They wed in 1943 and remained married until her death in 1951.) After this brief dalliance with Hollywood he returned to French cinema but would still find employment in various U.S. productions, notably in *Lili*, as the magician who attracts Leslie Caron's fancy; *The Devil at 4 O'Clock*, piloting a planeload of convicts; *Castle Keep*, as the proprietor of the title schloss; and *Mahogany*, as one of Diana Ross's lovers. In 1976 he published his autobiography, *Sun and Shadow*.

Screen (US releases only): 1936: Flight Into Darkness; 1938: Satan's Paradise; 1939: Three Hours; 1943: Assignment in Brittany; 1944: The Cross of Lorraine; 1946: Heartbeat; 1947: Song of Scheherezade; 1949: Siren of Atlantis; 1950: The Wicked City; 1953: Lili; The Gay Adventure; 1954: Charge of the Lancers; 1957: Royal Affair in Versailles; The Seventh Sin; 1959: John Paul Jones; 1960: The Enemy General; 1961: The Devil at 4 O'Clock; 1962: Seven Capital Sins; 1963: Five Miles to Midnight; 1969: Castle Keep; 1971: Cauldron of Blood; 1973: Day for Night; 1975: The Happy Hooker; Mahogany; 1976: Catherine & Co.; 1978: Cat and Mouse; Blackout; 1979: Something Short of Paradise; 1981: Don't Look in the Attic (dtv); 1983: Nana; 1987: Sweet Country; 1992: Becoming Colette; 1995: Jefferson in Paris; 1996: The Proprietor.

NY Stage: 1942: Rose Burke; 1949: My Name Is Aquilon; 1955: The Heavenly Twins; 1960: Second String; 1963: Tovarich; 1970: Camino Real; 1971: Murderous Angels; 1976: Days in the Trees; 1981: A Talent for Murder.

Select TV: 1951: No Time for Comedy (sp); A Christmas Gift (sp); 1952: A Softness in the Wind (sp); Letter to an Unknown Woman (sp); 1953: Arms and the Man (sp); 1956: Integrity (sp); 1957: Sing a Song (sp); 1958: World From a Sealed-Off Box (sp); 1960: The Imposter (sp); 1961: Intermezzo (sp); 1963: The Horse Without a Head; 1979: The French Atlantic Affair (ms); Beggarman Thief (ms); 1980: The Memory of Eva Ryker; A Time for Miracles; 1986: Sins (ms); 1988: Windmills of the Gods (ms); 1998: The Count of Monte Cristo.

GENE AUTRY

(ORVON GENE AUTRY) BORN: TIOGA, TX, SEPTEMBER 29, 1907. DIED: OCTOBER 2, 1998.

The screen's preeminent singing cowboy, Gene Autry got his start warbling on the radio and eventually fronted his own show, *National Barn Dance*, in 1931. Three years later he made his movie debut, in a Ken Maynard western for Mascot, *In Old Santa Fe*. The film also introduced the man who would be his comic sidekick for many years, Smiley Burnette. 1935 saw him take the reigns of his first starring vehicle, *Tumbling Tumbleweeds*, and for the next 12 years (usually astride his horse, Champion) he was the key moneymaker for his studio, Republic Pictures. He became the most successful of all cowboy stars, able to cross over into a respectable level of mainstream fame. In 1941, with *Back in the Saddle* — a standout among the many features he released at this time — he introduced the title tune that became his signature song and provided the title of his 1978 autobiography. He continued to be a prominent radio performer, hosting *Gene Autry's Melody Ranch* from 1940 to 1946. As Roy Rogers took over his berth at Republic in the late 1940s, Autry moved over to Columbia, where he ended his big-screen career with *Last of the Pony Riders*, in 1953. Thereafter he concentrated on television, formed Flying A Productions, and starred in *The Gene Autry Show* (1950–56). The owner of several radio and television stations, a record label (Challenger), and co-founder of the California Angels baseball team, Autry retired in the late 1950s, one of the richest men in show business. Although little of his work has been screened in recent years he is represented each Christmas as the vocalist on two of the holiday's most popular songs: "Rudolph the Red-Nosed Reindeer" and "Here Comes Santa Claus." He also has the distinction of holding the record for the most stars — five — on the Hollywood Walk of Fame.

Screen: **1934:** In Old Santa Fe; Mystery Mountain (serial); **1935:** The Phantom Empire (serial); Tumbling Tumbleweeds; Melody Trail; The Sagebrush Troubadour; The Singing Vagabond; **1936:** Red River Valley; Comin' Round the Mountain; The Singing Cowboy; Guns and Guitars; Oh Susanna!; The Big Show; Ride Ranger Ride; The Old Corral; **1937:** Round-Up Time in Texas; Git Along, Little Dogies; Rootin' Tootin' Rhythm; Yodelin' Kid From Pine Ridge; Public Cowboy No. 1; Boots and Saddles; Manhattan Merry-Go-Round; Springtime in the Rockies; **1938:** The Old Barn Dance; Gold Mine in the Sky; The Man From Music Mountain; Prairie Moon; Rhythm of the Saddle; Western Jamboree; **1939:** Home on the Prairie; Mexicali Rose; Blue Montana Skies; Mountain Rhythm; Colorado Sunset; In Old Monterey; Rovin' Tumbleweeds; South of the Border; **1940:** Rancho Grande; Shooting High; Men With Steel Faces; Gaucho Serenade; Carolina Moon; Ride, Tenderfoot, Ride; Melody Ranch; **1941:** Ridin' on a Rainbow; Back in the Saddle; The Singing Hills; Sunset in Wyoming; Under Fiesta Stars; Down Mexico Way; Sierra Sue; **1942:** Cowboy Serenade; Heart of the Rio Grande; Home in Wyomin'; Stardust on the Sage; Call of the Canyon; Bells of Capistrano; **1946:** Sioux City Sue; **1947:** Trail to San Antone; Twilight on the Rio Grande; Saddle Pals; Robin Hood of Texas; The Last Round-Up; **1948:** The Strawberry Roan; **1949:** Loaded Pistols; The Big Sombrero; Riders of the Whistling Pines; Rim of the Canyon; The Cowboy and the Indians; Riders in the Sky; **1950:** Sons of New Mexico; Mule Train; Cow Town; Beyond the Purple Hills; Indian Territory; The Blazing Sun; **1951:** Gene Autry and the Mounties; Texans Never Cry; Whirlwind; Silver Canyon; Hills of Utah; Valley of Fire; **1952:** The Old West; Night Stage to Galveston; Apache Country; Barbed Wire; Wagon Team; Blue Canadian Rockies; **1953:** Winning of the West; On Top of Old Smoky; Goldtown Ghost Riders; Pack Train; Saginaw Trail; Last of the Pony Riders; **1959:** Alias Jesse James.

Select TV: 1950–56: The Gene Autry Show (series).

FRANKIE AVALON

(Francis Avallone) Born: Philadelphia, PA, September 18, 1939.

Pompadoured Frankie Avalon became a hit recording artist (with two Number 1 Billboard songs: "Venus" and "Why") and pop idol while still a teen. Unlike many of his contemporaries he actually managed to parlay his juke-box fame into a successful movie career. His first acting assignment was an unheralded supporting role in a junior-league Alan Ladd western, *Guns of the Timberland*. He continued as an ensemble player in the higher profile *The Alamo*, as a green kid who survives the famous siege, and in *Voyage to the Bottom of the Sea*, which also allowed him to croon the title song over the credits. He showed up in a limp Ernie Kovacs comedy, *Sail a Crooked Ship*, and a small-budgeted affair from American International Pictures, *Panic in Year Zero*, a surprisingly good apocalyptic tale.

Also for AIP, who specialized in quickie fare for teens, he did the movies for which he is best remembered — teaming with Annette Funicello for a rather inane series of "beach" comedies, starting with *Beach Party* in 1963. Bursting with color and high spirits, these concoctions combined songs, gyrating dancers in skimpy bathing suits, brain-roasting plots, slapdash slapstick, and mugging in place of acting. Considering Avalon's limited thespian talents he seemed quite at home, and almost always got a chance to sing. These pictures — and their various hybrids — ended for Avalon in 1966 with the particularly woeful *Fireball 500*, a misguided attempt at something a little more serious. His heyday in decline, Avalon continued to perform his oldies in concert halls and clubs, more than once sharing the bill with two more former pop idols, Bobby Rydell and Fabian. In his guest spot as an angel in the smash-hit musical *Grease* and, more specifically, in his 1987 reteaming with Funicello, *Back to the Beach*, he good-naturedly lampooned his image.

Screen: **1957:** Jamboree; **1960:** Guns of the Timberland; The Alamo; **1961:** Alakazam the Great (voice); Voyage to the Bottom of the Sea; **1962:** Sail a Crooked Ship; Panic in Year Zero; The Castilian/Valley of the Swords; **1963:** Operation Bikini; Drums of Africa; Beach Party; **1964:** Bikini Beach; Pajama Party; Muscle Beach Party; **1965:** Beach Blanket Bingo; Ski Party; How to Stuff a Wild Bikini; I'll Take Sweden; Sergeant Deadhead; **1966:** Dr. Goldfoot and the Bikini Machine; Fireball 500; **1967:** The Million Eyes of Su-Muru; **1968:** Skidoo; **1970:** Horror House; **1974:** The Take; **1978:** Grease; **1982:** Blood Song/Dream Slayer (dtv); **1987:** Back to the Beach; **1994:** Stoned Age (dtv); **1995:** Casino.

NY Stage: 1997: Grease.

Select TV: 1976: Easy Does It…Starring Frankie Avalon (series); 1995: A Dream is a Wish Your Heart Makes: The Annette Funicello Story.

LEW AYRES

(Lewis Ayre) Born: Minneapolis, MN, December 28, 1908. ed: Univ of AZ. Died: December 30, 1996.

An actor who exuded a generic geniality that fell short of lighting up the screen, Lew Ayres starred in one of the first great classics of the sound era and played the most famous screen doctor of them all. Ironically, he was studying medicine at college when shifted his interest to music, joining the Ray West Band. An engagement in Los Angeles led to his 1929 movie debut, a bit part in Pathe's *The Sophomore*. The following year he won the role that made him a star, Paul Baumer, the young German soldier disillusioned by the realities of war, in Lewis Milestone's Oscar-winning classic *All Quiet on the Western Front*. The anti-war sentiments of the movie had such a profound effect on him that Ayres became a conscientious objector. The years following did not seem to fulfill the initial promise as Universal, who had released that movie and put him under contract, cast him in one uninspired film after another. Among these were *East Is West*, saving a Chinese Lupe Velez (!) from slavery; *Iron Man*, a boxing story; *Spirit of Notre Dame*, one of the many college football tales of the time; and *Okay America*, as a journalist involved in a kidnapping. At least *Night World*, an ensemble piece set in a night club, had some racy pre-code interest. Fox signed him to play in his next real hit, the folksy *State Fair*, where he shared the screen with two much bigger stars than himself, Will Rogers and Janet Gaynor. Because of it, Fox decided to put him under contract.

Fox, however, saw him as a "B" player, and buried him in such assignments as *Lottery Lover*, a stinker that included Billy Wilder among the writers; and *Silk Hat Kid*, which featured him as an ex-fighter-turned-bodyguard. Ayres had married Ginger Rogers in 1933 and her stardom certainly eclipsed his during their seven-year union. Undeterred, he showed determination by directing two movies for Republic: *The Leathernecks Have Landed*, starring himself, and *Hearts in Bondage*, with James Dunn and Mae Clarke. These only led to squabbles with the studio, however, after which Ayres was back to more second-features, mostly at Paramount. He was certainly a pleasant performer and finally got a break when Columbia hired him for *Holiday*, where he gave a standout performance as Katharine Hepburn's drunken wastrel brother. Soon afterwards MGM took him on and promptly gave him his signature role, that of the soft-spoken, too-good-to-be-true Dr. James Kildare in *Young Dr. Kildare*. This unremarkable hospital melodrama proved so popular that it spawned countless follow-ups, with Ayres on board for nine entries in the series. In between his medical assignments he could be seen on skates in *The Ice Follies of 1939*; was teamed with Jeanette MacDonald (on hiatus from Nelson Eddy) in *Broadway Serenade*; and got dumped by Greer Garson in favor of one of the studio's biggest stars, Robert Taylor, in *Remember?* His pacifist stance amid the fervent patriotism of World War II made him very unpopular at MGM. The studio expressed their feelings by replacing him in the "Kildare" series with Phillip Dorn.

Citing his religious beliefs, Ayres refused to take up arms and served instead as an orderly with the Army Medical Corps, a move that helped remove some of the anti-war stigma. After the war, he stayed with medical roles, first as a psychiatrist trying to help two different Olivia de Havillands in the noir *The Dark Mirror*, and then as the sympathetic doctor who aids deaf-mute Jane Wyman in *Johnny Belinda*, receiving an Oscar nomination for what was perhaps his best performance. The accolade failed to resuscitate his career, however, and he returned to "B" pictures, one of which, the 1953 release *Donovan's Brain*, was a science fiction movie of quality. Religion was clearly becoming his principal interest and he authored a book on the subject, *Altars of the East*, which he then produced in a film version, having written, financed, and narrated the project. In 1962 he returned to motion pictures with a quietly effective turn as the Vice President in the all-star *Advise and Consent*. His acting juices kept flowing well into his 80s, though mostly on television. On the big screen he could be seen as Earl Holliman's boss in Disney's *The Biscuit Eater*; under simian make-up in *Battle for the Planet of the Apes*; and getting sucked under the ice in *Damien: Omen II*. Before Ginger Rogers he was married (1931–33) to actress Lola Lane.

Screen: 1929: The Sophomore; The Kiss; 1930: All Quiet on the Western Front; Doorway to Hell; Common Clay; 1931: East Is West; Many a Slip; The Iron Man; Up for Murder; Heaven on Earth; The Spirit of Notre Dame; 1932: The Impatient Maiden; Night World; Okay America; 1933: State Fair; Don't Bet on Love; My Weakness; 1934: Cross Country Cruise; Let's Be Ritzy; She Learned About Sailors; Servants Entrance; 1935: Lottery Lover; Spring Tonic; Silk Hat Kid; 1936: The Leathernecks Have Landed (and dir.); Panic on the Air; Shakedown; Murder With Pictures; Lady Be Careful; 1937: The Crime Nobody Saw; Last Train From Madrid; Hold 'em Navy; 1938: Scandal Street; King of the Newsboys; Holiday; Rich Man, Poor Girl; Young Doctor Kildare; Spring Madness; 1939: The Ice Follies of 1939; Broadway Serenade; Calling Dr. Kildare; These Glamour Girls; The Secret of Dr. Kildare; Remember?; 1940: Dr. Kildare's Strange Case; Dr. Kildare Goes Home; The Golden Fleecing; Dr. Kildare's Crisis; 1941: Maisie Was a Lady; The People vs. Dr. Kildare; Dr. Kildare's Wedding Day; 1942: Dr. Kildare's Victory; Fingers at the Window; 1946: The Dark Mirror; 1947: The Unfaithful; 1948: Johnny Belinda; 1950: The Capture; 1951: New Mexico; 1953: No Escape; Donovan's Brain; 1962: Advise and Consent; 1964: The Carpetbaggers; 1972: The Biscuit Eater; The Man; 1973: Battle for the Planet of the Apes; 1977: End of the World; 1978: Damien: Omen II; 1979: Battlestar: Galactica.

Select TV: 1956: The Family Nobody Wanted (sp); 1958: Frontier Justice (series); 1968: Hawaii Five-O; 1969: Marcus Welby M.D./A Matter of Humanities; 1971: Earth II; 1972: She Waits; 1973: The Stranger; 1974: The Questor Tapes; Heatwave!; 1976: Francis Gary Powers: The True Story of the U-2 Spy Incident; 1978: Suddenly Love; 1979: Salem's Lot; Letters From Frank; Reunion; 1980: Of Mice and Men; 1985: Lime Street (series); 1986: Under Siege; 1994: Hart to Hart: Crimes of the Hart.

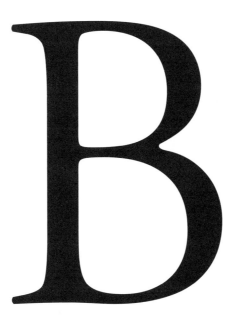

B

LAUREN BACALL

(Betty Joan Perske) Born: New York, NY, September 16, 1924. ed: AADA.

When 19-year-old Lauren Bacall sashayed her way through *To Have and Have Not*, cinema audiences had no option but to sit up and take notice of her inimitable 'come-hither' look and the way she purred, "You know how to whistle, don't you, Steve? You just put your lips together and ... blow," to a beguiled Humphrey Bogart. It was one of the most unforgettable film debuts of all time. Tested and signed by director Howard Hawks, whose wife spotted her on the cover of *Harper's Bazaar*, the striking model not only became an overnight sensation but captured the heart of her 45-year-old co-star. They married in 1945 and appeared, memorably, in three more films, each among the best noirs of the decade. The first was *The Big Sleep*, the bona fide masterpiece of the bunch, in which their bantering took sexual innuendo to a production code breaking point. *Dark Passage* followed. Part of the story was filmed from Bogart's point of view and required Bacall to speak directly to the camera. The last was *Key Largo*, where Bacall exhibited a touching vulnerability as the daughter of wheelchair-bound Lionel Barrymore. Bogart and Bacall propagated a simmering undercurrent of sensuality in all their exchanges, but there was speculation over whether Bacall could create sufficient spark on her own. In her first film without Bogart she was paired with Charles Boyer in *Confidential Agent*, a story of the Spanish Civil War. The very same critics who had lionized her before now expressed serious doubts about her acting ability. Undeterred, she continued to work independently of her famous husband, playing a very discreet lesbian in *Young Man With a Horn*, opposite Kirk Douglas, and a madam in a weak Gary Cooper western, *Bright Leaf*.

Frequent fights with Warners over the roles the studio offered her soon led to a buyout of her contract, so she signed up with 20th Century-Fox. She immediately scored a huge hit in *How to Marry a Millionaire*. Although she was billed below two of Fox's established players, Betty Grable and Marilyn Monroe, Bacall proved herself a fine light comedy player and showed the first real signs of her individuality as a screen personality *sans* Bogart. She followed up with another Fox ensemble piece, *Woman's World*, playing the wife of Fred MacMurray. From there she went to mgm, where she was lost amid the goings-on at a mental institution, in *The Cobweb*. Thankless roles in John Wayne's dreary anti-Commie adventure *Blood Alley*, and Douglas Sirk's florid soap opera *Written on the Wind*, as alcoholic Robert Stack's unhappy spouse, did little to enhance her reputation. Following Bogart's death in 1957, she wound up in a poor but popular romantic comedy with Gregory Peck, *Designing Woman*, followed by forgettable dramas like *The Gift of Love* and the British-made *Flame Over India*, her best-liked film of this period but a box-office failure. Disillusioned with Hollywood and hoping to start life anew she returned to her native New York, appearing in the Broadway comedy *Goodbye Charlie*. During the 1960s, while enduring a troubled marriage (1961–73) to actor Jason Robards, she became the toast of Broadway. She enjoyed back-to-back triumphs with the light romantic comedy *Cactus Flower* and *Applause*, a musical remake of *All About Eve*. For her reprise of Bette Davis's famous part of Margo Channing, Bacall won the Tony Award for Best Actress. 11 years later, she nabbed her second Tony for *Woman of the Year*, another musical based on a famous movie, this time recreating the role originated by Katharine Hepburn. She had, by this point, become the kind of star who could boost a film by her mere presence. She proved her worth in a standout supporting part, as an icy socialite none too concerned about her missing husband, in the Paul Newman detective thriller *Harper*, and in the asinine comedy *Sex and the Single Girl*, as Henry Fonda's jealous wife.

By the time her acclaimed autobiography *By Myself* (1979) was published, the sex symbol of the 1940s had become a legend. The exotic starlet whose future in show business had once been so tenuous had developed into a performer of intelligence and stature. She exhibited style in the hit whodunit *Murder on the Orient Express*; was emotionally affecting as John Wayne's ladyfriend in his final movie *The Shootist*; and even brought gravitas to the starring role in *The Fan* (1981), playing a Broadway diva being stalked by demented admirer Michael Biehn. In support, she added class to such films as *Health*, in a comical turn as a well-preserved but decidedly eccentric health nut; *Mr. North*, running a boarding house in this ensemble directed by Danny Huston, son of Bogart and Bacall's longime friend John; *Misery*, as James Caan's crusty publisher; *Ready to Wear*, as a noted dress designer; and *All I Want for Christmas*, as a grandmother, though she hardly looked the part. In 1996 she excelled as Barbra Streisand's insensitive mother in *The Mirror Has Two Faces*, for which she was Oscar-nominated as Best Supporting Actress — amazingly, her first such recognition. She was, apparently, deemed too independent of Hollywood to receive the requisite sentimentality votes to win. Almost 50 years after their first on-screen pairing, she showed up as a madam entertaining Kirk Douglas in *Diamonds*, a film that relied on nostalgia and good will to carry them through. A second memoir, entitled *Now*, was published in 1994.

Screen: 1944: To Have and Have Not; 1945: Confidential Agent; 1946: Two Guys From Milwaukee; The Big Sleep; 1947: Dark Passage; 1948: Key Largo; 1950: Young Man With a Horn; Bright Leaf; 1953: How to Marry a Millionaire; 1954: Woman's World; 1955: The Cobweb; Blood Alley; 1956: Written on the Wind; 1957: Designing Woman; 1958: The Gift of Love; 1960: Flame Over India/North West Frontier; 1964: Shock Treatment; Sex and the Single Girl; 1966: Harper; 1974: Murder on the Orient Express; 1976: The Shootist; 1981: Health (filmed 1979); The Fan; 1988: Appointment With Death; Mr. North; 1990: Innocent Victim/Tree of Hands (dtv); Misery; 1991: A Star for Two (nUSr); All I Want for Christmas; 1994: Ready to Wear/Prêt-à-Porter; 1996: The Line King: The Al Hirschfeld Story; The Mirror Has Two Faces; My Fellow Americans; 1997: Le Jour et la Nuit/Day and Night (nUSr); 1999: Diamonds; Presence of Mind (nUSr); 2000 The Venice Project (nUSr).

NY Stage: 1942: Johnny 2x4; 1961: Goodbye Charlie; 1967: Cactus Flower; 1970: Applause; 1981: Woman of the Year; 1999: Waiting in the Wings.

Select TV: 1955: The Petrified Forest (sp); 1956: Blithe Spirit (sp); 1973: Applause (sp); 1979: Perfect Gentlemen; 1989: Dinner at Eight; A Little Piece of Sunshine; 1993: The Portrait; A Foreign Field (sp); 1995: From the Mixed-Up Files of Mrs. Basil E. Frankweiler; 1999: Too Rich: The Secret Life of Doris Duke.

JIM BACKUS
BORN: CLEVELAND, OH, FEBRUARY 25, 1913. ED: AADA. DIED: JULY 3, 1989.

Although he may be forever associated with the cartoon character voice of the myopic Mr. Magoo (which he did for the first time in the 1949 short "Ragtime Bear"), Jim Backus's show business career dated all the way back to the 1930s, when he got his start on radio in his native Cleveland. He moved east to appear on Broadway in *Too Many Heroes*, after which he continued to find regular work in the New York radio market. Starting in 1949, he bounced back and forth between television (where he would be featured in no fewer than eight series over the next 20 years) and movies. Invariably, in the latter, he was most frequently seen in comical parts: an obnoxious motorist who picks up Jack Lemmon and June Allyson in *You Can't Run Away from It*; a nitwit military man in *The Horizontal Lieutenant*; a doddering story-book king in *The Wonderful World of the Brothers Grimm*; Lee Remick's insensitive boss in *The Wheeler Dealer*; and a drunken millionaire in *It's a Mad Mad Mad Mad World*. Ironically, his best-remembered big screen role was a dramatic one, playing James Dean's ineffectual father, unable to communicate with his restless son, in the 1955 classic *Rebel Without a Cause*. Most television viewers are quick to identify Backus as the pompous, lockjawed millionaire, Thurston Howell III, from one of the silliest of all sitcoms, *Gilligan's Island*. His many books

include *Only When I Laugh, Rocks on the Roof, What Are You Doing After the Orgy, Backus Strikes Back*, and *Forgive Us Our Digressions*.

Screen: 1949: One Last Fling; The Great Lover; Father Was a Fullback; Easy Living; A Dangerous Profession; 1950: Ma and Pa Kettle Go to Town; Customs Agent; Emergency Wedding; The Killer That Stalked New York; 1951: Bright Victory; The Hollywood Story; I Want You; Iron Man; Half Angel; The Man With a Cloak; M; His Kind of Woman; I'll See You in My Dreams; 1952: Pat and Mike; Deadline USA; Here Come the Nelsons; The Rose Bowl Story; Don't Bother to Knock; Androcles and the Lion; Above and Beyond; Angel Face; 1953: I Love Melvin; 1954: Geraldine; Deep in My Heart; 1955: Francis in the Navy; Rebel Without a Cause; The Square Jungle; 1956: The Great Man; Meet Me in Las Vegas; The Naked Hills; You Can't Run Away From It; The Opposite Sex; The Girl He Left Behind; 1957: Top Secret Affair; Man of a Thousand Faces; Eighteen and Anxious; 1958: The High Cost of Loving; Macabre; 1959: The Big Operator; The Wild and the Innocent; 1001 Arabian Knights (voice); A Private's Affair; Ask Any Girl; 1960: Ice Palace; 1962: The Wonderful World of the Brothers Grimm; The Horizontal Lieutenant; Boys' Night Out; Zotz!; Critic's Choice; 1963: Johnny Cool; The Wheeler Dealers; Sunday in New York; It's a Mad Mad Mad Mad World; Operation Bikini; My Six Loves; 1964: Advance to the Rear; John Goldfarb, Please Come Home; 1965: Fluffy; Billie; 1967: Hurry Sundown; Don't Make Waves; 1968: Where Were You When the Lights Went Out?; 1969: Hello Down There; 1970: The Cockeyed Cowboys of Calico County; Myra Breckinridge; 1972: Now You See Him, Now You Don't; 1975: Friday Foster; Crazy Mama; 1977: Pete's Dragon; 1978: Good Guys Wear Black; 1979: C.H.O.M.P.S.; 1980: Angels' Brigade; There Goes the Bride; 1984: Slapstick (of Another Kind); Prince Jack.

NY Stage: 1937: Too Many Heroes.

Select TV: 1949–50: Hollywood House (series); 1952–55: I Married Joan (series); 1958: The Pied Piper of Hamelin (sp); 1960: The Jim Backus Show/Hot Off the Wire (series); 1962: Talent Scouts (series); 1964–65: Famous Adventures of Mr. Magoo (series; voice); 1964–65: Gilligan's Island (series); 1966: Continental Showcase (series); 1968–69: Blondie (series); 1969: Wake Me When the War Is Over; 1972: Getting Away From It All; The Magic Carpet; 1973: The Girl Most Likely to…; Miracle on 34th Street; 1976: The Return of Joe Forrester/The Cop on the Beat; 1978: Rescue From Gilligan's Island; 1979: The Castaways on Gilligan's Island; The Rebels (ms); 1980: The Gossip Columnist; The Jayne Mansfield Story; 1981: The Harlem Globetrotters on Gilligan's Island.

HERMIONE BADDELEY
(HERMIONE CLINTON-BADDELY)
BORN: BROSELEY, SHROPSHIRE, ENGLAND, NOVEMBER 13, 1906. DIED: AUGUST 19, 1986.

Rubbery-faced, jocular Hermione Baddeley began performing while still in her teens and eventually became the star of a West End stage revue. She made a handful of movies in the 1920s and 1930s, but didn't really become a staple of British films until after World War II, when she came to embody everyone's idea of the blowsy, sassy cockney. Some of her memorable appearances were as a pier entertainer in the thriller *Brighton Rock*, seeking her revenge on killer Richard Attenborough, and in the whimsical comedy *Passport to Pimlico*, as a resident of a London neighborhood that declares independence from the rest of England after the discovery of an ancient charter. During the 1950s she continued to be a formidable presence on the British film scene with notable roles in *Dear Mr. Prohack*, opposite Cecil Parker; as Mrs. Cratchit in *A Christmas Carol*; and as Mrs. Pardell in *The Pickwick Papers*. She was, however, relatively unknown to American audiences until she received an unexpected Oscar nomination for her rather brief appearance in *Room at the Top*. (Her big moment came when she lashed out at self-involved Laurence Harvey after her friend, Simone Signoret, has been killed in a car accident.) Spurred on by her new-found fame she made her way to America to play in Universal's London-set Doris Day thriller *Midnight Lace*. Staying on in the States, she appeared as domestics in two Disney musicals, *Mary Poppins* and *The Happiest Millionaire*. Baddeley was curiously cast as Marie Dressler in the tawdry biopic *Harlow*; supported Day again on another sidetrip to England for *Do Not Disturb*; and tried desperately to inject some comedy into *Marriage on the Rocks*, as Deborah Kerr's bagpipe-playing mum. She reached a whole new fan base when she joined the cast of the hit television sitcom *Maude*, as Bea Arthur's hard-drinking maid. Her sister, Angela Baddeley, was best known for her role on the PBS series *Upstairs Downstairs*.

Screen: 1927: A Daughter in Revolt; 1928: The Guns of Loos; 1930: Caste; 1935: Royal Cavalcade; 1941: Kipps; 1947: It Always Rains on Sundays; Brighton Rock/Young Scarface; 1948: No Room at the Inn; Quartet; 1949: Passport to Pimlico; Dear Mr. Prohack; 1950: The Woman in Question; 1951: There Is Another Sun; Wall of Death; Tom Brown's Schooldays; Hell Is Sold Out; A Christmas Carol/Scrooge; 1952: Song of Paris; Time Gentlemen Please; The Pickwick Papers; 1953: Cosh Boy/The Slasher; Counter Spy/Double Agent; 1954: The Belles of St. Trinian's; Women Without Men; Blonde Bait; 1959: Room at the Top; Jet Storm; 1960: Expresso Bongo; Let's Get Married; Midnight Lace; 1961: Information Received; Rag Doll; Young, Willing and Eager; 1964: The Unsinkable Molly Brown; Mary Poppins; 1965: Do Not Disturb; Harlow; Marriage on the Rocks; 1967: The Adventures of Bullwhip Griffin; The Happiest Millionaire; 1970: The Aristocats (voice); 1972: Up the Front; 1974: The Black Windmill; 1979: C.H.O.M.P.S.; 1980: There Goes the Bride; 1982: The Secret of NIMH (voice).

NY Stage: 1961: A Taste of Honey; 1962: The Milk Trains Doesn't Stop Here Anymore; 1968: I Only Want an Answer (ob); 1969: Canterbury Tales; 1982: Whodunnit.

Select TV: 1965–66: Camp Runamuck (series); 1971: The Good Life (series); 1974–77: Maude (series); 1983: I Take These Men; This Girl for Hire; 1985: Shadow Chasers.

PEARL BAILEY

Born: Newport News, VA, March 29, 1918.
Died: August 17, 1990.

A true original, Pearlie Mae had a bluesy, insinuating way with a song, often interspersing witty asides into her singing, a trait that helped make her one of America's most beloved entertainers. She entered the business at 15, dancing and singing with various bands, eventually making a name for herself as a cabaret jazz singer in the 1940s. Her success in the 1946 Broadway musical *St. Louis Woman* brought her to the attention of the Hollywood studios. She made two brief appearances for Paramount, singing "Tired" in the all-star *Variety Girl*, and easily stealing the show with her rendition of "I Should Have Quit When I Was Ahead" in *Isn't It Romantic?* Over the years she would prove to be a mightily effective presence in such musicals as *Carmen Jones* (giving a memorable rendition of "Beat Out

That Rhythm on a Drum") and *Porgy and Bess* (lamenting "I Can't Sit Down"). Bailey occasionally essayed straight roles, such as a torch singer drowning her sorrows in drink in *All the Fine Young Cannibals*, or as one of Beau Bridges's tenants in *The Landlord*, but she was criminally underused for the most part. She returned to Broadway in the 1960s and won a Tony Award for the all-black version of *Hello, Dolly!* A frequent television performer, she hosted her own short-lived variety series and won an Emmy Award for her role in the Afterschool Special *Cindy Eller: A Modern Fairy Tale*. Her 1968 autobiography was entitled *The Raw Pearl*.

Screen: 1947: Variety Girl; 1948: Isn't It Romantic?; 1954: Carmen Jones; 1956: That Certain Feeling; 1958: St. Louis Blues; 1959: Porgy and Bess; 1960: All the Fine Young Cannibals; 1970: The Landlord; 1976: Norman...Is That You?; 1981: The Fox and the Hound (voice).

NY Stage: 1946: St. Louis Woman; 1950: Arms and the Girl; Bless You All; 1954: House of Flowers; 1967: Hello, Dolly! (and 1975 revival).

Select TV: 1971: The Pearl Bailey Show (series); 1983: The Member of the Wedding (sp); 1984–85: Silver Spoons (series); 1985: Cindy and Eller: A Modern Fairy Tale; 1989: Peter Gunn.

FAY BAINTER

Born: Los Angeles, CA, December 7, 1891.
Died: April 16, 1968.

Because she was a latecomer to the screen, Fay Bainter was already a middle-aged woman when she started portraying the sympathetic maternal types for which moviegoers will forever remember her. She had, in fact, been acting professionally since the age of six, eventually joining the Oscar Morosco stock company. She debuted on Broadway in 1912, before becoming a member of Minnie Madern Fiske's touring company. Her first movie role, in 1934, was as Lionel Barrymore's novelist wife in *This Side of Heaven*, which was followed by one of her most notable stage triumphs, playing the self-serving wife in *Dodsworth*. The Hollywood matriarchal roles started almost immediately with *The Soldier and the Lady*, as mother to Anton Walbrook. In *Make Way for Tomorrow* she was the selfish daughter-in-law to aging Beulah Bondi, though in reality the two ladies were less than a year apart in age. In 1938 Bainter made movie history by becoming the first performer to be nominated for Oscars in both the lead (*White Banners*) and supporting (*Jezebel*) categories. In the former she was an almost-too-good-to-be true servant for a small town family, harboring a secret about her sordid past. For the latter, playing Bette Davis's kindly Aunt Belle, she won the Academy Award. It was hardly a standout performance but Bainter was becoming such a dependable fixture in Hollywood that it seemed a fitting accolade. That same year she had an unsympathetic role in *The Shining Hour*, as the possessive spinster sister of Melvyn Douglas, whose hatred of his new bride, Joan Crawford, nearly causes tragedy.

Although she was the titular mother in *Mother Carey's Chickens*, she took fourth billing, but in 1939 she topped the bill in two films. The first, at Columbia, was *The Lady and the Mob*, in which she portrayed an aristocratic matron who forms her own vigilante group to combat the racketeers that are destroying her town. Then, at Paramount, she struggled against poverty with Frank Craven for the more serious *Our Neighbors — The Carters*. During the 1940s she signed a contract with MGM, where she was mother to a succession of actors, such as Mickey Rooney in both *Young Tom Edison* and, in one of her career high points, *The*

Human Comedy, valiantly holding down the homefront during World War II. Other studios made her matriarch to William Holden in *Our Town*, John Payne in *Maryland* (one of her favorite roles), and Jeanne Crain in *State Fair*. Back at MGM she helped Rooney and Judy Garland get into show business in *Babes on Broadway*, and played Katharine Hepburn's crusading aunt in *Woman of the Year*. She rated top billing as a selfish wartime woman in *The War Against Mrs. Hadley*, a bit of early-1940s patriotism, and in Paramount's remake of *Mrs. Wiggs of the Cabbage Patch*, playing a dirt-poor mom raising a brood of kids. In *Dark Waters* she had a rare shot at villainy, trying to drive Merle Oberon insane, and again in Warners's melodrama *Deep Valley*, turning a deaf era to her hated husband, Henry Hull. Bainter returned to films in 1961, after an eight-year absence, for her final role, as the deceived grandmother in William Wyler's *The Children Hour*, for which she received her third Academy Award nomination. She is buried in Arlington National Cemetery, her husband having been a lieutenant commander in the military.

Screen: 1934: This Side of Heaven; 1937: Quality Street; The Soldier and the Lady/Michael Strogoff; Make Way for Tomorrow; 1938: Jezebel; White Banners; Mother Carey's Chickens; The Arkansas Traveler; The Shining Hour; 1939: Yes, My Darling Daughter; The Lady and the Mob; Daughters Courageous; Our Neighbors the Carters; 1940: Young Tom Edison; A Bill of Divorcement; Our Town; Maryland; 1941: Babes on Broadway; 1942: Woman of the Year; The War Against Mrs. Hadley; Mrs. Wiggs of the Cabbage Patch; Journey for Margaret; 1943: The Human Comedy; Presenting Lily Mars; Salute to the Marines; Cry Havoc; The Heavenly Body; 1944: Dark Waters; Three Is a Family; 1945: State Fair/ It Happened One Summer; 1946: The Kid From Brooklyn; The Virginian; 1947: Deep Valley; The Secret Life of Walter Mitty; 1948: Give My Regards to Broadway; June Bride; 1951: Close to My Heart; 1953: The President's Lady; 1961: The Children's Hour.

NY Stage: 1912: The Rose of Panama; 1913: The Bridal Path; 1916: Arms and the Girl; 1917: The Willow Tree; 1918: The Kiss Burglar; East Is West; 1923: The Other Rose; 1924: The Dream Girl; 1925: The Enemy; 1926: The Two Orphans; First Love; 1927: Fallen Angels; 1928: She Stoops to Conquer; Beaux Stratagem; Jealousy; 1930: Lysistrata; 1931: The Admirable Crichton; 1933: For Services Rendered; Uncle Tom's Cabin; 1934: Dodsworth; 1945: The Next Half Hour; 1949: Gayden.

Select TV: 1948: Night Must Fall (sp); Kind Lady (sp) 1950: A Child Is Born (sp); 1951: Two Living and One Dead (sp); 1953: Jenny (sp); Black Rain (sp); Career (sp); 1954: The Happiest Day (sp); The Story of Ruth (sp); Guilty Is the Stranger (sp); The Runaway (sp); 1955: My Name Is Julia Ross (sp); 1956: The Sears Girl (sp); The Book of Ruth (sp); 1957: The Dark Corner (sp).

CARROLL BAKER

BORN: JOHNSTOWN, PA, MAY 28, 1931.
ED: ACTORS STUDIO

Before her brief period as a screen sex symbol, icy blonde Carroll Baker was a dancer in a traveling troupe and in New York night clubs. After a forgettable screen debut in an Esther Williams film, *Easy to Love*, she went back East and studied at the Actors Studio. There she met and married director Jack Garfein, and appeared in the Broadway play *All Summer Long*. Warner Bros. took an interest, assigning her a prime supporting role, as Elizabeth Taylor and Rock Hudson's daughter, who gets a crush on millionaire James Dean, in *Giant*, one of the major hits of the decade. This was immediately followed by her

signature role, as the thumb-sucking, child-like wife of Karl Malden in the steamy and controversial Tennessee Williams drama *Baby Doll*. She won an Academy Award nomination for the part, but subsequent performances proved her to be merely competent. In her first post-*Baby Doll* assignment she vied with Jean Simmons for the affections of Gregory Peck in the epic western *The Big Country*, though the gulf between the warmly appealing Simmons and the coolly distant Baker left the outcome in little doubt. Follow-up roles in such films as *The Miracle* (as a 19th century postulant nun) and *Bridge to the Sun* (as a wife adapting to life with Japanese husband James Shigeta) failed to ignite the interest of either the public or the critics. In between those dramas she appeared in a light comedy, *But Not for Me*, falling for the much older Clark Gable.

Baker's screen persona had a hint of petulant bitchiness, which hampered efforts at more sympathetic roles, such as the pioneering woman who wins the heart of James Stewart in the all-star *How the West Was Won*. Trying to cash in on her fading sex symbol image, she played the Harlow-like movie goddess in Paramount's red hot success *The Carpetbaggers*. She cartoonishly vamped George Peppard before finally self-destructing when the chandelier on which she was partying plunged to the ground. Sensing a good thing, Paramount cast Baker as Harlow herself in the less terrible of two competing 1965 biopics on the subject, but she was severely trounced by the critics and left Hollywood to drift into European filmmaking, appearing in movies with titles like *Her Harem*, *The Sweet Body of Deborah*, and *Baba Yaga — Devil Witch*. In the late 1970s, long after the luster had faded, she returned to star in two American productions: Andy Warhol's *Bad* (no doubt for camp appeal) as a woman running an organization that specialized in assassinating babies and animals; and Disney's troubled *The Watcher in the Woods*, in which she and Bette Davis experienced supernatural happenings in England. Her worn look, steeped in sadness, now gave credence to decent performances, as Mariel Hemingway's distressed mom in *Star 80*, and as the ex-wife of Jack Nicholson in *Ironweed*. Her autobiography was, inevitably, titled *Baby Doll* (1983).

Screen: 1953: Easy to Love; 1956: Giant; Baby Doll; 1958: The Big Country; 1959: The Miracle; But Not for Me; 1961: Something Wild; Bridge to the Sun; 1963: How the West Was Won; Station Six Sahara; 1964: The Carpetbaggers; Cheyenne Autumn; 1965: Sylvia; The Greatest Story Ever Told; Mister Moses; Harlow; 1967: Jack of Diamonds; 1968: Her Harem (nUSr); So Sweet…So Perverse (nUSr); 1969: The Sweet Body of Deborah; Paranoia/Orgasmo/A Quiet Place to Kill; 1970: The Spider (nUSr); 1971: The Fourth Mrs. Anderson (nUSr); Captain Apache; 1972: Silent Horror/Behind the Silence (nUSr); The Devil Has Seven Faces (nUSr); 1974: Baba Yaga — Devil Witch (nUSr); The Madness of Love (nUSr); 1975: Bloodbath/The Sky is Falling (dtc); The Private Lesson (nUSr); The Private Lesson (nUSr); 1976: James Dean: The First American Teenager; Bait (nUSr); Confessions of a Frustrated Housewife (nUSr); Rich and Respectable; The Flower With the Deadly Sting; 1977: The Body; Andy Warhol's Bad; Cyclone (nUSr); Valentina…The Virgin Wife; 1980: The World Is Full of Married Men; The Watcher in the Woods; 1983: Star 80; 1984: The Secret Diary of Sigmund Freud (dtv); 1986: Native Son; 1987: Ironweed; 1990: Kindergarten Cop; 1991: Blonde Fist (nUSr); 1993: Cyberdeen/Jackpot (nUSr); 1994: Gipsy Angel (nUSr); 1995: In the Flesh (dtv); 1996: Skeletons (dtv); 1997: Rag and Bone (nUSr); The Game; 1998: Nowhere to Go/Silent Hearts (dtv).

Select TV: 1969: Rain (sp); 1976: The Next Victim; 1983: Red Monarch; 1985: Hitler's SS — Portrait in Evil; 1987: On Fire; 1993: Judgment Day: The John List Story; Men Don't Tell; A Kiss to Die For; 1996: Dalva; 1997: Just Your Luck; North Shore Fish; 1997: Heart Full of Rain; 2000: Another Woman's Husband.

DIANE BAKER
BORN: HOLLYWOOD, CA, FEBRUARY 25, 1938.
ED: USC.

An underappreciated, appealing brunette with a vulnerable nature, Diane Baker (the daughter of actress Dorothy Harrington) was introduced to film audiences in 1959, as the older sister of Millie Perkins in *The Diary of Anne Frank*. Although little of the attention surrounding the film focused on her, 20th Century-Fox wasted no time in promoting their new star. She was quickly featured in supporting roles in two more big productions that year, *The Best of Everything* and *Journey to the Center of the Earth*. Fox afforded her the lead in *Tess of the Storm Country*, a remake of an old Mary Pickford melodrama, in which she played a Scottish girl coming to the Pennsylvania Dutch country in search of a husband. The film was a complete failure, so she was dumped into a childish fairytale, *The Wizard of Baghdad*, and a sword-and-sandal adventure, *The 300 Spartans*. Nonetheless, she continued to be a sympathetic and sensible presence during the 1960s. Her résumé included the limp espionage thriller *The Prize*, as the offspring of kidnapped scientist Edward G. Robinson; the intriguing *Mirage*, where she may or may not having been trying to help amnesiac Gregory Peck; Disney's advertising satire *The Horse in the Gray-Flannel Suit*; and the dormant volcano epic *Krakatoa — East of Java*. During the 1970s she starred in a flop television series, *Here We Go Again*, and later produced a documentary feature, *Ashyana*. After a long absence from the big screen she was seen as the senator whose daughter is kidnapped in the 1991 Best Picture Oscar-winner *The Silence of the Lambs*. This revitalized interest in her and she began popping up as moms in films like *The Net* (Sandra Bullock) and *The Cable Guy* (Matthew Broderick).

Screen: 1959: The Diary of Anne Frank; The Best of Everything; Journey to the Center of the Earth; 1960: Tess of the Storm Country; 1961: The Wizard of Baghdad; 1962: Hemingway's Adventures of a Young Man; The 300 Spartans; 1963: Nine Hours to Rama; Stolen Hours; The Prize; 1964: Strait-Jacket; Marnie; 1965: Mirage; 1966: Sands of Beersheba; 1968: The Horse in the Gray Flannel Suit; 1969: Krakatoa — East of Java/Volcano; 1976: Baker's Hawk; 1979: The Pilot/Danger in the Skies; 1991: The Silence of the Lambs; The Closer (dtv); 1993: The Joy Luck Club; Twenty Bucks; 1994: Imaginary Crimes; 1995: The Net; 1996: The Cable Guy; Courage Under Fire; 1997: Murder at 1600; 2002: Harrison's Flowers.

Select TV: 1959: Della (sp); In Lonely Expectation (sp); The Killers (sp); 1960: Arrowsmith (sp); 1965: Inherit the Wind (sp); 1966: The Dangerous Days of Kiowa Jones; 1969: Trial Run; The D.A.: Murder One; 1970: The Old Man Who Cried Wolf; 1971: Do You Take This Stranger?; Sarge: The Badge or the Cross; Congratulations It's a Boy!; A Little Game; 1972: Killer by Night; 1973: Here We Go Again (series); Police Story; 1974: A Tree Grows in Brooklyn; 1975: The Dream Makers; The Last Survivors; 1980: Fugitive Family; 1982: The Blue and the Gray (ms); 1983: A Woman of Substance; 1991: The Haunted; 1992: Perry Mason: The Case of the Heartbroken Bride; 1995: A Walton Wedding; 1998: About Sarah; 2000: Jackie Bouvier Kennedy Onassis.

STANLEY BAKER
BORN: FERANDLE, WALES, FEBRUARY 8, 1927.
DIED: JUNE 28, 1976.

A ruggedly macho star of British films, Stanley Baker became most closely associated in the international market with action and adventure dramas. He began acting as a teenager, debuting in the 1943 war movie *Undercover*, before his career was interrupted by military service. He turned his attention to the stage but soon committed to the movies full time in the 1950s. He played a succession of tough-guy roles: a whaling boat skipper marooned in the Antarctic in *Hell Below Zero*; a boxer who participates in a robbery in *The Good Die Young*; a soldier trapped behind enemy lines in *A Hill in Korea*; and Henry Tudor, who finally puts a stop to Laurence Olivier's tyranny, in *Richard III*. Americans began to take note of him in international costume epics such as *Knights of the Round Table*, *Helen of Troy*, and *Alexander the Great*. By the late 1950s he'd progressed to leads: playing a saboteur in *Checkpoint*; an ex-con battling fellow truck driver Patrick McGoohan in *Hell Drivers*; a dangerous military man in *Yesterday's Enemy*; and a police inspector on the trail of an escaped jewel thief in *Hell Is a City*. He was also featured in the Oscar-nominated *The Guns of Navarone*, as a knife-wielding commando in Gregory Peck's suicide squad. In the 1960s he became co-producer of his own starring vehicles, most notably the epic *Zulu*, as a British officer whose hopelessly outnumbered troops are ambushed by a tribe of African natives. In *Sands of the Kalahari*, he was one of a group of plane crash survivors, and in the true-life *Robbery*, he masterminded the Great Train Robbery of 1963. These entertainments proved that Baker knew what suited him best, although he was certainly up to the challenge of playing an atypical role, such as a college professor whose obsession with a young student causes much havoc, in *Accident*. Less successfully he was an Olympic runner in *The Games*; a mercenary in *The Last Grenade*; a thief in *The Butterfly Affair*; and an international agent searching for a Russian scientist in *Innocent Bystanders*. He was knighted in 1976 and died only a month later.

Screen: 1943: Undercover/Underground Guerillas; 1948: All Over the Town; 1949: Obsession/The Hidden Room; 1950: Your Witness/Eye Witness; 1951: The Rossiter Case; Captain Horatio Hornblower; Home to Danger; Cloudburst; Lilli Marlene; 1952: Whispering Smith Hits London/Whispering Smith Versus Scotland Yard; 1953: The Cruel Sea; Paratrooper/The Red Beret; Knights of the Round Table; 1954: Hell Below Zero; The Good Die Young; Beautiful Stranger/Twist of Fate; 1955: Helen of Troy; 1956: Alexander the Great; Richard III; Child in the House; A Hill in Korea/Hell in Korea; 1957: Checkpoint; 1957: Hell Drivers; Campbell's Kingdom; Violent Playground; 1958: Sea Fury; 1959: The Angry Hills; Blind Date/Chance Meeting; Jet Storm; Yesterday's Enemy; 1960: Hell Is a City; The Criminal/The Concrete Jungle; 1961: The Guns of Navarone; 1962: A Prize of Arms; Sodom and Gomorrah; The Man Who Finally Died; Eva; 1963: In the French Style; 1964: Zulu (and co-prod.); 1965: Dingaka; Sands of the Kalahari (and co-prod.); 1967: Accident; Robbery (and co-prod.); 1969: Girl With a Pistol; Where's Jack?; 1970: The Games; The Last Grenade; Perfect Friday; The Butterfly Affair/Popsy Pop; 1971: Schizoid/The Lizard in a Woman's Skin; 1973: Innocent Bystanders; 1975: Zorro; Pepita Jiminez/Bride to Be.

NY Stage: 1951: A Sleep of Prisoners.

Select TV: 1952: The Taming of the Shrew (sp); 1955: The Creature (sp) 1967: Who Has Seen the Wind? (sp); Code Name: Heraclitus (sp); 1974: Robinson Crusoe (sp); 1976: How Green Was My Valley (ms).

LUCILLE BALL

BORN: CELORON, NY, AUGUST 6, 1911.
DIED: APRIL 26, 1989.

For nearly 20 years, before *I Love Lucy* gave her an almost mystical level of immortality, Lucille Ball had been working quite steadily in movies. She possessed a sparkling screen presence that would still be remembered with fondness, even if popular opinion had never cast her as the Queen of the Television Sitcom. After attending the John Murray Anderson Drama School, her work as a chorus girl and model led to her first two movie roles, at 20th Century Pictures, doing unbilled bits in *Broadway Through a Keyhole* and *Blood Money*. She was then hired as a Goldwyn Girl and made her debut as such in an Eddie Cantor comedy, *Roman Scandals*, chained to the wall at a slave market with other blonde lovelies, her long wig strategically covering the naughty bits. More unbilled background parts followed until she finally got mentioned, playing a nurse in a Lee Tracy film for Columbia, *Carnival*. Signed by RKO, she continued in bit parts (she can be seen in a flower shop in *Top Hat*, for example) before making headway in 1937 as one of a group of aspiring actresses in the wonderful *Stage Door*, spitting out sardonic remarks with the rest of the girls. The studio rewarded her by assigning her the lead in a "B" comedy, *Go Chase Yourself*, as the level headed wife of nitwit bank teller Joe Penner.

Ball continued in second leads, experiencing a breakthrough of sorts when she played a temperamental actress opposite Jack Oakie in the lively *The Affairs of Annabel*. Her comic capablities proved popular enough to rate a sequel, *Annabel Takes a Tour*, but her dramatic follow-ups found her stranded in sundry jungles in *Five Came Back* and *Panama Lady*. She returned to comedy, opposite Red Skelton in his movie debut, *Having Wonderful Time*, and playing foil to the Marx Brothers in *Room Service*, though neither utilized her properly. She headlined the 1940 musical *Too Many Girls*, which was a professional flop but a personal success when she met Desi Arnaz, who became her husband later that year. In the same year she played dual roles as a drab housewife and a South American temptress in the minor comedy, *You Can't Fool Your Wife*. She won good notices as smart-mouthed chorus girl Bubbles in Dorothy Arzner's *Dance, Girl, Dance*, a film that has won a cult following among feminists over the years. Taking a step backwards, she played straight woman to some radio celebrities in *Look Who's Laughing* (Edgar Bergen and his dummy, Charlie McCarthy, as well as Fibber McGee and Molly), but when a great dramatic opportunity arose, she grabbed it. Her atypical role as a cruel and selfish nightclub singer blindly adored by Henry Fonda, in the Damon Runyon drama *The Big Street*, is one of her most interesting performances and was a personal favorite of Ball herself. Shortly after its release, however, her contract with RKO expired.

She went over to MGM, where she was initially treated as a star attraction. She took the lead in the lumpy 1943 adaptation of *DuBarry Was a Lady* (her red hair was perfect for Metro's glossy Technicolor look) and, although she was dubbed for most of the songs, it was her own voice that featured in the best number, "Friendship." She playfully sent herself up in *Best Foot Forward*, playing actress Lucille Ball on a visit to a boys' military school, and took a bright comical supporting part in *Easy to Wed* (a remake of *Libeled Lady*), in the Jean Harlow role. Another supporting role, this time in the Tracy and Hepburn vehicle *Without Love*, preceded her loan-out to Fox for a good noir, *The Dark Corner*, as the loyal secretary of gumshoe Mark Stevens. After leaving MGM, she freelanced as an amateur sleuth in *Lured*; as

Franchot Tone's meddling spouse in the oddball *Her Husband's Affairs*; and as the ideal leading lady for Bob Hope in his successful comedies *Sorrowful Jones* (a remake of *Little Miss Marker*) and *Fancy Pants* (a remake of *Ruggles of Red Gap*.) A three-picture deal at Columbia produced *Miss Grant Takes Richmond*, which foreshadowed her flaky "Lucy" television character; *The Fuller Brush Girl*, which attempted to milk more money out of Red Skelton's *The Fuller Brush Man*; and, most atypically, a trashy Arabian Nights pastiche called *The Magic Carpet*, which Ball considered her worst film.

In 1951 she made the historic decision to embark on a career in television. Using a radio show she'd done with Richard Denning, *My Favorite Husband*, as the basis, she and Arnaz created *I Love Lucy*. It became the blueprint for many sitcoms that followed, as Ball became the nation's most beloved clown, winning Emmy Awards for Best Comedienne in 1952 and Best Actress in 1955. As the scattered-brained, overzealous wife of Arnaz's longsuffering bandleader character, Ball showed a genuine skill at slapstick, which belied the scrupulously precise writing and the exacting work of rehearsal and performance. From this point on, millions of fans would wrongly dub her a comedienne, though she was, in fact, an actress playing comedy. She just happened to do it more brilliantly than most. During the run of the series, she and Arnaz did two comedies for MGM: *The Long Long Trailer*, an extension of their television characters, which was a hit, and *Forever, Darling*, which was not. At the end of the 1950s her relationship with RKO came full circle when she and her husband purchased the studio where she had languished as a bit player and renamed it Desilu. Following her divorce from Arnaz in 1960, Ball had a successful Broadway run in *Wildcat*, and paired with Bob Hope again for the somewhat serious *The Facts of Life*, and a rather poor film version of the Broadway hit *Critic's Choice*. On television, she had two more hit series, garnering Emmys in 1967 and 1968 for *The Lucy Show*. One of her biggest movie successes, *Yours, Mine and Ours*, teamed her with Henry Fonda, as the harried parents of a large brood of children. Her last big screen appearance was as the star of *Mame*, and though her singing voice was barely adequate, she disproved many critics who thought she was miscast in the role. By the time Ball returned to television in the ill-advised *Life with Lucy*, endless reruns of her first two series had made her one of the most recognizable entertainers in the world and an unparalleled show business legend. She is the mother of actors Lucie Arnaz and Desi Arnaz, Jr., both of whom appeared on her series, *Here's Lucy*.

Screen: 1933: Broadway Through a Keyhole; Blood Money; Roman Scandals; 1934: Moulin Rouge; Nana; Bottoms Up; Hold That Girl; Bulldog Drummond Strikes Back; The Affairs of Cellini; Kid Millions; Broadway Bill; Jealousy; Men of the Night; Fugitive Lady; 1935: Carnival; Roberta; Old Man Rhythm; Top Hat; The Three Musketeers; I'll Love You Always; I Dream Too Much; 1936: Chatterbox; Follow the Fleet; The Farmer in the Dell; Bunker Bean; That Girl From Paris; 1937: Don't Tell the Wife; Stage Door; 1938: Joy of Living; Go Chase Yourself; Having Wonderful Time; The Affairs of Annabel; Room Service; Next Time I Marry; Annabel Takes a Tour; 1939: Beauty for the Asking; Twelve Crowded Hours; Panama Lady; Five Came Back; That's Right-You're Wrong; 1940: The Marines Fly High; You Can't Fool Your Wife; Dance, Girl, Dance; Too Many Girls; 1941: A Girl, a Guy, and a Gob; Look Who's Laughing; 1942: Valley of the Sun; Seven Days' Leave; The Big Street; 1943: DuBarry Was a Lady; Best Foot Forward; Thousands Cheer; 1944: Meet the People; 1945: Without Love; Abbott and Costello in Hollywood; 1946: Ziegfeld Follies; Easy to Wed; The Dark Corner; Two Smart People; Lover Come Back; 1947: Lured; Her Husband's

Affairs; **1949:** Sorrowful Jones; Easy Living; Miss Grant Takes Richmond; **1950:** Fancy Pants; A Woman of Distinction; The Fuller Brush Girl; **1951:** The Magic Carpet; **1954:** The Long Long Trailer; **1956:** Forever, Darling; **1960:** The Facts of Life; **1963:** Critic's Choice; **1967:** A Guide for the Married Man; **1968:** Yours, Mine and Ours; **1974:** Mame.

NY Stage: 1960: Wildcat.

Select TV: 1951–57: I Love Lucy (series); **1957–60:** The Lucy-Desi Comedy Hour (series); **1962–68:** The Lucy Show (series); **1968–74:** Here's Lucy (series); **1977:** Lucy Calls on the President (sp); **1980:** Lucy Moves to NBC (sp); **1985:** Stone Pillow; **1986:** Life With Lucy (series).

MARTIN BALSAM

BORN: NEW YORK, NY, NOVEMBER 4, 1919. ED: ACTORS STUDIO. DIED: FEBRUARY 13, 1996.

Stocky Martin Balsam was a sterling addition to the roster of fine character players who made their names in the postwar era. A graduate of the Actors Studio, he was frequently seen in the early days of live television drama on such shows as *Philco Playhouse* and *Goodyear Playhouse*. He made his motion picture debut in 1954's Best Picture Oscar-winner, *On the Waterfront*, before delivering an exceptional turn as the jury foreman in *12 Angry Men*. He was outstanding as the doomed investigator who made the fateful trip up the stairs of the Bates house in *Psycho*; the fast-talking Hollywood agent in *Breakfast at Tiffany's*; Jason Robards's level-headed brother in *A Thousand Clowns* (for which he won an Academy Award); the stagecoach driver in *Hombre*; a con man who gets tarred and feathered in *Little Big Man*; Joanne Woodward's unfulfilled husband in *Summer Wishes Winter Dreams*; and the bespectacled subway hijacker with a bad cold in *The Taking of Pelham One Two Three*. He appeared in both the 1962 version of *Cape Fear* (as the police investigator) and the 1991 remake (as a judge). He did several "B" productions for an Italian company that included some juicy leading roles, like his good cop battling big city corruption in *Confessions of a Police Captain*. His stage work was recognized with a 1968 Tony Award for *You Know I Can't Hear You When the Water's Running* and a 1977 Obie Award for *Cold Storage*. In the late 1970s he became familiar to television viewers when he joined Carroll O'Connor on the *All in the Family* spinoff, *Archie Bunker's Place*. His daughter is actress Talia Balsam, from his very brief marriage (1959–62) to actress Joyce Van Patten.

Screen: 1954: On the Waterfront; **1957:** 12 Angry Men; Time Limit; **1958:** Marjorie Morningstar; **1959:** Al Capone; Middle of the Night; **1960:** Psycho; **1961:** Ada; Breakfast at Tiffany's; **1962:** Cape Fear; Everybody Go Home!; **1963:** Who's Been Sleeping in My Bed?; **1964:** Seven Days in May; The Carpetbaggers; Youngblood Hawke; **1965:** Harlow; The Bedford Incident; A Thousand Clowns; **1966:** The Captive City (It: 1962); After the Fox; **1967:** Hombre; **1969:** Me, Natalie; Trilogy; The Good Guys and the Bad Guys; **1970:** Catch-22; Tora! Tora! Tora!; Little Big Man; **1971:** The Anderson Tapes; Column of Infamy (nUSr); The True and the False (nUSr); **1972:** The Man; Suspected of Murder (nUSr); Eyes Behind the Stars (dtv); **1973:** The Stone Killer; Summer Wishes Winter Dreams; **1974:** Smiling Maniacs (nUSr); The Taking of Pelham One Two Three; Confessions of a Police Captain; Murder on the Orient Express; **1975:** Counselor at Crime; Mitchell; Time of the Assassin (nUSr); **1976:** Ready to Kill (nUSr); All the President's Men; Two Minute Warning; **1977:** Dirty Diamonds of Blood (nUSr); The Sentinel; **1978:** Death Rage; Silver Bears; Brother from Space (nUSr); **1979:** Gardenia

(nUSr); Cuba; **1980:** The Warning (dtv); Cry Onion; There Goes the Bride; **1983:** The Salamander; **1984:** The Goodbye People; **1985:** St. Elmo's Fire; Death Wish 3; **1986:** Brothers in Blood (nUSr); The Delta Force; Once Again (dtv) **1987:** Private Investigations; **1988:** Innocent Prey (dtv); **1990:** Opponent (nUSr) **1991:** Two Evil Eyes (The Black Cat); Cape Fear; **1994:** The Silence of the Hams (dtv); **1995:** Soldier Ignoto (nUSr); **1997:** Legend of the Spirit Dog (dtv).

NY Stage: 1941: Ghost For Sale; **1947:** The Wanhope Building; Lamp at Midnight; **1948:** Macbeth; Sundown Beach; **1949:** The Closing Door; **1950:** The Liar; **1951:** The Rose Tattoo; **1953:** Camino Real; **1956:** Middle of the Night; **1962:** Nowhere to Go but Up; **1967:** You Know I Can't Hear You When the Water's Running; **1977:** Cold Storage.

Select TV: 1954: Statute of Limitations (sp); **1954–55:** The Greatest Gift (series); **1958:** The Desperate Age (sp); Bomber's Moon (sp); **1959:** Man in Orbit (sp); Free Week-End (sp); Body and Soul (sp); Winterset (sp); **1960:** Sacco-Vanzetti Story (sp); **1970:** Hunters Are for Killing/Hard Frame; The Old Man Who Cried Wolf; **1972:** Night of Terror; **1973:** A Brand New Life; **1973:** The Six Million Dollar Man; **1974:** Trapped Beneath the Sea; **1975:** Miles to Go Before I Sleep; Death Among Friends; **1976:** The Lindbergh Kidnapping Case; **1977:** Raid on Entebbe; Contract on Cherry Street; The Storyteller; **1978:** Siege; Rainbow; The Millionaire; **1979:** The Seeding of Sarah Burns; House on Garibaldi Street; Aunt Mary; **1979–81:** Archie Bunker's Place (series); **1980:** Love Tapes; **1981:** The People vs. Jean Harris (ms); **1982:** Little Gloria...Happy at Last; **1983:** I Want to Live; **1985:** Murder in Space; James A. Michener's Space (ms); **1986:** Second Serve; Grown-Ups (sp); **1987:** Queenie (ms); Kids Like These. **1988:** The Child Saver.

ANNE BANCROFT

(ANNA MARIA LOUISA ITALIANO) BORN: BRONX, NY, SEPTEMBER 17, 1931. ED: AADA

A blueprint example of a terrific actress who was practically discarded by the studio system, Anne Bancroft managed to pull a complete about face, rising above the doldrums of her early career to become one of the most respected performers in the business. After studying at the American Academy of Dramatic Arts she made her professional debut (billed as Anne Marno) in a live television drama titled *Torrents of Spring*. The exposure led to a contract with 20th Century-Fox, for whom she debuted as a hotel lounge singer in *Don't Bother to Knock*. The mediocrity of her performance was a masterpiece next to that of the movie's star, Marilyn Monroe. Unlike Monroe, however, Bancroft wasn't being given the necessary care to nurture her into a major name, judging from the second-rate material the studio handed her. She was the composer's loyal wife in the Sol Hurok biopic *Tonight We Sing*; leading lady to Dan Dailey in a cute baseball flick, *The Kid from Left Field*; a courtesan in a big spectacle, *Demetrius and the Gladiators*; and a widow inadvertently harboring disguised Confederate officer Van Heflin in *The Raid*. She hit rock bottom with the hilariously cheesy *Gorilla at Large*, as a trapeze artist who specializes in doing her aerial act over a cage of gorillas (!). Encouraging notices notwithstanding, her impact on the moviegoing public was negligible. When her contract expired with Fox, she continued elsewhere with similarly unchallenging projects like *New York Confidential*, as the daughter of mobster Broderick Crawford; *Nightfall*, involved with fugitive Aldo Ray; *Walk the Proud Land*, as an Indian; and *The Restless Breed*, as a half-breed.

Her obvious talent was being dealt a disservice by such inferior product and she was justifiably unhappy with her position. As a result she turned her back on Hollywood and returned to New York. She took Broadway by storm with back-to-back triumphs, as the offbeat Manhattanite, Gittel Mosca, in *Two for the Seesaw*, and as Helen Keller's teacher, Annie Sullivan, in *The Miracle Worker*. She won Tony Awards for both roles. Now considered a star, she returned to the movies at the insistence of director Arthur Penn. Her performance as Annie Sullivan in the fine 1962 film version of *The Miracle Worker* won her a much-deserved Academy Award, playing this tough but compassionate lady. Now considered an actress of great power she further impressed with two more Oscar-nominated roles: the sad, unfulfilled British housewife in *The Pumpkin Eater*, and the cool, seductive Mrs. Robinson in the biggest comedy hit of the 1960s, *The Graduate*. By exposing the insecurity in a deceptively confident woman, she created an unforgettable portrait of a middle-aged predator, turning herslf into something of an icon along the way. In between these two fine roles she portrayed a desperate woman on the suicide hotline with Sidney Poitier in *The Slender Thread*, and replaced the ailing Patricia Neal as a doctor in director John Ford's final, critically lambasted film *7 Women*. Her failure to find a suitable follow-up to *The Graduate* resulted in only one film over the next eight years, a supporting part, as Jenny, the mother of Winston Churchill, in *Young Winston*. Bancroft finally secured another lead, this time as Jack Lemmon's nurturing wife in Neil Simon's *The Prisoner of Second Avenue*. (Lemmon later praised her as his favorite co-star.) She then landed an important part in a hit film, as a ballerina who sacrifices personal happiness for the sake of her career, in *The Turning Point*, for which she garnered her fourth nomination from the Academy.

The comedy *Fatso*, with Dom Deluise, was her sole attempt at directing and writing. The film was shrill, as was her own performance, but she followed that with a very gracious turn as a famed Victorian actress who befriends the deformed John Hurt in *The Elephant Man*. In the 1980s she was fortunate to get a solid run of meaty leading roles, an uncommon occurrence for actresses over the age of 50. She did a bright comical turn opposite her real-life husband Mel Brooks (they had married in 1964) in the surprisingly good remake of *To Be or Not to Be*, and played the eccentric, life-loving movie fan faced with her own mortality in the touchingly humorous *Garbo Talks*. As the pragmatic, chainsmoking Mother Superior in *Agnes of God*, she received her fifth Oscar nomination, before going one-on-one with suicidal daughter Sissy Spacek in the harrowing *'night, Mother*. She brought style to the story of a 20-year correspondence between real-life New York writer Helen Hanft and a London bookstore owner (Anthony Hopkins) in *84 Charing Cross Road*, and was crackling as Harvey Fierstein's domineering mother in *Torch Song Trilogy*. By the 1990s she began to settle into smaller roles for both comic (*Love Potion No. 9*, *Honeymoon in Vegas*) and dramatic (*Malice*) effect. Somewhat larger were her assignments in *How to Make an American Quilt*, as a woman devastated by husband Rip Torn's affair with her sister, and in *Home for the Holidays*, as Holly Hunter's meddlesome mom. Not one to shrink from some high emoting, she played to the gallery as a modern-day Miss Havisham in the 1998 remake of *Great Expectations*, and as a wealthy, garrulous American residing in Italy in *Up at the Villa*. After almost 50 years in the industry, Bancroft is one of the rare female stars whose steady employment stands as an affront to those skeptics from her early career.

Screen: 1952: Don't Bother to Knock; 1953: Treasure of the Golden Condor; Tonight We Sing; The Kid From Left Field; 1954: Demetrius and the Gladiators; The Raid; Gorilla at Large;

1955: A Life in the Balance; New York Confidential; The Naked Street; The Last Frontier; 1956: Nightfall; Walk the Proud Land; 1957: The Girl in Black Stockings; The Restless Breed; 1962: The Miracle Worker; 1964: The Pumpkin Eater; 1965: The Slender Thread; 1966: 7 Women; 1967: The Graduate; 1972: Young Winston; 1975: The Prisoner of Second Avenue; The Hindenberg; 1976: Lipstick; Silent Movie; 1977: The Turning Point; 1980: Fatso (and dir., wr.); The Elephant Man; 1983: To Be or Not to Be; 1984: Garbo Talks; 1985: Agnes of God; 1986: 'night, Mother; 1987: 84 Charing Cross Road; 1988: Torch Song Trilogy; 1989: Bert Rigby, You're a Fool; 1992: Honeymoon in Vegas; Love Potion No. 9; 1993: Point of No Return; Malice; Mr. Jones; 1995: How to Make an American Quilt; Home for the Holidays; Dracula: Dead and Loving It; 1996: The Sunchaser; 1997: G.I. Jane; Critical Care; 1998: Great Expectations; Antz (voice); 2000: Keeping the Faith; Up at the Villa; 2001: Heartbreakers.

NY Stage: 1958: Two for the See-Saw; 1959: The Miracle Worker; 1963: Mother Courage and Her Children; 1965: The Devils; 1967: The Little Foxes; 1968: A Cry of Players; 1977: Golda; 1981: Duet for One; 2002: Occupant (ob).

Select TV: 1950: Letter From Cairo (sp) 1953: To Live in Peace (sp); 1954: A Medal for Benny (sp); 1956: The Hired Wife (sp); The Corrigan Case (sp); Fear is the Hunter (sp); Key Largo (sp); 1957: Too Soon to Die (sp); Invitation to a Gunfighter (sp); The Mad Bomber (sp); Hostages of Fortune (sp); 1967: I'm Getting Married (sp); 1970: Annie: The Women in the Life of a Man (and dir.); 1974: Annie and the Hoods (sp); 1977: Jesus of Nazareth (ms); 1982: Marco Polo (ms); 1992: Neil Simon's Broadway Bound; Mrs. Cage (sp); 1994: Oldest Living Confederate Widow Tells All; 1996: Homecoming; 1999: Deep in My Heart; 2001: Haven.

GEORGE BANCROFT

BORN: PHILADELPHIA, PA, SEPTEMBER 30, 1882. ED: ANNAPOLIS. DIED: OCTOBER 2, 1956.

Unremarkable and doughy in appearance, tough guy actor George Bancroft hardly seemed star material, but unlike so many of his contemporaries, he easily made the transition from silence to sound, and it was during that all-important period that some of his most popular features were produced. A veteran of minstrel shows and the legitimate stage, he came to Hollywood in 1921, signing a contract with Paramount Pictures four years later. He bided his time with supporting appeances in such films as *The Pony Express*, and the nautical adventure *Old Ironsides*, until he teamed with director Josef Von Sternberg for four melodramas that finally put him on top. The first was *Underworld*, an Oscar-winning look at the world of Depression-era crime. Bancroft was a mob boss, making him the first actor to gain stardom in this genre. This success was followed by *The Drag Net*, playing a drunken ex-cop who thinks he may have mistakenly murdered a friend, and *The Docks of New York*, saving Betty Compson from the streets and going to jail for a murder she committed. For the last of the Von Sternberg quartet, *Thunderbolt*, he was nominated for an Academy Award for portraying a convict plotting to kill a fellow prisoner who has stolen Fay Wray from him. Paramount happily awarded him additional leads in such movies as *Ladies Love Brutes*, in which he romanced Mary Astor; *Scandal Sheet*, as a ruthless tabloid publisher; and *Lady and Gent*, as a washed-up boxer raising his late manager's son. His star began to fade during the mid-1930s and he shifted into supporting roles, playing Jean Arthur's editor in *Mr. Deeds Goes to Town*. He could also be seen conspiring with Humphrey

Bogart in *Angels With Dirty Faces*; as the sheriff who rode shotgun atop the title vehicle in John Ford's *Stagecoach*; and playing the great inventor's dad in *Young Tom Edison*. Having had his fill of acting, he retired from the business in 1942 to become a rancher.

Screen: 1921: Journey's End; 1922: The Prodigal Judge; 1923: Driven; 1924: The Deadwood Coach; Teeth; 1925: Code of the West; The Rainbow Trail; The Pony Express; The Splendid Road; 1926: The Enchanted Hill; Sea Horses; Old Ironsides; The Runaway; 1927: White Gold; The Rough Riders; Too Many Crooks; Underworld; Tell It to Sweeney; 1928: The Docks of New York; Showdown; The Dragnet; 1929: The Wolf of Wall Street; Thunderbolt; The Mighty; 1930: Ladies Love Brutes; Derelict; Paramount on Parade; 1931: Scandal Sheet; Rich Man's Folly; 1932: The World and the Flesh; Lady and Gent; 1933: Blood Money; 1934: Elmer and Elsie; 1936: Hell-Ship Morgan; Mr. Deeds Goes to Town; Wedding Present; 1937: John Meade's Woman; Racketeers in Exile; A Doctor's Diary; 1938: Submarine Patrol; Angels With Dirty Faces; 1939: Each Dawn I Die; Espionage Agent; Rulers of the Sea; Stagecoach; 1940: Green Hell; Young Tom Edison; When the Daltons Rode; North West Mounted Police; Little Men; 1941: Texas; The Bugle Sounds; 1942: Syncopation; Whistling in Dixie.

NY Stage: 1923: Cinders; The Rise of Rosie O'Reilly.

TALLULAH BANKHEAD

BORN: HUNTSVILLE, AL, JANUARY 31, 1903.
DIED: DECEMBER 12, 1968.

A legendary star of the Broadway theatre who never reached the same heights on the screen, husky-voiced Tallulah Bankhead was as well known for her uninhibited behavior offstage as her flamboyant performances on the boards. As a teenager she won a beauty contest and came to New York, where she made her stage debut with a small part in *The Squab Farm*. There followed a few movie roles before a run of plays during the 1920s made her a luminary of London's West End, including *The Dancers*, *Fallen Angels*, and *They Knew What They Wanted*. With the advent of the talkies, she was signed by Paramount, but her six starring roles for them, starting with *Tarnished Lady* and ending with the most notable of the bunch, *Devil and the Deep*, opposite Gary Cooper, were poorly received by critics and public alike. After another failure, *Faithless*, for MGM, she retreated to Broadway, where she would eventually win the greatest acclaim of her career, as the cold-hearted Regina Hubbard in the original 1939 production of *The Little Foxes*. Although Bette Davis played Regina in the film adaptation, Bankhead did venture back to Hollywood for her best role, the cynical, fur-coated journalist in Alfred Hitchcock's *tour de force* of confinement, *Lifeboat*. The remainder of her career was spent principally on the stage, on her own radio series (*The Big Show*), and in television guest spots (*The Lucy-Desi Comedy Hour* and *Batman*, among others.) By the time she made her final film, the gothic *Die, Die, My Darling*, her outrageous behavior had gained her a camp following among those who'd never actually witnessed her more serious work. Her tell-all autobiography, titled simply *Tallulah*, was published in 1952.

Screen: 1918: When Men Betray; Thirty a Week; Who Loved Him Best; 1919: The Trap; 1928: His House in Order; A Woman's Law; 1931: Tarnished Lady; My Sin; The Cheat; 1932: Thunder Below; Make Me a Star; Devil and the Deep; Faithless; 1943: Stage Door Canteen; 1944: Lifeboat; 1945: A Royal Scandal; 1952: Main Street to Broadway; 1965: Die, Die, My Darling/Fanatic; 1966: The Daydreamer (voice).

NY Stage: 1918: The Squab Farm; 1919: 39 East; 1920: Foot-Loose; 1921: Nice People; Everyday; 1922: The Exciters; 1933: Forsaking All Others; 1934: Dark Victory; 1935: Rain; Something Gay; 1936: Reflected Glory; 1937: Antony and Cleopatra; 1938: The Circle; 1939: The Little Foxes; 1941: Clash by Night; 1942: The Skin of Our Teeth; 1945: Foolish Notion; 1947: The Eagle Has Two Heads; 1948: Private Lives; 1954: Dear Charles; 1956: A Streetcar Named Desire; 1957: Eugenia; 1961: Midgie Purvis; 1964: The Milk Train Doesn't Stop Here Anymore.

Select TV: 1952–53: All Star Revue (series); 1953: Hedda Gabler (sp); 1962: A Man for Oona (sp).

IAN BANNEN

BORN: AIRDRIE, SCOTLAND, JUNE 29, 1928.
ED: RATCLIFFE COL., LEICESTERSHIRE.
DIED: NOVEMBER 3, 1999.

A successful portrayer of brash blokes, Ian Bannen was onstage from the 1940s, but it was not until the mid-1950s that he began appearing in films. His 1956 debut came in the popular Boulting Brothers comedy *Private's Progress*, as one of Ian Carmichael's slacker barracks-mates. He also appeared in the last production ever made at Ealing, *The Long Arm*. In both cases he was billed way down the cast list. The parts didn't get much larger until 1965, when he made a first big impression on U.S. audiences in a pair of rugged, male-dominated films: *The Hill*, as a prison camp officer with a conscience, and *The Flight of the Phoenix*, which earned him a Best Supporting Actor Oscar nomination for his portrayal of an optimistic survivor of a desert plane crash. His next American assignment, playing the romantic lead opposite Natalie Wood in *Penelope*, was bad enough to make him return to Europe. On his résumé during this period are *The Sailor from Gibraltar*, in which he left Vanessa Redgrave for an affair with mysterious Jeanne Moreau; *Lock Up Your Daughters!*, a lamentable bawdy romp; *Fright*, playing an asylum escapee out to kill Susan George; and, best of all, *The Offence*, intelligently portraying an accused child molester being brutally interrogated by Sean Connery. Back in America he was one of the participants in a horse race in *Bite the Bullet*; did a pair for Disney, *The Watcher in the Woods* and *Night Crossing*; and showed up as a police officer in the Oscar-winning *Gandhi*. He lapsed into an unremarkable standing among his peers until he received another dose of acclaim as the irascible grandfather in John Boorman's episodic homily to wartime England, *Hope and Glory*. Later he appeared as Jeremy Irons's lecherous dad in *Damage*, and Angus McFadyen's leper father in the Oscar-winning *Braveheart*. He then had what turned out to be the role of his career: the scheming Irish villager out to win the lottery in the delightful *Waking Ned Devine*. Alas, a year after its U.S. release, he was killed in a car accident while on location in Scotland for the film *Strictly Sinatra*.

Screen: 1956: Private's Progress; The Third Key/The Long Arm; 1957: Yangtse Incident/Battle Hell; Miracle in Soho; The Birthday Present; 1958: A Tale of Two Cities; She Didn't Say No!; Behind the Mask; Man in a Cocked Hat/Carlton-Browne of the F.O.; 1960: On a Friday at 11; A French Mistress; The World in My Pocket; The Risk; 1961: Station Six-Sahara; 1964: Psyche 59; 1965: Mister Moses; The Hill; Rotten to the Core; The Flight of the Phoenix; 1966: Penelope; 1967: The Sailor From Gibraltar; 1969: Lock Up Your Daughters!; 1970: Too Late the Hero; 1971: The Deserter; Fright; 1972: Doomwatch; 1973: The Offence; The Mackintosh Man; From Beyond the Grave/Creatures; The Driver's Seat/Psychotic; 1974: The Voyage; 1975: Bite the Bullet; 1976: Sweeney; 1978: Inglorious Bastards/Counterfeit

Commandos; **1979:** Ring of Darkness; **1980:** The Watcher in the Woods; **1981:** Eye of the Needle; **1982:** Night Crossing; Gandhi; **1983:** The Prodigal; Gorky Park; **1987:** Defence of the Realm; Hope and Glory; **1988:** The Courier; **1989:** Streghe/Superstition 2 (dtv); **1990:** Ghost Dad; **1991:** George's Island; Crossing the Line/The Big Man; The Gamble (dtv; filmed 1988); **1992:** Damage; **1993:** Speaking of the Devil (dtv); **1995:** Lamb (filmed 1985); Braveheart; **1998:** Something to Believe In (nUSr); Waking Ned Devine; **2000:** To Walk with Lions (dtv in US); Best (nUSr) **2002:** Taliesen Jones.

NY Stage: 1984: A Moon for the Misbegotten.

Select TV: 1961: Macbeth (sp); **1967:** Johnny Belinda (sp); **1971:** Jane Eyre (sp); **1974:** The Gathering Storm; **1977:** Jesus of Nazareth (ms); **1979:** Spooner's Patch (series); **1980:** Tinker, Tailor, Soldier, Spy (ms); **1981:** Dr. Jekyll and Mr. Hyde; **1989:** The Lady and the Highwayman; The Fifteen Streets; **1990:** Perry Mason: The Case of the Desperate Deception; **1991:** Uncle Vanya (sp); Murder in Eden (sp); Ashenden (ms); **1992:** Common Pursuit; **1993:** Doctor Finlay (series); **1994:** Measure for Measure (sp); **1995:** The Politician's Wife (ms); **1996:** Original Sin.

THEDA BARA

(THEODOSIA GOODMAN) BORN: CINCINNATI, OH, JULY 29, 1889. DIED: APRIL 7, 1955.

One of the most famous sirens of the silent screen, Theda Bara is also something of a mystery to modern audiences insomuch as almost no footage of her work survives. She first acted onstage under the name Theodosia de Coppet (including the 1908 New York production *The Devil*), before being spotted by movie director Frank Powell. A barrage of outrageously phony publicity (she was said to have been born "in the shadow of the Sphinx," among other things) gave her an exotic mystique. Producer William Fox capitalized on this when he sold her debut melodrama, *A Fool There Was*, to an eager public, circa 1914. From this film came, perhaps, the first famous movie quote or, in this case, title card: "Kiss Me, My Fool!" and Bara became the movie's first sex goddess, or vamp. Today photographs of the heavily made-up, droopy-lidded, and somewhat meaty actress are more likely to draw laughs than tingles of ecstasy and indeed, audiences of the time had had their fill of her by the end of the decade. In the space of five years she had played Carmen, Camille, and, of course, Cleopatra, in one of her biggest successes. In the early 1920s she tried theatre again before returning in one more unsuccessful film and two short subjects. Happily married to director Charles Brabain, she disappeared completely from view with the coming of sound.

Screen: 1914: A Fool There Was; The Kreutzer Sonata; **1915:** The Clemenceau Case; The Devil's Daughter; Lady Audley's Secret; Sin; The Two Orphans; Carmen; The Galley Slave; Destruction; The Stain; **1916:** The Serpent; Gold and the Woman; The Eternal Sappho; East Lynne; Under Two Flags; Her Double Life; Romeo and Juliet; The Vixen; **1917:** The Darling of Paris; The Tiger Woman; Her Greatest Love; Heart and Soul; Camille; Cleopatra; **1918:** Rose of Blood; Madame Dubarry; The Forbidden Path; The Soul of Buddha; Under the Yoke; When a Woman Sins; Salome; The She-Devil; **1919:** The Light; When Men Desire; The Siren's Song; A Woman There Was; Kathleen Mavourneen; La Belle Russe; The Lure of Ambition; **1925:** The Unchastened Woman.

BRIGITTE BARDOT

(CAMILLE JAVAL) BORN: PARIS, FRANCE, SEPTEMBER 28, 1934.

In the late 1950s the name Brigitte Bardot became synonymous with the sexually uninhibited freedom of the French cinema and remains well known to many who have never even seen one of her films. A former ballet student turned model, she came to the attention of screenwriter Roger Vadim, whom she married in 1952. That same year she made her debut in a Bourvil feature, *Le Trou Normand*. English language productions quickly followed: *Act of Love*, starring Kirk Douglas; the biblical spectacle *Helen of Troy*; and a substantial role in the British comedy, *Doctor at Sea*, with Dirk Bogarde. Worldwide attention came in 1956 with *And God Created Woman*, the story of a naughty wife getting her kicks in Saint-Tropez, directed and written by her husband (whom she divorced the following year). Censorship problems and the highly erotic content of the piece sealed Bardot's fate as a much-publicized sex kitten, and suddenly foreign-language films became extremely desirable to those who had previously avoided them.

Her work continued to be widely viewed, even if the attraction was more for her body than her acting skills. Among her more critically acclaimed efforts were *Love Is My Profession*, and the Oscar-nominated courtroom drama *The Truth*. By the time she teamed with another French superstar, Jeanne Moreau, in the mild adventure spoof *Viva Maria*, her heyday was in decline. 1965 marked the only time she appeared in an all-American production: *Dear Brigitte*, playing herself, although her scene was the only one not shot in the States. She did her first lead role in an English-language production, *Shalako*, in 1968, but her films no longer rated attention in those sexually liberated times. She retired in 1973 and later used her fame and money to help create the Foundation for the Protection of Distresed Animals.

Screen: (US releases only): 1953: Act of Love; **1956:** Helen of Troy; The Grand Maneuver; Doctor at Sea; **1957:** Please Mr. Balzac; And God Created Woman; The Light Across the Street (Fr: 1955); **1958:** The Night Heaven Fell; Mam'zelle Pigalle/That Naughty Girl (Fr: 1955); La Parisienne; The Girl in the Bikini (Fr: 1952); **1959:** A Woman Like Satan; Love Is My Profession; **1960:** Come Dance With Me; Crazy for Love (Fr: 1952); Babette Goes to War; **1961:** The Truth; **1962:** A Very Private Affair; **1963:** Please Not Now!; **1964:** Contempt; Love on a Pillow (Fr: 1962); **1965:** Dear Brigitte; Viva Maria; **1966:** Masculine-Feminine; **1967:** Two Weeks in September; **1968:** Shalako; **1969:** Spirits of the Dead; **1971:** The Bear and the Doll; **1973:** The Legend of Frenchie King (Fr: 1971); **1976:** Ms. Don Juan (Fr: 1973); The Novices (Fr: 1970); Rum Runner (Fr: 1970).

LYNN BARI

(MARGARET SCHUYLER FISHER) BORN: DECEMBER 18, 1913. DIED: NOVEMBER 20, 1989.

A cool brunette who came to Hollywood as a chorus player, Lynn Bari made her debut in that capacity in MGM's *Dancing Lady*, in 1933. She moved over to Fox in 1934, as a bit player, where she stayed for 12 years, fluctuating between second leads in "A" pictures and larger parts in "B" features. She played a big band vocalist in the musicals *Sun Valley Serenade* and *Orchestra Wives*, though her singing was dubbed, and, in *Hello, Frisco, Hello*, temporarily snatched John Payne away from Alice Faye. Meanwhile, she could be seen front and center in such second string features as *Return of the Cisco Kid*, as a rancher battling a crooked businessman; *News Is Made at Night*, as a reporter pursued by her editor, Preston Foster; *Pardon Our Nerve*, pushing waiter Guinn Williams into the boxing profession; *Free, Blonde and 21*, as the good girl at a hotel for women; *Pier 13*, as a waitress at a waterfront dive, hoping to clear her sister of a robbery charge; *We Go Fast*, back waiting tables again, while drawing the romantic interest of three different men; and *Secret Agent of Japan*, as a British spy in Shanghai. In a moment of good will the studio promoted her to leading lady in an "A" picture, *The Magnificent Dope*, where she lost her heart to goofball Henry Fonda. Despite her low ranking on the Fox star list, she was considered enough of a looker to be almost as popular as Betty Grable as a G.I. pinup. She kept working after leaving Fox, but film prospects weren't very promising, so she turned towards television, starring in two summer replacement series as well as many anthology dramas. In 1955 she married a doctor and divided her time between occasional acting assignments (which included one last trip back to Fox's "B" unit for a dilly called *The Women of Pitcairn Island*) and working as her husband's nurse.

Screen: 1933: Dancing Lady; Meet the Baron; 1934: Coming Out Party; Stand Up and Cheer; Search for Beauty; David Harum; Bottoms Up; Handy Andy; 365 Nights in Hollywood; Music in the Air; Caravan; 1935: George White's Scandals; Spring Tonic; My Marriage; The Man Who Broke the Bank at Monte Carlo; Charlie Chan in Paris; The Great Hotel Murder; Dante's Inferno; Welcome Home; The Gay Deception; Charlie Chan in Shanghai; Way Down East; Under Pressure; Ten Dollar Raise; Metropolitan; Orchids for You; Ladies Love Danger; Doubting Thomas; Redheads on Parade; Thanks a Million; Music Is Magic; 1936: Everybody's Old Man; Ladies in Love; The Song and Dance Man; King of Burlesque; The Great Ziegfeld; Private Number; Poor Little Rich Girl; Girls' Dormitory; Star for a Night; It Had to Happen; Fifteen Maiden Lane; Crack-Up; Pigskin Parade; Sing, Baby, Sing; 36 Hours to Kill; 1937: Wee Willie Winkie; This Is My Affair; Sing and Be Happy; Love Is News; Café Metropole; She Had to Eat; You Can't Have Everything; Woman-Wise; Wake Up and Live; Life Begins in College; The Lady Escapes; Fair Warning; Ali Baba Goes to Town; 45 Fathers; Lancer Spy; Wife Doctor and Nurse; On the Avenue; 1938: I'll Give a Million; Rebecca of Sunnybrook Farm; Josette; Speed to Burn; The Baroness and the Butler; Walking Down Broadway; Mr. Moto's Gamble; Battle of Broadway; Always Goodbye; Sharpshooters; Meet the Girls; 1939: Return of the Cisco Kid; Chasing Danger; News Is Made at Night; Pack Up Your Troubles; Elsa Maxwell's Hotel for Women; Charlie Chan in City of Darkness; Hollywood Cavalcade; Pardon Our Nerve; 1940: City of Chance; Free, Blonde and 21; Lillian Russell; Earthbound; Pier 13; Kit Carson; Charter Pilot; 1941: Blood and Sand; We Go Fast; Sun Valley Serenade; Moon Over Her Shoulder; The Perfect Snob; 1942: Secret Agent of Japan; Night Before the Divorce; The Falcon Takes Over; The Magnificent Dope; Orchestra Wives; China Girl; 1943: Hello, Frisco, Hello; 1944: The Bride of San Luis Rey; Tampico; Sweet and Lowdown; 1945: Captain Eddie; 1946: Shock; Home Sweet Homicide; Margie; Nocturne; 1948: The Man From Texas; The Spiritualist; 1949: The Kid From Cleveland; 1951: I'd Climb the Highest Mountain; On the Loose; Sunny Side of the Street; 1952: Has Anybody Seen My Gal?; I Dream of Jeannie; 1954: Francis Joins the WACs; 1955: Abbott and Costello Meet the Keystone Cops; 1956: The Women of Pitcairn Island; 1958: Damn Citizen; 1964: Trauma; 1968: The Young Runaways. **Select TV:** 1950: Detective's Wife (series); 1952: Boss Lady (series).

LEX BARKER
BORN: RYE, NY, MAY 8, 1919. DIED: MAY 11, 1973.

Blond and blandly handsome, Lex Barker found a temporary slot in the cinematic jungle hall of fame by being the first actor to replace Johnny Weissmuller in the role of Tarzan. He had done a few supporting parts (playing one of Loretta Young's Swedish brothers in *The Farmer's Daughter*, and a contractor in *Mr. Blandings Build His Dream House*, among others) before RKO producers decided he would look ideal in a loin cloth. Cast as the lord of the jungle in *Tarzan's Magic Fountain*, in 1949, he only stayed on for four more entries in the increasingly budget-conscious series before calling it quits in 1953 with *Tarzan and the She-Devil*. (The devil woman in this case was another personality hired strictly for her physique, Monique Van Vooren.) During this time he achieved a level of notoriety in the fan magazines when he married — and quickly divorced — two of Hollywood's glamour girls: Arlene Dahl (1951–52) and Lana Turner (1953–57). There was no great demand for him except as an action type and he spent the next few years in this capacity, mostly in "B" films like *The Girl in the Kremlin*, teamed for minimum results with Zsa Zsa Gabor; and *Jungle Heat*, which was not a return trip to the vines, but a drama that cast him as a doctor in Hawaii. When jobs became scarce in the States he started seeking employment overseas, working tirelessly in European features. He managed to land a role in one prestigious foreign production that was actually both a critical and box-office success worldwide, Federico Fellini's *La Dolce Vita*.

Screen: (US releases only): 1946: Doll Face; Do You Love Me?; Two Guys From Milwaukee; 1947: The Farmer's Daughter; Dick Tracy Meets Gruesome; Crossfire; Under the Tonto Rim; Unconquered; 1948: Mr. Blandings Builds His Dream House; Return of the Bad Men; The Velvet Touch; 1949: Tarzan's Magic Fountain; 1950: Tarzan and the Slave Girl; 1951: Tarzan's Peril; 1952: Tarzan's Savage Fury; Battles of Chief Pontiac; 1953: Tarzan and the She-Devil; Thunder Over the Plains; 1954: The Yellow Mountain; 1955: The Man From Bitter Ridge; Duel on the Mississippi; Mystery of the Black Jungle/The Black Devils of Kali; 1956: The Price of Fear; Away All Boats; 1957: War Drums; The Girl in the Kremlin; Jungle Heat; The Deerslayer; The Girl in Black Stockings; 1961: La Dolce Vita; 1963: Son of Red Corsair; 1965: Code 7 Victim 5; Treasure of Silver Lake; Apache Gold; 1966: A Place Called Glory; 1967: Woman Times Seven; Shatterhand/Apaches Last Battle.
NY Stage: 1938: The Merry Wives of Windsor.

BINNIE BARNES
(GITELLE GERTRUDE MAUDE BARNES)
BORN: LONDON, ENGLAND, MARCH 25, 1903. DIED: JULY 27, 1998.

A former chorus girl and dance hall hostess, erudite blonde Binnie Barnes first came to movies while in her native England, starring in a series of two-reelers with comedian Stanley Lupino. After making an impression as Catherine Howard in the international hit *The Private Life of Henry VIII*, and in the London stage production of *Cavalcade*, she was summoned to Hollywood in 1934. There she appeared as the mistress who gives up Frank Morgan for the good of his family in *There's Always Tomorrow*. Although she established herself as a fine comic performer, quick with a cutting remark, she was also comfortable in period pieces like *Diamond Jim*, as Lillian Russell; *The Last of the Mohicans*, being rescued from the Indians by scout Randolph Scott; *The Three Musketeers*, as Milady De Winter; and *The Adventures of Marco Polo*, as Alan Hale's overbearing wife. Among her more notable roles in comedy were as Charles Winninger's gold-digging fiancée in *Three Smart Girls*; as Katharine Hepburn's snobby cousin in *Holiday*; finding a dead body at her hotel in *Three Girls About Town*; playing wife to Fred Allen in *It's in the Bag*; and cracking wise along with Abbott and Costello in *The Time of Their Lives*. Barnes was always a welcome presence and guaranteed to receive favorable mention, but in all her years in Hollywood no one bothered to build a vehicle solely for her to carry. Married to Columbia executive Mike Frankovich from 1940 until his death in 1992, Barnes basically retired in 1955, but was coaxed back thrice, each time in Columbia productions: as a nun in *The Trouble With Angels*, alongside Rosalind Russell, whom she'd supported in *This Thing Called Love*, back in 1941; the sequel, *Where Angels Go…Trouble Follows*; and finally, *40 Carats*, as Liv Ullmann's mother, a role which, if nothing else, allowed her to dance with Gene Kelly.

Screen: 1931: A Night in Montmartre; Love Lies; Dr. Josser K.C.; Out of the Blue; Down Our Street; Murder at Covent Garden; 1932: Partners Please; Strip Strip Hooray!; The Last Coupon; Old Spanish Customers; Innocents of Chicago; 1933: Counsel's Opinion; Taxi to Paradise; Their Night Out; Heads We Go/The Charming Deceiver; The Private Life of Henry VIII; The Silver Spoon; The Lady Is Willing; 1934: Nine Forty-Five; No Escape; The Private Life of Don Juan; Forbidden Territory; Gift of Gab; There's Always Tomorrow; One Exciting Adventure; 1935: Diamond Jim; Rendezvous; 1936: Small Town Girl; Sutter's Gold; The Last of the Mohicans; The Magnificent Brute; Three Smart Girls; 1937: Breezing Home; Broadway Melody of 1938; 1938: The First Hundred Years; The Adventures of Marco Polo; The Divorce of Lady X; Holiday; Always Goodbye; Gateway; Tropic Holiday; Three Blind Mice; Thanks for Everything; 1939: Wife, Husband and Friend; The Three Musketeers; Man About Town; Frontier Marshal; Day-Time Wife; 1940: Till We Meet Again; 1941: New Wine; This Thing Called Love; Angels With Broken Wings; Tight Shoes; Skylark; Three Girls About Town; 1942: Call Out the Marines; I Married an Angel; In Old California; 1943: The Man From Down Under; 1944: Barbary Coast Gent; The Hour Before the Dawn; Up in Mabel's Room; 1945: It's in the Bag; The Spanish Main; Getting Gertie's Garter; 1946: The Time of Their Lives; 1947: If Winter Comes; 1948: The Dude Goes West; 1949: My Own True Love; The Pirates of Capri; 1951: Fugitive Lady; 1953: Decameron Nights; 1954: Fire Over Africa/Malaga; 1955: Shadow of the Eagle (Europe: 1951); 1966: The Trouble With Angels; 1968: Where Angels Go…Trouble Follows; 1973: 40 Carats.

WENDY BARRIE

(MARGARET WENDY JENKINS)
BORN: HONG KONG, APRIL 18, 1912.
RAISED IN ENGLAND. DIED: FEBRUARY 2, 1978.

One of several English ladies whose impressive appearance in the international smash *The Private Life of Henry VIII* brought her offers from Hollywood, Wendy Barrie optimistically went West, only to spend most of her career in second features and "B" movies. Fox launched her as Spencer Tracy's co-star in the largely unnoticed screwball comedy *It's a Small World*. She bounced about from studio to studio, collecting her paychecks for such ventures as *Love on a Bet*, as a golddigger who encounters Gene Raymond in his underwear; *Under Your Spell*, a quickie vehicle in

the waning movie career of opera star Lawrence Tibbett; *Breezing Home*, taking a shine to a horse named Galaxy; *Prescription for Romance*, as an American doctor in Budapest; *A Girl with Ideas*, suing and then taking ownership of Walter Pidgeon's newspaper; and *Newsboys' Home*, likewise becoming publisher of a big city paper. Between those and many other programmers were her two most famous Hollywood assignments: *Dead End*, as the rich girl who is desired by Joel McCrea, but is repelled by the squalor of his tenement life, and *The Hound of the Baskervilles*, the first Basil Rathbone-Sherlock Holmes film, as the Baskervilles' pretty neighbor. She appeared opposite George Sanders in two of his *Saint* mysteries, and then, when he gave up that series, in two of his *Falcon* outings. There were many who speculated that her movie career was cut short in the 1940s because of her involvement with notorious gangster Bugsy Siegel, but she was already deeply unhappy with most of the roles she was offered, so it hardly mattered. In any event, she found a second career as a hostess, first on radio and then in the very early days of television.

Screen: 1931: Collision; 1932: Threads; The Call Box Mystery; Where Is the Lady?; The Barton Mystery; Wedding Rehearsal; 1933: Cash/For Love or Money; It's a Boy; The Private Life of Henry VIII; This Acting Business; The House of Trent; 1934: Murder at the Inn; Without You; The Man I Want; Freedom of the Seas; There Goes Susie/Scandals of Paris; Give Her a Ring; 1935: It's a Small World; College Scandal; The Big Broadcast of 1936; A Feather in Her Hat; Millions in the Air; 1936: Love on a Bet; Speed; Ticket to Paradise; Under Your Spell; 1937: Breezing Home; What Pice Vengeance?; Wings Over Honolulu; Dead End; A Girl With Ideas; Prescription for Romance; 1938: I Am the Law; Pacific Liner; Newsboys' Home; 1939: The Saint Strikes Back; The Hound of the Baskervilles; Five Came Back; The Witness Vanishes; Day-Time Wife; 1940: The Saint Takes Over; Women in War; Cross-Country Romance; Men Against the Sky; Who Killed Aunt Maggie?; 1941: Repent at Leisure; The Saint in Palm Springs; The Gay Falcon; Public Enemies; A Date With the Falcon; Eyes of the Underworld; 1943: Forever and a Day; Follies Girl; Submarine Alert; 1954: It Should Happen to You; 1963: The Moving Finger.

NY Stage: 1942: Morning Star.

Select TV: 1948–49: Adventures of Oky Doky (series); Picture This (series); 1949–50: The Wendy Barrie Show (series).

GENE BARRY

(EUGENE KLASS) BORN: NEW YORK, NY, JUNE 14, 1921.

Following ten years of stage work and small roles on television, the personable but decidedly average Gene Barry came to the movies under contract to Paramount. He first starred in a well-liked "B" thriller, *The Atomic City*, as a distressed dad who goes after the Russian agents who kidnapped his son. This was followed by a run of mostly unremarkable second features, such as *The Girls of Pleasure Island*, as one of the marines who stumbles upon a trio of British beauties; the low-grade musical *Those Redheads From Seattle*, as a Yukon saloon keeper who sets his sights on Rhonda Fleming; *Alaska Seas*, a remake of *Spawn of the North*; and the excessively stylized western spoof *Red Garters*, as hero Guy Mitchell's nemesis. His most famous foray was in one of the top sci-fi flicks of the 1950s, George Pal's *The War of the Worlds*, although the cast took a back seat to the Oscar-winning special effects. After leaving Paramount his assignments remained on the second-feature level, including playing a greedy oilman in *The Houston Story*, and finding himself in possession of a capsule capable of destroying the world in *The 27th Day*, an offbeat sci-fi story/anti-Communist statement. It took television to bring him true stardom, playing the most dapper of all western heroes, *Bat Masterson*. This was followed by two other popular shows, *Burke's Law* and *The Name of the Game*, which left very little time for movies. When he returned to Broadway in 1983, he scored a solid success as the gay nightclub owner in the musical adaptation of *La Cage aux Folles*. He served as executive producer on the film *The Second Coming of Suzanne*, which was written and directed by his son, Michael Barry.

Screen: 1952: The Atomic City; 1953: The Girls of Pleasure Island; The War of the Worlds; Those Redheads From Seattle; 1954: Alaska Seas; Red Garters; Naked Alibi; 1955: Soldier of Fortune; The Purple Mask; 1956: The Houston Story; Back From Eternity; 1957: The 27th Day; China Gate; Forty Guns; 1958: Hong Kong Confidential; Thunder Road; 1967: Maroc 7; 1969: Subterfuge; 1974: The Second Coming of Suzanne (and exec. prod.); 1980: Guyana: Cult of the Damned.

NY Stage: 1942: New Moon; 1942: Rosalinda; 1943: The Merry Widow; 1944: Catherine Was Great; 1946: The Would-Be Gentleman; 1950: Happy as Larry; Bless You All; 1962: The Perfect Setup; 1983: La Cage aux Folles.

Select TV: 1955: Touch of Spring; 1955–56: Our Miss Brooks (series); 1956: The Women Who Dared; 1957: Ain't No Time for Glory (sp); Threat to a Happy Ending; 1959–61: Bat Masterson (series); 1963–66: Burke's Law (series); 1968: Prescription: Murder; Istanbul Express; 1968–70: The Name of the Game (series); 1971: Do You Take This Stranger?; The Devil and Miss Sarah; 1972: The Adventurer (series); 1977: Ransom for Alice!; Aspen/The Innocent and the Damned (ms); 1980: A Cry for Love; 1981: The Girl, the Gold Watch & Dynamite; The Adventures of Nellie Bly; 1987: Perry Mason: The Case of the Lost Love; 1989: Turn Back the Clock; 1991: The Gambler Returns: The Luck of the Draw; 1994–95: Burke's Law (series); 2001: These Old Broads.

ETHEL BARRYMORE

(ETHEL MAE BLYTHE) BORN: PHILADELPHIA, PA, AUGUST 15, 1879. DIED: JUNE 18, 1959.

Often referred to (along with Helen Hayes) as "the First Lady of the American Theatre," Ethel Barrymore did indeed carry herself like royalty. She made her professional debut at the age of 15, appearing with her uncle, John Drew, and first acted on the Broadway stage in 1901 in *Captain Jinks of the Horse Marines*. In time she would firmly establish herself as one of the stage's most commanding performers. Although she initially appeared in some silent films, beginning in 1915, she was soon back on the boards, making her mark in such plays as *Rose Bernd*, *A Royal Fandango*, *The Second Mrs. Tanqueray*, *The Constant Wife*, and *The Kingdom of God*. Once talking pictures arrived, she got her feet wet by appearing opposite her brothers, Lionel and John, in *Rasputin and the Empress*, though her stagy emoting was somewhat heavy-handed. It was not until 1944, following one of her greatest theatrical triumphs, in *The Corn Is Green*, that she decided to make a fulltime living as a character actress in Hollywood. She began on a high note, winning an Academy Award in 1944 for her portrayal of Cary Grant's cancer-stricken mother in *None But the Lonely Heart*. An authoritative, somewhat stern presence who could cut down an adversary with as little as a raised eyebrow, she received three additional nominations for her peerless supporting work: in *The Spiral Staircase* (taken care of by deaf-mute Dorothy McGuire), *The Paradine Case* (wed to

judge Charles Laughton), and *Pinky* (tended by servant Jeanne Crain). In addition to these she gave an outstanding performance as the art gallery owner who first recognizes Joseph Cotten's talent as a painter in *Portrait of Jennie*. She was awarded a starring role in the taut 1951 version of *Kind Lady*, in which she was held prisoner in her own home by Maurice Evans, followed by another lead in her last film, *Johnny Trouble*, as an invalid who believes Stuart Whitman is her long lost son, returned after a 27-year absence. A Broadway theatre was named in her honor in 1928. Her 1956 autobiography was titled *Memories*.

Screen: 1915: The Nightingale; The Final Judgment; 1916: The Kiss of Hate; The Awakening of Helen Richie; 1917: The White Raven; The Lifted Veil; The Eternal Mother; An American Widow; The Call of Her People; Life's Whirlpool; 1918: Our Mrs. McChesney; The Divorcee; 1932: Rasputin and the Empress; 1944: None But the Lonely Heart; 1946: The Spiral Staircase; 1947: The Farmer's Daughter; Moss Rose; Night Song; 1948: The Paradine Case; Moonrise; Portrait of Jennie; 1949: The Great Sinner; That Midnight Kiss; The Red Danube; Pinky; 1951: Kind Lady; The Secret of Convict Lake; It's a Big Country; 1952: Deadline USA; Just for You; 1953: The Story of Three Loves; Main Street to Broadway; 1954: Young at Heart; 1957: Johnny Trouble.

NY Stage: 1901: Captain Jinks of the Horse Marines (and 1907 revival); 1902: A Country Mouse; Carrots; 1903: Cousin Kate (and 1907 and 1911 revivals); 1904: Sunday; 1905: A Doll's House; Alice Sit-by-the-Fire (and 1911 revival); 1907: The Silver Box; His Excellency the Governor; Her Sister; 1908: Lady Frederick; 1910: Mid-Channel; 1911: Trelawny of the Wells; The Twelve Pound Look; 1912: A Slice of Life; 1913: Tante; 1914: A Scrap of Paper; 1915: The Shadow; Our Mrs. McChesney; 1917: The Lady of the Camellias; 1918: The Off Chance; Belinda; 1919: Declasse; Twelve Pound Look; 1921: Clair de Lune; Twelve Pound Look; 1922: Rose Bernd; Romeo and Juliet; 1923: The Laughing Lady; The School for Scandal; A Royal Fandango; 1924: The Second Mrs. Tanqueray; 1925: Hamlet; The Merchant of Venice; 1926: The Constant Wife; 1928: The Kingdom of God; 1929: The Love Duel; 1930: Scarlet Sister Mary; 1931: George White's Scandals; 1933: Under Glass; 1934: L'aiglen; 1935: Declasse; 1937: The Ghost of Yankee Doodle; London Assurance; 1938: Whiteoaks; 1939: Farm of Three Echoes; 1940: An International Incident; The Corn is Green; 1944: Embezzled in Heaven.

Select TV: 1953: Ethel Barrymore Theater (series); 1957: Eloise (sp).

JOHN BARRYMORE

(JOHN SIDNEY BLYTHE) BORN: PHILADELPHIA, PA, FEBRUARY 15, 1882. DIED: MAY 29, 1942.

John was the youngest and most famous of the three Barrymore siblings and the one who became a full-fledged movie star, earning the immortal nickname "The Great Profile." He originally worked as a cartoonist for a New York newspaper, but was easily lured into the family acting circle, filling in for another actor for one performance of his sister Ethel's play *Captain Jinks of the Horse Marines*, while in Philadelphia. His formal debut came in Chicago in 1903, in *Magda*, with his Broadway bow later that same year in *Glad of It*. After garnering his first serious attention with the play *The Fortune Hunter*, in 1909, his reputation for light comedy grew. This led, four years later, to his film debut for Famous Players, in *An American Citizen*. For them he did a film version of one of his plays, *The Dictator*, as well as such titles as *Are You a Mason?*, *The*

Incorrigible Dukane, and *The Red Widow*, which he hated. By the early 1920s he had soared to his peak as a matinee idol and leading man of both the stage and screen. Admired among his theatre performances of this period were *The Jest* (opposite brother Lionel), *Richard III*, and most notably, his *Hamlet*, which won raves on both sides of the Atlantic. On film he was hailed for *Dr. Jekyll and Mr. Hyde*, playing the famous transformation scene without the help of makeup; *Sherlock Holmes*, an adaptation of the William Gillette stage perennial and a role Barrymore had little interest in doing; and *Beau Brummel*, the success of which brought him a contract with Warner Bros.

For that studio he shot a distorted rendering of *Moby Dick*, retitled *The Sea Beast*, with an absurd love interest added in the person of Dolores Costello, who became one of his wives (1928–35). Next up was *Don Juan*, which had the added lure of being the first feature with synchronized music, thereby guaranteeing it great public interest and heavy box-office returns; and finally *When a Man Loves*, swashbuckling as an escaped prisoner wooing his real life wife again. Switching over to United Artists he romped through *The Beloved Rogue*, as poet François Villion; *Tempest*, which was not Shakespeare but a tale of the Russian revolution; and *Eternal Love*, which timidly entered into the talking picture era by providing sound effects but no dialogue. The silent era was, in fact, perfect for the actor whose sometimes too-flamboyant style could be quite colorful and exciting to watch in a medium devoid of sound, but pure ham with the microphone close by. As the sound era officially arrived, he was beginning to show the effects of years of heavy drinking and carefree hellraising but he was still a major name so Warners asked him back again. For them he did a speech from *Richard III* as part of the all-star omnibus *The Show of Shows*, which unfavorably emphasized his very theatrical style; returned to the Great White Whale for another minor version of *Moby Dick*, this time under its correct name, but still with that damn female subplot; had a hit playing a Scotsman in *The Man From Blankley's*; and did two extremely florid, similar turns, in the quirky *Svengali* and *The Mad Genius*, as a club-footed puppeteer who regrets not having become a ballet dancer (!).

Dropped by Warners, he signed with Metro, who placed him alongside older brother Lionel in *Arsene Lupin*, in the title role, as an elegant thief. There were admiring notices for his doomed jewel thief in *Grand Hotel*, though he was miscast in one of his most famous roles, the part calling for a much younger man; Katharine Hepburn's unbalanced father in *A Bill of Divorcement* (for RKO), though he was clearly outshone by her more controlled acting; the near-biographical part of the alcoholic actor in *Dinner at Eight*, adding much gloom to what was supposed to be a light piece of sophistication; the tormented Jewish lawyer in *Counsellor-at-Law* (at Universal), marvelously restrained in one of his most effective assignments on film; RKO's *Topaze*, an adaptation of the famous French play, as the timid schoolteacher used as a pawn in a business fraud who turns the financial scheming to his advantage; and the maniacal theatrical producer trying to con former protégé Carol Lombard in the frantic comedy *Twentieth Century* (for Columbia), one case where he really could have used a leash. Opposite Lionel and sister Ethel he played the Russian Prince who kills the mad monk in *Rasputin and the Empress*, his fairly ordinary performance being no match for Lionel's more enjoyable thesping.

Having passed 50 and showing every minute of his age, he segued into support, including his only full-fledged trek into Shakespeare on film, *Romeo and Juliet*, again too old, as was the entire cast, but under those circumstances an ideal Mercutio. He was very serious as the voice teacher in love with Jeannette

MacDonald in the vastly popular musical *Maytime*, and then wildly funny as a jealous husband in the Claudette Colbert comedy *Midnight*. He was not the famous British adventurer but his boss, Inspector Neilson of Scotland Yard, in *Bulldog Drummond Comes Back*, but in light of the fact that the bland John Howard had the lead, it was only fitting that Barrymore get top billing. He played the role twice more in the Paramount "B" series until he was replaced by H.B. Warner. There was a pleasant little programmer, which again cast him as a drunk, *The Great Man Votes*, after which he made an ill-advised return to Broadway, in *My Dear Children*, which audiences turned up to see because he was clearly making a spectacle of himself each night. Sadly, his career continued to peter out in a run of "B" films and he died broke. His name continues to be a very familiar one although it is doubtful that much of his highly expressive brand of acting would appeal to most modern audiences. His children, Diana and John (Drew) Jr., worked briefly as actors, both receiving their fair share of critical derision. John Jr.'s daughter is actress Drew Barrymore. John Barrymore's autobiography, *Confessions of an Actor*, was published in 1926.

Screen: 1913: An American Citizen; 1914: The Dictator; The Man From Mexico; 1915: Are You a Mason?; The Incorrigible Dukane; 1916: Nearly a King; The Lost Bridegroom; The Red Widow; 1917: Raffles — The Amateur Cracksman; 1918: On the Quiet; 1919: Here Comes the Bride; The Test of Honor; 1920: Dr. Jekyll and Mr. Hyde; 1921: The Lotus Eater; 1922: Sherlock Holmes; 1924: Beau Brummel; 1926: The Sea Beast; Don Juan; 1927: When a Man Loves; The Beloved Rogue; 1928: Tempest; 1929: Eternal Love; The Show of Shows; General Crack; 1930: The Man From Blankley's; Moby Dick; 1931: Svengali; The Mad Genius; 1932: Arsene Lupin; Grand Hotel; State's Attorney; A Bill of Divorcement; Rasputin and the Empress; 1933: Reunion in Vienna; Dinner at Eight; Night Flight; Topaze; Counsellor-at-Law; 1934: Long Lost Father; Twentieth Century; 1936: Romeo and Juliet; 1937: Maytime; Bulldog Drummond Comes Back; Night Club Scandal; True Confession; Bulldog Drummond's Revenge; 1938: Romance in the Dark; Bulldog Drummond's Peril; Marie Antoinette; Spawn of the North; Hold That Co-Ed; 1939: The Great Man Votes; Midnight; 1940: The Great Profile; 1941: The Invisible Woman; World Premiere; Playmates.

NY Stage: 1903: Glad of It; 1904: The Dictator; Yvette; 1905: Pantaloon; Alice Sit-by-the-Fire; 1907: His Excellency — The Governor; The Boys of Company B; 1908: Toddles; 1909: A Stubborn Cinderella; The Fortune Hunter; 1911: Uncle Sam; 1912: A Slice of Life; The Affairs of Anatol; 1913: Believe Me Xantippe; 1914: The Yellow Ticket; Kick-In; 1916: Justice; 1917: Peter Ibbetson; 1918: Redemption; 1919: The Jest; 1920: Richard III; 1921: Clair de Lune; 1922: Hamlet (and 1923 revival); 1940: My Dear Children.

LIONEL BARRYMORE

(Lionel Herbert Blythe)
Born: Philadelphia, PA, April 28, 1878.
Died: November 15, 1954.

Of all the acting Barrymores, sour-voiced, blustering Lionel was the one who almost did not become an actor, preferring at the outset to study art. Unlike most success stories, family pressure pushed him *towards* acting and he made his Broadway debut in 1900, in *Sag Harbor*. 11 years later he joined D.W. Griffith's Biograph studios, acting in over 50 shorts in a three year period, and making his "feature" (it was approximately 40 minutes long) debut doing various bit parts in the biblical spectacle *Judith of*

Bethulia, in 1914. While continuing to act both on film and stage, he dabbled in directing, debuting in this capacity (as well as receiving screenplay credit) with one of his sister Ethel's movies, *Life's Whirlpool*, in 1917. Shortly afterwards he and younger brother John showed up side by side onstage in *Peter Ibbetson* and *The Jest*. Back in movies, Lionel's 1918 Broadway success in *The Copperhead* was captured on film by Paramount two years later, allowing him a showy role as a much-hated resident in a small Illinois town who turns out to have been a Union spy, not the Southern sympathizer the townies pegged him to be. Unlike his siblings, the eldest Barrymore preferred the movies over theatre, making his final Broadway appearance in *Man or Devil* in 1925, and signing a contract with MGM the following year. With few exceptions (albeit two very important ones) he would remain exclusively at the studio until his death 28 years later. He was the husband cheated on by Greta Garbo in *The Temptress*, but, for the most part, was best known during the silent period for his sneering villainy in such films as *The Eternal City*, as a megalomaniac politician hoping to rule Italy; D.W. Griffith's epic box-office failure *America*, as a traitorous Captain in league with the Indians; *The Thirteenth Hour*, as a criminologist who kills by night; and *Body and Soul*, as an evil doctor lusting after Aileen Pringle. His last notable silent was *Sadie Thompson* (for United Artists), as the hypocritical clergyman who is tempted from the path of righteousness by South Seas slut Gloria Swanson.

When the talkies came Lionel really began to hit his stride as a character actor. His famous crotchety tones were first heard as a power-crazy financier in a semi-talkie at Warners, *The Lion and the Mouse*. He showed up as himself, directing a creaky rendition of the balcony scene from *Romeo and Juliet*, in the all-star *The Hollywood Revue of 1929*, and then promptly nabbed a Best Actor Oscar for playing the alcoholic lawyer in *A Free Soul*, his passionate peroration in defense of daughter Norma Shearer culminating in his collapse. He appeared with brother John for the first time on film in *Arsene Lupin*, with Lionel as the club-footed inspector on the trail of master thief John, and then stole the show as the dying clerk Kringelein in the all-star *Grand Hotel*, which also featured John among the cast. He was a lawyer who believes in justifiable homicide in *Guilty Hands*; Garbo's jealous ex-lover in *Mata Hari*; a lawyer who gets burned when he dabbles in politics in *The Washington Masquerade*; and an unappreciated country doctor in *One Man's Journey*. When he and his siblings got together for their only acting appearance as a trio on film, *Rasputin and the Empress*, it was Lionel who came off most triumphantly in a juicy turn as the slithery and calculating priest. In another popular MGM star-laden enterprise, *Dinner at Eight*, he was the wealthy husband of Billie Burke; was back for one last outing with John in *Night Flight*, as an airline inspector; lurched on as the drunken Billy Bones in *Treasure Island*; and was properly patriarchal as the head of a small town family in an adaptation of Eugene O'Neill's *Ah, Wilderness!* As the star of the horror fantasy *The Devil-Doll* he spent much of the movie disguised as a little old lady; gave a sour puss interpretation of President Andrew Jackson in *The Gorgeous Hussy*; played Robert Taylor's concerned dad in *Camille*; and was the first actor to play Judge Hardy, in *A Family Affair*, before Lewis Stone took up the part.

In 1937, while on the set of *Saratoga*, Barrymore fell and broke his hip, an accident that would cripple him. As a result he would appear for the remainder of his career, first on crutches (as in Frank Capra's Oscar-winning *You Can't Take It With You*, over at Columbia, a screwball comedy that featured one of his most satisfying performances) and then in a wheelchair. This did nothing to slow the actor down as he took on two of his most popular

roles: on radio, as Scrooge in an annual broadcast of *A Christmas Carol*, and as Dr. Gillespie, the grumpy patriarch of Blair General Hospital, in *Young Dr. Kildare* and the subsequent series. When Lew Ayres (Kildare) left the series, the emphasis simply shifted over to Barrymore, starting with *Calling Dr. Gillespie* in 1942. Also at MGM (he was studio head Louis B. Mayer's favorite contract player) there was one of his most fulfilling roles, as the stubborn old crone who traps death in a tree, in the fine film adaptation of *On Borrowed Time*. Although there was often a tendency to ham, Barrymore could still be quite effective, as he was in Capra's *It's a Wonderful Life*, as the despicable Mr. Potter (an RKO release that turned out to be his most enduring portrayal), and in John Huston's *Key Largo*, as Lauren Bacall's father-in-law. Not only did he author a memoir, *We Barrymores*, and a novel, *Mr. Cantonwine I* (both published in 1951), but he also composed a tone poem, *In Memoriam*, dedicated to his brother John. Among the features he directed are *Madame X* (1929), for which he received an Academy Award nomination, making him the first actor to be recognized in the director's category; *His Glorious Night* (1929), the movie credited with ruining John Gilbert's career; *The Unholy Night* (1929); *The Rogue Song* (1930), which brought an Oscar nomination to leading man, Lawrence Tibbett; and *Ten Cents a Dance* (1931).

Screen: 1914: Judith of Bethulia; The Seats of the Mighty; The Span of Life; The Woman in Black; Men and Women; Under the Gaslight; 1915: Wildfire; A Modern Magdalen; The Curious Conduct of Judge Legarde; The Flaming Sword; Dora Thorne; A Yellow Streak; 1916: Dorian's Divorce; The Quitter; The Upheaval; The Brand of Cowardice; 1917: The End of the Tour; His Father's Son; The Millionaire's Double; Life's Whirlpool (and dir.; wr.); 1919: The Valley of Night; 1920: The Copperhead; The Master Mind; The Devil's Garden; 1921: The Great Adventure; Jim the Penman; 1922: Boomerang Bill; The Face in the Fog; 1923: The Enemies of Women; Unseeing Eyes; The Eternal City; 1924: America; Meddling Women; Decameron Nights; I Am the Man; 1925: The Iron Man; Children of the Whirlwind; The Girl Who Wouldn't Work; The Wrongdoers; Fifty-Fifty; The Splendid Road; 1926: The Barrier; Brooding Eyes; The Lucky Lady; Paris at Midnight; The Bells; The Temptress; 1927: The Show; Women Love Diamonds; Body and Soul; The Thirteenth Hour; 1928: Sadie Thompson; Drums of Love; The Lion and the Mouse; Road House; West of Zanzibar; The River Woman; 1929: Alias Jimmy Valentine; The Hollywood Revue of 1929; The Mysterious Island; 1930: Free and Easy; 1931: A Free Soul; Guilty Hands; The Yellow Ticket; Mata Hari; 1932: Broken Lullaby/The Man I Killed; Arsene Lupin; Grand Hotel; Washington Masquerade; Rasputin and the Empress; 1933: Sweepings; Looking Forward; Dinner at Eight; The Stranger's Return; Night Flight; One Man's Journey; Christopher Bean; Should Ladies Behave?; 1934: This Side of Heaven; Carolina; Cardboard City; Treasure Island; The Girl From Missouri; 1935: David Copperfield; Mark of the Vampire; The Little Colonel; Public Hero No. 1; The Return of Peter Grimm; Ah, Wilderness!; 1936: The Voice of Bugle Ann; The Road to Glory; The Devil-Doll; The Gorgeous Hussy; 1937: Camille; Captains Courageous; A Family Affair; Saratoga; Navy Blue and Gold; 1938: Test Pilot; A Yank at Oxford; You Can't Take It With You; Young Dr. Kildare; 1939: Let Freedom Ring; Calling Dr. Kildare; On Borrowed Time; The Secret of Dr. Kildare; 1940: Dr. Kildare's Strange Case; Dr. Kildare Goes Home; Dr. Kildare's Crisis; 1941: The Bad Man; The Penalty; The People vs. Dr. Kildare; Lady Be Good; Dr. Kildare's Wedding Day; 1942: Dr. Kildare's Victory; Calling Dr. Gillespie; Dr. Gillespie's New Assistant; Tennessee Johnson; 1943: Thousands Cheer; Dr. Gillespie's Criminal Case; A Guy

Named Joe; **1944:** Three Men in White; Dragon Seed (narrator); Since You Went Away; Between Two Women; **1945:** The Valley of Decision; **1946:** Three Wise Fools; The Secret Heart; It's a Wonderful Life; Duel in the Sun; **1947:** Dark Delusion; **1948:** Key Largo; **1949:** Down to the Sea in Ships; Malaya; **1950:** Right Cross; **1951:** Bannerline; **1952:** Lone Star; **1953:** Main Street to Broadway.

NY Stage: 1900: Sag Harbor; **1901:** The Brixton Burglary; The Second in Command; **1902:** The Mummy and the Humming Bird; **1903:** The Best of Friends; The Other Girl; **1905:** Pantaloon; **1917:** Peter Ibbetson; **1918:** The Copperhead; **1919:** The Jest; **1920:** The Letter of the Law; **1921:** Macbeth; The Claw; **1923:** Laugh, Clown, Laugh; **1925:** The Piker; Taps; Man or Devil.

RICHARD BARTHELMESS

BORN: NEW YORK, NY, MAY 9, 1895.
ED: HUDSON RIVER MILITARY ACAD., TRINITY COL., HARTFORD. DIED: AUGUST 17, 1963.

Because the majority of his roles were done in the silent era, little of Richard Barthelmess's work is seen or discussed today. He was, in fact, one of the most popular motion picture actors of his time. After some minor stage work he came to films in a 1916 serial entitled *Gloria's Romance*. Soon he was in great demand as a leading man for some of the noted actresses of the period, including Marguerite Clark (*Snow White*, *The Valentine Girl*, *The Seven Swans*) and Anna Q. Nilsson (*The Moral Code*). In 1919 he signed up with D.W. Griffith and played the role that brought him fame, the Chinaman in love with Lillian Gish in *Broken Blossoms*, one of the two most revived of Barthelmess's silent pictures. Griffith loved the combination of male strength and sensitivity that made Barthelmess a matinee idol that both men and women felt they could trust. After *Blossoms* he was a bandit torn between two women in *Scarlet Days*; a beach bum in *The Idol Dancer*; and a seafarer who finds love with Carl Dempster on a desert island in *The Love Flower*. Teamed again with Gish in 1920, he had another major success with the melodrama *Way Down East*. He became a part of silent movie history by appearing in one of the most famous scenes of all, racing across the raging ice floes in order to save the woman he loves. (This is his other frequently silent revived film.) With Charles H. Duell he formed his own production company, called Inspiration, in 1921. Their first release was the hugely popular *Tol'able David*, wherein he played a gentle backwoods boys who must face a trio of convicts while trying to deliver the mail.

With three major releases in as many years, Barthelmess had now become one of the top stars in Hollywood. Among the more notable productions during this period were *Sonny*, in a dual role; *The Bond Boy*, in which his lecherous stepmother tried to have her way with him; *The Bright Shawl*, which paired him with the other Gish sister, Dorothy; *Fury*, avenging his mother's ruin in a follow-up with the second Gish; *The Enchanted Cottage*, finding love there with May McAvoy; *Shore Leave*, a version of the musical *Hit the Deck*, minus the songs (!); *Just Suppose*, as an English prince in America; and *The Drop Kick*, attending college, although Barthelemess had recently turned 30 in real-life. After his production company dissolved, he signed with First National where he played a prize fighter in *The Patent Leather Kid* and an innocent man sent to prison in *The Noose*, receiving Oscar nominations for both. As the sound era came he starred as a British pilot in one of the most popular films of the early talkie period, *The Dawn Patrol*. He also garnered favorable notices playing one of the "Lost Generation," dwelling in 1920s Paris, in director

William Dieterle's English-language debut, *The Last Flight*. He continued for a few years at Warners, but he was starting to look his age, which made him look very silly as the youth enamored of Bette Davis in *Cabin in the Cotton*. There were efforts to stretch, playing a drug addict in *Heroes for Sale*; an Indian in *Massacre*, which was a rare early examination of the plight of Native Americans; and *A Modern Hero*, as an opportunistic heartbreaker climbing the corporate ladder, but none of these worthy efforts drew much public interest. By the mid-1930s his box-office appeal had waned and he worked only sporadically towards the end of the decade, finding one last moment of glory in Howard Hawk's action film *Only Angels Have Wings*, as Rita Hayworth's disgraced husband. Following a stint in the Naval Reserve during War War II, he gladly retired from acting, knowing full well that his best years were long gone.

Screen: 1916: Gloria's Romance (serial); War Brides; Just a Song at Twilight; **1917:** Snow White; The Moral Code; Soul of a Magdalen; The Eternal Sin; Camille; Nearly Married; The Streets of Illusion; The Valentine Girl; Bab's Diary; Bab's Burglar; For Valor; **1918:** Seven Swans; Sunshine Nan; Wild Primrose; Richard Man Poor Man; Hit-the-Trail Holiday; **1919:** The Hope Chest; Boots; The Girl Who Stayed at Home; Three Men and a Girl; Peppy Polly; I'll Get Him Yet; Broken Blossoms; Scarlet Days; **1920:** The Idol Dancer; The Greatest Question; The Love Flower; Way Down East; **1921:** Experience; Tol'able David; **1922:** The Seventh Day; Just a Song at Twilight; Sonny; The Bond Boy; **1923:** The Bright Shawl; Fury; The Fighting Blade; Twenty-One; **1924:** The Enchanted Cottage; Classmates; **1925:** New Toys; Soul-Fire; Shore Leave; The Beautiful City; **1926:** Just Suppose; Ranson's Folly; The Amateur Gentleman; The White Black Sheep; **1927:** The Drop Kick; The Patent Leather Kid; **1928:** The Noose; The Little Shepherd of Kingdom Come; The Wheel of Chance; Out of the Ruins; Scarlet Seas; **1929:** Weary River; Drag; Young Nowheres; The Show of Shows; **1930:** Son of the Gods; The Dawn Patrol; **1931:** The Lash; The Finger Points; The Last Flight; **1932:** Alias the Doctor; Cabin in the Cotton; **1933:** Central Airport; Heroes for Sale; **1934:** Massacre; A Modern Hero; Midnight Alibi; **1935:** Four Hours to Kill; **1936:** A Spy of Napoleon; **1939:** Only Angels Have Wings; **1940:** The Man Who Talked Too Much; **1942:** The Mayor of 44th Street; The Spoilers.
NY Stage: 1936: The Postman Always Rings Twice.

FREDDIE BARTHOLOMEW

(FREDERICK LLEWELLYN) BORN: LONDON, ENGLAND, MARCH 28, 1924. DIED: JANUARY 23, 1992.

A polite, sensitive and gentlemanly child actor from an era when such a personality could actually become popular, Freddie Bartholomew was raised by an aunt who pushed him into show business. After bit roles in two British productions, he studied his craft with Italia Conti, who recommended the boy to director George Cukor, who was, in turn, engaged to direct David O. Selznick's classy production of *David Copperfield*. Tested and signed for the role, the 10-year-old Bartholomew and his aunt journeyed to Los Angeles, where the child did a commendable job carrying the first half of the lengthy Dickens story before growing up to be the much less interesting Frank Lawton. Signed to a contract by MGM, he first took a supporting role, as Garbo's son, in *Anna Karenina*, and then was borrowed by Selznick again for the role he was born to play, *Little Lord Fauntleroy*. MGM was now anxious to create vehicles for him and, in an effort to toughen his screen image, he was teamed most enjoyably with Mickey

Rooney and Jackie Cooper in *The Devil Is a Sissy*. Opposite Spencer Tracy he played the spoiled rich brat chastened by a Portuguese fisherman in his best movie, *Captains Courageous*, the role for which he is probably best remembered. Loaned out whenever another studio needed a young Englishman he was seen in the film versions of such classic stories as *Kidnapped*, *Swiss Family Robinson*, and *Tom Brown's School Days*. A custody battle between his parents and the aunt who raised him resulted in the loss of most of his movie earnings. At 18 he joined the Air Force and made only two more screen appearances after the war. The last of these was *St. Benny the Dip*, in which he played a priest, after which he happily left the business, in 1951. There was a brief fling at television hosting before he established himself in the world of advertising, eventually becoming vice president of the firm of Benton and Bowles. He married, moved his family to New Jersey, and never looked back.

Screen: 1930: Fascination; 1932: Lily Christine; 1935: David Copperfield; Anna Karenina; 1936: Professional Soldier; Little Lord Fauntleroy; The Devil Is a Sissy; Lloyds of London; 1937: Captains Courageous; 1938: Kidnapped; Lord Jeff; Listen, Darling; 1939: The Spirit of Culver; Two Bright Boys; 1940: Swiss Family Robinson; Tom Brown's Schooldays; 1941: Naval Academy; 1942: Cadets on Parade; A Yank at Eton; Junior Army; 1944: The Town Went Wild; 1947: Sepia Cinderella; 1951: St. Benny the Dip.

BILLY BARTY

(WILLIAM JOHN BERTANZETTI) BORN: MILLSBORO, PA, OCTOBER 25, 1924. ED: LA CITY COL., LA STATE UNIV. DIED: DECEMBER 23, 2000.

At three feet, nine inches in height, Billy Barty was certainly the most famous dwarf actor in the history of Hollywood. Only three years old when he entered movies, as Mickey Rooney's little brother in the "Mickey Maguire" shorts, he soon became a familiar sight to Depression-era audiences. He made fleeting, leering appearances in musical numbers at Warner Bros. including *Footlight Parade* and *Gold Diggers of 1933*, in the latter chasing after some chorines with a can opener. He dropped out of sight for many years but began showing up with increasing regularity on television in the 1950s and 1960s. During this time he helped to establish The Little People of America to oversee the rights of those hindered from working because of their height. Starting in the 1970s there suddenly seemed to be a great demand for Barty. He made notable appearances in *The Day of the Locust*, as part of Karen Black's clique of Hollywood losers, memorably coaching his pet fowl in a cock fight; *Foul Play*, misidentified as an assassin and being dropped out of a window by a terrified Goldie Hawn; and *Willow*, as the wise old wizard presiding over an entire village of small citizens. When Cannon embarked on their woeful attempt to musicalize several famous fairy tales, Barty got his one leading role, playing *Rumpelstiltskin*, opposite Amy Irving. Although he did not appear in the most famous "little people" movie of them all, *The Wizard of Oz*, he had the key role of the villain in the misguided 1981 spoof about the making of that film, *Under the Rainbow*.

Screen (features): 1930: Soup to Nuts; 1931: Goldie; Daddy Long Legs; Over the Hill; 1933: Gold Diggers of 1933; Out All Night; Roman Scandals; Footlight Parade; Alice in Wonderland; 1934: Gift of Gab; 1935: A Midsummer Night's Dream; Bride of Frankenstein; 1937: Nothing Sacred; 1942: Here We Go Again; 1950: Pigmy Island; 1952: The Clown; 1954: Fireman, Save My

Child; 1957: The Undead; 1962: Billy Rose's Jumbo; 1964: Roustabout; 1965: Harum Scarum; 1970: Pufnstuf; 1973: The Godmothers; 1975: The Day of the Locust; 1976: W.C. Fields and Me; Won Ton Ton, the Dog Who Saved Hollywood; 1977: The Amazing Dobermans; The Happy Hooker Goes to Washington; 1978: Rabbit Test; Foul Play; Lord of the Rings (voice); 1979: Firepower; Skatetown USA; 1981: Hardly Working; Under the Rainbow; 1984: Night Patrol; 1986: Legend; Tough Guys; 1987: Masters of the Universe; Off the Mark; Rumpelstiltskin; Body Slam; 1988: Willow; 1989: Snow White (dtv); UHF; 1990: Lobster Man From Mars; The Rescuers Down Under (voice); 1991: Digging Up Business (dtv); Life Stinks; 1992: Wishful Thinking (dtv); The Naked Truth; 1994: Radioland Murders; 1998: An Alan Smithee Film: Burn Hollywood Burn; I-O Error (nUSr).

NY Stage: 1991: Andre Heller's Wonderhouse

Select TV: 1951: Your Pet Parade; 1951–52: Ford Festival (series); 1954: The Spike Jones Show (series); 1956–58: Circus Boy (series); 1957: The Spike Jones Show (series); 1958: Club Oasis (series); 1969–71: H.R. Pufnstuf (series); 1970–72: The Bugaloos (series) 1973–75: Sigmund and the Sea Monsters (series); 1974: Punch and Jody; 1976: Twin Detectives; 1976–77: The Krofft Supershow (series); 1977–78: The Redd Foxx Comedy Hour (series); 1978–79: The Bay City Rollers Show (series); 1983: Ace Crawford — Private Eye (series); 1991: Vendetta: Secrets of a Mafia Bride.

RICHARD BASEHART

BORN: ZANESVILLE, OH, AUGUST 31, 1914. DIED: SEPTEMBER 17, 1984.

An intelligent, serious actor who snagged a few starring roles but who stays in the mind as a character player, Richard Basehart first worked as a radio announcer before debuting on Broadway, in 1943, in *Counterattack*. Two years later he scored a success, starring in *The Hasty Heart*, which brought Hollywood calling. His work as an unhinged cop killer in the "B" thriller *He Walked by Night* brought favorable notices. Other leads came with MGM's intriguing noir *Tension*, as a nebbish plotting to kill his wife's lover, and Universal's *Outside the Wall*, trying to go straight after doing a stretch in the pen. He gave perhaps his finest film performance in 1951's tense *Fourteen Hours*, as the disturbed young man threatening to jump off a building ledge. For 20th Century-Fox he played the evil guardian who marries Valentina Cortese in *The House on Telegraph Hill* (they also wed in real life); the American officer saved by German spy Oskar Werner in the Oscar-nominated *Decision Before Dawn*; and one of the unfortunate folks aboard the *Titanic*. 1956 found him in two of his best roles, as Ishmael in John Huston's impressive production of *Moby Dick*, and Fellini's superb *La Strada*, as the circus fool whose antics drive strongman Anthony Quinn to murder. There were roles in many overseas productions: the lead in a cheapie biopic of *Hitler*; supporting work in the Lana Turner soaper *Portrait in Black*; the Mayan epic *Kings of the Sun*, in which he sported a particularly silly hairdo; and the thriller *The Satan Bug*, where he had a bad accent for a reason. Starting in the 1960s, he was found more frequently on television, starring in Irwin Allen's sci-fi series *Voyage to the Bottom of the Sea*; acting in several telefilms; and winning an Emmy Award for narrating the special *Let My People Go*, in 1965. Back on the big screen he was buried under animal makeup for *The Island of Dr. Moreau*; had a starring role in a tepid heist comedy, *The Great Bank Hoax*; and showed up as a Russian diplomat in *Being There*.

Screen: 1947: Cry Wolf; Repeat Performance; 1948: He Walked by Night; 1949: The Black Book/Reign of Terror; Roseanna McCoy; Tension; 1950: Outside the Wall; 1951: Fourteen Hours; The House on Telegraph Hill; Fixed Bayonets; Decision Before Dawn; 1953: Titanic; 1954: The Stranger's Hand (nUSr); Avanzi di Galera/Jailbirds (nUSr); 1955: The Good Die Young; Canyon Crossroads; La Veno d'Oro/The Golden Touch (nUSr); Cartouche (nUSr); 1956: The Extra Day; The Intimate Stranger/Finger of Guilt; Moby Dick; La Strada; 1957: Time Limit; Arrivederci Dimas (nUSr); 1958: The Brothers Karamazov; 1959: The Ambitious Ones/The Restless and the Damned (nUSr); Jons und Erdme (nUSr); 1960: Five Branded Woman; Portrait in Black; For the Love of Mike; 1961: Passport to China; The Savage Guns; 1962: Hitler; The Swindle/Il Bidone (It: 1955); 1963: Kings of the Sun; 1964: Four Days in November (narrator); 1965: The Satan Bug; 1969: Un Homme Qui Me Plait/Love Is a Funny Thing (nUSr); 1972: Chato's Land; Rage; 1973: And Millions Will Die; 1976: Mansion of the Doomed; 1977: The Island of Dr. Moreau; 1978: The Great Bank Hoax; 1979: Being There.

NY Stage: 1943: Counterattack; 1944: Take It As It Comes; Hickory Stick; 1945: The Hasty Heart; 1948: The Survivors; 1958: The Day the Money Stopped.

Select TV: 1957: So Soon to Die (sp); 1959: A Dream of Treason (sp); 1960: The Hiding Place (sp); 1964–68: Voyage to the Bottom of the Sea (series); 1969: Hans Brinker (sp); 1970: Sole Survivor; The Andersonville Trial (sp); 1971: City Beneath the Sea; The Birdmen; The Death of Me Yet; 1972: Assignment: Munich; The Bounty Man; 1973: Maneater; 1974: Valley Forge (sp); 1976: Time Travelers; 21 Hours at Munich; Flood!; 1977: Stonestreet: Who Killed the Centerfold Model?; 1978: The Bastard (ms); WEB (series); 1979: The Rebels (ms); 1980: Marilyn: The Untold Story; 1981: Masada (ms; narrator); 1982: Knight Rider.

ALAN BATES

BORN: ALLESTREE, DERBYSHIRE, ENGLAND, FEBRUARY 17, 1934.

During the 1960s, rumpled, naturalistic-looking Alan Bates was one of the much-heralded young British actors who graced some of the most interesting international films of the decade. He studied at RADA, then made his professional bow in You and Your Wife, in Coventry, in 1955. It was then on to London where he gained attention in the original West End productions of Long Day's Journey Into Night (playing Edmund), Look Back in Anger (as Cliff), and Harold Pinter's The Caretaker (which he later played in a movie that went under the play's original title as well as The Guest). The theatre he belonged to, London's Royal Court, was involved in adapting The Entertainer to film and Bates made his debut in it as Laurence Olivier's son. Things really took off with Whistle Down the Wind, with Bates as an escaped con protected by some children who believe he is Jesus Christ, a potentially sticky subject nicely handled. He firmly made the leap to film stardom with his next, John Schlesinger's gritty look at a working class marriage in trouble, A Kind of Loving, a great success in Britain, less so in the U.S. He took third billing to Laurence Harvey and Lee Remick in a thriller, The Running Man, and did a bleak satire on the social structure, Nothing But the Best. In America he found his biggest audiences yet, as the young man taught to live life to the fullest by Anthony Quinn in Zorba the Greek, and as the energetic boyfriend who turns his attentions from bitchy Charlotte

Rampling to frumpish, unloved Lynn Redgrave in Georgy Girl.

In 1967 he starred in the French-made comedy King of Hearts, as the young soldier who stumbles upon a town overrun by the escaped asylum inmates. At the time it received little critical or public attention, but over the years it achieved stature as one of the ultimate cult movies. After playing the very patient shepherd who stands by Julie Christie in the lengthy Far From the Madding Crowd, he scored his only Oscar nomination, for The Fixer. His performance as a Jewish handyman unjustly imprisoned for the murder of a child was probably his least interesting film and performance to date, but his run of fine work until then definitely warranted some sort of recognition. His finest performance came soon afterwards, as the incarnation of D.H. Lawrence trying to unravel the complexities of male/female relationships in Ken Russell's Women in Love. The film gained some degree of notoriety for its notorious nude wrestling scene between Bates and Oliver Reed. Reteaming with Julie Christie, he was once again a man of the land carrying on a romantic correspondence with her, in The Go-Between, another film that got a better response in England than it did in the States.

There followed a successful performance in the taxing role of the father of a spastic child, who covers his pain with flippancy, in A Day in the Death of Joe Egg. A recreation of his acclaimed London stage role, as a homosexual teacher in Butley, and of In Celebration, an uncomfortable reunion of three brothers, were presented by the experimental American Film Theatre series, which inevitably reached a limited audience. As his prestige began to fade in the 1970s he popped up, bearded, in prominent supporting roles in two widely-seen American releases: An Unmarried Woman, at his most ingratiating as the artist who becomes Jill Clayburgh's lover, and The Rose, as Bette Midler's heartless manager. Back in British productions, he seduced Isabelle Adjani in Quartet, and developed amnesia in The Return of the Soldier, two films that found no audience outside of their initial engagements. Supposedly intended for a wider market was the grotesque remake of The Wicked Lady, with Bates looking puffy, aged, and disinterested as a highwayman. Later he would receive praise playing the real-life homosexual spy Guy Burgess in the television special An Englishman Abroad, and the immoral King Claudius in Mel Gibson's version of Hamlet. The strange projects of the late 1980s and early 1990s in which he had leads, including We Think the World of You, as a devotee of lover Gary Oldman's dog; the incomprehensible Secret Friends, as an amnesiac; and Silent Tongue, as a sleazy medicine show owner, were further instances of products failing to entice even those who were seeking such specialized fare. Finally ending up in something high profile, he played a butler with a shady past in director Robert Altman's Gosford Park, after which he reunited with Charlotte Rampling for a barely distributed version of The Cherry Orchard.

Screen: 1960: The Entertainer; 1961: Whistle Down the Wind; 1962: A Kind of Loving; 1963: The Running Man; 1964: The Caretaker/The Guest; Nothing But the Best; Zorba the Greek; 1966: Georgy Girl; King of Hearts; 1967: Far From the Madding Crowd; 1968: The Fixer; 1970: Women in Love; 1971: The Go-Between; 1972: A Day in the Death of Joe Egg; 1973: The Impossible Object/The Story of a Love Story; 1974: Butley; Three Sisters (UK: 1970); 1975: In Celebration; Royal Flash; 1978: An Unmarried Woman; 1979: The Shout; The Rose; 1980: Nijinsky; 1981: Quartet; Recedo Gory/Hands Up! (nUSr); 1982: Britannia Hospital; 1983: The Return of the Soldier; The Wicked Lady; 1986: Duet for One; 1987: A Prayer for the Dying; 1988: We Think the World of You; 1989: Force Majeur (nUSr); 1990: Doctor M/Club Extinction (nUSr); Mr. Frost; Hamlet; 1991:

Shuttlecock (nUSr); **1992:** Secret Friends; **1994:** Silent Tongue (filmed 1992); **1997:** Gentlemen Don't Eat Poets/The Grotesque (filmed 1995); **2001:** Gosford Park; **2002:** The Mothman Prophecies; The Cherry Orchard; The Sum of All Fears; Evelyn.
NY Stage: 1957: Look Back in Anger; **1961:** The Caretaker; **1964:** Poor Richard; **1965:** A Hero of Our Time; **2000:** The Unexpected Man.
Select TV: 1974: The Story of Jacob and Joseph; **1976:** The Collection (sp); **1978:** The Mayor of Casterbridge; **1980:** Very Like a Whale (sp; and dir.); **1981:** The Trespasser (sp); **1983:** An Englishman Abroad (sp); A Voyage Round My Father (sp); Separate Tables; Dr. Fisher of Geneva (sp); **1987:** Pack of Lies; **1988:** The Dog It Was That Died (sp); **1991:** Unnatural Pursuits; 102 Boulevard Haussmann; **1994:** Hard Times; **1996:** Oliver's Travels (ms); **1998:** Nicholas' Gift; **2000:** St. Patrick: The Irish Legend; Arabian Nights; The Prince and the Pauper; In the Beginning; **2001:** Love in the Cold Climate.

FLORENCE BATES

(FLORENCE RABE) BORN: SAN ANTONIO, TX, APRIL 15, 1888. DIED: JANUARY 31, 1954.

One of Hollywood's late bloomers, full-figured Florence Bates didn't venture into acting until she was 47. By the time she joined the Pasadena Playhouse, she had already had a career as an attorney and a period of running a bakery in Los Angeles with her second husband. She had, in fact, made the record books by becoming the first lady lawyer in Texas. She set the tone for many of her subsequent roles with her second film appearance, playing the yakety, selfish Mrs. Van Hopper in Alfred Hitchcock's *Rebecca*, an imperious dowager with a flamboyant manner. Among the highlights of her busy career over the next 14 years were *Love Crazy*, as Myrna Loy's self-satisfied mom; *The Tuttles of Tahiti*, living on a South Seas island with her champion fighting bird; *The Moon and Sixpence*, again residing in the islands, as a colorful innkeeper; *Saratoga Trunk*, as a pretentious society lady; *Heaven Can Wait*, being promptly dispatched to hell for her sins; *Tonight and Every Night*, as a jovial London theatre owner; *The Time, the Place and the Girl*, as S.Z. Sakall's henpecking wife; *The Secret Life of Walter Mitty*, as Danny Kaye's domineering future mother-in-law, who barks at him in one of his daydreams; *I Remember Mama*, in a memorable scene as a famous authoress trading advice and recipes with Irene Dunne; *Portrait of Jennie*, as a landlady; *On the Town*, as Vera-Ellen's ballet instructor; *County Fair*, as a hamburger stand proprietress; *Lullaby of Broadway*, once again nagging poor S.Z. Sakall; and the 1952 version of *Les Misérables*, as the hateful Mme. Bonnett who terrorizes poor little Cozette.
Screen: 1937: The Man in Blue; **1940:** Rebecca; Calling All Husbands; Son of Monte Cristo; Hudson's Bay; Kitty Foyle; **1941:** Road Show; Love Crazy; Strange Alibi; The Devil and Miss Jones; The Chocolate Soldier; **1942:** The Tuttles of Tahiti; Mexican Spitfire at Sea; We Were Dancing; The Moon and Sixpence; My Heart Belongs to Daddy; **1943:** They Got Me Covered; Slightly Dangerous; Mister Big; Mr. Lucky; Heaven Can Wait; His Butler's Sister; **1944:** The Mask of Dimitrios; Since You Went Away; Kismet; The Belle of the Yukon; **1945:** Tahiti Nights; Tonight and Every Night; Out of This World; San Antonio; Saratoga Trunk; **1946:** Whistle Stop; The Man I Love; Diary of a Chambermaid; Cluny Brown; Claudia and David; The Time, the Place and the Girl; **1947:** The Brasher Doubloon; Love and Learn; The Secret Life of Walter Mitty; Desire Me; **1948:** The Inside Story; I Remember Mama; Winter Meeting; River Lady; Texas, Brooklyn and Heaven; My Dear Secretary; Portrait of Jennie; **1949:** A Letter to Three Wives; The Judge Steps Out; The Girl From Jones Beach; On the Town; **1950:** Belle of Old Mexico; County Fair; **1951:** The Second Woman; Lullaby of Broadway; Father Takes the Air; The Tall Target; Havana Rose; **1952:** The San Francisco Story; Les Misérables; **1953:** Main Street to Broadway; Paris Model.

ANNE BAXTER

BORN: MICHIGAN CITY, IN, MAY 7, 1923.
RAISED IN BRONXVILLE, NY.
DIED: DECEMBER 12, 1985.

There was something so right about Anne Baxter's Oscar-nominated performance as Eve Harrington in *All About Eve*, so conniving and deeply despicable, that it is the part for which she will be forever remembered. It was also important that Eve was never shown onstage taking over for Margo Channing in the role that wins her raves, for no audience would ever believe that someone as ordinary Baxter could ever equal the dynamic Bette Davis. The granddaughter of architect Frank Lloyd Wright, Baxter studied acting with Maria Ouspenskaya, making her Broadway debut at age 13 in the short-lived *Seen But Not Heard*. After a few more Broadway roles she went to Hollywood to test for David Selznick and then for Alfred Hitchcock for the lead in *Rebecca*. Although nothing came of this, Darryl Zanuck liked the test and put her under contract to Fox. She was immediately loaned to MGM for her debut, as the ingénue in a Wallace Beery movie, *20 Mule Team*. Back on Fox turf she was the daughter of fugitive Walter Brennan in *Swamp Water*; a French girl helping Monty Woolley evacuate children in *The Pied Piper*; and the woman desired by both Tyrone Power and Dana Andrews in *Crash Dive*. Her two best early roles, however, were on loan-out, first to RKO, playing the daughter of Joseph Cotten, toying with Tim Holt's affections, in Orson Welles's *The Magnificent Ambersons*, and for Paramount, as the French barmaid assisting soldier Franchot Tone, in Billy Wilder's *Five Graves to Cairo*. At Fox she foreshadowed her *Eve* role in *Guest in the House*, insinuating herself into a family with charm but intending malice; and she was the homefront daughter who falls in love with John Hodiak when her family hosts *Sunday Dinner for a Soldier*. The romance also blossomed in real life, as the two were married in 1946. (They divorced in 1955, shortly before Hodiak died). In the showy role of the drug-addicted Sophie in the popular 1946 adaptation of Somerset Maugham's *The Razor's Edge*, she won an Academy Award as Best Supporting Actress for her somewhat overbaked performance.

Baxter got a few loan-out assignments (including playing second fiddle to Lana Turner in MGM's *Homecoming*) and, back at Fox, a pleasant fantasy, *The Luck of the Irish*; a good western, *Yellow Sky*; and a pair of fluffy musicals, *You're My Everything*, and *A Ticket to Tomahawk*. It seemed clear, however, that Fox was never going to sell a film on Baxter's name even after the tremendous success of *All About Eve* in 1950. There was very little to commend her during this period, which included the traditional loyal wife role in the biopic of golfer Ben Hogan, *Follow the Sun*; the "Last Leaf" segment of *O.Henry's Full House*, as Jean Peters's severely ill sister; a minor Hitchcock drama *I Confess*; and such melodramatic items as *Carnival Story*, as a German refugee who joins a traveling sideshow, and *One Desire*, in love with gambler Rock Hudson. Apart from *Eve*, her most notable role was one of her most flamboyant and unrestrained, temptress Nefretiri in Cecil B. DeMille's massive biblical specatcle *The Ten Commandments*, one of the most popular attractions of the 1950s.

As movie offers dwindled she returned to the stage, ironically playing the part of Margo Channing in the Broadway musical version of *All About Eve*, retitled *Applause*. Her last theatrical feature, *Jane Austen in Manhattan*, secured her a leading role, and although it attracted little interest, she at least got to appear alongside her daughter, Katrina Hodiak. She ended her career as one of the stars of a nighttime television drama, *Hotel*, dying during the run of the show. Her autobiography, *Intermission: A True Story*, was published in 1976.

Screen: 1940: 20 Mule Team; The Great Profile; 1941: Charley's Aunt; Swamp Water; 1942: The Magnificent Ambersons; The Pied Piper; 1943: Crash Dive; Five Graves to Cairo; The North Star/Armored Attack; 1944: The Sullivans; The Eve of St. Mark; Sunday Dinner for a Soldier; Guest in the House; 1945: A Royal Scandal; 1946: Smoky; Angel on My Shoulder; The Razor's Edge; 1947: Mother Wore Tights (narrator); Blaze of Noon; 1948: Homecoming; The Walls of Jericho; The Luck of the Irish; Yellow Sky; 1949: You're My Everything; 1950: A Ticket to Tomahawk; All About Eve; 1951: Follow the Sun; 1952: The Outcasts of Poker Flat; My Wife's Best Friend; O. Henry's Full House; 1953: I Confess; The Blue Gardenia; 1954: Carnival Story; 1955: Bedevilled; One Desire; The Spoilers; 1956: The Come-On; The Ten Commandments; Three Violent People; 1958: Chase a Crooked Shadow; 1960: Season of Passion/Summer of the 17th Doll; Cimarron; 1962: Walk on the Wild Side; 1963: Mix Me a Person; 1965: The Family Jewels; 1966: The Tall Women; 1967: The Busy Body; 1971: Fool's Parade; 1972: The Late Liz; 1980: Jane Austen in Manhattan.

NY Stage: 1936: Seen But Not Heard; 1938: There's Always a Breeze; Madame Carpet; 1957: The Square Root of Wonderful; 1971: Applause; 1974: Noel Coward in Two Keys.

Select TV: 1958: The Right Hand Man (sp); 1967: Stranger on the Run; 1968: The Challengers; Companions in Nightmare; 1969: Marcus Welby M.D./A Matter of Humanities (pilot); 1969–70: Marcus Welby M.D. (series); 1970: Ritual of Evil; 1971: If Tomorrow Comes; 1972: The Catcher; 1973: Lisa-Bright and Dark; 1976: Arthur Hailey's The Moneychangers; 1978: Little Mo; 1979: Nero Wolfe; 1981: East of Eden (ms); 1983–86: Hotel (series); 1984: The Masks of Death (sp).

WARNER BAXTER

BORN: COLUMBUS, OH, MARCH 29, 1891.
DIED: MAY 7, 1951.

A no-nonsense, scowling leading man with a pencil-thin moustache, Warner Baxter is probably best known for his portrayal of the hard-as-nails director in the landmark musical *42nd Street*, in which he barked the immortal command to Ruby Keeler, "You're going out there a youngster, but you've got to come back a star!" Between odd jobs he had acted on the legit stage and in vaudeville before joining the Morosco stock company in Los Angeles. While there he made his movie debut in *All Woman*, then found success on the New York stage in *Lombardi Ltd.*, which he also took on the road. Back in L.A. his movie career started for real in 1921, as he worked steadily throughout the decade, playing a small town citizen suspected of murder in *The Ninety and Nine*; a war vet fallen on hard times in *Blow Your Own Horn*; Lillian Rich's callous lover in *The Golden Bed*; a most unlikely island native in *Aloma of the South Seas*; the title role in *The Great Gatsby*, Paramount's first of three attempts to adapt Fitzgerald's classic novel; and the Indian Alessandro in the third version of *Ramona*. It was not until the transition from silence to sound that his status really soared, playing the grinning,

romantic Mexican bandit, the Cisco Kid, in Fox's *In Old Arizona*. He won an Academy Award and would later reprise the role on three occasions, starting with *The Arizona Kid* and *The Cisco Kid*. Signed to a contract he appeared in *Daddy Long Legs*, as Janet Gaynor's wealthy, secretive benefactor. He then went to MGM for the title role in the umpteenth DeMille version of *The Squaw Man*; did his immortal role as bombastic Broadway director Julian Marsh in Warners's *42nd Street*; returned to MGM for *Penthouse*, as a lawyer trying to put a big shot criminal in jail; was summoned to Columbia for Frank Capra's charming racetrack comedy *Broadway Bill*; and then back to his home lot, which was now called 20th Century-Fox, for one of his finest performances in John Ford's *The Prisoner of Shark Island*, an engrossing historical examination of the doctor who was sent to prison for assisting John Wilkes Booth.

Apparently Cisco kept him Hispanic in most people's minds because he played shameless variations on this character in both *Under the Pampas Moon* and *The Robin Hood of El Dorado*. He joined the casts of some popular adventures that kept him in the public eye. In *The Road to Glory*, he was a tough French captain during World War I, troubled by his unrequited love for June Lang and having to command his own dad, Lionel Barrymore, who has joined the regiment; in *Slave Ship*, he piloted the title vessel until his conscience overpowered his greed; and in *Kidnapped*, alongside Freddie Bartholomew, he was the Scottish adventurer Alan Breck, though he was starting to look a bit too old for such roles. He did *Wife, Doctor and Nurse*, made almost directly on top of *Wife, Husband and Friend*; and then played a millionaire disguised as a bum in *I'll Give a Million*, which played to dwindling audiences. Inevitably it was time to drag out the sure thing, so in 1939 he did *The Return of the Cisco Kid*, a year before his Fox contract came to a close with the fantasy *Earthbound*. He went over to Columbia for *Adam Had Four Sons*, in love with a much younger Ingrid Bergman, but dropped out of sight after suffering a nervous breakdown. He returned to work at the age of 50, settling into a "B" series for Columbia, as an amnesia victim who calls himself Dr. Ordway and becomes a top criminologist. The first of the batch, *Crime Doctor*, was released in 1943, and the series ended nine entries later with *Crime Doctor's Diary*, in 1949. In between these he did other second-feature assignments for the company, the last of which was *State Penitentiary*, playing a man imprisoned for embezzlement who escapes to find the real culprit.

Screen: 1918: All Woman; 1921: Sheltered Daughters; Cheated Hearts; The Love Charm; First Love; 1922: Her Own Money; The Girl in His Room; A Girl's Desire; If I Were Queen; The Ninety and Nine; 1923: Blow Your Own Horn; St. Elmo; In Search of a Thrill; 1924: Alimony; Those Who Dance; Christine of the Hungry Heart; The Female; The Garden of Weeds; 1925: The Golden Bed; The Air Mail; Welcome Home; Rugged Water; The Awful Truth; A Son of His Father; The Best People; 1926: Mannequin; Miss Brewster's Millions; The Runaway; Aloma of the South Seas; Mismates; The Great Gatsby; 1927: The Telephone Girl; Singed; Drums of the Desert; The Coward; A Woman's Way; 1928: Tragedy of Youth; Three Sinners; Ramona; Craig's Wife; Danger Street; 1929: West of Zanzibar; In Old Arizona; Linda; Thru Different Eyes; Behind That Curtain; The Far Call; Romance of the Rio Grande; 1930: Happy Days; Such Men Are Dangerous; The Arizona Kid; Renegades; 1931: Doctors' Wives; Daddy Long Legs; The Squaw Man; Their Mad Moment; Surrender; The Cisco Kid; 1932: Amateur Daddy; Man About Town; Six Hours to Live; 1933: 42nd Street; Dangerously Yours; I Loved You Wednesday; Paddy, the Next Best Thing; Penthouse; 1934: As Husbands Go; Such Women Are Dangerous; Stand Up

and Cheer; Grand Canary; Broadway Bill; Hell in the Heavens; **1935:** One More Spring; Under the Pampas Moon; King of Burlesque; **1936:** The Prisoner of Shark Island; The Robin Hood of El Dorado; The Road to Glory; To Mary With Love; White Hunter; **1937:** Slave Ship; Vogues of 1938; Wife, Doctor and Nurse; **1938:** Kidnapped; I'll Give a Million; **1939:** Wife, Husband and Friend; Return of the Cisco Kid; Barricade; **1940:** Earthbound; **1941:** Adam Had Four Sons; **1943:** Crime Doctor; Crime Doctor's Strangest Case; **1944:** Lady in the Dark; Shadows in the Night; **1945:** Crime Doctor's Courage; Crime Doctor's Warning; **1946:** Just Before Dawn; Crime Doctor's Man Hunt; **1947:** The Millerson Case; Crime Doctor's Gamble; **1948:** The Gentleman From Nowhere; **1949:** Prison Warden; The Devil's Henchman; Crime Doctor's Diary; **1950:** State Penitentiary.
NY Stage: 1917: Lombardi Ltd.; 1918: A Tailor Made Man.

JOHN BEAL

(James Alexander Bliedung)
Born: Joplin, MO, August 13, 1909.
ed: Univ. of PA. Died: April 26, 1997.

A compact, reliable actor with a strong, serious-sounding voice, who forever stayed on the second rung of stardom, John Beal began acting at college in the Mask and Wig Club. Through a meeting with director Jasper Newton Deeter, he joined the Hedgerow Theatre Rep Company and acted with them until his Broadway debut in 1930, via understudy work, in *That's Gratitude*. After his stage success in *Another Language*, Hollywood beckoned and he went west to repeat his role in the 1933 movie adaptation for MGM. As the sensitive young man falling hopelessly in love with sister-in-law Helen Hayes, it was clear from the start that he was an actor worth watching. He signed on with RKO that same year, finding his best leading roles in two period dramas, *The Little Minister*, with Katharine Hepburn, and George Stevens's *Laddie*, as a farm boy in love with his English neighbor. There was also the important role of Marius in the abbreviated but effective 1935 version of *Les Misérables*. When his RKO assignments became more decidedly "B," as with *The Man Who Found Himself* and *Border Cafe*, he moved back to MGM for the remake of *Madame X*, as the attorney who doesn't realize his client is his mother; and *Port of Seven Seas*, again playing a Frenchman named Marius, this time in a story that would later become better known as *Fanny*. Finding less and less fulfillment in the lowly assignments he was being giving by Hollywood, he chose to act in the theatre whenever possible (sometimes opposite his wife, Helen Craig), notably as one of the replacement cast members of the long running comedy *The Voice of the Turtle*. After World War II (during which he directed some training films) his movie roles became more sporadic with leads in the "B" horror *The Vampire* and the Disney adventure *Ten Who Dared*, leading an expedition down the Colorado river. He could still be found on Broadway in his 80s, as a member of Tony Randall's Broadway theatre company, and had a brief role as one of the law partners in the 1993 hit *The Firm*.
Screen: 1933: Another Language; 1934: Hat, Coat and Glove; The Little Minister; 1935: Les Misérables; Laddie; Break of Hearts; 1936: M'Liss; We Who Are About to Die; 1937: The Man Who Found Himself; Border Cafe; Danger Patrol; Double Wedding; Madame X; Beg, Borrow or Steal; 1938: Port of Seven Seas; I Am the Law; The Arkansas Traveler; 1939: The Great Commandment; The Cat and the Canary; 1941: Ellery Queen and the Perfect Crime; Doctors Don't Tell; 1942: Atlantic Convoy; Stand By All Networks; One Thrilling Night; 1943:

Edge of Darkness; Let's Have Fun; 1947: Key Witness; 1948: So Dear to My Heart (narrator); 1949: Alimony; Song of Surrender; Chicago Deadline; 1950: Messenger of Peace; 1952: My Six Convicts; 1953: Remains to Be Seen; 1954: The Country Parson; 1957: That Night!/The Long Way Home; The Vampire; 1959: The Sound and the Fury; 1960: Ten Who Dared; 1974: The House That Cried Murder; 1983: Amityville 3-D; 1993: The Firm.
NY Stage: 1930: That's Gratitude; 1931: Give Me Yesterday; No More Fronteirs; 1932: Wild Waves; Another Language; 1933: She Loves Me Not; 1936: Russet Mantle; 1938: Soliloquy; 1939: Miss Swan Expects; 1941: Liberty Jones; 1946: The Voice of the Turtle; 1949: Lend an Ear; 1955: The Teahouse of the August Moon; 1959: Our Town; 1962: Calculated Risk; 1966: Thornton Wilder's Triple Bill; 1969: To Be Young Gifted and Black; Billy; In the Matter of Robert J. Oppenheimer; Our Town; 1970: The Candyapple; 1971: Long Day's Journey Into Night; 1981: Rivers Return; 1991: The Crucible; 1992: A Little Hotel on the Side; The Master Builder; The Sea Gull; 1993: Three Men on a Horse.
Select TV: 1950: Hit the Deck (sp); 1952: Tigers Don't Sing (sp); 1953: Freedom Rings (series); The Intruder (sp); 1954: You Are Only Young Once (sp); 12 Angry Men (sp); 1957: The Princess Back Home (sp); Little Charlie Don't Want a Saddle (sp); 1958: Anxious Night (sp); 1959: Whisper of Evil (sp); 1960: Road to Reality (series); 1962: Farewell to Innocence (sp); 1966: The Easter Angel (sp); 1969: The Town Will Never Be the Same (sp); 1975: The Legend of Lizzie Borden; 1976: The Adams Chronicles (ms); 1977: Eleanor and Franklin: The White House Years; 1979: Jennifer: A Woman's Story; 1988: A Place at the Table (sp); 1990: The Kid Who Loved Christmas.

THE BEATLES

Born: Liverpool, England
Ringo Starr (Richard Starkey)
Born: July 7, 1940.
John Lennon Born: October 9, 1940.
Died: December 8, 1980.
Paul McCartney (James Paul McCartney)
Born: June 18, 1942.
George Harrison Born: February 25, 1943. Died: November 29, 2001.

So much has been written about the musical accomplishments of this rock band phenomenon that the Beatles are often overlooked as one of the more delightful pleasures of the British cinema of the 1960s. At the height of their smashing success in both the United Kingdom and America, they appeared in Richard Lester's rambunctious, delightfully comedic look at the hysteria surrounding them, *A Hard Day's Night*. The film took the cinema world by storm, helping to legitimize the Beatles in the eyes of many who initially took them for a passing fad. There followed another, wackier Lester comedy, *Help!*, and a brief participation in a groundbreaking animated feature that epitomized the psychedelia of the era, *Yellow Submarine*. The documentary, *Let It Be*, released after the group's official breakup in 1970, turned out to be a very sad examination of the disintegration of the Fab Four. For it, they were given the Academy Award for Music Scoring.

John Lennon was the first to venture into acting away from the band, in another Lester film, *How I Won the War*, but it was Ringo, often considered the most natural actor of the four, who was frequently hired for legit roles, notably in *The Magic Christian*, as Peter Seller's adopted son, and in the title role of *Caveman*. Paul McCartney did some film scores (*The Family Way*, *Beyond the Limit*) and songs (including the title tunes for the

James Bond film *Live and Let Die* and *Vanilla Sky*, both of which brought him Oscar nominations), and scripted his own starring feature, *Give My Regards to Broad Street*. George Harrison took up producing, starting with the Monty Python comedy *Life of Brian*, eventually forming Handmade Films. Among his other producing credits were *Time Bandits* (his biggest financial success), *The Missionary*, *A Private Function*, *Withnail and I*, *The Lonely Passion of Judith Hearne*, *How to Get Ahead in Advertising*, and *Nuns on the Run*. The Beatles' major contributions, however, were musical, and all four continued to find individual success in the recording field for years after the breakup. In 1995 Harrison, McCartney, and Starr came together to participate in *The Beatles Anthology*, a massive television and CD documentation of the group. New material was added to a pair of songs Lennon had written before his murder by a deranged fan in 1980.

Screen: BEATLES: **1964:** A Hard Day's Night (and songs); **1965:** Help! (and songs); **1968:** Yellow Submarine (and songs); **1970:** Let It Be (and songs).

LENNON: **1967:** How I Won the War; **1970:** Diaries Notes and Sketches; **1972:** Dynamite Chicken.

McCARTNEY: **1980:** Rockshow; **1984:** Give My Regards to Broad Street (and wr., songs); **1987:** Eat the Rich; **1991:** Get Back.

HARRISON: **1972:** The Concert for Bangladesh (and prod.); **1979:** The Life of Brian (and exec. prod.); **1986:** Water (and exec. prod.); Shanghai Surprise (and exec. prod.).

STARR: **1968:** Candy; **1970:** The Magic Christian; **1971:** 200 Motels; **1972:** Blindman; The Concert for Bangladesh; **1974:** Son of Dracula (and prod.); That'll Be the Day; **1975:** Lisztomania; **1978:** The Last Waltz; **1979:** Sextette; The Kids Are Alright; **1981:** Caveman; **1984:** Give My Regards to Broad Street; **1986:** Water.

Select TV: BEATLES: **1967:** Magical Mystery Tour (sp).

STARR: **1983:** Princess Daisy; **1985:** Alice in Wonderland; **1990–91:** Shining Time Station (series).

STARR AND HARRISON: **1978:** Ringo (sp).

HARRISON: **1978:** The Rutles/All You Need Is Cash (sp).

McCARTNEY: **1973:** James Paul McCartney (sp).

McCARTNEY; HARRISON, AND STARR: **1995:** The Beatles Anthology (sp).

WARREN BEATTY

(HENRY WARREN BEATY)

BORN: RICHMOND, VA, MARCH 30, 1937.

Considering his media reputation as a handsome lothario, Warren Beatty could have spent his career cashing in on his looks, playing vapid roles, or grinding out superficial romantic comedies. Instead he built a respectable résumé by appearing in (and sometimes producing, writing, and directing) mostly intelligent, often challenging commerical projects, and giving some fine performances in them. The younger brother of actress Shirley MacLaine, he studied acting with Stella Adler before debuting in a New Jersey stock production of *Compulsion*. For a brief period he was a cast regular on a sitcom, *The Many Loves of Dobie Gillis*, playing ladies' man Milton Armitage. By the time he left the show he had already made his sole New York stage appearance, in *A Loss of Roses*, which won him a Theatre World Award in 1960. The following year he was brought to Hollywood and never looked back, becoming a star with his very first film, *Splendor in the Grass*, in which he and Natalie Wood portray a young couple in 1920s Kansas whose relationship is destroyed by their meddlesome parents. Soon afterwards he gave one of his few misconceived performances,

playing an Italian gigolo to the much older Vivien Leigh in a botched Tennessee Williams story, *The Roman Spring of Mrs. Stone*. He followed that with a noble failure, *All Fall Down*, as the no-good brother of Brandon De Wilde. There was the weird, self-indulgent *Mickey One*, in which he was a paranoid comedian on the run, and two misfires made in England: *Kaleidoscope*, as a card-sharp who gets himself in trouble with a narcotics smuggler, and the tacky comedy *Promise Her Anything*, playing a Greenwich Village pornographer opposite Leslie Caron, one of the many actresses with whom his name was romantically linked over the years.

It was time for him to take control of a career that was beginning to fall apart, so he sought out Arthur Penn, his *Mickey One* director, for a gangster project he had in mind. The end result, his first credit as actor and producer, was *Bonnie and Clyde*. After an initially lukewarm response from audiences and critics, this mixture of black comedy and violence eventually took the world by storm. This controversial, somewhat fictionalized look at the notorious gangster couple of the Depression era, boasted an exceptional ensemble cast. Beatty himself, as the highly charming, girl-shy mobster, nabbed a pair of Oscar nominations for acting and producing. As *Bonnie and Clyde* came to be considered one of the most influential movies of its time, Beatty's stature in the industry soared and he was proclaimed one of the maverick talents of the day. Three years later he followed up with *The Only Game in Town*, a two-character bomb opposite Elizabeth Taylor and the unfortunate final movie of director George Stevens. But he redeemed himself in two interesting films: the deliberately-paced, hypnotic Robert Altman western, *McCabe and Mrs. Miller*, with Beatty as a gambler setting up a bordello in a snowbound mining town; and a top notch political thriller, *The Parallax View*. However, it was not until Beatty took to producing again that he had another sizeable hit with the sexy and vacuous satire *Shampoo*, playing a bed-hopping Beverly Hills hairdresser. He received his first writing credit (in collaboration with Robert Towne), earning an Oscar nomination for his script. Much better was the 1978 remake of *Here Comes Mr. Jordan*, now retitled *Heaven Can Wait*, in which he played a football star, untimely ripped from life, and desperately trying to reincarnate. He not only produced it but also made his debut as director (in collaboration with Buck Henry). He did a splendid job in updating the piece for modern consumption while still maintaining the light-hearted charm of the original. By receiving Oscar nominations in four categories, Beatty became the first person to achieve this feat since Orson Welles did so with *Citizen Kane*, back in 1941.

His most ambitious project was *Reds*, a lengthy but engrossing look at the growth and distortion of communism as seen through the eyes of journalist John Reed. Beatty actually managed to make the complex tale palatable for a commercial audience, something he always had in mind with any project he approached. The movie won him the Academy Award for Best Director of 1981, while once again bestowing him with nominations for acting, writing, and producing. As was becoming more common, he talked endlessly of ultimately unrealized projects and took far too much time between films. His next production, *Ishtar*, was a vain attempt by he and Dustin Hoffman to capture the fun of the Crosby-Hope *Road* pictures, and it became one of the most notorious flops of the 1980s. Safer fare soon followed, such as the live-action cartoon *Dick Tracy* (on which he also served as director and producer), and *Bugsy*, in which he portrayed another famed gangster of the past, Bugsy Siegel. Beatty's powerful and dangerous performance as the ruthless killer who had charmed his way into the Hollywood social scene was perhaps his best ever and he received another acting nomination to go with his nomination as producer. In addition, he married his leading lady, Annette Bening, in 1992, and then starred with her in the remake of *Love Affair*, which proved to be of little interest to modern audiences. Tackling another risky venture, he directed, wrote, and produced *Bulworth*, playing a politician whose conscience prompts him to tell the truth in the style of a rap artist. He received an Oscar nomination for his script and, despite the movie's mediocre box-office returns, proved that time had not tarnished his image as one of the most interesting personalities and creative minds to have graced the motion picture scene for the past 40 years. There was speculation, in 1999, that he would consider running for president. Unlike Ronald Reagan, the liberal Beatty did not act on this intriguing possibility.

Screen: 1961: Splendor in the Grass; The Roman Spring of Mrs. Stone; 1962: All Fall Down; 1964: Lilith; 1965: Mickey One; 1966: Promise Her Anything; Kaleidoscope; 1967: Bonnie and Clyde (and prod.); 1970: The Only Game in Town; 1971: McCabe and Mrs. Miller; 1972: $ (Dollars); 1974: The Parallax View; 1975: Shampoo (and prod.; co-wr.); The Fortune; 1978: Heaven Can Wait (and co-dir.; prod.; co-wr.); 1981: Reds (and dir.; prod.; co-wr.); 1985: George Stevens: A Filmmaker's Journey; 1987: Ishtar (and prod.); 1990: Dick Tracy (and dir.; prod.); 1991: Truth or Dare; Bugsy (and prod.); 1994: Love Affair (and prod.; co-wr.); 1998: Bulworth (and dir.; co-wr.; prod.); 2001: Town and Country.

NY Stage: 1959: A Loss of Roses.

Select TV: 1957: The Curly-Headed Kid (sp); The Night America Trembled (sp); 1959–60: The Many Loves of Dobie Gillis (series).

LOUISE BEAVERS

BORN: CINCINNATI, OH, MARCH 8, 1902.
DIED: OCTOBER 26, 1962.

Of the two famous black actresses to corner the market in playing maids in the 1930s and 1940s, Louise Beavers was more soft-spoken and less sassy than Hattie McDaniel, but no less welcome a presence. She did, in fact, start out in life as a maid to actress Leatrice Joy, before doing bit roles and extra work in silent movies. Finally securing a larger part, as a cook, in the 1927 film of *Uncle Tom's Cabin*, her legitimate movie career was launched. As an indication of how low a black performer's standing was in the industry at this period, Beavers not only portrayed Lilyan Tashman's maid in the film *Gold Diggers of Broadway*, but did that very task off screen for a spell to help supplement her income. She assumed literally dozens of domestic supporting parts, including *She Done Him Wrong*, in which she swapped some crisp dialogue with Mae West, and *Mr. Blandings Builds His Dream House*, in which her slogan for 'Wham' ham saves the day. She took a substantial role as the pancake maker whose daughter passes for white in the 1934 version of *Imitation of Life*, bringing considerable dignity and warmth to a character who was not without her infuriating traits. Unlike her co-star, Claudette Colbert, the success of the movie did absolutely nothing to change her position in Hollywood. There was another good-sized role in the Bobby Breen musical *Rainbow on the River*, playing the former slave whose love rescues the lad from a life with his crabby grandmother, May Robson; and she had a nice moment in *Holiday Inn*, where she got to participate in the number "Abraham." Although her television series, *Beulah*, had her back in an apron, it was at least a starring role. Not surprisingly, Hattie McDaniel had done the part on radio and even filled

in for Beavers during the show's television run.

Screen: 1927: Uncle Tom's Cabin; 1929: Coquette; Barnum Was Right; Glad Rag Doll; Gold Diggers of Broadway; Nix on Dames; Wall Street; 1930: Wide Open; She Couldn't Say No; Back Pay; True to the Navy; Our Blushing Brides; Manslaughter; Safety in Numbers; 1931: Party Husbands; Annabelle's Affairs; Heaven on Earth; Don't Bet on Women; Reckless Living; Girls About Town; Sundown Trail; Good Sport; Ladies of the Big House; Six Cylinder Love; Up for Murder; Millie; 1932: The Expert; Freaks; Night World; It's Tough to Be Famous; Young America; Street of Women; What Price Hollywood?; The Strange Love of Molly Louvain; Midnight Lady; The Dark Horse; Unashamed; Divorce in the Family; Wild Girl; Too Busy to Work; 1933: Pick-Up; What Price Innocence? A Shriek in the Night; Her Bodyguard; Girl Missing; 42nd Street; She Done Him Wrong; Central Airport; The Big Cage; The Phantom Broadcast; Midnight Mary; Hold Your Man; In the Money; Only Yesterday; Jimmy and Sally; Notorious But Nice; Bombshell; Her Splendid Folly; 1934: Bedside; In the Money; I've Got Your Number; Cheaters; Glamour; The Merry Frinks; Imitation of Life; I Believed in You; I Give My Love; Palooka; Hat, Coat and Glove; Merry Wives of Reno; A Modern Hero; Registered Nurse; 1935: West of the Pecos; Annapolis Farewell; 1936: Bullets or Ballots; Wives Never Know; General Spanky; The Gorgeous Hussy; Rainbow on the River; 1937: Make Way for Tomorrow; Wings Over Honolulu; Love in a Bungalow; The Last Gangster; 1938: Scandal Street; Life Goes On; Brother Rat; Reckless Living; The Headleys at Home; Peck's Bad Boy With the Circus; 1939: Made for Each Other; The Lady's From Kentucky; Reform School; 1940: Women Without Names; Parole Fixer; No Time for Comedy; I Want a Divorce; 1941: Virginia; Belle Starr; Sign of the Wolf; Shadow of the Thin Man; The Vanishing Virginian; 1942: Reap the Wild Wind; Young America; Holiday Inn; The Big Street; Tennessee Johnson; Seven Sweethearts; 1943: Good Morning Judge; Du Barry Was a Lady; Top Man; All by Myself; Jack London; There's Something About a Soldier; 1944: Follow the Boys; South of Dixie; Dixie Jamboree; Barbary Coast Gent; 1945: Delightfully Dangerous; 1946: Lover Come Back; Young Widow; 1947: Banjo; 1948: Good Sam; Mr. Blandings Builds His Dream House; For the Love of Mary; 1949: Tell It to the Judge; 1950: Girls' School; My Blue Heaven; The Jackie Robinson Story; 1952: Colorado Sundown; I Dream of Jeannie; Never Wave at a WAC; 1956: Goodbye, My Lady; You Can't Run Away From It; Teenage Rebel; 1957: Tammy and the Bachelor; 1958: The Goddess; 1960: All the Fine Young Cannibals; The Facts of Life.

Select TV: 1952–53: Beulah (series); 1955: Cleopatra Collins (sp); 1957: The Hostess With the Mostess (sp); 1959: Swamp Fox (series).

WALLACE BEERY

BORN: KANSAS CITY, MO, APRIL 1, 1885.
DIED: APRIL 15, 1949.

The most unlikely superstar of Hollywood's golden era, gravel-voiced Wallace Beery was a jowly, imposing, lovable lug who didn't mind hamming it for appreciative audiences. After a brief stint with the circus he followed older brother Noah into the theatre where, of all things, they worked as chorus boys in various musical touring shows. Ending up in Chicago, he was hired by Essany Pictures in 1914 to star in a series of one-reelers, outrageously dressed in drag as a Swedish housemaid named Swedie. After working as both an actor and director at Universal, he moved over to Keystone where he acted with Gloria Swanson, to whom he was briefly wed (1916–18). Soon he was being noticed for his villainous roles in movies like *Patria*, a serial; *The Unpardonable Sin*, where he tried to force himself upon the heroine, Blanche Sweet; and the 1920 version of *The Last of the Mohicans*, as the evil Indian, Magua. There was no predicting what nationality Beery would show up as: he was German in *Behind the Door* and *The Four Horsemen of the Apocalypse*; Chinese in *A Tale of Two Worlds* and *I Am the Law*; and Russian in *Bavu*. Douglas Fairbanks's big hit, *Robin Hood*, found him playing Richard the Lionheart (a role he repeated in a movie of that same name); *Three Ages* cast him as Buster Keaton's nemesis; and *The Man from Hell's River* found him in support of the cinema's most famous German Shepherd, Rin-Tin-Tin. He was busy but he was not yet a star. The parts started to improve, however, with Beery ending up in the star slot for *The Devil's Cargo*, as a stoker who turns out to be Satan; and as the leader of the expedition in the creaky dinosaur adventure *The Lost World*.

Paramount signed him to their roster in 1925 and he had a breakthrough with an army comedy, *Behind the Front*, in which he was teamed with Raymond Hatton. The movie was successful enough to indicate that he might not have to keep playing bad guys to pay the rent. There were several follow-ups with Hatton, starting with *We're in the Navy Now* and ending with *The Big Killing*, by which time there was zero public interest. So it was back to being bad for *Beggars of Life* and *Chinatown Nights* before the studio dropped him just as sound was coming in. MGM couldn't have made a wiser move when they snatched him up shortly thereafter, assigning him another bad guy role but one that would give his career a vital shot in the arm. For his ferociously full-bodied portrayal of the murderous convict Butch, in the prison drama *The Big House* (1930), he received an Oscar nomination. In *Min and Bill*, released that same year, he had an even more significant part. Sparring with Marie Dressler, he set the tone for all the worthless but loveable oafs that audiences would line up to see him play. He was, at last, a star. The following year he poured it on thick as the washed-up prizefighter, whose love of the bottle is surpassed only by his love for his ever-weeping kid, Jackie Cooper, in *The Champ*. One of the seminal tearjerkers of the period and an enormous box-office hit, it won Beery an Academy Award in the only tie in the Best Actor category to date. (He shared honors with Fredric March.) He also did quite well with *Hell Divers*, a routine aerial drama with Clark Gable, who also appeared with him in *The Secret Six*, in which Beery was an arrogant gangster rising to the top of his game.

He was now firmly fixed in MGM's firmament of stars and was being treated as such. He participated in *Grand Hotel*, as the bullying financier, another smash and the Oscar-winner for Best Picture of 1931–32. Continuing his run of good fortune, he did *Tugboat Annie*, another bullseye teaming with Dressler; *Dinner at Eight*, in which he and Jean Harlow — in the best of the movie's multiple subplots — were a wonderfully uncouth rich couple; *Viva Villa*, as the volatile Mexican revolutionary, which was a terrific meeting of actor and role if you overlooked his uncertain accent; and *Treasure Island*, as an effective Long John Silver to Jackie Cooper's Jim Hawkins. He was alongside Cooper again in a loan-out to 20th Century for the rousingly rude *The Bowery*. Also for that company he played the famed circus showman in *The Mighty Barnum*, a role he reprised from *A Lady's Morals*. Returning to Metro he was Robert Young's dad, trying to make a top flyer out of the kid, in *West Point of the Air*, after which he was up to no good again, in *China Seas*, where former co-star Clark Gable now rated billing above him. Beery was cast to perfection as the womanizing drunkard in the family drama *Ah,*

Wilderness!, before doing *O'Shaughnessy's Boy* — again with Jackie Cooper. This was a shameless rehash of *The Champ*, with the locale changed from the boxing world to the circus.

By 1936 he still had a loyal following, but MGM decided he was better off in programmers, usually westerns or adventure tales with a touch of roguish good spirits. The budgets had shrunk but he never strayed far from the slobs people came to expect of him, including *The Good Old Soak*, drunk again; *Bad Man of Brimstone*, as bandit "Trigger" Bill; *Stablemates*, with Mickey Rooney replacing Jackie Cooper, and proving to be a more ideal screen partner; and *Thunder Afloat*, as a tugboat captain. MGM tried out Marjorie Rambeau in a very Marie Dressler-like role opposite Beery in *20 Mule Team*, but they had better luck later that year when Marjorie Main showed up for a small part in *Wyoming*. Main's sassy ripostes, aimed at Beery's no-good lout, made for some broad knockabout fun. This crude duo added zing to five more films: *Barnacle Bill*; *The Bugle Sounds*; the memorably titled *Jackass Mail*; the topical *Rationing*; and *Bad Bascomb*, which gave Beery another sobbing child co-star in the form of Margaret O'Brien. Figuring enough years had passed since *The Champ*, MGM made a blatant attempt to recapture past glories by casting Beery as a prizefighter opposite boy star Dean Stockwell in *The Mighty McGurk*. The results were not encouraging. Beery had one last box-office hit, *A Date With Judy*, at one point dancing with Carmen Miranda, but it was really Jane Powell's showcase. By the time his last movie, *Big Jack*, was released in 1949, he was dead of a heart attack.

Screen (features): 1917: Patria (serial); The Little American; **1918:** Johanna Enlists; **1919:** The Unpardonable Sin; The Love Burglar; Soldiers of Fortune; Victory; Behind the Door; **1920:** The Virgin of Stamboul; The Mollycoddle; The Round-Up; The Last of the Mohicans; **1921:** The Rookie's Return; 813; The Four Horsemen of the Apocalypse; A Tale of Two Worlds; The Northern Trail; The Golden Snare; The Last Trail; **1922:** The Rosary; Wild Honey; The Man From Hell's River; I Am the Law; Trouble; Hurricane's Gal; Robin Hood; The Sagebush Trail; Only a Shopgirl; **1923:** The Flame of Life; Stormswept; Patsy; Bavu; Ashes of Vengeance; Drifting; The Three Ages; The Eternal Struggle; The Spanish Dancer; Richard the Lion-Hearted; White Tiger; **1924:** Drums of Jeopardy; The Signal Tower; Unseen Hands; Another Man's Wife; The Sea Hawk; The Red Lily; Dynamite Smith; Madonna of the Streets; **1925:** Let Women Alone; So Big; The Devil's Cargo; The Lost World; The Great Divide; Coming Through; Adventure; The Night Club; In the Name of Love; Rugged Water; The Wanderer; The Pony Express; **1926:** Behind the Front; Volcano; Old Ironsides; We're in the Navy Now; **1927:** Casey at the Bat; Fireman, Save My Child; Now We're in the Air; **1928:** Wife Savers; Partners in Crime; The Big Killing; Beggars of Life; **1929:** Chinatown Nights; Stairs of Sand; River of Romance; **1930:** The Big House; A Lady's Morals; Billy the Kid; Min and Bill; Way for a Sailor; **1931:** The Secret Six; The Champ; Hell Divers; **1932:** Grand Hotel; Flesh; **1933:** Tugboat Annie; Dinner at Eight; The Bowery; **1934:** Viva Villa!; Treasure Island; The Mighty Barnum; **1935:** West Point of the Air; China Seas; O'Shaughnessy's Boy; Ah, Wilderness!; **1936:** A Message to Garcia; Old Hutch; **1937:** The Good Old Soak; Slave Ship; Bad Man of Brimstone; **1938:** Port of Seven Seas; Stablemates; **1939:** Stand Up and Fight; Sergeant Madden; Thunder Afloat; **1940:** The Man From Dakota; 20 Mule Team; Wyoming; **1941:** The Bad Man; Barnacle Bill; **1942:** The Bugle Sounds; Jackass Mail; **1943:** Salute to the Marines; **1944:** Rationing; Barbary Coast Gent; **1945:** This Man's Navy; **1946:** Bad Bascomb; The

Mighty McGurk; **1948:** Alias a Gentleman; A Date With Judy; **1949:** Big Jack.
NY Stage: 1907: A Yankee Tourist.

ED BEGLEY

BORN: HARTFORD, CT, MARCH 25, 1901.
DIED: APRIL 28, 1970.

A relative latecomer to movies, the stocky, gruff Ed Begley nonetheless became one of the busier character actors of the postwar era. A former radio announcer, he made his New York stage debut in 1943, in *Land of Fame*. Four years later he came to movies in one of the fine docudramas of the period, *Boomerang!*, followed by another of that genre, *The Street With No Name*, and the hit comedy *Sitting Pretty*, as one of the town big shots exposed in Clifton Webb's tell-all book. His other Hollywood credits included *Dark City*, as an ill-fated gambler; *You're in the Navy Now*, as a port commander; *Deadline U.S.A.*, as a newspaper editor; and *Odds Against Tomorrow*, as a nasty, corrupt ex-cop. He won acclaim on Broadway for alternating both lawyer roles in *Inherit the Wind*, before returning to Hollywood to give his two best performances: in *Patterns*, as a businessman whose life is shattered when he is replaced by Van Heflin; and as the bigoted juror in *12 Angry Men*. His Academy Award came in 1962 for playing the powerful political boss in *Sweet Bird of Youth*, after which he did a bit of dancing in the musical *The Unsinkable Molly Brown*; was a Texas billionaire running an anti-communist organization in *Billion Dollar Brain*; led the lynch mob that tried to string up Clint Eastwood in *Hang 'em High*; and did the frug with Rita Hayworth in his farewell film, *Road to Salina*. His son is actor Ed Begley, Jr.
Screen: 1947: Boomerang!; The Roosevelt Story (narrator); The Web; **1948:** Sitting Pretty; Deep Waters; The Street With No Name; Sorry Wrong Number; **1949:** It Happens Every Spring; The Great Gatsby; Tulsa; **1950:** Saddle Tramp; Dark City; Stars in My Crown; Wyoming Mail; Backfire; Convicted; **1951:** You're in the Navy Now/USS Teakettle; The Lady From Texas; On Dangerous Ground; **1952:** Boots Malone; Deadline USA; Lone Star; The Turning Point; **1956:** Patterns; **1957:** 12 Angry Men; **1959:** Odds Against Tomorrow; **1961:** The Green Helmet; **1962:** Sweet Bird of Youth; **1964:** The Unsinkable Molly Brown; **1966:** The Oscar; **1967:** Warning Shot; Billion Dollar Brain; **1968:** Hang 'em High; Wild in the Streets; Firecreek; A Time to Sing; **1969:** The Monitors; The Violent Enemy; **1970:** The Dunwich Horror; **1971:** Road to Salina.
NY Stage: 1943: Land of Fame; Get Away Old Man; **1944:** Pretty Little Parlor; **1947:** All My Sons; **1954:** All Summer Long; **1955:** Inherit the Wind; **1957:** A Shadow of My Enemy; **1958:** Look Homeward Angel; **1960:** Semi-Detached; Advise and Consent; **1969:** Zelda; Our Town.
Select TV: 1952: Leave It to Larry (series); **1965:** Inherit the Wind (sp); **1969:** The Silent Gun.

BARBARA BEL GEDDES

BORN: NEW YORK, NY, OCTOBER 31, 1922.

Hollywood, apparently, didn't think very much of Barbara Bel Geddes and the feeling appeared to be mutual. Each time she scored a success on the stage, be it in *Cat on a Hot Tin Roof*, or in *Mary, Mary*, she was never asked to repeat her role in the movie adaptation. Bel Geddes, the daughter of a noted stage designer, debuted on Broadway in 1942,

in *Out of the Frying Pan*, and had her first major hit with *Deep Are the Roots* two years later, winning a Theatre World Award. A year after her first movie, *The Long Night*, as a girl trying to convince fugitive Henry Fonda to give himself up, she received an Academy Award nomination for her beautiful portrayal of the aspiring young writer, Katrin, in *I Remember Mama* (1948). After her effective work in two top notch dramas at Fox, *Panic in the Streets*, as Richard Widmark's wife, and *Fourteen Hours*, trying to talk suicidal Richard Basehart out of jumping from a window ledge, she was back on the stage where she remained a top attraction. When she did return to films, in Hitchcock's *Vertigo*, it was clearly in support. That James Stewart's character opted for Kim Novak over Bel Geddes is clearly a case of sex winning out over personality. She then played loyal spouse to Danny Kaye, as musician "Red" Nichols, in *The Five Pennies*, and did two unworthy melodramas: *5 Branded Women*, getting her head shaved for cavorting with the enemy, and *By Love Possessed*, reduced to supporting Lana Turner. She showed up unexpectedly in two 1971 films but decided thereafter to concentrate on television, where she won a whole new legion of admirers, and a 1980 Emmy Award, playing the matriarch Miss Ellie on the popular nighttime soap *Dallas*. She also wrote and illustrated children's books, including *I Like to Be Me* (1963) and *So Do I* (1972).
Screen: 1947: The Long Night; **1948:** I Remember Mama; Blood on the Moon; **1949:** Caught; **1950:** Panic in the Streets; **1951:** Fourteen Hours; **1958:** Vertigo; **1959:** The Five Pennies; **1960:** 5 Branded Women; **1961:** By Love Possessed; **1971:** Summertree; The Todd Killings.
NY Stage: 1941: Out of the Frying Pan; **1942:** Little Darling; **1943:** Nine Girls; **1944:** Mrs. January and Mr. X; **1945:** Deep are the Roots; **1950:** Burning Bright; **1951:** The Moon Is Blue; **1954:** The Living Room; **1955:** Cat on a Hot Tin Roof; **1956:** The Sleeping Prince; **1959:** Silent Night, Holy Night; **1961:** Mary, Mary; Luv; **1967:** Everything in the Garden; **1973:** Finishing Touches.
Select TV: 1950: Rebecca (sp); The Philadelphia Story (sp); **1957:** Fifty Beautiful Girls (sp); The Morning After (sp); **1958:** Rumors of Evening (sp); The Desperate Age (sp); The Hasty Heart (sp); **1977:** Our Town (sp); **1978–84/1985–90:** Dallas (series).

HARRY BELAFONTE

BORN: NEW YORK, NY, MARCH 1, 1927.
RAISED IN JAMAICA, WEST INDIES.

This velvet-voiced singing sensation of the 1950s made some very effective ventures into acting before opting to concentrate on recording and social issues. Early on, Belafonte was a nightclub performer and a regular on a forgotten television series, *Sugar Hill Times*. He began to draw attention as a folk singer in the Broadway revue *John Murray Anderson's Almanac*, winning a Tony Award in 1953. Soon he was a regular television attraction, helping to popularize calypso music. He gave a fine performance as the soldier ensnared by Dorothy Dandridge in the musical *Carmen Jones* (although his singing voice was, inexplicably, dubbed!); created an interracial stir by romancing Joan Fontaine in *Island in the Sun*; and thought he was the last man on earth for the first half hour of the atmospheric *The World, the Flesh, and the Devil*, until Inger Stevens and Mel Ferrer showed up. During the 1960s he became a fervent civil rights activist and experienced racism firsthand when a 1968 television appearance with Petula Clark sparked complaints from executives who were shocked when she touched him during a love duet. Among his later big screen appearances he had the title role in *The Angel Levine*, sent to earth to help Zero Mostel; did a broad Godfather parody in the 1974 comedy *Uptown Saturday Night*; returned after a long hiatus for a starring role in the interesting reverse racism parable *White Man's Burden*; and was the saving grace of a Robert Altman misfire, *Kansas City*, as a vicious Depression-era mobster. He also served as producer on the 1984 film *Beat Street* and of such stage plays as *To Be Young Gifted and Black*. He won an Emmy Award for the 1960 special *Tonight With Belafonte*. His daughter is model-actress Shari Belafonte.

Screen: 1953: Bright Road; 1954: Carmen Jones; 1957: Island in the Sun; 1959: The World, the Flesh, and the Devil; Odds Against Tomorrow; 1970: The Angel Levine; King: A Filmed Record…Montgomery to Memphis; 1972: Buck and the Preacher; 1974: Uptown Saturday Night; 1992: The Player; 1994: Ready to Wear/ Prêt-à-Porter; 1995: White Man's Burden; 1996: Kansas City.

NY Stage: 1953: John Murray Anderson's Almanac.

Select TV: 1949: Sugar Hill Times (series); 1955: Three for Tonight (sp); Winner by Decision (sp); 1960: Tonight With Belafonte (sp); 1981: Grambling's White Tiger; 1999: Swing Vote.

RALPH BELLAMY

BORN: CHICAGO, IL, JUNE 17, 1904.
DIED: NOVEMBER 29, 1991.

Best known for playing second leads who inevitably lost the girl to the star, Ralph Bellamy got his revenge, in a way, by surviving far longer than most of those stars he supported. The veteran of some 15 stock companies and founder of his own theatre group, the Ralph Bellamy Players, he made his Broadway debut in *Town Boy*, in 1929. Signed to a contract by producer Joseph Schenck in 1931 he made his film debut on loan-out to MGM in the gangster melodrama *The Secret Six*, getting shot in the back by Wallace Beery. After being loaned out again, this time to Paramount, he garnered some attention playing a blind soldier in love with Ruth Chatterton in *The Magnificent Lie*, but was dropped by Schenck. He did not have to wait long for work. Over the next six years he appeared in close to 50 movies, though usually as nothing more than a reliable stock player. Among his free-lance assignments during this period were *Young America*, as a good-hearted judge running a juvenile court; *Rebecca of Sunnybrook Farm*, as a doctor; *The Woman in Room 13*, as a politician swearing vengeance on his ex-wife; *Destination Unknown*, as a mysterious stowaway; *Picture Snatcher*, as James Cagney's editor; *Spitfire*, as a construction engineer watching out for mountain girl Katharine Hepburn; *The Healer* (for Monogram), as a doctor with miraculous powers; *Hands Across the Table*, as a crippled aviator in love with manicurist Carole Lombard; and *The Man Who Lived Twice*, as a fugitive who agrees to a rehabilitation experiment, a part that allowed him to take on a second pesonality. Appreciation came in the form of an Oscar nomination for his very funny performance as the charmingly brainless Oklahoman Daniel Leeson, losing Irene Dunne to Cary Grant in Leo McCarey's *The Awful Truth*. Although this marked a career highpoint, it also branded him as the ultimate "other man," ready to surrender the leading lady to the higher-salaried star as the script dictated.

He inevitably lost Ginger Rogers to Fred Astaire in *Carefree*; was the frustrated movie producer in *Boy Meets Girl*; played a psychologist held hostage in his home by some escaped cons in *Blind Alley*; and topped all other stints in the luckless boyfriend department with director Howard Hawks's delightful *His Girl*

Friday, when Grant (again!) plucked Rosalind Russell away from him. During the early 1940s he starred as the famous detective Ellery Queen in four lowly-regarded mysteries, and became part of horror-movie history playing Colonel Montford in Universal's *The Wolf Man*. Staying on at that studio he was the hero in another horror exercise, *The Ghost of Frankenstein*; didn't get Irene Dunne (again!) at the fade out of *Lady in a Jam*; and played dual roles as a German Baron and an Englishman in *The Great Impersonation*. Leaving the movies in 1945, he returned to the stage, scoring three hits on Broadway: *State of the Union*, *Detective Story*, and, most notably, *Sunrise at Campobello*. His uncanny, Tony Award-winning impersonation of Franklin Roosevelt, which he repeated in the 1960 movie adaptation, would, in a way, become his signature role. Over 20 years later he played FDR once again, in the massive mini-series *The Winds of War*. As he grew older Bellamy appeared sporadically on screen as a fine character actor, including roles in *The Professionals*, hiring Burt Lancaster to get his young bride back; *Rosemary's Baby*, as an evil doctor; and scoring a notable triumph as one of the scheming brothers in the 1983 comedy hit *Trading Places*. One of the founders of the Screen Actors Guild, he also served four terms (1952–64) as president of Actors Equity. He published his autobiography, *When the Smoke Hits the Fan*, in 1979, and was presented with a special Academy Award in 1986.

Screen: 1931: The Secret Six; The Magnificent Lie; Surrender; 1932: West of Broadway; Forbidden; Disorderly Conduct; Young America; The Woman in Room 13; Rebecca of Sunnybrook Farm; Almost Married; Wild Girl; Air Mail; 1933: Second Hand Wife; Parole Girl; Destination Unknown; Picture Snatcher; The Narrow Corner; Below the Sea; Headliner Shooter; Flying Devils; Blind Adventure; Ace of Aces; Ever in My Heart; 1934: Spitfire; This Man Is Mine; One to Every Woman; Before Midnight; One Is Guilty; Girl in Danger; The Crime of Helen Stanley; Woman in the Dark; 1935: Helldorado; The Wedding Night; Rendezvous at Midnight; Eight Bells; Air Hawks; The Healer; Gigolette; Navy Wife; Hands Across the Table; 1936: Dangerous Intrigue; Roaming Lady; Straight from the Shoulder; The Final Hour; Wild Brian Kent; The Man Who Lived Twice; Counterfeit Lady; 1937: Let's Get Married; It Can't Last Forever; The Awful Truth; 1938: The Crime of Dr. Hallet; Fools for Scandal; Boy Meets Girl; Carefree; Girls' School; Trade Winds; 1939: Let Us Live; Smashing the Spy Ring; Blind Alley; Coast Guard; 1940: His Girl Friday; Flight Angels; Brother Orchid; Queen of the Mob; Dance, Girl, Dance; Public Deb No. 1; Ellery Queen — Master Detective; Meet the Wildcat; 1941: Ellery Queen's Penthouse Mystery; Footsteps in the Dark; Affectionately Yours; Ellery Queen and the Perfect Crime; Dive Bomber; Ellery Queen and the Murder Ring; The Wolf Man; 1942: The Ghost of Frankenstein; Lady in a Jam; Men of Texas; The Great Impersonation; 1943: Stage Door Canteen; 1944: Guest in the House; 1945: Delightfully Dangerous; Lady on a Train; 1955: The Court-Martial of Billy Mitchell; 1960: Sunrise at Campobello; 1966: The Professionals; 1968: Rosemary's Baby; 1971: Doctors' Wives; 1972: Cancel My Reservation; 1977: Oh, God!; 1983: Trading Places; 1987: Disorderlies; Amazon Women on the Moon; 1988: Coming to America; The Good Mother; 1990: Pretty Woman.

NY Stage: 1929: Town Boy; 1930: Roadside; 1943: Tomorrow the World; 1945: State of the Union; 1949: Detective Story; 1958: Sunrise at Campobello.

Select TV: 1949–54: Man Against Crime (series); 1954: Fearful Decision (sp); 1955: Like Father, Like Son (sp); The Devil's Disciple (sp); 1956: The Starlet (sp); Honor (sp); The Film Maker (sp); Heritage of Anger (sp); 1957: The Locked Door (sp);

1957–59: To Tell the Truth (series); 1961: The Dispossessed (sp); Frontier Justice (series); 1963–64: The Eleventh Hour (series); 1967: Wings of Fire; 1969: The Immortal; 1969–70: The Survivors (series); 1970–71: The Most Deadly Game (series); 1971: Owen Marshall — Counsellor at Law/A Pattern of Morality; 1972: Something Evil; 1974: The Missiles of October (sp); 1975: Log of the Black Pearl; Adventures of the Queen; Search for the Gods; Murder on Flight 502; 1976: McNaughton's Daughter; Return to Earth; Nightmare in Badham County; The Boy in the Plastic Bubble; Arthur Hailey's The Moneychangers; 1976–77: Once an Eagle (ms); 1977: Hunter (series); Testimony of Two Men (ms) Charlie Cobb: Nice Night for a Hanging; 1978: Wheels (ms); The Clone Master; The Millionaire; 1979: The Billion Dollar Threat; 1980: Power (ms); The Memory of Eva Ryker; Condominium (ms); 1983: The Winds of War (ms); 1984: Love Leads the Way; 1985: Space (ms); 1989: Christine Cromwell: Things That Go Bump in the Night; War and Remembrance (ms).

JEAN-PAUL BELMONDO

BORN: NEUILLY-SUR-SEINE, FRANCE, APRIL 9, 1933.

This lanky French actor found his place in movie history starring in one of the most influential films of all time, director Jean-Luc Godard's new-wave classic *Breathless*. Epitomizing the anti-hero of the era, he became one of France's most cherished stars and a darling of the American art-house circuit. After studying at the Conservatoire he played a few movie roles and starred on the Paris stage in *Oscar*. 1959 brought him his first significant part, in *Classe Tous Risques* (*The Big Risk*) but everthing paled next to the Godard film which opened in Europe later that year. Belmondo's restless hoodlum Michel was the centerpiece of *Breathless/A Bout de Souffle*, which broke conventions with its spontaneous, jump cut, offhanded style of moviemaking, leading the way for generations of directors to imitate. Three of his most popular features during the 1960s were the powerful *Two Women* opposite Sophia Loren in her Oscar-winning role; the costume epic *Cartouche*; and the playful chase movie *That Man From Rio*, his biggest moneymaker. He was also found in such international all-star offerings as *Is Paris Burning?* and *Casino Royale*, but, unlike many foreign stars of the day, never risked a transition to American films. His output was smaller as he reached his 50s, many of his features not being exported to the U.S. After a long absence he did show up on the American art house screens in the update of *Les Misérables*, in 1995. His autobiography, published at the height of his popularity, when he was only 30, is entitled *Thirty Years and Twenty-Five Films* (1963).

Screen (US releases only): 1960: Breathless; 1961: Two Women; The Cheaters; Love and the Frenchwoman; Leda; 1962: La Viaccia; 1963: Monkey in Winter; 1964: Sweet and Sour; Cartouche; A Woman Is a Woman; That Man From Rio; Doulos — The Finger Man; Moderato Cantabile; 1965: Banana Peel; Male Hunt; Backfire; Weekend at Dunkirk; Greed in the Sun; 1966: Up to His Ears; The Winner; Is Paris Burning?; 1967: Casino Royale; Tender Scoundrel; The Thief of Paris; 1969: Pierrot Le Fou; The Brain; 1970: Love Is a Funny Thing; Mississippi Mermaid; Borsalino; 1972: The Burglars; 1973: The Inheritor; 1974: Stavisky; 1975: Night Caller; 1976: Le Magnifique; 1980: The Incorrigible; The Hunter (Will Get You!); 1995: Les Misérables.

Additional European Titles: 1957: Sois Belle et Tais-toi; 1959: A Double Tour; Classe Tous Risques; 1961: Leon Morin — Priest; 1972: Docteur Popaul; 1975: L'Alpageur (and exec. prod.; co-wr.); 1976: Le Corps de Mon Ennemi (and prod.); 1977: L'Animal; 1984: Joyeuses Paques (and prod.).

ROBERT BENCHLEY

BORN: WORCESTER, MA, SEPTEMBER 15, 1889. ED: HARVARD. DIED: NOVEMBER 21, 1945.

Immortal humorist and Algonquin Round Table member, Robert Benchley hadn't any intention of becoming a movie star but did just the same, first in a series of short subjects, and then as a sardonic supporting player who stole many a feature film in the early 1940s. Originally employed in advertising, Benchley rose to associate editor of the *New York Tribune* to editor of the *Tribune Graphic* to managing editor of *Vanity Fair*. His reputation was made, however, through his humorous columns in the *New York World*, theatre reviews in *The New Yorker*, and his series of bumbling comical lectures. The last led to his long running comical shorts, the "How to…" series, in which he gave amusingly wrong-headed advice on how to accomplish inane, everyday tasks. One of them, "How to Sleep," won the Academy Award for Best Live-Action Short Subject of 1935. Later he appeared in many features, usually cast as a slightly befuddled, quipping, self-depreciating fellow often with an eye for a pretty girl he had no chance of obtaining. In a memorable attempt to proposition Ginger Rogers in *The Major and the Minor*, he made the oft-quoted suggestion that she "slip out of that wet coat and into a dry martini." In a rare starring role of sorts he visited the Disney Studios for an inside look at the facilities in *The Reluctant Dragon*. He wrote the 1922 Broadway show *The 49ers*. Both his son, Nathaniel (*The Off Islanders*) and grandson Peter (*Jaws*) became writers.

Screen (shorts): 1928: The Treasurer's Report; The Sex Life of the Polyp; The Spellbinder; 1929: Furnace Trouble; Lesson Number One; Stewed Fried and Boiled; 1933: Your Technocracy and Mine; 1935: How to Sleep; How to Break 90 at Croquet; 1936: How to Behave; How to Train a Dog; How to Vote; How to Be a Detective; 1937: The Romance of Digestion; How to Start the Day; A Night at the Movies; 1938: Music Made Simple; How to Figure Income Tax; An Evening Alone; The Courtship of the Newt; Opening Day; Mental Poise; How to Raise a Baby; How to Read; How to Watch Football; How to Sub-let; 1939: How to Eat; An Hour for Lunch; Dark Magic; Home Early; The Day of Rest; See Your Doctor; 1940: Home Movies; That Inferior Feeling; The Trouble With Husbands; 1941: How to Take a Vacation; Waiting for Baby; Crime Control; The Forgotten Man; 1942: Nothing But Nerves; The Witness; The Man's Angle; Keeping in Shape; 1943: My Tomato; No News Is Good News; 1944: Important Business; Why Daddy?; 1945: I'm a Civilian Here Myself; Boogie Woogie.

Screen (features): 1932: The Sport Parade; 1933: Headline Shooter; Dancing Lady; 1934: Rafter Romance; Social Register; 1935: China Seas; 1936: Piccadilly Jim; 1937: Live, Love and Learn; Broadway Melody of 1938; 1940: Hired Wife; Foreign Correspondent; 1941: Nice Girl?; The Reluctant Dragon; Bedtime Story; You'll Never Get Rich; Three Girls About Town; 1942: Take a Letter, Darling; The Major and the Minor; I Married a Witch; 1943: Flesh and Fantasy; The Sky's the Limit; Song of Russia; Young and Willing; 1944: National Barn Dance; Her Primitive Man; Janie; Practically

Yours; See Here, Private Hargrove; **1945:** Duffy's Tavern; It's in the Bag; Kiss and Tell; Pan-American; Week-end at the Waldorf; The Stork Club; Snafu; **1946:** Road to Utopia; The Bride Wore Boots; Janie Gets Married.

NY Stage: 1927: Nantucket Follies.

WILLIAM BENDIX

BORN: BROOKLYN, NY, JANUARY 4, 1906.
DIED: DECEMBER 14, 1964.

Following in the footsteps that Wallace Beery had implanted on the cinematic landscape of the 1930s, William Bendix was the equivalent husky, seemingly slow-witted, and lovable lug of the 1940s. As a child he appeared in a Vitagraph short, the name of which seems to have been forgotten. He also played minor league baseball and managed a grocery store in Newark, NJ, while acting with the New Jersey Federal Project. This led to Broadway and the role of the cop in the original 1939 production of William Saroyan's *The Time of Your Life*, winning the attention of the film industry. He simultaneously debuted on screen in support of Tracy and Hepburn in their first teaming, *Woman of the Year*, as a friend of the former, and in a Hal Roach "B," *Brooklyn Orchid*. It was Paramount, however, who snatched him up and put him under contract, impressed by his work in two films for them, *Wake Island*, right at home as a Marine, and *The Glass Key*, where he really registered, as a brutish bodyguard. Since his contract fell into the non-exclusive category, Bendix could be seen all over, supporting Abbott and Costello in Universal's *Who Done It?*; returning to Roach for the starring role in another quickie, *Taxi Mister?*, and re-enlisting with the Marines for Fox's *Guadalcanal Diary*, which, like *Wake Island*, was a big war time hit. There were leads in failures like the film adaptation of Eugene O'Neill's *The Hairy Ape* (UA) and the sentimental Hollywoodized take on *The Babe Ruth Story* (AA), but also fine work in Hitchcock's superb ensemble at Fox, *Lifeboat*, as a hapless seaman whose leg has to be amputated.

Abroad With Two Yanks found him in drag, which was guaranteed for some laughs because he was about the last actor to look comfortable in a dress; *Don Juan Quilligan*, made him a bigamist, albeit a comical one; and *The Dark Corner*, cast him as a hired killer, which allowed to him appear with a performer who might be considered his polar opposite, the snooty Clifton Webb. When it came time to film *The Time of Their Life*, he ended up, ironically, playing a different role than his stage one; this time cast as the bartender. Not unexpectedly he could pour on the oaf routine a bit much and there was a touch of ham to his portrayal of Alan Ladd's unhinged buddy in the famous noir thriller *The Blue Dahlia*. He could be found giving solid comic support to Paramount's two biggest attractions, Bob Hope in *Where There's Life* and, better yet, Bing Crosby in *A Connecticut Yankee in King Arthur's Court*, wherein the sight of him in Prince Valiant wig added to his very funny performance. Having starred since 1944 on the popular radio series *The Life of Riley*, Bendix made a film of it in 1949 and then found television stardom taking over the part from Jackie Gleason in 1953. His movie work at that point became more sporadic and less distinguished, ranging from a slapstick baseball comedy, *Kill the Umpire*, to a tired teaming with Groucho Marx, *A Girl in Every Port*, to a pirate picture, *Blackbeard the Pirate*, though not in the title role. Certainly the best film he made during this period was *Detective Story*, supporting Kirk Douglas, as an understanding cop. He ended up in some A.C. Lyle "B" westerns in the 1960s before his death from pneumonia.

Screen: 1942: Woman of the Year; Brooklyn Orchid; Wake Island; The Glass Key; Who Done It?; Star Spangled Rhythm; The McGuerins from Brooklyn; **1943:** The Crystal Ball; Taxi Mister?; China; Hostages; Guadalcanal Diary; **1944:** Lifeboat; The Hairy Ape; Abroad With Two Yanks; Greenwich Village; **1945:** It's in the Bag; Don Juan Quilligan; Duffy's Tavern; A Bell for Adano; **1946:** Sentimental Journey; The Blue Dahlia; The Dark Corner; Two Years Before the Mast; White Tie and Tails; **1947:** I'll Be Yours; Blaze of Noon; Calcutta; The Web; Variety Girl; Where There's Life; **1948:** The Time of Your Life; Race Street; The Babe Ruth Story; **1949:** The Life of Riley; Streets of Laredo; A Connecticut Yankee in King Arthur's Court; Cover-Up; The Big Steal; Johnny Holiday; **1950:** Kill the Umpire; Gambling House; **1951:** Submarine Command; Detective Story; **1952:** Macao; A Girl in Every Port; Blackbeard the Pirate; **1954:** Dangerous Mission; **1956:** Crashout; Battle Stations; **1958:** The Deep Six; **1959:** Idle on Parade; The Rough and the Smooth/Portrait of a Sinner; **1961:** Johnny Nobody; The Phony American; **1962:** Boys' Night Out; **1963:** The Young and the Brave; For Love or Money; **1964:** Law of the Lawless; **1965:** Young Fury.

NY Stage: 1939: The Time of Your Life; **1960:** Take Me Along.

Select TV: 1953–58: The Life of Riley (series); **1959:** A Quiet Game of Cards (sp); The Ransom of Red Chief (sp); **1960:** The Overland Trail (series).

CONSTANCE BENNETT

BORN: NEW YORK, NY, OCTOBER 22, 1904.
DIED: JULY 24, 1965.

Despite being a much admired and popular star of the 1930s, Constance Bennett did not remain in the public's consciousness as vividly as her younger sister Joan did, which was a shame considering the high level of charm she could produce. The daughter of stage actor Richard Bennett, she got her first movie parts through his influence. There were large roles in silents like *Cytherea*, as a movie star; *The Goose Hangs High*, as a flapper; and the hit *Sally, Irene and Mary*, as Sally, a kept woman. She signed a contract with Pathe and made her talking-picture debut for them in *This Thing Called Love*, a successful comedy that paired her with Edmond Lowe. She then began to establish herself as a major name, first with the melodrama *Common Clay*, as a housekeeper who has a baby out of wedlock with Lew Ayres; and, more notably, the trend-setting filmland story *What Price Hollywood?*; as the young hopeful who rises to the top while the director who discovered her descends into alcoholism. Thereafter she became one of the highest paid actresses in the business (setting a record with $30,000 a week for her role in Warners's *Bought*, as a girl from the wrong side of the tracks who longs to be a socialite). However, there was little in her output over the next few years to indicate that greatness was being achieved or that her popularity warranted the hefty pay check. These assignments included *Rockabye*, a soap opera about a doting mother and a major disaster for RKO; *Bed of Roses*, stretching without success in an unsympathetic portrait of a bad girl; and *After Tonight*, as a Russian spy romanced by Gilbert Roland, who later became her fourth husband (1941–45). Over at 20th Century she took a back seat to Frank Morgan in *The Affairs of Cellini*.

She went over to MGM for a pair of films, *Outcast Lady*, wrongly suspected of killing her wimpy husband on their wedding night, and *After Office Hours*, where she got to trade quips with Clark Gable. Going over to England for *Everything Is Thunder* did not indicate a career in good shape. However, she returned to the U.S. in a pair of back to back comedies for Hal Roach that represented her at her peak: *Topper*, in perhaps, her best remembered role, as the ghostly, fun-loving Marion Kirby who enjoys teasing mortal Roland Young, and *Merrily We Live*, as a spoiled rich girl in a story clearly inspired by the popularity of *My Man Godfrey*. She returned to familiar haunts for *Topper Takes a Trip* (although her co-star from the first film, Cary Grant, was only seen in flashbacks), after which she began to slip from her star position in the industry eventually ending up below the title in Garbo's last film, *Two-Faced Woman*, in 1941. She turned to touring and performing on the radio, then returned to the screen with her own production, *Paris Underground*, which teamed her with Gracie Fields. There were notable supporting parts in *Centennial Summer*, as Jeanne Crain's aunt, and *As You As You Feel*, as a married woman charmed by Monty Wooley, in between which she was reduced to billing *below* Vera Ralston for *Angel on the Amazon*. In the late 1950s she started her own cosmetics company. The year after she died, Universal released her first film in 12 years, the remake of *Madame X*, with Bennett as Lana Turner's mother.

Screen: 1922: Reckless Youth; Evidence; What's Wrong With Women?; 1924: Cytherea; Into the Net; Married?; 1925: The Goose Hangs High; Code of the West; My Son; My Wife and I; The Goose Woman; Sally, Irene and Mary; Wandering Fires; 1926: The Pinch Hitter; 1929: This Thing Called Love; 1930: Son of the Gods; Rich People; Common Clay; Three Faces East; Sin Takes a Holiday; 1931: The Easiest Way; Born to Love; The Common Law; Bought; 1932: Lady With a Past; What Price Hollywood?; Two Against the World; Rockabye; 1933: Our Betters; Bed of Roses; After Tonight; 1934: Moulin Rouge; The Affairs of Cellini; Outcast Lady; 1935: After Office Hours; 1936: Everything Is Thunder; Ladies in Love; 1937: Topper; 1938: Merrily We Live; Service de Luxe; 1939: Topper Takes a Trip; Tail Spin; 1940: Escape to Glory; 1941: Law of the Tropics; Two-Faced Woman; Wild Bill Hickok Rides; 1942: Sin Town; Madame Spy; 1946: Paris Underground (and prod.); Centennial Summer; 1947: The Unsuspected; 1948: Smart Woman; 1949: Angel on the Amazon; 1951: As You As You Feel; 1954: It Should Happen to You; 1966: Madame X.

NY Stage: 1953: A Date With April.

Select TV: 1952: Sinora Isabel (sp); 1953: Twentieth Century (sp); 1956: Onions in the Stew (sp).

JOAN BENNETT

BORN: PALISADES, NJ, FEBRUARY 27, 1910.
DIED: DECEMBER 7, 1990.

The youngest of the three Bennett sisters, following Constance and Barbara, Joan Bennett, although not so much a star attraction in herself, wound up having the most extensive career, becoming the most famous member of the acting family. She came to movies as an extra (and a blonde), in 1923, then joined her father, actor Richard Bennett, on Broadway in *Jarnegan*. Goldwyn signed her to play opposite Ronald Colman in the highly popular *Bulldog Drummond*, where her lack of experience was as evident, as it was in one of the other big hits of 1929 in which she appeared, *Disraeli*. After such movies as *Puttin' on the Ritz* and John Barrymore's second attempt at *Moby Dick*, she became a temporary contract player at Fox but little of her work — including one she made with Spencer Tracy, *She Wanted Millionaire* — made much of an impression. Playing Amy in George Cukor's excellent version of *Little Women* at RKO at last brought her the sort of attention she'd been hoping for, as

well as a contract with independent producer Walter Wanger, and work in more visible product, including Claudette Colbert's *Private Worlds*, as Joel McCrea's jealous wife; and two with Bing Crosby: *Mississippi*, and *Two for Tonight*, as the soundboard for his love songs. Prior to these she had gotten nice reviews for her work in a period comedy at Paramount, *The Pursuit of Happiness*, but it had failed at the box office. She wasn't trusted to carry a movie without a stronger male co-star, which was the case with *Thirteen Hours by Air*, with Fred MacMurray; *Two in a Crowd*, with Joel McCrea; and two with Cary Grant: *Big Brown Eyes* and *Wedding Present*. Similarly it was Randolph Scott who was the attraction in *The Texans*, and Jack Benny in *Artists and Models Abroad*.

Wanger was still determined to push her into a high bracket of stardom, and figured the trick might be done if she got rid of the blonde hair color that made her look too much like her sister Constance, and changed into a brunette. Thereby the "new" Bennett was seen for the first time in the 1938 release *Trade Winds*, as a murder suspect pursued by Fredric March. The public response in the fan magazines was positive, so a brunette Bennett would remain from that point on. She and Wanger married in 1940. After appearing as Louis Hayward's leading lady in *The Man in the Iron Mask*, her husband produced for her the thriller *The House Across the Bay*, with Joan in danger from escaped convict husband George Raft because she'd been shacking up with Walter Pidgeon in his absence. Bennett then signed dual contracts with Columbia and Fox, where her most notable release was for the latter, *Man Hunt*, playing a cockney whore, though not very well. This had been directed by Fritz Lang and the two of them formed their own company together, teaming on three more productions: *Secret Beyond the Door*, the last and weakest of the lot; and two in which she played very wicked ladies with whom Edward G. Robinson becomes involved, *The Woman in the Window*, and *Scarlet Street*, her two personal favorites. She liked playing bad and did so again, with lesser results, in *Woman on the Beach* and *The Stolen Moment*. Back to being nice she was the patient wife of Spencer Tracy in the popular *Father of the Bride* and then was involved in a juicy Hollywood scandal when her husband tried to shoot her agent, Jennings Lang, in a fit of jealousy. There was reconciliation with Wanger (their last production together was *Navy Wife* in 1956) but the couple divorced in 1965. Her involvement with the bizarre vampire soap opera, *Dark Shadows*, won her a whole new generation of admirers and also brought her back to the big screen via a movie spinoff, *House of Dark Shadows*, in 1970. That same year she published her memoirs, *The Bennett Playbill*.

Screen: 1928: The Divine Lady; Power; 1929: Bulldog Drummond; Three Live Ghosts; Disraeli; The Mississippi Gambler; 1930: Puttin' on the Ritz; Crazy That Way; Moby Dick; Maybe It's Love; Scotland Yard; 1931: Doctors' Wives; Hush Money; Many a Slip; 1932: She Wanted a Millionaire; Careless Lady; The Trial of Vivienne Ware; Weekends Only; Wild Girl; Me and My Gal; Arizona to Broadway; 1933: Little Women; 1934: The Pursuit of Happiness; The Man Who Reclaimed His Head; 1935: Private Worlds; Mississippi; Two for Tonight; She Couldn't Take It; The Man Who Broke the Bank at Monte Carlo; 1936: Thirteen Hours by Air; Big Brown Eyes; Two in a Crowd; Wedding Present; 1937: Vogues of 1938; 1938: I Met My Love; The Texans; Artists and Models Abroad; Trade Winds; 1939: The Man in the Iron Mask; The Housekeeper's Daughter; 1940: Green Hell; The House Across the Bay; The Man I Married; The Son of Monte Cristo; 1941: She Knew All the Answers; Man Hunt; Wild Geese Calling; Cofirm or Deny; 1942: Twin Beds; The Wife Takes a Flyer; Girl Trouble; 1943: Margin for Error;

1944: The Woman in the Window; 1945: Nob Hill; Colonel Effingham's Raid; Scarlet Street; 1947: The Macomber Affair; Woman on the Beach; 1948: Secret Beyond the Door; Hollow Triumph; The Scar; 1949: The Reckless Moment; 1950: For Heaven's Sake; Father of the Bride; 1951: Father's Little Dividend; The Guy Who Came Back; 1954: Highway Dragnet; 1955: We're No Angels; 1956: There's Always Tomorrow; Navy Wife; 1960: Desire in the Dust; 1970: House of Dark Shadows; 1976: Suspiria.

NY Stage: 1928: Jarnegan; 1958: Love Me Too Late.
Select TV: 1954: The Man Who Came to Dinner (sp); 1957: The Thundering Wave (sp); Junior Miss (sp); 1959: Too Young to Go Steady (series); 1968–71: Dark Shadows (series); 1972: Gidget Gets Married; The Eyes of Charles Sand; 1978: Suddenly Love; 1981: This House Possessed; 1982: Divorce Wars: A Love Story.

JACK BENNY

(Benjamin Kubelsky) Born: Waukeegan, IL, February 14, 1894. Died: December 26, 1974.

Better known for his enormously successful career on both radio and television than for his contributions to cinema, the self-depreciating Jack Benny loved to poke fun at his failures as a movie star when, in fact, he was quite a pleasant addition to film comedy. Starting as a violinst for a local band, he was soon performing routines in vaudeville, first as part of a team, Salisbury and Benny, then as a single. Oddly it was his work as an emcee in New York nightclubs that won him attention and a contract with MGM, debuting as the host of the moldy all-star The Hollywood Revue of 1929. There were raves for his participation in the 1930 stage hit Earl Carroll's Vanities, followed by his successful radio debut in 1932. Here he cemented his characterization of the pompous and cowardly skinflint, surrounded by a collection of top notch supporting players including his wife Mary Livingston, raspy-voiced Eddie "Rochester" Anderson, and man of a thousand voices Mel Blanc. There were some popular comedies at Paramount cashing in on his radio success, including The Big Broadcast of 1937, College Holiday, and Artists and Models; and some blatant spin offs from the airwaves such as Love Thy Neighbor, dramatizing his mock radio feud with comedian Fred Allen, and Buck Benny Rides Again, in both cases playing himself. One of his biggest hits was the movie version of Charley's Aunt, the plot of which, of course, found him scampering about in drag. The following year, 1942, brought his most acclaimed screen work, as the arrogant, second-rate Polish actor who must face the Nazis in Ernst Lubitsch's To Be or Not to Be. The film that Benny would trounce mercilessly as the one that ruined his movie standing, The Horn Blows at Midnight, was indeed a box-office failure but actually much more enjoyable than the star's put-downs suggested. It did, however, mark the end of the Benny starring vehicles. As he took The Jack Benny Show triumphantly over to television (for a 15 year run, winning Emmy Awards in 1957 and 1959) he was seen on screen thereafter only in guest spots. He produced the film The Lucky Stiff, for United Artists, in 1949.

Screen: 1929: The Hollywood Revue of 1929; Chasing Rainbows; 1930: Medicine Man; 1933: Mr. Broadway; 1934: Transatlantic Merry-Go-Round; 1935: Broadway Melody of 1936; It's in the Air; 1936: The Big Broadcast of 1937; College Holiday; 1937: Artists and Models; 1938: Artists and Models Abroad; 1939: Man About Town; 1940: Buck Benny Rides Again; Love Thy Neighbor; 1941: Charley's Aunt; 1942: To Be or Not to Be; George Washington Slept Here; 1943: The Meanest Man in the World; 1944: Hollywood Canteen; 1945: It's in the Bag; The Horn Blows at Midnight; 1946: Without Reservations; 1949: The Great Lover; 1952: Somebody Loves Me; 1954: Susan Slept Here; 1957: Beau James; 1962: Gypsy; 1963: It's a Mad Mad Mad Mad World; 1967: A Guide for the Married Man; 1972: The Man.

NY Stage: 1926: The Great Temptations; 1930: Earl Carroll's Vanities; 1934: Bring on the Girls; 1963: Jack Benny.
Select TV: 1950–65: The Jack Benny Show (series); 1955–58: Shower of Stars (series); 1960: The Slowest Gun in the West (sp); 1974: Annie and the Hoods (sp).

EDGAR BERGEN

Born: Chicago, IL, February 16, 1903.
ed: Northwestern Univ.
Died: Septmber 30, 1978.

The most famous ventriloquist of all time, Edgar Bergen might not have been the best of the bunch, but he just happened to have created the sassiest and most lovable dummy of them all, and hence his alter ego, Charlie McCarthy. He had, in fact, introduced Charlie as far back as high school, eventually performing the act in vaudeville. Rudy Vallee asked him to join his radio program around the same time that Bergen began appearing in a handful of short subjects. In time he and Charlie were joined in their routines by another inspired creation, the dim-witted Mortimer Snerd. By the time of their feature debut, in the all-star The Goldwyn Follies in 1938, Bergen and McCarthy were among radio's most popular stars. Bergen had, in fact, already received a special Academy Award the year before, for the creation of Charlie, despite their limited involvement in motion pictures up to that time. Film only enhanced the enjoyment of seeing the polite and mild-mannered Bergen feed straight lines to the monocled, wisecracking McCarthy. The dummy sparred memorably with W.C. Fields in You Can't Cheat an Honest Man, and even had his own starring vehicle, Charlie McCarthy — Detective. Bergen and McCarthy were also seen sharing the screen with some other radio favorites, Fibber McGee and Molly, in both Look Who's Laughing and its follow-up, Here We Go Again. In later years Bergen branched out into straight acting, most notably in I Remember Mama, as the timid undertaker, and remained a popular guest on television. Fittingly, his last appearance was in The Muppet Movie, which was dedicated to his honor, Bergen having passed away shortly after filming his role. Charlie McCarthy now resides in the Smithsonian Institution. Bergen's daughter is actress Candice Bergen.

Screen (shorts): 1930: The Operation; The Office Scandal; 1933: Africa Speaks…English; Free and Easy; 1934: At the Races; Pure Feud; 1935: All American Drawback; Two Boobs in a Balloon; 1937: Double Talk; 1950: Charlie McCarthy and Mortimer Snerd in Sweden.
Screen (features): 1938: The Goldwyn Follies; A Letter of Introduction; 1939: Charlie McCarthy — Detective; You Can't Cheat an Honest Man; 1941: Look Who's Laughing; 1942: Here We Go Again; 1943: Stage Door Canteen; 1944: Song of the Open Road; 1947: Fun and Fancy Free; 1948: I Remember Mama; 1949: Captain China; 1965: One-Way Wahine; 1967: Don't Make Waves; Rogue's Gallery; 1970: The Phynx; 1976: Won Ton Ton, the Dog Who Saved Hollywood; 1979: The Muppet Movie.

Court (sp); **1962:** Who Killed Julie Greer? (sp); A Time
to Die (sp); **1956–57:** Do You Trust Your Wife? (series);
1964: The Hanged Man; **1971:** The Homecoming.

POLLY BERGEN

(NELLIE PAULINA BURGIN)
BORN: KNOXVILLE, TN, JULY 14, 1930.

A singer-actress of a pleasing if unremarkable personality, Polly Bergen had been
singing on radio since she was 14 years
old. Nightclub and summer stock led to
film work, starting with the Monogram cheapie *Across the
Rio Grande*, in which she was billed, for the only time, as
Polly Burgin. She next appeared as the sunny leading lady in
three Dean Martin and Jerry Lewis comedies (*At War With
the Army*, *That's My Boy*, and *The Stooge*), and then in a
batch of movies at M G M, including a 3-D rodeo story,
Arena, and *Fast Company*, as the owner of a dancing horse.
She did not achieve her own individual fame until she began
showing up regularly on television, not only as a panelist on
the popular game show *To Tell the Truth*, but on her own
variety series. She won an Emmy Award for starring in
Helen Morgan in 1957, ironically the same year in which Ann
Blyth received poor notices for her interpretation of the
singer on the big screen. In the 1960s she was back in
movies, curiously receiving "guest star" billing, though she
had the title role, in *Belle Somers*, an hour-long quickie for
Columbia; then as Gregory Peck's loyal wife in her best
known release, *Cape Fear*; and as the first female Chief
Executive in one of the coyest of all 1960s gimmick comedies, *Kisses for My President*. Retreating comfortably to
television and business (establishing a cosmetics line and a
culinary company) 20 years went by before she showed up
in the movies again, in the comedy spoof *Making Mr. Right*.
Her book, *Polly's Principles*, was published in 1974.

Screen: **1949:** Across the Rio Grande; **1950:** At War With the
Army; **1951:** That's My Boy; Warpath; **1953:** The Stooge; Arena;
Half a Hero; Cry of the Hunted; Fast Company; Escape From
Fort Bravo; **1961:** Belle Sommers; **1962:** Cape Fear; **1963:** The
Caretakers; Move Over, Darling; **1964:** Kisses for My President;
1967: A Guide for the Married Man; **1987:** Making Mr. Right;
1990: Cry-Baby; **1995:** Dr. Jekyll and Ms. Hyde; **1996:** Once
Upon a Time…When We Were Colored.

NY Stage: **1953:** John Murray Anderson's Almanac; **1955:**
Champagne Complex; **1959:** First Impressions; **2001:** Follies;
2002: Cabaret.

Select TV: **1952:** The Haunted Heart (sp); Autumn in New
York (sp); **1954–55:** Pepsi-Cola Playhouse (series); **1956–61:**
To Tell the Truth (series); **1957:** Helen Morgan (sp);
1957–58: The Polly Bergen Show (series); **1974:** Death
Cruise; **1975:** Murder on Flight 502; **1977:** 79 Park Avenue
(ms); Telethon; **1978:** How to Pick Up Girls; **1981:** The
Million Dollar Face; **1982:** Born Beautiful; **1983:** The Winds
of War (ms); **1984:** Velvet; **1988:** Addicted to His Love; She
Was Marked for Murder; **1989:** The Haunting of Sarah
Hardy; My Brother's Wife; **1991:** Lightning Field; **1991–92:**
Baby Talk (series); **1992:** Lady Against the Odds; **1993:** Perry
Mason: The Case of the Skin-Deep Scandal; **1994:** Leave of
Absence (and story; co-exec. prod.); **1995:** The Surrogate;
1996: In the Blink of an Eye; For Hope.

INGRID BERGMAN

BORN: STOCKHOLM, SWEDEN, AUGUST 29, 1915.
DIED: AUGUST 29, 1982.

When Ingrid Bergman first came to
Hollywood's attention in 1939, it was clear
that the movies had found the most exquisite female performer of the day, beautiful
and soft spoken, intelligent and sexy but never in a stark and
obvious manner. Her raw emotional display could often be heartbreaking. Shortly after graduation from the Royal Dramatic
Theatre School of Stockholm, she landed her first film role,
playing a hotel maid, in *Munkbrogreven*, in 1934. With her next
movie, *Branningar/Ocean Breakers*, she was upped to the female
leading role, as a fisherman's daughter who refuses to divulge the
name of the father of her illegitimate child. With this and her
next four movies, she became well-known in her native country,
the last of the group, *Intermezzo*, being the most famous, a
romantic melodrama about the affair between a married world-
famous violinist (Gosta Ekman) and a classical student pianist.
After four more Swedish films (one of which, *En Kvinnas Ansikte*,
was remade by MGM in 1941 as a Joan Crawford vehicle),
American producer David O. Selznick, impressed by what he'd
seen of her so far, signed her to a seven year contract. Her first
English-language assignment was a remake of *Intermezzo*, this
time opposite Leslie Howard and with the added subtitle *A Love
Story*. It brought her fine reviews, was a box-office success, and
made Bergman "The Next Big Thing." She actually had one
more Swedish film to do, *Juninatten*, before she returned to
Hollywood for the real star treatment.

At first things did not appear too promising, with her loan-out
to Columbia for the family saga *Adam and Her Four Sons*, as a
French governess; and to MGM for *Rage in Heaven*, coping with
psychotic husband Robert Montgomery's unstable behavior. Also
at Metro she did a muddled version of *Dr. Jekyll and Mr. Hyde*,
initially signed for the good-girl role but, in an effort to try something uncharacteristic, trading parts with Lana Turner, thereby
playing the tart Miriam Hopkins had played in the earlier, better
version. Then Warner Bros. asked her for services, putting her in
the wartime romantic drama against which all others would be
compared, *Casablanca*, the Best Picture Oscar winner of 1943. As
Ilsa, the woman who loved and had to leave Humphrey Bogart,
she played to perfection the role with which she would be most
closely identified. It was, in fact, she and not Bogart who spoke
the words "Play it, Sam," coming closest to the mythical distortion "Play it again, Sam." That same year she continued her good
fortune playing, superbly, the Spanish peasant girl in *For Whom
the Bell Tolls*, lighting up the screen in her love scenes with Gary
Cooper. As was usually the case in Hollywood, she was not
required to actually play the part with a Spanish accent, the
feeling being that an accent of any kind qualified you as any sort
of foreigner. In any event she received an Oscar nomination for
this lengthy and extremely popular adaptation of the Ernest
Hemingway novel. Though it may have seemed impossible that
things could have gotten better, they did, as she went on to win
the Academy Award for Best Actress of 1944, playing the threatened wife of Charles Boyer in the U.S. remake of *Gaslight*. As a
thriller it was rather antiquated and none too exciting, while her
performance, though the best thing in the film, was nowhere near
as interesting as the two she'd given the year before. It would be
fair to say the trophy was given more in recognition of her incredible level of popularity at the time.

She seemed very much at home in a nun's habit, teamed with
Bing Crosby in *The Bells of St. Mary's*, a sequel to the far-superior

Going My Way, and one of the massive box-office hits of the 1940s. It brought her another Oscar nomination. Finally doing another one for Selznick, she did her first of three under Alfred Hitchcock's direction, *Spellbound*, as Gregory Peck's sympathetic shrink, and then reteamed with Gary Cooper, for the boring *Saratoga Trunk*, ill at ease as an illegitimate half-Creole. They were hits, as was an inspired pairing with Cary Grant in one of Hitchcock's best thrillers, *Notorious*, playing the daughter of a German spy. Quickly forgotten among this bunch was *Arch of Triumph*, saved from suicide by Charles Boyer, but much noise was made about the fortune spent on *Joan of Arc*, not to mention its great amount of hype. This had been a dream role of hers ever since drama school and, as a sort of rehearsal, she had done it on Broadway in Maxwell Anderson's *Joan of Lorraine*. Everybody got an "A" for effort on the film, and Bergman got a fourth Oscar mention, but it was not the hoped-for masterpiece. The tepid reviews did not bode well for its run but, despite its reputation as a failure, it did, in fact, do more than respectable business. Her last for Hitchcock was the costumer *Under Capricorn*, which did nothing but prove that even the mightiest among the Hollywood elite were capable of turning out dogs. Soon after came the scandal that seems inconceivable and silly by today's standards. During production of Roberto Rossellini's *Stromboli* the still-married Bergman bore the director's child. As a result the press had a field day tearing her to shreds and she retreated to Europe, her reputation temporarily soiled among the more puritanical moviegoers.

During the early 1950s she appeared only in foreign-language productions, one of which found her back in familiar territory, playing Joan of Arc again, this time under her husband's direction, in *Joan at the Stake*. Of these movies, only two received any sort of U.S. bookings, *The Greatest Love*, and *Fear/Angst*, and none of them were well liked in Europe, helping to put her career into a terrible slump. After the venom had evaporated, her 1956 comeback, playing a Russian peasant claiming to be a member of the royal family, in *Anastasia*, was greeted with rapture, winning her a second Academy Award for a tour de force performace. More importantly, to Hollywood, it made money. Because of it, there was a brief resurgence of Bergman as a box-office attraction, with the light-hearted *Indiscreet*, where she was, yet again, perfect alongside Cary Grant, and the epic *The Inn of the Sixth Happiness*, as a very good-hearted woman helping to evacuate several Chinese when the Japanese attack. It should be noted that although these three movies were American productions, they were all made in England. Although Bergman's marriage to Rossellini ended in 1958, she had no reason to move back to the United States and continued to work in Europe, giving a good performance as an older woman caught up in a hopeless love affair with the much younger Anthony Perkins in *Goodbye Again*. She was the richest woman in the world in *The Visit*, an unfaithful rendering of the much-admired play, and was back with a younger man (Omar Sharif in this case) for the last segment of the all-star omnibus *The Yellow Rolls-Royce*.

By now she had secured a place as one of the medium's most admired stars, finally returning to Hollywood for the first time in two decades to give a sparkling performance as the nurse neglected by womanizing doctor Walter Matthau, in *Cactus Flower*, one of the top hits of 1969. A romantic drama with Anthony Quinn, *A Walk in the Spring Rain*, exited quickly but she had a showy character part as the shy and simple nursemaid in the all-star Agatha Christie mystery *Murder on the Orient Express*. For it she became the third performer (after Walter Brennan and Katharine Hepburn) to win three Academy Awards, and certainly the first to spend a majority of her acceptance speech apologizing

for winning, believing fellow-nominee Valentina Cortese was more deserving of the statuette. A role opposite Liza Minnelli, as a fading countess, in *A Matter of Time*, was greeted with ridicule but her final film role, as Liv Ullman's unfeeling mother in Ingmar Bergman's *Autumn Sonata*, was not only one of her best but brought her yet another Oscar nomination. On television she won Emmy Awards for *The Turn of the Screw* and (posthumously) *A Woman Called Golda*. She died from cancer on her 67th birthday, two years after the publication of her autobiography, *Ingrid Bergman: My Story*. There was no denying at the time of her passing that this was an actress who ranked high among the cinematic legends. Her daughters are news reporter Pia Lindstrom and actress Isabella Rossellini.

Screen: 1934: Munkbrogreven/The Count of Monk's Bridge (nUSr); 1935: Branningar/Ocean Breakers/The Surf (US: 1951); Swedenhielms/The Family Swendenhielms; 1936: Valborgsmassoafton/Walpurgis Night (US: 1941); Pa Solsidan/ On the Sunny Side (nUSr); Intermezzo (US: 1937); 1938: Dollar; En Kvinnas Ansikte/A Woman's Face (US: 1939); Die Vier Gesellen/The Four Companions (nUSr); 1939: En Enda Natt/Only One Night (US: 1942); Intermezzo — A Love Story; 1940: Juninatten/A Night in June; 1941: Adam Had Four Sons; Rage in Heaven; Dr. Jekyll and Mr. Hyde; 1943: Casablanca; For Whom the Bell Tolls; 1944: Gaslight; 1945: Spellbound; The Bells of St. Mary's; 1946: Saratoga Trunk; Notorious; 1948: Arch of Triumph; Joan of Arc; 1949: Under Capricorn; 1950: Stromboli; 1952: Europa '51/The Greatest Love (US: 1954); Siamo Donne/We the Women (nUSr); 1953: Viaggio in Italia/Journey to Italy (nUSr); Giovanna D'Arco al Rogo/Joan at the Stake (nUSr); 1954: Angst/Fear (US: 1956); 1956: Anastasia; 1957: Paris Does Strange Things; 1958: Indiscreet; The Inn of the Sixth Happiness; 1961: Goodbye Again; 1964: The Visit; 1965: The Yellow Rolls-Royce; 1967: Stimulantia/Fugitive in Vienna (The Necklace; nUSr); 1969: Cactus Flower; 1970: A Walk in the Spring Rain; 1973: From the Mixed-Up Files of Mrs. Basil E. Frankweiler/The Hideaways; 1974: Murder on the Orient Express; 1976: A Matter of Time; 1978: Autumn Sonata.

NY Stage: 1940: Liliom; 1946: Joan of Lorraine; 1967: More Stately Mansions; 1972: Captain Brassbound's Conversion; 1975: The Constant Wife.

Select TV: 1959: The Turn of the Screw (sp); 1961: 24 Hours in a Woman's Life (sp); 1963: Hedda Gabler (sp); 1967: The Human Voice (sp); 1982: A Woman Called Golda.

ELISABETH BERGNER

(ELISABETH ETTEL) BORN: DROHOBYCZ, AUSTRIA-HUNGARY, AUGUST 22, 1897. ED: VIENNA CONSERVATORY. DIED: MAY 12, 1986.

This blonde, elfin European actress was critically admired in her day but, by the time of her death, Elisabeth Bergner's work was largely forgotten. Having studied acting in Vienna, she soon became a busy stage actress before making her film debut in *Der Evangeliman*, in 1923. Gaining great international fame over the next ten years, she was asked to make her English-language debut in the British film *Catherine the Great*, in 1934. The following year she repeated her stage triumph, *Escape Me Never*, on film, as a poor thing blindly in love with her uncaring husband. She won an Oscar nomination but did not accept any Hollywood offers, and instead did two movies under contract to United Artists in Britain: *Dreaming Lips*, a remake of one of her German movies, *Der Traumende Mund*; and *Stolen Life*, in which she had a dual role. It was not until 1942 that she did her sole American-produced film, made at Universal. In the indifferently received melo-drama *Paris Calling*, she played a wealthy Parisienne who joins the French underground, only to discover that her former lover, Basil Rathbone, is in league with the Nazis. In later years she was occasionally coaxed away from the stage for screen appearances, such as the Vincent Price horror film *Cry of the Banshee*, as a witch, and Maximilian Schell's *The Pedestrian*, in 1974.

Screen (US releases only): 1934: Catherine the Great; 1935: Escape Me Never; 1937: As You Like It; Dreaming Lips; 1939: Stolen Life; 1942: Paris Calling; 1970: Cry of the Banshee; 1974: The Pedestrian.

NY Stage: 1935: Escape Me Never; 1943: The Two Mrs. Carrolls; 1946: The Duchess of Malfi; 1948: The Cup of Trembling.

MILTON BERLE

(MILTON BERLINGER) BORN: NEW YORK, NY, JULY 12, 1908. DIED: MARCH 27, 2002.

As one of the pioneering entertainers of the medium, Milton Berle earned the affec-tionate sobriquets "Mr. Television" and "Uncle Miltie." He brought entertainment to millions of home viewers, though his movie career — dating all the way back to silents — never commanded the same sort of attention. A member of New York's Professional Children's School, he was a child actor in two of the most famous titles of the silent era: *Tillie's Punctured Romance*, which starred Charlie Chaplin and Marie Dressler, and Pearl White's classic serial *The Perils of Pauline*. On the vaudeville circuit he initially teamed with Jack Duffy before gaining attention as a solo act at the Palace Theatre in 1931. He worked steadily as a radio and nightclub comic and starred in two 1940s comedy-mys-teries for Fox, *Whispering Ghosts* and *Over My Dead Body*, before breaking into the infant medium of television as the star of *The Texaco Star Theater*, in 1948. Suddenly he was a comic sensation, a goofy, grinning host whose outrageous antics often included wearing a dress. The series, which became the *Buick-Berle Show* and finally *The Milton Berle Show*, ran until 1956. He cashed in on his television success with only one film vehicle, *Always Leave Them Laughing*, a semi-biographical story of the rise and fall of an arrogant comic. Berle's later movie roles were in supporting or guest spots, with the excep-tion of the all-star *It's a Mad Mad Mad Mad World*, where he was memorably partnered with Terry-Thomas. Otherwise, he could be seen bickering with Margaret Leighton over their dead dog in *The Loved One*; helping to rob the U.S. treasury wearing a George Washington costume in *Who's Minding the Mint*; and playing it straight as Anjanette Comer's father in the gangster biopic *Lepke*. He authored the books *Out of My Trunk* (1945), *Earthquake* (1959), and *Milton Berle: An Autobiography* (1974).

Screen (features): 1914: Tess of the Storm Country; The Peril of Pauline (serial); Tillie's Punctured Romance; 1917: Rebecca of Sunnybrook Farm; The Little Brother; 1919: Wishing Ring Man; Eyes of Youth; 1920: Birthright; The Mark of Zorro; 1921: Love's Penalty; 1922: Divorce Coupons; 1923: Ruth of the Range (serial); 1937: New Faces of 1937; 1938: Radio City Revels; 1941: Tall, Dark and Handsome; Sun Valley Serenade; Rise and Shine; 1942: Whispering Ghosts; A Gentleman at Heart; 1943: Over My Dead Body; Margin of Error; 1949: Always Leave Them Laughing; 1960: Let's Make Love; The Bellboy; 1963: It's a Mad Mad Mad Mad World; 1965: The Loved One; 1966: The Oscar; Don't Worry, We'll Think of a Title; 1967: The Happening; Who's Minding the Mint?; 1968: Where Angels Go...Trouble

Follows; For Singles Only; 1969: Can Hieronymous Merkin Ever Forget Mercy Humppe and Find True Happiness?; 1974: Journey Back to Oz (voice; filmed 1964); 1975: Lepke; 1976: Won Ton Ton, the Dog Who Saved Hollywood; 1979: The Muppet Movie; 1983: Cracking Up/Smorgasbord (dtv); 1984: Broadway Danny Rose; 1985: Pee-wee's Big Adventure; 1989: Going Overboard; 1991: Driving Me Crazy/Trabbi Goes to Hollywood/Autobahn; 1995: Storybook (dtv).

NY Stage: 1932: Vanities; 1934: Saluta; Lost Paradise; 1939: See My Lawyer; 1943: Ziegfeld Follies; 1968: The Goodbye People; 1983: Goodnight Grandpa (ob).

Select TV: 1948–56: Texaco Star Theatre/Buick-Berle Show/The Milton Berle Show (series); 1958–59: Milton Berle Starring in the Kraft Music Hall (series); 1960–61: Jackpot Bowling Starring Milton Berle (series); 1966–67: The Milton Berle Show (series); 1969: Seven in Darkness; 1972: Evil Roy Slade; 1975: The Legend of Valentino; 1988: Side by Side.

TURHAN BEY

(TURHAN GILBERT SELAHETTIN SAHULTAVEY) BORN: VIENNA, AUSTRIA, MARCH 30, 1920.

Born of Turkish-Czech parentage, Turhan Bey became a leading purveyor of exotic foreigners during the 1940s. Coming to the United States in the 1930s, he studied acting at Ben Bard's School of Dramatic Art, then at the Pasadena Playhouse. After a brief stop at Warner Bros., he was signed by Universal, where he was first seen as an Arab in *Raiders of the Desert* and an Asian in *Burma Convoy*. He continued with secondary parts in such programmers as *Drums of the Congo*, *Bombay Clipper*, and *The Mummy's Tomb*, in which he was a High Priest killed off by a heavily-bandaged Lon Chaney, Jr. He was — unfortunately for him — perfect for Universal's idiotic Technicolor desert epics, such as *Arabian Nights*, and, in a bigger role, *Ali Baba and the Forty Thieves*. M G M fool-ishly cast him as a Chinaman opposite Katharine Hepburn in *Dragon Seed*, a movie that made even the talented per-formers look silly. More Universal costume flicks, like *Sudan*, as a bandit leading a slave revolt, and *A Night in Paradise*, as the fabled Aesop, did nothing to prevent his career from trickling down in the early 1950s. He returned to Vienna, where he became a photographer, and pro-duced the 1953 film *Stolen Identity*. Years after the industry had consigned him to nostalgia, he showed up in some direct-to-video titles.

Screen: 1941: Footsteps in the Dark; Raiders of the Desert; Burma Convoy; Shadows on the Stairs; The Gay Falcon; 1942: Junior G-Men of the Air (serial); The Falcon Takes Over; A Yank on the Burma Road; Bombay Clipper; Drums of the Congo; Arabian Nights; Destination Unknown; The Unseen Enemy; The Mummy's Tomb; 1943: Danger in the Pacific; Adventures of Smilin' Jack (serial); White Savage; The Mad Ghoul; Background to Danger; 1944: Follow the Boys; The Climax; Dragon Seed; Bowery to Broadway; Ali Baba and the Forty Thieves; 1945: Frisco Sal; Sudan; 1946: A Night in Paradise; 1947: Out of the Blue; 1948: The Amazing Mr. X; Adventures of Casanova; 1949: Parole Inc; Song of India; 1953: Prisoners of the Casbah; Healer (nUSr); 1995: The Skateboard Kid II (dtv); 1996: Virtual Combat (dtv).

RICHARD BEYMER

(GEORGE RICHARD BEYMER) BORN: AVOCA, IA, FEBRUARY 21, 1938.

A bright-faced and earnest young actor, Richard Beymer landed a coveted role in one of the great movie musicals, *West Side Story*, only to be singled out for critical scorn. Although his portrayal of Tony was adequate, he was overshadowed by the excellence of his fellow cast members and was criticized for being too wholesome to be a gang leader. He had debuted at age 12 on a Los Angeles children's television show before hitting the big screen in Vittorio De Sica's troubled 1953 production, *Indiscretion of an American Wife/Terminal Station*, as Jennifer Jones's nephew. A few years later he had the lead in Disney's revolutionary war drama, *Johnny Tremain*, and the important role of Anne's love interest, Peter, in a major release, *The Diary of Anne Frank*. Another lead, in *Hemingway's Adventures of a Young Man*, won him no new converts. Neither did a supporting role in a facile Terry-Thomas farce, *Bachelor Flat*, and, after playing the naïve, small-town lad who falls for failed actress Joanne Woodward in *The Stripper*, he left motion pictures to study acting in New York. He occasionally popped up in little-seen cheapies, like *Scream Free/Free Grass*, a drugs-and-motorcycles drama with *West Side Story* co-star Russ Tamblyn. He directed a short film, "A Very Special Day," and had a regular role on the 1990s cult television show, *Twin Peaks*.

Screen: 1953: Indiscretion of an American Wife/Terminal Station; So Big; 1957: Johnny Tremain; 1959: The Diary of Anne Frank; 1960: High Time; 1961: West Side Story; 1962: Five Finger Exercise; Hemingway's Adventures of a Young Man; Bachelor Flat; The Longest Day; 1963: The Stripper; 1969: Free Grass/Scream Free; 1974: Interview (and dir.; nUSr); 1983: Cross Country; 1989: Silent Night Deadly Night 3: Better Watch Out! (dtv); 1992: Black Belt (dtv); 1993: Under Investigation (dtv); 1994: My Girl 2; 1995: The Little Death (dtv); 1996: Foxfire; 1998: The Disappearance of Kevin Johnson (dtv); 2001: Home: The Horror Story (nUSr).

Select TV: 1958: Boston Tea Party (sp); 1959: Dark December (sp); 1984: Paper Dolls (series); 1985: Generation; 1990–91: Twin Peaks (series); 1992: Danger Island; 1994: State of Emergency; 1996: A Face to Die For; 1997: Elvis Meets Nixon.

CHARLES BICKFORD

BORN: CAMBRIDGE, MA, JANUARY 1, 1889.
ED: MIT. DIED: NOVEMBER 9, 1967.

Tough as sandpaper with a voice to match, authoritative character actor Charles Bickford was an intimidating presence who brooked no nonsense. He'd been a sailor before appearing onstage, first in burlesque then on Broadway, making his legit debut in 1919, in *Dark Rosaleen*. With a decade of theatre experience — notably the very popular *Outside Looking In* and co-authorship of *The Cyclone Lover* — he came to movies at the dawn of sound. Accepting an offer from Cecil B. DeMille and MGM, he played a coal miner married to Kay Johnson but in love with another woman, in *Dynamite*. Also at Metro, he played his most notable leading-man role, seaman Matt Burke, opposite Greta Garbo in her first talkie, *Anna Christie*. Although he was not officially under contract to them, MGM made every effort to build him into star. Unfortunately, he met with failure in the love-triangle, *Passion Flower*, and a disastrous adventure, *The Sea Bat*, as an escaped con. Bickford's

notorious temper frequently flared at the weak properties he was being offered, such as Universal's *East of Borneo*, as a long-lost physician whose wife finds him practicing in the jungles. He had no better luck with Columbia's *Pagan Lady*, as a bootlegger named Dingo Mike; *Vanity Street*, as a cop who rescues Helen Chandler from a life on the streets; and RKO's critically-reviled *Panama Flo*, trying to rape housekeeper Helen Twelvetrees before becoming her lover. Not surprisingly, he found himself better suited to character parts, like the mobster who changes his unsavory ways to rescue Shirley Temple in *Little Miss Marker*; the canal-boat bully who makes Henry Fonda's life miserable in *The Farmer Takes a Wife*; a gun-runner to the Indians in *The Plainsman*; an evil land developer in *Valley of the Giants*; and the level-headed ranch foreman, Slim, in *Of Mice and Men*.

In the early 1940s he had fallen into a rut at the lower-grade studios, including Monogram's *Mutiny in the Big House*, as the prison chaplain, and Republic's *Girl From God's Country*, as an Alaskan marshal on the trail of Chester Morris. DeMille came to his rescue by putting him in Paramount's "A" picture, *Reap the Wild Wind*, and suddenly Bickford really seemed to hit his stride. He won three Academy Award nominations: as the pragmatic Dean of Lourdes, who first scorns Jennifer Jones, then becomes her mentor, in *The Song of Bernadette*; as the household butler who becomes Loretta Young's confidante in *The Farmer's Daughter*; and, best of all, as Jane Wyman's stern but caring father in *Johnny Belinda*. He was equally memorable as the policeman who kills Linda Darnell in *Fallen Angel*; the ranch hand whose love for Jennifer Jones enrages Gregory Peck in *Duel in the Sun*; the convict who joins Burt Lancaster in his desperate prison-break in *Brute Force*; the hard-nosed newspaper correspondent in *Command Decision*; the sympathetic studio head in the 1954 remake of *A Star Is Born*; the battling rancher in *The Big Country*; and the father of alcoholic Lee Remick in *Days of Wine and Rose*, a role he reprised from the television production. He died during the run of the television series *The Virginian*, having taken over the role from Lee J. Cobb. His autobiography, published in 1965, was colorfully titled *Bulls, Balls, Bicycles, and Actors*.

Screen: 1929: Dynamite; South Sea Rose; 1930: Hell's Heroes; Anna Christie; The Sea Bat; Passion Flower; 1931: River's End; Squaw Man; East of Borneo; Pagan Lady; Men in Her Life; 1932: Panama Flo; Thunder Below; Scandal for Sale; Last Man; Vanity Street; 1933: No Other Woman; Song of the Eagle; This Day and Age; White Woman; 1934: Little Miss Marker; A Wicked Woman; 1935: A Notorious Gentleman; Under Pressure; The Farmer Takes a Wife; East of Java; 1936: Rose of the Rancho; Pride of the Marines; The Plainsman; 1937: Night Club Scandal; Thunder Trail; Daughter of Shanghai; High, Wide and Handsome; 1938: Valley of the Giants; Gangs of New York; The Storm; 1939: Stand Up and Fight; Of Mice and Men; Street of Missing Men; Romance of the Redwoods; Our Leading Citizen; One Hour to Live; Thou Shalt Not Kill; Mutiny in the Big House; 1940: Girl From God's Country; South to Karanga; Queen of the Yukon; 1941: Riders of Death Valley; Burma Convoy; 1942: Reap the Wild Wind; Tarzan's New York Adventure; 1943: Mr. Lucky; The Song of Bernadette; 1944: Wing and a Prayer; 1945: Captain Eddie; Fallen Angel; 1946: Duel in the Sun; 1947: The Farmer's Daughter; The Woman on the Beach; Brute Force; 1948: Four Faces West; The Babe Ruth Story; Johnny Belinda; Command Decision; 1949: Roseanna McCoy; Whirlpool; Guilty of Treason; 1950: Branded; Riding High; 1951: Jim Thorpe — All-American; The Raging Tide; Elopement; 1953: The Last Posse; 1954: A Star Is Born; 1955: Prince of Players; Not as a Stranger; The Court-Martial of Billy Mitchell; 1956: You Can't Run Away From It; 1957: Mister Cory;

1958: The Big Country; 1960: The Unforgiven; 1962: Days of Wine and Roses; 1966: A Big Hand for the Little Lady.

NY Stage: 1919: Dark Rosaleen; 1925: Houses of Sand; Outside Looking In; 1926: Glory Hallelujah; No More Women; Chicago; 1927: Bless You Sister; 1928: Gods of the Lightning; 1938: Casey Jones.

Select TV: 1952: Sunk (sp); 1955: The Woman at Fog Point (sp); The Man Behind the Badge (series); 1956: Forbidden Area (sp); Front Page Father (sp); Sincerely Willis Wade (sp); 1957: The Man Who Couldn't Wait (sp); Clipper Ship (sp); 1958: Days of Wine and Roses (sp); Free Weekend (sp); 1959: Out of Dust (sp); Winterset (sp); 1960: Tomorrow (sp); The Cradle Song (sp); 1962: The Farmer's Daughter (sp); 1966–67: The Virginian (ser.).

THEODORE BIKEL
BORN: VIENNA, AUSTRIA, MAY 2, 1924.
ED: RADA.

Colorful Theodore Bikel's peregrinations took him from his native Austria to Palestine (Israel), where he debuted onstage in *Tevye the Milkman*. (Later he would play Tevye in the musical, *Fiddler on the Roof*.) He then went to London to study at the Royal Academy of Dramatic Arts before making his film debut for John Huston, as a German sailor in 1951's *The African Queen*. In Spain he played a French general in *The Pride and the Passion* for producer-director Stanley Kramer and it was under his guidance that Bikel came to Hollywood for his first American-made film, *The Defiant Ones*. He received an Oscar nomination for playing the sheriff in pursuit of Tony Curtis and Sidney Poitier. He became as well known for his folk-singing as his acting, and made his Broadway musical debut in 1959, as Captain von Trapp, in the original production of *The Sound of Music*. There were key roles in two of the most entertaining films of the 1960s: *My Fair Lady*, as "that dreadful Hungarian," Zoltan Karparthy, and *The Russians Are Coming! The Russians Are Coming!*, as the non-English speaking commander of a grounded submarine. Canadian producer Robert Radnitz awarded him sizeable roles in two children's films: *My Side of the Mountain*, appropriately cast as a retired folk singer who befriends a young lad living in the wild, and *The Little Ark*, in which he rated top billing. He was also among the cast principals of the incomprehensible Frank Zappa and the Mothers of Invention mish-mash, *200 Motels*, which achieved cult status among fans of the bizarre.

Screen: 1951: The African Queen; 1953: Never Let Me Go; Melba; Desperate Moment; A Day to Remember; 1954: The Love Lottery; The Little Kidnappers; 1955: The Colditz Story; Chance Meeting; The Divided Heart; 1956: Forbidden Cargo; Above Us the Waves; Flight From Vienna; 1957: The Vintage; The Pride and the Passion; The Enemy Below; 1958: Fraulein; 1958: The Defiant Ones; I Want to Live; I Bury the Living; 1959: The Blue Angel; Woman Obsessed; The Angry Hills; 1960: A Dog of Flanders; 1964: My Fair Lady; 1965: Sands of the Kalahari; 1966: The Russians Are Coming! The Russians Are Coming!; 1968: Festival; Sweet November; The Desperate Ones; 1969: My Side of the Mountain; 1970: Darker Than Amber; 1971: 200 Motels; 1972: The Little Ark; 1984: Very Close Quarters (dtv); 1985: Prince Jack; 1987: Dark Tower (dtv); 1989: Lodz Ghetto (voice); See You in the Morning;

1991: Shattered; 1992: Crisis in the Kremlin (dtv); 1993: Benefit of the Doubt; My Family Treasure (dtv); 1997: Shadow Conspiracy; 1998: Trickle (dtv).

NY Stage: 1955: Tonight in Samarkand; The Lark; 1957: The Rope Dancers; 1959: The Sound of Music; 1964: Café Crown; 1966: Pousse-Cafe; 1979: The Inspector General; 1999: The Gathering (ob).

Select TV: 1955: Julius Caesar (sp); 1958: World From a Sealed Off Box (sp); 1960: The Dybbuk; 1965: Who Has Seen the Wind? (sp); 1966: Noon Wine (sp); 1967: The Diary of Anne Frank (sp); 1972: Killer by Night; 1975: Murder on Flight 502; 1976: Victory at Entebbe; 1977: Testimony of Two Men; 1978: Loose Change (ms); 1988: A Stoning in Fulham County; 1989: The Final Days; 1991: Memories of Midnight; 1998: Babylon 5: In the Beginning.

SIDNEY BLACKMER
BORN: SALISBURY, NC, JULY 13, 1895.
DIED: OCTOBER 5, 1973.

Something about Sidney Blackmer reminded people of Teddy Roosevelt, and he was asked to play the portly president on several occasions: *This Is My Affair*, *In Old Oklahoma*, *Buffalo Bill*, and *My Girl Tisa*. (Somehow he was overlooked for *Arsenic and Old Lace!*) With a career dating back to the silent serial *The Perils of Pauline*, Blackmer worked for years in frequently unsympathetic supporting roles. During the 1930s he was allotted a few leading-man spots: *It's a Wise Child*, as a lawyer in love with Marion Davies; *Woman Hungry*, marrying Lila Lee against her will; *Deluge*, a sci-fi story in which he established his own island amid the floods; *Great God Gold*, as a greedy financier; and *False Pretenses*, as a millionaire on the skids. However, he was not interesting or colorful enough to sustain leads, so he was more acceptably employed in support. Among these roles were: *The Little Colonel*, trying to steal land from Evelyn Venable; *In Old Chicago*, as General Phil Sheridan; *Suez*, as a French marquis; *Elsa Maxwell's Hotel for Women*, as Ann Sothern's agent; and *Dance, Girl, Dance*, as Virginia Field's husband, referred to as "Puss in Boots." During the 1940s he sank to such desperate fare as PCR's *The Panther's Claw* and *Gallant Lady/Prison Girls*, although he did show up briefly as the man shot by Jennifer Jones's jealous father in Selznick's big-budget *Duel in the Sun*. When he triumphed onstage in *Come Back, Little Sheba* (winning the Tony Award) and *Sweet Bird of Youth* (as Boss Finley) he wasn't asked to repeat the parts on film. His last movie role, however, was distinctive, playing the warlock next door in *Rosemary's Baby*.

Screen: 1914: The Perils of Pauline (serial); 1929: A Most Immoral Lady; 1930: The Love Racket; Strictly Modern; The Bad Man; Kismet; Little Caesar; Mothers Cry; Sweethearts and Wives; 1931: Woman Hungry; The Lady Who Dared; It's a Wise Child; One Heavenly Night; 1933: From Hell to Heaven; The Cocktail Hour; The Wrecker; Deluge; Goodbye Love; 1934: This Man Is Mine; Transatlantic Merry-Go-Round; The President Vanishes; Down to Their Last Yacht; The Count of Monte Cristo; 1935: Great God Gold; A Notorious Gentleman; Behind the Green Lights; The Little Colonel; Streamline Express; Smart Girl; The Girl Who Came Back; False Pretenses; Forced Landing; Woman Trap; 1936: The President's Mystery; Early to Bed; Missing Girls; The Florida Special; House of Secrets; Heart of the West; 1937: Shadows of the Orient; A Doctor's Diary; John Meade's Woman; This Is My Affair; Heidi; Wife, Doctor and Nurse; Charlie Chan at Monte Carlo; The Fire Trap; Thank You,

Mr. Moto; Girl Overboard; Women Men Marry; The Last Gangster; Michael O'Halloran; **1938:** In Old Chicago; Speed to Burn; Sharpshooters; Straight Place and Show; Suez; Orphans of the Street; Trade Winds; While New York Sleeps; **1939:** Convict's Code; Fast and Loose; It's a Wonderful World; Unmarried; Law of the Pampas; Elsa Maxwell's Hotel for Women; Trapped in the Sky; Within the Law; **1940:** Maryland; Framed; Third Finger, Left Hand; Dance, Girl, Dance; I Want a Divorce; **1941:** Murder Among Friends; Cheers for Miss Bishop; Rookies on Parade; The Great Swindle; Love Crazy; Angels With Broken Wings; Obliging Young Lady; Ellery Queen and the Perfect Crime; Down Mexico Way; The Feminine Touch; The Officer and the Lady; **1942:** Always in My Heart; Nazi Agent; Gallant Lady; Quiet Please, Murder; The Panther's Claw; Sabotage Squad; **1943:** Murder in Times Square; I Escaped From the Gestapo/No Escape; In Old Oklahoma/War of the Wildcats; **1944:** Buffalo Bill; Broadway Rhythm; The Lady and the Monster; Wilson; **1946:** Duel in the Sun; **1948:** My Girl Tisa; A Song Is Born; **1950:** Farewell to Yesterday (narrator); **1951:** People Will Talk; Saturday's Hero; **1952:** The San Francisco Story; Washington Story; **1954:** Johnny Dark; The High and the Mighty; **1955:** The View From Pompey's Head; **1956:** High Society; Beyond a Reasonable Doubt; Accused of Murder; **1957:** Tammy and the Bachelor; **1965:** Joy in the Morning; How to Murder Your Wife; **1967:** A Covenant With Death; **1968:** Rosemary's Baby.
NY Stage: **1917:** The Morris Dance; **1921:** The Mountain Man; **1922:** Love Child; **1923:** Scaramouche; **1924:** The Moonflower; **1925:** The Carolinian; **1926:** Love in a Mist; **1927:** Springboard; **1946:** Wonderful Journey; **1947:** Portrait in Black; **1950:** Come Back, Little Sheba; **1952:** Brass Ring; **1959:** Sweet Bird of Youth; **1960:** Take Me Along; **1963:** A Case of Libel.
Select TV: **1951:** The Pen (sp); **1952:** The Barker (sp); **1954:** The Notebook Warrior; **1956:** One Bright Day (sp); The Little Foxes (sp); **1959:** What Makes Sammy Run? (sp); **1971:** Do You Take This Stranger?

VIVIAN BLAINE

(VIVIAN STAPLETON) BORN: NEWARK, NJ, NOVEMBER 21, 1921. DIED: DECEMBER 9, 1995.

If not for her hilarious, much-imitated creation of the inimitable Miss Adelaide, Vivian Blaine might have been an unremarkable footnote in musical history. The former band singer was signed by 20th Century-Fox in 1942 and appeared in a string of their standard musical fare, including one in support of Laurel and Hardy, *Jitterbugs*; the bowdlerization of Cole Porter's *Something for the Boys*, singing with newcomer Perry Como; and her first and only genuine lead, *Doll Face*, where the budget did not extend to Technicolor. The most notable of her Fox assignments were Rodgers and Hammerstein's *State Fair*, as a band singer, introducing such numbers as "It's a Grand Night for Singing" and "That's for Me," and *Three Little Girls in Blue*, trying to nab a millionaire husband in *Atlantic City*. (The movie gave that seaside resort its signature tune, "On the Boardwalk in Atlantic City.") In 1950, she won the role of Adelaide, the brassy, nasal-voiced nightclub singer in Frank Loesser's smash hit, *Guys and Dolls*. She became the toast of Broadway, bringing down the house each night with her recitation of her many ailments in "Adelaide's Lament." She was invited to repeat her role in the 1955 movie adaptation, thereby preserving her performance for generations to come. Ironically, there was little left to her movie career. She was Red Skelton's leading lady in his last

starring vehicle, *Public Pigeon No. One*, but afterwards there was only sporadic work in little-seen or unreleased "B" films.
Screen: **1942:** Thru Different Eyes; Girl Trouble; **1943:** He Hired the Boss; Jitterbugs; **1944:** Greenwich Village; Something for the Boys; **1945:** Nob Hill; State Fair; Doll Face; **1946:** If I'm Lucky; Three Little Girls in Blue; **1952:** Skirts Ahoy; **1953:** Main Street to Broadway; **1955:** Guys and Dolls; **1957:** Public Pigeon No. One; **1972:** Richard; **1978:** The Dark.
NY Stage: **1950:** Guys and Dolls; **1956:** A Hatful of Rain; **1958:** Say Darling; **1963:** Enter Laughing; **1972:** Company; **1983:** Zorba.
Select TV: **1951–52:** Those Two (series); **1953:** Double Jeopardy (sp); **1955:** Pick the Winner (sp); Dream Girl (sp); **1978:** Katie — Portrait of a Centerfold; **1979:** The Cracker Factory; Fast Friends; Sooner or Later.

BETSY BLAIR

(ELIZABETH WINIFRED BOGER)
BORN: NEW YORK, NY, DECEMBER 11, 1923.

Affable, soft-spoken Betsy Blair seemed too wholesome to make it in the cut-throat world of show business, and she was, in fact, best known as Mrs. Gene Kelly, having married the dancer in 1940. She came to films in her own right in 1947, supporting Rosalind Russell in *The Guilt of Janet Ames*, but she made her first real impression as one of the asylum inmates in *The Snake Pit*. She was scheduled to play Desdemona in Orson Welles's troubled adaptation of *Othello*, but the part went to Suzanne Cloutier. When her big opportunity came, however, Blair seized it, with her role as the dowdy schoolteacher romanced by Ernest Borgnine, in the 1955 Academy Award-winner for Best Picture, *Marty*. Her heartfelt performance earned her an Oscar nomination but it also, ironically, heralded the end of her Hollywood career. After divorcing Kelly in 1957 she did a western, *The Halliday Brand*, as the daughter of bigoted Ward Bond, and then moved to Europe to work in films there. The next time she was seen Stateside it was some 15 years later, in the adaptation of Edward Albee's stage hit *A Delicate Balance*, where she and Joseph Cotten were the panic-stricken couple nest door. Another lengthy period lapsed before she showed up as Tom Berenger's mother in *Betrayed*. She was married briefly (1963–69) to director Karel Reisz and afterwards remarried and made her home in London.
Screen: **1947:** The Guilt of Janet Ames; A Double Life; **1948:** Another Part of the Forest; The Snake Pit; **1950:** Mystery Street; **1951:** Kind Lady; **1955:** Marty; **1957:** The Halliday Brand; **1958:** Calle Mayor/The Lovemaker; **1960:** The Dauphins (nUSr); **1961:** Senilita (nUSr); All Night Long (nUSr); **1962:** Il Grido/The Outrcy (It: 1957); **1969:** Marry Me!Marry Me!; **1973:** A Delicate Balance; **1986:** Descente aux Enfers (nUSr); **1987:** Flight of the Space Goose (nUSr); **1988:** Betrayed.
NY Stage: **1941:** The Beautiful People; **1951:** King Richard II; **1960:** Face of a Hero.
Select TV: **1950:** The Charmed Circle (sp); **1957:** A Will to Live (sp); **1988:** Suspicion; Marcus Welby — A Holiday Affair; **1994:** Scarlett (ms).

JANET BLAIR

(MARTHA JANET LAFFERTY)
BORN: ALTOONA, PA, APRIL 23, 1921.

A one-time band singer with no acting background, photogenic Janet Blair was signed to a movie contract in 1941 by Columbia Pictures to play the sister of Joan Blondell and Binnie Barnes in the farce *Three Girls About Town*. The following year she was the title character in the charming *My Sister Eileen*, as a pretty, aspiring actress who takes up residence in Greenwich Village with older and wiser sibling Rosalind Russell. That same year she was loaned out to Universal for her first full-fledged musical, *Broadway*, playing George Raft's dancing partner. Back at Columbia she was featured opposite Cary Grant in one of his least-famous movies, *Once Upon a Time*, about a dancing caterpillar; the Rita Hayworth musical drama, *Tonight and Every Night*, singing the Oscar-nominated "Anywhere;" *Tars and Spars*, which was more notable for featuring the movie debuts of Alfred Drake and Sid Caesar; and was Red Skelton's leading lady in his most popular comedy vehicle, *The Fuller Brush Man*. She shifted over to television in the 1950s, where she was a regular on three different series, including *Caesar's Hour* as Sid Caesar's wife. There was a successful tour of *South Pacific*; one late starring role, in the British witchcraft thriller, *Burn, Witch, Burn!*; the mom role in an unsuccessful Disney musical, *The One and Only Genuine Original Family Band*; and the television series *The Smith Family*, as Henry Fonda's wife. After that she pretty much dropped out of sight.

Screen: 1941: Three Girls About Town; 1942: Blondie Goes to College; Two Yanks in Trinidad; Broadway; My Sister Eileen; 1943: Something to Shout About; 1944: Once Upon a Time; 1945: Tonight and Every Night; 1946: Tars and Spars; Gallant Journey; 1947: The Fabulous Dorseys; 1948: I Love Trouble; The Black Arrow; The Fuller Brush Man; 1957: Public Pigeon No. One; 1962: Boys' Night Out; Burn, Witch, Burn!/Night of the Eagle; 1968: The One and Only Genuine Original Family Band; 1976: Won Ton Ton, the Dog Who Saved Hollywood.

NY Stage: 1953: A Girl Can Tell.

Select TV: 1949–54: Leave It to Girls (series); 1955: A Connecticut Yankee (sp); One Touch of Venus (sp); 1956–57: Caesar's Hour (series); 1958–59: The Chevy Show (series); 1959: Strawberry Blonde (sp); 1971–72: The Smith Family (series).

ROBERT BLAKE

(Michael Gubitosi) Born: Nutley, NJ, September 18, 1933.

When Robert Blake was at the peak of his television popularity, starring as the title character in the 1970s cop show *Baretta*, many people were not aware that his acting career had begun in childhood. He had started out as one of the Little Rascals, joining the *Our Gang* series with the 1939 short, "Joy Scouts," during its later, weaker period at MGM. Originally billed as Mickey Gubitosi, he became Mickey Blake and then Bobby Blake by the end of the series in 1944. He continued as a child star, appearing as the Indian Little Beaver in the Republic western series, *Red Ryder*. (In later life he looked back on that career move with much derision.) There were also notable roles as the young violinist who grows up to be John Garfield in *Humoresque*, and as the Mexican lad who sells Humphrey Bogart the lottery ticket in *Treasure of the Sierra Madre*. As he grew older, he took small parts in films and on television, gaining a reputation as an outspoken and difficult actor. In 1967 he landed the best film role of his career, playing the complex killer Perry Smith in the riveting true-life drama, *In Cold Blood*, portraying both the pathos and the monstrosity of this character. He followed up with three forgettable vehicles: *Tell Them Willie Boy Is Here*, as the fugitive Indian who kills a man in self-defense; *Corky*, as a race car driver; and *Electra Glide in Blue*, as a highway patrol officer. With *Baretta*, the self-consciously cool Blake became an Emmy Award-

winner and a media superstar. Unfortunately, the effort to carry this success to the big screen resulted in two horrendously bad comedies: *Coast to Coast*, as a trucker linked to wacko Dyan Cannon; and *Second Hand Hearts*, where he and Barbara Harris were a pair of married losers. Another television series, *Hell Town*, sank without trace and Blake went on a long hiatus before returning to give a very mannered portrayal of another real-life killer, in the telefilm *Judgment Day: The John List Story*. His last big screen appearances featured him as a subway supervisor in *Money Train*, and as a weirdly face-painted drifter in David Lynch's excruciating *Lost Highway*. In 2001–02, he was back in the news when he found himself charged with his wife's murder.

Screen (features): AS MICKEY GUBITOSI: 1940: I Love You Again.

AS BOBBY BLAKE: 1942: Mokey; China Girl; Andy Hardy's Double Life; 1943: Lost Angel; Salute to the Marines; Slightly Dangerous; 1944: The Cherokee Flash; Tuscon Raiders; Marshal of Reno; The Big Noise; The San Antonio Kid; The Woman in the Window; Meet the People; The Seventh Cross; Vigilantes of Dodge City; Cheyenne Wildcat; Sheriff of Las Vegas; 1945: The Great Stagecoach Robbery; The Horn Blows at Midnight; Bells of Rosarita; Colorado Pioneers; Wagon Wheels Westward; Lone Texas Ranger; Phantom of the Plains; Dakota; Marshal of Laredo; Pillow to Post; 1946: California Gold Rush; Santa Fe Uprising; Sheriff of Redwood Valley; Stagecoach to Denver; Conquest of Cheyenne; Humoresque; Home on the Range; Sun Valley Cyclone; Out California Way; In Old Sacramento; A Guy Could Change; 1947: The Last Round-Up; Oregon Trail Scouts; Homesteaders of Paradise Valley; Marshal of Cripple Creek; The Return of Rin Tin Tin; Rustlers of Devil's Canyon; Vigilantes of Boomtown; 1948: The Treasure of the Sierra Madre; 1950: The Black Rose; Black Hand; 1952: Apache War Smoke; 1953: Treasure of the Golden Condor; Veils of Bagdad; 1956: Screaming Eagles; Three Violent People; The Rack.

AS ROBERT BLAKE: 1956: Rumble on the Docks; 1957: The Beast of Budapest; The Tijuana Story; 1958: Revolt in the Big House; 1959: Battle Flame; The Purple Gang; Pork Chop Hill; 1961: Town Without Pity; 1963: PT 109; The Connection; 1965: The Greatest Story Ever Told; 1966: This Property Is Condemned; 1967: In Cold Blood; 1969: Tell Them Willie Boy Is Here; 1972: Corky; 1973: Electra Glide in Blue; 1974: Busting; 1975: Ripped-Off; 1980: Coast to Coast; 1981: Second Hand Hearts; 1995: Money Train; 1997: Lost Highway.

NY Stage: 1965: Harry Noon and Night.

Select TV: 1963–64: The Richard Boone Show (series); 1975–78: Baretta (series); 1981: The Big Black Pill (and exec. prod.); The Monkey Mission (and exec. prod.); Of Mice and Men (and exec. prod.); 1983: Blood Feud (ms); Murder 1 — Dancer 3 (and exec. prod.); 1985: Heart of a Champion: The Ray Mancini Story; Hell Town (series); 1993: Judgment Day: The John List Story.

JOAN BLONDELL

Born: New York, NY, August 30, 1906.
Died: December 25, 1979.

Sassy, wisecracking blondes were a dime a dozen in 1930s Hollywood, but there was none better than Joan Blondell. Her impeccable timing was complemented by an amiability that was most comforting, like a beneficent aunt. The daughter of vaudevillians, she joined her folks' act as a child, touring throughout the world. Back in the States, she got a solo part on Broadway, in *The Trial of Mary Dugan*, in 1927. While she was appearing with James Cagney in *Penny Arcade*, Warner Bros.

bought the property and took both actors with it. Renamed *Sinners' Holiday*, it was released after Blondell's next assignment for the studio, *The Office Wife*. Secondary parts as brassy babes followed: *God's Gift to Women*, as a Parisian named Fifi; *Other Men's Women*, as a waitress dumped by Grant Withers in favor of Mary Astor; and *The Public Enemy*, as a gangster's moll. Staying on at Warners for the duration of the 1930s, she added her special glow to many a musical, comedy, or drama. With the passing years, even her greatest admirers would be at a loss to distinguish most of these from one another, thinking instead of Blondell first and the film second. Fittingly, her first lead, in 1932, was opposite Cagney in *Blonde Crazy*, in which they were con artists. Blondell took it all in stride, making it seem like what they were doing was more jovial than criminal. They also made a terrific team in *Footlight Parade*, one of the reasons this was probably the most enjoyable of the Busby Berkeley musicals. Prior to that she had sung "My Forgotten Man" in *Gold Diggers of 1933*.

She was *Miss Pinkerton*, a nurse investigating a murder; *Blondie Johnson* (at Fox), turning bad after being victimized by her landlord; a chorus girl loved by out-of-towner Eric Linden in *Big City Blues*; and best friends with Ann Dvorak and Bette Davis who together made *Three on a Match*. She traded barbs with another of Warners's sharpest blondes, Glenda Farrell, in *Havana Widows* and *I've Got Your Number*; and had marital problems in *Smarty*, a movie that wanted audiences to believe that there was humor in physical abuse. She did *Convention City* with Dick Powell, whose path she had crossed in the Busby Berkeley films, and would again in *Dames*. For *Broadway Gondolier* it was Blondell who got Powell in the final clinch, as she did in real life, marrying him in 1936. Powell opted for Ruby Keeler over Blondell in *Colleen* and *Gold Diggers of 1937*, and for Jeannie Madden in *Stage Struck*, where Blondell was supposed to be the untalented one, stuck financing her own Broadway showcase. Blondell was then saddled with Fernand Gravet in *The King and the Chorus Girl*, a comedy that should have been funnier, considering one of its script writers was Groucho Marx. Some of her best notices came playing opposite Leslie Howard (who had specifically requested her services) in the delicious Hollywood satire, *Stand-In*, distributed by United Artists. Back at Warners she was a reporter in *Back in Circulation*, *The Perfect Specimen*, and *Off the Record*. Feeling pigeon-holed, both she and Powell left the company in 1939 after their contract demands were rejected.

Blondell freelanced, doing three comedies with Melvyn Douglas at Columbia: *There's Always a Woman*, *Good Girls Go to Paris*, and *The Amazing Mr. Williams*. She sparkled in such comedies as *Topper Returns*, as a ghost, and *Three Girls About Town*, trying to find out who left a dead body at the hotel where she and Binnie Barnes are employed. Two of her less noteworthy efforts, *Model Wife* and *I Want a Divorce*, paired her again with Powell. The title of the latter turned out to be prophetic when she appeared on Broadway in Mike Todd's production *The Naked Genius*. She and Powell divorced in 1945, and Todd became her next husband two years later (until 1950). Back in Hollywood, she showed wonderful versatility as Aunt Cissy in the excellent film of *A Tree Grows in Brooklyn*. There were good supporting roles in *Nightmare Alley*, as a carnival performer, and *The Blue Veil*, as a has-been vaudevillian, a performance that garnered her her only Oscar nomination. She had a starring role in *The Corpse Came C.O.D.* in 1947, but that marked the last time she would be called on to carry a movie. As she grew older and plumper she continued to provide stellar support to Katharine Hepburn in *Desk Set*, and to Edward G. Robinson in *The Cincinnati Kid*, dealing hands for the high-stakes poker players. She received a pair of Emmy nominations for her work on the television series

Here Come the Brides and, a year before her death, added much-appreciated *bonhomie* to the peripheral role of a soda shop owner in *Grease*. Her novel, *Center Door Fancy* (1972), was a thinly disguised version of her own life.

Screen: 1930: The Office Wife; Sinners' Holiday; 1931: Illicit; Millie; My Past; God's Gift to Women; Other Men's Women/The Steel Highway; The Public Enemy; Big Business Girl; Night Nurse; The Reckless Hour; Blonde Crazy; 1932: Union Depot; The Greeks Had a Word for Them; The Crowd Roars; The Famous Ferguson Case; Make Me a Star; Miss Pinkerton; Big City Blues; Three on a Match; Central Park; Lawyer Man; 1933: Blondie Johnson; Broadway Bad; Gold Diggers of 1933; Goodbye Again; Footlight Parade; Havana Widows; Convention City; 1934: I've Got Your Number; Smarty; Dames; He Was Her Man; Kansas City Princess; 1935: Traveling Saleslady; Broadway Gondolier; We're in the Money; Miss Pacific Fleet; 1936: Colleen; Sons o' Guns; Bullets or Ballots; Stage Struck; Three Men on a Horse; Gold Diggers of 1937; 1937: The King and the Chorus Girl; Back in Circulation; The Perfect Specimen; Stand-In; 1938: There's Always a Woman; Off the Record; 1939: East Side of Heaven; The Kid From Kokomo; Good Girls Go to Paris; The Amazing Mr. Williams; 1940: Two Girls on Broadway; I Want a Divorce; 1941: Topper Returns; Model Wife; Three Girls About Town; 1942: Lady for a Night; 1943: Cry Havoc; 1945: A Tree Grows in Brooklyn; Don Juan Quilligan; Adventure; 1947: The Corpse Came C.O.D.; Nightmare Alley; Christmas Eve; 1950: For Heaven's Sake; 1951: The Blue Veil; 1956: The Opposite Sex; 1957: Lizzie; This Could Be the Night; Desk Set; Will Success Spoil Rock Hunter?; 1961: Angel Baby; 1964: Advance to the Rear; 1965: The Cincinnati Kid; 1966: Paradise Road; Ride Beyond Vengeance; 1967: Waterhole No. 3; 1968: Kona Coast; Stay Away, Joe; 1970: The Phynx; 1971: Support Your Local Gunfighter; 1976: Won Ton Ton, the Dog Who Saved Hollywood; 1977: Opening Night; The Baron/Black Clue; 1978: Grease; 1979: The Champ; 1981: The Glove; The Woman Inside.

NY Stage: 1927: The Trial of Mary Dugan; Tarnish; 1929: Maggie the Magnificent; Penny Arcade; 1943: The Naked Genius; 1957: The Rope Dancers; 1972: The Effect of Gamma Rays on Man-in-the-Moon Marigolds (ob).

Select TV: 1955: Star in the House (sp); 1957: Child of Trouble (series); 1959: A Marriage of Strangers (sp); 1963: The Real McCoys (series); 1967: Winchester '73; 1968–70: Here Come the Brides (series); 1972–73: Banyon (series); 1975: The Dead Don't Die; Winner Take All; 1976: Death at Love House; 1978: Battered; The Rebels (ms).

CLAIRE BLOOM

BORN: LONDON, ENGLAND, FEBRUARY 15, 1931.

A sophisticated and intelligent actress, Claire Bloom was already on the London stage as a teen when the Rank Organisation decided to promote her as a starlet. After one film she retreated to the theatre, making an impression in such plays as *The Lady's Not for Burning* and *Ring Round the Moon*. As a result her movie career was relaunched with much hype as the ballerina fostered by Charlie Chaplin in his final American production, *Limelight*. She followed it by playing a woman who gains James Mason's affections to help her escape from East Berlin in *The Man Between*, and received acclaim for important roles in Laurence Olivier's *Richard III*, as Lady Anne; the lavish Hollywood production of *The Brothers Karamazov*, as Katya; and the film of the groundbreaking stage drama *Look Back in*

Anger, as Richard Burton's mistress. She went to Broadway in 1959 to star in *Rashomon* with Rod Steiger, whom she married that same year. Bloom became one of the less-heralded British names to appear in international productions during the 1960s, with an unrewarding role in the Cinerama family epic *The Wonderful World of the Brothers Grimm*, and a more fulfilling assignment, playing a sad nympho, in the glossy soap *The Chapman Report*. She was a tart-tongued lesbian in the talky ghost story *The Haunting*, which has earned a cult following over the years. This was followed by the misguided *The Outrage*, a *Rashomon*-like story in which she was presumably raped by Mexican bandit Paul Newman, and the deadly dull *The Spy Who Came in From the Cold*, as a communist librarian who falls for drab agent Richard Burton.

Perhaps her best-remembered role came when she replaced Anne Heywood in *Charly*. Bloom did a good job in a difficult part, as the therapist who helps retarded Cliff Robertson, only to reject him when she realizes that he is falling in love with her. Shortly after this, she and Steiger divorced, in 1969, the same year that their two film appearances together were released: *The Illustrated Man*, a distastrous attempt to film some Ray Bradbury stories, with Bloom in various roles; and *Three Into Two Won't Go*, which, appropriately, was about a disintegrating marriage. In *A Severed Head* she was a professor carrying on with her half-brother, Richard Attenborough, and then gave her best shot at a Southern accent, playing Richard Thomas's lonely mother in *Red Sky at Morning*. After playing Nora in a New York stage production of *A Doll's House*, she committed the role to film in 1973. Another adaptation, starring Jane Fonda, appeared around the same time, but Bloom received the better notices. She was a great asset to *Islands in the Stream*, showing up as the ex-wife of independent beachcomber George C. Scott, but seemed as uncomfortable as the rest of the starry guests, playing Hera to Olivier's Zeus, in the silly *Clash of the Titans*. Better things were happening for her in various British television dramas, including *Brideshead Revisited*, *Shadowlands*, and *Intimate Contact*. On screen she was involved in a relationship with Shashi Kapoor in *Sammy and Rosie Get Laid*, a film whose title was more intriguing than its plot, and was little more than background dressing as the wife deceived by Martin Landau in *Crimes and Misdemeanors*. Atypically she appeared in an action movie, *Daylight*, as one of the people trapped in a tunnel whom Sylvester Stallone hopes to save.

Screen: 1948: The Blind Goddess; 1952: Limelight; 1953: The Man Between; 1955: Innocents of Paris (UK: 1953); 1956: Richard III; Alexander the Great; 1958: The Brothers Karamazov; The Buccaneer; 1959: Look Back in Anger; 1961: Brainwashed; 1962: The Wonderful World of the Brothers Grimm; The Chapman Report; 1963: The Haunting; 80,000 Suspects (nUSr); 1964: Il Maesatro di Vigevano (nUSr); The Outrage; 1965: High Infidelity; The Spy Who Came in From the Cold; 1968: Charly; 1969: The Illustrated Man; Three Into Two Won't Go; 1971: A Severed Head; Red Sky at the Morning; 1973: A Doll's House; 1977: Islands in the Stream; 1981: Clash of the Titans; 1985: Dejavu; 1987: Sammy and Rosie Get Laid; 1989: Crimes and Misdemeanors; 1994: A Village Affair (nUSr); The Princess and the Goblin (voice); 1995: Mighty Aphrodite; 1996: Daylight; 1998: Wrestling with Alligators (dtv).

NY Stage: 1956: Romeo and Juliet; Richard II; 1959: Rashomon; 1971: A Doll's House (ob); Hedda Gabler; 1972: Vivat! Vivat! Regina; 1976: The Innocents; 1998: Electra.

Select TV: 1955: Romeo and Juliet (sp); 1961: Anna Karenina;

1973: The Going Up of David Lev; 1979: Backstairs at the White House (ms); 1982: Brideshead Revisted (ms); 1983: Separate Tables; 1984: Ghost Writer; Ellis Island (ms); Time and the Conways; Florence Nightingale; Promises to Keep; 1985: Shadowlands (sp); 1986: Liberty; Anastasia: The Mystery of Anna; 1987: Consenting Adults (ms); Queenie (ms); Hold the Dream; 1988: Beryl Markham: A Shadow in the Sun; 1989: The Lady and the Highwayman; 1997: Family Money (series); What the Deaf Man Heard; 1998: Imogene's Face; 1999: The Lady in Question; 2000: Love and Murder; Yesterday's Children.

ERIC BLORE

BORN: LONDON, ENGLAND, DECEMBER 23, 1887.
DIED: MARCH 2, 1959.

The Astaire-Rogers films could certainly stand on their own musical achievements, but having the terrific supporting talent of comical Eric Blore did them no harm. He appeared in no fewer than five in the series: *Flying Down to Rio*, as an assistant to hotel manager Franklin Pangborn; *The Gay Divorcee*, as a fractious waiter; *Top Hat*, as a butler, memorably introducing himself by proclaiming, "*We are Bates;*" *Swing Time*, as the impatient dance-school manager; and *Shall We Dance*, in which he hilariously tried to spell "Susquehanna" for Edward Everett Horton's benefit. Elsewhere, he carried on most winningly as Leslie Howard's ingratiating valet with a penchant for strange bird calls in Warners' *It's Love I'm After*. A former insurance agent, Blore first did a spell of acting in Australia, then in London, before coming to America in 1923. He launched his Hollywood career in the 1926 version of *The Great Gatsby* as Lord Digby. The diminutive, balding actor made a career out of variations on the haughty gentleman's gentleman, huffily reacting to situations for maximum effect. Following a rare lead role in his native country, called (of course) *A Gentleman's Gentleman*, he returned to Los Angeles where he was the fake Sir Alfred, a cardsharp, in *The Lady Eve*; a servant in the company of Fred Astaire in *The Sky's the Limit*; and the butler, Jamison, for ten episodes of *The Lone Wolf* series. As his career dwindled to less prestigious pictures, including the immortal *Bowery to Bagdad*, as a genie, he landed the plum assignment as the voice of Mr. Toad in Disney's *The Adventures of Ichabod and Mr. Toad*.

Screen: 1926: The Great Gatsby; 1930: Laughter; 1931: My Sin; Tarnished Lady; 1933: Flying Down to Rio; 1934: The Gay Divorcee; Limehouse Blues; 1935: Behold My Wife; Top Hat; Folies Bergere; To Beat the Band; The Good Fairy; Diamond Jim; Old Man Rhythm; The Casino Murder Case; I Live My Life; I Dream Too Much; Seven Keys to Baldpate; 1936: Swing Time; Two in the Dark; The Ex-Mrs. Bradford; The Smartest Girl in Town; Sons o'Guns; Piccadilly Jim; 1937: Quality Street; The Soldier and the Lady; Shall We Dance; Breakfast for Two; It's Love I'm After; Hitting a New High; 1938: Joy of Living; Swiss Miss; A Desperate Adventure; 1939: Island of Lost Men; A Gentleman's Gentleman; $1,000 a Touchdown; 1940: Music in My Heart; The Man Who Wouldn't Talk; Till We Meet Again; South of Suez; The Boys From Syracuse; The Earl of Puddlestone; The Lone Wolf Strikes; The Lone Wolf Meets a Lady; The Lone Wolf Keeps a Date; 1941: The Lady Eve; Sullivan's Travels; The Shanghai Gesture; Road to Zanzibar; Red Head; Lady Scarface; New York Town; Three Girls About Town; The Lone Wolf Takes a Chance; Secrets of Lone Wolf; 1942: The Moon and Sixpence; Confirm or Deny; Counter Espionage; 1943: Happy Go Lucky; The Sky's the Limit; Forever and a Day; Holy Matrimony; Submarine Base; Passport to Suez; One Dangerous Night; 1944: San Diego, I Love

You; **1945:** I Was a Criminal; Kitty; Penthouse Rhythm; Men in Her Diary; Easy to Look At; **1946:** Abie's Irish Rose; The Notorious Lone Wolf; **1947:** Winter Wonderland; The Lone Wolf in London; The Lone Wolf in Mexico; **1948:** Romance on the High Seas; **1949:** The Adventures of Ichabod and Mr. Toad (voice); Love Happy; **1950:** Fancy Pants; **1954:** Bowery to Bagdad.

NY Stage: 1923: Little Miss Bluebeard; 1926: Ghost Train; 1927: Mixed Doubles; Just Fancy!; 1928: Here's Howe!; Angela; 1929: Meet the Prince; 1930: Roar China; 1931: Give Me Yesterday; Here Goes the Bride; 1932: Gay Divorce.

Select TV: 1951: An Old Old Story (sp).

ANN BLYTH
BORN: MT. KISCO, NY, AUGUST 16, 1928.

She was groomed to be a singer, but it is for playing one of the screen's great spoiled brats that Ann Blyth will be best remembered. A child prodigy, she began singing professionally at age 5, performed on the radio, and studied with the San Carlos Opera Company. Her acting break came with the Broadway production of Watch on the Rhine, as Paul Lukas's daughter. When the play came to Los Angeles she was tested and signed by Universal. They started her as the second lead in some second-rate Donald O'Connor-Peggy Ryan musicals but, fortunately, she was borrowed by Warner Bros., who cast her as Joan Crawford's horrid, selfish daughter, Veda, in Mildred Pierce, a depiction that earned her an Oscar nomination and made her a star. Her follow-up roles weren't particularly impressive, ranging from a bitchy, younger version of Bette Davis in Another Part of the Forest (the prequel to The Little Foxes); to the silly fantasy, Mr. Peabody and the Mermaid, which attempted to sell her as a sex symbol; to a very lovely, but otherwise unremarkable colleen enchanted by Bing Crosby in one of his lesser vehicles, Top o' the Morning. She took a lead in the grandiose soap opera, Our Very Own, about an adopted girl who tracks down her birth mother, and was the standard "loving wife" in Mario Lanza's biggest hit, MGM's The Great Caruso. Metro tried to make her a major singing star, but properties like the tired remake of Rose Marie, the mummified The Student Prince, and the best of the lot, Kismet, arrived at the end of MGM's musical heyday and did little for her. She ended her movie career with two poorly received biopics, The Buster Keaton Story, as one of his wives; and The Helen Morgan Story, for which she was critically lambasted. She retired to occasional summer stock appearances and concerts, and did a brief stint in the 1970s as spokesperson for Hostess Cupcakes.

Screen: 1944: Chip Off the Old Block; The Merry Monahans; Babes on Swing Street; Bowery to Broadway; 1945: Mildred Pierce; 1947: Swell Guy; Brute Force; Killer McCoy; A Woman's Vengeance; 1948: Another Part of the Forest; Mr. Peabody and the Mermaid; 1949: Red Canyon; Once More, My Darling; Top o' the Morning; Free for All; 1950: Our Very Own; 1951: Katie Did It; The Great Caruso; Thunder on the Hill; The Golden Horde; I'll Never Forget You; 1952: The World in His Arms; Sally and Saint Anne; One Minute to Zero; 1953: All the Brothers Were Valiant; 1954: Rose Marie; The Student Prince; 1955: The King's Thief; Kismet; 1956: Slander; 1957: The Buster Keaton Story; The Helen Morgan Story.

NY Stage: 1941: Watch on the Rhine.

DIRK BOGARDE
(DEREK JULES GASPARD ULRIC NIVEN VAN DEN BOGAERD) BORN: LONDON, ENGLAND, MARCH 28, 1921. DIED: MAY 8, 1999.

One of Britain's most popular and respected stars, Dirk Bogarde began as a prettified, competent leading man before maturing into a complex and intriguing actor. Originally intent on being a commercial artist, he was bitten by the acting bug after winning a role in When We Are Married, at a suburban London theatre called Q. There was one film as an extra, Come on George, followed by war service, and finally, his London debut in Power Without Glory, in 1946. Soon the handsome, slightly aloof actor was signed by the Rank Organisation to play the footman who seduces the title heroine, in Esther Waters, after original choice Stewart Granger dropped out. His standing was greatly enhanced by starring in the very popular drama The Blue Lamp, as a crook who kills a policeman, and he was again on the lam in Hunted, only this time with an orphan boy in tow. The role won him his best reviews to date. It was a comedy, Doctor in the House, about a group of fun-seeking medical students, that turned him into a major box-office attraction. The film spawned several sequels, three of which he starred in, as "Dr. Sparrow," while guesting in another, We Joined the Navy. He put his sinister side to to good use as a Bluebeard in Cast a Giant Shadow; was unconvincing in the title role of The Spanish Gardener; and followed in Ronald Colman's footsteps to the guillotine for the remake of A Tale of Two Cities. There were two MGM-financed films made in England: George Bernard Shaw's The Doctor's Dilemma (not to be confused with the Doctor comedies), in which he was a dying scoundrel; and Libel, as an amnesia victim. His first foray in Hollywood, playing composer Franz Liszt in Song Without End, was enough of a failure to put a stop to any further work in the States. (This film is not to be confused with The Singer Not the Song, released soon afterwards, in which he was — of all things — a black leather-clad Mexican bandit attracted to clergyman John Mills.)

With the arrival of the 1960s, Bogarde took on a daring role in an important film, Victim. As a married barrister faced with the public exposure of his homosexuality, he partook in an exceptional film that proved to be a milestone for two reasons: it treated a delicate subject with intelligence and sympathy, and it featured a gay performer in the starring role, playing a gay character. He followed this with a complete volte-face, as the sadistic naval disciplinarian who challenges captain Alec Guinness in the rousing Damn the Defiant! A good teaming with Judy Garland, battling her for their illegitimate child, in her last film, I Could Go on Singing, preceded an enigmatic performance in the title role of Joseph Losey's somewhat unsatisfying The Servant. Bogarde won the BFA Award, the British film industry's highest honor, for his efforts. He teamed again with Losey to better effect, in the grim World War I drama, King and Country; was one of Julie Christie's many lovers in one of the seminal British films of the decade, Darling, winning another BFA Award; adopted a fey blond wig as the villain in Losey's disastrous spy spoof, Modesty Blaise; and, in the cryptic Accident, he effectively hid his passion for a young student. He was featured in the controversial and decadent examination of the Nazis, The Damned, for Italian director Luchino Visconti, who also cast him in the atmospheric Death in Venice, based on Thomas Mann's novel. As the tormented composer Gustav von Eschenbach, obsessed with a beautiful young boy, Bogarde gave a haunting performance. Working less frequently in films, he began to concentrate on writing. He published four volumes of his memoirs, *A Postillion Struck by Lightning* (1977), *Snakes and Ladders* (1978), *An Orderly Man* (1983), and *Cleared for Take Off* (1995), as well as the novels *A Gentle Occupation* (1980), *Voices in the Garden* (1981), and *West of Sunset* (1984). He was knighted in 1992.

Screen: 1939: Come on George; 1947: Dancing With Crime; 1948: Esther Waters; Quartet; Once a Jolly Swagman; 1949: Dear Mr. Prohack; Boys in Brown; 1950: The Blue Lamp; So Long at the Fair; The Woman in Question; 1951: Blackmailed; 1952: Hunted; Penny Princess; The Gentle Gunman; 1953: Appointment in London; Desperate Moment; 1954: They Who Dare; Doctor in the House; The Sleeping Tiger; For Better For Worse; The Sea Shall Not Have Them; 1955: Simba; Doctor at Sea; Cast a Dark Shadow; 1956: The Spanish Gardener; 1957: Ill Met By Moonlight/Night Ambush; Doctor at Large; Campbell's Kingdom; 1958: A Tale of Two Cities; The Wind Cannot Read; The Doctor's Dilemma; 1959: Libel; 1960: Song Without End; The Singer Not the Song; The Angel Wore Red; 1961: Victim; 1962: HMS Defiant/Damn the Defiant!; The Password Is Courage; We Joined the Navy; 1963: The Mind Benders; I Could Go on Singing; Doctor in Distress; The Servant; 1964: Hot Enough for June/Agent 8 3/4; King and Country; 1965: The High Bright Sun/McGuire Go Home!; Darling; 1966: Modesty Blaise; 1967: Accident; Our Mother's House; 1968: Sebastian; The Fixer; 1969: Oh! What a Lovely War; Justine; The Damned; 1971: Death in Venice; 1973: The Serpent; 1974: The Night Porter; 1975: Permission to Kill; 1977: Providence; A Bridge Too Far; 1978: Despair; 1991: Daddy Nostalgia.

Select TV: 1966: Blithe Spirit; 1973: Upon This Rock; 1982: The Patricia Neal Story; 1986: May We Borrow Your Husband?; 1987: The Vision.

HUMPHREY BOGART

BORN: NEW YORK, NY, JANUARY 23, 1899.
DIED: JANUARY 14, 1957.

Should a list of the five or ten most significant stars in movie history be drawn up for posterity, Humphrey Bogart's name would feature prominently on it. In fact, when the American Film Institute did just that, categorizing by sex, it was no great surprise that Bogart headed the male list. With his lisping speech and unglamorous face, Bogart defied all the leading-man conventions to become a charismatic and popular star on the sheer strength of his unique personality. He was one of the early anti-heroes, playing rogues to perfection, but even when playing the hero, his cocksure attitude and world-weariness remained. He was the guy you wanted on your side, whose gritty determination, integrity, and *savoir-faire* got the job done. Born to wealth, he was kicked out of Phillips Academy before joining the navy, where he received the injury to his lip that gave him that trademark lisp. After the war, a boyhood acquaintance got him a job as a stage manager, which led to a walk-on in *Experience*, and thence to his Broadway debut, in *Drifting*, in 1920. After a decade of stage he was spotted by a Fox talent scout in *It's a Wise Child*, was tested, and signed to a contract. He debuted in *A Devil with Women*, billed below Victor McLaglen, but winning the girl (Mona Maris) from him at the end. Next up was the largely comical prison movie, *Up the River*, which, although it featured Spencer Tracy in *his* debut, and John Ford as director, was not a highpoint for any of them.

After three more for Fox and a loan-out to Universal, playing a cad who marries, then dumps Sidney Fox in *Bad Sister*, he was dropped from his contract, prompting him to return to the stage.

Back in Hollywood, Columbia gave him his first official lead, as a pilot-inventor involved with heiress Dorothy Mackaill in the quickie *Love Affair*. Warners gave him his first gangster role, in *Three on a Match*, as a kidnapper named The Mug, but again he made his way back to New York. He finally got the break he needed, as low-life hoodlum Duke Mantee, holding a group of people hostage at a desert filling station, in the Robert Sherwood play *The Petrified Forest*. At co-star Leslie Howard's insistence, Bogart repeated the role in Warners's excellent 1936 movie adaptation and he signed with the studio as a contract player. He took mainly supporting parts, though he starred in one of the earliest movies to take a hard look at the Ku Klux Klan, *Black Legion*, and carried the remake of *Five Star Final*, redubbed *Two Against the World*, and set at a radio station. He clashed with Pat O'Brien in an acceptable prison film, *San Quentin*, then played a D.A. in one of the big Bette Davis hits of the day, *Marked Woman*. Despite the fact that he was one of the most exciting personalities on screen, Warners kept him lower down the cast list than he deserved.

In *Bullets or Ballots*, he was the dangerous gangster whom Edward G. Robinson tries to expose by infiltrating his gang; in *Kid Galahad*, as a fighter-manager/hoodlum, he again came after Robinson with guns blazing when he's double-crossed; and he completed his Eward G. trifecta in *The Amazing Dr. Clitterhouse*, as a jewel thief named Rocks Valentine. More impressively, he took on James Cagney in two of his best gangster flicks, *Angels With Dirty Faces*, as a lawyer-turned-nightclub owner who pays the price for his disloyalty, and *The Roaring Twenties*, as a rival bootlegger who goes from tough dog to sniveling coward when facing the other end of a gun barrel. Despite their urban personalities he and Cagney came off well in a western, *The Oklahoma Kid*, where Bogart was a particularly unsavory villain. Another good gangster role, made on loan-out, was in *Dead End*, a theatrical but powerful look at New York slum life and corruption. Based on Sidney Kingsley's play, it featured big shot Bogart returning to his neighborhood, where he gets a literal and figurative slap in the face from his mother and his old girlfriend, who's become a whore. A less typical role was as the whimsical, pooch-toting Hollywood producer, trying to salvage a sinking studio, in the sharp satire *Stand-In*. Back at Warners the actor had to contend with the silly role of a wrestling manager in *Swing Your Lady* (his own least favorite film); became a member of the walking dead in the career nadir *The Return of Dr. X*; and was very much ill at ease as an Irish stable boy in *Dark Victory*.

He was still taking secondary parts to "bigger" names as the 1940s began: George Raft in *Invisible Stripes* and *They Drive by Night*; Errol Flynn in the western *Virginia City*; and Edward G. Robinson, again, in *Brother Orchid*. This frustrating state of affairs might have continued indefinitely, had not everyone else turned down the role of Mad Dog Earle in *High Sierra*. As a killer on the run from the police, Bogart was riveting in a well-made and engrossing film that proved a box-office success. He was, at long last, declared a true star. Showing he could be just as convincing on the right side of justice, he played one of his signature roles, the ultimate hard-boiled private eye, Sam Spade, in director-writer John Huston's classic noir *The Maltese Falcon*. This marked the beginning of Bogart's reign at Warners. He followed it with the light-hearted *All Through the Night*, stumbling into a ring of Nazi spies while trying to locate his pal's murderer; the minor *The Big Shot*, which resembled one of his lesser 1930s assignments; and *Across the Pacific*, which brought together several of the names behind *Falcon* with less fruitful results. *Casablanca* not only brought him his first Oscar nomination, but presented Bogart's hitherto unexplored romantic side. As the cynical but heroic expatriate cafe owner, Rick Blaine, he sacrifices his love for Ingrid Bergman in the name of "the cause." Rick became one of the great characters of movie lore and is certainly one of the most-quoted. The film, intelligently scripted and superbly acted, became one of the box-office smashes of the day. As *the* seminal wartime romance it garnered Warners the Academy Award for Best Picture of 1943. With World War II at its height it was only natural that Bogart would go into battle. For Warners he was in *Action in the North Atlantic*, and for Columbia he outwitted the enemy at a desert oasis in the tense *Sahara*.

1944 paired him with not only his best leading lady, but his future wife, Lauren Bacall. In Howard Hawks's *To Have and Have Not*, their magnetic chemistry was unbeatable and they teamed three more times for maximum effect. *The Big Sleep*, perhaps their apogee together, was an adaptation of Raymond Chandler's densely plotted novel. With Bogart as L.A. gumshoe Philip Marlowe, it was the definitive noir film. In *Dark Passage* Bogart's face was obscured for much of the film, his looks changed by a plastic surgeon so he can hunt down the person who got him thrown in jail. Lastly, there was *Key Largo*, which pitted him once more against Edward G. Robinson, although Bogart now had top billing. It was not all good, however, and he played wife-killers in both *Conflict* and *The Two Mrs. Carrolls*, a film so bad it spent two years on the shelf. He rebounded with a good melodrama for Columbia, *Dead Reckoning*, with Lizabeth Scott as a Bacall *manqué*. He decided to form his own company, dubbed Santana and distributed through Columbia. Their output consisted of an interesting examination of juvenile delinquency, *Knock on Any Door*; a disappointing Hollywood noir-thriller, *In a Lonely Place*, with Bogart stretching as a temperamental screenwriter; and two middling adventures, *Tokyo Joe*, and *Sirocco*. Daring to challenge his box-office standing, Bogart appeared in John Huston's grimly uncommercial *The Treasure of the Sierra Madre*. His callous and greedy prospector, Fred C. Dobbs, won raves and the movie, though not a hit in its day, became one of his most enduring works. He ended his contract with Warners after *The Enforcer*, in which he was a D.A. out to expose Everett Sloane as the head of an assassination ring.

Huston next paired Bogart brilliantly with Katharine Hepburn in the crowd-pleasing classic *The African Queen*. Released in 1951, the film expanded Bogey's range as a grubby, comical drunk, Charley Allnutt, who steals a spinster's heart. He won a well-deserved and very popular Academy Award. He followed up with a tough newspaper drama, *Deadline USA*; was oddly teamed with June Allyson in a Korean War story, *Battle Circus*; and did a tepid spoof for Houston, *Beat the Devil*, that developed a cult following, although Bogart dismissed it as a stinker. Three years after *Queen*, he was in the running for another Oscar as Queeg, the unhinged commander, in *The Caine Mutiny*, the highlight of which was Bogart's famous breakdown on the witness stand. Defying the skeptics, he replaced Cary Grant in the romantic comedy *Sabrina* and his casting against type was one factor that made the film so delightful. There was little to be said for a trite Hollywood story, *The Barefoot Contessa*, though Bogart's work, as a melancholy director, was not to be faulted. A fluffy comedy at Paramount, *We're No Angels*, misfired, and in Fox's widescreen effort, *The Left Hand of God*, he seemed disinterested as a downed flyer posing as a priest in China. There was one more ruthless killer, in the engrossing hostage drama *The Desperate Hours*, opposite Fredric March. (Spencer Tracy backed out when Bogart would not take second billing.) He finished his career with another good film, playing a washed-up sportswriter horrified at the corruption in the fight game, in *The Harder They Fall*, released shortly before his death from lung cancer. As the world becomes less interested in

nostalgia, Bogart's style refuses to go out of fashion. Over 40 years after his death, the Bogey legend is as robust as ever.

Screen: 1930: A Devil With Women; Up the River; 1931: Body and Soul; Bad Sister; Women of All Nations; A Holy Terror; 1932: Love Affair; Big City Blues; Three on a Match; 1934: Midnight; 1936: The Petrified Forest; Bullets or Ballots; Two Against the World; China Clipper; Isle of Fury; Black Legion; 1937: The Great O'Malley; San Quentin; Marked Woman; Kid Galahad; Dead End; Stand-In; 1938: Swing Your Lady; Men Are Such Fools; Crime School; The Amazing Dr. Clitterhouse; Racket Busters; Angels With Dirty Faces; 1939: King of the Underworld; The Oklahoma Kid; Dark Victory; You Can't Get Away With Murder; The Roaring Twenties; The Return of Dr. X; 1940: Invisible Stripes; Virginia City; It All Came True; Brother Orchid; They Drive by Night; 1941: High Sierra; The Wagons Roll at Night; The Maltese Falcon; 1942: All Through the Night; The Big Shot; Across the Pacific; In This Our Life; 1943: Casablanca; Action in the North Atlantic; Sahara; Thank Your Lucky Stars; 1944: Passage to Marseille; To Have and Have Not; 1945: Conflict; 1946: Two Guys From Milwaukee; The Big Sleep; 1947: Dead Reckoning; The Two Mrs. Carrolls; Dark Passage; 1948: Always Together; The Treasure of the Sierra Madre; Key Largo; 1949: Knock on Any Door; Tokyo Joe; 1950: Chain Lightning; In a Lonely Place; 1951: The Enforcer; Sirocco; The African Queen; 1952: Deadline USA; 1953: Battle Circus; Beat the Devil; The Love Lottery; 1954: The Caine Mutiny; Sabrina; A Star Is Born (voice); The Barefoot Contessa; 1955: We're No Angels; The Left Hand of God; The Desperate Hours; 1956: The Harder They Fall.

NY Stage: 1922: Drifting; Swifty; 1923: Meet the Wife; 1924: Nerves; 1925: Hell's Bells; Cradle Snatchers; 1927: Saturday's Children; Baby Mine; 1929: The Skyrocket; It's a Wise Child; 1931: After All; 1932: I Loved You Wednesday; Chrysalis; 1933: Our Wife; The Mask and the Face; 1934: Invitation to a Murder; 1935: The Petrified Forest.

Select TV: 1955: The Petrified Forest (sp).

MARY BOLAND

BORN: PHILADELPHIA, PA, JANUARY 28, 1880.
DIED: JUNE 23, 1965.

In the 1930s, when fluttery, scatterbrained ladies were a staple of screwball comedies, none was more diligently ditzy than Mary Boland. Debuting on the New York stage in 1905, she gained a solid reputation for her theatre work in *Clarence* and *Meet the Wife*, while appearing in some silent films. With the coming of sound she did two supporting roles for Paramount, and the studio, which would gain a reputation for breezy comedies, snatched her up. Someone had the good sense to pair her with Charlie Ruggles in the episodic *The Night of June 13*, and so began a series of inspired outings. The garrulous Boland henpecked the long-suffering Ruggles through *Six of a Kind*, where they ran into Burns and Allen, and the classic Leo McCarey comedy *Ruggles of Red Gap*, as the Flouds, Old West employers of manservant Charles Laughton. The duo was sufficiently popular to carry their own vehicles, such as *People Will Talk*, in which Boland mistakenly believes that Ruggles is having an affair with a younger woman, and *Early to Bed*, in which she has to contend with his sleepwalking habit. Their cherished, 13-film partnership ended in 1939 with a pair of programmers, *Boy Trouble* and *Night Work*. During her lucrative stay with Paramount, Boland made rare excursions into drama, such as *A Son Comes Home*, as a restaurant owner out to prove that her accused offspring is innocent of murder, but there was no doubt that audiences and critics preferred her in comedy. After leaving Paramount in the late 1930s she freelanced, joining the distaff ensemble of *The Women*, as the countess, before shining as the meddlesome, mercenary matriarch in MGM's splendid adaptation of *Pride and Prejudice*. She returned to the stage, touring extensively with *Meet the Wife*, and made a few low-budget movies before retiring in the early 1950s.

Screen: 1915: The Edge of the Abyss; 1916: The Price of Happiness; The Stepping Stone; 1917: Mountain Dew; 1918: A Woman's Experience; The Prodigal Wife; 1919: The Perfect Lover; 1920: His Temporary Wife; 1931: Secrets of a Secretary; Personal Maid; 1932: The Night of June 13th; Evenings for Sale; If I Had a Million; 1933: Mama Loves Papa; Three-Cornered Moon; The Solitaire Man; 1934: Four Frightened People; Six of a Kind; Melody in Spring; Stingaree; Here Comes the Groom; Down to Their Last Yacht; The Pursuit of Happiness; 1935: Ruggles of Red Gap; People Will Talk; Two for Tonight; The Big Broadcast of 1936; 1936: A Son Comes Home; Early to Bed; Wives Never Know; College Holiday; 1937: Marry the Girl; Danger-Love at Work; Mama Runs Wild; There Goes the Groom; 1938: Artists and Models Abroad; Little Tough Guys in Society; 1939: Boy Trouble; The Magnificent Fraud; Night Work; The Women; 1940: He Married His Wife; New Moon; Pride and Prejudice; Hit Parade of 1941; One Night in the Tropics; 1944: in Our Time; Nothing But Trouble; They Shall Have Faith; 1948: Julia Misbehaves; 1950: Guilty Bystander.

NY Stage: 1905: Strongheart; 1907: The Ranger; 1908: Jack Straw; 1909: Inconstant George; 1910: Smith; 1911: A Single Man; 1912: The Perplexed Husband; 1913: Much Ado About Nothing; The Tyranny of Tears; 1914: A Scrap of Paper; My Lady's Dress; 1916: Backfire; 1917: The Case of the Lady Chamber; 1918: Sick-a-Bed; The Matinee Hero; 1919: Clarence; 1921: Alias Jimmy Valentine; 1922: The Torch Bearers; 1923: Meet the Wife; 1925: Cradle Snatchers; 1927: Women Go On Forever; 1928: Heavy Traffic; 1930: Ada Beats the Drum; The Vinegar; 1932: Face the Music; 1935: Jubilee; 1942: The Rivals; 1947: Open House; 1954: Lullaby.

Select TV: 1950: The Rivals (sp); 1954: The First Born (sp); 1955: The Women (sp); The Guardsman (sp).

JOHN BOLES
BORN: GREENVILLE, TX, OCTOBER 27, 1895.
ED: UNIV. OF TX. DIED: FEBRUARY 27, 1969.

With the coming of sound, singers were in big demand, and so it was that John Boles, who was operatically trained in Paris, came into his element. He made a name for himself in several New York operettas, including *Mercenary Mary* and *The Love Spell*, and even took some silent movie roles. But it was with his first sound film, the benchmark *The Desert Song*, that his reputation was secured. Other successes in that creaky transition period included RKO's big hit *Rio Rita*, sharing the screen with comedians Wheeler and Woolsey; *Captain of the Guard*; *Song of the West*; and the offbeat variety show *The King of Jazz*, in which he sang the hit "It Happened in Monterey." When the fad for operettas started to wane, he turned to drama, appearing in two of Universal's most famous movies of this period: *Frankenstein*, as the young hero, Victor Moritz, and *Back Street*, as the married paramour of Irene Dunne. Squarely handsome and often mustachioed, Boles's lack of personal charisma was compensated for by pairings with dynamic leading ladies, like Dunne (in *The Age of Innocence*, where he failed to express the complexities of the lovelorn Newland Archer), Loretta Young (*The White Parade*),

Rosalind Russell (*Craig's Wife*, in a much-maligned performance, as Craig), and Barbara Stanwyck (*Stella Dallas*, as her boorish husband). Paramount wisely returned him to his roots, teaming him with Metropolitan Opera star Gladys Swarthout, in *Rose of the Rancho*. The movie was, unfortunately, a bust, as was their follow-up, *Romance in the Dark*. By the end of the 1930s, he was concentrating on theatre appearances and only returned to movies for a Monogram quickie, *The Road to Happiness*, and to play Kathryn Grayson's dad in MGM's all-star *Thousands Cheer*. After a nine-year absence, he inexplicably appeared in the kitschy *Babes in Bagdad*, which may have been the deciding factor in driving Boles out of movies and into the oil business.

Screen: 1924: So This Is Marriage?; 1925: Excuse Me; 1927: The Love of Sunya; 1928: The Shepherd of the Hills; We Americans; The Bride of the Colorado; Fazil; The Water Hole; Virgin Lips; Man-Made Woman; Romance of the Underworld; 1929: The Last Warning; The Desert Song; Scandal; Rio Rita; 1930: Song of the West; Captain of the Guard; The King of Jazz; One Heavenly Night; 1931: Resurrection; Seed; Frankenstein; Good Sport; 1932: Careless Lady; Back Street; Six Hours to Live; 1933: Child of Manhattan; My Lips Betray; Only Yesterday; 1934: I Believed in You; Music in the Air; Beloved; Bottoms Up; Stand Up and Cheer; The Life of Vergie Winters; Wild Gold; The Age of Innocence; The White Parade; 1935: Orchids to You; Curly Top; Redheads on Parade; The Littlest Rebel; 1936: Rose of the Rancho; A Message to Garcia; Craig's Wife; 1937: As Good as Married; Stella Dallas; Fight for Your Lady; 1938: She Married an Artist; Romance in the Dark; Sinners in Paradise; 1942: The Road to Happiness; Between Us Girls; 1943: Thousands Cheer; 1952: Babes in Bagdad.

NY Stage: 1924: Little Jesse James; 1925: Mercenary Mary; 1926: Kitty's Kisses; 1943: One Touch of Venus.

RAY BOLGER
BORN: DORCHESTER, MA, JANUARY 10, 1904.
DIED: JANUARY 15, 1987.

Undeniably a legend of the musical theatre, Ray Bolger was assured screen immortality for his *pièce-de-résistance* as the Scarecrow in *The Wizard of Oz*. Biding his time as a bank clerk and salesman, he studied dance at Russakoff's Ballet School before joining Bob Ott's Musical Comedy Repertory. Starring in vaudeville as one-half of a dance team, Sanford and Bolger, he soon gained fame for his rubbery-limbed style of movement. After his Broadway debut in *The Merry World*, in 1926, he became a favorite in such shows as *Life Begins at 8:40*, and his star-making *On Your Toes*, in which he performed the ballet "Slaughter on Tenth Avenue." MGM didn't consider the lanky dancer with the oversized nose to be leading man material, but they sought him out for specialty bits in films like *The Great Ziegfeld*, as himself, and *Sweethearts*, clomping in a pair of wooden shoes. When Arthur Freed produced his adaptation of *The Wizard of Oz*, Bolger was the perfect match for the Scarecrow, and his most beloved creation was born. His rendition of "If I Only Had a Brain" became one of the highlights of a movie chock full of riches. Remaining a supporting player in the movies, he went back to the stage for the stardom he felt was his due, scoring two of his biggest triumphs with *By Jupiter* and *Where's Charley?* When he reprised the latter role for an English-made film adaptation, he finally got top billing. One of the show's songs, "Once in Love With Amy," became something of a signature and was the theme of his short-lived television series in the 1950s. One last musical role, as the villainous Barnaby in

Disney's *Babes in Toyland*, in 1961, was not the career highlight it should have been. In later life he was content to rest on his laurels, although he was coaxed before the cameras for the occasional character part.

Screen: 1936: The Great Ziegfeld; 1937: Rosalie; 1938: Sweethearts; 1939: The Wizard of Oz; 1941: Sunny; 1943: Forever and a Day; Stage Door Canteen; 1944: Four Jacks and a Jill; 1946: The Harvey Girls; 1949: Make Mine Laughs; Look for the Silver Lining; 1952: Where's Charley?; 1953: April in Paris; 1961: Babes in Toyland; 1966: The Daydreamer; 1979: Just You and Me, Kid; The Runner Stumbles; 1985: That's Dancing!

NY Stage: 1926: Ritz-Carlton Nights; 1929: Heads Up!; 1931: George White's Scandals of 1931; 1934: Life begins at 8:40; 1936: On Your Toes; 1940: Keep Off the Grass; 1942: By Jupiter; 1946: Three to Make Ready; 1948: Where's Charley?; 1962: All American; 1969: Come Summer.

Select TV: 1953–55: The Ray Bolger Show/Where's Raymond? (series); 1956–57: Washington Square (series); 1958: The Girl With the Flaxen Hair (sp); 1959: Silhouette (sp); 1976: The Entertainer; Captains and the Kings (ms); 1978: Three on a Date.

WARD BOND

(WARDELL BOND) BORN: DENVER, CO, APRIL 9, 1903. DIED: NOVEMBER 5, 1960.

Blessed with a commanding *basso profundo* voice, burly workaholic Ward Bond made over 175 movie appearances, ranging from substantial support to mere walk-ons, in a 30-year span. His first movie assignment came about when he and fellow USC football player John Wayne appeared as extras for director John Ford's *Salute*. The three became close friends and frequently worked together throughout the rest of their careers. Bond made a total of 19 films for Ford, including *Drums Along the Mohawk*, as one of the settlers of the Mohawk Valley; *The Long Voyage Home*, as a rugged seaman called Yank; *The Grapes of Wrath*, as a policeman; *Fort Apache*, as a sergeant major; *3 Godfathers*, on the trail of bank robber John Wayne; *Wagon Master*, as an opinionated Mormon elder; *The Quiet Man*, as the village priest; and, in their last collaboration, *The Wings of Eagles*, cleverly cast as Hollywood director John Dodge, clearly based on Ford himself. Among his non-Ford films in support of Wayne were *Tall in the Saddle*, as a skeptical judge; *Operation Pacific*, as a submarine skipper; and *Rio Bravo*, commandeering a wagonload of dynamite. Bond also appeared in some of the most popular movies of all time, including *Gone With the Wind*, as a Yankee captain; *The Maltese Falcon*, as a detective; and *It's a Wonderful Life*, as the friendly cop, Bert. The definitive Ward Bond performance, however, was in *Gentleman Jim*, where his rip-roaring interpretation of hell-raising prizefighter John L. Sullivan brought down the house. He finally received star billing, in his own television series, *Wagon Train*, but he died of a heart attack during its run.

Screen: 1929: Salute; Words and Music; 1930: Born Reckless; The Big Trail; 1931: Arrowsmith; Three Girls Lost; A Connecticut Yankee; Sob Sister; The Spider; 1932: Virtue; Flesh; Hello Trouble; Rackety Rax; White Eagle; High Speed; The Trial of Vivienne Ware; Sundown Rider; 1933: When Strangers Marry; Heroes for Sale; Lady for a Day; Wild Boys of the Road; The Wrecker; Police Car 17; Lucky Devils; The Fighting Code; State Trooper; Unknown Valley; Straightaway; Obey the Law; 1934: Whirlpool; Most Precious Thing in Life; The Poor Rich; Frontier Marshal; Broadway Bill; It Happened One Night; The Defense Rests; The Fighting Ranger; Death on the Diamond; Here

Comes the Groom; Chained; The Affairs of Cellini; Voice in the Night; A Man's Game; The Crime of Helen Stanley; Circus Clown; Against the Law; Girl in Danger; The Human Side; I'll Tell the World; Men of the Night; Kid Millions; 6 Day Bike Rider; 1935: Western Courage; The Crimson Trail; Devil Dogs of the Air; She Gets Her Man; Grand Old Girl; His Night Out; Black Fury; Fighting Shadows; Little Big Shot; The Last Days of Pompeii; Go Into Your Dance; Calm Yourself; Guard That Girl; Times Square Lady; Murder in the Fleet; Waterfront Lady; Mary Jane's Pa; The Headline Woman; Broadway Hostess; Justice of the Range; Too Tough to Kill; Under Pressure; One New York Night; Three Kids and a Queen; 1936: Cattle Thief; Muss 'em Up; The Bride Walks Out; Crash Donovan; They Met in a Taxi; Legion of Terror; Conflict; The Man Who Lived Twice; Fury; The Leathernecks Have Landed; Avenging Waters; Pride of the Marines; The Gorgeous Hussy; Colleen; Fatal Lady; Second Wife; Two in the Dark; White Fang; The Accusing Finger; The First Baby; High Tension; Without Orders; 1937: You Only Live Twice; Topper; The Soldier and the Lady; Souls at Sea; Dead End; The Devil's Playground; A Fight to the Finish; The Wildcatter; 23 1/2 Hours Leave; Escape by Night; Night Key; Park Avenue Logger; Mountain Music; Music for Madame; Fight for Your Lady; Marry the Girl; When's Your Birthday?; Woman Wise; 1938: Born to Be Wild; The Law West of Tombstone; Reformatory; Professor Beware; Gun Law; Hawaii Calls; Flight Into Nowhere; Mr. Moto's Gamble; The Amazing Dr. Clitterhouse; Over the Wall; Numbered Woman; Prison Break; Bringing Up Baby; You Can't Take It With You; Of Human Hearts; Penitentiary; The Adventures of Marco Polo; Going Places; Fugitives for a Night; Submarine Patrol; 1939: Dodge City; Made for Each Other; The Cisco Kid and the Lady; They Made Me a Criminal; Waterfront; Trouble in Sundown; The Return of the Cisco Kid; Frontier Marshal; The Kid From Kokomo; The Oklahoma Kid; The Girl From Mexico; Drums Along the Mohawk; Heaven With a Barbed-Wire Fence; Mr. Moto in Danger Island; Confessions of a Nazi Spy; Pardon Our Nerve; Gone With the Wind; Young Mr. Lincoln; 1940: Santa Fe Trail; Buck Benny Rides Again; Little Old New York; Virginia City; The Grapes of Wrath; The Mortal Storm; The Long Voyage Home; Sailor's Lady; Kit Carson; 1941: The Shepherd of the Hills; A Man Betrayed; Tobacco Road; Swamp Water; Sergeant York; Manpower; Doctors Don't Tell; Wild Bill Hickok Rides; The Maltese Falcon; 1942: The Falcon Takes Over; In This Our Life; Gentleman Jim; Sin Town; Ten Gentlemen From West Point; A Night to Remember; 1943: Hello, Frisco, Hello; A Guy Named Joe; They Came to Blow Up America; Hitler — Dead or Alive; Cowboy Commandos; Slightly Dangerous; 1944: Home in Indiana; The Sullivans; Tall in the Saddle; 1945: Dakota; They Were Expendable; 1946: Canyon Passage; My Darling Clementine; It's a Wonderful Life; 1947: The Fugitive; Unconquered; 1948: Fort Apache; 3 Godfathers; The Time of Your Life; Joan of Arc; Tap Roots; 1950: Wagonmaster; Riding High; Singing Guns; Kiss Tomorrow Goodbye; 1951: The Great Missouri Raid; Operation Pacific; Only the Valiant; On Dangerous Ground; 1952: The Quiet Man; Thunderbirds; Hellgate; 1953: Blowing Wild; The Moonlighter; Hondo; 1954: Gypsy Colt; The Bob Mathias Story; Johnny Guitar; The Long Gray Line; 1955: Mister Roberts; A Man Alone; 1956: The Searchers; Dakota Incident; Pillars of the Sky; 1957: The Wings of Eagles; The Halliday Brand; 1958: China Doll; 1959: Rio Bravo; Alias Jesse James.

Select TV: 1950: My Brother's Keeper (sp); 1952: Apple of His Eye (sp); 1953: Gun Job (sp); Winners Never Loose (sp); 1955: Rookie of the Year (sp); 1956: The Marshal and the Mob (sp);

Plague Ship (sp); Once a Hero (sp); 1957–61: Wagon Train (series).

BEULAH BONDI
BORN: CHICAGO, IL, MAY 3, 1889.
DIED: JANUARY 11, 1981.

Audiences perceived diminutive Beulah Bondi as the ultimate, hair-in-a-bun arche-type of motherhood, even when she was barely in her 40s. She had started out in the theatre, as a child, with the title role in *Little Lord Fauntleroy*, and worked in stock for over 20 years before finally making it to Broadway in 1925. When Elmer Rice's tenement-life drama, *Street Scene*, was bought for film adaptation, Bondi was one of a handful of the original stage cast to be asked to repeat their roles. Thus, her Hollywood career was launched. She rapidly appeared in a string of motherly roles, playing mom to Helen Hayes (*Arrowsmith*, though a mere 11 years older than that lady), Sylvia Sidney (*The Trail of the Lonesome Pine*), Martha Scott (*Our Town*), Fred MacMurray (*Remember the Night*), and Bette Davis (*The Sisters*). To prove she could play any age, the same year she played Lionel Barrymore's stepdaughter in *The Stranger's Return*, she then showed up as his coarse wife in *Christopher Bean*. She received Best Supporting Actress Oscar nominations for *The Gorgeous Hussy*, as the devoted, pipe-smoking wife of Andrew Jackson, and for *Of Human Hearts*, playing James Stewart's com-passionate, self-sacrificing mother. Altogether she was Stewart's ma in four films, the other three being *Vivacious Lady*, *Mr. Smith Goes to Washington*, and, most memorably, *It's a Wonderful Life*. (In perhaps the movie's most haunting scene, she refuses Stewart entry to her house when he returns to the world in which he'd never been born.) Her finest hour came with Leo McCarey's beautiful 1937 drama, *Make Way for Tomorrow*, as an elderly woman separated from her husband and placed in a nursing home. Still active in her 80s, she won a 1977 Emmy Award for guest starring on the television series *The Waltons*.

Screen: 1931: Street Scene; Arrowsmith; 1932: Rain; 1933: Christopher Bean; The Stranger's Return; 1934: Finishing School; Two Alone; Ready for Love; Registered Nurse; 1935: Bad Boy; The Good Fairy; 1936: The Invisible Ray; The Trail of the Lonesome Pine; The Moon's Our Home; The Case Against Mrs. Ames; Hearts Divided; The Gorgeous Hussy; 1937: Maid of Salem; Make Way for Tomorrow; 1938: The Buccaneer; Of Human Hearts; Vivacious Lady; The Sisters; 1939: On Borrowed Time; The Underpup; Mr. Smith Goes to Washington; 1940: Remember the Night; The Captain Is a Lady; Our Town; 1941: Penny Serenade; The Shepherd of the Hills; One Foot in Heaven; 1943: Watch on the Rhine; Tonight We Raid Calais; 1944: I Love a Soldier; And Now Tomorrow; Our Hearts Were Young and Gay; The Very Thought of You; She's a Soldier Too; 1945: The Southerner; Back to Bataan; 1946: Breakfast in Hollywood; Sister Kenny; It's a Wonderful Life; 1947: High Conquest; 1948: The Snake Pit; So Dear to My Heart; The Sainted Sisters; 1949: The Life of Riley; Reign of Terror/The Black Book; Mr. Soft Touch; 1950: The Baron of Arizona; The Furies; 1952: Lone Star; 1953: Latin Lovers; 1954: Track of the Cat; 1956: Back From Eternity; 1957: The Unholy Wife; 1959: The Big Fisherman; A Summer Place; 1961: Tammy Tell Me True; 1962: The Wonderful World of the Brothers Grimm; 1963: Tammy and the Doctor.

NY Stage: 1925: One of the Family; 1927: Saturday's Children; Mariners; 1928: Cock Robin; 1929: Street Scene; 1930: Milestones; 1932: Distant Drums; The Late Christopher Bean; 1934: Mother Lode; 1950: Hilda Crane; 1953: On Borrowed Time.

Select TV: 1953: Gran'ma Rebel (sp); 1957: Black Is for Grief (sp); On Borrowed Time (sp); 1960: Tomorrow (sp); Morning's at Seven (sp); 1972: She Waits.

PAT BOONE
(CHARLES EUGENE PATRICK BOONE)
BORN: JACKSONVILLE, FL, JUNE 1, 1934.
RAISED IN NASHVILLE, TN.

Exceedingly wholesome and purveying a whitewashed brand of parent-palatable, non-threatening pop, Pat Boone, like so many singers of his generation, tried to parlay his chart success into movie fame. And, like so many before and since, he proved to be decidedly mediocre. Already hosting his own radio show at 17, he made his first national impact as a winner on *Arthur Godfrey's Talent Scouts*, in 1954. The following year he became a regular on Godfrey's variety series and, ultimately, the host of his own television show, *The Pat Boone-Chevy Showroom*. He was at his pop star peak, and scored no fewer than six number one hits, including "Ain't That a Shame," "Love Letters in the Sand," and "April Love." Fox introduced him to movie audiences in an adaptation of the Broadway hit, *Bernardine*. They followed it with two sticky musicals: *April Love*, in which he was a decid-edly milquetoast juvenile delinquent sent to work on a farm; and *Mardi Gras*, as a cadet who wins a date with a Hollywood starlet. The highlight of his motion picture career came with the top-notch sci-fi adaptation of Jules Verne's *Journey to the Center of the Earth*, in which — incredibly — he rated billing *above* James Mason! The critically-maligned remake of *State Fair* had him as a farm boy enamored of sexy Ann-Margret, and an attempt to expand his range, as a singer whose child is kid-napped, in *The Yellow Canary*, landed with a dull thud. As he grew more deeply religious, his holier-than-thou image became a source of derision, as highlighted in the hit 1989 documentary, *Roger & Me*, in which he appeared briefly as himself. Confounding fans and critics alike, however, he broke his type-cast image in 1997, when he released an album of heavy metal songs, *No More Mr. Nice Guy*.

Screen: 1957: Bernardine; April Love; 1958: Mardi Gras; 1959: Journey to the Center of the Earth; 1961: All Hands on Deck; 1962: State Fair; The Main Attraction; 1963: The Yellow Canary; 1964: Never Put It in Writing; The Horror of It All; Goodbye Charlie; 1965: The Greatest Story Ever Told; 1967: The Perils of Pauline; 1970: The Cross and the Switchblade; 1989: Roger and Me.

Select TV: 1955–57: Arthur Godfrey and His Friends (series); 1957–60: The Pat Boone-Chevy Showroom (series); 1966–68: The Pat Boone Show (series); 1969: The Pigeon.

RICHARD BOONE
BORN: LOS ANGELES, CA, JUNE 18, 1917.
DIED: JANUARY 10, 1981.

Look up the word "craggy" in the dictionary and you will find a photo of leathery-skinned Richard Boone, a grizzled actor whose roles usually took him out west. He had been a boxer, an oilfield roughneck, and a World War II navy gunner before making his unlikely Broadway bow, in the Judith Anderson production of *Medea*, in 1947. Three years later he debuted on film for 20th Century-Fox, as a hardened soldier in *The Halls of Montezuma*. Under contract to the studio he made such movies as *Kangaroo*, trying to swindle Aussie rancher Finlay

Currie; *Return of the Texan*, as Dale Robertson's odious boss; *Way of a Gaucho*, as the officer out to capture outlaw Robert Mitchum; and *Vicki*, a remake of *I Wake Up Screaming*, in the Laird Cregar role of the obsessed detective. He might have continued as a reliable supporting player had it not been for television. He was first cast in the title role of *Medic*, and then, in his most famous part, as the gunslinger Paladin in the western series *Have Gun Will Travel*. His increased stature led to occasional leads in films, like the dopey horror opus *I Bury the Living*, as a cemetery manager who fears he may have the power over life and death; *Rio Conchos*, as a Rebel officer, determined to intercept a shipment of rifles bound for the Indians; and *Kona Coast*, as a fisherman hunting his daughter's killer. He was well-matched with John Wayne as Sam Houston in the lavish production of *The Alamo*, and as a sinister gunman in the Duke's farewell vehicle, *The Shootist*. On the other hand, his role in *The Arrangement*, as the senile dad of Kirk Douglas — an actor who was one year his senior — showed either considerable faith or considerable lack of judgment. He had his finest hour as a screen villain in the 1967 Paul Newman western *Hombre*, playing a despicable outlaw who terrorizes the stagecoach passengers. In the 1970s he returned to television to play a cowboy cop in *Hec Ramsey*.

Screen: 1950: Halls of Montezuma; 1951: Call Me Mister; The Desert Fox; 1952: Kangaroo; Red Skies of Montana; Return of the Texan; 1953: Way of a Gaucho; Beneath the 12-Mile Reef; City of Bad Men; Man on a Tightrope; The Robe; Vicki; 1954: The Siege at Red River; Dragnet; The Raid; 1955: Man Without a Star; Ten Wanted Men; Robbers' Roost; The Big Knife (narrator); 1956: Battle Stations; Away All Boats; Star in the Dust; 1957: The Garment Jungle; Lizzie; The Tall T; 1958: I Bury the Living; 1960: The Alamo; 1961: A Thunder of Drums; 1964: Rio Conchos; 1965: The War Lord; 1967: Hombre; 1968: Kona Coast; 1969: The Night of the Following Day; The Arrangement; 1970: The Kremlin Letter; Madron; 1971: Big Jake; 1975: Against a Crooked Sky; 1976: The Shootist; 1978: God's Gun; The Big Sleep; 1979: Winter Kills; 1981: The Bushido Blade.

NY Stage: 1947: Medea; 1950: The Man; 1959: The Rivalry

Select TV: 1954–56: Medic (series); 1955: Love Is Eternal (sp); Wuthering Heights (sp); 1956: A House of His Own (sp); Dead of Noon (sp); 1957–63: Have Gun Will Travel (series); 1959: Little Tin God (sp); The Tunnel (sp); 1960: Tomorrow (sp); 1962: John Brown's Body (sp); 1963–64: The Richard Boone Show (series); 1971: In Broad Daylight; 1972: Deadly Harvest; Hec Ramsey; Goodnight My Love; 1972–74: Hec Ramsey (series); 1974: The Great Niagara; 1977: The Last Dinosaur: 1978: The Hobbitt (voice).

SHIRLEY BOOTH

(THELMA BOOTH FORD) BORN: NEW YORK, NY, AUGUST 30, 1898. DIED: OCTOBER 16, 1992.

Plump, loveable, and possessed of a distinctively nasal New York accent, Shirley Booth had only five movie credits to her name, but her imprint on the big screen was undeniable. She had toiled happily and successfully on the Broadway stage for more than 25 years, where her theatrical triumphs included *Three Men on a Horse*; *The Philadelphia Story*; *My Sister Eileen*; *Goodbye, My Fancy*; and *The Time of the Cuckoo*, winning Tony Awards for the last two. Her first Tony Award-winning role, as the ill-bred but good-natured housewife in William Inge's *Come Back, Little Sheba*, was so applauded that Hollywood finally took an interest. Producer Hal Wallis signed her to a contract, allowing Booth to re-create this truly unforgettable character for posterity, a magnificent performance that won her a much-

deserved Academy Award for Best Actress of 1952. She proved difficult to cast, although Wallis presented her in a pair of gentle soap operas: *About Mrs. Leslie*, as a woman reflecting on an affair with Robert Ryan; and *Hot Spell*, as the exasperated wife of philandering Anthony Quinn. A comedy, *The Matchmaker*, in which she was ideally cast as meddlesome Dolly Levi, marked the end of her brief film career, but she went on to television fame by winning two Emmy Awards as the spirited maid *Hazel*, in the sitcom based on the *Saturday Evening Post* cartoon.

Screen: 1952: Come Back, Little Sheba; 1953: Main Street to Broadway; 1954: About Mrs. Leslie; 1958: Hot Spell; The Matchmaker.

NY Stage: 1925: Hell's Bells!; Laff That Off; 1926: Buy Buy Baby; 1928: The War Song; 1931: The School for Virtue; The Camels are Coming; Coastwise; 1933: The Music and the Face; 1934: After Such Pleasures; 1935: Three Men on a Horse; 1937: Excursion; Too Many Heroes; 1939: The Philadelphia Story; 1940: My Sister Eileen; 1943: Tomorrow the World; 1945: Hollywood Pinafore; 1946: Land's End; 1948: The Men We Marry; 1949: Love Me Long; 1950: Come Back, Little Sheba; 1951: A Tree Grows in Brooklyn; 1952: The Time of the Cuckoo; 1954: By the Beautiful Sea; 1955: The Desk Set; 1957: Miss Isobel; 1959: Juno; 1960: Second String; 1970: Look to the Lilies; Hay Fever.

Select TV: 1957: The Hostess With the Mostess (sp); 1961: Welcome Home (sp); The Haven (sp); 1961–66: Hazel (series); 1967: Do Not Go Gentle Into That Good Night (sp); 1968: The Smugglers; 1973: A Touch of Grace (series).

ERNEST BORGNINE

(ERMES EFRAN BORGNINO) BORN: HAMDEN, CT, JANUARY 24, 1917. ED: RANDALL SCHOOL OF DRAMATIC ART, HARTFORD.

No one could have predicted stardom for this round-bellied, raspy-voiced, un-handsome character player, so Ernest Borgnine's ascent in Hollywood was a most welcome surprise. After military duty in WWII, he studied acting under the G.I. Bill of Rights and became a member of Virginia's Barter Theatre. After some television work he was signed by Columbia Pictures and immediately cast as a villain, trying to steal a priceless collection of jade in a Jon Hall programmer, *China Corsair*. Neither his debut, nor his next few movies did much for him, but he gained considerable attention as the sadistic stockade sergeant who taunts Frank Sinatra in 1953's red-hot *From Here to Eternity*. He continued to work in the capacity of an effective movie "heavy" in such movies as *The Stranger Wore a Gun*, a 3-D Randolph Scott western; *Johnny Guitar*, getting shot down by hero Sterling Hayden; *Vera Cruz*, sharing villain duties with Charles Bronson and Jack Elam; and, most memorably, in *Bad Day at Black Rock*, making Spencer Tracy's life miserable in general. That same year, 1955, a self-described "fat, ugly man" was needed for the lead in the movie adaptation of Paddy Chayefsky's acclaimed television drama, *Marty*. Borgnine movingly became the lonely, self-deprecating Bronx butcher who tenderly woos a shy schoolteacher. He won the Academy Award for Best Actor, and the film won Best Picture.

Hollywood now had to sell their front-rank star's unglamorous mug in leads. He did well in a much-liked western *Jubal*, as a rancher devastated to learn of his wife's infidelities with Rod Steiger and Glenn Ford. This was followed by Paddy Chayefsky's less engrossing *The Catered Affair*, married to Bette Davis; and the Fox musical biopic *The Best Things in Life Are Free*, as songwriter Lew Brown, with Gordon MacRae as Buddy DeSilva and

Dan Dailey as Ray Henderson. His biggest hit at this time, *The Vikings*, found him unsympathetic as the barbarian dad of Kirk Douglas, who was, in fact, a year older than Borgnine. A routine Alan Ladd western, *The Badlanders*, was notable insomuch as it introduced him to Katy Jurado, who became his second wife (1959–64). A few more starring vehicles fared poorly: *The Rabbit Trap*, another one adapted from a television drama, as a businessman who neglects his son; the Australian-made *Summer of the 17th Doll/Season of Passion*, as a cane cutter in love with Anne Baxter; and *Man on a String*, as real-life spy Boris Morros, which was filmed in Italy, a sure sign in the 1960s of a career in crisis. Television rescued him, with his charming portrayal of the leader of a gang of military layabouts in the sitcom *McHale's Navy*, which spawned two theatrical features, although Borgnine was only in the first.

Following the run of the series, he was seen as an edgy plane-crash survivor in *The Flight of the Phoenix*; as a general in one of the biggest hits of the late 1960s, *The Dirty Dozen*; and in the controversial *The Wild Bunch*, where he was the most sympathetic member of a gang of violent outlaws. He was also in the popular *Willard*, as the mean boss attacked by Bruce Davison's trained rats, but nobody was too interested in seeing Borgnine and Bette Davis riding around in hippie garb on a motorcycle in *Bunny O'Hare*. Another massive box-office success, *The Poseidon Adventure*, found him pitted most explosively against Gene Hackman, which he followed with starring roles in *Emperor of the North Pole*, as a vicious train conductor out to kill hobo Lee Marvin, and *Law and Order*, forming a neighborhood vigilante group with Carroll O'Connor. He was top-billed as a silly Satanist in *The Devil's Rain*, and mugged uncomfortably as a Southern sheriff in *Convoy*. He was Muhammad Ali's trainer in *The Greatest*; a journalist in space in Disney's *The Black Hole*; and a cabbie in the futuristic *Escape from New York*, but many of his later films received no distribution in the U.S. He sensibly returned to television, first in a military drama, *Airwolf*, and, much later, in a secondary role in the sitcom, *The Single Guy*. In between these gigs he was enormously likeable as the easy-going Mafioso in the comedy, *Spike of Bensonhurst*. In one of the more puzzling unions in show business history, he was married for less than a year to Ethel Merman, in 1964.

Screen: 1951: China Corsair; The Whistle at Eaton Falls; The Mob; 1953: From Here to Eternity; The Stranger Wore a Gun; 1954: Johnny Guitar; Demetrius and the Gladiators; The Bounty Hunter; Vera Cruz; 1955: Bad Day at Black Rock; Marty; Run for Cover; Violent Saturday; The Last Command; The Square Jungle; 1956: Jubal; The Catered Affair; The Best Things in Life Are Free; 1957: Three Brave Men; 1958: The Vikings; The Badlanders; Torpedo Run; 1959: Rabbit Trap; 1960: Man on a String; Pay or Die; 1961: Season of Passion/Summer of the 17th Doll; Go Naked in the World; 1962: Barabbas; Il Re di Poggio Reale/Black City (nUSr); Il Giudizio Universale/The Last Judgment (nUSr); I Briganti Italiani/The Italian Brigands (nUSr); 1964: McHale's Navy; 1965: The Flight of the Phoenix; 1966: The Oscar; 1967: Chuka; The Dirty Dozen; 1968: The Legend of Lylah Clare; The Split; Ice Station Zebra; 1969: The Wild Bunch; 1970: The Adventurers; A Bullet for Sandoval; Suppose They Gave a War and Nobody Came; 1971: Willard; Bunny O'Hare; Rain for a Dusty Summer (nUSr); 1972: Hannie Caulder; The Revengers; The Poseidon Adventure; 1973: The Neptune Factor; Emperor of the North Pole; 1974: Law and Disorder; 1975: Ripped Off/Counter Punch; The Devil's Rain; Hustle; 1976: Shoot; 1977: The Greatest; 1978: Crossed Swords; Convoy; 1979: Ravagers; The Double McGuffin; Holiday Hookers/Love by Appointment; The Black Hole; 1980: When

Time Ran Out...; 1981: High Risk; Escape From New York; Deadly Blessing; Super Fuzz; 1983: Young Warriors; 1986: The Manhunt (dtv); Code Name: Wildgeese; 1988: Spike of Bensonhurst; 1989: The Opponent (dtv); Skeleton Coast (dtv); Real Men Don't Eat Gummy Bears (nUSr); Moving Target (dtv); 1990: Any Man's Death; Laser Mission (dtv); 1991: Mountain of Diamonds (nUSr); 1992: Mistress; 1995: Captiva Island (dtv); 1996: Merlin's Shop of Wonders (dtv); All Dogs Go to Heaven 2 (voice; dtv); 1997: McHale's Navy; Gattaca; 1998: 12 Bucks (dtv); Mel (dtv); Small Soldiers (voice); Baseketball; All Dogs Christmas Carol (voice; dtv); 1999: The Last Great Ride (dtv); The Lost Treasure of Sawtooth Island (dtv); Abilene (television); 2000: Hoover; Castlerock (nUSr); 2001: The Long Ride Home (dtv).

NY Stage: 1952: Mrs. McThing.

Select TV: 1962–66: McHale's Navy (series); 1971: Sam Hill: Who Killed the Mysterious Mr. Foster?; The Trackers; 1974: Love Leads the Way; Twice in a Lifetime; 1976: Future Cop; 1977: Jesus of Nazareth (ms); Fire!; 1978: The Ghost of Flight 401; The Cops and Robin; 1979: All Quiet on the Western Front; 1983: Blood Feud (ms); Carpool; 1984: The Last Days of Pompeii (ms); 1984–86: Airwolf (series); 1985: The Dirty Dozen: The Next Mission; Alice in Wonderland; 1987: The Dirty Dozen: The Deadly Mission; Treasure Island (ms); 1988: The Dirty Dozen: The Fatal Mission; 1989: Jake Spanner — Private Eye; 1990: Appearances; 1995–97: The Single Guy (series); 1997: All Dogs Go to Heaven (series; voice).

CLARA BOW

BORN: BROOKLYN, NY, JULY 29, 1905.
DIED: SEPTEMBER 27, 1965.

The vogue for Clara Bow may have been brief, but in the 1920s she was the quintessential flapper, with her cupid's bow lips, bobbed hair, and devil-may-care *joie de vivre*. Growing up in poverty, she won first prize in a beauty contest run by Motion Picture Classic magazine — a bit part in the film, *Beyond the Rainbow*. (Her appearance was edited out of the final print, but was later restored for the reissue). As consolation, she then got a substantial role, in *Down to the Sea in Ships*, and sufficiently impressed executive B.P. Schulberg that he signed her to a contract with his company, Preferred Pictures. Promoting her as the next big star, he started her in support, in *Maytime*, an odd case of an operetta being adapted for the silent screen, and gave her her first lead, in *Poisoned Paradise*, where she fell in love with Kenneth Harlan after trying to rob him. On loan to Universal she was top-billed for the first time, in *Wine*, changing from sweet young thing to wild party girl. Between loan-outs and assignments for her home studio she appeared in no fewer than 14 movies in 1925, ranging from *Parisian Lovers*, to the western *Scarlet West*, to *The Keeper of the Bees*, which had her inheriting some hives from a beekeeper. Her best known 1925 release was *The Plastic Age*, perhaps the definitive flapper portrayal, whose hedonistic ways nearly sink the big crew race at a co-ed college. It was this film that set Bow on the path to cinematic notoriety as the representative of all Jazz Babies.

She and Schulberg moved over to Paramount, where she got her best reviews, as a flapper (of course) who forsakes her boring backwoods husband for a city-slick lawyer in the big hit *Mantrap*. She then helped introduce stage sensation Eddie Cantor to the movie public, doing pratfalls with him in *Kid Boots*. However, it was a mild 1927 comedy, called *It*, about a shopgirl who entices her boss, that changed her life. Thanks to a massive publicity campaign, Bow became a sex symbol and was bestowed with the title "The It Girl." It became the rage to imitate her style and her popularity was further enhanced by her involvement in the first ever Academy Award-winner for Best Picture, *Wings*, though her role was secondary to newcomers Richard Arlen and Buddy Rodgers. Her naughty girl image continued with *Hula*, which required her to ride a horse in the house; *Get Your Man*, trying to seduce Buddy Rogers; *Red Hair*, as a manicurist who enjoys the attention of three suitors; and *The Fleet's In*, as a dance hall hostess. With the arrival of talking pictures her stature appeared secure, with vehicles like *The Wild Party*, as a college girl making a pass at professor Fredric March, and *The Saturday Night Kid*, as a salesgirl taking the fall for Jean Arthur's dirty deeds. However, her uninhibited off-screen lifestyle, which went far beyond what she was allowed to do on screen, resulted in some messy, adverse publicity. After press reports of her involvement in an embezzlement lawsuit filed against a former secretary, Bow's audience began to dwindle almost overnight, and Paramount dropped her in 1931. Two more film efforts at Fox, *Call Her Savage* and *Hoopla*, tried to simulate her successes of the past decade past, but her youth was vanishing as quickly as the ticket-buyers. She briefly (1937) ran a Hollywood nightclub called, not surprisingly, It, then moved to Nevada with her husband (1931–62), actor-turned-politician Rex Bell. She returned to California in the 1950s to live out her remaining years in seclusion as her health slowly faded.

Screen: 1922: Beyond the Rainbow; 1923: Down to the Sea in Ships; Enemies of Women; Maytime; Daring Years; 1924: Grit; Black Oxen; The Poisoned Paradise; Daughters of Pleasure; Wine; Empty Hearts; This Woman; Black Lightning; 1925: Capital Punishment; Helen's Babies; The Adventurous Sex; My Lady's Lips; Parisian Love; Eve's Lover; Kiss Me Again; The Scarlet West; The Primrose Path; The Plastic Age; Keeper of the Bees; Free to Love; The Best Bad Man; Lawful Cheaters; 1926: The Ancient Mariner; My Lady of Whims; Fascinating Youth; Shadow of the Law; Two Can Play; Dancing Mothers; The Runaway; Mantrap; Kid Boots; 1927: It; Children of Divorce; Rough House Rosie; Wings; Hula; Get Your Man; 1928: Red Hair; Ladies of the Mob; The Fleet's In!; Three Weekends; 1929: The Wild Party; Dangerous Curves; The Saturday Night Kid; 1930: Paramount on Parade; True to the Navy; Love Among the Millionaires; Her Wedding Night; 1931: No Limit; Kick In; 1932: Call Her Savage; 1935: Hoopla.

STEPHEN BOYD

(WILLIAM MILLAR) BORN: BELFAST, IRELAND, JULY 4, 1928. DIED: JUNE 2, 1977.

Rugged, serious, and cleft-chinned, Stephen Boyd was a proficient leading man in the 1960s, though his most famous role cast him as a villain. A child actor, he appeared on the Canadian stage in the 1940s, then toured in stock throughout the U.S. before finally making his way to England, where he began his film career. He hooked up with Fox and was seen in several international releases, such as *The Man Who Never Was*, as an Irishman who is also a German double agent; *Abandon Ship*, as a ship's officer adrift in an overcrowded lifeboat; and *Island in the Sun*, as one of Joan Collins's dalliances. In 1959 he had a breakthrough in the soap opera *The Best of Everything*, as an editor in love with secretary Hope Lange. More significantly, he was Messala, Charlton Heston's best friend-turned-enemy, in the epic *Ben-Hur*, playing the character as gay, though Heston was none the wiser. His memorable challenge to the hero in the famous chariot race was a signicant part of the multi Oscar-winning film's

huge worldwide success. Boyd was now much in demand. He starred in *Lisa*, as a Dutch police official, and in *Billy Rose's Jumbo*, as an uninspired leading man for Doris Day. (His singing voice was very obviously dubbed.) He was a solid hero in another costly production, *The Fall of the Roman Empire*; was virtually unrecognizable as Nimrod in John Huston's *The Bible*; and commanded a team of shrunken scientists traveling inside a human body in the memorable sci-fi adventure, *Fantastic Voyage*. He sank with the ship in the silly 1960s soap opera, *The Oscar*, ineptly playing an egotistical actor. Boyd spent the next decade mostly in telefilms and forgettable action or horror offerings until his death, at 49, of a heart attack.

Screen: 1955: Born for Trouble; An Alligator Named Daisy; 1956: The Man Who Never Was; Hell in Korea/A Hill in Korea; 1957: Abandon Ship/Seven Waves Away; Island in the Sun; Seven Thunders/The Beast of Marseilles; The Night Heaven Fell; 1958: The Bravados; 1959: Woman Obsessed; Ben-Hur; The Best of Everthing; 1961: The Big Gamble; 1962: Lisa/The Inspector; Billy Rose's Jumbo; 1963: Imperial Venus; 1964: The Fall of the Roman Empire; The Third Secret; Genghis Khan; 1966: The Oscar; Fantastic Voyage; The Bible; 1967: The Caper of the Golden Bulls; 1968: Assignment K; Shalako; 1969: Slaves; 1971: The Great Swindle (nUSr); The Manipulater/B.J. Lang Presents; 1972: Hannie Caulder; 1973: The Man Called Noon; 1974: Marta (filmed 1970); Kill! Kill! Kill!; Those Dirty Dogs; 1976: One Billion for a Blonde (nUSr); The Big Game; African Story (nUSr); Evil in the Deep; 1977: The Devil Has Seven Faces; One Man Against the Organization; The Squeeze; Lady Dracula; 1980: Impossible Love (nUSr).

Select TV: 1960: To the Sound of Trumpets (sp); 1962: The Wall Between (sp); 1964: War of Nerves (sp); 1966: The Poppy Is Also a Flower; 1970: Carter's Army; 1972: The Hands of Cormac (sp); 1973: Key West; 1975: The Lives of Jenny Dolan.

WILLIAM BOYD

BORN: CAMBRIDGE, OH, JUNE 5, 1895. RAISED IN OK. DIED: SEPTEMBER 12, 1972.

William Boyd became so identified with one particular character — Hopalong Cassidy — that his cinematic alter-ego's name has outlasted his own. Starting off as an extra for Cecil B. DeMille, in 1919's *Why Change Your Husband?*, he made a comfortable living in silent films like *The Volga Boatman* and *King of Kings*. As sound came he alternated between Pathe (including *Painted Desert*, as a cowboy who finds a baby in the desert) and RKO (including *Carnival Boat*, as a lumberjack in love with singer Ginger Rogers) before his fortunes changed in 1935. Originally cast as a villain in a Paramount programmer called *Hop-A-Long Cassidy* (the hyphens were soon dropped), he was promoted to the lead and rapidly became one of the screen's western legends. With his distinctive black outfit and prematurely gray hair, "Hoppy" was a good-natured hero who neither drank nor smoked. There were two immediate follow-ups that same year, *The Eagle's Brood* and *Bar 20 Rides Again*, "Bar 20" being a reference to Hoppy's ranch. He knocked off three films for Republic, but after playing *Go-Get-'Em-Haines* in 1936, he decided that Hoppy was too much of sure a thing, so he eschewed all other acting assignments and never again played any other character. Boyd continued in the role at Paramount for another 41 features until he switched over to United Artists in 1942 for 25 more, ending with *Borrowed Trouble*, in 1948. Towards the end of the series he had also become producer and cleverly bought up the rights to the entire Hopalong catalogue. With the dawn of television he starred in a weekly Hopalong series and made a small fortune via the frequent showings of the movies, making him a sensation all over again. Wealthy in the extreme, he quietly retired in the late 1950s.

Screen: 1918: Old Wives for New; 1919: Why Change Your Wife?; 1920: A City Sparrow; 1921: Brewster's Millions; Moonlight and Honeysuckle; The Affairs of Anatol; Exit the Vamp; A Wise Fool; 1922: Bobbed Hair; Nice People; The Young Rajah; Manslaughter; On the High Seas; 1923: Enemies of Children; The Temple of Venus; Michael O'Halloran; Hollywood; 1924: Tarnish; Changing Husbands; Triumph; 1925: Forty Winks; The Road to Yesterday; The Golden Bed; The Midshipman; 1926: The Last Frontier; Eve's Leaves; Her Man O'War; The Volga Boatman; Steel Preferred; 1927: Two Arabian Knights; King of Kings; Dress Parade; Wolves of the Air; Jim the Conqueror; Yankee Clipper; 1928: The Night Flyer; Power; Skyscraper; The Cop; 1929: High Voyage; Lady of the Pavements; The Flying Fool; The Leatherneck; Wolf Song; 1930: Those Who Dance; Officer O'Brien; His First Command; The Storm; 1931: The Gang Buster; The Painted Desert; Beyond Victory; The Big Gamble; Suicide Fleet; 1932: Carnival Boat; Men of America; The Wiser Sex; Madison Square Garden; 1933: Lucky Devils; Emergency Call; 1934: Port of Lost Dreams; Cheaters; Flaming Gold; 1935: The Lost City; Transatlantic Merry-Go-Round; Night Life of the Gods; Racing Luck; Hop-A-Long Cassidy; Bar 20 Rides Again; Eagle's Brood; Call of the Prairie; Go Get 'em Haines; 1936: Three on the Trail; Federal Agent; Burning Gold; Heart of the West; Hopalong Cassidy Returns; Trail Dust; Borderland; 1937: Hills of Old Wyoming; North of the Rio Grande; Rustlers' Valley; Hopalong Rides Again; Texas Trail; Partners of the Plains; Cassidy of Bar 20; 1938: Bar 20 Justice; Heart of Arizona; In Old Mexico; The Frontiersman; Pride of the West; Sunset Trail; 1939: Silver on the Sage; Law of the Pampas; Range War; Renegade Trail; 1940: Santa Fe Marshal; Showdown; Hidden Gold; Stagecoach War; Three Men From Texas; 1941: In Old Colorado; Doomed Caravan; Pirates on Horseback; Border Vigilantes; Wide Open Town; Secrets of the Wasteland; Stick to Your Guns; Twilight on the Trail; Outlaws of the Desert; Riders of the Timberline; 1942: Undercover Man; Lost Canyon; 1943: Leather Burners; Hoppy Serves a Writ; Border Patrol; False Colors; Colt Comrades; Bar 20; Riders of the Deadline; 1944: Texas Masquerade; Lumberjack; Forty Thieves; Mystery Man; 1946: The Devil's Playground; Fools' Gold; Unexpected Guest; Dangerous Venture; 1947: Hoppy's Holiday; The Marauders; 1948: Silent Conflict; The Dead Don't Dream; Strange Gamble; Sinister Journey; False Paradise; Borrowed Trouble; 1952: The Greatest Show on Earth.

NY Stage: 1915: Beverly's Balance; Our Mrs. Chesney; 1916: Come Out of the Kitchen.

Select TV: 1949–51: Hopalong Cassidy (series).

CHARLES BOYER

BORN: FIGEAC, LOT, FRANCE, AUGUST 28, 1897.
DIED: AUGUST 26, 1978.

Heavy-lidded, with dark eyebrows and a thick, Gallic voice that made every sentence sound seductive, Charles Boyer became Hollywood's ideal of the great French lover. Customarily mimicked with a line he never actually said ("Come wiz me to ze Casbah"), there was more to him than the parodies might suggest. While studying acting at the Paris Conservatoire, he began appearing in French silents as well as onstage, scoring a big success with

Le Voyageur. His first brush with Hollywood came when MGM hired him to appear in a French version of their 1930 prison drama *The Big House*, in the role played in English by Chester Morris. He made his English-language debut at Paramount, opposite Ruth Chatterton, in *The Magnificent Lie*, as an effete actor helping her to deceive a blind soldier Ralph Bellamy; followed by *The Man from Yesterday*, as Claudette Colbert's husband. MGM, who still had him under contract, cast him as Jean Harlow's chauffeur/lover in *Red-Headed Woman*, but he was billed far down the cast list. Discouraged, he returned to France, where he might have stayed had not Fox asked him back. (They had been impressed by his playing of a Japanese (!) naval commander in the English-language *Thunder in the Sun*, a version of Boyer's French film, *La Bataille*.) Although the Fox film *Caravan*, with Loretta Young, failed, Paramount's 1935 *Private Worlds*, which paired him again with French-born Colbert (contrast her non-existent accent with his thick, often indecipherable one), finally brought him some attention. The favorable reaction to Boyer's portrayal of a doctor at a mental institution led to his signing a contract with independent producer Walter Wanger.

For the next several years he carved out a solid niche in the American film industry. At RKO, he and Katharine Hepburn engaged in an uninspired romance in *Break of Hearts*, then he went to Selznick for *The Garden of Allah*. This kitschy melodrama, set in Algeria, cast him as a former monk looking for sin, but who finds Marlene Dietrich looking for God instead. The film became best known for its striking use of early Technicolor. Boyer displayed comedic flair in *History Is Made at Night*, as a headwaiter wooing Jean Arthur; and was the perfect Hollywood vision of Napoleon, playing the role with intelligence and conviction, in *Conquest*. This was one of the rare instances that the reviews for a Garbo film favored her leading man, and Boyer received an Oscar nomination for his performance. He immediately got a second one for that infamous "casbah" movie, *Algiers*, as the highly charismatic fugitive Pepe Le Moko. Back with Colbert, they played a pair of Russians who stoop to becoming servants in *Tovarich*, a comedy that was better in premise than execution. One of the definitive soap operas of the 1930s, *Love Affair*, featured Boyer falling in love with, and then parting from, Irene Dunne, and it was their sensitive playing that saved the film from being mawkish. He made another hit, Warner's long-winded *All This, and Heaven Too*, as Bette Davis's employer who falls in love with her. Unfortunately, there was little either could do to disguise hokum of the most specious sort. He stayed in the soap genre, appearing at Universal with Margaret Sullivan in the first remake of *Back Street*, one of the most dated of all stories, although this version was the most capably done of three. Less well known were another teaming with Dunne, *When Tomorrow Comes*, and another with Sullivan, *Appointment for Love*. There was often the touch of the charming scoundrel in many of these roles and most certainly in *Hold Back the Dawn* in which he seduced innocent Olivia de Havilland in order to get a US passport.

In 1944 he had a great big box-office success with *Gaslight*, earning his third Oscar nomination for playing the unscrupulous husband trying to drive poor Ingrid Bergman crazy, though there would be less and less to get excited over about this very stagy, very glossy film with the passing of the years. After this batch of high profile entertainments nothing seemed to go well, with a third, poorly received Dunne film, *Together Again*; an adaptation of Graham Greene, *Confidential Agent*, which neither the author nor anybody else liked; and another with Bergman, *Arch of Triumph*, as a refugee from Nazi Germany. In the late 1940s as he turned 50, he quietly moved into characters parts, in many cases with a beard, bouncing back and forth between American and French productions. The former included *Thunder in the East* (which had nothing to do with his earlier movie of the same title), in support of Alan Ladd; *The Happy Time*, as a member of a French-Canadian household; and *The Cobweb*, back at a mental institution. For his home country there was Marcel Ophuls's acclaimed romance *Madame de…/The Earrings of Madame de…*, and then a U.S. production made in France, the non-musical version of *Fanny*, as Leslie Caron's dad, giving the movie's best performance and nabbing a fourth and final Oscar nomination. His charm was still very much in evidence in *Barefoot in the Park*, romancing Mildred Natwick, and he was much acclaimed for his work opposite Jean-Paul Belmondo in the bio drama *Stavisky*, in 1974. Throughout the years he was one actor whose co-workers spoke almost consistently of a very conscientious and professional worker. In 1978 he committed suicide, a few days after the death of his beloved wife of 44 years, former actress Pat Paterson.

Screen: 1920: L'Homme du Large (nUSr); 1921: Chantelouve (nUSr); 1922: L'Esclave (nUSr); Le Grillon de Foyer (nUSr); 1927: Le Capitaine Fracasse (nUSr); 1928: Le Ronde Infernale (nUSr); 1930: Barcarolle d'Amour (nUSr); Revolte dans la Prison; 1931: Le Proces de Mary Dugan; The Magnficent Lie; Tumultes (nUSr); 1932: The Man From Yesterday; Red-Headed Woman; Sous d'Autres Cieux (nUSr); F.P.I. Ne Repond Pas (nUSr); 1933: Moi et L'Imperatrice (nUSr); Heart Song/The Only Girl; 1934: L'Epervier/Les Amoureux (US: 1940); La Bonheur (nUSr); La Bataille (nUSr); Thunder in the East/The Battle; Caravane (nUSr); Caravan; 1935: Liliom; Private Worlds; Break of Hearts; Shanghai; 1936: Mayerling; The Garden of Allah; 1937: History Is Made at Night; Conquest; Tovarich; 1938: Orage; Algiers; 1939: Love Affair; When Tomorrow Comes; 1940: All This, and Heaven Too; 1941: Back Street; Hold Back the Dawn; Appointment for Love; 1942: Tales of Manhattan; 1943: The Constant Nymph; Flesh and Fantasy (and co-prod.); 1944: Gaslight; Together Again; 1945: Confidential Agent; 1946: Cluny Brown; 1947: A Woman's Vengeance; 1948: Arch of Triumph; 1951: The Thirteenth Letter; The First Legion; 1952: The Happy Time; 1953: Thunder in the East; Madame de…/The Earrings of Madame De…; 1955: La Fortuna di Essere Donna (nUSr); Lucky to be a Woman (nUSr); The Cobweb; 1956: Around the World in Eighty Days; Paris Palace Hotel (nUSr); 1957: Nana (filmed 1954); 1958: La Parisienne; The Buccaneer; 1961: Les Demons de Minuit (nUSr); Adorable Julia (nUSr); Fanny; 1962: The Four Horsemen of the Apocalypse; Maxime (filmed 1957); 1963: Love Is a Ball; 1965: A Very Special Favor; 1966: How to Steal a Million; Is Paris Burning?; 1967: Casino Royale; Barefoot in the Park; 1969: The Day the Hot Line Got Hot; The April Fools; The Madwoman of Chaillot; 1973: Lost Horizon; 1974: Stavisky; 1976: A Matter of Time.

NY Stage: 1948: Red Gloves; 1951: Don Juan in Hell; 1953: Kind Sir; 1958: The Marriage-Go-Round; 1962: Lord Pengo.

Select TV: 1952–56: Four Star Playhouse (series); 1953: Charles Boyer Theater (series); 1957: There Shall Be No Night (sp); 1957–58: Alcoa Theatre (series); 1963: Man and Boy; 1964: The Rogues (series).

EDDIE BRACKEN
BORN: QUEENS, NY, FEBRUARY 7, 1915.
DIED: NOVEMBER 14, 2002

The standard Eddie Bracken characterization, that of the whining, eternally nervous dumb cluck, wasn't much varied during the actor's heyday in the early 1940s, but this shtick could be effective in moderation and in the right hands. He also had the good luck of being guided by Preston Sturges in two of that director's most enduring films. A graduate of New York's Professional Children's School, he appeared in some silent short subjects as a child. While a teenager he began acting on Broadway, making enough of an impact in the 1939 production of *Too Many Girls*, that he was asked to repeat his part in the RKO film version the following year where, among other things, he sang "I Didn't Know What Time It Was," to Desi Arnaz (!). In 1941 he was signed up by Paramount and began his six-year association with the studio, starring exclusively in comedies. He supported Bob Hope in the popular service farce *Caught in the Draft*; toured Paramount studios with his sailor buddies as part of the plot that tied all the acts together in the all-star *Star Spangled Rhythm*; and found that he possessed Bing Crosby's vocal chords in the gimmick musical *Out of This World*. 1944 was his peak year, with Sturges choosing him for two sharp comic showcases. The first, *The Miracle of Morgan's Creek*, cast him as a 4F ninny who agrees to take the credit for impregnating Betty Hutton, while the second, *Hail the Conquering Hero*, once again found him as a military reject, who reluctantly lets some marines pass him off as a war hero, a more serious film than the first and featuring Bracken's finest work. There followed more fluffy musicals including *Bring on the Girls* and *Hold That Blonde*, after which he freelanced, in Warners's *The Girl From Jones Beach*; MGM's *Summer Stock*, as Judy Garland's annoying boyfriend; and RKO's *Two Tickets to Broadway*, a minor affair despite the contributions of Busby Berkeley and Ann Miller, among others. In the early 1950s he backed away from movies, choosing to work on TV and stage. His New York theatre credits included one directorial effort, *How to Make a Man*, in 1961, and an unsuccessful musical that he produced and appeared in, *Beg, Borrow or Steal*. In the 1980s, long absent from the screen, he began showing up in supporting roles for the newer breed of comedy directors, including Harold Ramis and John Landis, in their films *National Lampoon's Vacation* and *Oscar*, respectively.

Screen: 1940: Too Many Girls; 1941: Life With Henry; Reaching for the Sun; Caught in the Draft; 1942: Sweater Girl; The Fleet's In; Star Spangled Rhythm; 1943: Happy Go Lucky; Young and Willing; 1944: The Miracle of Morgan's Creek; Hail the Conquering Hero; Rainbow Island; 1945: Out of This World; Bring on the Girls; Duffy's Tavern; Hold That Blonde; 1947: Ladies' Man; Fun on a Weekend; 1949: The Girl From Jones Beach; 1950: Summer Stock; 1951: Two Tickets to Broadway; 1952: We're Not Married; About Face; 1953: A Slight Case of Larceny; 1962: Always on a Sunday (nUSr); 1965: Wild Wild World (narrator); 1971: Shinbone Alley (voice); 1983: National Lampoon's Vacation; 1990: Preston Sturges: The Rise and Fall of an American Dreamer; 1991: Oscar; 1992: Home Alone 2: Lost in New York; 1993: Rookie of the Year; 1994: Baby's Day Out.

NY Stage: 1931: The Man on Stilts; 1933: The Lady Refuses; 1934: The Drunkard; 1935: Life's Too Short; 1936: So Proudly We Hail; Iron Men; 1938: Brother Rat; What a Life; 1939: Too Many Girls; 1952: The Seven Year Itch; 1957: Shinbone Alley; 1960: Beg, Borrow or Steal; 1966: The Odd Couple; 1978: Hello, Dolly!

Select TV: 1952: A Question of Rank (sp); I've Got a Secret (series); 1953: The Corporal and the Lady (sp); 1955: Suit Yourself (sp); A Likely Story (sp); Make the Connection (series); 1956: Mr. Belvedere (sp); Formosa Patrol (sp); The Marriage Plan (sp); 1957: Awake With Fear (sp); Masquerade Party (series); 1959: The Strawberry Blonde (sp); Archy and Mehitabel (sp); 1989: Show Beat (sp); 1993: The American Clock; 1994: Assault at West Point; Winnetka Road (series); 2000: The Ryan Interview (sp).

ALICE BRADY
BORN: NEW YORK, NY, NOVEMBER 2, 1892.
DIED: OCTOBER 28, 1939.

An actress whose career fell into two distinctive phases, as a star in silent movies, and then later, in a completely different vein, as a character actress par excellence, Alice Brady died while at the peak of the latter. The daughter of producer William A. Brady, she first won fame appearing in stage operettas under the name Rose Marie. After establishing herself on Broadway (mainly in Gilbert and Sullivan operettas) she came to movies in 1914, with *As Ye Sow*. Over the next nine years she became the highly paid star of such romantic melodramas as *Bought and Paid For*, *At the Mercy of Men*, and *Her Silent Sacrifice*. When she'd had enough, she went back to the stage in 1923, and stayed there for another ten years where her credits included *The Immoral Lady* and *Mourning Becomes Electra*. Asked back to Hollywood in 1933, she made her mark as a superb character comedienne in such films as *When Ladies Meet*, as a bemused widow; *The Gay Divorcee*, as Ginger Rogers's aunt; *One Hundred Men and a Girl*, as a socialite who agrees to finance Adolphe Menjou's orchestra then forgets; and, most memorably, *My Man Godfrey*, as perhaps the most delightfully scatter-brained matron in movie history. There were some starring roles too, including *Lady Tubbs*, as a railroad cook, and *The Harvester*, as an ambitious small town mom plotting to marry off her daughters to wealth. Her Oscar nominated work in *Godfrey* is impressively contrasted with the one that won her the Academy Award, *In Old Chicago*, as the very sensible and loving Ma O'Leary whose cow started the big blaze. Sadly, only two years later, she was dead of cancer, only a few months after the release of *Young Mr. Lincoln*, in which she was another 19th century Midwestern mama, refusing to testify against her sons in a murder trial.

Screen: 1914: As Ye Sow; 1915: The Boss; The Cup of Chance; The Lure of Women; 1916: The Rack; The Ballet Girl; The Woman in 47; Then I'll Come Back to You; Tangled Fates; La Boheme; Miss Petticoats; The Gilded Cage; Bought and Paid For; 1917: A Woman Alone; A Hungry Heart; The Dancer's Peril; Darkest Russia; Maternity; The Divorce Game; A Self-Made Widow; Betsy Ross; A Maid of Belgium; 1918: Her Silent Sacrifice; Woman and Wife; The Knife; The Spurs of Sybil; At the Mercy of Men; The Trap; The Whirlpool; The Death Dance; The Ordeal of Rosetta; The Better Half; In the Hollow of Her Hand; Her Great Chance; 1919: The Indestructible Wife; The World to Live In; Marie Ltd.; The Redhead; His Bridal Night; 1920: The Fear Market; Sinners; A Dark Lantern; The New York Idea; 1921: Out of the Chorus; The Land of Hope; Little Italy; Dawn of the East; Hush Money; 1922: Anna Ascends; The Leopardess; Missing Millions; 1923: The Snow Bride; 1933: When Ladies Meet; Broadway to Hollywood; Beauty for Sale; Stage Mother; Should Ladies Behave?; 1934: Miss Fane's Baby Is Stolen; The Gay Divorcee; 1935: Let 'em Have It; Gold Diggers of 1935; Lady Tubbs; Metropolitan; 1936: The Harvester; My Man Godfrey; Go West, Young Man; Mind Your Own Busines; Three Smart Girls; 1937: Call It a Day; Mama Steps Out; Mr. Dodd

Takes the Air; One Hundred Men and a Girl; Merry-Go-Round of 1938; In Old Chicago; 1938: Joy of Living; Goodbye Broadway; 1939: Zenobia; Young Mr. Lincoln.

NY Stage: 1911: H.M.S. Pinafore; 1912: Patience; The Pirates of Penzance; The Mikado; Little Women; The Family Cupboard; 1913: The Things That Count; School; 1914: What Is Love?; Sylvia Runs Away; 1915: Sinners; Gilbert & Sullivan Opera Co.; 1918: Forever After; 1920: Anna Ascends; 1921: The Love Letter; 1922: Drifting; 1923: Zander the Great; 1925: Oh Mama; 1926: Bride of the Lamb; Sour Grapes; The Witch; 1927: Lady Alone; The Thief; 1928: A Most Immoral Lady; 1929: Karl and Anna; The Game of Love and Death; 1930: Love, Honor and Betray; A Month in the Country; 1931: Brass Ankle; Mourning Becomes Electra; Bless You Sister; 1932: Mademoiselle.

SCOTT BRADY
(GERALD KENNETH TIERNEY) BORN: BROOKLYN, NY, SEPTEMBER 13, 1924. DIED: APRIL 16, 1985.

It was only natural that somebody who made a living as a lumberjack and a prizefighter would find his calling as a movie tough guy in various action films, westerns, and war stories. The younger brother of actor Lawrence Tierney, Scott Brady studied acting at the Beverly Hills Drama School, following military service in World War II. His first several credits were in starring roles, beginning with a "B" for Eagle-Lion, *Canon City*, as a con busting out of the Colorado State Penitentiary. He continued as a lead in what were basically programmers, like *He Walked by Night*, on the trail of killer Richard Basehart; *Port of New York*, as a customs bureau agent tracking a gang of drug smugglers led by a hirsute Yul Brynner; *Undertow*, the one about the guy framed for murder tracking down the real killers; and *I Was a Shoplifter*, as an undercover cop. Although there was a welcome break, playing a romantic lead, in Fox's *The Model and the Marriage Broker*, as an X-ray technician matched up with Jeanne Crain, it was soon back to action, only this time he was usually found in the saddle. These second string entertainments included *Bronco Buster*, as an arrogant rodeo rider; *The Law vs. Billy the Kid*, as Billy; *The Vanishing American*, a well-meaning film about the mistreatment of Indians, though Brady was hardly a convincing Native American; and *Mohawk*, this time trying to quash an Iroquis uprising. During these he did appear in a popular success, the campy cult favorite *Johnny Guitar*, as Dancin' Kid, the bad guy fought over by a very butch pair of ladies, Joan Crawford and Mercedes McCambridge. He tried his own television western, *Shotgun Slade*, and was later seen as a character player in several television films and occasional theatrical features, like *Marooned* and *The China Syndrome*.

Screen: 1948: Canon City; In This Corner; He Walked by Night; 1949: The Gal Who Took the West; Port of New York; Undertow; I Was a Shoplifter; 1950: Kansas Raiders; Undercover Girl; 1951: The Model and the Marriage Broker; Untamed Frontier; 1952: Montana Belle; Yankee Buccaneer; Bronco Buster; Bloodhounds of Broadway; 1953: A Perilous Journey; El Alamein; 1954: The Law vs. Billy the Kid; Johnny Guitar; 1955: White Fire/Three Steps to the Gallows; They Were So Young; Gentlemen Marry Brunettes; The Vanishing American; 1956: Terror at Midnight; The Maverick Queen; Mohawk; 1957: The Storm Rider; The Restless Breed; 1958: Ambush at Cimarron Pass; Blood Arrow; 1959: Battle Flame; 1963: Operation Bikini; 1964: Stage to Thunder Rock; 1965: John Goldfarb, Please Come Home; Black Spurs; 1966: Destination Inner Space; Nightmare in Wax; 1967: Red Tomahawk; Fort Utah; Castle of Evil; Journey to the Center of Time; **1968:** They Ran for Their Lives; Arizona Bushwhackers; **1969:** Road Hustlers; The Ice House; Cycle Savages; Marooned; **1970:** Hell's Bloody Devils/Smashing the Crime Syndicate; Satan's Sadists; **1971:** Cain's Way; Doctors' Wives; $ (Dollars); Five Bloody Graves; **1972:** The Loners; The Leo Chronicles; **1973:** Bonnie's Kids; Wicked, Wicked; **1979:** The China Syndrome; **1981:** Strange Behavior; **1984:** Gremlins.

NY Stage: 1959: Destry Rides Again.

Select TV: 1953: Just What the Doctor Ordered (sp); Tangier Lady (sp); **1954:** Rim of Violence (sp); Wonderful Day for a Wedding (sp); **1955:** Millions of Georges (sp); Night in the Big Swamp (sp); **1956:** Roustabout (sp); **1957:** Lone Woman (sp); **1959:** The Salted Mine (sp); **1959–61:** Shotgun Slade (series); **1969:** The D.A.: Murder One; **1973:** The Night Strangler; **1974:** Roll Freddy Roll; **1975:** The Kansas City Massacre; **1976:** Law and Order; **1978:** When Every Day Was the Fourth of July; To Kill a Cop; Suddenly Love; Arthur Hailey's Wheels (ms); **1979:** Women in White; The Last Ride of the Dalton Gang; **1980:** Power; **1981:** American Dream; **1983:** The Winds of War (ms); This Girl for Hire.

NEVILLE BRAND

BORN: KEWANEE, IL, AUGUST 13, 1920.
DIED: APRIL 16, 1992.

With his guttural voice and mean-looking face, Neville Brand couldn't help but find himself pigeon-holed as a bad guy throughout the 1950s, ending up with perhaps his most famous part, Al Capone, on the hit series *The Untouchables.* An army veteran who became the fouth most-decorated soldier during World War II, he made his big screen debut in *D.O.A.* playing a killer, and his future was pretty much set. He was a stand-out as the barracks leader in Billy Wilder's *Stalag 17,* and got himself top-billing in *Man Crazy,* marrying thief Christine White, and in director Don Siegel's hard hitting prison drama *Riot in Cell Block 11,* as a con leading his fellow inmates in a revolt, demanding better living conditions. That same year, 1954, he was given a more atypical assignment, playing opposite Jan Sterling in a love story, *Return to the Sea,* as a sailor on leave in San Diego who falls for a waitress. He carried a poor Allied Artist thriller, *Bobby Ware Is Missing,* and stayed in cheap programmers for *Fury at Gunsight Pass,* as a vicious outlaw holding a town hostage and threaten to kill one citizen every hour on the hour; *Gun Brothers,* as the bad sibling of Buster Crabbe; and *Badman's Country,* playing outlaw Butch Cassidy, being pursued by noted lawman Pat Garrett (George Montgomery). He also took supporting roles in "A-line" features such as the 3-D hit *The Charge at Feather River*; *The Tin Star,* challenging naïve sheriff Anthony Perkins to a showdown; *The Lonely Man,* trying to persuade former outlaw Jack Palace back to a life of crime; and *Five Gates to Hell,* as a Vietnamese man who abducts the staff of a hospital. He became so associated with playing Capone (despite his atrocious attempt an an Italian accent) that he was asked to reprise the role in *The George Raft Story.* Around that same time he had another notable assignment, as the prison guard who endures Burt Lancaster's indifference in *Birdman of Alcatraz.*

Screen: 1949: D.O.A.; Port of New York; **1950:** Kiss Tomorrow Goodbye; Where the Sidewalk Ends; Halls of Montezuma; **1951:** Only the Valiant; The Mob; Red Mountain; Flame of Araby; **1952:** Kansas City Confidential; The Turning Point; **1953:** The Man From the Alamo; Stalag 17; Man Crazy; The Charge at Feather River; Gun Fury; **1954:** Prince Valiant; The Lone Gun; Riot in Cell Block 11; Return from the Sea; **1955:** The Prodigal;

The Return of Jack Slade; Bobby Ware Is Missing; **1956:** Raw Edge; Fury at Gunsight Pass; Mohawk; Gun Brothers; Love Me Tender; Three Outlaws; **1957:** The Tin Star; The Way to the Gold; The Lonely Man; **1958:** Cry Terror!; Badman's Country; **1959:** Five Gates to Hell; **1960:** The Adventures of Huckleberry Finn; **1961:** The Last Sunset; The Scarface Mob (from television); The George Raft Story; **1962:** Hero's Island; Birdman of Alcatraz; **1965:** That Darn Cat!; **1968:** Three Guns for Texas; **1969:** The Desperados; Backtrack; **1970:** Tora! Tora! Tora!; **1973:** Cahill: U.S. Marshal; The Deadly Trackers; This Is a Hi-Jack; Scalawag; **1974:** The Mad Bomber; The Police Connection; **1975:** Psychic Killer; **1976:** Eaten Alive/Death Trap; **1978:** The Mouse and His Child (voice); Hi-Riders; Five Days From Home; **1979:** Angels' Brigade; **1980:** Twinkle, Twinkle, Killer Kane/The Ninth Configuration; The Return; Without Warning; **1983:** Evils of the Night.

NY Stage: 1962: Night Life.

Select TV: 1952: The Man Who Had Nothing to Lose (sp); **1954:** The Edge of Battle (sp); The Dumbest Man in the Army (sp); **1955:** Armed (sp); Ride With the Executioner (sp); Blow Up at Cortland (sp); On the Nose (sp); **1957:** Harbor Patrol (sp); **1958:** Run, Joe, Run (sp); All the King's Men (sp); The Coward of Fort Bennett (sp); Galvanized Yankee (sp); Goodbye...But It Doesn't Go Away (sp); **1959:** Body and Soul (sp); The Untouchables (sp; also theatrical release as The Scarface Mob); **1963:** Seven Miles of Bad Roads (sp); **1965–67:** Laredo (series); **1970:** Marriage: Year One; Lock, Stock and Barrel; **1971:** Hitched; **1972:** Two for the Money; No Place to Run; The Adventures of Nick Carter; **1974:** Killdozer; Death Stalk; **1975:** Barbary Coast; The Seekers (ms) **1976:** The Quest; Captains and the Kings; **1977:** Fire!; Captains Courageous.

MARLON BRANDO

BORN: OMAHA, NE, APRIL 3, 1924.

Few actors have warranted so many articles, books, and endless discussions on their impact and talent as Marlon Brando. Many have theorized that he *was* great once and thereafter mostly squandered his abilities in projects far beneath him, while others contend that he has only to walk on screen to grab your attention, effortlessly. He is one of the blessed, it is true, and if indeed he had as much disinterest in the profession as he stated so many times, then it remains a mystery as to why he continued to be so damn mesmerizing. His image as the sullen rebel was formed early on, having been expelled from military school. Following his older sister Jocelyn's interest in acting, he traveled to New York where he became Stella Adler's prized pupil. In no time he was creating a stir on Broadway in *Truckline Cafe* (which won him a Theatre World Award) and, more importantly, Tennessee Williams's searing drama *A Streetcar Named Desire.* His performance as the uncouth, hostile, and sexually magnetic Stanley Kowolski became a part of acting folklore, and there wasn't a soul in show business who did not have some opinion on the direction this independent and controversial performer was heading. Before he repeated the role in Eli Kazan's exceptional 1951 film version of *Streetcar,* he debuted on big screen the year before to glowing acclaim, as a paraplegic, in Fred Zinneman's melodramatic but gripping *The Men.* The movie of *Streetcar,* despite its compromised ending, was a groundbreaker in bringing a rawer form of adult drama to film and became one of the seminal motion pictures of its era. It preserved Brando's Stanley for further generations to be awed and influenced by, brought him the first of his many Oscar nominations, and made him a box-office attraction.

To prove his versatility he played the brooding Mexican revolutionary in the above-average biopic *Viva Zapata!*; conquered Shakespeare in *Julius Caesar*, participating in the ensemble as Marc Antony but taking top billing; and sang and danced charmingly in the colorful 1955 adaptation of the Broadway smash hit musical *Guys and Dolls*. There were more Oscar nominations for the first two and he finally grabbed the award for what is, to many, his greatest work in his best film, playing New Jersey longshoreman Terry Malloy, who speaks out against corruption in Elia Kazan's towering *On the Waterfront*, the Best Picture Oscar-winner of 1954. Certainly powerful but infinitely more dated was *the* motorcycle picture of the era, *The Wild One*, offering the sight of Brando in his leather jacket and white cap, which became one of the enduring images of that decade. Just to show that not all was rosy he was left at sea in a cardboard costume epic, *Desiree*, as a very solemn Napoleon Bonaparte. It didn't do badly, however, in so much as Brando was almost as popular as he was a critic's darling at this period in his career. This was further proven by his bizarre casting as an impish Japanese interpreter, acting under the usual unconvincing makeup given to Caucasians cast as Asians, in *The Teahouse of the August Moon*, which went on to gross impressive figures. He had, by this time, utterly rocked Hollywood from its foundations, with his naturalistic approach that made the dialogue sound fresh and spontaneous to some, mumbled to others. Off screen he was also breaking rules, being uncooperative with the press, savoring his image as a slovenly non-conformist, and speaking his mind about the superficiality of the very profession that had made him so famous.

There was another gigantic box-office hit, and a fifth Oscar nod, for *Sayonara*, an overlong look at relations between American soldiers and Japanese women at the close of World War II, with Brando holding it all together as the Southern officer whose prejudices collapse when he falls in love with a Matsubayashi actress. This was followed by a controversial turn as a sympathetic Nazi in *The Young Lions*, where, alas, he only shared a brief bit of on-screen time with another great actor, Montgomery Clift. His work as a loner in a snakeskin jacket, in *The Fugitive Kind*, showed him at his most brooding, which caused many a critic to carp about his $1 million salary (a record at the time). The film was not without interest, but coming from Brando and Tennessee Williams greater things were expected. Still at the top of his profession, he took his eccentricities behind the camera for his fascinatingly flawed sole directorial effort, *One-Eyed Jacks*. The cost delays, endless footage shot and search for perfection made the film the source of much derision and speculation as to whether he had become one of the industry's chief megalomaniacs. Despite undeniable moments of originality the movie lost money, as did the remake of *Mutiny on the Bounty*, which found him at his most alienating as an effete Fletcher Christian. Although it would wind up as one of 1962's Oscar nominees for Best Picture, this film deeply hurt his reputation and he soon fell into his bleakest period of failures, although in most cases he was still the best thing about each movie.

There was a cloudy political drama, *The Ugly Amercan*; an attempt at comedy, *Bedtime Story*, which gave him a wry con-artist partner in David Niven, an actor he adored working with; a World War II drama, *Morituri*, which marked the first time he began using cue-cards on the set, claiming they helped give the moment spontaneity when in fact he was becoming blatantly lazy about giving the script sufficient attention; *The Appaloosa*, a western almost unanimously referred to by the critical consensus as "pretentious;" *The Chase*, which boasted one of the best casts to ever fail at salvaging a sinking vessel; Charlie Chaplin's farewell disaster, *A Countess From Hong Kong*, an unhappy, antiquated romp in which Brando played an ambassador concealing stowaway Sophia Loren in his ship's cabin; a bleak and messy adaptation of the Carson McCuller's novel *Reflections in a Golden Eye*, with Brando making a daring attempt to portray a masochistic homosexual army officer; a no-holds barred cameo as a long-haired guru in the all-star sex romp *Candy*; *The Night of the Following Day*, a kidnapping drama, which, unlike most of the others, wasn't even anticipated with much fanfare; and one of his own personal favorites, *Burn!*, a downbeat political drama set in the Caribbean. There was still much respect for his talents but seldom had a star of his stature made such self-destructive choices in material with such dire box-office results. In Ireland he played the lewd groundskeeper in a prequel of sorts to *The Turn of the Screw*, called *The Nightcomers*, which was dismissed just as quickly as those in the 10 years prior. Few knew that a resurrection was just around the corner.

When, in 1972, he made his staggering comeback with *The Godfather*, his stature grew to God-like proportions. Although it was essentially a supporting role, his astounding work as the elderly Mafia don dominated an already terrific film and he was awarded his second Academy Award. In a controversial move that reminded people of just who they were dealing with, he refused the prize on behalf of the American Indians' mistreatment by Hollywood. By the time of the award ceremony, he was already getting another batch of raves for his raw portrayal of a tormented American who carries on a torrid, anonymous sexual affair with a French girl in the X-rated, hotly debated *Last Tango in Paris*. Like *Godfather* it not only brought him respect but box-office clout, since these were two of the most heavily attended movies of the time. With yet another Oscar nomination in his pocket, he was more in demand than ever but, for the most part, he would thereafter accept astronomical salaries and top billing for what were essentially supporting parts. This started with a role secondary to Jack Nicholson's in the over-hyped western *The Missouri Breaks*, which seemed to indicate that Brando wasn't about to take himself too seriously if he could have a little cheeky fun instead. Some were appalled by what they considered shameless mugging, while others marveled at his ability to take a failing script and infuse it with some degree of unpredictability, with the sort of acting quirks that were uniquely his own.

There were even smaller, high-salaried parts in such major events as *Superman*, as the hero's dad, establishing a certain credible tone to the fantasy in its opening scenes, and *Apocalypse Now*, as the bald, enigmatic, creepy Colonel Kurtz, not showing up until the last portion of the film, but worth all the anticipatory build-up in the story. Both were major box-office hits, which was not to be said of *The Formula*, a pairing with the other actor who had turned down *his* Oscar, George C. Scott. Again, Brando's few moments as a self-satisfied millionaire provided the only juice. Prior to this, in a rare television appearance, he won an Emmy Award for playing white supremacist George Lincoln Rockwell in the mini-series *Roots: The Next Generations*. Still proclaiming his disinterest in the whole acting business, he all but disappeared during the 1980s. Fortunately he was still in need of cash to pay expenses on his private South Seas island home, and returned to the profession in the little-seen anti-apartheid drama *A Dry White Season*, for which he received his ninth acknowledgement by the Academy. In the 1990s there were larger roles in a pair of gentle comedies, *The Freshman*, in which he played a parody of his *Godfather* character, and *Don Juan DeMarco*, as a soul-searching psychiatrist. The less substantial parts included a walk-through as Torquemada in the bomb *Christopher Columbus*, and the mad scientist in *The Island of Dr. Moreau*, immense in size and done up in white makeup. Many felt that he had really gone too far this time which was also the consensus on *Free Money*, a movie that skipped theatres altogether to premiere on cable television. In contrast, *The Score* found him in a relatively normal mode as the fence for thief Robert DeNiro. Ever controverisal, unpredictable and dynamic he published his autobiography, *Songs My Mother Taught Me*, in 1994, which, purposefully, kept many questions unanswered.

Screen: 1950: The Men; 1951: A Streetcar Named Desire; 1952: Viva Zapata!; 1953: Julius Caesar; The Wild One; 1954: On the Waterfront; Desiree; 1955: Guys and Dolls; 1956: The Teahouse of the August Moon; 1957: Sayonara; 1958: The Young Lions; 1960: The Fugitive Kind; 1961: One-Eyed Jacks (and dir.); 1962: Mutiny on the Bounty; 1963: The Ugly American; 1964: Bedtime Story; 1965: The Saboteur-Code Name: Morituri; 1966: The Chase; The Appaloosa; 1967: A Countess From Hong Kong; Reflections in a Golden Eye; 1968: Candy; 1969: The Night of the Following Day; 1970: Burn!; 1972: The Nightcomers; The Godfather; 1973: Last Tango in Paris; 1976: The Missouri Breaks; 1978: Superman; 1979: Apocalypse Now; 1980: The Formula; 1989: A Dry White Season; 1990: The Freshman; 1992: Christopher Columbus — The Discovery; 1995: Don Juan DeMarco; 1996: The Island of Dr. Moreau; 1997: The Brave (nUSr); 2001: The Score.

NY Stage: 1944: I Remember Mama; 1946: Truckline Café; Candida; A Flag Is Born; 1947: A Streetcar Named Desire.

Select TV: 1948: I'm No Hero (sp); 1979: Roots: The Next Generations (ms); 1999: Free Money.

ROSSANO BRAZZI

BORN: BOLOGNA, ITALY, SEPTEMBER 18, 1916.
DIED: DECEMBER 24, 1994.

About the only Italian leading man to be successfully imported by Hollywood, Rossano Brazzi enjoyed a comfortable period of fame in the 1950s. Abandoning his original intent to be a lawyer, he worked on the stage before making his movie debut in his native country in 1939. During the 1940s he became one of Italy's most popular leading men, eventually coming to the U.S. in 1949 for his Hollywood debut, playing Prof. Bhaer opposite June Allyson in the financially successful remake of *Little Women*. He did not, however, choose to continue in American films for another four years, when he returned in two of 1954's big productions, *Three Coins in the Fountain*, romancing Jean Peters in Rome, and *The Barefoot Contessa*, in which he was extremely tedious playing Ava Gardner's impotent husband. He was, however, at his most appealing as Katharine Hepburn's free-spirited lover in director David Lean's intelligent, adult romance *Summertime*, and starred in one of the most widely seen movies of the 1950s, the musical *South Pacific*, an understandable choice in so much as a middle-aged foreigner was required, although his singing voice was dubbed and his charisma at low ebb. Never abandoning Italian films altogether, he continued to appear less frequently in U.S. movies as the 1960s came, with the exception of some soap operas with Italian settings like *Rome Adventure*, wooing Suzanne Pleshette only to lose her to younger Troy Donahue, and *The Light in the Piazza*, as George Hamilton's dad. He made his directorial debut with the cheesy

children's film *The Christmas That Almost Wasn't*, in which he also played the lead, a black-garbed villain. Later roles included playing a balloonist in a bloated adventure, *Krakatoa — East of Java*, and far less illustrious, cheapjack productions such as *Frankenstein's Castle of Freaks*, as the Count; and *The Final Conflict*, as a monk trying to stop devil spawn Sam Neill from scoring in politics.

Screen (US releases only): 1949: Little Women; 1954: Three Coins in the Fountain; The Barefoot Contessa; 1955: Summertime; 1957: Interlude; The Story of Esther Costello; Legend of the Lost; 1958: South Pacific; A Certain Smile; 1959: Count Your Blessing; 1962: Light in the Piazza; Rome Adventure; 1963: Three Fables of Love; Dark Purpose; 1965: The Battle of the Villa Fiorita; 1966: Engagement Italiano; The Christmas That Almost Wasn't (and dir.); 1967: Woman Times Seven; The Bobo; 1968: One Step to Hell/King of Africa; 1969: Krakatoa — East of Java/Volcano; The Italian Job; 1970: The Adventurers; 1971: Psychout for Murder; Mr. Kingstreet's War/Heroes Die Hard; 1972: The Great Waltz; 1975: Frankenstein's Castle of Freaks; 1981: The Final Conflict; 1985: Fear City; Final Justice; 1986: Formula for Murder; 1988: We the Living (filmed 1942); 1989: Russicum/Third Solution.

Select TV: 1955: Big Nick (sp); 1969: Honeymoon With a Stranger; 1969–70: The Survivors (series); 1980: A Time for Miracles; 1984: The Far Pavilions (ms).

LUCILLE BREMER

BORN: AMSTERDAM, NY, FEBRUARY 21, 1917.
DIED: APRIL 16, 1996.

For someone considered one of Hollywood's failures, Lucille Bremer's short résumé has enough high points to make better and more enduring actresses envious. An accomplished ballet dancer with the Philadelphia Opera Company and, later, a Radio City Music Hall Rockette, she made her Broadway bow in the chorus of *Panama Hattie*, in 1940. After being spotted by producer Arthur Freed in a dinner club chorus line, she was signed by MGM with a great future promised by studio head Louis B. Mayer. Working in three successive Vincente Minnelli assignments, she certainly started at the top. First she played Judy Garland's older sister in one of the loveliest musicals ever made, *Meet Me in St. Louis*, though her own involvement in the music was restricted to a few bars of the title song and a bit of the "Skip to My Lou" sequence. She then got the chance to partner with Fred Astaire, not once but twice; first in two of the best segments of the episodic *Ziegfeld Follies*, as the desired prey of his suave jewel thief in "This Heart of Mine," and, most interestingly, as the Asian he fantasizes about in the evocative "Limehouse Blues" number; second, in the wobbly fantasy *Yolanda and the Thief*, which she did not possess the right level of innocence and wistfulness to pull off. While she was clearly a fine dancer, Bremer's acting abilities were adequate at best and the studio soon lost interest. After finishing her contract in three loan-out projects to the "B" studio Eagle-Lion, she married in 1948 and left the movie business, eventually opening a dress shop in La Jolla, California.

Screen: 1944: Meet Me in St. Louis; 1945: Yolanda and the Thief; 1946: Ziegfeld Follies; Till the Clouds Roll By; 1947: Dark Delusion; 1948: Adventures of Casanova; Ruthless; Behind Locked Doors.

NY Stage: 1940: Panama Hattie.

WALTER BRENNAN

BORN: SWAMPSCOTT, MA, JULY 25, 1894.
DIED: SEPTEMBER 21, 1974.

Of all the supporting players who were stars in their own right, Walter Brennan may well have had the greatest following. As soon as the Academy established an Oscar category for Best Supporting Actor, Brennan copped the award three times, the first performer to do so, the list since extending to only two other names (Ingrid Bergman and Jack Nicholson; Katharine Hepburn, of course, took home four). Long before these honors were bestowed upon him, he had carried jobs as a lumberjack and bank clerk while dabbling in vaudeville. Arriving in Hollywood in the 1920s he found work as an extra and stuntman (his first known credit in this capacity being *Lorraine of the Lions*, in 1925), gradually moving up to bit player (with *The Ridin' Rowdy*, in 1927) and, finally, chief supporting player. Even before he reached 50, he was adept at playing curmudgeonly old codgers, with or without his false teeth. There are so many different sources that list various credits for Brennan during the early 1930s that it is still almost impossible to determine whether or not he is indeed featured in certain motion pictures. Almost certainly his breakthrough came in 1935, with *Barbary Coast*, as a scuzzy barfly called Old Atrocity. The producer of that film, Samuel Goldwyn, kept him in mind for his next period drama, and Brennan's first Oscar was bestowed upon him for playing Edward Arnold's lively Swedish buddy, Swan Bostrom, in the lumber saga *Come and Get It*. That same year, 1936, his other roles ran the gamut from a small bit as a taxi driver in *These Three* to one of the leads in the first-rate western *Three Godfathers*, as the illiterate member of a gang of second-rate bank robbers who end up nursing a baby.

After Oscar number one, his position as a major addition to the Hollywood scene was solidified by his landing the lead in a "B," *The Affairs of Cappy Ricks*, as the head of a navigation company trying to solve his domestic problems; and being paired off with new child star Jane Withers, in *Wild and Wooly*, as her crusty old "gramps," who goes from drunk to town hero. In 1938 he won his second Oscar, for playing Loretta Young's cantankerous old Southern uncle in *Kentucky*, a highly colorful bit of acting that might be construed more as ham when seen today. He was a perfect choice to play the town drunk, Muff Potter, in Selnick's 1938 version of *The Adventures of Tom Sawyer*, and did the expected crotchety-but-loyal "sidekick" roles to Gary Cooper (*The Cowboy and the Lady*), Spencer Tracy (*Stanley and Livingstone, Northwest Passage*), and Fred Astaire and Ginger Rogers (*The Story of Vernon and Irene Castle*). In 1940 the third Academy Award came for perhaps the greatest performance of his career, playing the egomaniacal and dangerous Judge Roy Bean, who meets his match in Gary Cooper, in *The Westerner*, Brennan carefully finding the balance between a humorous degree of self-righteousness and out-and-out evil. There was even a fourth chance for the statuette, in 1941, when he was nominated for his boisterous turn as a mountain preacher, again opposite Cooper, in *Sergeant York*, but this time Donald Crisp beat him out. Since he and Cooper worked so well together there were other pairings in *Meet John Doe*, at his most ornery, as a railroad tramp with a contempt for "Heelots;" *Pride of the Yankees*, as a sports reporter; and *Task Force*, as Coop's best friend and fellow-aircraft flier.

In a marvelous display of his comical abilities he was a cackling half-wit named Featherhead, in Bob Hope's *The Princess and the Pirate*, then had the pivotal role of the innocent man on the run in *Swamp Water*. During the 1940s he essayed perhaps his most famous sidekick part, the alcoholic buddy of Humphrey Bogart in *To Have and Have Not*. And who else but Brennan could convincingly play an expert in the art of mule training as he did in the gentle rural drama *Scudda Hoo! Scudda Hay!* Nothing fit him, however, more comfortably than the old west and among the standouts in this genre were *My Darling Clementine*, in one of his nastiest roles, as Old Man Clanton, having no qualms about shooting Tim Holt in the back; and two with John Wayne, *Red River*, as the scruffy chuck wagon cook, and *Rio Bravo*, as Stumpy, one of his most delightfully crusty characterizations. By the 1950s he was so well known that he even got some starring roles, in *Goodbye, My Lady*, as Brandon De Wilde's uncle, in this boy and his dog story, and *God Is My Partner*, as a surgeon who hopes to find spiritual fulfillment by giving away his money. Thanks to television his stardom rose even higher as he played the leads in three series, *The Real McCoys*, *The Tycoon*, and *The Guns of Will Sonnett*. As a result of these, the now 70-year-old-plus actor once again rated top billing on the big screen, with two Disney features, *The Gnome-Mobile*, in a dual role, as a lumber tycoon and a pint-sized forest creature; and *The One and Only Genuine Original Family Band*, croaking out a few songs as the leader of a musically-inclined brood.

Screen: 1927: The Ridin' Rowdy; Blake of Scotland Yard (serial); 1928: Tearin' Into Trouble; The Ballyhoo Buster; The Lariat Kid; Silks and Saddles; 1929: One Hysterical Night; Smilin' Guns; The Long Long Trail; The Shannons of Broadway; 1930: The King of Jazz; 1931: Heroes of the Flames (serial); Dancing Dynamite; Neck and Neck; Is There Justice?; 1932: Law and Order; Cornered; Hello Trouble; Texas Cyclone; Two-Fisted Law; The All-American; Fighting for Justice; Honeymoon Lane; Speed Madness; The Airmail Mystery (serial); The Fourth Horseman; Parachute Jumper; 1933: One Year Later; Man of Action; From Headquarters; The Kiss Before the Mirror; Saturday's Millions; The Keyhole; The Birdcage; The Invisible Man; The Phantom of the Air (serial); Sing Sinner Sing; Silent Men; Sensation Hunters; Rustlers' Roundup; Strange People; 1934: Murder in the Private Car; Half a Sinner; The Life of Vergie Winters; Whom the Gods Destroy; Death on the Diamond; Good Dame; Riptide; Fugitive Lovers; The Painted Veil; Beloved; Cheating Cheaters; Tailspin Tommy (serial); Gridiron Flash; Great Expectations; I'll Tell the World; Murder in the Clouds; The Prescott Kid; There's Always Tomorrow; Uncertain Lady; A Wicked Woman; You Can't Buy Everything; 1935: Welcome Home; The Wedding Night; Lady Tubbs; Northern Frontier; The Mystery of Edwin Drood; Public Hero No. 1; Party Wire; Barbary Coast; Man on the Flying Trapeze; Seven Keys to Baldpate; Bride of Frankenstein; We're in the Money; Metropolitan; Law Beyond the Range; Spring Tonic; 1936: Three Godfathers; Fury; These Three; Come and Get It; Banjo on My Knee; The Moon's Our Home; Paradise Valley; 1937: She's Dangerous; When Love Is Young; The Affairs of Cappy Ricks; Wild and Woolly; 1938: The Adventures of Tom Sawyer; The Buccaneer; Kentucky; The Texans; Mother Carey's Chickens; The Cowboy and the Lady; 1939: Stanley and Livingstone; The Story of Vernon and Irene Castle; They Shall Have Music; Joe and Ethel Turp Call on the President; 1940: The Westerner; Northwest Passage; Maryland; 1941: Meet John Doe; Sergeant York; Swamp Water; Nice Girl?; This Woman Is Mine; Rise and Shine; 1942: Pride of the Yankees; Stand By for Action; 1943: Slightly Dangerous; Hangmen Also Die; The North Star/Armored Attack; 1944: The Princess and the Pirate; To Have and Have Not; Home in Indiana; 1945: Dakota; 1946: Nobody Lives Forever; Centennial Summer; My Darling Clementine; A Stolen Life; 1947: Driftwood; 1948: Red River; Scudda Hoo! Scudda Hay!; Blood on the Moon; 1949: Brimstone; Task Force; The Green Promise; 1950: Singing Guns; Curtain Call at Cactus

Creek; Surrender; A Ticket to Tomahawk; The Showdown; **1951:** The Wild Blue Yonder; Along the Great Divide; Best of the Bad Men; **1952:** Lure of the Wilderness; Return of the Texan; **1953:** Sea of Lost Ships; **1954:** Drums Across the River; Four Guns to the Border; **1955:** The Far Country; Bad Day at Black Rock; At Gunpoint; **1956:** Come Next Spring; Goodbye, My Lady; The Proud Ones; Glory; **1957:** The Way to the Gold; God Is My Partner; Tammy and the Bachelor; **1959:** Rio Bravo; **1962:** Shoot Out at Big Sag; **1963:** How the West Was Won; **1965:** Those Calloways; **1966:** The Oscar; **1967:** The Gnome-Mobile; Who's Minding the Mint?; **1968:** The One and Only Genuine Original Family Band; **1969:** Support Your Local Sheriff!; **1975:** Smoke in the Wind (filmed 1971).

Select TV: **1953:** Lucky Thirteen (series); **1955:** Mr. Ears (sp); **1956:** The Happy Sun (sp); Duffy's (sp); **1957–63:** The Real McCoys (series); **1964–65:** The Tycoon (series); **1967–69:** The Guns of Will Sonnett (series); **1970–71:** To Rome With Love (series); **1969:** The Over-the-Hill Gang; **1970:** The Young Country; The Over-the-Hill Gang Rides Again; **1972:** Two for the Money; Home for the Holidays.

GEORGE BRENT

(GEORGE BRENDAN NOLAN) BORN: SHANNONSBRIDGE, IRELAND, MARCH 15, 1904. DIED: MAY 26, 1979.

It is hard to imagine someone as consistently low in excitement as George Brent making an impact in his own solo starring vehicles. Instead he became know for patiently, competently partnering with some of the screen's great actresses in films that gave the women all the best moments. Gaining experience as a member of the Abbey Theatre, he came to America where his Broadway work brought interest from Hollywood. A few years after his debut, he signed on with Warner Bros. in 1932, and there he would make his mark, first as leading man to his then-off-screen spouse (1932–34) Ruth Chatterton in such dramas as *The Crash*, asking her to flirt with financiers in order to get stock tips; and *Lily Turner*, as a cab driver who becomes a carnival strongman. He then found his true niche as Bette Davis's frequent sounding board in some of her best remembered pictures of this period: *Jezebel*, as one of her Southern suitors; *Dark Victory*, in the most famous of all his roles, as the brain surgeon with whom suffering Bette falls in love; *The Old Maid*, being killed off early in the story; *The Great Lie*, leaving Mary Astor pregnant with the baby that Bette craves; and *In This Our Life*, as the husband she dumps in order to pursue her sister's spouse. He also lent his low-octane talents to Ann Sheridan (whom he briefly married, 1942–43) in *Honeymoon for Three*, improbably cast as an irresistible ladies' man; Joan Fontaine in *The Affairs of Susan*, just one of her less-than-scintillating batch of admirers; Barbara Stanwyck in *My Reputation*, as the man threatening to destroy just that; and Dorothy McGuire in *The Spiral Staircase*, as her deadly tormentor. Over at Fox he had one of the leads in the popular 1939 drama *The Rains Came*, but found his footage entirely eliminated from the 1955 remake, *The Rains of Ranchipur*. After Warners the assignments became considerably more "B" including such titles as *Slave Girl*, *Out of the Blue*, *Angel on the Amazon*, and *The Kid from Cleveland*, and he briefly dabbled in television before retiring in the late 1950s. There was one more role, in the little-seen religious biopic of political lawyer Charles Colson, *Born Again*, released shortly before his death.

Screen: **1931:** Under Suspicion; Lightning Warrior (serial); Once a Sinner; Fair Warning; Homicide Squad; Charlie Chan Carries On; Ex-Bad Boy; **1932:** So Big; The Rich Are Always With Us; Week-End Marriage; Miss Pinkerton; The Purchase Price; The Crash; They Call It Sin; **1933:** 42nd Street; The Keyhole; Luxury Liner; From Headquarters; Baby Face; Female; Lilly Turner; **1934:** Housewife; Stamboul Quest; Desirable; The Painted Veil; **1935:** Living on Velvet; Front Page Woman; The Goose and the Gander; Special Agent; In Person; The Right to Live; Stranded; **1936:** Snowed Under; The Golden Arrow; The Case Against Mrs. Ames; Give Me Your Heart; More Than a Secretary; **1937:** The Go Getter; Mountain Justice; God's Country and the Woman; Submarine D-1; **1938:** Jezebel; Racket Busters; Gold Is Where You Find It; Secrets of an Actress; **1939:** Dark Victory; The Old Maid; The Rains Came; Wings of the Navy; **1940:** The Man Who Talked Too Much; 'Til We Meet Again; The Fighting 69th; Adventure in Diamonds; South of Suez; **1941:** Honeymoon for Three; International Lady; The Great Lie; They Dare Not Love; **1942:** The Gay Sisters; In This Our Life; Twin Beds; You Can't Escape Forever; Silver Queen; **1944:** Experiment Perilous; **1945:** The Affairs of Susan; Mexican Manhunt; **1946:** My Reputation; The Spiral Staircase; Tomorrow Is Forever; Love Come Back; Temptation; **1947:** Slave Girl; Out of the Blue; The Corpse Came C.O.D.; Christmas Eve; **1948:** Luxury Liner; Angel on the Amazon; **1949:** Red Canyon; Illegal Entry; The Kid From Cleveland; Bride for Sale; **1951:** FBI Girl; **1952:** Man Bait/The Last Page; Montana Belle (filmed 1948); **1953:** Tangier Incident; **1956:** Death of a Scoundrel; **1978:** Born Again.

NY Stage: **1929:** Seven Year Love; **1930:** The Fatal Woman; Love Honor and Betray; A Month in the Country.

Select TV: **1953:** Double Exposure (sp); Medicine Woman (sp); **1954:** Unbroken Promise (sp); **1955:** Return in Triumph (sp); The Mativ Hat (sp); Diagnosis of a Selfish Lady (sp); Death Dream (sp); **1956–67:** Wire Service (series).

DAVID BRIAN

BORN: NEW YORK, NY, AUGUST 5, 1910. ED: CCNY. DIED: JULY 15, 1993.

A lead and supporting player of no standout abilities or traits, David Brian mostly worked on screen in deadly serious parts although his background was a musical one. A former chorus boy, he had spent time singing and dancing in clubs and vaudeville before serving in the Coast Guard during World War II. After the war he was signed up by Warner Bros. and got his most challenging assignments right off the bat, coming up against Joan Crawford in two melodramas, *Flamingo Road* and *The Damned Don't Cry*, and Bette Davis in another, *Beyond the Forest*, where he was the rich man with whom she has an extra-marital affair. Borrowed by MGM, he played the level-headed uncle of Claude Jarman in the fine racial tension drama *Intruder in the Dust*, which would turn out to be the most satisfying credit he'd have on his résumé. Back at Warners he rated some starring parts in a few lower-budgeted dramas like *Breakthrough*, as the captain in charge of a platoon preparing for the Normandy invasion, and *Inside the Walls of Folsom Prison*, as the head of the guards, trying to give the prisoners a fair shake; and was called to support bigger stars like Gary Cooper in *Springfield Rifle*, and John Wayne in *The High and the Mighty*. The fading Republic studios put him alongside Vera Ralston for programmers like *A Perilous Journey*, *Timberjack*, and *Accused or Murder*, while Columbia starred him as a man saving the Indians from the Swedes in *The White Squaw*, and Allied Artists cast him as a doctor trying to track down his son, who unknowingly has some deadly virus capsules in his possession, in *No Place to Hide*.

There was also a television series, *Mr. District Attorney*, before he returned to the big screen where his roles got increasingly smaller as he settled into character parts.

Screen: 1949: Flamingo Road; G Men (only in prologue of re-issue of 1935 film); Beyond the Forest; Intruder in the Dust; 1950: The Damned Don't Cry; Breakthrough; The Great Jewel Robbery; 1951: Inside Straight; Fort Worth; Inside the Walls of Folsom Prison; 1952: This Woman Is Dangerous; Million Dollar Mermaid; Springfield Rifle; 1953: Ambush at Tomahawk Gap; A Perilous Journey; 1954: The High and the Mighty; Dawn at Socorro; 1955: Timberjack; 1956: Fury at Gunsight Pass; The First Traveling Saleslady; The White Squaw; No Place to Hide; Accused of Murder; 1958: Ghost of the China Sea; 1959: The Rabbit Trap; 1961: Pocketful of Miracles; 1963: How the West Was Won; 1965: The Rare Breed; 1966: Castle of Evil; 1968: The Destructors; 1969: The Girl Who Knew Too Much; Childish Thing/Confessions of Tom Harris (filmed 1966); 1971: The Seven Minutes.

Select TV: 1953: 19 Rue Marie (sp); 1954: That Other Sunlight (sp); The Taming of the Shrew (sp); Mr. District Attorney (series); 1959: Shadow of Evil (sp); 1961: Labor of Love (sp); 1964: Who Is Jennifer? (sp); 1970–71: The Immortal (series); 1976: The Manhunter.

LLOYD BRIDGES

BORN: SAN LEANDRO, CA, JANUARY 15, 1913.
ED: UCLA. DIED: MARCH 10, 1998.

The patriarch of acting's most underrated family, Lloyd Bridges had to be content with being one of film's most ubiquitous, taken-for-granted supporting players whose brush with stardom did not come until the advent of television. His early days didn't show great promise as he did some Broadway; ran his own theatre, called The Playroom Club; and even taught drama at a private school in Darien, Connecticut. In 1941 he was signed to a contract by Columbia Pictures and worked for them over the next four years in nearly 50 features, many of them "B's" and mostly without causing any kind of stir. Among these were his debut, in an entry in a "B" movie series *The Lone Wolf Takes a Chance*; *Here Comes Mr. Jordan*, as a flier; *Shut My Big Mouth*, supporting Joe E. Brown in this western spoof; and *Sahara*, as a British soldier, a film that was remade as the western *Last of the Comanches*, a decade later, and *also* featured Bridges in the cast. Shortly before he left the studio they let him have one of the leads in *She's a Soldier Too*, engaging cabbie Nina Foch to find his son. Following this period, things looked rosier as he took the lead in a Universal serial, *Secret Agent X-9*, and performed effectively in two top-notch military dramas with more on their minds than gunplay, Lewis Milestone's anti-war piece, *A Walk in the Sun*, and Mark Robson's *Home of the Brave*, as the friendliest member of a platoon that otherwise treats their sole black member with scorn. Meanwhile there were some poverty row assignments like Republic's *Secret Service Investigator*, as a World War II vet involved with counterfeiters; Eagle-Lion's *Trapped*, which *also* involved illegal money making, and Monogram's *16 Fathoms Deep*, as a sponge diver; but at least these roles were more substantial than most of those he'd previously done.

If many of his assignments in the early 1950s looked no better, there were some peaks among the programmers, landing a part in one of the true peaks of the western genre, *High Noon*, excellent as Gary Cooper's stubborn deputy; *The Rainmaker*, as Katharine Hepburn's brother; and best of all, *The Goddess*, as Kim Stanley's second husband, who cannot get the love in return that his movie

star wife demands from him. However, the budgets couldn't be any smaller on those he carried, including the sci-fi adventure *Rocket Ship XM*; *Little Big Horn*, which did not focus on the famous battle but on the patrol trying to get to General Custer; and *Wetbacks*, about illegal immigration. By that time it was clear that the movies were never going to make him more than a good second lead so he plunged (literally) into television as underwater diver Mike Nelson in the hit series *Sea Hunt*. Thereafter he pretty much became a television regular, appearing on several other shows and in such big mini-series as *Roots* and *East of Eden*. In the 1980s he was one of the veteran performers who were allowed to reveal their comical talents in the smash hit comedy *Airplane!*, as an air traffic controller who reverts to substance abuse. Suddenly he was in demand again as a character player, and turned in some sparkling work, as the feisty grandfather in *Cousins* and the absent-minded commander in the comic spoof *Hot Shots!* There were also two with son Beau (*The Fifth Musketeer*, as Aramis; and *The Wild Pair*), and two with son Jeff (*Tucker* and *Blown Away*). His jokey appearance as a don in the spoof *Jane Austen's Mafia!* was released posthumously. His was one of the most successful and longlasting of Hollywood marriages, having wed actress Dorothy Simpson in 1938.

Screen: 1941: The Lone Wolf Takes a Chance; They Dare Not Love; Honolulu Lu; Son of Davy Crockett; Three Girls About Town; I Was a Prisoner on Devil's Island; Here Comes Mr. Jordan; The Medico of Painted Springs; Sing for Your Supper; Our Wife; Two Latins From Manhattan; The Royal Mounted Patrol; Harmon of Michigan; You Belong to Me; 1942: Alias Boston Blackie; Harvard, Here I Come; The Wife Takes a Flyer; Cadets on Parade; Underground Agent; Stand By All Networks; West of Tombstone; Blondie Goes to College; Shut My Big Mouth; Canal Zone; Flight Lieutenant; Atlantic Convoy; Tramp Tramp Tramp; The Daring Young Man; The Talk of the Town; Hello Annapolis; Riders of the Northland; Sweetheart of the Fleet; Meet the Stewarts; North of the Rockies; The Spirit of Stanford; Commandos Strike at Dawn; A Man's World; Pardon My Gun; 1943: Sahara; Hail to the Rangers; The Heat's On; Passport to Suez; Crime Doctor's Strangest Case; Destroyer; 1944: She's a Soldier Too; Two-Man Submarine; Louisiana Hayride; The Master Race; Once Upon a Time; Saddle Leather Law; 1945: A Walk in the Sun; Miss Susie Slagle's; Strange Confession; Secret Agent X-9 (serial); 1946: Canyon Passage; Abilene Town; 1947: Ramrod; The Trouble With Women; Unconquered; 1948: Secret Service Investigator; 16 Fathoms Deep; Moonrise; 1949: Red Canyon; Hideout; Home of the Brave; Calamity Jane and Sam Bass; Trapped; 1950: Colt .45; Rocket Ship XM; The White Tower; The Sound of Fury; 1951: Little Big Horn; Three Steps North; The Whistle at Eaton Falls; 1952: High Noon; Plymouth Adventure; Last of the Comanches; 1953: The Tall Texan; City of Bad Men; The Kid From Left Field; The Limping Man; 1954: Pride of the Blue Grass; Deadly Game/Third Party Risk; 1955: Wichita; Apache Woman; 1956: Wetbacks; The Rainmaker; 1957: Ride Out for Revenge; 1958: The Goddess; 1966: Around the World Under the Sea; 1968: The Daring Game; Attack on the Iron Coast; 1969: The Happy Ending; 1971: To Find a Man; 1973: Running Wild; 1979: The Fifth Musketeer; 1980: Bear Island; Airplane!; 1982: Airplane II: The Sequel; 1986: Weekend Warriors; 1987: The Wild Pair; 1988: Tucker: The Man and His Dream; 1989: Cousins; Winter People; 1990: Joe vs. the Volcano; 1991: Hot Shots!; 1992: Honey, I Blew Up the Kid; 1993: Mr. Bluesman (nUSr); Hot Shots! Part Deux; 1994: Blown Away; 1998: Meeting Daddy (dtv); Jane Austen's Mafia!

NY Stage: 1937: Othello; 1940: Suzanna and the Elders; 1953: Dead Pigeon; 1959: Guys and Dolls; 1967: Cactus Flower.

Select TV: 1952: International Incident (sp); This Plane for Hire (sp); 1953: A Long Way Home (sp); 1956: The Ainsley Case (sp); Tragedy in a Temporary Town (sp); The Regulators (sp); American Primitive (sp); Heritage of Anger (sp); 1957: Clash by Night (sp); They Never Forget (sp); Man on the Outside (sp); 1957–61: Sea Hunt (series); 1959: Lepke (sp); 1961: Who Killed Julie Greer? (sp); The Fortress (sp); Star Witness (sp); 1962–63: The Lloyd Bridges Show (series); 1963: A Hero of Our Times (sp); 1965–66: The Loner (series); 1968: A Case of Libel (sp); The People Next Door (sp); 1969: The Silent Gun; Lost Flight; Silent Night, Lonely Night; 1970: The Love War; 1970–71: San Francisco International Airport (series); 1971: Do You Take This Stranger?; A Tattered Web; The Deadly Dream; 1972: Haunts of the Very Rich; 1973: Trouble Comes to Town; Crime Club; Death Race; 1975: Stowaway to the Moon; The Return of Joe Forrester; 1975–76: Joe Forrester (series); 1977: Roots (ms); Telethon; 1978: The Great Wallendas; The Critical List; 1979: Disaster on the Coastliner; 1980: Moviola: This Year's Blonde; 1981: John Steinbeck's East of Eden (ms); 1982: Life of the Party: The Story of Beatrice; The Blue and the Gray (ms); 1983: Grace Kelly; 1984: George Washington (ms); Paper Dolls (series); 1986: Dress Gray; North & South Book II (ms); The Thanksgiving Promise; 1988: She Was Marked for Murder; 1989: Cross of Fire; 1990: Leona Helmsley: The Queen of Mean; Capital News (series); 1991: In the Nick of Time; 1992: Devlin; 1993–94: Harts of the West (series); 1994: Secret Sins of the Father; 1995: The Other Woman; Sidney Sheldon's Nothing Lasts Forever; 1996: The Deliverance of Elaine.

BARBARA BRITTON

(BARBARA BRANTINGHAM). BORN: LONG BEACH, CA, SEPTEMBER 26, 1919. ED: LONG BEACH CA COL. DIED: JANUARY 17, 1980.

An actress whose screen career didn't supply her with enough highlights to wipe away her dominating image as "the Revlon Lady," Barbara Britton was signed up by Paramount Pictures right out of college. The pretty redhead debuted in a Hopalong Cassidy western, Secrets of the Wasteland, and proceeded to decorate several of the studio's movies, including the nurse tribute So Proudly We Hail!, and the remake of Mrs. Wiggs of the Cabbage Patch, before landing her first real lead, in 1944's Till We Meet Again, as the nun who assists downed pilot Ray Milland. Shortly afterwards she was Joel McCrea's love interest in the promptly forgotten remake of The Virginian, and helped clear innocent Robert Lowery in a Pine-Thomas quickie, They Made Me a Killer, before Paramount sent her on her way. There were lots of roles in westerns and action programmers and she even had her own vehicles, The Fabulous Suzanne, a horse story, and The Bandit Queen, riding around in a mask seeking revenge on the thugs who murdered her parents. Champagne for Caesar was of a higher vintage than most of these, but her role as Ronald Colman's sister was secondary. In 1952 she appeared in one of the biggest hits of the year, Bwana Devil, the success of which had nothing to do with her, nor with the movie's quality in so much as it was fairly terrible, but with the fact that it was the first full-length feature filmed and distributed in 3-D. After her own television series, Mr. and Mrs. North, she did a few more features then put aside acting to be a spokesperson for Revlon cosmetics, in commercials that ran over a 12 year period.

Screen: 1941: Secrets of the Wasteland; Louisiana Purchase; 1942: The Fleet's In; Reap the Wild Wind; Beyond the Blue Horizon; Wake Island; Mrs. Wiggs of the Cabbage Patch; 1943: Young and Willing; So Proudly We Hail!; 1944: The Story of Dr. Wassell; Till We Meet Again; 1945: The Great John L; Captain Kidd; 1946: The Virginian; They Made Me a Killer; The Fabulous Suzanne; The Return of Monte Cristo; 1947: Gunfighters; 1948: Albuquerque; Mr. Reckless; The Untamed Breed; 1949: Loaded Pistols; I Shot Jesse James; Cover-Up; 1950: Champagne for Caesar; Bandit Queen; 1952: The Raiders; Ride the Man Down; Bwana Devil; 1954: Dragonfly Squadron; 1955: Ain't Misbehavin'; Night Freight; The Spoilers.

NY Stage: 1951: Getting Married; 1956: Wake Up Darling; 1961: How to Make a Man; 1965: Me and Thee; 1967: Spofford.

Select TV: 1950: Mrs. Mike (sp); Christopher Beach (sp); 1951: Haunted House (sp); 1952: Say Hello to Pamela (sp); Till Next We Meet (sp); 1952–54: Mr. and Mrs. North (series); 1955: The Stranger (sp); Twelve to Eternity (sp); The Fabulous Sycamores (sp).

HELEN BRODERICK

BORN: PHILADELPHIA, PA, AUGUST 11, 1891. DIED: SEPTEMBER 25, 1959.

A small and sassy character actress who could dish out a dead-pan wisecrack with the best of them, Helen Broderick started as a Ziegfeld girl before making her name on Broadway throughout the 1920s. In 1931 she came to the movies to recreate her stage role as an American tourist in Paris in the lousy adaptation of Fifty Million Frenchmen, returned to Broadway, then signed a contract with RKO in 1935. She had supported Fred Astaire onstage in The Band Wagon, and did it twice on screen, brilliantly, in Top Hat, at her funniest as Edward Everet Horton's wife, sitting back and observing her husband's jittery behavior with a bemused air, and Swing Time, as the dance studio receptionist who has some appropriately tart comments for Victor Moore. She was upped to leading roles for some "B's" including To Beat the Band, as a lawyer hoping to get her cut of a client's inheritance, and Murder on a Bridle Path, as amateur sleuth Hildegarde Withers. Due to their supporting success in Swing Time, Broderick and Victor Moore were reteamed for some minor comedies, We're on the Jury, pretty much taking the path Henry Fonda did years later in 12 Angry Men, swaying the other jurors to see her point; and Meet the Missus, as a finalist in a Mrs. America contest. In the mid-1940s Universal hoped she could create the same sort of magic she had for Astaire and Rogers by putting her in support of their big dance team of the day, Donald O'Connor and Peggy Ryan, in Chip Off the Old Block, and then dropped her into Her Primitive Man, which also had Edward Everet Horton among the cast members, but these clearly weren't on the same level. After one with Deanna Durbin, Because of Him, she bid the movie business farewell. Her son was Academy Award-winning actor Broderick Crawford.

Screen: 1931: Fifty Million Frenchmen; 1935: Top Hat; To Beat the Band; 1936: Love on a Bet; The Bride Walks Out; Murder on a Bridle Path; Swing Time; Smartest Girl in Town; 1937: We're on the Jury; Meet the Missus; The Life of the Party; She's Got Everything; 1938: Radio City Revels; The Rage of Paris; The Road to Reno; Service de Luxe; 1939: Stand Up and Fight; Naughty But Nice; Honeymoon in Bali; 1940: The Captain Is a Lady; No, No, Nanette; 1941: Virginia; Nice Girl?; Father Takes a Wife; 1942: Are Husbands Necessary?; 1943: Stage Door Canteen; 1944: Chip Off the Old Block; Her Primitive Man; Three Is a Family; 1945: Love, Honor and Goodbye; 1946: Because of Him.

NY Stage: 1907: Ziegfeld Follies of 1908; 1908: The Girl Question; 1911: Jumping Jupiter; 1923: Nifties of 1923; The Wild Westcotts; 1926: Mama Loves Papa; Oh Please; 1929: Fifty Milion Frenchmen; 1931: The Band Wagon; 1932: Earl Carroll Vanities; 1933: As Thousands Cheer.

CHARLES BRONSON

(CHARLES BUCHINSKI) BORN: EHRENFELD, PA, NOVEMBER 3, 1920.

Perhaps the prime example of "good things come to those who wait," squinty-eyed Charles Bronson had pretty much resigned himself to being a macho, un-handsome supporting player when suddenly, past the age of 50, he became a box-office draw. As one of 15 children, he worked in the the Pennsylvania coalmines until World War II came. After service he studied art and then acting under the G.I. Bill before enrolling at the Pasadena Playhouse. Thanks to a fellow student, he won an audition with director Henry Hathaway and got a role in *You're in the Navy Now*, in 1951, billed under his real name. And so he stayed in similar small parts for the next few years, sometimes in big hits, like Tracy and Hepburn's *Pat and Mike*, as a prizefighter, and the 3-D sensation *House of Wax*, as Vincent Price's mute assistant. In later years, when he'd become very famous, it was a constant source of surprise for the unenlightened to see the name "Buchinsky" in the opening credits only to have Charles Bronson show up in the course of the film. After changing his last name to Bronson in 1956, with the western *Drum Beat*, he actually landed some leads in two 20th Century-Fox "B" movies, *Gang War*, as a high school teacher who finds himself in danger after witnessing a gangland execution, and *Showdown at Boot Hill*, as a marshal who feels he may have been too hasty in killing a criminal. Most effective of all was being given the title role in Roger Corman's *Machine-Gun Kelly*, a medium gangster flick that had its share of devotees, with Bronson giving one of his better performances, as the real-life thug who wasn't as brave as he pretended to be.

In the 1960s he tried some television series but none of them took off. Meanwhile, in movies he was back in support, showing up in some of the decade's prime action hits, playing one of *The Magnificent Seven*; *The Great Escape*, as the one most responsible for carving out the tunnel to the outside world; and going on the suicide mission as one of *The Dirty Dozen*; in each instance his brooding presence being utilized to good advantage. In between these he could be seen trying to stop eccentric scientist Vincent Price in the action fantasy *Master of the World*; back in the ring as a prizefighter in Elvis Presley's *Kid Galahad*; giving Frank Sinatra and Dean Martin a hard time as a bandit in *4 for Texas*; and marrying a disenchanted Natalie Wood in *This Property Is Condemned*. Not unlike Clint Eastwood, it took a Sergio Leone spaghetti western to open the door to movie stardom. *Once Upon a Time in the West* gave Bronson the customary Eastwood role of the nameless hero in this overlong saga and suddenly he was in demand all over the place. However, all of his initial follow-up features were pretty dire, including *You Can't Win 'Em All*, teamed with Tony Curtis; *Someone Behind the Door*, as an amnesiac who becomes Anthony Perkins's pawn; and *Red Sun*, a western that brought him into contact with a samurai, played by Toshiro Mifune. *The Valachi Papers*, a tedious post-*Godfather* crime tale, gave him his first popular vehicle and, in due time, he was grinding out gritty action dramas pretty regularly. He never really could compete with Eastwood in this market, however, reaching a much smaller U.S. audience. And whereas Eastwood, for all his emotionless underacting, had an underlying charisma, Bronson's scowling, frozen-faced performing could be quite boring.

Because of *Valachi* it became quite the norm to see a Bronson action film or two popping up with regularity ever year. Despite him being considered a "draw" there wasn't much interest in *The Stone Killer* as a cop who uncovers a strange plot using Vietnam vets, and *Mr. Majestyk*, an attempt at something different in so much as he was a farmer, though still involved with the mob. In 1974 he made the one that stood out above the others, *Death Wish*, as a New York businessman who becomes a vigilante after his wife is murdered and his daughter is raped by a bunch of thugs. An engrossing and violent piece of mass entertainment, it was worth reams of news print and controversy and became the role for which Bronson would become forever identified. He did in fact drag the character out with laughable frequency in sequel after sequel until he was well into his 70s. At the time it was the one movie he did that had a large cross-over appeal at the box office. Afterwards, it was back to the old routine, with the customary westerns, including an attempt at something more lighthearted, *From Noon Till Three*, as second rate bank robber whose sexual exploits become exaggerated with the passing years; the critically-liked boxing picture *Hard Times*, as a bare-knuckle fighter; and one of the few in which he shared star billing, *Death Hunt*, with Lee Marvin, whom he had once supported in *The Dirty Dozen*. As the years passed he became an increasingly less dependable draw and it was likely even his most avid fans could detect the weariness in his crumpled face towards the constant lack of inspired material. He married actress Jill Ireland in 1968, after appearing with her in *Villa Rides*. She was his co-star on several occasions before her death of cancer in 1990.

Screen: AS CHARLES BUCHINSKY: 1951: U.S.S. Teakettle/You're in the Navy Now; The People Against O'Hara; The Mob; 1952: Red Skies of Montana; My Six Convicts; The Marrying Kind; Pat and Mike; Diplomatic Courier; Bloodhounds of Broadway; 1953: The Clown; House of Wax; Miss Sadie Thompson; 1954: Crime Wave; Tennessee Champ; Riding Shotgun; Apache; Vera Cruz.

AS CHARLES BRONSON: 1954: Drum Beat; 1955: Big House USA; Target Zero; 1956: Jubal; 1957: Run of the Arrow; 1958: Gang War; Showdown on Boot Hill; Machine Gun Kelly; When Hell Broke Loose; 1959: Never So Few; 1960: The Magnificent Seven; 1961: Master of the World; A Thunder of Drums; 1962: X-15; Kid Galahad; 1963: The Great Escape; 4 for Texas; 1965: The Sandpiper; Battle of the Bulge; 1966: This Property Is Condemned; 1967: The Dirty Dozen; 1968: Guns for San Sebastian; Villa Rides!; Farewell Friend (nUSr); 1969: Once Upon a Time in the West; Rider on the Rain; 1970: Lola/Twinky; You Can't Win 'em All; The Family; Cold Sweat; 1971: Someone Behind the Door; Red Sun; 1972: Chato's Land; The Mechanic; The Valachi Papers; 1973: Chino; The Stone Killer; 1974: Mr. Majestyk; Death Wish; 1975: Breakout; Hard Times; 1976: Breakheart Pass; From Noon Till Three; St. Ives; 1977: The White Buffalo; Telefon; 1979: Love and Bullets; 1980: Caboblanco; Borderline; 1981: Death Hunt; 1982: Death Wish II; 1983: Ten to Midnight; 1984: The Evil That Men Do; 1985: Death Wish 3; 1986: Murphy's Law; 1987: Assassination; Death Wish 4: The Crackdown; 1988: Messenger of Death; 1989: Kinjite: Forbidden Subjects; 1991: The Indian Runner; 1994: Death Wish V: The Face of Death.

Select TV: 1954: The Witness (sp); 1955: Woman in the Mine (sp); Chain of Hearts (sp); Prosper's Old Mother (sp); 1957: Outpost (sp); 1958–60: Man With a Camera (series); 1959: Rank and File (sp); 1960: The Cruel Day (sp); 1961: Memory in White (sp); 1963: Empire (series); 1963–64: Travels of Jamie McPheeters (series); 1977: Raid on Entebbe; 1986: Act of Vengeance; 1991: Yes Virginia, There Is a Santa Claus; 1993: The Sea Wolf; Donato and Daughter; 1995: Family of Cops; 1997: Breach of Faith: Family of Cops II; 1999: Family of Cops III.

CLIVE BROOK

(Clifford Hardman Brook) Born: London, England, June 1, 1887. Died: November 17, 1974.

Maybe because he was British, Clive Brook was one of the stars of the silent screen who made the transition to talkies with ease, becoming, among other things, Hollywood's first idea of what Sherlock Holmes would sound like. For a spell it seemed that acting wasn't even in the stars, as Brook made a living as an insurance clerk and a news reporter before finally achieving the rank of major during World War I. It wasn't until after military service that he decided to try his luck as an actor and soon was apearing on the London stage and in films. He came to the U.S. in 1924 to work for Paramount Pictures, achieving his most notable silent triumphs with Josef von Sternberg's 1927 gangster melodrama *Underworld*, as a broken down lawyer, and Rowland V. Lee's *Barbed Wire*, as a German prisoner of war who falls for French girl Pola Negri. As the movies began to speak he came to represent a certain deadly earnest, stiff British reserve, hence his casting as Holmes, first in Paramount's *The Return of Sherlock Holmes*, which sounded like a sequel, and then, somewhat confusingly, Fox's *Sherlock Holmes*. His two most notable pictures of this era don't stand the test of time particularly well. There was *Shanghai Express*, the height of Josef von Sternberg's photographic infatuation with Marlene Dietrich, in which Brook was possibly the dreariest leading man she ever had; and 1933's *Cavalcade*, in which he and Diana Wynyard led a British cast through three decades of history — probably the worst film to ever win the Best Picture Oscar. After 1934 he returned to Britan and continued appearing in movies for another 10 years or so, though his prime had clearly passed. He directed and starred in the 1944 comedy *On Approval*, as a stuck up Duke stranded on an island with Beatrice Lillie. In 1963, out of the blue, he was coaxed back once more, by John Huston, for *The List of Adrian Messenger*.

Screen: 1920: Trent's Last Case; Kissing Cup's Race; 1921: Her Penalty; The Loudwater Mystery; Daniel Deronda; A Sportsman's Wife/The Woman Who Came Back; Sonia; Christie Johnstone; 1922: Shirley; Married to a Mormon; Stable Companions; The Experiment; A Debt of Honor; Love and a Whirlwind; 1923: Through Fire and Water; This Freedom; Out to Win; The Royal Oak; Woman to Woman; The Money Habit; 1924: The White Shadow/White Shadows; The Recoil; Christine of the Hungry Heart; The Wine of Life; The Passionate Adventurer; The Mirage; The Money Habit; 1925: When Love Grows Cold; Enticement; Seven Sinners; Declassée; Playing With Souls; If Marriage Fails; The Woman Hater; Compromise; The Home Maker; The Pleasure Buyers; 1926: Why Girls Go Back Home; For Alimony Only; You Never Know Women; The Popular Sin; Three Faces East; 1927: Afraid to Love; Barbed Wire; Underworld; Hula; The Devil Dancer; French Dressing; 1928: Midnight Madness; The Yellow Lily; The Perfect Crime; Forgotten Faces; 1929: The Four Feathers; Interference; A Dangerous Woman; Charming Sinners; The Return of Sherlock Holmes; The Laughing Lady; 1930: Slightly Scarlet; Paramount on Parade; Sweethearts and Wives; Anybody's Woman; 1931: East Lynne; Tarnished Lady; Scandal Sheet; The Lawyer's Secret; Silence; 24 Hours; Husband's Holiday; 1932: The Man From Yesterday; Sherlock Holmes; The Night of June 13th; Shanghai Express; Make Me a Star; 1933: If I Were Free; Cavalcade; Midnight Club; 1934: Gallant Lady; Where Sinners Meet; Let's Try Again; 1935: Dressed to Thrill; Loves of a Dictator/The Dictator; 1936: Love in Exile; The Lonely Road/Scotland Yard

Commands; 1938: Action for Slander; The Ware Case; 1939: Return to Yesterday; 1940: Convoy; 1941: Freedom Radio/A Voice in the Night; Breach of Promise/Adventure in Blackmail; 1943: The Flemish Farm; The Shipbuilders; 1944: On Approval (and dir.); 1963: The List of Adrian Messenger.
NY Stage: 1951: The Second Threshold.

HILLARY BROOKE

(Beatrice Peterson) Born: Astoria, NY, September 8, 1914. Died: May 25, 1999.

A tall blonde with a wicked gleam in her eye that made her so right for playing bad girls and unsympathetic parts, Hillary Brooke came to films in 1937, in RKO's *New Faces of 1937*, following a brief modeling career. Initially a bit player used to look pretty while passing through a scene, she had a breakthrough in 1942 when she got the leading lady role in a "Lone Wolf" mystery at Columbia, *Counter Espionage*, and, over at Universal, played the heroine in another series entry, *Sherlock Holmes Faces Death*, in danger because she's in line for an inheritance. Throughout the 1940s she could be seen in secondary roles in "A" features like *Jane Eyre*, as Rochester's fiancée, Blanche; *Ministry of Fear*, on the side of evil in this tense Fritz Lang-Graham Greene espionage tale; *Road to Utopia*, as a femme fatale trying to seduce a Klondike treasure map away from Bing Crosby and Bob Hope; and *The Enchanted Cottage*, her own personal favorite, as Robert Young's betrothed. As a star she had the lead in a melodrama for Paramount's "B" unit, *Big Town*, as the helpful gal Friday to newspaper editor Philip Reed, a film popular enough in its small way to warrant three immediate sequels. She later became associated with Abbott and Costello, appearing with them in two features, *Africa Screams*, and *Abbott and Costello Meet Captain Kidd*, and on their television series. Around this time she'd really bottomed out in pictures, appearing with the Bowery Boys in *Lucky Losers*; in *Skipalong Rosenbloom*, a mock western with ex-boxer Maxie Rosenbloom; and the unintentionally funny *The Lost Continent*, searching for an atomic rocket while dodging animated dinosaurs. On television Brooke became well known for playing Roberta Townsend, Charles Farrell's much younger love interest, on *My Little Margie* before retiring from the limelight in the early 1960s.

Screen: 1937: New Faces of 1937; 1939: Eternally Yours; 1940: New Moon; Two Girls on Broadway; Florian; The Philadelphia Story; 1941: Dr. Jekyll and Mr. Hyde; Maisie Was a Lady; Mr. and Mrs. North; Married Bachelor; The Lone Rider Rides On; The Lone Rider in Frontier Fury; Unfinished Business; 1942: Born to Sing; Ship Ahoy; Sleepytime Gal; To the Shores of Tripoli; Wake Island; Counter Espionage; Calling Dr. Gillespie; Sherlock Holmes and the Voice of Terror; 1943: Happy Go Lucky; The Crystal Ball; Sherlock Holmes Faces Death; 1944: Lady in the Dark; And the Angels Sing; Practically Yours; Jane Eyre; Standing Room Only; Ministry of Fear; 1945: The Enchanted Cottage; The Crime Doctor's Courage; The Woman in Green; 1946: Road to Utopia; Up Goes Maisie; Strange Impersonation; Monsieur Beaucaire; The Gentleman Misbehaves; Earl Carroll's Sketchbook; Strange Journey; The Strange Woman; 1947: Big Town; I Cover Big Town; Big Town After Dark; 1948: Big Town Scandal; The Fuller Brush Man; Let's Live Again; 1949: Africa Screams; Bodyhold; Alimony; 1950: Unmasked; The Admiral Was a Lady; Beauty on Parade; Vendetta; Lucky Losers; 1951: Insurance Investigator; Skipalong Rosenbloom; The Lost Continent; 1952: Confidence Girl; Abbott and Costello Meet Captain Kidd; Never Wave at a WAC;

1953: The Lady Wants Mink; Mexican Manhunt; Invaders From Mars; The Maze; 1954: Heat Wave/The House Across the Lake; Dragon's Gold; 1955: Bengazi; 1956: The Man Who Knew Too Much; 1957: Spoilers of the Forest.

Select TV: 1951–52: The Abbott and Costello Show (series); 1952–55: My Little Margie (series); 1953: The Ladies on His Mind (sp); 1954: Backstage (sp); A Man's Home (sp); 1955: Luxurious Ladies (sp); 1956: The Sword of Villon (sp); 1957: Palm Springs Incident (sp).

LOUISE BROOKS

BORN: CHERRYVALE, KS, NOVEMBER 14, 1906. DIED: AUGUST 8, 1985.

There are those who might very well be under the mistaken impression that Louise Brooks was foreign, since her two most famous and revived silent pictures were made in Germany. She was in fact a Midwesterner, who danced in the George White Scandals and the Ziegfeld Follies before Paramount took note and signed her to a contract. She entered movies in a small part, in *The Street of Forgotten Men*, in 1925, and began to gather favorable notices over the next few years, especially for *Rolled Stockings*, as a collegiate wild girl and campus flirt, and *Beggars of Life*, as a fugitive who dresses as a boy to hide out among the hobos. Then came the two in Germany, for director G.W. Pabst, a pair of sexually startling dramas for which Brooks received glowing reviews: *Pandora's Box*, as Lulu, the nymphomaniac, and *Diary of a Lost Girl*. These made her the talk of Europe, so she refused to return to Hollywood on any terms but her own. Her stance backfired and they soon lost interest. When she finally did go back it was as a supporting player, but work was not plentifully and, in due time, she was filing for bankruptcy. She swallowed her pride and took jobs dancing in New York nightclubs. More surprisingly she can be seen as nothing more than a chorus girl in a 1937 Grace Moore musical, *When You're in Love*. She had been long out of the business when her work in the Pabst films began to bring a cult following and the dark-eyed girl with the bobbed hair was now looked on as one of the enduring images of silent film history. With Hollis Alpert she penned her autobiography, *Lulu in Hollywood*, in 1982.

Screen: 1925: The Street of Forgotten Men; 1926: The American Venus; A Social Celebrity; It's the Old Army Game; The Show-Off; Love 'em and Leave 'em; Just Another Blonde; 1927: Evening Clothes; Rolled Stockings; The City Gone Wild; Now We're in the Air; 1928: A Girl in Every Port; Beggars of Life; 1929: Pandora's Box; Diary of a Lost Girl; The Canary Murder Case; 1930: Prix de Beaute/Miss Europe; 1931: It Pays to Advertise; God's Gift to Women; 1936: Empty Saddles; 1937: When You're in Love; 1938: Overland Stage Raiders.

JOE E. BROWN

(JOSEPH EVAN BROWN) BORN: HOLGATE, OH, JULY 28, 1892. DIED: JULY 6, 1973.

As Warner Bros.'s major comedic offering at the dawn of the talkies, Joe E. Brown enjoyed his period as a money-making attraction, but since few of his vehicles were revived with the passing years, it is as a character comedian and supporting player most later generations know him best. A circus acrobat while still a child, he later made his name on the vaudeville circuit, which resulted in interest from the movies. His enormous mouth, from which he would often emit bellowing yells, along with his characterization of the innocent who triumphs in the end, made him a star attraction in the 1930s, with a series of broad comedies including *The Tenderfoot, You Said a Mouthful*, and *Fireman, Save My Child*. In the latter he had a thing for baseball and Brown's real-life love of the sport was the basis for two of his most notable outings of this period, *Elmer the Great* and *Alibi Ike*. *Elmer*, which he had done as a stage play in San Francisco, was a property he would visit again, not only onstage but on radio as well. Seen today, it is apt to produce stony silence in place of laughs. Around the same time he was part of the off-beat ensemble of the hit Shakespeare adaptation, *A Midsummer Night's Dream*, playing a very broad version of the slow-witted Flute. His contract at Warners came to an end with another sports themed vehicle, *Polo Joe*, and *Earthworm Tractors*, a strong contender for the least appealing movie title in history. As his popularity decreased, so did his budgets and, over at Columbia and Republic, the sophistication level of his films were indicated by the many titles that needed to remind audiences of the width of Brown's mouth, *So You Won't Talk, Shut My Big Mouth*, and *Chatterbox*. After the war he played the serious role of a minister in one of the earliest movies about animal rights, *The Tender Years*, and found himself onstage portraying Elwood P. Dowd in *Harvey*. As a result he got one of his best roles, as Cap'n Andy in the 1951 version of *Show Boat*, and later down the line, the part for which audiences cherish him the most, the nit-witted millionaire smitten with Jack Lemmon in Billy Wilder's *Some Like It Hot*, delivering the great closing line with panache. He published *Your Kids and Mine*, in 1944, and his autobiography, *Laughter Is a Wonderful Thing*, in 1956.

Screen: 1928: Crooks Can't Win; Hit of the Show; The Circus Kid; Take Me Home; 1929: Molly and Me; My Lady's Past; On With the Show; 1929: Sally; Painted Faces; 1930: Song of the West; Hold Everything; Top Speed; The Lottery Bride; Maybe It's Love; 1931: Going Wild; Sit Tight; Broad-Minded; Local Boy Makes Good; 1932: Fireman, Save My Child; The Tenderfoot; You Said a Mouthful; 1933: Elmer the Great; Son of a Sailor; 1934: A Very Honorable Guy; The Circus Clown; 6 Day Bike Rider; 1935: Alibi Ike; Bright Lights; A Midsummer Nght's Dream; 1936: Sons o'Guns; Earthworm Tractors; Polo Joe; 1937: When's Your Birthday?; Riding on Air; Fit for a King; 1938: Wide Open Faces; The Gladiator; Flirting With Fate; 1939: $1,000 a Touchdown; Beware Spooks!; 1940: So You Won't Talk; 1942: Shut My Big Mouth; Joan of Ozark; The Daring Young Man; 1943: Chatterbox; 1944: Casanova in Burlesque; Pin-Up Girl; Hollywood Canteen; 1947: The Tender Years; 1951: Show Boat; 1956: Around the World in Eighty Days; 1959: Some Like It Hot; 1963: The Comedy of Terrors; It's a Mad Mad Mad Mad World.

NY Stage: 1920: Jim Jam Jems; 1921: The Greenwich Village Follies (and 1922, 1923); 1924: Betty Lee; 1925: Captain Jinks; 1926: Twinkle Twinkle; 1948: Harvey; 1951: Courtin' Time; 1961: Show Boat.

Select TV: 1952–53: The Buick Circus Hour (series); 1955: Meet Mr. Justice (sp); The Silent Partner (sp); 1956: The Golden Key (sp).

CORAL BROWNE

BORN: MELBOURNE, AUSTRALIA, JULY 23, 1913.
DIED: MAY 29, 1991.

A brittle, sophisticated actress who specialized in playing character parts of
less-than-cuddly women, Coral Browne had
acted for years on the London stage (and in
secondary roles in a handful of British films) before coming to
Broadway in 1956 to play in *Tamburlaine the Great*. Two years
later she made a splash in the hit film of *Auntie Mame*, in a
bullseye performance as Rosalind Russell's arrogant and snippy
actress friend, Vera Charles. Later she played a bitchy journalist
nosing her way into Vivien Leigh's affairs in *The Roman Spring of
Mrs. Stone*; the nagging wife polished off by timid Donald
Pleasence in the true-life *Dr. Crippen*; a cunning lesbian with an
eye on Susannah York in *The Killing of Sister George*, participating
in a much talked about seduction scene; one of the victims of
crazed earl Peter O'Toole in *The Ruling Class*; and a caustic
drama critic electrocuted under a hair dryer by Vincent Price in
Theatre of Blood. She married Price that same year, 1973, and they
remained so until her death. In the 1980s she acted two of her
best roles, as herself in the acclaimed television drama *An
Englishman Abroad*, recreating her real-life meeting with exiled,
gay British spy Guy Burgess; and, on the big screen, in the off-
beat *Dreamchild*, as the grown-up Alice Liddell who had been the
inspiration for Lewis Carroll's *Alice in Wonderland*, and realized
too late the importance of the author to her life.

Screen: 1935: Line Engaged; Charing Cross Road; 1936: The
Amateur Gentleman; Guilty Melody; 1938: We're Going to be
Rich; Yellow Sands; Black Limelight; 1939: The Nursemaid
Who Disappeared; 1940: Let George Do It; 1946: Piccadilly
Incident; 1947: The Courtney Affair/The Courtneys of Curzon
Street; 1954: Twist of Fate; Beautiful Stranger; 1958: Auntie
Mame; 1961: The Roman Spring of Mrs. Stone; 1962: Go to
Blazes; 1964: Dr. Crippen; Tamahine; 1967: The Night of the
Generals; 1968: The Legend of Lylah Claire; The Killing of
Sister George; 1972: The Ruling Class; 1973: Theatre of Blood;
1975: The Drowning Pool; 1980: Xanadu (voice); 1984:
American Dreamer; 1985: Dreamchild.

NY Stage: 1956: Tamburlaine the Great; Macbeth; Troilus
and Cressida; 1963: The Rehearsal; 1965: The Right
Honorable Gentleman.

Select TV: 1972: Lady Windermere's Fan (sp); Mrs. Warren's
Profession; 1979: Time Express (series); 1982: Eleanor: First
Lady of the World; 1983: An Englishman Abroad (sp).

NIGEL BRUCE

(WILLIAM NIGEL BRUCE) BORN: ENSENADA,
MEXICO, FEBRUARY 4, 1895. RAISED IN ENGLAND.
DIED: OCTOBER 8, 1953.

This most welcome British import, with the
popping eyes and gray brush of mustache,
found his niche in Hollywood playing some-
what flustered types with a haughty upper class air, but was first
and foremost the screen's best remembered Dr. Watson. His
unlikely place of birth, Mexico, was simply a matter of being
born while his parents were on vacation. Back in England he
became an actor following service in World War I, during which
he had been injured in the leg (a la Dr. Watson). After stage work
in both London and New York, he began appearing in British
pictures until Fox asked him to repeat his Broadway role of the
cuckolded millionaire in the movie of *Springtime for Henry*, in

1934. Soon afterwards it seemed any time Hollywood tackled a
subject with a British background Bruce was there, including *The
Charge of the Light Brigade*, as Sir Benjamin Warrenton, the
incompetent commander whose miscalculation results in a massacre; *The Rains Came*, showing his meaner side, as Myrna Loy's
husband; *Rebecca*, as Major Lacy; *Suspicion*, as Beaky, the family
friend whom Joan Fontaine believes has been murdered by Cary
Grant; *This Above All*, as an inn keeper; and *Lassie Come Home*,
as the benign old gentleman from whom the pooch escapes. It
was 1939 when 20th Century-Fox first called on him to play the
loyal Dr. Watson to Basil Rathbone's Sherlock Holmes, in *The
Hound of the Baskervilles*. There followed one more for the studio,
The Adventures of Sherlock Holmes, and that might have been it
had Universal not decided to revive the team in modern day war-
related cases, starting in 1942 with *Sherlock Holmes and the Voice
of Terror*. In time Bruce's comical, befuddled interpretation of the
good doctor, contrasted with Rathbone's somber common sense,
would become the one by which all subsequent interpretations
would be measured. Altogether there were 14 mysteries with
Rathbone, ending with *Dressed to Kill*, in 1946. Among Bruce's
last films was *Bwana Devil*, the very first feature released in 3-D,
in which he ended up as lion food.

Screen: 1929: Red Aces; 1931: The Squeaker; Escape; The Perfect
Alibi/Birds of Prey; The Calendar/Bachelor's Folly; 1932: Lord
Camber's Ladies; The Midshipmaid; 1933: I Was a Spy; 1934:
Channel Crossing; Springtime for Henry; Coming Out Party;
Stand Up and Cheer; Murder in Trinidad; The Lady Is Willing;
Treasure Island; 1935: The Scarlet Pimpernel; She; Becky Sharp;
Jalna; The Man Who Broke the Bank at Monte Carlo; 1936: The
Trail of the Lonesome Pine; Under Two Flags; The White Angel;
The Charge of the Light Brigade; Follow Your Heart; The Man I
Marry; 1937: Thunder in the City; The Last of Mrs. Cheyney;
1938: Kidnapped; Suez; The Baroness and the Butler; 1939: The
Hound of the Baskervilles; The Adventures of Sherlock Holmes;
The Rains Came; 1940: Adventure in Diamonds; The Blue Bird;
Lillian Russell; Hudson's Bay; Rebecca; Susan and God; A
Dispatch From Reuters; Play Girl; 1941: This Woman Is Mine;
Free and Easy; The Chocolate Soldier; Suspicion; 1942: This
Above All; Journey for Margaret; Roxie Hart; Eagle Squadron;
Sherlock Holmes and the Voice of Terror; Sherlock Holmes and
the Secret Weapon; 1943: Crazy House; Sherlock Holmes in
Washington; Forever and a Day; Lassie Come Home; Sherlock
Holmes Faces Death; 1944: The Pearl of Death; Follow the Boys;
Gypsy Wildcat; The Spider Woman; The Scarlet Claw;
Frenchman's Creek; 1945: House of Fear; Son of Lassie; The Corn
Is Green; Pursuit to Algiers; The Woman in Green; 1946: Terror
by Night; Dressed to Kill; 1947: The Two Mrs. Carrolls; The
Exile; 1948: Julia Misbehaves; 1950: Vendetta; 1951: Hong Kong;
1952: Limelight; Bwana Devil; 1954: World for Ransom.

NY Stage: 1926: This Was a Man; 1931: Lean Harvest;
Springtime for Henry; 1937: Virginia; 1938: Knights of Song.

Select TV: 1954: A String of Beads (sp).

VIRGINIA BRUCE

(HELEN VIRGINIA BRIGGS) BORN: MINNEAPOLIS,
MN, SEPTEMBER 29, 1910. RAISED IN FARGO,
ND. DIED: FEBRUARY 24, 1982.

Blonde Virginia Bruce was a shining
example of a capable actress who kept more
than busy during Hollywood's golden era,
was well liked and considered quite attractive, yet never made it
to the top rank of actresses of her time. Before she could start
school at UCLA, she was spotted by director William Beaudine

who encouraged her to try her hand at films. She kicked off her career at the dawn of the talkies, appearing in bit roles, mostly for Paramount. Since this was getting her nowhere, she took off for New York where she worked in Ziegfeld shows. Again the movies took an interest and MGM signed her to a contract in 1931. Shortly afterwards her name became better known chiefly because she married (1932–34) fading film star John Gilbert. She was the star of an earlier, forgotten version of *Jane Eyre*, then played singer Jenny Lind in *The Mighty Barnum*, in 1934. In one of the stranger cases of movie logic she started getting cast in musicals even though she was often dubbed, landing roles in *Metropolitan*, as an aspiring opera singer; *The Great Ziegfeld*, as the one atop the giant wedding cake in the "Pretty Girl Is Like a Melody" number; and *Born to Dance*, in which she introduced "I've Got You Under My Skin." MGM also gave her leads as *Times Square Lady*, reluctantly inheriting a New York nightclub; *Society Doctor*, as the nurse fought over by Robert Taylor and Chester Morris; and *The First Hundred Years*, as a literary agent who refuses to give up her career when husband Robert Montgomery gets a better job offer. During the 1940s her assignments were often in lower budgeted productions including some for Universal, appearing, or rather dis-appearing as *The Insivible Woman*, and playing the kid's mom in *Butch Minds the Baby*, among others. In the 1950s she starred in *Istanbul*, which was directed, written and produced by her husband, Ali Ipar. After a hiatus she made her last movie, in 1960, *Strangers When We Meet*, playing Kim Novak's mother.

Screen: 1929: Fugitives; Blue Skies; Woman Trap; Illusion; The Love Parade; Why Bring That Up?; 1930: Lilies of the Field; Only the Brave; Slightly Scarlet; Paramount on Parade; Follow Thru; Raffles; Let's Go Native; Whoopee!; Young Eagles; Safety in Numbers; Social Lion; 1931: Hell Divers; 1932: The Miracle Man; Sky Bride; Winner Take All; Downstairs; Kongo; A Scarlet Week-End; 1934: Jane Eyre; The Mighty Barnum; Dangerous Corner; 1935: Times Square Lady; Society Doctor; Shadow of Doubt; Let 'Em Have It; Escapade; Here Comes the Band; The Murder Man; Metropolitan; 1936: The Garden Murder Case; The Great Ziegfeld; Born to Dance; 1937: Woman of Glamour; When Love Is Young; Between Two Women; Wife, Doctor and Nurse; Bad Man of Brimstone; 1938: The First Hundred Years; Arsene Lupin Returns; Yellow Jack; Woman Against Woman; There's That Woman Again; There Goes My Heart; 1939: Let Freedom Ring!; Society Lawyer; Stronger Than Desire; 1940: Flight Angels; The Man Who Talked Too Much; Hired Wife; The Invisible Woman; 1941: Adventure in Washington; 1942: Pardon My Sarong; Butch Minds the Baby; Careful — Soft Shoulders; 1944: Brazil; Action in Arabia; 1945: Love, Honor and Goodbye; 1948: Night Has a Thousand Eyes; 1949: State Dept. — File 649; 1953: Istanbul; 1957: Two Grooms for a Bride; The Reluctant Bride; 1960: Strangers When We Meet.

NY Stage: 1931: America's Sweetheart.

Select TV: 1950: Wedding Anniversary (sp); 1953: Something to Live For (sp); 1956: Who's Calling? (sp); People in Glass (sp); Mildred Pierce (sp).

YUL BRYNNER

BORN: VLADIVOSTOK, RUSSIA, JULY 7, 1915.
DIED: OCTOBER 10, 1985.

For some actors it is better to be forever identified with one specific role than not be remembered at all and obviously Yul Brynner had no qualms about returning to the role of "The King" from *The King and I*, again and again…and again, until the two became an inseparable part of show business lore.

The movie's first bald superstar was born in Russia of Swiss-Mongolian extraction. Raised in Paris, he performed, with no great distinction, as a trapeze artist and cafe guitarist before venturing forth to the U.S. in 1941. His legit acting debut came that same year, in a Connecticut production of *Twelfth Night*, and his theatrical connections allowed him to meet actress Virginia Gilmore, whom he wed (1944–60). After one Broadway role, in the musical *Lute Song*, and a feature film, *Port of New York*, as a drug smuggler (with hair) he settled into the early days of television, both directing and acting, until Rodgers and Hammerstein changed his fortunes forever. Cast opposite Gertrude Lawrence in the original 1951 Broadway production of *The King and I*, Brynner was an overnight sensation as the arrogant, domineering, sexy and quite human ruler of Siam, winning a Tony Award (in the featured, or supporting, category) and the attention of the movie industry. 1956 was his year at the top, first repeating his galvanizing performance as the King in 20th Century-Fox's lavish and fairly faithful adaptation of this classic show, winning a much-deserved Academy Award. There was also his forceful performance as the Egyptian Pharaoh, who stubbornly refuses to believe in a higher power, in the mightiest Biblical spectacle of them all, *The Ten Commandments*, and a charismatic turn as the Russian general who tries to pass Ingrid Bergman off as the daughter of the slain royal family in *Anastasia*. All were among the most popular and talked about films of the year.

It wasn't easy to come up with leads for so atypical a star but Brynner got to strut his stuff effectively in such good movies as *The Brothers Karamazov*, as Dimitri, in a game attempt to present an audience-friendly version of the classic Dostoyevsky novel, and *The Magnificent Seven*, creating an unforgettable iconic image as the black outfitted hero, leading a band of hired guns to save a besieged town. Something about his heavy accent and chrome dome (it was shaved) made casting directors think of him in terms of the past and it was more common to see him in period settings than in modern dress, ill-advised when he tried out-and-out comedy (*Once More With Feeling*, *Surprise Package*), and rare that he would show up with hair (*The Sound and the Fury*, *Solomon and Sheba*). By the mid-1960s such standard adventures as *Taras Bulba*, as a Cossack; *Kings of the Sun*, in skimpy garb as an Indian; *Flight From Ashiya*, as an aviator; and *Morituri*, as a German commander, battling with Marlon Brando, made it clear that he wasn't much of a box-office draw, but he kept at it in various international productions, lending his scowling, often riveting presence and staying very much the center of attention. He finally had another big hit, albeit in a supporting role, as the robot gunslinger (looking very much like his *Magnificent Seven* character) in 1973's *Westworld*, but after repeating the part in the sequel and notching up one more quickly forgotten credit, he decided he'd had enough of the big screen. He had already tried a television version of the King in 1972, when he brought the Rodgers and Hammerstein musical back to New York in 1977 to raves. In fact, he carted it back to Broadway yet again, in 1984, shortly before he died from lung cancer, pretty much taking the role with him, for all subsequent portrayals couldn't help but bring comparisons to Brynner.

Screen: 1949: Port of New York; 1956: The King and I; The Ten Commandments; Anastasia; 1958: The Brothers Karamazov; The Buccaneer; 1959: The Journey; The Sound and the Fury; Solomon and Sheba; 1960: Once More With Feeling; Surprise Package; The Magnificent Seven; 1962: Testament of Orpheus (filmed 1959); Escape From Zahrain; Taras Bulba; 1963: Kings of the Sun; 1964: Flight From Ashiya; Invitation to a Gunfighter; 1965: Morituri/The Saboteur-Code Name: Morituri; 1966: Cast a Giant Shadow; Return of the Seven; 1967: The Double Man;

Triple Cross; The Long Duel; **1968:** Villa Rides!; **1969:** The File of the Golden Goose; The Madwoman of Chaillot; **1970:** The Magic Christian; **1971:** The Battle of Neretva; The Light at the Edge of the World; Romance of a Horsethief; Adios Sabata/Indio Black; Catlow; **1972:** Fuzz; **1973:** The Serpent/Night Flight From Moscow; Westworld; **1976:** The Ultimate Warrior; Furtureworld; **1978:** Death Rage/Anger in His Eyes.

NY Stage: **1946:** Lute Song; **1951:** The King and I; **1976:** Home Sweet Homer; **1977:** The King and I (revival); **1984:** The King and I (revival).

Select TV: **1948:** Mr. And Mrs. (series); **1966:** The Poppy Is Also a Flower (also theatrical); **1972:** Anna and the King (series).

EDGAR BUCHANAN

(WILLIAM EDGAR BUCHANAN)
BORN: HUMANSVILLE, MO, MARCH 21, 1903.
DIED: APRIL 4, 1979.

A portly, grizzled character player with a scratchy voice, Edgar Buchanan spent almost his entire career either in westerns or pictures taking place in some such rural settings. He did not launch his career until he was in his 30s, joining the Pasadena Playhouse after making a successful living as a dentist. When he did make his debut, it was in a crime drama, *My Son Is Guilty*, shortly after which he was seen in his first western, *When the Daltons Rode*, in 1940. He then spent most of the 1940s at Columbia where he was a shipyard worker in *Good Luck, Mr. Yates*; supported Cary Grant both in *Penny Serenade*, as the devoted best buddy, Applejack, who stands by Grant and Irene Dunne through their years of tearful heartbreak, and *The Talk of the Town*. He was the usavory papa of a band of outlaw brothers in *Renegades*; teamed with Alan Hale to do some counterfeiting in *Perilous Holiday*; provided the ample frame for Friar Tuck in the Technicolor hit *The Bandit of Sherwood Forest*; was a shady lawyer in *The Walls Came Tumbling Down*; destroyed ships for profit in *The Wreck of the Hesperus*; and was the sheriff in the Randolph Scott oater, *Coroner Creek*. For all this hard work it was only fitting that Columbia gave him at least one vehicle of his own, *The Best Man Wins*, casting him as a no good gambler who returns to wife Anna Lee, just as she is about to divorce him for another. When television came along he played Red Connors, sidekick to William Boyd, in *Hopalong Cassidy*, and then later got a nice steady gig as layabout Uncle Joe on the long-running *Petticoat Junction*. His latter-day movie roles included *Chartroose Caboose*, as a retired train conductor sheltering a young couple; *Ride the High Country*, as a hard-drinking judge; and his last, *Benji*, where he shared the screen with his canine co-star from *Petticoat Junction*.

Screen: **1939:** My Son Is Guilty; **1940:** Tear Gas Squad; When the Daltons Rode; Three Cheers for the Irish; The Doctor Takes a Wife; The Sea Hawk; Submarine Zone/Escape to Glory; Too Many Husbands; Arizona; **1941:** The Richest Man in Town; Penny Serenade; Texas; You Belong to Me; Her First Beau; **1942:** The Talk of the Town; Tombstone — The Town Too Tough to Die; **1943:** City Without Men; The Desperadoes; Destroyer; Good Luck, Mr. Yates; **1944:** The Impatient Years; Buffalo Bill; Bride by Mistake; Strange Affair; **1945:** The Fighting Guardsman; **1946:** The Bandit of Sherwood Forest; If I'm Lucky; Renegades; Perilous Holiday; The Walls Came Tumbling Down; Abilene Town; **1947:** Framed; The Sea of Grass; **1948:** The Swordsman; Adventures in Silverado; The Best Man Wins; The Black Arrow; The Wreck of the Hesperus; Coroner Creek; The Untamed Breed; The Man From Colorado; **1949:** Red Canyon; Any

Number Can Play; Lust for Gold; The Walking Hills; **1950:** Devil's Doorway; Cheaper by the Dozen; The Big Hangover; Cargo to Capetown; The Great Missouri Raid; **1951:** Flaming Feather; Silver City; Rawhide; Cave of Outlaws; **1952:** The Big Trees; Toughest Man in Arizona; Wild Stallion; **1953:** It Happens Every Thursday; Shane; **1954:** She Couldn't Say No; Make Haste to Live; Human Desire; Dawn at Socorro; Destry; **1955:** Rage at Dawn; Wichita; The Silver Star; The Lonesome Trail; **1956:** Come Next Spring; **1957:** Spoilers of the Forest; **1958:** The Sheepman; Day of the Bad Man; **1959:** King of the Wild Stallions; It Started With a Kiss; Hound-Dog Man; Edge of Eternity; Four Fast Guns; **1960:** Stump Run; Chartroose Caboose; Cimarron; **1961:** The Comancheros; Tammy Tell Me True; **1962:** The Devil's Partner; Ride the High Country; **1963:** A Ticklish Affair; Donovan's Reef; Move Over, Darling; McLintock!; **1965:** The Rounders; The Man From Button Willow (voice); **1966:** Gunpoint; **1967:** Welcome to Hard Times; **1969:** Angel in My Pocket; **1974:** Benji.

Select TV: **1949–51:** Hopalong Cassidy (series); **1956:** Judge Roy Bean (series); **1963–70:** Petticoat Junction (series); **1969:** Something for a Lonely Man; The Over-the-Hill Gang; **1970:** The Over-the-Hill Gang Rides Again; **1971:** Yuma; **1971–72:** Cade's County (series).

JACK BUCHANAN

BORN: HELENSBURGH, SCOTLAND, APRIL 2, 1891.
DIED: OCTOBER 20, 1957.

A suave entertainer with a nasally singing voice, Jack Buchanan became something of a dancing sensation in the 1920s and 1930s on the British stage and in films, a kind of Englishman's Fred Astaire. After toiling on the boards in Glasgow, London, and on tour, and landing a few film parts, he finally made a name for himself in 1921, as a member of the *A to Z Revue*, which also featured Gertrude Lawrence. The show came to Broadway retitled *Charlot's Revue of 1924*, and he was suddenly a star on both sides of the Atlantic. He made his talkie debut in America with *Paris*, in 1929, followed by his best known film of this period, *Monte Carlo*, a creaky but charming musical for Ernst Lubitsch, where he was well-teamed with Jeanette MacDonald, playing a count who poses as a hairstylist (!) to get in her good graces. Despite favorable notices the movie was not a success, so it was back to London, where his popularity continued in movies like *That's a Good Girl* (which he directed and co-scripted himself); *Brewster's Millions*; and *This'll Make You Whistle*. He had become somewhat passé by the time he returned to Hollywood in 1953, to play the hilariously egotistical producer-director in *The Band Wagon*, where his gentle top hat and tails number with Astaire, "I Guess I'll Have to Change My Plans," was one of that musical's most unpretentious delights. Both he and director Preston Sturges brought their careers to an end with the failure *The French They Are a Funny Race*, with Buchanan cast as an Englishman coping with the culture shock of living in France. He served as producer on the 1938 film *Sweet Devil*.

Screen: **1917:** Auld Lange Syne; **1919:** Her Heritage; **1923:** The Audacious Mr. Squire; **1925:** The Happy Ending; Settled Out of Court; Bulldog Drummond's Third Round; **1927:** Confetti; Toni; **1929:** Paris; **1930:** Monte Carlo; **1931:** Man of Mayfair; **1932:** Goodnight Vienna; **1933:** Yes, Mr. Brown (and co-dir.); That's a Good Girl (and dir.; co-wr.); **1935:** Brewster's Millions; Come Out of the Pantry; **1936:** When Knights Were Bold; Backstage/Limelight; **1937:** This'll Make You Whistle; Smash and Grab (and prod.); The Sky's the Limit (and co-dir.; prod.; co-wr.); **1938**: Break the News (and prod.); **1939**: The Gang's All Here/The Amazing Mr. Forrest (and prod.; US: 1945); The Middle Watch; **1940**: Bulldog Sees It Through; **1953**: The Band Wagon; **1955**: As Long as They're Happy; Josephine and Men; **1956**: The French They Are a Funny Race/The Diary of Major Thompson.

NY Stage: 1924: Charlot's Revue of 1924; **1926**: Charlot's Revue of 1926; **1929**: Wake Up and Dream; **1937**: Between the Devil; **1948**: Don't Listen Ladies.

HORST BUCHHOLZ
BORN: BERLIN, GERMANY, DECEMBER 4, 1932.

Perhaps the first international star from post World War II Germany, Horst Buchholz had his brief period of fame in the late 1950s/early 1960s and, if he didn't quite take the world by storm, at least he got to work with Billy Wilder. Starting in German films as an extra, his first brush with fame came when he won the Cannes Film Festival Award for *Sky Without Stars*. After his role as the charming scoundrel in *The Confessions of Felix Krull* (in which he was billed as Henry Bookholt), the offers came in at a rapid clip for the handsome and intense young actor. His English-language debut was in a good film, *Tiger Bay*, as the killer who abducts young Hayley Mills, after which he came to the U.S. to play one of *The Magnificent Seven*. 1961 saw him in two high profile productions, *Fanny*, as Leslie Caron's lover, who leaves her pregnant when he goes off to sea, and the Wilder film, *One, Two, Three*, hilarious as a hotheaded communist clashing with American businessman James Cagney, a tension that carried through off screen as well. This was the peak, for it wasn't long before he slipped up playing the man who assassinated Gandhi in *Nine Hours to Rama*, and was soon appearing in heavily ridiculed efforts like *The Empty Canvas*, with Bette Davis as his domineering mother, and *Marco the Magnificent*, as Marco Polo, presented here as a callow fellow. By the end of the 1960s his hot period had long cooled off and he spent most of his time back in Europe, where occasionally a credit would be transported across the Atlantic to complete apathy, including the remake of *The Great Waltz*, as composer Johann Strauss; a caper movie, *The Catamount Killing*; and a World War II espionage thriller *Code Name: Emerald*. After being long off the public radar, he did show up in one of the most widely seen of all foreign language films, *Life Is Beautiful*, as the doctor who fails to help prisoner Roberto Benigni.

Screen (US releases only): 1957: The Confessions of Felix Krull; **1958**: Teenage Wolfpack; **1959**: Sky Without Stars; Mon Petit; Tiger Bay; **1960**: The Magnificent Seven; **1961**: Fanny; One, Two, Three; **1963**: Nine Hours to Rama; **1964**: The Empty Canvas; **1966**: That Man in Istanbul; Marco the Magnificent; **1969**: The Young Rebel; **1972**: The Great Waltz; **1975**: The Catamount Killing; **1979**: Avalanche Express; **1984**: Sahara; **1985**: Code Name: Emerald; **1987**: And the Violins Stopped Playing (dtv); **1992**: Aces: Iron Eagle III; **1993**: Faraway, So Close; **1998**: Life Is Beautiful.

Select TV: 1976: The Savage Bees; **1977**: Raid on Entebbe; **1978**: Return to Fantasy Island; **1979**: The French Atlantic Affair (ms); **1981**: Berlin Tunnel 21; **1998**: Voyage of Terror/The Fourth Horseman; **2001**: The Enemy.

VICTOR BUONO
BORN: SAN DIEGO, CA, FEBRUARY 3, 1938.
DIED: JANUARY 1, 1982.

Few character actors hammed it up as adeptly as Victor Buono, who used his 300 pounds to great effect, usually as oily, sniveling, effete villains. He had done a few roles in stock and on television before his memorable 1962 motion picture debut, as the mother-dominated pianist Edward Flagg, who agrees to be the accompanist for aging child star Bette Davis, in *What Ever Happened to Baby Jane?* His eccentric performance was a treat and he nabbed an Oscar nomination for Best Supporting Actor. Of course his girth meant he was basically reserved for supporting roles, so he popped up in two jokey Frank Sinatra films, *4 for Texas*, as a duplicitous banker scheming to take control of a gambling boat, and *Robin and the 7 Hoods*, as the gangland Chicago equivalent of the Sheriff of Nottingham. Working again for some of the same principals who put together *Baby Jane*, he showed up in the flashback sequences of *Hush...Hush, Sweet Charlotte*, as Bette Davis's Southern daddy. He did have two starring vehicles, *The Strangler*, again mom-dominated, but this time as a crazed killer, and the Italian-made cheapie *The Mad Butcher*, packaging his victims into sausages. Buono was perfect for playing comic book bad guys as in the first Matt Helm caper, *The Silencers*, and on television in *Batman*, as one of the funniest of all the guest villains, the outrageous King Tut. One of his more benign parts called for him to play a nutty seafarer who helps mastermind a heist by using carnival kiddie boats in *Who's Minding the Mint?* For his very last role, he parodied Sidney Greenstreet in the Hollywood-set caper *The Man With Bogart's Face*.

Screen: 1962: What Ever Happened to Baby Jane?; **1963**: My Six Loves; 4 for Texas; **1964**: The Stranger; Robin and the 7 Hoods; Hush...Hush, Sweet Charlotte; **1965**: The Greatest Story Ever Told; Young Dillinger; Big Daddy; Northeast to Seoul; **1966**: The Silencers; **1967**: Who's Minding the Mint?; **1969**: Boot Hill/Trinity Rides Again; **1970**: Beneath the Planet of the Apes; The Man With Icy Eyes (nUSr); Mother/Up Your Teddy Bear; **1972**: The Wrath of God; **1973**: Arnold; **1974**: Moon Child; The Mad Butcher; **1978**: The Evil; **1979**: Target: Harry/How to Make It (filmed 1969); **1980**: The Man With Bogart's Face/Sam Marlowe, Private Eye.

NY Stage: 1970: Camino Real.

Select TV: 1965: Asylum for a Spy (sp); **1972**: Goodnight My Love; **1973**: The Crime Club; **1976**: Brenda Starr, High Risk; **1977**: Man From Atlantis; **1977–78**: Man From Atlantis (series); **1979**: Backstairs at the White House (ms); The Return of the Mod Squad; Better Late Than Never; **1980**: Murder Can Hurt You!; More Wild Wild West.

BILLIE BURKE
(MARY WILLIAM ETHELBERT APPLETON BURKE)
BORN: WASHINGTON, DC, AUGUST 7, 1885.
RAISED IN LONDON. DIED: MAY 14, 1970.

Being in *The Wizard of Oz* has pretty much guaranteed its cast members screen immortality and, although Billie Burke was an absolute delight as the Good Witch Glinda, the role didn't really showcase what she was best known for, playing lovable, "bird witted" (her own term) excitable eccentrics. Since her parents were entertainers, she found herself touring Europe with her father's company at an early age. It was in London where she made her legit debut, in 1903, in *The School Girl*. Returning to America, she made her Broadway bow in *My Wife*, in 1907, and if her work over the next few years wasn't enough to make her a name, her marriage in 1914 to theatrical impressario Florenz Ziegfeld certainly did. Soon she was working in films, appearing in several for Paramount including *Good Gracious Annabelle!* and *The Misleading Widow*, but these didn't quite establish her as one of the legends of the silent screen. Back on Broadway she worked to help pay off some of Ziegfeld's growing debts and, about the time of his death, in 1932, her own career in the movies was about to blossom. An L.A. production of the play *The Vinegar Tree* revived Hollywood's interest and she played the very serious role of John Barrymore's uncaring, estranged wife in *A Bill of Divorcement*. The following year, 1933, she was the daffy society lady who threw the party in *Dinner at Eight*, pretty much setting the tone for her long line of wacky cinematic eccentrics, including those in *Finishing School, Forsaking All Others, Splendor*; *Doubting Thomas*, higher-billed than usual as Will Rogers's stage struck wife; and *Piccadilly Jim*.

Perhaps the peak of these jabbering, fluttery ladies came with *Topper*, playing the Mrs. opposite Roland Young, hen-pecking away at the poor fellow, trying to making him staid and well-behaved when all he's looking for is a little fun in his life, supplied by his ghostly friends, the Kerbys. Another high point came with *Merrily We Live*, in which she headed a whole family as flaky as she was; Burke's particular quirk being the desire to rehabilitate bums. For this film she received her only Oscar nomination. She was back with Roland Young for the somewhat more serious *The Young in Heart*; the dud *Dulcy*; the poor adaptation of the stage musical *Irene*; *They All Kissed the Bride*; and two *Topper* sequels. If her dithering could work off of Young's apologetic murmuring, then it certainly could bounce off of Frank Morgan's stammering hesitations as it did in *The Ghost Comes Home, Hullabaloo*, and *The Wild Man of Borneo*. Among her later successes were *The Man Who Came to Dinner*, as the woman who must play host to crabby, wheelchair-bound Monty Woolley; *In This Our Life*, in a rare serious part, as Bette Davis's invalid mother; and *Father of the Bride*, as the mother of the groom, a role she repeated in the sequel, *Father's Little Dividend*. Apparently these chirping biddies weren't close to her heart, as she declared Glinda to be her favorite movie role. There were two autobiographies: *With a Feather on My Nose* (1949) and *With Powder on My Nose* (1959).

Screen: 1916: Peggy; Gloria's Romance (serial); 1917: The Mysterious Miss Terry; Arms and the Girl; The Land of Promise; 1918: Eve's Daughter; Let's Get a Divorce; In Pursuit of Polly; The Make-Believe Wife; 1919: Good Gracious Annabelle!; The Misleading Widow; Sadie Love; Wanted: A Husband; 1920: Away Goes Prudence; 1921: The Frisky Mrs. Johnson; The Education of Elizabeth; 1929: Glorifying the American Girl; 1932: A Bill of Divorcement; 1933: Christopher Strong; Dinner at Eight; Only Yesterday; 1934: Finishing School; Where Sinners Meet; We're Rich Again; Forsaking All Others; 1935: After Office Hours; Society Doctor; Doubting Thomas; Becky Sharp; A Feather in Her Hat; She Couldn't Take It; Splendor; 1936: My American Wife; Piccadilly Jim; Craig's Wife; 1937: Parnell; Topper; The Bride Wore Red; Navy Blue and Gold; 1938: Everybody Sing; Merrily We Live; The Young in Heart; 1939: Topper Takes a Trip; Zenobia; Bridal Suite; The Wizard of Oz; Remember?; Eternally Yours; 1940: The Ghost Comes Home; And One Was Beautiful; The Captain Is a Lady; Dulcy; Hullabaloo; Irene; 1941: One Night in Lisbon; Topper Returns; The Wild Man of Borneo; The Man Who Came to Dinner;; 1942: What's Cookin'?; In This Our Life; They All Kissed the Bride; Girl Trouble; 1943: Hi Diddle Diddle; Gildersleeve on

Broadway; So's Your Uncle; You're a Lucky Fellow Mr. Smith; 1945: Swing Out, Sister; The Cheaters; 1946: Breakfast in Hollywood; The Bachelor's Daughters; 1949: The Barkleys of Broadway; Andy Baby Makes Three; 1950: Father of the Bride; Three Husbands; Boy From Indiana; 1951: Father's Little Dividend; 1953: Small Town Girl; 1959: The Young Philadelphians; 1960: Sergeant Rutledge; Pepe.

NY Stage: 1907: My Wife; 1908: Love Watches; 1910: Mrs. Dot; Suzanne; 1911: The Philosopher in the Apple Orchard; The Runaway; 1912: The Mind-the-Paint Girl; 1913: The Amazons; The Land of Promise; 1914: Jerry; 1917: The Rescuing Angel; 1918: A Marriage of Convenience; 1919: Caesar's Wife; 1921: The Intimate Stranger; 1922: Rose Briar; 1924: Annie Dear; 1925: Rose Briar (revival); 1927: The Marquise; 1928: The Happy Husband; 1929: Family Affairs; 1930: The Truth Game; 1943: This Rock; 1944: Mrs. January & Mr. X.

Select TV: 1951: Dear Amanda (sp); 1952: Doc Corkle (series); 1955: Arsenic and Old Lace (sp); 1956: Mother Was a Bachelor (sp); 1957: The Star-Wagon (sp); 1958: Rumors of Evening (sp).

GEORGE BURNS
(NATHAN BIRNBAUM) BORN: NEW YORK, NY, JANUARY 20, 1896. DIED: MARCH 9, 1996.
& GRACIE ALLEN
BORN: SAN FRANCISCO, CA, JULY 26, 1902. DIED: AUGUST 27, 1964.

Long before George Burns became show business's most beloved centenarian, he was half of the most successful husband and wife comedy team in history. He started in vaudeville with a children's singing group, eventually moving into comedy as he got older. It was on the circuits, in 1923, that he met Gracie Allen, who hadn't had much luck in an act with her sisters, and they began to develop their routines, Burns feeding the material to fluttery, scatterbrained Allen. They were a hit and solidified their union with marriage in 1926. They made their screen debuts in 1929, with a short subject for Warner Bros. called "Burns and Allen in Lambchops," named for one of their routines. Their fame grew through guest spots on radio, notably Gracie's on-going, program-to-program search for her "lost" brother, which resulted in their own show for NBC, *The Adventures of Gracie*, in 1934. In the meantime they were recreating some of their best vaudeville work in a series of two-reelers for Paramount in which Allen misused words and told the screwiest of stories, all of which seemed to make perfect sense to her, while Burns held his exasperation in check.

When the time came to move into features, Burns and Allen became part of the ensemble cast of *The Big Broadcast*, in 1932, with Burns taking a bigger role upfront as a radio station owner and Allen only joining him later in the story, as a bird-brained new receptionist. Initially, Paramount saw the team working best in this format, as part of a collection of comedians and singers, and presented them as such in other efforts like *College Humor, We're Not Dressing* and two more *Big Broadcast* entries. Gracie's non-stop prattle was often used to annoy the hell out of other comics like Franklin Pangborn in *International House*, and both Charlie Ruggles and W.C. Fields in *Six of a Kind*, where she and Burns answered an ad to drive cross-country with Ruggles and his unofficial screen partner, Mary Boland. When the team did rate their own starring vehicles, including *Many Happy Returns*, in which Burns was bribed into marrying meddling Allen; and *Here Comes Cookie*, with Allen trying to blow all the money she inherited on a flop rendition of *Romeo and Juliet*, they were not only more cheaply made but not among their better-received films.

Over at RKO, they did get a wonderful opportunity to support Fred Astaire in *A Damsel in Distress*, where the trio brought down the house with their charming "whisk broom" dance and an imaginative Oscar-winning number at a carnival fun house. Before they left movies to concentrate on radio, Gracie had a few solo appearances, most notably in the Philo Vance mystery with the attention-getting title *The Gracie Allen Murder Case*.

Their radio show transferred without a hitch to television in 1950, its gimmick of having Burns watch Allen's antics and then address the audience directly, making it a surreal milestone in the medium. *The George Burns and Gracie Allen Show* ran until Gracie decided to retire in 1958. Six years later she died of cancer. Burns began to develop a solo act where his comical abilities, so apparent as the act's straight man, would now blossom fully. When his good friend Jack Benny had to drop out of the movie version of *The Sunshine Boys* for health reasons, it proved to be a turning point in Burns's career. Replacing Benny as the gentle vaudevillain who reluctantly teams with his more volatile ex-partner (Walter Matthau), Burns was superb and won a very popular Academy Award for Best Supporting Actor, the oldest performer to do so up to that time. Suddenly he was a movie star all over again and continued to be a very welcome screen presence. His biggest hit was the 1977 comedy *Oh, God!*, in which he was cast as The Almighty himself and, for audiences, it was a casting that was somehow more than fitting. He could also be seen singing the Beatles' "Fixing a Hole" in the bizarre *Sgt. Pepper's Lonely Hearts Club Band*, and playing a retired performer sheltering runaway teen Brooke Shields in *Just You and Me, Kid*. He died in 1996, less than two months after his 100th birthday.

Screen (shorts): BURNS AND ALLEN: 1929: Burns and Allen in Lambchops; 1930: Fit to be Tied; Pulling a Bone; 1931: The Antique Shop; Once Over Light; One Hundred Percent Service; 1932: Oh My Operation; The Babbling Book; Hollywood on Parade #2; 1933: Let's Dance; Walking the Baby; Hollywood on Parade #12.

Screen (features): BURNS AND ALLEN: 1932: The Big Broadcast; 1933: International House; College Humor; 1934: Six of a Kind; We're Not Dressing; Many Happy Returns; 1935: Love in Bloom; Here Comes Cookie; The Big Broadcast of 1936; 1936: The Big Broadcast of 1937; College Holiday; 1937: A Damsel in Distress; 1938: College Swing; 1939: Honolulu.

ALLEN: 1939: The Gracie Allen Murder Case; 1941: Mr. and Mrs. North; 1944: Two Girls and a Sailor.

BURNS: 1956: The Solid Gold Cadillac (narrator); 1975: The Sunshine Boys; 1977: Oh, God!; 1978: Sgt. Pepper's Lonely Hearts Club Band; Movie Movie; 1979: Just You and Me, Kid; Going in Style; 1980: Oh, God! Book II; 1984: Oh, God! You Devil; 1988: 18 Again; 1994: Radioland Murders.

Select TV: BURNS AND ALLEN: 1950–58: The George Burns and Gracie Allen Show (series).

BURNS: 1958–59: The George Burns Show (series); 1964–65: Wendy and Me (series); 1982: Two of a Kind; 1985: George Burns Comedy Week (series).

RAYMOND BURR

BORN: NEW WESTMINSTER, BRITISH COLUMBIA, CANADA, MAY 21, 1917. ED: STANFORD UNIV., UNIV. OF CA, COLUMBIA UNIV. DIED: SEPTEMBER 12, 1993.

Television can make heroes of villains, and there is probably no better example than Raymond Burr. The hefty and imposing actor with the sonorously deep voice had established himself as one of the big screen's best bad guys, but when television called he became the small screen's most famous crusading lawyer. He had learned his trade onstage and radio, sometimes performing overseas, before making his movie debut in the 1946 prison melodrama *San Quentin*. For the next few years he was seen in some pretty trashy stuff with titles like *FBI Girl*, *The Whip Hand*, *Bandits of Corsica*, and *Tarzan and the She-Devil*, plus two pricelessly campy gorilla flicks, *Bride of the Gorilla* (top billed), as a plantation under a simian curse, and *Gorilla at Large*, as an amusement park owner married to Anne Bancroft. On a higher "A" scale he was the hammy prosecutor in *A Place in the Sun*, and played his most famous heavy, the creepy, bespectacled neighbor across the courtyard from James Stewart in Alfred Hitchcock's *Rear Window*. Pretty soon after completing one of his most famous and oddest assignments, playing the reporter in spliced-in U.S. footage in the original *Godzilla*, he started his nine-year run as *Perry Mason*, the crime-solving lawyer, winning a pair of Emmy Awards in 1959 and 1961. Only one year after *Mason* went off the air he was back in the crime fighting business, this time in a wheelchair, as *Ironside*, for another lengthy haul. Although he would return to films on occasion, including a remake of *Godzilla*, television had clearly become his bread and butter. Apparently audiences could never get enough of Perry Mason, because a 1985 reunion movie, *Perry Mason Returns*, was so popular that Burr churned out another 24 telefilms as the peerless lawyer until his death in 1993.

Screen: 1946: San Quentin; Without Reservations; 1947: Code of the West; Desperate; 1948: Pitfall; Raw Deal; Fighting Father Dunne; Sleep My Love; Ruthless; Adventures of Don Juan; I Love Trouble; Walk a Crooked Mile; Station West; 1949: Criss Cross; Bride of Vengeance; Black Magic; Abandoned; Red Light; Love Happy; 1950: Unmasked; Borderline; Key to the City; 1951: FBI Girl; M; The Magic Carpet; New Mexico; Bride of Gorilla; His Kind of Woman; A Place in the Sun; The Whip Hand; 1952: Meet Danny Wilson; Mara Maru; Horizons West; 1953: Tarzan and the She-Devil; Serpent of the Nile; The Blue Gardenia; Fort Algiers; Bandits of Corsica; 1954: Casanova's Big Night; Khyber Patrol; Gorilla at Large; Rear Window; Passion; Thunder Pass; 1955: They Were So Young/Violated/Party Girls for Sale; A Man Alone; Count Three and Pray; You're Never Too Young; 1956: Godzilla — King of the Monsters; Great Day in the Morning; A Cry in the Night; The Brass Legend; Secret of Treasure Mountain; Ride the High Iron; Please Murder Me; 1957: Crime of Passion; Affair in Havana; 1960: Desire in the Dust; 1968: P.J.; 1976: The Amazing World of Psychic Phenomena (narrator); 1977: Tomorrow Never Comes (dtc/dtv); 1980: The Return/The Alien's Return (dtv); 1982: Out of the Blue; Airplane II: The Sequel; 1985: Godzilla 1985; 1991: Delirious.

NY Stage: 1944: The Duke in Darkness.

Select TV: 1952: A Star Shall Rise; 1954: The Room (sp); 1955: The Ordeal of Dr. Sutton (sp); 1957: The Greer Case (sp); The Lone Woman (sp); 1957–66: Perry Mason (series); 1967: Ironside; 1967–75: Ironside (series); 1968: Split Second to an Epitaph; 1971: The Priest Killer; 1973: Portrait; A Man Whose Name Was John (sp); 1976: Mallory: Circumstantial Evidence; Kingston: The Power Play; 1977: Kingston: Confidential (series); 79 Park Avenue (ms); 1978: The Jordan Chance; 1978–79: Centennial (ms); 1979: Love's Savage Fury; Disaster on the Coastliner; 1980: The Curse of King Tut's Tomb; The Night the City Screamed; 1981: Peter and Paul; 1985: Perry Mason Returns; 1986: Perry Mason: The Case of the Notorious Nun; Perry Mason: The Case of the Shooting Star; 1987: Perry Mason: The Case of the Lost Love; Perry Mason: The Case of the Sinister Spirit; Perry Mason: The Case of the Murdered Madam; Perry Mason: The Case of the Scandalous Scoundrel; 1988: Perry Mason: The Case of the

Avenging Ace; Perry Mason: The Case of the Lady in the Lake; 1989: Perry Mason: The Case of the Lethal Lesson; Perry Mason: The Case of the Musical Murder; Perry Mason: The Case of the All-Star Assassin; 1989–90: Trial by Jury (series); 1990: Perry Mason: The Case of the Poisoned Pen; Perry Mason: The Case of the Desperate Deception; Perry Mason: The Case of the Silenced Singer; Perry Mason: The Case of the Defiant Daughter; 1991: Perry Mason: The Case of the Ruthless Reporter; Perry Mason: The Case of the Maligned Mobster; Perry Mason: The Case of the Glass Coffin; Showdown at Williams Creek; Perry Mason: The Case of the Fatal Fashion; 1992: Perry Mason: The Case of the Fatal Framing; Grass Roots; Perry Mason: The Case of the Reckless Romeo; Perry Mason: The Case of the Heartbroken Bride; 1993: Perry Mason: The Case of the Skin-Deep Scandal; The Return of Ironside; Perry Mason: The Case of the Killer Kiss.

RICHARD BURTON

(RICHARD JENKINS, JR.) BORN: PONTRHYDYFEN, SOUTH WALES, NOVEMBER 10, 1925. ED: OXFORD. DIED: AUGUST 5, 1984.

Thanks to the gossip columns of the 1960s, when everything from the British Isles was in vogue, Richard Burton was probably the best known actor from the United Kingdom. He wasn't the best, simply because when he did junk he didn't even bother to mask his boredom, but he was capable of great things. Encouraged by a teacher, he took up acting while a teenager, making his London debut with Emlyn Williams in The Druid's Rest. While at Oxford his reputation, helped greatly by a splendidly commanding speaking voice, began to grow and he was noticed both in Britain and the States when he played in The Lady's Not for Burning. There were a few British movies, starting with The Last Days of Dolwyn, in which he was the stepson of Edith Evans who refuses to sell her land to an evil developer. This was followed by a few more U.K. releases that went nowhere, and one American one, My Cousin Rachel, that did, to some degree. It was a dreary Daphne DuMaurier gothic in which Burton fell in love with the cousin, Olivia de Havilland, he suspected might actually be a murderer. He got a Best Supporting Actor Oscar nomination for it and then another one, this time in the leading category, for The Robe, the first CinemaScope feature and therefore a gigantic box-office success. These were hardly among his best performances, and his work in the latter film, as the centurion who finds religion, was especially wooden, but he was now in demand in Hollywood. Fox borrowed him from Korda, for whom he was contracted, finally buying out his contract altogether. None of the three subsequent films he did in the U.S. for that company was either widely seen or liked, they being The Rains of Ranchipur, as an Indian doctor in a reprise of the role Tyrone Power had done the first time out in The Rains Came; Prince of Players, as Edwin Booth; and, worst of all, Sea Wife, shipwrecked with Joan Collins.

It was back to sword and sandals for Alexander the Great, one of the major failures of the 1950s spectacles, though one that had its share of supporters. Since his reputation was starting to falter he returned to the stage where he had success in London in Henry V, and then on Broadway in Time Remembered. Returning to British films, he was the one chosen above all others to play Jimmy Porter in the film of the groundbreaking play Look Back in Anger, and although this in no way repeated the triumph of what had occurred with John Osborne's kitchen-sink life drama onstage, this was really the first suggestion of impressive film acting that Burton had done to date. Back on Broadway he fol-

lowed in Rex Harrison's footsteps as a non-singer in a musical, playing King Arthur in Lerner and Lowe's smash hit Camelot and was enthusiastically praised, winning a Tony Award in the process. Then came 20th Century-Fox's heavily hyped Cleopatra and the love affair to end all love affairs with his co-star Elizabeth Taylor, whom he married in 1963. Although the movie would be saddled with a bad rep due to its enormous costs and troubled production, the end result was neither camp nor classic but an intelligently conceived miss and Burton was quite good as the doomed Marc Antony. He and Taylor were back again for The V.I.P.s, which was really an ensemble piece, and one in which they were both upstaged by such folk as Maggie Smith and Margaret Rutherford. Burton, however, was in fine form as the soft spoken Becket, brilliantly opposing his King, Peter O'Toole, an example of how his underplaying could be enormously effective, and at last getting an Oscar nomination he actually deserved. There was another mention from the Academy for The Spy Who Came in From the Cold, an attempt to debunk all the glamour about spying that the James Bond films had created, but one that forgot to be entertaining while doing so.

Between those Burton did a nice job as the defrocked priest stirring up trouble at a Mexican resort in the downbeat The Night of the Iguana, and then frolicked with Taylor in The Sandpiper. Thanks to the acres of endless press on this union, they were so incredibly popular that audiences even showed up in sizable numbers for this superficial melodrama. Fortunately their clout managed to get Who's Afraid of Virginia Woolf? made as well. Adapted faithfully from Edward Albee's acclaimed, shattering Broadway drama, Warners took a risk by keeping the adult language intact, and the result was, by a landslide, the one true classic done by the famous couple. As the weary college professor who verbally and manipulatively gives his sluttish wife her due, Burton was simply magnificent, giving the performance of his career. It was the closest he came to finally getting that Oscar but had to be content with another nomination, 1966 being the year of Paul Scofield in A Man for All Seasons. The other good one the overexposed team of Taylor-Burton made was director Franco Zeffirelli's The Taming of the Shrew, in which Burton, never more lively or entertaining, was Petrucchio. There was also another with Taylor (in a brief appearance) which marked Burton's only time behind the cameras, Dr. Faustus, sharing the credit for this decidedly non-commercial fiasco with Nevill Coghill. Despite movies like that one and another weird item with the wife, Boom!, he had become something of a box-office draw, scoring a pair of hits in 1969 with the adventure film Where Eagles Dare, stoically participating in some pretty exciting action sequences with co-star Clint Eastwood, and the historical drama Anne of the Thousand Days, which gave him a good chance to chew into Henry VIII, which he did well enough to rate another Oscar nomination.

There began a run of really crummy movies with Staircase, grotesquely camping it as Rex Harrison's lover; Raid on Rommel, returning to familiar territory having appeared in the superior The Desert Rats two decades earlier; Villain, as a homosexual gangster, a movie made for God-knows-who; Bluebeard, killing off a bevy of international beauties; The Assaassination of Trotsky, as the murdered Russian upstart; and The Klansman, which he walked through like a zombie, badly hurting his popularity and reputation. Around this time he and Taylor divorced, remarried, then divorced again, having grown as tired of each other as the public had. Burton did get one more good chance when, after taking over the role on Broadway, he was selected to play the tormented psychiatrist in Sidney Lumet's movie of Equus. This very theatrical piece did not play well on screen but Burton was at least game and got one last bid for the Oscar. He lost, making him, along with Peter O'Toole, the actor to receive the most nominations without winning. His last glimpse of glory was a 1980 revival of *Camelot*, while a reunion with Taylor onstage, in *Private Lives*, was a disaster. Following his death in 1984 some of his movies received posthumous distribution and there were moments in *Nineteen Eighty-Four*, interrogating John Hurt, and *Absolution*, as a priest suppressing his homosexual desires, that suggest he was still willing to give it a go when he felt the urge. Melvyn Bragg's 1988 biography *Richard Burton: A Life*, contained extensive passages from Burton's own diaries and showed a perceptive, fascinating, and somewhat sad man. His daughter from his first marriage to Sybill Christopher is actress Kate Burton.

Screen: 1949: The Last Days of Dolwyn/The Woman of Dolwyn; Now Barabbas Was a Robber; 1950: Waterfront; 1951: The Woman With No Name; Green Grow the Rushes; 1952: My Cousin Rachel; 1953: The Desert Rats; The Robe; 1955: Prince of Players; The Rains of Ranchipur; 1956: Alexander the Great; 1957: Sea Wife; 1958: Bitter Victory; 1959: Look Back in Anger; 1960: The Bramble Bush; Ice Palace; 1961: A Midsummer Night's Dream (narrator); 1962: The Longest Day; 1963: Cleopatra; The V.I.P.s; 1964: Zulu (narrator); Becket; The Night of the Iguana; Hamlet; 1965: The Sandpiper; What's New, Pussycat?; The Spy Who Came in From the Cold; 1966: Who's Afraid of Virginia Woolf?; 1967: The Taming of the Shrew; The Comedians; 1968: Doctor Faustus (and co-dir.); Boom!; Candy; 1969: Where Eagles Dare; Staircase; Anne of the Thousand Days; 1971: Raid on Rommel; Villain; 1972: A Wall in Jerusalem (narrator); Hammersmith Is Out; Bluebeard; The Assassination of Trotsky; 1973: Under Milk Wood (voice); Massacre in Rome; 1974: The Klansman/The Burning Cross; 1976: The Battle of Sujetska/The Fifth Offensive (nUSr); 1977: The Voyage (filmed 1973); Exorcist II: The Heretic; Volcano (narrator); Equus; 1978: The Medusa Touch; The Wild Geese; 1979: Tristan and Isolde/Lovespell (nUSr); 1981: Breakthrough/Sergeant Steiner; Circle of Two; 1985: Nineteen Eighty-Four; 1988: Absolution (filmed 1979).

NY Stage: 1950: The Lady's Not For Burning; 1951: Legend of Lovers; 1957: Time Remembered; 1960: Camelot; 1964: Hamlet; 1976: Equus; 1980: Camelot (revival); 1983: Private Lives.

Select TV: 1958: Wuthering Heights (sp); 1960: The Fifth Column (sp); 1960: The Tempest (sp); A Subject of Scandal and Concern (sp); Winston Churchill — The Valiant Years (series); 1973: Divorce His, Divorce Hers; 1974: A Walk With Destiny (sp); 1976: Brief Encounter; 1983: Wagner (ms); Alice in Wonderland (sp); 1984: Ellis Island (ms).

CHARLES BUTTERWORTH

BORN: SOUTH BEND, IN, JULY 26, 1896.
DIED: JUNE 14, 1946.

A slim, long faced comedic actor, Charles Butterworth excelled at playing befuddled suitors with a tight-lipped, deadpan way of speaking that can seem positively strange and mannered to today's viewers. He came to Hollywood via such Broadway musical comedies as *Americana* and *Sweet Adeline*, debuting on the big screen in *The Life of the Party*, in 1930. Among his more notable movie assignments were *Love Me Tonight*, very funny as Jeanette MacDonald's nitwit suitor; *My Weakness*, as Lew Ayres's stuck-up cousin; *The Nuisance*, as a professional accident victim named Floppy; *My Weakness*, the title, in his case, referring to his craving for raw carrots (!); *Orchids to You*, as a clueless stockholder in love with Jean Muir; *Bulldog*

Drummond Strikes Back, as Drummond's buddy Algy; *Hollywood Party*, as a naïve Oklaohoma millionaire attending the movieland bash; *The Moon's Our Home*, as the brainless cousin Margaret Sullavan is ordered to marry; *Rainbow on the River*, as the butler who is the only one to give any attention to displaced Bobby Breen; *Every Day's a Holiday*, as Charles Winninger's butler; and his own starring vehicle, *Baby Face Harrington*, as Una Merkel's timid husband who is mistaken for a criminal. By the 1940s it was clear that Butterworth wasn't going to be asked to vary his shtick all that much, which did indeed have a tendency to grate if the material wasn't top notch. His films were pretty much cheapies by the time he died in an automobile accident.

Screen: 1930: The Life of the Party; 1931: Illicit; Side Show; The Bargain; The Mad Genius; 1932: Beauty and the Boss; Love Me Tonight; Manhattan Parade; 1933: The Nuisance; Penthouse; My Weakness; 1934: Student Tour; Hollywood Party; The Cat and the Fiddle; Forsaking All Others; Bulldog Drummond; Strikes Back; 1935: The Night Is Young; Baby Face Harrington; Orchids to You; Magnificent Obsession; 1936: Half Angel; We Went to College; Rainbow on the River; The Moon's Our Home; 1937: Swing High, Swing Low; 1938: Every Day's a Holiday; Thanks for the Memory; 1939: Let Freedom Ring; 1940: The Boys From Syracuse; 1941: Second Chorus; Road Show; Blonde Inspiration; Sis Hopkins; 1942: What's Cookin'?; Night in New Orleans; Give Out, Sisters; 1943: Always a Bridesmaid; The Sultan's Daughter; This Is the Army; 1944: Follow the Boys; Bermuda Mystery; Dixie Jamboree.

NY Stage: 1926: Americana; 1927: Allez-Oop; 1928: Good Boy; 1929: Sweet Adeline; 1932: Flying Colors; 1942: Count Me In; 1945: Brighten the Corner.

RED BUTTONS

(AARON CHWATT) BORN: BROOKLYN, NY, FEBRUARY 5, 1919.

A likeable if unremarkable comedian who dabbled succesfully in serious acting, Red Buttons had a tendency to pour on the corn at times with shticky routines and a personality that tried a bit too hard. Still, there was something comforting about having had him around for so long. His name, interestingly enough, came from one of his earliest jobs, when the redhead worked as a singing bellboy at a Bronx club and wore a loud uniform covered with red buttons. Soon he was doing his comedy act in the Catskills and joined the army stage production of *Winged Victory* during World War II. He made his motion picture debut in the film of it, in 1944, but it didn't lead to a movie career just yet. Stardom came with television when he landed his own series, which started out as a variety show and then mutated into a sitcom. After the show's demise it appeared uncertain just what direction Buttons's career would take until he surprised everyone by giving a fine performance as Marlon Brando's doomed army buddy in the 1957 hit *Sayonara*, winning an Academy Award for Best Supporting Actor. Now Buttons could be taken seriously as a film actor and would return to films over the years, usually in support, in such movies as *Hatari!*, as the most comical member of John Wayne's team of animal rustlers; the remake of *Stagecoach*, in the Donald Meek role, as the timid liquor salesman; *The Poseidon Adventure*, as one of the survivors of the capsized ocean liner; and, best of all, *They Shoot Horses, Don't They?*, as the old sailor who becomes Jane Fonda's temporary dance marathon partner. There was also top billing in the fun Jules Verne adventure *Five Weeks in a Balloon* and, in a wholly different vein, a low budget whodunit, *Who Killed Mary*

What's'ername?, as an ex-boxer trying to track down a prostitute's murderer. Another try at series television didn't work out but he was seen steadily in that medium whether as a guest star or participant in several telefilms.

Screen: 1944: Winged Victory; 1946: 13 Rue Madeleine; 1951: Footlight Varieties; 1957: Sayonara; 1958: Imitation General; 1959: The Big Circus; 1961: One, Two, Three; 1962: Hatari!; Five Weeks in a Balloon; The Longest Day; Gay Purr-ee (voice); 1963: A Ticklish Affair; 1964: Your Cheatin' Heart; 1965: Up From the Beach; Harlow; 1966: Stagecoach; 1969: They Shoot Horses, Don't They?; 1971: Who Killed Mary What's 'ername?; 1972: The Poseidon Adventure; 1976: Gable and Lombard; 1977: Viva Knievel!; Pete's Dragon; 1978: Movie Movie; 1979: C.H.O.M.P.S.; 1980: When Time Ran Out…; 1988: 18 Again!; 1990: The Ambulance (dtv); 1994: It Could Happen to You; 1999: The Story of Us.

NY Stage: 1942: Vickie; Wine, Women and Song; 1943: Winged Victory; 1947: Barefoot Boy With Cheek; 1948: Hold It!; 1995: Red Buttons on Broadway.

Select TV: 1952–55: The Red Buttons Show (series); 1956: The Tale of St. Emergency (sp); 1958: Hansel and Gretel (sp); 1959: The Tallest Marine (sp); A Marriage of Strangers (sp); 1966: The Double Life of Henry Phyfe (series); 1970: George M (sp); Breakout; 1975: The New Original Wonder Woman; 1976: Louis Armstrong: Chicago Style; 1977: Telethon; 1978: Vega$; The Users; 1980: Power; The Dream Merchants; 1981: Leave 'em Laughing; 1985: Reunion at Fairborough; Alice in Wonderland (sp); 1987: Knots Landing (series).

SPRING BYINGTON

BORN: COLORADO SPRINGS, CO, OCTOBER 17, 1893. DIED: SEPTEMBER 7, 1971.

This very pleasant, sweet-faced character actress was famous for portraying mothers, be they warm or wacky or both, and she started off her movie career playing one of literature's most famous, Marmee, in the 1933 version of *Little Women*. Prior to that Spring Byington had had a lengthy and successful stage career that started back when she joined a Denver touring company at the age of 18. In 1924 she made her Broadway bow in *Beggar on Horseback*, eventually achieving bigger roles there in such plays as *Once in a Lifetime* and *When Ladies Meet*. Once she established herself as one of the screen's most dependable character actresses, she was hardly ever in want of work. She was Mickey Rooney's mom in *Ah, Wilderness!*; gossipy biddies in *Way Down East* and *Theodora Goes Wild*; and then made the first of several appearances as the Mother of the Jones family in *Every Saturday Night*, a series of lowly-regarded "B" movies made for 20th Century-Fox. They ended with *On Their Own*, in 1941, with Byington upped to top-billing since her co-star, Jed Prouty, had exited after the previous installment. Had circumstances not dictated otherwise, she might have been the mom in another long-running series as well, having been cast as Mrs. Hardy in *A Family Affair*, before Fay Holden took over the part in the highly popular "Andy Hardy" movies, giving a less dithering interpretation of the role. The following year, 1938, Byington scored her one and only Oscar nomination, playing the mildly batty mom in the year's Best Picture winner, *You Can't Take It With You*. Ideally, she was Widow Douglas in *The Adventures of Tom Sawyer*, and was courted by Charles Coburn in *The Devil and Miss Jones*, having been married to him in *The Story of Alexander of Graham Bell*. This teaming worked well enough for her to be wooed by him again, in *Louisa*, a sweet

comedy made at Universal, in which she received 5th billing despite the fact that she had the title role! Around that same time she had another good part, as the music store clerk for whom S.Z. Sakall has lost his heart, in *In the Good Old Summertime*. In the 1950s she capped off her career by becoming a television star with the hit sitcom *December Bride*, which she had previously done on radio.

Screen: 1933: Little Women; 1935: Werewolf of London; Love Me Forever; Orchids to You; Way Down East; Mutiny on the Bounty; Ah, Wilderness!; Broadway Hostess; The Great Impersonation; 1936: The Charge of the Light Brigade; Every Saturday Night; The Voice of Bugle Ann; Educating Father; Back to Nature; Palm Springs; Stage Struck; The Girl on the Front Page; Dodsworth; Theodora Goes Wild; 1937: Green Light; Penrod and Sam; Off to the Races; The Jones Family in Big Business; Hot Water; Hotel Haywire; The Road Back; Borrowing Trouble; It's Love I'm After; Clarence; A Family Affair; 1938: Love on a Budget; A Trip to Paris; Safety in Numbers; The Buccaneer; Penrod and His Twin Brother; Jezebel; You Can't Take It With You; The Adventures of Tom Sawyer; Down on the Farm; 1939: The Jones Family in Hollywood; The Story of Alexander Graham Bell; Everybody's Baby; The Jones Family in Quick Millions; Chicken Wagon Family; Too Busy to Work; 1940: A Child Is Born; The Blue Bird; On Their Own; My Love Came Back; Young as You Feel; Lucky Partners; Laddie; 1941: Arkansas Judge; Meet John Doe; The Devil and Miss Jones; When Ladies Meet; Ellery Queen and the Perfect Crime; The Vanishing Virginian; 1942: Rings on Her Fingers; Roxie Hart; The Affairs of Martha; The War Against Mrs. Hadley; 1943: Presenting Lily Mars; Heaven Can Wait; The Heavenly Body; 1944: I'll Be Seeing You; 1945: Thrill of a Romance; Captain Eddie; Salty O'Rourke; The Enchanted Cottage; A Letter for Evie; 1946: Dragonwyck; Faithful in My Fashion; Meet Me on Broadway; Little Mr. Jim; My Brother Talks to Horses; 1947: Singapore; It Had to Be You; Cynthia; Living in a Big Way; 1948: B.F.'s Daughter; 1949: In the Good Old Summertime; The Big Wheel; 1950: Please Believe Me; Devil's Doorway; Louisa; Walk Softly Stranger; The Reformer and the Redhead (voice); The Skipper Surprised His Wife; 1951: Angels in the Outfield; Bannerline; According to Mrs. Hoyle; 1952: No Room for the Groom; Because You're Mine; 1954: The Rocket Man; 1960: Please Don't Eat the Daisies.

NY Stage: 1924: Beggar on Horseback; 1925: Weak Sisters; 1926: Puppy Love; The Great Adventure; 1927: Skin Deep; 1928: The Merchant of Venice; Tonight at 12; 1929: Ladies Don't Lie; Be Your Age; Jonesy; 1930: I Want My Wife; Once in a Lifetime; 1931: Ladies of Creation; 1932: We Are No Longer Children; When Ladies Meet; 1933: The First Apple; 1934: No Questions Asked; Jigsaw; Piper Paid.

Select TV: 1951: Charming Billy (sp); 1954: Wonderful Day for a Wedding (sp); 1954–59: December Bride (series); 1956: The Great Wide World (sp); 1960: Sitter's Baby (sp); The Matchmaker (sp); 1961–63: Laramie (series); 1964: The Timothy Heist (sp).

C

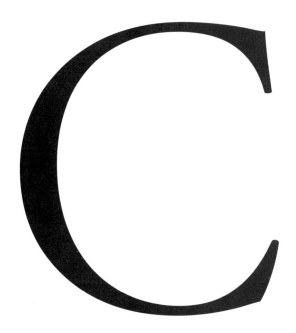

BRUCE CABOT

(Etienne Jacques de Bujac) Born: Carlsbad, NM, April 20, 1904. Died: May 3, 1972.

Because he rescued Fay Wray from the clutches of King Kong, stolid he-man Bruce Cabot's place in movie history is assured. A chance encounter with producer David O. Selznick led to a contract at RKO, where his roles gradually got bigger, first playing the killer in *Roadhouse Murder*, then a bandleader in *The Great Jasper*, and finally culminating in the mightiest of all 1930s adventures, *King Kong*. The studio allowed him to seduce Irene Dunne in *Ann Vickers*; support Edna May Oliver in a Hildegarde Withers mystery, *Murder on the Blackboard*; and carry a "B," *Shadows of Sing Sing*, before dropping him. Freelancing, he remained mostly second-lead material in films like *Let 'em Have It*, as a chauffeur-turned-criminal; *Show Them No Mercy!*, as a nasty kidnapper who gets his comeuppance courtesy of machine gun-toting mom Rochelle Hudson; and *Fury*, inciting violence among the townfolk. He was occasionally given leads, at companies ranging from the lowly Condor Pictures (*Love Takes Flight*) to the prestigious MGM (*Sinners in Paradise*). His rather dour personality made him suitable to play Magua in the 1936 version of *The Last of the Mohicans*, and he found his niche in action pictures or westerns from that point on. In the latter genre he would frequently play villains, as in *Bad Men of Brimstone*, Warners's top notch *Dodge City*, and *Gunfighters*, though he did get to play the hero in *Wild Bill Hickok Rides*. He also provided a lighter brand of ill-will in two Bob Hope comedies, *Sorrowful Jones* and *Fancy Pants*. Having tried to kill off John Wayne in *Angel and the Badman*, he was called on in his later years to support The Duke in such movies as *The Comancheros*, *McLintock!*, and *The Green Berets*.

Screen: 1931: Confessions of a Co-Ed; 1932: What Price Hollywood?; Lady With a Past; Roadhouse Murder; 1933: Lucky Devils; The Great Jasper; King Kong; Disgraced!; Flying Devils; Scarlet River; Midshipman Jack; Ann Vickers; 1934: Shadows of Sing Sing; Murder on the Blackboard; Finishing School; Their Big Moment; His Greatest Gamble; Men of the Night; Redhead; Night Alarm; 1935: Let 'em Have It; Show Them No Mercy!; Without Children; 1936: Legion of Terror; Three Wise Guys; Fury; Sinner Take All; Don't Gamble With Love; The Last of the Mohicans; Don't Turn 'em Loose; The Big Game; Robin Hood of El Dorado; 1937: Bad Guy; Bad Man of Brimstone; Love Takes Flight; 1938: Sinners in Paradise; Smashing the Rackets; Tenth Avenue Kid; 1939: Homicide Bureau; Dodge City; Traitor Spy/The Torso Murder Mystery; Mickey the Kid; Mystery of the White Room; My Son Is Guilty; 1940: Susan and God; Girls Under 21; Captain Caution; 1941: The Flame of New Orleans; Sundown; Wild Bill Hickok Rides; 1942: Silver Queen; Pierre of the Plains; 1943: The Desert Song; 1945: Divorce; Salty O'Rourke; Fallen Angel; 1946: Smoky; Avalanche; 1947: Angel and the Badman; Gunfighters; 1948: The Gallant Legion; 1949: Sorrowful Jones; 1950: Fancy Pants; Rock Island Trail; 1951: Best of the Badmen; 1952: Lost in Alaska; Kid Monk Baroni; 1956: Rommel's Treasure; Toto Lascia o Raddopia (nUSr); 1958: The Quiet American; The Sheriff of Fractured Jaw; 1959: The Love Specialist; Guardatele ma non Toccatele (nUSr); Goliath and the Barbarian; John Paul Jones; 1961: The Red Cloak (It: 1955); The Comancheros; 1962: Hatari!; 1963: McLintock!; 1964: Law of the Lawless; 1965: Black Spurs; In Harm's Way; Town Tamer; Cat Ballou; 1966: The Chase; 1967: The War Wagon; 1968: Hellfighters; The Green Berets; 1969: The Undefeated; 1970: WUSA; Chisum; 1971: Big Jake; Diamonds Are Forever.
NY Stage: 1940: Off the Record.
Select TV: 1951: Treasure Trove (sp); Driven Snow (sp).

SID CAESAR

Born: Yonkers, NY, September 8, 1922.
Ed: Juilliard.

One of television's comedy kings, Sid Caesar was too busy conquering that medium in the 1950s to concentrate on films. When he did make it to the silver screen, the general consensus was that he had passed his prime. His earliest recognition came during World War II, when he did his comedic impersonations in the revue *Tars and Spars*, which was later filmed in 1945. After the war he did another revue show, this time on Broadway, called *Make Mine Manhattan*. From that he almost immediately made the leap to television, appearing in *The Admiral Broadway Revue*, in 1949, working for the first time with Imogene Coca. They clicked so well that she became his partner on the program he would forever be associated with, *Your Show of Shows*. This freewheeling, hit-or-miss variety show made full use of Caesar's wild impersonations and he won his first Emmy Award for it in 1952. There were several follow-up shows, including *Caesar's Hour*, which won him another Emmy in 1956. When Stanley Kramer was rounding up his all-star comedy cast for *It's a Mad Mad Mad Mad World*, he gave one of the main roles to Caesar, who spent much of the movie, with Edie Adams, frantically trying to free himself from a hardware-store basement. It was easily Caesar's best movie role, and certainly more satisfying than two starring efforts he did for director William Castle, *The Spirit Is Willing* and *The Busy Body*, both released in 1967 on double-bills. His subsequent supporting roles were usually comical, but not in particularly funny movies, and his highest exposure came with the 1978 musical *Grease*, in which he played it relatively straight as a high school gym coach. His 1982 autobiography, *Where Have I Been?*, spoke frankly of a troubled personal life. A 1973 compilation, *Ten From Your Show of Shows*, made highlights of the famed series available for the first time in years.

Screen: 1945: Tars and Spars; 1947: The Guilt of Janet Ames; 1963: It's a Mad Mad Mad Mad World; 1967: The Busy Body; The Spirit Is Willing; A Guide for the Married Man; 1974: Airport 1975; 1976: Silent Movie; 1977: Fire Sale; 1978: Grease; The Cheap Detective; 1980: The Fiendish Plot of Dr. Fu Manchu; 1981: History of the World Part 1; 1982: Grease 2; 1984: Over the Brooklyn Bridge; Cannonball Run II; 1986: Stoogemania; 1989: The Emperor's New Clothes (dtv); 1997: Vegas Vacation; 1999: The Wonderful Ice Cream Suit (dtv).

NY Stage: 1944: Tars and Spars; 1948: Make Mine Manhattan; 1962: Little Me; 1971: Four on a Garden; 1989: Sid Caesar: The Legendary Genius of Comedy (ob); Sid Caesar & Company: Does Anybody Know What I'm Talking About?

Select TV: 1949: Admiral Broadway Revue (series); 1950–54: Your Show of Shows (series); 1954–57: Caesar's Hour (series); 1958: Sid Caesar Invites You (series); 1961: The Devil You Say (sp); 1963–64: The Sid Caesar Show (series); 1967: The Sid Caesar-Imogene Coca-Carl Reiner-Howard Morris Special (sp); 1977: Flight to Holocaust; Barnaby and Me; Curse of the Black Widow; 1981: The Munsters' Revenge; 1983: Found Money; 1985: Love Is Never Silent; Alice in Wonderland (sp); 1988: Freedom Fighter; Side by Side; 1995: The Great Mom Swap.

JAMES CAGNEY
BORN: NEW YORK, NY, JULY 17, 1899.
DIED: MARCH 30, 1986.

There is no doubt that the movies would have been a poorer medium without the frequently-mimicked James Cagney. A dynamic bundle of energy — sneering, cocky, fast-talking, cheekily self-assured — he brought an irresistible charm to the bad boy roles in which he specialized. History has proclaimed him one of the definitive movie gangsters, alongside Humphrey Bogart and Edward G. Robinson, but Cagney (just like his two famous contemporaries) displayed a much greater versatility than that, preferring to think of himself as a song-and-dance man. While still a young man, he appeared in an amateur production at the Lenox Hill Settlement House before going into vaudeville with the cast of *Every Sailor*, dressed in drag. Despite his lack of dancing skills he made his Broadway debut as part of the chorus of the 1920 musical *Pitter Patter*. His

unique, stiff-legged hoofing would be come as famous as his unmistakable, hand-jabbing gestures. Working on the road and in New York he received high praise for his tough character in the play *Outside Looking In*, followed by his punk murderer in *Penny Arcade*. Thanks to the insistence of Al Jolson, who bought the screen rights and sold them to Warner Bros., Cagney got to repeat his part in the 1930 movie adaptation (now called *Sinner's Holiday*), breaking down in melodramatic fashion when his ma finds out he's killed a man. Warner Bros. were unconvinced that he was a hot property, so they kept him in smaller roles, in *Doorway to Hell*, as henchman to a far-less convincing mobster, Lew Ayres; *Other Men's Women*, as a railroad worker; and the George Arliss vehicle, *The Millionaire*, showing up for one scene as a life insurance salesman.

Fortune stepped in when director William Wellman swapped Eddie Woods for Cagney in the lead of his new gangster movie, *The Public Enemy*. Gritty and fast-moving, the film made Cagney a star, playing the dangerous, arrogant hood who doesn't think twice about mashing half a grapefruit into his girlfriend's kisser. He gave the same actress, Mae Clarke, an equally rough time in *Lady Killer*, dragging her across the room by her hair, only that was supposed to be a comedy. He took one more secondary part, to Edward G. Robinson in *Smart Money*, before the Cagney bandwagon began rolling under its own power. His pugnacious personality afforded him the opportunity to spit out some tart banter, woo the ladies on his own terms, and slap around anybody who gave him a bit of lip. Partnered very nicely with Joan Blondell, he was a con artist seeking payback on Louis Calhern in the mostly-comedic *Blonde Crazy*. He was then a cabbie set on avenging his brother's murder in *Taxi!*; a race-car driver in *The Crowd Roars*; a prizefighter for the first of three trips to the ring, in *Winner Take All*; a photographer specializing in unsavory assignments in *Picture Snatcher*; a rip-roaring promoter, always looking for new angles to grab the suckers, in an unsung gem called *Hard to Handle*; and shared the spotlight with fellow hard-case Frankie Darro in *The Mayor of Hell*. Cagney finally talked the studio into allowing him to display his terpsichorean skills in the Busby Berkeley extravaganza *Footlight Parade*. Participating with Ruby Keeler in the "Shanghai Lil" finale, he made the whole sequence quite unforgettable.

He was a racketeer opposite a relatively unknown Bette Davis in *Jimmy the Gent*, a far more enjoyable teaming than their later, better-known *The Bride Came C.O.D.* The clumsy melodrama, *He Was Her Man*, wasted the Cagney-Blondell magic, but another pairing, this time with off-screen friend Pat O'Brien, led to eight successful outings. The first, *Here Comes the Navy*, with Cagney as a swaggering sailor, was a minor item that somehow became a Best Picture nominee at the 1934 Oscars. He demonstrated that a sharp blow from the head was just as effective as a closed fist, as a trucker in the tight little quickie *The St. Louis Kid*. In the era of the newly established Production Code, these last two movies demonstrated, much to the relief of his admirers, that Cagney was just as edgy and explosive without overt violence and could, in fact, be equally riveting on the right side of the law, as in the hit *G Men*. He even took on Shakespeare, effortlessly portraying Bottom — complete with ass's head — in Warners's weirdly hypnotic *A Midsummer Night's Dream*. Three more with O'Brien — *Devil Dogs of the Air*, *The Irish in Us* (the second prizefighter picture, featuring another of Cagney's real-life pals, Frank McHugh), and *Ceiling Zero* — weren't comparable to the less typical *Frisco Kid*, a period piece set on the Barbary Coast. He battled endlessly with Warners over his salary and even walked out for a spell, making some cheapies in the interim: *Great Guy*, and the musical, *Something to Sing About*. Financial issues resolved, he returned to the home lot, where he was about to reach his peak years as one of Hollywood's leading attractions.

A manic comic turn in 1938's *Boy Meets Boy* (again with Pat O'Brien) was followed by one of his signature gangster films, *Angels With Dirty Faces*. As the slum boy who resorts to crime while his pal, O'Brien, becomes a priest, he went screaming to the electric chair, giving the impression of a coward in an effort to deter others from following his criminal path. For this memorable creation he received his first Oscar nomination. Humphrey Bogart was also in the *Angels* cast and the two were together in another pair of hits: *The Roaring Twenties*, driven to bootlegging by the hard times, and *The Oklahoma Kid*, in which Cagney's bravado transferred surprisingly well to the Old West. In between, he made *Each Dawn I Die*, spending time in jail with fellow yardbird George Raft. Cagney was the bright spot in two otherwise standard war films, *The Fighting 69th*, with O'Brien and McHugh in an Irish battalion; and *Captains of the Clouds*, notable only for being his first Technicolor film. He demonstrated his light comedy touch in *The Strawberry Blonde*; and grew a moustache to turn up the heat in *Torrid Zone*, with another of his best co-stars, Ann Sheridan. They'd worked wonders paired off in *Roaring Twenties* and were back together for his last boxing flick, *City for Conquest*, to which was added the drama of Cagney's pugilist losing his eyesight. Having made a fortune for Warners with his fists, Cagney now wanted to show what he could do with his feet. *Yankee Doodle Dandy*, the story of Broadway performer-songwriter George M. Cohan, was no more authentic then any other biopic. But Cagney was dazzling, literally dancing off the proscenium arch of the theatre in a superb *tour de force* that was *the* patriotic smash of the war years. He won a highly popular Academy Award for Best Actor of 1942.

Eager for independence, Cagney left Warners immediately after his Oscar triumph to form his own production company with his brother, William, serving as producer, but the enterprise (distributed through United Artists) was not a successful one. Their first effort, *Johnny Come Lately*, presented Cagney as a philosophical wanderer fighting small-town corruption. It was a very minor film, as was *Blood on the Sun*, though this thriller set in Japan with Cagney as a reporter was more to the public's liking. The brothers purchased the Pulitzer Prize-winning *The Time of Their Life*, but the story of various oddballs at a San Francisco bar failed to duplicate the acclaim it had received on the stage. To keep body and soul together he went over to Fox for the wartime espionage docudrama, *13 Rue Madeleine*, but by the end the 1940s he was back at Warners under a new contract. There he created one of his most enduring characters, the sadistic, mother-obsessed killer, Cody Jarrett, in *White Heat*, one of the outstanding films of the gangster genre. Its fiery climax featured one of the most parodied lines in film history: "Top of the world, Ma!"

Though he was back with the studio that had made him a star, the early 1950s were not the best of times for the actor. *West Point Story* was an old-fashioned musical that seemed like a step backwards; *Kiss Tomorrow Goodbye*, produced by his own company, was a gangster drama that fared poorly; *Come Fill the Cup*, although the best of this lot, found most of the attention going to Gig Young; *What Price Glory?* (for Fox) was a misguided remake of the famed silent film; and *A Lion Is in the Streets* was one of his all time worst (again, from his own company) with Cagney sporting a particularly unconvincing Southern accent as a peddler-turned-politico. He left Warners and did a western at Paramount, *Run for Cover*, but it failed to rise above the morass. His box-office appeal had temporarily cooled, but in 1955 he starred in three big hits. He started with *Love Me or Leave Me*,

earning another Oscar nomination, as Doris Day's crippled, abusive husband in the true story of singer Ruth Etting and her involvement with gangster Marty "The Gimp" Snyder. Then he was effective as the unpopular ship's captain in *Mister Roberts*, which he played with the perfect mixture of bluster and petty evil. Finally, he reprised his George M. Cohan role for a guest spot in *The Seven Little Foys*, performing a delightful shoft-shoe routine with Bob Hope. He came to the rescue when Spencer Tracy was booted off the western *Tribute to a Bad Man*, and then brought some credibilty to a typical soap opera with Barbara Stanwyck, *These Wilder Years*, looking for the son he had given up for adoption.

In 1957, he donned a variety of disguises to emulate Lon Chaney in the above-average biography, *Man of a Thousand Faces*. That same year, his sole directorial attempt, a low budget remake of *This Gun for Hire* for Paramount, called *Short Cut to Hell*, went by without much comment. In his last musical, *Never Steal Anything Small*, he was done in by bad material, but a trip overseas to Ireland, for *Shake Hands with the Devil*, resulted in an interesting look at the IRA. For another of his buddies, Robert Montgomery, he made a rare television appearance in *Soldier From the War Returning*, an episode of Montgomery's anthology show. He also did a feature film under Montgomery's direction, *The Gallant Hours*, a biopic of Admiral "Bull" Halsey, then gave a breathlessly explosive performance as a Coca Cola executive, in Billy Wilder's wonderful *One, Two, Three*, proving he was still an invincible whirlwind of energy in his 60s. Then, in 1961, he abruptly retired. He was adamant about staying away from the spotlight until, on the advice of a physician, he came back to work for 1981's *Ragtime*. Noticeably frail, he was nevertheless mesmerizing in his brief role as a New York police commissioner, proving that among movie legends he was still the champ. He published his autobiography, *Cagney by Cagney*, in 1976, two years after he had received the American Film Institute Life Achievement Award. His relatively low-key private life means he has not been the subject of any scandal-mongering biographies and his work is rarely analyzed. He remains, nevertheless, one of Hollywood's genuine giants.

Screen: 1930: Sinner's Holiday; Doorway to Hell; 1931: Other Men's Women; The Millionaire; The Public Enemy; Smart Money; Blonde Crazy; 1932: Taxi!; The Crowd Roars; Winner Take All; 1933: Hard to Handle; Picture Snatcher; The Mayor of Hell; Footlight Parade; Lady Killer; 1934: Jimmy the Gent; He Was Her Man; Here Comes the Navy; The St. Louis Kid; 1935: Devil Dogs of the Air; G Men; The Irish in Us; A Midsummer Night's Dream; Frisco Kid; Ceiling Zero; 1936: Great Guy; 1937: Something to Sing About; 1938: Boy Meets Girl; Angels With Dirty Faces; 1939: The Oklahoma Kid; Each Dawn I Die; The Roaring Twenties; 1940: The Fighting 69th; Torrid Zone; 1941: City for Conquest; The Strawberry Blonde; The Bride Came C.O.D.; 1942: Captains of the Clouds; Yankee Doodle Dandy; 1943: Johnny Come Lately; 1945: Blood on the Sun; 1946: 13 Rue Madeleine; 1948: The Time of Your Life; 1949: White Heat; 1950: West Point Story; Kiss Tomorrow Goodbye; 1951: Come Fill the Cup; Starlift; 1952: What Price Glory?; 1953: A Lion Is in the Streets; 1955: Run for Cover; Love Me or Leave Me; Mister Roberts; The Seven Little Foys; 1956: Tribute to a Bad Man; These Wilder Years; 1957: Man of a Thousand Faces; Short Cut to Hell (and dir.); 1959: Never Steal Anything Small; Shake Hands With the Devil; 1960: The Gallant Hours; 1961: One, Two, Three; 1968: Arizona Bushwhackers (narrator); 1981: Ragtime.

NY Stage: 1920: Pitter Patter; 1925: Outside Looking In; 1926: Broadway; 1927: Women Go on Forever; 1928: The Grand Street

Follies of 1928; **1929:** The Grand Street Follies of 1929; Maggie the Magnificent; **1930:** Penny Arcade.
Select TV: **1956:** Soldier From the War Returning (sp); **1984:** Terrible Joe Moran.

LOUIS CALHERN

(CARL HENRY VOGT) BORN: BROOKLYN, NY, FEBRUARY 19, 1895. DIED: MAY 12, 1956.

An erudite character performer, with an imposing, beak-like nose, Louis Calhern did most of his best work after the age of 50. When he decided to become an actor he changed his name to avoid disgracing his family, and, after military service during World War I, he made his movie debut in the 1921 feature *What's Worth While?* After making no impact on the silent screen, he returned to the stage and carved out a respectable list of Broadway credits. He returned to the movies to provide ample support for comedians like the Marx Brothers (*Duck Soup*, as Groucho's rival and ruler of neighboring Sylvania), Wheeler and Woolsey (*The Nitwits*), Charlie McCarthy (*Charlie McCarthy — Detective*), and Danny Kaye (*Up in Arms*). He also took part in such prestigious dramas as *The Count of Monte Cristo*, as the magistrate who imprisons Robert Donat; *The Life of Emile Zola*; *Juarez*; and *Notorious*. He signed a contract with MGM in the late 1940s, and became a member of the studio's stock company. He had a sterling year in 1950, first playing Buffalo Bill and participating in the showstopper "There's No Business Like Show Business" in *Annie Get Your Gun*. Then he created one of his finest characterizations as the duplicitous legal mastermind in the classic caper film *The Asphalt Jungle*. Finally, he received an Oscar nomination for recreating his stage part of Chief Justice Oliver Wendell Holmes in *The Magnificent Yankee*, a standard "grand old man" role and performance that required him to age from 61 to 90. As one of Metro's elder statesmen he participated in such hits as *Executive Suite*, as a cynical board member; *Blackboard Jungle*, as a weary teacher; and *High Society*, as Grace Kelly's uncle. He even essayed Shakespeare, taking the title role of *Julius Caesar*, though he was dwarfed by a stellar cast that included James Mason and Marlon Brando. It was while filming *The Teahouse of the August Moon*, with Brando, that Calhern died of a heart attack. Paul Ford completed the picture.
Screen: **1921:** What's Worth While?; The Blot; Too Wise Wives; **1922:** Woman Wake Up!; **1923:** The Last Moment; **1931:** Stolen Heaven; Road to Singapore; Blonde Crazy; **1932:** They Call It Sin; Night After Night; Okay America!; Afraid to Talk; 20,000 Years in Sing Sing; **1933:** The Woman Accused; Frisco Jenny; Strictly Personal; The World Gone Mad; Diplomaniacs; Duck Soup; **1934:** The Affairs of Cellini; The Man With Two Faces; The Count of Monte Cristo; Sweet Adeline; **1935:** The Arizonan; Woman Wanted; The Last Days of Pompeii; **1936:** The Gorgeous Hussy; **1937:** Her Husband Lies; The Life of Emile Zola; **1938:** Fast Company; **1939:** Juarez; 5th Ave. Girl; Charlie McCarthy — Detective; **1940:** I Take This Woman; Dr. Ehrlich's Magic Bullet; **1943:** Heaven Can Wait; Nobody's Darling; **1944:** Up in Arms; The Bridge of San Luis Rey; **1946:** Notorious; **1948:** Arch of Triumph; **1949:** The Red Pony; The Red Danube; **1950:** Annie Get Your Gun; Nancy Goes to Rio; The Asphalt Jungle; Devil's Doorway; A Life of Her Own; The Magnificent Yankee; Two Weeks With Love; **1951:** The Man With a Cloak; It's a Big Country (narrator); **1952:** Invitation; We're Not Married; Washington Story; The Prisoner of Zenda; The Bad and the Beautiful (voice); **1953:** Confidentially Connie; Remains to Be Seen; Julius Caesar; Latin Lovers; Main Street to Broadway; **1954:**

Rhapsody; Executive Suite; The Student Prince; Men of the Fighting Lady; Betrayed; Athena; **1955:** Blackboard Jungle; The Prodigal; **1956:** Forever, Darling; High Society.
NY Stage: **1923:** Roger Bloomer; The Song and Dance Man; Cobra; **1925:** In a Garden; **1926:** Hedda Gabler; A Woman Disputed; Up the Line; **1927:** The Dark Savages; Under the Skin; **1928:** A Distant Drum; **1929:** Gypsy; The Love Duel; **1930:** The Tyrant; **1931:** Give Me Yesterday; Brief Moment; **1932:** Inside Story; **1933:** Dinner at Eight; **1934:** Birthday; **1935:** Hell Freezes Over; **1937:** Robin Landing; **1942:** The Great Big Doorstep; **1944:** Jacobowsky and the Colonel; **1946:** The Magnificent Yankee; **1948:** The Survivors; The Play's the Thing; **1950:** King Lear; **1955:** The Wooden Dish (and dir.).

RORY CALHOUN

(FRANCIS TIMOTHY McCOWAN) BORN: LOS ANGELES, CA, AUGUST 8, 1922. DIED: APRIL 28, 1999.

A stoically handsome leading man who found his calling in second-string westerns, Rory Calhoun was a very busy, though hardly first-rate actor. It was Alan Ladd who suggested he give acting a try, after Calhoun had spent time in various odd jobs, including mining and lumberjacking. Signed by Fox as Frank McCowan, he made little impact until he changed his name and began getting leads in "B" films. He was stranded on *Adventure Island*; hacked his way out of the jungle after a plane crash in *Miraculous Journey*; and was a racehorse owner in *County Fair*. He was promoted to such "A" movies as *With a Song in My Heart* and *How to Marry a Millionaire*, supplying the romantic interest for Susan Hayward and Betty Grable, respectively. After these it was back to grinding out action adventures and westerns, including *The Yellow Tomahawk*, as a heroic Indian guide; *A Bullet Is Waiting*, as a prisoner who falls for rancher's daughter Jean Simmons; *Red Sundown*, going from gunman to lawman; *The Hired Gun* (which he co-produced, with his agent), tracking innocent fugitive Anne Francis; *Utah Blaine*, battling Ray Teal over ranch rights; and *Ride Out for Revenge*, providing aide to Cheyenne Indians who were being forced from their land. Much of the 1960s was spent in European productions like *The Colossus of Rhodes*, *The Secret of Monte Cristo*, and *A Face in the Rain*. He later showed up as a white-haired, campy performer in such purposefully silly movies as *Motel Hell*, *Angel*, and *Hell Comes to Frogtown*.
Screen: AS FRANK McCOWAN: **1944:** Something for the Boys; Sunday Dinner for a Soldier; **1945:** The Bullfighters; Nob Hill; The Great John L.

AS RORY CALHOUN: **1947:** The Red House; Adventure Island; That Hagen Girl; **1948:** Miraculous Journey; **1949:** Sand; Massacre River; **1950:** A Ticket to Tomahawk; County Fair; Rogue River; Return of the Frontiersman; **1951:** Meet Me After the Show; **1952:** I'd Climb the Highest Mountain; With a Song in My Heart; Way of a Gaucho; **1953:** The Silver Whip; Powder River; How to Marry a Millionaire; **1954:** River of No Return; The Yellow Tomahawk; A Bullet Is Waiting; Dawn at Socorro; Four Guns to the Border; **1955:** The Looters; Ain't Misbehavin'; The Treasure of Pancho Villa; The Spoilers; **1956:** Red Sundown; Raw Edge; Flight to Hong Kong; **1957:** The Hired Gun; The Domino Kid; Utah Blaine; Ride Out for Revenge; The Big Caper; **1958:** Apache Territory; The Saga of Hemp Brown; **1960:** The Colossus of Rhodes; Thunder in Carolina/Hard Drivin'; **1961:** Marco Polo; The Secret of Monte Cristo; **1963:** A Face in the Rain; The Gun Hawk; The Young and the Brave; **1965:** Young

Fury; Operation Delilah; Black Spurs; **1966:** Apache Uprising; Finger on the Trigger; Our Man in Bagdad; **1967:** The Emerald of Artatama; **1968:** Dayton's Devils; **1969:** Operation Cross Eagles; **1972:** Night of the Lepus; **1975:** Mulefeathers/The West Is Still Wild; **1976:** Won Ton Ton, the Dog Who Saved Hollywood; **1977:** Kino, the Padre on Horseback/Mission to Glory; Love and the Midnight Auto Supply; **1979:** The Main Event; **1980:** Smokey and the Judge (dtv) Motel Hell; **1983:** Angel; **1984:** Avenging Angel; **1988:** Hell Comes to Frogtown; **1989:** Bad Jim; Roller Blade Warriors: Taken By Force (dtv); **1992:** Pure Country.
Select TV: **1954:** The Road Ahead; **1955:** Garrity's Sons (sp); Day is Done (sp); **1956:** Hot Cargo (sp); **1958:** Curfew at Midnight (sp); **1958–60:** The Texan (series); **1968:** Land's End (sp); **1977:** Flight to Holocaust; **1979:** Flatbed Annie & Sweetiepie: Lady Truckers; The Rebels (ms); **1982:** Capitol (series); The Blue and the Gray (ms).

MICHAEL CALLAN

(MARTIN CALINIEFF) BORN: PHILADELPHIA, PA, NOVEMBER 22, 1935.

A former nightclub entertainer in his home town of Philadelphia, Michael Callan first gained attention as a dancer, billed as Mickey Calin, in such stage musicals as *The Boy Friend*, and as Riff in the original cast of *West Side Story*. When he came to Hollywood, Columbia Pictures had other ideas for him and, aside from an exciting number in *Pepe*, did not bother to display his fancy footwork on screen. He started off as one of the questionable "heroes" in *They Came to Cordura*, and then jumped up to top billing, as the star circus aerialist in *The Flying Fontaines*. There was the teen ensemble *Because They're Young*, though he was too old to pass as a high schooler; *Gidget Goes Hawaiian*, as Deborah Walley's unsuccessful suitor; and Disney's *Bon Voyage*, where he was compensated by winning Walley's heart. He reached some degree of popularity with the hit 1962 medical soap opera, *The Interns*, where he was involved with two women between hospital duties. In its 1964 sequel, *The New Interns*, he was still a womanizer, but now officially a doctor. There were supporting roles in such entertaining films as the Jules Verne fantasy *Mysterious Island*, as a Union soldier battling giant monsters; *The Victors*, buying hooker Romy Schneider; and the jokey western *Cat Ballou*, as one of Jane Fonda's confederates in crime. His movie career came to an abrupt halt in the middle of the decade, though he would occasionally pop up in low-profile quickies, such as the thriller *Double Exposure*, which he also executive produced.
Screen: **1959:** They Came to Cordura; The Flying Fontaines; **1960:** Because They're Young; Pepe; **1961:** Mysterious Island; Gidget Goes Hawaiian; **1962:** 13 West Street; Bon Voyage; The Interns; **1963:** The Victors; **1964:** The New Interns; **1965:** Cat Ballou; You Must Be Joking!; **1972:** The Magnificent Seven Ride!; **1973:** Frasier — The Sensuous Lion; **1975:** Lepke; The Photographer; **1978:** Record City; **1982:** The Cat and the Canary; **1983:** Double Exposure (and prod.); Chained Heat; **1988:** Freeway; **1995:** Leprechaun 3 (dtv); **1997:** The Last Road (dtv).
NY Stage: AS MICKEY CALIN: **1954:** The Boyfriend; **1956:** Catch a Star; **1957:** West Side Story.
Select TV: **1966:** Occasional Wife (series); **1968:** Kiss Me Kate (sp); **1969:** In Name Only; **1973:** The Gift of Terror; **1978:** Blind Ambition (ms); Donner Pass: The Road to Survival; **1980:** Scruples (ms); **1984:** Last of the Great Survivors; **1985:** My Wicked, Wicked Ways — The Legend of Errol Flynn; **1985–87:** One Life to Live (series).

CORINNE CALVET

(CORINNE DIBOS) BORN: PARIS, FRANCE, APRIL 30, 1925. ED: UNIV. OF PARIS SCHOOL OF FINE ARTS. DIED: JUNE 23, 2001.

A sultry French actress who offered up Hollywood's version of European sex appeal, Corinne Calvet was appearing in films in her native country when Hal Wallis hired her to decorate a number of his early 1950s productions. She was, in fact, supposed to start her American career somewhat earlier, but this plan was derailed because her English was deemed inadequate. She improved sufficiently to make her official U.S. debut in *Rope of Sand*, as a con artist who falls in love with diamond thief Burt Lancaster. Her adequate performance encouraged Wallis to cast her opposite Martin and Lewis in *My Friend Irma Goes West* and *Sailor Beware*, in both cases as an actress; and she was given Marlene Dietrich's old role in the unnecessary remake of *Shanghai Express*, now called *Peking Express*. Her impressive lineup of leading men included James Cagney (*What Price Glory?*, with Dan Dailey also in contention for her hand), Danny Kaye (*On the Riviera*, taking a secondary position to Gene Tierney), and James Stewart (*The Far Country*, snatching him away from Ruth Roman). She was one of George Sanders's unlucky wives in *Bluebeard's Tenth Honeymoon*, and joined the cast of passé stars in an A.C. Lyles western, *Apache Uprising*. By the time she published her 1983 autobiography, *Has Corinne Been a Good Girl?*, her name was familiar only to avid movie nostalgists.
Screen (US releases only): **1949:** Rope of Sand; **1950:** When Willie Comes Marching Home; My Friend Irma Goes West; **1951:** Quebec; On the Riviera; Peking Express; Sailor Beware; **1952:** Thunder in the East; What Price Glory?; **1953:** Powder River; Flight to Tangier; **1954:** The Far Country; So This Is Paris; The Adventures of Casanova; The Girls of San Frediano; Four Women in the Night; Bonnes a tuer; **1955:** Napoleon; **1958:** The Plunderers of Painted Flats; **1960:** Bluebeard's Tenth Honeymoon; **1962:** Hemingway's Adventures of a Young Man; **1965:** Apache Uprising; **1970:** Pound; **1976:** Too Hot to Handle; **1980:** Dr. Heckyl and Mr. Hype; **1982:** The Sword and the Sorcerer; **1988:** Side Roads.
Select TV: **1952:** Legacy of Love (sp); **1953:** Babette (sp); **1958:** Balance of Terror (sp); **1974:** The Phantom of Hollywood; **1979:** The French Atlantic Affair (ms); She's Dressed to Kill.

ROD CAMERON

(NATHAN RODERICK COX) BORN: CALGARY, ALBERTA, CANADA, DECEMBER 7, 1910. DIED: DECEMBER 21, 1983.

A former stunt man, Rod Cameron successfully used his imposing height and rugged manner in a series of "B" adventures during the 1940s and 1950s. He came to Paramount in the 1930s as Fred MacMurray's stand-in and stayed there for several years, winning small roles in movies like *North West Mounted Police*, *Christmas in July*, *The Fleet's In*, and *Wake Island*. In the mid-1940s, he moved over to Universal to star in his own sagebrush sagas starting with *Boss of Boomtown*. He continued in that genre almost exclusively over the next 20 years, projecting virility but showing precious little animation. Among his offerings were a pair of westerns produced and written by future director Blake Edwards: *Panhandle*, in which Cameron avenged his brother's murder, and *Stampede*, as a cattle baron. He twice teamed with Yvonne De Carlo in *Frontier Gal*, a comedy in which he married her at gunpoint; and

River Lady, as a logger whose business she tries to ruin. A novelty 3-D offering, *Southwest Passage*, replaced horses with camels, and was followed by bad guy roles in *Dakota Lil*, as leader of a counterfeiting ring, and *Santa Fe Passage*, in league with the Apaches. He left Universal in 1948 to join Republic, where his diminishing assignments eventually forced him to take the inevitable European route in the 1960s. He also did a couple of television series, of which *State Trooper* had the longest run.

Screen: 1939: Heritage of the Desert; 1940: Christmas in July; North West Mounted Police; Rangers of Fortune; Stagecoach War; The Quarterback; 1941: Life With Henry; Henry Aldrich for President; The Monster and the Girl; I Wanted Wings (voice); Nothing But the Truth; Among the Living; The Parson of Panamint; Night of January 16th; Buy Me That Town; No Hands on the Clock; Pacific Blackout; 1942: The Fleet's In; The Remarkable Andrew; Priorities on Parade; Wake Island; True to the Army; Commandos Strike at Dawn; The Forest Rangers; Star Spangled Rhythm; 1943: Gung Ho!; G-Men vs. the Black Dragon (serial); Secret Service in Darkest Africa (serial); Riding High; The Good Fellows; Honeymoon Lodge; No Time for Love; The Kansan; 1944: Mrs. Parkington; Boss of Boomtown; Trigger Trail; Riders of the Santa Fe; The Old Texas Trail; 1945: Beyond the Pecos; Salome, Where She Danced; Frontier Gal; Renegades of the Rio Grande; Swing Out, Sister; 1946: The Runaround; 1947: Pirates of Monterey; 1948: River Lady; Panhandle; Strike It Rich; Belle Starr's Daughter; The Plunderers; 1949: Stampede; Brimstone; 1950: Stage to Tucson; Dakota Lil; Short Grass; 1951: The Sea Hornet; Oh Susanna!; Cavalry Scout; 1952: Ride the Man Down; Woman of the North Country; Wagons West; Fort Osage; The Jungle; 1953: San Antone; The Steel Lady; 1954: Southwest Passage; Hell's Outpost; 1955: Headline Hunters; Santa Fe Passage; The Fighting Chance; Double Jeopardy; Passport to Treason; 1956: Yaqui Drums; 1957: Spoilers of the Forest; 1958: The Man Who Died Twice; 1960: The Electronic Monster; 1963: The Gun Hawk; 1964: Las Pistoles no Discuten/Bullets Don't Lie (nUSr); Bullets and the Flesh (nUSr); 1965: The Bounty Killer; Requiem for a Gunfighter; 1967: Winnetou and His Friend Old Firehand (nUSr); 1971: Evel Knievel; The Last Movie; 1975: The Kirlian Force; Psychic Killer; 1976: Jesse's Girls; 1977: Love and the Midnight Auto Supply.

Select TV: 1953–55: City Detective (series); 1956–59: State Trooper (series); 1959: Coronado 9 (series); 1967: Ride the Wind (sp).

JUDY CANOVA

(JULIET CANOVA) BORN: JACKSONVILLE, FL, NOVEMBER 20, 1916. DIED: AUGUST 5, 1983.

A bellowing singer-comic whose lack of subtlety rivaled Martha Raye's, Judy Canova's act consisted of playing a hillbilly yokel, a role she perfected in an act with her siblings. Shelving her original aspirations to be a classical singer, Canova took her hayseed family to New York nightclubs and a Broadway revue, *Calling All Stars*. Judy was herself called to Hollywood to do a guest shot in Warners's *In Caliente*, giving her rendition of "The Lady in Red." She returned to New York for the hit musical *Yokel Boy*, before Republic Pictures gave her starring roles in a succession of low-brow comedies, designed to cash in on her radio popularity. In *Scatterbrain*, *Puddin' Head*, *Joan of Ozark*, *Chatterbox*, and *Honeychile*, country bumpkin Canova matched wits (!) with such slickers as movie moguls, New Yorkers, and even Nazis. Her movies continued throughout the early 1940s to the mid-1950s, ending with *Lay That Rifle Down*, after which she

was seen infrequently on screen (as the sheriff's wife in the 1960 version of *The Adventures of Huckleberry Finn*, for instance) and television. Her daughter is actress Diana Canova, who was probably best known for appearing on the television sitcom *Soap*.

Screen: 1935: In Caliente; Broadway Gondolier; Going Highbrow; 1937: Artists and Models; Thrill of a Lifetime; 1940: Scatterbrain; 1941: Sis Hopkins; Puddin' Head; 1942: Sleepytime Gal; True to the Army; Joan of Ozark; 1943: Chatterbox; Sleepy Lagoon; 1944: Louisiana Hayride; 1945: Hit the Hay; 1946: Singin' in the Corn; 1951: Honeychile; 1952: Oklahoma Annie; The WAC From Walla Walla; 1954: Untamed Heiress; 1955: Carolina Cannonball; Lay That Rifle Down; 1960: The Adventures of Huckleberry Finn; 1976: Cannonball.

NY Stage: 1934: Calling All Stars; 1936: Ziegfeld Follies of 1936; 1939: Yokel Boy.

EDDIE CANTOR

(EDWARD ISRAEL ISKOWITZ) BORN: NEW YORK, NY, JANUARY 31, 1892. DIED: OCTOBER 10, 1964.

Exuberant, wide-eyed, and ingratiating, comedian Eddie Cantor's brash, eager-to-please mannerisms have often been compared with Al Jolson's. Cantor remains infinitely more accessible and likeable, however, simply because he didn't take himself as seriously. A teen performer with Gus Edwards's "Kid Kabaret," Cantor later appeared in a vaudeville double act, first with Sammy Kessler and then with Al Lee, before going legit in a West Coast revue, *Canary Cottage*, in 1917. Soon he was one of the hits of the Ziegfeld Follies, wildly prancing about in a slightly effete manner, rolling his eyes and singing, often in blackface. His popularity led to two stage showcases being created specifically for him, *Kid Boots* and *Whoopee*, both of which were filmed. *Whoopee*, which was a talkie and in an early form of color, proved a solid success for producer Samuel Goldwyn. Cantor's charisma added sparkle to a rather creaky production that, if nothing else, gave moviegoers a chance to hear the comic's signature tune, "Making Whoopee." Cantor became Goldwyn's prize property during the early 1930s in a series of elaborate musical hodgepodges, usually featuring the Goldwyn Girls and an occasional tasteless blackface bit. There was *Palmy Days*, for which Cantor received a writing credit and sang another zippy number, "My Baby Said Yes, Yes;" *The Kid From Spain*, involving bullfighting; and *Strike Me Pink*, the weakest and least popular of the bunch. The best effort was *Roman Scandals*, with Cantor transported back to ancient Rome for some anachronistic fun, while another enjoyable romp, *Kid Millions*, found him en route to Egypt, cavorting through a song that was pure Cantor ("Okay, Toots!"), and concluding with a bizarre color fantasy sequence in a milk factory.

After breaking with Goldwyn, his movie career faltered somewhat, though his radio show maintained huge popularity. A one-shot deal with Fox, *Ali Baba Goes to Town*, had some of the Goldwyn zip, but *Forty Little Mothers* was too subdued for most fans, even though it was directed by Busby Berkeley, who had conceived most of the numbers in Cantor's previous pictures. He did have one last triumph, though, playing both himself and an Eddie Cantor look-alike, in Warners's all-star musical, *Thank Your Lucky Stars* — mercilessly making fun of himself as an old ham that nobody wants to hire. He produced a pair of teamings with Joan Davis at RKO. *Show Business* (in which he once again sang "Making Whoopee") did well, but *If You Knew Susie* (named after another one of his famous numbers) did not. As with so many agile comedians, advancing age caused his appeal to dwindle. Television kept him busy in the 1950s (most notably as one of the rotating hosts of *The Colgate Comedy Hour*), but a biopic, *The Eddie Cantor Story* (starring Keefe Brasselle and featuring Cantor himself in an epilogue) was a disaster. He wrote four show business memoirs: *My Life Is in Your Hands* (1928), *Take My Life* (1957), *The Way I See It* (1959), and *As I Remember Them* (1964).

Screen: 1926: Kid Boots; 1927: Special Delivery; 1929: Glorifying the American Girl; 1930: Whoopee; 1931: Palmy Days (and co-wr.); 1932: The Kid From Spain; 1933: Roman Scandals; 1934: Kid Millions; 1936: Strike Me Pink; 1937: Ali Baba Goes to Town; 1940: Forty Little Mothers; 1943: Thank Your Lucky Stars; 1944: Hollywood Canteen; Show Business; 1948: If You Knew Susie; 1952: The Story of Will Rogers; 1953: The Eddie Cantor Story.

NY Stage: 1917–19: Ziegfeld Follies; 1920: Broadway Brevities of 1920; 1921: The Midnight Rounders; 1922: Make It Snappy; 1923: Kid Boots; 1927: Ziegfeld Follies of 1927; 1928: Whoopee; 1941: Banjo Eyes.

Select TV: 1950–54: The Colgate Comedy Hour (series); 1955: Eddie Cantor Comedy Theatre (series); 1956: George Has a Birthday (sp); Seidman and Son (sp).

CAPUCINE

(GERMAINE LEFEBVRE) BORN: TOULON, FRANCE, JANUARY 6, 1931. DIED: MARCH 17, 1990.

Given her classical beauty and her icy quality, it is hardly surprising that Capucine began her career as a Paris fashion model. She had made a handful of French film appearances, purely as window dressing, when she decided to pursue her modeling career in New York in the 1950s. There she took on her new "single-name" moniker and studied acting with Gregory Ratoff before producer Charles Feldman brought her to Hollywood. She made her U.S. debut in the troubled 1960 biopic *Song Without End*, playing the princess loved by composer Franz Liszt (Dirk Bogarde). That same year, the better and more popular adventure *North to Alaska*, was released, wherein John Wayne stole her away from intended fiancé Stewart Granger. She was disappointing in the whorehouse drama *Walk on the Wild Side*, as a hooker loved by her madam, Barbara Stanwyck (both actresses were, in fact, lesbians), but she was quite funny as Peter Sellers's cheating wife in the comedy sensation *The Pink Panther*. She steamed up two jungle films with William Holden, *The Lion* and *The 7th Dawn*, before rejoining Sellers in *What's New, Pussycat?* Her calm demeanor in the last was a relief from all the mugging, and her character was named — for those in the know — Miss Lefebvre. She then joined the ensemble of the decidedly dry *The Honey Pot*, as one of Rex Harrison's former mistresses. It was her last major American production. By the end of the 1960s her star was in decline. She later appeared in little-seen international productions, including two misguided *Pink Panther* movies made *after* the death of co-star Peter Sellers. Suffering from depression and lacking work, she committed suicide in 1990, throwing herself from the window of her eighth-floor apartment in Lausanne, Switzerland.

Screen (US releases only): 1960: Song Without End; North to Alaska; 1962: Walk on the Wild Side; The Lion; 1964: The Pink Panther; The Seventh Dawn; 1965: What's New, Pussycat?; 1967: The Honey Pot; 1968: The Queens; 1969: Fraulein Doktor; 1970: Fellini Satyricon; 1972: Red Sun; 1973: Exquisite Cadaver; 1979: Nest of Vipers; Jaguar Lives!; Arabian Adventure; 1980: Incorrigible; 1981: The Con

Artists; 1982: Trail of the Pink Panther; 1983: Curse of the Pink Panther.

CLAUDIA CARDINALE

BORN: TUNIS, TUNISIA, NORTH AFRICA, APRIL 15, 1939. RAISED IN ITALY.

With her alluring eyes and husky voice, Claudia Cardinale was one of the more desirable European imports of the 1960s, and her hesitation with the English language only made her that much more appealing. After winning a beauty contest while still a teen, she decided to study acting and was soon seen in Italian films, including the international success *Big Deal on Madonna Street*. Stardom came by way of two acclaimed Luchino Visconti epics, *Rocco and His Brothers* and *The Leopard*. She also had a starring role in *Girl With a Suitcase*, as an enigmatic woman in love with her ex-lover's younger brother, and was among the many women in the supporting cast of one of Federico Fellini's most talked-about puzzles, *8 1/2*. American films now beckoned her and she appeared in two of 1964's major releases: *The Pink Panther*, as the princess who owns the title diamond, and *Circus World*, as Rita Hayworth's aerialist daughter. There was a supporting role, as George Segal's sister, in the Algerian war drama *Lost Command*, plus leading lady duties in the Gregory Peck thriller *Blindfold*, and the Tony Curtis beach comedy *Don't Make Waves*. Perhaps her best U.S. work was in the 1966 western *The Professionals*, as Ralph Bellamy's kidnapped wife who prefers the company of bandit Jack Palance. Returning to foreign shores, she made a notable appearance in Werner Herzog's *Fitzcarraldo*, confounding the skeptics and still looking quite beautiful. However, many of her efforts did not f i n d their way to the U.S., including *Claretta*, for which she won a Best Actress prize at the Venice Film Festival. She was one of several cast members from the original film who showed up in the posthumous Sellers sequel, *Son of the Pink Panther*.

Screen (US releases only): 1960: Big Deal on Madonna Street (It: 1958); 1961: Upstairs and Downstairs; Rocco and His Brothers; Girl With a Suitcase; 1962: La Viaccia/The Lovemakers; Bell'Antonio (It: 1960); 1963: 8 1/2; The Leopard; 1964: The Pink Panther; Cartouche; Bebo's Girl; Circus World; 1965: The Magnificent Cuckold; 1966: Time of Indifference; Sandra; Lost Command; Blindfold; The Professionals; 1967: Don't Make Waves; A Rose for Everyone; 1968: The Queens; The Hell With Heroes; 1969: Once Upon a Time in the West; A Fine Pair; 1970: Mafia; 1971: The Red Tent; 1973: The Legend of Frenchie King; Diary of a Telephone Operator; 1974: Popsy Pop/The Butterfly Affair; 1976: Conversation Piece; Midnight Pleasures; 1979: Escape to Athena; 1980: The Immortal Bachelor; 1982: Careless/Senilita; Fitzcarraldo; Burden of Dreams; 1983: The Gift; The Salamander; 1985: Henry IV; 1986: Next Summer; 1987: A Man in Love; 1988: Traffic Jam (filmed 1979); History; 1993: Son of the Pink Panther; 1999: My Best Fiend.

Select TV: 1977: Jesus of Nazareth (ms); 1983: Princess Daisy (ms); 1997: Nostromo (ms).

HARRY CAREY

BORN: BRONX, NY, JANUARY 16, 1878.
DIED: SEPTEMBER 21, 1947.

Though he is most often thought of as the dour, craggy-faced character actor of the 1930s and 1940s, Harry Carey was one of the biggest western stars of the silent era, with a movie history dating back to 1910. The son of a lawyer, Carey was also heading in that direction until the lure of acting proved too strong. He wrote his own starring stage vehicle, *Montana*, which he performed across the country in 1904. Back in his hometown of the Bronx, he joined D.W. Griffith's Biograph company, appearing in more than 100 two-reelers between 1910 and 1917. Moving over to Universal Studios, he joined forces with young director John Ford and his popularity steadily increased with such feature-length entries as *The Secret Man*, *A Marked Man*, *Straight Shooting* (as a character called Cheyenne Harry), *Phantom Riders*, and *Riders of Vengeance*. In perhaps his best-known film, *The Outcasts of Poker Flats*, he played both the gambling hall proprietor in love with Gloria Hope, and the fictional protagonist of Bret Harte's book who inspires him. By the end of the silent era he had begun drifting into smaller parts before he took a brief leave of absence.

Carey returned to films playing the title role in MGM's hit jungle epic, *Trader Horn*, which drew attention for actually having been filmed on location in Africa. He took leads for poverty row companies like Artclass, Mascot, and Ajax, and earned favorable mention for his variation on Doc Holliday in Universal's *Law and Order*, and as the comical old bandit who must face the modern world after a 25-year stretch in the pen in *The Last Outlaw*. He stayed busy as a character player in westerns such as *The Law West of Tombstone*, as an enigmatic lawman, with more than a passing resemblance to the legendary Judge Roy Bean; *The Shepherd of the Hills*, as a mysterious healer set on curing the inhabitants of an Ozark community; and *Angel and the Badman*, as the sheriff who takes an interest in John Wayne's life of crime. Off the prairie, he was in *The Prisoner of Shark Island* (his last for John Ford), as the commandant of a military prison; *You and Me*, as the department store owner who hires ex-cons Sylvia Sidney and George Raft; and *King of Alcatraz*, as the heroic freighter captain who guns down gangster J. Carroll Naish. He received an Oscar nomination for Frank Capra's *Mr. Smith Goes to Washington*, for his performance as the amused president of the senate. One of his last films, *Red River*, also featured his son, Harry Carey, Jr., who continued the family tradition by appearing mainly in westerns. A year after Carey Sr.'s death, Ford fittingly dedicated his film *3 Godfathers* to him, it being a remake of one of their earlier collaborations, *Marked Men*. Carey's second wife, with whom he had sometimes co-starred, was actress Olive Golden.

Screen (features): 1914: Judith of Bethulia; 1915: Judge Not, or The Woman of Mona Diggins; Just Jim; 1916: The Three Godfathers; Behind the Lines; A Knight of the Range; 1917: Hair-Trigger Burke; The Honor of an Outlaw; A 44-Caliber Mystery; The Golden Bullet; The Wrong Man; Six-Shooter Justice; The Soul Herder; The Almost Good Man; Red Saunders Plays Cupid; Beloved Jim; Two Guns; The Fighting Gringo; The Secret Man; Straight Shooting; A Marked Man; Bucking Broadway; 1918: Wild Women; Three Mounted Men; Thieves' Gold; Hell Bent; A Regular Fellow; Fighting Through; God's Outlaw; The Mayor of Filbert; The Scarlet Drop; The Phantom Riders; A Woman's Fool; 1919: Roped; Blind Husbands; Bare Fists; Riders of Vengeance; The Outcasts of Poker Flat; A Fight

for Love; Ace of the Saddle; A Gun Fightin' Gentleman; Rider of the Law; Marked Men; Sure Shot Morgan; The Fighting Brothers; By Indiana Post; The Rustlers; Gun Law; The Gun Packer; The Last Outlaw; 1920: Overland Red; West Is West; Sundown Slim; Hitchin' Posts; Human Stuff (and wr.); Bullet Proof; Blue Streak McCoy; 1921: If Only Jim; The Freeze Out; The Wallop; Hearts Up; Desperate Trails; The Fox; 1922: Man to Man; Canyon of the Fools; The Kickback; Good Men and True; 1923: Crashin' Thru; Desert Driven; The Night Hawk; The Miracle Baby; 1924: The Man From Texas; Roaring Rails; Tiger Thompson; The Lightning Rider; Flaming Forties; 1925: Beyond the Border; Soft Shoes; The Texas Trail; The Man From Red Gulch; The Prairie Pirate; The Bad Lands; Wanderer; Silent Sanderson; 1926: Driftin' Thru; Satan Town; The Frontier Trail; The Seventh Bandit; 1927: Johnny Cut Your Hair; Slide, Kelly, Slide; A Little Journey; 1928: The Trail of '98; Border Patrol; Burning Brides; 1931: Trader Horn; Bad Company; The Vanishing Legion (serial); Cavalier of the West; 1932: Border Devils; Without Honor; Law and Order; Last of the Mohicans (serial); The Devil Horse (serial); Night Rider; 1933: Man of the Forest; Sunset Pass; Thundering Herd; 1935: Rustler's Paradise; Powdersmoke Range; Barbary Coast; Wagon Trail; Wild Mustang; Last of the Clintons; 1936: Sutter's Gold; The Last Outlaw; The Accusing Finger; Valiant Is the Word for Carrie; The Prisoner of Shark Island; Little Miss Nobody; Aces Wild; Ghost Town; 1937: Racing Lady; Born Reckless; Kid Galahad; Souls at Sea; Border Cafe; Annapolis Salute; Danger Patrol; 1938: The Port of Missing Girls; You and Me; The Law West of Tombstone; Gateway; Sky Giant; King of Alcatraz; 1939: Burn 'em Up O'Connor; Street of Missing Men; Inside Information; Code of the Streets; Mr. Smith Goes to Washington; My Son Is Guilty; 1940: Outside the 3-Mile Limit; Beyond Tomorrow; They Knew What They Wanted; 1941: Among the Living; The Shepherd of the Hills; Sundown; Parachute Battalion; 1942: The Spoilers; 1943: Happy Land; Air Force; 1944: The Great Moment; 1945: China's Little Devils; 1946: Duel in the Sun; 1947: Angel and the Badman; The Sea of Grass; 1948: Red River; So Dear to My Heart.

NY Stage: 1940: Heavenly Express; 1941: Ah, Wilderness!; 1944: But Not Goodbye. ____

MACDONALD CAREY

(EDWARD MACDONALD CAREY)
BORN: SIOUX CITY, IA, MARCH 15, 1913.
ED: UNIV. OF IA. DIED: MARCH 21, 1994.

It is not uncommon for film stars to make their start in soap operas, but Macdonald Carey reversed the trend by surrendering his waning movie career for success on a daytime serial. He had started out singing in operettas before joining a company of would-be Shakespearean thespians calling themselves the Globe Players. He became a radio actor, first in Chicago and then New York, where he won a role in the 1941 Broadway hit *Lady in the Dark*. As a result, he was signed by Paramount, where he became one of their less colorful performers of the 1940s. They launched him with *Dr. Broadway*, as a Times Square physician, and then gave him the secondary role of a millionaire in a Rosalind Russell comedy, *Take a Letter, Darling*. He was featured in one of the studio's wartime ensembles, *Wake Island*, before going over to Universal for his best film, Alfred Hitchcock's *Shadow of a Doubt*, as one of the detectives on the trail of killer Joseph Cotten. During World War II he performed his military duty before returning to his home lot in 1945, but there was little reason to rejoice. His work in movies like the misguided *Dream Girl*; the notorious flop *Bride of Vengeance*, as Cesare Borgia; *Streets of Laredo*, as a grinning bad guy; and *The Great Gatsby*, as Nick Carraway, ranged from uninspired to barely adequate. He was soon relegated to second features, including Paramount's examination of racial discrimination towards Mexican-American fruit pickers, *The Lawless*, which became his own personal favorite of his films. As a character player he was Patrick Henry in the historical epic *John Paul Jones*, and Brandon de Wilde's distant dad in the noted teen-pregnancy drama, *Blue Denim*. In 1965 he signed on to play kindly Dr. Tom Horton on the daytime soap *Days of Our Lives*, where he achieved his greatest fame and won a pair of Emmy Awards. He stayed with the show until his death in 1994.

Screen: 1942: Dr. Broadway; Take a Letter, Darling; Wake Island; Star Spangled Rhythm; 1943: Shadow of a Doubt; Salute for Three; 1947: Suddenly It's Spring; Variety Girl; 1948: Hazard; Dream Girl; 1949: Streets of Laredo; Bride of Vengeance; The Great Gatsby; Song of Surrender; 1950: South Sea Sinner; Comanche Territory; The Lawless; Copper Canyon; Mystery Submarine; The Great Missouri Raid; 1951: Excuse My Dust; Meet Me After the Show; Cave of Outlaws; Let's Make It Legal; 1952: My Wife's Best Friend; 1953: Count the Hours; Outlaw Territory/Hannah Lee; 1954: Fire Over Africa/Malaga; 1956: Stranger at My Door; Odongo; 1958: Man or Gun; 1959: Blue Denim; John Paul Jones; 1962: Stranglehold; The Devil's Agent; These Are the Damned/The Damned; 1963: Tammy and the Doctor; 1966: The Redeemer (voice); 1977: End of the World/Foes; 1980: American Gigolo; 1984: Access Code (dtv); 1987: It's Alive III: Island of the Alive.

NY Stage: 1941: Lady in the Dark; 1954: Anniversary Waltz.

Select TV: 1952: Yellow Jack (sp); Edge of the Law (sp); 1953: The Sermon of the Gun (sp); The Inn of the Eagles (sp); Hired Mother (sp); 1955: Where You Love Me (sp); 1956: Cry Justice (sp); Times Like These (sp); Miracle on 34th Street (sp); Moments of Courage (sp); Easter Gift (sp); The Kill (sp); Dr. Christian (series); 1957: Broken Barrier (sp); 1958: The Lonely Stage (sp); Natchez (sp); False Impression (sp); 1959–61: Lock Up (series); 1961: Tangle of Truth (sp); 1965–94: Days of Our Lives (series); 1972: Gidget Gets Married; 1973: Ordeal; 1975: Who Is the Black Dahlia?; 1977: Roots (ms); 1978: Stranger in Our House; 1979: The Rebels; 1980: The Top of the Hill; The Girl, the Gold Watch and Everything; Condominium; 1992: A Message From Holly.

TIMOTHY CAREY

BORN: BROOKLYN, NY, MARCH 11, 1929.
DIED: MAY 11, 1994.

A fearful-looking, deep-voiced character player, Timothy Carey started out in small parts before he gained notoriety with his work in two Stanley Kubrick films. In *The Killing*, he was a chilling creep who shoots a racehorse during the big robbery, while in *Paths of Glory* he was positively heartbreaking as the soldier who wails and sobs while marching to his execution. He appeared as an illiterate Cajun bully who has lustful designs on a teenage girl in *Bayou*, which was later resold under the name *Poor White Trash*, in 1961. The movie became a drive-in classic, and Carey's bizarre, uninhibited contribution to the film is usually cited as the main reason for its continuing cult attraction. His singularly weird, edgy performances added an element of surprise to films like *One-Eyed Jacks*, where he tried to shoot Marlon Brando in the back, and *The Mermaids of Tiburon*,

a movie that had some nudie footage added to spice up its appeal. In the 1960s, Carey wrote, produced, and directed his own barely-seen vehicle *The World's Greatest Sinner*, as a salesman-turned-rock 'n' roll evangelist, and continued to appear in mostly off-beat entertainments like *Head*, terrorizing the Monkees; *Chesty Anderson USN*, as a wacko villain; *The Killing of a Chinese Bookie*, as one of gangster Morgan Woodward's henchmen; and *Echo Park*, as the proprietor of a greasy spoon. On television he appeared as a preacher in the mini-series version of *East of Eden*, having shown up as a bouncer in the original film. He has also been billed as Timothy Agoglia Carey.

Screen: 1951: Ace in the Hole; 1952: Hellgate; Bloodhounds of Broadway; 1953: White Witch Doctor; The Wild One; Crime Wave; 1954: Alaska Seas; 1955: East of Eden; Finger Man; I'll Cry Tomorrow; 1956: Francis in the Haunted House; The Naked Gun; The Last Wagon; The Killing; Flight to Hong Kong; Rumble on the Docks; 1957: Chain of Evidence; Paths of Glory; Bayou/Poor White Trash; 1958: Revolt in the Big House; Unwed Mother; 1959: Gunfight at Dodge City; 1960: The Boy and the Pirates; 1961: The Second Time Around; One-Eyed Jacks; 1962: Convicts 4; The Mermaids of Tiburon/The Aqua Sex; The World's Greatest Sinner (and dir.; wr.; prod.); 1964: Shock Treatment; Bikini Beach; Rio Conchos; 1965: Beach Blanket Bingo; 1967: A Time for Killing; Waterhole # 3; 1968: Head; 1969: Change of Habit; 1971: What's the Matter With Helen?; Minnie and Moskowitz; 1972: Get to Know Your Rabbit; 1973: The Outfit; 1975: Peeper; 1976: Chesty Anderson USN; The Killing of a Chinese Bookie; 1977: Speedtrap; 1982: Fast-Walking; 1983: D.C. Cab; 1986: Echo Park.

Select TV: 1971: Ransom for a Dead Man; 1973: The Bait; 1980: Nightshade; 1981: John Steinbeck's East of Eden (ms).

KITTY CARLISLE

(CATHERINE CONN) BORN: NEW ORLEANS, LA, SEPTEMBER 3, 1910. ED: RADA.

A trained opera singer, Kitty Carlisle came to the movies after performing in the Broadway shows *Rio Rita* and *Champagne Sec*. She appeared in three films for Paramount in 1934: *Murder at the Vanities*, as the leading lady whose life is in constant danger (the movie introduced "Cocktails for Two" but is better remembered for Duke Ellington's risqué "Marihuana"); *She Loves Me Not*, successfully vying for Bing Crosby's affections with Miriam Hopkins; and *Here Is My Heart*, as an exiled princess whom Crosby woos in order to obtain a valuable pistol (!). She co-starred with the Marx Brothers in one of their classic MGM comedies, *A Night at the Opera*, as the diva whose ambitions they help fulfill. Ironically, in light of the fondness with which she is remembered for her role, this movie essentially heralded the end of her screen career. Returning to the stage, her professional life soon took a back seat to being the wife of director-writer Moss Hart. (She was later billed as Kitty Carlisle Hart). In later years she became better known as a game show panelist on *To Tell the Truth*, and was chairman of the New York State Council on the Arts. Her reputation as a Manhattan socialite led to her final film appearance, basically playing herself, in *Six Degrees of Separation*.

Screen: 1934: Murder at the Vanities; She Loves Me Not; Here Is My Heart; 1935: A Night at the Opera; 1943: Larceny With Music; Hollywood Canteen; 1987: Radio Days; 1993: Six Degrees of Separation.

NY Stage: 1932: Rio Rita; 1933: Champagne Sec; 1936: White Horse Inn; 1937: Three Waltzes; 1940: Walk With Music; 1948: The Rape of Lucretia; 1954: Anniversary Waltz; 1956: Kiss Me

Kate; **1983:** On Your Toes.

Select TV: 1952–53: I've Got a Secret (series); **1954:** What's Going On? (series); **1956:** Holiday (sp); **1956–67; 1969–77:** To Tell the Truth (series).

RICHARD CARLSON
Born: Albert Lea, MN, April 29, 1912.
ed: Univ. of MN. Died: November 25, 1977.

A pleasant looking actor with the personality of an average schoolteacher (which, in fact, he had been), Richard Carlson came to Hollywood when David O. Selznick hired him as a writer. The producer changed his mind when he thought Carlson's acceptable looks and previous stage experience might serve him better in front of the camera. There followed some juvenile roles in comedies like *The Young in Heart*, as Janet Gaynor's poverty-stricken suitor; *The Ghost Breakers*, playing it straight to a fidgety Bob Hope in a haunted castle; and *Hold That Ghost*, doing much the same in support of Abbott and Costello. In a more dramatic context he played a young Thomas Jefferson in Columbia's Revolutionary War flop, *The Howards of Virginia*; and the fiancé Margaret Sullavan twice rejects in *Back Street*; while Goldwyn hired him for *The Little Foxes*, as Theresa Wright's intrusive love interest, a character that had not even appeared in the original play. During the 1940s he was a "B" picture lead of little distinction, a position he returned to following military service. He had his biggest success with the 1950 production of *King Solomon's Mines*, trekking fearlessly through the jungles with Stewart Granger and Deborah Kerr. Three sci-fi features, all in 3-D, followed: *It Came From Outer Space*, as an astronomer trying to save his small town from replicating aliens; *The Maze*, inheriting a possessed Scottish castle; and, most famously, *The Creature From the Black Lagoon*, rescuing Julie Adams from the Gill-Man. He directed himself in the dated space travel drama, *Riders to the Stars*, and the "B" western *Kid Rodelo*, but stayed exclusively behind the cameras for *Four Guns to the Border* (1954), *Appointment With a Shadow* (1958), and *The Saga of Hemp Brown* (1958).

Screen: 1938: The Young in Heart; The Duke of West Point; **1939:** Little Accident; Dancing Co-Ed; These Glamour Girls; Winter Carnival; **1940:** Beyond Tomorrow; Too Many Girls; The Ghost Breakers; No, No, Nanette; The Howards of Virginia; **1941:** West Point Widow; The Little Foxes; Back Street; Hold That Ghost; **1942:** My Heart Belong to Daddy; Highways by Night; White Cargo; Fly-by-Night/Secrets of G32; The Affairs of Martha; **1943:** Presenting Lily Mars; Young Ideas; A Stranger in Town; The Man From Down Under; **1947:** So Well Remembered; **1948:** The Amazing Mr. X/The Spiritualist; Behind Locked Doors; **1950:** Try and Get Me/The Sound of Fury; King Solomon's Mines; **1951:** The Blue Veil; Valentino; A Millionaire for Christy; **1952:** Whispering Smith vs. Scotland Yard/Whispering Smith Hits London; The Rose Bowl Story (narrator); Retreat, Hell!; **1953:** Magnetic Monster; The Maze; Flat Top; All I Desire; Seminole; It Came From Outer Space; **1954:** Riders to the Stars (and dir.); The Creature From the Black Lagoon; **1955:** The Last Command; Bengazi; An Annapolis Story; **1956:** Three for Jamie Dawn; **1957:** The Helen Morgan Story; **1960:** Tormented; **1966:** Kid Rodelo (and dir.); **1968:** The Power; **1969:** The Valley of Gwangi; Change of Habit.

NY Stage: 1937: Now You've Done It; The Ghost of Yankee Doodle; **1938:** Whiteoaks; **1939:** Stars in Your Eyes.

Select TV: 1950: The Canton Story (sp); The Road to Jericho (sp); **1951:** One Sunday Afternoon (sp); **1952:** Captain-General of the Armies (sp); The Playwright (sp); **1953:** Adventure in Connecticut (sp); Pursuit (sp); **1953–58:** I Led Three Lives (series); **1954:** All Dressed in White (sp); Hemmed In (sp); The Philadelphia Story (sp); **1955:** Haunted (sp); **1956:** The Billy Mitchell Court-Martial (sp); The Night They Won the Oscar (sp); **1958:** The Other Place (sp); **1958–59:** Mackenzie's Raiders (series); **1966:** The Doomsday Flight.

HOAGY CARMICHAEL
(Hoaglund Howard Carmichael)
Born: Bloomington, IN, November 22, 1899.
ed: Indiana Univ. Died: December 27, 1981.

Pianist, singer and songwriter, Hoagy Carmichael won the favor of the world with such compositions as "Georgia on My Mind," "The Nearness of You," and one of the most beloved songs of them all, "Star Dust." He then surprised everyone with his capable talents as a supporting actor. Carmichael had first appeared, fleetingly as himself, playing the piano and singing his own composition, "Old Man Moon," in *Topper*, with Joan Bennett and Cary Grant. Seven years later, the former lawyer-turned-bandleader was asked to portray the piano-playing Cricket in *To Have and Have Not* — hardly a stretch — but his presence was ingratiating enough that he repeated the performance (with variations) in other films. As the small-town saloon pianist in the Oscar-winning *The Best Years of Our Lives*, he dueted memorably at the keyboard with double amputee Harold Russell, and considerably brightened up the otherwise dreary western *Canyon Passage*, singing his own Oscar-nominated composition, "Ole Buttermilk Sky," on muleback. He vocalized on a Christmas song in the drama *Johnny Holiday*, filmed on location at the Indiana Boys' School in his home state, and he salvaged a Republic western, *Timberjack*, by singing a number he'd written with Johnny Mercer, "He's Dead But He Won't Lie Down." As a composer, his songs were heard in such films as *Sing, You Sinners*, *Mr. Bug Goes to Town*, and *Here Comes the Groom*, which won him an Oscar for the hit "In the Cool, Cool, Cool of the Evening" in 1951.

Screen: 1937: Topper (and songwr.); **1944:** To Have and Have Not (and songwr.); **1945:** Johnny Angel (and songwr.); **1946:** Canyon Passage (and songwr.); The Best Years of Our Lives; **1947:** Night Song (and songwr.); **1950:** Johnny Holiday; Young Man With a Horn; **1952:** Belles on Their Toes; The Las Vegas Story (and songwr.); **1955:** Timberjack (and songwr.).

Select TV: 1952: The Whale on the Beach (sp); **1953:** Saturday Night Revue (series); **1957:** Helen Morgan (sp); **1959–60:** Laramie (series).

IAN CARMICHAEL
Born: Hull, England, June 20, 1920.
ed: RADA.

A good-natured British actor who specialized in bumbling, nervous twits, Ian Carmichael reached his peak of fame in the late 1950s and early 1960s. A comedian, singer and dancer, he performed in revues before and after serving in the army during World War II. His film career was properly launched — after a few false starts — with the 1956 comedy *Simon and Laura*, a film version of the hit West End play, supporting Peter Finch and Kay Kendall, as a harried television producer. Rank gave him his own vehicle, *The Big Money*, but it sat on the shelf for two years, so the Boulting Brothers snatched him up to play the raw recruit in *Private's Progress*, a performance that set the tone for future expectations. A companion follow-up, *Brothers in Law*, set him down in the legal world, and in *Lucky Jim*, he was the university lecturer who butts heads with Terry-Thomas, opposite whom he'd be paired on several occasions. Two movies brought him prominence in the States: *I'm All Right, Jack*, as the innocent interloper who comes between the trade unions and the company bosses; and *School for Scoundrels*, in which he tried to learn the art of one-upmanship to best his rival. After his split with the Boultings his film career trickled down, but on television he was ideally cast as the aristocratic detective Lord Peter Wimsey in several mystery thrillers.

Screen: 1948: Bond Street; 1949: Trottie True/Gay Lady; Dear Mr. Prohack; 1952: Time Gentlemen Please!; Ghost Ship; 1953: Meet Mr. Lucifer; 1954: The Colditz Story; Betrayed; 1955: Simon and Laura; Storm Over the Nile; 1956: Private's Progress; Brothers in Law; The Big Money; 1957: Lucky Jim; Happy Is the Bride; 1959: Left Right and Center; I'm All Right Jack; School for Scoundrels; 1960: Light Up the Sky; 1961: Double Bunk; 1962: The Amorous Prawn; 1963: Heavens Above!; Hide and Seek; 1964: The Case of the 44s; 1967: Smashing Time; 1971: The Magnificent Seven Deadly Sins; 1973: From Beyond the Grave; 1980: The Lady Vanishes; 1991: Dark Obsession/ Diamond Skulls.

NY Stage: 1965: Boeing-Boeing.

Select TV: 1970: Bachelor Father (series); 1972: The Unpleasantness of the Bellona Club (ms); Clouds of Witness (ms); 1973: Murder Must Advertise (ms); 1975: Five Red Herrings (ms); 1995: The Great Kandinsky (sp).

LESLIE CARON

BORN: BOULOGNE-BILLANCOURT, FRANCE, JULY 1, 1931. ED: NATIONAL CONSERVATORY OF DANCE.

Leslie Caron came to Hollywood to be Gene Kelly's dance partner but, unlike many ballet performers before her, she proved that she was also a fine actress. Having studied dance since the age of 10, she eventually joined Roland Petit's Ballets des Champs-Elysses, where Kelly spotted her. She was signed by MGM to be his co-star in the 1951 Oscar-winner *An American in Paris*. The world fell in love with this elfin, enchanting creature who danced to the strains of the Gershwins' "Our Love Is Here to Stay" on the studio-built banks of the Seine. MGM was so impressed that they immediately bowed to her wish to appear in a non-musical, *The Man with a Cloak*, a 19th century melodrama in which she took fourth billing as Louis Calhern's grand-daughter. She followed it with an appearance in the "Mademoiselle" segment of *The Story of Three Loves*, directed by Vincente Minnelli, who had guided her through *An American in Paris*. However, her most popular success was in the semi-musical *Lili*, as the aimless waif who melts the heart of a crippled carnival puppeteer, Mel Ferrer. It was a slight piece, but her portrayal of the naïve girl avoided the cloying stereotypes and earned her an Oscar nomination. MGM took a gamble with her in an adult adaptation of the Cinderella story, told with ballet interludes, *The Glass Slipper*, but it didn't work on any level and ended up a box-office flop.

Fox borrowed her services to appear with Fred Astaire in the update of *Daddy Long Legs*, although they were not the ideal physical match that she and Kelly had been. However, her snappy number at the school dance, "Slue-Foot," was far more fun than her extended ballet fantasy, performed under the guidance of her mentor, Roland Petit. The central character in the 1940 version of

Waterloo Bridge had been a dancer, so MGM decided to cast Caron in the remake, *Gaby*, but it was another failure. She returned to stage work in Europe and appeared in the London production of *Gigi*, a straight play that MGM bought and converted to a musical. Caron was still under contract to the studio and they opted for her over the Broadway Gigi, Audrey Hepburn. Once more under Minnelli's assured hand, the motion picture adaptation of *Gigi*, with songs added by Lerner and Loewe, became the role of Caron's career. (Her vocals were dubbed, however, by Betty Wand). As the Parisian orphan training to be a courtesan she blossomed into womanhood, much to the confusion of smitten Louis Jourdan. The movie was a smash hit, a last hurrah of sophisticated, tastefully opulent entertainment, and won a then-record nine Academy Awards including Best Picture, although neither Caron nor any of the other cast members were even nominated. Disappointment followed with *The Man Who Understood Women*, and her last MGM assignment, *The Subterraneans*, so she opted again for Europe, winning good notices for her role as Dirk Bogarde's wife in the British-made *The Doctor's Dilemma*.

She scored another big hit with *Fanny*, as the pregnant girl who reluctantly marries the much older Maurice Chevalier when her lover Horst Buchholz goes off to sea. (Originally a stage musical, all the songs were dropped for the movie adaptation.) Her status as a respected actress was solidified by more raves and an Oscar nomination for *The L-Shaped Room*, portraying a lonely, pregnant woman who moves into a shabby London boarding house, with great conviction. One last Hollywood triumph, as an uptight schoolteacher, teamed delectably with Cary Grant in the comedy *Father Goose*, helped wash away the bad taste of such tacky farces as *A Very Special Favor* and *Promise Her Anything*. She began to work more in international productions, and her presence in these films often guaranteed them U.S. bookings, proving that she was still an alluring screen presence. Most notably she appeared in Truffaut's *The Man Who Loved Women*, as Charles Denner's ex-lover; the Swiss *Dangerous Moves*, which won the Oscar for Best Foreign Language Film in 1984; Louis Malle's *Damage*, as the astute mother of Juliette Binoche; the intriguingly strange British comedy *Funny Bones*, as the strong-willed parent of a demented young comedian; and the popular fable *Chocolat*, as a widow courted by John Wood. She was married (1956–66) to director-producer Peter Hall, among others.

Screen: 1951: An American in Paris; The Man With a Cloak; 1952: Glory Alley; 1953: The Story of Three Loves; Lili; 1955: The Glass Slipper; Daddy Long Legs; 1956: Gaby; 1958: Gigi; 1959: The Doctor's Dilemma; The Man Who Understood Women; 1960: The Subterraneans; Austerlitz (nUSr); 1961: Fanny; 1962: Guns of Darkness; 1963: Three Fables of Love; The L-Shaped Room; 1964: Father Goose; 1965: A Very Special Favor; 1966: Promise Her Anything; Is Paris Burning?; 1970: Madron; 1972: Chandler; 1973: Head of the Family (It: 1967); 1976: Serail; 1977: The Man Who Understood Women; Valentino; 1979: Goldengirl; 1980: Tous Vedettes (nUSr); 1981: Contract; Chanel Solitaire; 1984: The Unapproachable; Dangerous Moves; 1985: Imperative; 1989: Guerriers et Captives/Warriors and Sinners (nUSr); 1990: Courage Mountain; 1992: Damage; 1995: Funny Bones; 1999: The Reef/Passion's Way (dtv); 2000: Chocolat.

Select TV: 1974: QBVII (ms); 1984: Master of the Game (ms); 1988: Il Trenio di Lenin (sp); The Man Who Lived at the Ritz (ms); 1996: Danielle Steel's The Ring; 1998: Let It Be Me; 2000: The Last of the Blonde Bombshells; 2001: Murder on the Orient Express.

CARLETON CARPENTER
BORN: BENNINGTON, VT, JULY 10, 1926.
ED: NORTHWESTERN UNIV.

Lanky and goofily charming, Carlton Carpenter joined the MGM musical stock company in the early 1950s, following a career as a nightclub magician and Broadway actor. Leading roles in some minor vehicles highlighted his dopey innocence: in *Fearless Fagan*, he was a raw recruit who enlisted in the army with a circus lion in tow; and in *Sky Full of Moon*, he was an "aw-shucks" cowboy in love with worldly-wise Vegas gal Jan Sterling. His best-remembered moment, however, was his lightning-fast duet of "Abba-Dabba Honeymon" with Debbie Reynolds in *Two Weeks With Love*. (The couple had displayed similar camaraderie singing "I Wanna Be Loved By You" in the biopic *Three Little Worlds*, released earlier that year.) After the war movie *Take the High Ground*, MGM let him go and he returned to the stage. He did one last stint in the movie military, in Warners's *Up Periscope*, before quitting films to focus his attention on the theatre. Later, he wrote the music and lyrics for the 1985 Off Broadway show *Northern Boulevard*, and published several gay mystery novels.

Screen: 1949: Lost Boundaries; 1950: Father of the Bride; Three Little Words; Summer Stock; Two Weeks With Love; 1951: Vengeance Valley; The Whistle at Eaton Falls; 1952: Fearless Fagan; Sky Full of Moon; 1953: Take the High Ground; 1959: Up Periscope; 1971: Some of My Best Friends Are…; 1981: The Prowler.

NY Stage: 1944: Bright Boy; Career Angel; 1946: Three to Make Ready; 1947: The Magic Touch; 1953: John Murray Anderson's Almanac; 1957: A Box of Watercolors (ob); Hotel Paradiso; 1962: A Stage Affair (ob); 1966: Hello, Dolly!; 1970: Lyle (ob); The Boys in the Band (ob); 1972: Dylan (ob); 1973: The Greatest Fairy Story Ever Told (ob); 1974: What Is Making Gilda So Gray? or, It Just Depends on Who You Get (ob); 1975: A Good Old-Fashioned Revue (ob); 1979: Miss Stanwyck Is Still in Hiding (ob); 1981: Something for the Boys (ob); 1986: Light Up the Sky (ob); Murder at Rutherford House (ob); 1994: Crazy for You.

Select TV: 1954: Lady in the Dark (sp).

JOHN CARRADINE
(RICHMOND REED CARRADINE)
BORN: NEW YORK, NY, FEBRUARY 5, 1906.
DIED: NOVEMBER 27, 1988.

A strong contender for the busiest actor of all time, John Carradine racked up so many credits in his 58 years on screen that it is almost impossible to document them all. An eccentric, deep-voiced performer, whose gaunt appearance made him look almost cadaverous, Carradine made a living as an artist before making his stage debut in New Orleans, in 1925. He joined a Shakespearean stock company then made his way to Hollywood, where he first acted in bit parts under the name John Peter Richmond. Among the early films in which he can be spotted are *The Invisible Man*, as a villager who utters the immortal line "I've just seen the Invisible Man;" *Clive of India*, as a drunk; and *Les Misérables*, as a young radical. As his roles grew he began to make his mark as a hissable villain, shooting Tyrone Power in the back in *Jesse James* (a role he repeated in the sequel *The Return of Frank James*), and playing sadistic prison guards in two John Ford adventures, *The Prisoner of Shark Island* and *The Hurricane*.

In contrast, the same director made him the victimized Italian secretary of Katharine Hepburn in *Mary of Scotland*. It was Ford who supplied him with two of his most substantial parts: the suave, self-important gambler in *Stagecoach*, and the slightly loopy and ultimately doomed preacher, Casey, in *The Grapes of Wrath*. Carradine was also one of the many actors to portray Abraham Lincoln on screen, in a particularly hokey sequence in *Of Human Hearts*, virtually unrecognizable under tons of makeup. In 1937 he played his favorite screen role, as the super-stitious sailor Long Jack, in the much-loved adaptation of Rudyard Kipling's *Captains Courageous*, starting out as a typical Carradine creep and maturing into a much more humane creature as the film progressed.

During the 1940s he gravitated to poverty row productions like PRC's *Bluebeard*, taking the lead, as a crazed, homicidal puppeteer, and he began to dabble in horror films, including *Voodoo Man*, as Bela Lugosi's idiot henchman; *The Invisible Man's Revenge*, as a scientist assisting the transparent hero; *Captive Wild Women*, turning gorillas into sexy females; and two portrayals of a musta-chioed Count Dracula, in *House of Frankenstein* and *House of Dracula*. His involvement in these productions assured him an honorary place in the horror hall of fame, but too many of his performances in this genre only emphasized the hamminess to which he was prone. In the 1950s he resurfaced in big budget features like *Johnny Guitar*, as Joan Crawford's loyal employee, and *The Ten Commandments*, as Moses's brother, Aaron, both sympa-thetic performances. Aside from an occasional reunion with John Ford (*The Man Who Shot Liberty Valance*, as a pompous orator, and *Cheyenne Autumn*, as a card cheat), Carradine's movies got cheesier as he got older, with titles like *Invasion of the Animal People*, as a geologist trying to save his niece from an alien force; *Hillbillys in a Haunted House*, looking marginally healthier than co-stars Lon Chaney, Jr. and Basil Rathbone; *The Astro Zombies*, manufacturing the title creatures; *Billy the Kid vs. Dracula*, as the Count; *Vampire Hookers*, presiding over a harem of lusty babes; and *Satan's Cheerleaders*, as a crazed vagrant. Most of these dis-played the actor either shamelessly chewing the scenery or clearly disengaged. By the time of his death in 1988, he had been in countless features in which his footage was shot separately to be spliced into already completed projects. In the age of video, his name invariably appears on the box of yet another ignominious effort. At least two film assignments, *The McMasters* and *Boxcar Bertha*, featured his son David. Two of his other sons, Keith and Robert, are also actors.

Screen: 1930: Tol'able David; 1931: Bright Lights; Heaven on Earth; 1932: Forgotten Commandments; The Sign of the Cross; 1933: The Story of Temple Drake; This Day and Age; To the Last Man; The Invisible Man; 1934: The Black Cat; Cleopatra; The Meanest Gal in Town; 1935: Clive of India; Transient Lady; Cardinal Richelieu; Les Misérables; Bride of Frankenstein; Alias Mary Dow; The Crusades; She Gets Her Man; Bad Boy; The Man Who Broke the Bank at Monte Carlo; 1936: Anything Goes; The Prisoner of Shark Island; A Message to Garcia (voice); Captain January; Under Two Flags; White Fang; Mary of Scotland; Ramona; Dimples; Daniel Boone; Garden of Allah; Winterset; Laughing at Trouble; 1937: Nancy Steele Is Missing; Captains Courageous; This Is My Affair; Love Under Fire; Ali Baba Goes to Town; The Hurricane; The Last Gangster; Danger — Love at Work; Thank You, Mr. Moto; 1938: International Settlement; Of Human Hearts; Four Men and a Prayer; Kentucky Moonshine; Kidnapped; I'll Give a Million; Alexander's Ragtime Band; Gateway; Submarine Patrol; 1939: Jesse James; Mr. Moto's Last Warning; The Three Musketeers; Stagecoach; The Hound of the Baskervilles; Captain Fury; Five

Came Back; Frontier Marshal; Drums Along the Mohawk; **1940:** The Grapes of Wrath; The Return of Frank James; Brigham Young — Frontiersman; Chad Hanna; **1941:** Western Union; Blood and Sand; Man-Hunt; Swamp Water; **1942:** Son of Fury; Whispering Ghosts; Northwest Rangers; Reunion in France; **1943:** I Escaped From the Gestapo; Captive Wild Woman; Hitler's Madman; Silver Spurs; Revenge of the Zombies; Isle of Forgotten Sins; Gangway for Tomorrow; **1944:** Waterfront; Voodoo Man; The Black Parachute; The Adventures of Mark Twain; The Invisible Man's Revenge; Return of the Ape Man; The Mummy's Ghost; Barbary Coast Gent; Bluebeard; Alaska; House of Frankenstein; **1945:** It's in the Bag; Captain Kidd; House of Dracula; Fallen Angel; **1946:** Face of Marble; Down Missouri Way; **1947:** The Private Affairs of Bel Ami; **1949:** C-Man; **1954:** Casanova's Big Night; Thunder Pass; Johnny Guitar; The Egyptian; **1955:** Stranger on Horseback; The Kentuckian; Desert Sands; **1956:** Hidden Guns; The Court Jester; The Female Jungle; The Black Sleep; Around the World in Eighty Days; The Ten Commandments; Dark Venture; **1957:** The True Story of Jesse James; The Unearthly; The Story of Mankind; Hell Ship Mutiny; Half Human; **1958:** The Proud Rebel; Showdown at Boot Hill; The Last Hurrah; **1959:** The Cosmic Man; Invisible Invaders; The Oregon Trail; **1960:** The Incredible Petrified World; Tarzan the Magnificent; The Adventures of Huckleberry Finn; Sex Kittens Go to College; **1962:** Invasion of the Animal People; The Man Who Shot Liberty Valance; **1964:** The Patsy; Cheyenne Autumn; Curse of the Stone Hand; **1965:** House of the Black Death; The Wizard of Mars/Horrors of the Red Planet; **1966:** Munster Go Home; Night of the Beast; Billy the Kid vs. Dracula; Broken Sabre; Night Train to Mundo Fine; **1967:** Hillbillys in a Haunted House; Dr. Terror's Gallery of Horrors/Alien Massacre; La Senora Muerte/The Death Woman; The Hostage; **1968:** Pacto Diabolico/Pact With the Devil; They Ran for Their Lives (nUSr); The Astro-Zombies; Autopsy of a Ghost; The Helicopter Spies; Genesis (narrator); **1969:** Blood of Dracula's Castle; The Good Guys and the Bad Guys; The Trouble With Girls; Las Vampiras; **1970:** Cain's Cutthroats/Cain's Way; Hell's Bloody Devils/The Fakers; Blood of the Iron Maiden/Trip to Terror; The McMasters; Myra Breckinridge; Horror of the Blood Monsters/The Flesh Creatures/Vampire Men of the Lost Planet; Five Bloody Graves/The Lonely Man/Gun Raiders; **1971:** Shinbone Alley (voice); The Seven Minutes; **1972:** Boxcar Bertha; Portnoy's Complaint (voice); Blood of Ghastly Horror/Man With the Synthetic Brain; Everything You Always Wanted to Know About Sex But Were Afraid to Ask; Richard; **1973:** Bigfoot; Legacy of Blood; House of Dracula's Daughter (nUSr); The Gatling Gun; Terror in the Wax Museum; Bad Charleston Charlie; Superchick; Hex/The Shrieking; 1000 A.D. (nUSr); Silent Night, Bloody Night; **1974:** The House of Seven Corpses; Moonchild; **1975:** Mary Mary Bloody Mary; **1976:** Won Ton Ton, the Dog Who Saved Hollywood; The Killer Inside Me; The Shootist; The Last Tycoon; Crash; **1977:** The Sentinel; The White Buffalo; Satan's Cheerleaders; Journey Into the Beyond (narrator); Shock Waves/Death Corps; Golden Rendezvous; **1978:** Vampire Hookers/Sensuous Vampires; Sunset Cove; The Bees; The Mouse and His Child (voice); Satan's Mistress/Dark Eyes/Demon Rage; Missile X/Teheran Incident; **1979:** Monster; Nocturna: Granddaughter of Dracula; **1980:** The Boogey Man; The Monster Club; **1981:** The Howling; Dr. Dracula; The Nesting; Frankenstein Island; **1982:** The Secret of NIMH (voice); The Scarecrow/Klynham Summer; The Vals; **1983:** House of the Long Shadows; Boogey Man 2; **1984:** The Ice Pirates; **1985:** Evil of the Night; **1986:** The Tomb; Hollywood Ghost Stories; Revenge; Peggy Sue Got Married; Demented Death Farm Massacre; **1987:**

Monster in the Closet; Evil Spawn/The Alien Within; **1988:** Star Slammer/Prison Ship; **1989:** Buried Alive; **1995:** Jack-O.

NY Stage: **1946:** The Duchess of Malfi; **1947:** Galileo; **1948:** Volpone; The Cup of Trembling; **1949:** The Madwoman of Chaillot; **1962:** A Funny Thing Happened on the Way to the Forum; **1981:** Frankenstein.

Select TV: **1956:** The Rarest Stamp (sp); The House of Seven Gables (sp); **1957:** The Prince and the Pauper (sp); **1969:** Daughter of the Mind; **1970:** Crowhaven Farm; **1972:** Decisions, Decisions (sp); **1973:** The Night Strangler; The Cat Creature; **1975:** Stowaway to the Moon; **1976:** Death at Love House; **1977:** Tail Gunner Joe; Christmas Miracle in Caulfield USA/Christmas Coal Mine Miracle; **1978:** Greatest Heroes of the Bible (ms); **1979:** The Seekers; **1981:** Goliath Awaits.

LEO CARRILLO

BORN: LOS ANGELES, CA, AUGUST 6, 1880. DIED: SEPTEMBER 10, 1961.

A descendant of California's first governor (Leo Carrillo State Park is named after the politician, *not* the actor), Leo Carrillo left the newspaper business to be a stage comedian. After becoming a legit actor, he finally made it to the movies when he was nearing 50. At first he rated leads in melodramas like *The Guilty Generation*, as a gang leader; *Homicide Squad*, as "Big Louie" Grenado; *Obey the Law*, as a good-hearted Italian barber; and *Love Me Forever*, as a dim-witted racketeer in love with opera star Grace Moore. He was, however, more successful as a character player, often used for comic effect whenever someone was needed to mangle the English language. Among the highlights of his characters years were *Viva Villa*, as Wallace Beery's violent henchman, Sierra, who shoots poor Fay Wray; *The Gay Desperado*, as an opera-loving Mexican bandit; *History Is Made at Night*, as Grand Cesare, the chef; and *Too Hot to Handle*, as the assistant to shady newsreel journalist Clark Gable. In 1939 he co-starred with Fox child star Jane Withers in the unappetizingly titled *Chicken Family Wagon*, as a junk dealer who moves to New York. He spent much of the 1940s as part of Universal's stock company, appearing with Abbott and Costello in their debut, *One Night in the Tropics*; on *Horror Island*, where the cast was killed off one by one; in support of Donald O'Connor in *What's Cookin'?*; in two with Olsen and Johnson, *Crazy House* and *The Ghost Catchers*; and some Maria Montez kitsch, *Gypsy Wildcat*. United Artists signed him to play Pancho to Duncan Renaldo's Cisco Kid in a series of "B" westerns, which led to the *Cisco Kid* television series that ran from 1950 to 1956. His last film found him in familiar territory, as the title character in *Pancho Villa Returns*, and he had the dubious distinction of appearing in both *Moonlight and Pretzels* and *Moonlight and Cactus*. The year of his death, 1961, he published a book, *The California I Love*.

Screen: **1928:** The Dove; **1929:** Mr. Antonio; **1931:** Hell Bound; Lasca of the Rio Grande; The Guilty Generation; Homicide Squad; **1932:** The Broken Wing; Girl of the Rio; Deception; Men Are Such Fools; **1933:** Obey the Law; Before Morning; Moonlight and Pretzels; Racetrack; Parachute Jumper; **1934:** Viva Villa; Manhattan Melodrama; The Gay Bride; Four Frightened People; The Band Plays On; **1935:** The Winning Ticket; Love Me Forever; In Caliente; If You Could Only Cook; **1936:** It Had to Happen; Moonlight Murder; The Gay Desperado; **1937:** I Promise to Pay; History Is Made at Night; 52nd Street; Hotel Haywire; The Barrier; Manhattan Merry-Go-Round; **1938:** Girl of the Golden West; Too Hot to Handle; City Streets; Little Miss Roughneck; Flirting With Fate; Blockade; **1939:** Arizona Wildcat;

Fisherman's Wharf; The Girl and the Gambler; Society Lawyer; Chicken Wagon Family; Rio; **1940:** 20 Mule Team; Wyoming; Lillian Russell; Captain Caution; One Night in the Tropics; **1941:** Horror Island; Barnacle Bill; Riders of Death Valley (serial); Tight Shoes; The Kid From Kansas; Honolulu Lu; Road Agent; **1942:** What's Cookin'?; Unseen Enemy; Escape From Hong Kong; Men of Texas; Top Sergeant; Sin Town; Timber; American Empire; Danger in the Pacific; **1943:** Crazy House; Frontier Bad Men; Larceny With Music; Phantom of the Opera; Follow the Band; **1944:** Babes on Swing Street; Bowery to Broadway; The Ghost Catchers; Gypsy Wildcat; Moonlight and Cactus; **1945:** Under Western Skies; Crime Inc.; Mexicana; **1947:** The Fugitive; **1948:** Valiant Hombre; **1949:** The Gay Amigo; Satan's Cradle; The Daring Caballero; **1950:** The Girl From San Lorenzo; Pancho Villa Returns.

NY Stage: 1915: Fads and Fancies; **1916:** Upstairs and Down; **1917:** Lombardi Ltd..; **1923:** Mike Angelo; Magnolia; **1924:** Gypsy Jim; The Saint; **1926:** The Padre.

Select TV: 1950–56: The Cisco Kid (series).

DIAHANN CARROLL

(CAROL DIAHANN JOHNSON) BORN: BRONX, NY, JULY 17, 1935.

Attractive and classy, Diahann Carroll was living proof that 1950s Hollywood wasn't ready to make a black woman into a star, and her undeniable talent was squandered by the industry. Her first taste of show business success came courtesy of television, when she won a week's engagement at New York's Latin Quarter as the amateur talent prize on Dennis James's *Chance of a Lifetime* show. Soon she was singing in nightclubs and on Broadway, in *House of Flowers*, before landing film roles in *both* of Hollywood's big black operettas of the 1950s: *Carmen Jones* and *Porgy and Bess* (her vocals dubbed in both!). She had a good part, as Sidney Poitier's lover, in *Paris Blues* and returned to Broadway to win a Tony Award for the interracial musical *No Strings*. On television, she made her mark as the first black woman — who was not a domestic — to carry a series, *Julia*, in which she was a widowed nurse raising a young son. Her role as a resilient Harlem mother who falls for garbage man James Earl Jones in the gritty drama-comedy *Claudine* won her raves and a well-deserved Oscar nomination, but a lack of follow-up material left her movie career in the doldrums. She continued to sing and do television, including a role on the prime time soap *Dynasty*. Her autobiography, *Diahann*, was published in 1986, three years before her marriage to singer Vic Damone. After a long absence she showed up as a mother in a nostalgic look at a faux musical group, *The Five Heartbeats*, and then as an eccentric voodoo woman in *Eve's Bayou*.

Screen: 1954: Carmen Jones; **1959:** Porgy and Bess; **1961:** Goodbye Again; Paris Blues; **1967:** Hurry Sundown; **1968:** The Split; **1974:** Claudine; **1991:** The Five Heartbeats; **1997:** Eve's Bayou.

NY Stage: 1954: House of Flowers; **1962:** No Strings; **1983:** Agnes of God.

Select TV: 1968–71: Julia (series); **1975:** Death Scream; **1976:** The Diahann Carroll Show (series); **1979:** Roots: The Next Generations (ms); I Know Why the Caged Bird Sings; **1982:** Sister Sister; **1984–87:** Dynasty (series); **1989:** From the Dead of Night; **1990:** Murder in Black and White; **1994:** A Perry Mason Mystery: The Case of the Lethal Lifestyle; Lonesome Dove: The Series (series); **1998:** The Sweetest Gift; **1999:** Having Our Say: The Delany Sisters — The First 100 Years; Jackie's Back!; **2000:**

The Courage to Love; Sally Hemmings: An American Scandal; Livin' for Love: The Natalie Cole Story.

LEO G. CARROLL

BORN: WEEDON, NORTHANTS, ENGLAND, OCTOBER 25, 1891. DIED: OCTOBER 16, 1972.

A cartoonishly serious-looking British character player with an imposing brow, Leo G. Carroll made his name on both the London and New York stages, starting in 1912. For the next 20-some years he racked up credits on both sides of the Atlantic before his 1934 Hollywood debut in MGM's *What Every Woman Knows*, as a senate leader. He continued to work in the theatre while carving out a career in the movies, where he was especially at home in period pieces like *The Barretts of Wimpole Street*, as one of sickly Norma Shearer's doctors; *A Christmas Carol*, physically well-cast as Marley's Ghost; *The Private Lives of Elizabeth and Essex*, as Sir Edward Coke; *Wuthering Heights*, as a servant; and *Tower of London*, as Hastings. Alfred Hitchcock took a shine to Carroll and used him on no fewer than six occasions: *Rebecca*, as a doctor; *Suspicion*, as a police captain; *The Paradine Case*, as a barrister; *Strangers on a Train*, as Ruth Roman's dad; *North by Northwest*, as a professor with the CIA; and, most notably, *Spellbound*, as the shady mental institution director who is replaced by an unstable Gregory Peck. Amid these he could be seen in two Charlie Chan mysteries: *City of Darkness*, as a forger, and *Murder Cruise*, as an archeologist. His hangdog face also graced *Song of Love*, as Katharine Hepburn's overbearing father; *Father of the Bride*, as a pretentious caterer; *The Happy Time*, as a feared schoolmaster, dubbed "The Old Roman;" and *The Bad and the Beautiful*, as a grimly-mannered director, perhaps a backhanded tribute to Hitchcock. Later he had great success on television, appearing in the title role of *Topper*, and the 1960s spy hit *The Man From U.N.C.L.E.* He is fondly remembered by sci-fi aficionados as the scientist who mutates horribly in the cult favorite *Tarantula*.

Screen: 1934: What Every Woman Knows; Sadie McKee; Outcast Lady; Stamboul Quest; The Barretts of Wimpole Street; **1935:** Murder on a Honeymoon; The Right to Live; Clive of India; The Casino Murder Case; **1936:** The Man I Marry; **1937:** London by Night; Captains Courageous; **1938:** A Christmas Carol; **1939:** The Private Lives of Elizabeth and Essex; Wuthering Heights; Bulldog Drummond's Secret Police; Charlie Chan in City in Darkness; Tower of London; **1940:** Waterloo Bridge; Charlie Chan's Murder Cruise; **1941:** Scotland Yard; Bahama Passage; This Woman Is Mine; Suspicion; **1945:** The House on 92nd Street; Spellbound; **1947:** Forever Amber; Time Out of Mind; Song of Love; The Paradine Case; **1948:** Enchantment; So Evil My Love; **1950:** The Happy Years; Father of the Bride; **1951:** The First Legion; Strangers on a Train; The Desert Fox; **1952:** The Snows of Kilimanjaro; The Bad and the Beautiful; Rogue's March; **1953:** Treasure of the Golden Condor; Young Bess; **1955:** We're No Angels; Tarantula; **1956:** The Swan; **1959:** North by Northwest; **1961:** The Parent Trap; One Plus One; **1963:** The Prize; **1965:** That Funny Feeling; **1966:** The Spy With My Face; One of Our Spies Is Missing; One Spy Too Many; **1969:** From Nashville With Music.

NY Stage: 1912: Rutherford and Son; **1913:** Everyman; **1924:** Havoc (and dir.); **1925:** The Vortex; **1926:** The Constant Nymph; **1927:** Speak Easy; Diversion; **1928:** Heavy Traffic; The Perfect Alibi; **1929:** The Novice and the Duke; **1930:** Mrs. Moonlight; **1932:** Too True to Be Good; Troilus and Cressida; **1933:** For Services Rendered; The Mask and the Face; The Green Bay Tree;

1935: Petticoat Fever; 1936: Mainly for Lovers; Prelude to Exile; 1937: The Masque of the Kings; Storm Over Patsy; Love of Women; 1938: Save Me the Waltz; Two Bouquets; 1940: Love for Love; 1941: Anne of England; Angel Street; 1944: The Late George Apley; 1947: Druid Circle; 1948: You Never Can Tell; Jenny Kissed Me; 1951: Mary Rose; Lo and Behold!; 1953: On Borrowed Time; 1956: Someone Waiting.

Select TV: 1953–55: Topper (series); 1958: Angel Street (sp); Bellingham (sp); 1961: Bury Me Twice (sp); 1962: Dead on Nine (sp); 1962–63: Going My Way (series); 1964–68: The Man From U.N.C.L.E. (series); 1966–67: The Girl From U.N.C.L.E. (series); 1967: A Boy Called Nuthin' (sp).

MADELEINE CARROLL

(MARIE-MADELEINE BERNADETTE O'CARROLL)
BORN: WEST BROMWICH, ENGLAND, FEBRUARY 26, 1906. ED: BIRMINGHAM UNIV.
DIED: OCTOBER 2, 1987.

One of the most elegantly beautiful leading ladies of the 1930s, Madeleine Carroll transferred to Hollywood from her native England with reasonable success, though she chose to cut short her career. A brief early period as a hat model led to her London stage debut in 1927, in *The Lash*. The following year she was on screen in *The Guns of Loos* and was suddenly in demand for dramas that didn't see much life outside of England: *The W Plan, French Leave, The School for Scandal, Sleeping Car,* and *I Was a Spy,* among others. It was in a pair of thrillers for Alfred Hitchcock (*The 39 Steps*, as the woman reluctantly handcuffed to Robert Donat, and *Secret Agent,* pretending to be John Gielgud's wife) that she was at her best. These films brought her to Hollywood, where she signed contracts with independent producer Walter Wanger and with 20th Century-Fox. She was ideal for decorating such costume films as *Lloyd's of London,* unhappily married to George Sanders, and *The Prisoner of Zenda,* as Princess Flavia, torn between two Ronald Colmans. She paired off with Gary Cooper in a good adventure, *The General Died at Dawn,* and a pretty bad one, *North West Mounted Police.* Paramount took her on in the late 1930s, where she teamed on four occasions with Fred MacMurray, with *Honeymoon in Bali* the best of the bunch. In another MacMurray vehicle, the tiresome drama *Virginia,* the supporting cast featured Sterling Hayden, who was promoted to Carroll's leading man in *Bahama Passage,* (they married in 1942 and divorced four years later). She ended her stay at Paramount in a bright teaming with Bob Hope, *My Favorite Blonde,* after which she turned her back on films to work for war relief organizations. (She had lost a sister during the London blitz.) There were a few more credits in the late 1940s, including a final fling with MacMurray, in *Don't Trust Your Husband,* but she had lost interest in the business and retired soon afterwards.

Screen: 1928: The Guns of Loos; The First Born; What Money Can Buy; 1929: The Crooked Billet; L'Instinct (nUSr); The American Prisoner; Atlantic; 1930: Young Woodley; The W Plan; Escape; French Leave; The School for Scandal; Madame Guillotine; 1931: Kissing Cup Race; Fascination; The Written Law; 1933: Sleeping Car; I Was a Spy; 1934: The World Moves On; 1935: The Dictator/Loves of a Dictator; The 39 Steps; 1936: Secret Agent; The Case Against Mrs. Ames; The General Died at Dawn; Lloyd's of London; 1937: On the Avenue; The Prisoner of Zenda; It's All Yours; 1938: Blockade; 1939: Cafe Society; Honeymoon in Bali; 1940: My Son, My Son; Safari; North West Mounted Police; 1941: Virginia; One Night in Lisbon; 1942: Bahama Passage; My Favorite Blonde; 1947:

White Cradle Inn; 1948: Don't Trust Your Husband/An Innocent Affair; 1949: The Fan.

NY Stage: 1948: Goodbye, My Fancy.

Select TV: 1950: The Letter (sp); 1951: Women of Intrigue (sp); 1955: The Bitter Choice (sp).

NANCY CARROLL

(ANNA VERONICA LaHIFF) BORN: NEW YORK, NY, NOVEMBER 19, 1904. DIED: AUGUST 6, 1965.

Nancy Carroll was one of the most critically applauded leading ladies at the dawn of the talkies, but her erstwhile popularity is remembered only by her most loyal fans. After years as a chorus girl, the petite redhead signed with Paramount Pictures, and in 1928 garnered attention with the drama *Manhattan Cocktail,* as a Broadway hopeful disillusioned by the wicked city. In the first movie adaptation of that hoariest of stage plays, *Abie's Irish Rose,* she was the title colleen, marrying Jewish Buddy Rogers, and she entered the top realm with the romantic drama *The Shopworn Angel.* Co-starring with Gary Cooper, she played a selfish showgirl who discovers her romantic side when the naïve Cooper falls in love with her. She was equally adept at musicals and appeared with Buddy Rogers again in *Close Harmony,* as a vaudevillian; and *Follow Thru,* an early Technicolor offering, based on a Broadway hit, that gave the era one of its most famous songs, "Button Up Your Overcoat." At the height of her fame, in 1930, she received an Oscar-nomination, playing a gold-digging manicurist whose quest for a wealthy husband is sidetracked by true love, in *The Devil's Holiday.* She had another success with *Laughter,* preferring lover Fredric March to dull husband Frank Morgan, and then a major flop with *The Night Angel,* as the daughter of whorehouse madam Allison Skipworth. Her box-office appeal began to evaporate, notably with a somber anti-war drama, *The Man I Killed,* which was quickly withdrawn and re-titled *Broken Lullaby,* in hopes of attracting a different audience. After leaving Paramount in 1933 she freelanced in supporting roles, playing a reporter in the Deanna Durbin musical *That Certain Age,* and taking fifth billing below former leading man Fredric March in *There Goes My Heart.* She had retired by the end of the 1930s but she returned to the profession for a season on the television series *The Aldrich Family.* The year before she died she could be seen in the Off Broadway play *Cindy.*

Screen: 1927: Ladies Must Dress; 1928: Abie's Irish Rose; Easy Come, Easy Go; Chicken a la King; The Water Hole; Manhattan Cocktail; 1929: The Shopworn Angel; The Wolf of Wall Street; Sin Sister; Close Harmony; The Dance of Life; Illusion; Sweetie; 1930: Dangerous Paradise; Paramount on Parade; Follow Thru; The Devil's Holiday; Honey; Laughter; Two Against Death; 1931: Stolen Heaven; The Night Angel; Personal Maid; 1932: Broken Lullaby/The Man I Killed; Wayward; Scarlet Dawn; Hot Saturday; Under Cover Man; 1933: Child of Manhattan; The Woman Accused; The Kiss Before the Mirror; I Love That Man; 1934: Springtime for Henry; Transatlantic Merry-Go-Round; Jealousy; 1935: I'll Love You Always; After the Dance; Atlantic Adventure; 1938: That Certain Age; There Goes My Heart.

NY Stage: 1923: The Passing Show of 1923; Tropics of 1923; 1924: The Passing Show of 1924; 1925: Mayflowers; 1933: An Undesirable Lady; 1948: For Heaven's Sake Mother; 1964: Cindy (ob).

Select TV: 1950–51: The Aldrich Family (series); 1962: The Love of Claire Ambler (sp); A Man for Oona (sp).

JACK CARSON

BORN: CARMEN, MANITOBA, CANADA,
OCTOBER 27, 1910. RAISED IN MILWAUKEE, WI.
DIED: JANUARY 2, 1963.

Amiable oaf Jack Carson specialized in beefy lugs, by turns overbearing boors or hapless targets of derision. During his heyday at Warner Bros. in the 1940s he was used mainly for comedy, but could show an effective dramatic side when necessary. After moving from Canada to Milwaukee, Wisconsin, he went straight from college to vaudeville, which led, in turn, to radio work. In 1937 he was signed up by RKO Pictures who used him in a string of small roles (26 in 1937–38 alone!), some of which were in standout films like *Stage Door*, as a blind date; *Carefree*, as Dr. Fred Astaire's assistant; and *Bringing Up Baby*, as a roustabout. Working on a freelance basis, he was a reporter in *Mr. Smith Goes to Washington*, and a Wild West windbag in *Destry Rides Again*, until he returned to RKO for third billing, as Ginger Rogers's objectionable fiancé, in *Lucky Partners*. At MGM he tried to woo Myrna Loy away from William Powell in *Love Crazy*, before Warner Bros. signed him on in 1941, as a comedy attraction. His first part there was an unsympathetic one, as the egotistical contractor who wins Rita Hayworth from James Cagney in *The Strawberry Blonde*, but Cagney got revenge with *The Bride Came C.O.D.* by gaining the affections of Bette Davis. Carson perfected his patented blowhard routine as the former football star who can't help but showing off his famous moves to Olivia de Havilland in *The Male Animal*.

Another bright comedy, *Larceny, Inc.*, gave him the first of several teamings with Jane Wyman, which included his first top billing, in a weak 1944 spy picture, *Make Your Own Bed*. More successful was his pairing with the studio's resident singer, Dennis Morgan, also a Milwaukee native. In 1942 they fought over Ann Sheridan in *Wings for the Eagle*, and in *The Hard Way*, they were a pair of vaudevillians, Carson ending up a suicide after wife Joan Leslie abandons him. Carson and Morgan lightened up for several comedy/musicals, including *Two Guys From Milwaukee*; *The Time, the Place and the Girl*; and *Two Guys from Texas*. For *It's a Great Feeling*, the duo played themselves in a tour of the studio backlot, during which Carson good-naturedly kidded himself as a vain ham whom nobody at Warners will work with. On occasion Carson appeared in dramas, playing Joan Crawford's rejected suitor in *Mildred Pierce*, and the publicist whom James Mason antagonizes in *A Star Is Born*, a Warners film made after his contract with them had officially expired. After leaving the studio he took a few more leads in comedy vehicles, like *The Good Humor Man*, which introduced him to his third (1952–58) wife, Lola Albright; the cheesy wrestling farce, *Mr. Universe*, made for Eagle Lion; and the oddball, stylized musical *Red Garters*, winning leading lady Rosemary Clooney at the finale. But it was soon back to support, as the "other man" opposite Judy Holliday in *Phffft*; as a mechanic in *The Tarnished Angels*; and effectively playing Paul Newman's brother in *Cat on a Hot Tin Roof*.

Screen: 1937: You Only Live Once; Too Many Wives; On Again Off Again; The Toast of New York; It Could Happen to You; Reported Missing; Stage Door; Music for Madame; Stand-In; She's Got Everything; Quick Money; High Flyers; **1938:** Crashing Hollywood; Everybody's Doing It; Night Spot; Go Chase Yourself; Law of the Underworld; The Saint in New York; Vivacious Lady; This Marriage Business; Bringing Up Baby; Condemned Women; Maid's Night Out; Having Wonderful Time; Carefree; Mr. Doodle Kicks Off; **1939:** The Kid From Texas; Mr. Smith Goes to Washington; The Escape; Legion of

Lost Flyers; Destry Rides Again; The Honeymoon's Over; **1940:** I Take This Woman; Shooting High; Young As You Feel; Enemy Agent; Parole Fixer; Typhoon; Alias the Deacon; The Girl in 313; Queen of the Mob; Lucky Partners; Sandy Gets Her Man; Love Thy Neighbor; **1941:** Mr. and Mrs. Smith; The Strawberry Blonde; Love Crazy; The Bride Came C.O.D.; Navy Blues; Blues in the Night; **1942:** The Male Animal; Larceny, Inc.; Wings for the Eagle; The Hard Way; Gentleman Jim; **1943:** Thank Your Lucky Stars; Princess O'Rourke; **1944:** Shine On, Harvest Moon; Make Your Own Bed; The Doughgirls; Arsenic and Old Lace; Hollywood Canteen; **1945:** Roughly Speaking; Mildred Pierce; **1946:** One More Tomorrow; Two Guys From Milwaukee; The Time, the Place and the Girl; **1947:** Love and Learn; **1948:** Always Together; April Showers; Two Guys From Texas; Romance on the High Seas; **1949:** John Loves Mary; My Dream Is Yours; It's a Great Feeling; **1950:** Bright Leaf; The Good Humor Man; **1951:** Mr. Universe; The Groom Wore Spurs; **1953:** Dangerous When Wet; **1954:** Red Garters; A Star Is Born; Phffft; **1955:** Ain't Misbehavin'; **1956:** The Bottom of the Bottle; The Magnificent Roughnecks; **1957:** The Tattered Dress; The Tarnished Angels; **1958:** Cat on a Hot Tin Roof; Rally 'Round the Flag, Boys!; **1960:** The Bramble Bush; **1961:** King of the Roaring 20's — The Story of Arnold Rothstein.

NY Stage: 1952: Of Thee I Sing.

Select TV: 1950: Room Service (sp); 1950–52: All Star Revue (series); 1951: No Shoes (sp); 1952: For Heaven's Sake (sp); The U.S. Royal Showcase (series); 1954–55: The Jack Carson Show (series); 1955: The Man in the Corner (sp); The Gambler (sp); The Director (sp); 1957: Three Men on a Horse (sp); Huck Finn (sp); 1958: The Long March (sp); 1961: The Big Splash (sp); 1962: Sammy the Way Out Seal.

JOHN CASSAVETES

BORN: NEW YORK, NY, DECEMBER 9, 1929.
DIED: FEBRUARY 3, 1989.

John Cassavetes's trend-setting work as an audacious director of independent films has often overshadowed his fine contributions as an actor. He was one of the brood of young thespians who cut their teeth on live television in the 1950s and he developed a flair for intense, angst-ridden characters. He established himself in adaptations of three television dramas: *Edge of the City*, based on *A Man Is Ten Feet Tall*, in which Cassavetes was excellent as a dock worker who befriends beleaguered fellow-employee Sidney Poitier; *The Night Holds Terror*, holding Jack Kelly and his family hostage; and *Crime in the Streets*, playing a young hoodlum alongside another future director, Mark Rydell. *Edge of the City* resulted in a contract with MGM but only one movie came out of it, a western called *Saddle the Wind*, in which Cassavetes played Robert Taylor's wastrel brother. He also did a season on a television show, *Johnny Staccato*, as a part-time pianist/private eye. He made his directorial debut with *Shadows*, a gritty, crude, and improvisational effort that flew in the face of standard Hollywood fare, and won him raves upon its art house release in 1961. Suddenly a new career opened up to him and Hollywood gave him two assignments to helm, *Too Late Blues* and *A Child Is Waiting*. The first was an uncompromising depiction of the love between a jazz musician (Bobby Darin) and a singer (Stella Stevens) that unfolded on its own terms. The second was a more accessible, moving drama about mentally retarded children, starring Burt Lancaster and Judy Garland. Both were box-office failures, however, and the studios had second thoughts about him as a force behind the camera, so he returned to acting.

He managed to pick two very lucrative properties: First, he earned an Oscar nomination for Best Supporting Actor as a member of *The Dirty Dozen*, one of the most successful war movies of all time; then, he did his most notable acting work, as Mia Farrow's deceitful husband, in the disturbing and brilliant witchcraft film, *Rosemary's Baby*. The same year of its release, 1968, he had a directorial breakthrough with *Faces*, which examined a marriage in crisis and featured his real-life wife Gena Rowlands (they married in 1954 and remained wed until Cassavetes's death). The movie had a raw, riveting intensity but already exposed the weaknesses that marred so much of his work: self-indulgence and an elongated running time that detracted from the work's overall impact. His original screenplay for *Faces* won him an Oscar nomination, and from this point on (with one exception) he would write all of the movies he directed. In 1970, directing himself, along with real-life friends Ben Gazzara and Peter Falk, he had his biggest commercial success with the maddening *Husbands*, about three friends who go on a binge after the premature death of a buddy. The following year he helmed a mildly popular comedy, *Minnie and Moskowitz*, about an unconventional love affair between Gena Rowlands and hippie Seymour Cassel. (Cassavetes appeared uncredited as Rowlands's loutish married lover.) He received his sole directorial Oscar nomination, in 1974, for *A Woman Under the Influence*, but by now only the faithful were enjoying his work. Films like *The Killing of a Chinese Bookie* and *Gloria* (again, with Rowland) lacked focus and a compelling sense of narrative, and only served to antagonize the audience. To finance his own filmmaking he acted in second-rate fare like *Capone*, supporting Ben Gazzara in the title role, and the sniper thriller *Two Minute Warning*.

Some of his better roles for other filmmakers were as a mobster in Elaine May's *Mikey and Nicky*, a movie that divided audiences as much as one of Cassavetes's works; as Richard Dreyfuss's no-nonsense doctor in John Badham's *Whose Life Is It Anyway?*; and as an architect suffering a mid-life crisis in Paul Mazursky's curious updating of the Shakespeare tale, *Tempest*. His career hit a humiliating low in a commercial horror movie, *The Fury*, as the villain trying to manipulate a pair of telekinetic teens, and graphically getting blown to pieces for the finale. His last directorial effort, *Big Trouble*, was intended as a follow-up to the Peter Falk and Alan Arkin hit, *The In-Laws*, but the end result pleased neither the commercial audience nor the Cassavetes cult. His marriage to Rowlands produced a son, Nick Cassavetes, who also became an actor-director. He followed in his dad's footsteps by directing Rowlands in the 1996 release, *Unhook the Stars*, and dusted off one of the old man's un-filmed screenplays, *She's So Lovely*, in 1997. As with so much of his father's work, these films provoked a euphoric response from a few select admirers while sending the ticket-buying customers scurrying away.

Screen: 1953: Taxi; 1955: The Night Holds Terror; 1956: Crime in the Streets; 1957: Edge of the City; Affair in Havana; 1958: Saddle the Wind; 1960: Virgin Island; 1961: Shadows (and dir.; wr.); 1962: The Webster Boy (nUSr); 1964: The Killers; 1967: Devil's Angels; The Dirty Dozen; 1968: Rosemary's Baby; 1969: Bandits in Rome (nUSr); If It's Tuesday, This Must Be Belgium; 1970: Machine Gun McCain (filmed 1968); Husbands (and dir.; wr.); 1971: Minnie and Moskowitz (and dir.; wr.); 1975: Capone; 1976: Two Minute Warning; Mikey and Nicky; 1978: The Fury; Brass Target; 1979: Opening Night (and dir.; wr.); 1981: Whose Life Is It Anyway?; 1982: The Incubus; Tempest; 1984: Marvin and Tige; Love Streams (and dir.; wr.).

NY Stage: 1953: The Fifth Season.

Select TV: 1955: Ladder of Lies (sp); Crime in the Street (sp);

Time for Love (sp); A Room in Paris (sp); The Expendable House (sp); 1956: Bring Me a Dream (sp); The Last Patriarch (sp); 1957: Winter Dreams (sp); 1958: Kurishiki Incident (sp); The First Star (sp); 1959: Train for Tecumseh (sp); The Dreamer (sp); 1959–60: Staccato/Johnny Staccato (series); 1965: The Fliers (sp); 1967: Free of Charge (sp); 1979: Flesh and Blood.

JOAN CAULFIELD

(BEATRICE JOAN CAULFIELD) BORN: ORANGE, NJ, JUNE 1, 1922. ED: COLUMBIA UNIV. DIED: JUNE 18, 1991.

Wholesome, pretty, and blonde, Joan Caulfield was one of Paramount's pleasant-but-uninspired stars of the late 1940s. As a client of the Harry Conover Modeling Agency during World War II, she did a cover of *Life* magazine that brought her to the attention of director George Abbott, who cast her in the stage musical *Beat the Band* in 1942. She rated the lead in her follow-up show, *Kiss and Tell*, and won a contract with Paramount Pictures, where she debuted as a boarding-house maid in love with Sunny Tufts in a lukewarm comedy, *Miss Susie Slagle's*. Her fortunes improved when she co-starred with Bing Crosby and Fred Astaire in the big hit musical *Blues Skies*, dancing briefly with the latter and singing one song, "Serenade to an Old-Fashioned Girl." She was, however, not only upstaged by the leading men but by the other female lead, the more flamboyant Olga San Juan. Caulfield was a nimble partner for Bob Hope in the colorful period comedy, *Monsieur Beaucaire*, and then had her best role in the bright comedy *Dear Ruth*. The story of a woman, whose sister conducts a romantic correspondence in her name with soldier William Holden, it spawned a sequel, *Dear Wife*, in which Caulfield also appeared. In 1950 she left Paramount, did some stage work, and starred on the live television series *My Favorite Husband*, which went to tape after she left the cast. In the 1960s, looking considerably older, she did two of A.C. Lyles's cheapie westerns, *Red Tomahawk* and *Buckskin*, after which she retired to become vice-president in charge of television programming for Donnelly Communications.

Screen: 1945: Duffy's Tavern; 1946: Blue Skies; Miss Susie Slagle's; Monsieur Beaucaire; 1947: Dear Ruth; Welcome Stranger; The Unsuspected; Variety Girl; 1948: The Sainted Sisters; Larceny; 1950: Dear Wife; The Petty Girl; 1951: The Lady Says No; 1955: The Rains of Ranchipur; 1963: Cattle King; 1967: Red Tomahawk; 1968: Buckskin; 1973: The Daring Dobermans; 1976: Pony Express Rider.

NY Stage: 1942: Beat the Band; 1943: Kiss and Tell.

Select TV: 1950: Saturday's Children (sp); 1951: Girl in a Million (sp); 1953–55: My Favorite Husband (series); 1956: The Bankmouse (sp); Only Yesterday (sp); 1957–58: Sally (series); 1973: The Magician; 1975: The Hatfields and the McCoys.

GEORGE CHAKIRIS

BORN: NORWOOD, OH, SEPTEMBER 16, 1933.

Darkly handsome George Chakiris was a chorus dancer in films as far back as 1951's *The Great Caruso* (performing under the name George Kerris). He can be spotted in several 1950s musicals, usually gyrating behind the leading lady, notably in Marilyn Monroe's classic "Diamonds Are a Girl's Best Friend" number from *Gentlemen Prefer Blondes*. After one attempt at a straight acting part, in Fox's war movie, *Under Fire*, Chakiris went on the London stage to play Bernardo in *West Side Story*, a fortunate bit of casting that landed him the role of the Puerto Rican gang leader of the Sharks in the 1961 movie version. As Rita Moreno's brooding lover, his sizzling dancing in the opening street ballet and the exciting "America" number, demonstrated enough screen presence to snatch the Best Supporting Actor Oscar away from fellow nominee Montgomery Clift. Suddenly he was a heartthrob and he essayed some serious acting in dramas like *Diamond Head*, as Yvette Mimieux's Hawaiian lover; the robust adventure *Kings of the Sun*, as a Mayan king; and *Flight From Ashiya*, as a pilot helping to rescue some shipwreck survivors. It was clear, however, that Bernardo would remain his career highpoint, and, by the time he returned to musicals, with the taffy-colored French concoction *The Young Girls of Rochefort*, his popularity had faded. After giving Lana Turner LSD in *The Big Cube*, and participating in the Cold War flop *The Day the Hot Line Got Hot*, he spent most of his time onstage. In later years he was occasionally seen on television, including a recurring role for one season on the soap *Dallas*.

Screen: 1947: Song of Love; 1951: The Great Caruso; 1952: Stars and Stripes Forever; 1953: The 5,000 Fingers of Dr. T; Give a Girl a Break; Second Chance; Gentlemen Prefer Blondes; 1954: There's No Business Like Show Business; White Christmas; Brigadoon; 1955: The Girl Rush; 1956: Meet Me in Las Vegas; 1957: Under Fire; 1961: West Side Story; 1962: Two and Two Make Six; Diamond Head; 1963: Bebo's Girl; Kings of the Sun; 1964: McGuire, Go Home!/The High Bright Sun; Flight From Ashiya; 633 Squadron; 1966: Is Paris Burning?; 1967: Il Ladro della Gioconda/The Theft of the Mona Lisa (nUSr); The Young Girls of Rochefort; 1969: Sharon in Scarlet (nUSr); The Big Cube; The Day the Hot Line Got Hot; 1979: Why Not Stay for Breakfast? (nUSr); 1982: Jekyll & Hyde...Together Again; 1989: Pale Blood (dtv).

Select TV: 1976: Notorious Woman (ms); 1977: Return to Fantasy Island; 1985–86: Dallas (series).

RICHARD CHAMBERLAIN
(GEORGE RICHARD CHAMBERLAIN)
BORN: LOS ANGELES, CA, MARCH 31, 1935.
ED: L.A. CONSERVATORY OF MUSIC.

The man dubbed "the King of the Mini-Series," Richard Chamberlain was clearly more comfortable and appreciated on the small screen, though he carried his share of big screen vehicles. A student of actor/acting instructor Jeff Corey, he had appeared in guest roles on television in the late 1950s and had one "B" feature to his credit, *The Secret of the Purple Reef*, when his wholesome good looks won him the title role in *Dr. Kildare*. The 1960s television adaptation of MGM's famous medical series made him an overnight star and Chamberlain got a hit record out of the deal, "Three Stars Will Shine Tonight," the show's theme song. Screen roles in the movies soon followed, although *Twilight of Honor*, as a lawyer defending Nick Adams, and *Joy in the Morning*, as a young newlywed studying for the bar, were forgettable outings. Chamberlain proved himself a capable actor in a television production of *Hamlet*, and as Julie Christie's abusive husband in director Richard Lester's demanding drama, *Petulia*. His attempts to shine as the tormented homosexual composer Tchaikovsky, in *The Music Lovers*, were buried under director Ken Russell's visual overkill. He was part of a successful ensemble, as Aramis, in Lester's tongue-in-cheek version of *The Three Musketeers*, and was the cost-cutting scum responsible for *The Towering Inferno* catching fire. A lone chance to display his singing abilities, in *The*

Slipper and the Rose, in which he was the Prince to Gemma Craven's Cinderella, sank without trace, but his popularity soared to new heights with such widely-seen mini-series as *Centennial*, *Shogun*, *The Thorn Birds*, and *Dream West*. Figuring to cash in on his television fame, he did a pair of would-be action adventure movies as Allan Quatermain, in a remake of *King Solomon's Mines* and in *Allan Quatermain and the Lost City of Gold*, but the audience reception was decidedly negative.

Screen: 1960: The Secret of the Purple Reef; 1961: A Thunder of Drums; 1963: Twilight of Honor; 1965: Joy in the Morning; 1968: Petulia; 1969: The Madwoman of Chaillot; 1971: The Music Lovers; Julius Caesar; 1973: Lady Caroline Lamb; 1973: The Three Musketeers; The Towering Inferno; 1975: The Four Musketeers; 1976: The Slipper and the Rose; 1978: The Swarm; The Last Wave; 1981: Murder by Phone; 1984: King Solomon's Mines; 1987: Allan Quartermain and the Lost City of Gold; 1996: Bird of Prey; 1997: A River Made to Drown In (nUSr); 1999: The Pavilion (dtv).

NY Stage: 1966: Breakfast at Tiffany's; 1976: The Night of the Iguana; 1978: Fathers and Sons (ob); 1987: Blithe Spirit; 1993: My Fair Lady; 1999: The Sound of Music.

Select TV: 1961–66: Dr. Kildare (series); 1967: Portrait of a Lady (sp); 1970: Hamlet (sp); 1972: Portrait: The Woman I Love (sp); 1974: F. Scott Fitzgerald and The Last of the Belles; The Lady's Not for Burning (sp); 1975: The Count of Monte Cristo; 1977: The Man in the Iron Mask; 1979: Centennial (ms); 1980: Shogun (ms); 1983: The Thorn Birds (ms); Cook & Perry: The Race to the Pole; 1985: Wallenberg: A Hero's Story; 1986: Dream West (ms); 1987: Casanova; 1988: The Bourne Identity; 1989–90: Island Son (series; and co-exec. prod.); 1990: The Return of the Musketeers (theatrical in Europe); 1991: Aftermath: A Test of Love; The Night of the Hunter; 1993: Ordeal in the Arctic; 1996: The Thorn Birds: The Missing Years; 1997: The Lost Daughter; All the Winters That Have Been; 1999: Too Rich: The Secret Life of Doris Duke.

MARGE CHAMPION
(MARJORIE CELESTE BELCHER)
BORN: LOS ANGELES, CA, SEPTEMBER 2, 1919.
& GOWER CHAMPION
BORN: GENEVA, IL, JUNE 22, 1920. RAISED IN LOS ANGELES, CA. DIED: AUGUST 25, 1980.

Everybody's favorite smiling dance couple of the 1950s, Marge and Gower Champion's usual film formula was to wait in the background until called upon to do their big number, which they then performed with the expected exuberance and finesse. Gower had won a dance contest as a teenager, with a prize of a 13-week engagement at the Cocoanut Grove in Los Angeles with his then-partner, Jeanne Tyler. They were soon nightclub headliners, which led to specialty numbers in such stage shows as *Streets of Paris* and *Count Me In*. Marge had learned ballet from her father and was an artists' model for Walt Disney, her most famous assignment being Snow White. Bit parts in films and stage work, some of it dramatic, like *Dark of the Moon*, billed her as Marjorie Belle. After Gower's original partner retired, he did a solo bit in MGM's *Till the Clouds Roll By* and then sought out Marge, whom he had known from school, for his new partner. Married in 1947, the team was soon finding appreciative audiences in clubs, on the television series *Admiral Broadway Revue*, and, playing themselves, in Bing Crosby's film *Mr. Music*.

MGM came calling and in their first assignment the couple memorably played Frank and Ellie in the 1951 version of *Show Boat*, dancing enchantingly to "Life Upon the Wicked Stage" and

"I Might Fall Back On You." In *Lovely to Look At*, in which their parts were bigger, they glided gracefully through "Smoke Gets in Your Eyes," which Gower had previously performed with Cyd Charisse in *Till the Clouds Roll By*. Their one starring vehicle, *Everything I Have Is Yours*, was a box-office dud, so they returned to support in a bright, largely-forgotten musical, *Give a Girl a Break*, where their showstopper was a rooftop number. After being asked to dance with elephants in the deliriously kitschy *Jupiter's Darling*, they turned down an offer to renew with MGM and went to Columbia. There they effortlessly stole the show with their rehearsal dance to "Someone to Watch Over Me," in *Three for the Show*, before starring in their own short-lived television series. Gower went on to become one of Broadway's greatest choreographer-directors with the shows *Bye Bye Birdie*; *Carnival*; *My Mother, My Father and Me*; *Hello, Dolly!*; *Three Bags Full*; *I Do! I Do!*; *The Happy Time*; *A Flea in Her Ear*; *Sugar*; *Irene*; *Mack and Mabel*; *Rockabye Hamlet*; and *A Broadway Musical*. Altogether he won six Tony Awards for his efforts but two movie credits as director, *My Six Loves* and *Bank Shot*, won him little acclaim. In 1973 the dancing couple divorced and Gower died on the opening night of his last New York triumph, *42nd Street*, in 1980. Marge did some straight acting and choreographed a provocative nude dance number for the 1981 film *Whose Life Is It Anyway?*

Screen: MARGE AND GOWER: **1950:** Mr. Music; **1951:** Show Boat; **1952:** Lovely to Look At; Everything I Have Is Yours; **1953:** Give a Girl a Break; **1955:** Jupiter's Darling; Three for the Show. MARGE (AS MARJORIE BELLE): **1939:** Honor of the West; Sorority House; The Story of Vernon and Irene Castle; What a Life; All Women Have Secrets; (AS MARGE CHAMPION): **1968:** The Swimmer; The Party; **1970:** The Cockeyed Cowboys of Calico County.
GOWER: **1946:** Till the Clouds Roll By.

NY Stage: MARGE AND GOWER: **1955:** 3 for Tonight (and dir.; chor. for Gower). MARGE (AS MARJORIE BELLE): **1945:** Dark of the Moon; (AS MARGE CHAMPION): **2001:** Follies.
GOWER: **1939:** Streets of Paris; **1942:** The Lady Comes Across; Count Me In.

Select TV: MARGE AND GOWER: **1949:** Admiral Broadway Revue (series); **1953:** Bouquet for Millie (sp); **1955:** 3 For Tonight (sp); **1956:** The Rider on the Pale Horse (sp); **1957:** The Marge and Gower Champion Show (series); Mischief at Bandy Leg (sp).

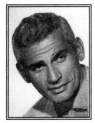

JEFF CHANDLER

(IRA GROSSEL) BORN: BROOKLYN, NY, DECEMBER 15, 1918. DIED: JUNE 17, 1961.

The epitome of 1950s virility, muscular, iron-jawed Jeff Chandler starred in a series of adventure films and romances that, like the star's gray hair, aged prematurely. Dropping his original intent of entering the restaurant business, he studied at the Feagin School of Dramatic Art in New York, then joined the army. Moving to L.A. after the war, his good looks got him a few bit parts in films, which led to a substantial role in a minor 1949 adventure, *Sword in the Desert*. The following year came the highpoint of his career, playing Cochise in the pro-Indian western *Broken Arrow* for 20th Century-Fox. His quiet dignity in the role earned him a supporting Oscar nomination back in the days when a Jew from Brooklyn playing a Native American was perfectly acceptable. The role made him a star and he would return to the part in two less prestigious westerns, *The Battle at Apache Pass*, and *Taza — Son of Cochise*, with Rock Hudson as the title offspring. Universal signed Chandler to a contract and pre-

sented him in such silly pictures as *Flame of Araby*, which referred to Maureen O'Hara and not the prize stallion he hoped to capture; *Sign of the Pagan*, as a Roman Centurion clashing with Jack Palance as a hammy Attila the Hun; and *Yankee Pasha*, with a supporting cast consisting mostly of Miss Universe contestants.

Chandler became the rugged and stoic leading man of such ladies as Loretta Young (*Because of You*, where he married her not realizing she'd been a drug smuggler's moll), Jane Russell (*Foxfire*, where he was a half-breed Apache mining engineer), Joan Crawford (*Female on the Beach*, where he had murderous intentions on Joan, his wife), and Lana Turner (*The Lady Takes a Flyer*, where he was a more plausible pilot than she was). These movies were hardly career peaks for any of the principals involved, and neither was a version of the oft-filmed *The Spoilers*. One of his bigger successes, *Away All Boats*, cast him as a World War II battleship captain, and a temporary change of pace found him in the comedy *Toy Tiger*, in which child actor Tim Hovey conned Chandler into pretending to be his dad. His own production company, Earlmar, made a western for United Artists, *Drango*, about the Reconstruction-era South. Despite constant battles over material, he re-signed with Universal to play a lawyer on trial in *The Tattered Dress*; an islander who gets plane crash survivor Esther Williams all hot under the swimsuit in *Raw Wind in Eden*; and an Air Force major being coerced to lie about a pilot's courage in *Stranger in My Arms*. Finally quitting Universal he did a western at Paramount, *The Jayhawkers*; a religious film at Warners, *A Story of David*; played a one-armed Civil War vet taking on some young hoods in *The Plunderers*; and published the famous best-seller of the title, in the sequel *Return to Peyton Place*. Following his early death from blood poisoning, a World War II adventure, *Merrill's Marauders*, helmed by cult director Samuel Fuller, was released.

Screen: **1947:** Johnny O'Clock; The Invisible Wall; Roses Are Red; **1949:** Mr. Belvedere Goes to College; Sword in the Desert; Abandoned; **1950:** Broken Arrow; Two Flags West; Double Crossbones (narrator); Deported; **1951:** Bird of Paradise; Smuggler's Island; Iron Man; Meet Danny Wilson; Flame of Araby; **1952:** The Battle of Apache Pass; Red Ball Express; Yankee Buccaneer; Son of Ali Baba (narrator); Because of You; **1953:** The Great Sioux Uprising; East of Sumatra; War Arrow; **1954:** Taza — Son of Cochise; Yankee Pasha; Sign of the Pagan; **1955:** Foxfire; Female on the Beach; The Spoilers; **1956:** Toy Tiger; Away All Boats; Pillars of the Sky; **1957:** Drango; The Tattered Dress; Jeanne Eagles; **1958:** Man in the Shadow; The Lady Takes a Flyer; Raw Wind in Eden; **1959:** Stranger in My Arms; Ten Seconds to Hell; Thunder in the Sun; The Jayhawkers; **1960:** The Plunderers; **1961:** Return to Peyton Place; **1962:** Merrill's Marauders; A Story of David (filmed 1960).

LON CHANEY

BORN: COLORADO SPRINGS, CO, APRIL 1, 1883. DIED: AUGUST 26, 1930.

One of the legendary names of the silent cinema, "the Man of a Thousand Faces" was able to create a multitude of memorable characters through body contortions, prosthetics, wigs, and make-up, all the while conveying some degree of emotional power underneath. Lon Chaney hid behind such a myriad of weird creations that many movie fans are still not sure what he looked like off screen. The son of deaf-mute parents, he began performing at an early age at his brother's theatre, and his vaudeville journeys eventually took him to Hollywood, where he found work as a bit player. His output during this early period, in both shorts and features, is almost impossible to chronicle, although it is certain that he directed some two-reelers in 1915. Universal was sufficiently impressed to offer him a contract and his first part of importance was as a politician, in 1917, in *Hell Morgan's Girl*. Two years later, on a loan-out to Paramount, came a star-making role, *The Miracle Man*, which required him to play a phony cripple. It was a highly profitable venture for the studio and Chaney soon had offers pouring in from all directions. Throughout the 1920s his reputation for versatility increased as he played Asians in *Bits of Life* and *Shadows*; Fagin in *Oliver Twist*, opposite Jackie Coogan; and sinister cripples in *The Penalty* (seeking revenge on the surgeon who had removed his legs) and *The Shock* (wheelchair-bound until the final reel). He would also take dual roles in films like *Treasure Island* (Blind Pew and Merry), *Outside the Law* (a gangster and a Chinaman), and *A Blind Bargain* (a mad scientist and an ape-creature).

In 1923 came the first of his two most famous roles. As the hideously deformed bell ringer Quasimodo, in Universal's lavish rendition of *The Hunchback of Notre Dame*, Chaney found a remarkable degree of pathos and humanity in this most pitiable of literary creations. MGM snatched him up for the very first film that the company produced and distributed, *He Who Gets Slapped*, a pretentious, but nonetheless fascinating story of a scientist who tries to escape his past by hiding behind clown makeup and calling himself "He." For his immediate follow-up, the tongue-in-cheek *The Monster*, Chaney looked oddly like Boris Karloff, playing a crazed surgeon who abducts innocent motorists in order to conduct experiments with reincarnation. *The Unholy Three* reunited him with director Tod Browning, with whom Chaney had often worked in the early days. This time the actor was part of a gang of criminals, spending most of the story dressed as a little old lady. But it was Universal who provided him with his signature part, the title role in *The Phantom of the Opera*. His startling facial make-up for the deformed and deranged Erik has never been surpassed in any of the numerous remakes, and the film remains one of the most frequently revived of all silent movies. He wore little special make up for *Tell It to the Marines*, but reverted to variations on earlier characters with *The Blackbird* (fake cripple), *Mr. Wu* (Oriental), and *Laugh, Clown, Laugh* (a clown, of course). He has been mistakenly labeled a horror actor by many, when in fact he only played a handful of characters that might qualify for that genre. One such was the creepy vampire in *London After Midnight*, a thriller that has become the most coveted of all the "lost" Chaney films. With the advent of sound it was intended that Chaney would reprise new versions of old hits, but only *The Unholy Three* was made, and shortly afterwards he died of throat cancer. (One of his planned films, *Dracula*, went to Bela Lugosi.) His son, Creighton, later became famous as Lon Chaney, Jr. An entertaining 1957 Universal biopic, *Man of a Thousand Faces*, starred James Cagney who, despite his own special talents, couldn't compete with Chaney's exclusive brand of magic.

Screen (features): 1915: Father and the Boys; 1916: The Grip of Jealousy; Tangled Hearts; The Gilded Spider; Bobbie of the Ballet; Grasp of Greed; The Mark of Cain; If My Country Should Call; Place Beyond the Winds; The Price of Silence; 1917: The Piper's Price; Hell Morgan's Girl; The Girl in the Checkered Coat; The Flashlight; A Doll's House; Fires of Rebellion; The Rescue; Triumph; Pay Me; The Empty Gun; Anything Once; The Scarlet Car; 1918: Broadway Love; The Kaiser — The Beast of Berlin; Fast Company; The Grand Passion; A Broadway Scandal; Riddle Gawne; The Devil Bateese; The Talk of the Town; Danger — Go Slow; 1919: The Wicked Darling; False Faces; A Man's Country; The Miracle Man; When Bearcat Went

Dry; Paid in Advance; Victory; 1920: Daredevil Jack (serial); Treasure Island; The Gift Supreme; Nomads of the North; The Penalty; 1921: Outside the Law; For Those We Love; Bits of Life; Ace of Hearts; 1922: The Trap; Voices of the City; Flesh and Blood; The Light in the Dark; Shadows; Oliver Twist; Quincy Adams Sawyer; A Blind Bargain; 1923: All the Brothers Were Valiant; While Paris Sleeps; The Shock; The Hunchback of Notre Dame; 1924: The Next Corner; He Who Gets Slapped; 1925: The Monster; The Unholy Three; The Phantom of the Opera; The Tower of Lies; 1926: The Blackbird; The Road to Mandalay; Tell It to the Marines; 1927: Mr. Wu; The Unknown; Mockery; London After Midnight; 1928: The Big City; Laugh, Clown, Laugh; While the City Sleeps; West of Zanzibar; 1929: Where East Is East; Thunder; 1930: The Unholy Three.

LON CHANEY, JR.

(CREIGHTON CHANEY) BORN: OKLAHOMA CITY, OK, FEBRUARY 10, 1906. DIED: JULY 12, 1973.

Although he became famous in his own right, Lon Chaney, Jr. forever lived in the shadow of his legendary father. Lon Sr. never wanted his son to go into show business and the younger Chaney planned on being a plumber, but less than two years after the old man's death Junior's film career began. Originally billed under his real name, he did bit parts without much success, and even after cashing in on dad's name his projects were no more distinguished. He did land a major role in a cheapie, *The Shadow of Silk Lennox*, as a crime boss, and was the principal villain in a Tom Tyler western, *Cheyenne Rides Again*, before becoming a contract player at 20th Century-Fox. In 1937 alone they put him in 16 features and a serial, and he was seen in everything from *Charlie Chan on Broadway* to a Ritz Brothers comedy (*Life Begins at College*) and a Sonja Henie skating musical (*Happy Landing*). The turning point came with his portrayal of the mentally weak, but physically powerful Lennie in a Los Angeles theatre production of John Steinbeck's *Of Mice and Men*. He repeated the role in Lewis Milestone's 1939 film version and won the best reviews of his career, but the hulking actor was hardly leading man material, so he signed with Universal, where he would make his reputation as a horror star. The first of the bunch, *Man Made Monster*, in which he was a circus performer capable of absorbing electricity, was fairly campy stuff. But in 1941 he starred in the film with which he would become most closely identified. With *The Wolf Man*, as the hapless Larry Talbot, who turns from man to beast at each full moon, he created a sympathetic character in a superior film of the genre.

He would reincarnate the Wolf Man in *Frankenstein Meets the Wolf Man*, *House of Frankenstein*, *House of Dracula*, and, most effectively, in *Abbott & Costello Meet Frankenstein*, in which his tragic plight contrasted surprisingly well with the comedians' low-jinks. In between he played any creature part Universal threw his way, including the Monster in *The Ghost of Frankenstein*; a vampire in *Son of Dracula*, where he was not the offspring of Lugosi's famous bloodsucker, as the title suggested, but one named Alucard; and the Mummy on three occasions, which required no dialogue but a lot of shuffling about under gauze. The studio also starred him in five low-budget horror/mysteries based on the popular *Inner Sanctum* radio show: *Calling Dr. Death*, using hypnotism to find his wife's murderer; *Weird Woman*, married to a witch; *Dead Man's Eyes*, feigning blindness after Acquanetta throws acid in his face in a jealous rage; *The Frozen Ghost*, as a mentalist who may have caused an audience member's death; and *Pillow of Death*, accused of killing his wife with said cushion. He returned to character acting, eventually landing a good role as the sad, retired sheriff in *High Noon*. He appeared in other "A" features like *Not as a Stranger* and *The Defiant Ones*, but he soiled his reputation with his heavy drinking and the often embarrassing way he mugged his way through such paltry fare as *The Black Sleep*, *Indestructible Man*, and *The Alligator People*. Unkempt, bloated, and speaking with an increasingly raspy voice, he abandoned whatever dignity he had by playing imbeciles in such career-ending films as *Spider Baby* (singing the title song!), *Hillbillys in a Haunted House*, and *Dracula vs. Frankenstein*.

Screen: AS CREIGHTON CHANEY: 1932: Bird of Paradise; The Last Frontier (serial); 1933: Lucky Devils; Scarlet River; Son of the Border; The Three Musketeers (serial); 1934: Sixteen Fathoms Deep; Girl O' My Dreams; The Life of Vergie Winters.

AS LON CHANEY, JR.: 1935: Captain Hurricane; Accent on Youth; The Shadow of Silk Lennox/The Silk Shadow; Scream in the Night; The Marriage Bargain/Within the Rock; Hold 'em Yale; 1936: The Singing Cowboy; Undersea Kingdom/Sharad of Atlantis (serial); Ace Drummond (serial); The Old Corral; Killer at Large; Rose Bowl; 1937: Cheyenne Rides Again; Midnight Taxi; Secret Agent X-9 (serial); That I May Live; Angel's Holiday; Slave Ship; Born Reckless; The Lady Escapes; One Mile From Heaven; Wild and Wooly; Thin Ice; Wife, Doctor and Nurse; Life Begins in College; Charlie Chan on Broadway; Second Honeymoon; Love and Hisses; Love Is News; 1938: City Girl; Happy Landing; Sally, Irene and Mary; Walking Down Broadway; Mr. Moto's Gamble; Josette; Passport Husband; Alexander's Ragtime Band; Speed to Burn; Straight Place and Show; Submarine Patrol; Road Demon; 1939: Jesse James; Union Pacific; Frontier Marshal; Charlie Chan in City of Darkness; Of Mice and Men; 1940: One Million B.C.; North West Mounted Police; 1941: Man Made Monster/The Atomic Monster; Too Many Blondes; Billy the Kid; San Antonio Rose; Riders of Death Valley; Badlands of Dakota; The Wolf Man; 1942: North to the Klondike; Overland Mail; The Ghost of Frankenstein; Sherlock Holmes and the Voice of Terror; The Mummy's Tomb; 1943: Eyes of the Underworld; Frankenstein Meets the Wolf Man; Frontier Badmen; Crazy House; Son of Dracula; Calling Dr. Death; 1944: Weird Woman; Ghost Catchers; Follow the Boys; Cobra Woman; The Mummy's Ghost; House of Frankenstein; Dead Man's Eyes; The Mummy's Curse; 1945: Here Come the Co-Eds; The Frozen Ghost; Strange Confession; The Daltons Ride Again; House of Dracula; Pillow of Death; 1947: My Favorite Brunette; 1948: Albuquerque; The Counterfeiters; 16 Fathoms Deep; Abbott and Costello Meet Frankenstein; 1949: There's a Girl in My Heart; Captain China; 1950: Once a Thief; 1951: Inside Straight; Only the Valiant; Behave Yourself!; Flame of Araby; Bride of the Gorilla; 1952: Thief of Damascus; High Noon; Springfield Rifle; The Black Castle; The Bushwhackers; The Battles of Chief Pontiac; 1953: Raiders of the Seven Seas; A Lion Is in the Streets; 1954: Jivaro; The Boy From Oklahoma; Casanova's Big Night; The Big Chase; Passion; The Black Pirates; 1955: Big House U.S.A.; The Silver Star; Not as a Stranger; I Died a Thousand Times; The Indian Fighter; 1956: Manfish; The Black Sleep/Dr. Cadman's Secret; Indestructible Man; Daniel Boone — Trail Blazer; Pardners; 1957: The Cyclops; 1958: The Defiant Ones; Money, Women and Guns; 1959: The Alligator People; 1961: Rebellion in Cuba; 1962: The Devil's Messenger; 1963: The Haunted Palace; 1964: Law of the Lawless; Witchcraft; Stage to Thunder Rock; Spider Baby/Cannibal Orgy; 1965: Face of the Screaming Werewolf/House of Terror (filmed 1959); Young Fury; Black Spurs; House of the Black Death/ Blood of the Man Beast; Town Tamer; 1966: Apache Uprising; Johnny Reno; 1967:

Welcome to Hard Times; Hillbillys in a Haunted House; Dr. Terror's Gallery of Horrors/The Blood Suckers/Alien Massacre; 1968: Buckskin; 1969: Fireball Jungle/Jungle Terror; 1970: Dracula vs. Frankenstein/Blood of Frankenstein/ Frankenstein's Bloody Terror; 1971: The Female Bunch.

Select TV: 1952: Frankenstein (sp); The Trial (sp); 1955: Stay on Stranger (sp); 1956: Ballad of Jubal Pickett (sp);1957: Hawkeye (series); 1959: The Family Man (sp); 1966–67: Pistols and Petticoats (series); 1969: A Stranger in Town/The Children's West (sp).

CAROL CHANNING

BORN: SEATTLE, WA, JANUARY 31, 1921.

A delightfully spacey performer, saucer-eyed and scratchy-voiced Carol Channing never played her most famous role, Dolly Levi, on film, but she toured endlessly in *Hello, Dolly!* to remind movie audiences of what they had missed. An entertainer in nightclubs during the 1940s, she found her initial fame on Broadway in *Lend an Ear* (winning a Theatre World Award) and for playing Lorelei Lee in the original *Gentlemen Prefer Blondes*, in 1949. She got two movie roles out of the deal, including supporting Ginger Rogers in one of RKO's last pictures, *The First Traveling Saleslady*, opposite an undiscovered Clint Eastwood. The 1964 Broadway musical *Hello, Dolly!* made her a household name, as well as winning her a Tony Award and propelling her to television fame, but Hollywood considered Barbra Streisand a safer box-office bet when it came time to making the movie version. With *Thoroughly Modern Millie*, however, Channing cut loose as the life-loving eccentric Muzzy Van Hossmere, displaying all the engaging qualities that had secured her popularity and nabbing an Oscar nomination in the process. Her follow-up, *Skidoo*, as the wife of gangster Jackie Gleason, was a bizarre artifact of the psychedelic 1960s, and a movie she always regretted making. There were a few screen credits since then, but it was in the theatre that her larger-than-life personality was most at home.

Screen: 1950: Paid in Full; 1956: The First Traveling Saleslady; 1967: Thoroughly Modern Millie; 1968: Skidoo; 1971: Shinbone Alley (voice); 1978: Sgt. Pepper's Lonely Hearts Club Band;1990: Happily Ever After (voice); 1994: Hans Christian Andersen's Thumbelina (voice); 1998: The Line King: The Al Hirschfeld Story.

NY Stage: 1941: No for an Answer; Let's Face It; 1942: Proof Through the Night; 1948: Lend an Ear; 1949: Gentlemen Prefer Blondes; 1954: Wonderful Town; 1955: The Vamp; 1961: Show Girl; 1964: Hello, Dolly!; 1971: Four on a Garden; 1974: Lorelei; or: Gentlemen Still Prefer Blondes; 1978: Hello, Dolly! (revival); 1995: Hello, Dolly! (revival).

Select TV: 1955: Svengali and the Blonde (sp); 1957: Three Men on a Horse (sp); 1985: Alice in Wonderland (sp).

CHARLES CHAPLIN

BORN: LONDON, ENGLAND, APRIL 16, 1889.
DIED: DECEMBER 25, 1977.

There is, perhaps, no more recognizable screen character than Charlie Chaplin's Little Tramp: the derby hat, the baggy pants, the funny walk, the bamboo cane, the brief moustache; this indelible everyman achieved a worldwide fame of immeasurable proportions. Because of this quintessential creation, comedy was raised to a more significant level, expanding all comedic aspirations, and drawing focus to the humanity behind the humor. Most importantly, despite every effort to elevate Chaplin to a God-like stature (one that he immodestly supported), he was and still is very funny. Born to poverty, he was already appearing onstage at the tender age of five, and though there were legit stage roles in plays like *Sherlock Holmes*, he perfected his craft in the music halls, joining the Fred Karno company when he was 17. As their chief attraction he journeyed with the group to America in 1910, touring a show called *A Night at an English Music Hall*. A second tour, three years later, caught the attention of Mack Sennett, and Chaplin was asked to join the Keystone Company. He debuted in the 1914 short, "Making a Living," wearing a light-colored top coat, a high hat, and a bushy moustache, but it was with his second one-reeler, "Kid Auto Races at Venice," that his beloved tramp character first appeared on screen. During that same year his popularity increased through a series of quickie comedies that paired him with some of Keystone's most famous names: Fatty Arbuckle, Mabel Normand, and Chester Conklin. "Caught in a Cabaret" gave him his first directorial credit (shared with Normand), while "Caught in the Rain" is his first solo credit for directing and writing.

His involvement with *Tillie's Punctured Romance*, often called the first feature-length comedy, was instrumental in making him a bona fide star. In it, he and Normand were a pair of con artists who schemed to drain Marie Dressler's bank account by having Chaplin marry her. He left Keystone — where he had made no fewer than 32 shorts in 1914 — when a better offer from Essanay came along in 1915. At Essanay his work included "A Night Out," his first teaming with Edna Purviance, who would be his leading lady until 1923's "The Pilgrim;" his first attempt at out-and-out sentiment, "The Tramp;" his extended drag act, "A Woman," which displayed him sans mustache; and his acclaimed spoof of *Carmen*, which was sometimes billed as "Charlie Chaplin's Burlesque on Carmen," and went the rounds in an extended, four-reel format. The Tramp, or "the Little Fellow" as Chaplin preferred to call him, was a superb creation, quick on his feet with an eyebrow raising contempt for his adversaries, a character who could be both playful and mean, forlorn or triumphant.

Now at the peak of his popularity, he accepted a very lucrative offer from Mutual that allowed him total freedom to direct, write, and act. This period (1916–17) is often considered his greatest, with one solid comedic gem following another: "The Pawnshop," "Behind the Screen," "The Immigrant," "Easy Street," "The Adventurer," and "The Rink" which displayed Chaplin's remarkable agility on skates and might be his finest two-reeler. His prodigious output also included experimental oddities like "One A.M.," in which, after a very brief exchange with a taxi driver, a drunken Chaplin is left alone on screen to battle the elements in his own home. Over at First National his artistic ambitions began to grow, first by extending his films to three reels, starting with "A Dog's Life," and followed by one of his most acclaimed comedies, "Shoulder Arms," the requisite army spoof that nearly every comedian in history would attempt to duplicate. It was for First National, in 1921, that he created his first genuine starring feature, *The Kid*. A hugely sentimental film and a box-office smash, the tale tells of how the Tramp finds an abandoned baby and raises him as his own son, only to have the authorities separate the two. The movie made a star of young Jackie Coogan, and proved that Chaplin knew how to create and maintain an extended storyline.

In 1919, Chaplin had joined Douglas Fairbanks, D.W. Griffith, and Mary Pickford in forming their own distribution company, United Artists. The first feature he wrote and directed for them

was *A Woman of Paris*, a dramatic showcase for Edna Purviance in which he had a walk-on. Released in 1923, it was pretty standard stuff and a financial failure. Two years later, however, Chaplin gave the world *The Gold Rush*, arguably his greatest feature, an assured mix of comedy, pathos, and adventure. (One of his gentlest moments, the dinner roll dance, is an inspired creation.) He had, by this point, become adamant about taking all the time he needed on his films, rather than churn out a batch of silents before that era came to an end. His next full-length feature, *The Circus*, was released in 1928, a year after the release of the first talkie. The Academy of Motion Picture Arts and Sciences found him worthy of an Oscar nomination for Best Actor and bestowed upon him a special award at their very first ceremony. The film, sadly, did not retain this degree of prestige with the passing years, despite being one of his most satisfying. In spite of the advent of sound, Chaplin made two more silent features: *City Lights*, in 1931, was an outstanding creation and featured the Tramp falling in love with a blind flower girl; and *Modern Times*, in 1936, embodies one of the screen's most indelible images as the Tramp gets trapped inside the cogs of a vast machine. The film briefly featured sound when Chaplin sang a nonsense ditty at the climax; paired him with his third wife, Paulette Goddard; and included the most enduring music Chaplin would ever compose for one of his films, a theme that became the song "Smile." Both movies did the unthinkable by becoming box-office smashes, confounding the skeptics who had predicted that Chaplin's stubbornness to move with the times would prove his downfall.

Goddard was his co-star again in *The Great Dictator*, Chaplin's official sound debut. Released in 1940, and another box-office hit, it featured the comic in the dual roles of a dictator (clearly modeled on Hitler) and a Jewish barber who, by a quirk of fate, replaces him. The film made a mighty statement against fascism, received Oscar nominations for Best Picture, Actor, and Original Screenplay, but today — despite moments of brilliance — looks surprisingly cheap and awkwardly staged. That Chaplin liked to talk was evident in his next feature, *Monsieur Verdoux*, a long and long-winded story of a wife killer that suffered the condemnation of many and gave him his first starring failure. The film was not helped when a heavily publicized paternity suit started a vast Chaplin backlash. He sold off the majority of his interest in United Artists in 1951 and, because of his controversial politics and failure to pay back taxes, was told he was no longer wanted in the U.S. Around the time of *Limelight*, a gentle but rather self-indulgent look at an aging comedian, he moved to Switzerland, where he would remain for the rest of his life. *Limelight* (which briefly teamed him with another silent movie immortal, Buster Keaton) was sporadically distributed in America, by-passing Los Angeles together. It was not officially released there until 1972, garnering Chaplin the Academy Award for Best Original Score two decades after its initial premiere. Two years earlier he had been welcomed back to the country to receive another special Oscar, one of the most significant tributes in the history of the award. Around that period his 1957 feature, *A King in New York*, which he had refused to be shown in the U.S., was at last released, revealing a rather weak satire that, like all of his talkies, seemed often naïve in content and old-fashioned in technique. Only worse was his last, *A Countess From Hong Kong*, distributed in 1967 to the most horrendous reviews of his career. Partially because of these setbacks and partially because of the public's rediscovery of Buster Keaton and Harold Lloyd, Chaplin's stature as the master comic of the silent era was suddenly being questioned. It became trendy to knock him for his old-world sentimentality, but one has only to view his output at Mutual to see that his comic brilliance speaks for itself. He published his autobiography in 1964. A son, Sydney, had some degree of success on Broadway, while a daughter, Geraldine, became a star after appearing in *Doctor Zhivago*.

Screen (shorts): 1914: Making a Living; Kid Auto Races at Venice; Mabel's Strange Predicament; Between Showers; A Film Johnnie; Tango Tangles; His Favorite Pastime; Cruel, Cruel Love; The Star Boarder; Mabel at the Wheel; Twenty Minutes of Love.

and director-writer: 1914: Caught in a Cabaret (co-dir; w/Mabel Normand); Caught in the Rain; A Busy Day; The Fatal Mallet (co-dir. w/Normand); Her Friend the Bandit (co-dir. w/Normand); The Knockout (actor only); Mabel's Busy Day (co-dir. w/Normand); Mabel's Married Life (and co-dir. w/Normand); Laughing Gas; The Property Man; The Face on the Barroom Floor; Recreation; The Masquerader; His New Profession; The Rounders; The New Janitor; Those Love Pangs; Dough and Dynamite (co-wr. w/Mack Sennett); Gentlemen of Nerve; His Musical Career; His Trysting Place; Getting Acquainted; His Prehistoric Past; **1915:** His New Job; A Night Out; The Champion; His Regeneration (actor only); In the Park; A Jitney Elopement; The Tramp; By the Sea; Work; A Woman; The Bank; Shanghaied; A Night in the Show; **1916:** Carmen/Charlie Chaplin's Burlesque on Carmen; Police; The Floorwalker; The Fireman; The Vagabond; One A.M.; The Count; The Pawnshop; Behind the Screen; The Rink; **1917:** Easy Street; The Cure; The Immigrant; The Adventurer; **1918:** Triple Trouble; A Dog's Life; The Bond; Shoulder Arms; **1919:** Sunnyside; A Day's Pleasure; **1921:** The Idle Class; **1922:** Pay Day; **1923:** The Pilgrim.

Screen (features): 1914: Tillie's Punctured Romance.

and director-writer-producer: 1921: The Kid; The Nut (actor only); **1923:** Hollywood (actor only); A Woman of Paris; **1925:** The Gold Rush (and music for 1942 reissue); **1928:** Show People (actor only); The Circus.

and director-writer-producer-music: 1931: City Lights; **1936:** Modern Times; **1940:** The Great Dictator; **1947:** Monsieur Verdoux; **1952:** Limelight; **1957:** A King in New York (US: 1973); **1967:** A Countess From Hong Kong.

CYD CHARISSE

(TULA ELLICE FINKLEA) BORN: AMARILLO, TX, MARCH 8, 1921.

Think of Cyd Charisse and you think of dancing. As an actress she was serviceable, but the moment she took her extraordinary long legs onto the dance floor she was as sensational as they come. As a child she studied dancing with Nico Charisse, whom she would later marry. Following a brief tour with the Ballet Russe around America and Europe, she debuted in films in 1943, under the name Lily Norwood, performing dances in *Mission to Moscow* and *Something to Sing About*. MGM came calling and her first assignment, in *Ziegfeld Follies*, allowed her a brief spin with future partner Fred Astaire. For the next several years the studio cast her in specialty numbers or supporting parts. There was a lovely trio with Judy Garland and Virginia O'Brien, singing "It's a Great Big World" in *The Harvey Girls*, though her voice was dubbed, as it would continue to be. In *Words and Music* she had a priceless bit, serving tea to her guests while dancing to the tune of "In the Blue Room," and she, Ricardo Montalban, and Ann Miller stole the notices with their fiery flamenco number that put a momentary spark into the lifeless musical *The Kissing Bandit*. There were occasional straight roles like *Tension*, falling in love with Richard Basehart's alternate persona; *East Side, West Side*, as one of phi-

landerer James Mason's many women; Universal's costume adventure *Mark of the Renegade*, as a señorita in old California; and *The Wild North*, as a half-breed canoeing through Canada with Stewart Granger, but the roles stretched her beyond her limitations.

Everything changed with *Singin' in the Rain*, in which she was so breathtaking enticing Gene Kelly in the "Broadway Melody" ballet that MGM at last awarded her some starring roles. She started out with her best ever, *The Band Wagon*, as the snobby classical dancer lured into show music, sparkling in her sumptuous dance with Fred Astaire, "Dancing in the Dark." Next it was back with Kelly for the stodgy movie of *Brigadoon*, where they performed "The Heather on the Hill" so enchantingly that they almost made you stop looking at the phony backdrops. There was a guest bit, dancing to "One Alone," in the biopic *Deep in My Heart*, and an uninspired tour of the casinos, *Meet Me in Las Vegas*, highlighted by her "Frankie and Johnny" number. In her third film with Kelly, *It's Always Fair Weather*, she had no duets with her co-star, instead performing a stunning number at a gymnasium with a bunch of grateful boxers. *Silk Stockings*, a remake of *Ninotchka* with Fred Astaire, was supposed to be a career peak. Her "Red Blues" number is one of the most enthralling ever put on film, but her acting performance as the icy Russian was no match for Greta Garbo's. MGM's golden era was coming to an end and Charisse bowed out in a drama, *Party Girl*, that nevertheless afforded her two show-stopping numbers. After that she would dance on screen only a few more times, notably in the ballet pastiche *Black Tights*. Most of her other work was in totally forgettable international productions in which, if nothing else, she continued to look stunning. There was some nightclub performing with her husband, singer Tony Martin, whom she had married in 1948, and, in 1991, she made her long-delayed Broadway debut in *Grand Hotel*, once again in a role made famous by Garbo.

Screen: AS LILY NORWOOD: 1943: Mission to Moscow; Something to Sing About.

AS CYD CHARISSE: 1943: Thousands Cheer; **1946:** Ziegfeld Follies; The Harvey Girls; Three Wise Fools; Till the Clouds Roll By; **1947:** Fiesta; The Unfinished Dance; **1948:** On an Island With You; Words and Music; The Kissing Bandit; **1949:** Tension; East Side, West Side; **1951:** Mark of the Renegade; **1952:** The Wild North; Singin' in the Rain; **1953:** Sombrero; The Band Wagon; Easy to Love; **1954:** Brigadoon; Deep in My Heart; **1955:** It's Always Fair Weather; **1956:** Meet Me in Las Vegas; **1957:** Silk Stockings; **1958:** Twilight of the Gods; Party Girl; **1961:** Five Golden Hours; **1962:** Black Tights; Two Weeks in Another Town; **1963:** Assassination in Rome (nUSr); **1966:** The Silencers; **1968:** Maroc 7; **1976:** Won Ton Ton, the Dog Who Saved Hollywood; **1978:** Warlords of Atlantis; **1994:** That's Entertainment! III.

NY Stage: 1991: Grand Hotel.

Select TV: 1980: Portrait of an Escort; **1989:** Swimsuit.

CHARLEY CHASE

(CHARLES PARROTT) BORN: BALTIMORE, MD, OCTOBER 20, 1893. DIED: JUNE 20, 1940.

Because his career consisted almost exclusively of short subjects and, perhaps, because he died long before the nostalgia craze, Charley Chase is one of the forgotten comedians of the silent era. A vaudeville performer from his teen years, he came to Hollywood in 1914 to work with Al Christie at Universal. He soon joined Mack Sennett's studio, doing bit parts and larger roles, and kept busy by occasionally directing, using his real name. By the end of the decade this seemed to be his preferred profession, but producer Hal Roach felt differently and hired Chase in 1924 to star in a series of one- and two-reel comedies. He established the image of a brash but well-bred young fellow prone to slapstick encounters, and often played variations on the obnoxious twit or the henpecked husband. He stayed with Roach for 12 years (from the end of 1933 until Chase parted with the studio, the comic directed all of his own comedies), before switching over to Columbia in 1937. In less-assured hands the shorts began to lose their sense of fun and spontaneity, and Chase took to the bottle, which was instrumental in bringing on the heart attack that killed him at age 46.

Screen (shorts): 1914: The Anglers (and dir.); The Knockout; The Masquerader; Dough and Dynamite; His New Profession; The Rounders; His Musical Career; Gentlemen of Nerve; Our Country Cousin; Mabel's New Job; Her Last Chance; Cursed By His Beauty; 1915: Only a Farmer's Daughter; Hash House Mashers; Love in Armor; Do-Re-Mi-Fa (and dir.); Love, Loot and Crash; Settled at the Seaside; A Versatile Villain; The Rent Jumpers; The Hunt (and dir.); His Father's Footsteps; Fatty and the Broadway Stars; The Little Teacher; Fatty's Reckless Fling; 1916: A Dash of Courage (and dir.); 1917: Her Torpedoed Love; Chased Into Love (and dir.); 1918: Hello Trouble (and dir.); 1919: Ship Ahoy! (and dir.); 1920: Kids Is Kids (and dir.); 1924: At First Sight; One of the Family; Just a Minute; A Perfect Lady; Hard Knocks; Powder and Smoke; Don't Forget; Love's Detour; April Fool; The Fraidy Cat; Publicity Pays; Why Husbands Go Mad; Position Wanted; Young Oldfield; Jeffries Jr.; Stolen Goods; Ten Minute Egg; Sweet Daddy; Seeing Nellie Home; Why Men Work; The Poor Fish; Sittin' Pretty; Outdoor Pajamas; Too Many Mamas; All Wet; Bungaloo Boobs; Accidental Accidents; The Royal Buzz; 1925: The Rat's Knuckles; Hello Baby; Fighting Fluid; Plain and Fancy Girls; Is Marriage the Bunk?; The Family Entrance; Looking for Sally; Big Red Riding Hood; Should Husbands Be Watched?; Hard Boiled; Bad Boy; Innocent Husbands; Isn't Life Terrible?; What Price Goofy?; No Father to Guide Him; The Caretaker's Daughter; Thundering Fleas; His Wooden Wedding; The Uneasy Three; 1926: There Ain't No Santa Claus; Charley My Boy; Dog Shy; Mama Behave; Mum's the Word; Love Fliv the King; Mighty Like a Moose; Bromo and Juliet; Crazy Like a Fox; Tell 'em Nothing; Be Your Age; 1927: Us; Many Scrappy Returns; A One-Mama Man; The Call of the Cuckoos; Are Brunettes Safe?; Bigger and Better Blondes; Forgotten Sweeties; Fluttering Hearts; What Women Did for Me; Now I'll Tell One; The String of Strings; Assistant Wives; The Lighter That Failed; The Way of All Pants; Never the Dames Shall Meet; 1928: Aching Youths; All for Nothing; Limousine Love; Imagine My Embarrassment; The Fight Pest; Is Everybody Happy?; The Booster; All Parts; Chasing Husbands; The Family Group; 1929: Ruby Love; Off to Buffalo; Movie Night; Thin Twins; The Big Squawk; Crazy Feet; Leaping Love; Snappy Sneezer; Stepping Out; Great Gobs; 1930: The Real McCoy; Whispering Whoopee; Fifty Million Husbands; Fast Work; All Teed Up; Girl Shock; Dollar Dizzy; Looser Than Loose; High Cs; 1931: Rough Seas; The Pip From Pittsburgh; Thundering Tenors; One of the Smiths; The Panic Is On; Skip the Maloo; Hasty Marriage; What a Bozo!; 1932: The Tabasco Kid; First in War; In Walked Charley; The Nickel Nurser; Young Ironsides; Girl Grief; Now We'll Tell One; Mr. Bride; 1933: Fallen Arches; Nature in the Wrong; Arabian Tights; His Silent Racket; Sherman Said It (and dir.); Midsummer Mush (and dir.); Luncheon at Twelve (and dir.); 1934: I'll Take Vanilla (and dir.); Another Wild Idea (and dir.); The Cracked Iceman (and dir.); Four Parts (and dir.); It Happened One Day (and dir.); Something Simple (and dir.);

You Said a Hatful! (and dir.); Fate's Fathead (and dir.); The Chases of Pimple Street (and dir.); 1935: The Four Star Boarder (and dir.); Okay Toots! (and dir.); Poker at Eight (and dir.); Manhattan Monkey Business (and dir.); Nurse to You (and dir.); Public Ghost No. 1 (and dir.); Southern Exposure (and dir.); 1936: Life Hesitates at 40 (and dir.); The Count Takes the Count (and dir.); Vamp 'Til Ready (and dir.); On the Wrong Trek (and dir.); Neighborhood House (and dir.); 1937: Hollywood Party; The Grand Hooter; From Bad to Worse; The Wrong Miss Wright; Calling All Doctors; The Big Squirt; Man Bites Lovebug; 1938: Time Out for Trouble; The Mind Needer; Many Sappy Returns; The Nightshirt Bandit; Pie a la Maid; 1939: The Sap Takes a Wrap; The Chump Takes a Bump; Rattling Romeo; Skinny the Moocher; Teacher's Pest; The Awful Goof; Mutiny on the Body (and dir.); 1940: The Heckler; South of the Boudoir; His Bridal Fright.

Screen (features): 1914: Tillie's Punctured Romance; 1923: Her Dangerous Path (serial); Long Live the King; King of the Wild Horses; 1929: Modern Love; You Can't Buy Love; 1933: Sons of the Desert; 1936: Kelly the Second; Neighborhood House.

RUTH CHATTERTON
BORN: NEW YORK, NY, DECEMBER 24, 1893.
DIED: NOVEMBER 24, 1961.

Although she was one of the top names of the early talkie years, very little of Ruth Chatterton's work has survived her heyday. She was a chorus girl before making her Broadway debut in The Great Name, in 1911. Over the next several years she became one of the big stars of the stage with vehicles like Daddy Long Legs, Mary Rose (which she also directed), and The Little Minister. She came to California to do some theatre and Emil Jannings asked her to join him on screen in Sins of the Father, which resulted in a contract with Paramount. With the advent of sound she became a star in such melodramas as The Laughing Lady and The Right to Love, in which she played both mother and daughter. She earned an Oscar nomination for the soggiest melodrama of them all, Madame X, as an outcast who is defended at a murder trial by a man who doesn't know she's his mother. There was a second nomination, for Sarah and Son, in which she searched for the son her cruel husband had sold off as a baby. Chatterton was at her box-office peak, but there followed a downswing with The Magnificent Lie and Tomorrow and Tomorrow, so she accepted an offer to go over to Warner Bros. The first at her new studio was a comedy, The Rich Are Always With Us, which featured Warner's future leading attraction, Bette Davis, and George Brent, who became Chatterton's second husband in 1932. She and Brent teamed thrice more: in The Crash, she flirted with men to get stock market tips for her husband; in Lily Turner, she was pregnant, abandoned, and working the carny circuit; and in Female, she was the disillusioned head of an automobile company. These failed to resuscitate her career and both her marriage and the Warners's contract ended in 1934. Two years later she gave her best performance, as Walter Huston's selfish wife, in William Wyler's Dodsworth, but instead of presaging a new phase of her career it was her final American movie. Two films in England preceded her return to stage work before she turned her attention towards writing.

Screen: 1928: Sins of the Fathers; 1929: The Doctor's Secret; The Dummy; Madame X; Charming Sinners; The Laughing Lady; 1930: Sarah and Son; Paramount on Parade; Lady of Scandal; Anybody's Woman; The Right to Love; 1931: Unfaithful; The Magnificent Lie; Once a Lady; 1932: Tomorrow and Tomorrow;

The Rich Are Always With Us; The Crash; **1933:** Frisco Jenny; Lilly Turner; Female; **1934:** Journal of a Crime; **1936:** Lady of Secrets; Girls' Dormitory; Dodsworth; **1938:** The Rat; The Royal Divorce.

NY Stage: 1911: The Great Name; **1912:** The Rainbow; **1914:** Daddy Long Legs (and 1918 revival); **1916:** Come Out of the Kitchen; **1918:** Perkins; **1919:** Moonlight and Honeysuckle; **1920:** Mary Rose (and dir.); A Marriage of Convenience; **1922:** La Tendresse; **1923:** The Changelings; **1924:** The Magnolia Lady; **1925:** The Little Minister; The Man With a Load of Mischief; **1940:** Leave Her to Heaven; Treat Her Gently; **1946:** Second Best Bed; **1951:** Idiot's Delight.

Select TV: 1950: Dodsworth (sp); **1951:** Old Acquaintance (sp); **1952:** The Paper Moon (sp); **1953:** Hamlet (sp).

MAURICE CHEVALIER

BORN: PARIS, FRANCE, SEPTEMBER 12, 1888.
DIED: JANUARY 1, 1972.

The epitome of French charm and suave innuendo, devil-may-care Maurice Chevalier's slyly playful song stylings made him the sort of singular entertainer who defied imitation, so unique and exclusive were his talents. Because of his worldwide popularity, he could also boast of having one of the most instantly recognizable voices in show business. Born into a life of poverty, he escaped while a young man by joining the Casino de Touelles, where he did impersonations. There were a few short film roles while he was making a name for himself as part of a dance team with the legendary Mistinguett (who was also his lover) in the Folies Bergère. Going solo he appeared in the London revue *Hullo America*, in 1919, and then became the star attraction at the Casino de Paris during the 1920s. His fame was so great that Hollywood decided to present him to U.S. audiences as a new musical star and he was signed by Paramount in 1929. His American debut, *Innocents of Paris*, was as clunky as most productions during the transitional silent-to-sound period, but it gave him one of his most famous songs, "Louise." In the technically crude, formative years of the movie musical, Chevalier became a rare bright spot, starting off with Ernst Lubitsch's *The Love Parade*, his first teaming with Jeanette MacDonald, which was much lighter and more assured than most contemporary offerings around. Chevalier was refreshingly roguish, charming the ladies with a tilt of his straw hat and a song, and his risque and sophisticated humor in these movies is still a delight to watch. For *The Love Parade* and his immediate follow-up, *The Big Pond* (in which he first sang "You Brought a New Kind of Love to Me"), he was honored with a pair of Oscar nominations. *The Love Parade* received five additional nominations, including one for Best Picture.

The Smiling Lieutenant, with Lubitsch at the helm, and *One Hour With You*, with Lubitsch sharing directorial credit with George Cukor, continued the high level of entertainment. (As was the custom at the time, there were also simultaneous French-made versions of these films.) In both cases Chevalier found himself the happy object of desire of two women (Claudette Colbert and Miriam Hopkins in the former; MacDonald and Genevieve Tobin in the latter). Both movies scored worthwhile financial returns, and competed against each other for the Best Picture Oscar. With *Love Me Tonight*, directed by Rouben Mamoulian in 1932, Chevalier and the screen musical reached their zenith. Innovative, witty, and without a trace of the static camera technique that had stymied so many films before it, this enchanting fairy tale found Chevalier as a tailor in love with princess Jeanette MacDonald. A brilliant Rodgers and Hart score

included "Mimi," and the song that would become the theme of Paramount Studios, "Isn't It Romantic?" In a typical Hollywood irony, the film was less popular than the others, and despite being the undisputed masterpiece of the bunch, was overlooked by the Academy in all departments.

After another good one, *A Bedtime Story*, in which Chevalier was stuck with abandoned toddler Baby LeRoy, there was a distinct critical backlash. *The Way to Love* went through filming difficulties, with Chevalier's co-star walking off the picture, to be replaced by Ann Dvorak. With box-office receipts falling Paramount had no qualms about letting him go. There was one last teaming with Lubitsch and MacDonald, *The Merry Widow*, at MGM, and then *Folies Bergère*, at 20th Century, playing a dual role as a millionaire and a night club entertainer hired to impersonate him. Public response was mild and Chevalier felt it was time to return to Europe. For more than two decades he would not be seen in an American-produced film, although there were two English-language features made in Britain, *The Beloved Vagabond*, and *Break the News*, which teamed him with Jack Buchanan. During World War II he was accused of Nazi collaboration, but it was later discovered that he had performed for the Germans only under the condition that ten Jewish prisoners be released.

He was a name from the past when he showed up playing Audrey Hepburn's father in Billy Wilder's 1957 comedy *Love in the Afternoon*. Distinctly older — he was just turning 70 — but no less disarming, he was suddenly in demand again and began the second phase of his Hollywood career. *Gigi* found him at his most engaging, as the elderly womanizer Honore Lachille. He supplied the movie with several of its highlights, introducing yet another of his signature songs, "Thank Heaven for Little Girls," dueting with Hermione Gingold on "I Remember It Well," and tipping the straw once more for the marvelous "I'm Glad I'm Not Young Anymore." The response was rapturous, the movie a smash hit that received all nine of the Oscars for which it was nominated, while Chevalier himself was given a special Academy Award. While continuing to perform his one-man stage shows he worked steadily in character parts, the best being the wealthy shopkeeper who marries the much younger Leslie Caron in *Fanny*. One last full-fledged musical, *Can-Can*, featured a duet with Frank Sinatra, but it was as heavy-handed as *Love Me Tonight* had been light. He had a hit with the Disney adventure *In Search of the Castaways*, and regained top billing for playing a priest in the fluffy farce *Monkeys, Go Home!* There were several memoirs including *The Man in the Straw Hat* (1949), *With Love* (1960), and the posthumously published *I Remember It Well* (1972).

Screen: 1921: Le Mauvais Garçon; **1929:** Innocents of Paris; The Love Parade; **1930:** Paramount on Parade; The Big Pond; Playboy of Paris; **1931:** The Smiling Lieutenant; **1932:** One Hour With You; Make Me a Star; Love Me Tonight; **1933:** A Bedtime Story; The Way to Love; **1934:** The Merry Widow; **1935:** Folies Bergère; **1936:** The Beloved Vagabond; **1939:** With a Smile/Avec le Sourire (Fr: 1936); **1940:** The Man of the Hour/L'Homme de Jour (Fr: 1936); **1941:** Break the News (Fr: 1938); Personal Column/Pieges (Fr: 1939); **1947:** Man About Town/Le Silence est D'Or (Fr: 1945); **1950:** A Royal Affair/Le Roi; Just Me/Ma Pomme; **1953:** Schlager-Parade (nUSr); **1954:** Cento Anni D'Amore (nUSr); **1956:** My Seven Little Sins/J'Avais Sept Filles; **1957:** The Happy Road (voice); Love in the Afternoon; **1958:** Gigi; **1959:** Count Your Blessings; **1960:** Can-Can; Black Tights (narrator); A Breath of Scandal; Pepe; **1961:** Fanny; **1962:** Jessica; In Search of the Castaways; **1963:** A New Kind of Love; **1964:** Panic Button; I'd Rather Be Rich; **1967:** Monkeys, Go Home!; **1970:** The

Aristocats (voice).
Select TV: 1967: Ce'st la Vie (sp).

JULIE CHRISTIE
BORN: CHUKUA, ASSAM, INDIA, APRIL 14, 1941.

The so-called 1960s "British Invasion" was, no doubt, dominated by the men, but the one motion picture performer who, perhaps, embodied it more than any other was Julie Christie. The beautiful actress with the full lips and sad eyes was born on her father's tea plantation in India but did her schooling in England, where she eventually attended the Central School of Music and Drama. There were three seasons with Frinton-on-Sea Rep, television work, and small parts in some films before director John Schlesinger chose her for a pivotal supporting role in *Billy Liar*, in 1963. As the liberated girl who offers Tom Courtenay the hope of a more interesting life, she was quite smashing. It was Schlesinger who gave her first starring role, in *Darling*, and Christie became the rage of the British cinema in 1965. It was hard to judge the depth and range of her performance since she was required to be an emotionally deadened, selfish, vacuous creature who sleeps her way to a position of total un-fulfillment. You certainly didn't like this detached character, but the critical world loved Christie as she won several honors including the Academy Award for Best Actress. The film itself became one of the seminal ones of the new British realism craze of the 1960s and even reached beyond the art houses to find a reasonable amount of success with audiences who didn't mind something this disturbing and bleak. To cap off the year she was in a monster hit, David Lean's *Doctor Zhivago*, as his lady love, Lara, the part most moviegoers would forever associate her with. She pulled off a dual role in the interesting film of the sci-fi parable *Fahrenheit 451*, then was back with Schlesinger again for *Far From the Madding Crowd*. Since her wishy-washy character made audiences want to tear their hair out, this lengthy, heavily publicized effort was a major box-office failure. There were attempts by fans to raise its stature in later years, and the same could be said for director Richard Lester's challenging *Petulia*, containing perhaps her best performance, as the sad, emotionally unhinged woman carrying on a hopeless affair with doctor George C. Scott.

During the 1970s she played the wealthy woman in love with poor Alan Bates in *The Go-Between*, and engaged in one of the more startling sex scenes of its day, with Donald Sutherland, in *Don't Look Now*, a creepy psychological thriller that was probably the most satisfying film of director Nicolas Roeg's often off-putting career. She received another Oscar nomination, as the madam who takes to drugs, in *McCabe and Mrs. Miller*, although the film was clearly dominated by her co-star, Warren Beatty. Since their names were privately linked during this period, she was again his leading lady, for *Shampoo*, where her outrageous behavior under a banquet table was crucial in the movie achieving notoriety and financial success, and for *Heaven Can Wait*, somewhat out of place with her staid performance in this otherwise sparkling fantasy-comedy. That was basically the end of her high profile movie career as she moved into more specialized, international productions. Among those films that had some degree of success on the art house circuit were Merchant Ivory's *Heat and Dust*, which brought her back to the country of her birth, and *Miss Mary*, playing a governess in this story filmed in Argentina. Her one big budget Hollywood film of the 1980s, *Power*, was a major washout, although she herself was still as watchable as ever in the secondary role of Richard Gere's wife.

After a long absence from mainstream movies she played David Thewlis's mother in the fantasy *Dragonheart*, bringing a certain dignity to it all, followed by her fine performance as Gertrude in Kenneth Branagh's full-length presentation of *Hamlet*. Happily there was another sensational role around the corner, in *Afterglow*, as a former movie star, who is slowly unraveling as she faces advancing age and a philandering husband. Her performance was another of her very best and she earned an Oscar nomination for it.

Screen: 1962: Crooks Anonymous; The Fast Lady; 1963: Billy Liar; 1965: Young Cassidy; Darling; Doctor Zhivago; 1966: Fahrenheit 451; 1967: Far From the Madding Crowd; 1968: Petulia; 1969: In Search of Gregory; 1971: The Go-Between; McCabe and Mrs. Miller; 1973: Don't Look Now; 1975: Shampoo; Nashville; 1977: Demon Seed; 1978: Heaven Can Wait; 1981: Memoirs of a Survivor; 1982: Les Quarantiemes Rugissants/The Roaring Forties (nUSr); The Return of the Soldier; 1983: Heat and Dust; 1986: Power; Miss Mary; La Memoire Tatouee/Secret Obsession (nUSr); 1988: The Gold Diggers (filmed 1983); Silent Memory (dtv); 1990: Fools of Fortune; 1996: Dragonheart; Hamlet; 1997: Afterglow; 2001: Bephegor: Phantom of the Louvre (nUSr); Snapshots (nUSr); 2002: No Such Thing; 2003: I'm With Lucy.
NY Stage: 1995: Uncle Vanya.
Select TV: 1983: Separate Tables (sp); 1988: Sins of the Fathers (ms); Dadah is Death (ms); 1992: The Railway Station Man; 1996: Karaoke (ms).

EDUARDO CIANNELLI
BORN: NAPLES, ITALY, AUGUST 30, 1887.
DIED: OCTOBER 8, 1969.

A former medical student and opera singer, Eduardo Ciannelli came to Hollywood in 1933 to repeat his stage role in *Reunion in Vienna*. His grim features and thick accent made him ideal for movie villains, starting with *Winterset*, as repulsive gangster Trock Estrella, intent on revenge against Burgess Meredith, a repeat of his Broadway role that he played, yet again, on television in the 1950s. He projected dark menace in *Marked Woman*, as a dangerous racketeer who orders Bette Davis beaten up; in *Super-Sleuth* his villainy was used in a lighter tone, threatening to kill actor Jack Oakie because his last movie was so bad; in *Angels Wash Their Faces*, he was an arsonist facing the Termite Club (the Dead End Kids); in *Bulldog Drummond's Bride*, he was a bank robber posing as a house painter; in *Foreign Correspondent*, he turned up as one of the Nazis; and, in his most memorable role, he was the evil Guru in *Gunga Din*. There was a lead in the Republic serial, *The Mysterious Dr. Satan*, and a regular role on the television series *Johnny Staccato* in the late 1950s. During World War II he changed his billing to "Edward" and took atypically benign roles, as a bar owner in *Kitty Foyle*, and as a mayor in *A Bell for Adano*, but as late as the 1960s he was still being called upon for his dangerous scowl such Mafia-related movies as *The Brotherhood* and *Stiletto*.

Screen: 1933: Reunion in Vienna; 1935: The Scoundrel; 1936: Winterset; 1937: Marked Woman; Hitting a New High; On Such a Night; Super Sleuth; The Girl From Scotland Yard; Criminal Lawyer; The League of Frightened Men; 1938: Law of the Underworld; Blind Alibi; 1939: Gunga Din; Society Lawyer; The Angels Wash Their Faces; Risky Business; Bulldog Drummond's Bride; 1940: Strange Cargo; Foreign Correspondent; Kitty Foyle; Zanzibar; Forgotten Girls; The Mummy's Hand; Outside the Three-Mile Limit; Mysterious Dr. Satan (serial); 1941: They Met in Bombay; I Was a Prisoner on Devil's Island; Ellery Queen's Penthouse Mystery; Paris Calling; Sky Raiders (serial); **1942:** Dr. Broadway; Cairo; You Can't Escape Forever; **1943:** The Constant Nymph; They Got Me Covered; Adventures of the Flying Cadets (serial); Flight for Freedom; **1944:** Passage to Marseille; The Mask of Dimitrios; The Conspirators; Storm Over Lisbon; **1945:** A Bell for Adano; Dillinger; Incendiary Blonde; Crime Doctor's Warning; **1946:** Heartbeat; California; Perilous Holiday; Gilda; The Wife of Monte Cristo; Joe Palooka-Champ; **1947:** The Lost Moment; Seven Keys to Baldpate; Crime Doctor's Gamble; Rose of Santa Rosa; **1948:** On Our Merry Way/A Miracle Can Happen; To the Victor; I Love Trouble; The Creeper; **1950:** Rapture; Inesorabili/Fighting Men (nUSr); **1951:** The People Against O'Hara; Fugitive Lady; E'lamore che mi Rovina (nUSr); Lt. Giorgio (nUSr); Prigionieri dele Tenebre (nUSr); **1953:** Volcano; I Vinti/The Vanquished (nUSr); **1954:** The City Stands Trial; Voice of Silence; Vomini ombra/Shadow Men (nUSr). Probito/Forbidden (nUSr); **1955:** Mambo; Helen of Troy; City of Condemned Women (nUSr); The Stranger's Hand; **1957:** Love Slaves of the Amazon; The Monster From Green Hell; Il Ricatto di un Padre (nUSr); **1958:** Houseboat; Attila; **1963:** 40 Pounds of Trouble; **1964:** The Visit; **1965:** Massacre at Grand Canyon; **1966:** The Chase; **1968:** The Brotherhood; **1969:** McKenna's Gold; Stiletto; Colpo Rovente (nUSr); Boot Hill; Syndicate; The Secret of Santa Vittoria.

NY Stage: 1920: Always You; **1924:** Rose Marie; **1928:** The Front Page; **1930:** Sari; This Man's Town; Uncle Vanya; The Inspector General; **1931:** The Wiser They Are; Reunion in Vienna; **1933:** Foolscap (and wr.); **1934:** Yellow Jack; Mahogany Hall (and dir.); **1935:** A Journey by Night; Winterset; **1961:** The Devil's Advocate.

Select TV: 1951: The Idol of San Vittore (sp); Winterset (sp); **1956:** The Fall of the House of Usher (sp); **1957:** Carriage from Britain (sp); **1959:** The Killers of Mussolini (sp); **1959–60:** Johnny Staccato (series).

DIANE CILENTO

Born: Rabaul, New Guinea, April 2, 1933. Raised in England. ed: AADA, RADA.

This earthy British actress was already appearing onstage in her teens prior to her film debut, in her native country, in *Wings of Danger*. She was seen principally in English productions for the next 10 years, and landed her first lead in the title role of the whimsical *The Angel Who Pawned Her Harp*. Some of the films surfacing in the U.S. included *The Admiral Crichton*, which was re-titled *Paradise Lagoon*, and Gary Cooper's last, *The Naked Edge*. There were some New York stage appearances as well, including *Tiger at the Gates*, which earned her a Theatre World Award. She made her name, albeit temporarily, with her lusty portrayal of the poacher's daughter, Molly, in the 1963 Academy Award-winning smash, *Tom Jones*. Cilento competed with two of her co-stars, Edith Evans and Joyce Redman, for the supporting actress Oscar but they all lost to Margaret Rutherford. Her other outstanding performance, in the underrated 1967 Paul Newman western *Hombre*, featured her as the most commendable member of a group of ambushed stagecoach passengers. In between she was a psychiatric patient suspected of murdering her shrink in *The Third Secret*, and the closest thing to a love interest in the epic *The Agony and the Ecstasy*, considering the principals were a pope and a homosexual. During the 1970s she appeared in commercially unsuccessful movies like the botched historical piece *Hitler: The Last Ten Days*, and the cult thriller *The Wicker Man*, where she led her followers

in a memorable fertility dance. In latter years she concentrated on writing, publishing the novels *The Manipulator* and *The Hybrid*. She was married (1962–73) to Sean Connery and is the mother of actor Jason Connery. Her marriage to playwright Anthony Shaffer lasted from 1985 to his death in 2001.

Screen: 1952: Dead on Course/Wings of Danger; Moulin Rouge; **1953:** Meet Mr. Lucifer; **1954:** The Angel Who Pawned Her Harp; The Passing Stranger; **1955:** Passage Home; The Woman for Joe; **1957:** Paradise Lagoon/The Admirable Crichton; **1958:** The Truth About Women; **1959:** Jet Storm; **1961:** Stop Me Before I Kill/The Full Treatment; The Naked Edge; **1962:** I Thank a Fool; **1963:** Tom Jones; **1964:** The Third Secret; Rattle of a Simple Man; **1965:** The Agony and the Ecstasy; **1967:** Hombre; **1969:** Negatives; **1972:** Z.P.G.; **1973:** Hitler: The Last Ten Days; The Wicker Man; **1975:** The Tiger Lily; **1981:** Duet for Four; **1985:** The Boy Who Had Everything.

NY Stage: 1955: Tiger at the Gates; **1959:** Heartbreak House; **1960:** The Good Soup.

Select TV: 1967: Another Moon Called Earth (sp); **1973:** Spell of Evil (sp); **1978:** Tycoon (series); **1982:** For the Term of His Natural Life (sp).

DANE CLARK

(Bernard Zanville) Born: New York, NY, February 18, 1913. ed: Cornell Univ., St. John's Univ. Died: September 11, 1998.

Following unsuccessful attempts to make a living as a lawyer, a model, a boxer, and a stage actor, diminutive tough guy Dane Clark came to Hollywood in 1942. Originally acting in small roles under his real name, he was signed by Warner Bros., who gave him the show business moniker for which he never developed any fondness. Used strictly as a supporting player, he appeared in such wartime films as *Destination Tokyo*, as a submarine crewman named Tin Can, and *Pride of the Marines*, as the best buddy of blinded John Garfield, an actor with whom Clark was often (unfavorably) compared. Also in uniform, he was a horny soldier in *God Is My Co-Pilot*, and danced with Joan Crawford in the all-star *Hollywood Canteen*. The studio finally awarded him starring roles in *That Way With Women*, where he was up-staged by Sidney Greenstreet, and *Deep Valley*, as an escaped con protected by Ida Lupino. It was in a loan-out to Republic that he gave his best performance, as an accidental killer on the run in the "B" thriller, *Moonrise*. Back at Warners he continued to appear in standard properties with standard titles like *Backfire*, *Barricade*, and *Whiplash*. Clearly not the stuff of star material, he made his living carrying second-string efforts like *Go, Man, Go*, playing Abe Saperstein, the creator of the Harlem Globetrotters. Some British-made features included *Highly Dangerous*, as a reporter teamed with scientist Margaret Lockwood, and *The Gambler and the Lady*, with Kathleen Byron. He then made the transition from the big screen to the small one, where he received a steady stream of work, including some unsuccessful weekly series.

Screen: as Bernard Zanville: 1942: The Glass Key; Sunday Punch; Pride of the Yankees; Wake Island; Tennessee Johnson; **1943:** Action in the North Atlantic.

as Dane Clark: 1943: Destination Tokyo; **1944:** The Very Thought of You; Hollywood Canteen; **1945:** God Is My Co-Pilot; Pride of the Marines; **1946:** Her Kind of Man; A Stolen Life; **1947:** That Way With Women; Deep Valley; **1948:** Moonrise; Embraceable You; Whiplash; **1949:** Without Honor; **1950:** Barricade; Backfire; Time Running Out/Gunman in the Streets; **1951:** Never Trust a Gambler; Fort Defiance; Highly Dangerous;

1952: The Gambler and the Lady; 1954: Go, Man, Go; Paid to Kill/ Five Days; Thunder Pass; Port of Hell; Blackout/Murder by Proxy; 1955: Toughest Man Alive; 1956: The Man Is Armed; Massacre; 1957: Outlaw's Son; 1968: The Whistle (nUSr); 1970: The McMasters; 1980: The Woman Inside; 1982: Blood Song; 1988: Last Rites.

NY Stage: AS BERNARD ZANVILLE: 1934: Sailors of Cattaro; 1935: Panic; Till the Day I Die; Waiting for Lefty; Dead End; Sweet Shadow.

AS DANE CLARK: 1951: The Number; 1954: Fragile Fox; 1962: A Thousand Clowns; Brecht on Brecht (ob); 1968: Mike Downstairs.

Select TV: 1955: One Life (sp); 1956–57: Wire Service (series); 1957: Reunion (sp); A Hero's Return (sp); 1958: The Enemy Within (sp); 1959: Bold Venture (series); The Killers (sp); 1961: No Exit (sp); The Devil Makes Sunday (sp); 1971: The Face of Fear; 1972: The Family Rico; Say Goodbye, Maggie Cole; 1973–74: Perry Mason (series); 1975: James Dean; Murder on Flight 502; 1976: The Return of Joe Forrester; 1976–77: Once an Eagle (ms); 1979: The French Atlantic Affair (ms); 1980: Condominium.

FRED CLARK

BORN: LINCOLN, CA, MARCH 9, 1914.
ED: STANFORD UNIV., AADA.
DIED: DECEMBER 5, 1968.

A bald, mustachioed character actor who specialized in crafty, short-tempered types, Fred Clark came to Hollywood in 1947 to play a detective in Warner Bros.'s *The Unsuspected*. He stayed on for 21, very busy years, playing roles as diverse as a hearing-impaired gangster in Universal's *Ride the Pink Horse*; the studio executive with a "set of ulcers" in *Sunset Blvd.*; Montgomery's Clift's lawyer in *A Place in the Sun*; movie producer Richard Conte's business partner in *Hollywood Story*; the married man who plans a weekend tryst with Betty Grable in *How to Marry a Millionaire*; the harried chief-of-staff working for Fred Astaire in *Daddy Long Legs*; a slimy board member trying to slicker stock holder Judy Holliday in *The Solid Gold Cadillac*; Jane Wyman's philandering boss in *Miracle in the Rain*; a sadistic cop who survives a plane crash in *Back from Eternity*; a detective investigating the kidnapping of movie star Jane Russell in *The Fuzzy Pink Nightgown*; the stuffy banker put ill at ease by flamboyant Rosalind Russell in *Auntie Mame*; and the military commander in *Don't Go Near the Water*. Highly adept at comedy, he made a great foil for such comedians as Bob Hope (*The Lemon Drop Kid, Here Come the Girls*), Abbott and Costello (*Abbott & Costello Meet the Keystone Cops*, doing a rotten Russian accent), and Jerry Lewis (*The Caddy, Living It Up, Visit to a Small Planet*). In his later years the quality of his work was diminished in feeble comedies like *Sergeant Deadhead* and *War, Italian Style*, in both instances playing opposite a tired Buster Keaton. On television he was best known as neighbor Harry Morton on *The George Burns-Gracie Allen Show*. He was married (1952–63) to actress Benay Venuta.

Screen: 1947: The Unsuspected; Ride the Pink Horse; 1948: Hazard; Fury at Furnace Creek; Mr. Peabody and the Mermaid; Two Guys From Texas; Cry of the City; 1949: Flamingo Road; The Younger Brothers; Task Force; Alias Nick Beal; The Lady Takes a Sailor; White Heat; 1950: Sunset Blvd.; The Eagle and the Hawk; Return of the Frontiersman; The Jackpot; Mrs. O'Malley and Mr. Malone; 1951: A Place in the Sun; The Lemon Drop Kid; Hollywood Story; Meet Me After the Show; 1952: Dreamboat; Three for Bedroom C; 1953: The Caddy; Here Come the Girls; How to Marry a Millionaire; The Stars Are Singing;

1954: Living It Up; 1955: How to Be Very, Very Popular; Abbott and Costello Meet the Keystone Cops; Daddy Long Legs; The Court-Martial of Billy Mitchell; 1956: The Solid Gold Cadillac; Miracle in the Rain; Back From Eternity; The Birds and the Bees; 1957: Joe Butterfly; Don't Go Near the Water; The Fuzzy Pink Nightgown; 1958: Mardi Gras; Auntie Mame; 1959: The Mating Game; It Started With a Kiss; 1960: The Passionate Thief; Visit to a Small Planet; Bells Are Ringing; 1961: A Porte Chuise/Behind Closed Doors (nUSr); 1962: Hemingway's Adventures of a Young Man; Wild Living (nUSr); Boys' Night Out; Zotz!; 1963: Move Over, Darling; 1964: The Curse of the Mummy's Tomb; 1965: John Goldfarb, Please Come Home; Sergeant Deadhead; When the Boys Meet the Girls; Dr. Goldfoot and the Bikini Machine; 1967: War, Italian Style; I Sailed to Tahiti With an All-Girl Crew; 1968: The Horse in the Gray Flannel Suit; Skidoo; 1969: Eve.

NY Stage: 1938: School House on the Lot; What a Life; 1939: See My Lawyer; 1956: Mister Roberts; 1957: Romanoff and Juliet; 1960: Viva Madison Avenue; 1964: Absence of a Cello.

Select TV: 1951–53: The George Burns-Gracie Allen Show (series); 1953: Twentieth Century (sp); 1956: Circle of Guilt (sp); President (sp); 1957: The Singin' Idol (sp); 1959: The Case of Two Sisters (sp); 1961: My Darling Judge (sp); 1962: The Hold-Out (sp); Male Call (sp); 1965: Mr. Governess (sp); 1966: The Double Life of Henry Phyfe (series); Olympus 7-0000 (sp).

PETULA CLARK

BORN: EWELL, SURREY, ENGLAND, NOVEMBER 15, 1932.

Although she had a movie career that dated back to the early 1940s, Petula Clark was relatively unknown in the United States until she began climbing the pop charts in the 1960s. Having started as a child singer during World War II, she was soon appearing in British films, including *I Know Where I'm Going!* and *Vice Versa*, opposite Anthony Newley, but few of her pictures made it across the sea. The handful that did included *The Promoter/The Card*, starring Alec Guinness; *My Heart Goes Crazy*, a British musical originally called *London Town*, made seven years before its U.S. release; and *Track the Man Down*, which had an American star, Kent Taylor. During the mid-1960s she became an enormously popular singer with such hits as "Downtown," "I Know a Place," "My Love," and "Don't Sleep in the Subway." Hollywood capitalized by casting her in two musicals: in *Finian's Rainbow*, as an Irish colleen, she danced a bit with Fred Astaire and sang such lilting numbers as "Look to the Rainbow" to perfection; and in *Goodbye, Mr. Chips* she reprised Greer Garson's old role, only now she was a musical hall entertainer. Although she was one of the brightest talents of the genre, musicals were on their way out and her film career foundered. She returned to England where she made several stage appearances, finally coming to Broadway in 1994 in *Bloodbrothers*, reminding audiences of what they'd been missing.

Screen: 1944: A Medal From the General; Strawberry Roan; 1945: Murder in Reverse; I Know Where I'm Going!; 1946: London Town/My Heart Goes Crazy; 1947: Vice Versa; Holiday Camp; 1948: Easy Money; Here Come the Huggetts; 1949: Vote for Huggett; The Huggetts Abroad; Don't Ever Leave Me; 1950: The Romantic Age; Dance Hall; 1951: White Corridors; Madame Louise; 1952: The Card/The Promoter; Made in Heaven; 1953: The Runaway Bus; The Gay Dog;

The Happiness of Three Women; 1955: Track the Man Down; 1957: That Woman Opposite; Six-Five Special; 1963: A Couteaux Tires/Daggers Drawn; 1965: Questi Pazzi Pazzi Italiani; 1966: The Big T.N.T. Show; 1968: Finian's Rainbow; 1969: Goodbye, Mr. Chips; 1980: Never Never Land.

NY Stage: 1994: Blood Brothers.

Select TV: 1968: Petula (sp).

MAE CLARKE

(VIOLET MARY KLOTZ) BORN: PHILADELPHIA, PA, AUGUST 16, 1907. DIED: APRIL 29, 1992.

In one fabulous year, Mae Clarke made a lasting contribution to film history. A cabaret dancer, she worked her way up to Hollywood in 1929, to appear in Fox's *Big Time*, in which she and Lee Tracy were vaudevillians, and *Nix on Dames*, as the romantic bone of contention between Robert Ames and William Harrigan. Two years later, in 1931, she had her *annus mirabilis*. First she was Molly, a prostitute in love with the mousey death-row inmate in the original version of *The Front Page*; then she was immortalized by getting a grapefruit-half shoved in her kisser by boyfriend James Cagney in Warners's classic gangster flick *The Public Enemy*; next she was Colin Clive's bride, confronted by the Monster on her wedding day in *Frankenstein*; and finally, she was a dancer-turned-streetwalker, in the first filming of *Waterloo Bridge*. These last two were stylishly directed by James Whale, at Universal, where Clarke was briefly under contract. After that remarkable run, her films became more routine. She was a doomed model in *Three Wise Girls*; a nightclub dancer in the juicy pre-code *Night World*; a whore in *Nana*; a schoolteacher in *Silk Hat Kid*; and another dame roughed up by Cagney in *Lady Killer*. By the end of the decade she was working at Republic in second features, and she would continue to find employment as an unbilled supporting player, in such movies as *Singin' in the Rain*, as a hairdresser; *The Catered Affair*, as a saleswoman; and *Thoroughly Modern Millie*, as a an office worker.

Screen: 1929: Big Time; Nix on Dames; 1930: The Dancers; The Fall Guy; Men on Call; 1931: Reckless Living; The Front Page; The Good Bad Girl; Waterloo Bridge; The Public Enemy; Frankenstein; 1932: Impatient Maiden; Three Wise Girls; Final Edition; Night World; Breach of Promise; The Penguin Pool Murder; As the Devil Commands; 1933: Parole Girl; Turn Back the Clock; Penthouse; Going Hollywood; Fast Workers; Lady Killer; Flaming Gold; 1934: This Side of Heaven; Let's Talk It Over; Nana; The Man With Two Faces; 1935: The Daring Young Man; Silk Hat Kid; Hitch Hike Lady; 1936: The House of 1,000 Candles; Wild Brian Kent; Hats Off; Hearts in Bondage; 1937: Great Guy; Trouble in Morocco; Outlaws of the Orient; 1940: Women in War; 1941: Sailors on Leave; 1942: Flying Tigers; The Lady From Chungking; 1944: And Now Tomorrow; Here Come the Waves; 1945: Kitty; 1948: Daredevils of the Clouds; 1949: Streets of San Francisco; Gun Runner; King of the Rocket Men (serial); 1950: Annie Get Your Gun; The Yellow Cab Man; Duchess of Idaho; 1951: The Unknown Man; The Great Caruso; Royal Wedding; The People Against O'Hara; Callaway Went Thataway; Three Guys Named Mike; Mr. Imperium; 1952: Thunderbirds; Love Is Better Than Ever; Skirts Ahoy!; Pat and Mike; Fearless Fagan; Singin' in the Rain; Because of You; Horizons West; 1953: Confidentially Connie; 1954: Magnificent Obsession; 1955: Women's Prison; Not as a Stranger; I Died a Thousand Times; Wichita; 1956: Come Next Spring; The Catered Affair; Mohawk; The Desperados Are in Town; Ride the High Iron; 1958: The Voice in the Mirror; 1959: Ask Any Girl; 1966: A Big Hand for the Little Lady; 1967: Thoroughly Modern Millie; 1970: Watermelon Man; 1989: Beverly Hills Brats.

NY Stage: 1924: Sitting Pretty; 1925: Gay Paree; 1926: The Noose; 1927: Manhattan Mary.

Select TV: 1954: The Man in the Cellar (sp); 1956: Front Page Father (sp).

STANLEY CLEMENTS

BORN: LONG ISLAND, NY, JULY 16, 1926. DIED: OCTOBER 16, 1981.

Pint-sized Stanley Clements's specialty was playing wise-guy teens of limited intelligence. His early work included a pivotal role in Fox's *Tall, Dark and Handsome*, as a teen hood befriended by two-bit gangster Cesar Romero; *On the Sunny Side*, as a bully giving British refugee Roddy McDowall a hard time; and two appearances with the East Side Kids, in *Smarts Alecks* and *'Neath Brooklyn Bridge*. (He later became the star of the series after the ensemble mutated into the Bowery Boys.) At Paramount he had a showy role as the street tough who helps Bing Crosby form his boys' choir in 1944's *Going My Way*, and landed his best role the following year, as the doomed jockey involved with racetrack corruption, in an entertaining Alan Ladd vehicle, *Salty O'Rourke*. He reverted to juvenile delinquency in the second-run features *Bad Boy*, *Johnny Holliday*, and *Military Academy*, before landing leads in Monogram/Allied Artists "B" pictures like *Army Bound*, as a racecar driver who ends up in the service; *White Lightning*, as an ace hockey player; and *Hot News*, as a boxer-turned-reporter, exposing a gambling operation. In 1956 he replaced Leo Gorcey in the declining Bowery Boys series, playing a character called Duke, starting with *Fighting Trouble* and ending with *In the Money*, two years later. He was briefly married (1945–48) to actress Gloria Grahame, and died only 11 days after she did, in 1981.

Screen: 1941: Tall, Dark and Handsome; Accent on Love; Down in San Diego; I Wake Up Screaming; 1942: Right to the Heart; Smart Alecks; On the Sunny Side; 'Neath Brooklyn Bridge; 1943: They Got Me Covered; The More the Merrier; Ghosts on the Loose; Sweet Rosie O'Grady; You're a Lucky Fellow Mr. Smith; Thank Your Lucky Stars; 1944: Girl in the Case; Going My Way; Cover Girl; 1945: Salty O'Rourke; See My Lawyer; 1947: Variety Girl; 1948: Hazard; Big Town Scandal; Canon City; Joe Palooka in Winner Take All; The Babe Ruth Story; Racing Luck; 1949: Mr. Soft Touch; Bad Boy; Johnny Holiday; Red Light; 1950: Military Academy With That Tenth Avenue Gang; Destination Murder; 1951: The Pride of Maryland; 1952: Jet Job; Army Bound; Boots Malone; 1953: Off Limits; White Lightning; Hot News; 1954: The Rocket Man; 1955: Air Strike; Robber's Roost; Last of the Desperadoes; Mad at the World; Fort Yuma; 1956: Wiretapper; Fighting Trouble; Hot Shots; 1957: Hold That Hypnotist; Spook Chasers; Looking for Danger; Up in Smoke; 1958: In the Money; A Nice Little Bank That Should Be Robbed; 1961: Sniper's Ridge; Saintly Sinners; 1963: Tammy and the Doctor; It's a Mad Mad Mad Mad World; 1965: That Darn Cat!; 1968: Panic in the City; 1973: Timber Tramp; 1978: Hot Lead, Cold Feet.

MONTGOMERY CLIFT

(EDWARD MONTGOMERY CLIFT) BORN: OMAHA, NE, OCTOBER 17, 1920. DIED: JULY 23, 1966.

In the 1950s, Montgomery Clift was one of the triumvirate of young men who were proclaimed the groundbreakers of the naturalistic style of acting. But unlike Marlon Brando, whose longevity ensured venerability, and James Dean, whose early death guaranteed legendary status, Clift lived just long enough to watch his career peter out due to ill health, alcoholism, and professional and personal instability. In any event, he was simply one of the most powerful, sensitive, and magnetic actors the screen has ever known. Through his parents' encouragement he was already onstage by age 14, in the summer stock production of *Fly Away Home*, which made it to Broadway in 1935. Clift spent the next ten years building an enviable reputation in theatre, appearing in such productions as *There Shall Be No Night*, with the Lunts; the original presentation of *The Skin of Our Teeth*, directed by Elia Kazan; and Lillian Hellman's *The Searching Wind*. After turning down several offers, he finally came to Hollywood to co-star as John Wayne's combative adopted son in the hit western *Red River*, an engrossing character study greatly enhanced by the sensitivity Clift brought to his role. Because of post-production delays, the film was released in 1948, *after* Clift's second venture, *The Search*, a moving story of a young G.I. who forms a relationship with a displaced boy in the aftermath of World War II. Clift's superb performance won him his first Oscar nomination and he became one of the most written-about and coveted new actors of the postwar era. He was not afraid to display his vulnerability and compassion, and although audiences were initially drawn in by his awesomely handsome appearance, it was his barely concealed torment that kept them riveted.

He displayed his cruel side, as the fortune-hunting lover of Olivia de Havilland in *The Heiress*, and then played perhaps his most famous role, the doomed George Eastman in *A Place in the Sun*. His sensational portrayal of a social climber trying to unload pregnant girlfriend Shelley Winters in favor of the rich and lovely Elizabeth Taylor, earned him a second Oscar nomination. The film was a box-office and critical smash, bringing Clift to the peak of his popularity. Better yet was *From Here to Eternity*, the Best Picture Oscar-winner of 1953 and one of the biggest moneymakers of the decade. He gave his finest performance, as a stubborn, non-conformist soldier at odds with the army, and it brought yet another Oscar nomination to the star. Overwhelmed by his fame and the media attention, he dabbled in noncommercial fare like Vittorio de Sica's *Indiscretion of an American Wife*. The film, which was little more than an extended dialogue with Jennifer Jones at a rail station, suffered from poor distribution and excessive studio tampering. He returned to the stage in a revival of *The Sea Gull*, part of a four-year sabbatical from the screen, which was unheard of for a major star in that era.

While filming his return assignment, the MGM Civil War epic *Raintree County*, he was badly injured in a car accident. The resulting reconstructive surgery distorted his once beautiful features, rendering many of his facial muscles immobile, and leaving him with a haunted appearance. It is a testament to his talent that the disfigurement did not interfere with his expressive ability. *Raintree* was often incomprehensible but it was a hit, despite the continuity problems of editing together the pre- and post-operative Clift throughout the story. He was outstanding in *The Young Lions*, as a Jewish G.I., although the film's structure robbed audiences of seeing him share more than a scant few seconds of screen time with Brando. His quiet authority stood out amid the showier performances of Elizabeth Taylor and Katharine Hepburn in Tennessee Williams's unappetizing *Suddenly, Last Summer*, although by this time his drinking was making him quite difficult to work with. He could, however, still come through gloriously, as he did in John Houston's messy *The Misfits*, as Clark Gable's sad rodeo buddy. More impressive was his brief sequence as a mentally unbalanced witness who has faced sterilization by the Nazis in *Judgment at Nuremberg*. Clift was at his most riveting, his naked vulnerability mixing with his own increasing instability, and he landed his fourth Oscar nomination for his incredible performance. Unfortunately, the successive failures of the ambitious *Wild River*; director John Huston's well-liked biography of *Freud*; and the jumbled espionage drama *The Defector*, made it difficult for Elizabeth Taylor to convince Warner Bros. to hire Clift for *Reflections in a Golden Eye*. They at last relented, but Clift died of a heart attack before filming began and was replaced by Brando. It would have been interesting to see Clift, whose inner demons included his struggle with his own sexual identity in a less tolerant age, tackle the part of the tormented, gay army major.

Screen: 1948: The Search; Red River; 1949: The Heiress; 1950: The Big Lift; 1951: A Place in the Sun; 1953: I Confess; From Here to Eternity; Indiscretion of an American Wife/Terminal Station; 1957: Raintree County; 1958: The Young Lions; Lonelyhearts; 1959: Suddenly, Last Summer; 1960: Wild River; 1961: The Misfits; Judgment at Nuremberg; 1962: Freud; 1966: The Defector.

NY Stage: 1935: Fly Away Home; Jubilee; 1938: Yr. Obedient Husband; Eye on the Sparrow; Dame Nature; 1939: The Mother; 1940: There Shall Be No Night; 1942: The Skin of Our Teeth; 1944: Our Town; The Searching Wind; 1945: Foxhole in the Parlor; You Touched Me!; 1954: The Sea Gull (ob).

COLIN CLIVE

(COLIN CLIVE-GRIEG) BORN: ST. MALO, FRANCE, JANUARY 20, 1898. RAISED IN ENGLAND. ED: STONEYHURST COL., RADA. DIED: JUNE 25, 1937.

There are few over-the-top performances as warmly cherished as Colin Clive's Doctor Henry Frankenstein. His strangled, exulted cries of "It's alive! It's alive!" have become a part of movie folklore. The thin British actor with the tormented visage was born to a military family and would have followed that route had it not been for an injury. Opting for the stage, he landed his breakthrough role of the frightened alcoholic, Captain Stanhope, in the 1929 London production of *Journey's End*. When the play's director, James Whale, went to Hollywood the following year, he requested Clive for the film version, which won raves for its grim view of war. Whale, who was as comfortable with his homosexuality as Clive was uncomfortable with his, then gave the actor his immortalizing role, as the doctor who dares experiment with bringing the dead to life, in *Frankenstein*. Crazed, pitiable, and high-strung, he was perfect for the part and would reprise it in the equally enjoyable 1935 sequel, *Bride of Frankenstein*. He was Katharine Hepburn's leading man in one of her box-office failures, *Christopher Strong*; Rochester, in the forgotten Monogram version of *Jane Eyre*; a cruel wife-beater in the Whale melodrama *One More River*; and the crazed pianist Orlac who, following an accident, receives a new pair of hands, in the cult horror film *Mad Love*. He appeared in the biography of his ancestor, Robert Clive, *Clive of India*, but not in the title role, which was taken by Ronald Colman. A long-time alcoholic, Clive's health had been deteriorating steadily by the time of his death from intestinal and pulmonary ailments at age 39.

Screen: 1930: Journey's End; 1931: The Strong Sex; Frankenstein; 1932: Lily Christine; 1933: Christopher Strong; Looking Forward; 1934: The Key; Jane Eyre; One More River; 1935: Clive of India; The Right to Live; Bride of Frankenstein; The Girl From 10th Avenue; Mad Love; The Man Who Broke the Bank at Monte Carlo; The Widow From Monte Carlo; 1937: History Is Made at Night; The Woman I Love.

NY Stage: 1930: Overture; 1933: Eight Bells; The Lake; 1935: Libel!

ANDY CLYDE

BORN: BLAIRGOWRIE, SCOTLAND, MARCH 25, 1892. DIED: MAY 18, 1967.

This bespectacled Scottish comedian, whose trademark was his bushy moustache, came to the U.S. in 1923. Thanks to his friend and fellow Scotsman Jimmy Finlayson, Clyde obtained work at the Mack Sennett studios, appearing in supporting parts in various short comedies. With the coming of sound he began his own series of star comedies in which he portrayed a naïve hayseed, usually called Pop. The series took him from the Sennett Studios to Educational Pictures and over to Columbia, continuing all the way to 1956. Simultaneously he made a living as a character actor in features like *Million Dollar Legs*, in the title role, as a champion marathon runner; *The Little Minister*, as a Scottish policeman with the colorful moniker Wearyworld. *The Village Tale*, as a small-town storekeeper; and *Abe Lincoln in Illinois*, as a stagecoach driver. Paramount gave him bigger parts in a pair of "B's," *McFadden's Flats*, as barber who saves his friend's business, and *Straight from the Shoulder*, as a rifle-manufacturer, while a poverty row company, Chesterfield, gave him top-billing in *Red Lights Ahead*, as a junk dealer who tests his family's appetite for money. Starting with *Three Men from Texas*, in 1940, he played the recurring comical role of cook California Carlson in many Hopalong Cassidy westerns. He later could be found on television as a regular on such series as *The Real McCoys*.

Screen: (features): 1925: Branded Man; The Goodbye Kiss; 1929: Should a Girl Marry?; Ships of the Night; Midnight Daddies; 1932: Million Dollar Legs; 1934: The Little Minister; 1935: Romance in Manhattan; McFadden's Flats; The Village Tale; Annie Oakley; 1936: Yellow Dust; Straight From Shoulder; Two in a Crowd; Red Lights Ahead; 1937: The Barrier; 1939: It's a Wonderful World; Bad Lands; 1940: Abe Lincoln in Illinois; Cherokee Strip; Three Men From Texas; 1941: In Old Colorado; Doomed Caravan; Pirates on Horseback; Border Vigilantes; Wide Open Town; Secrets of the Wasteland; Stick to Your Guns; Twilight on the Trail; Outlaws of the Desert; Riders of the Timberline; 1942: Undercover Man; Lost Canyon; This Above All; 1943: The Leather Burners; Hoppy Serves a Writ; Border Patrol; False Colors; Colt Comrades; Bar 20; Riders of the Deadline; 1944: Texas Masquerade; Lumberjack; Forty Thieves; Mystery Man; 1945: Roughly Speaking; Son of the Prairie; 1946: The Devil's Playground; Fools' Gold; The Green Years; Unexpected Guest; Dangerous Venture; The Plainsman and the Lady; That Texas Jamboree; Throw a Saddle on a Star; 1947: Hoppy's Holiday; The Marauders; 1948: The Silent Conflict; The Dead Don't Dream; Strange Gamble; Sinister Journey; False Paradise; Borrowed Trouble; 1949: Crashing Thru; Riders of the Dusk; Shadows of the West; Range Land; Haunted Trails; 1950: Gunslingers; Arizona Territory; Cherokee Uprising; Fence Riders; Outlaws of Texas; Silver Raiders; 1951: Abilene Trail; 1955: The Road to Denver; Carolina Cannonball.

Select TV: 1957–63: The Real McCoys (series); 1958–64: Lassie (series); 1964–65: No Time for Sergeants (series).

LEE J. COBB

(LEO JACOBY) BORN: NEW YORK, NY, DECEMBER 8, 1911. DIED: FEBRUARY 11, 1976.

A forceful character actor with an edgy, authoritative voice, scowling Lee J. Cobb was so convincing at playing men older than himself that he never seems to have been young. He carried that cantankerous image off screen too, claiming to have hated every single experience he had in front of a movie camera. His early attempts to be an actor took him to California, but he failed to find movie work, and, after appearing with the Pasadena Playhouse, he returned to New York, where he became a member of the Group Theatre. He began getting roles in films like the Hopalong Cassidy western *North of the Rio Grande*, and Eddie Cantor's *Ali Baba Goes to Town*, around the time he scored a stage triumph in *Golden Boy*, in 1937. Two years later he was asked to repeat his role in the film version and was entirely believable as William Holden's elderly Italian father, although he was only 28 years old and a mere seven years Holden's senior. In 1943 Cobb joined 20th Century-Fox, starting with *Tonight We Raid Calais*, playing a French peasant, again older than himself. Over the next seven years he became one of Fox's prime supporting players and created a strong gallery of work in movies like *The Song of Bernadette*, as the village doctor; *Anna and the King of Siam*, as the King's right-hand man, Kralahome; *Call Northside 777*, as James Stewart's editor; and *Boomerang!*, as the police chief tracking a priest's killer.

At the end of the 1940s he played his greatest stage role, the world-weary Willy Loman, in Arthur Miller's groundbreaking *Death of a Salesman*. He received raves for realistically portraying an older man without resorting to makeup, but when the 1951 film version was made Cobb lost the role to Fredric March. Fox compensated him with the lead in *The Man Who Cheated Himself*, as a San Francisco cop who gets himself in hot water when his mistress kills her husband. The film did little business but there were consolations. In *On the Waterfront*, he had a dynamic turn as the bullying labor boss, which earned him a richly deserved Oscar nomination, and in *12 Angry Men* he was riveting as the most stubborn of a group of jurors. In the cult gangster film *Party Girl*, he was bellowing racketeer Rico Angelo, beating the daylights out of the guest of honor at a testimonial dinner; but stumbled badly, applying stereotypical Oriental makeup to play a war lord in *The Left Hand of God*. Another geriatric role, Feodor, in *The Brothers Karamazov*, earned him a second Oscar nomination. (His "son" — Yul Brynner — was only four years younger than Cobb in real life.) Another of his larger roles was as the sympathetic psychiatrist who is made privy to Joanne Woodward's multiple personalities in *The Three Faces of Eve*, and he carried two Columbia crime melodramas: the cheapjack *Miami Expose*, and the better *The Garment Jungle*, under threat of violence for not cooperating with the labor bosses.

A dependable bad guy, he lured Gary Cooper back into his outlaw clutches in the underrated *Man of the West*, and was a dangerous killer who forces Richard Widmark to help him across the border in *The Trap*. There were attempts at comedy: as a drunken playwright in *But Not for Me*; as Frank Sinatra's Jewish papa in *Come Blow Your Horn*; and as the befuddled head of the spy organization, ZOWIE, in *Our Man Flint*, and its sequel, *In Like Flint*, which required him, at one point, to dress in drag. He was guilty of some serious scenery chewing as the bushy-haired patriarch in the disastrous remake of *The Four Horsemen of the Apocalypse*. During the 1960s he found success on television, starring in the long running western series *The Virginian* for four seasons, and finally got to preserve his *Salesman* performance when a production of it was taped for television. Towards the end of his career he rated occasional top billing, as with the racial drama *The Liberation of L. B. Jones*, playing an attorney, and the Italian-made cheapie *Blood, Sweat and Fear*, as a drug kingpin. His widest exposure, however, came with the 1973 horror sensation, *The Exorcist*. As with so many times in the past, his gruff approach, as the suspicious police investigator, helped take a lot of the inherent silliness out of the proceedings.

Screen: AS LEE COBB: **1934:** Vanishing Shadow (serial); **1937:** North of the Rio Grande; Rustler's Valley.

AS LEE COLT: **1937:** Ali Baba Goes to Town.

AS LEE J. COBB: **1938:** Danger on the Air; **1939:** The Phantom Creeps (serial); Golden Boy; **1941:** This Thing Called Love; Men of Boys Town; Paris Calling; **1943:** The Moon Is Down; Tonight We Raid Calais; The Song of Bernadette; Buckskin Frontier; **1944:** Winged Victory; **1946:** Anna and the King of Siam; **1947:** Boomerang!; Captain From Castile; Johnny O'Clock; **1948:** The Miracle of the Bells; Call Northside 777; The Luck of the Irish; **1949:** The Dark Past; Thieves Highway; **1950:** The Man Who Cheated Himself; **1951:** Sirocco; The Family Secret; **1952:** The Fighter; **1953:** The Tall Texan; **1954:** Yankee Pasha; Gorilla at Large; On the Waterfront; Day of Triumph; **1955:** The Racers; The Road to Denver; The Left Hand of God; **1956:** The Man in the Gray Flannel Suit; Miami Expose; **1957:** 12 Angry Men; The Three Faces of Eve; The Garment Jungle; **1958:** The Brothers Karamazov; Man of the West; Party Girl; **1959:** The Trap; Green Mansions; But Not for Me; **1960:** Exodus; **1962:** The Four Horsemen of the Apocalypse; **1963:** How the West Was Won; Come Blow Your Horn; **1966:** Our Man Flint; **1967:** In Like Flint; **1968:** Coogan's Bluff; **1969:** They Came to Rob Las Vegas; McKenna's Gold; **1970:** The Liberation of L.B. Jones; Mafia/The Day of the Owl (filmed 1968); Macho Callahan; **1971:** Lawman; **1973:** The Man Who Loved Cat Dancing; La Polizia sta a Guardare/Ransom! Police Is Watching (nUSr); The Exorcist; **1975:** The Last Circus Show (nUSr); That Lucky Touch; Blood Sweat and Fear; **1976:** Cross Shot (nUSr); Nick the Sting (nUSr); **1977:** Ultimatum; **1979:** Arthur Miller on Home Ground.

NY Stage: **1935:** Crime and Punishment; Waiting for Lefty; Till the Day I Die; The Mother; **1936:** Bitter Stream; Johnny Johnson; **1937:** Golden Boy; **1939:** The Gentle People; Thunder Rock; **1940:** The Fifth Column; **1941:** Clash by Night; **1943:** Winged Victory; **1949:** Death of a Salesman; **1952:** Golden Boy (revival); **1953:** The Emperor's New Clothes; **1968:** King Lear.

Select TV: **1951:** The Moon and Sixpence (sp); **1954:** Night Visitor (sp); **1955:** Darkness at Noon (sp); **1956:** A Patch on Faith (sp); **1957:** Panic Button (sp); No Deadly Medicine (sp); **1959:** Project Immortality (sp); I, Don Quixote (sp); **1960:** Lear vs. the Committeeman (sp); Men in White (sp); **1962:** The Unstoppable Gray Fox (sp); **1962–66:** The Virginian (series); **1966:** Death of a Salesman (sp); **1970–71:** The Young Lawyers (series); **1972:** Heat of Anger; **1973:** Double Indemnity; **1974:** Dr. Max; Trapped Beneath the Sea; The Great Ice Rip-Off.

CHARLES COBURN

BORN: SAVANNAH, GA, JUNE 19, 1877.
DIED: AUGUST 30, 1961.

It took Charles Coburn a long time to get to the movies, but when he did he became one of the most beloved and ubiquitous of character players. The plump, jowly actor had started as company manager to the Savannah Theatre before talking them into hiring him as a performer. Following his 1901 Broadway debut, in *Up York State*, he created his own stock company, the Coburn Players, which included Ivah Wills, who became his wife in 1906. They spent several years on tour and then on Broadway, eventually opening their own theatre in New York in 1928, which was a quick financial failure. With a solitary film credit to his name, Coburn accepted an offer to come to Hollywood following his wife's death in 1937. His first major appearance, as the hard-drinking but sensible village doctor in *Of Human Hearts*, gave audiences their first glimpse of the oft-present Coburn monocle. His roles included straight drama, as in *Kings Row*, where he played the spiteful doctor who cut off Ronald Reagan's legs, and *In This Our Life*, as Bette Davis's pathetic uncle who seems to exhibit an "unnatural" interest in his niece. But comedy was his forte, notably in *The Lady Eve*, as Barbara Stanwyck's cardsharp partner, and in MGM's *The Captain Is a Lady*, as an old blowhard forced into a ladies' retirement community. In 1941, he received his first Oscar nomination, as the store owner who learns humanity from shop girl Jean Arthur, in *The Devil and Miss Jones*, and two years later, reteamed with Arthur, he won the Academy Award for *The More the Merrier*. However, his overbearing millionaire, who shares Arthur's apartment in wartime Washington, was played with far less charm than he had shown in some of his other roles.

His Oscar success rated some starring parts in mild vehicles like *My Kingdom for a Cook*, as an English ambassador in search of a decent chef while visiting the U.S.; *Shady Lady*, again dealing a dirty game of cards; and *Colonel Effingham's Raid*, the gentle tale of a man who fights to save a historic courthouse. In the poor adaptation of the Broadway musical *Knickerbocker Holiday*, Coburn, as Peter Stuyvestant, failed to make an impression with the big hit number of the show, "September Song." Sporting a bushy beard and a Scottish brogue, he received a third Oscar nomination, in 1946, as Dean Stockwell's colorful and influential great-grandfather in *The Green Years*. (Although it was a starring role his nomination was once again in the supporting category.) In the romantic comedy *Louisa* he vied with fellow senior citizen Edmund Gwenn for the hand of Spring Byington, then pursued the much younger Marilyn Monroe, first as a scientist in *Monkey Business*, then as a millionaire in *Gentlemen Prefer Blondes*. He was the object of intended mayhem in the British production *How to Murder a Rich Uncle*, and, as he entered his 80s, he essayed some historical roles: Hippocrates in *The Story of Mankind*, and Ben Franklin in *John Paul Jones*. He was preparing to film *Advise and Consent* when he died of a heart attack at the age of 84.

Screen: **1935:** The People's Enemy; **1938:** Of Human Hearts; Vivacious Lady; Yellow Jack; Lord Jeff; **1939:** Idiot's Delight; Made for Each Other; The Story of Alexander Graham Bell; Bachelor Mother; In Name Only; Stanley and Livingstone; **1940:** Road to Singapore; Florian; Edison, the Man; The Captain Is a Lady; Three Faces West; **1941:** The Lady Eve; The Devil and Miss Jones; Our Wife; Unexpected Uncle; H.M. Pulham, Esq.; **1942:** Kings Row; In This Our Life; George Washington Slept Here; **1943:** The More the Merrier; The Constant Nymph; Heaven Can Wait; Forever and a Day; My Kingdom for a Cook; Princess

O'Rourke; **1944:** Knickerbocker Holiday; The Impatient Years; Together Again; Wilson; **1945:** A Royal Scandal; Over 21; Shady Lady; Rhapsody in Blue; Colonel Effingham's Raid; **1946:** The Green Years; **1947:** Lured; The Paradine Case; **1948:** B.F.'s Daughter; Green Grass of Wyoming; **1949:** Impact; The Doctor and the Girl; The Gal Who Took the West; Yes Sir,, That's My Baby; Everybody Does It; **1950:** Peggy; Louisa; Mr. Music; **1951:** The Highwayman; **1952:** Has Anybody Seen My Gal?; Monkey Business; **1953:** Trouble Along the Way; Gentlemen Prefer Blondes; **1954:** The Rocket Man; The Long Wait; **1955:** How to Be Very, Very Popular; **1956:** The Power and the Prize; Around the World in Eighty Days; **1957:** Town on Trial; The Story of Mankind; **1958:** How to Murder a Rich Uncle; **1959:** A Stranger in My Arms; The Remarkable Mr. Pennypacker; John Paul Jones; **1960:** Pepe.

NY Stage: **1901:** Up York State; **1905:** The Player Maid; **1907:** The Coming of Mrs. Patrick; **1916:** The Yellow Jacket (and 1928 revival); **1917:** The Imaginary Invalid; **1918:** The Better 'ole; **1920:** French Leave; **1922:** The Bronx Express (and prod.); **1924:** The Farmer's Wife; **1925:** Trelawny of the Wells; **1926:** The Right Age to Marry (and dir.); Old Bill M.P.; **1928:** Diplomacy; The Yellow Jacket (revival; and prod.); **1928:** Falstaff (and prod.); **1930:** The Plutocrat (and dir.; prod.); **1932:** Troilus and Cressida; **1933:** Kultur (and dir.); **1934:** The First Legion; **1936:** Three Wise Fools; The County Chairman; Around the Corner; **1937:** Sun Kissed.

Select TV: **1950:** You Can't Take It With You (sp); **1953:** The World's My Oyster (sp); **1954:** The Royal Family (sp); One for the Road (sp); The Cuckoo in Spring (sp); **1956:** A Difficult Age (sp); Mr. Kagle and the Baby Sitter (sp); **1959:** The Wicked Scheme of Jebel Deeks (sp).

JAMES COBURN
BORN: LAUREL, NE, AUGUST 31, 1928.
ED: LOS ANGELES CITY COL., USC.
DIED: NOVEMBER 18, 2002

Lean and deep-voiced, James Coburn parlayed his wicked grin and cocksure attitude into 1960s stardom, when "cool" was very much in favor with movie audiences. Finding an interest in acting while at L.A. City College, he pursued his drama studies at USC and in New York with Stella Adler. He began landing small parts on television and then in films, starting with a Randolph Scott western, *Ride Lonesome*, teamed with Pernell Roberts as outlaws. Three Steve McQueen films in a row kick-started his career: *The Magnificent Seven*, as a knife-throwing mercenary; *Hell Is for Heroes*, as a corporal; and *The Great Escape*, as an Australian POW with a less-than-convincing accent. He continued to impress with supporting parts in *Charade*, as one of the villains out to dispose of Audrey Hepburn; *The Americanization of Emily*, as James Garner's womanizing friend; and *Major Dundee*, as a one-armed Indian Scout. In 1965 he moved up to second billing, after Anthony Quinn, in the oddball pirate adventure *A High Wind in Jamaica*.

He was cast as the title character in one of the many James Bond spoofs, *Our Man Flint*, released in 1966. His tongue-in-cheek performance as the super-cool spy was the main reason to watch this silly movie and its equally silly sequel, *In Like Flint*, and although the films made Coburn a star, he declined to continue the series. He wasn't the box-office attraction producers had hoped for, but during the next decade he was sufficiently popular to obtain starring roles in such fare as the mild crime tale with the great title, *Dead Heat on a Merry-Go-Round*; the flaky western *Waterhole # 3*, as a hellraising gambler; the cult comedy *The*

President's Analyst, a satire that fell maddeningly short of brilliance; the late 1960s artifact, *Duffy*, as a layabout enlisted to rob millionaire James Mason; *The Last of the Mobile Hot Shots*, a Tennessee Williams Southern gothic, in which he was a dying property owner who marries hooker Lynn Redgrave; Sergio Leone's epic spaghetti western *Duck, You Sucker*, whose unappetizing title was changed to *A Fistful of Dynamite* after customers stayed away; *The Honkers*, which was compared unfavorably to 1972's two other rodeo movies, *J.W. Coop* and *Junior Bonner*; and two at MGM: Blake Edwards's *The Carey Treatment*, as a doctor investigating a murder, and Sam Peckinpah's *Pat Garrett & Billy the Kid*, as Garrett, the lawman responsible for the death of the infamous outlaw. (The financially troubled studio tampered extensively with both these movies, much to the outrage of their respective directors.)

He fared better in the intriguing mystery *The Last of Sheila*, where his murder set the plot in motion, and the horse race epic, *Bite the Bullet*, teamed for maximum effect with Gene Hackman. Between these he had two major box-office duds, with the pickpocket guide, *Harry in Your Pocket*, and *The Internecine Project*, an unappealing international espionage thriller. By the time of the war drama *Cross of Iron*, in which he was a Nazi sergeant, and *The Baltimore Bullet*, where he played a pool shark, the audiences for James Coburn pictures had long disappeared. He took second billing to former *Magnificent Seven* co-star Charles Bronson in *Hard Times*, as his fight promoter; to Charlton Heston in *The Last Hard Men*, as a villain; and to media-hyped model Susan Anton in *Goldengirl*. Likewise, nobody hungered for *Loving Couples*, as Shirley MacLaine's smarmy, cheating spouse, or for a fly-by-night adventure, *High Risk*, so it was off to television for a spell. There were a few low profile theatrical features during the 1980s and he reappeared, white-haired, in the 1990s as a character actor in movies like *Young Guns II*, *Hudson Hawk*, *Sister Act 2*, and *Maverick*, which reteamed him briefly with former *Great Escape* co-star James Garner. A showy but unsympathetic role as Nick Nolte's hateful, abusive father in the glum *Affliction* garnered him a Best Supporting Actor Oscar, awarded more for his longevity than for his rather superficial performance. It did not lead to any immediate career resurrection, but, four years later he gave an outstanding performance as a dying novelist collaborating with gigolo Andy Garcia in *The Man from Elysian Fields*, released shortly before he succumbed to a heart attack.

Screen: **1959:** Ride Lonesome; Face of a Fugitive; **1960:** The Magnificent Seven; **1962:** Hell Is for Heroes; **1963:** The Great Escape; Charade; **1964:** The Man From Galveston; The Americanization of Emily; **1965:** Major Dundee; A High Wind in Jamaica; The Loved One; **1966:** Our Man Flint; What Did You Do in the War, Daddy?; Dead Heat on a Merry-Go-Round; **1967:** In Like Flint; Waterhole # 3; The President's Analyst; **1968:** Duffy; Candy; **1969:** Hard Contract; **1970:** Last of the Mobile Hot Shots; **1972:** Duck, You Sucker/A Fistful of Dynamite; The Honkers; The Carey Treatment; **1973:** The Last of Sheila; Pat Garrett & Billy the Kid; Harry in Your Pocket; **1974:** A Reason to Live, A Reason to Die; The Internecine Project; **1975:** Bite the Bullet; Hard Times; **1976:** Sky Riders; The Last Hard Men; Midway; **1977:** White Rock; Cross of Iron; **1978:** California Suite; **1979:** Firepower; The Muppet Movie; Goldengirl; **1980:** The Baltimore Bullet; Mr. Patman/Crossover (dtv); Loving Couples; **1981:** High Risk; Looker; **1985:** Martin's Day; **1986:** Death of a Soldier; **1990:** Train to Heaven (nUSr); Young Guns II; **1991:** Hudson Hawk; **1992:** The Player; Hugh Hefner: Once Upon a Time (narrator); **1993:** Deadfall; Sister Act 2: Back in the Habit; **1994:** Maverick; **1996:** The Set-Up (dtv); Skeletons (dtv); Eraser; The Nutty Professor; **1997:** Keys to Tulsa; **1998:**

Affliction; 1999: Payback; 2000: Intrepid/Deep Water (dtv); 2001: Monsters Inc. (voice); The Texas Rangers (narrator); 2002: Snow Dogs; The Man from Elysian Fields; 2003: American Gun.

Select TV: 1960: Klondike (series); 1961: Acapulco (series); 1978: The Dain Curse (ms); 1981: Jacqueline Susann's Valley of the Dolls; 1981–82: Darkroom (series host); 1983: Malibu; Pinocchio (sp); 1984: Draw!; 1985: Sins of the Father; 1992: Crash Landing: The Rescue of Flight 232/A Thousand Heroes; The Fifth Corner (series); 1993: The Hit List; 1994: Greyhounds; Ray Alexander: A Taste for Justice; 1995: The Avenging Angel; Ray Alexander: A Menu for Murder; The Set Up; A Christmas Reunion; 1996: The Cherokee Kid; 1997: The Second Civil War; 1998: Dean Koontz's Mr. Murder; 1999: Noah's Ark; Shake, Rattle and Roll: An American Love Story; 2000: Missing Pieces; 2001: Proximity; Walter and Henry.

STEVE COCHRAN

(ROBERT ALEXANDER COCHRAN) BORN: EUREKA, CA, MAY 25, 1917. RAISED IN LARAMIE, WY. ED: UNIV. OF WY. DIED: JUNE 15, 1965.

Following a stage career that took him from stock to Broadway, Steve Cochran came to Hollywood in 1945 to work for Samuel Goldwyn, who had spotted him in a touring production of *Without Love*. He specialized in playing sleazy pretty boys, giving Danny Kaye a hard time on three occasions, in *Wonder Man*, *The Kid From Brooklyn*, and *A Song Is Born*, in the role Dana Andrews had done with more flair in the original, *Ball of Fire*. Cochran had two of his most effective roles playing Virginia Mayo's immoral lovers in both *The Best Years of Our Lives* and *White Heat*, where he paid dearly for crossing gangster James Cagney. Following a stint on Broadway, as Mae West's leading man in *Diamond Lil*, he officially joined the Warner Bros. stock company in 1949. He starred in his own vehicles for the studio, like *Highway 301*, as the leader of the Tri-State Gang; *Tomorrow Is Another Day*, as an ex-con unjustly accused of a crime; *Inside the Walls of Folsom Prison*, as one of the jailbirds; and *The Tanks Are Coming*, as an army sergeant. He was, however, more effective in support, playing unsympathetic parts in *Dallas*, teamed with Raymond Massey, and in *Storm Warning*, as Doris Day's abusive husband, his personal favorite of his roles. After Warners he continued to star in low-budget efforts like *Private Hell 36*, which achieved cult status with devotees of director Don Siegel. A low-keyed attempt to change his image, *Come Next Spring*, about a wanderer returning to his Arkansas home, was produced at Republic for his own company, Robert Alexander Productions. In Europe he got good notices for playing a man suffering a mental breakdown in director Michelangelo Antonioni's *Il Grido/The Outcry*, and joined the eclectic casts of two trashy Albert Zugsmith melodramas, *The Beat Generation* and *The Big Operator*. His sole directorial effort, *Tell Me in the Sunlight*, was posthumously released — he had died suddenly from swollen lung tissue while on a cruise with his all-female crew, though the boat did not return to port until days after the incident.

Screen: 1945: Wonder Man; The Gay Senorita; Boston Blackie Booked on Suspicion; Boston Blackie's Rendezvous; 1946: The Kid From Brooklyn; The Chase; The Best Years of Our Lives; 1947: Copacabana; 1948: A Song Is Born; 1949: White Heat; 1950: The Damned Don't Cry; Highway 301; Dallas; Storm Warning; Raton Pass; Inside the Walls of Folsom Prison; Tomorrow Is Another Day; Jim Thorpe — All-American; The Tanks Are Coming; 1952: The Lion and the Horse; Operation Secret; 1953: Back to God's Country; She's Back on Broadway;

The Desert Song; Shark River; 1954: Carnival Story; Private Hell 36; 1956: Come Next Spring (and prod.); The Weapon; 1957: Slander; 1958: Quantrill's Raiders; 1959: The Big Operator; I Mobster; The Beat Generation; 1962: The Outcry/Il Grido (It: 1957); The Deadly Companions; 1963: Of Love and Desire; 1966: Mozambique; 1967: Tell Me in the Sunlight (and dir.; co-music).

NY Stage: 1944: Hickory Stick; Broken Hearts of Broadway; 1948: Diamond Lil.

Select TV: 1953: Letter of Love (sp); 1954: The Role of Lover (sp); Trip Around the Block (sp); 1955: A Most Contagious Game (sp); 1957: Outlaw's Boots (sp); 1960: The Indian Captive (sp); 1963: Obituary for Mr. X (sp).

CLAUDETTE COLBERT

(LILY CLAUDETTE CHAUCHOIN) BORN: PARIS, FRANCE, SEPTEMBER 13, 1903. RAISED IN NEW YORK, NY. DIED: JULY 30, 1996.

Although she excelled at drama, it is for her seemingly effortless agility with comedy that Claudette Colbert will be long remembered. It was well known to movie enthusiasts that she insisted on being photographed from her left side, but none of that sort of superficiality comes across in her acting, which was direct and free of pretensions. Her family moved from Paris to New York when she was six and, while attending the Art Students League there, she met the author of a play, *The Wild Westcotts*, resulting in her stage debut in 1923. For the next few years she was a Broadway regular, most notably opposite Walter Huston in *The Barker*. This led to a contract with First National Pictures in 1927 that resulted in a single film, *For the Love of Mike*, directed by Frank Capra, with whom she'd later reap some of her greatest rewards. Unhappy with her movie experience, she went back to Broadway for a few more plays, including *Dynamo*, which prompted a movie contract offer from Paramount. She did not draw attention on screen until she paired with fellow French star Maurice Chevalier, first in *The Big Pond*, and then *The Smiling Lieutenant*, in which she gallantly gave him up to Miriam Hopkins. (Like Chevalier she did double duty by appearing in the French versions of these and other movies.) She fell in love with Fredric March in *Manslaughter*, even though he sent her to prison for the title crime, and in the less melodramatic *Honor Among Lovers*, she forsook March to marry Monroe Owsley.

She continued mostly in melodramas, including *His Woman*, with Gary Cooper, and *The Man From Yesterday*, with countryman Charles Boyer, although she also appeared in a minor comedy, *The Misleading Lady*, as a socialite who wants to be an actress, and the woeful George M. Cohan vehicle, *The Phantom President*. Her stature began to rise, thanks to a campy performance as the evil Poppea in Cecil B. DeMille's bizarre Biblical epic *The Sign of the Cross*, and then in a bright comedy, *Three-Cornered Moon*, about a family gamely making it through the Depression. It was another comedy, on loan to Columbia, that pushed her into the stratosphere of stardom. Legend has it that neither Colbert nor Clark Gable had wanted to do Frank Capra's *It Happened One Night* and expected nothing of it, but the movie was a smash, and was considered the forerunner of the whole genre of screwball comedies. The film made history by winning Academy Awards in all five of the top categories in 1934, including Best Actress for Colbert, who was superb as the heiress on the run, battling playfully with Gable and — in one of the film's most famous scenes — showing him how to hitchhike. Rounding out a great year she had another hit with DeMille, in the enjoyably kitschy version of *Cleopatra*, and carried one of the seminal tearjerkers of the decade, *Imitation of Life*, getting rich off of Louise Beavers's pancake recipe while clashing with daughter Rochelle Hudson because they are both interested in the same man. Somehow the performers made it more bearable than it sounds.

Another Oscar nomination was offered for her role as a doctor at a mental institution in *Private Worlds*, a movie that received attention in its day for its unique subject matter, but has since faded with time. She sparkled in several light romantic comedies of this era, including *The Gilded Lily*, marking the first of many collaborations with Fred MacMurray; *She Married Her Boss*, another successful loan-out to Columbia, playing secretary and bride to Melvyn Douglas; *The Bride Comes Home*, engaged to Robert Young but ending up with MacMurray; *Bluebeard's Eighth Wife*, reteamed charmingly with Gary Cooper; *Midnight*, one of her best, as a woman who agrees to seduce the lover of John Barrymore's wife; MGM's *It's a Wonderful World*, a fast-paced road comedy with James Stewart; *Skylark*, which featured a priceless scene in which she tries to make dinner on board a ship during a storm; and Preston Sturges's *The Palm Beach Story*, which was stolen from under her by Rudy Vallee. During this period, Colbert also had some dramatic highlights, including a game attempt to portray a New Englander accused of witchcraft in *Maid of Salem*; a popular reunion with Gable, in *Boom Town*; John Ford's exciting adventure *Drums Along the Mohawk*; and the cliché-ridden but profitable nurses-on-the-battlefront ensemble, *So Proudly We Hail!*. In the immensely popular drama *Since You Went Away*, she was a tower of strength as the mother who valiantly holds her family together on the home front, a performance for which she earned another Oscar nod. There were, of course, miscalculations, such as *Under Two Flags*, in which she was miscast as a Legionnaire's vamp named Cigarette, and *Tovarich*, where she and Boyer valiantly tried to squeeze out some laughs as a pair of Russian nobles forced into servitude.

She ended her Paramount contract with two more MacMurray teamings: *No Time for Love*, as a stylish lady in love with a sandhog; and *Practically Yours*, which was probably the most poorly reviewed of all their pairings. After the war she kept her career brewing with two popular comedies with MacMurray, *The Egg and I*, about city folk moving to a farm, and *Family Honeymoon*, as a widow with three children, but both films depended on the obvious for laughs. She turned down two hits (*State of the Union* and *All About Eve*) to do *Three Came Home*, a stark prison camp drama in which she gave what is considered by many to be her finest dramatic performance. But her movie career was clearly in decline, as evidenced by *Thunder on the Hill*, curiously cast as a nun trying to save innocent Ann Blyth from execution, and an uninspired comedy with the bland Macdonald Carey, *Let's Make It Legal*. She went to Europe for a British film, *Outpost in Malaya*, and two French ones, before returning to the U.S. for several television roles and her solitary western, *Texas Lady*. After her role as Troy Donahue's mother in the glossy 1961 soap opera *Parrish*, she never again returned to the big screen. She appeared frequently on Broadway, including two plays with Rex Harrison, *The Kingfisher* and *Aren't We All?*, and co-starred with Ann-Margret in the television mini-series *The Two Mrs. Grenvilles*, looking as chic and lovely as ever.

Screen: 1927: For the Love of Mike; 1929: The Hole in the Wall; The Lady Lies; L'Enigmatique Mr. Parkes; 1930: The Big Pond; Young Man of Manhattan; Manslaughter; Le Grande Mare (nUSr); 1931: Honor Among Lovers; The Smiling Lieutenant; Secrets of a Secretary; His Woman; 1932: The Wiser Sex; The

Misleading Lady; The Man From Yesterday; Make Me a Star; The Phantom President; The Sign of the Cross; 1933: Tonight Is Ours; I Cover the Waterfront; Three-Cornered Moon; Torch Singer; 1934: Four Frightened People; It Happened One Night; Cleopatra; Imitation of Life; 1935: The Gilded Lily; Private Worlds; She Married Her Boss; The Bride Comes Home; 1936: Under Two Flags; 1937: Maid of Salem; I Met Him in Paris; Tovarich; 1938: Bluebeard's Eighth Wife; 1939: Zaza; Midnight; It's a Wonderful World; Drums Along the Mohawk; 1940: Boom Town; Arise, My Love; 1941: Skylark; Remember the Day; 1942: The Palm Beach Story; 1943: No Time for Love; So Proudly We Hail!; 1944: Since You Went Away; Practically Yours; 1945: Guest Wife; 1946: Tomorrow Is Forever; Without Reservations; The Secret Heart; 1947: The Egg and I; 1948: Sleep My Love; Family Honeymoon; 1949: Bride for Sale; 1950: Three Came Home; The Secret Fury; 1951: Thunder on the Hill; Let's Make It Legal; 1952: Outpost in Malaya/The Planter's Wife; 1954: Daughters of Destiny/Destinées; 1955: Texas Lady; 1957: Royal Affairs in Versailles/Affair in Versailles (Fr: 1954); 1961: Parrish.

NY Stage: 1923: The Wild Westcotts; 1925: A Kiss in a Taxi; 1926: Ghost Train; 1927: The Barker; The Mulberry Bush; 1928: La Gringa; Within the Law; Fast Life; Tin Pan Alley; 1929: Dynamo; See Naples and Die; 1956: Janus; 1958: The Marriage-Go-Round; 1961: Julia Jake and Uncle Joe; 1963: The Irregular Verb to Love; 1978: The Kingfisher; 1981: A Talent for Murder; 1985: Aren't We All?

Select TV: 1954: The Royal Family (sp); 1955: Magic Formula (sp); The Guardsman (sp); Private Worlds (sp); While We're Young (sp); 1956: Blithe Spirit (sp); After All These Years (sp); 1957: One Coat of White (sp); 1958: Last Town Car (sp); 1959: The Bells of St. Mary's (sp); 1959–60: The Women (series host); 1987: The Two Mrs. Grenvilles.

CONSTANCE COLLIER

(Laura Constance Hardie) Born: Windsor, England, January 22, 1875. Died: April 25, 1955.

A noted thespian of the British stage, Constance Collier turned to films on a regular basis as she entered her later years. There had been a few credits in silent movies, including a 1916 version of *Macbeth*, but it was not until she came to MGM in 1935, first to play Ricardo Cortez's snobby aunt in *Shadow of Doubt*, then Countess Lidia in Garbo's *Anna Karenina*, that she began her official Hollywood career. In *Professional Soldier*, she sheltered kidnapped Freddie Bartholomew; played Lady Lorridale opposite Bartholomew in *Little Lord Fauntleroy*; was outstanding as a nasty teacher intent on destroying Simone Simon's plans in *Girls' Dormitory*; returned to Britain for *Thunder in the City*, as a Duchess whose daughter Edward G. Robinson wants to marry; was Joan Fontaine's toffee-nosed aunt in *A Damsel in Distress*; and had one of her most substantial roles, in a "B" for Universal, *Half a Sinner*, coming to the aide of schoolteacher Heather Angel. She was ideal for playing slightly haughty grande dames and ladies of position, as in costume pieces like *Kitty* and *Monsieur Beaucaire*. There were also roles as aging thespians, in *Stage Door*, opposite Katharine Hepburn, and *The Perils of Pauline*. One of her last roles found her as one of the guests at the sinister cocktail party in Alfred Hitchcock's *Rope*. She received screen credit for the 1935 adaptation of *Peter Ibbetson*, which she had written and directed on Broadway.

Screen: 1916: Macbeth; The Code of Marcia Gray; Tongues of Men; 1919: The Impossible Woman; 1920: Bleak House; 1922:

The Bohemian Girl; **1935:** Shadow of Doubt; Anna Karenina; **1936:** Professional Soldier; Girls' Dormitory; Little Lord Fauntleroy; **1937:** Wee Willie Winkie; Thunder in the City; Stage Door; A Damsel in Distress; Clothes and the Woman; **1939:** Zaza; **1940:** Susan and God; Half a Sinner; **1945:** Kitty; Weekend at the Waldorf; **1946:** The Dark Corner; Monsieur Beaucaire; **1947:** The Perils of Pauline; **1948:** Rope; The Girl From Manhattan; An Ideal Husband; **1949:** Whirlpool.

NY Stage: **1908:** Samson; **1909:** Israel; **1911:** Trelawny of the Wells; Thais; **1912:** Oliver Twist; The Explorer; **1913:** Nan; **1914:** Othello; **1916:** The Merry Wives of Windsor (and 1917); **1917:** Peter Ibbetson; **1918:** An Ideal Husband; **1925:** Hamlet; **1927:** Meet the Wife; John; The Spot on the Son; **1928:** Our Betters; **1929:** Serena Blandish; **1930:** The Matriarch; **1931:** Hay Fever; **1932:** Dinner at Eight; **1939:** Aries Is Rising; **1942:** Gratefully Yours (and dir.).

JOAN COLLINS
BORN: LONDON, ENGLAND, MAY 23, 1933. ED: FRANCIS HOLLAND SCHOOL IN LONDON, RADA.

Her early, superficial sex-kitten career was predicted by the critics to soon fade, but Joan Collins confounded the naysayers and was still going strong more than 40 years later. While still a teenager she made her stage debut in London, in 1946, in a production of *A Doll's House*. A few years later, she landed small parts in British films that capitalized on her looks and little else, including *Cosh Boy/The Slasher*, intent on suicide after being impregnated by hood James Kenney; *Turn the Key Softly*, as a hooker fresh out of prison; and the lead in *Our Girl Friday*, stuck on a desert island with three men. Her much-heralded American screen debut came in 1955 with Howard Hawks's lavish and highly entertaining epic *Land of the Pharaohs*. As an Egyptian villainess who gets her comeuppance in a memorable finale, she seemed to many like a second-rate Elizabeth Taylor, and the film took a nosedive at the box office. Nonetheless, she got a contract with 20th Century-Fox and took the key role of showgirl Evelyn Nesbit in *The Girl in the Red Velvet Swing*, as well as ensemble work in dramas like *The Wayward Bus*, as Rick Jason's possessive alcoholic wife, and the hit *Island in the Sun*. Over at MGM she proved a poor replacement for Joan Crawford in *The Opposite Sex*, the flimsy remake of *The Women*, and she went down with the ship in the heavy-handed comedy *Rally 'Round the Flag, Boys*, trying to seduce Paul Newman away from Joanne Woodward. The studio terminated her contract after casting her in an Italian-made Biblical saga, *Esther and the King*, which had even less success than her previous endeavor in this genre.

When Bing Crosby and Bob Hope reteamed for one last *Road* movie it was cruelly decided that Dorothy Lamour should be replaced by a younger actress. Collins took her spot in *The Road to Hong Kong*, which only made one look upon Lamour's contributions to the series with a newfound respect. She married actor-singer Anthony Newley in 1963 and seemed to fade from the scene for a while, though she showed up just before their 1970 divorce in his bizarre ego trip, *Can Hieronymous Merkin Every Forget Mercy Humppe and Find True Happiness?* Basically playing herself, she sang "Chalk and Cheese" while, in a cinematic lowpoint, Newley drifted naked around her. By the 1970s she was settled back in England where her film work included trash like *The Bawdy Adventures of Tom Jones*, as a highwaywoman; *Alfie Darling*, an unsanctioned sequel to the Michael Caine classic; *The Devil Within Her*, plagued by an evil dwarf; and a pair of stinkers based on novels by her equally talented sister, Jackie, *The*

Stud and *The Bitch*. There was an unexpected resurgence in her career when she was signed for a prime-time television soap, *Dynasty*, in 1981. As the manipulative, bitchy Alexis Carrington she reached new heights of campy superstardom and became the rage of the tabloids. Her career faltered again once the show went off the air, although she did appear briefly as an agent in a good film, *A Midwinter's Tale*. She also fulfilled some sort of destiny, reprising a role played by Elizabeth Taylor, in *The Flintstones in Viva Rock Vegas*. Following in the literary footsteps of her sister, she wrote a 1978 autobiography, *Past Imperfect*, which was updated after her comeback.

Screen: **1951:** Lady Godiva Rides Again; I Believe in You; **1952:** The Slasher/Cosh Boy/Tough Guys; **1953:** Turn the Key Softly; The Square Ring; Decameron Nights; **1954:** The Woman's Angle (UK: 1952); The Good Die Young; Our Girl Friday/The Adventures of Sadie; **1955:** Judgment Deferred (UK: 1952); Land of the Pharaohs; The Virgin Queen;The Girl in the Red Velvet Swing; **1956:** The Opposite Sex; **1957:** The Wayward Bus; Sea Wife; Island in the Sun; Stopover Tokyo; **1958:** The Bravados; Rally 'Round the Flag, Boys!; **1960:** Seven Thieves; Esther and the King; **1962:** The Road to Hong Kong; **1964:** La Congiuntura/Hard Time for Princes (nUSr); **1967:** Warning Shot; **1969:** Can Hieronymus Merkin Ever Forget Mercy Humppe and Find True Happiness?; If It's Tuesday, This Must Be Belgium; Subterfuge; L'Amore Breve/Besieged (nUSr); **1970:** The Executioner; Up in the Cellar; **1971:** Quest for Love;Revenge/Inn of the Frightened People; **1972:** Fear in the Night/Dynasty of Fear; Tales From the Crypt; **1973:** Tales That Witness Madness; Dark Places; **1974:** L'Arbitro/The Referee/Football Crazy; **1975:** Alfie Darling/Oh, Alfie; The Great Adventure; **1976:** The Devil Within Her/I Don't Want to Be Born; The Bawdy Adventures of Tom Jones; **1977:** Fearless/Fatal Charm/Magnum Cop; Empire of the Ants; **1978:** The Big Sleep; The Stud; Zero to Sixty; **1979:** The Bitch; Sunburn; Game for Vultures; **1982:** Homework; Nutcracker; **1994:** Decadence (dtv); **1996:** A Midwinter's Tale/In the Bleak Midwinter; The Line King: Al Hirschfeld; **1999:** The Clandestine Marriage (dtv; and assoc. prod.); **2000:** The Flintstones in Viva Las Vegas.

NY Stage: **1992:** Private Lives.

Select TV: **1972:** The Man Who Came to Dinner (sp); **1973:** Drive Hard, Drive Fast; **1976:** Arthur Hailey's The Moneychangers (ms); **1981–89:** Dynasty (series); **1982:** Paper Dolls; The Wild Women of Chastity Gulch; **1983:** The Making of a Male Model; **1984:** Her Life as a Man; **1985:** The Cartier Affair; **1986:** Sins (ms; and exec. prod.); Monte Carlo (and exec. prod.); **1991:** Dynasty: The Reunion; **1995:** Hart to Hart: Two Harts in Three-Quarters Time; **1996:** Annie: A Royal Adventure; **1997:** Pacific Palisades (series); **1998:** Sweet Deception; **2000:** Joseph and the Amazing Technicolor Dreamcoat; **2001:** These Old Broads.

RAY COLLINS
BORN: SACRAMENTO, CA, DECEMBER 10, 1889.
DIED: JULY 11, 1965.

A member of Orson Welles's Mercury Theatre company, Ray Collins had been on the stage since he was a child. He came to Hollywood for a bit part in *The Grapes of Wrath* and then joined Welles in the cast of *Citizen Kane*. His expert work as Kane's arch enemy, political boss Jim Gettys, who coolly exposes Kane's extra-marital dalliance, was followed by another fine performance, as Uncle Jack in Welles's adaptation of *The Magnificent Ambersons*. Over the next decade or so Collins became one of those characters actors who never seemed in want of work. His somewhat sour demeanor was used for good effect in comedies like *The Senator Was Indiscreet*, as the political boss trying to stop William Powell from naming names; *It Happens Every Spring*, as a professor; *Francis*, as a flustered colonel; three Ma and Pa Kettle entries, as the wealthy dad of the Kettle's daughter-in-law; and *The Solid Gold Cadillac*, as one of the unctuous businessman trying to hoodwink Judy Holliday. In more dramatic fare he made some sentimental ghostly appearances in *The Human Comedy*, as Mickey Rooney's dad; was a physician who repairs injured Warner Baxter in the premiere of the long-running series *Crime Doctor*; was William Eythe's folksy papa in *The Eve of St. Marks*; a corrupt politician in *The Racket*; the sheriff in *The Desperate Hours*; and showed up as an effete court chamberlain in the (presumably) tongue-in-cheek, *Night in Paradise*. By the time he returned to work for Welles, in *Touch of Evil*, he had already begun his long-running role of Lt. Tragg on the long-running television series *Perry Mason*.

Screen: 1940: The Grapes of Wrath; 1941: Citizen Kane; 1942: The Big Street; Highways by Night; The Navy Comes Through; Commandos Strike at Dawn; The Magnificent Ambersons; 1943: Crime Doctor; The Human Comedy; Madame Curie (voice); Slightly Dangerous; Salute to the Marines; Whistling in Brooklyn; 1944: See Here, Private Hargrove; The Hitler Gang; The Eve of St. Mark; The Seventh Cross; Barbary Coast Gent; Shadows in the Night; Can't Help Singing; 1945: Roughly Speaking; The Hidden Eye; Miss Susie Slagle's; The Unseen (narrator); Leave Her to Heaven; 1946: Up Goes Maisie; Badman's Territory; Boys' Ranch; Crack-Up; Three Wise Fools; Two Years Before the Mast; The Return of Monte Cristo; The Best Years of Our Lives; A Night in Paradise; 1947: The Bachelor and the Bobby-Soxer; The Red Stallion; The Senator Was Indiscreet; A Double Life; 1948: The Swordsman; Homecoming; Good Sam; For the Love of Mary; The Man From Colorado; Command Decision; 1949: Red Stallion of the Rockies; Hideout; It Happens Every Spring; The Fountainhead; The Heiress; Free for All; Francis; 1950: Paid in Full; Kill the Umpire; The Reformer and the Redhead; Ma and Pa Kettle Go to Town; Summer Stock; 1951: You're in the Navy Now/U.S.S. Teakettle; Ma and Pa Kettle Back on the Farm; Vengeance Valley; Reunion in Reno; I Want You; The Racket; 1952: Invitation; Dreamboat; Young Man With Ideas; Ma and Pa Kettle at the Fair; 1953: The Desert Song; Column South; Ma and Pa Kettle on Vacation; The Kid From Left Field; Bad for Each Other; 1954: Rose Marie; Athena; 1955: The Desperate Hours; Texas Lady; 1956: Never Say Goodbye; The Solid Gold Cadillac; 1957: Spoilers of the Forest; 1958: Touch of Evil; 1961: I'll Give My Life.

NY Stage: 1924: The Blue Bandana; Conscience; 1925: Eve's Leaves; The Bridge of Distances; 1926: The Half-Naked Truth; Donovan Affair; 1928: On Call; 1929: A Strong Man's House; A Comedy of Women; 1931: Paging Danger; 1941: Native Son.

Select TV: 1954: The Halls of Ivy (series); 1955: Miracle on 34th Street (sp); 1956: Gun in His Hand (sp); The Star Spangled Soldier (sp); Invitation to a Gunfighter (sp); 1957–65: Perry Mason (series).

RONALD COLMAN

BORN: RICHMOND, SURREY, ENGLAND, FEBRUARY 9, 1891. DIED: MAY 19, 1958.

The epitome of the classic British gentleman, and the possessor of, perhaps, the most beautiful speaking voice in film history, unpretentious Ronald Colman's charm and good breeding have survived surprisingly well in a more vulgar age. While working as a young man for the British Steamship Company, he began to dabble in amateur theatrics, but World War I intervened and he served with the London Scottish Regiment until an injury forced him back into civilian life. Through the urging of its star, Gladys Cooper, he was cast in a supporting role in the play *The Misleading Lady*, which was followed by other theatrical endeavors. A short subject, *The Live Wire*, never saw the light of day; while his first feature, *The Toilers*, in 1919, cast him as a young fisherman who deserts his village to seek his fortune in London. In his next two pictures, *A Daughter of Eve* and *Sheba*, he did not even receive billing. His first starring role came in 1920, in *A Son of David*, which cast him as a Jewish boxer, although Ronald Colman was hardly anyone's idea of a pugilist. That same year he came to the U.S. to work on Broadway, where he did a small part in *The Dauntless Three*, then toured with Fay Bainter in *East Is West*. He took time out to make his first American movie, playing a wealthy playboy, in a forgotten film with a memorable title, *Handcuffs or Kisses?*

It was his performance in another play, *La Tendresse*, opposite Ruth Chatterton, that really sparked interest from Hollywood. Lilian Gish requested him as her leading man in *The White Sister*, and he grew his famous mustache so that he would be more convincing as an Italian. The critical and public response was favorable and Colman's movie career took off. His dignity was immediately tested when he was required to wear tights and a shoulder-length wig in *Romola*, this time sharing the screen with both Gish sisters. Producer Samuel Goldwyn signed him to a contract and started him off as May McAvoy's co-star in *Tarnish*. His first great success, *The Dark Angel*, in 1925, featured him as blinded war veteran who allows the woman he loves, Vilma Banky, to believe he is dead. Goldwyn's follow-up melodrama, *Stella Dallas*, in which Colman wed then abandoned the title heroine, was equally popular, signifying that one of the screen's most romantic figures, and a fine actor to boot, had officially arrived. There followed a wordless Oscar Wilde adaptation, *Lady Windermere's Fan*; his most famous silent film, Paramount's *Beau Geste*, escaping with his brothers to the Foreign Legion; and then several more teamings with Banky, including *The Winning of Barbara Worth*, which placed him in an atypical Colman genre, the western; *The Night of Love*, in which he was a Spanish Gypsy; and *The Magic Flame*, in dual roles, as a heroic circus clown and a villainous prince.

When talkies arrived he became one of the few silent stars to effortlessly maintain his same level of stardom. His sly performance in the light-weight detective caper *Bulldog Drummond* was a resounding success, and it resulted in one of two Oscar nominations for him in 1929. The other, *Condemned*, saw him rather unconvincingly cast as a Devil's Island convict; certainly the most suave prisoner in the place. He then played one of his most famous early roles, a charming safecracker, in *Raffles*, which he followed with a bright comedy, *The Devil to Pay*, gleefully living the good life until Loretta Young captures his heart. In *Arrowsmith* he triumphed over miscasting as the dedicated doctor who journeys to the West Indies to cure the bubonic plague, but after playing another dual role, in *The Masquerader*, as a journalist and his drug-addicted politican cousin, he split unhappily with Goldwyn. Joining producer Joseph M. Schenk, he took on another *Bulldog Drummond* romp and played the title character in the historical epic *Clive of India*, which found him plus powdered wig but minus mustache for the first time since his American debut. He remained clean-shaven for one of his most famous roles, Sydney Carton, the cynical lawyer who makes the ultimate sacrifice during the French Revolution in the justifiably acclaimed 1935 version of *A Tale of Two Cities*. It was a role that required a great deal of introspection and proved that he was an actor capable of evoking much pathos through subtle gestures. He also spoke, unforgettably, one of the great exit lines in all of film history: "It is a far, far better thing that I do than I have ever done. It is a far, far better rest that I go to than I have ever known." He then unwisely returned to the Foreign Legion for *Under Two Flags*, where a promising cast, that included Claudette Colbert and Rosalind Russell, seemed ill at ease with the whole experience.

No longer under contract, he freelanced with great success, making three of his best movies in a row. First was Frank Capra's expensive *Lost Horizon*, in a definitive role, as the idealist entranced by the peace he finds in Shangri-La. Then came the most notable of his dual roles, in the best version of *The Prisoner of Zenda*, a superior swashbuckler with class and intelligence. He followed with *If I Were King*, in which he was simply wonderful as the carefree poet Francois Villon, a period piece given great energy and wit by Preston Sturges's sharp screenplay. He was (for the second time) a tragic, blinded hero, in Rudyard Kipling's *The Light That Failed*, after which he did a pair of lackluster comedies: *Lucky Partners*, with Ginger Rogers, and the very poor *My Life With Caroline*, sabotaged by an amateurish performance from leading lady Anna Lee. As he entered his 50s he found his popularity enhanced by two major hits, both released in 1942. He took third billing to Cary Grant and Jean Arthur in George Stevens's smart comedy, *The Talk of the Town*, but he stole the film, as a bearded professor whose views on the law are revised by suspected arsonist Grant. It was for this part that he should have received his third Oscar nomination rather than the dated romance *Random Harvest*, as Greer Garson's amnesiac husband. One of his rare out-and-out disasters was *Kismet*, a gaudy and flaccid Technicolor romp through old Baghdad, in which he gave his best shot as a crafty beggar. He still had one more career peak, in 1947, with George Cukor's *A Double Life*. Colman showed an unexpectedly dark side as the unbalanced actor whose portrayal of Othello drives him to murder, and he finally won a long overdue Academy Award. An enjoyable comedy, *Champagne for Caesar*, failed to catch on, so he turned to television, recreating his radio role as a college professor in *The Halls of Ivy*, starring his wife (since 1938), actress Benita Hume. A year before he died he played the Spirit of Man, one of the larger roles in Irwin Allen's all-star oddity *The Story of Mankind*. It was a testament to his impeccable capabilities and stature that, of all the horrible reviews heaped upon the film, not a bad word was said about him.

Screen: 1919: The Toilers; A Daughter of Eve; Sheba; Snow in the Desert; 1920: A Son of David; Anna the Adventuress; The Black Spider; 1921: Handcuffs or Kisses?; 1923: The White Sister; 1924: The Eternal City; 20 Dollars a Week; Romola; Tarnish; 1925: Her Night of Romance; A Thief in Paradise; His Supreme Moment; The Sporting Venus; Her Sister from Paris; The Dark Angel; Stella Dallas; Lady Windermere's Fan; 1926: Kiki; Beau Geste; The Winning of Barbara Worth; 1927: The Night of Love; The Magic Flame; 1928: Two Lovers; 1929: The Rescue; Bulldog Drummond; Condemned; 1930: Raffles; The Devil to Pay; 1931: The Unholy Garden; Arrowsmith; 1932: Cynara; 1933: The Masquerader; 1934: Bulldog Drummond Strikes Back; 1935: Clive of India; The Man Who Broke the Bank at Monte Carlo; A Tale of Two Cities; 1936: Under Two Flags; 1937: Lost Horizon; The Prisoner of Zenda; 1938: If I Were King; 1939: The Light That Failed; 1940: Lucky Partners; 1941: My Life With Caroline; 1942: The Talk of the Town; Random Harvest; 1944: Kismet/Oriental Dream; 1947: The Late George Apley; A Double Life; 1950: Champagne for Caesar; 1956: Around the World in Eighty Days; 1957: The Story of Mankind.

NY Stage: 1921: The Nightcap; 1922: La Tendresse.
Select TV: 1952: The Lost Silk Hat (sp); 1953: The Man Who Walked Out on Himself (sp); The Ladies on His Mind (sp); 1954: A String of Pearls (sp); The Halls of Ivy (series); 1956: The Chess Game (sp); 1957: A Perfect Likeness (sp).

JERRY COLONNA
(GERARDO COLONNA) BORN: BOSTON, MA, OCTOBER 17, 1904. DIED: NOVEMBER 21, 1986.

Bug-eyed, with a bushy mustache that suggested a reject from a barbershop quartet, Jerry Colonna's principal claim to fame was his siren-like bellowing voice, which could be alternately funny or annoying. Originally a bandleader, he found employment as a trombone player on CBS radio, working in comical routines between numbers. In 1938 he joined Bob Hope on radio as his second banana and it was in this role that he found his greatest success. As a result he popped up in supporting roles in five Hope films: *College Swing*, as a professor; *Road to Singapore*; *Star Spangled Rhythm*, adding a memorable punchline to a sketch; *Road to Rio*, leading a charging cavalry in a shaggy-dog running gag; and *The Road to Hong Kong*. He could also be counted on to lend unsubtle lunacy to cheapie musicals like *Priorities on Parade*, as a hot dog vendor at an aircraft factory; *Sis Hopkins*; and *True to the Army* (as a pigeon trainer!), where he joined Judy Canova for some unsophisticated drawing-room humor; *Ice Capades* and *Ice Capades Revue*; and *Atlantic City*, showing up dressed as King Neptune. Perfectly suited for voice work, he sang "Casey at the Bat" in Disney's *Make Mine Music*, and was the March Hare in *Alice in Wonderland*.

Screen: 1937: 52nd Street; Rosalie; 1938: College Swing; Little Miss Broadway; Garden of the Moon; Valley of the Giants; Port of Seven Seas; There Goes My Heart; 1939: Naughty But Nice;The Sweepstakes Winner; 1940: Road to Singapore; Comin' Round the Mountain; Melody and Moonlight; 1941: You're the One; Sis Hopkins; Ice Capades; 1942: True to the Army; Priorities on Parade; Ice-Capades Revue/Rhythm Hits the Ice; Star Spangled Rhythm; 1944: Atlantic City; 1945: It's in the Bag; 1946: Make Mine Music (voice); 1947: Road to Rio; 1951: Alice in Wonderland (voice); Kentucky Jubilee; 1956: Meet Me in Las Vegas; 1958: Andy Hardy Comes Home; 1962: The Road to Hong Kong.
Select TV: 1951: The Jerry Colonna Show (series); 1955–56: Super Circus (series); 1957: Pinocchio (sp); 1977: Don't Push — I'll Charge When I'm Ready (filmed 1969).

CHESTER CONKLIN
(JULES COWLES) BORN: OSKALOOSA, IA, JANUARY 11, 1888. DIED: OCTOBER 11, 1971.

One of the busiest of all silent movie comedians, pint-sized Chester Conklin, with his trademark walrus moustache, first worked as a clown with the Al G. Barnes Circus. This training made him ideal for Mack Sennett's Keystone Studios, which he joined in 1913, doing supporting bits in various shorts with Mabel Normand and Charlie Chaplin. There were also two-reelers which teamed him with massive Mack Swain, billing them as Ambrose and Walrus, and a stint with the Keystone Cops. Conklin eventually rose to starring solo work in his own short subject series, while earning steady employment as a character actor in features, most notably Erich von Stroheim's classic *Greed*, as ZaSu Pitts's father. When talkies came he went back to starring roles in a series of shorts for Paramount Pictures. As he grew older he lent his services to many features, mainly in tiny parts that were little more than extra work. He was a particular favorite of Preston Sturges, who found bits for him in several of his comedies including *Sullivan's Travels* and *The Palm Beach Story*.

Screen (shorts): 1914: Back to Nature Girls; Her Private Husband; The Great Nickel Robbery; Those Dangerous Eyes; Making a Living; Mabel's Strange Predicament; Between Showers; Tango Tangles; Cruel Cruel Love; Mabel at the Wheel; Twenty Minutes of Love; False Alarm; Business Is Business; Laughing Gas; The Piper; His Son's Wife; Caught in a Cabaret; The Face on the Barroom Floor; Dough and Dynamite; Mabel's Busy Day; Step Lively Please; The First Heir; Mabel's New Job; Those Love Pangs; Gentlemen of Nerve; Curses! They Remarked; The Love Thief; His Taking Ways; How Heroes Are Made; Home Rule; Soft Boiled Egg; Country Chicken; Perfect Villain; A Colored Girl's Love; Wild West Love; The Masquerader; The Anglers; 1915: Love Speed and Thrills; Hushing the Scandal; Ambrose's Sour Grapes; Hash House Mashers; A One Night Stand; The Best of Enemies; A Woman; Bulldog Yale; Shot in the Excitement; The Home Breakers; The Cannon Ball; Caught in a Park; Droppington's Devilish Dream; Willful Ambrose; When Ambrose Dared Walrus; A Bird's a Bird; Hearts and Planets; Ambrose's Fury; Droppington's Family Tree; Ambrose's Lofty Perch; A Hash House Fraud; Do-Re-Mi-Fa; The Battle of Ambrose and Walrus; Saved by the Wireless; 1916: Cinders of Love; Dizzy Heights and Daring Hearts; A Tugboat Romeo; Bucking Society; His First False Step; 1917: The Pullman Bride; A Clever Dummy; Dodging His Doom; An International Sneak; Cactus Nell; The Pawnbroker's Heart; 1918: It Pays to Exercise; Ladies First; The Village Chestnut; 1919: Yankee Doodle in Berlin; Uncle Tom Without a Cabin; 1920: Chicken a la Cabaret; Lightweight Lover; You Wouldn't Believe It; 1921: Skirts; 1930: Chester Conklin in The Master Sweeper; Cleaning Up; The Love Trader; 1931: Gents of Leisure; Studio Sap; Taxi; The New Yorker; Stout Hearts and Willing Hands; The Thirteenth Alarm; 1935: Keystone Hotel; La Fiesta de Santa Barbara; 1938: Flatfoot Stooges; A Nag in the Bag; 1939: Mutiny on the Body; The Teacher's Pet; 1940: You're Next; 1941: Dutiful But Dumb; 1942: Piano Mooner; College Belles; 1943: Phony Express; His Wedding Scare; 1945: Micro Phonies; 1948: A Pinch in Time; 1952: Happy Go Wacky; 1953: So You Want to Be a Musician.

Screen (features): 1914: Tillie's Punctured Romance; 1920: Uncle Tom's Cabin; Married Life; 1923: Desire; Anna Christie; Souls for Sale; Tea, With a Kick; 1924: Galloping Fish; The Fire Patrol; Another Man's Wife; North of Nevada; 1925: Greed; A Woman of the World; The Great Love; The Pleasure Buyers; The Masked Bride; The Phantom of the Opera; Battling Bunyon; Where Was I?; The Winding Stair; The Great Jewel Robbery; One Year to Live; My Neighbor's Wife; Under the Rouge; The Gold Rush; 1926: Behind the Front; The Wilderness Woman; Say It Again; We're in the Navy Now; The Duchess of Buffalo; More Pay Less Work; The Nervous Wreck; A Social Celebrity; Fascinating Youth; The Lady of the Harem; Midnight Lovers; Sybil; 1927: Rubber Heels; A Kiss in the Taxi; McFadden's Flats; Cabaret; Two Flaming Youths; Tell It to Sweeney; Silk Stockings; Drums of the Desert; 1928: Tillie's Punctured Romance (remake); Fools for Luck; Gentlemen Prefer Blondes; The Big Noise; Variety; Taxi 13; The Haunted House; Trick of Hearts; Feel My Pulse; Horseman of the Plains; Beau Broadway; 1929: Fast Company; The House of Horror; The Studio Murder Mystery; The Virginian; Marquis Preferred; Stairs of Sand; Sunset Pass; Shanghai Rose; The Show of Shows; 1930: Swing High; 1931: Her Majesty Love; 1933: Hallelujah, I'm a Bum; 1936:

Call of the Prairie; Modern Times; The Preview Murder Mystery; 1937: Sing Cowboy Sing; Hotel Haywire; Forlorn River; 1938: Every Day's a Holiday; 1939: Hollywood Cavalcade; Zenobia; Henry Goes Arizona; 1940: Li'l Abner; The Adventures of Red Ryder (serial); The Great Dictator; 1941: Honolulu Lu; Harmon of Michigan; Here Comes Mr. Jordan; Sullivan's Travels; 1942: In Old California; Valley of the Sun; The Palm Beach Story; Sons of the Pioneers; 1943: Around the World; Sagebrush Law; 1944: Knickerbocker Holiday; The Miracle of Morgan's Creek; The Yellow Rose of Texas; The Man From Frisco; Can't Help Singing; Goodnight Sweetheart; The Adventures of Mark Twain; Hail the Conquering Hero; Sunday Dinner for a Solider; The Great Moment; 1945: Abbott and Costello in Hollywood; 1946: She Wrote the Book; Smooth as Silk; The Hoodlum Saint; Singin' in the Corn; Little Giant; Fear; 1947: The Trouble With Women; Song of Scheherazade; The Perils of Pauline; Springtime in the Sierras; Song of the Wasteland; 1949: Jackpot Jitters; The Beautiful Blonde From Bashful Bend; Knock on Any Door; The Golden Stallion; 1950: Fancy Pants; Shakedown; Let's Dance; The Milkman; Joe Palooka in Humphrey Takes a Chance; Never a Dull Moment; 1951: Here Comes the Groom; 1952: Son of Paleface; 1955: The Beast With a Million Eyes; Apache Woman; 1958: Rock-a-Bye Baby; 1962: Paradise Alley (filmed 1957); 1966: A Big Hand for the Little Lady.

SEAN CONNERY

(THOMAS CONNERY) BORN: EDINBURGH, SCOTLAND, AUGUST 25, 1930.

True, he will always be James Bond, but Sean Connery escaped that typecasting to create a solid body of work that revealed him to be a fine actor of rugged appeal to both men and women. A playful glint in his eye also betrayed the fact that he obviously enjoying getting paid for what he was doing. Cashing in on his good looks, he started out as a body builder and a model, which got him work in the 1951 London production of *South Pacific*, decorating the background as a sailor. This led to small parts in films, but it was television that provided him with his juicier roles, first in *Anna Christie*, opposite Diane Cilento, whom he later married (1962–73), and then *Requiem for a Heavyweight*. The latter won him a contract with 20th Century-Fox but he mostly worked elsewhere, notably *Another Time, Another Place*, as Lana Turner's lover in a routine soap opera, and Disney's unsuccessful *Darby O'Gill and the Little People*, a leprechaun fantasy in which he even sang! He was also included in the vast international cast of Fox's D-Day epic, *The Longest Day*, though not in a starring role.

He really caught the attention of the movie-going public when he was chosen to play Ian Fleming's virile, super-cool secret agent, James Bond, in the adventure film that launched the series, *Dr. No*, in 1962 (1963 in the U.S.). The movie's success showed there was a demand for such fare, and the next entry, *From Russia With Love*, proved to be a bigger attraction than the first. Connery immediately became a 1960s pop culture icon, reaching his peak with the third installment, 1964's *Goldfinger*, the most entertaining film in the series, while the box-office grosses for the following year's *Thunderball* made it one of the top ten attractions of the decade. In between his Fleming forays Connery was in Hitchcock's *Marnie*, as an employer who falls for sexually-frigid kleptomaniac Tippi Hedren; Sidney Lumet's gritty *The Hill*, which presented him at his most powerful, as a defiant prisoner; and *A Fine Madness*, where he pulled off a difficult role as an unstable, womanizing poet. After returning as Bond in *You*

Only Live Twice, he dropped out of the series to do the 1971 hit thriller *The Anderson Tapes*; a poor western, *Shalako*; and the coal-mining drama *The Molly Maguires*, where he inexplicably took second billing to Richard Harris. But public response proved that it was as Bond that Connery was identified so, after some cutthroat negotiations with the producers, he consented to do *Diamond Are Forever*. (Albert Broccoli and Harry Saltzman were eager to accommodate him, due to the negative response to his wooden replacement, George Lazenby, in *On Her Majesty's Secret Service*.)

There was little interest in United Artists's *The Offense*, where he stretched as an unscrupulous police officer, so he returned to action and adventure in big-budget failures like *Zardoz*, trotting around in the distant future in a skimpy loin cloth; *The Wind and the Lion*, as a Moroccan sheik who kidnaps Candice Bergen; and *Meteor*, trying to save the world while bathed in mud. However, he received raves for his participation in John Huston's *The Man Who Would Be King*, as an adventurer with more nerve than brains, though, in truth, co-star Michael Caine seemed more at ease as his charlatan cohort. A more popular success was *Murder on the Orient Express*, where he was merely part of the starry ensemble of suspects. In Richard Lester's *Robin and Marian* he gave a touching performance as Robin Hood in his twilight years, and was at his most rakishly engaging as the mastermind behind *The Great Train Robbery*. His reputation stayed high, even though the box-office receipts fell short on *Outland*, a sci-fi twist on *High Noon*, in which he was as solidly heroic as ever. To improve his financial standing he donned his toupee for one more Bond, *Never Say Never Again*, essentially a retread of *Thunderball*. Even though the movie was made without the backing of Saltzman and Broccoli, the popular opinion was that it far outweighed Roger Moore's Bond contribution that same year, *Octopussy*, and that Connery was the sole possessor of the role.

Unpromising small parts in trashy international efforts followed: *Highlander*, as hero Christopher Lambert's mentor; and *Sword of the Valiant*, as a knight; plus the ambitious, but unfortunate flop adaptation of the cult novel, *The Name of the Rose*, as a sleuthing monk. Then, in 1987, Brian De Palma cast him as an Irish cop who teams with Elliot Ness (Kevin Costner) in *The Untouchables*. Given some meaty David Mamet dialogue, his magnetic performance stole the movie and he won a much-applauded Academy Award for Best Supporting Actor. Two years later he had a resounding success as Harrison Ford's befuddled father in *Indiana Jones and the Last Crusade*, displaying unexpected comical finesse, after which he was less believable as Dustin Hoffman's father in the caper film *Family Business*. He brought in huge audiences for the claustrophobic 1990 submarine epic, *The Hunt for Red October*. (He was supposed to be Russian, but Connery, stubbornly Scottish, never attempted an accent when playing another nationality.) A proven moneymaker once again, he started producing his own films and his popularity saved some weak dramas like *Medicine Man*, *Rising Sun*, *Just Cause*, and *The Rock*, a high-testosterone actioner that featured some droll interplay between Connery and co-star Nicolas Cage. Well into his 60s, his screen presence was as potent and assured as ever, though his mistaken belief that the public would accept him as a villain was part of the reason *The Avengers* hit the wall. Committing robbery for the thrill of it, however, was acceptable, as he proved with his usual flair in *Entrapment*. In a less taxing mode, he suffered through marital problems with Gena Rowlands in the ensemble *Playing by Heart*, and was an author living in seclusion in *Finding Forrester*. He had become one of the most formidable and respected of all great stars, and, more significantly to the Hollywood front offices, achieved the unheard

of, being bankable at the age of 70. He received a Tony Award as one of the producers of the play *Art*.

Screen: 1954: Lilacs in the Spring/Let's Make Up; 1957: No Road Back; Hell Drivers; Time Lock; Action of the Tiger; 1958: Another Time, Another Place; 1959: Darby O'Gill and the Little People; Tarzan's Greatest Adventure; 1961: The Frightened City; On the Fiddle/Operation Snafu; 1962: The Longest Day; 1963: Dr. No; 1964: From Russia With Love; Woman of Straw; Marnie; Goldfinger; 1965: The Hill; Thunderball; 1966: A Fine Madness; 1967: You Only Live Twice; 1969: Shalako; 1970: The Molly Maguires; 1971: The Anderson Tapes; The Red Tent; Diamonds Are Forever; 1972: The Offence; 1974: Zardoz; Murder on the Orient Express; 1975: The Terrorists; The Wind and the Lion; The Man Who Would Be King; 1976: Robin and Marian; The Next Man; 1977: A Bridge Too Far; 1979: The Great Train Robbery; Meteor; Cuba; 1981: Outland; Time Bandits; 1982: Wrong Is Right; Five Days One Summer; 1983: Never Say Never Again; 1984: Sword of the Valiant; 1986: Highlander; The Name of the Rose; 1987: The Untouchables; 1988: The Presidio; Memories of Me; 1989: Indiana Jones and the Last Crusade; Family Business; 1990: The Hunt for Red October;The Russia House; 1991: Robin Hood: Prince of Thieves; Highlander II: The Quickening; 1992: Medicine Man (and exec. prod.); 1993: Rising Sun (and exec. prod.); 1994: A Good Man in Africa; 1995: Just Cause (and prod.); First Knight; 1996: Dragonheart (voice); The Rock (and exec. prod.); 1998: The Avengers; Playing by Heart; 1999: Entrapment (and prod.); 2000: Finding Forrester (and prod.); 2003: The League of Extraordinary Gentlemen.

Select TV: 1957: Anna Christie (sp); Requiem for a Heavyweight (sp); 1961: Anna Karenina (sp).

WALTER CONNOLLY

BORN: CINCINNATI, OH, APRIL 8, 1887.
DIED: MAY 28, 1940.

Short and stocky, with a high-pitched voice and a mustache that pointed sharply downward, like an upside down letter "V," Walter Connolly crammed some notable film work into an eight-year period before his untimely death at 53. A former bank clerk, he spent years on the stage before finally coming to movies in 1932, under contract to Columbia Pictures. His work included four films for Frank Capra: *The Bitter Tea of General Yen*, as Nils Asther's oily financial advisor; *Lady for a Day*, as the wealthy dad of Jean Parker's fiancé; *Broadway Bill*, as the banker father-in-law of Warner Baxter; and, most notably, *It Happened One Night*, as Claudette Colbert's exasperated millionaire father. He was Myrna Loy's parent in another bright screwball comedy, *Libeled Lady*, and was Fredric March's short-tempered editor in *Nothing Sacred*. He snagged leads as two famous fictional sleuths, *Father Brown — Detective*, and Nero Wolfe in *The League of Frightened Men*, but although he played the title role in *The Great Victor Herbert*, he was given billing below the singers, Allan Jones and Mary Martin. His meatiest part was in Columbia's *Whom the Gods Destroy*, as a passenger who has disguised himself as a woman to escape a sinking ship, but must hide his true identity after he is proclaimed a dead hero.

Screen: 1932: No More Orchids; Washington Merry-Go-Round; Man Against Women; 1933: Lady for a Day; East of Fifth Avenue; The Bitter Tea of General Yen; Paddy — The Next Best Thing; Master of Men; Man's Castle; 1934: It Happened One Night; Once to Every Woman; Eight Girls in a Boat; Twentieth Century; Whom the Gods Destroy; Servant's Entrance; Lady by Choice; Broadway Bill; The Captain Hates the Sea; White Lies;

1935: Father Brown — Detective; She Couldn't Take It; So Red the Rose; One Way Ticket; 1936: The Music Goes 'Round; Soak the Rich; The King Steps Out; Libeled Lady; 1937: The Good Earth; Nancy Steele Is Missing; Let's Get Married; The League of Frightened Men; First Lady; Nothing Sacred; 1938: Penitentiary; Start Cheering; Four's a Crowd; Too Hot to Handle; 1939: The Girl Downstairs; The Adventures of Huckleberry Finn; Bridal Suite; Good Girls Go to Paris; Coast Guard; Those High Gray Walls; 5th Ave. Girl; The Great Victor Herbert.

NY Stage: 1916: Come Out of the Kitchen; 1920: Woman of Bronze; 1923: The Talking Parrott; 1925: Applesauce; 1926: Treat 'em Rough; 1927: The Love Thief; Praying Curve; The Springboard; Trigger; 1928: The Behavior of Mrs. Crane; The Happy Husband; Possession; Meet the Wife; 1929: Merry Andrew; Stepping Out; Paris Bound; Ladies Leave; Your Uncle Dudley; 1930: Uncle Vanya; 1931: Anatol; Six Characters in Search of an Author; The Good Fairy; 1932: The Late Christopher Bean; 1934: Gather Ye Rosebuds; 1935: The Bishop Misbehaves.

CHUCK CONNORS

(Kevin Joseph Connors) Born: Brooklyn, NY, April 10, 1921. ed: Seton Hall Col. Died: November 10, 1992.

Lean and squinty-eyed, with a face seemingly carved from solid stone, Chuck Connors was yet another on the long list of reliable supporting players who stepped up to stardom by way of television. A professional baseball player with the Chicago Cubs, among others, he decided to change his profession to acting in the early 1950s and obtained supporting parts in movies like *Pat and Mike*; *Good Morning, Miss Dove*; and *The Big Country*, where he was outstanding as Burl Ives's lecherous son. He landed an occasional lead in "B" programmers, including *Walk the Dark Street*, where he and Don Roos stalked each other with rifles, and *Hot Rod Girl*, as a cop who befriends teen racing enthusiasts. Then, in 1958, came the hit television series *The Rifleman*, with Connors as a widowed homesteader whose main concern, aside from maintaining law and order, was the well-being of his young son, played by Johnny Crawford. The show's success landed him the title role in the uninspired *Geronimo*, and in the boy-and-his-dolphin story *Flipper*, although he did not stay with this property when it became a television series. In *Synanon* he was an inmate at a drug rehabilitation clinic, and he took the lead in a routine, but extremely violent western, *Ride Beyond Vengeance*. He made several more television series and telefilms, and spent much of his later years appearing in foreign films and direct-to-video fare.

Screen: 1952: Pat and Mike; 1953: Trouble Along the Way; Code Two; South Sea Woman; 1954: Naked Alibi; Dragonfly Squadron; The Human Jungle; 1955: Target Zero; Good Morning, Miss Dove; Three Stripes in the Sun; 1956: Hold Back the Night; Hot Rod Girl; Walk the Dark Street; 1957: Tomahawk Trail; Designing Woman; Death in Small Doses; Old Yeller; The Hired Gun; 1958: The Lady Takes a Flyer; The Big Country; 1962: Geronimo; 1963: Flipper; Move Over, Darling; 1965: Synanon; 1966: Ride Beyond Vengeance; 1968: Kill Them All and Come Back Alone; 1970: Captain Nemo and the Underwater City; 1971: The Deserter; Support Your Local Gunfighter; 1972: The Proud and the Damned; 1973: The Mad Bomber/The Police Connection/Detective Geronimo; Soylent Green; Embassy; 1974: 99 and 44/100% Dead; 1975: Pancho Villa; 1978: The Legend of Sea Wolf/Wolf Larsen (filmed 1974); 1979: Tourist Trap; 1980: Virus/The End (dtv); 1981: Day of the Assassin (dtv); Garden of Venus (nUSr); 1982: Balboa; Airplane

II: The Sequel; 1984: Target Eagle (dtv); 1985: The Vals (dtv; filmed 1982); 1987: Summer Camp Nightmare/The Butterfly Revolution; Terror Squad (dtv); 1988: Sakura Killers (dtv); Trained to Kill (dtv); Taxi Killer (nUSr); Skinheads: The Second Coming of Hate (dtv); 1991: Last Flight to Hell (nUSr); 1994: Salmonberries.

Select TV: 1954: The Road to Edinburgh (sp); Vote of Confidence (sp); 1955: The Good Sisters (sp); O'Connor and the Blue-Eyed Felon (sp); Barbed Wire Christmas (sp); 1956: The Thread (sp); 1958–63: The Rifleman (series); 1963–64: Arrest and Trial (series); 1965–66: Branded (series); 1967–68: Cowboy in Africa (series); 1971: The Birdmen; 1972: Night of Terror; 1972–74: Thrill Seekers (series); 1973: Set This Town on Fire (filmed 1969); The Horror at 37,000 Feet; The Police Story; 1976: Banjo Hackett: Roamin' Free; Nightmare in Badham County; 1977: Roots (ms); The Night They Took Miss Beautiful; 1978: Standing Tall; 1982: The Capture of Grizzly Adams; 1983–84: The Yellow Rose (series); 1987–88: Werewolf (series); 1988: Once Upon a Texas Train/Texas Guns; 1989: High Desert Kill; 1991: The Gambler Returns: The Luck of the Draw; 3 Days to Kill.

MIKE CONNORS

(Krekor Ohanian) Born: Fresno, CA, August 15, 1925. ed: UCLA.

Before finding fame as one of television's tough-but-charming detectives, Mike Connors tried, unsuccessfully, to carve a niche as a movie star. He had studied to be a lawyer but found greater interest in acting, taking small parts on television and on the big screen under the improbable name "Touch" Connors. As Touch he could be seen in a wide-range of productions during the mid-1950s, from *The Ten Commandments* to *Shake Rattle and Rock*, as a deejay. Once he became "Mike" he landed the lead in a dreary AIP war film, *Suicide Battalion*, as part of a demolition team, and then his own, one-season television show, *Tightrope*. During the 1960s his film roles expanded, though they were unremarkable. He was Romy Schneider's ex-husband in the light comedy *Good Neighbor Sam*; partnered Robert Redford as a G.I. in the limp *Situation Hopeless — But Not Serious*; wandered aimlessly through two junky soaps, *Where Love Has Gone* and *Harlow*; recreated John Carradine's snooty gambler in the remake of *Stagecoach*; and carried an inane Bond spoof, *Kiss the Girls and Make Them Die*, in which he and Dorothy Provine try to stop Raf Vallone from sterilizing the world! Television came to his rescue with *Mannix*, and he played the hard-hitting hero for eight seasons. Indeed, the majority of his subsequent work was done on the small screen, with occasional cheapie movies like *Too Scared to Scream* and *Fistfighter* to help pay the rent.

Screen: as Touch Connors: 1952: Sudden Fear; 1953: Island in the Sky; The 49th Man; Sky Commando; 1954: Day of Triumph; 1955: Five Guns West; Swamp Women; The Twinkle in God's Eye; 1956: Oklahoma Woman; The Day the World Ended; Jaguar; Shake, Rattle and Rock; The Ten Commandments; Flesh and the Spur.

as Mike Connors: 1957: Voodoo Woman; 1958: Suicide Battalion; Live Fast, Die Young; 1960: The Dalton That Got Away; 1964: Panic Button; Good Neighbor Sam; Where Love Has Gone; 1965: Situation Hopeless — But Not Serious; Harlow; 1966: Stagecoach; Kiss the Girls and Make Them Die; 1979: Avalanche Express; 1980: Nightkill; 1984: Too Scared to Scream; 1989: Fistfighter; 1992: Armen and Bullik (nUSr); 1993: Public Enemy #2 (dtv); 1994: Downtown Heat (nUSr); 1996: Wild Bill:

Hollywood Maverick; **1997:** James Dean: Race With Destiny.
Select TV: **1955:** The Last Out (sp); No Trial by Jury (sp); **1959–60:** Tightrope (series); **1967–75:** Mannix (series); **1973:** Beg, Borrow or Steal; **1976:** The Killer Who Wouldn't Die; Revenge for a Rape; **1978:** Long Journey Back; **1979:** The Death of Ocean View Park; High Midnight; **1980:** Casino; **1981–82:** Today's FBI (series); **1988–89:** War and Remembrance (ms); **1989:** Crimes of the Century (series host); **1993:** Hart to Hart Returns; **1999:** Gideon.

WILLIAM CONRAD
BORN: LOUISVILLE, KY, SEPTEMBER 27, 1920.
ED: FULLERTON COL. DIED: FEBRUARY 11, 1994.

Jack-of-all-trades William Conrad appeared extensively in radio, television and movies before stardom finally came to him in the guise of a detective whose gimmick was his girth. The thickly-mustachioed, balding actor, with a most distrusting squint, made his film debut in 1946, in *The Killers*, and he was a solid supporting player in such films as *Tension*, as a Hispanic cop; *The Naked Jungle*, helping Charlton Heston battle rampaging soldier ants; and *The Conqueror*, as John Wayne's Mongolian sidekick. On radio his deep, dramatic voice was heard on many series, including *Gunsmoke* (1952–61), where no one gave a thought to the size of Marshal Matt Dillon's waistline. Moving to the small screen he produced such series as *Bat Masterson*, *Klondike*, and *77 Sunset Strip*, provided voice-over commentary for *The Bullwinkle Show* and *The Fugitive*, and, in the 1970s, finally became a full-fledged (visible) star, first as burly detective *Cannon*, then, in the late 1980s, as equally portly ex-cop Jason McCabe in *Jake and the Fat Man*. In the 1960s Conrad produced several unremarkable melodramas for Warner Bros.: *An American Dream* (1966), *A Covenant With Death* (1967), *First to Fight* (1967), *The Cool Ones* (1967), and *Assignment to Kill* (1968), and directed three mediocre thrillers: *My Blood Runs Cold*, *Brainstorm*, and *Two on a Guillotine*, all released in 1965.
Screen: **1946:** The Killers; **1947:** Body and Soul; **1948:** Arch of Triumph; Four Faces West; To the Victor; Sorry Wrong Number; Joan of Arc; **1949:** Any Number Can Play; Tension; East Side, West Side; **1950:** The Milkman; Dial 1119; One Way Street; **1951:** Cry Danger; The Sword of Monte Cristo; The Racket; **1952:** Lone Star; **1953:** Cry of the Hunted; The Desert Song; **1954:** The Naked Jungle; **1955:** 5 Against the House; The Naked Sea (narrator); The Cowboy (narrator); **1956:** The Conqueror; Johnny Concho; **1957:** The Ride Back; Zero Hour (narrator); **1959:** -30-; **1965:** Battle of the Bulge (narrator); **1976:** Moonshine County Express; **1985:** Killing Cars (dtv); **1991:** Hudson Hawk (narrator).
Select TV: **1959–73:** Rocky and His Friends/The Bullwinkle Show (series narrator); **1963–67:** The Fugitive (series narrator); **1970:** Brotherhood of the Bell; **1971:** The D.A.: Conspiracy to Kill; Cannon; O'Hara — United States Treasury: Operation Cobra; **1971–76:** Cannon (series); **1973–78:** The Wild, Wild World of Animals (series narrator); **1974:** The FBI Story: The FBI Verus Alvin Karpis — Public Enemy (narrator); **1976:** The Macahans (narrator); **1977:** The City (narrator); Tales of the Unexpected (series narrator); How the West Was Won (ms;narrator); **1978:** Night Cries; Keefer; **1979:** The Rebels (narrator); **1979–80:** Buck Rogers in the 25th Century (series narrator); **1980:** The Murder That Wouldn't Die; Turnover Smith (and exec. prod.); The Return of Frank Cannon; **1981:** Nero Wolfe (series); **1982:** Shocktrauma; **1985:** In Like Flynn; **1987:** Vengeance: The Story of Tony Cimo; **1987–92:** Jake and the

Fatman (series); **1988:** The Highwayman (series narrator).

HANS CONRIED
BORN: BALTIMORE, MD, APRIL 15, 1917.
ED: COLUMBIA UNIV. DIED: JANUARY 5, 1982.

A character actor *par excellence*, tall and slender Hans Conried put his aquiline nose, disdainful look, and clipped, aristocratic voice to good use in the creation of sundry snobs and eccentrics. It was his distinctive voice that got him started on the radio when he was only 18, eventually appearing on shows like *My Friend Irma* and *The Great Gildersleeve*. Meanwhile, he became a supporting actor, mostly in dramatic movies during World War II, where he sometimes portrayed Nazis. After the war he was used more satisfyingly for comical effect, as in *My Friend Irma*; *The Barkleys of Broadway*, as a pretentious artist; *Summer Stock*, as a hammy singer; *Texas Carnival*, as a hotel clerk; *You're Never Too Young*; *The Birds and the Bees*; and *The Patsy*, as a voice teacher. In 1953 he achieved his greatest success on the big screen, first as the voice of snarling Captain Hook in Disney's *Peter Pan*, then got top billing as the man whose television set comes to life in the sci-fi satire *The Twonky*. Best of all, he appeared as the evil piano instructor, Dr. Terwiliker, in the ultra-strange Dr. Seuss fantasy, *The 5,000 Fingers of Dr. T*. (His performance of "The Dressing Song" was a camp highlight.) He would go on to greater television success with his narration of other Seuss creations and, most of all, for playing the smart-mouthed Uncle Tonoose on the long-running sitcom, *The Danny Thomas Show*.
Screen: **1938:** Dramatic School; **1939:** It's a Wonderful World; Never Say Die; On Borrowed Time; **1940:** Dulcy; Bitter Sweet; **1941:** Maisie Was a Lady; Underground; The Gay Falcon; Unexpected Uncle; Weekend for Three; A Date With the Falcon; **1942:** Joan of Paris; Saboteur; The Wife Takes a Flyer; The Falcon Takes Over; Pacific Rendezvous; Blondie's Blessed Event; Journey Into Fear; Underground Agent; The Big Street; Nightmare; Once Upon a Honeymoon; **1943:** Hitler's Children; Hostages; A Lady Takes a Chance; Crazy House; His Butler's Sister; **1944:** Passage to Marseille; Mrs. Parkington; **1947:** The Senator Was Indiscreet; **1948:** Design of Death (narrator); **1949:** The Barkleys of Broadway; My Friend Irma; Bride for Sale; On the Town; **1950:** Nancy Goes to Rio; Summer Stock; **1951:** The Light Touch; Rich, Young and Pretty; Behave Yourself!; Texas Carnival; Too Young to Kiss; **1952:** Three for Bedroom C; The World in His Arms; Big Jim McLain; **1953:** Peter Pan (voice); Siren of Bagdad; The Twonky; The Affairs of Dobie Gillis; The 5,000 Fingers of Dr. T; **1955:** Davy Crockett — King of the Wild Frontier; You're Never Too Young; **1956:** The Birds and the Bees; Bus Stop; **1957:** The Monster That Challenged the World; Jet Pilot; **1958:** The Big Beat; Rock-a-Bye Baby; **1959:** Juke Box Rhythm; 1001 Arabian Nights (voice); **1963:** My Six Loves; **1964:** The Patsy; Robin and the 7 Hoods; **1970:** The Phantom Tollbooth (voice); **1973:** The Brothers O'Toole; **1976:** The Shaggy D.A.; **1978:** The Cat From Outer Space; **1980:** Oh, God! Book II.
NY Stage: **1953:** Can-Can; **1959:** Tall Story; **1971:** 70 Girls 70; **1974:** Irene; **1977:** Something Old Something New.
Select TV: **1950–52:** Pantomime Quiz (series); **1953:** Take a Guess (series); **1955–57:** Pantomime Quiz (series); **1957–58:** What's It For? (series); **1958:** Hansel and Gretel (sp); **1958–64:** The Danny Thomas Show/Make Room for Daddy; **1959–61:** Take a Good Look (series); **1959–62:** The Jack Paar Show (series); **1961:** Feathertop (sp); **1961–62:** The Bullwinkle Show (series; voice); **1962–63:** Pantomime Quiz (series); **1964:** Made in

America (series); **1969:** Wake Me When the War Is Over; **1970–71:** Make Room for Granddaddy (series); **1973:** Dr. Seuss on the Loose (sp; voice); **1977–78:** The Tony Randall Show (series); **1978:** The Hobbit (voice); **1980–81:** The Drack Pack (series; voice); **1981:** American Dream; American Dream (series); Through the Magic Pyramid; Barefoot in the Park (sp).

RICHARD CONTE

(NICHOLAS PETER CONTE) BORN: JERSEY CITY, NJ, MARCH 24, 1910. DIED: APRIL 15, 1975.

A tough, Italian-American actor, whose granite features and gritty delivery concealed a surprisingly likeable demeanor, Richard Conte was most at home in gangster films and noir dramas. Oddly, it was his work as a singing waiter at a resort that got him noticed by director Elia Kazan, who offered him a scholarship to New York's Neighborhood Playhouse. Conte made a single film appearance, playing a hobo in *Heaven With a Barbed Wire Fence*, before finding success on Broadway in the drama *Jason*, billed as Nicholas Conte. 20th Century-Fox signed him to a contract in 1943, changed his name, and added him to the ensemble of some top war movies: *Guadalcanal Diary*, as a Marine captain; *The Purple Heart*, as a captive flier who is brutally interrogated by the Japanese; and the engrossing *A Walk in the Sun*, which emphasized characterization over action. In between these he was given a star role in a "B" picture, *The Spider*, as a private eye tracking a killer in New Orleans's French Quarter. After the war he played an undercover Nazi in *13 Rue Madeleine*, and then gave a topnotch, sympathetic performance in *Call Northside 777*, as the wrongfully imprisoned man whom James Stewart tries to help. On loan to United Artists, he had his first romantic lead, in a soggy soap, *The Other Love*, dallying with dying pianist Barbara Stanwyck. In 1949 he was a standout as the son of Edward G. Robinson, imprisoned for his family's malfeasance in *House of Strangers*. He moved into leads with *Thieves Highway*, as a trucker seeking revenge on corrupt Lee J. Cobb, and *Whirpool*, as a psychiatrist whose wife, Gene Tierney, is a shoplifter.

In the early 1950s Conte left Fox for Universal, where he was assigned to low-budget mysteries and noir programmers like *The Sleeping City*, posing as an intern at Bellevue Hospital to investigate a narcotics ring; *Under the Gun*, as a very bad trustee at a Southern prison; *Hollywood Story*, as a movie producer shooting a picture based on an unsolved filmland murder; and *The Raging Tide*, as a racketeer stowaway on Charles Bickford's fishing boat. After his Universal contract expired his cunning dark side was effectively exposed in the superior Allied Artists noir, *The Big Combo*, and he was particularly sadistic as one of Susan Hayward's husbands in the popular biopic of Lillian Roth, *I'll Cry Tomorrow*. He could also be a comforting presence, which he proved as pregnant Judy Holliday's husband in the gentle *Full of Life*, and as the protective brother trying to save his siblings from harm in *The Brothers Ricco*. Moving back into ensemble work he was one of the cowardly Medal of Honor winners in *They Came to Cordura*, and added a certain dramatic edge to the Frank Sinatra heist romp *Ocean's Eleven*, as the doomed member of a group of thieves. This led to three more with Sinatra: *Assault on a Queen*, *Tony Rome*, and *Lady in Cement*. He supported John Wayne in *Circus World*; played Barabbas in the all-star religious epic *The Greatest Story Ever Told*; and blackmailed Michael Rennie in the glossy *Hotel*. In 1972, he received unparalleled exposure as Marlon Brando's enemy, Barzini, in *The Godfather*, but rather than it reviving his career, he worked on cheesy,

Italian-made crime films right up to his death.

Screen: AS NICHOLAS CONTE: **1939:** Heaven With a Barbed-Wire Fence.

AS RICHARD CONTE: **1943:** Guadalcanal Diary; **1944:** The Purple Heart; **1945:** A Bell for Adano; Captain Eddie; The Spider; A Walk in the Sun; **1946:** Somewhere in the Night; 13 Rue Madeleine; **1947:** The Other Love; **1948:** Call Northside 777; Cry of the City; **1949:** Whirlpool; House of Strangers; Thieves' Highway; Big Jack; **1950:** The Sleeping City; Under the Gun; **1951:** Hollywood Story; The Raging Tide; **1952:** The Raiders; The Fighter; **1953:** The Blue Gardenia; Desert Legion; Slaves of Babylon; **1954:** Highway Dragnet; Race for Life/Mask of Dust; **1955:** Target Zero; New York Confidential; The Big Combo; The Big Tip-Off; The Case of the Red Monkey; Bengazi; I'll Cry Tomorrow; **1956:** Full of Life; **1957:** The Brothers Rico; **1958:** This Angry Age; **1959:** They Came to Cordura; **1960:** Ocean's Eleven; Pepe; **1963:** Who's Been Sleeping in My Bed?; **1964:** The Eyes of Annie Jones; Circus World; **1965:** Synanon; The Greatest Story Ever Told; **1966:** Assault on a Queen; **1967:** Hotel; Tony Rome; Sentence of Death (nUSr); **1968:** Lady in Cement; **1970:** Operation Cross Eagles (and dir.); Explosion; **1972:** The Godfather; **1973:** The Big Family (nUSr); Big Guns (nUSr); Pete Pearl and the Pole (nUSr); The Inspector Is Killed (nUSr); Wipeout!/The Boss (nUSr); **1974:** Anna: The Pleasure the Torment (nUSr); My Brother Anastasia (nUSr); Shoot First Die Later/The Corrupt Cop (nUSr); **1975:** The Evil Eye (nUSr); Roma Violenta/Violent Rome/Street Killers (nUSr); Un Urlo dalle Tenebra/Return of the Exorcist/Naked Exorcism (nUSr); The Violent Professionals; No Way Out.

NY Stage: as Nicholas Conte: **1940:** Heavenly Express; **1941:** Walk Into My Parlor; **1942:** Jason; **1943:** The Family.

Select TV: **1953:** The Eye of the Beholder (sp); **1954:** Turn Back the Clock (sp); **1956:** The Silent Strangers (sp); Overnight Haul (sp); **1957:** End of a Gun (sp); **1959:** Four Just Men (series); **1966:** The Jean Arthur Show (series); **1969** The Challengers.

JACKIE COOGAN

(JOHN LESLIE COOGAN, JR.) BORN: LOS ANGELES, CA, OCTOBER 26, 1914. ED: VILLANOVA UNIV., USC. DIED: MARCH 1, 1984.

Often considered the movies' first child superstar, Jackie Coogan was a prime example of a young actor who lost favor with a fickle public that couldn't stand to see him grow up. Born to vaudevillians, he was already onstage by age two and followed that with a bit in a 1916 Essanay production called *Skinner's Baby*. Appearing in a revue with swimming star Annette Kellerman, Coogan was spotted by Charlie Chaplin, who felt the boy had star quality. After giving him a small part in the short *A Day's Pleasure*, Chaplin cast him as his scene-stealing co-star in the 1921 feature, *The Kid*, a successful mixture of comedy and pathos. As the orphan with the soulful eyes and bobbed locks, Coogan stole hearts the world over and was an overnight sensation. Over the next few years Jackie Coogan toys and merchandising would earn him over $4 million. Producer Sol Lesser took him under his wing and put him in such features as *Peck's Bad Boy*, *Long Live the King*, and *Oliver Twist*. Predictably, he was almost always cast as an orphan adrift in a cruel world, thereby affording him the necessary heartbreaking moments for maximum audience satisfaction. When, at age 12, he got a grown-up haircut, the studio capitalized on the publicity with a vehicle titled (unimaginatively) *Johnny, Get Your Hair Cut*.

With the coming of sound, the chunky, teenaged Coogan's

attempts to maintain his stardom with new versions of *Tom Sawyer* and *Huckleberry Finn* led nowhere. Following a car accident in which his father was killed, Coogan, now 21, expected to collect the fortune he had made as a child. To his horror he discovered that his mother and her new husband had no intention of turning over any of what was left. A highly publicized lawsuit, which netted Coogan a paltry $35,000 settlement, helped to establish the Child Actors Bill, which would protect future child stars from suffering a similar fate. (The bill became more popularly known as the Coogan Law.) He had married (1937–40) up-and-coming dancer Betty Grable and together they appeared in the features *College Swing* and *Million Dollar Legs*, although her position in the industry had clearly eclipsed his. Following a stint as a flight officer during World War II, Coogan tried nightclub shows and even worked as a salesman, but was lured back to acting in the early 1950s. Now balding and plump, with a high pitched voice, he gained some attention for his supporting work in such "A" features as *The Actress* and *The Joker Is Wild*, and made appearances in Albert Zugsmith potboilers like *High School Confidential* and *Sex Kittens Go to College*. He found his greatest latter-day fame playing the ghoulishly lovable Uncle Fester on the television series *The Addams Family*, which ran endlessly in syndication. He was hired, for the sake of nostalgia, to appear in oddball productions like *The Manchu Eagle Murder Caper Mystery* and *Won Ton Ton, the Dog Who Saved Hollywood*. His grandson is actor Keith Coogan.

Screen: 1916: Skinner's Baby; 1921: The Kid; Peck's Bad Boy; 1922: My Boy; Oliver Twist; Trouble; 1923: Daddy; Circus Days; 1924: Long Live the King; A Boy of Flanders; Little Robinson Crusoe; The Rag Man; 1925: Old Clothes; 1927: Johnny, Get Your Hair Cut; The Bugle Call; Buttons; 1930: Tom Sawyer; 1931: Huckleberry Finn; 1935: Home on the Range; 1938: College Swing; 1939: Million Dollar Legs; Sky Patrol; 1947: Kilroy Was Here; 1948: French Leave; 1951: Skipalong Rosenbloom; Varieties on Parade; 1952: Outlaw Women; 1953: The Actress; 1954: Mesa of Lost Women; 1956: The Proud Ones; 1957: The Buster Keaton Story; The Joker Is Wild; Eighteen and Anxious; 1958: High School Confidential; Lonelyhearts; No Place to Land; The Space Children; 1959: Night of the Quarter Moon; The Big Operator; The Beat Generation; 1960: Sex Kittens Go to College; Platinum High School; Escape From Terror; 1965: John Goldfarb, Please Come Home; Girl Happy; 1966: A Fine Madness; 1968: Silent Treatment; Rogue's Gallery; The Shakiest Gun in the West; 1969: Marlowe; 1973: Cahill — U.S. Marshal; 1975: The Manchu Eagle Murder Caper Mystery; 1976: Won Ton Ton, the Dog Who Saved Hollywood; 1980: Human Experiments; Dr. Heckyl and Mr. Hype; 1982: The Escape Artist; 1983: The Prey.

Select TV: 1950–55: Pantomime Quiz (series); 1952: Cowboy G-Men (series); 1956: The Old Payola (sp); Forbidden Area (sp); 1957: The Troublemakers (sp); 1958: Trial by Slander (sp); 1959: The Indian Giver (sp); 1962–63: McKeever & the Colonel (series); 1964–66: The Addams Family (series); 1972: Cool Million; 1974: The Phantom of Hollywood; 1975: The Specialists; 1976: Sherlock Holmes in New York; 1977: Halloween With the New Addams Family (sp); 1980: The Kids Who Knew Too Much.

ELISHA COOK, JR.
BORN: SAN FRANCISCO, CA, DECEMBER 26, 1903. DIED: MAY 18, 1995.

Saucer-eyed and neurotic, Elisha Cook, Jr. became everybody's favorite film weasel. He started acting onstage as a teen but didn't make regular movie appearances until the late 1930s. His diminutive stature allowed him to play characters

much younger than his actual years, in such movies as *Pigskin Parade*, as a Commie college student; *They Won't Forget*, as the boyfriend of the murdered girl; and *Newsboys' Home*, as a newsie. His greatest fame came in 1941, playing the bullying gunsel Wilmer in the private eye classic *The Maltese Falcon*, while he had another solid role, as the mousey racetrack cashier who gets revenge on his two-timing wife, in Stanley Kubrick's superb 1956 heist film, *The Killing*. In between, he was a plantation overseer with murderous designs on Merle Oberon in *Dark Waters*; a piano player in *Sergeant York*; the weird desk clerk suspected of murder in *I Wake Up Screaming*; a twitchy jazz drummer in *Phantom Lady*; a doomed stoolpigeon in *The Big Sleep*; a shifty radio disc jockey in *The Falcon's Alibi*; Lawrence Tierney's devoted pal who gets stabbed in *Born to Kill*; a hotel elevator operator and uncle of unhinged Marilyn Monroe in *Don't Bother to Knock*; and one of Jack Palance's unfortunate victims in *Shane*. Busy well into his 70s, Cook was called back to reprise Wilmer in the shoddy 1975 *Maltese Falcon* sequel/spoof, *The Black Bird*. He was frequently billed without the "Jr."

Screen: 1930: Her Unborn Child; 1936: Two in a Crowd; Pigskin Parade; 1937: Wife, Doctor and Nurse; They Won't Forget; The Devil Is Driving; Thoroughbreds Don't Cry; Life Begins in College; Love Is News; Breezing Home; Danger — Love at Work; 1938: Submarine Patrol; Three Blind Mice; My Lucky Star; Newsboys' Home; 1939: Grand Jury Secrets; 1940: Stranger on the Third Floor; He Married His Wife; Public Deb No. 1; Tin Pan Alley; 1941: Man at Large; Love Crazy; Sergeant York; The Maltese Falcon; I Wake Up Screaming; Hellzapoppin'; Ball of Fire; 1942: A Gentleman at Heart; In This Our Life; A-Haunting We Will Go; Sleepytime Gal; Manila Calling; Wildcat; 1944: Up in Arms; Casanova Brown; Dark Waters; Phantom Lady; Dark Mountain; 1945: Dillinger; Why Girls Leave Home; 1946: The Big Sleep; Blonde Alibi; Cinderella Jones; The Falcon's Alibi; Joe Palooka — Champ; Two Smart People; 1947: Born to Kill; The Fall Guy; The Long Night; The Gangster; 1949: Flaxy Martin; The Great Gatsby; 1951: Behave Yourself!; 1952: Don't Bother to Knock; 1953: Thunder Over the Plains; I, the Jury; Shane; 1954: The Outlaw's Daughter; Drum Beat; 1955: Timberjack; The Indian Fighter; Trial; 1956: The Killing; Accused of Murder; 1957: The Lonely Man; Voodoo Island; Baby Face Nelson; Plunder Road; Chicago Confidential; 1958: House on Haunted Hill; 1959: Day of the Outlaw; 1960: Platinum High School; College Confidential; 1961: One-Eyed Jacks; 1963: Papa's Delicate Condition; The Haunted Palace; Black Zoo; Johnny Cool; 1964: Blood on the Arrow; The Glass Cage; 1967: Welcome to Hard Times; 1968: Rosemary's Baby; 1969: The Great Bank Robbery; 1970: El Condor; 1972: The Great Northfield Minnesota Raid; Blacula; 1973: Emperor of the North Pole; Electra Glide in Blue; The Outfit; 1974: Messiah of Evil/Dead People; 1975: The Black Bird; 1976: Winterhawk; St. Ives; 1979: The Champ; 1941; 1980: Tom Horn; Carny; 1981: Harry's War; National Lampoon Goes to the Movies (dtv); 1982: Hammett.

NY Stage: 1925: The Crooked Friday; 1926: Hello Lola!; Henry-Behave; Gertie; 1928: Her Unborn Child; Kingdom of God; 1930: Many a Slip; 1931: Privilege Car; 1932: Lost Boy; Merry-Go-Round; Chrysalis; 1933: Three-Cornered Moon; Ah, Wilderness!; 1935: Crime Marches On; 1936: Come Angel Band; 1963: Arturo Ui.

Select TV: 1970: The Movie Murderer; Night Chase; 1972: The Night Stalker; 1974: The Phantom of Hollywood; 1977: Mad Bull; 1979: Salem's Lot; 1981: Leave 'em Laughing; 1982: Terror at Alcatraz; 1983: This Girl for Hire; 1983–88: Magnum P.I. (series); 1984: Off Sides; It Came Upon the Midnight Clear; 1987: The Man Who Broke 1,000 Chains.

GARY COOPER

(FRANK JAMES COOPER) BORN: HELENA, MT, MAY 7, 1901. ED: WESLEYAN COL., GRINNELL COL. DIED: MAY 13, 1961.

Without realizing it, Gary Cooper was a trendsetter. His quiet hesitancy, natural speech patterns, and uncanny use of stillness, represented a huge leap forward in screen acting for audiences accustomed to florid gestures. Yet there was nothing studied about Cooper's acting style. Doing his work with conviction and strength, carrying no pretentious bag of tricks, and having received no formal instruction in his craft, he became one of the movies' most enduring and beloved stars. Raised on a Montana ranch, Cooper returned with his family to his father's native England in 1910, where he was schooled until the outbreak of World War I. While attending Grinnell College his interest leaned towards art, but attempts to sell his work proved mostly futile. After moving to Los Angeles to join his recently relocated parents, a chance meeting with some friends from Montana, who were doing stunt work for westerns, resulted in his introduction to the movies. There were countless stunt and extra appearances, only some of which have been verified, including *The Vanishing American*, and *The Eagle*, starring Rudolph Valentino. His big break came in 1926, when he took a substantial supporting role as a young engineer in the modern-day western *The Winning of Barbara Worth*. Paramount signed him to a contract, opening the doors for bigger parts, including *Children of Divorce*, as a spoiled socialite, and another western, *Arizona Bound*, in which he had the lead as a young drifter recovering a shipment of stolen gold. A fortuitous supporting role cast him as a doomed pilot in the first Academy Award-winner for Best Picture, *Wings*.

Now primed for stardom, he began to carve his niche in both westerns and romantic dramas opposite such leading ladies as Fay Wray (*The Legion of the Condemned*, their first of four together), Colleen Moore (*Lilac Time*, for First National); Lupe Velez (*Wolf Song*), with whom he had a much-publicized off-screen relationship; and Nancy Carroll (*The Shopworn Angel*, which featured their speaking voices in the final scenes.) His first all-talking picture, *The Virginian*, cemented the laconic Gary Cooper image of the strong, silent hero of few words (namely "yep" and "nope"). In later years it became one of the more widely screened movies from the very early, primitive first year of sound pictures. He was becoming a major attraction with roles as a romantic Foreign Legionnaire in Marlene Dietrich's *Morocco*; a gangster in Rouben Mamoulian's well-liked *City Streets*; and, most importantly, as a soldier in love with nurse Helen Hayes in the first film version of Hemingway's *A Farewell to Arms*, which earned an Oscar nomination for Best Picture. Time hasn't been kind to any of these, but Cooper's smooth underplaying was instrumental to the success of each. He brightened the otherwise glum period romance, *One Sunday Afternoon*, but fell with a crash in the dreary attempt to put Noel Coward's *Design for Living* on screen. Metro borrowed him for *Today We Live*, which featured a William Faulkner script and Joan Crawford as leading lady, but little else, and the ludicrous *Operator 13*, as a Southerner in love with Northern spy Marion Davies, doing a pretty unconvincing impression of a black maid. Goldwyn used him for one of his many failed efforts to make a star out of Anna Sten, *The Wedding Night*, and, back on his home lot, he and Carol Lombard held their own against rising child star Shirley Temple, in *Now and Forever*.

As a dashing adventurer he scored a smashing success with *The Lives of a Bengal Lancer*, in 1935, playfully sparring with Franchot Tone in Northwestern India, and setting his feet on the path to Hollywood greatness. (Fortunately for him, all trace of the follow-up, *Peter Ibbetson*, a woefully misguided romantic whimsy with Ann Harding, was wiped clean.) In 1936, Frank Capra found his perfect "everyman" in Cooper for *Mr. Deeds Goes to Town*. As the naïve Midwesterner who inherits a fortune and becomes disillusioned when his attempts at philanthropy are met with cynicism, Cooper gave his most flawless performance. The film's perfect mixture of gentle humor and social commentary received Oscar nominations for Best Picture, Best Actor (for Cooper), and Best Director, which Capra won. Cooper followed it with the odd but engrossing adventure, *The General Died at Dawn*, as a soldier of fortune in Northern China, and DeMille's robust *The Plainsman*, playing Wild Bill Hickok, with his *Deeds* co-star, Jean Arthur, as Calamity Jane. He easily coasted through three enjoyable comedies: *Desire*, back with Dietrich in more light-hearted surroundings; *Bluebeard's Eighth Wife*, playing off another peerless interpreter of light comedy, Claudette Colbert; and *The Cowboy and the Lady*, falling for arrogant Merle Oberon. *Souls at Sea* found him acting macho with George Raft, and for Goldwyn (with whom he had signed a contract) he did the poorly received, tongue-in-cheek *The Adventures of Marco Polo*. He rebounded in 1939 with the best-remembered version of the ultimate Foreign Legion story, *Beau Geste*, by which time he was commanding the highest salary in the business at $500,000 a year.

He was matched marvelously with Walter Brennan in two films: *The Westerner*, in which Cooper shrewdly manipulated Brennan's Judge Roy Bean; and Capra's *Meet John Doe*, as a ballplayer-turned-hobo, who is picked to represent the country's underprivileged in a cynical political scheme, against the better-judgment of Brennan, his happily unemployed sidekick. In 1941, his status soared to new heights, first for his brilliant comedic work as a tongue-tied professor in love with showgirl Barbara Stanwyck, in the classic *Ball of Fire*, then as the backwoods turkey shooter who becomes World War I's greatest hero, in *Sergeant York*. The latter film won him an Academy Award for Best Actor and proved to be a great inspiration to America as it entered World War II. He was nominated for the Oscar again for his superb portrayal of baseball star Lou Gehrig in Goldwyn's sudsy biopic *The Pride of the Yankees*. (Cooper's final public speech as the dying ball-player is one of the memorable moments of his career.) At the author's request, he carried the film of Hemingway's *For Whom the Bell Tolls*, creating a beautifully believable relationship with Ingrid Bergman, earning another Oscar nomination, and scoring his greatest box-office success of all. Other big money-makers during this period included three for Cecil B. DeMille: *North West Mounted Police* (Cooper's first in Technicolor); *The Story of Dr. Wassell*; and the rather preposterous, though lively, *Unconquered*. Cooper reteamed with Bergman for the plodding New Orleans saga, *Saratoga Trunk*, and effortlessly pulled off a pair of mild comedies for the newly-formed International Pictures, *Casanova Brown* and *Along Came Jones*, the latter carrying the actor's only on-screen credit for producing.

In the immediate postwar years he stumbled badly in a misguided attempt to film Ayn Rand's *The Fountainhead*, and merely went through the motions in a clichéd war drama, *Task Force*. He phoned in a trio of routine westerns (*Bright Leaf*, *Dallas* and *Distant Drums*), but followed these with one of the classics of the genre, *High Noon*. Filmed in real time, the movie — a thinly disguised allegory for America's apathy to the McCarthy Senate hearings — showed Cooper at his most subtle and sympathetic, as retiring sheriff Will Cain, who must face a group of gunmen, only to find himself being deserted by the townspeople on whom he thought he could depend. A solid box-office hit, it earned him a second Academy Award and became the movie with which his name would be most readily identified. He was at his charming best in William Wyler's gentle look at Quaker life, *Friendly Persuasion*, and in Billy Wilder's May-December romance, *Love in the Afternoon*, as an aging Casanova falling for Audrey Hepburn. (There was much mention of how extreme shading was used to disguise Cooper's features.) He found potent box-office success with Burt Lancaster in *Vera Cruz*, though both *Man of the West*, as a former bandit drawn back into Lee J. Cobb's dangerous gang, and *The Hanging Tree*, as a doctor with a tragic past, were superior in quality. He showed up in the glossy Fox CinemaScope soaper, *Ten North Frederick*, and displayed emotional depth as a branded coward who shows his true courage in the complex *They Came to Cordura*. At the 1961 Academy Award ceremony James Stewart picked up a special trophy for "Coop," whom everyone knew was dying from cancer. His final movie, a mediocre mystery with Deborah Kerr, *The Naked Edge*, was released posthumously, climaxing more than 30 years as one of the industry's sterling attractions.

Screen: 1925: The Thundering Herd; Wild Horse Mesa; The Lucky Horseshoe; The Vanishing American; The Eagle; 1926: The Enchanted Hill; Watch Your Wife; The Winning of Barbara Worth; 1927: It; Children of Divorce; Arizona Bound; Wings; Nevada; The Last Outlaw; 1928: Beau Sabreur; The Legion of the Condemned; Doomsday; Half a Bride; Lilac Time; The First Kiss; The Shopworn Angel; 1929: Wolf Song; Betrayal; The Virginian; 1930: Only the Brave; Paramount on Parade; The Texan; Seven Days Leave; A Man From Wyoming; The Spoilers; Morocco; 1931: Fighting Caravans; City Streets; I Take This Woman; His Woman; 1932: Make Me a Star; Devil and the Deep; If I Had a Million; A Farewell to Arms; 1933: Today We Live; One Sunday Afternoon; Design for Living; Alice in Wonderland; 1934: Operator 13; Now and Forever; 1935: The Wedding Night; The Lives of a Bengal Lancer; Peter Ibbetson; 1936: Desire; Mr. Deeds Goes to Town; Hollywood Boulevard; The General Died at Dawn; The Plainsman; 1937: Souls at Sea; 1938: The Adventures of Marco Polo; Bluebeard's Eighth Wife; The Cowboy and the Lady; 1939: Beau Geste; The Real Glory; 1940: The Westerner; North West Mounted Police; Meet John Doe; 1941: Sergeant York; Ball of Fire; 1942: The Pride of the Yankees; 1943: For Whom the Bell Tolls; 1944: The Story of Dr. Wassell; Casanova Brown; 1945: Along Came Jones (and prod.); Saratoga Trunk; 1946: Cloak and Dagger; 1947: Unconquered; Variety Girl; 1948: Good Sam; 1949: The Fountainhead; It's a Great Feeling; Task Force; 1950: Bright Leaf; Dallas; 1951: U.S.S. Teakettle/You're in the Navy Now; Starlift; It's a Big Country; Distant Drums; 1952: High Noon; Springfield Rifle; 1953: Return to Paradise; Blowing Wild; 1954: Garden of Evil; Vera Cruz; 1955: The Court-Martial of Billy Mitchell; 1956: Friendly Persuasion; 1957: Love in the Afternoon; 1958: Ten North Frederick; Man of the West; 1959: The Hanging Tree; Alias Jesse James; They Came to Cordura; The Wreck of the Mary Deare; 1961: The Naked Edge.

Select TV: 1961: The Real West (sp; voice).

GLADYS COOPER

BORN: LEWISHAM, ENGLAND, DECEMBER 18, 1888. DIED: NOVEMBER 17, 1971.

Few were better than Gladys Cooper at portraying the sort of aristocratic lady who thought highly of herself and little of anyone else. Like so many other English stage actors, she did not make regular movie appearances until she was past 50. Her theatrical bow came at 17, in *Bluebelle in Fairyland*, followed by work as a chorus girl whose refined beauty made her a popular pin-up for the soldiers during World War I. Her legitimate London stage career soon began and she established her reputation in such plays as *The Admirable Crichton* and *The Second Mrs. Tanqueray*. There were some British silents and then several Broadway appearances in the 1930s, including *The Shining Hour* and *Call It a Day*. She made the trip to Hollywood in 1940, at Alfred Hitchcock's request, to play Laurence Olivier's sister in *Rebecca*, and made a good enough impression to receive many offers of work. Her reputation was enhanced by two superb performances, both of which earned her Oscar nominations. First, she was at her meanest as the selfish, destructive mother of Bette Davis in *Now, Voyager*, cruelly referring to her daughter as her "ugly duckling." Then she was the immoveable nun who jealously discounted Jennifer Jones's miraculous claims in *The Song of Bernadette*. The recognition got her signed by MGM, where she filled a succession of *grande dame* roles in such movies as *The White Cliffs of Dover*, *The Valley of Decision*, *The Pirate*, and *Madame Bovary*. After her contract ended she triumphantly returned to Broadway, in *The Chalk Garden*, and co-starred briefly in the television series *The Rogues*. Other film highlights include her domineering mother to dowdy daughter Deborah Kerr in *Separate Tables*, a role not unlike her *Now, Voyager* one, and the sensible maternal influence on Rex Harrison in *My Fair Lady*, a performance that earned her a final Oscar nomination. (Coincidentally, she had played the same role the year before in a television version of *Pygmalion*.) Although she did not sing in *Fair Lady*, she did a bit of warbling a few years later in Disney's *The Happiest Millionaire*. Her autobiography was published in 1931, and she was created a Dame Commander of the British Empire in 1967. One of her stepsons was actor Robert Morley.

Screen: 1913: The Eleventh Commandment; 1914: Dandy Donovan, the Gentleman Cracksman; 1917: The Sorrows of Satan; Masks and Faces; 1918: My Lady's Dress; 1920: Unmarried; 1922: Headin' North; 1923: Bonnie Prince Charles; The Bohemian Girl; 1935: The Iron Duke; 1940: Rebecca; Kitty Foyle; 1941: That Hamilton Woman; The Black Cat; The Gay Falcon; 1942: This Above All; Eagle Squadron; Now, Voyager; 1943: Forever and a Day; Mr. Lucky; Princess O'Rourke; The Song of Bernadette; 1944: The White Cliffs of Dover; Mrs. Parkington; 1945: The Valley of Decision; Love Letters; 1946: The Green Years; The Cockeyed Miracle; 1947: Green Dolphin Street; The Bishop's Wife; Beware of Pity; 1948: Homecoming; The Pirate; 1949: The Secret Garden; Madame Bovary; 1951: Thunder on the Hill; 1952: At Sword's Point; 1955: The Man Who Loved Redheads; 1958: Separate Tables; 1963: The List of Adrian Messenger; 1964: My Fair Lady; 1967: The Happiest Millionaire; 1969: A Nice Girl Like Me.

NY Stage: 1934: The Shining Hour; 1935: Othello; Macbeth; 1936: Call It a Day; 1938: Spring Meeting; 1942: The Morning Star; 1955: The Chalk Garden; 1962: A Passage to India.

Select TV: 1957: Circle of the Day (sp); The Mystery of 13 (sp); 1958: Verdict of Three (sp); 1959: The Stray Cat (sp); 1963: Pygmalion (sp); 1964–65: The Rogues (series).

JACKIE COOPER

(JOHN COOPER, JR.) BORN: LOS ANGELES, CA, SEPTEMBER 15, 1922.

Of all the many Little Rascals who contributed to the Our Gang series, only Jackie Cooper could claim to having had a truly successful movie career outside of those famous two-reelers. It was Cooper's grandmother, a film extra, who got him started in movies when he was barely four years old. In 1929, at age seven, he was signed by Hal Roach to a two-year contract to join the popular Our Gang shorts, and by 1931 Cooper had made a total of 15 appearances, starting with *Boxing Gloves* and ending with *Bargain Day*. The beaming youngster was particularly adept at instantly switching from an overbearing enthusiasm to a tearful, quivery-lipped sadness. The boy's uncle, director Norman Taurog, cast Cooper in *Skippy* and launched him into stardom. This utterly beguiling story of a boy trying to earn money to buy a license for his captured dog brought Taurog the Best Director Oscar and earned Cooper a nomination for Best Actor. (He is the youngest person ever to be nominated in that category.) Legend has it that the lad was fast asleep at the Oscar ceremony by the time Lionel Barrymore was announced as the winner. Signed to a contract by MGM, the youngster became a star attraction in the early 1930s, thanks in large part to his teaming with Wallace Beery in three consecutive hits: the gooey tearjerker, *The Champ*, where he broke hearts around the world with his overwrought crying scene; the studio's colorful adaptation of *Treasure Island*; and the rowdy turn-of-the-century drama *The Bowery*, for United Artists. Metro gave him top billing for tearjerkers like *When a Feller Needs a Friend*, as a crippled child who just wants to play ball with the other kids, and *Divorce in the Family*, with Conrad Nagel as his rejected step-dad. At Paramount, a sequel to *Skippy*, called *Sooky*, referred to the character of Cooper's best buddy in both films, as played by Robert Coogan. Fox borrowed him to cash in on his ability to tug at the heartstrings in a new version of *Peck's Bad Boy*.

As he grew into a teenager he began to lose favor with the public, and he ended his term at MGM with the delightful *The Devil Is a Sissy*, where he and Mickey Rooney were a couple of tough New Yorkers who take sophisticated Freddie Bartholomew under their wing. He acquitted himself nicely in a supporting role in Warners's *White Banners*, as Claude Rains's fellow-inventor, before descending into low budget teen dramas like *Gangster's Boy*, *Newsboys' Home*, and the serial *Scouts to the Rescue*. Paramount cast him as hapless teen Henry Aldrich in *What a Life!*, which, despite his whiney, annoying performance, led to a successful series of comedies. Cooper bowed out after only one more entry, *Life With Henry*, giving the part over to affable Jimmy Lydon. After serving in the Navy during World War II, Cooper returned to acting, strengthening his skills with stage work, but the movies had little to offer except such "B" material as Monogram's *French Leave*, which featured another former child star, Jackie Coogan. The rebirth of Cooper's career came through television, with a pair of self-produced sitcoms that he also occasionally directed: *The People's Choice*, featuring a voice-over commentary by a basset hound, and *Hennesey*. He left acting briefly to serve as vice-president in charge of production at Screen Gems television from 1964 to 1969. Throughout the 1970s and 1980s he made his reputation as an accomplished television director, winning Emmy Awards for his work on the series *M*A*S*H* and *The White Shadow*. His one big-screen directorial effort, the feminist comedy *Stand Up and Be Counted*, made little impact, but he made a welcome return to the movies as the exasperated *Daily Planet* editor Perry White in the blockbuster, *Superman*, a role he reprised for three sequels before retiring in 1989. The title of his 1981 autobiography, *Please Don't Shoot My Dog*, was a direct reference to *Skippy*.

Screen (shorts): 1929: Boxing Gloves; Bouncing Babies; Moan & Groan, Inc.; Shivering Shakespeare; 1930: The First Seven Years; When the Wind Blows; Bear Shooters; A Tough Winter; Pups Is Pups; Teacher's Pet; School's Out; 1931: Helping Grandma; Love Business; Little Daddy; Bargain Day; Jackie Cooper's Christmas; 1932: The Stolen Jools; Hollywood on Parade No. 3; 1942: Soaring Stars.

Screen (features): 1929: William Fox Movietone Follies of 1929; Sunny Side Up; 1931: Skippy; Sooky; Young Donovan's Kid; The Champ; 1932: When a Feller Needs a Friend; Divorce in the Family; 1933: Broadway to Hollywood; The Bowery; 1934: Lone Cowboy; Treasure Island; Peck's Bad Boy; 1935: Dinky; O'Shaughnessy's Boy; 1936: The Devil Is a Sissy; Tough Guy; 1938: White Banners; Gangster's Boy; That Certain Age; Newsboys' Home; Boy of the Streets; 1939: Scouts to the Rescue (serial); Spirit of Culver; Streets of New York; What a Life!; Two Bright Boys; The Big Guy; 1940: Seventeen; The Return of Frank James; Gallant Sons; 1941: Life With Henry; Ziegfeld Girl; Her First Beau; Glamour Boy; 1942: Syncopation; Men of Texas; The Navy Comes Thru; 1943: Where Are Your Children?; 1947: Stork Bites Man; Kilroy Was Here; 1948: French Leave; 1961: Everything's Ducky; 1971: The Love Machine; 1974: Chosen Survivors; 1978: Superman; 1981: Superman II; 1983: Superman III; 1987: Superman IV: The Quest for Peace; Surrender.

NY Stage: 1949: Magnolia Alley; 1951: Remains to Be Seen; 1954: King of Hearts.

Select TV: 1952: A Message for Janice (sp); Something Old Something New (sp); 1953: Jim's Big Boy (sp); Birthright (sp); The Middle Son (sp); Hound Dog Man (sp); Westward the Sun (sp); 1954: A Dreamer of Summer (sp); 1955: Yellow Jack (sp); Yankee Peddler (sp); I Found 60 Million Dollars (sp); It Depends on You (sp); The Pardon-Me Boy (sp); 1955–58: The People's Choice (series; and dir.); 1956: The Old Lady Shows Her Medals (sp); 1958: The Fair-Haired Boy (sp); Mid-Summer (sp); The Hasty Heart (sp); 1959–62: Hennesey (series; and dir.); 1962: Special Assignment (sp); 1968: Shadow on the Land; 1971: Maybe I'll Come Home in the Spring; 1972: The Astronaut; 1974: The Dean Martin Comedy World (series); The Day the Earth Moved; 1975: The Invisible Man; 1975: Mobile One; Mobile Two (series); 1977: Operation Petticoat.

MELVILLE COOPER

BORN: BIRMINGHAM, ENGLAND, OCTOBER 15, 1896. ED: KING EDWARD'S SCHOOL. DIED: MARCH 29, 1973.

One of Hollywood's busiest English imports, stocky Melville Cooper brought his bassett-hound eyes to the movies in 1931 after nearly 20 years of making a reputation on the British stage. After his fine work in the British version of *The Scarlet Pimpernel*, and two Broadway appearances, he came to Hollywood in 1936 to appear as Reginald Owen's chauffeur in MGM's *The Bishop Misbehaves*. Ideal for costume pictures, and invariably cast in pompous roles, he was seen in *The Gorgeous Hussy*, *The Adventures of Robin Hood* (as the Sheriff of Nottingham), *Moonfleet*, and *Pride and Prejudice*, in the showy role of Mr. Collins, Greer Garson's spurned suitor. His adept comedy playing was on display in *Gold Diggers of Paris*, as a dance festival coordinator charmed by Rosemary Lane; *Four's a Crowd*, as Walter Connolly's butler; *Garden of the Moon*, as the maître'd at the title nightclub; *Tovarich*, as the banker who hires impoverished nobles Claudette Colbert and Charles Boyer; *The Lady Eve*, as a cardsharp; and *Life Begins at 8:30*. He had one of his largest roles in Universal's 1939 "B" offering, *Two Bright Boys*, enlisting Freddie Bartholomew in a scheme to swindle Jackie Cooper out of his property. In the 1940 Oscar-winner *Rebecca* he showed up as a coroner who hilariously regales his fellow diners with grisly details of his profession.

Screen: 1931: Black Coffee; 1932: Bachelor's Folly/The Calendar; Wives Beware/Two White Arms; 1933: Forging Ahead; Leave It to Me; To Brighton With Gladys; 1934: The Private Life of Don

Juan; 1935: The Scarlet Pimpernel; The Bishop Misbehaves; Rendezvous; 1936:The Gorgeous Hussy; 1937: The Last of Mrs. Cheyney; Thin Ice; The Great Garrick; Tovarich; 1938: Women Are Like That; The Adventures of Robin Hood; Hard to Get; Gold Diggers in Paris; Four's a Crowd; The Dawn Patrol; Comet Over Broadway; Dramatic School; Garden of the Moon; 1939: I'm From Missouri; Two Bright Boys; The Sun Never Sets; Blind Alley; 1940: Pride and Prejudice; Too Many Husbands; Rebecca; Murder Over New York; Escape to Glory; 1941: Scotland Yard; Flame of New Orleans; The Lady Eve; You Belong to Me; 1942: This Above All; The Affairs of Martha/Once Upon a Thursday; Life Begins at Eight-Thirty; Random Harvest; 1943: Hit Parade of 1943; The Immortal Sergeant; Holy Matrimony; My Kingdom for a Cook; 1946: Heartbeat; 13 Rue Madeleine; 1947: The Imperfect Lady; 1948: Enchantment; 1949: The Red Danube; Love Happy; And Baby Makes Three; 1950: Father of the Bride; The Underworld Story; The Petty Girl; Let's Dance; 1953: It Should Happen to You; 1955: Moonfleet; The King's Thief; 1956: Diane; Bundle of Joy; Around the World in Eighty Days; 1957: The Story of Mankind; 1959: From the Earth to the Moon.

NY Stage: 1935: Laburnum Grove; Jubilee; 1943: The Merry Widow; 1944: The Maid as Mistress; While the Sun Shines; 1945: Firebrand of Florence; Pygmalion; 1946: Gypsy Lady; The Haven; 1947: An Inspector Calls; 1950: The Liar; The Day After Tomorrow; 1951: Make a Wish; 1952: Much Ado About Nothing; 1953: Escapade; 1957: The Merry Widow; 1960: My Fair Lady; 1963: The Importance of Being Earnest (ob); 1966: Hostile Witness; 1970: Charley's Aunt.

Select TV: 1950: The Merry Widow (sp); 1951: Mme. Modiste (sp); 1952: Angel Street (sp); Jenny Kissed Me (sp); A Kiss for Cinderella (sp); 1953: The Marmalade Scandal (sp); A Christmas Carol (sp); Return to Ballygally (sp); 1956: The Corn Is Green (sp); Keely's Wonderful Machine (sp); 1957: Charley's Aunt (sp); 1959: Night of Betrayal (sp).

JEFF COREY
BORN: NEW YORK, NY, AUGUST 10, 1914.
DIED: AUGUST 16, 2002

Gaunt and bushy-browed, Jeff Corey's 50-year career as a stellar character actor was interrupted in the 1950s when he became a victim of blacklisting. During this time of enforced retirement he set up his own acting school in Hollywood, where he became one of the most respected teachers of the craft to young students like Jack Nicholson. On the big screen he could be seen as a sympathetic psychiatrist in *Home of the Brave*; a wino in *Lady in a Cage*; the mysterious man who brokers John Randolph's transformation into Rock Hudson in *Seconds*; a sheriff in both *Butch Cassidy and the Sundance Kid* and its prequel, *Butch and Sundance — The Early Days*; a collegiate official in *Getting Straight*; and Wild Bill Hickok in *Little Big Man*. On television he directed episodes of *Night Gallery* and *Police Story*.

Screen: 1940: Third Finger, Left Hand; Bitter Sweet; You'll Find Out; 1941: All That Money Can Buy/The Devil and Daniel Webster; The Reluctant Dragon; North to the Klondike; Paris Calling; Small Town Deb; Petticoat Politics; You Belong to Me; 1942: The Man Who Wouldn't Die; Roxie Hart; Tennessee Johnson; The Postman Didn't Ring; Girl Trouble; 1943: The Moon Is Down; Frankenstein Meets the Wolf Man; My Friend Flicka; 1946: The Killers; Somewhere in the Night; California; It Shouldn't Happen to a Dog; 1947: Ramrod; The Gangster;

Hoppy's Holiday; Miracle on 34th Street; Unconquered; Brute Force; The Flame; 1948: The Wreck of the Hesperus; Homecoming; Alias a Gentleman; Canon City; Let's Live Again; Kidnapped; Wake of the Red Witch; A Southern Yankee; Joan of Arc; I, Jane Doe; 1949: City Across the River; Roughshod; Black Shadows (narrator); Follow Me Quietly; The Hideout; Bagdad; Home of the Brave; 1950: The Outriders; Rock Island Trail; The Nevadan; Singing Guns; The Next Voice You Hear; Bright Leaf; Rawhide/Desperate Siege; 1951: The Prince Who Was a Thief; Red Mountain; Superman and the Mole-Men; Fourteen Hours; Only the Valiant; New Mexico; Never Trust a Gambler; 1963: The Balcony; The Yellow Canary; 1964: Lady in a Cage; 1965: Once a Thief; The Cincinnati Kid; Mickey One; 1966: Seconds; 1967: In Cold Blood; 1968: The Boston Strangler; 1969: True Grit; Butch Cassidy and the Sundance Kid; 1970: Impasse; Beneath the Planet of the Apes; Cover Me Babe; Getting Straight; They Call Me Mister Tibbs!; Little Big Man; 1971: Shoot-Out; Catlow; Clay Pigeon; 1975: Paper Tiger; 1976: The Premonition; The Last Tycoon; 1977: Moonshine County Express; Oh, God!; 1978: Jennifer; The Wild Geese; 1979: Butch and Sundance: The Early Days; 1980: Battle Beyond the Stars; 1982: The Sword and the Sorcerer; 1983: Rooster: Spurs of Death (dtv); 1984: Conan the Destroyer; 1985: Creator; 1988: Messenger of Death; 1990: Bird on a Wire; Up River (filmed 1979; dtv); 1992: The Secret Ingredient (dtv); 1993: Ruby Cairo; Beethoven's 2nd; 1994: The Judas Project (dtv); Surviving the Game; Color of Night; 1998: Ted (nUSr).

Select TV: 1970: The Movie Murderer; A Clear and Present Danger; 1972: Something Evil; 1973: Set This Town on Fire; 1974: The Gun and the Pulpit; 1976: Banjo Hackett: Roamin' Free; 1977: Testimony of Two Men (ms); Curse of the Black Widow; Captains Courageous; 1978: Harold Robbins' The Pirate; 1980: Homeward Bound; 1982: Cry for the Strangers; 1985: Hell Town; Hell Town (series); Final Jeopardy; 1986: Morningstar/Eveningstar; Second Serve; 1989: A Deadly Silence; 1990: To My Daughter; The Rose and the Jackal; 1991: Payoff; 1992: Sinatra; 1996: The Lottery.

WENDELL COREY
BORN: DRACUT, MA, MARCH 20, 1914.
DIED: NOVEMBER 8, 1968.

An all-purpose second lead or supporting player, steadfastly serious Wendell Corey lacked the necessary charisma for true stardom. Ten years' work in the theatre, culminating in the successful 1945 Broadway production of *Dream Girl*, warranted a contract with producer Hal Wallis. He started out in a pair of melodramas starring fellow Wallis contractees Burt Lancaster and Lizabeth Scott: *Desert Fury*, as John Hodiak's seemingly gay henchman; and *I Walk Alone*, as Lancaster's book-keeper brother, killed by mob boss Kirk Douglas. Passed over for the film version of *Dream Girl*, he was groomed as emotional fodder for some of the screen's great leading ladies. In *The File on Thelma Jordan* he was a D.A. brought down by troublemaker Barbara Stanwyck; in *Harriet Craig* he was Joan Crawford's ineffectual husband; and in *No Sad Songs for Me* dying wife Margaret Sullavan tried to match-make him with Viveca Lindfors before she checked out. Corey did land top billing in *Hell's Half Acre* and *The Bold and the Brave*, but the former was nothing more than a Republic "B," and the latter was stolen by Mickey Rooney. He lent solid support in *The Search*, a strong performance as Montgomery Clift's cynical army buddy; *Rear Window*, as James Stewart's detective friend; *The Big Knife*, as Rod Steiger's flunky;

The Rack, reprising his television role as a prosecuting attorney; *The Killer Is Loose*, doing some commendable work as a pathetic killer out to get Rhonda Fleming; and *Alias Jesse James*, in the title role of this Bob Hope spoof. In the 1960s he served as president of the Academy of Motion Picture Arts and Sciences, which sufficiently piqued his interest in politics that he served on the Santa Monica City Council before running unsuccessfully for congress in 1966. Voters were doubtlessly discouraged by the titles of his movie output around that time: *Women of the Prehistoric Planet*, *Cyborg 2087*, and *The Astro-Zombies*.

Screen: 1947: Desert Fury; I Walk Alone; 1948: The Search; Man-Eater of Kumaon; Sorry Wrong Number; The Accused; 1949: Any Number Can Play; The File on Thelma Jordan; Holiday Affair; 1950: No Sad Songs for Me; The Furies; Harriet Craig; The Great Missouri Raid; 1951: Rich, Young and Pretty; The Wild Blue Yonder; 1952: The Wild North; Carbine Williams; My Man and I; 1953: Jamaica Run; 1954: Laughing Anne; Hell's Half Acre; Rear Window; 1955: The Big Knife; 1956: The Bold and the Brave; The Killer Is Loose; The Rack; The Rainmaker; 1957: Loving You; 1958: The Light in the Forest; 1959: Alias Jesse James; 1964: Blood on the Arrow; 1966: Agent for H.A.R.M.; Waco; Women of the Prehistoric Planet; Picture Mommy Dead; 1967: Red Tomahawk; Cyborg 2087; 1968: Bucksin; 1969: The Astro-Zombies.

NY Stage: 1942: Comes the Revelation; 1943: The First Million; Manhattan Nocturne; 1944: Jackpot; But Not Goodbye; 1945: The Wind Is Ninety; Dream Girl; 1956: Night of the Auk; 1959: Jolly's Progress.

Select TV: 1951: Susan and God (sp); 1952: The Animal Kingdom (sp); The Lucky Coin (sp); 1953: A Tale of Two Cities (sp); 1955: Donovan's Brain (sp); The Rack (sp); 1956: The Lou Gehrig Story (sp); 1957–58: Harbor Command (series); 1959: Peck's Bad Girl (series); 1961: Westinghouse Playhouse (series); 1962–63: The Eleventh Hour (series).

VALENTINA CORTESE

(VALENTINE CORTESE) BORN: MILAN, ITALY, JANUARY 1, 1925.

A performer in Italian films during the 1940s, teenager Valentina Cortese built a career there in such movies as *A Yank in Rome*, *A Bullet for Stefano*, and *Les Misérables*. Her role in the 1948 British release *The Glass Mountain* brought her to the attention of American producers, who changed the last "e" in her name to an "a." A brief period of activity in U.S. films in the late 1940s and early 1950s included *Thieves' Highway*, as a femme fatale out to trap gangster Richard Conte; *Malaya*, as a refugee helping Spencer Tracy; and *House on Telegraph Hill*, which introduced her to her future husband (1951–60), actor Richard Basehart. Returning to Europe she appeared in a smattering of US-distributed pictures, including the British-made *The Secret People*, which featured an as yet undiscovered Audrey Hepburn; and *Angels of Darkness*, starring Anthony Quinn, with whom she appeared thrice more, in *Barabbas*, *The Visit*, and *The Secret of Santa Vittoria*. In 1973, she landed the plum role of a problematic film star who can't remember her lines in Francois Truffaut's *Day for Night*, earning an Oscar nomination for Best Actress. (The award that year went to Ingrid Bergman, who graciously acknowledged Cortese's work in her acceptance speech and apologized for winning!) Rather than parlaying her success into a crop of major parts, the actress was not seen again on U.S. screens until she did a small role in Irwin Allen's all-star disaster, *When Time Ran Out...* After

another long break, she appeared as the Queen of the Moon in the overblown fantasy *The Adventures of Baron Munchausen*.

Screen (US releases only): 1948: The Glass Mountain; 1949: Black Magic; Thieves' Highway; 1950: Malaya; 1951: House on Telegraph Hill; 1952: The Secret People; 1954: The Barefoot Contessa; 1955: Shadow of the Eagle; 1956: Magic Fire; Angels of Darkness; 1958: The Rocket From Calabuch; 1962: Barabbas; 1964: Evil Eye; The Visit; 1965: Juliet of the Spirits; 1968: The Legend of Lylah Clare; 1969: Listen — Let's Make Love; The Secret of Santa Vittoria; 1970: Give Her the Moon; First Love; 1972: The Assassination of Trotsky; 1973: Brother Sun, Sister Moon; Day for Night; 1976: Kidnap Syndicate (dtv); 1977: Widow's Nest (dtv); 1980: When Time Ran Out...; 1989: The Adventures of Baron Munchausen.

Select TV: 1957: Adam Had Four Sons (sp); 1958: Night of the Stranger (sp); 1977: Jesus of Nazareth.

RICARDO CORTEZ

(JACOB KRANTZ) BORN: VIENNA, AUSTRIA, SEPTEMBER 19, 1899. DIED: APRIL 28, 1977.

The former Jacob Krantz (a.k.a. Jack Crane) inadvertently owed his career to Rudolph Valentino. Krantz was dancing a tango at the Cocoanut Grove in Los Angeles when he was spotted by producer Jesse L. Lasky, who was having contractual problems with Valentino. Lasky thought Krantz bore a close resemblance to the movie star and hired the unknown to join Paramount with the intention of making him the screen's next great lover. After changing his name to Ricardo Cortez, the studio cast him in a supporting part in the comedy, *Sixty Cents an Hour*. Since audiences didn't know his true identity, they were fooled into believing Cortez was another smoldering Latin Lover, an image he propagated in a tango with Bebe Daniels in *Argentine Love*, and in a bullfight in *The Spaniard*. On loan-out to MGM, Cortez had the distinction of being Greta Garbo's leading man in her 1926 Hollywood debut, *The Torrent*. With the advent of sound he continued to work steadily, despite his rather dull personality, and originated roles that would later be made famous by other actors: detective Sam Spade in the 1931 version of *The Maltese Falcon*; and lawyer Perry Mason in *The Case of the Black Cat*. In 1938, 20th Century-Fox tagged him to direct the newspaper drama *Inside Story*, and he went on to helm six more "B" efforts: *Chasing Danger*, *The Escape*, *City of Chance* (all 1939), *Heaven With a Barbed Wire Fence*, *Free, Blonde and 21*, and *Girl in 313* (all 1940). During the 1950s he left acting to join a brokerage firm, returning only once for a small part in John Ford's *The Last Hurrah*. His brother, Stanley Cortez, was an admired cinematographer, whose credits included *The Magnificent Ambersons* and *The Night of the Hunter*.

Screen: 1923: Sixty Cents an Hour; Children of Jazz; Hollywood; The Call of the Canyon; 1924: The Next Corner; A Society Scandal; The Bedroom Window; The City That Never Sleeps; Feet of Clay; This Woman; Argentine Love; 1925: The Swan; The Spaniard; Not So Long Ago; In the Name of Love; The Pony Express; 1926: The Cat's Pajamas; The Torrent; Volcano; The Sorrows of Satan; The Eagle of the Sea; 1927: New York; Mockery; By Whose Hand?; The Private Life of Helen of Troy; 1928: Prowlers of the Sea; The Grain of Dust; Ladies of the Night Club; Excess Baggage; The Gun Runner; 1929: The Younger Generation; New Orleans; Mid-Stream; Phantom at the House; 1930: The Lost Zeppelin; Montana Moon; Her Man; 1931: Illicit; Ten Cents a Dance; Behind Office Doors; The Maltese Falcon; White Shoulders; Transgression; Big Business

Girl; Reckless Living; Bad Company; **1932:** Men of Change; No One Man; Thirteen Women; Symphony of Six Million; Is My Face Red?; The Phantom of Crestwood; Flesh; **1933:** Broadway Bad; Midnight Mary; Torch Singer; Big Executive; The House on 56th Street; **1934:** The Big Shakedown; Mandalay; Wonder Bar; The Man With Two Faces; Hat, Coat and Glove; A Lost Lady; Firebird; **1935:** I Am a Thief; The White Cockatoo; Shadow of a Doubt; Special Agent; Frisco Kid; **1936:** Murder of Dr. Harrigan; Man Hunt; The Walking Dead; Postal Inspector; The Case of the Black Cat; **1937:** Her Husband Lies; Talk of the Devil; The Californian; West of Shanghai; City Girl; **1939:** Mr. Moto's Last Warning; Charlie Chan in Reno; **1940:** Murder Over New York; **1941:** Romance of the Rio Grande; A Shot in the Dark; World Premiere; I Killed That Man; **1942:** Who Is Hope Schuyler?; Rubber Rackateer; Tomorrow We Live; **1944:** Make Your Own Bed; **1946:** The Inner Circle; The Locket; **1947:** Blackmail; **1948:** Mystery in Mexico; **1950:** Bunco Squad; **1958:** The Last Hurrah.

DOLORES COSTELLO

BORN: PITTSBURGH, PA, SEPTEMBER 17, 1905.
DIED: MARCH 1, 1979.

A delicately pretty blonde actress of the silent era, Dolores Costello, along with older sister Helen, came to movies as a child in 1911, appearing with their father, actor Maurice Costello. After the two girls danced on Broadway in *George White Scandals of 1924*, they were signed by Warner Bros. in 1925, and featured together in *Bobbed Hair*. The following year Dolores took the lead opposite John Barrymore in a re-working of *Moby Dick*, re-titled *The Sea Beast*. She not only became a star, but also the volatile actor's wife (1928–35). Costello featured in some of the studio's hand-wringing melodramas, including *Old San Francisco*, as part of a family of Spanish aristocrats; *The Heart of Maryland*, as a Southern belle in love with Union soldier Jason Robards (Sr.) during the Civil War; and *When a Man Loves*, which paired her again with Barrymore in a film based on Proust's *Manon Lescaut*. In 1928 she had two of her most prestigious offerings, with the period romance *Glorious Betsy*, as the commoner in love with Napoleon's younger brother, and *Noah's Ark*, a big budget attempt to contrast the diluvian Biblical event with a World War I story. By the 1930s, feeling uncomfortable in talking pictures, she dropped out of the public eye, only to return later in the decade for *Little Lord Fauntleroy*, as Freddie Bartholomew's darling mum, "Dearest," and in *The Beloved Brat*, as a schoolmistress at odds with troublemaker Bonita Granville. Her re-emergence led to the role for which she is best remembered, as Isabel Amberson in Orson Welles's *The Magnificent Ambersons*. She gave a fine performance as the gentle mother whose love for Joseph Cotten is thwarted by her spoiled son, Tim Holt, but she retired shortly afterwards. Her son is actor John Barrymore, Jr., also known as John Drew Barrymore, and her granddaughter is actress Drew Barrymore.
Screen: 1911: The Meeting of the Ways; His Sister's Children; The Child Crusoes; A Geranium; 1912: A Juvenile Love Affair; Wanted, a Grandmother; Ida's Christmas; The Money King; The Troublesome Stepdaughters; 1913: The Hindoo Charm; Fellow Voyagers; 1915: How Cissy Made Good; 1923: The Glimpses of the Moon; Lawful Larceny; 1925: Greater Than a Crown; Bobbed Hair; 1926: Mannequin; The Little Irish Girl; The Sea Beast; Bride of the Storm; The Third Degree; 1927: When a Man Loves; Old San Francisco; A Million Bid; The Heart of Maryland; The College Widow; 1928: Glorious Betsy; Tenderloin; 1929: Glad Rag Doll; The Redeeming Sin; Madonna of Avenue A; Hearts in

Exile; The Show of Shows; Noah's Ark; **1930:** Second Choice; **1931:** Expensive Women; **1936:** Yours for the Asking; Little Lord Fauntleroy; **1938:** The Beloved Brat; Breaking the Ice; **1939:** Whispering Enemies; Outside These Walls; King of the Turf; **1942:** The Magnificent Ambersons; **1943:** This Is the Army.

JOSEPH COTTEN

BORN: PETERSBURG, VA, MAY 15, 1905.
ED: HICKMAN SCHOOL OF EXPRESSION, DC.
DIED: FEBRUARY 6, 1994.

Few would claim that Joseph Cotten was a great actor, but he lent his dry, intelligent presence with commendable competence to some of the most famous movies of the 1940s. He was working as a drama critic for the *Miami Herald* when he first started acting professionally. He left Florida for New York and took jobs as a stage manager before winning roles in productions of *Jezebel* and *The Postman Always Rings Twice*. In 1937 he joined the Mercury Theatre Co., beginning his prosperous association with Orson Welles. For Welles he made an unreleased short film, "Too Much Johnson," while achieving Broadway success as Katharine Hepburn's ex-husband in the original production of *The Philadelphia Story*. He was passed over in favor of Cary Grant for the movie version but came to Hollywood with Welles and Company in 1941 to be part of the legendary production of *Citizen Kane*. Like everyone else in that exceptional cast, he was as assured as any film veteran, playing Jedediah Leland, Kane's closest friend, who becomes drunkenly disillusioned with his buddy's megalomania. (In a nod to his own past, Cotten was cast as a newspaper drama critic.) The next year he was at his sympathetic best in Welles's other great achievement of the decade, *The Magnificent Ambersons*. As Dolores Costello's gentlemanly suitor, Cotten stoically endured the verbal abuse of her selfish son, Tim Holt. A third collaboration with Welles, *Journey Into Fear*, was a muddled, verbose tale of wartime intrigue that Cotten himself had adapted from Eric Ambler's novel.

Meager box-office returns on each of Cotten's films didn't deter David O. Selznick from signing him to a contract in 1942, promptly loaning him out to Universal for one of Alfred Hitchcock's personal favorites, *Shadow of a Doubt*. As Teresa Wright's charming but dangerous uncle, Cotten delivered a performance of subtle ambiguity. His first big financial success came in the romantic Deanna Durbin vehicle, *Hers to Hold*, which he followed with Paramount's phony melodrama, *Love Letters*. A series of Selznick soaps garnered mixed results. In *Since You Went Away* he gave a heartfelt performance as a lovesick swain who nobly sacrifices Claudette Colbert to his friend, but in *I'll Be Seeing You*, as a shell-shocked soldier in love with jailbird Ginger Rogers, he lacked the necessary complexity for the role. His inherent decency was used to good effect when he came to Ingrid Bergman's aid in MGM's glossy thriller, *Gaslight*; as a foil for ne'er-do-wells Gregory Peck and Jennifer Jones in *Duel in the Sun*; as the virtuous Congressman who falls in love with his servant, Loretta Young, in *The Farmer's Daughter*; and as a painter obsessed with other-worldly Jennifer Jones in the lyrical fantasy *Portrait of Jennie*. Cotten's naturally impassive quality was particularly effective in director Carol Reed's *The Third Man*, later voted by the British Film Institute as the greatest British film ever made. As Holly Martins, a world-weary writer tracking the mysterious Harry Lime through the sewers of post-WWII Vienna, he had the film stolen from under him by Orson Welles.

Hitchcock's woeful *Under Capricorn* and Bette Davis's dreary melodrama *Beyond the Forest* signaled the end of Cotten's time at the top. During the 1950s, most of his assignments were uninspired, including *Peking Express*, a misguided remake of *Shanghai Express*; *The Steel Trap*, as a bank employee who has second thoughts about the money he has stolen; and *The Bottom of the Bottle*, as the brother of alcoholic Van Johnson. He recovered slightly with an unsympathetic leading role opposite Marilyn Monroe in the popular *Niagara*, plotting her demise by the great falls; a thriller, *The Killer Is Loose*, which developed a cult following in later years when its director, Budd Boetticher was rediscovered as an unsung talent; and a brief reunion with Welles in the latter's *Touch of Evil*, though Cotten was unbilled for his tiny part. With stardom a thing of the past, he switched to support, occasionally rating some meatier roles. He schemed with Olivia de Havilland in the gothic thriller *Hush...Hush, Sweet Charlotte*; portrayed Richard Chamberlain's unpleasant father in the cryptic *Petulia*; and tried to save his son from evil Vincent Price in *The Abominable Dr. Phibes*. When he rated star billing again it was in horror cheapies like *Baron Blood* and as the mad doctor in the cheesy, Italian-made *Lady Frankenstein*. In 1960 he married actress Patricia Medina (they appeared together in *Latitude Zero* and *Timber Tramps*), and in 1987 he published his autobiography, *Vanity Will Get You Somewhere*.

Screen: 1941: Citizen Kane; Lydia; 1942: The Magnificent Ambersons; Journey Into Fear (and co-wr); 1943: Shadow of a Doubt; Hers to Hold; 1944: Gaslight; Since You Went Away; I'll Be Seeing You; 1945: Love Letters; 1946: Duel in the Sun; 1947: The Farmer's Daughter; 1948: Portrait of Jennie; 1949: Under Capricorn; Beyond the Forest; The Third Man (US: 1950); 1950: Walk Softly Stranger; Two Flags West; The Wild Heart (narrator); September Affair; 1951: Half Angel; Peking Express; The Man With a Cloak; 1952: Untamed Frontier; The Steel Trap; 1953: Niagara; A Blueprint for Murder; 1955: Special Delivery; 1956: The Killer Is Loose; The Bottom of the Bottle/Beyond the River; 1957: The Halliday Brand; 1958: From the Earth to the Moon; Touch of Evil; 1960: The Angel Wore Red; 1961: The Last Sunset; 1964: Hush...Hush, Sweet Charlotte; 1965: The Great Sioux Massacre; 1966: The Oscar; The Money Trap; The Tramplers; 1967: Brighty of the Grand Canyon; The Hellbenders; Jack of Diamonds; 1968: Petulia; White Comanche (nUSr); 1969: Gangster '70/Days of Fire (nUSr); 1970: The Grasshopper; Tora!Tora!Tora!; Latitude Zero; 1971: The Abominable Dr. Phibes; 1972: The Scientific Cardplayer (dtv); Baron Blood; 1973: Soylent Green; Lady Frankenstein; A Delicate Balance; 1975: Timber Tramps; 1976: Il Giustiziere sfida la Cita/Rambo's Revenge/Syndicate Sadists (nUSr); A Whisper in the Dark (nUSr); 1977: Twilight's Last Gleaming; Airport '77; F for Fake; 1978: L'Ordre et la Securite du Monde/Last In Last Out (nUSr); Caravans; 1979: The Crime of the Century/The Perfect Crime (dtv); 1980: Guyana: Cult of the Damned; The Hearse; The Concorde Affair (dtv); Heaven's Gate; 1981: The Survivor (nUSr); Delusion/The House Where Death Lives; Screamers/The Fish Men (filmed 1977).

NY Stage: 1932: Absent Father; 1933: Jezebel; 1935: Loose Moments; 1936: The Postman Always Rings Twice; 1936: Horse Eats Hat; 1937: Julius Caesar; 1938: The Shoemaker's Holiday; Danton's Death; 1939: The Philadelphia Story; 1953: Sabrina Fair; 1958: Once More With Feeling; 1962: Calculated Risk.

Select TV: 1954: High Green Wall (sp); State of the Union (sp); 1955: Broadway (sp); 1955–56: The 20th Century-Fox Hour (series); 1956: Man Without Fear (sp); HMS Marlborough (sp); The Man in the Black Robes (sp); 1956–57: On Trial/The Joseph Cotten Show (series); 1957: Edge of Innocence (sp); 1961: The Hitch-Hiker (sp); Notorious (sp); 1963–64: Hollywood and the Stars (series); 1967: Some May Live; 1968: Split Second to an Epitaph; 1969: The Lonely Profession; 1970: Cutter's Way; 1971: Assault on the Wayne; Do You Take This Stranger?; City Beneath the Sea; 1972: The Screaming Woman; Doomsday Voyage; 1973: The Devil's Daughter; 1976: The Lindbergh Kidnapping Case; 1977: Aspen/The Innocent and the Damned; 1978: Return to Fantasy Island; 1979: Churchill and the Generals; 1980: Casino.

TOM COURTENAY

BORN: HULL, YORKSHIRE, ENGLAND, FEBRUARY 25, 1937. ED: RADA.

Perhaps the least publicized of the crop, Tom Courtenay was one of the many fine British actors who stamped their imprint on films in the 1960s. Upon graduating from RADA, he was accepted by the Old Vic in London, debuting with them at the 1960 Edinburgh Festival in *The Sea Gull*. After taking over the starring role from Albert Finney in the West End production of *Billy Liar*, he won the lead in Tony Richardson's gripping film *The Loneliness of the Long Distance Runner*. His superlative performance as a rebellious reform-school boy ensured that it was he, and not Finney, who was cast in the movie version of *Billy Liar*. Playing the role with which he would become most closely identified, the gaunt young actor with the haunted eyes brilliantly portrayed Billy Fisher, a funeral director's assistant from the North of England whose vivid fantasies replace the dreariness of his real world. Continuing his run of celluloid non-conformists, he won a Venice Film Festival Award for his work as the doomed deserter in the grim WWI drama *King and Country*. He made a quantum leap from grainy British spoolers to big-budget international productions with his standout performance as the bespectacled rebel Pasha in *Doctor Zhivago*, a part that won him an Oscar nomination in the supporting category. But he sabotaged his standing as a movie attraction with a succession of ambitious flops: *The Night of the Generals*, giving easily the best performance in the film, as the corporal who exposes Peter O'Toole's evil deeds; *The Day the Fish Came Out*, a risible disaster that required him to spend part of the movie scampering about with his underwear on his head; *Otley*, one of the many spy spoofs of the 1960s; and *One Day in the Life of Ivan Denisovich*, a highly un-commercial — though critically-lauded — attempt to film Alexander Solzhenitsyn's novella. Preferring to work in the theatre, Courtenay stayed away from the big screen until his triumphant return (with old pal Albert Finney) in *The Dresser*, repeating his stage role as the sad, prissy title character and earning an Oscar nomination in the process. He seemed to haphazardly choose his parts, as evidenced by the notorious Bill Cosby fiasco, *Leonard Part 6*, but once again proved his worth in the true-life crime story *Let Him Have It*. His tightly controlled, emotional portrayal of the father of a simple-minded lad who is unjustly condemned to death, was one of his most masterful depictions.

Screen: 1962: The Loneliness of the Long Distance Runner; Private Potter; 1963: Billy Liar; 1964: King and Country; 1965: Operation Crossbow; King Rat; Doctor Zhivago; 1967: The Night of the Generals; The Day the Fish Came Out; 1968: A Dandy in Aspic; 1969: Otley; 1971: One Day in the Life of Ivan Denisovich; Catch Me a Spy/To Catch a Spy; 1983: The Dresser; 1987: Happy New Year; Leonard Part VI; 1991: Let Him Have It; 1993: The Last Butterfly; 2001: Whatever Happened to Harold Smith?; Last Orders; 2002: Nicholas Nickleby.

NY Stage: 1977: Otherwise Engaged; 1981: The Dresser; 1994: Uncle Vanya; 1995: Moscow Stations (ob).

Select TV: 1973: I Heard the Owl Call My Name; 1985: Absent

Friends; **1991**: Redemption; **1995**:The Old Curiosity Shop (sp); **1998**: A Rather English Marriage.

JEROME COWAN

BORN: NEW YORK, NY, OCTOBER 6, 1897.
DIED: JANUARY 24, 1972.

In a 33-year span, hard-working, musta-chioed character actor Jerome Cowan knocked off more than 120 movie roles. A lengthy stage career culminated in three suc-cessive hit productions in 1934–35, and he made his film bow in 1936 for Samuel Goldwyn, as an Irish patriot, in *Beloved Enemy*. He was seen thereafter as the schooner captain who employs native Jon Hall in *The Hurricane*; a shady nightclub owner in *The Gracie Allen Murder Case*; the suitor spurned by Bette Davis, who consequently ends up as *The Old Maid*; a radio mystery writer in Abbott and Costello's *Who Done It?*; the Emperor Napoleon in *The Song of Bernadette*; a ruthless killer who dis-patches Doris Lloyd for her tires (!) in *No Place for a Lady*; another of Davis's romantic cast-offs, in *Mr. Skeffington*; a Nazi spy running a night spot in *Joan of Ozark*; and a wealthy indus-trialist whose plane Edward G. Robinson predicts will crash in *Night Has a Thousand Eyes*. His two most recognizable roles were as Humphrey Bogart's murdered partner, Miles Archer, in *The Maltese Falcon*, and the skeptical attorney out to prove that Edmund Gwenn is not Santa Claus in *Miracle on 34th Street*. By the mid-1940s he rated top billing in a pair of Warners's private-eye capers, *Find the Blackmailer* and *Crime by Night*, but was too valuable in the supporting category and promptly returned there. He also appeared as Dagwood's boss, George Radcliffe, in the popular Blondie series, starting in 1946 with *Blondie Knows Best*, and ending with *Blondie's Big Deal*, three years later.

Screen: 1936: Beloved Enemy; **1937**: You Only Live Once; Shall We Dance; New Faces of 1937; The Hurricane; Vogues of 1938; **1938**: The Goldwyn Follies; There's Always a Woman; **1939**: St. Louis Blues; The Gracie Allen Murder Case; The Great Victor Herbert; The Saint Strikes Back; East Side of Heaven; She Married a Cop; The Old Maid; Exile Express; **1940**: Framed; The Wolf of New York; Ma, He's Making Eyes at Me; Meet the Wildcat; Torrid Zone; City for Conquest; Castle on the Hudson; Street of Memories; The Quarterback; Melody Ranch; **1941**: Victory; High Sierra; The Roundup; Affectionately Yours; One Foot in Heaven; Kisses for Breakfast; Kiss the Boys Goodbye; Rags to Riches; Too Many Blondes; Mr. and Mrs. North; The Great Lie; Singapore Woman; Out of the Fog; The Maltese Falcon; The Bugle Sounds; **1942**: Street of Chance; Frisco Lil; Moontide; Thru Different Eyes; Girl From Alaska; Joan of Ozark; Who Done It?; A Gentleman at Heart; **1943**: The Song of Bernadette; No Place for a Lady; Ladies' Day; Mission to Moscow; Silver Spurs; Hi Ya, Sailor; Find the Blackmailer; Crime Doctor's Strangest Case; **1944**: Sing a Jingle; Guest in the House; Crime by Night; Mr. Skeffington; South of Dixie; Minstrel Man; **1945**: Fog Island; Divorce; Getting Gertie's Garter; The Crime Doctor's Courage; Behind City Lights; Jungle Captive; G.I. Honeymoon; Hitchhike to Happiness; Blonde Ransom; One Way to Love; **1946**: My Reputation; Murder in the Music Hall; Claudia and David; The Kid From Brooklyn; Flight to Nowhere; One Exciting Week; Blondie Knows Best; Mr. Ace; Deadline at Dawn; A Night in Paradise; The Perfect Marriage; **1947**: Blondie's Holiday; Driftwood; Riffraff; Miracle on 34th Street; The Unfaithful; Cry Wolf; Dangerous Years; Blondie's Anniversary; Blondie's Big Moment; Blondie in the Dough; **1948**: So This Is New York; Wallflower; Night Has a Thousand Eyes;

Blondie's Reward; Arthur Takes Over; June Bride; **1949**: Scene of the Crime; Blondie's Secret; Blondie Hits the Jackpot; Blondie's Big Deal; The Girl From Jones Beach; The Fountainhead; Always Leave Them Laughing; **1950**: Young Man With a Horn; Joe Palooka Meets Humphrey; The Fuller Brush Girl; Peggy; When You're Smiling; West Point Story; Dallas; **1951**: The Fat Man; Criminal Lawyer; Disc Jockey; **1953**: The System; **1959**: Have Rocket Will Travel; **1960**: Visit to a Small Planet; Private Property; **1961**: All in a Night's Work; Pocketful of Miracles; **1963**: Critic's Choice; Black Zoo; **1964**: The Patsy; **1965**: John Goldfarb, Please Come Home; **1966**: Frankie and Johnny; Penelope; **1967**: The Gnome-Mobile; **1969**: The Comic.

NY Stage: 1923: We've Got to Have Money; **1930**: Frankie and Johnny; **1932**: Little Black Book; **1933**: Marathon; Both Your Houses; As Thousands Cheer; **1934**: Ladies' Money; **1935**: Paths of Glory; Boy Meets Girl; **1953**: My 3 Angels; **1954**: Lunatics and Lovers; **1957**: Rumple; **1958**: Say Darling.

Select TV: 1951–52: Not for Publication (series); **1953–57**: Valiant Lady (series); **1960–61**: The Tab Hunter Show (series); **1964–65**: The Tycoon (series).

NOËL COWARD

BORN: TEDDINGTON, MIDDLESEX, ENGLAND, DECEMBER 16, 1899. DIED: MARCH 26, 1973.

England's poster boy for upper-crust sophis-tication, Noël Coward was a playwright, composer, actor, director, and wit. His effete, erudite manner prevented him from becoming a bona fide leading man, and he took leading roles in only three movies. The first was Ben Hecht and Charles MacArthur's wittily unique *The Scoundrel*, with Coward letter-perfect as a caustically cynical publisher, oblivious to the pain he inflicts on others. The next project was the patriotic World War II drama, *In Which We Serve*. Coward wrote, produced, and co-directed the film with David Lean, as well as providing the musical score. His own performance was somewhat stiff, but the film was acclaimed as a masterpiece of British propaganda and earned Coward a special Academy Award for "outstanding pro-duction achievement," as well as a nomination as writer. His third lead was in *The Astonished Heart*, replacing Michael Redgrave, as a psychiatrist whose extra-marital fling with Margaret Leighton leads to tragedy. This was the only time he appeared in a movie version of one of his own plays, though it was far from his best. He made no contribution to the motion picture adaptations of his stage works *Cavalcade, Tonight Is Ours, Design for Living, This Happy Breed, Tonight at 8:30*, and *Bitter Sweet*, but he served as screenwriter and producer of *Blithe Spirit*. He also adapted the exquisite *Brief Encounter* from his one-act, *Still Life*. This deeply moving tale (directed by David Lean) of an unrequited affair between a doctor and a married woman is arguably Coward's shining contribution to cinema. His supporting roles include playing a member of David Niven's stuffy gentlemen's club in *Around the World in Eighty Days*; a secret service boss who recruits reluctant Alec Guinness in *Our Man in Havana*; an old queen known as The Witch of Capri in *Boom!*; and a criminal who masterminds a heist from prison in *The Italian Job*. He published a pair of autobiographies, *Present Indicative* (1933) and *Future Indefinite* (1949), and was knighted in 1970.

Screen: 1918: Hearts of the World; **1935**: The Scoundrel; **1942**: In Which We Serve (and co-dir.; wr.; music); **1950**: The Astonished Heart; **1956**: Around the World in Eighty Days; **1960**: Our Man in Havana; Surprise Package; **1964**: Paris — When It

Sizzles; 1965: Bunny Lake Is Missing; 1968: Boom!; 1969: The Italian Job.

NY Stage: 1925: The Vortex (and wr.); 1928: This Year of Grace (and wr.); 1930: Private Lives (and wr.); 1933: Design for Living (and wr.;dir.); 1936: Tonight at 8:30 (and wr.); 1957: Nude With Violin (and wr.;dir.); 1958: Present Laughter (and wr.; dir.).

Select TV: 1955: Together With Music (sp; and dir.; wr.; songwr.); 1956: Blithe Spirit (sp; and dir.);This Happy Breed (sp); 1967: Androcles and the Lion (sp).

LARRY "BUSTER" CRABBE

(CLARENCE LINDEN CRABBE) BORN: OAKLAND, CA, FEBRUARY 17, 1907. RAISED IN HI. ED: USC. DIED: APRIL 23, 1983.

Buster Crabbe spent more time in the saddle than in space, but he will be remembered first and foremost as the movies' earliest sci-fi hero, Flash Gordon. He became an accomplished swimmer as a young man, eventually winning a gold medal in the 1932 Olympics in the 400-meter free-style event, ironically breaking the record of another swimmer who turned to movies, Johnny Weissmuller. His Hollywood debut was as a bit player in the musical *Good News*, followed by a more unusual assignment, serving as Joel McCrea's swimming double in *The Most Dangerous Game*. He then signed a contract with Paramount Pictures in 1933. A quick cash-in on MGM's current Tarzan success, called *King of the Jungle*, was his official launch by the studio, and then, for independent producer Sol Lesser, he did a serial playing Tarzan himself, *Tarzan the Fearless*. Since Weissmuller was clearly everyone's favorite Ape Man, Crabbe came out of the water and found his niche in westerns like *Thundering Herd*, *Nevada*, and *The Wanderer of the Wasteland*. In 1936 he made his first appearance as the blond-haired, intergalactic adventurer *Flash Gordon*. The serial proved so popular that Universal ordered two more: *Flash Gordon's Trip to Mars* and *Flash Gordon Conquers the Universe*. Crabbe was also assigned to two other Universal serials, as detective *Red Barry*, and *Buck Rogers*, another interplanetary hero. In the 1940s the brawny actor appeared in countless poverty row westerns from PRC, including *Billy the Kid — Wanted*, *Sheriff of Sage Valley*, *Cattle Stampede*, and *Thundering Gun Slingers*. Over at Paramount's "B" unit he played a villain in *Swamp Fire*, notable as his only teaming with Johnny Weissmuller, who had grown too old by that point to play Tarzan. Two more serials at Columbia, *Pirates of the High Seas* and *King of the Congo*; a television series, *Captain Gallant of the French Foreign Legion*; and a few more westerns preceded his retirement from movies. In addition to his involvement in the swimming pool business, he served as athletic director at a summer resort and wrote the book *Energetics* (1970) about physical fitness for those over 50.

Screen: 1930: Good News; 1932: The Most Dangerous Game; That's My Boy; 1933: King of the Jungle; Man of the Forest; Tarzan the Fearless (serial); To the Last Man; The Sweetheart of Sigma Chi; The Thundering Herd; 1934: Search for Beauty; You're Telling Me; Badge of Honor; We're Rich Again; She Had to Choose; The Oil Raider; 1935: Hold 'em Yale; The Wanderer of the Wasteland; Nevada; 1936: Drift Fence; Desert Gold; Arizona Raiders; Flash Gordon (serial); Rose Bowl; Lady Be Careful; Arizona Mahoney; 1937: Murder Goes to College; King of Gamblers; Forlorn River; Sophie Lang Goes West; Thrill of a Lifetime; Daughter of Shanghai; 1938: Flash Gordon's Trip to Mars (serial); Red Barry (serial); Tip-Off Girls; Hunted Men; Illegal Traffic; 1939: Buck Rogers (serial); Unmarried; Million Dollar Legs; Colorado Sunset; Call a Messenger; 1940: Flash

Gordon Conquers the Universe (serial); Sailor's Lady; 1941: Jungle Man; Billy the Kid — Wanted; Billy the Kid's Roundup; 1942: Billy the Kid Trapped; Billy the Kid's Smoking Guns; Law and Order; Jungle Siren; Wildcat; Mysterious Rider; Sheriff of Sage Valley; Queen of Broadway; 1943: The Kid Rides Again; Fugitive of the Plains; The Renegade/Code of the Plains; Western Cyclone; Cattle Stampede; Blazing Frontier; Devil Riders; 1944: Thundering Gunslingers; Nabonga; Frontier Outlaws; Valley of Vengeance; The Contender; The Drifter; Fuzzy Settles Down; Wild Horse Phantom; Oath of Vengeance; 1945: Gangster's Den; His Brother's Ghost; Shadows of Death; Border Badmen; Rustler's Hideout; Stagecoach Outlaws; Fighting Bill Carson; Lightning Raiders; Prairie Rustlers; 1946: Gentlemen With Guns; Ghost of Hidden Valley; Terrors on Horseback; Overland Raiders; Outlaw of the Plains; Swamp Fire; Prairie Badmen; 1947: The Last of the Redmen; The Sea Hound (serial); 1948: Caged Fury; 1950: Captive Girl; Pirates of the High Seas (serial); 1952: King of the Congo (serial); 1956: Gun Brothers; 1957: The Lawless Eighties; 1958: Badman's Country; 1960: Gunfighters at Abilene; 1965: The Bounty Killer; Arizona Raiders; 1979: Swim Team (dtv); It Fell From the Sky/The Alien Dead; 1982: The Comeback Trail (filmed 1971).

Select TV: 1952: A Cowboy for Chris (sp); 1955: The Cornered Man (sp); 1955–56: Captain Gallant (series).

JAMES CRAIG

(JOHN HENRY MEADOR) BORN: NASHVILLE, TN, FEBRUARY 4, 1911. ED: RICE INST. DIED: JUNE 28, 1985.

A routine leading man of mostly routine films, James Craig's movie career came courtesy of a chance encounter with Hollywood talent scout Oliver Hinsdell, who was struck by actor's resemblance to Clark Gable. After some regional theatre work around Houston, Craig wound up under contract, first at Paramount, then Columbia, and finally Universal. He made little impact at any of those studios, despite an occasional "B" lead like the western *Thunder Trail* in 1937. He attracted some attention when RKO picked him to be one of Ginger Rogers's two leading men in her 1940 Oscar-winning tour de force, *Kitty Foyle*. RKO also cast him as farmer Jabez Stone, whose soul is at stake in a debate between the Devil and Daniel Webster, in *All That Money Can Buy*, an interesting fantasy where Craig was seriously outgunned by veteran performers Walter Huston and Edward Arnold. The movie did win Craig a contract at MGM, but it was clear that he was there to fill in for the studio's top stars who had gone off to war. His best efforts at Metro were two gentle dramas of rural America: *The Human Comedy*, as the town's telegraph operator; and *Our Vines Have Tender Grapes*, as a friendly newspaperman. His starring assignments came in programmers such as *The Omaha Trail*, helping bring a locomotive westward; *Northwest Rangers*, a western reworking of *Manhattan Melodrama*, in the role, fittingly, that Gable had played; *Dangerous Partners*, surviving a plane crash; and *Boys' Ranch*, overseeing Butch Jenkins and other youngsters. His MGM contract expired in 1951 with *The Strip*, but he continued to work in cheap fare like *The Women of Pitcairn Island* and *The Cyclops*, finally descending to A.C. Lyles's westerns like *Hostile Guns* and *Fort Utah* in the 1960s.

Screen: 1937: Sophie Lang Goes West; Thunder Trail; Born to the West; 1938: Pride of the West; The Big Broadcast of 1938; The Buccaneer; 1939: Blondie Meets the Boss; Cafe Hostess; Good Girls Go to Paris; The Lone Wolf Spy Hunt; Missing Daughters; North of Shanghai; Romance of the Redwoods; A

Woman Is the Judge; Behind Prison Gates; Taming of the West; The Man They Could Not Hang; Flying G-Men (serial); Overland With Kit Carson (serial); 1940: The House Across the Bay; Winners of the West (serial); Konga the Wild Stallion; Scandal Sheet; Zanzibar; South to Karanga; I'm Nobody's Sweetheart Now; Seven Sinners; Law and Order; Kitty Foyle; 1941: All That Money Can Buy/The Devil and Daniel Webster; Unexpected Uncle; 1942: Valley of the Sun; Friendly Enemies; The Omaha Trail; Northwest Rangers; Seven Miles From Alcatraz; 1943: The Human Comedy; Swing Shift Maisie; Lost Angel; The Heavenly Body; 1944: Kismet; Marriage Is a Private Affair; Gentle Annie; 1945: Our Vines Have Tender Grapes; Dangerous Partners; She Went to the Races; 1946: Boys' Ranch; Little Mr. Jim; 1947: Dark Delusion; 1948: The Man From Texas; Northwest Stampede; 1949: Side Street; A Lady Without Passport; 1951: The Strip; Drums in the Deep South; 1952: Hurricane Smith; 1953: Code Two; Fort Vengeance; 1955: Last of the Desperados; 1956: While the City Sleeps; Massacre; The Women of Pitcairn Island; 1957: Shootout at Medicine Band; The Persuader; The Cyclops; Ghost Diver; Naked in the Sun; 1958: Man or Gun; 1959: Four Fast Guns; 1967: Hostile Guns; Fort Utah; Doomsday Machine; 1968: The Devil's Brigade; Arizona Bushwhackers; 1969: If He Hollers, Let Him Go!; 1970: The Revenge of Dr. X; 1971: Bigfoot; 1986: Tormentors (dtv; filmed 1971).

Select TV: 1954: Wedding March (sp); Cubs of the Bear (sp); 1955: The Westerner (sp).

JEANNE CRAIN

BORN: BARSTOW, CA, MAY 25, 1925.

20th Century-Fox's resident "sweet young thing" for over 10 years, petite Jeanne Crain's limitations as an actress were compensated for by her genial personality. After winning some beauty contests and working as a model, she came to the attention of Fox, who gave her the starlet treatment and a bit in their 1943 musical, The Gang's All Here. Her first real role was in the horse story Home in Indiana, as one of the girls in Lon McCallister's life, after which she was featured in Winged Victory, as Barry Nelson's worried, homefront bride. Two pictures she made in 1945 brought her fame. State Fair was a popular musical remake of the earlier Janet Gaynor film, with Crain playing the country girl who falls in love with Dana Andrews. She introduced the Oscar-winning Rodgers and Hammerstein song "It Might as Well Be Spring," although her singing voice was dubbed by Louanne Hogan. An even bigger box-office success was the entertaining melodrama Leave Her to Heaven, as the sweet sister whom bitchy Gene Tierney tries to destroy, even from beyond the grave. She used her star status to sell two more agreeable musicals: Centennial Summer, which bore more than a passing resemblance to State Fair; and Margie, an affectionate glance back at the 1920s. Staying in that decade, she was allowed to play someone more mature in You Were Meant for Me, married to bandleader Dan Dailey.

Shortly afterwards she got to shine in three of her best films. Apartment With Peggy, with William Holden, was a touching comedy-drama about a young couple struggling to make it after the war; Joseph L. Mankiewicz's A Letter to Three Wives, an incisive multi-story look at marriage, examined her relationship with husband Jeffrey Lynn; and Pinky gave her the most challenging part of her career, playing a light-skinned black girl passing for white. Her competent performance resulted in her sole Oscar nomination, though the film's director, Elia Kazan, considered

her work below par. The acclaim the movie received didn't translate into better roles, however, and Fox cast her as the eldest daughter in the nostalgic Cheaper by the Dozen, where her coy behavior was especially unctuous. A pleasant George Cukor comedy, The Model and the Marriage Broker, was stolen by Thelma Ritter, after which Crain and Farley Granger enacted the famous "The Gift of the Magi" episode from the weak compilation O. Henry's Full House. She teamed with Cary Grant in People Will Talk, as a suicidal medical student whom he marries; was the center of attention in Belles on Their Toes, a sequel to Cheaper by the Dozen; and played Vicki, a remake of I Wake Up Screaming. She left Fox and went over to Universal, where she appeared in a Kirk Douglas western, Man Without a Star, and as lawyer Jeff Chandler's estranged wife in The Tattered Dress. By now it was clear that the bloom was off her rose; she was just another working actress, reading her lines, professionally but without inspiration. After The Joker Is Wild, with Frank Sinatra, she made some Italian epics before returning to the U.S. for Madison Avenue and the motorcycle melodrama Hot Rods to Hell, both of which reteamed her with Dana Andrews. She did a horror movie, The Night God Screamed, and a disaster flick, Skyjacked, retiring in the 1970s before she'd even reached the age of 50.

Screen: 1943: The Gang's All Here; 1944: Home in Indiana; In the Meantime Darling; Winged Victory; 1945: State Fair; Leave Her to Heaven; 1946: Centennial Summer; Margie; 1948: You Were Meant for Me; Apartment for Peggy; 1949: A Letter to Three Wives; The Fan; Pinky; 1950: Cheaper by the Dozen; I'll Get By; 1951: Take Care of My Little Girl; People Will Talk; The Model and the Marriage Broker; 1952: Belles on Their Toes; O. Henry's Full House; 1953: City of Bad Men; Dangerous Crossing; Vicki; 1954: Duel in the Jungle; 1955: Man Without a Star; Gentlemen Marry Brunettes; The Second Greatest Sex; 1956: The Fastest Gun Alive; 1957: The Tattered Dress; The Joker Is Wild; 1960: Guns of the Timberland; 1961: Queen of the Nile; With Fire and Sword; Pontius Pilate; Twenty Plus Two; 1962: Madison Avenue; 1967: Hot Rods to Hell; 1971: The Night God Screamed; 1972: Skyjacked.

Select TV: 1955: The Girl Who Wasn't Wanted (sp); 1958: The Great Gatsby (sp); The Trouble With Ruth (sp); 1959: Meet Me in St. Louis (sp); 1960: The Man Who Knew Tomorrow (sp); Journal of Hope (sp); 1962: The Other Woman (sp).

BRODERICK CRAWFORD

(WILLIAM BRODERICK CRAWFORD) BORN: PHILADELPHIA, PA, DECEMBER 9, 1911. DIED: APRIL 26, 1986.

Burly, brutish Broderick Crawford was an imposing character player who used his harsh voice to bark opposing souls into submission. The son of character actress Helen Broderick, he began appearing on radio while very young before a meeting with the Lunts resulted in his 1935 Broadway debut, in Point Valaine. While performing in Punches and Judy, he was spotted by Samuel Goldwyn and given his first film part, in the 1937 screwball comedy Woman Chases Man. After two more movies he played Lennie in the Broadway hit Of Mice and Men, but didn't get to repeat the part on film. Back in Hollywood he was kept in character parts in such movies as Beau Geste, as a legionnaire, and The Real Glory, as a lieutenant in the Philippines, supporting Gary Cooper in both. He signed with Universal, who put him into action pictures or westerns, usually as tough guys, gangsters, villains, or lovable lugs. On a few low-budget occasions he was the lead, as in Tight Shoes, a Damon Runyon comedy; North to the

Klondike, exacting revenge on Lon Chaney, Jr. (no doubt for getting the role of Lennie in the screen version of *Of Mice and Men*); *Butch Minds the Baby*, as an ex-con softened by a toddler; and *The Runaround*, with wooden Rod Cameron, trying to stop heiress Ella Raines for eloping.

He was firmly entrenched in this routine when, in 1949, director Robert Rossen cast him as politician Willy Stark, who mutates from a foursquare guy into a fascist egomaniac in *All the King's Men*. It was a forceful and gripping performance in an intelligent, critically acclaimed movie that won an Academy Award for Best Picture and Best Actor for Crawford. A Columbia Pictures contract had come with the role, thus making him available when director George Cukor was casting the part of junk tycoon Harry Brock in the 1950 film version of the Broadway sensation *Born Yesterday*. Crawford was a dangerous, dimwitted bully, but he also showed a surprising vulnerability and a deft comic touch, making this his second great performance in a two-year span. Columbia felt obliged to promote him as star material, but most of his vehicles were programmers meant for limited audiences. In *The Mob*, he was a cop posing as a hood; in *Scandal Sheet*, a bombastic newspaper editor; in Warners's *Stop, You're Killing Me*, he played Edward G. Robinson's old role in a semimusical remake of *A Slight Case of Murder*; in *The Last of the Comanches*, he reprised Bogart's part in a satisfying western rethinking of *Sahara*; and in *The Last Posse*, he was an honest sheriff, wounded while tracking a gang of robbers. His Columbia contract ended as the jealous husband of slutty Gloria Grahame in *Human Desire*, a melodrama based on an Emile Zola story.

He did some noirs, a genre he fit into with ease, playing an FBI agent avenging the murder of colleague Kennth Tobey in *Down Three Dark Streets*, and the head of a crime operation in *New York Confidential*. He ended up in the slammer in *Big House USA*, before breaking out to recover some ransom money. In the hit *Not as a Stranger*, he showed up in a supporting part as a doctor; went to Italy for Fellini's *Il Bibone/The Swindle*; and suggested a hidden sexual agenda as Robert Wagner's sadistic commanding officer in *Between Heaven and Hell*. His star was fading on the big screen, but Crawford found four solid years of television employment on the hit syndicated series *Highway Patrol*. By the end of the 1950s he was playing big-screen bad guys again in *The Fastest Gun Alive* and *The Decks Ran Red*, but when the 1960s arrive, he became one of the many performers who crossed the Atlantic in search of a paycheck. He appeared in trash like *Hell's Bloody Devils*, which found room for bikers, Nazis, and Colonel Sanders, and took the title role in the little-seen *The Private Files of J. Edgar Hoover*, a campy look at the FBI director. Despite his lengthy list of credits, he was practically bankrupt by the time he died in 1986.

Screen: 1937: Woman Chases Man; Submarine D-1; 1938: Start Cheering; 1939: Sudden Money; Ambush; Undercover Doctor; Beau Geste; Island of Lost Men; The Real Glory; Eternally Yours; 1940: Slightly Honorable; I Can't Give You Anything But Love, Baby; When the Daltons Rode; Seven Sinners; Trail of the Vigilantes; Texas Rangers Ride Again; 1941: The Black Cat; Tight Shoes; Badlands of Dakota; South of Tahiti; 1942: North to Klondike; Larceny, Inc.; Butch Minds the Baby; Broadway; Men of Texas; Sin Town; 1946: The Runaround; Black Angel; 1947: Slave Girl; The Flame; 1948: The Time of Your Life; Sealed Verdict; 1949: Bad Men of Tombstone; A Kiss in the Dark; Night Unto Night; Anna Lucasta; All the King's Men; 1950: Cargo to Capetown; Convicted; Born Yesterday; 1951: The Mob; 1952: Scandal Sheet; Lone Star; Stop, You're Killing Me; The Last of the Comanches; 1953: The Last Posse; 1954: Night People; Human Desire; Down Three Dark Streets; 1955: New York Confidential;

Big House USA; Not as a Stranger; Il Bidone/The Swindlers; 1956: The Fastest Gun Alive; Between Heaven and Hell; 1958: The Decks Ran Red; 1960: Goliath and the Dragon; 1961: Square of Violence; 1962: Convicts 4; 1963: The Castilian; 1964: A House Is Not a Home; 1965: Up From the Beach; 1966: Kid Rodelo; The Oscar; The Texican; 1967: Red Tomahawk; The Vulture; Per Un Dollaro di Gloria/Mutiny at Fort Sharp (nUSr); 1970: Hell's Bloody Devils/The Fakers; How Did a Nice Girl Like You Get Into This Business? (nUSr); Gregorio and His Angel (filmed 1966; nUSr); 1971: Ransom Money; 1972: Embassy/Target: Embassy; 1973: Terror in the Wax Museum; 1976: Won Ton Ton, the Dog Who Saved Hollywood; 1977: Proof of a Man (nUSr); 1978: The Private Files of J. Edgar Hoover; 1979: A Little Romance; 1980: There Goes the Bride; Harlequin; 1981: Liar's Moon; 1982: The Uppercrust (nUSr).

NY Stage: 1935: Pointe Valaine; Punches and Judy; Sweet Mystery of Life; 1937: Of Mice and Men.

Select TV: 1952: Ride the River (sp); 1953: Hunt the Man Down (sp); The Widow Makes Three (sp); 1954: Man From Outside (sp); Dancing Dan's Christmas (sp); 1955–59: Highway Patrol (series); 1961–62: King of Diamonds (series); 1966: Brilliant Benjamin Boggs (sp); 1970: The Challenge; 1970–71: The Interns (series); 1971: A Tattered Web; 1972: The Adventures of Nick Carter; 1974: The Phantom of Hollywood; 1976: Look What's Happened to Rosemary's Baby?; Mayday at 40,000 Feet.

JOAN CRAWFORD

(LUCILLE FAY LeSUEUR) BORN: SAN ANTONIO, TX, MARCH 23, 1904. DIED: MAY 10, 1977.

There is no denying that Joan Crawford was one of Hollywood's greatest stars; how good an actress she was is subject for debate. Arch, self-involved, and unpleasant, she could march through a scene with the dead earnestness of a woman devoid of the slightest sense of humor about herself. Alternatively, she could be resilient, distinctive, vulnerable, romantic, and possessed of a rare ability to deliver crisp, hard-boiled dialogue with wit and irony. She had started as a dancer, calling herself Billie Cassin (using her stepfather's surname), appearing in nightclubs in Chicago and Detroit, before making it to the Broadway revue *Innocent Eyes*. She was discovered by an MGM executive and signed to a contract, making her movie bow in 1925, as Norma Shearer's stand-in for *Lady of the Night*. She followed with some bit roles; a larger part in a Jackie Coogan film, *Old Clothes*; and, finally, her first significant role, as Irene, in *Sally, Irene and Mary*, playing — appropriately — a chorus girl. Now billed as Joan Crawford, she dutifully fulfilled her silent era assignments for Metro, including *The Understanding Heart*, with Francis X. Bushman, Jr.; *The Unknown*, as a circus girl, in one of Lon Chaney's bizarre attractions; *Twelve Miles Out*, entangled with bootleggers and John Gilbert; a silent (!) version of the famous operetta *Rose Marie*; and *Our Modern Maidens*, with Douglas Fairbanks, Jr., who became her first husband (1929–33). In 1928, she landed the vehicle that made her one of the studio's big attractions, *Our Dancing Daughters*, as the embodiment of a jazz-happy flapper.

Although she possessed the terpsichorean grace of a mule, she was frequently called upon to dance during the dawn of sound, as in *The Hollywood Revue of 1929*, singing "Gotta Feelin' for You;" *Our Blushing Brides*; and *Dance, Fools, Dance*, the first of her many teamings with Clark Gable. In 1930's *Paid* she gave the first indication of her dramatic flair, as a shop-girl who resorts to a life of crime after being unfairly dismissed. Gable talked her into joining the Salvation Army in *Laughing Sinners*, and she nearly scandalized his political career in *Possessed*, their biggest hit to date. She was one of the many stars featured in the Best Picture Oscar-winner of 1932, *Grand Hotel*, giving a good performance as Wallace Beery's secretary. She made history as Fred Astaire's very first on-screen dancing partner, in *Dancing Lady*, which also featured Gable and another future husband (1933–39), Franchot Tone. The newlyweds teamed for *Sadie McKee*, with Crawford faring better opposite Tone than she did Gary Cooper, in *Today We Live*. But it was her collaboration with Gable that really pleased audiences, and *Chained* and *Forsaking All Others* were among the top attractions of 1934. The pair clicked beautifully, sparring and swapping insults, hiding their true feelings behind tough facades. Tone was with her in *No More Ladies*; the period romance *The Gorgeous Hussy*; *Love on the Run*; and *The Bride Wore Red*, but only won her in the final reel of the second and fourth of these, allowing her to gravitate to the higher-billed Robert Montgomery and Clark Gable in the first and third respectively. *Bride* laid an egg at the box office, as did *Mannequin*, with Spencer Tracy, and *The Shining Hour*, which co-starred her with Margaret Sullavan, who was always more of a critical favorite than a public one. Crawford's appeal seemed to have hit bottom with the goofy extravaganza *The Ice Follies of 1939*, but she was rescued later that same year with one of her great bitchy roles, as gold-digger Crystal Allen, who delights in luring away Norma Shearer's man, in George Cukor's smashing version of *The Women*.

She appeared in two more lush Cukor soap operas, *Susan and God*, and *A Woman's Face*, her last great moment in the sun at Metro, as a scarred woman given a second chance through plastic surgery. In between these two she'd done her last — and her favorite — film with Gable, *Strange Cargo*. The remake of *When Ladies Meet*, with Robert Taylor and Greer Garson, was a dud, and she herself despised *Reunion in France*, a wartime propaganda vehicle with John Wayne, in which she was supposed to be French. With the routine spy yarn *Above Suspicion*, she happily bid goodbye to the studio that had paid her bills for 18 years. By the mid-1940s it was generally believed that her best years were over, and, when she signed with Warner Bros. she took a substantial cut in salary. But it was for Warners, in 1945, that she played the role of her career, in *Mildred Pierce*, as the determined waitress who sacrifices all for ungrateful daughter Ann Blyth. The picture was a fast-paced and enjoyable melodrama, with a tasty script and memorable characters, and she was awarded her long-coveted Academy Award for Best Actress. Three more meaty dramas followed: *Humoresque*, as an unhappy society woman with a dependency on the bottle; *Possessed* (no relation to the Gable picture), earning another Oscar nomination, as a woman driven mad by her love for Van Heflin; and *Flamingo Road*, at her toughest, as a former carny dancer going head to head with power-hungry politician Sidney Greenstreet.

In the 1950s her soaps became increasingly florid, and the advent of Technicolor emphasized her darkened lipstick and the prominent severity of her penciled eyebrows. There were *Sudden Fear*, which brought her another Oscar nomination, as a playwright who realizes that husband Jack Palance intends to murder her; *Torch Song*, as a selfish entertainer softened by blind pianist Michael Wilding (the film embarrassingly featured an eye-popping dark-face production number); *Johnny Guitar*, everybody's favorite feminist western with Crawford, in pants, battling an equally butch Mercedes McCambridge; *Female on the Beach*, suspecting younger lover Jeff Chandler of foul play; and *Autumn Leaves*, tending another younger man, Cliff Robertson, until she realizes he has severe mental problems. Less agreeable were her

viperish turns in the remake of *Craig's Wife*, now called *Harriet Craig*; *The Damned Don't Cry*, finding wealth and power as a gangster's moll; and *Queen Bee*, manipulating and destroying the members of a wealthy Southern family. This was probably the nastiest role of her career and epitomized her grotesque side that made her reviled by some, beloved by others, the gay community making up the largest constituency of the latter.

She was merely part of the ensemble in 20th Century-Fox's glossy *The Best of Everything*, but scored one last starring triumph when director Robert Aldrich cast her opposite Bette Davis in the low-budget psychological thriller, *What Ever Happened to Baby Jane?* A new genre of 1960s gothics, starring aging ladies of the golden era, began, but the original was the best. Crawford was at her most sympathetic, as the crippled one-time movie star tormented by her unhinged sister. Crawford now entered the campiest stage of her career, teaching judo in a mental hospital in *The Caretakers*; toting an axe in *Strait-Jacket*; running a circus whose members meet horrible deaths in *Berserk*; and acting opposite a Neanderthal Man in *Trog*. After her death of cancer in 1977, her adopted daughter, Christina, published the unflattering memoir by which all others are measured, *Mommie Dearest*, painting the late star as a manipulative egotist and child abuser, an image that has tarnished the memory of her work. However, the revelations could hardly have come as surprise to anyone familiar with her screen persona. Crawford's own version of the story, *Portrait of Joan*, appeared in 1962, while Roy Newquist published *Conversation With Joan* (1980), an extensive interview with the actress, in which she gave her opinions on each of her films. In addition to Fairbanks and Tone, her third husband (1942–46), Phillip Terry, was also an actor. She had also been married (1955–59) to Pepsi chairman Alfred Steele and remained on the board of directors until an ouster in 1972.

Screen: AS LUCILLE LESUEUR: 1925: Lady of the Night; Pretty Ladies; The Only Thing.

AS JOAN CRAWFORD: 1925: Old Clothes; Sally, Irene and Mary; 1926: The Boob; Tramp, Tramp, Tramp; Paris; 1927: The Taxi Driver; Winners of the Wilderness; The Understanding Heart; The Unknown; Twelve Miles Out; Spring Fever; 1928: West Point; Rose Marie; Across to Singapore; The Law of the Range; Four Walls; Our Dancing Daughters; Dream of Love; 1929: The Duke Steps Out; Our Modern Maidens; The Hollywood Revue of 1929; Untamed; 1930: Montana Moon; Our Blushing Brides; Paid; 1931: Dance, Fools, Dance; Laughing Sinners; This Modern Age; Possessed; 1932: Letty Lynton; Grand Hotel; Rain; 1933: Today We Live; Dancing Lady; 1934: Sadie McKee; Chained; Forsaking All Others; 1935: No More Ladies; I Live My Life; 1936: The Gorgeous Hussy; Love on the Run; 1937: The Last of Mrs. Cheyney; The Bride Wore Red; 1938: Mannequin; The Shining Hour; 1939: The Ice Follies of 1939; The Women; 1940: Strange Cargo; Susan and God; 1941: A Woman's Face; When Ladies Meet; 1942: They All Kissed the Bride; Reunion in France; 1943: Above Suspicion; 1944: Hollywood Canteen; 1945: Mildred Pierce; 1946: Humoresque; 1947: Possessed; Daisy Kenyon; 1949: Flamingo Road; It's a Great Feeling; 1950: The Damned Don't Cry; Harriet Craig; 1951: Goodbye, My Fancy; 1952: This Woman Is Dangerous; Sudden Fear; 1953: Torch Song; 1954: Johnny Guitar; 1955: Female on the Beach; Queen Bee; 1956: Autumn Leaves; 1957: The Story of Esther Costello; 1959: The Best of Everything; 1962: What Ever Happened to Baby Jane?; 1963: The Caretakers; 1964: Strait-Jacket; 1965: I Saw What You Did; 1967: Berserk; 1970: Trog.

NY Stage: 1924: Innocent Eyes; The Passing Show of 1924.

Select TV: 1954: The Road to Edinburgh (sp); 1958: Strange Witness (sp); 1959: And One Was Loyal (sp);Della (sp).

LAIRD CREGAR

(SAMUEL LAIRD CREGAR) BORN: PHILADELPHIA, PA, JULY 28, 1916. ED: WINCHESTER COL. DIED: DECEMBER 9, 1944.

A jumbo-sized character player, adept at providing menace, Laird Cregar had a brief but busy career. A scholarship to the Pasadena Community Playhouse led to two small film roles, but it was his acclaimed performance in a stage production of *Oscar Wilde* that won him a contract with 20th Century-Fox, where he started off by playing a French fur-trapper in *Hudson's Bay*. He distinguished himself in supporting parts in such hit films as *Charley's Aunt*, reacting to the flirtations of Jack Benny in drag with comic flair; and, more significantly, *I Wake Up Screaming*, stealing the show as the sinister and unscrupulous detective in pursuit of Carole Landis's murderer. On loan to Paramount he appeared in another big one, *This Gun for Hire*, as the double-crossing nightclub owner who becomes hit man Alan Ladd's target. Back at Fox there were colorful turns in *The Black Swan*, as the pirate Captain Morgan; *Heaven Can Wait*, as a very elegant devil; and *Holy Matrimony*, as a crafty art dealer. The studio cast him as the title character in *The Lodger*, based loosely on the story of Jack the Ripper. Cregar was third billed (after Merle Oberon and George Sanders) but he commanded all the attention as the bloodthirsty monster who roamed the streets of London, disposing of women he deemed unworthy to live. It was successful enough for Cregar to receive a follow-up vehicle, *Hangover Square*, this time given top-billing, as a deranged pianist who goes into a homicidal rage whenever he hears certain discordant noises. In an effort to escape typecasting, Cregar began a crash diet that, tragically, resulted in a fatal heart attack.

Screen: 1940: Granny Get Your Gun; Oh Johnny, How Can You Love; Hudson's Bay; 1941: Blood and Sand; Charley's Aunt; I Wake Up Screaming; 1942: Joan of Paris; Rings on Her Fingers; This Gun for Hire; Ten Gentlemen From West Point; The Black Swan; 1943: Hello, Frisco, Hello; Heaven Can Wait; Holy Matrimony; 1944: The Lodger; 1945: Hangover Square.

RICHARD CRENNA

BORN: LOS ANGELES, CA, NOVEMBER 30, 1927. ED: USC. DIED: JANUARY 17, 2003.

An all-purpose actor who played sinners and saints with equal aplomb, Richard Crenna's continuing stardom owed immensely to his frequent exposure on the small screen. While still a teen he began acting on radio, where he became a regular player on such series as *A Date With Judy* and *Our Miss Brooks*. When the latter came to television in 1952 he followed with it, playing Eve Arden's dumbest pupil, Walter Denton. Shortly after that series left the air he was back starring in his own sitcom, *The Real McCoys*, which had a healthy six-year run. He'd done a handful of movies, including a 1956 theatrical spin-off of *Our Miss Brooks*, but it was not until the 1960s that he began to cultivate a more interesting film career, beginning with the very popular war adventure *The Sand Pebbles*, as a dignified navy gunboat captain. He was suitably menacing in the ace thriller *Wait Until Dark*, but as a thug terrorizing blind Audrey Hepburn he also revealed an unexpectedly sympathetic side. Roles in big-budgeted films like *Star!*, as the true love of Julie Andrews's life, and *Marooned*, as an unfortunate astronaut, were little more than serviceable. On television he became a staple in telefilms, winning an Emmy Award for playing an insufferable cop who must face humiliation after

being sexually assaulted in *The Rape of Richard Beck*. In the 1980s his movie career was jump-started by the pseudo-noir *Body Heat*, as Kathleen Turner's husband, murdered by her lover, William Hurt. The following year he had a plum role as Sylvester Stallone's commanding officer in the hit *First Blood*, which gave him steady work for two more sequels. Best of all was the delightful 1984 comedy, *The Flamingo Kid*, in which Crenna, as a wealthy car dealer, entices cabana boy Matt Dillon to enjoy the good life. He has directed television episodes of several series and the telefilm *Better Late Than Never* (1979).

Screen: 1952: Red Skies of Montana; The Pride of St. Louis; It Grows on Trees; 1956: Our Miss Brooks; Over-Exposed; 1965: John Goldfarb, Please Come Home; 1966: Made in Paris; The Sand Pebbles; 1967: Wait Until Dark; 1968: Star!/Those Were the Happy Times; 1969: Midas Run; Marooned; 1971: Red Sky at Morning; Doctors' Wives; Catlow; The Deserter; 1972: Dirty Money; A Man Called Noon; 1973: Jonathan Livingston Seagull (voice); 1976: Breakheart Pass; 1978: The Evil/House of Evil; 1979: Wild Horse Hank; 1980: Stone Cold Dead; Death Ship; 1981: Body Heat; 1982: First Blood; 1983: Table for Five; 1984: The Flamingo Kid; 1985: Rambo: First Blood Part II; Summer Rental; 1988: Rambo III; 1989: Leviathan; 1993: Hot Shots! Part Deux; 1995: A Pyromaniac's Love Story; Jade; Sabrina; 1998: Wrongfully Accused.

Select TV: 1952–55: Our Miss Brooks (series); 1957–63: The Real McCoys (series); 1963: The Long Life of Edward Smalley (sp); 1964–65: Slattery's People (series); 1971: Thief; 1972: Footsteps; 1973: Double Indemnity; 1974: Double Solitaire (sp); Nightmare; Shootout in a One-Dog Town; Honky Tonk; 1975: A Girl Named Sooner; 1976–77: All's Fair (series); 1977: The War Between the Tates; 1978: Centennial (ms); Devil Dog: The Hound of Hell; First You Cry; 1979: Mayflower: The Pilgrim's Adventure; 1980: Fugitive Family; 1981: The Ordeal of Billy Carney; 1982: The Day the Bubble Burst; 1982–83: It Takes Two (series); 1984: Passions; 1985: The Rape of Richard Beck; Doubletake; 1986: A Case of Deadly Force; On Wings of Eagles (ms); The Price of Passion; 1987: Police Story: The Freeway Killings; Kids Like These; Plaza Suite (sp); 1988: Plaza Suite (sp); Internal Affairs; 1989: The Case of the Hillside Stranglers; Stuck With Each Other; 1990: Murder in Black and White; Montana; Last Flight Out; Murder Times Seven; 1991: And the Sea Will Tell; 1991–92: Pros & Cons (series); 1992: Intruders; Terror on Track 9; 1993: A Place to Be Loved; 1994: Janek: The Forget-Me-Not Murders; Jonathan Stone: Threat of Innocence; Janek: A Silent Betrayal; 1995: In the Name of Love: A Texas Tragedy; 1996: Texas Graces; Race Against Time: The Search for Sarah; 1997: 20,000 Leagues Under the Sea; Deep Family Secrets; Heart Full of Rain; 1999: To Serve and Protect; 2000: By Dawn's Early Light; Murder She Wrote: A Story to Die For; 2001: The Day Reagan Was Shot.

DONALD CRISP

BORN: ABERFELDY, SCOTLAND, JULY 27, 1880. DIED: MAY 25, 1974.

By the time he won his Oscar in 1941, character actor Donald Crisp had been in Hollywood for over 30 years. Following some stage credits he worked for D.W. Griffith on the 1910 short, *The Two Paths*, and on the first significant silent feature, *The Birth of a Nation*, as General Grant. His most prominent role of this period was as Lillian Gish's miserable bastard of a father in the 1919 melodrama *Broken Blossoms*. In the meantime, Crisp had made his directorial debut with the 1916 version of *Ramona*, and would go on to helm a total of 46 films, most notably the Douglas Fairbanks adventure *Don Q — Son of Zorro*, and one of the most popular of all the Buster Keaton comedies, *The Navigator*, sharing credit with the star. With the coming of sound, the distinguished looking, white-haired Scottish actor became a highly visible presence in period pieces, including *Mutiny on the Bounty*, as one of the mutineers; *The Life of Emile Zola*, as a lawyer assisting Paul Muni in his defense of Joseph Schildkraut; *The Private Life of Elizabeth and Essex*, as Francis Bacon; and *The Sea Hawk*, as one of Queen Elizabeth's court advisors. Something in his bearing suggested the medical profession, as evidenced by doctoral roles in *The Little Minister*, *Jezebel*, *Wuthering Heights* and *The Old Maid*. He usually projected a wise, benign presence, but he could be equally effective when being strict or stern, as in *A Woman Rebels*, as Katharine Hepburn's domineering judicial father; *That Certain Woman*, keeping Bette Davis away from the child she has had with Henry Fonda; or *Dr. Erlich's Magic Bullet*, as the health minister who curtails government funding for Edward G. Robinson's experiments.

He reached his peak in 1941 as the strong and decent patriarch of a coal-mining family in John Ford's classic mood piece, *How Green Was My Valley*, winning the Academy Award for Best Supporting Actor. He also played fathers in two of the best-loved animal pictures of the 1940s, *Lassie Come Home* and *National Velvet*, making him the quintessential pipe-smoking, advice-dispensing movie papa. He would appear in three more features with the famous collie at MGM: *Son of Lassie*, *Hills of Home*, and *Challenge to Lassie*, and partnered with other canine co-stars late in his career in *A Dog of Flanders*, and Disney's *Greyfriars Bobby*, which was the first time in years he had received top billing. As approached his 80th year, he could be seen playing Tyrone Power's Irish da in *The Long Gray Line*; a Cardinal in *The Last Hurrah*; a small town mayor in Disney's *Pollyanna*; and Henry Fonda's old man in *Spencer's Mountain*. As if he weren't busy enough in show business, Crisp also cultivated a substantial fortune maintaining an additional career as a director of the Bank of America.

Screen: 1914: The Battle of the Sexes; The Great Leap: Until Death Do Us Part; The Escape; Home Sweet Home; The Avenging Conscience; 1915: The Birth of a Nation; The Love Route; The Blue or the Gray; Girl of Yesterday; The Foundling; The Commanding Officer; The Mountain Rat; May Blossom; 1916: Ramona; 1917: Joan the Woman; 1919: Broken Blossoms; 1921: The Bonnie Brier Bush; 1925: Don Q — Son of Zorro (and dir.); 1926: The Black Pirate; 1928: The Viking; Stand and Deliver; The River Pirate; 1929: Trent's Last Case; The Pagan; The Return of Sherlock Holmes; 1930: Scotland Yard; 1931: Svengali; Kick In; 1932: Red Dust; Passport to Hell; 1933: Broadway Bad; 1934: What Every Woman Knows; The Little Minister; British Agent; The Life of Vergie Winters; The Key; Crime Doctor; 1935: Mutiny on the Bounty; Oil for the Lamps of China; Vanessa — Her Love Story; Laddie; 1936: The Charge of the Light Brigade; Mary of Scotland; A Woman Rebels; Beloved Enemy; The White Angel; 1937: The Life of Emile Zola; Parnell; Confession; That Certain Woman; The Great O'Malley; 1938: Jezebel; The Sisters; The Dawn Patrol; The Amazing Dr. Clitterhouse; Valley of the Giants; Comet Over Broadway; Sergeant Murphy; The Beloved Brat; 1939: Wuthering Heights; Juarez; The Old Maid; The Private Lives of Elizabeth and Essex; Daughters Courageous; The Oklahoma Kid; 1940: Dr. Ehrlich's Magic Bullet; The Sea Hawk; Brother Orchid; City for Conquest; Knute Rockne: All-American; 1941: How Green Was My Valley; Dr. Jekyll and Mr. Hyde; Shining Victory; 1942: The Gay Sisters; 1943: Forever and a Day; Lassie Come Home; 1944:

The Adventures of Mark Twain; The Uninvited; 1945: National Velvet; The Valley of Decision; Son of Lassie; 1947: Ramrod; 1948: Hills of Home; Whispering Smith; 1949: Challenge to Lassie; 1950: Bright Leaf; 1951: Home Town Story; 1954: Prince Valiant; 1955: The Man From Laramie; The Long Gray Line; 1957: Drango; 1958: The Last Hurrah; Saddle the Wind; 1959: A Dog of Flanders; 1960: Pollyanna; 1961: Greyfriars Bobby; 1963: Spencer's Mountain.

Select TV: 1959: The Raider (sp).

RICHARD CROMWELL

(ROY RADABAUGH) BORN: LONG BEACH, CA, JANUARY 8, 1910. ED: CHOUINARD ART SCHOOL. DIED: OCTOBER 11, 1960.

Sweet-faced Richard Cromwell made his living playing sensitive, pretty-boy types during the 1930s, after winning the lead in the talking picture remake of *Tol'able David*. Although his main interest had been in the arts, which included painting murals for the Pantages Theatre in Hollywood, he was chosen over more experienced candidates to star as young Virginia lad David Kinemon, who is unfairly branded a coward until he proves his worth delivering the U.S. mail. Because of the good response towards the picture, Cromwell won leading roles in such movies as *Maker of Men* and *That's My Boy*, in both rather unconvincingly cast as football heroes; *Above the Clouds*, as newsreel cameraman Robert Armstrong's eager assistant; and Cecil B. DeMille's *This Day and Age*, as a juvenile district attorney (!) who brings down criminal Charles Bickford. Never really star material, he was appreciated for supporting bigger stars, as in *Emma*, playfully ribbing Marie Dressler, as the only stepchild who genuinely cares for her; *The Lives of a Bengal Lancer*, as the weak-willed commanding officer's son, foisted upon Gary Cooper and Franchot Tone; *Poppy*, in love with W.C. Fields's daughter; *Jezebel*, in which he dared to duel with George Brent; and *Young Mr. Lincoln*, in which he and Eddie Quillan faced a murder rap until Henry Fonda saved their necks. Inevitably he was demoted to the poverty row circuit, starring as a drifter who helps a rural radio station in *Village Barn Dance*; an intern infiltrating a gang of criminals in *Riot Squad*; and, most appropriately, the title role in the gangster spoof *Baby Face Morgan*, as a country yokel engaged to lead his late father's gang. After the war he briefly married (1945–46) actress Angela Lansbury, though it was well known that he was gay, before quitting show business to return to the art world, where he specialized in ceramics after reverting to his real name.

Screen: 1930: The King of Jazz; Tol'able David; 1931: Fifty Fathoms Deep; Shanghaied Love; Are These Are Children?; Maker of Men; 1932: Strange Love of Molly Louvain; The Age of Consent; Emma; Tom Brown of Culver; That's My Boy; 1933: This Day and Age; Above the Clouds; Hoopla; 1934: Among the Missing; When Strangers Meet; The Most Precious Thing in Life; Name the Woman; Carolina; 1935: Life Begins at 40; The Lives of a Bengal Lancer; Annapolis Farewell; Men of the Hour; McFadden's Flats; Unknown Woman; 1936: Poppy; 1937: The Road Back; The Wrong Road; 1938: Jezebel; Come On Leathernecks; Storm Over Bengal; Our Fighting Navy/Torpedoed; 1939: Young Mr. Lincoln; 1940: Enemy Agent; The Villain Still Pursued Her; Village Barn Dance; 1941: Riot Squad; Parachute Battalion; 1942: Baby Face Morgan; 1943: Cosmo Jones in the Crime Smasher; 1948: Bungalow 13.

NY Stage: 1936: So Proudly We Hail.

HUME CRONYN

BORN: LONDON, ONTARIO, CANADA,
JULY 18, 1911.

There are two distinct phases to Hume
Cronyn's film career. In the 1940s he excelled
at playing quiet, bookish types, appearing
much older than his years. Later, as a gen-
uine senior citizen, he was a memorable screen partner to his
real-life wife, Jessica Tandy. Leaving behind a career in law, he
joined the National Theatre Stock Company in Washington,
making his stage bow in *Up Pops the Devil*. Following studies at
the American Academy of Dramatic Arts, he first stepped on the
Broadway stage in 1934, in a small bit in *Hipper's Holiday*.
Establishing a respectable career there with such hits as *Room
Service* and *High Tor*, he soon met up with Tandy, whom he married in 1942. The next year he went to Hollywood to make his
first movie appearance, in Hitchcock's fine thriller *Shadow of a
Doubt*, playing a nebbishy amateur sleuth. Not only did Cronyn
act for the great director again, as the ship's radio operator in
another of his best offerings, *Lifeboat*, but he collaborated on the
screenplays of Hitch's *Rope* and *Under Capricorn*. In the meantime, he had signed with MGM, where he earned his sole Oscar
nomination, portraying a German who wakes up to the realities
of Nazism in the 1944 release *The Seventh Cross*. It also marked his
first on-screen pairing with Tandy, playing his wife. Two years
later they had a more curious connection on screen in *The Green
Years*, with Cronyn playing Tandy's father. Also during this period
Cronyn could be seen, sans Tandy, in Universal's *Phantom of the
Opera*, assisting Edgar Barrier in investigating the horrific crimes;
Ziegfeld Follies, as Fanny Brice's twittery husband in the
"Sweepstakes Ticket" sequence; *The Postman Always Rings Twice*,
as the lawyer who gets killers John Garfield and Lana Turner off
the hook; *The Beginning or the End*, as physicist Dr. J. Robert
Oppenheimer, the man behind the Manhattan Project; and, back
at Universal, *Brute Force*, a standout as a sadistic prison guard.

For the next four decades the Cronyns gave much attention to
the stage, where their many teamings would include *The
Fourposter*, *A Delicate Balance*, *The Gin Game*, and *Foxfire*.
Sporadically Cronyn would return to the big screen, including
roles in *Sunrise at Campobello*, playing adviser Louis Howe to
Ralph Bellamy's Franklin Roosevelt; the over-publicized
Cleopatra, as the Queen of the Nile's counselor Sosigenes, who is
memorably disposed of by Roddy McDowall; the hurriedly-pro-
duced Richard Burton version of *Hamlet*, repeating his stage role
as Polonius; *There Was a Crooked Man...*, as an effete prison
inmate, presumably John Randolph's lover; and the underrated
political thriller, *The Parallax View*, receiving second-billing, as
Warren Beatty's skeptical editor. In the 1980s Cronyn and Tandy
came together memorably as Glenn Close's dismayed parents in
The World According to Garp, while Cronyn was a delight as the
septuagenarian whose rejuvenation causes him to cheat on Tandy
in the sci-fi hit *Cocoon*. Another sci-fi flick, **batteries not included*,
saw them as a pair of oldsters being helped by teeny aliens to
combat a corrupt landlord. On television Cronyn won Emmy
Awards for his work in two telefilms, *Broadway Bound*, and *To
Dance With the White Dog*, and, following Tandy's death in 1994,
he returned to the screen, as the bedridden Marvin, in the adaptation of *Marvin's Room*. His autobiography, *A Terrible Liar*, was
published in 1992.

Screen: 1943: Shadow of a Doubt; Phantom of the Opera; The
Cross of Lorraine; 1944: The Seventh Cross; Main Street After
Dark; Blonde Fever; Lifeboat; 1945: A Letter for Evie; The Sailor
Takes a Wife; 1946: Ziegfeld Follies; The Green Years; The

Postman Always Rings Twice; The Secret Heart (voice); 1947: The
Beginning or the End; Brute Force; 1948: The Bride Goes Wild;
1949: Top o' the Morning; 1951: People Will Talk; 1956: Crowded
Paradise; 1960: Sunrise at Campobello; 1963: Cleopatra; 1964:
Hamlet; 1969: Gaily, Gaily; The Arrangement; 1970: There Was a
Crooked Man...; 1974: Conrack; The Parallax View; 1981: Honky
Tonk Freeway; Rollover; 1982: The World According to Garp;
1984: Impulse; 1985: Brewster's Millions; Cocoon; 1987: Batteries
Not Included; 1988: Cocoon: The Return; 1993: The Pelican
Brief; 1994: Camilla; 1996: Marvin's Room.

NY Stage: 1934: Hipper's Holiday; Boy Meets Girl; 1937: High
Tor; Room Service; 1938: There's Always a Breeze; Escape This
Night; 1939: Off to Buffalo; The Three Sisters; 1940: The Weak
Link; Retreat to Pleasure; 1941: Mr. Big; 1948: The Survivors;
1951: The Fourposter; 1955: The Honeys; A Day By the Sea; 1958:
The Man in the Dog Suit; 1959: Triple Play; 1961: Big Fish, Little
Fish; 1964: Hamlet; The Physicists; 1966: A Delicate Balance;
1972: Promenade All!; Samuel Beckett Festival (ob); 1974: Noel
Coward in Two Keys; 1977: The Gin Game; 1982: Foxfire (and
co-wr.); 1986: The Petition.

Select TV: 1950: The Reluctant Landlord (sp); 1954: The
Marriage (series); 1955: The Fourposter (sp); Christmas 'til
Closing (sp); 1957: The Five Dollar Bill (sp); A Member of the
Family (sp); 1958: The Bridge of San Luis Rey (sp); 1959: The
Moon and Sixpence (sp); A Doll's House (sp); 1960: Juno and the
Paycock (sp); 1981: The Gin Game (sp); 1987: Foxfire (also co-
wr.); 1989: Day One; Age-Old Friends; 1991: Christmas on
Division Street; 1992: Broadway Bound; 1993: To Dance With
the White Dog; 1997: 12 Angry Men; Alone; 1998: Seasons of
Love; 1999: Sea People; Santa and Pete; 2000: Yesterday's
Children; 2001: Off Season.

BING CROSBY

(HARRY LILLIS CROSBY) BORN: TACOMA, WA,
MAY 3, 1903. ED: GONZAGA UNIV.
DIED: OCTOBER 14, 1977.

Since the dawn of the talkies, singers have
tried their hand at movie acting with varying
degrees of success. Certainly the first great
vocalist to become an equally great movie star was Bing Crosby.
Nobody ever merged the artistry of song so effortlessly with the
technique of acting. It was as if he taught a whole generation of
performers the appeal of appearing relaxed on screen. His early
career found him teamed with Al Rinker, and, after joining Paul
Whiteman's orchestra, they added a third member, Harry Barris,
to become the Rhythm Boys. It was as part of this group that Bing
made his feature debut in Universal's all-star musical revue, *King
of Jazz*, where he performed "So the Bluebirds and the Blackbirds
Got Together." He was soon famous enough as a solo recording
artist that Mack Sennett signed him for a series of comical shorts,
distributed by Educational Pictures, each of which was designed to
highlight one of Crosby's hit songs, such as "I Surrender, Dear"
and "Just One More Chance." In 1931 he began his amazingly successful career on radio, and parlayed this the following year into his
first official starring feature, *The Big Broadcast*, singing his theme
song, "Where the Blue of the Night (Meets the Gold of the Day)."
This marked the beginning of his long and fruitful reign at
Paramount where, during the 1940s, he would become the undisputed king of the lot.

In the meantime, he was sly and charming in a series of light
and often-forgettable comedies that would give him an excuse to
croon a tune to the leading lady. Often included in the cast were
comedians like Burns and Allen (*College Humor*, *We're Not*

Dressing), Jackie Oakie (*College Humor, Too Much Harmony, The Big Broadcast of 1936*), W.C. Fields (*Mississippi*), and Martha Raye (*Double or Nothing, Rhythm on the Range*), and, although he played off most of them beautifully, Crosby rarely needed the support of comic relief. Few people were so adept at spinning a line for a laugh as Bing, and he was rapidly building a peerless reputation as a light comic actor. There were also some serious roles, as in *Sing, You Sinners*, playing a shiftless gambler who would rather spend his time at the racetrack, easily his best movie of this period. Among the hit songs that the public showed up to hear Crosby sing were "Learn to Croon" (*College Humor*), "Temptation" (from his loan-out to MGM, *Going Hollywood*), "Love in Bloom" (*She Loves Me Not*), "Love is Just Around the Corner" (*Here Is My Heart*), "It's Easy to Remember" (*Mississippi*), "I'm an Old Cowhand" (*Rhythm on the Range*), "Pennies from Heaven" (the title song from his loan-out to Columbia), "Sweet Leilani" (marking the first time he introduced an Oscar-winning song, from the film *Waikiki Wedding*), and "Small Fry" (*Sing, You Sinners*).

In 1940 history was made by way of an unremarkable movie called *Road to Singapore*. The cast included Dorothy Lamour but, more significantly, it marked the first time Crosby would share the screen with Paramount's other great asset, comedian Bob Hope. In addition to many guest appearances and countless pairings on radio and television, they would co-star in seven *Road* pictures, reaching some sort of manic pinnacle with the hilarious *Road to Utopia*, in 1946. There may never have been a funnier duo in the history of movies, and they traded quips and insults as if they were making them up on the spot. The barbs were always winningly delivered with a hint of affection behind them. Crosby was, in fact, one performer who could click quite comfortably with many other top stars. A pair of musicals with the woefully underused Mary Martin, *Rhythm on the River* and *Blues in the Night*, were among the most pleasant of his 1940s vehicles, and in 1942, he scored a gigantic hit with Fred Astaire in the breezy *Holiday Inn*. He earned himself a certain degree of immortality when he sang Irving Berlin's "White Christmas" for the first (but certainly not the last) time. It not only became his most popular song but the best-selling single of all time, and the second Oscar-winning song he introduced on screen.

Dixie, his first full Technicolor musical, covered some shaky territory, and only someone with Crosby's affability could diminish the unpleasant connotations of the title song and the focus on blackface minstrel shows of the 1800s. During this period everything he touched turned to gold, and that was never truer than *Going My Way*. Leo McCarey's beautifully restrained story of two very human priests (Barry Fitzgerald was the other) in a New York City parish proved irresistible to wartime audiences. It not only resulted in more hit records, with the Oscar-winning "Swinging on a Star" and "Too-Ra-Loo-Ra-Loo-Ra," but Crosby's subtle acting skills had never before been so effectively displayed. He won the Academy Award for Best Actor of 1944, while the film took a total of seven trophies, including Best Picture. The following year Crosby became the first performer to receive a second nomination for playing the same character, Father O'Malley, in *The Bells of St. Mary's*. This sequel may have been a pale reflection of the original, but it was an even bigger moneymaker, this time for RKO. In between, he paired off with Paramount's biggest female attraction, Betty Hutton, in *Here Come the Waves*. The highlight was another Crosby smash tune, "Ac-cent-u-ate the Positive," which was, alas, another foray into blackface. Knowing a good thing when he saw it, Crosby reteamed with Astaire for another Irving Berlin tunefest, *Blue Skies*, where their rendition of "A Couple of Song and Dance

Men" was a joyous highpoint. This, in turn, was followed by a pleasant variation on the *Going My Way* formula, with Crosby and Barry Fitzgerald competing as small town doctors in *Welcome Stranger*.

He was fortunate to be under Billy Wilder's guidance for an intelligent comment on prejudice, *The Emperor Waltz*, about a phonograph salesman in Austria, and he was perfectly cast as the misplaced hero of *A Connecticut Yankee in King Arthur's Court*. He teamed felicitously with director Frank Capra for the fine remake of *Broadway Bill*, now titled *Riding High*, while a second Capra movie, *Here Comes the Groom*, took in more cash though it offered little beyond a great duet with Jane Wyman, "In the Cool Cool Cool of the Evening." He stumbled in a third teaming with Fitzgerald, *Top O' the Morning*, about the theft of the Blarney Stone, but had one of his most appealing leading ladies, Nancy Olsen, in one of his least appreciated films, *Mr. Music*. Paramount produced their final entry in the "Road" show, *Road to Bali*, which generated good returns, before Crosby returned to drama in *Little Boy Lost*, as a former war correspondent searching for his son. More famously, he gave a powerful performance as a drunken, self-pitying entertainer in *The Country Girl*, earning himself a third Oscar nomination. Between those two came his biggest financial success, *White Christmas*, a Technicolor variation on *Holiday Inn*, with more Irving Berlin songs and Danny Kaye instead of Fred Astaire.

He ended his Paramount contract in 1956 with a dud, *Anything Goes*, which was even further removed from the Broadway musical than the earlier film of the same name that Crosby had made for the studio back in 1936. MGM then cast him in the Cary Grant role for the musical version of *The Philadelphia Story*, now called *High Society*. With Grace Kelly at his side it was a sophisticated delight, and he and Frank Sinatra harmonized divinely on "Well Did You Evah?" Crosby was becoming less concerned with maintaining a steady movie career than he was with performing on television specials and playing golf. The 1960s found him providing dollops of the patented Crosby charm to the back-to-college romp *High Times*, marking the last time he introduced a famous number, "The Second Time Around;" a final *Road* film (*to Hong Kong*); and the musical *Robin and the 7 Hoods*, which he stole from Sinatra and his Rat Pack. His final big screen appearance was in the remake of *Stagecoach*, receiving favorable comment for reprising Thomas Mitchell's Oscar-winning role as the drunken doctor. When he died of a heart attack on a golf course in Spain in 1977 it was clear that the world had lost one of its most cherished and significant entertainers of the century. When Gary, his eldest son from his first marriage, penned his memoirs, portraying Bing as a cold, unfeeling lout, the public didn't want to hear of it. Bing's second, happier marriage to actress Kathryn Grant produced three children, including Mary Frances Crosby, best known for her role on the television serial *Dallas*; Harry, who appeared in the 1980 horror film *Friday the 13th*; and Nathaniel who took up dad's favorite pastime by becoming a pro golfer. Crosby's own memoir, *Call Me Lucky*, was published in 1953 and embodied his ever-present self-effacing attitude about his importance to show business.

Screen: 1930: King of Jazz; Reaching for the Moon; 1931: Confessions of a Co-Ed; 1932: The Big Broadcast; 1933: College Humor; Too Much Harmony; Going Hollywood; 1934: We're Not Dressing; She Loves Me Not; Here Is My Heart; 1935: Mississippi; Two for Tonight; The Big Broadcast of 1936; 1936: Anything Goes/Tops Is the Limit; Rhythm on the Range; Pennies From Heaven; 1937: Waikiki Wedding; Double or Nothing; 1938: Doctor Rhythm; Sing, You Sinners; 1939: Paris Honeymoon; East Side of Heaven; The Star Maker; 1940: Road to Singapore;

If I Had My Way; Rhythm on the River; **1941:** Road to Zanzibar; Birth of the Blues; **1942:** My Favorite Blonde; Holiday Inn; Road to Morocco; Star Spangled Rhythm; **1943:** Dixie; **1944:** The Princess and the Pirate; Going My Way; Here Come the Waves; **1945:** Duffy's Tavern; The Bells of St. Mary's; Out of This World (voice); **1946:** Road to Utopia; Blue Skies; **1947:** Welcome Stranger; My Favorite Brunette; Variety Girl; Road to Rio; **1948:** The Emperor Waltz; **1949:** A Connecticut Yankee in King Arthur's Court; Top o' the Morning; The Adventures of Ichabod and Mr. Toad (narrator); **1950:** Riding High; Mr. Music; **1951:** Here Comes the Groom; Angels in the Outfield; **1952:** The Greatest Show on Earth; Just for You; Road to Bali; Son of Paleface; **1953:** Little Boy Lost; Scared Stiff; **1954:** White Christmas; The Country Girl; **1956:** Anything Goes; High Society; **1957:** Man on Fire; **1959:** Say One for Me; Alias Jesse James; **1960:** High Time; Let's Make Love; Pepe; **1962:** The Road to Hong Kong; **1964:** Robin and the 7 Hoods; **1965:** Cinerama's Russian Adventure/Bing Crosby's Cinerama Adventure (narrator); **1966:** Stagecoach; **1972:** Cancel My Reservation; **1974:** That's Entertainment!

NY Stage: 1976: Bing Crosby on Broadway.

Select TV: 1956: High Tor (sp); 1964–65: The Bing Crosby Show (series); 1964–70: The Hollywood Palace (series; frequent host); 1971: Dr. Cook's Garden.

PAT CROWLEY

BORN: OLYPHANT, PA, SEPTEMBER 17, 1929

Not long after attending New York's High School of the Performing Arts, perkily pleasant Patricia Crowley got jobs in two Broadway short runs, *Southern Exposure* and *Four Twelves Are 48*, and the lead in a television adaptation of *A Date With Judy*. Paramount Pictures signed her to a contract in 1953 and promoted her as the newest "girl next door" type, debuting her as the leading lady in a weak Martin and Lewis comedy, *Money From Home*. She got her main showcase with the theatre-based comedy, *Forever Female*, as the ingénue who wins a role from aging star Ginger Rogers. She was a very appealing and likeable actress who got few chances to shine, as evidenced when, three years later, she played straight woman to Dean and Jerry, again, in *Hollywood or Bust*. In between, she was one of boxer Tony Curtis's women in *The Square Jungle*, and Indian agent Audie Murphy's wife in *Walk the Proud Land*. She found her biggest success on television, reprising Doris Day's role in the small screen version of *Please Don't Eat the Daisies*, after which she maintained a fairly low profile in that medium with roles on such lesser soaps as *Generations* and *Port Charles*.

Screen: 1953: Money From Home; 1954: Forever Female; Red Garters; 1956: The Square Jungle; There's Always Tomorrow; Walk the Proud Land; Hollywood or Bust; 1960: Key Witness; 1963: The Wheeler Dealers; 1966: To Trap a Spy; 1972: The Biscuit Eater.

NY Stage: 1950: Southern Exposure; 1951: Four Twelves Are 48.

Select TV: 1950: Sixteen (sp); 1951–52: A Date With Judy (series); 1952: Fairy Tale (sp); Caprice (sp); 1954: Two (sp); Guilty Is the Stranger (sp); 1957: Girl With a Glow (sp); 1958: Time to Go Now (sp); 1959: The Untouchables (sp; released theatrically as The Scarface Gang); 1965–67: Please Don't Eat the Daisies (series); 1975: The Return of Joe Forrester; 1975–76: Joe Forrester (series); 1978: Return to Fantasy Island; A Family Upside Down; The Millionaire; 1985: International Airport; 1986: Dynasty (series); 1989–90: Generations; 1997: Port

Charles (series); 2001: 61*.

CONSTANCE CUMMINGS

(CONSTANCE CUMMINGS HALVERSTADT)
BORN: SEATTLE, WA, MAY 15, 1910.

An American actress who spent much of her life in England, Constance Cummings started as a chorus girl, made her Broadway debut in *Treasure Girl* in 1928, and came to Hollywood, in 1931, to play Walter Huston's daughter in the prison drama *The Criminal Code*. She stayed for the next five years, appearing as gangster Leo Carrillo's daughter in *The Guilty Generation*, secretly romancing rival hood Boris Karloff's son, Robert Young; playing Harold Lloyd's leading lady in the best of his few talking pictures, *Movie Crazy*; falling for escaped con Jack Holt in *Behind the Mask*; taking billing over newcomer Mae West, as the woman whom George Raft wishes to impress in *Night After Night*; and portraying a nightclub performer of questionable talent, helped by singer Russ Columbo, in *Broadway Thru a Keyhole*. (The movie had enough parallels to the real life story of Ruby Keeler to prompt a violent reaction from Keeler's husband, Al Jolson.) Cummings declared *This Man Is Mine*, as the sex-hungry ex-lover of Ralph Bellamy, luring him away from good wife Irene Dunne; supported Huston again in Frank Capra's *American Madness*; tried to get charlatan Warren William to go straight in *The Mind Reader*; and went on an alcoholic binge with Robert Young in the curious comedy-mystery, *Remember Last Night?* After marrying British playwright Benn Levy she moved to England, where she would play her most famous screen role, as Rex Harrison's new spouse who is haunted by the ghost of his first wife, in David Lean's supernatural comedy, *Blithe Spirit*. She appeared sporadically in features like *The Intimate Stranger/Finger of Guilt*, as a temperamental movie star, and *The Battle of the Sexes*, as an efficiency expert whom Peter Sellers tries to bump off. During the 1970s she became a member of Britain's National Theatre Company and received a Tony Award for her 1979 performance in *Wings*.

Screen: 1931: The Criminal Code; The Last Parade; Lover Come Back; The Guilty Generation; Traveling Husbands; 1932: Behind the Mask; The Big Timer; Movie Crazy; Night After Night; American Madness; The Last Man; Attorney for the Defense; Washington Merry-Go-Round; 1933: The Mind Reader; The Billion Dollar Scandal; Broadway Thru a Keyhole; The Charming Deceiver/Heads We Go; 1934: Channel Crossing; Looking for Trouble; Glamour; This Man Is Mine; 1935: Remember Last Night?; 1936: The Wrecker/Seven Sinners; 1937: Strangers on a Honeymoon; 1940: The Haunted Honeymoon/Busman's Holiday; 1941: This England; 1942: The Foreman Went to France/Somewhere in France; 1945: Blithe Spirit; 1950: Into the Blue; 1956: John and Julie; The Intimate Stranger/Finger of Guilt; 1960: The Battle of the Sexes; 1963: A Boy Ten Feet Tall/ Sammy Going South; In the Cool of the Day.

NY Stage: 1928: Treasure Girl; 1929: The Little Show; 1930: This Man's Town; June Moon; 1934: Accent on Youth; 1937: Young Madame Conti; Madame Bovary; 1938: If I Were You; 1945: One Man Show; 1960: The Rape of the Belt; 1969: Hamlet; 1978: Wings (ob; Bdwy 1979); 1982: The Chalk Garden (ob).

Select TV: 1952: Lady From Washington (sp); 1956: Bitter Waters (sp); 1957: Night Drive (sp); 1973: Long Day's Journey Into Night (sp); 1985: Love Song; 1986: Dead Man's Folly.

ROBERT CUMMINGS

(CLARENCE ROBERT CUMMINGS) BORN: JOPLIN, MO, JUNE 9, 1908. ED: CARNEGIE INST. OF TECHNOLOGY, AADA. DIED: DECEMBER 1, 1990.

Although he was adept at drama, Robert Cummings's everyman appeal and bright speaking voice made him ideal for light comedy, the genre most audiences associate him with. Amusingly, he tried to start his acting career posing as an Englishman, using the bogus name Blade Stanhope Conway. When this didn't work out he re-christened himself Brice Hutchens, and appeared under that name in *Ziegfeld Follies of 1934*. The following year he signed a film contract with Paramount and made his official on-screen debut in their flop Civil War drama, *So Red the Rose*, as a smitten young Texan who proposes to Southern belle Maragaret Sullavan before being killed in battle. His second assignment, the cheaply produced *The Virginia Judge*, as Walter C. Kelly's wastrel stepson, actually received distribution first. He was upped to second billing for the light-hearted western *Arizona Mahoney*, as a circus performer; was the love interest of the forgotten Eleanore Whitney in the cheapie musical *Three Cheers for Love*; and co-starred with Shirley Ross in *Hideaway Girl*, as a man-about-town who falls for an accused jewel thief. He could not seem to get the essential breakthrough role and the studio continued to use him as a secondary player in films ranging from *Hollywood Boulevard* (as a screenwriter) to *Last Train from Madrid* (as a sensitive Spanish soldier, eager to exit the war-torn city) to *Wells Fargo* (as a prospector). When his contract expired, he jumped at the opportunity to transfer to Universal, where he found himself in the first of three movies he would make with Deanna Durbin, *Three Smart Girls Grow Up*, though he ultimately paired off with Nan Grey at the fade out.

By the end of 1939 he had worked with Gloria Jean in *The Under-Pup*, again matched with Nan Grey; Basil Rathbone in *Rio*, as the lover of Rathbone's wife, Sigrid Gurie; Sonja Henie in *Everything Happens at Night*, on loan at Fox; and the most famous dummy of them all in *Charlie McCarthy — Detective*. MGM borrowed him for his first top-billed part, in a "B" feature, *And One Was Beautiful*, playing a fashionably dapper playboy. He went back with Durbin for *Spring Parade*, this time as her love interest since she was now officially a "grown-up," and provided part of the triangle in *One Night in the Tropics*, which was stolen by Abbott and Costello in their movie debuts. Fortunately, Cummings's easy-going style was making an impression and he was borrowed by RKO for the comedy *The Devil and Miss Jones*, though in this instance carrying the dramatic end of the plot, as a union organizer. 20th Century-Fox used him for *Moon Over Miami*, where he got Carole Landis in the final clinch, because star Betty Grable was reserved for contractee Don Ameche. Back at Universal he displayed his knack for gentle comedy in the last (and best) of his Deanna Durbin films, *It Started With Eve*. The screenplay was written by Norman Krasna, who also supplied the scripts for *The Devil and Miss Jones*, and Warners's *Princess O'Rourke*, featuring Cummings as a pilot in love with royal Olivia de Havilland. In director Sam Wood's fine rendering of the best-seller *Kings Row*, at Warner Bros., Cummings was at his best, as the kindly young man who becomes a disillusioned medical student, and in Alfred Hitchcock's tense *Saboteur*, as an innocent man on the run, he ended up atop the Statue of Liberty in one of the master's most memorable finales. Cummings finished his stay at Universal with the anthology film, *Flesh and Fantasy*, falling in love with a masked Betty Field.

After the war he cornered the market on decent types, playing opposite some strong leading ladies, in *The Bride Wore Boots* (Barbara Stanwyck), *The Accused* (Loretta Young), *Sleep My Love* (Claudette Colbert), and *The Lost Moment* (Susan Hayward). For Columbia he did a slew of mild comedies, including *Tell It to the Judge*, with Rosalind Russell in the title role; *The Petty Girl*, as a calendar artist getting prudish professor Joan Caulfield to pose for him; *The Barefoot Mailman*, as a con man trekking along the first U.S. postal route; and *The First Time*, in which he and Barbara Hale were parents having their first baby (who narrated). In 1954, although the director claimed dissatisfaction with Cummings's previous work, he was back with Hitchcock for the gripping *Dial M for Murder*. Around this time he shifted his interest to television, winning an Emmy Award for the original presentation of *Twelve Angry Men*, in the part Henry Fonda made famous on film. He also starred in his own sitcom, *The Bob Cummings Show*, which he frequently directed. He returned to the big screen for such 1960s hits as *Beach Party*, as a professor studying teenagers, and the sexsational, *The Carpetbaggers*, billing himself as "Bob." In 1966 he reprised Berton Churchill's embezzling banker in the remake of *Stagecoach*, and had one last starring role, in the British-made espionage film, *Five Golden Dragons*. A well-known health advocate, he wrote a book called *How to Stay Young and Vital*, and spent the rest of his days trying to live up to the title.

Screen: 1933: Sons of the Desert (extra); 1935: The Virginia Judge; So Red the Rose; Millions in the Air; 1936: Arizona Mahoney; Forgotten Faces; Desert Gold; Border Flight; Three Cheers for Love; Hollywood Boulevard; Lady Be Careful; The Accusing Finger; Hideaway Girl; 1937: Wells Fargo; Last Train From Madrid; Sophie Lang Goes West; Souls at Sea; 1938: College Swing; Touchdown Army; You and Me; The Texans; I Stand Accused; 1939: Three Smart Girls Grow Up; The Under-Pup; Rio; Everything Happens at Night; Charlie McCarthy — Detective; 1940: And One Was Beautiful; Private Affairs; Spring Parade; One Night in the Tropics; 1941: The Devil and Miss Jones; Free and Easy; Moon Over Miami; It Started With Eve; 1942: Kings Row; Saboteur; Between Us Girls; 1943: Forever and a Day; Princess O'Rourke; Flesh and Fantasy; 1945: You Came Along; 1946: The Bride Wore Boots; The Chase; 1947: Heaven Only Knows; The Lost Moment; 1948: Sleep My Love; The Accused; Let's Live a Little; 1949: Free for All; Reign of Terror/The Black Book; Tell It to the Judge; 1950: Paid in Full; The Petty Girl; For Heaven's Sake; 1951: The Barefoot Mailman; 1952: The First Time; 1953: Marry Me Again; 1954: Lucky Me; Dial M for Murder; 1955: How to Be Very, Very Popular; 1962: My Geisha; 1963: Beach Party; 1964: The Carpetbaggers; What a Way to Go!; 1966: Promise Her Anything; Stagecoach; 1967: Five Golden Dragons.

NY Stage: AS BLADE STANHOPE CONWAY: 1931: The Roof; 1933: Strange Orchestra.

AS BRICE HUTCHENS: 1934: Ziegfeld Follies of 1934.

AS ROBERT CUMMINGS: 1951: Faithfully Yours.

Select TV: 1952: Pattern for Glory (sp); 1952–53: My Hero (series); 1954: Twelve Angry Men (sp); 1955–59: The Bob Cummings Show/Love That Bob (series; and dir.); 1956: Special Announcement (sp); 1957: One Left Over (sp); 1958: Bomber's Moon (sp); 1961–62: The Bob Cummings Show (series); 1963: Last of the Private Eyes (sp); 1964–65: My Living Doll (series); 1969: Gidget Grows Up; 1973: The Great American Beauty Contest; Partners in Crime; 1978: Three on a Date.

TONY CURTIS

(BERNARD SCHWARTZ) BORN: BRONX, NY, JUNE 3, 1925.

The epitome of the postwar studio-manufactured star, handsome, dark-haired Tony Curtis, with his distinctive Bronx accent, worked his way up from the celluloid assembly line to prove himself a bona fide 1950s box-office attraction and a fine actor on several occasions. His was not, however, a dependable talent, and there were many missteps along the way, with Curtis only adding to the mediocrity. After serving in the navy during World War II, he studied at the Dramatic Workshop in New York, followed by stock company and Off Broadway work. His performance in a revival of *Golden Boy* led to an offer from Universal, who intended to groom him for big things, changing his name to Anthony Curtis and first giving him billing in the mild juvenile delinquent drama, *City Across the River*. He followed with several bit roles, including two hits: *Francis*, the first of the talking mule sagas, given two lines as a captain; and *Winchester '73*, a James Stewart western. With the studio public relations department working overtime, his face was becoming famous in fan magazines long before he'd made an impact on the big screen. When Universal decided to give him leads, they were in costume kitsch like *The Prince Who Was a Thief*, in which he donned earrings and a turban to romance Piper Laurie; *Son of Ali Baba*, a sequel of sorts, with Laurie again; and the Medieval romp, *The Black Shield of Falworth*, for which he was mercilessly ribbed because of his inappropriate, hard-to-conceal accent. He was cast as a boxer in programmers like *Flesh and Fury* and *The Square Jungle*; a football player in *All American*; a racecar driver in *Johnny Dark*; and a hood who pulls off a robbery based on the famous Brinks job in *Six Bridges to Cross*. At Paramount he did the entertaining, if inaccurate biopic, *Houdini* (they were both Hungarian after all), which was significant because it marked his first teaming with wife Janet Leigh, whom he had married in 1951.

Rescue came by way of Burt Lancaster, who asked Curtis to co-star with him in the circus drama, *Trapeze*, one of 1956's big hits. The following year, back with Lancaster in the hardboiled masterpiece *Sweet Smell of Success*, Curtis was at his best, playing an oily, fawning press agent and receiving unexpected praise. Suddenly he was on the "A" list, co-starring in the bloody *The Vikings*, clashing with Kirk Douglas and having his hand lopped off in the process; *Kings Go Forth*, where it was Frank Sinatra's turn to lose an appendage; and, most impressively, in Stanley Kramer's important racial drama, *The Defiant Ones*. As the bigoted Southern convict chained to Sidney Poitier, Curtis was impressive enough to earn an Oscar nomination. He peaked in 1959 when he and Jack Lemmon donned dresses for Billy Wilder's classic farce, *Some Like It Hot*. Most of the acclaim was heaped on Lemmon and Marilyn Monroe, but Curtis was no less brilliant, performing three deftly drawn characterizations, including a bespectacled millionaire with a voice suspiciously like Cary Grant's. He actually teamed with Grant in a second comedy release that year, *Operation Petticoat*, which made even more money. These were sandwiched in between three more with Leigh, *The Perfect Furlough*, *Who Was That Lady?*, and *Pepe*, the last two released in 1960, two years before they divorced.

Alongside Debbie Reynolds he gave a fine performance as a struggling musician in the worthwhile comedy-drama, *The Rat Race*, and then played Laurence Olivier's slaveboy in Stanley Kubrick's mighty spectacle, *Spartacus*. Two Universal star vehicles followed: the lightweight *The Great Impostor*, which allowed him

to don various disguises in this account of real-life con man Ferdinand Demara; and *The Outsider*, a somber look at the American Indian who helped raise the flag at Iwo Jima, for which he received some of his best reviews. (The movie failed badly and was re-edited in hopes of pulling in a different audience.) Curtis now began to rely on comedies, most of them of the fluffy 1960s variety, like *40 Pounds of Trouble*, a remake of *Little Miss Marker*, notable for its chase through Disneyland; *Wild and Wonderful*, which involved a French poodle and Curtis's second wife (1963–67), Christine Kaufman; the wretched *Goodbye Charlie*, in which he fell in love with former-man Debbie Reynolds; and *Sex and the Single Girl*, as a book editor in pursuit of Natalie Wood. In the drama-comedy, *Captain Newman, M.D.*, he supplied most of the humor as a fast-talking orderly, and in *The Great Race*, he amusingly sent up comic book heroes, as a daredevil dressed in white. He began to slide with European-made sex farces like *Arrivederci, Baby!* and *On My Way to the Crusades I Met a Girl Who…*, which was also known as *The Chastity Belt*. A temporary respite from this slump came with what would turn out to be his last hit, *The Boston Strangler*, in which he gave an engrossing and complex interpretation of its deranged protagonist, real-life accused serial killer Albert DeSalvo.

He failed to find an audience with an international all-star auto race movie, *Those Daring Young Men in Their Jaunty Jalopies*; an anti-war comedy, *Suppose They Gave a War and Nobody Came*; or a buddy flick with Charles Bronson, *You Can't Win 'em All*. In the 1970s his standing had fallen far enough that he turned to television, but the series, *The Persuaders*, with Roger Moore, didn't make it. There were still leads, in trashy fare like *Lepke*, as the real-life Jewish gangster; *The Manitou*, a horror tale in which he was a fake spiritualist; and a woeful sequel, *The Bad News Bears Go to Japan*. Not surprisingly he started taking supporting parts, playing the villain in another version of *Little Miss Marker*, and a character closely modeled on Senator Joseph McCarthy, in *Insignificance*. At least these were released to theatres, which was more than can be said for such career killers as *Alien X Factor* and *The Mummy Lives*. By now he'd lost most of the respect he'd earned from any commendable work he'd done in the past, and in interviews he came off as self-deluded. He could still rise to the occasion, as he did in *Naked in New York*, well-cast as a slick Broadway producer, but credits like *The Continued Adventures of Reptile Man* suggested a man who had no qualms about tossing dignity right out the window. Dabbling in writing, his works have included the novel *Kid Andrew Cody & Julie Sparrow* (1977), and *Tony Curtis: The Autobiography* (1994). One of his daughters, from his marriage to Leigh, is actress Jamie Lee Curtis.

Screen: AS ANTHONY CURTIS: 1949: Criss Cross; Take One False Step; City Across the River; The Lady Gambles; Johnny Stool Pigeon; Francis; 1950: Sierra; I Was a Shoplifter; Winchester '73. AS TONY CURTIS: 1950: Kansas Raiders; 1951: The Prince Who Was a Thief; 1952: Flesh and Fury; Meet Danny Wilson; No Room for the Groom; Son of Ali Baba; 1953: Houdini; All American; Forbidden; 1954: Beachhead; Johnny Dark; The Black Shield of Falworth; So This Is Paris; 1955: The Purple Mask; Six Bridges to Cross; The Square Jungle; 1956: Trapeze; The Rawhide Years; 1957: Mister Cory; The Midnight Story; Sweet Smell of Success; 1958: The Vikings; Kings Go Forth; The Defiant Ones; The Perfect Furlough; 1959: Some Like It Hot; Operation Petticoat; 1960: Who Was That Lady?; The Rat Race; Spartacus; Pepe; 1961: The Great Impostor; The Outsider; 1962: Taras Bulba; 1963: 40 Pounds of Trouble; The List of Adrian Messenger; Captain Newman, M.D.; 1964: Paris — When It Sizzles; Wild and Wonderful; Goodbye Charlie; Sex and the

Single Girl; **1965:** The Great Race; Boeing Boeing; **1966:** Not With My Wife You Don't!; Chamber of Horrors; Arrivederci, Baby!/Drop Dead Darling; **1967:** Don't Make Waves; **1968:** Rosemary's Baby (voice); The Boston Strangler; **1969:** On My Way to the Crusades I Met a Girl Who… /The Chastity Belt; Those Daring Young Men in Their Jaunty Jalopies/Monte Carlo or Bust; **1970:** Suppose They Gave a War and Nobody Came?; You Can't Win 'em All; **1975:** Lepke; **1976:** The Last Tycoon; **1978:** The Manitou; The Bad News Bears Go to Japan; Sextette; **1979:** Some Like It Cool/Casanova & Co./Sex on the Run; It Rained All Night the Day I Left (dtv); Double Take (nUSr); **1980:** Little Miss Marker; The Mirror Crack'd; **1981:** Title Shot; **1982:** Othello the Black Commando (nUSr); **1983:** Brainwaves; **1984:** Where Is Parsifal? (nUSr); **1985:** Insignificance; **1986:** Balboa (dtv); Club Life; **1988:** The Last of Philip Banter; Welcome to Germany (nUSr); **1989:** Midnight; Walter & Carlo in America (nUSr); **1990:** Lobster Man From Mars; **1991:** Prime Target; **1992:** Center of the Web; **1993:** The Mummy Lives (dtv); **1994:** Naked in New York; **1995:** The Immortals (dtv); **1996:** The Celluloid Closet; **1997:** Hardball (dtv); Brittle Glory/The Continued Adventures of Reptile Man (nUSr); Alien X Factor (dtv); **1998:** Louis and Frank (dtv); Stargames (nUSr); **1999:** Play It to the Bone.

Select TV: **1957:** Cornada (sp); **1958:** Man on a Rock (sp); **1959:** The Stone (sp); **1971–72:** The Persuaders (series); **1973:** The Third Girl From the Left; **1975:** The Count of Monte Cristo; The Big Rip-Off; **1975–76:** McCoy (series); **1978:** The Users; **1978–81:** Vega$ (series); **1980:** Moviola: The Scarlett O'Hara War; **1981:** Inmates: A Love Story; The Million Dollar Face; **1982:** Portrait of a Showgirl; **1985:** Half Nelson; **1986:** Mafia Princess; Agatha Christie's Murder in Three Acts; **1989:** Tarzan in Manhattan; **1990:** Thanksgiving Day; **1992:** Christmas in Connecticut; **1994:** A Perry Mason Mystery: The Case of the Grimacing Governor; Bandit: Beauty and the Bandit; **1997:** Elvis Meets Nixon.

PETER CUSHING

BORN: KENLEY, SURREY, ENGLAND, MAY 26, 1913. ED: GUILDHALL SCHOOL OF MUSIC AND DRAMA. DIED: AUGUST 11, 1994.

Gaunt and elegant, with coldly calculating eyes, Peter Cushing had been acting for over 20 years when he became a top name in the field of horror, a genre to which he brought considerable intelligence and dignity. Although he spent most of his career working in his native country, he actually made his movie debut in Hollywood, in 1939, in *The Man in the Iron Mask*. (He was hired to be Louis Hayward's stand-in when the actor was required to "share" a scene with his double, but he got a bit part as well.) A handful of other American productions preceded his return to England during World War II, where he appeared with the Entertainment National Services Association. His debut in a British film was in Laurence Olivier's 1948 Oscar-winning version of *Hamlet*, as the foppish Osric. He toured with the Old Vic, and was extraordinarily busy during the early days of live television. On the big screen, his roles ranged from his brief bit as a racing spectator in John Huston's made-in-England *Moulin Rouge*, to the central role of Deborah Kerr's cuckolded husband in the first attempt to film Graham Greene's *The End of the Affair*. His fortunes changed forever in 1957 when he was cast as Dr. Frankenstein in Hammer Studios's color version of the famous Shelley novel. Given the expanded title of *The Curse of Frankenstein*, it featured Christopher Lee as the Monster, and the success of the film was such that both Cushing's and Lee's names

would become synonymous with the studio. They co-starred in countless horror movies and were much-loved by those who found these frequently verbose, frequently bloody offerings to their taste. Other classics tales were dusted off, resulting in *Horror of Dracula*, with Cushing as Dr. Van Helsing, and *The Mummy*, as the archaeologist who revives the title character.

Eager to tap the vein for all it was worth, Hammer asked Cushing to reprise Van Helsing in *The Brides of Dracula*; *Dracula A.D. 1972*, which modernized the tale and therefore meant Cushing was playing a descendant of the famed vampire hunter; *Legend of the Seven Golden Vampires*, which brought martial arts into the mix; and *The Satanic Rites of Dracula/Count Dracula and His Vampire Bride*. Meanwhile Dr. Frankenstein reemerged no fewer than five times in *The Revenge of Frankenstein*, hiding under the name of Dr. Stein; *The Evil of Frankenstein*; *Frankenstein Created Woman*, in which the reincarnated creature was played by a Playboy centerfold; *Frankenstein Must Be Destroyed!*; and *Frankenstein and the Monster From Hell*. Hammer also allowed him to play Sherlock Holmes, in a remake of *The Hound of the Baskervilles*, but the character was never revived for a studio series, although Cushing would later play him again on television. The actor would occasionally be invited to essay a straight role in outside productions like *John Paul Jones* and *The Naked Edge*, but it was clear where his fame rested. When he wasn't stitching together monsters or staking out vampires, the studio made him a doctor in league with real-life body snatchers Burke and Hare in *Mania/The Flesh and the Fiends*, one of Hammer's most popular offerings; a notorious smuggler in *Captain Clegg/Night Creatures*; the Sheriff of Nottingham in *Sword of Sherwood Forest*; the absent-minded Dr. Who in two features based on the cult British television series; and a Scrooge-like bank manager in one of his personal favorites, *Cash on Demand*. In 1977 he received his widest exposure ever when he played the evil Grand Moff Tarkin in the enormously successful *Star Wars*. Far from the sinister characters he played on screen, Cushing was frequently spoken of by colleagues as a gentle and gentlemanly actor. Following his retirement he published a pair of autobiographies: *Peter Cushing — An Autobiography* (1986); and *Past Forgetting: Memoirs of the Hammer Years* (1988).

Screen: **1939:** The Man in the Iron Mask; **1940:** A Chump at Oxford; Vigil in the Night; Laddie; Women in War; **1941:** They Dare Not Love; **1948:** Hamlet; **1952:** Moulin Rouge; **1954:** The Black Knight; **1955:** The End of the Affair; **1956:** Magic Fire; Alexander the Great; Time Without Pity; **1957:** The Curse of Frankenstein; The Abominable Snowman of the Himalayas; **1958:** Violent Playground; Horror of Dracula/Dracula; The Revenge of Frankenstein; **1959:** The Hound of the Baskervilles; John Paul Jones; The Mummy; **1960:** Mania/The Flesh and the Fiends; The Brides of Dracula; **1961:** The Risk/Suspect; Trouble in the Sky/Cone of Silence; The Naked Edge; Sword of Sherwood Forest; The Hellfire Club; **1962:** Cash on Demand; Night Creatures/Captain Clegg; The Man Who Finally Died; **1964:** The Evil of Frankenstein; Fury at Smugglers' Bay (UK: 1961); **1965:** She; The Gorgon; Dr. Terror's House of Horrors; The Skull; **1966:** Dr. Who and the Daleks; Daleks — Invasion Earth 2150 A.D.; **1967:** Island of Terror; Frankenstein Created Woman; **1968:** The Mummy's Shroud (narrator); Torture Garden; Corruption; The Vampire Beast Craves Blood/The Blood Beast Terror; **1970:** Frankenstein Must Be Destroyed!; One More Time; Scream and Scream Again; The Vampire Lovers; **1971:** The House That Dripped Blood; The Bloodsuckers/Incense for the Damned; **1972:** Tales From the Crypt; Dr. Phibes Rises Again; Twins of Evil; Asylum; Dracula A.D. 1972; **1973:** Island of the Burning Damned/Island of the Burning Doomed/Night of the

Big Heat (UK: 1967); The Creeping Flesh; And Now the Screaming Starts; **1974:** Frankenstein and the Monster From Hell; Horror Express; Madhouse; I, Monster (UK: 1971); Fear in the Night (UK: 1972); The Beast Must Die; **1975:** Tender Dracula; The Ghoul; Legend of the Werewolf (nUSr); Call Him Mr. Shatter; Nothing But the Night/The Resurrection Syndicate (UK: 1972); From Beyond the Grave/The Creatures From Beyond the Grave (UK: 1973); **1976:** At the Earth's Core; Dirty Knight's Work/Trial by Combat; **1977:** Star Wars; Shock Waves/Death Corps (UK: 1975); Land of the Minotaur/The Devil's Men; The Uncanny (nUSr); Battle Flag (nUSr); **1978:** Hitler's Son/Son of Hitler (nUSr); Touch of the Sun (nUSr); Count Dracula and His Vampire Bride/Satanic Rites of Dracula (UK: 1973); **1979:** The Seven Brothers Meet Dracula/Legend of the 7 Golden Vampires (UK: 1974); Arabian Adventure; **1981:** Monster Island; Black Jack (nUSr); **1984:** House of the Long Shadows; Top Secret!; Sword of the Valiant; **1988:** Biggles: Adventures in Time (filmed 1985).

NY Stage: 1941: The Seventh Trumpet.

Select TV: 1965: Monica (sp); 1966: Some May Live/In Saigon Some May Live; 1967: Sherlock Holmes; 1976: The Great Houdinis; 1980: A Tale of Two Cities; 1984: Helen Keller: The Miracle Continues; Masks of Death.

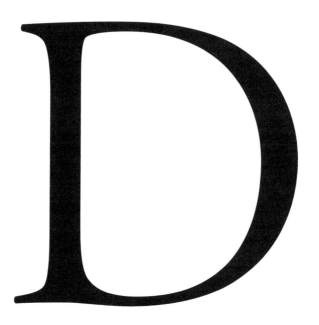

ARLENE DAHL

BORN: MINNEAPOLIS, MN, AUGUST 11, 1924.

It was clear to even the least demanding of audiences that Arlene Dahl's career was based more on her looks than on any special gifts as an actress. In fact, she wrote a regular column on the subject of beauty and held a position as National Beauty Advisor for Sears Roebuck & Company. An early job as a buyer for Marshall Field department stores led to modeling assignments in New York that, in turn, took her to a Broadway flop, *Mr. Strauss Goes to Boston*. Chorus work at the Latin Quarter nightclub won her a contract with Warner Bros., where she was featured as the inspiration for that famous tune in the songwriter biopic, *My Wild Irish Rose*. MGM picked up her contract and promptly put her into three Red Skelton films, of which *Three Little Words* was the standout, allowing her to sing such Kalmar and Ruby songs as "I Love You So Much." But her roles at MGM were no more interesting than those at Warners and she was soon looking elsewhere for work. There were bland programmers like *Caribbean*, with John Payne; *Jamaica Run*, with Ray Milland; and two with Fernando Lamas, *Sangaree* and *The Diamond Queen*, both released in 1953. (She and Lamas married the next year.) Dahl got a rare chance to shine, as Rhonda Fleming's ex-con sister in *Slightly Scarlet*, and got top-billing in the colorful 1959 adaptation of Jules Verne's *Journey to the Center of the Earth*. In the 1960s she began to publish her line of Beautyscope books, which combined beauty care with astrology, and although this was the more dominant part of her career, she still pursued occasional acting jobs. She appeared on Broadway in *Applause*, in the daytime serial *One Life to Live*, and the quickie feature *Night of the Warrior*, which starred her son, Lorenzo Lamas. Prior to her marriage to Fernando Lamas (which ended in 1960) she had been wed (1951–52) to actor Lex Barker.

Screen: 1947: Life With Father; My Wild Irish Rose; 1948: The Bride Goes Wild; A Southern Yankee; 1949: Reign of Terror/The Black Book; Scene of the Crime; Ambush; 1950: The Outriders; Three Little Words; Watch the Birdie; 1951: Inside Straight; No Questions Asked; 1952: Caribbean; 1953: Jamaica Run; Desert Legion; Sangaree; The Diamond Queen; Here Come the Girls; 1954: Woman's World; Bengal Brigade; 1956: Slightly Scarlet; 1957: Wicked as They Come; 1958: She Played With Fire/Fortune Is a Woman; 1959: Journey to the Center of the Earth; 1964: Kisses for My President; 1968: Le Poneyettes (nUSr); 1969: The Road to Katmandu (nUSr); 1970: Land Raiders; 1972: Sotto a Chi Tocca! (nUSr); 1991: Night of the Warrior.

NY Stage: 1945: Mr. Strauss Goes to Boston; 1953: Cyrano de Bergerac; 1972: Applause.

Select TV: 1953: Pepsi Cola Playhouse (series); 1954: Wedding March (sp); September Affair (sp); 1958: Opening Night (series); 1981–84: One Life to Live (series).

DAN DAILEY

BORN: NEW YORK, NY, DECEMBER 14, 1914.
DIED: OCTOBER 16, 1978.

Dan Dailey's towering height seemed to preclude any success as a dancer, but he was a most capable hoofer in some of Fox's major musicals, in addition to being quite a decent actor. A former vaudevillian and minstrel man, he came to Broadway (as Dan Dailey, Jr.) as part of the ensemble of *Babes in Arms*, in 1937, then advanced to a bigger part in *Stars in Your Eyes*, two years later. MGM signed him up, initially casting him as a Nazi in *The Mortal Storm*; then as a juvenile lead in a Charles Coburn comedy, *The Captain Is a Lady*; and as a supporting player in three Frank Morgan vehicles, *Hullabaloo*, *Washington Melodrama*, and *The Wild Man of Borneo*. He was way down the cast lists of *Lady Be Good* and *Ziegfeld Girl*, but took starring roles in a pair of "B" films: *Mokey*, as a newly-remarried dad with a petulant child, Robert Blake; and *Sunday Punch*, as a boxer battling William Lundigan over Jean Rogers. After five years of war service he returned to a new studio, 20th Century-Fox, to co-star with Betty Grable in *Mother Wore Tights*, a nostalgic story about a couple of vaudevillians. The studio put them together three more times, starting with *When My Baby Smiles at Me*, which gave Dailey a meaty dramatic role as an alcoholic burlesque comedian. The performance was good enough to earn him an Oscar nomination and he later reprised the part on television in

Burlesque, the original title of the play on which the movie was based. More typical of the Grable/Dailey pairings were *My Blue Heaven*, where they were radio stars, and *Call Me Mister*, which involved a USO troupe.

Having proven himself as a serious actor, Dailey continued in dramatic roles in such films as *I Can Get It for You Wholesale* (although the ambitious social climber of the novel was re-written for Susan Hayward), and *The Pride of St. Louis*, as baseball great Dizzy Dean, whose flaw, according to the script, was immaturity. Dailey's musical assignments were in familiar fare like *You're My Everything*, trying to keep daughter Shari Robinson out of the limelight; *Give My Regards to Broadway*, where he and Charles Winninger were a father-and-son juggling team; and *The Girl Next Door*, as a cartoonist who falls for June Haver. He was lost in the all-star cast of *There's No Business Like Show Business*, where he married Ethel Merman and produced Donald O'Connor and Mitzi Gaynor as offspring, but he really shone as a disillusioned ad-man in MGM's Gene Kelly-Stanley Donen project, *It's Always Fair Weather*. (At one point he joined Kelly and Michael Kidd in a glorious dance using garbage can lids.) He played composer Ray Henderson in the biopic *The Best Things in Life Are Free*; fell for stripper Jayne Mansfield as a passenger on *The Wayward Bus*; and was a boozy movie director in the star-laden *Pepe*, dancing for the last time on screen, with Maurice Chevalier and Cantinflas. He ended his career in nightclubs and on television, where he starred in such series as *The Governor* and *J.J.* and *Faraday and Company*. His sister was actress Irene Dailey, best known for starring in the original Broadway production of *The Subject Was Roses*.

Screen: 1940: The Mortal Storm; The Captain Is a Lady; Hullabaloo; Keeping Company; Dulcy; Susan and God; 1941: Ziegfeld Girl; Washington Melodrama; The Wild Man of Borneo; The Get-Away; Lady Be Good; Down in San Diego; Moon Over Her Shoulder; 1942: Mokey; Sunday Punch; Panama Hattie; Timber; Give Out, Sisters; 1947: Mother Wore Tights; 1948: You Were Meant for Me; Give My Regards to Broadway; Chicken Every Sunday; When My Baby Smiles at Me; 1949: You're My Everything; 1950: When Willie Comes Marching Home; A Ticket to Tomahawk; I'll Get By; My Blue Heaven; 1951: I Can Get It for You Wholesale; Call Me Mister; 1952: The Pride of St. Louis; What Price Glory?; 1953: Meet Me at the Fair; Taxi; The Girl Next Door; The Kid From Left Field; 1954: There's No Business Like Show Business; 1955: It's Always Fair Weather; 1956: Meet Me in Las Vegas; The Best Things in Life Are Free; 1957: The Wings of Eagles; Oh, Men! Oh, Women!; The Wayward Bus; 1958: Underwater Warrior; 1960: Pepe; 1962: Hemingway's Adventures of a Young Man; 1978: The Private Files of J. Edgar Hoover.

NY Stage: 1937: Babes in Arms; 1939: Stars in Your Eyes; 1965: Catch Me If You Can; 1969: Plaza Suite.

Select TV: 1955: Burlesque (sp); 1956: Paris in the Springtime (sp); 1959: Four Just Men (series); 1969–70: The Governor and J.J. (series); 1971: Mr. and Mrs. Bo Jo Jones; 1972: Michael O'Hara the Fourth (sp); 1973–74: Faraday and Company (series); 1975: The Daughters of Joshua Cabe Return; 1977: Testimony of Two Men (ms).

JOHN DALL

(JOHN JENNER THOMPSON) BORN: NEW YORK, NY, MAY 26, 1918. ED: COLUMBIA UNIV. DIED: JANUARY 15, 1971.

Tall and thin, with a slightly superior air, John Dall had a short but interesting film résumé. With a few years of Broadway credits behind him, including one of the leads in the popular comedy *Dear Ruth*, he won the plum role of the Welsh coal miner whose limited life is improved by schoolteacher Bette Davis in *The Corn Is Green*. Dall was perhaps a bit too polished to lend credence to his lowly origins, but his performance resulted in a 1945 Oscar nomination for Best Supporting Actor. Warners, who released the film, did not use him again for another three years, so he starred in Universal's *Something in the Wind*, with two of that studio's biggest attractions, Donald O'Connor and Deanna Durbin, where Dall, not O'Connor, got to be her leading man. Back at Warners he played to his strength as Farley Granger's sinister and deadly lover in Alfred Hitchcock's experimental *Rope*. (He had been cast because the director had wanted an actual gay man in the role.) The following year he led a life of crime with Peggy Cummins in one of the true cult noir classics of the period, *Gun Crazy*, then spent much of the next decade on the small screen. He returned to the movies as the snooty Roman, Glabrus, who is defeated and humiliated by Kirk Douglas's army of slaves in the epic *Spartacus*, and was the villain in the period costumer, *Atlantis — The Lost Continent*, a fantasy aimed principally at children.

Screen: 1945: The Corn Is Green; 1947: Something in the Wind; 1948: Rope; Another Part of the Forest; 1949: Gun Crazy; 1950: The Man Who Cheated Himself; 1960: Spartacus; 1961: Atlantis — The Lost Continent.

NY Stage: 1942: Janie; R.U.R.; 1944: Dear Ruth; 1948: Red Gloves; 1955: Champagne Complex.

Select TV: 1952: The Doctor's Wife (sp); Outward Bound (sp); 1953: The Hasty Heart (sp); 1958: The Coward of Fort Bennett (sp); 1959: And Practically Strangers (sp).

DOROTHY DANDRIDGE

BORN: CLEVELAND, OH, NOVEMBER 9, 1923. DIED: SEPTEMBER 8, 1965.

A groundbreaking performer, whose personal life was steeped in sadness and cut tragically short, Dorothy Dandridge was in show business by the age of four, singing with her sister in a stage act called The Wonder Children. This led to the sisters appearing in some guest spots and Dorothy's solo debut, for Metro, singing in a shanty town in the Marx Brothers' *A Day at the Races*. She took the female lead in a Mantan Moreland comedy, *Four Shall Die*; played an African native in *Drums of the Congo*; and performed the famous "Chattanooga Choo-Choo" number with the Nicholas Brothers in *Sun Valley Serenade*. She was unhappily wed (1942–49) to one of the brothers, Harold, and the couple produced a mentally handicapped daughter. Dandridge was able to establish herself as a nightclub singer, although racism resulted in such indignities as not being permitted to use the facilities of the Las Vegas hotel where she was performing. A successful engagement at the Mocambo in the early 1950s, led to a second stint in Hollywood, where she rated substantial roles in such movies as *The Harlem Globetrotters*, as the love interest of real-life basketball star Billy Brown; *Tarzan's Peril*, giving the role of a native queen more than it deserved; and *Bright Road*, as a kindly schoolteacher opposite Harry Belafonte. In 1954, teamed again with Belafonte, she played the title role in Otto Preminger's adaptation of the operetta *Carmen Jones*, giving a fiery, sexy performance as the heartless, flirtatious tramp. She made history by becoming the very first black performer to receive an Oscar nomination for a leading role, but this did not mean that work came fast and furious. It was another three years before she showed up on the big screen again, in the interracial soaper *Island in the Sun*, which once again featured Belafonte, although her love interest was Caucasian John Justin. She was Preminger's natural choice for Bess in his 1959 version of *Porgy and Bess*, although, as in *Carmen*, her singing voice was dubbed. By 1962 she had declared bankruptcy, and three years later she was found dead of a drug overdose in her Hollywood apartment. In 1970 her autobiography, *Everything and Nothing: The Dorothy Dandridge Tragedy*, was published.

Screen: 1936: Easy to Take; 1937: A Day at the Races; It Can't Last Forever; 1940: Irene; Four Shall Die; 1941: Lady From Louisiana; Sundown; Sun Valley Serenade; Bahama Passage; 1942: Drums of the Congo; Lucky Jordan; 1943: Hit Parade of 1943; 1944: Since You Went Away; Atlantic City; 1945: Pillow to Post; 1947: Ebony Parade; 1951: Tarzan's Peril; The Harlem Globetrotters; 1953: Bright Road; Remains to Be Seen; 1954: Carmen Jones; 1957: Island in the Sun; 1958: The Decks Ran Red; 1959: Porgy and Bess; Tamango (filmed 1957); 1960: Malaga/Moment of Danger.

NY Stage: 1939: Swingin' the Dream.

Select TV: 1962: The Murder Men (sp).

HENRY DANIELL

(CHARLES HENRY DANIELL) BORN: LONDON, ENGLAND, MARCH 5, 1894. DIED: OCTOBER 31, 1963.

Was there ever a character actor whose immediate appearance was so adamantly unfriendly as Henry Daniell? Suave and cold-eyed, with a down-turned mouth and a withering voice, he was one of the movies' best villains. His London stage career began as England went to war in 1914, and in the 1920s he sailed to America, working in such Broadway plays as *The Second Mrs. Tanqueray* and *Serena Blandish*. At the dawn of sound he made his film debut, as a murder suspect in the 1929 Fredric March vehicle, *Jealousy*, and later that same year starred opposite Ina Claire, who was recreating her stage role, in *The Awful Truth*. After a handful of other movie assignments he returned to the stage to score a great success playing a killer in *Kind Lady*, which immediately landed him back in Hollywood. His memorable performance as the sarcastic Baron de Varville in George Cukor's hit costume melodrama, *Camille*, easily stole the notices from leading man Robert Taylor. Cukor became a great admirer of Daniell's skills and called on him again for *Holiday*, as Katharine Hepburn's self-righteous cousin; *The Philadelphia Story*, as the insensitive *Spy* magazine editor; and *A Woman's Face*, as a lawyer. In *Under Cover of Night*, he played a callous physicist whose ambition leads him to commit multiple murders, even coaxing Sara Haden's dog to leap out a window to its death!

He conspired to break up Errol Flynn's romance with Bette Davis in *The Private Lives of Elizabeth and Essex*, and engaged Flynn in the memorable, shadow-enhanced duel in the grand adventure film *The Sea Hawk*. He made an ideal Nazi, first in a satirical vein, as Chaplin's right-hand man, Herr Garbitsch, in *The Great Dictator*, and then, more seriously, in *Reunion in France*, *Watch on the Rhine*, and *Mission to Moscow*, as the real-life von Ribbentrop. At his peak in the mid-1940s, he was perfectly cast as Professor Moriarty in *The Woman in Green*; got his just desserts for blackmailing murderer Charles Laughton in *The Suspect*; and reached a pinnacle of loathsomeness as the sadistic schoolmaster, Brocklehurst, in *Jane Eyre*. In 1945 he played his largest role, as the doctor who foolishly employs Boris Karloff as a grave robber in Val Lewton's chiller, *The Body Snatchers*. Two historical roles, as King William III in *Captain Kidd*, and Franz

Liszt in MGM's dreary *Song of Love*, preceded a pair of forgettable late-1940s efforts: *The Bandit of Sherwood Forest*, wickedly plotting to kill the young King Henry III; and *Wake of the Red Witch*, as Gail Russell's dad. When he was asked to support Maria Montez and Yvonne de Carlo in the kitschy costume spectacles *Siren of Atlantis* and *Buccaneer's Girl*, respectively, it was apparent that his best years were over. By the 1950s his assignments got smaller, although he could still be counted on for his colorful delivery in such good movies as *Lust for Life*, as Van Gogh's father, and *Witness for the Prosecution*, as a barrister. Back with Cukor again, he had a minuscule role as the Prince of Transylvania in *My Fair Lady*, but collapsed on the set and died during production.

Screen: 1929: Jealousy; The Awful Truth; 1930: The Last of the Lone Wolf; 1934: Path of Glory; 1936: The Unguarded Hour; Camille; 1937: The Thirteenth Chair; Madame X; Under Cover of Night; The Firefly; 1938: Marie Antoinette; Holiday; 1939: The Private Lives of Elizabeth and Essex; We Are Not Alone; 1940: The Philadelphia Story; The Great Dictator; All This, and Heaven Too; The Sea Hawk; 1941: A Woman's Face; The Feminine Touch; Dressed to Kill; Four Jacks and a Jill; 1942: Random Harvest; Reunion in France; The Great Impersonation; Nightmare; Castle in the Desert; Sherlock Holmes and the Voice of Terror; 1943: Watch on the Rhine; Mission to Moscow; Sherlock Holmes in Washington; 1944: Jane Eyre; The Suspect; 1945: The Body Snatcher; Hotel Berlin; The Woman in Green; Captain Kidd; The Chicago Kid; 1946: The Bandit of Sherwood Forest; 1947: Song of Love; The Exile; 1948: Wake of the Red Witch; Siren of Atlantis; 1949: The Secret of St. Ives; 1950: Buccaneer's Girl; 1954: The Egyptian; 1955: The Prodigal; 1956: Diane; Lust for Life; The Man in the Gray Flannel Suit; 1957: Les Girls; The Sun Also Rises; The Story of Mankind; Mister Cory; Witness for the Prosecution; 1958: From the Earth to the Moon; 1959: The Four Skulls of Jonathan Drake; 1961: Voyage to the Bottom of the Sea; The Comancheros; 1962: The Chapman Report; The Notorious Landlady; Madison Avenue; Five Weeks in a Balloon; Mutiny on the Bounty; 1964: My Fair Lady.

NY Stage: 1921: Clair de Lune; 1924: The Second Mrs. Tanqueray; 1929: Serena Blandish; 1935: Kind Lady; 1943: Murder Without Crime; Lovers and Friends; 1946: The Winter's Tale; 1946: Lady Windermere's Fan; 1949: That Lady; 1953: My Three Angels; 1963: Lord Pengo.

Select TV: 1950: The Marriages (sp); 1951: The Target (sp); 1955: The Smuggler (sp); 1956: The Barretts of Wimpole Street (sp); Confession (sp); 1957: The Little Minister (sp); 1959: The Wings of the Dove (sp); My Three Angels (sp); 1960: Tory Vengeance (sp).

BEBE DANIELS

(PHYLLIS DANIELS) BORN: DALLAS, TX, JANUARY 14, 1901. DIED: MARCH 16, 1971.

An actress whose long career took her through many phases, Bebe Daniels started out as a child performer in her dad's own company, even doing a bit of Shakespeare. Her mom, a casting director, was instrumental in helping her start in films, and as early as 1908 she was working in short subjects. She was a mere 14 years old when she first appeared as Harold Lloyd's leading lady in his "Lonesome Luke" comedies, starting with *Luke Laughs Out*, in 1916. She would act in more than 40 entries in the one-reeler series over a two-year period, and, when Lloyd dropped the character of Luke, he retained Daniels's services for dozens of other shorts, finally ending their successful partnership in 1919. Cecil B. DeMille signed her to a contract that same year, and throughout the 1920s she would become a dependable addition to Paramount, bouncing between comedy and drama, in such movies as *The Affairs of Anatol*, as a naughty lady called Satan Synne; *Nice People*, with Wallace Reid; *The World's Applause*, a showbiz murder mystery; *The Glimpses of the Moon*, from an Edith Wharton novel; *Monsieur Beaucaire*, supporting Rudolph Valentino, in one of his biggest hits; *Dangerous Money*, as a naïve heiress; *The Crowded Hour*, a backstage drama; *Miss Brewster's Millions*, a distaff variation on the oft-filmed tale; *Senorita* and *She's a Shiek*, in both instances donning mannish garb for some swashbuckling adventures; and *Feel My Pulse*, as a hypochondriac.

When talkies came she was no longer considered a significant asset to the company and her contract was ended, prompting her to sign up with the newly established RKO. Fortunately, her first sound feature, a cumbersome musical based on a Broadway show, *Rio Rita*, in which she sang and spoke with a Spanish accent, was one of the big hits of 1929. A follow-up, *Dixiana*, which, like the previous film, had comedians Wheeler and Woolsey around for box-office insurance, did not find much favor and, after a brief stay, RKO sent her on her way. Among the more notable of her early 1930s films were *Alias French Gertie*, which teamed her with Ben Lyon, whom she married in 1930, and the earlier, lesser version of *The Maltese Falcon*, as femme fatale Bridget Shaughnessy. In 1933 she played to the hilt the part that would give her lasting fame, temperamental stage star Dorothy Brock, whose sprained ankle allows Ruby Keeler to take her place in the groundbreaking musical, *42nd Street*. That same year she was at her best as John Barrymore's loyal and loving secretary in the potent drama *Counsellor-at-Law*, before taking her last Hollywood role, one not unlike Dorothy Brock, playing a fading actress who is replaced by Alice Faye, in *Music Is Magic*. With Lyon she sailed to England where the couple hosted the wartime radio show, *Hi Gang!*, and, afterwards, *Life With the Lyons*, which transferred to television and spawned minor movie spin-offs. During a brief return to the U.S., Daniels wrote and produced the comedy *The Fabulous Joe*.

Screen (features): 1919: Male and Female; Everywoman; 1920: Why Change Your Wife?; Dancin' Fool; Sick Abed; The Fourteenth Man; You Never Can Tell; Oh Lady Lady; 1921: Two Weeks With Pay; She Couldn't Help It; Ducks and Drakes; The March Hare; One Wild Week; The Affairs of Anatol; The Speed Girl; 1922: Nancy From Nowhere; A Game Chicken; North of the Rio Grande; Nice People; Pink Gods; Singed Wings; 1923: The World's Applause; The Glimpses of the Moon; The Exciters; His Children's Children; 1924: Heritage of the Desert; Daring Youth; Unguarded Women; Monsieur Beaucaire; Sinners in Heaven; Dangerous Money; Argentine Love; 1925: Miss Bluebeard; The Crowded Hour; The Manicure Girl; Wild Wild Susan; Lovers in Quarantine; The Splendid Crime; 1926: Miss Brewster's Millions; Volcano; The Palm Beach Girl; The Campus Flirt; Stranded in Paris; 1927: A Kiss in a Taxi; Senorita; Swim, Girl, Swim; She's a Sheik; 1928: The Fifty-Fifty Girl; Hot News; Feel My Pulse; Take Me Home; What a Night!; 1929: Rio Rita; 1930: Love Comes Along; Alias French Gertie; Lawful Larceny; Dixiana; 1931: Reaching for the Moon; My Past; The Maltese Falcon; Honor of the Family; 1932: Silver Dollar; 1933: 42nd Street; Cocktail Hour; The Song You Gave Me; A Southern Maid; Counsellor-at-Law; 1934: Registered Nurse; 1935: Music Is Magic; 1939: Not Wanted on Voyage; The Return of Carol Dean; 1941: Hi Gang!; 1953: Life With the Lyons/Family Affair; 1954: The Lyons in Paris.

Select TV: 1955: Life With the Lyons (series).

ROYAL DANO

BORN: NEW YORK, NY, NOVEMBER 16, 1922.
DIED: MAY 15, 1994.

Cadaverous-looking, with a wobbly, unsettling voice to match, Royal Dano came to films in 1950 following some stage work in New York. For the next 40 years he racked up extensive television and film credits, often in unsympathetic roles, and usually in westerns or rural settings. His appearances out West include *The Red Badge of Courage*, as the Tattered Man; *Bend of the River*, as one of the gunmen out to kill James Stewart; *Johnny Guitar*, as a sickly outlaw gunned down by Ernest Borgnine; *Man of the West*, as the mute member of Lee J. Cobb's gang; *Cimarron*, as a photographer; the fantasy *7 Faces of Dr. Lao*, as a troublemaker who unleashes a giant sea serpent; *The Undefeated*, as a one-armed Confederate major; and *Skin Game*, ideally cast as abolitionist John Brown. In other genres he could be seen as the deputy sheriff in Alfred Hithcock's missing corpse comedy, *The Trouble With Harry*; a whaler on board the Pequod in *Moby Dick*; and apostle Peter in the 1961 version of *King of Kings*. His least-known and most widely attended role is an uncredited one: supplying the voice of the animatronic Abraham Lincoln in the Hall of Presidents in the Disney theme parks.

Screen: 1950: Undercover Girl; Under the Gun; 1951: The Red Badge of Courage; Flame of Araby; 1952: Bend of the River; Carrie; 1954: Johnny Guitar; 1955: The Far Country; The Trouble With Harry; 1956: Tribute to a Bad Man; Moby Dick; Santiago; Tension at Table Rock; 1957: All Mine to Give; Man in the Shadow; Crime of Passion; Trooper Hook; 1958: Saddle the Wind; Handle With Care; Man of the West; 1959: Never Steal Anything Small; These Thousand Hills; Hound-Dog Man; The Boy and the Bridge; Face of Fire; 1960: The Adventures of Huckleberry Finn; Cimarron; 1961: King of Kings; Posse From Hell; 1962: Savage Sam; 1964: 7 Faces of Dr. Lao; 1965: Gunpoint; 1967: Welcome to Hard Times; The Last Challenge; 1968: Day of the Evil Gun; If He Hollers, Let Him Go; 1969: The Undefeated; Death of a Gunfighter; 1970: Machismo/40 Graves for 40 Guns; 1971: Chandler; Skin Game; The Great Northfield Minnesota Raid; 1972: The Culpepper Cattle Co.; Howzer; 1973: Ace Eli and Rodger of the Skies; Cahill — U.S. Marshal; Electra Guide in Blue; 1974: Big Bad Mama; Messiah of Evil/Dead People; 1975: The Wild Party; Capone; 1976: The Killer Inside Me; Drum; The Outlaw Josey Wales; 1977: Hughes and Harlow: Angels in Hell; 1978: Bad Georgia Road; One Man Jury; 1980: In Search of Historic Jesus; 1981: Take This Job and Shove It; 1982: Hammett; 1983: Something Wicked This Way Comes; The Right Stuff; 1984: Teachers; 1986: Cocaine Wars; Red-Headed Stranger; 1987: House II: The Second Story; 1988: Ghoulies 2; Killer Klowns From Outer Space; 1990: Spaced Invaders; 1991: Joey Takes a Cab; 1993: The Dark Half.

NY Stage: 1947: Finian's Rainbow; 1949: Mrs. Gibson's Boys; Metropole; She Stoops to Conquer; 1951: Four Twelves Are 48; 1952: Three Wishes for Jamie.

Select TV: 1952: Mr. Lincoln (sp); 1962: Mr. Magoo's Christmas Carol (sp; voice); 1965: The Dangerous Days of Kiowa Jones (sp); Backtrack (sp); 1970: Run, Simon, Run; 1972: Moon of the Wolf; 1975: Huckleberry Finn; 1976: The Manhunter; 1977: Murder in Peyton Place; How the West Was Won (ms); 1978: A Love Affair: The Eleanor and Lou Gehrig Story; Crash; Donner Pass: The Road to Survival; 1979: The Last Ride of the Dalton Gang; Strangers: The Story of a Mother and Daughter; 1983: Will There Really Be a Morning?; Murder 1, Dancer 0; 1987: LBJ: The Early Years; 1988: Once Upon a Texas Train.

HELMUT DANTINE

BORN: VIENNA, AUSTRIA, OCTOBER 7, 1917.
ED: UNIV. OF CA. DIED: MAY 3, 1982.

It is pure Hollywood irony that Helmut Dantine would escape the German Anschluss in his native country so that he could come to America to play Nazis. Arriving in California in 1938, he acted with the Pasadena Playhouse before debuting in 1941, for Warner Bros., in a Ronald Reagan vehicle, *International Squadron*. The following year, over at MGM, he played a memorable role as the German soldier who confronts Greer Garson after crashing his plane in *Mrs. Miniver*, before returning to Warners to play the newlywed gambler who seeks Humphrey Bogart's help in *Casablanca*. Thus, he participated in two Academy Award-winning Best Pictures in consecutive years. He played Nazis in such features as *Edge of Darkness*, *Northern Pursuit*, and *Escape in the Desert*, which updated the plot of *The Petrified Forest* to World War II; and, for variation, was an underground agent fighting against the SS in *Berlin Hotel*, which gave him a lead alongside Raymond Massey and Peter Lorre. He finished his Warners contract in a dud "B" thriller, *Shadow of a Woman*, married to helpless Andrea King and starving his own son to death for an inheritance. With the end of World War II he expanded his nationalities to Greek in the cheapie *Guerilla Girl*; the title alien in *Stranger From Venus*, trying to warn Americans against nuclear war; a Russian in *War and Peace*; an imprisoned French journalist in *Hell on Devil's Island*; and Marc Antony to Virginia Mayo's Cleopatra in the all-star flop *The Story of Mankind*. In 1957 he directed the Fox "B" actioner, *Thundering Jets*, and later acted in two Sam Peckinpah films on which he served as executive producer: *Bring Me the Head of Alfredo Garcia* and *The Killer Elite*.

Screen: 1941: International Squadron; 1942: Desperate Journey; To Be or Not to Be; Mrs. Miniver; The Pied Piper; The Navy Comes Through; 1943: Casablanca; Edge of Darkness; Mission to Moscow; Watch on the Rhine; Northern Pursuit; 1944: Passage to Marseille; Hollywood Canteen; 1945: Hotel Berlin; Escape in the Desert; 1946: Shadow of a Woman; 1948: Whispering City; 1953: Guerilla Girl; Call Me Madam; 1954: Immediate Disaster/Stranger From Venus; 1956: War and Peace; Alexander the Great; 1957: The Story of Mankind; Hell of Devil's Island; 1958: Fraulein; Tempest; 1965: Operation Crossbow; 1974: Bring Me the Head of Alfredo Garcia (and exec. prod.); 1975: The Wilby Conspiracy (and exec. prod.); The Killer Elite (and exec. prod.); 1979: The Fifth Musketeer.

Select TV: 1951–52: Shadow of a Cloak (series); 1953: The Bet (sp);1957: Clipper Ship; 1959: A Source of Irritation (sp); 1960: The Hiding Place (sp); 1969: The File on Devlin (sp).

RAY DANTON

BORN: NEW YORK, NY, SEPTEMBER 19, 1931. ED: CARNEGIE TECH. INST. DIED: FEBRUARY 11, 1992.

A stock-in-trade virile type, with dark hair and cleft-chin, Ray Danton made his name playing villains and gangsters in "B" films of the late 1950s and early 1960s. After working in radio dramas and stock, he came to Universal in 1955 to debut in the western, *Chief Crazy Horse*, as a character named Little Big Man. That same year he was the bad guy in the plane crash drama *The Looters*, co-starring Julie Adams, who became his wife (1954–81). In 1959 he showed up in two Albert Zugsmith exploitation dramas: *Beat Generation*, as a rapist called The Aspirin Kid;

and *The Big Operator*, as a criminal cohort of Mickey Rooney's, disposing of a witness in a cement mixer. His signature role followed in *The Rise and Fall of Legs Diamond*, an enjoyable, highly fictionalized biopic of the prohibition era gangster. This led to the lead role in *The George Raft Story*, a movie that was based even less in reality than *Legs*. (Danton's only resemblance to Raft was his inability to bring much emotional color to a part.) The inevitable journey to Europe followed, grinding out international cheapies, before directing three horror films, *The Deathmaster* (1972), *Crypt of the Living Dead* (1973), and *Psychic Killer* (1976), the last of which he co-scripted. He also helmed the telefilm, *The Return of Mike Hammer*.

Screen: 1955: Chief Crazy Horse; The Looters; The Spoilers; I'll Cry Tomorrow; 1956: Outside the Law; 1957: The Night Runner; 1958: Too Much, Too Soon; Onionhead; Tarawa Beachhead; 1959: The Beat Generation; The Big Operator; Yellowstone Kelly; 1960: The Rise and Fall of Legs Diamond; Ice Palace; 1961: A Fever in the Blood; The George Raft Story; Portrait of a Mobster; A Majority of One; 1962: The Chapman Report; The Longest Day; 1964: Sandokan Fights Back; FBI Code 98; Sandokan Against the Leopard of Sarawak (nUSr); 1965: The Spy Who Went to Hell/Code Name: Jaguar (nUSr); 1966: Secret Agent Super Dragon; Ballata da Milliardo (nUSr); 1967: Lucky the Inscrutable (nUSr); 1970: The Last Mercenary; 1971: Triangle (nUSr); 1974: Centerfold Girls; 1976: Six-Pack Annie.

Select TV: 1957: Eye of the Storm (sp); 1959–60: The Alaskans (series); 1971: Banyon; 1972: A Very Missing Person; 1973: Runaway!

BOBBY DARIN

(WALDEN ROBERT CASSOTTO) BORN: BRONX, NY, MAY 14, 1936. ED: HUNTER COL. DIED: DECEMBER 20, 1973.

Charismatic pop singer Bobby Darin burst on the scene in the late 1950s with such hit recordings as "Splish Splash" and "Dream Lover," performing in a style that was exciting enough for the teen audience, yet smooth enough for their parents to give a listen. By 1959 he topped the charts with "Mack the Knife," and was famous enough to appear as himself, the following year, in the all-star comedy *Pepe*, wherein he belted out the snappy number "That's How It Went Alright." In 1960 he married actress Sandra Dee, with whom he would co-star in three ultra-fluffy comedies for Universal: *Come September*, *If a Man Answers*, and *That Funny Feeling*. In between these he was a wisecracking soldier in *Hell is for Heroes*, and Pamela Tiffin's love interest in the remake of *State Fair*, which, if nothing else, allowed him to sing Rodgers and Hammerstein's "That's for Me." He was handed some meaty dramatic roles, giving a solid performance as a jazz musician in John Cassavetes's *Too Late Blues*; an acceptable one as an imprisoned racist challenging shrink Sidney Poitier in the hokey *Pressure Point*; and a superb one as a shell-shocked soldier in *Captain Newman, M.D.*, which landed him an Oscar nomination for Best Supporting Actor. He continued his recording career, drifting away from rock 'n' roll and branching out into standards and, eventually, spiritual music. Following his 1967 divorce from Dee, he appeared, billed as Robert Darin, in *The Happy Ending*, as a phony Italian gigolo, and starred in a pair of his own television variety series. Plagued by lifelong heart problems, he died shortly after the run of the second series, in 1973, following surgery. He was only 37.

Screen: 1960: Pepe; 1961: Come September; 1962: Too Late Blues; State Fair; Pressure Point; Hell Is for Heroes; If a Man Answers; 1963: Captain Newman, M.D.; 1965: That Funny

Feeling; **1967:** Gunfight in Abilene; **1968:** Cop-Out/Stranger in the House; **1969:** The Happy Ending; **1973:** Happy Mother's Day, Love George/Run, Stranger, Run.

Select TV: 1961: Bobby Darin and Friends (sp); **1967:** Rodgers and Hart Today (sp); **1972:** Dean Martin Presents The Bobby Darin Amusement Company (series); **1973:** The Bobby Darin Show (series).

LINDA DARNELL

(MONETTA ELOYSE DARNELL) BORN: DALLAS, TX, OCTOBER 16, 1921. DIED: APRIL 10, 1965.

Linda Darnell came to Hollywood's attention strictly on the basis of her looks, and was only just starting to show signs of improvement when her stay on the "A" list came to an end. An offer of a contract with 20th Century-Fox came when she was still in her teens, after dancing and modeling work got her noticed by a talent scout. She started off in a starring part, *Elsa Maxwell's Hotel for Women*, in 1939, and fulfilled leading-lady duties opposite some of the studio's major contract players, including Henry Fonda in *Chad Hanna*, going from frump to glamour girl after joining the circus. With Tyrone Power, she appeared on four separate occasions: *Day-Time Wife*, as his neglected spouse; *Brigham Young — Frontiersman*, in which she nearly starved to death as one of the Mormon settlers; *The Mark of Zorro*, as the niece of his arch enemy; and *Blood and Sand*, where she was no match for the more colorful Rita Hayworth. Fittingly, she played a young contractee hoping to achieve movie stardom in *Star Dust*, supposedly inspired by her own experiences. Unbilled, and filmed mostly in long shot, she played the Virgin Mary in *The Song of Bernadette*, before turning to more convincing roles as bad girls. In UA's *Summer Storm*, she was Edward Everett Horton's flirtatious wife; in *Hangover Square*, a trollop in Victorian London; and in *Fallen Angel*, a slutty waitress. In all three cases she paid mightily for her sins. She was also added to the mix of the tepid Fox musical, *Centennial Summer*, an attempt to copy the nostalgic charms of MGM's *Meet Me in St. Louis*.

There were supporting roles in two good movies: *Anna and the King of Siam*, in which she was sentenced to the stake; and *My Darling Clementine*, easily the weakest performance in this John Ford classic, as a saloon singer named Chihuahua. Then director Otto Preminger brought her in to replace Peggy Cummins in his lavish adaptation of the steamy best seller, *Forever Amber*. The source material's notoriety guaranteed a box-office smash, but Darnell played the tedious heroine, a courtesan who rises to prominence in the court of King Charles II, in a thoroughly tedious manner. Preston Sturges's *Unfaithfully Yours* was a comedy built upon Rex Harrison's adroit playing, rather than Darnell's contributions, but in 1949 she gave one of her better performances, as Paul Douglas's money-hungry wife, in one of the studio's most prestigious projects, *A Letter to Three Wives*. Likewise, opposite Douglas, she was thoroughly convincing as a scheming opera diva in *Everbody Does It*, and as the slatternly wife of a hoodlum who dies under doctor Sidney Poitier's care in *No Way Out*. By 1951, Fox had terminated her contract and she went first to Universal, for the Vegas comedy *The Lady Pays Off*; then to Britain, to romp with a very attractive Tab Hunter on *Saturday Island*, and to play the heroine of *Blackbeard the Pirate*; and finally to Italy. Returning to the U.S., she continued on her downward slide with a Dale Robertson western, *Dakota Incident*, and a Paramount programmer, *Zero Hour*, the inspiration for the spoof *Airplane!* By the late 1950s she

had retired, although she was coaxed back in 1965 to lend her name to an A.C. Lyles western, *Black Spurs*. She may have continued as part of his stock company had it not been for her tragic death that same year in a fire, presumably caused when she fell asleep with a cigarette in her hand.

Screen: 1939: Elsa Maxwell's Hotel for Women; Day-Time Wife; **1940:** Star Dust; Brigham Young — Frontiersman; The Mark of Zorro; Chad Hanna; **1941:** Blood and Sand; Rise and Shine; **1942:** The Loves of Edgar Allan Poe; **1943:** City Without Men; The Song of Bernadette; **1944:** It Happened Tomorrow; Buffalo Bill; Summer Storm; Sweet and Low Down; **1945:** Hangover Square; The Great John L.; Fallen Angel; **1946:** Centennial Summer; Anna and the King of Siam; My Darling Clementine; **1947:** Forever Amber; **1948:** The Walls of Jericho; Unfaithfully Yours; **1949:** A Letter to Three Wives; Slattery's Hurricane; Everybody Does It; **1950:** No Way Out; Two Flags West; **1951:** The 13th Letter; The Guy Who Came Back; The Lady Pays Off; **1952:** Island of Desire/Saturday Island; Night Without Sleep; Blackbeard the Pirate; **1953:** Second Chance; **1954:** This is My Love; **1955:** Angels of Darkness; Gli Ultimi Cinque Minuti/The Last Five Minutes (nUSr); **1956:** Dakota Incident; **1957:** Zero Hour; **1965:** Black Spurs.

Select TV: 1956: All for a Man (sp); **1957:** Terror in the Streets (sp); Homeward Borne (sp).

JAMES DARREN

(JAMES ERCOLANI) BORN: PHILADELPHIA, PA, JUNE 8, 1936.

Discovered by talent agent Joyce Selznick, brooding but benign James Darren was taken on by Columbia studios and marketed to teenage girls as a hunky pin-up. Displaying a swaggering, urban appeal, he was first showcased as a gang leader in *Rumble on the Docks*, then as a hoodlum trying to spare sibling Richard Conte from the mob's wrath in *The Brothers Ricco*. His popularity soared with the lightweight 1959 teen comedy, *Gidget*, in which he played a surfer with the memorable moniker Moondoggie, and sang the title song to Sandra Dee. This led to a concurrent recording career that produced two top ten hits, "Goodbye Cruel World" (1961) and "Her Royal Majesty" (1962). He played the nice guy in a platoon of bigots in *All the Young Men*; a slum kid hoping to become a concert pianist in *Let No Man Write My Epitaph*, which was stolen from him by Shelley Winters, as his drug-addicted mom; and then returned to play opposite different actresses than Ms. Dee in *Gidget Goes Hawaiian* (Deborah Walley) and *Gidget Goes to Rome* (Cindy Carol). He was rewarded by Columbia with a role in their 1961 action hit, *The Guns of Navarone*, as part of Gregory Peck's daredevil team sent to blow up the title weapons. A competent but hardly indispensable actor, his fame waned as he grew older and he found most of his later work on television, including a regular role in the 1980s series *T.J. Hooker*, and directing jobs on such shows as *The 'A' Team* and *Hunter*.

Screen: 1956: Rumble on the Docks; **1957:** The Brothers Ricco; The Tijuana Story; Operation Mad Ball; **1958:** Gunman's Walk; **1959:** The Gene Krupa Story; Gidget; **1960:** All the Young Men; Because They're Young; Let No Man Write My Epitaph; **1961:** Gidget Goes Hawaiian; The Guns of Navarone; **1962:** Diamond Head; **1963:** Gidget Goes to Rome; **1964:** For Those Who Think Young; The Lively Set; **1970:** Venus in Furs/Paroxismus; **1978:** The Boss' Son; **2001:** Random Acts (nUSr).

Select TV: 1966–67: The Time Tunnel (series); **1971:** City Beneath the Sea; **1975:** The Lives of Jenny Dolan; **1980:** Turnover

Smith; **1981:** Scruples; **1982:** Aliens From Another Planet; **1983–86:** T.J. Hooker (series); **1999:** Melrose Place (series).

FRANKIE DARRO

(FRANK JOHNSON) BORN: CHICAGO, IL,
DECEMBER 22, 1917. DIED: DECEMBER 25, 1976.

A feisty, small-framed performer who literally grew up in the movies, Frankie Darro (originally billed as Darrow) started out as a child actor in silent movies. (His many roles included playing a street urchin saved by William Haines in *Fighting the Flames*.) In the 1930s, he parlayed his tough-guy personality into some standout portrayals of bad boys and troublemakers, most notably in director William A. Wellman's effective examination of teenage vagrancy, *Wild Boys of the Road*, in which he gave a dynamic performance. He butted heads with James Cagney in the reform school drama *The Mayor of Hell*, more than holding his own against this powerhouse talent. (Earlier Darro had played the younger version of Cagney's brother, Eddie Woods, in the classic *The Public Enemy*.) He surfaced in such self-explanatory titles as *Juvenile Court*, as Rita Hayworth's no-good brother; *Born to Fight*, as an up-and-coming boxer named "Baby Face" Madison; *Wanted by the Police*, unwillingly involved in a stolen car racket; and *Reformatory*, not to be confused with *Boys Reformatory*. (In the former Darro was a bad egg; in the latter he was a good kid unjustly sent to the slammer.) His diminutive size made him perfect for playing jockeys, as he did in *The Ex-Mrs. Bradford*, *A Day at the Races*, *Thoroughbreds Don't Cry*, and *Riding High*. Fittingly, he lent his voice to the most famous animated juvenile delinquent in history, the cigar-smoking Lampwick, in Disney's *Pinocchio*. Finding a home at Monogram, he was top billed in such cheapies as *Chasing Trouble* and *Laughing at Danger*; fell in with the Bowery Boys in *Angels Alley* and *Fighting Fools*; then worked his way down to tinier parts in *The Ten Commandments* (as a slave), *Operation Petticoat* (as one of Cary Grant's submarine crew), and *The Carpetbaggers* (as a bellhop). His long list of credits failed to provide him with adequate income, however, and he died in poverty.

Screen: AS FRANKIE DARROW: **1924:** Judgment of the Storm; Roaring Rails; The Signal Tower; So Big; Racing for Life; Half-a-Dollar Bill; **1925:** Confessions of a Queen; The People Vs. Nancy Preston; Let's Go Gallagher; The Midnight Flyer; The Phantom Express; Wandering Footsteps; The Wyoming Wildcat; The Cowboy Musketeer; The Fearless Lover; Women and Gold; Fighting the Flames; Bustin' Through; Memory Lane; **1926:** Kiki; The Cowboy Cop; Flaming Waters; The Carnival Girl; The Arizona Streak; Memory Lane; Mike; Out of the West; Tom and His Pals; Red Hot Hoofs; Wild to Go; The Thrill Hunter; Born to Battle; The Masquerade Bandit; Flesh and the Devil; Hearts and Spangles; Her Husband's Secret; **1927:** Long Pants; Lightning Lariats; Cyclone of the Range; Judgment of the Hills; Her Father Said No; The Flying U Ranch; Little Mickey Grogan; Tom's Gang; The Desert Pirate; The Cherokee Kid; Moulders of Men; **1928:** The Texas Tornado; Tyrant of Red Gulch; When the Law Rides; The Circus Kid; The Avenging Rider; Phantom of the Range; Terror; **1929:** The Pride of Pawnee; Trail of the Horse Thieves; Rainbow Man; Gun Law; Blaze o' Glory; Idaho Red.
AS FRANKIE DARRO: **1931:** The Mad Genius; The Sin of Madelon Claudet; The Vanishing Legion (serial); Way Back Home; The Public Enemy; **1932:** Cheyenne Cyclone; Amateur Daddy; The Lightning Warrior (serial); Three on a Match; **1933:** Tugboat Annie; Wild Boys of the Road; Laughing at Life; The Mayor of Hell; The Wolf Dog (serial); The Big Race; **1934:** The Devil

Horse (serial); The Merry Frinks; No Greater Glory; Broadway Bill; Burn 'em Up Barnes (serial); Little Men; **1935:** Men of Action; Valley of Wanted Men; Stranded; The Phantom Empire (serial); Three Kids and a Queen; The Unwelcome Stranger; Red Hot Tires/Racing Luck; The Pay-Off; **1936:** Black Gold; The Ex-Mrs. Bradford; Racing Blood; Mind Your Own Business; Charlie Chan at the Race Track; Born to Fight; Headline Crasher; **1937:** Devil Diamond; A Day at the Races; Tough to Handle; Saratoga; Anything for a Thrill; Thoroughbreds Don't Cry; Young Dynamite; **1938:** Reformatory; Wanted by the Police; Juvenile Court; Tough Kid; **1939:** The Great Adventures of Wild Bill Hickok; Boys Reformatory; Irish Luck; **1940:** Chasing Trouble; On the Spot; Pinocchio (voice); Laughing at Danger; Up in the Air; Men With Steel Faces; **1941:** Gang's All Here; You're Out of Luck; Let's Go Collegiate; Tuxedo Junction; **1942:** Junior G-Men of the Air (serial); **1946:** Freddie Steps Out; Her Sister's Secret; High School Hero; Junior Prom; **1947:** That's My Man; Vacation Days; Sarge Goes to College; **1948:** Smart Politics; Angels' Alley; Heart of Virginia; Trouble Makers; Hold That Baby!; **1949:** Fighting Fools; **1950:** A Life of Her Own; Riding High; Wyoming Mail; Sons of New Mexico; **1951:** Pride of Maryland; Across the Wide Missouri; The Sellout; Westward the Women; **1952:** Pat and Mike; **1953:** Two-Gun Marshal; **1954:** The Lawless Rider; Living It Up; Racing Blood; **1956:** The Ten Commandments; **1958:** The Perfect Furlough; **1959:** Operation Petticoat; **1964:** The Carpetbaggers; **1969:** Hook, Line, and Sinker.
Select TV: **1974:** The Girl on the Late, Late Show.

JANE DARWELL

(PATTI WOODWARD) BORN: PALMYRA, MO,
OCTOBER 15, 1879. DIED: AUGUST 13, 1967.

By the time she won her well-deserved Academy Award, in 1940, Jane Darwell had been acting professionally for over 30 years. A veteran of the Henry Duff stock company, she came to films in 1914 but returned to the stage before settling down in Hollywood for good with the coming of talkies. The doe-eyed, matronly Darwell became a busy supporting player with such memorable portrayals as the self-righteous Dolly Merriwether in *Gone With the Wind*; the tough and terrifying Ma Grier, who happily joins the lynching party in *The Ox-Bow Incident*; and the "Old Doll" helped by Bob Hope in *The Lemon Drop Kid*. A frequent favorite of John Ford, she was seen in *3 Godfathers*, *Wagonmaster*, and *The Last Hurrah*, among others, and it was for Ford that she played the formidable Ma Joad in his 1940 film of *The Grapes of Wrath*. Her Oscar-winning performance is one of the greatest portraits of maternal strength, familial warmth, and iron-willed perseverance in the history of film. During the 1940s a few "B" movie leads came her way with *Private Nurse*, helping Ann Todd reconcile with her ex-hood father, and *Captain Tugboat Annie*, reprising Marie Dressler's famous role. She ended her career with a poignant cameo in Disney's *Mary Poppins*, playing the Bird Woman who sells breadcrumbs for "Tuppence a Bag" on the steps of St. Paul's Cathedral.

Screen: **1914:** Rose of the Rancho; Ready Money; The Only Son; After Five; Master Mind; Brewster's Millions; Man on the Box; **1915:** The Goose Girl; Hypocrites; The Reform Candidate; **1916:** The Rug Maker's Daughter; **1930:** Tom Sawyer; **1931:** Huckleberry Finn; Fighting Caravans; Ladies of the Big House; **1932:** Back Street; Hot Saturday; No One Man; Murders in the Zoo; **1933:** Bondage; Jennie Gerhardt; Bed of Roses; Ann Vickers; Only Yesterday; Air Hostess; One Sunday Afternoon; Before

Dawn; Women Won't Tell; Design for Living; Emergency Call; Child of Manhattan; He Couldn't Take It; Aggie Appleby, Maker of Men; The Past of Mary Holmes; Roman Scandals; **1934:** Once to Every Woman; Finishing School; David Harum; Wake Up and Dream; Desirable; The Scarlet Empress; Heat Lightning; The Firebird; Fashions of 1934; Let's Talk It Over; Happiness Ahead; Wonder Bar; Change of Heart; Most Precious Thing in Life; Blind Date; Embarrassing Moments; Journal of a Crime; Gentlemen Are Born; Jimmy the Gent; Million Dollar Ransom; The White Parade; One Night of Love; Bright Eyes; Tomorrow's Youth; **1935:** Life Begins at 40; Curly Top; McFadden's Flats; One More Spring; Navy Wife; Metropolitan; We're Only Human; **1936:** Paddy O'Day; Captain January; Little Miss Nobody; The Country Doctor; White Fang; Ramona; Private Number; Star for a Night; Poor Little Rich Girl; The First Baby; Craig's Wife; Laughing at Trouble; **1937:** The Great Hospital Mystery; Dangerously Yours; Wife, Doctor and Nurse; The Singing Marine; Nancy Steel Is Missing; Slave Ship; Love Is News; Fifty Roads to Town; **1938:** The Jury's Secret; Five of a Kind; Change of Heart; Time Out for Murder; Little Miss Broadway; Three Blind Mice; Battle of Broadway; Up the River; **1939:** Inside Story; Jesse James; Unexpected Father; The Zero Hour; The Rains Came; Grand Jury Secrets; Miracle on Main Street; Gone With the Wind; 20,000 Men a Year; **1940:** The Grapes of Wrath; Chad Hanna; Brigham Young — Frontiersman; Youth Will Be Served; Untamed; **1941:** All That Money Can Buy/The Devil and Daniel Webster; Thieves Fall Out; Small Town Deb; Private Nurse; **1942:** Young America; The Loves of Edgar Allan Poe; Men of Texas; It Happened in Flatbush; The Great Gildersleeve; All Through the Night; On the Sunny Side; Highways by Night; **1943:** The Ox-Bow Incident; Tender Comrade; Gildersleeve's Bad Day; Government Girl; Stage Door Canteen; **1944:** Sunday Dinner for a Soldier; She's a Sweetheart; Music in Manhattan; Reckless Age; The Impatient Years; **1945:** Captain Tugboat Annie; A Yank in London/I Live in Grosvenor Square; **1946:** Three Wise Fools; My Darling Clementine; Dark Horse; **1947:** Red Stallion; Keeper of the Bees; **1948:** 3 Godfathers; Train to Alcatraz; **1949:** Red Canyon; **1950:** Wagon Master; The Daughter of Rosie O'Grady; Caged; Redwood Forest Trail; Surrender; Three Husbands; The Second Face; Father's Wild Game; **1951:** The Lemon Drop Kid; Excuse My Dust; Journey Into Light; Fourteen Hours; **1952:** We're Not Married; **1953:** The Sun Shines Bright; It Happens Every Thursday; Affair With a Stranger; The Bigamist; **1955:** Hit the Deck; A Life at Stake; **1956:** There's Always Tomorrow; Girls in Prison; **1958:** The Last Hurrah; **1959:** Hound-Dog Man; **1964:** Mary Poppins.
NY Stage: 1921: Swords; 1944: Suds.
Select TV: 1952: Josie (sp); 1954: Slide Darling Slide (sp); 1955: The Mumbys (sp); 1956: The Prima Donna (sp); Sincerely Willis Wayde (sp); The Greer Case (sp); 1957: Three Men on a Horse (sp); 1958: A Dead Ringer (sp); A Boy Grows Up (sp); 1961: The Fawn (sp).

HOWARD DA SILVA

(HAROLD SILVERBLATT) BORN: CLEVELAND, OH, MAY 4, 1909. ED: CARNEGIE TECH. INST. DIED: FEBRUARY 16, 1986.

A deep-voiced character actor adept at playing shifty characters and villains, Howard Da Silva learned stagecraft with the Group Theatre and Orson Welles's Mercury Theatre. His impressive credits in *Waiting for Lefty*, *Golden Boy*, and the controversial *The Cradle Will Rock* brought him to Hollywood in 1940, where he repeated his stage role as the bully who battles then ultimately befriends Raymond Massey in *Abe Lincoln in Illinois*. He returned to New York to become a part of musical theatre history by creating the role of Jud Frye in the original production of *Oklahoma!*, which got him a contract with Paramount Pictures. He exuded a strong presence in such roles as the sympathetic bartender in *The Lost Weekend*; the sadistic sea captain in *Two Years Before the Mast*; and the wicked slave trader in DeMille's *Unconquered*, pretty much stealing the film from Gary Cooper and company. He was a violent ex-con who coaxed Farley Granger back to a life of crime in *They Live by Night*; a self-righteous rancher smuggling Mexicans into the U.S. in *Border Incident*; Eve Arden's jealous spouse in *Three Husbands*; and a policeman tracking crazed David Wayne in the remake of *M*. His career was interrupted by the McCarthy blacklist and Da Silva was abruptly fired from the RKO film *Slaughter Trail*, replaced by Brian Donlevy. He stayed off the screen for 12 years, returning in 1963 in the gentle drama, *David and Lisa*, as the doctor who counsels damaged youngsters Keir Dullea and Janet Margolin. Movie roles still proved hard to find, so he went back to Broadway to score a triumph as the irascible Ben Franklin in the hit musical, *1776*. Reprising the role in the 1972 movie version became the actor's crowning film achievement. His appearance as Meyer Wolfsheim in the 1974 version of *The Great Gatsby* was noteworthy because he had also acted in the 1949 film adaptation, as Wilson. His final movie, *Garbo Talks*, gave him some effective scenes as a grizzled old photographer hired to track down the elusive actress. He won an Emmy Award in 1978 for the PBS special *Verna: U.S.O. Girl*.

Screen: 1935: Once in a Blue Moon; 1939: Golden Boy; 1940: I'm Still Alive; Abe Lincoln in Illinois; 1941: The Sea Wolf; Steel Against the Sky; Strange Alibi; Navy Blues; Sergeant York; Bad Men of Missouri; Nine Lives Are Not Enough; Blues in the Night; Wild Bill Hickok Rides; 1942: Bullet Scars; The Big Shot; Native Land; Juke Girl; Keeper of the Flame; Reunion in France; The Omaha Trail; 1943: Tonight We Raid Calais; 1945: The Lost Weekend; Duffy's Tavern; Five Were Chosen; 1946: The Blue Dahlia; Two Years Before the Mast; 1947: Unconquered; Blaze of Noon; Variety Girl; 1949: They Live by Night; The Great Gatsby; Border Incident; 1950: The Underworld Story; Wyoming Mail; Tripoli; Three Husbands; 1951: Fourteen Hours; M; 1963: David and Lisa; 1964: The Outrage; 1966: Nevada Smith; 1972: 1776; 1974: The Great Gatsby; I'm a Stranger Here Myself (narrator); 1976: Hollywood on Trial; 1978: The Private Files of J. Edgar Hoover; 1981: Mommie Dearest; 1984: Garbo Talks.

NY Stage: 1930: Romeo & Juliet; The Green Cockatoo; Siegfried; Alison's House; 1932: Liliom; Dear Jane; Alice in Wonderland; 1933: The Cherry Orchard; 1934: The Sailors of Cattaro; 1935: Black Pit; 1937: Golden Boy; The Cradle Will Rock; 1938: Casey Jones; Abe Lincoln in Illinois; 1939: Summer Night; 1940: Two on an Island; 1943: Oklahoma!; 1950: Burning Bright; 1953: The World of Sholom Aleichem (ob); 1956: The Adding Machine (ob); Diary of a Scoundrel (ob); 1957: Volpone (ob); Compulsion; 1959: Fiorello!; 1962: Romulus; In the Counting House; 1963: Dear Me the Sky Is Falling; 1964: Hamlet; 1967: The Unknown Soldier and His Wife; 1969: 1776.

Select TV: 1964: Hamlet (sp); 1965: For the People (series); 1967: The Beggars Opera (sp); 1974: Smile Jenny, You're Dead; The Missiles of October (sp); 1978: Verna: U.S.O. Girl (sp); 1980: Power (ms); 1984: The Cafeteria (sp).

HARRY DAVENPORT

BORN: NEW YORK, NY, JANUARY 19, 1866.
DIED: AUGUST 9, 1949.

One of the movies' distinguished "old men," white-haired Harry Davenport dabbled in films during the silent era, where he also amassed considerable directorial credits, including the "Mr. Jarr" series of short subjects. He returned to feature films to work strictly as an actor, starting with *Her Unborn Child* in 1930, and he remained eternally busy from that point to the end of his life, appearing in 18 features and one serial in 1937 alone. Among his many roles were a philosopher driven to suicide by Noël Coward's cynicism in *The Scoundrel*; a decrepit Confederate Soldier dwelling on the past in *They Won't Forget*; a retiring physics professor in *Under Cover of Night*; the chief of staff in *The Life of Emile Zola*; Monsieur de Cosse in *Marie Antoinette*; an opera director in *Maytime*; an archduke under Joe E. Brown's surveillance in *Fit for a King*; a railroad owner facing ruin by a rival business in *Paradise Express*; the Judge in *You Can't Take It With You*; King Louis XI in *The Hunchback of Notre Dame*; Dr. Meade in *Gone With the Wind*; the sensible Davies, who tries to stop the lynching, in *The Ox-Bow Incident*; the level-headed lawyer, Colonel Skeffington, in *Kings Row*; and Grandpa Smith in *Meet Me in St. Louis*. Davenport grabbed the spotlight in some "B" pictures, including *Granny Get Your Gun*, wherein he and fellow senior citizen May Robson brought crooked gambling-house owner Clay Clement to justice; and *Grandpa Goes to Town*, discovering a gold mine in a ghost town and saving it from a bunch of greedy gangsters. His daughter was silent screen actress Dorothy Davenport.

Screen: 1914: Fogg's Millions; 1915: C.O.D.; Father and the Boy; 1917: One Night; The Wheel of the Law; 1917: The False Friend; A Man's Law; The Planter; Sowers and Reapers; 1919: A Girl at Bay; Dawn; The Unknown Quantity; 1930: Her Unborn Child; 1931: My Sin; His Woman; 1933: Get That Venus; 1935: The Scoundrel; 1936: Three Men on a Horse; The Case of the Black Cat; Legion of Terror; Three Cheers for Love; King of Hockey; 1937: Fly Away Baby; The Life of Emile Zola; Under Cover of Night; Her Husband's Secretary; White Bondage; They Won't Forget; Four Days' Wonder; Maytime; Radio Patrol (serial); The Great Garrick; Mountain Justice; Mr. Dodd Takes the Air; First Lady; The Perfect Specimen; Paradise Express; Wells Fargo; As Good as Married; Armored Car; Fit for a King; 1938: The Sisters; Saleslady; Gold Is Where You Find It; The Long Shot; The First Hundred Years; Marie Antoinette; The Cowboy and the Lady; Man Proof; Young Fugitives; The Rage of Paris; Reckless Living; You Can't Take It With You; The Higgins Family; Tail Spin; 1939: Juarez; Orphans of the Street; My Wife's Relatives; Made for Each Other; Should Husbands Work?; The Covered Trailer; Money to Burn; Exile Express; The Story of Alexander Graham Bell; Death of a Champion; Gone With the Wind; The Hunchback of Notre Dame; 1940: Granny Get Your Gun; Too Many Husbands; Grandpa Goes to Town; All This, and Heaven Too; Lucky Partners; Foreign Correspondent; Earl of Puddlestone; I Want a Divorce; Dr. Ehrlich's Magic Bullet; 1941: That Uncertain Feeling; I Wanted Wings; Hurricane Smith; The Bride Came C.O.D.; One Foot in Heaven; 1942: Kings Row; Larceny, Inc.; Ten Gentlemen From West Point; Tales of Manhattan; Son of Fury; 1943: The Ox-Bow Incident; Shantytown; Headin' for God's Country; We've Never Been Licked; Gangway for Tomorrow; The Amazing Mrs. Holliday; Government Girl; Jack London; Princess O'Rourke; 1944: The Impatient Years; The Thin Man Goes Home; Kismet;

Music for Millions; Meet Me in St. Louis; 1945: The Enchanted Forest; Too Young to Know; This Love of Ours; Adventure; 1946: She Wouldn't Say Yes; A Boy, a Girl and a Dog; Pardon My Past; Courage of Lassie; Faithful in My Fashion; Three Wise Fools; G.I. War Bride; Claudia and David; Lady Luck; 1947: Stallion Road; The Farmer's Daughter; That Hagen Girl; The Bachelor and the Bobby-Soxer; Keeper of the Bees; Sport of Kings; The Fabulous Texan; 1948: Three Daring Daughters; Man From Texas; For the Love of Mary; That Lady in Ermine; The Decision of Christopher Blake; 1949: Down to the Sea in Ships; Little Women; That Forsyte Woman; Tell It to the Judge; 1950: Riding High.
NY Stage: 1914: Sari; 1918: The Squab Farm; Lightnin'; Three Wise Fools.

MARION DAVIES

(MARION CECILIE DOURAS) BORN: BROOKLYN, NY, JANUARY 3, 1897. DIED: SEPTEMBER 22, 1961.

Because of *Citizen Kane*, Marion Davies will be forever unfairly equated with the untalented character portrayed by Dorothy Comingore in Orson Welles's masterpiece. As the mistress of William Randolph Hearst, it has been naturally assumed that it was Davies who was being raked over the coals in the thinly disguised expose of the infamous newspaper magnate, but in reality the blonde, spunky star was considered by critics and industry members to be one of the brighter lights of the silent cinema. She had started as a chorus girl in the Ziegfeld Follies and appeared in a 1917 movie directed by her brother-in-law, George Lederer, called *Runaway Romany*. During her chorine days she made the acquaintance of Hearst who converted a Harlem casino into a movie studio with the sole purpose of making Davies a star. Their maiden venture, *Cecilia of the Pink Roses*, was — unsurprisingly — greeted with rapturous notices in the Hearst papers, and was followed by such vehicles as the spy story, *The Burden of Proof*, and *The Belle of New York*, with Davies as a Salvation Army girl. A distribution agreement between Paramount and Hearst resulted in a production company called Cosmopolitan putting out titles like *The Restless Sex*; *Bride's Play*, with Davies playing a dual role in two time periods; and the very lavish costume drama *When Knighthood Was in Flower*. Audience response was mixed, but she had become a well-known name nonetheless, because Hearst had instructed his newspapers to mention her name on a daily basis. The critics may have resented these tactics, but they usually had nice things to say about Davies, if not the pictures themselves.

Hearst and Cosmopolitan moved over to Goldwyn for *Little Old New York*, which had Davies passing as a male in order to inherit some money. In 1924, she and her mentor were gleefully received by MGM, who were only too happy to be in Hearst's good graces. In no time Davies became the most beloved socialite on the Hollywood scene, hosting parties on the Hearst yacht, *Oneida*, and at the imposing San Simeon castle. Her box office had improved too, through such films as *Lights of Old Broadway*, again in a dual role, as rich and poor twins; and *Beverly of Graustark*, which reprised the cross-dressing ploy. *The Red Mill* was strictly for those who wanted to experience the noted Victor Herbert operetta *without* the songs, though it had the added historical interest of being directed by "Fatty" Arbuckle, using the alias William Goodrich, following his career-ruining scandal. *Tillie the Toiler* was based on a popular comic strip that ran in Hearst's newspapers, about a bubble-headed office girl. It was clear that comedy was Davies's forte, being the genre that garnered her the most praise. She was particularly good as a flapper in *The Patsy*, mimicking several of her contemporaries, including Lillian Gish and Pola Negri; and *Show People*, making it big in movies while leaving the reg'lar folks behind. When the talkies came, she made a singing guest appearance in *The Hollywood Revue of 1929*, but interest in her began to dim shortly thereafter, with two of her films, *Rosalie* and *Five O'Clock Girl* being shut down in mid-production. The early 1930s were not a prime period for Davies, even though she appeared opposite strong co-stars in *Five and Ten* (Leslie Howard), *Polly of the Circus* (Clark Gable), *Going Hollywood* (Bing Crosby), and *Operator 13* (Gary Cooper), in a particularly embarrassing performance that required her to wear blackface for half the film. After a disagreement over her roles with MGM, she went over to Warner Bros. to partner Dick Powell in both *Page Miss Glory* and in the period comedy, *Hearts Divided*, as an American wooed by Napoleon's brother! She reteamed with Gable for a schizophrenic combination of boxing and music, *Cain and Mabel*, and ended her career with an inconsequential comedy, *Ever Since Eve*, in 1937, the year she turned 40. Ever loyal to Hearst, she came to his financial aid when his fortunes began to fade. She married for the first time shortly after Hearst's death in 1951 and lived comfortably in seclusion for her remaining years.

Screen: 1917: Runaway Romany; 1918: Cecilia of the Pink Roses; The Burden of Proof; 1919: The Belle of New York; Getting Mary Married; The Dark Star; 1920: The Cinema Murder; April Folly; The Restless Sex; 1921: Buried Treasure; Enchantment; 1922: Bride's Play; Beauty's Worth; The Young Diana; When Knighthood Was in Flower; 1923: Adam and Eva; Little Old New York; 1924: Yolanda; Janice Meredith; 1925: Zander the Great; Lights of Old Broadway; 1926: Beverly of Graustark; 1927: The Red Mill; Tillie the Toiler; Quality Street; The Fair Co-ed; 1928: The Patsy; The Cardboard Lover; Show People; 1929: The Hollywood Revue of 1929; Marianne; 1930: Not So Dumb; The Floradora Girl; 1931: The Bachelor Father; It's a Wise Child; Five and Ten; 1932: Polly of the Circus; Blondie of the Follies; 1933: Peg O' My Heart; Going Hollywood; 1934: Operator 13; 1935: Page Miss Glory; 1936: Hearts Divided; Cain and Mabel; 1937: Ever Since Eve.

NY Stage: 1915: Stop! Look! Listen!; 1916: Ziegfeld Follies of 1916; Betty; 1917: Oh Boy!; Miss 1917; Words and Music; 1920: Ed Wynn's Carnival.

BETTE DAVIS

(RUTH ELIZABETH DAVIS) BORN: LOWELL, MA, APRIL 5, 1908. DIED: OCTOBER 6, 1989.

Dynamic, fearless, eccentric, fascinating, Bette Davis is thought by many to be the greatest female star Hollywood ever produced, an actress who believed in giving her audience their money's worth. And though she often went over the top with those wonderfully wide, hypnotic eyes and that clipped, defiant speech pattern, she was not the self-parody that a million female impersonators have tried to portray. After a stint with the Provincetown Players in *The Earth Between*, she got the lead on Broadway in *Broken Dishes*, in 1929, which landed her a screen test with Universal. Her first film for them was *Bad Sister*, and, although Davis would soon play plenty of those, the title role, in this instance, was essayed by Marianne Madison. The studio wasted her in minor assignments in *Seed*, as John Boles's daughter, and *Waterloo Bridge*, as Douglass Montgomery's sister, but it was due to another thankless role, in Columbia's *The Menace*, that George Arliss requested she star opposite him in the

1932 melodrama *The Man Who Played God*. Her performance as the much younger music student who wants to marry Arliss won her a contract with Warner Bros. where, in due time, she would become the undisputed queen of the lot. She had a secondary role, albeit one she liked, as an artist who won't marry Hardie Albright, in *So Big*, and a more important one in the soap opera *The Rich Are Always With Us*, trying to snatch George Brent away from Ruth Chatterton. Brent had also been in *So Big* and would later become Davis's most frequent leading man.

In *Cabin in the Cotton* she spoke her first quotable line of dialogue ("I'd love to kiss ya but ah just washed ma hair.") and went on to appear in *Three on a Match*, as one of the title trio, although Ann Dvorak got the juiciest part; and *20,000 Years in Sing-Sing*, which gave her a good opportunity to act opposite Spencer Tracy. Davis, however, was dissatisfied with the direction her career was heading. *Ex-Lady* gave her top billing but little else; *Fashions of 1934* found her uncharacteristically cast as a glamorous designer; *Jimmy the Gent* put her very much in support, although it was the better of her two pairings with James Cagney; and although *Fog Over Frisco* brought her a fat part as a socialite dabbling in vice, but it was strictly a "B" programmer. Warners were reluctant to let RKO cast her as the crude, selfish waitress who nearly destroys Leslie Howard in *Of Human Bondage*, but they finally agreed and she gleefully seized the opportunity. Her full-throttle performance won absolute raves, marking her emergence as a true Hollywood "name." Back at Warners she got a big mad scene in *Bordertown*, and enlivened the conventional 1935 drama, *Dangerous*, playing an alcoholic actress. This brought her her first Oscar nomination and her first win. More worthwhile, however, was her subdued work in *The Petrified Forest*, as the waitress with big dreams, teamed again quite beautifully with Leslie Howard. Her Oscar-winner status did not save her from being dumped into wretched fare like *Satan Met a Lady*, an earlier version of *The Maltese Falcon*. She expanded her range with the bright comedy, *It's Love I'm After*, in which she was a howl as Leslie Howard's temperamental girlfriend, but shortly afterward came her celebrated battle with Warners over better scripts, which led to her suspension. Although she lost the suit filed on her by the studio she had won a moral victory when Warners, anxious to placate her, handed her the script of *Marked Woman*, about a dance hall hostess who faces hell for agreeing to testify against a powerful racketeer. The eventual success of the movie proved that Davis was a *bona fide* leading attraction.

In 1938 came *Jezebel* and the beginning of Bette's golden period. As the self-centered Southern belle who foolishly ruins her relationship with Henry Fonda, she gave her finest, most detailed performance to date and picked up a second Academy Award. Her follow-up, *The Sisters* (with Jane Bryan and Anita Louise as her siblings), found her as the loyal wife of top-billed Errol Flynn, with the 1906 San Francisco earthquake thrown in for good measure. Her next Oscar nominations were for two glossy melodramas that benefited greatly from her handling of the material: *Dark Victory*, one of the definitive soap operas of the 1930s, cast her as an irresponsible socialite sadly facing her own mortality when she is diagnosed with a brain tumor; and *The Letter* featured one of the great opening scenes in Warners history, with Davis emptying a gun into her lover. In between these she became increasingly infuriating as she aged through the plodding *The Old Maid*, and sniped grandly as the Queen, who cannot stand to see leading man Errol Flynn dare to usurp her authority, in *The Private Lives of Elizabeth and Essex*, her first color picture. In *Juarez*, she brought a smattering of public interest to a difficult and un-commercial product, generously awarding the best scenes to Paul Muni and Brian Aherne, and, in a similar vein, gave Mary

Astor the meatiest moments in *The Great Lie*. She took a back seat to Monty Woolley in the adaptation of the stage hit *The Man Who Came to Dinner*, and to Paul Lukas in *Watch on the Rhine*, although her presence in both assured them respectable box-office receipts.

The Davis faithful endured the endless costumer *All This, and Heaven Too*, watching her sacrifice her own happiness as the governess who fawns over employer Charles Boyer, while he suffers through marriage to bitchy Barbara O'Neill. Borrowed by Goldwyn Studios, she gave a towering performance as the greedy Regina Hubbard, who gladly watches her crippled husband die, in the potent adaptation of Lillian Hellman's *The Little Foxes*, which brought her another Oscar nomination. She was in the running again for one of the pinnacles of all 1940s soap operas, *Now, Voyager*, in which she was unforgettable as a timid ugly duckling who blossoms with the help of kindly psychiatrist Claude Rains and finds some degree of contentment with suave Paul Henreid. (The film afforded her another quotable line: "Oh Gerry, don't let's ask for the moon — we have the stars.") A disappointing comedy with James Cagney, *The Bride Came C.O.D.*, was followed by a stint as a selfish bitch who steals Dennis Morgan away from her sister, Olivia de Havilland, in *In This Our Life*, a Hollywoodization of a Pulitzer Prize-winning novel. Her role as Miriam Hopkins's best friend in *Old Acquaintance* was not mirrored off screen; the relationship between the two was notoriously icy, Davis later referring to her as one of the most uncooperative and difficult of all actresses. After introducing the wartime hit song "They're Either Too Young or Too Old," in *Thank Your Lucky Stars*, Davis received her seventh Oscar nomination for the overlong drama *Mr. Skeffington*, in which she endured both a marriage of convenience to Claude Rains and a bad case of diphtheria. She made a noble effort playing the inspirational schoolteacher Miss Moffett in *The Corn Is Green*, but was clearly too young for a part made famous onstage by Ethel Barrymore. (Later, at a more appropriate age, she dusted it off as a stage musical, which closed prior to its New York run). Serving as her own producer for the high melodrama *A Stolen Life*, she cast herself opposite her own favorite actress, Bette Davis, playing good and bad twins, a premise that lost all sense of plausibility after a while. Suddenly the good years came to an end and she saw herself caught in a string of failures starting with *Deception*, a florid reunion with Rains; continuing through *Winter Meeting* and the comedy *June Bride*; and ending with a crash, with the critically-panned effort, *Beyond the Forest*. This last film, in which she vamped in a black fright wig, got an abortion, shot Minor Watson on a hunting trip, misapplied her lipstick for her big death scene, and uttered the immortal cry "What a dump!," was instrumental in Davis asking to be released from her Warners contract.

Davis may have been down, but she was far from out, and she rose again, magnificently, with *All About Eve*, giving her greatest performance in her greatest film. As the petulant, insecure actress Margo Channing, who has to contend with her fading youth and the conniving tactics of her understudy, Anne Baxter, she delivered her stinging lines peerlessly, but also found the deeply human side of this difficult woman. The performance earned her another Oscar nomination and has accorded her great respect with the passing of the years. The film also introduced her to Gary Merrill, who became her fourth husband (1950–60), and the two were seen together in two less-well known movies, *Another Man's Poison* and *Phone Call from a Stranger*. Playing a movie star for Fox in the hokey *The Star*, she was awarded nomination number nine before reprising Queen Elizabeth, in a secondary role, in *The Virgin Queen*. She was a small-town librarian in *Storm Center*, which dealt with book censorship; and tried to pass herself off as a Bronx housewife in *The Catered Affair*, a role played on television by Thelma Ritter with far more conviction. In England she supported *two* Alec Guinnesses in the disappointing *The Scapegoat*, playing most of her scenes in bed as his drug-addicted mother. A remake of *Lady for a Day*, now called *Pocketful of Miracles*, was intended to restore her to box-office favor, but difficulty on the set with co-star Glenn Ford and the end result, with Davis as the street vendor turned into a society lady, did not erase memories of May Robson in the earlier movie. Acclaim came unexpectedly with a low budget "horror" film that paired her with an actress she had always held in low esteem, Joan Crawford. *What Ever Happened to Baby Jane?* was Davis's last real motion picture peak, giving an appropriately bizarre performance that tottered on the brink of *grand guignol* and earned her a then-record tenth Oscar nomination.

An immediate follow-up, *Hush…Hush, Sweet Charlotte*, in which she was a crazed former belle being duped by sister Olivia de Havilland, also did agreeable business but wasn't nearly as good. Because of these movies Davis became a *grande dame* of the grotesque, participating in nonsensical films like *The Anniversary* (in which she sported an eye-patch) and *Bunny O'Hare* (robbing banks in hippie duds while carousing around on a motorcycle with Ernest Borgnine). Now past 60 and not receiving many film offers, she kept her name before the public on television, where she won an Emmy Award for *Strangers: The Story of a Mother and Daughter*. Movies like *Connecting Rooms* and *The Scientific Cardplayer* didn't find U.S. distribution, but Davis recovered some dignity with roles in the Agatha Christie thriller *Death on the Nile*, as one of the suspects, and *The Whales of August*, showing some of her old fire as Lillian Gish's blind, cantankerous sister. It was brave of her to continue acting, after becoming partially paralyzed as the result of a stroke a few years earlier, but Davis was just about the last actor anyone expected to quit before her time was up. She walked off her final movie, *Wicked Stepmother*, in disgust, and the film received very little distribution in a truncated, incoherent form in 1989, the same year that Davis died. There were three memoirs: *The Lonely Life* (1962); *Mother Goddamn* (1974), an extended interview within Whitney Stein's text in which she gave her opinions on each of her films; and *This 'n' That* (1987), a response to her daughter's unflattering book published a few years earlier. In 1977 she became the first female recipient of the American Film Institute's Life Achievement Award, a fitting honor for one as irreplaceable as Davis.

Screen: 1931: Bad Sister; Seed; Waterloo Bridge; 1932: Way Back Home; The Menace; Hell's House; The Man Who Played God; So Big; The Rich Are Always With Us; The Dark Horse; Cabin in the Cotton; Three on a Match; 1933: 20,000 Years in Sing Sing; Parachute Jumper; The Working Man; Ex-Lady; Bureau of Missing Persons; 1934: Fashions of 1934; The Big Shakedown; Jimmy the Gent; Fog Over Frisco; Of Human Bondage; Housewife; 1935: Bordertown; The Girl From 10th Avenue; Front Page Woman; Special Agent; Dangerous; 1936: The Petrified Forest; The Golden Arrow; Satan Met a Lady; 1937: Marked Woman; Kid Galahad; That Certain Woman; It's Love I'm After; 1938: Jezebel; The Sisters; 1939: Dark Victory; Juarez; The Old Maid; The Private Lives of Elizabeth and Essex; 1940: All This, and Heaven Too; The Letter; 1941: The Great Lie; The Bride Came C.O.D.; The Little Foxes; The Man Who Came to Dinner; 1942: In This Our Life; Now, Voyager; 1943: Watch on the Rhine; Thank Your Lucky Stars; Old Acquaintance; 1944: Mr. Skeffington; Hollywood Canteen; 1945: The Corn Is Green; 1946: A Stolen Life; Deception; 1948: Winter Meeting; June

Bride; **1949:** Beyond the Forest; **1950:** All About Eve; **1951:** Payment on Demand; **1952:** Another Man's Poison; Phone Call From a Stranger; The Star; **1955:** The Virgin Queen; **1956:** The Catered Affair; Storm Center; **1959:** John Paul Jones; The Scapegoat; **1961:** Pocketful of Miracles; **1962:** What Ever Happened to Baby Jane?; **1964:** Dead Ringer; The Empty Canvas; Where Love Has Gone; Hush…Hush, Sweet Charlotte; **1965:** The Nanny; **1968:** The Anniversary; **1971:** Bunny O'Hare; **1972:** Connecting Rooms (filmed 1970; nUSr); The Scientific Cardplayer (nUSr); **1976:** Burnt Offerings; **1978:** Return From Witch Mountain; Death on the Nile; **1980:** The Watcher in the Woods; **1987:** The Whales of August; **1989:** Wicked Stepmother.

NY Stage: **1929:** The Earth Between; Broken Dishes; **1930:** Solid South; **1952:** Two's Company; **1960:** The World of Carl Sandburg; **1961:** The Night of the Iguana.

Select TV: **1957:** With Malice Toward One (sp); For Better For Worse (sp); Footnote on a Doll (sp); **1958:** That Cold Touch (sp); The Starmaker (sp); **1972:** Madame Sin; The Judge and Jake Wade; **1973:** Scream Pretty Peggy; **1976:** The Disappearance of Aimee; **1978:** The Dark Secret of Harvest Home; **1979:** Strangers: The Story of a Mother and Daughter; **1980:** White Mama; Skyward; **1981:** Family Reunion; **1982:** A Piano for Mrs. Cimino; Little Gloria…Happy at Last (ms); **1983:** Right of Way; Arthur Hailey's Hotel; **1985:** Murder With Mirrors; **1986:** As Summers Die.

JOAN DAVIS

(MADONNA JOSEPHINE DAVIS) BORN: ST. PAUL, MN, JUNE 29, 1907. DIED: MAY 22, 1961.

At a time when physically funny women were not the norm, Joan Davis was one of the few to throw herself into knockabout slapstick comedy. The pointy-nosed, rubbery-faced comedienne started out in vaudeville with husband Seranus "Sy" Wills, as the comedy team Wills and Davis. Signed by 20th Century-Fox in 1937, she was used extensively for specialty spots and supporting roles in musicals like *Wake Up and Live* (dancing to "I Love You Much Too Much Muchacha"); *You Can't Have Everything*; *Thin Ice* (singing "Olga From the Volga"); *Life Begins in College*; *On the Avenue*; and *Sally, Irene and Mary* (as Irene). She certainly garnered her share of audience attention, since most of these were very profitable for the studio, but Fox didn't give her any vehicles of her own, using her instead in noticeably low-budget fare like *Manhattan Heartbeat* and *Sailor's Lady*. After a beneficial stop at Universal, playing a professional radio screamer in a good Abbott and Costello comedy, *Hold That Ghost*, she finally started getting leads, at Columbia, in quickie titles like *Two Latins From Manhattan*, *Sweethearts of the Fleet*, and *Two Senoritas From Chicago*, Jinx Falkenberg being senorita number two. Over at RKO she teamed up with Eddie Cantor for *Show Business*, which drew enough positive feedback from both the fans and from Cantor that she was asked to reunite with him four years later for *If You Knew Susie*, which met with less favorable results. After a lame 1952 Columbia farce, *Harem Girl*, she formed her own production company and came up with her own hit television series, *I Married Joan*, finally getting the success she deserved.

Screen: **1935:** Millions in the Air; **1936:** Bunker Bean; **1937:** The Holy Terror; Time Out for Romance; Nancy Steel Is Missing; Wake Up and Live; You Can't Have Everything; Sing and Be Happy; Angel's Holiday; The Great Hospital Mystery; Thin Ice; On the Avenue; Life Begins in College; Love and Hisses; **1938:** Sally, Irene and Mary; Josette; My Lucky Star; Hold That Co-

Ed; Just Around the Corner; **1939:** Tailspin; Daytime Wife; Too Busy to Work; **1940:** Free, Blonde and 21; Manhattan Heartbeat; Sailor's Lady; **1941:** For Beauty's Sake; Sun Valley Serenade; Hold That Ghost; Two Latins From Manhattan; **1942:** Yokel Boy; Sweethearts of the Fleet; **1943:** He's My Guy; Two Senoritas From Chicago; Around the World; **1944:** Show Business; Beautiful But Broke; Kansas City Kitty; **1945:** She Gets Her Man; George White's Scandals; **1946:** She Wrote the Book; **1948:** If You Knew Susie; **1949:** Make Mine Laughs; **1950:** Traveling Saleswoman; Love That Brute; **1951:** The Groom Wore Spurs; **1952:** Harem Girl.

Select TV: **1952–55:** I Married Joan (series).

NANCY DAVIS

(ANNE FRANCIS ROBBINS) BORN: NEW YORK, NY, JULY 6, 1921. ED: SMITH COL.

Better-known under her later married name, Nancy Davis started off in summer stock before moving on to Broadway, making her bow in the 1946 musical *Lute Song*, supporting Mary Martin. After some more regional theatre work, she won a contract with MGM and debuted for them, in 1949, in *The Doctor and the Girl*, the girl being Janet Leigh, not Davis. A handful of pictures followed, but she made little impression as an actress, co-starring with James Whitmore in two dramas, *Shadow in the Sky*, and the odd fantasy *The Next Voice You Hear…*, about God speaking on the radio, a movie less ridiculous than its premise might lead one to think; and in one with future California Senator George Murphy, *Talk About a Stranger*, in 1952. That same year she made her own indirect move into politics by marrying Ronald Reagan. The next year she featured in her most famous movie, the interesting sci-fi thriller *Donovan's Brain*, as scientist Lew Ayres's concerned wife. Later, she and Reagan gave the world a chance to see them playing lovers in *Hellcats of the Navy*, but she retired from movies in 1958, only to return to the limelight when Reagan served as governor of California, and then when she became First Lady in 1981. This did not cause a great rush on the public's part to rent *Hellcats of the Navy*, for to many she was no more a personality worth enthusing over than she had been in her acting days.

Screen: **1949:** The Doctor and the Girl; East Side, West Side; **1950:** Shadow in the Sky; The Next Voice You Hear …; **1951:** Night Into Morning; It's a Big Country; Shadow in the Sky; **1952:** Talk About a Stranger; **1953:** Donovan's Brain; **1957:** Hellcats of the Navy; **1958:** Crash Landing; **1996:** Wild Bill: Hollywood Maverick; **1998:** Off the Menu: The Last Days of Chasen's.

NY Stage: **1946:** Lute Song.

Select TV: **1953:** 22 Sycamore Road (sp); First Born; **1954:** The Pearl Street Incident; **1958:** Turkey for the President (sp); **1961:** Money and Minister (sp).

OSSIE DAVIS

BORN: COGDELL, GA, DECEMBER 18, 1917. ED: HOWARD UNIV.

In a quieter way than Sidney Poitier, the superb Ossie Davis was an important contributor in the struggle for black actors to break away from the evils of Hollywood stereotyping. The two, in fact, made their debuts in the same movie, 1950's *No Way Out*. Davis had established himself on the New York stage in the title role of the short-lived 1946 play *Jeb*, which featured Ruby Dee, who became his wife two years later.

During the 1950s his theatre credits included *The Wisteria Trees* and *The Green Pastures*, and he had his first work as a playwright, *The Big Deal*, produced in 1953. He really came into his own when he wrote for himself the role of the fiery preacher in the 1961 Broadway hit, *Purlie Victorious*. Two years later, a very low budget movie adaptation, re-titled *Gone Are the Days*, would preserve his performance. Because of his stage success, Davis secured supporting parts in Otto Preminger's *The Cardinal*, as a priest facing the violence of the Ku Klux Klan, and *The Hill*, as a prisoner who finally blows his cool under Harry Andrews's bigoted taunts. He got his best film role in the genial western *The Scalphunters*, as the ingenious runaway slave who is more than a match for crude fur trapper Burt Lancaster. Less interestingly, he teamed with Burt Reynolds for another light-hearted look at the Old West, in *Sam Whiskey*, this time as a blacksmith.

A prime part as an outspoken slave who stands up to wicked Stephen Boyd in the trashy melodrama *Slaves*, reflected the post-civil rights era in which it was made. Davis then turned to directing, receiving favorable notices for the popular urban comedy *Cotton Comes to Harlem*, which he also co-scripted; the domestic drama, *Black Girl*; and the actioner, *Gordon's War*. He starred in *Countdown at Kusini*, a production co-financed by a black fraternity, but it was barely distributed. As a graying, intelligent, and dignified character player he was well served by director Spike Lee in such movies as *Do the Right Thing*, as the neighborhood drunk, romancing Ruby Dee; *Jungle Fever*, as the self-righteous father of drug addict Samuel L. Jackson; and *Get on the Bus*, as an old-timer traveling to the Million Man March in Washington, DC. He had a wonderful cameo as the judge in the 1994 film adaptation of *The Client*, a part he would repeat on the subsequent television series the next year, and another substantial co-starring part, in *I'm Not Rappaport*, reprising his stage role as a building superintendent who forms an unlikely friendship with radical Walter Matthau. On television, he chalked up writing credits on series like *East Side, West Side* and *The Eleventh Hour*, and wrote and directed the special *Today Is Ours*.

Screen: 1950: No Way Out; 1951: Fourteen Hours; 1953: The Joe Louis Story; 1963: Gone Are the Days (and wr.); The Cardinal; 1964: Shock Treatment; 1965: The Hill; 1966: A Man Called Adam; 1968: The Scalphunters; 1969: Sam Whiskey; Slaves; 1972: Malcolm X (voice); 1975: Let's Do It Again; 1976: Countdown at Kusini (and dir.; prod.); 1979: Hot Stuff; House of God (dtc); 1984: Harry and Son; 1985: Avenging Angel; 1988: School Days; 1989: Do the Right Thing; 1990: Joe Versus the Volcano; 1991: Jungle Fever; 1992: Gladiator; Malcolm X (voice); 1993: Grumpy Old Men; 1994: The Client; 1996: Get on the Bus; I'm Not Rappaport; 1997: 4 Little Girls; 1998: Doctor Dolittle; 2000: Dinosaur (voice); Here's to Life! (nUSr).

NY Stage: 1946: Jeb; Anna Lucasta; 1948: Leading Lady; 1949: Smile of the World; 1950: The Wisteria Trees; 1951: The Royal Family; The Green Pastures; Remains to Be Seen; 1953: Touchstone; 1955: The Wisteria Trees (revival); 1956: No Time for Sergeants; 1957: Jamaica; 1960: A Raisin in the Sun; 1961: Purlie Victorious; 1963: Ballad of Bimshire (ob); 1965: The Zulu and the Zayda; 1979: Take It From the Top (ob; and dir.); 1986: I'm Not Rappaport.

Select TV: 1951: Green Pastures (sp); 1955: The Emperor Jones (sp); 1960: John Brown's Raid (sp); Seven Times Monday (sp); 1967: The Outsider; 1969: Night Gallery; Teacher, Teacher; 1971: The Sheriff; 1977: Billy: Portrait of a Street Kid; 1978: King (ms); 1979: Roots: The Next Generations (ms); Freedom Road (ms); 1980: All God's Children; 1981: Don't Look Back; 1989–90: B.L. Stryker (series); 1990–94: Evening Shade (series); 1993: The Ernest Green Story; Queen (ms); 1994: Ray Alexander: A Taste

for Justice; Stephen King's The Stand (ms); 1995: Ray Alexander: A Menu for Murder; The Android Affair; 1995–96: John Grisham's The Client (series); 1996: Home of the Brave; 1996–98: Promised Land (series); 1997: Miss Evers' Boys; 12 Angry Men; 1999: The Secret Path; The Soul Collector; A View to Cherish; 2000: Finding Buck McHenry; 2001: Anne Rice's The Feast of All Saints.

SAMMY DAVIS, JR.
BORN: NEW YORK, NY, DECEMBER 8, 1925.
DIED: MAY 16, 1990.

One of the most dynamic all-around entertainers in the last half of the 20th century, Sammy Davis, Jr. never achieved the status of a true movie star, but he did carve out his own unmistakable niche on the big screen. The pint-sized singer-dancer was already onstage as a child in a trio with his father and his uncle, Will Mastin, and appeared in a pair of short subjects, *Rufus Jones for President* and *Season's Greetings*. By the end of World War II, Sammy was the star attraction of the act, dabbling in song, mimicry, comedy, dancing, and musicianship, and became an in-demand nightclub headliner and recording artist. It looked as if his career had come to an end when Davis lost an eye in an automobile accident, but instead, in the aftermath of this tragic event, he flourished, overcoming physical and racial barriers to become one of the most popular entertainers of the 1950s. In the midst of his rising fame he made his adult screen debut, as Eartha Kitt's sailor lover, in the 1958 version of *Anna Lucasta*. The following year he stopped the show in a role he was born to play, Sportin' Life, in *Porgy and Bess*, selling "It Ain't Necessarily So" in his inimitable style. His friendship with Frank Sinatra made him one of the much-publicized "Rat Pack" and he was called on to brighten up several of their "home movies." He crooned "E-O-Eleven" as a garbage man/demolitions expert in the Vegas heist caper, *Ocean's Eleven*; played a Civil War version of Gunga Din in *Sergeant's 3*; and gave a powerhouse performance singing "Bang! Bang!" in *Robin and the 7 Hoods*.

As the field for black performers opened wider and wider in the 1960s, Davis was given a showcase as an embittered jazz trumpeter in *A Man Called Adam*, but it was cheaply done and made little impact. With another former Rat Pack member, Peter Lawford, he starred in an innocuous comedy set in England, *Salt and Pepper*, the principal joke of which was that Davis was named "Salt" and Lawford was "Pepper." Davis was at his full capacity in his nightclub act or on his frequent television variety show appearances, though he did get another scene-stealing number on screen, as a groovy street preacher belting out "Rhythm of Life" in Bob Fosse's *Sweet Charity*. Having had hit records with "What Kind of Fool Am I?" and "The Candy Man" by Leslie Bricusse and Anthony Newley, he starred in a Broadway revival of their musical, *Stop the World — I Want to Get Off*, which was curiously filmed (and promptly ignored) under the title *Sammy Stops the World*. In the crummy car chase movie, *The Cannonball Run*, he and Dean Martin livened up the proceedings as a pair of priests, and his last role, as an aging hoofer in *Tap*, reminded audiences of what a fine actor he had always been. There were three autobiographies: *Yes I Can* (1965); *Hollywood in a Suitcase* (1980); and *Why Me?* (1989).

Screen: 1958: Anna Lucasta; 1959: Porgy and Bess; 1960: Ocean's Eleven; Pepe; 1962: Sergeants 3; Convicts 4; The Threepenny Opera; 1963: Johnny Cool; 1964: Nightmare in the Sun; Robin and the 7 Hoods; 1966: A Man Called Adam; 1968: Salt and

Pepper; 1969: Sweet Charity; 1970: Elvis; That's the Way It Is!; One More Time; 1971: Diamonds Are Forever; 1972: Gone With the West/Little Moon & Jud McGraw (filmed 1969); 1973: Save the Children; 1976: James Dean: The First American Teenager; 1978: Sammy Stops the World; 1981: The Cannonball Run; 1982: Heidi's Song (voice); 1983: Cracking Up/ Smorgasbord; 1984: Cannonball Run II; 1985: That's Dancing; 1986: The Perils of P.K.; 1988: Moon Over Parador; 1989: Tap.

NY Stage: 1956: Mr. Wonderful; 1964: Golden Boy; 1978: Stop the World — I Want to Get Off!

Select TV: 1958: Auf Wiedersehn (sp); 1961: Memory in White (sp); 1962: The Legend (sp); 1966: The Sammy Davis, Jr. Show (series); Alice in Wonderland: or What's a Nice Kid Like You Doin' in a Place Like This? (sp; voice); 1969: The Pigeon; 1971: The Trackers; 1973: Poor Devil; NBC Follies (series); 1975–77: Sammy and Company (series); 1985: Alice in Wonderland; 1990: The Kid Who Loved Christmas.

DORIS DAY

(DORIS MARY ANN VON KAPPELHOFF)
BORN: CINCINNATI, OH, APRIL 3, 1924.

In an increasingly cynical world it became very easy to pour contempt on Doris Day's sunny, virginal film persona, but there is much to enjoy in her bright singing voice, smart penchant for light comedy, and surprisingly assured attempts at drama. She began by singing on local radio stations before moving to the big time with Bob Crosby's band and then Les Brown's, scoring a chart hit with "Sentimental Journey." Warner Bros. took an interest in her on the recommendation of composer Jule Styne, and studio director Michael Curtiz gave her a part (fourth-billed) in the musical comedy *Romance on the High Seas*, wherein she introduced another hit, "It's Magic." She stayed with the studio into the mid-1950s, mainly in light musicals, but occasionally, as in *Young Man With a Horn*, impressively showing a serious side. In *Storm Warning*, a drama with Ginger Rogers, she not only didn't sing a note but was killed off by the Ku Klux Klan! On a lighter note, in *My Dream Is Yours*, she was reteamed with her *High Seas* co-star, Jack Carson, in a remake of *20 Million Sweethearts*, followed in quick succession by *It's a Great Feeling*, as a Hollywood hopeful sharing the screen with several Warner Bros. guest stars; *Tea for Two*, a reworking of the old stage hit *No, No, Nanette*, and the first of five with Gordon MacRae; and *West Point Story*, a botched opportunity to work with James Cagney, something that was rectified down the line.

She was enjoyable in the lively western *Calamity Jane*, belting out the Oscar-winning "Secret Love," as the butch and spunky heroine, and was charming in a pair of nostalgic pieces based on Booth Parkington's "Penrod" stories, *On Moonlight Bay* and *By the Light of the Silvery Moon*, both with MacRae. More typically, she played the loving wife in biopics of songwriter Gus Kahn (Danny Thomas) in *I'll See You in My Dreams*, and baseball player Grover Cleveland Alexander (Ronald Reagan) in *The Winning Team*, which at least allowed her to become temporarily intolerant when she walked out on him, mistaking his epilepsy for alcoholism. A remake of *Four Daughters*, called *Young at Heart*, gave her some emotional grist opposite Frank Sinatra, but with only one brief opportunity to sing together. Day was eager to move on and her contract was dissolved, so she went to MGM for the Ruth Etting biopic, *Love Me or Leave Me*, singing some fabulous torch songs while being slapped around by James Cagney, as her hoodlum spouse. At Paramount she paired with James Stewart in Alfred Hitchcock's superior remake of his own *The Man Who Knew Too Much*, delivering an excellent performance, particularly in a scene where Stewart sedates her before telling her their son has been kidnapped. She also introduced the Oscar-winning song that she would be forever identified with, "Que Sera Sera (Whatever Will Be Will Be)."

Because she was now more interested in proving her capabilities in straight acting, she rarely performed again in full-fledged musicals. There were, in fact, only two more of these: Stanley Donen's delightful *The Pajama Game*, in which she did sterling work in a cast consisting mostly of the original Broadway company, and the less-enjoyable *Billy Rose's Jumbo*, in 1962. Oddly enough, these were among her least popular movies at a time when she was the biggest female draw around. In the melodramatic *Julie*, she suspected psychotic husband Louis Jourdan of wanting to kill her and ended up having to pilot an airplane in the hokey climax, and in the glossy thriller *Midnight Lace*, she was terrorized in a backlot fog-bound London. She was much more at ease with lighter fare like *Teacher's Pet*, a witty comedy about journalism teamed surprisingly well with the much-older Clark Gable, and *It Happened to Jane*, in which she took on some crooked railroad executives, cast opposite another actor she clicked with beautifully, Jack Lemmon. Despite the two of them being among the most popular stars of the time, the movie, curiously, did weak business. The gargantuan hit that set her on the throne as the queen of perky comedies was Universal's *Pillow Talk*, a sharp and sassy battle of the sexes with Rock Hudson. She received her lone Oscar nomination for her portrayal of an icy Manhattan decorator duped into romance because of a crossed phone line. Despite the tendency of some modern audiences to point to these particular Day films as a low point of that era, many, in fact remain smart and satisfying. Probably her two best were *Please Don't Eat the Daisies*, in which she and drama critic husband David Niven move to a large house in the suburbs, and *Lover Come Back*, replaying her love-hate deception game with Rock Hudson in the world of advertising.

She played the stonewall virginal act a bit too coyly with Cary Grant in *That Touch of Mink*, but the film was another huge moneymaker for Universal. James Garner proved another ideal co-star in *The Thrill of It All*, in which Day sent her marital life into an uproar by becoming a spokesperson for a soap company. But the cutesy *Move Over, Darling*, again with Garner, took most of the wit out of its original source, *My Favorite Wife*, falling flat on its face, while a final Hudson teaming, *Send Me No Flowers*, was decidedly sub-par. Filling the vacancy left by Hudson and Garner was virile Rod Taylor in both *Do Not Disturb*, which set Day down in a British backdrop to give things a different twist, and the slapstick *The Glass Bottom Boat*, where she was mistaken for a secret agent. Audiences were still paying to see her, but things started to get downright desperate with the clumsy spy spoof *Caprice*, and the sex farce *Where Were You When the Light Went Out?*, set against the notorious 1965 New York City blackout. A pale western spoof, *The Ballad of Josie*, and a very mild family comedy, *With Six You Get Eggroll*, seemed to indicate it was time to quit as there was no place for her kind of wholesomeness in the movies of the late 1960s. Much to her displeasure, her husband-manager Marty Melcher signed her to do a television series, *The Doris Day Show*, which became an expected ratings winner. After their divorce it was revealed that he had been robbing her blind, and she won a very hefty lawsuit against him that made headlines. In 1975 she published her autobiography, *Doris Day: Her Own Story*, which became a bestseller. Aside from a mid-1980s cable series devoted to her love of animals, she disappeared from the entertainment scene altogether, leaving fond memories of a simpler era for her very loyal legion of devotees.

Screen: 1948: Romance on the High Seas; 1949: My Dream is Yours; It's a Great Feeling; 1950: Young Man With a Horn; Tea for Two; West Point Story; 1951: Storm Warning; Lullaby of Broadway; On Moonlight Bay; Starlift; I'll See You in My Dreams; 1952: The Winning Team; April in Paris; 1953: By the Light of the Silvery Moon; Calamity Jane; 1954: Lucky Me; Young at Heart; 1955: Love Me or Leave Me; 1956: The Man Who Knew Too Much; Julie; 1957: The Pajama Game; 1958: Teacher's Pet; The Tunnel of Love; 1959: It Happened to Jane; Pillow Talk; 1960: Please Don't Eat the Daisies; Midnight Lace; 1961: Lover Come Back; 1962: That Touch of Mink; Billy Rose's Jumbo; 1963: The Thrill of It All; Move Over, Darling; 1964: Send Me No Flowers; 1965: Do Not Disturb; 1966: The Glass Bottom Boat; 1967: Caprice; The Ballad of Josie; 1968: Where Were You When the Lights Went Out?; With Six You Get Egg Roll.

Select TV: 1968–73: The Doris Day Show (series); 1975: Doris Day Today (sp); 1984: Doris Day's Best Friends (series).

LARAINE DAY

(LARAINE JOHNSON) BORN: ROOSEVELT, UT, OCTOBER 13, 1917.

Pleasant but lacking the magnetism required of a front-rank actress, Laraine Day lucked out by latching onto a signature role in a hit film series that kept her name in the public eye, albeit temporarily. Joining the Long Beach Players, she took her stage name from the theatre's manager, Elias Day, and was spotted there by a talent scout who got her a brief bit in the 1937 version of *Stella Dallas*, billed under her real name. She was signed by MGM to play Wallace Beery's daughter in *Sergeant Madden*, in 1939, and that same year, now called Laraine Day, she joined the hospital staff of *Calling Dr. Kildare*, as the likeable nurse Mary Lamont. She was called back to play the role on five more occasions, ending with *Dr. Kildare's Wedding Day*, in 1941. During this period she had some worthy assignments, notably Alfred Hitchcock's fine thriller *Foreign Correspondent*, helping Joel McCrea search for an assassin, and *Journey for Margaret*, in which she suffered from emotional trauma. There were sizeable roles in hits like *Mr. Lucky*, with Cary Grant, and, as a throwback to *Kildare*, nurse duties in *The Story of Dr. Wassell*, with Gary Cooper, but these were not among those stars' better pictures. In 1947 she became the wife of Leo Durocher, manager of the New York Giants baseball team, a relationship that would last until 1960. Top billed as the *Bride by Mistake*, she posed as her own secretary; was a destructive kleptomaniac in the noir *The Locket*; was Kirk Douglas's office help in *My Dear Secretary*; and was the "I" in *I Married a Communist*, an earnest but dated anti-Red melodrama. During the 1950s she appeared in one hit film, *The High and the Mighty*, as a passenger aboard a damaged plane; had her own short-lived television series, *Daydream With Laraine*; and wrote a book, *Day With the Giants*, in 1953. When MGM revived *Doctor Kildare* as a television series in the 1960s, the character of Mary Lamont was not a part of the regular cast.

Screen: AS LARAINE JOHNSON: 1937: Stella Dallas; 1938: Border G-Men; Scandal Street; Painted Desert; 1939: Arizona Legion.

AS LARAINE DAY: 1939: Sergeant Madden; Calling Dr. Kildare; Tarzan Finds a Son!; Secret of Dr. Kildare; 1940: My Son, My Son; I Take This Woman; And One Was Beautiful; Dr. Kildare's Strange Case; Foreign Correspondent; Dr. Kildare Goes Home; Dr. Kildare's Crisis; 1941: The Bad Man; The Trial of Mary Dugan; The People vs. Dr. Kildare; Dr. Kildare's Wedding Day; Unholy Partners; Kathleen; 1942: Journey for Margaret; Fingers at the Window; A Yank on the Burma Road; 1943: Mr. Lucky; 1944: The Story of Dr. Wassell; Bride by Mistake; 1945: Those Endearing Young Charms; Keep Your Powder Dry; 1946: The Locket; 1947: Tycoon; 1948: My Dear Secretary; 1949: I Married a Communist/The Woman on Pier 13; Without Honor; 1954: The High and the Mighty; 1956: Toy Tiger; Three for Jamie Dawn; 1960: The Third Voice.

Select TV: 1951: The Crisis (sp); Day Dreaming With Laraine Day (series); It's a Promise (sp); 1952: So Many Things Happen (sp); 1953: Women Who Wait (sp); 1954: Turn Back the Clock (sp); Double Indemnity (sp); 1955: Final Tribute (sp); 1956: Prima Donna (sp); Now, Voyager (sp); Woman Who Dared (sp); 1959: Alone (sp); Dark as the Night (sp); 1975: Murder on Flight 502; 1978: Return to Fantasy Island.

JAMES DEAN

BORN: MARION, IN, FEBRUARY 8, 1931.
DIED: SEPTEMBER 30, 1955.

With only three starring roles to his credit, James Dean has become one of the lasting icons of Hollywood. Intense, handsome, vulnerable, and highly original, he mesmerized moviegoers in the mid-1950s and continues to fascinate them to this day. After winning a drama contest in high school, he went to UCLA to partake of James Whitmore's acting classes. While in Los Angeles he managed to get bit parts in four movies (he can be seen at a sweet-shop counter in *Has Anybody Seen My Gal?*, for example) before he went east to join the Actors Studio. There was much television work and two Broadway roles, including *The Immoralist*, as a homosexual Arab, which earned him a Theatre World Award. Back in Hollywood he won the role of tormented teen Cal Trask in Elia Kazan's adaptation of *East of Eden*. Although he was billed below Julie Harris, and the movie contained fine work from the likes of Jo Van Fleet and Raymond Massey, it was Dean who riveted audiences. His strange, uncompromising performance ranged from childlike sincerity to volatile pain and it earned him an Oscar nomination.

The success of the picture made him nothing less than a sensation and, with his second movie, *Rebel Without a Cause*, he became a restless symbol of teen angst. By the time of its release, in October of 1955, Dean was dead, killed in a car accident while driving in his Porsche en route to Salinas. The following year he was seen in his last role, playing ranch hand Jett Rink in George Steven's superb epic, *Giant*. Dean was required to metamorphose from a young, inarticulate stud, mooning over Elizabeth Taylor, to an egomaniacal, drunken millionaire, and he did it so impressively that he was again Oscar-nominated, thus making him the only performer to receive posthumous recognition from the Academy *twice*. Soon after, his cult began to grow, prompting Warners (who had released all three movies) to throw together a curious documentary, *The James Dean Story*, under the guidance of then-unknown director Robert Altman. (25 years later, Altman would direct the stage play *Come Back to the Five and Dime, Jimmy Dean, Jimmy Dean*, as well as its film adaptation.) Countless books on Dean have poured onto the market, including several which acknowledged his homosexuality, and almost all of which speak of his neuroses and flashes of cruelty. There are posters, buttons, mugs, t-shirts, and figurines available in most nostalgia and junk shops, and an annual gathering in his hometown of Fairmount, Indiana. Best of all, there are his starring films available for viewing, all worthwhile achievements, which seem to justify all the hype.

Screen: 1951: Sailor Beware; Fixed Bayonets; 1952: Has Anybody

Seen My Gal?; 1953: Trouble Along the Way; 1955: East of Eden; Rebel Without a Cause; 1956: Giant.
NY Stage: 1952: See the Jaguar; 1954: The Immoralist.
Select TV: 1951: Hill Number One (sp); 1952: Prologue to Glory (sp); 1953: Something for an Empty Briefcase (sp); Sentence of Death (sp); A Long Time Till Dawn (sp); Life Sentence (sp); Keep Our Honor Bright (sp); The Bells of Cockaigne (sp); Harvest (sp); 1954: Run Like a Thief (sp); The Unlighted Road (sp).

ROSEMARY DeCAMP

BORN: PRESCOTT, AZ, NOVEMBER 14, 1910.
DIED: FEBRUARY 20, 2001.

Because of her warm and matronly personality, Rosemary DeCamp played mother to performers who were often her own age, not young enough for her to have possibly sired them, or even, as in the case of James Cagney, older than she was! She came to films in 1940, after many years on radio, to appear as a naïve immigrant in the Martha Scott vehicle, *Cheers for Miss Bishop.* Although she worked at various studios it was at Warners Bros., where she was under contract, that she did her most notable work, starting with the one where she played Cagney's mom, *Yankee Doodle Dandy,* and then the George Gershwin biopic, *Rhapsody in Blue,* as parent to Robert Alda. She was Zachary Scott's cuckolded wife in the successful soaper *Nora Prentiss,* and Doris Day's ma in the charming period musicals *On Moonlight Bay* and *By the Light of the Silvery Moon,* but had to be content with being given secondary roles in all of her films. For Universal she was William Bendix's wife in the expanded version of the radio hit *The Life of Riley,* a role she later played on television with Jackie Gleason as Riley. After playing the mom in the campy William Castle horror film, *13 Ghosts,* she was off the big screen for over 20 years, finally returning in the little-seen spoof, *Saturday the 14th.* Among her frequent television appearances was a recurring role as Marlo Thomas's mother on the series *That Girl.*
Screen: 1941: Cheers for Miss Bishop; Hold Back the Dawn; 1942: Jungle Book; Yankee Doodle Dandy; Eyes in the Night; Commandos Strike at Dawn; Smith of Minnesota; 1943: City Without Men; This Is the Army; 1944: The Merry Monahans; Bowery to Broadway; Practically Yours; 1945: Blood on the Sun; Pride of the Marines; Week-end at the Waldorf; Rhapsody in Blue; Danger Signal; Too Young to Know; 1946: From This Day Forward; Two Guys From Milwaukee; 1947: Nora Prentiss; 1949: Night Unto Night; The Life of Riley; Look for the Silver Lining; The Story of Seabiscuit; 1950: The Big Hangover; 1951: Night Into Morning; On Moonlight Bay; 1952: Treasure of the Lost Canyon; Scandal Sheet; 1953: By the Light of the Silvery Moon; Main Street to Broadway; So This is Love; 1955: Strategic Air Command; Many Rivers to Cross; 1960: 13 Ghosts; 1981: Saturday the 14th.
Select TV: 1949–50: The Life of Riley (series); 1953: Alias Nora Hale (sp); 1954: Good of His Soul (sp); 1955: Nobody's Fool (sp); 1955–59: The Bob Cummings Show/Love That Bob (series); 1958: Trial by Slander (sp); No Place to Run (sp); 1966–70: That Girl (series); 1978: The Time Machine; 1979: Blind Ambition (ms).

YVONNE DE CARLO

(PEGGY YVONNE MIDDLETON) BORN: VANCOUVER, BRITISH COLUMBIA, CANADA, SEPTEMBER 1, 1922.

There is little to be said for most of the turgid movies Yvonne De Carlo appeared in during her tenure as the "B" queen at Universal, and she is instead better known to most audiences for her two-year stint as Lily on the syndicated television series, *The Munsters.* Trained as a dancer, she journeyed to Hollywood several times with her mother, but failed to get a break in the movie business. She got work as a nightclub chorine and was eventually signed by Paramount, where she spent most of her time filling the background in movies like *This Gun for Hire, Road to Morocco, For Whom the Bell Tolls,* and *The Story of Dr. Wassell.* Over at Republic she had her first notable part, playing an Indian in the cheaply made 1943 version of *The Deerslayer.* Her big chance came when she won the lead in Universal's *Salome, Where She Danced,* which, despite its Biblical title, was set principally in Arizona. As a Viennese dancer-turned-spy, she was saddled with a ridiculous script and a dull leading man, Rod Cameron, and the picture was dismissed as rubbish by the press. It seemed dangerous to pair her again with Cameron for her follow-up, *Frontier Gal,* but at least this one was intentionally funny.

She plugged away in various Technicolor costume pictures and westerns, most of which garnered awful reviews. In *Song of Scheherazade,* she was the exotic inspiration for composer Rimsky-Korsakov, as played by Jean-Pierre Aumont; *Slave Girl,* which was intended as a parody, featured a talking camel; *Calamity Jane and Sam Bass* cast her opposite Howard Duff; *Buccaneer's Girl* found her as a stowaway in love with pirate Philip Friend; in the musical *Casbah,* she sang the hit song, "For Every Man There's a Woman;" and, in *The Desert Hawk,* she returned as the actual Scheherezade. DeCarlo's notices were never particularly favorable, although her good looks were often commented upon. In the melodrama, *Criss Cross,* she turned in a fine performance as Burt Lancaster's scheming ex-wife, but after that one it was back to potboilers with a stop in Britain, playing Alec Guinness's Moroccan girlfriend in *The Captain's Paradise,* a movie whose premise was more engaging than its execution. She took an above-average assignment as Charlton Heston's noble wife, Sephora, in the monster 1956 hit, *The Ten Commandments,* and showed her comical side as the housekeeper in John Wayne's *McLintock!,* invoking jealousy in Maureen O'Hara. Then came the role of the stylishly vampiric housewife Lily Munster in the television series, *The Munsters,* and a spin-off theatrical feature, *Munster, Go Home!,* which brought her lifelong fame. Most of her latter-day movies were undistinguished, although she got a prime moment in the Broadway spotlight, singing "I'm Still Here" in the original production of the cult musical *Follies.* Her autobiography, *Yvonne,* was published in 1987.
Screen: 1942: Harvard, Here I Come; This Gun for Hire; Road to Morocco; Lucky Jordan; Youth on Parade; 1943: Rhythm Parade; The Crystal Ball; Salute for Three; For Whom the Bell Tolls; So Proudly We Hail!; Let's Face It; True to Life; The Deerslayer; 1944: Standing Room Only; The Story of Dr. Wassell; Rainbow Island; Kismet; Practically Yours; Here Come the Waves; 1945: Bring on the Girls; Salome, Where She Danced; Frontier Gal; 1947: Song of Scheherazade; Brute Force; Slave Girl; 1948: Black Bart; Casbah; River Lady; 1949: Calamity Jane and Sam Bass; The Gal Who Took the West; Criss Cross; 1950: Buccaneer's Girl; The Desert Hawk; 1951: Tomahawk; Hotel Sahara; Silver City; 1952: The San Francisco Story; Scarlet Angel; Hurricane Smith; 1953: Sombrero; Seal Devils; Fort Algiers; The Captain's Paradise; 1954: Border River; Passion; Tonight's the Night/Happy Ever After; The Contessa's Secret (nUSr); 1955: Shotgun; Flame of the Islands; 1956: Magic Fire; Raw Edge; Death of a Scoundrel; The Ten Commandments; 1957: Band of Angels; 1959: Timbuktu; 1960: Mary Magdalene; 1963: McLintock!; 1964: A Global Affair; Law of the Lawless; 1965: Tentazioni Proibiti (nUSr); 1966: Munster, Go Home!; 1967:

Hostile Guns; **1968:** The Power; Arizona Bushwhackers; **1971:** The Delta Factor; The Seven Minutes; **1975:** Arizona Slim; **1976:** It Seemed Like a Good Idea at the Time; Won Ton Ton, the Dog Who Saved Hollywood; House of Shadows; Blazing Stewardesses/Texas Layover; **1977:** Satan's Cheerleaders; **1978:** Nocturna: Granddaughter of Dracula; **1980:** Guyana: Cult of the Damned; Silent Scream; The Man With Bogart's Face/Sam Marlowe, Private Eye; **1981:** Play Dead; Liar's Moon; **1983:** Vultures in Paradise; **1987:** Cellar Dweller (dtv); **1988:** American Gothic; **1990:** Mirror, Mirror; **1991:** Oscar; **1992:** The Naked Truth (dtv); Desert Kickboxer (dtv); **1993:** The Sorority House Murders (dtv); Season of the Heart (dtv; voice).

NY Stage: 1971: Follies.

Select TV: 1956: Hot Cargo (sp); 1964–66: The Munsters (series); 1974: The Girl on the Late, Late Show; The Mark of Zorro; 1981: The Munster's Revenge; 1986: A Masterpiece of Murder; 1995: Here Come the Munsters; The Barefoot Executive.

FRANCES DEE

(JEAN FRANCES DEE) BORN: LOS ANGELES, CA, NOVEMBER 26, 1907. RAISED IN CHICAGO, IL.

A serenely beautiful actress of Hollywood's golden era, Frances Dee stayed firmly on the second tier throughout her career. She exuded modest charm in every assignment she took, but she lacked the necessary chops to carry the show. Starting as an extra, she got her big break when Maurice Chevalier requested her for his leading lady in *Playboy of Paris*, as the boss's daughter who loves Maurice, a waiter. Paramount ideally cast her as the ravishing rich girl Phillips Holmes commits murder for in *An American Tragedy*, and she continued to play the love interest to leading men like Richard Arlen in *Caught*, George Bancroft in *Rich Man's Folly*, and Jack Oakie in *June Moon*, as the sweet lady who nearly loses him to the evils of show business. In 1933 she co-starred with Buster Crabbe in Paramount's pseudo-Tarzan epic, *King of the Jungle*, and did her best work to date as Meg in RKO's sterling adaptation of *Little Women*. That same year she was featured in *The Silver Cord*, in support of Joel McCrea, whom she promptly wed, beginning one of the most enduring marriages in Hollywood history. With him she would appear in the Goldwyn logging drama *Come and Get It*; the popular but otherwise unremarkable western, *Wells Fargo*; and one of his later programmers, *Four Faces West*. She provided serenity for Leslie Howard in the midst of his obsession with fiery Bette Davis in *Of Human Bondage*; and took a back seat to Miriam Hopkins in *Becky Sharp*, where her beauty was captured in the new Technicolor process. Her rare top billing came in minor items like *Finishing School*, uncharacteristically getting pregnant by Bruce Cabot; *Coming Out Party*, as a society deb; and *Half Angel*, hiding out from reporters after being acquitted of murder. Opposite Ronald Colman she was at her most pleasing in the delightful *If I Were King*, and was the star of one of Val Lewton's overrated RKO cult thrillers, *I Walked With a Zombie*. She retired from the screen in 1954. McCrea passed away in 1990. Their son, Jody, became an actor.

Screen: 1929: Words and Music; 1930: A Man From Wyoming; Follow Thru; Monte Carlo; Manslaughter; Playboy of Paris; Along Came Youth; True to the Navy; 1931: An American Tragedy; Caught; Rich Man's Folly; June Moon; Working Girls; 1932: If I Had a Million; The Strange Case of Clara Deane; Nice Women; Love Is a Racket; This Reckless Age; Sky Bride; The Night of June 13th; 1933: The Crime of the Century; King of the Jungle; The Silver Cord; One Man's Journey; Headline

Shooter; Blood Money; Little Women; 1934: Keep 'em Rolling; Finishing School; Coming Out Party; Of Human Bondage; 1935: The Gay Deception; Becky Sharp; 1936: Half Angel; Come and Get It; 1937: Wells Fargo; Souls at Sea; 1938: If I Were King; 1939: Coast Guard; 1941: So Ends Our Night; A Man Betrayed; 1942: Meet the Stewarts; 1943: I Walked With a Zombie; Happy Land; 1945: Patrick the Great; 1947: The Private Affairs of Bel Ami; 1948: Four Faces West; 1951: Payment on Demand; Reunion in Reno; 1952: Because of You; 1953: Mister Scoutmaster; 1954: Gypsy Colt.

Select TV: 1951: Child in the House (sp); The Green Convertible (sp); 1954: Unbroken Promise (sp).

RUBY DEE

(RUBY ANN WALLACE) BORN: CLEVELAND, OH, OCTOBER 27, 1924. RAISED IN NEW YORK, NY. ED: HUNTER COL.

At a time when it was rare for a black actress to play anything other than a domestic, Ruby Dee could count herself among the few who found fairly steady work in substantial roles. While learning her craft with the American Negro Theatre she made her 1943 Broadway debut in a play called *South Pacific*, which is not to be confused with the musical of the same name. Three years later she was in *Jeb*, which introduced her to future husband, Ossie Davis, and played the lead in *Anna Lucasta*. She made her movie debut in 1950, as the wife of the first black major league ballplayer in *The Jackie Robinson Story*, acting opposite Robinson himself. That same year she joined her husband for his big screen bow in *No Way Out*, and was back in the sports genre for the story of The Harlem Globetrotters, *Go, Man, Go!* She showed intelligence and strength as Sidney Poitier's wife in *Edge of the City*, and repeated her stellar performance from the original stage version of *A Raisin in the Sun* for the excellent 1961 movie adaptation, again as Poitier's spouse. With Davis she scored with the Broadway run of *Purlie Victorious* and was also seen in the movie version, re-titled *Gone Are the Days*. After playing a subway victim in the overwrought *The Incident*, she helped adapt *The Informer* into an urban ghetto drama called *Up Tight*, in which she played a welfare mother who turns tricks to survive. Dee scored more stage kudos for *Boesman and Lena* and appeared in two movies directed by her husband, *Black Girl* and *Countdown at Kusini*. She appeared to good effect in a pair of Spike Lee films: *Do the Right Thing*, as a world-weary Brooklyn resident known as Mother Sister; and *Jungle Fever*, superb as the distraught mother of crackhead Samuel L. Jackson. On television she appeared in her own adaptation of *Zora Is My Name* and won an Emmy Award for the drama *Decoration Day*, in 1991. When not performing she was an active crusader for civil rights.

Screen: 1950: The Jackie Robinson Story; No Way Out; 1951: The Tall Target; 1954: Go, Man, Go!; 1957: Edge of the City; 1958: St. Louis Blues; 1959: Take a Giant Step; 1960: Virgin Island; 1961: A Raisin in the Sun; 1963: Gone Are the Days; The Balcony; 1968: The Incident; 1969: Uptight (and co-wr.); 1972: Buck and the Preacher; Black Girl; 1976: Countdown at Kusini; 1982: Cat People; 1989: Do the Right Thing; 1990: Love at Large; 1991: Jungle Fever; 1993: Cop and a Half; 1995: Just Cause; 1997: A Simple Wish; 1999: Baby Geniuses; A Time to Dance (narrator).

NY Stage: 1943: South Pacific; 1944: Walk Hard (ob); 1946: Jeb; Anna Lucasta; 1948: A Long Way From Home (ob); 1949: A Smile of the World; 1953: The World of Sholom Aleichem (ob); 1959: A Raisin in the Sun; 1961: Purlie Victorious; 1970:

Boesman and Lena (ob); 1972: Wedding Band (ob); 1975: Hamlet (ob); 1988: Checkmates; 1998: My One Good Nerve: A Visit With Ruby Dee (ob; and wr.).

Select TV: 1960: Seven Times Monday (sp); 1961: Black Monday (sp); 1968–69: Peyton Place (series); 1969: Deadlock; 1971: The Sheriff; 1972: To Be Young, Gifted and Black (sp); 1974: It's Good to Be Alive; 1979: Roots: The Next Generations (ms); I Know Why the Caged Bird Sings; 1980: All God's Children; 1980–81: Ossie and Ruby! (series); 1982: Long Day's Journey Into Night (sp); 1985: Go Tell It on the Mountain (sp). The Atlanta Child Murders; 1988: Windmills of the Gods (ms); Gore Vidal's Lincoln (ms); 1990: Zora Is My Name (and wr.); The Court-Martial of Jackie Robinson; Decoration Day; 1993: The Ernest Green Story; 1994: Stephen King's The Stand (ms); 1996: Mr. & Mrs. Loving; Captive Heart: The James Mink Story; 1998: The Wall; 1999: Passing Glory; Having Our Say: The Delany Sisters' First 100 Years; 2000: A Storm in Summer; Finding Buck McHenry; 2001: Anne Rice's The Feast of All Saints; Taking Back Our Town.

SANDRA DEE

(ALEXANDRA ZUCK) BORN: BAYONNE, NJ, APRIL 23, 1942.

Blonde, perky, virginal Sandra Dee was less an actress than she was a representation of a bygone era of wholesome teen romance. Her early career as a model led to commercial spots and a contract with producer Ross Hunter, who intended to use her in his glossy remake of *Imitation of Life*, for Universal Pictures. Before that, she made two films at MGM, debuting as the kid sister in *Until They Sail*, in 1957, and then landing the title role in *The Reluctant Debutante*, holding her own next to pros Rex Harrison and Kay Kendall. Finally, for Universal, she began playing the roles that would land her in the fan magazines, including *The Restless Years*, in which she was concerned about losing her virginity to John Saxon, and *Imitation of Life*, a huge hit and the prime example of Ross Hunter's lush, silly soap operas, with Dee as the daughter at odds with actress mother Lana Turner. For Columbia she made *Gidget*, an unremarkable movie about a spirited beach-girl that spawned endless sequels and television spin-offs, though none starred Dee. She was an untamed western gal in Audie Murphy's *The Wild and the Innocent*, where, at 17, she coaxed him away from the more age-appropriate Joanne Dru. She hit the peak of her fame in the glossily entertaining melodrama with which her name would become forever linked, *A Summer Place*, falling in love with Troy Donahue to Max Steiner's memorable theme music.

Her recognition factor was raised considerably by her 1960 wedding to singing idol Bobby Darin, with whom she did a series of pin-headed Universal comedies: *Come September*, carrying the subplot for stars Rock Hudson and Gina Lollobrigida; *If a Man Answers*, with Dee trying to invoke jealousy in new husband Darin by inventing a lover; and *That Funny Feeling*, as a maid who doesn't realize the man she's picked up is her employer. She supported Lana Turner in another Ross Hunter soaper, *Portrait in Black*, and was given to director-star Peter Ustinov as "box-office assurance" for the tame adaptation of his successful stage play *Romanoff and Juliet*. Rather than carry on as Gidget, she picked up where Debbie Reynolds had left off in the *Tammy* series with *Tammy Tell Me True*, which sent the winsome country hick to college, and *Tammy and the Doctor*, as an angelic nurse's aide. A brainless Fox comedy with James Stewart, *Take Her, She's Mine*, made her Universal films look like pinnacles of wit; and

her last under her contract with them, a limp spy flick, *A Man Could Get Killed*, saw her shunted back into a secondary role. By 1967 her marriage to Darin had ended and it was clear that Dee was on her way out of favor in Hollywood. The bubble-headed romp, *Doctor, You've Got to Be Kidding* was a low point for leering, cutesy comedies, and her last theatrical feature, *The Dunwich Horror*, was a poor AIP concoction. Her stardom officially ended before she had even turned 30. During the 1970s there were occasional television movies and then she faded from view. A biography of her and Darin, written by their son, spoke of her bout with alcoholism.

Screen: 1957: Until They Sail; 1958: The Reluctant Debutante; The Restless Years; 1959: A Stranger in My Arms; Imitation of Life; The Wild and the Innocent; Gidget; The Snow Queen (voice); A Summer Place; 1960: Portrait in Black; 1961: Romanoff and Juliet; Tammy Tell Me True; Come September; 1962: If a Man Answers; 1963: Tammy and the Doctor; Take Her, She's Mine; 1964: I'd Rather Be Rich; 1965: That Funny Feeling; 1966: A Man Could Get Killed; 1967: Doctor, You've Got to Be Kidding; Rosie!; 1970: The Dunwich Horror; 1971: Ad Est di Marsa Matruh (nUSr); 1983: Lost (dtv).

Select TV: 1972: The Daughters of Joshua Cabe; 1974: Houston We've Got a Problem; 1976: The Manhunter; 1977: Fantasy Island.

DON DeFORE

BORN: CEDAR RAPIDS, IA, AUGUST 25, 1913. ED: UNIV. OF IA. DIED: DECEMBER 22, 1993.

Amiable, stocky character player Don DeFore exhibited much of Jack Carson's similarly oafish quality, but the soft, unimposing nature of his personality limited him almost exclusively to second leads. A student of the Pasadena Community School Theatre, he came to Hollywood in 1937 to join the Warner Bros. stock company in such films as *Garden of the Moon*, as a cowboy, and *Brother Rat*, as the catcher on the school baseball team. He made some Broadway appearances, including a supporting part in *The Male Animal*, as a dim football captain, which brought him back to Hollywood, where he tried out the name "Don Deforest" at Fox, playing a motorcycle cop in a "B" film, *We Go Fast*. Returning to "DeFore" he repeated his *Male Animal* role when Warners brought the property to the screen in 1942, and even showed up in the 1952 musical version, *She's Working Her Way Through College*. For Paramount, he was one of Joan Fontaine's many boyfriends in *The Affairs of Susan*, and a singing soda jerk in *My Friend Irma*, the movie that introduced Martin and Lewis to film audiences. At Warners he shared the screen with Jack Carson in *Romance on the High Seas*, as the husband of jealous Janis Paige, and took on Carson's old role in *One Sunday Afternoon*, a musical retelling of *The Strawberry Blonde*. He landed some lower-grade leads, as an ex-GI befriending hobo Victor Moore in *It Happened on 5th Avenue*, the first official release from Allied Artists; and *Southside 1-1000*, as a treasury agent on the trail of counterfeiters. With television he found his greatest fame, first as Thorny Thornberry on *The Adventures of Ozzie and Harriet*, and then as the head of the household on *Hazel*.

Screen: 1937: Kid Galahad; Submarine D-1; 1938: Brother Rat; Garden of the Moon; Freshman Year; 1941: We Go Fast; 1942: The Male Animal; You Can't Escape Forever; Right to the Heart; Wings for the Eagle; 1943: The Human Comedy; City Without Men; A Guy Named Joe; 1944: Thirty Seconds Over Tokyo; And Now Tomorrow; 1945: The Affairs of Susan; You Came Along;

The Stork Club; **1946:** Without Reservations; **1947:** Ramrod; It Happened on 5th Avenue; **1948:** Romance on the High Seas; One Sunday Afternoon; **1949:** Too Late for Tears; My Friend Irma; **1950:** Dark City; Southside 1-1000; **1951:** The Guy Who Came Back; **1952:** A Girl in Every Port; No Room for the Groom; She's Working Her Way Through College; And Now Tomorrow; Jumping Jacks; **1957:** Battle Hymn; **1958:** A Time to Live and a Time to Die; **1960:** The Facts of Life; **1981:** A Rare Breed.
NY Stage: **1938:** Where Do We Go From Here? (ob); **1939:** Steel; **1940:** The Male Animal; **1951:** Dream Girl.
Select TV: **1950:** Mr. & Mrs. Detective (sp); **1951:** A Woman's Privilege (sp); **1952:** The Marriage of Lit-Lit (sp); **1952–58:** The Adventures of Ozzie & Harriet (series); **1954:** The Power of Suggestion (sp); **1955:** Time Is Just a Place (sp); A Gift of Life (sp); **1959:** The Philadelphia Story (sp); **1961–65:** Hazel (series); **1968:** A Punt, a Pass and a Prayer (sp); **1978:** Black Beauty (ms).

GLORIA DeHAVEN
BORN: LOS ANGELES, CA, JULY 23, 1924.

Although she was qualified to enter MGM's illustrious stable of musical stars during that studio's golden era of song, Gloria DeHaven was just not exciting enough to reach the genre's upper echelons. The daughter of actor Carter DeHaven, she got her earliest film work by way of dad's role as Charlie Chaplin's assistant, supposedly appearing as an extra in *Modern Times* and *The Great Dictator*. She studied at the Ken-Mar Professional School and did some more bit roles before joining first the Bob Crosby band, then the Jan Savitt Orchestra, as a singer. This led to a contract with MGM, joining June Allyson and Nancy Walker for the exuberant "The Three B's" number in *Best Foot Forward*; performing "In a Little Spanish Town" with Virginia O'Brien in *Thousands Cheer*; dancing to "Pretty Baby" in *Broadway Rhythm*; and getting her biggest showcase in *Two Girls and a Sailor*, again teamed with Allyson and singing the sprightly "My Mother Told Me." Retiring briefly while married (1944–50) to actor John Payne, she returned in 1948 in the pleasant, but unpopular, *Summer Holiday*, as Mickey Rooney's sweetheart, and in *Summer Stock*, as Judy Garland's disagreeable sister. That same year, she was in a Red Skelton comedy, *The Yellow Cab Man*, and played her own mother, Flora Parker DeHaven, in the biopic of Kalmar and Ruby, *Three Little Words*, singing their most enduring song, "Who's Sorry Now?" Her MGM years were over but she hung on through the early 1950s in minor musicals at other studios, including RKO's *Two Tickets to Broadway* and Paramount's *The Girl Rush*, where she at least got to sing the best song, "An Occasional Man." This marked her last big screen appearance for 21 years while she opted for stage and television work, including a stint on the soap *As the World Turns*, and hostess chores for the *ABC Prize Movie*. In 1976 she was one of the countless retiree guest stars who were seen in the spoof *Won Ton Ton, the Dog Who Saved Hollywood*, and, after another long break from theatrical releases, she joined the cast of senior stars for the comedy *Out to Sea*, being romanced by Jack Lemmon.
Screen: **1936:** Modern Times; **1940:** The Great Dictator; Susan and God; Keeping Company; **1941:** Two-Faced Woman; The Penalty; **1943:** Best Foot Forward; Thousands Cheer; **1944:** Broadway Rhythm; Two Girls and a Sailor; Step Lively; The Thin Man Goes Home; Between Two Women; **1948:** Summer Holiday; **1949:** Scene of the Crime; The Doctor and the Girl; Yes Sir, That's My Baby; **1950:** The Yellow Cab Man; Three Little Words; Summer Stock; I'll Get By; **1951:** Two Tickets to

Broadway; **1953:** Down Among the Sheltering Palms; **1955:** So This Is Paris; The Girl Rush; **1976:** Won Ton Ton, the Dog Who Saved Hollywood; **1978:** Bog!; **1994:** The Legend of O.B. Taggart (dtv); **1997:** Out to Sea.
NY Stage: **1955:** Seventh Heaven; **1968:** Have I Got One For You (ob).
Select TV: **1951:** Miss Liberty (sp); **1956:** The Briefcase (sp); **1957:** Mr. Broadway (sp); **1966–67:** As the World Turns (series); **1969:** ABC Prize Movie (series); **1972:** Call Her Mom; **1974:** Nakia (series); **1976:** Who Is the Black Dahlia?; Banjo Hackett: Roamin' Free; **1977:** Sharon: Portrait of a Mistress; **1978:** Evening in Byzantium; **1983–87:** Ryan's Hope (series); **1984:** Off Sides.

OLIVIA DE HAVILLAND
BORN: TOKYO, JAPAN, JULY 1, 1916.
RAISED IN CA.

Starting out as one of Warner Bros.'s most charming ingénues of the 1930s, Olivia de Havilland rose to many challenges as an actress, eventually winning her place among the most admired ladies of the screen. Born in Tokyo to British parents, she was brought to California when her folks separated, and was raised by her mother, along with her younger sister who would become Joan Fontaine. Although they are probably the most famous movie star sisters, their much-publicized rivalry and mutual antagonism was legendary. De Havilland first found success while still in college, acting in a production of *A Midsummer Night's Dream* in Saratoga, which led to an offer to appear in Max Reinhardt's lavish staging of the piece for the Hollywood Bowl. When Reinhardt made a film of it in 1935, de Havilland was asked to repeat her role as Hermia, putting her alongside such notables as James Cagney and Dick Powell. It was an auspicious debut and, although Warners regarded her as little more than sweet and decorative, they did sign her to a contract. She could have done better than a Joe E. Brown clinker, *Alibi Ike*, or one of the weaker Cagneys, *The Irish in Us*, though she did get to play the heroine in *Captain Blood*, one of the best of the swashbuckling genre and a hefty moneymaker. The public and the studio liked her pairing with Errol Flynn so much that the two performers would share the screen seven more times, finally calling it quits in 1941 with *They Died With Their Boots On*.

Most of these Flynn-de Havilland duets were grand entertainments, including the much-loved *The Adventures of Robin Hood*, with de Havilland as Maid Marian, prior to which she had provided the rather intrusive love interest in *The Charge of the Light Brigade*. Setting aside their costume frills, the pair took on a comedy, *Four's a Crowd*, set in the newspaper world, while, sans Flynn, de Havilland also showed her comedic side as a fan who pesters Leslie Howard in the delightful *It's Love I'm After*. She was the co-star of the expensive and top-heavy *Anthony Adverse*, going from cook's daughter to mistress of Napoleon, and then it was back to Flynn for a superior western, *Dodge City*, and the historical romance *The Private Lives of Elizabeth and Essex*, supporting the formidable Bette Davis who became an off-screen friend. She got her best chance in the decade's biggest hit of all, *Gone With the Wind*, on loan to Selznick for this highly honored production. As the relentlessly good-hearted Melanie, she painted an admirable portrait of human decency, which earned her a well-deserved supporting Oscar nomination. It would keep her name before the public for years to come, all the latter-day press attention focusing on her, since she would outlive the other principals by decades. Her immediate follow-ups hardly reflected the new status this movie had brought: a loan-out to Goldwyn, *Raffles*; a light comedy, *My Love Came Back*; and her weakest Flynn teaming, *Santa Fe Trail*.

A bright and popular comedy with James Cagney, *The Strawberry Blonde*, was followed by a good soap opera made on loan to Paramount, *Hold Back the Dawn*, in which she played a mousey schoolteacher married to unscrupulous Charles Boyer, who is using her to get a visa. This time she got an Oscar nod in the Best Actress category, losing to sister Joan (for *Suspicion*), which really added fire to their never-ending family feud. De Havilland declined a number of roles before backing up Bette Davis in *In This Our Life*, an engrossing melodrama that took liberties with its Pulitzer Prize-winning source. She also played the wife of timid college professor Henry Fonda in the mild, stagebound domestic comedy, *The Male Animal*, and starred with Robert Cummings in a light romance, *Princess O'Rourke*, in which she caused a diplomatic uproar by falling in love with an American pilot. Around this time there was a very public legal battle with Warner Bros. over the length of her contract and the number of times she'd been on suspension for refusing work. Ultimately the ruling was in her favor, a decision that led to an industry rule that seven years would be the limit to any performer's contract, including suspensions. In any case, she was through with Warners, and she went over to Paramount to play an unwed mother in *To Each His Own*. Her performance was a sterling example of how a fine actress can overcome soggy material, and she finally equaled her sister by winning the Academy Award for Best Actress of 1946. That same year she got to live every actor's dream, sharing the screen with herself, playing good and evil twins in *The Dark Mirror*, one of the less entertaining examples of this kind of melodramatic plotline.

She landed consecutive powerhouse roles, first in Fox's *The Snake Pit*, a bold film for its day, showing the harrowing conditions of mental institutions. De Havilland was excellent as the sympathetic, unhinged heroine, earning another Oscar nomination for this major box-office success. Her second, *The Heiress*, was less of a popular hit but that hardly mattered since it was one of the most acclaimed films of 1949, if indeed the decade. De Havilland gave the performance of her career as the plain spinster who suffers mistreatment by suitor Montgomery Clift and domineering father Ralph Richardson, and she received her second Academy Award for what still ranks as a highly regarded movie and one of the best cinematic interpretations of Henry James. After some Broadway work she returned for the boring costume piece *My Cousin Rachel*, and then took a secondary role, as Robert Mitchum's Swedish wife, in *Not as a Stranger*. *The Proud Rebel* won fine reviews for her performance as a pioneer woman who helps Alan Ladd and his mute son, made between trips to England for some unremarkable dramas with up-and-coming British stars Paul Scofield (*That Lady*) and Dirk Bogarde (*Libel*). There was a tired MGM soaper, *Light in the Piazza*, as a rich lady trying to find a husband for her mentally disturbed daughter, made prior to her becoming one of the ladies of 1960s *grand guignol*, first in the unpleasant *Lady in a Cage*, trapped in an elevator, and then in a rare nasty role as Bette Davis's scheming relative, in *Hush…Hush, Sweet Charlotte*. From then on she was merely an ensemble player in such lousy all-star dramas as *The Adventurers*, taking younger Bekim Fehmiu to bed; *Airport '77*, sharing some corny scenes with Joseph Cotten; and *The Swarm*, ditto, with Fred MacMurray, but even these failed to dim the glow of her earlier achievements. In 1963 she published *Every Frenchman Has One*, a book about her years in Paris.

Screen: 1935: A Midsummer Night's Dream; Alibi Ike; The Irish in Us; Captain Blood; 1936: Anthony Adverse; The Charge of the Light Brigade; 1937: Call It a Day; The Great Garrick; It's Love I'm After; 1938: Gold Is Where You Find It; The Adventures of Robin Hood; Four's a Crowd; Hard to Get; 1939: Wings of the Navy; Dodge City; The Private Lives of Elizabeth and Essex; Gone With the Wind; 1940: Raffles; My Love Came Back; Santa Fe Trail; 1941: The Strawberry Blonde; Hold Back the Dawn; They Died With Their Boots On; 1942: The Male Animal; In This Our Life; 1943: Thank Your Lucky Stars; Princess O'Rourke; Government Girl; 1946: The Well-Groomed Bride; To Each His Own; Devotion; The Dark Mirror; 1948: The Snake Pit; 1949: The Heiress; 1952: My Cousin Rachel; 1955: That Lady; Not as a Stranger; 1956: The Ambassador's Daughter; 1958: The Proud Rebel; 1959: Libel; 1962: Light in the Piazza; 1964: Lady in a Cage; Hush…Hush, Sweet Charlotte; 1970: The Adventurers; 1972: Pope Joan; 1977: Airport '77; 1978: The Swarm; 1979: The Fifth Musketeer.

NY Stage: 1951: Romeo & Juliet; 1952: Candida; 1962: A Gift of Time.

Select TV: 1967: Noon Wine (sp); 1972: The Screaming Woman; 1979: Roots: The Next Generations (ms); 1982: Murder Is Easy; The Royal Romance of Charles and Diana; 1986: North and South Book II (ms); Anastasia: The Mystery of Anna; 1988: The Woman He Loved.

ALBERT DEKKER

(ALBERT VAN DEKKER) BORN: BROOKLYN, NY, DECEMBER 20, 1905. ED: NOWDOIN COL. DIED: MAY 5, 1968.

A supporting player with an occasional lead to his credit, imposing, sinister-looking Albert Dekker had ten years of stage work behind him when he came to Warner Bros. in 1937 to appear (under his real name) in *The Great Garrick*. He soon began his journey into unsympathetic parts, as the Comte de Provence in *Marie Antoinette*; a blackmailer in both *The Lone Wolf in Paris* and *The Last Warning*; a Roman soldier in the religious curiosity, *The Great Commandment*; King Louis XIII in *The Man in the Iron Mask*; and a murder victim in *Extortion*. At Paramount he played the title character in a Technicolor sci-fi thriller *Dr. Cyclops*, and his name would be forever associated with the evil bald scientist with the Coke-bottle glasses who shrinks people to the size of dolls. In the "B" *Among the Living* he played a dual role, as an escaped lunatic and his innocent brother accused of murder. He stayed on for character roles at Paramount, with occasional star parts in Republic Pictures fare, such as *The French Key*, as a detective, and *The Pretender*, as a financier. He later appeared as the wicked doctor who gets his hands on the mysterious case in the cult classic *Kiss Me Deadly*; an unscrupulous medico with designs on Katharine Hepburn's money in *Suddenly, Last Summer*; and the railroad executive who hires Robert Ryan to capture *The Wild Bunch*. Latter-day leads came in undistinguished films like *Machete*, as a plantation owner who suspects wife Maria Blanchard of infidelity, and one of those daft Japanese monster films, *Gammera, the Invincible*, as the U.S. Secretary of Defense, battling a fire-breathing turtle. He achieved a creepy notoriety by way of his strange death, a probable suicide that was ruled accidental. As detailed in Kenneth Anger's *Hollywood Babylon*, Dekker was found hanging by his neck in his bathroom, with needles protruding from his arms.

Screen: AS ALBERT VAN DEKKER: 1937: The Great Garrick; She Married an Artist; 1938: Marie Antoinette; The Lone Wolf in Paris; Extortion.

AS ALBERT DEKKER: 1939: The Last Warning; Paris Honeymoon; Never Say Die; Hotel Imperial; Beau Geste; The Man in the Iron

Mask; The Great Commandment; 1940: Dr. Cyclops; Strange Cargo; Rangers of Fortune; Seven Sinners; 1941: You're the One; Blonde Inspiration; Reaching for the Sun; Buy Me That Town; Honky Tonk; Among the Living; 1942: Night in New Orleans; Wake Island; Once Upon a Honeymoon; The Lady Has Plans; In Old California; Yokel Boy; The Forest Rangers; Star Spangled Rhythm; 1943: The Woman of the Town; In Old Oklahoma/War of the Wildcats; Buckskin Frontier; The Kansan; 1944: Experiment Perilous; The Hitler Gang (narrator); 1945: Incendiary Blonde; Hold That Blonde; Salome, Where She Danced; 1946: Two Years Before the Mast; The French Key; The Killers; California; Suspense; 1947: The Pretender; Gentleman's Agreement; Wyoming; Cass Timberlane; Slave Girl; The Fabulous Texan; 1948: Fury at Furnace Creek; Lulu Belle; 1949: Search for Danger; Bride of Vengeance; Tarzan's Magic Fountain; 1950: The Kid From Texas; Destination Murder; The Furies; 1951: As Young as You Feel; 1952: Wait Till the Sun Shines, Nellie; 1954: The Silver Chalice; 1955: East of Eden; Kiss Me Deadly; Illegal; 1957: She Devil; 1958: Machete; 1959: Suddenly, Last Summer; The Sound and the Fury; These Thousand Hills; Middle of the Night; The Wonderful Country; 1965: Gammera, the Invincible; 1967: Come Spy With Me; 1969: The Wild Bunch.

NY Stage: AS ALBERT VAN DEKKER: 1928: Marco Millions; Volpone; 1930: Conflict; Sisters of the Chorus; 1931: Napi; 1934: Brittle Heaven; 1935: Fly Away Home; 1936: Johnny Johnson; 1937: An Enemy of the People.

AS ALBERT DEKKER: 1930: Troika; 1935: Journey by Night; Squaring the Circle; 1952: Gertie; 1959: The Andersonville Trial; 1960: Face of a Hero; 1961: A Man for All Seasons; 1965: The Devils.

Select TV: 1950: The Human Touch (sp); 1951: Valley Forge (sp); 1952: The Housekeeping (sp); Treasure Island (sp); 1955: The Answer (sp); The Chivington Road (sp); All My Sons (sp); 1960: Emmanuel (sp); 1961: The Dispossessed (sp); 1966: Death of a Salesman (sp); Ten Blocks on the Camino Real (sp).

ALAIN DELON

BORN: SCEAUX, FRANCE, NOVEMBER 8, 1935.

A pretty-faced French actor, Alain Delon made his reputation in the 1960s art house scene with films by René Clement and Luchino Visconti, before trying to escape his image as a looker by producing his own vehicles, many of them tough action flicks. With no formal training, he ingratiated himself with the filmmaking crowd at the Cannes Film Festival and was cast in *Quand la Femme s'en Mele*. He was soon getting steady work and moved up to a lead in 1960's *3 Murderesses*, the first movie to give him exposure in the United States. In Clement's adaptation of *The Talented Mr. Ripley*, called *Purple Noon*, Delon essayed one of his most famous roles, as a man who schemes to murder Maurice Ronet and take his place. In 1961 he appeared as the boxer, Rocco, in Visconti's *Rocco and His Brothers*, a lengthy movie that has been trimmed and hacked over the years, but still maintains a stellar reputation. The same was true of his other Visconti epic, *The Leopard*, co-starring Burt Lancaster and Claudia Cardinale, in a tale of Sicilian aristocracy and the unification of Italy. He appeared in international efforts like *Joy House*, with Jane Fonda; *The Yellow Rolls-Royce*, with Shirley MacLaine and George C. Scott; *Once a Thief*, with Ann-Margret; and *Texas Across the River*, a Dean Martin comedy. He had, by this point, produced his first vehicle back in Europe, *L'Insoumis*, in 1964, but it never reached American shores. In the early 1970s he focused on making gangster and action pictures,

which kept him popular in his native country for many years, including *Borsalino*, which matched him with his French box-office peer, Jean-Paul Belmondo, though the latter was always considered the superior actor. (A real-life scandal around this time, involving murder, drugs, and underworld characters only enhanced Delon's reputation as a hard case.) Dispiriting efforts like *Red Sun*, with Charles Bronson, and *Scorpio*, with Lancaster again, preceded his last American lead in the dismal *The Concorde — Airport 1979*. By the 1980s distributors saw no reason to import Delon films to the U.S., including his directorial efforts, *For a Cop's Hide* and *The Cache*. He was seen supporting Jeremy Irons in *Swann in Love*, as a rouged homosexual, and in 1996 *Purple Noon* was successfully reissued to the art houses, 36 years after its initial U.S. engagement.

Screen (US releases only): 1960: 3 Murderesses; Purple Noon; 1961: Rocco and His Brothers; 1962: Eclipse; 1963: Any Number Can Win/The Big Grab/Melodie en Sous-Sol; The Leopard; 1964: Joy House/The Love Cage; 1965: Once a Thief; The Yellow Rolls-Royce; 1966: Lost Command; Texas Across the River; Is Paris Burning?; 1968: Girl on a Motorcycle; 1969: The Last Adventure; Spirits of the Dead; 1970: The Sicilian Clan; Borsalino (and prod.); The Swimming Pool; 1972: Red Sun; The Godson; The Assassination of Trotsky; 1973: Scorpio; 1974: The Widow Couderc; Shock; 1975: No Way Out; Icy Breasts; 1976: The Love Mates; Two Against the Law; 1977: Dirty Money; La Samourai; Zorro; Mr. Klein (and prod.); 1978: Indian Summer; 1979: The Concorde — Airport 1979; 1984: Swann in Love; 1999: Hundred and One Nights.

DOLORES DEL RIO

(LOLITA DOLORES MARTINEZ ASUNSOLO LOPEZ NEGRETTE) BORN: DURANGO, MEXICO, AUGUST 3, 1905. DIED: APRIL 11, 1983.

With a passive face that seemed to be dipped in porcelain, Dolores Del Rio was one of the great beauties of the early talkies. Indeed, she held on to those stunning features long into her 60s and used them to great effect as the first Latin actress to become a genuine Hollywood star. A second cousin of actor Ramon Novarro, she was born to riches and enhanced her financial stature by marrying the wealthy Jaime Del Rio at age 16. A chance meeting with director Edwin Carewe led to a small part in 1925's *Joanna*, and she made her first big impression in the hit *What Price Glory?*, playing the beautiful Charmaine. Also for Carewe she had her first notable vehicle, *Resurrection*, based on Tolstoy, and made her entrance into sound with *Evangeline*, singing the title song. After her first husband's death, she married (1930–41) MGM art director Cedric Gibbons. At RKO she starred as a Polynesian girl, opposite Joel McCrea, in *Bird of Paradise*, perhaps her most famous film of this era, though hard to take seriously nowadays. She got top billing over Fred Astaire and Ginger Rogers in *Flying Down to Rio*, though anyone who was watching her instead of them was simply blind. There followed another hit musical, *Wonder Bar*, in which she danced with whip-wielding Ricardo Cortez, a stoic performer as severely limited as Del Rio. She decorated such unremarkable fare as *The Widow From Monte Carlo*, trying to escape her English life of luxury, and *Lancer Spy*, seducing George Sanders for information, but by the outbreak of World War II there was very little interest in her in the U.S. She returned to Mexico where she made several films with actor Pedro Armendariz, only one of which, *Portrait of Maria*, received extensive distribution. She remained mostly in foreign films, with occasional English-language productions like the John Ford features *The Fugitive*, in 1947, and *Cheyenne Autumn*, in 1964 — in both instances cast as an Indian. Likewise she was Elvis Presely's Indian mother in one of his better features, *Flaming Star*.

Screen (US releases only): 1925: Joanna; 1926: High Steppers; Pals First; The Whole Town's Talking; What Price Glory?; 1927: Resurrection; The Loves of Carmen; 1928: The Gateway to the Moon; The Trail of '98; No Other Woman; The Red Dance; Revenge; 1929: Evangeline; 1930: The Bad One; 1932: The Girl of the Rio; Bird of Paradise; 1933: Flying Down to Rio; 1934: Wonder Bar; Madame Du Barry; 1935: In Caliente; I Live for Love; The Widow From Monte Carlo; 1936: Accused; 1937: The Devil's Playground; Lancer Spy; International Settlement; 1940: The Man From Dakota; 1942: Journey Into Fear; 1945: Portrait of Maria; 1947: The Fugitive; 1960: Flaming Star; 1961: La Cucaracha/The Soldiers of Pancho Villa; 1964: Cheyenne Autumn; 1967: More Than a Miracle; 1976: Salsa.

Select TV: 1957: Old Spanish Custom (sp); 1958: The Public Prosecutor (sp).

WILLIAM DEMAREST

BORN: ST. PAUL, MN, FEBRUARY 27, 1892.
DIED: DECEMBER 28, 1983.

No one perfected the role of the loveable curmudgeon like William Demarest, who sarcastically snapped his way through over 100 movies, usually while maintaining a pricelessly disdainful look on his face. A former vaudevillian, boxer, and stock theatre actor, he made his film debut in 1926, making little impression despite appearing in both the first all-talking short, *A Night in Coffee Dan's*, and the first feature with sound, *The Jazz Singer*. He took time away from movies to work as a talent agent for a five-year stretch, returning to his minor status as a lowly supporting player in 1934. During the 1940s he really hit his stride, thanks mainly to Preston Sturges, who directed him splendidly on several occasions, including *Christmas in July*, mulling over a coffee slogan; *The Lady Eve*, as Henry Fonda's valet, who is not taken in by Barbara Stanwyck's con act; *Sullivan's Travels*, as a member of the boisterous Ale & Quail hunting club; *Hail the Conquering Hero*, as the Sergeant who helps Eddie Bracken pass himself off as a war hero; *The Great Moment*, providing some broad humor to a mostly serious bio, as the first patient to use ether; and *The Miracle of Morgan's Creek*, in a wild slapstick turn as Betty Hutton's exasperated policeman dad, a strong contender for the greatest role of his career. A disagreement with Sturges in the late 1940s ended their alliance, but Demarest went on to earn an Oscar nomination for giving some bite to the clichéd loyal friend role in *The Jolson Story*, in 1946. He helped Humphrey Bogart track down Nazis in *All Though the Night*; pursued Abbott and Costello for stealing a bus in *Pardon My Sarong*; saddled up as Gary Cooper's sidekick in *Along Came Jones*; and introduced a hit song (!), "A Kiss to Build a Dream On," in *The Strip*. Late in his career, taking over from William Frawley, he gained a whole new following as the cantankerous Uncle Charlie on the hit television series *My Three Sons*, playing opposite Fred MacMurray, with whom he'd shared the screen in *Never a Dull Moment* and *The Far Horizons*.

Screen: 1926: When the Wife's Away; 1927: Don't Tell the Wife; Fingerprints; The Gay Old Bird; Simple Sis; A Million Bid; In Old San Francisco; The Bush Leaguer; A Sailor's Sweetheart; The Jazz Singer; Matinee Ladies; What Happened to Father?; The Black Diamond Express; The First Auto; A Reno Divorce; 1928: Five and Ten Cent Annie; The Butter and Egg Man; The Escape; Sharp Shooters; The Crash; Pay As You Enter; 1934: White Lies;

Circus Clown; Fog Over Frisco; Fugitive Lady; Many Happy Returns; 1935: The Murder Man; The Casino Murder Case; After Office Hours; Diamond Jim; Bright Lights; Hands Across the Table; 1936: The Great Ziegfeld; Love on the Run; Wedding Present; Mind Your Own Business; 1937: Charlie Chan at the Opera; Don't Tell the Wife; The Great Hospital Mystery; Big City; Rosalie; Blonde Trouble; The Great Gambini; Oh Doctor!; The Hit Parade; Easy Living; Time Out for Romance; Wake Up and Live; 1938: Rebecca of Sunnybrook Farm; Josette; One Wild Night; Romance on the Run; Peck's Bad Boy With the Circus; 1939: King of the Turf; The Gracie Allen Murder Case; Mr. Smith Goes to Washington; The Great Man Votes; While New York Sleeps; Cowboy Quarterback; Miracles for Sales; Laugh It Off; 1940: Tin Pan Alley; Little Men; Wolf of New York; The Great McGinty; The Farmer's Daughter; Christmas in July; Comin'Round the Mountain; 1941: Ride on Vaquero; Glamour Boy; Dressed to Kill; Rookies on Parade; The Lady Eve; Country Fair; The Devil and Miss Jones; 1942: Pardon My Sarong; Sullivan's Travels; All Through the Night; True to the Army; My Favorite Spy; The Palm Beach Story; Life Begins at Eight-Thirty; Behind the Eight Ball; Johnny Doughboy; 1943: Stage Door Canteen; True to Life; Dangerous Blondes; 1944: The Miracle of Morgan's Creek; Nine Girls; Hail the Conquering Hero; Once Upon a Time; 1945: Duffy's Tavern; Along Came Jones; Salty O'Rourke; Pardon My Past; 1946: Our Hearts Were Growing Up; The Jolson Story; 1947: Variety Girl; The Perils of Pauline; 1948: The Sainted Sisters; Night Has a Thousand Eyes; On Our Merry Way/A Miracle Can Happen; Whispering Smith; 1949: Jolson Sings Again; Sorrowful Jones; Red, Hot and Blue; 1950: Never a Dull Moment; When Willie Comes Marching Home; Riding High; He's a Cockeyed Wonder; 1951: The First Legion; Excuse My Dust; The Strip; Behave Yourself!; 1952: The Blazing Forest; What Price Glory?; 1953: Dangerous When Wet; Here Come the Girls; The Lady Wants Mink; Escape From Fort Bravo; 1954: The Yellow Mountain; 1955: Jupiter's Darling; The Far Horizons; The Private War of Major Benson; Lucy Gallant; Sincerely Yours; Hell on Frisco Bay; 1956: The Mountain; The Rawhide Years; 1960: Pepe; 1961: King of the Roaring 20's — The Story of Arnold Rothstein; Twenty Plus Two; 1962: Son of Flubber; 1963: It's a Mad Mad Mad Mad World; 1964: Viva Las Vegas; 1965: That Darn Cat; 1975: The Wild McCullochs; 1976: Won Ton Ton, the Dog Who Saved Hollywood.

NY Stage: 1920: Silks and Satins; 1929: Sketch Book; 1931: Vanities.

Select TV: 1959–60: Love and Marriage (series); 1961–62: Tales of Wells Fargo (series); 1965–72: My Three Sons (series); 1973: Don't Be Afraid of the Dark; 1978: The Millionaire.

RICHARD DENNING

(LOUIS ALBERT HEINDRICH DENNINGER)
BORN: POUGHKEEPSIE, NY, MARCH 27, 1914.
DIED: OCTOBER 11, 1998.

Neither inept nor terribly exciting, tall, blond Richard Denning serviceably did his job, got his paycheck, and moved on to the next assembly line assignment. Following his debut in 1937, he spent a very busy few years under contract to Paramount in such movies as *The Big Broadcast of 1938*, as a ship's officer; *King of Chinatown*, as a hospital intern; and *I'm from Missouri*, as a pilot. He did three for DeMille, *The Buccaneer*, *Union Pacific*, and *North West Mounted Police*, and finally moved out from the background to get the leading lady at the finale of *The Farmer's Daughter*, even if that lady was Martha Raye. He took top-billing in a "B," *Golden Gloves*, as an amateur fighter; was borrowed by

Columbia to play one of the offspring in *Adam Had Four Sons*; and was the main non-skating performer in a Republic cheapie, *Ice-Capades Revue*, prior to his military service. After the war, he moved up to star roles in such low-budget features as *Disaster*, as an innocent man framed for murder; *Harbor of Missing Men*, as a smuggler battling crime boss George Zucco; *Flame of Stamboul*, again as Zucco's nemesis, this time as an intelligence agent; *Target Hong Kong*, as an American mercenary fighting the Commies; *The Creature From the Black Lagoon*, certainly his most famous film, rescuing Julie Adams from the title monster; *The Creature With the Atom Brain*, fighting atomic zombies; and *The Day the World Ended*, the movie that officially launched everybody's favorite low-budget studio, AIP. On radio he starred opposite Lucille Ball in *My Favorite Husband*, the forerunner of her classic sitcom *I Love Lucy*. On television he kept busy with the series *Mr. and Mrs. North* and, later, *Hawaii Five-0*, settling in for a comfortable 12-year run in the recurring role of the governor of the state to which he and real-life wife, actress Evelyn Ankers, had moved in the early 1960s.

Screen: 1937: Hold 'em Navy; 1938: King of Alcatraz; The Texans; Her Jungle Love; The Buccaneer; College Swing; Campus Confessions; Illegal Traffic; The Big Broadcast of 1938; You and Me; Say It in French; 1939: Grand Jury Secrets; Some Like It Hot; King of Chinatown; Ambush; The Star Maker; Million Dollar Legs; I'm From Missouri; Persons in Hiding; Night of Nights; Television Spy; Geronimo; Hotel Imperial; The Gracie Allen Murder Case; Union Pacific; Sudden Money; Disputed Passage; Undercover Doctor; 1940: The Farmer's Daughter; Parole Fixer; Emergency Squad; Golden Gloves; Seventeen; Queen of the Mob; Love Thy Neighbor; Those Were the Days; North West Mounted Police; 1941: Adam Had Four Sons; West Point Widow; 1942: Beyond the Blue Horizon; Quiet Please, Murder; The Glass Key; Ice-Capades Revue; 1946: Black Beauty; The Fabulous Suzanne; 1947: Seven Were Saved; 1948: Unknown Island; Caged Fury; Disaster; Lady at Midnight; 1950: Double Deal; Harbor of Missing Men; No Man of Her Own; 1951: Flame of Stamboul; Insurance Investigator; Weekend With Father; 1952: Okinawa; Scarlet Angel; Hangman's Knot; 1953: The 49th Man; The Glass Web; Target Hong Kong; 1954: Jivaro; The Creature From the Black Lagoon; Why Men Leave Home; Battle of Rogue River; Target Earth; 1955: The Magnificent Matador; Air Strike; Creature With the Atom Brain; The Crooked Web; The Gun That Won the West; 1956: The Day the World Ended; Million Dollar Manhunt/Assignment Redhead; Girls in Prison; Oklahoma Woman; 1957: Naked Paradise/Thunder Over Hawaii; An Affair to Remember; Buckskin Lady; The Black Scorpion; The Lady Takes a Flyer; 1958: Desert Hell; 1963: Twice Told Tales.

Select TV: 1952–54: Mr. & Mrs. North (series); 1953: The Doctor's Downfall (sp); 1954: Tapu (sp); The Legal Beagles (sp); 1955: All That Glitters (sp); 1956: On the Beach (sp); 1957: The Idea Man (sp); Eyes of a Stranger (sp); 1958: The Laughing Willow (sp); 1960–61: Michael Shayne (series); 1964–65: Karen (series); 1966: Alice Through the Looking Glass (sp); 1968–80: Hawaii Five-O (series).

REGINALD DENNY
(REGINALD LEIGH DAYMORE) BORN: RICHMOND, SURREY, ENGLAND, NOVEMBER 20, 1891. DIED: JUNE 16, 1967.

A silent film star who survived long enough to still be playing small roles in the 1960s, Reginald Denny came to the U.S. in 1915.

He made his stage debut in *Rosalind*, followed by his movie debut, four years later, in *The Oakdale Affair*. His initial fame came via a series of Universal two-reelers called "The Leather Pushers," in which he played boxer Kid Robertson, and he stayed in the ring for the feature *The Abysmal Brute*. In *Sporting Youth* he was a chauffeur mistaken for race car driver, but his forte became light comedy, scoring in such Universal offerings as *Where Was I?*, in which he was confronted by a strange woman claiming to be his wife; *What Happened to Jones*, posing as both a woman and a bishop; *Skinner's Dress Suit*, as a henpecked husband who leads his wife to believe he's received a raise; *On Your Toes*, as a dancer who turns to boxing; and *That's My Daddy*, based on a story he himself wrote. He was still under contract as a leading player when his sound debut, the part-talkie *Clear the Decks*, arrived but soon slipped into secondary or supporting parts. During the 1930s he was seen in the bizarre dirigible-set *Madame Satan*; honeymooning with Norma Shearer in the film adaptation of Noël Coward's *Private Lives*; carrying on with trollop Bette Davis in *Of Human Bondage*; facing his doom as one of *The Lost Patrol*; playing Garbo's brother in *Anna Karenina*; drinking to murderous excess in *Remember Last Night?*; and spouting Shakespeare, as Benvolio, in *Romeo and Juliet*. Starting in 1937 he became best known for portraying Algy, the hero's friend and fellow investigator, in the *Bulldog Drummond* series. Off screen he designed the first radio-controlled aircraft to be flown without a pilot and operated his own hobby shop on Hollywood Boulevard.

Screen: 1919: The Oakdale Affair; Bringing Up Betty; 1920: 39 East; A Dark Lantern; Experience; 1921: Footlights; Disraeli; Paying the Piper; The Iron Trail; Tropical Love; The Price of Possession; 1922: The Kentucky Derby; Sherlock Holmes; 1923: The Thrill Chaser; The Abysmal Brute; 1924: Sporting Youth; The Reckless Age; The Fast Worker; Captain Yearless; 1925: I'll Show You the Town; Oh Doctor!; California Straight Ahead; Where Was I?; 1926: Skinner's Dress Suit; What Happened to Jones; Take It From Me; Rolling Home; 1927: Jaws of Steel; Out All Night; Fast and Furious; The Cheerful Fraud; On Your Toes; 1928: The Night Bird; Good Morning, Judge; That's My Daddy; 1929: Red Hot Speed; Clear the Decks; His Lucky Day; One Hysterical Night; 1930: Embarrassing Moments; Madam Satan; What a Man!; Those Three French Girls; A Lady's Morals; Oh, for a Man; 1931: Private Lives; Kiki; Stepping Out; Parlor, Bedroom and Bath; 1932: Strange Justice; The Iron Master; 1933: The Barbarian; Only Yesterday; The Big Bluff; Fog; 1934: The Lost Patrol; One More River; The Richest Girl in the World; Of Human Bondage; Dancing Man; The Little Minister; We're Rich Again; The World Moves On; 1935: Anna Karenina; Lottery Lover; Vagabond Lady; No More Ladies; Here's to Romance; Midnight Phantom; Remember Last Night?; Without Children/Penthouse Party; The Lady in Scarlet; 1936: It Couldn't Have Happened (But It Did); Two in a Crowd; More Than a Secretary; Romeo and Juliet; The Rest Cure; The Preview Murder Mystery; 1937: Bulldog Drummond Comes Back; The Great Gambini; Join the Marines; Beg, Borrow or Steal; Bulldog Drummond Escapes; Women of Glamour; Let's Get Married; Jungle Menace (serial); 1938: Bulldog Drummond's Revenge; Four Men and a Prayer; Bulldog Drummond's Peril; Blockade; Bulldog Drummond in Africa; Arrest Bulldog Drummond!; 1939: Everybody's Baby; Bulldog Drummond's Bride; Bulldog Drummond's Secret Police; 1940: Spring Parade; Rebecca; Seven Sinners; 1941: Appointment for Love; International Squadron; One Night in Lisbon; 1942: Thunder Birds; Sherlock Holmes and the Voice of Terror; Over My Dead Body; Captains of the Clouds; Eyes in the Night; 1943: Crime Doctor's Strangest Case;

1944: Song of the Open Road; 1945: Love Letters; 1946: Tangier; The Locket; 1947: My Favorite Brunette; The Macomber Affair; The Secret Life of Walter Mitty; Escape Me Never; Christmas Eve; 1948: Mr. Blandings Builds His Dream House; 1950: The Iroquois Trail; 1953: The Hindu/Sabaka; Fort Vengeance; Abbott and Costello Meet Dr. Jekyll and Mr. Hyde; 1954: World for Ransom; 1955: Escape to Burma; 1956: Around the World in Eighty Days; 1964: Advance to the Rear; 1965: Cat Ballou; 1966: Assault on a Queen; Batman.

NY Stage: 1915: Rosalind; 1917: The Professor's Love Story.
Select TV: 1950: The Invisible Wound (sp); 1952: All's Well With Lydia (sp); 1953: The Stolen General (sp); 1954: Mason-Dixon Line (sp); 1955: Roberta (sp); 1957: Helen Morgan (sp); 1960: The Scarlet Pimpernel (sp); 1964: The Timothy Heist (sp).

JOHN DEREK

(DEREK SULLIVAN HARRIS) BORN: HOLLYWOOD, CA, AUGUST 12, 1926. DIED: MAY 22, 1998.

Long before John Derek became known for marrying some of the most beautiful women in show business, he used his own good looks to acquire a following as a teen idol. The son of director Lawson Harris and actress Dolores Johnson, he started as a bit player in Selznick's 1944 hit, *Since You Went Away*, under his real name. Five years later, as John Derek, he was launched as a new discovery with Columbia's *Knock on Any Door*, impressively playing a juvenile delinquent defended for murder by Humphrey Bogart. He also did strong work in the Oscar-winning *All the King's Men*, as Broderick Crawford's adopted, football-playing son, who ends up in a wheelchair after trying to please his image-conscious dad. As Columbia's new star he surfaced in frothy costume adventures like *Rogues of Sherwood Forest*, as Robin Hood's offspring, and *The Mask of the Avenger*, as a faux Count of Monte Cristo; as well as in meatier fare like *Saturday's Hero*, as a young jock who realizes that his college is more interested in his brawn than his brain. It was hard to take him serious in things like *Prince of Pirates* and *The Adventures of Hajji Baba*, while his performance as the unhinged John Wilkes Booth in the biopic *Prince of Players* was very bad indeed. He appeared as Joshua in the all-star cast of Hollywood's grand epic *The Ten Commandments*, and as a friendly Arab whose open-mindedness causes his doom in *Exodus*. After marrying Ursula Andress he co-starred with her, as a hitchhiker, in *Nightmare in the Sun*, which he also produced, and again in *Once Before I Die*, which marked his directorial debut. After taking up photography he shot some nudes of his wife that appeared in *Playboy*, but divorced her to move on to Linda Evans, whom he directed in *Childish Things*, before finally settling down with Mary Cathleen Collins. She would become his "greatest creation," under the name Bo Derek, with John directing her — when she was all of 16 — in a cheapie called *Fantasies*, which got a delayed release in 1981. Because of Bo's popularity in the 1979 comedy "*10*," John Derek was suddenly famous again as her Svengali-like mentor, taking charge of both directorial and cinematographic chores for her starring vehicles, *Tarzan the Ape Man*, *Bolero*, and *Ghosts Can't Do It*, amassing some of the worst reviews ever aimed at a director.

Screen: AS DEREK HARRIS: 1944: Since You Went Away; 1945: I'll Be Seeing You.

AS JOHN DEREK: 1947: A Double Life; 1949: Knock on Any Door; All the King's Men; 1950: Rogues of Sherwood Forest; 1951: Saturday's Hero; The Mask of the Avenger; The Family Secret; 1952: Scandal Sheet; Thunderbirds; 1953: Mission Over Korea; The Last Posse; Prince of Pirates; Ambush at Tomahawk

Gap; Sea of Lost Ships; 1954: The Outcast; The Adventures of Hajji Baba; 1955: Run for Cover; Prince of Players; An Annapolis Story; 1956: The Leather Saint; The Ten Commandments; 1957: Omar Khayyam; Fury at Showdown; The Flesh Is Weak; 1958: High Hell; The Volga Boatman/Prisoners of the Volga; 1959: Il Corsaro della Mezzaluna/Pirate of the Half Moon (nUSr); 1960: Exodus; 1963: Nightmare in the Sun (and prod.); 1966: Once Before I Die (and dir.; prod.); 1969: Childish Things (and dir.).

Select TV: 1953: Tomorrow's Men (sp); 1956: Black Jack Hawk (sp); Massacre at Sand Creek (sp); 1961–62: Frontier Circus (series).

VITTORIO DE SICA

BORN: SORA, ITALY, JULY 7, 1902.
DIED: NOVEMBER 13, 1974.

Better remembered as a director than an actor, Vittorio De Sica had an enormous list of film credits as a performer dating back to the silent movie era. After a brief period with Tatiana Pavlova's stage company, he formed his own theatrical group, gradually making a name for himself as a leading man in Italian cinema. He began directing in 1940 with *Rose Scarlatte*, but it was not until after World War II that he leaped to the forefront of filmmakers with two of the most acclaimed movies of the so-called Italian neo-realism period, *Shoeshine* and *The Bicycle Thief*. Both films were honored with Academy Awards for Best Foreign Langauge Film, as were his later works, *Yesterday, Today and Tomorrow* and *The Garden of the Finzi-Continis*. Equally well known were *Umberto D* and *Two Women*, which earned an Oscar for Sophia Loren. During the 1950s De Sica began showing up as an actor on the art house circuit in such imports as *Frisky*, with Gina Lollobrigida, and *Too Bad She's Bad*, with Loren. In 1957 he made his American acting debut in the unwieldy remake of *A Farewell to Arms*, scoring an Oscar nomination from an industry no doubt impressed that the great director was also a capable thespian. He was a colorful asset to the World War II epic as Rock Hudson's cynical-but-good-natured friend who winds up on the end of a firing squad. Thereafter he could be found in international productions, both high (*It Started in Naples*, *The Shoes of the Fisherman*) and low (*The Amorous Adventures of Moll Flanders*, *Snow Job*, *Andy Warhol's Dracula*).

Screen (US releases only): 1953: Times Gone By (The Trial of Frine segment); 1954: Bread, Love and Dreams; Hello Elephant; 1955: Frisky; 1956: Too Bad She's Bad; 1957: Scandal in Sorrento; The Monte Carlo Story; The Gold of Naples (and dir., co-wr.); It Happend in the Park; A Farewell to Arms; The Miller's Beautiful Wife; 1958: A Plea for Passion/The Bigamist; 1959: Holiday Island; The Tailor's Maid; Anatomy of Love; It Happened in Rome; 1960: It Started in Naples; The Angel Wore Red; Fast and Sexy; General Della Rovere; 1961: The Millionairess; The Wonders of Aladdin; 1963: Lafayette; 1965: The Amorous Adventures of Moll Flanders; 1968: The Biggest Bundle of Them All; The Shoes of the Fisherman; 1969: If It's Tuesday, This Must Be Belgium; 1972: Snow Job; 1974: Andy Warhol's Dracula.

ANDY DEVINE

(JEREMIAH SCHWARTZ) BORN: FLAGSTAFF, AZ, OCTOBER 7, 1905. ED: UNIV. OF SANTA CLARA. DIED: FEBRUARY 18, 1977.

With a voice that sounded as if his throat needed oiling, not to mention his ever-expanding belly and distinctively unsubtle persona, Andy Devine become one of filmdom's best-remembered character actors. Arriving in Hollywood in 1928, fresh from playing college football, he sought work as a bit player, landing his first part in *We Americans*, at Universal, a studio he would be a part of for some 20 years. Various films required him to display his gridiron skills, such as *The Spirit of Notre Dame*, *The All American*, and *Saturday's Millions*, and he did the first of many westerns, *Law and Order*, in 1932. His raspy-voiced rube characterization was a welcome screen presence to some, an irritable nuisance to others. In any event, he was never long out of work, playing a hypochondriac soda jerk in Will Rogers's *Doctor Bull*; an informant named Careful in *Million Dollar Ransom*; a delivery boy suspected of foul play in *The President Vanishes*; and a bumpkin in *The Farmer Takes a Wife*. It was downright bizarre to hear him doing Shakespeare in the famed 1936 production of *Romeo and Juliet*, and he was far more believable as an out-of-work assistant director who puts Janet Gaynor at ease in *A Star is Born*, or as the loyal friend who dies in the Chicago fire while trying to rescue Don Ameche in *In Old Chicago*. In 1939 he played perhaps his most famous role of all, as Buck, the driver of John Ford's *Stagecoach*. During the war years he frequently showed up as Richard Arlen's sidekick in a series of "B" adventures, including *Mutiny on the Blackhawk*, *Black Diamond*, *Devil's Pipeline*, *The Leather Pushers*, and *Raiders of the Desert*. His lively and sometimes overbearing comic skills gave some zing to Maria Montez desert epics like *Ali Baba and the Forty Thieves* and *Sudan*, while the Technicolor western *Canyon Passage* also featured Devine's two sons as his on-screen children. Moving over to Republic in the late 1940s, he lent support to Roy Rogers as Cookie Bullfincher, before appearing on television as Jingles, yet another sidekick, on *The Adventures of Wild Bill Hickok*, for seven seasons. In later years the portly, bushy-browed actor showed up as an ineffectual sheriff in *The Man Who Shot Liberty Valance*; a judge in *The Ballad of Josie*; and a priest in *Won Ton Ton, the Dog Who Saved Hollywood*. The Walt Disney Company used his unforgettable voice in the animated feature *Robin Hood*, as Friar Tuck.

Screen: 1928: We Americans; Lonesome; Red Lips; 1929: Naughty Baby; Hot Stuff; 1931: Spirit of Notre Dame; The Criminal Code; Danger Island (serial); 1932: Law and Order; The Impatient Maiden; The Man From Yesterday; Man Wanted; Tom Brown of Culver; Radio Patrol; Three Wise Girls; Destry Rides Again; Fireman, Save My Child; Fast Companions; The All American; 1933: Doctor Bull; Chance at Heaven; Song of the Eagle; Midnight Mary; Saturday's Millions; The Big Cage; Horseplay; The Cohens and Kellys in Trouble; 1934: Upper World; The Gift of Gab; Stingaree; Hell in the Heavens; Million Dollar Ransom; The Poor Rich; Let's Talk It Over; 1935: The President Vanishes; Way Down East; The Farmer Takes a Wife; Straight From the Heart; Hold 'em Yale; Fighting Youth; Coronado; Chinatown Squad; 1936: Romeo and Juliet; Small Town Girl; Flying Hostess; The Big Game; Yellowstone; Mysterious Crossing; 1937: A Star Is Born; The Road Back; Double or Nothing; You're a Sweetheart; 1938: Men With Wings; Yellow Jack; In Old Chicago; Dr. Rhythm; The Storm; Strange Faces; Personal Secretary; Swing That Cheer; 1939: Never Say Die; The Spirit of Culver; Mutiny on the Blackhawk; Stagecoach; Tropic Fury; Legion of Lost Flyers; Geronimo; The Man From Montreal; 1940: Margie; Little Old New York; Buck Benny Rides Again; Danger on Wheels; Torrid Zone; Hot Steel; When the Daltons Rode; The Leather Pushers; Black Diamonds; Devil's Pipeline; Trail of the Vigilantes; 1941: A Dangerous Game; Lucky Devils; The Flame of New Orleans; Mutiny in the Arctic; Men of the Timberland; Badlands of Dakota; South of Tahiti; Road Agent; The Kid from Kansas; Raiders of the Desert; 1942: Top

Sergeant; Unseen Enemy; North to the Klondike; Escape From Hong Kong; Timber; Danger in the Pacific; Between Us Girls; Sin Town; 1943: Rhythm of the Islands; Frontier Badmen; Corvette K-225; Crazy House; 1944: Ali Baba and the Forty Thieves; Follow the Boys; Ghost Catchers; Babes on Swing Street; Bowery to Broadway; 1945: Sudan; Frisco Sal; That's the Spirit; Frontier Gal; 1946: Canyon Passage; 1947: The Michigan Kid; Bells of San Angelo; Springtime in the Sierras; Slave Girl; The Fabulous Texan; The Marauders; On the Old Spanish Trail; The Vigilantes Return; 1948: The Gay Ranchero; Old Los Angeles; Under California Skies; Eyes of Texas; Grand Canyon Trail; Nighttime in Nevada; The Gallant Legion; The Far Frontier; 1949: The Last Bandit; 1950: The Traveling Saleswoman; Never a Dull Moment; 1951: New Mexico; The Red Badge of Courage; Slaughter Trail; 1952: Montana Belle; 1953: Island in the Sky; 1954: Thunder Pass; 1955: Pete Kelly's Blues; 1956: Around the World in Eighty Days; 1960: The Adventures of Huckleberry Finn; 1961: Two Rode Together; 1962: The Man Who Shot Liberty Valance; 1963: How the West Was Won; It's a Mad Mad Mad Mad World; 1965: Zebra in the Kitchen; 1968: The Ballad of Josie; The Road Hustlers; 1970: Myra Breckinridge; The Phynx; 1973: Robin Hood (voice); 1976: Won Ton Ton, the Dog Who Saved Hollywood; A Whale of a Tale; 1978: The Mouse and His Child (voice).

Select TV: 1951–58: The Adventures of Wild Bill Hickok (series); 1964–65: Flipper (series); 1969: Ride a Northbound Horse (sp); 1969: The Over-the-Hill Gang.

BRANDON DE WILDE

(ANDRE BRANDON DE WILDE) BORN: BROOKLYN, NY, APRIL 9, 1942. DIED: JULY 6, 1972.

A thoroughly engaging child actor, Brandon De Wilde grew up to become one of the most sensitive, beautiful-looking performers of his generation, but too little of him was recorded on film before his untimely death. The son of a stage manager, he was a mere seven years old when he made his Broadway debut in 1950 as the quirky little boy next door in *The Member of the Wedding*. Two years later, he and co-stars Julie Harris and Ethel Waters repeated their roles — to much acclaim — in the movie adaptation. De Wilde's most memorable role as a youngster came in the 1953 western classic *Shane*, as the wide-eyed son of pioneers Van Heflin and Jean Arthur who is in awe of gunfighter Alan Ladd, shouting "Shane! Come back! Come back, Shane!" in the famous finale. At 11 years old he was the youngest actor nominated for an Oscar in the supporting category up to that time, although the story goes that his parents did not even bother to inform him of the honor until four years after the fact. By that time De Wilde had starred in his own short-lived television series, *Jamie*. He grew through his teen years and into manhood right before the audience's eyes in such minor movies as the pleasant boy-and-his-dog tale *Goodbye, My Lady*, and the James Stewart western *Night Passage*. His next notable film was *Blue Denim*, which, despite being quite ordinary in every way, was significant as the forerunner of all the cinematic teen pregnancy dramas. John Frankenheimer's intriguing but ultimately unsatisfying *All Fall Down* gave him a good role as a youngster hero-worshipping no-good older brother Warren Beatty. It was a part he repeated to some degree in the far superior *Hud*, blindly idolizing his wastrel uncle, Paul Newman, until he sees him for the scoundrel that he is. His fine work in that film should have signaled a great future as a leading adult player, but aside from his appealing work in the underrated

Disney drama *Those Calloways*, and a role as John Wayne's son in Otto Preminger's cluttered war epic, *In Harm's Way*, he never quite achieved such heights. On his way to appear in a Denver theatre production of *Butterflies Are Free*, he rammed his van into a parked car and was killed.

Screen: 1952: The Member of the Wedding; 1953: Shane; 1956: Good-bye, My Lady; 1957: Night Passage; 1958: The Missouri Traveler; 1959: Blue Denim; 1962: All Fall Down; 1963: Hud; 1965: Those Calloways; In Harm's Way; 1971: The Deserter; 1972: Wild in the Sky/Black Jack.

NY Stage: 1950: The Member of the Wedding; 1952: Mrs. McThing; 1953: The Emperor's Clothes; 1958: Comes a Day; 1965: A Race of Hairy Men.

Select TV: 1951: No Medals on Pop (sp); 1952: A Cowboy for Chris (sp); 1953: Jamie (sp); 1953–54: Jamie (series); 1955: The Day They Gave the Babies Away/All Mine to Give (sp); 1956: Bend to the Wind (sp); 1957: The Locked Door (sp); 1959: Man of His House (sp); 1960: My Theory About Girls (sp); 1964: The Tenderfoot (sp); 1966: The Confession (sp).

BILLY DE WOLFE

(WILLIAM ANDREW JONES) BORN: WOLLASTON, MA, FEBRUARY 18, 1907. DIED: MARCH 5, 1974.

With his pencil moustache, whiney voice, and supercilious air, Billy De Wolfe specialized in prissy suitors and buffoons, though he only worked in a handful of Hollywood films. He spent a good deal of his childhood in Wales, from where his parents hailed, before returning to the U.S. to be in vaudeville as a dancer, taking his show business name from a stage manager he'd encountered. Back in the British Isles, he began perfecting his comedy act, which included mimicking women, and Bing Crosby, who caught his show in New York, recommended to Paramount that he be tested. De Wolfe was duly signed to partner the crooner in the Technicolor musical *Dixie*, providing comic relief in this biopic of songwriter Dan Emmett. He would later support Crosby in the 1946 hit *Blue Skies*, doing his famous "Mrs. Murgatroyd" routine, playing an old lady getting tipsy in a nightclub. In the droll comedy *Dear Ruth*, he was Joan Caulfield's fiancé, fated to be dumped once William Holden entered the picture, a part he repeated in both sequels. Also for Paramount he popped up as a Greenwich Village artist in *Our Hearts Were Growing Up*, and as a hammy Shakespearean actor in *The Perils of Pauline*. There were parts in two minor Doris Day musicals for Warner Bros., *Tea for Two* and *Lullaby of Broadway* (as a dancer-turned-servant), and a role in the Fox adaptation of *Call Me Madam*, as a State Department attaché. He worked principally on television and in theatre after that, although he was seen as the mayor in a Patty Duke vehicle, *Billie*, and in Disney's *The World's Greatest Athlete*.

Screen: 1943: Dixie; 1945: Duffy's Tavern; 1946: Miss Susie Slagle's; Blue Skies; Out Hearts Were Growing Up; 1947: The Perils of Pauline; Dear Ruth; Variety Girl; 1948: Isn't It Romantic?; 1949: Dear Wife; 1950: Tea for Two; 1951: Dear Brat; Lullaby of Broadway; 1953: Call Me Madam; 1965: Billie; 1973: The World's Greatest Athlete.

NY Stage: 1953: Jon Murray Anderson's Almanac; 1957: Ziegfeld Follies; 1966: How to Succeed in Business Without Really Trying.

Select TV: 1967: The Pruitts of Southampton (series); 1967–68: Good Morning World (series); 1969: The Queen and I (series); Arsenic and Old Lace (sp).

ANGIE DICKINSON

(ANGELINE BROWN) BORN: KULM, ND, SEPTEMBER 30, 1931. RAISED IN EDGLEY, ND, AND GLENDALE, CA. ED: GLENDALE COL.

Blonde and bright, with an engaging smile, cat-eyed Angie Dickinson, who was equal parts sweet and sexy, had to wait for television to find her signature role after a lengthy career on film ranging from supporting bits to leads. While still in college she married Gene Dickinson and took up secretarial work until she entered a beauty contest on a whim and won. This led to chorus girl work on television's *Colgate Comedy Hour* and a bit in the Doris Day movie *Lucky Me*. Over the next few years she was seen in low-budget westerns and action fare, including the hostage drama *Cry Terror!*, playing Rod Steiger's tough gun moll. Her first significant part was in Howard Hawks's first rate western, *Rio Bravo*, playing Feathers, the dancehall hostess who waits for John Wayne to realize he's in love with her. One of the big hits of 1959, the movie was instrumental in landing her a contract with Warner Bros., which brought such roles as Frank Sinatra's wife in the heist drama *Ocean's Eleven*, and the lead in the glossy soap opera *The Sins of Rachel Cade*, as a missionary who gives birth to an illegitimate child. Over at United Artists she had the title role in *Jessica*, as a midwife who drives the men in an Italian village to distraction. It did not win her any new admirers. Better was Universal's *Captain Newman, M.D.*, though she didn't have much to do, playing a nurse. In the 1960s she did two poor Dick Van Dyke comedies, *The Art of Love* and *Some Kind of a Nut*; a flat Burt Reynolds western, *Sam Whiskey*, and an all-star misfire, *The Chase*, as Marlon Brando's wife. She was seen to good effect in John Boorman's tough thriller, *Point Blank*, and won a cult following when she appeared in the nude in Roger Corman's trashy and enjoyable *Big Bad Mama*. Around that time she started a four-year run on *Police Woman*, which marked the first time an hour-long television drama centered on the exploits of a female cop. As a result, the role of Sgt. Suzanne "Pepper" Anderson made her one of the hottest stars on the tube and gave her her best-remembered role. Most of her subsequent work has been on the small screen, but she had a sensational movie role in Brian DePalma's 1980 hit thriller, *Dressed to Kill*, as an unfulfilled wife whose adulterous fling has deadly consequences. In later years she played Lauren Holly's wealthy mom in the remake of *Sabrina*; a former Vegas showgirl in *Duets*; and, looking appropriately horrid, Helen Hunt's alcoholic, vagrant mother in *Pay It Forward*. She was married (1965–80) to composer Burt Bacharach.

Screen: 1954: Lucky Me; 1955: Man With the Gun; Tennessee's Partner; The Return of Jack Slade; 1956: Hidden Guns; Gun the Man Down; Tension at Table Rock; The Black Whip; 1957: Shoot-Out at Medicine Bend; Calypso Joe; Run of the Arrow (voice); China Gate; 1958: Cry Terror!; 1959: I'll Give My Life; Rio Bravo; 1960: The Bramble Bush; Ocean's Eleven; 1961: A Fever in the Blood; The Sins of Rachel Cade; 1962: Rome Adventure; Jessica; 1963: Captain Newman, M.D.; 1964: The Killers; 1965: The Art of Love; 1966: The Chase; Cast a Giant Shadow; 1967: Point Blank; The Last Challenge; 1969: Sam Whiskey; Some Kind of a Nut; Young Billy Young; 1971: The Resurrection of Zachary Wheeler; Pretty Maids All in a Row; 1973: The Outside Man; 1974: Big Bad Mama; 1978: L'Homme en Colere/Jigsaw (nUSr); 1980: Klondike Fever; Dressed to Kill; 1981: Charlie Chan and the Curse of the Dragon Queen; Death Hunt; 1987: Big Bad Mama II; 1994: Even Cowgirls Get the Blues; 1995: Sabrina; 1996: The Maddening (dtv); The Sun, the

Moon and the Stars (nUSr); **2000**: Duets; Pay It Forward; **2001**: Ocean's Eleven; **2002**: Big Bad Love.

NY Stage: **1962**: The Perfect Setup.

Select TV: **1966**: The Poppy Is Also a Flower; **1970**: The Love War; **1971**: Thief; See the Man Run; **1973**: The Norliss Tapes; **1974**: Pray for the Wildcats; **1974–78**: Police Woman (series); **1977**: A Sensitive Passionate Man; **1978**: Overboard; Pearl (ms); **1979**: The Suicide's Wife; **1981**: Dial M for Murder; **1982**: Cassie & Company (series); One Shoe Makes It Murder; **1984**: Jealousy; A Touch of Scandal; **1985**: Hollywood Wives (ms); **1987**: Stillwatch; Police Story: The Freeway Killings; **1988**: Once Upon a Texas Train; **1989**: Prime Target; **1992**: Treacherous Crossing; **1993**: Wild Palms (ms); **1996**: Danielle Steel's Remembrance; **1997**: Deep Family Secrets; The Don's Analyst; **1999**: Sealed With a Kiss; **2001**: The Last Producer.

MARLENE DIETRICH

(Maria Magdalena Dietrich) Born: Berlin, Germany, December 27, 1901.
Died: May 6, 1992.

Being one of Hollywood's true legends does not necessarily entail being one of its great talents, as proven by Marlene Dietrich's high standing. Undeniably shapely, seductive, and enigmatic, with a sultry air of boredom, Dietrich did little more than strike poses in much of her early work. As she matured, her world weariness was put to good effect, allowing her to suggest deeper levels of character, and the striking way in which she to seemed to defy the passing years kept her always fascinating. She started as a chorus girl while studying drama at the Deutsche Theaterschule, and by 1923 she was appearing in small parts in films. She continued to act on the big screen over the next six years without achieving much in the way of fame, but that changed when director Josef von Sternberg spotted her in a stage revue, *Zwei Kravatten*, and cast her as the sluttish saloon singer Lola-Lola, who destroys fawning school teacher Emil Jannings, in the classic *The Blue Angel*. Straddling a chair, wearing top hat and garter belt, she throatily intoned "Falling in Love Again" and carved out her own territory on the map of movie history. Hollywood, figuring they could refine her for the American masses, came calling for both her and von Sternberg, and Paramount Pictures cast her in a similar role in 1930's *Morocco*, as a cabaret singer in love with legionnaire Gary Cooper. She donned a man's tux and playfully planted a kiss on a woman in the audience, before throwing off her high heels to follow Coop into the desert, earning an Oscar nomination in the process. It was the kind of turgid kitsch she and von Sternberg would ostentatiously produce for the studio over the next few years and the public lapped it up.

She was a hooker-turned-spy in *Dishonored*, outfoxing the likes of Warner Oland and Victor McLaglen, before facing a firing squad for her troubles, and she followed this with the inimitable Shanghai Lily in *Shanghai Express*, still the golden-hearted whore, giving herself to Oland in order to save lover Clive Brook and a trainload of passengers trapped amid some political unrest in China. The film was just as superficial and tedious as most of her vehicles, but it became her biggest hit during her stay at Paramount and was an Oscar nominee for Best Picture. She was another nightclub singer in *Blonde Venus*, the highlight of which had her singing "Hot Vodoo" in a gorilla costume, before the studio suggested a break from von Sternberg, and put her under the direction of the more talented Rouben Mamoulian. However, the finished product, *Song of Songs*, was just more of the same ponderous melodramatics, the storyline requiring her to pose

nude for sculptor Brian Aherne. By this point the audience was glutted on the exotic German sensation and had no interest in her most eccentrically entertaining collaboration with von Sternberg, *The Scarlet Empress*, which found her betrothed to a bizarrely hammy Sam Jaffe as the Grand Duke Peter. (Playing the Empress as a young girl was Dietrich's real-life daughter, Maria Riva.) Her final von Sternberg effort, *The Devil Is a Woman*, a dull love triangle with Lionel Atwill and Cesar Romero, was critically panned, so she wisely reteamed with Gary Cooper in a lighthearted comedy, *Desire*, which suggested that she had possibilities in this genre. However, a second attempt to mine the humor in her persona, in Ernst Lubitsch's *Angel*, was positively deadly. She went over to Selznick for his foolish Technicolor extravaganza *The Garden of Allah*, trekking to the Sahara desert in search of fulfillment, then to England for *Knight Without Armour*, paired with Robert Donat. Soon after, Paramount quietly cancelled their new contract with her.

By the end of the decade she was considered washed up when Universal came to her rescue, hiring her for the western comedy-drama, *Destry Rides Again*. In one of her best-remembered roles, the irrepressible saloon entertainer Frenchie, she was a bad lady in love with a good man, sheriff James Stewart. She sang another of her signature songs, "See What the Boys in the Backroom Will Have," to a barroom full of appreciative rowdies, and had an unforgettable knock-down, drag-out battle with Una Merkel. The movie was one of the top hits of 1939 and Dietrich temporarily escaped the box-office poison label. Suddenly she was in demand again, appearing in director Rene Clair's U.S. debut, *The Flame of New Orleans*, and causing a rift between Warners's tough guys, Edward G. Robinson and George Raft, in *Manpower*. She teamed on three occasions with John Wayne: *Seven Sinners*, as yet another cabaret entertainer in this South Seas adventure; the umpteenth version of the western *The Spoilers*; and *Pittsburgh*, as an unlikely product of the coalmines. Most moviegoers still considered her an icy, inaccessible icon, and it was obviously Wayne who was the box-office lure. She did, however, win the admiration of the American public during World War II, speaking out against Hitler and her homeland, and refusing all offers to continue her film career under the Nazi regime. That her star status was faltering again was evident when she accepted billing below the title for the overstuffed costume melodrama *Kismet*, which found her famous shapely legs covered in gold for one dance sequence.

A presumably tongue-in-cheek adventure, *Golden Earrings*, had her playing a Gypsy who helps undercover intelligence officer Ray Milland, and something about this goofy movie appealed to the public, giving her status yet another boost just when she needed it. On a more respectable level, Billy Wilder used her brilliantly for the 1948 postwar comedy *A Foreign Affair*, on familiar terrain as a cabaret performer, but this time with ties to the Nazi party, a part diametrically opposite her actual political stance. Dietrich was beginning to show signs of becoming an interesting and complex actress. She was a temperamental stage star, singing Cole Porter's "The Laziest Gal in Town," in Hitchcock's *Stage Fright*; the improbable hostess of an outlaw hideout in the routine western *Rancho Notorious*; and reteamed with James Stewart for the engaging thriller, *No Highway in the Sky*, as a famous actress aboard a crippled airplane. Stunningly well preserved, she made headlines around this time when she became a grandmother. Wilder used her splendidly for a second time, in *Witness for the Prosecution*, pulling off a very tricky role as murder suspect Tyrone Power's cold-hearted wife. In 1961 she joined Stanley Kramer's all-star production of *Judgment at Nuremberg*, giving her most effective performance, as the widow of a Nazi general who befriends American judge Spencer Tracy, in the hope that he will see the humanity of the German people. That, however, brought down the curtain on her movie career, although she resurfaced nearly 20 years later in the weird, limited release *Just a Gigolo*, co-starring with rocker David Bowie, singing the title song and looking rather frail. Before this there had been several live concerts, including some that brought her back to Germany. One of her co-stars from *Judgment at Nuremberg*, Maximilian Schell, directed a documentary on her, *Marlene*, although she refused to be photographed during her interview portions of the film. She came off as a difficult, cranky old woman who looked back on her career with a mixture of egotism and contempt.

Screen: 1923: Der Kleine Napoleon/The Little Napoleon; Tragodie der Liebe/Tragedy of Love; Der Mensch am Wege/The Man by the Wayside; 1924: Der Sprung ins Leben/Leap Into Life; 1926: Manon Lescaut; Eine DuBarry von Heute/A Modern DuBarry; Madame Wunscht Keine Kinder/Madame Doesn't Want Children; Kopf Hoch Charly!/Heads Up Charly!; 1927: Der Juxbaron/The Imaginary Baron; Sein Grosser Bluff/His Greatest Bluff; Cafe Electric; 1928: Princess Olala/Art of Love; 1929: Ich Kusse Ihre Hand Madame/I Kiss Your Hand Madame; Die Frau nach der Man Sich Sehnt/The Woman Men Long For; Das Schiff der Verloren en Menschen/The Ship of Lost Men; Gefahren der Brautzeit/Dangers of the Engagement; 1930: The Blue Angel; Morocco; 1931: Dishonored; 1932: Shanghai Express; Blonde Venus; 1933: Song of Songs; 1934: The Scarlet Empress; 1935: The Devil Is a Woman; 1936: Desire; The Garden of Allah; 1937: Knight Without Armor; Angel; 1939: Destry Rides Again; 1940: Seven Sinners; 1941: The Flame of New Orleans; Manpower; 1942: The Lady Is Willing; The Spoilers; Pittsburgh; 1944: Follow the Boys; Kismet; 1946: Martin Roumagnac/The Room Upstairs; 1947: Golden Earrings; 1948: A Foreign Affair; 1949: Jigsaw/Gun Moll; 1950: Stage Fright; 1951: No Highway in the Sky; 1952: Rancho Notorious; 1956: Around the World in Eighty Days; 1957: The Monte Carlo Story; Witness for the Prosecution; 1958: Touch of Evil; Das Gab's nur Einmel/It Only Happened Once (nUSr); 1961: Judgment at Nuremberg; 1962: The Black Fox (narrator); 1964: Paris — When It Sizzles; 1981: Just a Gigolo; 1985: Marlene (voice).

NY Stage: 1967: Marlene Dietrich; 1968: Marlene Dietrich.

Select TV: 1973: Marlene Dietrich — I Wish You Love (sp).

BRADFORD DILLMAN

BORN: SAN FRANCISCO, CA, APRIL 14, 1930.
ED: YALE UNIV.

Tall, slim, and serious-looking, Bradford Dillman, a graduate of the Actors Studio, made a splash on Broadway in the original 1956 production of *Long Day's Journey Into Night*, playing the younger, tubercular son, Edmund, a role that earned him a Theatre World Award. Signed up by 20th Century-Fox, he made his film debut in 1958 in a pair of glossy soap operas: *A Certain Smile*, supporting Joan Fontaine; and *In Love and War*, as one of a trio of soldiers, who leaves his steady girl for Hawaiian nurse France Nuyen. He then got the role of a lifetime, the aloof, dangerous rich boy who forms an unholy alliance with his buddy, and probable bedmate, Dean Stockwell, in order to commit the perfect crime, in *Compulsion*. Both leads were exceptional in an engrossing thriller based on the real-life Leopold and Loeb case of the 1920s. Director Richard Fleischer engaged him for another courtroom drama, *Crack in the Mirror*, which had Dillman and his co-stars, Orson Welles and Juliette Greco, each

playing two roles, a somewhat pretentious and confusing device. He had a sympathetic role in the much-maligned version of Faulkner's *Sanctuary*, and was beatific as the animal-loving *Francis of Assisi*. In 1966 he starred in an unsuccessful television series *Court Martial*, and then appeared in such ensemble films as *The Bridge at Remagen* and *Suppose They Gave a War and Nobody Came?* As a supporting player he was featured in two hits of the early 1970s, *Escape From the Planet of the Apes*, as a human scientist, and *The Way We Were*, as Robert Redford's college friend. He never repeated his role from *Long Day's Journey* in the movie adaptation (his *Compulsion* co-star Dean Stockwell did it) but he did play Willie Oban in John Frankenheimer's 1973 version of another O'Neill marathon, *The Iceman Cometh*. He took top billing in William Castle's yucky final production, *Bug*, and showed up as John Wilkes Booth in the cheesy Sun Classics docudrama, *The Lincoln Conspiracy*. He was seen in many telefilms, won an Emmy Award for the daytime special *The Last Bride of Salem*, in 1975, and had a one-season recurring role on the nighttime soap *Falcon Crest*. In 1963 he married former model-actress Suzy Parker. He published a book on his love of football, *Inside the New York Giants*, and a memoir, *Are You Anybody?: An Actor's Life* (1987).

Screen: 1958: A Certain Smile; In Love and War; 1959: Compulsion; 1960: Crack in the Mirror; 1961: A Circle of Deception; Sanctuary; Francis of Assisi; 1965: A Rage to Live; 1966: The Plainsman; 1968: Jigsaw; Sergeant Ryker (from TV); 1969: The Bridge at Remagen; 1970: Suppose They Gave a War and Nobody Came?; 1971: The Mephisto Waltz; Escape From the Planet of the Apes; The Resurrection of Zachary Wheeler; 1972: Brother John; 1973: The Iceman Cometh; The Way We Were; 1974: A Black Ribbon for Deborah (nUSr); Chosen Survivors; 99 and 44/100% Dead; Gold; 1975: Bug; 1976: Mastermind; The Enforcer; 1977: The Lincoln Conspiracy; 1978: The Amsterdam Kill; The Swarm; Piranha; 1979: Love and Bullets; 1980: Guyana: Cult of the Damned; Running Scared/Desperate Men (dtv); 1983: Sudden Impact; 1985: The Treasure of the Amazon (dtv); 1988: Man Outside; 1989: Lords of the Deep; Heroes Stand Alone.

NY Stage: 1953: The Scarecrow (ob); 1955: Third Person (ob); 1956: Long Day's Journey Into Night; 1962: The Fun Couple.

Select TV: 1954: Strangers in Hiding (sp); 1957: There Shall Be No Night (sp); 1963: The Case Against Paul Ryker (sp); 1966: Court-Martial (series); 1967: The Helicopter Spies; 1969: Fear No Evil; 1970: Black Water Gold; 1971: Longstreet; Five Desperate Women; Revenge; 1972: The Eyes of Charles Sand; The Delphi Bureau; Moon of the Wolf; 1973: Deliver Us From Evil; 1974: Murder or Mercy; The Disappearance of Flight 412; 1975: Adventures of the Queen; Force Five; The Last Bride of Salem (sp); 1976: Widow; Street Killing; Kingston: The Power Play; 1977: The Hostage Heart; 1979: Jennifer: A Woman's Story; Before and After; 1980: The Memory of Eva Ryker; Tourist; 1982: King's Crossing (series); The Legend of Walks Far Woman; 1982–83: Dynasty (series); 1985: Covenant; 1993: The Heart of Justice.

RICHARD DIX

(ERNEST CARLTON BRIMMER) BORN: ST. PAUL, MN, JULY 18, 1894. DIED: SEPTEMBER 20, 1949.

A forceful, rugged leading man with a flamboyant acting style that is often a bit hard for modern audiences to digest, Richard Dix carried his stardom from silents to sound before fading into "B" features. Originally a medical student, he turned to acting and made the rounds with various stock companies before his Broadway bow in *The Hawk*, in 1919. After some stage work in L.A., he landed a dual role in the 1921 movie *Not Guilty*, resulting in a contract with Samuel Goldwyn. He stayed there for two years until tempted by a better offer from Paramount, who started him off with *Racing Hearts*, a melodrama that had been intended for the late Wallace Reid. There were parts as irresponsible rich boys in such films as *Manhattan*, *Paradise for Two*, and *Let's Get Married*, and as sportsmen, in *The Quarterback*, *Knockout Reilly*, and *Warming Up*, which involved baseball. Two of his biggest hits of this period were DeMille's first version of *The Ten Commandments*, appearing as the good brother in the modern portion, and *The Vanishing American*, his stern features allowing him to play an Indian more convincingly than most Caucasians. Dix made the transition to sound in *Nothing But the Truth*, a farce about a man who makes a bet that he cannot lie, but after two more assignments a contract dispute caused him to accept a more lucrative offer over at RKO. He made an adaptation of a popular stage comedy, *Seven Keys to Baldpate*, as a writer who cannot get his manuscript finished because of all the frantic activity occurring around him, followed by two vehicles that passed quickly into obscurity: *Lovin' the Ladies*, as an electrician posing as a gentleman; and *Shooting Straight*, as a gambler who mistakenly thinks he's committed murder.

Then came the 1931 Academy Award winner for Best Picture, *Cimarron*, an epic western about the Oklahoma land rush. Dix was at his most colorful as the strong-willed husband, Yancy Cravat, who cannot control his wanderlust, and he earned an Oscar nomination. He followed this career high with a batch of movies that were no better than programmers, including *The Lost Squadron*, as an aerial ace working as a Hollywood stunt flyer; *Hell's Highway*, unjustly sentenced to a chain gang; and *Young Donovan's Kid*, a sentimental story featuring child star Jackie Cooper. Another attempt to repeat the epic scope of *Cimarron*, entitled *The Conquerors*, spanned some 60 years of the American banking business, and he reteamed with *Cimarron* co-star Irene Dunne for *Stingaree*, which found him as a bandit in love with an opera singer. By the end of the 1930s his busy output consisted mostly of "B" melodramas and westerns, including *Man of Conquest*, as Sam Houston; *The Round-Up*, which had a slightly bigger budget that most of these; *Badlands of Dakota*, as Wild Bill Hickok; and *Tombstone — The Town Too Tough to Die*, as Wyatt Earp. He played a crazed captain in Val Lewton's *Ghost Ship*, before embarking on a series of low budget detective thrillers at Columbia, based on the long-running radio program, *The Whistler*. The first of these, *The Whistler*, was released in 1944, and he stayed on for six more offerings, ending in 1947 with *The Thirteenth Hour*.

Screen: 1921: Not Guilty; The Sin Flood; Dangerous Curve Ahead; All's Fair in Love; The Poverty of Riches; 1922: The Glorious Fool; Yellow Men and Gold; The Wallflower; Fools First; The Bonded Woman; 1923: The Christian; Souls for Sale; Racing Hearts; The Woman With Four Faces; To the Last Man; Call of the Canyon; The Ten Commandments; Quicksands; 1924: The Stranger; Icebound; Unguarded Women; Sinners in Heaven; Manhattan; 1925: A Man Must Live; Too Many Kisses; Men and Women; The Shock Punch; The Lucky Devil; The Vanishing American; 1926: Woman-Handled; Let's Get Married; Say It Again; Fascinating Youth; The Quarterback; 1927: Paradise for Two; Knockout Reilly; Man Power; Shanghai Bound; 1928: The Gay Defender; Robin Hood of El Dorado; Sporting Goods; The Travelling Salesman; Easy Come, Easy Go; Warming Up; Moran of the Marines; 1929: Redskin; Nothing But the Truth; The Wheel of Life; The Love Doctor; Seven Keys to Baldpate;

1930: Lovin' the Ladies; Shooting Straight; 1931: Cimarron; Young Donovan's Kid; The Public Defender; Secret Service; 1932: The Lost Squadron; The Roar of the Dragon; Hell's Highway; The Conquerors; 1933: The Great Jasper; No Marriage Ties; Day of Reckoning; The Ace of Aces; 1934: Stingaree; His Greatest Gamble; West of the Pecos; 1935: The Arizonan; Transatlantic Tunnel/The Tunnel; 1936: Yellow Dust; Special Investigator; Devil's Squadron; 1937: The Devil's Playground; The Devil Is Driving; It Happened in Hollywood; 1938: Blind Alibi; Sky Giant; 1939: Twelve Crowded Hours; Man of Conquest; Here I Am a Stranger; Reno; 1940: The Marines Fly High; Men Against the Sky; Cherokee Strip; 1941: The Roundup; Badlands of Dakota; 1942: Tombstone — The Town Too Tough to Die; American Empire; 1943: Eyes of the Underworld; Buckskin Frontier; The Kansan; Top Man; The Ghost Ship; 1944: The Whistler; The Mark of the Whistler; 1945: Power of the Whistler; Voice of the Whistler; 1946: The Mysterious Intruder; Secret of the Whistler; 1947: The Thirteenth Hour.

NY Stage: 1914: The Hawk; 1920: Night Lodging; 1925: Lamb's Gambol.

TROY DONAHUE

(MERLE JOHNSON, JR.) BORN: NEW YORK, NY, JANUARY 27, 1937. DIED: SEPTEMBER 2, 2001.

Known more for his pin-up image than his acting range, blond, blandly handsome Troy Donahue became a fixture of late-1950s and early-1960s pop culture. Like many before and since, his looks got his movie career started, via a contract with Universal, while he was still acting in summer stock. He was featured in supporting roles in two Blake Edwards comedies, *This Happy Feeling* and *The Perfect Furlough*; the creature feature, *Monster on the Campus*; and the hit 1959 Sandra Dee soaper, *Imitation of Life*, with Donahue as the brutal boyfriend of passing-for-white Susan Kohner. Co-starring opposite Dee that same year in another glossy success, *A Summer Place*, over at Warner Bros., made Donahue a major heartthrob. Signed by that studio, he kept busy on the big screen in lush dramas like *Parrish*, as a tobacco grower with girl troubles, and *Susan Slade*, as a horse doctor who saves Connie Stevens from her checkered past. He also had back-to-back television series with *Surfside Six* and *Hawaiian Eye*. In 1962 he starred in *Rome Adventure*, with Suzanne Pleshette, who became his wife for less than a year, in 1964. There was a respite from the suds with a mild comedy, *Palm Springs Weekend*, followed by *A Distant Trumpet*, where he played a cavalryman out west in his usual drab manner. By the mid-1960s his popularity started to fade, and when, in 1974, he showed up in Francis Ford Coppola's Oscar-winning sequel, *The Godfather Part II*, most audiences were surprised to see his name on the cast list of so prestigious a project. As an inside joke, Donahue portrayed a character named Merle Johnson, his real name. This credit did nothing to improve his reputation and he spent most of his time thereafter in direct-to-video cheapies with titles like *The Chilling*, *Assault of the Party Nerds*, *Nudity Required*, and *Merchants of Venus*.

Screen: 1957: Man Afraid; The Tarnished Angels; 1958: This Happy Feeling; Voice in the Mirror; Summer Love; Live Fast, Die Young; Wild Heritage; Monster on the Campus; 1959: The Perfect Furlough; Imitation of Life; A Summer Place; 1960: The Crowded Sky; 1961: Parrish; Susan Slade; 1962: Rome Adventure; 1963: Palm Springs Weekend; 1964: A Distant Trumpet; 1965: My Blood Runs Cold; 1967: Come Spy With Me; Those Fantastic Flying Fools/Blast-Off; 1971: Sweet Saviour; 1974:

Cockfighter/Born to Kill; Seizure; The Godfather Part II; **1977:** The Legend of Frank Woods; **1983:** Tin Man (dtv); **1984:** Grandview, U.S.A.; **1986:** Low Blow/Savage Sunday; **1987:** Cyclone; Deadly Prey (dtv); Hollywood Cop (dtv); **1988:** Hawkeye (dtv); Dr. Alien/I Was a Teenage Sex Mutant (dtv); Sexpot (dtv); A Woman Obsessed (dtv); **1989:** Deadly Spygames (dtv); Assault of the Party Nerds (dtv); The Chilling (dtv); Bad Blood (dtv); **1990:** Terminal Force (dtv); Cry-Baby; Omega Cop (dtv); Nudity Required (dtv); Shock 'em Dead (dtv); **1991:** Deadly Diamonds (dtv); Sounds of Silence (dtv); The Pamela Principle (dtv); **1992:** Double Trouble; **1993:** Showdown (dtv); **1998:** Merchants of Venus (dtv).

Select TV: **1960–62:** Surfside Six (series); **1962–63:** Hawaiian Eye (series); **1968:** Split Second to an Epitaph; **1969:** The Lonely Profession; **1970:** The Secret Storm (series); **1983:** Malibu; **1998:** Legion; **1999:** Shake, Rattle and Roll: An American Love Story.

ROBERT DONAT

BORN: MANCHESTER, ENGLAND, MARCH 18, 1905. DIED: JUNE 9, 1958.

Self-effacing, timid, and fragile, Robert Donat seemed the most unlikely person to pursue a career requiring one to emote before the masses, but in doing so he became one of Great Britain's best loved and most admired stars. His entrance into dramatics came via elocution lessons intended to cure his stuttering, and he debuted in *Julius Caesar* in 1921, in Birmingham. He joined the Benson Company and the Liverpool Rep, acted in Cambridge, and finally made his London debut, in 1930, in *Knave and Queen*. Two years later his success in *Precious Bane* earned him a contract with film producer Alexander Korda, who started him with *Men of Tomorrow*, in 1933, followed by his first leading role, as an embezzler, in *That Night in London*. That same year, playing the king's squire, Thomas Culpepper, he supported Charles Laughton in *The Private Life of Henry VIII*, which became the most popular British movie shown in the U.S. up to that time. Because of it, he received an American offer and made a highly entertaining version of *The Count of Monte Cristo*, playing the wrongly imprisoned hero Edmond Dantes. It was a big box-office success, but was, in fact, the only Hollywood-based production he would ever film. Returning to Britain he appeared in one of his most famous roles, the innocent man on the run in Alfred Hitchcock's grand adventure *The 39 Steps*, before taking a dual role as a Scottish ghost and his descendant in the comedy *The Ghost Goes West*. Marlene Dietrich, whose Hollywood career was waning, joined him for *Knight Without Armour*, which, despite its title, was an espionage thriller, with Donat as a British Agent posing as a Russian.

He signed a contract with MGM in the late 1930s, but the terms of the agreement stipulated that his movies were to be made in England. The first two were major triumphs for him. *The Citadel* cast him as a doctor, and his subtle metamorphosis from idealist to cynic nabbed him an Oscar nomination in 1938. The following year he won the coveted trophy for the role that made him a part of Hollywood legend. As the shy schoolteacher who blossoms when he falls for Greer Garson, in *Goodbye, Mr. Chips*, he had to age from stoic youth to a doddering, white-haired senior. His performance, seen today, seems a little contrived, but it was a very popular Oscar choice, beating out Gable as Rhett Butler. For Fox's British unit he did a biopic, *The Young Mr. Pitt*, as the man who became Prime Minister at age 24, but World War II delayed the completion of his MGM contract, ultimately fulfilled by Donat doing *Tartu*, a wartime adventure, and the perceptive

Vacation From Marriage/Perfect Strangers, in which he and Deborah Kerr were a happily married couple who find themselves physically and emotionally separated by the war. The latter won an Academy Award for its script, but interest in Donat from the U.S. studios had waned. Because he was asthmatic, Donat limited himself to those projects he felt would be no strain, which included *The Winslow Boy*, as the defense counsel for a young school boy accused of stealing a postal order; *Cure for Love*, which he also found the strength to direct; *The Magic Box*, playing William Friese-Green, the man the British felt was responsible for the creation of motion pictures; and, finally, a Chinese mandarin in *The Inn of the Sixth Happiness*, a lengthy Ingrid Bergman Hollywood production filmed overseas. The year it was released, 1958, he died, nearly broke, having spent most of his money on medical fees over the course of his distinguished career.

Screen: **1933:** Men of Tomorrow; Overnight/That Night in London; For Love or Money/Cash; The Private Life of Henry VIII; **1934:** The Count of Monte Cristo; **1935:** The 39 Steps; **1936:** The Ghost Goes West; **1937:** Knight Without Armour; **1938:** The Citadel; **1939:** Goodbye, Mr. Chips; **1942:** The Young Mr. Pitt; **1943:** Tartu/The Adventures of Tartu; **1945:** Vacation From Marriage/Perfect Strangers; **1947:** Captain Boycott; **1948:** The Winslow Boy; **1949:** Cure for Love (and dir.; co-wr.; prod.); **1951:** The Magic Box; **1954:** Lease of Life; **1958:** The Inn of the Sixth Happiness.

BRIAN DONLEVY

(WALDO BRUCE DONLEVY) BORN: PORTADOWN, COUNTY ARMAGH, IRELAND, FEBRUARY 9, 1899. RAISED IN SHEBOYGAN FALLS, WI. ED: ST. JOHN'S MILITARY ACAD. DIED: APRIL 5, 1972.

A strong actor whose no-nonsense countenance suggested a man you didn't want to mess with, Brian Donlevy specialized in character work. He was occasionally called upon to play leads, which he did quite effectively, though it was often hard to warm up to a performer who was so good at displaying meanness. While Donlevy was still a baby his family moved to America, and, after some military experience as a youth, he entered the U.S. Naval Academy. He soon lost interest in the service and moved to New York to make it as a writer, but he wound up posing for Arrow Collar ads, which led to his 1924 movie debut in a tiny part in *Jamestown*. That same year he made his Broadway bow in *What Price Glory?* and would continue to work quite steadily there for the next decade. He arrived in Hollywood in 1935, scoring a part in Edward G. Robinson's melodrama *Barbary Coast*, playing the first of many villainous roles, a murderous henchmen named Knuckles Jacoby, who gets hanged by a gang of vigilantes. He followed this with *Mary Burns — Fugitive*, as a gangster shot down by G-Men, before signing up with 20th Century-Fox. He took leads in "B" movies like *Half Angel*, as a reporter who believes Frances Dee is innocent of poisoning her father; *Human Cargo*, again as a newsman, teamed with Claire Trevor to do an expose on illegal aliens; and *High Tension*, as a cable engineer trying to get Glenda Farrell to marry him. The studio bumped him up to big-budget productions like *This Is My Affair*, *In Old Chicago*, and *Jesse James*, but always as the bad guy, robbing a bank in the first; getting justifiably trampled by a cattle stampede in the second, and killing off Jane Darwell in the last. In 1939, Donlevy reached his peak with *Destry Rides Again*, as James Stewart's nemesis, a saloon owner who hopes to get rich by stealing land and charging tolls, and with the remake of *Beau Geste*, earning his sole Oscar nomination for his superb playing of the despicable, scar-faced commander Sgt. Markoff, one of the most hissable curs in celluloid history. Because of his work in the latter, Paramount signed him to a non-exclusive contact. For them he immediately played his most famous leading role, as the bum who becomes governor in the Preston Sturges comedy *The Great McGinty*. His gruff bravado gave this somewhat tame satire its kick and he would reprise the character, briefly, in Sturges's *The Miracle of Morgan's Creek*.

He was a flight instructor in *I Wanted Wings*, and had one of his best roles, as the iron major in charge of the Marine battalion, in *Wake Island*, a fairly standard war film that became one of the year's top hits and an Oscar nominee for Best Picture. He was top-billed in the mystery *The Glass Key*, as a corrupt politician, but most of the attention went to co-stars Alan Ladd and Veronica Lake. Universal gave him a lead as both hero and lover, playing gambler Daniel Shayne in the 1942 drama *Nightmare*, which was Donlevy's personal favorite of all his roles. Another major assignment featured him as an immigrant who becomes a powerful tycoon, in MGM's *An American Romance*, inheriting the part after Spencer Tracy's departure. This problematic film became one of that studio's major underachievers of the war years, being rejected off the bat as overlong and eventually being trimmed by nearly a half-hour, to no avail. Back at Paramount Donlevy somehow escaped being cast as the sadistic captain in *Two Years Before the Mast*, instead playing the sailor who writes an exposé on the disgraceful conditions of seafaring in the 1830s, but in the 1946 remake of *The Virginian*, he was mean again, as Trampas, the part Walter Huston had done in the better-known 1929 version. He was a comical bootlegger in *Our Hearts Were Growing Up*, and fulfilled his Paramount obligation supporting Ray Milland in *The Trouble With Women*. For MGM he headed the cast of *The Beginning or the End*, about the development of the Atom bomb; was a hot shot gambler involved in the fight game in *Killer McCoy*; and was a brigadier general in the all-star military hit *Command Decision*. At the start of the 1950s he began a radio series, *Dangerous Assignment*, which transferred to television with Donlevy as producer. During that decade he played a gangster with a hearing-aid in the hard-hitting *The Big Combo*, after which he went to England to star as Dr. Quatermass in *The Quatermass Experiment/The Creeping Unknown*, an intelligently conceived sci-fi thriller that gained a cult following. Later years were spent in A.C. Lyles's "B" westerns and low-grade productions like the Japanese *Gammera the Invincible*, about a rampaging giant turtle, but his acute alcoholism had taken its toll and he often had trouble memorizing dialogue. His life-long ambition to be a writer was partially realized in the 1940s when he published a book of poems, *Leaves in the Wind*, under the pen name of Porter Down.

Screen: 1923: Jamestown; 1924: Damaged Hearts; Monsieur Beaucaire; 1925: School for Wives; 1926: A Man of Quality; 1929: Mother's Boy; Gentlemen of the Press; 1935: Barbary Coast; Mary Burns — Fugitive; Another Face; 1936: Strike Me Pink; 13 Hours by Air; Human Cargo; Half Angel; High Tension; 36 Hours to Kill; 1937: Crack-Up; 1937: Midnight Taxi; This Is My Affair; Born Reckless; In Old Chicago; 1938: Battle of Broadway; We're Going to Be Rich; Sharpshooters; 1939: Jesse James; Union Pacific; Beau Geste; Behind Prison Gates; Allegheny Uprising; Destry Rides Again; 1940: The Great McGinty; When the Daltons Rode; Brigham Young — Frontiersman; 1941: I Wanted Wings; Billy the Kid; Hold Back the Dawn; Birth of the Blues; South of Tahiti; 1942: The Remarkable Andrew; A Gentleman After Dark; The Great Man's Lady; Two Yanks in Trinidad; Wake Island; The Glass Key; Nightmare; Stand by for Action; 1943: Hangmen Also Die; The City That Stopped Hitler: Heroic Stalingrad (narrator); 1944: The Miracle of Morgan's Creek; An

American Romance; 1945: Duffy's Tavern; 1946: The Virginian; Our Hearts Were Growing Up; Canyon Passage; Two Years Before the Mast; 1947: Song of Scheherazade; The Beginning or the End; The Trouble With Women; Kiss of Death; Heaven Only Knows; Killer McCoy; 1948: A Southern Yankee; Command Decision; 1949: The Lucky Stiff; Impact; 1950: Shakedown; Kansas Raiders; 1951: Fighting Coast Guard; Slaughter Trail; 1952: Hoodlum Empire; Ride the Man Down; 1953: The Woman They Almost Lynched; 1955: The Big Combo; 1956: The Creeping Unknown/The Quatermass Experiment; A Cry in the Night; 1957: Enemy From Space/Quatermass II; 1958: Escape From Red Rock; Cowboy; 1959: Juke Box Rhythm; Never So Few; 1961: Girl in Room 13; The Errand Boy; 1962: The Pigeon That Took Rome; 1965: Gammera, the Invincible; Curse of the Fly; How to Stuff a Wild Bikini; The Fat Spy; 1966: Waco; 1967: Hostile Guns; Five Golden Dragons; 1968: Arizona Bushwhackers; Rogue's Gallery; 1969: Pit Stop.

NY Stage: 1924: What Price Glory?; 1927: Hit the Deck!; Ringside; 1928: Rainbow; 1929: Queen Bee; 1930: Up Pops the Devil; 1931: Peter Flies High; Society Girl; 1932: The Inside Story; The Boy Friend; 1933: Three-Cornered Moon; Three and One; 1934: No Questions Asked; The Perfumed Lady; The Milky Way; Life Begins at 8:40.

Select TV: 1950: The Pharmacist's Mate (sp); 1952: Dangerous Assignment (series); 1953: Tunnel Job (sp); 1955: The Great McGinty (sp); 1956: Home Is the Hero (sp).

JEFF DONNELL

(JEAN MARIE DONNELL) BORN: SOUTH WINDHAM, ME, JULY 10, 1921. ED: YALE UNIV. DIED: APRIL 11, 1988.

A character actress with a perky personality, it was Jeff Donnell's fate to be declared second-lead material, earning distinction only by her unusual first name. She was working with the Farragut Playhouse in New Hampshire when she was signed up by Columbia Pictures, and she started out in the 1942 comedy hit *My Sister Eileen*, playing the girl who lives above Rosalind Russell and Janet Blair. (There was a similar role in *A Night to Remember*, the following year.) She partnered Larry Parks in the horror-comedy *The Boogie Man Will Get You*, supporting Boris Karloff and Peter Lorre, and continued to fill out the cast lists of such minor war-time entertainments as *What's Buzzin', Cousin?*; *Nine Girls*, a murder mystery set at a girls' college; *There's Something About a Soldier*; and *Edie Was a Lady*, as Anne Miller's roommate. She stayed with Columbia for the remainder of the 1940s, moving up to leading lady when she paired off with "B" cowboy star Ken Curtis in such western musicals as *Throw a Saddle on a Star*, *Singin' on the Trail*, and *That Texas Jamboree*. Rare "A" movie parts came her way in Irene Dunne's *Over 21*, and *In a Lonely Place*, with Humphrey Bogart. In the classic *Sweet Smell of Success*, she was seen as Tony Curtis's long-suffering secretary, but was back at Columbia in the 1960s to populate the adult side of *Gidget Goes Hawaiian* and *Gidget Goes to Rome*, as Gidget's mother. Television audiences knew her best as George Gobel's wife, Alice, on *The George Gobel Show*. She was briefly (1954–56) wed to actor Aldo Ray.

Screen: 1942: My Sister Eileen; The Boogie Man Will Get You; 1943: What's Buzzin', Cousin?; A Night to Remember; There's Something About a Soldier; Doughboys in Ireland; City Without Men; 1944: She's a Soldier Too; Nine Girls; Stars on Parade; Three Is a Family; Carolina Blues; Mr. Winkle Goes to War; Once Upon a Time; Cowboy Canteen; 1945: Power of the

Whistler; Eadie Was a Lady; Dancing in Manhattan; Over 21; Song of the Prairie; **1946:** Tars and Spars; Throw a Saddle on a Star; The Phantom Thief; Night Editor; That Texas Jamboree; The Unknown; Singing on the Trail; It's Great to Be Young; Cowboy Blues; **1947:** Mr. District Attorney; **1949:** Roughshod; Stagecoach Kid; Easy Living; Post Office Investigator; Outcasts of the Trail; **1950:** In a Lonely Place; Hoedown; Walk Softly Stranger; The Fuller Brush Girl; Redwood Forest Trail; Big Timber; **1951:** Three Guys Named Mike; **1952:** Skirts Ahoy!; Thief of Damascus; The First Time; Because You're Mine; **1953:** So This Is Love; Flight Nurse; The Blue Gardenia; **1954:** Massacre Canyon; **1956:** Magnificent Roughnecks; **1957:** The Guns of Fort Petticoat; Destination 60,000; Sweet Smell of Success; My Man Godfrey; **1961:** Force of Impulse; Gidget Goes Hawaiian; **1963:** Gidget Goes to Rome; **1964:** The Swingin' Maiden/The Iron Maiden; **1969:** The Comic; **1970:** Tora!Tora!Tora!; **1972:** Stand Up and Be Counted.

Select TV: 1953: Girl of My Dreams (sp); **1954:** One for the Road (sp); **1954–58:** The George Gobel Show (series); **1956:** Sincerely Willis Wayde (sp); **1959:** Little Tin God (sp); **1960:** Game of Hearts (sp); Uncle Harry (sp); **1962:** Farewell to Innocence (sp); **1964:** Bristle Face (sp); **1971:** Love Hate Love; Congratulations, It's a Boy!; **1973:** The Gift of Terror (sp); **1975–76:** Matt Helm (series); **1976:** McNaughton's Daughter; **1977:** Spider-Man/The Amazing Spiderman; **1979:** Murder by Natural Causes; Rendezvous Hotel; Portrait of a Stripper.

RUTH DONNELLY

BORN: TRENTON, NJ, MAY 17, 1896.
DIED: NOVEMBER 17, 1982.

As a member of the Warner Bros. stock company in the 1930s, Ruth Donnelly cracked wise, but age restricted her to smaller roles than those given to younger fellow quipsters Joan Blondell or Glenda Farrell. She started as a chorus girl in her teens, working her way up to larger Broadway roles in such 1920s fare as *The Meanest Man in the World*, *As You Were*, and *Cheaper to Marry*. She made her film debut in the 1927 silent *Rubber Heels*, went back to the stage, and finally returned to movies in 1931, for Fox's *Transatlantic*. Warner Bros. took her on the following year, starting her off as a maid in the melodrama *Jewel Robbery*, and over the next few years her credits included *Hard to Handle*, as Mary Brian's hilariously money-hungry mom; *Ladies They Talk About*, behind bars in a woman's prison; *Havana Widows*, supporting Blondell and Farrell; *Happiness Ahead*, as Josephine Hutchinson's maid; and *Footlight Parade* and *Convention City*, in both instances as the wife of Guy Kibbee. In 1933 alone she added her witty presence to no fewer than 13 features. She played off Edward G. Robinson to good effect in the 1938 comedy, *A Slight Case of Murder*, as his wife, and participated in celluloid matrimony to Kibbee once again, in the 1939 classic *Mr. Smith Goes to Washington*. Last seen at Warners in *Pillow to Post* and *Cinderella Jones*, in 1946, she bid farewell to the big screen 11 years later with the Fox "B" western, *The Way to the Gold*, after which she retired and spent much of her time composing songs.

Screen: 1927: Rubber Heels; **1931:** Transatlantic; The Spider; Wicked; **1932:** The Rainbow Trail; Blessed Event; Jewel Robbery; Make Me a Star; **1933:** Hard to Handle; Employees' Entrance; Ladies They Talk About; Lilly Turner; Goodbye Again; Private Detective 62; Sing, Sinner, Sing; Bureau of Missing Persons; Footlight Parade; Ever in My Heart; Female; Havana Widows; Convention City; **1934:** Wonder Bar; Heat Lightning; Mandalay;

Merry Wives of Reno; Housewife; Romance in the Rain; Happiness Ahead; **1935:** The White Cockatoo; Maybe It's Love; Traveling Saleslady; Alibi Ike; Red Salute; Metropolitan; Personal Maid's Secret; Hands Across the Table; **1936:** The Song and Dance Man; 13 Hours by Air; Mr. Deeds Goes to Town; Fatal Lady; Cain and Mabel; More Than a Secretary; **1937:** Roaring Timber; Portia on Trial; **1938:** A Slight Case of Murder; Army Girl; Meet the Girls; The Affairs of Annabel; Annabel Takes a Tour; Personal Secretary; **1939:** The Family Next Door; The Amazing Mrs. Williams; Mr. Smith Goes to Washington; **1940:** My Little Chickadee; Scatterbrain; Meet the Missus; **1941:** Model Wife; Petticoat Politics; The Roundup; The Gay Vagabond; Sailors on Leave; Rise and Shine; You Belong to Me; **1942:** Johnny Doughboy; **1943:** This Is the Army; Thank Your Lucky Stars; Sleepy Lagoon; **1945:** Pillow to Post; The Bells of St. Mary's; **1946:** Cross My Heart; Cinderella Jones; In Old Sacramento; **1947:** The Ghost Goes Wild; Little Miss Broadway; The Fabulous Texan; **1948:** Fighting Father Dunne; The Snake Pit; **1950:** Where the Sidewalk Ends; **1951:** I'd Climb the Highest Mountain; The Secret of Convict Lake; The Wild Blue Yonder; **1955:** A Lawless Street; The Spoilers; **1956:** Autumn Leaves; **1957:** The Way to the Gold.

NY Stage: 1914: A Scrap of Paper; **1917:** Going Up; **1918:** One of Us; A Prince There Was; **1920:** As You Were; The Meanest Man in the World; **1922:** Madeleine and the Movies; **1923:** The Crooked Square; **1924:** Cheaper to Marry; **1926:** If I Was Rich; **1930:** So Was Napoleon; **1931:** She Means Business; **1963:** The Riot Act; **1971:** No, No, Nanette.

DIANA DORS

(DIANA FLUCK) BORN: SWINDON, WILTSHIRE, ENGLAND, OCTOBER 23, 1931. ED: RADA.
DIED: MAY 4, 1984.

Britain's so-called "sex symbol" of the 1950s, Diana Dors had the misfortune of being more figure than talent, and her reputation wasn't helped by the mostly second-rate films in which she appeared. While attending RADA she was offered a bit in a 1946 film, *The Shop at Sly Corner*, followed by a contract with Rank, where she had a run of insignificant parts until she attracted attention for her role as the sexy niece in *Here Come the Huggetts*, a sequel to her earlier movie, *Holiday Camp*. Her subsequent motion picture work was mostly routine, with such films as *Worm's Eye View*, *Lady Godiva Rides Again* (which referred to Pauline Stroud, not Dors), and *Is Your Honeymoon Really Necessary?*, but she attracted publicity for her very obvious sexuality. In the mid-1950s she began to appear in higher-budgeted films which got exported to the U.S., including *The Weak and the Wicked*, as one of the bad girls in prison; *A Kid for Two Farthings*, as a Londoner blessed by a magical goat; *Value for Money*, as a gold-digging showgirl; and *Yield to the Night/Blonde Sinner*, which de-glamorized her in hopes of getting her some serious attention. Financially strapped RKO was curious enough to offer her *The Unholy Wife*, wherein she attempted to kill husband Rod Steiger, and *I Married a Woman*, searching in vain for laughs, opposite television comedian George Gobel. By the 1960s she was getting blowsier and plumper, so she turned to character acting in such international efforts as *Berserk*, with Joan Crawford; *There's a Girl in My Soup*; *Deep End*, as a hefty bath house customer looking for stimulation in a movie that became a cult favorite; *Hannie Caulder*, as a madam in the Old West; *Theatre of Blood*, in which she was strangled by Jack Hawkins; and *Steaming*, back in the bathhouse, this time as the manager, in

Joseph Losey's last movie. One of her husbands was actor Richard Dawson.

Screen: 1946: The Shop at Sly Corner; 1947: Dancing with Crime; Holiday Camp; 1948: Good Time Girl; The Calendar; My Sister and I; Oliver Twist; Penny and the Pownall Case; Here Come the Huggetts; 1949: Vote for Huggett; It's Not Cricket; A Boy, a Girl and a Bike; Diamond City; 1950: Dance Hall; 1951: Worm's Eye View; Lady Godiva Rides Again; 1952: The Last Page/Man Bait; My Wife's Lodger; 1953: The Great Game; Is Your Honeymoon Really Necessary?; It's a Grand Life; The Saint's Return; 1954: The Weak and the Wicked/Young and Willing; As Long as They're Happy; 1955: A Kid for Two Farthings; Value for Money; An Alligator Named Daisy; 1956: Yield to the Night/Blonde Sinner; 1957: The Unholy Wife; The Long Haul; 1958: I Married a Woman; La Ragazza del Palio/The Love Specialist; Tread Softly Stranger; 1959: Passport to Shame; 1960: Scent of Mystery; 1961: On the Double; King of the Roaring 20's — The Story of Arnold Rothstein; Encontra a Mallorca; 1962: Mrs. Gibbon's Boys; 1963: West Eleven; 1964: Allez France/The Counterfeit Constable; 1966: The Sandwich Man; 1967: Berserk; Danger Route; 1968: Hammerhead; 1969: Baby Love; 1970: There's a Girl in My Soup; 1971: Deep End; Hannie Caulder; 1972: The Piped Piper; Nothing but the Night/The Resurrection Syndicate; The Amazing Mr. Blunden; 1973: Theatre of Blood; Steptoe and Son Ride Again; 1974: From Beyond the Grave; Craze; 1975: The Groove Room/What the Swedish Butler Saw; Bedtime with Rosie; Three for All; The Amorous Milkman; 1976: Keep It Up Downstairs; Adventures of a Taxi Driver; 1977: Adventures of a Private Eye; 1979: Confessions from the David Galaxy Affair; 1985: Steaming.

Select TV: 1981: Dick Turpin.

KIRK DOUGLAS

(Issur Danielovitch) Born: Amsterdam, NY, December 9, 1916. ed: St. Lawrence Univ., AADA.

In many ways Kirk Douglas was the first anti-hero superstar of the postwar era. He eased effortlessly from flawed good guys to charismatic bad guys, with scant regard for audience approval. The owner of the movies' most famous cleft chin won his first stage part, in *Spring Again*, after studying at the American Academy of Dramatic Arts in New York. Following a few more Broadway credits, he was recommended to producer Hal Wallis by Lauren Bacall. Wallis gave him the flashy part of Barbara Stanwyck's alcoholic husband in the 1946 melodrama, *The Strange Love of Martha Ivers*, and the offers started pouring in. At RKO he played Rosalind Russell's lover in the troubled and ultimately disastrous attempt to present *Mourning Becomes Electra* to the general public, and a hood duped by femme fatale Jane Greer in the notable noir *Out of the Past*. At Fox, he was part of the ensemble of the critically-admired *A Letter to Three Wives*, as Ann Sothern's English professor husband. That same year, 1949, marked his breakthrough to the top, with the grim prizefighting drama *Champion*. Douglas was at his most uncompromisingly ugly, as a ruthless boxer with no concern for anyone else in his climb to fame. He grabbed his first, well-deserved Oscar nomination, and signed a contract with Warner Bros., for whom he was a brash trumpeter driven to drink in *Young Man With a Horn*, and the Gentleman Caller in *The Glass Menagerie*, giving a nice, subdued performance in a movie that was not always faithful to its source material. At Paramount, he played an unscrupulous reporter in Billy Wilder's neglected masterpiece,

Ace in the Hole, which fared so badly at the box office that its title was changed to *The Big Carnival*. He was also excellent as the investigator being pushed over the edge by the daily workings at a Manhattan police station in the better-attended *Detective Story*.

MGM cast him as a hard-edged movie producer, more misunderstood than hateful, in Vincent Minnelli's skewered look at Hollywood, *The Bad and the Beautiful*. The movie was a flat-out hit and Douglas came away with a second Oscar nomination. In order to qualify for tax emption he did a few productions outside the U.S., including an interesting look at Israel in its early years, *The Juggler*, and *Ulysses*, a partially dubbed Italian spectacle. Back in the States he formed his own production company, Bryna, named after his mom, but their first effort, *The Indian Fighter*, in which he helped protect a wagon train from the likes of Lon Chaney, Jr. and Walter Matthau, was not a hit. Douglas had, in the meantime, made a huge box-office success, Disney's colorful *20,000 Leagues Under the Sea*, at his most likeable as adventurer Ned Land. In addition to battling a giant squid in the movie's most famous sequence, he also sang "A Whale of a Tale" while strumming a guitar. He reached his acting pinnacle with another fine Minnelli film, *Lust for Life*, with Douglas perfectly cast as the tormented painter Vincent van Gogh, a towering, no-holds-barred performance that earned him one last Oscar nomination, in 1956. The next year he had a solid hit when he reteamed with Burt Lancaster (they had co-starred for Wallis in 1947's *I Walk Alone*) for *Gunfight at the O.K. Corral*, where Douglas got the juicier role as the tubercular Doc Holliday. His next film did not bring in the crowds, but has since risen in stature to be considered one of the great anti-war films. Director Stanley Kubrick's *Paths of Glory* was a brutal and uncompromising look at the stupidity of the military mind, with Douglas at his sympathetic best as the officer who tries to save three soldiers from the firing squad. He returned to villainy as the chief barbarian, who has his eye gouged out by a falcon, in the popular epic *The Vikings*, made for his own company. It was obvious that audiences preferred the Old West to Shaw, showing up for *Last Train from Gun Hill*, but ignoring a truncated but highly entertaining adaptation of *The Devil's Disciple*, where producer Lancaster gave Douglas the plum role of Dick Dudgeon.

Back with Kubrick, he made *Spartacus*, the movie with which his name has become synonymous, giving an impassioned performance as the slave who leads a doomed revolt against the Romans. It was a massive moneymaker and still remains the most thrilling and intelligent of all the thundering and lengthy spectacles of that time. Also released around the same time, and popular in its own way, was *Strangers When We Meet*, the story of adulterous affair in which he was paired with the uninspiring Kim Novak. In 1962 he made a simple black-and-white drama for Universal, *Lonely Are the Brave*, playing a modern day cowboy on the run from the law. It was a quietly effective study of a man out of synch with the times and the actor's own favorite of his movies. *For Love or Money* found him attempting comedy, Universal/1960s-style, before returning to his element as the hero of the well-scripted paranoia classic, *Seven Days in May*, with Lancaster as his nemesis. His popularity began to dwindle and his most widely seen offerings of this period, *In Harm's Way* and *The War Wagon*, owed more to the participation of co-star John Wayne. Among his less successful films were the Norwegian Resistance adventure, *The Heroes of Telemark*; *Cast a Giant Shadow*, his second movie set in Israel; *Is Paris Burning?*, in which he made a far less compelling General Patton than George C. Scott later did; *The Way West*, which proved that Robert Mitchum and Richard Widmark were *also* on their way out as name attractions; *The Brotherhood*, which tackled the Mafia three years before *The*

Godfather did it with far more panache; and *The Arrangement*, a self-indulgent mid-life crisis mess from director Elia Kazan. Douglas, however, gave one of his most spirited performances as a wily, bespectacled prisoner in the lively western comedy-drama, *There Was a Crooked Man...* , but had to wait until the silly 1975 soaper, *Once Is Not Enough*, for something akin to another hit. In between, he reluctantly faced fellow gunfighter Johnny Cash in *A Gunfight*; did some European films; and appeared with some regularity in television movies. A marginally popular horror thriller, *The Fury*, featured Douglas as the hero in this tale of telekinesis, after which he hit a career low-point as a human Wiley Coyote in the horrendous spoof *The Villain*.

Twice during the 1970s, he attempted directing, but neither *Scalawag*, in which he was a crusty old pirate, or the western *Posse*, as a marshal held prisoner by outlaw Bruce Dern, did any business. He found solace in television, including the first movie for HBO, *Draw!*, and *Amos*, which found him in a mental home. (Earlier, he had hoped to turn another piece with the same setting into a film, but his son Michael ended up with the rights to *One Flew Over the Cuckoo's Nest*, which Kirk had done on Broadway, and cast the younger and more bankable Jack Nicholson instead.) On the big screen he played a dual role in the actioner *The Man From Snowy River*, which was very popular in its native Australia, but not in America. *Tough Guys* had the idea of pairing Douglas and Lancaster as a pair of old crooks, released into the real world after a lifetime in jail. The execution was too low-brow and the jokes too obvious, but Douglas, feisty as ever at age 69, proved that he had no qualms about showing his bare butt. The weak ensemble comedy *Greedy*, for which he spent most of the film in a wheelchair, marked his last appearance prior to a stroke in early 1996. That same year he made a poignant appearance at the Oscars, accepting a special award, and reminding audiences that this was truly one of the major contributors to cinema of the past 50 years. There was one, tailor-made starring role left in him, playing a boxer recovering from a stroke in *Diamonds*, but even though he played some scenes opposite the lady who helped get him started in the business, Lauren Bacall, it was a sorry affair. After much talk he and son Michael, who had become as big a star as his dad had, finally teamed for a project, *It Runs in the Family*, which also featured Kirk's grandson, Cameron. Douglas published three memoirs, *The Ragman's Son* (1988), *Climbing the Mountain* (1997), and *My Stroke of Luck* (2002), as well as three novels: *Dance With the Devil* (1990), *The Gift* (1992), and *Last Tango in Brooklyn* (1994). In 1991 he received the American Film Institute Life Achievement Award.

Screen: 1946: The Strange Love of Martha Ivers; 1947: Mourning Becomes Electra; Out of the Past; I Walk Alone; 1948: The Walls of Jericho; My Dear Secretary; 1949: A Letter to Three Wives; Champion; 1950: Young Man With a Horn; The Glass Menagerie; 1951: Ace in the Hole/The Big Carnival; Along the Great Divide; Detective Story; 1952: The Big Trees; The Big Sky; The Bad and the Beautiful; 1953: The Story of Three Loves; Act of Love; The Juggler; 1954: Ulysses; 20,000 Leagues Under the Sea; 1955: Man Without a Star; The Racers; The Indian Fighter; 1956: Lust for Life; 1957: Top Secret Affair; Gunfight at the O.K. Corral; Paths of Glory (and prod.); 1958: The Vikings; 1959: Last Train From Gun Hill; The Devil's Disciple; 1960: Strangers When We Meet; Spartacus (and exec. prod.); 1961: The Last Sunset; Town Without Pity; 1962: Lonely Are the Brave; Two Weeks in Another Town; 1963: The Hook; The List of Adrian Messenger; For Love or Money; 1964: Seven Days in May; 1965: In Harm's Way; The Heroes of Telemark; 1966: Cast a Giant Shadow; Is Paris Burning?; 1967: The Way West; The War

Wagon; 1968: A Lovely Way to Die; The Brotherhood (and prod.); 1969: The Arrangement; 1970: There Was a Crooked Man ...; 1971: A Gunfight; The Light at the Edge of the World (and prod.); To Catch a Spy/Catch Me a Spy; 1973: Scalawag (and dir.); 1974: The Master Touch; 1975: Jacqueline Susann's Once Is Not Enough; Posse (and dir.; prod.); 1978: The Chosen/Holocaust 2000; The Fury; 1979: The Villain; 1980: Saturn 3; Home Movies; The Final Countdown; 1983: The Man From Snowy River; Eddie Macon's Run; 1986: Tough Guys; 1991: Oscar; 1992: Veraz (nUSr); 1994: Greedy; 1999: Diamonds; 2003: It Runs in the Family.

NY Stage: 1941: Spring Again; 1942: The Three Sisters; 1944: Kiss and Tell; Trio; 1945: Alice in Arms; The Wind Is Ninety; 1946: Woman Bites Dog; 1963: One Flew Over the Cuckoo's Nest.

Select TV: 1968: The Legend of Silent Night (sp; narrator); 1973: Dr. Jekyll and Mr. Hyde (sp); 1974: Mousey; 1976: Arthur Hailey's The Moneychangers; Victory at Entebbe; 1982: Remembrance of Love; 1984: Draw!; 1985: Amos; 1987: Queenie; 1988: Inherit the Wind; 1991: Two-Fisted Tales (sp); 1992: The Secret; 1994: Take Me Home Again.

MELVYN DOUGLAS

(MELVYN EDOUARD HESSELBERG) BORN: MACON, GA, APRIL 5, 1901. DIED: AUGUST 4, 1981.

There are two halves to Melvyn Douglas's long career: the romantic lead and the elderly character actor. He was so good in the latter that people sometimes forget the intelligence and light-hearted charm he brought to the former. The son of noted concert pianist Edouard Hesselberg, he made his stage bow in Chicago in 1919. For the next several years he worked in stock and touring companies until making his Broadway debut in *A Free Soul*, in 1928. Two years later he scored enough of a success in another play, *Tonight or Never*, that he was asked by Samuel Goldwyn to repeat the part in the 1931 film version, playing an agent for the Metropolitan Opera, opposite Gloria Swanson. That same year he married his co-star from the original stage production, Helen Gahagan, whose only screen role would be the lead in the 1935 fantasy *She*. Although Douglas was officially under contract to Goldwyn, no work was forthcoming, so he starred opposite Greta Garbo for the first time, in MGM's *As You Desire Me*, emoting too heavily as her Italian lover; paired with Claudette Colbert in Paramount's *The Wiser Sex*, as an attorney framed for murder; played the young hero amid the colorful cast of weirdos in James Whale's cult horror film, *The Old Dark House*; and supported John Barrymore in the excellent *Counsellor-at-Law*, as Barrymore's wife's lover. In 1934 he directed two Broadway plays, *Moor Born* and *Within the Gates*, before finding his Hollywood niche with a sophisticated comedy, *She Married Her Boss*, co-starring once again with Claudette Colbert, in a film that had him marrying her for her mind. As a result of this movie he was signed to a contract with Columbia Pictures, who attempted to make him the new "Michael Lanyard" in the *Lone Wolf* series, but he did only one picture, *The Lone Wolf Returns*, before passing the part on to Francis Lederer. On loan to RKO he lost Barbara Stanwyck to Preston Foster in *Annie Oakley*, while at Paramount he played part of his role in *Mary Burns: Fugitive* as a blind man, until plot complications restored his sight in time for his clinch with Sylvia Sidney. Back at Columbia he was in a fairly mediocre but popular screwball comedy, *Theodora Goes Wild*, playing a book illustrator who loosens up Irene Dunne and then regrets it.

His solid work in MGM's starry period picture *The Gorgeous Hussy*, as the object of Joan Crawford's affections, was good enough for the studio to offer to share his contract with Columbia. He did some of his best work around this time, though he often had to take outside offers, including a reteaming with Colbert, *I Met Him in Paris*, at Paramount, and *That Certain Age*, at Universal, in which Deanna Durbin had a crush on him. Taking a cue from the popular *Thin Man* comedies, Columbia found Douglas a delightful co-star in Joan Blondell for *There's Always a Woman*, in which they were a sleuthing couple, but Blondell was unavailable for the follow-up, *There's That Woman Again*, and was replaced by Virginia Bruce. Back at MGM he played the relatively small part of Freddie Bartholomew's dad in *Captain's Courageous*, before being paired with Garbo again for his most memorable movie of that era, *Ninotchka*, as the womanizer who dissuades Greta from her Communist ways. It was such a hit that Columbia shamelessly cashed in on it with *He Stayed for Breakfast*, casting Douglas as a Communist organizer hiding out in Loretta Young's apartment. Another comedy with Garbo, *Two-Faced Woman*, is best remembered as the movie that sent her running from Hollywood. Following a stint in the army during World War II, he returned to movies as the "other man" in the weakest of the Tracy-Hepburn teamings, *The Sea of Grass*. He was Rosalind Russell's leading man in *The Guilt of Janet Ames*, and gave a wonderfully sly performance as the sardonic family friend in *Mr. Blandings Builds His Dream House*. He was third-billed for *The Great Sinner* and *My Forbidden Past*, while the RKO programmer *On the Loose* found him playing a neglectful dad. He retreated to the stage, where he found greater satisfaction in such Broadway plays as *Inherit the Wind*, *The Waltz of the Toreadors*, and *The Best Man*, for which he won a Tony Award.

When he returned to the movies after an 11-year absence, in 1962's *Billy Budd* (looking decidedly older), a new phase of his career began, as one of the exemplary character players of his time. He promptly won an Academy Award as Best Supporting Actor for his brilliant performance as Paul Newman's stubborn, dying rancher father in *Hud*. On a lighter level he played comedic military men in *Advance to the Rear* and *The Americanization of Emily*, and received top billing for the French-made love story *Rapture*, though the romance certainly didn't focus on him. In *I Never Sang for My Father*, as Gene Hackman's selfish dad, he once again played a character facing the end of his life and for it he nabbed another Oscar nomination, this time in the lead category. He perfectly played aging politicians in *The Candidate*, as Robert Redford's father, and *The Seduction of Joe Tynan*, going senile in front of his fellow senators, then brought great dignity to 1979's dark satire, *Being There*, as Shirley MacLaine's sickly millionaire husband, and won himself a second Academy Award for Best Supporting Actor. He died shortly afterwards, his final movie, *Ghost Story*, being released posthumously. Among his many television roles was the *CBS Playhouse* presentation of *Do Not Go Gentle Into That Good Night*, for which he won an Emmy Award. His wife served as a Congresswoman during the 1940s and died in 1980.

Screen: 1931: Tonight or Never; 1932: Prestige; As You Desire Me; The Wiser Sex; The Broken Wing; The Old Dark House; 1933: The Vampire Bat; Nagana; Counsellor-at-Law; 1934: Dangerous Corner; Woman in the Dark; 1935: The People's Enemy; She Married Her Boss; Annie Oakley; Mary Burns — Fugitive; The Lone Wolf Returns; 1936: And So They Were Married; Theodora Goes Wild; The Gorgeous Hussy; 1937: Women of Glamour; I Met Him in Paris; I'll Take Romance; Angel; Captains Courageous; 1938: Arsene Lupin Returns; Fast Company; The Toy Wife; There's Always a Woman; The Shining Hour; That Certain Age; 1939: There's That Woman Again; Tell No Tales; Ninotchka; Good Girls Go to Paris; The Amazing Mr.

Williams; 1940: Too Many Husbands; He Stayed for Breakfast; This Thing Called Love; Third Finger, Left Hand; 1941: That Uncertain Feeling; A Woman's Face; Our Wife; Two-Faced Woman; 1942: We Were Dancing; They All Kissed the Bride; Three Hearts for Julia; 1947: The Sea of Grass; The Guilt of Janet Ames; 1948: Mr. Blandings Builds His Dream House; My Own True Love; 1949: A Woman's Secret; The Great Sinner; 1951: My Forbidden Past; On the Loose; 1962: Billy Budd; 1963: Hud; 1964: Advance to the Rear; The Americanization of Emily; 1965: Rapture; 1967: Hotel; 1970: I Never Sang for My Father; 1972: One Is a Lonely Number; The Candidate; 1976: The Tenant; 1977: Twilight's Last Gleaming; 1979: The Seduction of Joe Tynan; Being There; 1980: The Changeling; Tell Me a Riddle; 1981: Ghost Story.

NY Stage: 1928: A Free Soul; Back Here; 1929: Now-a-Days; 1930: Recapture; Tonight or Never; 1934: No More Ladies; Mother Lode (and dir.); 1935: Deluxe; Tapesty in Gray; 1949: Two Blind Mice; 1950: The Bird Cage; 1951: The Little Blue Light; 1951: Glad Tidings (and dir.); 1952: Time Out for Ginger; 1955: Inherit the Wind; 1958: Waltz of the Toreadors; 1959: Juno; The Gang's All Here; 1960: The Best Man; 1967: Spofford.

Select TV: 1950: Cause for Suspicion (sp); 1951: Roughly Speaking (sp); 1952: Reunion in Vienna (sp); 1952–53: Hollywood Off Beat/Steve Randall (series); 1953: Your Big Moment/Blind Date (series); 1955: Letters Marked Personal (sp); The Chess Game (sp); 1957: The Greer Case (sp); The Legacy (sp); 1958: The Plot to Kill Stalin (sp); The Return of Ansel Gibbs (sp); 1959: Frontier Justice (series); 1965: Inherit the Wind (sp); 1966: Lamp at Midnight (sp); 1967: The Crucible (sp); Do Not Go Gentle Into That Good Night (sp); 1968: Companions in Nightmare; 1970: Hunters Are for Killing; 1971: Death Takes a Holiday; 1973: The Going Up of David Lev; 1974: The Death Squad; Murder or Mercy?; 1977: Intimate Strangers; 1982: Hot Touch.

PAUL DOUGLAS

BORN: PHILADELPHIA, PA, NOVEMBER 4, 1907.
ED: YALE UNIV. DIED: SEPTEMBER 11, 1959.

A burly, dark-browed, down-to-earth actor who was a prominent "character star" of the 1950s, Paul Douglas's intimidating appearance belied his predilection for playing likeable lugs in the tradition of Wallace Beery and William Bendix. He played professional football with the Fighting Yellow Jackets before moving over to sports commentary, and finally acting on radio. Garson Kanin chose him to play the brutish junk tycoon opposite Judy Holliday in the original 1948 Broadway production of *Born Yesterday*, which led his movie debut in Joseph L. Mankiewicz's *A Letter to Three Wives*, as Linda Darnell's husband. Fox put him under contract for his own comedy vehicle, *Everybody Does It*, as an executive who becomes a singer, although it is his wife, Celeste Holm, with aspirations in that direction. The humor was limited to a dubbed operatic voice emanating from this lummox's mouth. Equally gimmicky was *It Happens Every Spring*, about a wood that resists the impact of baseballs, with Douglas in the sidekick role to catcher Ray Milland. It was down to more serious business as a tough sergeant in postwar Germany in *The Big Life*, one of Montgomery Clift's lesser movies, while another tailor-made vehicle, *Love That Brute*, found racketeer Douglas wooing sweet young thing Jean Peters. Top notch roles in the early 1950s included *Panic in the Streets*, teamed with Richard Widmark, trying to stop a plague from spreading in New Orleans, and *Fourteen Hours*, at his most authoritative, in one of his best performances, as a good-hearted policeman who tries to talk Richard Basehart out of jumping from a building.

MGM starred him in the baseball fantasy *Angels in the Outfield*, as a hot-tempered manager who gets some help from heaven, and the sentimental *When in Rome*, as a con man whose outlook changes when he disguises himself as a priest. Over at RKO, a heavy Clifford Odets drama, *Clash by Night*, had him portraying a cuckolded husband with uncertainty, but he came off better in two with William Holden: the Paramount comedy *Forever Female*, in love with Ginger Rogers; and *Executive Suite*, blackmailed by ruthless Fredric March for dabbling with Shelley Winters. A trip to Great Britain produced *The Maggie*, a minor Ealing Studios comedy in which he was a rich American clashing with the small town Scots, and a strange updating of Shakespeare, *Joe Macbeth*, as a gangster driven to murder by opportunistic wife Ruth Roman. He missed out on the movie version of *Born Yesterday* (although he did a television adaptation for *Hallmark Hall of Fame*) but he was reteamed with Judy Holliday, giving a bright performance as the only honest member of the board of directors, in *The Solid Gold Cadillac*, a smart satire on big business. Another trip to Britain yielded a sci-fi thriller, *The Gamma People*, where he discovered a country of children whose minds are being controlled; then to Italy for the lead in *Fortunella*, opposite Giulietta Masina, before returning Stateside for his last role, as Debbie Reynolds's dad in a flat farce, *The Mating Game*. He was scheduled to play another business executive, in Billy Wilder's *The Apartment*, but died of a heart attack just before filming began and was replaced by Fred MacMurray. He was survived by his fifth wife, actress Jan Sterling, whom he had married in 1950. They had done no official movie acting together, although Douglas made a cameo at the end of her film *Rhubarb*.

Screen: 1949: A Letter to Three Wives; It Happens Every Spring; Everybody Does It; 1950: The Big Lift; Love That Brute; Panic in the Streets; 1951: Fourteen Hours; The Guy Who Came Back; Rhubarb; Angels in the Outfield; 1952: When in Rome; Clash by Night; We're Not Married; Never Wave at a WAC; 1953: Forever Female; 1954: Executive Suite; The Maggie/High and Dry; Green Fire; 1955: Joe Macbeth; 1956: The Leather Saint; The Solid Gold Cadillac; The Gamma People; 1957: This Could Be the Night; Beau James; 1958: Fortunella; 1959: The Mating Game.

NY Stage: 1948: Born Yesterday; 1957: A Hole in the Head.

Select TV: 1955: Casablanca (sp); Numbers and Figures (sp); 1956: The Man in the Black Robe (sp); Adventure Theatre (series); Born Yesterday (sp); 1958: The Honor System (sp); The Dungeon (sp); The Chain and the River (sp); 1959: The Raider (sp); The Incorrigibles (sp).

TOM DRAKE

(Alfred Alderice) Born: Brooklyn, NY, August 5, 1918. ed: Mercersburg Acad. Died: August 11, 1982.

No one deserved the description "the boy next door" more than handsome, friendly-looking Tom Drake. Indeed, his lasting claim to fame was to have those very words sung about him by Judy Garland in *Meet Me in St. Louis*. Following work with stock companies, he came to Broadway, in 1938, for *June Night*, billed under his real name. One movie role, billing him as Richard Alden, in *The Howards of Virginia*, preceded his return to the stage, where his success in the hit 1942 comedy, *Janie*, landed him a contract with MGM. The studio put the newly dubbed "Tom

Drake" into a lot of small roles playing soldiers, but then came *Meet Me in St. Louis* and his very sweet, soft-spoken performance made him a fan magazine favorite. High profile roles for MGM included *The Green Years*, about an Irish lad's devotion to his feisty old granddad, Charles Coburn, and *Courage of Lassie*, as a soldier who trains a dog named Bill to become a killer. He slipped back into smaller roles with *Cass Timberlane* and *The Beginning or the End*, which told of the development of the atomic bomb, before being partnered with Mickey Rooney in the unfortunate biopic *Words and Music*, giving a non-descript interpretation of one of the 20th century's greatest composers, Richard Rodgers. After another pleasant Lassie film, *Hills of Home*, he left Metro to appear in *The Great Rupert*, notable as the first movie directed by special effects wizard George Pal. Later down the line he was back at Metro for *Raintree County*, as Elizabeth Taylor's brother; and *The Sandpiper*, once again in support of Ms. Taylor and directed by Vincente Minnelli, who had guided him through *Meet Me in St. Louis*. In later years he dabbled in sales to compensate for the lack of acting work.

Screen: AS RICHARD ALDEN: 1940: The Howards of Virginia. AS TOM DRAKE: 1944: Two Girls and a Sailor; Maisie Goes to Reno; The White Cliffs of Dover; Marriage Is a Private Affair; Mrs. Parkington; Meet Me in St. Louis; 1945: This Man's Navy; 1946: The Green Years; Courage of Lassie; Faithful in My Fashion; 1947: I'll Be Yours; Cass Timberlane; The Beginning or the End; 1948: Alias a Gentleman; Hills of Home; Words and Music; 1949: Mr. Belvedere Goes to College; Scene of the Crime; 1950: The Great Rupert; 1951: Never Trust a Gambler; Disc Jockey; FBI Girl; 1953: Sangaree; 1955: Sudden Danger; Betrayed Women; 1957: The Cyclops; Date With Disaster; Raintree County; 1958: Money, Women and Guns; 1959: Warlock; 1960: The Bramble Bush; 1965: The Sandpiper; House of the Black Death/Blood of the Man Devil; 1966: The Singing Nun; Johnny Reno; 1967: Red Tomahawk; 1968: Warkill; 1973: The Spectre of Edgar Allan Poe; Savage Abduction/Cycle Psycho.

NY Stage: AS ALFRED ALDERICE: 1938: June Night; Dance Night; Run, Sheep, Run; 1939: Clean Bed; 1942: Janie.

Select TV: 1950: The Little Minister (sp); Murder at the Mardi Gras (sp); 1952: A String of Beads (sp); 1954: The Secret (sp); Girl in Flight (sp); 1955: The Man Nobody Wanted (sp); 1956: Rope Enough (sp); 1970: The Boy Who Stole the Elephant (sp); 1971: City Beneath the Sea; 1975: The Return of Joe Forrester/Cop on the Beat; 1976: A Matter of Wife…and Death; Mayday at 40,000 Feet.

MARIE DRESSLER

(Leila von Koerber) Born: Coburg, Ontario, Canada, November 9, 1869. Died: July 28, 1934.

By a happy accident, the elderly, shapeless, and far-from-pretty Marie Dressler became one of the true superstars of the early sound era, proving that audiences will respond, on occasion, to a performer's beguiling personality and talent. Dressler's brief popularity in the final years of her life was, in fact, part of her second wave of fame. Her early show business career consisted of chorus work with an opera troupe, a stock company production of *Under Two Flags*, and her Broadway debut, in 1892, in *The Robber of the Rhine*. She did some vaudeville engagements and gained quite a reputation as a comic actress, hitting her peak with a piece called *Tillie's Nightmare*, in 1910. While touring on the West Coast she was invited by Mack Sennett to make a "Tillie" film and the result, *Tillie's Punctured Romance*, was considered the first official feature-length American comedy. With Dressler, Charlie Chaplin, and Mabel Normand in the cast it became a smashing success. Dressler followed it with some shorts, including "Tillie's Tomato Surprise" and "Tillie Wakes Up," while she continued to work in vaudeville, but her popularity was waning. By 1928 she was basically broke, so when director Allan Dwan offered her another movie part, in *The Joy Girl*, he had to pay her way to Hollywood. A friend of Dressler's, Francis Marion, wrote a script for her, *The Callahans and the Murphys*, and sold it to MGM, who put her under contract. The film also featured comic Polly Moran and Metro teamed the two fleshy ladies on four occasions, in *Bringing Up Father*, *Caught Short*, *Reducing*, and *Politics*, all broadly played and noisily low-brow.

Dressler made the transition to talkies with *The Divine Lady*, as the mother of Corinne Griffith, and then stole *The Vagabond Lover* away from its novice star, Rudy Vallee. She appeared in the creaky vaudeville hodgepodge *The Hollywood Revue of 1929*, singing "For I'm the Queen," and in *Chasing Rainbows*, where she and Moran supported Bessie Love and Charles King, in this follow-up to the Oscar-winning *The Broadway Melody*. She impressively proved her worth as a serious thespian as the broken down Marthy in *Anna Christie*, drawing her share of attention away from its star, Greta Garbo. That same year, 1930, MGM brilliantly paired Dressler with the equally unattractive Wallace Beery in the drama-comedy *Min and Bill*. The movie was a mixed bag, alternating between scrappy comedy and maudlin sentimentality, but it was a huge hit and Dressler won a very popular Academy Award for Best Actress. She was once again a star attraction, so MGM scrambled to come up with vehicles for a stout, 60-something -year-old lady. She played a maid who marries her employer in *Emma*, bringing sufficient empathy to another of the cinema's frustrating, self-sacrificing ladies to earn another Oscar nomination. She was memorably reteamed with Beery for *Tugboat Annie*, another mix of laughs and tears, and the movie most closely associated with the actress. The two actors were not given much time on screen together in *Dinner at Eight*, although Dressler was one of the better things about this uneven all-star gathering, zinging the famous final line at Jean Harlow. She was a housekeeper again, in *Christopher Bean*, an adaptation of the play *The Late Christopher Bean*, co-starring Lionel Barrymore, but she died a mere six months after its release, of cancer. She penned two memoirs: *The Life Story of an Ugly Duckling* (1924) and *My Own Story* (1934).

Screen (features): 1914: Tillie's Punctured Romance; 1926: The Joy Girl; 1927: The Callahans and the Murphys; Breakfast at Sunrise; 1928: Bringing Up Father; The Patsy; 1929: The Divine Lady; The Vagabond Lover; The Hollywood Revue of 1929; 1930: Chasing Rainbows; Anna Christie; The Girl Said No; One Romantic Night; Caught Short; Let Us Be Gay; Min and Bill; 1931: Reducing; Politics; 1932: Emma; Prosperity; 1933: Tugboat Annie; Dinner at Eight; The Late Christopher Bean.

NY Stage: 1892: The Robber of the Rhine; 1900: Miss Print; 1901: The King's Carnival; 1902: The Hall of Fame; King Highball; 1904: Higgledy-Piggledy; 1906: Twiddle-Twaddle; 1909: The Boy and the Girl; 1910: Tillie's Nightmare; 1912: Roly Poly; Without the Law; 1913: Marie Dressler's All-Star Gambol (and wr.); 1914: A Mix-Up; 1920: The Passing Show of 1921; 1923: The Dancing Girl.

ELLEN DREW

(Terry Ray) Born: Kansas City, MO, November 23, 1915.

Just one of the plethora of pretty girls who brought pulchritude but little presence to many a Hollywood feature, Ellen Drew came to Los Angeles, as so many before her, as a beauty contest winner. In 1936, she was signed to a contract by Paramount Pictures. Although she would stay with them for nine years, it was clear that she had great difficulty making any initial impression, appearing in 25 features under her original name, before she finally decided to change it and start anew. And so she became "Ellen Drew" with the 1938 release, *Sing, You Sinners*, in which she played Fred MacMurray's fiancée. Thereafter the smaller the budget, the higher Drew's billing, with prominent parts in such "B's" as *Women Without Names*, as a waitress sent to prison on a frame-up; *The Monster and the Girl*, as a woman sold into prostitution, resulting in vengeance from a killer ape; and *The Mad Doctor*, as a suicidal girl who agrees to marry scheming, murderous Basil Rathbone. *Christmas in July* was one of Preston Sturges's most charming comedies, with Drew as Dick Powell's faithful girlfriend, and she took roles in the higher-budgeted *Buck Benny Rides Again* and *Reaching for the Sun*, although the focus was clearly on Jack Benny and Joel McCrea, respectively. She finished her contract with Paramount with a cheapie for the Pine-Thomas programmer department, *Dark Mountain*, in 1944, then went looking for work elsewhere. There was a lead opposite Boris Karloff in a mediocre Val Lewton chiller, *Isle of the Dead*, but most of her latter career was spent in westerns, including *The Baron of Arizona*, marrying megalomaniac Vincent Price; *Stars in My Crown*, as parson Joel McCrea's loving wife; and *Outlaw's Son*, which was her last film before she retired.

Screen: AS TERRY RAY: 1936: Yours for the Asking; College Holiday; Rhythm on the Range; The Return of Sophie Lang; My American Wife; Hollywood Boulevard; Lady Be Careful; Big Broadcast of 1937; Murder With Pictures; Wives Never Know; Rose Bowl; 1937: The Crime Nobody Saw; Night of Mystery; Internes Can't Take Money; Make Way for Tomorrow; Turn Off the Moon; Hotel Haywire; Mountain Music; This Way Please; Murder Goes to College; 1938: Coconut Grove; The Buccaneer; Dangerous to Know; Bluebeard's Eighth Wife; You and Me.

AS ELLEN DREW: 1938: Sing, You Sinners; If I Were King; 1939: The Lady's From Kentucky; The Gracie Allen Murder Case; Geronimo; 1940: Women Without Names; Buck Benny Rides Again; French Without Tears; Christmas in July; The Texas Rangers Ride Again; 1941: The Monster and the Girl; The Mad Doctor; Reaching for the Sun; The Parson of Panamint; Night of January 16th; Our Wife; 1942: The Remarkable Andrew; My Favorite Spy; Ice-Capades Revue; Star Spangled Rhythm; 1943: Night Plane From Chungking; 1944: The Imposter; Dark Mountain; That's My Baby!; 1945: China Sky; Isle of the Dead; Man Alive; 1946: Sing While You Dance; Crime Doctor's Man Hunt; 1947: Johnny O'Clock; The Swordsman; 1948: The Man From Colorado; 1949: The Crooked Way; 1950: The Baron of Arizona; Cargo to Capetown; Davy Crockett — Indian Scout; Stars in My Crown; The Great Missouri Raid; 1951: Man in the Saddle; 1957: Outlaw's Son.

Select TV: 1952: Birth of a Hero (sp); 1953: The Governess (sp); 1954: Go Away a Winner (sp); 1955: Visitor in the Night (sp); The Brain of John Emerson (sp); 1961: The Sisters (sp).

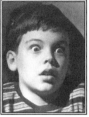

BOBBY DRISCOLL

BORN: CEDAR RAPIDS, IA, MARCH 3, 1937.
DIED (REPORTED): MARCH 30, 1968.

Hollywood's most chilling casualty of child stardom, Bobby Driscoll, in his sunnier days, had been Walt Disney's first successful non-animated star. His family had moved to California when he was only six and he was promptly hired by MGM for the feature, *Lost Angel*, seen briefly as a child on a train. He kept busy in small roles over the next several years, achieving fame as the co-star of the beguiling part cartoon/part live-action Disney feature, *Song of the South*, as the little boy befriended by Uncle Remus (James Baskett). An immediate follow-up, *So Dear to My Heart*, preceded the lead in a gripping RKO "B" thriller, *The Window*, which earned the young actor a special juvenile Academy Award. He was the natural choice for Jim Hawkins in Disney's 1950 remake of *Treasure Island*, and he supplied the voice of *Peter Pan* in the 1953 animated classic. Over at Columbia he had a nice role as part of the family ensemble of *The Happy Time*, but that marked the end of the line. In 1956 he was arrested for possession of narcotics, and three years later for heroin. Not long afterwards he was jailed for assault with a deadly weapon and robbery before he finally entered a drug rehab clinic in the early 1960s. He had made one final attempt to restart his movie career, appearing in the juvenile delinquent drama *The Party Crashers*, which was also notable as the last movie appearance of the equally troubled Frances Farmer. Nothing more was heard from Driscoll until 1968, when his corpse was found in a deserted tenement on Manhattan's Lower East Side, the result of a drug overdose. (Ironically the opening scene of *The Window* finds Driscoll lying on the floor of an abandoned building.) The body was not identified until some 19 months after it was found, by which time the former child star had been buried in a pauper's grave on Hart Island.

Screen: 1943: Lost Angel; 1944: The Sullivans; Sunday Dinner for a Soldier; The Big Bonanza; 1945: Identity Unknown; 1946: Miss Susie Slagle's; From This Day Forward; So Goes My Love; O.S.S.; 1947: Song of the South; 1948: If You Knew Susie; Melody Time; So Dear to My Heart; 1949: The Window; 1950: Treasure Island; 1951: When I Grow Up; 1952: The Happy Time; 1953: Peter Pan (voice); 1955: The Scarlet Coat; 1958: The Party Crashers.

Select TV: 1952: Early Space Conqueror (sp); 1955: The Double Life of Barney Peters (sp); A Matter of Life and Death (sp); Ah, Wilderness! (sp); Too Late to Run (sp); 1956: No Horse, No Wife, No Mustache (sp); I Do (sp).

JOANNE DRU

(JOANNE LETITIA LA COCK) BORN: LOGAN, WV, JANUARY 31, 1923. DIED: SEPTEMBER 10, 1996.

A former model, Joanne Dru was first known in show business circles as the wife (1941–49) of singer-actor Dick Haymes. She made her film debut in the misguided 1946 remake of the dated stage hit *Abie's Irish Rose*, as the Irish girl loved by Jewish Richard Norris, but after this bumpy introduction, the early stage of her new-found career met mostly with success. First she was the object of Montgomery Clift's affections in the classic western, *Red River*, a lady so tough she barely flinched when having an arrow pulled from her shoulder. Then she played the woman taken in by Broderick Crawford's rise to power in the Oscar-winning *All the King's Men*. Both films fea-

tured John Ireland, to whom she was married from 1949 to 1956. She was the heroine of two John Ford westerns: *She Wore a Yellow Ribbon*, involved in an extraneous love triangle; and the lesser-known *Wagon Master*, as a medicine show performer. After these prestigious assignments, things got more routine, as she played opposite such diverse leading men as Dan Dailey in *The Pride of St. Louis*; Clifton Webb in *Mr. Belvedere Rings the Bell*; James Stewart in *Thunder Bay*; Martin and Lewis in *3 Ring Circus*; and even Liberace in *Sincerely Yours*. She returned to the range in such westerns as *Vengeance Valley*; *Outlaw Territory/Hannah Lee*, taking top billing as a saloon proprietress in love with killer Harry Carey, Jr., in this programmer directed in 3-D by Ireland; *The Siege at Red River*; and *Drango*. She retired from movies after her supporting role in 1965's *Sylvia*, only to return once more, unexpectedly and without the slightest fanfare, in a 1981 sci-fi adventure called *Super Fuzz*. Her brother was performer Peter Marshall, best known for hosting the television game show *Hollywood Squares*.

Screen: 1946: Abie's Irish Rose; 1948: Red River; 1949: She Wore a Yellow Ribbon; All the King's Men; 1950: Wagon Master; 711 Ocean Drive; 1951: Vengeance Valley; Mr. Belvedere Rings the Bell; 1952: Return of the Texan; The Pride of St. Louis; My Pal Gus; 1953: Thunder Bay; Forbidden; Hannah Lee/Outlaw Territory; 1954: Duffy of San Quentin; The Siege at Red River; Southwest Passage; 3 Ring Circus; Day of Triumph; 1955: The Warriors/The Dark Avenger; Sincerely Yours; Hell on Frisco Bay; 1957: Drango; 1958: The Light in the Forest; 1959: The Wild and the Innocent; 1960: September Storm; 1965: Sylvia; 1981: Super Fuzz.

NY Stage: 1955: Deadfall.

Select TV: 1951: The Silver Cord (sp); 1953: Richard and the Lion (sp); 1954: Yours for a Dream (sp); 1955: Celebrity (sp); A Kiss for Mr. Lincoln (sp); 1956: Gentle Stranger (sp); Flamingo Road (sp); 1957: The Blackwell Story (sp); 1958: All I Survey (sp); 1960–61: Guestward Ho! (series).

HOWARD DUFF

BORN: BREMERTON, WI, NOVEMBER 24, 1913.
DIED: JULY 8, 1990.

A solid actor whose face often suggested a tinge of worry or dismay, Howard Duff's path to potential stardom was hampered by too many run-of-the-mill films. Having studied acting with the Seattle Repertory Playhouse, he became a noted radio actor on a local station in the 1930s. Following war service his radio fame spread when he played Detective Sam Spade, from 1946 to 1949, during which time he received a contract with Universal Studios. He debuted with a bang in *Brute Force*, as a convict serving time for a murder his wife committed, and then appeared as a con man in the gripping *The Naked City*. *Illegal Entry*, a 1949 programmer, found him top billed as a vet recruited to crack down on illegal aliens. The melodrama *Woman in Hiding* was notable for introducing Duff to his future wife, Ida Lupino, a union that lasted from 1951 to 1968. In the meantime, Duff continued on Universal's "B" list with *Calamity Jane and Sam Bass*, opposite Yvonne De Carlo; *Johnny Stool Pigeon*, as a Federal agent; *Shakedown*, at his most convincing, as a backstabbing newspaper photographer on the rise; and *The Lady From Texas*, coming to the aide of widow Josephine Hull. He and Lupino teamed up for some second features of their own, including *Jennifer*, set in an eerie mansion; *Private Hell 36*, co-written by Lupino; *Women's Prison*, with Duff as a helpful doctor; and *While the City Sleeps*, a crime story where they shared no scenes together. The couple went to television to star in a sitcom, *Mr. Adams and Eve*, but it only ran a single season. During the 1960s Duff accepted work in some foreign-language offerings and had a long run of telefilms. He briefly resurfaced in American theatrical features in the late 1970s as an effective character actor, in *The Late Show*, as detective Art Carney's partner, whose murder sets the plot in motion; *A Wedding*, as a lecherous doctor; and, best of all, *Kramer vs. Kramer*, as Dustin Hoffman's intimidating lawyer. He spent much of the 1980s working on three nighttime television soaps: *Flamingo Road*, *Knots Landing*, and *Dallas*.

Screen: 1947: Brute Force; 1948: The Naked City; All My Sons; 1949: Illegal Entry; Calamity Jane and Sam Bass; Johnny Stool Pigeon; Red Canyon; Woman in Hiding; 1950: Spy Hunt; Shakedown; 1951: The Lady From Texas; Steel Town; 1952: Roar of the Crowd; Models, Inc.; 1953: Spaceways; Tanganyika; Jennifer; 1954: The Yellow Mountain; Private Hell 36; 1955: Women's Prison; Flame of the Islands; 1956: While the City Sleeps; Blackjack Ketchum — Desperado; The Broken Star; 1957: Sierra Stranger; 1962: Boys' Night Out; War Gods of Babylon (nUSr); 1963: Sardanapalus the Great (nUSr); La Congiura dei Borgia/Conspiracy of the Borgias (nUSr); 1968: Panic in the City; 1977: The Late Show; 1978: A Wedding; 1979: Kramer vs. Kramer; 1980: Oh, God Book II; 1986: Double Negative/Deadly Companion (filmed 1980); 1987: Monster in the Closet; No Way Out; 1991: Too Much Sun.

Select TV: 1953: The Ming Lama (sp); 1954: A Season to Love (sp); Woman Expert (sp); 1955: The Confessions of Henry Pell (sp); 1956: The Payoff (sp); 1957: Pride Is the Man (sp); 1957–58: Mr. Adams and Eve (series); 1960–61: Dante (series); 1966–69: Felony Squad (series); 1969: The D.A.: Murder One; 1971: In Search of America; A Little Game; 1972: The Heist; 1973: Snatched; 1977: In the Glitter Palace; 1978: Ski Lift to Death; Battered; 1980: Valentine Magic on Love Island; Flamingo Road; The Dream Merchants; 1981: East of Eden (ms); 1981–82: Flamingo Road (series); 1982: The Wild Women of Chastity Gulch; 1983: This Girl for Hire; 1984–85: Knots Landing (series); 1987: Rose Are for the Rich; 1988–89: Dallas (series); 1989: Settle the Score; War and Remembrance (ms); 1990: Love on the Run.

PATTY DUKE

(ANNA MARIE DUKE) BORN: NEW YORK, NY, DECEMBER 14, 1946.

Although she made movie history as the youngest recipient (at that time) of an Oscar, Patty Duke's career blossomed instead on television and, judging from her fine work in that medium, it has been the big screen's loss. A graduate of the Quintano School for Young Professionals, her early assignments included a recurring role on a short-lived daytime serial based on the film *Kitty Foyle*. In 1959 she won the demanding part of the deaf and blind Helen Keller in the Broadway production of *The Miracle Worker*, receiving raves and a Theatre World Award. Three years later, she and her co-star, Anne Bancroft, sensationally repeated their roles on film. Duke's animal-like Helen was amazing, and it won her the Academy Award as Best Supporting Actress. Instead of doing another film, the hottest young performer in the business then surprised everyone by opting for a television series sitcom in which she played down-to-earth American Patty and her twin British cousin Cathy, in *The Patty Duke Show*. (Another show biz record: Duke was the youngest person to ever have a series named after her.) Three theatrical vehicles, *Billie*, as an aspiring

athlete; *Me Natalie*, as an unfulfilled New Yorker; and *You'll Like My Mother*, a thriller, all failed despite her better intentions, but *Valley of the Dolls* made money, even though it was one of most notoriously bad movies of the 1960s. Duke received some of the worst notices of her career for her overwrought impersonation of a self-destructive star, but she atoned for that one when she won a 1970 Emmy Award for the acclaimed telefilm *My Sweet Charlie*. It seemed clear that her destiny was the small screen. She won two more Emmys, for the mini-series *Captains and the Kings*, and for the remake of *The Miracle Worker*, this time playing Bancroft's role of teacher Annie Sullivan. A telefilm based on her own best-selling 1987 autobiography, *Call Me Anna*, recounted her unhappy childhood and bouts with depression. As a result of her marriage to actor John Astin she billed herself as Patty Duke Astin from 1973 to 1982. They are the parents of two very talented actors, Sean and Mackenzie Astin. Continuing to make history, Duke became the first woman to serve as president of the Screen Actors Guild (1985–88). After a long absence, she showed up in major a theatrical release, *Prelude to a Kiss*, though it was hard to accept the fact that she'd been around long enough to convincingly play the mother of Meg Ryan. Another book she authored, *Surviving Sexual Assault*, was published in 1983.

Screen: 1955: I'll Cry Tomorrow; 1956: Somebody Up There Likes Me; 1958: The Goddess; Country Music Holiday; 1959: Happy Anniversary; The 4-D Man; 1962: The Miracle Worker; 1965: Billie; 1966: The Daydreamer (voice); 1967: Valley of the Dolls; 1969: Me, Natalie; 1971: You'll Like My Mother; 1978: The Swarm (AS PATTY DUKE ASTIN); 1982: By Design (AS PATTY DUKE ASTIN); 1986: Something Special/Willy Milly; 1989: The Hitchhikers (dtv); 1992: Prelude to a Kiss; 1999: Kimberly (nUSr).

NY Stage: 1959: The Miracle Worker; 1962: Isle of Children; 2002: Oklahoma!

Select TV: 1958: Kitty Foyle (series); Wuthering Heights (sp); Swiss Family Robinson; 1958–59: The Brighter Day (series); 1959: Meet Me in St. Louis (sp); Once Upon a Christmas Fable (sp); 1961: The Power and the Glory (sp); 1963–66: The Patty Duke Show (series); 1970: My Sweet Charlie; 1971: Two on a Bench; If Tomorrow Comes; 1972: She Waits; Deadly Harvest; 1974: Miss Kline, We Love You (sp); Nightmare; 1976: Look What's Happened to Rosemary's Baby; Captains and the Kings (ms); 1977: Fire!; Rosetti and Ryan: Men Who Love Women; Curse of the Black Widow; Killer on Board; The Storyteller; 1978: Having Babies III; A Family Upside Down; 1979: Women in White; Hanging by a Thread; Before and After; The Miracle Worker; 1980: The Women's Room; Mom, the Wolfman and Me; The Babysitter; 1981: The Violation of Sarah McDavid; Please Don't Hit Me Mom! (sp); 1982: Something So Right; 1982–83: It Takes Two (series); 1983: September Gun; 1984: Best Kept Secrets; George Washington (ms); 1985: Hail to the Chief (series); 1986: A Time to Triumph; George Washington: The Forging of a Nation (ms); 1987: Fight for Life; Karen's Song (series); 1988: Perry Mason: The Case of the Avenging Ace; Fatal Judgment; 1989: Everybody's Baby: The Rescue of Jessica McClure; Amityville 4: The Evil Escapes; 1990: Call Me Anna; Always Remember I Love You; 1991: Absolute Strangers; 1992: Last Wish; Grave Secrets: The Legacy of Hilltop Drive; A Killer Among Friends; 1993: A Family of Strangers; No Child of Mine; A Matter of Justice; 1994: One Woman's Courage; Cries From the Heart; 1995: Amazing Grace (series); When the Vows Break; 1996: Race Against Time: The Search for Sarah; Harvest of Fire; To Face Her Past; 1997: A Christmas

Memory; **1998:** When He Didn't Come Home; **1999:** The Patty Duke Show: Still Rockin' in Brooklyn Heights; A Season for Miracles; **2000:** Miracle on the Mountain: The Kincaid Family Story; Love Lessons.

KEIR DULLEA

BORN: CLEVELAND, OH, MAY 30, 1936.
ED: RUTGERS UNIV., SAN FRANCISCO ST. COL.

The owner of the most vacant stare in movies, Keir Dullea came to acting after studying at the Neighborhood Playhouse. He made his New York stage debut in a 1956 revue, *Sticks and Stones*, followed by regional work and an Off Broadway role in *Season of Choice*. His first two movie roles were most impressive. He was the troubled delinquent whose life clergyman Don Murray hopes to save in the effective *The Hoodlum Priest*, and then he nabbed a San Francisco Film Festival Award for playing the mentally disturbed teenager in love with Janet Margolin in the art house hit *David and Lisa*. He played a young soldier in a truncated adaptation of James Jones's *The Thin Red Line*; Carol Lynley's incestuous brother in *Bunny Lake Is Missing*; and the lawyer who doesn't realize the old wreck he's defending is his mom, in the umpteenth remake of *Madame X*. Dullea then took his most famous part, as the emotionless astronaut, Dave Bowman, in Stanley Kubrick's sci-fi classic, *2001: A Space Odyssey*, and the sight of his frozen face streaking through the unknown at the movie's climax became a key image of the late 1960s. That same year he came between lesbian lovers Anne Heywood and Sandy Dennis in another (surprisingly) popular movie, *The Fox*, once again bringing an icy, unsympathetic quality to the part. After that he appeared in oddball projects that went virtually unseen, including *De Sade*, as the noted author and advocate of sexual deviance; *Paperback Hero*, as a hockey player who imagines himself a gunslinger; and the Harlequin Romance production *Leopard in the Snow*. He had been long out of the minds of most moviegoers when he repeated his role as cinema's most famous space case in *2010*, the follow-up to Kubrick's triumph.

Screen: 1961: The Hoodlum Priest; **1963:** David and Lisa; **1964:** The Thin Red Line; Mail Order Bride; The Naked Hours; **1965:** Bunny Lake Is Missing; Madame X; **1968:** 2001: A Space Odyssey; The Fox; **1969:** De Sade; **1972:** Pope Joan/The Devil's Imposter; **1973:** Il Diavolo nel Cervello/Devil in the Brain (nUSr); Paperback Hero; **1974:** Paul and Michelle; Black Christmas/Silent Night, Evil Night; **1977:** Welcome to Blood City (nUSr); **1978:** Leopard in the Snow; **1981:** The Haunting of Julia/Full Circle (filmed 1976); **1982:** Brain Waves; **1984:** The Next One; Blind Date; 2010; **1993:** Oh, What a Night (dtv); **2000:** 3 Days of Rain (nUSr).

NY Stage: 1959: Season of Choice (ob); **1967:** Dr. Cook's Garden; **1969:** Butterflies Are Free; **1974:** Cat on a Hot Tin Roof; **1975:** P.S. Your Cat Is Dead; **1985:** Doubles; **1992:** The Other Side of Paradise (ob).

Select TV: 1959: Mrs. Miniver (sp); **1961:** Give Us Barabbas (sp); All Summer Long (sp); **1962:** Far From the Shade Tree (sp); **1963:** The Young Avengers (sp); **1970:** Black Water Gold; **1973:** The Starlost (series); **1976:** Law and Order; **1978:** Because He's My Friend; **1979:** Legend of the Gold Gun; **1980:** Brave New World; The Hostage Tower; **1981:** No Place to Hide; **1986:** Guiding Light (series); **2000:** The Audrey Hepburn Story; Songs in Ordinary Time.

DOUGLASS DUMBRILLE

BORN: HAMILTON, ONTARIO, CANADA, OCTOBER 13, 1889. DIED: APRIL 2, 1974.

Hardly a household name, Douglass Dumbrille was, nevertheless, one of the screen's greatest villains. With his shifty eyes, pencil mustache, and cool sense of control, he could be deliciously hateful. Leaving the banking business to join a stock company, he appeared in a solitary silent feature before making his 1924 Broadway bow in a production of *Macbeth*. Summoned to Hollywood, he made his talkie debut in 1931's *His Woman*, for Paramount. Over at Warners he was a lawyer in both *I Am a Fugitive From a Chain Gang* and *Hard to Handle*; and had Bette Davis bumped off in *Fog Over Frisco*. The Lives of a Bengal Lancer, starring Gary Cooper, shot Dumbrille to the forefront of movie nasties, and it was he, as Mohammed Khan, who uttered the immortal threat "We have ways of making men talk." His second leap into movie infamy was also with Cooper, in the superb *Mr. Deeds Goes to Town*, as the unctuous lawyer who tries to prove Deeds insane in order to deprive him of his millions. He began his reign as chief nemesis to some of the top comedians in the business when he twice tried to give the Marx Brothers a hard time, in *A Day at the Races* and *The Big Store*; took on Abbott and Costello on three occasions, *Ride 'em Cowboy*, *Lost in a Harem*, and *Abbott and Costello in the Foreign Legion*; and oozed menace at Bob Hope in *Road to Zanzibar*, *Monsieur Beaucaire*, *Road to Utopia*, and *Son of Paleface*. He played the role of the bookie in Frank Capra's 1934 racehorse comedy, *Broadway Bill*, and its 1950 remake, *Riding High*. Dumbrille not only rated top billing in the 1938 "B" western, *The Mysterious Rider*, but was the hero of sorts, playing outlaw Pecos Bill, a man driven to crime after being framed for murder who then spends the film trying to right some wrongs. That this did not lead to similar assignments obviously meant that audiences had trouble accepting him as a good guy.

Screen: 1916: What 80 Million Women Want; **1931:** His Woman; **1932:** I Am a Fugitive From a Chain Gang; The Wiser Sex; Blondie of the Follies; That's My Boy; Pride of the Legion; **1933:** Laughter in Hell; Lady Killer; Heroes for Sale; The World Changes; Voltaire; Baby Face; Elmer the Great; Female; Hard to Handle; The Silk Express; Convention City; King of the Jungle; Smoke Lightning; Rustlers' Roundup; The Big Brain; The Man Who Dared; The Way to Love; **1934:** Treasure Island; Fog Over Frisco; Massacre; Broadway Bill; Hi, Nellie!; Journal of a Crime; Operator 13; Stamboul Quest; Harold Teen; The Secret Bride; **1935:** The Lives of a Bengal Lancer; Naughty Marietta; Love Me Forever; Crime and Punishment; Peter Ibbetson; Cardinal Richelieu; The Lone Wolf Returns; The Public Menace; Air Hawks; Unknown Woman; The Calling of Dan Matthew; **1936:** The Princess Comes Across; Mr. Deeds Goes to Town; The Music Goes 'Round; You May Be Next; End of the Trail; The Witness Chair; M'liss; Counterfeit Lady; **1937:** The Emperor's Candlesticks; The Firefly; A Day at the Races; Ali Baba Goes to Town; Woman in Distress; **1938:** The Buccaneer; Kentucky; Stolen Heaven; The Mysterious Rider; Storm Over Bengal; Crime Takes a Holiday; Fast Company; Sharpshooters; **1939:** Tell No Tales; Captain Fury; Thunder Afloat; The Three Musketeers; Rovin' Tumbleweeds; Charlie Chan at Treasure Island; Mr. Moto in Danger Island; City of Darkness; **1940:** Slightly Honorable; Virginia City; South of Pago Pago; Michael Shayne — Private Detective; **1941:** Washington Melodrama; Road to Zanzibar; The Roundup; The Big Store; Murder Among Friends; Ellery Queen and the Perfect Crime; **1942:** Ten Gentlemen From West Point;

King of the Mounties (serial); I Married an Angel; Stand by for Action; Castle in the Desert; A Gentleman After Dark; Ride 'em Cowboy; **1943:** DuBarry Was a Lady; False Colors; **1944:** Uncertain Glory; Gyspy Wildcat; Lost in a Harem; Forty Thieves; Jungle Woman; Lumberjack; **1945:** A Medal for Benny; The Frozen Ghost; Flame of the West; The Daltons Ride Again; Jungle Queen (serial); **1946:** Road to Utopia; Monsieur Beaucaire; A Night in Paradise; Pardon My Past; The Cat Creeps; Spook Busters; Under Nevada Skies; The Catman of Paris; **1947:** Dishonored Lady; The Dragnet; Christmas Eve; The Fabulous Texan; It's a Joke, Son; Blonde Savage; **1948:** Last of the Wild Horses; **1949:** Dynamite; Alimony; Tell It to the Judge; The Lone Wolf and His Lady; Riders of the Whistling Pines; Joe Palooka in the Counterpunch; **1950:** Riding High; Buccaneer's Girl; Rapture; The Savage Horde; The Kangaroo Kid; Her Wonderful Lie; Abbott and Costello in the Foreign Legion; **1951:** A Millionaire for Christy; **1952:** Son of Paleface; Scaramouche; Apache War Smoke; Sky Full of Moon; Sound Off; **1953:** Plunder of the Sun; Julius Caesar; Captain John Smith and Pocahontas; **1954:** World for Ransom; Lawless Rider; The Key Man/A Life at Stake; **1955:** Jupiter's Darling; Mobs Inc.; **1956:** Shake, Rattle and Rock; The Ten Commandments; **1958:** The Buccaneer; **1960:** High Time; **1962:** Air Patrol; **1963:** Johnny Cool; **1964:** Shock Treatment; What a Way to Go!

NY Stage: 1924: Macbeth; 1925: The Call of Life; Princess Flavia; 1928: The Three Musketeers; 1929: Chinese O'Neil; 1930: Joseph; A Month in the Country; 1931: As You Desire Me.

Select TV: 1950: The Devil's Due (sp); 1954: The Fugitives (sp); 1952–55: China Smith (series); 1953–58: The Life of Riley (series); 1956: Young Andy Jackson (sp); 1958–59: The Grand Jury (series); 1963–64: The New Phil Silvers Show (series).

MARGARET DUMONT

(MARGARET BAKER) BORN: BROOKLYN, NY, OCTOBER 20, 1889. DIED: MARCH 6, 1965.

The screen's great dowager, Margaret Dumont, stood straight-faced and took abuse from some of the best comedians in the business, but she will first and foremost be associated with the Marx Brothers. Starting out as a singer under the name Daisy Dumont, she toured Europe before coming to Broadway, where she appeared on three occasions with comic Lew Fields. Her marriage to millionaire John Moller, Jr. sent her into temporary retirement, but his death a few years later brought her back to the stage. Her role as the wealthy, haughty Mrs. Potter in the 1925 Broadway production of The Cocoanuts, was the beginning of her legendary teaming with the Marxes. Groucho alternately romanced and insulted her, much to the delight of theatre audiences, and it was only natural that she be asked back for their follow-up hit, Animal Crackers. When both comedies were preserved on film, Dumont, happily, came with the package. She went on to appear with the Brothers in five more films, most deliciously in Duck Soup, singing the immortal national anthem, "Hail, Hail, Fredonia," and in A Night at the Opera, where she provided the punchline for the classic stateroom scene. She did not deviate much from her huffy, grande dame character as she provided an easy target for other comics, such as Abbott and Costello (Little Giant), Laurel and Hardy (The Dancing Masters), Danny Kaye (Up in Arms), and W.C. Fields (Never Give a Sucker an Even Break, where she was given the memorable moniker Mrs. Hemoglobin). She was woefully underused in most of the films she made, sometimes showing up for the briefest of scenes. Happily, her last public appearance

reunited her with Groucho Marx, on a television skit, only days before she died. It reminded audiences that theirs was one of the most perversely satisfying male-female relationships in movie history.

Screen: 1917: A Tale of Two Cities; 1929: The Cocoanuts; 1930: Animal Crackers; 1931: Girl Habit; 1933: Duck Soup; 1934: Kentucky Kernels; Fifteen Wives; Gridiron Flash; 1935: A Night at the Opera; Orchids to You; After Office Hours; Rendezvous; 1936: The Song and Dance Man; Anything Goes; 1937: The Life of the Party; A Day at the Races; Wise Girl; Youth on Parole; High Flyers; 1938: Dramatic School; 1939: At the Circus; The Women; 1941: The Big Store; Never Give a Sucker an Even Break; For Beauty's Sake; 1942: About Face; Born to Sing; Rhythm Parade; Sing Your Worries Away; Tales of Manhattan (restored print only); 1943: The Dancing Masters; 1944: Up in Arms; Bathing Beauty; Seven Days Ashore; 1945: The Horn Blows at Midnight; Billy Rose's Diamond Horseshoe; Sunset in El Dorado; 1946: Little Giant; Susie Steps Out; 1952: Three for Bedroom C; Stop, You're Killing Me; 1956: Shake, Rattle and Rock; 1958: Auntie Mame; 1962: Zotz!; 1964: What a Way to Go!

NY Stage: 1921: The Fan; 1922: Go Easy Mabel; 1923: The Rise of Rosie O'Reilly; 1925: The Four Flusher; 1925: The Cocoanuts; 1928: Animal Crackers; 1931: Shoot the Works; 1932: Tell Her the Truth.

Select TV: 1952–53: My Friend Irma (series).

JAMES DUNN

BORN: NEW YORK, NY, NOVEMBER 2, 1905. DIED: SEPTEMBER 3, 1967.

Despite being a top-billed leading man for several years during the 1930s, James Dunn is best remembered for his comeback role in the following decade. After making his 1930 Broadway debut in His Majesty's Car, Dunn was signed to a contract by Fox, who immediately put him into Bad Girl, where he gave a very effective performance as a radio salesman who marries Sally Eilers only to subject her to a life of hardship because of his foolhardy behavior. This unheralded film wound up with Academy Awards for its director (Frank Borzage) and screenwriter (Edwin Burke). The Dunn-Eilers teaming clicked in four more films, Dance Team, where they were amateur hoofers; Over the Hill, in which Dunn came from a no-good family; Sailor's Luck; and Hold Me Tight, as a couple struggling with his unemployment. Oddly enough, one of Dunn's other starring vehicles, Jimmy and Sally, did not pair him with Ms. Eilers, as the title promised, but with Claire Trevor. Occasionally used by the studio in musicals, the actor thrice starred alongside the up-and-coming Shirley Temple, in Stand Up and Cheer; Baby Take a Bow; and Bright Eyes, as a friendly pilot to whom she sings "On the Good Ship Lollipop." Leaving Fox in 1935, he and Eilers found themselves teamed yet again, in Universal's Don't Get Personal and We Have Our Moments. The actor's stardom, however, was on the wane and he was soon working at bottom-of-the-barrel companies like Monogram and PRC, starring with his then-wife (1938–42) Frances Gifford, in Mercy Plane and Hold That Woman. He was rescued from near-oblivion by director Elia Kazan, who gave him the key role of the charming but undependable alcoholic father in the beautiful 1945 adaptation of the best seller A Tree Grows in Brooklyn, made for Dunn's old studio, Fox. He played the role with such conviction that he won the Academy Award as Best Supporting Actor of 1945. Alas, this did not jump start his career and he was soon right back to cheapies like That Brennan Girl and The Golden Gloves Story, although 20th Century-Fox gave him the lead in a "B," The Caribbean Mystery, as a detective from Brooklyn. In his later years he was seen on the short-lived television sitcom *It's a Great Life*.

Screen: 1931: Bad Girl; Sob Sister; Over the Hill; 1932: Dance Team; Society Girl; Handle With Care; 1933: Hello, Sister!; Hold Me Tight; Girl in 419; Sailor's Luck; Jimmy and Sally; Take a Chance; Arizona to Broadway; 1934: Hold That Girl; Stand Up and Cheer; Change of Heart; Baby Take a Bow; 365 Nights in Hollywood; Have a Heart; Bright Eyes; She Learned About Sailors; 1935: George White's 1935 Scandals; The Daring Young Man; The Pay-Off; Welcome Home; Bad Boy; 1936: Don't Get Personal; Hearts in Bondage; Two-Fisted Gentleman; Come Closer Folks; 1937: Mysterious Crossing; We Have Our Moments; Venus Makes Trouble; Living on Love; 1938: Shadows Over Shanghai; 1939: Pride of the Navy; Mercy Plane; 1940: Son of the Navy; Hold That Woman; 1942: The Living Ghost; 1943: The Ghost and the Guest; Government Girl; 1944: Leave It to the Irish; 1945: A Tree Grows in Brooklyn; The Caribbean Mystery; 1946: That Brennan Girl; 1947: Killer McCoy; 1948: Texas, Brooklyn and Heaven; 1950: The Golden Gloves Story; 1951: A Wonderful Life; 1960: The Bramble Bush; 1962: Hemingway's Adventures of a Young Man; 1966: The Oscar.

NY Stage: 1930: His Majesty's Car; 1940: Panama Hattie; 1948: Harvey.

Select TV: 1952: The Summer People (sp); I Want to Be a Star (sp); 1953: Medal in the Family (sp); 1954: The Treasure of Santa Domingo (sp); 1954–55: It's a Great Life (series); 1955: A Picture in the Paper (sp); 1957: Mr. Broadway (sp); Law and Order Inc. (sp); 1959: The Nine Lives of Elfego Baca (ms); 1960: Journey to the Day; 1968: Shadow Over Elveron.

IRENE DUNNE

Born: Louisville, KY, December 20, 1898.
ed: Chicago Col. of Music.
Died: September 4, 1990.

She could sing, play comedy, excel at soaps, adapt to whatever period of time a film called for, and act up a storm, effortlessly looking comfortable in any genre. Irene Dunne was, in fact, one of the nicest pleasures of moviegoing during the 1930s and 1940s. Her early reputation was made as a singer where, fittingly enough, her first big professional assignment was touring in the musical *Irene*. In 1923 she made her Broadway debut in *The Clinging Vine*, and found steady work there over the next few years. However, it was her performance in another touring production, *Show Boat*, as Magnolia, that brought her to the attention of RKO. They signed her to a contract in 1930 and cast her as a society girl in the musical *Leathernecking*, which co-starred Eddie Foy, Jr. The original Rodgers and Hart stage score was dumped in favor of a new one and the film failed, but Dunne didn't have to wait long to find celluloid success. Richard Dix requested her to portray his strong-willed wife in the epic western *Cimarron*, and she convincingly aged from young pioneer to elderly Congresswoman, carrying many of the picture's scenes. Her role earned her the first of several Oscar nominations for Best Actress and the movie itself took the accolade for Best Picture of the year. Having established herself as a tower of strength, she went on to become the definitive Fannie Hurst heroine, first with *Symphony of Six Million*, as a schoolteacher in love with doctor Ricardo Cortez, and then in Universal's seminal weepie, *Back Street*, as the loyal mistress of banker John Boles. She stayed in these kinds of melodramas with *The Secret of Madame Blanche*, as a musical hall singer accused of murder; *The Silver Cord*, battling smothering mother Laura Hope Crewes for the love of Joel McCrea; *Ann Vickers*, as the man-hating head of a women's correctional facility; *Stingaree*, as an aspiring singer, opposite her *Cimarron* co-star Richard Dix; and *The Age of Innocence*, rejoining Boles in a very minor adaptation of Edith Wharton's major novel.

The musical side of Dunne was shown to its best advantage yet in *Roberta*, singing the haunting "Smoke Gets in Your Eyes," although it was hard to take your eyes off of her co-stars, Fred Astaire and Ginger Rogers. There was very little good to say about the tedious *Sweet Adeline*, however, which clumsily combined warbling and spying. Finished with RKO, she signed dual contracts with Universal and Columbia and immediately had a hit with another memorable soap opera, *Magnificent Obsession*, accidentally blinded by irresponsible Robert Taylor, who woos his way into her heart in hopes of making amends. She triumphantly repeated her stage performance in Universal's prestigious production of *Show Boat*, singing "Make Believe" and other gems in the second movie version of the immortal Jerome Kern-Oscar Hammerstein II musical, which got bogged down in its unwieldy second half. That same year she made her breakthrough as a comedy performer with Columbia's *Theodora Goes Wild*, playing the author of a hot bestseller. She received her second Oscar nomination, presumably for showing contrasting personalities to the character, timid and extroverted, though, in fact, she was battling a pretty mediocre script the whole way through. Her third nomination came for the famous screwball comedy *The Awful Truth*, teamed to perfection with Cary Grant, as a pair of separating lovers who don't really want to spend their time with anyone else. There were two disappointing Jerome Kern musicals, Paramount's *High, Wide and Handsome*, and RKO's *Joy of Living*, before another career peak with *Love Affair*, opposite Charles Boyer, in 1939. She cleverly combined her skills at both tearjerkers and sophisticated comedy, keeping everything nicely in balance until the frustrating final scenes following her crippling accident. She was once again nominated for an Oscar. That same year she reteamed with Boyer for *When Tomorrow Comes*, in which she was a waitress carrying on with him, despite his marriage to deranged Barbara O'Neill.

Another fine comedy with Grant, *My Favorite Wife*, in which she came back into his life after being presumed dead, preceded the more serious, often maudlin *Penny Serenade*, which found them adopting a child after their own unborn baby has died, a soggy story that was made palatable by their formidable talents. This lady's exceptional grace and intelligent were instrumental in giving credibility to two of the more heavy-handed tear-jerkers of the war years, *A Guy Named Joe*, in which she abandons her memories of a dead Spencer Tracy for the much less appealing Van Johnson, and *The White Cliffs of Dover*, a saga spanning both World Wars, during which Dunne loses both husband and son while growing to love England nonetheless. Both films were among the biggest moneymakers of the war years. After another teaming with Boyer, as a small town mayor in the light comedy, *Together Again*, she did three of her best movies in a row. For 20th Century-Fox there was *Anna and the King of Siam* (the non-musical version of *The King and I*), where Dunne was perfect as the British schoolteacher who clashes with Siamese ruler Rex Harrison, earning his respect in the process. Then she was the level-headed mother in Warner Bros.'s charming adaptation of the longest running stage play of the decade, *Life With Father*, a nostalgic glimpse of old New York that was a prime example of the sort of proficient studio product of the time, and a movie that took its place among the highest grossing movies to date. Most noteworthy was her work in *I Remember Mama*, George Stevens's tasteful and touching look at a Norwegian family in turn-of-the-century San Francisco. Dunne's convincing accent and her interpretation of an intellectually limited but loving woman, rated a sixth and final nod from the Academy but, alas, no win. It would be her last hurrah. After a game, but inadequate attempt to play Queen Victoria in *The Mudlark*, and two unpopular comedies — *Never a Dull Moment*, with Fred MacMurray, and *It Grows on Trees*, a fantasy in which money did just that — she announced her retirement. One of the best-liked people in Hollywood, Dunne used her special glow to win a seat in the UN General Assembly in 1957.

Screen: 1930: Leathernecking; 1931: Cimarron; Bachelor Apartment; The Great Lover; Consolation Marriage; 1932: Symphony of Six Million; Thirteen Women; Back Street; 1933: No Other Woman; The Secret of Madame Blanche; The Silver Cord; Ann Vickers; If I Were Free; 1934: This Man Is Mine; The Age of Innocence; Stingaree; 1935: Roberta; Sweet Adeline; Magnificent Obsession; 1936: Show Boat; Theodora Goes Wild; 1937: High, Wide and Handsome; The Awful Truth; 1938: Joy of Living; 1939: Love Affair; Invitation to Happiness; When Tomorrow Comes; 1940: My Favorite Wife; 1941: Penny Serenade; Unfinished Business; 1942: Lady in a Jam; 1943: A Guy Named Joe; 1944: The White Cliffs of Dover; Together Again; 1945: Over 21; 1946: Anna and the King of Siam; 1947: Life With Father; 1948: I Remember Mama; 1950: The Mudlark; Never a Dull Moment; 1952: It Grows on Trees.

NY Stage: 1923: The Clinging Vine; 1924: Lollipop; 1926: Sweetheart Time; 1927: Yours Truly; 1928: She's My Baby; Luckee Girl.

Select TV: 1954: Sister Veronica (sp); 1955: Touch of Spring (sp); 1956: On the Beach (sp); Sheila (sp); 1962: Go Fight City Hall (sp).

MILDRED DUNNOCK

BORN: BALTIMORE, MD, JANUARY 25, 1901.
ED: COLUMBIA UNIV. DIED: JULY 5, 1991.

Stage veteran Mildred Dunnock came to films relatively late in life, but the sharp-nosed, frail-looking actress gave some impressive performances, usually as elderly biddies and motherly types. She originally studied to become a teacher, so it was only fitting that her movie debut was as a school instructor, in the 1945 adaptation of the play *The Corn Is Green*, repeating her 1940 stage role. This was followed by one of her most famous movie assignments, as the wheelchair-bound woman whom giggling psychotic Richard Widmark shoves down the stairs in *Kiss of Death*. Back on Broadway she played the part for which she would become best-known, Willy Loman's long-suffering wife, Linda, in the original staging of Arthur Miller's classic *Death of a Salesman*. She repeated the role in the fine 1951 movie adaptation opposite Fredric March, receiving an Oscar nomination, and again, in the 1966 television version, with the original Willy, Lee J. Cobb. In the meantime she was a señora in *Viva Zapata!*; Danny Thomas's Jewish mama in *The Jazz Singer* remake; Carroll Baker's flaky Aunt Rose in *Baby Doll*, a performance that in no way drew attention away from the many other colorful characters in this red hot Tennessee Williams piece, but one that rated another Oscar nomination nonetheless; Elvis Presley's Southern mama in *Love Me Tender*; a beloved school-teacher fired at the outset of *Peyton Place*; one of the Sisters in *The Nun's Story*; and, repeating another of her stage roles, Aunt Nonnie, in *Sweet Bird of Youth*, gently telling the overbearing Ed Begley to go to hell, in the revised finale. Her assignments dwin-

dled by the late 1960s, though she could still be seen as late as 1987, playing a sickly old lady in a forgettable teen comedy, *The Pick-Up Artist*. Her countless television appearances include the 1981 telefilm, *The Patricia Neal Story*, in which Ms. Dunnock played herself.

Screen: 1945: The Corn Is Green; 1947: Kiss of Death; 1951: I Want You; Death of a Salesman; 1952: The Girl in White; Viva Zapata!; 1953: The Jazz Singer; Bad for Each Other; 1954: Hansel and Gretel (voice); 1955: The Trouble With Harry; 1956: Love Me Tender; Baby Doll; 1957: Peyton Place; 1959: The Nun's Story; The Story on Page One; 1960: Butterfield 8; 1961: Something Wild; 1962: Sweet Bird of Youth; 1964: Behold a Pale Horse; Youngblood Hawke; 1965: 7 Women; 1969: What Ever Happened to Aunt Alice?; 1975: The Spiral Staircase; 1976: Dragonfly/One Summer Love; 1987: The Pick-Up Artist.

NY Stage: 1932: Life Begins; 1938: The Hill Between; 1940: The Corn Is Green; The Cat Screams; Vickie; 1943: Richard III; 1944: Only the Heart; 1945: Foolish Notion; 1946: Lute Song; Another Part of the Forest; 1948: The Hallams; The Leading Lady; 1949: Death of a Salesman; 1950: Pride's Crossing; 1951: The Wild Duck; Peer Gynt; 1953: In the Summer House; 1955: Cat on a Hot Tin Roof; 1956: Child of Fortune; 1960: Farewell, Farewell, Eugene; 1963: The Milk Train Doesn't Stop Here Anymore; The Trojan Women (ob); 1964: Traveler Without Luggage; 1966: Phaedra (ob); 1967: Willie Doesn't Live Here Anymore (ob); 1970: Colette (ob); A Place Without Doors (ob); 1976: Days in the Trees; 1977: Tartuffe.

Select TV: 1950: The Last Step (sp); 1953: Mark of Cain (sp); 1954: Game of Hide and Seek (sp); Uncle Harry (sp); The Happy Journey (sp); A Child Is Born (sp); 1955: A Business Proposition (sp); 1956: The Wonderful Gifts (sp); 1957: The Traveling Lady (sp); Winter Dreams (sp); The Play Room (sp); The Sound of Trouble (sp); 1959: Diary of a Nurse (sp); 1961: Night of the Story (sp); The Power and the Glory (sp); 1966: Death of a Salesman (sp); 1968: The Hamster of Happiness (sp); 1973: A Brand New Life; A Summer Without Boys; 1974: Murder or Mercy; 1975: The Shopping Bag Lady (sp); 1979: The Best Place to Be; And Baby Makes Six; 1980: Baby Comes Home; 1981: The Patricia Neal Story; Isabel's Choice.

JIMMY DURANTE

BORN: NEW YORK, NY, FEBRUARY 10, 1893.
DIED: JANUARY 28, 1980.

He had a big nose and he never let you forget it. Jimmy Durante's act consisted of exagger-ated exasperation, a uniquely throaty way with a song, and jovial good spirits, all punc-tuated by countless references to the size of his proboscis, or, as he dubbed it, his "schnozzola." It was a limited, often strained persona, but he got by on the infectious joy he clearly got from providing entertainment, and simply because he was one of the nicest guys in the business. He started off as a ragtime pianist, playing in nightclubs while still a teen, adding songs and comedy to his act, and eventually creating a trio with Lou Clayton and Eddie Jackson. By the time he opened his own nightclub in 1930, he was famous in vaudeville and the legit theatre, making catch-phrases of such expressions as "Everybody wants to get into the act!" and "I've got a million of 'em." He made his movie debut that year, pretty much playing an extension of himself, a comic-singer at the titular hood's hideout in *Roadhouse Nights*, before signing with MGM. They teamed him with Buster Keaton for a series of comedies, although Durante's frantic delivery clashed awkwardly with the great comedian's deadpan demeanor. At

Paramount he teamed with Broadway legend George M. Cohan in a misguided satire, *The Phantom President*, and, by 1934, started getting his own solo projects. The oddball romp *Hollywood Party*, found him cast as a movieland jungle hero named "Schnarzan," and in *Palooka*, playing fight manager Knobby Walsh, he interpolated his immortal theme song, "Inka Dinka Doo." It was clear, however, that Durante was not movie star material, so he became a supporting or specialty act, backing up Shirley Temple in *Little Miss Broadway*; Alice Faye in *Sally, Irene and Mary*; and Gene Autry in *Melody Ranch*. Another lead, in the early 1940s, in the service comedy *You're in the Army Now*, had him mugging away with Phil Silvers, as a pair of vacuum cleaner salesman who are drafted.

In the 1941 adaptation of *The Man Who Came to Dinner* he was a less-than-inspired choice to play the irascible Banjo, a character based on Harpo Marx. He added some spunk to a few lesser MGM musicals, including *Music for Millions*, singing his self-composed "Umbriago," as well as "Toscanini, Iturbi and Me;" *Two Sisters From Boston*, as a saloon pianist, belting out "G'wan, You're Mudder's Callin';" *It Happened in Brooklyn*, dueting marvelously with Frank Sinatra on "The Song's Gotta Come From the Heart;" and Esther Williams's *On an Island With You*, again performing his own composition, "I Can Do Without Broadway, But Can Broadway Do Without Me?" He landed another lead, in producer/special effects wizard George Pal's first feature, *The Great Rupert*, starring opposite a squirrel, but it was strictly a "B" feature. A second burst of stardom came via television, as he hosted three variety shows in a row: *All Star Revue*, which earned him an Emmy Award; *The Colgate Comedy Hour*; and, finally, his own showcase, *The Jimmy Durante Show*. His sign-off, "Goodnight, Mrs. Calabash, wherever you are," was a carry-over from his successful radio show, and became one of the most famous lines in show business history. The name, it turned out, referred to the owner of a Chicago boarding house where Durante and his wife lived following their marriage in 1916. He adopted it as a nickname for Mrs. Durante, who had died in 1943. There were two more notable movie roles: in *Billy Rose's Jumbo*, which he'd done on the stage in 1935, his famous "What elephant?" reaction to getting caught stealing a pachyderm was one of the film's few highlights; and he set the all-star *It's a Mad Mad Mad Mad World* plot in motion by, literally, kicking the bucket. He was forced to retire in the early 1970s when a series of strokes confined him to a wheelchair. Visitors to Hollywood are reminded of Mr. Durante's most famous feature, immortalized in cement in the forecourt of Grauman's Chinese Theatre.

Screen: 1930: Roadhouse Nights; 1931: The Cuban Love Song; The New Adventures of Get-Rich-Quick Wallingford; 1932: The Wet Parade; The Passionate Plumber; Speak Easily; The Phantom President; Blondie of the Follies; 1933: Hell Below; What No Beer?; Meet the Baron; Broadway to Hollywood; 1934: George White's Scandals; Hollywood Party; Strictly Dynamite; Palooka/Joe Palooka; Student Tour; 1935: Carnival; 1936: Forbidden Music/Land Without Music; 1938: Start Cheering; Little Miss Broadway; Sally, Irene and Mary; 1940: Melody Ranch; 1941: You're in the Navy Now; The Man Who Came to Dinner; 1944: Two Girls and a Sailor; Music for Millions; 1946: Two Sisters From Boston; 1947: It Happened in Brooklyn; This Time for Keeps; 1948: On an Island With You; 1950: The Great Rupert; The Milkman; 1957: Beau James; 1960: Pepe; 1961: The Last Judgment/Il Giudizio Universale; 1962: Billy Rose's Jumbo; 1963: It's a Mad Mad Mad Mad World.

NY Stage: 1929: Show Girl; 1930: The New Yorkers; 1933: Strike Me Pink; 1935: Jumbo; 1936: Red Hot and Blue!; 1939: Stars in Your Eyes; 1940: Keep Off the Grass.

Select TV: 1950–53: All Star Revue (series); 1953–54: The Colgate Comedy Hour (series); 1954–56: The Jimmy Durante Show (series); 1966: Alice Through the Looking Glass (sp); 1969–70: Jimmy Durante Presents The Lennon Sisters (series); 1971: Frosty the Snowman (sp; voice).

DEANNA DURBIN

(EDNA MAE DURBIN) BORN: WINNIPEG, CANADA, DECEMBER 4, 1921. RAISED IN LOS ANGELES, CA.

It may be impossible for the more crass and cynical among modern movie audiences to consider that a demure teenager with a beautiful soprano voice ideal for light arias was once among the most popular motion picture attractions of the 1930s and 1940s. It is also a testament to the skills of Deanna Durbin that her sweetness and style have aged well. She moved to Los Angeles shortly after she was born and, by the time she was a teen, had gained enough of a reputation as a fine singer that she auditioned for Walt Disney for the voice of Snow White. She didn't get the part, but she was noticed by an MGM talent scout who signed her to a contract with the intention of featuring her in a biopic of opera singer Eva Schumann-Heink. Instead she appeared in a short, *Every Sunday*, a historic event because it marked the only teaming on film of Durbin and Judy Garland. (Legend has it that Louis B. Mayer ordered Garland dumped in favor of Durbin, but due to a misunderstanding, things worked out the opposite.) Producer Joe Pasternak snatched Durbin up and, in 1936, she was signed by Universal for whom she would work exclusively over the next 12 years. Her maiden effort, *Three Smart Girls*, was not a starring role, nor was it a very good movie, but it was a hit. Durbin, as the youngest sister, was billed as "Universal's new singing discovery," and made an immediate impact, warbling contemporary songs like "My Heart Is Singing," and some operatic arias. This would be her usual pattern: a simple vocal rendition, sometimes at the piano, with Durbin center stage, rather than featuring her in large-scale production numbers, and it proved to be exactly what audiences wanted. With her next movie, *One Hundred Men and a Girl*, it was clear that the teen was big box office and her prestige was enhanced when her first two films rated Oscar nominations for Best Picture. In 1938 she was awarded a special juvenile Academy Award. That year had seen the release of *Mad About Music*, which cast her as the daughter of image-conscious actress Gail Patrick, with Durbin singing "Ave Maria" for the first time on screen; and *That Certain Age*, where she swooned over older Melvyn Douglas but opted for someone her own age, Jackie Cooper.

There was a sequel to her first hit, *Three Smart Girls Grow Up*, but this time she received top billing, and in *First Love*, a charming update on "Cinderella," her first screen kiss came courtesy of newcomer Robert Stack, making headlines in the process. She sang "Ave Maria" for the second time, in *It's a Date*, then co-starred for the first time with Franchot Tone, in 1941's *Nice Girl?* She was still considered too young to be romantically linked with him (he was 16 years her senior), and she ended up with Stack again. However, in her two subsequent Tone pairings, *His Butler's Sister*, in 1943, and *Because of Him*, in 1946, there was no longer any hesitation in accepting them as lovers, Durbin having "matured" in the interim. *It Started With Eve*, often considered her first official adult role, was not only another delight, but revealed that she had blossomed into an adept comedic actress. *Hers to Hold* was yet another sequel to *Three Smart Girls*, while *The Amazing Mrs. Holliday* afforded her a dramatic role, as a missionary trying to rescue Chinese orphans. She was a disillusioned saloon singer married to troubled Gene Kelly in *Christmas Holiday*, a darker movie than some audiences were expecting from her, though the piece was toned down considerably from the original Somerset Maugham novel, in which her character was a prostitute. *Can't Help Singing* was her only movie in color; *Lady in a Train*, a routine mystery, found Durbin as a blonde for a change; and *Something in the Wind* teamed her with the studio's other young musical star, Donald O'Connor, though not romantically, which would have made sense. Instead she was matched up for more typical results with Jon Dall. Her box-office appeal had cooled considerably by this point, and her last two, *Up in Central Park* and *For the Love of Mary*, were written off as financial failures. In 1948, her Universal contract ended and, despite other offers, including one from MGM, where her original producer, Joe Pasternak, was now situated, she announced her retirement from show business. Durbin moved to France with her third husband and refused all requests for interviews, severing all connections with the entertainment world for over 50 years. Despite the self-exile she retained a strong and devoted core of admirers.

Screen: 1936: Three Smart Girls; 1937: One Hundred Men and a Girl; 1938: Mad About Music; That Certain Age; 1939: Three Smart Girls Grow Up; First Love; 1940: It's a Date; Spring Parade; 1941: Nice Girl?; It Started With Eve; 1943: The Amazing Mrs. Holliday; Hers to Hold; His Butler's Sister; 1944: Christmas Holiday; Can't Help Singing; 1945: Lady on a Train; 1946: Because of Him; 1947: I'll Be Yours; Something in the Wind; 1948: Up in Central Park; For the Love of Mary.

DAN DURYEA

BORN: WHITE PLAINS, NY, JANUARY 23, 1907.
ED: CORNELL UNIV. DIED: JUNE 7, 1968.

The perpetually sarcastic look on Dan Duryea's face made him perfect for playing creeps, cynics, and the kind of outright villains you couldn't wait for the hero to slap around. After spending six years in the advertising business he took up acting, first in summer stock, and then on Broadway. He appeared in the original 1935 production of *Dead End*, which was written by former classmate Sidney Kingsley, but it was his performance as the scheming nephew, Leo Hubbard, in the 1939 stage hit *The Little Foxes*, that brought him his greatest attention. He repeated his part splendidly in the 1941 film version, and that same year was memorable as Dana Andrews's henchman in *Ball of Fire*, famously addressed by Gary Cooper as "you very ugly young man." He was a cynical sports reporter in *Pride of the Yankees*; a tank soldier trapped under fire in *Sahara*; a no-good relative of Greer Garson's in *Mrs. Parkington*; Gregory Peck's uncooperative brother in *The Valley of Decision*; and irked Cooper again as the main villain in *Along Came Jones*, finally meeting his demise at the hands of heroine Loretta Young. In 1945 he joined Universal, where he would spend most of the next decade or so. He stole Edward G. Robinson's paintings in *Scarlet Street*, and was so loathsome that the audience cheered when he went to the electric chair for a murder he *didn't* commit. This was his third assignment for director Fritz Lang, following Paramount's *Ministry of Fear*, and RKO's *The Woman in the Window*, as a slimy blackmailer.

He took a rare sympathetic role in Deanna Durbin's murder-mystery, *Lady on a Train*; topped the bill in the underrated noir *Black Angel*, in a tricky role as the alcoholic songwriter husband of murdered Constance Dowling, giving one of his very best per-

formances; and was in the lead again in *White Tie and Tails*, unconvincingly cast as a butler pretending to be a gentleman. He was the only *Little Foxes* cast member to appear in the 1948 prequel, *Another Part of the Forest*, this time playing Leo's father. The bad guy roles kept coming, including *Criss Cross*, at his most hateful as a jealous gangster who shoots both leads, Burt Lancaster and Yvonne de Carlo; *Johnny Stool Pigeon*, in the title role, as an Alcatraz inmate feeding information to narcotics agent Howard Duff; *Too Late for Tears*, as a blackmailer poisoned by Lizabeth Scott; and a pair of James Stewart westerns, *Winchester '73* and *Night Crossing*. Stewart, perhaps to atone for whacking Duryea's head on a bar in *Winchester*, had him cast in a sympathetic role in *Thunder Bay*, but Duryea was never quite as compelling in that vein. By the 1960s his movies had cheaper budgets, including *Taggart, Incident at Phantom Hill*, and his last, *The Bamboo Saucer*. When Universal did a television remake of *Winchester '73*, Duryea was back, but playing a different character. At the time of his death, in 1968, he had a recurring role in the nighttime soap *Peyton Place*.

Screen: 1941: The Little Foxes; Ball of Fire; 1942: That Other Woman; The Pride of the Yankees; 1943: Sahara; 1944: Ministry of Fear; None But the Lonely Heart; Mrs. Parkington; The Woman in the Window; Main Street After Dark; Man From Frisco; 1945: The Valley of Decision; The Great Flamarion; Along Came Jones; Lady on a Train; Scarlet Street; 1946: Black Angel; White Tie and Tails; Larceny; 1948: Black Bart; Another Part of the Forest; River Lady; 1949: Criss Cross; Too Late for Tears; Manhandled; Johnny Stool Pigeon; 1950: One Way Street; Winchester '73; The Underworld Story; 1951: Chicago Calling; Al Jennings of Oklahoma; 1953: Thunder Bay; Sky Commando; 1954: Ride Clear of Diablo; World for Ransom; This is My Love; Silver Lode; Rails Into Laramie; Terror Street/36 Hours; 1955: The Marauders; Foxfire; Storm Fear; 1957: Battle Hymn; The Burglar; Night Passage; Slaughter on Tenth Avenue; 1958: Kathy O'; 1960: Platinum High School; 1961: Six Black Horses; 1964: He Rides Tall; Walk a Tightrope; 1965: Taggart; Do You Know This Voice?; The Bounty Killer; The Flight of the Phoenix; 1966: Incident at Phantom Hill; The Hills Run Red; 1967: Five Golden Dragons; 1968: The Bamboo Saucer.

NY Stage: 1935: Dead End; 1937: Many Mansions; 1938: Missouri Legend; 1939: The Little Foxes.

Select TV: 1952: Singapore Souvenir (sp); 1952–55: China Smith (series); 1953: Double Exposure (sp); 1955: The Lie (sp); 1956: The Road That Led Afar (sp); 1957: The Frightened Witness (sp); 1959: Showdown at Sandoval/Gunfight at Sandoval (sp); Comeback (sp); 1960: Mystery at Malibu (sp); Shadow of a Pale Horse (sp); 1963: The Many Ways of Heaven (sp); 1967: Winchester '73; Stranger on the Run; 1967–68: Peyton Place (series).

ANN DVORAK

(ANN McKIM) BORN: NEW YORK, NY,
AUGUST 2, 1911. DIED: DECEMBER 10, 1979.

Unlike fellow contracee Bette Davis, Ann Dvorak saw her career at Warners going nowhere, fought for better work, and still got nowhere. She started out as a child actor — thanks to the influence of her mother, actress Anna Lehr, and her father, a Biograph studio manager — billed as Baby Anna Lehr in a pair of silent movies. At the dawn of the sound era she became a chorus dancer in a handful of MGM movies before Howard Hughes decided to turn her into a star. He cast her opposite Spencer Tracy in his airplane epic, *Sky Devils*, and, more significantly, in the gangster tale *Scarface*, as the sister towards whom Paul Muni has some pre-Code incestuous feelings. Hughes sold her contract to Warner Bros., where she took the lead in *The Strange Love of Molly Louvain*, playing an abandoned woman with a newborn baby who is loved by three different men. In *Three on a Match*, with Bette Davis and Joan Blondell, Dvorak gave an impassioned performance as a slum girl who becomes a socialite, then slides downhill. For the most part, however, she was second lead material, playing off James Cagney in both *The Crowd Roars* and *G Men*, and decorating such features as *Massacre*, *Heat Lightning*, and *The Friends of Mr. Sweeney*. The great roles in front rank features never came so she was reduced to carrying "B" fare at Columbia, like *Cafe Hostess* and *Girls of the Road*, about female hobos. By the late 1940s she rated a good-sized role as a saloon singer in the Randolph Scott western, *Abilene Town*, but after such efforts as *The Private Affairs of Bel Ami*, as one of the women in George Sanders's life, and 1951's *I Was an American Spy*, as a cabaret singer battling the Japanese, she retired from the screen. She had been married (1932–46) to British actor-director Leslie Fenton, who guided her through the 1939 MGM melodrama *Stronger Than Desire*, as a woman who believes she has killed her blackmailer.

Screen: AS BABY ANNA LEHR: 1916: Ramona; 1920: The Five Dollar Plate.

AS ANN DVORAK: 1929: The Hollywood Revue of 1929; 1930: Free and Easy; Way Out West; Love in the Rough; Lord Byron of Broadway; 1931: Son of India; Susan Lenox (Her Fall and Rise); The Guardsman; Politics; This Modern Age; Dance, Fools, Dance; Just a Gigolo; 1932: Sky Devils; The Crowd Roars; Scarface; The Strange Love of Molly Louvain; Love Is a Racket; Stranger in Town; Crooner; Three on a Match; 1933: The Way to Love; College Coach; 1934: Massacre; Heat Lightning; Midnight Alibi; Friends of Mr. Sweeney; Housewife; Side Streets; Gentlemen Are Born; I Sell Anything; Murder in the Clouds; 1935: Sweet Music; G Men; Bright Lights; Dr. Socrates; Thanks a Million; 1936: We Who Are About to Die; 1937: Racing Lady; Midnight Court; She's No Lady; The Case of the Stuttering Bishop; Manhattan Merry-Go-Round; 1938: Merrily We Live; Gangs of New York; 1939: Blind Alley; Stronger Than Desire; 1940: Cafe Hostess; Girls of the Road; 1941: Don Winslow of the Navy; 1942: This Was Paris; 1943: Squadron Leader X; 1944: Escape to Danger; There's a Future in It; 1945: Flame of the Barbary Coast; Masquerade in Mexico; 1946: The Bachelor's Daughters; Abilene Town; 1947: The Private Affairs of Bel Ami; The Long Night; Out of the Blue; 1948: The Walls of Jericho; 1950: A Life of Her Own; Our Very Own; The Return of Frank James; Mrs. O'Malley and Mr. Malone; 1951: I Was an American Spy; The Secret of Convict Lake.

Select TV: 1950: Close-Up (sp); 1951: Flowers for John (sp); 1952: Street Scene (sp); The Trial of Mary Dugan (sp).

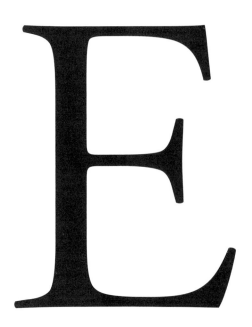

BUDDY EBSEN
(CHRISTIAN RUDOLPH EBSEN)
BORN: BELLEVILLE, IL, APRIL 2, 1908.
ED: UNIV. OF FL, ROLLINS COL.

It is often forgotten that one of the most delightful talents of Buddy Ebsen, a performer whose greatest fame was due to his work in television, was his inimitable, eccentric dancing style, captured in some of his earliest movie appearances. Learning to hoof at his father's dance studio, he wound up on Broadway in the chorus of the Ziegfeld hit *Whoopee*. His sister, Vilma, soon joined him as a duo, and they made their movie debuts in that capacity in MGM's *Broadway Melody of 1936*, where their teaming with Eleanor Powell for the roof-top number "Sing Before Breakfast," was one of the movie's highlights. Ebsen's tall, lanky frame, smiling rube persona, and wonderfully rubbery gyrations and body movements really made him stand out, but no one knew what to do with him outside of letting him brighten up some musicals with a specialty dance or two. He supported Ms. Powell again, in *Born to Sing*, and then in *Broadway Melody of 1938*, where he danced a few steps with Judy Garland in the finale. He almost got to join Garland on screen a second time, but in one of film history's well-known twists of fate, had to drop out of *The Wizard of Oz*, where he was cast as the Tin Man, because he was allergic to the silver makeup. Instead he supported Jeanette MacDonald and Nelson Eddy in *The Girl of the Golden West* and, over at Fox, Shirley Temple in *Captain January* (performing the charming "At the Cod Fish Ball") and Sonja Henie in *My Lucky Star*. After scoring back on Broadway in *Yokel Boy*, he turned down a long-term contract at MGM and wound up at RKO in cheaper fare, like *Sing Your Worries Away*, playing comedy off of Bert Lahr, and *Parachute Battalion*, performing in a rare dramatic role at this stage of his career.

After that he left Hollywood temporarily and returned in the 1950s, achieving great success on television playing Fess Parker's sidekick, George Russel, in Disney's mini-series *Davy Crockett* (the programs were so popular that they were combined into two theatrical features for future showings). On the big screen he displayed his worth as a serious actor in the grim war film *Attack* and in *Breakfast at Tiffany's*, where he appeared as Audrey Hepburn's hayseed ex-husband. Then a pair of hit television shows came along, making him more famous than ever: *The Beverly Hillbillies*, playing amiable backwoods millionaire Jed Clampett in one of the most widely seen sitcoms of the 1960s, and, the following decade, *Barnaby Jones*, where he had the title role of the low-keyed, grandfatherly detective. There was one last opportunity to dance, in Disney's little-seen 1968 musical *The One and Only Genuine Original Family Band*. Another 25 years passed before he showed up on the big screen again, in the movie version of *The Beverly Hillbillies*, playing, of course, Barnaby Jones. He co-wrote the title song for a 1951 comedy in which he did not appear, *Behave Yourself!*, and published his memoirs, *The Other Side of Oz*, in 1993.

Screen: 1935: Broadway Melody of 1936; 1936: Born to Dance; Captain January; Banjo on My Knee; 1937: Broadway Melody of 1938; 1938: Yellow Jack; The Girl of the Golden West; My Lucky Star; 1939: Four Girls in White; 1941: Parachute Battalion; They Met in Argentina; 1942: Sing Your Worries Away; 1950: Under Mexicali Skies; 1951: Silver City Bonanza; Rodeo King and the Senorita; Thunder in God's Country; Utah Wagon Train; 1954: Night People; Red Garters; 1955: Davy Crockett — King of the Wild Frontier (from TV); 1956: Davy Crockett and the River Pirates (from TV); Between Heaven and Hell; Attack; 1961: Breakfast at Tiffany's; 1962: The Interns; 1964: Mail Order Bride; 1968: The One and Only Genuine Original Family Band; 1993: The Beverly Hillbillies.

NY Stage: 1928: Whoopee; 1932: Flying Colors; 1934: Ziegfeld Follies; 1939: Yokel Boy; 1946: Show Boat.

Select TV: 1952: Burlesque (sp); The Nervous Wreck (sp); Seven Keys to Baldpate (sp); The Pussyfooting Rocks (sp); 1954–55: Disneyland: Davy Crockett (sp); 1956: My Baby Boy (sp); 1958–59: Northwest Passage (series); 1959: A Trip to Paradise (sp); Free Weekend (sp); 1960: Graduation Dress (sp); 1962–71: The Beverly Hillbillies (series); 1970: The Andersonville Trial (sp); 1972: The Daughters of Joshua Cabe; 1973: Horror at 37,000 Feet; Tom Sawyer; The President's Plane Is Missing; 1973–80: Barnaby Jones (series); 1976: Smash-Up on Interstate 5; 1978: Leave Yesterday Behind; The Critical List; The Bastard (ms); 1979: The Paradise Connection; 1981: Fire on the Mountain; The Return of the Beverly Hillbillies; **1984–85:** Matt Houston (series); **1987:** Stone Fox; **1990:** Working Trash.

NELSON EDDY

BORN: PROVIDENCE, RI, JUNE 29, 1901.
DIED: MARCH 6, 1967.

Back when Hollywood made such things as operettas, Jeanette MacDonald and Nelson Eddy ruled the genre. They were not an official team, but they are eternally linked as icons of a bygone era. Eddy began singing while a boy but headed towards a career in copywriting after moving to Philadelphia. Some amateur theatre work encouraged him to audition, successfully, for the Philadelphia Civic Opera, which eventually led to his New York debut, in *Pagliacci* at the Met. He branched out on his own, singing in concerts and on the radio, making enough of a name for himself that MGM signed the baritone to a contract in 1933, giving him specialty numbers in three musicals, including *Dancing Lady*, where he showed up to sing Rodgers and Hart's "That's the Rhythm of the Day." In 1935 the studio cast Eddy as MacDonald's leading man in *Naughty Marietta*, and although he hadn't been her equal as a film star at that point in time, the end result certainly made him so. As the Yankee scout who falls in love with a French princess, he sang with bravado and sparred playfully with his co-star, showing more animation than he was usually credited with. The movie featured one of the pair's most famous duets, "Ah, Sweet Mystery of Life," and one of Eddy's signature numbers, "Tramp Tramp Tramp." The response was so good that the singers were immediately reteamed for what were probably their two best films. The first, *Rose-Marie*, found Eddy in the garb he would forever be associated with, a Mountie's uniform, singing "Indian Love Call," a number that marked perhaps the ultimate MacDonald-Eddy moment on screen. Their next, *Maytime*, was potentially sticky material that somehow worked, a doomed love affair between two singers, with another of the team's immortal duets, "Will You Remember," sending the fans into ecstasy. Just to show things needn't all be so serious, Eddy also did a spoof number, "Ham and Eggs."

For a break, he got a new partner, Eleanor Powell, in *Rosalie*, looking great in a cadet uniform and introducing the classic "In the Still of the Night." Back with MacDonald, he was a Mexican bandit in *The Girl of the Golden West*, followed by their first Technicolor opus, *Sweethearts*, as a Broadway couple driven to separation by one of those idiotic plot twists all too prevalent in musicals of the day. Wishing to work with others, Eddy teamed with Virginia Bruce in *Let Freedom Ring*, and Ilona Massey in *Balalaika*, but it was clear that the fans preferred him with MacDonald. They were back again three more times, with *New Moon*, which provided Eddy with another seminal moment, singing "Stout Hearted Men;" the Technicolor *Bitter Sweet*, an adaptation of a Noël Coward work that discarded so much of the source material that it made the author swear off Hollywood; and their swan song, *I Married an Angel*, another adaptation that tossed away most of the original Broadway score. The box office had cooled off somewhat by the last picture, and the critics were less than kind, saving most of their criticism for Eddy's limitations as an actor. He was, it should be noted, hired first and foremost for his singing abilities, and this he did most impressively. However, his future as a movie attraction without Jeanette seemed questionable. As it turned out, he made only three more on-screen appearances, the most famous and popular being the remake of *Phantom of the Opera*, which, seen today, usually makes horror fans uneasy because there is too much singing in it, while opera fans resent the intrusion of the gothic plot. *Knickerbocker Holiday*, yet another adaptation of a Broadway hit that wreaked havoc with much of the score, and *Northwest Outpost*, were both produced and distributed on the cheap, so Eddy's exit from the picture business was a quiet one. He continued to sing in concerts, for recordings, and on TV, reuniting in 1959 for an album with MacDonald that sold quite well. In the 1960s he sang in nightclubs, teamed on occasion with Gale Sherwood, and died shortly after giving a performance in Miami Beach. Modern movie audiences may give little thought to them, but the supporters of MacDonald and Eddy are among the most ardent and loyal of followers, continuing fan clubs to this day.

Screen: 1933: Broadway to Hollywood; Dancing Lady; 1934: Student Tour; 1935: Naughty Marietta; 1936: Rose-Marie; 1937: Maytime; Rosalie; 1938: The Girl of the Golden West; Sweethearts; 1939: Let Freedom Ring; Balalaika; 1940: New Moon; Bitter Sweet; 1941: The Chocolate Soldier; 1942: I Married an Angel; 1943: Phantom of the Opera; 1944: Knickerbocker Holiday; 1946: Make Mine Music (voice); 1947: Northwest Outpost.

Select TV: 1955: The Desert Song (sp).

BARBARA EDEN

(BARBARA JEAN MOORHEAD)
BORN: TUCSON, AZ, AUGUST 23, 1934. RAISED IN SAN FRANCISCO, CA. ED: SAN FRANCISCO ST. COL. CONSERVATORY OF MUSIC.

A perky, pretty actress, adept at combining sex appeal with a certain degree of friendliness, Barbara Eden was a nice addition to several 1960s entertainments, but she didn't pass the stardom test until she took steady work on the small screen. She grew up in San Francisco, where she studied drama and voice before heading to Hollywood to find work. She made her debut in 1956 in one of the very last movies produced by RKO, *Back From Eternity*, in a small part. The following year she got her first glimpse of stardom, playing the Marilyn Monroe role in the television adaptation of *How to Marry a Millionaire*, which ran in syndication. She was given some movie roles at Fox, working her way up to the female lead in a "B" thriller, *Twelve Hours to Kill*, followed by a typical military comedy with Pat Boone, *All Hands on Deck*, and one of the more serious Elvis Presley vehicles, *Flaming Star*, though not as his love interest. Also for Fox there were two enjoyable Irwin Allen adventures, *Voyage to the Bottom of the Sea* (which also featured Michael Ansara, to whom she was married from 1958 to 1973) and *Five Weeks in a Balloon*; and one of the limp teamings of Tommy Noonan and Peter Marshall, *Swingin' Along*. Elsewhere she was an aggressive beach cutie in *Ride the Wild Surf*, a more serious sun-and-sand romp than most of those that were popular at the time but no less trivial, and two 1964 fantasies with Tony Randall. The first, *The Brass Bottle*, was prophetic because it involved a genie (Burl Ives), while the second, *7 Faces of Dr. Lao*, gave her the intriguing role of a prim schoolmarm whose hidden desires are unleashed by the God Pan (Randall). The next year she herself was taking up residence in a genie's bottle, playing the role with which she would become forever identified, the sunny and vivacious lead of the hit sitcom *I Dream of Jeannie*. From that point on she was basically a television name, returning to the movies for a couple of cheapies, *The Amazing Dobermans*, which at least gave her a chance to appear with Fred Astaire, and the bird-brained *Harper Valley P.T.A.*, which was successful enough in certain rural areas to rate a television spin-off for Eden. She reteamed with her *Jeannie* co-star, Larry Hagman, for the 1971 telefilm *A Howling in the Woods*, and again, briefly in 1990, when she joined the cast of his soap series *Dallas*. He did not, however, partner with her for her two *Jeannie* telefilm reunions in which, having reached her 50s, she still looked pretty terrific.

Screen: 1956: Back From Eternity; 1957: The Wayward Girl; Will Success Spoil Rock Hunter?; 1959: A Private's Affair; 1960: Twelve Hours to Kill; From the Terrace; Flaming Star; 1961: All Hands on Deck; Voyage to the Bottom of the Sea; 1962: Swingin' Along/Double Trouble; Five Weeks in a Balloon; The Wonderful World of the Brothers Grimm; 1963: The Yellow Canary; 1964: The Brass Bottle; The New Interns; 7 Faces of Dr. Lao; Ride the Wild Surf; 1971: Quick, Let's Get Married/The Confession/Seven Different Ways (filmed 1964); 1976: The Amazing Dobermans; 1978: Harper Valley P.T.A.; 1984: Chattanooga Choo Choo (dtv); 1996: A Very Brady Sequel; 2003: Carolina.

Select TV: 1957–59: How to Marry a Millionaire (series); 1965–70: I Dream of Jeannie (series); 1971: The Feminist and the Fuzz; A Howling in the Woods; 1972: The Woman Hunter; 1973: Guess Who's Sleeping in My Bed; 1974: The Stranger Within; 1975: Let's Switch; 1976: How to Break Up a Happy Divorce; 1977: Stonestreet: Who Killed the Centerfold Model?; 1979: The Girls in the Office; 1980: Condominium; 1981: Return of the Rebels; 1981–82: Harper Valley P.T.A. (series); 1985: I Dream of Jeannie: 15 Years Later; 1987: The Stepford Children; 1988: The Secret Life of Kathy McCormick (and co-prod.); 1989: Your Mother Wears Combat Boots; A Brand New Life (series); 1990: Opposites Attract; 1990–91: Dallas (series); 1991: Her Wicked Ways/Lethal Charm; Hell Hath No Fury; I Still Dream of Jeannie; 1993: Visions of Murder; 1994: Eyes of Terror; 1996: Dead Man's Island; Nite Club Confidential.

CLIFF EDWARDS

BORN: HANNIBAL, MO, JUNE 14, 1895.
DIED: JULY 17, 1971.

The man known as "Ukulele Ike" would probably not mean a thing to today's audiences were it not for the fact that he introduced two of the best-loved songs in motion picture history. He made his initial living as a saloon singer and ukulele player, adopting his nickname when a cafe proprietor who could not remember his name kept calling him "Ike." He was soon a star of both vaudeville and recordings, boasting such hit tunes as "Sleepy Time Gal" and "Toot Toot Tootsie Goodbye." This led to an offer to make his movie debut in MGM's extravaganza *The Hollywood Revue of 1929*, in which he sang the immortal "Singin' in the Rain." Thereafter he was called on to provide comedy and songs in several early musicals, including *Lord Byron of Broadway*, *So This Is College*, *Good News*, and *Take a Chance*. His bizarre singing style usually required him to break from the vocals to go into a high-pitched series of scat-like noises and nonsense phrases. He had become a standard supporting and bit player by the end of the 1930s, appearing in such "A" movies as *The Girl of the Golden West*, *Gone With the Wind* (heard as a wounded soldier), and *His Girl Friday*. His greatest cinematic moment came, however, when Walt Disney hired him to supply the voice of Jiminy Cricket in the 1940 animated classic, *Pinocchio*, opening the film by singing one of the most beautiful songs ever written for the big screen, the Academy Award-winning "When You Wish Upon a Star." Although Disney would use his voice again, in *Dumbo*, as one of the Crows, singing the delightful "When I See an Elephant Fly," and *Fun and Fancy Free*, reprising Jiminy Cricket, he afterwards moved on to "B" westerns, including *Prairie Stranger* and *Lawless Plainsmen*. It was all

downhill from there, with Edwards long unemployed and virtually forgotten when he died in 1971.

Screen: 1929: The Hollywood Revue of 1929; So This Is College?; Marianne; 1930: Montana Moon; Way Out West; Those Three French Girls; Good News; Doughboys; Lord Byron of Broadway; 1931: Parlor, Bedroom and Bath; The Great Lover; The Sin of Madelon Claudet; Dance, Fools, Dance; Stepping Out; The Prodigal; Shipmates; Sidewalks of New York; Laughing Sinners; 1932: Hell Divers; Young Bride; Fast Life; 1933: Flying Devils; Take a Chance; 1934: George White's Scandals; 1935: George White's 1935 Scandals; Red Salute; 1936: The Man I Marry; 1937: They Gave Him a Gun; Between Two Women; Saratoga; Bad Guy; The Women Men Marry; The Bad Man of Brimstone; 1938: The Girl of the Golden West; The Little Adventuress; 1939: Maisie; Smuggled Cargo; Gone With the Wind; 1940: High School; His Girl Friday; Pinocchio (voice); Millionaires in Prison; Flowing Gold; She Couldn't Say No; Friendly Neighbors; 1941: The Monster and the Girl; Power Dive; Knockout; International Squadron; Dumbo (voice); Riders of the Badlands; Thunder Over the Prairie; Prairie Stranger; 1942: West of Tombstone; Sundown Jim; Lawless Plainsmen; Riders of the Northland; Bad Men of the Hills; Seven Miles from Alcatraz; Pirates of the Prairie; Overland to Deadwood; American Empire; Bandit Ranger; 1943: Fighting Frontier; Sagebrush Law; The Falcon Strikes Back; Red River Robin Hood; Salute for Three; The Avenging Rider; 1947: Fun and Fancy Free (voice); 1965: The Man From Button Willow (voice).

NY Stage: 1921: The Mimic World of 1921; 1924: Lady Be Good; 1925: Sunny; 1935: George White's Scandals.

Select TV: 1949: The Cliff Edwards Show (series).

VINCE EDWARDS

(VINCENTO EDUARDO ZOINO) BORN: NEW YORK, NY, JULY 9, 1928. DIED: MARCH 11, 1996.

A brooding actor of no special qualities, Vince Edwards had his flash of fame in the 1960s when he became one of two hot young doctors on TV. He had originally hoped to enter the Olympics as a swimmer, but instead wound up studying acting at the American Academy of Dramatic Arts. In due time he began popping up all over television and on the big screen in small roles in films like *Sailor Beware* and *Rogue Cop*, while knocking off a lead in one 1952 cheapie, *Hiawatha*, as an Indian chief in this very loose adaptation of the Longfellow poem. He had a dark quality so right for playing thugs and did so in *The Night Holds Terror*, terrorizing Jack Kelly and his family, and in director Stanley Kubrick's tense *The Killing*, as the mobster lover of Marie Windsor. There were plenty of bottom-of-the-barrel programmers that followed, such as *Island Woman*, a Calypso-scored romance that reteamed him with Windsor; *City of Fear*, where he played an escaped con hunted by the cops; and *Murder by Contract*, as a hit man hired to bump off Caprice Toriel. None of these films did much except supply him with an occasional paycheck. Then came the ABC medical drama *Ben Casey*, in 1961, and Edwards finally found himself on the covers of the fan magazines, as the young doctor whom audiences were only too willing to have perform surgery on them. The show was such a hit that Edwards was able to get an album out of the deal, *Vince Edwards Sings*, although it didn't exactly chase Elvis off the charts. He was seen in two all-star war movies, the underrated *The Victors* and the all-too-typical *The Devil's Brigade*, and in the British-produced *Hammerhead*, one of the many attempts to cash in on the espionage/secret agent craze started by the James Bond adventures. The rest of his sporadic film career consisted mostly of quickies and direct-to-video titles like *Return to Horror High* and *Cellar Dweller*. On television he directed episodes of such series as *Fantasy Island* and *Police Story*, and tried his hand at writing with the 1973 telefilm *Maneater*.

Screen: 1951: Mr. Universe; Sailor Beware; 1952: Hiawatha; 1954: Rogue Cop; 1955: The Night Holds Terror; Cell 2455 Death Row; 1956: The Killing; Serenade; 1957: Hit and Run; The Hired Gun; The Three Faces of Eve; Ride Out for Revenge; 1958: Island Woman; Murder by Contract; 1959: City of Fear; The Scavengers; 1961: The Outsider; 1962: Too Late Blues; 1963: The Victors; 1968: The Devil's Brigade; Hammerhead; 1969: The Desperados; 1972: The Mad Bomber/The Police Connection; 1982: The Seduction; 1983: Space Raiders; Deal of the Century; 1984: The Fix/The Agitators (dtv); 1986: Sno-Line; 1987: Return to Horror High; 1988: Cellar Dwellar (dtv); 1989: Andy and the Airwave Rangers (dtv); 1990: The Gumshoe Kid; 1991: Son of Darkness: To Die For II (dtv); Original Intent (dtv); 1993: Motorama; 1994: The Fear (dtv).

NY Stage: 1947: High Button Shoes.

Select TV: 1955: Garity's Sons (sp); 1957: Bitter Choice (sp); 1961–66: Ben Casey (series); 1970: Sole Survivor; Dial Hot Line; 1970–71: Matt Lincoln (series); 1971: Do Not Fold, Spindle or Mutilate; 1973: Firehouse; 1975: Death Stalk; 1977: The Rhinemann Exchange (ms); Cover Girls; 1978: The Courage and the Passion (and exec. prod.); Evening in Byzantium; 1987: The Dirty Dozen: The Deadly Mission; 1988: The Return of Ben Casey; 1991: Dillinger; 1994: Jailbreakers.

RICHARD EGAN

BORN: SAN FRANCISCO, CA, JULY 29, 1921.
ED: UNIV. OF SAN FRANCISCO, STANFORD UNIV.
DIED: JULY 20, 1987.

The ever-squinting Richard Egan was called on to project a level of stoic virility during the 1950s, but he lacked that extra something — perhaps charm?, mobility in his facial muscles? — that would have made him a true movie star, and little of his work is given much thought anymore. Following military service during World War II, he became an instructor of public speaking at Northwestern University. This encouraged him to try Hollywood, where he found small parts in seven features in his premiere year, 1950. The roles gradually increased in size until he finally got some leads in a trio of "B" movies made for United Artists in 1954: *Wicked Woman*, where he played a bar owner seduced by a blonde temptress from out-of-town; *Gog*, a 3-D sci-fi about a rebellious robot; and *Khyber Patrol*, where he was captain of a Lancer regiment battling Raymond Burr. Around this time 20th Century-Fox decided to add him to the payroll, and he went from fighting Tyrone Power over Susan Hayward in *Untamed* to starring roles in the adventure *Seven Cities of Gold*, as an unlikely Spanish Conquistador, and *The View From Pompey's Head*, as a lawyer facing prejudice in the deep South in this failed adaptation of a best seller. There followed the melodramatic *The Revolt of Mamie Stover*, as an author trying to save Jane Russell from a wicked life as a saloon singer (clearly a prostitute in the original novel) and *Love Me Tender*, top-billed as the older brother of Elvis Presley (who was the *real* reason people turned up to see this). Away from Fox he fared somewhat better in two Universal dramas, *Slaughter on Tenth Avenue*, though it was a minor imitation of *On the Waterfront*, and *Voice in the Mirror*, a sincere effort about a man falling into alcoholism after the death of his child. He also participated in one of 1959's biggest hits, *A Summer Place*, as Sandra Dee's father, carrying on illicitly with Dorothy McGuire, and then went over to Disney to play Jane Wyman's former squeeze in *Pollyanna*. Following some second rate historical epics, *Esther and the King* and *The 300 Spartans*, Egan took on some unsuccessful television series before his star began to fade. Little of the work he did in the latter half of his career would be called high profile, until he ended up as a regular on a daytime serial, *Capitol*, which gave him steady employment in the last five years of his life.

Screen: 1950: The Damned Don't Cry; The Good Humor Man; The Killer That Stalked New York; Wyoming Mail; Kansas Raiders; Undercover Girl; Highway 301; 1951: Bright Victory; Hollywood Story; Up Front; The Golden Horde; Flame of Araby; 1952: The Battle at Apache Pass; The Devil Makes Three; One Minute to Zero; Cripple Creek; Blackbeard the Pirate; 1953: Split Second; The Glory Brigade; The Kid From Left Field; 1954: Wicked Woman; Gog; Demetrius and the Gladiators; Khyber Patrol; 1955: Underwater!; Untamed; Violent Saturday; Seven Cities of Gold; The View From Pompey's Head; 1956: The Revolt of Mamie Stover; Love Me Tender; Tension at Table Rock; 1957: Slaughter on Tenth Avenue; 1958: Voice in the Mirror; The Hunters; 1959: These Thousand Hills; A Summer Place; 1960: Pollyanna; Esther and the King; 1962: The 300 Spartans; 1968: The Destructors; Chubasco; 1969: The Big Cube; 1970: Moonfire; 1973: Day of the Wolves; 1978: The Amsterdam Kill; 1980: Mission to Glory/ Kino, the Padre on Horseback/The Father Kino Story (dtv); 1982: The Sweet Creek County War (dtv).

Select TV: 1953: Double Bet (sp); 1954: Go Away a Winner (sp); 1962–63: Empire (series); 1963: Redigo (series); 1966: Valley of Mystery (sp); 1970: The House That Would Not Die; 1974: Shoot-Out in a One-Dog Town; Throw Out the Anchor (sp); 1982–87: Capitol (series).

SALLY EILERS

(DOROTHEA SALLY EILERS) BORN: NEW YORK, NY, DECEMBER 11, 1908. DIED: JANUARY 5, 1978.

A blonde star attraction for a brief period in the early 1930s, Sally Eilers had come to Hollywood several years earlier and started out working in a few shorts for Pathé and in features like *Cradle Snatchers* and *The Show of Shows*. In 1930 her name became better known in the movie social scene when she married cowboy star Hoot Gibson. The following year she found stardom of her own playing the title role in *Bad Girl*, a box-office hit and an Oscar winner for director Frank Borzage, with Eilers as a dress model who becomes attracted to James Dunn because he's standoffish enough to make *her* chase *him*. Fox decided to take advantage of her newfound success by reteaming her with Dunn on several occasions. They worked together in *Dance Team*, trying to make it big in show business, going from one seedy establishment to the next; *Over the Hill*, portraying childhood sweethearts; and *Hold Me Tight*, with Eilers as a pregnant store clerk trying to support her out-of-work husband. Theirs was not the most inspired of celluloid pairings, with Dunn registering more strongly of the two. However, these years at Fox, which included playing the trapeze artist who breaks Norman Foster's heart in the Oscar-nominated *State Fair*, would be Eilers's golden ones. Once she left the studio in 1934, there was little to get excited about in most of her subsequent assignments, including two reunions with Dunn at Universal, *Don't Get Personal* and *We Have Our Moments*; although RKO did offer her a few juicy roles in potboilers like *Condemned Women*, as a former nurse sent up the river for larceny; *Tarnished Angel*, as a showgirl-turned-evangelist; and *They Made Her a Spy*, with a title that speaks for itself. The 1950 "B" western *Stage to Tucson* marked her film farewell, although she remained on the Hollywood social scene for several years after that. Her marriage to Gibson had ended in 1933, and that same year she married producer Harry Joe Brown. They divorced in 1943.

Screen: 1927: The Red Mill; Sunrise; Paid to Love; Cradle Snatchers; Slightly Used; 1928: Dry Martini; Broadway Daddies; Fazil; The Goodbye Kiss; 1929: Broadway Babies; Trial Marriage; The Show of Shows; The Long, Long Trail; Weary River; Sailor's Holiday; 1930: Let Us Be Gay; She Couldn't Say No; Doughboys; Trigger Tricks; Roaring Ranch; 1931: Reducing; Quick Millions; The Black Camel; Clearing the Range; Parlor, Bedroom and Bath; Bad Girl; Over the Hill; Holy Terror; 1932: Dance Team; Disorderly Conduct; Hat Check Girl; 1933: Second-Hand Wife; State Fair; Made on Broadway; I Spy/The Morning After; Sailor's Luck; Central Airport; Hold Me Tight; Walls of Gold; 1934: She Made Her Bed; Three on a Honeymoon; 1935: Carnival; Pursuit; Alias Mary Dow; Remember Last Night?; 1936: Strike Me Pink; Don't Get Personal; Without Orders; Florida Special; 1937: We Have Our Moments; Danger Patrol; Talk of the Devil; 1938: Lady Behave; Condemned Women; The Nurse From Brooklyn; Tarnished Angel; Everybody's Doing It; 1939: They Made Her a Spy; Full Confession; 1941: I Was a Prisoner on Devil's Island; 1944: A Wave, a WAC and a Marine; 1945: Out of the Night/ Strange Illusion; 1948: Coroner Creek; 1950: Stage to Tucson.

ANITA EKBERG

(Kirsten Anita Marriane Ekberg)
Born: Malmo, Sweden, September 29, 1931.

This tall and icy Swedish beauty was a staple in American films of the 1950s, where she was almost always around just to exhibit an exaggerated European sexuality. She continued into the 1960s, working back and forth between unexceptional Hollywood fare and European product until she faded away, to be seen on occasion in mostly un-exported films. She first came to the U.S. in 1951, after being proclaimed Miss Sweden, and was promptly put under contract by Howard Hughes. However, Universal used her first, as a handmaiden in a Rock Hudson swashbuckler, *The Golden Blade*, and as one of the shapely inhabitants of Venus in *Abbott and Costello Go to Mars*, which was not the last time she would be around to supply material for a leering comic co-star. Following a few more bit parts, she was featured in John Wayne's *Blood Alley*, trying to pass for Chinese. She then did two with Dean Martin and Jerry Lewis, *Artists and Models* and *Hollywood or Bust*. She was known well enough by this point to play herself in the latter, presumably due more to fan magazines than her screen achievements. There was a slight leap into more-prestigious offerings when she joined the huge cast of Dino DeLaurentiis's 1956 production of *War and Peace*, playing Helene. Then it was back to the comedians, playing opposite Bob Hope in one of his weaker efforts, *Paris Holiday*, and being asked back for a second go-round five years later for *Call Me Bwana*. Ekberg played the title role in a western-set courtroom drama, *Valerie*, and finally got top billing for a mild Universal melodrama more notable for its title, *Screaming Mimi*, as a nightclub dancer under the spell of a psychiatrist. Around this time she began to gravitate toward foreign productions, eventually ending up in the most popular import of its day, Fellini's *La Dolce Vita*, as the actress who takes a stroll into the fountain in one of the film's many famous

moments. For the same director she starred in his notably bizarre episode of *Boccaccio '70*, as the sexy poster that comes to life in "The Temptation of Dr. Antonio." Then it was a reunion of sorts with Martin and Lewis, first with Dean in *4 for Texas*, and then Jerry in *Way…Way Out*, hardly material worth crossing the Atlantic for. Very little of what she did afterwards found any American distribution, among the exceptions being two guest bits she did for Fellini, in *The Clowns*, and then, much later, *Intervista*, shocking audiences unaware of how portly she had become in the intervening years.

Screen (US releases only): 1953: The Golden Blade; Abbott and Costello Go to Mars; Take Me to Town; The Mississippi Gambler; 1955: Blood Alley; Artists and Models; 1956: Man in the Vault; War and Peace; Hollywood or Bust; Back From Eternity; Zarak; 1957: Pick-Up Alley/Interpol; Valerie; 1958: Paris Holiday; Screaming Mimi; The Man Inside; 1961: La Dolce Vita; 1962: Boccaccio '70; 1963: Call Me Bwana; 4 for Texas; 1966: The Alphabet Murders; Way…Way Out; 1967: Woman Times Seven; 1968: The Cobra; 1969: If It's Tuesday, This Must Be Belgium; 1971: The Clowns; 1974: Fangs of the Living Dead/Malenka (It: 1968); 1975: Death Knocks Twice (It: 1969); 1980: Daisy Chain; 1992: Intervista (It: 1987); 1999: The Red Dwarf.

Select TV: 1955: Casablanca (sp); 1979: Gold of the Amazon Women; 1980: S*H*E.

DENHOLM ELLIOTT

Born: London, England, May 31, 1922.
ed: Malvern Col. Died: October 6, 1992.

Minus any fanfare or efforts to push him as a star, Denholm Elliott became one of Britain's most stellar, unsung performers, carving out a movie career that lasted over 40 years, during which he usually played character roles, hence the lack of public or media focus. He became better known with the passing of each decade, appearing in enough popular movies that even younger audiences were familiar with him by the time of his death. Following a stint in the military during World War II that ended dramatically, with him spending three years in a German prisoner of war camp, Elliott made his stage debut, in 1945, and then his movie bow, in a small role in 1949's *Dear Mr. Prohack*. Three years down the line he had a pivotal role in the 1952 British Oscar winner, *Breaking The Sound Barrier*, as Ann Todd's brother who is killed when his plane crashes. He played Ralph Richardson's son in the ensemble Christmastime drama *The Holly and the Ivy*; the civil servant carrying on with Trevor Howard's wife in *The Heart of the Matter*, from Graham Greene's novel; and paired off with Dirk Bogarde as one of the military survivors of a raid on Rhodes in *They Who Dare*. Staying in uniform he finally got a lead role, albeit in a very minor production, *Pacific Destiny*, as real-life Arthur Grimble, who tried to end a native uprising in the South Seas. His other starring role was more memorable, if only because the movie was Mike Todd, Jr.'s strange *Scent of Mystery*, which had the distinction of being the first (and last) picture in Smell-o-vision. At that point Elliott wasn't all that well known outside his native country, but in the 1960s he became more widely seen, appearing in the prison camp drama *King Rat*; *Alfie*, as an efficient abortionist; *The Night They Raided Minsky's*, as the head of the Society for the Suppression of Vice; and Sidney Lumet's take on *The Sea Gull*, as Dr. Dorn.

In 1974 he seized one of his best opportunities when he

played the down-on-his-luck, drunken filmmaker who shoots a hilariously pretentious Bar Mitzvah movie in *The Apprenticeship of Duddy Kravitz*. This, in turn, was followed by his interpretation of the aging Will Scarlett in *Robin and Marian*, and apperances in such big budget international productions as *Voyage of the Damned*, *A Bridge Too Far*, and *The Boys From Brazil*. In 1981 he had the small role of Harrison Ford's colleague in *Raiders of the Lost Ark*, which turned out to be the most widely seen movie he'd ever do (he repeated the part in the second sequel, *Indiana Jones and the Last Crusade*), and then a meaty part in the weird *Brimstone and Treacle*, as an unfaithful husband whose daughter lies in a coma. The movie that gave the biggest boost to his popularity with the general American public was *Trading Places*, where he gave a winning performance as the sardonic valet of greedy Don Ameche and Ralph Bellamy, who takes up sides with Eddie Murphy and Dan Aykroyd to get revenge on the old geezers. Then he effortlessly stole scenes repeating the Clifton Webb role in the highly unpopular remake of *The Razor's Edge*, before reaching one of his acting peaks as the life-loving Mr. Emmerson in the art house sensation of 1986, *A Room With a View*. It earned him his sole Oscar nomination, in the supporting category. Afterwards he was the family doctor called on to "cure" James Wilby of his homosexuality in *Maurice*; Mia Farrow's timid suitor in *September*; and, finally, a bumbling actor in the farcical *Noises Off*. Sadly, he passed away later that same year, 1992, of AIDS-related tuberculosis. His first wife (1954–56) was actress Virginia McKenna.

Screen: 1949: Dear Mr. Prohack; 1952: Breaking the Sound Barrier; The Holly and the Ivy; 1953: The Ringer; The Cruel Sea; They Who Dare; 1954: The Heart of the Matter; Lease of Life; 1955: The Man Who Loved Redheads; The Night My Number Came Up; 1956: Pacific Destiny; 1960: Scent of Mystery; 1962: Station Six Sahara; 1964: Nothing But the Best; 1965: You Must Be Joking!; King Rat; 1966: McGuire Go Home/The High Bright Sun; Alfie; The Spy With a Cold Nose; 1968: Maroc 7; Here We Go Round the Mulberry Bush; The Night They Raided Minsky's; 1969: The Sea Gull; 1970: Too Late the Hero; The Rise and Rise of Michael Rimmer; 1971: The House That Dripped Blood; Percy; Quest for Love; 1973: A Doll's House; Vault of Horror; 1974: It's Not the Size That Counts/Percy's Progress; The Apprenticeship of Duddy Kravitz; 1975: Russian Roulette; 1976: To the Devil — A Daughter/Child of Satan; Robin and Marian; Partners; Voyage of the Damned; 1977: A Bridge Too Far; 1978: Sweeney 2; The Little Girl in Blue Velvet; The Boys From Brazil; Watership Down (voice); 1979: Game for Vultures; Saint Jack; Cuba; 1980: The Hound of the Baskervilles; Zulu Dawn; Rising Damp; Bad Timing: A Sensual Obsession; 1981: Sunday Lovers; Raiders of the Lost Ark; 1982: Brimstone and Treacle; The Missionary; 1983: Trading Places; The Wicked Lady; 1984: The Razor's Edge; 1985: A Private Function; Underworld/ Transmutations; 1986: A Room With a View; The Whoopee Boys; 1987: Defence of the Realm; Maurice; September; 1989: Stealing Heaven; Killing Dad; Return From the River Kwai; Indian Jones and the Last Crusade; 1991: Toy Soldiers; 1992: Scorchers (dtv); Noises Off.

NY Stage: 1950: Ring 'Round the Moon; 1951: Green Bay Tree; 1957: Monique; 1961: Write Me a Murder; 1964: The Sea Gull; The Crucible; 1967: The Imaginary Invalid; A Touch of the Poet; Tonight at 8:30; 1977: The New York Idea; The Three Sisters.

Select TV: 1951: One Pair of Hands (sp); 1957: Twelfth Night (sp); The Lark (sp); 1958: The Winslow Boy (sp); A Tale of Two Cities (sp); 1959: The Moon and Sixpence (sp); 1963: The Invincible Mr. Disraeli (sp); 1965: The Holy Terror (sp); 1968: Dracula (sp); 1972: Madame Sin; The Sextet: Follow the Yellow Brick Road (sp); 1980: Blade on the Feather (sp); 1981: Rude Awakening (sp); 1982: The Two Faces of Evil (sp); 1983: The Hound of the Baskervilles (sp); 1984: Camille; 1985: Bleak House (sp); 1986: Hotel du Lac (sp); Mrs. Delafield Wants to Marry; 1988: The Bourne Identity (sp); 1990: The Love She Sought; 1991: Codename Kyril (sp); A Murder of Quality (sp); One Against the Wind.

HOPE EMERSON

BORN: HAWARDEN, IA, APRIL 29, 1897.
DIED: APRIL 25, 1960.

With her six-foot-plus height, beak-like nose, broad bottom, and sour features, it was hard to miss Hope Emerson. She'd worked for years in vaudeville before making her Broadway bow in *Lysistrata* in 1930. Past the age of 50, she came to Hollywood, in 1948, to knock off a few credits for Fox, starting with *Cry of the City*, a Victor Mature vehicle in which she played a killer masseuse. The following year she made a memorable impression as Olympia La Pere, proving her strength by lifting Spencer Tracy in the air in the middle of the courtroom, in *Adam's Rib*. Then came *Caged*, and anyone who saw this stark melodrama of life in a women's lock-up couldn't possibly forget Emerson's cruel and raw performance as the hateful prison matron, the one by which all other cinematic interpretations must be measured. It earned her an Oscar nomination for Best Supporting Actress. There weren't a lot of roles for a woman of her size to fill comfortably, though she did portray pirate Ann Bonney in the comedy *Double Crossbones*; then took charge of the range, playing pioneer ladies in the westerns *Westward the Women* and *The Guns of Fort Petticoat*, helping Audie Murphy to hold off an Indian rampage.

Screen: 1948: Cry of the City; That Wonderful Urge; 1949: House of Strangers; Dancing in the Dark; Adam's Rib; Roseanna McCoy; Thieves' Highway; 1950: Caged; Copper Canyon; Double Crossbones; 1951: Belle le Grande; Westward the Women; 1953: The Lady Wants Mink; Champ for a Day; A Perilous Journey; 1954: Casanova's Big Night; 1955: Untamed; 1957: The Guns of Fort Petticoat; All Mine to Give; 1958: Rock-a-Bye Baby.

NY Stage: 1930: Lysistrata; 1932: Smiling Faces; 1936: Swing Your Lady; 1944: Chicken Every Sunday; 1947: Street Scene; The Magic Touch; 1948: The Cup of Trembling.

Select TV: 1948–49: Kobb's Korner (series); 1952: Doc Corkle (series); 1952–53: I Married Joan (series); 1958: Peter Gunn (series); 1959–60: The Dennis O'Keefe Show (series).

LEIF ERICKSON

(WILLIAM WYCLIFFE ANDERSON) BORN: ALAMEDA, CA, OCTOBER 27, 1911. ED: GLENN TAYLOR MILITARY ACAD., UCLA. DIED: JANUARY 29, 1986.

An actor whose strapping build and deep voice were ideal for unsympathetic parts, Leif Erickson did these and more-benign secondary roles without any exceptional quirks or notable traits, filling his parts as called for. He attended UCLA and studied singing, eventually joining Ted Fio Rito's orchestra, where he was given his curious name, inspired by the real life explorer (and pronounced "life"). He thereafter appeared in Max Reinhardt's famous stage production of *A Midsummer Night's Dream*, although he was not cast in the movie version, instead joining comedians Olsen and

Johnson on tour. Then Paramount offered him a contract, starting in 1935, initially billing him as "Glenn Erickson." Taking back his "Leif," he worked in musical comedies like *College Holiday* and *The Big Broadcast of 1938*, in both playing the romantic juvenile in support of the more colorful comedic talents on hand; the adventure *Ride a Crooked Mile*, as the rebellious son of Cossack Akim Tamiroff; and the social drama *…One Third of a Nation*, as a tenement landlord wracked with guilt. He married another studio contractee, Frances Farmer, in 1936, and their turbulent six-year marriage was chronicled in the many books later written about the troubled actress. In the meantime Erickson went over to Universal, where he sparred with Abbott and Costello in *Pardon My Sarong*; visited a spooky mansion in *Night Monster*; fought Jon Hall for Maria Montez in *Arabian Nights*; and flew over Britain in the wartime success *Eagle Squadron*. After the war years he managed to land an occasional supporting role in some good films, including *The Snake Pit*; *Show Boat*, as the troublemaker who gets Ava Gardner fired; and *On the Waterfront*, urging Marlon Brando to testify against his bosses. During the 1950s he was seen in two of his most famous movies. First, he played the average dad who is made into a zombie by Martians in the sci-fi classic *Invaders From Mars*; then he teamed with Deborah Kerr to repeat his stage role as the loutish husband who hides his closeted yen for other guys in *Tea and Sympathy*, though this aspect was pretty much obliterated from the film version. There was still time to play straight man to comedians such as Martin and Lewis in *Sailor Beware*; Abbott and Costello, again, in *Abbott and Costello Meet Captain Kidd*; and even Rowan and Martin in their first film, *Once Upon a Horse*. As have many actors with less-than-exciting personalities, he found stardom on the tube, as the patriarch of the Cannon clan in the western series *The High Chaparral*.

Screen: AS GLENN ERICKSON: 1933: The Sweetheart of Sigma Chi; 1935: Wanderer of the Wasteland; Nevada; 1936: Desert Gold; Drift Fence.

as LEIF ERICKSON: 1936: Girl of the Ozarks; College Holiday; 1937: Conquest; Waikiki Wedding; 1938: Thrill of a Lifetime; The Big Broadcast of 1938; Ride a Crooked Mile/Escape From Yesterday; 1939: Crisis (narrator); …One Third of a Nation; 1941: H.M. Pulham, Esq.; Nothing but the Truth; The Blonde From Singapore; 1942: Are Husbands Necessary?; The Fleet's In; Night Monster; Arabian Nights; Eagle Squadron; Pardon My Sarong; 1947: The Gangster; Blonde Savage; 1948: The Gay Intruders; Sorry, Wrong Number; Miss Tatlock's Millions; Joan of Arc; The Snake Pit; 1949: Johnny Stool Pigeon; The Lady Gambles; 1950: Stella; Three Secrets; Dallas; Mother Didn't Tell Me; Love That Brute; The Showdown; 1951: The Tall Target; Reunion in Reno; The Cimarron Kid; Sailor Beware; Show Boat; 1952: With a Song in My Heart; Carbine Williams; My Wife's Best Friend; Abbott and Costello Meet Captain Kidd; Never Wave at a WAC; 1953: Trouble Along the Way; Fort Algiers; A Perilous Journey; Born to the Saddle; Paris Model; Invaders From Mars; Captain Scarface; 1954: On the Waterfront; 1956: Star in the Dust; Tea and Sympathy; The Fastest Gun Alive; 1957: The Vintage; Istanbul; Kiss Them for Me; 1958: Twilight for the Gods; Once Upon a Horse; 1963: A Gathering of Eagles; 1964: The Carpetbaggers; Strait-Jacket; Roustabout; 1965: I Saw What You Did; Mirage; 1972: Man and Boy; 1975: Abduction; 1976: Winterhawk; 1977: Twilight's Last Gleaming.

NY Stage: AS WILLIAM ANDERSON: 1938: Golden Boy.

AS LEIF ERICKSON: 1938: All the Living; Rocket to the Moon; 1939: The Gentle People; Margin for Error; 1940: Higher and Higher; Retreat to Pleasure; 1941: The Cream in the Well; 1953:

Tea and Sympathy; 1960: The World of Carl Sandburg.

Select TV: 1951: The Marquis (sp); 1952: Homecoming (sp); 1957: One Coat of White (sp); Panic Button (sp); 1958: The Vigilante (sp); 1959: The Raider (sp); 1960: The Shape of the River (sp); 1967–71: The High Chaparral (series); 1971: Terror in the Sky; The Deadly Dream; 1972: The Family Rico; The Daughters of Joshua Cabe; 1980: Wild Times; 1983: Savage: In the Orient.

JOHN ERICSON

(JOSEPH MEIBES) BORN: DUSSELDORF, GERMANY, SEPTEMBER 25, 1926. RAISED IN NY. ED: AADA.

A blond, nice-looking, but often ineffectual addition to MGM's roster of stars of the early 1950s, German-born John Ericson came to the U.S. with his family when he was only three years old. Following college he worked with some stock companies and made his entrance into movies pretty easily after responding to an open audition for director Fred Zinnemann's movie *Teresa*. He won the leading male role of the sensitive young G.I. who is disturbed by the prejudice he and his Italian war bride are subjected to when they return to his home in New York. Ericson was never again quite as compelling as he was playing this emotionally vulnerable character. Despite that, the critical and public reaction was lukewarm at best, a fact that didn't much faze Ericson, who had already won another plum lead (the role William Holden would play in the movie version) in the original Broadway production of *Stalag 17* that same year, 1951. Afterwards he returned to Hollywood with a contract with MGM, where he played the pianist in love with Elizabeth Taylor in the glossy soap opera *Rhapsody*; emphasized his Germanic roots as Count von Astberg in the fairly deadly rendering of *The Student Prince*; and was Grace Kelly's no-good brother in *Green Fire*. None of these movies did much to bring Ericson any sort of fame, nor were they any more than secondary roles. This was also true of *Bad Day at Black Rock*, where he was one of the wicked townspeople, convincingly mean but overshadowed by most of the other, more colorful cast members.

With MGM no longer interested, he went the independent route. He finally got himself leads, albeit in "B's," like *The Return of Jack Slade*, as a son avenging his dad; *The Cruel Tower*, as a steeplejack battling over Mari Blanchard; *Oregon Passage*, as a cavalry officer who invokes the hostility of the Shoshone tribe; and, perhaps his best-known film, *Pretty Boy Floyd*, as the 1930s gangster. After a trip back to his old studio to play the likeable newspaper editor in *7 Faces of Dr. Lao*, he wound up in European productions or in barely released fare, with a side trip to Disney for *Bedknobs and Broomsticks*, playing a Nazi battling an army of enchanted armor.

Screen: 1951: Teresa; 1954: Rhapsody; The Student Prince; Green Fire; 1955: Bad Day at Black Rock; The Return of Jack Slade; 1956: The Cruel Tower; 1957: Forty Guns; Oregon Passage; 1958: Day of the Bad Man; 1960: Under Ten Flags; Pretty Boy Floyd; 1962: Slave Queen of Babylon/I Am Semiramis (nUSr); 1964: 7 Faces of Dr. Lao; 1965: Operation Atlantis (nUSr); 1967: Treasure of Pancho Villa/Seven for Pancho Villa (nUSr); 1968: The Destructors; Bamboo Saucer/Collision Course; The Money Jungle; 1969: Heads or Tails (nUSr); 1971: Bedknobs and Broomsticks; 1976: Hustler Squad; 1977: Crash!; 1980: House of the Dead/Alien Zone (dtv); 1986: Final Mission (dtv); 1989: Primary Target (dtv).

NY Stage: 1951: Stalag 17.

Select TV: 1951: Saturday's Children (sp); England Made Me (sp); **1956:** Heritage of Anger (sp); **1958:** The Innocent Sleep (sp); **1965–66:** Honey West (series); **1972:** The Bounty Man; **1973:** Tenafly; **1974:** Hog Wild; **1985:** Robert Kennedy and His Times (ms).

LEON ERROL

BORN: SYDNEY, AUSTRALIA, JULY 3, 1881.
DIED: OCTOBER 12, 1951.

Bald, pinch-faced, quivery Leon Errol kept a multilevel career going for close to 20 years. There were his short subjects in which he was a bona fide star, released concurrently with some features in which he was usually a supporting player. In addition, for RKO, there was a series of second string, unsophisticated "Mexican Spitfire" pictures that teamed him (in a dual role) with Lupe Velez. Finally, there was an even cheaper-budgeted run of "Joe Palooka" comedies for Monogram. He had performed in circuses and Shakespearean rep in Australia and then emigrated to the U.S., in his early 20s, eventually establishing his comic persona of the wobbly-legged, nervous drunk in vaudeville and in the Ziegfeld Follies, where he appeared from 1911 to 1915. His film debut came in 1924 in *Yolanda*, followed by a few supporting roles, which he continued to do when talkies arrived. At Paramount he could be found among the ensemble of *We're Not Dressing*, responsible for the shipwreck that stranded the cast on a deserted island; in *Alice in Wonderland*, as Uncle Gilbert; and in his own vehicles, like *Finn and Hattie*, teamed with ZaSu Pitts as a pair of vulgar Americans abroad, and *Only Saps Work*. In 1933 he began his long-running career in shorts, playing his stock nervous drunk, forever the target of his henpecking wife. (One title, "Should Wives Work?," received an Oscar nomination in 1937.) Six years later he found himself over at RKO lending support to excitable Latin actress Lupe Velez in a flimsy comedy called *The Girl From Mexico*, which proved popular enough to encourage the studio to develop it into a series. The next year came *Mexican Spitfire*, with Errol given full reign over the farcical proceedings, playing both Donald Woods's well meaning Uncle Matt and British whisky baron Lord Epping. Six more entries with self-explanatory titles followed, with Errol ultimately adding on a third character, Epping's valet. It all ended in 1943 with *Mexican Spitfire's Blessed Event*, which turned out to be a baby ocelot. Errol, in the meantime, had been keeping busy, not only in his two-reelers but also over at Universal in such memorably titled quickies as *Hat Check Honey* and *Babes on Swing Street*. The 1946 Monogram "B" *Joe Palooka Champ* found the comedian cast as manager Knobby Walsh and gave him another run of steady employment for four years, climaxing with *Joe Palooka in Humphrey Takes a Chance*. He was all ready to take on TV when he died of a heart attack in 1951.

Screen (shorts): 1930: Let's Merge; The Mashie Niblick; **1933:** Poor Fish; Three Little Swigs; Hold Your Temper; **1934:** No More Bridge; Autobuyography; Service With a Smile; Good Morning Eve; Perfectly Mismated; Fixing a Stew; One Too Many; **1935:** Hit and Rum; Salesmanship Ahoy; Home Work; Honeymoon Bridge; Counselitis; **1936:** Down the Ribber; Pirate Party on Catalina Isle; Wholesailing Along; One Live Ghost; **1937:** Wrong Romance; Should Wives Work?; A Rented Riot; **1938:** Dummy Owner; His Pest Friend; The Jitters; Stage Fright; Major Difficulties; Berth Quakes; **1939:** Crime Rave; Home Boner; Moving Vanities; Ring Madness; Wrong Room; Truth Aches; **1940:** Scrappily Married; Bested by a Beard; He Asked for It; Tattle Television; **1941:** The Fired Man; When Wife's Away; A Polo Phony; A Panic in the Parlor; Man-I-Cured; Who's a

Dummy?; **1942:** Home Work; Wedded Blitz; Hold 'Em Jail; Framing Father; Mail Trouble; Dear! Deer!; Pretty Dolly; **1943:** Double Up; Family Feud; Gem Jams; Radio Runaround; Seeing Nellie Home; Cutie on Duty; Wedtime Stories; **1944:** Say Uncle; Poppa Knows Worst; Prices Unlimited; Girls Girls Girls; Triple Trouble; He Forgot to Remember; **1945:** Birthday Blues; Let's Go Stepping; It Shouldn't Happen to a Dog; Double Honeymoon; Beware of Redheads; **1946:** Oh Professor Behave; Maid Trouble; Twin Husbands; I'll Take Milk; Follow That Blonde; **1947:** Borrowed Blonde; Wife Tames Wolf; In Room 303; Hired Husband; Blondes Away; The Spook Speaks; **1948:** Bet Your Life; Bachelor Blues; Don't Fool Your Wife; Secretary Trouble; Uninvited Blonde; Backstage Follies; **1949:** Dad Always Pays; Cactus Cut-Up; I Can't Remember; Oils Well That Ends Well; Sweet Cheat; Shocking Affair; **1950:** High and Dizzy; Texas Tough Guy; Spooky Wooky; **1951:** Chinatown Chump; Punchy Pancho; One Wild Night; Deal Me In; Lord Epping Returns; Too Many Wives.

Screen (features): 1924: Yolanda; **1925:** Clothes Make the Pirate; Sally; **1927:** The Lunatic at Large; **1930:** Paramount on Parade; Only Saps Work; **1931:** One Heavenly Night; Finn and Hattie; Her Majesty Love; **1933:** Alice in Wonderland; **1934:** We're Not Dressing; The Notorious Sophie Lang; The Captain Hates the Sea; **1935:** Princess O'Hara; Coronado; **1937:** Make a Wish; **1939:** The Girl From Mexico; Career; Dancing Co-Ed; **1940:** Mexican Spitfire; Pop Always Pays; Mexican Spitfire Out West; The Golden Fleecing; **1941:** Six Lessons From Madame La Zonga; Where Did You Get That Girl?; Hurry, Charlie, Hurry; Mexican Spitfire's Baby; Melody Lane; Moonlight in Hawaii; Never Give a Sucker an Even Break; **1942:** Mexican Spitfire at Sea; Mexican Spitfire Sees a Ghost; Mexican Spitfire's Elephant; **1943:** Strictly in the Groove; Cowboy in Manhattan; Follow the Band; Gals Inc.; Mexican Spitfire's Blessed Event; Higher and Higher; **1944:** Hat Check Honey; The Invisible Man's Revenge; Slightly Terrific; Twilight on the Prairie; Babes on Swing Street; **1945:** She Gets Her Man; What a Blonde!; Under Western Skies; Mama Loves Papa; **1946:** Riverboat Rhythm; Joe Palooka — Champ; Gentleman Joe Palooka; **1947:** Joe Palooka in the Knockout; **1948:** Joe Palooka in Fighting Mad; The Noose Hangs High; Variety Time; **1949:** Joe Palooka in the Big Fight; Joe Palooka in the Counterpunch; **1950:** Joe Palooka Meets Humphrey; Joe Palooka in Humphrey Takes a Chance.

NY Stage: 1911–15: Ziegfeld Follies; **1912:** A Winsome Widow; **1916:** The Century Girl; **1917:** Hitchy-Koo; **1918:** Hitchy-Koo of 1918; **1920:** Sally; **1921:** Ziegfeld Midnight Frolic; **1925:** Louis the 14th; **1927:** Yours Truly; **1929:** Fioretta.

STUART ERWIN

BORN: SQUAW VALLEY, CA, FEBRUARY 14, 1903.
ED: UNIV. OF CA. DIED: DECEMBER 21, 1967.

The specialty of this wide-eyed, fair-haired actor was portraying amiable, none-too-bright hayseeds and innocents, which he did first in his own vehicles and then, more successfully, as a second lead. After a brief stage career he came to movies in 1928, in *Mother Knows Best*, at Fox, where he filled a few more roles, including a lead in *Speakeasy*, until he signed up with Paramount at the start of the talkie era. There he provided support in both comedies and dramas, including *Dangerous Curves, Sweetie, Along Came Youth*, and *Dude Ranch*, which, if nothing else, introduced him to actress June Collyer. He married her in 1931, and they would remain so until his death, 36 years later. In 1932 he was bumped up to bigger parts, co-starring with

Bing Crosby in *The Big Broadcast*, and playing "Merton of the Movies" in *Make Me a Star*, from the stage farce about a country boy who becomes a film luminary. He had one of the larger roles in the all-star comedy *International House*, as an electric company rep in Shanghai, and then had another lead, in *He Learned About Women*, as a bookworm, before Paramount dropped him. With that he went over to MGM, joining Crosby again in *Going Hollywood*, and then proving his worth as a straight dramatic actor with *Viva Villa!*, as the American reporter who covers the exploits of scene-chewing Wallace Beery. Meanwhile, in 1934, he was the first actor to play the comic book prizefighter Palooka Joe, in *Palooka*. Then, playing his usual slow-witted rube bit, he somehow landed himself a supporting Oscar nomination for Fox's *Pigskin Parade*. That studio kept him on for a few more comedies, including some showcases of his own: *Checkers*, in which he was teamed with child-star Jane Withers; *It Could Happen to You*, a more serious piece, about an adman charged with murder; and *The Honeymoon's Over*. These were nothing more than mild "B" fillers, however, and he went back to supporting work, including a bit as the milkman in *Our Town*, and as straight man to infant-attraction Baby Sandy in *Sandy Gets Her Man*. He ended up over at the poverty-row studios for *Kill Dill* and *Heading for Heaven*, among others. At that point television had arrived, and Erwin moved over to that medium with much success, starring opposite his wife in *Life With the Erwins*. The show soon became *The Stu Erwin Show*, with the actor playing a character named Stu Erwin, though in fact he was portraying a bumbling high school principal, not a movie star. From then on he would bill himself as Stu.

Screen: 1928: Mother Knows Best; 1929: Speakeasy; The Exalted Flapper; New Year's Eve; Thru Different Eyes; Sweetie; The Cock-eyed World; The Trespasser; This Thing Called Love; Dangerous Curves; The Sophomore; 1930: Happy Days; Men Without Women; Paramount on Parade; Young Eagles; Dangerous Nan McGrew; Love Among the Millionaires; Playboy of Paris; Only Saps Work; Along Came Youth; Maybe It's Love; No Limit; 1931: Up Pops the Devil; Dude Ranch; The Magnificent Lie; Working Girls; 1932: Two Kinds of Women; Strangers in Love; Misleading Lady; Make Me a Star; The Big Broadcast; 1933: Face in the Sky; Crime of the Century; He Learned About Women; Under the Tonto Rim; The Stranger's Return; Hold Your Man; International House; Before Dawn; Day of Reckoning; Going Hollywood; 1934: Palooka; Viva Villa!, The Party's Over; Bachelor Bait; Chained; The Band Plays On; Have a Heart; 1935: After Office Hours; Ceiling Zero; 1936: Exclusive Story; Absolute Quiet; Women Are Trouble; All American Chump; Pigskin Parade; 1937: Dance, Charlie, Dance; Small Town Boy; Slim; Second Honeymoon; I'll Take Romance; 1938: Checkers; Mr. Boggs Steps Out; Three Blind Mice; Passport Husband; 1939: Back Door to Heaven; It Could Happen to You; Hollywood Cavalcade; The Honeymoon's Over; 1940: Our Town; When the Daltons Rode; Sandy Gets Her Man; A Little Bit of Heaven; 1941: Cracked Nuts; The Bride Came C.O.D.; 1942: The Adventures of Martin Eden; Drums of the Congo; Blondie for Victory; 1943: He Hired the Boss; 1944: The Great Mike; 1945: Pillow to Post; 1947: Kill Dill; Heading for Heaven; Heaven Only Knows; 1948: Strike It Rich; 1950: Father Is a Bachelor; 1960: For the Love of Mike; 1963: Son of Flubber; 1964: The Misadventures of Merlin Jones.

NY Stage: 1942: Mr. Sycamore; 1950: Great to Be Alive!

Select TV: 1950–55: Life With the Erwins/The Stu Erwin Show/Trouble With Father (series); 1952: The Lucky Suit (sp); 1957: Snow Shoes (sp); 1958: The Right Hand Man (sp); 1959: A Diamond Is a Boy's Best Friend (sp); 1962: The Friendly Thieves (sp); 1963–64: The Greatest Show on Earth (series); 1968: Shadow Over Elveron.

EDITH EVANS

BORN: LONDON, ENGLAND, FEBRUARY 8, 1888.
DIED: OCTOBER 14, 1976.

She was Britain's grande dame, first and foremost of the theater, and then, once she had passed the age of 60, on the screen. With a weathered, skeptical face, rich voice, and imperial sense of command, she could effortlessly steal a scene or a whole film. While apprenticing to be a hat maker, she acted in a production of *Much Ado About Nothing* and was encouraged to go professional. She eventually did, landing some stage work in the West End and parts in three silent movies, including two starring Florence Turner, the later of these, *East Is East*, released in 1916. For the next 31 years she turned her back on the picture business, making her name as one of the supreme talents of the British theater through such plays as *Back to Methuselah*, *The Apple Cart*, and *Heartbreak House*. She also had several acclaimed seasons at the Old Vic, where her credits included *The Taming of the Shrew*, *The Merchant of Venice*, and *The Cherry Orchard*. During World War II she played the impossible, stubbornly self-righteous Lady Bracknell in Oscar Wilde's masterpiece *The Importance of Being Earnest*, one of the great examples of an actor fulfilling a role they were born to play. In 1948 she began her film career proper with one of the leads in the oddball fantasy *The Queen of Spades*, as an old lady whose knack for winning at cards is coveted by Anton Wolbrook. This was followed by a role in an Emlyn Williams production, *The Last Days of Dolwyn*, as a villager who tries to stop Williams from buying up her land.

Then came the charming 1952 film version of *Earnest*, and fortunately for all, Evans was allowed to preserve her great performance, making this the reference point for all subsequent interpretations of the part. Next it was back to the theater for *The Dark Is Light Enough* and *The Chalk Garden*, among others. She repeated her role from the latter in the 1964 movie, earning her an Oscar nod, perhaps just for being her usually compelling self since there was nothing special about this particular performance. There were, in fact, far more notable accomplishments in *Look Back in Anger*, as the cockney old lady to whom Richard Burton remains loyal, providing all the best scenes in this unsteady adaptation of the ground-breaking John Osborne play; *The Nun's Story*, subtly commanding the screen in her very brief part as the Mother Superior; and *Tom Jones*, hilarious as Hugh Griffith's pestering, dotty sister. She did earn a supporting Oscar nomination for the last and then another, in the lead category, for *The Whispers*, her last top-billed role on film, playing a lonely old woman whose life is made more miserable by the return of her selfish husband. It is perhaps the grimmest movie on the subject of old age ever made and therefore not much of a box-office attraction. There was another sizable role, in the gentle comedy *Crooks and Coronets*, in which she was the intended prey of thieves Telly Savalas and Warren Oates, and then much-welcomed bits in *Scrooge*, as the Ghost of Christmas Past; *A Doll's House*, as the nurse; *The Slipper and the Rose*, as the prince's grandmother; and *Nasty Habits*, as the dying abbess, looking very frail indeed. She had, in fact, passed away just a few months after filming her scenes. She was made a Dame of the British Empire in 1945.

Screen: 1915: A Honeymoon for Three; A Welsh Singer; 1916: East Is East; 1947: The Queen of Spades; 1949: The Last Days of Dolwyn/Woman of Dolwyn; 1952: The Importance of Being Earnest; 1959: Look Back in Anger; The Nun's Story; 1963: Tom Jones; 1964: The Chalk Garden; 1965: Young Cassidy; 1967: The Whisperers; Fitzwilly; 1968: Prudence and the Pill; 1969: The

Madwoman of Chaillot; Crooks and Coronets/Sophie's Place; 1970: Scrooge; 1973: A Doll's House; 1974: Craze; 1976: The Slipper and the Rose; 1977: Nasty Habits.

NY Stage: 1931: The Lady With the Lamp; 1932: Evensong; 1933: Tattle Tales; 1935: Romeo and Juliet; 1950: Daphne Laureola.

Select TV: 1961: Time Remembered (sp); 1970: David Copperfield; 1971:The Gambler (sp); 1973: Upon This Rock (sp); 1974: QB VII (ms).

MADGE EVANS

BORN: NEW YORK, NY, JULY 1, 1909.
DIED: APRIL 26, 1981.

A virtually forgotten star who had two separate periods of stardom, Madge Evans began her career as a child model for print ads for products like Fairy Soap. By the time she was five, she had already made both her Broadway and Hollywood debuts, in The Highway of Life and Sign of the Cross, respectively, billed as Baby Madge. It was under this billing that she was signed by Paramount, where she would star until 1919 in such films as Seven Sisters, The Little Duchess, The Little Patriot, Maternity, and Gates of Gladness. A few years later she returned to the screen as a teen, under her real name, in On the Banks of the Wabash and Classmates, before retreating back to the stage. After establishing herself as a legitimate adult thespian of the theater, she basically started her film career all over again with a contract with MGM, in 1931. As a result she became a star of melodramas such as Son of India, as a Boston girl romanced by Ramon Novarro; and Heartbreak, as an Austrian countess, as well as such lighter fair as Sporting Blood, a horseracing story with Clark Gable. Among her better-known credits around this time were Al Jolson's rhyming musical Hallelujah, I'm a Bum, as a woman suffering from amnesia after attempting suicide, and the all-star Dinner at Eight, carrying on a doomed affair with John Barrymore, and being completely overshadowed by the more interesting actors in the cast. After playing the scheming woman who steals Helen Hayes's husband in What Every Woman Knows, and Frank Lawton's love interest, Agnes Wickfield, in David Copperfield, MGM began to lose interest, as did Evans, who returned to the stage in 1938, never again to appear in a film. Her last release, Republic's Army Girl, wasn't so much about Evans, as the title implied, but about tanks. In 1939 she settled in Suffern, NY with her new husband, playwright Sidney Kingsley.

Screen: AS BABY MADGE: 1914: The Sign of the Cross; Shore Acres; 1915: Zaza; Alias Jimmy Valentine; The Garden of Lies; 1916: Seven Sisters; The Revolt; Seventeen; Husband and Wife; Sudden Riches; The Little Patriot; The Hidden Scar; Broken Chains/The New South; 1917: Beloved Adventuress; The Little Duchess; The Burglar; The Volunteer; Web of Desire; The Corner Grocer; The Adventures of Carol; Maternity; 1918: Gates of Gladness; Woman and Wife; The Golden Wall; The Power and the Glory; Stolen Orders; Neighbors; Wanted: A Mother; The Love Nest; 1919: Seventeen; Home Wanted; The Love Defender; 1921: Heidi.

AS MADGE EVANS; 1923: On the Banks of the Wabash; 1924: Classmates; 1931: Son of India; Sporting Blood; Guilty Hands; Heartbreak; 1932: West of Broadway; Are You Listening?; Lovers Courageous; The Greek Had a Word for Them; Huddle; Fast Life; 1933: Hell Below; Hallelujah, I'm a Bum; Made on Broadway; Dinner at Eight; The Nuisance; The Mayor of Hell; Broadway to Hollywood; Beauty for Sale; Day of Reckoning; 1934: Fugitive Lovers; The Show-Off; Stand Up and Cheer; Death on the Diamond; Grand Canary; Paris Interlude; What

Every Woman Knows; 1935: Helldorado; David Copperfield; Age of Indiscretion; Transatlantic Tunnel; Calm Yourself; Men Without Names; 1936: Moonlight Murder; Exclusive Story; Piccadilly Jim; Pennies From Heaven; 1937: Espionage; The Thirteenth Chair; 1938: Sinners in Paradise; Army Girl.

NY Stage: AS BABY MADGE: 1914: The Highway of Life; 1917: Peter Ibbetson.

AS MADGE EVANS: 1926: Daisy Mayne; 1927: The Marquise; 1928: Our Betters; 1929: Dread; 1931: Philip Goes Forth; 1938: Here Come the Clowns; 1943: The Patriots.

Select TV: 1950: Sense and Sensibility (sp); 1951: Deception (sp); 1953: Judgment (sp); 1954: Fear Is No Stranger (sp); The Magic Monday (sp).

MAURICE EVANS

BORN: DORCHESTER, ENGLAND, JUNE 3, 1901.
DIED: MARCH 12, 1989.

Most of the major acting accomplishments of Maurice Evans took place on the stage, where Shakespeare was his forte, although later audiences probably remember him best for two roles in the realm of fantasy. His initial forays into theater came via his father's own adaptations of Thomas Hardy novels. This led to professional work and his 1927 London debut. Journey's End, in 1929, marked his first stage triumph, and in 1934 he became a member of the Old Vic. The next year he came to Broadway in Romeo and Juliet, and it was there that he would continue his career with notable interpretations of Richard II, Macbeth, and Hamlet. (He toured with Hamlet extensively during World War II.) Evans had a handful of parts in British films in the early 1930s, including Raise the Roof, in the starring role of a rich man's son who winds up owning a failed theatrical company; By-Pass to Happiness, which was not about heart surgery but a highway extension; and the 1935 version of Scrooge, as a pauper. After a long break, he resumed his career on the big screen with a major role, opposite Ethel Barrymore, in MGM's Kind Lady. This was arguably his finest hour in this medium, as a scoundrel who takes charge of the old lady's life, charming his way into her good graces before his true psychopathic nature becomes evident. Back in Britain he was composer Arthur Sullivan to Robert Morley's W.S. Gilbert in The Story of Gilbert and Sullivan, minus, of course, any indication of that man's probable homosexuality. Meanwhile there were more theatrical endeavors like Dial M for Murder and the musical Tenderloin, in addition to serving as one of the producers behind television's Hallmark Hall of Fame specials, which allowed him to strut his stuff in everything from Hamlet to The Devil's Disciple. In the late 1960s he suddenly became familiar to a whole different audience, playing Elizabeth Montgomery's charming warlock dad in the hit series Bewitched. On the big screen, he made his mark in sci-fi history playing a role in which he was buried under orangutan makeup, Dr. Zaius, in the 1968 smash Planet of the Apes. That same year he was also one of the few trustworthy characters surrounding imperiled Mia Farrow in the thriller Rosemary's Baby.

Screen: 1930: White Cargo; Raise the Roof; Should a Doctor Tell?; 1932: Wedding Rehearsal; Marry Me; 1933: The Only Girl/Heart Song; 1934: The Path of Glory; 1935: Checkmate; By-Pass to Happiness; Scrooge; 1951: Kind Lady; 1953: Androcles and the Lion; The Story of Gilbert and Sullivan/The Great Gilbert and Sullivan; 1965: The War Lord; 1966: One of Our Spies Is Missing (dtv); 1967: Traitors of San Angel (nUSr); Jack of Diamonds; 1968: Planet of the Apes; Rosemary's Baby; 1970: The Body Stealers/Thin Air; Beneath the Planet of the Apes; 1973:

Terror in the Wax Museum; **1979:** The Jerk.

NY Stage: 1935: Romeo and Juliet; **1936:** St. Helena; Saint Joan; **1937:** Richard II; **1938:** Hamlet; **1939:** Henry IV; **1940:** Richard III; Twelfth Night; **1941:** Mabeth; **1945:** Hamlet; **1947:** Man and Superman; **1948:** The Linden Tree; **1949:** Man and Superman; The Browning Version; Harlequinade; **1950:** The Devil's Disciple; **1951:** The Wild Duck; **1952:** Dial M for Murder; **1956:** The Apple Cart; **1959:** Heartbreak House; **1960:** Tenderloin; **1962:** The Aspern Papers.

Select TV: 1953: Hamlet (sp); **1954:** King Richard II (sp); Macbeth (sp); **1955:** The Devil's Disciple (sp); **1956:** The Taming of the Shrew (sp); Man and Superman (sp); **1957:** Twelfth Night (sp); **1958:** Dial M for Murder (sp); **1959:** Caesar and Cleopatra (sp); No Leave for the Captain (sp); **1960:** The Tempest (sp); Macbeth (sp); **1962:** The Loves of Claire Ambler (sp); **1964–72:** Bewitched (series): **1965:** The Game (sp); **1966:** The War of the Roses (sp); Heartbreak House (sp); **1969:** U.M.C.; **1970:** Brotherhood of the Bell; **1980:** The Girl, the Gold Watch, and Everything; **1983:** Agatha Christie's A Caribbean Mystery.

TOM EWELL

(Yewell Tompkins) Born: Owensboro, KY, April 29, 1909. Died: September 12, 1994.

A deft comic performer with an oafish, everyman aura about him, Tom Ewell started acting as a teenager but found little luck at that point in his life, dropping the idea temporarily to become a salesman. Undaunted, he decided to give acting another try, winding up on Broadway in the 1934 production *They Shall Not Die*. He would stay in theatre for the next 15 years, with two very minor side trips to the movies. In 1949, following a Broadway success in *John Loves Mary*, he made his first cinematic impact in *Adam's Rib*, as the philandering husband whom Judy Holliday tries to shoot. One of his other co-stars was David Wayne, and the two of them made an engaging team in the 1951 filmization of Bill Mauldin's military cartoon creations, Willie and Joe, in *Up Front*. For the same studio, Universal, he played an ex-con dad in a piffling comedy, *Finders Keepers*; mugged along with Abbott and Costello in *Lost in Alaska*; and played Willie once again, in *Back at the Front*, with Harvey Lembeck replacing Wayne. Ewell then returned to Broadway to score his greatest success, as the tempted husband in *The Seven Year Itch*. He won the Tony Award and, more surprisingly, the role in the 1955 movie adaptation, despite the fact that director Billy Wilder wanted Walter Matthau instead. 20th Century-Fox, figuring they had enough box-office insurance by casting Marilyn Monroe as the very friendly neighbor, went with Ewell and it proved to be his shining cinematic moment. Left in New York by his vacationing wife and son and attempting in vain to get something going with Monroe, the girl upstairs, Ewell managed to make the character sweet instead of smarmy. Hoping to cash in on the huge success of the film, Fox placed him alongside pseudo-bombshells Sheree North in *The Lieutenant Wore Skirts* and Jayne Mansfield in *The Girl Can't Help It*, with less-than-thrilling results. The truth was the doughy Ewell looked more like a farmer than a leading man, so he naturally slipped into character work. He played the alcoholic composer in *Tender Is the Night*, and was the dad in the remake of *State Fair*, where at one point he sang to a hog. In the late 1970s the plumper and much older-looking actor had another brush with fame as Billy Truman, who ran the hotel in which Robert Blake lived, in the popular detective series *Baretta*.

Screen: 1940: They Knew What They Wanted; **1941:** Desert Bandit; **1949:** Adam's Rib; **1950:** An American Guerilla in the Philippines; Mr. Music; A Life of Her Own; **1951:** Up Front;

Finders Keepers; **1952:** Lost in Alaska; Back at the Front; **1955:** The Seven Year Itch; The Lieutenant Wore Skirts; **1956:** The Great American Pastime; The Girl Can't Help It; **1958:** A Nice Little Bank That Should Be Robbed; **1962:** Tender Is the Night; State Fair; **1970:** Suppose They Gave a War and Nobody Came/War Games; **1972:** To Find a Man; They Only Kill Their Masters; **1974:** The Great Gatsby; **1983:** Easy Money.

NY Stage: 1934: They Shall Not Die; Geraniums in My Window; **1935:** Let Freedom Ring; **1936:** Ethan Frome; Stage Door; **1938:** The Merchant of Yonkers; **1939:** Family Portrait; **1941:** Liberty Jones; Sunny River; **1946:** Apple of His Eye; **1947:** John Loves Mary; **1948:** Small Wonder; **1952:** The Seven Year Itch; **1957:** The Tunnel of Love; **1958:** Patate; **1960:** A Thurber Carnival; **1965:** Xmas in Las Vegas.

Select TV: 1951: Mighty Like a Rogue (sp); **1955:** Daisy Daisy (sp); **1959:** The Square Egghead (sp); The Day of the Hanging (sp); **1960–61:** The Tom Ewell Show (series); **1975:** Promise Him Anything…; **1975–78:** Baretta (series); **1979:** The Return of Mod Squad; **1981–82:** Best of the West (series); **1982:** Terror at Alcatraz.

WILLIAM EYTHE

(John Joseph Eythe) Born: Mars, PA, April 7, 1918. ed: Carnegie Tech. Died: January 26, 1957.

Hired by 20th Century-Fox after his stage success in *The Moon Is Down* (although he did not repeat his role in that particular movie adaptation), William Eythe had stolid, photographable good looks but no staying power. Originally an aspiring set designer, he took speech instruction to cure his stuttering, and it led to his switching his interest to acting. He did the revue *Lend an Ear* in stock and then started his own company, the Fox Chapel Players, in Pittsburgh. Eventually he sought work in New York, which led to *The Moon Is Down* and that offer from Fox. His first part for that studio was a good one, as the sensitive son forced by his fanatical dad to participate in a lynching, in hopes that it will make a man out of him, in the masterful *The Ox-Bow Incident*, and it didn't hurt that he followed this one with a role in another of the best movies of 1943, *The Song of Bernadette*. As star material in the making, he was cast as Anne Baxter's country boyfriend, who is sent off to an uncertain fate as a soldier in the Philippines, in *The Eve of St. Mark*, and he had top billing in one of the engrossing docudramas of the postwar period, *The House on 92nd Street*, as an FBI agent posing as a member of a spy ring in Manhattan. Little of the acclaim the film received had much to do with Eythe's contribution to it. His stay at Fox came to a close with the musical *Centennial Summer*, where his vocals were dubbed despite the fact that he had a perfectly acceptable singing voice, and *Meet Me at Dawn*, where he headed a supporting cast of British players. What few movies assignments he took after that were in "B" efforts, like *Mr. Reckless* and *Customs Agent*. On the other hand he found himself in two hits when he returned to Broadway, first with his old revue, *Lend an Ear*, and then in Cole Porter's *Out of This World*. He was only 38 when he died of acute hepatitis, following a long battle with alcoholism.

Screen: 1943: The Ox-Bow Incident; The Song of Bernadette; **1944:** The Eve of St. Mark; Wilson; Wing and a Prayer; **1945:** A Royal Scandal; The House on 92nd Street; Colonel Effingham's Raid; **1946:** Centennial Summer; **1948:** Meet Me at Dawn; Mr. Reckless; **1949:** Special Agent; **1950:** Customs Agent.

NY Stage: 1942: The Moon Is Down; **1948:** Lend an Ear (and co-prod.); **1950:** The Liar; Out of This World.

Select TV: 1951: Fog Station (sp); **1952:** The Haunted Heart (sp).

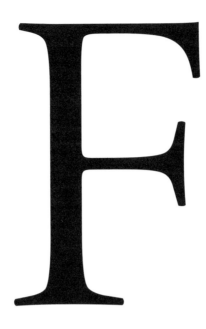

F

FABIAN

(FABIAN ANTHONY FORTE) BORN: PHILADELPHIA, PA, FEBRUARY 6, 1943.

This wavy-haired pop singer of the late 1950s seemed to take to the big screen more easily than many others in his profession, although most of his notable assignments were not starring vehicles. He had few outstanding traits as an actor, yet he was actually more adept in that field than he was as a singer, his output as a recording artist rating little mention today. Like Frankie Avalon and Bobby Rydell, he sang as a teen in Philadelphia, where he was signed to a record contract by the time he was 14. In 1959, on the heels of the top-ten hits "Turn Me Loose" and "Tiger," he made his movie debut in *Hound-Dog Man* for 20th Century-Fox, placed in a rural setting as Elvis Presley had been for his first movie. Roles supporting older stars like John Wayne, in *North to Alaska*, and James Stewart, in *Mr. Hobbs Takes a Vacation* followed, both of which were good movies and box-office successes, although it would be a stretch to say that Fabian's work in them was in any way a contributing factor. He was bumped up to leads in typical teen fare of the day, like the memorably titled *Love in a Goldfish Bowl*, and the sand-and-surf offering *Ride the Wild Surf*, but things were less than rosy financially speaking. He took another secondary role to Stewart in a less-appealing comedy, *Dear Brigitte*; got quickly bumped off near the beginning of *Ten Little Indians*; paired up with Avalon for the deadly *Fireball 5000*; and got roped into the Italian-made *Dr. Goldfoot and the Girl Bombs*, which was everything its title proclaimed it to be. As the music of the 1960s changed, interest in the vocally challenged Fabian evaporated. By 1970 he decided he would change his image and revert to his full name in order to be taken more seriously as an actor. He hoped to be accepted as a tough guy in the violent gangster melodrama *A Bullet for Pretty Boy*, but it only led to further cheap-jack productions. After the acting offers stopped coming, he teamed with Avalon and Rydell in the 1980s and toured successfully in nightclubs and casinos as the Golden Boys of Rock 'n' Roll, the trio singing their old songs to their faithful fans.

Screen: AS FABIAN: 1959: Hound-Dog Man; 1960: North to Alaska; High Time; 1961: Love in a Goldfish Bowl; 1962: Mr. Hobbs Takes a Vacation; The Longest Day; Five Weeks in a Balloon; 1964: Ride the Wild Surf; 1965: Dear Brigitte; 1966: Ten Little Indians; Fireball 500; Dr. Goldfoot and the Girl Bombs; 1967: Thunder Alley; 1968: Maryjane; The Wild Racers; 1969: The Devil's 8.
AS FABIAN FORTE: 1970: A Bullet for Pretty Boy; 1972: Lovin' Man; 1973: Little Laura and Big John; 1976: Soul Hustler/The Day the Lord Got Busted; 1978: Disco Fever; 1981: Kiss Daddy Goodbye; 1983: Get Crazy; 1996: Up Close and Personal.
Select TV: 1977: Getting Married; 1978: Katie: Portrait of a Centerfold; 1979: Crisis in Mid-Air; 1994: Runaway Daughters.

DOUGLAS FAIRBANKS

(DOUGLAS ELTON ULMAN) BORN: DENVER, COLO., MAY 23, 1883. DIED: DECEMBER 12, 1939.

It is not unreasonable to suggest that beaming, swarthy, mustachioed Douglas Fairbanks was the first movie hero to put the fun into adventure. Rather than tackle his assignments with a stoic seriousness, he had a grand time as he leapt about with astonishing athletic finesse and was smart enough to let the audiences in on his infectious spirits. Though born "Douglas Ulman," Fairbanks actually grew up with his famous last name because his mother chose to revert to the surname of her previous husband when Doug's father walked out on the family. As a young man he drifted about Europe, dropped out of Harvard, and tried his hand at various jobs, including a spell at acting with Frederick Warde's touring company, in 1900. This led to Broadway and then more touring, where he began to get leading roles in such plays as *As Ye Sow* and *The Man of the Hour*. In time he was sought by Hollywood, eventually making his debut for D.W. Griffith in *The Lamb*, in 1915, which was based on a play he had done, called *The New Henrietta*. The early part of his screen career found him playing carefree swells and playboys, men with much money and little concern for anyone else, until something in the storyline ignites a spark of human decency. These movies included *His Picture in the Papers*, *Reggie*

Mixes In, Manhattan Madness, and *The Matrimaniac*. Soon he had become popular and wealthy enough to establish his own production company, releasing *In Again, Out Again*, in 1917, as its maiden effort. During this period he tried his hand first at screenwriting, starting with *Down to Earth* and *The Man From Painted Post*, and then at directing, with *Arizona*, a western that was not considered one of his better works.

His exuberant and spirited screen persona placed Fairbanks at the top of his profession, and he joined up with three of the other giants of the day, his real-life love interest Mary Pickford, Charlie Chaplin, and Griffith, to establish their own distribution company in 1919. The result, of course, was United Artists, which gave these four creative talents freedom and, eventually, the ability to become involved in all kinds of independent productions. Fairbanks was the first of the four founders to give his new organization something to distribute, thereby making *His Majesty, the American* the very first United Artist release. The film was also the premiere attraction at what was at that time the world's largest movie theater, the Capitol, in New York. He played a smiling (of course) American who discovers he is heir to the throne of a European kingdom. He also served as producer and writer, working under the pseudonym Elton Banks (in time this credit would change to Elton Thomas). The next vehicle marked the directorial debut of Victor Fleming, *When the Clouds Roll By*, a critical look at psychiatry, featuring a dream sequence that had the star being pursued by giant servings of food!

1920 was a banner year for Fairbanks. There was his marriage to Mary Pickford, the first great storybook union of two movie legends, the couple being dubbed the King and Queen of Hollywood. Then came his opportunity to show his physicality as a swashbuckler with *The Mark of Zorro*. This film began the spectacular series of costume adventures for which he would become best known. It was only natural that he would play D'Artagnan in *The Three Musketeers*, as well as the title role in *Robin Hood*. Both films feature Fairbanks in his prime and were profitable ventures for United Artists. *Robin Hood* also had the distinction of utilizing the largest, most spectacular sets ever built for a movie up to that time. This was followed by the movie that is probably most closely associated with him, *The Thief of Baghdad*, another triumphant production with the star bounding about the imaginatively designed sets in headband, earring, and pajama bottoms with a mad enthusiasm that is captivating enough to overcome the plot's more plodding moments.

His next films included an inevitable sequel, *Don Q: Son of Zorro*, the very first full-length two-tone Technicolor feature; *The Black Pirate*, with its famous stunt that had Fairbanks descending down a ship's sail by ripping it with his sword; *The Gaucho*, a Mexican twist on Robin Hood that featured a brief appearance by Pickford; and *The Iron Mask*, a silent film in which he reprised D'Artagnan and which did well amid the talkie-dominated year of 1929. The film itself, in fact, had a prologue and epilogue spoken by Fairbanks. That same year, to launch his full-fledged debut in sound, he and Pickford co-starred at last, in *The Taming of the Shrew*. The movie was profitable but seemed ill advised since their reading of Shakespeare only emphasized how less-than-appealing both their speaking voices were. There was also trouble off screen in their rapidly deteriorating marriage, which would come to an end in 1935. Sound was not kind to Fairbanks, who returned to modern dress for the first time since *The Nut*, back in 1921, with *Reaching for the Moon*, playing a girl-shy millionaire in this weak comedy that had nothing to do with his 1917 film of the same name. After that he co-directed and hosted a documentary travelogue, *Around the World in 80 Minutes*. *Mr. Robinson Crusoe* placed him on a tropical isle and required him to

solo it for a hefty portion of the film, and *The Private Life of Don Juan* found him as a retired rogue trying to prove his true existence after staging his own funeral. The latter was made in Britain for Alexander Korda and was a critical and box-office disaster. Shortly after marrying Lady Sylvia Ashley in 1936, Fairbanks announced his retirement from acting and was on the brink of launching a new production company when he died of a heart attack in 1939. His son from his first marriage (to Betty Sully), Douglas Fairbanks, Jr., had already started his own career, and, although he would dabble from time to time in swashbuckling roles, his father's act was a tough one to follow.

Screen: 1915: The Lamb; Double Trouble; 1916: His Picture in the Papers; The Habit of Happiness; The Good Bad Man; Reggie Mixes In; Flirting With Fate; The Half-Breed; The Mystery of the Leaping Fish; Manhattan Madness; American Aristocracy; The Matrimaniac; The Americano; 1917 (and producer from this point on unless otherwise noted): In Again, Out Again; Wild and Wooly; Down to Earth (and wr.); The Man From Painted Post (and wr.); Reaching for the Moon; 1918: A Modern Musketeer; Headin' South; Mr. Fix-It; Say! Young Fellow; Bound in Morocco; He Comes Up Smiling; Arizona (and dir.; wr.); 1919: The Knickerbocker Buckaroo (and wr.); His Majesty the American (and co-wr. **AS ELTON BANKS**); When the Clouds Roll By (and co-wr.) The Mollycoddle (and co-wr.); 1920: The Mark of Zorro (and co-wr. **AS ELTON THOMAS**); 1921: The Nut; The Three Musketeers; 1922: Robin Hood (and wr. **AS ELTON THOMAS**); 1924: The Thief of Baghdad (and co-wr. **AS ELTON THOMAS**); 1925: Don Q — Son of Zorro; 1926: The Black Pirate (and co-wr. **AS ELTON THOMAS**); 1927: A Kiss from Mary Pickford (cameo only); The Gaucho (and co-wr. **AS ELTON THOMAS**); 1928: Show People (cameo only); 1929: The Iron Mask (and wr. **AS ELTON THOMAS**); The Taming of the Shrew; 1930: Reaching for the Moon (actor only); Around the World in 80 Minutes (and co-dir.); 1932: Mr. Robinson Crusoe (and co-wr. **AS ELTON THOMAS**); 1934: The Private Life of Don Juan (actor only).

NY Stage: 1902: Her Lord and Master; A Rose o' Plymouth-Town; 1904: The Pit; Two Little Sailor Boys; 1905: Fantana; A Case of Frenzied Finance; As Ye Sow; 1906: Clothes; The Man of the Hour; 1908: All for a Girl; A Gentleman from Mississippi; 1910: The Cub; 1911: The Lights o' London; A Gentleman of Leisure; 1912: Hawthorne of the USA; 1913: The New Henrietta; 1914: He Comes Up Smiling; The Show Shop.

DOUGLAS FAIRBANKS, JR.

BORN: NEW YORK, NY, DECEMBER 9, 1909.
DIED: MAY 7, 2000.

Carrying around the same name as a famous father can either hamper or help a career, and for Douglas Fairbanks, Jr. it succeeded in doing both. He did, indeed, become very much a star in his own right, but since his old man was one of the pioneering legends of the silver screen, he always had an also-ran stigma to deal with. Following his parents' divorce, he grew up with his mother. His first involvement with the film world came via Paramount's blatant attempt to cash in on his father's name by putting the teenager into an adventure story, *Stephen Steps Out*, in 1923. Its failure put him right back to square one, but he had a desire to stay in the business and continued to do roles of varying sizes, the most notable being the boyfriend of Stella's daughter (Lois Moran) in the 1925 version of *Stella Dallas*, and the cub reporter in *The Power of the Press*, directed by a not-yet-famous Frank Capra. Even if he wasn't making more than a marginal impact on the big screen, he was becoming better known on the social scene, where his name was linked with Joan Crawford's. They married in 1928 and appeared together in *Our Modern Maidens*, which included a sequence in which young Fairbanks did an imitation of his dad. Things began to get better in 1930. Signed to a long-term contract with Warner Bros., he was featured in three of their major releases that year: *The Dawn Patrol*, an anti-war aerial drama directed by Howard Hawks; *Outward Bound*, in which he awkwardly played the key role of the young suicide who decides he wants a second chance after experiencing the afterlife; and best of all, *Little Caesar*, as a gigolo, holding his own against the powerhouse Edward G. Robinson.

He was steadily employed at Warner Bros. for the next three years. His jobs there included the curious assignment of taking the lead in French versions of two Joe E. Brown movies; *Union Depot*, portraying a bum who finds some money; *It's Tough to Be Famous*, satirizing the process of media adulation; and *Parachute Jumper*, once again facing poverty and getting involved with smuggling. His best-known role of this period, however, was at RKO, where he portrayed the young playwright in *Morning Glory*, opposite Katharine Hepburn in her Oscar-winning performance. A battle with Warner Bros. lost him his contract, while constant battles with Crawford cost them their marriage (in 1933), so he left America temporarily behind and traveled to England with his father with whom he had at last formed a bond. Junior took the role of the Czar in the Elisabeth Bergner version of *Catherine the Great*, stayed in London for some stage work, and then decided to form his own production company there. Only the first of his efforts, *The Amateur Gentleman*, had anything close to success (there was also one in which he did not appear, *Crime Over London*), so he returned to the U.S. in 1937.

Fortunately some of his best roles were to come. For Selznick he was an appropriately nasty Rupert of Hentzau in one of the era's most enjoyable adventures, *The Prisoner of Zenda*, and he played the son of a family of confidence tricksters in the screwball comedy *The Young in Heart*. At RKO, along with Victor McLaglen and Cary Grant, he made up the colorful trio of soldiers in George Stevens's grand *Gunga Din*, which continues to be his most widely seen performance. He had far less box-office success with some minor action films: *Rulers of the Sea*, a Scottish tale of the first steamship; *Green Hell*, notable only because it was directed by the once-esteemed James Whale; and *Safari*, a jungle romance with Madeline Carroll. Once again he took a crack at producing, with *Angels Over Broadway*, doing a good job playing a debonair gambler in this multi-character drama by Ben Hecht. He then had a dual role in *The Corsican Brothers*, a swashbuckler in the tradition of the movies of you-know-who.

With the outbreak of World War II, Fairbanks took a break from his film career, attaining the impressive military rank of Lieutenant Commander, serving as Presidential envoy to several South American nations, and helping to organize the British War Relief. After the war ended, he romped again, in *Sinbad the Sailor*, a solid box-office hit, and wrote the scripts for two other vehicles, *Exile* and *The Fighting O'Flynn*. His love affair with England brought him an honorary knighthood in 1949, for helping to promote good relations between that country and the U.S. It was in England that he made *State Secret/The Great Manhunt*, an acclaimed thriller, and *Mr. Drake's Duck*, a light comedy about a duck that lays radioactive eggs. It was his last official leading role in a theatrically released feature for 30 years. During this period he became better known as one of London's leading socialites and also sat in with the U.S. delegation at SEATO. In the 1950s he executive produced the feature *Moment of Danger/Malaga*, and produced, hosted and occasionally acted in the anthology television series *Douglas Fairbanks, Jr. Presents*.

(Several episodes of the show were edited together into theatrical features for distribution in England under these titles: *The Genie, Three's Company, Destination Milan, Forever My Heart*, and *The Last Moment*.) In 1981, he returned one last time to the big screen, teamed with some other cinematic old-timers, including Fred Astaire, for the thriller *Ghost Story*, still looking as suave as ever. He published two autobiographies, *Salad Days* (1988) and *A Hell of a War* (1993), and co-authored *The Fairbanks Album* (1975).

Screen: 1923: Stephen Steps Out; 1925: The Air Mail; Wild Horse Mesa; Stella Dallas; 1926: Padlocked; Broken Hearts of Hollywood; Man-Bait; 1927: A Texas Steer; Women Love Diamonds; Is Zat So?; 1928: Dead Man's Curve; Modern Mothers; The Toilers; The Power of the Press; The Barker; A Woman of Affairs; 1929: The Jazz Age; Fast Life; Our Modern Maidens; The Careless Age; The Show of Shows; The Forward Pass; 1930: Party Girl; The Dawn Patrol; Loose Ankles; Little Accident; The Way of All Men; Outward Bound; One Night at Susie's; Little Caesar; 1931: L'Aviateur (nUSr); Chances; I Like Your Nerve; L'Athlete Incomplet (nUSr); 1932: Union Depot; It's Tough to Be Famous; Love Is a Racket; Scarlet Dawn; 1933: Parachute Jumper; Morning Glory; The Life of Jimmy Dolan; The Narrow Corner; Captured!; 1934: Catherine the Great; Success at Any Price; 1935: Mimi; Man of the Moment; 1936: The Amateur Gentleman (and prod.); Accused (and prod.); 1937: Jump for Glory/When Thief Meets Thief (and prod.); The Prisoner of Zenda; 1938: Joy of Living; Having Wonderful Time; The Rage of Paris; The Young in Heart; 1939: Gunga Din; The Sun Never Sets; Rulers of the Sea; 1940: Green Hell; Safari; Angels Over Broadway (and assoc. prod.); 1941: The Corsican Brothers; 1947: Sinbad the Sailor; The Exile (and wr.; prod.); 1948: That Lady in Ermine; 1949: The Fighting O'Flynn (and co-wr.; prod.); 1950: State Secret/The Great Manhunt; 1951: Mr. Drake's Duck; 1957: Chase a Crooked Shadow (and exec. prod.); 1967: The Funniest Man in the World (narrator); Red and Blue; 1981: Ghost Story; 1985: George Stevens: A Filmmaker's Journey.
Select TV: 1953–57: Douglas Fairbanks, Jr. Presents (series; and prod.); 1972: The Crooked Hearts; 1980: The Hostage Tower; 1986: Strong Medicine.

PETER FALK

BORN: NEW YORK, NY, SEPTEMBER 16, 1927.
ED: SYRACUSE UNIV.

It was hard not to associate Peter Falk with the world of cops and robbers. This small, tough, charismatic actor with the garbled voice and distinctive glass eye started out excelling at bad guys both serious and comical before switching sides, becoming one of the small screen's most celebrated detectives. His first job came as an efficiency expert for the Connecticut Budget Bureau until he sought greater fulfillment in the world of acting, studying under Eva LaGalliene and Sanford Meisner. This led to a whole slew of Off Broadway work, starting in 1956 with *Don Juan* and a revival of *The Iceman Cometh*. Soon he was busy in television and films as well, making his debut in the latter medium in the 1958 conservation drama *Wind Across the Everglades*. After that he had a larger role, as the sick leader of a beatnik gang, serving a hamburger full of broken glass to a kid, in the Canadian-made *The Bloody Brood*. What really established him were back-to-back Oscar nominations, contrasting his dramatic and comical sides: *Murder, Inc.*, in 1960, found him as that organization's foremost gangster, Abe Reles, while *Pocketful of Miracles*, in 1961, featured him as an affable Damon Runyon hood, standing out amid an impressive supporting cast. Shortly after these he won his first Emmy Award, for his performance on an episode of *The Dick Powell Show*, entitled "The Price of Tomatoes." Back on movie screens he had one of his biggest roles to date, as the chief of police in the poorly received adaptation of Jean Genet's *The Balcony*. He then went back to comedy for *It's a Mad Mad Mad Mad World*, showing up late in the story as a greedy cabbie; *Robin and the 7 Hoods*, another fun turn as a lovable gangster, this time getting his own song, "All for One; " and *The Great Race*, well teamed with Jack Lemmon, as his none-too-bright henchman. Less successfully he and Lemmon were back together for the abrasive film version of the oddball play *Luv*.

He found himself alongside John Cassavetes in an Italian-made cheapie *Machine Gun McCain*, which led to his being featured in a couple of that man's off-beat, self-indulgent film projects, *Husbands* and *A Woman Under the Influence*, with Falk showing a more serious side than most of his other work had allowed. In the former, Falk, Cassavetes and Ben Gazzara improvised their way through a drunken night of middle-aged angst, while the latter found him trying to deal with the emotional breakdown of wife Gena Rowlands. In between the two came *Columbo*, a rotating series under the *NBC Sunday Mystery Movie* umbrella, which gave Falk undreamed-of fame. Playing the gruff, raincoat-clad, cigar-chomping private detective, whose first name was never uttered, he became one of the medium's indelible icons and won three Emmy Awards, in 1972, 1975, and 1976. When he brought the show back in the late 1980s, first as a series and then as an occasional telefilm, he found himself with yet another Emmy, in 1990.

The show helped revitalize his movie career as well. For Neil Simon he did a funny send-up of Bogart in the all-star spoof *Murder by Death*, then played a less-impressive variation on it for the limp follow-up, *The Cheap Detective*. Teamed marvelously with Alan Arkin, he was a scatterbrained father-in-law-to-be, presumably working on a case for the CIA, in the hit *The In-Laws*, a pairing so right that the two looked for years for a follow-up project, unwisely adding Cassavetes to the mix for a resulting disaster, *Big Trouble*. Audiences were also not interested in Falk as the small-time hood teamed with Cassavetes in Elaine May's troubled *Mikey and Nicky*, or as the mastermind behind the famed Boston robbery in a somber recreation of *The Brink's Job*; and certainly not as the manager of a team of lady wrestlers in *…All the Marbles*. Under tons of makeup, he was a crook in *Happy New Year* and a feisty septuagenarian in *Roommates*. He bared his behind in the flaky caper *In the Spirit* and tried his best to instill some life into poor comedies like *Vibes, Cookie, Tune in Tomorrow …*, and *Corky Romano*. In most of these instances, his sly presence was a joy and a relief to have around.

Screen: 1958: Wind Across the Everglades; 1959: The Bloody Brood; 1960: Pretty Boy Floyd; The Secret of the Purple Reef; Murder, Inc.; 1961: Pocketful of Miracles; 1962: Pressure Point; 1963: The Balcony; It's a Mad Mad Mad Mad World; 1964: Robin and the 7 Hoods; 1965: Italiano Brava Gente/Attack and Retreat; The Great Race; 1966: Penelope; 1967: Luv; 1968: Anzio; 1969: Castle Keep; 1970: Operation Snafu/Situation Normal All Fouled Up; Machine Gun McCain; Husbands; 1974: A Woman Under the Influence 1976: Murder by Death; Mikey and Nicky; 1978: The Cheap Detective; The Brink's Job; 1979: Opening Night (filmed 1977); The In-Laws; 1981: The Great Muppet Caper; …All the Marbles/The California Dolls; 1986: Big Trouble; 1987: Happy New Year; The Princess Bride; 1988: Wings of Desire; Vibes; 1989: Cookie; 1990: In the Spirit; Tune in Tomorrow…; 1992: The Player; 1993: Faraway So Close!; 1995: Roommates; Cops 'n' Roberts (nUSr); 2000: Enemies of Laughter (nUSr); 3 Days of Rain (nUSr); 2001: Lakeboat; Made;

Corky Romano; 2002: Undisputed.

NY Stage: 1956: Don Juan (ob); The Iceman Cometh (ob); Saint Joan (ob); Diary of a Scoundrel (ob); 1957: The Lady's Not for Burning (ob); Purple Dust (ob); 1958: Comic Strip (ob); Bonds of Interest (ob); 1964: The Passion of Josef D; 1971: The Prisoner of Second Avenue; 1998: Mr. Peters' Connections (ob).

Select TV: 1957: The Mother Bit (sp); Rudy (sp); 1958: The Power and the Glory (sp); The Emperor's Clothes (sp); 1962: The Price of Tomatoes (sp); 1965–66: The Trials of O'Brien (series); 1966: Brigadoon (sp); Dear Deductible (sp); 1968: A Hatful of Rain (sp); Prescription Murder; 1971: A Step Out of Line; Ransom for a Dead Man; 1971–77: Columbo (series); 1976: Griffith and Phoenix: A Love Story; 1989–90: Columbo (series; and exec. prod.); 1990: Columbo Goes to College; 1991: Caution: Murder Can Be Hazardous to Your Health; Columbo and the Murder of a Rock Star; Death Hits the Jackpot; 1992: Columbo: No Time to Die; Columbo: A Bird in the Hand (and exec. prod.); 1993: Columbo: It's All in the Game (and wr.; exec. prod.); 1994: Columbo: Butterfly in Shades of Grey (and exec. prod.); Columbo: Undercover; 1995: Columbo: Strange Bedfellows (and exec. prod.); 1996: Columbo: A Trace of Murder; 1997: Pronto; The Sunshine Boys; 1998: Columbo: Ashes to Ashes; Vig/Money Kings; 2000: A Storm in Summer; Columbo: Murder With Too Many Notes; 2001: A Town Without Christmas; 2002: Columbo: Murder by Suicide; Columbo: The Man Who Murdered Himself; The Lost World.

FRANCES FARMER
BORN: SEATTLE, WA, SEPTEMBER 19, 1913.
ED: UNIV. OF WA. DIED: AUGUST 1, 1970.

There is probably no better example of a star whose turbulent off-screen life has given them more lasting fame than their film work than Frances Farmer. The attractive actress had talent and was determined to prove it, but she simply would not play Hollywood games and went down in flames as a result. While in college she took an interest in drama, which led her to New York, where she hoped to join the Group Theatre. Instead a friend got her a test with Paramount that resulted in starring roles in a pair of "B's," *Too Many Parents*, as a receptionist at a boys' military school, and *Border Flight*, which paired her with Robert Cummings. She moved into an "A" production, playing leading lady to Bing Crosby in *Rhythm on the Range*, but when Crosby wasn't on screen, his other female co-star, Martha Raye, was coaxing all the attention her way. Therefore her big break came elsewhere when Goldwyn borrowed her for a dual role in the logging epic *Come and Get It*, first playing a saloon singer and then, in the latter half of the story, her daughter. It was her best chance on screen and her most notable motion picture credit.

Back at her home lot, she complained about the work she was being given: *Exclusive*, as Charles Ruggles's daughter, who takes a job at a rival paper, and *Ebb Tide*, a color drama in which she took a back seat to Barry Fitzgerald and Oscar Homolka. She retreated to New York, where at last she got to join the Group Theatre, participating in the original 1937 production of Clifford Odets's *Golden Boy*. Returning to Hollywood, she starred with her then-husband Leif Erickson in yet another unremarkable production, *Ride a Crooked Mile*, as the niece of Cossack Akim Tamiroff. More "B" films followed including *World Premiere*, with a declining John Barrymore, and the thriller *Among the Living*, which belonged to Albert Dekker in a dual role. It was around this time that she was arrested for drunken driving; her temper and physical resistance landed her in jail. In 1944 she was placed in a sanitarium. The horrors she suffered in various mental hospitals, culminating in a partial lobotomy, are well documented in various books, including her own memoir, *Will There Really Be a Morning?* Following her release she took a job as a receptionist and then made an embarrassing appearance on the patronizing *This Is Your Life* series, where her deteriorated condition was hard to overlook. There was one more movie role, in the cheap teen drama *The Party Crashers*, released, ironically, by the studio she had battled so fervently with in the past, Paramount. Her memoirs were published posthumously in 1972, while movie audiences got a glimpse into her tragic life via the 1982 biopic *Frances*, starring Jessica Lange.

Screen: 1936: Too Many Parents; Border Flight; Rhythm on the Range; Come and Get It; **1937:** The Toast of New York; Exclusive; Ebb Tide; **1938:** Ride a Crooked Mile; **1940:** South of Pago Pago; Flowing Gold; **1941:** World Premiere; Badlands of Dakota; Among the Living; **1942:** Son of Fury; **1958:** The Party Crashers.

NY Stage: 1937: Golden Boy.

Select TV: 1958: Reunion (sp).

CHARLES FARRELL

BORN: EAST WALPOLE, MA, AUGUST 9, 1901.
ED: BOSTON UNIV. DIED: MAY 6, 1990.

The name of Charles Farrell is inevitably linked to his co-star of no less than a dozen films, Janet Gaynor. From the late silent era into the early talkies, they were the movies' favorite couple, though more credit has always been given to her than to him for their popularity. Farrell had come to films in 1923, starting as an extra, in *The Cheat*. He continued in this capacity for the next few years until he moved into romantic leads with *Wings of Youth*, and one of the big adventures of 1928, *Old Ironsides*. One year earlier he found true stardom playing Ms. Gaynor's love interest, sewer worker Chico, in one of the most famous of all of the slushy melodramas of the silent era, *7th Heaven*. They were quickly reteamed for *Street Angel*, with Farrell as the sensitive painter Gaynor meets while on the run from the law. They had become such a solid success for their studio that Fox, figuring audiences would accept them in anything, decided to make their all-talking debut a musical. The result, *Sunnyside Up*, was just another creaky songfest and Farrell proved to be a washout as a singer, though he and Gaynor got to introduce the hit "If I Had a Talking Picture of You." Away from Gaynor, Farrell was having less success in such pictures as *Liliom*, which was *Carousel* without the music, and *The Princess and the Plumber*, which gave him Maureen O'Sullivan as a co-star. Things were rosier at the box office with Gaynor on hand for the musicals *High Society Blues* and *Delicious* (where Farrell was not asked to sing any of the Gershwin numbers), and in the heavier dramas, *The Man Who Came Back*, in which he became a drunk, and *Tess of the Storm Country*.

Shortly after the duo played newlyweds in *The First Year*, Farrell dissolved his contract with Fox. There was one more pairing with Gaynor, in *Change of Heart*, in 1934, and then he came back to the studio under its new banner, 20th Century-Fox, to play Shirley Temple's dad in *Just Around the Corner*, in 1938. The fact was that Farrell was a somewhat ineffectual performer and wasn't much in demand once the days of working with Gaynor had come to a close. Choosing temporary retirement during the early 1940s, he wound up making a great deal more money for himself running the Palm Springs Racquet Club than he might have had he continued in movies. He did return to

acting, on television in the 1950s, in one of the most dated of all sitcoms of that era, *My Little Margie*. During that time he also served as mayor of Palm Springs. He was married to actress Virginia Valli from 1932 until her death in 1968.

Screen: 1923: The Cheat; Rosita; The Hunchback of Notre Dame; The Ten Commandments; **1925:** The Love Hour; The Freshman; Wings of Youth; Clash of the Wolves; **1926:** Old Ironsides; Sandy; A Trip to Chinatown; **1926:** The Rough Riders; **1927:** 7th Heaven; **1928:** Street Angel; The Red Dance; The River; Fazil; **1929:** City Girl; Sunnyside Up; Lucky Star; **1930:** Happy Days; Liliom; The Princess and the Plumber; High Society Blues; **1931:** The Man Who Came Back; Body and Soul; Heart Break; Merely Mary Ann; Delicious; **1932:** After Tomorrow; Tess of the Storm Country; The First Year; Wild Girl; **1933:** Girl Without a Room; Aggie Appleby: Maker of Men; The Big Shakedown; **1934:** Change of Heart; Falling in Love/Trouble Ahead; **1935:** Fighting Youth; Forbidden Heaven; **1936:** The Flying Doctor; **1937:** Moonlight Sonata; Midnight Menace/Bombs Over London; **1938:** Flight to Fame; Just Around the Corner; Tail Spin; **1941:** The Deadly Game.

Select TV: 1952–55: My Little Margie (series); **1956:** The Charlie Farrell Show (series).

GLENDA FARRELL

BORN: ENID, OK, JUNE 30, 1904.
DIED: MAY 1, 1971.

Warner Bros. certainly knew how to showcase wisecracking dames, and squinty-eyed Glenda Farrell was among the best of the lot. A former member of various stock companies, she came to Broadway in 1929, in *Skidding*. That same year she made her motion picture debut, in a small part in *Lucky Boy*, for Tiffany Pictures. She arrived at Warners in 1930 to appear in one of their most enduring productions of that period, *Little Caesar*, as a gangster's moll. Two years later she was in another top film, *I Am a Fugitive From a Chain Gang*, in which she turned ex-con Paul Muni over to the law when he tried to escape her clutches. Soon the sassy blonde was all over the Warners lot, in such productions as *Mystery of the Wax Museum*, as a tart-tongued reporter; *Mary Stevens, M.D.* as a nurse; and *Go Into Your Dance* as Al Jolson's sister. She was teamed with the equally acerbic Joan Blondell in *Kansas City Princess*, as manicurists involved with gangsters, and *We're in the Money*, as process servers. Finally, after years of solid work in mostly supporting or secondary roles, Farrell was allowed by the studio to carry a vehicle of her own, *Smart Blonde*, playing intrepid ace reporter Torchy Blane. The 1936 release was successful enough to rate seven sequels, starting with *Fly-Away Baby*, then continuing with *The Adventurous Blonde*, *Blondes at Work*, *Torchy Gets Her Man*, *Torchy Blane in Chinatown*, and finally, at least as far as Farrell was concerned, *Torchy Runs for Mayor*. A much different personality, Jane Wyman, took over the part for the last installment, *Torchy Plays With Dynamite*, in 1939. Farrell left Warners that same year. Aside from some secondary parts in occasional "A's" like *The Talk of the Town* and *Johnny Eager*, she resigned herself to such programmers as *A Night for Crime*, *Ever Since Venus*, and *Mary Lou*, most of these made for Columbia. The 1950s and 1960s found her working a great deal on TV, including a guest appearance on *Ben Casey* that won her an Emmy Award in 1962. Returning infrequently to the big screen, audiences saw a much more subdued persona (as Kim Novak's mother in *Middle of the Night*, Jerry Lewis's supervisor in *The Disorderly Orderly*, and Elvis Presley's mom in *Kissin' Cousins*) than they had seen in the old days.

Screen: 1929: Lucky Boy; 1930: Little Caesar; 1932: Scandal for Sale; Life Begins; I Am a Fugitive From a Chain Gang; Three on a Match; The Match King; 1933: Grand Slam; Mystery of the Wax Museum; Girl Missing; The Keyhole; Gambling Ship; Lady for a Day; Mary Stevens, M.D.; Bureau of Missing Persons; Havana Widows; Central Airport; Man's Castle; 1934: I've Got Your Number; The Big Shakedown; Heat Lightning; Hi, Nellie!; Dark Hazard; Merry Wives of Reno; The Personality Kid; Kansas City Princess; The Secret Bride; 1935: Gold Diggers of 1935; Traveling Saleslady; Little Big Shot; Go Into Your Dance; In Caliente; We're in the Money; Miss Pacific Fleet; 1936: Snowed Under; The Law in Her Hands; Nobody's Fool; High Tension; Gold Diggers of 1937; Smart Blonde; Here Comes Carter; 1937: Fly-Away Baby; Dance, Charlie, Dance; You Live and Learn; Breakfast for Two; The Adventurous Blonde; Hollywood Hotel; 1938: Blondes at Work; Stolen Heaven; The Road to Reno; Prison Break; Torchy Gets Her Man; Exposed; 1939: Torchy Blane in Chinatown; Torchy Runs for Mayor; 1942: Johnny Eager; Twin Beds; The Talk of the Town; A Night for Crime; 1943: Klondike Kate; City Without Men; 1944: Ever Since Venus; 1947: Heading for Heaven; Mary Lou; 1948: I Love Trouble; Lulu Belle; 1952: Apache War Smoke; 1953: Girls in the Night; 1954: Secret of the Incas; Susan Slept Here; 1955: The Girl in the Red Velvet Swing; 1959: Middle of the Night; 1964: The Disorderly Orderly; Kissin' Cousins; 1968: Tiger by the Tail.

NY Stage: 1929: Skidding; Divided Honors; 1930: Recaptured; Love, Honor and Betray; A Month in the Country; On the Spot; 1932: Life Begins; 1940: Separate Rooms; 1945: The Overtons; 1949: Mrs. Gbbons' Boys; 1954: Home Is the Hero; 1959: Masquerade; 1968: 40 Carats.

Select TV: 1951: Ruggles of Red Gap (sp); 1955: Miss Turner's Decision (sp); The Expendable House (sp); 1957: The Old Ticker (sp); 1958: The Other Place (sp); The Edge of Truth (sp); 1959: Night Club (sp); The Killers (sp); The Bells of St. Mary's (sp); 1960: Queen of the Orange Bowl (sp); A Palm Tree in a Rose Garden (sp); 1961: A String of Beads (sp); Summer Rhapsody (sp); 1963: Moment of Rage (sp).

ALICE FAYE

(ALICE JEANNE LEPPERT) BORN: NEW YORK, NY, MAY 4, 1912. DIED: MAY 9, 1998.

Her name is unquestionably linked with 20th Century-Fox, where, in the late 1930s and early 1940s, she was their reigning singing star until Bette Grable came along and pushed her out of the spotlight. If comparisons need to be made, Alice Faye was a better vocalist than Grable, though not all that much better an actress. There is something hard about her looks that make her seem less attractive today than she was meant to be, but there was also something tough about her personality that makes her much easier to take now than many of the more gooey warbling ingénues of that time. As a teen she joined the Chester Hale Dance Group, which led to chorus work in the 11th Broadway edition of George White's Scandals. Its star, Rudy Vallee, liked her voice enough to give her a regular spot on his radio show. He was also instrumental in getting her cast as his leading lady in the 1935 film version of George White's Scandals, which was made by Fox. As a result of this, she was signed to a contract with the studio and put in a dramatic movie, Now I'll Tell, though she was safely cast as a cabaret singer. Ironically, her most notable contribution during her first few years in Hollywood occurred not at Fox but while on loan to Paramount, where she introduced the hit "I Feel a Song Coming On" in the musical Every Night at

Eight.

Back at the home lot, things began to brighten when she and Jack Hayley teamed as a couple of vaudevillians in the Shirley Temple opus Poor Little Rich Girl, where they helped cut back some of the Temple goo. She was saddled with the Ritz Brothers for Sing, Baby, Sing and was back with Temple again for Stowaway. Then she was paired with Dick Powell for another hit, On the Avenue, where she sang a batch of Irving Berlin tunes, including "I've Got My Love to Keep Me Warm." The music was a relief from the bird-brained backstage plot, which was also true for both Wake Up and Live, a radio tale that included columnist Walter Winchell among the cast, and You Can't Have Everything, a particularly rotten concoction that had her playing the great-granddaughter of Edgar Allen Poe! All three of these were among the year's top-grossing releases. 1938 was a banner year for Faye, finding her in two of the biggest hits of her career, and the films which most readily come to mind in conjunction with her name: In Old Chicago, an entertaining period musical, climaxed by a stunning recreation of the great fire, and her own personal favorite, Alexander's Ragtime Band, which once again had her selling a slew of Berlin songs, including the title tune.

Now one of the top stars on the lot, she kept giving the fans what they wanted, with occasional, less-successful forays into straight drama like Tail Spin, playing an aviatrix, and Barricade, as a singer involved in a murder rap. More to the liking of audiences of the time were Rose of Washington Square, which paralleled the life of Fanny Brice so closely that that lady sued, and Hollywood Cavalcade, a Technicolor look at silent movies that at one point had her doing slapstick with the Keystone Kops, before the plot spiraled downward into the usual show business clichés. Further moneymakers followed with Little Old New York, not a musical but something akin to the biography of steamboat inventor Robert Fulton, Hollywood-style; Lillian Russell, another superficial biopic, about the turn-of-the-century stage performer; and Tin Pan Alley, a historical occasion of sorts because her co-star was Betty Grable, on her way up. So many of Faye's films had been set nostalgically in the past, but Fox decided it was time to place her back in the present, starring her in some colorful, gaudy extravaganzas which the studio became notorious for in the 1940s. She could be found spending That Night in Rio, a remake of Folies Bergere, in which a great deal of the spotlight was taken from her by the irrepressible Carmen Miranda and Don Ameche in a dual role; and selling a tune or two on The Great American Broadcast, which was also stolen from her, this time by the dynamic Nicholas Brothers. Miranda was back again for Week-end in Havana, in which Faye was cast as a Macy's shopgirl who is given the title holiday as a gift. These were followed by two of her biggest successes, another period piece, Hello, Frisco, Hello (notable only because it gave her one of her signature numbers, the Oscar-winning "You'll Never Know"), and perhaps the epitome of trashy Fox musicals of the wartime era, The Gang's All Here, yet again taking a back seat to Miranda at her campiest.

Although she was at a peak of sorts, she decided to back off from this kind of fluff to try something different with Fallen Angel, as a wealthy woman married to fortune hunter Dana Andrews. Supposedly her part had been shortened by the front office, and this gave her another reason to put an end to her relationship with the studio. She had married bandleader Phil Harris in 1941, following a brief union (1937–40) with singer Tony Martin, and she wanted to settle down and raise her children. In 1945 she retired from pictures, although she and her husband could be heard on radio and later seen sporadically on television. After a 17-year break from the big screen, her old studio asked her back to play the Fay Bainter role in the 1962 remake of State Fair, singing one of the new numbers supplied by Richard Rodgers, "Never Say No." Although this did not indicate that she was looking for steady employment, there were a few more assignments over the years, including a flop Broadway revival of *Good News*, and the quickly forgotten children's movie, *The Magic of Lassie*, which marked the last time she sang on screen. With that she once again settled into happy retirement with Harris, who died in 1995.

Screen: 1934: George White's Scandals; Now I'll Tell; She Learned About Sailors; 365 Nights in Hollywood; 1935: George White's 1935 Scandals; Every Night at Eight; Music Is Magic; King of Burlesque; 1936: Poor Little Rich Girl; Sing, Baby, Sing; Stowaway; 1937: On the Avenue; Wake Up and Live; You Can't Have Everything; You're a Sweetheart; In Old Chicago; 1938: Sally, Irene and Mary; Alexander's Ragtime Band; 1939: Tail Spin; Rose of Washington Square; Hollywood Cavalcade; Barricade; 1940: Little Old New York; Lillian Russell; Tin Pan Alley; 1941: That Night in Rio; The Great American Broadcast; Week-end in Havana; 1943: Hello, Frisco, Hello; The Gang's All Here; 1944: Four Jills in a Jeep; 1945: Fallen Angel; 1962: State Fair; 1976: Won Ton Ton, the Dog Who Saved Hollywood; 1978: The Magic of Lassie; Every Girl Should Have One; 1994: Carmen Miranda: Bananas Is My Business.

NY Stage: 1931: George White's Scandals; 1974: Good News.

NORMAN FELL

(NORMAN FELD) BORN: PHILADELPHIA, PA, MARCH 24, 1924. ED: TEMPLE UNIV. DIED: DECEMBER 14, 1998.

A character performer whose depressed-looking face and sardonic way with a line were used with minimal effect in movies, Norman Fell was probably more recognizable for his countless television appearances. After serving as a tail gunner during World War II, he studied with Stella Adler and, later, at the Actors Studio. In time he was seen all over TV in dramas, specials, guest parts, and in a few series as a regular. He made his big-screen debut as one of the sergeants in *Pork Chop Hill*, after which he was a radio announcer commenting on the trial in *Inherit the Wind*. He played one of Frank Sinatra's gang of thieves, a demolitions expert, in *Ocean's Eleven*; the detective on the tail of Jimmy Durante at the beginning of *It's a Mad Mad Mad Mad World*; the suspicious boarding-house owner with an intense dislike for resident Dustin Hoffman in *The Graduate*; and a police captain in *Bullitt*. He was one of the whirlwind vacationers in *If It's Tuesday, This Must Be Belgium*; Sergeant Towser in the all-star adaptation of *Catch-22*; a district attorney in *Charley Varrick*; the Gypsy father of leading lady Joan Prather in the chaotic comedy *Rabbit Test*; did an amusing bit as a New York City tour guide in the Burt Reynolds vehicle *Paternity*; and showed up as the owner of the topless dance club in the sleaze-cheapie *Stripped to Kill*. Television viewers probably most identify him as the easily irritated landlord in the hit 1970s sitcom *Three's Company*, which in turn gave him his own spin-off, *The Ropers*.

Screen: 1957: The Violators (AS NORMAN FELD); 1959: Pork Chop Hill; 1960: The Rat Race; Inherit the Wind; Ocean's Eleven; 1963: PT-109; It's a Mad Mad Mad Mad World; 1964: The Killers; Quick, Before It Melts; 1967: The Young Warriors; Fitzwilly; The Graduate; 1968: The Secret War of Harry Frigg; Bullitt; The Young Runaways; 1969: If It's Tuesday, This Must Be Belgium; 1970: The Boatniks; Catch-22; 1973: The Stone Killer; Charley Varrick; 1974: Airport 1975; 1975: Cleopatra Jones and the Casino of Gold; 1978: Rabbit Test; Guardian of the

Wilderness; The End; 1981: The Kinky Coaches and the Pom Pom Pussycats/Heartbreak High (dtv); On the Right Track; Paternity; 1985: Transylvania 6-5000; 1987: Stripped to Kill; 1989: C.H.U.D. II — Bud the Chud (dtv); 1990: The Boneyard (dtv); 1991: For the Boys; 1992: The Naked Truth (dtv); 1993: Hexed; 1995: Beachhouse (dtv); 1996: The Destiny of Marty Fine (dtv).

Select TV: 1956: Joe & Mabel (series); 1961–62: 87th Precinct (series); 1963: Sergeant Ryker (sp); 1964: The Hanged Man; 1967:The Movie Maker; 1969: Three's a Crowd; 1970–71: Dan August (series); 1972: The Heist; 1973: Needles and Pins (series); 1974: Thursday's Game; 1975: Death Stalk; 1976: Rich Man, Poor Man (ms); Richie Brockelman: Missing 24 Hours; 1977–79: Three's Company (series); 1979–80: The Ropers (series); 1980: Moviola: This Year's Blonde; For the Love of It; 1982–83: Teachers Only (series); 1983: Uncommon Valor; 1984: The Jesse Owens Story; 1995: Family Reunion: A Relative Nightmare.

JOSE FERRER

(JOSE VICENTE FERRER DE OTERO Y CINTRÓN) BORN: SANTURCE, PUERTO RICO, JANUARY 8, 1912. ED: PRINCETON UNIV. DIED: JANUARY 26, 1992.

A versatile actor who believed there was nothing he could not accomplish, Jose Ferrer left behind a colorful film career of highs and lows, despite a late start. His family moved from Puerto Rico to New York when he was six years old. He attended college with the idea of become an architect but changed his mind to study acting, making his debut on a Long Island showboat and later joining Joshua Logan's theater company in upstate New York. His Broadway debut came with a walk-on in the comedy *A Slight Case of Murder* and, five years down the line, he become a star via his performances in a 1940 revival of *Charley's Aunt*, and a production of *Othello*, as Iago, opposite Paul Robeson. He missed out on the lead in director Billy Wilder's Oscar-winning film *The Lost Weekend* when he refused to sign a contract with Paramount, who had wanted Wilder to cast a "name" anyway. In the meantime he was branching out to behind-the-scenes jobs in the theater, serving as co-director of *Vickie* and as director-producer of *Strange Fruit*. Then came his greatest theatrical triumph yet, starring as the lovelorn *Cyrano de Bergerac*, which brought him the very first Tony Award ever given a lead actor and resulted in his long-overdue movie debut, in 1948, for producer Walter Wanger, in his lavish *Joan of Arc*. As the weak-willed Dauphin, Ferrer was one of the few things critics liked about this uneven spectacle, and he received an Oscar nomination in the supporting category. Over at Fox he hypnotized Gene Tierney into carrying out his foul deeds in *Whirlpool*, and, at MGM, he played an ailing South American dictator, opposite Cary Grant, in one of that actor's more serious assignments, *Crisis*. In 1950 producer Stanley Kramer decided to film *Cyrano de Bergerac* and, although made on the cheap with a less-than-thrilling supporting cast, the movie captured Ferrer's stage performance, as the witty, charismatic swordsman with the oversized nose, in all its glory, and he won himself an Academy Award. It would become his signature role, Ferrer having already done it on television in 1949, later reviving it Off Broadway in 1953, doing it yet again on the tube in 1955, and finally playing a variation on the part for the European feature *Cyrano and D'Artagnan*, in 1964.

In the meantime he scored another Broadway hit directing, producing, and starring with Gloria Swanson in a revival of *Twentieth Century*. He followed that by directing the original stage productions of *The Four Poster* and *Stalag 17*, winning Tony Awards for both. His next motion picture was one of his greatest triumphs, with Ferrer giving another superb interpretation of a physically deformed and tormented Frenchman, artist Toulouse-Lautrec, searching in vain for love, in the atmospheric and surprisingly popular 1952 biopic *Moulin Rouge*. He received his third and final Oscar nomination for it. With that he was on the Hollywood "A" list, choosing to play the tortured Reverend in *Miss Sadie Thompson* (not his finest hour on film), and then the small but pivotal role of the defense counselor in *The Caine Mutiny*, giving a memorable climactic speech and justifiably tossing champagne in smug Fred MacMurray's face. *Deep in My Heart* was just another composer biopic, in this instance the story of Sigmund Romberg, but Ferrer was a delight singing "Mr. and Mrs." with real-life wife (1953–67) Rosemary Clooney (prior to Clooney, he had been married to actress Uta Hagen from 1938 to 1948) and stopping the show by acting out an entire production at a breakneck pace for a group of stunned backers. Then he debuted as a film director with *The Shrike*, repeating another role that had won him Tony Awards on Broadway, both for directing and acting, playing a henpecked husband. The film did not repeat its previous success. Undaunted, he followed it with another movie that he directed and acted in, the British-made *Cockleshell Heroes*, as a major training a group of soldiers for an attack on the Germans. He co-wrote as well as helmed *The Great Man*, playing a reporter investigating the demise of a beloved TV star in what turned out to be the most effective of all his directorial credits. Then he appeared in *I Accuse!*, good as the sad, wrongly imprisoned Jewish officer Alfred Dreyfuss in this honorable attempt to fully dramatize what had been touched on only marginally in *The Life of Emile Zola*. None of these went over with the public, and a domestic comedy, more serious than funny, that he did with Gena Rowlands, *The High Cost of Loving*, pretty much cooled down Hollywood's interest in him both behind and in front of the cameras.

He returned to the stage to direct two musicals, *Oh Captain!*, an adaptation of the Alec Guinness film *The Captain's Paradise*, for which he co-wrote the book, and *Juno*. He sang opera in Santa Fe and directed, but didn't appear in, two heavily panned films, the second remake of *State Fair*, and *Return to Peyton Place*, a sequel to one of Fox's blockbusters, and, therefore, the most popular of all his directorial jobs. Around this time he did a small part as the creepy Turkish Bey, who desires and then beats Peter O'Toole in the Oscar-winning blockbuster *Lawrence of Arabia*. Despite the minimal amount of screen time, it was Ferrer's favorite of all his movie performances. Going the all-star cast route, he was Herod in *The Greatest Story Ever Told*, and one of the villains, a vocal anti-Semite, aboard the *Ship of Fools*. He was just right as a hammy actor in Carl Reiner's sprightly comedy *Enter Laughing*, but soon afterwards began his long and winding journey through bit roles, telefilms, dubious European productions, trash cinema, and countless hard-to-trace jobs (wherever the money could be found or whether a particular location might seem worth the trip). Among the more high-profile projects were the disaster movie spoof *The Big Bus*, playing the villain who resides in an iron lung; the all-star *Voyage of the Damned*, portraying a corrupt immigration official in a movie that bore more than a passing resemblance to *Ship of Fools*, only it wasn't half as good; and *The Swarm*, getting blown up in a nuclear power plant because of rampaging bees. He also appeared in *The Fifth Musketeer*, a revision of *The Man in the Iron Mask*, as an aged Athos; *The Big Brawl*, as a Chicago gangster in this early attempt to get the general public interested in martial arts master Jackie Chan; *Fedora*, as Marthe Keller's ominous physician; Woody Allen's *A Midsummer Night's Sex Comedy*, as a philosophizing professor; the remake of *To Be or Not to Be*, as the chief Nazi; and

The Evil That Men Do, as another vile baddie in one of Charles Bronson's flops. He did manage to get another leading role, late in the game, but it was in the barely released *Old Explorers*, with James Whitmore. There were also some final visits to the New York theatre, producing and starring in the Off Broadway play *White Pelicans* in 1978 and directing the Broadway musical *Carmelina* the following year, neither of which ran very long. One of his sons from his marriage to Rosemary Clooney, Miguel Ferrer, also became an actor.

Screen: 1948: Joan of Arc; 1949: Whirlpool; 1950: The Secret Fury; Crisis; Cyrano de Bergerac; 1952: Anything Can Happen; Moulin Rouge; 1953: Miss Sadie Thompson; 1954: The Caine Mutiny; Deep in My Heart; 1955: The Shrike (and dir.); Cockleshell Heroes (and dir.); 1956: The Great Man (and dir.; co-wr.); 1958: I Accuse! (and dir.); The High Cost of Loving (and dir.); 1961: Forbid Them Not (narrator); 1962: Lawrence of Arabia; 1963: Nine Hours to Rama; Cyrano and D'Artagnan (nUSr); 1964: Stop Train 349; 1965: The Greatest Story Ever Told; Ship of Fools; 1967: Enter Laughing; 1969: The Young Rebel/Cervantes; 1975: Orders to Kill; 1976: Paco; The Big Bus; Voyage of the Damned; 1977: Crash!; The Sentinel; Forever Young, Forever Free/Lollipop (filmed 1975); 1978: The Private Files of J. Edgar Hoover; Dracula's Dog/Zoltan: Hound of Dracula; The Swarm; 1979: Fedora; The Fifth Musketeer; Natural Enemies; 1980: Who Has Seen the Wind? (filmed 1977); The Big Brawl; 1982: A Midsummer Night's Sex Comedy; Blood Tide/The Red Tide; And They're Off (nUSr); 1983: The Being; To Be or Not To Be; 1984: The Evil That Men Do; Dune; 1986: Bloody Birthday (filmed 1980); The Violins Came With the Americans/The Sun and the Moon (nUSr); 1990: Hired to Kill (dtv); Old Explorers; 1991: A Life of Sin (dtv); 1992: Arrest the Restless (nUSr).

NY Stage: 1935: A Slight Case of Murder; Stick in the Mud; 1936: Spring Dance; Brother Rat; 1937: In Clover; 1938: How to Get Tough About It; Missouri Legend; 1939: Mamba's Daughters; Key Largo; 1940: Charley's Aunt; 1942: Let's Face It; 1943: Othello; 1946: Cyrano de Bergerac; 1948: Volpone (ob; and adapt.); Angel Street (ob); The Bear (ob); On the Harmfulness of Tobacco (ob); The Alchemist (ob); S.S. Glencairn: The Long Voyage Home (ob; and dir.); The Insect Comedy (ob; and dir.); The Silver Whistle; 1950: Twentieth Century (and dir.; prod.); 1952: The Shrike (and dir.); 1953: Cyrano de Bergerac (ob; and dir.); The Shrike (ob; and co-dir.); Richard III (ob); Charley's Aunt (ob; and dir.); 1958: Edwin Booth (and dir.); 1963: The Girl Who Came to Supper; 1967: Man of La Mancha; 1978: A Life in the Theatre (ob); White Pelicans (ob; and prod.).

Select TV: 1949: Cyrano de Bergerac (sp); 1955: Cyrano de Bergerac (sp); 1959: Survival (sp); 1967: Kismet (sp); 1968: A Case of Libel (sp); 1970: The Aquarians; 1971: Banyon; Gideon (sp); The Cable Car Murder/Crosscurrent; 1973: The Marcus-Nelson Murders; 1975: The Missing Are Deadly; Medical Story; The Art of Crime; 1976: Meeting at Potsdam (sp); 1977: Exo-Man; The Rhinemann Exchange (ms); 1978: The Amazing Captain Nemo; 1979: The French Atlantic Affair (ms); 1980: Pleasure Palace; Gideon's Trumpet; The Murder That Wouldn't Die; The Dream Merchants (ms); 1981: Evita Peron; Peter and Paul; Berlin Tunnel 21; 1983: Blood Feud; This Girl for Hire; 1984: Samson and Delilah; George Washington (ms); 1985: Hitler's SS: Portrait in Evil; Christopher Columbus (ms); Covenant; Seduced; 1986: Blood and Orchids; Bridges to Cross (series); 1987: Young Harry Houdini; 1988: Strange Interlude (sp); 1989: Mother's Day; 1991: The Perfect Tribute.

MEL FERRER

(MELCHIOR GASTON FERRER) BORN: ELBERON, NJ, AUGUST 25, 1917.

When it comes to exploring Mel Ferrer's place in Hollywood history, it is not unjust to say that he was something of an also-ran. The gaunt actor with the dark eyes had star roles and served as director and producer on several occasions, but his work was often no more than serviceable and, on many instances, downright dull. Dropping out of Princeton, he joined the Cape Playhouse in Dennis, Massachusetts, eventually making it to Broadway as a chorus boy in two 1938 musicals. While continuing to act onstage he did some directing and producing for radio. This led to a contract with Columbia to serve in several behind-the-scenes jobs, resulting in his directorial debut, 1945's hour-long melodrama *The Girl of the Limberlost*. Back on the stage his path crossed with Jose Ferrer when Jose directed him in *Strange Fruit*, after which Mel returned the favor by directing Jose in his most famous role, *Cyrano de Bergerac*. (Although Mel's father's name was Jose, he was in no way related to his more famous acting namesake.) Mel Ferrer's film acting debut finally took place in 1949, in the independently made, socially conscious *Lost Boundaries*, playing a black doctor passing for white in a small New England town. Two more directorial efforts followed, *The Secret Fury*, which starred Claudette Colbert, and *Vendetta*, which he came aboard to do after several other directors had dropped off. Concentrating on his acting, he went back to Columbia to give one of his best performances, as the matador who loses his nerve, in *The Brave Bulls*, and then accepted a contract with MGM. There he dueled memorably with Stewart Granger in the fast-paced swashbuckler *Scaramouche*, and then played perhaps his most memorable role, the crippled and unpleasant puppeteer, who can only express kindness through his characters, in *Lili*. It was a surprise success, as was the clunky costume epic *Knights of the Round Table* (MGM's first film in CinemaScope), where he made for a very uninspired King Arthur. Around this time he met Audrey Hepburn and convinced her to join him on Broadway in the fantasy *Ondine*. They became an item and were married in 1954.

The press began to accuse Ferrer, the lesser light of the pair, of coasting on the fame of his better-known and better-liked wife. She was, in fact, instrumental in getting him the part of Prince Andrey in *War and Peace*, but Hepburn and her other co-star, Henry Fonda, made a better match. Ferrer and Hepburn also joined forces on television for a mediocre version of *Mayerling*, and then he made the sorry mistake of directing her in *Green Mansions*, which did absolutely nothing to enhance his career behind the camera. On screen he joined the too-old cast of *The Sun Also Rises*, back in the bullring, and battled Harry Belafonte over Inger Stevens in the intriguingly stark end-of-the-world drama *The World, the Flesh, and the Devil*. At this point, Ferrer retreated to Europe, where his stardom trickled away via such international fare as *The Devil and the Ten Commandments*, and the incredibly dull biopic of painter *El Greco*. While across the sea, he participated in *The Longest Day*, the smash hit epic about the D-Day invasion, and in *The Fall of the Roman Empire*, as a blind prophet who poisons Alec Guinness. He made a stop back in the U.S. to leer his way through *Sex and the Single Girl*, proving that comedy was not his forte. After serving as producer for one of Hepburn's biggest hits, *Wait Until Dark*, the couple split in 1968. Things never did pick up for Ferrer as far as film work was concerned. What few of his movies played on this side of the Atlantic included non-entities as the "John Wayne in London" vehicle *Brannigan*; *Eaten Alive*, where he provided dinner for a hungry crocodile; *The Norseman*, hiding behind a bushy beard, as a Viking kidnapped by Indians; and *The Fifth Floor*, where he played a doctor at an unorthodox mental asylum. His last directorial effort, *Every Day Is a Holiday*, was based on a story that he wrote. His name could be found as producer on such films as *The Night Visitor* and *W*.

Screen: 1949: Lost Boundaries; 1950: Born to Be Bad; 1951: The Brave Bulls; 1952: Rancho Notorious; Scaramouche; 1953: Lili; Saadia; Knights of the Round Table; 1955: Oh…Rosalinda!; 1956: War and Peace; 1957: The Vintage; Paris Does Strange Things/Elena and Her Men; The Sun Also Rises; 1958: Fraulein; 1959: The World, the Flesh, and the Devil; 1960: The Hands of Orlac (nUSr); L'Homme a Femmes/Ladies Man (nUSr); 1961: Blood and Roses; Legge di Guerra (nUSr); Forbidden/Proibito (nUSr); 1962: The Devil and the Ten Commandments (nUSr); The Longest Day; 1963: I Lancieri Neri/Charge of the Black Lancers (nUSr); 1964: The Fall of the Roman Empire; Paris — When It Sizzles; Sex and the Single Girl; El Senor de la Salle (nUSr); 1966: El Greco (and prod.; Sp: 1964); 1969: Who Are My Own? (nUSr); 1971: A Time for Loving/Paris Was Made for Lovers (and prod.; nUSr); 1975: Brannigan; 1976: The Black Pirate (nUSr); The Girl From the Red Cabaret (Sp: 1973); 1977: Eaten Alive/Death Trap; Das Netz (nUSr); The Girl in the Yellow Pyjamas (nUSr); 1978: Hi-Riders; The Norseman; The Tempter/The Antichrist (It: 1974); Yesterday's Tomorrow (nUSr); 1979: The Visitor; 1980: The Fifth Floor; Sfida all'ultimo Paradiso (nUSr); Emerald Jungle/Eaten Alive by Cannibals (dtv); Nightmare City/City of the Walking Dead (dtv); Buitres sobre la Ciudad (nUSr); 1981: Screamers/The Fish Men; Lili Marleen; Mille Milliards de Dollars (nUSr); Deadly Game (nUSr); The Great Alligator (dtv).

NY Stage: 1938: You Never Know; Everywhere I Roam; 1940: Kind Lady; Cue for Passion; 1945: Strange Fruit; 1954: Ondine.

Select TV: 1953: The Vigilantes (sp); 1957: Mayerling (sp); 1963: The Fifth Passenger (sp); 1973: Tenafly; 1977: Sharon: Portrait of a Mistress; 1978: Black Beauty (ms); 1980: The Top of the Hill; The Memory of Eva Ryker; Fugitive Family; 1981–82: Behind the Screen (series); 1981–84: Falcon Crest (series); 1982: One Shoe Makes It Murder; 1985: Seduced; 1986: Peter the Great (ms); Outrage!; Dream West (ms); 1988: Wild Jack; 1989: Christine Cromwell: Things That Go Bump in the Night; 1995: Catherine the Great.

STEPIN FETCHIT

(LINCOLN PERRY) BORN: KEY WEST, FL, MAY 30, 1902. DIED: NOVEMBER 19, 1985.

One of the most controversial actors in the history of film, Stepin Fetchit's stock portrayal of a slow-talking, wide-eyed, shuffling, almost moronic black man in countless supporting parts of the 1930s has made his name synonymous with Hollywood's insensitive, racist attitude towards African-Americans. His entrance into show business came in 1914, performing in minstrel shows and vaudeville, where he originally partnered an actor named Ed Lee, the two men billing themselves as Step and Fetchit. Once the team broke up, Perry combined the names and adapted it for his own. This led to film work, starting in 1927 in *In Old Kentucky*, and a contract with Fox Films, where he supported such star attractions as Janet Gaynor (*Carolina*) and Shirley Temple (*Stand Up and Cheer*). Will Rogers was so enamored of his talents that he used him as a comical foil on four different occasions: *David Harum*,

Judge Priest (which at least allowed him to play off of Hattie McDaniel), *The County Chairman*, and Rogers's last, *Steamboat 'Round the Bend*. In time he became one of the more frequently employed black actors, ultimately becoming quite well-to-do financially, although his carelessness with cash and the eventual collapse of his career caused him to file for bankruptcy in 1947. There were a few more jobs in the 1950s before Fetchit began to fade from the show business scene. During the 1960s he converted to Islam, became a member of Muhammad Ali's entourage, and made two later film appearances, in *Amazing Grace* and *Won Ton Ton, the Dog Who Saved Hollywood*, before once again disappearing from view, though never from motion picture notoriety.

Screen: 1927: In Old Kentucky; 1928: Nameless Men; The Tragedy of Youth; The Devil's Skipper; 1929: Show Boat; Hearts in Dixie; Big Time; Salute; Fox Movietone Follies of 1929; Thru Different Eyes; The Kid's Clever; The Ghost Talks; 1930: Cameo Kirby; Swing High; La Fuerzer del Querer/Face of Desire (nUSr); The Big Fight; 1931: Neck and Neck; The Wild Horse; The Prodigal; The Galloping Ghost (serial); 1934: David Harum; The World Moves On; Stand Up and Cheer; Carolina; Judge Priest; Bachelor of Arts; Marie Galante; 1935: Helldorado; One More Spring; The Virginia Judge; The County Chairman; Steamboat 'Round the Bend; Charlie Chan in Egypt; 1936: 36 Hours to Kill; Dimples; 1937: On the Avenue; Love Is News; Fifty Roads to Town; 1938: His Exciting Night; 1939: Zenobia; 1947: Miracle in Harlem; 1952: Bend of the River; 1953: The Sun Shines Bright; 1974: Amazing Grace; 1976: Won Ton Ton, the Dog Who Saved Hollywood.

NY Stage: 1940: Walk With Music.

Select TV: 1972: Cutter.

BETTY FIELD

BORN: BOSTON, MA, FEBRUARY 8, 1918.
ED: AADA. DIED: SEPTEMBER 13, 1973.

A celebrated stage actress with sad, sultry eyes, Betty Field leaned heavily toward playing neurotic types and won some plum roles as a result, although she had an annoying tendency to take things way over the top. Her stage debut came in Newark, NJ, in a production of *The Shanghai Gesture*, and, when she was only 16, she made her Broadway bow in *Page Miss Glory*. Several onstage teen roles followed, including the part of Henry Aldrich's girlfriend in *What a Life*. Paramount hired her to repeat her part in the 1939 movie version, where she and Jackie Cooper made a most unappetizing twosome. That same year, she was seen to much better advantage in Hal Roach's acclaimed production of *Of Mice and Men*, as Curley's sad, slatternly wife. Back at Paramount she and Cooper were paired again for an adaptation of Booth Tarkington's *Seventeen*, and then she played leading lady to Fredric March in *Victory*, another attempt to bring the un-cinematic writings of Joseph Conrad to the screen. Warner Bros. borrowed her to play Claude Rains's disturbed daughter in *Kings Row*, where her heavy emoting was one of the few minuses in an otherwise compelling film. In 1943 she wed playwright Elmer Rice, for whom she had acted in his plays *Two on an Island* and *Flight to the West*. He would continue to give her meaty stage roles, in *A New Life* and *Dream Girl*. After giving a nice performance as the wife of farmer Zachary Scott in *The Southerner*, she was off screen for four years before returning to play Daisy Buchanan and bearing the brunt of the harsh criticism aimed at Paramount's second version of *The Great Gatsby*. After another period away to concentrate on theater, she was back

in Hollywood, looking older and devoid of any glamour, for *Picnic*, as Kim Novak's mother; *Bus Stop*, as a waitress; and *Peyton Place*, at her most mannered, as the low-class wife of Arthur Kennedy who eventually hangs herself in Lana Turner's closet. On a more restrained note, she essayed the part of Burt Lancaster's patient wife in *Bird Man of Alcatraz* quite effectively, and ended her career with a small role as Don Stroud's mother in the Clint Eastwood thriller *Coogan's Bluff*. Her marriage to Rice ended in divorce in 1956.

Screen: 1939: What a Life; Of Mice and Men; 1940: Seventeen; Victory; 1931: The Shepherd of the Hills; Blues in the Night; 1942: Kings Row; Are Husbands Necessary?; 1943: Flesh and Fantasy; 1944: The Great Moment; Tomorrow, the World!; 1945: The Southerner; 1949: The Great Gatsby; 1955: Picnic; 1956: Bus Stop; 1957: Peyton Place; 1959: Hound-Dog Man; 1960: Butterfield 8; 1962: Bird Man of Alcatraz; 1966: 7 Women; 1968: How to Save a Marriage (And Ruin Your Life); Coogan's Bluff.

NY Stage: 1934: Page Miss Glory; 1937: Room Service; Angel Island; 1938: If I Were You; What a Life; Primrose Path; 1940: Two on an Island; Flight to the West; 1943: A New Life; 1944: The Voice of the Turtle; 1945: Dream Girl; 1949: The Rat Race; 1951: Not for Children; 1952: The Four Poster; 1953: The Ladies of the Corridor; 1955: Festival; 1958: Waltz of the Toreadors; A Touch of the Poet; 1959: A Loss of Roses; 1963: Strange Interlude; 1966: Where's Daddy?; 1971: Landscape (ob); All Over.

Select TV: 1948: Street Scene (sp); 1950: Six Characters in Search of an Author (sp); 1951: Local Storm (sp); Grace (sp); 1952: They Knew What They Wanted (sp); 1953: Before I Wake (sp); 1956: Happy Birthday (sp); The Breach (sp); 1957: The Lie (sp); 1959: Ah, Wilderness! (sp); 1960: Uncle Harry (sp); 1961: All Summer Long (sp); 1962: Focus (sp).

W.C. FIELDS

(WILLIAM CLAUDE DUKENFIELD)
BORN: PHILADELPHIA, PA, JANUARY 29, 1880.
DIED: DECEMBER 25, 1946.

He is one of the most distinctive talents in cinema folklore, still highly revered and endlessly imitated, even by those who have never seen one of his films. The plump comedian with the bulbous nose and the one-of-a-kind, deliberately mannered speaking voice — from which came all sorts of put downs, witticisms, and strange observations on human behavior, delivered from the side of his mouth — was a hero to the downtrodden, even though there was rarely more than self-interest at stake. W.C. Fields was a scalawag, a liar, a drunk, a con man, a braggart, and a cheat, always at odds with a world that would not step to his peculiar rhythm, but somehow coming out triumphant in the end. His early life did not start out so rosy either. Running away from home when he was 11, he found jobs at amusement piers and vaudeville houses as a juggler. By the turn of the century, he was becoming fairly well known in this profession, touring various parts of the globe before ending up at the Palace in New York, in 1913. Two years later he became a part of the Ziegfeld Follies, where his routines included his pool-table bit, captured on film in the 1915 short "Pool Sharks." Leaving Ziegfeld in 1921, he acted in a book show, *Poppy*, which Paramount bought and made into *Sally of the Sawdust* (with D.W. Griffith, of all people, as director), a financially successful film but inferior to the later sound version. Signed to a contract by Paramount, Fields continued in silent films, where the mild impression he made was not about to place him among the screen immortals. In silence (and sporting the small fake mustache that was part of his look at the time) he played the drunken dad of Carol Dempster in a melodrama, again helmed by Griffith, *That Royle Girl*; and a Florida druggist, in his first starring vehicle, *It's the Old Army Game*, which set the tone for the typical Fields entry, involving the minor dilemmas descending upon a beleaguered, lazy dreamer with outrageous schemes. He was a Jersey optometrist with an impatient, henpecking wife (for the first time, but certainly not the last) in *So's Your Old Man*; a shady businessman in *Fools for Luck*, which gave him Chester Conklin as his comic foil; and played a variation of the old Charlie Chaplin role in the disastrous re-do of *Tillie's Punctured Romance*.

Sound would change the moribund state of his career. The new phase of his movie life began with four Mack Sennett shorts, "The Dentist," "The Fatal Glass of Beer," "The Pharmacist" (a remake, of sorts, of *It's the Old Army Game*), and "The Barber Shop," all of which had moments of inspired brilliance. Hearing that glorious, sardonic voice made his film persona that much better, and Paramount re-hired him for what would prove to be an inspired six-year period of creativity, with movies both sublime and surreal. *Million Dollar Legs*, in which he took billing *after* Jack Oakie, was a demented masterpiece about a mythical country competing in the Olympics, with Fields at his most deliriously obtuse as the Indian-wrestling President. This was followed by some more ensemble comedies: *If I Had a Million*, which had Fields teamed for the first time with his best co-star, the no-nonsense Allison Skipworth, taking out his driving woes on all the road hogs by deliberately running them off the streets in one of the good episodes of this hit-or-miss omnibus; *International House*, a weird hodgepodge about an early demonstration of television; *Alice in Wonderland*, which perfectly cast the actor as Humpty Dumpty, though only his voice made him recognizable under the makeup; and *Six of a Kind*, where Fields once again partnered with Skipworth, though they both showed up late in the film. She and Fields were also the stars of the 58-minute quickie *Tillie and Gus*, a sweet and simple tale of two cardsharps and the first of his talkies to be sold on his name. This film gave Fields yet another memorable foil, Baby LeRoy, leading to all sorts of legendary tales about the great comedian's nasty attitude towards children in general and this child specifically.

LeRoy was back to get booted in the behind by Fields in *The Old-Fashioned Way*, a milder, more nostalgic piece than most of those before it, about a troupe of actors, with Fields as the modestly nicknamed "Great McGonigle." There was a babysitting sequence with LeRoy in *It's a Gift*, a delightful, near-plotless romp highlighted by a hilariously tasteless encounter with a blind man, Mr. Muckle. The film is often singled-out by Fields aficionados as the most satisfying of all his vehicles. He was then borrowed by MGM to play a more restrained version of his movie persona, Mr. Micawber, in the hit 1935 version of *David Copperfield*, replacing Charles Laughton (at Laughton's request) and fulfilling a dream of interpreting his favorite author, Charles Dickens. Back at Paramount he shared screen time with a top-billed Bing Crosby in the period musical *Mississippi*, though it often seemed like two separate movies spliced together. *Man on the Flying Trapeze* was back to prime Fields territory, and, indeed, it is another of his funniest works. In it the comedian played befuddled memory expert Ambrose Wolfinger, trying to survive a nagging wife, played to perfection by Kathleen Howard, who had henpecked him previously in *It's a Gift*. Like most Fields movies, the critics were more enthusiastic about it than the general public. Once again he got *Poppy* made for the big screen, though barely, since he was ill during much of its production, and

a double was used in certain sequences. His Paramount contract came to an end, in a money dispute, with another all-star concoction, *The Big Broadcast of 1938*, which began with Fields obliviously blowing up a filling station and ended with a race between a pair of gigantic ocean liners. In it he played twin brothers, roles originally intended for Jack Benny. There was an offer for Fields to do the title role in MGM's *The Wizard of Oz*, but after some negotiations he decided to turn it down, much to the benefit of Frank Morgan.

Fields went over to Universal for four comedies, which are probably among his best-known pictures, although none of them can touch his Paramount output for sheer effortless lunacy. *You Can't Cheat an Honest Man* was a continuation of his noted mock-radio feud with dummy Charlie McCarthy, a cause for much bickering on-set with director George Marshall, and displeasure from the comedian with the finished product. *My Little Chickadee* had the seemingly brilliant idea of placing him alongside Mae West. It marked the first time his actual name would appear in the writing credits (usually he was not credited or wrote under a pseudonym, the most persistent being "Charles Bogle"), although more of the script was West's than his. In any event the pairing was one that worked better in theory than execution because the two performers did not click off screen or on, sharing very little time before the camera. *The Bank Dick* was probably the best of the Universal comedies, with Fields's most famous screen-credit nom de plume, Mahatma Kane Jeeves; while *Never Give a Sucker an Even Break* was so uneven that it even spoofed its own silliness within its plot. Since none of these were box-office bonanzas, Fields was hardly in great demand once his contract came to an end. In any event he was no longer in the best of health, so he confined himself to guest star bits, including another pairing with Edgar Bergen and Charlie McCarthy, *Song of the Open Road*, and a segment of *Tale of Manhattan*, which wound up on the cutting room floor (it was finally restored on video in 1996). In 1946 his legendary drinking caught up with him, and he died of a liver ailment on Christmas day, leaving a void that no one would even dare think of trying to fill. His one book, *Fields for President*, was published in 1940.

Screen (shorts): 1915: Pool Sharks; His Lordship's Dilemma; 1930: The Golf Specialist; 1932: The Dentist; 1933: The Fatal Glass of Beer; The Pharmacist; Hip Action; Hollywood on Parade B-2; 1934: Hollywood on Parade B-10.

Screen (features): 1924: Janice Meredith; 1925: Sally of the Sawdust; That Royle Girl; 1926: It's the Old Army Game; So's Your Old Man; 1927: The Potters; Running Wild; Two Flaming Youths; 1928: Tillie's Punctured Romance; Fools for Luck; 1931: Her Majesty Love; 1932: Million Dollar Legs; If I Had a Million; 1933: International House; Tillie and Gus; Alice in Wonderland; 1934: Six of a Kind; You're Telling Me; The Old-Fashioned Way (and story AS CHARLES BOGLE); Mrs. Wiggs of the Cabbage Patch; It's a Gift (and story AS CHARLES BOGLE); 1935: David Copperfield; Mississippi; Man on the Flying Trapeze (and co-story AS CHARLES BOGLE); 1936: Poppy; 1938: The Big Broadcast of 1938; 1939: You Can't Cheat an Honest Man (and story AS CHARLES BOGLE); 1940: My Little Chickadee (and co-wr.); The Bank Dick (and wr. AS MAHATMA KANE JEEVES); 1941: Never Give a Sucker an Even Break (and story AS OTIS CRIBLECOBLIS); 1944: Follow the Boys; Song of the Open Road; Sensations of 1945.

NY Stage: 1905: The Ham Tree; 1915–21: Ziegfeld Follies; 1922: George White's Scandals; 1923: Poppy; 1925: The Comic Supplement; Ziegfeld Follies of 1925; 1928: Earl Carroll Vanities of 1928–29; 1930: Ballyhoo.

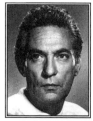

PETER FINCH

(FREDERICK PETER INGLE FINCH) BORN: LONDON, ENGLAND, SEPTEMBER 28, 1916. DIED: JANUARY 14, 1977.

By the time Peter Finch became an international star, he had been around for quite some time, earning a reputation as a strong performer, bringing a bit of world-weariness, punctuated by a depth of sensitivity, to his characters. In his own understated way, he was one of the best actors England had to offer. Although he was born in that country, he was raised in France, India, and ultimately Australia, where he worked in vaudeville before making his legitimate stage debut in *While Parents Sleep*, in 1935. Over the next ten years he acted in a handful of Australian films, including the well-liked war story *Rats of Tobruk*; made a name for himself on radio; and started his own theatrical company, called Mercury. It was the last that brought him to the attention of Laurence Olivier, who suggested he come to London. After a role in a made-in-Australia Ealing Studios film, *Eureka Stockade*, he went to England to work for that film company on *Train of Events*, as an actor who has murdered his wife; and then to MGM for *The Miniver Story*, as a Polish officer. For Olivier he appeared onstage in *Daphne Laureolla*, and then returned to the movies to play the Sheriff of Nottingham in Disney's made-in-England *The Story of Robin Hood and His Merrie Men*, and theatrical manager D'Oyly Carte in the biopic *The Story of Gilbert and Sullivan*. His first actual movie lead came in 1954 with an American production, *Elephant Walk*, as a tea planter who neglects his wife and then has a herd of pachyderms stampede his home. It was not a hit, so he went back to supporting parts in *Father Brown*, as a thief who steals a precious cross from Alec Guinness, and in *The Dark Avenger*, as the French villain in this flop Errol Flynn vehicle. Things picked up greatly with *A Town Called Alice*, as an Australian in love with Virginia McKenna, a role for which he won the British Film Award, and a popular war movie, *The Battle of the River Plate/Pursuit of the Graf Spee*, as the captain of the notorious German battleship. In 1959 he finally made a major impact on the international market with his fine work as the doctor whom Audrey Hepburn assists in the Belgian Congo in the prestigious and popular *The Nun's Story*.

Following this came the lead in a minor Disney adventure, a remake of *Kidnapped*, and more beneficially, *The Trials of Oscar Wilde*, the more lavishly produced and better-liked of two films on the writer released at that time, earning a second British Film Award for his performance. This was followed by a third BFA, for *No Love for Johnnie*, with Finch as a single-minded political climber. He got involved in some soapy productions, like the American *The Sins of Rachel Cade*, which brought him back to the Belgian Congo; the British-made Susan Hayward melodrama, *I Thank a Fool*; and the Sophia Loren-in-Israel dud, *Judith*. Amid these, though, were two gritty British dramas, *Girl With Green Eyes*, with Finch as Rita Tushingham's older lover in one of his best-ever performances, and *The Pumpkin Eater*, with the actor as a philandering writer, battling fiercely with unhappy wife Anne Bancroft.

He found himself stranded in the desert in *The Flight of the Phoenix*, and then in the snow in the expensive international production *The Red Tent*. Between these he played the uptight squire in John Schlesinger's overlong *Far From the Madding Crowd*, which was not the great work one would have hoped for from these talents, and *The Legend of Lylah Claire*, a grotesque glimpse at Hollywood stardom that seemed to be a big put-on. None of these went over well at the box office, but the former led to

another teaming with Schlesinger in 1971, *Sunday, Bloody Sunday*, with Finch giving a frank and touching performance as a homosexual doctor whose younger lover is leaving him. This was virtually the first time a major name actor agreed to enact gay love scenes on film. It brought him a fourth British Film Award and his first Oscar nomination. Although this gave him a high standing in the film community, it was followed by more disasters. These included the musical remake of *Lost Horizon*, in which, among other detriments, his singing voice was badly dubbed; *The Nelson Affair*, with Finch and Glenda Jackson having no luck visiting territory traveled by Laurence Olivier and Vivien Leigh previously; and *The Abdication*, with Finch as a cardinal falling in love with Liv Ullmann. His movie career came to a close on a very high note, however, when he played the newsman driven to madness — and therefore high ratings — in the 1976 hit *Network*. Ranting brilliantly about the dangers of television, his line "I'm mad as hell and I'm not going to take it anymore!" became a pop culture catchphrase, turning Finch into a temporary cult figure. Sadly, only a few months after the picture's release, he died of a heart attack in the lobby of the Beverly Hills Hotel. He became the first actor to win the Academy Award posthumously; his wife gave a tearful acceptance speech at that year's ceremony.

Screen: 1936: Dad and Dave Come to Town; Red Sky at Morning/Escape at Dawn; 1938: Mr. Chedworth Steps Out; 1942: The Power and the Glory; 1944: Jungle Patrol (narrator); 1946: A Son Is Born; Rats of Tobruk; 1948: Eureka Stockade/Massacre Hill; The Hunt (narrator); 1949: Train of Events; 1950: The Wooden Horse; The Miniver Story; 1952: The Story of Robin Hood and His Merrie Men; 1953: The Great Gilbert and Sullivan/The Story of Gilbert and Sullivan; The Heart of the Matter; 1954: Elephant Walk; Father Brown/The Detective; 1955: Make Me an Offer; The Dark Avenger/The Warriors; Passage Home; Simon and Laura; Josephine and Men; 1956: A Town Like Alice; The Battle of the River Plate/Pursuit of the Graf Spee; 1957: The Shiralee; Robbery Under Arms; 1958: Windom's Way; 1959: Operation Amsterdam; The Nun's Story; 1960: Kidnapped; The Trials of Oscar Wilde; 1961: The Sins of Rachel Cade; No Love for Johnnie; 1962: I Thank a Fool; 1963: In the Cool of the Day; 1964: Girl With Green Eyes; First Men in the Moon; The Pumpkin Eater; 1965: The Flight of the Phoenix; 1966: Judith/Conflict; 10:30 P.M. Summer; 1967: Far From the Madding Crowd; 1968: The Legend of Lylah Clare; 1971: The Red Tent; Sunday, Bloody Sunday; 1972: Something to Hide; England Made Me; 1973: Lost Horizon; The Nelson Affair/Bequest to the Nation; 1974: The Abdication; 1976: Network.

Select TV: 1976: Raid on Entebbe.

JAMES FINLAYSON

BORN: FALKIRK, SCOTLAND, AUGUST 27, 1887. DIED: OCTOBER 9, 1953.

It is impossible to think of this bald, bushy-mustached comic without Laurel and Hardy coming to mind. Starting with the 1927 short "Love 'em and Weep," he became a frequent foil and supporting player in so many of their two-reelers and features that he is regarded by the comedy team's fans with the same reverence and affection with which Margaret Dumont is held by Marx Brothers aficionados. Coming to America with a Scottish theater troupe, he appeared on Broadway in *Bunty Pulls the String*, and then journeyed to Los Angeles, in 1919, to try his luck in the movies. There he worked for Thomas Ince and Mack Sennett before joining Hal Roach in 1923, as a star and feature player of various short subjects. With his trademark hot temper and exaggerated exasperation, punctuated by a raised brow on one side and an eye squeezed shut on the other, he had his finest moment with Laurel and Hardy in the 1929 short "Big Business," maniacally destroying Stan and Ollie's automobile while they gleefully and violently dismantled his home. He could also be seen opposite the comedians playing a drunken millionaire in "Sugar Daddies," a soda jerk in "Men o' War," a governor who ends up coated in paint in "The Hoose-Gow," a big game hunter whom Hardy impersonates in "Another Fine Mess," Hardy's two-faced butler in "Chickens Come Home," the sergeant of their regiment in *Bonnie Scotland*, and the sadistic captain of the guard in *The Bohemian Girl*. In 1940 he made his last appearance opposite the duo with their final Hal Roach feature, *Saps at Sea*. In total, they had done 33 on-screen appearances together. Outside the comedy team, his roles were often unbilled or quick bits like the bill collector in *Julia Misbehaves*, and a London cabby in *Royal Wedding*.

Screen (shorts): 1919: Love's False Faces; Why Beaches Are Popular; 1921: You Wouldn't Believe It; 1922: Home Made Movies; The Counter Jumper; 1923: White Wings; Roughest Africa; Where's My Wandering Boy Tonight?; Pitfalls of a Big City; The Soilers; The Barnyard; No Wedding Bells; 1924: Near Dublin; Wide Open Spaces; Brothers Under the Chin; Smithy; Rupert of Hee-Haw; 1925: Official Officers; Mary Queen of Tots; Yes, Yes, Nanette; Unfriendly Enemies; Moonlight and Noses; Hard Boiled; Thundering Fleas; Husbands; The Caretaker's Daughter; 1926: Madame Mystery; Never Too Old; The Merry Widower; Wise Guys Prefer Brunettes; Raggedy Rose; The Nickel Hopper; 1927: Seeing the World; With Love and Hisses; Love 'em and Weep; Do Detectives Think?; Hats Off; Flying Elephants; Sugar Daddies; The Call of the Cuckoos; The Second Hundred Years; 1928: Should Tall Men Marry?, Galloping Ghosts; 1929: Liberty; Big Business; Men o' War; The Hoosegow; Fast Freight; 1930: Dollar Dizzy; Night Owls; Another Fine Mess; 1931: One of the Smiths; False Roomers; A Melon-Drama; Catch as Catch Can; Oh! Oh! Cleopatra; Scratch as Catch Can; One Good Turn; Our Wife; Chickens Come Home; The Hasty Marriage; Stout Hearts and Willing Hands; 1932: The Chimp; Boy Oh Boy; Trouble From Abroad; The Iceman's Ball; So This Is Harris; Thru Thin and Thicket; The Millionaire Cat; Union Wages; Jitters the Butler; 1933: Mush and Milk; Me and My Pal; His Silent Racket; Hokus Fokus; The Druggist's Dilemma; The Gay Nighties; 1935: Thicker Than Water; Manhattan Monkey Business; 1936: Life Hesitates at 40.

Screen (features): 1920: Married Life; Down on the Farm; 1921: A Small Town Idol; Home Talent; 1922: The Crossroads of New York; 1923: Hollywood; A Man About Town; 1925: Welcome Home; Innocent; 1927: No Man's Law; 1928: Lady Be Good; Ladies' Night in a Turkish Bath; Show Girl; Bachelor's Paradise; 1929: Two Weeks Off; Hard to Get; Wall Street; 1930: For the Defense; Young Eagles; Flight Commander; The Dawn Patrol; 1931: Big Business Girl; Pardon Us; 1932: Pack Up Your Troubles; Thunder Below; 1933: The Devil's Brother/Fra Diavolo; The Girl in Possession; Dick Turpin; Strictly in Confidence; 1934: What Happened to Harkness; Oh! No Doctor; Father and Son; Nine Forty Five; Trouble in Store; 1935: Handle With Care; Who's Your Father?; Bonnie Scotland; 1936: The Bohemian Girl; Our Relations; 1937: All Over Town; Pick a Star; Way Out West; Toast of New York; Angel; 1938: Carefree; Block-Heads; Wise Girl; 1939: The Great Victor Herbert; The Flying Deuces; Hollywood Cavalcade; 1940: A Chump at Oxford; Raffles; Foreign Correspondent; Saps at Sea; 1941: Nice Girl?; One Night in Lisbon; 1942: To Be or Not to Be; 1943: Yanks Ahoy!; 1946:

Till the Clouds Roll By; 1947: The Perils of Pauline; Thunder in the Valley; 1948: Grand Canyon Trail; Julia Misbehaves; 1951: Royal Wedding; Here Comes the Groom.
NY Stage: 1916: Bunty Pulls the Strings.

ALBERT FINNEY
BORN: LANCASHIRE, ENGLAND, MAY 9, 1936.
ED: RADA.

Despite a tendency over the years to drift in and out of films, Albert Finney probably held onto his stardom longer than most of the crop of exciting young British actors to hit the cinema in the 1960s. Burly, tussle-haired and undeniably manly he started out as a brashly handsome, brooding lad and continued to impress as the year's went by, ending up a somewhat ruddy-looking, stocky version of himself, but no less thrilling a presence. Joining Birmingham Rep after school at RADA, he made his stage debut with them in *Julius Caesar*, in 1956, moving on to London in 1960 for Charles Laughton's production of *The Party*. From there it was off to Stratford where he was seen in *A Midsummer Night's Dream*, *King Lear*, and *Coriolanus*, among others, impressing director Tony Richardson enough with the last that he offered Finney a small role as Laurence Olivier's son, who gets sent off to military service near the beginning of the film version of *The Entertainer*. Richardson, being the producer of *Saturday Night and Sunday Morning*, may have been instrumental in Finney getting the lead in this adaptation of the acclaimed Alan Sillitoe novel. In any case this was his launching pad to film stardom, giving a ferociously watchable performance as the aimless young factory worker torn between two women, becoming one of the celluloid representatives of the kind of working class youth British audiences were happy to see portrayed on screen. Its great success made him a hot property, hot enough, in fact, for him to turn down *Lawrence of Arabia* and opt for the theatre again, with back-to-back successes in *Billy Liar* and *Luther*, eventually bringing the latter to New York in 1963.

In the meantime he made an even greater leap up the ladder of movie stardom with another Richardson production, *Tom Jones*, playing the devilishly sexy rogue who beds various ladies in 18th century England. His magnetic presence, not to mention his ability to bypass any of the character's potential smarminess, was essential in turning this delightful romp into one of the gigantic hits of 1963. It also won an Academy Award for Best Picture and a nomination for Finney. He himself served as producer for his follow-up film, a remake of *Night Must Fall*, as the deranged killer Robert Montgomery had played in the earlier version, but it was a dreary thing and got a thumbs-down from both press and public. With that Finney dropped out of the movies for a while, concentrating onstage instead, as a member of the National Theatre, before returning triumphantly in 1967 for Stanley Donen's bittersweet and brilliant look at the highs and lows of a marriage, *Two for the Road*. This was Finney at his most charming and complex, teamed superbly with Audrey Hepburn with whom he was romantically linked for a spell. Forming his own company he decided to try his hand at directing with *Charlie Bubbles*, an overly artsy and ultimately maddening, yet sometimes perceptive look at a writer whose personal life is falling apart. Another project, *The Picasso Summer*, was so blatantly un-commercial that it didn't even play in cinemas in most countries, being sold directly to television. In the musical *Scrooge* he shattered tradition by playing Ebenezer in both his younger *and* older incarnations; portrayed a bingo caller obsessed with private eye movies in the cultish *Gumshoe*; recorded a Royal Court production of *Alpha Beta*, for minimal cinematic consumption; then reached another film high point, making himself virtually unrecognizable as master sleuth Hercule Poirot in the 1974 hit *Murder on the Orient Express*, a much-heralded performance that landed him another Oscar nomination. Once again defying the assumptions that an actor naturally followed a high profile movie with further films, he returned again to the British stage, doing some Shakespearean roles at the National.

Starting in 1981 there came a whole slew of Albert Finney films including the moody urban horror thriller *Wolfen*; the sad domestic drama *Shoot the Moon*, breaking up painfully with Diane Keaton; and the over-publicized and expensive musical *Annie*, bald-headed as Daddy Warbucks and easily one of the better things in it. He then gave a bombastic performance as a hammy old Shakespearean actor on his last legs in *The Dresser*, earning another Oscar nomination, after which he was nominated yet again, playing an alcoholic ex-consul in Mexico in the little seen *Under the Volcano*. *Orphans* gave him another meaty role, as a gangster kidnapped by a pair of brothers, but it too was barely distributed. This was often the case with many of the films Finney did in the 1990s, productions that gave him some terrific roles to sink his teeth into but seemed to be made strictly for smaller-than-average audiences on the art house circuits. *Miller's Crossing* was one of the more widely seen, with the actor in what was basically a supporting role, but a good one, as a tough Irish mobster not afraid to take on some gunmen who have interrupted his quiet evening at home. In *The Playboys* he was at his most powerfully bull-like as a police officer in love with the much younger Robin Wright; brought a quiet sadness to the updated version of *The Browning Version*, as a schoolteacher who has alienated most of the people in his life; and created a touching portrait of a lonely, gay bus conductor in Dublin, given to quoting Oscar Wilde, in *A Man of No Importance*. It was a testament to his talents that despite the mild commercial response to most of this work, certain filmmakers were insistent on hiring Finney. He probably would have been wise to skip the horrid *Breakfast of Champions*, as a crazed pornographer, at one point wading through toxic waste, or *Simpatico*, as a racing commissioner whose career is ruined. However, it was great to see him as a lawyer locking horns with Julia Roberts in a huge commercial entertainment, *Erin Brockovich*, which brought him another Oscar mention, in the supporting category.

Screen: 1960: The Entertainer; 1961: Saturday Night and Sunday Morning; 1963: Tom Jones; The Victors; 1964: Night Must Fall (and prod.); 1967: Two for the Road; 1968: Charlie Bubbles (and dir.); 1969: The Picasso Summer; 1970: Scrooge; 1972: Gumshoe; 1973: Alpha Beta; 1974: Murder on the Orient Express; 1975: The Adventure of Sherlock Holmes' Smarter Brother; 1978: The Duellists; 1981: Wolfen; Loophole; Looker; 1982: Shoot the Moon; Annie; 1983: The Dresser; 1984: Under the Volcano; 1987: Orphans; 1990: Miller's Crossing; 1992: The Playboys; 1993: Rich in Love; 1994: The Browning Version; A Man of No Importance; 1995: The Run of the Country; 1997: Washington Square; 1999: Breakfast of Champions; Simpatico; 2000: Erin Brockovich; Traffic; 2001: Delivering Milo (nUSr).

NY Stage: 1963: Luther; 1968: A Day in the Death of Joe Egg.

Select TV: 1975: Forget-Me-Not Lane (sp); 1984: Pope John Paul II; The Biko Inquest (and dir.); 1990: Endless Game; The Image; 1991: The Green Man; 1996: Karaoke (ms); Cold Lazarus (ms); 1997: Nostromo (ms); 1998: A Rather English Marriage; 2001: Hemingway: The Hunter of Death; 2002: The Gathering Storm.

BARRY FITZGERALD

(WILLIAM JOSEPH SHIELDS) BORN: DUBLIN, IRELAND, MARCH 10, 1888. ED: CIVIL SERVICE COL. DIED: JANUARY 4, 1961.

To many he was Hollywood's very embodiment of Ireland, a lovable pint-sized actor with a playful, expressive face and a thick brogue that conjured up comforting images of a tweedy old soul talking blarney with St. Patrick himself. Indeed Barry Fitzgerald was so well thought of during his heyday in the 1940s that he was nominated by the Motion Picture Academy in *both* the lead and supporting categories for his signature role in *Going My Way*. For a few years he worked as a junior executive in the unemployment insurance division of the British Civil Service until boredom caused him to seek after-hours work as an actor. In 1915 he joined Dublin's Abbey Theatre, while continuing his day job. Eventually he came to Broadway, starting with *Cartney and Kevney* in 1928, and would appear there in two of the most noted Irish plays, *The Plough and the Stars* and *Juno and the Paycock*. It was in Alfred Hitchcock's 1930 film version of the latter that Fitzgerald made his movie debut. Six years later he came to Hollywood, where he was featured, along with several other members of the Abbey Theatre (including his brother, Arthur Shields), in the movie version of *The Plough and the Stars*, the first of several films Fitzgerald would do for John Ford.

He stayed on in Hollywood as a supporting actor of little note, though he did get to participate in one of the screwball classics of the period, *Bringing Up Baby*, as the drunken groundskeeper. It was not until John Ford called on him again, for *The Long Voyage Home*, as the crabby ship's steward, and for *How Green Was My Valley*, as one of the Welsh villagers who beat up Roddy McDowall's insensitive teacher, that he began to stand out from the pack. He remained seaworthy for *The Sea Wolf*, in which he lost a leg to a shark, and for two contemporary wartime dramas at Universal, *The Amazing Mrs. Holliday* and *Corvette K-225*, having the enemy torpedo his ship in both. Then, in 1944, his status changed forever when Paramount signed him up to play the irascible Catholic priest who clashes with young upstart Bing Crosby in *Going My Way*. His Father FitzgGibbons became one of the best-loved and most-imitated characters of all 1940s films, and with it Fitzgerald pulled off that Oscar-historical feat of the double nomination, winning in the supporting category. As a result he became one of the studio's prime character players, with roles in such box-office successes as *Incendiary Blonde*, as Betty Hutton's father; *Two Years Before the Mast*; and *California*, to name a few. *The Stork Club*, with Fitzgerald playing a millionaire whom Betty Hutton mistakes for a derelict, and *Easy Come, Easy Go*, with the actor playing a gambler (brother Arthur Shields showed up as his on-screen sibling), gave him actual star parts, but it was his reunion with Crosby, this time with the two playing doctors, in the charming *Welcome Stranger*, that gave him his biggest hit at the time.

Over at Universal he was given top billing in one of the best crime dramas of the 1940s, *The Naked City*, as the quick-thinking detective trying to solve a murder amid some splendid on-location backdrops of Manhattan. Another noted assignment away from his home studio displayed a darker side, with Fitzgerald playing the doctor who becomes one of the murder victims in the classic adaptation of Agatha Christie's *Ten Little Indians*, re-titled *And Then There Were None*. Back at Paramount he and Crosby had a third teaming, which turned out to be one reunion too many, with the limp *Top O' the Morning*, with Fitzgerald as an

Irish cop and Crosby as an investigator trying to figure out who stole the Blarney Stone. At Warners he starred in a minor horserace drama, *The Story of Seabiscuit*, his authentic brogue showing up Shirley Temple's fake one, and he played a bad guy in his last Paramount offering, *Silver City*. His final assignment with John Ford turned out to be another high point, *The Quiet Man*, where he was one of the colorful Irish villagers who welcome home ex-fighter John Wayne. After a turn as Bette Davis's brother in *The Catered Affair*, he returned to his beloved Ireland for two more films, which included playing the oldest man in the world in *Broth of a Boy*. He died there in 1961 following brain surgery.

Screen: 1930: Juno and the Paycock/The Shame of Mary Boyle; 1936: When Knights Were Bold; The Plough and the Stars; 1937: Ebb Tide; 1938: Bringing Up Baby; Four Men and a Prayer; The Dawn Patrol; 1939: Pacific Liner; The Saint Strikes Back; Full Confession; Marie Antoinette; 1940: The Long Voyage Home; 1941: San Francisco Docks; The Sea Wolf; How Green Was My Valley; Tarzan's Secret Treasure; 1943: Two Tickets to London; The Amazing Mrs. Holliday; Corvette K-225; 1944: Going My Way; I Love a Soldier; None But the Lonely Heart; 1945: Incendiary Blonde; And Then There Were None; Duffy's Tavern; The Stork Club; 1946: Two Years Before the Mast; California; 1947: Easy Come, Easy Go; Welcome Stranger; Variety Girl; 1948: The Sainted Sisters; The Naked City; Miss Tatlock's Millions; 1949: Top O' the Morning; The Story of Seabiscuit; 1950: Union Station; 1951: Silver City; 1952: The Quiet Man; Il Filo D'erba (nUSr); 1954: Tonight's the Night/Happy Ever After; 1956: The Catered Affair; 1958: Rooney; 1959: Broth of a Boy.

NY Stage: 1928: Cartney and Kevney; 1932: Things That Are Caesar's; The Far-Off Hills; 1934: The Plough and the Stars; Look at the Heffernans; The Playboy of the Western World; The Shadow of the Glen; Church Street; The Well of the Saints; Juno and the Paycock; 1935: The Silver Tassie; 1939: The White Steed; 1940: Juno and the Paycock (revival); 1941: Taynard Street.

Select TV: 1952: The Man Who Struck It Rich (sp); 1954: The White Steed (sp).

GERALDINE FITZGERALD
BORN: DUBLIN, IRELAND, NOVEMBER 24, 1913.

A fine and passionate actress, with an early career as a stalwart but unappreciated leading lady and a latter one as a feisty character player, Geraldine Fitzgerald got her start at Dublin's Gate Theatre. In 1934 she began appearing in several British films of little note, including *Blind Justice*, as a young woman threatened by blackmail; *Lieutenant Daring R.N.*, as a lady kidnapped by pirates; and a version of *The Mill on the Floss*, as the Tulliver daughter in love with the son of her family's arch enemy. She moved to New York in 1938, and a previous acquaintance with Orson Welles got her work there in his Mercury Theatre production of Shaw's *Heartbreak House*. This stirred up interest from Hollywood, and Fitzgerald debuted there in 1939 in two big productions, *Dark Victory*, where she gave a nice performance as Bette Davis's devoted best friend, and *Wuthering Heights*, where she was by far the best thing in the film, as Isabella, whom Laurence Olivier marries on the rebound. It brought her her one and only Oscar nomination, in the supporting category. Under contract to Warners, she made herself difficult, turning down roles (notably Mary Astor's part in *The Maltese Falcon*) and winding up on suspension. Among those she did accept were two with Jeffrey Lynn: *A Child Is Born*, as a convicted killer about to give birth in a maternity ward in this remake of *Life Begins*, and *Flight*

From Destiny, as Lynn's cheated-on wife. She was also seen in the romantic melodrama *Shining Victory*, assisting and falling in love with doctor James Stephenson, and in *The Gay Sisters*, bitching it up, in a monocle no less, as the cinematic sibling of Barbara Stanwyck and Nancy Coleman. Certainly her most prestigious picture at the studio was the film of the Broadway hit *Watch on the Rhine*, once again taking a secondary role to Davis, as the wife of villain George Coulouris. Still not officially under contract, she spent most of the remaining decade elsewhere, trying to kill off her sister in Universal's *The Strange Affair of Uncle Harry*; teaming with Alan Ladd for the Paramount spy drama *O.S.S.*; and, perhaps most famously, playing First Lady Edith Wilson, just the sort of noble, colorless lady she claimed to loathe portraying, in Fox's ambitious, long-winded and award-laden 1944 biopic *Wilson*.

Her two remaining jobs with Warner Bros. consisted of perhaps her best star part for them, the deserted wife who forms an odd alliance with Sidney Greenstreet and Peter Lorre, sharing a sweepstakes ticket, in *Three Strangers*, and the role of a woman swindled by John Garfield, until love steps in, in *Nobody Lives Forever*. Due to a mutual lack of interest, she left Hollywood, doing a single movie back in Britain, *The Late Edwina Black/The Obsessed*, in which she was accused of murdering the title character. After a break she returned to acting, via the New York stage, which brought her a sole Hollywood offer, Fox's *Ten North Frederick*, where she played Gary Cooper's cold-hearted, ambitious wife. Entering her character-actress phase, she got one of her best roles ever, in *The Pawnbroker*, where she was touching as the nice, lonely woman who tries to break through to emotionally deadened Rod Steiger. Shortly afterwards she formed Theatre of the People, which actually performed drama on the streets of New York City. A 1971 Off Broadway production of *Long Day's Journey Into Night* reminded audiences of her talents, and suddenly Fitzgerald began to pop up more steadily onstage, television and the big screen. In the last category she was a fire-and-brimstone preacher in *Rachel, Rachel*; Jeff Bridges's mom in *The Last American Hero*; Art Carney's dotty former lover in *Harry and Tonto*; Dudley Moore's wealthy aunt in the smash hit *Arthur*; and Rodney Dangerfield's crotchety mother-in-law in *Easy Money*. In addition to her many theatre roles, she also directed such works for the New York stage as *Mass Appeal*, *The Return of Herbert Bracewell*, *To Whom It May Concern*, and *Sharon*, a musical for which she also wrote the book and lyrics. Her son, from her first marriage, is director Michael Lindsay-Hogg, best known for the Beatles' *Let It Be* and the TV mini-series *Brideshead Revisited*.

Screen: 1934: Blind Justice; Open All Night; 1935: The Lad; The Ace of Spades; Three Witnesses; Lieutenant Daring R.N.; Turn of the Tide; Radio Parade of 1935; Department Store/Bargain Basement; 1936: Debt of Honor; Cafe Mascot; 1937: The Mill on the Floss; 1939: Dark Victory; Wuthering Heights; 1940: A Child Is Born; 'Til We Meet Again; 1941: Flight From Destiny; Shining Victory; 1942: The Gay Sisters; 1943: Watch on the Rhine; 1944: Ladies Courageous; Wilson; 1945: The Strange Affair of Uncle Harry; 1946: Three Strangers; O.S.S.; Nobody Lives Forever; 1948: So Evil My Love; 1951: Obsessed/The Late Edwina Black; 1958: Ten North Frederick; 1961: The Fiercest Heart; 1965: The Pawnbroker; 1968: Rachel, Rachel; 1973: The Last American Hero; 1974: Harry and Tonto; 1976: Echoes of a Summer; 1977: The Mango Tree; 1978: Bye Bye Monkey; 1979: Lovespell/Tristan and Isolde (dtv); 1981: Arthur; 1982: Blood Link/The Link (nUSr); 1983: Easy Money; 1986: Poltergeist II; 1988: Arthur 2: On the Rocks.

NY Stage: 1938: Heartbreak House; 1943: Sons and Soldiers;

1955: The Doctor's Dilemma; 1956: King Lear; 1957: Hide and Seek; 1961: The Cave Dwellers (ob); 1965: Pigeons (ob); 1971: Long Day's Journey Into Night (ob); 1975: Ah, Wilderness!; 1976: Songs of the Street (and wr.; later ob as Streetsongs in 1979; 1980; 1989); 1977: The Shadow Box; A Touch of the Poet; 1987: Danger: Memory (ob).

Select TV: 1952: The Daughter (sp); The Gallows Tree (sp); Fear (sp); 1953: Babylon Revisited (sp); 1954: Dark Possession (sp); The Lawn Party (sp); 1955: The Secret of Emily (sp); The Barretts of Wimpole Street (sp); Like Father, Like Son (sp); Isobel (sp); 1956: Dodsworth (sp); 1959: The Moon and Sixpence (sp); 1965: Our Private World (series); 1970: The Best of Everything (series); 1974: The Widowing of Mrs. Holroyd (sp); 1975: Forget-Me-Not Lane (sp); Beyond the Horizon (sp); 1976: Ah, Wilderness! (sp); 1977: Yesterday's Child; The Quinns; 1978: Tartuffe (sp); 1980: The Jilting of Granny Weatherall (sp); 1983: Dixie: Changing Habits; Kennedy (ms); 1985: Do You Remember Love?; 1986: Night of Courage; Circle of Violence: A Family Drama; 1991: Bump in the Night.

RHONDA FLEMING

(MARILYN LOUIS) BORN: HOLLYWOOD, CA, AUGUST 10, 1923.

Let's face it, Rhonda Fleming was a terrifically glamorous movie star name, and the lady was certainly beautiful, but there's a good chance that moviegoers remember her more for her striking red hair than for her acting abilities. Almost as soon as she was finished with school, she sought work in films, starting off as an extra, rising to supporting parts in *Spellbound* and *Out of the Past*, and then gaining leading-lady status in a Randolph Scott western, *Abilene Town*. Signed to a contract by Paramount in 1947, the studio started her out in a Pine-Thomas "B," *Adventure Island*, and then deemed her worthy of pairing off with their two hottest stars for their 1949 releases. She appeared with Bing Crosby in *A Connecticut Yankee in King Arthur's Court*, as the King's niece, looking luscious in Technicolor, and with Bob Hope in *The Great Lover*, as the daughter of impoverished duke Roland Culver. From there it was over to western territory and Glenn Ford for the aptly titled *The Redhead and the Cowboy*, although, curiously, it was filmed in black and white. Then she was sent back to the Pine-Thomas "B" unit for three with Ronald Reagan: *The Last Outpost, Hong Kong,* and *Tropic Zone*. For that sector of the studio, she was top billed for another film extolling the virtues of her hair, *Those Redheads From Seattle*, a puny musical that at least was allotted Technicolor in its budget. Elsewhere her assignments were pretty much on the same programmer level; costumed kitsch with titles that seemed left over from silent era melodramas, including *Little Egypt*, which was not about the famed carny dancer but a con artist from New Jersey; *Serpent of the Nile*; *Yankee Pasha*, sold into a Moroccan harem consisting of several Miss Universe contestants; and *Odongo*, where she was one of the more glitzy veterinarians around. In the wake of these there was a well-received potboiler for RKO, *Slightly Scarlet*, which found her opposite another auburn lady, Arlene Dahl; an "A" western, *Gunfight at the O.K. Corral*; and a worthy reunion with Bob Hope, *Alias Jesse James*. She later devoted a great deal of her time to charity work, opening the Rhonda Fleming Mann Resource Center for Women with Cancer at the UCLA Medical Center.

Screen: 1943: In Old Oklahoma; 1944: Since You Went Away; When Strangers Marry/Betrayed; 1945: Spellbound; 1946: The Spiral Staircase; Abilene Town; 1947: Adventure Island; Out of the Past; 1949: A Connecticut Yankee in King Arthur's Court; The Great Lover; 1950: The Eagle and the Hawk; The Redhead and the Cowboy; 1951: Cry Danger; The Last Outpost; Little Egypt; Crosswinds; Hong Kong; 1952: The Golden Hawk; 1953: Tropic Zone; Pony Express; Serpent of the Nile; Inferno; Those Redheads From Seattle; 1954: Jivaro; Yankee Pasha; 1955: Tennessee's Partner; 1956: The Queen of Babylon; The Killer Is Loose; Slightly Scarlet; While the City Sleeps; Odongo; 1957: The Buster Keaton Story; Gunfight at the O.K. Corral; Gun Glory; 1958: Bullwhip; Home Before Dark; 1959: Alias Jesse James; The Big Circus; 1960: The Crowded Sky; 1961: Revolt of the Slaves; 1964: The Patsy; 1966: Run for Your Wife; 1976: Won Ton Ton, the Dog Who Saved Hollywood; 1980: The Nude Bomb.

NY Stage: 1973: The Women.

Select TV: 1955: Stage Door (sp); South of Selanger (sp); 1968: Backtrack; 1975: The Last Hours Before Morning; 1979: Love for Rent.

ERROL FLYNN

BORN: HOBART, TASMANIA, JUNE 20, 1909. DIED: OCTOBER 14, 1959.

Apart from Douglas Fairbanks, the word "swashbuckler" brings no star more quickly to mind than Errol Flynn. This handsome, slyly smiling actor excelled at swordplay and adventure in the movie heyday of the 1930s and 1940s, his devil-may-care lady-killer movie image flowing out of the fiction and into his personal life as well. Despite all the joy he gave us up there on the screen, his physical deterioration and early death are among Hollywood's great tragedies. There has been much speculation on how he spent his pre-film days, but one fact is that he worked as a shipping clerk, which took him to New Guinea. It was there that he played Fletcher Christian in a pseudo-documentary called *In the Wake of the Bounty*, in 1933. From there he went to England, joining the Birmingham Rep and co-starring as a reporter in a "B" film, *Murder at Monte Carlo*, which won him a contract with Warner Bros. Arriving in America, he played two more roles of little note before he won the part that would make him a star, the doctor-turned-buccaneer in *Captain Blood*, one of the screen's most glorious pirate epics. It was a smash, and the public responded so enthusiastically to Flynn's teaming with Olivia de Havilland that they were called back together again on many occasions. *The Charge of the Light Brigade* was the next such event, a highly fictitious interpretation of history, set in India, memorable mainly for its rousing staging of its titular event. Then he went modern for *Green Light*, as a self-sacrificing physician, which did well enough to prove that audiences would accept him outside of costume adventures. It was, however, in this genre that he was most adept, and, following a secondary part in *The Prince and the Pauper* (the Mauch twins had most of the footage, with Flynn showing up about half-way through the story), he starred in the film with which his name would forever be happily linked, *The Adventures of Robin Hood*. A rousing Technicolor joy, it presented Flynn at his most charming and daring-do best, with de Havilland once again by his side, as Maid Marian, and Basil Rathbone around to cross swords with our hero in one of the screen's great duels. Prior to that he donned a uniform to spend time in the Sahara, not so much for adventure, but to complete a love triangle, in *Another Dawn*, and took a stab at comedy with *The Perfect Specimen*, as a sheltered, rich boy.

He took on Richard Barthlemess's old role in the 1938 remake of *The Dawn Patrol*, which wound up getting better notices than the original, and then went west for the highly enjoyable *Dodge City*, playing a quick-witted Irishman who tames that lawless town. DeHavilland was back with him for the least remembered of their pairings, *Four's a Crowd*, a comedy, and there were two with Bette Davis, *The Sisters* and *The Private Lives of Elizabeth and Essex*, despite the fact that she didn't care much for him as an actor. In any event, he held his own against the mighty Bette in *The Private Lives of Elizabeth and Essex*, playfully engaging in a game of power until their mutual stubbornness turns to tragedy. There was another western, *Virginia City*, which clearly aimed for a repeat of the success of *Dodge City*, though Miriam Hopkins was a far cry from the sort of heroine that de Havilland played, and another magnificent pirate epic, *The Sea Hawk*, which managed to be as entertaining in its own way as *Captain Blood*, though it was a shame the budget did not allow for Technicolor. *Santa Fe Trail* was Flynn-de Havilland again, but the interesting part of the film involved Raymond Massey as John Brown. With the country being on the brink of war, Flynn took to the air again in the dullish flying film *Dive Bomber!*, after which there was one final teaming with de Havilland, for *They Died With Their Boots On*, with Flynn somehow ideally cast as the arrogant, pig-headed General Custer, facing his famous finale at Little Big Horn. Around this time he was tried and acquitted for the rape of two underage girls, which only served to enhance his reputation as a sexual hellion. In later years it became known that his appetites did not stop at women. In the meantime, he continued to fight the war on screen (after being labeled 4-F in real life), appearing in *Desperate Journey*, patriotism at its most shameless, as part of a diverse Allied crew shot down over Nazi Germany; *Edge of Darkness*, as a Norwegian leading his village in a revolt against the Nazis; and *Objective, Burma!*, as a paratrooper taking on the Japanese, in the best and most popular of this group. Despite his convincing gung-ho portrayals of men in battle, his most winning work around the war years was the boxing bio *Gentleman Jim*, as James J. Corbett, a personal favorite of Flynn's, a combination of nostalgia, humor, and roughhousing that really clicked.

The lavish but decidedly second rate western *San Antonio*, was his last hit for a while, as the fans backed away from *Cry Wolf* and *Escape Me Never*. Flynn was unsympathetic in both films, in the former trying to deny Barbara Stanwyck her rightful inheritance, and in the latter, as a composer, cheating on wife Ida Lupino. *Adventures of Don Juan* was more like the old stuff, with a tongue wisely implanted in cheek, but it was clear that the aging Flynn was descending from his peak. Away from Warners, on loan to MGM, he was top billed for *That Forsyte Woman*, ill at ease as Greer Garson's stuffy and demanding husband, and he still found his name at the head of the cast list in what was clearly a supporting role as a red-bearded horse traitor in the lifeless Kipling adventure *Kim*. Warners had only routine westerns to offer, including *Rocky Mountain*, which was notable only because Flynn's co-star, Patrice Wymore, became his last wife the year of its release, 1950. Then he ended his relationship with his home studio with an all-too-typical film, *Mara Maru*, as a deep-sea diver. Looking decidedly less youthful, no doubt caused by his drinking, he continued in a lot of mediocre fare that attempted to rekindle the old spirit, such as *Adventures of Captain Fabian*, which he himself wrote; *The Master of Ballantrae*, which wound up being released by Warners, despite their split; *King's Rhapsody*, where he played opposite his wife; and *The Warriors/The Dark Avenger*, which was made, like most of his films during this period, in Europe. Things picked up a bit when Hollywood asked him back for a trio of drunk roles, starting with *The Sun Also Rises*, too old like the rest of the cast, but a scene stealer

nonetheless; then *Too Much, Too Soon*, too ironically cast as the deteriorating John Barrymore; and John Huston's elephant adventure, *The Roots of Heaven*. With his last girlfriend, Beverly Aadland, he wound up in a very strange cheapie called *Cuban Rebel Girls*, which was distributed in 1959 shortly after his death of a heart attack at 50. Also released that same year was his auto-biography, playfully titled *My Wicked, Wicked Ways*. His first marriage (1935–43) to actress Lili Damita produced a son, Sean Flynn, who tried to follow in his father's footsteps with the shamelessly titled 1963 feature *Son of Captain Blood*. Sean was later reported missing in Vietnam while serving as a photojournalist.

Screen: 1933: In the Wake of the Bounty; 1935: Murder at Monte Carlo; The Case of the Curious Bride; Don't Bet on Blondes; Captain Blood; 1936: The Charge of the Light Brigade; 1937: Green Light; The Prince and the Pauper; Another Dawn; The Perfect Specimen; 1938: The Adventures of Robin Hood; Four's a Crowd; The Sisters; The Dawn Patrol; 1939: Dodge City; The Private Lives of Elizabeth and Essex; 1940: Virginia City; The Sea Hawk; Santa Fe Trail; 1941: Footsteps in the Dark; Dive Bomber!; They Died With Their Boots On; 1942: Desperate Journey; Gentleman Jim; 1943: Edge of Darkness; Thank Your Lucky Stars; Northern Pursuit; 1944: Uncertain Glory; 1945: Objective, Burma!; San Antonio; 1946: Never Say Goodbye; 1947: Cry Wolf; Escape Me Never; Always Together; 1948: Silver River; Adventures of Don Juan; 1949: That Forsyte Woman; It's a Great Feeling; 1950: Montana; Rocky Mountain; Kim; 1951: Hello God (nUSr); Adventures of Captain Fabian (and wr.); 1952: Mara Maru; Against All Flags; 1953: The Master of Ballantrae; Crossed Swords; 1955: Let's Make Up/Lilacs in the Spring; King's Rhapsody; The Warriors/The Dark Avenger; 1957: Istanbul; The Big Boodle; The Sun Also Rises; 1958: Too Much, Too Soon; The Roots of Heaven; 1959: Cuban Rebel Girls (and wr.).

Select TV: 1956: The Sword of Villon (sp); 1957: Without Incident (sp); The Errol Flynn Theatre (series); 1959: The Golden Shanty (sp).

NINA FOCH

(Nina Consuelo Maud Fock) Born: Leyden, Holland, April 20, 1924. Raised in New York, NY. ed: AADA.

Refined and self-assured, Nina Foch (bearing a passing resemblance to Marlene Dietrich from certain angles) came to the movies after some stock and touring company work to fulfill a contract with Columbia Pictures. Following her 1943 debut as the heroine in a decent thriller, *The Return of the Vampire*, she became a dependable lead for the "B" unit, playing a Gypsy cursed by lycanthropy in *Cry of the Werewolf*; a cabbie in *She's a Soldier Too*; a Navy nurse in the thriller *Escape in the Fog*; and, best of all, the secretary hired by a mysterious family who wants to bump her off, in *My Name Is Julia Ross*, where her performance gave some weight to the rather implausible proceedings. In between these assignments she was allowed to do smaller roles in more elaborate productions like *A Song to Remember*, *The Guilt of Janet Ames*, and *Johnny O'Clock*, where her character's murder set the plot in motion. Soon she began co-starring in movies that were a cut or two above "B" pictures, including *The Dark Past*, as the girlfriend of escaped con William Holden, and *Johnny Allegro*, as the wife of counterfeiter George MacReady. From there she had a brief spell at MGM, starting out very nicely as the sophisticated lady who takes a shine to Gene Kelly's paintings, and to Kelly himself, in the Oscar-winning *An American in Paris*. There was a brief appearance as Marie Antoinette in the colorful swashbuckling adventure *Scaramouche*, and then a somewhat larger role, as the loyal secretary of the suicidal businessman in *Executive Suite*. Although it was hardly a standout performance, especially in light of the all-star ensemble surrounding her, Foch was the sole cast member to receive an Oscar nomination. The honor didn't do much for her career, however, as she was relegated to playing straight woman for Dean Martin and Jerry Lewis (*You're Never Too Young*) and then was lost amid the spectacle of *The Ten Commandments*, as Pharaoh's daughter, Bithinia. After an effective bit as a wealthy, bitchy Roman who demands to see Kirk Douglas and Woody Strode battle to the death in *Spartacus*, she was off the screen for a long time. An older Foch continued to bring a welcome lift to such later films as *Skin Deep*, as Allyson Reed's mother; *Sliver*, as an imperiled tenant; and *'Til There Was You*, as a pioneering lady architect.

Screen: 1943: The Return of the Vampire; 1944: Nine Girls; Cry of the Werewolf; She's a Soldier Too; Shadows in the Night; She's a Sweetheart; The Strange Affair; 1945: A Song to Remember; I Love a Mystery; Boston Blackie's Rendezvous; Escape in the Fog; My Name Is Julia Ross; Prison Ship; 1947: Johnny O'Clock; The Guilt of Janet Ames; 1948: The Dark Past; 1949: The Undercover Man; Johnny Allegro; 1951: St. Benny the Dip; An American in Paris; 1952: Scaramouche; Young Man With Ideas; 1953: Fast Company; Sombrero; 1954: Executive Suite; Four Guns to the Border; 1955: You're Never Too Young; Illegal; 1956: The Ten Commandments; 1957: Three Brave Men; 1959: Cash McCall; 1960: Spartacus; 1971: Such Good Friends; 1975: Salty; Mahogany; 1978: Jennifer; 1981: Rich and Famous; 1987: Dixie Lanes (dtv); 1989: Skin Deep; 1993: Sliver; Morning Glory; 1996: It's My Party; 1997: 'Til There Was You; 1998: Hush; Shadow of a Doubt (dtv); 2002: Pumpkin.

NY Stage: 1947: John Loves Mary; 1949: Twelfth Night; 1950: A Phoenix Too Frequent; King Lear; 1957: Measure for Measure; The Taming of the Shrew; 1960: A Second String.

Select TV: 1950: The Rose and the Shamrock (sp); 1951: Ice Bound (sp); Q.E.D. (series); The Skin of Our Teeth (sp); 1952: World So Wide (sp); The Jungle (sp); The Magnolia Touch (sp); 1953: Ski Story (sp); Trapped (sp); 1954: A Guest at the Embassy (sp); It's News to Me (series); State of the Union (sp); 1955: Roberta (sp); 1956: Manhattan Duet (sp); Yacht on the High Seas (sp); The Undiscovered Country (sp); Heritage of Anger (sp); 1957: The Playroom (sp); 1958: The Laughing Willow (sp); Much Ado About Nothing (sp); Free Weekend (sp); 1959: Ten Little Indians (sp); The Case of Julia Walton (sp); 1960: A Time to Decide (sp); 1962: Hercule Poirot (sp); Rebecca (sp); 1966: And Baby Makes Five (sp); 1968: Prescription Murder; 1969: Gidget Grows Up; 1972: The Scarecrow (sp); 1973: Female Artillery; 1976: The Great Houdinis; 1978: Child of Glass; 1979: Ebony, Ivory and Jade; 1985–86: Shadow Chasers (series); 1988: Outback Bound; 1988–89: War and Remembrance (ms); 1992: In the Arms of a Killer; 1993: Armistead Maupin's Tales of the City (ms); 1994: Alien Nation: Dark Horizon; 1999: Family Blessing; 2000: Bull (series).

HENRY FONDA

BORN: GRAND ISLAND, NE, MAY 16, 1905.
DIED: AUGUST 12, 1982.

Many have referred to him as the very best actor there ever was, and in his quiet, unmannered, straightforward way, Henry Fonda was certainly a front-runner for that honor. A star for over 45 years, he was the very embodiment of an idealistic level of integrity, shy yet forceful, manly yet sensitive,

deliberate of speech with both thought and feeling behind each word, and stubbornly All-American. His earliest acting credits were with the Omaha Community Playhouse, which included Marlon Brando's mother among its troupe. From there he became a member of the Provincetown Players and University Players Guild, where he would meet lifelong friend James Stewart and his first wife Margaret Sullavan (they married in 1931). Building a reputation in the New York theatre, he received his greatest attention with *New Faces* (of 1934), which led to a movie contract with independent producer Walter Wanger. It was not for Wanger that he made his film debut, however. After scoring a hit on Broadway in *The Farmer Takes a Wife*, he was asked by Fox to repeat his role in the 1935 movie version, playing a gentle man of the soil who romances Janet Gaynor. Thanks to the good notices, his career took off quite nicely, so Fox quickly made plans for a reunion with Gaynor in a remake of the silent classic *Way Down East*, until she was injured on the set and replaced by Rochelle Hudson. The film certainly did not erase memories of the earlier version and an assignment as leading man to opera diva Lily Pons, in *I Dream Too Much*, was just as quickly forgotten. His official boss, Wanger, finally found some jobs for him. The first was in a good drama about feuding Kentuckians, *The Trail of the Lonesome Pine*, the first three-strip Technicolor production released by Paramount. The next was in *The Moon's Our Home*, which marked the first of two times that he acted on screen with Sullavan (the other was *Let Us Live*), who was already his ex-wife — she having divorced Fonda in 1933 to marry his agent, Leland Hayward. Chalking up another technical milestone, he was in the first British Technicolor film, *Wings of the Morning*, portraying a Canadian; then was an ex-con whose attempts to go straight add up to naught in a socially conscious message picture, albeit a fairly hokey one, *You Only Live Once*.

At Warner Bros. he did one forgotten Bette Davis picture, *That Certain Woman*, and one of her best-loved and best-remembered films, *Jezebel*. In the latter, as the man Davis foolishly drives away, you actually believed that Fonda was strong enough to put her in her place, as he did in the famous ballroom scene. After wrapping up his contract with Wanger with the Spanish Civil War drama, *Blockade*, and starring with George Raft in a decent adventure epic at Paramount, *Spawn of the North*, he had his best film yet with *Jesse James*, a fine bit of movie fiction about the notorious outlaw with Fonda as James's brother, Frank. It was followed by more Americana, Hollywood-style, with *The Story of Alexander Graham Bell* as Mr. Watson, on the receiving end of the famous first phone call; *Young Mr. Lincoln*, perfectly cast as the great man during his lawyer years (a role he was initially intimidated by); and John Ford's thrilling outdoor adventure *Drums Along the Mohawk*, as an early settler who outruns the Indians in a memorable chase sequence. These were all made at Fox, where he finally consented to sign a contract, mainly to assure that he'd be cast in one of the studio's most-talked-about upcoming projects, *The Grapes of Wrath*, from John Steinbeck's novel. The film was a somber, de-glamorized, and compelling look at a poor dust bowl family, with Fonda in a towering, Oscar-nominated performance as the wandering son, Tom Joad. Despite its mild box-office performance at the time, it has since come to be regarded as a classic achievement from one of the most highly regarded of all directors, John Ford, and one of the key roles on the Fonda résumé. He was called on for a sequel to *Jesse James*, *The Return of Frank James*, the focus now being on him since Jesse (Tyrone Power) had bitten the dust in the original, and to support Alice Faye in an all-too-typical biopic, *Lillian Russell*, which made him only too happy to accept an offer from Paramount to pair off with Barbara Stanwyck for *The Lady Eve*. His hopelessly klutzy millionaire, taken for a ride by a sexy cardsharp, was a comic revelation and one of his most enduring performances.

Because of it he was quickly called on by Warners to play another mild mannered type in *The Male Animal*, showing a surer comic touch under these circumstances than either of his co-stars, Olivia de Havilland and Jack Carson. He was also a nice guy, used, chewed up and spit out by a bitchy Lucille Ball in RKO's Runyon tale, *The Big Street*, and then another naïve rube, adrift in the big city, in *The Magnificent Dope*, back on his home lot. Just when his roles at Fox were starting to drive him to rebellion, along came William Wellman's masterful *The Ox-Bow Incident*, with Fonda playing an honest cowboy trying desperately to stop a lynching. It barely made a dime, but it is a strong contender for the most satisfying, haunting western ever made. Following a stint in the Navy, there was another top-notch entry in this genre, Ford's *My Darling Clementine*, with Fonda as a no-nonsense Wyatt Earp, and the same director's less-accomplished *Fort Apache*, which was interesting only because Fonda got to play a dislikeable character for a change, the cold-hearted fort commander. In between, the two men collaborated on something less assured for both of them, *The Fugitive*, a version of Graham Greene's *The Power and the Glory*, a brooding work that was as liked by Ford aficionados as it was hated by fans of Greene. A segment in the multi-episode film *On Our Merry Way* was notable only for teaming him for the first time on screen with pal James Stewart. After that he took a lengthy, seven-year break from acting in films (with the exception of a guest spot in *Main Street to Broadway*), returning to his theatrical roots for his greatest Broadway triumph, *Mister Roberts*, which was followed by a smaller role, as the attorney, in *The Caine Mutiny Court-Marital*. He came back to movies in a fanfare of glory with the 1955 film version of *Mister Roberts*, and, despite battles on the set that caused John Ford to walk off the project and Mervyn LeRoy to take his place, it marked another high-water mark in Fonda's career. His levelheaded Naval officer, yearning to see action while waiting out World War II on a laundry ship, was a beautiful creation. Though he was not even nominated for an Oscar, the film itself became much honored and was a massive box-office hit.

Somehow, despite the obvious miscasting, Fonda brought off playing Pierre in the costly 1956 interpretation of *War and Peace*, proving that he could pretty much make anything work. He took on a good role in one of Alfred Hitchcock's starker, less-popular offerings, *The Wrong Man*, a documentation of a musician who endures the hell of a false arrest. Then he moved over to more familiar territory with *12 Angry Men*, as the persuasive voice of reason in a film that he produced by himself. It was another of his finest hours, believably persuading a roomful of stubborn jurors to see his point of view in a film that riveted its audiences through meaningful words and fine performances, being confined to a single setting. Fonda got an Oscar nomination for this one, but in the Best Picture category, not for acting. There were some decent westerns, *The Tin Star*, where he played a bounty hunter helping terrified new sheriff Anthony Perkins; and *Warlock*, which took another look at mob violence; then a remake of *Morning Glory*, renamed *Stage Struck*, with Fonda in the role Adolphe Menjou had played (and since Susan Strasberg was certainly no match for Katharine Hepburn, Fonda easily came out on top). He again took a trip back to Broadway for another hit, *Two for the Seesaw*, though he was not asked to appear in the film version; Robert Mitchum got the job. Instead he took on three outstanding political roles: in *Advise and Consent*, as the controversial cabinet member whose selection for office sets the whole plot in motion; in *The Best Man*, as a presidential candidate trying in vain to stay away from mudslinging, giving one of his

most finely honed performances; and in *Fail-Safe*, moving up to the office of the President, and spending most of his screen time in a tense hot-line conversation with Russia. He showed up, surprisingly, as Buffalo Bill, sporting long locks, in the all-star *How the West Was Won*; was right at home in the rural family drama, *Spencer's Mountain*, which was the basis for the better-known television series *The Waltons*; but seemed embarrassed by the comical low-jinks in *Sex and the Single Girl*, taking a back seat to Natalie Wood and Tony Curtis.

Having passed 60, he was a rare star in his age group to still rate some leads, starring in the pleasant comic-western *A Big Hand for the Little Lady*, getting roped into a high-stakes poker game; reuniting with Lucille Ball for the hugely popular family comedy *Yours, Mine and Ours*; and joining James Stewart for *Firecreek*, with Fonda as the bad guy. Taking billing *below* Claudia Cardinale (!) he was seen in the endless spaghetti western *Once Upon a Time in the West*, which was notable only because he never played a character so hateful, a man not above murdering an innocent child. He played a bearded warden, battling with convict Kirk Douglas in a most enjoyable prison lark, *There Was a Crooked Man...*, and offered up some goofy comic relief alongside Stewart in the whorehouse comedy *The Cheyenne Social Club*. *Sometimes a Great Notion* found him deliciously ornery as Paul Newman's stubborn dad, but thereafter he mostly went the guest route in things like *Tentacles*, which proved that even actors as revered and frequently employed as Fonda still took jobs for the money; and *Rollercoaster*, where he was there strictly to add another star name to the advertising, as he did in a previous production also presented in Sensurround, *Midway*. He was easily the best thing in the silly bee attack flick *The Swarm*, as a scientist who sacrifices his own life, and found his way back to the White House for *Meteor*, an end-of-the-world disaster. Son Peter directed him in *Wanda Nevada*, as a grizzled prospector, but it was hardly shown. Daughter Jane, acting as producer, did him proud, however. *On Golden Pond* was a touching examination of the estrangement between a cantankerous father and his distant daughter (Jane) that cut close enough to the bone for them to give their heartfelt best. It was a resounding smash hit and Henry, already ill by the time of the award ceremony, at last won a very popular Academy Award, only months before his death. America had lost a true celluloid hero. Fonda collaborated with Howard Teischmann on his memoirs, *Fonda: My Life*, published in 1981. He had received a special Academy Award, awarded only a year before he won his competitive trophy, as well as the American Film Institute Award, in 1978.

Screen: 1935: The Farmer Takes a Wife; Way Down East; I Dream Too Much; 1936: The Trail of the Lonesome Pine; The Moon's Our Home; Spendthrift; 1937: Wings in the Morning; You Only Live Once; Slim; That Certain Woman; 1938: I Met My Love Again; Jezebel; Blockade; Spawn of the North; The Mad Miss Manton; 1939: Jesse James; Let Us Live; The Story of Alexander Graham Bell; Young Mr. Lincoln; Drums Along the Mohawk; 1940: The Grapes of Wrath; Lillian Russell; The Return of Frank James; Chad Hanna; 1941: The Lady Eve; Wild Geese Calling; You Belong to Me; 1942: The Male Animal; Rings on Her Fingers; The Magnificent Dope; Tales of Manhattan; The Big Street; 1943: The Immortal Sergeant; The Ox-Bow Incident; 1946: My Darling Clementine; 1947: The Long Night; The Fugitive; Daisy Kenyon; 1948: On Our Merry Way/A Miracle Can Happen; Fort Apache; 1949: Jigsaw; 1953: Main Street to Broadway; 1955: Mister Roberts; 1956: War and Peace; The Wrong Man; 1957: The Tin Star; 12 Angry Men (and prod.); 1958: Stage Struck; 1959: Warlock; The Man Who Understood Women; 1962: Advise and Consent; The Longest Day; 1963:

How the West Was Won; Spencer's Mountain; **1964:** The Best Man; Fail-Safe; Sex and the Single Girl; **1965:** The Rounders; In Harm's Way; Battle of the Bulge; **1966:** A Big Hand for the Little Lady; The Dirty Game; **1967:** Welcome to Hard Times; **1968:** Firecreek; Yours, Mine and Ours; Madigan; The Boston Strangler; **1969:** Once Upon a Time in the West; **1970:** Too Late the Hero; The Cheyenne Social Club; There Was a Crooked Man…; **1971:** Sometimes a Great Notion/Never Give an Inch; **1973:** The Serpent/Night Flight From Moscow; Ash Wednesday; My Name Is Nobody; Mussolini: Dead or Alive/The Last Four Days; **1976:** Midway; **1977:** Rollercoaster; Tentacles; The Great Smokey Roadblock/The Last of the Cowboys; **1978:** The Swarm; **1979:** Fedora; City on Fire; Wanda Nevada; Meteor; The Greatest Battle/Battle Force; **1981:** On Golden Pond.

NY Stage: 1929: The Game of Life and Death; **1932:** I Loved You Wednesday; **1933:** Forsaking All Others; **1934:** New Faces; The Farmer Takes a Wife; **1937:** Blow Ye Winds; **1948:** Mister Roberts; **1951:** Point of No Return; **1954:** The Caine Mutiny Court-Martial; **1958:** Two for the Seesaw; **1959:** Silent Night, Lonely Night; **1960:** Critic's Choice; **1962:** A Gift of Time; **1965:** Generation; **1969:** Our Town; **1974:** Clarence Darrow; **1978:** First Monday in October.

Select TV: 1953: The Decision at Arrowsmith (sp); **1955:** Clown (sp); The Petrified Forest (sp); The Star and the Story (series); **1959–61:** The Deputy (series); **1963:** Tissue of Hate (sp); **1967:** Stranger on the Run; **1971–72:** The Smith Family (series); **1973:** The Red Pony; The Alpha Caper; **1975:** Collision Course; **1976:** Captains and the Kings (ms); **1978:** Home to Stay; Clarence Darrow (sp); **1979:** Roots: The Next Generations (ms); **1980:** The Oldest Living Graduate (sp); Gideon's Trumpet; **1981:** Summer Solstice.

JANE FONDA

Born: New York, NY, December 21, 1937.
ed: Vassar Col.

There have been countless examples of children following in the acting footsteps of their famous parents, but inevitably one is usually the more shining talent of the two. Only a handful of times has greatness begat greatness and Henry Fonda's daughter Jane is perhaps the outstanding example of this. If Henry was one of the best actors of his generation, then Jane was certainly among the best of hers. She and younger brother Peter were born to Henry's second wife, Frances Brokaw, who would eventually take her own life. While at school Jane began acting and made her professional bow with her father in a production of *The Country Girl*, in his home town of Omaha. After studying for a spell at the Actors' Studio, she landed the lead opposite Anthony Perkins in the slight basketball comedy *Tall Story*, no doubt helped by the fact that the director, Joshua Logan, was a good friend of her dad's. Nevertheless there were others who saw her potential and she was greatly in demand, doing some short-lived Broadway plays during the early 1960s including *There Was a Little Girl*, which won her a Theatre World Award. Back at the movies she was one of the better things about the tepid melodrama *Walk on the Wild Side*, as a whore named Kitty Twist, but was less appealing playing a frigid widow in the ensemble *The Chapman Report*. Nor was her performance as a newlywed in Tennessee Williams's atypical stab at comedy *Period of Adjustment* anything more than a game effort. *In the Cool of the Day*, was the sort of soap opera set against a lush backdrop (Greece, in this case) that did little to enhance the careers of any of the talents involved. She was, however, more relaxed in the stage-bound romantic comedy *Sunday in New York*, as an innocent in the big city, pursued by an eager Rod Taylor.

Around this time she dabbled in some French films, which emphasized her sex appeal, marrying the director, Roger Vadim, of one of them, *La Ronde*, in 1965. Back in Hollywood she had her biggest hit to date, the spoof western *Cat Ballou*, as a sweet thing who turns to crime after her father is murdered. She was sharp, sexy and strong, but it was hard to draw attention away from co-star Lee Marvin, playing two roles opposite her. There followed some more dips in her rollercoaster career with a typical 1960s sex comedy *Any Wednesday*, as Jason Robards's mistress, and the overheated Southern melodrama *Hurry Sundown*, where most people remarked upon her suggestive playing of a saxophone. Thankfully these were followed by her terrific work in a big moneymaker, *Barefoot in the Park*, again as a newlywed, this time trying to keep the fun in her marriage to stuffed-shirt Robert Redford. Vadim also put her in a film that would forever keep her in camp-cult heaven, *Barbarella*, a far-out and fun comic book come to life, overdressed with kitschy costumes and gaudy sets, which required Jane to strip over the opening credits while floating in air. Lest this sort of thing mean she wasn't to be taken serious as an actress, she blew everybody away with the next two. *They Shoot Horses, Don't They?* gave her a gritty role as a severely pessimistic marathon dancer, banking all her hopes on one last contest, and she nabbed her first Oscar nomination for this strikingly grim movie. Two years later the award was hers for her outstanding, down-to-earth portrayal of a hard-as-nails call girl stalked by a killer in the 1971 success *Klute*, an otherwise fairly average thriller, which found her easily wiping the screen up with a very stiff Donald Sutherland in the title role.

She did not, however, cash in on this high level of show business heat, choosing to make more of a name for herself with her outspoken criticisms of President Nixon and the Vietnam War, earning herself a great many unforgiving enemies for decades to come. In the cinemas at this period her work included barely seen efforts like *Steelyard Blues*, as another streetwalker, in this muddled anti-establishment comedy, and the heavily panned remake of *The Blue Bird*, as if the original wasn't bad enough. More promising on the outset was an adaptation of *A Doll's House*, which wound up on television in most markets once Claire Bloom's version beat it into theatres. Just when the skeptics were ready to write her career off as past its heyday, she suddenly became America's premiere actress, starting with a pair of 1977 hits. First up was the caper comedy *Fun With Dick and Jane*, with Fonda once and for all showing her skill at comedy, turning to a life of crime with husband George Segal to retaliate for his job loss, and then the somber *Julia*, as writer Lillian Hellman, a combination of strength and vulnerability that got her another Oscar nomination. In *Coming Home* she was a timid wife who blossoms through her highly erotic relationship with paraplegic Jon Voight. The film was much talked about though only mildly popular at first, until both she and Voight took home Academy Awards for 1978. That year ended with a dull western *Comes a Horseman*, as an iron-willed rancher battling evil Jason Robards, and an ultra-serious bit in the all-star comedy *California Suite*, trading bitter insults with ex-husband Alan Alda. The former hurt her momentum not at all and the latter was one of the year's top moneymakers. She was on a roll. *The China Syndrome* was an excellent drama, and a strong contender for the best film she ever appeared in, a cautionary tale about a near-disaster at a nuclear plant with Fonda as the newswoman awakened by the seriousness of the issues at hand. Shortly after the release of the movie a similar incident took place for real at Three Mile Island, causing the film to become a must-see event, with Jane only too eager to talk about the problems of nuclear power wherever she could find a soap box. It also brought her another Oscar nod.

A reunion with Redford, *The Electric Horseman*, a lazy romance with some satirical swipes at media adoration thrown in, was a missed opportunity but it did nice business, while a frisky comedy about secretaries taking vengeance on their boss, *Nine to Five*, was the biggest hit Fonda ever had. Then came *On Golden Pond*, a project she had pursued for herself and her father. Taking a secondary part, she had some superb moments opposite him, trying to connect desperately before it is too late, and the press made much of the real-life parallel to her equally strained relationship with her famous dad. This time her Oscar nomination came in the supporting category. The film was such a phenomenon that it wiped out any notice of her colorless romantic thriller, *Rollover*, which opened around the same time. During all this high profile work she had carved out a second career for herself as an exercise guru with a best selling book and video tape, leading the way for a legion of copycat celebrities marketing similar products. It made her so rich that she didn't need to work and was, in fact, off the big screen for four years, pausing to act on television in *The Dollmaker*, as a backwoods mother in 1940s Kentucky, and winning herself an Emmy Award. Her return to theatrical features came with *Agnes of God*, as fine as ever as a chain smoking psychiatrist, and a mild melodrama, *The Morning After*, bolstered considerably by her Oscar-nominated work as a drunken, washed up actress. Apparently losing interest in her craft, she came up with two major disappointments, *Old Gringo*, as a virgin involved in political dissension south of the border, and *Stanley and Iris*, hoping to educate illiterate Robert De Niro. By the time the last was released in early 1990 she had declared her retirement from acting with the intention of playing wife to television executive Ted Turner, and counting the cash from her exercise empire. When the couple split a decade later, she stood her ground, telling the press that her show business life was a thing of the past, depriving the world of years worth of potentially brilliant work. In 1974 she put together a documentary with then-husband Tom Hayden, *Introduction to the Enemy/Vietnam Journey*, and later served as executive producer for the television series adaptation of *9 to 5*.

Screen: 1960: Tall Story; 1962: Walk on the Wild Side; The Chapman Report; Period of Adjustment; 1963: In the Cool of the Day; 1964: Sunday in New York; Joy House/The Love Cage; 1965: Cat Ballou; Circle of Love/La Ronde; 1966: The Chase; Any Wednesday; 1967: The Game Is Over; Hurry Sundown; Barefoot in the Park; 1968: Barbarella; 1969: Spirits of the Dead; They Shoot Horses, Don't They?; 1971: Klute; 1972: F.T.A. (and prod.; co-wr.); 1973: Tout va Bien; Steelyard Blues; A Doll's House; 1976: The Blue Bird; 1977: Fun With Dick and Jane; Julia; 1978: Coming Home; Comes a Horseman; California Suite; 1979: The China Syndrome; The Electric Horseman; 1980: No Nukes; Nine to Five; 1981: On Golden Pond; Rollover; 1985: Agnes of God; 1986: The Morning After; 1987: Leonard Part 6; 1989: Old Gringo; 1990: Stanley and Iris.

NY Stage: 1960: There Was a Little Girl; Invitation to a March; 1962: The Fun Couple; 1963: Strange Interlude.

Select TV: 1961: A String of Beads (sp); 1984: The Dollmaker.

JOAN FONTAINE

(Joan de Beauvoir de Havilland)
Born: Tokyo, Japan, October 22, 1917.

Because of Joan Fontaine's long-time rivalry with her older sister Olivia de Havilland, it is difficult not to assess them together as actresses, with Olivia coming out ahead in overall impact. Fontaine, however, was a fine performer in her own right, with an unforced sense of poise and an appealing vul-

nerability that came through the often patrician air many of her characters carried. Shortly after both girls were born, their mother divorced and moved to America, where she remarried a man named Fontaine, thereby giving Joan her stage name. A brief tenure with a San Jose theater group, under the name Joan Burfield, won her a screen test with MGM and a part in a 1935 Joan Crawford film, *No More Ladies*, as one of the women used by wolf Robert Montgomery. Producer Jesse Lasky caught one of her stage performances, signed her to a contract and then sold it to RKO, where her first role was in support of Katharine Hepburn, in *Quality Street*. That studio decided to make her a leading lady in "B" films, including *You Can't Beat Love*, as the daughter of a mayor campaigning for re-election; *Maid's Night Out*, as an impoverished deb; *The Man Who Found Himself*, as a nurse trying to help disgraced doctor John Beal; and *Sky Giant*, as the woman fought over by pilots Richard Dix and Chester Morris. In between, she got to be Fred Astaire's co-star in his non-Ginger Rogers film of this period, *A Damsel in Distress*. To play it safe, the studio gave the great dancer Burns and Allen for added insurance because Fontaine, nice as she was, didn't know a thing about hoofing, her one number being obscured by trees. There was also a small role in another big RKO picture, *Gunga Din*, as Douglas Fairbanks, Jr.'s fiancée (though she hardly made much of an impression amid the male hijinks and action), and one over at MGM, as one of *The Women*, a confused young thing who has dumped her husband and run off to Reno.

In 1939 she married her first husband (1939–45), actor Brian Aherne, who had appeared in the earlier film version of one of her later films, *The Constant Nymph*. Stardom came in 1940, when Fontaine was chosen by producer David O. Selznick and director Alfred Hitchcock to play Laurence Olivier's shy bride, whose first name is never mentioned, in *Rebecca*. She rose above the character's potentially annoying timidity to make her deeply sympathetic and engaging, earning an Oscar nomination in the process. The film itself became one of the year's top box-office hits, established Hitchcock in America, and won the Academy Award for Best Picture of 1940. Almost immediately, she followed it up with a second Hitchcock outing, *Suspicion*, as yet another nervous wife, in this case one who thinks her husband, Cary Grant, is trying to bump her off. It was not one of the cinema's great acting triumphs, nor was it one of that great director's outstanding films, but it did solidify her standing in the industry when she won the Academy Award for Best Actress of 1941. One of those that she beat out for the trophy was sister Olivia, which may have been the genesis for their life-long feud. In addition to getting that coveted industry accolade, these were her most lucrative years at the box office, as she skipped between various studios, on loan from Selznick. There was a popular wartime romantic teaming with Tyrone Power, *This Above All*, at Fox; a gentle drama that found her playing a teen convincingly enough to receive another Oscar nod, *The Constant Nymph*, for Warners; and Fox's splendid 1944 version of *Jane Eyre*, which almost certainly contained her very best performance, as the plain but determined governess who falls in love with the moody Rochester (Orson Welles) while employed at his estate on the Yorkshire moors. This was followed by the Technicolor pirate epic, *Frenchman's Creek*, an expensive but profitable endeavor made for Paramount, and the sort of superficial, idiotic movie that gives costume adventures a bad name. Also for that studio, she got a chance to show her knack for comedy in the cute *The Affairs of Susan*, as an actress who changes her personality according to the taste of her four suitors.

At this point she terminated her contract with Selznick, since most of her work had been done for others anyway. She played a wicked lady in *Ivy*, trying to kill off her husband and lover; a snobby countess wooed by Bing Crosby in the musical *The Emperor Waltz*; and a woman pining for her lost love, Louis Jourdan, in *Letter From an Unknown Woman*, a film that became more highly-regarded over the years because of the strong cult following for its director, Max Ophuls. During the late 1940s and early 1950s Fontaine began to lose her stature, though there were some hits, like the romantic *September Song*, in which she and lover Joseph Cotten realized they are on the reported "dead" list of their crashed air flight, and *Ivanhoe*, in which she basically took a back seat to the pageantry and sword fighting. For director George Stevens she had an effective role as an alcoholic in *Something to Live For*, but it was not one of his more notable films. In *Casanova's Big Night* and *Serenade*, she was simply there to fill in the leading-lady roles, for Bob Hope and Mario Lanza, respectively. Becoming an ensemble player, she carried on a forbidden romance with Harry Belafonte in *Island in the Sun*, and its interracial theme made this Fox-made potboiler a hot property at the time. There was also an above-average soap opera about four sisters in wartime New Zealand, *Until They Sail*; the sci-fi adventure *Voyage to the Bottom of the Sea*, with Fontaine looking very efficient as a scientist who is ultimately done in by a shark; and the much-disliked 1962 version of *Tender Is the Night*, where she played Jennifer Jones's money-obsessed sister. Although she ended her movie career in 1967, as the star of a Hammer horror film, *The Devil's Own*, she continued to act onstage and in a few telefilms. In 1978 she published her autobiography, *No Bed of Roses*.

Screen: AS JOAN BURFIELD: 1935: No More Ladies.

AS JOAN FONTAINE: 1937: Quality Street; You Can't Beat Love; The Man Who Found Himself; Music for Madame; A Million to One; A Damsel in Distress; 1938: Maid's Night Out; Blonde Cheat; Sky Giant; The Duke of West Point; 1939: Gunga Din; Man of Conquest; The Women; 1940: Rebecca; 1941: Suspicion; 1942: This Above All; 1943: The Constant Nymph; 1944: Jane Eyre; Frenchman's Creek; 1945: The Affairs of Susan; 1946: From This Day Forward; 1947: Ivy; 1948: The Emperor's Waltz; Letter From an Unknown Woman; Kiss the Blood Off My Hands; You Gotta Stay Happy; 1950: Born to Be Bad; September Affair; 1951: Darling, How Could You!; 1952: Something to Live For; Ivanhoe; Othello; 1953: Decameron Nights; Flight to Tangier; The Bigamist; 1954: Casanova's Big Night; 1956: Serenade; Beyond a Reasonable Doubt; 1957: Island in the Sun; Until They Sail; 1958: A Certain Smile; 1961: Voyage to the Bottom of the Sea; 1962: Tender Is the Night; 1967: The Devil's Own/The Witches.

NY Stage: 1954: Tea and Sympathy; 1970: 40 Carats.

Select TV: 1953: Girl on a Park Bench (sp); 1955: Trudy (sp); 1956: In Summer Promise (sp); The Shadowy Third (sp); 1957: The Victorian Chaise Lounge (sp); 1959: Perilous (sp); 1960: Closed Set (sp); The Story of Judith (sp); 1978: The Users; 1986: Crossings (ms); Dark Mansions; 1994: Good King Wenceslas.

DICK FORAN

(JOHN NICHOLAS FORAN) BORN: FLEMINGTON, NJ, JUNE 18, 1910. ED: PRINCETON UNIV. DIED: AUGUST 10, 1979.

This tall, red-haired, long-faced cowboy from New Jersey was a star of "B" westerns (and much more affable and animated than so many in this genre), while chalking up a few supporting roles in some mainstream releases. Despite his screen image of a hayseed, westerner, or rube, he was Princeton-educated, originally set on becoming a geologist before his interest in singing steered

him towards show business. He wound up on the radio as a vocalist and bandleader, eventually signing a contract with Fox in 1934, billed as Nick Foran. Warners hired him the following year to carry a series of singing cowboy cheapies, starting with *Moonlight on the Prairie*, but it was his role as the oafish Boze in that studio's adaptation of the stage hit *The Petrified Forest* that brought him his greatest attention so far. There were also supporting parts in the anti-Klan drama *Black Legion*, as Humphrey Bogart's co-worker who tries to blow the whistle on a hate group, with tragic results; *Boy Meets Girl*, in a very funny turn as an egotistical movie star; *Four Daughters*, as Gale Page's goofy suitor; and *The Fighting 69th*, as a member of the regiment. In 1940 he was hired by Universal, where he was the crusading newspaper man in love with Mae West in *My Little Chickadee*; the unnecessary love interest in the studio's take on *The House of the Seven Gables*; archaeologist Steve Banning in both *The Mummy's Hand* and *The Mummy's Tomb*; and straight man to Abbott and Costello in *In the Navy*, *Keep 'Em Flying*, and *Ride 'Em Cowboy* (in which he sang the hit "I'll Remember April"). He was the star of a pair of western serials, *Winners of the West* and *Riders of Death Valley*, and had leads in some "B" second-string musicals, *Hi, Buddy* and *He's My Guy*. In the 1950s and 1960s he was seen as a character actor in films like *Chicago Confidential* and *Donovan's Reef*, while co-starring in programmers like *Violent Road*, carrying high explosives through dangerous territory, and *The Atomic Submarine*, encountering an underwater spaceship.

Screen: AS NICK FORAN: 1934: Stand Up and Cheer; Change of Heart; Gentlemen Are Born; 1935: Lottery Lover; One More Spring; It's a Small World; Ladies Love Danger; Accent on Youth.

AS DICK FORAN: 1935: Moonlight on the Prairie; The Farmer Takes a Wife; Shipmates Forever; Dangerous; 1936: The Petrified Forest; Song of the Saddle; Treachery Rides the Range; Trailin' West; The Case of the Velvet Claws; The Big Noise; The Golden Arrow; Earthworm Tractors; California Mail; Public Enemy's Wife; Black Legion; 1937: Guns of the Pecos; Land Beyond the Law; Blazing Sixes; The Devil's Saddle Legion; Empty Holsters; Prairie Thunder; Cherokee Strip; The Perfect Specimen; 1938: She Loved a Fireman; Over the Wall; Cowboy From Brooklyn; Love, Honor and Behave; Four Daughters; Secrets of a Nurse; Heart of the North; Boy Meets Girl; The Sisters; 1939: Daughters Courageous; Hero for a Day; Inside Information; I Stole a Million; Four Wives; Private Detective; 1940: The Fighting 69th; My Little Chickadee; The House of the Seven Gables; Rangers of Fortune; The Mummy's Hand; Winners of the West (serial); 1941: Four Mothers; In the Navy; Horror Island; Mob Town; Riders of Death Valley (serial); Unfinished Business; Keep 'Em Flying; The Kid From Kansas; Road Agent; 1942: Ride 'Em Cowboy; The Mummy's Tomb; Butch Minds the Baby; Behind the Eight Ball; Private Buckaroo; 1943: Hi, Buddy; He's My Guy; 1945: Guest Wife; 1947: Easy Come, Easy Go; 1948: Fort Apache; 1949: Deputy Marshal; El Paso; 1951: Al Jennings of Oklahoma; 1954: Treasure of Ruby Hills; 1956: Please Murder Me!; 1957: Sierra Stranger; Chicago Confidential; 1958: Thundering Jets; The Fearmakers; Violent Road; 1959: Atomic Submarine; 1960: The Big Night; Studs Lonigan; 1962: Donovan's Reef; 1964: Taggart; 1967: Brighty of Grand Canyon.

NY Stage: 1943: A Connecticut Yankee.

Select TV: 1950: The Loud Red Patrick (sp); 1951: Treasure Trove (sp); Screwball (sp); Tremolo (sp); 1954: Detective's Holiday (sp); The Philadelphia Story (sp); 1955: Billy and the Bride (sp); Cardboard Casanova (sp); Face of Danger (sp); Miracle on 34th Street (sp); 1957: Sweet Charlie (sp); 1959: The

Sounds of Eden (sp); The Swamp Fox (ms); **1960:** The Redcoat Strategy (sp); **1965–66:** O.K. Crackerby (series).

GLENN FORD

(Gwyllyn Samuel Newton Ford)
Born: Quebec, Canada, May 1, 1916.
Raised in Santa Monica, CA.

The career of Glenn Ford was long, varied, and very busy. Although he often seemed no more exciting than someone's average uncle who just happened to be a movie actor, there were varying moods he conveyed, with a fierce and full determination, that made him quite effective in certain parts. Ford could be brooding, mean, heroic, taciturn, wise, foolish, amiable, dull, or sardonic, and, for a period in the 1950s, he had just the right persona to make him a box-office attraction as well. Growing up in Southern California, he had his first taste of show business working as a stable boy for Will Rogers. He joined the Santa Monica Players, which resulted in a short film, "Night in Manhattan," and offers from Broadway. It was, however, another play back in California, *Judgment Day*, which won him a contract with Columbia Pictures, although they did not give him his first film assignment. That came from the 20th Century-Fox "B" unit, where he played a department store clerk traveling west to Arizona in *Heaven With a Barbed Wire Fence*. Apparently Columbia didn't think any more highly of him, since they basically stuck him in one "B" film after another, including *Convicted Women*, as a reporter; *Babies for Sale*, ditto, only this time in the lead; and *Blondie Plays Cupid*, paired with Luana Walters, as a couple helped by Penny Singleton. As was customary for second-string players who showed some promise, the studio rewarded him with occasional "A" jobs. These included *The Lady in Question*, which was notable for teaming him with Rita Hayworth for the first time, and *Texas*, where he acted alongside William Holden, who would become a lifelong friend. Not unexpectedly he got his best break elsewhere, with the independently produced *So Ends Our Night*, an intelligent drama about a trio of disparate types fleeing Nazi Germany, with Ford cast as a half Aryan, half Jew.

Back at Columbia he got to play Jack London's hero in *The Adventures of Martin Eden*, and he appeared in the requisite wartime dramas, *Flight Lieutenant* and *Destroyer*, before joining the Marines for real. When he came back from the service, his career got a terrific shot in the arm when he reteamed with Hayworth for one of the hottest films of 1946, *Gilda*, as her brooding, angry ex-lover and an employee of jealous club-owner George Macready. That same year Bette Davis personally selected him to play opposite two of her in the silly soap opera *A Stolen Life*, and it looked as if Ford had at last made it to the top. As far as Columbia was concerned, though, it didn't mean that he got assigned the greatest material, what with a mild comedy, *The Mating of Millie*, and a reunion with Hayworth, *The Loves of Carmen*, where he was cast most implausibly as Don Jose. He did get to play up his bad side, as a nasty judge in a western with Holden, *The Man From Colorado*, and as the killer of Ida Lupino and Gig Young, driven by his selfish desire for wealth, in *Lust for Gold*. More of the films that kept his résumé lengthy but short of great titles followed, including *The Doctor and the Girl*, the girl being Janet Leigh; *The Redhead and the Cowboy*, with Rhonda Fleming's locks being the hair in question; *The Secret of Convict Lake*, with Ford as an escaped con stumbling upon a settlement of women; *Follow the Sun*, a biopic of golfer Ben Hogan, the drama stemming from his having endured a near-tragic car accident; *Affair in Trinidad*, a deadly dull fourth teaming with

Hayworth; and *The Man From the Alamo*, with the actor at his most stolid as the man who chooses to leave the fort and is branded a coward.

Many of these were made for other studios, but *The Big Heat*, directed by Fritz Lang, was done back at Columbia, and it turned out to be one of Ford's very best assignments, a tense melodrama in which he effectively played an ex-cop trying to destroy Lee Marvin's crime syndicate. Even though he was relentlessly busy, he managed to work in another Lang film, *Human Desire*, with one of his *Big Heat* co-stars, Gloria Grahame, though this time the magic wasn't there. He appeared in two drab South American offerings for RKO, *Appointment in Honduras* and *The Americano*, and in a western with Barbara Stanwyck and Edward G. Robinson, *The Violent Men*. Then he went over to MGM for three major 1955 releases that made him a box-office draw: *Blackboard Jungle*, giving a fine performance as the decent, nervous teacher who takes on a class of juvenile delinquents in what is probably his most famous film; *Interrupted Melody*, a biopic that is very much a dated product of the 1950s, as the devoted husband of polio-inflicted opera singer Marjorie Lawrence (Eleanor Parker); and the engrossing *Trial*, portraying a lawyer defending a Mexican boy tried for murder. Because of these, he was signed up by MGM, who put him in *Ransom!*, with the actor really delivering the emotional goods as a father coping with his son's kidnapping. Metro then gave him two big hit service farces: *The Teahouse of the August Moon*, where he showed his flair for gentle comedy as an army officer building the title structure, though he quarreled off screen with co-star Marlon Brando, and the much weaker *Don't Go Near the Water*, in which he played a Navy officer building a recreation hall on a South Pacific island. Meanwhile, back at Columbia, he did a pair of superior westerns: *Jubal*, as a cowpoke who finds himself in a mess of trouble when he gets involved with jealous Ernest Borgnine's wife, and *3:10 to Yuma*, in perhaps his most convincing bad guy performance, taunting the sheriff (Van Heflin) who is trying to take him into custody. He tried for something a tad different with *Cowboy*, which dispensed with guns and shootouts to concentrate on a cattle roundup.

It appeared at this point that he was becoming most relaxed in nice-guy roles and comedies, as with *The Sheepman*, with Shirley MacLaine; *It Started With a Kiss*, a marital romp set in Spain, with Debbie Reynolds; *The Gazebo*, an amusing black farce involving blackmail, also with Reynolds; and *The Courtship of Eddie's Father*, the story of a widower whose son, Ronny Howard, is trying to find him a wife. Less effectively, he took on some ill-advised remakes with *Cimarron*, which did not do for MGM what the update of *Ben-Hur* had done; *Pocketful of Miracles*, in which he caused endless problems off-set with director Frank Capra and was out of his element as a Ramon Runyon character in this remake of *Lady for a Day*; and director Vincente Minnelli's disastrous *The Four Horsemen of the Apocalypse*, with Ford as the last actor you'd expect to be following in Valentino's footsteps. The "heat" he'd managed to generate for that brief five-year period in the 1950s had started to cool off. Most of his 1960s films were of little consequence, such as an implausible thriller, *Experiment in Terror*; a forced Civil War comedy, *Advance to the Rear*; a sad, final teaming with Hayworth, *The Money Trap*; the all-star dud, *Is Paris Burning?*, as General Omar Bradley; and one of the poorest box-office performers for the usually lucky Disney Studio, *Smith!*, a well-meaning pro-Indian tale. Ford's pleasant New York romance with Geraldine Page, *Dear Heart*, received little attention, though there was some degree of interest in *The Rounders*, where he and Henry Fonda teamed as a pair of down-and-dirty cowpokes. Inevitably he turned to television, where he starred in two short-lived series, *Cade's County* and *The Family Holvak*. There were occasional returns to the cinema, but most of these were stuff made strictly for the cash, like *The Visitor*, an Italian sci-fi cheapie; *Happy Birthday to Me*, a slasher film; and *Raw Nerve*, a thriller minus any thrills. There was one worthwhile production during this period, *Superman*, in which he was very touching as the farmer who becomes the Man of Steel's earthling father. He was married (1943–59) to dancer Eleanor Powell, and to two lesser-known actresses, Kathryn Hays and Cynthia Howard. In 1970 he published his autobiography *Glenn Ford, R.F.D. Beverly Hills*.

Screen: 1939: Heaven With a Barbed Wire Fence; My Son Is Guilty; 1940: Convicted Women; Men Without Souls; Babies for Sale; Blondie Plays Cupid; The Lady in Question; 1941: So Ends Our Night; Texas; Go West, Young Lady; 1942: The Adventures of Martin Eden; Flight Lieutenant; 1943: The Desperadoes; Destroyer; 1946: Gilda; A Stolen Life; Gallant Journey; 1947: Framed; 1948: The Mating of Millie; The Loves of Carmen; The Return of October; The Man From Colorado; 1949: The Undercover Man; Lust for Gold; Mr. Soft Touch; The Doctor and the Girl; 1950: The White Tower; Convicted; The Redhead and the Cowboy; The Flying Missile; 1951: Follow the Sun; The Secret of Convict Lake; 1952: The Green Glove; Affair in Trinidad; Young Man With Ideas; 1953: Time Bomb; The Man From the Alamo; Plunder of the Sun; The Big Heat; Appointment in Honduras; 1954: Human Desire; 1955: The Americano; The Violent Men; Blackboard Jungle; Interrupted Melody; Trial; 1956: Ransom!; Jubal; The Fastest Gun Alive; The Teahouse of the August Moon; 1957: 3:10 to Yuma; Don't Go Near the Water; 1958: Cowboy; The Sheepman; Imitation General; Torpedo Run; 1959: It Started With a Kiss; The Gazebo; 1960: Cimarron; 1961: Cry for Happy; Pocketful of Miracles; 1962: The Four Horsemen of the Apocalypse; Experiment in Terror; 1963: Love Is a Ball; The Courtship of Eddie's Father; 1964: Advance to the Rear; Fate Is the Hunter; Dear Heart; 1965: The Rounders; 1966: The Money Trap; Is Paris Burning?; Rage; 1967: A Time for Killing; The Last Challenge; 1968: Day of the Evil Gun; 1969: Heaven With a Gun; Smith!; 1973: Santee; 1976: Midway; 1978: Superman; 1979: The Visitor; 1980: Virus; 1981: Happy Birthday to Me; Day of the Assassin (nUSr); 1988: Casablanca Express (dtv); 1990: Border Shootout (nUSr); 1992: Our Hollywood Education (nUSr); Raw Nerve.

NY Stage: AS GWYLLYN FORD: 1938: Soliloquy.

Select TV: 1970: The Brotherhood of the Bell; 1971–72: Cade's County (series); 1973: Jarrett; 1974: The Disappearance of Flight 412; The Greatest Gift; Punch and Jody; 1975: Friends of Man (series narrator); The Family Holvak (series); 1977: Once an Eagle (ms); The Three Thousand Mile Chase; 1978: When Havoc Struck (series narrator); Evening in Byzantium; 1979: The Sacketts; Beggarman, Thief; The Gift; 1991: Final Verdict.

PAUL FORD

(PAUL FORD WEAVER) BORN: BALTIMORE, MD, NOVEMBER 2, 1901. DIED: APRIL 12, 1976.

This bulbous-nosed, jowly character player, who was so good at playing blustery windbags in various states of befuddlement and exasperation, came into the public consciousness once he was past the age of 50. Paul Ford did not, in fact, get started in the business until he was in his 40s, working with a puppet theater sponsored by the WPA. From there he acted on radio and debuted on Broadway in *Decision*, in 1944, and in films with *The House on 92nd Street*, in 1945, way down the cast

list, as a sergeant. It was television that made him famous when he joined *You'll Never Get Rich* (later known as *The Phil Silvers Show* or by its lead character's name, *Sgt. Bilko*) as Col. Hall, the flustered, consistently outwitted superior of fast-talking army con man Phil Silvers. This role was, no doubt, inspired by his scene-stealing turn as another confused military man, Colonel Purdy, in the 1953 Broadway hit *The Teahouse of the August Moon*. Due to the tragic passing of Louis Calhern while on location, Ford got the chance to resume his movie career with the 1956 film version, once again getting raves. Over the years the Ford shtick was used to great effect as grouchy Horace Vandergelder in *The Matchmaker*, a rather ideal mating of actor and part; speech-spouting blowhard Mayor Shinn in *The Music Man* (he had followed David Burns in the part onstage); the nit-witted air traffic controller in *It's a Mad Mad Mad Mad World*; and the gung-ho townie eager to fight the enemy in *The Russians Are Coming! The Russians Are Coming!* One of his larger roles came when he repeated his stage part as the senior citizen facing fatherhood in the typical 1960s comedy *Never Too Late*. He could be seen in a somewhat quieter, more serious vein in such movies as *Advise and Consent*, as a senator, and *The Comedians*, in which he and Lillian Gish were health food advocates pitching their product to the Haitians.

Screen: 1945: The House on 92nd Street; 1948: The Naked City; 1949: Lust for Gold; All the King's Men; 1950: The Kid From Texas; Perfect Strangers; 1956: The Teahouse of the August Moon; 1958: The Missouri Traveler; The Matchmaker; 1962: The Music Man; Advise and Consent; Who's Got the Action?; 1963: It's a Mad Mad Mad Mad World; 1965: Never Too Late; 1966: The Russians Are Coming! The Russians Are Coming!; A Big Hand for the Little Lady; The Spy With a Cold Nose; 1967: The Comedians; 1970: Lola/Twinky; 1972: Richard; 1974: Journey Back to Oz (voice; filmed in 1964).

NY Stage: 1944: Decision; Lower North; 1945: Kiss Them for Me; 1946: Flamingo Road; Another Part of the Forest; 1947: As We Forgive Our Debtors; Command Decision; 1952: Brass Ring; 1953: The Teahouse of the August Moon; 1957: Good as Gold; 1958: Whoop-Up; 1959: The Music Man; 1960: A Thurber Carnival; 1962: Never Too Late; 1966: 3 Bags Full; 1967: What Did We Do Wrong?; 1969: Three Men on a Horse; The Front Page; 1972: Fun City.

Select TV: 1955–59: You'll Never Get Rich/The Phil Silvers Show (series); 1956: The Tale of St. Emergency (sp); Bloomer Girl (sp); 1957: A Man's Game (sp); 1960: The Girls in 509 (sp); The Right Man (sp); Babes in Toyland (sp); 1961: Open House (sp); 1962: The Teahouse of the August Moon (sp); 1963: Don't Shake the Family Tree (sp); 1964–65: The Baileys of Balboa (series); 1969: In Name Only.

WALLACE FORD

(SAMUEL JONES GRUNDY) BORN: BOLTON, LANCASHIRE, ENGLAND, FEBRUARY 12, 1898. DIED: JUNE 11, 1966.

An earthy character player with a tendency to chomp down on a part to both good and bad effect, Wallace Ford pretty much disguised his British roots, although he would return to his native dialect when called for. Running away from a childhood spent mostly in foster homes, he wound up in vaudeville and then the legitimate stage, eventually coming to Broadway, where he made his name throughout the 1920s. Hollywood, looking for theater people at the dawn of the talkies, beckoned and Ford debuted there in 1930, in two short subjects. He then made his feature bow at MGM, in *Possessed*, as the dull fiancé Joan Crawford dumps for Clark Gable. There were some leads, such as the wisecracking reporter getting the scoop on an escaped killer in *Night of Terror*; the sympathetic clown in Todd Browning's startling *Freaks*, which became one of the most notorious "horror" movies of its day; the selfish song and dance man who abandons the woman who stood by him in *My Woman*; the truck driver determined to make his marriage to Gloria Shea work in *Money Means Nothing*; the second-rate director who turns his bad Sheik film into a comedy in *The Nut House*; the injured racecar driver in *In Spite of Danger*; and the racketeer who ends up in the military in the British film *You're in the Army Now*. For director John Ford, he was properly British as one of the nervous soldiers under siege in the gripping *The Lost Patrol*, and had his most famous role of the 1930s, in *The Informer*, as the rebel whom best friend Victor McLaglen sells out for the price of a drink. He would jam pack his schedule over the next three decades with such roles as an archeologist in *The Mummy's Hand*; a detective on the trail of killer Joseph Cotten in *Shadow of a Doubt*; the cab driver who helps save James Stewart from being "cured" in *Harvey*; the sheriff in *The Rainmaker*; and his last part, as Elizabeth Hartman's sad, drunken old grandfather, in *A Patch of Blue*.

Screen: 1931: Possessed; X Marks the Spot; 1932: Skyscraper Souls; Freaks; Beast of the City; Prosperity; Hypnotized; Central Park; Are You Listening?; The Wet Parade; City Sentinel; 1933: Goodbye Again; East of Fifth Avenue; The Big Cage; Employees' Entrance; Headline Shooter; My Woman; Night of Terror; Three-Cornered Moon; She Had to Say Yes; 1934: Money Means Nothing; A Woman's Man; Men in White; The Man Who Reclaimed His Head; I Hate Women; The Lost Patrol; 1935: Another Face; The Whole Town Is Talking; The Nut Farm; The Informer; Swell Head; In Spite of Danger; She Couldn't Take It; Men of the Hour; Get That Man; Mary Burns — Fugitive; One Frightened Night; The Mysterious Mr. Wong; Sanders of the River; 1936: Rogues' Tavern; Two in the Dark; Absolute Quiet; A Son Comes Home; 1937: You're in the Army Now/OHMS; Dark Sands/Jericho; He Loved an Actress/Mad About Money/Stardust; Exiled to Shanghai; 1938: Swing It Sailor; 1939: Back Door to Heaven; 1940: Isle of Destiny; Two Girls on Broadway; Love, Honor and Oh Baby!; Give Us Wings; The Mummy's Hand; Scatterbrain; 1941: A Man Betrayed; The Roar of the Press; Blues in the Night; Murder by Invitation; 1942: Scattergood Survives a Murder; Inside the Law; All Through the Night; Seven Days' Leave; The Mummy's Tomb; 1943: The Marines Come Through; Shadow of a Doubt; The Cross of Lorraine; The Ape Man; 1944: Secret Command; Machine Gun Mama; 1945: The Great John L.; Spellbound; They Were Expendable; Blood on the Sun; On Stage Everybody; 1946: The Green Years; A Guy Could Change; Rendezvous With Annie; Crack-Up; The Black Angel; Lover Come Back; 1947: Dead Reckoning; Magic Town; T-Men; 1948: Shed No Tears; Coroner Creek; The Man From Texas; Embraceable You; Belle Starr's Daughter; 1949: Red Stallion of the Rockies; The Set-Up; 1950: The Breaking Point; Dakota Lil; The Furies; Harvey; 1951: Warpath; He Ran All the Way; Painting the Clouds With Sunshine; 1952: Flesh and Fury; Rodeo; 1953: The Nebraskan; The Great Jesse James Raid; 1954: She Couldn't Say No; The Boy From Oklahoma; Destry; 3 Ring Circus; 1955: The Man From Laramie; The Spoilers; Lucy Gallant; A Lawless Street; Wichita; 1956: Johnny Concho; The Maverick Queen; The First Texan; Stagecoach to Fury; Thunder Over Arizona; The Rainmaker; 1958: The Last Hurrah; The Matchmaker; Twilight for the Gods; 1959: Warlock; 1961: Tess of the Storm Country; 1965: A Patch of Blue.

NY Stage: 1918: Seventeen; 1919: Abraham Lincoln; 1921: The

Poppy God; 1922: Broken Branches; Abie's Irish Rose; 1923: Nobody's Business; 1924: Gypsy Jim; Nancy Ann; Pigs; 1929: Gypsy; The Nut Farm; 1937: Of Mice and Men; 1939: Kindred.
Select TV: 1952: Come What May (sp); 1953: The Happy Rest (sp); 1954: Runaway (sp); 1955: The Ox-Bow Incident (sp); 1957: Snow Shoes (sp); 1958: The Last Man (sp); Silent Thunder (sp); 1959–60: The Deputy (series); 1964: Bristle Face (sp).

STEVE FORREST

(WILLIAM FORREST ANDREWS)
BORN: HUNSTVILLE, TX, SEPTEMBER 29, 1924.
ED: UCLA

15 years younger than his more famous and more interesting brother, Dana Andrews, Steve Forrest managed to carve out a lengthy, if less-than-distinguished, career of his own. Under his real name he worked in bit parts, starting with *Crash Dive*, which featured his brother. Pausing for military service and radio performing, he tried to re-establish himself again in the early 1950s, still using his real name, but decided to change it to "Steve Forrest" in 1952, with *The Bad and the Beautiful*, where he was glimpsed playing a movie actor. He continued at MGM in small parts, rising up the cast list for *So Big*, as farmer Jane Wyman's son who goes off to the big bad city (Chicago); *Rogue Cop*, as the brother of corrupt policeman Robert Taylor, who bites the dust, for plot purposes; and *Prisoner of War*, second billed to Ronald Reagan, as one of the incarcerated G.I.'s tortured by the Koreans. Finally, in 1955, he was upped to co-star, playing a would-be priest who shelters on-the-run Anne Baxter in the melodrama *Bedevilled*. When Forrest worked in films, it was usually in roles that would not detract from the stars, such as *It Happened to Jane*, hoping to sway Doris Day away from Jack Lemmon; *Flaming Star*, as Elvis Presley's older brother in one of the singer's better movies; and *The Second Time Around*, marrying sheriff Debbie Reynolds. He did get top billing for Disney's *Rascal*, but the real stars of that one were young Billy Mumy and his pet raccoon. On the tube he found steady work, including jobs as a series regular in *S.W.A.T.* and *Dallas*. Back on the big screen, he was seen as one of the men in Joan Crawford's life in *Mommie Dearest*, and then made fun of his stoic image in the space movie spoof in *Amazon Women on the Moon*. After another spell away from movies, he showed up as the warden in the little-seen *Killer: A Journal of Murder*.

Screen: AS WILLIAM ANDREWS: 1943: Crash Dive; The Ghost Ship; 1951: Geisha Girl; Sealed Cargo; 1952: Last of the Comanches.
AS STEVE FORREST: 1952: The Bad and the Beautiful; 1953: Dream Wife; Battle Circus; The Clown; So Big; Take the High Ground; The Band Wagon; 1954: Rogue Cop; Prisoner of War; Phantom of the Rue Morgue; 1955: Bedevilled; 1957: The Living Idol; 1959: It Happened to Jane; 1960: Heller in Pink Tights; Flaming Star; 5 Branded Women; 1961: The Second Time Around; 1962: The Longest Day; 1963: The Yellow Canary; 1969: Rascal; 1971: The Wild Country; The Late Liz; 1979: North Dallas Forty; 1981: Mommie Dearest; 1984: Sahara; 1985: Spies Like Us; 1987: Amazon Women on the Moon; 1992: Storyville; 1996: Killer: A Journal of Murder.
NY Stage: 1958: The Body Beautiful.
Select TV: 1957: Clipper Ship (sp); The Armed Venus (sp); 1958: You'll Have to Die Now (sp); Third Son (sp); 1960: Minister Accused (sp); 1966: The Baron (series); 1974: The Hanged Man; 1975: The Hatfields and the McCoys; 1975–76: S.W.A.T. (series); 1976: Wanted: The Sundance Woman; 1977: Testimony of Two Men (ms); Last of the Mohicans; 1978: Maneaters Are Loose!; The Deerslayer; 1979: Captain America; 1980: Roughnecks; A

Rumor of War; Condominium; **1981:** The Manions of America (ms); **1982:** Hotline; **1983:** Malibu; **1985:** Hollywood Wives (ms); **1986:** Dallas (series); **1987:** Gunsmoke: Return to Dodge; **1992:** Columbo: A Bird in the Hand.

JOHN FORSYTHE

(JOHN LINCOLN FREUND) BORN: PENNS GROVE, NJ, JANUARY 29, 1918. ED: UNIV. OF NC.

A smooth, pleasantly handsome leading man with an attractive speaking voice, John Forsythe owed most of his fame to television, where men of such a mild nature can make a bigger impression. Growing up in New York City and the Connecticut suburbs, he hoped to become a sportswriter. During college he spent his summers as a sports announcer for the Brooklyn Dodgers, which led to acting work on radio in various soap operas. There was also a supporting part in a big war film, *Destination Tokyo*, where he was cast, of course, as a radio operator, and then a bit as a soldier in *Northern Pursuit*, but these didn't lead to a studio contract or any further movies for the time being. Instead some stage work and duty with the U.S. Army Air Corps followed, after which he studied with the Actors Studio. Playing the title character in the road company of *Mister Roberts*, he was eventually allowed to follow Henry Fonda in the role on Broadway, which was a definite sign of progress. By this time he'd begun working frequently on television and had a Broadway hit of his own, *The Teahouse of the August Moon*, in the part Glenn Ford would play in the movie version, although Forsythe got a chance to reprise it on the small screen. In 1952 he landed the lead in a tense melodrama, *The Captive City*, as an honest reporter exposing small-town corruption, and was back at the news desk for *It Happens Every Thursday*, as Loretta Young's husband, the latter made at Universal, where he was under contract.

Obviously Hollywood pictured him as someone who seemed like he could write, for he played another such role, this time as a TV script writer, framed for murder, in *The Glass Web*. Over at MGM, in a grittier mode, he was the Confederate officer who forces William Holden to pursue him and his fellow prisoners in *Escape From Fort Bravo*. For a man with relatively few movie credits, he lucked out in getting to work with Alfred Hitchcock not once but twice, in *The Trouble With Harry*, and, later down the line, *Topaz*, though both ranked among the Master's less-accomplished efforts. He had his first TV success in 1957, with *Bachelor Father*, and, after several more attempts, he would find his longest-lasting job as the distinguished lead of the nighttime soap *Dynasty*. He also had the distinction of starring in what is considered, officially, to be the first made-for-television film, *See How They Run*, in 1964. Back at the movies, he was mired in the rubbishy *Kitten With a Whip*, as a politician kept under Ann-Margret's taunting thumb; appeared in the outstanding *In Cold Blood*, at his authoritative best as the main investigator of the heinous crimes; was convincingly slimy as the judge being defended by Al Pacino in *...And Justice for All*; and was totally unrecognizable under tons of icky makeup as the modern equivalent of Marley's Ghost in Bill Murray's *Scrooged*.

Screen: **1943:** Destination Tokyo; **1952:** The Captive City; **1953:** It Happens Every Thursday; The Glass Web; **1954:** Escape From Fort Bravo; **1955:** The Trouble With Harry; **1956:** The Ambassador's Daughter; Everything But the Truth; **1964:** Kitten With a Whip; **1966:** Madame X; **1967:** In Cold Blood; **1969:** The Happy Ending; Topaz; **1978:** Goodbye and Amen; **1979:** ...And Justice for All; **1988:** Scrooged; **1991:** Stan and George's New Life (nUSr); **2000:** Charlie's Angels (voice); **2003:** Charlie's Angels:

Full Throttle (voice).

NY Stage: **1942:** Yankee Point; Vickie; **1943:** Winged Victory; **1944:** Yellow Jack; **1946:** Woman Bites Dog; **1947:** It Takes Two; **1950:** Mister Roberts; **1953:** The Teahouse of the August Moon; **1968:** Weekend.

Select TV: **1951:** Dark Victory (sp); Three Hours Between Planes (sp); The American Leonardo (sp); The Monument (sp); I Am Jonathan Scrivener (sp); **1953:** Conflict (sp); **1956:** Return to Cassino (sp); **1957:** Girl With a Glow (sp); **1957–62:** Bachelor Father (series); **1959:** What Makes Sammy Run? (sp); **1962:** The Teahouse of the August Moon (sp); **1964:** See How They Run; **1965–66:** The John Forsythe Show (series); **1967:** A Bell for Adano (sp); **1968:** Shadow on the Land; **1969–71:** To Rome With Love (series); **1971:** Murder Once Removed; **1971–77:** The World of Survival (series narrator); **1973:** The Letters; Lisa — Bright and Dark; **1974:** Cry Panic; The Healers; Terror on the 40th Floor; **1975:** The Deadly Tower; **1976:** Amelia Earhart; **1976–81:** Charlie's Angels (series; voice); **1977:** Tail Gunner Joe; Never Con a Killer; **1978:** Cruise Into Terror; With This Ring; The Users; **1980:** A Time for Miracles; Sizzle; **1981–89:** Dynasty (series); **1982:** The Mysterious Two; **1987:** On Fire; **1990:** Opposites Attract; **1991:** Dynasty: The Reunion; **1992–93:** The Powers That Be (series); **1993–94:** I Witness Video (series); **1999:** Journey to the Center of the Earth.

BOB FOSSE

BORN: CHICAGO, IL, JUNE 23, 1927.
DIED: SEPTEMBER 23, 1987.

In addition to being one of the most distinctive and innovative choreographers in dance history, as well as an original and exciting film director, Bob Fosse was also a charming on-screen performer. He began dancing as a kid, entertained in burlesque shows, and then formed a nightclub dance team with his first wife (1949–51), Mary-Ann Niles. Because of their appearances, Fosse was hired as a dancer at MGM in the last years of its musical heyday, making his debut in a forgettable semi-musical *The Affairs of Dobie Gillis*, where he revealed a highly likeable personality. He could also dance with the best of them, as witnessed by his sensationally sexy movements in the "From This Moment On" number in *Kiss Me Kate*, and his plucky cavorting in the park with Debbie Reynolds to the song "In Our United State," in *Give a Girl a Break*. Over at Columbia he not only got to play Janet Leigh's suitor in the 1955 remake of *My Sister Eileen*, but also received his first on-screen credit as choreographer, staging a particularly exciting dance between himself and Tommy Rall. Around that same time he scored his first significant success on Broadway, as choreographer of *The Pajama Game*, winning the first of eight Tony Awards. With *Redhead*, in 1959, starring Gwen Verdon (whom he married the following year), he served as director *and* choreographer, his finger-snapping, hip-thrusting style of movement becoming part of theater legend. When his work for *The Pajama Game* and *Damn Yankees* was adapted for the screen, he not only received choreographer credit on both films but had perhaps his most exciting on-screen moment, dancing (unbilled) with Verdon in *Damn Yankees* to the playful "Who's Got the Pain?"

In 1969 he turned his attention to film directing with the snappy adaptation of *Sweet Charity*, which he had done onstage. With his second assignment, *Cabaret*, he surpassed all expectations and came up with a bold and dazzling work, winning the Academy Award for Best Director of 1972. Within a few months of that triumph, he also netted two Tonys for *Pippin* and an

Emmy for the TV special *Liza With a Z*. There were additional Oscar nominations for directing the grim, non-musical biography, *Lenny* (Bruce), and directing and writing the thinly veiled, autobiographical *All That Jazz*, about a bed-hopping director/choreographer driving himself to a heart attack. His final film, *Star 80*, about the murder of centerfold Dorothy Stratton, was another brilliant examination of the underside of show business. In 1974 he showed how sparkling a performer he still was when he played The Snake in the otherwise misguided adaptation of *The Little Prince*, and stole the notices hands down with his gyrating solo number. Although he and Verdon separated in 1970, they remained each other's trusted confidante and friend. She was, in fact, with him when he collapsed of a heart attack while on the road for the revival of *Sweet Charity*, in 1987.

Screen: 1953: The Affairs of Dobie Gillis; Give a Girl a Break; Kiss Me Kate; 1955: My Sister Eileen (and choreog.); 1958: Damn Yankees (and choreog.); 1974: Lenny (voice; and dir.); The Little Prince; 1977: Thieves.

NY Stage: (performer only): 1961: Pal Joey.

PRESTON FOSTER

BORN: OCEAN CITY, NJ, AUGUST 24, 1900.
DIED: JULY 14, 1970.

Both star and supporting player, hero and villain, Preston Foster brought his (ultimately) mustachioed machismo to a long list of films, but he was nothing more than a standard performer, without a strong enough personality to suggest that he should have or could have achieved higher heights. A former opera singer, he switched to legitimate stage work in the 1920s, appearing on Broadway in *Congratulations* and *Ladies All*, among others. He then made his name in Hollywood with the prison picture *The Last Mile*, as "Killer" Mears. Warners signed him to a contract, and he played a murderous lab assistant in the Technicolor thriller *Doctor X*; an evangelist who puts Barbara Stanwyck in jail and then marries her in *Ladies They Talk About*; and a killer loved by Aline MacMahon in *Heat Lightning*. When the Brothers Warner were through with him, RKO took him on for *The People's Enemy*, as a gangster who deserts his wife and child; *The Last Days of Pompeii*, as a blacksmith affected by his run-in with Jesus, a la Ben-Hur, (and no match at all in the memorable acting department against Basil Rathbone as Pontius Pilate); and *Annie Oakley*, as Toby Walker (not Frank Butler, as in real-life), the fellow-marksman who falls in love with Barbara Stanwyck. For RKO he also appeared in director John Ford's troubled production of *The Plough and the Stars*, opposite Stanwyck yet again, as an officer during the Irish Rebellion, and *The Outcasts of Poker Flat*, as author Brett Harte's gold-rush-era gambler. From there it was over to Universal, where he played detective Bill Crane in three B-movie mysteries: *The Westland Case*, *The Lady in the Morgue*, and *The Last Warning*, which in no way stood out from the dozens of other whodunits being produced around town. Still studio-hopping as the 1930s came to a close, he ended up at 20th Century-Fox, where he rated sizable roles on occasion, like the shady nightclub owner who winds up fighting both the Japanese *and* the Nazis in *Secret Agent of Japan*; the chaplain in the hit war film *Guadalcanal Diary* (just another entry in a crowded genre); Roddy McDowall's rancher dad in the seminal horse picture *My Friend Flicka* (there was also a sequel, *Thunderhead: Son of Flicka*); and a real-life Chicago hood in *Roger Touhy, Gangster*. During the 1950s the actor, by then playing supporting parts in films, landed his own series,

Waterfront, which eked out a respectable run.

Screen: 1928: Pusher-in-the-Face; 1929: Nothing but the Truth; 1930: Follow the Leader; Heads Up; 1931: His Woman; 1932: Life Begins; The All-American; You Said a Mouthful; Two Seconds; The Last Mile; Doctor X; I Am a Fugitive From a Chain Gang; 1933: Ladies They Talk About; Elmer the Great; Corruption; Dangerous Crossroads; The Man Who Dared; Hoopla; The Devil's Mate; 1934: Sensation Hunters; Heat Lightning; Sleepers East; Wharf Angel; The Band Plays On; 1935: The People's Enemy; Strangers All; The Informer; Annie Oakley; The Arizonan; The Last Days of Pompeii; We're Only Human; 1936: Love Before Breakfast; The Plough and the Stars; Muss 'em Up; We Who Are About to Die; 1937: The Outcasts of Poker Flat; Sea Devils; You Can't Beat Love; First Lady; The Westland Case; 1938: Everybody's Doing It; Submarine Patrol; Double Danger; The Lady in the Morgue; Up the River; The Last Warning; White Banners; Army Girl; The Storm; 1939: Society Smugglers; Twenty Thousand Men a Year; Chasing Danger; Missing Evidence; News Is Made at Night; Geronimo; 1940: Cafe Hostess; North West Mounted Police; Moon Over Burma; 1941: The Roundup; Unfinished Business; 1942: Secret Agent of Japan; Little Tokyo USA; Night in New Orleans; A Gentleman After Dark; Thunder Birds; American Empire; 1943: My Friend Flicka; Guadalcanal Diary; 1944: Roger Touhy, Gangster; Bermuda Mystery; 1945: Thunderhead — Son of Flicka; Abbott and Costello in Hollywood; The Valley of Decision; Twice Blessed; 1946: Tangier; The Harvey Girls; Inside Job; Strange Triangle; Blonde From Brooklyn; 1947: Ramrod; King of the Wild Horses; 1948: The Hunted; Thunderhoof; 1949: The Big Cat; I Shot Jesse James; 1950: The Tougher They Come; 1951: Tomahawk; Three Desperate Men; The Big Gusher; The Big Night; 1952: Montana Territory; Kansas City Confidential; 1953: Law and Order; I, the Jury; The Marshal's Daughter; 1957: Destination 60,000; 1964: Advance to the Rear; The Time Travelers; The Man From Galveston; 1967: You've Got to Be Smart; 1968: Chusbasco.

NY Stage: 1929: Congratulations; Seven; 1930: Ladies All; 1931:Two Seconds; 1932: Adam Had Two Sons.

Select TV: 1953: Manhattan Robin Hood (sp); The Lady and the Champ (sp); 1953–56: Waterfront (series); 1956: The Guardian (sp); 1961: Gunslinger (series).

SUSANNA FOSTER

(SUSANNA DELEE FLANDERS LARSON)
BORN: CHICAGO, IL, DECEMBER 6, 1924.

The short screen career of Susanna Foster was over and done with before she reached the age of 21, and yet this strawberry-blonde soprano managed to squeeze in a dozen film credits, including a few vehicles of her own. She'd been singing professionally since she was a child, and she made her Hollywood debut for Paramount, in 1939, as part of the cast of the biopic *The Great Victor Herbert*, singing "Kiss Me Again." This was followed by a starring role in *There's Magic in Music*, as a burlesque star who winds up at the real-life Interlochen Music Camp and becomes one of the "nice" kids. Once that studio had no further use for her, she was signed by Universal, supposedly as a threat to keep their main singing star, Deanna Durbin, in line. Pleasant as she was, she fell short of the sort of star quality Ms. Durbin so obviously possessed. There were two teamings with teenage dancing star Donald O'Connor, in *Top Man* and *This Is the Life*. In between, she did the movie she is most closely associated with, the 1943 remake of *Phantom of the Opera*, playing the imperiled heroine Christine. Since this was the first sound version of the story, the musical side was emphasized, which delighted fans of Ms. Foster and her co-star Nelson Eddy, but left horror aficionados deeply disappointed. A very similar tale followed, *The Climax*, this time with Boris Karloff, instead of Claude Rains, as the creepy fellow worshiping Foster's singing talents. After the 1945 vehicle *That Night With You*, she concentrated on performing in operettas and married her partner, Wilbur Evans. By the time they divorced in 1956, she'd put show business behind her completely, choosing to work as a clerk in a brokerage firm.

Screen: 1939: The Great Victor Herbert; 1941: There's Magic in Music; Glamour Boy; 1942: Star Spangled Rhythm; 1943: Top Man; Phantom of the Opera; 1944: Follow the Boys; This Is the Life; The Climax; Bowery to Broadway; 1945: Frisco Sal; That Night With You.

EDDIE FOY, JR.
BORN: NEW ROCHELLE, NY, FEBRUARY 4, 1905. DIED: JULY 13, 1983.

As the one enduring trouper to come out of the vaudeville family act "The Seven Little Foys," Eddie Foy, Jr. branched off on his own in the late 1920s, debuting on Broadway in *Show Girl*, in 1929. Over the years he would pop up in supporting roles in films, mostly musicals, including *Leathernecking*, as a buck private trying to impress newcomer Irene Dunne; *Broadway Through a Keyhole*, as the partner of Constance Cummings in her nightclub act; *Myrt and Marge*, as an egotistical comedian; and *Four Jacks and a Jill*, as one of the Jacks. Over at cheapie studio Republic, he was thrown into four Judy Canova vehicles: *Scatterbrain*, *Puddin' Head*, *Joan of Ozark*, and *Honeychile*, and won the title role in the 1942 film version of the Broadway success *Yokel Boy*, which tossed out the original plot, most of the songs, and Canova, for whom the property was purchased in the first place. There were also at least four occasions where he was called on to play his dad: *Frontier Marshal*, being rescued by Randolph Scott as Wyatt Earp; *Lillian Russell*; *Yankee Doodle Dandy*, memorably confronting James Cagney playing Foy's "rival," George M. Cohan; and *Wilson*. All the while he chalked up some credits on the New York stage with *At Home Abroad*, *The Red Mill*, and, most significantly, *The Pajama Game*. He repeated his role in the 1957 version of the last, playing the ultra-jealous factory foreman Heinzy, singing the title song and a performing a delightful soft shoe number, "I'll Never Be Jealous Again," with Reta Shaw. Four years later he had a showstopper, "It's a Simple Little System," in the movie adaptation of *Bells Are Ringing*, where he played a bookie disguised as a record salesman. He was last seen on screen tossing custard pies with Morey Amsterdam in the slapstick flop *Won Ton Ton, the Dog Who Saved Hollywood*. Brother Bryan Foy was a film director and producer, his most famous credit in the former category being the first all-talking full-length motion picture, *Lights of New York*.

Screen: 1929: Queen of the Night Clubs; 1930: Leathernecking; 1933: Broadway Through a Keyhole; 1934: Myrt and Marge; 1936: College Holiday; 1937: Turn Off the Moon; 1939: Secret Service of the Air; Frontier Marshal; Code of the Secret Service; Women in the Wind; The Cowboy Quarterback; Smashing the Money Ring; 1940: Lillian Russell; Scatterbrain; A Murder in the Air; Fugitive From Justice; The Texas Rangers Ride Again; 1941: Rookies on Parade; Country Fair; The Case of the Black Parrot; Puddin' Head; 1942: Four Jacks and a Jill; Yokel Boy; Yankee Doodle Dandy; Powder Town; Joan of Ozark; Moonlight Masquerade; 1943: Dixie Dugan; Dixie; 1944: Wilson; And the

Angels Sing; 1951: Honeychile; 1953: The Farmer Takes a Wife; 1954: Lucky Me; 1957: The Pajama Game; 1960: Bells Are Ringing; 1961: Gidget Goes Hawaiian; 1968: 30 Is a Dangerous Age, Cynthia; 1976: Won Ton Ton, the Dog Who Saved Hollywood.

NY Stage: 1929: Show Girl; 1930: Ripples; Smiles; 1931: The Cat and the Fiddle; 1935: At Home Abroad; 1937: Orchids Preferred; 1945: The Red Mill; 1954: The Pajama Game; 1957: Rumple; 1961: Donnybrook.

Select TV: 1957: Mr. Broadway (sp); 1962–63: Fair Exchange (series); 1977: The Girl in the Empty Grave; Deadly Game.

ANTHONY FRANCIOSA
(ANTHONY PAPALEO) BORN: NEW YORK, NY, OCTOBER 25, 1928.

An affable Italian-American who was very good at projecting sensitivity beneath a strong exterior, Anthony Franciosa was treated to some excellent roles during his first few years in Hollywood, before he settled into television and more routine fare. Almost directly out of high school, he was getting work off Broadway, eventually making his Broadway debut in the 1953 production of *End as a Man*. He made a major impact two years later as Polo Pope, whose main concern is getting drugs for his junkie brother, in *A Hatful of Rain*, winning a Theatre World Award in the process. The sudden demand for him was such that he was utilized by four major studios in 1957, with MGM's *This Could Be the Night*, as a nightclub operator who sets his sights on innocent Jean Simmons; Warners's *A Face in the Crowd*, as an opportunistic office boy who becomes Andy Griffith's agent; Paramount's *Wild Is the Wind*, as Anna Magnani's younger lover, a role he purportedly played off screen as well, despite his marriage that year to Shelley Winters; and, most importantly, in Fox's outstanding film version of *A Hatful of Rain*, in which he was heartbreakingly good, earning an Oscar nomination for his work. There were additional worthy parts, as Franciosa appeared in *The Long Hot Summer*, playing Orson Welles's weakling son, and in *Career*, giving a sharp performance as a determined stage actor. These pretty much obliterated memories of the ghastly *The Naked Maja*, in which he made an unconvincing Francisco Goya. In 1960 he divorced Shelley Winters, just around the time he realized that his film career was beginning to lose steam. There was a ponderous melodrama that hoped to gain attention with its steamy title, *Go Naked in the World*; a stagy Tennessee Williams comedy with Jane Fonda, *Period of Adjustment*; and then, following a bad-guy role as a Mexican bandit, in *Rio Conchos*, a television series that didn't make it, *Valentine's Day*. The material he was being offered on the big screen was getting fluffier than his earlier stuff, as witnessed by a flat caper-flick, *Assault on a Queen*; James Garner's poor spy-spoof, *A Man Could Get Killed*; the excruciating Ann-Margret vehicle *The Swinger*, where he played a smut-magazine editor; and the cheeky Raquel Welch romp, *Fathom*. In 1968 he began a second TV series, this time landing himself a hit, with *The Name of the Game*, playing reporter Jeff Dillon. From that point on the small screen supplied his paycheck, with occasional trips back to the movies for foreign productions and little-seen efforts like *Firepower* and *Backstreet Dreams*. After years away from "A" products, he showed up as a Mafia boss seeking justice for his son's death in *City Hall*. He has also been billed as Tony Franciosa.

Screen: 1957: A Face in the Crowd; This Could Be the Night; A Hatful of Rain; Wild Is the Wind; 1958: The Long Hot Summer; 1959: The Naked Maja; The Story on Page One; Career; 1961: Go

Naked in the World; Senilita/Careless; **1962:** Period of Adjustment; **1964:** Rio Conchos; The Pleasure Seekers; **1966:** Assault on a Queen; A Man Could Get Killed; The Swinger; **1967:** Fathom; **1968:** The Sweet Ride; In Enemy Country; **1969:** A Man Called Gannon; **1970:** Web of the Spider/ In the Grip of the Spider; **1972:** Across 110th Street; **1974:** Ghost in the Noonday Sun (nUSr); **1975:** The Drowning Pool; **1979:** Firepower; The World Is Full of Married Men; **1980:** La Cicala (nUSr); Texas Legend; **1981:** Aiutami a Sognare/Help Me Dream (nUSr); **1982:** Julie Darling/Daughter of Death (dtv); Death Wish II; Tenebrae/Unsane; Kiss My Grits/Summer Heat (dtv); **1988:** Death House; **1989:** La Morte di Moda/Fashion Crimes (nUSr); **1990:** Backstreet Dreams; **1992:** Double Threat (dtv); **1996:** City Hall.

NY Stage: 1948: Hamlet (ob); 1949: Yes Is for a Very Young Man (ob); 1953: End as a Man; 1954: Wedding Breakfast; 1955: A Hatful of Rain.

Select TV: 1954: The Arena (sp); 1955: It Might Happen Tomorrow (sp); 1956: The Cradle Song (sp); 1960: Heaven Can Wait (sp); 1964–65: Valentine's Day (series); 1967: Fame Is the Name of the Game; 1968–71: The Name of the Game (series); 1971: The Deadly Hunt; Earth II; 1972: The Catcher; 1972–73: Search (series); 1974: This Is the West That Was; 1975: Matt Helm; 1975–76: Matt Helm (series); 1977: Curse of the Black Widow; Aspen/The Innocent and the Damned (ms); 1978: Wheels (ms); 1981: Side Show; 1984–85: Finder of Lost Loves (series); 1986: Stagecoach; 1987: Blood Vows: The Story of a Mafia Wife; 1990: Ghost Writer; 1992: Till Death Do Us Part.

ANNE FRANCIS
BORN: OSSINING, NY, SEPTEMBER 16, 1930.

Delicately beautiful on the surface but backed up by a determined, no-nonsense demeanor, Anne Francis was best known for her tenure at MGM in the mid-1950s, where her work was solid rather than remarkable. Most of her life was spent in front of a camera, having started modeling for magazine covers from the age of five. From there she acted on radio serials; appeared on Broadway playing the young Gertrude Lawrence in Lady in the Dark; and landed what turned out to be her first MGM contract, in 1946. They gave her tiny roles in This Time for Keeps and Summer Holiday then promptly dropped her off the studio roster. After appearing in the color finale of Portrait of Jennie, she found herself working as one of the Bonny Maid Versatile Varieties Girls, which was little more than being an on-screen saleslady, on the NBC series Versatile Varieties, in 1949. This was followed by a cheaply produced but juicy reform school drama, So Young, So Bad, in which she created quite an impression as juvenile hellraiser. That same year 20th Century-Fox decided to take a crack at her and put her under contract, labeling her "The Palomino Blonde." There she twice played the daughter of snooty Clifton Webb, in Elopement and Dreamboat, and then got the title role in Lydia Bailey, as an aristocrat joining the Haitian rebels, which drew nothing more than negative notices. After playing James Cagney's mistress, Flamingo, in one of his poorest films, A Lion Is in the Streets, and supporting George "Foghorn" Winslow in the Lenny Bruce (!) scripted curio The Rocket Man, she wound up back under MGM's employ. During this busy period she was George Raft's mistress in Rogue Cop; Glenn Ford's helpless pregnant wife, taunted over the phone by his students in Blackboard Jungle; and Paul Newman's widowed sister-in-law in The Rack. She also had her most famous role, Aleria, the scantily clad daughter of Walter

Pidgeon and best friend of Robby the Robot, in the sci-fi classic Forbidden Planet. She was one of the distrustful townsfolk in Bad Day at Black Rock, and played opposite Ford again in the soft but successful comedy Don't Go Near the Water. There was one starring vehicle over at Warners, Girl of the Night, where she explained to psychiatrist Lloyd Nolan how she became a hooker, but it was a flop-and-run programmer. She went back to supporting roles in The Satan Bug and Funny Girl, where precious little of her ended up in the final print, supposedly because of a run-in with Barbra Streisand. In the meantime she had starred as a sexy private eye in the series Honey West, which became something of a cult item in certain circles in later years, then went back to the movies for thankless straight-woman roles in The Love God? and Hook, Line & Sinker, for comedians Don Knotts and Jerry Lewis, respectively, at their least inspired. Throughout the 1970s and 1980s, she received most of her employment from made-for-TV films.

Screen: 1947: This Time for Keeps; 1948: Summer Holiday; Portrait of Jennie; 1950: So Young, So Bad; 1951: The Whistle at Eaton Falls; Elopement; 1952: Dreamboat; Lydia Bailey; 1953: A Lion Is in the Streets; 1954: The Rocket Man; Susan Slept Here; Rogue Cop; 1955: Bad Day at Black Rock; Battle Cry; Blackboard Jungle; The Scarlet Coat; 1956: Forbidden Planet; The Rack; The Great American Pastime; 1957: The Hired Gun; Don't Go Near the Water; 1960: Girl of the Night; The Crowded Sky; 1965: The Satan Bug; Brainstorm; 1968: Funny Girl; More Dead Than Alive; 1969: Impasse; The Love God?; Hook, Line & Sinker; 1972: Pancho Villa; 1976: Survival; 1978: Born Again; 1988: Return (dtv); 1990: Little Vegas; 1993: The Double O Kid (dtv); 1996: Lover's Knot (dtv).

NY Stage: 1940: Lady in the Dark.

Select TV: 1949–50: Versatile Varieties (series); 1950: Good Housekeeping (sp); 1954: I Like It Here (sp); 1960: Queen of the Orange Bowl (sp); The Yum Yum Girl (sp); 1965–66: Honey West (series); The Further Adventures of Gallegher (sp); 1970: Wild Women; The Intruders; 1971: The Forgotten Man; Mongo's Back in Town; 1971–72: My Three Sons (series); 1972: Fireball Forward; Haunts of the Very Rich; 1974: Cry Panic; FBI Story: The FBI vs. Alvin Karpis — Public Enemy Number One; 1975: The Last Survivors; A Girl Named Sooner; 1976: Banjo Hackett: Roamin' Free; 1978: Little Mo; 1979: The Rebels; Beggarman, Thief; 1980: Detour to Terror; 1981: Dallas (series); 1982: Rona Jaffe's Mazes and Monsters; 1984: Riptide (series); 1986: A Masterpiece of Murder; 1987: Poor Little Rich Girl: The Barbara Hutton Story (ms); Laguna Heat; 1988: My First Love; 1992: Love Can Be Murder; 1996: Have You Seen My Son?

KAY FRANCIS
(KATHARINE EDWINA GIBBS)
BORN: OKLAHOMA CITY, OK, JANUARY 13, 1903.
DIED: AUGUST 26, 1968.

This brunette leading lady with the sad eyes and a tendency to mispronounce her R's, was very much a product of the early 1930s, glamorous to behold but more than a tad artificial when held up to close scrutiny, missing the depth and commitment that might have carried her name beyond its era. She followed her vaudevillian mother into the business, understudying Katharine Cornell in The Green Hat, and making her Broadway debut proper (as Katharine Francis) in a 1925 production of Hamlet, as the Player Queen. By this time she had married a man named James Francis, and she kept his name for her professional one even after their divorce. It was through her co-star in the 1928 stage production of *Elmer the Great*, Walter Huston, that she got into the movies, winning a contract at Paramount. She made her screen debut (now billed as Kay) opposite Huston in *Gentlemen of the Press*, as his secretary and mistress. They no doubt liked each other as acting partners, for they would pair up on three more occasions over the years, in *The Virtuous Sin*, where she was torn between him and Kenneth MacKenna (who became her third husband, 1931–33); *Storm at Daybreak*; and *Always in My Heart*. In the meantime, Paramount let her get verbally bashed by the Marx Brothers in *The Cocoanuts*, one of the handful of supporting assignments she made prior to her breakthrough, playing gangster William Powell's gun moll in *Street of Chance*, in 1930. It was, in fact, their second teaming, following *Behind the Makeup*, but it was far from the last. They were paired multiple times over the years, although they did not have the greatest on-screen chemistry. They were seen together in the Paramount melodramas *For the Defense*, with Francis as an actress guilty of drunk driving, and *Ladies' Man*, as a married socialite who becomes Powell's lover. After she moved over to Warners, they teamed for *Jewel Robbery*, where she was a bored baroness, thrilled to have met a charming thief, and *One-Way Passage*, perhaps the most famous of their movies together and certainly their most popular, with Francis as the terminally ill lady who falls for Powell, who is scheduled to be executed. Seen today, her unimpressive emoting seems to diminish his lighter, more proficient style.

Around this time she did appear in the brightest of all her pictures, Ernst Lubitsch's sparkling *Trouble in Paradise* (for Paramount), as the unsuspecting, wealthy lady whom Herbert Marshall tries to fleece but falls in love with instead. Her home studio, Warners, however, continued to try to sell her in heavy dramas like *The House on 56th Street*, a turn-of-the-century soap opera, made even less appetizing by giving her Ricardo Cortez as her leading man. There were also several forgettable properties with George Brent, including *The Keyhole* and *Stranded*; as well as the biography *The White Angel*, which cast her to little effect as Florence Nightingale. The ultra-weepy *I Found Stella Parish*, in which she hoped to prevent her daughter from discovering her sordid past, proved to be the one hit in this bunch, so the studio tried once again to make her part of a team. In this case her co-star had been Ian Hunter, so she found herself alongside him again for *Stolen Holiday*, marrying him because Claude Rains turned out to be a bad man; *Another Dawn*, with Francis opting for the better-billed Errol Flynn at the finale; *Confession*, abandoning Hunter for a fling with Basil Rathbone; and *Comet Over Broadway*, where he was her producer and she a rising stage actress, although a less blazing star one couldn't hope to find. By the end of the 1930s, it was clear that Francis had done little to keep the studio's coffers plentifully supplied, and she began taking secondary roles, playing Cary Grant's insufferable wife in *In Name Only* and Deanna Durbin's mother in *It's a Date*. She was featured in the popular 1941 adaptation of *Charley's Aunt*, but audiences showed up not for her but to see Jack Benny in a dress. There was a USO tour during World War II with Carole Landis, Mitzi Mayfair, and Martha Raye that became a weak Fox musical, *Four Jills in a Jeep*, and she ended her career at Monogram, in 1946, in *Wife Wanted*, as, ironically, a washed-up film star. After that she was seen in a few stage productions before quietly retiring.
Screen: 1929: Gentlemen of the Press; The Cocoanuts; Dangerous Curves; Illusion; The Marriage Playground; 1930: Behind the Makeup; Street of Chance; Paramount on Parade; A Notorious Affair; Raffles; Let's Go Native; For the Defense; The Virtuous Sin; Passion Flower; 1931: Scandal Sheet; Ladies' Man; Vice Squad; Transgression; Guilty Hands; 24 Hours; Girls About Town; The False Madonna; 1932: Strangers in Love; Man

Wanted; Street of Women; Jewel Robbery; One Way Passage; Trouble in Paradise; Cynara; 1933: The Keyhole; Storm at Daybreak; Mary Stevens, M.D.; I Loved a Woman; 1934: The House on 56th Street; Mandalay, Wonder Bar; Dr. Monica; British Agent; 1935: Stranded; Living on Velvet; The Goose and the Gander; I Found Stella Parish; 1936: The White Angel; Give Me Your Heart; 1937: Stolen Holiday; Another Dawn; Confession; First Lady; 1938: Women Are Like That; My Bill; Secrets of an Actress; Comet Over Broadway; 1939: King of the Underworld; Women in the Wind; In Name Only; 1940: It's a Date; Little Men; When the Daltons Rode; Play Girl; 1941: The Man Who Lost Himself; Charley's Aunt; The Feminine Touch; 1942: Always in My Heart; Between Us Girls; 1944: Four Jills in a Jeep; 1945: Divorce; Allotment Wives; 1946: Wife Wanted.
NY Stage: AS KATHARINE FRANCIS: 1925: Hamlet; 1927: Crime; Venus; 1928: Elmer the Great.
AS KAY FRANCIS: 1946: State of the Union.
Select TV: 1950: Call It a Day (sp).

ARTHUR FRANZ
BORN: PERTH AMBOY, NJ, FEBRUARY 29, 1920.

A fairly non-descript, second-string star of the 1950s, Arthur Franz had a few years of Broadway credits to his name when he made enough of an impact in the military stage drama *Command Decision* that he was brought to Hollywood in 1948. He did not, however, repeat his part in MGM's film version of that play, but wound up as one of the stars of a Fox "B," *Jungle Patrol*, as a flier, and continued in this capacity at Eagle-Lion for *Red Stallion in the Rockies*; Republic for *Tarnished*, as an ex-marine who can't live down his checkered past; and in one of the last features produced for Monogram, *Flight to Mars*, in which he and Cameron Mitchell took a voyage to the Red Planet, while wearing spacesuits left over from *Destination Moon*. In *Abbott and Costello Meet the Invisible Man*, he wasn't seen much at all, being the Invisible Man, a boxer trying to clear himself of murder. Between the many programmers he took occasional assignments in support of more distinctive performers in such "A" productions as *Sands of Iwo Jima*, and *Submarine Command*, serving under John Wayne and William Holden, respectively; *The Member of the Wedding*, as Julie Harris's older brother, Jarvis; *The Caine Mutiny*, as the ship's medical officer; and *The Young Lions*, as a lieutenant. He earned his degree of cult fame via his participation in *Invaders From Mars*, as the astronomer who tries to help little Jimmy Hunt battle the body-snatching aliens, in what is probably his best-known part; *Back From the Dead*, as a man whose dead wife takes over the body of new spouse Peggie Castle; and *Monster on the Campus*, as a college professor with a bad habit of turning into a beast (although Eddie Parker took over the part once Franz went from professor to monster). In later years he was still called on for countless television guest spots and to essay small parts in such movies as *The Sweet Ride* and *That Championship Season*.
Screen: 1948: Jungle Patrol; 1949: The Doctor and the Girl; Sands of Iwo Jima; Red Stallion in the Rockies; Red Light; Roseanna McCoy; 1950: Three Secrets; Tarnished; 1951: Abbott and Costello Meet the Invisible Man; Submarine Command; Strictly Dishonorable; Flight to Mars; 1952: Rainbow 'Round My Shoulder; The Member of the Wedding; The Sniper; Eight Iron Men; 1953: Bad for Each Other; The Eddie Cantor Story; Invaders From Mars; 1954: Flight Nurse; The Caine Mutiny; The Steel Cage; 1955: Battle Taxi; New Orleans Uncensored; Bobby Ware Is Missing; 1956: Beyond a Reasonable Doubt; The Wild

Party; Running Target; 1957: The Devil's Hairpin; The Unholy Wife; Hellcats of the Navy; Back From the Dead; 1958: The Young Lions; The Flame Barrier; Monster on the Campus; 1959: The Atomic Submarine; Woman Obsessed; 1964: The Carpetbaggers; 1966: Alvarez Kelly; 1968: Anzio; The Sweet Ride; 1970: Dream No Evil; 1973: So Long Blue Boy; 1975: The Human Factor; 1976: Sisters of Death; 1977: Jaws of Death; 1982: That Championship Season.

NY Stage: 1941: Hope for a Harvest; 1942: The Witch; Little Darling; 1943: The Moon Vine; 1946: Little Brown Jug; 1947: Command Decision.

Select TV: 1953: The Devil's Other Name (sp); Camille (sp); 1954: By-Line (sp); 1955: The 99th Day (sp); Too Late to Run (sp); The Late George Apley (sp); 1956: Once for Every Woman (sp); Pattern for Pursuit (sp); 1959: World of Giants (series); 1965–67: The Nurses (series); 1974: Murder or Mercy; The Missiles of October (sp); 1976: F. Scott Fitzgerald in Hollywood; 1977: The Last Hurrah; The Amazing Howard Hughes; 1979: Jennifer: A Woman's Story; 1980: Bogie.

WILLIAM FRAWLEY

BORN: BURLINGTON, IA, FEBRUARY 26, 1887.
DIED: MARCH 3, 1966.

First and foremost he was Fred Mertz, but his television work was only the capstone to a long and active career for bald, blustery, and stocky William Frawley. Spending his early days in vaudeville, he formed an act with his then-wife Louise Broedt, making his mark as the performer who introduced the enduring song "Carolina in the Morning." From there he moved to the legitimate stage, beginning with *Merry Merry*, in 1925, and ending with *Ghost Writer*, in 1933. The same year as the latter, he made his film debut at Universal, in *Moonlight and Pretzels*, but spent the majority of the decade under contract to Paramount, where he was called on to play eyebrow-lifting cops, shady hooligans, fast talking con men, skeptical sidekicks, and assorted blowhards, often giving emphasis to a line by chomping on a cigar. There were roles in both versions of *The Lemon Drop Kid* (a con artist called The Professor in the first one, and a mug coaxed into playing a sidewalk Santa in the second) and in one that featured his future co-star, Lucille Ball, *Ziegfeld Follies*, although they shared no scenes together. Instead Frawley was seen in "The Sweepstakes Ticket" sketch with Fanny Brice. Among his many assignments, he showed up as a gossip columnist in *Shoot the Works*; an unorthodox dentist named Painless in *Welcome Home*; Milton Shakespeare, the head of a theatrical troupe, in *Three Cheers for Love*; a football coach in *Rose Bowl*; and a drunk who gets Harold Lloyd in trouble with the police in *Professor Beware*. He played a school bully still taunting meek Charlie Ruggles in *Night Work*; The "Duke" in Mickey Rooney's interpretation of *The Adventures of Huckleberry Finn*; and a hood employing Abbott and Costello to do his dirty work in *One Night in the Tropics*. Perhaps his most widely seen roles were in *Going My Way*, making Bing Crosby some dough by buying his song, "Swingin' on a Star; " and *Miracle on 34th Street*, advising judge Gene Lockhart and trying to steer him clear of doing any wrong to Santa Claus. In 1951 he began his stint as the lovably lazy, wisecracking landlord Fred Mertz on *I Love Lucy*, continuing through some "Lucy-Desi" specials, in a role that made him one of the legendary figures in the history of that medium. After that he had another hit show, *My Three Sons*, playing the sardonic housekeeper, Bub, and a substantial role in a baseball film aimed at kids, *Safe at Home*, which featured real-life Yankees Roger Maris and Mickey Mantle.

Screen: 1933: Moonlight and Pretzels; Hell and High Water; 1934: Miss Fane's Baby Is Stolen; Bolero; The Witching Hour; Shoot the Works; Here Is My Heart; The Lemon Drop Kid; Crime Doctor; 1935: Car 99; Hold 'em Yale; College Scandal; Ship Cafe; Alibi Ike; Welcome Home; Harmony Lane; 1936: Strike Me Pink; Desire; The Princess Comes Across; F-Man; Three Cheers for Love; Three Married Men; The General Died at Dawn; Rose Bowl; 1937: High, Wide and Handsome; Double or Nothing; Blossoms on Broadway; Something to Sing About; 1938: Mad About Music; Professor Beware; Sons of the Legion; Touchdown Army; 1939: Persons in Hiding; St. Louis Blues; Ambush; Grand Jury Secrets; Night Work; The Adventures of Huckleberry Finn; Rose of Washington Square; Stop, Look and Love; Ex-Champ; 1940: The Farmer's Daughter; Opened by Mistake; Untamed; Golden Gloves; Rhythm on the River; The Quarterback; One Night in the Tropics; Sandy Gets Her Man; Dancing on a Dime; Those Were the Days; 1941: Blondie in Society; The Bride Came C.O.D.; Public Enemies; Cracked Nuts; Footsteps in the Dark; Six Lessons From Madame La Zonga; 1942: Treat 'em Rough; Roxie Hart; It Happened in Flatbush; Give Out, Sisters; Moonlight in Havana; Wildcat; Gentleman Jim; 1943: Larceny With Music; We've Never Been Licked; Whistling in Brooklyn; 1944: Minstrel Man; Going My Way; Lake Placid Serenade; The Fighting Seabees; 1945: Flame of the Barbary Coast; Lady on a Train; Hitchhike to Happiness; 1946: The Virginian; Rendezvous With Annie; Ziegfeld Follies; The Inner Circle; Crime Doctor's Man Hunt; 1947: Mother Wore Tights; Miracle on 34th Street; My Wild Irish Rose; I Wonder Who's Kissing Her Now; Monsieur Verdoux; Blondie's Anniversary; Down to Earth; Hit Parade of 1947; 1948: The Babe Ruth Story; Good Sam; Joe Palooka in Winner Take All; Texas, Brooklyn and Heaven; Chicken Every Sunday; The Girl From Manhattan; 1949: Home in San Antone; The Lady Takes a Sailor; East Side, West Side; Red Light; The Lone Wolf and His Lady; 1950: Kiss Tomorrow Goodbye; Pretty Baby; Kill the Umpire; Blondie's Hero; 1951: The Lemon Drop Kid; Rhubarb; Abbott and Costello Meet the Invisible Man; 1952: Rancho Notorious; 1962: Safe at Home.

NY Stage: 1925: Merry, Merry; 1927: Bye Bye Bonnie; 1928: She's My Baby; Here's Howe!; 1929: Carry On; Sons o' Guns; 1931: She Lived Next to the Firehouse; 1932: Tell Her the Truth; Twentieth Century; 1933: The Ghost Writer.

Select TV: 1950: The First Hundred Years (sp); 1951–57: I Love Lucy (series); 1957–60: The Lucy-Desi Comedy Hour (sp); 1959: Comeback (sp); 1960–64: My Three Sons (series).

KATHLEEN FREEMAN

BORN: CHICAGO, IL, FEBRUARY 17, 1919.
DIED: AUGUST 23, 2001.

A character actress whose career stretched across a 50-year span, Kathleen Freeman played good-hearted working women and domestics, but could be a peerless comic performer, playing a more abrasive, earthy sort of character, often with a brassy mouth and sour puss. She was seen as early as 1948, as the star of a short subject "Annie Was a Wonder" and doing mere bits in such films as *The Naked City*, as a subway passenger, and *Casbah*, as a nurse. Over the years Freeman was the patient vocal coach ("and I *Cahn't* stand him!") of Jean Hagen in *Singin' in the Rain*; a gossip in *Houseboat*; the perplexed maid sent hunting for insects in *The Fly*; a Swedish immigrant in *North to Alaska*; a Salvation Army member in *Mail Order Bride*; John

Huston's missus in *Myra Breckinridge*; a policewoman in Disney's *The Strongest Man in the World*; an abusive nun in *The Blues Brothers*; a cooking show host terrorized by the vicious critters in *Gremlins 2: The New Batch*; and Fred Ward's hoodlum mom in *Naked Gun 33 1/3: The Final Insult*. However, she is probably most closely associated with Jerry Lewis, for whom she provided stellar support on 12 separate occasions, starting in 1954 with *3 Ring Circus*, where she was pelted with custard, through *The Nutty Professor* (as college secretary Millie Lemon), and ending with *Which Way to the Front?*, in 1970. In 2000, already past 80, she made a long-overdue Broadway debut in the musical *The Full Monty*, but passed away during its run.

Screen: 1948: The Naked City; The Saxon Charm; Casbah; Behind Locked Doors; 1949: Mr. Belvedere Goes to College; 1950: The House by the River; A Life of Her Own; Lonely Heart Bandits; The Reformer and the Redhead; Once a Thief; No Man of Her Own; Cry Danger; 1951: Appointment With Danger; A Place in the Sun; Cause for Alarm!; Behave Yourself!; The Wild Blue Yonder; The Company She Keeps; Love Is Better Than Ever; Let's Make It Legal; 1952: The Greatest Show on Earth; Talk About a Stranger; Singin' in the Rain; The Bad and the Beautiful; Kid Monk Baroni; O. Henry's Full House; Skirts Ahoy!; The Prisoner of Zenda; Monkey Business; 1953: She's Back on Broadway; The Magnetic Monster; Half a Hero; The Glass Web; The Affairs of Dobie Gillis; Dream Wife; The Glass Wall; A Perilous Journey; 1954: Athena; 3 Ring Circus; 1955: The Far Country; Artists and Models; 1956: Hollywood or Bust; 1957: The Midnight Story; Kiss Them for Me; Pawnee; 1958: The Fly; Houseboat; Too Much, Too Soon; The Buccaneer; The Missouri Traveler; 1960: North to Alaska; 1961: The Ladies' Man; Wild Harvest; The Errand Boy; 1962: Madison Avenue; 1963: The Nutty Professor; Who's Minding the Store?; 1964: Mail Order Bride; The Patsy; The Disorderly Orderly; 1965: The Rounders; That Funny Feeling; Marriage on the Rocks; 1966: Three on a Couch; 1967: Point Blank; 1969: Hook, Line & Sinker; Support Your Local Sheriff!; The Good Guys and the Bad Guys; Death of a Gunfighter; So Evil My Sister; 1970: Myra Breckinridge; The Ballad of Cable Hogue; Which Way to the Front?; 1971: Head On; Support Your Local Gunfighter; 1972: Where Does It Hurt?; Stand Up and Be Counted; 1973: Unholy Rollers; Your Three Minutes Are Up; 1975: The Strongest Man in the World; 1978: The Norsemen; 1980: The Blues Brothers; 1981: Heartbeeps; 1986: The Best of Times; Malibu Bikini Shop; 1987: Dragnet; Innerspace; In the Mood; Teen Wolf Too; 1988: The Wrong Guys; 1989: Chances Are; 1990: Hollywood Chaos (dtv); Gremlins 2: The New Batch; 1991: Joey Takes a Cab; Dutch; The Willies (dtv); 1992: FernGully: The Last Rain Forest (voice); Little Nemo: Adventures in Slumberland (voice); 1993: Hocus Pocus; 1994: Reckless Kelly; Naked Gun 33 1/3: The Final Insult; 1995: Two Guys Talkin' About Girls (dtv); 1996: Carpool (voice); 1997: Hercules (voice); 1998: Blue Brothers 2000; I'll Be Home for Christmas; Richie Rich's Christmas Wish (dtv); 2000: Ready to Rumble; Nutty Professor II: The Klumps; Seven Girlfriends; 2001: Joe Dirt; Shrek (voice).

NY Stage: 2000: The Full Monty.

Select TV: 1953–54: Topper (series); 1954–55: Mayor of the Town (series); 1966–67: It's About Time (series); 1968: Helicopter Spies; 1969–71: The Beverly Hillbillies (series); 1970: But I Don't Want to Get Married!; 1971: Funny Face (series); 1972: Call Her Mom; 1973–74: Lotsa Luck (series); 1974: The Daughters of Joshua Cabe Return; 1978: The Last Ride of the Dalton Gang; 1988: Bring Me the Head of Dobie Gillis; Glitz; 1999: Detention (series; voice).

MONA FREEMAN
(MONICA FREEMAN) BORN: BALTIMORE, MD, JUNE 9, 1926.

A plump-cheeked, tiny actress, Mona Freeman came to the movies directly from high school, having worked as a model during her teen years. At first she was seen in very small parts, finally moving up to leading roles in 1946 in Fox's version of *Black Beauty*, which became a standard girl-and-her-horse story, and in a Republic production, *That Brennan Girl*, in which she played an irresponsible young mother. Signed to a contract by Paramount, she first won attention for her lively turn as Joan Caulfield's troublemaking younger sister, whose letters to William Holden set the whole plot rolling, in the 1947 comedy hit *Dear Ruth*. That same year, at Fox, she made an attractive contribution to a good Betty Grable musical, *Mother Wore Tights*, as Grable's eldest daughter. Paramount didn't do much with her that was out of the ordinary, asking her to repeat her most famous role in a pair of *Dear Ruth* sequels, *Dear Wife* and *Dear Brat*, the latter title referring to her, Freeman having been upped to top billing. There were also leading-lady roles in some westerns: *Streets of Lardeo*, where she, not Holden, shot the bad guy in the final reel; *Copper Canyon*, looking more at ease in the genre than lead Hedy Lamarr; and *Branded*, falling for Alan Ladd while he pretended to be her long-lost brother. Following the requisite straight-woman stint to Martin and Lewis, in *Jumping Jacks*, she acted elsewhere, mostly in programmers like the British-made *Shadow of Fear*, and two with John Payne, *Hold Back the Night* and *The Road to Denver*. She was always a very pleasant person to have around, but that just wasn't enough to keep audiences, or Freeman herself, interested in prolonging her film career, and after the 1958 drama *The World Was His Jury*, she left movies, working for the next decade or so in television.

Screen: 1944: Our Hearts Were Young and Gay; Till We Meet Again; Here Come the Waves; Together Again; 1945: National Velvet; Roughly Speaking; Junior Miss; Danger Signal; 1946: Black Beauty; That Brennan Girl; Our Hearts Were Growing Up; 1947: Variety Girl; Dear Ruth; Mother Wore Tights; 1948: Isn't It Romantic?; 1949: Streets of Laredo; The Heiress; Dear Wife; 1950: Branded; Copper Canyon; I Was a Shoplifter; 1951: Dear Brat; Darling, How Could You!; The Lady From Texas; 1952: Flesh and Fury; The Greatest Show on Earth; Jumping Jacks; Angel Face; Thunderbirds; 1955: Battle Cry; The Road to Denver; 1956: The Way Out/Dial 999; Shadow of Fear/Before I Wake; Hold Back the Night; Huk; 1957: Dragoon Wells Massacre; 1958: The World Was His Jury.

Select TV: 1956: The Baxter Boy (sp); Seidman and Son (sp); Men Against Speed (sp); 1957: Three Men on a Horse (sp); Christmas in Connecticut (sp); 1958: The Long March (sp); 1960: The Women of Hadley (sp); Operation Northstar (sp); 1961: The Two Worlds of Charlie Gordon (sp); 1972: Welcome Home, Johnny Bristol.

GERT FROBE
(KARL-GERHART FROEBER) BORN: PLANITZ, GERMANY, FEBRUARY 25, 1913.
DIED: SEPTEMBER 4, 1988.

This portly, growling German character actor with the imposing brow, had a thick résumé of mostly unseen film credits from his home country when he became internationally known for playing the title role in the 1964 James Bond smash *Goldfinger*, perhaps the most enjoyable entry in the long-running series. Although he wasn't even the most menacing foil in the film itself (that honor went to silent Harold Sakata as Oddjob), he made an unmistakable impression and an unforgettable exit, getting sucked out a hole in an airplane. After that he was seen in several international productions, usually in a lighter vein, including *Those Magnificent Men in Their Flying Machines*, as the pompous General who duels with Jean-Pierre Cassel, via hot air balloons; *A High Wind in Jamaica*, as the ship's captain who is killed by a little girl; and *Chitty Chitty Bang Bang*, much too cutesy as the none-too-villainous King of Vulgaria. He was in *Those Daring Young Men in Their Jaunty Jalopies*, in pretty much a reprise of his *Flying Machines* role, though with a different name, and he played a Nazi in both *Is Paris Burning?* and *Triple Cross*. His bank was robbed by Warren Beatty and Goldie Hawn in *$*; in the remake of *Ten Little Indians*, he had the role previously played by Roland Young and Stanley Holloway; and in *Sidney Sheldon's Bloodline*, he was the inspector investigating the whole sordid affair.

Screen (US releases only): 1953: Man on a Tightrope; 1955: Special Delivery; Mr. Arkadin/Confidential Report; 1958: He Who Must Die; 1959: Eternal Waltz; 1960: It Happened in Broad Daylight; Rosemary; Prisoner of the Volga; 1962: The Longest Day; 1963: Threepenny Opera; 1964: Goldfinger; 1965: Banana Peel; Backfire; Those Magnificent Men in Their Flying Machines or How I Flew From London to Paris in 25 Hours 11 Minutes; A High Wind in Jamaica; Greed in the Sun; 1966: Enough Rope; Is Paris Burning?; 1967: Those Fantastic Flying Fools/Blast Off!; Triple Cross; The Upper Hand; 1968: Tonio Kroger; Chitty Chitty Bang Bang; 1969: Those Daring Young Men in Their Jaunty Jalopies/Monte Carlo or Bust; 1971: $ (Dollars); 1972: Ludwig; 1975: Ten Little Indians; 1977: The Serpent's Egg; 1979: Sidney Sheldon's Bloodline; 1980: Daisy Chain.

DWIGHT FRYE

BORN: SALINA, KS, FEBRUARY 22, 1899.
DIED: NOVEMBER 7, 1943

This small, intense character actor achieved his place in film history via a pair of roles in two of Universal's all-time classic horrors, *Dracula* and *Frankenstein*, both distributed in 1931. Having come from the New York stage, where his credits included *A Man's Man* and the immortal *Devil in the Cheese*, Dwight Frye made his official motion picture debut in the gangster film *The Doorway to Hell*, for Warners, in 1930. The following year he played the pathetic Renfield, Bela Lugosi's bugmunching slave, in *Dracula*, giving a gloriously strange, unforgettable performance, punctuated by a sinister laugh that seemed to be heaving forth from his chest, like the last gasps of breath. As a follow-up, he was Fritz, the cruel hunchbacked assistant to Colin Clive, a skanky little fellow who delighted in torturing the Monster (Boris Karloff), in *Frankenstein*. Although few of his other films would remain as high profile as these, he was seen throughout the 1930s in many other genres and even preceded Elisha Cook, Jr. in the role of gunsel, Wilmer, in the original 1931 version of *The Maltese Falcon*. Having created so indelible an impression as Renfield, he was borrowed by a poverty-row company to basically reprise the part in *Vampire Bat*, where he was accused of murder because of his hobby of raising bats as pets. Not wanting to proceed with the *Frankenstein* series without him, Universal resurrected Frye as Karl, Dr. Praetorious's assistant, for *Bride of Frankenstein*, where he behaved in a manner

similarly heinous to Fritz, before being tossed off the top of a tower. However by the early 1940s, much of the actor's work was so insignificant and the parts so peripheral that he was a mere bit player in *Son of Frankenstein*, *Frankenstein Meets the Wolf Man*, and *The Ghost of Frankenstein*. During the war years he overworked himself by taking additional jobs outside the show business field to supplement his income. This may have resulted in the heart attack that killed him when he was only 44 years old.

Screen: 1927: The Night Bird; 1930: The Doorway to Hell; Man to Man; 1931: Dracula; The Maltese Falcon; The Black Camel; Frankenstein; 1932: Attorney for the Defense; By Whose Hand?; The Western Code; A Strange Adventure; 1933: The Vampire Bat; The Invisible Man; The Circus Queen Murder; 1935: Bride of Frankenstein; Atlantic Adventure; The Great Impersonation; The Crime of Dr. Crespi; 1936: Florida Special; Alibi for Murder; Beware of Ladies; Great Guy; Tough Guy; 1937: Sea Devils; The Man Who Found Himself; The Road Back; Something to Sing About; Renfrew of the Royal Mounted; The Shadow; 1938: Who Killed Gail Preston?; The Invisible Enemy; Sinners in Paradise; Fast Company; The Night Hawk; Adventure in Sahara; 1939: Son of Frankenstein; The Man in the Iron Mask; Conspiracy; I Take This Woman; 1940: Drums of Fu Manchu (serial); Gangs of Chicago; Phantom Raiders; Sky Bandits; The Son of Monte Cristo; 1941: Mystery Ship; The People vs. Dr. Kildare; The Blonde From Singapore; The Devil Pays Off; 1942: Sleepytime Gal; The Ghost of Frankenstein; Danger in the Pacific; Prisoner of Japan; 1943: Frankenstein Meets the Wolf Man; Dead Men Walk; Hangmen Also Die; Submarine Alert; Dangerous Blondes.

NY Stage: 1922: The Plot Thickens; Six Characters in Search of an Author; 1923: Rita Coventry; The Love Habit; 1923: Sitting Pretty; So This Is Politics; 1925: Puppets; A Man's Man; 1926: Goat Song; The Chief Thing; Devil in the Cheese; 1927: Ink; 1928: The Queen's Husband; Mima; 1933: Keeper of the Keys; 1934: Queer People.

ANNETTE FUNICELLO

BORN: UTICA, NY, OCTOBER 22, 1942.

Outside of their animated superstars, Annette Funicello is probably the performer most closely associated with the Walt Disney Company. The relentlessly perky brunette had moved to California with her family when she was a youngster and was spotted in a school production by a Disney talent scout who asked her to audition for a new children's TV show being created by the studio. She thereby became the standout star of *The Mickey Mouse Club* and the only one of the kids from that series to be kept under contract after its cancellation. Billed simply as "Annette," she had scored two Top 10 recordings, "Tall Paul" and "O Dio Mio," despite the fact that she wasn't much of a singer, and had popped up in several Disney features and television mini-series, although she wasn't all that hot an actress either. There was, however, something exceedingly likable and comfortable about her personality that made audiences care. She found herself as Mary Contrary in the studio's lavish but disappointing version of *Babes in Toyland*, and co-star to Tommy Kirk in three other productions, *The Shaggy Dog*, *The Misadventures of Merlin Jones*, and *The Monkey's Uncle*, singing the unforgettable title songs for the last two. Her place as an icon of 1960s kitsch was solidified by her work outside Disney when American International Pictures teamed her with Frankie Avalon for the inane-but-popular teen comedy *Beach Party*, in 1963. She was called back to sing and look alternately sweet or pouty — depending on how

Frankie was treating her at that moment — in a few other lively but often excruciatingly stupid romps, including *Bikini Beach*, *Pajama Party* (Kirk filling in for a cameoing Avalon), and, perhaps the most famous title of them all, *Beach Blanket Bingo*. After this era came to an end, she made TV guest appearances, became a commercial pitch person for Jif peanut butter, and was called on to host or speak on various Disney-related programs and videos. In 1987, serving with Avalon as co-executive producer, the duo did a colorful send-up of their old beach pictures, *Back to the Beach*, with Annette good-naturedly kidding herself as an airhead mom, but it wasn't very popular. Shortly afterwards she announced that she was suffering for multiple sclerosis, detailing her struggle in her 1994 autobiography, *A Dream Is a Wish Your Heart Makes*. The book was made into a typical TV bio-film, with Annette playing her older self.

Screen: 1959: The Shaggy Dog; 1961: Babes in Toyland; 1963: Beach Party; 1964: The Misadventures of Merlin Jones; Muscle Beach Party; Bikini Beach; Pajama Party; 1965: Dr. Goldfoot and the Bikini Machine; The Monkey's Uncle; Beach Blanket Bingo; How to Stuff a Wild Bikini; Ski Party; 1966: Fireball 500; 1967: Thunder Alley; 1968: Head; 1987: Back to the Beach (and coexec. prod.); 1989: Troop Beverly Hills.

Select TV: 1955–59: The Mickey Mouse Club (series); 1959: The Danny Thomas Show (series); 1961: The Horsemasters; 1962: Escapade in Florence; 1976: Easy Does It…Starring Frankie Avalon (series); 1985: Lots of Luck; 1995: A Dream Is a Wish Your Heart Makes.

G

JEAN GABIN

(Jean-Alexis Moncorge)
Born: Mereil, France, May 17, 1904.
Died: November 15, 1976.

In the 1930s Jean Gabin became the most famous international star France had created up until then. The strong, stoic-faced actor followed a stint in the military with roles in some musical revues and operettas, eventually becoming a legitimate stage actor in Paris. He made his film debut in 1930 in *Chacun sa Chance*. In 1934 he appeared opposite Josephine Baker in *Zouzou* and had his breakthrough role in *Maria Chapdelaine*, playing a fur trapper pursued by the police. His stardom came with *La Bandera*, a French Foreign Legion tale, and with an ineffective version of *The Lower Depths*, in which he played a pickpocket. It was further solidified by his two most famous roles, the charming crook in *Pepe Le Moko* (overshadowed in Hollywood the following year when Charles Boyer did the remake, *Algiers*), and the French officer who bonds with German commandant Erich von Stroheim in *Grand Illusion*. The latter film made such an impact on the international market that it became the first foreign-language movie to be nominated for an Oscar for Best Picture. It was followed by *Quai des Brumes*, another tale of doomed love, with Gabin as a deserter and Michelle Morgan his love interest, and a film that was banned in several countries over the decade, *Le Jour se Levre*, with the actor on the run after committing murder. Inevitably Hollywood made offers, and his attempts to establish himself in American products were among the least successful of any famous European star. *Moontide*, made for Fox in 1942, co-starred Ida Lupino, and found Gabin as a seaman who thinks he may have murdered someone, while *The Impostor*, over at RKO, cast him as an escaped murderer who turns hero when he joins the army. The 1940s would prove to probably be his weakest period of productivity, but he began to reestablish himself in the 1950s with *The Walls of Malapaga* and with *French Can-Can/Only the French Can*, as a cabaret owner; *Les Misérables*, as Jean Valjean; *Inspector Maigret*, as the noted detective, a part he would later reprise; and *The Possessors*, as a domineering millionaire. By the 1960s his reliability as a draw on the international art-house cir-

cuit had cooled down. He had become something of an institution in his native country, however, continuing to act as a white-haired character player right up to *L'Annee Sainte*, released the year he died, 1976. Needless to say, the role found him once again dabbling in crime, Gabin having made a career of playing, on so many occasions, criminals, thieves, murderers, and anti-heroes.

Screen (US releases only): 1935: They Were Five; The Lower Depths; **1936:** Pepe Le Moko; **1937:** Grand Illusion; Port of Shadows; **1938:** Daybreak; **1942:** Moontide; **1943:** The Imposter; **1949:** The Room Upstairs; **1950:** The Walls of Malapaga; **1951:** Marie du Port; **1954:** Le Plaisir/House of Pleasure; The Moment of Truth; **1956:** Only the French Can/French Can-Can; **1957:** Razzia; Four Bags Full; **1958:** The Most Dangerous Sin; The Case of Dr. Laurent; Inspector Maigret; **1959:** The Possessors; Love Is My Profession; The House on the Waterfront; Speaking of Murder; **1960:** Rue de Paris; **1962:** Night Affair; The Magnificent Tramp; **1963:** Monkey in Winter; Any Number Can Win; **1964:** The Gentleman from Epsom; **1967:** The Upper Hand; **1970:** The Sicilian Clan; **1975:** Le Chat; Verdict/Jury of One; **1976:** Two Against the Law.

CLARK GABLE

(William Clark Gable) Born: Cadiz, OH,
February 1, 1901. Died: November 16, 1960.

When you've been called "The King," it's safe to say that your place in history is assured, and "The King" is exactly the nickname Clark Gable earned during his reign as Hollywood's number-one leading man of the 1930s. Relentlessly virile, with a smile that could charm the most hardened of moviegoers, he didn't vary much from his stock image: sardonic, fast-talking, tough, and impatient with nonsense and fools. He was a dependable boss or leader, yet everybody's best pal. As much as the women in the audience went crazy for him, he always made himself accessible to the men as well, and that was the secret to his long and undying stature as the epitome of male movie stardom. It was while earning a living as a telephone repairman that he met Josephine Dillon, a drama coach 14 years his senior, who became his first wife and his acting teacher. Through her he got extra work in some films and a role in a touring production of *The Copperhead*, which starred Lionel Barrymore. From there he went on to chalk up a few Broadway credits and the lead in a California production of *The Last Mile*, playing a hardened convict. Ironically he failed his screen test at MGM, but did get to play a bad guy in a William Boyd western for Pathé, *The Painted Desert*. He ended up back at MGM in a supporting role as Anita Page's husband in *The Easiest Way*, and that convinced the studio that they had made a miscalculation before. Signed by them in 1931, his name would ultimately become synonymous with the company in its heyday.

Gable was soon one of the most ubiquitous employees on the lot, playing gangsters in both *Dance, Fools, Dance*, opposite Joan Crawford, and in *A Free Soul*, which was one of the year's big ones since it starred Norma Shearer, Lionel Barrymore, and Leslie Howard. He took up with Crawford again for *Possessed*, playing a politician; and inherited a role meant for the declining John Gilbert, in *Susan Lennox (Her Fall and Rise)*, as Garbo's disenchanted lover. It was worth noting that despite playing second-fiddle to his more esteemed female co-star, he dominated every one of their scenes together. By this point he had received his first top-billed role, in *Sporting Blood*, a racing story, and scored a major box-office hit with *Hell Divers*, second billed to Wallace Beery, both playing squabbling Naval Air Force fliers.

Gable played a minister in *Polly of the Circus*, but since he wasn't exactly the first actor who came to mind when casting a clergyman role, it was not considered a beneficial assignment. Nor was the adaptation of *Strange Interlude*, where he and co-star Norma Shearer expressed some of their longings in voice-overs in an effort to find a cinematic equivalent of the asides in Eugene O'Neill's stage original. *Red Dust*, one of the year's top box-office hits, found him as an independent rubber plantation owner caught between two women, Mary Astor and Jean Harlow, splendidly trading barbs with the latter, which, of course, meant they were crazy for one another and destined to end up in a final clinch at the fade-out. It was clear that within the course of one year, the studio had discovered and nurtured a major star. He was borrowed by Paramount in 1932, for a pleasant romantic comedy, *No Man of Her Own*, which would prove fortuitous since it co-starred Carole Lombard whom he would marry seven years later. This would mark their only screen teaming. Harlow and Gable were back at it again for *Hold Your Man*, which really belonged to her, with Gable disappearing for the middle portion while she went off to a women's detention home. He played a barbaric stage director trying to make a star out of Crawford in *Dancing Lady*, wherein he got to introduce Fred Astaire to the cinema audiences, and he teamed with Helen Hayes in *The White Sister*, both of them trying to pass for Italians, and then again in *Night Flight*, where he was third billed, after John Barrymore and Hayes, in this all-star aerial drama that was not a moneymaker as expected.

There was another loan-out, this time to Columbia, supposedly as punishment for refusing work, and it provided him an unexpectedly happy circumstance. The film was director Frank Capra's *It Happened One Night*, and it was instrumental in launching the "screwball comedy" genre of the 1930s. Gable was never more wittily adept or assured as a smart-aleck reporter who falls in love with runaway heiress Claudette Colbert. One of the movies of that era that can still evoke a smile, it was a critical and financial sensation in its day, sweeping the Oscars with Best Picture, Best Actress, Best Director, and Best Screenplay wins, and the Academy Award to Gable as Best Actor of 1934. That same year he gave another excellent performance, as the devil-

may-care gangster resigned to his life as a bad but wealthy man, in *Manhattan Melodrama*, and had two more hits with Crawford, *Chained*, playing a South American rancher, and the brighter *Forsaking All Others*, picking her up on the rebound from Robert Montgomery. From this red-hot peak he found himself in *China Seas*, in a situation similar to *Red Heat*, fought over by Harlow and the more ladylike Rosalind Russell. It's worth noting that just three years after *Hell Divers*, he was now billed *above* Wallace Beery.

Maintaining this high level he made one of his finest films, *Mutiny on the Bounty*, minus his famous mustache, and doing a commendable job as Fletcher Christian, leading the ship's revolt against sadistic Charles Laughton. It was a thoroughly satisfying performance, good enough to earn him another Oscar nomination, and make audiences forget that he didn't even bother to attempt a British accent. With it he became the first star to be seen in back-to-back Academy Award winners for Best Picture. From there he went into a zippy newsroom comedy with Constance Bennett, *After Office Hours*, then was back with two of his most dependable leading ladies, Harlow and Myrna Loy, for one of his lesser efforts, *Wife vs. Secretary*. Then he had his biggest hit to date, *San Francisco*, finding redemption after the great earthquake, as a Barbary Coast saloon owner campaigning for public office. It didn't hurt the box office at all that his co-stars were Spencer Tracy and Jeanette MacDonald, though he was, in fact, more comfortably partnered with him than with her. Borrowed by Warners for *Cain and Mabel*, this minor show business/boxing picture was significant only because it was the last time audiences would see him sans mustache. *Love on the Run* was perhaps the least famous of his multiple teamings with Crawford, a comedy in which he pinched her away from her real-life husband, Franchot Tone. It was followed by his most notorious misfire, the biopic of the Irish nationalist leader *Parnell*, showing his stubbornness or his inability to play anything outside what the Gable audiences loved. *Saratoga* was a cursed production, with co-star Lionel Barrymore injuring himself on the set and Harlow dying during the shoot, but it became a curio that made money, as did the routine flier love triangle, *Test Pilot*, with Tracy and Loy, an inexplicable Oscar nominee for Best Picture and a prime example of star power over standard material. Loy was back for the more enjoyable *Too Hot to Handle*, in which Gable was a newsreel cameraman on the make. Then he made *Idiot's Delight*, famous for his cheeky song-and-dance rendering of "Puttin' on the Ritz," a moment that holds up far better than most of the dramatic passages in this awkward mix of romance and pacifism.

Gable reached the Mount Olympus of movie stardom when audiences demanded at any cost that he play Rhett Butler in the much anticipated film of *Gone With the Wind*. His reluctant participation resulted in MGM being allowed to distribute the Selznick production, and there is no doubt that his performance is one of the crucial elements that has carried the movie into immortality. A blockbuster in its day (holding the top spot as the highest-grossing movie of all time for over 25 years), it continues to enthrall movie lovers and has come to symbolize the studio era at its best. Gable's work is everything it's cracked up to be: charming, powerful, and unexpectedly complex, even allowing for him to have an effective crying scene. He received an Oscar nomination but lost to Robert Donat's Mr. Chips. After this triumph, he was back with Crawford one last time for the allegorical adventure *Strange Cargo*, and with Tracy and Colbert for the easy-to-take *Boom Town*. Then the studio found him another profitable partner, Lana Turner, although their four movies together — *Honky Tonk*, a western; *Somewhere I'll Find*

You, in which he was far more believable as a war correspondent than she was; *Homecoming*, a romance on the battlefront; and *Betrayed*, a World War II tale set in the Netherlands — were nothing to get excited about. He enlisted in the army during World War II and became the most famous widower in Hollywood history when third wife Carole Lombard (they had married in 1939) was killed in an air crash in 1942.

After a three-year absence, he returned with *Adventure*, with its much-quoted ad line, "Gable's Back and Garson's got him." He and Greer made an awkward team, though, and he was at his all-time least likeable as a stubborn seaman. *The Hucksters* was better by far, a witty look at advertising with that nice girl vs. easy girl set-up again, this time with Deborah Kerr and Ava Gardner, respectively. There was a well liked but extremely talky war movie, *Command Decision*, from the hit Broadway play, and then a slump period. During this time he showed up wearing a Little Lord Fauntleroy outfit in the dreadful *Key to the City*; raced cars against a rear projection screen in *To Please a Lady*; and fell for a Russian Gene Tierney in *Never Let Me Go*, one of the many Iron Curtain dramas churned out in the early 1950s. Relief came with a sharp remake of *Red Dust*, now called *Mogambo*. The graying actor was beginning to show his age, but there was still a lot of spirit left in him. His co-stars, Ava Gardner and Grace Kelly, both nabbed Oscar nominations for their work, and the movie was a top grosser in 1953. It did not, however, mean that Gable was back on top to stay. The public still went for him on occasion, but, oddly, one of his more popular movies of the 1950s, *The Tall Men*, was one of his least interesting, an uninspired western with Jane Russell. He had ended his 23-year stay at Metro with the final Turner teaming (*Betrayed*), in 1954, and spent the rest of his career freelancing.

The King and Four Queens was an obvious attempt to get some mileage out of that crown bestowed upon him decades before, while *Band of Angels* returned him to the Deep South of *Gone With the Wind*, with shabby results. *Run Silent, Run Deep* gave him an interesting role as a submarine commander whose obsessive need for revenge has his crew looking upon him like Captain Bligh, but the film itself never rose to expected heights, despite Burt Lancaster as his second in command. There was a surprisingly good teaming with Doris Day, *Teacher's Pet*, possibly his best latter-day film; *But Not for Me*, a pleasant comedy that made no bones about commenting on the age difference between Gable and Carroll Baker; and *It Started in Naples*, which kept him right up-to-date by matching him with the hottest female star of the day, Sophia Loren. This was also the case with *The Misfits*, which co-starred him with Marilyn Monroe. It is now famous for being the last movie for both of them, but despite a troubled script and overall feeling of sadness rather than compelling drama, it does offer some of the best acting Gable ever did. Shortly after his death, his last wife, Kay Spreckels, gave birth to his only child, a son, John Clark Gable, who made a half-hearted attempt to follow in his father's footsteps by starring in the low-budget film *Big John*, in 1990. It is worth noting that to this day audiences at showings of *Gone With the Wind* still let out a sigh at the first sight of Rhett Butler staring at Scarlett from the bottom of the stairs, a testament to Gable's power if ever there was one.

Screen: 1924: Forbidden Paradise; White Man; 1925: The Pacemakers (serial); The Merry Widow; Déclassée; The Plastic Age; North Star; 1926: The Johnstown Flood; 1931: The Painted Desert; Dance, Fools, Dance; The Easiest Way; Night Nurse; The Finger Points; The Secret Six; A Free Soul; Laughing Sinners; Sporting Blood; Susan Lennox (Her Fall and Rise); Possessed; Hell Divers; 1932: Polly of the Circus; Strange Interlude; Red Dust; No Man of Her Own; 1933: The White Sister; Hold Your Man; Night Flight; Dancing Lady; 1934: It Happened One Night; Men in White; Manhattan Melodrama; Chained; Forsaking All Others; 1935: After Office Hours; The Call of the Wild; China Seas; Mutiny on the Bounty; 1936: Wife vs. Secretary; San Francisco; Cain and Mabel; Love on the Run; 1937: Parnell; Saratoga; 1938: Test Pilot; Too Hot to Handle; 1939: Idiot's Delight; Gone With the Wind; 1940: Strange Cargo; Boom Town; Comrade X; 1941: They Met in Bombay; Honky Tonk; 1942: Somewhere I'll Find You; 1945: Adventure; 1947: The Hucksters; 1948: Homecoming; Command Decision; 1949: Any Number Can Play; 1950: Key to the City; To Please a Lady; 1951: Across the Wide Missouri; Callaway Went Thataway; 1952: Lone Star; 1953: Never Let Me Go; Mogambo; 1954: Betrayed; 1955: Soldier of Fortune; The Tall Men; 1956: The King and Four Queens; 1957: Band of Angels; 1958: Run Silent, Run Deep; Teacher's Pet; 1959: But Not for Me; 1960: It Started in Naples; 1961: The Misfits.

NY Stage: 1928: Machinal; 1929: Hawk Island; 1930: Love, Honor and Betray.

ZSA ZSA GABOR

(Sari Gabor) Born: Budapest, Hungary, February 6, 1917.

Famous for being famous, Zsa Zsa Gabor was known by people who were not even sure what she did for a living. Over the years her silly name, penchant for getting married too many times, outlandish behavior on TV talk shows, varying dates of birth, and, finally, her notorious run-in with a Beverly Hills cop, whom she slapped for giving her a speeding ticket, made her a juicy celebrity, but not an actress of any serious note. A former Miss Hungary beauty pageant winner, she made her movie debut in 1952 for MGM, in *Lovely to Look At*. That same year she had her most famous film role, French cabaret performer Jane Avril, "sort of" singing the hit song "Where Is Your Heart" (she was dubbed), in the Oscar-nominated Toulouse-Lautrec biopic *Moulin Rouge*. It was followed by another major film, *Lili*, with Gabor as the magician's assistant; her glamorous persona there to contrast with Leslie Caron's more drab, but certainly more sincere, one. By the end of the 1950s, she was descending into campy products like the peerless *Queen of Outer Space*, as the Venusian who helps the astronauts battle the title character; *The Girl in the Kremlin*, as both Stalin's mistress and her twin; and *Country Music Holiday*, as herself. In the 1960s she was the Dead Mommy in *Picture Mommy Dead*, and the annoying wife of Tony Curtis, whom he has launched into space, in the limp comedy *Arrivederci, Baby!* By the 1980s it was hard to take her seriously playing anyone but herself, which is how she turned up in *A Nightmare on Elm Street 3: The Dream Warriors*, getting devoured by Freddy Krueger, and *The Naked Gun 2 1/2: The Smell of Fear*, parodying her confrontation with that police officer. The most famous of her husbands (1949–57) was actor George Sanders, with whom she appeared in *Death of a Scoundrel*. Her younger sister, Eva Gabor (1921–95), was best known for her role as Louis Jourdan's flighty mistress in *Gigi*, and as the socialite-turned-farm girl in the popular 1960s TV series *Green Acres*.

Screen: 1952: Lovely to Look At; We're Not Married!; Moulin Rouge; 1953: Lili; The Story of Three Loves; The Most Wanted Man in the World/Public Enemy No. 1; 1954: 3 Ring Circus; Love in a Hot Climate/Sang et Lumieres (nUSr); Ball der Nationen/Ball of the Nations (nUSr); 1956: Death of a

Scoundrel; 1957: The Girl in the Kremlin; 1958: The Man Who Wouldn't Talk; Touch of Evil; Queen of Outer Space; Country Music Holiday; 1959: For the First Time; 1960: La Contessa Azzurra (nUSr); Pepe; 1962: Boys' Night Out; 1966: Picture Mommy Dead; Arrivederci, Baby!/Drop Dead Darling; 1967: Jack of Diamonds; 1972: Up the Front (nUSr); 1976: Won Ton Ton, the Dog Who Saved Hollywood; 1978: Every Girl Should Have One; 1985: Frankenstein's Great Aunt Tillie; 1986: Movie Maker/Smart Alec (dtv); 1987: A Nightmare on Elm Street 3: The Dream Warriors; 1991: The Naked Gun 2 1/2: The Smell of Fear; 1992: The Naked Truth; 1993: Happily Ever After (voice); The Beverly Hillbillies; 1996: A Very Brady Sequel.

Select TV: 1956: The Honest Man (sp); The Tall Dark Stranger (sp); 1957: The Greer Case (sp); Circle of the Day (sp); The Last Voyage (sp); The Subpoena (sp); The Two Mrs. Carrolls (sp); 1960: Ninotchka (sp); 1965: Double Jeopardy (sp); 1966: Alice in Wonderland: or What's a Nice Kid Like You Doin' in a Place Like This? (sp; voice); 1985: California Girls.

GRETA GARBO

(GRETA LOUISA GUSTAFSSON)
BORN: STOCKHOLM, SWEDEN,
SEPTEMBER 18, 1905. DIED: APRIL 15, 1990.

There is no need to have to say the first name. "Garbo" alone was, and is, a magical word for anyone in love with the cinema, though it is doubtful that there are many actresses who enter the profession hoping to emulate her. Hauntingly beautiful, with sad, searching eyes and a face, even when blank, that could say volumes, her talking-picture style is, nonetheless, highly theatrical, too richly overwrought for modern audiences. She will moan her words to express pain, then throw back her head archly when happy, melodramatically emoting to the heavens. Yet somehow all of this is fascinating to watch. She almost effortlessly sweeps her sometimes more-adept co-stars off the screen because you cannot help but be mesmerized. Appearances in some short films led to a scholarship to the Royal Stockholm Theatre School where she met director Mauritz Stiller. He became her mentor, offering her up to the movie-going public for the first time with the 1924 melodrama The Atonement of Gosta Berling, in which she played an Italian countess. From that came a smaller part, in The Joyless Street, and an offer from MGM, who were actually more interested in Stiller than her. On his insistence, she came along as part of the deal. After the requisite Hollywood makeover, a more glamorous Garbo emerged, and thus she was sold as an enigmatic beauty opposite the stoic Ricardo Cortez, in The Torrent, in which she left him after an unrequited romance to become an opera singer. The film that brought her to prominence was Flesh and the Devil, in which she tempted John Gilbert into some passionate lovemaking and ended up on an ice floe. Its success made the studio begin to treat her as their prize property, and, after meeting some salary demands, they put her together with Gilbert again for Love, which would mark the first time she would play Anna Karenina on screen, and for A Woman of Affairs, in which her reckless life led to her inevitable demise. Less successful were The Divine Woman, her first to give her top billing, in which she played a character somewhat based on Sarah Bernhardt, and Mysterious Lady, a silly thing in which she was a Russian spy, though it was agreed that she still looked sensational, if nothing else!

Talkies had arrived and no star's transition to sound was ever as heralded. The notable ad line "Garbo talks!" referred to Anna Christie, a rather sluggish film in which she played Eugene

O'Neill's waterfront dweller to great acclaim and substantial box-office success. It earned her an Oscar nomination in 1930, the same year she was up for her work in Romance, a moldy old melodrama in which she was cast for the second time as an opera singer. The high dramatics continued with Susan Lennox (Her Fall and Rise), playing a runaway who ends up sleeping her way to the top after being separated from her true love, Clark Gable, and with Mata Hari, portraying a spy in this colorful pabulum with a less-than-exciting leading man in Roman Novarro. This was followed by one of her greatest triumphs, the all-star Grand Hotel, which gave her the line most closely associated with her, "I want to be alone!" She enchanted jewel thief John Barrymore, although they were both miscast, their ages being reversed from the original novel in which there was an older woman/younger man plot line. In any case it was Barrymore's brother, Lionel, who stole the show from both of them. The film was the Academy Award winner for Best Picture of 1932, yet was the only Oscar winner in the history of this coveted trophy that didn't receive a single nomination in any other category. That same year Garbo had one of her stronger co-stars in Erich von Stroheim in As You Desire Me, but the film lost its footing in the latter half when she changed from platinum blonde to her natural color and fell in love with Melvyn Douglas. Queen Christina was Garbo in pants, with heavy suggestions of lesbianism despite her love for leading man John Gilbert, whom she insisted on as co-star to help his ailing career. Her wordless close-up at the ship's railing is one of the most famous scenes in cinema history, while the film itself is probably the most watchable, dramatically engrossing, and least dated of all of the Garbo dramas.

She returned to Tolstoy for the second version of Anna Karenina. Though still heavily melodramatic, the film offered a highly suitable role for her nonetheless. She then played perhaps her most famous part, in Camille. As the dying courtesan in love with Robert Taylor, she received some of her most rapturous praise and a third Oscar nomination. Today it is probably the epitome of high-gloss MGM melodrama from that era, which is half good, half bad. More interesting was Conquest, because she was challenged for once by a stronger role for her leading man, Charles Boyer, who played Napoleon to her Marie Walewska. Then someone had the bright idea to utilize the serious Garbo mystique in a comedy. The result, director Ernst Lubitsch's Ninotchka, worked like a charm, reteaming her, more rewardingly than the last time, with Melvyn Douglas, who toiled to bring a spark of humanity and fire to her stern-faced Russian emissary with hilarious results. She received her fourth and final Oscar nomination, and the film itself remains the finest and most enduring of all her films. Hoping that lightning would strike a second time, MGM stuck with comedy and Douglas for Two-Faced Woman, offering the actress as twins, but the final product pleased no one, least of all Garbo, who had no desire to leap into another film at that point. Her temporary retirement turned out to be permanent, and she drifted so thoroughly out of the limelight that she became the most famous ex-movie star of them all. In time, photos of her walking about Manhattan, hoping to enjoy her solitude, would become newsworthy events as the world refused to lessen its interest in her. All offers for film work were refused, and a special Academy Award bestowed upon her at the 1954 Oscar ceremony failed to bring her back before the public. All of this only deepened the mystery as the legend continues to surpass most of the work itself.

Screen: 1924: The Atonement of Gosta Berling/The Story of Gosta Berling; 1925: The Joyless Street/The Street of Sorrow; 1926: The Torrent/The Temptress; 1927: Flesh and the Devil; Love; 1928: The Divine Woman; The Mysterious Lady; 1929: A

Woman of Affairs; Wild Orchids; The Single Standard; The Kiss; A Man's Man; 1930: Anna Christie; Romance; 1931: Inspiration; Susan Lennox (Her Fall and Rise); 1932: Mata Hari; Grand Hotel; As You Desire Me; 1933: Queen Christina; 1934: The Painted Veil; 1935: Anna Karenina; 1937: Camille; Conquest; 1939: Ninotchka; 1941: Two-Faced Woman.

REGINALD GARDINER

(WILLIAM REGINALD GARDINER) BORN: WIMBELDON, SURREY, ENGLAND, FEBRUARY 27, 1903. ED: RADA. DIED: JULY 7, 1980.

With arched-eyebrow and frequent cigarette in hand, debonair, pencil-mustached Reginald Gardiner usually took a sardonic view of whatever events were going on around him, while playing various cads, snobs, wits, and fools to perfection. Most of his early work on the London stage was in dramas, such as *The Prisoner of Zenda* and *Blackmail*, but in America he made his reputation with the revues *At Home Abroad* and *The Show Is On*. From these came film offers, and he made his U.S. debut in the 1936 musical *Born to Sing*, as a cop who really wants to be a symphony conductor. This part was amusing enough that he played a variation on it right afterwards, in *A Damsel in Distress*, as a butler who secretly sings opera. There were straight-man parts opposite Laurel and Hardy in *The Flying Deuces*, as an officer in the French Foreign Legion, and opposite Charlie Chaplin in *The Great Dictator*, as the German soldier who turns his back on Nazism. Although he would be called on for serious fare like *Marie Antoinette*, as Artois, and the war films *Captains of the Clouds* (his own personal favorite) and *Halls of Montezuma*, it was in comedy that he is most fondly remembered. In that capacity he was the second-rate sculptor with designs on Anna Lee in *My Life With Caroline*; Loretta Young's opportunistic publisher in *The Doctor Takes a Wife*; and a thinly disguised version of Noël Coward in *The Man Who Came to Dinner* (a part he would later play on television as well). Other comedic roles were Barbara Stanwyck's fake "husband" in *Christmas in Connecticut*; a Duke pursued by Betty Grable in *Sweet Rosie O'Grady*, the first of four in support of that lady; and a genuine orchestra conductor in *Do You Love Me?* Continuing to work right up until the mid-1960s (later roles include William Shakespeare in *The Story of Mankind*, a painter in *What a Way to Go!*, and a lieutenant in *Sergeant Deadhead*), he was forced to retire after being injured in a fall.

Screen: 1931: The Perfect Lady; 1932: Flat No. 9; Josser on the River; 1933: Radio Parade; Just Smith/Leave It to Smith; 1934: Borrow a Million; How's Chances?; Virginia's Husband; 1935: Opening Night; A Little Bit of Bluff; Royal Cavalcade/Regal Cavalcade; 1936: Born to Dance; 1937: A Damsel in Distress; 1938: Everybody Sing; Marie Antoinette; Sweethearts; The Girl Downstairs; 1939: The Flying Deuces; The Night of Nights; 1940: The Doctor Takes a Wife; Dulcy; The Great Dictator; 1941: My Life With Caroline; A Yank in the RAF; Sundown; The Man Who Came to Dinner; 1942: Captains of the Clouds; 1943: Forever and a Day; The Immortal Sergeant; Sweet Rosie O'Grady; Claudia; 1945: Molly and Me; The Horn Blows at Midnight; Christmas in Connecticut; The Dolly Sisters; 1946: Do You Love Me?; Cluny Brown; One More Tomorrow; 1947: I Wonder Who's Kissing Her Now; 1948: That Wonderful Urge; Fury at Furnace Creek; That Lady in Ermine; 1950: Wabash Avenue; I'll Get By; Halls of Montezuma; 1951: Elopement; 1952: Androcles and the Lion; 1954: Black Widow; 1955: Ain't Misbehavin'; 1956: The Birds and the Bees; 1957: The Story of

Mankind; 1958: Rock-a-Bye Baby; 1961: Back Street; 1962: Mr. Hobbs Takes a Vacation; 1964: What a Way to Go!; 1965: Sergeant Deadhead; Do Not Disturb.

NY Stage: 1935: At Home Abroad; 1936: The Show Is On; 1952: An Evening With Beatrice Lillie; 1956: The Little Glass Clock; 1964: My Fair Lady.

Select TV: 1954: The Man Who Came to Dinner (sp); 1955: The Guardsman (sp); Alice in Wonderland (sp); 1956: Mr. Belvedere (sp); 1958: No Time at All; 1966–67: The Pruitts of Southampton (series).

AVA GARDNER

BORN: GRABTOWN, NC, DECEMBER 24, 1922. DIED: JANUARY 25, 1990.

In the 1940s there were few stars so blatantly sold on their looks as Ava Gardner was. In fact, Hollywood was so sure that there wasn't much more to her, that she spent the first four years of her movie career doing little more than decorating the background of various films. She was, at that time, more famous for her marriages to Mickey Rooney and Artie Shaw than for any of her screen credits. Later she was given some chances and showed definite signs of talent. Once her heyday was gone, she often looked back on her career with disdain and disinterest, as if the whole thing wasn't worth her time, and, unfortunately, that indifference often came across in her work. Born in poverty on a farm in North Carolina, she came to New York as a teenager to visit her sister and wound up as a photographer's model. Her picture caught the attention of someone from MGM, and she was signed to a contract, making her debut in 1941, in a Pete Smith Specialty short, "Fancy Answers," followed by a bit as a socialite in the feature *H.M. Pulham, Esq.* The following year came her marriage to Rooney, which lasted less than two years but brought her plenty of newsprint. In the meantime she got fifth billing in *Three Men in White*, one of the Dr. Gillespie quickies of the period, and then landed a bigger part, as a woman returning to her small town after becoming city-wise, in *Whistle Stop*, for United Artists. It was, in fact, another studio, not her own, that gave her her breakthrough part, in *The Killers*, a Universal release in which she played a double-crossing vixen in the life of doomed prizefighter Burt Lancaster (in his film debut). Sensing that they might be passing up a good thing, MGM let her play the bad girl opposite Clark Gable in a popular and good film, *The Hucksters*, which made it clear that something could be made of her provocative way of delivering a line. A period of unsuccessful films, hoping to cash in on her sudden stardom, followed. These included *Singapore*, a tired pseudo-*Casablanca* drama in which she had amnesia; *One Touch of Venus*, where she was the department store mannequin come-to-life in this ruinous adaptation of the Broadway musical hit; *The Bribe*, a failed noir stolen by Charles Laughton; The *Great Sinner*, where Gardner played a Russian countess; and *Pandora and the Flying Dutchman*, a beautifully photographed, British-made fantasy of some cult appeal in which she was ideal as a good-time gal, using up men like Kleenex until she finds herself falling for mysterious James Mason.

Since it was the general consensus that she was not an actress of great range, it was risky for MGM to give her the meaty part of tragic half-caste Julie in the 1951 version of *Show Boat*. Despite the fact that her actual singing voice ended up only on the soundtrack album and not in the film itself, she gave a strong and touching performance, certainly her best so far. There was another hit film, for Fox, *The Snows of Kilimanjaro*, which wasn't very good but did have added star power in Gregory Peck and Susan Hayward (who took second billing, though Gardner had the better role). Next came one of the very best parts of her career, in *Mogambo*, with the actress at her sassy best, her sharp tongue barely covering up a multitude of insecurities, as the showgirl sharing the jungle with Clark Gable. It earned her her sole Oscar nomination and gave her more credibility as an actress than ever before, admirably following in the footsteps of Jean Harlow, who had done the part in her own inimitable way opposite Gable in the original version, *Red Dust*. On top of all the attention she got for this film, Gardner was a red-hot item in the gossip columns because of her tumultuous marriage (1951–57) to Frank Sinatra. Back on the screen, it appeared for a while as if the Oscar nod had been a fluke, with her less-than-scintillating work in *Knights of the Round Table*, as nobody's idea of Lady Guinevere; and the colossally boring *The Barefoot Contessa*, in which she showed little of the magnetism her character was meant to have, her supposedly eye-catching dance being done off screen. She was happy to do *Bhowani Junction*, once again playing a half-caste, because George Cukor directed it, but she hated *The Little Hut*, a desert-island comedy in which she played house with David Niven and Stewart Granger. It would be hard to image that she was very satisfied with *The Naked Maja*, a soggy load of romantic claptrap in which she was the Duchess of Alba, having an unhappy affair with Anthony Franciosa as Francisco Goya. It marked the end of her MGM contract. Much better were Fox's *The Sun Also Rises*, too old to play Hemingway's Lady Brett, but making her scenes count nonetheless, and UA's surprisingly lucrative end-of-the-world drama, *On the Beach*, giving a very gentle, effective performance as Gregory Peck's lover.

As the 1960s arrived she started off on a sour note, playing a prostitute in love with priest Dirk Bogarde in *The Angel Wore Red*. Thereafter she began to work her way down the cast lists, taking a backseat to Charlton Heston and some impressive battle scenes in *55 Days at Peking*, and likewise stepping aside while the men got all the best moments in *Seven Days in May*, as Burt Lancaster's mistress. Her part in *The Night of the Iguana* was officially a supporting role, but she put a great deal of zing into the proceedings as the seen-it-all hotel proprietress, giving an outstanding performance. In the all-star, episodic *The Bible*, she was Sarah, supplying star power and little else; while the remake of *Mayerling* found her as dreary as the rest of the cast, as the Empress Elizabeth. There was a lead in a barely released oddity, called, alternately, *Tam Lin* and *The Devil's Widow*, the only novelty of it being that Roddy McDowall directed it. She went back to supporting parts, showing up as Lily Langtry in *The Life and Times of Judge Roy Bean*; and looking worn and disinterested in the Sensurround hit *Earthquake*, improbably cast as Lorne Greene's daughter. Not masking her waning disinterest in the whole profession, she was in director George Cukor's misfire fantasy, *The Blue Bird*, as Luxury; *The Cassandra Crossing*, as a wealthy train passenger carrying on with gigolo Martin Sheen; the cheesy Canadian disaster film, *City on Fire*, as an alcoholic; and one that aspired to a more literary crowd, *Priest of Love*, as an admirer of author D.H. Lawrence. Most of her later years were spent in telefilms; her last theatrical production, *Regina*, never made it to American cinemas.

Screen: 1941: H.M. Pulham, Esq.; 1942: We Were Dancing; Joe Smith — American; This Time for Keeps; Kid Glove Killer; Sunday Punch; Calling Dr. Gillespie; Reunion in France; 1943: Pilot #5; DuBarry Was a Lady; Hitler's Madman; Ghosts on the Loose; Young Ideas; Lost Angel; Swing Fever; 1944: Three Men in White; Maisie Goes to Reno; Music for Millions; Blonde Fever; Two Girls and a Sailor; 1945: She Went to the Races; 1946:

Whistle Stop; The Killers; 1947: The Hucksters; Singapore; 1948: One Touch of Venus; 1949: The Bribe; The Great Sinner; East Side, West Side; 1951: Pandora and the Flying Dutchman; My Forbidden Past; Show Boat; 1952: Lone Star; The Snows of Kilimanjaro; 1953: Ride, Vaquero!; The Band Wagon; Mogambo; Knights of the Round Table; 1954: The Barefoot Contessa; 1956: Bhowani Junction; 1957: The Little Hut; The Sun Also Rises; 1959: The Naked Maja; On the Beach; 1960: The Angel Wore Red; 1963: 55 Days at Peking; 1964: Seven Days in May; The Night of the Iguana; 1966: The Bible; 1969: Mayerling; 1971: Tam Lin/The Devil's Widow; 1972: The Life and Times of Judge Roy Bean; 1974: Earthquake; 1975: Permission to Kill; 1976: The Blue Bird; 1977: The Sentinel; The Cassandra Crossing; 1979: City on Fire; 1980: The Kidnapping of the President; 1981: Priest of Love; 1982: Regina/Regina Roma (dtv).

Select TV: 1985: A.D.; The Long Hot Summer; Knots Landing (series); 1986: Harem.

JOHN GARFIELD

(JACOB JULIUS GARFINKLE) BORN: NEW YORK, NY, MARCH 4, 1913. DIED: MAY 21, 1952.

Before the onslaught of rebellious young actors of the postwar years, there was John Garfield, tough, cynical, edgy, not unlike his real-life self. During the 1940s he was one of Warner Bros.'s more interesting young actors, even though some of the material he was handed seems dated today and at times prompted him to try too hard to impress you with his intensity. After receiving a scholarship to the Ouspenskaya Drama School, he became a member of Eva La Gallienne's company. During a break, he went to Hollywood and landed a bit at the studio that would later become his home, Warners, in the musical *Footlight Parade*, where he can be glimpsed as a sailor in the "Shanghai Lil" number. Since nothing more came of this trip, he went back to New York and joined the Group Theatre. Among the plays he performed in for them were *Johnny Johnson* and *Golden Boy*, though he didn't have the leads. He did, however, star on Broadway in *Having Wonderful Time*, at which point he signed a contract with Warner Bros. His debut for them, playing the doomed and moody musician loved by Priscilla Lane in 1938's *Four Daughters*, was much commented on. It was one case where the audience truly felt they were watching an exciting new talent, and he received a well-deserved supporting Oscar nomination as a result. The film was a hit, and the studio didn't waste much time giving him the big push. To this end, there immediately followed his first starring role, a boxer on the run, in *They Made Me a Criminal*, which found him teamed with the Dead End Kids in a film directed by Busby Berkeley, of all people. *Blackwell's Island* wasn't originally supposed to have featured Garfield in a lead, having been started before *Four Daughters*, but because of the potential so evident, even in the daily rushes, his part, as a reporter who has himself thrown in prison, was beefed up. Although he had died in *Four Daughters*, the follow-up, *Daughters Courageous*, brought him back just the same, although in a different role. Then, because the studio liked him teamed with Priscilla Lane, they were together once more for *Dust Be My Destiny*, with Garfield ending up behind bars yet again.

Staying in the slammer, he starred in *Castle on the Hudson*, which referred to Sing Sing prison, and remained on the wrong side of the law for *East of the River*, the one about the good and bad brothers both in love with the same girl. As a break from all this criminal activity, Garfield got to play an inventor in *Saturday's Children*, and proved heroic opposing evil Edward G.

Robinson in the highly enjoyable 1941 version of *The Sea Wolf*, in a role not in the original novel. He was a bad guy again in *Out of the Fog*, as a petty hood terrorizing Thomas Mitchell and John Qualen. It was a part that was prime Garfield, cocky, snide, and menacing. Other studios came calling, so he went to MGM to play a none-too-convincing paisano, a hot-tempered but relatively decent guy, in *Tortilla Flat*, and then to RKO for *The Fallen Sparrow*, as a man who survived being tortured in a prison camp (which resulted in some fairly theatrical tics). Being the early 1940s, he was sent to do battle on screen in one of the dozens of look-alike war dramas, *Air Force*, not surprisingly cast as the maverick, scoffing at authority until patriotism makes him a hero. He also appeared in the much better *Destination Tokyo*, the definite submarine drama of the era, co-starring alongside Cary Grant. The remake of *Outward Bound*, renamed *Between Two Worlds*, saw him going at it in hammy fashion, as the reporter who finds out that he and the other passengers aboard ship are dead. After this he had one of his best-remembered roles, the young soldier who loses his eyesight during the war, in *Pride of the Marines*. MGM borrowed him again, this time for one of the hot melodramas of the day, James M. Cain's *The Postman Always Rings Twice*, in which he and Lana Turner were extremely unsympathetic as the illicit lovers/murderers. With a plot far too similar to the same author's *Double Indemnity*, its melodramatic affectations couldn't help but pale in comparison. After a topnotch soaper, *Humoresque*, in which he was surprisingly believable as a determined violinist, he ended his contract with Warners.

For his own production company he did a well-regarded but talky film, *Body and Soul*, playing a dim boxer trying to help his poor mom and facing the expected gangsters in the process. It earned him his second Oscar nomination. That same year, 1947, he took a supporting role as Gregory Peck's best friend, a Jewish soldier, in the Best Picture winner, *Gentleman's Agreement*, because he believed so strongly in the movie's message about anti-Semitism. There were more raves for his work as a racketeer's lawyer in the highly un-commercial *Force of Evil*, directed by a promptly blacklisted Abraham Polonsky. Then, back at Warners for a spell, he did Humphrey Bogart's old part in *The Breaking Point*, a remake of *To Have and Have Not*, which didn't have anything near the success of the original, despite being the more faithful rendering of the Hemingway novel. In fact, besides *Gentleman's Agreement*, none of the films he'd done around this time were potent box-office pictures, so he found himself returning to the stage for greater acting satisfaction with *The Skipper Next to God* and *The Big Knife*. (He had already made a famous miscalculation when he turned down the lead in the original production of *A Streetcar Named Desire*.) By the early 1950s, he was under scrutiny as a Communist sympathizer and was finding his services less in demand. He therefore took it upon himself to set up his own production, the 1951 release *He Ran All the Way*, in which he held Shelley Winters and her family hostage. The following year he was dead of a heart attack at the age of 39. Only a month before he had been back on Broadway with *Golden Boy*, only this time in the title role.

Screen: 1933: Footlight Parade; 1938: Four Daughters; 1939: They Made Me a Criminal; Blackwell's Island; Juarez; Daughters Courageous; Dust Be My Destiny; Four Wives; 1940: Castle on the Hudson; Saturday's Children; Flowing Gold; East of the River; 1941: The Sea Wolf; Out of the Fog; 1942: Dangerously They Live; Tortilla Flat; 1943: Air Force; The Fallen Sparrow; Thank Your Lucky Stars; Destination Tokyo; 1944: Between Two Worlds; Hollywood Canteen; 1945: Pride of the Marines; 1946: The Postman Always Rings Twice; Nobody Lives Forever; Humoresque; 1947: Body and Soul; Daisy Kenyon;

Gentleman's Agreement; **1948:** Force of Evil; **1949:** We Were Strangers; Jigsaw; **1950:** Under My Skin; The Breaking Point; **1951:** He Ran All the Way.

NY Stage: 1935: Awake and Sing; Weep for the Virgins; 1936: Johnny Johnson; 1937: Having Wonderful Time; Golden Boy; 1940: Heavenly Express; 1948: The Skipper Next to God; 1949: The Big Knife; 1951: Peer Gynt; 1952: Golden Boy (revival).

WILLIAM GARGAN

BORN: BROOKLYN, NY, JULY 17, 1905.
DIED: FEBRUARY 17, 1979.

A decidedly run-of-the-mill character actor and an even less-exciting lead, William Gargan came to Hollywood in the early 1930s, mainly to repeat his performance as the reluctant servant in the 1932 adaptation of *The Animal Kingdom*. From there he played best buddy to William Boyd in both *Lucky Devils* and *Emergency Cal*, and supported such loose women as Joan Crawford in *Rain* and Miriam Hopkins in *The Story of Temple Drake*. Over at Universal he was given leads in some long-forgotten "B's" including *Flying Hostesses*, as an aerial instructor; *Breezing Home*, as a horse trainer; *Behind the Mike*, about rival radio stations; *Reported Missing*, on the trail of a plane saboteur; *The Devil's Party*, which had him growing up to be a cop while his childhood friend (Victor McLaglen) became a criminal; and *House of Fear*, as a detective who poses as a Broadway producer in order to find out who offed an actor. In 1940 his career got a major boost when he received a most undeserving Oscar nomination for seducing mail-order bride Carole Lombard in *They Knew What They Wanted*. The following year he took over the role of Ellery Queen from Ralph Bellamy for three "B" capers at Columbia, and continued sleuthing during the early days of TV with the series *Martin Kane, Private Eye*. Between episodes, he continued to grind out second features such as the musical *Song of the Sarong*, as a pearl hunter on a tropical island; *Behind Green Lights*, as a cop falling for murder suspect Carole Landis; *Night Editor*, as a misbehaving cop who finds redemption by solving a murder he's been falsely accused of; and *Rendezvous 24*, as an American agent saving Paris from a Nazi attack. His career came to an end following an operation that caused him to lose the use of his voice. Thereafter he campaigned extensively for the American Cancer Society and published a book on his battle, *Why Me?*, in 1969. His brother was character actor Edward Gargan, who shared the screen with his sibling in *Follow That Woman*.

Screen: 1917: Mother's Darling; 1929: Lucky Boy; 1930: Follow the Leader; 1931: His Woman; 1932: The Misleading Lady; Rain; The Sport Parade; The Animal Kingdom; Rain; 1933: Lucky Devils; Sweepings; The Story of Temple Drake; Emergency Call; Headline Shooter; Night Flight; Aggie Appleby — Maker of Men; 1934: Four Frightened People; Strictly Dynamite; The Lineup; British Agent; Things Are Looking Up; 1935: Black Fury; A Night at the Ritz; Traveling Saleslady; Bright Lights; Don't Bet on Blondes; Broadway Gondolier; 1936: Man Hunt; The Sky Parade; Alibi for Murder; Blackmailer; The Milky Way; Navy Born; Flying Hostess; 1937: Breezing Home; Fury and the Woman/Lucky Corrigan; You Only Live Once; Wings Over Honolulu; Some Blondes Are Dangerous; Behind the Mike; Reported Missing; She Asked for It; You're a Sweetheart; 1938: The Crowd Roars; The Devil's Party; Personal Secretary; The Crime of Dr. Hallet; 1939: Women in the Wind; Within the Law; Broadway Serenade; The Housekeeper's Daughter; Three Sons; House of Fear; Adventures of Jane Arden; Joe and Ethel Turp Call on the President; 1940: Isle of Destiny; They Knew What They

Wanted; Turnabout; Star Dust; Sporting Blood; Double Alibi; **1941:** Flying Cadets; Sealed Lips; Cheers for Miss Bishop; I Wake Up Screaming; Keep 'Em Flying; **1942:** Bombay Clipper; Miss Annie Rooney; A Close Call for Ellery Queen; Who Done It?; Destination Unknown; The Mayor of 44th Street; A Desperate Chance for Ellery Queen; Enemy Agents Meet Ellery Queen; **1943:** No Place for a Lady; Swing Fever; Harrigan's Kid; **1944:** The Canterville Ghost; **1945:** She Gets Her Man; One Exciting Night/Midnight Manhunt; Song of the Sarong; The Bells of St. Mary's; Follow That Woman; **1946:** Behind Green Lights; Strange Impersonation; Night Editor; Murder in the Music Hall; Hot Cargo; Rendezvous 24; Till the End of Time; Swell Guy; **1948:** The Argyle Secrets; Waterfront at Midnight; **1949:** Dynamite; **1956:** Miracle in the Rain; The Rawhide Years.

NY Stage: **1925:** Aloma of the South Seas; **1928:** War Song; **1929:** Headquarters; **1930:** Out of a Blue Sky; Roar China!; **1931:** She Lived Next Door to a Firehouse; He; **1932:** The Animal Kingdom.

Select TV: **1949–51:** Martin Kane, Private Eye (series); **1955:** Favorite Son (sp); Man on a Ledge (sp); **1958:** The McTaggart Succession (sp).

BEVERLY GARLAND

(Beverly Fessenden) Born: Santa Cruz, CA, October 17, 1926.

Something of a cult favorite, Beverly Garland was a good-looking, highly engaging blonde with a crisp delivery, who brightened up many "B" productions of the 1950s, somehow managing to retain her dignity despite appearing in some prime claptrap. She made her debut under the name Beverly Campbell, in 1949's *D.O.A.*, the first of her films to grow in stature with the passing years, and then went over to MGM as a small-part player, creating little impact. Instead she found much work on television and became a favorite of independent filmmakers, where her credits included many in the fantasy/sci-fi genre. She supported George "Foghorn" Winslow in a comedy/fantasy co-written by Lenny Bruce, *The Rocket Man*; played a movie star being led by Bomba the Jungle Boy to find her husband in *Killer Leopard*; and was killed off while trying to battle one of the silliest-looking of all budget-conscious 1950s monsters in *It Conquered the World*. She appeared in *Swamp Women*, as an escaped convict ("Branded Women! Notorious Women! Scarlet Women!" proclaimed the ads); *Curucu, Beast of the Amazon*, as a doctor searching South America for a so-called "monster;" and *Not of This Earth*, as a nurse unwittingly supplying blood specimens to an alien. In the unforgettable *The Alligator People*, she was understandably dismayed to find out that her husband had become an upright reptile (!), while in the omnibus *Twice Told Tales*, she was paired with Vincent Price for a mini-version of *The House of Seven Gables*. The occasional "A" film included *The Desperate Hours*, as a school teacher; *The Joker Is Wild*, as Eddie Albert's wife; and the cult item *Pretty Poison*, as Tuesday Weld's mean mom who is shot down by her offspring. Her many TV series included *My Three Sons*, as Fred MacMurray's new wife, joining the show late in the run; *Scarecrow and Mrs. King*, as Kate Jackson's mother; and *Lois and Clark: The New Adventures of Superman*, as Lois's mom. Her name remained prominent in the Hollywood area for years as the proprietress of the Beverly Garland Hotel.

Screen: **1949:** D.O.A. (as Beverly Campbell); **1950:** A Life of Her Own; **1951:** Strictly Dishonorable; **1952:** Fearless Fagan; **1953:** The Glass Web; Problem Girls; The Neanderthal Man; **1954:** Bitter Creek; The Go-Getter; The Desperado; Two Guns and a

Badge; The Rocket Man; The Miami Story; Killer Leopard; **1955:** New Orleans Uncensored; The Desperate Hours; Sudden Danger; **1956:** It Conquered the World; Gunslinger; Swamp Women; Curucu, Beast of the Amazon; The Steel Jungle; **1957:** Not of This Earth; Naked Paradise; The Joker Is Wild; Chicago Confidential; Badlands of Montana; **1958:** The Saga of Hemp Brown; **1959:** The Alligator People; **1963:** Twice Told Tales; Stark Fear; **1968:** Pretty Poison; **1969:** The Mad Room; **1974:** Where the Red Fern Grows; Airport 1975; **1977:** Sixth and Main; **1979:** Roller Boogie; **1980:** It's My Turn.

Select TV: **1954:** Bourbon Street (sp); **1955:** Too Late to Run (sp); **1956:** Touch and Go (sp); Second Chance (sp); **1957:** Decoy (series); **1958:** The Nine Lives of Elfego Baca (ms); **1959:** Coronado 9 (series); Move Along Mustangers (sp); Gunfight at Sandoval (sp); **1964:** Charlie — He Couldn't Kill a Fly (sp); **1964–65:** The Bing Crosby Show (series); **1967:** Trial by Error (sp); **1969–72:** My Three Sons (series); **1970:** Cutter's Trail; **1972:** Say Goodbye, Maggie Cole; The Weekend Nun; **1973:** The Voyage of the Yes; **1974:** Unwed Father; The Healers; The Day the Earth Moved; **1983:** This Girl for Hire; **1983–87:** Scarecrow and Mrs. King (series); **1990:** The World's Oldest Living Bridesmaid; **1991:** Finding the Way Home; **1995–97:** Lois & Clark: The New Adventures of Superman (series); **1995:** Hellfire/Blood Song/Haunted Symphony; **1997:** Port Charles (series).

JUDY GARLAND

(Frances Ethel Gumm) Born: Grand Rapids, MN, June 10, 1922. Died: June 22, 1969.

Was there anything Judy Garland couldn't do well? Aside from her magical prowess with a song, she played comedy effortlessly, swept most of the reigning dramatic actresses right under the rug, more than held her own with the screen's two greatest male dancers, and had a bright wit that made her endlessly fascinating, even when she was simply sitting still for an interview. The press tried for years to color her image by focusing on the negative: the pill addiction, the many marriages, suicide attempts, the financial hardships, on-set difficulties, the lost jobs. If, in the end, what finally matters is the work, then there is little but praise, because most of what she did, she did magnificently. A child of the stage, she teamed with her two older sisters for a singing act called The Gumm Sisters. They toured vaudeville and even appeared in some early shorts, but it was clear that Judy was the one with the talent, and the trio soon broke up, allowing her to continue solo. She was screen-tested and signed by MGM, who put her in a short film, "Every Sunday," opposite a pre-stardom Deanna Durbin. Legend has it that studio head Louis B. Mayer's orders to get rid of Garland and keep Durbin were misunderstood. In any event, MGM got Judy, although it was Fox who debuted her in her first feature, the foolishly enjoyable 1936 musical *Pigskin Parade*, where, ninth billed, she was merely part of the ensemble cast, playing a backwoods gal and singing in three of the musical numbers. It didn't exactly make her the next big thing, but that would come soon enough.

Back at her home studio, she remained a team player for *Broadway Melody of 1938*, and this time she stood out, singing "You Made Me Love You" to a photo of Clark Gable, with a special introduction written by her close friend Roger Edens. There followed a pleasant horse picture, *Thoroughbreds Don't Cry*, which was important in her career because it teamed her for the first time with Mickey Rooney. A funny, screwball-family comedy of the sort popular in the 1930s, *Everybody Sing*, kept her in support, but she was more prominent in a quickie, *Listen, Darling*, where she and Freddie Bartholomew played matchmaker for their single mom, Mary Astor. That one became famous as the movie where Garland sang "Zing Went the Strings of My Heart," though in a different arrangement than the one she became associated with. Back with Rooney, she joined the studio's hit series, *Love Finds Andy Hardy*, though she was not the love of the title, since he treated her like a kid while pursuing the far less likable Lana Turner. The third Rooney-Garland pairing, *Babes in Arms*, would mark the beginning of the inimitable "putting on a show" format, with Mickey a rambunctious bundle of energy and Judy keeping him in check with her underplaying and common sense. In the meantime, she made the movie that would keep her famous for generations to come, even if she had never made another film, *The Wizard of Oz*. Her determination and genuine sense of wonderment were essential for making this potentially strange work so beautiful and forever enchanting, and she was given a special juvenile Oscar as a result. Of course it also gave the world one of the greatest songs ever written for a motion picture, the Academy Award-winning "Over the Rainbow," which became Garland's signature number. Officially a star, she was still willing to appear in a secondary capacity in two more Andy Hardy offerings, not to mention three more musicals with Rooney: *Strike Up the Band*; *Babes on Broadway*, in which they did a charming bit of hoofing to "How About You?;" and their best together, *Girl Crazy*, which included another enchanting Garland moment when she sang "Embraceable You" to a roomful of adoring men. In each she had to endure Rooney's self-centered indifference to her until common sense got the best of him. *Little Nellie Kelly* offered two Garlands for the price of one, mother and daughter in different eras, though an unbearably pious Charles Winninger hindered this one considerably. *Ziegfeld Girl* was one of her rare missteps, a grotesque soap opera with songs, in which she, Lana Turner, and Hedy Lamarr were showgirls striving to make it in the biz. At least the script had the good sense to have Garland be the one to make it in the end.

For Me and My Girl, sold as her first adult role, with her name solo above the title, gave her another great partner in screen newcomer Gene Kelly. Their gentle rendition of the title number was one of the nice, understated highlights of both their careers. There wasn't a great deal left of the original Booth Tarkington story in *Presenting Lily Mars*, but she had some fine moments, comical and musical, as a show business hopeful, bugging Van Heflin to help her along. She had become one of the surest box-office draws in the business, and her popularity skyrocketed with the 1944 release of *Meet Me in St. Louis*, a joyous slice of nostalgia directed with taste and skill by Vincente Minnelli. He became Garland's second husband, and the film, one of the true classics of the studio era, allowed her to sing such enduring melodies as "The Trolley Song" and "Have Yourself a Merry Little Christmas." As proof of her high standing with the public, she managed to bring in the crowds for the one dramatic film she did during the 1940s, *The Clock*, a sweet romance with Robert Walker, directed by Minnelli, in which she didn't sing a note. *The Harvey Girls*, the story of waitresses in the untamed West, was another success, and it gave her another Oscar-winning hit song, "On the Atchison, Topeka, and Santa Fe," although it co-starred her least-appealing leading man, John Hodiak. Minnelli tried to do something offbeat with the fantasy *The Pirate*, but it never quite achieved the artistic heights it was aiming for, although Garland and Kelly did get to introduce the unforgettable "Be a Clown." A third Kelly teaming, *Easter Parade*, wasn't realized once he injured himself, but his replacement, Fred Astaire, was all the compensation one could hope for. He and Garland were pure gold together, and their tramp number, "A Couple of Swells," was

among the best-loved musical sequences captured on film. It was around this point that Garland began having difficulties in showing up for work. As a result she was fired from both *The Barkleys of Broadway* (an intended reteaming with Astaire) and, more regrettably, *Annie Get Your Gun*, which went to Betty Hutton instead. The two she did make, *In the Good Old Summertime* and *Summer Stock*, both had their moments, especially the latter, which ended with one of the killer Garland moments of all time, the sensational "Get Happy." That, however, marked the parting of the ways with MGM, who no longer were willing to wait around until their frequently ill and undependable star got her act together.

She'd divorced Minnelli in the meantime and found solace from her stagnant film career in live performing, first in London and then at the Palace Theatre in New York, both of which were the beginning of a series of concerts that would be spoken of with awe by audiences for years to come. Because of these she was once again a hot property, so her third husband, Sid Luft, planned her comeback by signing her with Warner Bros. for the 1954 remake of *A Star Is Born*. It was just the sort of showcase most performers only dream of, providing an electrifying three hours of all facets of the Garland talent. There was another signature song, "The Man That Got Away," and, despite the controversial trimming of the film after its initial run, healthy box-office returns and an Oscar nomination. There would not be another on-screen appearance for seven years, but in the meantime, she continued to shine in one live engagement after another, as well as in some television specials. When she did return to the movies, it was as a frumpy German housewife in the powerful all-star drama *Judgment at Nuremberg*, an effective cameo that earned her another Oscar nod, in the supporting category. Earlier that year, 1961, she played her historical concert at Carnegie Hall. The best-selling record from that event won the Grammy Award and has preserved the live Judy at her best.

1963 was a year of triumphs, if not in financial terms. She was enormously moving in another straight role, as a music teacher who finds work at a school for retarded children, in *A Child Is Waiting*. She then had another great showcase in *I Could Go on Singing*, playing a beloved singer going through a personal crisis. With concert footage shot at the London Palladium and a sequence scripted from Garland's own feelings about the sacrifices she'd made for show business, the whole film had a riveting, semi-autobiographical feel. That same year she carried a superior TV variety show, *The Judy Garland Show*, that allowed her to rip into a wealth of great songs, even if it ranked low in the ratings and was cancelled after a season. Amid much touring, she was sacked from another film, *Valley of the Dolls*, which was ultimately for the better, but she seemed to be running herself ragged, often looking rail thin and haggard, and working continuously, partly to pay bills and partly for the sheer enjoyment she got out of it. Still, the world was shocked and saddened when she died of an accidental drug overdose at the age of 47. She left behind two daughters, Liza Minnelli and Lorna Luft, who displayed impressive singing talents of their own, and a legacy that is without equal. The world still responds to her with wide-eyed reverence and beaming admiration, realizing that most performers can only hope to achieve a portion of what she was capable of attaining.

Screen: 1936: Pigskin Parade; 1937: Broadway Melody of 1938; Thoroughbreds Don't Cry; 1938: Everybody Sing; Listen, Darling; Love Finds Andy Hardy; 1939: The Wizard of Oz; Babes in Arms; 1940: Andy Hardy Meets Debutante; Strike Up the Band; Little Nellie Kelly; 1941: Ziegfeld Girl; Life Begins for Andy Hardy; Babes on Broadway; 1942: For Me and My Girl;

1943: Presenting Lily Mars; Girl Crazy; Thousands Cheer; 1944: Meet Me in St. Louis; 1945: The Clock; 1946: The Harvey Girls; Ziegfeld Follies; 1947: Till the Clouds Roll By; 1948: The Pirate; Easter Parade; Words and Music; 1949: In the Good Old Summertime; 1950: Summer Stock; 1954: A Star Is Born; 1960: Pepe (voice); 1961: Judgment at Nuremberg; 1962: Gay Purr-ee (voice); 1963: A Child Is Waiting; I Could Go on Singing.
Select TV: 1963–64: The Judy Garland Show (series).

JAMES GARNER

(JAMES SCOTT BAUMGARNER)
BORN: NORMAN, OK, APRIL 7, 1928.

Few actors have made it all seem so effortless as James Garner. Audiences never seemed to tire of his combination of ruggedness and twinkling good humor, demanding little of him but getting 100 percent professionalism just the same. Following military service in Korea and a brief spell at the University of Oklahoma, he traveled to California, where a former acquaintance, who had become a producer, got him a walk-on in the 1954 Broadway production of The Caine Mutiny Court-Martial. This led to work on television and a contract with Warner Bros., debuting for them in the 1956 aviation drama Toward the Unknown, as a test pilot. There was also a supporting role in one of the big hits of 1957, Sayonara, sharing a few scenes with Marlon Brando, as a fellow-officer. Then came the television series that made him famous, Maverick, a jokey western that depended a great deal on his amiability and light touch. Hoping to spin off his popularity into the movies, the studio gave him three starring roles: the leader of a U.S. commando unit in wartime Britain in Darby's Rangers; the demolitions expert clashing with submarine commander Edmond O'Brien in Up Periscope; and the smooth business tycoon in Cash McCall. The impact of each was minor, but they proved he was quite capable of carrying a feature film. He did a good job in the difficult role of the man who questions the close relationship between his lover, Audrey Hepburn, and her friend, Shirley MacLaine, in The Children's Hour, then got to show his flair for light comedy for the first time on the big screen with a fair MGM comedy, Boys' Night Out, fortunate to have Tony Randall to play off of, to make up for Kim Novak being his leading lady. He was at his rugged best in The Great Escape, one of the finest films he ever appeared in, trying to make it to the outside, with Donald Pleasence along for the ride. Next he teamed with Doris Day for two comedies, the frothy The Thrill of It All, and the dreadful Move Over, Darling. The latter was a remake of My Favorite Wife, with Garner coming up short in the old Cary Grant role, though no one would argue that Garner had his own degree of smooth charm.

Staying in comedy, he did a flat satire on Texas millionaires, The Wheeler Dealers, which was a shame because he and Lee Remick hinted at great possibilities as a team. The next one was the darkly comedic The Americanization of Emily, in which he played a cowardly soldier more interested in women than battle, giving his best performance to date in his own personal favorite among his films. He had done his share of box-office hits, but attendance in this instance might be attributed to the red hot Julie Andrews, as it would be previously to Doris Day. Garner's own dramatic vehicle, the interesting 36 Hours, in which he was captured by the Nazis and led to believe that the war was over, did not create much of a stir. After getting stuck in some badly botched comedies, The Art of Love, as a con man in Paris, and the spy spoof A Man Could Get Killed, it was up to him to carry the lengthy racecar epic, Grand Prix, which was more notable for its

thrilling point-of-view photography than its clichéd drama. There was the undeniably intriguing but much-disliked amnesia drama Mister Buddwing, drifting through an unfriendly Manhattan in an effort to retrace his past, and some westerns, the muddled Duel at Diablo, which gave him Sidney Poitier as his co-star to no avail; the umpteenth telling of the shoot-out at the O.K. Corral, Hour of the Gun, in which he played Wyatt Earp; and A Man Called Sledge, which offered a more vicious Garner than expected. Someone had the better notion of Garner taking that genre lightly, as he'd done in the past. This resulted in one of his bigger hits, the frisky Support Your Local Sheriff!, as a lawman using gentle logic over gunplay, and Skin Game, as a con man presenting buddy Louis Gossett, Jr. as his "slave." In the mid-1970s, Garner returned to TV with great success in the lighthearted (of course) detective series The Rockford Files, which won him an Emmy Award in 1977 and proved to be one of his best-loved properties, being revised on several occasions two decades later in a series of telefilms. In the meantime he was faring less well in movies, doing two fairly obscure Disney films, One Little Indian and The Castaway Cowboy, plus two with Lauren Bacall, the scattershot ensemble spoof Health and the thriller The Fan, in which he comforted her while she was being stalked by a nutty admirer.

Once Rockford wrapped up its run, Garner jumped back into movies with a bang, in Victor/Victoria, teamed again with Julie Andrews and displaying his genius as a deft "reaction" actor, as the macho gangster perplexed by the free-spirited sexuality around him. Searching for a far less sophisticated audience, he was a military man causing havoc with his Tank, and then played an amiable druggist in love with Sally Field in Murphy's Romance, where he was so damn charming that he got an Oscar nomination at last, no doubt a tribute to his whole career. His dependability was an asset to the dire Sunset, portraying Wyatt Earp again, this time in Hollywood, and then he good naturedly kidded the part that had made him famous, Maverick, in a popular big-budget movie version of the show, although it was Mel Gibson who now had the title role. Teamed with another master of light comedy, Jack Lemmon, he was an ex-president in a coarse comedy, My Fellow Americans, and then got a chance to act opposite another great contemporary he'd somehow missed crossing paths with up to that point, Paul Newman, in Twilight, though Garner's name and image did not even appear on the advertisements. Then he played a man of the cloth returning to his previous career as an astronaut in Space Cowboys, showing his years alongside Clint Eastwood and Donald Sutherland, in a "seniors in space" gimmick that attracted the crowds. He counted on finding more dependable, challenging fare on television during his later years, doing several well-regarded television films, including Promise, Decoration Day, and Breathing Lessons.

Screen: 1956: Toward the Unknown; The Girl He Left Behind; 1957: Shoot-Out at Medicine Bend; Sayonara; 1958: Darby's Rangers; 1959: Up Periscope; Alias Jesse James; Cash McCall; 1961: The Children's Hour; 1962: Boys' Night Out; 1963: The Great Escape; The Thrill of It All; The Wheeler Dealers; Move Over, Darling; 1964: The Americanization of Emily; 36 Hours; 1965: The Art of Love; 1966: Duel at Diablo; A Man Could Get Killed; Mister Buddwing; Grand Prix; 1967: Hour of the Gun; 1968: The Pink Jungle; How Sweet It Is!; 1969: Marlowe; Support Your Local Sheriff!; 1970: A Man Called Sledge; 1971: Support Your Local Gunfighter; Skin Game; 1972: They Only Kill Their Masters; 1973: One Little Indian; 1974: The Castaway Cowboy; 1981: Health; The Fan; 1982: Victor/Victoria; 1984: Tank; 1985: Murphy's Romance; 1988: Sunset; 1992: The Distinguished Gentleman; 1993: Fire in the Sky; 1994: Maverick; 1996: Wild Bill: Hollywood Maverick; My Fellow Americans; 1998: Twilight;

2000: Space Cowboys; **2001**: Atlantis: The Lost Empire (voice); **2002**: Divine Secrets of the Ya-Ya Sisterhood; **2003**: The Notebook.

NY Stage: AS JIM BUMGARNER: **1954**: The Caine Mutiny Court-Martial.

Select TV: **1957–60**: Maverick (series); **1971–72**: Nichols (series); **1974**: The Rockford Files; **1974–80**: The Rockford Files (series); **1978**: The New Maverick; **1981**: Bret Maverick; **1981–82**: Bret Maverick (series); **1982**: The Long Summer of George Adams; **1984**: The Glitter Dome; Heartsounds; **1985**: James A. Michener's Space (ms); **1986**: Promise (and exec. prod.); **1989**: My Name Is Bill W (and exec. prod.); **1990**: Decoration Day; **1991**: Man of the People (series); **1993**: Barbarians at the Gate; **1994**: Breathing Lessons; The Rockford Files: I Still Love L.A. (and co-exec. prod.); **1995**: The Rockford Files: A Blessing in Disguise (and co-exec. prod.); Larry McMurtry's Streets of Laredo; **1996**: The Rockford Files: If the Frame Fits…; The Rockford Files: Godfather Knows Best; The Rockford Files: Friends and Foul Play; The Rockford Files: Crime and Punishment; **1997**: Dead Silence; The Rockford Files: Murder and Misdemeanors; Legalese; **1999**: The Rockford Files: If It Bleeds…It Leads (and prod.); Shake, Rattle; and Roll: An American Love Story; One Special Night; **2000**: God, the Devil, and Bob (series; voice); The Last Debate; **2002**: First Monday (series); Roughing It.

PEGGY ANN GARNER

BORN: CANTON, OH, FEBRUARY 3, 1931.
DIED: OCTOBER 16, 1984.

A noted child star of the 1940s, whose success never really carried into adulthood, Peggy Ann Garner had a wistful innocence about her that made her very engaging for her brief moment in the spotlight. She made her stage debut with the Olney Theatre stock company at the age of five in a production of *Mrs. Wiggs of the Cabbage Patch*, but it was her work as a John Powers model that was actually more instrumental in leading to her 1938 film debut, at Warner Bros., in *Little Miss Thoroughbred*, in an unbilled bit. Larger parts followed in *Blondie Brings Up Baby*, as a wealthy crippled girl, and *In Name Only*, as Carole Lombard's daughter. In 1942 she was signed up by 20th Century-Fox, who cast her and Roddy McDowall as the main children being cared for by grumpy Monty Woolley in *The Pied Piper*. The studio then gave her the bulk of the opening half hour of *Jane Eyre*, where she was highly sympathetic as the younger version of Joan Fontaine, enduring the hell of orphanage life under the iron hand of Henry Daniell. For her reward she won the role for which she is best known, optimistic Francie Nolan, somehow finding the good in life despite her poverty-stricken upbringing, in the marvelous 1945 film of Betty Smith's novel, *A Tree Grows in Brooklyn*. She was so right in the part that she received a special juvenile Academy Award. The studio put her in five more films, including the starring vehicles *Junior Miss*, from the Broadway success, as a meddlesome youngster who plays matchmaker for the girl she mistakenly believes her father is having an affair with, and *Home, Sweet Homicide*, as a mystery writer's daughter, solving a murder. After Fox she went over to some of the cheaper companies for her teen years, appearing in Monogram's *Bomba, the Jungle Boy*, the premiere entry in a long-running series, playing a photographer's daughter saved by Johnny Sheffield, and Eagle-Lion's *The Big Cat*, falling in love with Lon McCallister, whose family is feuding with her clan. After 1954, she found more work onstage and in TV, eventually dropping out the business to work in real estate and sales,

although she did venture back to the movies in 1978, as part of the large ensemble of Robert Altman's *A Wedding*, where she was barely noticed. One of her husbands (1956–63) was actor Albert Salmi.

Screen: **1938**: Little Miss Thoroughbred; **1939**: In Name Only; Blondie Brings Up Baby; **1940**: Abe Lincoln in Illinois; **1942**: The Pied Piper; Eagle Squadron; **1944**: Jane Eyre; The Keys of the Kingdom; **1945**: A Tree Grows in Brooklyn; Nob Hill; Junior Miss; **1946**: Home, Sweet Homicide; **1947**: Daisy Kenyon; Thunder in the Valley; **1948**: Sign of the Ram; **1949**: The Lovable Cheat; Bomba, the Jungle Boy; The Big Cat; **1951**: Teresa; **1954**: Black Widow; The Black Forest; **1966**: The Cat; **1978**: A Wedding.

NY Stage: **1950**: The Man; **1951**: The Royal Family; **1952**: First Lady; **1954**: Home Is the Hero.

Select TV: **1950**: Eight Witnesses (sp); **1951**: Two Girls Named Smith (series); **1952**: Salad Days (sp); Mr. Thayer (sp); **1955**: Stage Door (sp); Strange Companion (sp); **1958**: The Velvet Trap (sp); The Unfamiliar (sp); **1959**: We Wish on the Moon (sp); **1963**: The Patriots (sp); **1978**: Betrayal.

BETTY GARRETT

BORN: ST. JOSEPH, MO, MAY 23, 1919.
ED: NEIGHBORHOOD PLAYHOUSE.

There was too little of Betty Garrett captured on film. This vibrant, highly ingratiating actress got to strut her stuff in a mere seven films, but much of what is there is to be cherished. She danced with Martha Graham's company and then sang in nightclubs before appearing on Broadway in *Let Freedom Ring* and *Call Me Mister*. It was in the latter that she stopped the show, singing "South America, Take It Away," and she won a contract with MGM as a result, debuting for them in support of Margaret O'Brien in *The Big City*, in 1948. That same year she became the love interest of a fictionalized, heterosexual version of lyricist Lorenz Hart (Mickey Rooney) in the biopic *Words and Music*, where, if nothing else, she got to sing "There's a Small Hotel." 1949 proved to be her big year, with Garrett first appearing in the period musical *Take Me Out to the Ball Game*, in hot pursuit of reluctant Frank Sinatra, a role she virtually reprised to splendid effect in the much better *On the Town*, as a cabbie enticing him with her exuberant rendition of "Come Up to My Place." The latter was one of the top hits of 1949, among the most highly regarded of all MGM musicals, and her most enduring film role. Wedged between the two was *Neptune's Daughter*, where, along with her fellow cast members, she sang the Oscar-winning hit "Baby, It's Cold Outside." Garrett found that she was no longer wanted by the industry when she chose to stand loyally by her husband, actor Larry Parks (whom she had married in 1944), who was branded a Communist sympathizer. Instead they went overseas and did a stage act together. After the witch-hunt era had passed, Garrett did get another motion picture part, in a sprightly musical version of *My Sister Eileen*, ideally cast opposite Jack Lemmon. After the hostage thriller *Shadow on the Window*, she stuck to theater and TV, where she later gained fame with a whole new generation of admirers through her recurring roles on two hit series, *All in the Family* and *Laverne and Shirley*. Parks died in 1975, having spent much of his later years as a successful businessman.

Screen: **1948**: The Big City; Words and Music; **1949**: Take Me Out to the Ball Game; Neptune's Daughter; On the Town; **1955**: My Sister Eileen; **1957**: Shadow on the Window.

NY Stage: **1938**: Danton's Death; **1941**: Of V We Sing; **1942**: Let

Freedom Ring; **1943:** Something for the Boys; **1944:** Jackpot; Laffing Room Only; **1946:** Call Me Mister; **1957:** Bells Are Ringing; **1960:** Beg, Borrow or Steal; **1963:** Spoon River Anthology; **1964:** A Girl Could Get Lucky; **1981:** The Supporting Cast; **1989:** Meet Me in St. Louis; **2001:** Follies.

Select TV: 1957: The Penlands and the Poodle (sp); **1973–75:** All in the Family (series); **1976–81:** Laverne & Shirley (series); **1998:** The Long Way Home.

GREER GARSON

(EILEEN EVELYN GREER GARSON)
BORN: LONDON, ENGLAND, SEPTEMBER 29, 1903.
DIED: APRIL 6, 1996.

MGM's great lady of the war years, the strikingly red-haired Greer Garson, didn't have a diverse bag of goods to offer, but she did instill a great deal of integrity and believability into some dangerously hokey material. She exuded a sense of good breeding and maturity, not to mention a degree of comfort and warmth that made her very nice to have around in troubling times. In order to promote the image of her as an authentic Irish colleen, the Hollywood publicity machine insisted for years that she was born in Ireland, when in fact she came into the world in London. It was in England that she made her professional stage debut, with Birmingham rep, in *Street Scene*, which led to theater work in her native city, including *Golden Arrow*, with Laurence Olivier, and a starring role in *Old Music*. Louis B. Mayer, head of MGM, happened to catch her performance in the last and offered her a job back at the studio in California. Her trip there, however, proved futile, since they had nothing there for her to work on. When she did venture into her first project for them, *Goodbye, Mr. Chips*, it was filmed in England. She made for a lovely Mrs. Chips, making a solid impression on audiences and critics alike, convincing us all that she could indeed instill some love and life into the stuffy, passive schoolteacher (Robert Donat). For her performance she received a 1939 Oscar nomination in the lead category, although her screen time was relatively small. Between 1939 and 1945 she would be nominated for the Oscar annually, except for 1940. That year she gave what is probably her most enchanting performance of all, as the eldest and smartest of the Bennett sisters in the sparkling adaptation of *Pride and Prejudice*, once again playing opposite Olivier, who was no big fan of hers. (Prior to this she had done an amnesia comedy with Robert Taylor, *Remember?*, in which she gave a very arch performance.) Her second nomination was for her role in the soggy Technicolor soap opera *Blossoms in the Dust*, standing up for the rights of illegitimate children and starring for the first of eight times with Walter Pidgeon. She and Robert Taylor then made a second unsuccessful stab at humor, the remake of *When Ladies Meet*, considered inferior to the 1933 version.

Pidgeon and Garson were husband and wife again in her most famous film, *Mrs. Miniver*, a fine piece of war propaganda about a patriotic British family that had nothing whatsoever to do with real life but was certainly more intelligently conceived and dramatically compelling than most of her vehicles, thanks in no small part to the assured guiding hand of director William Wyler. It won the Academy Award as Best Picture of 1942, and she herself received the trophy, making Hollywood history by giving the longest acceptance speech on record, running over 5 1/2 minutes, although Oscar folklore has stretched it out between 30 minutes to an hour. Following the release of the film, she married (1943–47) the actor who had played Mrs. Miniver's son, Richard Ney. Her box-office standing was cemented that year with her

role in a second potent hit, *Random Harvest*, as a music hall entertainer in love with amnesiac Ronald Colman, a stellar example of two pros giving their all to infuse some weight into a fairly flimsy story. *Madame Curie* teamed her again with Pigeon, and, since she was one actress who could get away with playing a scientist with total conviction, she was again Oscar nominated. It must be said in her favor that not many stars could have mined healthy box-office figures out of this kind of dry material. The third with Pigeon/fourth with Oscar, the plodding epic *Mrs. Parkington*, gave her the chance to age from young girl to old lady; and *The Valley of Decision*, her sixth Oscar nomination, gave her a chance to speak with an Irish accent on screen (which many assumed was the real Garson), playing the servant girl in love with wealthy Gregory Peck. All of these were hits, as was *Adventure*, in which she was uncomfortably teamed with Clark Gable. This one, however, started her critical downslide.

Desire Me gave her another unlikely co-star, Robert Mitchum, and a director, George Cukor, so unhappy with the finished result that he asked that his name be taken off the print, thereby making it one of the rare pictures of the studio era to have no directorial credit. Hoping to have fun with her straight-laced image, Garson tried a comedy, *Julia Misbehaves*, with Pigeon around for moral support, but it wasn't very funny. They were back again for *That Forsyte Woman*, although her main leading man was Errol Flynn, with Pidgeon in a secondary part as the man who loves her from afar while she turns her attentions to Robert Young. The star power did nothing to keep it from being spoiled goods. She and Pidgeon then did a too-late sequel, the U.K.-made *The Miniver Story*, which nobody bothered with; the war having been over for five years, thereby removing the topicality of these characters. Their final pairing, *Scandal at Scourie*, released in 1953, proved that Garson's heyday was long gone, and the following year, after a poorly done boys' school story, *Her 12 Men*, she asked to be released from her contract. The gentle western *Strange Lady in Town* marked her first movie ever outside of MGM (it was done for Warners). Its failure encouraged her to try TV, including adaptations of *Captain Brassbound's Conversion* and *The Little Foxes*, and to make her long-delayed Broadway bow, succeeding Rosalind Russell in *Auntie Mame*. When she did return to the movies, it was in heavy makeup, giving a very mannered, vocally annoying interpretation of Eleanor Roosevelt in *Sunrise at Campobello*, which, nonetheless, brought her Oscar nominations up to a total of seven. After supporting roles as the Mother Superior in *The Singing Nun*, and as the wife of Fred MacMurray in Disney's musical *The Happiest Millionaire* (her one song was chopped from the final print), she put an end to her movie career. Garson did some more stage work and a telefilm of *Little Women*, playing Aunt March, a role resumed by Mildred Natwick when it spun-off into a weekly series. Having married millionaire E.E. Fogelson in 1949, she lived quite comfortably, keeping active as a civic leader and establishing the Greer Garson Theatres at the College of Santa Fe and Southern Methodist University in Dallas.

Screen: 1939: Goodbye, Mr. Chips; Remember?; **1940:** Pride and Prejudice; **1941:** Blossoms in the Dust; When Ladies Meet; **1942:** Mrs. Miniver; Random Harvest; **1943:** The Youngest Profession; Madame Curie; **1944:** Mrs. Parkington; **1945:** The Valley of Decision; Adventure; **1947:** Desire Me; **1948:** Julia Misbehaves; **1949:** That Forsyte Woman; **1950:** The Miniver Story; **1951:** The Law and the Lady; **1953:** Julius Caesar; Scandal at Scourie; **1954:** Her 12 Men; **1955:** Strange Lady in Town; **1960:** Sunrise at Campobello; Pepe; **1966:** The Singing Nun; **1967:** The Happiest Millionaire.

NY Stage: 1958: Auntie Mame.

Select TV: 1955: Reunion in Vienna (sp); 1956: Career (sp); The Little Foxes (sp); 1957: The Earring (sp); The Glorious Gift of Molly Malloy (sp); 1960: Captain Brassbound's Conversion; 1963: The Invincible Mr. Disraeli (sp); 1968: The Little Drummer Boy (voice); 1978: Little Women.

VITTORIO GASSMAN

Born: Genoa, Italy, September 1, 1922.
ed: Acad. of Dramatic Art, Rome.
Died: June 29, 2000.

One of the most prestigious of all Italian actors, Vittorio Gassman came to prominence as a romantic hero before showing his versatility in comedy as well. Having studied at the Accademia Nazionale Arte Dramatica, he made his stage debut in *La Nemica* in 1943, in Milan. After countless plays he switched to films in 1946, playing a sailor in *Preludio d'Amore*. His first taste of international fame came with *Bitter Rice*, as the lover of Silvana Mangano, a movie that received a considerable publicity boost after condemnation from the Catholic Legion of Decency. He and Mangano were teamed again for *Anna*, this time with Gassman in a villainous role. In 1952, he came to the U.S., where he married Shelley Winters and signed a contract with MGM. As is usually the case with acclaimed foreigner actors hoping for fame in Hollywood, his material proved pretty mediocre, including *Sombrero*, as a Mexican villager; *Cry of the Hunted*, as an escaped con; and the soapy romance *Rhapsody*, as a violinist in love with Elizabeth Taylor. Meanwhile he made one back in Italy with Winters, *Mambo*, a romantic drama set in Venice. A year before its 1955 American release, they were divorced. Back on his home turf, he played Anatole in the costly 1956 version of *War and Peace*, and co-directed, co-scripted, and acted in *Kean Genio o Sregolatezza/Kean — Genius or Scoundrel*, which never opened in the U.S. He then had his biggest international success so far, *Big Deal on Madonna Street*, a comical and influential caper film, in which he was a former boxer involved with a bunch of bumbling crooks. This was followed by some more international productions, such as *Tempest*, which had nothing to do with Shakespeare (unlike his 1982 film *Tempest*, which was sort-of based on The Bard); *The Miracle*, where Gassman played a Gypsy in love with Carroll Baker; and *Barabbas*, a religious epic with Anthony Quinn. In the meantime he was finding his greatest success in his own language in comedies like *Let's Talk About Women* and *The Easy Life*. During the 1970s his films were exported less to this country, with some exceptions: *Scent of a Woman*, with Gassman playing a blind soldier (and made 17 years before the better-known Al Pacino version), and *We All Loved Each Other So Much*. In the late 1970s, Hollywood showed a sudden renewal of interest in the actor, with Robert Altman's *A Wedding*, in which he played the father of groom Desi Arnaz, Jr.; Altman's futuristic flop, *Quintet*; *The Nude Bomb*, with Gassman as a comic book villain; and the Burt Reynolds vehicle *Sharky's Machine*, as a somewhat more serious villain. Then it was back to Italy to do a whole new crop of movies that did not come to America. This string was broken by *Life Is a Bed of Roses*, for Alain Resnais; *The Family*, in which he was the strong patriarch of a large brood over an 80 year period, a performance that won him a Donatello Award in Italy; and *The Sleazy Uncle*, in the title role. He returned once last time to American films to play a Mafioso figure in the ensemble drama *Sleepers*.

Screen (US releases only): 1950: Bitter Rice; Lure of the Sila; 1952: Streets of Sorrow; 1953: Anna; Sombrero; The Glass Wall; Cry of the Hunted; 1954: Rhapsody; 1955: Mambo; 1956: War

and Peace; 1958: Beautiful But Dangerous; 1959: Tempest; The Love Specialist; The Miracle; The Great War; 1960: Big Deal on Madonna Street; 1962: Barabbas; 1964: Let's Talk About Women; And Suddenly It's Murder; The Easy Life/Il Sorpasso; 1965: Il Successo; The Eye of the Needle; 1966: The Dirty Game; 1967: Woman Times Seven; A Maiden for a Prince; The Tiger and the Pussycat; 1968: 15 From Rome; The Devil in Love; Catch as Catch Can; 1969: Ghosts — Italian Style; 1970: 12 Plus 1/The Thirteen Chairs; 1976: Scent of a Woman; Midnight Pleasures; 1977: We All Loved Each Other So Much; 1978: Viva Italia!; A Wedding; 1979: Quintet; 1980: The Immortal Bachelor; The Nude Bomb; 1981: Sharky's Machine; 1982: Tempest; 1984: Life Is a Bed of Roses; 1988: The Family; 1991: The Sleazy Uncle; The Palermo Connection (dtv).; 1996: Sleepers.
Select TV: 1994: Abraham.

JOHN GAVIN

(John Anthony Golenor)
Born: Los Angeles, CA, April 8, 1928.
ed: Stanford Univ.

Squarely handsome romantic lead John Gavin was very much a fixture of the glossy productions made at Universal in the late 1950s and early 1960s. After studying political science at college, he entered the Navy, serving during the Korean War. A meeting with film producer Bryan Foy led him to Hollywood agent Henry Willson, who got him a screen test and, ultimately, a contract with Universal Studios. Although he had no previous acting experience to speak of, the company launched him in a big role in *Behind the High Wall*, as a getaway driver for a gang of cons, who clashes with a greedy warden. The one that was supposed to make him a major name was the 1958 adaptation of Erich Maria Remarque's anti-war novel, *A Time to Love and a Time to Die*, but the general consensus declared Gavin colorless and difficult to care about as the doomed German soldier in love with Lilo Pulver. Instead, he garnered a lot of attention through his next four films, each among the most popular movies of the period. The 1959 remake of the Fannie Hurst tearjerker *Imitation of Life* found him playing a photographer loved by both Lana Turner and her daughter Sandra Dee. In *Psycho*, where his services were basically forced upon an unimpressed Alfred Hitchcock, he was Janet Leigh's lover and Vera Miles's eleventh hour rescuer. *Spartacus* allowed him to look very appealing in a Roman toga as Julius Caesar, and he once again popped up as a last-minute hero, in this case a construction foreman, in *Midnight Lace*, with Doris Day. There was no great desire to make vehicles around him, so he was back playing lover to Sandra Dee in both *Tammy Tell Me True* and *Romanoff and Juliet*, and providing very little fire as the married man carrying on with Susan Hayward in another slushy remake of a Fannie Hurst story, *Back Street*. Having been raised by a Mexican mother, Gavin was fluent in Spanish, which was instrumental in his being appointed special advisor to Secretary General Jose Mora of the Organization of American States in 1961, a post he continued for the next 12 years. In 1962 he was assigned to help organize a program to bring aid to Latin America, called Alliance for Progress. Although he would continue to act off and on over the years — amusingly sending up his wooden image in *Thoroughly Modern Millie*, for example — Gavin's interests were clearly steering him elsewhere. During the Reagan administration, he served as ambassador to Mexico for five years. He married actress Constance Towers in 1974.

Screen: 1956: Behind the High Wall; Four Girls in Town; 1957: Quantez; 1958: A Time to Live and a Time to Die; 1959:

Imitation of Life; 1960: Psycho; Spartacus; Midnight Lace; A Breath of Scandal; 1961: Romanoff and Juliet; Tammy Tell Me True; Back Street; 1967: Thoroughly Modern Millie; Pedro Paramo (nUSr); 1968: OSS 117: Double Agent; 1969: The Madwoman of Chaillot; 1970: Pussycat, Pussycat, I Love You; 1973: Keep It in the Family/Les Cocus (nUSr); 1976: House of Shadows; 1978: Jennifer; 1997: The P.A.C.K. (dtv).

NY Stage: 1973: Seesaw.

Select TV: 1964: A Truce to Terror (sp); 1964: Destry (series); 1965: Convoy (series); 1970: Cutter's Trail; 1978: The New Adventures of Heidi; 1979: Doctors' Private Lives (series); 1980: Sophia Loren: Her Own Story.

JANET GAYNOR

(Laura Gainor) Born: Philadelphia, PA, October 6, 1906. Died: September 14, 1984.

Because she won the very first Academy Award for Best Actress, Janet Gaynor is forever a part of motion picture history. Although she is no longer held in high esteem for her acting abilities, in her heyday she was much loved and a top box-office draw, one of the few performers to make the transition from silence to sound with nary a hitch. There was something sweet and wistful about her that made audiences want to be on her side, as she enacted resilience in the face of suffering. As she reached her 30s, she herself seemed to sense that she was not keeping up with the changing times, and she gracefully bowed out. While a teen, her family had moved to Los Angeles, where she worked as a movie extra until she found bigger parts in the two-reelers "The Spooney Age" and "The Haunted Honeymoon." After the lead in the western short, "The Cloud Rider," she made her official feature debut, in support of George O'Brien, in the 1926 epic *The Johnstown Flood*. This was made for Fox, who promptly signed her to a contract and gave her starring roles in, among others, two directed by John Ford, *The Shamrock Handicap* and *The Blue Eagle*. Then came three in a row that made her a bona fide star. The first was the box-office sensation *7th Heaven*, with Gaynor playing a Paris streetwalker in love with Charles Farrell. This film was one of the seminal romantic weepies of the silent era and the first Oscar winner for Best Director (Frank Borzage). Next came *Sunrise*, with the actress as a simple farm wife who discovers that husband George O'Brien intends to kill her, then manages to fall in love with him all over again when he reneges on his shameful plan. It was one of the most haunting and masterfully directed (F. W. Murnau) of all motion pictures, certainly one of the handful of silent films that retains its power to this day, and a recipient of a one-time only Academy Award for Best Unique and Artistic Production. Then there was the effective *Street Angel*, with Gaynor running from the police and joining a circus, where she meets Farrell. For the whole lot of them, she was awarded that Oscar, the only time an actress won for her body of work rather than for a single film.

There were talking segments in *Four Devils* and *Lucky Star* (the third pairing with Farrell), and then came Gaynor and Farrell's full-fledged talkie debut, in *Sunny Side Up*, which was a musical, despite the fact that neither of them could sing. In this particular case, it was questionable whether or not Gaynor could even act, but it was another smash. (Like many a silent star, what seemed appealing and moving with the sound missing seemed less so when given dialogue to speak.) She also had big successes with *The Man Who Came Back* (Farrell again), as a cabaret performer succumbing to drugs in her least favorite of her movies; *Daddy Long Legs*, as an orphan who falls in love with her benefactor,

Warner Baxter, in a remake of an old Mary Pickford vehicle; and *Delicious* (Farrell), as a Scottish lass in America in yet another primitive musical. *State Fair* had her teamed with Will Rogers, as her dad, in a much-loved and much-revisited story. With *Carolina*, she received some of her better reviews of this period, starring alongside Robert Young in a story of a poor family.She had her twelfth and final teaming with Farrell in *Change of Heart*, and then helped introduce Henry Fonda to movie audiences in the gentle period piece *The Farmer Takes a Wife*. In 1936 she made her first film away from her home lot since becoming a star, *Small Town Girl*, made at MGM, with Robert Taylor, then returned to the newly christened 20th Century-Fox for one more film, *Ladies in Love*, receiving less money than she was used to and therefore deciding to venture elsewhere.

Fortunately, she began her new, post-Fox life on a high note, playing the sweet thing who falls for drunken Fredric March while rising to movie stardom, in the 1937 version of *A Star Is Born*. It was not a bad performance at all, and it was even deemed worthy of an Oscar nomination, but it suffers when compared with Judy Garland's towering work in the remake. Unlike Garland, or Streisand in the 1976 version, you never believed for a minute that Gaynor possessed any special talents that would skyrocket her to the top of her profession so quickly. The following year she did another well-liked film, the screwball comedy *The Young in Heart*, and then promptly retired at the age of 31. She did however stay in the Hollywood social scene, after marrying noted dress designer Adrian in 1939. There were some live television dramas and then her old studio welcomed her back in 1957, for the Pat Boone vehicle *Bernardine*, but the response to her performance was pretty chilly. Following Adrian's death in 1959, she began to seek more work on television and stage, making a much-maligned Broadway debut in a 1980 adaptation of the movie *Harold and Maude*. Following a 1984 car accident, in which actress Mary Martin was also injured, she was hospitalized, never fully recovering and ultimately dying from pneumonia.

Screen: 1926: The Johnstown Flood; The Shamrock Handicap; The Midnight Kiss; The Blue Eagle; The Return of Peter Grimm; 1927: Two Girls Wanted; 7th Heaven; Sunrise; 1928: Street Angel; 1929: Christina; Four Devils; Lucky Star; Sunny Side Up; 1930: Happy Days; High Society Blues; 1931: The Man Who Came Back; Daddy Long Legs; Merely Mary Ann; Delicious; 1932: The First Year; Tess of the Storm Country; 1933: State Fair; Adorable; Paddy — The Next Best Thing; 1934: Carolina; Change of Heart; Servants' Entrance; 1935: One More Spring; The Farmer Takes a Wife; 1936: Small Town Girl; Ladies in Love; 1937: A Star Is Born; 1938: Three Loves Has Nancy; The Young in Heart; 1957: Bernardine.

NY Stage: 1980: Harold and Maude.

Select TV: 1953: Dear Cynthia (sp); 1954: Two-Dozen Roses; 1959: The Flying Wife (sp).

MITZI GAYNOR

(Franceska Mitzi von Gerber) Born: Chicago, IL, September 4, 1930.

Very much a product of the glossy, non-threatening 1950s, Mitzi Gaynor was perky and eager to please in the less-than-scintillating musicals she made for 20th Century-Fox during that decade. Her limitations as an actress and her lack of any distinguishing traits as a singer-dancer, however, have kept her from being spoken of with the great talents in that genre. Following in her mother's footsteps, she learned to dance by joining the Los Angeles Light Opera Co. A role in *The Great Waltz* resulted in a contract with Fox, who gave her a showy part in support of Betty Grable, in *My Blue Heaven*, singing "Live Hard, Work Hard, Love Hard." In time she had her own vehicle, *Golden Girl*, one of those biopics about relatively obscure entertainers of days gone by, in this case Lotta Crabtree, who made her name while the country was fighting the Civil War. That was followed by *Bloodhounds of Broadway*, with the unappetizing premise of Gaynor as a hillbilly who makes it to the Great White Way, and *The I Don't Care Girl*, another biography, this time about the somewhat better-known Eva Tanguay. None of them established Gaynor as the studio's hoped-for replacement for Betty Grable. Instead she joined the all-star cast of *There's No Business Like Show Business*, where her French rendition of "Alexander's Ragtime Band" was *not* among the more arresting moments in the history of movie musicals. She then went over to Paramount for Bing Crosby's wobbly remake of *Anything Goes*, where, if nothing else, she at least got to sing the title song. She also participated in a better bio than the previous ones she'd done, *The Joker Is Wild*, as the wife of Joe E. Lewis, played by Frank Sinatra. Following these she made her one appearance for MGM, in *Les Girls*, being outshone by both Gene Kelly and Kay Kendall, making her biggest impact in a spoof of *The Wild One* to the tune of "Why Am I So Gone About That Girl?" Thanks to Mary Martin being passed over for the part, she landed the role of her career, nurse Nellie Forbush, in the 1958 adaptation of *South Pacific*, where she gave one of the better performances in this uneven but extremely popular movie. She finished her motion picture career with three weak comedies, then concentrated completely on television, nightclubs, and touring shows. She carried on the brassy, old-fashioned tradition of hard sell, show biz pizzazz for as long as audiences were willing to show up.

Screen: 1950: My Blue Heaven; 1951: Take Care of My Little Girl; Golden Girl; 1952: We're Not Married!; Bloodhounds of Broadway; 1953: The I Don't Care Girl; Down Among the Sheltering Palms; 1954: Three Young Texans; There's No Business Like Show Business; 1956: Anything Goes; The Birds and the Bees; 1957: The Joker Is Wild; Les Girls; 1958: South Pacific; 1959: Happy Anniversary; 1960: Surprise Package; 1963: For Love or Money.

Select TV: 1968: Mitzi (sp); 1969: Mitzi's Second Special (sp); 1973: Mitzi…The First Time (sp); 1974: Mitzi: A Tribute to the American Housewife (sp); 1975: Mitzi and a Hundred Guys (sp); 1976: Roarin' in the 20's (sp); 1977: Mitzi…Zings Into Spring (sp); 1978: Mitzi…What's Hot, What's Not (sp).

BEN GAZZARA

(BIAGIO ANTHONY GAZZARA)
BORN: NEW YORK, NY, AUGUST 28, 1930.

A gritty, Italian-American actor with a forceful presence, Ben Gazzara was also capable of showing a warm side, though underneath it there usually seemed to be a constant sense of restlessness and rage. Earning an acting scholarship to study with Erwin Piscator, he joined the Actors Studio. That group put together a stage adaptation of Calder Willingham's disturbing novel, *End as a Man*, which premiered on Broadway in 1953. Playing a sadistic, domineering military student, Gazzara won raves, a Theatre World Award, and two other major roles, in *Cat on a Hot Tin Roof* and in *A Hatful of Rain*. His Hollywood debut came in 1957, in Columbia's re-titled film version of *End as a Man*, called *The Strange One*, with most of its homosexual overtones softened by the censors. It was still

an effective debut, and Gazzara followed it up with a movie that also ran into censorship problems, *Anatomy of a Murder*, as a husband accused of murdering the man who tried to rape his wife (Lee Remick), giving a cocky and shrewd performance in a big box-office hit. There was another popular movie, *The Young Doctors*, where Gazzara, as the new physician on staff, clashed with veteran Fredric March, bringing some edge to potentially soapy material. Some Italian-made ventures, *The Passionate Thief* and *Conquered City*, followed, and then an odd prison movie-biopic, *Convicts 4*, about as an inmate turning to painting while in the slammer, that disappeared fairly quickly. He opted to try television at that point, landing in a hit series, *Run for Your Life*, and directing some of the episodes. That medium would keep him busy over the years in telefilms and mini-series, including the first big one in the latter category, *QB VII*, as a writer sued by Anthony Hopkins. This was compensation for his big-screen projects of the late 1960s: a trashy pot boiler, *A Rage to Live*, as one of Suzanne Pleshette's lovers, and a clichéd war film, *The Bridge at Remagen*.

Too many of his subsequent ventures into theatrical films showed a decided lack of taste, although his virile, no-nonsense presence occasionally came through. *Husbands* marked the first of three for buddy John Cassavetes, with Gazzara giving the most interesting performance in this rambling, maddening film, as a man going through a middle-age crisis. That one brought him some degree of attention and acclaim, which was not the case with the other two Cassavetes endeavors: the unappetizing *The Killing of a Chinese Bookie*, in which he played a strip-club owner, and *Opening Night*, which had trouble getting bookings by exhibitors burned by past Cassavetes projects. Among the other projects seemingly designed to empty theaters were the underwater adventure *The Neptune Factor*; the gangster biopic *Capone*; the muddled sex-thriller *Bloodline*, in which he came to Audrey Hepburn's rescue; and the notorious "Moonie-produced" bomb *Inchon*. There were also two failures for director Peter Bogdanovich, *Saint Jack*, in which Gazzara played a pimp in Singapore, and *They All Laughed*, a pleasant diversion in which he was quite appealing as a detective trailing Ms. Hepburn. Amid these there were more of those Italian-made efforts that he couldn't seem to stay away from, most of which never saw the light of day in America; and then a typical villain role in support of Patrick Swayze, in *Road House*, his first widely distributed American movie in some time. It took nearly another decade before he began popping up with more regularity in American features, his talents suddenly appreciated by those aware of what he was capable of. As a result, he was a porno king in the jokey *The Big Lebowski*; Campbell Scott's unscrupulous boss in the quixotic *The Spanish Prisoner*; Vincent Gallo's confrontational dad in *Buffalo 66*; and a philandering husband facing his mistress's illness in *Happiness*. Joining two interesting ensemble pieces, he was a Mafioso chief in the *Summer of Sam*, and an aging stock-company actor in *Illuminata*. He managed to score a leading role in an independent quickie, *Blue Moon*, as a man trying to put some zing back into his marriage to Rita Moreno, but it was a poor thing that disappeared in a flash. He was married from 1961 to 1979 to actress Janice Rule.

Screen: 1957: The Strange One; 1959: Anatomy of a Murder; 1961: The Young Doctors; The Passionate Thief; 1962: Convicts 4; 1965: A Rage to Live; 1966: Conquered City/The Captive City (filmed 1962); 1969: If It's Tuesday, This Must Be Belgium; The Bridge at Remagen; 1970: King: A Filmed Record… Montgomery to Memphis; Husbands; 1973: The Neptune Factor; 1975: Capone; 1976: The Killing of a Chinese Bookie; High Velocity; Voyage of the Damned; 1977: The Sicilian

Connection/Afyon Oppio (filmed 1973); **1979:** Opening Night (filmed 1977); Saint Jack; Sidney Sheldon's Bloodline; **1981:** They All Laughed; **1982:** Tales of Ordinary Madness; Inchon; **1983:** La Ragazza di Trieste/The Girl from Trieste (nUSr); **1984:** La Donna delle Meraviglie/Woman of Wonders (nUSr); **1985:** Uno Scandolo Perbene/A Proper Scandal (nUSr); **1986:** The Professor/Il Camorrista (nUSr); **1987:** Figlio mio Infinitemente Caro/My Dearest Son (nUSr); **1988:** Quicker Than the Eye (dtv); Don Bosco (nUSr); Secret Obsession/La Memoire Tatouee (dtv); **1989:** Road House; **1990:** Beyond the Ocean (nUSr); **1991:** Per Sempre/Forever (nUSr); **1994:** Nefertiti: Daughter of the Sun (nUSr); Swallows Never Die in Jerusalem (nUSr); **1995:** The Dogfighters (dtv); Banditi (nUSr); **1996:** Ladykiller (dtv); **1997:** Farmer and Chase; Shadow Conspiracy; Vicious Circles (dtv); **1998:** The Big Lebowski; The Spanish Prisoner; Too Tired to Die (dtv); Buffalo 66; Happiness; Shark in a Bottle (dtv); Los de Enfrente (nUSr); **1999:** Summer of Sam; The Thomas Crown Affair; Illuminata; Undertaker's Paradise (nUSr); **2000:** Jack of Hearts (nUSr); Nella Terra di Nessano; The List (dtv); Very Mean Men (nUSr); Blue Moon; Believe (dtv); **2001:** Home Sweet Hoboken (nUSr); **2002:** Dogville (dtv).

NY Stage: 1953: End as a Man; 1955: Cat on a Hot Tin Roof; A Hatful of Rain; 1958: Night Circus; 1963: Strange Interlude; 1964: Traveler Without Luggage; 1975: Hughie/Duet; 1976: Who's Afraid of Virginia Woolf?; 1992: Shimada.

Select TV: 1954: The Alibi Kid (sp); 1957: The Troublemakers (sp); 1958: The Violent Heart (sp); 1961: Cry Vengeance (sp); 1963–64: Arrest and Trial (series); 1964: Carol for Another Christmas (sp); 1965–68: Run for Your Life (series); 1972: When Michael Calls/Shattered Silence; Fireball Forward; The Family Rico; Pursuit; 1973: Maneater; 1974: QB VII (ms); 1977: The Death of Richie; The Trial of Lee Harvey Oswald; 1982: A Question of Honor; 1985: An Early Frost; A Letter to Three Wives; 1987: Police Story: The Freeway Killings; Control; Downpayment on Murder; 1990: People Like Us; 1991: Lies Before Kisses; 1993: Blindsided; Love, Honor and Obey: The Last Mafia Marriage; The Window Over the Way; 1994: Parallel Lives; Fatal Vows: The Alexandra O'Hara Story; 1995: Convict Cowboy; 1996: Scene of the Crime; 1997: Stag; 1998: Protector/Valentine's Day; 2001: Brian's Song; 2002: Hysterical Blindness.

LEO GENN

BORN: LONDON, ENGLAND, AUGUST 9, 1905.
ED: CAMBRIDGE UNIV. DIED: JANUARY 26, 1978.

Erudite, smooth Britisher Leo Genn intended to become a lawyer and had actually begun a legal practice when the stage caught his fancy. He made his professional theatrical debut in 1930 and began in films five years later with the curious *Immortal Gentleman*, helping to act out scenes from Shakespeare. Over the years he played small roles in such notable British features as *Pygmalion*, as a Prince at the ball; *The Way Ahead*, as a captain; *Henry V*, as the Constable of France; and *Caesar and Cleopatra*, as Bel Affiris. Following service in the Royal Artillery during World War II, he returned briefly to the legal profession, serving as a prosecutor of war criminals at the Belsen concentration camp. In 1946 he scored a success on Broadway in *Another Part of the Forest* and was asked by RKO to appear in two films that starred Rosalind Russell, *The Velvet Touch* and *Mourning Becomes Electra*, playing Captain Brant in the latter. He was called on to lend a sure-hand to such movies as *The Snake Pit*, as Olivia de Havilland's kindly doctor, and *Quo Vadis?*, as Petronius, keeping Nero's nutty behavior in check,

giving the closest thing to a real performance in the film, and earning an Oscar nomination in the process. Back in Britain, he had a leading role in *The Wooden Horse*, a true-life story of some prisoners escaping from a German POW camp; was the father of *The Girls of Pleasure Island*, confronted by a battalion of Marines; and played an officer in the British parachute regiment in *The Red Beret/Paratrooper*, supporting Alan Ladd. He appeared in *Moby Dick*, as Starbuck, once again trying to supply reason to a raving lunatic, in this instance Gregory Peck as Captain Ahab. In *The Steel Bayonet*, he commanded a company under siege at an abandoned farmhouse; played a Scotland Yard Inspector in the thriller *Psycho-Circus/Circus of Fear*; joined Flora Robson and Robert Helpmann as a trio of unconvincing Asians in *55 Days at Peking*; and reprised the role C. Aubrey Smith had done in *And Then There Were None*, in the 1966 remake, *Ten Little Indians*.

Screen: 1935: Immortal Gentleman; 1937: The Cavalier of the Streets; Jump for Glory/When Thief Meets Thief; The Rat; 1938: The Drum/Drums; Kate Plus Ten/The Vanishing Train; Dangerous Medicine; Pygmalion; 1939: Ten Days in Paris/Missing Ten Days; 1940: Law and Disorder; Contraband/Blackout; 1941: The Young Mr. Pitt; 1943: The Bells Go Down (narrator); 1944: The Way Ahead; Henry V; 1945: Caesar and Cleopatra; 1946: Green for Danger; 1947: Mourning Becomes Electra; 1948: The Velvet Touch; The Snake Pit; 1949: No Place for Jennifer; 1950: The Wooden Horse; The Miniver Story; 1951: The Magic Box; Quo Vadis?; 1952: Plymouth Adventure; Affair in Monte Carlo/24 Hours in a Woman's Life; 1953: The Girls of Pleasure Island; The Red Beret/Paratrooper; Personal Affair; 1954: The Green Scarf; 1955: The Lowest Crime/Chantage; Lady Chatterley's Lover; 1956: Beyond Mombasa; Moby Dick; 1957: The Steel Bayonet; I Accuse!; 1958: Tank Force/No Time to Die; 1960: Playgirl After Dark/Too Hot to Handle; Era notte a Roma/Escape by Night (nUSr); 1962: The Longest Day; 1963: 55 Days at Peking; 1964: The Death Ray of Dr. Mabuse (nUSr); 1965: Ten Little Indians; Circus of Fear/Psycho-Circus; Khartoum (narrator); 1969: Connecting Rooms; 1970: The Bloody Judge; 1971: Die Screaming Marianne; Lizard in a Woman's Skin (nUSr); Endless Night; 1973: The Mackintosh Man; The Silent One/The Great Manhunt; 1974: The Matryr; 1975: Frightmare.

NY Stage: 1938: The Flashing Stream; 1946: Another Part of the Forest; 1957: Small War on Murray Hill; 1961: The Devil's Advocate; 1964: Fair Game for Lovers; 1968: The Only Game in Town.

Select TV: 1955: Salome (sp); 1960: Mrs. Miniver (sp); 1968: Dr. Jekyll and Mr. Hyde (sp).

GLADYS GEORGE

(GLADYS ANNA CLARE) BORN: HATTON, ME,
SEPTEMBER 13, 1900. DIED: DECEMBER 8, 1954.

When it came to playing floozies, broads, drunks, and impudent women, Gladys George had few equals. An actress from the age of three, she became a part of her parents' touring stock company, working her way to New York, making her stage debut there in 1918, in *The Betrothal*. The next year marked her first film appearance, and although there would be a handful of silents, she did not really become known until she scored a few hits on Broadway in the 1930s, including *The Milky Way* and *Personal Appearance*. Because of the latter, she was invited to Paramount to play the lead in the tearjerker *Valiant Is the World for Carrie*, as a woman who belies her bad reputation by taking care of a pair of orphans. For rising above such mush she was rewarded with an Oscar nomination. Figuring her to be soap opera material, MGM put her in the 1937 remake of *Madame X*, falling into ill-repute after a sordid affair, and then cast her as the wife of hired killer Franchot Tone in the melodramatic *They Gave Him a Gun*. In a less-typical setting, she could be found in their lavish production of *Marie Antoinette*, as John Barrymore's mistress, Madame du Barry. In 1939 she journeyed over to Warner Bros. to play perhaps her most famous role, James Cagney's moll, Panama Smith, in the exciting gangster flick *The Roaring Twenties*, where she uttered the immortal eulogy over his dead body, "He used to be a tough guy." Also for that studio she was the flirtatious widow of Humphrey Bogart's murdered partner in *The Maltese Falcon*, and had a juicy bit as an arrogant, hard-drinking actress whom Ida Lupino plots to replace with her sister, Joan Leslie, in *The Hard Way*. In the 1946 Oscar-winner for Best Picture, *The Best Years of Our Lives*, she was once again a wreck, playing Dana Andrews's blowsy stepmother. Staying on the sauce, she was another drunken thespian, Doris Day's mom, in *Lullaby of Broadway*, and then played John Garfield's neglectful, boozy mother in his last film, *He Ran All the Way*. It addition to these supporting parts, she got top billing for a "Little Tough Guys" programmer, *Hit the Road*, and took the lead in a Columbia "B," *Millie's Daughter*, trying to keep her own off-spring from ending up as badly as she did.

Screen: 1919: Red Hot Dollars; 1920: Woman in the Suitcase; Below the Surface; Home Spun Folks; 1921: Chickens; The Easy Road; The House That Jazz Built; 1934: Straight Is the Way; 1936: Valiant Is the Word for Carrie; 1937: They Gave Him a Gun; Madame X; 1938: Love Is a Headache; Marie Antoinette; 1939: I'm From Missouri; Here I Am a Stranger; The Roaring Twenties; 1940: A Child Is Born; The House Across the Bay; The Way of All Flesh; 1941: The Lady From Cheyenne; The Maltese Falcon; Hit the Road; 1942: The Hard Way; 1943: The Crystal Ball; Nobody's Darling; 1944: Minstrel Man; Christmas Holiday; 1945: Steppin' in Society; 1946: The Best Years of Our Lives; 1947: Millie's Daughter; 1948: Alias a Gentleman; 1949: Flamingo Road; 1950: Bright Leaf; Undercover Girl; 1951: Lullaby of Broadway; Detective Story; He Ran All the Way; Silver City; 1953: It Happens Every Thursday.

NY Stage: 1918: The Betrothal; 1934: Queer People; The Milky Way; Personal Appearance; 1940: Lady in Waiting; 1941: The Distant City; 1943: The Skin of Our Teeth.

Select TV: 1953: Rocking Horse (sp); 1954: Sal (sp).

JOHN GIELGUD

(ARTHUR JOHN GIELGUD) BORN: LONDON, ENGLAND, APRIL 14, 1904. DIED: MAY 21, 2000.

He was one of the most highly regarded actors in the history of the profession, but for the most part, cinemagoers had to wait until he was past the age of 50 to begin seeing Gielgud on screen on a fairly regular basis. As one of those thespians who always preferred the theater to the sound stage, there is too little of the younger Gielgud recorded on film. What we do have captures the smooth, authoritative presence, punctuated by the gorgeous cadence of his voice; when he speaks nearly everything he says sounds like poetry. There was acting in his family tree, one of his great-aunts being the celebrated Ellen Terry. While still a teen, he began studying at Lady Constance Bennett's Drama School, which led to his London debut, in a walk-on, in *Henry V*, at the Old Vic. This was followed by a scholarship to the Royal Academy of Dramatic Arts and some West End roles, including Romeo

in *Romeo and Juliet*, and Charley in *Charley's Aunt*. After three seasons with the Oxford Rep, he made his New York stage debut in 1928, in *The Patriot*, which did nothing whatsoever for him. His reputation began to grow the following year when he joined the Old Vic, where his countless Shakespearean triumphs would include a Who's Who of the Bard's greatest roles: Macbeth, Prospero, Antony, Romeo, Shylock, and even King Lear, which he played before he was 40. His few dalliances in the cinema during the 1930s included two notable efforts, the popular Jessie Matthews musical *The Good Companions*, as a music teacher, and Hitchcock's *The Secret Agent*, in the title role, as a writer assigned to kill a German spy. The talent was evident though he would later dismiss his work in these early efforts. Back onstage he achieved his greatest theatrical fame to date when he played Hamlet, in both London (1934) and New York (1936). Meanwhile, on film, he played Benjamin Disraeli in a quickly forgotten biopic, *The Prime Minister*, which turned out to be his sole motion-picture credit during the 1940s. During the 1950–51 season at Stratford-on-Avon, he won raves for his Cassius in *Julius Caesar* and found himself in Hollywood two years later, recreating the role for Joseph Mankiewicz's acclaimed all-star film adaptation. This, the widest exposure Gielgud had received in America up to that time, clearly indicated what film audiences had been missing.

Two more Shakespeare film adaptations followed, with the 1954 version of *Romeo and Juliet*, for which he supplied the narration only, and Olivier's *Richard III*, as the unfortunate Clarence, who is drowned in a cask of wine. He was thought of for only the classiest of roles at that point, so he played the stern father of sickly Elizabeth Barrett (Jennifer Jones) in the remake of the dated *The Barretts of Wimpole*, and Warwick in director Otto Preminger's famously troubled production of Shaw's *Saint Joan*. He supplied the voice of the Ghost in Richard Burton's quickly filmed *Hamlet*, adapted from the production Gielgud had directed on Broadway in 1964. That same year he won his first Oscar nomination, for his sly and amusing interpretation of King Louis VII of France, in *Becket*. Soon a period began in which Gielgud would pop up in all sorts of roles to lend a certain prestige to various projects, good and bad, often stealing the show. These included the title role in the dark Hollywood satire *The Loved One*, at one point appearing as a corpse; Henry IV in *Chimes at Midnight*; the incompetent Lord Raglan in the 1960s re-interpretation of *The Charge of the Light Brigade*; the title role in the 1971 version of *Julius Caesar*, and the only cast member to escape critical scorn; Richard Widmark's servant in the all-star whodunit *Murder on the Orient Express*; and the rigid hospital administrator in *The Elephant Man*. There was a starring part in director Alain Resnais's muddled talkfest, *Providence*, and a terrific role as Dudley Moore's sardonic manservant and conscience in the smash-hit 1981 comedy *Arthur*. The Academy Award it earned him for Best Supporting Actor was a very popular one, and it brought him a whole new generation of admirers.

After that, it was back to cameos again as various authoritative gentlemen, notably the Viceroy who has trouble keeping Ben Kingsley in line, in the Oscar-winning *Gandhi*. He was not, however, above slumming, donning motorcycle leather for a terrible comedy, *Scandalous*, and playing the lead in the ghastly *Prospero's Books*, which required him to appear nude, albeit in long shot. Even as he reached the age of 90, there seemed to be no signs of slowing down and among his assignments in these twilight years were two films that were Oscar nominated: *Shine*, in which he played Noah Taylor's piano teacher, and *Elizabeth*, showing up as Pope Paul IV. His last Shakespearean film, Kenneth Branagh's full-length *Hamlet*, found him without a word of dialogue, playing Priam. He published several memoirs, *Early Stages* (1939), *Stage Directions* (1963), *Distinguished Company* (1973), and *An Actor and His Time* (1979). His awards included a 1961 Tony for directing the play *Big Fish, Little Fish* and a 1991 Emmy for appearing on TV in the special *Summer Lease*.

Screen: 1924: Who Is the Man?; 1929: The Clue of the New Pin; 1932: Insult; 1933: The Good Companions; 1936: The Secret Agent; 1941: The Prime Minister; 1953: Julius Caesar; 1954: Romeo and Juliet (voice); 1956: Richard III; Around the World in Eighty Days; 1957: The Barretts of Wimpole Street; Saint Joan; 1964: Hamlet (voice); Becket; 1965: The Loved One; To Die in Madrid (voice); 1967: Chimes at Midnight/Falstaff; October Revolution (narrator); 1968: Sebastian; The Charge of the Light Brigade; The Shoes of the Fisherman; 1969: Assignment to Kill; Oh! What a Lovely War; 1971: Julius Caesar; 1972: Eagle in a Cage; 1973: Lost Horizon; 1974: 11 Harrowhouse; Gold; Murder on the Orient Express; 1975: Galileo; 1976: Aces High; 1977: Providence; Joseph Andrews; 1979: Murder by Decree; A Portrait of the Artist as a Young Man; 1980: Caligula; The Human Factor; The Orchestra Conductor/The Conductor; The Elephant Man; The Formula; 1981: Sphinx; Lion of the Desert; Arthur; Priest of Love; Chariots of Fire; 1982: Gandhi; 1983: The Wicked Lady; 1984: Scandalous; Invitation to the Wedding (nUSr); 1985: The Shooting Party; Plenty; Leave All Fair (nUSr); 1987: The Whistle Blower; 1988: Appointment With Death; Bluebeard, Bluebeard (nUSr); Arthur 2: On the Rocks; 1989: Getting It Right; 1990: Strike It Rich; 1991: Prospero's Books; 1992: Shining Through; The Power of One; 1995: First Knight; Haunted (dtv); 1996: Dragonheart (voice); The Leopard Son (narrator); Looking for Richard; Shine; Hamlet; The Portrait of a Lady; 1998: Quest for Camelot (voice); Elizabeth; 1999: The Tichborne Claimant (nUSr).

NY Stage: 1928: The Patriot; 1936: Hamlet; 1947: The Importance of Being Earnest; Love for Love; Medea (and dir.); Crime and Punishment; 1951: The Lady's Not for Burning (and dir.); 1958: Ages of Man; 1959: Much Ado About Nothing (and dir.); 1963: The School for Scandal (and dir.); 1963: Ages of Man (revival); 1964: Tiny Alice; 1966: Ivanov (and dir.; adpt.); 1970: Home; 1976: No Man's Land.

Select TV: 1959: The Browning Version (sp); 1966: Ages of Man (sp); The Love Song of Barney Kempinsky (sp); 1967: Ivanov (sp); 1968: From Chekhov With Love (sp); The Mayfly and the Frog (sp); 1970: Hamlet (sp); 1972: Home (sp); Probe; 1973: Frankenstein: The True Story; 1974: QB VII (ms); 1975: Edward the King (ms); 1978: King Richard the Second (sp); Les Misérables; 1980: Why Didn't They Ask Evans? (sp); 1982: Brideshead Revisited (ms); The Hunchback of Notre Dame; Inside the Third Reich (ms); Marco Polo (ms); The Seven Dials Mystery (sp); 1983: The Scarlet and the Black; 1984: The Master of Ballantrae; The Far Pavilions (ms); Oedipus the King (sp); Frankenstein; Camille; Antigone; 1985: Romance on the Orient Express; Wagner; 1986: Time After Time; The Canterville Ghost (sp); Quartermaine's Terms (sp); 1988: A Man for All Seasons; 1988–89: War and Remembrance (ms); 1991: Summer Lease (sp); The Strauss Dynasty (ms); 1994: Scarlett (ms); The Best of Friends; 1996: Gulliver's Travels; 1997: A Dance to the Music of Time (ms); 1998: Merlin; 2000: Catastrophe.

BILLY GILBERT

(WILLIAM GILBERT BARON)
BORN: LOUISVILLE, KY, SEPTEMBER 12, 1894.
DIED: SEPTEMBER 23, 1971.

A supporting character comedian who didn't usually spend his given time on screen quietly in the background, Billy Gilbert, flabby-faced with often-unruly hair, was adept at bombastic, flustered types. A veteran of vaudeville, where for a brief period he teamed with a pre-Costello Bud Abbott, Gilbert came to the movies in the 1920s. There were several assignments with Laurel and Hardy, notably the two-reelers "County Hospital," as an abused doctor, and "The Music Box," as the man whose piano is given a beating by the duo. Then producer Hal Roach unsuccessfully attempted to pair him with twig-thin Ben Blue in some two-reelers where they were known as "The Taxi Boys." Ever since vaudeville, Gilbert's main shtick relied on an extended build-up to whether or not he was going to let go with an overpowering sneeze, which, of course, he ultimately did. He could be seen doing this as one of W.C. Fields's cabinet members in the comedy classic *Million Dollar Legs*, and could be heard, off screen, as the most famous sneezer of them all, Sneezy, in Walt Disney's first feature length cartoon, *Snow White and the Seven Dwarfs*. The irritable Gilbert could be seen in *One Hundred Men and a Girl*, giving Adolph Menjou and his orchestra a hard time about rehearsing in his building, while the gentle, befuddled Gilbert was on hand in *His Girl Friday*, carrying a reprieve from the governor. Top billed, he teamed with Maxie Rosenbloom and Shemp Howard for three Monogram cheapies in the 1940s: *Three of a Kind*, playing vaudevillians; the requisite haunted house romp, *Crazy Knights*; and *Trouble Chasers*, foiling a gang of jewel thieves. For the stage, Gilbert served not only as actor and director (*The Red Mill*, in 1945, and *Sally*, in 1948) but playwright as well, debuting in this capacity in 1952 with *Buttrio Square*.

Screen (shorts): 1927: Smith's Pony; 1930: The Doctor's Wife; The Beauties; 1931: Dogs Is Dogs; Shiver My Timbers; The Panic Is On; The Hasty Marriage; One Good Turn; A Melon-Drama; Catch as Catch Can; The Pajama Party; 1932: Free Eats; Spanky; The Tabasco Kid; What Price Taxi?; Young Ironsides; Just a Pain in the Parlor; Strange Inner-Tube; Never the Twins Shall Meet; The Nickel Nurser; In Walked Charley; First in War; You're Telling Me; County Hospital; Their First Mistake; The Chimp; Strictly Unreliable; The Music Box; Seal Skins; Sneak Easily; On the Loose; Red Noses; Towed in a Hole; Taxi Barons; 1933: Fallen Arches; The Rummy; Wreckety Wrecks; Thundering Taxis; Luncheon at Twelve; Maids a la Mode; Call Her Sausage; The Bargain of the Century; Forgotten Babies; Bring 'em Back a Wife; Asleep in the Fleet; One Track Minds; Rhapsody in Brew; 1934: Another Wild Idea (voice); The Cracked Iceman; Them Thar Hills; Men in Black; Music in Your Hair; Movie Daze; Mrs. Barnacle Bill; Apples to You!; The Caretaker's Daughter; Soup and Fish; Roamin' Vandals; Tripping Through the Tropics; Next Weekend; Get Along Little Hubby; 1935: Just Another Murder; Nurse to You; His Bridal Sweet; Pardon My Scotch; His Old Flame; 1936: Violets in Spring; So and Sew; 1937: Swing Fever; 1938: Once Over Lightly; 1941: Meet Roy Rogers; 1943: Shot in the Escape; 1944: Crazy Like a Fox; Wedded Bliss.

Screen (features): 1916: Bubbles of Trouble; 1921: Dynamite Allen; 1929: Noisy Neighbors; Woman From Hell; 1931: Chinatown After Dark; First Aid; 1932: Pack Up Your Troubles; Blondie of the Follies; Skyscraper Souls; Million Dollar Legs; 1933: This Day and Age; Sons of the Desert (voice); The Girl in

419; Made on Broadway; **1934:** Happy Landing; Peck's Bad Boy; Eight Girls in a Boat; Cockeyed Cavaliers; The Merry Widow; Evelyn Prentice; **1935:** Coronado; A Night at the Opera; Millions in the Air; Mad Love; Escapade; Curly Top; Hail Brother; Here Comes the Band; The Night Is Young; I Dream Too Much; **1936:** Sutter's Gold; Parole!; Love on the Run; Three of a Kind; Dangerous Waters; The Bride Walks Out; Grand Jury; The Big Game; Love on a Bet; Early to Bed; Night Waitress; Kelly the Second; Pepper; Hi Gaucho!; Give Us This Night; The First Baby; Poor Little Rich Girl; F-Man; The Devil-Doll; My American Wife; One Rainy Afternoon; **1937:** The Man Who Found Himself; The Outcasts of Poker Flat; Live, Love and Learn; Rosalie; We're on the Jury; Sea Devils; Music for Madame; China Passage; The Toast of New York; The Life of the Party; The Firefly; On the Avenue; Espionage; Broadway Melody of 1938; One Hundred Men and a Girl; Captains Courageous; Maytime; Fight for Your Lady; When You're in Love; Snow White and the Seven Dwarfs (voice); She's Got Everything; **1938:** Mr. Doodle Kicks Off; My Lucky Star; The Girl Downstairs; Maid's Night Out; Joy of Living; Block-Heads; Happy Landing; Breaking the Ice; Peck's Bad Boy With the Circus; Army Girl; **1939:** Forged Passport; Destry Rides Again; Rio; The Under-Pup; The Star Maker; Million Dollar Legs; **1940:** Sing, Dance, Plenty Hot; His Girl Friday; Women in War; Scatterbrain; Safari; A Night at Earl Carroll's; Sandy Is a Lady; Seven Sinners; A Little Bit of Heaven; Queen of the Mob; Cross Country Romance; The Villain Still Pursued Her; Lucky Partners; Tin Pan Alley; No, No, Nanette; The Great Dictator; **1941:** Reaching for the Sun; New Wine; One Night in Lisbon; Angels With Broken Wings; Model Wife; Week-end in Havana; Our City; **1942:** Mr. Wise Guy; Sleepytime Gal; Valley of the Sun; Song of the Islands; Arabian Nights; **1943:** Shantytown; Crazy House; Spotlight Scandals; Always a Bridesmaid; Stage Door Canteen; **1944:** Three of a Kind/Cooking Up Trouble; Crazy Knights/Ghost Knights; Ever Since Venus; **1945:** Anchors Aweigh; Trouble Chasers; **1947:** Fun and Fancy Free (voice); **1948:** The Kissing Bandit; **1949:** Bride of Vengeance; **1952:** Down Among the Sheltering Palms; **1961:** Paradise Alley; **1962:** Five Weeks in a Balloon.

NY Stage: **1947:** The Chocolate Soldier; **1952:** Buttrio Square (and wr.).

JOHN GILBERT

(JOHN CECIL PRINGLE) BORN: LOGAN, UT, JULY 10, 1895. ED: HITCHCOCK MILITARY ACAD. DIED: JANUARY 9, 1936.

The mention of John Gilbert's name inevitably brings up legendary tales of how the mighty star of the silent era was destroyed by the coming of talkies, which cruelly exposed his vocal flaws. It is true that Gilbert never reached the peak he had achieved sans sound, but it is clear, watching him in his most famous sound feature, Queen Christina, that there was absolutely nothing strange or unpleasant about his speaking voice. He had started out in the business as a stage manager for a theatrical company in Spokane and managed to get extra work in films via his stepfather's friendship with director Walter Edwards. Starting out in a bit part in Matrimony, in 1915, he eventually worked his way up to billing, the following year, in Bullets and Brown Eyes, listed as "Jack" Gilbert. His first leading role, as a handicapped man in Princess of the Dark, came the next year. He worked for the Thomas Ince Company for a while before moving over to Parlata for One Dollar Bid, which co-starred his future wife (1923–24), Leatrice Joy. With a pair of 1920 releases, The White Circle and

The Great Redeemer, he expanded his interests, serving not only as actor but also as co-writer and assistant director of both. There were additional writing credits on The Bait, Deep Waters, and Love's Penalty, the last-named marking his only credit as director, although the end result evoked no fondness from the actor. That same year, 1921, brought Shame, notable because it was the first movie to bill him as "John" Gilbert. Signing with Fox in 1922, the actor continued to work at a furious rate, although he always seemed to just miss being considered one of the front-rank attractions. All that changed in 1924 when he signed up with MGM, who hoped to promote him as a smoldering love interest (despite a distinctively pointy nose, he was thought of as a rather handsome item). The promotion worked, as his stature rose through such films as His Hour and The Wife of the Centaur, playing opposite Aileen Pringle in both; the popular circus triangle, He Who Gets Slapped, supporting Lon Chaney; and the song-less Erich von Stroheim-directed version of The Merry Widow. These were followed by the blockbuster that he is invariably associated with, The Big Parade, director King Vidor's still-compelling look at a young wastrel whose eyes are opened to the horrors of war. It became, after The Birth of a Nation, the second most popular movie made in the silent era.

The next few years were the prime Gilbert years, and the studio cashed in on his success by reuniting him with his Big Parade co-star, Renee Adoree, for the carnival tale The Show, and the Tolstoy-inspired The Cossacks; and by putting him under Vidor's guidance again for La Boheme, which offered not only Adoree but also Lillian Gish as his other leading lady. He and Vidor teamed for a third, Bardelys the Magnificent, a swashbuckler, but the response was less enthusiastic this time out. It was his three romantic melodramas with Greta Garbo that really made him one of the most sterling examples of the silent movie lover: Flesh and the Devil, where he was Garbo's true love, despite her marriages to two other men; Love, which was Anna Karenina, given a more "commercial" title; and A Woman of Affairs, where his role was considerably smaller than hers. Their popularity was only enhanced by the fact that the two were supposedly an item off screen as well.

When the transition to sound finally came, Gilbert debuted with an uninspired reading of the balcony scene (with Norma Shearer) from Romeo and Juliet, in The Hollywood Revue of 1929, prompting little mention. His first starring talkie, His Glorious Night, is generally considered the one that ruined him; a florid melodrama that laid a colossal egg at the box office. There was speculation that Louis B. Mayer was out to destroy the star because of a previous argument, and this may have had much to do with the studio's lack of support at this point, as his next several movies, including Gentleman's Fate and West of Broadway (he played a drunk in the latter), continued to do poorly. It was with great reluctance that MGM bowed to Garbo's wishes to have him as her leading man in probably the finest of her melodramas, Queen Christina, replacing Laurence Olivier, as the Queen's Spanish lover, the supposed reason why this lady never chose to marry. His work was quite adequate, but the studio was eager to let him go. By this time, he was drinking heavily and made his last appearance, as a slave to the bottle, in The Captain Hates the Sea, over at Columbia. He died of a heart attack in 1936 at the age of 40. His other wives included actresses Ina Claire (1929–31) and Virginia Bruce (1932–34).

Screen: AS JACK GILBERT: **1915:** Matrimony; The Coward; Aloha Oe; **1916:** Hell's Hinges; Civilization; The Aryan; Bullets and Brown Eyes; The Apostle of Vengeance; The Phantom; Eye of the Night; Shell 43; The Sin Ye Do; **1917:** The Weaker Sex; Princess of the Dark; The Dark Road; Happiness; The

Millionaire Vagrant; Hater of Men; The Mother Instinct; Golden Rule Kate; The Devil Dodger; Up or Down?; **1918:** One Dollar Bid; Nancy Comes Home; Shackled; Wedlock; More Trouble; The Mask of Riches; Three X Gordon; Sons of Men; The Dawn of Understanding; **1919:** The Busher; The White Heather; The Man Beneath; The Red Viper; Widow by Proxy; The Heart o' the Hills; Should a Woman Tell?; **1920:** The White Circle (and co-wr.); The Great Redeemer (and co-wr.); Deep Waters (and wr.); **1921:** The Servant in the House.

AS JOHN GILBERT: 1921: Shame; Ladies Must Live; **1922:** Gleam o' Dawn; Arabian Love; The Yellow Stain; Honor First; Monte Cristo; Calvert's Valley; The Love Gambler; A California Romance; **1923:** Truxton King; The Madness of Youth; While Paris Sleeps/The Glory of Love; St. Elmo; The Exiles; Cameo Kirby; **1924:** Just Off Broadway; The Wolf Man; The Lone Chance; A Man's Mate; His Hour; Romance Ranch; He Who Gets Slapped; Married Flirts; The Snob; The Wife of the Centaur; **1925:** The Merry Widow; The Big Parade; **1926:** La Boheme; Bardelys the Magnificent; **1927:** Flesh and the Devil; The Show; Twelve Miles Out; Love; Man, Woman and Sin; **1928:** The Cossacks; Four Walls; Show People; The Masks of the Devil; **1929:** A Woman of Affairs; Desert Nights; A Man's Man; The Hollywood Revue of 1929; His Glorious Night; **1930:** Redemption; Way for a Sailor; **1931:** Gentleman's Fate; The Phantom of Paris; West of Broadway; **1932:** Downstairs (and co-wr.); **1933:** Fast Workers; Queen Christina; **1934:** The Captain Hates the Sea.

CONNIE GILCHRIST

(ROSE GILCHRIST) BORN: BROOKLYN, NY, FEBRUARY 2, 1901. ED: ASSUMPTION ACAD. DIED: MARCH 3, 1985.

MGM's down-to-earth character actress of the 1940s, Connie Gilchrist, so distinctly a product of Brooklyn, specialized in domestics and unrefined broads who didn't mind dishing out some sass or good common sense. Her acting career began in Europe, first on the London stage and then in France, where she was part of a touring company. Returning to America, she made her Broadway debut in 1935, in *Mulatto*. It was a role in *Ladies and Gentleman*, however, that led to a contract in 1940 with Metro, who premiered her in *Hullabaloo*, as one of Frank Morgan's ex-wives. She first made her mark the following year, battling with Marjorie Main over Wallace Beery in *Barnacle Bill*, an assignment she was asked to repeat for both *Rationing* and *Bad Bascomb*. The studio had no limitations as to what she'd play or where she'd show up, so she was seen as a hard-edged criminal in *A Woman's Face*; an Indian squaw in *Apache Trail*, which was about as convincing as her being cast as an Italian in *Tortilla Flat*; a wartime nurse in *Cry Havoc*; a maid in *The Valley of Decision*; and a campus cook in *Good News*. Although she played a charwoman in *Presenting Lily Mars*, the film gave her one of her finest moments when she sang a duet with Judy Garland, "Every Little Movement." After finishing her contract with MGM, she ended up over at Fox playing Linda Darnell's boozy mom in the Oscar-winning *A Letter to Three Wives*, and at Universal, appearing in a pair of Charles Coburn comedies, *Peggy* and *Louisa*. She did some more housekeeping in *Auntie Mame*, *Say One for Me*, *The Misadventures of Merlin Jones*, and *Fluffy*, to name but a few, and she was seen on television as Purity Pinker in *Long John Silver*, among many other assignments.

Screen: 1940: Hullabaloo; **1941:** Down in San Diego; Billy the Kid; Dr. Kildare's Wedding Day; The Wild Man of Borneo; A

Woman's Face; H.M. Pulham, Esq.; Barnacle Bill; Married Bachelor; **1942:** Johnny Eager; We Were Dancing; This Time for Keeps; Sunday Punch; Tortilla Flat; Grand Central Murder; Apache Trail; Born to Sing; The War Against Mrs. Hadley; **1943:** Thousands Cheer; Presenting Lily Mars; Swing Shift Maisie; Cry Havoc; The Heavenly Body; The Human Comedy; **1944:** Rationing; See Here, Private Hargrove; Nothing but Trouble; Music for Millions; The Seventh Cross; **1945:** The Valley of Decision; Junior Miss; **1946:** Young Widow; Bad Bascomb; Faithful in My Fashion; Up Goes Maisie; **1947:** The Hucksters; Song of the Thin Man; The Unfinished Dance; Good News; **1948:** Tenth Avenue Angel; The Bride Goes Wild; The Big City; Luxury Liner; Chicken Every Sunday; **1949:** Act of Violence; A Letter to Three Wives; Little Women; The Story of Molly X; **1950:** Stars in My Crown; Buccaneer's Girl; A Ticket to Tomahawk; Louisa; Peggy; Undercover Girl; Tripoli; The Killer That Stalked New York; **1951:** Here Comes the Groom; Thunder on the Hill; Chain of Circumstances; **1952:** One Big Affair; The Half-Breed; Flesh and Fury; **1953:** Houdini; The Great Diamond Robbery; **1954:** It Should Happen to You; **1955:** The Far Country; Long John Silver; **1956:** The Man in the Gray Flannel Suit; **1958:** Machine Gun Kelly; Auntie Mame; Some Came Running; **1959:** Say One for Me; **1962:** The Interns; Swingin' Along; **1964:** A Tiger Walks; The Misadventures of Merlin Jones; A House Is Not a Home; **1965:** Two on a Guillotine; Sylvia; Fluffy; Tickle Me; The Monkey's Uncle; **1969:** Some Kind of a Nut.

NY Stage: 1935: Mulatto; **1937:** Excursion; Work Is for Horses; **1938:** How to Get Tough About It; **1939:** Ladies and Gentlemen.

Select TV: 1954: Under the Black Flag (sp); **1955:** Long John Silver (series).

HERMIONE GINGOLD

BORN: LONDON, ENGLAND, DECEMBER 9, 1897. DIED: MAY 24, 1987.

This eccentric and witty character actress, with the nasally, comically aristocratic voice, took a long time coming to the attention of the American public, but when she did at last, she was a presence to be treasured. She had been acting since childhood but did not gain much notice until the 1930s when she became a popular attraction in various London revues, where her droll delivery and outrageously colorful outfits were a welcome delight. In 1953 she came to Broadway to appear in *John Murray Anderson's Almanac* and found herself winning over the U.S. as well. She had been popping up irregularly in British films since 1932, the most notable credit being an adaptation of *The Pickwick Papers*, as Miss Tomkins, and finally made her American movie debut, albeit in a sequence shot in England, in the all-star Oscar-winner *Around the World in Eighty Days*, as an aging London tart. Her Hollywood debut proper came in 1958, when she was ideally cast as a witch in Columbia's comic fantasy *Bell Book and Candle*. This was followed by her most memorable screen role, as Maurice Chevalier's former flame in *Gigi*, where she made her mark on musical film history when she joined him for Lerner and Loewe's sparkling "I Remember It Well." Alas, it was difficult for filmmakers to find suitable roles for such an odd duck of advancing years, and she was seen only sporadically over the next three decades. She was notable as the Mayor's pretentious wife in *The Music Man*, and got to repeat her stage role as the snooty, wheelchair-bound grandmother in *A Little Night Music*, although her solo, "Liaisons," was not included in the celluloid version. Gingold was last seen playing a doddering actress trying to help Ron Silver find the elusive film star in *Garbo Talks*. Her 1958 autobiography was entitled *The World Is Square.*

Screen: 1932: Dance, Pretty Lady; 1936: Someone at the Door; 1937: Merry Comes to Town; 1938: Meet Mr. Penny; 1943: The Butler's Dilemma; 1952: The Pickwick Papers; 1953: The Slasher/Cosh Boy; Our Girl Friday/The Adventures of Sadie; 1956: Around the World in Eighty Days; 1958: Bell Book and Candle; Gigi; 1961: The Naked Edge; 1962: The Music Man; Gay Purree (voice); 1964: I'd Rather Be Rich; 1965: Harvey Middleman — Fireman; 1966: Promise Her Anything; Munster, Go Home!; 1967: Blast-Off!/Those Fantastic Flying Fools; 1977: A Little Night Music; 1984: Garbo Talks.

NY Stage: 1953: John Murray Anderson's Almanac; 1959: First Impressions; 1960: From A to Z (and co-wr.); 1963: Oh Dad, Poor Dad, Mama's Hung You in the Closet and I'm Feelin' So Sad; 1973: A Little Night Music; 1978: Side by Side by Sondheim.

Select TV: 1954–55: One Minute Please (series); 1955: She Stoops to Conquer (sp); 1958–62: The Jack Paar Show (series); 1963: A Cry of Angels (sp); 1967: Before the Fringe (series; and co-wr.); 1969: Winter of the Witch (sp); 1971: Banyon; 1983: How to Be a Perfect Person in Just Three Days (sp).

LILLIAN GISH

(Lillian Diana de Guiche)
Born: Springfield, OH, October 14, 1893.
Died: February 27, 1993.

Hers is perhaps the defining face of silent films: sad-looking, poised, and heart-shaped, with pursed lips and yearning eyes she could evoke great emotion through nothing more than a glance. Being part of the silent school of acting, she could be just as guilty of hand wringing over-emoting as many of her fellow actors of the period. There was, however, a delicate sensitivity that has made her stand out from so many of the others. She and her younger sister Dorothy (1898–1968) began acting onstage as children, at which time they became acquainted with Mary Pickford. It was through her that they were introduced to D.W. Griffith, with whom Lillian's name would be forever linked in film history. Griffith debuted the sisters in a 1912 short, "An Unseen Enemy," and both continued to appear, together or apart, in one- and two-reelers for the director over the next two years. When he moved up to features with *Judith of Bethulia*, Lillian was part of the cast. Her roles grew bigger, and she reached stardom when she was chosen to play the heroine, the Northern girl rescued (!) by the Ku Klux Klan, in Griffith's still-controversial Civil War epic *The Birth of a Nation*. It became the biggest hit of the early days of film, changed the way the world looked at movies, and continues to keep Gish's name before generations of film students. She did more work for Griffith, becoming queen of the ripe melodrama through such movies as the self-explanatory *Daphne and the Pirate*; *Sold for Marriage*, playing a Russian immigrant; *Intolerance*, rocking the cradle in the scenes connecting the four storylines in another of the director's hotly debated productions; *The House Built Upon Sand*, behaving like a spoiled brat until she wakes up to her husband's virtues; and *Hearts of the World*, separated from lover Robert Harron by the First World War. *Broken Blossoms*, was another of her most famous and frequently revived silent films, a downbeat plea for racial tolerance, in which she was a waif whose love for an Asian man (Richard Barthelmess) leads to tragedy. *Way Down East*, perhaps the *second* best remembered of all her films, reteamed her with Barthelmess in a story of an outcast orphan who finds love with a farm boy, and contained the classic sequence of Gish trapped on the raging ice floe, an indelible part of motion pic-

ture folklore. *Orphans of the Storm*, the most famous pairing with sister Dorothy, was set during the French Revolution and went so far as to include Lillian's last minute rescue from the guillotine from Danton (Monte Blue). The previous year, 1921, she became one of the rare female stars of her day to try her hand at directing, guiding Dorothy through *Remodeling Her Husband*.

Shortly after this period, she left Griffith over a salary disagreement. There were two teamings with Ronald Colman and director Henry King, both made in Italy: *The White Sister*, in which Gish became a nun, thinking her lover had died in the war, and the lavish costume piece *Romola*, in which she wed wicked William Powell, who did her dirt by impregnating sister Dorothy. Signing a contract with the newly formed MGM, she did two literary adaptations, *La Boheme*, with John Gilbert, as star-crossed Parisian lovers, and an engrossing adaptation of *The Scarlet Letter*, as the shamed adulteress Hester Prynne, in a much-acclaimed performance. This would prove to be the last of her triumphs, financially. The next three films, *Annie Laurie*, a story of bickering Scottish clans; *The Enemy*, a melodrama about a wife (Lillian) turning to the streets, while her husband (Ralph Forbes) is away at war; and *The Wind*, an atmospheric tale of an innocent girl out West, driven to murder, all lost money. (*The Wind* has since been proclaimed one of the most underrated and magnificent of all silent films.) After these disappointments, MGM had no regrets seeing her sign up with United Artists instead. For them she made her talkie debut, 1930s *One Romantic Night*, the second of three film versions of the play *The Swan*, and it made no impact whatsoever on American box offices, prompting her to ask that the agreement be dissolved. She decided it was time to return to the theater, where, with the exception of one film, she would stay exclusively for the next 12 years. That film was 1933's *His Double Life*, an independently made comedy that was distributed by Paramount with so little fanfare that it was clear that Gish's name was suddenly synonymous with a bygone era. On Broadway she did productions of *Uncle Vanya* and a notable *Hamlet*, appearing as Ophelia opposite John Gielgud in the title role.

When she did return to the big screen, it was in a supporting role in an undistinguished war film, *Commandos Strike at Dawn*, as a Norwegian villager. This did, however, mark a period of renewed interest from Hollywood, and the more mature Gish proved that she was still a worthy addition to the film scene through her work in *Miss Susie Slagle's*, as the kindly old lady running a Baltimore boarding house for medical students (sister Dorothy would later play the part on television); the steamy box-office smash *Duel in the Sun*, as Lionel Barrymore's sickly wife, an Oscar-nominated role and one of the movie's few sympathetic characterizations; and *Portrait of Jennie*, as the Mother Superior. Then it was back to the stage again, performing on Broadway in *The Trip to Bountiful*, the same year (1953) she did it on television. Later she appeared in such plays as *All the Way Home*; a production of *Romeo and Juliet* (as the Nurse); and *I Never Sang for My Father*. Television saw her in productions of *Grandma Moses*, *The Day Lincoln Was Shot*, *Morning's at Seven*, *The Grass Harp*, and *Arsenic and Old Lace*. She chose to return to the movies only on very rare occasions, sometimes with worthwhile results, most specifically *The Night of the Hunter*, where she was marvelous as the formidable spinster who proves a challenge to murderous Robert Mitchum in this disturbing film that came to be recognized as a gothic masterpiece. Other later movies roles included the stern pioneering mother of Burt Lancaster in *The Unforgiven*; a health enthusiast in *The Comedians*; the family matriarch who expires during the reception in *A Wedding*; and Alan Alda's doddering mom in *Sweet Liberty*. She had a leading role for her final film, the moody and melancholy *The Whales of August*, putting up with her blind and abrasive sister, Bette Davis, with great dignity and understanding, a relationship that was supposedly echoed off screen as well. By the time she died, on the brink of reaching her 100th birthday, she was looked on as something of a treasure, a link between modern cinema and its origins. She received a special Academy Award in 1971 and the American Film Institute Life Achievement Award in 1984. She published two autobiographies, *Life and Lillian Gish*, in 1932; and *The Movies, Mr. Griffith and Me*, in 1969.

Screen (features): 1914: Judith of Bethulia; The Battle of the Sexes; Lord Chumley; The Quicksands; Man's Enemy; Home Sweet Home; The Rebellion of Kitty Belle; The Tear That Burned; 1915: The Birth of the Nation; The Lost House; Captain Macklin; Enoch Arden; The Lily and the Rose; 1916: Daphne and the Pirate; Sold for Marriage; An Innocent Magdalene; Intolerance; Diane of the Follies; Pathways of Life; The Children Pay; 1917: The House Built Upon Sand; Souls Triumphant; 1918: Hearts of the World; The Great Love; 1919: The Greatest Thing in Life; A Romance of Happy Valley; Broken Blossoms; True-Heart Susie; The Greatest Question; 1920: Way Down East; 1921: Orphans of the Storm; 1923: The White Sister; 1924: Romola; 1926: La Boheme; The Scarlet Letter; 1927: Annie Laurie/Ladies From Hell; 1928: The Enemy; The Wind; 1930: One Romantic Night; 1934: His Double Life; 1942: Commandos Strike at Dawn; 1943: Top Man; 1946: Miss Susie Slagle's; Duel in the Sun; 1948: Portrait of Jennie; 1955: The Cobweb; The Night of the Hunter; 1958: Orders to Kill; 1960: The Unforgiven; 1966: Follow Me, Boys!; 1967: Warning Shot; The Comedians; 1978: A Wedding; 1984: Hambone and Hillie; 1986: Sweet Liberty; 1987: The Whales of August.

NY Stage: 1913: A Good Little Devil; 1930: Uncle Vanya; 1932: Camille; 1933: Nine Pine Street; 1934: The Joyous Season; 1936: Hamlet; 1937: The Star Wagon; 1939: Dear Octopus; 1942: Mr. Sycamore; 1947: Crime and Punishment; 1950: The Curious Savage; 1953: The Trip to Bountiful; 1958: A Family Reunion (ob); 1960: All the Way Home; 1963: Too True to Be Good; 1965: Anya; 1968: I Never Sang for My Father; 1973: Uncle Vanya; 1975: A Musical Jubilee.

Select TV: 1949: The Late Christopher Bean (sp); Outward Bound (sp); 1951: Ladies in Retirement (sp); Detour (sp); The Joyous Season (sp); 1952: Grandma Moses (sp); 1953: The Trip to Bountiful (sp); 1954: The Quality of Mercy (sp); The Corner Drugstore (sp); 1955: I Mrs. Bibb (sp); The Sound and the Fury (sp); 1956: The Day Lincoln Was Shot (sp); Morning's at Seven (sp); 1960: The Grass Harp (sp); 1961: The Spiral Staircase (sp); 1969: Arsenic and Old Lace (sp); 1976: Twin Detectives; 1977: Sparrow; 1981: Thin Ice; 1983: Hobson's Choice; 1985: Adventures of Huckleberry Finn.

JACKIE GLEASON

(HERBERT JOHN GLEASON) BORN: BROOKLYN, NY, FEBRUARY 26, 1916. DIED: JUNE 24, 1987.

On television, Jackie Gleason was revered as one of the medium's most cherished and important performers, a comedian of seemingly limitless range who could get a laugh with a wide-eyed bellow or a wordless piece of pantomime. In the movies, his best work found him playing it straight, revealing a deft character actor with a smooth demeanor who could be tough or soft, lovable or downright mean. Born into poverty, he worked his way up from pool-hall hustler to nightclub comic, eventually landing a contract with Warner Bros. As a result he could be seen giving capable but uninspired support in such features as *Larceny,*

Inc. and *All Through the Night*, playing one of Humphrey Bogart's pals in the latter. The lead in a Columbia quickie, *Tramp, Tramp, Tramp*, did nothing but offer further discouragement, so he found comfort back on the nightclub circuit before giving the new medium of television a shot. This must have seemed even less promising than the movies after his first attempt at a series, *The Life of Riley*, flopped. (It wasn't until William Bendix brought it back later on that it became a hit.) It was on his second show, *Cavalcade of Stars*, that his most famous character was introduced, bombastic bus driver Ralph Kramden, and Gleason at last began to cultivate a wide audience. From this came his own variety series, *The Jackie Gleason Show*, which not only continued to showcase his various other characters, such as Reggie Van Gleason and The Poor Soul, but also gave ample room to the Kramden character and *The Honeymooners*. That, in turn, became so successful that Gleason broke from the variety format for an entire season just to present *The Honeymooners* skit on a weekly basis. In time it would be considered one of TV's most quotable classic comedies.

Busy on the small screen for the rest of the 1950s, he made a stop-off on Broadway for *Take Me Along*, winning the Tony Award for this musical version of *Ah, Wilderness!* It was not until 1961 that he returned to theatrical features, as pool shark Minnesota Fats, a secondary but pivotal role, in the gritty drama *The Hustler*. His cool, fastidious characterization was superb, and he earned an Oscar nomination, launching the second phase of his film career. There was another excellent supporting role, as Anthony Quinn's sleazy, exploitive and self-loathing manager in *Requiem for a Heavyweight*, then some starring vehicles, of which *Gigot*, from a story by Gleason himself, was the noblest attempt. In it he played, quite nicely, a mute, slow-witted Parisian janitor, but the extreme sentimentality of the whole piece turned off both critics and public. *Papa's Delicate Condition* had similar problems, with Gleason as a well-meaning drunk, though it did allow him to introduce the Academy Award-winning song "Call Me Irresponsible." The further failures of the all-star *Skidoo*, which required him at one point to indulge in an acid trip; *Don't Drink the Water*, in which he was miscast as a Jewish tourist behind the Iron Curtain; *How to Commit Marriage*, a strained teaming with Bob Hope; and *How Do I Love Thee?*, which examined a troubled marriage, put him out of the movie scene for a while. He returned in 1977 in a huge hit, the goofy car chase flick *Smokey and the Bandit*, giving a performance as a short-tempered Southern sheriff that was barn broad to say the least. Once again it made him a hot film property and, following two *Smokey* sequels and a poor Richard Pryor comedy, *The Toy*, he got himself one last worthwhile movie, *Nothing in Common*, uncompromisingly good as Tom Hanks's selfish, blowhard father who reluctantly turns to his estranged son for help. Ironically, he never won an Emmy Award in the medium in which he excelled, but there were few who would dispute the title bestowed upon him by Orson Welles, "The Great One."

Screen: AS JACKIE C. GLEASON: 1941: Navy Blues; Steel Against the Sky; 1942: Larceny, Inc.; All Through the Night; Escape From Crime.

AS JACKIE GLEASON: 1942: Lady Gangster; Tramp, Tramp, Tramp; Orchestra Wives; Springtime in the Rockies; 1950: The Desert Hawk; 1961: The Hustler; 1962: Requiem for a Heavyweight; Gigot (and co-wr.; music); 1963: Papa's Delicate Condition; Soldier in the Rain; 1968: Skidoo; 1969: How to Commit Marriage; Don't Drink the Water; 1970: How Do I Love Thee?; 1977: Mr. Billion; Smokey and the Bandit; 1980: Smokey and the Bandit II; 1982: The Toy; 1983: The Sting II; Smokey and the Bandit 3; 1986: Nothing in Common.

NY Stage: 1940: Keep Off the Grass; 1943: Artists and Models; 1944: Follow the Girls; 1949: Along Fifth Avenue; 1959: Take Me Along.

Select TV: 1949–50: The Life of Riley (series); 1950–52: Cavalcade of Stars (series); 1952–55: The Jackie Gleason Show (series); 1953: The Laugh Maker (sp); 1954: Peacock City (sp); Short Cut (sp); 1955: The Show-Off (sp); Uncle Ed and Circumstances (sp); 1955–56: The Honeymooners (series); 1956–59: The Jackie Gleason Show (series); 1958: The Time of Your Life (sp); 1961: The Million Dollar Incident (sp); You're in the Picture (series); The Jackie Gleason Show (series); 1962–70: Jackie Gleason and His American Scene Magazine/The Jackie Gleason Show (series); 1974: Julie and Jackie: How Sweet It Is (sp); 1983: Mr. Halpern and Mr. Johnson (sp); 1985: Izzy and Moe.

JAMES GLEASON

BORN: NEW YORK, NY, MAY 23, 1886.
DIED: APRIL 12, 1959.

This long-faced, balding character player, with the pencil moustache and the suspicious whine in his voice was one of Hollywood's most formidable and ubiquitous performers, chalking up more than 100 film appearances in some 30 years. Choosing to pursue his parents' profession, he worked in their stock company for many years, taking a break for military service during World War I. After the war he began making a name for himself, not so much as an actor but as a playwright, where his credits included *Is Zat So?*, *Mammy*, and *The Fall Guy*. He came to Hollywood in 1928, officially launching his career by playing a fight manager in *The Count of Ten*, then appearing in the big-screen version of his own play, *The Shannons of Broadway*, opposite his wife, Lucille Webster (Gleason), to whom he'd been married since 1905. In addition to a fleeting on-screen appearance in the opening scene, he was credited as co-writer of the Oscar-winning musical *The Broadway Melody*, (which did not exactly indicate any special talents in that field). Amid a burgeoning career, he took on some continuing roles in some minor film series. First he was smart-alecky Inspector Oscar Piper in the Hildegarde Withers mysteries — *Penguin Pool Murder*, *Murder on the Blackboard*, *The Plot Thickens*, and *Forty Naughty Girls*. He was then in five Republic Pictures Higgins Family quickies (acting alongside wife Lucille and son Russell) — *The Higgins Family*, *My Wife's Relatives*, *Should Husbands Work?*, *The Covered Trailer*, and *Money to Burn*. Further down the line, he took over the part of boxing manager Knobby Walsh from Leon Errol in the "Z" budgeted *Joe Palooka* films.

His screen career reached its zenith in 1941, first with Frank Capra's still-potent expose of media frenzy and fascism, *Meet John Doe*, as Barbara Stanwyck's exasperated editor, and then with one of the best-liked fantasies of the era, *Here Comes Mr. Jordan*, as Robert Montgomery's bewildered fight manager, in a splendidly funny and touching performance that earned him an Oscar nomination in the supporting category. Capra, who once called him his "favorite character actor," used him again in *Arsenic and Old Lace*, as a perplexed police inspector, and *Riding High*, as a racetrack official. Gleason's other significant works included *Crash Dive*, as an ailing C.P.O. who sacrifices his life during the big battle; *The Clock*, as a milkman who takes young lovers Judy Garland and Robert Walker on his early morning rounds; *The Bishop's Wife*, as a friendly cabbie; *Come Fill the Cup*, as a recovering alcoholic; and *The Night of the Hunter*, as a broken down, boozed-up riverboat captain. A life-long asthmatic, Gleason died from it in 1959, 12 years after the death of his beloved wife and 14

years after his son, Russell, was accidentally killed in a fall. Gleason also directed the 1932 short "Off His Base," co-directed the 1935 feature *Hot Tip*, and scripted (sometimes without credit) such movies as *The Bowery*, *The World Moves On*, and *Servant's Entrance*.

Screen: 1922: Polly of the Follies; 1928: The Count of Ten; 1929: The Shannons of Broadway; The Broadway Melody (and co-wr.); The Flying Fool; Oh Yeah!; 1930: Her Man; The Matrimonial Bed; Big Money; Puttin' on the Ritz; Dumbbells in Ermine; The Swellhead; 1931: A Free Soul; Sweepstakes; The Big Gamble; Suicide Fleet; It's a Wise Child; Beyond Victory; 1932: Penguin Pool Murder; Fast Companions; The Crooked Circle; The All-American; Lady and Gent; Blondie of the Follies; The Devil Is Driving; 1933: Hoopla; Clear All Wires; Billion Dollar Scandal; 1934: Orders Is Orders; Helldorado; The Meanest Gal in Town; Murder on the Blackboard; Search for Beauty; Change of Heart; 1935: We're Only Human; Hot Tip; Murder on a Honeymoon; West Point of the Air; 1936: Murder on a Bridal Path; The Ex-Mrs. Bradford; Don't Turn 'em Loose; The Plot Thickens; The Big Game; Yours for the Asking; 1937: Manhattan Merry-Go-Round; Forty Naughty Girls; 1938: Army Girl; The Higgins Family; 1939: My Wife's Relatives; Should Husbands Work?; On Your Toes; The Covered Trailer; Money to Burn; 1940: Earl of Puddlestone; Grandpa Goes to Town; 1941: Affectionately Yours; Meet John Doe; Nine Lives Are Not Enough; Here Comes Mr. Jordan; Tanks a Million; Babes on Broadway; A Date With the Falcon; Hay Foot; 1942: My Gal Sal; Tales of Manhattan; Footlight Serenade; Manila Calling; The Falcon Takes Over; 1943: Crash Dive; A Guy Named Joe; 1944: Arsenic and Old Lace; The Keys of the Kingdom; Once Upon a Time; 1945: The Clock; Captain Eddie; A Tree Grows in Brooklyn; This Man's Navy; 1946: The Hoodlum Saint; Lady Luck; The Well-Groomed Bride; Home, Sweet Homicide; 1947: Down to Earth; The Homestretch; Tycoon; The Bishop's Wife; 1948: When My Baby Smiles at Me; The Return of October; Smart Woman; The Dude Goes West; 1949: Take One False Step; The Life of Riley; Bad Boy; Miss Grant Takes Richmond; 1950: Key to the City; Riding High; The Yellow Cab Man; Joe Palooka in the Squared Circle; The Jackpot; 1951: Come Fill the Cup; Joe Palooka in the Triple Cross; Two Gals and a Guy; I'll See You in My Dreams; 1952: What Price Glory?; We're Not Married; The Story of Will Rogers; 1953: Forever Female; 1954: Suddenly; Hollywood Thrill-Makers/Hollywood Stunt Man; 1955: The Night of the Hunter; The Girl Rush; 1956: Star in the Dust; 1957: Spring Reunion; Loving You; Man in the Shadow; 1958: The Female Animal; Once Upon a Horse; Man or Gun; Rock-a-Bye Baby; Money, Women and Guns; The Last Hurrah.

NY Stage: 1919: It Happens to Everybody; The Five Million; 1920: The Charm School; 1921: Like a King; 1923: The Deep Tangled Wildwood; 1924: The Lady Killer; 1925: Is Zat So? (and wr.); Lambs Gambol; 1927: The Shannons of Broadway (and wr.).

Select TV: 1954: The Frame Up (sp); 1955: Burlesque (sp); The Big Umbrella (sp); Rookie of the Year (sp); 1957: Shark of the Mountain (sp).

PAULETTE GODDARD

(PAULINE MARION GODDARD LEVEE)
BORN: WHITESTONE LANDING, NY, JUNE 3, 1905.
DIED: APRIL 23, 1990.

It's obvious that Paulette Goddard owed her screen career to Charlie Chaplin, but there's a good chance that she'd have made it anyway. Although she was not versatile and persevered more through sheer spunk, beauty, and a lively determination than great talent, it should be noted that she and Claire Bloom were the only leading ladies of the great comedian to later have full-blown careers on their own. A former Ziegfeld Girl, she came to Hollywood in the early 1930s, making her debut in *The Girl Habit* and then becoming a Goldwyn Girl, albeit for one time only, in Eddie Cantor's *The Kid From Spain*. (Some sources list *The Locked Door, City Streets, Roman Scandals* and *Kid Millions* among her credits, though these appearances have never been substantiated.) She signed a contract with Hal Roach and showed up in some of his short-subjects, but a chance meeting with Charlie Chaplin changed her lowly status when he bought her contract and became her Svengali, creating a satisfying screen image, a spirited girl of the gutter, not easily given to surrender. They were quietly married in 1936, the same year that he brought forth *Modern Times*, which featured Goddard as the street gamine to whom Charlie loses his heart. Her performance was thoroughly engaging, signaling the emergence of an appealing new star. Producer David O. Selznick signed her up with the intention of having her play Scarlett O'Hara, but instead she was seen in supporting roles in *The Young in Heart*, as Richard Carlson's boss and love interest; and, over at MGM, in *Dramatic School*, as an acting student jealous of Luise Rainer, and *The Women*, as a wife on her way to Reno for a divorce, engaging in a memorable battle with Rosalind Russell. (In the later television adaptation Goddard would take Russell's part). A co-starring role with Bob Hope in the horror comedy *The Cat and the Canary* not only resulted in a follow-up, *The Ghost Breakers*, but also a contract with Paramount. She fell flat on her face playing a Gypsy in DeMille's clunky Technicolor adventure, *North West Mounted Police*, but gave her best shot dancing with Fred Astaire in one of his weakest films, *Second Chorus*. In the meantime Chaplin gave her another good part in his first sound feature, *The Great Dictator*, a role not unlike the one she'd played in *Modern Times*, a determined peasant girl loved by the Little Tramp. The couple divorced in 1942, and Goddard's career continued to soar with plum parts in *Hold Back the Dawn*, as Charles Boyer's gold-digging girlfriend; another for DeMille, *Reap the Wild Wind*, as a Southern belle desired by both Ray Milland and John Wayne; and one more with Hope, *Nothing but the Truth*.

She reached a career high with the ponderous but popular nurses-at-war drama, *So Proudly We Hail!*, as the toughest of the ladies, tossing off flip remarks during the battle for Bataan, and earning an Oscar nomination in the supporting category. Staying topical in the midst of the war, she and Fred MacMurray endured the D.C. housing shortage in *Standing Room Only*, while she did some shipyard welding on the home front in *I Love a Soldier*, the G.I. being the less-than-exciting Sonny Tufts. Her Oscar nomination encouraged Paramount to star her in a lavish costume drama, *Kitty*, as a London guttersnipe who goes the Eliza Doolittle route, becoming a duchess through the coaching of Ray Milland. The film was mildly enjoyable, highly successful, and thoroughly forgettable entertainment. In 1944 she married her other *Second Chorus* co-star, Burgess Meredith, and starred with him in his 1946 production of *Diary of a Chambermaid*, playing an outspoken maid, to good notices but meager audiences. Back with DeMille, she tried too hard to impress as a rambunctious slave girl on the run with Gary Cooper in *Unconquered*; hopped over to England to play the scheming Mrs. Chevely in *An Ideal Husband*; and then returned home, where she made some missteps instrumental in turning her career downward. First came *Hazard*, which gave her another of Paramount's drearier leading men, Macdonald Carey, as a co-star. Then there was the studio's

notorious bomb (the last film Goddard under her contract), *Bride of Vengeance*, where she played the wicked Lucreatia Borgia, dressed to the nines and flaring her nostrils in what was probably the worst performance of her career. For Columbia she sank in a version of *Anna Lucasta*, in which all the principals reverted back to the story's original Polish origins, having been changed to black for the famous stage production.

No longer in demand, Goddard wrapped up her career in a handful of quickly forgotten cheapies, including *The Torch*, portraying a Mexican in a production shot south of the border; *Babes in Bagdad*, playing a fairly long-in-the-tooth babe; and the British-made *A Stranger Came Home/The Unholy Four*, finding out that her presumed-deceased husband is alive. Having divorced Meredith in 1950, she married once more, in 1958, to author Erich Maria Remarque (he died in 1970) and retired into wealth, returning with no fanfare whatsoever for one last theatrical film appearance, the Italian-made *Time of Indifference*, and a television movie, *The Snoop Sisters*.

Screen: 1931: The Girl Habit; 1932: The Mouthpiece; The Kid From Spain; 1936: Modern Times; 1938: The Young in Heart; Dramatic School; 1939: The Women; The Cat and the Canary; 1940: The Ghost Breakers; The Great Dictator; North West Mounted Police; 1941: Second Chorus; Pot o' Gold; Hold Back the Dawn; Nothing but the Truth; 1942: The Lady Has Plans; Reap the Wild Wind; The Forest Rangers; Star Spangled Rhythm; 1943: The Crystal Ball; So Proudly We Hail!; 1944: Standing Room Only; I Love a Soldier; 1945: Kitty; Duffy's Tavern; 1946: Diary of a Chambermaid; 1947: Suddenly It's Spring; Variety Girl; Unconquered; An Ideal Husband; 1948: Hazard; On Our Merry Way; 1949: Bride of Vengeance; Anna Lucasta; 1950: The Torch; 1952: Babes in Bagdad; 1953: Vice Squad; Paris Model; Sins of Jezebel; 1954: A Stranger Came Home/The Unholy Four; The Charge of the Lancers; 1964: Time of Indifference/Gli Indifferenti.

NY Stage: 1926: No Foolin'.

Select TV: 1972: The Snoop Sisters/The Female Instinct.

THOMAS GOMEZ

(SABINO TOMAS GOMEZ) BORN: NEW YORK, NY, JULY 10, 1905. DIED: JUNE 18, 1971.

This fleshy, oily character player was almost always called upon to ooze menace, which was just as well, since even his benign roles failed to evoke much in the way of sympathy or prolonged interest. Debuting on the New York stage in a 1924 production of *Cyrano de Bergerac*, he made his living there for the next 19 years, dabbling mainly in the classics until signed to a contract by Universal Pictures. Called upon to kill off Evelyn Ankers in his very first film, *Sherlock Holmes and the Voice of Terror*, Gomez was pretty much typecast from the get-go, playing rotters in such movies as *Frontier Badmen*; *The Daltons Ride Again*; two Abbott and Costello comedies, *Who Done It?* and *In Society*; and the costume epic *A Night in Paradise*, as the wicked Croesus, betrothed to a reluctant Merle Oberon. Shortly before his contract expired, he received an Oscar nomination playing, with total conviction, the hearty, simple Mexican peasant in charge of the merry-go-round in *Ride the Pink Horse*. After Universal, he could still be found in a bad mood in *Key Largo*, as a henchman of Edward G. Robinson's, while he discovered in *Force of Evil* that there were more dangerous operators than himself, playing a small time bookie rubbed out by the mob. Occasionally, however, he could also be found on the side of good, as he was in Fox lavish Technicolor epic *Captain From*

Castile, as a Padre. In the 1950s his most interesting assignment came with the sports film *The Harlem Globetrotters*, which told the tale of the famous black basketball team and gave Gomez top billing as their team manager Abe Saperstein.

Screen: 1942: Sherlock Holmes and the Voice of Terror; Arabian Nights; Pittsburgh; Who Done It?; 1943: White Savage; Corvette K-225; Frontier Badmen; Crazy House; 1944: The Climax; Phantom Lady; Dead Man's Eyes; Follow the Boys; In Society; Bowery to Broadway; Can't Help Singing; 1945: Patrick the Great; I'll Tell the World; The Daltons Ride Again; Frisco Sal; 1946: A Night in Paradise; Swell Guy; 1947: Singapore; Ride the Pink Horse; Captain From Castile; Johnny O'Clock; 1948: Casbah; Angel in Exile; Key Largo; Force of Evil; 1949: Come to the Stable; Sorrowful Jones; That Midnight Kiss; The Woman on Pier 13/I Married a Communist; 1950: Kim; The Eagle and the Hawk; The Furies; 1951: Anne of the Indies; The Harlem Globetrotters; 1952: The Sellout; The Merry Widow; Macao; Pony Soldier; 1953: Sombrero; 1954: The Gambler From Natchez; The Adventures of Haji Baba; 1955: The Looters; The Magnificent Matador; Las Vegas Shakedown; Night Freight; 1956: Trapeze; The Conqueror; 1959: John Paul Jones; But Not for Me; 1961: Summer and Smoke; 1968: Stay Away, Joe; 1970: Beneath the Planet of the Apes.

NY Stage: 1925: Hamlet; 1928: Cyrano de Bergerac; 1929: Richelieu; 1936: Idiot's Delight; 1937: Robin Landing; Western Waters; 1938: The Sea Gull; 1940: There Shall Be No Night; The Taming of the Shrew; 1953: Sherlock Holmes; 1956: Cat on a Hot Tin Roof; 1960: The Visit; 1962: A Man for All Seasons.

Select TV: 1953: Life With Luigi (series); 1954: The Worthy Opponent (sp); 1955: The Great McGinty (sp); 1956: This Business of Murder (sp); Caesar and Cleopatra (sp); 1961: Power and the Glory (sp); 1968: Shadow Over Elveron.

LEO GORCEY

BORN: NEW YORK, NY, JUNE 3, 1915.
DIED: JUNE 2, 1969.

This runty, benign mug with the exaggerated "youse guys" dialect became the leader and center of attention of the long-running Dead End Kids/Bowery Boys comedies, spitting out his low-life slang, malapropisms, and disdainful asides until he had long outgrown his punk act. The son of actor Bernard Gorcey (who later acted in support of his son, as soda-shop owner Louie, in the same series), Leo was among the young teens who became the talk of Broadway by performing in Sidney Kingsley's searing glimpse at New York slum life, *Dead End*. He, along with his young co-stars, Billy Halop, Bobby Jordan, Bernard Punsley, Huntz Hall, and Gabriel Dell, came to Hollywood to appear in the slightly softened but nonetheless still-powerful 1937 Samuel Goldwyn production of the play, with Gorcey upped from his less-important stage role to that of Spit, the kid who rats on Halop. It wasn't unfair to say that Gorcey, like most of his youthful cast mates, had already appeared in the best film he'd ever get offered. The gang made such a splash that they were signed up by Warner Bros., dubbed The Dead End Kids, and reteamed for two more dramas with one of their *Dead End* co-stars, Humphrey Bogart, for *Crime School*, and another outstanding product, *Angels With Dirty Faces*, in which they played impressionable adolescents in awe of hoodlum James Cagney.

After three more films, the group left Warners and pretty much split up. Gorcey and Jordan ended up at Monogram, where they starred in a lighter series of entertainments under the name

The East Side Kids, featuring Gorcey as Muggs (his first appearance was in the second installment, *Boys of the City*). There were solo assignments for Gorcey outside of this programmer studio, such as MGM's *Born to Sing* and *Down in San Diego*, where his wisecracking, lowbrow persona could be quite funny. In time he took center stage of the East Side quickies, eventually rejoined by Huntz Hall as his comic sidekick. When that series was retired in 1945 with *Come Out Fighting*, Gorcey found himself under a new classification as one of The Bowery Boys, beginning with *Live Wires*. The budgets were just as paltry as the previous series, while the running times averaged about an hour. The humor continued to get broader and dopier, with an eye on the least sophisticated of moviegoers. By the 1950s, Gorcey's Brooklynese tough guy (now called Slip Mahoney) was losing his luster, while heavy drinking and a hellraising lifestyle were beginning to affect the actor's health. Too long-in-the-tooth to be considered much of a "Boy" anymore, he left the series in 1956 after *Crashing Las Vegas*. 14 years later, he and Hall made a fleeting appearance wearing their trademark Bowery Boys attire, in the bizarre comedy *The Phynx*, released after Gorcey's death. His brother, David Gorcey, had acted in some films with him but gave up the profession to join the clergy.

Screen: 1937: Dead End; Portia on Trial; Mannequin; Headin' East; 1938: Beloved Brat; Crime School; Angels With Dirty Faces; 1939: They Me Made a Criminal; Hell's Kitchen; The Angels Wash Their Faces; The Dead End Kids On Dress Parade; Private Detective; Invisible Stripes; 1940: Boys of the City; That Gang of Mine; Hullabaloo; Gallant Sons; 1941: Pride of the Bowery; Angels With Broken Wings; Flying Wild; Bowery Blitzkrieg; Out of the Fog; Down in San Diego; Road to Zanzibar; Spooks Run Wild; 1942: Mr. Wise Guy; Sunday Punch; Let's Get Tough; Smart Alecks; 'Neath Brooklyn Bridge; Born to Sing; Maisie Gets Her Man; 1943: Kid Dynamite; Clancy Street Boys; Ghosts on the Loose; Mr. Muggs Steps Out; Destroyer; 1944: Million Dollar Kid; Follow the Leader; Block Busters; Bowery Champs; 1945: One Exciting Night/Midnight Manhunt; Docks of New York; Mr. Muggs Rides Again; Come Out Fighting; 1946: Live Wires; In Fast Company; Bowery Bombshell; Spook Busters; Mr. Hex; 1947: Hard-Boiled Mahoney; News Hounds; Bowery Buckaroos; 1948: Angels' Alley; Jinx Money; So This Is New York; Smugglers' Cove; Trouble Makers; 1949: Fighting Fools; Hold That Baby!; Angels in Disguise; Master Minds; 1950: Blonde Dynamite; Lucky Losers; Triple Trouble; Blues Busters; 1951: Bowery Battalion; Ghost Chasers; Let's Go Navy; Crazy Over Horses; 1952: Hold That Line; Here Come the Marines; Feudin' Fools; No Holds Barred; 1953: Jalopy; Loose in London; Clipped Wings; Private Eyes; 1954: Paris Playboys; The Bowery Boys Meet the Monsters; Jungle Gents; 1955: Bowery to Bagdad; High Society; Jail Busters; Spy Chasers; 1956: Dig That Uranium; Crashing Las Vegas; 1963: It's a Mad Mad Mad Mad World; 1965: Second Fiddle to a Steel Guitar; 1970: The Phynx.

NY Stage: 1935: Dead End.

RUTH GORDON

(RUTH GORDON JONES) BORN: WOLLASTON, MA, OCTOBER 30, 1896. ED: AADA.
DIED: AUGUST 28, 1985.

Tiny, outspoken Ruth Gordon had at least one false start as a movie attraction, during which time she had earned her place as one of the preeminent theater actresses of her day. It looked as if she would become best known in Hollywood as a screenwriter, until she returned to films on the brink of 70 and became the movies' best-loved spunky old lady. She grew up in New England as the daughter of a retired sea captain (described in her 1946 stage memoir, *Years Ago*, and in the 1953 film version, *The Actress*) and made her professional debut in New York, in support of Maud Adams, in a 1915 production of *Peter Pan*. This was followed by such plays as *Serena Blandish*, *Saturday's Children*, *Here Today*, *They Shall Not Die*, and three in which she served as both writer and star, *Over 21*, *Leading Lady*, and *A Very Rich Woman*. Her first brush with movies came with bits in two silent films, *Camille* and *The Whirl of Life*, both released the year of her Broadway bow. Another 25 years passed before she was asked in front of the cameras again, to play the strong wives of two historical figures. In *Dr. Ehrlich's Magic Bullet* she was married to the bacteriologist who cured syphilis, and in *Abe Lincoln in Illinois* she created a memorably unsentimental Mary Lincoln. After a few more acting roles, including one in *Edge of Darkness*, which found her and another notable lady of the theater, Judith Anderson, playing Norwegian villagers battling the Nazis, she opted for screenwriting in collaboration with Garson Kanin, whom she had married in 1942. They received Oscar nominations for three of their four efforts: *A Double Life*, which brought Ronald Colman his Academy Award; the finest of the Spencer Tracy-Katharine Hepburn teamings, *Adam's Rib*; and *Pat and Mike*. Their fourth, *The Marrying Kind*, was a prime vehicle for Judy Holliday. Back onstage, Gordon had a great success playing Dolly Levi in Thornton Wilder's *The Matchmaker*.

Returning to the movies in 1965 (22 years after her last film), the actress promptly received an Oscar nomination for playing Natalie Wood's dotty old mom in *Inside Daisy Clover*. Her clever performance in the gothic classic *Rosemary's Baby*, as the nosey next-door neighbor who just happens to be a witch, was a triumph in every way, earning her an Academy Award as Best Supporting Actress of 1968 and landing her three sizable roles as follow-ups. *Whatever Happened to Aunt Alice?* found her investigating the mysterious murders of sinister Geraldine Page's former housekeepers; *Where's Poppa?*, a hit-or-miss black comedy, required her to annoyingly repeat the title query as George Segal's senile mom; and *Harold and Maude* had her sharing a bed with 20-year-old Bud Cort. After a disappointing initial run, the last of the trio became one of the genuine cult favorites of the 1970s, recognized as one of the most satisfying black comedies of all time, and was considered by many, including the lady herself, to be the finest role of Gordon's movie career. There was a telefilm follow-up to her Oscar role, *Look What's Happened to Rosemary's Baby*, and then she played wacky old biddies ad nauseam, including those in the lowbrow Clint Eastwood comedies *Every Which Way But Loose* and *Any Which Way You Can*, where she gave the co-starring orangutan a run for its money in the mugging department. There were gentler roles in *My Bodyguard*, as Chris Makepeace's understanding grandmother, and in *Boardwalk*, top billed along with Lee Strasberg, as an elderly couple facing the decline of their urban neighborhood. There was one last leading role, in a barely distributed comedy called, alternately, *Mugsy's Girls* and *Delta Pi*, as an old dame in charge of a group of mud-wrestlers, which must be looked upon as something of a comedown from playing Mary Lincoln. In 1980 she and Kanin collaborated on the script of a TV movie, *Hardhat and Legs*. Gordon wrote three other volumes of memoirs, *Myself Among Others* (1971), *My Side* (1976), and *An Open Book* (1980), as well as a novel, *Shady Lady* (1982).

Screen: 1915: Camille; The Wheel of Life; 1940: Dr. Ehrlich's Magic Bullet; Abe Lincoln in Illinois; 1941: Two-Faced Woman; 1943: Edge of Darkness; Action in the North Atlantic; 1965: Inside Daisy Clover; 1966: Lord Love a Duck; 1968: Rosemary's Baby; 1969: Whatever Happened to Aunt Alice?; 1970: Where's Poppa?; 1971: Harold and Maude; 1976: The Big Bus; 1978: Every Which Way But Loose; 1979: Boardwalk; Scavenger Hunt; 1980: My Bodyguard; Any Which Way You Can; 1983: Jimmy the Kid; 1985: Delta Pi/Mugsy's Girls; Maxie; 1987: The Trouble With Spies; 1988: Voyage of the Rock Aliens (dtv).

NY Stage: 1915: Peter Pan; 1918: Seventeen; 1923: Tweedles; 1925: Mrs. Partridge Presents; The Fall of Eve; 1927: Saturday's Children; 1929: Serena Blandish; Lady Fingers; 1930: Hotel Universe; The Violet; 1931: The Wiser They Are; A Church Mouse; 1932: Here Today; 1933: Three-Cornered Moon; 1934: They Shall Not Die; A Sleeping Clergyman; 1936: The Country Wife; Ethan Frome; 1937: A Doll's House; 1942: The Strings My Lord Are False; The Three Sisters; 1944: Over 21 (and wr.); 1948: Leading Lady (and wr.); 1949: The Smile of the World; 1954: The Matchmaker; 1960: The Good Soup; 1963: My Mother, My Father and Me; 1965: A Very Rich Woman (and wr.); 1966: The Loves of Cass McGuire; 1974: Dreyfus in Rehearsal; 1976: Mrs. Warren's Profession.

Select TV: 1950: Over 21 (sp); 1973: Isn't It Shocking?; 1976: The Great Houdini; Look What's Happened to Rosemary's Baby; 1977: The Prince of Central Park; 1978: Perfect Gentlemen; 1982: Don't Go to Sleep.

MICHAEL GOUGH

BORN: MALAYA, INDIA, NOVEMBER 23, 1917. ED: ROSE HILL SCHOOL, KENT, ENGLAND; OLD VIC SCHOOL.

A gaunt, mean-looking, British character actor with a very carefully modulated voice, Michael Gough (rhymes with "cough") debuted professionally with the Old Vic in 1936. 11 years later he made his film debut in the 1947 soaper *Blanche Fury*, marrying reluctant governess Valerie Hobson. His sinister manner and dispiriting tone of voice soon equated him with U.K. horror films, such as the Hammer version of the classic vampire legend *Horror of Dracula*, where he joined Peter Cushing in battling the bloodsucker; *Horrors of the Black Museum*, as an evil journalist, hypnotizing his assistant to commit murder; and in the unintentionally funny *Konga*, where he was carried around London by a rampaging giant gorilla. After a while this genre became his bread and butter, with *What a Carve Up!/ No Place Like a Homicide*, a spoof of thrillers, as a club-footed butler in the requisite old dark house; the 1962 remake of *The Phantom of the Opera*, as the evil impresario who steals Herbert Lom's music; *Black Zoo*, at his scenery-chewing worst as an animal worshipper, clad in a kitschy tiger-print robe, who uses his powers over the critters to dispose of his enemies; *Dr. Terror's House of Horrors*, where his severed hand terrorized art critic Christopher Lee; two Joan Crawford clinkers, *Berserk* and *Trog*; *Horror Hospital*, as the disfigured head of a health clinic; and *Satan's Slave*, as an evil sorcerer. During this reign of terror, he was called on every now and then to give support in some non-horrific "A" fare like *Women in Love*, *The Dresser*, and *Out of Africa*. In 1989 he found himself reaching his largest American audience yet when he was cast as the loyal butler, Alfred Pennyworth, in the smash hit *Batman*, returning to the part for three sequels. He won a 1979 Tony Award for his role in the Broadway comedy *Bedroom Farce*.

Screen: 1947: Blanche Fury; 1948: Anna Karenina; Bond Street; Saraband for Dead Lovers; 1949: The Small Black Room/Hour of Glory; 1950: Blackmailed; Ha'penny Breeze; 1951: No Resting Place; The Man in the White Suit; Night Was Our Friend; 1953: Twice Upon a Time; Rob Roy, The Highland Rogue; The Sword and the Rose; 1955: Richard III; 1956: Reach for the Sky; 1957: Night Ambush/Ill Met by Moonlight; 1958: Horror of Dracula/Dracula; 1959: The Horse's Mouth; The House in the Woods; Model for Murder; Horrors of the Black Museum; 1961: Konga; I Like Money/Mr. Topaze; 1962: Home Sweet Homicide/What a Carve Up!; Candidate for Murder; The Phantom of the Opera; 1963: Black Zoo; 1964: Tamahine; Game for Three Losers; 1965: Dr. Terror's House of Horrors; The Skull; 1967: They Came From Outer Space; Berserk; 1968: Crimson Cult; One Night … A Train (nUSr); 1969: A Walk With Love and Death; 1970: Women in Love; Trog; The Corpse; 1971: Julius Caesar; The Go-Between; 1973: Horror Hospital; The Legend of Hell House; 1975: Galileo; 1976: Satan's Slave; 1978: The Boys From Brazil; 1979: L'amour en Question/A Question of Love (nUSr); 1982: Venom; 1983: The Dresser; 1984: Top Secret!; Oxford Blues; 1985: Out of Africa; 1986: Caravaggio; 1987: Memed My Hawk (filmed 1984); The Fourth Protocol; 1988: The Serpent and the Rainbow; 1989: Batman; 1990: Strapless; The Garden (narrator); 1991: Let Him Have It; 1992: Batman Returns; Little Nemo: Adventures in Slumberland (voice); 1993: Wittgenstein; The Age of Innocence; 1994: The Advocate/Hour of the Pig; Nostradamus; A Village Affair (nUSr); Uncovered (nUSr); 1995: Batman Forever; 1997: Batman and Robin; 1998: What Rats Won't Do (dtv); 1999: St. Ives (nUSr); Sleepy Hollow; 2002: The Cherry Orchard.

NY Stage: 1937: Love of Women; 1959: The Fighting Cock; 1979: Bedroom Farce; 1987: Breaking the Code.

Select TV: 1972: The Six Wives of Henry VIII; The Search for the Nile (ms); The Man Who Came to Dinner (sp); 1974: QB VII (ms); 1982: Brideshead Revisited (ms); Inside the Third Reich (ms); 1984: Mistral's Daughter (ms); 1985: Lace II; 1989: After the War (ms); The Shell Seekers; 1991: The Wanderer; Sleepers (ms); 1995: The Haunting of Helen Walker; 1996: Young Indiana Jones: Travels with Father.

BETTY GRABLE

(Ruth Elizabeth Grasle) Born: St. Louis, MO, December 18, 1916. ed: Mary St., Hollywood Professional School. Died: June 27, 1973.

Her name instantly evokes a bygone era — World War II, when pinup girls could capture a soldier's fancy with nothing more revealing than a shapely pair of legs. Betty Grable herself was the first to admit that those appendages of hers were her fortune, and indeed it is very difficult today to see what else could have made her the hottest female box-office attraction of the 1940s. Her acting was little more than perfunctory, and her singing voice wasn't memorable. There were certainly better looking stars and more-adept dancers. Perhaps it was nothing more than her lack of pretentiousness and her uncomplicated dependability that made audiences feel comfortable. It was certainly not an instant love affair, since Grable was in features for an entire decade before stardom hit. She had come to Los Angeles as a teen, accompanied by her mother, who had hoped to see her achieve something as a dancer. At the age of 14, she made her film debut for Fox, the studio over which she would later reign, in a blackface number in *Let's Go Places*, in 1930. For the next few years she popped up in some Educational Pictures shorts (billed as "Frances Dean") while continuing in chorus parts and bits, most memorably a duet with Edward Everett Horton, "Let's K-nock K-nees," in the Astaire-Rogers vehicle *The Gay Divorcee*, which won her a contract with RKO in 1934. She had some bigger roles, playing a co-ed in *Old Man*

Rhythm, one of the many campus musicals of the time, and, on loan to Paramount, in *Collegiate*, which was more of the same. In 1937, still not very well known, she married former child star Jackie Coogan, and around that time, Paramount signed her up, figuring to give her a try. She did supporting work for them in *College Swing*, which put Burns and Allen and Bob Hope in the spotlight, and in Hope's *Give Me a Sailor*. Prior to those, she got pushed into the lead in a "B," *This Way Please*, when Shirley Ross dropped out, but she had to take billing under the Yacht Boys for another musical, *Thrill of a Lifetime*, cast as the love interest of Leif Erickson. There was another starring role, in *Campus Confessions*, yet another college comedy, in which she was cast as a reporter, and in *Million Dollar Legs*, which might have referred to her attributes or to the school basketball team, depending on who appealed to you more. Coogan appeared with her in the latter film, a year before they divorced (1940). Real stardom, however, seemed to be out of her grasp, so she went to Broadway after the studio dropped her, appearing in *DuBarry Was a Lady*, taking the second lead to Ethel Merman.

Because of this show, 20th Century-Fox expressed interest in making her a star and did so by casting her in a Technicolor musical originally designed for Alice Faye, *Down Argentine Way*. Gaudy and unmemorable, it did good business and set the ball rolling. As a follow-up, she partnered with Faye in the better *Tin Pan Alley*, which was in black and white, and then did *Moon Over Miami*, which, like *Down Argentine Way*, featured Don Ameche. There was a break for some straight films, *A Yank in the RAF*, where she played a chorus girl, and therefore still got to sing, and the memorably titled *I Wake Up Screaming*, where she tried to find out who killed her sister, Carole Landis. Then it was back to the color extravaganzas with *Song of the Islands*, the only novelty being its South Seas setting, and *Springtime in the Rockies*, her first time getting top billing in a Fox extravaganza. These look-alike entertainments are something of a chore to get through today with trite plots, heavy-handed direction, uninteresting leading men, sometimes tastelessly staged numbers, and Grable's often abrasive nature, always pouting and playing hard to get, as if that sort of thing made her endearing. *Coney Island* was a marginal improvement over, say, *Billy Rose's Diamond Horseshoe* (though this one had one of the biggest hits to come from a Grable opus, "The More I See You"), while *The Shocking Miss Pilgrim* at least offered some newly uncovered Gershwin songs, as well as a twist of feminism to the plot about a groundbreaking lady typist. To cash in on her famous over-the-shoulder pinup, there was, of course, one called *Pin Up Girl*, with its endless all-women army drill finale, and then a biopic pairing her with an even less-exciting blonde, June Haver, *The Dolly Sisters*, which was poor even by these standards. Criticism be damned, these films made money, so Fox must have been doing something right.

In the postwar era, a genuinely nice film emerged, *Mother Wore Tights*, a period piece that also benefited from a talented co-star, Dan Dailey. It was Dailey, in fact, who easily stole the show in their follow-up, *When My Baby Smiles at Me*, as her alcoholic burlesque partner. In the meantime, two Grable vehicles attempted to present her in a different light: *That Lady in Ermine*, a costume picture set in a mythical kingdom, started by Ernst Lubitsch and finished by Otto Preminger when the former died, and the Preston Sturges western spoof *The Beautiful Blonde of Bashful Bend*, a tired movie that the once-great director made during his declining years. Fox was running out of ideas, which was evident when the 1950 production *Wabash Avenue* turned out to be a remake of the seven-year-old *Coney Island*. She and Dailey were together again for the gooey *My Blue Heaven*, which included another up-and-coming musical star on the studio roster, Mitzi Gaynor. Fox bought the rights to a Broadway hit, *Call Me Mister*, for the Grable-Dailey combo, but like too many adaptations of the time, it bore little resemblance to what audiences had enjoyed onstage. By the early 1950s the sparkle was fading fast, so the studio teamed her up with Lauren Bacall and its newest attraction, Marilyn Monroe, in the enjoyable *How to Marry a Millionaire*, which only emphasized that Grable, despite top billing, lacked all the know-how that the other two women had possessed since birth. Despite the enormous success of *Millionaire*, she only did one more film for Fox, the badly received *How to Be Very, Very Popular*, following a mediocre loan-out to Columbia, *Three for the Show*. With no further offers on the horizon, she chose to do Vegas with her latest husband (1945–65) Harry James, and some touring in regional theaters. She had one final moment of glory as one of the replacement Dollys in *the* Broadway smash of the 1960s, *Hello, Dolly!*, and then faded back into the memories of millions of Americans to whom she had meant so much during a turbulent yet more innocent period.

Screen: 1930: Let's Go Places; Happy Days; New Movietone Follies of 1930; Whoopee; 1931: Kiki; Palmy Days; 1932: The Greeks Had a Word for Them; The Kid From Spain; Probation; Hold 'em Jail; The Age of Consent; 1933: Cavalcade; Child of Manhattan; What Price Innocence?; Melody Cruise; Sweetheart of Sigma Chi; 1934: Student Tour; The Gay Divorcee; Hips Hips Hooray!; By Your Leave; 1935: The Nitwits; Old Man Rhythm; 1936: Collegiate; Follow the Fleet; Don't Turn 'em Loose; Pigskin Parade; 1937: This Way Please; Thrill of a Lifetime; 1938: College Swing; Give Me a Sailor; Campus Confessions; 1939: Man About Town; Million Dollar Legs; The Day the Bookies Wept; 1940: Down Argentine Way; Tin Pan Alley; 1941: Moon Over Miami; A Yank in the RAF; I Wake Up Screaming; 1942: Song of the Islands; Footlight Serenade; Springtime in the Rockies; 1943: Coney Island; Sweet Rosie O'Grady; 1944: Four Jills in a Jeep; Pin Up Girl; 1945: Billy Rose's Diamond Horseshoe; The Dolly Sisters; 1946: Do You Love Me?; 1947: The Shocking Miss Pilgrim; Mother Wore Tights; 1948: That Lady in Ermine; When My Baby Smiles at Me; 1949: The Beautiful Blonde From Bashful Bend; 1950: Wabash Avenue; My Blue Heaven; 1951: Call Me Mister; Meet Me After the Show; 1953: The Farmer Takes a Wife; How to Marry a Millionaire; 1955: Three for the Show; How to Be Very, Very Popular.

NY Stage: 1939: Du Barry Was a Lady; 1967: Hello, Dolly!
Select TV: 1956: Cleopatra Collins (sp); Twentieth Century (sp).

GLORIA GRAHAME

(GLORIA HALLWARD) BORN: LOS ANGELES, CA, NOVEMBER 28, 1925. DIED: OCTOBER 5, 1981.

With her pouting upper lip and an arched brow that could speak volumes, Gloria Grahame was just about the sexiest thing to come along in the 1940s. She also happened to be a terrific actress who could play sweet, cunning, dumb, brash, or pathetic with equal aplomb. The daughter of stage actress Jean Grahame, she made her theatre debut with the Pasadena Playhouse, at the age of nine, in a production of *The Bluebird*, and ultimately made it to Broadway in 1943, as an understudy to Miriam Hopkins in *The Skin of Our Teeth*. Two flop plays followed, but it didn't matter, since she'd already been spotted by an MGM talent agent who signed her to a studio contract. There were small parts in *Blonde Fever*, as a waitress giving Philip Dorn that malady, and Tracy and Hepburn's *Without Love*, as a flower girl; a brief marriage (1945–48) to actor Stanley

Clements; and a memorable bit for Frank Capra in *It's a Wonderful Life*, as good-time gal Violet, who is arrested for her loose ways in James Stewart's vision of the world without him. The next year her career really began to cook after she played a cheap dance-hall floozie questioned by the police in RKO's powerful *Crossfire*, a performance good enough to earn her an Oscar nomination. Back at MGM, she was upped to second billing for the Red Skelton comedy *Merton of the Movies*, playing a temperamental actress, after which she married (1948–52) director Nicholas Ray. From this union came parts in his *A Woman's Secret*, as a tramp trained to be a singer by Maureen O'Hara, and *In a Lonely Place*, perfectly matched with Humphrey Bogart, as the compassionate neighbor who tries to break through his near-pathological fits of anger. She had a banner year in 1952, first with the Oscar winner for Best Picture, *The Greatest Show on Earth*, which required her to rest her head under an elephant's foot, as a showgirl who drives partner Lyle Bettger to jealousy; then with *Sudden Fear*, where she was at her bitchiest, scheming with Jack Palance to bump off Joan Crawford; and, finally, with director Vincente Minnelli's sharp look at Hollywood, *The Bad and the Beautiful*. She didn't show up in the last one until well into the film, but her performance as Dick Powell's perky Southern wife was liked enough to win her the Academy Award for Best Supporting Actress.

Despite this coveted accolade, she still wasn't considered worthy of carrying a film on her own, taking second billing in *The Glass Wall*, helping Vittorio Gassman run from the immigration authorities, and in *Man on a Tightrope*, cheating on husband Fredric March. She did get one of her best parts ever at this point, as Lee Marvin's unfortunate moll, ending up with hot coffee heaved in her face and reciprocating in kind, in director Fritz Lang's top-notch noir *The Big Heat*. There was a lesser follow-up, which also featured Glenn Ford, with Lang at the helm, *Human Desire*, and a junky costumer that gave her star billing, *Prisoners of the Casbah*. She had another floozie role, as the nightclub singer sheltering her criminal lover (Gene Barry) from cop Sterling Hayden, in *Naked Alibi*. In 1955 she showed up in some higher-profile projects, starting with the all-star mental institution dud, *The Cobweb*, as the unhappy wife of doctor Richard Widmark, fighting with him over a pair of window drapes. In *Not as a Stranger*, she was a bored widow dallying with Robert Mitchum, and she did a delightful turn as the sexed-up Ado Annie in the Rodgers and Hammerstein musical *Oklahoma!*, a part she had balked at doing when first offered it. Sadly, her career began to lose its footing. She received a rare barrage of bad reviews for the made-in-England *The Man Who Never Was*; and slipped down the cast list for the heist drama *Odds Against Tomorrow*; while only her most ardent followers could distinguish *Ride Out for Revenge* from *Ride Beyond Vengeance*. During the 1960s, she spent a good deal of her time raising her family. Later she appeared in a horror quickie, *Blood and Lace*, and then did small parts in *Chilly Scenes of Winter*, as John Heard's suicidal mother, and the Oscar-winning *Melvin and Howard*, thoroughly wasted as Mary Steenburgen's mom. She had divorced Nicholas Ray in 1952, married (1954–57) director Cy Howard, and then raised a few eyebrows when she wed the man who had been her stepson while married to Ray.

Screen: 1944: Blonde Fever; 1945: Without Love; 1946: It's a Wonderful Life; 1947: It Happened in Brooklyn; Crossfire; Song of the Thin Man; Merton of the Movies; 1949: A Woman's Secret; Roughshod; 1950: In a Lonely Place; 1952: The Greatest Show on Earth; Macao; Sudden Fear; The Bad and the Beautiful; 1953: The Glass Wall; Man on a Tightrope; East of Sumatra; The Big Heat; Prisoner of the Casbah; 1954: Human Desire; The

Naked Alibi; **1955:** The Good Die Young; The Cobweb; Not as a Stranger; Oklahoma!; **1956:** The Man Who Never Was; **1957:** Ride Out for Revenge; **1959:** Odds Against Tomorrow; **1965:** Ride Beyond Vengeance; **1971:** Blood and Lace; The Todd Killings; **1972:** Chandler; The Loners; **1974:** Tarots; **1975:** Mama's Dirty Girls; **1976:** Mansion of the Doomed/Eyes; **1979:** Head Over Heels/Chilly Scenes of Winter; **1980:** Melvin and Howard; **1981:** The Nesting; A Nightingale Sang in Berkeley Square/The Big Scam (UK: 1979; dtv).

NY Stage: AS GLORIA HALLWARD: **1943:** The World Is Full of Girls; **1944:** A Highland Fling.

Select TV: **1970:** Escape; **1971:** Black Noon; **1974:** The Girl on the Late, Late Show; **1976:** Rich Man, Poor Man (ms); **1977:** Seventh Avenue (ms); **1981:** Mr. Griffin and Me.

FARLEY GRANGER

BORN: SAN JOSE, CA, JULY 1, 1925.

Never a great threat to the scores of more forceful actors of the postwar years, Farley Granger was an attractive-looking performer who could bring a certain conviction to some roles, while grossly overestimating his abilities in others. He stepped into movies directly out of college with Samuel Goldwyn's pro-Russia war film, *The North Star*, as Anne Baxter's boyfriend. Following military service he ended up in two impressive films, Alfred Hitchcock's experimental *Rope*, as John Dall's fellow killer and nervous lover, and, more significantly, Nicholas Ray's *They Drive by Night*, as a young man forced deeper into criminal activities, in a critically lauded performance. Because of these, Goldwyn made sure he put Granger under contract, but those pictures the actor made for the producer, including *Roseanna McCoy*, loving Joan Evans despite his family's feud with her brood, and *Edge of Doom*, wanted for murdering a priest, were hardly hot box office. Instead, Granger was luckier on loan to MGM, where he did a decent thriller set in New York, *Side Street*, as a financially strapped husband who gets into trouble with gangsters after turning to robbery. The Goldwyn properties he did that fared better with the public, the Ann Blyth soap opera, *Our Very Own*, and the Danny Kaye musical, *Hans Christian Andersen*, with Granger as a gratingly unpleasant ballet impresario, did not spotlight the young star.

Meanwhile RKO borrowed him for a farce, *Behave Yourself!*, which only went to prove that he was completely ill at ease in this genre. It was Hitchcock who gave him the film he would earn the most attention for, the smashing *Strangers on a Train*, as the appropriately rattled young tennis player who gets trapped in a deadly alliance with psychotic homosexual Robert Walker. He did two unsuccessful episode films, *O. Henry's Full House*, in a poorly executed version of that author's best-loved story, "The Gift of the Magi," and *The Story of Three Loves*, in the "Mademoiselle" segment with Leslie Caron, as a grown-up version of Ricky Nelson. Accepting an offer from Italian director Lucino Visconti, he received admirable notices for his work in *Senso*, as a selfish Austrian soldier. After playing an unappealing playboy in the Jane Powell musical *Small Town Girl*, and killer Harry Thaw in *The Girl in the Red Velvet Swing*, he took the hint that Hollywood was losing interest and confined himself to the stage for the next decade. His subsequent movie career consisted almost exclusively of foreign-made products that nobody bothered to import to America; blink-and-you-miss-'em efforts of little interest to anyone; and television films.

Screen: **1943:** The North Star/Armored Attack; **1944:** The Purple Heart; **1948:** Rope; Enchantment; **1949:** They Live by Night; Roseanna McCoy; Side Street; **1950:** Our Very Own; Edge of Doom; **1951:** Strangers on a Train; Behave Yourself!; I Want You; **1952:** O. Henry's Full House; Hans Christian Andersen; **1953:** The Story of Three Loves; Small Town Girl; **1954:** Senso/The Wanton Contessa; **1955:** The Naked Street; The Girl in the Red Velvet Swing; **1968:** Rogue's Gallery; **1970:** Qualcosa Striscia nel Buio/Something Is Crawling in the Dark (nUSr); **1971:** They Call Me Trinity; **1972:** La Rossa dalla pelle che Scotta/The Red Headed Corpse/Sweet Spirits (nUSr); **1973:** Arnold; The Man Called Noon; The Serpent/Night Flight From Moscow; **1974:** Savage Lady/Death Shall Have Your Eyes; **1975:** The Slasher/Revelations of a Sex Maniac; **1978:** Amuck/Leather and Whips (filmed 1972); **1980:** The Co-Ed Murders/The Police Want Help; **1981:** The Prowler; **1984:** Deathmask; **1986:** Very Close Quarters (dtv); The Imagemaker; **1996:** The Celluloid Closet; **2001:** The Next Big Thing (nUSr).

NY Stage: **1955:** The Carefree Tree (ob); **1959:** First Impressions; The Warm Peninsula; **1960:** The King and I; **1962:** Brigadoon; **1964:** The Seagull; The Crucible; **1965:** The Glass Menagerie; **1979:** Sweet Main Street (ob); A Month in the Country (ob); **1981:** Deathtrap; **1984:** Outward Bound (ob); **1985:** Tally & Son (ob).

Select TV: **1955:** Incident in an Alley (sp); **1956:** Caesar and Cleopatra (sp); Seidman and Son (sp); **1957:** The Bottle Imp (sp); Circle of Fear (sp); The Clouded Image (sp); Beyond This Place (sp); Come to Me (sp); **1958:** The Hidden River (sp); The Wound Within (sp); **1960:** Arrowsmith (sp); **1961:** The Prisoner of Zenda (sp); The Heiress (sp); **1967:** Blind Man's Bluff (sp); **1968:** Laura (sp); **1969:** The Challengers; **1972:** The Lives of Jenny Dolan; **1976:** Widow; **1976–77:** One Life to Live (series); **1977:** Seventh Avenue (ms); **1978:** Black Beauty; **1986–87:** As the World Turns (series).

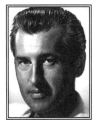

STEWART GRANGER

(JAMES LABLANCHE STEWART) BORN: LONDON, ENGLAND, MAY 6, 1913. ED: EPSOM COL., WEBBER-DOUGLAS SCH. OF DRAMATIC ART. DIED: AUGUST 16, 1993.

The suave Stewart Granger sounded and behaved as if he would be better suited for drawing room comedies, lounging about in a smoking jacket, swilling martinis, and making bedroom eyes at the ladies. Instead he became almost exclusively associated with costume romps and adventure films. Indeed, it is as difficult to picture him in a suit and tie, as it is to *not* picture him in the jungle or some exotic locale, wearing a panama hat and toting a rifle, or slashing a rapier in period clothing. After he completed his schooling, he did extra work and stage roles in rep before making his London debut in *Autumn*, in 1937. Two years later he got his official film career rolling with a supporting part in the comedy *So This Is London*, as the juvenile second lead to comedians Alfred Drayton and Robertson Hare. When World War II began, he joined the military but was soon wounded, so it was back to the movies, where, in 1943, he made his first impression in the lush Gainsbourgh melodrama *The Man in Grey*, as an actor scheming Margaret Lockwood hopes will take Phyllis Calvert away from James Mason. It was for this studio that Granger made such other romantic dramas as *Fanny by Gaslight*, bringing together most of the cast of that first hit, minus Lockwood; and *Love Story*, going blind and falling for Lockwood, who was counting the days to her demise. There was also *The Magic Bow*, a biopic of Paganini, and the kitschy *Madonna of the Seven Moons*, in which Granger was about as convincing an Italian as the rest of the British cast.

Amid these he participated in England's most lavish production of the time, *Caesar and Cleopatra*, as Apollodorous. The film was a break from his other critically reviled properties, though it too received its share of pans. After Gainsborough, he continued in florid melodramas like *Blanche Fury*, trying to claim Valerie Hobson's estate and ending up on the end of a hangman's rope, and *Saraband for Dead Lovers*, having a doomed affair with Joan Greenwood. In 1949 he tried light comedy with *Woman Hater* and *Adam and Evelyne/Adam and Evalyn*, the latter introducing him to Jean Simmons, who became his wife in 1950.

That same year the two of them came to Hollywood, and Granger hit it big the first time out with the rousing African adventure *King Solomon's Mines*. He was a solid hero, and the movie not only made lots of money but also received an Oscar nomination for Best Picture. Signed up by MGM, he was immediately put into a series of adventures, none of which did half as well as *King Solomon*, including *Soldiers Three*, from a Kipling story; *The Wild North*, in which he played a fur trapper; the zippy swashbuckler *Scaramouche*, probably the most enjoyable of all his films; the remake of *The Prisoner of Zenda*, where he was no match for the original's Ronald Colman; and *Young Bess*, where he once again appeared with Simmons. Over at Columbia, he was in the grotesque Biblical spectacle, *Salome*, as Rita Hayworth's boring lover, and then he went back to MGM for *All the Brothers Were Valiant*, as a whaler; *Beau Brummell*, as the famous dandy; and the made-in-Britain *Moonfleet*, a costly box-office disappointment. *Bhowani Junction*, with Ava Gardner, did decent business, but an attempt at comedy for the both of them, *The Little Hut*, showed that they were not in the same class as their co-star, David Niven. Granger tried some westerns, *The Last Hunt* and *Gun Glory*, and then went back to the jungle for *Harry Black and the Tiger*, before taking star billing (but a supporting role) in a prime John Wayne picture, *North to Alaska*, his last film credit worth discussing. It was released in 1960, the same year he and Simmons split. Since there was little interest anymore from Hollywood, he went overseas for such non-events as *Sodom and Gomorrah*, *The Secret Invasion*, and *The Last Safari*, barely hiding his boredom. Returning to America, he became a TV series star with *The Men From Shiloh*, and, when seen back on the big screen, it was in a small role in *The Wild Geese*. Following some more telefilms, he made his long-delayed Broadway debut, opposite Glynis Johns and Rex Harrison, in a 1989 production of *The Circle*, receiving a Theatre World Award. But one wonders how fulfilling his career could have been; he was once quoted as saying he wasn't proud of a single film he'd ever done. His autobiography, *Sparks Fly Upward*, was published in 1981.

Screen: 1933: A Southern Maid; 1934: Give Her a Ring; Over the Garden Wall; 1939: So This Is London; 1940: Convoy; 1942: Secret Mission; 1943: Thursday's Child; The Man in Grey; The Lamp Still Burns; 1944: Fanny by Gaslight; Love Story/A Lady Surrenders; Madonna of the Seven Moons; Waterloo Road; 1945: Caesar and Cleopatra; 1946: Caravan; The Magic Bow; 1947: Captain Boycott; 1948: Blanche Fury; Saraband for Dead Lovers; Woman Hater; 1949: Adam and Evelyne/Adam and Evalyn; 1950: King Solomon's Mines; 1951: Soldiers Three; The Light Touch; 1952: The Wild North; Scaramouche; The Prisoner of Zenda; 1953: Salome; Young Bess; All the Brothers Were Valiant; 1954: Beau Brummell; Green Fire; 1955: Moonfleet; Footsteps in the Fog; 1956: Bhowani Junction; The Last Hunt; 1957: The Little Hut; Gun Glory; 1958: The Whole Truth; Harry Black and the Tiger; 1960: North to Alaska; 1961: The Secret Partner; 1962: Swordsman of Siena; 1963: Sodom and Gomorrah; I Giorno piu Corto/The Shortest Day (nUSr); 1964: The Secret Invasion; Commando (Sp: 1962); 1965: The Crooked Road; 1966: Frontier

Hellcat; Rampage at Apache Wells; Target for Killing (nUSr); 1967: Requiem for a Secret Agent (nUSr); Red Dragon/Code Name Alpha; Killer's Carnival (nUSr); The Last Safari; 1968: Flaming Frontier/Old Surehand; 1969: The Trygon Factor; 1978: The Wild Geese; 1987: Hell Hunters (dtv).
NY Stage: 1989: The Circle.
Select TV: 1969: Any Second Now; 1970–71: The Men From Shiloh (series); 1972: The Hound of the Baskervilles; 1982: The Royal Romance of Charles and Diana; 1986: Crossings (ms); 1987: A Hazard of Hearts; 1989: Chameleons; 1990: Fine Gold.

CARY GRANT

(ARCHIBALD ALEXANDER LEACH)
BORN: BRISTOL, ENGLAND, JANUARY 18, 1904.
DIED: NOVEMBER 29, 1986.

The impact that handsome, charming, peerless Cary Grant made on acting is such that performers are still being compared to him whenever they attempt light comedy. Although he was no slouch as a dramatic actor, it is in comedy that he was and still is most loved. His acting deftly combined self-deprecating humor with a smooth, gentlemanly air, and it must have been hard to do, because it looks so effortless. Unlike his screen image, he was born in less-than-classy surroundings, escaping his poor home to join a group of acrobats, whose journeys took them to the U.S. Returning to England, he began getting jobs onstage and found himself back on this side of the Atlantic when he came to Broadway for the 1927 musical *Golden Dawn*. Still billed under his real name, he did a few more plays, including *Nikki*, where he was inspired to change his name after playing a character called "Cary Lockwood." Around this time, he made his film debut, in a one-reel short made in New York, "Singapore Sue." This led to a contract with Paramount, for whom he made his first appearance as "Cary Grant," fifth billed in *This Is the Night*, as the javelin-throwing husband of philandering Thelma Todd. He remained in support for a while and then got to play opposite some of the studio's top actresses. In *Blonde Venus*, he was a millionaire who nearly stole Marlene Dietrich away from dull scientist husband Herbert Marshall, and, in a songless *Madame Butterfly*, he played Lieutenant Pinkerton, opposite Sylvia Sidney. Most important was *She Done Him Wrong*, where he was the mission worker ensnared by Mae West, who coaxed him with one of the great come-on lines in cinema history, "Come up some time and see me." This film was such a hit that West asked for Grant again for her immediate follow-up, *I'm No Angel*, which was a better movie and even more popular. It was tough to register against the irrepressible West though, so for a time, he just went on working like any other contract player, not yet considered the important star that he would become later on.

Among the films that kept him busy throughout the early 1930s were *The Eagle and the Hawk*, as the aviation buddy who saves Fredric March's reputation; *Alice in Wonderland*, masked as the Mock Turtle; *Gambling Ship*, top billed for the first time; *Thirty Day Princess*, as a newspaper publisher who thinks he's in love with royalty (Sylvia Sidney again); and *Wings in the Dark*, as a pilot who loses his sight. Before his contract was up, he was borrowed by RKO for *Sylvia Scarlett*, which marked his first and least-liked teaming with Katharine Hepburn, and by MGM for *Suzy*, which became notable again years later via the documentary *That's Entertainment!*, because of the scene where he sings "Did I Remember?" to Jean Harlow. A trip to England in 1936, to make *Romance and Riches*, was ill advised, but when he returned to Hollywood, he was about to embark on the beginning of his three-decade reign as one of the cinema's top attractions. The first comedy to do the trick was *Topper*, in which he and Constance Bennett were friendly ghosts trying to help Roland Young put some zest into his drab life. This was followed by the Oscar-winning *The Awful Truth*, in which he traded insults marvelously with estranged wife Irene Dunne until good sense brought them back together again. Then came two with Hepburn, *Bringing Up Baby*, a strong contender for the funniest comedy of the screwball era and indeed among the greatest of all farces, with Grant as a timid, bespectacled professor mixed up with a scatterbrain heiress, a feisty leopard, and a precious dinosaur bone; and the classy *Holiday*, with the actor as a nonconformist who finds a kindred soul in Hepburn just as he is about to marry her sister. He followed these with two adventure films, *Gunga Din* and *Only Angels Have Wings*; wisely, both movies had a good amount of humor sprinkled in, so the witty side of Grant was still in evidence. The former was especially popular and became one of the most influential and lauded of all such pictures of the studio era. The latter found him playing the sort of tough-talking, cynical man of independence and action that was more suited to Clark Gable. The year was rounded out by one that turned out to be something of a missed opportunity, *In Name Only*. Somebody had the great idea of putting him opposite Carole Lombard, but then made a film that was little more than a passable soap opera.

Nonetheless, he was on a roll, and he knocked off three sparkling comedies in one year, 1940. *His Girl Friday* was a masterpiece of precision comic timing with Grant delivering dialogue at machine-gun speed in this remake of *The Front Page*, with Rosalind Russell matching him line for line as his ex. In *My Favorite Wife*, he was back again with Dunne, as a presumed-widower now remarried, only to have his first spouse show up alive; and in the stagy-but-smart *The Philadelphia Story*, he slyly won back ex-wife Katharine Hepburn with the sort of graceful underplaying that was already making him one of the most admired artists in the business. In typical Hollywood fashion, he received his first Oscar nomination, not for any of these, but for the somber *Penny Serenade*, wherein he and Dunne coped with the loss of their child. He was an unlikely potential murderer in Hitchcock's *Suspicion*, but fared better as a suspected arsonist in the intelligent *The Talk of the Town*, in which he, Ronald Colman, and Jean Arthur were a triumphant trio.

After two misfires — *Once Upon a Honeymoon*, trying to escape from the Nazis with Ginger Rogers, in an awkward combination of humor and more serious issues, and *Mr. Lucky*, playing a gambler — he made the definitive submarine movie of the war years, *Destination Tokyo*. He mugged shamelessly through the otherwise classic farce *Arsenic and Old Lace*, as a playwright horrified to realize that his sweet old aunts are murderers; a movie held-up from distribution for nearly three years because the Broadway original was still playing to packed houses. Once again for playing it dead serious, he got his other Oscar nod, for the very moody and blatantly un-commercial *None But the Lonely Heart*, as a cockney drifter, a worthy attempt rather than a towering achievement. It could be said that he was playing it straight yet again for *Night and Day*, since this extremely silly biopic of songwriter Cole Porter didn't even hint at that composer's preference for men. Working for Hitchcock again to much better effect, he and Ingrid Bergman created sparks in *Notorious*, hunting down spies in Rio de Janeiro, in one of the great director's best works. This was followed by a jolly run at the box office with a series of sweet and light comedies: *The Bachelor and the Bobby-Soxer*, with Grant pursued by an eager Shirley Temple; *Mr. Blandings Builds His Dream House*, as a harried

advertiser coping with constructing a new home; and *The Bishop's Wife*, in which he pulled off playing an angel as only Cary Grant could. The crowds even showed up for the coy and archaic *Every Girl Should Be Married*, where he was a pediatrician relentlessly pursued by Betsy Drake. She also nabbed him off screen as well.

Fox's mild *I Was a Male War Bride* was one of his biggest hits of all, not surprisingly since it had the hook of putting him in drag for the final part of the film, which was no less awkward than believing he was a French officer. This lucrative high point brought him into the early 1950s where he suffered a brief box-office slump. During this time, he was back to drama for *Crisis*, as a physician forced to operate on an ailing South American dictator, and *People Will Talk*, an ambitious piece by Joseph L. Mankiewicz, again as a man of medicine, a doctor who believes in treating his patients with humanity. With Drake, he appeared in a pleasant family comedy, *Room for One More*, that did badly enough to have its title changed at one point to *The Easy Way*. He was also in a fairly tiresome farce about a rejuvenation formula, *Monkey Business*, which had the distinction of allowing him to work with Marilyn Monroe, and the very weak and very minor *Dream Wife*, bickering with ex-fiancée Deborah Kerr. The success of the lightweight Hitchcock romp, *To Catch a Thief*, in which he was the screen's most agreeable cat burglar, started him cooking once again, and even his uncomfortable participation in Colonial garb, in the adventure epic *The Pride and the Passion*, did not prevent it from scoring big. This one had Sophia Loren as his leading lady, but they were more happily paired in the comedic *Houseboat*, where he was a widower falling for his housekeeper. He and Deborah Kerr waded easily through the slushier moments of the tear-jerker *An Affair to Remember*, a remake of the better *Love Affair*, and perhaps *the* definitive CinemaScope soaper of the 1950s; while he and Bergman had a nice reunion with an airy, sophisticated comedy, *Indiscreet*, filmed in London. This was followed by his last and best for Hitchcock, *North by Northwest*, the ultimate innocent-man-on-the-run adventure and one of the true peaks in the history of entertainment, a blatantly commercial film that was even revered among those pretending to favor only high art. That same year, 1959, brought him the highest grossing movie of his career, *Operation Petticoat*, back on a submarine, albeit with a crew of mostly women, in a jolly farce that hit all the right buttons for the paying masses.

Entering the 1960s he was hotter than ever, a commendable accomplishment considering the ever-changing taste of the American public. *The Grass Is Greener* had a topnotch cast with Kerr, Jean Simmons, and Robert Mitchum, but was perhaps too stage-bound for wide interest. Faring far better were the Doris Day comedy *That Touch of Mink*, which he managed to keep from lapsing into coyness, as a devil-may-care playboy eagerly enticing the virginal miss, and the fine comic-thriller *Charade*, which placed him in a rollicking sort of danger with the other great Hepburn, Audrey. In the amusing *Father Goose*, he was surprisingly convincing as a beach bum, reluctantly coming to the rescue of Leslie Caron and her students, and in *Walk, Don't Run*, a fair-to-middling remake of a movie that was never that special to begin with (*The More the Merrier*), Grant, now considered too old for leading lady Samantha Eggar, played matchmaker for her and Jim Hutton. With that he announced his retirement, remaining on the social scene but adamantly refusing all film offers. He did, fortunately, make himself available for his fans, with a traveling one-man show, *A Conversation With Cary Grant*, which always attracted a crowd — people being only too aware that he was one of the cinema's irreplaceable stars. He died shortly before one of these presentations, in Davenport, Iowa. Despite speculation that he and Randolph Scott were lovers (having shared a home together in the 1930s), Grant's five marriages included those to actresses Virginia Cherrill (1933–35), Betsy Drake (1949–62), and Dyan Cannon (1965–68), who bore him his only child. In 1970 he received a special Academy Award.

Screen: 1932: This Is the Night; Sinners in the Sun; Merrily We Go to Hell; Devil and the Deep; Blonde Venus; Hot Saturday; Madame Butterfly; 1933: She Done Him Wrong; Woman Accused; The Eagle and the Hawk; Gambling Ship; I'm No Angel; Alice in Wonderland; 1934: Thirty Day Princess; Born to Be Bad; Kiss and Make Up; Ladies Should Listen; 1935: Enter Madame; Wings in the Dark; The Last Outpost; 1936: Sylvia Scarlett; Big Brown Eyes; Suzy; Wedding Present; 1937: When You're in Love; Romance and Riches/The Amazing Quest of Ernest Bliss/Amazing Adventure; Topper; The Toast of New York; The Awful Truth; 1938: Bringing Up Baby; Holiday; 1939: Gunga Din; Only Angels Have Wings; In Name Only; 1940: His Girl Friday; My Favorite Wife; The Howards of Virginia; The Philadelphia Story; 1941: Penny Serenade; Suspicion; 1942: The Talk of the Town; Once Upon a Honeymoon; 1943: Mr. Lucky; Destination Tokyo; 1944: Once Upon a Time; None But the Lonely Heart; Arsenic and Old Lace; 1946: Night and Day; Notorious; Without Reservations; 1947: The Bachelor and the Bobby-Soxer; The Bishop's Wife; 1948: Mr. Blandings Builds His Dream House; Every Girl Should Be Married; 1949: I Was a Male War Bride; 1950: Crisis; 1951: People Will Talk; 1952: Room for One More/The Easy Way; Monkey Business; 1953: Dream Wife; 1955: To Catch a Thief; 1957: The Pride and the Passion; An Affair to Remember; Kiss Them for Me; 1958: Indiscreet; Houseboat; 1959: North by Northwest; Operation Petticoat; 1961: The Grass Is Greener; 1962: That Touch of Mink; 1963: Charade; 1964: Father Goose; 1966: Walk Don't Run; 1970: Elvis: That's the Way It Is; 1985: George Stevens: A Filmmaker's Journey.

NY Stage: AS ARCHIE LEACH: 1927: Golden Dawn; 1929: Boom Boom; Wonderful Night; 1931: Nikki.

BONITA GRANVILLE

BORN: NEW YORK, NY, FEBRUARY 2, 1923.
DIED: OCTOBER 11, 1988.

Sharp-nosed, brazen child-star Bonita Granville was born to show business parents and made her film debut at age nine, playing the daughter of Ann Harding in *Westward Passage*, which featured her father, Bernard Granville. She continued to land supporting roles in such movies as *Ah, Wilderness!* and *Cavalcade*, until she became the talk of Hollywood, playing the monstrous brat whose vicious gossip ruins the lives of Miriam Hopkins, Joel McCrea, and Merle Oberon in *These Three*. Fot it, she became only the second youngster (after Jackie Cooper) up to that time to be nominated for an Oscar. She wound up getting some other brash roles, in *Maid of Salem*, causing all the hysteria by pretending to be possessed by witches; and in her first starring feature, aptly titled *Beloved Brat*, playing a neglected rich kid who causes a fatal car accident. Under contract to Warner Bros., she was chosen to play everybody's favorite girl sleuth in *Nancy Drew — Detective*, a serviceable effort that did well enough to rate three sequels. She shuttled between leading roles in teen pictures like *Gallant Sons*, *Syncopation*, and *Down in San Diego*, while continuing to provide support to stars such as Bette Davis in *Now, Voyager*, as her snooty niece, and Margaret Sullavan in *The Mortal Storm*. In the latter, she was given a hard time by the Nazis, a situation repeated in an enormously successful piece of propaganda trash, *Hitler's Children*, where she even endured a public whipping. Efforts to keep the now-over 21-year-old

Granville cooking as a lead attraction found her playing *The Beautiful Cheat* at Universal; being Mickey Rooney's girlfriend in *Love Laughs at Andy Hardy*; and starring in a Monogram cheapie, *The Guilty*, as twin sisters both in love with a mentally unstable war vet. The last proved to be fateful in that oil tycoon John Devereaux Wrather, Jr., who produced it, became her husband in 1947. There were two low-budget items from Mr. and Mrs. Wrather, *Strike It Rich* and *Guilty of Treason*, which only proved that the public wasn't particularly interested in the grown-up Bonita. The next phase of her career turned out to be on the production side as she and her husband purchased the lucrative *Lassie* TV series, with Granville not only serving as producer but as occasional director and performer. In 1978, long absent from a Hollywood she considered morally objectionable, she produced the G-rated *The Magic of Lassie*, which only proved how out of touch she was with the current times.

Screen: 1932: Westward Passage; Silver Dollar; 1933: Cavalcade; Cradle Song; 1934: The Life of Vergie Winters; Anne of Green Gables; A Wicked Woman; 1935: Ah, Wilderness!; 1936: These Three; Song of the Saddle; The Garden of Allah; The Plough and the Stars; 1937: Maid of Salem; Quality Street; Call It a Day; It's Love I'm After; 1938: Beloved Brat; Merrily We Live; White Banners; My Bill; Hard to Get; Nancy Drew — Detective; 1939: Nancy Drew — Reporter; Nancy Drew — Trouble Shooter; The Angels Wash Their Faces; Nancy Drew and the Hidden Staircase; 1940: Those Were the Days; Forty Little Mothers; Third Finger, Left Hand; The Mortal Storm; Escape; Gallant Sons; 1941: The Wild Man of Borneo; The People vs. Dr. Kildare; Down in San Diego; H.M. Pulham, Esq.; 1942: Syncopation; Now, Voyager; The Glass Key; Seven Miles From Alcatraz; 1943: Hitler's Children; 1944: Youth Runs Wild; Song of the Open Road; Andy Hardy's Blonde Trouble; 1945: Senorita of the West; The Beautiful Cheat; 1946: Breakfast in Hollywood; Suspense; The Truth About Murder; Love Laughs at Andy Hardy; 1947: The Guilty; 1948: Strike It Rich; 1949: Guilty of Treason; 1956: The Lone Ranger.

Select TV: 1951: Make Your Bed (sp); 1952: Annual Honeymoon (sp); One Strange Day (sp); 1953: Guest in the House (sp); The Son-in-Law (sp); 1957: Shadow in the Sky (sp); 1958: The Fair-Haired Boy (sp); 1959: The Velvet Alley (sp).

CHARLEY GRAPEWIN

BORN: XENIA, OH, DECEMBER 20, 1869.
DIED: FEBRUARY 2, 1956.

One of cinema's great, wheezy old codgers, Charley Grapewin did not start his film career until he was over 60, but he still managed to chalk up more than 100 roles over the next 21 years. Among his most prominent parts were the petty employer who accuses Fred Stone of stealing his glue formula in *Alice Adams*; Wallace Ford's trucking business partner in *In Spite of Danger*; the feisty Gramps with whom Bette Davis runs her wayside filling station and diner in *The Petrified Forest*; and Old Father, done up in Chinese makeup along with the many other Caucasians in the cast, in the Oscar-winning *The Good Earth*. Some of his other significant roles included the owner of the sued newspaper in the sprightly comedy *Libeled Lady*; the publisher of the Carvel paper in the first Andy Hardy movie, *A Family Affair*; kindly Uncle Henry in the classic musical fantasy *The Wizard of Oz*; the formidable Pa Joad in *The Grapes of Wrath*; and, repeating a role he had done with great success stage, the shiftless Jeeter Lester in *Tobacco Road*, pouring it on thick as the comedic epitome of poor white trash. Love it or hate it, this was

Grapewin's one big chance to seize the spotlight, playing a lazy, lying, and utterly worthless old coot in this strange bit of cinema that was flung in the face of an unsuspecting public by director John Ford of all people. Taking a break from the rural roles, he became Inspector Queen, father of sleuth Ellery, in seven murder mysteries for Columbia, starting with *Ellery Queen — Master Detective*, in 1940, and ending with *Enemy Agents Meet Ellery Queen*, two years later.

Screen: 1929: The Shannons of Broadway; 1930: Only Saps Work; 1931: The Millionaire; Gold Dust Gertie; Heaven on Earth; 1932: Hell's House; The Big Timer; Disorderly Conduct; The Woman in Room 13; Lady and Gent; No Man of Her Own; Huddle; Wild Horse Mesa; The Night of June 13th; American Madness; Are You Listening?; Washington Masquerade; 1933: Heroes for Sale; Wild Boys of the Road; Midnight Mary; Beauty for Sale; Pilgrimage; Don't Bet on Love; Turn Back the Clock; Torch Singer; Hell and High Water; Hello, Everybody!; Female; The Kiss Before the Mirror; 1934: Two Alone; Anne of Green Gables; Judge Priest; She Made Her Bed; The President Vanishes; The Quitter; The Loudspeaker; Return of the Terror; Caravan; 1935: One Frightened Night; In Spite of Danger; Party Wire; Shanghai; Alice Adams; King Solomon of Broadway; Rendezvous; Ah, Wilderness!; Eight Bells; Super-Speed; 1936: The Petrified Forest; The Voice of Bugle Ann; Small Town Girl; Libeled Lady; Sinner Take All; Without Orders; 1937: The Good Earth; A Family Affair; Captains Courageous; Between Two Women; Bad Guy; Big City; Broadway Melody of 1938; Bad Man of Brimstone; 1938: Of Human Hearts; The Girl of the Golden West; Three Comrades; Three Loves Has Nancy; Listen, Darling; The Shopworn Angel; Artists and Models Abroad; 1939: Stand Up and Fight; Burn 'em Up O'Connor; The Wizard of Oz; City in Terror/The Man Who Dared; Sudden Money; Hero for a Day; Dust Be My Destiny; Sabotage; 1940: Johnny Apollo; Earthbound; The Grapes of Wrath; Rhythm on the River; Texas Rangers Ride Again; Ellery Queen — Master Detective; 1941: Ellery Queen's Penthouse Mystery; Tobacco Road; Ellery Queen and the Perfect Crime; Ellery Queen and the Murder Ring; They Died With Their Boots On; 1942: A Close Call for Ellery Queen; A Desperate Chance for Ellery Queen; Enemy Agents Meet Ellery Queen; 1943: Crash Dive; 1944: Follow the Boys; Atlantic City; The Impatient Years; 1947: Gunfighters; 1948: The Enchanted Valley; 1949: Sand; 1951: When I Grow Up.

PETER GRAVES

(PETER AURNESS) BORN: MINNEAPOLIS, MN, MARCH 18, 1926. ED: UNIV. OF MN.

Years before he found television immortality as Mr. Phelps, Peter Graves was a familiar, fair-haired, emotionally reserved, manly player of 1950s features. The younger brother of actor James Arness, he lent his concise vocal tones to radio announcing before making his way to Hollywood. There he did some TV before co-starring in a pair of low-budget westerns, *Rogue River* and *Fort Defiance*, in the latter playing Dane Clark's blinded brother. Graves excelled as the two-faced prisoner, Price, in Billy Wilder's classic *Stalag 17*; remained bad as Edward G. Robinson's cellmate in *Black Tuesday*; and portrayed the father who goes to the gallows in *The Night of the Hunter*. There were occasional leads too, in "B" product, which included the western *Fort Yuma*, as a cavalry officer; *Death in Small Doses*, as an FDA investigator trying to find out why truckers are getting hooked on uppers; and *Bayou*, which became a drive-in hit when it was reissued in 1961 as *Poor White Trash*. Since there was no danger of

him upstaging the aliens, he was also asked to star in a quartet of silly sci-fi thrillers: *Red Planet Mars*, as a scientist communicating with the Martians; *Killers From Space*, with its memorable pop-eyed extra-terrestrials; *It Conquered the World*, battling something that resembled a mean vegetable; and *Beginning of the End*, saving the world from giant grasshoppers. While his brother was winning solid fame on the tube in the long-running *Gunsmoke*, Graves began to find more work on television as well, finally hitting pay dirt as Jim Phelps, head of the spy team on the long-running *Mission: Impossible*. Thereafter, most of his employment came from the small screen, with an occasional appearance in a theatrical release, most notably *Airplane!*, as a pilot with a thing for gladiator movies. He received a steady paycheck for years serving as host for A&E's *Biography* series.

Screen: 1950: Rogue River; 1951: Fort Defiance; 1952: Red Planet Mars; 1953: Stalag 17; East of Sumatra; War Paint; Beneath the 12 Mile Reef; 1954: Killers From Space; The Raid; The Yellow Tomahawk; Black Tuesday; 1955: The Long Gray Line; The Naked Street; Robbers' Roost; Wichita; The Night of the Hunter; The Court-Martial of Billy Mitchell; Fort Yuma; 1956: Hold Back the Night; Canyon River; It Conquered the World; 1957: Death in Small Doses; Bayou/Poor White Trash; Beginning of the End; 1958: Wolf Larsen; 1959: Stranger in My Arms; 1965: A Rage to Live; 1966: Texas Across the River; 1968: The Ballad of Josie; Sergeant Ryker (from TV); 1970: The Five Man Army; 1975: Sidecar Racers; 1976: The Mysterious Monsters (narrator); 1978: Cruise Missile/Missile X: The Neutron Bomb Incident; High Seas Hijack; 1979: Parts: The Clonus Horror; 1980: Survival Run; Airplane!; 1982: Savannah Smiles; Airplane II: The Sequel; 1983: The Guns and the Fury (dtv); 1984: Aces Go Places III: Our Man From Bond Street (dtv); 1987: Number One With a Bullet; 1993: Addams Family Values; 1999: House on Haunted Hill.

NY Stage: 1962: The Captains and the Kings.

Select TV: 1953: Melody in Black (sp); Part of the Game (sp); 1954: Beyond the Cross (sp); Sauce for the Gander (sp); 1955: Bitter Grapes (sp); 1955–59: Fury (series); 1956: Circle of Guilt (sp); 1960–61: Whiplash (series); 1963: The Case Against Paul Ryker (sp); 1966: Court-Martial (series); Showdown With the Showdown Kid (sp); 1967: Valley of Mystery; 1967–73: Mission: Impossible (series); 1973: A Call to Danger; The President's Plane Is Missing; 1974: Scream of the Wolf; The Underground Man; Where Have All the People Gone?; 1975: Dead Man on the Run; 1977: SST — Death Flight; 1979: The Rebels; Death on the Freeway; 1980: The Memory of Eva Ryker; 1981: 300 Miles for Stephanie; 1983: The Winds of War (ms); 1987: If It's Tuesday, It Still Must Be Belgium; Best of Friends; 1987–94: Biography (series); 1988–89: War and Remembrance (ms); 1988–90: Mission: Impossible (series); 2001: These Old Broads.

COLEEN GRAY

(DORIS JENSEN) BORN: STAPLEHURST, NE, OCTOBER 23, 1922. ED: HAMLINE UNIV.

Petite and pretty Coleen Gray (note the missing "l") was signed to a contract by 20th Century-Fox, in 1945, following some regional theater work. After some minor roles, she landed a good part in the cult noir *Nightmare Alley*, as Tyrone Power's wife and partner in his phony spiritualist act. This led to some horsey pictures, such as *Sand*, in which she helped Mark Stevens track down his missing stallion, and Paramount's Bing Crosby racetrack vehicle, *Riding High*, where she made for a very pleasant leading lady. She dabbled in the world of crime with *The Sleeping City*, as a Bellevue nurse involved in illegal drug trafficking; *Lucky Nick Cain*, as a gambler accused of murder, in one of the relentlessly second-rate programmers George Raft kept churning out to keep his name before the public; the taut *Kansas City Confidential*, as the daughter of bank robber Preston Foster; and *Las Vegas Shakedown*, about a casino trying to stay legit. Big-time stardom refused to happen, and she became a staple of second features, mainly westerns, falling for deserter Sterling Hayden in *Arrow in the Dust*, which was not to be confused with *Star in the Dust*, where she was the lover of hired gunman Richard Boone; and *Copper Sky*, where she and Jeff Morrow were the sole survivors of an Indian massacre. There were also parts in "B" horrors like *The Vampire*, as the nurse who realizes doctor John Beal is trying to put the bite on her; and the immortal *The Leech Woman*, as a woman who kills men for their hormones. Stuck among these was actually a satisfying quality feature, the heist thriller *The Killing*, where she was Sterling Hayden's loyal girlfriend. Later years found her acting on some TV soaps and doing various series guest shots.

Screen: 1945: State Fair; 1946: Three Little Girls in Blue; 1947: Kiss of Death; Nightmare Alley; 1948: Red River; Fury at Furnace Creek; 1949: Sand; 1950: Riding High; Father Is a Bachelor; The Sleeping City; 1951: Apache Drums; Lucky Nick Cain/I'll Get You For This; 1952: Models, Inc.; Kansas City Confidential; 1953: The Fake; Sabre Jet; The Vanquished/The Gallant Rebel; 1954: Arrow in the Dust; 1954: Las Vegas Shakedown; The Twinkle in God's Eye; Tennessee's Partner; 1956: Star in the Dust; The Wild Dakotas; The Killing; Frontier Gambler; Death of a Scoundrel; The Black Whip; 1957: Destination 60,000; The Vampire; Copper Sky; 1958: Hell's Five Hours; Johnny Rocco; 1960: The Leech Woman; 1962: The Phantom Planet; 1965: Town Tamer; 1968: P.J.; 1972: The Late Liz; 1986: Cry From the Mountain.

NY Stage: 1949: Leaf and Bough.

Select TV: 1961–62: Window on Main Street (series); 1967–68: Days of Our Lives (series); 1969–70: Bright Promise (series); 1971: Ellery Queen: Don't Look Behind You; 1979: The Best Place to Be.

KATHRYN GRAYSON

(Zelma Kathryn Hedrick) Born: Winston-Salem, NC, February 9, 1922.

MGM's reigning soprano during its musical heyday, Kathryn Grayson, button-nosed and sweet, was never known for her masterful acting range, but she remains an attractive presence for fans of the genre. She was discovered at the St. Louis Opera House by an MGM talent scout, who signed her up and then put her through the usual studio training until she made her debut in the title role of *Andy Hardy's Private Secretary*. When she finally got a musical showcase, she had to take a back seat to Abbott and Costello in the rather forgettable remake of *Rio Rita*. Her next film, *Seven Sweethearts*, was constructed to make her more the center of attention, but it wasn't anything special either. She and Gene Kelly were asked to carry the ponderous plot of the all-star war morale booster *Thousands Cheer*, and then were paired with more pleasing results (she somehow rated billing above him) in the huge hit *Anchors Aweigh*, which allowed her to sing "Jealousy," while playing a young Hollywood hopeful. There were two guest appearances, both of which were notable: *Ziegfeld Follies*, because she was not able to hit the final high note in the finale and had to be dubbed, and *Till the Clouds Roll By*, because it allowed her to play Magnolia in a "Show Boat" sequence, per-

haps serving as the ultimate audition for the real thing.

There were minor pairings with Frank Sinatra, in *It Happened in Brooklyn*, as a schoolteacher with a nice set of pipes, and in *The Kissing Bandit*, one of the studio's most notorious miscalculations, before she served as leading lady to Mario Lanza in his first two films, *That Midnight Kiss* and *The Toast of New Orleans*. Although these weren't particularly popular, it was fortunate that she stuck around on the payroll because the studio did allow her to play Magnolia for real in their lovely 1951 version of *Show Boat*, where she acquitted herself quite nicely. Her co-star was Howard Keel, and they teamed again for *Lovely to Look At*, the remake of *Roberta*, which meant she got to sing "Smoke Gets in Your Eyes," and, more impressively, *Kiss Me Kate*, containing Grayson's best screen work, as the feisty Lilly/Katharine in this surprisingly faithful and sprightly adaptation of the Cole Porter Broadway success. Despite this being a high point, it marked the end of her stay at MGM, and she was in only one more film, *The Vagabond King*, an unsuccessful operetta for Paramount, made in 1956, by which time these things were no longer of much interest to movie audiences. There were occasional nightclub gigs (including some with Keel) and operetta appearances (*The Merry Widow*, *Naughty Marietta*) over the next several years, but she had pretty much backed away from the business by the end of the 1960s.

Screen: 1941: Andy Hardy's Private Secretary; The Vanishing Virginian; 1942: Rio Rita; Seven Sweethearts; 1943: Thousands Cheer; 1945: Anchors Aweigh; 1946: Ziegfeld Follies; Two Sisters From Boston; 1947: Till the Clouds Roll By; It Happened in Brooklyn; 1948: The Kissing Bandit; 1949: That Midnight Kiss; 1950: The Toast of New Orleans; Grounds for Marriage; 1951: Show Boat; 1952: Lovely to Look At; 1953: The Desert Song; So This Is Love; Kiss Me Kate; 1956: The Vagabond King.

Select TV: 1955: Shadow on the Heart (sp); The Invitation (sp); 1957: Lone Woman (sp); 1958: A Game of Hate (sp).

MITZI GREEN

(Mitzi Keno) Born: Bronx, NY, October 22, 1920. Died: May 24, 1969.

A precocious child star of the early talkie era, Mitzi Green, with her Louise Brooks bangs and talent for mimicry, was born the child of vaudevillians, who in best show business fashion, made her part of the act, billing her as "Little Mitzi." Connections with both Elsie Janis and Jackie Coogan landed the youngster (now using her mother's maiden name) work at Paramount, playing one of Mary Brian's sisters in *The Marriage Playground*. From this came a contract with the studio and a scene-stealing role in *Honey*, as a society brat who reports all the gossip she sees from her tree outpost. The studio was eager to cash in on her success and added her to their all-star revue, *Paramount on Parade*, in which she impersonated Maurice Chevalier. From this it was on to imitating Clara Bow (she played her little sister) in *Love Among the Millionaires*; taunting pesky cousin Jackie Searl in *Finn and Hattie*; and playing Becky Thatcher in *Tom Sawyer*, which reunited her with family friend Jackie Coogan. After a bit in the studio's charming *Skippy*, she went over to RKO, who promptly starred her as *Little Orphan Annie*, which did nice business, though Green was already too old for the part. Unsatisfied with RKO's contract offer, her parents chose to return their daughter to vaudeville, thereby putting an end to her film stardom. There was a stage success in the original production of Rodgers and Hart's *Babes in Arms*, introducing the durable standards "Where or When," "My Funny Valentine," and "The Lady Is a Tramp;" and, in 1945, she had another Broadway long run with *Billion Dollar Baby*. By this point, she had married director Joe Pevney and was focusing her interests more towards raising a family rather than spending time in the footlights. Unheralded, she returned to movies in two 1952 releases, Abbott and Costello's *Lost in Alaska*, as a dance hall girl, and the Fox musical, *Bloodhounds of Broadway*, supporting another Mitzi, Gaynor. She also appeared briefly in a short-lived sitcom, *So This Is Hollywood*, playing a movie stuntwoman, and did some summer theatre.

Screen: 1929: The Marriage Playground; 1930: Honey; Paramount on Parade; Love Among the Millionaires; Tom Sawyer; Santa Fe Trail; 1931: Finn and Hattie; Dude Ranch; Newly Rich; Huckleberry Finn; Skippy; 1932: Girl Crazy; Little Orphan Annie; 1934: Transatlantic Merry-Go-Round; 1952: Lost in Alaska; Bloodhounds of Broadway.

NY Stage: 1937: Babes in Arms; 1940: Three After Three; Walk With Music; 1942: Let Freedom Ring; 1945: Billion Dollar Baby.

Select TV: 1955: So This Is Hollywood (series).

RICHARD GREENE

BORN: PLYMOUTH, ENGLAND, AUGUST 25, 1918.
DIED: JUNE 1, 1985.

A somewhat neutral addition to the acting scene throughout his career, Richard Greene was born into a theatrical family and followed in his parents' tracks, debuting with the Old Vic in a production of *Julius Caesar*. In 1934 he made his film debut with a teensy bit in a Gracie Fields vehicle, *Sing As You Go*, and then returned to the theater as a member of the Brandon-Thomas Rep Company. His first stage success came in London, in *French Without Tears*, and resulted in offers from both British and U.S. film studios, with Greene opting for 20th Century-Fox in America. For that company, he was one of the brothers investigating their father's murder in the John Ford-directed *Four Men and a Prayer*. After being put on ice with Sonja Henie in *My Lucky Star*, he was promptly overshadowed by Walter Brennan in *Kentucky*, by Shirley Temple in *The Little Princess*, by Basil Rathbone as Sherlock Holmes in *The Hound of the Baskervilles* (Greene was young Baskerville), and by Spencer Tracy in *Stanley and Livingstone*. Although he took third billing to Alice Faye and Fred MacMurray, he had the key role in *Little Old New York*, playing determined steamboat inventor Robert Fulton in this slice of fictionalized history. Following *I Was an Adventuress*, as the husband of con artist-ballerina Zorina, Greene was released from his contract, allowing him to enlist in the Royal Armoured Corps of the 27th Lancers to fight during World War II. Back in England he resumed his movie career and then was called back to Fox following the war to appear in their expensive, lumbering costume romance *Forever Amber*, as Cornel Wilde's sardonic buddy, a role originally intended for Vincent Price. He stuck around for the uninspired filming of Oscar Wilde's *The Fan*, and a Douglas Fairbanks, Jr. swashbuckler, *The Fighting O'Flynn*, as the villain's henchman. He began to create a niche in costume quickies like *Captain Scarlett* and *The Bandits of Corsica*, and he became more famous than ever when his Anglo TV series, *The Adventures of Robin Hood*, became a hit here in America in the 1950s. He was married (1941–51) to actress Patricia Medina, with whom he appeared in *The Fighting O'Flynn*.

Screen: 1934: Sing as You Go; 1938: Four Men and a Prayer; My Lucky Star; Submarine Patrol; Kentucky; 1939: The Little Princess; The Hound of the Baskervilles; Stanley and Livingstone; Here I Am a Stranger; 1940: Little Old New York; I

Was an Adventuress; 1942: Unpublished Story; Flying Fortress; 1943: The Yellow Canary; 1944: Don't Take It to Heart; 1946: Showtime/Gaiety George; 1947: Forever Amber; 1948: The Fighting O'Flynn; 1949: The Fan; If This Be Sin/That Dangerous Age; Now Barabbas Was a Robber; 1950: The Desert Hawk; Operation X/My Daughter Joy; Shadow of the Eagle; 1951: Lorna Doone; 1952: The Black Castle; 1953: Rogue's March; Captain Scarlett; The Bandits of Corsica; 1955: Contraband Spain; 1960: Beyond the Curtain; 1961: Sword of Sherwood Forest; 19647: Dangerous Island/Island of the Lost; 1968: The Blood of Fu Manchu; 1972: Castle of Fu Manchu; Tales From the Crypt.

Select TV: 1951: Berkeley Square (sp); Peter Ibbetson (sp); Coriolanus (sp); Stolen Years (sp); 1955: The Return of Gentleman Jim (sp); 1955–58: The Adventures of Robin Hood (series); 1959: The Wayward Widow (sp); 1960: Hot Footage (sp).

SYDNEY GREENSTREET

BORN: SANDWICH, ENGLAND, DECEMBER 27, 1879. DIED: JANUARY 18, 1954.

A massive, imposing figure of 1940s cinema, Sydney Greenstreet's hooded glare and sinister chuckle have caused him to be endlessly mimicked. Early on he took up tea planting in Ceylon and then managed a brewery in England before giving in to the lure of the stage. He acted with the Ben Greet Company, and in 1904, they came to America, where Greenstreet would make his home from then on. He toiled exclusively in the theater for the next 37 years. It was in a Los Angeles production of *There Shall Be No Night*, with the Lunts, that director John Huston first saw him, asking him to play the suave villain Casper Guttman in the classic noir *The Maltese Falcon*. It was one of the great movie debuts of all time, with Greenstreet creating so indelible an impression that he was nominated for an Oscar in the supporting category. As a result Warner Bros. put him under contract, reteaming him with his *Falcon* co-star, Humphrey Bogart, in both *Across the Pacific*, and the Academy Award-winning *Casablanca*, as a rival bar owner anxious to purchase Bogart's establishment. It was not Bogart, however, whom the studio fancied teaming their rotund star with, but another *Falcon* alumnus, Peter Lorre. With Lorre, he did supporting work in *Background to Danger*, where he was in league with the Nazis; *Passage to Marseille* (again with Bogart), as a French colonial governor; *The Conspirators*; and the all-star *Hollywood Canteen*. They were then promoted as the star attractions of a weak thriller, *The Mask of Dimitrios*, with Greenstreet once again supplying the villainy. There were lighter roles in *Pillow to Post* and *Christmas in Connecticut*, followed by a couple more with Lorre, *Three Strangers* (Geraldine Fitzgerald was the other), as a financially strapped lawyer sharing a winning sweepstakes ticket, and *The Verdict*, as a police superintendent gone bad. Over at MGM he was as commanding as ever in *The Hucksters*, as a pompous soap tycoon, memorably spitting on the boardroom table to make a point about advertising. There was no lack of work, because it was clear that the actor was an added plus to whatever film he appeared in, notably *The Woman in White*, where his treacherous Count Fosco effortlessly outshone his younger co-stars. After another memorable villain role, as the corrupt political boss in one of the best Joan Crawford vehicles, *Flamingo Road*, and another loan-out to MGM, for *Malaya*, he retired in 1952, two years before his death from complications from diabetes.

Screen: 1941: The Maltese Falcon; They Died With Their Boots On; 1942: Across the Pacific; In This Our Life; Casablanca; 1943:

Background to Danger; **1944:** Passage to Marseille; Between Two Worlds; The Mask of Dimitrios; The Conspirators; Hollywood Canteen; **1945:** Pillow to Post; Conflict; Christmas in Connecticut; **1946:** Three Strangers; Devotion (filmed 1943); The Verdict; **1947:** That Way With Women; The Hucksters; **1948:** Ruthless; The Woman in White; The Velvet Touch; **1949:** Flamingo Road; It's a Great Feeling; Malaya.

NY Stage: **1905:** Everyman; **1907:** Ben Greet Repertory; **1909:** The Goddess of Reason; **1911:** Thais; Speed; **1912:** What Ails You?; **1914:** Lady Windermere's Fan; **1915:** She's in Again; A World of Pleasure; **1916:** A King of Nowhere; King Henry VIII; Colonel Newcome; The Merry Wives of Windsor; **1917:** Friend Martha; **1918:** The Rainbow Girl; **1920:** Lady Billy; **1923:** The Magic Ring; **1925:** The Student Prince; **1926:** The Humble; **1927:** Junk; Lady in Love; **1928:** The Madcap; **1930:** R.U.R.; Volpone; Lysistrata; **1931:** The Admirable Crichton; Berlin; **1932:** The Good Earth; **1933:** Roberta; **1935:** The Taming of the Shrew (and 1940); **1936:** Idiot's Delight; **1937:** Amphitryon 38; **1938:** The Sea Gull; **1940:** There Shall Be No Night.

CHARLOTTE GREENWOOD

(FRANCES CHARLOTTE GREENWOOD)
BORN: PHILADELPHIA, PA, JUNE 25, 1890.
DIED: JANUARY 18, 1978.

A gangly, uninhibited, beanpole-shaped comic, whose shtick was to kick out her long legs in eccentric dances and movements, Charlotte Greenwood made her name in nightclubs and vaudeville and on the legit stage, where she clowned her way through such shows as *Music Box Revue* and *Hassard Short's Ritz Revue*. With the coming of talkies, she was called on by Warner Bros. to repeat her stage role of Letty Pepper in *So Long Letty*, but there wasn't any demand for more vehicles. Instead she thrashed around with Buster Keaton in one of his unsatisfying early talkies, *Bedroom, Parlor and Bath*, and with Eddie Cantor in *Palmy Days*, in an often-exhausting effort to make an impression. In the "B" drama *Cheaters at Play*, she was a wealthy ex-chorus girl who had her jewels stolen, and she was part of a disruptive American film crew in the British-made *Orders Is Orders*. Older and calmer, she joined the 20th Century-Fox stock company in 1940, her presence there being a decided asset to such bland musicals as *Moon Over Miami*, *Springtime in the Rockies*, *The Gang's All Here*, and *Wake Up and Dream*. On a far cheaper level, she was the money-hungry mother of Lynn Bari, and thereby the title character, in a "B," *The Perfect Snob*; the mom of *Dixie Dugan*, an unsuccessful attempt to bring a comic strip to life; and she ventured over to UA to participate in an ancient bedroom farce, *Up in Mabel's Room*. Her role as a farmer in *Home in Indiana* not only gave her a chance to be serious, but showed how comfortably she fit into rural settings, which paved the way for the part moviegoers remember her most fondly for, Aunt Eller, a model of folksy common sense and good humor, in the Rodgers and Hammerstein musical *Oklahoma!* (She had been the first choice for the part in the original 1943 stage production, but was unavailable). After two more films she devoted most of her time to practicing the Christian Science religion. Her 1947 autobiography was entitled *Never Too Tall*.

Screen: **1915:** Jane; **1928:** Baby Mine; **1929:** So Long Letty; **1931:** Parlor, Bedroom and Bath; Stepping Out; The Man in Possession; Flying High; Palmy Days; **1932:** Cheaters at Play; **1933:** Orders Is Orders; **1940:** Star Dust; Young People; Down Argentine Way; **1941:** Tall, Dark and Handsome; Moon Over Miami; The Perfect Snob; **1942:** Springtime in the Rockies; **1943:**

Dixie Dugan; The Gang's All Here; **1944:** Up in Mabel's Room; Home in Indiana; **1946:** Wake Up and Dream; **1947:** Driftwood; **1949:** The Great Dan Patch; Oh, You Beautiful Doll; **1950:** Peggy; **1953:** Dangerous When Wet; **1955:** Oklahoma!; **1956:** Glory; The Opposite Sex.

NY Stage: **1912:** The Passing Show of 1912; **1913:** The Man With Three Wives; The Passing Show of 1913; **1914:** Pretty Mrs. Smith; **1916:** So Long Letty; **1919:** Linger Longer Letty; **1922:** Letty Pepper; Music Box Revue; **1924:** Hassard Short's Ritz Revue; **1927:** Rufus Le Maire's Affairs; **1950:** Out of This World.

JOAN GREENWOOD

BORN: LONDON, ENGLAND, MARCH 4, 1921.
DIED: FEBRUARY 28, 1987.

Was there ever a more blatantly sexy, meltingly husky voice than that of Joan Greenwood? This wittily alluring British actress made a killing playing seductresses and bitches, but could be a gentle lass as well. She debuted on the London stage as a teen in *Le Malade Imaginaire*, in 1938, and made her film bow two years later, in *John Smith Wakes Up*. Roles in both films and theater kept her busy for the next few years until she finally got noticed on screen, as a model in *Latin Quarter*, and as a woman who goes from mute to jabber-mouth in *A Girl in a Million*. These led to a contract with Rank, where she aided amnesiac John Mills in *The October Man*, and played Lady Caroline Lamb, getting all the good notices, in *The Bad Lord Byron*. Her reputation began to grow with the success of *Kind Hearts and Coronets*, in which she was the naughty wife who desired murderer Dennis Price, and two other Ealing comedies: *Whisky Galore*, where she was the island telephone operator; and *The Man in the White Suit*, as the boss's daughter, in love with inventor Alec Guinness. These were followed by another perfect part, the self-satisfied Gwendolen, in the bright movie version of *The Importance of Being Earnest*. She had offers from other countries, so she went to France for *Knave of Hearts*, and to America for the costume picture *Moonfleet*, playing a wicked lady, and for *Stage Struck*, portraying a self-centered actress. She took some time to do television and theater, so it was a while before she was back on screen again, in the Jules Verne fantasy *Mysterious Island*, and in another of her all-time best roles, Lady Bellaston, in the Oscar-winning *Tom Jones*, very elegant and all-too-willing to get Albert Finney into bed. After the Disney adventure *The Moon-Spinners*, where she was Hayley Mills's aunt, she pretty much bid goodbye to her movie career, popping up here and there on occasion, evoking little comment in a spoof of *The Hound of the Baskervilles*, and in the two-part adaptation of *Little Dorrit*, released posthumously.

Screen: **1940:** John Smith Wakes Up; **1941:** My Wife's Family; He Found a Star; **1943:** The Gentle Sex; **1945:** They Knew Mr. Knight; **1946:** Latin Quarter; A Girl in a Million; The Man Within/The Smugglers; **1947:** The October Man; The White Unicorn/Bad Sister; **1948:** Saraband for Dead Lovers; **1949:** The Bad Lord Byron; Whisky Galore/Tight Little Island; Kind Hearts and Coronets; **1950:** Flesh and Blood; **1951:** Young Wives' Tale; The Man in the White Suit; **1952:** Mr. Peek-a-Boo; The Importance of Being Earnest; **1954:** Knave of Hearts/Lover Boy; Father Brown/The Detective; **1955:** Moonfleet; **1958:** Stage Struck; **1961:** Mysterious Island; **1962:** The Amorous Prawn; **1963:** Tom Jones; **1964:** The Moon-Spinners; **1971:** Girl Stroke Boy; **1978:** The Hound of the Baskervilles; The Uncanny; **1979:** The Water Babies; **1988:** Little Dorrit.

NY Stage: 1954: Confidential Clerk; 1966: Those That Play the Clowns.
Select TV: 1954: The King and Mrs. Candle (sp); 1956: Man and Superman (sp); 1979: The Flame Is Love; 1981: Triangle (series); 1983: Wagner (ms); 1984: Ellis Island (ms); 1986: At Bertram's Hotel; 1987: Melba (ms).

JANE GREER

(BETTEJANE GREER) BORN: WASHINGTON, DC, SEPTEMBER 9, 1924. DIED: AUGUST 24, 2001.

A wide-eyed beauty, Jane Greer had a career that never brought her as much fame as expected, despite an obvious talent and a fairly consistent excellence that more enduring actresses couldn't claim. She had been a band singer and photographers' model, but was first known in Hollywood as Rudy Vallee's much younger wife. The couple divorced after two years of marriage, in 1945, the same year Greer started at R K O, in *Pan Americana*, using her real first name. Starting with *Dick Tracy*, it was shortened to a simpler "Jane," after which the actress was used mostly as decoration, as in the western *Sunset Pass*, and the swashbuckler *Sinbad the Sailor*. Things then changed for the better when she played the woman abandoned by heel Robert Young in *They Won't Believe Me*, and the icy femme fatale in the noir cult film *Out of the Past*, which really turned out to be the role of a lifetime. Keeping her bad, R K O made her a wicked gambling-house proprietress in *Station West*; reteamed her with her *Out of the Past* co-star, Robert Mitchum, as a couple in pursuit of the man who has stolen from him, in *The Big Steal*; and presented her as an ex-con snatching away the lover of her parole officer, Lizabeth Scott, in *The Company She Keeps*. Exiting R K O, she was the female relief in the male-dominated Gary Cooper comedy *You're in the Navy Now*; the heroine of M G M's *The Prisoner of Zenda* remake; a nurse with man trouble in the mild comedy *You for Me*; and the ex-wife of drunken vaudevillian Red Skelton in *The Clown*, a variation on *The Champ*. After playing the second, nicer wife of Lon Chaney in the biopic *Man of a Thousand Faces*, she cut back her screen appearances considerably. She was too long out of the spotlight when she was asked to play a variation of the role of the mother of the character she had played in *Out of the Past*, now updated and called *Against All Odds*. Looking sensational, she proved to be just as coolly effective, leading one to hope there would be some more good roles to make up for so many lost years. Instead there were small, unremarkable mother parts in *Just Between Friends* (Mary Tyler Moore) and *Immediate Family* (James Woods).
Screen: AS BETTEJANE GREER: 1945: Pan Americana; Two O' Clock Courage; George White's Scandals.
AS JANE GREER: Dick Tracy; 1946: The Falcon's Alibi; The Bamboo Blonde; Sunset Pass; 1947: Sinbad the Sailor; They Won't Believe Me; Out of the Past; 1948: Station West; 1949: The Big Steal; 1950: The Company She Keeps; 1951: You're in the Navy Now/U.S.S. Teakettle; 1952: The Prisoner of Zenda; Desperate Search; You for Me; 1953: The Clown; Down Among the Sheltering Palms; 1956: Run for the Sun; 1957: Man of a Thousand Faces; 1964: Where Love Has Gone; 1965: Billie; 1973: The Outfit; 1984: Against All Odds; 1986: Just Between Friends; 1989: Immediate Family; 1996: Perfect Mate (dtv).
Select TV: 1953: Look for Tomorrow (sp); 1955: One Man Is Missing (sp); 1957: Moment of Decision (sp); 1958: No Time at All (sp); 1982: Louis L'Amour's The Shadow Riders.

VIRGINIA GREY

BORN: LOS ANGELES, CA, MARCH 22, 1917.

There are few ladies who kept as busy as Virginia Grey and yet it is doubtful she would make any lists of the best-remembered stars of the 1930s and 1940s, despite her competence and endurance. She got her first role in a 1927 production of *Uncle Tom's Cabin*, at Universal, where her mother worked as a film cutter. After a few more parts, she left acting to study nursing but was drawn back to the movies, doing bit roles until MGM signed her to a contract in 1936. There she was destined to make more fleeting appearances until cast as Bruce Cabot's love interest in a "B" movie, *Bad Guy*. This only meant that her supporting roles would now be somewhat bigger, showing up as one of Clark Gable's chorus girls in *Idiot's Delight*, and C. Aubrey Smith's adopted daughter, who isn't the nice girl she appears to be, in *Another Thin Man*. The leads she obtained were still in back-of-the-line product like *Blonde Inspiration*, serving as muse for writer John Shelton. Otherwise she was called on to keep a straight face while ogled by the likes of the Marx Brothers (*The Big Store*) and Red Skelton (*Whistling in the Dark*), or to play the ingénues in support of older stars like Charles Coburn (*The Captain Was a Lady*) and Marjorie Main (*Tish*). After Metro it was over to Republic for programmers like *Bells of Capistrano*, a Gene Autry western, and *Idaho*, which paired her with Roy Rogers. She pretty much remained on this level of visibility into the 1950s, her starring credits including such titles as *Blonde Ransom*, about a faked kidnapping; *Swamp Fire*, where she shared the screen with both Johnny Weissmuller and Buster Crabbe; *Who Killed Doc Robin?*, Hal Roach, Jr.'s failed attempt to create a new Our Gang series; and *Glamour Girl*, in which she played a musical talent scout. She also starred in an unintentionally funny dinosaur adventure, *Unknown Island*; the launch of Weissmuller's formulaic series, *Jungle Jim*; and one of her better low-budgeters, *The Threat*, in which she played a cafe singer held hostage by convict Charles McGraw. By the late 1950s she moved down to supporting roles, getting a lot of needed work from producer Ross Hunter, including *The Restless Years*, as a lonely spinster; *Back Street*, as Susan Hayward's sister; and *Tammy Tell Me True*, as a headmistress. She had a tiny role as a passenger in Hunter's 1970 hit *Airport*, after which she retired.
Screen: 1927: Uncle Tom's Cabin; 1928: Heart to Heart; The Michigan Kid; Jazz Mad; 1931: Misbehaving Ladies; Palmy Days; 1933: Secrets; 1934: St. Louis Kid; Dames; The Firebird; 1935: She Gets Her Man; Gold Diggers of 1935; 1936: Old Hutch; The Great Ziegfeld; 1937: Secret Valley; Bad Guy; Rosalie; 1938: Test Pilot; Rich Man, Poor Girl; Ladies in Distress; Youth Takes a Fling; Dramatic School; The Shopworn Angel; 1939: Idiot's Delight; Broadway Serenade; The Hardys Ride High; Thunder Afloat; Another Thin Man; The Women; 1940: Three Cheers for the Irish; The Captain Is a Lady; Hullabaloo; The Golden Fleecing; Keeping Company; 1941: Blonde Inspiration; Washington Melodrama; The Big Store; Whistling in the Dark; Mr. and Mrs. North; 1942: Tarzan's New York Adventure; Grand Central Murder; Tish; Bells of Capistrano; Secrets of the Underground; 1943: Idaho; Stage Door Canteen; Sweet Rosie O'Grady; 1944: Strangers in the Night; 1945: Grissly's Millions; Flame of the Barbary Coast; Blonde Ransom; The Men in Her Diary; 1946: Smooth as Silk; Swamp Fire; House of Horrors; 1947: Wyoming; Unconquered; 1948: Who Killed "Doc" Robin?; Glamour Girl; So This Is New York; Unknown Island; Miraculous Journey; Mexican Hayride; Leather Gloves; Jungle Jim; 1949: The Threat; 1950: Highway 301; 1951: Bullfighter and

the Lady; Three Desperate Men; Slaughter Trail; **1952:** Desert Pursuit; **1953:** A Perilous Journey; The Fighting Lawman; Captain Scarface; **1954:** The Forty-Niners; Target Earth; **1955:** The Eternal Sea; The Last Command; All That Heaven Allows; The Rose Tattoo; **1956:** Accused of Murder; **1957:** Crime of Passion; Jeanne Eagles; **1958:** The Restless Years; **1959:** No Name on the Bullet; **1960:** Portrait in Black; **1961:** Tammy Tell Me True; Flower Drum Song; Back Street; Bachelor in Paradise; **1963:** Black Zoo; **1964:** The Naked Kiss; **1965:** Love Has Many Faces; Madame X; **1968:** Rosie!; **1970:** Airport.

Select TV: **1952:** Dante's Inferno (sp); **1953:** The Lady and the Champ (sp); **1955:** The 99th Day (sp); **1956:** Crack-Up (sp); **1958:** Tapes for Geoffrey (sp); The Great Gatsby (sp); **1960:** R.S.V.P. (sp); **1975:** The Lives of Jenny Dolan; **1976:** Arthur Hailey's The Moneychangers (ms).

ANDY GRIFFITH

BORN: MOUNT AIRY, NC, JUNE 1, 1926.
ED: UNIV. OF NC.

Television's favorite folksy actor, Andy Griffith, came to show business via a traveling act he and his wife, actress Barbara Edwards, had conceived that included singing, dancing, guitar playing, and amusing monologues spoken by Andy. One of these pieces, entitled "What It Was Was Football," was eventually recorded and brought him his first taste of fame. After an appearance on The Ed Sullivan Show, he won the lead in a television version of Mac Hayman's novel No Time for Sergeants, on the U.S. Steel Hour, followed by the smash Broadway adaptation, playing the hillbilly who wins over the U.S. Air Force with his unpretentious, dopey charm. He won a Theatre World Award and a chance to repeat the part in Warner Bros.'s pleasing and highly successful 1958 movie version. Before that he was permitted to show his dramatic strength as the backwoods guitarist who reveals his egomaniacal side on his rise to the top in the excellent A Face in the Crowd, certainly his most satisfying work in motion pictures. There were two less-exciting movie assignments, with another service comedy, Onionhead, and a minor Debbie Reynolds vehicle, The Second Time Around, before Griffith found unparalleled fame on the small screen, as the nice-guy sheriff of the little town of Mayberry, on The Andy Griffith Show. The program made him one of the legendary names of the tube, where he wound up spending most of his career, later on finding another hit series, Matlock, as a down-to-earth lawyer, in the late 1980s. Occasionally visiting the movies during these years, he was an aging Hollywood cowboy in Hearts of the West, and comical villains in both Rustler's Rhapsody and Spy Hard.

Screen: **1957:** A Face in the Crowd; **1958:** No Time for Sergeants; Onionhead; **1961:** The Second Time Around; **1969:** Angel in My Pocket; **1975:** Hearts of the West; **1985:** Rustler's Rhapsody; **1996:** Spy Hard; **2001:** Daddy and Them.

NY Stage: **1955:** No Time for Sergeants; **1959:** Destry Rides Again.

Select TV: **1955:** No Time for Sergeants (sp); **1958:** Never Know the End (sp); The Male Animal (sp); **1960–68:** The Andy Griffith Show (series); **1970–71:** The Headmaster (series); **1971:** The New Andy Griffith Show (series); **1972:** Strangers in 7A; **1973:** Go Ask Alice; **1974:** Pray for the Wildcats; Winter Kill; Savages; **1976:** Street Killing; **1977:** The Girl in the Empty Grave; Washington: Behind Closed Doors (ms); Deadly Games; **1978–79:** Centennial (ms); **1979:** Salvage; Salvage (series); From Here to Eternity (ms); Roots: The Next Generations (ms); **1981:** Murder in Texas; **1982:**

For Lovers Only; **1983:** Murder in Coweta County; The Demon Murder Case; **1984:** Fatal Vision; **1985:** Crime of Innocence; **1986:** Diary of a Perfect Murder; Return to Mayberry; Under the Influence; **1986–95:** Matlock (series); **1992:** Matlock: The Vacation (and co-exec. prod.); **1994:** The Gift of Love; **1995:** Gramps; **1998:** Scattering Dad; **1999:** A Holiday Romance.

HUGH GRIFFITH

BORN: MARIAN-GLAS, ANGLESEY, NORTH WALES, MAY 30, 1912. DIED: MAY 14, 1980.

One of England's gleefully energetic scene-stealers of the postwar era, gruff, demonic-looking Hugh Griffith, usually sputtering with disapproval under a bushy pair of brows, had come to the profession after a spell as a bank clerk. He made his film debut in the 1940 production Neutral Port, and then disappeared from that medium until after the war. He began to gain attention in some of the prime Ealing Studios comedies of the day, including Kind Hearts and Coronets, as the Lord High Steward; A Run for Your Money, hilarious as a harp-totting street vagrant; and The Titfield Thunderbolt, priceless as a train stoker living in a derailed railroad car. His American debut came with the mammoth spectacle Ben-Hur, adding a dash of color as Sheik Ilderim and winning an Academy Award in the process, no doubt part of the juggernaut that swept up a record 11 trophies for that film. Now an international attraction, he was seen in such big films as The Story on Page One, as the judge presiding over a murder case; Exodus, as a Cypriot shipping magnate; the remake of Mutiny on the Bounty; How to Steal a Million, as Audrey Hepburn's befuddled art forger dad; and Oliver!, as a tipsy magistrate. The crowning achievement of his career came with his splendidly daft portrayal of the grouchy, exasperated Squire Weston in the Academy Award-winning romp Tom Jones, a role that earned him an Oscar nomination and one that he reprised several years later for a brief sequence in Joseph Andrews. By the time of the latter, he'd associated himself with a lot of misguided projects, including Oh Dad, Poor Dad…, where he played an oversexed suitor; director Pier Pasolini's grotesque, X-rated version of The Canterbury Tales; and junky horror films like Craze and Legend of the Werewolf, all of which he did with a twinkle in his eye.

Screen: **1940:** Neutral Port; **1947:** Silver Darlings; **1948:** So Evil My Love; The Three Weird Sisters; The First Gentleman/Affairs of a Rogue; Dulcimer Street/London Belongs to Me; **1949:** The Last Days of Dolwyn/Woman of Dolwyn; Kind Hearts and Coronets; Dr. Morelle — The Case of the Missing Heiress; A Run for Your Money; **1950:** Gone to Earth/The Wild Heart; **1951:** The Galloping Major; Laughter in Paradise; **1953:** The Beggar's Opera; The Titfield Thunderbolt; **1954:** Man With a Million/The Million Pound Note; The Sleeping Tiger; **1955:** Passage Home; **1957:** The Good Companions; Lucky Jim; **1959:** Ben-Hur; The Story on Page One; **1960:** Exodus; The Day They Robbed the Bank of England; **1962:** The Counterfeit Traitor; Term of Trial; Mutiny on the Bounty; Lisa/The Inspector; **1963:** Hide and Seek; Tom Jones; **1964:** The Bargee; **1965:** The Amorous Adventures of Moll Flanders; **1966:** How to Steal a Million; **1967:** Oh Dad, Poor Dad, Mama's Hung You in the Closet and I'm Feeling So Sad; Marito e mio e L'Ammazzo quando mi Pare/Drop Dead, My Love (nUSr); Brown Eye, Evil Eye; The Sailor From Gibraltar; **1968:** The Fixer; Oliver!; **1969:** The Chastity Belt/On My Way to the Crusades I Met a Girl Who…; **1970:** Cry of the Banshee; Start the Revolution Without Me; **1971:** Wuthering Heights; The Abominable Dr. Phibes; Who Slew Auntie Roo?; The Canterbury Tales; **1972:** Crescete e

Moltioplicatevi (nUSr); Dr. Phibes Rises Again; What?; **1973:** The Last Days of Man on Earth/The Final Programme; Craze; Luther; Take Me High/Hot Property; **1974:** Legend of the Werewolf; The Visitor/Cugini Carnali (nUSr); **1976:** The Passover Plot; Casanova & Co./Sex on the Run; **1977:** Joseph Andrews; The Last Remake of Beau Geste; **1978:** The Hound of the Baskervilles; **1980:** A Nightingale Sang in Berkeley Square (dtv).

NY Stage: **1951:** Legend of Lovers; **1957:** Look Homeward Angel; **1963:** Andorra.

Select TV: **1966:** Dare I Weep, Dare I Mourn (sp); **1978:** Grand Slam.

HARRY GUARDINO

Born: Brooklyn, NY, December 23, 1925.
Died: July 17, 1995.

The kind of regular-Joe, macho actor whose movie career basically put him in secondary roles, Harry Guardino came to films after studying at New York's Dramatic Workshop. For Columbia Pictures he did bits in *Purple Heart Diaries*, and Humphrey Bogart's *Sirocco*. He acted on Broadway in *A Hatful of Rain*, guested on several television series, and got his best movie role up until then, as the friendly handyman with an eye on Sophia Loren in the hit comedy *Houseboat*. After that he was Danny Kaye's fellow-musician and best friend in the biopic of Red Nichols, *The Five Pennies*, and looked right at home in battle fatigues in *Pork Chop Hill* and *Hell Is for Heroes*, where he tried to command a small unit pinned down by the Germans. He was also seen to good effect as Barabbas in the spectacle *King of Kings*; as a big game hunter in *Rhino!*; as a slick saloonkeeper in Disney's *The Adventures of Bullwhip Griffin*; and as Richard Widmark's fellow detective in *Madigan*. Over in Italy, he participated in one of the many caper films of the 1960s, *The Treasure of San Gennaro*; played one of the plane crash survivors in an expanded telefilm, *Valley of Mystery*, that received some token theatrical play-dates; and was in a similar situation with *Jigsaw*, top billed in this remake of the all-too-recent *Mirage*, that by-passed the tube to spend a little time in cinemas. By then television was consuming most of Guardino's time, and he chalked up three failed series and a load of TV movies. Back in theatres, he was part of the family ensemble of *Lovers and Other Strangers*, and appeared as Clint Eastwood's supervising officer in the hit *Dirty Harry*, a part he later repeated in *The Enforcer*. On Broadway he twice showed his less-known musical side, in *Anyone Can Whistle* and *Woman of the Year*.

Screen: **1951:** Purple Heart Diary; Sirocco; **1952:** Flesh and Fury; **1955:** The Big Tip Off; Hold Back Tomorrow; **1958:** Houseboat; **1959:** Pork Chop Hill; The Five Pennies; **1960:** 5 Branded Women; **1961:** King of Kings; **1962:** The Pigeon That Took Rome; Hell Is for Heroes; **1964:** Rhino!; **1966:** The Treasure of San Gennaro; **1967:** The Adventures of Bullwhip Griffin; **1968:** Jigsaw; Madigan; The Hell With Heroes; **1970:** Lovers and Other Strangers; **1971:** Red Sky at Morning; Slingshot; Dirty Harry; **1972:** They Only Kill Their Masters; **1975:** Capone; Whiffs; **1976:** St. Ives; The Enforcer; **1977:** Rollercoaster; **1978:** Matilda; **1979:** Goldengirl; **1980:** Any Which Way You Can; **1991:** Under Surveillance (dtv); **1992:** Fist of Honor (dtv).

NY Stage: **1953:** End as a Man; **1955:** A Hatful of Rain; **1960:** One More River; **1963:** Natural Affection; **1964:** Anyone Can Whistle; **1966:** The Rose Tattoo; **1968:** The Seven Descents of Myrtle; **1981:** Woman of the Year.

Select TV: **1957:** The Deadly Silence (sp); The Mother Bit (sp);

1958: Run, Joe, Run (sp); **1959:** Made in Japan (sp); The Killers of Mussolini; **1962:** Chez Rouge (sp); **1964:** The Reporter (series); **1966:** Valley of Mystery (and cinemas); **1969:** The Lonely Profession; **1971:** Monty Nash (series); The Last Child; **1973:** Police Story; Partners in Crime; **1973–74:** Perry Mason (series); **1974:** Indict and Convict; Get Christie Love!; **1976:** Street Killing; Having Babies; **1977:** Contract on Cherry Street; **1978:** Evening in Byzantium; **1979:** Pleasure Cove; Double Take; **1981:** Sophisticated Gents; **1989:** The Neon Empire.

ALEC GUINNESS

(Alec Guinness de Cuffe) Born: London, England, April 2, 1914. Died: August 5, 2000.

Because they were equated with drama and, more specifically, Shakespeare, Laurence Olivier and John Gielgud have often been cited as Great Britain's finest thespians, but for the sheer scope and enjoyment of his motion picture work, Alec Guinness might very well be the crowning import from the British Isles. Somewhat self-effacing in personality, prematurely bald, and possessing a pinched, nasal voice, he nonetheless commanded the screen through sheer versatility, becoming a master of disguises and alter-personas, excelling at heavy drama but remaining most dear to our hearts for his witty comedic finesse. He first took acting lessons at Fay Compton's school, but, after making his London stage bow in *Libel* and doing extra work in the film *Evensong*, he found himself under Gielgud's tutelage. In time he became one of the brightest names at the Old Vic during the pre- and postwar years, racking up such credits as *Hamlet*, *King Lear*, and *Saint Joan*. Having played Herbert Pocket in his own stage adaptation of *Great Expectations*, he was engaged by director David Lean to repeat the part in his 1946 version of the Dickens novel, which opened to universal acclaim, earning an Oscar nomination in the Best Picture category. As a follow-up Lean asked Guinness to play Fagin in his even-better film of *Oliver Twist*, and the actor's stunning, Chameleon-like transformation into the grubby street criminal had the motion picture industry abuzz. This was topped by his portrayal of eight different members (including one female) of the D'Ascoyne family, killed off for their fortune, in *Kind Hearts and Coronets*, one of the true pleasures of the famous Ealing Studios period of British comedy. It was for this company that Guinness would solidify his growing reputation for creating rich and varied characterizations. His output there came to include *A Run for Your Money*, as an impatient newspaper man, asked to show two contest winners around London, in one of his less-flamboyant characterizations; *The Lavender Hill Mob*, as a meek bank employee planning a heist, a performance that won enough favor in America to earn him an Oscar nomination; the decidedly one-note *The Man in the White Suit*, as an inventor whose indestructible fabric puts the clothing industry in an uproar; and *The Captain's Paradise*, as a man shuttling between two different wives, a movie whose premise has given it a better reputation than it deserves.

Indeed, not everything he did was first rate or comedic. Around this time he essayed some dramatic roles as well, playing a most formidable Prime Minister Benjamin Disraeli in *The Mudlark*, a British-made production for 20th Century-Fox; a man who learns he has only a few months to live in *Last Holiday*; and an imprisoned Cardinal in the stark *The Prisoner*, adapted from a play he had done. There was gentle humor in *Father Brown/The Detective*, where he brought G.K. Chesterton's stories to life, although Peter Finch, as the villain, was the one who got to don various disguises; while *To Paris With Love*, where he took his son on holiday to show him the good life, was probably the slimmest of all the Ealing assignments. However, he reached his Ealing peak with the next one, the very black and very funny *The Ladykillers*, wearing especially grotesque makeup as the mastermind behind a robbery foiled by a harmless little old biddy; the film is a strong contender for the most satisfying comedy to come out of Great Britain.

Shortly afterwards he made one of his rare journeys to Hollywood, for the classy but flatfooted *The Swan*, as a stodgy prince betrothed to an unwilling Grace Kelly. Rejoining David Lean, he pulled off the incredibly difficult role of the stubborn colonel, whose ambition causes him to forget that he is fighting a war, in the international smash *The Bridge on the River Kwai*, becoming that much more familiar to the moviegoing public and winning the Academy Award for Best Actor of 1957. The movie itself took the Oscar as the year's Best Picture and became something of a model for commercial filmmaking at its most exceptional. Back at Ealing, he was a timid naval officer (and several of his ancestors) in the lightweight *All at Sea/Barnacle Bill*, his last for the company shortly before it closed its doors for good. He received a producer credit for the drab drama *The Scapegoat*, which also found him playing a dual role; and he did the writing himself for *The Horse's Mouth*, giving another of his very best performances, as the grizzled and cantankerous painter/non-conformist Gulley Jimson, a man too brilliant and original to dwell comfortably in the real world. This time he earned an Oscar nomination for his script.

Our Man in Havana was an awkward Graham Greene adaptation, with Guinness as a timid every-man roped into spy work, but *Tunes of Glory* was another critical triumph, in which he was absolutely magnificent as the foolish but popular Scottish officer who clashes with stern martinet John Mills. His second Hollywood production, *A Majority of One*, found him uncomfortably cast as a Japanese industrialist in an overlong version of a Broadway success, starring opposite an equally out-of-place Rosalind Russell, as a Jewish widow. In the meantime, he continued to flourish in his West End stage career where his credits included *The Cocktail Party* and *Dylan*, both of which he did in New York as well, and *Hotel Paradiso*, which he brought to film with far less success, giving one of his most undisciplined performances in this noisy bedroom farce. On screen there were starring parts, as the sensible naval officer in the fine adventure epic *Damn the Defiant/HMS Defiant*, and as the strange little German holding two soldiers hostage long after the war is over in the misbegotten comedy *Situation Hopeless — But Not Serious*. He did supporting work in such grand epics as Lean's *Lawrence of Arabia*, as a very dignified Prince Feisal, in the 1962 Academy Award winner for Best Picture and one of the seminal movies of its day; *The Fall of the Roman Empire*, as Emperor Marcus Aurelius, being killed off early on in the story; *Doctor Zhivago*, framing the film as Omar Shariff's brother in one of the highest-grossing pictures of all time and his fifth under Lean's direction; and *Cromwell*, in a somewhat larger part, as the sympathetic King Charles, whose position is usurped by Puritan fanatic Richard Harris, in the title role. He also made an effectively creepy Marley's Ghost in the musical version of *Scrooge*, croaking his way through one song; showed up as the pope in a flower-child take on the story of St. Francis of Assisi, *Brother Sun, Sister Moon*; and took his final big screen lead, albeit in an illadvised project, *Hitler: The Last Ten Days*, as the Führer.

In the late 1970s his visibility as a film actor ascended with the hit Neil Simon comedy *Murder by Death*, as a blind butler, in his third and last made-in-Hollywood effort, and then soared to undreamed of heights with the phenomenal worldwide sensation of *Star Wars*. As the sage-like Obi Wan Kenobi, he added immeasurable class to the whole endeavor, earned an Oscar nomination in the supporting category, and became something of a sci-fi pop folk-hero for the ages. Wisely he had arranged for a percentage of the profits, making him very well off for the rest of his life. He repeated the part in the equally popular sequels *The Empire Strikes Back* and *Return of the Jedi*, despite having been killed off in the original. Thereafter he was seen getting more-fulfilling assignments on television, with *Tinker, Tailor, Soldier, Spy* and *Smiley's People*, than on the big screen, where he had little to work with in *Lovesick*, as Sigmund Freud, and *A Passage to India*, as an Indian. In the latter Guinness worked for the last time with the director who had started his film career in first place, David Lean (who didn't seem to realize that casting a Caucasian as an Indian was no longer acceptable). For his work in the two-part *Little Dorrit*, in which he was condemned to debtors' prison, he was awarded a fourth Oscar nomination, certainly the only participant in that project to emerge triumphant. Continuing in upscale productions, he portrayed the eccentric jungle hermit who made James Wilby an unwilling captive in *A Handful of Dust*, and was last seen playing Jeremy Irons's boss in the curious *Kafka*. Few audiences caught his final glimpse on screen, an unbilled cameo in the thriller *Mute Witness*, which had been filmed in 1985, 10 years (!) before the movie's limited release. He received a special career award from the Academy of Motion Picture Arts and Sciences, given in 1980, which marked the only time he showed up for an Oscar ceremony. He published his autobiography, *Blessings in Disguise*, in 1985, and it confirmed his reputation as a soft-spoken man who let his vast talent speak for him. There were two follow-up memoirs, *My Name Escapes Me* (1997) and *My Absolute Final Performance* (1998).

Screen: **1934:** Evensong; **1946:** Great Expectations (US: 1947); **1948:** Oliver Twist (US: 1951); **1949:** Kind Hearts and Coronets (US: 1950); A Run for Your Money; **1950:** Last Holiday; The Mudlark; **1951:** The Lavender Hill Mob; The Man in the White Suit (US: 1952); **1952:** The Card/The Promoter; **1953:** Malta Story (US: 1954); The Captain's Paradise; **1954:** Father Brown/The Detective; To Paris With Love (US: 1955); The Prisoner; **1955:** The Ladykillers (US: 1956); **1956:** The Swan; **1957:** Barnacle Bill/All at Sea; The Bridge on the River Kwai; **1958:** The Horse's Mouth (and wr.); **1959:** The Scapegoat (and prod.); **1960:** Our Man in Havana; Tunes of Glory; **1961:** A Majority of One; **1962:** H.M.S. Defiant/Damn the Defiant; Lawrence of Arabia; **1964:** The Fall of the Roman Empire; **1965:** Situation Hopeless — But Not Serious; Doctor Zhivago; **1966:** Hotel Paradiso; The Quiller Memorandum; **1967:** The Comedians; **1970:** Cromwell; Scrooge; **1972:** Brother Sun, Sister Moon; **1973:** Hitler: The Last Ten Days; **1976:** Murder by Death; **1977:** Star Wars; **1980:** The Empire Strikes Back; Raise the Titanic; **1983:** Lovesick; Return of the Jedi; **1984:** A Passage to India; **1987:** Little Dorrit (US: 1988); **1988:** A Handful of Dust; **1991:** Kafka; **1995:** Mute Witness (filmed 1985).

NY Stage: **1942:** Flare Path; **1950:** The Cocktail Party; **1964:** Dylan.

Select TV: **1959:** The Wicked Scheme of Jebel Deeks (sp); **1970:** Twelfth Night (sp); **1974:** Caesar and Cleopatra (sp); **1979:** Tinker, Tailor, Soldier, Spy (sp); **1980:** Little Lord Fauntleroy; **1982:** Smiley's People (sp); **1984:** Edwin (sp); **1985:**

Monsignor Quixote; 1992: Tales From Hollywood (sp); 1993: A Foreign Field; 1996: Interview Day/Eskimo Day (sp).

EDMUND GWENN

BORN: GLAMORGAN, WALES, SEPTEMBER 26, 1875.
ED: KING'S COL. DIED: SEPTEMBER 6, 1959.

The man who set the standard by which all other screen Santas must be measured, Edmund Gwenn, the short Welshman with the friendly face and gentle voice, was banished from his home as a teen because of his acting ambitions. In due time he made it to the London stage as one of the cast members of George Bernard Shaw's original 1902 production of *Man and Superman*. For the next 30 years he was primarily know as a stage actor, although he did make some film appearances in England, starting with the 1916 short subject "The Real Thing at Last," and including the 1920 production of *The Skin Game*, in a role he'd played onstage and would repeat in Alfred Hitchcock's sound version of the same story 11 years later. With the coming of talkies, film jobs began to take precedence over theater. Amid some supporting work, there were leads in *The Admiral's Secret*, as an old seaman in possession of a valuable diamond; the hit musical *The Good Companions*, as part of a trio who help form a traveling theater company; *Smithy*, as a clerk mistakenly thought to have come into a large sum of money; and *Father and Son*, as the Father, an ex-con. Gwenn was in such demand that America beckoned, and he arrived in 1935 for the Broadway production of *Laburnum Grove* and the MGM mystery *The Bishop Misbehaves*, the first of many lovable old codgers he'd play in Hollywood over the years. He was Katharine Hepburn's dad and partner in crime in *Sylvia Scarlett*, and then returned to England to repeat his *Laburnum Grove* role on film, playing a counterfeiter. He laid the ham on thick as Fredric March's employer, Bonnyfeather, in Warners's lavish *Anthony Adverse*; was Robert Montgomery's gentle butler in *The Earl of Chicago*; and turned effectively wicked in Hitchcock's *Foreign Correspondent*, trying to kill Joel McCrea and taking a fall as a result. That same year, 1940, he had one of his best roles, as Greer Garson's rational father, who must endure wife Mary Boland's excessive prattle, in *Pride and Prejudice*. Nearing the age of 70, the best of Gwenn's movie career was yet to come.

He had the hots for a cross-dressing Jack Benny in *Charley's Aunt*, and carried one lovely segment of *Lassie Come Home*, as the lonely peddler who befriends the collie when his own pooch is killed. Promoted to top-billing, he returned as the collie's co-star to great effect twice more, in *Challenge to Lassie* and *Hills of Home*. He then played the role of his life, the sweet eccentric who really believes he is Kris Kringle in the Christmas classic (originally released in June!), *Miracle on 34th Street*. His very human interpretation of Santa Claus was a masterpiece in the genre of whimsy, and he won a much-deserved Academy Award in the supporting category, though there was no doubt as to who was really carrying the film. As a follow-up, the same studio (Fox) and director (George Seaton) gave him another wonderful film and role, *Apartment for Peggy*, as the retired professor who rents his attic to William Holden and Jeanne Crain, while blithely planning to do himself in. Also at Fox he was another crafty counterfeiter, in *Mister 880*, earning another Oscar nomination. There was a superior sci-fi tale, *Them!*, as an entomologist who helps combat an army of gigantic ants, and his last canine opus, *It's a Dog's Life*, a story told from the point of view of a bull terrier. It was a rare actor who could land starring parts at 80, but Gwenn got just that in his last Hitchcock effort, the feeble black comedy *The Trouble With Harry*, as one of the New Englanders trying to dispose of a body. No doubt needing or wanting to work, his final credit was in an Italian-Spanish cheapie called *The Rocket From Calabuch*, which received a few playdates in the U.S. two years after its foreign release, and one year before Gwenn's death.

Screen: 1920: Unmarried; The Skin Game; 1931: Hindle Wakes; Money for Nothing; The Skin Game; Frail Women; Condemned to Death; 1932: Love on Wheels; Tell Me Tonight/Be Mine Tonight; 1933: The Good Companions; Cash/For Love or Money; Early to Bed; I Was a Spy; Channel Crossing; Smithy; Friday the Thirteenth; Marooned; 1934: The Admiral's Secret; Passing Shadows; Waltzes From Vienna/Strauss's Great Waltz; Warn London; Java Head; Father and Son; Spring in the Air; 1935: The Bishop Misbehaves; Sylvia Scarlett; 1936: All-American Chump; The Walking Dead; Anthony Adverse; Mad Holiday; Laburnum Grove; 1937: Parnell; 1938: A Yank at Oxford; South Riding; Penny Paradise; 1939: An Englishman's Home/Mad Men of Europe; Cheer, Boys, Cheer; 1940: The Earl of Chicago; The Doctor Takes a Wife; Pride and Prejudice; Foreign Correspondent; 1941: Cheers for Miss Bishop; One Night in Lisbon; The Devil and Miss Jones; Scotland Yard; Charley's Aunt; 1942: A Yank at Eton; 1943: The Meanest Man in the World; Forever and a Day; Lassie Come Home; 1944: Between Two Worlds; 1945: The Keys of the Kingdom; Dangerous Partners; Bewitched; She Went to the Races; 1946: Of Human Bondage; Undercurrent; 1947: Miracle on 34th Street; Life With Father; Thunder in the Valley; Green Dolphin Street; 1948: Apartment for Peggy; Hills of Home; 1949: Challenge to Lassie; 1950: Pretty Baby; Louisa; Mister 880; For Heaven's Sake; A Woman of Distinction; 1951: Peking Express; 1952: Sally and Saint Anne; Les Misérables; Bonzo Goes to College; Something for the Birds; 1953: Mister Scoutmaster; The Bigamist; 1954: Them!; The Student Prince; 1955: The Trouble With Harry; It's a Dog Life; 1959: The Rocket From Calabuch/Calabuch.

NY Stage: 1922: The Voice From the Minaret; Fedora; 1935: Laburnum Grove; 1941: The Wookey; 1944: Sheppey; 1945: You Touched Me!

Select TV: 1952: Heart of Gold (sp); 1953: Guardian of the Clock (sp); 1954: Come on Red (sp); 1955: The Great Shinin' Saucer of Paddy Faneen (sp); The Strange Dr. Lorenz (sp); 1957: The Greer Case (sp); A Man's Game (sp); Winter Dreams (sp).

BUDDY HACKETT

(Leonard Hacker) Born: Brooklyn, NY, August 31, 1924.

This fleshy, mush-mouthed comedian made a name for himself throughout the 1950s and 1960s in contrasting personas: as a rather racy nightclub entertainer, and as a more family-suitable lovable lug, which he pretty much reserved for his motion picture appearances. Starting in the late 1940s, he developed a stand-up routine, playing various Brooklyn clubs, the Catskills, and, finally, Los Angeles. From these engagements he ended up in two films at Universal, *Walking My Baby Back Home*, a Donald O'Connor musical; and *Fireman, Save My Child*, called on to replace an ailing Lou Costello and thereby ending up with one of the leads. After that, a chance meeting with playwright Sidney Kingsley enabled him to expand his horizons to legit theater when he won a role in the writer's Broadway farce *Lunatics and Lovers*. He landed his own short-lived series, *Stanley*, co-starring a pre-famous Carol Burnett; got good notices playing the lovelorn Pluto in the disposable film version of the spicy bestseller *God's Little Acre*; and continued to be in demand for appearances on various TV variety shows, winning a semi-regular spot on Jack Paar's series. In the 1960s he played his three best-known movie roles. First he was Robert Preston's buddy, small town blacksmith Marcellus Washburn, in the hit musical *The Music Man*, getting his moment in the spotlight singing the snappy "Shipoopi." After that he and Mickey Rooney were memorably paired as the two bunglers who are left at the controls of a private airplane in their quest for stolen cash in the all-star *It's a Mad Mad Mad Mad World*. As the decade came to a close, he was Dean Jones's mechanic pal in a third box-office winner, *The Love Bug*, about a Volkswagen with a mind of its own (made for Disney, of course). From there on it was basically Vegas and television, where Hackett could be found making a game attempt to play the actor for whom he once filled in, Lou Costello, in the telefilm *Bud and Lou*. In 1989 he was heard as the friendly seagull in the much-loved Disney animated film, *The Little Mermaid*, his distinct voice more likely recognized by parents than by kids in the audience.

Screen: 1953: Walking My Baby Back Home; 1954: Fireman, Save My Child; 1958: God's Little Acre; 1961: All Hands on Deck; Everything's Ducky; 1962: The Wonderful World of the Brothers Grimm; The Music Man; 1963: It's a Mad Mad Mad Mad World; 1964: Muscle Beach Party; 1965: The Golden Head; 1969: The Love Bug; The Good Guys and the Bad Guys; 1981: Loose Shoes/Coming Attractions; 1988: Scrooged; 1989: The Little Mermaid; 1998: Paulie; 2000: Little Mermaid II: Return to the Sea (dtv).

NY Stage: 1954: Lunatics and Lovers; 1960: Viva Madison Avenue!; 1964: I Had a Ball; 1967: Buddy Hackett — Eddie Fisher.

Select TV: 1949: School House (series); 1956–57: Stanley (series); 1958–59: The Jackie Gleason Show (series); 1978: Bud and Lou; 1980: You Bet Your Life (series); 1992: Fish Police (series; voice); 1999: Action (series).

JEAN HAGEN

(Jean Shirley Ver Hagen) Born: Chicago, IL, August 3, 1923. Raised in Elkhart, IL. Ed: Lake Forrest Col., Northwestern Univ. Died: August 29, 1977.

In a brief career spanning many genres, Jean Hagen was responsible for one of the greatest performances ever given in a musical film, even though the role didn't require her to either sing or dance. Her earliest show biz work was on radio dramas of the late 1940s, before she won a replacement role in the Broadway show *Swan Song*, in 1946. This led to more theater work, including *The Traitor*, which was responsible for her contract with MGM. She started off well, in a key role in the Tracy-Hepburn classic, *Adam's Rib* (the first movie she filmed, *Side Street*, was released afterwards), as the woman with whom married Tom Ewell has a fling, and she got involved in another fine film, *The Asphalt Jungle*, as criminal Sterling Hayden's girlfriend. She didn't rise above the supporting cast, but one such role was the gem she'd be remembered for, Lina Lamont, the arrogant, pin-headed silent film star with the grating voice, in one of the greatest of them all, *Singin' in the Rain*. She received a well-deserved Oscar nomination and most certainly should have won, but the award went to Gloria

Grahame that year. As a consolation, her performance allowed her name to be spoken of with rapture by generations of fans of musical films for decades to come. After that she played nice, uncomplicated wives in *Carbine Williams* (James Stewart), *Half a Hero* (Red Skelton), and the Disney hit *The Shaggy Dog*, opposite Fred MacMurray. By this time she had become well known to TV audiences as another wife, that of Danny Thomas, in the sitcom *Make Room for Daddy*. Following roles in a good sci-fi film, *Panic in Year Zero*, in which she and Ray Milland tried to survive after a nuclear attack wiped out most of the population, and the Bette Davis melodrama, *Dead Ringer*, she quietly retired from the business, eventually returning for a small part in a telefilm, *Alexander: The Other Side of Dawn*, aired only three months before her death of throat cancer in 1977.

Screen: 1949: Adam's Rib; Ambush; Side Street; 1950: The Asphalt Jungle; A Life of Her Own; 1951: Night Into Morning; No Questions Asked; Shadow in the Sky; 1952: Singin' in the Rain; Carbine Williams; 1953: Latin Lovers; Arena; Half a Hero; 1955: The Big Knife; 1957: Spring Reunion; 1959: The Shaggy Dog; 1960: Sunrise at Campobello; 1962: Panic in Year Zero; 1964: Dead Ringer.

NY Stage: 1946: Swan Song; Another Part of the Forest; 1948: Ghosts; 1949: The Traitor.

Select TV: 1953–56: Make Room for Daddy/The Danny Thomas Show (series); 1956: The Lou Gehrig Story (sp); 1959: Symbol of Authority (sp); Six Guns for Donegan (sp); 1960: The Snows of Kilimanjaro (sp); 1977: Alexander: The Other Side of Dawn.

WILLIAM HAINES

BORN: STAUNTON, VA, JANUARY 2, 1900.
DIED: DECEMBER 26, 1973.

A personable, light-hearted leading man of the silent era who eventually found his calling elsewhere, William Haines was an office boy on Wall Street when he decided to enter a "New Faces" contest in 1922. He won a contract with the Samuel Goldwyn Company and made his film bow in *Brothers Under the Skin*. He was promptly snatched up by MGM, who began to spotlight him in such films as *Wine of Youth*, *The Denial*, and *Sally, Irene and Mary*, as Mary's neglected beau. Moving up to leads, Haines was seen in a cross-country romance, *A Little Journey*, and *Brown of Harvard*, which was the Haines image personified, playing the smart-aleck ladies' man of the campus. He was similarly cocky while playing baseball in *Slide Kelly Slide*, football in *West Point*, and golf in *Spring Fever*. There was also a military role opposite Lon Chaney in the highly popular *Tell It to the Marines*, which really pushed him to the forefront of star attractions. Around the same time he was playing Marion Davies's sassy fellow-actor in *Show People*, he became Metro's first star to experiment in sound with the drama *Alias Jimmy Valentine*. He more or less kept giving his fans what they expected as he entered his talkie period, with *Navy Blues*, romancing dance-hall hostess Anita Page; *The Girl Said No*, still passing for a college boy at 30; *The New Adventures of Get-Rich-Quick Wallingford*; and his last for the studio, *Fast Life*, playing a speed boat enthusiast, in 1932. Ironically, he bade farewell to the movies with *The Marines Are Coming*, serving in the same celluloid branch of the military he'd been with in one of his earlier triumphs. Haines had already begun to dabble in outside interests — antiques and decorating — with his companion, Jimmy Shields. In 1936 both their names were in the news when a guest at one of their house parties was accused of molesting a neighbor's six-year-old boy. Haines, who had been fairly open about his

homosexuality, suffered physical abuse and was basically run out of town. Continuing his business as a decorator, he became a respected name in this field, where his clients included mogul Jack Warner and U.S. Ambassador Walter H. Annenberg.

Screen: 1922: Brothers Under the Skin; 1923: Three Wise Fools; Souls for Sale; Lost and Found; Six Days; 1924: The Gaiety Girl; The Desert Outlaw; Married Flirts; Circe the Enchantress; Three Weeks; Wine of Youth; The Midnight Express; True as Steel; Wife of the Centaur; 1925: The Denial; Fighting the Flames; The Tower of Lies; Who Cares?; A Fool and His Money; Little Annie Rooney; Sally, Irene and Mary; A Slave of Fashion; 1926: Brown of Harvard; Mike; Lovey Mary; Memory Lane; The Thrill Hunter; Tell It to the Marines; 1927: Spring Fever; Slide, Kelly, Slide; West Point; A Little Journey; 1928: The Smart Set; Show People; Excess Baggage; Telling the World; Alias Jimmy Valentine; 1929: A Man's Man; Speedway; The Duke Steps Out; The Hollywood Revue of 1929; Navy Blues; 1930: The Girl Said No; Free and Easy; Remote Control; Way Out West; 1931: A Tailor Made Man; Just a Gigolo; The New Adventures of Get-Rich-Quick Wallingford; 1932: Are You Listening?; The Fast Life; 1934: Young and Beautiful; The Marines Are Coming.

ALAN HALE

(RUFUS ALAN McKAHN)
BORN: WASHINGTON, DC, FEBRUARY 10, 1892.
ED: UNIV. OF PA. DIED: JANUARY 23, 1950.

Among the most ubiquitous character players from the 1920s through the 1940s was beefy, hearty Alan Hale, an imposing fellow with a bushy mustache and a sturdy bass voice, who went from playing silent movie villains to mostly jovial types, with occasional forays back to brutish menace. Originally an aspiring opera singer, he wound up on the legit stage instead. From there he joined the Lubin Film Studio, making his 1911 debut before the cameras in the short, "The Cowboy and the Lady." Three years later came his feature-length bow, with *The Power of the Press*, after which he played starring parts in literary adaptations like the short-subject *Martin Chuzzlewit*, and the feature-length *Jane Eyre* (as Rochester). With *The Four Horsemen of the Apocalypse*, in 1921, he began to be typed as a villain, getting throttled by Will Rogers in *One Glorious Day*, stealing Lon Chaney's mining claim in *The Trap*, and trying to kill J. Warren Kerrigan in the classic western *The Covered Wagon*. In 1922 he put aside villainy to play the role that he would become most closely identified with, Little John, supporting Douglas Fairbanks in his take on *Robin Hood*, though Hale would not truly solidify his claim to the part for another 16 years. In the meantime, there were some excursions behind the cameras, serving as a director for the Cecil B. DeMille Company, where his credits in this capacity included *The Wedding Stone*, *Risky Business* and *Rubber Tires*. Starting with *Skyscraper* in 1928, he did a quartet of films playing sidekick to William Boyd, which led into the sound era with the part-talkie *The Leatherneck*. He returned to meanness with *Susan Lennox (Her Fall and Rise)*, trying to rape Greta Garbo; *Destination Unknown*, as a Swedish bosun trying to steal liquor from Pat O'Brien; and *The Sin of Madelon Claudet*, thoughtlessly dumping Helen Hayes in her time of need. The lighter side of Hale was seen in *It Happened One Night*, as a garrulous motorist giving a lift to hitchhiking Claudette Colbert, and *Imitation of Life*, selling furniture to the same lady. He then showed up in period costume for *The Crusades*, *The Last Days of Pompeii*, and *The Prince and the Pauper*, the last marking his first time sharing the screen with

Errol Flynn, although, in this case, finding himself on the receiving end of Flynn's sword. After playing the hapless slob who pines for Barbara Stanwyck in *Stella Dallas*, he returned to Flynn and Sherwood Forest, making his robust reprise of Little John in the thrilling *The Adventures of Robin Hood* a part of film history.

As a contractee for Warner Bros., he played a similar role, as Flynn's loyal sidekick, in a highly enjoyable western, *Dodge City*, and then opposed him in battle as the Earl of Tyrone in *The Private Lives of Elizabeth and Essex*. Still in swashbuckling costume, he was Porthos in *The Man in the Iron Mask* (for UA), then basically dusted off his Little John shtick for another grand Flynn epic, *The Sea Hawk*. Just to keep the routine in balance, he was then back out West with Flynn again, for *Virginia City*. Ida Lupino disposed of him in *They Drive by Night*, after which he played the father of James Cagney in *The Strawberry Blonde*, and the dad of boxer Errol Flynn in *Gentleman Jim*. Also with Cagney, he was a sergeant in the war film *The Fighting 69th*; teamed with Marjorie Rambeau in an ill-advised effort to replace Wallace Beery, in *Tugboat Annie Sails Again*; and was called on for Flynn-support, yet again, for *Desperate Journey*. He did a delightful song and dance with Jack Carson in the all-star *Thank Your Lucky Stars* and had a funny bit not getting his hair cut in *Destination Tokyo*, as the submarine's chatty cook. At the close of the 1940s, he returned to familiar territory as Flynn's swashbuckling partner, in *Adventures of Don Juan*, appearing a bit long in the tooth for this sort of thing by now, and paid a final visit to the role of Little John in Columbia's *Rogues of Sherwood Forest*. As if he wasn't busy enough, during his lifetime Hale was credited with inventing such things as the sliding theater seat and the portable fire extinguisher. His son, Alan Hale, Jr., was also an actor, gaining TV immortality as the Skipper in the series *Gilligan's Island*.

Screen (features): 1914: The Power of the Press; The Woman in Black; Jane Eyre; 1915: Dora Thorne; East Lynne; 1916: Pudd'nhead Wilson; The Purple Lady; Rolling Stones; The Love Thief; The Scarlet Oath; The Woman in the Case; The Beast; 1917: The Price She Paid; Life's Whirlpool; One Hour; The Eternal Temptress; 1918: Moral Suicide; 1919: Love Hunger; 1921: A Wise Fool; The Four Horsemen of the Apocalypse; Over the Wire; The Fox; The Great Impersonation; The Barbarian; A Voice in the Dark; 1922: Shirley of the Circus; One Glorious Day; The Dictator; The Trap/Heart of a Wolf; Robin Hood; A Doll's House; 1923: The Covered Wagon; Cameo Kirby; Hollywood; The Eleventh Hour; Quicksands; Main Street; Long Live the King; The Cricket; 1924: Black Oxen; Code of the Wilderness; Girls Men Forget; Troubles of a Bride; One Night in Rome; For Another Woman; 1925: Dick Turpin; The Crimson Runner; Flattery; Ranger of the Big Pines; 1926: Hearts and Fists; 1927: Vanity; The Wreck of the Hesperus; 1928: The Cop; Oh Kay!; Skyscraper; The Leopard Lady; Sal of Singapore; Power; The Spieler; 1929: Sailor's Holiday; Red Hot Rhythm; The Leatherneck; The Sap; 1930: She Got What She Wanted; 1931: Aloha; Susan Lennox (Her Fall and Rise); Rebound; The Night Angel; The Sin of Madelon Claudet; Sea Ghost; 1932: Union Depot; So Big; Rebecca of Sunnybrook Farm; The Match King; 1933: Picture Brides; What Price Decency?; Destination Unknown; The Eleventh Commandment; 1934: Of Human Bondage; The Little Minister; It Happened One Night; The Lost Patrol; Imitation of Life; Fog Over Frisco; Great Expectations; Little Man, What Now?; Broadway Bill; Miss Fane's Baby Is Stolen; The Scarlet Letter; There's Always Tomorrow; Babbitt; 1935: Grand Old Girl; The Last Days of Pompeii; The Crusades; The Good Fairy; Another Face; 1936: Two in the Dark; A

Message to Garcia; Yellowstone; Our Relations; Parole!; The Country Beyond; 1937: God's Country and the Woman; High, Wide and Handsome; Stella Dallas; The Prince and the Pauper; Thin Ice; Music for Madame; 1938: The Adventures of Robin Hood; Algiers; Four Men and a Prayer; Valley of the Giants; Listen, Darling; The Adventures of Marco Polo; The Sisters; 1939: Dodge City; The Man in the Iron Mask; Dust Be My Destiny; Pacific Liner; The Private Lives of Elizabeth and Essex; On Your Toes; 1940: Virginia City; Three Cheers for the Irish; The Fighting 69th; They Drive by Night; Santa Fe Trail; Tugboat Annie Sails Again; The Sea Hawk; Green Hell; 1941: The Strawberry Blonde; Manpower; Thieves Fall Out; The Great Mr. Nobody; The Smiling Ghost; Footsteps in the Dark; 1942: Juke Girl; Captains of the Clouds; Gentleman Jim; Desperate Journey; 1943: Action in the North Atlantic; Destination Tokyo; Thank Your Lucky Stars; This Is the Army; 1944: The Adventures of Mark Twain; Make Your Own Bed; Hollywood Canteen; Janie; 1945: God Is My Co-Pilot; Escape in the Desert; Roughly Speaking; Hotel Berlin; 1946: Perilous Holiday; The Time, the Place and the Girl; Night and Day; The Man I Love; 1947: Pursued; Cheyenne; My Wild Irish Rose; That Way With Women; 1948: My Girl Tisa; Whiplash; Adventures of Don Juan; 1949: South of St. Louis; The Younger Brothers; The Inspector General; Always Leave Them Laughing; The House Across the Street; 1950: Colt .45; Stars in My Crown; Rogues of Sherwood Forest.

NY Stage: 1912: The Poor Little Rich Girl; 1919: A Lonely Romeo.

BARBARA HALE

BORN: DEKALB, IL, APRIL 18, 1921.
ED: CHICAGO ACAD. OF FINE ARTS.

This innocuously nice, attractive, brunette leading lady of the late 1940s-early 1950s was too lightweight to set the cinema ablaze, so she found her place in show business history, not on the big screen but in the TV courtroom. A former model, she was hired by RKO in 1943, made her debut in a bit in *Gildersleeve's Bad Day*, and thereafter decorated the casts of similar programmers like *Mexican Spitfire's Blessed Event* and *The Falcon in Hollywood*. She did get a lead in a "B" western, *West of the Pecos*, disguising herself as a boy and falling for Robert Mitchum. It was notable to Hale for personal reasons, because one of the other cast members, Bill Williams, became her husband in 1946. Moving up a notch or two, she appeared in the allegorical *The Boy With Green Hair*, and in a superior "B," *The Window*, in which she played the mother of terrorized Bobby Driscoll. By this point her contract had ended so she went over to Columbia for the highly popular sequel *Jolson Sings Again*, as the "second" Mrs. Al Jolson, Ellen Clark, though in fact the singer never married anyone by this name, and the number of spouses was decreased for your entertainment pleasure. At Fox she was the wife in a mild James Stewart comedy, *The Jackpot*, while at Warners she provided blank support to tenacious politician James Cagney in *A Lion Is in the Streets*. Back at Columbia she starred in a trio of fluffy comedies: *And Baby Makes Three*, pregnant on her way to the alter, albeit with ex-hubby Robert Young's child; *Emergency Wedding*, as Larry Parks's doctor wife; and *The First Time*, in which she and Robert Cummings portrayed a couple going through the joy and turmoil of having a baby. Top billed, she proved a colorless heroine in the swashbuckler *Lorna Doone* and was part of the ensemble of characters stranded in the desert and surrounded by hostile Indians in *Last of the Comanches*. She finally found her niche on the small screen, playing Raymond Burr's loyal secretary, Della Street, in the prototype of all TV lawyer shows, *Perry Mason*, winning an Emmy Award for the part in 1959. Following the demise of the series, she was seen only sporadically on the big screen, including *Airport*, where she was Dean Martin's neglected wife, and the surfing flick *Big Wednesday*, which starred her son, actor William Katt. In the 1980s she and Raymond Burr returned to television in countless *Perry Mason* telefilms.

Screen: 1943: Gildersleeve's Bad Day; Higher and Higher; Gildersleeve on Broadway; Government Girl; The Iron Major; Mexican Spitfire's Blessed Event; The Seventh Victim; Around the World; 1944: The Falcon Out West; Belle of the Yukon; Heavenly Days; Goin' to Town; The Falcon in Hollywood; 1945: West of the Pecos; First Yank in Tokyo; 1946: Lady Luck; 1947: A Likely Story; 1948: The Boy With Green Hair; 1949: The Clay Pigeon; The Window; Jolson Sings Again; And Baby Makes Three; 1950: The Jackpot; Emergency Wedding; 1951: Lorna Doone; 1952: The First Time; Last of the Comanches; 1953: Seminole; Lone Hand; A Lion Is in the Streets; 1955: Unchained; The Far Horizons; 1956: The Houston Story; Seventh Cavalry; 1957: The Oklahoman; Slim Carter; 1958: Desert Hell; 1968: Buckskin; 1970: Airport; 1972: Soul Soldier; 1975: The Giant Spider Invasion; 1978: Big Wednesday.

Select TV: 1952: The Divided Heart (sp); 1954: Remember to Live (sp); 1955: The Windmill (sp); 1956: Behind the Mask (sp); The Guardian (sp); The Country Husband (sp); 1957–66: Perry Mason (series); 1959: Night Club (sp); 1985: Perry Mason Returns; 1986: Perry Mason: The Case of the Notorious Nun; Perry Mason: The Case of the Shooting Star; 1987: Perry Mason: The Case of the Lost Love; Perry Mason: The Case of the Sinister Spirit; Perry Mason: The Case of the Murdered Madam; Perry Mason: The Case of the Scandalous Scoundrel; 1988: Perry Mason: The Case of the Avenging Ace; Perry Mason: The Case of the Lady in the Lake; 1989: Perry Mason: The Case of the Lethal Lesson; Perry Mason: The Case of the Musical Murder; Perry Mason: The Case of the All-Star Assassin; 1990: Perry Mason: The Case of the Poisoned Pen; Perry Mason: The Case of the Desperate Deception; Perry Mason: The Case of the Silenced Singer; Perry Mason: The Case of the Defiant Daughter; 1991: Perry Mason: The Case of the Ruthless Reporter; Perry Mason: The Case of the Maligned Mobster; Perry Mason: The Case of the Glass Coffin; Perry Mason: The Case of the Fatal Fashion; 1992: Perry Mason: The Case of the Fatal Framing; Perry Mason: The Case of the Reckless Romeo; Perry Mason: The Case of the Heartbroken Bride; 1993: Perry Mason: The Case of the Skin-Deep Scandal; Perry Mason: The Case of the Killer Kiss; A Perry Mason Mystery: The Case of the Wicked Wives; 1994: A Perry Mason Mystery: The Case of the Lethal Lifestyle; A Perry Mason Mystery: The Case of the Grimacing Governor; 1995: A Perry Mason Mystery: The Case of the Jealous Jokester.

JACK HALEY

BORN: BOSTON, MA, AUGUST 10, 1898.
DIED: JUNE 6, 1979.

Of Judy Garland's three peerless companions on the road to Oz, Jack Haley had the most extensive film career, dating back to the 1927 silent *Broadway Madness*. Prior to that, the apple-cheeked, cheerful-looking, wavy-haired entertainer plugged tunes in Philadelphia, was a song-and-dance man in vaudeville, and had made his Broadway debut in *Round the Town*, in 1924. He came to Paramount in 1930 to preserve his stage role

in the musical *Follow Thru* on film, though in typical fashion much of the material from the original had been discarded. For that studio he partnered with Jack Oakie as a team of song writers in *Sitting Pretty*; headlined the comedy *Here Comes the Groom*, pretending to be a radio crooner while fleeing the police; and was featured as a sailor in a feeble concoction called *Coronado*. He then settled in over at Fox, where he and Alice Faye were a pair of vaudevillians in one of the nicer Shirley Temple efforts, *Poor Little Rich Girl*. Although they gave him a pair of "B's" to star in, *Danger — Love at Work* and *She Had to Eat*, he was strictly ensemble material when it came the studio's bigger budgeted fare, appearing in such well-attended musicals as *Pigskin Parade, Wake Up and Live* (where his vocals were inexplicably dubbed by Buddy Clark), *Alexander's Ragtime Band*, and *Thanks for Everything*.

Fate handed him the role he became most famous for when Buddy Ebsen developed an allergic reaction to the silver makeup used for the Tin Man in *The Wizard of Oz*. Haley stepped in and brought an enduring sweetness to the character in search of a heart, making it inconceivable that someone else nearly had the part. After that high point of musical cinema, it was back to basics with seen-it-before offerings like *Moon Over Miami* and *Navy Blues*. He was asked to repeat his role from the 1940 Broadway show *Higher and Higher*, but since the whole Rodger and Hart score was scrapped, it was pretty much another fish altogether. As the 1940s rolled on, he led the cast of some Pine-Thomas quickies distributed by Paramount, including a pair of comedy chillers, *One Body Too Many* and *Scared Stiff*, plus *People Are Funny*, based on a popular radio show of the time. When RKO released the compilation *Make Mine Laughs*, featuring clips of Haley in *George White's Scandals*, both he and former *Oz* co-star Ray Bolger filed suit, causing the movie to be withdrawn from circulation. Having invested wisely in real estate, the actor took it easy once he'd reached his half-century mark, choosing to appear only occasionally on TV, and not showing up in a theatrical release again until *Norwood*, in 1970. It was directed by his son, Jack Haley, Jr., who was best known for the compilation celebrating MGM's golden age of musicals, *That's Entertainment!* The older Haley was seen briefly in *New York, New York* (opposite then-daughter-in-law Liza Minnelli), but only in the longer 1981 reissue print, having been excised from the original 1977 version.

Screen: 1927: Broadway Madness; 1930: Follow Thru; 1933: Sitting Pretty; Mr. Broadway; 1934: Here Comes the Groom; 1935: The Girl Friend; Coronado; Redheads on Parade; Spring Tonic; 1936: F-Man; Poor Little Rich Girl; Mister Cinderella; Pigskin Parade; 1937: Wake Up and Live; Pick a Star; She Had to Eat; Ali Baba Goes to Town; Danger — Love at Work; 1938: Rebecca of Sunnybrook Farm; Alexander's Ragtime Band; Hold That Co-Ed; Thanks for Everything; 1939: The Wizard of Oz; 1941: Moon Over Miami; Navy Blues; 1942: Beyond the Blue Horizon; 1943: Higher and Higher; 1944: One Body Too Many; Take It Big; 1945: George White's Scandals; People Are Funny; Scared Stiff; Sing Your Way Home; 1946: Vacation in Reno; 1970: Norwood; 1977: New York, New York (in 1981 reissue print only).

NY Stage: 1924: Round the Town; 1925: Gay Paree; 1926: Gay Paree of 1926; 1929: Follow Thru; 1931: Free for All; 1932: Take a Chance; 1940: Higher and Higher; 1942: Show Time; 1948: Inside U.S.A.

Select TV: 1950–51: Ford Star Revue (series); 1953: Uncle Jack (sp); 1958: No Time at All (sp); 1972: Rolling Man.

HUNTZ HALL

(HENRY RICHARD HALL) BORN: BOSTON, MA, AUGUST 15, 1920. DIED: JANUARY 30, 1999.

As the dopey-looking, fidgety member of the Dead End Kids/Bowery Boys, Huntz Hall would, along with Leo Gorcey, become the most famous performer from that varied and long-running series of films. A veteran of the Professional Children's School, he had sung with the Madison Square Quintette before making his legit stage bow as Dippy, one of the aimless slum kids, in *Dead End*. Along with his youthful fellow cast members (Gorcey, Billy Halop, Bobby Jordan, Gabriel Dell, and Bernard Punsley), he made his motion picture debut in the outstanding 1937 film adaptation made for Samuel Goldwyn. At first the gang did variations of this juvenile delinquent formula at Warners, with *Crime School* and *Angels With Dirty Faces*, the latter perhaps the most famous of the serious movies Hall and his chums appeared in. In time they went from Dead End Kids to Little Tough Guys (where Hall's character was indelicately dubbed Pig) to East Side Kids (as Glimpy) or variations of the same; the tone getting goofier and the target audience being far less sophisticated, to say the least. The whole endeavor actually managed to shoot lower, starting in 1946, with *Live Wires*. From this point on the gang was known as The Bowery Boys and Hall was dubbed Satch (a.k.a. Horace Debussy Jones). With this character he would take his mugging to new heights and become the comical centerpiece, of great appeal mainly to undemanding children. Hall carried on valiantly, being upped to front billing after Gorcey's departure, finishing the series in 1958, with *In the Money*. In later years he had character parts in a few films, notably *Valentino*, cast as studio head Jesse Lasky, and the sexploitation cheapie, *Gas Pump Girls*, surrounded by a few centerfolds masquerading as actresses.

Screen: 1937: Dead End; 1938: Crime School; Little Tough Guy; Angels With Dirty Faces; 1939: Hell's Kitchen; Call a Messenger; The Angels Wash Their Faces; The Return of Dr. X; They Made Me a Criminal; The Dead End Kids on Dress Parade; 1940: Give Us Wings; Junior G-Men (serial); You're Not So Tough; 1941: Hit the Road; Bowery Blitzkrieg; Sea Raiders (serial); Zis Boom Bah; Spooks Run Wild; Mob Town; 1942: Junior Army; Private Buckaroo; Mr. Wise Guy; Tough as They Come; Smart Alecks; 'Neath Brooklyn Bridge; Junior G-Men of the Air (serial); Let's Get Tough; 1943: Clancy Street Boys; Mug Town; Kid Dynamite; Mr. Muggs Steps Out; Keep 'Em Slugging; Ghosts on the Loose; 1944: Block Busters; Bowery Champs; Follow the Leader; Million Dollar Kid; 1945: Wonder Man; A Walk in the Sun; Bring on the Girls; Mr. Muggs Rides Again; Docks of New York; Come Out Fighting; 1946: Live Wires; In Fast Company; Bowery Bombshell; Spook Busters; Mr. Hex; 1947: Hard Boiled Mahoney; News Hounds; Bowery Buckaroos; 1948: Angels' Alley; Jinx Money; Smugglers' Cove; Trouble Makers; 1949: Fighting Fools; Hold That Baby!; Angels in Disguise; Master Minds; 1950: Blonde Dynamite; Lucky Losers; Triple Trouble; Blues Busters; 1951: Bowery Battalion; Ghost Chasers; Let's Go Navy!; Crazy Over Horses; 1952: Hold That Line; Here Come the Marines; Feudin' Fools; No Holds Barred; 1953: Jalopy; Loose in London; Clipped Wings; Private Eyes; 1954: Paris Playboys; The Bowery Boys Meet the Monsters; Jungle Gents; Bowery to Bagdad; 1955: High Society; Spy Chasers; Jail Busters; 1956: Dig That Uranium; Crashing Las Vegas; Fighting Trouble; Hot Shots; 1957: Hold That Hypnotist; Spook Chasers; Looking for Danger; Up in Smoke; 1958: In the Money; 1965: Second Fiddle to a Steel Guitar; 1967: Gentle Giant; 1970: The Phynx; 1973: The

Manchu Eagle Murder Caper Mystery; 1974: Herbie Rides Again; 1976: Won Ton Ton, the Dog Who Saved Hollywood; 1977: Valentino; 1979: Gas Pump Girls; 1982: The Escape Artist; 1987: Cyclone; 1991: Auntie Lee's Meat Pies (dtv).

NY Stage: 1935: Dead End.

Select TV: 1971: Escape; The Chicago Teddy Bears (series); 1984: The Ratings Game.

JON HALL

(CHARLES HALL LOCHER) BORN: FRESNO, CA, FEBRUARY 23, 1913. DIED: DECEMBER 13, 1979.

Not unlike his frequent co-star, Maria Montez, the extremely limited Jon Hall was kept going because Hollywood thought he photographed well in Technicolor. The virile and bland star of countless swashbucklers, fairy tales, and South Sea Island adventures started working in pictures as a bit player, using his real name. Paramount gave him a try under the name "Lloyd Crane" for two films, *Mind Your Own Business* and *The Girl From Scotland Yard*, and then dropped him. He was, therefore, treated as a new discovery when he and Dorothy Lamour starred as a pair of simple island natives desperately in love in director John Ford's epic *The Hurricane*, where they were upstaged by the incredible, excitingly staged storm that wiped out most of the cast at the climax. The duo returned to their sarongs for *Aloma of the South Seas*, this time in color; but while Lamour stayed on at Paramount, Hall went over to Universal where he would make a career in similarly silly fare. After going to war for *Eagle Squadron*, and disappearing for much of *Invisible Agent* (it was 1942, so it had a war background), he was cast opposite Ms. Montez for a piece of exotica called *Arabian Knights*, the studio's very first three-color Technicolor production. It was the sort of garish trash in which opulent set design substituted for wit and directorial flair, and it became the blueprint for their subsequent teamings. Hall's roles in these kitschy outings included a fisherman in *White Savage*; Mr. Baba in *Ali Baba and the Forty Thieves*; the man desired by a pair of twin Montez sisters in *Cobra Woman*; the king's messenger, who captures Maria's untamed heart, in *Gypsy Wildcat*; and a slave trader in *Sudan*. In each, Montez's acting made Hall look good in comparison, but there was little to recommend in these turgid adventures despite the efforts of certain fans to elevate them to some exalted level of irresistible camp. After leaving Universal, Hall pretty much stayed in this genre, with a few westerns thrown in for some variety. There was also a syndicated TV series aimed at the youngsters, *Ramar of the Jungle*, and a directorial effort, the low budget *The Beach Girls and the Monster*, with Hall himself as the monster. Suffering from cancer, he shot himself to death in 1979.

Screen: AS CHARLES LOCHER: 1935: Women Must Dress; Charlie Chan in Shanghai; Here's to Romance; 1936: The Amazing Exploits of the Clutching Hand (serial); The Mysterious Avenger; The Lion Man; Winds of the Wasteland.

AS LLOYD CRANE: 1936: Mind Your Own Business; 1937: The Girl From Scotland Yard.

AS JON HALL: 1937: The Hurricane; 1940: South of Pago Pago; Sailor's Lady; Kit Carson; 1941: Aloma of the South Seas; 1942: The Tuttles of Tahiti; Eagle Squadron; Invisible Agent; Arabian Nights; 1943: White Savage; 1944: Ali Baba and the Forty Thieves; Lady in the Dark; Cobra Woman; Gypsy Wildcat; The Invisible Man's Revenge; San Diego, I Love You; 1945: Men in Her Diary; Sudan; 1947: The Michigan Kid; Last of the Redmen; The Vigilantes Return; 1948: The Prince of Thieves; 1949: The Mutineers; Zamba; Deputy Marshal; 1950: On the Isle of Samoa;

1951: When the Redskins Rode; China Corsair; Hurricane Island; 1952: Brave Warrior; Last Train From Bombay; 1953: White Goddess; Eyes of the Jungle; 1955: Phantom of the Jungle; Thunder Over Sangoland; 1957: Hell Ship Mutiny (and exec. prod.); 1959: Forbidden Island; 1965: The Beach Girls and the Monster (and dir.).

Select TV: 1952–54: Ramar of the Jungle (series).

PORTER HALL

(CLIFFORD PORTER HALL) BORN: CINCINNATI, OH, SEPTEMBER 19, 1888. ED: UNIV. OF CINCINNATI. DIED: OCTOBER 6, 1953.

Small, sour-faced Porter Hall was a character player for whom audiences had little sympathy. If not playing out-and-out villains, he was often shifty, grouchy, difficult, or cowardly. Originally a steel-mill worker, he took up acting, joined a traveling Shakespeare company, and finally made it to Broadway in 1926. After another eight years of theater credits, he came to Hollywood and made his debut in one of the watershed productions of the 1930s, the lighthearted murder mystery *The Thin Man*, in a key role as a lawyer. There followed such weasel-like characterizations as the crooked father of Madeleine Carroll in *The General Died at Dawn*, and the murderer of Wild Bill Hickok (Gary Cooper) in *The Plainsman*. He was the self-righteous dad of Bette Davis in *The Petrified Forest*; the selfish son-in-law of senior citizens Beulah Bondi and Victor Moore in *Make Way for Tomorrow*; the warden of *Prison Farm*; and, calling a spade a spade, The Weasel in *Tennessee Johnson*. He played the atheist who blithely tosses Bing Crosby's baseball under a truck in *Going My Way*; the seemingly timid head of the oddball family of murderers in the black comedy *Murder, He Says*; the self-important psychiatrist who tries to declare Edmund Gwenn nuts in *Miracle on 34th Street*; and the leader of the racist lynch mob in *Intruder in the Dust*. On a less-malevolent note, he was the studio boss in *Sullivan's Travels*; the train passenger who temporarily holds up Fred MacMurray's murder plans in *Double Indemnity*; and President Franklin Pierce in *The Great Moment*. He also appeared as the judge who gets shot in the ass on three separate occasions by trigger-happy Betty Grable in *The Beautiful Blonde from Bashful Bend*, and the small-town newspaper editor who wears both suspenders and a belt in *Ace in the Hole*.

Screen: 1934: The Thin Man; Murder in the Private Car; 1935: The Case of the Lucky Legs; 1936: The Petrified Forest; Too Many Parents; And Sudden Death; The Princess Comes Across; The Story of Louis Pasteur; The General Died at Dawn; Satan Met a Lady; Snowed Under; The Plainsman; Let's Make a Million; 1937: Souls at Sea; Make Way for Tomorrow; Wild Money; True Confession; Bulldog Drummond Escapes; King of Gamblers; Hotel Haywire; This Way Please; Wells Fargo; 1938: Scandal Street; Dangerous to Know; Prison Farm; Stolen Heaven; Bulldog Drummond's Peril; King of Alcatraz; Tom Sawyer — Detective; The Arkansas Traveler; Men With Wings; 1939: Grand Jury Secrets; They Shall Have Music; Mr. Smith Goes to Washington; Henry Goes Arizona; 1940: His Girl Friday; Arizona; Dark Command; Trail of the Vigilantes; 1941: The Parson of Panamint; Mr. and Mrs. North; Sullivan's Travels; 1942: The Remarkable Andrew; Butch Minds the Baby; Tennessee Johnson; 1943: A Stranger in Town; The Woman of the Town; The Desperadoes; 1944: The Miracle of Morgan's Creek; Standing Room Only; Going My Way; The Great Moment; Double Indemnity; The Mark of the Whistler; 1945: Blood on the Sun; Bring on the Girls; Kiss and Tell; Murder, He Says;

Week-end at the Waldorf; 1947: Miracle on 34th Street; Singapore; Unconquered; 1948: You Gotta Stay Happy; That Wonderful Urge; 1949: Chicken Every Sunday; The Beautiful Blonde From Bashful Bend; Intruder in the Dust; 1951: Ace in the Hole/The Big Carnival; 1952: Carbine Williams; Holiday for Sinners; The Half-Breed; 1953: Vice Squad; Pony Express; 1954: Return to Treasure Island/Long John Silver.

NY Stage: 1926: The Great Gatsby; Naked; 1927: Loud Speaker; 1928: Night Hostess; 1929: It's a Wild Child; 1932: Collision; 1933: The Dark Tower; 1934: Bring on the Girls.

Select TV: 1952: The Man Who Had Nothing to Lose (sp); My Wife Geraldine (sp); Moses and Mr. Aiken (sp).

BILLY HALOP

BORN: BROOKLYN, NY, FEBRUARY 11, 1920. DIED: NOVEMBER 9, 1976.

When the Dead End Kids first came to Hollywood, sensitive tough-guy Billy Halop was their unofficial leader, having been the focus of the stage drama, *Dead End*, that introduced the gang. Halop had been acting on radio since he was six years old, in various dramas and on the children's series *Let's Pretend*. When the *Dead End* movie was ready to go before the cameras for Goldwyn, Halop and most of his young co-stars were asked to repeat their parts, with Sylvia Sidney cast as the teen's older sister. The success of the film brought Halop further supporting gigs at Warners and a title role for him at Universal, in *Little Tough Guy*, this time playing the misbehaving younger brother of Helen Parrish. This led to the "Little Tough Guy" series for the studio, where he was supported by most of the *Dead End* bunch. Halop, however, was not anxious to be typecast in these swaggering delinquent roles, so he left the group before they began to indulge in their increasingly silly outings. Unfortunately his career didn't take him beyond "B" productions, including various cheap-jack serials like *Junior G-Men* and *Sky Raiders*, and he had pretty much given up on the movies by the end of the 1940s, becoming a salesman. There followed hard times including a drunk driving arrest and a nervous breakdown, after which he took employment as a male nurse. In the 1960s he began to appear in small, unbilled roles in such movies as *A Global Affair* and *Mister Buddwing*, in both instances playing cab drivers; and he was seen by millions of viewers when he joined the cast of the smash hit series *All in the Family*, as Archie's buddy, Bert Munson, a role he was still playing at the time of his death. His younger sister, Florence, worked frequently on radio and TV, where her series included *Meet Millie* and *St. Elsewhere*. Billy's autobiography was titled *There's No Dead End*.

Screen: 1937: Dead End; 1938: Crime School; Little Tough Guy; Angels With Dirty Faces; 1939: Hell's Kitchen; Dust Be My Destiny; The Angels Wash Their Faces; Call a Messenger; The Dead End Kids on Dress Parade; You Can't Get Away With Murder; They Made Me a Criminal; 1940: Junior G-Men (serial); Tom Brown's School Days; Give Us Wings; Sea Raiders (serial); You're Not So Tough; 1941: Mob Town; Blues in the Night; Sky Raiders (serial); Hit the Road; 1942: Tough as They Come; Junior Army; Junior G-Men of the Air (serial); 1943: Mug Town; 1946: Gas House Kids; 1947: Dangerous Years; 1949: Challenge of the Range; Too Late for Tears; 1955: Air Strike; 1962: Boys' Night Out; 1963: For Love or Money; The Courtship of Eddie's Father; The Wheeler Dealers; Move Over, Darling; 1964: A Global Affair; 1966: Mister Buddwing; 1967: Fitzwilly.

NY Stage: 1935: Dead End.

Select TV: 1952: Crossroads (sp); 1954: The Pale Blonde of Sand

Street (sp); 1972–77: All in the Family (series); 1974: The Phantom of Hollywood.

GEORGE HAMILTON

BORN: MEMPHIS, TN, AUGUST 12, 1939.

Because he never suggested any great range as an actor, George Hamilton's dark good looks were given more credit for his frequent employment in the early 1960s than his talent. Over time he would give some better-than-average performances and show a flair for good-natured self-parody, but, as he aged, he seemed to become better known for his ever-present tan than for his contributions to cinema. Fresh out of high school (where he'd won a Florida state acting contest), he came to Los Angeles to seek work and wound up winning the lead in a 1959 Allied Artists update of Dostoyevsky, called *Crime & Punishment, U.S.A.*, as a law student who winds up involved in murder. MGM put him under contract, debuting him as the weakling son of Robert Mitchum in the lengthy *Home From the Hill*, where George Peppard acted him right off the screen. This was followed by the much-despised drama *All the Fine Young Cannibals*, in which he floundered as the Texas millionaire who marries Natalie Wood, and the popular-but-vapid *Where the Boys Are*, in which he once again represented shallow wealth, as a rich college boy hitting on Dolores Hart. Back at Allied Artists, he was top billed again for *Angel Baby*, as the promoter of a backwoods evangelist group; then he dropped down the cast list for one of the vacuous Lana Turner soaps of the day, *By Love Possessed*, as the son of Efrem Zimbalist, Jr., charged with rape. For his home studio he did some more soaps: *Light in the Piazza*, in a particularly misguided turn as Yvette Mimieux's Italian suitor, and an overwrought Vincente Minnelli drama, *Two Weeks in a Another Town*, as an overly sensitive Hollywood actor. At Columbia, he appeared in a movie that was much better than any of these, *The Victors*, a multi-story piece about some American soldiers in Europe, as a nice boy falling in love with violinist Romy Schneider, who turns out to be less innocent then he thinks. But he didn't benefit at all from being given the lead in a Warners film, *Act One*, providing very little insight into playwright Moss Hart and receiving some of the worst notices of his career.

Perhaps to make up for this, MGM gave him another biopic to carry, and he wound up giving his best performance to date, playing alcoholic country-music superstar Hank Williams in *Your Cheatin' Heart*, which, alas, didn't bring in enough box-office returns for the studio to justify producing it in the first place. MGM finished him off with a French farce that put him between Jeanne Moreau and Bridget Bardot, *Viva Maria!*; and tepid fare like the Sandra Dee vehicle *Doctor, You've Got to Be Kidding*, and the caper flick *Jack of Diamonds*. Television was the next logical step, but he had the dubious distinction of having two series, *The Survivors* and *Paris 7000*, cancelled in the same season. There was a minor big screen success with Hamilton giving a playful performance as the gaudy motorcycle daredevil *Evel Knievel*, and then some excursions into camp, intentional or otherwise, with *Jacqueline Susann's Once Is Not Enough*, as one of Deborah Raffin's lovers; Mae West's bizarre farewell, *Sextette*, as a gangster; and *The Happy Hooker Goes to Washington*. When he popped up clowning wittily in the pleasant vampire spoof *Love at First Bite*, as a disco dancing Count Dracula in New York City, it was looked on as some kind of comeback, suggesting that Hamilton had a cheeky sense of humor, a knack for comedy, and some degree of awareness about his limitations. The surprise success of the film inspired him to try again with *Zorro, the Gay*

Blade, but this time absolutely nothing went right. He retreated to television again, making occasional theatrical appearances, as in *The Godfather Part III*, as a Mafia attorney, and *Doc Hollywood*, where he played a plastic surgeon. After a while he seemed to get hired just to show up as himself (*Meet Wally Sparks*, *Bullworth*), suggesting that he was being ribbed for representing a somewhat superficial example of a Hollywood celebrity.

Screen: 1959: Crime & Punishment, USA; 1960: Home From the Hill; All the Fine Young Cannibals; Where the Boys Are; 1961:Angel Baby; By Love Possessed; A Thunder of Drums; 1962: Light in the Piazza; Two Weeks in Another Town; 1963: The Victors; Act One; 1964: Looking for Love; Your Cheatin' Heart; 1965: Viva Maria!; 1967: Doctor, You've Got to Be Kidding; Jack of Diamonds; That Man George!/Our Man in Marrakech; A Time for Killing; 1968: The Power; 1970: Togetherness; Elvis: That's the Way It Is; 1971: Evel Knievel (and prod.); 1973: The Man Who Loved Cat Dancing; 1974: Medusa; 1975: Jacqueline Susann's Once Is Not Enough; 197: The Happy Hooker Goes to Washington; 1978: Sextette; 1979: Love at First Bite (and exec prod.); From Hell to Victory; 1981: Zorro, the Gay Blade (and prod.); 1990: The Godfather Part III; 1991: Doc Hollywood; 1992: Once Upon a Crime; 1993: Amore! (dtv); 1994: Double Dragon; 1995: Playback (dtv); 1997: Meet Wally Sparks; 8 Heads in a Duffel Bag; 1998: Bulworth; She's Too Tall (nUSr); 1999: Pets (nUSr); The Little Unicorn (dtv); 2001: Crocodile Dundee in Los Angeles; 2002: Hollywood Ending.

NY Stage: 2001: Chicago.

Select TV: 1964: The Turncoat (sp); 1969–70: The Survivors (series); 1970: Paris 7000 (series); 1975: The Dead Don't Die; 1977: Roots (ms); The Strange Possession of Mrs. Oliver; Killer on Board; 1978: The Users; 1979: Institute for Revenge; Express to Terror/Supertrain; Death on the Freeway; The Seekers; 1980: The Great Cash Giveaway Getaway; 1983: Malibu; 1985: Two Fathers' Justice; 1985–86: Dynasty (series); 1986: Monte Carlo; 1987: Spies (series); Poker Alice; 1991: Caution: Murder Can Be Hazardous to Your Health; 1992: The House on Sycamore Street; 1994: Two Fathers: Justice for the Innocent; 1995: Danielle Steel's Vanished; 1995–96: George and Alana (series; and prod.); 1996: Hart to Hart: Till Death Do Us Hart; 1997: Rough Riders; Jenny (series); 1998: Casper Meets Wendy; 1999: P.T. Barnum.

MARGARET HAMILTON

BORN: CLEVELAND, OH, DECEMBER 9, 1902. DIED: MAY 16, 1985.

With her sour-apple expression and beak-like nose, Margaret Hamilton was so unforgettable-looking that she would, no doubt, be ranked high among the more-distinctive character players of all time, even if she hadn't gained unparalleled immortality as the greatest villain in celluloid history. Before acting claimed her, she taught kindergarten and ran her own nursery school. She joined the Cleveland Playhouse and spent three years with that company before moving on to New England, where she won a role in the play *The Hallams*. When the show, re-titled *Another Language*, moved to Broadway in 1932, Hamilton came with it, playing a brittle-tongued wife dominated by the family matriarch. She recreated her performance in the 1933 MGM film version, which starred Helen Hayes. Similarly she was asked to repeat another of her New York stage roles, for Fox, in *The Farmer Takes a Wife*, alongside Henry Fonda, in his film debut. In time she would corner the movie market playing spinsters, gossips, schoolmarms, and acerbic old buzzards. She provided one truly glorious moment in *These Three*, when she gave audiences what they were longing for, hauling off and smacking bratty Bonita Granville in the face. There were more crabby ladies in *Nothing Sacred*, *A Slight Case of Murder*, and *Mother Carey's Chickens*, but they were nothing compared to her still-mesmerizing dual performance as Miss Gulch and the Wicked Witch of the West in the 1939 classic *The Wizard of Oz*. As a replacement for Gale Sondergaard, she proved to be both deliciously entertaining and truly terrifying as she stopped at nothing to gain possession of Judy Garland's ruby slippers. Since the movie was not yet legendary upon its initial release, there was, alas, no Oscar nomination for Hamilton's peerless work. Instead, she went back to basics, disapproving of Mae West in *My Little Chickadee*; giving Anne Baxter a hard time in *Guest in the House*; and hen-pecking husband Porter Hall in *The Beautiful Blonde from Bashful Bend*. She provided a funny sight gag, wearing a pair of horn-rimmed glasses, to play Harold Lloyd's look-alike sister, in *The Sin of Harold Diddlebock*, and tried to put a spell on Lou Costello in *Comin' Round the Mountain*, as a sorceress. By the late 1950s *Oz* had taken TV by storm, and filmmakers didn't mind cashing in on Hamilton's connection with that movie, as in *13 Ghosts*, where she played a witchy housekeeper, and *Brewster McCloud*, where, after being bumped off, she was seen wearing those red slippers at long last.

Screen: 1933: Another Language; 1934: Hat, Coat and Glove; There's Always Tomorrow; Broadway Bill; By Your Leave; 1935: The Farmer Takes a Wife; Way Down East; 1936: Chatterbox; These Three; The Moon's Our Home; The Witness Chair; Laughing at Trouble; 1937: You Only Live Once; When's Your Birthday?; Good Old Soak; Mountain Justice; Nothing Sacred; Saratoga; I'll Take Romance; 1938: A Slight Case of Murder; The Adventures of Tom Sawyer; Mother Carey's Chickens; Four's a Crowd; Breaking the Ice; Stablemates; 1939: The Wizard of Oz; The Angels Wash Their Faces; Babes in Arms; Main Street Lawyer; 1940: My Little Chickadee; The Villain Still Pursued Her; I'm Nobody's Sweetheart Now; The Invisible Woman; 1941: Play Girl; The Gay Vagabond; The Shepherd of the Hills; 1942: Twin Beds; Meet the Stewarts; The Affairs of Martha; 1943: City Without Men; The Ox-Bow Incident; Johnny Come Lately; 1944: Guest in the House; 1945: George White's Scandals; 1946: Janie Gets Married; Faithful in My Fashion; 1947: The Sin of Harold Diddlebock/Mad Wednesday; Dishonored Lady; Driftwood; 1948: State of the Union; Texas, Brooklyn and Heaven; Bungalow 13; 1949: The Sun Comes Up; The Red Pony; The Beautiful Blonde From Bashful Bend; 1950: Riding High; The Great Plane Robbery; Wabash Avenue; 1951: People Will Talk; Comin' Round the Mountain; 1960: 13 Ghosts; 1962: Paradise Alley (filmed 1957); 1966: The Daydreamer; 1967: Rosie!; 1969: Angel in My Pocket; 1970: Brewster McCloud; 1971: The Anderson Tapes; 1974: Journey Back to Oz (voice; filmed 1964).

NY Stage: 1932: Another Language; 1933: The Dark Tower; 1934: The Farmer Takes a Wife; 1943: Outrageous Fortune; 1948: The Men We Marry; 1952: Fancy Meeting You Again; 1956: The Adding Machine (ob); Diary of a Scoundrel (ob); 1958: Annie Get Your Gun; Goldilocks; 1963: Save Me a Place at Forest Lawn (ob); 1966: UTBU; Show Boat; 1969: Come Summer; Oklahoma!; Our Town; 1977: The New York Idea (ob); The Three Sisters (ob); 1978: The Devil's Disciple (ob).

Select TV: 1950: Papa Romani (sp); 1953–54: The Paul Winchell-Jerry Mahoney Show (series); 1954: Man of Extinction (sp); An Eye for an Eye (sp); The Fifth Wheel (sp); The Man Who Came to Dinner (sp); 1955: The Silent Woman (sp); The Guardsman (sp); Beloved Stranger (sp); The Devil's Disciple (sp); 1957: The Trial of Lizzie Borden (sp); The Staring Match (sp); On Borrowed Time (sp); You Can't Win (sp); 1959: Once Upon a

Christmas Time (sp); The Silver Whistle (sp); 1960: The Bat (sp); 1967: Ghostbreaker (sp); 1973: The Night Strangler; 1973–75: Sigmund and the Sea Monsters (series); 1979: Letters From Frank.

MURRAY HAMILTON

BORN: WASHINGTON, NC, MARCH 24, 1923.
DIED: SEPTEMBER 1, 1986.

An all-purpose character player of the postwar era with a few notable roles to his credit, Murray Hamilton debuted on the New York stage, in 1945, in *Strange Fruit*. Following work in the original production of *Mister Roberts*, he came to Hollywood to make his bow in the 1951 Universal film *Bright Victory*, ironically playing a character named Hamilton, a blinded soldier who describes his night on the town. His more high-profile roles during this period included three films in support of James Stewart, *The Spirit of St. Louis*, as Charles Lindbergh's buddy; *Anatomy of a Murder*, as the town bartender; and *The FBI Story*, as his fellow investigator; while one of his lesser-known assignments, William Castle's cheesy spy caper, *13 Frightened Girls*, gave him top billing, as a CIA Agent. In *Tall Story*, he was Tony Perkins's basketball coach, and he gave one of the many fine performances in one of the top films of the early 1960s, *The Hustler*, as the tobacco tycoon who challenges Paul Newman to a high-stakes billiard game in his basement. His film fame was cemented later on when he played the cuckolded Mr. Robinson in the 1967 classic *The Graduate*, creepily confronting Dustin Hoffman at his boarding house. He then played the closest thing to a human villain in the 1975 blockbuster *Jaws*, as the stubborn mayor who refuses to close the beaches after the shark attacks; repeating the part, with higher billing, in the sequel, *Jaws 2*, which was *not* directed by Steven Spielberg as the first one was. Instead, he returned to Spielberg under somewhat dire circumstances for the bombastic farce *1941*, in which he and Eddie Deezen were stuck on a runaway Ferris wheel.

Screen: 1951: Bright Victory; The Whistle at Eaton Falls; 1956: Toward the Unknown; The Girl He Left Behind; 1957: Jeanne Eagles; The Spirit of St. Louis; 1958: Darby's Rangers; Too Much, Too Soon; No Time for Sergeants; Houseboat; 1959: Anatomy of a Murder; The FBI Story; 1960: Tall Story; 1961: The Hustler; 1963: Papa's Delicate Condition; 13 Frightened Girls; The Cardinal; 1966: Seconds; An American Dream; 1967: Danger Has Two Faces; The Graduate; 1968: No Way to Treat a Lady; The Boston Strangler; The Brotherhood; 1969: If It's Tuesday, This Must Be Belgium; 1973: The Way We Were; 1975: Jaws; The Drowning Pool; 1977: Damnation Alley; 1978: Casey's Shadow; Jaws 2; 1979: The Amityville Horror; 1941; 1980: Brubaker; 1983: Hysterical; 1985: Too Scared to Scream; 1988: Whoops Apocalypse.

NY Stage: 1945: Strange Fruit; 1948: Mister Roberts; 1952: The Chase; 1954: Stockade (ob); 1960: Critic's Choice; 1962: Mary, Mary; 1963: The Heroine; 1964: Absence of a Cello; 1968: 40 Carats.

Select TV: 1953: The Glorification of Al Toolum (sp); 1955: The Spongers (sp); 1958: Girl in the Subway (sp); 1959–60: Love and Marriage (series); 1963: Sergeant Ryker (sp); 1966–67: The Man Who Never Was (series); 1971: Vanished; Cannon; A Tattered Web; The Harness; The Failing of Raymond; 1972: Deadly Harvest; 1973: Incident on a Dark Street; Murdock's Gang; 1976: Rich Man, Poor Man (ms); 1977: Murder at the World Series; Killer on Board; 1979: A Last Cry for Help; Donovan's Kid; 1980: Swan Song; 1981: B.J. and the Bear (series); All the Way Home;

1982: Rona Jaffe's Mazes and Monsters; 1983: Summer Girl; 1985: Hail to the Chief (series); 1986: The Last Days of Patton.

NEIL HAMILTON

(JAMES NEIL HAMILTON) BORN: LYNN, MA, SEPTEMBER 9, 1899. DIED: SEPTEMBER 24, 1984.

From D.W. Griffith to Batman, Neil Hamilton's career was a long one of highs and lows, semi-stardom and relative obscurity. He had started out as a film extra at various East Coast studios, modeled as an Arrow Collar man, and acted with a few stock companies before Griffith gave him his big break. For the famed director he appeared as a young Southern lad in *The White Rose*; the colorless hero of the Revolutionary War epic *America*, acted right off the screen by wicked Lionel Barrymore; and a Polish refugee facing life on the streets of Berlin in the ironically titled *Isn't Life Wonderful?* All three films proved to be major box-office disappointments in their time, but Hamilton did manage to land a contract with Paramount Pictures. For that company, his most notable roles would be Digby Geste in the famous Foreign Legion epic *Beau Geste*, opposite Ronald Colman; and Nick Carraway in the first film version of *The Great Gatsby*. When sound arrived, he found himself securing secondary roles in some major releases, playing the alcoholic major in *The Dawn Patrol*; the thoughtless lover of Helen Hayes in the soapy *The Sin of Madelon Claudet*; the bland explorer who loses Jane (Maureen O'Sullivan) to a more swingin' lifestyle in *Tarzan the Ape Man*; and a man blinded by drink in *The Wet Parade*. He played the socialite husband of Constance Bennett in the trend-setting melodrama *What Price Hollywood?*; Leslie Howard's lawyer in the excellent adaptation of the stage hit *The Animal Kingdom*; and the man who stole Fay Wray from Gary Cooper in *One Sunday Afternoon*. Hamilton's film persona was soft and, frankly, rather wimpy, so he did not find himself in demand as a leading man. By the early 1940s he was doing more than his share of "B's" for Monogram, Republic, and PCR. When he did get a part in a big production, Selznick's *Since You Went Away*, he ended up on the cutting room floor, seen in the finished print in photographs only. In the mid-1940s he left Hollywood for a spell, working on the stage. Unexpectedly he became famous all over again in the 1960s, when he played the ultra-square Commissioner Gordon in the smash hit TV series *Batman*, retiring three years after its cancellation.

Screen: 1918: The Beloved Impostor; 1919: The Great Romance; 1923: The White Rose; 1924: America; The Sixth Commandment; The Side Show of Life; Isn't Life Wonderful?; 1925: The Street of Forgotten Men; Men and Women; The Golden Princess; The Little French Girl; New Brooms; 1926: The Splendid Crime; Desert Gold; Diplomacy; Beau Geste; The Great Gatsby; 1927: The Music Master; Ten Modern Commandments; The Joy Girl; The Spotlight; The Shield of Honor; 1928: Mother Machree; The Showdown; Don't Marry; Something Always Happens; The Grip of the Yukon; Hot News; The Patriot; Take Me Home; Three Week-Ends; What a Night!; 1929: Why Be Good?; A Dangerous Woman; The Studio Murder Mystery; The Mysterious Dr. Fu Manchu; The Love Trap; The Kibitzer; 1930: Darkened Rooms; Command Performance; The Return of Dr. Fu Manchu; Anybody's War; The Dawn Patrol; Ladies Must Play; The Cat Creeps; The Widow From Chicago; 1931: Ex-Flame; Strangers May Kiss; The Spy; Laughing Sinners; The Great Lover; This Modern Age; The Sin of Madelon Claudet; 1932: Tarzan the Ape Man; The Wet Parade; Are You Listening?; The Woman in Room 13; What Price Hollywood?;

Two Against the World; The Animal Kingdom; As the Devil Commands; 1933: The World Gone Mad; The Silk Express; Terror Aboard; One Sunday Afternoon; Ladies Must Love; 1934: Tarzan and His Mate; Here Comes the Groom; Once to Every Bachelor; Blind Date; Two Heads on a Pillow; One Exciting Adventure; Fugitive Lady; By Your Leave; 1935: Keeper of the Bees; Honeymoon Limited; Mutiny Ahead; The Daring Young Man; 1936: You Must Get Married; Southern Roses; Everything in Life; 1937: Secret Lives/I Married a Spy; Mr. Stringfellow Says No; Portia on Trial; Lady Behave!; 1938: The Hollywood Stadium Mystery; Army Girl; 1939: The Saint Strikes Back; 1940: Queen of the Mob; 1941: Federal Fugitives; King of the Texas Rangers (serial); They Meet Again; Father Takes a Wife; Look Who's Laughing; Dangerous Lady; 1942: Too Many Women; X Marks the Spot; The Lady Is Willing; Secrets of the Underground; 1943: All By Myself; The Sky's the Limit; Bombardier; 1944: When Strangers Marry; 1945: Brewster's Millions; 1959: The Devil's Hand/The Naked Goddess; 1961: The Little Shepherd of Kingdom Come; 1964: Good Neighbor Sam; The Patsy; 1965: The Family Jewels; 1966: Madame X; Batman; 1970: Which Way to the Front?

NY Stage: 1945: Many Happy Returns; The Deep Mrs. Sykes; 1947: State of the Union; 1948 The Men We Marry; 1952: To Be Continued; 1953: Late Love.

Select TV: 1948–53: Hollywood Screen Test (series); 1949–50: That Wonderful Guy (series); 1952: The Night of January 16th (sp); 1954: Panama Hattie (sp); King's Pawn (sp); 1965: In Darkness Waiting (sp); 1966–68: Batman (series); 1971: Vanished.

ANN HARDING

(DOROTHY WALTON GATLEY) BORN: FORT SAM HOUSTON, TX, AUGUST 7, 1901. ED: BRYN MAWR. DIED: SEPTEMBER 1, 1981.

An accomplished actress with sleek blonde hair and a dignified air about her, Ann Harding's fame did not carry on beyond the timeline of her career. While working in Paramount's reading department, she joined the Provincetown Players in 1921, the same year she made her Broadway debut in *Like a King*. She would find great success on the New York stage during the 1920s, culminating in the 1927 drama *The Trial of Mary Dugan*. From this came Hollywood offers, and she signed with Pathé for *Paris Bound*, opposite Fredric March. She stayed with the studio for *Her Private Affair* and *Holiday*, among others, the latter being forced into obscurity by the Katharine Hepburn remake eight years later. Harding, however, received an Oscar nomination for her part. When Pathé was consumed by RKO, she toiled for that company, playing a faux-cockney governess in *Devotion*; a divorcée opposite a very young Laurence Olivier in *Westward Passage*, which, despite its title, was *not* a western; and the true love of soul-searching Leslie Howard in *The Animal Kingdom*, where she gave an exceptional performance. For MGM she appeared opposite her *Animal Kingdom* rival, Myrna Loy, in *When Ladies Meet*, an intelligent if stage-bound drama, with Harding sympathetically playing Frank Morgan's cuckolded wife; then reported back to her home lot for the soaps *The Life of Vergie Winters* and *The Fountain*, both of which proved that she was losing her popularity. After *Enchanted April* didn't go over, she went to Paramount for the heavy-handed Gary Cooper romance *Peter Ibbetson*, followed by a low-budget effort for RKO, *The Witness Chair*, which signaled that it was time to leave Hollywood.

She took off for England, appearing onstage in *Candida* and in a film, *Love From a Stranger*, suspecting the worst of husband Basil Rathbone. When she resurfaced in Hollywood in the 1940s, it was in supporting roles in two pro-Russia pieces, *Mission to Moscow* and *The North Star*, both of which were looked back upon with suspicion and scorn during the blacklisting era; as well as in a lead in a "B" mystery for Columbia, *Nine Girls*; and one over at Monogram, *It Happened on 5th Avenue*, a semi-musical about a group of vagrants taking over her abandoned society mansion. She was next seen playing the standard biopic "tower-of-strength" wife, in this case the spouse of Supreme Court Justice Oliver Wendell Holmes, in *The Magnificent Yankee*, growing old with Louis Calhern, a role that contrasted effectively with her bitter, ex-wife of corporate executive Fredric March in the hit *The Man in the Gray Flannel Suit*. She made her last New York stage appearance in 1964, in *Abraham Cochrane*, remaining very much a critic's favorite to the end.

Screen: 1929: Paris Bound; Her Private Affair; Condemned; 1930: Holiday; The Girl of the Golden West; 1931: East Lynne; Devotion; 1932: Prestige; Westward Passage; The Conquerors; The Animal Kingdom; 1933: When Ladies Meet; Double Harness; The Right to Romance; 1934: Gallant Lady; The Life of Vergie Winters; The Fountain; 1935: Biography of a Bachelor Girl; The Flame Within; Enchanted April; Peter Ibbetson; 1936: The Lady Consents; The Witness Chair; 1937: Love From a Stranger; 1942: Eyes in the Night; 1943: Mission to Moscow; The North Star; 1944: Nine Girls; Janie; 1945: Those Endearing Young Charms; 1946: Janie Gets Married; 1947: It Happened on 5th Avenue; Christmas Eve; 1950: Two Weeks With Love; The Magnificent Yankee; 1951: The Unknown Man; 1956: The Man in the Gray Flannel Suit; I've Lived Before; Strange Intruder.

NY Stage: 1921: Like a King; 1923: Tarnish; 1924: Thoroughbreds; 1925: Stolen Fruit; The Taming of the Shrew; 1926: Schweiger; The Eskimo; A Woman Disputed; 1927: The Trial of Mary Duggan; 1949: Goodbye, My Fancy; 1962: General Seeger; 1964: Abraham Cochrane.

Select TV: 1952: Years of Grace (sp); 1953: There's No Place Like Home (sp); Miracle in the Night (sp); 1954: The Great Lady (sp); The Queen's English (sp); 1955: An Act of Murder (sp); P.J. and the Lady (sp); Lonely Heart (sp); Progress and Minnie Sweeney (sp); The Late George Apley (sp); 1956: The Center of the Maze (sp); The Great Lady (sp); 1957: The House of Empty Rooms (sp); Young Man From Kentucky (sp); 1960: Morning's at Seven (sp); 1963: The Embezzler (sp).

CEDRIC HARDWICKE

BORN: LYE, STOURBRIDGE, ENGLAND, FEBRUARY 19, 1893. ED: RADA. DIED: AUGUST 6, 1964.

British character player Cedric Hardwicke came to Hollywood in the mid-1930s to lend his commanding yet often sour personality to countless films, frequently playing glowering men of authority or despicable villains. Sometimes he acted with a touch of ham, which, depending on the film, could be just right for the occasion. In 1912 he made his London stage bow in *The Monk and the Woman*, a year before his film debut in a two-reeler called "Riches and Rogues." It was another 13 years before he tried movies again, occupying the majority of his time with the stage, which included playing Cap'n Andy in the London version of *Show Boat*. With the arrival of sound, he was seen in such British films as *The Ghoul*, with Boris Karloff; *Nell Gwynn*, with Anna Neagle; and *The King of Paris*, in which he had the starring role of an egotistical actor in love with a Russian girl. Hollywood had been interested ever since his stage success in *The Barretts of*

Wimpole Street, back in 1930. At last they got him for two period films, *Becky Sharp*, as the Marquis of Steyne, who accepts Miriam Hopkins's offer for sex if he will pay her gambling debts, and *Les Misérables*, as the compassionate Bishop who aids escaped con Fredric March. Then it was back to England (he was knighted in 1934) for *Things to Come*, chewing the scenery to the max, as he spoke against the scientific age; and the hit *Tudor Rose*, scheming as the Earl of Warwick. He made his Broadway debut with *Promise* in 1936; returned to England for a film lead, far from ideally casted as adventurer Allan Quartermain in the earlier, less-effective version of *King Solomon's Mines*; and then finally settled down in Hollywood, where he took on a role that he played with relish, the incarnation of death in MGM's effective fantasy *On Borrowed Time*. That same year, Spencer Tracy searched for him in *Stanley and Livingstone*, and he played one of his finest villain parts, Frollo, in the masterful 1939 version of *The Hunchback of Notre Dame*. He was the bad guy in Universal's sequel, *The Invisible Man Returns*, after which he signed a contract with RKO, though he went straight over to Paramount, where he got all the best reviews for *Victory*, as a woman-hating thief. Apparently feeling he fit right into the supernatural genre, Universal cast him as the *other* son of the mad doctor in *The Ghost of Frankenstein*, and dumped him into another one of their see-through entries, *Invisible Agent*, as a spy.

It was Hardwicke who instigated the all-star *Forever and a Day* to aid British War Relief, and he not only played a comical plumber opposite Buster Keaton but directed that particular sequence of this multi-episode film as well. He signed with Fox, which resulted in a major leading role, the Nazi commander who captures a Norwegian village in *The Moon Is Down*, and supporting roles in other big projects, including *Wilson*, as Henry Cabot Lodge, and *The Keys of the Kingdom*, as a priest. Back in England he played one of his meanest parts, Ralph Nickleby, in *Nicholas Nickleby*, making you forget how inadequate Derek Bond was in the title role. Hardwicke then returned to America for some benign roles, including the boarder who skips out on the family in *I Remember Mama*; the father of the murdered young man in Alfred Hitchcock's experimental *Rope*; and King Arthur in *A Connecticut Yankee in King Arthur's Court*, joining Bing Crosby and William Bendix for a lively duet, "Busy Doing Nothing." Prior to this he had been in England to film another starring part, the sickly father battling for his son's honor in the adaptation of the stage hit *The Winslow Boy*. He could still be counted on to lend a certain authoritative, sometimes royal, manner as he did in *Salome*, as Tiberius; *Bait*, fittingly cast as the Devil; *Richard III*, as Edward IV, thereby expiring early on in the story; *Helen of Troy*, as Priam; and *The Ten Commandments*, as the Pharaoh, once again exiting a lengthy tale in its first half. He presided over the bizarre "all-star history lesson" as a heavenly judge in *The Story of Mankind*, and was in charge of the expedition in the enjoyable adventure *Five Weeks in a Balloon*. His final role was an effective bit as Anne Bancroft's sickly father in *The Pumpkin Eater*, released the year that he died, 1964. Three years earlier he had published his autobiography, *A Victorian in Orbit*. On Broadway he had directed several plays, including *Lorelei, An Inspector Calls*, and *Miss Isobel*. His son, Edward Hardwicke, found his greatest fame playing Watson in the successful BBC dramatization of the Sherlock Holmes cases.

Screen: 1926: Nelson; 1931: Dreyfus/The Dreyfus Case; 1932: Rome Express; 1933: Orders Is Orders; 1934: The Ghoul; The Lady Is Willing; Bella Donna; Nell Gwynn; Power/Jew Suss; The King of Paris; 1935: Becky Sharp; Les Misérables; Peg of Old Drury; 1936: Things to Come; Tudor Rose; Laburnum Grove; 1937: Green Light; King Solomon's Mines; 1939: On Borrowed

Time; Stanley and Livingstone; The Hunchback of Notre Dame; 1940: The Invisible Man Returns; Tom Brown's Schooldays; The Howards of Virginia; Victory; 1941: Suspicion; Sundown; 1942: The Ghost of Frankenstein; Valley of the Sun; Invisible Agent; Commandos Strike at Dawn; 1943: Forever and a Day (and co-dir.; prod.); The Moon Is Down; The Cross of Lorraine; 1944: The Lodger; Wing and a Prayer; Wilson; The Keys of the Kingdom; 1945: The Picture of Dorian Gray (narrator); 1946: Sentimental Journey; Beware of Pity; 1947: Nicholas Nickleby; The Imperfect Lady; Ivy; Lured; Song of My Heart; Tycoon; 1948: A Woman's Vengeance; I Remember Mama; Rope; 1949: A Connecticut Yankee in King Arthur's Court; Now Barabbas Was a Robber; 1950: The Winslow Boy (UK: 1948); The White Tower; 1951: Mr. Imperium; The Desert Fox; 1952: The Green Glove; Caribbean; 1953: Salome; Botany Bay; The War of the Worlds (narrator); 1954: Bait; 1956: Helen of Troy; Diane; Richard III; Gaby; The Vagabond King; The Power and the Prize; The Ten Commandments; Around the World in Eighty Days; 1957: The Story of Mankind; Baby Face Nelson; 1962: Five Weeks in a Balloon; 1964: The Magic Fountain (narrator; filmed 1961); The Pumpkin Eater.

NY Stage: 1936: Promise; 1937: The Amazing Dr. Clitterhouse; 1938: Shadow and Substance; 1946: Antigone; Candida; 1949: Caesar and Cleopatra (and dir.); 1951: Don Juan in Hell; 1953: Horses in Midstream (and dir.); 1954: The Burning Glass; 1959: A Majority of One; 1963: Too True to Be Good.

Select TV: 1952: Crossroads (sp); 1953: Best Seller (sp); In the Pincers (sp); The Thirteen Clocks (sp); 1955: The Barretts of Wimpole Street (sp); Dr. Jekyll and Mr. Hyde (sp); 1956: Tunnel of Fear (sp); Caesar and Cleopatra (sp); 1957: Mr. and Mrs. McAdam (sp); Shadow and Substance (sp); Mr. Krane (sp); The Prince and the Pauper (sp); 1958: The Other Place (sp); 1959: Who Pays? (series); 1960: The Women of Hadley (sp); 1961–62: Mrs. G. Goes to College/The Gertrude Berg Show (series).

JEAN HARLOW

(HARLEAN CARPENTER) BORN: KANSAS CITY, MO, MARCH 3, 1911. DIED: JUNE 7, 1937.

Her life was tragically short, her career as a star lasting no more than seven years, and yet Jean Harlow is one of the handful of never-to-be-forgotten names that immediately conjure up images of a glamorous, art deco, otherworldly 1930s Hollywood. The reigning bombshell of that decade, she was a platinum blonde with a suggestive gaze and a sassy way with a line, often accentuated by a hand to the hip. If she was limited in her acting, it didn't matter, for what she did she did definitively. Married at 16, she quickly divorced and ended up as a movie extra, the first such credit to be verified being *Moran of the Marines*. There was a notable bit in a Laurel and Hardy short, "Double Whoopee," having her skirt torn away, and then she lucked out when Howard Hughes dropped Greta Nissen, his original choice for the female lead of his aerial epic *Hell's Angels*, because her accent was too thick. Harlow got the role, playing a supposedly British girl in love with flier Ben Lyon while carrying on with his brother, James Hall. The male leads left something to be desired, but there was great excitement over the impressive aerial sequences and the picture retains a certain degree of enjoyment, even today. Harlow, although both her look and acting would be fine tuned in time, made a tremendous impact as the ultimately heartless trollop. Officially she was under contract to Hughes, but she worked elsewhere, at MGM for *The Secret Six*, still very evidently struggling at her craft, as a gangster's moll; at

Universal for *Iron Man*, as Lew Ayres's money-hungry wife; at Warner Bros. for *The Public Enemy*, again as a gun moll, but hardly one of the standout aspects of this seminal gangster movie; and at Fox for *Goldie*, as another tramp, a carnival diver desired by both Spencer Tracy and Warren Hymer. She then made the film (at Columbia) that became one of the signature titles of her career, director Frank Capra's *Platinum Blonde*, a comedy about a society girl who weds reporter Robert Williams but doesn't realize he wants to be a regular guy, thereby losing him to top-billed Loretta Young. Of course it was a stretch accepting Harlow in this snooty role, since she had a bit of the street in her.

At that point, realizing Hughes hadn't a single thing lined up for her, she signed a contract with an anxious MGM. They gave her a secondary part in *The Beast of the City*, and then the lead in *Red-Headed Woman*, where she set out to snare boss Chester Morris while wearing his photo in her garter. She made a real splash opposite Clark Gable in the jungle melodrama *Red Dust*, at her wise-cracking best, as the tart swapping insults with him until he finally comes to his senses and realizes that if he wants to have a little fun in his life, he'd do far better with Harlow than with the more-refined Mary Astor. They played off one another so well that they were immediately reunited for *Hold Your Man*, which was really *her* movie, having to spend a good portion of the story enduring a stretch in a women's detention home. After that came another defining Harlow title, *Bombshell*, with the actress at her brashest, in a satire on the movie business that substituted high energy for out-and-out laughs. Opposite Harlow was Lee Tracy, another actor who could spin off a one-liner or banter with the best of them. This was followed by the all-star *Dinner at Eight*, where her performance as the trashy wife of Wallace Beery was a great asset to an uneven film. Staying comedic she was another fortune hunter in *The Girl From Missouri*, going after Lionel Barrymore, but ending up (of course) with the much younger Franchot Tone. *Reckless* found her playing a chorus girl (albeit with a dubbed singing voice) and was notable in that it introduced her to William Powell, to whom she was nearly wed in 1936. There was another big hit with Gable and Beery, *China Seas*, which seemed an awful lot like *Red Dust*, what with Harlow playing a brassy babe named China Doll who bides her time waiting for Gable to dump the classier Rosalind Russell.

A middling comedy-drama with Spencer Tracy, *Riff Raff*, was followed by a medium drama, *Wife vs. Secretary*, which gave her Gable again and another of the studio's biggest stars, Myrna Loy. As the loyal secretary who almost coaxes Gable away from an unappreciative Loy, she showed that she had clearly grown into an actress who was not only a deft comedienne but also one capable of some dramatic substance. Popular as she was, it seemed as if MGM never quite trusted her to carry something on her own, so there was always another major contract player alongside her for insurance. Following that rule, next up she was joined by Powell, Loy, and Tracy, providing an outstanding example of star power that was further enhanced by a top-notch screenplay, in perhaps the brightest film she ever made, *Libeled Lady*, as Tracy's impatient girlfriend, roped into a scheme to marry Powell. Paired with Robert Taylor, she was a poor widow scheming to marry his brother until the obvious happens, in *Personal Property*. Things were going quite splendidly and another seemingly sure thing was lined up with Gable, *Saratoga*. During filming she was rushed to the hospital with uremic poisoning and died of cerebral edema at the age of 26. She left behind a shocked and grieving industry and public, not to mention an unfinished film. The released product, a box-office hit, is a curious thing to view, as many of Harlow's scenes are enacted by a double hiding her eyes with binoculars and other props, or simply turning her face from the camera. Her fame did not subside, and she became the topic of a best-selling biography and two back-to-back film biopics released in 1965, emphasizing the tawdry side of her life, including her awkward marriage to MGM executive Paul Bern who committed suicide a few months after their wedding.

Screen (features): 1928: Moran of the Marines; 1929: The Love Parade; The Saturday Night Kid; Fugitives; Close Harmony; This Thing Called Love; New York Nights; 1930: Hell's Angels; 1931: The Secret Six; Iron Man; The Public Enemy; Goldie; Platinum Blonde; 1932: Three Wise Girls; The Beast of the City; Red-Headed Woman; Red Dust; 1933: Hold Your Man; Bombshell; Dinner at Eight; 1934: The Girl From Missouri; 1935: Reckless; China Seas; 1936: Riff Raff; Wife vs. Secretary; Suzy; Libeled Lady; 1937: Personal Property; Saratoga.

JULIE HARRIS

BORN: GROSSE POINTE, MI, DECEMBER 2, 1925. ED: YALE DRAMA SCHOOL.

With a record five Tony Award wins, plain-looking, heartbreakingly sincere Julie Harris was considered one of the premiere stage actresses of her time. Fortunately her occasional travels to the big screen provided her with a few choice cinematic roles as well. Not yet 20, she went from studying drama at Yale to the 1945 Broadway production *It's a Gift*, after which she kept busy in a variety of plays (winning a Theatre World Award for *Sundown Beach*), taking the time in between to join the Actors Studio. What made her the most exciting new name on Broadway were back-to-back triumphs, first convincingly playing pre-adolescent Frankie in Carson McCuller's *The Member of the Wedding*, and then unconventional Sally Bowles in *I Am a Camera*. The latter would account for her first Tony Award. Amazingly, she was asked to recreate her roles in both film adaptations, looking much too old in close-up for the first, although she earned an Oscar nomination, and then going to Britain to film the other, easily upstaging co-star Laurence Harvey. Between the two, she gave a beautiful performance as the girl loved by James Dean in *East of Eden*, making one wish that every young movie actress was as interesting as this one (her voice, so vulnerable, sounds as if she is on the verge of crying).

There was Tony number two for *The Lark*, playing Joan of Ark (a role she repeated on television); two more movies, made overseas; and then another fine part, as the employment counselor helping Anthony Quinn, in *Requiem for a Heavyweight*. Her fidgety performance as an unstable spinster in the intellectual chiller *The Haunting* was certainly memorable, and she followed it with other neurotic parts in *You're a Big Boy Now* and *Reflections in a Golden Eye*, although most everybody in the cast was off-kilter in those films. In the first she was Peter Kastner's landlady; in the latter she was so unhinged she ultimately mutilated herself with a pair of pruning shears. Returning to Broadway, she picked up her next three Tonys, for *40 Carats*, *The Last of Mrs. Lincoln*, and *The Belle of Amherst*. Harris made several telefilms, got top billing as a Christian woman aiding the Jews in the theatrical release *The Hiding Place*, and had a regular role on the nighttime soap *Knots Landing*. She also had some supporting roles where she was little more than just a welcome presence, including *Gorillas in the Mist*, and in *Housesitter*, as Steve Martin's mother. After a long stretch, she received another starring role, as an old lady befriending a child, in *The First of May*, a tiny movie meant for a few test markets. On television she won Emmy Awards for *Little Moon of Alban* and *Victoria Regina*.

Screen: 1952: The Member of the Wedding; 1955: East of Eden; I Am a Camera; 1958: The Truth About Women; 1960: The Poacher's Daughter/Sally's Irish Rogue; 1962: Requiem for a Heavyweight; 1963: The Haunting; 1966: Harper; You're a Big Boy Now; 1967: Reflections in a Golden Eye; 1968: The Split; 1970: The People Next Door; 1975: The Hiding Place; 1976: Voyage of the Damned; 1979: The Bell Jar; 1983: Brontë; 1986: Nutcracker — The Motion Picture (voice); 1988: Gorillas in the Mist; 1992: Housesitter; 1993: The Dark Half; 1996: Carried Away; 1998: Passage to Paradise (nUSr); Bad Manners; 2001: The First of May.

NY Stage: 1945: It's a Gift; 1946: The Playboy of the Western World; 1947: Alice in Wonderland; 1948: Macbeth; Sundown Beach; The Young and Fair; 1949: Magnolia Alley; Montserrat; 1950: The Member of the Wedding; 1951: I Am a Camera; 1954: Mademoiselle Colombe; 1955: The Lark; 1957: The Country Wife; 1959: The Warm Peninsula; 1960: Little Moon of Alban; 1961: A Shot in the Dark; 1963: Marathon '33; 1964: Hamlet; Ready When You Are C.B.!; 1965: Skyscraper; 1968: 40 Carats; 1971: And Miss Reardon Drinks a Little; 1972: Voices; The Last of Mrs. Lincoln; 1973: The Au Pair Man; 1974: In Praise of Love; 1976: The Belle of Amherst; 1979: Break a Leg; 1980: Mixed Couples; 1991: Lucifer's Child; 1993:The Fiery Furnace (ob); 1994: The Glass Menagerie; 1997: The Gin Game.

Select TV: 1951: Bernice Bobs Her Hair (sp); October Story (sp); 1953: The Happy Rest (sp); 1955: A Wind From the South (sp); 1956: The Good Fairy (sp); 1957: The Lark (sp); 1958: Johnny Belinda (sp); Little Moon of Alban (sp); 1959: A Doll's House (sp); 1960: Ethan Frome (sp); Turn the Key Softly (sp); 1961: The Heiress (sp); Night of the Storm (sp); He Who Gets Slapped (sp); The Power and the Glory (sp); Victoria Regina (sp); 1963: Pygmalion (sp); 1964: Hamlet (sp); 1965: The Holy Terror (sp); 1967: Anastasia (sp); 1968: Journey Into Midnight; 1970: The House on Greenapple Road; How Awful About Allan; 1972: Home for the Holidays; 1973: Thicker Than Water (series); 1974: The Greatest Gift; 1975: The Family Holvak (series); 1976: The Last of Mrs. Lincoln (sp); The Belle of Amherst (sp); 1978: Stubby Pringle's Christmas (sp); 1979: Backstairs at the White House (ms); The Gift; 1981–87: Knots Landing (series); 1988: The Woman He Loved; Too Good to Be True; The Christmas Wife; 1989: Single Women, Married Men; 1993: They've Taken Our Children: The Chowchilla Kidnapping; When Love Kills: The Seduction of John Hearn; 1994: Scarlett (ms); One Christmas; 1995: Secrets; Lucifer's Child (sp); Little Surprises; 1996: The Christmas Tree; 1997: Ellen Foster; 1998: Love Is Strange.

PHIL HARRIS

BORN: LINTON, IN, JUNE 24, 1904. RAISED IN NASHVILLE, TN. DIED: AUGUST 11, 1995.

Bearish, good-natured Phil Harris started out as a drummer before forming his own band in 1931. His film debut came two years later, in a junior-grade RKO musical, *Melody Cruise*, second billed to Charlie Ruggles, as a playboy juggling two women during an ocean voyage. By the time he returned to movies, in another Ruggles film, *Turn Off the Moon*, he was more famous as a bandleader and therefore played himself. He had become well known on radio, frequently clowning with Jack Benny, and once again played himself, in Benny's big-screen vehicle *Buck Benny Rides Again*. At Columbia Harris actually managed to land his own starring quickie, *I Love a Bandleader*, as a painter who gets amnesia and becomes a guess-what? After playing a con man in Betty Grable's *Wabash Avenue*, he decided to concentrate on straight acting and gave some decent performances in such movies as the highly popular airplane-in-peril adventure *The High and the Mighty*, and *Good-bye, My Lady*, a doggie story starring Brandon De Wilde. It was for Walt Disney, however, that he would find his greatest movie role, as the voice of the swingin' bear Baloo in *The Jungle Book*, giving a classic rendering of the Oscar-nominated song "The Bare Necessities." Harris was thought to be a key to that movie's huge success, so his vocal talents were featured in two more Disney cartoons, *The Aristocats*, and the all-animal *Robin Hood*, where he was appropriately cast as Little John. His 1941 marriage to actress-singer Alice Faye lasted until his death; although they teamed frequently on both radio and television, they did no movies together.

Screen: 1933: Melody Cruise; 1937: Turn Off the Moon; 1939: Man About Town; 1940: Buck Benny Rides Again; Dreaming Out Loud; 1945: I Love a Bandleader; 1950: Wabash Avenue; 1951: Here Comes the Groom; Starlift; The Wild Blue Yonder; 1954: The High and the Mighty; 1956: Anything Goes; Goodbye, My Lady; 1963: The Wheeler Dealers; 1964: The Patsy; 1967: The Cool Ones; The Jungle Book (voice); 1970: The Aristocats (voice); 1973: The Gatling Gun; Robin Hood (voice); 1992: Rock-a-Doodle (voice).

Select TV: 1956: Manhattan Tower (sp).

RICHARD HARRIS

BORN: LIMERICK, IRELAND, OCTOBER 1, 1930.
ED: LAMDA. DIED: OCTOBER 25, 2002

From a whisper to a shout, the very colorful Richard Harris could run the gamut within the same film from meditative mumbler to bombastic bellower. Like many of those from Great Britain who made their mark in the 1960s, he was as well known for his lusty, hard-drinking, off-screen exploits as he was for his acting, which could be pure ham when he was saddled with tripe or strikingly good when he decided the material warranted his respect. After school he joined John Littlewood's acting company in the late 1950s, making his film debut around this period in a comedy, *Alive and Kicking*. In 1959 he had his first taste of success on the London stage with *The Ginger Man*, and was starting to be seen by a wider movie-going audience via some films made in England with major American names, *Shake Hands With the Devil* (James Cagney); *The Wreck of the Mary Deare* (Gary Cooper), in a showy villain role; and *A Terrible Beauty* (Robert Mitchum). There was also a secondary part as a brutish corporal in an unsuccessful film adaptation of a West End hit, *The Long and the Short and the Tall*, in support of Laurence Harvey. After that there were two big budget international adventures, *The Guns of Navarone*, seen prior to the big mission, as a squadron leader; and the remake of *Mutiny on the Bounty*, giving a standout performance as the head of the mutineers. He got his chance to make his contribution to the spate of "angry young man" films coming out of England with *This Sporting Life*, an overlong look at the life of a restless coal miner-turned-rugby player, a part he played with total conviction and brooding magnetism, earning an Oscar nomination and becoming one of the leading names in the very exciting new breed of British leading men. He followed this peak with a pair of foreign productions, *Red Desert*, a typical love-it-or-hate-it Michelangelo Antonioni offering which Harris himself regretted doing, and *Three Faces of a Woman*, which never reached the U.S. He acquitted himself magnificently in the tampered-with western *Major Dundee*, co-starring (as a Confederate officer) with former *Mary Deare* lead Charlton Heston. There were small parts in two big spectacles, *The Bible*, as the murderous Cain, and *Hawaii*, as the ship's cap-

tain, in love with Julie Andrews; then a misguided attempt at a wacky espionage comedy with *Caprice*, opposite Doris Day.

One of his most famous films of this time, *Camelot*, wasn't all that good either but his own performance as King Arthur was quite commendable. Having sung in that picture, he decided to record some records and entered the pop charts in 1968 with the lengthy single "MacArthur Park," a rare case of a non-singer scoring a top ten hit. After a three year absence, there were three showcase roles in 1970: *The Molly Maguires*, in a strong performance as detective infiltrating Sean Connery's secret rebel forces; *A Man Called Horse*, as a Englishman inducted into the Sioux tribe in a stomach turning initiation ceremony requiring Harris to be hung up by the skin on his chest; and the title role as a deeply unsympathetic *Cromwell*, taking over the throne of England from Charles II (Alec Guinness). Only the second one made money and, indeed, throughout the 1970s, the actor would wind up in some of the least-attended attractions of the decade, including *The Hero/Bloomfield*, as an aging soccer star, which he himself co-wrote and directed; a violent western, *The Deadly Trackers*, as a sheriff bent on revenge; *Echoes of a Summer*, co-starring with Jodie Foster; an unnecessary sequel, *The Return of a Man Called Horse*; and the blatantly silly *Jaws* rip-off, *Orca*, having a showdown with an angry whale. Faring somewhat better were some action attractions, *Juggernaut*, as a sardonic bomb expert trying to save a booby-trapped ship; *The Cassandra Crossing*, trying to stop a train on the brink of disaster; and *The Wild Geese*, as a mercenary in Africa. Also among his non-hits were three with his second wife (1974–82), Ann Turkel: *99 and 44/100% Dead*, as a hit-man; *Golden Rendezvous*, trapped aboard a hijacked gambling ship; and *Ravagers*, searching for life in a devastated futuristic world. When at last he did appear in another movie that had some success at the box office, it was perhaps the worst of them all, *Tarzan the Ape Man*, where his over-the-top playing was at least a relief from the excruciating boredom. After that he retreated back to something more appealing to audiences, spending a good deal of time reprising his *Camelot* role, on Broadway and in multiple tours.

Around the time of the *Ape* film there were more movies whose distribution was spotty or nil including *Your Ticket is No Longer Valid*, *Danny Travis*, and *Highpoint*. He was looking quite thin and worn by this point but career relief came in the 1990s when he was chosen to play a character role, a bearded, bull-headed landowner, in *The Field*, which reminded the industry of his capabilities and earned him another Oscar nomination. From that he secured a few more good parts, with the Academy Award Best Picture winner *Unforgiven*, as a pretentious gunfighter who takes a beating from sheriff Gene Hackman; *Wrestling Ernest Hemingway*, as a pushy senior citizen trying to relieve his loneliness by making friends with Robert Duvall; *Cry, the Beloved Country*, as a wealthy South African bigot; and *Trojan Eddie*, heading a band of Gaelic gypsies. Despite these being followed by some more films that skipped distribution in the U.S., he ended up in a huge hit and another Oscar winner for Best Picture, *Gladiator*, excellent as the Roman Emperor slain by his own son (Joaquin Phoenix), and in one of the most charming fantasy movies in years, *Harry Potter and the Sorcerer's Stone*, as the head wizard, Professor Dumbledore, a part he was called on to reprise in the first sequel, released posthumously. Harris published a book of poetry, *I, in the Membership of My Days*, in 1973, and a novel, *Honor Bound*, in 1982. His son is actor Jared Harris whose credits include playing Andy Warhol in *I Shot Andy Warhol*.

Screen: 1958: Alive and Kicking; 1959: Shake Hands With the Devil; The Wreck of the Mary Deare; 1960: A Terrible Beauty/The Night Fighters; 1961: The Long and the Short and the Tall/

Jungle Fighters; The Guns of Navarone; **1962:** Mutiny on the Bounty; **1963:** This Sporting Life; **1965:** Red Desert; I Tre Volti/ Three Faces of a Woman (nUSr); Major Dundee; The Heroes of Telemark; **1966:** The Bible; Hawaii; **1967:** Caprice; Camelot; **1970:** The Molly Maguires; A Man Called Horse; Cromwell; **1971:** Man in the Wilderness; **1972:** The Hero/Bloomfield (and dir.; co-wr.); **1973:** The Deadly Trackers; **1974:** 99 and 44/100% Dead; Juggernaut; **1976:** Robin and Marian; Echoes of a Summer (and co-exec. prod.); The Return of a Man Called Horse (and co-exec. prod.); **1977:** The Cassandra Crossing; Golden Rendezvous (nUSr); Orca; **1978:** The Wild Geese; **1979:** Ravagers; **1980:** The Last Word; A Game for Vultures; **1981:** Gulliver's Travels (filmed 1977); Your Ticket Is No Longer Valid (dtc); Tarzan the Ape Man; **1984:** Triumphs of a Man Called Horse; Highpoint (filmed 1980); **1985:** Martin's Day; **1990:** Mack the Knife; The Field; **1982:** Patriot Games; Unforgiven; **1993:** King of the Wind (filmed 1989; dtv); Wrestling Ernest Hemingway; **1994:** Silent Tongue; **1995:** Cry, the Beloved Country; **1997:** Smilla's Sense of Snow; Trojan Eddie; Savage Hearts (dtv); **1998:** This Is the Sea (nUSr); The Barber of Siberia (nUSr); **1999:** To Walk with Lions (dtv in US); Grizzly Falls; **2000:** Gladiator; **2001:** Harry Potter and the Sorcerer's Stone/Harry Potter and the Philosopher's Stone; **2002:** My Kingdom (nUSr); The Count of Monte Cristo; Harry Potter and the Chamber of Secrets; My Kingdom; **2003:** Kaena: The Prophecy.

NY Stage: 1981: Camelot.

Select TV: 1964: Carol for Another Christmas (sp); 1971: The Snow Goose (sp); 1982: Camelot (sp); 1988: Maigret; 1994: Abraham; 1995: The Great Kandinsky; 1997: The Hunchback; 2002: Julius Caesar; The Apocalypse.

REX HARRISON

(REGINALD CAREY HARRISON) BORN: HUYTON, LANCASHIRE, ENGLAND, MARCH 5, 1908. ED: LIVERPOOL COL. DIED: JUNE 2, 1990.

Suave and charismatic, Rex Harrison had talents so assured that he prospered as one of the best-loved of all British thespians, despite the fact that most of his roles emphasized his somewhat aloof, snobbish air. (Offstage he was said to have been one of the most self-involved of all actors, intolerant of being anything but the center of everyone's attention.) A peerless interpreter of drawing-room comedy, he also broke ground of sorts by creating one of the greatest, most original characterizations in the history of the musical, even though he didn't have the faintest knack for singing. After completing his education, he joined Liverpool Rep, toured with various acting companies, and made his London stage debut in 1930, in *Getting George Married*. That same year he began to get small film parts, but it was not until his stage success in *French Without Tears*, in 1936, that movie producers saw him as star potential. He signed a contract with Alexander Korda and was cast opposite Vivien Leigh in *Storm in a Teacup*, wittily playing a reporter who gets a kick out of causing trouble. They were teamed again in *St. Martin's Lane/Sidewalks of London*, in which he had a somewhat prophetic role, rescuing her lowlife character from the gutter and helping her become more refined. After this film, he had his widest exposure in the U.S., playing a snobby doctor in the Oscar-nominated *The Citadel*. A West End success, in a production of Noel Coward's *Design for Living*, enhanced his growing reputation as one of the best light comedians around. This was followed by leads in two of the biggest British imports of the early 1940s, *Night*

Train (to Munich), as a government agent trying to help Margaret Lockwood recover her father from the Nazis, and the acclaimed film version of Shaw's *Major Barbara*, as the young professor who joins the Salvation Army because he is smitten with Wendy Hiller. Hollywood desperately wanted him, but it was wartime, and he joined the RAF instead. When he returned, he gave an impeccable performance as the haunted husband in Coward's silly but popular *Blithe Spirit*, another crossover success in the U.S., and was at his most caddish in *The Rake's Progress/Notorious Gentleman*, as a self-centered womanizer, a part many likened to his off-screen self.

In 1946, he finally came to Hollywood, signing a contract with 20th Century-Fox. He started off splendidly, playing the vain ruler in *Anna and the King of Siam*, holding his own quite nicely in comparison with Yul Brynner's definitive interpretation of the part in the later musical version, even if Harrison was rather tall for an Asian. He did, however, possess the arrogance and self-satisfaction the part called for, and the movie was very popular. It was followed by one of his best-remembered roles, the romantic sea captain who happens to be dead, in the pleasant fantasy romance *The Ghost and Mrs. Muir*, falling in love with mortal Gene Tierney. There was a third consecutive box-office hit with the tiresome Southern melodrama *The Foxes of Harrow*, again playing a rather selfish character; but his first attempt at American comedy, Preston Sturges's *Unfaithfully Yours*, a sporadically funny farce with Harrison as an egomaniacal orchestra conductor plotting his wife's demise, did poorly. His position as one of the hot "new" stars of the day was diminished greatly after his involvement with actress Carole Landis who, shortly afterwards, committed suicide. Because of the scandal, his Fox contract came to an end, and Harrison figured it was time to go back to his theater roots. He went to Broadway, scoring a hit with then-wife (1943–57) Lilli Palmer in *Bell Book and Candle*. He and Palmer didn't do as well in the movies, appearing as the only two cast members of the film version of the play *The Four Poster*, a series of marital vignettes taking place exclusively in a bedroom and therefore meant for very specialized audiences. Perhaps because there were bills to pay, he took part in a nonsensical historical epic, *King Richard and the Crusaders*, looking like he'd rather be anywhere else, playing a jewel-laden Moorish physician. Any memory of that film was soon wiped away by the acclaim for the mightiest musical of them all, Lerner and Loewe's *My Fair Lady*. Opening on Broadway in 1956, it reaped the sort of reviews and box office that all producers dream of, and Harrison's performance as the snappish, self-involved Henry Higgins became legendary, his style of talk-singing the part being much imitated and admired. He won the Tony Award and became more famous than ever, returning to the movies as a newly minted star attraction, to act opposite his new wife (1957–59) Kay Kendall (they had met while working in *The Constant Husband*) in the stylish but often empty comedy *The Reluctant Debutante*. Despite the shortcomings of the material, Harrison and Kendall proved to be a delectable team on screen.

My Fair Lady, both in New York and London, continued to occupy most of his time during the late 1950s, but he was in great demand again for films and, in 1960, appeared in the glossy Doris Day hit *Midnight Lace*, pretending to be concerned about her while she's being driven crazy by threatening phone calls. Replacing Peter Firth as Caesar, he became part of the most over-hyped movie of its day, *Cleopatra*, and he turned out to be the one unanimously acclaimed aspect of the film, giving a commanding and nuanced performance, which earned him an Oscar nomination. He later spoke of it as the most satisfying movie role of his career, and he played Caesar yet again, on the Broadway stage in 1977, in Shaw's *Caesar and Cleopatra*. His newfound movie star status helped him secure the role of Higgins in the 1964 movie version of *My Fair Lady*, although it is unthinkable that anyone else could have been offered the part. His brilliance as this egotistical but magnetic figure was forever captured on film, winning him the Academy Award and helping the movie become a massive success, nab the Oscar for Best Picture, and assure its place in history as one of the best adaptations (and certainly the most faithful) of a Broadway musical in Hollywood history. This, like *Cleopatra*, had been a costly production, and Harrison found himself in two more budget breakers: *The Agony and the Ecstasy*, as a warring Pope bickering with Michelangelo (Charlton Heston) over the painting of the ceiling of the Sistine Chapel, and the musical fantasy *Doctor Dolittle*, as the eccentric veterinarian with a knack for conversing with animals, another one of the roles most closely associated with him. He was fine in these, but stumbled badly playing an aging homosexual living a hellish relationship with Richard Burton in *Staircase*, a rare example of Harrison completely losing his grasp on a part. After that failure it was back to the stage, with a few cameo film spots along the way, and some television roles, including *The Adventures of Don Quixote*. He enjoyed his stardom and knew that the theater was the one place to retain it, finding work right into his 80s. He reprised Higgins again in the early 1980s and had just finished a run in *The Circle* on Broadway when he passed away in 1990, a year after being knighted. His fourth (1962–71) of six wives was actress Rachel Roberts. He published two memoirs, *Rex* (1975) and *Comedy: A Damn Serious Business* (1990), and a collection of poems, *If Love Be Love* (1979).

Screen: 1930: The Great Game; The School for Scandal; 1934: Get Your Man; Leave It to Blanche; 1935: All at Sea; 1937: Men Are Not Gods; Storm in a Teacup; Over the Moon; 1938: School for Husbands; The Citadel; St. Martin's Lane/Sidewalks of London (US: 1940); 1939: The Silent Battle/Continental Express; Ten Days in Paris/Missing Ten Days; 1940: Night Train to Munich/Night Train; Over the Moon; 1941: Major Barbara; 1945: I Live in Grosvenor Square/A Yank in London; Blithe Spirit; The Rake's Progress/Notorious Gentleman; 1946: Anna and the King of Siam; 1947: The Ghost and Mrs. Muir; The Foxes of Harrow; 1948: Escape; Unfaithfully Yours; 1951: The Long Dark Hall; 1952: The Four Poster; 1953: Main Street to Broadway; 1954: King Richard and the Crusaders; 1955: The Constant Husband; 1958: The Reluctant Debutante; 1960: Midnight Lace; 1962: The Happy Thieves; 1963: Cleopatra; 1964: My Fair Lady; The Yellow Rolls-Royce; 1965: The Agony and the Ecstasy; 1967: The Honey Pot; Doctor Dolittle; 1968: A Flea in Her Ear; 1969: Staircase; 1978: Crossed Swords/The Prince and the Pauper; Shalimar/Deadly Thief; 1979: The Fifth Musketeer/Behind the Mask (filmed 1977); Ashanti; 1983: A Time to Die/Seven Graves for Rogan (filmed 1978).

NY Stage: 1936: Sweet Aloes; 1948: Anne of the Thousand Days; 1950: Bell Book and Candle; 1952: Venus Observed; 1953: The Love of Four Colonels (and dir.); 1956: My Fair Lady; 1959: The Fighting Cock; 1973: Emperor Henry IV; 1974: In Praise of Love; 1977: Caesar and Cleopatra; 1978: The Kingfisher; 1981: My Fair Lady (revival); 1983: Heartbreak House; 1985: Aren't We All?; 1989: The Circle.

Select TV: 1953: The Man in Possession (sp); 1973: The Adventures of Don Quixote (sp); 1974: Rex Harrison Presents Stories of Love (sp); 1982: The Kingfisher (sp); 1986: Anastasia: The Mystery of Anna; Heartbreak House.

WILLIAM S. HART
BORN: NEWBURGH, NY, DECEMBER 6, 1869.
DIED: JUNE 23, 1946.

The positively grim-looking William S. Hart, with a countenance not unlike that of a cigar-store Indian, became an unlikely movie star at the age of 50. Following a stage career that found him performing Shakespeare and portraying bad guys in such productions as *Ben-Hur* and *The Squaw Man*, he came to Hollywood in 1914 to appear in some two-reelers. In no time his friend, producer Thomas H. Ince, gave him the chance to star in his own westerns, and he became one of the first great stars of that genre. Hart went for a more serious, earthy approach to the form than most filmmakers had attempted to that point, usually appearing as a man of low repute who found a conscience along the way. From 1914 to 1925, he would remain a potent figure in Hollywood, often directing his own films, getting additional credits as storywriter and/or executive producer, right up to his final starring feature, the independently produced *Tumbleweeds*. By 1919 he had broken off with Ince and signed up with Famous Players-Lasky, but it wasn't long before he realized that he was being eclipsed in popularity by such other stars as Tom Mix. He retired before the coming of the sound era, although there was one last release of sorts, a 1939 reissue of *Tumbleweeds* with a new prologue. In 1929 he published his autobiography, *My Life — East and West*.

Screen (features): 1914: The Bargain; The Passing of Two-Gun Hicks (and dir.); His Hour of Manhood; Jim Cameron's Wife; 1915: The Sheriff's Streak of Yellow.

and director: Scourge of the Desert; Pinto Ben (and wr.); On the Night Stage (actor only); In the Sagebrush Country; The Man From Nowhere; The Grudge; The Taking of Luke McVane; Mr. Silent Haskins; Cash Parrish's Pal; The Roughneck; The Conversion of Frosty Blake; Keno Bates — Liar; The Disciple; Between Men; The Darkening Trail; Tools of Providence; A Knight of the Trails; Bad Buck of Santa Ynez; The Ruse; 1916: Hell's Hinges (and co-dir.); The Aryan; The Primal Lure; The Apostle of Vengeance; The Captive God (actor only); The Dawn Maker; The Return of Draw Egan; The Patriot; The Devil's Double; Truthful Tulliver; 1917: The Gun Fighter; The Square Deal Man; The Desert Man; Wolf Lowry; The Cold Deck.

and director/executive producer: The Silent Man; The Narrow Trail (actor; wr.; exec. prod.); 1918: Wolves of the Rail (and wr.); Blue Blazes Rawden; The Tiger Man; Selfish Yates; Shark Monroe; Riddle Gawne; The Border Wireless; Branding Broadway; 1919: Breed of Men (actor; wr.; exec. prod.); The Poppy Girl's Husband; The Money Corral (actor; dir.; wr.); Square Deal Sanderson.

and executive producer: Wagon Tracks; John Petticoats; 1920: The Toll Gate (and co-wr.); Sand; The Cradle of Courage; The Testing Block (and wr.); 1921: O'Malley of the Mounted; The Whistle; The Three-Word Brand; White Oak (and wr.); 1922: Travelin' On (and wr.); 1923: Hollywood (cameo); Wild Bill Hickok (actor; wr.); 1924: Singer Jim McKee (and wr.); 1925: Tumbleweeds; 1928: Show People (actor).

NY Stage: 1899: Ben-Hur; 1903: Hearts Courageous; 1904: Love's Pilgrimage; Home Folks; 1905: Strolling Players; The Squaw Man; 1910: The Barrier; 1911: The Silent Call; 1912: The Trail of the Lonesome Pine.

LAURENCE HARVEY

(Larushka Mischa Skikne) Born: Jonishkis, Lithuania, October 1, 1928. Raised in South Africa. Died: November 25, 1973.

It is interesting to note that the two most acclaimed and enduring performances of cold, aloof, and threateningly handsome Laurence Harvey required him to play emotionally deadened human beings. Having been brought up in South Africa, he served with their army during World War II and made his first notable stage appearance in Johannesburg. From there he moved to England, very briefly attending RADA and acting with both Manchester Rep and the Shakespearean Memorial Theatre. He landed a starring role in a "B" psychological thriller, *House of Darkness*, as a wicked and greedy brother haunted by his evil deeds. This led to a contract with Associated British Films. For the next few years, he worked for them in fairly undistinguished product that included *A Killer Walks*, again playing a bad brother, this one murdering his grandmother for cash. That particular movie did spark some industry interest, as did *Women of Twilight/Twilight Women*, with Harvey playing a condemned killer in a film that would find a minor degree of notoriety for becoming Britain's first release to receive an "X" certification, and one of the lesser-known screen versions of *Romeo and Juliet*, as Romeo. Around this time he made his Broadway debut, in *Island of Goats*, winning a Theatre World Award for his work.

Hollywood, always on the look-out for someone new, was taking note of his progress, and so Warner Bros. gave him the lead in one of the most idiotic of all 1950s costume epics, *King Richard and the Crusaders*, as a heroic Scottish knight. It is little wonder he retreated back to England for *The Good Die Young*, where he played opposite Margaret Leighton who later (1957–61) became the first of his three wives. He was the British tutor living in 1932 Berlin in *I Am a Camera*, before that tale became better known when it was musicalized as *Cabaret*; a blinded soldier in *Storm Over the Nile*; a Navy diver named Buster Crabb in the war film *The Silent Enemy*; a fast-talking promoter in *Expresso Bongo*; and one of the *Three Men in a Boat*, a comedy that achieved a certain level of popularity in Britain. One of that movie's producers was Jack Clayton, and when he made his transition to director with *Room at the Top*, he gave Harvey the lead and put him firmly on the cinema map. The role of the misguided opportunist, who realizes too late that he's sacrificed real love for position, required him to be more than a bit icy and ultimately pathetic, which he did well enough to earn an Oscar nomination. The film, a great achievement in itself, became one of the landmarks of the British "angry young man" cinema, bringing a new degree of gritty, working class authenticity to the film scene, and it made Harvey red hot.

Hollywood came calling once again, only with more lucrative offers, and he accepted roles in two of 1960s biggest box-office attractions, *The Alamo*, as the determined-but-doomed Colonel William Travis, and *Butterfield 8*, as the lover causing his share of havoc in Elizabeth Taylor's shambles of a life. After this he returned home to get the lead in the film version of the much-admired stage hit *The Long and the Short and the Tall*, which did not repeat its previous success at all. Back in the U.S., he was deeply dislikable in both *Summer and Smoke*, as the neighbor who thoughtlessly ignores pining Geraldine Page, and *Walk on the Wild Side*, miscast as a Texas drifter and sparking no fire whatsoever with the equally distant Capucine. Nor was he the warmest person to carry the story side of the expensive children's film *The Wonderful World of the Brothers Grimm*, as the famous fairy tale author. It was evident that Harvey worked best playing

impenetrable types, which meant audiences had a tough time embracing his screen persona. He was no better liked by those who worked with him, his arrogance and difficult behavior garnering some of the most vocal condemnations from co-stars and fellow-workers of any film actor. Therefore he was exactly right as the zombie-like vet being used as a pawn for diabolical political means in the original and daring *The Manchurian Candidate*, a movie that continued to rise in stature with the passing of the years. Shortly afterwards he made his debut as a director with *The Ceremony*, an opaque crime drama that was almost universally panned for its pretensions and murky cinematography. His career began to slip up badly with the ill-advised remake of *Of Human Bondage*, further brought down by having Kim Novak as his leading lady; *Life at the Top*, in a reprise of his breakthrough role in this uncalled for sequel to *Room at the Top*; and *A Dandy in Aspic*, which he finished directing after Anthony Mann died during production. Amid these, he was another cool character in a good film, *Darling*, but most of the praise for that one went to Julie Christie. He ended up in some minimally circulated European product and in a supporting role in the American flop *WUSA*, as a charlatan preacher. He tried to revitalize interest in himself by directing a horror movie, *Welcome to Arrow Beach*, in which he played a cannibal, which explained its unappetizing alternate title, *Tender Flesh*. By the time it showed up in the U.S. in 1974, Harvey was dead of cancer.

Screen: 1948: House of Darkness; Man on the Run; The Dancing Years; 1949: The Man From Yesterday; Landfall; 1950: Cairo Road; The Black Rose; 1951: Scarlet Thread; There Is Another Sun/Wall of Death; 1952: A Killer Walks; I Believe in You; Women of Twilight/Twilight Women; 1953: Innocents of Paris; 1954: Romeo and Juliet; King Richard and the Crusaders; 1955: The Good Die Young; I Am a Camera; 1956: Storm Over the Nile; 1957: Three Men in a Boat; After the Ball; 1958: The Truth About Women; The Silent Enemy; 1959: Room at the Top; Expresso Bongo; 1960: Butterfield 8; The Alamo; 1961: The Long and the Short and the Tall/Jungle Fighters; Two Loves; Summer and Smoke; 1962: Walk on the Wild Side; The Manchurian Candidate; The Wonderful World of the Brothers Grimm; A Girl Named Tamiko; 1963: The Running Man; The Ceremony (and dir.; prod.); 1964: Of Human Bondage; The Outrage; 1965: Darling; Life at the Top; 1966: The Spy With a Cold Nose; 1968: A Dandy in Aspic (and co-dir.); The Winter's Tale; Rebus (nUSr); 1969: Kampf um Rom/The Last Roman (nUSr); She and He (and prod.; nUSr); 1970: The Magic Christian; WUSA; 1972: Escape to the Sun; 1973: Night Watch; 1974: Welcome to Arrow Beach/Tender Flesh (and dir.; exec. prod.); 1977: F for Fake.

NY Stage: 1955: Island of Goats; 1957: The Country Wife; 1958: Henry V.

Select TV: 1950: Othello (sp); 1953: As You Like It (sp); 1955: The Secret Servant (sp).

HURD HATFIELD

(William Rukard Hurd Hatfield) Born: New York, NY, December 7, 1918. ed: Bard Col., Chekhov Drama School. Died: December 25, 1998.

Lean, smooth, and austere Hurd Hatfield attended acting school in Devonshire, England, studying with Michael Chekhov before coming to Broadway for a flop, *The Possessed*, followed by some Shakespeare. A mutual acquaintance got him a screen test with director Albert Lewin, and he was signed to a contract with MGM, hailed as a potentially exciting new discovery. He debuted in *Dragon Seed*, as Walter Huston's son who begins to enjoy killing the enemy, looking a bit more convincingly Chinese than most of the Caucasian cast in this monumentally silly epic. This was followed by the part for which he is best remembered, the depraved aristocrat in the extremely satisfying 1945 adaptation of Oscar Wilde's classic *The Picture of Dorian Gray*, a role that required him to be fairly aloof, cold-blooded, and eerily expressionless, which he did quite marvelously. Despite his triumph in that film, he didn't stick around MGM very long, exiting the studio after playing one of the men behind the atomic bomb in *The Beginning or the End*. Elsewhere he was the sickly rich son killed off by valet Francis Lederer in UA's *Diary of a Chambermaid*; Audrey Totter's drunken husband in Warners Bros.'s *The Unsuspected*, a role he particularly hated; and a priest in RKO's expensive epic *Joan of Arc*. By this point, what little public interested his MGM push had generated had vanished, so he appeared in some "B's": *The Checkered Coat*, as a psychotic mental patient; *Chinatown at Midnight*, as a killer on the run in San Francisco; and *Tarzan and the Slave Girl*, as the leader of a lion-worshiping tribe. After that he worked infrequently, popping up in character roles in various movies, including *King of Kings*, as Pontius Pilate; the obtuse *Mickey One*, as a possessive nightclub owner; and *The Boston Strangler*, as a gay man questioned by policeman Henry Fonda. It should be noted that at this stage in his life he still looked incredibly well preserved, leading one to believe that there was truly something inspired, if not downright prophetic, about his casting as Dorian Gray.

Screen: **1944:** Dragon Seed; **1945:** The Picture of Dorian Gray; **1946:** Diary of a Chambermaid; **1947:** The Beginning or the End; The Unsuspected; **1948:** The Checkered Coat; Chinatown at Midnight; Joan of Arc; **1950:** Tarzan and the Slave Girl; Destination Murder; **1958:** The Left-Handed Gun; **1961:** King of Kings; El Cid; **1965:** Mickey One; Harlow; The Double-Barreled Detective Story; **1968:** The Boston Strangler; **1971:** Von Richtofen and Brown; **1985:** King David; Waiting to Act (dtv); **1986:** Crimes of the Heart; **1989:** Her Alibi.

NY Stage: **1939:** The Possessed; **1941:** Twelfth Night; **1942:** The Strings My Lord Are False; **1949:** The Ivy Green; **1952:** Venus Observed; **1953:** Love's Labour's Lost; Camino Real; **1954:** Bullfight; Anastasia; **1955:** Julius Caesar (ob); The Tempest (ob); **1956:** The Lovers; **1957:** The Duchess of Malfi; **1959:** Much Ado About Nothing.

Select TV: **1950:** The Rivals (sp); The Importance of Being Earnest (sp); Hollywood Screen Test (series); **1952:** The Nativity Play (sp); **1953:** Greed (sp); Seventh Heaven (sp); The Hasty Heart (sp); **1954:** The Hunchback of Notre Dame (sp); **1955:** The King's Bounty (sp); I Was Accused (sp); **1956:** Lamp at Midnight (sp); **1957:** The Prince and the Pauper (sp); **1958:** The Last Man (sp); The Count of Monte Cristo (sp); **1959:** Various Temptations (sp); I Don Quixote (sp); **1963:** The Invincible Mr. Disraeli (sp); One Day in the Life of Ivan Denisovich (sp); A Cry of Angels (sp); **1966:** The Movers (sp); Ten Blocks on the Camino Real (sp); Don Juan in Hell (sp); **1971:** Thief; **1973:** The Norliss Tapes; **1978:** The Word (ms); **1979:** You Can't Go Home Again; **1981:** The Manions of America (sp); **1991:** Lies of the Twins.

JUNE HAVER

(JUNE STOVENOUR) BORN: ROCK ISLAND, IL, JUNE 10, 1926.

Groomed by 20th Century-Fox to be "the next Betty Grable," June Haver had been in show business since she was a child, eventually becoming a band vocalist at age 14. She

sang in two Universal shorts and made her official feature debut for Fox in 1943, playing a hatcheck girl in the Alice Faye musical *The Gang's All Here*. The following year she was upped to the lead in one of those bio-musicals of the time about little-known composers, *Irish Eyes Are Smiling*, opposite Dick Haymes as Ernest R. Ball. Then she was paired with Grable herself in one of the least-appealing films of the studio's shaky musical output, *The Dolly Sisters*, a highly fictionalized account of a once popular vaudeville act, that became a smash hit. Next she teamed with Fred MacMurray in *Where Do We Go From Here?*, losing him in the movie to Joan Leslie, although real life would soon dictate otherwise. She continued in such lightweight entertainments as *I Wonder Who's Kissing Her Now*, about another trivia-question composer, Joe Howard; and some that did not require her to sing, including one about mules, *Scudda Hoo! Scudda Hay!* Haver was blandly pretty and could get by with a song and dance, but was sorely missing that extra spark of charisma to breathe life into the mostly routine material she was given. There were two visits to Warners for similar properties: *Look for the Silver Lining*, which was yet another biopic, but at least one in which she was the principal subject matter, playing Broadway star Marilyn Miller, and in no way suggesting that this lady might have been interesting enough to rate her story being told on film; and *The Daughter of Rosie O'Grady*, in which just about every other cast member (from S.Z. Sakall to Gene Nelson) had more to offer than she did. She returned to her home lot to finish to her contract with *The Girl Next Door*, as a stage performer who settles down with cartoonist Dan Dailey. After that she briefly entered a convent but gave up that idea, marrying Fred MacMurray in 1955, and settling into retirement on their ranch. MacMurray died in 1991.

Screen: **1943:** The Gang's All Here; **1944:** Home in Indiana; Irish Eyes Are Smiling; **1945:** Where Do We Go From Here?; The Dolly Sisters; **1946:** Three Little Girls in Blue; Wake Up and Dream; **1947:** I Wonder Who's Kissing Her Now; **1948:** Scudda Hoo! Scudda Hay!; **1949:** Oh, You Beautiful Doll; Look for the Silver Lining; **1950:** The Daughter of Rosie O'Grady; I'll Get By; **1951:** Love Nest; **1953:** The Girl Next Door.

JUNE HAVOC

(ELLEN EVANGELINE HOVICK)
BORN: SEATTLE, WA, NOVEMBER 8, 1916.

It is quite understandable for modern audiences to respond with confusion when hearing the names of 1940s blondes June Haver and June Havoc. The latter's distinction was being the Baby June immortalized in the classic Broadway musical *Gypsy*, not to mention having a bit more range and sparkle as an actress than the other June. Her vaudeville years as a child performer were followed by appearances with the Anna Pavlova dance troupe and the St. Louis Municipal Opera Company. Starting in 1936, she began achieving some success on Broadway in such shows as *Forbidden Melody*, *Pal Joey*, and *Mexican Hayride*. She came to Hollywood in 1941, debuting as a nightclub performer in the RKO musical *Four Jacks and a Jill*. There were some other musical appearances, including *Sing Your Worries Away* and *Hello, Frisco, Hello*, but Havoc was not the center of attention in either. She began to concentrate on her more dramatic side with *Intrigue*, as the head of a black market operation, and participated in the 1947 Oscar-winner for Best Picture, *Gentleman's Agreement*, as Gregory Peck's self-loathing Jewish secretary, enacting a good scene explaining how she Anglicized her name to avoid job discrimination. There were also a handful of top billing assignments, playing tough dames in *The*

Story of Molly X, as an ex-con; and *Once a Thief* as a shoplifter; and then landing the title role in *Lady Possessed*, suffering an identity crisis after a miscarriage. She never achieved the heights of stardom that her sister, Gypsy Rose Lee, did (though she was, certainly, the more talented of the two) but kept quite busy over the years, including directing and writing the short-lived 1963 Broadway comedy *Marathon '33*, and another for Off Broadway, *Oh Glorious Tintinnabulation*, in 1974.

Screen: 1942: Four Jacks and a Jill; Powder Town; My Sister Eileen; Sing Your Worries Away; 1943: Hello, Frisco, Hello; Timber Queen; No Time for Love; Hi Diddle Diddle; 1944: Casanova in Burlesque; 1945: Brewster's Millions; 1947: Intrigue; Gentleman's Agreement; 1948: When My Baby Smiles at Me; The Iron Curtain; 1949: The Story of Molly X; Red, Hot and Blue; Chicago Deadline; 1950: Mother Didn't Tell Me; Once a Thief; 1951: Follow the Sun; 1952: Lady Possessed; 1956: Three for Jamie Dawn; 1978: The Private Files of J. Edgar Hoover; 1980: Can't Stop the Music; 1987: Return to Salem's Lot.

NY Stage: 1936: Forbidden Melody; 1940: Pal Joey; 1944: Mexican Hayride; Sadie Thompson; 1945: The Ryan Girl; Dunnigan's Daughter; 1946: Dream Girl; 1950: Affairs of State; 1958: The Infernal Machine (ob); 1959: The Beaux Stratagem (ob); The Warm Peninsula; 1966: Dinner at Eight; 1975: Habeas Corpus; 1982: Annie.

Select TV: 1951: Cakes and Ale (sp); 1952: Anna Christie (sp); Daisy Mayme (sp); 1953: The Bear (sp); Mrs. Union Station (sp); 1954–55: Willy (series); 1956: Robin Dow (sp); 1957: Mr. Broadway (sp); The Mother Bit (sp); 1959: The Pink Burrow (sp); 1964: The June Havoc Show (series); 1970: The Boy Who Stole the Elephants (sp)

JACK HAWKINS

BORN: LONDON, ENGLAND, SEPTEMBER 14, 1910.
DIED: JULY 18, 1973.

One of Britain's least-likely stars of the postwar era, Jack Hawkins had a rugged, earthy, working-class quality about him; with his growlingly throaty voice, furrowed brows, and imposing, powerful physicality, he looked more like a hearty drinking buddy from the corner pub than a leading man. He had started out as a child performer, debuting as a frog in a children's play, in London in 1923, and followed this with the leading role (!) in a production of *Saint Joan*. His theater career extended to New York as well, where he made his American bow in *Journey's End*, in 1929. The next year he had a bit part in the film *Birds of Prey/The Perfect Alibi*, then returned to the London stage for *Autumn Crocus*, marrying one of its cast members, Jessica Tandy, in 1932 (they divorced in 1940). He continued to accept movie assignments, which ranged from donning 18th century garb to participate in a duel with Anna Neagel, in *Peg of Old Drury*, to romancing Judy Gunn in a sinking comedy, *Beauty and the Barge*, to tracking down a secret band of criminals known as The Fellowship of the Frog in *The Frog*. However, the bulk of his work at this point was in the theater, and he did a stint as the head of England's USO equivalent, ENSA, while serving in the Royal Welsh Fusiliers during World War II. Afterward, it was back to secondary parts in the movies, including *The Fallen Idol*, as the inspector investigating the death of Ralph Richardson's shrewish wife (he would later play the lead in a television adaptation), and *State Secret*, as the Iron Curtain chief of police. Around that time he had a taste of international filmmaking, playing Tyrone Power's bowman buddy in Fox's ponderous costume epic *The Black Rose*, then won great acclaim as the teacher who helps

a deaf-mute child in *Mandy/Crash of Silence*. This one, along with *The Cruel Sea*, in which he played the commander of a torpedoed World War II warship, made him one of Britain's most-respected actors and a sudden box-office attraction in his native country.

He was Alec Guinness's interrogator in *The Prisoner*, and then headed Howard Hawks's lively spectacle *Land of the Pharaohs*, as Egypt's self-proclaimed "living God," done in by wicked Joan Collins. He had the good fortune of appearing in two of the monster hits of the late 1950s, both Academy Award winners for Best Picture as well: *The Bridge on the River Kwai*, as the major leading a team of saboteurs into the jungle in order to destroy the title structure (and somehow rating billing *above* Alec Guinness), and *Ben-Hur*, as the Roman whose life is saved by Charlton Heston during the famous sea battle sequence. Meanwhile, on native soil, he was in hot pursuit of a master safecracker in *The Long Arm/The Third Key*, which was notable for being the last Ealing movie made at Ealing Studios; starred in director John Ford's look at a day in the life of a police inspector, *Gideon of Scotland Yard*, which was greeted with equal degrees of applause or snoring by critics; infiltrated the Nazis during World War II in *The Two-Headed Spy*, a true story; and was on the other side of the law as a former army colonel masterminding a bank heist in the acclaimed *The League of Gentlemen*.

He was featured in his third Academy Award-winner for Best Picture, *Lawrence of Arabia*, as Peter O'Toole's superior officer, General Allenby, and from that point on he pretty much stayed in secondary roles, often in middling 1960s fare where his presence was always a great asset, including *The Third Secret*, as a judge suspected of murder; *Guns at Batasi*, stationed at an African outpost; and *Judith*, as a British officer aiding Sophia Loren in this very bad Israeli drama. Unbeknownst to many filmgoers, Hawkins's screen voice from 1967 on was no longer his own. Plagued by throat cancer, he had his voice box removed in an operation in 1966. Determined to keep acting and still in demand, he appeared quite regularly in supporting parts in such all-star attractions as *Oh! What a Lovely War*, *Waterloo*, and *Theater of Blood*, his voiced usually dubbed by either Charles Gray or Robert Rietty.

Screen: 1930: The Perfect Alibi/Birds of Prey; 1932: The Lodger/The Phantom Fiend (US: 1935); 1933: The Lost Chord; The Good Companions; I Lived With You; The Jewel; A Shot in the Dark; 1934: Autumn Crocus; Death at Broadcasting House; 1935: Peg of Old Drury; 1937: Beauty and the Barge; The Frog; 1938: Who Goes Next?; A Royal Divorce; 1939: Murder Will Out; 1940: The Flying Squad; 1942: Next of Kin; 1948: The Fallen Idol; Bonnie Prince Charlie; 1949: The Small Black Room; 1950: The Black Rose; The Elusive Pimpernel; The Great Manhunt/State Secret; 1951: The Great Adventure/The Adventurers; No Highway in the Sky/No Highway; 1952: Outpost in Malaya/The Planter's Wife; Murder on Monday/Home at Seven; Angels One Five; 1953: Crash of Silence/Mandy; The Cruel Sea; Twice Upon a Time; Malta Story; The Intruder; Front Page Story; 1954: Land of Fury/The Seekers; 1955: Land of the Pharaohs; The Prisoner; Touch and Go/The Light Touch; 1956: The Long Arm/The Third Key; The Man in the Sky/Decision Against Time; 1957: The Bridge on the River Kwai; 1958: She Played With Fire/Fortune Is a Woman; The Two-Headed Spy; Gideon of Scotland Yard/Gideon's Day; 1959: Ben-Hur; 1961: The League of Gentlemen; Two Loves; 1962: Five Finger Exercise; Lawrence of Arabia; 1963: Lafayette; Rampage; 1964: The Third Secret; Guns at Batasi; Zulu; 1965: Lord Jim; Masquerade; 1966: Judith; 1968: Great Catherine; Shalako; 1969: Those Daring Young Men in Their Jaunty Jalopies/Monte Carlo or Bust; Oh! What a Lovely War; 1970: Twinky/Lola; Waterloo; 1971: When Eight Bells Toll;

The Adventures of Gerard; The Beloved/Sin (nUSr); Kidnapped; Nicholas and Alexandra; 1972: Young Winston; 1973: Theater of Blood; Escape to the Sun; Tales That Witness Madness.

NY Stage: 1929: Journey's End; 1939: Dear Octopus; 1951: Romeo and Juliet.

Select TV: 1956: Caesar and Cleopatra (sp); 1959: The Fallen Idol (sp); 1963: To Bury Caesar (sp); 1965: Back to Back (sp); 1966: The Open Door (sp); The Poppy Is Also a Flower (also theatrical); 1970: Jane Eyre (sp); 1974: QB VII (ms).

SESSUE HAYAKAWA

(Kintaro Hayakawa) Born: Nanaura, Chiba, Japan, June 10, 1889. Died: November 23, 1973.

The first Asian performer to attain any degree of film stardom in the United States, Sessue Hayakawa had come from Japan to study banking at the University of Chicago, but ended up on the stage instead. A Los Angeles production of the play The Typhoon gained him some note, and when Thomas H. Ince decided to film it, Hayakawa came with the package. It was this film and one for DeMille, The Cheat, in which he played an evil playboy who brands heroine Gladys Brockwell when she will not succumb to his desires, that made the actor a movie attraction. Although these were no better than "wicked-Oriental" roles, he also was given star parts in comedies like Hashimura Togo and romances like Alien Souls. In time he tried his hand at writing (specifically A Heart in Pawn) and formed his own film company (starting with The Beggar Prince and continuing up to The Vermillion Pencil), acting with his wife Tsuru Aoki on several occasions. By the coming of sound, he was appearing less frequently, opting to work in French movies and eventually moving to that country during World War II. At the end of the 1940s, he was surprised to find that Hollywood was still interested in him, and he landed some substantial villain parts in Tokyo Joe, with Humphrey Bogart, and Three Came Home, in which he played a colonel questioning his own sense of decency while keeping Claudette Colbert prisoner. His most memorable movie role was one of his last, the tormented Colonel Saito, who locks horns with stubborn prisoner Alec Guinness, in the classic The Bridge on the River Kwai, a part that earned him an Oscar nomination. He did a spoof of this in a sequence of the Jerry Lewis comedy The Geisha Boy; was the jungle chief in the disastrous attempt to film Green Mansions; and led his band of pirates in attacking the Swiss Family Robinson, in the very successful Disney rendering of the story. He retired in 1964 to study Zen Buddhism, becoming an ordained priest. His book, Zen Showed Me the Way, was published the same year.

Screen (US features only): 1914: The Wrath of the Gods; The Typhoon; 1915: After Five; The Clue; The Secret Sin; The Cheat; Temptation; 1916: Alien Souls; The Honorable Friend; The Soul of Kura San; The Victoria Cross; 1917: Each to His Kind/The Rajah's Amulet; The Bottle Imp; The Jaguar's Claws; Forbidden Paths; Hashimura Togo; The Call of the East; The Secret Game; 1918: The Hidden Pearls; The Honor of His House; The City of Dim Faces; The Temple of Dusk; The White Man's Law; The Bravest Way; His Birthright (and co-wr.); 1919: Bonds of Honor; A Heart in Pawn (and wr.); His Debt; The Courageous Coward; The Man Beneath; The Dragon Painter; The Illustrious Prince; The Tong Man; 1920: The Beggar Prince; The Brand of Lopez; The Devil's Claim; Li Ting Lang; An Arabian Knight; 1921: The First Born; Black Roses; Where Lights Are Low; The Swamp (and co-wr.); 1922: Five Days to Live; The Vermilion Pencil; 1924: The Danger Line/La Bataille; The Great Prince Shan; Sen Yan's

Devotion; 1931: Daughter of the Dragon; 1949: Tokyo Joe; 1950: Three Came Home; 1955: House of Bamboo; 1957: The Bridge on the River Kwai; 1958: The Geisha Boy; 1959: Green Mansions; 1960: Hell to Eternity; Swiss Family Robinson; 1962: The Big Wave; 1966: The Daydreamer (voice).

NY Stage: 1959: Kataki.

Select TV: 1958: Kurishika Incident (sp).

STERLING HAYDEN

(Sterling Relyea Walter) Born: Montclair, NJ, March 26, 1916. Died: May 23, 1986.

The studio system didn't do right by massive, deep-voiced Sterling Hayden, for here was a performer utilized initially for his looks and written off as a stiff, who grew more interesting the further he got away from the Hollywood gloss. His first love was the sea, and he spent many of his teen years on shipboard before someone convinced him his physical attributes were striking enough that the movies might have some use for him. Apparently they were right, for he was tested and signed by Paramount in 1941 with nary an acting lesson behind him. As "Stirling" Hayden, he was put into two Technicolor productions, both of which starred Madeleine Carroll, Virginia and Bahama Passage, upped to leading man in the latter, as a hunky islander who gets Carroll's fires burning. His reviews were poor, but he did get a wife out of the deal; he and Carroll taking the vows in 1942, only to divorce four years later. After service in the Marines during World War II, he returned to Paramount, with his name now correctly spelled, and appeared in Blaze of Noon, a mawkish melodrama, playing William Holden's pilot brother who pines for sister-in-law Anne Baxter; El Paso, a Pine-Thomas cheapie; and Manhandled, an attempt to sell Dorothy Lamour in a noir thriller. It was not until he went elsewhere, over to MGM, that he found his first good part, playing the doomed gangster involved in a misguided heist in the taut and influential John Huston-directed crime thriller The Asphalt Jungle. There was still a monolithic quality to his acting, so he was put into westerns where this sort of thing seemed less noticeable, including the remake of So Big, as the husband of formidable Jane Wyman; Arrow in the Dust, as a deserter who redeems himself by leading a wagon train to safety; The Last Command, as Jim Bowie, in Republic Pictures's version of the siege at the Alamo; and the cult item Johnny Guitar, as the laconic gunman loved by a butch Joan Crawford. Outside this genre, he went swashbuckling (looking, not unexpectedly, ill at ease) in The Golden Hawk; provided some comfort to temperamental movie actress Bette Davis in a superficial glance at Hollywood, The Star; and tried to reason with quick-tempered assassin Frank Sinatra in Suddenly.

Another film about a robbery-gone-wrong film, The Killing, proved to be his next outstanding property. His stony persona was never so effectively utilized as it was in this movie in which he played the ex-con who organizes a heist at a racetrack. After that it was back to westerns like The Iron Sheriff, trying to track down the real killer before his son hangs for a crime he didn't commit; and Terror in a Texas Town, which had the novelty of featuring a harpoon in the requisite shootout sequence. There was Crime of Passion, where he was paired up with an actress past her prime, Barbara Stanwyck, presumably because, as with Bette Davis, there was no chance that his under-emoting would upstage her histrionics. Having pretty much called it quits by the early 1960s, Hayden looked as if he'd left the motion picture sound stages behind for good when The Killing's director, Stanley Kubrick, called on him and gave him the greatest role of his career, the coolly demented, paranoid General Jack D. Ripper, whose impotence causes world destruction, in the black comedy to end them all, *Dr. Strangelove or: How I Learned to Stop Worrying and Love the Bomb*. Oddly, after this triumph, several more years lapsed before he did another film, *Hard Contract*, as a former hit man targeted by assassin James Coburn. After that he popped up in some effective character roles, as the crooked cop who is slain by Al Pacino in *The Godfather*, in one of that classic film's many memorable set pieces, and as an alcoholic novelist, slapped around by tiny Henry Gibson, in the modern Phillip Marlowe noir, *The Long Goodbye*. He'd become a more interesting actor than he'd ever been, with suggestions of neuroses and complexities in these men that he would have been incapable of at the launch of his career. Hayden, now bushy-bearded and very imposing in height, was seen in a leading role, as the head of a clan of vagabonds, in *King of the Gypsies*, and then popped up briefly to play the chairman of the board in the hit comedy *Nine to Five*. Despite a certain degree of industry respect he had managed to attain with the passing of the years, his principal interest remained sailing, his movie jobs being done strictly for the cash as far as he was concerned. He focused on his life at sea in his autobiography, *Wanderer* (1963) and in his 700-page novel, *Voyager* (1977). There was also a 1983 French documentary about his life and travels, *Lighthouse of Chaos*.

Screen: AS STIRLING HAYDEN: 1941: Virginia; Bahama Passage. AS STERLING HAYDEN: 1947: Variety Girl; Blaze of Noon; 1949: El Paso; Manhandled; 1950: The Asphalt Jungle; 1951: Journey Into Light; Flaming Feather; 1952: The Denver and Rio Grande; The Golden Hawk; Flat Top; Hellgate; The Star; 1953: Take Me to Town; Kansas Pacific; Fighter Attack; So Big; 1954: Crime Wave; Arrow in the Dust; Prince Valiant; Johnny Guitar; Naked Alibi; Suddenly; 1955: Battle Taxi; Timberjack; The Eternal Sea; Shotgun; The Last Command; Top Gun; 1956: The Come-On; The Killing; 1957: 5 Steps to Danger; Crime of Passion; The Iron Sheriff; Valerie; Zero Hour; Gun Battle at Monterey; 1958: Terror in a Texas Town; Ten Days to Tulara; 1964: Dr. Strangelove or: How I Learned to Stop Worrying and Love the Bomb; 1969: Hard Contract; Sweet Hunters (nUSr); 1970: Loving; 1971: Cobra/Le Saut de l'ange (dtv); 1972: The Godfather; Le Grand Depart (nUSr); 1973: The Long Goodbye; 1974: The Last Days of Man on Earth/The Final Programme; Deadly Strangers (dtv); 1975: Cipolla Colt/Cry Onion (nUSr); 1977: 1900; 1978: King of the Gypsies; 1979: Winter Kills; 1980: The Outsider; Nine to Five; 1981: Gas; 1982: Venom; 1983: Lighthouse of Chaos.

Select TV: 1954: Delay at Fort Bess (sp); 1957: A Sound of Different Drummers (sp); The Last Man (sp); Iron Horse (sp); 1958: The Long March (sp); Old Man (sp); 1960: Ethan Frome (sp); 1964: Carol for Another Christmas (sp); 1982: The Blue and the Gray (ms).

RICHARD HAYDN
BORN: LONDON, ENGLAND, MARCH 10, 1905.
DIED: APRIL 25, 1985.

There were two versions of Richard Haydn: the lightweight, straightforward character performer and, more distinctly, the reedy-voiced, slightly stooped, prissy caricature, which he dubbed "Edwin Carp." The latter creation is what made him famous in London stage revues of the 1930s and brought him to Broadway, for *Two for the Show* in 1940. The following year he made his movie debut in his regular guise, in *Charley's Aunt*, then brought the "Carp" side of himself to life on screen with delightful results, as the mousey professor still in love with a girl named Genevieve in the classic screwball comedy *Ball of Fire*.

Thereafter, he was a constant pleasure in such appearances as Jennifer Jones's boorish fiancé in *Cluny Brown*; the ailing Emperor in *The Emperor Waltz*, buried under tons of makeup to age him; and the nosey neighbor who meets his match in bitchy Clifton Webb in *Sitting Pretty*. While all of this was going on, he directed three comedies for Paramount: *Miss Tatlock's Millions* (1948), *Dear Wife* (1949), and *Mr. Music* (1950), in each case making cameos under amusing, made-up monikers. In a more subdued style, he was seen in such serious fare as *Adventure*, *The Beginning or the End*, and the classic mystery *And Then There Were None*, as the house servant who is among the first of the frightened victims to be killed off. His familiar, nasal tones were heard as the voice of the hookah-puffing caterpillar ("Who-o-o A-r-r-r-e Y-o-o-ou?") in Disney's *Alice in Wonderland*, and he appeared in two of his biggest hits late in his career with *The Sound of Music*, as Max, the impresario who gets the Von Trapp family their bookings, and *Young Frankenstein*, as the professor who convinces Gene Wilder to follow in his family's footsteps.

Screen: 1941: Charley's Aunt; Ball of Fire; 1942: Are Husbands Necessary?; Thunder Birds; 1943: Forever and a Day; No Time for Love; 1944: Henry Aldrich — Boy Scout; 1945: Tonight and Every Night; And Then There Were None; Adventure; 1946: Cluny Brown; The Green Years; 1947: The Late George Apley; The Beginning or the End; Singapore; Forever Amber; The Foxes of Harrow; 1948: Sitting Pretty; The Emperor Waltz; Miss Tatlock's Millions (AS RICHARD RANCYD; and dir.); 1949: Dear Wife (AS STANLEY STAYLE; and dir.); 1950: Mr. Music (AS CLAUD CURDLE; and dir.); 1951: Alice in Wonderland (voice); 1952: The Merry Widow; 1953: Never Let Me Go; Money From Home; 1954: Her 12 Men; 1955: Jupiter's Darling; 1956: Toy Tiger; 1958: Twilight for the Gods; 1960: Please Don't Eat the Daisies; The Lost World; 1962: Five Weeks in a Balloon; Mutiny on the Bounty; 1965: The Sound of Music; Clarence, the Cross-Eyed Lion; 1967: The Adventures of Bullwhip Griffin; 1974: Young Frankenstein.

NY Stage: 1939: Set to Music; 1940: Two for the Show.

Select TV: 1979: The Return of Charlie Chan/Happiness Is a Warm Clue (filmed 1970).

GEORGE "GABBY" HAYES
BORN: WELLSVILLE, NY, MAY 7, 1885.
DIED: FEBRUARY 9, 1969.

The most famous western sidekick of them all, whiskered, toothless "Gabby" Hayes became one of the most fondly remembered and mimicked characters of the genre. A vaudevillian, he appeared in a sole silent film, *Why Women Marry*, in 1923, before resuming his movie career proper at the dawn of the sound era. There were exceptions (*Dragnet Patrol*, *Mr. Deeds Goes to Town*, etc.), but nearly all of his many film credits would be in the horse opera category. The majority of his work in the early 1930s was done at Monogram; however his first great fame came when he was cast in the 1935 Paramount feature *Hop-A-Long Cassidy*, as a supporting character named Uncle Ben. Although Ben was killed off, Hayes made enough of an impression for the producers to find him another role in the sequel, *Bar 20 Rides Again*, as Windy Halliday, an old desert coot who proved so popular that he stayed with the series until 1939. That same year he teamed up with Roy Rogers at Republic in *Southward Ho!*, in which the two of them returned from the Civil War to take possession of a ranch, and the character of "Gabby" was born. Together he and Rogers would appear in 40 films, ending with *Helldorado*, in 1946. After his film career ended, Hayes went to television, hosting showings of his old films.

Screen: 1923: Why Women Marry; 1929: The Rainbow Man; Big News; Smiling Irish Eyes; 1930: For the Defense; 1931: Big Business Girl; God's Country and the Man; Nevada Buckaroo; Cavalier of the West; Dragnet Patrol; 1932: Riders of the Desert; Without Honor; From Broadway to Cheyenne; Klondike; Texas Buddies; The Boiling Point; Ghost Valley; The Fighting Champ; The Night Rider; Border Devils; Hidden Valley; The Man From Hell's Edges; Winner Take All; Self-Defense; Wild Horse Mesa; 1933: Phantom Broadcast; Trailing North; Breed of the Border; Crashin' Broadway; The Return of Casey Jones; The Sphinx; The Gallant Fool; Fighting Texans; Skyway; Devil's Mate; Ranger's Code; The Fugitive; Galloping Romeo; Riders of Destiny; 1934: The Lost Jungle (serial); The Lucky Texan; West of the Divide; Beggars in Ermine; Mystery Liner; City Limits; Monte Carlo Nights; Blue Steel; The Man From Utah; Randy Rides Alone; The Star Packer; In Old Santa Fe; 'Neath Arizona Skies; The Lawless Frontier; The Man From Hell; 1935: The Brand of Hate; The Lost City; Death Flies East; Rainbow Valley; The Hoosier Schoolmaster; Justice of the Range; Honeymoon Limited; Hop-A-Long Cassidy; Smokey Smith; Thunder Mountain; Tumbling Tumbleweeds; Eagle's Brood; Bar 20 Rides Again; $1,000 a Minute; The Throwback; Swifty; The Headline Woman; Welcome Home; Ladies Crave Excitement; The Outlaw Tamer; Texas Terror. Tombstone Terror; 1936: Valley of the Lawless; Call of the Prairie; I Married a Doctor; Mr. Deeds Goes to Town; The Lawless Nineties; Three on the Trail; Hearts in Bondage; The Texas Rangers; Heart of the West; Hopalong Cassidy Returns; Valiant Is the Word for Carrie; Trail Dust; Song of the Trail; The Lonely Trail; Silverspurs; 1937: Borderland; Hills of Old Wyoming; North of Rio Grande; The Plainsman; Mountain Music; Hopalong Rides Again; Rustler's Valley; Texas Trail; 1938: Heart of Arizona; Gold Is Where You Find It; Bar 20 Justice; In Old Mexico; Pride of the West; Sunset Trail; The Frontiersman; 1939: Silver on the Sage; Fighting Thoroughbreds; Let Freedom Ring; Man of Conquest; In Old Caliente; Saga of Death Valley; In Old Monterey; The Renegade Trail; Wall Street Cowboy; The Arizona Kid; Days of Jesse James; Southward Ho!; 1940: Dark Command; Young Buffalo Bill; Wagons Westward; The Carson City Kid; The Ranger and the Lady; Colorado; Young Bill Hickok; The Border Legion; Melody Ranch; 1941: Robin Hood of the Pecos; In Old Cheyenne; Sheriff of Tombstone; Nevada City; Jesse James at Bay; Bad Man of Deadwood; Red River Valley; 1942: Man From Cheyenne; Sunset on the Desert; South of Santa Fe; Heart of the Golden West; Ridin' Down the Canyon; Romance on the Range; Sons of the Pioneers; Sunset Serenade; 1943: Calling Wild Bill Elliott; Bordertown Gunfighters; Death Valley Manhunt; Overland Mail Robbery; Wagon Tracks West; In Old Oklahoma; The Man From Thunder River; 1944: Lights of Old Santa Fe; Tucson Raiders; Mojave Firebrand; The Big Bonanza; Tall in the Saddle; Marshal of Reno; Hidden Valley Outlaws; 1945: Bells of Rosarita; The Man From Oklahoma; Along the Navajo Trail; Utah; Don't Fence Me In; Sunset in El Dorado; Out California Way; 1946: Home in Oklahoma; My Pal Trigger; Song of Arizona; Badman's Territory; Roll On, Texas Moon; Rainbow Over Texas; Under Nevada Skies; Helldorado; 1947: Trail Street; Wyoming; 1948: Albuquerque; The Untamed Breed; Return of the Bad Men; 1949: El Paso; 1950: The Cariboo Trail.

HELEN HAYES

(HELEN HAYES BROWN) BORN: WASHINGTON, DC, OCTOBER 10, 1900. DIED: MARCH 17, 1993.

For someone whose stature in the theater was so dominant, diminutive, sweet-voiced Helen Hayes didn't do too badly in her sporadic movie career either, preserving her

stellar talent on film and winning a pair of Oscars in the process. "The First Lady of the American Theater" (a title tossed about in Ethel Barrymore's presence as well) was only five years old when she made her professional stage debut, in her birthplace, playing Prince Charles in *The Royal Family*. In 1909 she made her first Broadway appearance, in *Old Dutch*, and, three years later, she was first seen on film, in a short called "Jean and the Calico Doll." There was one silent feature, *The Weavers of Life*, and then it was back to Broadway, where she made her reputation in such acclaimed productions as *Clarence*, *Caesar and Cleopatra*, *What Every Woman Knows*, and *Coquette*. MGM took an interest in her and signed her to a contract a few years into the sound revolution. Her talkie debut was the sort of heavy melodrama prevalent in that period, *The Sin of Madelon Claudet*, about a wronged woman who goes from society to the streets, never telling her son who she really is. That Hayes brought more than a degree of credibility and even some heartbreak to such a turgid thing was remarkable, and she was rewarded with an Academy Award. She then went off the Metro lot for adaptations of two famous novels, Sinclair Lewis's *Arrowsmith* (for Goldwyn), the better of the two movies, adding considerable spunk to the role of physician Ronald Colman's wife, and Ernest Hemingway's *A Farewell to Arms* (Paramount), a fairly soggy affair, portraying Catherine, the nurse in love with soldier Gary Cooper, in this Oscar nominee for Best Picture. This meant three box-office successes in a row, so she was bound to trip up at some point and did so in a big way with the jaw-dropper *The Son-Daughter*, as a Chinese girl in love with Roman Novarro, proving that even Helen Hayes could do rotten work in impossible material. Much better was her role in *Another Language*, as the daughter-in-law who begins to regret her marriage to Robert Montgomery, because his mother is so selfish. Then there was *What Every Woman Knows*, in which she played a Scottish lass married to doltish Brian Aherne; the only time she repeated one of her theatrical roles on film, giving more to the writing than it gave back to her. It was then back with Montgomery for *Vanessa — Her Love Story*, a melodrama in which they wed others although they were obviously crazy about each other, asking audiences to wait patiently till the climax when they realized this. This ended her Metro contract and she was only too happy to go back to the theater, not accepting another featured role in a movie for 17 years.

In the meantime she solidified her reputation as one of the great names of the stage with such triumphs as *Victoria Regina*; *The Merchant of Venice*; *Happy Birthday*, for which she very fittingly won the very first Tony Award ever given in the dramatic category; *Mrs. McThing*, and *Time Remembered*, which brought her a second Tony Award. She returned to motion pictures during the 1950s, with two major roles: the small town mom who discovers that beloved son Robert Walker is a Communist, in the ultra-patriotic, ultra-silly *My Son John*, and, in far more intelligent circumstances, the skeptical Grand Duchess in *Anastasia*, looking splendidly regal in the role as few actresses could. She then disappeared from movies once again, returning with a bang in 1970, as the carefree stowaway, stealing every moment of the all-star blockbuster *Airport*, and getting the Academy Award for Best Supporting Actress of the year, thereby making her the first performer to win Oscars in both the lead and supporting category. This also began her run of chipper "little-old-lady" roles, which included a short-lived TV series, *The Snoop Sisters*, and her last three theatrical releases, all of which were done for Disney: *Herbie Rides Again*, the only real hit of the batch, about a Volkswagen with a mind of its own; *One of Our Dinosaurs Is Missing*, an unrealized teaming with Peter Ustinov; and the most satisfying of them, *Candleshoe*, in which David Niven attempted to con her out of her fortune. Hayes, as ever, was a continuous joy, the sort of performer you hoped would just keep on acting forever. She retired, however, after the 1985 telefilm *Murder With Mirrors*. Among her many accolades was an Emmy Award, given for the body of her 1952 TV work. Despite the many sources that credit Rita Moreno as the first performer to receive all four major show business awards, Hayes beat her by a year, earning a Grammy Award for Best Spoken Word Recording in 1976 for *Great American Documents*. Her marriage to playwright Charles MacArthur (*The Front Page*) lasted until his death in 1956. They adopted a son, James, who became an actor. (She did a cameo opposite him in *Third Man on the Mountain*.) Hayes published three memoirs, *A Gift of Joy* (1965), *On Reflection* (1969), and *My Life in Three Acts* (1990).

Screen: 1917: The Weavers of Life; 1931: The Sin of Madelon Claudet; Arrowsmith; 1932: A Farewell to Arms; The Son-Daughter; 1933: The White Sister; Another Language; Night Flight; 1934: What Every Woman Knows; Crime Without Passion; 1935: Vanessa — Her Love Story; 1943: Stage Door Canteen; 1952: My Son John; 1953: Main Street to Broadway; 1956: Anastasia; 1958: Third Man on the Mountain; 1970: Airport; 1974: Herbie Rides Again; 1975: One of Our Dinosaurs Is Missing; 1978: Candleshoe.

NY Stage: 1909: Old Dutch; 1910: The Summer Widowers; 1911: The Never Homes; 1914: The Prodigal Husband; 1918: Penrod; Dear Brutus; 1919: Clarence; 1920: Bab; 1921: The Wren; Golden Days; 1922: To the Ladies!; 1923: We Moderns; 1924: Dancing Mothers; Quarantine; 1925: Caesar and Cleopatra; The Last of Mrs. Cheyney; Young Blood; 1926: What Every Woman Knows; 1927: Coquette; 1930: Mr. Gilhooley; Petticoat Influence; 1931: After All; The Good Fairy; 1933: Mary of Scotland; 1935: Victoria Regina; 1940: Twelfth Night; 1941: Candle in the Wind; 1943: Harriet; 1946: Happy Birthday; 1950: The Wisteria Trees; 1952: Mrs. McThing; 1954: What Every Woman Knows (revival); 1955: The Wisteria Trees (revival); The Skin of Our Teeth; 1956: The Glass Menagerie; 1957: Time Remembered; 1958: A Touch of the Poet; 1964: The White House; 1966: The School for Scandal; Right You Are (If You Think You Are); We Comrades Three; 1967: The Show-Off; 1969: The Front Page; 1970: Harvey.

Select TV: 1950: The Late Christopher Bean (sp); The Barretts of Wimpole Street (sp); 1951: Victoria Regina (sp); Mary of Scotland (sp); Not a Chance (sp); The Lucky Touch (sp); Dark Fleece (sp); 1952: The Twelve Pound Look (sp); The Christmas Tie (sp); The Happy Journey (sp); 1954: Side by Side (sp); Welcome Home (sp); The Royal Family (sp); 1955: Arsenic and Old Lace (sp); The Skin of Our Teeth (sp); 1956: Dear Brutus (sp); Cradle Song (sp); 1957: Four Women in Black (sp); Mrs. Gilling and the Skyscraper (sp); 1958: Mrs. McThing (sp); One Red Rose for Christmas (sp); 1959: Ah, Wilderness! (sp); The Cherry Orchard (sp); 1960: The Bat (sp); The Cradle Song (sp); The Velvet Glove (sp); 1969: Arsenic and Old Lace (sp); 1971: Do Not Fold, Spindle or Mutilate (sp); 1972: Harvey (sp); The Snoop Sisters/The Female Instinct; 1973–74: The Snoop Sisters (series); 1976: Arthur Hailey's The Moneychangers (ms); Victory at Entebbe; 1978: A Family Upside Down; 1982: Agatha Christie's Murder Is Easy; 1983: Agatha Christie's A Caribbean Mystery; 1985: Agatha Christie's Murder With Mirrors.

DICK HAYMES

BORN: BUENOS AIRES, ARGENTINA, SEPTEMBER 13, 1916. ED: LOYOLA UNIV. DIED: MARCH 28, 1980.

This toothy, slick-haired singer represented a certain crooner image of the 1940s, one that suggested a hint of insincerity behind the eager-to-please baritone, and one that hasn't dated too well with the passing of the years. Coming to America in 1936, Haymes began singing professionally with Freddie Martin and Orin Tucker's orchestras while also working as a radio announcer. In the early 1940s he finally found solid success as a singer for Harry James and his orchestra. With them he ended up at MGM in *DuBarry Was a Lady*, and soon became a hit recording artist, his biggest seller being "Little White Lies." 20th Century-Fox, thinking they could have another Bing Crosby on their hands, signed him to a contract, putting him in three Technicolor hits, *Irish Eyes Are Smiling*, playing forgotten composer Ernest R. Ball; the Betty Grable vehicle *Billy Rose's Diamond Horseshoe*, singing the enduring ballad "The More I See You;" and Rodgers and Hammerstein's *State Fair*, performing "It's a Grand Night for Singing." Although he didn't sing it in the film, he also got a hit recording out of that movie's Oscar-winning tune, "It Might as Well Be Spring." These were typical Fox products, slick and bland, and Haymes, with his waxy superficiality, added little to them except a nice, albeit undistinguished singing voice. There was another with Grable, *The Shocking Miss Pilgrim*, which had the plus of featuring some previously un-produced Gershwin music in it, and then his only one for the company that gave him top billing, *Carnival in Costa Rica*. After his Fox contract ended in 1947, he went over to Universal where he won over few converts with Deanna Durbin's swan song, *Up in Central Park*, and the emasculated film version of *One Touch of Venus*. By 1949 his marriage to actress Joanne Dru (they had wed in 1941) had ended, and his career was pretty much going nowhere. After his final movie role, in *Cruisin' Down the River* in 1953, he briefly (until 1954) became the latest husband of Rita Hayworth and ran afoul of the law when he was temporarily deported as an undesirable alien. Haymes spent the remainder of his career doing a nostalgic nightclub act and occasional TV guest appearances, ending up, as did many stars of the past, in the all-star flop *Won Ton Ton, the Dog Who Saved Hollywood*.

Screen: 1938: Dramatic School; 1943: DuBarry Was a Lady; 1944: Four Jills in a Jeep; Irish Eyes Are Smiling; 1945: Billy Rose's Diamond Horseshoe; State Fair; 1946: Do You Love Me?; 1947: The Shocking Miss Pilgrim; Carnival in Costa Rica; 1948: Up in Central Park; One Touch of Venus; 1951: St. Benny the Dip; 1953: All Ashore; Cruisin' Down the River; 1976: Won Ton Ton, the Dog Who Saved Hollywood.

Select TV: 1952: National Honeymoon (sp); Song for a Banjo (sp); 1953: Sweet Talk Me Jackson (sp); 1956: Cry Justice (sp); The Lord Don't Play Favorites (sp); 1972: The Fabulous Fordies (sp); 1974: Betrayal.

LOUIS HAYWARD

(SEAFIELD GRANT) BORN: JOHANNESBURG, SOUTH AFRICA, MARCH 19, 1909. RAISED IN LONDON, ENGLAND. DIED: FEBRUARY 21, 1985.

Never a money attraction and certainly no threat to the more memorable leading men of his day, urbane Louis Hayward, with the aloof smirk, made a comfortable living in Hollywood as a swashbuckling hero and a light second lead, lacking the strong personality that separates the mere journeymen from the greats. After some stage work in England, he made his film debut in the 1931 production *Self-Made Lady*, as the man Heather Angel eventually marries. There were a few more roles in British movies, including the lead in *Chelsea Life*, as a young painter, and then his Broadway debut in 1935, in *Point Valaine*. That same year he came to Hollywood for MGM's Ann Harding vehicle *The Flame Within*, as an alcoholic loved by Maureen

O'Sullivan, and for Columbia's *A Feather in Her Hat*, as an aristocrat in search of his real mother. The next year he made a greater impression, as the mysterious highwayman Denis Moore, killed in a duel by Claude Rains early on in the Warner Bros. epic *Anthony Adverse*. He then became the first actor to play sophisticated crime-stopper Simon Templar, in *The Saint in New York*, but what might have become his signature role ended up being subsequently played by George Sanders in the follow-up adventures.

In 1939 he made his first splash in the swashbuckling genre, playing the dual role of Louis XIV and his wicked brother Philippe, in *The Man in the Iron Mask*, for United Artists. That same year he married Ida Lupino, whom he would later appear with in the psychological thriller *Ladies in Retirement*, before divorcing in 1945. He picked up a sword again for *The Son of Monte Cristo*, fopping his way through the role; played a spoiled brat in *My Son, My Son*; and had the main male role in the women-focused *Dance, Girl, Dance*. There was supposed to have been a featured part in Orson Welles's *The Magnificent Ambersons*, but it all ended up on the cutting room floor, save for some fleeting glimpses of him in the ballroom sequence. In 1945 he was handed perhaps his most enduring role, as the young man who watches most of the guests at a mysterious mansion meet their doom, in the superb adaptation of Agatha Christie's *Ten Little Indians*, renamed by Fox *And Then There Were None*. After that it was back to some standard Columbia swashbucklers like *The Return of Monte Cristo*, taking the family lineage a generation further by playing the Count's grandson; *The Black Arrow*, which put him in shining armor; *Fortunes of Captain Blood*, and *Captain Pirate*, both of which had him treading unsuccessfully in the footsteps of Errol Flynn, as Peter Blood. In most cases Hayward took a percentage of the profits; one of the first performers to do so. 16 years after he had created the part, he played Simon Templar again, in the British-made *The Saint's Girl Friday*. That same year, 1954, he starred in *Lone Wolf*, the first of three short-lived TV shows.

Screen: 1932: Self-Made Lady; 1933: The Thirteenth Candle; The Man Outside; I'll Stick to You; Chelsea Life; Sorrell and Son; 1934: The Love Test; 1935: The Flame Within; A Feather in Her Hat; 1936: Absolute Quiet; Trouble for Two/The Suicide Club; Anthony Adverse; The Luckiest Girl in the World; 1937: The Woman I Love; 1938: Midnight Intruder; The Rage of Paris; The Saint in New York; Condemned Women; The Duke of West Point; 1939: The Man in the Iron Mask; 1940: My Son, My Son; Dance, Girl, Dance; The Son of Monte Cristo; 1941: Ladies in Retirement; 1942: The Magnificent Ambersons; 1945: And Then There Were None; 1946: Young Widow; The Strange Woman; The Return of Monte Cristo; 1947: Repeat Performance; 1948: Ruthless; The Black Arrow; Walk a Crooked Mile; 1949: The Pirates of Capri/Captain Sirocco; 1950: House by the River; Fortunes of Captain Blood; 1951: The Lady and the Bandit; The Son of Dr. Jekyll; 1952: Lady in the Iron Mask; Captain Pirate; 1953: The Royal African Rifles/Storm Over Africa; 1954: The Saint's Girl Friday/The Saint's Return; Duffy of San Quentin; 1956: The Search for Bridey Murphy; 1967: Chuka; The Christmas Kid/Joe Navidad; 1970: The Phynx; 1973: Terror in the Wax Museum.

NY Stage: 1935: Point Valaine.

Select TV: 1952: Crossed and Double-Crossed (sp); 1954: The Lone Wolf (series); 1955: So Evil My Love; The Voyage of Captain Tom Jones — Pirate (sp); 1958: Balance of Terror (sp); 1960: Dead on Nine (sp); 1961: The Picture of Dorian Gray (sp); 1963: The Pursuers (series); 1969–70: The Survivors (series).

SUSAN HAYWARD

(EDYTHE MARRENNER) BORN: BROOKLYN, NY, JUNE 30, 1917. DIED: MARCH 14, 1975.

A surprisingly enduring star, who projected a granite-hard, Brooklynese spirit not unlike Barbara Stanwyck, Susan Hayward often showed a fierce determination rather than a stunning innate talent, but she could scale some mighty impressive heights under the right circumstances. From the slums to the stenographers' pool to a modeling agency, she ultimately landed on the cover of *The Saturday Evening Post*, which impressed the Selznick studio enough to test her for the coveted role of Scarlett O'Hara. Although that didn't work out, Warners liked her sufficiently to give her some walk-ons and bits, the first being *Hollywood Hotel*, though her exact whereabouts in the finished film have never been verified. The studio did give her billing for a "B" melodrama, *Girls on Probation*, pressing charges against Jane Bryan after her dress has been "borrowed" from the cleaners. When that led to nothing, Paramount got hold of her and allowed her to play the main woman's role in a good and significant film, *Beau Geste*. Going virtually unnoticed at the same time were leading lady parts opposite comedians Bob Burns (*Our Leading Citizen*) and Joe E. Brown (*$1,000 a Touchdown*). Columbia took her on for *Adam Had Four Sons*, where she got a good response, playing a bitch who tries to take over the household. Back at Paramount, she was still considered "B" material (*Among the Living*, a well-liked thriller, was the most notable of these) or worthy of secondary parts in "A" releases, like *Reap the Wild Wind*, as the girlfriend of wicked Robert Preston, and *The Forest Rangers*, as Paulette Goddard's competition for Fred MacMurray (Hayward loses out, as is obvious from the billing). Paramount had no qualms about loaning her out and sent her to Republic to play a songwriter in *Hit Parade of 1943*, and John Wayne's love interest in the war film *The Fighting Seabees*. They then sent her over to United Artists to play the loyal and loving wife of *Jack London* (Michael O'Shea), in a biopic based on the real Mrs. London's memoirs.

It was a vicious bitch role, on loan again to UA, that brought Hayward her best reviews so far, albeit in a movie not much liked otherwise, the adaptation of Eugene O'Neill's difficult *The Hairy Ape*. Nevertheless Paramount still saw her as a second lead and, after giving her yet another such part, in a popular soap, *And Now Tomorrow*, supporting Loretta Young, she quit. Over at RKO she played a dancer helping Bill Williams prove his innocence in a murder rap in *Deadline at Dawn*, which was of interest because it was the only motion picture collaboration between two prominent theater partners, writer Clifford Odets and director Harold Clurman. Hayward signed a contract with producer Walter Wanger at Universal, which resulted in a popular but dull western, *Canyon Passage*, and then a showy role as a former nightclub singer who ends hitting the sauce after giving up her career for Lee Bowman, in *Smash Up — The Story of a Woman*. It wasn't much of a movie, but Hayward gave it her all and earned herself an Oscar nomination. After nearly a decade in the business, she was finally someone producers thought of for dramatic roles of some weight. In the meantime she had to knock off a few for Universal, including *The Saxon Charm*, as John Payne's wife, and the Technicolor Southern soap opera *Tap Roots*, as something akin to Scarlett O'Hara, at long last. Then Goldwyn took her on to play another lady who curls up with the bottle, in *My Foolish Heart*. Again she was considered the standout performer in a movie of questionable merit and got a second Oscar nomination. This one was also a box-office winner, so 20th Century-Fox decided to put her under contract, hoping she'd bring in some customers if they stuck her in similarly glossy fare. At first there was little to get excited over with her role in *I'd Climb the Highest Mountain*, as a minister's wife, but she was on track as the ruthless business woman who goes from model to successful dress designer in *I Can Get It for You Wholesale*, based on the Jerome Weidman novel in which the main protagonist was male. This was followed by an enormously successful biblical epic, *David and Bathsheba*, giving into the desires of her king, Gregory Peck, though her part could have been played by just about anyone. Just as popular was *With a Song in My Heart*, the first of her three signature biopic roles of the 1950s and the weakest of the lot; all brave smiles and goodness as singer Jane Froman, crippled in a plane crash and valiantly finding the strength to perform again. The movie brought her Oscar nomination number three, after which she was back with Peck for another big box-office attraction, the sluggish rendering of Hemingway's *The Snows of Kilimanjaro*, where Ava Gardner lost him to Hayward but had the better role.

There was another slump in material, including a pair with Robert Mitchum, *The Lusty Men* and *White Witch Doctor*; the popular sequel to *The Robe*, *Demetrius and the Gladiator*, in which she played a villainess; and a Gary Cooper western, *Garden of Evil*, where she was determined to rescue ungrateful husband Hugh Marlowe from a cave-in. Then came a career peak and another Oscar nod with her role in *I'll Cry Tomorrow*, again as a real-life lady, singer Lillian Roth (and another alcoholic), giving a strong and harrowing performance as a woman who can't seem to help hitting bottom again and again. This was followed by two major miscalculations, the stupefyingly silly Genghis Khan adventure *The Conqueror*, with Hayward as the object of John Wayne's barbarian affections, and *Top Secret Affair*, with the actress ill at ease playing comedy with Kirk Douglas. Thankfully there was another great role on the way, her third big portrayal of a real woman in torment, convicted murderer Barbara Graham, who must face the gas chamber in *I Want to Live!* Despite lapses into standard 1950s histrionics, it was overall a fine, full-throttle performance in an engrossing film (albeit as factually questionable as most) and the one that finally won her the Academy Award.

From there she got stuck being one of the prime representatives of the soap opera gloss and goo of the late 1950s and 1960s, and she simply wasn't up to raising the level of these to anything more than the sludge that they were. She played a Basque immigrant in *Thunder in the Sun*; a former tramp prodding Dean Martin into the governor's mansion in *Ada*; carried on with married John Gavin in the third, unnecessary version of the hoary old tearjerker *Back Street*; faced a fatal illness in a remake of *Dark Victory*, now called *Stolen Hours*; and played a sculptress in the grotesque *Where Love Has Gone*, some Harold Robbins trash based on the Lana Turner scandal, in which Turner's daughter supposedly stabbed her mother's lover. It was a wiser move to take a part opposite Rex Harrison in the mild but classy *The Honey Pot*, than it was taking over from Judy Garland in *Valley of the Dolls*, sadly entering camp movie history with her hair-pulling battle royal with Patty Duke. There was only one more film role, in 1972, in the western *The Revengers*, in support of William Holden (with whom she had starred in *Young and Willing*, near 30 years earlier). After that, there were two leads in a pair of telefilms, and this might have been the medium in which she would stake her claim for the next few years had she not died of cancer in 1975, almost certainly a direct result of filming *The Conqueror* near an atomic test site.

Screen: 1937: Hollywood Hotel; 1938: The Sisters; Girls on Probation; Comet Over Broadway; 1939: Beau Geste; Our

Leading Citizen; $1,000 a Touchdown; 1941: Adam Had Four Sons; Sis Hopkins; Among the Living; 1942: Reap the Wild Wind; The Forest Rangers; I Married a Witch; Star Spangled Rhythm; 1943: Young and Willing; Hit Parade of 1943; Jack London; 1944: The Fighting Seabees; The Hairy Ape; And Now Tomorrow; 1946: Deadline at Dawn; Canyon Passage; 1947: Smash-Up — The Story of a Woman; They Won't Believe Me; The Lost Moment; 1948: The Saxon Charm; Tap Roots; 1949: Tulsa; House of Strangers; My Foolish Heart; 1951: I'd Climb the Highest Mountain; Rawhide; I Can Get It for You Wholesale; David and Bathsheba; 1952: With a Song in My Heart; The Snows of Kilimanjaro; The Lusty Men; 1953: The President's Lady; White Witch Doctor; 1954: Demetrius and the Gladiators; Garden of Evil; 1955: Untamed; Soldier of Fortune; I'll Cry Tomorrow; 1956: The Conqueror; 1957: Top Secret Affair; 1958: I Want to Live!; 1959: A Woman Obsessed; Thunder in the Sun; 1960: The Marriage-Go-Round; 1961: Ada; Back Street; 1962: I Thank a Fool; 1963: Stolen Hours; 1964: Where Love Has Gone; 1967: The Honey Pot; Valley of the Dolls; 1972: The Revengers.
Select TV: 1972: Heat of Anger; Say Goodbye, Maggie Cole.

RITA HAYWORTH

(MARGARITA CARMEN CANSINO)
BORN: BROOKLYN, NY, OCTOBER 17, 1918.
DIED: MAY 14, 1987.

During the 1940s, there was possibly no screen personality as beautifully vivacious, sexy, and desirable as Rita Hayworth. With her sleek moves, on or off the dance floor, stunning auburn hair, and combination sunny smile and come-hither glint in her eye, she was truly the "Love Goddess" the publicity machines proclaimed her to be. Acting wasn't a priority, but she wasn't exactly a washout in that department, proving herself fairly proficient the older she got, imbued with a world weariness that made her quite watchable. The daughter of noted Latin American dancer Eduardo Cansino, she started dancing professionally at the age of 14. In time she was signed to a contract with Fox, under the name Rita Cansino, and given small roles in mostly second-string features, sometimes dancing, sometimes not. The first was *Under the Pampas Moon*, in which she played a cantina girl who exchanges a few words with star Warner Baxter, then takes to the floor for a few steps. She was an Egyptian in *Charlie Chan in Egypt*; a Russian in a Jane Withers vehicle, *Paddy O'Daddy*; and an illegal immigrant in *Human Cargo*. After the folks at Fox disposed of her, she wound up doing some more "B" films, including some in which she had leads, such as *Rebellion*, as a Mexican whose father has been killed by Americans, and *Old Louisiana*. Both were made for a company called Crescent Pictures and both starred Tom Keene. In 1937 she married Edward Judson, a businessman, who decided it was time to launch her as "the next big attraction," and gave her the name by which she would become famous. She was signed to a contract with Columbia, but in the meantime, she remained strictly "B" material, despite receiving top billing in the circus mystery *The Shadow*, which had nothing to do with the famous radio serial of the same name, and being the victim in question in *Who Killed Gail Preston?*, where, as a temperamental singer, she had her vocals dubbed for what would not be the last time.

The long-awaited breakthrough came with a secondary role in an "A" film, Howard Hawks's *Only Angels Have Wings*, a critical and financial hit, with Rita as disgraced pilot Richard Barthlemess's wife, who happens to have been in love with Cary Grant once upon a time. This, and the fact that Hayworth was becoming one of the hottest pinups of the fan magazines, encouraged the studio to try her out in other substantial fare like *The Lady in Question*, which marked the first of five pairings with Glenn Ford, and *Angels Over Broadway*, in which she played gambler Douglas Fairbanks, Jr.'s girlfriend in a curious and not altogether successful Ben Hecht story about a batch of sad souls. At this point everybody wanted Rita and Warners got her to play *The Strawberry Blonde*, a superior remake of *One Sunday Afternoon*, opposite James Cagney; and Fox snagged her for *Blood and Sand*, an inferior re-do of the Valentino film, as the heartless socialite who proves to be Tyrone Power's downfall. Back on the home lot somebody had the great idea to let her dance with Fred Astaire, and they did so twice, profitably, in the military-themed *You'll Never Get Rich*, and the better *You Were Never Lovelier*. Her voice, again, was dubbed, but it is arguable that no one ever looked so right in Astaire's arms. Over at Fox, she replaced pregnant Betty Grable in one of that studio's typical musical offerings, *My Gal Sal*, and was featured in one of the poor segments of *Tales of Manhattan*, with Charles Boyer. Then Columbia gave her the two roles that would become her signature ones. The first was in *Cover Girl*, a better-than-average-for-that-studio musical in which she looked breathtaking and, in one sequence, memorably partnered Gene Kelly to dance to one of the great songs of the 1940s, "Long Ago and Far Away." The second was in a talky noir, *Gilda*, as the sensuous wife of nightclub owner George Macready, who finds herself drawn to former lover Glenn Ford. This was Hayworth at her naughty best, and her sizzling, strutting rendition of "Put the Blame on Mame," delivered in a strapless black dress, was one of the prime movie moments of the decade. In between was a very conventional movie about a potentially interesting topic, *Tonight and Every Night*, the story of a British theater (based on the real-life Windmill) that endured even during the blitz. Despite the London setting, Hayworth was conveniently made American in the storyline so as not to tax her talents too much.

Now at the apex of her popularity, she chose to do a musical sequel to *Here Comes Mr. Jordan*, called *Down to Earth*, appropriately cast as the goddess Terpsichore, but failing to produce much sparkle from leading man Larry Parks or the material itself. The movie was a pretty safe bet in terms of what the fans had come to expect, but it was followed by something more daring and complex, and easily one of her very best films, *The Lady From Shanghai*. This was made at the end of her marriage (1943–47) to Orson Welles, and he coaxed a tough and believable performance out of her as a dangerous blonde vixen. It was a box-office failure, and things were not helped by two sorry reunions with Glenn Ford, *The Loves of Carmen* and *Affair in Trinidad*. She got a lot of publicity out of her marriage to Prince Aly Kahn, but that was over in no time, likewise her marriages to singer Dick Haymes (1953–54) and producer James Hill (1958–61). In the meantime she continued to sizzle at Columbia in the atrociously garish *Salome* and the better *Miss Sadie Thompson*, in which she looked especially stunning as the island temptress. She seemed tired while being fought over by Robert Mitchum and Jack Lemmon in *Fire Down Below*, but was quite good as the nightclub owner in love with Frank Sinatra in the hit *Pal Joey*, one of the highlights of which included her (dubbed) rendition of Rodgers and Hart's strippers' ode "Zip." There were also good, mature performances in *Separate Tables*, top billed among the all-star cast as an aging beauty, and *They Came to Cordura*, as the only lady along for a trek through the desert led by Gary Cooper. The latter was her last at Columbia, and she began to slow down, appearing in tights for the lavish John Wayne vehicle *Circus World*; partnering Glenn Ford one last time for a quickly for-

gotten thriller, *The Money Trap*; and finishing up in some supporting parts in *Road to Salina*, and the western *The Wrath of God*, where most of the reviews concentrated on mentioning how great she still looked in her fifties. Alzheimer's disease caused her to retire, and she spent the rest of her life under the care of her daughter, Yasmin.

Screen: AS RITA CANSINO: 1934: Cruz Diablo/The Devil's Cross; 1935: Under the Pampas Moon; Charlie Chan in Egypt; Dante's Inferno; Paddy O'Day; 1936: Human Cargo; Meet Nero Wolfe; Rebellion; 1937: Trouble in Texas; Old Louisiana; Hit the Saddle. AS RITA HAYWORTH: 1937: Criminals of the Air; Girls Can Play; The Shadow; The Game That Kills; Paid to Dance; 1938: Who Killed Gail Preston?; There's Always a Woman; Convicted; Juvenile Court; The Renegade Ranger; 1939: Homicide Bureau; The Lone Wolf Spy Hunt; Special Inspector; Only Angels Have Wings; 1940: Music in My Heart; Blondie on a Budget; Susan and God; The Lady in Question; Angels Over Broadway; 1941: The Strawberry Blonde; Affectionately Yours; Blood and Sand; You'll Never Get Rich; 1942: My Gal Sal; Tales of Manhattan; You Were Never Lovelier; 1944: Cover Girl; 1945: Tonight and Every Night; 1946: Gilda; 1947: Down to Earth; 1948: The Lady From Shanghai; The Loves of Carmen; 1952: Champagne Safari; Affair in Trinidad; 1953: Salome; Miss Sadie Thompson; 1957: Fire Down Below; Pal Joey; 1958: Separate Tables; 1959: They Came to Cordura; The Story on Page One; 1962: The Happy Thieves; 1964: Circus World; 1966: The Money Trap; 1969: Sons of Satan (nUSr); 1971: The Rover (filmed 1967); Road to Salina; The Naked Zoo/The Hallucinators; 1972: The Wrath of God. **Select TV:** 1966: The Poppy Is Also a Flower (sp).

EILEEN HECKART

(ANNA ECHART HERBERT) BORN: COLUMBIA, OH, MARCH 29, 1919. ED: OH STATE UNIV. DIED: DECEMBER 31, 2001.

Her stage and television credits outweighed her movie roles by far, but long-faced character actress Eileen Heckart brought her considerable, if sometimes heavily theatrical, talents to film, with some occasionally winning results. A student of the American Theatre Wing, she made her New York debut in 1943, in *Tinker's Dam*, but it was not until a decade later that she received due praise and attention with her work in *Picnic*, a Theatre World Award-winning role as the desperate spinster, and in *The Bad Seed*, as the distressed neighbor, Mrs. Daigle. She did not get to preserve the former on film (Rosalind Russell played it) but did go to Warners to reprise the latter, an overly hysterical turn, but one that earned her an Oscar nomination nonetheless. In the meantime, she had already been in *Miracle in the Rain*, excellent as Jane Wyman's devoted friend, and *Somebody Up There Likes Me*, convincingly cast as Paul Newman's mother despite a mere six-year age difference. She had one of her best parts as a strong and supportive waitress in *Bus Stop*, but found herself working less frequently in films over the next several years, supporting Debbie Reynolds in a cutesy comedy, *My Six Loves*; providing a solid presence as one of the teachers surviving the urban jungle in *Up the Down Staircase*; and pouring it on a bit too thick as George Segal's overbearing mother in *No Way to Treat a Lady*. After that she achieved perfection, recreating another of her stage triumphs in the 1972 film version of *Butterflies Are Free*, as the author who doesn't realize she's being too protective of her blind son. It earned her the Academy Award for Best Supporting Actress; but most of her subsequent job offers came from TV or stage, and her remaining film credits were few. They included roles as Burgess Meredith's sister in the horror film *Burnt Offerings*; a friendly bar owner in Clint Eastwood's *Heartbreak Ridge*; and Diane Keaton's mom in *The First Wives Club*. On television she won a 1994 Emmy Award for guesting on the series *Love and War*.

Screen: 1956: Miracle in the Rain; Bus Stop; The Bad Seed; Somebody Up There Likes Me; 1958: Hot Spell; 1960: Heller in Pink Tights; 1963: My Six Loves; 1967: Up the Down Staircase; 1968: No Way to Treat a Lady; 1969: The Tree; 1972: Butterflies Are Free; 1974: Zandy's Bride; 1975: The Hiding Place; 1976: Burnt Offerings; 1986: Heartbreak Ridge; 1996: The First Wives Club.

NY Stage: 1942: Tinker's Dam (ob); 1944: Our Town; 1947: Trial Honeymoon; 1950: Hilda Crane; 1952: In Any Language; 1953: Picnic; 1954: The Bad Seed; 1955: A View From the Bridge; A Memory of Two Mondays; 1957: The Dark at the Top of the Stairs; 1960: Invitation to a March; 1961: Pal Joey; Everybody Loves Opal; 1962: A Family Affair; 1963: Too True to Be Good; 1965: And Things That Go Bump in the Night; Barefoot in the Park; 1967: You Know I Can't Hear You When the Water's Running; 1969: The Mother Lover; Butterflies Are Free; 1973: Veronica's Room; 1977: Ladies at the Alamo; 1989: Eleemosynary (ob); 1990: The Cemetery Club; 2000: The Waverly Gallery (ob).

Select TV: 1950: Black Sheep (sp); Zone Four (sp); Saturday's Children (sp); 1953: The Haven (sp); 1954: A Little Child Shall Lead Them (sp); 1955: My Lost Saints (sp); Christmas 'til Closing (sp); 1956: The Little Foxes (sp); 1957: No License to Kill (sp); The Out-of-Towners (sp); 1959: The Blue Men (sp); A Corner of the Garden (sp); A Doll's House (sp); 1960: Morning's at Seven (sp); The House of Bernarda Alba (sp); 1966: Save Me a Place at Forest Lawn (sp); The Effect of Gamma Rays on Man-in-the-Moon Marigolds (sp); 1968: Secrets (sp); 1971: All the Way Home (sp); 1972: The Victim; 1974: The FBI Story: The FBI Versus Alvin Karpas — Public Enemy Number One; 1977: Sunshine Christmas; 1978: Suddenly Love; 1979: Backstairs at the White House (ms); Out of the Blue (series); 1980: White Mama; FDR: The Last Year; 1981: The Big Black Pill; 1982: Games Mother Never Taught You; 1983: Trauma Center (series); 1984: Partners in Crime (series); 1986: Seize the Day; 1988: Annie McGuire (series); 1989: Stuck With Each Other; 1992: One Life to Live (series); 1994: Ultimate Betrayal; Breathing Lessons; 1994–95: The 5 Mrs. Buchanans (series); 1996: Murder One (series).

TIPPI HEDREN

(NATHALIE HEDREN) BORN: LAFAYETTE, MN, JANUARY 19, 1935.

Aloof, attractive, and soft-spoken, Tippi Hedren owed her cinematic fame entirely to Alfred Hitchcock. Looking for a newcomer to be his latest "cool blonde" leading lady, the great director was said to have noticed her on a TV commercial, which led to her being cast as the young lady who seems to bring on a destructive plague of feathered fiends in the highly effective thriller *The Birds*. Despite the good box-office figures and the film's eventual acceptance as another of Hitchcock's masterful accomplishments, Hedren's personal reception was, critically, somewhat cold and downright hostile for her next film under Hitch's guidance, *Marnie*, in a more demanding role, as a habitual thief haunted by her past. She did, in fact, give a decent try in both movies but simply lacked experience and the star quality her mentor had hoped she possessed. After these high profile productions, she was featured in mostly obscure fare, perhaps the best known being the notorious Charlie Chaplin flop, *A Countess From Hong Kong*, and the teen oriented *The Harrad Experiment*, which featured her real-life daughter Melanie Griffith. Her own interests over the years had shifted from acting to wild animals, and she spent a great deal of her time taking care of big cats most specifically, a life she hoped to capture in the 1981 film *Roar*. She was still called on from time to time to act, as she did in *Pacific Heights*, which also featured her daughter, and the TV sequel *The Birds II: Land's End*. She played a pro-choice activist in *Citizen Ruth*, and was involved in a fleeting bird sight gag in the screwy *I Woke Up Early the Day I Died*.

Screen: 1950: The Petty Girl; 1963: The Birds; 1964: Marnie; 1965: Satan's Harvest; 1967: A Countess From Hong Kong; 1968: Tiger by the Tail (nUSr); 1971: Mr. Kingstreet's War; 1973: The Harrad Experiment; 1975: Adonde Mucre el Viento/Where the Wind Dies (nUSr); 1981: Roar (and prod.); 1984: Foxfire Light (dtv); 1989: Deadly Spygames (dtv); In the Cold of the Night (dtv); 1990: Pacific Heights; 1994: Teresa's Tattoo (dtv); Inevitable Grace (dtv); 1996: Citizen Ruth; 1997: Mulligans! (nUSr); 1998: The Break Up (dtv); Exposé/Footsteps (dtv); 1999: The Storytellers (nUSr); I Woke Up Early the Day I Died; The Hand Behind the Mouse; 2000: Internet Love (nUSr); Mind Rage/Mind Lies (dtv).

Select TV: 1991: Shadow of a Doubt; 1992: Through the Eyes of a Killer; 1993: Perry Mason: The Case of the Skin-Deep Scandal; 1994: The Birds II: Land's End; Treacherous Beauties; 1998: Replacing Dad; 1999: The Darklings.

VAN HEFLIN

(EMMET EVAN HEFLIN, JR.)
BORN: WALTERS, OK, DECEMBER 13, 1910.
ED: UNIV. OF OK. DIED: JULY 23, 1971.

Because he didn't possess conventional leading-man looks, earnest, dependable Van Heflin wasn't thought of as one of MGM's more glamorous stars, which turned out to be a blessing. Instead his exceptional talents carried him through an active career in which he seemed to be one of the more under-appreciated actors around. With no real acting experience, he read for and got a role in the 1928 Broadway flop *Mr. Moneypenny*, billed as Evan Heflin. After that he studied acting and returned to the New York theatre as Van Heflin, starting with *The Bride of Torozko*. The success of another play, *End of Summer*, brought him to the attention of Katharine Hepburn, who asked RKO to include him in the cast of her 1936 film *A Woman Rebels*, as the married man who impregnates her. There were a few more assignments for that studio, including *The Outcasts of Poker Flat*, as the preacher who tries to save the sinful titular town, and then another boost via Hepburn when he was cast opposite her as the journalist in her 1939 Broadway hit, *The Philadelphia Story*. Although James Stewart got the part in the movie version, Heflin did wind up with a contract from MGM, where his first role was in the Rosalind Russell comedy *The Feminine Touch*, in 1941.

Just a year later he was handed a plumb role as the boozy, philosophical pal of Robert Taylor in *Johnny Eager*, and he proved, effortlessly, to be the best thing about the film, winning the Academy Award as Best Supporting Actor. From this he won top billing, albeit in a "B," *Kid Glove Killer*, as a scientist-criminologist, after which he was upped to a more expensive project, *Tennessee Johnson*, as Andrew Johnson, Lincoln's nearly impeached successor. That one didn't go over as hoped, but he was quite winning as one of Judy Garland's non-singing leading men, in *Presenting Lily Mars*, as a playwright. He was off the screen for a few years serving in the Air Force, after which he came back in some hits, including Paramount's *The Strange Love of Martha Ivers*, maintaining a certain dignity in contrast to the hysterical behavior of Barbara Stanwwyck and Kirk Douglas, and over at Warners in one of the best Joan Crawford soaps of the 1940s, *Possessed*, playing the lover whose growing disinterest in her affections drives her to madness. Back at MGM he gave some foundation of strength to the lengthy soap opera *Green Dolphin Street*, desired by sisters Lana Turner and Donna Reed; was oddly cast as Athos in the 1948 version of *The Three Musketeers*; then finished off his contract with one of his best assignments, playing Charles Bovary, the good-hearted physician chewed up and spit-out by selfish Jennifer Jones in *Madame Bovary*.

From there he ended up in some undemanding Universal productions, including *Tomahawk*, as Indian sympathizer Jim Bridger, and the family comedy *Weekend With Father*. For Paramount he was the investigator in the shameless anti-Red *My Son John*, once again bringing some credibility to superficial material, and then gave one of his finest performances, as the honest homesteader in the classic western *Shane*. This was one of the big box-office winners of the 1950s and so was Warners Bros.'s *Battle Cry*, with Heflin top billed in the ensemble cast, as the doomed Marine leader. There were some other worthy assignments like *Patterns*, playing a tough business executive in this small but effective drama expanded from a popular Rod Serling TV play, and a superior western, *3:10 to Yuma*, again outstanding as a man of decency, at odds with ruthless Glenn Ford. His days as a leading man came to a climax in some odd international productions like *Tempest*, heavily bearded as Russian revolutionist Pugachev, and *Under Ten Flags*, as a Nazi commander; and in an unmemorable programmer *Cry for Battle*. The last-named won its place in history as the movie that was playing in the Dallas theater where John Kennedy's alleged assassin, Lee Harvey Oswald, was captured. Heflin was seen in support, playing the lawman (reprising George Bancroft's role) in the remake of *Stagecoach*; and ended his movie career with a bang, literally, as the crazed passenger who sets off a bomb in the all-star blockbuster *Airport*. His sister, actress Frances Heflin, was perhaps best known for her work on the daytime serial *All My Children*.

Screen: 1936: A Woman Rebels; 1937: The Outcasts of Poker Flat; Flight From Glory; Saturday's Heroes; Annapolis Salute; 1939: Back Door to Heaven; 1940: Santa Fe Trail; 1941: The Feminine Touch; H.M. Pulham, Esq.; 1942: Johnny Eager; Kid Glove Killer; Seven Sweethearts; Grand Central Murder; Tennessee Johnson; 1943: Presenting Lily Mars; 1946: The Strange Love of Martha Ivers; 1947: Till the Clouds Roll By; Possessed; Green Dolphin Street; 1948: Tap Roots; B.F.'s Daughter; The Three Musketeers; The Secret Land (narrator); 1949: Act of Violence; Madame Bovary; East Side, West Side; 1951: Tomahawk; The Prowler; Week-End With Father; 1952: My Son John; 1953: Wings of the Hawk; Shane; 1954: Tanganyika; The Golden Mask; The Raid; Woman's World; Black Widow; 1955: Count Three and Pray; Battle Cry; 1956: Patterns; 1957: 3:10 to Yuma; 1958: Gunman's Walk; 1959: They Came to Cordura; Tempest; 1960: 5 Branded Women; Under Ten Flags; 1963: Cry of Battle; 1964: The Wastrel (It: 1961); 1965: The Greatest Story Ever Told; Once a Thief; 1966: Stagecoach; The Ruthless Four (nUSr); 1969: The Big Bounce; The Man Outside; 1970: Airport.

NY Stage: AS EVAN HEFLIN: 1928: Mr. Moneypenny.

AS VAN HEFLIN: 1934: The Bride of Torozko; 1936: End of Summer; 1938: Casey Jones; 1939: The Philadelphia Story; 1955: A View From the Bridge; A Memory of Two Mondays; 1963: A Case of Libel.

Select TV: 1950: A Double-Dyed Deceiver (sp); Arrowsmith (sp); 1957: The Dark Side of the Earth (sp); 1959: Rank and File (sp); 1960: The Cruel Day (sp); 1963–65: The Great Adventure (series narrator); 1968: A Case of Libel (sp); Certain Honorable Men (sp); 1970: Neither Are We Enemies (sp); 1971: The Last Child.

WANDA HENDRIX

(DIXIE WANDA HENDRIX) BORN: JACKSONVILLE, FL, NOVEMBER 3, 1928. DIED: FEBRUARY 1, 1981.

Tiny, serious-looking Wanda Hendrix wasn't bad at her craft, but she was presented as just another Paramount postwar pretty and probably gained more notoriety for her brief (1949–50) and unpleasant marriage to actor-war hero Audie Murphy. She went directly from working with the Jacksonville Little Theatre to a contract with Warners, who gave her supporting roles in *Confidential Agent*, as a British hotel maid, and *Nora Prentiss*, as Kent Smith's daughter. Right after that studio dropped her, Paramount took her on and gave her a nice bit as a small town youngster in a Bing Crosby vehicle, *Welcome Stranger*, but she was better served over at Universal, convincingly playing a Mexican peasant girl who aides Robert Montgomery in *Ride the Pink Horse*. Back at the home lot she was the daughter of widower Melvyn Douglas in *My Own True Love*; a farm girl who regrets marrying older Claude Rains in *Song of Surrender*; and an Italian in the long-forgotten movie that introduced the hit song "Mona Lisa," *Captain Carey, USA*. As the 1950s arrived, she was through with Paramount and jumped around from one programmer to the next, mainly westerns like *Sierra*, in which she was an unlikely lawyer in her one film with husband Murphy; and an A.C. Lyles cheapie, *Stage to Thunder Rock*, her last to received any sort of distribution.

Screen: 1945: Confidential Agent; 1947: Nora Prentiss; Welcome Stranger; Variety Girl; Ride the Pink Horse; 1948: Miss Tatlock's Millions; My Own True Love; 1949: Prince of Foxes; Song of Surrender; 1950: Captain Carey, USA; Saddle Tramp; Sierra; The Admiral Was a Lady; 1951: My Outlaw Brother; The Highwayman; 1952: Montana Territory; 1953: The Last Posse; Sea of Lost Ships; 1954: Highway Dragnet; The Golden Mask; The Black Dakotas; 1961: The Boy Who Caught a Crook; 1963: Johnny Cool; 1964: Stage to Thunder Rock; 1974: The Oval Portrait/One Minute Before Dark (nUSr).

Select TV: 1950: The Token (sp); 1951: The Happy Journey (sp); 1952: The American Leonardo (sp); 1953: A Tale of Two Cities (sp); Fresh Start (sp).

SONJA HENIE

BORN: OSLO, NORWAY, APRIL 8, 1912. DIED: OCTOBER 12, 1969.

Sonja Henie was to ice skating what Esther Williams was to swimming. Both were in the movies to do their stuff, which they did spectacularly, hoping to steer attention away from the fact that they could not act. Skating since the age of 8, Henie won her first significant trophy at 11 and took the World Figure Skating Championship title three years later. There was a forgotten movie role in her native country and then gold medals for her participation in the 1928, 1932, and 1936 Olympics. World famous, she was signed to a contract by 20th Century-Fox, who debuted her in 1936 as part of the musical grab bag *One in a Million*, the plot of which had her competing for the Olympics, so as not to tax her abilities too much. Henie was perky, with a fractured accent, delivering her lines stiffly and unconvincingly, but a large percentage of the audience took to her just the same. The film was a hit, as were the next two, *Thin Ice* and *Happy Landing*, and things were just fine until the novelty of it all began to wear off quicker than the studio had expected. *Second Fiddle* and *Everything Happens at Night* did just fair business, but there was a brief upswing with *Sun Valley Serenade*, possibly because it featured one of the most famous songs of the 1940s, "Chattanooga Choo-Choo." After *Wintertime*, in 1943, she ended her stay with Fox. There were two additional, cheaper films before she decided she could draw bigger audiences with her live appearances.

Screen: 1927: Syv Dager for Elisabeth/Seven Days for Elizabeth (nUSr); 1936: One in a Million; 1937: Thin Ice; 1938: Happy Landing; My Lucky Star; 1939: Second Fiddle; Everything Happens at Night; 1941: Sun Valley Serenade; 1942: Iceland; 1943: Wintertime; 1945: It's a Pleasure; 1948: The Countess of Monte Cristo; 1958: Hello, London.

PAUL HENREID

(PAUL GREGORY JULIUS HENREID RITTER VON WASEL-WALDINGAU). BORN: TRIESTE, HUNGARY, JANUARY 10, 1908. ED: MARIA THERESIANTISHE ACAD. INST. DIED: MARCH 29, 1992.

Suave, sleepy-eyed, rigid Paul Henreid had a passing vogue in the 1940s as a desirable, continental lover, appearing in two of the seminal romances of the era, thereby solidifying his place in movie history. A member of Max Reinhardt's Vienna Theatre, he worked with them until fleeing for England in the 1930s. There, billed as Paul von Henreid, he was seen in a few roles, with two of his movies, *Goodbye, Mr. Chips* and *Night Train/Night Train to Munich*, receiving wide distribution in the U.S. He made his official American debut for RKO, in 1942, with *Joan of Paris*, as a French flier trying to escape the Nazis. This was followed by the two movies for which he would become best known: *Now, Voyager*, as Bette Davis's suitor, whose seductive trademark is lighting two cigarettes at once before handing one over to the lady in question, and *Casablanca*, as freedom fighter Victor Laszlo, not realizing he is second-in-line to Humphrey Bogart, but nonetheless winning Ingrid Bergman in the end. Warners had something of a hot property on their hands, so they made him the star of *In Our Time*, as a Polish nobleman in love with Ida Lupino; *The Conspirators*, as a Dutch guerilla leader in love with Hedy Lamar; *Between Two Worlds*, too old to play the suicidal lover in this ensemble remake of *Outward Bound*; and two confusing titles, *Devotion*, supposedly portraying an Irishman (!), and *Deception*, back with Bette Davis, but with less success.

He went over to RKO for a color swashbuckler, *The Spanish Main*, and that did well enough to sentence him to similar material over the next few years, including *Last of the Buccaneers*, *Thief of Damascus*, and *Siren of Baghdad*. Just for a break, he starred as an understanding psychiatrist, trying to stop such questionable practices as group hosings and impromptu haircuts at a reform school for girls, in a juicy programmer, *So Young, So Bad*. By the end of the 1950s, he had segued into character roles in such disposable entertainments as *Ten Thousand Bedrooms*, and the woeful remake of *The Four Horsemen of the Apocalypse*. He had started his second career, as a director, in 1952, with *For Men Only/The Tall Lie*, about a fraternity hazing, playing one of the leads himself. It was marketed as a "B," and his subsequent directorial efforts weren't much more high-profile, the titles being *A Woman's Devotion*, a murder mystery with Henreid again taking

a featured role; *Girls on the Loose* and *Live Fast, Die Young*, both of which involved naughty ladies involved in crime; *Dead Ringer*, with former co-star Bette Davis playing a pair of twins; and *Ballad in Blue*. He also directed episodes of such television programs as *Bonanza*, *Thriller*, and *The Big Valley*.

Screen (US releases only): AS PAUL VON HENREID: 1937: Victoria the Great; 1939: Goodbye, Mr. Chips; Madmen of Europe/An Englishman's Home; 1940: Under Your Hat; Night Train/Night Train to Munich.

AS PAUL HENREID: 1942: Joan of Paris; Now, Voyager; Casablanca; 1944: In Our Time; Between Two Worlds; The Conspirators; Hollywood Canteen; 1945: The Spanish Main; 1946: Devotion; Of Human Bondage; Deception; 1947: Song of Love; 1948: Hollow Triumph/The Scar (and prod.); 1949: Rope of Sand; 1950: So Young, So Bad; Last of the Buccaneers; 1951: Pardon My French; 1952: For Men Only/The Tall Lie (and dir.; prod.); A Stolen Face; Thief of Damascus; 1953: Man in Hiding/Mantrap; Siren of Baghdad; 1954: Deep in My Heart; Kabarett; 1955: Pirates of Tripoli; 1956: Meet Me in Las Vegas; A Woman's Devotion (and dir.); 1957: Ten Thousand Bedrooms; 1959: Holiday for Lovers; Never So Few; 1962: The Four Horsemen of the Apocalypse; 1965: Operation Crossbow; 1969: The Madwoman of Chaillot; 1977: Exorcist II: The Heretic.

NY Stage: 1940: Flight to the West; 1955: Festival; 1973: Don Juan in Hell.

Select TV: 1953: The Jewel (sp); 1955: Mimi (sp); 1957: One Coat of White (sp); 1971: The Failing of Raymond; 1975: Death Among Friends/Mrs. R — Death Among Friends.

CHARLOTTE HENRY

(CHARLOTTE VIRGINIA DEMPSEY) BORN: BROOKLYN, NY, MARCH 3, 1913. DIED: APRIL 11, 1980.

A lovely, blonde-haired actress with a chipper speaking voice, Charlotte Henry came to Hollywood to repeat her 1928 stage role in *Courage*, for Warners, in 1930. A certain winsome quality made her ideal for literary adaptations like *Huckleberry Finn*, as one of the sisters whom Eugene Pallette (as the Duke of Bilgewater) tries to con; *Rebecca of Sunnybrook Farm*; and her two most famous movies, Paramount's notable box-office flop, *Alice in Wonderland*, as the title character, more than holding her own against the weirdly costumed guest stars; and, for Hal Roach, *Babes in Toyland*, sympathetic and charming as Bo-Peep, who tearfully agrees to wed villain Barnaby until Laurel and Hardy come to her rescue. Outside of these, most of the 1930s was spent in low-budget efforts like *Forbidden Heaven*, as a member of London's homeless; *The Hoosiers Schoolmaster*, as a rural servant girl; *The Mandarin Mystery*, as the heroine accused of murder in this Ellery Queen opus; *Hearts in Bondage*, as a Civil War belle; and *The Return of Jimmy Valentine*, as a small-town girl kidnapped by J. Carrol Naish. After a pair of Monogram quickies, *Bowery Blitzkrieg*, in support of the East Side Kids, and *She's in the Army*, a tribute to the WACs, she retired from the business.

Screen: 1930: Harmony at Home; On Your Back; Courage; 1931: Huckleberry Finn; Arrowsmith; 1932: Lena Rivers; Rebecca of Sunnybrook Farm; Forbidden; 1933: Man Hunt; Rasputin and the Empress; Alice in Wonderland; 1934: Babes in Toyland/March of the Wooden Soldiers; The Last Gentleman; The Human Side; 1935: The Hoosier Schoolmaster; Three Kids and a Queen; Forbidden Heaven; Laddie; 1936: The Gentleman From Louisiana; Hearts in Bondage; The Mandarin Mystery; The Return of Jimmy Valentine; 1937: Charlie Chan at the

Opera; Jungle Menace (serial); God's Country and the Man; Young Dynamite; **1941:** Bowery Blitzkrieg; **1942:** I Live on Danger; She's in the Army.

NY Stage: 1928: Courage; **1931:** Hobo.

AUDREY HEPBURN

(ANDREY KATHLEEN VAN HEEMSTRA RUSTON)
BORN: BRUSSELS, BELGIUM, MAY 4, 1929.
DIED: JANUARY 20, 1993.

One of the glowing lights of the postwar cinema, pencil-thin, doe-eyed, ravishingly beautiful Audrey Hepburn was the epitome of class without snobbery, artistry without pretensions. The lady with the heartbreaking lilt to her voice was accessible yet never one of the sure box-office draws, critically loved yet somehow underrated in her acting abilities; she has become one of the great stars that other performers talk about with envy and awe. Raised in the Netherlands, while training as a ballet dancer in England, she eventually appeared in a short travel documentary, "Nederlands in 7 Lessen/Dutch in Seven Lessons," in 1948, the same year she won a role in the chorus of the London production of *High Button Shoes*. There followed two revue shows, *Sauce Tartare* and *Sauce Piquante*, plus some bits in the films *One Wild Oat*, as a hotel receptionist, supporting future co-star Stanley Holloway; the very funny *Laughter in Paradise*, as a cigarette girl; and *The Lavender Hill Mob*, popping up early in the story, as a girlfriend of on-the-lam Alec Guinness. There were bigger parts in *Young Wives' Tale*, as a lodger scared of men; *Secret People* (the only one of her films to show her ballet dancing), as the younger sister of Valentina Cortese; and *Monte Carlo Baby*, as an actress. It was while filming the last, an otherwise forgettable comedy, that she was spotted by author Colette, who was looking for a new face to play the title role in the stage version of her novel *Gigi*. The 1951 Broadway production made Hepburn the most talked about newcomer of the season and won her a Theatre World Award.

It was time for the right motion picture vehicle to launch this exceptionally appealing young talent, and the perfect role was found in *Roman Holiday*, with Hepburn beautifully portraying the lonely princess who spends a few happy days incognito with reporter Gregory Peck. Peck insisted she share above the title billing, and by the end of 1953, there was no one else the press and public wanted to talk about more than the new Hepburn. While appearing on Broadway in *Ondine* with Mel Ferrer (who became her first husband, 1954–68), she won the Academy Award and became the most in-demand performer in the business. There was a Tony Award for *Ondine*, and then another ideal film showcase, *Sabrina*, with Hepburn as the sad chauffeur's daughter pining for millionaire William Holden until she grows up and gets over him, only to move on to older brother Humphrey Bogart. This was another hit topped off by a second Oscar nomination, and, just to add icing to the cake, Hepburn never looked so stunning, stylishly dressed at one point by Givenchy, the designer with whom her name would become synonymous.

War and Peace was a genuinely impressive spectacle for those not in love with Tolstoy's novel, after which someone at Paramount had the great idea to partner her with Fred Astaire for one of the supreme pleasures of the 1950s, *Funny Face*, where she played a book clerk who reluctantly becomes a fashion model. Their dances together were charming, and Hepburn was even allowed to do her own singing, putting her own personal stamp on Gershwin's "How Long Has This Been Going On?" There was

another May-December romance, this time with Gary Cooper, in *Love in the Afternoon*, which, although directed by Billy Wilder, was not the classic it should have been. But, compared to almost everything else around, it was nice enough. She decided to try something a bit heavier and scored a triumph both critically and financially with *The Nun's Story*, a tastefully crafted study of a young girl's journey from novice to nun until disillusionment takes over. Hepburn's was a deceptively simple but deeply nuanced portrayal of a woman internally conflicted, and she earned another Oscar nomination. That helped wipe out the memory of her other 1959 release, a misbegotten filmization of the blatantly un-cinematic novel *Green Mansions*, directed by Ferrer, with poor Audrey looking lost as mystic jungle girl Rima. Nor was she entirely at ease as a half-breed in the western *The Unforgiven*, a problematic production during which she sustained a back injury after falling from a horse.

Luckily she followed that one with another success, playing the part that would become her signature role, in the brightest comedy of 1961, *Breakfast at Tiffany's*. Despite complaints from the original author, Truman Capote, Hepburn made the role of free-spirited Manhattanite Holly Golightly very much her own, racking up a fourth Oscar nod for suggesting the insecurity beneath the uninhibited individualism. To add to her achievements, she also introduced the film's hit song, "Moon River." Her work in *The Children's Hour*, as one of the teachers whose life is destroyed by allegations of lesbianism, was very much underrated, but everybody loved her playful cavorting in the lightweight thriller *Charade*, which brought her together with Cary Grant, a match as perfect as one would expect. A second teaming with William Holden, *Paris — When It Sizzles*, was one of the true rotten eggs in her career, a leaden send-up of screenwriting, but it was followed by another high point, *My Fair Lady*. Controversy over her casting as guttersnipe-turned-lady Eliza Dolittle, in place of stage original Julie Andrews, filled acres of newsprint at the time and the debate continues to this day. Since Warner Bros. had no intention of giving the role to the cinematically un-tested Andrews, it is hard to imagine anyone else but Hepburn in the part. And, despite dubbed vocals, she was outstanding, making it another role with which she would be forever associated. The film, the most faithful of all transfers of a beloved Broadway musical, went on to rake in a fortune and won the Academy Award for Best Picture of 1964, though much attention was brought to the fact that Hepburn didn't even score a nomination, perhaps some sort of "punishment" for accepting so plum a part.

In the decade-plus since her Oscar, she had sustained her position as one of the biggest and most revered names in the business and any filmmaker lucky enough to land her services knew that her name could add endless prestige to a picture even if the exhibitors never considered her a dependable draw. She therefore brought a great deal of pizzazz to an unapologetically light-hearted caper film, *How to Steal a Million*, co-starring with Peter O'Toole. She scored a double bulls-eye in 1967, with *Two for the Road*, a harsh and perceptive look at a marriage told non-chronologically over the course of several years, with Hepburn giving a deep and incisive performance, while *Wait Until Dark*, the more popular of the two, was a taut thriller in which she was heart wrenching as a blind woman terrorized by some thugs. It brought her a fifth Oscar nomination.

At that point, her marriage to Ferrer at an end, she turned her back on movies, remarried, moved to Rome and concentrated on raising her family. Fortunately she was lured back to films four more times. The first was the best, *Robin and Marian*, a bitter-sweet look at two aging storybook legends (Sean Connery was

Robin Hood), followed by the worst, *Bloodline*, a crass and incoherent thriller that she fought valiantly to rise above. *They All Laughed*, was a pleasant, if odd comedy about cheating wives and detectives, where she was part of an ensemble, while her final role, in 1989, *Always*, found her doing an extended guest bit, most appropriately cast an angel. By that point she had become more interested in her position as UNICEF ambassador, traveling extensively to aid the children of the world. When she died of bowel cancer after returning from one of these trips, the entertainment industry and the world in general knew that her sort would never be seen again. A few months after her death, she was honored with the Jean Hersholt Humanitarian Award from the Academy of Motion Picture Arts and Sciences.

Screen: 1951: One Wild Oat; Laughter in Paradise; Young Wives' Tale (US: 1952); The Lavender Hill Mob (US: 1952); **1952:** Secret People; **1953:** Monte Carlo Baby/We Will Go to Monte Carlo (US: 1954); Roman Holiday; **1954:** Sabrina; **1956:** War and Peace; **1957:** Funny Face; Love in the Afternoon; **1959:** Green Mansions; The Nun's Story; **1960:** The Unforgiven; **1961:** Breakfast at Tiffany's; The Children's Hour; **1963:** Charade; **1964:** Paris — When It Sizzles; My Fair Lady; **1966:** How to Steal a Million; **1967:** Two for the Road; Wait Until Dark; **1976:** Robin and Marian; **1979:** Sidney Sheldon's Bloodline; **1981:** They All Laughed; **1989:** Always.

NY Stage: 1951: Gigi; 1954: Ondine.

Select TV: 1952: Rainy Day in Paradise Junction (sp); 1957: Mayerling (sp); 1987: Love Among Thieves; 1991: Gardens of the World (series host).

KATHARINE HEPBURN
BORN: HARTFORD, CT, MAY 12, 1907.
ED: BRYN MAWR.

Proclaiming Katharine Hepburn the greatest of all film actresses, one is unlikely to receive much disagreement. This patrician, fiercely original, ever-memorable, and often brilliant talent was among the most enduring figures in cinema history, as much a major star in the 1930s as she was 60 years later. After her professional stage debut in a 1928 Baltimore production of *The Czarina*, she came to Broadway later that year, in *These Days*. Following a few more parts of little distinction, she scored a hit with *The Warrior's Husband*, in 1932. By the end of that year she had been snatched up by RKO to play John Barrymore's daughter in *A Bill of Divorcement*, evoking an immediately enthusiastic response. With her breathy cadence and unbridled enthusiasm and drive, she was truly exciting to watch, certainly the one performance in the film that makes this fairly dated, stage-bound family drama worth a look today. RKO put her under contract, and she followed her initial triumph with *Christopher Strong*, a failure about an aviatrix, and *Morning Glory*, an above-average look at the New York stage, playing a determined young actress. The latter, combined with her definitive Jo in the best screen version of *Little Women*, made 1933 the year of Hepburn, and she scored an Academy Award for *Morning Glory*, although, of course, it is the other film and performance that has always been held in higher esteem. She went back to Broadway for what would become one of her notable career missteps, *The Lark*, receiving the sort of harsh notices that suggested a backlash over the great acclaim she'd received to date.

Returning to Hollywood, she loved John Beal in *The Little Minister*, but preferred Charles Boyer to Beal in *Break of Hearts*, lifting both above the potential sludge level but without box-office success. Things were brighter with *Alice Adams*, where she

was superb as a small-town girl trying to rise above her lowly station in life, a performance fully deserving of its Oscar nomination. That, however, was followed by one of her most awkward roles and a film she openly detested, *Sylvia Scarlett*, unconvincingly dressing up as a boy, despite her off-screen mannish habit of dressing in slacks. After the cold audience reception of three period pieces, *Mary of Scotland*, with Hepburn as the tragic would-be monarch; *A Woman Rebels*, where she played a Victorian non-conformist; and *Quality Street*, in which she desperately tried to snare herself a husband, RKO was starting to doubt the lady's staying power. The talent, however, was still there, for these were followed by roles in two of her best: *Stage Door*, brilliantly alive as an ambitious actress, mouthing the most famous line of her career ("The calla lilies are in bloom again."), and the funniest of all screwball comedies, *Bringing Up Baby*, removing all the potentially annoying characteristics of this loose wire and managing to make this man-hungry heiress an absolute delight, the standard by which all such similar attempts to create lovable scatterbrains should be judged. Sadly this failed too, and she and the studio parted company. With that film's leading man, Cary Grant, she did another good one, over at Columbia, *Holiday*, and then asked its author, Philip Barry, to write a play for her. It would help resuscitate her career.

The Philadelphia Story opened in New York, in 1939, to raves. When MGM bought the property, Hepburn made sure that she came with it, having purchased the rights. The movie, directed with a sure hand by George Cukor, with every ounce of the Metro gloss working in it's favor, gave Hepburn one of her best-remembered roles, spoiled rich girl Tracy Lord, caught between two very desirable men on the eve of her wedding to a total dolt. With Cary Grant and James Stewart by her side it became one of the top hits of the year, brought Hepburn another Oscar nod, and a contract with the studio. She stayed aloft for the next, which would prove to be one of the most significant movies of her career, *Woman of the Year*. As journalist Tess Harding, the embodiment of feminine assuredness, she was very much in her element and found the partner of a lifetime in Spencer Tracy, sparring warmly but exuding a respect and affection for one another that would make them the greatest of all screen couples. Hepburn got a fourth Oscar nomination and followed it up with two more (lesser) teamings with Tracy, *Keeper of the Flame* and *Without Love* (she had done the stage version of the latter without much success). Between these was one of her all-time embarrassing acting jobs, playing the gentle Chinese peasant girl in *Dragon Seed*, which only went to prove that even the mightiest of actors have their days off. Without Tracy, she seemed to be having a rough time at MGM, with two notable misfires, the silly melodrama *Undercurrent*, suspecting Robert Taylor of trying to do her in, and a lumpy composer biopic, *Song of Love*, as Clara Schumann to Robert Walker's Johannes Brahms. Even she and Tracy were off-track in the heavy-handed western family drama *The Sea of Grass*, but they ended the 1940s with the fine *State of the Union*, a literate political drama, and their very best teaming, the still-captivating comedy *Adam's Rib*, as married lawyers on opposite sides of a murder case, an outstanding example of the wit and affection so evident in their playing.

Back on an upswing, she created gold as a prim missionary, sailing along with Humphrey Bogart in what was essentially a two-character piece, *The African Queen* — one of the most satisfying of all movie experiences and a rare case of two great stars coming together and turning out a movie every bit as good as one might hope. This film brought her Oscar nomination number five, followed by another top-notch comedy with Tracy, *Pat and Mike*, in which she was ideally cast as an all-around athlete. Her sixth and seventh Oscar nominations came for spinster roles, in the memorable *Summertime*, playing a schoolteacher falling in love with Rossano Brazzi while vacationing in Venice, and *The Rainmaker*, looking far too old to play the country tomboy loosened up by Burt Lancaster, but giving it every bit of poignancy that one had come to expect from her. With Tracy, she appeared in a sprightly CinemaScope comedy for Fox, *Desk Set*, as an information whiz putting a new computer to shame; as with *Summertime*, taking over a role Shirley Booth had created onstage. There was a substantial but decidedly secondary role in the grotesque Tennessee Williams melodrama, *Suddenly, Last Summer*, as Elizabeth Taylor's shady and ultimately unhinged aunt, and that got her further recognition from the Oscar committee, after which she earned her ninth nomination, in 1962, for a far more deserving performance, as the sad, drug addicted Mary Tyrone in the faithful, harrowing movie version of O'Neill's *Long Day's Journey Into Night*, made for limited audiences.

Having taken time off to nurse Tracy, whose health was failing, she returned to the screen with him one last time, in 1967, with the box-office smash *Guess Who's Coming to Dinner*, as a well-to-do liberal couple questioning their own beliefs as they come to terms with their daughter's engagement to a black man (Sidney Poitier). The two were as perfect together as ever, and Hepburn was given her second Academy Award, perhaps more in honor of Tracy than for her somewhat undemanding role, he having died shortly after filming. The following year she made history, winning an Academy Award for the third time in the lead category for her witty, wearied Eleanor of Aquitaine in *The Lion in Winter*, proving in her 60s that she had few peers. Ironically, the back-to-back success of those movies put her on many box-office lists as a bankable attraction, something that hadn't happened before, the healthy financial returns for her pairings with Tracy always being credited more to him than her. The flop of the heavy-handed whimsy *The Madwoman of Chaillot* put a dent in things, so she was back onstage, in the musical *Coco*, wanting to prove herself in this genre as well. After another big screen disaster, *The Trojan Women*, she found more fulfilling projects on the home screen, including a faithful rendering of *The Glass Menagerie*, and *Love Among the Ruins*, a romance that allowed her to team with Laurence Olivier. She received an Emmy Award for the latter. On the big screen, the cryptic and stagy adaptation of Edward Albee's *A Delicate Balance* was scantly distributed and coolly received, and a teaming with another long-lasting legend, John Wayne, in *Rooster Cogburn*, brought in few customers.

The whole world *did* seem to want to see *On Golden Pond*, with Hepburn facing the twilight of her life with husband Henry Fonda, another long-overdue combination of two great actors brilliantly realized. In an amazing feat she broke her own record, becoming the only four-time Academy Award-winning performer and bringing her number of nominations up to 12. (Meryl Streep would eventually tie the latter figure, though two of hers were achieved in the supporting category.) There was one last Broadway play, *The West Side Waltz*, which proved that Hepburn, live and in full-force, could still bring in the crowds, and one more movie lead, *Grace Quigley*, a black comedy about euthanasia, which was hacked at after a bad film festival reception and barely noticed upon release. She kept busy with more telefilms and was coaxed back to movies by Warren Beatty to play what would be the only genuine supporting role of her film career (her only smaller part was a brief appearance as herself in *Stage Door Canteen*), his philosophical, frail, and lonely aunt in the 1994 remake of *Love Affair*. If Beatty had wanted someone truly without peer to give that role an extra kick, he got his wish, for there was no one more special and certainly no one who was

more of a living legend. She authored two memoirs: *The Making of the African Queen or How I Went to Africa With Bogart, Bacall and Huston and Almost Lost My Mind* (1987) and *Me: Stories of My Life* (1991).

Screen: 1932: A Bill of Divorcement; 1933: Christopher Strong; Morning Glory; Little Women; 1934: Spitfire; The Little Minister; 1935: Break of Hearts; Alice Adams; Sylvia Scarlett; 1936: Mary of Scotland; A Woman Rebels; 1937: Quality Street; Stage Door; 1938: Bringing Up Baby; Holiday; 1940: The Philadelphia Story; 1942: Woman of the Year; Keeper of the Flame; 1943: Stage Door Canteen; 1944: Dragon Seed; 1945: Without Love; 1946: Undercurrent; 1947: The Sea of Grass; Song of Love; 1948: State of the Union; 1949: Adam's Rib; 1951: The African Queen; 1952: Pat and Mike; 1955: Summertime; 1956: The Rainmaker; The Iron Petticoat; 1957: Desk Set; 1959: Suddenly, Last Summer; 1962: Long Day's Journey Into Night; 1967: Guess Who's Coming to Dinner; 1968: The Lion in Winter; 1969: The Madwoman of Chaillot; 1971: The Trojan Women; 1973: A Delicate Balance; 1975: Rooster Cogburn; 1978: Olly, Olly, Oxen Free/The Great Balloon Adventure; 1981: On Golden Pond; 1985: Grace Quigley/The Ultimate Solution of Grace Quigley; George Stevens: A Filmmaker's Journey; 1994: Love Affair; 1996: The Line King: The Al Hirschfeld Story (voice).

NY Stage: 1928: These Days; 1930: Art and Mrs. Bottle; 1932: The Warrior's Husband; 1933: The Lake; 1939: The Philadelphia Story; 1942: Without Love; 1950: As You Like It; 1952: The Millionairess; 1969: Coco; 1976: A Matter of Gravity; 1981: The West Side Waltz.

Select TV: 1973: The Glass Menagerie; 1975: Love Among the Ruins; 1979: The Corn Is Green; 1986: Mrs. Delafield Wants to Marry; 1988: Laura Lansing Slept Here; 1992: The Man Upstairs; 1994: This Can't Be Love; One Christmas.

HUGH HERBERT

BORN: BINGHAMTON, NY, AUGUST 10, 1885.
DIED: MARCH 12, 1952.

A former vaudeville comedian-writer, Hugh Herbert, with his hesitant speech pattern, fidgety body language, and trademark "woo-woo" catchphrase, was one of the more ubiquitous performers at Warner Bros. in the 1930s and also one of the most annoyingly mannered of all actors. He came to Hollywood in the late 1920s, writing for such films as the first all-talkie, *Lights of New York*, and debuting before the cameras at Warners in *Husbands for Rent*. He could be seen doing his shtick in support of Dick Powell in *College Coach*, *Footlight Parade*, *Convention City*, *Dames*, *The Singing Marine*, and *Hollywood Hotel*, at his most irritating as Lola Lane's idiotic relative. He "woo-wooed" his way through Shakespeare, as Snout, in *A Midsummer Night's Dream*, and was considered a valuable enough addition to the studio to rate starring vehicles like *That Man's Here Again*, which sounded like a hazard sign posted for those immune to Herbert's lack of restraint, and *Sh! The Octopus*, which was a damp comical thriller memorable only for its bizarre title. In the 1940s, Universal starred him in quickies like *La Conga Nights*, *Meet the Chump*, and *Hello Sucker*, while Columbia featured him in two-reelers with such you-were-warned titles as "Woo Woo" and "Get Along Little Zombie," before he returned to supporting parts in such lowly regarded "A" features as *One Touch of Venus*, *A Song Is Born*, and *The Beautiful Blonde From Bashful Bend*.

Screen: 1927: Husbands for Rent; 1928: Caught in the Fog; 1930: Danger Lights; Hook, Line and Sinker; Second Wife; 1931:

The Sin Ship; Laugh and Get Rich; Traveling Husbands; Friends and Lovers; 1932: Faithless; The Lost Squadron; Million Dollar Legs; 1933: Goldie Gets Along; Goodbye Again; Bureau of Missing Persons; Footlight Parade; College Coach; From Headquarters; She Had to Say Yes; Convention City; Strictly Personal; Diplomaniacs; 1934: Fashions of 1934; Easy to Love; Dames; Kansas City Princess; Wonder Bar; Harold Teen; Merry Wives of Reno; Sweet Adeline; Fog Over Frisco; The Merry Frinks; 1935: The Traveling Saleslady; Gold Diggers of 1935; A Midsummer Night's Dream; We're in the Money; Miss Pacific Fleet; To Beat the Band; 1936: Colleen; Love Begins at Twenty; One Rainy Afternoon; We Went to College; 1937: Sing Me a Love Song; That Man's Here Again; The Singing Marine; Marry the Girl; The Perfect Specimen; Sh! The Octopus; Hollywood Hotel; Top of the Town; 1938: Men Are Such Fools; Gold Diggers in Paris; Four's a Crowd; The Great Waltz; 1939: Eternally Yours; Little Accident; The Family Next Door; The Lady's From Kentucky; 1940: La Conga Nights; Private Affairs; Slightly Tempted; A Little Bit of Heaven; The Villain Still Pursued Her; Hit Parade of 1941; 1941: Meet the Chump; The Black Cat; Hello Sucker; Badlands of Dakota; Hellzapoppin'; 1942: There's One Born Every Minute; Don't Get Personal; Mrs. Wiggs of the Cabbage Patch; 1943: Stage Door Canteen; It's a Great Life; 1944: Ever Since Venus; Kismet; Music for Millions; 1945: One Way to Love; 1947: Blondie in the Dough; Carnegie Hall; 1948: A Miracle Can Happen/On Our Merry Way; So This Is New York; A Song Is Born; The Girl From Manhattan; 1949: The Beautiful Blonde From Bashful Bend; 1951: Havana Rose.

NY Stage: 1927: Polly of Hollywood; 1945: Oh Brother!

JEAN HERSHOLT

BORN: COPENHAGEN, DENMARK, JULY 12, 1886. DIED: JUNE 2, 1956.

His name pops up every so often at the Academy Awards, but few modern audiences are aware of the actor behind the honorary humanitarian statuette given in his honor. The accented, often-mustachioed actor, who frequently played wise or kindly Old World types, had come from Copenhagen's Dagmar Theatre. In 1914 he moved to Los Angeles, finding work first with the Triangle Film Company, then at Universal. During the 1920s he became increasingly better known by way of his appearances in such productions as *Tess of the Storm Country*, as a murderer; *Greed*, as ZaSu Pitts's suitor; and the 1925 version of *Stella Dallas*, as a salesman. A few years into the sound era he became a contract player at MGM, where he landed a major role as the inventor who marries housekeeper Marie Dressler against the wishes of his snobby children in *Emma*. Around that same time he was seen as the eager desk clerk in *Grand Hotel*; a janitor in *Night Court*; an art dealer in *Christopher Bean*; and a theatrical producer in *Dinner at Eight*. His greatest success came over at 20th Century-Fox when he portrayed Dr. John Luke in the film that cashed in on the newspaper headlines about the Dionne quintuplets, *The Country Doctor*, featuring the quints as themselves. The success of the picture resulted in a pair of sequels, *Reunion* and *Five of a Kind*, both at Fox, where Hersholt was now under contract. Staying in the medical profession, he began a popular radio show playing kindly small town Dr. Paul Christian, which he brought to the big screen for RKO, in 1939, with *Meet Dr. Christian*. There were five sequels and a subsequent television series on which Hersholt only showed up in the opening episode, the role being taken over by Macdonald Carey. He had founded the Motion Picture Relief Fund, served as pres-

ident of the Academy of Motion Picture Arts and Sciences, and was bestowed with three special Oscars for his humanitarian work. At the Oscar ceremony in 1957, a few months after the actor's death, the very first Jean Hersholt Humanitarian Award was given, to producer Y. Frank Freeman.

Screen: 1915: The Disciple; 1916: The Aryan; Hell's Hinges; The Desert; Kinkaid — Gambler; Bullets and Brown Eyes; The Apostle of Vengeance; 1917: Fighting for Love; Love Aflame; The Terror; The Soul Herder; The Saintly Sinner; The Show-Down; Southern Justice; The Greater Law; Stormy Knights; 49–17; 1918: Princess Virtue; Madame Spy; 1919: In the Land of the Setting Sun; 1920: The Servant in the House; The Red Lane; Merely Mary Ann; 1921: The Four Horsemen of the Apocalypse; A Certain Rich Man; The Deceiver; Golden Trail; Man of the Forest; The Servant in the House; 1922: Golden Dreams; The Gray Dawn; Tess of the Storm Country; When Romance Rides; Heart's Haven; The Stranger's Banquet; 1923: Jazzmania; Quicksand; Red Lights; 1924: Torment; The Woman on the Jury; Sinners in Silk; Her Night of Romance; Cheap Kisses; So Big; 1925: Greed; Fifth Avenue Models; Dangerous Innocence; A Woman's Faith; If Marriage Fails; Don Q — Son of Zorro; Stella Dallas; 1926: My Old Dutch; Greater Glory; It Must Be Love; Flames; The Old Soak; 1927: The Wrong Mr. Wright; The Student Prince in Old Heidelberg; 1928: Alias the Deacon; 13 Washington Square; The Secret Hour; The Battle of the Sexes; Jazz Mad; Give and Take; 1929: Abie's Irish Rose; The Younger Generation; Modern Love; The Girl on the Barge; 1930: Hell Harbor; Climax; The Case of Sergeant Grischa; Mamba; Viennese Nights; The Cat Creeps; East Is West; Third Alarm; 1931: Daybreak; A Soldier's Plaything; Susan Lennox (Her Fall and Rise); Phantom of Paris; Transatlantic; The Sin of Madelon Claudet; Private Lives; 1932: Beast of the City; Emma; Are You Listening?; Grand Hotel; Night Court; New Morals for Old; Skyscraper Souls; Unashamed; Hearts of Humanity; Flesh; The Mask of Fu Manchu; 1933: Crime of the Century; Dinner at Eight; Song of the Eagle; Christopher Bean; 1934: The Cat and the Fiddle; Men in White; The Fountain; The Painted Veil; 1935: Mark of the Vampire; Murder in the Fleet; Break of Hearts; 1936: Tough Guy; The Country Doctor; Sins of Man; His Brother's Wife; Reunion; One in a Million; 1937: Seventh Heaven; Heidi; 1938: Happy Landing; Alexander's Ragtime Band; I'll Give a Million; Five of a Kind; 1939: Mr. Moto in Danger Island; Meet Dr. Christian; 1940: Courageous Dr. Christian; Dr. Christian Meets the Women; Remedy for Riches; 1941: Melody for Three; They Meet Again; 1943: Stage Door Canteen; 1955: Run for Cover.

CHARLTON HESTON

(JOHN CHARLES CARTER) BORN: EVANSTON, IL, OCTOBER 4, 1923. ED: NORTHWESTERN UNIV.

With his booming voice, no-nonsense countenance, and sculpted physique, Charlton Heston became one of the truly commanding figures of the cinema. His larger-than-life stature made him *the* dominant star of the movie spectacle, a man at ease in action, game for adventure, heading a cast of thousands, leading the troops, or possibly saving the world. As a result he seemed so incongruous wearing a suit, sitting at a desk, or simply having dinner that he was never quite as interesting when the trappings around him weren't big. His resonant vocal tones got him work on various Chicago radio stations before he did some acting with a few North Carolina stock companies. Coming to New York, he made his Broadway debut in *Antony and Cleopatra*, after which he received a Theatre World Award for his performance in *Design for a Stained Glass Window*, in 1950. By that time he had done some amateur film productions of *Peer Gynt* and *Julius Caesar* (as Marc Antony) and won great acclaim playing Rochester in a TV version of *Jane Eyre*. From this he obtained a contract with Hal Wallis, who brought him to Paramount to play a cynical gambler in the noir *Dark City*.

It was the next film that put him on the Hollywood map, Cecil B. DeMille's Oscar-winning, all-star circus spectacular, *The Greatest Show on Earth*, in which he played the hard-as-nails manager, still snapping orders at his company of show folk while receiving a blood transfusion after the famous train wreck. From there he played a white man raised by Indians in *The Savage*; Jennifer Jones's lover in the over-heated Southern melodrama *Ruby Gentry*; and Andrew Jackson in *The President's Lady*, which was not one of the more popular biopics around. There were programmer westerns like *Pony Express*, where he was cast as Buffalo Bill, and *Arrowhead*, with Heston as an Apache-hating scout, plus a standard jungle tale, *The Naked Jungle*, which was made memorable by its ant-attack finale, courtesy of special effects producer George Pal. To show that he wasn't always the unsmiling, stick-in-the-mud that he often played, he did a comedy, *The Private War of Major Benson*, although the plot involved the loosening up of a tight-ass commander by a bunch of boys at a military school, so he still got to keep his granite-like reserve. Thanks to DeMille, his career soared once again when he played Moses in the 1956 blockbuster *The Ten Commandments*, probably the most entertaining of all the Biblical epics of that time, with Heston one of the few actors around who could pull off parting the Red Sea while sporting a flowing gray beard. He was improbably cast as a Mexican in *Touch of Evil*, but he was the one who got Orson Welles hired on as director, so the movie's special place in cult history owes much to him.

He showed a less-nice side as Gregory Peck's rival in *The Big Country*, one of his best performances up to that point, and then returned to sandals for his signature role. *Ben-Hur* was the biggest production of its day, costing some $15 million in 1959 dollars, a gamble by MGM that paid off big time. The audiences came in droves, and the reviews were quite exceptional, despite the expected overdone religious touches that make the film very much of its period. When the Academy handed out a record 11 awards to the film, Heston was included for his very respectable work. The film's undeniable place in Hollywood history gave Heston a sort of iconic status that he maintained over many bad movies and rough periods of questionable bankability. It was followed by a teaming with Gary Cooper, *The Wreck of the Mary Deare*, and a short-lived Broadway play, *The Tumbler*, after which he returned with another huge production, this time for money-spending producer Samuel Bronston, the underrated *El Cid*, again ideal as a real-life hero, driving the Moors out of Spain. It was now starting to look strange to see him in anything as small as the feather-weight comedy *The Pigeon That Took Rome*, or the soap opera *Diamond Head*, as Yvette Mimieux's overbearing brother, so he was back in period costume for *55 Days at Peking*, another ambitious but less-popular entry from Bronston, made in the days when Hollywood's idea of a commercial film involved the 1900 Chinese Boxer Rebellion, and for *The Greatest Story Ever Told*, part of the vast cast, as John the Baptist.

He went out west for the ambitious *Major Dundee*, a movie that was hacked to pieces without consideration for director Sam Pekinpah's original intention, then gave a good performance as the determined Michelangelo, at odds with his Pope (Rex Harrison) in another expensive film, *The Agony and the Ecstasy*.

These movies were losing a great deal of money, as did another under-appreciated piece, *The War Lord*, with Heston as a Norman warrior in a movie that stressed intimacy over scope, and *Khartoum*, where he was the real-life General "Chinese" Gordon, who battled the Arabs only to end up with his head on a stick. There was a well-liked western, *Will Penny*, in which he played a vulnerable cowboy in an intimate, moody piece that couldn't be given away, and his first massive hit in some time, the memorable sci-fi adventure *Planet of the Apes*, where he showed off his still-impressive pecs as an astronaut taunted and studied by simians with human characteristics. Although this one rescued his box-office standing, it was only temporary relief, followed by more duds, *Number One*, in which he was an aging footballer, and the tedious *The Hawaiians*; an unnecessary sequel, *Beneath the Planet of the Apes*; and two critically lambasted attempts at Shakespeare, *Julius Caesar*, and *Antony and Cleopatra*, which he himself directed, in both instances reprising one of his earliest roles, Marc Antony. Between some negligible ventures into the sci-fi genre, *The Omega Man*, battling zombies as one of the last survivors of world annihilation, and *Soylent Green*, living in the over-crowded future, there was a minor success with a trashy disaster movie, *Skyjacked*, so he did two more of this genre, *Airport 1975*, playing a heroic pilot, and the Sensurround extravaganza *Earthquake*, which gleefully disposed of much of the cast as Los Angeles collapsed around them, Heston included.

The aging Heston, as the rugged action star of the western *The Last Hard Men*; the sniper-in-the-stadium thriller *Two Minute Warning*; and the submerged-sub adventure *Gray Lady Down*, wasn't exactly what the younger audiences were keen to see, nor was there an iota of interest in his second attempt at directing, *Mother Lode*, written by his own son, Fraser, which found him in a dual role. He kept himself before the public with small-screen versions of some classic tales like *A Man for All Seasons*, which he also directed; *Treasure Island*, doing a surprisingly engaging turn as Long John Silver; and a Sherlock Holmes story, *The Crucifer of Blood*. There was also a short-lived nighttime serial *The Colbys*, which somehow seemed unworthy of him, despite his career-long involvement in some pretty shabby projects. Back on the big screen, he was accepting small roles from productions that wanted him around for his "history," like *Tombstone*, as Henry Hooker; *True Lies*, as Arnold Schwarzenegger's eye-patch wearing boss; and *In the Mouth of Madness*, as a book publisher. His son gave him a job as a bad guy in a children's adventure, *Alaska*, after which he was back doing Shakespeare again, as the Player King in Kenneth Branagh's full-text version of *Hamlet*, perhaps the most impressive of the American guest stars. His ever-recognizable and authoritative voice was heard in Disney's *Hercules* and in *Armageddon*, and he showed up briefly as a football commissioner in *Any Given Sunday*; as Andie MacDowell's gun-happy dad in *Town & Country*; and as an ape in the remake of one of his most famous films, *Planet of the Apes*. A mostly liberal Hollywood had no qualms about employing him despite the tarnishing his reputation received when he became a very vocal supporter of the right to carry firearms. He authored two autobiographies: *The Actor's Life* (1978) and *In the Arena* (1995).

Screen: 1941: Peer Gynt; 1950: Julius Caesar; Dark City; 1952: The Greatest Show on Earth; The Savage; Ruby Gentry; 1953: The President's Lady; Pony Express; Arrowhead; Bad for Each Other; 1954: The Naked Jungle; Secret of the Incas; 1955: The Far Horizons; The Private War of Major Benson; Lucy Gallant; 1956: The Ten Commandments; Three Violent People; 1958: Touch of Evil; The Big Country; The Buccaneer; 1959: Ben-Hur; The Wreck of the Mary Deare; 1961: El Cid; 1962: The Pigeon That Took Rome; Diamond Head; 1963: 55 Days at Peking; 1965: The

Greatest Story Ever Told; Major Dundee; The Agony and the Ecstasy; The War Lord; 1966: Khartoum; 1968: Counterpoint; Will Penny; Planet of the Apes; 1969: Number One; 1970: The Hawaiians; King: A Filmed Record…Montgomery to Memphis; Beneath the Planet of the Apes; 1971: Julius Caesar; The Omega Man; 1972: Skyjacked; 1973: Antony and Cleopatra (and dir.); Call of the Wild; Soylent Green; 1974: The Three Musketeers; Airport 1975; Earthquake; 1975: The Four Musketeers; 1976: The Last Hard Men; Midway; Two Minute Warning; 1978: Gray Lady Down; Crossed Swords/The Prince and the Pauper; 1980: The Mountain Men; The Awakening; 1982: Mother Lode (and dir.); 1990: Almost an Angel; 1991: Solar Crisis/Starfire (dtv); 1993: Wayne's World 2; Tombstone; 1994: True Lies; 1995: In the Mouth of Madness; 1996: Alaska; Lord Protector (narrator; dtv); Hamlet; 1997: Hercules (voice); 1998: Armageddon (voice); 1999: Toscano (nUSr); Any Given Sunday; 2001: Town & Country; Cats & Dogs (voice); Planet of the Apes; 2002: The Order (dtv); Bowling for Columbine.

NY Stage: 1947: Antony and Cleopatra; 1949: Leaf and Bough; Cock-a-Doodle-Do (ob); 1950: Design for a Stained Glass Window; 1956: Mister Roberts; 1960: The Tumbler.

Select TV: 1949: Jane Eyre (sp); 1950: The Taming of the Shrew (sp); Hear My Heart Speak (sp); 1951: Macbeth (sp); A Bolt of Lightning (sp); 1952: The Wings of the Dove (sp); 1953: Elegy (sp); A Day in Town (sp); 1955: The Renaissance (sp); The Seeds of Hate (sp); 1956: Forbidden Area (sp); 1957: The Trial of Captain Wirz (sp); Switch Station (sp); 1958: Beauty and the Beast (sp); Point of No Return (sp); 1961: The Fugitive Eye (sp); 1963: The Patriots (sp); 1968: Elizabeth the Queen (sp); 1983: Chiefs (ms); 1984: The Nairobi Affair; 1985–87: The Colbys (series); 1987: The Proud Men; 1988: A Man for All Seasons (and dir.); 1989: Original Sin; 1990: Treasure Island; The Little Kidnappers; 1991: The Crucifer of Blood; 1992: Crash Landing: The Rescue of Flight 232/A Thousand Heroes; 1994: James A. Michener's Texas (narrator; ms); 1995: The Avenging Angel; 1999: Gideon.

WENDY HILLER

BORN: BRAMHILL, CHESHIRE, ENGLAND, AUGUST 15, 1912.

One of the most dependably outstanding actresses the British Isles ever had to offer, compact, stern-looking Wendy Hiller kept her film roles down to a minimum, saving her rare appearances in front of the cameras for those cases when she found something worth sinking her teeth into. She studied with Manchester rep, after which she played the lead in both the London and New York productions of Love on the Dole, making her greatly in demand. Her movie debut came with Lancashire Luck, in 1937, as a commoner whose father suddenly strikes it rich, followed shortly by the film that won her well-deserved critical acclaim and audience fame, not only in her homeland but in America as well, Pygmalion. She was sensationally good as guttersnipe-turned-lady Eliza Doolittle, playing opposite the ideal Higgins, Leslie Howard; both of them earned Oscar nominations for their work, back when it was rare for actors in a British film to break into those categories. That was followed by another equally successful filming of Shaw, Major Barbara, with Hiller in the title role, as the strong-willed Salvation Army girl whose principals are challenged by her own father (Robert Morley). It was a long break between that and the next one, I Know Where I'm Going!, but that love story, set in Scotland, and shot by the highly original team of Michael Powell and Emeric Pressburger, con-

tinued her steady track record of appearing in some of the highest quality productions the British film industry had to offer.

There was a Broadway triumph in The Heiress, in 1947, but she did not make an American film until ten years later, with a supporting part in Something of Value, an underrated drama examining the non-commercial topic of Apartheid. She joined the ensemble of Separate Tables, playing Burt Lancaster's mistress and the proprietress of the hotel at which the cast gathered. It was hardly one of her greatest roles, but she was, as ever, nothing less than first rate and she received the Academy Award as Best Supporting Actress for it. More impressive was her performance as the embittered mother of Dean Stockwell in Sons and Lovers, while she added a certain level of respectability to the less-than-inspired filming of Lillian Hellman's Toys in the Attic, as one of Dean Martin's spinster sisters. There came another Oscar nomination, for her amusingly stone-faced interpretation of Paul Scofield's wife, in the 1966 Academy Award-winner for Best Picture, A Man for All Seasons, after which she basically popped up in star-laden efforts, bringing much color to Murder on the Orient Express, as a homely countess, and Voyage of the Damned, as one of the doomed ship's many passengers. Showing she could do wonders with any role, she was in fine form as the head nurse in The Elephant Man, after which she played the kindly best friend of Michael Ontkean and Kate Jackson in Making Love. In 1975 she was made a Dame of the British Empire.

Screen: 1937: Lancashire Luck; 1938: Pygmalion; 1940: Major Barbara; 1945: I Know Where I'm Going!; 1952: Outcast of the Islands; 1953: Sailor of the King/Single Handed; 1957: Something of Value; How to Murder a Rich Uncle; 1958: Separate Tables; 1960: Sons and Lovers; 1963: Toys in the Attic; 1966: A Man for All Seasons; 1974: Murder on the Orient Express; 1976: Voyage of the Damned; 1979: The Cat and the Canary; 1980: The Elephant Man; 1982: Making Love; 1987: The Lonely Passion of Judith Hearne; 1992: The Countess Alice (nUSr).

NY Stage: 1936: Love on the Dole; 1947: The Heiress; 1957: A Moon for the Misbegotten; 1959: Flowering Cherry.

Select TV: 1957: Traveling Lady (sp); Ann Veronica (sp); 1958: Eden End (sp); 1970: David Copperfield (theatrical in UK); 1972: Peer Gynt (sp); Clochemerle (series); 1978: King Richard the Second (sp); 1980: The Curse of King Tut's Tomb; 1981: The Importance of Being Earnest (sp); 1982: The Kingfisher (sp); Witness for the Prosecution; 1983: Attracta; 1986: The Last Viceroy; 1987: Anne of Green Gables: The Sequel; 1989: Ending Up; A Taste for Death (ms); 1994: The Best of Friends.

PAT HINGLE

(MARTIN PATTERSON HINGLE) BORN: DENVER, CO, JULY 19, 1924. ED: UNIV. OF TX.

Burly, bushy-browed Pat Hingle, who ran the gamut from rural dads to self-satisfied creeps, was a student of the Herbert Berghof Studio and the Actors Studio. He made his 1953 Broadway debut in End as a Man, and repeated his part in the 1957 film version, re-dubbed The Strange One, although in close-up he seemed like a rather elderly cadet. In contrast, looking old enough for the part, he was Warren Beatty's dad in one of the important films of 1961, Splendor in the Grass, and then Robert Preston's ineffectual brother in All the Way Home (a role he would reprise on television). He played the judge in Clint Eastwood's western Hang 'em High, and was called back to support that actor in both The Gauntlet and Sudden Impact. Amid these he was the millionaire kidnapped by Shelley Winters and her motley brood in Bloody Mama, and had a starring part as a Mennonite dad in a curio called *Happy as the Grass Was Green*, a movie that got its widest play at the visitors center in Pennsylvania's Amish Country. There were sad dad roles in *Norma Rae*, keeling over on the job from a heart attack, and in *The Falcon and the Snowman*, seeing son Timothy Hutton dragged off to prison for spying. There was little to do as Commissioner Gordon in the enormously popular *Batman* films, but he had a showy role as the sadistic mobster who bullies Anjelica Huston in *The Grifters*. Surprisingly he did wind up with another lead, in his late 70s no less, in *Road to Redemption*, playing an old codger being chased by the mob while on his way to his favorite fishing hole, in this religious piece financed by Billy Graham's evangelistic organization. And perhaps only Hingle himself knew if there was some deliberate intention to him being asked to appear in *Running Wild*, *Running Scared*, and *Running Brave*.

Screen: 1954: On the Waterfront; 1957: The Strange One; No Down Payment; 1960: Wild River (narrator); 1961: Splendor in the Grass; 1963: The Ugly American; All the Way Home; 1964: Invitation to a Gunfighter; 1966: Nevada Smith; 1968: Hang 'em High; Sol Madrid; Jigsaw; 1970: Bloody Mama; Norwood; WUSA; 1972: The Carey Treatment; 1973: One Little Indian; Running Wild; Happy as the Grass Was Green; 1974: The Super Cops; Deadly Honeymoon/Nightmare Honeymoon; 1977: The Gauntlet; 1979: When You Comin' Back, Red Ryder?; Norma Rae; 1980: Running Scared; 1982: Bless 'em All/The Act; 1983: Running Brave; Going Berserk; Sudden Impact; 1985: The Falcon and the Snowman; Brewster's Millions; 1986: Maximum Overdrive; 1987: Baby Boom; 1988: The Land Before Time (voice); 1989: Batman; 1990: The Grifters; 1992: Batman Returns; 1994: Lightning Jack; 1995: The Quick and the Dead; Batman Forever; 1996: Larger Than Life; 1997: Batman and Robin; A Thousand Acres; 1999: Hunter's Moon (dtv); Muppets from Space; 2000: Shaft; Morning (nUSr); Angel Doll (dtv); 2001: Road to Redemption; The Greatest Adventure of My Life (dtv).

NY Stage: 1953: End as a Man; 1955: Festival; Cat on a Hot Tin Roof; 1956: Girls of Summer; 1957: The Dark at the Top of the Stairs; 1958: J.B.; 1960: The Deadly Game; 1963: Strange Interlude; 1964: Blues for Mister Charlie; A Girl Could Get Lucky; 1965: The Glass Menagerie; 1966: The Odd Couple; 1967: Johnny No-Trump; 1968: The Price; 1970: Child's Play; 1972: The Selling of the President; 1973: That Championship Season; 1976: Lady From the Sea; 1980: A Life; 1997: 1776.

Select TV: 1955: Do It Yourself (sp); Black Frost (sp); The Expendable House (sp); 1956: This Land Is Mine (sp); 1957: Inspired Alibi (sp); A Child Is Waiting (sp); The Human Barrier (sp); 1959: The Last Autumn (sp); 1961: Black Monday (sp); 1963: The Name of the Game (sp); 1964: Carol for Another Christmas (sp); 1966: The Glass Menagerie (sp); 1969: The Ballad of Andy Crocker; 1970: A Clear and Present Danger; 1971: The City; Sweet Sweet Rachel; If Tomorrow Comes; All the Way Home (sp); 1973: Trouble Comes to Town; 1974: The Last Angry Man; 1976: The Secret Life of John Chapman; 1977: Escape From Bogen County; Sunshine Christmas; Tarantulas: The Deadly Cargo; 1979: Elvis; Stone; Disaster on the Coastliner; 1980: Stone (series); Wild Times; 1981: Of Mice and Men; The Private History of a Campaign That Failed (sp); 1982: Washington Mistress; 1983: The Fighter; 1985: Noon Wine (sp); The Rape of Richard Beck; Lady From Yesterday; Broken Badge; 1986: Casebusters; Manhunt for Claude Dallas; 1987: LBJ: The Early Years; Kojak: The Price of Justice; 1988: Stranger on My Land; Blue Skies (series); The Town Bully; 1989: War and Remembrance (ms); Everybody's Baby: The Rescue of Jessica McClure; 1990: The Kennedys of Massachusetts (ms); 1991: Not

of This World; 1992: Gunsmoke: To the Last Man; Citizen Cohn; The Habitation of Dragons; 1993: Simple Justice; 1994: Against Her Will: The Carrie Buck Story; One Christmas; 1995: Truman; 1996: Bastard Out of Carolina; 1997: The Shining (ms); Member of the Wedding; 2000: The Runaway; 2002: The Court (series).

VALERIE HOBSON
BORN: LARNE, COUNTY ANTRIM, IRELAND, APRIL 14, 1917. ED: RADA.
DIED: NOVEMBER 13, 1998.

Lady-like Valerie Hobson was revered as one of Britain's freshest offerings in the postwar era, although she had in fact been on the scene for some time. While still a teen, she played onstage in *Ball at the Savoy* and as a lead in some minor films, including *Eyes of Fate* and *Badger's Green*, about an endangered cricket field. In 1935 she accepted an offer to work for Universal in Hollywood, where she was seen in *The Mystery of Edwin Drood*, as Helena Landless, an orphan from Ceylon; *Bride of Frankenstein*, as Colin Clive's wife; and *Werewolf of London*, married to lycanthropic Henry Hull, after which she was soon dropped. Back in Britain she finally began to gain some notice with *Jump for Glory/When Thief Meets Thief*, as Glory, accused of murdering fiancé Alan Hale; and in an Alexander Korda production, *The Drum*, as the wife of Captain Roger Livesey. She married producer Anthony Havelock-Allen in 1939 and bided her time in such films as *The Spy in Black*, posing as a schoolmistress to stop evil Conrad Veidt; and *Atlantic Ferry*. She became a highly sought-after property following *Great Expectations*, where she gave her most memorable performance, as grown-up Estella, stringing along lovestruck Pip (John Mills), per her aunt's instructions. For her husband's production company she was held for ransom in *The Small Voice*, then was at her most charming as the wife of one of Dennis Price's multiple Alec Guinness victims in the classic comedy *Kind Hearts and Coronets*. She was the mother of the obsessed child in the oddball *The Rocking Horse Winner*, and leading lady to Guinness in *The Card/The Promoter*. Shortly after this, in 1952, she divorced Havelock-Allen; made one last film, for Rene Clement, *Knave of Hearts*; and triumphed in the London production of *The King and I*. She retired to marry politician John Profumo, who became well known via a 1963 headline-making sex scandal.

Screen: 1933: Eyes of Fate; 1934: Two Hearts in Waltztime; Path of Glory; Badger's Green; The Man Who Reclaimed His Head; 1935: Strange Wives; Oh What a Night; Rendezvous at Midnight; The Mystery of Edwin Drood; Bride of Frankenstein; Werewolf of London; Chinatown Squad; The Great Impersonation; 1936: August Weekend; Tugboat Princess; Secret of Stamboul; No Escape; 1937: Jump for Glory/When Thief Meets Thief; 1938: Drums/The Drum; This Man Is News; Life Returns (filmed 1935); 1939: Q Planes/Clouds Over Europe; This Man in Paris; Spy in Black/U-Boat 29; The Silent Battle/Continental Express; 1940: Contraband/Blackout; 1941: Atlantic Ferry/Sons of the Sea; 1942: Unpublished Story; 1943: The Adventures of Tartu/Tartu/Sabotage Agent; 1946: The Years Between; 1947: Great Expectations; Blanche Fury; 1948: The Small Voice/Hideout; 1949: Kind Hearts and Coronets; Train of Events; The Interrupted Journey; 1950: The Rocking Horse Winner; 1952: The Card/The Promoter; Who Goes There?/The Passionate Sentry; Meet Me Tonight; The Voice of Merrill/Murder Will Out; 1953: Background; 1954: Monsieur Ripois/Knave of Hearts/Lovers, Happy Lovers.

FAY HOLDEN

(DOROTHY FAY HAMMERTON)
BORN: BIRMINGHAM, ENGLAND,
AUGUST 20, 1893. DIED: JUNE 23, 1973.

MGM's embodiment of levelheaded, all-American motherliness, Fay Holden was, in fact, born in England, where she was known in her early days as Gaby Fay (as well as Dorothy Clyde, having married comedian Andy Clyde's brother). There were roles on Broadway in the late 1920s before she temporarily returned to England. Drawn back to the States, she ended up at the Pasadena Playhouse, around which time she made her movie debut in an exploitation quickie, *The Pace That Kills*, one of those silly anti-drug movies that became camp favorites in the more permissive 1970s, this one taking on the sensationalistic new title of *The Cocaine Fiends*. Her legit film work started with Warners's *I Married a Doctor*, while over at Paramount she played a mother in a Bing Crosby comedy, *Double or Nothing*, which was instrumental in landing her the role that made her famous, "Ma" Hardy in the long-running "Andy Hardy" series. Signed by MGM, Holden picked up in the sequel, *You're Only Young Once*, where Spring Byington had left off in the original film (*A Family Affair*), giving the part a more down-to-earth approach. After that one she was called on to repeat the role another 13 times, ending, temporarily, with *Love Laughs at Andy Hardy*, in 1946. There were other parts at the studio during this period, not surprisingly many that found her providing further maternal support, including *Bitter Sweet* (Jeanette MacDonald) and *Ziegfeld Girl* (Lana Turner), but she was first and foremost Mrs. Hardy, returning to the character after a 12-year break, one last time, for *Andy Hardy Comes Home*, in 1958.

Screen: AS GABY FAY: 1935: The Pace That Kills/The Cocaine Fiends; 1936: I Married a Doctor; The White Angel.

AS FAY HOLDEN: 1936: Wives Never Know; Polo Joe; 1937: Bulldog Drummond Escapes; Internes Can't Take Money; King of Gamblers; Double or Nothing; Souls at Sea; Exclusive; Guns of the Pecos; You're Only Young Once; 1938: Judge Hardy's Children; Love Is a Headache; Hold That Kiss; Test Pilot; Love Finds Andy Hardy; Out West With the Hardys; Sweethearts; 1939: Sergeant Madden; The Hardys Ride High; Andy Hardy Gets Spring Fever; Judge Hardy and Son; 1940: Andy Hardy Meets Debutante; Bitter Sweet; 1941: Ziegfeld Girl; Andy Hardy's Private Secretary; Washington Melodrama; I'll Wait for You; Blossoms in the Dust; Life Begins for Andy Hardy; H.M. Pulham, Esq.; 1942: The Courtship of Andy Hardy; Andy Hardy's Double Life; 1944: Andy Hardy's Blonde Trouble; 1946: Little Miss Big; Canyon Passage; Love Laughs at Andy Hardy; 1948: Whispering Smith; 1949: Samson and Delilah; 1950: The Big Hangover; 1958: Andy Hardy Comes Home.

NY Stage: AS GABY FAY: 1927: Murray Hill; 1928: The Bellamy Trial; 1929: Dinner Is Served.

Select TV: 1956: Mr. Kagle and the Baby Sitter (sp).

WILLIAM HOLDEN

(WILLIAM FRANKLIN BEEDLE, JR.)
BORN: O'FALLON, IL, APRIL 17, 1918. RAISED IN
PASADENA, CA. DIED: NOVEMBER 16, 1981.

There was a "regular guy" quality to William Holden that made him one of the most subtly persuasive, unpretentious of all film actors. Without resorting to a bag of tricks or tics, he projected a solid integrity with a touch of sardonic charm that carried him

through more than 40 years of stardom. While at Pasadena Junior College he acted in radio plays, after which he joined the Pasadena Workshop Theatre, playing the 80-year-old father-in-law of Marie Curie. Spotted by a Paramount Pictures talent scout, he was tested and signed by that studio and promptly given his new name. They gave him bits in two films (his first credit is purportedly *Prison Farm*, where he was among the inmates, though several sources leave this out) before Columbia borrowed him for the coveted lead in the 1939 film version of the stage sensation *Golden Boy*. As the young boxer who really wishes to be a professional musician, Holden's earnest performance made him a star. Because of it, Columbia took on half his contract for the next 14 years. Quickly he was borrowed by Warners for a gangster drama, *Invisible Stripes*, as the brother George Raft tries to steer away from crime, and, more notably, by UA for their version of *Our Town*, as George Gibbs, the young man who wins and woos Martha Scott before watching her face an early death (Holden made a noble attempt at this portrayal, but it was hardly ideal casting in the long run). Back at his home lot he was put in a college drama, *Those Were the Days*, and a popular World War II aerial adventure, *I Wanted Wings*. Over at Columbia he was hired for a pair of westerns: *Arizona*, a lavish one with Jean Arthur (who was 18 years his senior) as his love interest, and *Texas*, with off-screen friend Glenn Ford. Paramount then gave him lightweight parts in *The Fleet's In*, paired off with Dorothy Lamour, although most of the attention went to newcomer Betty Hutton, and in the fantasy *The Remarkable Andrew*, receiving advise from the ghosts of past historical figures. Both of these roles made him distinctly unhappy with the direction his career was going in. He married (1941–70) actress Brenda Marshall and joined the army, which kept him off movie screens for four years.

He returned to Paramount for another aerial drama, *Blaze of Noon*, about a family of fliers. Then he appeared in a gentle but highly satisfying comedy, *Dear Ruth*, as the soldier who returns home, thinking Joan Caulfield has been writing him letters. Even better was *Apartment for Peggy*, a superior comedy-drama made at Fox, about a young couple (Jeanne Crain was the wife) struggling to make it after the war. It was certainly better than anything Columbia had to offer — *The Dark Past*, with Holden stretching and failing as a criminal with psychological problems; *The Man From Colorado*, another western with buddy Glenn Ford; and some comedies, *Miss Grant Takes Richmond*, with Lucille Ball, and *Father Is a Bachelor*. Paramount, in the meantime, gave him a typical but Technicolored western, *Streets of Laredo*, and the inevitable sequel to *Dear Ruth*, called *Dear Wife*.

It was stacking up as a fairly average film career up to that point; then something spectacular happened. Montgomery Clift changed his mind about appearing in *Sunset Blvd.*, so director Billy Wilder cast Holden in his place, although he seemed a bit too old for the role. As the Hollywood writer whose career is going down the drain until he grabs a chance at notoriety by becoming the lover of fading silent star Gloria Swanson, he was excellent, suggesting a world-weariness and maturity that had seemed untapped thus far. The movie was, of course, the industry's greatest film about itself, and Holden was Oscar nominated, with a newfound respectability. With the passing years it became the norm to look upon the film as Gloria Swanson's vehicle, when in fact Holden had the higher billing and the central role. The same year, 1950, he was the bespectacled tutor hired to brighten up dim bulb Judy Holliday in another winner, *Born Yesterday*, certainly the best thing Columbia gave him during his employment for them. (It competed against *Sunset Blvd.* for the Best Picture Oscar, but *All About Eve* took home the prize). After these twin peaks, he did some routine dramas for Paramount, including the disappointing kidnapping thriller *Union Station* and *The Turning Point*, and then a pleasant racetrack story for Columbia, *Boots Malone*. It was up to Billy Wilder to find him another great one, as he did with *Stalag 17*, the prisoner-of-war film by which all others will be measured, with Holden brilliant as the mocking con artist who proves his worth in the end. For it, he won the Academy Award as Best Actor of 1953.

Now one of the biggest names in the business, the films kept coming fast and furious: *The Moon Is Blue*, a mild but popular comedy considered "naughty" in its time because of its casual use of the word "virgin;" *Forever Female*, a bright look at the theater with Ginger Rogers; and *Executive Suite*, an all-star corporate drama with Holden top billed above such stalwarts as Fredric March, an actor he idolized, and Barbara Stanwyck, whom he often credited with getting him his big break in *Golden Boy*. There was a third Wilder gem with *Sabrina*, one of the most joyous of all romantic comedies; the actor's hair dyed blond to play an irresponsible playboy trying to snare chauffeur's daughter Audrey Hepburn. Taking third-billing he was in another of the big ones of the decade, *The Country Girl*, in a fine, unsung performance, often over-shadowed by the acclaim for Bing Crosby's work, as the theatrical director who finds himself falling for Grace Kelly. This preceded *The Bridges at Toko-Ri*, a surprisingly downbeat war adventure; and *Love Is a Many Splendored Thing*, a wildly popular love story with Jennifer Jones, memorable only for its title song that swept the airwaves in 1955. There was another significant production that ranked high on his memorable list of credits, *Picnic*, even though he was again far too old for the part, a drifter who swoops into town and gets everybody's libido up. After that he did one that didn't fare too well, *Toward the Unknown*, as a disgraced pilot, made for his own company, Toluca Productions.

Holden then made history by becoming one of the first performers to accept a percentage of the profits as payment, and since the movie in question, *The Bridge on the River Kwai*, was one of the financial blockbusters of the 1950s, he got very rich indeed. He took top billing as the POW who escapes from a hellish Ceylon only to have to trek back through the jungles to destroy the title structure, although his role was secondary to that of Alec Guinness. In addition to its many other accolades and honors, the film won the Academy Award for Best Picture of 1957. After this towering achievement, it was inevitable that he would start to lose ground, as he did with *The Key*, a teaming with Sophia Loren; *The Horse Soldiers*, an uninspired western with John Wayne that was very costly, mainly because of the two stars' salaries; and *The World of Suzie Wong*, a glossy soap that got slaughtered by the critics though it would become Holden's last genuine moneymaker for some time.

In the 1960s he seemed to be marking time with *Satan Never Sleeps*, playing a priest; *The Lion*, celebrating his real-life love of big game hunting; *Paris — When It Sizzles*, a moronic comedy about screenwriting with Audrey Hepburn; *The 7th Dawn*, a dull adventure set in Malaya; and *Alvarez Kelly*, an uninspired Civil War tale. In the chaotic James Bond send-up *Casino Royale*, he appeared briefly as part of a spy unit sent to coax David Niven out of retirement, then did his macho act for *The Devil's Brigade*, a blatant copy of the better *The Dirty Dozen*, whipping a squad of misfits into shape, followed by a grim French-made father-and-son story with a misleadingly cheerful title, *The Christmas Tree*. Amid these was an intelligent spy thriller, *The Counterfeit Traitor*, and he ended the decade appearing in a much-discussed project, the violent western *The Wild Bunch*, giving a good performance as a cynical, saddle-worn outlaw leading a band of doomed gunmen in a film that still divides

audiences as to its value. Similarly he was another battered cowboy in the disappointing *Wild Rovers* (a film reportedly tampered with by the studio) and was certainly beginning to project a worn-out demeanor. He was still getting work but did not bother to hide his waning interest in the whole business, often bad-mouthing the profession as something he felt embarrassed about and did strictly for the money.

Money, therefore, can be credited as his reason for participating in another blood-drenched western, *The Revengers*, out to kill those who massacred his family, and in a dopey May-December romance, *Breezy*, as a man in crisis hopping into bed with teenager Kay Lenz. He was part of the starry cast of a big hit, *The Towering Inferno*, as the builder of the firetrap, and then had a final hurrah with a great part in a great film, *Network*, as the level-headed, ethical TV executive who finds himself caught up in an affair with the much younger Faye Dunaway, the embodiment of soullessness. The latter brought him his final Oscar nomination and earned him leads in a few more films, including the junky horror sequel *Damien: Omen II*, playing the guardian of a satanic little boy; *The Earthling*, reluctantly roaming through the Australian Bush with little Ricky Schroder; and *S.O.B.*, again projecting a degree of integrity, as a veteran Hollywood director, which was necessary amid the deliberately tasteless goings on. A few months after it was released, he died tragically, having passed out while drinking, and hitting his head. His body was not discovered until days after the fact. The movies had lost a major star, one who never seemed to make a big deal about just how valuable to the industry he had been. Although his television appearances were few, he did nab himself an Emmy Award for the mini-series *The Blue Knight*.

Screen: **1938:** Prison Farm; **1939:** Million Dollar Legs; Each Dawn I Die; Golden Boy; Invisible Stripes; **1940:** Our Town; Those Were the Days; Arizona; **1941:** I Wanted Wings; Texas; **1942:** The Remarkable Andrew; The Fleet's In; Meet the Stewarts; **1943:** Young and Willing; **1947:** Blaze of Noon; Dear Ruth; Variety Girl; **1948:** Rachel and the Stranger; Apartment for Peggy; The Dark Past; The Man From Colorado; **1949:** Streets of Laredo; Miss Grant Takes Richmond; Dear Wife; **1950:** Father Is a Bachelor; Sunset Blvd.; Union Station; Born Yesterday; **1951:** Force of Arms; Submarine Command; **1952:** Boots Malone; The Turning Point; **1953:** Stalag 17; The Moon Is Blue; Forever Female; Escape From Fort Bravo; **1954:** Executive Suite; Sabrina; The Country Girl; **1955:** The Bridges at Toko-Ri; Love Is a Many Splendored Thing; Picnic; **1956:** The Proud and Profane; Toward the Unknown; **1957:** The Bridge on the River Kwai; **1958:** The Key; **1959:** The Horse Soldiers; **1960:** The World of Suzie Wong; **1962:** Satan Never Sleeps; The Counterfeit Traitor; The Lion; **1964:** Paris — When It Sizzles; The 7th Dawn; **1966:** Alvarez Kelly; **1967:** Casino Royale; **1968:** The Devil's Brigade; **1969:** The Wild Bunch; The Christmas Tree; **1971:** Wild Rovers; **1972:** The Revengers; **1973:** Breezy; **1974:** Open Season; The Towering Inferno; **1976:** Network; **1978:** Damien: Omen II; **1979:** Ashanti; Fedora; Escape to Athena; **1980:** When Time Ran Out…; **1981:** The Earthling; S.O.B.

Select TV: **1973:** The Blue Knight (ms); **1976:** 21 Hours at Munich.

JUDY HOLLIDAY

(JUDITH TUVIM) BORN: NEW YORK, NY, JUNE 21, 1921. DIED: JUNE 7, 1965.

Her résumé is short, but Judy Holliday remains one of the best-loved and most important film stars of the 1950s. With her crackling voice and sparkling comedic delivery, she could bring down the house with just a twitch of her mouth or the widening of her eyes. With Alvin Hammer, Adolph Green, and Betty Comden, she started out as part of a nightclub act called The Revuers that played New York and, later, Hollywood. While in Hollywood, she was signed to a contract by 20th Century-Fox, appearing briefly in three movies, one of which, *Greenwich Village*, featured a fleeting glimpse of The Revuers, most of their footage being dropped from the finished movie. Returning to New York, she appeared onstage in *Kiss Them for Me*, before landing a job as Jean Arthur's understudy in Garson Kanin's *Born Yesterday*. Fate stepped in when Arthur got sick and Holliday took the play to Broadway, where she became the toast of the town as the sweetly stupid junk-dealer's mistress, Billie Dawn. From that she got a terrific supporting role as a ditsy wife on trial for trying to murder her husband in *Adam's Rib*, nearly plucking the film away from Spencer Tracy and Katharine Hepburn at their very best. When it came time to film *Born Yesterday*, Columbia seriously considered Rita Hayworth to play Billie, but wisely went with Holliday instead after coming to their senses. It became, of course, the screen's definitive portrait of the dumb blonde, vulgar but well meaning and vulnerable, her political awareness brought to life by instructor William Holden. Holliday was perfect, and, in a highly competitive year that included Bette Davis and Gloria Swanson among the nominees, won the Academy Award for Best Actress.

Not surprisingly she was put under contract by a thrilled Columbia, who kept her on safe ground, giving her her *Born Yesterday* director, George Cukor, to guide her through the next two. *The Marrying Kind*, which had serious overtones, was a flashback look at the ups and down of a couple on the verge of divorce, while the delightful *It Should Happen to You*, in which she put her name up on a billboard in Columbus Circle and became the rage of New York, managed to be in the same class as *Born Yesterday*, a prime example of the sophisticated, metropolitan humor of the era. That film introduced audiences to Jack Lemmon, and he and Holliday made such an engaging pair that they were together again for the memorably titled *Phffft* (the movie itself, however, was less memorable). Luckily the good material kept coming, and she was enchanting in a part originally written for the older Shirley Booth, upsetting the crooked board of directors as an inquisitive stockholder in *The Solid Gold Cadillac*. Then there was another attempt at something a little more serious, *Full of Life*, in which she and Richard Conte prepared for the arrival of their new baby. Although she was a critic's favorite, none of these made the top of the box-office lists. Her movie career temporarily done with, she returned to Broadway for another triumph, the musical *Bells Are Ringing*, winning a Tony Award for it. She repeated her role as the good-hearted, meddling telephone operator in the bright, faithful film adaptation, which captured her inimitable renditions of "The Party's Over" and the show-stopping "I'm Going Back." Two years after the failure of another stage musical, *The Hot Spot*, she was dead at the age of 43, leaving a small but worthy legacy behind her. Her final screen credit was an unexpected one, co-writing (with friend Gerry Mulligan) the title song for the 1965 film *A Thousand Clowns*, released posthumously.

Screen: 1944: Greenwich Village; Something for the Boys; Winged Victory; 1949: Adam's Rib; 1950: Born Yesterday; 1952: The Marrying Kind; 1954: It Should Happen to You; Phffft; 1956: The Solid Gold Cadillac; Full of Life; 1960: Bells Are Ringing.

NY Stage: 1945: Kiss Them for Me; 1946: Born Yesterday; 1951: Dream Girl; 1956: Bells Are Ringing; 1963: Hot Spot.

Select TV: 1954: The Huntress (sp).

EARL HOLLIMAN

BORN: DELHI, LA, SEPTEMBER 11, 1928. ED: USC.

Adept at "aw shucks" hayseeds and rural nice guys, Earl Holliman came to movies after a stint in the Navy and a period of studying at the Pasadena Playhouse. He debuted for Paramount, doing a brief bit as an elevator operator in a Martin and Lewis comedy, *Scared Stiff*, and continued in unheralded supporting parts in *The Bridges at Toko-Ri*, as a sailor buddy of William Holden and Mickey Rooney, and in the sci-fi cult classic *Forbidden Planet*, as the spaceship's cook. Things improved with *The Big Combo*, in which he was a (presumably) gay hoodlum; *The Rainmaker*, where he was Katharine Hepburn's love-struck yokel brother; and a pair of box-office hits, *Gunfight at the O.K. Corral* and *Don't Go Near the Water*, back in the navy for the latter. He was getting plenty of work on TV as well, including two short-lived series, but took the time to play a bad guy being brought to justice by Kirk Douglas in *Last Train From Gun Hill*; Jerry Lewis's straight man in *Visit to a Small Planet*; and the kindly fellow who brings some hope to Geraldine Page at the climax of *Summer and Smoke*, adding to the best scene in the film. He was one of the bickering brothers in the highly entertaining and popular western *The Sons of Katie Elder*, after which he spent much more of his time on the small screen in telefilms and a hit series, *Police Woman*, as the boss of crime-fighting Angie Dickinson. He did rate top billing on the big screen in Disney's 1972 remake of *The Biscuit Eater*, but the selling points were the dog and the kids.

Screen: 1953: Scared Stiff; The Girls of Pleasure Island; Destination Gobi; East of Sumatra; Devil's Canyon; 1954: Tennessee Champ; Broken Lance; 1955: The Bridges at Toko-Ri; The Big Combo; I Died a Thousand Times; 1956: Forbidden Planet; Giant; The Burning Hills; The Rainmaker; 1957: Gunfight at the O.K. Corral; Trooper Hook; Don't Go Near the Water; 1958: Hot Spell; 1959: The Trap; Last Train From Gun Hill; 1960: Visit to a Small Planet; 1961: Armored Command; Summer and Smoke; 1965: The Sons of Katie Elder; 1967: A Covenant With Death; 1968: The Power; Anzio; 1972: The Biscuit Eater; 1978: Good Luck, Miss Wyckoff; 1981: Sharky's Machine; 2000: Bad City Blues (dtv); The Perfect Tenant (dtv).

Select TV: 1957: The Dark Side of the Earth (sp); 1958: The Sea Is Boiling Hot (sp); The Man With Pointed Toes (sp); The Lady Died at Midnight (sp); The Return of Ansel Gibbs (sp); 1959–60: Hotel de Paree (series); 1961: The Dispossessed (sp); 1962: The Troubled Heart (sp); 1962–63: The Wide Country (series); 1970: Tribes; 1971: Alias Smith and Jones; Cannon; The Desperate Mission; 1973: Trapped; 1974: Cry Panic; I Love You…Goodbye; 1974–78: Police Woman (series); 1977: Alexander: The Other Side of Dawn; 1979: The Solitary Man; 1980: Where the Ladies Go; 1982: Country Gold; 1983: The Thorn Birds (ms); 1987: American Harvest; Gunsmoke: Return to Dodge; 1991–92: P.S. I Love You (series); 1992–93: Delta (series); 1997: Night Man (series).

STANLEY HOLLOWAY

BORN: LONDON, ENGLAND, OCTOBER 1, 1890. DIED: JANUARY 30, 1982.

The personification of the brash English Music Hall star, toothy, ruddy-faced cockney Stanley Holloway had a long and well-regarded career in his native country, but owes his fame in America almost entirely to "Alfred P. Dolittle." His early days were spent entertaining at concert parties. After serving in World War I, he acted in West End musicals, becoming famous as part of the cast of *The Co-Optimists*, where he sang comical ditties and did monologues. This was made into a film in 1929, but movies were of secondary interest to Holloway, who felt more at home onstage or making records. Despite his apathy, he was invited to make some of his own film vehicles and, as such, appeared in *Song of the Forge*, in a dual role, as father and son; *The Vicar of Bray*, in the title role; and *Sam Small Leaves Town*, as an actor hiding out to win a bet. In the 1940s he began doing character parts with great success including *Major Barbara*, as a policeman; *Champagne Charlie*, appropriately cast as a music hall performer, engaging in some sparring with rival entertainer Tommy Trinder; *Brief Encounter*, as the train station attendant, chatting up Joyce Carey; *Nicholas Nickelby*, brilliant as Crummles, the self-deluded ham actor; and in Olivier's Oscar-winning *Hamlet*, as the gravedigger. He was lucky to join the stock company at Ealing Studios, where he was featured in three of their best-remembered comedies: *Passport to Pimlico*, as the neighborhood grocer who finds a troublesome charter; *The Lavender Hill Mob*, as Alec Guinness's partner in crime; and *The Titfield Thunderbolt*, as a tipsy town official. In 1956 he made musical-comedy history playing the irascible, hard-drinking Dolittle in *My Fair Lady*, eventually preserving the role to perfection in the equally classic 1964 film version, which earned him an Oscar nomination in the supporting category. It wasn't exactly a springboard to a new film career, although he did pop up in the remake of *Ten Little Indians*, portraying the inspector (the part originally played by Roland Young); the all-star *In Harm's Way*, as an Australian coast guard assisting the U.S. navy; the Herman's Hermits musical *Mrs. Brown, You've Got a Lovely Daughter*, singing a song with Peter Noone; and in director Billy Wilder's *The Private Life of Sherlock Holmes*, once again playing a gravedigger, in a nod to *Hamlet*. His 1969 autobiography was entitled *Wiv a Little Bit of Luck*, in tribute to one of his songs from *My Fair Lady*.

Screen: 1921: The Rotters; 1929: The Co-Optimists; 1933: Sleeping Car; Lily of Killarney/Bride of the Lake; The Girl From Maxim's; 1934: Road House; Love at Second Sight/The Girl Thief; Sing As We Go; D'Ye Ken John Peel/Captain Moonlight; In Town To-Night; 1935: Squibs; Play Up the Band; 1937: Song of the Forge; The Vicar of Bray; Sam Small Leaves Town; Cotton Queen; 1941: Major Barbara; 1942: Salute John Citizen; 1944: This Happy Breed; The Way Ahead; Champagne Charlie; 1945: The Way to the Stars/Johnny in the Clouds; Caesar and Cleopatra; 1946: Brief Encounter; Wanted for Murder; Carnival; 1947: Meet Me at Dawn; Nicholas Nickleby; 1948: One Night With You; Hamlet; Snowbound; Silk Noose; Another Shore; 1949: The Winslow Boy; Passport to Pimlico; The Perfect Woman; 1950: Midnight Episode; 1951: One Wild Oat; The Lavender Hill Mob; The Magic Box; Lady Godiva Rides Again; 1952: The Happy Family/Mr. Lord Says No; Meet Me Tonight/Tonight at 8:30; 1953: The Beggar's Opera; The Titfield Thunderbolt; A Day to Remember; Meet Mr. Lucifer; 1954: Fast and Loose; 1955: An Alligator Named Daisy; 1956: Jumping for Joy; 1958: Hello, London; Alive and Kicking; 1959: No Trees in the Street; 1961: No Love for Johnnie; Operation Snafu/On the Fiddle; 1964: My Fair Lady; 1965: In Harm's Way; Ten Little Indians; 1966: The Sandwich Man; 1968: Mrs. Brown, You've Got a Lovely Daughter; 1969: How to Make It/Target Harry; 1970: The Private Life of Sherlock Holmes; 1971: Flight of the Doves; 1972: Up the Front; 1976: Journey Into Fear.

NY Stage: 1954: A Midsummer Night's Dream; 1956: My Fair Lady; 1960: Laughs and Other Events.

Select TV: 1960: The Mikado (sp); 1962–63: Our Man Higgins (series); 1968: Thingumybob (series); 1969: Run a Crooked Mile

1973: Dr. Jekyll & M. Hyde (sp).

STERLING HOLLOWAY

BORN: CEDARTOWN, GA, JANUARY 4, 1905.
ED: GA MILITARY ACAD., AADA.
DIED: NOVEMBER 22, 1992.

With a distinctive voice that sounded as if he was wheezing for air, a beak-like nose, and a bushy pile of hair, Sterling Holloway was one of the most instantly recognizable of all eccentric character players. In New York he acted with the Theatre Guild, gaining attention in three editions of *The Garrick Gaieties*, where his activities in the earliest of the revues included singing the Rodgers and Hart standard "Manhattan." Shortly afterwards he made his motion picture debut in the silent feature adaptation of the classic poem "Casey at the Bat," as Casey's manager. During the five years between that one and his second movie, *Blonde Venus*, he acted with the Pasadena Playhouse. On screen he was a sailor in the unforgettably titled "She Was a China Teacup and He Was Just a Mug" number from *International House*; a frog (of course) in *Alice in Wonderland*; a feisty playwright in *Dancing Lady*; one of the street kids in *Wild Boys of the Road*; and a gambler-stowaway in *Down to Their Last Yacht*. He was a sneezing caddy in *When Ladies Meet*; a dance marathon finalist in *Hard to Handle*; a bridegroom in *Professor Beware*; and a cow herder in *Maid of Salem*. Holloway always left an unmistakable, sometimes over-the-top impression, his mannerisms either allowing him to be excitably nervous and disagreeably cantankerous, or to float about lugubriously, as if he had just inhaled some illegal substance. He had one of his nicest roles, as an amiable farm hand sharing Christmas with Fred MacMurray's family in *Remember the Night*; and one of his rare serious assignments, as the platoon medic in the superior war picture *A Walk in the Sun*, his own favorite of his films. His unmistakable vocals were used to great effect by Walt Disney in *Dumbo*, as the stork; *Bambi*, as Flower the skunk; *Alice in Wonderland*, as the Cheshire Cat; and *The Jungle Book*, as Kaa the snake. However, his most famous voice role of all was as Winnie-the-Pooh in Disney's series of short subjects based on the famous A.A. Milne stories.

Screen: 1927: Casey at the Bat; 1932: Blonde Venus; American Madness; Lawyer Man; Faithless; Rockabye; 1933: Elmer the Great; International House; When Ladies Meet; Hell Below; Gold Diggers of 1933; Professional Sweetheart; Blondie Johnson; Wild Boys of the Road; Female; Hard to Handle; Adorable; Picture Snatcher; Going Hollywood; Alice in Wonderland; Advice to the Lovelorn; Dancing Lady; Fast Workers; 1934: The Merry Widow; Gift of Gab; Down to Their Last Yacht; A Wicked Woman; Strictly Dynamite; Murder in the Private Car; Tomorrow's Children; The Back Page; Girl o' My Dreams; Operator 13; The Cat and the Fiddle; 1935: $1,000 a Minute; The Lottery Lover; I Live My Life; Rendezvous; Life Begins at 40; Doubting Thomas; 1936: Avenging Waters; Career Woman; Palm Springs; 1937: Behind the Mike; Join the Marines; Maid of Salem; The Woman I Love; When Love Is Young; Varsity Show; 1938: Spring Madness; Doctor Rhythm; Professor Beware; Of Human Hearts; 1939: St. Louis Blues; Nick Carter — Master Detective; 1940: Remember the Night; The Blue Bird; Street of Memories; Hit Parade of 1941; Little Men; 1941: Cheers for Miss Bishop; New Wine; Top Sergeant Mulligan; Dumbo (voice); Meet John Doe; Look Who's Laughing; 1942: Don't Get Personal; Iceland; Bambi (voice); Here We Go Again; The Lady Is Willing; Star Spangled Rhythm; 1945: The Three Caballeros (voice); Wildfire; A Walk in the Sun; 1946: Sioux City Sue; Make

Mine Music (voice); Death Valley; **1947:** Saddle Pals; Twilight on the Rio Grande; Robin Hood of Texas; Trail to San Antone; **1949:** The Beautiful Blonde From Bashful Bend; **1950:** Her Wonderful Lie/Addio Mimi!; **1951:** Alice in Wonderland (voice); **1956:** Kentucky Rifle; **1957:** Shake, Rattle and Rock; **1960:** The Adventures of Huckleberry Finn; **1961:** Alakazam the Great (voice); **1963:** My Six Loves; It's a Mad Mad Mad Mad World; **1966:** Batman; **1967:** The Jungle Book (voice); **1968:** Live a Little, Love a Little; **1970:** The Aristocats (voice); **1976:** Won Ton Ton, the Dog Who Saved Hollywood; **1977:** Thunder and Lightning.

NY Stage: **1923:** The Evil Doers of Good; The Failures; Roseanne; Fata Morgana; **1925:** The Garrick Gaieties (and 1926; 1930 editions); **1928:** Get Me in the Movies; **1929:** The Shoestring Revue; **1952:** The Grass Harp.

Select TV: **1953–58:** The Life of Riley (series); **1955:** Willy (series); **1960:** The Land of Oz (sp); **1964–65:** The Baileys of Balboa (series).

CELESTE HOLM

BORN: NEW YORK, NY, APRIL 29, 1919.

A warm and clever actress, as comfortable in drama as she was in comedy, Celeste Holm was one of the darlings of the postwar film era. Hollywood saw her as mostly second-lead material, but she took what she got and made magic with it. Debuting professionally with a Pennsylvania stock company in 1936, she came to Broadway two years later, in *Gloriana*. There were several roles after that, culminating in her acclaimed Ado Annie in the original production of Rodgers and Hammerstein's groundbreaking musical *Oklahoma!*, which made her the talk of the New York theater. It was followed by her own stage vehicle, *Bloomer Girl*, and a contract with 20th Century-Fox, who started her off with *Three Little Girls in Blue*, where she showed up the rest of the cast with her rendition of "Always a Lady." From that she got a bigger role in similarly routine assignment, *Carnival in Costa Rica*, and seemed doomed to be wasted in such trivia until she got cast in the studio's big attempt at a message picture, *Gentleman's Agreement*. Holm was effortlessly good as a magazine fashion editor, who stands loyally by crusading writer Gregory Peck in his efforts to expose anti-Semitism, but fails to get him to love her in the end. The movie became one of the most talked about dramas of the year, a surprise moneymaker, and the Oscar-winner for Best Picture, while Holm took home the Academy Award as Best Supporting Actress of 1947.

Now considered worthy of prestige productions, she was effective as an inmate in the mental institution drama *The Snake Pit*, and charming as a tennis playing nun with a French accent in *Come to the Stable*, earning a second Oscar nomination for the latter. There were also light comedy parts in *Chicken Every Sunday*, as the wife of Dan Dailey in turn-of-the-century Tucson, and the disappointing *Everybody Does It*, as an aspiring opera singer married to Paul Douglas, who steals her thunder with his baritone voice. She also contributed greatly to one of the studio's best films of the late 1940s, *A Letter to Three Wives*, although only her voice was heard, as the lady in question who plans to run off with someone's husband, thereby setting all the flashbacks in motion. She made an ideal foil for Ronald Colman in the independently produced comedy *Champagne for Caesar*, and then became part of the classic ensemble of one of the all-time greats, *All About Eve*, as playwright Hugh Marlowe's good-hearted wife, who gets burned after helping aspiring thespian Anne Baxter. On set she was also singed by star Bette Davis whose best friend she portrayed in the movie but with whom she didn't get along at all. Nonetheless, Holm was part of its overall triumph, and it

brought her another Oscar nomination for being nothing short of superb in one of the less-showy roles in the film.

Surprisingly, after this peak she turned her back on Hollywood to return to theater, until asked back to appear in two MGM releases opposite Frank Sinatra: *The Tender Trap*, getting tossed aside for the younger Debbie Reynolds, and *High Society*, where they memorably dueted on Cole Porter's "Who Wants to Be a Millionaire." Alas, she wasn't interested in a steady movie career, preferring the stage, and her only roles in the 1960s were in two stale sex comedies, *Bachelor Flat*, as Terry-Thomas's fiancée, and *Doctor, You've Got to Be Kidding*, trying in vain to salvage this sinking ship, as Sandra Dee's mother. In 1973 she returned to movies in a worthy role, Aunt Polly, in a nice musical version of *Tom Sawyer*, receiving glowing reviews from critics thrilled to have her back. After that it was mostly telefilms and more theater, although she did play Ted Danson's mom for a brief scene in the hit *Three Men and a Baby*, reminding filmgoers of what they'd been missing for too long. She was married to actor Wesley Addy from 1961 until his death in 1996.

Screen: **1946:** Three Little Girls in Blue; **1947:** Carnival in Costa Rica; Gentleman's Agreement; **1948:** Road House; The Snake Pit; Chicken Every Sunday; **1949:** Come to the Stable; A Letter to Three Wives (voice); Everybody Does It; **1950:** Champagne for Caesar; All About Eve; **1955:** The Tender Trap; **1956:** High Society; **1961:** Bachelor Flat; **1967:** Doctor You've Got to Be Kidding; **1973:** Tom Sawyer; **1976:** Bittersweet Love; **1978:** The Private Files of J. Edgar Hoover; **1987:** Three Men and a Baby; **1996:** Once You Meet a Stranger (dtv); **1998:** Still Breathing.

NY Stage: **1938:** Gloriana; **1939:** The Time of Your Life; **1940:** Another Sun; Return of the Vagabond; **1941:** Eight O'Clock Tuesday; My Fair Ladies; **1942:** Papa Is All; All the Comforts of Home; The Damask Cheek; **1943:** Oklahoma!; **1944:** Bloomer Girl; **1949:** She Stoops to Conquer; **1950:** Affairs of State; **1952:** Anna Christie; The King and I; **1954:** His and Hers; **1958:** Interlock; Third Best Sport; **1960:** Invitation to a March; **1963:** A Month in the Country (ob); **1967:** Mame; **1970:** Candida; **1975:** Habeas Corpus; **1979:** The Utter Glory of Morrissey Hall; Paris Was Yesterday (ob); **1982:** With Love and Laughter (ob); **1991:** I Hate Hamlet.

Select TV: **1951:** The Pacing Goose (sp); **1952:** Four's a Family (sp); **1954:** Honestly Celeste (series); **1955:** The Bogey Man (sp); **1956:** Jack and the Beanstalk (sp); **1957:** Wedding Present (sp); The Yeoman of the Guard (sp); **1959:** Who Pays? (series); **1960:** The Man in the Dog Suit (sp); The Right Man (sp); **1965:** Kilroy (sp); Cinderella (sp); Meet Me in St. Louis (sp); **1970–71:** Nancy (series); **1972:** The Delphi Bureau; **1974:** The Underground Man; Death Cruise; **1976:** Captains and the Kings (ms); **1977:** The Love Boat II; **1979:** Backstairs at the White House (ms); **1981:** Midnight Lace; **1983:** This Girl for Hire; The Shady Hill Kidnappings; **1984:** Jessie (series); **1985:** Falcon Crest (series); **1987:** Murder by the Book; **1989:** Polly; **1989–90:** Christine Cromwell (series); **1990:** Polly — Comin' Home!; **1991–92:** Loving (series); **1996–97:** Promised Land (series); Home of the Brave; **2000:** The Beat (series).

PHILLIPS HOLMES

BORN: GRAND RAPIDS, MI, JULY 22, 1907.
ED: PRINCETON UNIV. DIED: AUGUST 12, 1942.

The son of actor Taylor Holmes and brother of actor Ralph Holmes, blond, blandly pretty Phillips Holmes was one of the luckier lightweight talents in movie history, being tested and signed by Paramount Pictures after a single

New York stage appearance, in the Princeton Triangle Show's production of *Napoleon Passes*. After some fairly small parts, the studio upped him to secondary leads in *Stairs of Sand*, a flop western, and *The Return of Sherlock Holmes*, as a kidnapping victim. He was a songwriter in the part-color *Pointed Heels*; a Confederate captain, supporting Gary Cooper, in *Only the Brave*; and Nancy Carroll's suitor, finally being promoted to leading-man status, in *The Devil's Holiday*, which brought him his best notices to date. He and Carroll were reteamed for *Stolen Heaven*, and then he got his best chance, albeit in one of the company's most-notorious failures of the early 1930s, *An American Tragedy*, giving an utterly inadequate performance as the young man who rises from poverty only to be tried for the murder of his pregnant girlfriend (Sylvia Sidney). Another film with Sidney, *Confessions of a Co-Ed*, was also poorly attended, as was *The Man I Killed*, in which he played a French war vet who contacts the family of a German soldier he had killed. This film did so badly that its title was changed to the deceptive *Broken Lullaby*. In 1932 he went over to MGM, but, aside from the all-star *Dinner at Eight*, his assignments there were hardly memorable. He wound up doing some pictures overseas and returning to the theater. His movie career was four years behind him when he was killed in a dual plane crash while serving with the Royal Canadian Air Force.

Screen: AS PHILLIPS R. HOLMES: 1928: Varsity; His Private Life; 1929: Illusion; The Wild Party; Stairs of Sand; The Return of Sherlock Holmes; Pointed Heels.

AS PHILLIPS HOLMES: 1930: Only the Brave; Paramount on Parade; The Devil's Holiday; Grumpy; Her Man; Man to Man; The Dancers; 1931: The Criminal Code; Stolen Heaven; Confessions of a Co-Ed; An American Tragedy; 1932: The Man I Killed/ Broken Lullaby; Two Kinds of Women; Make Me a Star; 70,000 Witnesses; Night Court; 1933: The Secret of Madame Blanche; Men Must Fight; Looking Forward; Storm at Daybreak; The Big Brain; Dinner at Eight; Penthouse; Beauty for Sale; Stage Mother; 1934: Private Scandal; Nana; Caravan; Great Expectations; Million Dollar Ransom; No Ransom; 1935: The Divine Spark/Casta Diva; Ten-Minute Alibi; 1936: Chatterbox; The House of the Thousand Candles; General Spanky; 1937: The Dominant Sex; 1938: Housemaster.

NY Stage: 1927: Napoleon Passes.

TIM HOLT

(CHARLES JOHN HOLT, JR.) BORN: BEVERLY HILLS, CA, FEBRUARY 5, 1918. ED: CULVER MILITARY ACAD., USC. DIED: FEBRUARY 15, 1973.

First and foremost he was just one of the many "B" western stars who rode across the motion picture plains in countless low-budget oaters, but mild-mannered Tim Holt also chalked up three of the greatest movies of the 1940s to his credit, and for those his name has survived. The son of actor Jack Holt, he made his debut in his father's movie, *The Vanishing Pioneer*, in 1928. After he finished school, he joined the Westwood Theatre Guild then won a contract with producer Walter Wanger who lent him to Goldwyn for *Stella Dallas*, in the pivotal role of the rich guy whom Anne Shirley marries. The next year he went west for *Law West of Tombstone*, as a young outlaw dubbed The Tonto Kid; played opposite Ginger Rogers in the flimsy comedy *5th Ave. Girl*; and had the relatively minor role of a cavalry lieutenant in John Ford's famed *Stagecoach*. As part of the RKO roster of stars, he played the eldest son in the 1940 version of *Swiss Family Robinson*; the

lead in the third cinematic incarnation of *Laddie*; and Charles Boyer's disapproving son in the second reprisal of *Back Street*. By this point the studio had begun showcasing him as a western star in such quickies as *Dude Cowboy*, *Robbers of the Range*, and *Cyclone on Horseback*. His greatest chance to date came when Orson Welles cast him as the spoiled, selfish George Amberson Minifer, who destroys his mother's chance at happiness, in the brilliant adaptation of Booth Tarkington's *The Magnificent Ambersons*. Holt's clipped delivery and chilling immovability as the character surprised the skeptics and seemed to point him towards great things.

The box-office failure of the Welles film, however, meant business as usual, and Holt was soon back on the range with *Bandit Ranger*, *Sagebrush Law*, and *Red River Robin Hood*. Between these there was a surprise hit, the tacky *Hitler's Children*, where he was a Nazi realizing the error of his misguided ways. Following service in the Air Force, he was Virgil Earp in the excellent *My Darling Clementine*, a western that was a definite leap up from his customary low-budget offerings, it being directed by John Ford. But, once again, he couldn't seem to advance despite these occasional high points. Instead he then returned to the same RKO sagebrush fare he'd specialized in before the war, including the 1948 release *The Arizona Ranger*, which had the distinction of pairing him with his dad, the two generations of Holts playing father and son ranchers quibbling over how to dispatch justice. That same year came his third great film experience, playing the sensitive Curtin, who teams up with unsavory Humphrey Bogart and adventure-loving Walter Huston to make their fortune, in *The Treasure of the Sierra Madre*. Not unlike *Ambersons*, it was better liked by critics than the public and did nothing to change Holt's career at the time. He continued making westerns for RKO until 1952, when they released his last in this genre, *Desert Passage*, bringing his total to 46 for the company. He later spent time tending to his Oklahoma ranch and working as sales manager for an Oklahoma City radio station.

Screen: 1928: The Vanishing Pioneer; 1937: Stella Dallas; 1938: Gold Is Where You Find It; Law West of Tombstone; I Met My Love Again; Sons of the Legion; The Renegade Ranger; 1939: The Spirit of Culver; Stagecoach; The Girl and the Gambler; 5th Ave. Girl; The Rookie Cop; 1940: Swiss Family Robinson; Laddie; Wagon Train; The Fargo Kid; 1941: Back Street; The Bandit Trail; Riding the Wind; Dude Cowboy; Robbers of the Range; Along the Rio Grande; Six-Gun Gold; Land of the Open Range; Cyclone on Horseback; Thundering Hoofs; 1942: The Magnificent Ambersons; Come on Danger!; Pirates of the Prairie; Bandit Ranger; 1943: Hitler's Children; The Avenging Rider; Sagebrush Law; Fighting Frontier; Red River Robin Hood; 1946: My Darling Clementine; 1947: Thunder Mountain; Under the Tonto Rim; Wild Horse Mesa; 1948: The Treasure of the Sierra Madre; Indian Agent; The Arizona Ranger; Western Heritage; Gun Smugglers; Guns of Hate; 1949: The Stagecoach Kid; Rustlers; Brothers in the Saddle; Masked Raiders; The Mysterious Desperado; 1950: Riders of the Range; Border Treasure; Dynamite Pass; Storm Over Wyoming; Rider From Tucson; Law of the Badlands; Rio Grande Patrol; 1951: Gunplay; Saddle Legion; His Kind of Woman; Pistol Harvest; Hot Lead; Overland Telegraph; 1952: Target; Trail Guide; Road Agent; Desert Passage; 1957: The Monster That Challenged the World; 1963: The Yesterday Machine; 1971: This Stuff'll Kill Ya!

Select TV: 1954: Adventure in Java (sp).

OSCAR HOMOLKA

BORN: VIENNA, AUSTRIA, AUGUST 12, 1898.
ED: VIENNA'S ROYAL DRAMATIC ACAD.
DIED: JANUARY 27, 1978.

With his heavy Viennese accent and distinctively bushy eyebrows, Oscar Homolka was a character player who almost always made an impression. A student of impresario Max Reinhardt, he acted on both the Viennese and German stage, starting in 1918, before making his movie debut eight years later in *Das Abenteur Eines*. As the Nazis rose to power, he fled to England, where he was featured in three films for Gaumont-British, including a star part in Alfred Hitchcock's *Sabotage/The Woman Alone*, in the unsympathetic role of a spy who inadvertently gets his brother-in-law killed. After that it was on to America, where he was once again cast in a lead role that required no sympathy, an unscrupulous ship's captain, in Paramount's Technicolor adventure *Ebb Tide*. His guttural voice and imposing presence made him an ideal villain, so he was a jealous knife thrower in *Seven Sinners*; a leader of a gang of crooks in *The Invisible Woman*; and an escaped con running an antique shop in the British-made *The Shop at Sly Corner/The Code of Scotland Yard*. The benign side of Homolka was seen to good effect as one of the professors enchanted by Barbara Stanwyck in *Ball of Fire*, and he was one of the friendly Russians, his famous brows covered in white make-up, in the propaganda piece *Mission to Moscow*. In 1948 he repeated his Broadway role of bombastic Uncle Chris in the splendid film of *I Remember Mama*, earning an Oscar nomination in the supporting category. In later years he was seen as General Kutuzov in *War and Peace*; a creepy one-eyed servant in *Mr. Sardonicus*; Colonel Stock in two Harry Palmer thrillers, *Funeral in Berlin* and *Billion Dollar Brain*; and one of the wicked businessmen disposed of by Katharine Hepburn in *The Madwoman of Chaillot*. He was married to actress Joan Tetzel from 1949 until her death in 1977.

Screen (US releases only): 1930: Dreyfus/The Dreyfus Case; **1936:** Rhodes/Rhodes of Africa; Everything Is Thunder; Sabotage/The Woman Alone; **1937:** Ebb Tide; **1940:** Comrade X; Seven Sinners; The Invisible Woman; **1941:** Rage in Heaven; Ball of Fire; **1943:** Mission to Moscow; Hostages; **1946:** The Code of Scotland Yard/The Shop at Sly Corner; **1948:** I Remember Mama; **1949:** Anna Lucasta; **1950:** The White Tower; **1953:** Mr. Potts Goes to Moscow/Top Secret; **1954:** The House of the Arrow; Prisoner of War; **1955:** The Seven Year Itch; **1956:** War and Peace; **1957:** A Farewell to Arms; **1958:** The Key; Tempest; **1961:** Mr. Sardonicus; **1962:** Boys' Night Out; The Wonderful World of the Brothers Grimm; **1964:** The Long Ships; **1965:** Joy in the Morning; **1966:** Funeral in Berlin; **1967:** The Happening; Billion Dollar Brain; **1968:** Assignment to Kill; **1969:** The Madwoman of Chaillot; **1970:** The Executioner; Song of Norway; **1974:** The Tamarind Seed.

NY Stage: 1940: Grey Farm; 1943: Innocent Voyage; 1944: I Remember Mama; 1948: The Last Dance; Bravo!; 1955: The Master Builder (and dir.); 1959: Rashomon.

Select TV: 1954: Love Song (sp); 1955: Darkness at Noon (sp); 1957: The Master Builder (sp); You Touched Me (sp); Murder in the House (sp); 1958: The Plot to Kill Stalin (sp); Heart of Darkness (sp); 1960: Arrowsmith (sp); In the Presence of Mine Enemies (sp); Assassination Plot at Teheran (sp); Victory (sp); The Ugly Duckling (sp); Rashomon; 1962: The Mooncussers (sp); 1968: Dr. Jekyll and Mr. Hyde (sp); 1975: One of Our Own.

BOB HOPE

(LESLIE TOWNES HOPE)
BORN: ELTHAM, ENGLAND, MAY 29, 1903.
RAISED IN CLEVELAND, OH.

Round-faced and slope-nosed, with a puckish sense of mischief in his eyes, Bob Hope became one of the half-dozen most-recognizable names and faces in show business history. A legend in his own lifetime, he conquered stage, radio, films, and TV as the king of the topical one-liner, bringing a sometimes predictable comfort to audiences with his sly but never stinging commentary on the world at large. In films his image was that of the boastful coward, a con man who wasn't too successful at the game but who, somehow, won the girl and saved the day. Perhaps it was through sheer luck or simply because none of the other cast members (apart from Bing Crosby) could ever keep up with his wit. Despite his stature as one of America's great institutions, Hope was, in fact, born in England. When he was four years old, however, his family moved to Ohio, where he took an interest in show business, forming a dance act with Lloyd Durbin. Later with a new partner, George Byrne, he played vaudeville, which led to Hope's Broadway debut in 1927, in *Sidewalks of New York*. He drifted between vaudeville and legit theater, including chorus work in *Smiles*, in support of Fred and Adele Astaire. It was his role in the hit Jerome Kern musical *Roberta*, in 1933, that finally brought him the attention he deserved. Because of this he was signed to make a series of short subjects for Educational Pictures, Warners, and Universal, but these did not immediately lead to features. With his wife, Dolores DeFina, whom he married in 1934, he returned to vaudeville, did some radio work for NBC, and then went back to the stage for *Ziegfeld Follies of 1936* (he sang "I Can't Get Started With You") and *Red, Hot and Blue!* (he shared the spotlight with Ethel Merman as they introduced Cole Porter's "It's De-Lovely").

There was renewed interest in Hope as star material, and in 1938 he made a double splash starting his long-running radio show for Pepsodent and debuting for Paramount in the all-star feature *The Big Broadcast of 1938*, where he and Shirley Ross shared a lovely, quiet moment amid the hectic plot, singing what would become Hope's theme song, the Oscar-winning "Thanks for the Memory." Paramount did a quickie cash-in on this one by reteaming him and Ross in *Thanks for the Memory* and in *Some Like It Hot*, which had nothing to do with the later classic of the same name, and which Hope considered his worst film. There were also teamings with brash Martha Raye, in *College Swing*, *Give Me a Sailor*, and *Never Say Die*, but these were not prime vehicles. Instead it was a pair of comic thrillers with Paulette Goddard, *The Cat and the Canary* and *The Ghost Breakers*, that first put him on the path to box-office success. There was another film, released in 1940, that was instrumental in making Hope a full-fledged movie attraction, a mild comedy in which he was billed after Bing Crosby and Dorothy Lamour, *Road to Singapore*. He and Crosby worked so flawlessly off of one another that it became one of the year's biggest hits, and the three stars would be teamed repeatedly with even better results in the future.

The writers began fine tuning Hope's scripts so that *Caught in the Draft*, a service farce; *Nothing But the Truth*, about a guy who will win a bet if he doesn't lie; and *My Favorite Blonde*, which had Hope on the run from spies with Madeleine Carroll, were improvements over his 1930s films and reflected his growing popularity as well. These were made amid *Road to Zanzibar*, one of the lesser in the follow-ups with Crosby and Lamour, and

Road to Morocco, which really set the silly tone for which that series would become fondly remembered. With World War II on, the comedian began his legendary trips abroad to entertain the troops, something he would continue to do for decades to come. Back at Paramount there was a bowdlerized filmization of the Broadway musical *Louisiana Purchase*, salvaged by Hope's spoof of *Mr. Smith Goes to Washington*, then two loan-outs to Goldwyn. The first, *They Got Me Covered*, was average wartime fare, but the second, the Technicolor romp *The Princess and the Pirate*, was one of Hope's classics, with the comic as a vain traveling actor hilariously pitted against cutthroat Victor McLaglen. Placing him incongruously in period clothes proved such an inspiration that he was back in stockings and ruffled lace, playing a cowardly French barber, in *Monsieur Beaucaire*, which put him pretty far from the previous interpreter of this part, Rudolph Valentino, and from the original Booth Tarkington source material. Then he and Crosby reached their peak as the cinema's funniest duo with *Road to Utopia*, the one that brought all the wisecracking asides and inside jokes to some sort of frenzied perfection. There was a fun comic thriller with Lamour, *My Favorite Brunette*; the most financially popular of the *Road* films, *Road to Rio*; and recognition in 1946 with a Medal of Merit from Dwight D. Eisenhower.

Hope did another splendidly funny spoof, *The Paleface*, out west as a dentist mistaken for a gunfighter; memorably partnered with a smug Jane Russell, he introduced another Oscar-winning song, "Buttons and Bows," and wound up with his greatest box-office hit ever. He found another prime leading lady in Lucille Ball with a pair of remakes: *Sorrowful Jones*, which was a bit gentler than the typical Hope film, being an update of Damon Runyon's *Little Miss Marker*, about an irresponsible gambler softened by an orphan, and *Fancy Pants*, where he was an English butler out west, reprising Charles Laughton's role in this weaker version of *Ruggles of Red Gap*. Back in Runyon-land he was *The Lemon Drop Kid*, which not only allowed him to dress as both Santa Claus and a little old lady, but let him introduce a Christmas classic, "Silver Bells." He and Crosby were still making merry in *Road to Bali*, and a sequel, *Son of Paleface*, had some moments of fun, but things started to slip with *My Favorite Spy* and *Here Come the Girls*, both of which seemed to indicate that the good ideas were running low.

It was now the 1950s, and Hope had comfortably transferred his stand-up act from radio to television. As a change of pace, the now past-50 comedian decided to try a more adult approach to his comedy with two biopics, *The Seven Little Foys*, as vaudevillian Eddie Foy (in an entertainment better than anyone had a right to expect), and the less-inspired *Beau James*, as flamboyant New York mayor Jimmy Walker. *Alias Jesse James*, perhaps the last of the presentable Hope vehicles, found him sending up the old west one last time, and *The Facts of Life* re-united him with Lucille Ball in a semi-serious tale of two people contemplating adultery, another departure from the normal formula, which earned them both high praise. By the 1960s there was a certain mechanical quality creeping into the Hope comedies, and *Bachelor in Paradise*, *A Global Affair*, and *I'll Take Sweden* just looked like any other of the leering farces of the day. By the time he rolled out three numb efforts with Phyllis Diller, *Boy, Did I Get a Wrong Number!*, *Eight on the Lam*, and *The Private Navy of Sgt. O'Farrell*, not only had audiences diminished but the critics had become downright murderous. After *Cancel My Reservation*, in 1972, he confined himself to his television specials, which would continue to gather good ratings right up until the comedian reached his 90s.

Over the years, Bob Hope received many awards and honors, including two Emmys, in 1959 for the "high quality of his televi-

sion programs through the years," and as star and executive producer of his 1966 Christmas special. He received four special Oscars, given in 1940, 1944, 1952, and 1965; an honorary title of Commander of the British Empire (Hope had early on become a U.S. Citizen); and various humanitarian awards. He became one of the wealthiest people in show business with an estimated worth somewhere between $400 and $700 million. Like anybody that famous, he had his detractors, and indeed by the 1970s he was being carried by a lot of good will, making it all too obvious on his television specials that he was reciting the jokes off of cue cards. But one only has to check out some of the prime Hope comedies of the 1940s to see that he was indeed one of our truly great movie comedians, one whose self-deprecating everyman qualities allowed him to be accepted by a wider demographic than most of his breed. Among the many books he published were an account of his years of touring for the troops, *The Last Christmas Show* (1974), and a lighthearted look at his movie career, *The Road to Hollywood: My Forty Year Love Affair With the Movies* (1977).

Screen: 1938: The Big Broadcast of 1938; College Swing; Give Me a Sailor; Thanks for the Memory; 1939: Never Say Die; Some Like It Hot/Rhythm Romance; The Cat and the Canary; 1940: Road to Singapore; The Ghost Breakers; 1941: Road to Zanzibar; Caught in the Draft; Nothing but the Truth; Louisiana Purchase; 1942: My Favorite Blonde; Road to Morocco; Star Spangled Rhythm; 1943: They Got Me Covered; Let's Face It; 1944: The Princess and the Pirate; 1946: Road to Utopia; Monsieur Beaucaire; 1947: My Favorite Brunette; Variety Girl; Where There's Life; Road to Rio; 1948: The Paleface; 1949: Sorrowful Jones; The Great Lover; 1950: Fancy Pants; 1951: The Lemon Drop Kid; My Favorite Spy; 1952: The Greatest Show on Earth; Son of Paleface; Road to Bali; 1953: Off Limits; Scared Stiff; Here Come the Girls; 1954: Casanova's Big Night; 1955: The Seven Little Foys; 1956: That Certain Feeling; The Iron Petticoat; 1957: Beau James; 1958: Paris Holiday (and prod.; co-wr.); 1959: The Five Pennies; Alias Jesse James (and exec prod.); 1960: The Facts of Life; 1961: Bachelor in Paradise; 1962: The Road to Hong Kong; 1963: Critic's Choice; Call Me Bwana; 1964: A Global Affair; 1965: I'll Take Sweden; 1966: The Oscar; Boy, Did I Get a Wrong Number!; Not With My Wife You Don't!; 1967: Eight on the Lam; 1968: The Private Navy of Sgt. O'Farrell; 1969: How to Commit Marriage; 1972: Cancel My Reservation (and prod.); 1979: The Muppet Movie; 1985: Spies Like Us; 1994: That Little Monster (dtv); 1998: Off the Menu: The Last Days of Chasen's.

NY Stage: 1927: Sidewalks of New York; 1928: Ups-a-Daisy; 1930: Smiles; 1932: Ballyhoo of 1932; 1933: Roberta; 1934: Say When; 1936: Ziegfeld Follies; 1936: Red, Hot and Blue!

Select TV: 1951–52: Chesterfield Sound Off Time (series); 1952–53: Colgate Comedy Hour (series); 1958: Roberta (sp); 1963–67: Bob Hope Presents the Chrysler Theatre (series); 1986: A Masterpiece of Murder.

MIRIAM HOPKINS

BORN: BAINBRIDGE, GA, OCTOBER 18, 1902.
DIED: OCTOBER 9, 1972.

An aggressive, watchable leading lady whose star shone brightest in the 1930s, Miriam Hopkins was a spirited blonde who has her vocal supporters and detractors, the price to be paid for throwing herself into a part, sometimes with the subtlety of a wrestler. The most negative trait of her acting would have to be the lack of sympathy she brought to so many of her characters, though her reputation among her colleagues was not too warm either, Hopkins being thought of as extremely difficult to work with. Assisted by an uncle who was in show business, she became a chorus girl on Broadway in the 1921 production of *Music Box Revue*. Two years later she was moved up to legitimate acting parts in *Little Jesse James* and maintained a solid stream of employment through such plays as *An American Tragedy* and *Lysistrata*. It was while appearing in the latter that she was signed up by Paramount, who cast her as a rebellious daughter in *Fast and Loose*, in 1930. The following year she had one of her more likable roles (and got to sing "Jazz Up Your Lingerie" with Claudette Colbert), as the princess whom Maurice Chevalier is told he must wed, in one of the French singer's charming musicals of the period, *The Smiling Lieutenant*. That part, along with the role of barmaid Ivy in the hit horror film *Dr. Jekyll and Mr. Hyde*, pushed Hopkins closer to full-fledged stardom.

After playing a taxi dancer in *Dancers in the Dark*, among other undistinguished fare, she ended up in one of the most sparkling of all 1930s comedies, Ernst Lubitsch's *Trouble in Paradise*, partnered with Herbert Marshall, as a jewel thief hoping to fleece Kay Francis. This was Hopkins at her best, and it helped to wash away the memory of two 1933 films that were reviled for trashing their original sources, *The Story of Temple Drake*, watered down from Theodore Dreiser's *Sanctuary*, yet still causing a stir among the censors with Hopkins leaving little to the imagination as a lady who is kidnapped, raped, and then falls into a life of degeneration; and *Design for Living*, a deadly dull adaptation of one of Noel Coward's most famous stage plays. Finishing her contract with Paramount, she played a rich woman involved with thief George Raft in the melodrama *All of Me*, and leading lady to Bing Crosby in *She Loves Me Not*, hiding out after witnessing a murder. She then went back to Broadway to star in *Jezebel*, which later became one of Bette Davis's most famous movie vehicles.

Samuel Goldwyn signed her up once she returned to Hollywood, but first he loaned her out to RKO for *Becky Sharp*. Her energetic performance, as William Thackeray's determined social climber, left critics and audiences sharply divided as to its merits, but it marked her one and only Oscar nomination. The movie did, however, find its place in history as the first three-strip Technicolor movie, which did not guarantee it box-office success. For Goldwyn, she was a dance-hall gal caught between Edward G. Robinson and Joel McCrea in *Barbary Coast*; McCrea's bride, marrying into his snooty family, in *Splendor*; a schoolteacher secretly in love with McCrea in *These Three*; and an architect with designs on McCrea in *Woman Chases Man*. The best of these was *These Three*, which distorted its original source, *The Children's Hour*, by dropping the lesbianism, but came up with a gripping adult drama nonetheless. This was her one peak during this period, after which she starred in some minor fare like the British *Men Are Not Gods*, and *Wise Girl*, with Ray Milland.

She went over to Warners to play a pair of secondary parts, in *The Old Maid*, with Bette Davis, with whom she most certainly did not get along, and the western *Virginia City*, with Errol Flynn. Two more leads, in *Lady With Red Hair*, as actress Mrs. Leslie Carter, and *Gentleman After Dark*, as Brian Donlevy's no-good wife, only showed that she was losing her leading-lady status. Her last success was once again opposite Bette Davis, playing her friendly rival, in *Old Acquaintance*, after which she retreated back to the stage. When she returned to movies, it was as a character player, doing a very efficient job as the foolish aunt in *The Heiress*. There were only a few more roles, but some were standouts, playing Gene Tierney's difficult mom in *The Mating Season*; Laurence Olivier's bitchy, destructive wife in *Carrie*; and another stupid lady, whose refusal to testify on Shirley MacLaine's behalf causes tragedy, in *The Children's Hour*. This, of course, was

These Three back in its original form, with the same director (William Wyler), and with Hopkins cast as the aunt of the character she had played the first time around. There were larger parts in an oft-banned version of *Fanny Hill* and in *Savage Intruder*, about a fading movie star, a film that was mostly seen, if at all, after her death of a heart attack in 1972. Her four husbands included (1937–39) director Anatole Litvak who had worked with her on *The Woman I Love*.

Screen: 1930: Fast and Loose; 1931: The Smiling Lieutenant; 24 Hours; 1932: Dr. Jekyll and Mr. Hyde; Two Kinds of Women; Dancers in the Dark; The World and the Flesh; Trouble in Paradise; 1933: The Story of Temple Drake; The Stranger's Return; Design for Living; 1934: All of Me; She Loves Me Not; The Richest Girl in the World; 1935: Becky Sharp; Barbary Coast; Splendor; 1936: These Three; 1937: Men Are Not Gods; The Woman I Love; Woman Chases Man; Wise Girl; 1939: The Old Maid; 1940: Virginia City; Lady With Red Hair; 1942: Gentleman After Dark; 1943: Old Acquaintance; 1949: The Heiress; 1951: The Mating Season; 1952: The Outcasts of Poker Flat; Carrie; 1961: The Children's Hour; 1965: Fanny Hill: Memoirs of a Woman of Pleasure; 1966: The Chase; 1976: Savage Intruder/The Comeback/Hollywood Horror Home (filmed 1968).

NY Stage: 1921: Music Box Revue; 1923: Little Jesse James; 1925: Puppets; Lovely Lady; 1926: The Matinee Girl; An American Tragedy; 1927: Thou Desperate Pilot; The Garden of Eden; Excess Baggage; 1929: Flight; The Camel Through the Needle's Eye; Ritzy; 1930: Lysistrata; His Majesty's Car; 1931: Anatol; 1933: Jezebel; 1943: The Skin of Our Teeth; 1944: The Perfect Marriage; 1947: A Message for Margaret; 1958: Look Homeward Angel.

Select TV: 1951: Ned McCobb's Daughter (sp); Long Distance (sp); 1954: Desert Crossing (sp); 1955: Sunset Boulevard (sp); Summer Pavilion (sp); 1957: Woman Alone (sp); 1962: A Very Special Girl (sp).

MICHAEL HORDERN

BORN: BERKHAMPSTEAD, ENGLAND, OCTOBER 3, 1911. ED: BRIGHTON COL. DIED: MAY 2, 1995.

Bulbous-nosed, balding Michael Hordern was one of those British players who seemed to be around forever, although it was not until he was well into his 50s that he began to find some of his most notable movie roles. Originally a teacher, he made his professional stage debut in 1937. Three years later he made his movie bow in a small part in the Margaret Lockwood drama *The Girl in the News*. During the 1950s his roles began to grow in size, with such parts as Marley's Ghost in *Scrooge/A Christmas Carol*; the inspector hoping to bring Nigel Patrick to justice in *Grand National Night/Wicked Wife*; and an island headman in *The Beachcomber*. He was used for comical effect in such military farces as *The Baby and the Battleship* and *Girls at Sea*, honing his befuddled buffoon characterization for which he would become best known. His best part to date came in 1956 with *The Spanish Gardener*, as the insecure diplomat who disapproves of his son's relationship with Dirk Bogarde. His participation in some major international productions of the 1960s increased audience awareness, including *Sink the Bismarck!*, *El Cid*, and *Cleopatra* (as Cicero). Director Richard Lester cast him to perfection in *A Funny Thing Happened on the Way to the Forum*, as the henpecked Sennex, after which he shone in *The Taming of the Shrew*, as Baptista; *Anne of the Thousand Days*, as Anne Boleyn's father; *England Made Me*, as a reporter; and *The Slipper and the Rose*, as the ditsy king. His distinctive, resonant voice was sometimes heard off screen, most notably as the narrator of Stanley Kubrick's *Barry Lyndon.* He was knighted in 1983.

Screen: 1940: The Girl in the News; 1946: The Years Between; A Girl in a Million; School for Secrets/Secret Flight; 1947: Mine Own Executioner; 1948: Third Time Lucky; Portrait From Life/The Girl in the Painting; The Small Voice/Hideout; 1949: Good Time Girl; Train of Events; Passport to Pimlico; 1950: The Astonished Heart; Trio; Highly Dangerous; Tom Brown's Schooldays; 1951: Flesh and Blood; The Magic Box; Scrooge/A Christmas Carol; 1952: The Card/The Promoter; The Story of Robin Hood and His Merrie Men; The Hour of 13; 1953: Street Corner/Both Sides of the Law; Wicked Wife/Grand National Night; The Heart of the Matter; Personal Affair; You Know What Sailors Are; 1954: The Beachcomber; Forbidden Cargo; 1955: The Night My Number Came Up; The Constant Husband; The Warriors/The Dark Avenger; Storm Over the Nile; 1956: Alexander the Great; The Man Who Never Was; Pacific Destiny; The Baby and the Battleship; The Spanish Gardener; 1957: No Time for Tears; 1958: I Accuse!; Windom's Way; The Spaniard's Curse; I Was Monty's Double; Girls at Sea; 1960: Sink the Bismarck!; Malaga/Moment of Danger; Man in the Moon; 1961: El Cid; 1963: Cleopatra; The V.I.P.s; 1964: The Yellow Rolls-Royce; 1965: Genghis Khan; The Spy Who Came in From the Cold; 1966: Cast a Giant Shadow; Khartoum; A Funny Thing Happened on the Way to the Forum; 1967: The Taming of the Shrew; The Jokers; How I Won the War; 1968: I'll Never Forget What's 'is Name; Prudence and the Pill; 1969: The Bed Sitting Room; Where Eagles Dare; Anne of the Thousand Days; 1970: Futtock's End; Some Will, Some Won't; 1971: Up Pompeii; Girl Stroke Boy; 1972: The Pied Piper; Demons of the Mind; The Possession of Joel Delaney; Alice's Adventures in Wonderland; 1973: England Made Me; Theater of Blood; The Mackintosh Man; 1974: Juggernaut; 1975: Mr. Quilp; Royal Flash; Barry Lyndon (narrator); Lucky Lady; 1976: The Slipper and the Rose; 1977: Joseph Andrews; 1978: The Medusa Touch; Watership Down (voice); 1980: The Wildcats of St. Trinian's; 1982: The Missionary; Gandhi; 1983: Yellowbeard; 1984: Boxer (narrator); 1985: Young Sherlock Holmes (narrator); 1986: Lady Jane; Labyrinth (voice); 1987: The Trouble With Spies (filmed 1984); 1988: Comrades; 1991: Dark Obsession/Diamond Skulls; The Fool; 1992: Freddie as F.R.O.7 (voice).

NY Stage: 1959: Moonbirds.

Select TV: 1955: The Merchant of Venice (sp); 1959: Oliver Twist (sp); 1960: Macbeth (sp); 1963: Dr. Syn: Alias the Scarecrow (theatrical in UK); 1966: Lamp at Midnight (sp); 1971: Don Juan in Hell (sp); Tartuffe (sp); 1975: King Lear (sp); Edward the King (sp); 1980: Gaugin the Savage; Shogun (ms); 1982: Oliver Twist; 1984: The Zany Adventures of Robin Hood; 1987: Scoop; The Secret Garden; 1988: Suspicion; 1989: Danny, the Champion of the World; 1992: Memento Mori (sp).

LENA HORNE

BORN: BROOKLYN, NY, JUNE 30, 1917.

Despite the movies' mistreatment of her, the ethereally beautiful Lena Horne, with the inimitably lucid singing voice, still managed to become one of the most widely hailed talents of the 20th century. Abandoned by her father as a child, she traveled with her mother, who was a performer. In time Lena took an interest in the business, debuting as a chorus girl at the famed Cotton Club in Harlem. There were similar jobs on Broadway in *Dance With Your Gods* and *Blackbirds of 1939*; she had a role in an all-black feature, *The Duke Is Tops*; and did some vocalizing with the Charlie Barnett band. It was

while performing at Cafe Society Downtown in New York that she was discovered by MGM musical supervisor Roger Edens. The studio signed her to a contract in 1941 and put her in two numbers ("Just One of Those Things" and "The Spring") in their adaptation of Cole Porter's *Panama Hattie*, but didn't let her blend in with the plot. Furthermore, they allowed racist theater owners to hack out her segments in unwelcoming areas of the country, and used makeup to lighten her already light skin tone, all of which was a bad omen of her tenure at the studio. There was, however, an all-black musical production, Vincente Minnelli's lively rendering of the stage hit *Cabin in the Sky*, where she had her best screen part, as the temptress sent by Satan to steer Eddie Anderson wrong. It was another all-black production, made on loan to 20th Century-Fox, that would allow her to sing what would become her signature song, the title number of *Stormy Weather*, a movie that was almost all tunes and little plot, the latter aspect being carried by Horne and Bill "Bojangles" Robinson.

At Metro, it was back to glorified guest appearances, including *Two Girls and a Sailor*, singing "Paper Doll;" *Ziegfeld Follies*, sizzling through "Love;" and *Words and Music*, getting two great Rodgers and Hart hits, "Where or When" and "The Lady Is a Tramp" (another of her key songs). The closest she came to the role she was born to play, the tragic Julie in *Show Boat*, was in the lengthy prologue to the Jerome Kern biopic *Till the Clouds Roll By*, but when the time came for the studio to actually film the whole musical, in 1951, they chickened out and gave the part to Ava Gardner. Turning her back on all this insulting nonsense, she continued to create magic in nightclubs, on albums, and in television appearances. There was a hit Broadway musical, *Jamaica*, in 1957, and a semi-breakthrough motion picture part, post-civil rights, in her first movie in some time, *Death of a Gunfighter*, as Richard Widmark's mistress. After another long absence, she was coaxed back to the movies by her then-son-in-law, director Sidney Lumet, for a scene-stealing bit as Glinda the Good Witch in the all-black musical *The Wiz*. In 1981 which she scored an unprecedented smash with her one-woman Broadway show, *Lena Horne: The Lady and Her Music*, which fully captured Horne's great artistry.

Screen: 1938: The Dukes Is Tops; 1942: Panama Hattie; 1943: Cabin in the Sky; Stormy Weather; I Dood It; Thousands Cheer; Swing Fever; 1944: Broadway Rhythm; Two Girls and a Sailor; 1946: Ziegfeld Follies; 1947: Till the Clouds Roll By; 1948: Words and Music; 1950: Duchess of Idaho; 1956: Meet Me in Las Vegas; 1969: Death of a Gunfighter; 1978: The Wiz; 1994: That's Entertainment! III.

NY Stage: 1934: Dance With Your Gods; 1939: Blackbirds of 1939; 1957: Jamaica; 1974: Tony Bennett & Lena Horne Sing; 1981: Lena Horne: The Lady and Her Music.

EDWARD EVERETT HORTON

BORN: BROOKLYN, NY, MARCH 18, 1886. ED: COLUMBIA UNIV. DIED: SEPTEMBER 29, 1970.

Like many of the great character players, beak-nosed, pained-looking Edward Everett Horton never strayed too far from his patented shtick, which suited audiences just fine. The jittery-voiced actor was usually the nervous ("Oh, dear!" was a stock response), duped dummy who would find himself insulted or sassed, only to reply most cordially to the affirmative, stopping himself in mid-sentence when awareness had set in, replying with an exasperated "now see here." Dropping out of college, he joined a Staten Island stock company specializing in Gilbert and Sullivan, then made his Broadway debut in 1908 in *The Man Who Stood Still*. There was possibly some extra or bit work in movies, but his first recorded appearance seems to be in 1922's *The Ladder Jinx*, as a bank teller. The next year he landed the lead in the 1923 version of *Ruggles of Red Gap*, a property made more famous by Charles Laughton 12 years later. This was followed by additional star parts in *To the Ladies*, *Try and Get It*, and the film adaptation of the stage hit *Beggar on Horseback*, as a composer torn between two women. Though busy on screen, he took the time to form his own stage company, which operated in Los Angeles. As the talkies came, he was appearing as frequently in two-reelers as he was in features.

At Warner Bros. his days as a leading attraction came to a halt after *The Hottentot*, as a horse fan who winds up a reluctant jockey, and *Wide Open*, as a man in love with his boss's daughter. In 1930 he appeared in *Holiday*, playing the hero's friend, Nick Potter, so successfully that he was asked to repeat his performance in the better-known Cary Grant-Katharine Hepburn remake in 1938. The pivotal role of the prissy feature writer, in whose desk the accused murderer, hides in the first film version of *The Front Page*, supplied Horton with the basis for his new career as a supporting fuss-budget par excellence. After taking time off to star in the West Coast production of *Springtime for Henry* (which he would play off and on for two decades), he was back on screen helping Maurice Chevalier take care of Baby LeRoy in *A Bedtime Story*; trying to remember where he'd seen Herbert Marshall before in *Trouble in Paradise*; and landing one of the few roles in the 1933 production of *Alice in Wonderland* that didn't entirely obscure a cast member with makeup, the Mad Hatter.

Then the best thing yet happened to Horton when he was cast as Fred Astaire's lawyer friend in *The Gay Divorcee*, which not only gave him a delightful number with Betty Grable, "Let's Knock K-nees," but paved the way for him to shine even more so in two other Fred Astaire-Ginger Rogers gems, *Top Hat* and *Shall We Dance*, in the latter finding great laughs with comic foil Eric Blore while memorably trying to shush a theatre audience. There were unsuitable roles, like the Spanish police chief in *The Devil Is a Woman*, and perfect ones, like the timid paleontologist who falls in love with Shangri-La in *Lost Horizon*. His popularity as a bright supporting player meant there were occasions when Horton found himself returning to top-billing, appearing in some vehicles made on the cheap, including *Your Uncle Dudley*, as a citizen putting the good of his community before his business and thereby incurring debt; *His Night Out*, as a hypochondriac; and *Her Master's Voice*, as a fake butler.

In the 1940s he was seen to good effect as Messenger 7013 in the highly popular fantasy *Here Comes Mr. Jordan*, and as the head of the funny farm in the energetic adaptation of the stage smash *Arsenic and Old Lace*. He was brought on board in hopes of brightening up some limp musicals like *Ziegfeld Girl*, *Springtime in the Rockies*, and *The Gang's All Here*, but the material just wasn't there. In 1944 he was surprisingly cast in a serious role, as a decadent nobleman in *Summer Storm*, but the film barely caused a ripple. Republic Pictures gave him one last screen lead in a poverty-row production, *Steppin' in Society*, in 1945, two years after which he decided to devote himself to the stage again. His later movie roles were fairly small, although he was part of the distinguished supporting cast of *Pocketful of Miracles*, as a proper butler. Looking quite frail, Horton had a recurring role as an Indian medicine man named Roaring Chicken on the 1960s TV series *F Troop*, and had passed away by the time his final movie, *Cold Turkey* (in which he didn't utter a single line), was released. A street in Encino, where part of his estate, Belleigh ("Belly") Acres, once stood, bears his name.

Screen: AS EDWARD HORTON: 1922: The Ladder Jinx; Too Much Business; A Front Page Story; 1923: Ruggles of Red Gap; To the Ladies; 1924: Try and Get It; Flapper Wives.

AS EDWARD EVERETT HORTON: 1924: The Man Who Fights Alone; Helen's Babies; 1925: Marry Me; Beggar on Horseback; The Business of Love; 1926: La Boheme; The Nut-Cracker; Poker Faces; The Whole Town's Talking; 1927: Taxi! Taxi!; 1928: The Terror; 1929: Sonny Boy; The Hottentot; The Sap; The Aviator; 1930: Take the Heir; Wide Open; Holiday; Once a Gentleman; Reaching for the Moon; 1931: Kiss Me Again; Lonely Wives; The Front Page; Six Cylinder Love; Smart Woman; The Age for Love; 1932: But the Flesh Is Weak; Roar of the Dragon; Trouble in Paradise; 1933: It's a Boy; A Bedtime Story; The Way to Love; Design for Living; Alice in Wonderland; 1934: The Woman in Command/Soldiers of the King; Easy to Love; Sing and Like It; The Poor Rich; Smarty; All the King's Horses; Success at Any Price; Uncertain Lady; Kiss and Make Up; The Merry Widow; Ladies Should Listen; The Gay Divorcee; 1935: The Private Secretary; Biography of a Bachelor Girl; The Night Is Young; The Devil Is a Woman; Your Uncle Dudley; In Caliente; Ten Dollar Raise; Going Highbrow; Little Big Shot; Top Hat; His Night Out; 1936: The Singing Kid; Her Master's Voice; Hearts Divided; Nobody's Fool; Man in the Mirror; 1937: The King and the Chorus Girl; Let's Make a Million; Lost Horizon; Shall We Dance; Oh Doctor!; Wild Money; Angel; The Perfect Specimen; Danger — Love at Work; The Great Garrick; Hitting a New High; 1938: Bluebeard's Eighth Wife; College Swing; Holiday; Little Tough Guys in Society; 1939: Paris Honeymoon; That's Right — You're Wrong; The Amazing Mr. Forrest/The Gang's All Here; 1941: You're the One; Ziegfeld Girl; Sunny; Bachelor Daddy; Here Comes Mr. Jordan; Weekend for Three; The Body Disappears; 1942: I Married an Angel; The Magnificent Dope; Springtime in the Rockies; 1943: Forever and a Day; Thank Your Lucky Stars; The Gang's All Here; 1944: Summer Storm; Her Primitive Man; San Diego, I Love You; Arsenic and Old Lace; Brazil; The Town Went Wild; 1945: Steppin' in Society; Lady on a Train; 1946: Cinderella Jones; Faithful in My Fashion; Earl Carroll Sketchbook; 1947: The Ghost Goes Wild; Down to Earth; Her Husband's Affairs; 1957: The Story of Mankind; 1961: Pocketful of Miracles; 1963: It's a Mad Mad Mad Mad World; 1964: Sex and the Single Girl; 1967: The Perils of Pauline; 1969: 2,000 Years Later; 1971: Cold Turkey.

NY Stage: 1908: The Man Who Stood Still; 1910: The Cheater; 1912: Elevating a Husband; The Governor's Lady; 1951: Springtime for Henry; 1965: Carousel.

Select TV: 1950: Holiday Hotel (series); Father Dear Father (sp); 1952: The Nightcap (sp); 1953: Whistling in the Dark (sp); The Front Page (sp); The Canterville Ghost (sp); Arsenic and Old Lace (sp); 1955: The Merry Widow (sp); Time Out for Ginger (sp); 1956: Manhattan Tower (sp); 1957: Three Men on a Horse (sp); 1961–62: The Bullwinkle Show (series; voice).

JOHN HOWARD

(JOHN R. COX, JR.) BORN: CLEVELAND, OH, APRIL 14, 1913. ED: WESTERN RESERVE UNIV. DIED: FEBRUARY 19, 1995.

Sly looking John Howard had little to distinguish him from a hundred other serviceable actors of his day, although he did attach himself to a famed series of detective films. It was while performing dramatic readings on the radio during college that he received an offer of a contract from Paramount Pictures. He debuted for them in 1935 under the name "John Cox, Jr." in *Car 99*, then changed his name to John Howard for his third movie appearance, in *Annapolis Farewell*. In 1937 Columbia and Frank Capra cast him in the role of Ronald Colman's selfish brother in the classic fantasy *Lost Horizon*, which gave someone back at Paramount the idea of Howard continuing the role Colman had made famous, intrepid investigator Bulldog Drummond. It was for this series that Howard grew his moustache, and his sleuthing chores began with *Bulldog Drummond Comes Back*, in 1937 and ended with *Arrest Bulldog Drummond*, in 1939. These were "B" features, as were many of the actor's other leads, such as *Touchdown Army*, as a West Point quarterback, and *Prison Farm*, as that institution's doctor. He was requested by director George Cukor to appear in support in perhaps his most famous film, *The Philadelphia Story*, in the most unappetizing part in the piece, George Kittridge, Katharine Hepburn's bland, foolish fiancé whom the audience waits eagerly for her to dump. When TV came he starred in the dramatic series *Dr. Hudson's Secret Journal*. By the 1970s he had given up acting to teach English at a high school in the San Fernando Valley.

Screen: AS JOHN COX, JR.: **1935:** Car 99; Four Hours to Kill!

AS JOHN HOWARD: **1935:** Annapolis Farewell; Millions in the Air; **1936:** Soak the Rich; Thirteen Hours by Air; Border Flight; Easy to Take; Valiant Is the Word for Carrie; **1937:** Let Them Live; Mountain Music; Hold 'em Navy; Hitting a New High; Lost Horizon; Bulldog Drummond Comes Back; Bulldog Drummond's Revenge; **1938:** Penitentiary; Touchdown Army; Bulldog Drummond's Peril; Bulldog Drummond in Africa; Prison Farm; **1939:** Bulldog Drummond's Secret Police; Disputed Passage; Bulldog Drummond's Bride; Grand Jury Secrets; What a Life; Arrest Bulldog Drummond; **1940:** Green Hell; The Man From Dakota; Texas Rangers Ride Again; The Philadelphia Story; The Invisible Woman; **1941:** The Mad Doctor; Father Takes a Wife; Tight Shoes; Three Girls About Town; **1942:** A Tragedy at Midnight; The Man Who Returned to Life; Submarine Raider; Isle of Missing Men; The Undying Monster; **1947:** Love From a Stranger; **1948:** Le Bataillon du Ciel/They Are Not Angels (nUSr); I, Jane Doe; **1949:** The Fighting Kentuckian; **1950:** Experiment Alcatraz; Radar Secret Service; **1952:** Models, Inc.; **1954:** Make Haste to Live; The High and the Mighty; **1957:** The Unknown Terror; **1966:** Destination Inner Space; **1968:** The Destructors; So Evil My Sister/Le Sorelle; **1975:** Capone.

NY Stage: **1953:** Hazel Flagg.

Select TV: **1951:** Crawford Mystery Theatre (series); **1955–57:** Dr. Hudson's Secret Journal (series); **1958–59:** The Adventures of the Sea Hawk (series); **1965–67:** My Three Sons (series).

LESLIE HOWARD

(LESLIE HOWARD STAINER) BORN: LONDON, ENGLAND, APRIL 3, 1893. ED: DULWICH COL. DIED: JUNE 2, 1943.

Leslie Howard's cultivated sensitivity belonged very much to a bygone era. His range took him from drawing-room comedy to Shakespeare to heavy soap opera, and he brought an intelligence and respect for the spoken word to all of it. Prior to serving in World War I, he worked as a banker, but changed his mind while recuperating from a war wound and joined a theatrical company. He toured in *Peg o' My Heart* and got small parts in two silent features and the leads in two short subjects, "Five Pounds Reward" and "Bookworms" (both 1920). He received an offer to appear on Broadway in *Just Suppose*, in 1920, and it was on the American stage that he was to create a name for himself during the next decade, with the hits *Aren't We All?*, *Outward Bound*, *Her Cardboard Lover*, and *Berkeley Square*, which he also directed and

produced, triumphing in London with it as well. (He would also write two plays in which he did not appear, *Out of a Blue Sky*, which he also directed, in 1930, and *Elizabeth Sleeps Out*, in 1935). When Warners decided to film *Outward Bound* in 1930, they asked for Howard as part of the package, although he played a different character than he had on Broadway (the drunk, as opposed to the young lover, now played by Douglas Fairbanks, Jr.). It was a performance too theatrical in technique, but he was nonetheless an arresting film presence.

MGM offered him a contract, and he did four films for them. He was pretty much left along the wayside in the 1931 hit *A Free Soul*, which was dominated by Norma Shearer and Lionel Barrymore, in his Oscar-winning role, and he wasn't given the choicest of material with two forgettable melodramas, *Never the Twain Shall Meet*, having a forbidden love for island girl Conchita Montenegro, and *Five and Ten*, falling for spoiled heiress Marion Davies. He took third billing to Norma Shearer and Fredric March in one of the smashes of 1932, *Smilin' Through*, but they were all defeated by the slushy material, with Howard hidden under white hair and old-age makeup, disapproving floridly of niece Norma's love for March. He went back to the stage in 1932 and scored again with *The Animal Kingdom*. RKO recorded it for posterity and released it by the end of that same year. It turned out to be the best Howard on film so far, with the actor playing a man regretting his marriage to Myrna Loy when his former lover, Ann Harding, reenters his life. This was the sort of witty, incisive material that he excelled at, as was another adaptation of his stage work, *Berkeley Square*, made for Fox, where he was transported back in time to 1784. It earned him his first Oscar nomination. He was well cast as the club-footed doctor obsessed with slut Bette Davis in *Of Human Bondage*, although this was an extremely truncated version of Somerset Maugham's lengthy and brilliant novel. A second teaming with Davis fared better, *The Petrified Forest*, with Howard once again repeating a role he had done on Broadway, the wandering poet who comes face to face with the brutish Humphrey Bogart at a lonely roadside station. He was superb in a role tailor-made for his talents, and the film remains one of his best.

In the meantime, he had returned to Britain for *The Scarlet Pimpernel*, playing the foppish Sir Percy who leads a double life, rescuing revolutionaries from the guillotine. Back in Hollywood it was a joy to hear him speaking the words of the Bard in the respectable MGM version of *Romeo and Juliet*, although he was absurdly overage at 43 to be playing the part of the tragic young teenage lover. At Warners, where he was under contract, he showed his flair for comedy with *It's Love I'm After*, hilariously energetic as an arrogant actor battling with wife Bette Davis, and then he paired up delightfully with Joan Blondell in the independently produced *Stand In*, as a straight-arrow financial analyst who winds up running a movie studio. In England, where he had formed his own company, he co-directed himself in what would turn out to be his greatest film role, the snobbish, sharp-witted Henry Higgins in the 1938 adaptation of Shaw's *Pygmalion*. Howard was so good that he actually makes it possible to temporarily forget Rex Harrison's perfection in the part years later. The film was one of the best British efforts of the decade, earning a second Oscar nomination for Howard and winning the screenplay adaptation award for Shaw himself. This was followed by the role that future film audiences would most readily identify him with, Ashley Wilkes, in the mightiest epic of them all, *Gone With the Wind*. He was not comfortable in the part, however, initially refusing the role and showing little interest in it during production. In the end he was never less than professional in his performance, but was probably the character subsequent audiences found least engaging.

He was far more at home with *Intermezzo*, as the violinist who can't help falling in love with his child's piano tutor, Ingrid Bergman. Howard was not only the rare star who really did seem like he could play the violin, but he also kept his character both sympathetic and understandable as he engaged in this doomed affair. After that he returned to Britain, hoping to keep that country's film industry afloat during World War II. As producer and director, he played a variation on an old role in *Pimpernel Smith*, professor by day/spy by night; and he directed himself in *Spitfire/The First of the Few*, portraying the man who invented the famed fighter plane of the title. He stayed behind the cameras for *The Gentle Sex*, co-directing, producing, and narrating, and *The Lamp Still Burns*, producing only. As actor only, he appeared in an extended cameo, as a camper confronting fleeing Nazi Eric Portman, in a major propaganda piece, *49th Parallel*. It was shown in a shortened form in the U.S. as *The Invaders*, and wound up with an Oscar nomination in the Best Picture category. Sadly, Howard (along with Carole Lombard) became one of the industry's most-famous wartime casualties when his plane was shot down while he was on his way back from a meeting in Lisbon. The movies, on either side of the Atlantic, could have continued to benefit from his panache. His son, Ronald Howard (1916–96), enjoyed a certain level of success in British films.

Screen: 1917: The Happy Warrior; 1919: The Lackey and the Lady; 1930: Outward Bound; 1931: A Free Soul; Never the Twain Shall Meet; Five and Ten; Devotion; 1932: Reserved for Ladies/Service for Ladies; Smilin' Through; The Animal Kingdom; 1933: Secrets; Captured!; Berkeley Square; 1934: The Lady Is Willing; Of Human Bondage; British Agent; 1935: The Scarlet Pimpernel; 1936: The Petrified Forest; Romeo and Juliet; 1937: It's Love I'm After; Stand-In; 1938: Pygmalion (and co-dir.); 1939: Intermezzo (and assoc. prod.); Gone With the Wind; 1942: Pimpernel Smith/Mister V (and dir.; prod.); 49th Parallel/The Invaders; Spitfire/The First of the Few (and dir.); 1943: The Gentle Sex (narrator; and co-dir.; prod.).

NY Stage: 1920: Just Suppose; 1921: The Wren; Danger; 1922: The Truth About Blayds; A Serpent's Tooth; The Romantic Age; The Lady Cristilinda; 1923: Anything Might Happen; Aren't We All?; 1924: Outward Bound; The Werewolf; 1925: Shall We Join the Ladies?; Isabel; The Green Hat; 1927: Her Cardboard Lover; Murray Hill (and dir.; wr.); Escape; 1929: Candle Light; Berkeley Square (and dir.; prod.); 1932: The Animal Kingdom (and prod.); 1933: This Side Idolatry (and prod.); 1934: The Petrified Forest (and prod.); 1936: Hamlet (and dir.; prod.).

RON HOWARD
BORN: DUNCAN, OK, MARCH 1, 1954.

Americans saw fresh-faced, boyish Ron Howard grow up right on their TV and movie screens, which brought him a warm following, and then watched him mature into an accomplished film director, which brought him glowing admiration. The son of actors Rance and Jean Howard, he made his acting debut with them at age two, in a production of *The Seven Year Itch*, at Baltimore's Hilltop Theatre. As "Ronny Howard" he was soon appearing all over television and in a minor part in the 1959 film *The Journey*, as Anne Jackson's son. The following year he entered the public consciousness in a strong way, playing the bright and ingratiating offspring of sheriff Andy Taylor on the sitcom *The Andy Griffith Show*. Memorably named Opie, he aged from 6 to 14 as the show ran through most of the 1960s. During its run he acted winningly

as the lisping Winthrop Paroo in the classic musical *The Music Man*, giving his unforgettable rendition of "Gary, Indiana;" as the motherless Eddie, trying to find a mate for dad Glenn Ford in the pleasant MGM comedy *The Courtship of Eddie's Father*; and as the kid scientist who makes the bad teens grow to enormous proportions in one of the all-time wonderfully awful movies, *Village of the Giants*.

As the 1970s came, he played a pioneer teen in one of Disney's least-successful movies of this period, *The Wild Country*, and Cloris Leachman's abused son in the thriller *Happy Mother's Day, Love George*. Then he got himself into the ensemble of a highly worthwhile film, *American Graffiti*, as the popular teen having romantic troubles with his sweetheart Cindy Williams, in this hauntingly atmospheric glimpse of a past era (1962). The movie's enormous popularity led to the TV series on which he would next count the passing years, *Happy Days*, a superficial look at the 1950s with Howard as all-American nice guy Richie Cunningham. It became one of the longest running sitcoms in the history of television. During its time on the air, he had a good role as the lad who hero worships aging gunfighter John Wayne in *The Shootist*, and the lead in a bit of prime drive-in fare, the memorably titled *Eat My Dust!* That one did well enough for its intended market, so Howard asked its producer, Roger Corman, if he could direct as well as star in the 1977 follow-up, *Grand Theft Auto*, thereby making his debut in this capacity. Back on television he directed the films *Cotton Candy* (and co-wr.; 1978), *Skyward* (and co-exec. prod.; 1980), and *Through the Magic Pyramid* (1981; and exec. prod.), having decided that this was the course he wanted his career to take, if only he could land more important, big-screen projects.

Working strictly behind the camera, he helmed *Night Shift* (1982), a mixed bag about a mortuary-turned-whorehouse, with his *Happy Days* co-star Henry Winkler, which did better on cable than in theaters. The one that really set him on the right path was *Splash* (1984), about a mermaid in Manhattan, which was directed with the right touch of fantasy and romance and resulted in a huge hit. The next, the witty and touching sci-fi *Cocoon* (1985), did even better, making him one of the most in-demand of all 1980s directors. His commercial sense was impeccable, and, in addition to these, the best of his efforts were *Parenthood* (1989), a very funny ensemble capturing the pains and joys of families, for which he also co-wrote the story; *The Paper* (1994), a fast-moving look at New York journalism; *Apollo 13* (1995), a gripping dramatization of the near-disastrous space trip (nominated for the Oscar for Best Picture of 1995); *Ransom* (1996), an exciting remake of an old Glenn Ford kidnapping thriller; and *A Beautiful Mind*, the fictionalized story of scientist John Nash's battle with schizophrenia. The last was an example of something potentially un-commercial made perfectly acceptable to mainstream audiences and Howard wound up with a pair of Oscars, for Best Director and Best Picture. His other directorial credits were *Gung Ho* (and exec. prod.; 1986); *Willow* (1988); *Backdraft* (1991); *Far and Away* (and co-story, prod.; 1992); *Ed TV* (and prod.; 1999); and *Dr. Seuss's How the Grinch Stole Christmas* (and prod.; 2000), his poorest effort and biggest moneymaker.

With Brian Glazer he founded Imagine Entertainment, which produced his films. For them he has served as executive producer or producer on several titles he did not direct: *Leo and Lance* (1980), *No Man's Land* (1987), *Clean and Sober* (1988), *Vibes* (1988), *The 'Burbs* (1989), *Closet Land* (1991), *The Chamber* (1996), *Inventing the Abbotts* (1997), and *Beyond the Mat* (1999). His younger brother, Clint Howard, has appeared in most of his films, as has his dad.

Screen: AS RONNY HOWARD: 1959: The Journey; 1961: Door-to-

Door Maniac/Five Minutes to Live; **1962:** The Music Man; **1963:** The Courtship of Eddie's Father; **1965:** Village of the Giants; **1971:** The Wild Country; **1973:** American Graffiti.

AS RON HOWARD: 1973: Happy Mother's Day, Love George/Run, Stranger, Run; **1974:** The Spikes Gang; **1976:** The First Nudie Musical; Eat My Dust!; The Shootist; **1977:** Grand Theft Auto (and dir.; co-wr.); **1979:** More American Graffiti; **1980:** Roger Corman: Hollywood's Wild Angel; **1992:** The Magical World of Chuck Jones; **2001:** Osmosis Jones (voice); The Independent.

Select TV: 1959: Black December (sp); **1960–68:** The Andy Griffith Show (series); **1961:** Tippy-Top (sp); **1967:** A Boy Called Nuthin' (sp); **1970:** Smoke (sp); **1971–72:** The Smith Family (series); **1974:** The Migrants; Locusts; **1974–80:** Happy Days (series); **1975:** Huckleberry Finn; **1980:** Act of Love; **1981:** Bitter Harvest; Fire on the Mountain; **1986:** Return to Mayberry.

TREVOR HOWARD

(TREVOR HOWARD-SMITH) BORN: CLIFTONVILLE, KENT, ENGLAND, SEPTEMBER 29, 1913. ED: RADA. DIED: JANUARY 7, 1988.

Without pretension or show, gruff-voiced, crag-faced Trevor Howard was undeniably one of the strongest, most consistently excellent actors England had to offer, making his mark as a star, minus conventional good looks; sometimes working as a supporting player, while usually showing up the better-known leads. His professional stage debut came in 1934, in Revolt in a Reformatory. Over the next ten years he was seen without great success in the West End and at Stratford-upon-Avon. After being wounded while serving with the Royal Artillery during World War II, he starred in London in A Soldier for Christmas, with Helen Cherry, whom he married in 1944. From this play he got his first film roles, in The Way Ahead and The Way to the Stars, in both cases playing military officers. It was his third film that made him a star, Brief Encounter, the most sophisticated of all screen love stories, tastefully written by Noel Coward and played with great intelligence and conviction by Howard, as the married doctor who falls for married Celia Johnson. Thanks to its tremendous success, he was featured in some of the better-known British productions of the late 1940s: The Adventuress/I See a Dark Stranger, as a naval officer convincing Deborah Kerr not to hate the British; So Well Remembered, as an alcoholic doctor; and The Third Man, shrewd and intimidating as the British liaison officer. This last one, which became one of the most acclaimed British exports of its day, was directed by Carol Reed and written by Graham Greene. For Reed, Howard did Outcast of the Islands, as an embezzler taken to a remote trading post in the Far East where his life falls apart, and, working again from Greene material, there came The Heart of the Matter, with Howard giving one of his most-admired performances, as the hated Sierra Leone deputy police commissioner Scobie, who has an affair with a refugee (Maria Schell). It was Howard's own favorite of his films.

By the end of the 1950s he had accepted an offer for a Hollywood film, the remake of The Most Dangerous Game, now called Run for the Sun, playing the villain, hunting down writer Richard Widmark. Roles in international productions like The Key, as a tugboat captain who becomes one of Sophia Loren's lovers, and The Roots of Heaven, as an idealist trying to protect a herd of elephants from poachers, made him that much better known in the U.S. His excellence was at last noted by Hollywood when he received an Oscar nomination for his solid work as the angry and brutish alcoholic father in the acceptable adaptation of D.H. Lawrence's Sons and Lovers, easily the film's best performance.

He also came through superbly in the troubled remake of Mutiny on the Bounty, as the cruel and stubborn Captain Bligh, a subtler interpretation than Charles Laughton's in the original but memorable nonetheless.

Then it was back to stalwart support, often as military men, as in Father Goose, as the Australian naval commander enlisting the help of beach bum Cary Grant; the exciting Von Ryan's Express, in which he and Frank Sinatra played off one another splendidly; The Charge of the Light Brigade, as an arrogant and determined British general; and Battle of Britain, one of several star cameos that added up to naught. He started out the 1970s with an excellent performance, as the village priest in the lengthy epic Ryan's Daughter, from David Lean, who had directed him in Brief Encounter so many years before. He was called on for many costume and period pictures, including Mary, Queen of Scots, as Lord Burleigh; the remake of Kidnapped; Pope Joan, as Pope Leo; and Ludwig, as Richard Wagner. As he grew older he did his guest bits in a occasional decent film like Superman, as a Krypton elder, or Gandhi, as a judge, but for the most part he steadfastly carried on through mountains of junk or barely-released productions, including Who?, as a Soviet spy; The Bawdy Adventures of Tom Jones, as Squire Western, following in the mighty footsteps of Hugh Griffith; Hurricane, once again as a village priest, the role played by C. Aubrey Smith the first, better time around; Sword of the Valiant, as King Arthur; and The Unholy, as a holy man again, only this time minus sight. Among these was a top-billed role as an Indian returned from the dead in a curio, Windwalker, which was spoken in the Cheyenne and Crow languages, and he was one of the thoughtless aristocrats residing in Kenya in the kinky White Mischief, where he, thankfully, was not asked to participate in the cross-dressing party scene.

Screen: 1944: The Way Ahead; **1945:** The Way to the Stars/ Johnny in the Clouds; **1946:** Brief Encounter; The Adventuress/ I See a Dark Stranger; Green for Danger; **1947:** So Well Remembered; I Became a Criminal/They Made Me a Fugitive; **1948:** One Woman's Story/Passionate Friends; **1949:** The Third Man; The Golden Salamander; **1950:** Odette; The Clouded Yellow; **1951:** Outcast of the Islands; Lady Godiva Rides Again; **1952:** Glory at Sea/Gift Horse; **1953:** The Heart of the Matter; The Stranger's Hand; Les Amants du Tage/The Lovers of Lisbon; **1955:** Cockleshell Heroes; **1956:** Run for the Sun; Around the World in Eighty Days; **1957:** Interpol/Pickup Alley; Stowaway Girl/Manuela; **1958:** The Key; The Roots of Heaven; **1960:** Malaga/Moment of Danger; Sons and Lovers; **1962:** Mutiny on the Bounty; The Lion; **1964:** Man in the Middle; Father Goose; **1965:** Operation Crossbow; Von Ryan's Express; Morituri; **1966:** The Liquidator; **1967:** Triple Cross; The Long Duel; A Matter of Innocence/Pretty Polly; **1968:** The Charge of the Light Brigade; **1969:** Battle of Britain; **1970:** Lola/Twinky; Ryan's Daughter; **1971:** The Night Visitor; Catch Me a Spy/To Catch a Spy; Mary, Queen of Scots; **1972:** Kidnapped; Pope Joan; **1973:** Ludwig; The Offence; A Doll's House; **1974:** Craze; 11 Harrowhouse; Persecution/The Terror of Sheba; **1975:** Hennessy; Conduct Unbecoming; **1976:** The Bawdy Adventures of Tom Jones; Eliza Fraser; Albino/Whispering Death; **1977:** Slavers; The Last Remake of Beau Geste; Aces High; **1978:** Who? (filmed 1974); Stevie; Superman; **1979:** Hurricane; Meteor; **1980:** Sir Henry at Rawlinson End; Windwalker; **1981:** The Sea Wolves; Light Years Away; **1982:** The Missionary; Gandhi; **1984:** Sword of the Valiant; **1985:** Dust; **1986:** Foreign Body; **1988:** White Mischief; The Dawning; The Unholy.

Select TV: 1954: Tonight at 8:30 (sp); **1956:** Flower of Pride (sp); **1959:** Muder in Gratitude (sp); **1960:** The Hiding Place (sp); **1963:** The Invincible Mr. Disraeli (sp); Hedda Gabler (sp); **1965:**

Eagle in a Cage (sp); **1966:** The Poppy Is Also a Flower; **1973:** Catholics; **1976:** The Count of Monte Cristo; **1980:** The Shillingbury Blowers/... And the Band Played On (sp); Staying On (sp); **1981:** A Country of Old Men (sp); Inside the Third Reich; Deadly Game; **1984:** George Washington (ms); **1985:** Time After Time; **1986:** Peter the Great (ms); Shaka Zulu; Christmas Eve.

ROCHELLE HUDSON

Born: Oklahoma City, OK, March 6, 1914. Died: January 17, 1972.

A small and attractive ingénue, with an intrinsic timidity that kept her from over-shadowing most anyone with whom shared the screen, Rochelle Hudson entered motion pictures at the age of 16, working for RKO. Her first starring role came outside the studio with the independently produced *Savage Girl*, in which she was a lost youngster raised in the jungle. Shortly afterwards she joined Fox/20th Century-Fox, where she was usually relegated to the "B" unit. There she was held captive by some kidnappers in *Show Them No Mercy*; loved a Mountie (Paul Kelly) in *The Country Beyond*; played a spoiled rich girl in *Everbody's Old Man*; and conned people for food money in the Jack Haley comedy *She Had to Eat*. On a decidedly higher budget, she could be seen being upstaged by Shirley Temple in *Curly Top*, and by the Dionne quintuplets in *Reunion*. It was in four movies done elsewhere that she received some of her best-known parts: Paramount's *She Done Him Wrong*, as the young runaway who winds up under Mae West's wing; Universal's *Imitation of Life*, as Claudette Colbert's daughter, falling in love with her mother's suitor, Warren William; UA's *Les Misérables*, as Cosette, in the best of the many screen adaptations of the classic novel; and another for Paramount, *Poppy*, at her most appealing as the daughter of irascible circus performer W.C. Fields. During the 1940s she moved over to Columbia's cheapie unit, then to the real poverty-row outlets, finishing up her leading-lady days in the Lippert production *Sky Liner*, in 1949. Due to increasing health problems, she limited her movie appearances thereafter, her most notable later role being Natalie Wood's ineffectual mom in *Rebel Without a Cause*. During World War II she and her husband had been stationed in Central America where they worked for Naval Intelligence.

Screen: **1931:** Laugh and Get Rich; Fanny Foley Herself; Are These Our Children?; Public Defender; **1932:** Hell's Highway; Beyond the Rockies; Penguin Pool Murder; Secrets of the French Police; The Savage Girl; **1933:** She Done Him Wrong; Love Is Like That; Notorious but Nice; Doctor Bull; Walls of Gold; Wild Boys of the Road; Mr. Skitch; Lucky Devils; The Past of Mary Holmes; Scarlet River; **1934:** Harold Teen; Such Women Are Dangerous; Judge Priest; Bachelor Bait; The Mighty Barnum; Imitation of Life; I've Been Around; **1935:** Life Begins at 40; Les Misérables; Way Down East; Curly Top; Show Them No Mercy; **1936:** The Music Goes 'Round; Everybody's Old Man; The Country Beyond; Poppy; Reunion; **1937:** Woman-Wise; That I May Live; Born Reckless; She Had to Eat; **1938:** Rascals; Mr. Moto Takes a Chance; Storm Over Bengal; **1939:** Pride of the Navy; Missing Daughters; A Woman Is the Judge; Smuggled Cargo; Pirates of the Skies; Konga — The Wild Stallion; **1940:** Convicted Woman; Men Without Souls; Babies for Sale; Island of Doomed Men; Girls Under 21; **1941:** Meet Boston Blackie; The Officer and the Lady; The Stork Pays Off; **1942:** Rubber Racketeers; Queen of Broadway; **1947:** Bush Pilot; **1948:** Devil's Cargo; **1949:** Sky Liner; **1955:** Rebel Without a Cause; **1964:** Strait-Jacket; **1965:** The Night Walker; **1967:** Dr. Terror's Gallery

of Horrors/Return From the Past.

Select TV: **1954–59:** That's My Boy (series); **1965:** Broken Sabre (sp).

ROCK HUDSON

(Roy Harold Scherer, Jr.) Born: Winnetka, IL, November 17, 1925. Died: October 2, 1985.

During the 1950s and early 1960s, Rock Hudson was burdened with being the screen's ideal of manliness — tall, handsome, wavy-haired, solidly built. All of this would have made him just another lifeless pinup of the studio system had he not also projected a warmth and charm that made audiences glad to be in his presence. Often dismissed as a second-rate actor, he triumphed on several occasions, leaving behind his beefcake image to give some performances of depth, and proving himself quite adept at light comedy. Following Navy service he worked at a variety of jobs, including postman, and it was on his route that he was discovered by agent Henry Willson, who secured him a screen test that resulted in a tiny role as a pilot in *Fighter Squadron*, at Warners, after which he signed a contract with Universal. For the next few years he was just another nice-looking contract player, popping up in the background in support of James Mason in *One-Way Street*; Donald O'Connor in *Double Crossbones*; Arthur Kennedy in *Bright Victory*, seen driving a jeep; and James Stewart in a pair of westerns, *Winchester '73*, as an Indian, and *Bend of the River*, in a bigger than usual role, as a gambler. These led to co-starring parts in minor fare like *Has Anybody Seen My Gal?*, where he and a very young Piper Laurie showed little promise of better things to come, and *The Scarlet Angel*, where he played Yvonne DeCarlo's sea captain lover in one of her many flimsy Technicolor melodramas.

Moving slowly through the ranks he was upped to star billing for some programmers like *Horizons West*, as the sensible brother of greedy Robert Ryan; *Seminole*, as a West Point officer sympathetic towards the Indians; *The Golden Blade*, stranded alongside Ms. Laurie again in one of the studio's many trashy costume adventures of the era; and *Taza — Son of Cochise*, once again playing an Indian. That made a total of 26 movies to his credit before he got his breakthrough role, playing the selfish playboy who accidentally blinds Jane Wyman in one of the seminal soaps of the 1950s, *Magnificent Obsession*. It proved so popular that they were reteamed for *All That Heaven Allows*, an equally lush and implausible concoction with the same director, Douglas Sirk, who would inexplicably earn a cult following for these things in later years. In this one Hudson was the affable landscaper who causes a scandal when he becomes Wyman's socially unacceptable younger lover. There were three more Hudson-Sirk teamings: *Battle Hymn*, about a military minister; *Written on the Wind*, in which he was desired by both Lauren Bacall and Dorothy Malone, but was upstaged by both them and a drunken Robert Stack; and *The Tarnished Angel*, from a Faulkner novel, where he played a reporter who falls in love with married Malone. Amid these were two loan-outs that were better than anything he'd done on his home lot, the mighty *Giant*, giving a fine Oscar-nominated performance as the cattle tycoon who sees his swaggering ways changed by humanity and the passing of time, and *Something of Value*, a noble attempt to shed light on Apartheid, with Hudson as the colonial farmer (minus a British accent) disgusted by the mistreatment of the blacks in Kenya. The former became one of the highest-grossing films of all time and would remain one of the seminal motion pictures of the decade.

By the end of the 1950s Hudson had become a full-fledged

box-office attraction, even carrying the stiff and endless remake of *A Farewell to Arms* to reasonable success for 20th Century-Fox. Back at Universal he was a disgraced, alcoholic captain trying to save his leaking boat in *Twilight of the Gods*, and a Napa Valley vintner in *This Earth Is Mine*, a family saga hoping in vain to duplicate the artistic and box-office success of *Giant*. Having proven himself to some degree in drama, it was time to try a comedy, and he chose well with *Pillow Talk*, playing a lecherous songwriter, wickedly teasing a flustered Doris Day while pretending to romance her as an effete Texan, a plot turn that would later be looked back on as some kind of inside joke. The film was a smash, and he and Day (along with supporting player Tony Randall) reteamed twice more, for the equally smart advertising spoof *Lover Come Back*, and the far less-satisfying *Send Me No Flowers*, with Hudson as a spineless hypochondriac. Between these were a western with Kirk Douglas, *The Last Sunset*; the overlong *The Spiral Road*, in which he became a missionary; and the aerial drama *A Gathering of Eagles*, in one of his less sympathetic performances, as a perfectionist colonel. None of these fared as well as the Day comedies. Likewise some other attempts at humor had less-than-impressive results, including the limp Howard Hawks satire *Man's Favorite Sport?*, and *A Very Special Favor*, which again involved Hudson pretending to be gay at one point.

Blindfold, a lighthearted thriller, was an improvement over most of these, but after one more, the war film *Tobruk*, Universal decided they were finished with him, for now. His box-office power having faded, he chose to do a risky sci-fi parable, *Seconds*, appearing late in the film as the re-crafted version of elderly John Rudolph and giving perhaps the best performance of his career, as a man trying to hang on to his youth and paying dearly for his bargain with the devil. Sadly, but not unexpectedly, the very weirdness that made it so engrossing alienated mainstream audiences, and it was a major flop. *Ice Station Zebra* was an adventure tale that did O.K., as did a fairly ordinary John Wayne western, *The Undefeated*, with Hudson performing behind a moustache, as a Confederate officer. After the old-fashioned aerial epic-romance *Darling Lili*, and the R-rated *Pretty Maids All in a Row* both took a dive, Universal offered him a TV series, *McMillan and Wife*, which rotated its time slot with *Columbo*, among others. It helped to re-establish Hudson as an audience favorite and ran for several years despite the fact that the star hated it.

There were a few more film appearances of little note, including *The Mirror Crack'd*, which reunited him with his *Giant* co-star and close friend, Elizabeth Taylor; some regional theater roles; and a brief return to weekly TV, as a recurring character on the popular soap *Dynasty*. His final burst of media fame was tragic. In 1985 he went public with the fact that he had contracted AIDS, and his death that year probably drew more attention to the epidemic to those outside the gay community than anyone else's passing. It also shattered many people's misconceptions of gay stereotypes and brought further awareness to the unfortunate need for so many stars to remain closeted in order to keep working in an unforgiving business.

Screen: 1948: Fighter Squadron; 1949: Undertow; 1950: I Was a Shoplifter; One-Way Street; Winchester '73; Peggy; The Desert Hawk; Shakedown; 1951: Double Crossbones; Tomahawk; Air Cadet; The Fat Man; Iron Man; Bright Victory; 1952: Here Come the Nelsons; Bend of the River; Scarlet Angel; Has Anybody Seen My Gal?; Horizons West; The Lawless Breed; 1953: Seminole; Sea Devils; The Golden Blade; Back to God's Country; Gun Fury; 1954: Taza — Son of Cochise; Magnificent Obsession; Bengal Brigade; 1955: Captain Lightfoot; One Desire; All That Heaven Allows; 1956: Never Say Goodbye; Giant;

Written on the Wind; Four Girls in Town; 1957: Battle Hymn; Something of Value; The Tarnished Angels; A Farewell to Arms; 1958: Twilight for the Gods; 1959: This Earth Is Mine; Pillow Talk; 1961: The Last Sunset; Come September; Lover Come Back; 1962: The Spiral Road; 1963: A Gathering of Eagles; Marilyn; 1964: Man's Favorite Sport?; Send Me No Flowers; 1965: Strange Bedfellows; A Very Special Favor; 1966: Blindfold; Seconds; 1967: Tobruk; 1968: Ice Station Zebra; 1969: A Fine Pair; The Undefeated; 1970: Darling Lili; Hornets' Nest; 1971: Pretty Maids All in a Row; 1973: Showdown; 1976: Embryo; 1978: Avalanche; 1980: The Mirror Crack'd; 1985: The Ambassador.

Select TV: 1971: Once Upon a Dead Man; 1971–77: McMillan and Wife/McMillan (series); 1978: Arthur Hailey's Wheels (ms); 1980: The Martian Chronicles (ms); 1981: The Star Maker; The Patricia Neal Story; 1982: World War III; The Devlin Connection (series); 1984: The Vegas Strip Wars; 1984–85: Dynasty (series).

HENRY HULL

BORN: LOUISVILLE, KY, OCTOBER 3, 1890.
ED: CCNY, COLUMBIA UNIV.
DIED: MARCH 8, 1977.

Thin, with a furrowed brow, Henry Hull specialized in practical oldsters and crotchety types, with performances that ranged from reasonably effective to garrulously self-important. He worked in the mining and mineralogy business and then turned to the stage, making his New York debut in 1911. He came to films in 1917, in *The Volunteer*, and dabbled there between theater assignments, including taking the lead in the 1924 version of *The Hoosier School Master*. Having made a major impact as Jeeter Lester in one of the longest running of all Broadway hits, *Tobacco Road*, he was summoned to Hollywood in 1934 to appear for Universal in a minor adaptation of *Great Expectations*, receiving top billing as the convict Magwitch. For the same company he played his most famous lead, in the granddaddy of all lycanthropy movies, *Werewolf of London*, before beginning his long career in character parts. Although he was skipped over for the 1941 film version of *Tobacco Road*, he was seen as the kindly pawnbroker who helps Spencer Tracy finance *Boys Town*; Emperor Franz Josef in *The Great Waltz*; and newspaper editor Major Rufus Todd in *Jesse James* and its sequel, *The Return of Frank James*. (A decade later he was seen in *The Return of Jesse James*, but was cast as Hank Younger). He was the town drunk in *Bad Little Angel*; one of the survivors in *Lifeboat*; an old salt who leads Joseph Cotten to the lighthouse at the climax of *Portrait of Jennie*; and a backwoodsman named Dirty Jim in *The Fool Killer*, among so many other credits. He was also the author of the 1922 Broadway play *Manhattan*.

Screen: 1917: The Volunteer; The Family Honor; Rasputin the Black Monk; A Square Deal; 1919: Little Women; 1922: One Exciting Night; 1923: The Last Moment; A Bride for a Knight; 1924: The Hoosier School Master; For Woman's Favor; Roulette; 1925: The Wrong-Doers; Wasted Lives; 1934: Midnight; Great Expectations; 1935: Werewolf of London; Transient Lady; Justice of the Range; 1936: Murder at Glen Athol; 1938: Yellow Jack; Boys Town; Three Comrades; Paradise for Three; Port of Seven Seas; The Great Waltz; 1939: Jesse James; Return of the Cisco Kid; Stanley and Livingstone; The Spirit of Culver; Miracles for Sale; Babes in Arms; Bad Little Angel; Nick Carter — Master Detective; Judge Hardy and Son; 1940: The Return of Frank James; My Son, My Son; 1941: High Sierra; 1942: Queen of

Broadway; The Big Shot; **1943:** The Woman of the Town; The West Side Kid; Seeds of Freedom (narrator); **1944:** What a Man; Lifeboat; Goodnight Sweetheart; Voodoo Man; **1945:** Objective, Burma!; **1947:** High Barbaree; Deep Valley; Mourning Becomes Electra; **1948:** Scudda Hoo! Scudda Hay!; The Walls of Jericho; Belle Starr's Daughter; Portrait of Jennie; Fighter Squadron; **1949:** The Fountainhead; Song of Surrender; Colorado Territory; El Paso; Rimfire; The Great Dan Patch; The Great Gatsby; **1950:** The Return of Jesse James; **1951:** Hollywood Story; **1952:** The Treasure of Lost Canyon; **1953:** The Last Posse; Inferno; Thunder Over the Plains; **1955:** Man With the Gun; **1956:** Kentucky Rifle; **1957:** The Buckskin Lady; **1958:** The Sheriff of Fractured Jaw; The Buccaneer; The Proud Rebel; **1959:** The Oregon Trail; **1961:** Master of the World; **1965:** The Fool Killer/ Violent Journey; **1966:** The Chase; **1967:** A Covenant With Death.

NY Stage: **1911:** Green Stockings; **1913:** Believe Me, Xantippe; **1916:** The Man Who Came Back; **1919:** 39 East; **1920:** When We Are Young; **1921:** The Trial of Joan of Arc; Everyday; **1922:** The Cat and the Canary; **1923:** Roger Bloomer; In Love With Love; The Other Rose; **1924:** The Youngest; **1926:** Lulu Belle; **1927:** Ivory Door; **1928:** The Grey Fox; **1929:** Young Alexander; Congratulations; Ladies Leave; Veneer; Michael and Mary; **1930:** Grand Hotel; **1931:** The Roof; The Bride the Sun Shines On; **1932:** The Moon in the Yellow River; Foreign Affairs; **1933:** Springtime for Henry; Tobacco Road; **1936:** Plumes in the Dust; The Masque of Kings; **1937:** Places Please!; **1945:** Foolish Notion; **1949:** Mister Roberts.

Select TV: **1951:** Ghost Town (sp); **1952:** Mr. Finchley Versus the Bomb (sp); Brigadier (sp); **1954:** The Test Case (sp); The Almighty Dollar (sp); **1955:** Freighter (sp); **1959:** Face of a Hero (sp); **1961:** The Wooden Dish (sp).

JOSEPHINE HULL

(JOSEPHINE SHERWOOD)
BORN: NEWTONVILLE, MA, JANUARY 3, 1886.
ED: RADCLIFFE. DIED: MARCH 12, 1957.

Short, adorably plump and downright huggable, Josephine Hull had only five movies to her credit, but two of them made her a major contributor in the annals of classic film comedy. Debuting onstage in 1900, she worked with various stock and touring companies, eventually joining the Actor's Theatre in New York. Adopting her husband's surname after marrying Shelley Hull (brother of actor Henry Hull), she appeared on Broadway in such plays as *Craig's Wife*, *An International Incident*, and *After Tomorrow*, making her feature film debut in the 1932 adaptation of the last-named, as Charles Farrell's jealous mother. In 1941 she scored a major stage triumph as Abby Brewster, one of the dotty old sisters who takes pleasure in poisoning lonely old men, in what became one of the longest-running plays of all time, *Arsenic and Old Lace*. Both she and her fellow cast member Jean Adair were considered so essential to the tone of the piece that Frank Capra cast them in the film version with extremely happy results. There was an even bigger success to come with another of the all-time Broadway attendance record holders, *Harvey*, playing Veta, the excitable sister of delirious Elwood P. Dowd, first in the original 1944 New York production, and then repeating her part in the exceptional 1950 movie version. Her wide-eyed, hilarious performance as this fluttery bundle of nerves was a joy, and it won her the Academy Award as Best Supporting Actress, against some formidable competition. Universal hoped to cash in on her accolade with a starring vehicle, *The Lady From Texas*, in which she was an eccentric Civil War widow, but it didn't make enough of

an impact to proceed with further films. She returned to Broadway for one last hit, *The Solid Gold Cadillac*, but left the show due to illness.

Screen: **1932:** After Tomorrow; **1933:** Careless Lady; **1944:** Arsenic and Old Lace; **1950:** Harvey; **1951:** The Lady From Texas.

NY Stage: **1906:** The Law and the Man; **1909:** The Bridge; **1923:** Neighbors; **1924:** Fata Morgana; The Habitual Husband; **1925:** Rosmersholm; Craig's Wife; **1926:** Daisy Mayme; **1927:** The Wild Man of Borneo; **1928:** March Hares; Hot Bed; **1929:** Before You're 25; **1930:** Those We Love; Midnight; **1931:** Unexpected Husband; After Tomorrow; **1932:** A Thousand Summers; **1933:** American Dream; A Divine Drudge; **1934:** By Your Leave; **1935:** On to Fortune; Seven Keys to Baldpate; A Night in the House; **1936:** You Can't Take It With You; **1940:** An International Incident; **1941:** Arsenic and Old Lace; **1944:** Harvey; **1948:** Minnie and Mr. Williams; **1950:** The Golden State; **1952:** Whistler's Grandmother; **1953:** The Solid Gold Cadillac.

Select TV: **1949:** Arsenic and Old Lace (sp); **1950:** Give Us Our Dream (sp); Dear Guests and Ghost (sp); **1951:** Grandma Was an Actress (sp); **1952:** Clean Sweep for Lavinia (sp); **1955:** The Meanest Man in the World (sp).

MARSHA HUNT

(MARCIA VIRGINIA HUNT) BORN: CHICAGO, IL, OCTOBER 17, 1917.

One of Hollywood's more-unfortunate also-rans, Marsha Hunt had both the good looks (especially her alluring eyes) and the good reviews, but she was either thought of as a "B" star or secondary player in top-of-the-line products, spending a major portion of her career under contract to MGM. She had studied acting at the Theodore Irving School of Dramatics but was noticed first by Paramount because of some modeling assignments. They signed her to a contract in 1935, starting with the quickie *The Virginia Judge*, as the girl loved by Robert Cummings. She stayed with that studio for two years in similar fare until MGM took her on. There she was cast as one of Greer Garson's sisters in the first-rate adaptation of *Pride and Prejudice*; a suicide in another Garson vehicle, *Blossoms in the Dust*; James Craig's fiancée in the beautifully realized home-front drama *The Human Comedy*; and one of the nurses in the flag-waving *Cry Havoc*. She headlined such "B's" as *Joe Smith — American*, as Robert Young's all-American wife; the murder mystery *Kid Glove Killer*; *The Affairs of Martha*, one of her own favorite roles, as a maid who marries her boss and writes a tell-all best seller; and *A Letter for Evie*, as a woman romancing soldier Hume Cronyn through the mail. After Metro, things stayed pretty much in the second tier, although she played mothers on some notable occasions, including *The Happy Time* (Bobby Driscoll), *Blue Denim* (Brandon de Wilde), and *Johnny Got His Gun* (Timothy Bottoms). After the last film she pretty much turned away from acting, preferring to concentrate on charity work.

Screen: **1935:** The Virginia Judge; **1936:** The Accusing Finger; Gentle Julia; Desert Gold; The Arizona Raiders; Hollywood Boulevard; Easy to Take; College Holiday; **1937:** Murder Goes to College; Thunder Trail; Annapolis Salute; Easy Living; The Long Shot; **1938:** Come on Leathernecks; **1939:** Born to the West; The Hardys Ride High; The Star Reporter; These Glamour Girls; Joe and Ethel Turp Call on the President; Winter Carnival; **1940:** Pride and Prejudice; Flight Command; Irene; Ellery Queen: Master Detective; **1941:** Blossoms in the Dust; I'll Wait for You; The Trial of Mary Dugan; The Penalty; Cheers for Miss Bishop;

Unholy Partners; 1942: Kid Glove Killer; Joe Smith — American; The Affairs of Martha; Panama Hattie; Seven Sweethearts; 1943: Thousands Cheer; Pilot # 5; The Human Comedy; Cry Havoc; Lost Angel; 1944: Bride by Mistake; None Shall Escape; Music for Millions; 1945: The Valley of Decision; A Letter for Evie; 1947: Smash Up: The Story of a Woman; Carnegie Hall; 1948: The Inside Story; Raw Deal; 1949: Jigsaw; Take One False Step; Mary Ryan — Detective; 1952: Actors and Sin; The Happy Time; 1956: Diplomatic Passport; No Place to Hide; 1957: Bombers B-52; Back From the Dead/Bury Me Dead; 1959: Blue Denim; 1960: The Plunderers; 1971: Johnny Got His Gun.

NY Stage: 1948: Joy to the World; 1950: The Devil's Disciple; Borned in Texas (sp); Legend of Sarah; 1967: The Paisley Convertible.

Select TV: 1949: Quality Street (sp); 1950: Willow Cabin (sp); 1951: The Secret Front (sp); 1957: Man of the Law (sp); 1959: Peck's Bad Girl (series); 1969: Fear No Evil; 1972: Jigsaw; 1981: Terror Among Us.

IAN HUNTER

BORN: KENILWORTH, SOUTH AFRICA, JUNE 13, 1900. DIED: SEPTEMBER 24, 1975.

A standard, indistinctive, but well-spoken British actor whose journey to Hollywood in the 1930s netted him work in an occasionally interesting film, South African Ian Hunter had moved to England, where he joined the army, in 1917. After the war he studied acting, making his London stage debut in 1919 in *Jack O'Jingles*. Five years later he made his film bow in the British *Not for Sale*, and in 1925 he first came to Broadway for a production of *School for Scandal*. There was a sole American film, *Syncopation*, amid all the British ones, but his official Hollywood career did not begin until he went to Warners in 1935, appearing opposite Bette Davis in *The Girl From 10th Avenue*, as a jilted New York socialite who marries her while both are intoxicated, and lending his crisp diction to the role of the King in *A Midsummer Night's Dream*. Afterward, he was saddled with Kay Francis for no less than seven pictures, including *I Found Stella Parish*, as the journalist who does the finding, and *The White Angel*, as a reporter chronicling the exploits of Florence Nightingale in this questionable biopic. He was King Richard in the grand *The Adventures of Robin Hood*, paling alongside the flamboyant styles of Basil Rathbone and Claude Rains; the boss who was supposed to marry Bette Davis at the climax of *The Sisters* (as in the original novel), until test audiences decided Errol Flynn was more to their liking; and the military dad separated from Shirley Temple in one of her better films, *The Little Princess*, for Fox. He soon found himself on the Metro lot where amid such dismissible assignments as *Tarzan Finds a Son* and *Ziegfeld Girl*, he had perhaps his best screen role, as the mysterious penal colony inmate who just might be Christ himself, in *Strange Cargo*. Elsewhere he was the dying King Edward in Universal's *Tower of London* and the alcoholic seaman in UA's *The Long Voyage Home*. After appearing on Broadway in *Edward, My Son*, he traveled to England to repeat his role in the film version (as the friend falling for the already-married Deborah Kerr) and stayed there for the remainder of his movie career, doing few pictures of any note.

Screen: 1924: Not for Sale; 1925: Confessions; A Girl of London; 1927: Downhill; Easy Virtue; The Ring; 1928: His House in Order; The Thoroughbred; Valley of the Ghosts; 1929: Syncopation; The Physician; 1930: Escape; 1931: Cape Forlorn/The Love Storm; Sally in Our Alley; 1932: The Water

Gypsies; The Sign of Four; Marry Me; 1933: The Man From Toronto; Skipper of the Osprey; Orders Is Orders; 1934: The Night of the Party; The Silver Spoon; Something Always Happens; No Escape; Death at the Broadcasting House; 1935: The Phantom Light; Lazybones; The Morals of Marcus; The Church Mouse; The Girl From 10th Avenue; Jalna; A Midsummer Night's Dream; I Found Stella Parish; 1936: The White Angel; To Mary With Love; The Devil Is a Sissy; Stolen Holiday; 1937: Call It a Day; Another Dawn; Confession; That Certain Woman; 52nd Street; 1938: The Adventures of Robin Hood; Comet Over Broadway; The Sisters; Secrets of an Actress; Always Goodbye; 1939: Broadway Serenade; Yes, My Darling Daughter; Tarzan Finds a Son; The Little Princess; Tower of London; Bad Little Angel; Maisie; 1940: Broadway Melody of 1940; Strange Cargo; The Long Voyage Home; Dulcy; Bitter Sweet; Gallant Sons; 1941: Come Live With Me; Andy Hardy's Private Secretary; Ziegfeld Girl; Dr. Jekyll and Mr. Hyde; Billy the Kid; Smilin' Through; 1942: A Yank at Eton; 1943: It Comes Up Love; Forever and a Day; 1946: Bedelia; White Cradle Inn/High Fury; 1947: The White Unicorn/Bad Sister; 1949: Edward, My Son; 1952: It Started in Paradise; 1953: Appointment in London; Eight O'Clock Walk; 1954: Don't Blame the Stork; 1956: The Door in the Wall; 1957: Battle of the River Plate/Pursuit of the Graf Spee; She Played With Fire/Fortune Is a Woman; 1958: Rockets Galore/Mad Little Island; 1959: Northwest Frontier/Flame Over India; 1960: The Bulldog Breed; 1961: Dr. Blood's Coffin; The Treasure of Monte Cristo/The Secret of Monte Cristo; The Queen's Guards; 1962: Guns of Darkness; 1963: Kali Yug — Goddess of Vengeance; Kali Yug — The Mystery of the Indian Tomb.

NY Stage: 1925: The School for Scandal; 1928: Olympia; 1948: Edward, My Son.

Select TV: 1955–58: The Adventures of Robin Hood (series).

JEFFREY HUNTER

(HENRY HERMAN McKINNIES, JR.)
BORN: NEW ORLEANS, LA, NOVEMBER 25, 1925. RAISED IN MILWAUKEE, WI. ED: NORTHWESTERN UNIV. DIED: MAY 27, 1969.

His erratic film career consisted of many second leads and a lot of standard adventure fare, but since his early death, good-looking Jeffrey Hunter, with the beautifully piercing eyes, is probably most readily identified with having played Jesus Christ. Starting as a radio performer, he moved on to summer stock and then enrolled in drama courses at UCLA. In 1950 he made his film debut there, along with Charlton Heston, in a barely distributed film made of a production of *Julius Caesar*. The next year he was signed to a contract by 20th Century-Fox, who put him into all sorts of small roles in such films as *Fourteen Hours*, appearing in a somewhat intrusive subplot, and *Belles on Their Toes*, playing the doctor who marries Jeanne Crain. He had a bigger part as a young firefighter at odds with Richard Widmark in *Red Skies of Montana*, then rated top billing for the first time in the British-made *Sailor of the King*, as the offspring of Wendy Hiller and Michael Rennie. But the studio didn't see him as anything more than pretty decoration for costume pictures like *Princess of the Nile*, or for westerns like *Three Young Texans* and *White Feather*. He was loaned out for *A Kiss Before Dying*, helping to track down killer Robert Wagner in this above average thriller; Disney's *The Great Locomotive Chase*, unofficially following in the footsteps of Buster Keaton, as the conductor who relentlessly pursues Fess Parker in an effort to get his train back, in an adventure covering some of the same ground as *The General*; and John Ford's *The Searchers*, where his scenes bickering with Vera Miles seemed to get in the way of the rest of the movie. His status on his home lot improved somewhat when he was cast as Frank James in *The True Story of Jesse James*; the husband who murders rapist Cameron Mitchell in *No Down Payment*; and one of the young marines in *In Love and War*, although in each case he was not trusted to carry the movie on his own. Those he did, *Count Five and Die*, as an American agent working with the British; and *The Way to the Gold*, suggested that Hunter had no drawing power.

Leaving Fox he was made the lead in some gritty thrillers, *Key Witness*, terrorized by a gang of thugs, and *Man-Trap*, married to nympho Stella Stevens; and in a grim war drama at Universal, *No Man Is an Island*, but his work was never more than competent. His casting as the lead in the remake of *King of Kings* was controversial, but in fact he played Christ with admirably tasteful restraint. The film was not among the more-popular biblical epics of its day, and that may have been the reason that it pretty much marked the end for Hunter in Hollywood. There was a foray into television for a one-season series, *Temple Houston*, and he almost became a part of sci-fi history when he played Kirk in the pilot for *Star Trek*, being replaced by William Shatner when it was picked up as a regular series. He was appearing in oddities and foreign films, and playing straight man to Bob Hope (*The Private Navy of Sgt. O'Farrell*) when he hurt himself badly in a fall. He died during the subsequent brain surgery. He was married (1950–55) to actress Barbara Rush (who appeared with him in *No Down Payment* after their divorce) and, for a few months before his death, to soap-star Emily McLaughlin.

Screen: 1950: Julius Caesar; 1951: Fourteen Hours; Call Me Mister; Take Care of My Little Girl; The Frogmen; 1952: Red Skies of Montana; Belles on Their Toes; Dreamboat; Lure of the Wilderness; 1953: Sailor of the King/Single-Handed; 1954: Three Young Texans; Princess of the Nile; 1955: Seven Angry Men; White Feather; Seven Cities of Gold; 1956: The Searchers; The Great Locomotive Chase; The Proud Ones; A Kiss Before Dying; Four Girls in Town; 1957: Gun for a Coward; The True Story of Jesse James; No Down Payment; The Way to the Gold; 1958: Count Five and Die; The Last Hurrah; In Love and War; Mardi Gras; 1960: Key Witness; Hell to Eternity; Sergeant Rutledge; 1961: Man-Trap; King of Kings; 1962: No Man Is an Island; The Longest Day; 1964: The Man From Galveston; Gold for the Caesars; 1965: Murieta; Brainstorm; 1967: Dimension 5; A Witch Without a Broom; A Guide for the Married Man; The Christmas Kid; 1968: Custer of the West; The Private Navy of Sgt. O'Farrell; Sexy Susan Sings Again (nUSr); Joe — Find a Place to Die (nUSr); Viva America (nUSr); 1969: Super Colt 38 (dtv).

Select TV: 1955: South of the Sun (sp); 1956: The Empty Room (sp); 1961: The Secret Mission (sp); 1963: Seven Miles of Bad Road (sp); 1963–64: Temple Houston (series); 1965: The Trains for Silence (sp).

KIM HUNTER

(JANET COLE) BORN: DETROIT, MI, NOVEMBER 12, 1922. DIED: SEPTEMBER 11, 2002.

A fine, intelligent, no-frills actress with too few movies to her credit, Kim Hunter had hoped to be a concert pianist but found acting more to her liking. She joined a stock company that called themselves the Theatre of the Fifteen, which led to membership with the Pasadena Playhouse. While there she was spotted by a talent scout for producer David Selznick, but he did little more than give her her stage name. Hunter's film debut

was at RKO in a lead, playing the innocent out-of-towner who discovers that her sister is part of a Greenwich Village devil-cult, in one of the weakest of the noted Val Lewton thrillers, *The Seventh Victim*. Remaining at RKO, she did a pivotal role supporting Ginger Rogers, as her coyly naïve housemate, in the patriotic *Tender Comrade*; went over to Monogram to star in *When Strangers Marry*, as a young bride worried that her husband is a killer; and then on to Paramount to play Lizabeth Scott's sister in the soapy *You Came Along*. Fortunately British filmmakers Michael Powell and Emeric Pressburger took an interest in her and cast her in one of the most imaginative of all screen fantasies, *A Matter of Life and Death/Stairway to Heaven*, where she gave a beautiful performance as the WAC who falls in love with semi-dead soldier David Niven.

At this point she went to Broadway to play the role for which she would become best known, Stella Kowalski, who endures the brutish behavior of her husband Stanley (Marlon Brando) for the sideline carnal pleasures, in the groundbreaking *A Streetcar Named Desire*. Hunter returned to Hollywood for the classic 1951 film version and preserved her performance in all its perfection, winning the Academy Award for Best Supporting Actress. As a result she was cast as the wife of Humphrey Bogart in *Deadline U.S.A.*, and of Jose Ferrer in *Anything Can Happen*, but found film offers eventually drying up due to blacklisting because of her pro-civil-rights stance. After this period had passed there was memorable work on TV for *Playhouse 90*, in *The Comedian* and *Requiem for a Heavyweight*, while back at the movies she played the mother of troubled teen James MacArthur in the admirable *The Young Stranger*. There was one more great film role for Hunter, and it was the strangest one of her career, buried under monkey makeup to play, with surprising dignity and a playful sense of fun, the sympathetic scientist who comes to Charlton Heston's aide in the enormously popular and influential sci-fi adventure *Planet of the Apes*. She repeated the part in two sequels, the better of which was *Escape From the Planet of the Apes*, which put her front and center of the story when she and fellow-ape Roddy McDowall become freak celebrities after returning to modern-day Earth. In 1975 she published an "autobiographical cookbook," *Loose in the Kitchen*.

Screen: 1943: The Seventh Victim; Tender Comrade; 1944: When Strangers Marry; 1945: You Came Along; 1946: Stairway to Heaven/A Matter of Life and Death; 1951: A Streetcar Named Desire; 1952: Deadline U.S.A.; Anything Can Happen; 1956: Bermuda Affair; Storm Center; 1957: The Young Stranger; 1958: Money, Women and Guns; 1964: Lilith; 1968: Planet of the Apes; The Swimmer; 1970: Beneath the Planet of the Apes; 1971: Escape From the Planet of the Apes; 1976: Dark August; 1986: The Kindred; 1991: Two Evil Eyes; 1997: Midnight in the Garden of Good and Evil; 1998: A Price Above Rubies; 1999: Abilene (dtv); Out of the Cold (nUSr); 2000: A Smaller Place (nUSr); Here's to Life! (nUSr).

NY Stage: 1947: A Streetcar Named Desire; 1951: Darkness at Noon; 1952: The Chase; The Children's Hour; 1954: The Tender Trap; 1961: Write Me a Murder; 1966: Come Slowly Eden (ob); 1968: Weekend; Hello and Goodbye (ob); 1969: The Penny Wars; 1973: The Women; All Is Bright (ob); 1976: The Cherry Orchard (ob); 1981: To Grandmother's House We Go; 1982: When We Dead Awaken (ob); 1983: Territorial Rights (ob); 1985: Faulkner's Bicycle (ob); 1987: Man and Superman (ob); 1988: A Murder of Crows (ob); 1993: The Eye of the Beholder (ob); 1996: An Ideal Husband.

Select TV: 1952: Rise Up and Walk (sp); The Petrified Forest (sp); 1955: The Trial of St. Joan (sp); A Midsummer's Daydream (sp); 1956: Try to Remember (sp); Moment of Courage (sp);

Orphans (sp); Requiem for a Heavyweight (sp); **1957:** The Comedian (sp); Perfect Likeness (sp); The Dark Side of the Earth (sp); Before I Die (sp); **1958:** Ticket to Tahiti (sp); Free Week-End (sp); **1959:** The Sounds of Eden (sp); **1960:** The Closing Door (sp); Alas, Babylon (sp); **1961:** The Sound of Murder (sp); Give Us Barabbas (sp); **1962:** Wanted: Someone Innocent (sp); **1966:** Lamp at Midnight (sp); **1968:** The Young Loner (sp); The People Next Door (sp); **1970:** Dial Hot Line; **1971:** In Search of America; **1973:** The Magician; **1974:** Unwed Father; Bad Ronald; Born Innocent; **1975:** Ellery Queen/Too Many Suspects; **1976:** The Dark Side of Innocence; **1977:** Once an Eagle (ms); **1978:** Stubby Pringle's Christmas (sp); **1979:** Backstairs at the White House (ms); The Golden Gate Murders/Specter on the Bridge; **1979–80:** The Edge of Night (series); **1980:** F.D.R.: The Last Year; **1981:** Skokie; **1985:** Private Sessions; Three Sovereigns for Sarah; **1988:** Drop-Out Mother; **1989:** Cross of Fire; **1993:** Bloodlines: Murder in the Family; Triumph Over Disaster: The Hurricane Andrew Story; **1997:** As the World Turns (series); **1999:** Blue Moon.

TAB HUNTER

(Arthur Gelien) Born: New York, NY, July 1, 1931. Raised in Los Angeles, CA.

Blond and extremely handsome in a boyish, friendly way, Tab Hunter was saddled with one of those phony 1950s names and had a hard time being taken seriously because of it. In truth he was never an actor of great range, but he possessed an enormously likable, self-effacing personality that could make him very appealing in certain roles. At one time he intended to become a professional ice skater, but through circumstances that have remained vague, he instead ended up getting cast in a film, The Lawless, in 1950, although he was deleted from the final print. Acquiring the same agent who launched Rock Hudson's career, Henry Willson, he was cast as a young marine stranded on an island with Linda Darnell in the British-made Island of Desire/Saturday Island, which at least meant you got to see him with his shirt off. Similarly, he had leads in other programmers like Gun Belt, turning bad to avenge his father's death, and Return to Treasure Island, playing an archeologist in a modern-day take on the classic story. Despite the low prominence of these, he did manage to get a contract with Warner Bros., who put him into the ensemble of one of the big films of 1955, Battle Cry, at his most engaging as a gosh-gee-wiz soldier. Because of its success, he was starred in two misfires opposite Natalie Wood, The Burning Hills and The Girl He Left Behind, plus William Wellman's final film, the quickly forgotten aerial drama Lafayette Escadrille.

His best Warners role came when he was added to what was principally the original cast from the Broadway production, in the 1958 film version of Damn Yankees, gamely singing and dancing alongside Gwen Verdon in a bright but not-particularly-popular musical. Despite the fact that he was one of the hottest faces in the fan magazines and even got himself a record contract, his box-office clout at the movies was questionable. Asking to be released from his Warners contract, he played opposite Sophia Loren in That Kind of Woman; was effectively unsympathetic in They Came to Cordura, as one of the medal of honor soldiers who aren't what they're cracked up to be; and was blandly nice as Debbie Reynolds's fiancé in The Pleasure of His Company. He slipped into foreign territory with The Golden Arrow; did the beach route with Ride the Wild Surf; and wound up in support of Soupy Sales in the juvenile Birds Do It. By the end of the 1960s he was pretty much out of the mainstream, and his roles at this

point included a killer with woman problems in The Arousers. In the 1980s he began showing up in films where he was mainly cast for his nostalgic appeal, including Polyester, romancing transvestite Divine (as he would again in the horrid Lust in the Dust), and the campy musical Grease 2, playing a high school teacher. There were the expected cheap horror movies and a horsy picture called Dark Horse, for which he himself supplied the story, but it barely received distribution. History's final judgment of Tab Hunter's abilities as an actor won't be all that important; he maintained a reputation for being one of the few truly nice people in the business, a much more admirable achievement.

Screen: **1952:** Island of Desire/Saturday Island; **1953:** Gun Belt; The Steel Lady; **1954:** Return to Treasure Island; Track of the Cat; **1955:** Battle Cry; The Sea Chase; **1956:** The Burning Hills; The Girl He Left Behind; **1958:** Lafayette Escadrille; Gunman's Walk; Damn Yankees; **1959:** That Kind of Woman; They Came to Cordura; **1961:** The Pleasure of His Company; **1962:** The Golden Arrow; **1963:** Operation Bikini; **1964:** Ride the Wild Surf; Troubled Waters/Man With Two Faces (nUSr); **1965:** The Loved One; City Under the Sea/War Gods of the Deep; **1966:** Birds Do It; **1967:** The Fickle Finger of Fate; Hostile Guns; **1968:** Scaccio Internationale/The Last Chance (nUSr); La Vendetta e il mio Perdona/Vengeance Is My Forgiveness (nUSr); **1969:** Quel Maledetto Ponte sull'Elba/The Legion of No Return (nUSr); **1971:** The Arousers/Sweet Kill/A Kiss From Eddie; **1972:** The Life and Times of Judge Roy Bean; **1975:** Timber Tramps; **1976:** Won Ton Ton, the Dog Who Saved Hollywood; **1981:** Polyester; **1982:** Pandemonium; Grease 2; **1985:** Lust in the Dust (and co-prod.); **1988:** Grotesque; **1989:** Cameron's Closet; Out of the Drak; **1991:** Dark Horse (and story); **1996:** Wild Bill: Hollywood Maverick.

NY Stage: **1964:** The Milk Train Doesn't Stop Here Anymore.

Select TV: **1955:** While We're Young (sp); Fear Strikes Out (sp); **1956:** Forbidden Area (sp); **1958:** Hans Brinker (sp); Portrait of a Murderer (sp); **1959:** Meet Me in St. Louis (sp); **1960–61:** The Tab Hunter Show (series); **1970:** San Francisco International Airport; **1971:** Hacksaw (sp); **1977–78:** Mary Hartman, Mary Hartman (series); **1978:** Katie: Portrait of a Centerfold; **1979:** The Kid From Left Field.

RUTH HUSSEY

(Ruth Carol O'Rourke) Born: Providence, RI, October 30, 1914. ed: Brown Univ., Univ. of MI School of Drama.

Second-string player Ruth Hussey had a bright, sophisticated delivery but was never considered by the front office to be anything more than reliable support. A former radio fashion-commentator and model, she wound up in some stage productions, including the touring company of Dead End, which won her a contract with MGM in 1937. There she was an unscrupulous lobbyist who uses innocent Cecilia Parker in Judge Hardy's Children; Edward G. Robinson's wife in Blackmail; Maureen O'Sullivan's college chum in Spring Madness; the girl Robert Young leaves behind to go on his Northwest Passage; and the lead in a "B," Within the Law, playing a shop girl wrongly sent to prison. She got her best chance and gave it all she had as wisecracking reporter Liz Imbrie in one of the enduring sophisticated entertainments of the era, The Philadelphia Story, earning an Oscar nomination in the supporting category. From this she was given leading-lady duties opposite some Roberts: Taylor (Flight Command), Cummings (Free and Easy), and Young (H.M. Pulham, Esq.). She left MGM in 1942 and found a good role over at Paramount, ghost hunting with Ray Milland in the atmospheric thriller *The Uninvited*, and ending up with Alan Napier at the climax. For UA she was a doctor in *Bedside Manner* and went French for a low-budget melodrama at Republic, *I, Jane Doe*. Back at Paramount she played Jordan Baker in the unpopular 1949 version of *The Great Gatsby*, after which her movie roles became less frequent. She was Jerry Lewis's mother in *That's My Boy*, a mink breeder in *The Lady Wants Mink*, and the wife on whom Bob Hope contemplates committing adultery in *The Facts of Life*. After that film, when she was seen at all, it was in TV guest appearances.

Screen: 1937: The Big City; Madame X; 1938: Judge Hardy's Children; Man-Proof; Marie Antoinette; Hold That Kiss; Rich Man, Poor Girl; Time Out for Murder; Spring Madness; 1939: Honolulu; Within the Law; Maisie; The Women; Another Thin Man; Blackmail; Fast and Furious; 1940: Northwest Passage; Susan and God; The Philadelphia Story; Flight Command; 1941: Free and Easy; Our Wife; Married Bachelor; H.M. Pulham, Esq.; 1942: Pierre of the Plains; Tennessee Johnson; 1943: Tender Comrade; 1944: The Uninvited; Marine Raiders; 1945: Bedside Manner; 1948: I, Jane Doe; 1949: The Great Gatsby; 1950: Louisa; Mr. Music; 1951: That's My Boy; 1952: Woman of the North Country; Stars and Stripes Forever; 1953: The Lady Wants Mink; 1960: The Facts of Life.

NY Stage: 1945: State of the Union; 1949: Goodbye, My Fancy; 1951: The Royal Family.

Select TV: 1950: The Magnificent Ambersons (sp); 1951: Counsellor-at-Law (sp); 1953: This Is My Heart (sp); 1954: To Lift a Feather (sp); The Boy Who Changed the World (sp); 1955: The Women (sp); 100 Years Younger (sp); Time Out for Ginger (sp); 1956: The Magic Glass (sp); Old Acquaintance (sp); 1957: Payment in Kind (sp); 1973: My Darling Daughters' Anniversary.

JOHN HUSTON
Born: Nevada, MO, August 5, 1906.
Died: August 28, 1987.

He was one of the screen's most-respected writers who became one of its great directors, but tall, long-faced, guttural-voiced John Huston was such an unpredictable, imposing, colorful character off screen that it only made sense that he would eventually step before the camera and succeed as impressively as he did behind it. The son of actor Walter Huston and his first wife, Reah Gore, young John grew up between New York, where his dad had gone to find work, and Arizona, where his mother settled after their divorce in 1913. The young Huston dabbled in painting, acting, and reporting. Through an acquaintance, he got a job as a writer for Goldwyn studios, though nothing came of the position. Instead he ended up at Universal Pictures, where his first credit, in 1931, was writing dialogue for *A House Divided*, which starred his father. Over the next ten years his reputation grew with his work on *Law and Order, Murders in the Rue Morgue* (both 1932), *Death Drives Through, It Happened in Paris* (both 1935), *Jezebel, The Amazing Dr. Clitterhouse* (both 1938), *Juarez* (1939), *Dr. Ehrlich's Magic Bullet* (1940; Oscar nomination), *High Sierra* (1941), *Sergeant York* (1941; Oscar nomination), and *Three Strangers* (1946).

In 1941 he launched his directorial career brilliantly with his literate, faithful adaptation of Dashiell Hammett's *The Maltese Falcon*, which became the detective noir by which all others would be measured. It netted him an Oscar nomination for his script. For the next 46 years he would experience the highs and lows of any director, but a good deal of his output was most impressive. Perhaps the peak for him, personally, came with *The*

Treasure of the Sierra Madre, in which both he and his dad stood proudly at the podium accepting their 1948 Academy Awards (two for John, for both directing and writing) for this gritty and downbeat morality tale. His other credits behind the camera were *In This Our Life* (and co-wr.; 1942), *Across the Pacific* (1942), *Key Largo* (and co-wr.; 1948), *We Were Strangers* (and co-wr.; 1949), *The Asphalt Jungle* (and co-wr.; 1950; Oscar nominations for dir. and wr.); *The Red Badge of Courage* (and wr.; 1951); *The African Queen* (and co-wr.; Oscar nominations for dir. and wr.; 1951), probably his finest achievement and certainly his most enduring work; *Moulin Rouge* (and co-wr.; 1952; Oscar nomination for dir.), *Beat the Devil* (and co-wr., co-prod.; 1954), *Moby Dick* (and co-wr.; 1956), *Heavens Knows, Mr. Allison* (and co-wr.; Oscar nomination for wr.), *The Barbarian and the Geisha* (1958), *The Roots of Heaven* (1958), *The Unforgiven* (1960), *The Misfits* (1961), *Freud* (1962), *The List of Adrian Messenger* (1963), *The Night of the Iguana* (and co-wr., co-prod.; 1964), *The Bible* (1966), *Casino Royale* (co-dir.; 1967), *Reflections in a Golden Eye* (1967), *Sinful Davey* (1969), *A Walk With Love and Death* (1969), *The Kremlin Letter* (and co-wr.; 1970), *Fat City* (1972), *The Life and Times of Judge Roy Bean* (1972), *The Mackintosh Man* (1973), *The Man Who Would Be King* (and co-wr.; Oscar nomination for wr.; 1975), *Wise Blood* (1980), *Phobia* (1980), *Victory* (1981), *Annie* (1982), *Under the Volcano* (1984), *Prizzi's Honor* (Oscar nomination; 1985), and *The Dead* (1987).

He had done some acting in a handful of features in his early years in Hollywood and first popped up in one of his own pictures, *The Treasure of the Sierra Madre*, as the man dressed in white who is repeatedly panhandled by Humphrey Bogart. In 1963 director Otto Preminger asked him to play an elderly man of the cloth in *The Cardinal*, and he stole the notices, earning a supporting-actor Oscar nomination in the process. Because of this, Huston was now considered for acting parts in other people's movies as well as his own. These roles ranged from the aging cowboy Buck Loner in the ghastly *Myra Breckinridge*, to a chimpanzee in the sci-fi sequel *Battle for the Planet of the Apes*, to Jeff Bridge's duplicitous father in *Winter Kills*. Best of all, he was the incestuous Los Angeles businessman in *Chinatown*, a brilliantly conceived portrayal of self-righteous evil. He continued to show up in several of his own movies: *We Were Strangers*, as a Cuban bank clerk stuck on Jennifer Jones; *The List of Adrian Messenger*; leading a fox hunt; *Casino Royale*, as the formidable "M" in this James Bond spoof; *A Walk With Love and Death*; *The Kremlin Letter*, as an admiral; *The Life and Times of Judge Roy Bean*, as Grizzly Adams; *Wiseblood*, seen in flashbacks as Brad Dourif's grandfather; and, most prominently, as both the narrator and the ark-building Noah in what turned out to be the most impressive sequence of the long-winded *The Bible*. He had guided his dad through cameos in *The Maltese Falcon* and *In This Our Life*, and directed daughter Anjelica in *Sinful Davey, A Walk With Love and Death, Prizzi's Honor*, and his final film, *The Dead*. Huston also directed and wrote the World War II documentaries *Report From the Aleutians, Battle of San Pietro*, and *Let There Be Light*. In 1983 he was given the American Film Institute Life Achievement Award. His autobiography, *An Open Book*, was published in 1981.

Screen: 1928: The Shakedown; 1930: Hell's Heroes; The Storm; 1945: Know Your Enemy (narrator); 1948: The Treasure of the Sierra Madre (and dir.; wr.); 1949: We Were Strangers (and dir.; co-wr.); 1962: Freud (narrator; and dir.); 1963: The List of Adrian Messenger (and dir.); The Cardinal; 1966: The Bible (and dir.); 1967: Casino Royale (and co-dir.); 1968: Candy; 1969: De Sade; A Walk With Love and Death (and dir.); 1970: The Kremlin Letter (and dir.; co-wr.); Myra Breckinridge; 1971: The Bridge in the Jungle; The Deserter; Man in the Wilderness; 1972: The Life and Times of Judge Roy Bean (and dir.); 1973: Battle for the Planet of the Apes; 1974: Chinatown; 1975: Breakout; The Wind and the Lion; 1976: Hollywood on Trial (narrator); 1977: Tentacles; 1978: Battleforce/The Great Battle; The Bermuda Triangle (dtv); 1979: Winter Kills; The Visitor; Jaguar Lives!; 1980: Wise Blood (and dir.); Agee; 1982: Cannery Row (narrator); 1983: Lovesick; A Minor Miracle (dtv); 1984: Angela (filmed 1977); 1985: Head On/Fatal Attraction (filmed 1980); Momo (nUSr); George Stevens: A Filmmaker's Journey; The Black Cauldron (narrator).

Select TV: 1976: Sherlock Holmes in New York; 1977: The Rhinemann Exchange (ms); 1978: The Word (ms); The Hobbit (voice); 1980: The Return of the King (voice); 1987: Mr. Corbett's Ghost.

WALTER HUSTON

(WALTER HOUGHSTON) BORN: TORONTO, CANADA, APRIL 6, 1884. DIED: APRIL 7, 1950.

With minor flash and flare, effortlessly segueing between leads and support, lean, tall, and formidable Walter Huston was one of the most consistently impressive actors for the two decades he spent in movies. Fluctuating between a career in engineering or acting, he made his stage debut in New York in 1905, in *In Convict Stripes*, but was working in the other business when his son (and future director) John was born the following year. He returned to the theater soon afterwards, doing a vaudeville act with a woman named Bayonne Whipple to whom he was married for a period. In 1924 he was back on Broadway in *Mr. Pitt*, followed by a triumph in Eugene O'Neill's *Desire Under the Elms*. With the coming of talkies, he was offered work in movies and debuted under contract for Paramount as a reporter carrying on with secretary Kay Francis in *Gentlemen of the Press*, filmed at Astoria Studios. The same year, 1929, he went to the West Coast for what would be his first impressive movie part, the villain Trampas, in the Gary Cooper western *The Virginian*. He finished up at Paramount with a melodrama that reunited him with Kay Francis, *The Virtuous Sin*, made the same year he played the title role in one of the last D.W. Griffith dramas, *Abraham Lincoln*, a creaky item but a part for which he was physically well suited.

For a while he found himself employed at various studios, including Universal, playing an old sailor who is crippled in *A House Divided*, and a variation on Wyatt Earp in *Law and Order*, both co-written by his son. He signed up with MGM, where he scored as a police captain determined to bring mobster Jean Hersholt to justice in *The Beast of the City*; a drunk in the odd *The Wet Parade*; and a chief executive who sees the error of his ways in *Gabriel Over the White House*, a drama just unconventional enough to maintain interest even today. He also did the Frank Capra film *American Madness* (for Columbia) one of that director's lesser-known movies of the 1930s, and *Rain* (for UA), a somewhat toned-down version of the Sadie Thompson story, with Huston as the self-righteous preacher. It was a return to theater that gave him his best part to date, the millionaire who begins to question his life and his relationship with his pushy social-climbing wife in *Dodsworth*. When Samuel Goldwyn filmed it, Huston came with the package and brought his quiet excellence to an outstanding film, earning an Oscar nomination, making up in prestige for its weak box-office returns. It was followed by a somewhat smaller role in *Of Human Hearts*, as James Stewart's religious father, miraculously avoiding making this character the foolish villain he could have become. Heading east again, he had another

Broadway triumph, this time in a musical, *Knickerbocker Holiday*, playing peg-legged Peter Stuyvesant, introducing the classic Kurt Weill tune "September Song." Returning to Hollywood he was the star of the soap *Always in My Heart*, in which he also sang. He then appeared in *All That Money Can Buy*, in one of his best-remembered roles, as Mr. Scratch, a tour de force as the Devil who battles Daniel Webster (Edward Arnold) for James Craig's soul. It resulted in a second Oscar nomination. There was a third one, in the supporting category, for his lively turn as James Cagney's vaudevillian dad in *Yankee Doodle Dandy*, one of the major hits of the war years.

Back to leads, he played Doc Holliday in the controversial western dud *The Outlaw*, which got shelved and chopped at by the censors because of all the uproar over Jane Russell's bosom. He was an American ambassador discovering why the Russians should be our allies in Warners's blatant piece of propaganda *Mission to Moscow*, not so much acting as giving speeches, and a Russian doctor in Goldwyn's *The North Star*, which earned some acclaimed despite screenwriter Lillian Hellman disowning it. (Both movies caused some discomfort during the McCarthy years for their pro-Russia slant, the latter re-edited for television to change its focus and re-titled *Armored Attack*.) Huston was seen in a light Asian makeup in the ridiculous *Dragon Seed*, then got top billing for the superb mystery ensemble *And Then There Were None*, as the judge. After playing the father in the pleasant musical version of *Ah, Wilderness!*, called *Summer Holiday*, his son gave him the role of his career when he cast him as Howard, the crusty old prospector in *The Treasure of the Sierra Madre*. As played brilliantly by Huston he was levelheaded, brash, bursting with enthusiasm, and absolutely unforgettable; earning the actor a much-applauded Academy Award for Best Supporting Actor of 1948. There were only two more parts, playing fathers to Ava Gardner and Barbara Stanwyck in *The Great Sinner* and *The Furies*, respectively; the latter released the year of his death, 1950.

Screen: 1929: Gentlemen of the Press; The Lady Lies; The Virginian; 1930: Abraham Lincoln; The Bad Man; The Virtuous Sin; 1931: The Criminal Code; The Star Witness; The Ruling Voice; 1932: The Woman from Monte Carlo; A House Divided; Law and Order; The Beast of the City; The Wet Parade; Night Court; American Madness; Rain; Kongo; 1933: Gabriel Over the White House; Hell Below; Storm at Daybreak; Ann Vickers; The Prizefighter and the Lady; 1934: Keep 'em Rolling; 1935: The Tunnel; 1936: Rhodes of Africa; Dodsworth; 1938: Of Human Hearts; 1939: The Light That Failed; 1941: All That Money Can Buy/The Devil and Daniel Webster; The Maltese Falcon; Swamp Water; The Shanghai Gesture; 1942: Always in My Heart; In This Our Life; Yankee Doodle Dandy; 1943: Edge of Darkness; The Outlaw; Mission to Moscow; The North Star; 1944: Dragon Seed; 1945: And Then There Were None; 1946: Dragonwyck; Duel in the Sun; 1948: Summer Holiday; The Treasure of the Sierra Madre; 1949: The Great Sinner; 1950: The Furies.

NY Stage: 1905: In Convict Stripes; 1924: Mr. Pitt; Desire Under the Elms; 1925: The Fountain; 1926: Kongo; 1927: The Barker; 1928: Elmer the Great; 1929: The Commodore Marries; 1934: Dodsworth; 1936: Othello; 1938: Knickerbocker Holiday; 1940: A Passenger to Bali; Love's Old Sweet Song; 1946: Apple of His Eye.

BETTY HUTTON

(ELIZABETH JUNE THORNBURG) BORN: BATTLE CREEK, MI, FEBRUARY 26, 1921.

Few stars ever hit the heights with such a bang as Betty Hutton. She was loud, raucous, eager to make an impression, and, for some, she could be quite hard to take. For others she had the sort of unforgettable brio and brass that was a welcome antidote to the many colorless ingénues who decorated the screen in the 1940s. While still a teen, she landed a job singing with Vincent Lopez's band, performing with them in New York nightclubs and appearing in a handful of short subjects shot in Manhattan, including one called, simply, "Vincent Lopez and His Orchestra." Going solo, she got a part in the Broadway revue *Two for the Show*, followed by *Panama Hattie*, in support of Ethel Merman. She made enough of an impression on one of that show's writers, Buddy de Sylva, that he asked her to join Paramount when he became the studio's head of production. Put into the musical comedy *The Fleet's In*, to support Dorothy Lamour and William Holden, she made an immediate impact as Lamour's manic roommate, performing the playful "Arthur Murray Taught Me Dancing in a Hurry." Her direct co-star was Eddie Bracken, and with him she was seen as part of the connecting plot in the all-star *Star Spangled Rhythm*, a tour of the Paramount backlot featuring almost every name on the studio roster, and the Technicolor *Happy Go Lucky*, which still had her in a secondary role, in support of Mary Martin and Dick Powell, but gave her another of her best-known show stoppers, "Murder, He Says."

She got upped to leading lady to play opposite the studio's biggest star attractions in a pair of military-themed musical comedies, *Let's Face It*, with Bob Hope, and *Here Come the Waves*, with Bing Crosby. Unlike most of their female co-stars, she did not take a back seat to them, belting out another powerhouse number, Cole Porter's "Let's Not Talk About Love," in the Hope film, and going so far as to play twins in the Crosby movie. In between, she had her defining film of the war years, the frenetic, risqué *The Miracle of Morgan's Creek*, playing the irresponsible good-time gal who ends up pregnant by a soldier she can't identify. Eddie Bracken (as her spineless admirer) was again her co-star, and director Preston Sturges kept things moving along at a pace that was often hilarious. There was a pleasant ensemble with *And the Angels Sing*, where her now-expected comic song set piece, bellowed at full throttle, was "His Rocking Horse Ran Away." Hutton was proving to be a box-office draw, carrying two biopics to success, *Incendiary Blonde*, as nightclub hostess Texas Guinan, and *The Perils of Pauline*, as silent movie star Pearl White. There was also a relatively low-budget affair, *The Stork Club*, in which she was nicely teamed with Barry Fitzgerald, and her first taste of flat-out disaster with the adaptation of Elmer Rice's *Dream Girl*, giving a monotonous and, frankly, wretched performance as a daydreaming heiress.

Fortunately a dream role landed in her lap courtesy of MGM, when the studio, fed up with Judy Garland's undependable behavior, borrowed Hutton for the 1950 screen version of *Annie Get Your Gun*. Brightly directed by George Sidney, this property and character fit her bombastic personality to a tee, becoming a box-office smash and the peak of her career. That same year, in *Let's Dance*, she proved to be an uncomfortable match with Fred Astaire, whose stylishness was, of course, in complete contrast to her indelicacies. She was back in form, however, as the trapeze artist (performing most of her own stunts) in love with disinterested big-top manager Charlton Heston in the blockbuster circus film *The Greatest Show on Earth*, which won the Academy Award for Best Picture of 1952 and became one of the top-grossing movies of all time. Shortly afterwards she married choreographer Charles Curran and wound up walking out of her contract when the studio would not agreed to him directing her next picture. It proved to be a self-destructive move from which her career never recovered. There were nightclub engagements; one last post-Paramount movie, UA's *Spring Reunion*, in 1957; a short-lived TV

series; and a noted flop television spectacular, *Satins and Spurs*. By 1967 she was filing for bankruptcy. She ended up working as a housekeeper at a rectory, eventually returning to Broadway to play Miss Hannigan in the hit musical *Annie* to very little fanfare; the comet that had scorched the screen in the 1940s was a name that meant little to modern audiences. Her sister, Marion Hutton, was also an actress.

Screen: 1942: The Fleet's In; Star Spangled Rhythm; 1943: Happy Go Lucky; Let's Face It; 1944: The Miracle of Morgan's Creek; And the Angels Sing; Here Come the Waves; 1945: Incendiary Blonde; Duffy's Tavern; The Stork Club; 1946: Cross My Heart; 1947: The Perils of Pauline; 1948: Dream Girl; 1949: Red, Hot and Blue; 1950:Annie Get Your Gun; Let's Dance; 1952: The Greatest Show on Earth; Sailor Beware; Somebody Loves Me; 1957: Spring Reunion; 1990: Preston Sturges: The Rise and Fall of an American Dreamer.

NY Stage: 1940: Two for the Show; Panama Hattie; 1964: Fade Out, Fade In; 1980: Annie.

Select TV: 1954: Satins and Spurs (sp); 1959–60: The Betty Hutton Show (series).

JIM HUTTON

(DANA JAMES HUTTON) BORN: BINGHAMTON, NY, MARCH 31, 1934. RAISED IN ALBANY, NY. DIED: JUNE 2, 1979.

Tall and gangly like a basketball player, the amiable, boyishly good-looking Jim Hutton found himself associated with too many of the bubble-headed romantic farces of the early 1960s, which caused him to be underrated for his natural capabilities at light comedy. It was while serving in the military in Germany that he began acting, being discovered shortly afterwards by director Douglas Sirk. Billed as "Dana J. Hutton," he was cast in a small part in Sirk's World War II epic, *A Time to Love and a Time to Die*, released by Universal. MGM signed him to a contract in 1960, and he became one of *The Subterraneans*, the studio's wrong-headed attempt to film Jack Kerouac's view of the beatnik world. After that he played a college student named TV Thompson, obsessed with sex in general and Paula Prentiss specifically, in *Where the Boys Are*. The movie was inane but fairly popular, so he was back with Prentiss, playing off of her very nicely in the air-light concoctions *The Honeymoon Machine*, in which he and Steve McQueen were sailors trying to outwit a roulette table; *Bachelor in Paradise*, where they supported Bob Hope; *The Horizontal Lieutenant*, which marked his first actual lead; and *Looking for Love*, an especially insipid pop musical in which he was a short-tempered inventor.

He at least got a chance to play a Tennessee Williams script, albeit one that was still pretty much in this vein, *Period of Adjustment*, opposite Jane Fonda. Leaving MGM, he went into more serious properties with *Major Dundee*, though still called on to provide some humor, as a cavalry lieutenant, and the heavily criticized Vietnam War epic *The Green Berets*, as a sergeant. There were still comedy roles, including two for Columbia: *Walk, Don't Run*, which, if nothing else, allowed him to play scenes with the master, Cary Grant, and *Who's Minding the Mint?*, a heist comedy that was probably the most enjoyable of all of Hutton's films. In the early 1970s he became a pretty regular face on TV, eventually playing one of literature's great sleuths in his own series, *The Adventures of Ellery Queen*. There was one last, ill-advised return to theatrical features, *Psychic Killer*, a fairly embarrassing attempt to squash his nice guy image, as a mental patient on a killing rampage. He passed away from cancer of the liver one year before his son, Timothy, found motion picture fame with *Ordinary People*.

Screen: AS DANA J. HUTTON: 1958: A Time to Love and a Time to Die.

AS JIM HUTTON: 1959: Ten Seconds to Hell; 1960: The Subterraneans; Where the Boys Are; 1961: The Honeymoon Machine; Bachelor in Paradise; 1962: The Horizontal Lieutenant; Period of Adjustment; 1964: Looking for Love; 1965: Major Dundee; The Hallelujah Trail; Never Too Late; 1966: Walk, Don't Run; The Trouble With Angels; 1967: Who's Minding the Mint?; 1968: The Green Berets; 1969: Hellfighters; 1975: Psychic Killer.

Select TV: 1971: The Deadly Hunt; The Reluctant Heroes; They Call It Murder; 1972: Call Her Mom; 1973: Don't Be Afraid of the Dark; 1974: The Underground Man; Nightmare at 43 Hillcrest; 1975: Ellery Queen/Too Many Suspects; 1975–76: The Adventures of Ellery Queen (series); 1978: Flying High.

MARTHA HYER
BORN: FORT WORTH, TX, AUGUST 10, 1924.
ED: NORTHWESTERN UNIV.,
PASADENA PLAYHOUSE.

Another of Hollywood's innocuous but singularly unspectacular talents, Martha Hyer came to the movies from the Pasadena Playhouse, signing a contract with RKO. That studio gave her one uneventful assignment after another, the most substantial work they had to offer being the leading lady to Tim Holt in a pair of his "B" westerns, *Gun Smugglers* and *Rustlers*. Even after leaving RKO, she stayed out west for a spell, with breaks to play the girlfriend in the sci-fi *Riders to the Stars*; William Holden's shallow fiancée in *Sabrina*, and a moll in the crime thriller *Down Three Dark Streets*. Universal made her the human in Donald O'Connor's life in *Francis in the Navy*; a movie star in *Kelly and Me*; and straight woman to comedians Rowan and Martin in their first vehicle, *Once Upon a Horse*. Since she seemed unlikely to be accused of upstaging anyone, she was placed alongside Jerry Lewis in *The Delicate Delinquent* and Bob Hope in *Paris Holiday*, attending to her leading lady chores dutifully. A career highlight of sorts was *Some Came Running*, where she was, inexplicably, Oscar-nominated for her very average work as the teacher with an interest in wanderer Frank Sinatra. It was back to being the "other woman" in *Houseboat*, followed by star parts for Fox in *Desire in the Dust*, falling in love with convict Ken Scott, and *The Right Approach*. She was soon back to supporting work for the sensationalized box-office hit *The Carpetbaggers*; *Bikini Beach*, doing a study on teen intelligence; and *The Sons of Katie Elder*, holding her own very nicely against the mostly male cast. In 1966 she married producer Hal Wallis (he died in 1986) after which she cut down on her acting jobs considerably. She published her autobiography, *Finding My Way*, as Martha Hyer Wallis, in 1990.

Screen: 1946: The Locket; 1947: Thunder Mountain; Born to Kill; Woman on the Beach; 1948: The Velvet Touch; Gun Smugglers; 1949: The Clay Pigeon; The Judge Steps Out; Roughshod; Rustlers; 1950: The Lawless; Outcasts of Black Mesa; Salt Lake Raiders; The Kangaroo Kid; Frisco Tornado; 1951: The Invisible Mr. Unmei/Oriental Evil; 1952: Geisha Girl; Wild Stallion; Yukon Gold; 1953: Abbott and Costello Go to Mars; So Big; 1954: Riders to the Stars; Lucky Me; Wyoming Renegades; The Scarlet Spear; The Battle of Rogue River; Sabrina; Down Three Dark Streets; Cry Vengeance; 1955: Francis in the Navy; Kiss of Fire; Paris Follies of 1956; 1956: Red Sundown; Showdown at Abilene; 1957: Battle Hymn; Kelly and Me; Mister Cory; The Delicate Delinquent; My Man Godfrey; 1958: Houseboat; Paris Holiday; Once Upon a Horse; Some Came

Running; 1959: The Big Fisherman; The Best of Everything; 1960: Ice Palace; Desire in the Dust; Mistress of the World; 1961: The Right Approach; The Last Time I Saw Archie; 1962: A Girl Named Tamiko; 1963: The Man From the Diner's Club; Wives and Lovers; 1964: The Carpetbaggers; Pyro; Blood on the Arrow; Bikini Beach; First Men in the Moon; 1965: The Sons of Katie Elder; 1966: The Chase; The Night of the Grizzly; Picture Mommy Dead; 1967: The Happening; War — Italian Style; Lo Scatenato/Catch as Catch Can (nUSr); La Mujerde Otro/Another Man's Wife (nUSr); 1968: House of 1,000 Dolls; 1969: Once You Kiss a Stranger; 1970: Crossplot (nUSr); 1973: Day of the Wolves.

Select TV: 1953: Exit — Linda Davis (sp); 1954: Meet a Lonely Man (sp); 1955: Broadway (sp); 1956: Ivy (sp); Jezebel (sp); 1958:Reunion (sp); 1964: Doesn't Anybody Know Who I Am? (sp); 1967: Some May Live.

REX INGRAM

BORN: CAIRO, IL, OCTOBER 20, 1895.
DIED: SEPTEMBER 19, 1969.

One of the few black performers to actually receive some substantial roles during Hollywood's "golden age," Rex Ingram had graduated from medical school but ended up doing extra work in silent movies. Roles didn't get any bigger as the sound era came, so he busied himself with some theater. In 1936 Warner Bros. helped boost his standing when they cast him as De Lawd in their all-black fantasy *The Green Pastures*, an odd blend of parables and whimsy that, although looked on today as patronizing, provided the actor with a chance to show just how effortlessly he could seize the screen with his deep voice and commanding presence. From there he was cast as Jim in the Mickey Rooney version of *The Adventures of Huckleberry Finn*, which was fitting since Ingram was himself born on a riverboat near Cairo, Illinois. It also happened to be one of the better attempts to put this frustratingly unfilmable work of fiction on the screen. His best-remembered role came with the lavish 1940 British production of *The Thief of Baghdad*, stealing every minute of this sometimes magical, sometimes heavy-handed bit of escapism, as the giant genie on whose ponytail Sabu rides. In another all-black production, MGM's *Cabin the Sky*, he was miles from his previous position in heaven, this time repeating his Broadway role as Lucifer, trying to tempt Eddie Anderson by sending Lena Horne his way. In later years he could be seen playing such supporting parts as the African guide in *Watusi*, reprising the character once played by Paul Robeson in the earlier version of the same story, *King Solomon's Mines*; Eartha Kitt's father in *Anna Lucasta*, Uncle Felix in *God's Little Acre*, and a wizened instructor trying to educate the locals in a racist Southern town in *Hurry Sundown*. He is not to be confused with the silent film director (1892–1950) of the same name.

Screen: 1918: Tarzan of the Apes; 1933: The Emperor Jones; 1934: Harlem After Midnight; 1936: The Green Pastures; 1939: The Adventures of Huckleberry Finn; 1940: The Thief of Baghdad; 1942: The Talk of the Town; 1943: Sahara; Cabin the Sky; Fired Wife; 1944: Dark Waters; 1945: A Thousand and One

Nights; Adventure; 1948: Moonrise; 1955: Tarzan's Hidden Jungle; 1956: Congo Crossing; 1957: Hell on Devil's Island; 1958: God's Little Acre; Anna Lucasta; 1959: Escort West; Watusi; 1960: Elmer Gantry; Desire in the Dust; 1964: Your Cheatin' Heart; 1967: Hurry Sundown; 1968: Journey to Shiloh.

NY Stage: 1929: Lulu Belle; 1934: Theodora the Queen; Stevedore; Dance With Your Gods; 1935: Stick-in-the-Mud; 1937: Marching Song; 1938: Haiti; Sing Out the News!; 1940: Cabin in the Sky; 1946: St. Louis Woman; Lysistrata; 1957: Waiting for Godot; 1961: Kwamina.

Select TV: 1955: The Emperor Jones (sp); The Intolerable Portrait (sp).

JOHN IRELAND

BORN: VANCOUVER, CANADA, JANUARY 30, 1914.
RAISED IN NY. DIED: MARCH 21, 1992.

Straddling somewhere between leads and character parts was John Ireland, his slightly angst-ridden features suggesting inner torment or out-and-out villainy. Originally a swimmer in water carnivals, he eventually took up legitimate acting, ending up in several stage productions in the early 1940s. As a result 20th Century-Fox signed him to a contract, starting him off in one of the best war films of the period, *A Walk in the Sun*, in which he was cast as a soldier named Windy. Although he also got involved in another outstanding project, *My Darling Clementine*, as one of the Clanton brothers, he found he could get actual leads elsewhere and left Fox to star in Eagle-Lion's *Railroaded!*, as a vicious gangster out to kill poor Sheila Ryan; *Open Secret*, a rare movie of the era that confronted anti-Semitism; and in Screen Guild's *I Shot Jesse James*, in which he played Bob Ford, the "I" of the title. Staying out west, he suggestively compared guns with Montgomery Clift in the hit *Red River*, which also featured Joanne Dru among the cast. She and Ireland married in 1949 (they divorced in 1958), the same year they both had a smash success in the Academy Award-winner for Best Picture, *All the King's Men*. Ireland was the newspaperman initially taken in by megalomaniac politician Broderick Crawford, and his fine performance earned him an Oscar nomination in the supporting category. After this high point, he returned to familiar fare with *The Return of Jesse James*, only this time he was cast as a Jesse James look-alike, in a movie that pretty much reflected the budget level of most of the films Ireland was asked to carry. Others included *The Basketball Fix*, as a sportswriter helping a college jock fend off gangsters; *The Bushwhackers*, as a peace-seeking vet reluctantly involved in a range war; *Security Risk*, as a federal agent tracking down commie spies at the Big Bear resort; *Outlaw Territory*, which he co-directed and co-produced with Lee Garmes; and *The Fast and the Furious*, another of his co-director credits and a film that was at least historically significant, being the first movie made for the independent company that would become American International Pictures.

Ireland was seen in larger-budgeted movies like *Queen Bee*, ill at ease as Joan Crawford's extra-marital fling; *Gunfight at the O.K. Corral*, covering some of the same ground as in *My Darling Clementine*, but this time playing Johnny Ringo; *Spartacus*, portraying a fellow-slave who joins Kirk Douglas in the revolt; and two for producer Samuel Bronston, *55 Days at Peking*, as Charlton Heston's sardonic second-in-command, and *The Fall of the Roman Empire*, as a bearded barbarian. In one of his last leads, he was the killer tormented by a pair of teens in *I Saw What You Did*, after which he went the foreign-market route, churning out all kinds of un-exportable films, the actual existence of many of them being hard to substantiate. There was also the expected grind-house fare like *Satan's Cheerleaders*, as a sheriff heading a satanic cult, and *Guyana: Cult of the Damned*, cashing in on the Jim Jones tragedy; not to mention a fair amount of made-for-TV films and guest spots, all of which hopefully kept him busy enough that he never actually had to watch this stuff.

Screen: 1945: A Walk in the Sun; 1946: Behind Green Lights; It Shouldn't Happen to a Dog; My Darling Clementine; Wake Up and Dream; Somewhere in the Night (voice); 1947: Railroaded!; The Gangster; Repeat Performance (narrator); 1948: Open Secret; I Love Trouble; Raw Deal; A Southern Yankee; Joan of Arc; Red River; 1949: I Shot Jesse James; Roughshod; The Walking Hills; Anna Lucasta; Mr. Soft Touch; The Doolins of Oklahoma; All the King's Men; The Undercover Man (narrator); 1950: Cargo to Capetown; The Return of Jesse James; 1951: Vengeance Valley; The Scarf; Little Big Horn; The Basketball Fix; Red Mountain; This Is Korea (narrator); 1952: The Bushwhackers; Hurricane Smith; 1953: The 49th Man; Combat Squad; Outlaw Territory/Hannah Lee (and co-dir.; co-prod.); 1954: The Good Die Young; Security Risk; The Fast and the Furious (and co-dir.); Southwest Passage; The Steel Cage; 1955: Glass Tomb/The Glass Cage; Queen Bee; Hell's Horizon; 1956: Gunslinger; 1957: Gunfight at the O.K. Corral; Stormy Crossing/Black Tide; 1958: No Place to Land; Party Girl; 1960: Faces in the Dark; Spartacus; 1961: Wild in the Country; Return of a Stranger; 1962: Brushfire!; 1963: No Time to Kill (W Ger: 1959); 55 Days at Peking; The Ceremony; 1964: The Fall of the Roman Empire; 1965: I Saw What You Did; Day of the Nightmare; 1967: Fort Utah; Flight From the Hawk; War Devils (nUSr); Tutto per Tutto/Copperface (nUSr); Odio per Odio/Hate for Hate (nUSr); 1968: Arizona Bushwhackers; Villa Rides!; Corri Uomo Corri/Run, Man, Run (nUSr); El Che Guevara/Rebel With a Cause/Diary of a Rebel (nUSr); A Pistol for a Hundred Coffins (nUSr); Quel caldo Maledetto Giorno di Fuocco/Damned Hot Day of Fire (nUSr); 1969: Quanto Costa Morire (nUSr); Zenadel (nUSr); The Insatiables/Carnal Circuit (nUSr); Ulna Sull'altra/One on Top of the Other (nUSr); T'ammazzo!/Trusting Is Good ... Shooting Is Better (nUSr); 1970: The Adventurers; 1971: Dirty Heroes; Escape to the Sun;

The Challenge of the Mackennas/Badlands Drifter (nUSr); 1972: Northeast of Seoul (nUSr); 1973: One on Top of the Other; 1974: The House of Seven Corpses; Welcome to Arrow Beach/Tender Flesh; The Mad Butcher; 1975: Farewell, My Lovely; Il Letto in Piazza/Sex Diary (nUSr); Noi Non Siamo Angeli/We Are No Angels (nUSr); 1977: Satan's Cheerleaders; Ransom/Maniac/Assault on Paradise; The Perfect Killer (dtc); Madame Kitty; The Swiss Conspiracy; Kino, the Padre on Horseback (nUSr); Taste of Death (dtv); Tomorrow Never Comes; 1978: Verano Sangriento (nUSr); Love and the Midnight Auto Supply; 1979: Delta Fox; Bordello (dtv); On the Air Live with Captain Midnight (filmed 1976); The Shape of Things to Come; 1980: Guyana — Cult of the Damned; Las Mujeres de Jeremias/Garden of Venus (nUSr); 1982: The Incubus; 1984: The Treasure of the Amazon (dtv); 1985: Martin's Day; 1986: Thunder Run; 1988: Miami Horror (dtv); Sundown: The Vampire in Retreat (dtv); Terror Night/Final Curtain (dtv); Messenger of Death; 1990: Graveyard Story (nUSr); 1991: Waxwork II: Lost in Time (dtv).

NY Stage: 1941: Fiddler's House; Not in Our Stars; Macbeth; 1942: Native Son; 1943: Counterattack; Richard III; A New Life; Doctors Disagree; 1944: A Highland Fling; 1948: The Rats of Norway; 1955: Deadfall.

Select TV: 1952: The Man I Marry (sp); 1954: Prisoner in the Town (sp); Time Bomb (sp); 1955: The Bridge (sp); Murder in Paradise (sp); Lonely Man (sp); 1956: Dealer's Choice (sp); Ordeal (sp); 1957: Without Incident (sp); A Sound of Different Drummers (sp); 1963: A Hero for Our Times (sp); 1974: The Phantom of Hollywood; The Girl on the Late, Late Show; 1978: The Millionaire; 1979: Crossbar; 1980: The Courage of Kavik the Wolf Dog; Tourist; Marilyn: The Untold Story; 1982: Cassie & Co. (series); 1986: Seasons in the Sun; 1988: Bonanza: The Next Generation; Perry Mason: The Case of the Lady in the Lake.

BURL IVES

BORN: HUNT, IL, JUNE 14, 1909.
DIED: APRIL 14, 1995.

Hefty, bearded Burl Ives, with the honeyed quaver to his voice, could easily have made his reputation on his singing alone, but someone had the great idea to hire him for character parts too, unveiling one of the most charismatic and scene-stealing of actors. His early years were spent wandering, traveling across the country performing odd jobs and singing for pay. After employment on an Indiana radio station and some professional musical training in New York, he began to concentrate on warbling the folk ballads that would make him famous. He became well known on both the airwaves and in nightclubs, also appearing on Broadway in the revue *Sing Out Sweet Land*, which featured his inimitable rendition of "Blue Tail Fly." 20th Century-Fox debuted him on the big screen in two of their rural Technicolor dramas, *Smoky* and *Green Grass of Wyoming*, while Disney made him one of the stars of *So Dear to My Heart*, as the town blacksmith who helps young Bobby Driscoll enter his pet sheep in the county fair. The movie also supplied him with a lovely Oscar-nominated ballad, "Lavender Blue," sung to Beulah Bondi. He continued to build praise for his acting in *East of Eden*, as the sheriff, and *The Power and the Prize*, as a business tycoon, and made an appearance as himself in the acclaimed *A Face in the Crowd*.

Then came the role that would put him on the acting map forever. As the bellowing, fearsome yet sympathetic and practical Big Daddy in Tennessee Williams's original 1955 Broadway production of *Cat on a Hot Tin Roof*, Ives won raves. Three years later he would make 1958 the peak of his movie career, repeating his role in MGM's hit adaptation and doing equally smashing work as the crude farmer in *Desire Under the Elms*; a swamp dweller in *Winds Across the Everglades*; and, best of all, the overbearing, stubborn patriarch feuding with Charles Bickford in the fine western epic *The Big Country*, making a memorable entrance interrupting a posh soiree. For the last he won the Academy Award for Best Supporting Actor of 1958. Hollywood continued to utilize his glowering presence in such movies as *Let No Man Write My Epitaph*, as a Chicago judge; *The Spiral Road*, as Rock Hudson's physician mentor; *Ensign Pulver*, following in James Cagney's footsteps as the unreasonable captain, giving a far more unpleasant interpretation of the part; and *The Brass Bottle*, as an amiable genie in this piffling comedy. Best of this period was another Disney offering, *Summer Magic*, in which he once again stole the show, singing a delightful number, "The Ugly Bug Ball." In 1964 he made his mark in television history as the narrator of the classic animated special *Rudolph the Red-Nosed Reindeer*, which gave him another signature song, "Holly Jolly Christmas." In later years there were star parts in *The McMasters*, running a farm with former slave Brock Peters, and *Earthbound*, befriending a family of aliens, but these films weren't widely seen to say the least.

Screen: 1946: Smoky; 1948: Green Grass of Wyoming; Station West; 1949: So Dear to My Heart; 1950: Sierra; 1955: East of Eden; 1956: The Power and the Prize; 1957: A Face in the Crowd; 1958: Desire Under the Elms; Cat on a Hot Tin Roof; The Big Country; Wind Across the Everglades; 1959: Day of the Outlaw; 1960: Our Man in Havana; Let No Man Write My Epitaph; 1962: The Flying Clipper (narrator); The Spiral Road; 1963: Summer Magic; 1964: The Brass Bottle; Ensign Pulver; 1966: The Daydreamer (voice); 1967: Blast Off!/Those Fantastic Flying Fools; 1970: The McMasters; 1976: Baker's Hawk; Hugo the Hippo (voice); 1979: Just You and Me, Kid; 1981: Earthbound; 1982: White Dog; 1986: Uphill All the Way; 1988: Two-Moon Junction.

NY Stage: 1938: The Boys From Syracuse; 1940: Heavenly Express; 1942: This Is the Army; 1944: Sing Out Sweet Land!; 1949: She Stoops to Conquer; 1952: Paint Your Wagon; 1954: Show Boat; 1955: Cat on a Hot Tin Roof; 1967: Dr. Cook's Garden.

Select TV: 1957: To Die Alone (sp); The Miracle Worker (sp); High-Low (series); 1959: Absalom, My Son (sp); 1964: Rudolph the Red-Nosed Reindeer (sp); 1965–66: O.K. Crackerby (series); 1968: The Sound of Anger; Pinocchio (sp); 1969: The Whole World Is Watching; 1969–70: The Lawyers (series); 1970: The Man Who Wanted to Live Forever; 1976: Captains and the Kings (ms); 1977: Roots (ms); 1978: The Bermuda Depths; The New Adventures of Heidi; 1984: The Ewok Adventure (narrator); 1987: Poor Little Rich Girl: The Barbara Hutton Story.

J

RICHARD JAECKEL

BORN: LONG BEACH, NY, OCTOBER 10, 1926.
DIED: JUNE 14, 1997.

Possessing a certain boyish quality about him, character player Richard Jaeckel started in movies at such a young age that it is not incorrect to think of him as having been around forever. He was all of 17 when he was spotted in the mailroom of 20th Century-Fox and asked to audition for the part of Private Johnny Anderson in one of that studio's major war epics, *Guadalcanal Diary*. He not only won the role but seemed to continue his association with war movies for as long as they were being regularly made, including some of the best known: *Sands of Iwo Jima*, *Battleground*, *Attack*, *The Naked and the Dead*, and *The Dirty Dozen*, finally promoted from private to sergeant with the last. Something about his small but sturdy figure screamed "manliness," and when he wasn't on the battlefields, he was usually out west in such films as *The Gunfighter*, as a would-be gunslinger taunting Gregory Peck and paying for it; *Apache Ambush*; *The Violent Men*, as one of the gunmen hired by land-hungry Edward G. Robinson; *3:10 to Yuma*, trying to snatch fellow outlaw Glenn Ford away from rancher Van Heflin; *Cowboy*; Elvis Presley's *Flaming Star*; and *Ulzana's Raid*. Perhaps his best-known role outside these genres was that of Terry Moore's athletic boyfriend, who makes aging Burt Lancaster jealous of his youth, in *Come Back, Little Sheba*. It would be hard to find anyone who had anything harsh to say about the actor, but few imagined him as an exciting enough performer to carry a movie, although he did have leads in the Japanese sci-fi junk film *The Green Slime*, as an astronaut battling the silly title creatures; and in *Jaws of Death*, where he was a shark activist driven to violence. After years of hard work he was honored with an Oscar nomination for his memorable death-by-drowning sequence in *Sometimes a Great Notion*, playing Paul Newman's cousin. In later years his résumé consisted of a lot of direct to video action titles, the most notable release during this period being Columbia's big-budget sci-fi adventure *Starman*, in which he had the clichéd role of the single-minded military skeptic out to destroy the friendly alien (Jeff Bridges).

Screen: 1943: Guadalcanal Diary; 1944: Wing and a Prayer; 1948: Jungle Patrol; 1949: City Across the River; Sands of Iwo Jima; Battleground; 1950: The Gunfighter; Wyoming Mail; 1951: Fighting Coast Guard; The Sea Hornet; 1952: Hoodlum Empire; My Son John; Come Back, Little Sheba; 1953: Big Leaguer; Sea of Lost Ships; 1954: The Shanghai Story; 1955: The Violent Men; Apache Ambush; 1956: Attack; 1957: 3:10 to Yuma; 1958: Cowboy; The Lineup; The Naked and the Dead; When Hell Broke Loose; The Gun Runners; 1960: The Gallant Hours; Platinum High School; Flaming Star; 1961: Town Without Pity; 1963: The Young and the Brave; 4 for Texas; 1965: Nightmare in the Sun; Town Tamer; 1966: Once Before I Die; 1967: The Dirty Dozen; 1968: The Devil's Brigade; 1969: The Green Slime; 1970: Chisum; Latitude Zero; 1971: Sometimes a Great Notion/Never Give an Inch; 1972: Ulzana's Raid; 1973: Pat Garrett and Billy the Kid; The Kill; 1974: The Outfit; Chosen Survivors; 1975: Gold Seekers/Surabaya Conspiracy (filmed 1970); The Drowning Pool; Part 2, Walking Tall; 1976: Grizzly; The Jaws of Death/ Mako: The Jaws of Death; 1977: Twilight's Last Gleaming; Day of the Animals; 1978: Speedtrap; 1979: The Dark; Delta Fox (filmed 1976); Pacific Inferno; 1980: Herbie Goes Bananas; 1981: ...All the Marbles; Mr. No Legs (nUSr); 1982: Cold River (filmed 1979); Blood Song/Dream Slayer (dtv); Airplane II: The Sequel; 1984: Killing Machine; The Fix/The Agitators (dtv); Starman; 1986: Black Moon Rising; 1989: Ghetto Blaster (dtv); 1990: Delta Force 2: Operation Stranglehold (dtv); 1991: The King of the Kickboxers (dtv); 1993: Martial Outlaw (dtv).

Select TV: 1951: TKO (sp); 1953: The Squeeze (sp); 1954: The Last Notch (sp); The Big Man (sp); 1955: The Petrified Forest (sp); 1956: Night Must Fall (sp); Smoke Jumpers (sp); 1957: Aftermath (sp); Ain't No Time for Glory (sp); 1958: The Days of November (sp); 1961–62: Frontier Circus (series); 1971: Deadly Dream; 1972–73: Banyon (series); 1973: Firehouse; The Red Pony; Partners in Crime; 1974: Firehouse (series); Born Innocent; 1975: The Last Day; 1978: Go West, Young Girl; 1979: Champions: A Love Story; Salvage; Salvage 1 (series); 1980: The $5.20 an Hour Dream; Reward; 1983: At Ease (series); The Awakening of Chandra; 1985: The Dirty Dozen: The Next Mission; 1985–87: Spenser: For Hire (series); 1988: Supercarrier (series); 1989: Baywatch: Panic at Malibu Pier; 1991–94: Baywatch (series).

SAM JAFFE

(SHALOM JAFFE) BORN: NEW YORK, NY,
MARCH 8, 1891. ED: COLUMBIA UNIV.
DIED: MARCH 24, 1984.

Whether you picture him with frizzy
hair or wearing dark make-up and a
turban, there was no mistaking tiny,
popeyed Sam Jaffe for anyone else. A one-time math
teacher, he joined the Washington Square Players in 1915,
making his New York stage debut for them in *The Clod*. 19
years later he made a memorable first impression on screen,
overacting outrageously (and bearing a certain off-putting
resemblance to Harpo Marx) as the nutty Grand Duke
Peter in the irresistible costume spectacle *The Scarlet
Empress*, opposite Marlene Dietrich. This was followed by
two career peaks, *Lost Horizon*, as the wise and ancient
High Lama, and the grand 1939 adventure *Gunga Din*, as
the heroic Indian water boy, his most famous movie role of
all, making audiences forget that he was, in fact, a 48-year-
old Jew from New York. These did not lead to an avalanche
of subsequent work, and Jaffe returned to New York where
he co-founded the Equity Library Theatre. Back in the
movies he was mesmerizing as the mastermind behind the
ill-fated robbery in the classic *The Asphalt Jungle*, earning
an Oscar nomination in the supporting category, and then
played the soft-spoken scientist enlightened by his
encounter with alien Michael Rennie in one of the outstanding sci-fi films of the genre, *The Day the Earth Stood
Still*. Certainly the most popular film in which he
appeared was the 1959 multi-Oscar-winner, *Ben-Hur*, as
Charlton Heston's loyal steward, Simonides, who ends up
imprisoned and lame after trying to clear his master's
name. In the early 1960s he created one of his best-
remembered characters, the title physician's wise old
mentor, Dr. Zorba, on the hit medical series *Ben Casey*,
which also featured his second wife, actress Bettye Ackerman.

Screen: 1934: The Scarlet Empress; We Live Again; 1937: Lost
Horizon; 1939: Gunga Din; 1943: Stage Door Canteen; 1946: 13
Rue Madeleine; 1947: Gentleman's Agreement; 1948: The
Accused; 1949: Rope of Sand; 1950: Under the Gun; The Asphalt
Jungle; 1951: I Can Get It for You Wholesale; The Day the Earth
Stood Still; 1957: Les Epions/The Spies; 1958: The Barbarian and
the Geisha; 1959: Ben-Hur; 1967: A Guide for the Married Man;
1968: Guns for San Sebastian; 1969: The Great Bank Robbery;
1970: The Dunwich Horror; 1971: Bedknobs and Broomsticks;
1980: Battle Beyond the Stars; 1983: On the Line/Downstream;
1984: Nothing Lasts Forever.

NY Stage: 1915: The Clod; 1918: Mrs. Warren's Profession;
1920: Samson and Delilah; 1921: The Idle Inn; 1922: The God
of Vengeance; 1924: The Main Line; Izzy; 1925: The Jazz Singer;
1930: Grand Hotel; 1934: The Bride of Torozko; 1937: The
Eternal Road; A Doll's House; 1939: The Gentle People; 1941:
King Lear (ob); 1942: Café Crown; 1944: Thank You Svoboda;
1947: This Time Tomorrow; 1954: Mademoiselle Colombe; The
Sea Gull (ob); 1956: The Adding Machine (ob); 1979: A
Meeting by the River.

Select TV: 1959: The Dingaling Girl (sp); The Final
Ingredient (sp); 1960: The Sound of Trumpets (sp); In the
Presence of Mine Enemies (sp); Legend of Lovers (sp);
1961–65: Ben Casey (series); 1969: Night Gallery; 1970:
Quarantined; The Old Man Who Cried Wolf; 1971: Sam Hill:
Who Killed the Mysterious Mr. Foster?; 1974: QB VII (ms);
1980: Gideon's Trumpet.

DEAN JAGGER

BORN: LIMA, OH, NOVEMBER 7, 1903.
DIED: FEBRUARY 5, 1991.

A soft-spoken, distinguished actor, Dean
Jagger is remembered principally for his later
incarnation as the bald-headed, fatherly sort,
a fountain of reason and restraint, although
his film roles dated back as far as the silent era. He originally
worked as an elementary school teacher before opting for the theater, joining a stock company in Grand Rapids, Michigan. In
time he ended up in vaudeville and on the radio, then made a
handful of movie appearances, starting with *Handcuffed*, in 1928.
On Broadway he appeared in the smash hit *Tobacco Road*, followed by *They Shall Not Live*, and interest from Hollywood was
reawakened as a result. Signed by Paramount, he played an
Indian in *Behold My Wife!*; a football coach in *College Rhythm*;
and a state trooper in *Car 99*, before finally landing himself top
billing, in a "B" western, *Wander of the Wasteland*, as an innocent
man on the lam from the law. This was a decidedly undistinguished period of his motion picture career, so he went back to
the theater after having churned out such low-budget fare as
Revolt of the Zombies and *Exiled to Shanghai*. Things began to
look up somewhat when he got to play the Mormon leader in the
Hollywood biopic *Brigham Young*, his quiet demeanor so perfect
for the role, although he was required to take a backseat in the
advertising and billing to the more glamorous Tyrone Power and
Linda Darnell, as the intrusive Hollywood love interest. From
there he was the baddie in an RKO western, *Valley of the Sun*, and
part of the vast cast of Goldwyn's pro-Russia epic, *The North Star*.

It was his role as the levelheaded Major Stovall, the bespectacled, pipe-smoking Air Force officer of *Twelve O'Clock High*, that
suddenly snapped his movie career into high gear. His gentle sense
of authority in the part won him the Academy Award for Best
Supporting Actor of 1949. From this point on Hollywood looked
on him to lend a certain decency or pious reverence to many a
project. In *It Grows on Trees* he watched as wife Irene Dunne's
newly planted trees sprouted cash, and in *My Son John* he was cast
as the self-righteous dad of evil Commie Robert Walker. He
coaxed Richard Burton to be a follower of Jesus in *The Robe*;
played the retired, too-good-to-be-true General in *White
Christmas*, referred to as the "Old Man" by an actor of the same
age, Bing Crosby; and was properly self-loathing as the ineffectual, conscience-stricken sheriff in *Bad Day at Black Rock*. There
was a starring role in the intellectual British-made sci-fi film *X the
Unknown*, battling monster mud; a stand-out part as Elvis
Presley's spineless dad in *King Creole*; and two of his best performances, as the father of novice Audrey Hepburn in *The Nun's
Story*, and as the sincere head of the evangelist organization that
welcomes Burt Lancaster into its tent in *Elmer Gantry*. By the late
1960s the work was becoming less "A," and he was seen as a nutty
old Indian trader in *Day of the Evil Gun*; a prospector in the drive-
in fave *Vanishing Point*; a crazed scientist in *God Bless Dr. Shagetz*,
a horror film that had additional scenes added to it, years after the
fact, so it could be shown as *Evil Town*; and a doctor in *Game of
Death*, this time appearing in the newly shot sequences into which
were spliced clips of the long-dead Bruce Lee.

Screen: 1928: Handcuffed; 1929: The Woman From Hell; 1930:
Whoopee!; 1934: You Belong to Me; College Rhythm; 1935:
Behold My Wife; Home on the Range; Wanderer of the
Wasteland; Car 99; Wings in the Dark; It's a Great Life!; Men
Without Names; People Will Talk; 1936: Woman Trap; Thirteen
Hours by Air; Revolt of the Zombies; Star for a Night; Pepper;
1937: Woman in Distress; Song of the City; Under Cover of

Night; Dangerous Number; Escape by Night; Exiled to Shanghai; **1940:** Brigham Young; **1941:** The Men in Her Life; Western Union; **1942:** Valley of the Sun; The Omaha Trail; **1943:** The North Star/Armored Attack; I Escaped From the Gestapo; **1944:** Alaska; When Strangers Marry; **1945:** A Yank in London/I Live in Grosvenor Square; **1946:** Sister Kenny; **1947:** Pursued; Driftwood; **1949:** Twelve O' Clock High; C Man; **1950:** Sierra; Dark City; **1951:** Rawhide; Warpath; **1952:** My Son John; Denver and Rio Grande; It Grows on Trees; **1953:** The Robe; **1954:** Executive Suite; Private Hell 36; White Christmas; **1955:** Bad Day at Black Rock; The Eternal Sea; It's a Dog's Life; **1956:** Red Sundown; On the Threshold of Space; X The Unknown; The Great Man; Three Brave Men; **1957:** 40 Guns; Bombers B-52; Bernardine; **1958:** The Proud Rebel; King Creole; **1959:** The Nun's Story; Cash McCall; **1960:** Elmer Gantry; **1961:** Parrish; The Honeymoon Machine; **1962:** Billy Rose's Jumbo; **1967:** First to Fight; **1968:** Firecreek; Tiger by the Tail; Day of the Evil Gun; **1969:** Smith!; **1970:** The Kremlin Letter; **1971:** Vanishing Point; **1975:** The Great Lester Boggs; So Sad About Gloria/Visions of Doom; **1977:** God Bless Dr. Shagetz/Evil Town; End of the World; **1979:** Game of Death; **1980:** Alligator.

NY Stage: **1933:** Tobacco Road; **1934:** They Shall Not Die; **1938:** Missouri Legend; Everywhere I Roam; **1939:** The Brown Danube; Farm of Three Echoes; **1940:** The Unconquered; **1948:** Doctor Social.

Select TV: **1952:** Our 200 Children (sp); **1955:** Visibility Zero (sp); My Son Is Gone (sp); **1956:** Night Call (sp); Smoke Jumpers (sp); **1957:** The Dark Side of the Earth (sp); **1962:** Mr. Doc (sp); **1963–65:** Mr. Novak (series); **1969:** The Lonely Profession; **1970:** The Brotherhood of the Bell; **1971:** Incident in San Francisco; **1972:** Truman Capote's The Glass House; The Delphi Bureau; **1973:** The Stranger; I Heard the Owl Call My Name; **1974:** The Hanged Man; **1976:** The Lindbergh Kidnapping Case; **1980:** Gideon's Trumpet.

EMIL JANNINGS

(THEODOR FRIEDRICH EMIL JANENZ)
BORN: RORSCHACH, SWITZERLAND,
JULY 23, 1884. RAISED IN NY, GERMANY.
DIED: JANUARY 3, 1950.

Significantly the first winner of the Academy Award for Best Actor, burly, versatile German thespian Emil Jannings was hailed in his day as one of film's consummate craftsmen, only to fall from grace when he refused to turn his back on his homeland. He was born in Switzerland to German parents who took him to live in New York for a spell (Jannings himself, in his 1928 autobiography, *How I Got Into Movies*, gave the false impression that he was American born) before he ended up in Germany. He studied acting under Max Reinhardt and made his movie debut as a bit player, beginning in 1914 with *Im Banne der Leidenschaft*. Over the next four years he worked himself up to leads in *Fuhrmann Henschel*, and in some pictures directed by Ernst Lubitsch, *Madame Dubarry* (as King Louis XV) and *Anna Boleyn* (as King Henry VIII), which came to the U.S. as *Passion* and *Deception*, respectively. His reputation began to grow around the world during a period when German cinema was at its most revered. Those films that brought him fame included *The Brothers Karamazov, Danton/All for a Woman, Loves of Pharaoh, Peter the Great, Quo Vadis?* (as Nero), and *Waxworks*. The last-named was an impressionistic episode film in which he showed up in the first installment, an Oriental fairytale. The two that turned him into the master of tragedy were F.W. Murnau's brief and brilliant

The Last Laugh, with Jannings as the hotel doorman who winds up as a washroom attendant (a tale told with a single title card), and *Variety*, with the actor as a trapeze artist whose unhappy marriage leads to murder. Hollywood eagerly awaited his arrival, and he signed a deal with Paramount Pictures.

He began his American film career at the stratosphere with *The Way of All Flesh*, as a bank cashier destroyed by a blonde temptress, and *The Last Command*, as a Czarist commander who ends up doing extra work in Hollywood, being directed by his former, vengeful rival. For the two he won the Academy Award at its first ceremony (both films were also runners-up for the Best Picture award), and follow-ups to these hits were quickly ordered. He was a criminal who begins to change his dirty ways under Fay Wray's influence in *The Street of Sin*; crazed Russian Czar Paul I in Lubitsch's *The Patriot*, one of the era's most coveted "lost" films; and, less successfully, a restaurateur in *Sins of the Fathers*, and part of a tragic triangle in *Betrayal*. The pattern was pretty much set, with Jannings usually being made to suffer because of a woman. This was the basis for the movie he made when he first returned to Germany, the one for which he would become forever associated, director Josef von Sternberg's haunting *The Blue Angel*, with Jannings at his most heartbreaking as the foolish professor obsessed with and ultimately degraded by nightclub tramp Marlene Dietrich. Because his thick accent made him completely unsuitable for American talking films, Jannings figured it was more beneficial to his career to remain in German, which would turn out to be a ghastly mistake as far as his reputation was concerned. Persuaded by Nazi minister of propaganda Herman Goebbels, he became head of the Tobis Film Company, making movies that were often blatantly anti-Semitic. In 1940 he became head of Germany's top film company, UFA, and was honored as "Artist of the State." Once the war ended he was promptly blacklisted and disappeared to Austria, a bitter and disgraced man.

Screen: **1914:** Im Banne der Leidenschaft; **1915:** Passionels Tagebuch; Arme Eva; Nacht des Grauens; **1916:** Die Ehe der Luise Rohrbach; **1917:** Klingendes Leben; Lulu; Das Leven ein Traum; Seeschlacht; Wenn Vier Dasselbe Machen; Ein Fideles Gefagnis; **1918:** Der Mann der Tat; Rose Bernd; Fuhrmann Henschel; Die Augen der mumie Maa; **1919:** Madame Dubarry/Passion; **1920:** Kolhiesels Tochter; Anna Boleyn/Deception; Danton/All for a Woman; The Brothers Karamazov; Algol; Der Stier von Olivera; **1921:** Die Ratten; Vendetta; Loves of Pharaoh; **1922:** Othello; August der Stark; **1923:** Die Grafin von Paris; Alles fur Geld/Fortune's Fool; **1924:** Tragodie der Liebe; Nju/Husbands or Lovers; Waxworks; Quo Vadis?; The Last Laugh; **1925:** Liebe Macht Blind; Variety; Tartuff; **1926:** Faust; **1927:** The Way of All Flesh; **1928:** The Last Command; The Street of Sin; The Patriot; **1929:** Sins of the Fathers; Betrayal; **1930:** The Blue Angel; Liebling der Gotter; **1931:** Sturme der Leidenschaf; **1932:** Konig Pausole/The Merry Monarch; **1934:** Der Schwarze Walfisch; **1935:** Der Alte und der Junge Konig; **1937:** Der Herrscher; Der Zerbrochene Krug; **1939:** Robert Koch der Beckampfer des Todes; **1940:** Ohm Kruger; **1942:** Die Entlassing; Altes Herz Wird Wieder Jung.

DAVID JANSSEN

(DAVID HAROLD MEYER) BORN: NAPONEE, NE,
MARCH 27, 1930. DIED: FEBRUARY 13, 1980.

With his grim-sounding voice and serious countenance, David Janssen was an actor who didn't seem to be having much fun but somehow managed to draw attention with his brooding presence. Despite a good number of movie credits, most people think of him first and foremost as a star of television. With his mother, a former Ziegfeld girl, he worked as a child with a traveling circus before they settled in Los Angeles, where mom's second marriage was to a man named Janssen. As a teenager he landed two movie roles, one as Johnny Weismuller's brother, in *Swamp Fire*, before returning to school where he nearly steered his future towards athletics. He returned to movies under contract to Universal in 1951, and remained very much in the supporting category, backing up a monkey in *Bonzo Goes to College*; the famous talking mule in three *Francis* installments, though as different characters in each; and precocious youngster Tim Hovey in both *The Private War of Major Benson* and *Toy Tiger*, to name a few. Audiences finally got to know who he was when his own TV series, *Richard Diamond — Private Detective*, aired in the late 1950s. Because of this, his movie roles got bigger, including *Hell to Eternity*, as a Marine; the notoriously bad live-action version of the comic strip *Dondi*, as an American G.I. taking care of a cutesy Italian orphan; and *King of the Roaring 20's*, oddly cast as gangster Arnold Rothstein.

His greatest claim to fame came with his next TV series, *The Fugitive*, playing Dr. Richard Kimble, searching for his wife's killer. Its final episode, aired in August of 1967, was the most-watched single program up to that time. Again, because of his small-screen success, Janssen got another chance at a movie career, faring well with a good thriller, *Warning Shot*, but ending up in some of the late 1960s biggest bores, *The Green Berets*, as a war correspondent following John Wayne and his troops into battle; *The Shoes of the Fisherman*, as a television reporter chronicling Anthony Quinn's ascent to Pope-hood; and *Marooned*, where he came to the rescue of his stranded fellow-astronauts. During the 1970s almost all of his work was on television, although he did venture into big-screen assignments with the glossy soap *Once Is Not Enough*; the sniper-in-the-stadium epic *Two Minute-Warning*; and *Inchon*, the Moonie-backed catastrophe which he was spared seeing the unveiling of, having died of a heart attack two years before its aborted release.

Screen: 1945: It's a Pleasure; 1946: Swamp Fire; 1952: Yankee Buccaneer; Untamed Frontier; Francis Goes to West Point; Bonzo Goes to College; 1955: Chief Crazy Horse; The Private War of Major Benson; Cult of the Cobra; To Hell and Back; Francis in the Navy; The Square Jungle; All That Heaven Allows; 1956: Never Say Goodbye; Away All Boats; Toy Tiger; Francis in the Haunted House; Showdown at Abilene; The Girl He Left Behind; 1958: Lafayette Escadrille; Darby's Rangers; 1960: Hell to Eternity; Dondi; 1961: Twenty Plus Two; Man-Trap; Ring of Fire; King of the Roaring 20's — The Story of Arnold Rothstein; 1962: Belle Sommers; 1963: My Six Loves; 1967: Warning Shot; 1968: The Green Berets; The Shoes of the Fisherman; 1969: Where It's At; Generation; Marooned; 1970: Macho Callahan; 1975: Once Is Not Enough; 1976: Two Minute Warning; 1977: Warhead/ Prisoner in the Middle; The Swiss Conspiracy; Golden Rendezvous/Nuclear Terror; 1980: Covert Action; 1982: Inchon.
Select TV: 1956: It Started With Eve (sp); 1957–60: Richard Diamond — Private Detective (series); 1957: Cupid Wore a Badge (sp); 1962: Shadow of a Hero (sp); 1963–67: The Fugitive (series); 1970: Night Chase; 1971: O'Hara: United States Treasury: Operation Cobra; 1971–72: O'Hara: U.S. Treasury (series); 1972: The Longest Night; Moon of the Wolf; 1973: Birds of Prey; Hijack!; Pioneer Woman; 1974: Smile, Jenny, You're Dead; Fer-de-Lance; 1974–76: Harry O (series); 1976: Stalk the Wild Child; Mayday at 40,000 Feet; 1977: A Sensitive Passionate Man; 1978: Superdome; Nowhere to Run; The Word (ms); 1978–79: Centennial (ms); 1979: S.O.S. Titanic; The Golden Gate Murders; 1980: High Ice; City in Fear.

CLAUDE JARMAN, JR.

BORN: NASHVILLE, TN, SEPTEMBER 27, 1934.
ED: VANDERBILT UNIV.

A lanky, blond cutie who projected a rural sincerity, Claude Jarman, Jr. was spotted in his fifth grade classroom by director Clarence Brown who was looking for someone inexperienced and natural to carry a certain MGM project. The film was the 1946 production of Marjorie Kinnan Rawling's novel *The Yearling*, and Jarman's love for his pet fawn was so endearing that he not only helped make this into an enduring family classic but received a special Academy Award as a result. To finish out his MGM contract, the studio made him the young version of Van Johnson in *High Barbaree*; an orphan befriending both Lassie and Jeanette MacDonald in *The Sun Comes Up*; and, best of all, the young Southern lad whose eyes are opened to the realities of prejudice when he sees an innocent black man face an angry mob in the fine Faulkner-based drama *Intruder in the Dust*. He spent most of the rest of his career in period settings, including the westerns *The Outriders*, as a doomed member of a wagon train; *Rio Grande*, as John Wayne's son; and *Hangman's Knot*, as one of Randolph Scott's band of Confederate soldiers, stunned to find out too late that the Civil War is over. By the mid-1950s he chose to leave acting behind and focus on school. He studied law, joined the Navy, and later became the executive director of the San Francisco Film Festival, receiving credit as producer of the rock concert film *Fillmore*. After years away from the camera, he appeared, unheralded, in 1977's massive mini-series, *Centennial*.
Screen: 1946: The Yearling; 1947: High Barbaree; 1949: The Sun Comes Up; Roughshod; Intruder in the Dust; 1950: The Outriders; Rio Grande; 1951: Inside Straight; 1952: Hangman's Knot; 1953: Fair Wind to Java; 1956: The Great Locomotive Chase.
Select TV: 1977–78: Centennial (ms).

LIONEL JEFFRIES

BORN: LONDON, ENGLAND, JUNE 10, 1926.
ED: RADA.

Bald, beak-nosed British character player Lionel Jeffries specialized in excitable types, nincompoops, and bureaucratic dolts, usually twitching his moustache or raising an eyebrow for maximum mugging effect. The son of Salvation Army social workers, he spent some time in the Far East where he worked on a radio station. This led to an interest in acting and schooling at RADA. His movie career began with a tiny part in a hypnotism comedy, *Will Any Gentleman ... ?* Two years later the British film industry began to take note when, at 29, he pulled off playing an elderly shopkeeper who finds a case full of cash in the "B" movie *Windfall*. Despite this being a lead, he pretty much stayed in supporting parts, and he could be spotted in several international productions, including *Lust for Life* and *The Nun's Story*, in both instances playing doctors. His fortunes really rose with his inspired comical performances as officious ninnies in a pair of Peter Sellers comedies, *Two Way Stretch* and *The Wrong Arm of the Law*, playing Inspector Nosey Parker in the latter. On a more malevolent note he did some grave robbing for Peter Cushing in *The Revenge of Frankenstein*, and was the ignorant and vindictive Marquis of Queensberry, who makes Peter Finch pay for his liaison with his son, in *The Trials of Oscar Wilde*. With the coming of the 1960s, he became well known to American audiences through his bumbling codger roles in such movies as *First Men in the Moon*, making an 1899 journey into space with Edward Judd; *Camelot*, as dotty old Pelinore; and *Chitty Chitty Bang Bang*, as the whacked-out grandfather who is mistakenly kidnapped. His ripe comic playing could be an asset or an endurance according to one's tolerance, and he certainly huffed and puffed what life he could into such weak fare as *Murder Ahoy!*, as a ship's captain reluctant to have Margaret Rutherford's sleuthing Miss Marple along for the trip; *The Secret of My Success*, in a variety of parts; and *Arrivederci, Baby!* In 1971 he made his directorial debut with the gentle *The Railway Children* (which he also wrote) and followed in this field with such barely seen projects as *The Amazing Mr. Blunden* (1972; and wr.), *Baxter* (1972), *Wombling Free* (1977; and wr.), and *The Water Babies* (1978; and wr.).

Screen: 1953: Will Any Gentleman…?; 1954: The Colditz Story; The Black Rider; 1955: Windfall; No Smoking; The Quatermass Experiment/The Creeping Unknown; All for Mary; 1956: Jumping for Joy; Eyewitness; Bhowani Junction; Lust for Life; The Baby and the Battleship; Up in the World; The High Terrace; The Man in the Sky/Decision Against Time; 1957: The Circle/Vicious Circle; Hour of Decision; Doctor at Large; All at Sea/Barnacle Bill; Blue Murder at St. Trinian's; 1958: Law and Disorder; Dunkirk; Orders to Kill; Up the Creek; The Revenge of Frankenstein; Girls at Sea; Behind the Mask; Nowhere to Go; Life Is a Circus; Further Up the Creek; 1959: The Nun's Story; Idol on Parade/Idle on Parade; Please Turn Over; 1960: Bobbikins; Two Way Stretch; The Trials of Oscar Wilde; Jazz Boat; Let's Get Married; Tarzan the Magnificent; 1961: The Hellions; Fanny; 1962: Operation Snatch; Mrs. Gibbons' Boys; Kill of Cure; The Notorious Landlady; The Wrong Arm of the Law; 1963: Call Me Bwana; The Crimson Blade/The Scarlet Blade; 1964: The Long Ships; First Men in the Moon; Murder Ahoy!; 1965: The Truth About Spring; You Must be Joking!; 1966: The Spy With a Cold Nose; Arrivederci, Baby!/Drop Dead Darling; 1967: Oh Dad, Poor Dad, Mama's Hung You in the Closet and I'm Feeling So Sad; Blast Off!/Those Fantastic Flying Fools; Camelot; 1968: Chitty Chitty Bang Bang; 1970: 12+1/The Thirteen Chairs; Lola/Twinky; Sudden Terror; 1971: Who Slew Auntie Roo?; 1974: What Changed Charley Farthing?/The Bananas Boat; 1975: Royal Flash; 1977: Wombling Free (voice; and dir.; wr.); 1978: The Water Babies (voice; and dir.; wr.); 1979: The Prisoner of Zenda; 1982: Better Late Than Never; 1989: A Chorus of Disapproval.

NY Stage: 1987: Pygmalion.

Select TV: Father Charlie (series); 1989: Danny, the Champion of the World; 1990: Jekyll & Hyde; 1992: Look at It This Way (ms); 1998: Heaven on Earth.

ALLEN JENKINS

(ALFRED McGONEGAL) BORN: NEW YORK, NY, APRIL 9, 1900. ED: AADA. DIED: JULY 20, 1974.

The inimitable, disgruntled, nasal delivery of Allen Jenkins made him one of the screen's perfect mugs, whether he played out-and-out villainous hoods, lighthearted lackeys, or dopey sidekicks. Born to theatrical parents, he initially worked backstage before segueing into acting, making his way to Broadway where he was seen in such notable plays as *The Front Page* and *Five Star Final*. Although he didn't end up in the film versions of either one of these, he was signed to a contract by Warner Bros., where he would become a cherished member of the studio that became synonymous with the gangster melodrama. He started out as a prisoner in *I Am a Fugitive From a Chain Gang*, appeared as a gunman sent to pressure Lee Tracy in the comedic *Blessed Event*; and then provided sidekick duties to James Cagney in such movies as *Jimmy the Gent* and *The Major of Hell*. Less expectedly, he was a volatile Communist sympathizer in *The Merry Frinks*, and a children's show performer in *Twenty Million Sweethearts*; and was twice called on to play Perry Mason's assistant, Spudsy, in *The Case of the Curious Bride* and *The Case of the Lucky Legs*. When Sam Levene and Teddy Hart were asked to repeat their stage roles, Jenkins, as box-office insurance of sorts, filled in the third spot for the droll comedy *Three Men on a Horse*. He then had two of his best-remembered sidekick roles, opposite a very dangerous Humphrey Bogart in the classic *Dead End*, and a relatively benign Edward G. Robinson in the very funny *A Slight Case of Murder*. He was so well known by the mid-1930s that Warners made him the star of the grade "C" mystery *Sh! The Octopus*, mugging outrageously with the spectacularly unfunny Hugh Herbert, and then gave him another substantial role, as Jane Wyman's dense police lieutenant boyfriend in *Torchy Blane…Playing with Dynamite*. Jenkins then reported for sidekick duty again, as George Sanders's chauffeur, "Goldy" Locke, in *The Gay Falcon*, *A Date With the Falcon* and *The Falcon Takes Over*; helped Gary Cooper learn about jive, playing a garbage man in the delightful *Ball of Fire*; and spent the whole of *Tortilla Flat* in a state of passive inebriation. By the late 1940s his assignments were mainly in cheap fare like *The Hat Box Mystery* and *The Case of the Baby-Sitter*, in both playing a clueless detective's assistant named Harvard Quinlan; and, most low-budget of all, *Chained for Life*, the only starring vehicle of Siamese twins Daisy and Violet Hilton. As he grew older, there were still a few "A" filmmakers willing to hire him for his peerless, snappish delivery, so he appeared as an elevator operator who takes a fancy to Thelma Ritter in *Pillow Talk*; a mug named Vermin in the musical *Robin and the 7 Hoods*; and a telegraph operator in the 1974 version of *The Front Page*, released posthumously.

Screen: 1931: The Girl Habit; 1932: Three on a Match; I Am a Fugitive From a Chain Gang; Blessed Event; Rackety Rax; 1933: Lawyer Man; 42nd Street; Bureau of Missing Persons; The Mayor of Hell; The Keyhole; Hard to Handle; Employees' Entrance; The Silk Express; Tomorrow at Seven; Professional Sweetheart; Blondie Johnson; The Mind Reader; Havana Widows; 1934: Jimmy the Gent; The St. Louis Kid; The Big Shakedown; The Case of the Howling Dog; I've Got Your Number; The Merry Frinks; Twenty Million Sweethearts; Happiness Ahead; Bedside; Whirlpool; 1935: The Case of the Curious Bride; The Case of the Lucky Legs; Page Miss Glory; Sweet Music; While the Patient Slept; A Night at the Ritz; I Live for Love; Miss Pacific Fleet; The Irish in Us; Broadway Hostess; 1936: Three Men on a Horse; Cain and Mabel; Sins of Man; The Singing Kid; 1937: Sing Me a Love Song; Dead End; Marked Woman; Ever Since Eve; The Singing Marine; Talent Scout; The Perfect Specimen; Sh! The Octopus; Ready, Willing and Able; Dance, Charlie, Dance; Marry the Girl; 1938: A Slight Case of Murder; The Amazing Dr. Clitterhouse; Gold Diggers in Paris; Swing Your Lady; Racket Busters; Fools for Scandal; Hard to Get; Heart of the North; Going Places; 1939: Five Came Back; Naughty but Nice; Destry Rides Again; Sweepstakes Winner; Torchy Blane…Playing With Dynamite; 1940: Tin Pan Alley; Brother Orchid; Margie; Meet the Wildcat; Oh Johnny, How You Can Love; 1941: Dive Bomber!; Ball of Fire; Footsteps in the Dark; The Gay Falcon; Time Out for Rhythm; Go West, Young Lady; A Date With the Falcon; 1942: Eyes in the Night; Tortilla Flat; They All Kissed the Bride; The Falcon Takes Over; Maisie Gets Her Man; 1943: Stage Door Canteen; 1945: Lady on a Train; Wonder Man; 1946: The

Dark Horse; Meet Me on Broadway; Singin' in the Corn; **1947:** Wild Harvest; The Senator Was Indiscreet; Easy Come, Easy Go; Fun on a Weekend; The Hat Box Mystery; The Case of the Babysitter; **1948:** The Inside Story; **1949:** The Big Wheel; Bodyhold; **1951:** Behave Yourself!; Chained for Life; Let's Go Navy; Crazy Over Horses; **1952:** Oklahoma Annie; The WAC from Walla Walla; **1959:** Pillow Talk; **1964:** Robin and the 7 Hoods; I'd Rather Be Rich; For Those Who Think Young; **1967:** Doctor, You've Got to Be Kidding; **1974:** The Front Page.

NY Stage: 1920: Floradora; **1922:** Secrets; **1926:** Glory Hallelujah; Potash and Perlmutter — Detectives; **1928:** The Front Page; **1930:** Five Star Final; **1931:** Wonderboy; **1932:** Blessed Event; **1943:** Something for the Boys.

Select TV: 1952: The Officer and the Lady (sp); **1953–56:** Waterfront (series): **1954:** Here Comes Calvin (sp); The Duke (series); **1955:** Numbers and Figures (sp); Honorary Degree (sp); **1956–57:** Hey Jeannie (series); **1957:** Three Men on a Horse (sp): **1961–62:** Top Cat (voice; series); **1971:** Getting Away from It All.

GLYNIS JOHNS

BORN: DURBAN, SOUTH AFRICA,
OCTOBER 5, 1923. RAISED IN ENGLAND.

With a husky voice that was part sexy, part flaky, Glynis Johns became one of the nicest additions to both the British and American postwar movie scenes. The daughter of character actor Mervyn Johns (*Jamaica Inn*, *Went the Day Well?*, *Dead of Night*, etc.), she began acting and dancing while a child and made her film debut playing a schoolgirl in *South Riding*, in 1938. Without attaining any great level of fame, she was seen as a Hutterite girl in the hit *49th Parallel/The Invaders*; played the daughter of an innkeeper (portrayed by her father) in the fantasy *The Halfway House*; was Deborah Kerr's wartime acquaintance in *Vacation From Marriage/Perfect Stranger*; and won the leads in *This Man Is Mine*, and in *Miranda*, the latter an uninspired story of a mermaid. After this period she began to get roles in movies that received substantial distribution in America because of their leading men: *State Secret*, a thriller with Douglas Fairbanks, Jr.; *No Highway in the Sky*, in which she was at her most beguiling as the stewardess who takes pity on eccentric James Stewart; *Appointment with Venus*, where she helped David Niven to rescue a cow from an island, hence its more-literal U.S. name, *Island Rescue*; and *The Card/The Promoter*, in which she was one of the women in the life of Alec Guinness. The British Disney unit called on her to play costumed ladies in *The Sword and the Rose* (Mary Tudor) and *Rob Roy, the Highland Rogue*, after which she continued to be the brightest thing about such movies as the remake of *The Beachcomber*, in the part Elsa Lanchester had played originally; *Loser Takes All*, as Rosanno Brazzi's fiancée; and *The Seekers*, ending up in an unfriendly New Zealand with Jack Hawkins.

Shortly after co-starring in Danny Kaye's finest hour, *The Court Jester*, she moved to America, playing *Major Barbara*, on Broadway, and taking star billing (although she died midway through the story) in a sentimental family film, *All Mine to Give*, which was also known by its more literal title, *The Day They Gave the Babies Away*. Almost immediately she went right back to England for the Lana Turner soaper *Another Time, Another Place*, and the I.R.A. drama *Shake Hands With the Devil*, which starred James Cagney. If there was a breakthrough American role it would probably be considered *The Sundowners*, in which she was a friendly Australian innkeeper romancing Peter Ustinov, a nice performance for which she received her sole Oscar nomination, in the supporting category. From this she got the star part in a

horror movie called *The Cabinet of Dr. Caligari*, which had nothing to do with the famous silent movie of the same name; carried the comical segment of the multi-character *The Chapman Report*; patiently endured Jackie Gleason's drinking in a mild piece of nostalgia, *Papa's Delicate Condition*; and then played her best-known role, the flighty mom in Disney's blockbuster smash *Mary Poppins*, singing "Sister Suffragette," but forsaking her freedom to give attention to her family. Ironically this didn't lead to an impressive run of work, and she seemed wasted playing James Stewart's wife in *Dear Brigitte*, while movies like *Don't Just Stand There* and *Lock Up Your Daughters!*, showed a decidedly poor judgment of scripts. In 1972 she made a triumphant return to the stage with *A Little Night Music*, introducing the hit song "Send in the Clowns" and winning a Tony Award. There was occasional TV and stage work and, later down the line, a role in another hit film, *While You Were Sleeping*, doing her stock scatterbrain act, as Peter Gallagher's mother-in-law.

Screen: 1938: South Riding; Murder in the Family; Prison Without Bars; **1939:** On the Night of the Fire; **1940:** The Briggs Family; Under Your Hat; **1941:** The Prime Minister; 49th Parallel/The Invaders (US: 1942); **1943:** The Adventures of Tartu/Tartu; **1944:** The Halfway House; **1945:** Perfect Strangers/Vacation From Marriage; **1946:** This Man Is Mine; **1947:** Frieda; An Ideal Husband; **1948:** Miranda; Third Time Lucky; **1949:** Dear Mr. Prohack; Helter Skelter; **1950:** The Blue Lamp; State Secret; **1951:** Flesh and Blood; No Highway in the Sky/No Highway; Appointment With Venus/Island Rescue; Encore; The Magic Box; **1952:** The Card/The Promoter; **1953:** The Sword and the Rose; Rob Roy, the Highland Rogue; Personal Affairs; The Weak and the Wicked/Young and Willing; **1954:** The Seekers/Land of Fury; The Beachcomber; Mad About Men; **1955:** Josephine and Men; **1956:** The Court Jester; Loser Takes All; All Mine to Give/The Day They Gave the Babies Away; Around the World in Eighty Days; **1958:** Another Time, Another Place; **1959:** Shake Hands With the Devil; **1960:** The Sundowners; The Spider's Web; **1962:** The Cabinet of Dr. Caligari; The Chapman Report; **1963:** Papa's Delicate Condition; **1964:** Mary Poppins; **1965:** Dear Brigitte; **1967:** Don't Just Stand There; **1969:** Lock Up Your Daughters!; **1972:** Under Milk Wood; **1973:** Vault of Horror; **1988:** Zelly and Me; **1993:** Nukie (dtv); **1994:** The Ref; **1995:** While You Were Sleeping; **1999:** Superstar.

NY Stage: 1952: Gertie; **1956:** Major Barbara; **1963:** Too True to be Good; **1972:** A Little Night Music; **1989:** The Circle.

Select TV: 1952: Lily — The Queen of the Movies (sp); **1953:** Two for Tea (sp); **1961:** The $200 Parlay (sp); **1963:** Windfall (sp); **1963:** Glynis (series); **1982:** Little Gloria — Happy at Last; **1984:** Spragghe; **1988–89:** Coming of Age (series).

BEN JOHNSON

BORN: PAWNEE, OK, JUNE 13, 1920.
DIED: APRIL 8, 1996.

Few actors seemed so authentically a part of the American West as Ben Johnson, and he was wise enough not to stray too often from the milieu into which he fit so comfortably. A former rodeo rider, he came to Hollywood when his horse was needed for the film *The Outlaw*, eventually serving as a stunt rider and double. (His actual on-screen appearances during this period are open to debate, with different sources listing different films). Director John Ford, feeling Johnson had real presence, made him a member of his stock company with parts in *3 Godfathers*, *She Wore a Yellow Ribbon*; *Wagon Master*, his largest role, guiding a group of Mormons out west; and *Rio Grande*. Between these he was the bashful leading man in love with Terry Moore, who happens to own an oversized ape, in the famous children's fantasy *Mighty Joe Young*. Johnson continued to take his small roles without complaint, appearing in some major works like *Shane*, where he taunted Alan Ladd for ordering "sody pop;" Marlon Brando's *One-Eyed Jack*; and Ford's epic *Cheyenne Autumn*, as a trooper. There was also a Monogram quickie in which he actually got top-billing, *Wild Stallion*, playing a cavalry officer who ends up at the army post where he grew up after being orphaned during an Indian attack.

He finally achieved some degree of fame when director Sam Peckinpah cast him as one of the hell-raisin' members of *The Wild Bunch*. Two years later Peter Bogdanovich had the inspired idea of using Johnson and his sturdy, laconic aura for the role of pool hall-movie theater proprietor Sam the Lion in *The Last Picture Show*, and the veteran actor came through gloriously, providing the heart and soul of the film's dying Texas town, and winning the Academy Award for Best Supporting Actor of 1971. This made him much in demand, and despite the paucity of westerns being made at the time, he kept busy as men of the law in *Dillinger*, as real-life G-Man Melvis Purvis; *The Sugarland Express*, in which he pursued kidnapper Goldie Hawn; and *Breakheart Pass*, as the U.S. marshal transporting supposed criminal Charles Bronson aboard a train. The less appealing side of Johnson was seen in *The Getaway*, as the sleazy politician who makes Ali MacGraw sleep with him before he'll parole Steve McQueen; and *Tex*, as Jennifer Tilly's overbearing father. He also got some starring roles in a pair of horror films, *The Town That Dreaded Sundown*, as a Texas ranger out to stop a hooded killer; and *Terror Train* as a conductor on the titular vehicle, aboard which a group of college kids are being murdered one by one.

Screen: 1943: Bordertown Gunfighters; 1944: Nevada; 1945: The Naughty Nineties; 1946: Badman's Territory; 1947: Wyoming; 1948: Gallant Legion; 3 Godfathers; 1949: She Wore a Yellow Ribbon; Mighty Joe Young; 1950: Wagon Master; Rio Grande; 1951: Fort Defiance; 1952: Wild Stallion; 1953: Shane; 1956: Rebel in Town; 1957: War Drums; Fort Bowie; Slim Carter; 1960: Ten Who Dared; 1961: Tomboy and the Champ; One-Eyed Jacks; 1964: Cheyenne Autumn; 1965: Major Dundee; 1966: The Rare Breed; 1968: Will Penny; Hang 'em High; 1969: The Wild Bunch; The Undefeated; 1970: Chisum; 1971: The Last Picture Show; Something Big; 1972: Corky; Junior Bonner; The Getaway; 1973: The Train Robbers; Dillinger; Kid Blue; 1974: The Sugarland Express; 1975: Bite the Bullet; Hustle; 1976: Breakheart Pass; 1977: The Town That Dreaded Sundown; The Greatest; Grayeagle; 1978: The Swarm; 1980: The Hunter; Terror Train; 1982: Soggy Bottom USA; Ruckus; Tex; 1983: Champions; 1984: Red Dawn; 1986: Let's Get Harry; 1988: Cherry 2000; 1989: Dark Before Dawn; 1990: Back to Back; 1991: My Heroes Have Always Been Cowboys; 1992: Radio Flyer; 1994: Angels in the Outfield; The Legend of O. B. Taggart (dtv); 1996: The Evening Star.

Select TV: 1966–67: The Monroes (series); 1969: Ride a Northbound Horse (sp); 1973: The Red Pony; Runaway!; Blood Sport; 1974: Locust; 1976: The Savage Bees; 1979: The Sacketts; 1980: Wild Times; 1982: Louis L'Amour's The Shadow Riders; 1985: Wild Horses; 1986: Dream West (ms); 1988: Stranger on My Land; 1991: The Chase; 1993: Bonanza: The Return; 1995: Bonanza: Under Attack; 1996: Ruby Jean and Joe.

CELIA JOHNSON

BORN: RICHMOND, SURREY, ENGLAND, DECEMBER 18, 1908. ED: RADA. DIED: APRIL 26, 1982.

This wide-eyed lady appeared, on the surface, a bit too aloof with her English gentility and good breeding, when in fact she possessed an accessible vulnerability that

took any potential stuffiness out of her characters. With only a handful of movies to her credit, she became one of her country's most highly regarded female thespians and, through a single film, won a legion of admirers in America as well. After studying at RADA, she made her 1929 London stage bow in *A Hundred Years Old*, and stayed exclusively in theatre for the next decade until she appeared in some short subjects made during World War II. Her official feature-length debut came with her role as Noel Coward's wife in the very British slice of patriotism *In Which We Serve*. It was Coward, along with director David Lean, who would make her known in films, first with Coward's admirable adaptation of his own play about 20 years in the life of one family, *This Happy Breed*, as the working-class wife of Robert Newton, and then with the movie for which Johnson would become best known and greatly revered, *Brief Encounter*, adapted from a one-act from his stage omnibus *Still Life*. A masterpiece of simplicity, it told the story of a sad, unhappily married woman who looks back on her aborted love affair with an understanding doctor, played by Trevor Howard. It offered Johnson the opportunity to break hearts, and her great performance earned her an Oscar nomination, one of only a handful of stars from a British film to do so up to that time. Despite the worldwide acclaim, she neither followed it up immediately with another vehicle, nor made any American films to widen her international appeal. Instead she waited until another Coward-scripted film popped up, *The Astonished Heart*, acting opposite Coward himself, though to a much less enthusiastic response this time out. Her few other films included *The Captain's Paradise*, where she played the genteel wife in the life of bigamist Alec Guinness; Carol Reed's colorful ensemble *A Kid for Two Farthings*, as the working class mum of a rambunctious little boy; and *The Prime of Miss Jean Brodie*, as the school head mistress.

Screen: 1942: In Which We Serve; 1943: Dear Octopus/The Randolph Family; 1944: This Happy Breed; 1946: Brief Encounter; 1950: The Astonished Heart; 1952: I Believe in You; The Holly and the Ivy; 1953: The Captain's Paradise; 1955: A Kid for Two Farthings; 1957: The Good Companions; 1969: The Prime of Miss Jean Brodie.

Select TV: 1971: The Cherry Orchard (sp); 1978: Romeo and Juliet; Les Misérables; 1980: The Hostage Tower; Staying On (sp); 1981: All's Well That Ends Well (sp).

VAN JOHNSON

(CHARLES VAN JOHNSON) BORN: NEWPORT, RI, AUGUST 25, 1916.

The popularity during the 1940s of freckle-faced, red-haired Van Johnson, not to mention the surprising longevity of his career overall, can perhaps be attributed to his non-threatening nature. There was nothing risky or shaded or unique about him or his work, certainly nothing that would allow you to overlook the often sub-par material he was asked to carry. Sometimes a degree of safe neutrality is the key to survival. While studying acting and dancing in New York, he got chorus work in three Broadway shows, including *Too Many Girls* (the 1940 film adaptation marked his movie debut), and *Pal Joey*, where he understudied Gene Kelly. By a stroke of luck, a Warners talent scout caught one of Johnson's performances when he took over the lead and signed him to a contract. After one movie he was dropped by them and taken on by MGM, who gave him supporting parts in "A" productions like *Somewhere I'll Find You*, as a soldier, and *The Human Comedy*, again sent to war, as Mickey Rooney's older brother, an important role in an important film.

He also became the squeaky clean substitute for Lew Ayres when that actor had had enough of the *Dr. Kildare* series, only now, since Lionel Barrymore was still around, the titles had *Dr. Gillespie* in them: *Dr. Gillespie's New Assistant* and *Dr. Gillespie's Criminal Case*.

Johnson's big break came when he was cast as the nice young soldier who wins Irene Dunne's heart after she loses Spencer Tracy to the war in *A Guy Named Joe*. A car accident put Johnson out of commission and almost cost him the role, had it not been for Tracy's insistence that the production be held up until the young actor recovered. The movie, now little more than a pious artifact of its day, was one of the smash hits of the war years, making Johnson a major motion picture attraction. There was a lighthearted war-themed musical, *Two Girls and a Sailor*, which marked the first of five teamings with June Allyson (*High Barbaree*, *The Bride Goes Wild*, *Too Young to Kiss*, and *Remains to Be Seen* were the others); another big war movie with Tracy, *Thirty Seconds Over Tokyo*, although this time Johnson was the real star of the film, as the principal airman leading the raid; and one of the undemanding Esther Williams efforts, *Thrill of a Romance*, where he smiled wholesomely while showing off his red hair and freckles in Technicolor. He followed these films with an all-star hit, *Week-end at the Waldorf*, where he was paired up with Lana Turner, making the Ginger Rogers-Walter Pidgeon storyline more interesting by default; and a forgettable remake of *Libeled Lady*, called *Easy to Wed*, proving a poor substitute for William Powell in the original.

All of these movies were popular enough to make him red hot at the box office, although his teaming with Lucille Bremer in *Till the Clouds Roll By* (dueting on "I Won't Dance") only showed how much more talented everyone else in that movie was. Similarly, he was merely adequate opposite Tracy and Hepburn in a smart political drama-comedy, *State of the Union*, but more than held his own against Gable and the very manly cast of the stage-bound war film *Command Decision*. He had the good fortune to be cast in one of the best war movies of its day, *Battleground*, as a sardonic soldier participating in the Battle of the Bulge; then he once again paled in comparison to a much stronger actor, James Stewart, whose role he took over in the remake of *The Shop Around the Corner*, now musicalized and rechristened *In the Good Old Summertime*. As the 1950s came, his stock dropped through such routine fare as the domestic comedy *Grounds for Marriage*; a sappy soap opera, *Invitation*, confessing to Dorothy McGuire that he was paid handsomely to marry her because her days were numbered; *Go for Broke!*, which had the interesting premise of Johnson commanding a squad of Japanese-Americans, but turned out to be just another war movie; and an Esther Williams dud, *Easy to Love*, set in picturesque Cypress Gardens. Columbia Pictures came to his rescue when they cast him as the officer who seizes the troubled ship from unhinged Humphrey Bogart in *The Caine Mutiny*. It proved to be not only a major box-office smash but contained the most assured performance of his career.

In 1954 he ended his MGM contract and tried to expand his image, playing an alcoholic fugitive in *The Bottom of the Bottle*, and a blind playwright in the London-based *23 Paces to Baker Street*, but they didn't win over the detractors. He also got work in Europe in such programmers as *Subway in the Sky*, in which he was accused of drug trafficking; *Beyond This Place*, trying to clear his imprisoned father of a murder charge; and *The Last Blitzkrieg*, playing against type as a German spy. Returning to the U.S., he had his last real movie lead, in 1963, playing a writer moving to suburbia, in the slick comedy *Wives and Lovers*. Following some secondary roles in the comedies *Divorce American Style*, as Jean

Simmons's ex, and *Yours, Mine and Ours*, as Henry Fonda's best pal, he spent most of the next two decades on television or in foreign features made strictly to pay the bills. By the time he appeared in a small role in the black and white film-within-the-film in Woody Allen's *The Purple Rose of Cairo*, it was certain that all but the most die-hard movie fans had not seen him up on the big screen in quite a spell.

Screen: 1940: Too Many Girls; 1942: Murder in the Big House; Somewhere I'll Find You; The War Against Mrs. Hadley; Dr. Gillespie's New Assistant; 1943: The Human Comedy; Pilot #5; Dr. Gillespie's Criminal Case; Madame Curie; A Guy Named Joe; 1944: The White Cliffs of Dover; Two Girls and a Sailor; Three Men in White; Between Two Women; Thirty Seconds Over Tokyo; 1945: Thrill of a Romance; Week-end at the Waldorf; 1946: Easy to Wed; No Leave, No Love; 1947: Till the Clouds Roll By; 1947: High Barbaree; The Romance of Rosy Ridge; 1948: The Bride Goes Wild; State of the Union; Command Decision; 1949: Mother Is a Freshman; In the Good Old Summertime; Scene of the Crime; Battleground; 1950: The Big Hangover; The Duchess of Idaho; Grounds for Marriage; 1951: Three Guys Named Mike; Go for Broke!; Too Young to Kiss; It's a Big Country; 1952: Invitation; When in Rome; Washington Story; Plymouth Adventure; 1953: Confidentially Connie; Remains to Be Seen; Easy to Love; 1954: The Siege at Red River; Men of the Fighting Lady; The Caine Mutiny; Brigadoon; The Last Time I Saw Paris; 1955: The End of the Affair; 1956: The Bottom of the Bottle; Miracle in the Rain; 23 Paces to Baker Street; Slander; 1957: Kelly and Me; Action of the Tiger; 1958: The Last Blitzkrieg; 1959: Subway in the Sky; Beyond This Place; 1960: The Enemy General; 1963: Wives and Lovers; 1967: Divorce American Style; 1968: Yours, Mine and Ours; Where Angels Go…Trouble Follows; 1969: The Professional/El Largo dia Del (nUSr); 1970: Company of Killers; La Battaglia d'Inghilterra/ Battle Squadron (nUSr); Il Prezzo del Potere/The Price of Power (nUSr); 1971: L'Occhio del Ragno/Eye of the Spider (nUSr); 1979: Concorde Affaire 79; From Corleone to Brooklyn; 1980: The Kidnapping of the President; 1981: Absurd!; 1982: The Mystery of the Etruscans/Scorpion with Two Tails (nUSr); 1985: The Purple Rose of Cairo; Down in the Jungle (nUSr); Killer Crocodile (nUSr); Taxi Killer (dtv); 1990: Delta Force Commando (dtv); 1991: Three Days to Kill (dtv); 1992: Clowning Around (dtv).

NY Stage: 1936: New Faces of 1936; 1939: Too Many Girls; 1940: Pal Joey; 1962: Come on Strong; 1965: Mating Dance; 1966: On a Clear Day You Can See Forever; 1985: La Cage aux Folles.

Select TV: 1957: The Pied Piper of Hamelin (sp); 1960: At Our Service (sp); 1967: Doomsday Flight; 1970: San Francisco International Airport; 1972: Call Her Mom; 1974: The Girl on the Late, Late Show; 1976: Rich Man, Poor Man (ms); 1978: Superdome; Black Beauty (ms); Getting Married; 1984: Glitter; 1988: Escape From Paradise.

AL JOLSON

(ASA YOELSON) BORN: ST. PETERSBURG, RUSSIA, MAY 26, 1886. RAISED IN NEW YORK, NY. DIED: OCTOBER 23, 1950.

He helped make motion picture history and for years was spoken of by those who had seen him perform live as one of the giants of the entertainment world. Today, with only motion pictures and recordings by which to judge, it appears as if Al Jolson was trying much too hard to be loved. He came to America as a child and was already performing in vaudeville houses as a teenager. By 1909 he was appearing as a headliner in legit theater and over the next decade or so became a stage sensation in such shows as *Robinson Crusoe Jr.*, *Sinbad* (introducing one of his signature songs, "Swanee"), and *Bombo*. His enthusiastic, highly mannered style was looked on as an antidote to the stiff, restrained singers who had trod the boards before him. Like many performers of his day, he adapted the minstrel tradition of entertaining in blackface, something he would continue to do in many of his movie roles, an unfortunate practice that would keep much of his work out of the public eye as the country became more sensitive to such things. When talking pictures were in the experimental stage, he did two short films to test the waters, "April Showers" and "The Plantation Act," then took the plunge in a big way. George Jessel had priced himself out of a property he had created onstage, so Jolson was offered *The Jazz Singer*, which would be Warner Bros.'s big gamble, the first feature with sound sequences. The movie, which was mainly silent, was scattered with musical interludes, the most famous being "My Mammy." Weak as the whole thing was, the world embraced both it and the new technology. Both the picture and Jolson, who certainly did his best to liven up the moldy proceedings, became a part of movie folklore, with the star uttering the prophetic line, "You ain't heard nothin' yet."

His follow-up was another semi-talkie, *The Singing Fool*, and it became an even bigger smash, in fact raking in grosses second only to *The Birth of a Nation*, and giving Jolson another song hit with "Sonny Boy." Awash in sentimentality and punctuated by the actor's overly ripe personality, his films would quickly become dated. His reputation off screen did not help compensate for the shortcomings in his work — his monstrous behavior and uncontrollable ego became the stuff of legend. *Mammy* presented him as a minstrel performer, while *Big Boy* went one step further, having him play the entire film in blackface, an act of awesomely bad taste, guaranteed to cause shudders in modern audiences. Moving over to United Artists, he tried a novelty musical, *Hallelujah, I'm a Bum*, much of which was done in rhyme to a Rodgers and Hart score. Jolson was more restrained than usual and the picture maintains a certain degree of oddball interest today, but it wasn't something the public wanted to see. He went back to Warners for the all-star *Wonder Bar* (he'd done a version of it on Broadway), which ended with a jaw-dropping blackface number called "Goin' to Heaven on a Mule," and he appeared for the only time on screen with then-wife (1928–39) Ruby Keeler in *Go Into Your Dance*, playing, appropriately, an arrogant singer. After their divorce Keeler looked back on the marriage with such disdain that she would not allow her name to be used in the biopic *The Jolson Story*.

In the meantime, Jolson went over to Fox to do three films, *Rose of Washington Square*, pretty much playing a variation of himself; *Hollywood Cavalcade*, this time actually playing himself, recreating the "Kol Nidre" sequence from *The Jazz Singer*; and *Swanee River*, portraying pioneering minstrel singer E.P. Christy. It was worth noting that he was not the top-billed attraction in any of these. By the mid-1940s he was considered a respected name from the past, but hardly a vibrant part of the current scene. Nobody, therefore, could have predicated just how popular *The Jolson Story* would turn out to be when Columbia released it in 1946. Jolson himself provided the vocals for Larry Parks's barn-broad impersonation and for the sequel, *Jolson Sings Again*, which was an even bigger moneymaker. When he died, only a year after the release of the latter, he was no doubt content in his belief that the world remained very much in love with his style. Within a decade of his passing, tastes had changed so enormously that he was looked on as little more than a curio from another age.

Screen: 1927: The Jazz Singer; 1928: The Singing Fool; 1929: Say It With Songs; New York Nights; 1930: Mammy; Big Boy; 1933: Hallelujah, I'm a Bum; 1934: Wonder Bar; 1935: Go Into Your Dance; 1936: The Singing Kid 1939: Rose of Washington Square; Hollywood Cavalcade; 1940: Swanee River; 1945: Rhapsody in Blue; 1946: The Jolson Story (voice); 1949: Jolson Sings Again (voice).
NY Stage: 1911: La Belle Paree; Vera Violetta; 1912: Whirl of Society; 1913: The Honeymoon Express; 1914: Dancing Around; 1916: Robinson Crusoe Jr.; 1918: Sinbad; 1921: Bombo; 1925: Big Boy; 1926: Artists and Models; 1931: Wonder Bar; 1940: Hold on to Your Hats.

ALLAN JONES

BORN: OLD FORGE, PA, OCTOBER 14, 1907.
ED: SYRACUSE UNIV. DIED: JUNE 27, 1992.

An appealing tenor and competent actor, with wavy hair and a friendly smile, Allan Jones had his moment in the musical sun, then faded from the scene long before such entertainments went out of fashion. As a young lad, it was expected that he would follow in his father's footsteps by working in a coal mine, but instead he received a music scholarship and studied at college and in Paris. He sang at Carnegie Hall and began acting in stage musicals, including the Broadway production of *Bitter Sweet*, which earned him a contract with MGM. Following his debut in *Reckless*, he was asked to join the Marx Brothers as a replacement of sorts for their recently retired sibling, Zeppo, in *A Night at the Opera*. He not only introduced the hit tune "Alone," but turned out to be the only male ingénue in the Brothers' films that audiences ever really gave a damn about. He was also the only one asked back for a second time, as he was for *A Day at the Races*. Both films were very popular and kept him famous for years, as did *The Firefly*, in which he was leading man to Jeanette MacDonald (on a break from Nelson Eddy), with Jones warbling what became his signature song, "The Donkey Serenade," and the 1936 version of *Show Boat* (for Universal), where the glorious Kern–Hammerstein score now included a lovely addition, "I Have the Room Above."

After a bright comedy with Judy Garland, *Everybody Sing*, he took a stop off at Paramount for the biopic *The Great Victor Herbert* (not playing the composer, but cast as a temperamental singer) and then hitched up with Universal. Things were supposed to start well with the starring role in the 1940 film version of the Broadway hit *The Boys From Syracuse*, but most of the Rodgers and Hart score was jettisoned, as was the dubious custom back then, and the end result had little to do with the original. The cast featured Irene Hervey, whom Jones had married in 1936. Universal also put Jones in *One Night in the Tropics*, which was stolen by supporting-players Abbott and Costello in their film debuts, and then such cheapies as *When Johnny Comes Marching Home*, as the Johnny in question, a soldier on leave; *You're a Lucky Fellow, Mr. Smith*; *Larceny with Music*; and *Senorita from the West*, all of which, if nothing else, gave him a chance to sing. By the end of the 1940s Hollywood had lost interest, and Jones left the picture business to appear in summer stock and nightclubs. He and Hervey divorced in 1957, shortly before their son Jack's singing career took off.

Screen: 1935: Reckless; A Night at the Opera; 1936: The Great Ziegfeld (voice); Rose-Marie; Show Boat; 1937: A Day at the Races; The Firefly; 1938: Everybody Sing; 1939: The Great Victor Herbert; Honeymoon in Bali; 1940: The Boys From Syracuse; One Night in the Tropics; 1941: There's Magic in Music; 1942: True to the Army; Moonlight in Havana; When Johnny Comes

Marching Home; **1943:** Rhythm of the Islands; Larceny with Music; You're a Lucky Fellow, Mr. Smith; Crazy House; **1944:** The Singing Sheriff; Sing a Jingle; **1945:** Honeymoon Ahead; The Senorita from the West; **1964:** Stage to Thunder Rock; **1965:** A Swingin' Summer.

NY Stage: 1931: Boccaccio; **1934:** Bitter Sweet; **1944:** Jackpot.

CAROLYN JONES

BORN: AMARILLO, TX, APRIL 28, 1929.
DIED: AUGUST 3, 1983.

It took television to give the delectable Carolyn Jones a place in entertainment history, for as often as the movies employed this talented lady with the enticing eyes, you couldn't help but wish there was more. Moving to Hollywood from Texas, she joined the Pasadena Playhouse, after which she was seen in a production of *The Live Wire*, directed by Aaron Spelling, whom she would marry (1953–65). She began getting very small parts in films like *The War of the Worlds* and *Road to Bali*, and a crucial one in the 3-D horror hit *House of Wax*, as the poor girl who is covered in wax in order to substitute for Vincent Price's sculpture of Joan of Arc. This didn't lead to anything substantial, but she could be seen walking Frank Sinatra's dog in *The Tender Trap*, and in one of Tom Ewell's fantasies in *The Seven Year Itch*. She had another bigger-than-average role, playing one of the earthlings fighting the pod people in the sci-fi classic *Invasion of the Body Snatchers*, and then things improved greatly after her scene-stealing bit as a sad bohemian who tries to seduce Don Murray in *The Bachelor Party*. Playing a character simply called Existentialist, she was nominated for an Oscar and was suddenly being added to movies because filmmakers knew she was going to add some sizzle to every scene she was in, as she did in *Marjorie Morningstar*, as the goodtime gal friend of Natalie Wood; *King Creole*, one of the best Elvis Presley films, as Walter Matthau's vulnerable moll; and *Last Train to Gun Hill*, as a saloon girl.

She was Sinatra's kooky girlfriend in *A Hole in the Head*, and a theatrical agent in *Career*, both of which kept her very much in the supporting position. The closest things she got to leading roles were playing Mickey Rooney's girlfriend in the low-budget gangster flick *Baby Face Nelson*; Alan Ladd's nympho wife, whose murder he's accused of, in *The Man in the Net*; and the woman wanted by neither Richard Burton nor Robert Ryan in the Alaska-set epic *Ice Palace*, a film that was not the hoped for success for Warners. She went back to secondary parts, providing some small pleasures to some weak comedies, *Sail a Crooked Ship* and *A Ticklish Affair*, until television came to her rescue. Looking to turn Charles Addams's brilliantly black *New Yorker* cartoons into a weekly TV series, ABC came up with *The Addams Family*, with Jones perfect as the mordantly sexy Morticia Addams. The show aired in first-run for two seasons and in syndication forever and Moritica became Jones's signature role. Unfortunately nobody had any great plans for her in the movies once the series ended its run. Aside from playing a saloon owner with her eye on Glenn Ford in the unmemorable western *Heaven With a Gun*, the offers were few and uninspired. She did some TV guest appearances and ended up as a regular on the short-lived daytime soap *Capitol*, dying of cancer during its run.

Screen: 1952: The Turning Point; **1953:** Road to Bali; Off Limits; House of Wax; The War of the Worlds; The Big Heat; **1954:** Geraldine; Make Haste to Live; The Saracen Blade; Three Hours to Kill; Shield for Murder; Desiree; **1955:** The Seven Year Itch; The Tender Trap; **1956:** The Man Who Knew Too Much; Invasion of the Body Snatchers; The Opposite Sex; **1957:** Johnny

Trouble; Baby Face Nelson; The Bachelor Party; **1958:** Marjorie Morningstar; King Creole; **1959:** A Hole in the Head; Last Train From Gun Hill; Career; The Man in the Net; **1960:** Ice Palace; **1961:** Sail a Crooked Ship; **1963:** How the West Was Won; A Ticklish Affair; **1969:** Heaven With a Gun; **1969:** Color Me Dead; **1976:** Eaten Alive/Death Trap; **1979:** Good Luck, Miss Wyckoff.

Select TV: 1954: Account Closed (sp); Double in Danger (sp);The Answer (sp); **1955:** The Black Sheep's Daughter (sp); Diagnosis of a Selfish Lady (sp); **1957:** The Girl in the Grass (sp); The Disappearance of Amanda Hale (sp); High Barrier (sp); **1958:** The Last Man (sp); **1962:** The Sea Witch (sp); **1964–66:** The Addams Family (series); **1977:** Little Ladies of the Night; Roots (ms); Halloween with the New Addams Family (sp); **1979:** The French Atlantic Affair (ms); **1980:** The Dream Merchants; **1981:** Midnight Lace; **1982–83:** Capitol (series).

DEAN JONES

BORN: DECATAUR, AL, JANUARY 25, 1931.

The epitome of the wholesome, family-oriented nice guy, Dean Jones, with the bright but quavery speaking voice, became synonymous with the lightweight Disney comedies of the 1960s and was pretty much limited in his options as a result. Having sung as a teenager, he studied voice in college before joining the Navy. After being discharged, he continued to sing at various establishments in Southern California, including Knotts Berry Farm where he was spotted by an MGM talent scout. Signed by the studio, he appeared in a whole slew of insignificant parts, which included playing a private in *Somebody Up There Likes Me* and a college student in *Tea and Sympathy*. His one lead for them, *Handle With Care*, found him cast as an impressionable young law student who thinks he has stumbled upon corruption in a small town, in this very minor "B" feature. In 1960 he went to Broadway where he scored a hit in a frothy adult comedy, *Under the Yum Yum Tree*, playing a college student who decides to live with his girlfriend *before* they get married, a part he repeated (at age 32!) in the 1963 film version, which was promptly stolen from him by Jack Lemmon. Around this time he also starred in his own short-lived series, *Ensign O'Toole*, reprising the role that had made Lemmon famous, thereby giving Jones some inevitable comparisons against which he failed. He found himself among the ensemble of a popular soaper, *The New Interns*, as an obstetrician who is aghast to discover that he himself is sterile, and in a disposable haunted-house offering, *Two on a Guillotine*.

Disney came along in 1965, giving him the male lead, as a detective investigating a kidnapping, in one of that company's biggest hits of the decade, *That Darn Cat!* Pleased by Jones's wide-eyed comic bumbling and unthreatening personality, the studio made him their top star attraction as it faced its potentially rocky transition period, brought on by Walt Disney's death and the collapse of the censorship code. Jones stuttered and blundered through several moneymakers for the company, including *The Ugly Dachshund*, as an illustrator, attempting to raise a disruptive Great Dane; *Monkeys, Go Home!*, as an American in France, trying to train monkeys to pick crops; and *Blackbeard's Ghost*, keeping an eye on mischievous pirate Peter Ustinov. In the very tame *The Love Bug*, his biggest hit of all, he was a racecar driver whose Volkswagen has a mind of its own; in *The Million Dollar Duck*, he was a professor whose bird lays golden eggs; and in *Snowball Express*, he was an accountant involved in a snowmobile race with the expected slapstick results. After a break, he inherited Tommy Kirk's old role, as a hexed fellow with a tendency to turn into a sheep dog, in the sequel *The Shaggy D.A.*

During this period he won the lead in the landmark Steven Sondheim stage musical, *Company*, but left shortly after it opened because of disagreements with the creators. By the late 1970s he had become a born-again Christian and hoped to celebrate his religious rebirth by playing the real-life Senator Charles Colson, who went through a similar voyage to enlightenment after his involvement in the Watergate scandal, in the little-seen *Born Again*. After a long period off the screen, he suddenly began popping up in secondary roles — in *Other People's Money*, as Gregory Peck's business partner, and in *Clear and Present Danger*, as a judge. He played the villain in a hit doggy movie, *Beethoven*, which was not unlike the movies he made in his younger days, only now there were urination jokes. When Disney did its tired remake of *That Darn Cat!*, someone at least had the nice idea to ask Jones to join the project, playing a role that was not in the original film.

Screen: 1956: Tea and Sympathy; These Wilder Years; The Rack; The Opposite Sex; The Great American Pastime; Somebody Up There Likes Me; 1957: Ten Thousand Bedrooms; Designing Woman; Until They Sail; Jailhouse Rock; 1958: Handle With Care; Imitation General; Torpedo Run; 1959: Night of the Quarter Moon; Never So Few; 1963: Under the Yum Yum Tree; 1964: The New Interns; 1965: Two on a Guillotine; That Darn Cat!; 1966: Any Wednesday; The Ugly Dachshund; 1967: Monkeys, Go Home!; 1968: Blackbeard's Ghost; The Horse in the Gray Flannel Suit; 1969: The Love Bug; 1971: The Million Dollar Duck; 1972: Snowball Express; 1973: Mister Superinvisible; 1976: The Shaggy D.A.; 1977: Herbie Goes to Monte Carlo; 1978: Born Again; 1991: Other People's Money; 1992: Beethoven; 1994: Clear and Present Danger; 1996: A Spasso nel Tempo/Adrift in Time (nUSr); 1997: That Darn Cat!

NY Stage: 1960: There Was a Little Girl; Under the Yum Yum Tree; 1970: Company; 1986: Into the Light.

Select TV: 1960: The Sunday Man (sp); 1962–63: Ensign O'Toole (series); 1965: The Rise and Fall of Eddie Carew (sp); 1969: What's It All About World? (series); 1971: The Chicago Teddy Bears (series); 1973: The Great Man's Whiskers; Guess Who's Sleeping in My Bed?; 1977: Once Upon a Brothers Grimm (sp); 1978: When Every Day Was the Fourth of July; 1980: The Long Days of Summer; 1982: Herbie the Love Bug (series); 1989: Fire and Rain; 1992: Saved by the Bell — Hawaiian Style; 1994–95: Beethoven (series; voice); 1995: The Computer Wore Tennis Shoes; 1996: Special Report: Journey to Mars; Jonny Quest: The New Adventures (series; voice); 1997: The Love Bug; 2001: Scrooge and Marley (sp).

JENNIFER JONES

(PHYLLIS FLORA ISLEY) BORN: TULSA, OK, MARCH 2, 1919. ED: AADA.

Jennifer Jones's fragility was both her strength and weakness as an actress. She could be touching, sensitive, and delicately enchanting, and yet she seemed to lack a certain thick skin that would allow her to survive the passing of time with the toughest and best of the leading ladies. Seen today, some of her most ambitious performances come up short: her attempts to convey a fiery spirit suggesting a certain degree of hollowness at the center. The child of acting parents, she was a part of their stock company while still very young, eventually going to New York to study acting at the American Academy of Dramatic Arts. There she met up-and-coming actor Robert Walker, whom she married in 1939. Trying their luck in Hollywood, they both did some insignificant work. Jones, under her real name, worked at

Republic Pictures in a John Wayne *Three Mesquiteers* western (*New Frontier*) and a *Dick Tracy* serial before returning to New York. She auditioned for producer David O. Selznick in hopes of landing the lead in the film of *Claudia* (Dorothy McGuire, who'd done it onstage, got the part), and he considered her for a role in *The Keys of the Kingdom* (Selznick eventually sold off the rights to this film to Fox). In any case, he saw her potential and signed her to a contract, a move that would ultimately change her fortunes and her personal life. Renaming her "Jennifer Jones," Selznick loaned her to 20th Century-Fox for the role of the French peasant girl, who claims to be visited by the Virgin Mary, in *The Song of Bernadette*, where she was treated in the pre-publicity as a newcomer. The film itself was a superbly controlled handling of a potentially icky subject, and Jones managed to capture the wide-eyed wonder and sincerity of this girl with a total, heartfelt conviction. The movie became one of the biggest hits of 1943, made Jones a full-fledged star, and capped its across-the-board triumph by winning her the Academy Award for Best Actress. Since the ceremonies took place on the 2nd of March of that year, she became the only performer to date to win the Oscar on their birthday.

She was back in the Oscar-running the following year, in another enormous hit, only this time in a supporting role, as the impatient and wishy-washy daughter of Claudette Colbert, in a well-meaning but over-long Selznick film about life on the home front, *Since You Went Away*. It was her only movie opposite her husband, and although there was a definite sweetness to their scenes together, Jones couldn't prevent the character from seeming infuriatingly self-involved. Over at Paramount she continued her winning streak with *Love Letters*, as an amnesiac, and the Academy just couldn't stop throwing Oscar nominations her way, despite the fact that this was soapsuds at their most superficial. It happened again with another Selznick biggie, *Duel in the Sun*, in which she stretched by playing a wicked, half-breed temptress, although it would have been hard for anyone to pull off the melodramatic finale, an extended crawl in the dirt towards the lover she has just plugged with a bullet, Gregory Peck. In between these she did a comedy for Ernst Lubitsch, *Cluny Brown*, as a maid who falls in love with impoverished refugee Charles Boyer; it was a relief to see her in something more lighthearted though it was not among the great director's more notable pictures.

Much better than any of her post-*Bernadette* dramas was the haunting *Portrait of Jennie*, with Jones in fine form as the mysterious girl whom artist Joseph Cotten meets in a wintry Central Park. She was required to start the film as a young girl and then age over the course of the movie, and that she did most convincingly. As bad luck would have it, *Jennie* did not find great success at the box office any more than did another of her more enduring projects, the lavish Vincente Minnelli production of *Madame Bovary*, in which she destroyed everyone around her in her pursuit of position as the self-centered, ruthless wife of doctor Van Heflin. Jones did a great deal of eye shifting to indicate scheming and treachery, but in this particular instance it worked quite effectively. Her marriage to Walker having ended (in 1945), she became Selznick's wife, in 1949, and remained so until his death in 1965. Paramount's adaptation of Theodore Dreiser's *Sister Carrie*, simplified to *Carrie*, found her again playing a woman whose quest for respectability causes destruction, in this case that of Laurence Olivier. Most critics complained that she'd taken all of the juice out of the original character and made her too sympathetic. There was little good to be said about the overheated melodrama *Ruby Gentry*, with Jones once again cast as a bad lady, or the lopsided satire *Beat the Devil*, with the actress playing (with blonde hair) Humphrey Bogart's lying wife. Nothing but bad luck seemed to plague *Indiscretion of an American*

Wife, a collaboration between Selznick and Italian director Vittorio DeSica; essentially a two-character piece with Jones having a brief encounter with Montgomery Clift. Much as a previous European endeavor, the British *Gone to Earth*, had gone through poor previews and delayed release, *Wife* was hacked at, shelved, and finally greeted with confusion when it opened in America in 1954.

Following these setbacks, the box office jumped way up with what was little more than a lushly photographed but uninspired romance, *Love Is a Many Splendored Thing*, made famous by its theme song, with Jones as a Eurasian doctor in love with William Holden. It was hardly her most interesting performance, but the great fondness the public felt for this movie in the mid-1950s helped to carry her into the Oscar nominees' circle one last time. She was pretty stiff as a New England schoolteacher in *Good Morning, Miss Dove*; gave it her best shot playing a housewife who is slowly unraveling in *The Man in the Gray Flannel Suit*; and then took a dive with two remakes, *The Barretts of Wimpole Street*, as the sickly Elizabeth Barrett, once again having trouble making audiences care about an insufferable character; and *A Farewell to Arms*, as the Army nurse in love with soldier Rock Hudson, which was her husband's last project and perhaps his weakest. Nonetheless it had a fair amount of box-office success, perhaps due to Hudson's great popularity at the time.

After disappearing for four years, Jones turned up as Nicole in the poorly received adaptation of *Tender Is the Night*, which turned out to be her last starring role in a major studio production. After Selznick died she was seen in two exploitive quickies that found her dallying with younger men, *The Idol* and *Angel, Angel, Down We Go*. She played a one-time porn star in the latter, a movie that fared badly in its scattered trade screenings, then pretty much sat on the shelf for two years before showing up on the bottom half of double bills as *Cult of the Damned*. In between these two, she made headlines when she attempted suicide and was found unconscious on the beach in Malibu. Years after this incident, she had one last role, in a high-profile film, *The Towering Inferno*, getting to dance with Fred Astaire but being cruelly disposed of by falling from a glass elevator. Shortly before this, she had married a millionaire and found no reason to work any further. Her eldest son, Robert Walker, Jr., was seen in such movies as *The Hook* and *Ensign Pulver*.

Screen: AS PHYLLIS ISLEY: **1939:** New Frontier; Dick Tracy's G-Men.

AS JENNIFER JONES: **1943:** The Song of Bernadette; **1944:** Since You Went Away; **1945:** Love Letters; **1946:** Cluny Brown; Duel in the Sun; **1948:** Portrait of Jennie; **1949:** We Were Strangers; Madame Bovary; **1952:** The Wild Heart/Gone to Earth (UK: 1950); Carrie; **1953:** Ruby Gentry; **1954:** Indiscretion of an American Wife/Terminal Station; Beat the Devil; **1955:** Love Is a Many Splendored Thing; Good Morning, Miss Dove; **1956:** The Man in the Gray Flannel Suit; **1957:** The Barretts of Wimpole Street; A Farewell to Arms; **1961:** Tender Is the Night; **1966:** The Idol; **1969:** Angel, Angel, Down We Go/Cult of the Damned; **1974:** The Towering Inferno.

NY Stage: **1954:** Portrait of a Lady; **1966:** The Country Girl (ob).

SHIRLEY JONES

BORN: SMITHTON, PA, MARCH 31, 1934.

One of the last of Hollywood's musical sweethearts, Shirley Jones set out to prove that there was more to her than a good set of pipes. She did just that and then achieved a third career, as every preteen's idea of a hip mom. Demonstrating her impressive vocal qualities at an early age, she trained with a singing coach in Pittsburgh. While there she also studied acting, at the Pittsburgh Playhouse, and performed with the Pittsburgh Civic Light Opera. Traveling to New York, her former voice teacher arranged an audition with Richard Rodgers that turned out to be the most fortuitous meeting of her life. The composer was so taken with her that he not only put her in the chorus of both *South Pacific* and *Me and Juliet*, but also gave her the lead in the road tour of the latter and, most significantly, the coveted part of Laurey in the long-awaited 1955 film version of *Oklahoma!* She was more impressive in her singing than her acting, but she nonetheless got awarded with another Rodgers assignment, *Carousel*, as the long-suffering Julie. It was a more difficult role dramatically, and she was still not quite ideal, but her skills were improving. The same year as that film's release, 1956, she married her co-star in a stage production of *The Beggar's Opera*, Jack Cassidy.

She became Pat Boone's leading lady in *April Love*; partnered James Cagney in an inferior musical, *Never Steal Anything Small*; and went to England to star as the mother of a talking infant in *Bobbikins*. Feeling the need to stretch, she played an alcoholic in a *Playhouse 90* presentation called *The Big Slide*, which was instrumental in her getting the role of the vengeful prostitute who participates in causing Burt Lancaster's downfall in *Elmer Gantry*. It was at best a competent performance, but the Academy of Motion Picture Arts and Sciences, always impressed at seeing someone try something atypical, gave her the Academy Award for Best Supporting Actress of 1960. Since her next drama, *Two Rode Together*, evoked little praise, it was wise that she didn't write off musicals altogether. As Marian the Librarian, in the four-star adaptation of the much-loved *The Music Man*, she gave the most satisfying performance of her career, singing such beauties as "Goodnight My Someone" and showing real charm for the first time. She was likewise a very nice presence in *The Courtship of Eddie's Father*, as the neighbor who becomes the best prospect for widower Glenn Ford, and *Bedtime Story*, as a contest winner whom Marlon Brando and David Niven hope to con. However, her own romantic comedy vehicle, *A Ticklish Affair*, in which she was a widower romanced by Navy commander Gig Young, was a complete washout. She seemed to be going nowhere by the late 1960s and returned to Broadway to star opposite her husband in the short-lived musical *Maggie Flynn*.

Thanks to television, she suddenly became famous all over again, as the "groovy" widowed mom who, with her children, forms a wholesome pop band in the hit TV series *The Partridge Family*. Her stepson, David Cassidy (playing her television offspring), received all the press and attention, with Jones relegated to background vocals on the concurrent albums issued along with the show. Although she returned to the hooking business, now as a madam, in *The Cheyenne Social Club*, the movies had very little use for her anymore, and most of her subsequent career was spent singing in Vegas or acting on TV. Having divorced Cassidy in 1974, she married actor-agent Marty Ingels, with him writing a joint biography, *Shirley & Marty: An Unlikely Love Story* (1990). Two of her sons with Jack Cassidy, Shaun and Patrick, are also actors.

Screen: **1955:** Oklahoma!; **1956:** Carousel; **1957:** April Love; **1959:** Never Steal Anything Small; **1960:** Bobbikins; Elmer Gantry; Pepe; **1961:** Two Rode Together; **1962:** The Music Man; **1963:** The Courtship of Eddie's Father; A Ticklish Affair; Dark Purpose; **1964:** Bedtime Story; **1965:** Fluffy; The Secret of My Success; **1969:** El Golfo (nUSr); The Happy Ending; **1970:** The Cheyenne Social Club; **1979:** Beyond the Poseidon Adventure; **1984:** Tank; **1985:** There Were Times Dear (dtv); **1994:** Cops 'n'

Roberts (dtv); 2000: Shriek If You Know What I Did Last Friday the 13th (dtv); Ping! (nUSr); The Adventures of Cinderella's Daughter (dtv); 2002: Manna from Heaven.

NY Stage: 1953: South Pacific; Me and Juliet; 1968: Maggie Flynn.
Select TV: 1951: Hired Girl (sp); 1956: The Big Slide (sp); 1957: Dark Victory (sp); Shadow of Evil (sp); 1958: The Red Mill (sp); 1964: The Shattered Glass (sp); 1969: Silent Night, Lonely Night; 1970–74: The Partridge Family (series); 1970: But I Don't Want to Get Married!; 1973: The Girls of Huntington House; 1975: The Family Nobody Wanted; Winner Take All; The Lives of Jenny Dolan; 1977: Yesterday's Child; 1978: Evening in Byzantium; Who'll Save Our Children; 1979: A Last Cry for Help; 1979–80: Shirley (series); 1980: The Children of An Lac; 1981: Inmates: A Love Story; 1989: Charlie; 1994–95: Burke's Law (series); 1997: Dog's Best Friend; 1999: Gideon.

VICTOR JORY

BORN: DAWSON CITY, YUKON TERRITORY, AK, NOVEMBER 28, 1902. DIED: FEBRUARY 12, 1982.

A tall, menacing character actor with a furrowed brow and richly creepy voice, Victor Jory joined the Pasadena Playhouse in 1923. From there he became part of Chamberlain Brown's stock company in New York, leading to his movie debut for Fox in 1930. There were some efforts to sell him as a leading man, in *The Devil's in Love*, as a French Army doctor; the earliest version of the horse tale *Smoky*, as a broncobuster; and *Escape From Devil's Island*, trying to spring fellow spy Norman Foster by disguising himself as a prison guard. Further down the line he played the title role in the Columbia serial *The Shadow* and was seen as late as 1957 carrying the cheap horror film *The Man Who Turned to Stone*, as a 200-year-old scientist rejuvenated by women's energy cells. He was, however, a character player at heart and his many familiar roles included Oberon, the King of the Fairies, in Warner Bros.'s richly atmospheric version of *A Midsummer Night's Dream*; Grace Moore's lover in *The King Steps Out*; and Injun Joe in *The Adventures of Tom Sawyer* (because of his stony features and pronounced cheekbones, he was called on several times to portray Indians, including *Cheyenne Autumn* and *Flap*). Making the best of his deeply unsympathetic nature, he played the overseer who tries to purchase the devastated Tara only to have dirt heaved in his face by Vivien Leigh in the blockbuster *Gone With the Wind*; the corrupt parole board head who takes glee in keeping innocent James Cagney in prison in *Each Dawn I Die*; Bruce Cabot's henchman, who nearly gets lynched, in *Dodge City*; and Anna Magnani's nasty, bed-ridden husband in *The Fugitive Kind*. One of his best roles found him playing the stern but loving father of Helen Keller (Patty Duke) in *The Miracle Worker*.

Screen: 1930: Renegades; 1932: Pride of the Legion; Handle With Care; 1933: Sailor's Luck; State Fair; Infernal Machine; Broadway Bad; Trick for Trick; Second Hand Wife; I Loved You Wednesday; My Woman; The Devil's in Love; Smoky; 1934: He Was Her Man; I Believed in You; Murder in Trinidad; Madame DuBarry; White Lies; Pursued; 1935: Mills of the Gods; Party Wire; Streamline Express; A Midsummer Night's Dream; Escape From Devil's Island; Too Tough to Kill; 1936: Hell-Ship Morgan; The King Steps Out; Meet Nero Wolfe; 1937: Glamorous Night; First Lady; Bulldog Drummond at Bay; 1938: The Adventures of Tom Sawyer; 1939: Blackwell's Island; Dodge City; Wings of the Navy; Man of Conquest; Women in the Wind; Susannah of the Mounties; Men With Whips; Rangle River (Australia: 1936); Each Dawn I Die; I Stole a Million; Call a Messenger; Gone

With the Wind; 1940: The Shadow (serial); The Green Archer (serial); Knights of the Range; The Light of Western Stars; The Lone Wolf Meets a Lady; River's End; Girl From Havana; Cherokee Strip; Lady With Red Hair; Give Us Wings; 1941: Border Vigilantes; Wide Open Town; Charlie Chan in Rio; Bad Men of Missouri; Secrets of the Lone Wolf; Riders of the Timberline; The Stork Pays Off; 1942: Shut My Big Mouth; Tombstone — The Town Too Tough to Die; 1943: Hoppy Serves a Writ; Buckskin Frontier; The Leather Burners; The Kansan; Bar 20; Colt Comrades; The Unknown Guest; Power of the Press; 1948: The Loves of Carmen; The Gallant Blade; 1949: A Woman's Secret; South of St. Louis; Canadian Pacific; Fighting Man of the Plains; 1950: The Capture; Cariboo Trail; 1951: Cave of the Outlaws; Flaming Feather; The Highwayman; 1952: Son of Ali Baba; The Toughest Man in Arizona; 1953: Cat Women of the Moon; The Hindu/Sabaka; The Man From the Alamo; 1954: Valley of the Kings; 1956: Manfish; Blackjack Ketchum; Desperado; Death of a Scoundrel; 1957: The Man Who Turned to Stone; The Last Stagecoach West; 1959: The Fugitive Kind; 1962: The Miracle Worker; 1964: Cheyenne Autumn; 1968: Jigsaw; 1969: Mackenna's Gold (narrator); 1970: Flap; 1971: A Time for Dying; 1973: Papillon; 1974: Frasier the Sensuous Lion; 1977: Kino, The Padre on Horseback/Mission to Glory; 1980: The Mountain Men.

NY Stage: 1943: The Two Mrs. Carrolls; 1944: The Perfect Marriage; 1945: Therese; 1946: Henry VII; John Gabriel Boorkman; Androcles and the Lion; 1947: Yellow Jack; 1950: The Devil's Disciple.

Select TV: 1950: The Second Oldest Profession (sp); 1952: Angel Street (sp); Captain-General of the Armies (sp); International Incident (sp); The Hospital (sp); 1953: The Mirror (sp); 1954: Moby Dick (sp); Exit for Margo (sp); The Man Who Escaped From Devil's Island (sp); A Connecticut Yankee in King Arthur's Court (sp); 1955–56: King's Row (series); 1956: Profile in Courage (sp); Prairie Night (sp); Key Largo (sp); 1957: Mr. and Mrs. McAdam (sp); The Still Trumpet (sp); Moment of Decision (sp); Galvanized Yankee (sp); 1958: Johnny Belinda (sp); 1959: Diary of a Nurse (sp); Manhunt (series); 1965: That Time in Havana (sp); Who Has Seen the Wind?; 1976: Perilous Journey; 1978: Devil Dog: The Hound of Hell; 1980: Power.

ALLYN JOSLYN

BORN: MILFORD, PA, JULY 21, 1901. DIED: JANUARY 21, 1981.

A welcome character player known for his pencil moustache, strangled speaking voice, and often jittery portrayals, Allyn Joslyn had been onstage for some 15 years before he came to Warner Bros. in 1937, a direct result of his performance in the Broadway production of *Boy Meets Girl*. For Warners he made his debut in a serious role, as the restless reporter eager to expose Southern bigotry, in that studio's uneven indictment of mob violence, *They Won't Forget*. It wasn't long before Hollywood realized that Joslyn's field of expertise was comedy, and in no time he was bringing his panache to such roles as a movie press agent in *Hollywood Hotel*; an acerbic society columnist in *Cafe Society*, a favorite role of his; a snooty social climber in *If I Had My Way*; the outspoken theater director who hates James Stewart's play in *No Time for Comedy*; and a stuffy banker in *Bedtime Story*. Returning to Broadway he scored his greatest success as the startled Mortimer Brewster in the smash hit *Arsenic and Old Lace*, but, needless to say, he was not asked to repeat his role in the movie version (Cary Grant got the job).

Columbia cast him as a reporter with an eye on lovely Janet Blair in *My Sister Eileen*, and, topically, a heel-clicking Nazi in the comedy *The Wife Takes a Flyer*. They also threw a lead role his way, the novelist-turned-sleuth in the "B" mystery *Dangerous Blondes*, which did well enough to produce a follow-up of sorts, *Strange Affair*. Fox signed him to a contract, letting him play a British soldier in *The Immortal Sergeant*; a priggish lawyer engaged to Gene Tierney until Don Ameche shows up in *Heaven Can Wait*; and, in one of the standout roles of his career, the exasperated father of meddlesome Peggy Ann Garner in *Junior Miss*. Fox allowed him a sole starring vehicle as well, *It Shouldn't Happen to a Dog*, playing a reporter teamed with police lady Carole Landis and her pooch. He was memorable as a tic-ridden fallen angel in the Jack Benny fantasy *The Horn Blows at Midnight*; played it straight as a thoughtful sheriff in pursuit of killer Dane Clark in the well-liked Republic "B" *Moonrise*; and was the cowardly passenger who dresses in drag to escape the sinking *Titanic*. By the mid-1950s his film work became sporadic, and he was much more prominent at that point on television, where he had his own short-lived situation comedy, *McKeever and the Colonel*.

Screen: 1937: They Won't Forget; Expensive Husbands; Hollywood Hotel; 1938: The Shining Hour; Sweethearts; 1939: Cafe Society; Only Angels Have Wings; Fast and Furious; 1940: If I Had My Way; The Great McGinty; Spring Parade; No Time for Comedy; 1941: This Thing Called Love; Bedtime Story; I Wake Up Screaming; 1942: The Affairs of Martha; The Wife Takes a Flyer; My Sister Eileen; 1943: Young Ideas; The Immortal Sergeant; Heaven Can Wait; Dangerous Blondes; 1944: Bride by Mistake; Sweet and Low-Down; The Imposter; Strange Affair; 1945: The Horn Blows at Midnight; Junior Miss; Colonel Effingham's Raid; 1946: It Shouldn't Happen to a Dog; The Thrill of Brazil; 1947: The Shocking Miss Pilgrim; 1948: If You Knew Susie; Moonrise; 1949: The Lady Takes a Sailor; 1950: Harriet Craig; 1951: As Young as You Feel; 1953: The Jazz Singer; I Love Melvin; Island in the Sky; Titanic; 1956: The Fastest Gun Alive; You Can't Run Away From It; 1957: Public Pigeon No. One; 1964: Nightmare in the Sun; 1972: The Brothers O'Toole.

NY Stage: 1922: Johannes Kreisler; 1923: Sandro Botticelli; Scaramouche; 1924: Man and the Masses; The Firebrand; 1926: The Moon Is a Gong; Head or Tail; 1927: A Lady in Love; One for All; 1928: The Mystery Man; 1929: Vermont; 1935: Boy Meets Girl; 1938: All That Glitters; 1941: Arsenic and Old Lace; 1952: Collector's Item.

Select TV: 1953–54: The Ray Bolger Show (series); 1957–58: The Eve Arden Show (series); 1962–63: McKeever and the Colonel (series).

LOUIS JOURDAN

(Louis Gendre) Born: Marseilles, France, June 19, 1919.

A handsome Frenchman who gave Maurice Chevalier a run for his money in debonair Gallic charm, Louis Jourdan did not dabble in weighty roles, preferring to ply his trade in airier fare. After studying acting in Paris with Rene Simon, he almost immediately found himself getting movie roles, making his debut in 1939 in the Charles Boyer film *Le Corsaire*. When World War II intervened, he joined the French Underground, then returned to movies, including a version of *Tess of the D'Urbervilles*. David O. Selznick was looking for an attractive Frenchman for his 1947 production of *The Paradine Case*, so Jourdan made his American debut in this second-rate Hitchcock drama, his performance as the tormented valet being greeted with sufficient praise. From there he played the musician loved by

Joan Fontaine in *Letter From an Unknown Woman*; Rodolphe Boulanger, the unscrupulous lover of Jennifer Jones, in *Madame Bovary*; and the ne'er-do-well brother in *The Happy Time*, now sharing star billing with the actor he had once supported, Charles Boyer. Clearly a pleasure to have around, he was Maggie McNamara's Italian (!) suitor in *Three Coins in the Fountain*, and the tutor in love with princess-to-be Grace Kelly in *The Swan*. He was infinitely more convincing in these two films than he was as the menacing killer in the hokey Doris Day vehicle *Julie*.

The role of a lifetime came along when director Vincente Minnelli cast him alongside Chevalier himself in the sparkling 1958 Oscar-winner *Gigi*. As Gaston, the ladies' man who is bored with his lifestyle until Leslie Caron relights his flame, he was never more assured in the art of sophisticated comedy, and he made musical history with his incomparable "talk-sing" version of Lerner and Loewe's lilting Academy Award-winning title song. There was an inferior follow-up with Chevalier, *Can-Can*, with Jourdan as an insufferably prudish judge. His star began to fade with *The V.I.P.s*, as Elizabeth Taylor's lover, in one of the less-interesting subplots of this multi-character drama; *Made in Paris*, as a world-famous dress designer; and *A Flea in Her Ear*, as the only French cast member in this flat Feydeau farce. During this period he made some occasional trips back to his homeland for such movies as *The Story of the Count of Monte Cristo*, in the title role, and *Cervantes*, as a cardinal. Still dapper and well preserved in his 60s, the movies suddenly asked him back to play some villains in the cable camp classic *Swamp Thing*, eventually turning into a monster for the finale; the James Bond adventure *Octopussy*; and the tongue-in-cheek *Year of the Comet*.

Screen (US releases only): 1939: Corsaire; 1941: Her First Affair; 1943: Heart of a Nation; 1945: Twilight; 1947: The Paradine Case; 1948: Letter From an Unknown Woman; No Minor Vices; 1949: Madame Bovary; 1951: Bird of Paradise; Anne of the Indies; 1952: The Happy Time; 1953: Decameron Nights; 1954: Three Coins in the Fountain; 1956: The Swan; Julie; The Bride Is Too Beautiful; 1958: Gigi; Dangerous Exile; 1959: The Best of Everything; 1960: Can-Can; The Virgins of Rome/Amazons of Rome; 1962: The Story of the Count of Monte Cristo; 1963: The V.I.P.s; 1964: Disorder; 1966: Made in Paris; 1968: A Flea in Her Ear; 1969: The Young Rebel/Cervantes; 1970: To Commit a Murder; 1978: Silver Bears; 1982: Swamp Thing; 1983: Octopussy; 1984: Double Deal (dtv; filmed 1981); 1986: For the Love of Angela (dtv); 1987: Counterforce (dtv); 1989: The Return of Swamp Thing; 1992: Year of the Comet.

NY Stage: 1954: The Immoralist; 1955: Tonight in Samarkand; 1978: 13 Rue de L'Amour.

Select TV: 1954: Wages of Fear (sp); 1955: Paris Precinct (series); Passage of Arms (sp); 1956: Journey by Moonlight (sp); Eloise (sp); 1958: The Falling Angel (sp); 1964: War of Nerves (sp); Graffiti (sp); A Crash of Cymbals (sp); 1969: Fear No Evil; Run a Crooked Mile; 1970: Ritual of Evil; 1973: The Great American Beauty Contest; 1975: The Count of Monte Cristo; 1977: The Man in the Iron Mask; 1979: The French Atlantic Affair (ms); 1982: Romance Theatre (series); 1984: The First Olympics — Athens 1896; Cover-Up; 1986: Beverly Hills Madam; 1988: Grand Larceny.

KATY JURADO

(Maria Christina Jurado Garcia) Born: Guadalajara, Mexico, January 16, 1924. Died: July 5, 2002.

Full-lipped, sad-eyed Katy Jurado was the Mexican actress most often called on to play moody women with heavy hearts and a multitude of burdens upon them. Making her movie debut in her native country, in *No Maturas* in 1943, she spent the next eight years there before Hollywood asked to be one of the supporting ladies in its first genuinely serious look at the world of the toreador, *Bullfighter and the Lady*. Her success in the U.S. was solidified by *High Noon*, playing the sultry woman from Gary Cooper's past who reluctantly sees him move on to good girl Grace Kelly, and *Broken Lance*, getting a surprise Oscar-nomination for her far from memorable performance as the loving Indian wife of Spencer Tracy. More impressively she was seen at her emotional best as the distraught mother of the young boy (Rafael Campos) accused of murder in *Trial*, and took another of her trips west for *The Badlanders*, a variation on *The Asphalt Jungle*, which introduced her to Ernest Borgnine, who became her husband (1959–64). In Marlon Brando's sole directorial effort, *One-Eyes Jacks*, she was the level-headed wife of sheriff Karl Malden, but her run of acceptable work had pretty much ended by the time she was cast as Elvis Presley's Indian mom in the ghastly *Stay Away, Joe*. For the next several years little was seen of her in American films save for appearances in John Huston's *Under the Volcano*, and the Woody Harrelson vehicle *The Hi-Lo Country*.

Screen (US releases only): 1951: Bullfighter and the Lady; 1952: High Noon; 1953: Arrowhead; San Antone; 1954: Broken Lance; 1955: The Racers; Trial; 1956: Trapeze; Man From Del Rio; 1957: Dragoon Wells Massacre; 1958: The Badlanders; 1961: One-Eyed Jacks; Seduction of the South; 1962: Barabbas; 1966: Smoky; A Covenant With Death; 1968: Stay Away, Joe; 1971: The Bridge in the Jungle; 1973: Pat Garrett and Billy the Kid; Once Upon a Scoundrel; 1979: Children of Sanchez; 1983: El Bruto (Mex: 1952); 1984: Under the Volcano; 1989: Fearmaker/House of Fear (dtv); 1998: The Hi-Lo Country.

NY Stage: 1956: The Best House in Naples.

Select TV: 1957: Four Women in Black (sp); 1969: Any Second Now; 1971: A Little Game; 1981: Evita Peron; 1984: A.K.A. Pablo (series); 1985: Lady Blue.

CURT JURGENS

(Curd Gustav Andreas Gottlieb Franz Jürgens) Born: Munich, Germany, December 12, 1912. Died: June 18, 1982.

A formidable German actor with a stiff, glowering, militaristic air about him, Curt Jurgens was a former reporter who turned to acting in the 1930s, making his debut in *Konigswalzer/The Imperial Waltz*. He continued making films in Germany, including a biography of Mozart, until he was placed in a concentration camp as a "political unreliable" toward the end of World War II. Another decade passed before he earned favorable notice for the film *The Devil's General*, thereby invoking the interest of the film industry in both Hollywood and England, as well as all sorts of international producers. In America he made an immediate impression as a U-boat commander who plays a deadly game of war with Robert Mitchum in the engrossing *The Enemy Below*, which treated Jurgens as a multifaceted character and not a mere villain. This was followed by another hit, *The Inn of the Sixth Happiness*, with the actor playing an unlikely Chinese officer with whom Ingrid Bergman falls in love. In no time Jurgens was racking up the credits fast and furious, playing a bigoted officer opposite Danny Kaye in *Me and the Colonel*; reprising Emil Jannings's role in the skewered redo of *The Blue Angel*; portraying scientist Werner von Braun in *I Am at the Stars*; and MacHeath in an obscure adaptation of *The Threepenny*

Opera. He returned to the military for *Battle of Britain* and *The Battle of Neretva*; was a dying pianist in the weird *The Mephisto Waltz*; and had his largest late-career exposure as the villain in one of the James Bond blockbusters, *The Spy Who Loved Me*. He received directorial credit on the films *Pramien auf den Tod* (and co-wr.; 1950), *Gangsterpremiere* (and co-wr.; 1951), and *Ohne Dich Wird es Nacht* (1956).

Screen (US releases only): 1942: The Mozart Story; 1955: The Devil's General; 1957: And God Created Woman; The Enemy Below; 1958: This Happy Feeling; Me and the Colonel; The Inn of the Sixth Happiness; Circus of Love; Bitter Victory; 1959: The Blue Angel; Tamango; Heroes and Sinners; House of Intrigue; 1960: I Aim at the Stars; Michael Strogoff; 1961: Ferry to Hong Kong; Brainwashed; An Eye for an Eye; Time Bomb; 1962: The Longest Day; 1963: The Miracle of the White Stallions; Of Love and Desire; The Threepenny Opera; 1964: Disorder; Hide and Seek; Psyche 59; Nutty, Naughty Chateau; 1965: Lord Jim; 1969: Battle of Britain; 1970: Hello-Goodbye; 1971: The Mephisto Waltz; The Battle of Neretva; Nicholas and Alexandra; 1973: Vault of Horror; 1974: Kill! Kill! Kill!; The Mafia Wants Your Blood; 1975: Slap in the Face; Undercovers Hero; 1976: Female for Hire/Nurses for Sale; 1977: The Spy Who Loved Me; Cagilostro; 1979: Goldengirl; 1980: Daisy Chain; 1981: Just a Gigolo; Breakthrough.

NY Stage: 1966: The Great Indoors.

Select TV: 1982: Smiley's People (ms).

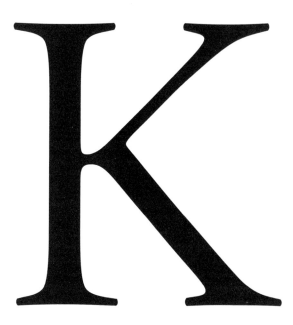

BORIS KARLOFF

(WILLIAM HENRY PRATT) BORN: EAST DULWICH, SOUTH LONDON, ENGLAND, NOVEMBER 23, 1887. ED: LONDON UNIV. DIED: FEBRUARY 2, 1969.

Everything about the movie's greatest ghoul, Boris Karloff (including his name!), was perfect for sending chills down your spine — dark, sinister brows, a gaunt, stooped figure, and an eerily gentleman-like voice that suggested menace behind the manners. At the same time there was something comforting about his presence, and he became one of the most beloved, affectionately mimicked performers in the history of film, a true hero to anyone who embraced the horror genre. In 1909 he moved to Canada where he became interested in acting, joining a traveling stock company, the Jean Russell Players. Crossing into America, he continued with several other troupes for the next few years until he ended up in Los Angeles, making his motion picture debut doing a bit part in the 1916 release *The Dumb Girl of Portici*, made, appropriately, at Universal, the studio that would change his fortunes 15 years down the line. For the remainder of the silent era and through the beginning of the talkies, he would fluctuate between bit parts and more sizable roles, usually as villains. Because of his dark complexion he was often seen as an Indian or an Arab, as he was in *The Last of the Mohicans*, *Without Benefit of Clergy*, *The Hope Diamond Mystery*, and *The Man From Downing Street*. He was also an Indian in *Omar the Tentmaker*, but it was notable in that it was his first sympathetic role.

After that he was back to being nasty with *Parisian Nights*, as a brutish Apache; *Forbidden Cargo*, as a rumrunner; *The Prairie Wife*, as a Mexican half-breed; and *Her Honor the Governor*, as a drug addict. His part as the side-show mesmerist in *The Bells* was one of his few silent era performances to rate any mention, while the best known of his films during this period were *Old Ironsides*, appearing as a Saracen pirate, and the first (and last) Oscar-winner for Best Comedy Direction, *Two Arabian Knights*, in which he was a ship's purser. When sound came there were some noteworthy roles in *The Criminal Code*, repeating the part of a murderous convict that he'd done in a Los Angeles stage production, and *Five Star Final*, posing as a clergyman to get a news story. It was not until his 80th film credit that Karloff at last became a star.

The role of "The Monster," in Universal's 1931 production of *Frankenstein*, had been turned down by Bela Lugosi because it would not allow the newly-established star any dialogue. Karloff, knowing that a good actor can say volumes without a single line, accepted the challenge, making the creature creepy, pathetic, and unforgettable. He was acclaimed as the greatest actor of his type since Lon Chaney and instantly became a part of horror film lore. The movie was a box-office success and continued to be one of the most widely viewed works from its era for decades to come. Universal decided to keep a shroud of mystery around their "new" find, often billing him simply as "Karloff." Although there were parts in straight "A" films like *Scarface*, as a hood murdered memorably at a bowling alley; *The House of Rothschild*, as an anti-Semitic Baron; and *The Lost Patrol*, grotesquely over the top as a religious fanatic; it was decided that horror would be the field in which he would dwell and the area in which audiences would most readily accept him. As a result he became almost exclusively associated with the genre, starring on occasion in accomplished chillers that ranked among the best in their category, but often showing up in programmer junk salvaged only by his participation. Among the films he appeared in soon after the *Frankenstein* triumph were *The Old Dark House*, a cultish, none-too-serious film from *Frankenstein* director James Whale, in which he was a bearded, mute butler (just one of the many weirdoes on hand); *The Mummy*, a somewhat talky piece that required him to wear bandage and gauze only for its opening scene; and *The Mask of Fu Manchu*, where he did an outlandish turn as the evil Asian, in this awesomely racist bit of kitsch. In *The Ghoul*, his first production made back in his homeland, he was seen rising from the dead, and in *The Black Cat* he was at his most evil, as a Satanist, playing opposite Bela Lugosi for the first of several times.

He returned successfully to The Monster for a smashing sequel, *Bride of Frankenstein*, this time speaking some dialogue and playing for both pathos and an occasional wry chuckle in a movie whose devoted followers outnumber the original. He went over to Columbia to play twins, one wicked and one good-hearted, in *The Black Room*; found himself being facially disfigured by Lugosi in *The Raven*, a role he didn't think much of; and played a scientist whose original good intentions turn him bad in *The Invisible Ray*, a situation he would venture into on too many occasions. Over at Warners he was *The Walking Dead*, a title that could easily be confused with the British picture he made around the same time, *The Man Who Lived Again*. He returned to Asian makeup to play a warlord in *West of Shanghai*, and then went over to a poverty-row studio, Monogram, to play another Eastern character, a Charlie Chan-type sleuth, in *Mr. Wong, Detective*, a shabbily conceived programmer that did enough business to rate four sequels. Back at Universal he gave the monster one last go on the big screen in *Son of Frankenstein*, which was the last of the series to be worthy of the original, although it seemed a bit of a setback on his part, since both Lugosi and Basil Rathbone had more substantial roles than he did. There were four "mad doctor" parts for Columbia, *The Man They Could Not Hang*, *The Man With Nine Lives*, *Before I Hang*, and *The Devil Commands*, in each case trying to develop some new device to better mankind, but ending up dead as punishment for tampering with the unknown. Between these he had one of his most fearsome roles, as the bald, club-footed executioner in *Tower of London*, easily stealing the show from a formidable cast (Bathbone, Vincent Price, et al.), and then he did one of the few films in which he didn't end up dead or on his way to the gallows, *Devil's Island*.

By this point Karloff was so famous in the fright genre that there were spoof parts making light of his image, as in *The Boogie Man Will Get You*, teamed with Peter Lorre, and *You'll Find Out*, which not only featured Lorre and Lugosi, but threw Ish Kabbible and the Kay Kyser band into the mix. However the cheesiness of many of his assignments, including *The Ape*, which had him donning a gorilla skin to kill his victims, meant it wasn't any great loss to leave the cinema behind and retreat to the stage for a while. His Broadway debut in the 1942 sensation *Arsenic and Old Lace* would become one of his greatest triumphs, and although he would return to it on radio and television, Raymond Massey got the part in Warner Bros.'s 1944 film version. Back in Hollywood he graduated from monster makeup to looking like his natural self in *House of Frankenstein*, giving the creature role over to the younger Glenn Strange. He was then fortunate to hook up with producer Val Lewton, who gave him parts in three atmospheric films with an emphasis on the power of suggestion over visual scares, *The Body Snatcher*, in one of his finest performances, as the intimidating grave robber who wields power over doctor Henry Daniell; *Isle of the Dead*, the weakest of the trio, as a general on a plague-infested island; and *Bedlam*, as the cruel warden of the notorious London insane asylum. Having reached 60, it seemed less likely that there would be starring vehicles, so he accepted offers from the major studios to play Indians in *Tap Roots* and in DeMille's Technicolor hit *Unconquered*, and to torment Danny Kaye as a fake psychiatrist in the comedy *The Secret Life of Walter Mitty*.

There was little to be said for his participation in a pair of Abbott and Costello films made back at his alma mater, Universal. The curiously named *Abbott and Costello Meet the Killer, Boris Karloff*, might have been considered something of an honor that he'd become famous enough to have his name featured in a title, were it not for the fact that it was an inaccurate one, while *Abbott and Costello Meet Dr. Jekyll and Mr. Hyde*, was dishonest in its own way, since Karloff was *not* Mr. Hyde, a stunt man playing the more physically demanding role of his evil alter ego. Also at Universal he did a pair of poorly received costume thrillers, *The Strange Door*, with Charles Laughton, and *The Black Castle*. Nor was there any advantage to Karloff signing on for such 1950s fare as *Voodoo Island* or *Frankenstein 1970*, as an

ancestor to the inventor, opening his castle for a television crew. He appeared at that point in much better reviewed work on television; onstage, with *Peter Pan*, as Captain Hook, and *The Lark*, as Bishop Cauchon; and in some made-in-England films that tried to aim for higher quality, *The Haunted Strangler*, in which he was a criminologist on the trail of a killer, and *Corridors of Blood*, a fictionalized account of the creation of anesthesia.

By the early 1960s television reruns of Karloff's old movies had turned him into a revered living legend to horror aficionados, who relished not only the grand sense of fun that he instilled in acting, but also the fact that he was clearly quite accomplished at his craft, something that could not always be said about such other genre names as Lugosi and Lon Chaney, Jr. Because of his "rediscovery" he was recruited for some lighthearted appearances over at American International, including *The Raven*, as a sorcerer dueling with Vincent Price, and *The Comedy of Terrors*, going for laughs as a doddering old man. There was a cheapie, *The Terror*, made on the standing sets of *The Comedy of Terrors*; *Black Sabbath*, one of Mario Bava's cult works; and *Die, Monster, Die!*, where, crippled by the effects of a meteor, his character used a wheelchair, drawing attention to his real physical deterioration. There was voice-over work in what would become one of the best loved of all television specials, *Dr. Seuss's How the Grinch Stole Christmas!*, and one final great movie role, pretty much playing himself, in *Targets*. The official debut feature of director Peter Bogdanovich, it was a dual story of a crazed gun-happy youth (Tim O'Kelly) who has casually murdered his family, and a classic horror star confronting a violent society that has made him feel passé. It was a marvelous testimonial to a figure who was by now looked on as one of the cinema's handful of one-of-a-kind immortals, and it should have, by all rights, been his last movie. Instead, never one to stop working, the very sickly Karloff was employed in six more productions, including four Mexican-produced cheapies, all of which were released after his death in 1969.

Screen: 1916: The Dumb Girl of Portici; 1919: The Lightning Raider (serial); The Masked Raider; His Majesty the American; The Prince and Betty; 1920: The Deadlier Sex; The Courage of Marge O'Doone; The Last of the Mohicans; 1921: Without Benefit of Clergy; The Hope Diamond Mystery (serial); Cheated Hearts; The Cave Girl; 1922: The Man From Downing Street; The Infidel; The Altar Stairs; Omar the Tentmaker; Nan of the North; A Woman Conquers; 1923: The Gentleman from America; The Prisoner; 1924: Riders of the Plains (serial); The Hellion; Dynamite Dan; 1925: Perils of the Wild (serial); Forbidden Cargo; The Prairie Wife; Parisian Nights; Never the Twain Shall Meet; Lady Robin Hood; 1926: The Greater Glory; Her Honor — The Governor; The Bells; The Golden Web; The Eagle of the Sea; Flames; Old Ironsides; Flaming Fury; The Man in the Saddle; Valencia; 1927: Tarzan and the Golden Lion; Let It Rain; The Meddlin' Stranger; The Princess From Hoboken; The Phantom Buster; Soft Cushions; Two Arabian Knights; The Love Mart; 1928: Vanishing Rider (serial); Vultures of the Sea (serial); Little Wild Girl; 1929: Burning the Wind; Little Wild Girl; The Fatal Warning (serial); The Devil's Chaplain; Phantom of the North; Two Sisters; Behind That Curtain; Anne Against the World; King of the Kongo (serial); The Unholy Night; 1930: The Bad One; The Sea Bat; The Utah Kid; Mothers Cry; 1931: The Criminal Code; The Last Parade; Dirigible; Cracked Nuts; Young Donovan's Kid; King of the Wild (serial); Smart Money; The Public Defender; Pardon Us; Five Star Final; I Like Your Nerve; Graft; The Mad Genius; The Yellow Ticket; The Guilty Generation; Frankenstein; Tonight or Never; 1932: Behind the Mask; Alias the Doctor; Business and Pleasure; Scarface; The Cohens and Kellys in Hollywood; The Miracle Man; Night

World; The Old Dark House; The Mask of Fu Manchu; The Mummy; 1933: The Ghoul; 1934: The Lost Patrol; The House of Rothschild; The Black Cat; Gift of Gab; 1935: Bride of Frankenstein; The Black Room; The Raven; 1936: The Invisible Ray; The Walking Dead; The Man Who Lived Again/The Man Who Changed His Mind; Juggernaut; 1937: Charlie Chan at the Opera; Night Key; West of Shanghai; 1938: The Invisible Menace; 1938: Mr. Wong — Detective; 1939: Son of Frankenstein; The Mystery of Mr. Wong; Mr. Wong in Chinatown; The Man They Could Not Hang; Tower of London; 1940: The Fatal Hour; British Intelligence; Black Friday; The Man With Nine Lives; Devil's Island; Doomed to Die; Before I Hang; The Ape; You'll Find Out; 1941: The Devil Commands; 1942: The Boogie Man Will Get You; 1944: The Climax; House of Frankenstein; 1945: The Body Snatcher; Isle of the Dead; 1946: Bedlam; 1947: The Secret Life of Walter Mitty; Lured; Unconquered; Dick Tracy Meets Gruesome; 1948: Tap Roots; 1949: Abbott and Costello Meet the Killer, Boris Karloff; 1951: The Strange Door; The Emperor's Nightingale (narrator); 1952: The Black Castle; 1953: Abbott and Costello Meet Dr. Jekyll and Mr. Hyde; 1955: Sabaka/The Hindu (filmed 1953); 1957: Monster of the Island (filmed 1953); Voodoo Island; 1958: The Haunted Strangler/Grip of the Strangler; Frankenstein 1970; 1963: The Raven; Corridors of Blood/Doctor From Seven Dials (filmed 1958); The Terror; The Comedy of Terrors; 1964: Black Sabbath; Bikini Beach; 1965: Die, Monster, Die!; 1966: Ghost in the Invisible Bikini; The Daydreamer (voice); 1967: The Venetian Affair; Mondo Balordo (narrator; filmed 1963); The Sorcerers; Mad Monster Party? (voice); 1968: Targets; 1970: The Crimson Cult; 1971: The Snake People/Isle of the Snake People; The Incredible Invasion/Alien Terror; Cauldron of Blood/Blind Man's Bluff; The Fear Chamber; 1972: House of Evil.

NY Stage: 1941: Arsenic and Old Lace; 1948: The Linden Tree; 1949: The Shop at Sly Corner; 1950: Peter Pan; 1955: The Lark.
Select TV: 1949: Starring Boris Karloff (series); 1950: Uncle Vanya (sp); 1951: The Kimballs (sp); Mutiny on the Nicolette (sp); The Lonely Place (sp); The Jest of Hahalaba (sp); 1952: Don Quixote (sp); Memento (sp); Soul of the Great Bell (sp); Death House (sp); 1953: The Invited Seven (sp); The Black Prophet (sp); Burden of Proof (sp); The Chase (sp); The Signal Man (sp); House of Death (sp); The White Carnation (sp); 1954–55: Colonel March of Scotland Yard (series); 1955: Arsenic and Old Lace (sp); The Sting of Death (sp); A Connecticut Yankee (sp); Mr. Blue Ocean (sp); Counterfeit (sp); 1956: Even the Weariest River (sp); Bury Me Later (sp); Rendezvous in Black (sp); 1957: The Lark (sp); The Man Who Played God (sp); The Deadly Game (sp); 1958: Vestris (sp); Legend of Sleepy Hollow (sp; narrator); Shadow of a Genius (sp); Heart of Darkness (sp); 1959: Indian Giver (sp); 1960: To the Sound of Trumpets (sp); Treasure Island (sp); 1960–62: Thriller (series); 1962: Out of This World (series); Arsenic and Old Lace (sp); The Paradine Case (sp); 1966: Dr. Seuss's How the Grinch Stole Christmas! (sp; voice).

DANNY KAYE

(David Daniel Kaminsky) Born: Brooklyn, NY, January 18, 1913. Died: March 3, 1987.

Alternately manic and soothing, Danny Kaye was the best combination of music and comedy that the movies had to offer. The excitable, red-headed entertainer could mug and cavort hilariously and then let go with one of his brilliant patter songs, delivered in a lightning-quick style with deliciously nonsensical lyrics, or sell a ballad as beautifully as

anybody on the pop charts. He began as part of a street singing duo with friend Louis Eisen while traveling through Florida. From there they worked their way up to jobs in the Catskills resorts, after which they split and Kaye helped form a dance trio called "The Three Terpsichoreans." It was with this group that he joined a touring show, La Vie Paris, and began to develop his mix of broad comical abandon and gibberish singing. Back in New York he was featured in vaudeville and on radio, becoming well enough known to be starred in some two-reelers, performing with a heavy Yiddish dialect. Needless to say, Kaye did not look back on these shorts with any fondness. Shortly afterwards he appeared in a revue called Sunday Night Varieties, which was staged at a resort in the Pocono Mountains. It was during this show that he met composer Sylvia Fine, who would not only write some of his best-remembered material, but also became his wife, in 1940.

Kaye debuted on Broadway, in 1939, in The Straw Hat Revue, and then, two years later, stole the show as part of the supporting cast of Lady in the Dark, performing his unforgettable patter number "Tchaikovsky," which required him to sing the names of various Russian composers in record time. He rejected an offer from MGM, then got himself a lead onstage in Let's Face It, where his big number (interpolated by his wife into an otherwise all-Cole Porter score) was "Melody in Four F." It was Samuel Goldwyn who finally grabbed him for the big screen, signing him to a five-year contract in 1943. Therefore Kaye started out as the star of his own lavish Technicolor showcase, Up in Arms, as a hypochondriac drafted into the Army. It wasn't much different from a hundred other service comedies, but the comedian was an immediate hit with the moviegoing public, bringing down the house with "The Lobby Number" and, for safe measure, "Melody in Four F."

The next two were more of the same — slick, popular, and, save for some priceless Kaye shtick, ultimately forgettable — Wonder Man, playing twins, one bad, one good, and The Kid From Brooklyn, reprising Harold Lloyd's old role from The Milky Way, as a timid milkman turned boxer. The next, however, was something more inspired. The Secret Life of Walter Mitty, adapted from the James Thurber character, had Kaye playing a meek daydreamer, therefore allowing him to cut loose with a variety of fanciful characters and to sing another of his classics, "Anatole of Paris," about an effete milliner. It became the role the majority of his fans would cherish most, even if Thurber himself went on record as hating the end result. After A Song Is Born, a weak re-do of Ball of Fire, he left Goldwyn for Warners, but his one film there, The Inspector General, in which he was cast as an illiterate carny stooge mistaken for the title character, fared poorly. This was a shame, for it was funnier than anything he'd done up to that time and included some of his musical peaks, with the droll "Gypsy Drinking Song" and the dazzling "Soliloquy for Three Heads." A stopover at Fox, for On the Riviera, found him once again playing a dual role and reprising a property done previously (in this case Chevalier's Folies Bergère and Don Ameche's That Night in Rio). It also had the same sort of blandness that was the hallmark of too many Fox musicals and featured a coy number called "Poppo the Puppet" that showed what a turnoff Kaye could be with the wrong material.

Back at Goldwyn he played what had been a dream part, the immortal teller of fairy tales, Hans Christian Andersen. The film bore next to no relation to fact and was pretty much a fairy tale itself, but Kaye was given an unforgettable score by Frank Loesser ("Thumbelina," "Anywhere I Wander," etc.) that more than made up for the dry balletic interludes and the Farley

Granger subplot. Surprisingly, it turned out to be one of the biggest hits of the year, giving Kaye another of his most enduring roles. From there it was over to Paramount for *Knock on Wood*, as a ventriloquist chased by spies (his own favorite of his films), and the holiday perennial and box-office colossus, *White Christmas*, which, despite a spin with Vera-Ellen that proved he could dance with the best of them, pretty much had him playing second fiddle to Bing Crosby. Around this time he brought attention to his work on behalf of aiding the world's underprivileged children for UNICEF, appearing in a 20-minute documentary called "Assignment Children." This was capped off by an honorary Academy Award (given in 1955) and his crowning film achievement, *The Court Jester*, a perfect blend of pageantry, hilarity, and music, in which Kaye created something of a classic with standout numbers like "Never Unfox the Fox," and a routine that became part of comic folklore, "The Chalice from the Palace." After a circus romp at MGM, *Merry Andrew*, he decided to play it straight for *Me and the Colonel*, bringing attention to his Jewish background for the first time on screen, as he tried to flee Nazi-occupied Paris in the company of a Polish anti-Semite (Curt Jurgens). This did not go over with the public, but the standard biopic *The Five Pennies* (about trumpeter Red Nichols) did, the highlight being Kaye's duet with the inimitable Louis Armstrong.

By the time of his last two farces, *On the Double* and *The Man From the Diner's Club*, it was clear that he was getting a mite old for such zany behavior, and he made the natural segue over to television. After his own series ran successfully for several seasons (he himself won an Emmy Award for it in 1964), he returned one last time to the movies in yet another straight role, the Rag Picker, in the all-star rendering of *The Madwoman of Chaillot*, and promptly stole a fairly disappointing movie from his talented co-stars. He returned to Broadway to star as Noah in Richard Rodgers's *Two by Two*, and what started as a triumph ended up a notorious part of theater history. Having broken his leg during the run, he kept playing the role in a wheelchair and then on crutches, ultimately losing interest in the piece and ad-libbing his way through it, much to the horror of his fellow cast members and the show's creators, turning the musical into something akin to vaudeville shtick. The remainder of his career was spent doing sporadic appearances on television, including children's specials, and one final dramatic turn, for which he received raves, as the concentration camp survivor who battles a Neo-Nazi group's plans to march in *Skokie*. After his death there were those who spoke of an insecure man with a cruel streak, but the legacy he left behind was that of a consummate professional who had only to walk on screen and make millions smile.

Screen: 1944: Up in Arms; 1945: Wonder Man; 1946: The Kid From Brooklyn; 1947: The Secret Life of Walter Mitty; 1948: A Song Is Born; 1949: The Inspector General; It's a Great Feeling; 1951: On the Riviera; 1952: Hans Christian Andersen; 1954: Knock on Wood; White Christmas; 1956: The Court Jester; 1958: Merry Andrew; Me and the Colonel; 1959: The Five Pennies; 1961: On the Double; 1963: The Man From the Diner's Club; 1969: The Madwoman of Chaillot.

NY Stage: 1939: The Straw Hat Revue; 1941: Lady in the Dark; Let's Face It; 1970: Two by Two.

Select TV: 1960: Danny Kaye (sp); 1962: The Danny Kaye Show (sp); 1963–67: The Danny Kaye Show (series); 1971: Here Comes Peter Cottontail (sp; voice); 1972: The Enchanted World of Danny Kaye: The Emperor's New Clothes (sp; voice); 1975: Peter Pan (sp); 1976: Pinocchio (sp); 1981: An Evening With Danny Kaye and the New York Philharmonic (sp); Skokie.

BUSTER KEATON

(JOSEPH FRANK KEATON) BORN: PIQUA, KS, OCTOBER 4, 1895. DIED: FEBRUARY 1, 1966.

Though he fell from the heights of silent movie stardom to the depths of alcoholism and bit roles that wasted his genius, Buster Keaton is now often regarded as the most inventive comedic artist of his era. Given a run in his day by Charlie Chaplin (the critics' darling) and Harold Lloyd (whose box-office appeal was usually a step or two ahead of Keaton's), his creativity with sight gags and physical comedy, as well as his often bleak and surreal view of the world, have won the unsmiling comic a continuing admiration that has, in many ways, outshone his one-time rivals. He joined his parents in vaudeville when he was only three years old, allowing himself to be tossed about onstage like a medicine ball. In time he became one of the most admired physical performers in the business, which made him a natural for the slapstick comedies of the silent era. His motion picture debut took place in 1917 when he was asked to join Fatty Arbuckle's ensemble of players for the two-reeler *The Butcher Boy*, participating in some knockabout shenanigans as a customer who shows up at Fatty's store to purchase some molasses. He stayed with the corpulent comic for another three years, co-starring in 15 short subjects in total, ending with *The Garage*, in 1920.

Soon he was popular enough to branch out on his own and was hired by Metro to star in a feature, *The Saphead*, playing a part Douglas Fairbanks had done onstage, that of a wealthy bumbler. A great deal more creative freedom was being offered by the same producer of Arbuckle's films, Joseph Schenck, whose contract allowed Keaton total control over his own two-reelers, with the comedian co-scripting and co-directing in collaboration with Eddie Cline. Keaton extended his power to include some nepotism as well, often finding roles for his dad, Joe Keaton. Made over a two year period (1921–23), these shorts included such weirdly inventive farces as "One Week" (building a do-it-yourself house with disastrous results), "The Boat" (putting his family through one seafaring catastrophe after another), "The Scarecrow" (living in an ingeniously decorated cottage), "The Playhouse" (at one point playing all of the cast members), "The Electric House" (using technical wizardry and imaginative props for sight gags), and "Cops" (being chased by an entire city police force in what is probably his most breathtaking and famous short film).

His official move into features came in 1923 with one of his lesser efforts, *The Three Ages*, which was basically three shorts combined to show Buster through different periods in history — prehistoric, Roman, and modern day. The follow-up, *Our Hospitality*, was a genteel spoof of the Old South, climaxing with an exciting waterfall rescue. In his subsequent features Keaton would create some of the great comic set pieces of the era: the amazing, elongated pursuit by a church full of anxious brides at the climax of *Seven Chances*; the lavish hurricane sequence that blew the comedian about like a tumbleweed in *Steamboat Bill Jr.*; the surreal, three-dimensional interactive movie in *Sherlock, Jr.*, with Buster as a love-smitten projectionist who finds himself jumping from scene to scene in a film within his film; and the sustained pursuit of *The General*, as Buster attempts to regain his captured locomotive in what is certainly his finest effort.

In addition to these he and co-star Kathryn McGuire spent the bulk of *The Navigator* going it alone on an abandoned steamship, in what proved to be among his biggest box-office successes; *Go West* offered him for the last time in his traditional garb of porkpie hat, slap shoes, baggy trousers, and vest; *Battling Butler* allowed him to roll out some slapstick in a boxing ring; and *College* found him going from shy nebbish to hero, as he tried to become an athlete to impress a girl. Keaton is credited as director or co-director on many of these as well as writer, though even without credit he was always instrumental in coming up with ideas. *College* and *Steamboat Bill Jr.* saw his box-office appeal slipping somewhat, so a change was suggested, resulting in Keaton signing a contract with Schenck's brother and joining the roster of stars over at MGM. He would later call this move the biggest professional mistake of his life, as it proved to be his downfall, his creative freedom slowly being yanked away from him.

Things did start out, however, on a high note with *The Cameraman*, a smart and charming piece that pretty much kept in the Keaton comic tradition with the extra-added attraction of on-location shooting in New York City. Trouble began almost immediately, though, with *Spite Marriage*, with too many studio advisers putting in their two cents. As the talkies arrived he started off on an uninspired but innocuous note with the Hollywood-set *Free and Easy*, which even required him to sing and dance. But such follow-ups as a tired service comedy, *Doughboys*, and *Parlor, Bedroom and Bath*, which hoped to find humor by having him play off of rubber-limbed Charlotte Greenwood, were just not funny enough, and there was something decidedly uncomfortable about the mating of Keaton and the microphone. In what they thought was a solution to his declining box-office receipts, MGM saw fit to team him on three successive occasions (*The Passionate Plumber*, *Speak Easily*, and *What! No Beer?*), with manic Jimmy Durante, a pairing that left Buster and the public cold. His unhappiness during this period led to his bout with the bottle and the eventual collapse of his career. Once the Metro contract was dissolved, he appeared in a series of very poor shorts, first for Educational ("The Gold Ghost" to "Love Nest on Wheels") and then Columbia ("Pest From the West" to "She's Oil Mine"). The low profile of these two-reelers meant that Keaton's status in the industry slipped dangerously during the 1930s, until he was thought of principally as a misused performer trying in vain to recapture the glory of his heyday. Once he came to accept that his days as the star of his own vehicles were over, he sought sideline work as a gag writer and found himself in an occasional supporting role in major studio productions, starting with Fox's *Hollywood Cavalcade*, a look back at the silent movie era that required him to heave some custard pies, despite the fact that this was never really his style of comedy.

Among his more substantial acting assignments were roles in Universal's *San Diego, I Love You*, as a bus driver who decides to detour from his usual route (it would mark one of the few times on screen that audiences ever saw him smile), and MGM's Judy Garland musical *In the Good Old Summertime*, as a hapless music store employee who, in his big slapstick scene, inadvertently destroys S.Z. Sakall's precious Stradivarius. There was even a small but significant bit of knockabout business in *Limelight*, memorable simply because it marked the only scene on film featuring both Keaton and Charlie Chaplin. It was much less fulfilling to see him play an Indian in a grotesque live-action adaptation of *Li'l Abner*; a short-order cook in a Susannah Foster musical, *That Night With You*; or a mountain man in the cheapjack "C" picture *God's Country*. During the 1950s film lovers began to unearth the Keaton classics and hail the work of an underappreciated talent. As a result, there was a great deal of work on television in guest shots, commercials, and an occasional dramatic role, plus cameos in such major productions as *Sunset Blvd.*, pretty much playing himself, as one of Gloria Swanson's card-playing cronies, and the Oscar-winning *Around the World in Eighty Days*, as a train conductor. Filmmakers were eager to pay tribute to one of the geniuses of the silent era and came up with parts for the aging comedian that were probably accepted by Keaton simply to pay the bills. These included roles in *Ten Girls Ago*, an aborted project with Bert Lahr that went unreleased; *It's a Mad Mad Mad Mad World*, in which he was barely visible in a pointless sequence; four brain-dead "Beach Party" movies, with Buster looking fairly pathetic in the teen surroundings, often dressed in Indian garb; and the experimental Samuel Beckett-scripted short "Film," in which he spent most of the movie with his back to the camera. He was last seen running around the Seven Hills of Rome in the farcical musical *A Funny Thing Happened on the Way to the Forum*, released several months after his death. In 1959 he was bestowed with a special Academy Award and published his autobiography *My Wonderful World of Slapstick* the following year.

Screen (shorts): 1917: The Butcher Boy; A Reckless Romeo; The Rough House; His Wedding Night; Oh Doctor!; Fatty at Coney Island; A Country Hero; 1918: Out West; The Bell Boy; Moonshine; Good Night Nurse; The Cook; 1919: Back Stage; The Hayseed; The Garage/Fire Chief; *And co-director and co-writer on the next 19 titles:* 1920: One Week; Convict 13; The Scarecrow; Neighbors; 1921: The Haunted House; Hard Luck; The High Sign; The Goat; The Playhouse; The Boat; 1922: The Paleface; Cops; My Wife's Relations; The Blacksmith; The Frozen North; The Electric House; Daydreams; 1923: The Balloonatic; The Love Nest; *Actor:* 1934: The Gold Ghost; Allez Oop; 1935: Palooka From Paducah; One-Run Elmer; Hayseed Romance; Tars and Stripes; The E-Flat Man; The Timid Young Man; 1936: Three on a Limb; Grand Slam Opera (and co-story); Blue Blazes; The Chemist; Mixed Magic; 1937: Jail Bait; Ditto; Love Nest on Wheels; 1939: Pest From the West; Mooching Through Georgia; 1940: Nothing but Pleasure; Pardon My Berth Marks; The Taming of the Snood/Four-Thirds Off; The Spook Speaks; His Ex Marks the Spot; 1941: So You Won't Squawk; General Nuisance/The Private General; She's Oil Mine; 1965: The Railrodder; Film.

Screen (features): 1920: The Saphead; 1923: The Three Ages (and co-dir.; co-wr.); Our Hospitality (and co-dir.); 1924: Sherlock, Jr. (and dir.); The Navigator (and co-dir.); 1925: Seven Chances (and dir.); Go West (and dir.; story); 1926: Battling Butler (and dir.); 1927: The General (and co-dir.; co-wr.); College; 1928: Steamboat Bill Jr.; The Cameraman; 1929: Spite Marriage; The Hollywood Revue of 1929; 1930: Free and Easy; Doughboys (and prod.); 1931: Parlor, Bedroom and Bath (and prod.); Sidewalks of New York; 1932: The Passionate Plumber; Speak Easily; 1933: What! No Beer?; 1934: The Champ of the Champs-Elysees; 1936: The Invader/An Old Spanish Custom; 1939: Hollywood Cavalcade; 1940: The Villain Still Pursued Her; Li'l Abner; 1943: Forever and a Day; 1944: San Diego, I Love You; 1945: That's the Spirit; That Night With You; 1946: God's Country; El Moderno Barba Azul/Boom in the Moon; 1949: The Lovable Cheat; In the Good Old Summertime; 1950: Sunset Blvd.; 1952: Limelight; 1956: Around the World in Eighty Days; 1960: The Adventures of Huckleberry Finn; 1962: Ten Girls Ago (unreleased); 1963: It's a Mad Mad Mad Mad World; 1964: Pajama Party; 1965: Beach Blanket Bingo; How to Stuff a Wild Bikini; Sergeant Deadhead; 1966: A Funny Thing Happened on the Way to the Forum; 1967: War Italian Style (It: 1966).

Select TV: 1954: The Awakening (sp); The Man Who Came to Dinner (sp); 1956: The Silent Partner (sp); 1958: The Innocent Sleep (sp).

LILA KEDROVA

BORN: LENINGRAD, RUSSIA, OCTOBER 9, 1918.
RAISED IN FRANCE. DIED: FEBRUARY 16, 2000.

Only the most perceptive fans of foreign films were aware of Lila Kedrova before her brief brush with international cinematic fame. Raised in France from the age of ten, she began acting in movies starting with the 1953 German release *Weg ohne Umkehr/No Way Back*, and was first seen on American screens in 1957 with the stateside distribution of the French production *Razzia*. In 1964 she made her big splash, playing the flamboyant, pitiable, aging courtesan, Madame Hortense, in *Zorba the Greek*, giving an unforgettable, smashing performance that was equal parts grotesque exuberance and sad longing. The film was one of the great successes of the year, and it won her the Academy Award as Best Supporting Actress. She was said to have been learning English while the film was being made, and that was fortunate since there was a temporary desire to cash in on her triumph by those looking for a pinch of color with a broken accent. There was another go with *Zorba* co-star Anthony Quinn, in *A High Wind in Jamaica*, after which she helped Paul Newman and Julie Andrews escape from behind the Iron Curtain in Hitchcock's *Torn Curtain*, and played Virna Lisi's mom in *The Girl Who Couldn't Say No*. Soon the post-Oscar excitement had passed and she was just another player in various uninspired international productions. She did, however, rate one more substantial role, as the dying wife of Melvyn Douglas in *Tell Me a Riddle*, after which she was called on to reprise Madame Hortense, opposite Quinn again, for the Broadway revival of the musical *Zorba*. Still the lucky role of a lifetime, Kedrova won a Tony Award for the part, making her the only performer to pull off this reverse order feat.

Screen (US releases only): 1957: Razzia; 1958: The Lovemaker; 1959: A Woman Like Satan; 1960: Human Cargo; 1964: Zorba the Greek; 1965: A High Wind in Jamaica; 1966: Torn Curtain; Penelope; 1970: The Kremlin Letter; The Girl Who Couldn't Say No; 1971: Escape to the Sun; 1975: Undercovers Hero/Soft Beds, Hard Battles; 1976: Night Child; The Tenant; Eliza's Horoscope; 1980: Clair de Femme; Practice Makes Perfect; Tell Me a Riddle; 1982: Blood Tide/Red Tide; Sword of the Valiant; 1988: Some Girls.

NY Stage: 1983: Zorba.

Select TV: 1972: Cool Millions.

HOWARD KEEL

(HAROLD CLIFFORD LEEK)
BORN: GILLESPIE, IL, APRIL 13, 1917.

MGM's macho baritone par excellence, Howard Keel was one of the unsung heroes of the genre. He possessed a big booming singing voice that could deliver a number gloriously, offset by an unpretentious personality that made audiences feel like he was just a regular guy who happened to be blessed with a great set of pipes. During the early 1950s he contributed greatly in keeping the Hollywood musical at a high-water mark. It was while working in an aircraft factory in California that he began winning competitions and prizes for his singing prowess. In time he joined the American Music Theater in Pasadena, studying under George Huston, and won an audition with Oscar Hammerstein II, who gave him the lead in the London production of *Oklahoma!* While doing the show over there, he quietly made his movie debut, in 1948, in a straight film, *The Small Voice/Hideout*, as an escaped con. Back in the United States he landed one of the choicest assignments ever for a relative unknown, the role of cocky marksman Frank Butler in MGM's lavish big-screen adaptation of the Broadway smash *Annie Get Your Gun*, which became one of the highest grossing pictures of the year. His renditions of such great numbers as "My Defenses Are Down" and "The Girl That I Marry" were ideal, and he was an instant success. Two immediate follow-ups, the South Seas saga *Pagan Love Song*, producer Arthur Freed's least favorite of his impressive slate of musicals, and the comedy *Three Guys Named Mike*, in which Keel romanced airline hostess Jane Wyman, were quickly forgotten.

Returning to classic material from the theater was a wise move indeed, for *Show Boat* was another smash with Keel making a sturdier Gaylord than Allan Jones in the 1936 version. His teaming with Kathryn Grayson was well liked enough to rate a follow-up, the garish remake of *Roberta*, now called *Lovely to Look At*, where his big solo was Jerome Kern's title tune. Amid all the singing he did some comedy in *Callaway Went Thataway*, in a dual role, as an arrogant, boozing ex-cowboy star and his guileless look-alike in this gentle spoof of how early television resuscitated many a career; and some dramatic acting in the horse race story, *Fast Company*, and the western *Ride, Vaquero!*, among others, making the transition between each genre with ease.

Warner Bros. borrowed him from Metro for another enjoyable romp, *Calamity Jane*, as a singing Wild Bill Hickok, opposite a butch Doris Day, and then he had his finest moment in the MGM spotlight, as the vain Shakespearean actor battling it out with estranged wife Grayson in the exuberant *Kiss Me Kate*, just about the most faithful adaptation of a Broadway musical done on screen up to that time. His vocals ranged from the playful "Where Is the Life That Late I Led?" to the haunting "So in Love," handling all facets of the material with equal skill. If *Rose Marie* had to be remade, then Keel was the one to do it, reluctantly reprising Nelson Eddy's part as the intrepid Mountie in this cumbersome offering. It was followed by another of his peaks, the role of the impetuous mountain man who marries and then wins the heart of Jane Powell in *Seven Brides for Seven Brothers*. Despite the emphasis on the magnificent dancing by the performers playing his brothers, it was Keel who added immeasurable strength and weight to the story. There were two more lavish musicals, the kitschy *Jupiter's Darling*, in which he made an eye-popping entrance warbling atop an elephant, and *Kismet*, with Keel in fine form as the beggar-poet, but the cool reception afforded both signaled the beginning of the end for the studio's heyday in this genre.

Leaving Metro, he took a variety of offers that included a minor religious film, *The Big Fisherman*, playing St. Peter, and the well-regarded British sci-fi thriller *The Day of the Triffids*, saving the world from a plant attack. By the end of the 1960s he was one of the past-their-prime stars of A.C. Lyles's cheapie westerns, including *Red Tomahawk* and *Arizona Bushwhackers*, between which he played an Indian in something a bit more high profile, *The War Wagon*, a John Wayne vehicle. The next several years were spent doing summer theater productions, including a stage version of *Seven Brides for Seven Brothers* alongside Jane Powell again, the illusion of theater perhaps disguising the fact that Keel was now 60. There was a sudden reemergence into the limelight when he was asked to appear on one of the hottest of the nighttime soaps, *Dallas*, playing millionaire Clayton Farlow. In 1994 he was seen on the big screen for the first time in more than 25 years, helping to host a look at the heyday of the MGM musical and, therefore, his best screen years, *That's Entertainment! III*.

Screen: AS HAROLD KEEL: 1948: The Small Voice/Hideout.
AS HOWARD KEEL: 1950: Annie Get Your Gun; Pagan Love Song; 1951: Three Guys Named Mike; Show Boat; Texas Carnival; Across the Wide Missouri (narrator); Callaway Went Thataway; 1952: Lovely to Look At; Desperate Search; 1953: Fast Company; Ride, Vaquero!; I Love Melvin; Calamity Jane; Kiss Me Kate; 1954: Rose Marie; Seven Brides for Seven Brothers; Deep in My Heart; 1955: Jupiter's Darling; Kismet; 1959: Floods of Fear; The Big Fisherman; 1961: Armored Command; 1963: The Day of the Triffids; 1965: The Man From Button Willow (voice); 1966: Waco; 1967: Red Tomahawk; The War Wagon; 1968: Arizona Bushwhackers; 1994: That's Entertainment! III.

NY Stage: 1957: Carousel; 1959: Saratoga; 1963: No Strings; 1972: Ambassador.

Select TV: 1957: Gift for a Gunman (sp); 1958: Roberta (sp); 1963: Kiss Me Kate (sp); 1981–91: Dallas (series); 1999: Hart to Hart: Home Is Where the Hart Is.

RUBY KEELER

(ETHEL HILDA KEELER) BORN: HALIFAX, NOVA SCOTIA, CANADA, AUGUST 25, 1909. RAISED IN NEW YORK, NY. DIED: FEBRUARY 28, 1993.

No tribute to the movie musical would be complete without the mention of her name, yet even her greatest admirers had to admit that Ruby Keeler wasn't exactly overflowing with talent. As a singer she could barely squeak by, her acting was best left unmentioned, while her specialty, dancing, had a clod-hopping nature that is singularly unattractive to view. But there was a sincerity about her that somehow made audiences wish her no great ill will. While growing up in New York she took an interest in dancing and was enrolled in the Professional Children's School. Her Broadway debut came in 1923 in the chorus of a George M. Cohan show, *The Rise of Rosie O'Reilly*. After that she restricted her entertaining to nightclubs for a few years until she was put into *Bye Bye Bonnie* and given a specialty number of her own. By the time she was seen supporting Eddie Cantor in his 1928 hit *Whoopee!*, she had already been introduced to one of the biggest stars of the era, Al Jolson. They married that year, and Keeler did one more Broadway show, *Show Girl*, before heading out to Hollywood where Jolson expected her to settle down and play wife. Instead she wound up a part of film history when she was chosen to play the sweet young thing who takes over the lead from the injured star in the groundbreaking Warner Bros. musical *42nd Street*. She and Dick Powell helped introduce one of the score's Harry Warren-Al Dubin gems, "Shuffle Off to Buffalo," and the huge success of the film made them a hot team.

They were seen in *Gold Diggers of 1933*, where Keeler performed "Pettin' in the Park;" *Footlight Parade*, where her big moment came when she, as a highly unlikely Asian, danced upon a bar with James Cagney to the tune of "Shanghai Lil;" *Dames*, with a portrait of her face made into an interlocking puzzle in one of those dazzlingly inventive Busby Berkeley numbers; and *Flirtation Walk*, the popularity of which can be the only possible reason something this limp was nominated for an Oscar for Best Picture. For a break she was given Jolson as her leading man in *Go Into Your Dance*; then returned to Powell for *Shipmates Forever* and *Colleen*; and finished off her stay at Warners with *Ready, Willing and Able*, notable for her cavorting with Lee Dixon on the keys of a giant typewriter. By the end of the 1930s her stay in the limelight and her turbulent marriage to Jolson were over. In 1941 she remarried and temporarily retired,

refusing to have her name used in Columbia's biopic *The Jolson Story*, and giving no public comment on that relationship, which she apparently looked back on with regret. Despite an occasional TV guest spot and a stage tour, she was long out of the minds of most audiences when there was suddenly a resurgence of interest in the Warner Bros. musical era and she became everyone's favorite figure of nostalgic camp. In one final, unexpected jolt of good fortune, she agreed to do a 1971 Broadway revival of the old stage hit *No, No, Nanette* after much coaxing, and wound up being the toast of the town. Afterwards she settled back into the retirement life, one she much preferred to show business.

Screen: 1933: 42nd Street; Gold Diggers of 1933; Footlight Parade; 1934: Dames; Flirtation Walk; 1935: Go Into Your Dance; 1936: Shipmates Forever; Colleen; 1937: Ready, Willing and Able; 1938: Mother Carey's Chickens; 1941: Sweetheart of the Campus; 1970: The Phynx.

NY Stage: 1923: The Rise of Rosie O'Reilly; 1927: Bye Bye Bonnie; Lucky; 1928: The Sidewalks of New York; Whoopee!; 1929: Show Girl; 1940: Hold Onto Your Hats; 1971: No, No, Nanette.

BRIAN KEITH

(ROBERT BRIAN KEITH) BORN: BAYONNE, NJ, NOVEMBER 14, 1921. DIED: JUNE 24, 1997.

A master of low-key acting, Brian Keith's specialty was the gruff guy with a soft spot. The son of noted character actor Robert Keith, he had first appeared on screen as a three-year-old, in *Pied Piper Malone*, billed as Robert Keith, Jr. Following service with the Navy, he started his legit acting career when he joined dad onstage in *Mister Roberts*, and purportedly did bits and extra work in films, not all of which have been substantiated. While securing guest parts on television he also began his movie career proper, at Paramount, in three adventure films, *Arrowhead*, in support of Charlton Heston; *Jivaro*, desiring Rhonda Fleming as they trekked through the jungle; and *Alaska Seas*, upped to one of the leads, as a salmon boat captain fighting with Robert Ryan over Jan Sterling. Following these he went over to Columbia for pretty much of the same while carrying his own one-season TV series, *Crusader*. Back at the movies he got top billing, albeit in a programmer, *Chicago Confidential*, as a state attorney battling a gambling syndicate, then was the social worker trying to help troubled teen Sal Mineo in *Dino*, and a French Foreign Legionnaire in the Fox "B" *Desert Hell*. He was convincingly cast as the father of Paul Newman in *The Young Philadelphians*, despite being only four years his senior, and put some grit into the Disney adventure *Ten Who Dared*, wearing beard and buckskins while exploring the Colorado River.

It was Disney, in fact, who saw some star potential in Keith and made him the likable dad of the two Hayley Millses in the hit *The Parent Trap*; the uncle who tries to save Tommy Kirk from the Indians in the doggie movie *Savage Sam*; the small-town sheriff trying to capture a roving critter in *A Tiger Walks*; and the New Englander intent on protecting endangered geese in *Those Calloways*, one of the best but least popular movies from the studio during their lucrative 1960s heyday. He went from playing it barn broad as a Scottish cattle baron in *The Rare Breed* to the epitome of level-headedness, as the police chief in the highly popular comedy *The Russians Are Coming! The Russians Are Coming!*, before being offered the role of the uncle raising three orphans in the sitcom *Family Affair*. The show ran five years and solidified his stardom, making him a television staple for years to come, eventually landing him another popular series, *Hardcastle and McCormick*, in the 1980s. On the big screen his expertise was still evident in *Reflections in a Golden Eye*, playing Julie Harris's military husband in this grim Southern gothic, and *With Six You Get Eggroll*, taking some of the cutesyness out of this Doris Day comedy. Buried behind whiskers again, he portrayed a stubborn rancher in Disney's *Scandalous John*; put on specs and mustache to play Teddy Roosevelt in *The Wind and the Lion*; was an amusingly dim-witted producer in the nostalgic *Nickelodeon*; and cameoed as a colorful old gunman taking on Billy the Kid and his gang in *Young Guns*. Suffering from cancer, he shot himself in 1997.

Screen: AS ROBERT KEITH, JR.: **1924:** Pied Piper Malone; **1947:** Boomerang!

AS BRIAN KEITH: **1948:** Portrait of Jennie; **1951:** Fourteen Hours; **1953:** Arrowhead; Jivaro; **1954:** Alaska Seas; The Bamboo Prison; **1955:** The Violent Men; Tight Spot; 5 Against the House; **1956:** Storm Center; Nightfall; **1957:** Run of the Arrow; Chicago Confidential; Hell Canyon Outlaws; Dino; **1958:** Sierra Baron; Villa!; Violent Road; Fort Dobbs; Appointment with a Shadow; Desert Hell; **1959:** The Young Philadelphians; **1960:** Ten Who Dared; **1961:** The Parent Trap; The Deadly Companions; **1962:** Moon Pilot; **1963:** Savage Sam; The Raiders; **1964:** A Tiger Walks; The Pleasure Seekers; **1965:** Those Calloways; The Hallelujah Trail; **1966:** The Russians Are Coming! The Russians Are Coming!; The Rare Breed; Way…Way Out; Nevada Smith; **1967:** Reflections in a Golden Eye; **1968:** With Six You Get Eggroll; **1969:** Krakatoa: East of Java/Volcano; Gaily, Gaily; **1970:** Suppose They Gave a War and Nobody Came; The Mackenzie Break; **1971:** Scandalous John; Something Big; **1975:** The Yakuza; The Wind and the Lion; **1976:** Joe Panther; Nickelodeon; **1978:** Hooper; **1979:** Meteor; **1980:** The Mountain Men; **1981:** Charlie Chan and the Curse of the Dragon Queen; Sharky's Machine; **1987:** Death Before Dishonor; **1988:** Young Guns; After the Rain/The Passage; **1989:** Welcome Home; **1993:** Wind Dancer (dtv); **1996:** Entertaining Angels: The Dorothy Day Story; **1997:** Walking Thunder (narrator; dtv); **1998:** Follow Your Heart (dtv).

NY Stage: AS ROBERT KEITH, JR.: **1948:** Mister Roberts; **1951:** Darkness at Noon; Out West of Eighth.

AS BRIAN KEITH: **1978:** Da.

Select TV: **1953:** Westward the Sun (sp); **1954:** Journey to Java (sp); **1955:** Pals to the End (sp); The Haven Technique (sp); Rescue (sp); Branded (sp); **1955–56:** Crusader (series); **1957:** Possessed (sp); **1958:** Elfego Baca (sp); **1959:** Move Along, Mustangers (sp); **1960:** The Westerner (series); **1961:** The Breaking Point (sp); **1963:** Johnny Shiloh (sp); **1964:** Bristle Face (sp); The Tenderfoot (sp); **1966–71:** Family Affair (series); **1972:** Second Chance; **1972–74:** The Little People/The Brian Keith Show (series); **1975:** Archer (series); The Zoo Gang (ms); **1976:** The Quest/The Longest Drive; The Loneliest Runner; **1977:** The Court-Martial of George Armstrong Custer (sp); In the Matter of Karen Ann Quinlan; **1978–79:** Centennial (ms); **1979:** The Chisholms (ms); The Seekers; **1980:** Power; Moviola: The Silent Lovers; **1982:** World War III; Cry for the Strangers; **1983–86:** Hardcastle and McCormick (series); **1984:** The Murder of Sherlock Holmes; **1986:** The B.R.A.T. Patrol; **1987:** The Alamo: Thirteen Days to Glory; **1987–88:** Pursuit of Happiness (series); **1989:** Perry Mason: The Case of the Lethal Lesson; Heartland (series); Lady in a Corner; **1991:** The Gambler Returns: The Luck of the Draw; **1991–92:** Walter & Emily (series); **1993:** The Secrets of Lake Success (ms); **1995:** Picture Windows: Lightning (sp); National Lampoon's Favorite Deadly Sins; The Return of Hunter: Everyone Walks in L.A.; **1997:** The Second Civil War; Spider-Man (series; voice); Rough Riders.

CECIL KELLAWAY

BORN: CAPETOWN, SOUTH AFRICA,
AUGUST 22, 1893. DIED: FEBRUARY 28, 1973.

A jovial, stocky, white-haired character actor with a kindly speaking voice, Cecil Kellaway was busy onstage and on screen in Australia before coming to Hollywood in 1938, under contract to RKO. He debuted almost concurrently in a pair of Preston Foster films, *Everybody's Doing It*, as the head of a cereal company, and *Double Danger*, as Foster's valet. He was soon free-lancing with *Wuthering Heights*, as Mr. Earnshaw; *Mexican Spitfire*, as Leon Errol's business associate, a role he would repeat again in the follow-up; *The Invisible Man Returns*, as a police inspector; and *The Mummy's Hand*, as a magician, before ending up at Paramount, where he would spend most of the war years, solidifying his position as one of filmdom's most ingratiatingly befuddled or raffish old gentlemen. For that company he was a dad who spends too much time with his fraternity lodge in the "B" *The Good Fellows*; a playful warlock in *I Married a Witch* (a picture shot at the studio but eventually released by UA); Thomas Gainsborough in the costumer *Kitty*; and Paulette Goddard's con man dad in *Unconquered*. Leaving that studio, he did some of his best-remembered roles, as the unwanted husband of Lana Turner in *The Postman Always Rings Twice*, more sympathetic in the part than intended; a mischievous leprechaun (ideally cast and earning an Oscar nomination in the process) in *The Luck of the Irish*; and the sanatorium head who covets James Stewart's invisible rabbit for his own in the classic whimsy *Harvey*. Still busy as he approached his 70s, he found himself once again on the Oscar eligibility list as the levelheaded Monsignor in the enormously popular *Guess Who's Coming to Dinner*.

Screen: **1933:** The Hayseeds; **1937:** It Isn't Done; **1938:** Mr. Cedworth Steps Out; Everybody's Doing It; Double Danger; Night Spot; Maid's Night Out; This Marriage Business; Blonde Cheat; Tarnished Angel; **1939:** Gunga Din; Man About Town; Wuthering Heights; The Sun Never Sets; The Under-Pup; We Are Not Alone; Intermezzo; **1940:** Mexican Spitfire; The Invisible Man Returns; Adventure in Diamonds; Brother Orchid; Phantom Raiders; The Mummy's Hand; The House of the Seven Gables; Mexican Spitfire Out West; The Letter; South of Suez; Diamond Frontier; Lady With Red Hair; **1941:** West Point Widow; The Night of January 16th; A Very Young Lady; Birth of the Blues; New York Town; Burma Convoy; Small Town Deb; Bahama Passage; Appointment for Love; **1942:** The Lady Has Plans; Take a Letter, Darling; I Married a Witch; Are Husbands Necessary?; My Heart Belongs to Daddy; Night in New Orleans; Star Spangled Rhythm; **1943:** The Crystal Ball; Forever and a Day; It Ain't Hay; The Good Fellows; **1944:** Frenchman's Creek; Mrs. Parkington; And Now Tomorrow; Practically Yours; **1945:** Love Letters; Kitty; **1946:** Monsieur Beaucaire; The Cockeyed Miracle; The Postman Always Rings Twice; Easy to Wed; **1947:** Unconquered; Variety Girl; **1948:** Always Together; The Decision of Christopher Blake; The Luck of the Irish; Joan of Arc; Portrait of Jennie; **1949:** Down to the Sea in Ships; **1950:** The Reformer and the Redhead; Kim; Harvey; **1951:** Half Angel; Francis Goes to the Races; Katie Did It; The Highwayman; **1952:** Just Across the Street; My Wife's Best Friend; **1953:** Young Bess; Thunder in the East; Cruisin' Down the River; The Beast from 20,000 Fathoms; Paris Model; **1954:** Hurricane at Pilgrim Hill; **1955:** Interrupted Melody; Female on the Beach; The Prodigal; **1956:** Toy Tiger; **1957:** Johnny Trouble; **1958:** The Proud Rebel; **1959:** The Shaggy Dog; **1960:** The Private Lives of Adam and Eve; **1961:** Tammy Tell Me True; Francis of Assisi; **1962:** Zotz!; **1963:** The Cardinal; **1964:** Hush…Hush, Sweet Charlotte; **1965:** The

Confession/Quick, Let's Get Married; **1966**: Spinout; **1967**: Fitzwilly; Guess Who's Coming to Dinner; **1970**: Getting Straight.
NY Stage: 1960: Greenwillow.
Select TV: 1954: Day of Good News (sp); **1955**: Visa for "X" (sp); Private History (sp); **1958**: A Source of Irritation (sp); Verdict of Three (sp); Birthday Party (sp); **1959**: Destination Space (sp); **1965**: Connery's Hands (sp); **1967**: Kismet (sp); **1972**: The Wacky Zoo of Morgan City.

DeFOREST KELLEY

(JACKSON DEFOREST KELLEY) BORN: ATLANTA, GA, JANUARY 20, 1920. DIED: JUNE 11, 1999.

Pretty much acting in anonymity for most of his career, lean, sour-pussed character actor DeForest Kelley found lasting fame via one of the most famous TV series of them all. The son of a Baptist minister, he moved to California as a teen, working at various odd jobs until he joined the Long Beach Community Players. After a break for military service during World War II, he was signed to a contract by Paramount Pictures where he debuted in a Pine-Thomas "B," *Fear in the Night*, followed by a more noticeable role, as one of the leading actors in *Variety Girl*, a film with a plot line that tied together a slew of guest appearances by the studio's big names. Little he did over the next several years was remarked upon, although he was seen in occasional "A" productions, including *The Men* and *The Man in the Gray Flannel Suit*, in both cases playing doctors. He did have one showy role, as the villainous Ike Clanton, in the 1957 hit *Gunfight at the O.K. Corral*, followed by many more visits to the saddle (mainly in A.C. Lyles's "B" westerns), until he was offered the role of Dr. Leonard "Bones" McCoy on the sci-fi series *Star Trek*. Even after cancellation, the show's cult continued to grow to staggering proportions, and he and the rest of the series's principals were called back for a big-screen reunion in 1979, *Star Trek: The Motion Picture*. The movie, despite a pervading dullness, was popular enough to rate several, livelier sequels, and, along with stars William Shatner and Leonard Nimoy, Kelley was considered an irreplaceable asset to fans who enjoyed his deadpan, sardonic delivery. He lived off these films quite comfortably for the remainder of his career.
Screen: 1947: Fear in the Night; Variety Girl; **1948**: Canon City; **1949**: The Duke of Chicago; Malaya; **1950**: The Men; **1953**: Taxi; **1955**: House of Bamboo; The View from Pompey's Head; Illegal; **1956**: Tension at Table Rock; The Man in the Gray Flannel Suit; **1957**: Gunfight at the O.K. Corral; Raintree County; **1958**: The Law and Jake Wade; **1959**: Warlock; **1964**: Gunfight at Comanche Creek; Where Love Has Gone; **1965**: Marriage on the Rocks; Black Spurs; Town Tamer; **1966**: Apache Uprising; Waco; **1972**: Night of the Lepus; **1979**: Star Trek: The Motion Picture; **1982**: Star Trek: The Wrath of Khan; **1984**: Star Trek III: The Search for Spock; **1986**: Star Trek IV: The Voyage Home; **1989**: Star Trek V: The Final Frontier; **1991**: Star Trek VI: The Undiscovered Country; **1999**: Trekkies.
Select TV: 1957: The Velvet Alley (sp); **1966–69**: Star Trek (series); **1973–75**: Star Trek (series; voice).

GENE KELLY

(EUGENE CURRAN KELLY) BORN: PITTSBURGH, PA, AUGUST 23, 1912. ED: UNIV. OF PITTSBURGH. DIED: FEBRUARY 2, 1996.

It was to the benefit of appreciative audiences everywhere that the movies gave us not one but two great male dancers who became household names. If Gene Kelly was fated to always be mentioned second to Fred Astaire, it is nonetheless remarkable that anyone even came near enough to the Master's heights in the first place. Kelly's style, of course, was miles from Astaire's, with more emphasis on both the athletic and the balletic. He also had a sweet sandpapery singing and speaking voice that was very much his own, and greater aspirations as far as cinema was concerned, crossing over to the director's chair with some commendable results. Between odd jobs in Pittsburgh he performed as part of a dance team with his brother Fred, eventually teaching his own dance classes. Traveling to New York to find work, he became a chorus boy in Mary Martin's *Leave It to Me*, then worked his way up to the starring role of Rodgers and Hart's classic *Pal Joey*, as a womanizing louse, giving a performance that made him the toast of Broadway. David O. Selznick signed him to a film contract as a result, but nothing ever came of that, so he lent Kelly to MGM to star opposite Judy Garland in *For Me and My Gal*, in which he played another dancing heel, one who tries to avoid being drafted. The two sparkled in their duet of the title number, and Kelly was an instant hit. MGM bought his contract from Selznick and saw great things in his future.

In the meantime he did a serious role in a disposable war movie, *Pilot # 5*, and, in order to prove his range, he would return time and again to straight drama between musical assignments. His work in this field was earnest, though there were times one detected a great deal of extended effort. In contrast, Kelly's performances in the musical genre had a lighter-than-air, relaxed quality many dramatic actors would kill to possess. He was bogged down by too much plot in both *DuBarry Was a Lady*, where he had to give over too much of the screen to Red Skelton and Lucille Ball, and the all-star *Thousands Cheer*, where he was part of the storyline that led up to all the guest appearances. After another war film, *The Cross of Lorraine*, Kelly was loaned to Columbia for one of the big wartime box-office attractions, *Cover Girl*, which paired him with the red-hot Rita Hayworth. This was considered a milestone in his career in that he and fellow-choreographer Stanley Donen were responsible for concocting a number that received a great deal of well-deserved attention, "The Alter Ego Ballet," a tricky bit that had Kelly dancing with himself. There was another loan-out, to Universal, to play another no-goodnick, in *Christmas Holiday*, a toned-down version of a Maugham novel, opposite that studio's biggest star of the day, Deanna Durbin.

Needing to provide their emerging star with something worthwhile to outshine all of these, Metro gave him a smashing showcase in *Anchors Aweigh*, with Kelly as a cocky sailor on leave in Hollywood. Although he was (inexplicably) billed *after* Frank Sinatra and Kathryn Grayson, it was all his show, with an exciting swashbuckling routine and a now-classic dance with the animated Jerry the Mouse among the highlights. The movie was among the highest-grossing releases of the 1940s and earned an Academy Award nomination for Best Picture. As for Kelly, he was so well liked at this point that he was nominated for an Oscar for the first and last time. *Ziegfeld Follies* gave him a dream chance to dance with Astaire in the memorable "The Babbit and the Bromide" number, probably the only time on screen his movements seemed (in comparison) less than perfect. Reunited with Garland, he was an traveling actor posing as *The Pirate*, mugging shamelessly in the comedy scenes but performing breathtakingly in the "Mack the Black" ballet and in a show-stopping trio with the brilliant Nicholas Brothers to the tune of "Be a Clown." There was a clever, non-musical use of his athletic abilities by casting him as D'Artagnan in *The Three Musketeers*, after which he and Vera-Ellen sizzled in the "Slaughter on Tenth Avenue" ballet from the Rodgers and Hart biopic *Words and Music*.

Following the popular-but-routine *Take Me Out to the Ballgame*, which once again had him unjustly taking third billing, this time to Sinatra and Esther Williams, Kelly took the opportunity to branch out and do some experimentation with the musical genre. With Stanley Donen co-directing, he took on the film version of the Broadway hit *On the Town*. Despite the fact that most of the fine score was tossed out, this was more than compensated by some innovative on-location shooting in Manhattan, set to the rousing "New York, New York" number, and an effervescent quality that made it one of the brightest entertainments to come out of MGM to date. More important, as far as the studio was concerned, it was a box-office smash. There was another drama, a dark, engrossing look at the Mafia, *Black Hand*, and then a final teaming with Garland, in *Summer Stock*, where his solo highlight found him dancing with a newspaper, while the low point had him playing a hillbilly alongside Phil Silvers. He then approached the front office with another pet project, which turned into a masterpiece. *An American in Paris*, as stylishly directed by Vincente Minnelli, was a delightful piece of romance set to the music of Gershwin, with Kelly as a painter who falls in love with Leslie Caron. What made it push the genre to an artistic high was the daring 18-minute ballet that climaxed the movie, retelling the story to the title tune amid backdrops representing the styles of some of the great French artists. The gamble worked, for not only was the movie a box-office sensation, but it did the unthinkable by winning the Academy Award for Best Picture of 1951. Kelly himself was awarded a special Oscar at the same ceremony.

Amazingly, Kelly (working again as co-director with Donen) managed to top this career peak with the film by which all other movie musicals would be forever measured, *Singin' in the Rain*. Working in a lighter tone than *Paris*, the result was a breathlessly funny look at Hollywood's transition from silence to sound with one magical moment after another. With co-star Donald O'Connor he brought down the house with the tongue-twisting "Moses Supposes," turned up the heat with Cyd Charisse amid the spectacular "Broadway Melody" ballet, and created one of the most indelible images on celluloid by joyously dancing to the title song in the middle of a downpour. Had he never worked again his place in movie history would have been assured, but continue he did with some European-made war-themed dramas, *The Devil Makes Three* and *The Crest of the Wave*. These were followed by a disappointing screen transfer of *Brigadoon*, foolishly filmed indoors, though Kelly and Charisse again had some lovely moments dancing in front of the cardboard backdrops; and a guest bit in another biopic, *Deep in My Heart*, in which he danced with brother Fred to Sigmund Romberg's "I Love to Go Swimmin' With Wimmen." There was one last teaming with Donen, *It's Always Fair Weather*, a downbeat tale of three former G.I.'s meeting for a bittersweet reunion ten years after the war. At the time the movie was pretty much written off as a failure, its difficult production bringing the partnership of Kelly and Donen to a bitter end, but it was probably the most imaginative employment of the CinemaScope screen up to that time, making full use of the rectangular image (which Kelly hated) to enhance such brilliant numbers as Kelly, Dan Dailey, and Michael Kidd romping with garbage can lids on their feet, and Kelly's glorious spree through the city on roller skates.

A similar blow to Kelly was the even bigger flop of his long-cherished all-dance project, *Invitation to the Dance*, three unrelated ballet episodes without dialogue, finally distributed years after being shelved. Initially he was to have served as director only, but the studio had no intention of financing a Kelly musical *sans* Kelly, therefore prompting him to find his way

into each of the segments, the best of which had him again in sailor garb, acting against some animated figures. The overall result was far better than its battered reputation has led audiences to believe. With musicals no longer a sure thing, Kelly did his first straight directorial project, *The Happy Road*, in which he also starred, as an unfeeling father tracking down his runaway son, but neither it nor the Cole Porter musical *Les Girls* was very popular, and he ended his bond with MGM in 1957. There was a serious role as a summer camp entertainer, in *Marjorie Morningstar*, though he was not ideally cast as a Jew, and probably his most satisfying non-musical part, as the cynical reporter, in *Inherit the Wind*. As a director he stumbled with such properties as *The Tunnel of Love*, *Gigot*, and *The Cheyenne Social Club* (also serving as producer of the last), but found his footing with the hilarious adultery comedy *A Guide for the Married Man*, and the lavish screen transfer of the Broadway sensation *Hello, Dolly!*, a movie that looks better and better with each passing year.

Although he was no longer a top attraction, there was still great fondness for his carefree charm, so he was occasionally called upon to brighten the screen with his presence, dancing briefly in *What a Way to Go!*, as Shirley MacLaine's hoofer husband in the best sequence of this multi-part comedy; doing some welcomed steps with co-host Astaire in the MGM celebration *That's Entertainment, Part 2*; emoting heavily in *Viva Knievel!*, his career low point, as a former racer-turned-boozer; and playing a character named Danny Maguire (a direct tribute to the part he had played in *Cover Girl*) in the garish disco extravaganza *Xanadu*. There was a credit as director for the Broadway musical *Flower Drum Song*; various TV specials including *Jack and the Beanstalk*, for which he received an Emmy Award as producer; and some well-deserved honors like the American Film Institute Life Achievement Award, in 1985. Following his death, Donen was quick to paint Kelly as an egotist and difficult collaborator, an assessment that was irrelevant in light of all the high spirits he brought to the screen and the even higher spirits he left audiences in as a result.

Screen: 1942: For Me and My Gal; 1943: Pilot # 5; DuBarry Was a Lady; Thousands Cheer; The Cross of Lorraine; 1944: Cover Girl; Christmas Holiday; 1945: Anchors Aweigh; 1946: Ziegfeld Follies; 1947: Living in a Big Way; 1948: The Pirate; The Three Musketeers; Words and Music; 1949: Take Me Out to the Ball Game (and co-wr.); On the Town (and co-dir.); 1950: Black Hand; Summer Stock; 1951: An American in Paris; It's a Big Country; 1952: Singin' in the Rain (and co-dir.); The Devil Makes Three; Love Is Better Than Ever; 1954: Brigadoon; Crest of the Wave/Seagulls Over Sorrento; Deep in My Heart; 1955: It's Always Fair Weather (and co-dir.); 1956: Invitation to the Dance (and dir.; wr.; choreog.); 1957: The Happy Road (and dir.; prod.); Les Girls; 1958: Marjorie Morningstar; 1960: Inherit the Wind; Let's Make Love; 1964: What a Way to Go!; 1968: The Young Girls of Rochefort; 1973: 40 Carats; 1974: That's Entertainment!; 1976: That's Entertainment; Part 2 (and dir.); 1977: Viva Knievel!; 1980: Xanadu; 1985: That's Dancing!; 1994: That's Entertainment! III.

NY Stage: 1938: Leave It to Me; 1939: One for the Money; The Time of Your Life; 1940: Pal Joey.

Select TV: 1957: The Life You Save (sp); 1958: Omnibus: Dancing — A Man's Game (sp); 1959: The Gene Kelly Pontiac Special (sp); The Gene Kelly Show (sp); 1962–63: Going My Way (series); 1966: Gene Kelly in New York, New York (sp); 1967: Jack and the Beanstalk (and dir.; prod.); 1970: Gene Kelly's Wonderful World of Girls (sp); 1971: The Funny Side (series); 1976: Dick Cavett's Backlot USA (sp); America Salutes Richard Rodgers: The Sound of His Music (sp); 1978: Gene Kelly…An American in Pasadena (sp); 1985: North and South (ms); 1986: Sins (ms).

GRACE KELLY

BORN: PHILADELPHIA, PA, NOVEMBER 12, 1929.
ED: AADA. DIED: SEPTEMBER 14, 1982.

Apart from Audrey Hepburn, there was no one in Hollywood who could have more effortlessly gone from actress to royalty than Grace Kelly. She was serenely beautiful, graceful, and intelligent, with a crisp, ladylike poise and, despite her somewhat aloof air, could be very sexy indeed. Coming from a well-to-do Philadelphia family with theatrical connections (her uncle was playwright George Kelly, best known for writing *Craig's Wife*), she took an interest in acting and, after studying at the American Academy of Dramatic Arts, began appearing on television in various commercials and on live drama series. There was a role on Broadway, in 1949, in *The Father* (for which she received a Theatre World Award), more television appearances, and then a supporting role in the 1951 Fox film *Fourteen Hours*, in a somewhat intrusive subplot, as a woman wanting a divorce, while poor Richard Basehart stands outside threatening to jump off a nearby window ledge. It wasn't long before she began rising straight to the top, first by appearing as Gary Cooper's gentle Quaker wife in the classic western *High Noon*, playing a very important part in the movie's final confrontation. From this she got a contract with MGM and reprised Mary Astor's *Red Dust* role in the worthy remake, *Mogambo*, as the proper married lady who finds herself being turned on by adventurer Clark Gable. For it she was nominated for an Oscar in the supporting category.

1954 was her zenith year, starting with parts in two of Alfred Hitchcock's best, *Dial M for Murder*, as the poor, unsuspecting wife who is nearly murdered and then faces charges for killing her assailant, and, better yet, *Rear Window*, as James Stewart's very passionate and very helpful girlfriend, who has no qualms about investigating a possible murder in the apartment across the way. By this point the critics were absolutely in love with Kelly. There was something breathtakingly right about her, and everything she did typified class. For her next movie she took on the unlikely role of Bing Crosby's dowdy, protective wife in *The Country Girl*. Because she triumphed over her miscasting by giving it all she had, there were raves topped by an Academy Award, much to the dismay of Judy Garland fans everywhere (Kelly's upset over Garland's tour-de-force performance in *A Star Is Born* still provokes arguments and some unfair Kelly-bashing). It should be noted that all of these movies were done outside her employer, MGM, and the one that she did that year for them, *Green Fire*, a routine Stewart Granger adventure, was the only flop among them.

A third for Hitchcock, *To Catch a Thief*, was mild, with greater emphasis on romance and pretty scenery than thrills, but since it paired her so perfectly with Cary Grant, nobody cared. More importantly, during filming on the Riviera, she met Prince Rainier of Monaco with whom her name soon became linked in the press. Back home she played her only celluloid princess in one of her weakest, *The Swan*, repeating a part she'd done earlier on TV, as the lady reluctantly arranged to wed Alec Guinness while really loving tutor Louis Jourdan. She then reprised Katharine Hepburn's role in the musical remake of *The Philadelphia Story*, now called *High Society*. It was crazy to make comparisons, but she was an inspired choice nonetheless and partnered Bing Crosby on the lovely Cole Porter ballad "True Love," thereby participating in a best-selling record. By the time it was released she had become Princess Grace of Monaco, and there she would stay, living a charmed life for over 25 years. Alas the fairy tale ended tragically when she died from a brain hemorrhage after being injured in a car crash. This sad event reminded the mourning world of how much joy she had brought to moviegoers during her very brief six-year reign in the cinema of the 1950s.

Screen: 1951: Fourteen Hours; 1952: High Noon; 1953: Mogambo; 1954: Dial M for Murder; Rear Window; The Country Girl; Green Fire; 1955: The Bridges at Toko-Ri; To Catch a Thief; 1956: The Swan; High Society; 1978: The Children of Theatre Street (narrator).

NY Stage: 1949: The Father; 1952: To Be Continued.

Select TV: 1948: Old Lady Robbins (sp); 1950: The Rockingham Tea Set (sp); Ann Rutledge (sp); The Swan (sp); Summer Had Better Be Good (sp); Leaf Out of a Book (sp); 1951: Berkeley Square (sp); 1952: The Big Build-Up (sp); The Kill (sp); Don Quixote (sp); Recapture (sp); 1953: The Way of the Eagle (sp); Boy of Mine (sp); 1954: The Thankful Heart (sp); 1966: The Poppy Is Also a Flower (sp); 1968: Monte Carlo: C'est La Rose (sp).

NANCY KELLY

BORN: LOWELL, MA, MARCH. 25, 1921.
DIED: JANUARY 2, 1995.

Nancy Kelly had to punch in a lot of time as she worked her way towards her most famous role, and, despite her attractive screen presence, there was always a feeling that Hollywood wasn't exactly throwing great challenges her way. The daughter of actress Nan Kelly Yorke, she was already appearing in silent movies as a child. Following some work on radio and stage, she came to 20th Century-Fox in 1938, where her better, and better-known, movies included *Jesse James* and *Stanley and Livingstone*, in which she lent a feminine touch to what were basically male-dominated films. When the studio did give her top billing, it was in "B" products like *Sailor's Lady*, ogled by the Navy, and *Scotland Yard*, an espionage tale in which Edmund Gwenn and John Loder actually had the more important roles. By the mid-1940s her résumé was containing such titles as *Women in Bondage*, *Tarzan's Desert Mystery*, and *Song of the Sarong*, which probably hastened her flight to the theater. There she had her greatest triumph, winning a Tony Award for playing the mother who is shattered when she realizes her little girl is a murderer in *The Bad Seed*. Most of the original cast was asked to repeat their roles in the 1956 movie version, including Kelly, who earned an Oscar nomination, even though the whole enterprise seems overheated and silly to today's audiences. Oddly this turned out to be her swan song as far as movies were concerned, and she went back to work onstage. She was married very briefly (1941–42) to Edmond O'Brien, with whom she appeared in the programmer *Parachute Battalion*.

Screen: 1926: Mismates; The Great Gatsby; Untamed Lady; 1929: Girl on the Barge; 1934: Convention Girl; 1938: Submarine Patrol; 1939: Tail Spin; Jesse James; Frontier Marshal; Stanley and Livingstone; 1940: He Married His Wife; Private Affairs; Sailor's Lady; One Night in the Tropics; 1941: Scotland Yard; A Very Young Lady; Parachute Battalion; 1942: Fly by Night; To the Shores of Tripoli; Friendly Enemies; 1943: Tornado; Women in Bondage; Tarzan's Desert Mystery; 1944: Show Business; Gambler's Choice; Double Exposure; 1945: Song of the Sarong; Betrayal from the East; The Woman Who Came Back; Follow That Woman; 1946: Murder in the Music Hall; 1956: Crowded Paradise; The Bad Seed.

NY Stage: 1931: Give Me Yesterday; 1935: One Good Year; 1937: Susan and God; 1942: Flare Path; 1949: The Big Knife; 1950: Season in the Sun; 1951: Twilight Walk; 1954: The Bad Seed; 1957: The Genius and the Goddess; 1959: The Rivalry; 1960: A

Mighty Man Is He; **1962:** Giants, Sons of Giants; **1968:** Quotations From Chairman Mao Tse-Tung.
Select TV: 1950: Minor Incident (sp); **1953:** The Fathers (sp); Conflict (sp); **1954:** Flowers in a Book (sp); The Secret Self (sp); Time Bomb (sp); **1958:** Office Party (sp); **1975:** The Impostor; **1977:** Murder at the World Series.

PATSY KELLY

(SARAH VERONICA ROSE KELLY)
BORN: BROOKLYN, NY, JANUARY 12, 1910.
DIED: SEPTEMBER 24, 1981.

One of the screen's most proudly lowbrow ladies of mirth, Patsy Kelly was always nice to have around for a biting barb and a disgruntled look. Although she originally studied to be a dancer, she was too naturally funny for her comic timing to go unnoticed, so she was hired by Frank Fay to join him in some comedy routines in his vaudeville act. With him she made her Broadway debut, in 1927, in *Harry Delmar's Revels*, then went off on her own to make her name in several musical comedies. Producer Hal Roach was looking for someone to replace ZaSu Pitts in the two-reeler series she'd been doing with Thelma Todd, and he convinced Kelly that she'd be ideal. Starting with "Beauty and the Bus," in 1933, there were 21 shorts in all, ending when Ms. Todd was found dead in 1935. An attempt to continue Kelly alongside Lyda Roberti only made it through two shorts and a feature, *Nobody's Baby*.

By this time Kelly was already being enlisted for some supporting roles in features like *Go Into Your Dance*, which starred one of her old pals from her dance-school days, Ruby Keeler; *Every Night at Eight*, as the cut-up in the singing trio featuring Alice Faye and Frances Langford; and *Pigskin Parade*, at her most hilariously butch, as a football coach. By the late 1930s she was dividing her time between assignments at Fox, including *Wake Up and Live*, as assistant to Walter Winchell, and *The Gorilla*, as comic foil to the Ritz Brothers at their least funny; and working for Roach, in such films as *Merrily We Live*, as the caustic cook to a family of eccentrics, and *Topper Returns*, mugging for maximum impact as a maid. In what seemed to be the blink of an eye, she slipped into the "B" unit, doing *In Old California* for Republic, and *Danger! Women at Work*, for the lowest of the low, PRC. After the latter, in 1943, she wasn't seen in a movie for another 17 years. During that period she worked mostly in stock and television, spending some of her time as personal assistant (and, as she herself later admitted, sexual companion) to actress Tallulah Bankhead. She returned to the movies stouter but no less amusing, as the housekeeper in *Please Don't Eat the Daisies*, and as one of the Manhattan witches in *Rosemary's Baby*. There was one last peak, reuniting her with Ruby Keeler, for the 1971 Broadway revival of *No, No, Nanette*, a surprise smash for which Kelly won a Tony Award, for once again playing an acerbic domestic. Her last two movies, *Freaky Friday* and *The North Avenue Irregulars*, were made for Disney.
Screen (shorts): 1931: Grand Dame; **1933:** Beauty and the Bus; Air Fright; Backs to Nature; **1934:** Maid in Hollywood; Soup and Fish; Babes in the Goods; I'll Be Suing You; Roamin' Vandals; Three Chumps Ahead; Opened by Mistake; One Horse Farmers; Done in Oil; Bum Voyage; **1935:** Treasure Blues; The Tin Man; Sing, Sister, Sing; The Misses Stooge; Slightly Static; Top Flat; Hot Money; Twin Triplets; All American Toothache; **1936:** Pan Handlers; Hill-Tillies; At Sea Ashore; **1940:** The Happiest Man on Earth; **1942:** Screen Snapshots #99.
Screen (features): 1933: Going Hollywood; **1934:** The Countess of Monte Cristo; The Party's Over; The Girl From

Missouri; Transatlantic Merry-Go-Round; **1935:** Go Into Your Dance; Page Miss Glory; Every Night at Eight; Thanks a Million; **1936:** Private Number; Sing, Baby, Sing; Kelly the Second; Pigskin Parade; **1937:** Nobody's Baby; Wake Up and Live; Pick a Star; Ever Since Eve; **1938:** Merrily We Live; There Goes My Heart; The Cowboy and the Lady; **1939:** The Gorilla; **1940:** Hit Parade of 1941; **1941:** Road Show; Topper Returns; Broadway Limited; Playmates; **1942:** Sing Your Worries Away; In Old California; **1943:** My Son the Hero; Ladies' Day; Danger! Women at Work; **1960:** Please Don't Eat the Daisies; The Crowded Sky; **1964:** The Naked Kiss; **1966:** The Ghost in the Invisible Bikini; **1967:** C'mon, Let's Live a Little; **1968:** Rosemary's Baby; **1970:** The Phynx; **1976:** Freaky Friday; **1979:** The North Avenue Irregulars.
NY Stage: 1927: Harry Delmar's Revels; **1928:** Three Cheers; **1929:** Earl Carroll's Sketch Book; **1930:** Earl Carroll's Vanities; **1931:** The Wonder Bar; **1932:** Flying Colors; Earl Carroll's Vanities; **1971:** No, No, Nanette; **1973:** Irene.
Select TV: 1969: The Pigeon; **1975–76:** The Cop and the Kid (series).

PAUL KELLY

BORN: BROOKLYN, NY, AUGUST 9, 1899.
DIED: NOVEMBER 6, 1956.

A second-tier player whose off-screen life was as dramatic as his on screen one (if not more so), lean Paul Kelly was already appearing on the Broadway stage as a child, in 1907, in *The Grand Army Man*. Employment at the New York-based Vitagraph Studios followed, notably in some 50 installments of "The Jarr Family" shorts. He became an official grown-up lead with the 1919 production of *Anne of Green Gables* and fluctuated between Broadway and films for a few years. His career, however, was stopped short in 1927 when he was sentenced to prison on a manslaughter charge after severely beating his mistress's husband, resulting in that man's death. Kelly spent two years in San Quentin, but as luck would have it, he managed to get work on the stage again, in *Bad Girl*, and his success in that play seemed to sweep the past under the rug.

He rejoined the Hollywood scene in 1933 with *Broadway Thru a Keyhole*, playing a gangster, and certainly not for the last time. His bigger roles were in *Speed Devils*, as a garage mechanic involved in corruption; *The Song and Dance Man*, atypically cast in the title role; *Parole Racket*, as an honest police lieutenant who winds up in jail; and *Join the Marines*, as a police officer who does just that. In 1940 his life was thrown another curve ball when the woman he'd committed murder for (now his wife) was killed in an auto accident. Kelly continued to rack up the motion picture credits, mainly in support when it came to "A's," but headlining some programmers, including *Not a Ladies Man*, portraying a man whose romance with Fay Wray is nearly destroyed by his son's meddling; *The Glass Alibi*, as a con man who marries Anne Gwynne to get at her money; and *Faces in the Fog*, acting alongside teenage Jane Withers. In the late 1940s he returned to New York for two more theatrical triumphs, *Command Decision* (earning a Tony Award) and *The Country Girl*, being passed over in favor of the far more bankable and interesting Clark Gable in the former and Bing Crosby in the latter when they were both committed to celluloid. In a bit of Hollywood irony one of his last film roles, in *Duffy of San Quentin*, found him playing the warden of the very facility at which he had done time.
Screen (features): 1917: Knights of the Square Table; **1918:** Fit to Fight; **1919:** Anne of Green Gables; **1920:** Uncle Sam of Freedom Ridge; **1921:** The Great Adventure; The Old Oaken

Bucket; 1926: The New Klondike; 1927: Slide, Kelly, Slide; Special Deliver; 1932: The Girl from Calgary; 1933: Broadway Thru a Keyhole; 1934: Side Streets; Blind Date; Death on the Diamond; The Love Captive; School for Girls; The President Vanishes; 1935: When a Man's a Man; Public Hero # One; Star of Midnight; Silk Hat Kid; Speed Devils; 1936: My Marriage; It's a Great Life; Here Comes Trouble; The Song and Dance Man; The Country Beyond; Women Are Trouble; Murder With Pictures; The Accusing Finger; 1937: Parole Racket; Join the Marines; It Happened Out West; The Frame-Up; Fit for a King; Navy Blue and Gold; 1938: The Nurse From Brooklyn; Torchy Blane in Panama; Island in the Sky; The Devil's Party; The Missing Guest; Juvenile Court; Adventure in Sahara; 1939: Forged Passport; The Flying Irishman; Within the Law; 6,000 Enemies; The Roaring Twenties; Invisible Stripes; 1940: Queen of the Mob; The Howards of Virginia; Wyoming; Girls Under 21; Flight Command; 1941: Ziegfeld Girl; I'll Wait for You; Parachute Battalion; Mystery Ship; Mr. and Mrs. North; 1942: Call Out the Marines; Tarzan's New York Adventure; Tough as They Come; The Secret Code (serial); Flying Tigers; Not a Ladies Man; 1943: The Man From Music Mountain; 1944: The Story of Dr. Wassell; Dead Man's Eyes; Faces in the Fog; 1945: China's Little Devils; Grissly's Millions; Allotment Wives; San Antonio; 1946: The Cat Creeps; The Glass Alibi; Deadline for Murder; Strange Journey; 1947: Fear in the Night; Spoilers of the North; Crossfire; Adventure Island; 1949: The File on Thelma Jordan; Guilty of Treason; Side Street; 1950: The Secret Fury; Frenchie; 1951: The Painted Hills; 1952: Springfield Rifle; 1953: Gunsmoke; Split Second; 1954: Duffy of San Quentin; Johnny Dark; The High and the Mighty; The Steel Cage; 1955: The Square Jungle; 1956: Storm Center; 1957: Curfew Breakers; Bail Out at 43,000.

NY Stage: 1907: Grand Army Man; 1911: The Confession; 1916: Little Women; 1918: Seventeen; Penrod; 1921: Honors Are Even; 1922: Up the Ladder; Whispering Wires; 1923: Chains; 1924: The Lady Killer; Nerves; 1925: Houses of Sand; The Sea Woman; 1926: Find Daddy; 1930: The Nine-Fifteen Revue; Bad Girl; 1931: Hobo; Just to Remind You; 1932: Adam Had Two Sons; The Great Magoo; 1945: The Beggars Are Coming to Town; 1947: Command Decision; 1950: The Country Girl.

Select TV: 1952: Melville Goodwin USA (sp); Street Scene (sp); Precinct (sp); 1954: His Father's Keeper (sp); 1955: One Foot in Heaven (sp); Marked for Death (sp); Jury of One (sp); 1956: Instant of Truth (sp).

KAY KENDALL

(JUSTINE McCARTHY) BORN: WITHERNSEA, ENGLAND, MAY 21, 1926. DIED: SEPTEMBER 6, 1959.

Mention the great ladies of British comedy, and Kay Kendall's name is not only guaranteed to come up, but to bring a warm smile to the face of anyone who has seen this sophisticated, lovely, and witty woman at work. At 12 she began appearing in revues at the London Palladium, graduating to an act with her sister. As a result she was asked to do bit work in films, working her way up to leading lady, opposite Sid Field, in the flop musical London Town, in 1946. After retreating to the legit theater she came back to movies, again in small parts, but she was starting to steal scenes in films like Lady Godiva Rides Again and It Started in Paradise. Because of the latter, she was signed by Rank, who made her a star with the breezy auto-race comedy Genevieve, enduring the contest for Kenneth More's sake and bringing a great deal of wry observation to the whole affair. There were parts in two minor

Stanley Holloway comedies and then a teaming with Rex Harrison in The Constant Husband, which led to their real life marriage, in 1957. Hollywood was eager to use her, and MGM gave her roles in some made-in-England productions, casting her opposite Robert Taylor in one of the more underrated costume pictures of the era, Quentin Durward; as one of Les Girls, easily the brightest thing in the film, joining Gene Kelly for the snappy "You're Just Too Too" number; and in a mild stage-to-screen comedy with Harrison, The Reluctant Debutante, where Kendall made her snobbery both hilarious and pathetic. Just when things were really on an upswing, it was revealed that she was dying of leukemia. Her last movie, a poorly received comedy with Yul Brynner, Once More With Feeling, was released after her death.

Screen: 1944: Fiddlers Three; Champagne Charlie; 1945: Dreaming; Caesar and Cleopatra; Waltz Time; 1946: London Town; 1950: Dance Hall; 1951: Happy Go Lovely; Lady Godiva Rides Again; 1952: Wings of Danger; Curtain Up; It Started in Paradise; 1953: Mantrap; Street of Shadows; The Square Ring; Genevieve; Meet Mr. Lucifer; 1954: Fast and Loose; Doctor in the House; 1955: The Constant Husband; Abdullah the Great; Quentin Durward; Simon and Laura; 1957: Les Girls; 1958: The Reluctant Debutante; 1960: Once More With Feeling.

ARTHUR KENNEDY

(JOHN ARTHUR KENNEDY) BORN: WORCESTER, MA, FEBRUARY 17, 1914. ED: CARNEGIE TECH. DIED: JANUARY 5, 1990.

One actor whose career really ran the gamut, light-haired, average-looking Arthur Kennedy zigzagged easily between leads and support, nice guys and villains, quality fare and junk, screen and stage. He never really became a leading attraction but was recognized with more than a fair share of respect for his work. Studying drama in college, he did some regional theater before making his Broadway bow in 1937, in Maurice Evans's production of Richard II, billed under his real name, John Kennedy. Some more stage work followed as he went from J. Arthur Kennedy to simply Arthur Kennedy. It was under that name that he came to Warner Bros. in 1940, for a major role, as James Cagney's piano-playing brother in City for Conquest, proving no contest for Cagney's magnetism but holding his own nonetheless. Although there was a starring role as an undercover cop in a "B," Strange Alibi, among others, the studio pictured him as reliable support, so he was one of Humphrey Bogart's henchmen in High Sierra; one of the Younger Brothers in Bad Men of Missouri; and one of the military ensemble in the clichéd but profitable war drama Air Force.

Following his stint in the real service during World War II, he came back to Hollywood and landed some prime roles, in the gripping docudrama Boomerang!, as a man accused of killing a minister; The Window, as Bobby Driscoll's disbelieving dad; Champion, earning his first Oscar nomination, as the crippled brother the otherwise self-involved Kirk Douglas cares for; and The Glass Menagerie, doing a nice job as Tom in this hot-and-cold attempt to film Tennessee Williams's classic. The last of these pretty much rated as a lead, which is what Universal gave him for real in the moving Bright Victory, with Kennedy as a soldier who faces an uncertain future after he is blinded. His portrait of an inconsiderate man strengthened by his ordeal was good enough to land him his only Oscar nomination in the Best Actor category. Around this time he won plaudits on Broadway in the original productions of three Arthur Miller classics, All My Sons; Death of a Salesman, for which he won the Tony Award; and The

Crucible, none of which he was permitted to preserve on screen.

Back in the movies he was fine as James Stewart's two-faced traveling companion in *Bend of the River*, and was a decided asset to another western, *Rancho Notorious*, looking for the man responsible for murdering his wife. There was a lead in a British quickie, *Impulse*, getting involved with femme fatale Constance Smith; a less-effective reteaming with Stewart, in another western, *The Man From Laramie*; and one of the less showy parts in *The Desperate Hours*, as the policeman trying to capture Humphrey Bogart. His brilliant performance in *Trial*, as the cynical lawyer who uses the trial of a young Mexican boy wanted for murder for his own means to preach Communist propaganda, netted him Oscar nod number three. There were two far less deserving nominations from the Academy, for the box-office smash *Peyton Place*, a touch heavy-handed as Hope Lange's disgusting father, whom she kills after he has raped her; and for *Some Came Running*, doing serviceable work with the unremarkable role of Frank Sinatra's brother.

He was Troy Donahue's neglected dad in the hit *A Summer Place*, and was at his caustic best as a cynical atheist in *Elmer Gantry*. He played a journalist based on Lowell Thomas in 1962's Oscar-winner for Best Picture, *Lawrence of Arabia*, and jumped back to a relatively big role, as Dr. Quimper, in the first and best of the Margaret Rutherford/Miss Marple movies, *Murder, She Said*. By the late 1960s he began to accept work in foreign productions amid such big American attractions as *Nevada Smith*, as a villain, and *Fantastic Voyage*, as one of the shrunken scientists traveling through the human body. There was a fourth Arthur Miller play, *The Price*, and then a long period of extreme movie junk, including *Shark!*, *The Cauldron of Death*, *Emmanuelle on Taboo Island*, and *The Sentinel*. Shortly before his death, he managed to get one last lead, in the barely distributed *Signs of Life*, as the patriarch of a family whose business is facing its demise.

Screen: 1940: City for Conquest; 1941: High Sierra; Strange Alibi; Knockout; Highway West; Bad Men of Missouri; They Died With Their Boots On; 1942: Desperate Journey; 1943: Air Force; 1946: Devotion (filmed 1943); 1947: Boomerang!; Cheyenne; 1949: The Walking Hills; Champion; Too Late for Tears; The Window; Chicago Deadline; 1950: The Glass Menagerie; 1951: Bright Victory; Red Mountain; 1952: Bend of the River; Rancho Notorious; The Girl in White; The Lusty Men; 1954: Impulse; 1955: Crashout; The Man From Laramie; The Naked Dawn; Trial; The Desperate Hours; 1956: The Rawhide Years; 1957: Peyton Place; 1958: Twilight for the Gods; Some Came Running; 1959: A Summer Place; 1960: Elmer Gantry; 1961: Home Is the Hero (UK: 1958); Claudelle Inglish; 1962: Murder, She Said; Hemingway's Adventures of a Young Man; Barabbas; Lawrence of Arabia; 1964: Cheyenne Autumn; 1965: Italiani Brava Gente/Attack and Retreat; Joy in the Morning; Murieta; 1966: Nevada Smith; Fantastic Voyage; 1967: Monday's Child (nUSr); 1968: A Minute to Pray, a Second to Die/Dead or Alive; Anzio; Day of the Evil Gun; 1969: Hail, Hero!; 1970: Shark!; 1971: Glory Boy/My Old Man's Place; 1975: Killer Cop (nUSr); Family Killer/Ferrante (filmed 1973); 1976: Don't Open the Window/The Living Dead at Manchester Morgue (filmed 1974); Emmanuelle on Taboo Island (nUSr); Nine Guests for a Crime (nUSr); 1977: The Sentinel; As of Tomorrow/Rich and Respectable (nUSr); Last Angels (nUSr); Cyclone (nUSr); 1978: The Antichrist/The Tempter (filmed 1974); Brutal Justice/Assault With a Deadly Weapon (filmed 1976); Cave of the Sharks/Shark's Cave (nUSr); Porco Mondo (nUSr); 1979: The Cauldron of Death/Ricco/The Dirty Mob (filmed 1973); The Humanoid (nUSr); 1980: Covert Action (filmed 1978); 1989: Signs of Life.

NY Stage: AS JOHN KENNEDY: 1937: Richard II; 1938: The Life and Death of an American (ob; and Bdwy 1939).
AS J. ARTHUR KENNEDY: 1939: Henry IV Part 1.
AS ARTHUR KENNEDY: 1940: An International Incident; 1947: All My Sons; 1949: Death of a Salesman; 1952: See the Jaguar; 1953: The Crucible; 1956: Time Limit!; The Loud Red Planet; 1961: Becket; 1968: The Price; 1973: Veronica's Room.
Select TV: 1954: Night Visitor (sp); 1956: This Is Villa (sp); 1959: The Sound of Gunfire (sp); 1960: The Web of Guilt (sp); In the Presence of Mine Enemies (sp); 1962: The Forgery (sp); 1964: Leviathan Five (sp); 1965: F.D.R. (series; narrator); 1966: The Confession (sp); 1969: Appalachian Autumn (sp); 1970: The Movie Murderer; 1971: A Death of Innocence; 1972: Crawlspace; 1973: The President's Plane Is Missing; 1974: Nakia; Nakia (series).

EDGAR KENNEDY

BORN: MONTEREY, CA, APRIL 26, 1890.
DIED: NOVEMBER 9, 1948.

Gruff, bald, and stocky comedian Edgar Kennedy was the undisputed master of the "slow burn," being driven mad by the likes of Laurel and Hardy and the Little Rascals, as well as on-screen wife Florence Lake in a long-running series of shorts. A veteran of minstrel shows and vaudeville, he came to movies in 1913 as a member of the Keystone Company but didn't really begin to shine until Hal Roach took him on in 1927. Stan and Ollie drove him crazy in two separate traffic jams, in "Leave 'em Laughing" and "Two Tars," while he took on the directorial reigns for two of their 1928 shorts, "From Soup to Nuts" and "You're Darn Tootin'," under the name of "E. Livingston Kennedy." With the Our Gang kids he played bumbling Kennedy the Cop in such two-reelers as "Moan and Groan, Inc." and "When the Wind Blows." In 1931 he went over to RKO for his own starring shorts (known as "Mr. Average Man"), as an exasperated husband enduring his fluttery wife. He racked up over 100 of these titles until his death in 1948. On the feature front he was seen as the detective beaten up by Carole Lombard in *Twentieth Century*; Daddy Warbucks in a cheapie version of *Little Orphan Annie*; the Sheriff in MGM's blockbuster hit *San Francisco*; a detective with a fondness for music in *Unfaithfully Yours*; and, best of all, the Freedonia lemonade vendor foolish enough to challenge Harpo Marx in *Duck Soup*.

Screen (shorts): 1913: Mabel's Dramatic Career; 1914: The Star Boarder; Twenty Minutes of Love; Caught in a Cabaret; Those Love Pangs; Dough and Dynamite; Gentlemen of Nerve; The Knockout; Our Country Cousin; The Noise of Bombs; Getting Acquainted; 1915: A Game Old Knight; The Great Vacuum Robbery; Fatty's Tin Type Tangle; Fickle Fatty's Fall; 1916: His Hereafter; His Bitter Pill; Madcap Ambrose; A Scoundrel's Tale; Bombs; Ambrose's Cup of Woe; Bucking Society; 1917: Her Fame and Shame; Her Torpedoed Love; Oriental Love; 1918: She Loved Him Plenty; 1925: The Marriage Circus; 1927: Wedding Bill$; The Wrong Mr. Right; 1928: A Pair of Tights; Two Tars; The Finishing Touch; Leave 'em Laughing; The Family Group; Limousine Love; The Fight Pest; Imagine My Embarrassment; Is Everybody Happy?; All Parts; The Booster; Chasing Husbands; Should Married Men Go Home?; 1929: Moan and Groan, Inc.; Great Gobs; Hotter Than Hot; Bacon Grabbers; Dad's Day; Hurdy Gurdy; Unaccustomed As We Are; A Perfect Day; Angora Love; Why Is a Plumber?; Thundering Toupees; Off to Buffalo; Dumb Daddies; 1930: Night Owls; The First Seven Years; Shivering Shakespeare; When the Wind Blows; The Real McCoy; All Teed Up; Fifty Million Husbands; Dollar Dizzy; Girl Shock;

Looser Than Loose; The Head Guy; The Big Kick; Bigger and Better; Doctor's Orders; Ladies Last; **1931:** All Gummed Up; The Midnight Patrol; High Gear; Love Fever; Lemon Meringue; Rough House Rhythm; Thanks Again; Camping Out; **1932:** Parlor, Bedroom and Wrath; Bon Voyage; Giggle Water; The Golf Chump; Fish Feathers; Never the Twins Shall Meet; **1933:** Art in the Raw; The Merchant of Menace; Good Housewrecking; Quiet Please; What Fur; Grin and Bear It; **1934:** Wrong Direction; In-Laws Are Out; Love on a Ladder; A Blasted Event; Poisoned Ivory; Brick-a-Brac; **1935:** A Night at the Biltmore Bowl; South Seasickness; Edgar Hamlet; Sock Me to Sleep; Happy Tho' Married; In Love at 40; Gobs of Trouble; **1936:** Gasoloons; Will Power; High Beer Preasure; Vocalizing; Dummy Ache; **1937:** Locks and Bonds; Bad Housekeeping; Dumb's the Word; Hillbilly Goat; Tramp Trouble; Morning Judge; Edgar and Goliath; **1938:** Beaux and Errors; Ears of Experience; False Roomers; Kennedy's Castle; Fool Coverage; A Clean Sweep; **1939:** Maid to Order; Kennedy the Great; Clock Wise; Baby Daze; Feathered Pests; Act Your Age; **1940:** Mutiny in the County; Slightly at Sea; Taint Legal; Sunk by the Census; Trailer Tragedy; **1941:** Drafted in the Depot; It Happened All Night; Mad About Moonshine; An Apple in His Eye; Westward Ho-Hum; I'll Fix It; A Quiet Fourth; **1942:** Cooks and Crooks; Inferior Decorator; Heart Burn; Two for the Money; Duck Soup; Rough on Rents; **1943:** Hold Your Temper; Indian Signs; Hot Foot; Not on My Account; Unlucky Dog; Prunes and Politics; **1944:** Love Your Landlord; Radio Rampage; Kitchen Cynic; Feather Your Nest; **1945:** Alibi Baby; You Drive Me Crazy; Sleepless Tuesday; What? No Cigarettes?; It's Your Move; The Big Beef; Mother-in-Law's Day; **1946:** Wall Street Blues; Motor Maniacs; I'll Build It Myself; Trouble or Nothing; Social Terrors; Do or Diet; **1947:** Noisy Neighbors; Heading for Trouble; Television Turmoil; Mind Over Mouse; Host to a Ghost; **1948:** No More Relatives; Brother Knows Best; How to Clean House; Dig That Gold; Home Canning; Contest Crazy.

Screen (features): 1914: Tillie's Punctured Romance; **1921:** Skirts; **1922:** The Leather Pushers; **1924:** The Night Message; The Battling Fool; **1925:** Proud Heart/His People; The Golden Princess; **1926:** My Old Dutch; The Better 'Ole; Across the Pacific; Going Crooked; Oh! What a Nurse; **1927:** Finger Prints; The Gay Old Bird; The Chinese Parrot; **1929:** Trent's Last Case; They Had to See Paris; **1931:** Bad Company; Quick Millions; **1932:** Carnival Boat; Hold 'Em Jail; Westward Passage; Rockabye; Penguin Pool Murder; Little Orphan Annie; **1933:** Professional Sweetheart; Duck Soup; Tillie and Gus; Scarlet River; Crossfire; Son of the Border; **1934:** Kid Millions; All of Me; Twentieth Century; Flirting With Danger; Heat Lightning; Murder on the Blackboard; The Silver Streak; We're Rich Again; Money Means Nothing; Gridiron Flash; King Kelly of the U.S.A.; The Marines Are Coming; **1935:** Cowboy Millionaire; Living on Velvet; Little Big Shot; Woman Wanted; In Person; $1,000 a Minute; The Bride Comes Home; Rendezvous at Midnight; **1936:** The Return of Jimmy Valentine; Three Men on a Horse; Small Town Girl; Mad Holiday; Fatal Lady; San Francisco; Yours for the Asking; The Robin Hood of El Dorado; **1937:** A Star Is Born; When's Your Birthday?; Super Sleuth; Double Wedding; True Confession; Hollywood Hotel; **1938:** Hey! Hey! U.S.A.; Peck's Bad Boy With the Circus; The Black Doll; Scandal Street; **1939:** Little Accident; Everything's on Ice; Charlie McCarthy, Detective; Laugh It Off; It's a Wonderful World; **1940:** Dr. Christian Meets the Women; Sandy Is a Lady; The Quarterback; Margie; Remedy for Riches; Li'l Abner; Who Killed Aunt Maggie?; Sandy Gets Her Man; **1941:** Public Enemies; Blondie in Society; The Bride Wore Crutches; **1942:** Snuffy Smith/Yard Bird; Pardon My Stripes; There's One Born Every Minute; In Old California; Hillbilly Blitzkrieg; **1943:** Cosmo Jones — Crime Smasher; The Falcon Strikes Back; Air Raid Wardens; Hitler's Madman; The Girl from Monterey; Crazy House; **1944:** It Happened Tomorrow; The Great Alaskan Mystery (serial); **1945:** Anchors Aweigh; Captain Tugboat Annie; **1947:** The Sin of Harold Diddlebock/Mad Wednesday; Heaven Only Knows; **1948:** Variety Times; Unfaithfully Yours; **1949:** My Dream Is Yours.

DEBORAH KERR

(DEBORAH JANE KERR-TRIMMER)
BORN: HELENSBURGH, SCOTLAND,
SEPTEMBER 30, 1921.

The very epitome of English good-breeding and refinement, Deborah Kerr also happened to be one of the most ingratiating of all actresses during her heyday in the 1950s, although her emoting might seem at times a tad florid by today's standards. She had studied ballet while a youngster but switched her interest to acting, receiving her theatrical training at her aunt's drama school in Bristol and at Oxford rep. Her initial film appearance, in *Contraband*, was sliced from the final print, so her official movie debut came in something more famous, the fine 1941 film adaptation of Shaw's *Major Barbara*, as Sgt. Jenny Hill; it was directed by Gabriel Pascal, with whom she signed a long-term contract. This was followed by important roles in *Hatter's Castle*, as Robert Newton's daughter, and the fantasy *The Life and Death of Colonel Blimp*, portraying three different women throughout the adventures of Roger Livesey. She was promoted to Robert Donat's leading lady for the observant *Perfect Strangers*, which, when it was distributed in America, by MGM in 1946, as *Vacation From Marriage*, did well enough to earn an Oscar for its story of a tedious couple who spring to life when separated by their wartime affairs. That same year she was seen as an Irish girl with a hatred for the British in *I See a Dark Stranger*, which showed up in America in a shortened form as *The Adventuress*; and then, the following year, she played a nun facing all sorts of mystical happenings at a desolate mountain top monastery in the moody, Technicolored *Black Narcissus*, a movie that really helped put her on the map.

MGM had made some overtures, buying part of Kerr's contract from Pascal but initially finding no reason to use her until they cast her as the nice lady who entices Clark Gable away from bad girl Ava Gardner in a witty look at the world of advertising, *The Hucksters*. Between two that were quickly forgotten, *If Winter Comes* and *Please Believe Me*, she was the troubled wife of millionaire Spencer Tracy in the filmed-in-England *Edward, My Son*, driven to drink and sinking her teeth into a few juicy scenes in the latter half of the story. It resulted in the first of six Oscar nominations. She would, alas, go on to hold the record in the leading female category for most nominations without a win. In the meantime she had the great fortune to be cast in two of the biggest blockbusters that MGM had to offer during the early 1950s, *King Solomon's Mines*, a fairly exciting adventure in which she searched Africa for diamonds with Stewart Granger; and the extremely expensive *Quo Vadis?*, a so-so Biblical spectacle where, at one point, she was tied to a pole to be attacked by a bull. In addition to grossing high figures for the studio, both movies wound up with Oscar nominations in the Best Picture category. There was a remake of *The Prisoner of Zenda*, with Kerr in the Madeleine Carroll role; a very minor comedy that marked her first teaming with Cary Grant, *Dream Wife*; and a bit of Shakespeare in the small role of Portia in the studio's prestigious production of *Julius Caesar*.

In 1953, she got her chance to shatter her genteel image when she replaced Joan Crawford as the adulterous officer's wife in *From Here to Eternity*. The film, based on James Jones's red-hot best-seller, was one of the year's big attractions and the Academy Award-winner for Best Picture of the year. (It competed with *Julius Caesar* for the trophy.) Kerr played the part of the bored, sexy, and flirtatious lady with bite and conviction, earning her an Oscar nomination as a result. She also entered the realms of motion picture iconography when she and Burt Lancaster embraced as the tide gushed about them, in one of the most unforgettable of all movie images. She chose to go to Broadway at this point and scored a big hit as another restless wife driven to adultery, in *Tea and Sympathy*, only this time her lover, John Kerr (no relation), was accused of being gay. It was brought to the screen in 1956 with the two Kerrs and many other cast principals intact, but with some minor censorship changes. In close-up, with the MGM gloss of Technicolor and CinemaScope, whatever merits the work had onstage were nowhere in evidence in this heavy-handed, superficial film. Prior to it she had gone back to England for an unsatisfying version of Graham Greene's *The End of the Affair*, again committing adultery, but with the unappetizing Van Johnson as her lover. These were instantly overshadowed by a much better movie, *The King and I*, a stage-bound but extremely pleasing adaptation of one of the most beloved of all Rodgers and Hammerstein musicals. She was so good (Oscar nomination number three) as the strong-willed, levelheaded schoolteacher who instills a conscience in the arrogant Yul Brynner, that nobody seemed to care that most of her singing was dubbed. It was yet another huge moneymaker and an Oscar nominee in the Best Picture category, once again indicating how important a part of the 1950s Kerr was. Her good fortune continued with *Heaven Knows, Mr. Allison*, sharing almost the entire screen time with only one other actor, Robert Mitchum. As the nun who must keep her reserve while stranded on an island with a soldier, she was once again splendid, bringing the Oscar count up to four. This was followed by one of her most famous movies, *An Affair to Remember*, a slick, 20th Century-Fox remake of the superior *Love Affair*, meeting and falling in love with Cary Grant until a car accident separates them. The two stars held it all together until the whole thing got far too gooey in the latter half.

Her fifth Oscar nod came for playing the pathetically repressed spinster attracted to a phony major, David Niven, in *Separate Tables*, an effective portrait of a childlike woman whose connection to real life has been thoroughly destroyed by her monstrously intimidating mother. She reteamed with Brynner for *The Journey*, notable in that she married one of its writers, Peter Viertel, then did the highly publicized *Beloved Infidel*, playing Sheila Graham to Gregory Peck's F. Scott Fitzgerald. It was an unexpected flop, but *The Sundowners* turned out to be one of the nicest things she'd ever done. As the strong and loving wife of sheep drover Robert Mitchum, she did a commendable job of making audiences believe she was an Australian woman who spent her life getting her hands dirty. For it she got her final recognition from Oscar and was certainly a better choice for the trophy in 1960 than its ultimate winner, Elizabeth Taylor.

Kerr gave another excellent performance as a repressed lady, a governess driven to the brink by a pair of odd children, in the often too-stately version of *The Turn of the Screw*, renamed *The Innocents*. She had a standard "terrified wife" role in *The Naked Edge*, which was of note only because it marked Gary Cooper's last appearance on film, and another frustrated governess part, in *The Chalk Garden*, this time suggesting a hint of steeliness and notoriety beneath the surface, though there was hardly anything

of interest or believability going on in this adaptation of the popular stage play. Her performance in *The Night of the Iguana* was something of a reprise of her *Separate Tables* role, playing a timid old maid who gets hot over defrocked minister Richard Burton. After that she had a run of bad luck in some broad comedies, *Marriage on the Rocks*, bickering with Frank Sinatra; *Casino Royale*, doing some slapstick as a horny Scottish heiress; and *Prudence and the Pill*, cheating on David Niven, and worried that she's gotten pregnant as a result. By the time she bedded Burt Lancaster again in *The Gypsy Moths*, or stood by while Kirk Douglas strayed from *her* in *The Arrangement*, it was clear that the oncoming coarseness of the modern cinema was at odds with this bastion of good taste. What work she did accept after that was mostly for television, including a remake of *Witness for the Prosecution*, where she played the Elsa Lanchester part of the nurse; and *Reunion at Fairborough*, which reteamed her with Robert Mitchum. Her sole theatrical release during this period, *The Assam Garden*, found her playing yet another repressed woman, a widow who befriends an Indian neighbor, but it came and went without much fanfare. In 1994 she was awarded with a special Academy Award, as was often the case with great stars who were denied the trophy in competition.

Screen: 1941: Major Barbara; Love on the Dole; Penn of Pennsylvania/The Courageous Mr. Penn; Hatter's Castle; 1942: The Day Will Dawn/The Avengers; 1943: The Life and Death of Colonel Blimp; 1945: Perfect Strangers/Vacation From Marriage (US: 1946); 1946: I See a Dark Stranger/The Adventuress; 1947: Black Narcissus; The Hucksters; If Winter Comes; 1949: Edward, My Son; 1950: Please Believe Me; King Solomon's Mines; 1951: Quo Vadis?; 1952: The Prisoner of Zenda; 1953: Thunder in the East (filmed 1951); Dream Wife; Young Bess; Julius Caesar; From Here to Eternity; 1955: The End of the Affair; 1956: The Proud and Profane; The King and I; Tea and Sympathy; 1957: Heaven Knows, Mr. Allison; An Affair to Remember; 1958: Bonjour Tristesse; Separate Tables; 1959: The Journey; Count Your Blessings; Beloved Infidel; 1960: The Sundowners; The Grass Is Greener; 1961: The Naked Edge; The Innocents; 1964: The Chalk Garden; The Night of the Iguana; 1965: Marriage on the Rocks; 1967: Eye of the Devil; Casino Royal; 1968: Prudence and the Pill; 1969: The Gypsy Moths; The Arrangement; 1985: The Assam Garden.

NY Stage: 1953: Tea and Sympathy; 1975: Seascape.

Select TV: 1973: A Song at Twilight (sp); 1982: Witness for the Prosecution; 1984: A Woman of Substance (ms); 1985: Reunion at Fairborough; 1986: Hold the Dream.

JOHN KERR

BORN: NEW YORK, NY, NOVEMBER 15, 1931.

Watery-eyed, boyish-looking John Kerr specialized in sensitive, handsome young males in states of angst, during a very brief period of filmic activity in the late 1950s. The son of screenwriter-playwright Geoffrey Kerr and actress June Walker, he began acting in stock productions as a teen, which led to a starring role on Broadway in *Bernardine*, winning a Theatre World Award. The 1953 production of *Tea and Sympathy* made him a star, playing the sensitive student accused of being gay, who rushes into the arms of married, unhappy, teacher's wife Deborah Kerr. MGM bought the rights to the play, but before they filmed it, they cast Kerr as a disturbed young man in the disappointing mental hospital ensemble *The Cobweb*. That film's director, Vincente Minnelli, guided him through the movie version of *Tea*, which turned out to be a flaccid, silly, and shallow soap opera, with both Kerrs doing what they could under the overheated circumstances.

He was a soldier in love with ballerina Leslie Caron in *Gaby*, which was the third and least-liked filming of *Waterloo Bridge*, and a Navy man falling for islander France Nuyen in the very popular 1958 adaptation of the Rodgers and Hammerstein stage sensation *South Pacific*. Although he often looked as beautiful as the scenery, his singing voice was rather unconvincingly dubbed, and he could not count this among his greater triumphs. Shortly after playing the young hero in the Vincent Price thriller *The Pit and the Pendulum*, he went over to TV, where his role on *Peyton Place*, as an attorney, inspired him to quit the business and try law for real. In 1970 he passed his bar exam and opened his own practice in West Los Angeles, returning to acting on very few occasions.

Screen: 1955: The Cobweb; 1956: Gaby; Tea and Sympathy; 1957: The Vintage; 1958: South Pacific; 1960: The Crowded Sky; Girl of the Night; 1961: The Pit and the Pendulum; Seven Women From Hell.

NY Stage: 1952: Bernardine; 1953: Tea and Sympathy; 1954: All Summer Long; 1958: The Infernal Machine (ob); Cue for Passion; 1967: The Tenth Man (ob).

Select TV: 1953: End of the Honeymoon (sp); 1955: The Bold and the Brave (sp); Combat Medic (sp); Undertow (sp); 1956: The Corn Is Green (sp); A Fair Shake (sp); 1957: Mr. and Mrs. McAdam; 1957: Killer's Pride (sp); The Years in Between (sp); 1958: Rumors of Evening (sp); Strange Occurrence at Roksay (sp); A Question of Romance (sp); 1959: Berkeley Square (sp); 1960: Friendly Enemies at Law (sp); 1962: Honor in Love (sp); Dry Rain (sp); 1963–64: Arrest and Trial (series); 1965–66: Peyton Place (series); 1971: Yuma; 1972: The Longest Night; 1973: Incident on a Dark Street; 1977: Washington: Behind Closed Doors (ms); 1986: The Park Is Mine.

EVELYN KEYES

BORN: PORT ARTHUR, TX, NOVEMBER 20, 1919. RAISED IN ATLANTA, GA.

A not untalented actress who was treated for the most part like just another of Hollywood's standard blonde leading ladies, Evelyn Keyes later looked back on her career with little enthusiasm for most of her assignments. A nightclub dancer, she won a beauty contest from Universal Pictures that resulted in absolutely nothing. Instead, it was a chance encounter with one of Cecil B. DeMille's screenwriters, Jeanie MacPherson, that got her into the movies, signing a contract with Paramount. There, among other jobs, she was seen in the DeMille epics *The Buccaneer* and *Union Pacific*. Her most enduring role came when she was chosen to play the relatively small part of Scarlett O'Hara's self-involved sister, Suellen, in the mightiest production of 1939 and the most-widely attended movie of its day, *Gone With the Wind*, resulting in a contract with Columbia.

At Columbia she was featured in *Lady in Question*, notable in that in was directed by one of her future husbands (1943–45), Charles Vidor; *Before I Hang*, as the daughter of convicted scientist Boris Karloff; *The Face Behind the Mask*, as the blind girl loved by facially scared Peter Lorre; and one of her best remembered films, *Here Comes Mr. Jordan*, as the love interest, Bette Logan, making little impact amid the more colorful characters on hand. After playing a genie in the fantasy *A Thousand and One Nights*, she portrayed a fictionalized version of Ruby Keeler (who refused to allow her name to be used) in the extremely popular biopic *The Jolson Story*, and ended her stay at the studio in an effective bit as a smallpox victim spreading terror in *The Killer That Stalked New*

York. Her favorite role came in the UA release *The Prowler*, carrying on an affair with Van Heflin, who wants to bump off her husband, and she acted up a storm in her big scene in the noir *99 River Street*, as an aspiring actress explaining how she murdered a lecherous producer. Right around the time she unofficially retired from movies (1957), she became bandleader Artie Shaw's eighth wife. Prior to that she had been briefly wed (1946–50) to director John Huston, though he never bothered to use her in one of his films. After a period away from the big screen, she had some roles in *Return to Salem's Lot* and *Wicked Stepmother*, though little mention was made of the fact, and she offered commentary in documentaries on both Shaw and Huston. She wrote the novel *I Am a Billboard* (1971) and a pair of autobiographies, *Scarlett O'Hara's Younger Sister* (1977) and *I'll Think About That Tomorrow* (1991).

Screen: 1938: The Buccaneer; Men With Wings; Sons of the Legion; Dangerous to Know; Artists and Models Abroad; 1939: Union Pacific; Paris Honeymoon; Sudden Money; Gone With the Wind; 1940: Slightly Honorable; The Lady in Question; Before I Hang; Beyond the Sacramento; 1941: The Face Behind the Mask; Here Comes Mr. Jordan; Ladies in Retirement; 1942: The Adventures of Martin Eden; Flight Lieutenant; 1943: Dangerous Blondes; The Desperadoes; There's Something About a Soldier; 1944: Nine Girls; Strange Affair; 1945: A Thousand and One Nights; 1946: The Thrill of Brazil; Renegades; The Jolson Story; 1947: Johnny O'Clock; 1948: The Mating of Millie; Enchantment; 1949: Mr. Soft Touch; Mrs. Mike; 1950: The Killer That Stalked New York; 1951: Smuggler's Island; Iron Man; The Prowler; 1952: One Big Affair; 1953: Rough Shoot/Shoot First; 99 River Street; 1954: Hell's Half Acre; It Happened in Paris; 1955: Top of the World; The Seven Year Itch; 1956: Around the World in Eighty Days; 1987: Return to Salem's Lot; 1989: Wicked Stepmother.

Select TV: 1951: Wild Geese (sp); 1955: Wild Stallion (sp).

GUY KIBBEE

BORN: EL PASO, TX, MARCH 6, 1882. RAISED IN ROSWELL, NM. DIED: MAY 24, 1956.

Bald and pot-bellied with rosy cheeks, Guy Kibbee was one of the staples of the Warners stock company in the 1930s, playing jovial millionaires, roaming husbands with a thing for chorus girls, enthusiastic dolts, or the occasional obnoxious lout. An actor since the age of 13, he had spent time working in road companies and entertaining on riverboats before he ended up on Broadway. His success in the 1930 production of *Torch Song* brought him to Hollywood the following year, where he made his debut at Paramount, playing a police commissioner, in *Stolen Heaven*. At that same studio he was Sylvia Sidney's mobster stepfather in *City Streets*, before going over to Warner Bros. In a mere six years he would rack up a lengthy list of credits there, including *Blonde Crazy*, as a con artist; *Taxi!*, as Loretta Young's father; *Fireman, Save My Child*, as a baseball manager; *The Dark Horse*, as an incredibly stupid political candidate; and *42nd Street*, in one of his key roles, as Bebe Daniels's sugar daddy, backing the show. He was called on to play variations of this blustering character in many of the lavish musicals spun from the success of that movie. There was also the lead in the highly unsatisfying adaptation of *Babbitt*, partnered well enough with Aline MacMahon that they ended up in several other films together. Outside his home studio, at Columbia, he had a fine role, as the pool hall denizen asked to pose as May Robson's husband, in Frank Capra's *Lady for a Day*.

Leaving Warners in 1937 he was the star of the "B" *Jim Hanvey — Detective*, and also *Don't Tell the Wife*, another low budget programmer, in which he played a naïve news editor hired to pose as a fake financier. He had the title role in *Captain January*, as a lighthouse keeper, although he wasn't so deluded as to believe that audiences showed up for him when his co-star was Shirley Temple. Capra placed him among the peerless supporting cast of *Mr. Smith Goes to Washington*, and this was Kibbee at his very best, as the easily manipulated governor pushed around by millionaire Edward Arnold. The more serious Kibbee was on hand to portray the small town father of Martha Scott in *Our Town*, while he good-naturedly presided over the "putting on a show" atmosphere of two Mickey Rooney-Judy Garland musicals, *Babes in Arms* and *Girl Crazy*, in the latter as Judy's granddad. In 1941 he rose up to top billing again, playing the philosophical small-town storeowner *Scattergood Baines*, who solves the problems of others with good, old-fashioned common sense. Made for Pyramid Pictures Corporation for distribution through RKO, there were four follow-ups, ending with *Scattergood Survives a Murder*. He retired from the screen after taking on some roles for director John Ford in the westerns *Fort Apache*, as a doctor, and *3 Godfathers*, as a judge.

Screen: 1931: Stolen Heaven; Man of the World; City Streets; Laughing Sinners; Side Show; The New Adventures of Get-Rich-Quick Wallingford; Blonde Crazy; Flying High; 1932: Union Depot; Fireman, Save My Child; Taxi!; The Strange Love of Molly Louvain; Crooner; Central Park; The Mouthpiece; High Pressure; Play Girl; The Crowd Roars; Two Seconds; Man Wanted; So Big; Winner Take All; The Dark Horse; Big City Blues; Rain; Scarlet Dawn; The Conquerors; 1933: 42nd Street; They Just Had to Get Married; Gold Diggers of 1933; The Life of Jimmy Dolan; Lady for a Day; The World Changes; Convention City; Girl Missing; Lilly Turner; The Silk Express; Footlight Parade; Havana Widows; 1934: Harold Teen; Big-Hearted Herbert; Merry Wives of Reno; Babbitt; The Merry Frinks; Wonder Bar; Dames; Easy to Love; 1935: Mary Jane's Pa; While the Patient Slept; Don't Bet on Blondes; Going Highbrow; I Live for Love; Captain Blood; 1936: Captain January; Earthworm Tractors; Three Men on a Horse; M'liss; Little Lord Fauntleroy; I Married a Doctor; The Captain's Kid; The Big Noise; 1937: Mama Steps Out; Riding on Air; Jim Hanvey — Detective; Bad Man of Brimstone; Don't Tell the Wife; The Big Shot; Mountain Justice; 1938: Three Comrades; Of Human Hearts; Rich Man, Poor Girl; Three Loves Has Nancy; Joy of Living; 1939: It's a Wonderful World; Bad Little Angel; Babes in Arms; Let Freedom Ring; Mr. Smith Goes to Washington; Henry Goes Arizona; 1940: Chad Hanna; Our Town; Street of Memories; 1941: Scattergood Baines; It Started With Eve; Design for Scandal; Scattergood Pulls the Strings; Scattergood Meets Broadway; 1942: Sunday Punch; Scattergood Rides High; There's One Born Every Minute; Tish; Whistling in Dixie; Scattergood Survives a Murder; Miss Annie Rooney; This Time for Keeps; 1943: Girl Crazy; Cinderella Swings It; Power of the Press; 1944: Dixie Jamboree; 1945: White Pongo; The Horn Blows at Midnight; 1946: Singing on the Trail; Cowboy Blues; Gentleman Joe Palooka; Lone Star Moonlight; 1947: Over the Santa Fe Trail; The Red Stallion; The Romance of Rosy Ridge; 1948: Fort Apache; 3 Godfathers.

NY Stage: 1930: Torch Song; Marseilles; 1946: A Joy Forever.

PERCY KILBRIDE

BORN: SAN FRANCISCO, CA, JULY 16, 1888.
DIED: DECEMBER 11, 1964.

Scrawny and sad-eyed, with an amusingly lugubrious speaking voice, Percy Kilbride was Hollywood's ideal rube and, indeed, found his place in movie history playing one of the most rustic fellers of them all. A stock player for years, he

was already approaching 40 by the time he came to Broadway in 1928, in *The Buzzard*. He was a theater staple for years with only two quick movie roles during the 1930s. What finally got him settled into films for good was his being asked by Warner Bros. to repeat his stage role as the slow-talking housing contractor in *George Washington Slept Here*. He was thereafter called upon for such rural entertainments as *The Adventures of Mark Twain*, *State Fair*, and *Welcome Stranger*. Late in life, his fortunes rose to unexpected heights when he was cast as Pa Kettle in *The Egg and I*, playing to perfection the lazy, soft-spoken husband of the domineering Marjorie Main. The duo stole the film from stars Claudette Colbert and Fred MacMurray, convincing Universal to give them their own showcase, titled simply *Ma and Pa Kettle*, which did well enough to encourage a series to spring forth. These proudly low-brow entries took the couple and their large brood from New York (*Ma and Pa Kettle Go to Town*) to Paris (*Ma and Pa Kettle on Vacation*) to Hawaii (*Ma and Pa Kettle at Waikiki*), getting a lot of barn-broad laughs by putting the hayseeds in incongruous settings. A car accident forced Kilbride to retire shortly after the last, the character being ignored altogether for *The Kettles in the Ozarks*, and then played by Parker Fennelly in the last of the films, *The Kettles on Old MacDonald's Farm*.

Screen: 1933: White Woman; 1936: Soak the Rich; 1942: George Washington Slept Here; Keeper of the Flame; 1943: Crazy House; The Woman of the Town; 1944: The Adventures of Mark Twain; Guest in the House; She's a Soldier Too; Knickerbocker Holiday; 1945: State Fair; She Wouldn't Say Yes; The Southerner; Fallen Angel; 1946: The Well-Groomed Bride; 1947: Welcome Stranger; Riffraff; The Egg and I; 1948: You Gotta Stay Happy; You Were Meant for Me; Black Bart; Feudin', Fussin' and A-Fightin'; 1949: Ma and Pa Kettle; Mr. Soft Touch; Free for All; The Sun Comes Up; 1950: Ma and Pa Kettle Go to Town; Riding High; 1951: Ma and Pa Kettle Back on the Farm; 1952: Ma and Pa Kettle on Vacation; Ma and Pa Kettle at the Fair; 1954: Ma and Pa Kettle at Home; 1955: Ma and Pa Kettle in Waikiki.

NY Stage: 1928: The Buzzard; 1929: Adam's Apple; Getting Even; 1930: Those We Love; The Up and Up; 1931: Louder Please; 1932: Lilly Turner; 1934: Whatever Possessed Her; Goodbye Please; Post Road; 1935: The Ragged Edge; 1936: Stork Mad; 1938: Sun Up to Sundown; Censored; 1940: George Washington Slept Here; 1941: Cuckoos on the Hearth; 1943: Little Brown Jug.

RICHARD KILEY

BORN: CHICAGO, IL, MARCH 31, 1922.
ED: LOYOLA UNIV. DIED: MARCH 5, 1999.

The movies could have been a lot kinder to someone as talented as Richard Kiley, but instead he had to make do with occasional assignments on screen while he secured his lasting fame onstage and depended on steadier, more lucrative employment on television. Discovering that he had a pretty impressive singing voice at an early age, he accepted a scholarship to Chicago's Barnum Dramatic School, after which he spent some time in the Navy. Returning to Chicago after the war, he utilized his equally splendid, cultured speaking voice as a radio actor before heading to New York to try his luck onstage. His debut there was in 1947's *The Trojan Women*, but his first major success in was in Shaw's *Misalliance* in 1953, winning a Theatre World Award for his performance. That same year he played the romantic lead in the musical *Kismet*, introducing the song "Stranger in Paradise" among others. He had already made his movie bow by this point, as part of the cast of Columbia's gangster melodrama, *The Mob*, as an undercover cop helping

Broderick Crawford investigate waterfront corruption, and did an overheated turn as the bad guy in Fox's *Pickup on South Street*. This was followed by perhaps his best-remembered movie role, the painfully naïve teacher whose precious record collection is destroyed by his hoodlum students in the seminal juvenile delinquent drama *Blackboard Jungle*, and by a key role in the sleeper independent film *The Phenix City Story*, as the son of the attorney general. A starring assignment in a Paramount cheapie, *Spanish Affair*, a love triangle, did nothing for him, so he went back to Broadway where he solidified his position as one of the major stars of the musical theater with the hits *Redhead* (Tony Award), *No Strings*, and his crowning achievement as a performer, *Man of La Mancha* (Tony Award), in which he sang one of the most famous of all show songs, "The Impossible Dream." Alas, Hollywood still had no idea what to do with him, although he did get to do a film musical when Frank Sinatra proved unavailable for Lerner and Lowe's adaptation of *The Little Prince*. Kiley was quite good as The Pilot and was one of the better-liked things about this roundly panned fantasy. There was another juicy role, as Diane Keaton's crippled, demanding father in *Looking for Mr. Goodbar*, and plenty of television work, resulting in three Emmy Awards, for his series *A Year in the Life*, the mini-series *The Thorn Birds*, and for guesting on *Picket Fences*. Another of his small-screen assignments was providing narration for countless *National Geographic* specials.

Screen: 1951: The Mob; 1952: The Sniper; Eight Iron Men; 1953: Pickup on South Street; 1955: Blackboard Jungle; The Phenix City Story; 1958: Spanish Affair; 1968: Pendulum; 1970: a.k.a. Cassius Clay (narrator); 1974: The Little Prince; 1977: Looking for Mr. Goodbar; 1981: Endless Love; 1986: Howard the Duck (voice); 1993: Jurassic Park (voice); 1998: Patch Adams.

NY Stage: 1947: The Trojan Women (ob); 1949: The Sun and I (ob); 1953: Misalliance; Kismet; 1954: Sing Me No Lullaby (ob); 1956: Time Limit!; 1959: Redhead; 1960: Advise and Consent; 1962: No Strings; 1964: Here's Love; I Had a Ball; 1965: Man of La Mancha; 1968: Her First Roman; 1971: The Incomparable Max; 1972: Voices; Man of La Mancha (revival); 1974: Absurd Person Singular; 1976: The Heiress; 1977: Knickerbocker Holiday; Man of La Mancha (revival); 1987: All My Sons.

Select TV: 1950: The Champion (sp); 1951: The Guinea Pig (sp); 1952: The Paper Moon (sp); Season of Divorce (sp); 1953: Two-Faced (sp); Salt of the Earth (sp); Flowers From a Stranger (sp); 1953: P.O.W. (sp); 1954: A Criminal Decision (sp); Paul's Apartment (sp); Arrowsmith (sp); The Warrior's Notebook (sp); The Small Door (sp); The Cuckoo in Spring (sp); 1955: Patterns (sp); The Day He Got Fired (sp); A Chance at Love (sp); 1956: The Landlady's Daughter (sp); 1957: The Discoverers (sp); Homeward Borne (sp); Shadow in the Sky (sp); Act of Mercy (sp); The Other Wise Man (sp); 1958: Before I Die (sp); The Hidden River (sp); Guy in Ward 4 (sp); 1960: The Women of Hadley (sp); Bride of the Fox (sp); 1961: Trial Without Jury (sp); Brandenburg Gate (sp); 1964: Charlie — He Couldn't Kill a Fly (sp); 1969: Night Gallery; 1971: Incident in San Francisco; Murder Once Removed; All the Way Home (sp); 1972: Jigsaw; Ceremony of Innocence (sp); 1975: Friendly Persuasion; 1976: The Macahans; 1980: Angel on My Shoulder; 1981: Golden Gate; Isabel's Choice; 1982: Pray TV; 1983: The Thorn Birds (ms); 1984: George Washington (ms); 1985: The Bad Seed; A.D. (ms); Do You Remember Love?; The Adventures of Huckleberry Finn (ms); 1986: Planet Earth (series narrator); If Tomorrow Comes (ms); 1987–88: A Year in the Life (series); 1988: My First Love; 1989: The Final Days; 1990: Gunsmoke: The Last Apache; 1991: Separate but Equal; Absolute Strangers; 1992: Mastergate (sp); 1994: The Cosby Mysteries; A Passion for Justice: The Hazel Brannon Smith Story; 1995: The Great Defender (series); Secrets; 1996: The Rockford Files: Crime and Punishment; Mary & Tim; 1999: Blue Moon.

PHYLLIS KIRK

(PHYLLIS KIRKEGAARD) BORN: SYRACUSE, NY, SEPTEMBER 18, 1926.

Bright-eyed Phyllis Kirk was exclusively a part of the 1950s as far as her movie career was concerned. A former model, she'd made two appearances on Broadway before being spotted in a play while in Philadelphia by the wife of movie executive Samuel Goldwyn. For his company she made her movie debut, in *Our Very Own*, as the best friend of Ann Blyth, a rich girl from a broken home, but she did not accept the mogul's offer of an exclusive contract. She continued in secondary parts, first at MGM and then over at Warners where she supported Alan Ladd in *The Iron Mistress*, although the title referred to his knife, not her. It was at that studio that she got the role that has kept her name prominent over the years, the heroine who realizes crazy sculptor Vincent Price wants to turn her into a statue of Marie Antoinette, in the 3-D smash *House of Wax*. From there she went west, playing leading lady to Randolph Scott in *Thunder Over the Plains*, and to Frank Sinatra in *Johnny Concho*, an assignment she particularly disliked. In between these two she had her only top-billed role, in a British "B" called *River Beat*, as a shipboard radio operator who gets involved in diamond smuggling. After playing Jerry Lewis's love interest in *The Sad Sack*, she left movies to do television, having a two-year run repeating Myrna Loy's role in the television version of *The Thin Man*. Nobody was ever going to compare Kirk to Loy, but the show gave her another level of brief fame. It was, in fact, her last major assignment. After a few more guest spots on the small screen, she found that her physical ailments (caused by an earlier bout with polio) were giving her trouble walking, which meant she could no longer effectively function in front of a camera. In the 1970s she started a new career in public relations, eventually working for CBS News.

Screen: 1950: Our Very Own; A Life of Her Own; Two Weeks With Love; Mrs. O'Malley and Mr. Malone; 1951: Three Guys Named Mike; 1952: About Face; The Iron Mistress; 1953: House of Wax; Thunder Over the Plains; 1954: Crime Wave; River Beat; 1955: Canyon Crossroads; 1956: Johnny Concho; Back From Eternity; 1957: City After Midnight/That Woman Opposite; The Sad Sack.

NY Stage: 1949: My Name Is Aquilon; 1951: Point of No Return.

Select TV: 1952: Devil in Velvet (sp); 1953: Wish on the Moon (sp); Candle in a Bottle (sp); P.O.W. (sp); 1954: The Inward Eye (sp); Prelude to Murder (sp); 1955: The Great Gatsby (sp); The Red Buttons Show (series); Heart Song (sp); 1956: The Bounty Hunters (sp); The Waiting House (sp); Made in Heaven (sp); 1957: Mrs. Wane Comes to Call (sp); Exclusive (sp); Men in Her Life (sp); 1957–59: The Thin Man (series).

TOMMY KIRK

BORN: LOUISVILLE, KY, DECEMBER 10, 1941. RAISED IN CA.

Definitely one of the unsung bright lights of Disney's early live-action period, sensitive Tommy Kirk made for an engaging hero of some lightweight fare but wasn't really given the chance to show his value in meatier material. He won a role in a Pasadena Playhouse production of *Ah, Wilderness!* when he was 12 and this resulted in several guest spots on TV. From there he was signed by Disney, in 1956, to partner Tim Considine in the sleuthing "Hardy Boys" segment of their highly popular *Mickey Mouse Club*, and he stayed under contract for the next eight years. His big-screen bow for them came in 1957, playing the rural lad who befriends and then must kill a stray pooch in *Old Yeller*, a superior dog picture in which he was quite moving. The studio saw him as more suited for comedies, however, so he was the likeable high schooler who turns into *The Shaggy Dog*, in this surprisingly popular gimmick fantasy that set the standard for all similar Disney family fare for decades to come; the dopey all-American college kid in *The Absent Minded Professor*, and its sequel *Son of Flubber*; and the genius inventor in *The Misadventures of Merlin Jones* and *The Monkey's Uncle*, both of which starred him alongside Annette Funicello. He was called on to partner Annette again, in a dim-witted AIP "Beach Party" credit, *Pajama Party*, as an alien visiting the California shore, shortly before his contract with Disney was suddenly terminated. It was not until years later that Kirk revealed that he had been fired because word had gotten out about his homosexuality, an image that the studio didn't feel comfortable with. Similarly he lost a role in *The Sons of Katie Elder* after a publicized marijuana arrest. By the end of the 1960s he had struck rock bottom with the quality of his material and eventually left the business to start his own carpet cleaning company, returning for occasional appearances in direct-to-video movies for filmmakers with fond memories of his past work.

Screen: 1957: Down Liberty Road; Old Yeller; 1959: The Shaggy Dog; 1960: The Snow Queen (voice); Swiss Family Robinson; 1961: The Absent Minded Professor; Babes in Toyland; 1962: Moon Pilot; Bon Voyage; 1963: Son of Flubber; Savage Sam; 1964: The Misadventures of Merlin Jones; Pajama Party; 1965: The Monkey's Uncle; Village of the Giants; 1966: The Ghost in the Invisible Bikini; 1967: Mother Goose-a-Go-Go/Unkissed Bride; It's a Bikini World; 1968: Catalina Caper; Track of Thunder; 1971: Blood of Ghastly Horror/Man With the Synthetic Brain/Psycho a Go-Go (filmed 1965); 1987: Streets of Death (dtv); 1995: Attack of the 60 Foot Centerfold (dtv); 1997: Little Miss Magic (dtv); 1998: Billy Frankenstein (dtv); 2001: The Education of a Vampire (dtv).

Select TV: 1956–57: The Mickey Mouse Club (series; segment: The Hardy Boys); 1961: The Horsemasters (theatrical in Europe); 1962: Escapade in Florence (theatrical in Europe); 1966: Mars Needs Women; 1968: It's Alive.

EARTHA KITT

Born: Columbia, SC, January 26, 1928.

The appropriately named Eartha Kitt became famous for her cat-like eyes and her purring intonations, which were exquisite or maddeningly affected, depending on your tolerance for so mannered, yet so unforgettable a show business figure. A former dancer with the Katherine Dunham group (with whom she appeared in the film *Casbah*), she dropped out of the company to stay on in Paris where she began singing in nightclubs. Her act came to Manhattan, which led to her being introduced as one of the *New Faces of 1952*. There was a 20th Century-Fox movie of that show, that added one of her signature numbers, the delightfully sexy holiday novelty "Santa Baby." She then played one of the women in the life of Nat King Cole in the Paramount biopic *St. Louis Blues*, followed by the leading role in *Anna Lucasta*, well cast as a waterfront hooker. Over the years she continued to enjoy her greatest fame as a nightclub entertainer, while guesting on television and sporadically appearing in such films as the obscure German-made version of *Uncle Tom's Cabin*, and one of those 1970s blaxploitation flicks, *Friday Foster*. In later years her increasingly bizarre tics were used to play a sorceress in *Erik the Viking*; a flirtatious business executive in *Boomerang*; a judge in *Fatal Instinct*; eccentric ladies in both *Ernest Scared Stupid* and *Harriet the Spy*; the voice of a meteor (!) in *The Pink Chiquitas*; and a long overdue role as the voice of a Disney villainess, in *The Emperor's New Groove*. She authored several memoirs: *Thursday's Child* (1956), *A Tart Is Not a Sweet* (1976), *Alone With Me* (1976), and *I'm Still Here: Confessions of a Sex Kitten* (1992).

Screen: 1948: Casbah; 1954: New Faces; 1958: St. Louis Blues; The Mark of the Hawk/Shaka Zulu; Anna Lucasta; 1961: The Saint of Devil's Island; 1965: Synanon; 1969: Uncle Tom's Cabin/White Trash Woman (filmed 1965); 1971: Up the Chastity Belt/Naughty Knights; 1975: Friday Foster; 1982: All by Myself; 1983: Serpent Warriors/Golden Viper (dtv); 1986: The Pink Chiquitas (voice; dtv); 1987: Dragonard (dtv); The Master of Dragonard Hill (dtv); 1989: Living Doll (dtv); Erik the Viking; 1991: Ernest Scared Stupid; 1992: Boomerang; 1993: Fatal Instinct; 1995: Unzipped; 1996: Harriet the Spy; 1997: Ill Gotten Gains (voice); 1999: I Woke Up Early the Day I Died; 2000: The Emperor's New Groove (voice).

NY Stage: 1946: Bal Negre; 1952: New Faces of 1952; 1954: Mrs. Patterson; 1957: Shinbone Alley; 1959: Jolly's Progress; 1978: Timbuktu!; 2000: The Wild Party.

Select TV: 1958: Heart of Darkness (sp); 1961: The Wingless Victory (sp); 1972: Lt. Schuster's Wife; 1978: To Kill a Cop; 2001: Feast of All Saints.

JACK KLUGMAN

Born: Philadelphia, PA, April 27, 1922.
ed: Carnegie Tech.

A rumpled, scratchy-voiced, regular kind of guy, Jack Klugman was a very gifted supporting actor with a perfectly respectable career who, suddenly, as he was pushing 50, achieved the extra perk of becoming a bona fide star. After studying drama in college he came to New York, where he roomed with fellow aspiring thespian Charles Bronson. He did some stage work and began appearing pretty regularly on TV, doing guest shots on series like *Captain Video* and *The Naked City*; a recurring role on a quickly forgotten soap, *The Greatest Gift*; and acclaimed work in anthology programs like *U.S. Steel Hour* and *Playhouse 90*. Amid all this he made his big-screen debut, in *Timetable*, then had a good role as an amiable, easily intimidated juror in *12 Angry Men*, one of the Oscar nominees for Best Picture of 1957. He was one of Rod Steiger's thugs in *Cry Terror!*, then had his best-remembered stage role, as the put-upon Herbie, in the original production of *Gypsy*, joining Ethel Merman in the hit song "Together, Wherever We Go." Back in the movies he was an alcoholics counselor in *Days of Wine and Roses* and loyally stood by Judy Garland and her demands in *I Could Go on Singing*, a role not unlike that in *Gypsy*. There was an Emmy Award for guesting on *The Defenders*, in 1964; a role portraying a ruthless hired killer in a French-made gangster film, *Hail, Mafia*; and then the best movie role of his career, playing Ali MacGraw's easy-going but protective dad in the box-office success *Goodbye, Columbus*. Shortly after the release of that movie, television made him a star, when he was cast as lovable slob Oscar Madison opposite Tony Randall in the sitcom adaptation of Neil Simon's *The Odd Couple*, Klugman having succeeded Walter Matthau in the role on Broadway. He won two more Emmys for the part and followed it with another long-running series, *Quincy, M.E.* Years later, despite his vocal chords having been damaged by throat cancer, he and Randall appeared together on Broadway in another Neil Simon piece, *The Sunshine Boys.*

Screen: 1956: Timetable; 1957: 12 Angry Men; 1958: Cry Terror!; 1962: Days of Wine and Roses; 1963: I Could Go on Singing; The Yellow Canary; Act One; 1965: Hail, Mafia; 1968: The Detective; The Split; 1969: Goodbye, Columbus; 1971: Who Says I Can't Ride a Rainbow?; 1976: Two Minute Warning; 1996: Dear God.

NY Stage: 1949: Saint Joan (ob); Stevedore (ob); 1952: Golden Boy; 1954: Coriolanus (ob); 1956: A Very Special Baby; 1959: Gypsy; 1963: Tchin-Tchin; 1966: The Odd Couple; 1968: The Sudden and Accidental Re-Education of Horse Johnson; 1987: I'm Not Rappaport; 1993: Three Men on a Horse; 1997: The Sunshine Boys.

Select TV: 1954: Good for You (sp); Presento (sp); 1954–55: The Greatest Gift (series); 1955: The Petrified Forest (sp); A Terrible Day (sp); The Expendable House (sp); Number Four with Flowers (sp); 1956: Rise Up and Walk (sp); The Third Ear (sp); The Ninth Hour (sp); 1957: The Thundering Wave (sp); 1958: The Lonely Stage (sp); Young and Scared (sp); The Man Who Asked for a Funeral (sp); The Time of Your Life (sp); Kiss Me Kate! (sp); 1959: The Velvet Alley (sp); 1961: The Million Dollar Incident (sp); 1964: The Threatening Eye (sp); A Crash of Symbols (sp); 1964–65: Harris Against the World (series); 1966: A Time of Flight (sp); Fame Is the Name of the Game; 1970–75: The Odd Couple (series); 1973: Poor Devil; 1974: The Underground Man; 1976: One of My Wives Is Missing; 1976–83: Quincy, M.E. (series); 1986–87: You Again? (series); 1989: Around the World in 80 Days (ms); 1993: The Odd Couple: Together Again; 1994: Parallel Lives.

SHIRLEY KNIGHT

BORN: GOESSEL, KS, JULY 5, 1936.

Opting for respect and awards over actual stardom, Shirley Knight spent her early years as an attractive, emotional blonde and always came through, even when the work didn't warrant attention. In later years she was stouter, world-wearier, but no less vulnerable or watchable. A student of the Pasadena Playhouse, she first came upon the scene in 1959, making several TV guest appearances as well as her big-screen debut, in Fox's *Five Gates to Hell*, as a nurse stationed in Vietnam. The following year she was quite good as the plain daughter whose neurotic date commits suicide in *The Dark at the Top of the Stairs*, earning an Oscar nomination in the supporting category. Two years later she was in the running again, for playing the former girlfriend of Paul Newman, who hates her father for having destroyed their relationship, in one of the lesser Tennessee Williams adaptations, *Sweet Bird of Youth*. It was shortly after showing up as one of *The Group* that she moved temporarily to Britain, appearing in the two-character *Dutchman*, as a tough tramp confronting Al Freeman, Jr. on a subway. There was a supporting role as George C. Scott's ex-wife in the disturbing *Petulia* and then probably her finest leading role in a movie, *The Rain People*, where she was outstanding as the Long Island housewife who abandons her family only to meet with tragedy on the road. She was off the screen for some time, concentrating on television, where she would earn three Emmy Awards, for guesting on *thirtysomething* and *NYPD Blue*, and for the telefilm *Indictment: The*

McMartin Trial. Back on the big screen she was Brooke Shields's free-spirited mama in *Endless Love*, and she had some other good roles as the timid mother of Al Franken in the underrated comedy-drama *Stuart Saves His Family*, and the skeptical mom of Helen Hunt in the popular *As Good As It Gets.*

Screen: 1959: Five Gates to Hell; 1960: Ice Palace; The Dark at the Top of the Stairs; 1962: The Couch; Sweet Bird of Youth; House of Women; 1964: Flight From Ashiya; 1966: The Group; Dutchman; 1968: Petulia; 1969: The Rain People; 1974: Juggernaut; 1978: Secrets (filmed 1971); 1979: Beyond the Poseidon Adventure; 1981: Endless Love; 1982: The Sender; 1991: Prisoners (dtv); 1994: Color of Night; 1995: Stuart Saves His Family; Death in Venice CA (nUSr); 1996: Diabolique; Somebody Is Waiting (dtv); 1997: As Good As It Gets; 1998: Little Boy Blue; 2000: 75 Degrees in July (nUSr); 2001: The Center of the World; Angel Eyes; 2002: The Salton Sea; Divine Secrets of the Ya-Ya Sisterhood; 2003: P.S. Your Cat Is Dead.

NY Stage: 1963: Journey to the Day (ob); 1964: The Three Sisters; 1966: Rooms: Better Luck Next Time/A Walk in Dark Places (ob); We Have Always Lived in the Castle; 1969: The Watering Place; 1975: Kennedy's Children; 1977: Happy End (ob); Landscape of the Body (ob); 1979: A Lovely Sunday for Creve Coeur (ob); Losing Time (ob); 1984: Come Back, Little Sheba (ob); 1986: Colette in Love (ob); 1987: The Depot (ob); 1997: The Young Man from Atlanta; 2002: Necessary Targets (ob).

Select TV: 1960: The Shape of the River (sp); 1962: You Can't Escape (sp); 1963: The Takers (sp); The Broken Year (sp); 1966: The Faceless Man (sp); 1967: The Outsider; 1968: Shadow Over Elveron; The Counterfeit Killer; 1975: Friendly Persuasion; Medical Story; 1976: Return to Earth; 21 Hours at Munich; 1978: The Defection of Simas Kudirka; 1979: Champions: A Love Story; 1980: Playing for Time; 1984: With Intent to Kill; 1987: Billionaire Boys Club; 1991: Bump in the Night; Shadow of a Doubt; 1992: To Save a Child; 1993: When Love Kills: The Seduction of John Hearn; Angel Falls (series); A Mother's Revenge; 1994: Baby Brokers; Hoggs' Heaven; The Yarn Princess; A Part of the Family; The Secret Life of Houses; 1995: Children of the Dust; A Good Day to Die; Indictment: The McMartin Trial; Stolen Memories: Secrets from the Rose Garden; Dad, the Angel & Me; 1996: Mary & Time; A Promise to Carolyn; The Uninvited; If These Walls Could Talk; 1997: Convictions; Dying to Be Perfect: The Ellen Hart Pena Story; 1998: The Wedding; A Father for Brittany; Maggie Winters (series); A Marriage of Convenience; 2001: My Louisiana Sky.

DON KNOTTS

(JESSE DONALD KNOTTS) BORN: MORGANTOWN, W V, JULY 21, 1924. ED: UNIV. OF AZ.

Everyone's favorite bag of nervous tics, Don Knotts stuck his neck our like a chicken and popped his eyes, and audiences lapped it up. While serving in the military during World War II, he joined a revue called *Stars and Gripes*, then went to New York to appear as a nightclub ventriloquist. This led to his Broadway debut in 1955, as a corporal in *No Time for Sergeants*, which resulted in his repeating his role for Warners in the hit film version (and, more important, introduced him to its star, Andy Griffith). Steve Allen made Knotts a regular on his show, and he became fairly well known by the time Griffith invited him to join the cast of *The Andy Griffith Show*, in 1960. As the boastful, dimwitted, and lovable mass of quivering jelly, Deputy Barney Fife, Knotts created one of television's classic characters and won an unprecedented five Emmy Awards for the role (1961, 1962,

1963, 1966, 1967). Because of his fame during the 1960s, he began to appear in his own big-screen vehicles, which were pretty much an extension of the Fife character and of appeal mainly to kids. The best of these was the one in which he was least seen, *The Incredible Mr. Limpet*, turning into an animated fish for most of the story. Others included the requisite haunted house tale, *The Ghost and Mr. Chicken*; *The Shakiest Gun in the West*, a remake of Bob Hope's far better *The Paleface*; and an attempt to move with the times with *The Love God?*, which had him involved with a girlie magazine. There were also welcome bits in *Move Over, Darling*, as a shoe salesman roped into pretending he was Doris Day's island mate, and *It's a Mad Mad Mad Mad World*, as a motorist who gives Phil Silvers a lift. In the 1975 Disney comedy *The Apple Dumpling Gang* he partnered effectively enough with another TV favorite, Tim Conway, for them to appear together on the big screen on four more occasions. After this he found another comfortable job as a regular on the popular smut-com *Three's Company*. Years later he rejoined his old co-star off and on for a few seasons of Griffith's lawyer series, *Matlock*, and showed up as a mysterious TV repairman in the fantasy *Pleasantville*. Nostalgists couldn't have been happier.

Screen: 1958: No Time for Sergeants; 1960: Wake Me When It's Over; 1961: The Last Time I Saw Archie; 1963: The Incredible Mr. Limpet; It's a Mad Mad Mad Mad World; Move Over, Darling; 1966: The Ghost and Mr. Chicken; 1967: The Reluctant Astronaut; 1968: The Shakiest Gun in the West; 1969: The Love God?; 1971: How to Frame a Figg; 1975: The Apple Dumpling Gang; 1976: No Deposit, No Return; Gus; 1977: Herbie Goes to Monte Carlo; 1978: Hot Lead and Cold Feet; 1979: The Apple Dumpling Gang Rides Again; The Prize Fighter; 1980: The Private Eyes; 1984: Cannonball Run II; 1987: Pinocchio and the Emperor of the Night (voice); 1996: Big Bully; 1997: Cats Don't Dance (voice); 1998: Pleasantville; 2001: Heart of Love (nUSr).

NY Stage: 1955: No Time for Sergeants.

Select TV: 1953–55: Search for Tomorrow (series); 1956–60: The Steve Allen Show (series); 1960–65: The Andy Griffith Show (series); 1970–71: The Don Knotts Show (series); 1972: The Man Who Came to Dinner (sp); 1973: I Love a Mystery; 1979–84: Three's Company (series); 1986: Return to Mayberry; 1987: What a Country! (series); 1989–92: Matlock (series); 1991: Doug (series; voice); 2000: Quints.

PATRIC KNOWLES

(REGINALD LAWRENCE KNOWLES)
BORN: HORSFORTH, YORKSHIRE, ENGLAND, NOVEMBER 11, 1911. DIED: DECEMBER 23, 1995.

He seemed like a pleasant enough fellow, but Patric Knowles was strictly second-fiddle material, which meant he chalked up a lot of credits, hardly ever getting singled out for the good ones, and seldom taking the blame for the stinkers. From the Abbey and Oxford rep companies he went into films in his native land in 1932, starting with the *Men of Tomorrow*. Four years later he came to America to play Kay Francis's married lover in *Give Me Your Heart* and stayed on at Warners for the next few years. His credits there included *The Charge of the Light Brigade*, as Errol Flynn's younger brother, getting Flynn properly peeved when he took Olivia de Havilland away from him; *It's Love I'm After*, as de Havilland's neglected fiancé; *The Patient in Room 18*, as Detective Lance O'Leary, a starring role; and *The Adventures of Robin Hood*, as Will Scarlett. After stopping off at Fox to portray one of the many brothers of Roddy McDowall in the Oscar-winning *How Green Was My Valley*, he joined Universal, where he

played the good guys in *The Wolf Man* and *Frankenstein Meets the Wolf Man*; and was straight man to Abbott and Costello in both *Who Done It?* and *Hit the Ice*. At Paramount he was there for Paulette Goddard to reject in favor of Ray Milland in *Kitty*, and to make sure audiences showing up for Bob Hope weren't distracted by anyone else in *Monsieur Beaucaire*. He pretty much played out the rest of his career in this unremarkable fashion. He published a novel, *Even Steven*, in 1960.

Screen: 1932: Men of Tomorrow; 1934: The Girl in the Crowd; Irish Hearts/Norah O'Neale; The Poisoned Diamond; 1935: Abdul the Damned; Royal Cavalcade/Regal Cavalcade; The Student's Romance; Honours Easy; Mr. Hobo/The Guv'nor; 1936: The Brown Wallet; Crown vs. Stevens; Wrath of Jealousy/Wedding Group; Two's Company; Fair Exchange; Irish for Luck; Give Me Your Heart; The Charge of the Light Brigade; 1937: It's Love I'm After; Expensive Husbands; 1938: The Patient in Room 18; The Adventures of Robin Hood; Four's a Crowd; Storm Over Bengal; The Sisters; Heart of the North; 1939: Torchy Blane in Chinatown; Beauty for the Asking; Five Came Back; Another Thin Man; The Spellbinder; The Honeymoon's Over; 1940: Married and in Love; A Bill of Divorcement; Women in War; Anne of Windy Poplars; 1941: How Green Was My Valley; The Wolf Man; 1942: Mystery of Marie Roget; The Strange Case of Dr. Rx; Lady in a Jam; Who Done It?; Sin Town; 1943: Frankenstein Meets the Wolf Man; Forever and a Day; All By Myself; Hit the Ice; Always a Bridesmaid; Crazy House; 1944: Chip Off the Old Block; This Is My Life; Pardon My Rhythm; 1945: Kitty; Masquerade in Mexico; 1946: O.S.S.; The Bride Wore Boots; Monsieur Beaucaire; Of Human Bondage; 1947: Variety Girl; Ivy; 1948: Dream Girl; Isn't It Romantic?; 1949: The Big Steal; 1950: Three Came Home; 1951: Quebec; 1952: Tarzan's Savage Fury; Mutiny; 1953: Jamaica Run; Flame of Calcutta; 1954: World for Ransom; Khyber Patrol; 1955: No Man's Woman; 1957: Band of Angels; 1958: From the Earth to the Moon; Auntie Mame; 1967: The Way West; 1968: In Enemy Country; The Devil's Brigade; 1970: Chisum; 1972: The Man; 1973: Terror in the Wax Museum; Arnold.

NY Stage: 1940: Goodbye to Love

Select TV: 1956: The Empty Room (sp); 1958: Elfego Baca; 1969: The D.A.: Murder One.

ALEXANDER KNOX

BORN: STRATHROY, ONTARIO, CANADA, JANUARY 16, 1907. ED: UNIV. OF WESTERN ONTARIO. DIED: APRIL 25, 1995.

Lofty character player Alexander Knox made his theatrical debut in Boston before heading to England for further stage work and some insignificant film roles, including one "A" production, *The Four Feathers*. Returning to America to support Laurence Olivier and Vivien Leigh in *Romeo and Juliet* on Broadway, he was then engaged by Warner Bros. to play the shipwrecked intellectual forced to be Edward G. Robinson's cabin boy in the best screen version of *The Sea Wolf*, and was certainly impressive in the part. He did not, however, get a contract out of the deal and went on to supporting parts in Columbia's *Commandos Strike at Dawn*, as a Nazi captain, and *This Above All*, as a priest. The latter was made for 20th Century-Fox, where he was chosen to carry Darryl F. Zanuck's patriotic pride and joy production, *Wilson*, a lengthy tribute to the 28th President. The film received a great deal of publicity but couldn't bring in enough customers to make back its enormous cost. Knox was a recipient of one of the movie's ten Oscar nominations for his work, although he played Woodrow

Wilson as an icon rather than a human being. That same year, with less fanfare but far more interesting results, he was top-billed as a vile Nazi war criminal looking back on his monstrous past, in Columbia's *None Shall Escape*. Columbia put him under contract, though Hollywood really wasn't quite sure what to do with someone who looked older than his years, as Knox did. Borrowed by RKO, he supported Rosalind Russell, as a doctor, in *Sister Kenny*, which he helped script; then actually did get another leading role (again, having collaborated on the writing), in *The Judge Steps Out*, leaving his selfish family behind and finding solace with Ann Sothern. He took second leads in *Tokyo Joe*, as the lawyer who has taken up with Humphrey Bogart's ex-wife, and *Two of a Kind*, remaining in the legal profession, as an unscrupulous attorney out to fleece an elderly couple. By the mid-1950s he'd gone back to England, where he was a psychiatrist who tries to help petty criminal Dirk Bogarde in *The Sleeping Tiger*; another shrink, in *Alias John Preston*, trying to cure troubled Christopher Lee; another Nazi, in *The Two-Headed Spy*; a scientist experimenting with a group of radioactive children in *These Are the Damned*; an American general in *How I Won the War*; and the U.S. Ambassador in *Nicholas and Alexandra*. In 1949 he starred on Broadway in a play he himself had written, *The Closing Door*.

Screen: 1938: The Phantom Strikes/The Gaunt Stranger; 1939: Cheer Boys Cheer; The Four Feathers; 1941: The Sea Wolf; 1942: Commandos Strike at Dawn; This Above All; 1944: None Shall Escape; Wilson; 1945: Over 21; 1946: Sister Kenny (and co-wr.); 1948: The Sign of the Ram; 1949: The Judge Steps Out (and co-wr.); Tokyo Joe; 1951: I'd Climb the Highest Mountain; Saturday's Hero; Two of a Kind; Man in the Saddle; Son of Dr. Jekyll; 1952: Paula; Europa 1951; 1954: The Sleeping Tiger; One Just Man; The Divided Heart; 1955: The Night My Number Came Up; 1956: Reach for the Sky; Alias John Preston; 1957: High Tide at Noon; Davy; Hidden Fear; 1958: Chase a Crooked Shadow; The Vikings; Passionate Summer; The Two-Headed Spy; Operation Amsterdam; Intent to Kill; 1959: The Wreck of the Mary Deare; 1960: Crack in the Mirror; Oscar Wilde; 1962: These Are the Damned/The Damned; The Share Out; The Longest Day; 1963: In the Cool of the Day; 1964: Man in the Middle; Woman of Straw; 1965: Mister Moses; Bikini Paradise; Crack in the World; 1966: The Psychopath; Modesty Blaise; Khartoum; 1967: Accident; How I Won the War; The 25th Hour; You Only Live Twice; 1968: Villa Rides!; Shalako; Fraulein Doktor; 1970: Skullduggery; Puppet on a Chain; 1971: Nicholas and Alexandra; 1978: The Chosen/Holocaust 2000; 1983: Gorky Park; 1985: Joshua Then and Now.

NY Stage: 1940: Romeo and Juliet; Jupiter Laughs; 1942: Jason; The Three Sisters; 1949: The Closing Door (and wr.).

Select TV: 1969: Run a Crooked Mile; 1973: Man Above Men (sp); 1976: Truman at Potsdam (sp); 1979: Churchill and the Generals (sp); 1980: Oppenheim (ms); Tinker, Tailor, Soldier, Spy (ms); Cry of the Innocent; 1983: Helen Keller: The Miracle Continues; 1985: The Last Place on Earth (ms).

ERNIE KOVACS
BORN: TRENTON, NJ, JANUARY 23, 1919.
ED: AADA. DIED: JANUARY 13, 1962.

As far as television was concerned, the sardonic, cigar-chomping comedian Ernie Kovacs was one of the true originals, creating a surreal, anything-goes kind of humor that has made him revered as a nonconformist visionary to this day. The movies, on the other hand, liked giving him occasional

jobs but weren't sure what to do with him in a controlled, carefully scripted format. Originally a disc jockey on a local New Jersey station, he segued over to television in Philadelphia where he had his first program offering his brand of deliberately silly gags. In time, during the 1950s, he was all over the tube in various comical grab-bag shows (sometimes doing more than one series at the same time) that mainly consisted of a series of blackout gags and Kovacs's weird characters like lisping Percy Dovetonsils and an all-ape band. It all ranged from sublimely inspired to flat-out lame. Kovacs got his first big-screen assignment when he signed an agreement with Columbia Pictures, playing the obnoxious commanding officer in the amusing military farce *Operation Mad Ball*. This pretty much set the tone for the sort of movie role he would play — the unctuous blowhard or jerky authority figure. He was a drunken writer in *Bell Book and Candle*; a railroad chairman dubbed "the meanest man in the world" by Doris Day in *It Happened to Jane*; a con man in John Wayne's *North to Alaska*; and an incompetent burglar who winds up commanding a vessel in *Sail a Crooked Ship*. Despite his proficiency for playing oily men with cheeky good humor, none of these would lead modern-day audiences to believe they were watching a comic referred to by many as a "genius." The last of these was released after his untimely death in a car accident. His widow was actress Edie Adams, who had appeared with him on several of his television shows and whom Kovacs had married in 1954.

Screen: 1957: Operation Mad Ball; 1958: Bell Book and Candle; 1959: It Happened to Jane/Twinkle and Shine; 1960: Our Man in Havana; Wake Me When It's Over; Strangers When We Meet; Pepe; North to Alaska; 1961: Five Golden Hours; 1962: Sail a Crooked Ship.

Select TV: 1951: Kovacs on the Corner (series); It's Time for Ernie (series); Ernie in Kovacsland (series); 1952–54: Kovacs Unlimited (series); 1952–53: The Ernie Kovacs Show (series); 1953: Take a Guess (series); 1954: Time Will Tell (series); 1954–55: One Minute Please (series); 1955–56: The Ernie Kovacs Show (series); 1956: The Ernie Kovacs Show (series); 1956–57: Tonight Show (series); 1959–61: Take a Good Look (series); 1961: Silents Please (series).

OTTO KRUGER
BORN: TOLEDO, OH, SEPTEMBER 6, 1885.
DIED: SEPTEMBER 6, 1974.

White-haired, long-faced Otto Kruger had a lengthy list of film credits in which he often played suave villains or shady fellows who simply couldn't be trusted. It was not a varied act, and as impressive as he was on occasion, he could be just as easily forgettable on others. Following some stock theater work, he made his Broadway debut in 1915 in *The Natural Law*, the same year he first showed up on movie screens, in *When the Call Came*. There was only one other silent feature, Kruger being too occupied with the stage to bother. It was not until 1933 that he officially came to Hollywood to lend support in MGM's *Turn Back the Clock*, after which he was Barbara Stanwyck's German husband who turns spy in *Ever in My Heart*. He finished off that year by receiving top billing in *The Women in His Life*, as a hard-drinking, unscrupulous, womanizing lawyer. There were also leads in *Crime Doctor* (which had nothing to do with the later series starring Warner Baxter); *Springtime for Henry*, getting the role so closely identified onstage with Edward Everett Horton, that of a self-centered playboy, terrified of marriage; and *Dracula's Daughter*, falling under the spell of the title character. His shifty persona was simply better suited to villains, and his vast gallery of them included crooked lawyers (*Exposed, Counsel for Crime, Disbarred*), Nazis (*The Man I Married, Saboteur, Hitler's Children, Tarzan's Desert Mystery*), and more benign types, such as the publisher in *Cover Girl*, and the judge who skips town in *High Noon*. He retired after a stroke and died on his 89th birthday.

Screen: 1915: The Runaway Wife; A Mother's Confession; 1923: Under the Red Robe; 1933: Turn Back the Clock; Beauty for Sale; Ever in My Heart; The Prizefighter and the Lady; The Women in His Life; 1934: Gallant Lady; Chained; Men in White; Treasure Island; Paris Interlude; Crime Doctor; Springtime for Henry; 1935: Vanessa: Her Love Story; Two Sinners; 1936: Dracula's Daughter; Lady of Secrets; Living Dangerously; 1937: They Won't Forget; Counsel for Crime; The Barrier; 1938: I Am the Law; Exposed; Glamorous Night; Thanks for the Memory; Housemaster; Star of the Circus/Hidden Menace; 1939: Disbarred; The Zero Hour; A Woman Is the Judge; Another Thin Man; Black Eyes; The Amazing Mr. Forrest/The Gang's All Here; Scandal Sheet; 1940: Dr. Ehrlich's Magic Bullet; A Dispatch From Reuters; The Man I Married; Seventeen; 1941: The Big Boss; The Men in Her Life; Mercy Island; 1942: Saboteur; Friendly Enemies; Secrets of a Co-Ed; 1943: Hitler's Children; Corregidor; Power of the Press; Night Plane From Chungking; Tarzan's Desert Mystery; Stage Door Canteen; 1944: Murder, My Sweet; Cover Girl; Storm Over Lisbon; They Live in Fear; Knickerbocker Holiday; 1945: The Great John L.; Jungle Captive; Wonder Man; The Woman Who Came Back; On Stage Everybody!; The Chicago Kid; Escape in the Fog; Allotment Wives; Earl Carroll's Vanities; 1946: The Fabulous Suzanne; Duel in the Sun; 1947: Love and Learn; 1948: Lulu Belle; Smart Woman; 1950: 711 Ocean Drive; 1951: Payment on Demand; Valentino; 1952: High Noon; 1954: Magnificent Obsession; Black Widow; 1955: The Last Command; 1958: The Colossus of New York; 1959: The Young Philadelphians; Cash McCall; 1962: The Wonderful World of the Brothers Grimm; 1964: Sex and the Single Girl.

NY Stage: 1915: The Natural Law; Young America; 1916: Seven Chances; Captain Kidd Jr.; Merry Christmas Daddy!; Editha's Burglar; 1917: Here Comes the Bride; 1919: Adam and Eva; 1921: Nobody's Money; Sonya; The Straw; Alias Jimmy Valentine; 1922: To the Ladies!; 1923: Will Shakespeare; The Was; The Nervous Wreck; 1925: Easy Come, Easy Go; 1928: Trelawney of the Wells; The Royal Family; 1929: Karl and Anna; The Game of Love and Death; 1930: The Boundry Line; They Never Grow Up; The Long Road; As Good As New; 1931: The Great Barrington; Private Lives; 1932: Counsellor-at-Law; 1942: The Moon Is Down; 1947: Little A; Laura; 1948: A Time for Elizabeth; 1949: The Smile of the World.

Select TV: 1950: The Happy Ending (sp); 1951: Outstation (sp); 1953: Something to Live For (sp); Woman's World (sp); 1954: Prelude to Murder (sp); The Face Is Familiar (sp); 1955: The Desert Song (sp); 1955–56: Lux Video Theatre (series); 1957: Miller's Millions (sp); 1961: Up Jumped the Devil (sp).

NANCY KWAN
BORN: HONG KONG, MAY 19, 1939.

A pretty, strong-willed lady who stood out simply because she was getting leading roles when no other Asian women were, Nancy Kwan had trained to be a dancer and performed for the British Royal Ballet. She was an unknown when she was chosen to play the feisty prostitute who falls for William Holden in the 1960 film version of the stage hit *The World of Suzie Wong*. The success of this soap opera was such that this became, like it or not, the role for which she would forever be identified. There was also a good follow-up part, playing the nightclub entertainer in the bright Rodgers and Hammerstein musical *Flower Drum Song*, performing such numbers as "I Enjoy Being a Girl," although her vocals were dubbed. There was the title role in the British comedy, *Tamahine*, as a Polynesian girl causing a ruckus at a men's college, followed by roles in too many other bird-brained farces, where her comical touch was often on the shrill side: the door-slamming farce *Honeymoon Hotel*; *Arrivederci, Baby!*, as one of the women on Tony Curtis's hit list; Disney's *Lt. Robin Crusoe, USN*, as Dick Van Dyke's female version of Friday; and the backwards-thinking military comedy *Nobody's Perfect*, as a nurse. For a time she returned to Hong Kong for some films, then commanded an all-female army of killers in the adventure *Wonder Women*; and showed up on television for a few jobs, including the mini-series *Noble House*. After a long absence from the big screen, she played one of Bruce Lee's employers in the hit biopic *Dragon: The Bruce Lee Story*.

Screen (US releases only): 1960: The World of Suzie Wong; 1961: Flower Drum Song; 1962: The Main Attraction; 1964: Tamahine; The Wild Affair; Fate Is the Hunter; Honeymoon Hotel; 1966: Arrivederci, Baby!/Drop Dead Darling; Lt. Robin Crusoe, USN; The Corrupt Ones; 1968: Nobody's Perfect; 1969: The Wrecking Crew; The Girl Who Knew Too Much; 1970: The McMasters; 1973: Wonder Women/The Deadly and the Beautiful; 1975: Supercock/Fowl Play; 1976: Project: Kill; 1978: Out of the Darkness/Night Creature; Fortress in the Sun; 1985: Walking the Edge; 1989: Night Children (dtv); 1990: Cold Dog Soup (dtv); 1993: Dragon: The Bruce Lee Story; 1997: Soul of the Avenger (dtv).

Select TV: 1983: The Last Ninja; 1985: Blade in Hong Kong; 1988: Noble House (ms); 1990: Miracle Landing.

ALAN LADD

Born: Hot Springs, AZ, September 3, 1913.
Raised in CA. Died: January 29, 1964.

Short, blond and nice-looking, Alan Ladd's tight-lipped, humorless persona was precisely what 1940s audiences were looking for in their tough guys, and, as a result, he became a star, if not a critic's darling. There was a sameness to his work, his expressionless emoting often leaving one cold, and yet his quietly unassuming manner made him hard to thoroughly dislike. He became a diving champion while a teen, then a lifeguard, before singing a contract with Universal in 1932. There he studied acting and got extra work in a single film (*Once in a Lifetime*) before they dropped him. Then it was over to Warners to work as a grip, followed by some acting on radio. There was a long list of movies in which he appeared as an extra or bit player; indeed, he is one of a handful of actors who started this way who actually worked his way up to superstardom. These assignments included *Pigskin Parade*, *The Goldwyn Follies*, *Citizen Kane* (glimpsed as a reporter in the screening room after the opening newsreel has ended), and Disney's *The Reluctant Dragon*. Between these there was a substantial role (credited as "Allan" Ladd) as a Nazi resistance fighter in *Beasts of Berlin* and actual billing over at Paramount for *Light of Western Stars*, as the lover of Esther Estrella. During this period he met up with agent Sue Carol (whom he would marry), who was instrumental in pushing him to the top. In 1942 she landed him a contract with Paramount, who immediately gave him a good role, as the laconic gunman in *This Gun for Hire*. Fourth billed, it was Ladd, however, who made the greatest impression, and his teaming with Veronica Lake encouraged the studio to put them together again in an immediate follow-up, *The Glass Key*, which was just as popular. After a decade's worth of credits, Ladd was a star.

Lucky Jordan was the first film to be sold exclusively on his name, with the actor playing a gangster who winds up fighting a gang of Nazi spies, while *And Now Tomorrow* found him trying to cure Loretta Young's oncoming deafness and falling in love with her. Wartime audiences loved this gooey stuff, so it was a hit, as was the much better *Salty O'Rourke*, with Ladd as a gam-

bler involved in horseracing, the whole movie being stolen from him by young Stanley Clements as a tough jockey. There was a famous noir, *The Blue Dahlia*, in which he reteamed with Lake, a movie that has not stood the test of time, unlike so many of this genre that have. He appeared in the more entertaining *Two Years Before the Mast*, as a sailor experiencing abuse from sadistic captain Henry da Silva. Only Ladd could so stoically withstand a whipping, teeth clenched and no suggestion of vulnerability whatsoever. Things began to fall into the numbingly routine with titles like *Calcutta* and *Saigon*, which were not to be confused with an earlier film he did entitled *China*, while *Beyond Glory* was notable only for being filmed on location at West Point. There was a welcome display of fun with Ladd and Dorothy Lamour singing "Tallahassee" in his guest spot in *Variety Girl*; a western for which Robert Preston easily drew all the attention away from the star, *Whispering Smith*, Ladd's biggest hit in a while; and a much-disliked version of *The Great Gatsby*, which was probably his biggest flop during this time. *Captain Carey, USA* was a dull postwar drama that is remembered only as the movie that introduced the enduring song "Mona Lisa," and *Branded*, in which he pretended to be the long lost heir of Charles Bickford, was another popular western, released just before his box-office power started to cool off.

He signed a contract with Warners in 1952, but in the meantime there were three more films on the way from Paramount. The first two, *Thunder in the East*, in which he was an adventurer falling in love with blind Deborah Kerr while in India, and *Botany Bay*, which was set in the Australian penal colony, were quickly forgotten, but the third turned out to be the biggest hit of his career and the one with which his name would be forever linked. *Shane* was a beautifully told, simple story about a mysterious gunman who rides into town, befriends a homesteader and his family, and rides off only after justice has been restored. Ladd's low-keyed personality was used to great effect, and the relationship he develops with young Brandon De Wilde showed the best acting he had attempted in his entire career.

In addition to his deal with Warners, there were suddenly multiple offers with various studios because of the staggering success of this film. But nobody was really faked into believing that Ladd had developed any great range, so the movies went right back to the routine with *Saskatchewan*, in which he played a Mountie in one of his more popular post-*Shane* offerings, and a batch made in England. These included *The Black Knight*, the most atypical of the bunch, with Ladd looking silly in medieval attire; *Paratrooper*, with the actor as a guilt-ridden American officer training alongside the British; and *Hell Above Zero*, trying to solve a murder mystery while aboard a whaling vessel. *Boy on a Dolphin* is best remembered for its offbeat teaming with Sophia Loren, while *The Proud Rebel* was a small triumph, a gentle western in which his real-life offspring David played his mute son, but it didn't bring in the crowds. Falling off into programmers (*The Badlanders*, *Guns of the Timberland*, et al). and a made-in-Italy spectacle (*Duel of Champions*), his career had reached an all-time low. *13 West Street*, a revenge drama made for his own Ladd Enterprises did little to help. There were bouts of depression, alcoholism, and injuries from a gunshot wound, a situation that was declared accidental. His death in 1964 was also declared accidental, the actor having been found with a mix of sedatives and alcohol in his system. Released soon after was *The Carpetbaggers*, in which he played a broken-down former movie star, and it proved to be the first widely seen movie he'd done in years. His sons Alan, Jr. and David both became motion picture executives.

Screen: 1932: Once in a Lifetime; Tom Brown of Culver; 1933: Island of Lost Souls; Saturday's Millions; 1936: Pigskin Parade; 1937: Last Train from Madrid; Hold 'em Navy; Souls at Sea; All Over Town; 1938: The Goldwyn Follies; Come on, Leathernecks!; Freshman Year; 1939: Rulers of the Sea; Beasts of Berlin; The Green Hornet (serial); 1940: Light of Western Stars; Those Were the Days; In Old Missouri; Gangs of Chicago; Captain Caution; Widcat Bus; Meet the Missus; Her First Romance; Brother Rat and a Baby; Cross-Country Romance; Victory; 1941: Petticoat Politics; Citizen Kane; The Black Cat; They Met in Bombay; The Reluctant Dragon; Great Guns; Cadet Girls; Gangs Inc/Paper Bullets; 1942: Joan of Paris; This Gun for Hire; The Glass Key; Lucky Jordan; Star Spangled Rhythm; 1943: China; 1944: And Now Tomorrow; 1945: Salty O'Rourke; Duffy's Tavern; 1946: The Blue Dahlia; O.S.S.; Two Years Before the Mast; 1947: Calcutta; Variety Girl; My Favorite Brunette; Wild Harvest; 1948: Saigon; Beyond Glory; Whispering Smith; 1949: The Great Gatsby; Chicago Deadline; 1950: Captain Carey, USA; Branded; 1951: Appointment with Danger; Red Mountain; 1952: The Iron Mistress; 1953: Thunder in the East; Botany Bay; Shane; Desert Legion; The Red Beret/Paratrooper; 1954: Saskatchewan; Hell Below Zero; The Black Knight; Drum Beat; 1955: The McConnell Story; Hell on Frisco Bay; 1956: Santiago; A Cry in the Night (narrator); 1957: The Big Land; Boy on a Dolphin; 1958: The Deep Six; The Proud Rebel; The Badlanders; 1959: The Man in the Net; 1960: Guns of the Timberland; All the Young Men; One Foot in Hell; 1961: Duel of Champions; 1962: 13 West Street; 1964: The Carpetbaggers.

Select TV: 1954: Committed (sp); 1958: Silent Ambush (sp).

BERT LAHR

(IRVING LAHRHEIM) BORN: NEW YORK, NY, AUGUST 13, 1895. DIED: DECEMBER 4, 1967.

Due to one great movie role, Bert Lahr is looked upon as one of the immortals of the screen, but there is no doubt that this baggy-eyed, balding comic's heart belonged to live theater. Joining an act called the Seven Frolics while still a teen, he was soon making a name for himself on the vaudeville and burlesque circuits, with one of his shows, *Folly Town*, moving to Broadway in 1920. His official Broadway career started with *Harry Delmar's Revels* in 1927, after which he was the star of *Hold Everything* and *Flying High*. MGM asked him to repeat his role in the film version of the last-named, with Lahr playing an inept aviator, but it didn't duplicate its stage success. He played himself in *Mr. Broadway* and portrayed a vaudevillian named Bert in *Merry-Go-Round of 1938*, meanwhile finding a warmer reception back onstage in New York, where his broad style of humor was perhaps better suited, in such hits as *Life Begins at 8:40*, *The Show Is On*, and *DuBarry Was a Lady*. After playing Claudette Colbert's stage partner in *Zaza*, he donned fur and a tail to be the Cowardly Lion in the greatest musical of them all, *The Wizard of Oz*. His priceless comic timing and unforgettable rendition of "If I Were King of the Forest" were key aspects in creating one of the best-loved characters in film history. This did not mean, however, that MGM let him appear in the *DuBarry* movie (Red Skelton got the role); instead he starred in *Sing Your Worries Away* at RKO, bouncing comic bits off of Buddy Ebsen, and did some specialties in MGM's *Meet the People*, and the unnecessary remake of *Rose Marie*, among others. Fittingly, his last movie role found him playing an old burlesque performer, in *The Night They Raided Minsky's*, but he died before he completed it, leaving his character but a vague background figure. He won a Tony Award for his final Broadway appearance, in the musical *Foxy*. His son John Lahr wrote a 1969 biography on his dad entitled *Notes on a Cowardly Lion*.

Screen: 1931: Flying High; 1933: Mr. Broadway; 1938: Merry-Go-Round of 1938; Love and Hisses; 1938: Josette; Just Around the Corner; 1939: Zaza; The Wizard of Oz; 1942: Sing Your Worries Away; Ship Ahoy; 1944: Meet the People; 1949: Always Leave Them Laughing; 1951: Mr. Universe; 1954: Rose Marie; 1955: The Second Greatest Sex; 1962: Ten Girls Ago (unreleased); 1968: The Night They Raided Minsky's.

NY Stage: 1920: Folly Town; 1927: Harry Delmar's Revels; 1928: Hold Everything; 1930: Flying High; 1932: Hot-Cha!; 1933: George White's Music Hall Varieties; 1934: Life Begins at 8:40; 1936: George White's Scandals; The Show Is On; 1939: DuBarry Was a Lady; 1944: Seven Lively Arts; 1946: Burlesque; 1951: Two on the Aisle; 1956: Waiting for Godot; 1957: Hotel Paradiso; 1959: The Girls Against the Boys; 1962: The Beauty Part; 1964: Foxy.

Select TV: 1951: Burlesque (sp); Flying High (sp); 1954: Anything Goes (sp); The Man Who Came to Dinner (sp); The Great Waltz (sp); 1956: School for Wives (sp); 1957: The Big Heist (sp); 1959: Mr. O'Malley (sp); 1960: The Greatest Man Alive (sp); 1964: The Fantasticks (sp); 1965: Cops and Robbers (sp).

ARTHUR LAKE

(ARTHUR SILVERLAKE) BORN: CORBIN, KY, APRIL 17, 1905. DIED: JANUARY 9, 1987.

Youthful-looking, goofily manic, wavy-haired Arthur Lake was first and foremost Dagwood Bumstead in Columbia's highly lucrative, long-running series, but his career dated back further than one might think. The child of a family of circus acrobats ("The Flying Silverlakes"), he made his movie debut as a 12-year-old in a pair of all-youngster fairy tale spoofs, *Jack and the Beanstalk* and *Aladdin and the Wonderful Lamp*, then joined his family in vaudeville. His sister Florence helped get him work in a series of two-reel comedies produced at Universal, which went under the banner of "Sweet Sixteen." During this period he began getting parts in feature films, including *The Cradle Snatchers*, as a naïve Swedish college student; *The Air*

Circus, as an arrogant flier; and *Harold Teen*, as a cocky student in the first of his assignments to be based on a comic strip. When sound arrived he did the expected creaky musicals (*On With the Show, Tanned Legs*) and collegiate capers (*Cheer Up and Smile*). He spent most of the 1930s as a serviceable supporting player, showing up as a footballer in *Girl o' My Dreams*; an insurance salesman in *I Cover Chinatown*; a dumb cadet in *Annapolis Salute*; and a nervous elevator operator in *Topper*. In 1938, his fortunes changed when he was chosen to play the inept, accident prone Dagwood, opposite Penny Singleton, in Columbia's budget-conscious version of Chic Young's incredibly popular, long-running comic strip *Blondie*. The movie was such a smash that the studio continued churning out more "B" entries over the next 12 years, with Lake's increasingly unsubtle performance, as the hyperactive husband with the annoying squeaky voice, testing the patience of all but the most avid fans. Following the 27 sequels, nobody was much interested in hiring Lake for anything else, so he briefly revived the part on TV, in 1954, with Pamela Britton in the Blondie role. He and Singleton were reteamed two decades later when they did one of the many road tours of the nostalgic musical *No, No, Nanette*. In 1948 he escaped from Dagwood temporarily when he appeared for Monogram in a remake of *16 Fathoms Deep*, which was the sole offering from his own Arthur Lake Productions. His sister Florence Lake (1904–80), whose career mainly consisted of bits, short subjects, and television guest spots, had appeared with her brother on a single occasion, in the film *Midshipman Jack*.

Screen (features): 1917: Jack and the Beanstalk; Aladdin and the Wonderful Lamp; **1925:** Where Was I?; Sporting Life; Smoldering Fires; California Straight Ahead; **1926:** Skinner's Dress Suit; **1927:** The Cradle Snatchers; The Irresistible Lover; **1928:** Stop That Man; The Count of Ten; Harold Teen; The Air Circus; Lilac Time; **1929:** On With the Show!; Dance Hall; Tanned Legs; **1930:** Cheer Up and Smile; She's My Weakness; **1931:** Indiscreet; **1933:** Midshipman Jack; **1934:** Silver Streak; Girl o' My Dreams; **1935:** Women Must Dress; Orchids to You; **1936:** I Cover Chinatown; **1937:** Annapolis Salute; 23 1/2 Hours Leave; Topper; Exiled to Shanghai; True Confession; **1938:** Everybody's Doing It; Double Danger; There Goes My Heart; Blondie; **1939:** Blondie Meets the Boss; Blondie Takes a Vacation; Blondie Brings Up Baby; **1940:** Blondie on a Budget; Blondie Has Servant Trouble; Blondie Plays Cupid; **1941:** Blondie Goes Latin; Blondie in Society; **1942:** Blondie Goes to College; Blondie's Blessed Event; The Daring Young Man; Blondie for Victory; **1943:** It's a Great Life; Footlight Glamour; **1944:** Sailor's Holiday; The Ghost That Walks Alone; Three Is a Family; **1945:** The Big Show-Off; Leave It to Blondie; Life With Blondie; **1946:** Blondie Knows Best; Blondie's Lucky Day; **1947:** Blondie's Holiday; Blondie's Big Moment; Blondie in the Dough; Blondie's Anniversary; **1948:** Blondie's Reward; 16 Fathoms Deep (and prod.); Blondie's Secret; **1949:** Blondie's Big Deal; Blondie Hits the Jackpot; **1950:** Blondie's Hero; Beware of Blondie.

Select TV: 1957: Blondie (series).

VERONICA LAKE

(CONSTANCE FRANCES MARIE OCKELMAN)
BORN: BROOKLYN, NY, NOVEMBER 14, 1919.
DIED: JULY 7, 1973.

An actress forever rooted in the war years of the 1940s, blonde, sultry, sexy Veronica Lake probably contributed more through her famous hair style than her acting talent and, as was so often the case with the limited lookers, faded from the scene as she

aged. Following her father's death, her mother remarried a man named Keane, hence the name "Constance Keane," which Lake originally used when she entered some Florida beauty contests. Encouraged to try acting, her family traveled to Hollywood where the young teen enrolled in the Bliss Hayden School of Acting. It was through an acquaintance there that she landed a bit part in RKO's *Sorority House*. Billing in Paramount's *All Women Have Secrets* followed, as did a bigger part in a Leon Errol short, "The Wrong Room." Paramount saw a screen test she had made and cast her as the vixen who causes some commotion between Ray Milland and William Holden in *I Wanted Wings*. It was just another war story set among the clouds but it became a big hit, and the newly dubbed "Veronica Lake" created a sensation with her peek-a-boo bang that drooped down one side of her face.

Signed to a contract by the excited studio, they immediately put her in what is certainly her best movie, director-writer Preston Sturges's perceptive and beautifully conceived comedy-drama *Sullivan's Travels*, as the girl who joins filmmaker Joel McCrea on his journey to find out what Americans want out of a movie. Just to play down her beauty and focus on her efforts to act, the plot required her to be dressed in men's clothing for a substantial portion of the film. This was followed by another good one, *This Gun for Hire*, where the audience responded enthusiastically to her teaming with the taciturn Alan Ladd. They were no Bogart and Bacall, but there was a certain deadpan look of desire between them that seemed ideal for the noir dramas of the day. Lake was paired with Ladd again in the remake of *The Glass Key*, and then she had a suitable role as a desirable witch in a highly enjoyable comedy, *I Married a Witch*, made for Paramount but ultimately distributed by United Artists. Her pinup was plastered over barrack lockers everywhere, prompting the spoof song "A Sweater, a Sarong and a Peek-a-Boo Bang," performed by the ladies being referred to, Paulette Goddard, Dorothy Lamour, and Lake, in *Star Spangled Rhythm*. Ironically it was at this point that she got rid of those famous locks, since too many women emulating the look were getting their hair caught in factory machinery. As a good-will gesture she changed her style and lost an awful lot.

She was one of the nurses in the flag-waving *So Proudly We Hail!*; a poor choice for the role of the Nazi spy in the adaptation of Somerset Maugham's *The Hour Before the Dawn*; and one of the ladies at a turn-of-the-century boarding house in an instantly forgettable bit of nostalgia, *Miss Susie Slagle's*. There were mild comedies with Eddie Bracken, made to contrast her stunning looks with his dorky quivering, *Bring on the Girls, Out of This World*, and *Hold That Blonde*; and two uninspired reteamings with Ladd, *The Blue Dahlia* and *Saigon*, by which time the late 1940s had arrived and Lake was no longer wanted by Paramount nor anyone else. There were roles in some summer stock productions, and, after disappearing from the show business scene altogether, she turned up working as a barmaid in a Manhattan cocktail lounge. When news of this leaked out, she got some offers from sympathetic producers, including one to appear Off Broadway in a revival of *Best Foot Forward*. Then she herself co-produced a cheap horror movie, *Flesh Feast*, which played the expected drive-in markets. Her second husband (1944–52) was director Andre De Toth, under whom she worked in *Slattery's Hurricane*.

Screen: AS CONSTANCE KEANE: 1939: Sorority House; All Women Have Secrets; Dancing Co-Ed; **1940:** Young as You Feel; Forty Little Mothers.

AS VERONICA LAKE: 1941: I Wanted Wings; Hold Back the Dawn; Sullivan's Travels; **1942:** This Gun for Hire; The Glass

Key; I Married a Witch; Star Spangled Rhythm; **1943:** So Proudly We Hail!; **1944:** The Hour Before the Dawn; **1945:** Bring on the Girls; Out of This World; Duffy's Tavern; Hold That Blonde; **1946:** Miss Susie Slagle's; The Blue Dahlia; **1947:** Ramrod; Variety Girl; **1948:** Saigon; The Sainted Sisters; Isn't It Romantic?; **1949:** Slatter's Hurricane; **1952:** Stronghold; **1967:** Footsteps in the Snow (nUSr); **1970:** Flesh Feast (and exec. prod.).

NY Stage: 1963: Best Foot Forward (ob).
Select TV: 1950: Shadow of the Heart (sp); 1951: The Facts of Life (sp); 1952: Brief Moment (sp); Better Than Walking (sp); 1953: Thanks for a Lovely Evening (sp); 1954: Gramercy Ghost (sp).

HEDY LAMARR

(HEDWIG EVA MARIA KIESLER)
BORN: VIENNA, AUSTRIA, NOVEMBER 9, 1913.
DIED: JANUARY 19, 2000.

Certainly one of Hollywood's true beauties, Hedy Lamarr was lucky to have her looks, for when it came to lighting up the screen with her acting capabilities, she had precious little to offer. While still in school she got some bit parts at the Sascha Film Studio, then studied acting with Max Reinhardt in Berlin. It was because of a 1933 German film, known in America as *Ecstasy*, that she became world famous, since there was a sequence that had her swimming and running through the woods in the nude. After it was distributed in the U.S. in 1937, there was an offer for a contract from MGM, which she accepted. First she did one on loan-out, *Algiers*, as the classy lady attracted to petty criminal Charles Boyer. It was a good start, as opposed to her first two for Metro, the troubled *I Take This Woman*, marrying Spencer Tracy after attempting suicide, and *Lady of the Tropics*, causing no sparks whatsoever while romancing Robert Taylor.

She was dropped down to fourth billing for a better project, *Boom Town*, unworthy of her trio of co-stars, Tracy, Clark Gable, and Claudette Colbert. With Gable she did a pseudo-*Ninotchka* story, *Comrade X*, as a Russian street car conductor, and she almost made Lana Turner look good, playing a failed *Ziegfeld Girl*, in this glossy musical soap opera package. Tracy got her again for *Tortilla Flat*, though she was, in fact, paired off with John Garfield, playing a Hispanic cannery worker, and then she took on one of her most famous and campiest temptress roles, Tondelayo in *White Cargo*, getting the workers at an African plantation all hot and bothered, Walter Pidgeon especially. There were two comedies, *The Heavenly Body*, in which she really showed her limitations in this field opposite a pro like William Powell, and *Her Highness and the Bellboy*, with Robert Walker. It was clear to MGM that she was hardly an asset to the box office, and she went elsewhere for some flops, including *Dishonored Lady*, which placed her alongside husband number three, John Loder, and *Let's Live a Little*, which was made for the budget-impaired Eagle-Lion Classics, an indication of how far her stock had fallen.

Just when everyone was ready to count her out, she was hired by Cecil B. DeMille to play the world's most notorious hair stylist in his expensive and lavish kitsch-fest, *Samson and Delilah*, and the movie was so popular that it became her signature role, if indeed she had one. Her low standing hardly improved after this financial peak though, with a routine western with Ray Milland, *Copper Canyon* (the two stars did not enjoy each other's company) and one of the weakest Bob Hope comedies of the time, *My Favorite Spy*. After that she was off to Europe to play Helen of Troy in *The Face That Launched a Thousand Ships*, and then back to America where she was a most unlikely Joan of Arc in one

of the silliest all-star cast productions of them all, *The Story of Mankind*. That same year, 1957, marked her final big-screen appearance, in a Universal soap opera, *The Female Animal*, as Jane Powell's mother. After that she pretty much stayed out of sight, except for two separate arrests for shoplifting and a lawsuit directed at Mel Brooks for using her name as a joke in the spoof *Blazing Saddles*. She published her autobiography, *Ecstasy and Me*, in 1966.

Screen: AS HEDY KIESLER; 1930: Sturme im Wasserglas/Die Blumenfrau von Lindenau (nUSr); Geld auf der Strasse/Money on the Street (nUSr); 1931: Mein Braucht Kein Geld/No Money Is Needed/His Majesty King Ballyhoo (nUSr); Die Koffer des Herrn O.F./The Trunks of Mr. O.F.; 1933: Symphonie Der Liebe/Ecstasy (US: 1937).

AS HEDY LAMARR: 1938: Algiers; 1939: Lady of the Tropics; 1940: I Take This Woman; Boom Town; Comrade X; 1941: Come Live With Me; Ziegfeld Girl; H.M. Pulham, Esq.; 1942: Tortilla Flat; Crossroad; White Cargo; 1943: The Heavenly Body; 1944: The Conspirators; Experiment Perilous; 1945: Her Highness and the Bellboy; 1946: The Strange Woman; 1947: Dishonored Lady; 1948: Let's Live a Little; 1949: Samson and Delilah; 1950: A Lady Without a Passport; Copper Canyon; 1951: My Favorite Spy; 1954: The Face That Launched a Thousand Ships; 1957: The Story of Mankind; The Female Animal.

FERNANDO LAMAS

BORN: BUENOS AIRES, ARGENTINA,
JANUARY 9, 1915. DIED: OCTOBER 8, 1982.

Apparently the MGM of the early 1950s wasn't content to have one "Latin lover" type around, so, in addition to Ricardo Montalban, they grabbed hold of Fernando Lamas, who wasn't as good an actor and didn't fare as well in the long run. He began his career in his native country on the radio and in films, including the lead in a version of Oscar Wilde's *Lady Windermere's Fan*, called *Historia de una Mala Mujer*, opposite Dolores Del Rio. He made his first American appearance in a Republic film, *The Avengers*, which was shooting on location in South America. The wife of its star, John Carroll, got Lamas a screen test with MGM, who cast him opposite Danielle Darrieux in *Rich, Young and Pretty*. Lana Turner got him as her leading man in the fairly popular remake of *The Merry Widow*, and since Lamas really sang (Turner was dubbed), he got to solo on the hit "Vilia." Then he was leading man to Esther Williams in one of her better movies, *Dangerous When Wet*, and although she would re-enter his life in the future, it was his co-star in Paramount's programmer *Sangaree*, Arlene Dahl, whom he married in 1954. Their union lasted until 1960, during which time he was the fur trapper in the plodding remake of *Rose Marie* and lent his scowling presence and thick accent to the cheesy Irwin Allen re-do of *The Lost World*. In 1961 he directed himself and Esther Williams in *The Magic Fountain*, and although it never played in the U.S., they did get a marriage out of the deal, which lasted from 1967 until Lamas's death. In the meantime there was another directorial effort, the grim *The Violent Ones*, with the actor also taking the leading role, as a deputy, and some television work. He last appeared on screen as one of the villains of the Neil Simon spoof *The Cheap Detective*, still possessing that certain mixture of ruggedness and suavity that had been his trademark. A son by his marriage to Dahl, Lorenzo Lamas, became an actor, principally of "B" action thrillers.

Screen (US releases only): 1948: The Story of a Bad Woman/Lady Windermere's Fan; 1950: The Avengers; 1951: Rich, Young and Pretty; The Law and the Lady; **1952:** The Merry Widow; **1953:** The Girl Who Had Everything; Dangerous When Wet; Sangaree; Diamond Queen; **1954:** Rose Marie; Jivaro; **1955:** The Girl Rush; **1960:** The Lost World; **1963:** Revenge of the Musketeers; **1967:** The Violent Ones (and dir.); Kill a Dragon; **1969:** 100 Rifles; Backtrack; **1976:** Won Ton Ton, the Dog Who Saved Hollywood; **1978:** The Cheap Detective.

NY Stage: **1956:** Happy Hunting.

Select TV: **1958:** Spider Web (sp); **1966:** Valley of Mystery; **1968:** For Love or $$$ (sp); **1969:** The Lonely Profession; **1971:** Powderkeg; **1975:** Murder on Flight 502; **1980:** The Dream Merchants.

DOROTHY LAMOUR

(MARY LETA DOROTHY SLATON)
BORN: NEW ORLEANS, LA, DECEMBER 10, 1914.
DIED: SEPTEMBER 22, 1996.

She came to Hollywood from New Orleans by way of New York, but something about Dorothy Lamour's full lips, long dark hair, and sleepy eyes made producers think of her as a South Seas Island girl, and hence the movies' most famous sarong-wearer was born. As a teen she won a "Miss New Orleans" contest and moved to Chicago where she auditioned to sing with the Herbie Kaye orchestra. She not only got the job but also married Kaye, and they moved to New York where she became a singer at the famous Stork Club. This landed her a job on radio's *The Dreamer of Songs*, which eventually moved to Los Angeles with Lamour tagging along. Spotted in a club by a Paramount executive, she was screen-tested and signed to a contract. The sarong films started immediately when she was cast in the title role of *The Jungle Princess*, as Ulah, a tropical babe who wins the heart of British hunter Ray Milland while singing "Moonlight and Shadows" and cavorting with her pet chimp, Bogo. Apparently this was all taken quite seriously back then and didn't do badly at the box office. From there she went to second leads in the musicals *Swing High, Swing Low* and *High, Wide and Handsome*, followed by the most famous and enduring of all her South Seas romps, *The Hurricane*, which was actually made elsewhere, for Goldwyn Studios. Back on the home lot there were two follow-ups with Milland, the Technicolored *Her Jungle Love*, which didn't stray too far from the earlier film's plot, only this time Lamour was named Tura and the monkey called Gaga, and *Tropic Holiday*, which took them to Mexico. Between the musicals and exotic settings, she made a game attempt as a serious actress in the adventure *Spawn of the North*, then kidded her image in *St. Louis Blues*, playing a stage actress sick of wearing sarongs who joins a Mississippi riverboat.

In 1939 she divorced Kaye and went exotic again the following year, this time for a comedy, *Road to Singapore*, where she was billed *after* Bing Crosby and *before* Bob Hope. No one could have predicted it, but this very mild offering was so popular that the three stars would be reteamed on six more occasions over the next 22 years, the only difference being that Lamour was dropped to third billing with the follow-up, *Road to Zanzibar*. There is no denying that it was these movies that kept Lamour's name alive with the passing years. In the meantime, there were more silly jungle epics with *Typhoon*; *Moon Over Burma*, where she played a nightclub singer stranded in Rangoon; *Aloma of the South Seas*, which reunited her with *Hurricane* co-star Jon Hall; and *Beyond the Blue Horizon*, in which she turned out to be a jungle dweller who is heir to a fortune. There were also separate teamings with Hope (*Caught in the Draft* and *They Got Me Covered*, the latter for Goldwyn) and Crosby

(*Dixie*). She was seen to better effect in a pair of musicals, *The Fleet's In*, as an aloof nightclub singer (she helped to introduce a big wartime hit, "I Remember You") romanced by sailor William Holden, and *And the Angels Sing*, as part of a sister act, singing "It Should Happen to You." There were two "Road" peaks with *Road to Morocco*, piping in on "Moonlight Becomes You," and *Road to Utopia*, in which she sang another chart-topper, "Personality," and appeared at one point in a sarong in the frozen north for a sight gag. Between these there was a sincere but icky drama, *A Medal for Benny*, where she played the unseen Benny's fiancée.

After another with Hope, *My Favorite Brunette*, and the most popular "Road" romp, *Road to Rio*, she did some dramas elsewhere, *Lulu Belle* and *The Lucky Stiff*, which went nowhere, then came back to Paramount in 1952 for one of the biggest box-office successes of them all, *The Greatest Show on Earth*, as a tough circus aerialist whose specialty it is to hang by her teeth in midair. After the first and last color entry in the series, *Road to Bali*, she and Paramount parted company. For the next decade she stuck to television and nightclubs before someone decided to do one last "Road" picture. *The Road to Hong Kong* (released by United Artists) had its share of bright ideas but making Joan Collins the star while reducing Lamour to a guest appearance was not among them. The remainder of her movie roles weren't much bigger, going back to the South Seas one last time to play a madam in the John Wayne comedy *Donovan's Reef*; belting out a song in a dress shop in the inane AIP teen romp *Pajama Party*; and doing walk-ons in the cameo-studded oddities *The Phynx*, and *Won Ton Ton, the Dog Who Saved Hollywood*. There was also the lead in a touring production of the Broadway smash *Hello, Dolly!*, and some scattered TV spots. She was considered by many to be a part of the campier side of the golden era of movies, so it wasn't likely that anyone was going to hire her for anything too serious at this stage of the game. Her 1980 autobiography was entitled *My Side of the Road*.

Screen: **1936:** The Jungle Princess; **1937:** Swing High, Swing Low; Last Train From Madrid; High, Wide and Handsome; The Hurricane; Thrill of a Lifetime; **1938:** The Big Broadcast of 1938; Her Jungle Love; Tropic Holiday; Spawn of the North; **1939:** St. Louis Blues; Man About Town; Disputed Passage; **1940:** Johnny Apollo; Typhoon; Road to Singapore; Moon Over Burma; Chad Hanna; **1941:** Road to Zanzibar; Caught in the Draft; Aloma of the South Seas; **1942:** The Fleet's In; Beyond the Blue Horizon; Road to Morocco; Star Spangled Rhythm; **1943:** They Got Me Covered; Dixie; Riding High; **1944:** And the Angels Sing; Rainbow Island; **1945:** A Medal for Benny; Duffy's Tavern; Masquerade in Mexico; **1946:** Road to Utopia; **1947:** My Favorite Brunette; Variety Girl; Wild Harvest; Road to Rio; **1948:** On Our Merry Way/A Miracle Can Happen; Lulu Belle; The Girl From Manhattan; **1949:** Manhandled; The Lucky Stiff; Slightly French; **1951:** Here Comes the Groom; **1952:** The Greatest Show on Earth; Road to Bali; **1962:** The Road to Hong Kong; **1963:** Donovan's Reef; **1964:** Pajama Party; **1970:** The Phynx; **1976:** Won Ton Ton, the Dog Who Saved Hollywood; **1987:** Creepshow II.

Select TV: **1952:** The Singing Years (sp); **1955:** The Mink Doll (sp); **1976:** Death at Love House.

BURT LANCASTER

(BURTON STEPHEN LANCASTER)
BORN: NEW YORK, NY, NOVEMBER 2, 1913.
DIED: OCTOBER 20, 1994.

A tower of physical strength, robust energy, and beaming self-assurance, Burt Lancaster was one of the truly great stars of the postwar era, an actor who wasn't content to be pigeonholed and tried absolutely everything. No one seemed to mind that he stumbled on occasion; he was still exciting to watch and made the movies that much more interesting because of his ambitions. He had spent several years as a circus acrobat, traveling with partner Nick Cravat who later appeared in some of his films. After serving in the Army, a chance encounter got him an audition for the Broadway play *A Sound of Hunting*, and few stars ever rose so swiftly to the top. Although the play didn't run very long, it won him a Theatre World Award, got him an agent, Harold Hecht, and an offer to sign a contract with movie producer Hal Wallis. He accepted the deal with Wallis but was actually seen first in two Mark Hellinger productions for Universal, *The Killers*, an over-extended version of a Hemingway story, with Lancaster impressive as a washed-up boxer awaiting his inevitable demise, and *Brute Force*, a well-done take on all the prison clichés, as an angry inmate. His first two for Wallis (distributed by Paramount) were less interesting, *Desert Fury* and *I Walk Alone*, both co-starring Lizabeth Scott, although it was more notable that Kirk Douglas was in the latter. He and Lancaster would team again on several occasions, with more memorable results.

Wallis cast Lancaster as the sinister husband in another film that expanded a short piece more than it needed to be, *Sorry, Wrong Number*, while Universal gave him a good role as the decent son who exposes his corrupt father, Edward G. Robinson, in *All My Sons*, adapted from the play by Arthur Miller. With Hecht he formed his own production company, in 1948, before such things were common with stars. Unfortunately their first film, the melodrama *Kiss the Blood off My Hands*, distributed by Universal, was one of their least-accomplished efforts. Also for that studio he was an armored car driver who ends up involved in a robbery in *Criss Cross*, then returned to Wallis for another noirish entry, *Rope of Sand*, as a thief trying to get to his stash before others beat him to it. The next Hecht-Lancaster venture (for Warner Bros.) fared far better than their maiden project, being the first movie that showed Lancaster in a lighthearted vein, the tongue-in-cheek medieval adventure *The Flame and the Arrow*, which was more popular than most of the serious stuff he was doing at the time. It greatly enhanced his box-office appeal, and he would return to this sort of romp with *The Crimson Pirate*, which was probably the pinnacle of these adventures; *Ten Tall Men*, set in the Foreign Legion; *South Sea Woman*; and *His Majesty O'Keefe*. All of these films found a devoted following even among those who weren't crazy about the more straightforward Lancaster work.

In the meantime he wanted to show he could tackle all kinds of roles, and since Wallis needed a name to help the adaptation of the Broadway drama *Come Back, Little Sheba* make a profit, Lancaster was cast as the alcoholic husband of Shirley Booth, bitter over his lost youth. Many critics spoke of miscasting, but his work in the film was, in fact, quite good; he more than held his own against Booth at her most magnificent. And if one looked past the fact that Lancaster had no Indian blood in him, his casting as Olympic great *Jim Thorpe — All American* was ideal, he being the most naturally athletic of all leading men. He was far less happy with MGM's western *Vengeance Valley*, where Robert Walker got the showier role, as his no-good brother. The one that really put Lancaster on top was Columbia's highly anticipated blockbuster, *From Here to Eternity*. This turned out to be an exceptional rendering of James Jones's much-read novel, and everyone involved benefited from its enormous box-office success. Top-billed Lancaster, as the levelheaded sergeant dallying with married Deborah Kerr on the side, was forceful and sympa-

thetic, receiving his first Oscar nomination. He played another Indian, in *Apache*, back when that sort of casting was perfectly acceptable, and had fun playing a mischievous bad guy opposite Gary Cooper in the otherwise routine western *Vera Cruz*. Not unlike *Sheba*, Wallis again asked him to lend his services to an adaptation of a stage play with a great actress, Anna Magnani, so he'd help bring in the customers to chancy material. The film was one of the best Tennessee Williams's adaptations, *The Rose Tattoo*, though Lancaster's portrayal of the lustful, spirited truck driver was a bit much at times.

Around the same time his first attempt at directing, *The Kentuckian*, in which he also starred as a peaceful settler who gets involved in a long-standing feud, received little attention despite being a most respectable effort. Instead there were big audiences for the colorful *Trapeze*, which allowed him to show off the sort of thing he did for a living before he became famous, and *Gunfight at the O.K. Corral*, an enjoyable rendition of the Wyatt Earp legend that teamed him again with Kirk Douglas. There was another lively, chest-beating turn, as the traveling charlatan Starbuck, in *The Rainmaker*, the third instance of Wallis casting him opposite an older actress (Katharine Hepburn) for money reasons, while the leading lady got all the acclaim. This bombastic performance was contrasted brilliantly with his low-keyed gossip columnist in the cult classic *Sweet Smell of Success*, a mesmerizing portrait of megalomania and evil, with the smooth-talking Lancaster calmly causing his share of destruction through words rather than actions. It was among his finest performances, but its lukewarm reception in 1957 assured that a certain amount of time would have to pass before most people came to this realization.

By this point he and Hecht were joined in their filmmaking endeavors by Harold Hill, and their company had won a Best Picture Oscar for *Marty*. Since Lancaster's name never appeared in the credits of any of these films as a producer, however, the award did not go to him. Hecht-Hill-Lancaster also presented a decent version of the Terence Rattigan play *Separate Tables*, but Lancaster took a back seat to the meatier, more interesting roles of David Niven, Deborah Kerr, et al. This film ended up with an Oscar nomination for Best Picture. He and Douglas were together again in a paired-down but lively rendering of Shaw's *The Devil's Disciple*, which allowed Lancaster to engage in a bit of two-fisted action, even though he was playing The Reverend Anderson. Alas it was chalked up as a failure, as was his teaming with Audrey Hepburn in the troubled western *The Unforgiven*, as the brother who is devastated to find out that she is a half-breed.

Then came the part that encapsulated all the brilliance, magnetism, and bravado of the actor, the title role of the bogus tent-show evangelist in *Elmer Gantry*. The film, a big, boisterously exciting cinematic rethinking of the Sinclair Lewis novel, was a huge hit, and Lancaster won a much-applauded Academy Award as Best Actor of 1960. After that he did the first of five directed by John Frankenheimer, *The Young Savages*, as a lawyer prosecuting a bunch of street hoods. The other four were *Birdman of Alcatraz*, another Lancaster peak, in which he gave an Oscar-nominated performance as an angry convict who becomes a gentle bird expert during a life-long stay behind bars; *Seven Days in May*, with the actor in a suave bad guy role, as a popular general trying to take over the government; *The Train*, in which he was a resistance leader trying to save some art work from the Nazis; and the only weak one of the bunch, *The Gypsy Moths*, as a traveling aerialist. Between these he was not at his best as a conscience-stricken Nazi in the otherwise exemplary *Judgment at Nuremberg*, but he gave a fine, understated performance in his own production, *A Child Is Waiting* (another sadly underrated failure), running an institution for mentally retarded children.

The expansive Italian production *The Leopard* cast him as the head of an aristocratic family and was heavily cut and dismantled over the years, nevertheless finding much favor among critics and with Lancaster himself, who proclaimed it among his best work. There was a badly misguided, overlong western comedy, *The Hallelujah Trail*, and a topnotch adventure film, *The Professionals*, which teamed him well with Lee Marvin. These were followed by one of the most interesting works of his career, *The Swimmer*, cast as a cocky, affluent suburbanite who swims his way home one afternoon, only to see all the failures of his life unfold before him. Needless to say, unadventurous audiences weren't about to line up for this one, but the playful western *The Scalphunters* did decently. His participation in *Airport*, as the head of same, kept him on top since it was one of the gigantic hits of the early 1970s, despite Lancaster's less than enthusiastic feelings about the film. Everything else that followed failed, including the westerns *Valdez Is Coming*, in which he was a grizzled old Mexican gunman, and *Ulzana's Raid*, which tried to make a statement in favor of the Indians.

He shared direction, script, and production credit on the routine cop film *The Midnight Man*, but its reception was no more illustrious than his last effort behind the lens. Another foray into foreign filmmaking, *Conversation Piece*, died the death after much editing and a long-delayed release date. It was time to go to television, where he played *Moses* in a mini-series that was actually edited down for distribution in theaters later on. On the big screen he was now relegated to the supporting cast for *Buffalo Bill and the Indians*, as the great showman's mythologizer, and *The Cassandra Crossing*, presiding over the disaster from afar, as he'd done in *Airport*, only this time the crowds stayed home. The leads that he did have included the crazed doctor in the unnecessary remake of *The Island of Dr. Moreau*; a former general holding weapons for ransom in *Twilight's Last Gleaming*; a military adviser serving in Vietnam in *Go Tell the Spartans*; and an aging outlaw in *Cattle Annie and Little Britches*. None of these fared well, which for the last two was a shame, for his own work was nicely commented on.

There was one last great film role to come, however, playing the petty gangster living in a changing *Atlantic City*. Both he and the film, a moody piece contrasting a dying world with a slicker soulless one, were superb, and Lancaster received some of the best notices of his career. Unfortunately, as was the fate of too many of his finest ventures, the movie only found an audience in select markets, though he did wind up with one last Oscar nomination and the sort of latter-day signature part all great actors deserve. Most of his subsequent work was on television, but there were two more leads on the big screen, *Tough Guys*, as a crook released into society after years in jail, a final teaming with Douglas that relied on cheap laughs, and the poorly distributed *Rocket Gibraltar*, as a dying patriarch. There were also supporting parts in two films that benefited greatly from his participation, *Local Hero*, as a businessman, and *Field of Dreams*, as the spirit of a dead ballplayer. When he appeared on screen in each, audiences knew immediately that they were in the hands of a confident performer, a presence larger than life, which ultimately is what being a movie star is all about.

Screen: 1946: The Killers; 1947: Brute Force; Desert Fury; Variety Girl; 1948: I Walk Alone; All My Sons; Sorry, Wrong Number; Kiss the Blood Off My Hands; 1949: Criss Cross; Rope of Sand; 1950: The Flame and the Arrow; Mister 880; 1951: Vengeance Valley; Jim Thorpe — All American; Ten Tall Men; 1952: The Crimson Pirate; Come Back, Little Sheba; 1953: South Sea Woman; From Here to Eternity; Three Sailors and a Girl; His Majesty O'Keefe; 1954: Apache; Vera Cruz; 1955: The Kentuckian (and dir.); The Rose Tattoo; 1956: Trapeze; The Rainmaker; 1957: Gunfight at the O.K. Corral; Sweet Smell of Success; 1958: Run Silent, Run Deep; Separate Tables; 1959: The Devil's Disciple; 1960: The Unforgiven; Elmer Gantry; 1961: The Young Savages; Judgment at Nuremberg; 1962: Birdman of Alcatraz; 1963: A Child Is Waiting; The List of Adrian Messenger; The Leopard; 1964: Seven Days in May; 1965: The Train; The Hallelujah Trail; 1966: The Professionals; 1968: The Scalphunters; The Swimmer; 1969: Castle Keep; The Gypsy Moths; 1970: Airport; King: A Filmed Record...Montgomery to Memphis; 1971: Valdez Is Coming; Lawman; 1972: Ulzana's Raid; 1973: Scorpio; Executive Action; 1974: The Midnight Man (and co-dir.; co-wr.; co-prod.); 1976: Buffalo Bill and the Indians, or Sitting Bull's History Lesson; 1977: Conversation Piece (filmed 1974); The Cassandra Crossing; Twilight's Last Gleaming; The Island of Dr. Moreau; 1900; 1978: Go Tell the Spartans; 1980: Zulu Dawn; 1981: Atlantic City; Cattle Annie and Little Britches; La Pelle/The Skin (nUSr); 1983: Local Hero; The Osterman Weekend; 1985: Little Treasure; 1986: Tough Guys; 1988: Rocket Gibraltar; 1989: Field of Dreams.

NY Stage: 1945: A Sound of Hunting.

Select TV: 1975: Moses the Lawgiver (ms; and theatrical in 1976); 1976: Victory at Entebbe; 1982: Marco Polo (ms); 1985: Scandal Sheet; 1986: On Wings of Eagles; Barnum; 1987: Control; 1988: Sins of the Fathers; 1989: The Jeweler's Shop; The Betrothed (Italian tv); 1990: The Phantom of the Opera; Voyage of Terror: The Achille Lauro Affair; 1991: Separate but Equal.

ELSA LANCHESTER

(ELIZABETH SULLIVAN)
BORN: LONDON, ENGLAND, OCTOBER 28, 1902.
DIED: DECEMBER 26, 1986.

A vibrantly batty actress, whose eyes popped and voice quavered, making her characters that much more eccentric and that much more delightful, Elsa Lanchester hailed from an unorthodox set of parents who did not believe in marriage. Her mother's name was Lanchester, hence the origin of Elsa's last name. As a child she took dancing classes, at one point studying under Isadora Duncan, then became an instructor herself. While still in her teens she opened an acting school for children that served as a theater/nightclub called "The Cave of Harmony." In 1922 Lanchester made her West End debut in *Thirty Minutes in a Street*, followed by several other productions including *Mr. Prohack*, in 1926, which featured Charles Laughton. Despite his homosexuality (which was not evident to her until a few years later), the two became man and wife in 1929, a union that lasted until his death in 1962. She began appearing in films, including three short comedies directed by Ivor Montagu, "Bluebottles," "The Tonic," and "Daydreams," then did another play with Laughton, *Payment Deferred*, which traveled to Broadway. Because of this, Laughton not only got a contract with Paramount but also got a chance to repeat his role in MGM's version of *Payment*, where Lanchester's part was played by Maureen O'Sullivan. Lanchester headed back to England, waiting for her husband to return for Alexander Korda's production of *The Private Lives of Henry VIII*, an incredibly popular film in which she had the funniest role, as Anne of Cleeves, beating an exasperated Henry in a game of cards.

Hollywood now took interest, and she came to MGM to play Clickett in *David Copperfield*, where she was supposed to be acting opposite Laughton as Micawber, until he was replaced by

W. C. Fields, upon Laughton's own request. That same year Lanchester played a very limited role that, curiously, would become perhaps her most famous, the Monster's mate in *Bride of Frankenstein*. There was also an intrusive opening prologue in which she was seen as Mary Shelley, but it was her tiny final scene, done up in an outrageous bouffant hairdo, hissing at Boris Karloff, that left an indelible impression on movie audiences. Lanchester followed this with two more teamings with Laughton, in *Rembrandt*, playing it absolutely straight as his housekeeper-mistress who provides the self-destructive artist with temporary happiness, and in *The Beachcomber/Vessel of Wrath*, a predecessor of *The African Queen*, as a missionary trying to reform crude beach bum Laughton in what was, no doubt, her most substantial, fulfilling big-screen assignment. In support, she was one of the weird sisters in *Ladies in Retirement*; the wife of symphony conductor Laughton in one of the better *Tales of Manhattan*; the bitchy mother of Roddy McDowall in the seminal family film *Lassie Come Home*; and the drunken cook in *The Spiral Staircase*. For RKO she got her sole top-billed role, as a charwoman intent on killing Hitler, in the "B" movie *Passport to Destiny*. Three of her best roles came in the late 1940s: the ditsy painter in *The Big Clock*, again in support of Laughton; her Oscar-nominated performance in *Come to the Stable*, once again as an artist, donating her stable to two nuns; and the Mayor's libidinous wife in the rollicking Danny Kaye comedy *The Inspector General*.

As the sort of character player who could be relied upon to provide some zing to even the least inspired of efforts she was Alan Young's henpecking wife in the flop film of Shaw's *Androcles and the Lion*, and donned whiskers to appear as The Bearded Lady in Martin and Lewis's *3 Ring Circus*. There was one last great role alongside Laughton, playing his relentlessly pushy nurse in *Witness for the Prosecution*, a part not in the original play. This was Lanchester's comic timing at its finest, and she should by all rights have won the Best Supporting Actress Oscar she was nominated for. She was appropriately cast as a ditsy witch (which in her later years was an apt description of her weird, bohemian look) in *Bell Book and Candle*, then did a one-woman show staged by her husband, *Elsa Lanchester — Herself*, shortly before Laughton's death. Throwing integrity to the winds, she took some broad roles in some idiotic comedies, *Honeymoon Hotel* and *Pajama Party*, and had a brief bit as the uppity nanny who quits at the beginning of the blockbuster musical *Mary Poppins*. This was done for Disney, and she stayed with them to play a nosy neighbor in *That Darn Cat!*; an old biddy in *Blackbeard's Ghost*; and a disagreeable housekeeper in *Rascal*. Going the horror route, she was Bruce Davison's mother who becomes rat food in *Willard*, and then had one last sizable role, spoofing Miss Marple, in the hit Neil Simon send-up *Murder by Death*. Her memoir, *Charles Laughton and I*, was published in 1939, but her contributions to Charles Higham's later bio on her husband are more frank and revealing about their often turbulent relationship.

Screen: 1927: One of the Best; 1928: The Constant Nymph; 1930: Comets; 1931: The Love Habit; The Stronger Sex; Her Strange Desire/Potiphar's Wife; The Officer's Mess; 1933: The Private Life of Henry VIII; 1935: David Copperfield; Naughty Marietta; Bride of Frankenstein; 1936: The Ghost Goes West; Rembrandt; 1938: The Beachcomber/Vessel of Wrath; 1941: Ladies in Retirement; 1942: Son of Fury; Tales of Manhattan; 1943: Forever and a Day; Thumbs Up; Lassie Come Home; 1944: Passport to Destiny; 1946: The Spiral Staircase; The Razor's Edge; 1947: Northwest Outpost; The Bishop's Wife; 1948: The Big Clock; 1949: The Secret Garden; Come to the Stable; The Inspector General; 1950: Buccaneer's Girl; Mystery Street; The Petty Girl; Frenchie; 1952: Dreamboat; Les Misérables; Androcles

and the Lion; 1953: The Girls of Pleasure Island; 1954: Hell's Half Acre; 3 Ring Circus; 1955: The Glass Slipper; 1957: Witness for the Prosecution; 1958: Bell Book and Candle; 1964: Honeymoon Hotel; Mary Poppins; Pajama Party; 1965: That Darn Cat!; 1967: Easy Come, Easy Go; 1968: Blackbeard's Ghost; 1969: Rascal; Me, Natalie; 1971: Willard; 1973: Arnold; Terror in the Wax Museum; 1976: Murder by Death; 1980: Die Laughing.

NY Stage: 1931: Payment Deferred; 1941: They Walk Alone; 1961: Elsa Lanchester — Herself (ob).

Select TV: 1953: Music and Mrs. Pratt (sp); The Baker of Barnbury (sp); 1955: Stage Door (sp); Heidi (sp); Alice in Wonderland (sp); 1956: Miss Mabel (sp); Stranger in the Night (sp); 1958: Mother Goose (sp); 1961: Cat in the Cradle (sp); 1965–66: The John Forsythe Show (series); 1969: My Dog, the Thief; In Name Only; 1971: Nanny and the Professor (series).

ELISSA LANDI
(ELIZABETH MARIE CHRISTINE KÜHNELT)
BORN: VENICE, ITALY, DECEMBER 6, 1904.
DIED: OCTOBER 21, 1948.

Born to aristocracy, Elissa Landi attained a period of steady employment for the first half of the 1930s, but despite her better efforts became one of Hollywood's less-celebrated stars of that decade. Supposedly descended from Franz Josef of Austria, her stepfather was an Italian count. She studied dance in England and made her stage debut in 1923 in *Dandy Dick*. After further work on the London stage, she became a star in England via such films as *Bolibar* and *Underground*, as a shopgirl in love with Brian Aherne. She continued to make films both in that country and elsewhere, including Sweden (*Sin*) and France (*The Parisian*), before venturing to America to star on the New York stage in a production of *A Farewell to Arms*. Because of it she was signed to a contract with Fox, who put her alongside Charles Farrell in the aviation drama *Body and Soul*. There were a few others — including *The Yellow Ticket* (her own favorite of her movies), in which she played a Jewish schoolteacher facing anti-Semitism in Czarist Russia; *Devil's Lottery*; and *The Woman in Room 13* — all of which, attendance-wise, only went to show the studio that perhaps they had made a mistake in signing her up. Paramount asked for her to play the heroine in DeMille's lush and silly *The Sign of the Cross*, but no one was watching her when Claudette Colbert and Charles Laughton were chewing up the scenery. Likewise, *The Masquerader* offered two Ronald Colmans to enjoy, and despite Landi ending up in a good and popular film like *The Count of Monte Cristo*, none of the credit was given to her. She returned to Europe for some films, then came back to Hollywood as a supporting player in *After the Thin Man*, as Myrna Loy's distraught cousin. Leads in the "B" films *The Thirteenth Chair* and *Corregidor* did nothing to reverse her fortunes, and she died of cancer when she was only 43. She authored the novels *Neilsen* (1925), *The Helmers* (1930), *House for Sale* (1933), *The Ancestor* (1934), and *The Pear Tree* (1944), as well as some plays.

Screen: 1926: London; 1928: Underground; Bolibar; 1929: The Inseparables; The Betrayal/Le Leurre sur la Cime; Sin; 1930: The Parisian; Knowing Men; 1931: The Price of Things; Children of Chance; Body and Soul; Always Goodbye; Wicked; The Yellow Ticket; 1932: Devil's Lottery; The Woman in Room 13; A Passport to Hell; The Sign of the Cross; 1933: The Masquerader; The Warrior's Husband; I Loved You Wednesday; By Candlelight; 1934: Sister Under the Sky; Man of Two Worlds; The Great Flirtation; The Count of Monte Cristo; 1935: Enter Madame; Without Regret; 1936: Koenigsmark/Crimson

Dynasty; The Amateur Gentleman; Mad Holiday; After the Thin Man; 1937: The Thirteenth Chair; 1943: Corregidor.

NY Stage: 1930: A Farewell to Arms; 1935: Tapestry in Gray; 1937: The Lady Has a Heart; 1938: The Empress of Destiny; 1943: Apology; 1944: The Dark Hammock.

CAROLE LANDIS

(FRANCES LILLIAN MARY RIDSTE)
BORN: FAIRCHILD, WI, JANUARY 1, 1919.
DIED: JULY 5, 1948.

Yet another of Hollywood's long list of unhappy endings, Carole Landis was a World War II pinup favorite with a lot of mediocre films to her credit, good looks, and a thoroughly undistinguished acting talent. Starting her professional career as a San Francisco nightclub dancer, she made her way to Hollywood at 18 and began getting bits in pictures like *Boy Meets Girl*, as a cashier; *Gold Diggers in Paris*, as one of the diggers; and *Hollywood Hotel*, as a hat check girl. She got a bigger part in one of the "Three Mesquiteers" westerns, *Cowboys From Texas*, but it wasn't until Hal Roach hired her that she became a star. For him she was a cave girl in the fairly silly *One Million B.C.*; a wife swapping personalities with her husband in *Turnabout*; and a carnival owner named Penguin in *Road Show*. Since everyone agreed that she had nice legs, her capabilities as an actress seemed of secondary interest. 20th Century-Fox added her to their roster to play the murder victim in *I Wake Up Screaming*, perhaps her most popular film, due to its star, Betty Grable; a band singer in the cheapie *Cadet Girl*; an art shop manager in *A Gentleman at Heart*; an entertainer helping to fight the Japanese in *Manila Calling*; and an inspector in *It Shouldn't Happen to a Dog*. She was strictly "B" material and was continuing on this level elsewhere after the studio dropped her, when she was found dead from an overdose of sleeping pills. She was said to be despondent over the breakup of her affair with Rex Harrison, causing a great deal of scandal within the industry, and prompting Harrison to return to England to avoid the fallout.

Screen: 1937: A Star Is Born; A Day at the Races; Broadway Melody of 1938; The Adventurous Blonde; Alcatraz Island; The Emperor's Candlesticks; Varsity Show; 1938: Hollywood Hotel; Blondes at Work; Gold Diggers in Paris; Boy Meets Girl; Men Are Such Fools; Girls on Probation; A Slight Case of Murder; Over the Wall; Four's a Crowd; When Were You Born?; Love, Honor and Behave; 1939: Daredevils of the Red Circle (serial); Reno; Three Texas Steers; Cowboys From Texas; 1940: One Million B.C.; Turnabout; Mystery Sea Raider; 1941: Road Show; Topper Returns; Dance Hall; Moon Over Miami; I Wake Up Screaming; Cadet Girl; 1942: A Gentleman at Heart; It Happened in Flatbush; My Gal Sal; Orchestra Wives; Manila Calling; The Powers Girl; 1943: Wintertime; 1944: Secret Command; Four Jills in a Jeep; 1945: Having Wonderful Crime; 1946: Behind Green Lights; It Shouldn't Happen to a Dog; Scandal in Paris; 1947: Out of the Blue; 1948: The Silk Noose/Noose; Lucky Mascot/The Brass Monkey.

NY Stage: 1945: A Lady Says Yes.

JESSIE ROYCE LANDIS

(JESSIE ROYCE MEDBURY) BORN: CHICAGO, IL, NOVEMBER 25, 1904. DIED: FEBRUARY 2, 1972.

A bright supporting player, Jessie Royce Landis had a whole slew of theater credits to her name when she came to Hollywood in 1949 to corner the market on playing snooty or dizzy moms, the sort of ladies who wore pearl necklaces and gloves and had chatty lunches with their friends. She made her Broadway debut in 1926 in *Honor of the Family*, and her credits there would include *Merrily We Roll Along*, *Love's Old Sweet Song*, and *Kiss and Tell*, she being one of those lucky actors who seemed to go from play to play with nary a break in between. There was a sole movie credit in 1930, in Paramount's *Derelict*, opposite George Bancroft, but nearly 20 years passed before she came west to play Tom Drake's mom in *Mr. Belvedere Goes to College*. She was then the mother of Susan Hayward (*My Foolish Heart*), Grace Kelly (*To Catch a Thief*, stubbing out her cigarette in a soft-boiled egg in homage to director Alfred Hitchcock who claimed to have hated them), Tab Hunter (*The Girl He Left Behind*), and Anthony Perkins (*Goodbye Again*). There was no need for Universal to remake *My Man Godfrey* in 1957, but since it did, Landis was the perfect choice to follow in the footsteps of the inimitable Alice Brady as the scatterbrained matriarch. She also had a memorable part as Cary Grant's mom, casually asking his kidnappers if they were trying to kill her son, in *North by Northwest*. It must have been dismaying to her, however, that she was playing the mother of an actor she was several months younger than. She was last seen on the big screen as the pretentious lady trying to smuggle jewels aboard a plane in her dog's necklace, in the blockbuster hit *Airport*, released two years before her death from cancer.

Screen: 1930: Derelict; 1949: Mr. Belvedere Goes to College; It Happens Every Spring; My Foolish Heart; 1950: Mother Didn't Tell Me; 1952: Tonight at 8:30/Meet Me Tonight; 1955: To Catch a Thief; 1956: The Girl He Left Behind; The Swan; 1957: My Man Godfrey; 1958: I Married a Woman; 1959: North by Northwest; A Private Affair; 1961: Goodbye Again; 1962: Bon Voyage!; Boys' Night Out; 1963: Critic's Choice; Gidget Goes to Rome; 1970: Airport.

NY Stage: 1926: The Honor of the Family; 1928: Command Performance; 1929: Young Alexander; Stripped; Damn Your Honor; 1930: Solid South; 1931: Colonel Satan; Peter Ibbetson; Marriage for Three; Little Women; 1932: Domino; 1933: Before Morning; 1934: Merrily We Roll Along; 1935: Substitute for Murder; 1936: Pre-Honeymoon; Love From a Stranger; 1937: Miss Quis; 1938: Dame Nature; 1939: Where There's a Will; The Brown Danube; 1940: Love's Old Sweet Song; 1942: Papa Is All; 1943: Kiss and Tell; 1946: The Winter's Tale; 1947: Little A; 1948: The Last Dance; 1949: Magnolia Alley; 1953: Richard III; 1954: Sing Me No Lullaby; 1956: Someone Waiting; 1964: Roar Like a Dove; I Knock at the Door (ob).

Select TV: 1953: Fadeout (sp); Lost Tour (sp); 1954: Papa Is All (sp); Late Date (sp); 1956: Career Girl (sp); 1960: A Girl in the Gold Bathtub (sp); 1971: Mr. and Mrs. Bo Jo Jones; 1972: The Ceremony of Innocence (sp).

PRISCILLA LANE

(PRISCILLA MULLICAN)
BORN: INDIANOLA, IA, JUNE 12, 1917.
ED: SIMPSON COL. DIED: APRIL 4, 1995.

She was one of a trio of acting sisters who came to prominence through a gimmick bit of casting, but Pricilla Lane had the most engaging personality of the group and therefore reached a higher level of fame. Following Lola (1909–81) and Rosemary (1913–74), she was the youngest, and it was with Rosemary that she sang with Fred Waring's Pennsylvanians. When that group came to Hollywood in 1937 to appear in the Warner Bros. musical *Varsity Show*, Priscilla made her film debut. The studio immediately made her the leading lady to Wayne Morris in two minor films,

Love, Honor and Behave and *Men Are Such Fools*, as an ambitious secretary, but the one that made her famous was *Four Daughters*, in which she, Lola, and Rosemary (plus Gale Page) were on-screen sisters in a well-written look at the small town lives of a music professor's family. Priscilla was the one in love with John Garfield, and it was the two of them who stood out from the ensemble with their subtle and believable playing. Lane was upped to top billing for the male-dominated military comedy *Brother Rat*, and then played the singer who breaks James Cagney's heart in one of the big successes of 1939, *The Roaring Twenties*. There were the inevitable sequels to *Daughters*, namely *Daughters Courageous*, *Four Wives*, and *Four Mothers*, and one for *Brother Rat* as well. Before she left the studio she did one of her best-remembered films, *Arsenic and Old Lace*, as Cary Grant's fiancée, providing a nice degree of sanity to the loony antics on hand. Off the lot she started well by landing the lead in a good Hitchcock thriller, *Saboteur*, helping innocent man-on-the-run Robert Cummings, but soon she and Hollywood mutually lost interest, and she retired in 1948. She was last seen trying to clear Lawrence Tierney's name in an RKO melodrama, *Bodyguard*.

Screen: 1937: Varsity Show; 1938: Love, Honor and Behave; Cowboy From Brooklyn; Men Are Such Fools; Four Daughters; Brother Rat; 1939: Yes, My Darling Daughter; Daughters Courageous; Dust Be My Destiny; The Roaring Twenties; Four Wives; 1940: Three Cheers for the Irish; Brother Rat and a Baby; Ladies Must Live; 1941: Four Mothers; Million Dollar Baby; Blues in the Night; 1942: Saboteur; Silver Queen; 1943: The Meanest Man in the World; 1944: Arsenic and Old Lace; 1947: Fun on a Weekend; 1948: Bodyguard.

HARRY LANGDON
BORN: COUNCIL BLUFFS, IA, JUNE 15, 1884.
DIED: DECEMBER 22, 1944.

Pale, baby-faced comedian Harry Langdon belonged exclusively to the silent cinema, and despite his one-time popularity, he is not quite in the same class as Chaplin, Keaton, and Lloyd, as many once tried to place him. His actions are that of a blank-faced innocent, and his characterization is rather grotesque and somewhat cutesy by today's standards. A veteran of the medicine show and minstrel circuits, he joined a vaudeville act called "Johnny's New Car," which consisted of a collapsible auto. It was with this group that he met Rose Mensoff, who, in 1903, became his wife. Staying in vaudeville for some 20 years, he was finally asked to join Mack Sennett for some short films, starting with "Picking Peaches," in 1924, and taking him to "Soldier Man" two years later. One of the chief writers of these comedies was a young Frank Capra, who chose to emphasize the more human side of Langdon rather than overwhelm him with gags. These shorts made Langdon popular enough that he accepted an offer from First National to make features, of which *Tramp, Tramp, Tramp*, about a foot race, was the first. This was followed by two that Capra himself directed, *The Strong Man*, with Langdon as a Belgian soldier who comes to America to find his pen pal during the war, and *Long Pants*, which cast the 43-year-old as a daydreaming teen who wants to cut his mother's apron strings. All three did good business.

It was at this point that the comedian decided he would dispose of Capra and his frequent director Harry Edwards. As a result he helmed three features for himself: the highly sentimental *Three's a Crowd*; *The Chaser*, swapping places with his estranged wife; and the spy spoof *Heart Trouble*. All of these promptly turned the critics against him and saw rapidly dwindling audi-

ences. His descent was swift and painful. Hal Roach hired him for eight two-reelers that were his introduction to talkies, but the alliance was short-lived and unprofitable. There was a pair of features, *See America Thirst*, where he teamed with lanky Slim Summerville, and *A Soldier's Plaything*, in which his part was more or less secondary to Ben Lyon. It was clear that the comedian's days as a big-screen attraction were over. He went back to vaudeville and then, badly in need of money, accepted an offer to appear in some shorts for the poverty-row company Educational Pictures. These were followed by two-reelers for Paramount and then Columbia, for whom he would work up to his death. In the meantime he supported Al Jolson in the strange, all-rhyming box-office flop, *Hallelujah, I'm a Bum*, which, ironically, would become Langdon's most widely available title in later years. Roach also utilized him as a gag writer (*A Chump at Oxford*, *Road Show*, *Saps at Sea*) and even placed him opposite Oliver Hardy in a mild comedy minus Stan Laurel, *Zenobia*, with Langdon as an elephant owner. After that it was down to Monogram Pictures, first in leads, then in support of the East Side Kids in *Block Busters*. He died, in virtual poverty, of a cerebral hemorrhage.

Screen (shorts): 1924: Picking Peaches; Smile Please; Feet of Mud; Shanghaied Lovers; Flickering Youth; The Luck of the Foolish; All Night Long; The Cat's Meow; His New Mamma; The First Hundred Years; The Hansom Cabman; 1925: Boobs in the Wood; Plain Clothes; Lucky Stars; There He Goes; The Sea Squawk; His Marriage Wow; Remember When?; Horace Greeley Junior; The White Wing's Bride; 1926: Saturday Alfternoon; Soldier Man; 1927: Fiddlesticks; 1929: Hotter Than Hot; Shy Boy; Skirt Shy; 1930 : The Head Guy; The Fighting Parson; The Big Kick; The King; The Shrimp; 1932: The Big Flash; 1933: Amateur Night; The Hitch Hiker; Knight Duty; Tied for Life; Hooks and Jabs; Tired Feet; Marriage Humor; The Stage Hand (and wr.); Leave It to Dad; 1934: No Sleep on the Deep; On Ice; A Roaming Romeo; A Circus Hoodoo; Petting Preferred; Council on De Fence; Trimmed in Furs; Shivers; Hollywood on Parade B-6; 1935: The Leather Necker; His Marriage Mix-Up; His Bridal Sweet; I Don't Remember; 1938: A Doggone Mixup; Sue My Lawyer (and wr.); 1940: Sitting Pretty; Goodness a Ghost (and wr.); Cold Turkey; 1941: Beautiful Clothes; 1942: What Makes Lizzie Dizzy; Carry Harry; Piano Mooner (and wr.); Tireman, Spare My Tires; 1943: A Blitz on the Fritz; Here Comes Mr. Zerk; Blonde and Groom (and wr.); 1944: Mopey Dope; Defective Detectives; To Heir Is Human; 1945: Pistol Packin' Nitwits (and co-wr.); Snooper Service.

Screen (features): 1926: Ella Cinders; Tramp, Tramp, Tramp; The Strong Man; Long Pants; 1927: His First Flame; Three's a Crowd (and dir.); The Chaser (and dir.); Heart Trouble (and dir.; wr.); 1930: See America Thirst; A Soldier's Plaything; 1933: Hallelujah, I'm a Bum; My Weakness; 1935: Atlantic Adventure; 1937: He Loved an Actress/Mad About Money; 1938: There Goes My Heart; 1939: Zenobia; 1940: Misbehaving Husbands; 1941: All-American Co-ed; Double Trouble; 1942: House of Errors (and co-wr.); 1943: Spotlight Scandals; 1944: Hot Rhythm; Block Busters; 1945: Swingin' on a Rainbow.

HOPE LANGE
BORN: REDDING RIDGE, CT, NOVEMBER 28, 1931.

A very comforting, sensible presence, Hope Lange was not, unfortunately, considered star material on the big screen and had to be content with secondary or supporting roles. The daughter of a musician and an actress, she was 11 when she made her Broadway debut, in *The Patriots*.

Under orders of her parents, she took a break from the business until she resumed acting in 1950. A good deal of stock work and some early television (including two stints as a game show assistant) followed before she was signed to a contract by 20th Century-Fox, in 1956. She started off well, playing a young woman who befriends Marilyn Monroe while traveling by bus in *Bus Stop*, and also marrying the leading man, Don Murray, that same year (earlier in 1956 he had starred in the Broadway flop *The Hot Corner*, in which Lange served as an understudy). This was shortly followed by the role of the dirt-poor daughter, who kills sleazy father Arthur Kennedy after he rapes her, in *Peyton Place*, giving one of the better performances in this over-heated movie and earning an Oscar nomination in the supporting category. She was rewarded with the role of Montgomery Clift's love interest in the engrossing World War II epic *The Young Lions*, and then, in a similar fashion, loved another soldier, Jeffrey Hunter, in *In Love and War*. Staying in ensemble casts, she was Joan Crawford's secretary in the glossy soap *The Best of Everything*, and the counselor who rescues Elvis Presley in *Wild in the Country*. She divorced Murray in 1961, then played the lead, opposite Glenn Ford, in *Love Is a Ball*, a comedy that was more popular in later years due to repeated television showings than in its initial release in the movies. She temporarily retired in 1963 when she married director Alan J. Pakula, but returned triumphantly to television in the sitcom version of *The Ghost and Mrs. Muir*, winning a pair of Emmy Awards. She spent a majority of her later career on TV, although there were occasional movies roles, including *Death Wish*, as Charles Bronson's wife who is horribly assaulted, thereby setting the plot in motion; *Blue Velvet*, as Laura Dern's mom (a fairly worthless part); and *Clear and Present Danger*, as a senator. She and Pakula divorced in 1969. In 1977 she returned to Broadway, opposite ex-husband Murray, in *Same Time, Next Year*.

Screen: 1956: Bus Stop; 1957: The True Story of Jesse James; Peyton Place; 1958: The Young Lions; In Love and War; 1959: The Best of Everything; 1961: Wild in the Country; Pocketful of Miracles; 1963: Love Is a Ball; 1968: Jigsaw; 1974: Death Wish; 1983: I Am the Cheese; 1984: The Prodigal; 1985: A Nightmare on Elm Street 2: Freddy's Revenge; 1986: Blue Velvet; 1990: Tune in Tomorrow…; 1994: Clear and Present Danger; 1995: Just Cause.

NY Stage: 1943: The Patriots; 1977: Same Time, Next Year; 1981: The Supporting Cast.

Select TV: 1953: Back That Fact (series); 1954–55: The Sky's the Limit (series); 1956: Snap Finger Creek (sp); 1957: For I Have Loved Strangers (sp); 1958: Point of No Return (sp); The Innocent Sleep (sp); 1962: Cyrano de Bergerac (sp); 1966: Shipwrecked (sp); 1967: Dear Friends (sp); 1968–70: The Ghost and Mrs. Muir (series); 1970: Crowhaven Farm; 1971–74: The New Dick Van Dyke Show (series); 1972: That Certain Summer; 1973: The 500 Pound Jerk; 1974: I Love You — Goodbye; Ferde-Lance; 1975: The Secret Night Caller; 1977: The Love Boat II; 1979: Like Normal People; 1980: The Day Christ Died; Beulah Land (ms); Pleasure Palace; 1985: Private Sessions; 1987: Ford: The Man and the Machine; 1989: Knight & Daye (series); 1993: Dead Before Dawn; Cooperstown; Danielle Steel's Message from Nam; 1998: Before He Wakes.

FRANCES LANGFORD

BORN: LAKELAND, FL, APRIL 4, 1914.
ED: SOUTHERN COL.

Generally thought of as a singer, diminutive, blonde Frances Langford also had a substantial number of movies to her credit, and, in many of them, she got to sell some pretty memorable Hollywood showstoppers. Having sung in vaudeville, in nightclubs, on radio, in a short subject, "The Subway Symphony," and on Broadway, she made a most auspicious feature movie debut in 1935's *Every Night at Eight*, introducing one of the enduring songs of all, "I'm in the Mood for Love." Later that same year she helped perform two more gems, "You Are My Lucky Star" and "Broadway Rhythm" in *Broadway Melody of 1936*. This pretty much set the pattern, with Langford called on for her voice so that little attention was paid to her acting limitations. Therefore, her starring vehicles, *Palm Springs*, as the daughter of an impoverished earl, and *The Hit Parade*, as a parolee-turned-singer, were greeted less than rapturously. Back to support, she helped sing "Over There" with James Cagney in *Yankee Doodle Dandy*, and was given the solo "What Does He Look Like?", among others, in the patriotic smash *This Is the Army*. All the while she had great success on the radio and helped to entertain the servicemen during World War II, reenacting this by playing herself in the 1954 biopic *The Glenn Miller Story*. Outside of her success as a vocalist she is probably most cherished by radio fans for starring opposite Don Ameche in the series *The Bickersons*, as the distaff half of a perpetually sniping couple. There was a marriage (1938–55) to actor Jon Hall (they appeared together in the film *Deputy Marshal*), followed by another to a millionaire, which enabled her to basically retire and limit her entertaining exclusively to her own Florida resort.

Screen: 1935: Every Night at Eight; Broadway Melody of 1936; 1936: Collegiate; Palm Springs; Born to Dance; 1937: The Hit Parade of 1937/I'll Reach for a Star; 1938: Hollywood Hotel; 1940: Dreaming Out Loud; Too Many Girls; Hit Parade of 1941; 1941: Swing It Soldier; All American Co-Ed; 1942: Mississippi Gambler; Yankee Doodle Dandy; 1943: Follow the Band; Cowboy in a Manhattan; Never a Dull Moment; This Is the Army; 1944: The Girl Rush; Dixie Jamboree; Career Girl; 1945: Radio Stars on Parade; 1946: People Are Funny; The Bamboo Blonde; 1947: Beat the Band; 1948: Melody Time (voice); 1949: Deputy Marshal; Make Mine Laughs; 1951: Purple Heart Diary; 1954: The Glenn Miller Story.

NY Stage: 1931: Here Goes the Bride; 1934: The Purple in Heart.

Select TV: 1950–51: Star Time (series); 1951–52: The Frances Langford-Don Ameche Show (series).

ANGELA LANSBURY

BORN: LONDON, ENGLAND, OCTOBER 16, 1925.

The success of Angela Lansbury was so instantaneously that it may have seemed that her subsequent career would be an anti-climax. Nothing was further from the truth. Without ever being a great beauty or a genuine box-office star, and despite lulls and misuses of her abilities, she maintained an impressive career for more than a half a century, amassing awards, raves, and the sort of stardom and appreciation her one-time contemporaries could never have hoped to achieve. The daughter of actress Moyna MacGill, she enrolled at the Webber-Douglas School of Singing and Dramatic Art, before her mother decided to abandon war-torn London and settle in the U.S. Lansbury continued her dramatic studies and worked up a nightclub act that she did in Montreal. When her mother went to Los Angeles to find film work, Angela joined her, eventually landing a role in *Gaslight*. She added some needed spunk to the film, as a cockney maid, looking older than her 18 years, and nabbed not only a contract with MGM but also a surprise Oscar nomination for Best Supporting Actress of 1944. As if this weren't enough, she was up for the award the very next year as well, for a far more impressive performance, playing the sad music-hall singer, Sibyl Vane, in the studio's fine adaptation of *The Picture of Dorian Gray*. Instead of boosting her to the star category, MGM let her be Elizabeth Taylor's restless older sister in *National Velvet*; a bitchy nightclub entertainer in the hit musical *The Harvey Girls*; and an especially unpleasant wife to Walter Pigeon in the soapy *If Winter Comes*. There was a song highlight, "How'd You Like to Spoon With Me?" in the all-star Jerome Kern tribute, *Till the Clouds Roll By*, and then she was supposed to be a bad lady again, in *The Three Musketeers*, playing Milady, but MGM foolishly gave the part to Lana Turner, reducing Lansbury to the less-demanding role of Queen Anne.

Staying in support, she had a good role, scheming for political power, in the Tracy-Hepburn drama-comedy *State of the Union*, then went over to Paramount to be on the receiving end of a spear in the blockbuster *Samson and Delilah*. There was no doubt that she was an asset to everything she was in, effortlessly outshining some of the star-level women she supported, like Turner, Esther Williams, or Hedy Lamarr. After her MGM contract ended with a Van Johnson movie, *Remains to Be Seen*, she seemed to be fading from view. There were nothing roles, in the Tony Curtis swashbuckler *The Purple Mask* and a Randolph Scott western *A Lawless Street*; a secondary part as an aloof princess in the Danny Kaye comedy *The Court Jester*; and top billing in a quickly forgotten "B," *Please Murder Me*. Supporting parts in *The Reluctant Debutante*, marvelously funny as a gossipy "friend" of Kay Kendall, and *The Long Hot Summer*, very restrained and likable as Orson Welles's mistress, seemed to remind Hollywood that this exceedingly talented lady should not go to waste.

There was a sizable role, as the girlfriend of John Mills in the Australian-made *Season of Passion/Summer of the 17th Doll*, and then she was at her very best as the beautician with words of wisdom for Dorothy McGuire in *The Dark at the Top of the Stairs*, and as the deadly mom of Laurence Harvey (she was only three years older than him in real life) in the weirdly hypnotic *The Manchurian Candidate*. The last-named especially proved that she just kept getting better and better, and she earned a third, much-deserved Oscar nomination. (Her performance, like that in another of her 1962 releases, *All Fall Down*, hinted at a mother's rather unsavory feelings for her offspring.) Thanks to these she could certainly be forgiven for her shamelessly hammy turn as Elvis Presley's pinheaded mamma in one of his money-makers, *Blue Hawaii*. By this point she had already gotten raves for her work on Broadway, as Joan Plowright's mom (another performer only a few years younger than Lansbury), in *A Taste of Honey*, and returned to movies to give another impressive performance, as the bored New York wife committing adultery with egotistical pianist Peter Sellers in *The World of Henry Orient*. It was good to have her around for the less crummy of the concurrent films about *Harlow*, as Carroll Baker's mama; the flat farce *The Amorous Adventures of Moll Flanders*, as a society lady; and the intriguing *Mister Buddwing*, as one of the neurotics encountered by amnesiac James Garner.

With a single role she became one of the great ladies of Broadway, playing the stylish, life-loving *Mame* in the hit musical version of *Auntie Mame*. She earned a much-applauded Tony Award and followed it by nabbing three more of the coveted trophies, for *Dear World*, the revival of *Gypsy*, and *Sweeney Todd: The Demon Barber of Fleet Street*. Thanks to these the New York theater community embraced her as one of the reigning performers of the American stage, making her a bigger star than she'd ever been considered in motion pictures. Because of her newfound status, Hollywood was briefly re-interested and gave her the lead in a bizarre, underrated black comedy, *Something for Everyone*, as

an impoverished countess hungry for young servant Michael York, and in Disney's mediocre musical *Bedknobs and Broomsticks*, as a would-be witch. She did some outrageous scene-chewing as a gaudily weird novelist in the Agatha Christie thriller *Death on the Nile*, and then stayed with Christie to play Miss Marple in the less-popular *The Mirror Crack'd*. There was another musical part, as Ruth, in the spirited, studio-bound adaptation of *The Pirates of Penzance*, and then, just when most actresses her age would have retired, the role of amateur sleuth Jessica Fletcher in the amazingly successful TV series *Murder, She Wrote*, which ran an unexpected 11 seasons, with Lansbury ultimately becoming executive producer as well. During the run she introduced the Oscar-winning title song in Disney's animated classic *Beauty and the Beast*, supplying the voice for an enchanted teapot. There was an exercise book and video for seniors, *Positive Moves*, and a made for television musical, *Mrs. Santa Clause*, in which she was just as warm and enchanting as ever. Her brothers Bruce and Edgar Lansbury both became producers. Her first marriage (1945–46) was to actor Richard Cromwell.

Screen: 1944: Gaslight; 1945: National Velvet; The Picture of Dorian Gray; 1946: The Harvey Girls; The Hoodlum Saint; 1947: Till the Clouds Roll By; The Private Affairs of Bel Ami; If Winter Comes; 1948: Tenth Avenue Angel; State of the Union; The Three Musketeers; 1949: The Red Danube; Samson and Delilah; 1951: Kind Lady; 1952: Mutiny; 1953: Remains to Be Seen; 1954: Key Man/A Life at Stake; 1955: The Purple Mask; A Lawless Street; 1956: Please Murder Me; The Court Jester; 1958: The Reluctant Debutante; The Long Hot Summer; 1960: The Dark at the Top of the Stairs; A Breath of Scandal; 1961: Blue Hawaii; Season of Passion/Summer of the 17th Doll (Australia 1959); 1962: The Four Horsemen of the Apocalypse (voice); All Fall Down; The Manchurian Candidate; 1963: In the Cool of the Day; 1964: The World of Henry Orient; Dear Heart; 1965: The Greatest Story Ever Told; Harlow; The Amorous Adventures of Moll Flanders; 1966: Mister Buddwing; 1970: Something for Everyone; 1971: Bedknobs and Broomsticks; 1978: Death on the Nile; 1980: The Lady Vanishes; The Mirror Crack'd; 1981: The Last Unicorn (voice); 1983: The Pirates of Penzance; 1985: The Company of Wolves; 1991: Beauty and the Beast (voice); 1997: Anastasia (voice); Beauty and the Beast: The Enchanted Christmas (dtv); 2000: Fantasia 2000.

NY Stage: 1957: Hotel Paradiso; 1960: A Taste of Honey; 1964: Anyone Can Whistle; 1966: Mame; 1969: Dear World; 1974: Gypsy; 1978: The King and I; 1979: Sweeney Todd: The Demon Barber of Fleet Street; 1982: A Little Family Business; 1983: Mame (revival).

Select TV: 1950: The Citadel (sp); The Wonderful Night (sp); 1952: Stone's Throw (sp); 1953: Cakes and Ale (sp); Dreams Never Lie (sp); The Ming Lama (sp); 1954: A String of Beads (sp); The Crime of Daphne Rutledge (sp); 1955: Madeira! Madeira! (sp); The Indiscreet Mrs. Jarvis (sp); Billy and the Bride (sp); 1956: The Rarest Stamp (sp); 1956: The Force of Circumstance (sp); Instant of Truth (sp); Claire (sp); The Brown Leather Case (sp); 1957: The Devil's Brook (sp); 1958: Verdict of Three (sp); 1959: The Grey Nurse Said Nothing (sp); 1982: Little Gloria…Happy at Last; 1983: Sweeney Todd: The Demon Barber of Fleet Street (sp); The Gift of Love: A Christmas Story; 1984: Lace (ms); The First Olympics: Athens 1896 (ms); A Talent for Murder; 1984–95: Murder, She Wrote (series); 1986: Rage of Angels: The Story Continues; 1988: Shootdown; 1989: The Shell Seekers; 1990: The Love She Sought; 1992: Mrs. 'arris Goes to Paris; 1996: Mrs. Santa Claus; 1997: Murder, She Wrote: South by Southwest; 1999: The Unexpected Mrs. Pollifax; 2000: Murder, She Wrote: A Story to Die For; 2001: Murder, She Wrote: The Last Free Man.

MARIO LANZA

(ALFRED ARNOLD COCCOZA) BORN: PHILADELPHIA, PA, JANUARY 31, 1921. DIED: OCTOBER 7, 1959.

The soaring tenor voice of Mario Lanza made him one of the legendary names in music, and Hollywood was quick to cash in on his success. His career was brief, and his output unvaried, while his unruly behavior towards his colleagues branded him as one of the most unpleasant cases of ego run amok in the history of the business. He trained to be an opera singer as a boy, but was already becoming a trouble-maker, being expelled from high school shortly before graduation. Through his music teacher he auditioned for and received a scholarship to study and perform at the Berkshire Music Festival at Tanglewood in Massachusetts. He was inducted into the Army, which led to his joining the chorus of the touring show *Winged Victory*. Coming to Hollywood with it, he was one of the few stars-to-be that didn't end up in Fox's 1944 film version. In any event, in the postwar 1940s, he began to build a reputation as a recording artist and concert performer. It was one of his concerts at the Hollywood Bowl that caught the attention of MGM executives who signed him to a contract. Producer Joe Pasternak, who had a thing for operettas and trained voices, was the obvious choice to guide Lanza through his debut. *That Midnight Kiss* found him as a singing truck driver with aspirations towards opera, a Hollywoodized version of how Lanza himself went from piano mover to star. It was the usual Pasternak mishmash of song and corn, leadenly directed by Norman Taurog, with the star singing "Celeste Aida" and joining Kathryn Grayson for "They Didn't Believe Me." The box-office response was encouraging but not outstanding.

Lanza and Grayson were teamed again for *The Toast of New Orleans*, their most memorable moment being their duet of the beautiful "Be My Love," which became one of Lanza's best-known numbers. This was followed by the biopic of Lanza's boyhood idol, Enrico Caruso, and, although it was just as glossy and suspect in accuracy as any Hollywood look at the life of a famous performer, it was reasonably entertaining and the biggest hit Lanza ever had. The next one, *Because You're Mine*, put him in the Army and had him sing "The Lord's Prayer," among other numbers. He was unhappy, however, with the material, and his uncouth behavior on set was making him a terror to work with. In fact, he proved so thoroughly uncooperative during the making of *The Student Prince* that he was fired from the film and only his vocals used. His replacement, Edmund Purdom, was so stiff that he made Lanza seem positively breathtaking as an actor. MGM got rid of Lanza, but he was back before the cameras with *Serenade* for Warners, and then two made in Europe for a production company called Titanus, *Seven Hills of Rome* and *For the First Time*. Oddly enough they wound up being distributed in America by MGM. By the time the last film was released, Lanza had died in Rome of a heart attack at age 38. He had been drinking heavily and suffered from weight problems.

Screen: **1949:** That Midnight Kiss; **1950:** The Toast of New Orleans; **1951:** The Great Caruso; **1952:** Because You're Mine; **1954:** The Student Prince (voice); **1956:** Serenade; **1958:** Seven Hills of Rome; **1959:** For the First Time.

CHARLES LAUGHTON

BORN: SCARBOROUGH, ENGLAND, JULY 1, 1899. ED: STONYHURST COL., RADA. DIED: DECEMBER 15, 1962.

Versatile, inimitable, unforgettable, Charles Laughton was one of the most colorful and exciting of all actors to have graced motion picture screens. Fleshy, with a jowly face and beady eyes, he was nobody's idea of your average leading man, but there was no doubt that he was nothing less than a star, from the minute he set foot in Hollywood. Because he wasn't afraid to go to any and all extremes with a part, he was accused of being a real lip-smacking ham at times, when in fact he was simply making sure that if anyone was going to make an impression in the good, bad, or indifferent material on hand, he would be the one. On many occasions he was nothing less than superb, though several of his colleagues wondered if all the suffering, methodical self-analysis, and on-set dissension was worth it. Following military service in World War II, he studied at RADA, which led to a brief bit in a production of *Liliom*. He became a busy player of London's West End in such works as *The Great Love*; *Mr. Prohack*, which featured Elsa Lanchester, whom he married in 1929; *A Man With Red Hair*; and his greatest triumph of them all, *On the Spot*, where he played a deranged killer. It was with Lanchester that he was first seen on screen, in a pair of short subjects, "Bluebottles" and "Daydreams," after which he had a tiny part, indulging in a meal, in his feature debut, *Piccadilly*. He and Lanchester were back onstage in *Payment Deferred*, which, despite a mild West End response, traveled to Broadway in 1931, where its run was equally short-lived. Nevertheless, MGM bought the rights to the play with the intention of Laughton repeating his role, though it was Paramount with whom Laughton actually signed a contract. They started him off in the highly melodramatic *Devil and the Deep*, as a vengeful submarine commander jealous of wife Tallulah Bankhead's interest in Gary Cooper. Prior to this he had been loaned out to Universal to play one of the more normal characters in the eccentric *The Old Dark House*, and then to MGM for the film of *Payment Deferred*, where he was excellent as the tormented murderer who sees his fortunes change for the better after he gets away with his crime.

Not slowing down for a second, he was Nero in Cecil B. DeMille's wildly undisciplined epic, *The Sign of the Cross*, giving perhaps the screen's first consciously campy performance. He had a priceless few minutes as a meek employee getting his revenge, in the best sequence of the multipart *If I Had a Million*, and was a broodingly weird mad scientist experimenting with turning animals into men in the truly creepy *Island of Lost Souls*, a failure in its day but certainly one of the most effective of all 1930s horror thrillers. He made a very productive return to England in 1933, to film *The Private Life of Henry VIII* for producer Alexander Korda, giving a full-bodied, earthy, and altogether marvelous performance as the egotistical King, tapping into both the serious and comical sides of his marital life. The movie became the most popular British import to play in the U.S. to date, and Laughton received the first Academy Award to go to a performer in a non-American film.

Back across the Atlantic he was the only reason to sit through the ludicrous *White Woman*, as a sarcastic, wicked jungle overseer. He then went over to MGM where he convincingly played the overbearing father of Norma Shearer (who was but a year younger than him in real life) in the stuffy movie version of *The Barretts of Wimpole Street*, and then gallantly bowed out of playing Micawber in *David Copperfield*, suggesting W. C. Fields as his replacement when he realized he wasn't producing the required results. 1935 was his peak year, starting with one of the sweetest comedies of its day, *Ruggles of Red Gap*, with Laughton perfect as the very proper Englishman who insists on maintaining his reserve after being brought west by vulgar millionaire Charlie Ruggles. This was followed by his appearance in the abbreviated but engrossing and best-remembered version of *Les Misérables*, as the relentless Javert, whose single-minded pursuit of Fredric March causes his own psychological destruction. Rounding out the year was perhaps his most famous and certainly his most-mimicked performance, the unflappable martinet Captain Bligh in the Academy Award winner for Best Picture, *Mutiny on the Bounty*. This was one of the screen's greatest portrayals of stubbornness and cruelty, earning Laughton another Oscar nomination and a place among the screen immortals.

He left Hollywood for some interesting, if not financially lucrative, assignments, including the title role in one of the most respected bios of its day, *Rembrandt*, a quirky and fascinating glimpse at a relentlessly individualistic and self-destructive original, then the most famous unfinished movie of the 1930s, *I Claudius*, clashing unpleasantly on the set with director Josef von Sternberg before co-star Merle Oberon's car accident shut the whole project down anyway. This was followed by three films for his own production company, Mayflower, which he formed with producer Erich Pommer. The first, *The Beachcomber/Vessel of Wrath*, gave Lanchester her only starring role opposite him, playing a prim missionary to his beach bum, while the second, *Sidewalks of London/St. Martin's Lane*, found him as a busker, losing his partner, Vivien Leigh, to the high-class Rex Harrison. For the third, he hired Alfred Hitchcock for the director's last British production before his initial journey to Hollywood. An adventure about a group of cutthroat pirateers, *Jamaica Inn*, earned Hitchcock some of his poorest reviews to date but Laughton was a treat as the crafty, pompous villain.

With the war breaking out in England, Laughton and Lanchester up and moved back to Southern California, where they felt their work would boost morale for their native country. Laughton's first feature as part of a deal with RKO turned out to be another of his career high points, playing the pathetic Quasimodo in the best of the many adaptations of *The Hunchback of Notre Dame*. Buried under effective makeup, he gave a heart-wrenching performance in a lavish, atmospheric and popular production. He was broadly, stereotypically Italian for *They Knew What They Wanted*, playing for the umpteenth time an unattractive man pining for a pretty lady, and battling with his director, Garson Kanin, who had no tolerance for Laughton's precise methods for getting under the skin of a character. In more pleasant circumstances, under a ton of white hair and aging makeup, was a cantankerous geezer in one of the nicest of the Deanna Durbin movies, *It Started With Eve*, and carried one of the better segments of the omnibus *Tales of Manhattan*, humiliating himself while trying to conduct an orchestra wearing an uncooperative waistcoat. He was a meek villager who rises to the occasion in the ultrapatriotic *This Land Is Mine*; a cowardly spirit in the undisciplined adaptation of Oscar Wilde's *The Canterville Ghost*; and a timid soul driven to kill his shrewish wife in *The Suspect*, like *Payment Deferred* another examination of a man wracked with guilt over his dastardly deed.

Getting older and fleshier, he began to trickle down in billing for a weak Hitchcock entry, *The Paradine Case*, as a judge; the fine noir *The Big Clock*, as a publisher covering up the murder he's committed (this time, guilt be damned!), supporting Ray Milland but stealing the film; *The Bribe*, as a drunken, morally bankrupt flunky, backing up Robert Taylor and Ava Gardner and

easily sweeping them right off the screen; and *The Blue Veil*, wonderful as an elderly widower hoping to win nurse maid Jane Wyman. Those he starred in at this time, *The Man on the Eiffel Tower*, as Inspector Maigret, and *The Strange Door*, as an evil squire, co-starring opposite Boris Karloff, had little to recommend. He was yet again one of the better things about another failed episode film, *O. Henry's Full House*, as a bum trying to get arrested; then he returned to a role he'd done before, this time for comical effect, in *Abbott and Costello Meet Captain Kidd*, which he made simply because he had always enjoyed the two comedians so much. He hammed it up horribly in a worthless costume film, *Salome*, as Herod; reprised his Henry VIII role for *Young Bess*, exiting the film early on and causing it to suffer as a result; and had a roaring good time bullying his daughters as the pig-headed, alcoholic boot-maker in *Hobson's Choice*, finding the right degree of humor and repugnance in the character. Next he tackled one exclusively as director with highly original results, *The Night of the Hunter*, a moody, startlingly bleak Gothic chiller that died at the box office but has remained a cult favorite.

This was followed by his last great starring performance, as the barrister fighting bad health while trying to win a murder case, in Billy Wilder's excellent version of the Agatha Christie play *Witness for the Prosecution*. Lanchester was back as his meddlesome nurse, and their sparring was simply glorious, earning Oscar nominations for both. Finally he was part of the large casts of two other worthy movies, in both cases as a senator: *Spartacus*, back in ancient Rome and sharing the screen briefly with his long-time acting rival, Laurence Olivier, and *Advise and Consent*, in a spot-on, memorable turn as the earthy, outspoken southerner Seab Cooley. He died of cancer prior to its release, remaining married to Lanchester to the end despite his homosexuality, which she spoke of in her later autobiography. There was also an appreciation of Laughton written by actor Simon Callow, a look at a body of work full of peaks most actors couldn't begin to climb. In New York he directed two Broadway productions in which he did not appear, *John Brown's Body* (which he also adapted) and *The Caine Mutiny Court-Martial*. He published two compilations of essays, *Tell Me a Story* (1957) and *The Fabulous Country* (1962).

Screen: 1929: Piccadilly; 1930: Wolves/Wanted Men (US: 1936); 1931: Down River; 1932: Devil and the Deep; The Old Dark House; Payment Deferred; The Sign of the Cross; If I Had a Million; 1933: Island of Lost Souls; The Private Life of Henry VIII; White Woman; 1934: The Barretts of Wimpole Street; 1935: Ruggles of Red Gap; Les Misérables; Mutiny on the Bounty; 1936: Rembrandt; 1939: The Beachcomber/Vessel of Wrath (UK: 1938); Jamaica Inn; The Hunchback of Notre Dame; 1940: Sidewalks of London/St. Martin's Lane (UK: 1938); They Knew What They Wanted; 1941: It Started With Eve; 1942: The Tuttles of Tahiti; Stand by for Action; Tales of Manhattan; 1943: Forever and a Day; The Man From Down Under; This Land Is Mine; 1944: The Canterville Ghost; The Suspect; 1945: Captain Kidd; 1946: Because of Him; 1947: The Paradine Case; 1948: Arch of Triumph; The Big Clock; The Girl From Manhattan; 1949: The Bribe; The Man on the Eiffel Tower; 1951: The Blue Veil; The Strange Door; 1952: O. Henry's Full House; Abbott and Costello Meet Captain Kidd; 1953: Salome; Young Bess; 1954: Hobson's Choice; 1957: Witness for the Prosecution; 1960: Under Ten Flags; Spartacus; 1962: Advise and Consent.

NY Stage: 1931: Payment Deferred; 1932: The Fatal Alibi; 1947: Galileo (and co-wr.); 1951: Don Juan in Hell (and dir.); 1956: Major Barbara (and dir.).

Select TV: 1953: This Is Charles Laughton (series); 1956: The Day Lincoln Was Shot (sp); 1958: Stopover in Bombay (sp); New

York Knight (sp); **1959:** The Last Lesson (sp); **1960:** In the Presence of Mine Enemies (sp).

STAN LAUREL
(ARTHUR STANLEY JEFFERSON)
BORN: ULVERSTON, ENGLAND, JUNE 16, 1890.
DIED: FEBRUARY 23, 1965.
& OLIVER HARDY
(NORVELL HARDY) BORN: HARLEM, GA,
JANUARY 18, 1892. DIED: AUGUST 7, 1957.

They are probably everybody's immediate example of a movie comedy team, but Laurel and Hardy have always sharply divided public opinion. It is often said that men enjoy them far more than women, that some find their slapstick caustic and crude, their characterizations arch and mannered. Their strongest supporters, including an organization proudly calling themselves "The Sons of the Desert" (after one of their best movies), have elevated them to a peak above all other film comics, noting the grace of their timing, the pure, unpretentious straight-for-the-gut level of their humor, and their dark, abrasive view of the world — the struggle of two amiable nitwits representing a little part of us all. Stan, though playing the dimmer of the two, was in fact the guiding force behind the team. Much in the tradition of Chaplin, he came to the U.S. after years in the British music halls, via Fred Karno's Company. It was while doing his vaudeville act in Los Angeles that he was signed to appear in a two-reeler, "Nuts in May," in 1918. There was a brief spell under contract Universal, more stage work, and then another short film, called "Lucky Dog." Significantly, it not only got him a contract with actor-turned-producer Bronco Billy Anderson, but also featured a bit player named Oliver Hardy. Hardy had gone from running a cinema to doing extra work in the movies, starting with "Outwitting Dad." His solo credits are not easy to verify, but he had supposedly popped up in more than 100 shorts before being elevated to the leads in some comedies for Larry Semon in the 1920s. There were some feature films around this time, including a long-forgotten version of *The Wizard of Oz*, in which he played the Tin Man.

Laurel had worked off and on for producer Hal Roach, officially becoming a member of his stock company in 1926, the same year Hardy joined the studio. Although they were assigned to several of the same short subjects, they were not at first an official team. Some important elements were coming together though. "Love 'em and Weep" featured them with their frequent exasperated foil, James Finlayson; "Why Girls Love Sailors" is pointed out as the one in which Hardy first used his shtick of fluttering his tie; and "Do Detectives Think?" debuted their trademark bowler hats. With "The Second Hundred Years," which cast them as escaping convicts, they were at last a genuine comic duo. This late 1920s period was a very successful one for them, as they were seen in some of their most inspired works, including "The Battle of the Century," featuring one of the screen's great, full-scale pie fights; "Should Married Men Go Home?," covering similar territory only with a mud brawl; "Two Tars," finding themselves destroying a traffic jam full of automobiles; and "Liberty," ending up atop a real skyscraper while trying to change their pants. In one of their best and best-remembered shorts, "Big Business," they vindictively tear apart Finlayson's home as he makes a mess of their car.

There were also examples of the strain in their work, including "Berth Marks," with its interminable sequence of the two trying to settle down for a night's sleep aboard a train. Since this particular two-reeler was done in both silent and sound versions, it is considered their first talkie. The first one they did strictly in an all-talking format was the 1929 short "Unaccustomed as We Are," followed by a guest spot in their first feature, the clunky, all-star *The Hollywood Revue of 1929*. It might be said that no silent movie comedians made the transition to sound as effortlessly as did Laurel and Hardy. Their voices, Stan's soft, inquisitive British drawl, and Ollie's pompous, impatient sniping, gave their comedy an added spark. Their high points in the two- or three-reel department in the early 1930s included "Brats," playing their own children, thereby prompting Hardy to ditch his Chaplinesque mustache; "Hog Wild," trying to fix a radio aerial; "Laughing Gravy," hoping to conceal a dog from their landlord; "Our Wife," with Ollie attempting to elope with Finlayson's hefty daughter; "Helpmates," hiding the remnants of a wild party from Ollie's wife; and "The Music Box," pushing a piano up a long flight of stairs with disastrous results. The last is among their most famous shorts and, despite the repetition of it all, an Academy Award winner for Best Short Subject (Live Action).

They began popping up in longer films, providing comic relief to the operettas *The Rogue Song* and *Fra Diavolo/The Devil's Brother*; and starring in the prison spoof *Pardon Us* and the requisite Army romp, *Pack Up Your Troubles*. The response was good enough that Roach began to wean them off of two-reelers to concentrate on full-length productions. They made their two best features almost back-to-back: *Sons of the Desert*, a marvelously sustained gem in which they steal off to their fraternal convention much to the displeasure of their wives, and *Babes in Toyland*, a genuinely baroque and enchanting fantasy in which they played inept toy makers who help save their town from the evil Barnaby. The latter would play endlessly on television under the title *March of the Wooden Soldiers*, and become their best-known work. They ended their two-reeler output in 1935 with "Thicker Than Water," the amusing ending of which saw the two switching personalities after a blood transfusion.

There were some more worthy entries with *The Bohemian Girl*, another semi-operetta in which they were gypsies raising an orphan girl; the often hilarious *Way Out West*, most of which had them trying to deliver a deed to a gold mine; and *Blockheads*, in which Stan unleashed his usual innocent havoc on Ollie while adjusting to civilian life after 20 years in the military. The last two (along with *Our Relations*) were made for Stan Laurel Productions instead of bearing the customary Hal Roach label, and the duo ended their partnership with the great comedy producer in 1940 with two very mild offerings, *A Chump at Oxford* and *Saps at Sea*. They should have, by rights, called in quits after these but instead signed up for some fairly lame features distributed by Fox, of which *Jitterbugs* was probably the most bearable. There was one more, rather strange reteaming, in the French-made *Atoll K/Utopia*, an attempt at social satire released in many truncated forms under various titles, with Hardy looking grotesquely obese and Laurel thin and sickly. Hardy did some solo parts, in John Wayne's *The Fighting Kentuckian* and Bing Crosby's *Riding High*, and the two were seen on a rather uncomfortable *This Is Your Life* TV presentation in which an angered Laurel refused to speak. Despite their long and seemingly busy motion picture careers, both men were badly in need of money at the time of their deaths. Shortly after Laurel's passing in 1965, MGM distributed three compilation films showing some of their best moments, *Laurel and Hardy's Laughing Twenties*, *The Crazy World of Laurel and Hardy*, and *The Further Perils of Laurel and Hardy*. Their faithful fans were vindicated — the clips, representing the peaks of an admittedly varied output, showed just how funny these two clowns could be. In 1960 Laurel was given an honorary Oscar.

Screen (shorts): LAUREL AND HARDY: **1917:** Lucky Dog; **1926:** Forty-Five Minutes From Hollywood; **1927:** Duck Soup; Slipping Wives; Love 'em and Weep; Why Girls Love Sailors; With Love and Hisses; Sailors Beware; Do Detectives Think?; Flying Elephants; Sugar Daddies; Call of the Cuckoo; The Second Hundred Years; Hats Off; Putting Pants on Philip; The Battle of the Century; **1928:** Leave 'em Laughing; The Finishing Touch; From Soup to Nuts; You're Darn Tootin'; Their Purple Moment; Should Married Men Go Home?; Early to Bed; Two Tars; Habeas Corpus; We Faw Down; **1929:** Liberty; Wrong Again; That's My Wife; Big Business; Double Whoopee; Berth Marks; Men o' War; A Perfect Day; They Go Boom; Bacon Grabbers; Angora Love; Unaccustomed as We Are; Hoosegow; **1930:** Night Owls; Blotto; Be Big; Brats; Below Zero; The Laurel and Hardy Murder Case; Hog Wild; Another Fine Mess; **1931:** Chickens Come Home; Laughing Gravy; Our Wife; Come Clean; One Good Turn; Beau Hunks; Helpmates; **1932:** Any Old Port; The Music Box; The Chimp; County Hospital; Scram; Their First Mistake; **1933:** Towed in a Hole; Twice Two; Me and My Pal; The Midnight Patrol; Busy Bodies; Wild Poses; Dirty Work; **1934:** The Private Life of Oliver the Eighth; Going Bye Bye; Them Thar Hills; The Live Ghost; Tit for Tat; **1935:** The Fixer Uppers; Thicker Than Water; **1936:** On the Wrong Trek; **1943:** The Tree in a Test Tube.

Screen (features): LAUREL AND HARDY: **1929:** The Hollywood Revue of 1929; **1930:** The Rogue Song; **1931:** Pardon Us; **1932:** Pack Up Your Troubles; **1933:** Fra Diavolo/The Devil's Brother; Sons of the Desert; **1934:** Hollywood Party; Babes in Toyland/March of the Wooden Soldiers; **1935:** Bonnie Scotland; **1936:** The Bohemian Girl; Our Relations; **1937:** Way Out West; Pick a Star; **1938:** Swiss Miss; Block-Heads; **1939:** The Flying Deuces; **1940:** A Chump at Oxford; Saps at Sea; **1941:** Great Guns; **1942:** A-Haunting We Will Go; **1943:** Air Raid Wardens; Jitterbugs; The Dancing Masters; **1944:** The Big Noise; Nothing but Trouble; **1945:** The Bullfighters; **1955:** Atoll K/Utopia/Robinson Crusoeland (filmed 1951).

HARDY: **1922:** Fortune's Masks; The Little Wildcat; **1923:** One Stolen Night; Three Ages; The King of the Wild; **1924:** The Girl in the Limousine; **1925:** The Wizard of Oz; The Perfect Clown; Stop, Look and Listen; **1926:** Gentle Cyclone; **1939:** Zenobia; **1949:** The Fighting Kentuckian; **1950:** Riding High.

PIPER LAURIE

(ROSETTA JACOBS) BORN: DETROIT, MI, JANUARY 22, 1932.

Not unlike Anne Bancroft, red-headed Piper Laurie was almost done in by the Hollywood studio system that couldn't see what this gifted lady had to offer. She toiled in programmers, fluff, and out-and-out garbage for years until suddenly she showed them all what they'd been misusing. She was all of 18 years of age when she was signed to a contract by Universal Pictures, in 1950, starting off as the love interest of ex-child star Scotty Beckett in *Louisa*. The next year she was the decorative leading lady to Tony Curtis in a lush and silly Arabian Knights-type adventure, *The Prince Who Was a Thief*, which did well enough that she was placed in similar fare like *Son of Ali Baba* (Curtis again) and *The Golden Blade* (Rock Hudson). There was a charmless small town comedy, *Has Anybody Seen My Gal?*, in which she seemed to be glumly enduring it all; a Francis (The Talking Mule) comedy, *Francis Goes to the Races*; the decently popular Tyrone Power yarn *The Mississippi Gambler*, in which she competed with Julie Adams for his affections; and another with

Curtis, *Johnny Dark*, which placed them in modern times, in and around the world of auto racing. She ended her contract with *Kelly and Me*, which presented her with the challenge of feeling ga-ga over Van Johnson, and she was no doubt only too happy to be let go. Over at MGM there was an improvement over this stuff with a role in an acceptable soap opera, *Until They Sail*, as one of four sisters involved with four soldiers in New Zealand. It was television, however, that provided her with her first breakthrough role, playing the sad, alcoholic wife of Cliff Robertson in *Days of Wine and Roses*, winning an Emmy Award in the process.

She went off to do some theater and then returned to the movies with a bang, playing the cynical, hard-drinking woman who shacks up with Paul Newman in the gritty *The Hustler*. Hollywood was taken aback by just how good Laurie was and, despite the relatively small size of her role, gave her an Oscar nomination in the leading category. Unfortunately, rather than cash in on this fame, she chose to retire, having just married critic Joseph Morgenstern. After a 15-year hiatus she showed up in an eye-popping role, as the mad, religious-ranting mother of Sissy Spacek in the hit horror movie *Carrie*, creating such a shattering impression that she earned another Oscar nomination. Having been rediscovered all over again, she spent a great deal of time on the small screen (including *Promise*, for which she received a second Emmy), but came back to the movies for *Return to Oz*, as Dorothy's aunt in this grim revisionist take on the Baum tales; *Children of a Lesser God*, as the mother of deaf Marlee Matlin, a rather unremarkable turn for which she was, nevertheless, given her third Oscar nomination; *Other People's Money*, as Gregory Peck's lover, giving a fine, understated performance; *Wrestling Ernest Hemingway*, as the lonely lady responding to Richard Harris's flirtations; and best of all *The Grass Harp*, as the delicate, free-spirited Southern lady who takes to living in a tree house, playing a genuine lead for the first time in ages. Curiously she had now graduated to playing Sissy Spacek's sister.

Screen: **1950:** Louisa; The Milkman; **1951:** The Prince Who Was a Thief; Francis Goes to the Races; **1952:** Has Anybody Seen My Gal?; No Room for the Groom; Son of Ali Baba; **1953:** The Mississippi Gambler; The Golden Blade; **1954:** Dangerous Mission; Johnny Dark; Dawn at Socorro; **1955:** Smoke Signal; Ain't Misbehavin'; **1957:** Kelly and Me; Until They Sail; **1961:** The Hustler; **1976:** Carrie; **1977:** Ruby; **1978:** The Boss's Son; **1981:** Tim (Australia: 1979); **1985:** Return to Oz; **1986:** Children of a Lesser God; **1987:** Distortions (dtv); **1988:** Appointment With Death; Tiger Warsaw; **1989:** Dream a Little Dream; **1991:** Other People's Money; **1992:** Storyville; **1993:** Rich in Love; Trauma (dtv); Wrestling Ernest Hemingway; **1995:** The Crossing Guard; **1996:** The Grass Harp; **1998:** The Faculty; **1999:** St. Patrick's Day; Palmer's Pick Up (nUSr); The Mao Game (nUSr).

NY Stage: **1958:** Rosemary (ob); The Alligators (ob); **1965:** The Glass Menagerie; **1980:** Biography (ob); **1992:** The Destiny of Me (ob); **2002:** Morning's at Seven.

Select TV: **1955:** Broadway (sp); **1956:** Winter Dreams (sp); The Road That Led Afar (sp); **1957:** Mr. and Mrs. McAdam (sp); Twelfth Night (sp); The Deaf Heart (sp); **1958:** Days of Wine and Roses (sp); **1959:** The Innocent Assassin (sp); Caesar and Cleopatra (sp); Winterset (sp); **1960:** You Can't Have Everything (sp); Legend of Lovers (sp); **1961:** A Musket for Jessica (sp); Come Again to Carthage (sp); **1963:** Something About Lee Wiley (sp); **1977:** In the Matter of Karen Ann Quinlan; **1978:** Rainbow; **1980:** Skag; Skag (series); **1981:** The Bunker; **1982:** Mae West; **1983:** The Thorn Birds (ms); **1985:** Love Mary; Tender Is the Night (ms); Toughlove; **1986:** Promise; **1988:** Go to the Light; **1990:** Rising Son; **1990–91:** Twin Peaks (series); **1993:** Lies and Lullabies; **1994:** Shadows of Desire; **1995:** Fighting for My Daughter; **1996:** Road to Galveston;

In the Blink of an Eye; **1997:** Dean Koontz's Intensity; Truman Capote's A Christmas Memory; Horton Foote's Alone; **1999:** Inherit the Wind; Partners (series); **2000:** Possessed; **2001:** Midwives; The Last Brickmaker in America.

PETER LAWFORD

(PETER SYDNEY ERNEST AYLEN)
BORN: LONDON, ENGLAND, SEPTEMBER 7, 1923.
DIED: DECEMBER 24, 1984.

Part suave, part smarmy, with thick brows and lounge lizard good looks, Peter Lawford appeared in all kinds of films and yet was in no way exceptional in any particular genre. He pretty much fit in everywhere, did his job with competence, and became more famous simply for being a personality than for his performances. The son of character actor Sydney Lawford, the young Lawford made his motion picture debut in 1930, at the age of seven, in a British film, *Poor Old Bill*, starring comedian Leslie Fuller. Eight years later the family traveled to the U.S., where Lawford auditioned for and got a role supporting Mickey Rooney and Freddie Bartholomew in MGM's *Lord Jeff*. Opting to finish his education, he wound up living in Florida for a spell until he decided to give Hollywood a try again. MGM took him on in 1942, giving him several small military roles, including *Mrs. Miniver*, as a pilot, and *Son of Lassie*, as an RAF flier. Between home lot assignments and loan-outs he could be found in no less than 15 releases in 1943, though always in small parts.

Following the war things picked up somewhat as his roles got bigger, with *My Brother Talks to Horses*, Lawford being the "my," the brother being young Butch Jenkins; *Two Sisters from Boston*, as the guy both June Allyson and Kathryn Grayson have their eye on; and *Good News*, as a popular college football star, delightfully croaking his way through such songs as "Be a Ladies' Man" and "The French Lesson." In *Easter Parade*, he was in love with Judy Garland, this time warbling Irving Berlin's "A Fella With an Umbrella," and in *It Happened in Brooklyn*, he was an aspiring songwriter, taking billing below Frank Sinatra but winning the leading lady, Kathryn Grayson, in the end. The labored *Julia Misbehaves* had him romantically linked with Elizabeth Taylor, and, in *On an Island with You*, he played a pilot stealing Esther Williams away from her film location. The studio tried him out in more dramatic fare with *Little Women*, as Laurie, and *The Red Danube*, helping Janet Leigh escape from the Russians, but they felt safer not having him carry the load, as in *Royal Wedding*, in which he was the love interest of Jane Powell. In 1952 he began topping the cast list at last with the "B's" *You for Me*, as a stuck-up millionaire pursuing nurse Jane Greer; *The Hour of 13*, as a London thief; and *Rogue's March*, as a soldier trying to prove his worth to his father.

After this batch he left the studio for television and starred in two series, including a fairly popular version of *The Thin Man*, where he dared not even try to compete with the more polished playing of William Powell in the same part. There was a bright comedy at Columbia, *It Should Happen to You*, in which he portrayed a wealthy businessman putting the moves on Judy Holliday, and then a five-year lapse before he returned to the big screen in *Never So Few*, providing support to off-screen buddy Frank Sinatra. In the 1960s he bounced back upon the movie scene as one of the evil Brits in *Exodus* and, more significantly, as a member of the gang of war vets turned thieves in *Ocean's Eleven*, which was the cinematic coming together of the so-called "Rat Pack" that consisted of Lawford, Sinatra, Sammy Davis, Jr., and Dean Martin, among others. Lawford would join them again in

Sergeants 3, before falling out of Sinatra's favor, and later partner Davis in the loose, made-in-Britain comedy, *Salt and Pepper*, which prompted a sequel, *One More Time*.

During the early 1960s he found himself a part of American "royalty," having married Patricia Kennedy, the sister of President John F. Kennedy, back in 1954 (they divorced in 1966). Also during that era he was seen as a playboy senator in *Advise and Consent*; represented the British at Normandy in the all-star blockbuster *The Longest Day*; was Carol Baker's inadequate husband in *Harlow*; and thought himself the father of Gina Lollobrigida's child in *Buona Sera, Mrs. Campbell*. By the 1970s audiences were used to seeing Lawford all over the television dials, where he had become a bushy-haired, smoky-voiced poster boy for casual acting. He also operated his own production company, Chrislaw, responsible for *The Patty Duke Show* and the films *Johnny Cool* (1963) and *Billie* (1965). His son is actor Christopher Lawford.

Screen: **1930:** Poor Old Bill; **1931:** A Gentleman of Paris; **1938:** Lord Jeff; **1942:** Mrs. Miniver; Eagle Squadron; Thunder Birds; Junior Army; A Yank at Eton; London Blackout Murders; Random Harvest; **1943:** Girl Crazy; The Purple V; The Immortal Sergeant; Pilot # 5; Above Suspicion; The Man From Down Under; Someone to Remember; Sherlock Holmes Faces Death; The Sky's the Limit; Paris After Dark; Flesh and Fantasy; Assignment in Brittany; Sahara; West Side Kid; Corvette K-225; **1944:** The Canterville Ghost; The Adventures of Mark Twain; The White Cliffs of Dover; Mrs. Parkington; **1945:** Son of Lassie; The Picture of Dorian Gray; **1946:** Ziegfeld Follies (voice); Two Sisters From Boston; Cluny Brown; My Brother Talks to Horses; **1947:** It Happened in Brooklyn; Good News; **1948:** On an Island With You; Easter Parade; Julia Misbehaves; **1949:** Little Women; The Red Danube; **1950:** Please Believe Me; **1951:** Royal Wedding; **1952:** Just This Once; Kangaroo; You for Me; The Hour of 13; Rogue's March; **1954:** It Should Happen to You; **1959:** Never So Few; **1960:** Ocean's Eleven; Exodus; Pepe; **1962:** Sergeants 3; The Longest Day; Advise and Consent; **1964:** Dead Ringer; **1965:** Harlow; Sylvia; **1966:** The Oscar; A Man Called Adam; **1968:** Salt and Pepper; Buona Sera, Mrs. Campbell; Skidoo; **1969:** Dead Run (filmed 1967); The April Fools; Hook Line & Sinker; **1970:** One More Time; Togetherness; **1971:** Clay Pigeon; **1972:** They Only Kill Their Masters; **1974:** Journey Back to Oz (voice; filmed 1964); That's Entertainment!; **1975:** Rosebud; **1976:** Won Ton Ton, the Dog Who Saved Hollywood; **1980:** Angels' Brigade; **1981:** Gypsy Angels (dtv); Body and Soul; **1983:** Where's Parsifal? (dtv).

Select TV: **1953:** The Son-in-Law (sp); Woman's World (sp); **1954:** For Value Received (sp); Mason-Dixon Line (sp); **1954–55:** Dear Phoebe (series); **1955:** Tom and Jerry (sp); **1956:** Once Upon a Time (sp); Sincerely, Willis Wayde (sp); **1957:** Ruggles of Red Gap (sp); **1957–59:** The Thin Man (series); **1959:** Point of Impact (sp); **1962:** The Armer's Daughter (sp); **1965:** March From Camp Tyler (sp); **1967:** How I Spent My Summer Vacation; **1971:** A Step Out of Line; The Deadly Hunt; Ellery Queen: Don't Look Behind You; **1974:** The Phantom of Hollywood; **1977:** Fantasy Island; **1979:** Highcliffe Manor (series; narrator); Mysterious Island of Beautiful Women.

FRANCIS LEDERER

(FRANTISEK LEDERER) BORN: PRAGUE, CZECHOSLOVAKIA, NOVEMBER 6, 1899.
DIED: MAY 25, 2000.

A Czech import who came to Hollywood after a brief career in German films, wavy-haired Francis Lederer had been acting with a Czech rep company before he went to Berlin to appear onstage in *Romeo and Juliet*. What really brought him fame was his role in the 1931 London production of *Autumn Crocus*, which came to Broadway the following year to repeat its great success. As a result, RKO signed him up to play an Eskimo (!) in *A Man of Two Worlds*, after which he was borrowed by Paramount for *Pursuit of Happiness*, as a deserter during the Revolutionary War who falls for Joan Bennett. Since RKO kept loaning him elsewhere or dropping him from their projects at the last minute (including *Break of Hearts*), he left that studio to find work on his own. He was the suave jewel thief in *The Lone Wolf in Paris*; and the lover of married Mary Astor in the charming *Midnight*; then gave his best performance, in Warners's red-hot melodrama *Confessions of a Nazi Spy*, as an American soldier working for the Gestapo. Since World War II was at hand, he played another Nazi in *The Man I Married*, which was no doubt preferable to supporting Judy Canova in *Puddin'head*. He got to play twins in the 1944 version of *The Bridge of San Luis Rey*, but the movie was a critical and commercial flop. This was followed by a Czech role for once, in *Voice in the Wind*, this time being persecuted by the Nazis, and then the role of the evil valet in *Diary of a Chambermaid*. With that he began to fade into smaller roles until another pair of star parts came along, playing the Count in California in *The Return of Dracula*, and a variation of Dr. Moreau in *Terror Is a Man*, two films he looked back upon with disdain. He was married (1937–40) to actress Margo and was one of a handful of noted film actors to live to the ripe old age of 100.

Screen (US releases only): 1929: Pandora's Box; 1934: A Man of Two Worlds; Pursuit of Happiness; Romance in Manhattan; 1935: The Gay Deception; 1936: One Rainy Afternoon; My American Wife; 1938: It's All Yours; The Lone Wolf in Paris; 1939: Midnight; Confessions of a Nazi Spy; 1940: The Man I Married; 1941: Puddin'head; 1944: The Bridge of San Luis Rey; Voice in the Wind; 1946: The Madonna's Secret; Diary of a Chambermaid; 1948: Million Dollar Weekend; 1950: Captain Carey, USA; A Woman of Distinction; Surrender; 1953: Stolen Identity; 1956: The Ambassador's Daughter; Lisbon; 1958: Maracaibo; The Return of Dracula; 1959: Terror Is a Man.

NY Stage: 1932: Autumn Crocus; 1939: No Time for Comedy; 1950: Parisienne; Arms and the Man.

Select TV: 1950: The Long Run (sp); 1954: No Rescue (sp); 1958: A Delicate Affair (sp); 1960: Arrowsmith (sp); Turn the Key Softly (sp); 1965: The Safe House (sp).

ANNA LEE

(JOAN BONIFACE WINNIFRITH)
BORN: IGTHAM, KENT, ENGLAND, JANUARY 2, 1913. ED: CENTRAL SCHOOL OF SPEECH TRAINING AND DRAMATIC ART.

A petite, blonde leading lady of British films who moved her life and career across the Atlantic during World War II, Anna Lee had started out with the London Rep Theatre before being burdened with the title of "Britain's Glamour Girl" of the 1930s. She made her motion picture debut in *Ebb Tide*, in 1932, in a supporting part, and stayed in the background for the next several films before playing one of the women in the life of fake artist Louis Hayward in *Chelsea Life*, and the ambitious beautician in *Faces*. Her better-known film appearances of this period were in *The Passing of the Third Floor Back*, as a rooming house boarder; *The Man Who Changed His Mind/The Man Who Lived Again*, desired by evil Boris Karloff; and the 1937 version of *King Solomon's Mines*. She came to America in 1939 and started off badly, being chucked way down

the cast list of *Seven Sinners*, followed by a fairly poor performance as Ronald Colman's young wife in *My Life with Caroline*. Things improved when she was cast as one of the daughters in director John Ford's classic *How Green Was My Valley*, the Academy Award-winner for Best Picture of 1941. Over at RKO she received her best-remembered screen role, as the heroine who tries to expose the horrid conditions of London's notorious insane asylum and winds up an inmate, in the fine Val Lewton production *Bedlam*. It wasn't long before she was inching back down the cast roster, performing in several films for John Ford (*The Horse Soldiers, The Man Who Shot Liberty Valance*, etc.); playing the friendly next-door neighbor of Bette Davis in *What Ever Happened to Baby Jane?*; and a heroic nun in her second Oscar-winner for Best Picture, *The Sound of Music*. Late in her career she reached her greatest level of fame when she was cast as the kindly patriarch Lila Quartermaine on the hit daytime soap *General Hospital*, eventually playing the role in a wheelchair. Her first husband (1933–44) was director Robert Stevenson; their daughter is actress-producer Venetia Stevenson.

Screen: 1932: Ebb Tide; Yes, Mr. Brown; Say It With Music; 1933: Mayfair Girl; King's Cup; Chelsea Life; Mannequin; Faces; The Bermondsey Kid; 1934: Lucky Loser; The Camels Are Coming; Rolling in Money; 1935: Heat Wave; The Passing of the Third Floor Back; First a Girl; 1936: The Man Who Lived Again/The Man Who Changed His Mind; You're in the Army Now/O.H.M.S.; 1937: King Solomon's Mines; Non-Stop New York; 1939: The Secret Four/The Four Just Men; Young Man's Fancy; Return to Yesterday; 1940: Seven Sinners; 1941: My Life With Caroline; How Green Was My Valley; 1942: Flying Tigers; Commandos Strike at Dawn; 1943: Hangmen Also Die; Flesh and Fantasy; Forever and a Day; 1944: Summer Storm; 1946: Bedlam; G.I. War Brides; 1947: High Conquest; The Ghost and Mrs. Muir; 1948: Best Man Wins; Fort Apache; 1949: Prison Warden; 1958: The Last Hurrah; Gideon of Scotland Yard/Gideon's Day; 1959: The Horse Soldiers; This Earth Is Mine; The Big Night; 1960: The Crimson Kimono; Jet Over the Atlantic; 1961: Two Rode Together; 1962: Jack the Giant Killer; The Man Who Shot Liberty Valance; What Ever Happened to Baby Jane?; 1963: The Prize; 1964: The Unsinkable Molly Brown; For Those Who Think Young; 1965: The Sound of Music; 1966: 7 Women; Picture Mommy Dead; 1967: In Like Flint; 1968: Star!; 1984: Clash (dtv); 1987: The Right-Hand Man; 1989: Listen to Me; Beverly Hills Brats; 1994: What Can I Do? (nUSr).

Select TV: 1951: A Date With Judy (series); 1951–54: It's News to Me (series); 1973: My Darling Daughters' Anniversary; 1976: Eleanor and Franklin; 1977: Eleanor and Franklin: The White House Years; 1978: The Beasts Are in the Streets!; 1978– : General Hospital (series); 1979: The Night Rider; 1980: Scruples (ms).

CHRISTOPHER LEE

BORN: LONDON, ENGLAND, MAY 27, 1922.

This tall, gaunt, and sinister-looking star of the British Hammer horror films built up a résumé so mind-bogglingly long it was a wonder Christopher Lee had time to spend even so much as a week off from making movies. Following service in the Air Force during World War II, he decided to pursue acting and, through a contact at Two Cities Films, got a screen test that landed him a contract with their parent company, the Rank Organization. They gave him a bit in the 1948 fantasy *Corridor of Mirrors*, which was released in the U.S. the following year by Universal. Aside from being seen as a

Spanish captain in the Gregory Peck adventure *Captain Horatio Hornblower*; as Seraut in *Moulin Rouge*; and in the well-liked war film *The Battle of the River Plate/Pursuit of the Graf Spee*, there was very little of what he did up to this point that would constitute high-profile material. His fortunes changed when he was chosen to play The Monster opposite Peter Cushing in Hammer's 1957 version of the Frankenstein story, *The Curse of Frankenstein*. The film, done in a style quite unlike the beloved Universal interpretation, was an international success, and Lee was immediately starred as the bloodthirsty count in *Horror of Dracula/Dracula*, which made him nearly as closely identified with the character as Bela Lugosi had been. After playing a grave robber in support of Boris Karloff in *Corridors of Blood*, Hammer made him Sir Henry Baskerville opposite Cushing as Holmes in their remake of *The Hound of the Baskervilles*, although Lee seemed a more logical choice to play Holmes (he played the role later, in a German film, *Sherlock Holmes and the Deadly Necklace*, but his voice was dubbed). Looking for another previous Universal horror film to remake, the studio dragged out the gauze, made Lee *The Mummy*, and had themselves another hit.

By now Lee had become synonymous with both Hammer and frequent co-star Cushing, making a name for himself in the thriller-fantasy field with such movies as *The Man Who Could Cheat Death*, reluctantly helping Anton Diffring stay young; *House of Fright/The Two Faces of Dr. Jekyll*, crushed to death by a python for dallying with Mr. Hyde's wife; and *The Hands of Orlac*, playing a crazed magician. Elsewhere he was at his chilling best as the devil worshiper in one of the most atmospheric of all horror films, *Horror Hotel/City of the Dead*; then returned to Hammer to play an evil Asian in *Terror of the Tongs*, which may have led to his later being cast as Fu Manchu in *The Face of Fu Manchu* and its sequels. There was *Psycho-Circus*, with Lee as a lion tamer hiding his scarred visage with a mask; *The Gorgon*, where he was a heroic professor battling a snake-haired woman; and *Rasputin — The Mad Monk*, which offered give-away beards at matinee showings, indicating that this probably wasn't a version of the Rasputin story to be taken with complete seriousness. He was a good guy battling witches in *The Devil Rides Out/The Devil's Bride*, one of his own favorite roles, and he dug up the count yet again for *Dracula — Prince of Darkness*, and various sequels.

Away from the horror genre he could be seen as a Soho club owner in the Brit teen flick *Beat Girl/Wild for Kicks*; Maycroft Holmes in *The Private Life of Sherlock Holmes*, working under the direction of Billy Wilder; a Confederate gunsmith in *Hannie Caulder*; Rochefort in *The Three Musketeers*, and its sequel, *The Four Musketeers*; the triple-nippled villain in the James Bond adventure *The Man with the Golden Gun*; one of the trapped passengers in the goofy *Airport '77*; a gay motorcyclist in *Serial*; and, in a surprise lead, the founder of Pakistan in *Jinnah*. Returning to the terror scene, he had a small bit as a burgomaster in the 1999 box-office success *Sleepy Hollow* and then thrilled aficionados of the fantasy genre when he did wicked turns in the *The Lord of the Rings* trilogy, as Ian McKellen's nemesis, Saruman, and in *Star Wars Episode II: Attack of the Clones*, as Count Dooku, at one point engaging in a laser sword battle with the pint-sized Yoda.

Screen: 1948: Corridor of Mirrors; One Night With You; A Song for Tomorrow; Saraband for Dead Lovers; Hamlet; My Brother's Keeper; Penny and the Pownall Case; Scott of the Antarctic; 1949: Trottie True/The Gay Lady; 1950: Prelude to Fame; They Were Not Divided; 1951: Captain Horatio Hornblower; Valley of Eagles; 1952: Top Secret/Mr. Potts Goes to Moscow; Babes in Bagdad; Paul Temple Returns; The Crimson Pirate; Moulin Rouge; 1953: Innocents in Paris; 1954: The Death of Michael Turbin; Destination Milan (TV in US); 1955: The

Warriors/The Dark Avenger; That Lady; Storm Over the Nile; Man in Demand; Cockleshell Heroes; The Final Column (TV in US); Police Dog; 1956: Private's Progress; 1956: Port Afrique; Pursuit of the Graf Spee/The Battle of the River Plate; Beyond Mombasa; Ill Met by Moonlight/Night Ambush; Alias John Preston; 1957: The Curse of Frankenstein; She Played With Fire/Fortune Is a Woman; The Traitor/The Accursed; Bitter Victory; 1958: A Tale of Two Cities; The Truth About Women; Unseen Heroes/Battle of the V-1; Horror of Dracula/Dracula; Corridors of Blood (US: 1962); 1959: The Mummy; The Hound of the Baskervilles; The Man Who Could Cheat Death; The Treasure of San Teresa/Long Distance; Wild for Kicks/Beat Girl; 1960: Horror Hotel/City of the Dead; House of Fright/The Two Faces of Dr. Jekyll; Too Hot to Handle/Playgirl After Dark; Hands of Orlac/Hands of a Strangler; 1961: Uncle Was a Vampire/Hard Times for Vampires; Terror of the Tongs; Scream of Fear/Taste of Fear; Hercules in the Haunted World; Secret of the Red Orchid; 1962: The Pirates of Blood River; The Devil's Daffodil/The Daffodil Killer; The Devil's Agent; 1963: Crypt of Horror/Terror in the Crypt; Horror Castle/Castle of Terror; Night Is the Phantom/What!; Faust '63/Catharsis; Sherlock Holmes and the Deadly Necklace/Valley of Fear; 1964: The Devil Ship Pirates; The Gorgon; Castle of the Living Dead; 1965: Dr. Terror's House of Horrors; The Face of Fu Manchu; She; The Skull; Ten Little Indians (voice); 1966: Dracula — Prince of Darkness; Rasputin — The Mad Monk; The Brides of Fu Manchu; 1967: Five Golden Dragons; Psycho-Circus/Circus of Fear; Theatre of Death/Blood Fiend; The Vengeance of Fu Manchu; Blood Demon/The Torture Chamber of Dr. Sadism; Island of the Burning Doomed/Night of the Big Heat/Island of the Burning Damned; 1968: The Devil's Bride/The Devil Rides Out; Dracula Has Risen From the Grave; Castle of Fu Manchu; Eve/The Face of Eve; Kiss and Kill/The Blood of Fu Manchu; Crimson Cult/Curse of the Crimson Altar; 1969: The Oblong Box; Eugenie...The Story of Her Journey Into Perversion/Philosophy of the Boudoir; 1970: The Magic Christian; Scream and Scream Again; One More Time; Taste the Blood of Dracula; The Scars of Dracula; The Private Life of Sherlock Holmes; Night of the Blood Monster/Bloody Judge; 1971: The House That Dripped Blood; Julius Caesar; Count Dracula; I Monster; Hannie Caulder; 1972: Dracula A.D. 1972; Horror Express; The Creeping Flesh; Raw Meat/Death Line; Nothing but the Night/The Resurrection Syndicate/The Devil's Undead; Dark Places; 1973: Dracula and His Vampire Bride/The Satanic Rites of Dracula; The Butcher, the Star and the Orphan; The Wicker Man; 1974: The Three Musketeers; The Man With the Golden Gun; 1975: The Four Musketeers; Killer Force/Diamond Mercenaries; 1976: The Keeper; To the Devil — A Daughter; Death in the Sun/Albino; Dracula and Son; 1977: Airport '77; End of the World; Meat Cleaver Massacre; Starship Invasions/Alien Encounter; 1978: Return From Witch Mountain; Caravans; 1979: Jaguar Lives!; The Passage; Circle of Iron/The Silent Flute; Arabian Adventure; Nutcracker Fantasy (voice); 1941; 1980: Bear Island; Serial; 1981: The Salamander; Safari 3000; An Eye for an Eye; 1982: The Last Unicorn (voice); The Return of Captain Invincible; House of the Long Shadows; 1985: Mask of Murder; Howling II: Your Sister Is a Werewolf (dtv); The Rosebud Beach Hotel; Jocks; 1986: The Girl; Shaka Zulu; 1987: Mio in the Land of Faraway; 1988: Dark Mission (dtv); Murder Story (dtv); 1990: The French Revolution; Gremlins 2: The New Batch; Honeymoon Academy; Fall of the Eagles (dtv); The Rainbow Thief (nUSr); The Miser (nUSr); 1991: Shogun Mayeda/Journey of Honor (dtv); Curse III: Blood Sacrifice (dtv); 1993: Cybereden/Jackpot (dtv); 1994: Police Academy 7: Mission to Moscow; Funny Man (dtv); **1995:** A Feast at Midnight; **1996:** The Stupids; Soul Music (dtv); **1998:** Tale of the Mummy (dtv); Jinnah; **1999:** Sleepy Hollow; **2001:** The Lord of the Rings: The Fellowship of the Ring; **2002:** Star Wars Episode II: Attack of the Clones; The Lord of the Rings: The Two Towers; **2003:** The Lord of the Rings: The Return of the King.

Select TV: **1953:** The Triangle; **1954:** Destination Milan; **1955:** The Final Column; **1955:** Stranglehold; **1974:** Diagnosis Murder; **1978:** Harold Robbins' The Pirate; **1979:** Captain America II: Death Too Soon; **1980:** Once Upon a Spy; **1981:** Goliath Awaits; The Boy Who Left Home to Find Out About the Shivers (sp); **1982:** Charles and Diana: A Royal Love Story; Massarati and the Brain; **1983:** Shaka Zulu (ms); **1984:** The Far Pavilions (ms); **1989:** Around the World in 80 Days (ms); Treasure Island (theatrical in UK); The Care of Time; **1991:** The Return of the Musketeers (theatrical in UK); **1992:** Sherlock Holmes and the Incident and Victoria Falls; Sherlock Holmes and the Leading Lady; **1993:** Death Train/Detonator; Double Vision; **1996:** Moses; Wyrd Sisters (series; voice); **1997:** The Odyssey; Ivanhoe; **2000:** In the Beginning; **2001:** Gormenghast.

GYPSY ROSE LEE

(ROSE LOUISE HOVICK) BORN: SEATTLE, WA, JANUARY 9, 1913. DIED: APRIL 26, 1970.

Although hers is one of the classic names in show business history, the film career of Gypsy Rose Lee leaves much to be desired, while her actual "accomplishments" onstage have been overshadowed by the musical retelling of her life. Entering vaudeville as a child, she performed with her sister (who became actress June Havoc) as part of "Madame Rose's Dancing Daughters," among other names, eventually becoming famous in burlesque as the best-known stripper of them all. Under the name "Louise Hovick," she was signed by 20th Century-Fox, who featured her in the all-star musical You Can't Have Everything, and in the Eddie Cantor comedy Ali Baba Goes to Town, where she proved to be a fairly inept actress. Under her more famous stage name of "Gypsy Rose Lee," she appeared as herself in Stage Door Canteen; had the lead in the RKO musical Belle of the Yukon; and was one of the past-their-prime Babes in Bagdad. In 1957 she published her autobiography, Gypsy, which two years later became one of the great Broadway musicals, keeping her name alive for years to come. In a bit of ironic casting her last movie was The Trouble With Angels, which involved nuns and starred Rosalind Russell, who had played Lee's mother in the film of Gypsy. She wrote the novel The G-String Murders that became the basis for the film Lady of Burlesque.

Screen: AS LOUISE HOVICK: **1937:** You Can't Have Everything; Ali Baba Goes to Town; **1938:** Sally, Irene and Mary; Battle of Broadway; **1939:** My Lucky Star.

AS GYPSY ROSE LEE: **1943:** Stage Door Canteen; **1945:** Belle of the Yukon; **1952:** Babes in Bagdad; **1958:** Screaming Mimi; Wind Across the Everglades; **1963:** The Stripper; **1966:** The Trouble With Angels.

NY Stage: **1936:** Spring Tonic; Ziegfeld Follies; **1942:** Star and Garter; **1961:** A Curious Evening with Gypsy Rose Lee (ob; and dir.; wr.; prod.).

Select TV: **1950:** Think Fast (series); **1956:** Sauce for the Goose (sp); **1958:** The Charmer (sp); The Gypsy Rose Lee Show (series); **1965:** Who Has Seen the Wind? (sp); Gypsy (series); **1966–67:** The Pruitts of Southampton (series); **1969:** The Over-the-Hill Gang.

JANET LEIGH

(JEANETTE HELEN MORRISON) BORN: MERCED, CA, JULY 6, 1927.

Absolutely a star but never the sort of performer whose name was used as the main drawing power for the films in which she appeared, bright, blonde Janet Leigh was one of the least pretentious of actresses. Whether playing ingénues, comical foils, tragic heroines, or levelheaded ladies, she was almost always proficiently on the mark and a pleasure to have around. Without any real training Leigh was signed by MGM, after a photo of her had been spotted by the right people at MCA. Metro entrusted her with the role of the Missouri farm girl in love with Van Johnson in The Romance of Rosy Ridge, and were sufficiently impressed to keep giving her work. There was a part in one of the best of the Lassie movies, Hills of Home, after which she was the loyal lady in the life of composer Richard Rodgers (Tom Drake) in Words and Music; Meg in the 1949 version of Little Women; the girl in question to Glenn Ford's physician in The Doctor and the Girl; and a ballerina-turned-nun (!) in The Red Danube. Borrowed by RKO, she was a widow being romanced by Robert Mitchum in the low-keyed Christmas perennial Holiday Affair, then got stuck in one of Howard Hughes personal projects, Jet Pilot, out of her element as a Russian spy in a movie filmed in 1950 but not released until 1957. Her position in the industry was greatly boosted when she became romantically linked with up-and-coming Tony Curtis, whom she married in 1951. Staying sweet, she was a naïve Southerner stuck on opera singer Ezio Pinza in Strictly Dishonorable; Gene Kelly's girlfriend in the episodic It's a Big Country; and Carleton Carpenter's love interest in the lion-joins-the-army comedy Fearless Fagan. She then did her best work to date, as the tough girlfriend of escaped killer Robert Ryan, in the finest of the James Stewart-Anthony Mann westerns of the 1950s, The Naked Spur. With that and Robert Taylor's Rogue Cop, she ended her contract with MGM.

She and Curtis got together for the highly colorful, highly fictitious biopic Houdini; a knight-in-armor adventure, The Black Shield of Falworth; the popular and brutal adventure tale, The Vikings; a strained slapstick sequence in Pepe; and a pair of mild comedies, The Perfect Furlough and Who Was That Lady?, the last stolen from them by Dean Martin. She and Curtis worked off one another most pleasantly, but, by the early 1960s their marriage was falling apart, and they divorced in 1962. In the meantime Leigh had fared quite nicely as the lovely Eileen in the 1955 musical version of My Sister Eileen, and endured the abuse of some thugs while stuck at an isolated motel in Orson Welles's stark and unforgettable Touch of Evil. There were even worse things in store for her at an even creepier roadside inn, in the film with which she would be forever associated — Alfred Hitchcock's dazzling, influential masterpiece, Psycho. As the nervous clerk who absconds with some cash and pays dearly for it, she gave a searing, intense, and sympathetic performance, culminating in her participation in one of the most famous and terrifying scenes in film history as she is brutally attacked in the shower. She received an Oscar nomination for her work and by all rights should have gotten the trophy that went to Shirley Jones instead.

From this peak she went into another fine film, The Manchurian Candidate, albeit in a relatively small role, as the mysterious lady whom Frank Sinatra meets on a train, and then had perhaps her showiest movie role, as Dick Van Dyke's neglected girlfriend, in the dandy 1963 film adaptation of the Broadway musical hit Bye Bye Birdie. Top billed at last, she made for a very pleasing trio with Ann-Margret and Bobby Rydell, singing "One Boy," and energetically cavorted through "The Shriners Ballet." Following another star part, in one of those many frothy 1960s comedies, *Wives and Lovers*, she found herself slipping down the "A" list, playing leading lady to Jerry Lewis in one of his poorest films, *Three on a Couch*; showing up in the international caper film *Grand Slam*; living in an underwater home with Tony Randall in the campy *Hello Down There*; and battling giant killer bunnies in the unintentionally funny *Night of the Lepus*. Spending much of the 1970s on television, she returned to the big screen alongside her daughter, Jamie Lee Curtis, in the thriller *The Fog*, then allowed another 18 years to pass before Jamie coaxed mom back to cinemas for *Halloween H20*. There were two memoirs, *There Really Was a Hollywood* (1984) and *Behind the Scenes of Psycho* (1995), as well as a novel, *House of Destiny* (1995).

Screen: 1947: The Romance of Rosy Ridge; If Winter Comes; 1948: Hills of Home; Words and Music; Act of Violence; 1949: Little Women; That Forsyte Woman; The Doctor and the Girl; The Red Danube; Holiday Affair; 1951: Strictly Dishonorable; Angels in the Outfield; Two Tickets to Broadway; It's a Big Country; 1952: Just This Once; Scaramouche; Fearless Fagan; 1953: Confidentially Connie; The Naked Spur; Houdini; Walking My Baby Back Home; 1954: Prince Valiant; Living It Up; The Black Shield of Falworth; Rogue Cop; 1955: Pete Kelly's Blues; My Sister Eileen; 1956: Safari; 1957: Jet Pilot (filmed 1950); 1958: Touch of Evil; The Vikings; The Perfect Furlough; 1960: Who Was That Lady?; Psycho; Pepe; 1962: The Manchurian Candidate; 1963: Bye Bye Birdie; Wives and Lovers; 1966: Kid Rodelo; Three on a Couch; Harper; An American Dream; 1968: Grand Slam; 1969: Hello Down There; 1972: One Is a Lonely Number; Night of the Lepus; 1979: Boardwalk; 1980: The Fog; 1998: Halloween H20: 20 Years Later; 2000: A Fate Totally Worse Than Death (dtv).

Select TV: 1957: Carriage From Britain (sp); 1964: Murder in the First (sp); 1966: Dear Deductible (sp); 1968: For Love or Money (sp); 1969: The Monk; Honeymoon With a Stranger; 1970: The House on Green Apple Road; 1971: Deadly Dream; 1973: Murdock's Gang; 1977: Murder at the World Series; Telethon; 1979: Mirror Mirror; 1997: In My Sister's Shadow.

VIVIEN LEIGH

(VIVIAN MARY HARTLEY)
BORN: DARJEELING, INDIA, NOVEMBER 5, 1913.
DIED: JULY 8, 1967.

She played perhaps the two most famous Southern women in the history of drama, and for that achievement alone Vivien Leigh ranks high among the greatest of all motion picture actresses. Her output was relatively small, but her emotional fire, classiness, and delicate beauty have kept a fervent interest in her among film aficionados. For those who have had the chance to search out the rest of her work, comes the verification that this was a lady who was extremely good at her craft. Born to British parents who were living in India, she received her education throughout Europe, ending up at RADA, where she studied acting. She very quickly received a film offer, appearing as a schoolgirl in *Things Are Looking Up*, in 1934. By the following year she was already bumped up to top billing, for the cheap and quickly forgotten *Gentleman's Agreement*, as an unemployed typist falling for a man she thinks is wealthy. Not getting anywhere in films, she tried the stage and received her first taste of fame in the West End comedy *The Mask of Virtue*, which resulted in a contract with producer Alexander Korda. For him she made *Fire Over England*, romanti-

cally paired with Laurence Olivier, who became her love interest off screen as well. They reteamed for *21 Days*, in which he accidentally kills her husband and sweats out the title period awaiting trial. Leigh then found a very pleasant co-star in Rex Harrison, first in the bright satire *Storm in a Teacup*, with Leigh as the daughter of blustering politician Cecil Parker, and then in *St. Martin's Lane*, where she was a street busker who becomes a famous entertainer, leaving behind partner Charles Laughton, who secretly pines for her. There was a brush with Hollywood when she was cast in the made-in-Britain Robert Taylor vehicle, *A Yank at Oxford*, reduced from original leading-lady status to playing a don's flirtatious wife.

This was released by MGM, who also snagged the distribution rights to *Gone With the Wind*, although it was up to producer David O. Selznick to pick the woman who would play the resilient, headstrong Scarlett O'Hara, the most coveted role of all time in the most anticipated motion picture of them all. Legend has it that Leigh was not even in the running until she came to Hollywood to visit Olivier, who was working on *Wuthering Heights* at the time, and met with Selznick. Every established American actress and many film fans were aghast at the announcement that someone from Britain was going to play this icon of Dixie, but Leigh, of course, came through with flying colors, having to carry the bulk of the nearly four-hour epic, despite top-billing being given to Clark Gable. She was simply sensational, behaving instinctively, plotting her rise, swooping about the proceedings like a whirlwind and yet remaining sympathetic, even sad in her misdirected passion. This was a great star at work, and the very mention of any of the other actresses who were even considered for the role now seems inconceivable. The movie was, needless to say, the blockbuster of its era, the epitome of studio-era storytelling at its most compelling. Leigh won the Academy Award as Best Actress of 1939 and became just about the best-known actress in the world.

Shortly afterwards *St. Martin's Lane* (newly christened *Sidewalks of London*) arrived in America, to cash in on her new fame, as did *21 Days*, which added the word *Together* to its title, perhaps in an effort to make it sound more romantic. Neither film prompted much interest, but her American follow-up to *GWTW*, the remake of *Waterloo Bridge*, was a triumph. As the ballerina who falls in love with soldier Robert Taylor, loses track of him, then takes to prostitution to survive, she had another field day, lifting this potentially eye-rolling material to a watchable, always engaging, level. The year of its release, 1940, she married Olivier and made her Broadway debut with him in *Romeo and Juliet*, which was not the hoped-for critical success. They decided to make another film together, a bit of British propaganda filmed in Hollywood, *That Hamilton Woman*, a fairly stodgy romance between Lord Admiral Nelson and Emma Hamilton. Perhaps carried by their fan magazine status, it fared well at the box office.

Although the movie industry would have been happy to keep her in Southern California, she and her husband returned to Britain where she did only two more movies during the 1940s. The first was the extremely costly Gabriel Pascal production of *Caesar and Cleopatra*, where she was well cast as Shaw's Queen of the Nile, convincingly making the leap from girlish enthusiasm to a viper-like sense of authority, in this surprisingly popular film that unfortunately left most critics cold. This was followed by the remake of *Anna Karenina*, which was immediately rejected as inferior to Garbo's version. Despite her constant poor health she kept busy on the stage, including the London production of Tennessee Williams's riveting *A Streetcar Named Desire*. When Warner Bros. took all of the Broadway principals save Jessica

Tandy for the 1951 movie adaptation, they invited Olivia de Havilland to join the cast; after she declined, they offered it to Leigh. As the faded, desperate Southern belle who cracks under the stress of living in the real world with her lower class sister and brutish brother-in-law, she was almost frighteningly good. She won her second Academy Award and found her second spot on the map of film immortality in what was, despite a compromised ending, one of the towering motion pictures of the 1950s.

Around the time of its run she played Cleopatra again, on Broadway, opposite Olivier and then had to leave the movie she was filming, *Elephant Walk*, because of illness, being replaced by Elizabeth Taylor (supposedly that is Leigh in some of the long shots in the finished print). There were only three more movies; in each she played women facing middle age. These were the British *The Deep Blue Sea*, from Terence Rattigan's play; another Tennessee Williams piece, albeit an inferior one, *The Roman Spring of Mrs. Stone*, in which she portrayed an actress taking up with Italian gigolo Warren Beatty; and, best of the lot, *Ship of Fools*, where she was part of the fine ensemble, as a wearied divorcée confronting vulgar baseball player Lee Marvin. She had divorced Olivier in 1960 and, three years later, risked taking on a musical role in *Tovarich*, which earned her a Tony Award. She died in 1967 of tuberculosis just as *Gone With the Wind* was about to be launched on its most successful reissue yet, reminding audiences of the thrill that Leigh brought to the screen on too few occasions.

Screen: 1934: Things Are Looking Up; 1935: The Village Squire; Gentleman's Agreement; Look Up and Laugh; 1937: Fire Over England; Dark Journey; Storm in a Teacup; 21 Days/21 Days Together (US: 1940); 1938: A Yank at Oxford; St. Martin's Lane/Sidewalks of London (US: 1940); 1939: Gone With the Wind; 1940: Waterloo Bridge; 1941: That Hamilton Woman/Lady Hamilton; 1945: Caesar and Cleopatra; 1948: Anna Karenina; 1951: A Streetcar Named Desire; 1955: The Deep Blue Sea; 1961: The Roman Spring of Mrs. Stone; 1965: Ship of Fools.

NY Stage: 1940: Romeo and Juliet; 1951: Caesar and Cleopatra; Antony and Cleopatra; 1960: Duel of Angels; 1963: Tovarich; 1966: Ivanov.

MARGARET LEIGHTON

BORN: BARNT GREEN, WORCESTERSHIRE, ENGLAND, FEBRUARY 26, 1922. DIED: JANUARY 13, 1976.

An elegantly lovely British actress with alluring, wide eyes and high cheekbones, Margaret Leighton had made her professional stage debut at the age of 16. She became a member of the Old Vic Company in the late 1940s, shortly before she made her first film appearances, in *The Winslow Boy*, as Cedric Hardwicke's strong-willed daughter, and the highly unsuccessful *Bonnie Prince Charlie*, as the commoner who helps David Niven evade the enemy. She was sinister playing a maid in one of the poorest of the Hitchcock films, *Under Capricorn*, which featured Michael Wilding, whom she would marry in 1963. In the meantime she was leading lady to David Niven (*The Elusive Pimpernel*), Walter Pidgeon (*Calling Bulldog Drummond*), and Rex Harrison (*The Constant Husband*, as a barrister). In between she joined the ensemble of the family Christmas drama *The Holly and the Ivy*, and the heist film *The Good Die Young*, which featured Laurence Harvey, to whom she was briefly wed (1957–61). She came to Hollywood in 1959 to play Joanne Woodward's nympho mom in *The Sound and the Fury*, and had a few more brief roles there, as Henry Fonda's wearied wife in *The Best Man*; the bickering spouse of Milton Berle in *The Loved One*; and a

major part as an unforgiving missionary locking horns with Anne Bancroft in the over-heated *7 Women*. Amid some ill-advised international efforts — including *The Madwoman of Chaillot*; *X, Y & Zee*; and *Lady Caroline Lamb* — she scored an Oscar nomination for *The Go-Between*, a tribute to years of reliable work, playing the bitchy, class-conscious mother of Julie Christie who destroys her daughter's unacceptable affair with farmer Alan Bates. She won Tony Awards for her performances in *Separate Tables* and *The Night of the Iguana*.

Screen: 1948: The Winslow Boy; Bonnie Prince Charlie; 1949: Under Capricorn; 1950: The Astonished Heart; The Elusive Pimpernel/The Fighting Pimpernel; 1951: Calling Bulldog Drummond; 1952: Home at Seven/Murder on Monday; The Holly and the Ivy; 1954: The Good Die Young; The Teckman Mystery; Court Martial/Carrington V.C.; 1955: The Constant Husband; 1957: The Passionate Stranger/A Novel Affair; 1959: The Sound and the Fury; 1962: Waltz of the Toreadors; 1964: The Best Man; 1965: The Loved One; 1966: 7 Women; 1969: The Madwoman of Chaillot; 1971: The Go-Between; 1972: X, Y & Zee/Zee and Co.; 1973: Lady Caroline Lamb; Bequest to the Nation/The Nelson Affair; From Beyond the Grave; 1975: Galileo; 1976: Dirty Knights' Work/Trial by Combat.

NY Stage: 1946: Uncle Vanya; Henry IV Part 1; Henry IV Part 2; Oedipus; The Critic; 1956: Separate Tables; 1959: Much Ado About Nothing; 1961: The Night of the Iguana; 1962: Tchin-Tchin; 1964: The Chinese Prime Minister; Homage to Shakespeare; 1966: Slapstick Tragedy; 1967: The Little Foxes.

Select TV: 1957: The Sparkle of Diamonds (sp); 1959: The Second Man (sp); The Browning Version (sp); 1962: The First Day (sp); A Month in the Country (sp); 1966: Heartbreak House (sp); 1969: An Ideal Husband (sp); 1970: Hamlet (sp); 1973: Frankenstein: The True Story; 1974: Great Expectations.

HARVEY LEMBECK

BORN: BROOKLYN, NY, APRIL 15, 1923. ED: UNIV. OF AL, NYU. DIED: JANUARY 5, 1982.

Very Brooklyn and very broad, Harvey Lembeck came to Broadway after a stint in the armed forces during World War II. He was first seen as part of the crew in *Mister Roberts*, then landed a plumb role in the 1951 stage production of *Stalag 17*. Having done some movies, including naval roles in *The Frogmen* and *You're in the Navy Now*, he won a rare lead when David Wayne bailed out of the "Willie and Joe" sequel, *Back at the Front*, playing the cinematic incarnation of Bill Maudlin's military comic-strip character Joe to Tom Ewell's Willie. When *Stalag 17* was adapted into a motion picture in 1953, Lembeck was one of the original cast members who came with the package, and he was once again hilarious teamed opposite Robert Strauss as the most clownish of the American prisoners. There were a few more military roles in such films as *Mission Over Korea* and *Between Heaven and Hell*, and he stayed in the Army for the hit series *You'll Never Get Rich/The Phil Silvers Show*, as Silvers's faithful sidekick, Corporal Rocco Barbella. After a relatively serious role as one of Raf Vallone's fellow workers in the film of *A View From the Bridge*, he was hired to play the part he would, for better or worse, probably be most identified with, the inept motorcycle gang leader Eric von Zipper in the pea-brained box-office hit *Beach Party*. This role was dragged out for most of the subsequent sequels and follow-ups, with Lembeck called on to mug excruciatingly. After this series came to a merciful end, he was rarely heard from save for some TV guest spots. His son is actor Michael Lembeck.

Screen: 1951: The Frogmen; You're in the Navy Now/U.S.S. Teakettle; Finders Keepers; Fourteen Hours; 1952: Back at the Front; Just Across the Street; 1953: Girls in the Night; Stalag 17; Mission Over Korea; 1954: The Command; 1956: Between Heaven and Hell; 1961: Sail a Crooked Ship; The Last Time I Saw Archie; 1962: A View From the Bridge; 1963: Beach Party; Love With the Proper Stranger; 1964: Bikini Beach; The Unsinkable Molly Brown; Pajama Party; 1965: Sergeant Deadhead; Beach Blanket Bingo; How to Stuff a Wild Bikini; Dr. Goldfoot and the Bikini Machine; 1966: Fireball 500; The Ghost in the Invisible Bikini; 1967: The Spirit Is Willing; 1969: Hello Down There; 1976: There Is No Thirteen; 1980: The Gong Show Movie.

NY Stage: 1948: Mister Roberts; 1951: Stalag 17; 1954: Wedding Breakfast; 1955: Phoenix '55 (ob); 1957: South Pacific; 1958: Oklahoma!

Select TV: 1955–59: You'll Never Get Rich/The Phil Silvers Show (series); 1958: Kiss Me Kate! (sp); 1961–62: The Hathaways (series); 1962–63: Ensign O'Toole (series); 1977: Raid on Entebbe.

JACK LEMMON

(JOHN UHLER LEMMON III) BORN: BOSTON, MA, FEBRUARY 8, 1925. ED: HARVARD. DIED: JUNE 27, 2001.

There were few actors so thoroughly comforting as Jack Lemmon. An affable everyman with a touch of neuroses, he was an undisputed master of light comedy who, not wanting to be pigeonholed, also showed the world that he was equally good at modern tragedy and pathos. As a result he held onto his stardom for over 40 years. Following drama studies at school, he knocked on the usual doors in New York, finding most of his initial jobs in live television during the late 1940s-early 1950s. There was a role in a failed Broadway revival of *Room Service*, and his own short-lived television series, *That Wonderful Guy* and *Heaven for Betsy* (which featured his first wife, Cynthia Stone), before Columbia asked him to test for a Judy Holliday comedy, *It Should Happen to You*, to be directed by George Cukor. Lemmon got the role of Ms. Holliday's friend, who disapproves of the fame she obtains via a publicity stunt, and his skills were more than evident in carrying his end of this bright and snappy entertainment. He and Holliday were immediately paired off again for the intriguingly title *Phffft!*, providing equally sparkling teamwork with a weaker script.

Signed to a Columbia contract, he proved himself a pleasing vocalist in two musicals, *Three for the Show*, a remake of *Too Many Husbands*, in which Betty Grable discovers she is married both to Lemmon and Gower Champion, and the much better *My Sister Eileen*, in which he played a New York publisher with an eye on Betty Garrett. In between these two he landed the coveted role of the amiably lazy Ensign Pulver in Warner's enormously popular 1955 movie adaptation of *Mister Roberts*, and wound up nearly stealing the show from the likes of Henry Fonda, James Cagney, and William Powell, winning the Academy Award for Best Supporting Actor. Columbia didn't exactly serve Lemmon well after this high point, putting him in another musical, the ill-advised remake of *It Happened One Night*, now called *You Can't Run Away from It*, with June Allyson as an inadequate substitute for Claudette Colbert. Lemmon's easy-going style was of a totally different tempo than Clark Gable's brusque machismo, so comparisons were not forthcoming. He then showed up in his first flat-out dramatic role, in *Fire Down Below*, where his dilemma of being trapped in a damaged ship was more involving than anything Rita Hayworth or Robert Mitchum had

to offer in their scenes. *Operation Mad Ball* was a half-enjoyable service comedy, with Lemmon leading an ensemble of fun-loving soldiers, but he hated playing the secondary role of Kim Novak's warlock brother in the hit *Bell Book and Candle*, finding little of interest in the part as written. The studio also allowed him to do a western, *Cowboy*, where he looked less uncomfortable on horseback than one might have expected, and a pairing with Doris Day, *It Happened to Jane*, a nice, gentle piece that was one of those inexplicable box-office failures from two stars who had just the sort of chemistry that should have guaranteed audience appreciation.

At this point Lemmon's career needed that one additional shot in the arm to take him up to that higher level that constitutes the ascension of a great star, and he got it, with a double punch from director Billy Wilder. Wilder first put him and Tony Curtis in drag for the funniest comedy of its day, if indeed all time, *Some Like It Hot*. Despite third billing (Marilyn Monroe, whose role was smaller, led the cast list), it was Lemmon who got the lion's share of the laughs, going from comic humiliation to perverse enjoyment in his womanly guise. It remains one of the great performances recorded on film, and he earned his first Oscar nomination in the lead category and a place in movie history. After this box-office smash, Wilder solidified Lemmon's growing level of importance with the more serious *The Apartment*, an incisive skewering of the corporate world, in which he was at his most complex as a lonely worker who must choose between power and morality. The movie never missed a beat in shifting from wry laughs to out and out sadness, and it became the blueprint for many subsequent filmmakers on how to combine comedy and drama without letting the seams show. The film won the Oscar for Best Picture of 1960, made a fortune, and got Lemmon another Oscar nomination. At this point he was just about the most admired talent in Hollywood.

There were still some comedies to knock off under his Columbia agreement, including one that mixed humor and seriousness with less dexterity, *The Wackiest Ship in the Army*, and *The Notorious Landlady*, which, if nothing else, allowed him to act opposite Fred Astaire. There were roles in two comedies he disliked, *Under the Yum Yum Tree*, playing a lecherous landlord, and the reasonably entertaining *Good Neighbor Sam*, pretending to be married to lovely Romy Schneider and getting into all sorts of trouble because of it. Despite Lemmon's negative feelings, they both were instrumental in maintaining his position as one of the top box-office draws of his day. More to his liking was the one that showed he could stretch, *Days of Wine and Roses*, with Lemmon in a shattering performance as a decent guy who drags his wife (Lee Remick) into a world of booze and misery. This resulted in Oscar nomination number three, but it would be a while before he would attempt such stark drama again. Instead he had another smash under Wilder's supervision, *Irma Le Douce*, being about the only actor who could pull off playing a pimp with charm.

He followed these with the relentlessly sexist black comedy *How to Murder Your Wife*, as a cartoonist who ends up accidentally married to sexy Virna Lisi, and the lavish spoof *The Great Race*, in a controversial turn as a maniacally exaggerated, mustache-twirling villain, purposefully playing to the rafters and getting more laughs than one might imagine, once again proving to be the rare actor who could achieve the seemingly impossible. Back with Wilder he let Walter Matthau steal the show in *The Fortune Cookie*, Lemmon spending most of the film in a state of incapacity for plot purposes. This pairing was too good to leave at that, so they became *The Odd Couple*, with Lemmon in top form as fuss-budget Felix Unger in a bull's-eye comedy that became one of the major hits of the 1960s. Staying on the lighter side, he stumbled with the strained and shrill *Luv*, an example of a loony stage farce not playing well for the cameras, and the charmless romantic comedy *The April Fools*. He faired better with Neil Simon's I-Hate-New-York farce *The Out of Towners*, as a particularly caustic Midwesterner facing every discomfort Manhattan has to offer; then directed Matthau as an old man in *Kotch*, receiving his share of favorable notices but not attempting it a second time.

Unlike so many of his era, he proved that he was willing to move with the times, shedding his clothes for an overlong Wilder comedy, *Avanti!*, then went serious again, with dire financial results but critical kudos galore, in *Save the Tiger*, a grim thing about a conscience-stricken businessman who questions his increasingly corrupt lifestyle. It was a reminder to many of just how superb Lemmon was when thrown something corrosive and sad, and he became the first male star to win an Academy Award in the lead category after having done so earlier in support. Wilder made him Hildy Johnson opposite Matthau's Walter Burns in the third filming of *The Front Page*, once again proving that these two were peerless when it came to grumpy camaraderie. Lemmon became the suffering everyman again for another bitter Neil Simon rant, *The Prisoner of Second Avenue*, and then foundered in the misguided *Alex and the Gypsy*, which only proved that he had really lost his box-office standing as far as 1970s audiences were concerned. Needing a hit, he got it with the topical and brilliant *The China Syndrome*, as a nuclear plant worker who, in best Lemmon fashion, must question his ethics when his business nearly suffers a meltdown. He received his sixth Oscar nomination and received two more, for *Tribute*, successfully recreating his Broadway role, as a life force who must face his somber, alienated son as well as his own eminent demise, and for the downbeat, political statement *Missing*, playing a father whose faith in government falls apart as he searches for his son in a disrupted South American country.

There were other worthy performances, strong and assured enough to keep his stature high even if there was no ultimate payoff at the turnstiles, including his perceptive turn as the much-loved priest who comforts his parish with superficialities until he is challenged by a younger, more honest cleric, in *Mass Appeal*; the self-centered, desperately unhappy man terrified of facing his mortality — basically becoming director Blake Edwards's alter ego — in the dramedy *That's Life!*; and an old codger in his last days, in *Dad* (with Lemmon convincingly made-up to look years older). As part of the ensemble of *Glengarry Glen Ross*, he was absolutely marvelous as the pathetic real estate salesman desperately afraid of losing his job, but, alas, this was the 1990s, and even dramas as good as this one were relegated to distribution from independent companies, with little rewards financial or otherwise, awaiting them at the end of the year.

Perhaps disillusioned, he and Matthau agreed to do a crass comedy, *Grumpy Old Men*, and something about it caught the public fancy, providing Lemmon with his first starring-role hit in years. As a result there were other broad vehicles allowing the aging actors to play dirty, including the inevitable sequel *Grumpier Old Men*; *My Fellow Americans* (this time opposite James Garner), as an ex-President; *Out to Sea*; and, after a 30-year break, the unnecessary *The Odd Couple II*. It didn't matter that none of these could touch Lemmon's best work; it was still nice to have someone around whose very presence gave audiences hope for a Hollywood that hadn't quite given up on an actor who had set trends in the art of comedic acting. He was last seen on the big screen, unbilled, as the golfing narrator of *The Legend of Bagger Vance*. Much of his later life was spent doing some rewarding roles on television, including versions of *Long Day's Journey Into Night* (which he'd done on Broadway), *12 Angry Men*, and *Inherit the Wind*. He finally received a long overdue Emmy Award for playing another fellow facing his final days, in *Tuesdays With Morrie*. His second wife was actress Felicia Farr, whom he married in 1962 and appeared with in *That's Life!*, which also featured his son, actor Chris Lemmon. In 1988 he received the American Film Institute Life Achievement Award.

Screen: 1954: It Should Happen to You; Phffft; 1955: Three for the Show; Mister Roberts; My Sister Eileen; 1956: You Can't Run Away From It; 1957: Fire Down Below; Operation Mad Ball; 1958: Cowboy; Bell Book and Candle; 1959: Some Like It Hot; It Happened to Jane; 1960: The Apartment; Pepe; 1961: The Wackiest Ship in the Army; 1962: Stowaway in the Sky (narrator); The Notorious Landlady; Days of Wine and Roses; 1963: Irma La Douce; Under the Yum Yum Tree; 1964: Good Neighbor Sam; 1965: How to Murder Your Wife; The Great Race; 1966: The Fortune Cookie; 1967: Luv; 1968: The Odd Couple; 1969: The April Fools; 1970: The Out of Towners; 1971: Kotch (and dir.); 1972: The War Between Men and Women; Avanti!; 1973: Save the Tiger; 1974: The Front Page; 1975: The Prisoner of Second Avenue; 1976: Alex and the Gypsy; 1977: Airport '77; 1979: The China Syndrome; 1980: Tribute; 1981: Buddy Buddy; 1982: Missing; 1984: Mass Appeal; 1985: Macaroni; 1986: That's Life!; 1989: Dad; 1991: JFK; 1992: The Player; Glengarry Glen Ross; 1993: Short Cuts; Grumpy Old Men; 1995: Grumpier Old Men; 1996: Getting Away With Murder; The Grass Harp; My Fellow Americans; Hamlet; 1997: Out to Sea; 1998: The Odd Couple II; Off the Menu: The Last Days of Chasen's; 2000: The Legend of Bagger Vance.

NY Stage: 1953: Room Service; 1960: Face of a Hero; 1978: Tribute; 1986: Long Day's Journey Into Night.

Select TV: 1949: June Moon (sp); 1949–50: That Wonderful Guy (series); 1950: Toni Twin Time (series); 1951: The Happy Journey (sp); Sparrow Cop (sp); Ad Libbers (series); The Easy Mark (sp); 1952: Size Twelve Tantrum (sp); Heaven for Betsy (series); 1953: Duet (sp); Snooksie (sp); Dinah Kip and Mr. Barlow (sp); The Checkerboard Heart (sp); The Grand Cross of the Crescent (sp); 1954: The Marriageable Male (sp); 1956: The Day Lincoln Was Shot (sp); 1957: The Three Graves (sp); Lost and Found (sp); The Mystery of 13 (sp); Voices in the Fog (sp); Souvenir (sp); 1957–58: Alcoa Theatre (series); 1958: The Victim (sp); The Days of November (sp); Loudmouth (sp); Most Likely to Succeed (sp); Disappearance (sp); 1959: Face of a Hero (sp); 1972: Jack Lemmon in 'S Wonderful 'S Marvelous 'S Gershwin (sp); 1973: Get Happy: The Music of Harold Arlen (sp); 1976: The Entertainer (sp); 1987: Long Day's Journey Into Night (sp); 1988: The Murder of Mary Phagan (ms); 1992: For Richer For Poorer; 1993: A Life in the Theatre; 1996: A Weekend in the Country; 1997: 12 Angry Men; 1998: The Long Way Home; 1999: Inherit the Wind; Tuesdays With Morrie.

SHELDON LEONARD

(SHELDON LEONARD BERSHOD)
BORN: NEW YORK, NY, FEBRUARY 22, 1907.
ED: SYRACUSE UNIV. DIED: JANUARY 10, 1997.

Back in the 1940s, if you were looking for someone to signify "gangster," there was no one who fit the bill better than Sheldon Leonard, with his shifty sneer and nasally Brooklynesque tones. Originally intending to make a career on Wall Street, he wound up acting on Broadway in such shows as *Hotel Alimony* and *Kiss the Boys Goodbye*. Although he had been seen playing an overseer in a British voodoo film, alternately called *Drums of the Jungle* and *Ouanga*, his official (Hollywood) motion picture bow came in 1939, in *Another Thin Man*, as the chief murder suspect. He went right to the hoodlum parts with *Tall, Dark and Handsome*, as Cesar Romero's nemesis, a Chicago mug named Pretty Willie; Alan Ladd's hit *Lucky Jordan*; *Born to Sing*, trying to stop Ray McDonald and his pals from putting on a show; *The Falcon in Hollywood*; and, of course, *The Gangster*. Since he could effortlessly shift his menace to a lighter vein, he was seen terrorizing the likes of such comedians as Abbott and Costello (*Hit the Ice*, *Abbott and Costello Meet the Invisible Man*), the Bowery Boys (*Bowery Bombshell*; *Jinx Money*, as a character named Lippy), and Martin and Lewis (*Money From Home*), as well as participating in the musical *Guys and Dolls*, as Harry the Horse. Outside the rackets he was an unlikely Indian in *The Iroquois Trail*, and played the bartender who cruelly squirted H. B. Warner with seltzer in *It's a Wonderful Life*.

Starting with *Make Room for Daddy/The Danny Thomas Show*, he began to establish himself as a significant behind-the-scenes contributor, as both producer and director, eventually winning two Emmys for that show. In time he found a second career as one of the foremost television producer-directors in the business, his credits encompassing such programs as *The Dick Van Dyke Show*, *The Andy Griffith Show*, and *My World and Welcome to It*, which brought him a third Emmy. He returned to the screen, after a long absence, to play F.B.I. director J. Edgar Hoover in *The Brink's Job*, perhaps a way of atoning for all those criminal roles he'd essayed in the past.

Screen: 1934: Ouanga/Drums of the Jungle; 1939: Another Thin Man; 1941: Tall, Dark and Handsome; Buy Me That Town; Married Bachelor; Rise and Shine; Week-end in Havana; Private Nurse; 1942: Born to Sing; Tortilla Flat; Lucky Jordan; Pierre of the Plains; Tennessee Johnson; The McGuerrins of Brooklyn; Street of Chance; 1943: Klondike Kate; City Without Men; Hit the Ice; Taxi Mister; Passport to Suez; Harvest Melody; 1944: Timber Queen; Uncertain Glory; To Have or Have Not; The Falcon in Hollywood; Gambler's Choice; Trocadero; 1945: Girls Who Leave Home; Zombies on Broadway; Frontier Gal; Radio Stars on Parade; Captain Kidd; River Gang; Crime, Inc.; 1946: Decoy; Bowery Bombshell; The Last Crooked Mile; Somewhere in the Night; The Gentleman Misbehaves; Her Kind of Man; Rainbow Over Texas; It's a Wonderful Life; 1947: Sinbad the Sailor; The Fabulous Joe; Violence; The Gangster; 1948: If You Knew Susie; Open Secret; Jinx Money; Joe Palooka in Winner Take All; Madonna of the Desert; Alias a Gentleman; Shep Comes Home; 1949: Take One False Step; My Dream Is Yours; Daughter of the Jungle; 1950: The Iroquois Trail; 1951: Abbott and Costello Meet the Invisible Man; Behave Yourself!; Come Fill the Cup; Young Man with Ideas; 1952: Here Come the Nelsons; Breakdown; Stop, You're Killing Me; 1953: Money From Home; Diamond Queen; 1955: Guys and Dolls; 1961: Pocketful of Miracles; 1978: The Brink's Job.

NY Stage: 1934: Hotel Alimony; The Night Remembers; 1935: Fly Away Home; 1937: Having Wonderful Time; Siege; 1938: Kiss the Boys Goodbye.

Select TV: 1954: The Duke (series); 1959–61: The Danny Thomas Show (series); 1964–69: Linus the Lionhearted (series; voice); 1975: Big Eddie (series); 1978: The Islander; Top Secret.

JOAN LESLIE
(JOAN AGNES THERESA SADIE BRODEL)
BORN: DETROIT, MI, JANUARY 26, 1925.

Sweet, perky young things were a dime a dozen back in Hollywood's heyday, but Joan Leslie stood out as a highly appealing, engaging young actress with some flashes of genuine talent. Success happened very quickly for her, and she had passed her peak before she'd reached the age of 21. She sang as one of "The Three Brodels," along with her two sisters; did some modeling; and earned a contract with MGM following a nightclub engagement in New York. Under her real name she debuted in 1936, in a major film in a very minor role, playing Robert Taylor's little sister in *Camille*, but the studio had no further use for her and dropped her. There were similarly small roles elsewhere, playing an autograph hound in *Love Affair*; Joel McCrea's sister in *Foreign Correspondent*; and a farmer's daughter in *Laddie*. In 1941 Warners decided to take her on and promote her as an exciting new discovery. As a result they rechristened her "Joan Leslie" and put her into a big hit, *High Sierra*, as a club-footed girl whose dilemma touches a soft spot in the heart of hoodlum Humphrey Bogart. After being Eddie Albert's co-star in a pair of "B's," *Thieves Fall Out* and *The Great Mr. Nobody*, she got another satisfying part in one of the studio's great successes of the day, *Sergeant York*, as the charming young bride of war hero Gary Cooper. On a roll, she kept popping up in some of the big ones of the war years. In *The Male Animal*, she was Olivia de Havilland's independent sister; in *Yankee Doodle Dandy*, she had a typical warm and loving wife role, in this case the "Mary" for whom George M. Cohan wrote his famous song of that name (despite the fact that Cohan was never married to anyone named "Mary"); and in *The Hard Way*, she had her most challenging assignment, as the sister Ida Lupino pushes to the top of the show business profession until Leslie becomes sick of her interference.

She then appeared in a rush of big patriotic musicals, the hugely popular *This Is the Army*, "singing" (she was dubbed by Sally Sweetland) "No You, No Me" with Dennis Morgan; *Thank Your Lucky Stars*, as part of the storyline in this all-star look into the Warners roster of celebrities, once again sharing the spotlight with Morgan, for "I'm Ridin' for a Fall;" *Hollywood Canteen*, as herself and the focus of soldier Robert Hutton's obsession; and *Rhapsody in Blue*, as one of George Gershwin's women, according to Hollywood's take on the great composer's life. Best of all was *The Sky's the Limit*, over at RKO, where she partnered Fred Astaire quite nicely for the lovely "My Shining Hour" duet. Back at the home lot she got top billing for the comical musical *Cinderella Jones*, in which she must marry brainy Robert Alda to win money, and *Janie Gets Married*, a sequel to a film in which Leslie hadn't appeared (Joyce Reynolds had done the part). Soon afterwards she finished her association with Warners, from that point on ending up in nothing but programmers and grade "B" fare like the fantasy *Repeat Performance*, reliving the year before she murdered her husband, and *The Woman They Almost Lynched*, playing the title role. By the mid-1950s she was growing less interested in acting and instead concentrated on raising her family and dabbling in dress designing with some degree of success. Although she and the motion picture industry parted company in 1956, after she supported Jane Russell in *The Revolt of Mamie Stover*, she did, however, pop up randomly on television in guest appearances and in some telefilms.

Screen: AS JOAN BRODEL: 1936: Camille; 1938: Men With Wings; 1939: Two Thoroughbreds; Nancy Drew — Reporter; Winter Carnival; Love Affair; 1940: Susan and God; Foreign

Correspondent; Young as You Feel; Star Dust; High School; Military Academy; Laddie

AS JOAN LESLIE: **1941:** High Sierra; The Great Mr. Nobody; The Wagons Roll at Night; Thieves Fall Out; Sergeant York; **1942:** The Male Animal; Yankee Doodle Dandy; The Hard Way; **1943:** This Is the Army; The Sky's the Limit; Thank Your Lucky Stars; **1944:** Hollywood Canteen; **1945:** Where Do We Go From Here?; Rhapsody in Blue; Too Young to Know; **1946:** Cinderella Jones; Janie Gets Married; Two Guys From Milwaukee; **1947:** Repeat Performance; **1948:** Northwest Stampede; **1950:** The Skipper Surprised His Wife; Born to Be Bad; **1951:** Man in the Saddle; **1952:** Hellgate; Toughest Man in Arizona; **1953:** The Woman They Almost Lynched; **1954:** Flight Nurse; Jubilee Trail; Hell's Outpost; **1956:** The Revolt of Mamie Stover.

Select TV: 1951: Flowers for John (sp); Black Savannah (sp); **1952:** The Imposter (sp); The Von Linden File (sp); **1953:** Dream Job (sp); The Old Man's Bride (sp); **1954:** Wonderful Day for a Wedding (sp); **1956:** Smoke Jumpers (sp); **1959:** The Day of the Hanging (sp); **1976:** The Keegans; **1986:** Charley Hannah; **1989:** Turn Back the Clock; **1991:** Fire in the Dark.

OSCAR LEVANT

BORN: PITTSBURGH, PA, DECEMBER 27, 1906.
DIED: AUGUST 14, 1972.

Not really an actor and not officially a comedian, America's favorite neurotic hypochondriac, Oscar Levant, was nonetheless an often hilarious addition to the movies, popping up periodically as a sardonic sidekick or naysayer with a slew of cynical remarks or a self-deprecating crack, customarily punctuated by a world-weary sigh. He had studied piano under Sigismond Stokowski and composition with Arnold Schönberg, becoming a pianist in various New York nightclubs and in theater orchestras. His early claim to fame was being the first person to record Gershwin's *Rhapsody in Blue*, and he became a well-known concert pianist over the years, also dabbling in song writing and composing scores for films (including *Leathernecking, Tanned Legs, Side Street*). Debuting as an actor in the 1927 Broadway hit *Burlesque*, he was first seen on screen in the 1929 movie version, retitled *The Dance of Life*, but another 11 years passed before he did a follow-up. In the meantime, in addition to his musical performances, he was making a name for himself on radio with his witty comments as a participant on the show *Information Please*. He was summoned back to movies in 1940 for the Bing Crosby vehicle *Rhythm on the River*, playing the assistant of composer Basil Rathbone.

As himself he was called on to pound out the title number on the keyboards for the Gershwin biopic *Rhapsody in Blue*, then pretty much set the blueprint for his subsequent roles when he played John Garfield's quipping, cynical piano-playing buddy in *Humoresque*. It was clear that Levant wasn't worth much when called on to act straightforward scenes, so he was basically utilized to make wisecracks and to alleviate the more saccharine qualities the scripts might possess. In *You Were Meant for Me* he performed *Concert in F*, a piece he revisited more memorably in the 1951 Oscar-winner *An American in Paris*, imaging himself as all the members of the orchestra in a funny dream sequence. In the last of the Fred Astaire-Ginger Rogers movies, *The Barkleys of Broadway*, he joined them for a sprightly number called "A Weekend in the Country," and was back with Astaire again for perhaps his most enduring role, the alter ego of writer-lyricist Adolph Green ("I can stand anything but failure") in one of the brightest entertainments of them all, *The Band Wagon*, at one

point helping to introduce the classic song "That's Entertainment!" That film's director, Vincente Minnelli, called on him again for a more serious part in *The Cobweb*, as a mother-obsessed patient, a character who had been gay in the original novel. His teaming with the equally sour-pussed Fred Allen, for the "Ransom of Red Chief" sequence of *O. Henry's Full House*, was a promise unfilled in light of the poor quality of this omnibus film. With the advent of television Levant continued to subject the world to his stinging barbs, usually as a high-strung, seemingly unstable, but nonetheless effortlessly funny raconteur on various talk shows. There were three acerbic autobiographies, *A Smattering of Ignorance* (1940), *Memoirs of an Amnesiac* (1965), and *The Unimportance of Being Oscar* (1968).

Screen: 1929: The Dance of Life; **1940:** Rhythm on the River; **1941:** Kiss the Boys Goodbye; **1945:** Rhapsody in Blue; **1946:** Humoresque; **1948:** You Were Meant for Me; Romance on the High Seas; **1949:** The Barkleys of Broadway; **1951:** An American in Paris; **1952:** O. Henry's Full House; **1953:** The I Don't Care Girl; The Band Wagon; **1955:** The Cobweb.

NY Stage: 1927: Burlesque.

Select TV: 1951: General Electric Guest House (series); **1958:** The Oscar Levant Show (series).

SAM LEVENE

BORN: RUSSIA, AUGUST 28, 1905.
DIED: DECEMBER 26, 1980.

Bringing with him an authentic feel of a working-class New York character actor, Sam Levene came to Hollywood in 1936 to repeat his acclaimed Broadway role as the crude gambler Patsy in the comedy hit *Three Men on a Horse*. Although he would continue to travel back east to his stage roots, he was asked back to the movies pretty regularly, playing police lieutenant Abrams of San Francisco homicide in both *After the Thin Man* and *Shadow of the Thin Man*; a soldier used as part of a malaria experiment in *Yellow Jack*, again repeating his role from the stage; one of the fliers tortured by the Japanese in *The Purple Heart*; the important role of the Jew who is murdered by anti-Semitic soldier Robert Ryan in the Oscar-nominated *Crossfire*; a doctor in *Dial 1119*; the manager of Martin Milner's jazz quintet in *Sweet Smell of Success*; and various mugs and thugs. There were many occasions when he landed some golden roles onstage but was not asked to repeat his performance on film, including *Room Service* and *The Sunshine Boys*, as well as his most famous part of all, good old reliable Nathan Detroit in *Guys and Dolls*, a character altered for the talents of Frank Sinatra in the 1955 movie adaptation. He showed up on Broadway playing Patsy once again in *Let It Ride*, a flop 1961 musical version of *Three Men on a Horse*, as well as in the straightforward 1969 revival of the show.

Screen: 1936: Three Men on a Horse; After the Thin Man; **1938:** Yellow Jack; The Shopworn Angel; The Mad Miss Manton; **1939:** Golden Boy; **1941:** Married Bachelor; Shadow of the Thin Man; **1942:** Sing Your Worries Away; Sunday Punch; Grand Central Murder; The Big Street; Destination Unknown; **1943:** I Dood It; Action in the North Atlantic; Whistling in Brooklyn; Gung Ho!; **1944:** The Purple Heart; **1946:** The Killers; **1947:** Boomerang!; Brute Force; Crossfire; A Likely Story; Killer McCoy; **1948:** Leather Gloves; The Babe Ruth Story; **1950:** Dial 1119; Guilty Bystander; **1953:** Three Sailors and a Girl; **1956:** The Opposite Sex; **1957:** Designing Woman; Sweet Smell of Success; Slaughter on Tenth Avenue; **1958:** Kathy O; **1963:** Act One; **1969:** A Dream of Kings; **1972:** Such Good Friends; **1976:** The Money; Demon/God Told Me To; **1979:**

Last Embrace; …And Justice for All.

NY Stage: 1927: Wall Street; 1928: Jarnegan; 1929: Headquarters; Street Scene; 1930: This Man's Town; 1931: Three Times the Hour; Wonder Boy; 1932: Dinner at Eight; 1934: Yellow Jack; Spring Song; 1935: Three Men on a Horse; 1937: Room Service; 1939: Margin for Error; 1945: A Sound of Hunting; 1948: Light Up the Sky; 1950: Guys and Dolls; 1954: The Matchmaker; 1956: Hot Corner; 1957: Fair Game; 1958: Make a Million; 1959: Heartbreak House; 1960: The Good Soup; 1961: The Devil's Advocate; Let It Ride; 1962: Seidman and Son; 1964: Café Crown; The Last Analysis; 1966: Nathan Weinstein — Mystic, Connecticut; 1969: Three Men on a Horse (revival); 1970: Paris Is Out!; A Dream Out of Time (ob); 1972: The Sunshine Boys; 1974: Dreyfus in Rehearsal; 1975: The Royal Family; 1980: Horowitz and Mrs. Washington.

Select TV: 1954: The Alibi Kid (sp); Johnny Blue (sp); 1957: The Mother Bit (sp); The Old Ticker (sp); 1958: Mrs. McThing (sp); 1959: The World of Sholom Aleichem (sp); 1966: A Small Rebellion (sp).

JERRY LEWIS

(Jerome Levitch) Born: Newark, NJ, March 16, 1926.

No one has a neutral opinion of Jerry Lewis and the comedian-actor-director-writer-producer wouldn't have had it any other way. From the time he came crashing upon the scene in the late 1940s, his manic, anything goes approach to getting a laugh caused his fans to hail him as some kind of genius, while his detractors have cursed the day he was allowed in front of a movie camera. Lewis wanted to be heard and make his mark in show business, which he certainly did. The son of second-tier nightclub performers, it was almost a given that he would follow them into the business. He eventually quit school to work in the Catskills, where he developed an act, pantomiming to records. It was while sharing a bill with singer Dean Martin in Atlantic City in 1946 that the two decided to develop a joint act, with Martin as suave straight man and Lewis as a hyperactive geek with a squeaky voice and the mannerisms of an idiotic child. In time they were the hit of the nightclub circuit, their explosive act taking them to Slapsie Maxie's Café, a Hollywood hot spot, resulting in a contract with producer Hal Wallis. He distributed his productions through Paramount, and Lewis (save for one cameo spot, running over Spencer Tracy's hat, in UA's *It's a Mad Mad Mad Mad World*) would make movies exclusively for that company from 1949 to 1965. The first two Martin and Lewis big screen assignments, *My Friend Irma* and *My Friend Irma Goes West*, put them in support of Marie Wilson, who starred with great success in *Irma* on radio. Both movies did well, with the team garnering most of the attention, especially Jerry, whose scene chewing was especially appreciated by kids. *At War With the Army* was their first starring vehicle, made on the cheap for their own York Productions banner. It was another smash, and it was clear that Martin and Lewis were taking the movies by storm. That same year, 1950, they became rotating hosts of *The Colgate Comedy Hour* on TV, which meant they were available pretty regularly in both mediums.

Their movies weren't much more than the same stock plots and situations that other comedians had gone through in the past, taking them to the navy (*Sailor Beware*), a haunted house (*Scared Stiff*), the race track (*Money from Home*), a golf course (*The Caddy*), and the big top (*3 Ring Circus*). There were remakes with sex changes to accommodate Lewis: *Living It Up*, which had

been *Nothing Sacred*, with the actor playing the Carole Lombard part, and *You're Never Too Young*, brushing off *The Major and the Minor*, with Lewis following in Ginger Rogers's footsteps. Needless to say these movies pretty much jettisoned a good deal of the wit and charm that had made the originals among the most admired comedies of their day. *Artists and Models* took the title of an old Jack Benny movie from the 1930s but was not a remake, instead involving Martin's dependency on Lewis for inspiring his comic book creations, while Bing Crosby's *Rhythm on the Range* mutated into *Pardners*, with Lewis's role deriving loosely from the one Frances Farmer had done the first time out. There were some that were more serious: *That's My Boy*, with Lewis as a sensitive lad forced into sports by his blowhard dad, and *The Stooge*, a painful account of an egotistical singer whose act fails after he dumps his loony partner. This had been part of the problem for Martin, who felt shoved into the background by his more aggressive teammate. Indeed, the writers had no qualms about giving Lewis the lion's share of the attention in the stories, figuring it was his antics that moviegoers were coming to see. The audiences never did stop coming either, despite the fact that eyewitnesses of their stage act claim that the movies couldn't even begin to capture by half what had made them so funny in person. The team split after *Hollywood or Bust*, in 1956, with Lewis taking the separation much harder, although his future seemed more secure at this point than did Martin's.

Serving as his own producer, he simply cast Darren McGavin in the Dean Martin role, as the police officer befriending Lewis who becomes a rookie cop, in *The Delicate Delinquent*. Its success kept him on the right track as far as fans were concerned, and he kept on this mediocre level through the next few, including a version of the famed comic strip *The Sad Sack*, and three more that he produced, *Rock-a-Bye Baby*, in which he was at his most cutesy, minding some babies; *The Geisha Boy*, where he played a magician in Japan befriending an orphan boy; and *Cinderfella*, a grotesque reworking of the fairytale in which he hoped to spotlight his musical side, having had a hit record with his remake of Jolson's "Rock-a-Bye Your Baby." In 1960 he asked the studio to allow him to direct, proving he could knock off a vehicle quickly and cheaply. The result, *The Bellboy*, represented a more inventive and surreal Lewis than had been seen before, with a plotless series of often inspired gags centered around Florida's posh Fontainebleau Hotel, with the star not speaking a word until the climax. It was certainly more acceptable than another of his films from the same year, *Visit to a Small Planet*, which had taken Gore Vidal's satirical stage play about an extraterrestrial visitor and turned it into a typical Lewis romp, with a lot of body contortions and facial tics substituting for wit.

The next few years would offer some other comedies that had moments of great creativity amid some sloppy sentimentality and excess, including *The Ladies' Man*, shot on a bizarre, doll house-like set, with Lewis as the caretaker at a women's boarding facility, and *The Errand Boy*, a romp through the Paramount studios backlot. Others were *Who's Minding the Store?*, where he was let loose in a department store; *The Patsy*, with the actor trained for stardom to replace a dead entertainer; and *The Disorderly Orderly*, in which he caused havoc in a hospital. His peak among this batch was *The Nutty Professor*, a sometimes-brilliant twist on Jekyll and Hyde with Lewis as a nebbishy college professor who turns himself into a slick, unpleasant lounge lizard to attract Stella Stevens. It was his greatest box-office hit. He ended his stay with Paramount with *The Family Jewels*, which gave audiences seven Jerrys for the price of one, some far funnier than others, and something less typical, *Boeing Boeing*, in which he toned down his mugging to play opposite Tony Curtis in a sex farce involving too many stewardesses, derived from a West End play.

By the mid-1960s the studio couldn't depend on him to keep the budgets down, so when he received offers elsewhere he jumped ship. But the best years were over, and his first two away from Paramount, Columbia's *Three on a Couch*, in which he donned various disguises to cure psychiatrist Janet Leigh's patients, and Fox's *Way…Way Out*, a shrill space-travel spoof, were among his very worst. By the time of 1970's *Which Way to the Front?*, bookings were becoming slim. He was simply getting too old for the spastic "jerk" act, so he began to concentrate on other areas. In the 1960s he started his annual Labor Day Telethon to raise money to fight muscular dystrophy, which like everything else he did, became an event that was heavily criticized by some, applauded by others. There was a chain of Jerry Lewis Cinemas, which ultimately faced bankruptcy, and the expected nightclub appearances and TV guest spots.

He continued to be one of the most controversial figures in the business, his temperament and staggering ego the subject of much bad press. Among the experiences that badly hurt his reputation were a serious film about a clown in a concentration camp, *The Day the Clown Cried*, which was halted prior to distribution and has never seen the light of day in America, and a Broadway-bound revival of Olsen and Johnson's *Hellzapoppin'*, which closed out of town due to endless battles between Lewis and others parties involved. In 1983 he was hired by director Martin Scorsese to play the straightforward role of a TV entertainer who is kidnapped by loony fan Robert DeNiro in *The King of Comedy*, and later did another interesting variation on his persona, playing the famous show business dad of failed comic Oliver Platt, in *Funny Bones*. These films, along with his appearances on several episodes of the series *Wiseguys*, suggesting a calmer Lewis was worth a look as a character actor. He did have a later-day triumph, coming to Broadway at last, in 1995, as the Devil in a revival of *Damn Yankees*, finally winning the approval of some of the skeptics. Certainly the most memorable moment of his annual telethon was his impromptu reunion with Dean Martin in 1976, although it was later revealed that neither star was in a completely coherent state during the event. Lewis published the books *The Total Filmmaker* (1971) and *Jerry Lewis in Person* (1982); directed one film in which he did not appear, *One More Time*, featuring pals Sammy Davis, Jr. and Peter Lawford; and created an animated series, *Will the Real Jerry Lewis Please Sit Down*, for which David Lander supplied the comedian's voice. His son Gary Lewis had a brief period in the musical spotlight in the 1960s with his rock group Gary Lewis and the Playboys, and played his dad in a flashback sequence in *Rock-a-Bye Baby*. In one of his more curious credits, Jerry was heard singing the title song in the 1960 feature *Raymie*.

Screen: 1949: My Friend Irma; 1950: My Friend Irma Goes West; At War With the Army; 1951: That's My Boy; Sailor Beware; 1952: Jumping Jacks; Road to Bali; 1953: The Stooge; Scared Stiff; The Caddy; Money From Home; 1954: Living It Up; 3 Ring Circus; 1955: You're Never Too Young; Artists and Models; 1956: Pardners; Hollywood or Bust; 1957: The Delicate Delinquent (and prod.); The Sad Sack; 1958: Rock-a-Bye Baby (and prod.); The Geisha Boy (and prod.); 1959: Li'l Abner; Don't Give Up the Ship; 1960: Visit to a Small Planet; The Bellboy (and dir.; wr.; prod.); Cinderfella (and prod.); 1961: The Ladies' Man (and dir.; co-wr.; prod.); The Errand Boy (and dir.; co-wr.; prod.); 1962: It's Only Money; 1963: The Nutty Professor (and dir.; co-wr.; prod.); It's a Mad Mad Mad Mad World; Who's Minding the Store?; 1964: The Patsy (and dir.; co-wr.); The Disorderly Orderly (and exec. prod.); 1965: The Family Jewels (and dir.; co-wr.; prod.); Boeing-Boeing; 1966: Three on a Couch

(and dir.; co-wr.; prod.); Way…Way Out; 1967: The Big Mouth (and dir.; co-wr.; prod.); 1968: Don't Raise the Bridge, Lower the River; 1969: Hook, Line & Sinker (and prod.); 1970: Which Way to the Front? (and dir.; prod.); 1972: The Day the Clown Cried (and dir.; co-wr.; nUSr); 1981: Hardly Working (and dir.; co-wr.); 1983: The King of Comedy; Smorgasbord/Cracking Up (and dir.; co-wr.); 1984: Slapstick (of Another Kind); Retenez-Moi…Ou je Fais un Malheur/Hold Me Back or I'll Have an Accident (nUSr); Par ou t'es Rentre? On t'as vu Sortir/How Did You Get In? No One Saw You Leave (nUSr); 1989: Cookie; 1992: Mr. Saturday Night; 1994: Arizona Dream; 1995: Funny Bones.
NY Stage: 1995: Damn Yankees.
Select TV: 1950–55: The Colgate Comedy Hour (series); 1957: The Jerry Lewis Show (sp); 1958: The Jerry Lewis Show (sp); 1959: The Jazz Singer (sp); 1962: The Jerry Lewis Show (series); 1967–69: The Jerry Lewis Show (series); 1984: The Jerry Lewis Show (series); 1987: Fight for Life.

BEATRICE LILLIE

(CONSTANCE SYLVIA MUNSTON)
BORN: TORONTO, ONTARIO, CANADA,
MAY 29, 1894. DIED: JANUARY 20, 1989.

Hardly much of a film star, tiny Beatrice Lillie was one of Great Britain's most revered entertainers, making her name in live theater via revues and cabaret appearances, acclaimed as a comic of stinging wit with a knack for getting laughs through mere facial expressions and a simple twitch of her limbs. Moving to London at 19, she soon got work as a chorus girl, but was finally encouraged by impresario Andre Charlot to concentrate on comedy. During the 1920s she became a stage star in both England and America, which resulted in her own silent vehicle, *Exit Smiling*, the highlight of which had her vamping the villain of the piece, Harry Myers. She also entered the aristocracy, via marriage to Lord Peel in 1920, hence her frequently being referred to as Lady Peel. Going to Hollywood at the dawn of the sound era, she was one of the unfortunate participants in the moldy all-star film *The Show of Shows*; did some short films, "Beatrice Lillie and Her Boy Friends" and "The Roses Have Made Me Remember;" and made another starring film (for Fox), *Are You There?*, that flopped, prompting her to retreat back to the theater. Asked to support Bing Crosby in Paramount's *Doctor Rhythm*, she effortlessly stole the show by interpolating her famous "Two Dozen Double Damask Dinner Napkins" routine, then returned to England where she entertained the troops during World War II.

There was one last movie lead, as a widow swapping boyfriends with her pal in *On Approval*, then it was back to live performing for her solo show *An Evening With Beatrice Lillie*. Movie audiences saw her as a Salvationist, nearly keeping David Niven from winning his bet towards the climax of *Around the World in Eighty Days*, and cherished her playing the evil white slaver in *Thoroughly Modern Millie*, where she gave a spry performance despite her poor health during most of the filming. She published her autobiography *Every Other Inch a Lady* in 1972. A stroke in 1976 left her bedridden for the remainder of her life.
Screen: 1926: Exit Smiling; 1929: The Show of Shows; 1931: Are You There?/Exit Laughing; 1938: Doctor Rhythm; 1943: Welcome to Britain; 1944: On Approval; 1949: Scrapbook for 1933; 1956: Around the World in Eighty Days; 1967: Thoroughly Modern Millie.
NY Stage: 1924: Andre Charlot's Revue; 1925: Charlot Revue; 1926: Oh Please!; 1928: She's My Baby; This Year of Grace; 1931: The Third Little Show; 1932: Too True to Be Good; I Walk a

Little Faster; **1935:** At Home Abroad; **1936:** The Show Is On; **1939:** Set to Music; **1944:** Seven Lively Arts; **1948:** Inside U.S.A.; **1952:** An Evening With Beatrice Lillie; **1957:** Ziegfeld Follies of 1957; **1958:** Auntie Mame; **1964:** High Spirits.

VIVECA LINDFORS

(Elsa Viveca Torstensdotter Lindfors) Born: Uppsala, Sweden, December 29, 1920. ed: Royal Dramatic School, Stockholm. Died: October 25, 1995.

One actress who got more interesting the further she got away from her glamorous ingénue stage, Viveca Lindfors came to films at age 19, first appearing in her native country in *The Spinning Family*, in 1940. She stayed busy in Swedish films during the early 1940s, making enough of a name for herself that Warner Bros. took an interest and signed her to a contract. She debuted for them in *To the Victor* in 1948, playing a woman with a past who falls in love with Dennis Morgan, and did one of the later Errol Flynn swashbucklers, *Adventures of Don Juan*, looking ravishing in the Oscar-winning period costumes. In 1949 she was directed by Don Siegel, in a failed romantic drama, *Night Unto Night*, and they married later that same year. Warners dropped her, and she continued to get work in mostly routine projects, in both the U.S. and back in Europe, including *Four in a Jeep*, as a Viennese housewife; *The Raiders*, as a Mexican woman, in this Gold Rush tale; *The Flying Missile*, as the love interest of Glenn Ford; and *Run for Cover*, as a farmer's daughter romanced by James Cagney. There were also roles in some of the costlier productions of their day like *Tempest*, as Russian Empress Catharine II; *King of Kings*, as Claudia; and *The Story of Ruth*; as well as an award at the Berlin Film Festival for *No Exit*. By the 1970s she was winning notice for her work as a character player, in such pictures as *The Way We Were* and *A Wedding*, having aged considerably but looking, nonetheless, striking and distinctive. By the 1980s she was adding her colorful presence to *Creepshow*, as a woman tormented by the living dead; *The Sure Thing*, as a college instructor; and *Stargate*, as a scientist. She died shortly before the release of a real showcase, *Last Summer in the Hamptons*, as a beloved, aging actress, watching clips of herself in old movies and sharing scenes with real-life son, actor Kristoffer Tabori, from her marriage to Siegel. She received an Emmy Award in 1990 for guesting on *Life Goes On*.

Screen (US releases only): 1940: The Spinning Family; **1945:** Black Roses; Marie at the Windmill; **1946:** Interlude; **1948:** To the Victor; Adventures of Don Juan; **1949:** Night Unto Night; The Mask and the Sword; **1950:** Backfire; This Side of the Law; No Sad Songs for Me; Dark City; Four in a Jeep; **1951:** The Flying Missile; Gypsy Fury/ Singoalia/The Wind Is My Lover; Journey Into Light; **1952:** The Raiders; No Time for Flowers; **1954:** Run for Cover; **1955:** Moonfleet; **1956:** The Halliday Brand; **1958:** I Accuse!; Tempest; Weddings and Babies; **1960:** The Story of Ruth; **1961:** King of Kings; **1962:** These Are the Damned/The Damned; No Exit; **1964:** An Affair of the Skin; **1965:** Sylvia; Brainstorm; **1969:** Coming Apart; **1970:** Puzzle of a Downfall Child; Cauldron of Blood/Blind Man's Bluff; **1973:** The Way We Were; **1977:** Welcome to L.A.; **1978:** Girlfriends; A Wedding; **1979:** Voices; Natural Enemies; **1981:** The Hand; **1982:** Creepshow; **1983:** Silent Madness; **1985:** The Sure Thing; **1987:** Lady Beware; Unfinished Business (and dir.; wr.); **1988:** Going Undercover; **1989:** Rachel River; Forced March; **1990:** Zandalee (dtv); Exiled in America (dtv); The Exorcist III; **1991:** Misplaced; Goin' to Chicago (dtv); **1992:** The Linguini Incident; **1993:**

Backstreet Justice (dtv); **1994:** Stargate; **1995:** Last Summer in the Hamptons; **1996:** Looking for Richard.

NY Stage: 1952: I've Got Sixpence; **1954:** Anastasia; **1956:** King Lear; Miss Julie (ob); **1963:** Pal Joey (ob); **1965:** Postmark Zero; **1968:** Cuba Si (ob); Guns of Carrar (ob); **1971:** Dance of Death (ob); **1974:** I Am a Woman (ob; and co-wr.); **1979:** Are You Now of Have You Ever Been? (ob); **1980:** An Evening With Viveca Lindfors and Kristoffer Tabori (ob); **1992:** Anna the Gypsy Swede (ob; and wr.).

Select TV: 1953: The Bet (sp); Autumn Nocturne (sp); The Vanishing Point (sp); **1955:** The Passport (sp); **1957:** They Never Forget (sp); The Last Tycoon (sp); **1958:** The Bridge of San Luis Rey (sp); The Spell of the Tigress (sp); **1959:** Dangerous Episode (sp); **1960:** The Emperor's Clothes (sp); **1962:** The Paradine Case (sp); **1967:** The Diary of Anne Frank (sp); **1978:** A Question of Guilt; **1980:** Marilyn: The Untold Story; Playing for Time; Mom, the Wolfman and Me; **1981:** The Best Little Girl in the World; For Ladies Only; **1982:** Divorce Wars: A Love Story; Inside the Third Reich; **1984:** A Doctor's Story; Passions; The Three Wishes of Billy Grier; **1985:** Secret Weapons; **1988:** The Ann Jillian Story; **1991:** Child of Darkness, Child of Light; **1993:** Zelda.

MARGARET LINDSAY

(Margaret Kies) Born: Dubuque, IA, September 19, 1910. Died: May 9, 1981.

If million dollar smiles could guarantee front-rank stardom, Margaret Lindsay might have become that much better known. Having started out on the British stage, it was understandable that many mistook her for an English thespian, especially since her first big role found her playing Englishwoman Edith Harris, who ends up on the Titanic, in the 1933 Oscar-winner for Best Picture, *Cavalcade*. Prior to that she had she had been leading lady to Tom Mix in *The Fourth Horseman*, and faked being a Brit in the Monogram production *West of Singapore*. Signed to a contract by Warners in 1933, she was Leslie Howard's unfaithful wife in *Captured!*, and the society gal who marries Donald Cook in *The World Changes*; and she played opposite James Cagney in four pictures: *Lady Killer*, *Devil Dogs of the Air*, *G Men*, and *Frisco Kid*. She backed up Bette Davis on both occasions when that lady won the Oscar, in *Dangerous*, where Davis lost Franchot Tone to her, and in *Jezebel*, where Lindsay won Henry Fonda from the irrepressible Bette, though it was the latter who accompanied him on the quarantine wagon in the movie's famous climax. On film Lindsay may have snatched men away from Davis, but, in truth, she couldn't compete with someone of Davis's stature. When Lindsay got top billing, it was in "B" films, like *When Were You Born?*, a murder mystery with an astrological twist, and *On Trial*, in which she was implicated in a murder by her own daughter. After finishing up her stay at Warners, she made some stops at Universal, where she played Hepzibah in the 1940 version of *The House of Seven Gables*, then signed up with Columbia. There she essayed her most famous role, mystery writer-secretary Nikki Porter in seven "Ellery Queen" quickies. She returned to supporting work before leaving the big screen behind after 1963's *Tammy and the Doctor*.

Screen: 1932: Okay America!; The All-American; Once in a Lifetime; Afraid to Talk; The Fourth Horseman; **1933:** West of Singapore; Cavalcade; Christopher Strong; Private Detective 62; Baby Face; The House on 56th Street; Captured!; Voltaire; Paddy, the Next Best Thing; The World Changes; From Headquarters; Lady Killer; **1934:** Merry Wives of Reno; Fog Over Frisco; The Dragon Murder Case; Gentlemen Are Born; **1935:** Bordertown;

Devil Dogs of the Air; The Florentine Dagger; The Case of the Curious Bride; G Men; Personal Maid's Secret; Frisco Kid; Dangerous; 1936: The Lady Consents; The Law in Her Hands; Public Enemy's Wife; Isle of Fury; Sinner Take All; 1937: Green Light; Song of the City; Slim; Back in Circulation; 1938: Jezebel; When Were You Born?; Gold Is Where You Find It; There's That Woman Again; Broadway Musketeers; Garden of the Moon; 1939: Hell's Kitchen; On Trial; The Under-Pup; 20,000 Men a Year; 1940: Double Alibi; British Intelligence; Honeymoon Deferred; The House of Seven Gables; Meet the Wildcat; Ellery Queen: Master Detective; 1941: Ellery Queen's Penthouse Mystery; There's Magic in Music; Ellery Queen and the Perfect Crime; Ellery Queen and the Murder Ring ; 1942: A Close Call for Ellery Queen; A Tragedy at Midnight; The Spoilers; Enemy Agents Meet Ellery Queen; A Desperate Chance for Ellery Queen; 1943: Crime Doctor; Let's Have Fun; No Place for a Lady; 1944: Alaska; 1945: The Adventures of Rusty; Scarlet Street; Club Havana; 1946: Her Sister's Secret; 1947: Seven Keys to Baldpate; Louisiana; Cass Timberlane; The Vigilantes Return; 1948: B.F.'s Daughter; 1956: Emergency Hospital; The Bottom of the Bottle; 1958: The Restless Years; 1960: Please Don't Eat the Daisies; Jet Over the Atlantic; 1963: Tammy and the Doctor.

Select TV: 1950: The Importance of Being Earnest (sp); 1953: Take a Guess (series); 1956: Indiscreet (sp); Mrs. Snyder (sp); 1974: The Chadwick Family.

HAROLD LLOYD
BORN: BURCHARD, NE, APRIL 20, 1893.
DIED: MARCH 8, 1971.

Always placed third after Chaplin and Keaton in the pantheon of great silent comedians, Harold Lloyd has been treated as something of an underdog, underappreciated and less of a household name with the passing of the years. The fact is that he was extremely popular in his day and left behind a worthy legacy of very funny movies. What's more, his brand of humor and his characterization of the bespectacled nebbish in peril was distinguishable enough from those other men, so no comparison is necessary. As a teen, Lloyd made his stage debut with the Burwood Stock Company, which led to further such work in various parts of the country. There were some unsubstantiated movie assignments, including bits and extra work that resulted in a meeting with Hal Roach. When Roach decided to set up his own company, he tried to introduce Lloyd as a character called "Willie," which just didn't catch on. After a brief period over at Essanay, Lloyd returned to Roach, and they came up with something more to the public's liking, "Lonesome Luke," whose main characteristic was wearing clothing that seemed too small for him. In the course of two years Lloyd starred in approximately 75 of these shorts, which were financially if not artistically fulfilling, since the comedian make it no secret that he hated the character.

In 1917 he changed his screen image to that of a mild-mannered fellow with a pair of round spectacles with no lenses, dubbing him "The Glass Character," and the Harold Lloyd the world came to love was born. Lloyd's steady leading lady up to this point, Bebe Daniels, left to find work elsewhere, and she was replaced by Mildred Davis, who debuted opposite the comedian in "From Hand to Mouth" in 1919. She stayed with him in front of the cameras for another four years when they became man and wife, causing her to retire from acting. 1919 was also a year of tragedy when a small prop bomb went off during a photo shoot, causing the loss of Lloyd's thumb and forefinger on his right

hand. This fact was not well known to most of the world, and the stunts the actor would perform with the use of a prosthetic device and a flesh-colored glove were that much more impressive. After a period of recovery he returned to work for Pathe, his popularity growing as he went from one-reelers to two with 1919's "Bumping Into Broadway." Also significant was the short "High and Dizzy" because it is often considered the first of his offerings to put Harold in a sequence of comical peril, with the comedian treading cautiously in high places with a minimum of trick effects and only an occasional stunt man involved. This successful ploy was repeated to even better effect in "Never Weaken," which found him atop a building under construction as girder after girder narrowly escapes his grasp.

Released in 1921 and clocking in at just under one-hour, *A Sailor-Made Man* became Lloyd's first official feature, with the star playing an idle playboy toughened up by the Navy. It was a Lloyd staple to take the character from spinelessness or carefree hedonism to some sort of growth or feeling of triumph, as was evident in *Grandma's Boy*, overcoming cowardice as he faces a town bully, and, in a flashback sequence, portraying a similarly nervous relative in Civil War days. It was one of his milder works but his own personal favorite. He followed this by playing *Dr. Jack*, an optimistic small-town physician who dispenses more wisdom than pills. These films were now full-fledged features, and he was reaching the zenith of his popularity. In 1923 he came up with his undisputed masterpiece, *Safety Last*, going off to the big city to seek his fortune and winding up as part of a publicity stunt requiring him to climb up the side of a building. The movie was one sustained laugh sequence after another, and its high-rise climax was one of the most amazing ever put on film. It also resulted in one of the enduring images of movie folklore, with the wide-eyed comic hanging off the hands of a large clock high above street level. He kept spinning them out with *Why Worry?*, as a hypochondriac getting involved in a South American revolution; *Girl Shy*, trying to stop the leading lady from marrying another man, leading to a thrilling chase scene; and *The Freshman*, going from college dork to football hero in another of his most fondly remembered films.

Around this point he was so in demand that he could accept a better offer from Paramount, which resulted in the sprightly *For Heaven's Sake*, portraying another member of the idle rich, helping a skid row mission; *The Kid Brother*, covering familiar territory, as a weakling and coward who finds courage via his love for leading lady Jobyna Ralston; and *Speedy*, playing a cab driver in New York in another of his finest accomplishments, punctuated by a nostalgic trip to Coney Island and a smashing on-location chase through Manhattan. Around this time sound arrived, so *Welcome Danger* added a soundtrack to the already finished silent movie. It did encouragingly, Lloyd's mild-mannered voice matching nicely with his image, but the next, *Feet First*, showed a dropping off of attendance despite having another of his cliffhanging sequences that Lloyd aficionados rank among his best, with Harold stuck on a scaffold in a sack. There was one last feature that received an ample amount of praise, *Movie Crazy*, a sweet entry about a poor schnook who goes to Hollywood under the impression that he is wanted as a leading man. The truth was Lloyd was starting to get too old for his young-innocent routine, and many moviegoers thought of him as someone from a bygone era.

Things pretty much bottomed out with *The Cat's Paw*, made for Fox and involving a crooked mayoral race and the criminal underworld of Chinatown, but he had roles in two more for Paramount that were a cut above this, *The Milky Way*, as a milkman who ends up as a boxer, and *Professor Beware*, as an

Egyptologist involved in scandal. Both lost money and Lloyd felt it was time to retire, having amassed an impressive fortune. His wealth was best reflected by his Beverly Hills estate, Greenacres, perhaps the most famous and largest of the grandiose movie mansions of the silent era. For RKO he became a producer and was responsible for two poorly received comedies, *A Girl, a Guy, and a Gob* (1941) and *My Favorite Spy* (1942). Then director-writer Preston Sturges coaxed him out of retirement for what turned out to be a disheartening experience, *The Sin of Harold Diddlebock*, which wound up being seen by most people in a cut version retitled *Mad Wednesday*. Sturges's attempt to capture some of the magic that had made Lloyd one of the heroes of his era was heartfelt, but the script just wasn't very funny. There was a special Oscar awarded in 1952 and then, a decade later, a successful compilation, produced and edited by Lloyd himself, *Harold Lloyd's World of Comedy*, which, along with its follow-up, *The Funny Side of Life*, was firm justification for Lloyd's reputation as one of the geniuses of film comedy.

Screen (shorts):: 1913: Algy on the Force; The Old Monk's Tale; His Chum, the Baron; A Little Hero; Cupid in the Dental Parlor; Hide and Seek; Twixt Love and Fire; 1914: The Wizard of Oz; Willie; Willie's Haircut; From Italy's Shores; Curses They Remarked; The Hungry Actors; 1915: Willie at Sea; Willie Runs the Park; Once Ever Ten Minutes; Soaking the Clothes; Terribly Stuck Up; Some Baby; Giving Them Fits; Tinkering with Trouble; Just Nuts; Ragtime Snap Shots; Ruses Rhymes and Roughnecks; Spit Ball Sadie; Pressing His Suit; A Mix-up for Maisie; Fresh From the Farm; Bughouse Bellhops; Great While It Lasted; A Foozle at a Tea Party; Peculiar Patients' Pranks; Lonesome Luke; Lonesome Luke — Social Gangster; 1916: Lonesome Luke Leans to the Literary; Luke Lugs Luggage; Lonesome Luke Lolls in Luxury; Luke the Candy Cut-Up; Luke Foils the Villain; Luke and the Rural Roughnecks; Luke Pipes the Pippens; Lonesome Luke — Circus King; Luke's Double; Them Was the Happy Days; Luke and the Bomb Throwers; Luke's Late Lunchers; Luke Laughs Last; Luke's Fatal Flivver; Luke's Society Mixup; Luke's Washful Waiting; Luke Rides Rough-Shod; Luke — Crystal Gazer; Luke's Lost Lamb; Luke Does the Midway; Luke Joins the Navy; Luke and the Mermaids; Luke's Speedy Club Life; Luke and the Bangtails; Luke the Chauffeur; Luke's Preparedness Preparations; Luke the Gladiator; Luke — Patient Provider; Luke's Newsie Knockout; Luke's Movie Muddle; Luke — Rank Impersonator; Luke's Fireworks Fizzle; Luke Locates the Loot; Luke's Shattered Sleep; 1917: Luke's Lost Liberty; Luke's Busy Day; Luke's Trolley Troubles; Lonesome Luke — Lawyer; Luke Wins Ye Ladye Fair; Lonesome Luke's Lively Life; Lonesome Luke on Tin Can Alley; Lonesome Luke's Honeymoon; Lonesome Luke — Plumber; Stop! Luke! Listen!; Lonesome Luke — Messenger; Lonesome Luke — Mechanic; Lonesome Luke's Wild Women; Over the Fence (and dir.); Lonesome Luke Loses Patients; Pinched; By the Sad Sea Waves; Birds of a Feather; Bliss; Lonesome Luke in From London to Laramie; Rainbow Island; Lonesome Luke in Love Laughs and Lather; The Flirt; Clubs Are Trump; All Aboard; We Never Sleep; Move On; Bashful; 1918: The Tip; The Big Idea; The Lamb; Hit Him Again; Beat It; A Gasoline Wedding; Look Pleasant Please; Here Come the Girls; Let's Go; On the Jump; Follow the Crowd; Pipe the Whiskers; It's a Wild Life; Hey There; Kicked Out; The Non-Stop Kid; Two-Gun Gussie; Fireman, Save My Child; The City Slicker; Sic 'em Towser; Somewhere in Turkey; Are Crooks Dishonest?; An Ozark Romance; Kicking the Germ Out of Germany; That's Him; Bride and Gloom; Two Scrambled; Bees in His Bonnet; Swing Your Partners; Why Pick on Me?; Nothing but Trouble; Hear 'em Rave; Take a Chance; She Loves Me Not;

1919: Wanted — $5000; Going! Going! Gone; Ask Father; On the Fire; I'm on My Way; Look Out Below!; The Dutiful Dub; Next Aisle Over; A Sammy in Siberia; Just Dropped In; Crack Your Heels; Ring Up the Curtain; Young Mr. Jazz; Si Senor; Before Breakfast; The Marathon; Back to the Woods; Pistols for Breakfast; Swat the Crook; Off the Trolley; Spring Fever; Billy Blazes, Esq.; Just Neighbors; At the Old Stage Door; Never Touched Me; A Jazzed Honeymoon; Count Your Change; Chop Suey & Co.; Heap Big Chief; Don't Shove; Be My Wife; The Rajah; He Leads, Others Follow; Soft Money; Count the Votes; Pay Your Dues; His Only Father; Bumping Into Broadway; Captain Kidd's Kids; From Handed to Mouth; 1920: His Royal Shyness; Haunted Spooks; An Eastern Westerner; High and Dizzy; Get Out and Get Under; Number Please; 1921: Now or Never; Among Those Present; I Do; Never Weaken; 1931: Screen Snap Shots No. 38.

Screen (features): 1921: A Sailor-Made Man; 1922: Grandma's Boy (and co-wr.); Dr. Jack; 1923: Safety Last; Why Worry?; 1924: Girl Shy; Hot Water; 1925: The Freshman; 1926: For Heaven's Sake; 1927: The Kid Brother; 1928: Speedy; 1929: Welcome Danger; 1930: Feet First; 1932: Movie Crazy; 1934: The Cat's Paw; 1936: The Milky Way; 1938: Professor Beware; 1947: The Sin of Harold Diddlebock/Mad Wednesday.

GENE LOCKHART

BORN: LONDON, ONTARIO, CANADA, JULY 18, 1891. DIED: MARCH 31, 1957.

Plump, soft-voiced Gene Lockhart had a look you couldn't help but distrust to some degree, and he was therefore called on to play sneaks, windbags, and fools. His benign side was less interesting, so it was just as well when they gave him some juice to squeeze. A one-time singer and journalist, he made his professional stage debut performing Gilbert and Sullivan. In 1917 he came to Broadway in *The Riviera Girl*, and, apart from a single silent movie credit, in the 1922 version of *Smilin' Through*, he pretty much stayed in the theater for the next 17 years. It was his performance as the hard-drinking Uncle Sid, in the 1933 Broadway production of *Ah, Wilderness!*, that brought him a steady stream of Hollywood offers, although he would not get to repeat his role in the 1936 movie version of *Wilderness* (Wallace Beery played it). Instead he essayed another drunken part, in RKO's *By Your Leave*, which marked his sound debut. Starting in 1936, his wife, actress Kathleen Lockhart, began joining him on screen, the first such occasion being *Brides Are Like That*, in which they portrayed man and wife. Gene continued to make an impression, as a meddlesome best man (named Pighead) in *Times Square Playboy*; as an unctuous producer in *Something to Sing About*; and, best of all, as the weasely informer who causes all sorts of trouble for Charles Boyer and pays for it with his life in *Algiers*. The last earned him his sole Oscar nomination. More snaky characters followed with *Sinners in Paradise*, as a politician stranded on a desert island, and *Blackmail*, as a lout who sends Edward G. Robinson to prison twice for the crime he himself committed. Between these he was at his kindest, as Bob Cratchit, in MGM's uninspired 1938 rendering of *A Christmas Carol*, playing opposite not only his real-life wife but daughter June as well.

Lockhart was ideally cast physically as orator Stephen A. Douglas in *Abe Lincoln in Illinois*, then took abuse from Edward G. Robinson in *The Sea Wolf*, before playing another pompous fellow, giving reverend Fredric March grief in *One Foot in Heaven*. Being wartime, he was asked to play an informer again, this time working for the Nazis, in *Hangmen Also Die*, a position he carried on in a more famous thriller of the 1940s, *The House on 92nd Street*. He was a decent sort of fellow in one of the big films of the war years, *Going My Way*, offering assistance to priest Bing Crosby; wound up murdered by Louis Hayward in *Strange Woman*; was an officious manager making demands of feminist Betty Grable in *The Shocking Miss Pilgrim*; and was the mayor taken in by Danny Kaye's deception in *The Inspector General*. At his funniest he was the spineless judge coached by William Frawley in the holiday classic *Miracle on 34th Street*, then went back to being victimized in a cheapie called *Red Light*, in which he met his demise getting crushed to death under a trailer. In a similarly low-budget vein he had a fairly large part as the bad guy in a Dan Duryea noir, *World for Ransom*, and received his last roles of any note in *Carousel*, as the Starkeeper, and in *The Man in the Grey Flannel Suit*, as one of Gregory Peck's fellow commuters.

Screen: 1922: Smilin' Through; 1934: By Your Leave; The Gay Bride; I've Been Around; 1935: Crime and Punishment; Star of Midnight; Captain Hurricane; Thunder in the Night; Storm Over the Andes; 1936: The Gorgeous Hussy; Brides Are Like That; Times Square Playboy; The Devil Is a Sissy; Earthworm Tractors; The First Baby; Career Woman; The Garden Murder Case; Wedding Present; Mind Your Own Business; Come Closer Folks; 1937: Make Way for Tomorrow; Mama Steps Out; Too Many Wives; Something to Sing About; The Sheik Steps Out; 1938: Of Human Hearts; Blondie; Algiers; Sweethearts; Men Are Such Fools; Listen, Darling; Penrod's Double Trouble; Meet the Girls; A Christmas Carol; Sinners in Paradise; 1939: The Story of Alexander Graham Bell; Blackmail; Geronimo; Hotel Imperial; Our Leading Citizen; I'm From Missouri; Tell No Tales; Bridal Suite; 1940: Edison, the Man; Abe Lincoln in Illinois; His Girl Friday; A Dispatch from Reuters; Dr. Kildare Goes Home; We Who Are Young; South of Pago Pago; Keeping Company; 1941: International Lady; The Sea Wolf; Meet John Doe; Steel Against the Sky; Billy the Kid; All That Money Can Buy; They Died With Their Boots On; One Foot in Heaven; 1942: The Gay Sisters; You Can't Escape Forever; Juke Girl; 1943: Mission to Moscow; Hangmen Also Die; Northern Pursuit; Forever and a Day; The Desert Song; Find the Blackmailer; 1944: Action in Arabia; Going My Way; Man From Frisco; 1945: Leave Her to Heaven; The House on 92nd Street; That's the Spirit; 1946: The Strange Woman; A Scandal in Paris/Thieves' Holiday; Meet Me on Broadway; 1947: The Foxes of Harrow; The Shocking Miss Pilgrim; Miracle on 34th Street; Honeymoon; Cynthia; Her Husband's Affairs; 1948: That Wonderful Urge; Joan of Arc; Apartment for Peggy; The Inside Story; I, Jane Doe; 1949: Madame Bovary; Down to the Sea in Ships; The Inspector General; Red Light; 1950: The Big Hangover; Riding High; 1951: I'd Climb the Highest Mountain; The Lady From Texas; Seeds of Destruction/The Sickle or the Cross; Rhubarb; 1952: A Girl in Every Port; Face to Face; Androcles and the Lion; Apache War Smoke; Bonzo Goes to College; Hoodlum Empire; 1953: Down Among the Sheltering Palms; Confidentially Connie; Francis Covers the Big Town; The Lady Wants Mink; 1954: World for Ransom; 1955: The Vanishing American; 1956: The Man in the Gray Flannel Suit; Carousel; 1957: Jeanne Eagels.

NY Stage: 1916: The Riviera Girl; 1921: Skylark; 1923: Sun-Up; 1924: The Handy Man; 1926: The Bunk of 1926; 1927: Faust; 1930: Little Father of the Wilderness; 1931: The Way of the World; 1933: Uncle Tom's Cabin; Ah, Wilderness!; 1935: Sweet Mystery of Life; 1937: Virginia; 1945: Happily Ever After; 1950: Death of a Salesman.

Select TV: 1950: The Barretts of Wimpole Street (sp); A Child Is Born (sp); 1951: The House of Seven Gables (sp); 1952: The

Bishop Misbehaves (sp); The Rose (sp); An Afternoon in Caribou (sp); 1953: My Daughter's Husband (sp); The Bells of Cockaigne (sp); The Closed Door (sp); 1954: The Test Case (sp); The Sins of the Fathers (sp); The Queen's English (sp); 1955: Homer Bell (series); The Late Christopher Bean (sp); 1956: Has Anybody Seen My Gal? (sp); 1957: It Happened on Fifth Avenue (sp).

JUNE LOCKHART

BORN: NEW YORK, NY, JUNE 25, 1925.

She probably had her bad days at home, but on camera June Lockhart always came across as the just about the nicest of the nice ladies. The daughter of actors Gene and Kathleen Lockhart, she made her film debut as one of their children (they were the Cratchits) in the 1938 version of *A Christmas Carol*. Over the next decade she was seen as one of Bette Davis's charges in *All This, and Heaven Too*; one of Gary Cooper's siblings in *Sergeant York*; the socialite New Yorker who turns out to be not so bad after all in *Meet Me in St. Louis*; and, prophetically, the grown-up version of the character Elizabeth Taylor had played in *Lassie Come Home*, in the sequel, *Son of Lassie*. There was also the starring role in a tepid chiller for Universal, *She-Wolf of London*, but she didn't seem to be going anywhere special on screen, so she went to Broadway where she received a Theatre World Award for her 1947 Broadway debut in *For Love or Money*. Around this time television arrived, and it was in that medium that Lockhart at last became famous, thanks to that inimitable collie, playing the kindly Ruth Martin on the series adaptation of *Lassie* for six seasons. This was followed by a stint as space mother Maureen Robinson in the deliberately goofy sci-fi series *Lost in Space*. With the exception of 1957's *Time Limit*, she was away from movies for some three decades but returned there in the 1980s in such oddities as the sci-fi spoof *Strange Invaders* and *Troll* (featuring her daughter Anne), no doubt cast by baby boomers with fond memories of their TV upbringing. There was an interesting role amid this bunch, as a pretentious actress, interacting with the mostly younger cast members of the comedy-drama *Sleep With Me*, and then a cameo in an overblown big-screen revision of *Lost in Space*.

Screen: 1938: A Christmas Carol; 1940: All This, and Heaven Too; 1941: Adam Had Four Sons; Sergeant York; 1942: Miss Annie Rooney; 1943: Forever and a Day; 1944: The White Cliffs of Dover; Meet Me in St. Louis; 1945: Keep Your Powder Dry; Son of Lassie; 1946: Easy to Wed; She-Wolf of London; The Yearling; 1947: Bury Me Dead; It's a Joke, Son; T-Men; 1957: Time Limit; 1982: Butterfly; Deadly Games; 1983: Strange Invaders; 1986: Troll; 1988: Rented Lips; 1989: The Big Picture; C.H.U.D. II: Bud the Chud (dtv); 1991: Dead Women in Lingerie; 1994: Sleep With Me; 1998: Lost in Space; 2000: Deterrence; The Thundering 8th (dtv).

NY Stage: 1947: For Love or Money; 1955: The Grand Prize.

Select TV: 1951: The Just and the Unjust (sp); One Sunday Afternoon (sp); For Love or Money (sp); 1952: Apple of His Eye (sp); But Not Forever (sp); The Doctor's Wife (sp); 1952–55: Who Said That? (series); 1953: The Burtons (sp); At Midnight on the 31st of March (sp); 1954: Goodbye…But It Doesn't Go Away (sp); The Deserter (sp); 1956: Rise Up and Walk (sp); Jack Be Nimble (sp); Morning's at Seven (sp); The Night They Won the Oscar (sp); The Confession (sp); 1957: Fear Has Many Faces (sp); The Grand Prize (sp); The Man Who Played God (sp); A Matter of Guilt (sp); A Loud Laugh (sp); 1958: Balance of Terror (sp); 1958–64: Lassie (series); 1959: The Square Egghead (sp); Night Club (sp); 1965–68: Lost in Space (series); 1968–70: Petticoat

Junction (series); 1970: But I Don't Want to Get Married; 1973: The Bait; 1975: Who Is the Black Dahlia?; 1977: Curse of the Black Widow; 1978: Loose Change (ms); The Gift of Love; A Double Life; 1979: Walking Through the Fire; 1982: The Capture of Grizzly Adams; 1984–86: General Hospital (series); 1984: The Night They Saved Christmas; 1988: Perfect People; A Whisper Kills; Never Say Goodbye; 1992: Danger Island; 1995: The Colony; Out There; 2001: Au Pair II.

MARGARET LOCKWOOD

(MARGARET DAY) BORN: KARACHI, INDIA, SEPTEMBER 15, 1916. ED: RADA. DIED: JULY 15, 1990.

In Britain she was one of the most popular stars of the postwar era, but she had a decidedly lesser impact on America, no doubt because the sort of lush romances in which she specialized were very much fashioned for native audiences. While quite young she took an interest in acting, studying at the Italia Conti School before making her professional stage bow in a 1928 production of *A Midsummer Night's Dream*. After some further dramatic studies at RADA she made her movie debut in 1934, in *Lorna Doone*, in support of Victoria Hopper. Signed by British Lion, she had her first lead, in *Midshipman Easy/Men of the Sea*, and played opposite Douglas Fairbanks, Jr. in *The Amateur Gentleman*, and George Arliss in *Dr. Syn*, the participation of these men guaranteeing some distribution in the United States. The one that really made her name, *The Lady Vanishes*, as the passenger trying to locate the missing Dame May Whitty, was also instrumental in bringing further attention to its director, Alfred Hitchcock. Now under contract to Gainsborough, the studio allowed Lockwood to go to Hollywood. However, neither film made there, a Shirley Temple vehicle, *Susannah of the Mounties*, or another with Fairbanks, *Rulers of the Sea*, suggested any reason for her to hang around that town.

Back home she landed good roles in *The Stars Look Down*, playing Michael Redgrave's shallow wife, and *Night Train to Munich*, escaping from the Nazis along with Rex Harrison and Paul Henreid. These were followed by the melodrama that helped make her a box-office attraction, *The Man in Grey*, in which she was the scheming governess who tries to make her employer, James Mason, her husband. This was topped by the 1945 version of *The Wicked Lady*, where she starred alongside Mason again, this time playing a treacherous woman who takes to highway robbery during the 17th century. The public loved watching her play these bitchy roles, and there was more with *Bedelia*, poisoning three husbands and trying to do away with number four. Moving away from villainy, she was falsely accused of wrongdoing in *Jassy*, then did some badly received comedies, *Look Before You Love* and *Cardboard Cavalier*. By the 1950s her heyday was trickling away, although she received encouraging notices for her sassy performance as the woman who thinks she's on to Dirk Bogarde's devious intentions in *Cast a Dark Shadow*. At that point, 1955, she offered up her autobiography, *Lucky Me*, and then backed away from motion pictures. There was stage work, television, and then, out of the blue, the role of the wicked (of course!) stepmother in the musical *The Slipper and the Rose*.

Screen: 1934: Lorna Doone; 1935: The Case of Gabriel Perry; Some Day; Honors Easy; Midshipman Easy/Men of the Sea; Man of the Moment; The Amateur Gentleman; Jury's Evidence; 1936: The Beloved Vagabond; Irish for Luck; 1937: The Street Singer; Who's Your Lady Friend?; Melody and Romance; Dr. Syn; Owd Bob/To the Victor; 1938: Bank Holiday/Three on a

Weekend; The Lady Vanishes; 1939: A Girl Must Live; Susannah of the Mounties; Rulers of the Sea; The Stars Look Down; 1940: Night Train to Munich; The Girl in the News; 1941: Quiet Wedding; 1942: Alibi; 1943: The Man in Grey; Dear Octopus/The Randolph Family; 1944: Give Us the Moon; Love Story/A Lady Surrenders; 1945: A Place of One's Own; I'll Be Your Sweetheart; The Wicked Lady; 1946: Bedelia; Hungry Hill; 1947: Jassy; The White Unicorn/Bad Sister; 1948: Look Before You Love; 1949: Madness of the Heart; Cardboard Cavalier; 1950: Highly Dangerous; 1952: Trent's Last Case; 1953: Laughing Anne; 1954: Trouble in the Glen; 1955: Cast a Dark Shadow; 1976: The Slipper and the Rose.

Select TV: 1965: The Flying Swan (series); 1972: Justice (series).

GINA LOLLOBRIGIDA

(LUIGINA LOLLOBRIGIDA) BORN: SUBIACO, ITALY, JULY 4, 1927.

A striking personality with an unforgettable name, Gina Lollobrigida became a sex symbol/star of the international cinema in the 1950s much as her fellow Italian Sophia Loren did. But whereas Sophia was magnetically one of a kind and a fine actress as well, Gina had to get by on her pouting presence more than a wide range of talent. Clearly her endowments got her into the business, since it was a chance meeting with director Mario Costa that got things rolling. Minus any acting studies, she debuted in *Elisir d'Amore* in 1946, and was upped to the title role, four years later, in *Miss Italia*, which starred American actor Richard Ney. It was 1952 when she was first imported to America in one of those foreign episode films that were popular in their day, *A Tale of Five Women*. There was an aborted attempt by Howard Hughes to sign her to a Hollywood contract, after which she returned to Europe to be Errol Flynn's leading lady in one of his later swashbucklers, *Crossed Swords*, and Humphrey Bogart's wife in the mediocre spoof *Beat the Devil*; and to fill out a period costume in the French adventure *Fan-Fan the Tulip*. She was already becoming a name in the international market, and this was enhanced by the success of *Bread, Love and Dreams*, in which she was a sexy villager with her eye on police chief Vittorio de Sica.

There was a rush to begin importing her films to the U.S., and such titles as *The Wayward Wife*, *Frisky*, and *Flesh and the Women* (in a dual role), clearly wanted audiences to believe that they were getting something naughty for their money. She made her official crossover into Hollywood movies with *Trapeze*, which turned out to be a good choice since this circus love-triangle featuring Burt Lancaster and Tony Curtis was one of the big hits of 1956. Lollobrigida, of course, looked alluring in a pair of tights. She was seemingly well cast as Esmeralda in the latest version of *The Hunchback of Notre Dame* (Anthony Quinn), but failed to wipe away memories of Maureen O'Hara in the previous, better rendition. Back in Italy she had appeared in her biggest hit, *La Donna piu Bella del Mondo*, which came to the U.S. in 1958 as *Beautiful but Dangerous*, the title suggesting something more interesting than the standard biopic it was — that of singer Lina Cavalieri. Following these, she had roles in two more major American films, both of which received a certain degree of audience interest despite being major yawns: *Solomon and Sheba*, appearing opposite Yul Brynner, and the World War II tale *Never So Few*, paired with Frank Sinatra, with whom she did not click off screen. In fact, her choice of English language vehicles continued to do nothing to raise her reputation as anything more than an international curiosity, including two tepid Universal comedies with Rock Hudson, *Come September* and *Strange Bedfellows* (at one point asked to portray Lady Godiva); a flop British soap opera with Sean Connery, *Woman of Straw*; and a terrible sex farce with Alec Guinness, *Hotel Paradiso*.

By the 1960s the distributors weren't so keen to import her foreign language offerings, and *Bambole/The Dolls*, another of those episode movies, was one of the few to open in America. Instead she ended up in one of Bob Hope's tired 1960s comedies, *The Private Navy of Sgt. O'Farrell*, still enduring the obvious jokes about her bustline, and the better *Buona Sera, Mrs. Campbell*, probably the most watchable of her English-speaking assignments during this period, as an unmarried mother having to confront three former G.I.'s, one of whom might be the father of her child. That pretty much spelled the end of high profile Lollobrigida releases. There was an effort to sell Cervantes to the youth crowd as *The Young Rebel*, in which she dabbled with Horst Buccholz, and a caper movie with David Niven that barely saw the light of day, *King, Queen, Knave*. Otherwise she was but a faint memory to most television viewers when she popped up for a season of *Falcon Crest* in the mid-1980s, followed by a miniseries, *Deceptions*. She seemed to add just the sort of glossy glamour that these kinds of entertainment required.

Screen (US releases only): 1952: A Tale of Five Women; **1953:** Crossed Swords; Beat the Devil; Fan-Fan the Tulip; The Young Caruso; Time Gone By; **1954:** Bread, Love and Dreams; **1955:** The Wayward Wife; Frisky; **1956:** Trapeze; Woman of Rome; **1957:** The Hunchback of Notre Dame; **1958:** Flesh and the Woman; Beautiful but Dangerous; **1959:** Solomon and Sheba; Never So Few; **1960:** Fast and Sexy; Where the Wind Blows!; The Unfaithfuls; **1961:** Go Naked in the World; Come September; **1964:** Woman of Straw; **1966:** Strange Bedfellows; Bambole/The Dolls; **1966:** Hotel Paradiso; **1968:** The Private Navy of Sgt. O'Farrell; Buona Sera, Mrs. Campbell; **1969:** The Young Rebel/Cervantes; **1971:** That Splendid November; **1975:** Bad Man's River; **1977:** King, Queen, Knave; The Lonely Woman; **1999:** Hundred and One Nights (filmed 1995).

Select TV: 1984–85: Falcon Crest (series); **1985:** Deceptions (ms).

HERBERT LOM

(HERBERT CHARLES ANGELO KUCHACEVICH ZE SCHLUDERPACHERU) BORN: PRAGUE, CZECHOSLOVAKIA, JANUARY 9, 1917.

Suavely sinister in both looks and voice, Herbert Lom left his native country as the Nazis approached and settled in England, where he made a successful career before moving into the international movie market. In Czechoslovakia he hade made his stage bow in 1936 and the following year appeared in the film *Zena pod Krizem*, before going to London to take up additional training with the Old Vic. His first British movie part of note was in *The Young Mr. Pitt*, where he was ideally cast as Napoleon, so much in fact that he would reprise the part in the 1956 version of *War and Peace*. This was followed by a breakthrough performance as an evil hypnotist in *The Dark Tower*, in 1943. There were supporting parts, as a psychiatrist in *The Seventh Veil*, and a gang leader in *Appointment with Crime*; and then a flashy lead in a "B" melodrama, *Dual Alibi*, playing twin French trapeze artists. His roles in two 1950s productions with American stars, *State Secret* (Douglas Fairbanks, Jr.) and *Night and the City* (Richard Widmark), helped bring him more attention outside Britain. In 1955 he reached his peak in England, playing the one potentially dangerous member of Alec Guinness's gang of second-rate thieves in the delightfully black *The Ladykillers*. After his second stint as Napoleon he

became a familiar face in international productions like *Spartacus*, *El Cid*, and *Gambit*, and even played Simon Legree in a multi-country production of *Uncle Tom's Cabin*. His unfriendly glare meant he was ideally employed for such horror offerings as the 1962 version of *The Phantom of the Opera*, *Count Dracula* (as Prof. Van Helsing), and *Mark of the Devil*, which had the dubious distinction of offering vomit bags to offended patrons. In 1964 he played (hilariously) the role of Peter Sellers beleaguered chief, Charles Dreyfuss, in the funniest of all the Inspector Clouseau comedies, *A Shot in the Dark*. He would become most closely identified with this part after director Blake Edwards decided to revive the series in 1975 with *The Return of the Pink Panther* and five other occasions for Lom to mug fearlessly.

Screen: 1937: Zena pod Krizem (nUSr); **1940:** Mein Kampf, My Crimes; **1942:** The Young Mr. Pitt; Secret Mission; Tomorrow We Live/At Dawn We Die; **1943:** The Dark Tower; **1944:** Hotel Reserve; **1945:** The Seventh Veil; Night Boat to Dublin; **1946:** Appointment With Crime; **1947:** Dual Alibi; **1948:** Snowbound; Good Time Girl; Portrait From Life/The Girl in the Painting; Lucky Mascot/The Brass Monkey; **1949:** Golden Salamander; **1950:** Night and the City; State Secret/The Great Manhunt; The Black Rose; Cage of Gold; **1951:** Hell Is Sold Out; Two on the Tiles; Mr. Denning Drives North; Whispering Smith Hits London/ Whispering Smith Versus Scotland Yard; **1952:** The Ringer; The Net/Project M7; The Man Who Watched Trains Go By/The Paris Express; **1953:** Rough Shoot/Shoot First; The Love Lottery; Star of India; **1954:** Twist of Fate/Beautiful Stranger; **1955:** The Ladykillers; **1956:** War and Peace; **1957:** Fire Down Below; Hell Drivers; Action of the Tiger; **1958:** I Accuse!; Chase a Crooked Shadow; The Roots of Heaven; Intent to Kill; **1959:** No Trees in the Street; The Big Fisherman; Passport to Shame/Room 43; Northwest Frontier/Flame Over India; Third Man on the Mountain; **1960:** I Aim at the Stars; Spartacus; **1961:** Mr. Topaze/I Like Money; El Cid; Mysterious Island; The Frightened City; **1962:** The Phantom of the Opera; Treasure of Silver Lake; Tiara Tahiti; **1964:** A Shot in the Dark; **1965:** Uncle Tom's Cabin/White Trash Woman (US: 1969); Return From the Ashes; **1966:** Bang, Bang, You're Dead!/Our Man in Marrakesh; Gambit; **1967:** Assignment to Kill; **1968:** Eve/The Face of Eve; Villa Rides!; 99 Women/Island of Despair; **1969:** Journey to the Far Side of the Sun/Doppelganger; **1970:** Count Dracula (US: 1973); Dorian Gray; **1971:** Mark of the Devil; Murders in the Rue Morgue; **1972:** Asylum; **1973:** Dark Places; And Now the Screaming Starts; **1975:** Ten Little Indians; The Return of the Pink Panther; **1976:** The Pink Panther Strikes Again; **1977:** Charleston; **1978:** Revenge of the Pink Panther; **1980:** The Lady Vanishes; The Man with Bogart's Face; Hopscotch; **1982:** Trail of the Pink Panther; **1983:** Curse of the Pink Panther; The Dead Zone; **1984:** Memed My Hawk (US: 1987); **1985:** King Solomon's Mines; **1987:** Whoops Apocalypse!; Skeleton Coast (dtv); Master of Dragonard Hill (dtv); **1988:** Going Bananas; The Crystal Eye (dtv); **1989:** River of Death; Ten Little Indians; **1990:** The Masque of the Red Death; **1991:** The Devil's Daughter (dtv); The Pope Must Die; **1993:** Son of the Pink Panther.

Select TV: 1963: The Horse Without a Head; **1963–64:** The Human Jungle (series); **1967:** The Karate Killers; **1969:** Mister Jericho; **1981:** Peter and Paul; **1987:** Scoop; **1998:** Marco Polo.

CAROLE LOMBARD

(JANE ALICE PETERS) BORN: FORT WAYNE, IN, OCTOBER 6, 1908. RAISED IN LOS ANGELES, CA. DIED: JANUARY 16, 1942.

Perhaps because of her tragic, early death, or maybe because she was blonde and gorgeous, Carole Lombard is revered even to this day as the crowning female practitioner of sophisticated 1930s comedy. She did indeed have a casual, sly way of bringing a lighter-than-air quality to good material. But she also had a habit of going into shrill decibels to achieve a laugh, her technique a mite frantic at times when a little more restraint would have sufficed. There is certainly no reason why Myrna Loy, Joan Blondell, or Claudette Colbert cannot be said to have given her more than a run for her money. While quite young her divorced mother moved her and her siblings to Los Angeles. There a chance meeting with director Allan Dwan led to Lombard being cast, in 1921, in a supporting part, as Monte Blue's daughter, in *A Perfect Crime*, using her real name, Jane Peters. Four years later she was signed to a contract by Fox under the new name of "Carol Lombard" (adding the "e" to "Carol" when she joined Paramount five years later). She started at Fox with a leading role in *Marriage in Transit*, starring Edmund Lowe, and was soon off the screen while recovering from facial injuries sustained in an automobile accident. Her contract with Fox was dissolved, so she instead went to work for Mack Sennett in three short comedies, "The Girl From Everywhere," "His Unlucky Night," and "The Swim Princess." She continued to find employment here and there, eventually landing a contract with Pathe, but making little impact until she reached Paramount in 1930, as part of the cast of a Buddy Rogers comedy, *Safety in Numbers*, playing a Follies girl. The studio was impressed enough to add her to the payroll, putting her in a pair of sophisticated comedies with William Powell, both of which had him playing gigolos, *Man of the World* and *Ladies' Man*, with Lombard as one of the women stuck on him. They married in 1931 and spent two years as man and wife.

Paramount continued to let her strut her stuff, opposite Norman Foster (*Up Pops the Devil*, as a jealous dancer), Gary Cooper (*I Take This Woman*, as an heiress who marries a cowboy) and Ricardo Cortez (*No One Man*, torn between him and Paul Lukas). These didn't quite push her into the upper echelons of stardom but she did get a chance to sparkle alongside Clark Gable on his one loan-out to Paramount, *No Man of Her Own*, in which she was a librarian intrigued by his interest in her. This was 1932, so it would be another seven years before they became one of Hollywood's most celebrated, albeit short-lived, married couples. In the meantime she got top billing in an ensemble, *From Hell to Heaven*, inspired by the multi-character format of *Grand Hotel*, as a woman whose faith in her ex is riding on a horse race; a war film, *The Eagle and the Hawk*, billed simply as "The Beautiful Lady" and being denied any opportunity to emote opposite one of its stars, Cary Grant; and a thriller, *Supernatural*, as an heiress possessed by her dead sister, who had gone to the electric chair for murder. She was also in a trashy jungle melodrama, *White Woman*, proving just how bad she could be in a dramatic role, and *Bolero*, which brought attention to her dancing abilities. There was the requisite leading-lady duty opposite the studio's big singing star, Bing Crosby, in *We're Not Dressing*, pairing off with him very nicely in this story of a shipwrecked snob finding love with a common sailor. Columbia borrowed her on several occasions with middling results, including *Virtue*, trying to leave behind her life as a hooker; *No More Orchids*, another case of casting her as an upper class lady in love with someone "beneath" her station, in this case Lyle Talbot; and *Brief Moment*, in a misconceived turn, as a nightclub singer battling with tycoon husband Gene Reynolds, in characters based on Libby Hollman and tobacco millionaire Smith Reynolds.

The one that changed her fortunes was Howard Hawks's high adrenalin comedy *Twentieth Century*, made over at Columbia. Lombard was the spoiled actress being pressured back into the business during a train trip by her egotistical mentor John Barrymore, and their frantic sparring went from sublime to downright exhausting in what turned out to be a smash hit at the box office. This did not mean that everything went swimmingly for Lombard from thereafter. For her home studio she and Gary Cooper had to share the screen with attention-grabbing moppet Shirley Temple in *Now and Forever*, and a sequel to *Bolero* was ordered, *Rumba*, which meant she was stuck with the unappetizing George Raft again. At MGM she got another batch of bad reviews playing a gold-digging showgirl trying to snare her share of bootlegger Nat Pendleton's dough in *The Gay Bride*. Better was a pleasant teaming with Fred MacMurray, *Hands Across the Table*, in which she was a manicurist trying to trap a man. Around the time her contract with Paramount was coming to an end, she went over to Universal for the quickly forgotten *Love Before Breakfast*, and one of her finest, *My Man Godfrey*. As the ditsy, pampered millionaire's daughter with a desperate crush on servant William Powell, she was at her most inspired, receiving her one and only Oscar nomination. The movie is one of the peaks of the screwball comedy genre of the decade, as is *Nothing Sacred*. This was made for Selznick in color, with Lombard taken to the big city by opportunistic Fredric March, who makes her a celebrity because everyone thinks she is dying of radiation poisoning. A smart satire on the media, Lombard was once again caught working overtime for laughs in more than one moment, the customarily more hammy March giving the more restrained and clever performance of the two.

Between these films Paramount decided to put her back with MacMurray for a shipboard romantic farce, *The Princess Comes Across*; a melodrama, *Swing High, Swing Low*, a version of the stage hit *Burlesque*, which became better known years later as the Betty Grable-Dan Dailey vehicle *When My Baby Smiles at Me*; and a stinker, *True Confessions*, with Lombard floundering as a pathological liar. Free from her Paramount contract, she went over to Warner Bros. for another limp one, *Fools for Scandal*, as an actress battling with impoverished nobleman Fernand Gravet, in a curious entertainment that inserted rhyming dialogue in a few places. There were surely better co-stars to be found than Gravet, and she got two of the best with James Stewart in *Made for Each Other* and Cary Grant in *In Name Only*, but, alas, these films both concentrated more on the serious despite light moments in each. Staying in a dramatic vein, she was ill at ease as Charles Laughton's mail-order bride in *They Knew What They Wanted*, and then did the cute but instantly forgettable *Mr. and Mrs. Smith*, notable only because it was a romantic comedy directed by Alfred Hitchcock. Her next film turned out to be another of her high points, Ernst Lubitsch's cult classic *To Be or Not to Be*, in which she was surprisingly well cast alongside Jack Benny as a pair of squabbling actors challenging the Nazis. Sadly, by the time it was released she was dead, having been killed in a plane crash while flying to sell war bonds, and leaving behind a grieving widower in Gable (they had married in 1939). Along with Leslie Howard, she was mourned as the greatest of Hollywood's casualties of World War II, and one can only speculate on the direction her career might have gone from the apex she had clearly reached at that point.

Screen: AS JANE PETERS: **1921:** A Perfect Crime; **1924:** Gold Heels. AS CAROL LOMBARD: **1925:** Marriage in Transit; Gold and the Girl; Hearts and Spurs; Durand of the Badlands; **1926:** The Road to Glory; **1928:** Me, Gangster; The Divine Sinner; Power; Show Folks; Ned McCobb's Daughter; **1929:** High Voltage; Big News; The Racketeer; **1930:** The Arizona Kid.

AS CAROLE LOMBARD: Safety in Numbers; Fast and Loose; **1931:** It Pays to Advertise; Man of the World; Ladies' Man; Up Pops the Devil; I Take This Woman; **1932:** No One Man; Sinners in the

Sun; Virtue; No More Orchids; No Man of Her Own; **1933:** From Hell to Heaven; Supernatural; The Eagle and the Hawk; Brief Moment; White Woman; **1934:** Bolero; We're Not Dressing; Twentieth Century; Now and Forever; Lady by Choice; The Gay Bride; **1935:** Rumba; Hands Across the Table; **1936:** Love Before Breakfast; The Princess Comes Across; My Man Godfrey; **1937:** Swing High, Swing Low; Nothing Sacred; True Confession; **1938:** Fools for Scandal; **1939:** Made for Each Other; In Name Only; **1940:** Vigil in the Night; They Knew What They Wanted; **1941:** Mr. and Mrs. Smith; **1942:** To Be or Not to Be.

SOPHIA LOREN

(SOFIA VILLANI SCICOLONE) BORN: ROME, ITALY, SEPTEMBER 20, 1934.

In the postwar cinema all sorts of luscious, sultry, buxom women were imported from overseas in hopes of catching the public's fancy, if for only a fleeting period of time, before the boys in the front offices came up with the next hopeful. Italy's Sophia Loren stood miles above all the rest, not only because she was so impossibly beautiful but because audiences genuinely fell in love with her, cared about her, were charmed by her, even before they realized she also happen to be a fine actress in her own right. At age 14 she won a beauty contest, which encouraged her to become a movie extra and a model. Using her real name, she was supposedly glimpsed in a handful of unsubstantiated credits, starting with *Curoi sul Mare*, in 1950. A meeting with producer Carlo Ponti, 24 years her senior, was crucial in the direction her career would take, for he became her mentor and lover, eventually marrying her in 1957. In the meantime he changed her name to Sophia Loren and gave her more substantial roles, in *La Tratta della Bianche/Girls Marked for Danger* and the opera *Aida*, in which her singing voice was dubbed. There was a brief role in *Attila the Hun*, which had Anthony Quinn as the star and, therefore, was supposed to give her more exposure overseas (but it was just another costume epic in a market crowded with them and didn't show up in America until 1958). Ponti tried again, putting her in the starring role of *Woman of the River*, in which she divided her passions between two different men. This time there was fairly wide art-house distribution in the United States, and her name was beginning to be heard in the right places, her face adorning the covers of the right magazines. There were some more Italian productions, including the trilogy *Scandal in Sorrento*, and *The Miller's Beautiful Daughter*, both of which came to America in 1957 when the craze for Loren began.

At last Hollywood wanted in on the growing interest, and 20th Century-Fox put her alongside Alan Ladd in a standard adventure, *Boy on a Dolphin*, the main attraction being Loren in wet swimwear. More popular was *The Pride and the Passion*, with the actress as a Spanish peasant, more believably cast than Frank Sinatra as same. Then came *Legend of the Lost*, one of the usually popular John Wayne's lesser box-office offerings of the time. Paramount signed her up to a contract and put her into their version of Eugene O'Neill's *Desire Under the Elms*. Although it was much panned, she gave it a game try as the immigrant who regrets marrying bullying farmer Burl Ives and falls in love with his sensitive son, Tony Perkins. Better, and by far her most popular film to date, was *Houseboat*, an enjoyable, well-scripted domestic comedy in which she was superbly teamed with Cary Grant (more comfortably than they had been in *The Pride and the Passion*), playing the housekeeper who comes to care for his children and winds up in love with their widowed dad. There were some mild box-office performers with *That Kind of Woman*,

with Loren falling in love with soldier Tab Hunter, although she's already attached to wealthy George Sanders, and the soap opera *Black Orchid*, a better reteaming with Anthony Quinn than the garish, lumbering period piece *Heller in Pink Tights*. Paramount gave her another older screen legend to be romanced by with Clark Gable, in *It Started in Naples*, then laid an egg with the expensive *A Breath of Scandal*, with Loren costumed to the nines as a princess in love with John Gavin. In England she teamed up with Peter Sellers for *The Millionairess*, where their performances were better than the end result. There was no doubt that everybody liked Sophia, if only she could attach herself to a really fine film to prove herself once and for all.

Back to Italy she went and found just the film she was looking for, *Two Women*, a powerful and somber story of a widow who sees herself and her daughter nearly destroyed by the brutality of war. She proved to be completely up to the challenge of the depths of the role and won over the remaining skeptics. Loren was now an "actress," and the accolades started to pour in, leading up to the Academy Award for Best Actress of 1961, the first (and, for 37 years, only) time a performer won the Oscar for a foreign-language performance. That same year she helped decorate a superior and popular spectacle, *El Cid*, with Charlton Heston, but seemed to be back to picking inferior material with *Five Miles to Midnight*, scheming with husband Anthony Perkins to collect some insurance money, and *The Condemned of Altona*, playing the wife of dying Fredric March.

There was another gargantuan spectacle, *The Fall of the Roman Empire*, which lost a small fortune, and then a return to Italy, where she seemed to get all her best reviews during that period. There were two with that country's leading *male* star, Marcello Mastroianni, whom she played off of beautifully: *Yesterday, Today and Tomorrow*, a three-episode film, which featured her famous striptease scene, and *Marriage Italian-Style*, as his eager-to-wed mistress, a former whore looking for respect. The latter really allowed her to show her range, taking her from naïve young thing to a hardened, middle-aged survivor, taping every vein from broad humor to flat out pathos It brought her a second Oscar nomination. At this point she was simply one of the most famous ladies in the world, so nobody seemed to take note of the fact that she had little to do in the World War II adventure *Operation Crossbow*, or that both *Judith*, about the Israeli underground, or *Lady L*, a strained comedy about a whore who rises to aristocracy, weren't very good, to say the least. She did a fun, tongue-in-cheek adventure with Gregory Peck, *Arabesque*, certainly her most entertaining American movie since *Houseboat*, but that and a lot of good will must have been the reason audiences forgave her for Charlie Chaplin's dead-on-arrival swan song, *A Countess from Hong Kong*, and the lead-footed fairy tale *More Than a Miracle*. Her bad luck continued through two weak ones with Mastroianni, *Sunflower* and *The Priest's Wife*; *Lady Liberty*, a one-joke comedy in which she tried to get some cheese through customs; and *Man of La Mancha*, in which she would have been ideally cast as slatternly kitchen wench Aldonza had this not been the poor musical version of Don Quixote that it was.

Her box office but not her public reputation crumbled to a point where there was no longer a rush to bring her films to America. Those that did show up included such second rate international adventures as *The Cassandra Crossing*, *Brass Target*, and *Firepower*, in which the critics were more inclined to talk about her sustained beauty than anything else. Fortunately there was another good one with Mastroianni, *A Special Day*, with Loren as a bored housewife trying to seduce him despite his homosexual inclination. By the 1980s she confined most of her work to the small screen, including an adaptation of her autobiography, *Sophia: Her Own Story*, playing herself in the latter part of the saga. When she did return to the big screen it was in a homage of sorts to one of her *Yesterday, Today and Tomorrow* roles, stripping for Mastroianni in the all-star *Ready to Wear/Pret-a-Porter*. Fans were happy to have her back, even in something as weak as this or *Grumpier Old Men*, looking fabulous at 60 and reminding us all of an undimmed star quality that burned luminously through years of easily disposable and unworthy properties. In 1993 she was given a special Academy Award.

Screen: AS SOFIA SCICOLONE: 1950: Cuori sul Mare; Il Voto; Toto Tarzan; Le Sei Mogli di Barablu/Bluebeard's Seven Wives; Io Sono il Capataz; Anna; 1951: Milano Miliardaria; Quo Vadis?; Il Padrone del Vapore; Lebra Bianca/Brief Rapture; Il Mago per Forza; Il Sogno di Zorro/The Dream of Zorro; 1952: E'Arrivato l' Accordatore; Era Lui…Si Si/It's Him … Yes Yes.

AS SOPHIA LOREN: 1952: La Favorita; La Tratta della Bianche/Girls Marked for Danger/Ship of Condemned Women; 1953: Africa Sotto i Mari/Woman of the Red Sea; Aida (US: 1955); Ci Troviamo in Galleria; La Domenica della Buona Gente/Good Folks' Sunday; Due Notti con Cleopatra/Two Nights With Cleopatra; 1954: Tempi Nostri/The Anatomy of Love; Neapolitan Carousel (US: 1959); Il Paese dei Campanelli; Pellegrini d'Amore; Un Giorno in Pretura/A Day in Court (US: 1965); Miseria e Nobilita/Poverty and Nobility; 1955: Attila (US: 1958); L'Oro di Napoli/Gold of Naples (US: 1957); La Donna del Fiume/Woman of the River (US: 1957); Peccato che Sia una Canaglia/Too Bad She's Bad (US: 1956); Il Segno di Venere/The Sign of Venus; La Bella Mugnaia/The Miller's Beautiful Wife (US: 1957); Pane Amore e…/Scandal in Sorrento (US: 1957); La Fortuna di Essera Donna/Lucky to Be a Woman; 1957: Boy on a Dolphin; The Pride and the Passion; Legend of the Lost; 1958: Desire Under the Elms; The Key; Houseboat; 1959: The Black Orchid; That Kind of Woman; 1960: Heller in Pink Tights; It Started in Naples; A Breath of Scandal; 1961: The Millionairess; Two Women; El Cid; 1962: Boccaccio '70; Madame/Madame Sans-Gene; 1963: Five Miles to Midnight; The Condemned of Altona; 1964: Yesterday, Today and Tomorrow; The Fall of the Roman Empire; Marriage Italian-Style; 1965: Operation Crossbow; Lady L; 1966: Judith; Arabesque; 1967: A Countess From Hong Kong; More Than a Miracle/Cinderella: Italian Style; 1968: Ghosts — Italian Style (US: 1969); 1970: Sunflower; 1971: The Priest's Wife; 1972: Lady Liberty/La Mortadella; Man of La Mancha; 1973: White Sister; 1974: The Voyage (US: 1977); 1975: Verdict/Jury of One; 1975: La Pupa del Gangster/Oopsie Poopsie (US: 1978); 1977: Angela (US: 1984); The Cassandra Crossing; A Special Day; 1978: Brass Target; Blood Feud/Revenge (US: 1980); 1979: Firepower; 1990: Saturday, Sunday and Monday (nUSr); 1994: Ready to Wear/Pret-a-Porter; 1995: Grumpier Old Men; 1997: Soleil (nUSr); 2002: Francesca and Nunziata (nUSr); Between Strangers (nUSr).

Select TV: 1964: Sophia Loren in Rome (sp); 1967: With Love — Sophia (so); 1968: Sophia: A Self Portrait (sp); 1974: Brief Encounter; 1980: Sophia Loren: Her Own Story; 1984: Aurora; 1986: Courage; 1988: Mario Puzo's The Fortunate Pilgrim (ms); La Ciociara/Running Away.

PETER LORRE

(LÁSZLÓ LOWENSTEIN) BORN: ROSENBERG, AUSTRIA-HUNGARY, JUNE 26, 1904. DIED: MARCH 23, 1964.

The actor with the most instantly recognizable, sinister speaking voice in movie history, heavy-lidded (and later on, heavy)

Peter Lorre was a joy to watch, alternately brilliant and campy, thrillingly eccentric and world-wearily sardonic. Moving to Vienna as a youngster, he joined a theatrical company and performed in cafés and nightclubs. In 1929 he journeyed to Berlin and won the lead in a play, *Die Pioniere von Inglostadt*. Other theatre followed, including *Spring's Awakening*, in 1930, which led to Lorre being cast as the child murderer in director Fritz Lang's still powerful and disturbing *M*, the film that made him into a star. He stayed on in Germany for a few years but got out before the Nazis took charge, traveling to Austria for *Schluss im Morgengrauen*, then to France for *Du Haut en Bas*, and finally to England, where he made another favorable impression, playing the bad guy in director Alfred Hitchcock's first version of *The Man Who Knew Too Much*, in 1934.

Hollywood had wanted him ever since *M*, so he accepted an offer from MGM to play the weird Doctor Gogol in the melodramatic but effective *Mad Love*, at one point appearing, unforgettably, in neck brace, eyeshades, and metal hands in order to freak out Colin Clive. This one certainly got him noticed, and he followed it with the lead in Columbia's version of *Crime and Punishment*, winning more raves for this sincere, Josef von Sternberg-directed attempt to film the florid Dostoyevsky novel, with Lorre as the student racked with guilt over the murder he has committed. He went back to Britain and Hitchcock for *Secret Agent*, pretty much stealing the show as a fidgety, womanizing spy alternately called "The Mexican" and "The General," though he was, in fact, neither. He then came to 20th Century-Fox under contract to play another character with dual monikers, a spy called "Colonel Gimpy" and "Baron Tagger," in a "B" film, *Crack-Up*. The studio sought something unusual for him to play and found it in the 1937 release *Think Fast, Mr. Moto*, in which he was cast as an ingenious Japanese detective, back when such casting of a Caucasian as an Asian was acceptable to the public at large. He made such an impact as this character that the studio asked him to repeat the part seven more times in a mere two year span, ending with *Mr. Moto Takes a Vacation*. During this period the studio utilized him in only three non-Moto films, including *I'll Give a Million*, as a millionaire posing as a bum.

With his contract up, he went elsewhere to continue his growing gallery of nasties and weirdoes. He appeared in *Strange Cargo*, as a weasel named Monsieur Pig; *Island of Doomed Men*, whipping his prisoners with sadistic delight; *I Was an Adventuress*, teamed with Erich von Stroheim as a pair of jewel thieves; and *Stranger on the Third Floor*, as a mysterious, possible killer in this sleeper "B." In *You'll Find Out*, he shared the screen with Boris Karloff and Bela Lugosi and was thereby elevated to their position as a "horror" star in the minds of many, and in *The Face Behind the Mask*, he was at his creepiest, sporting an expressionless recreation of his real face. That same year, 1941, he went to Warners to play perhaps his most famous character, the effete cohort of Sidney Greenstreet in the classic *The Maltese Falcon*, the screen's perfect interpretation of the sniveling weasel, one who thinks he is tough until confronted by the real thing, Humphrey Bogart. Because of this he was signed to a contract by Warners, where he reteamed with Bogart for the lighthearted, highly entertaining wartime thriller *All Through the Night*, as one of the evil Nazis, and, even more memorably, *Casablanca*, once again as a spineless character, this one with a pair of stolen visas. It was not a large role, but the movie became so famous and so imitated that it was looked on as one of his most accomplished performances.

There was another definitive Lorre role, as the forever-nervous Doctor Einstein in the hit film adaptation of the Broadway smash *Arsenic and Old Lace*, giving a sublime comic performance. The studio also saw potential in reteaming him with the jumbo, equally menacing Greenstreet, and they had starring roles in the mediocre mystery *The Mask of Dimitrios*, with Lorre as a nebbishy mystery writer. They were also seen in *The Conspirators*, in support of *Casablanca* co-star Paul Henreid; guesting in *Hollywood Canteen*; in *Three Strangers*, rounding off the title trio with Geraldine Fitzgerald, sharing a winning lottery ticket, in the best of this batch; and in *The Verdict*, with Lorre uncovering Greenstreet's perfect murder plot in 1890s London. Lorre and Warners parted company after another thriller, *The Beast With Five Fingers*, which like *Mad Love*, involved severed hands.

After some more supporting Hollywood roles, including villain duty in the Bob Hope hit *My Favorite Brunette*; a seemingly unsavory club owner in *Black Angel*; a police inspector in *Casbah*; a slithery criminal named Toady in *Rope of Sand*; and a shady arcade owner in *Quicksand*, he returned to Germany where he directed, wrote, produced, and starred in *Der Verlorene/The Lost One*, a study of Nazism that was barely distributed. A heftier, more tired Lorre returned to the screen for an inferior reteaming with Bogart, *Beat the Devil*; and he was one of the reluctant guests of Captain Nemo in the Walt Disney smash *20,000 Leagues Under the Sea*. He showed up for cameo as a ship's steward in the all-star Oscar-winner *Around the World in Eighty Days*; played an uncooperative movie director in *The Buster Keaton Story*; did a bit of unexpected singing and hoofing to the song "Siberia" in *Silk Stockings*; and portrayed Nero in Irwin Allen's strange all-star campfest *The Story of Mankind*. He had some fun sending up the horror genre along with Boris Karloff in both *The Raven* and *The Comedy of Terrors*, in which he did, after all, get the girl in the end. He couldn't help but look slightly bored during his participation in many of his later assignments, including Jerry Lewis's *The Sad Sack*, as an Arab villain; *The Big Circus*, in clown makeup; and *Voyage to the Bottom of the Sea*, as a submarine commodore. But then, even the disgruntled look of ennui when coming from someone as distinctive as Peter Lorre could somehow give audiences a jolt of pleasure. He passed away of a stroke, awaiting his fourth divorce, in 1964. He died before the release of another Jerry Lewis film in which he essayed a very undemanding part, *The Patsy*, and *Muscle Beach Party*, in which he didn't even receive billing.

Screen: 1930: M; Bomben auf Monte Carlo/Bombs Over Monte Carlo (nUSr); Die Koffer des Herrn O.F./The Trunks of Mr. O.F. (nUSr); 1932: Funf von der Jazzband/Five of the Jazzband (nUSr); Der Weisse Damon/The White Demon (nUSr); FP1 Antwortet Nicht/FP1 Doesn't Answer (nUSr); 1933: Was Frauen Traumen/What Women Dream (nUSr); Unsichtbare Gegner/Invisible Opponent (nUSr); Schuss im Morgengrauen/A Shot at Dawn (nUSr); 1934: Du Haut en Bas/From Top to Bottom (nUSr); The Man Who Knew Too Much; 1935: Mad Love; Crime and Punishment; 1936: Secret Agent; Crack-Up; 1937: Nancy Steele Is Missing!; Think Fast, Mr. Moto; Lancer Spy; Thank You, Mr. Moto; 1938: Mr. Moto's Gamble; Mr. Moto Takes a Chance; I'll Give a Million; The Mysterious Mr. Moto; 1939: Mr. Moto's Last Warning; Mr. Moto in Danger Island; Mr. Moto Takes a Vacation; 1940: Strange Cargo; I Was an Adventuress; Island of Doomed Men; Stranger on the Third Floor; You'll Find Out; 1941: Mr. District Attorney; The Face Behind the Mask; They Met in Bombay; The Maltese Falcon; 1942: All Through the Night; The Boogie Man Will Get You; Invisible Agent; 1943: Casablanca; The Constant Nymph; Background to Danger; The Cross of Lorraine; 1944: Arsenic and Old Lace; Passage to Marseille; The Mask of Dimitrios; The Conspirators; Hollywood Canteen; 1945: Confidential Agent; Hotel Berlin; 1946: Three Strangers; Black Angel; The Chase; The Verdict; The Beast With Five Fingers; 1947: My Favorite Brunette; 1948: Casbah; 1949:

Rope of Sand; 1950: Quicksand; Double Confession; 1951: Der Verlorene/The Lost One (and dir.; wr.; prod.); 1953: Beat the Devil; 1954: 20,000 Leagues Under the Sea; 1956: Congo Crossing; Meet Me in Las Vegas; Around the World in Eighty Days; 1957: The Buster Keaton Story; Silk Stockings; Hell Ship Mutiny; The Story of Mankind; The Sad Sack; 1959: The Big Circus; 1960: Scent of Mystery; 1961: Voyage to the Bottom of the Sea; 1962: Tales of Terror; Five Weeks in a Balloon; 1963: The Raven; The Comedy of Terrors; 1964: Muscle Beach Party; The Patsy.

Select TV: 1952: Taste (sp); 1953: The Vanishing Point (sp); 1954: Casino Royale (sp); 1955: Arsenic and Old Lace (sp); Reunion in Vienna (sp); A Promise to Murder (sp); 1956: The Finishers (sp); The Fifth Wheel (sp); The Man Who Lost His Head (sp); Seidman and Son (sp); Operation Cicero (sp); 1957: The Last Tycoon (sp); The Jet-Propelled Couch (sp); 1960: The Cruel Day (sp); 1963: The End of the World Baby (sp).

ANITA LOUISE

(ANITA LOUISE FREMAULT) BORN: NEW YORK, NY, JANUARY 9, 1915. DIED: APRIL 25, 1970.

Just another pretty lady from the 1930s, whose résumé was full but whose lasting impression on the cinema is questionable, Anita Louise was encouraged to go into show business by her mom. Only seven years, old she debuted under her real name in the 1922 film version of *Down to the Sea in Ships*, and continued to be seen in youth roles until the dawn of the talkies. Starting with *Square Shoulders*, for Pathe in 1929, she changed her name to Anita Louise and started getting more mature parts despite the fact that she was still just a teenager. There were leads in *Heaven on Earth*, as a poor Mississippi girl; *Everything's Rosie*, as a foster child being raised by comedian Robert Woolsey; and *Bachelor of Arts*, as a co-ed in love with Tom Brown. For the most part, however, she was better known for her secondary assignments in higher profile films, including *Madame Du Barry*, dressed to the nines as Marie Antoinette; *Judge Priest*, as the romantic interest of Will Rogers's son; *A Midsummer Night's Dream*, as Titania, Queen of the Fairies; *The Story of Louis Pasteur*, as the scientist's daughter; *Anthony Adverse*, as the title character's philandering mom, who causes the death of lover Louis Hayward; *The Sisters*, as the sibling of Bette Davis who marries for wealth; *Marie Antoinette*, this time as Marie's friend, Princess de Lamballe; and *Casanova Brown*, in which she was jilted by Gary Cooper. In the 1940s she went over to Columbia where she was a staple of their "B" unit in such movies as *Harmon of Michigan*, as the wife of real-life football hero Tom Harmon; an entry in the "I Love a Mystery" series, *The Devil's Mask*; and the fairly popular adventure *The Bandit of Sherwood Forest*, as the leading lady to Cornel Wilde. Having married producer Buddy Adler in 1940, she eventually retired from movies, though she was seen from time to time on television.

Screen: AS ANITA FREMAULT: 1922: Down to the Sea in Ships; 1924: The Sixth Commandment; Lend Me Your Husband; 1927: The Music Master; 1928: Four Devils; A Woman of Affairs; 1929: The Spirit of Youth; Wonder of Women.

AS ANITA LOUISE: 1929: Square Shoulders; The Marriage Playground; 1930: What a Man!; The Florodora Girl; Just Like Heaven; The Third Alarm; 1931: Millie; The Great Meadow; The Woman Between; Everything's Rosie; Heaven on Earth; 1932: The Phantom of Crestwood; 1933: Our Betters; 1934: Most Precious Thing in Life; Are We Civilized?; I Give My Love; Cross Streets; Judge Priest; Madame Du Barry; The Firebird; Bachelor of Arts; **1935:** Lady Tubbs; Here's to Romance; A Midsummer Night's Dream; Personal Maid's Secret; **1936:** The Story of Louis Pasteur; Brides Are Like That; Anthony Adverse; **1937:** Call It a Day; Green Light; The Go-Getter; First Lady; That Certain Woman; Tovarich; **1938:** My Bill; Marie Antoinette; Going Places; The Sisters; **1939:** The Gorilla; Hero for a Day; Reno; These Glamour Girls; Main Street Lawyer; The Little Princess; **1940:** Wagons Westward; The Villain Still Pursued Her; Glamour for Sale; **1941:** The Phantom Submarine; Two in a Taxi; Harmon of Michigan; **1943:** Dangerous Blondes; **1944:** Nine Girls; Casanova Brown; **1945:** Love Letters; The Fighting Guardsman; **1946:** Shadowed; The Bandit of Sherwood Forest; The Devil's Mask; Personality Kid; **1947:** Blondie's Big Moment; Bulldog Drummond at Bay; **1952:** Retreat, Hell!

Select TV: **1952:** Heart of Gold (sp); **1953:** The Juror (sp); **1954:** The Fugitives (sp); **1956–58:** My Friend Flicka (series); **1957:** The Greer Case (sp); **1962:** Far From a Shade Tree (sp).

BESSIE LOVE

(JUANITA HORTON) BORN: MIDLAND, TX, SEPTEMBER 10, 1898. DIED: APRIL 26, 1986.

A tiny, spunky little blonde who achieved stardom in the silent era, saw it wane, returned to it for a bit during the crucial transition to talkies, and finally left it behind when she took off to live in Britain, Bessie Love had started seeking film work while in high school. In 1916 she was one of the zillions of extras in *Intolerance* and promptly became leading lady to William S. Hart in *The Aryan*, and to Douglas Fairbanks in *Reggie Mixes In*. Among her other early leads were *The Matinee Idol*, heading a troupe of actors; *The Song and Dance Man*, as a stage star torn between two men; *Lovey Mary*, a very Mary Pickford-like role, portraying an orphan girl much younger than herself; and *Anybody Here Seen Kelly?*, as an immigrant searching New York for Tom Moore. By the time talkies came she was hardly at her peak, but she nevertheless landed the starring role in the first all-talking, all-singing, all-dancing musical, *The Broadway Melody*, in 1929. The film is horribly dated, and Love's own high-decibel performance is tough to take, but at the time the movie was a phenomenon, earning the Academy Award for Best Picture and an Oscar nomination for Love. Although she was hardly a stellar addition to this genre, she was featured in other musicals such as *Chasing Rainbows* (the inevitable flop *Broadway Melody* sequel, best known for introducing the classic song "Happy Days Are Here Again"); *They Learned About Women*; and *Good News*, which had a livelier incarnation years later with June Allyson. After this period of activity dried up she went to London to do a play and moved there in 1935. Starting in the 1950s and continuing for the next 35 years, she began showing up as a supporting player in all sorts of productions made in England, including *Isadora*, as Vanessa Redgrave's mom; *The Ritz*, as a bathhouse accountant; and *Ragtime*, as a befuddled old lady whose home is staked out by the cops. She wrote several plays, including *Homecoming*, which she also acted in, in London, in 1958.

Screen: **1916:** Intolerance; Reggie Mixes In; The Aryan; The Flying Torpedo; The Good Bad Man; Hell-to-Pay Austin; A Sister of Six; Acquitted; Stranded; The Heiress at Coffee Dan's; **1917:** Wee Lady Betty; Nina the Flower Girl; Cheerful Givers; Pernickety Polly Ann; A Daughter of the Poor; Sawdust Ring; **1918:** How Could You, Caroline?; The Great Adventure; Carolyn of the Corners; A Little Sister of Everybody; The Dawn of Understanding; **1919:** Over the Garden Wall; The Enchanted

Barn; A Yankee Princess; Cupid Forecloses; A Fighting Colleen; The Wishing Ring Man; The Little Boss; **1920:** Pegeen; Bonnie May; The Midlanders; **1921:** The Spirit of the Lake; Penny of Top Hill Trail; The Sea Lion; The Swamp; The Honor of Ramirez; **1922:** Bulldog Courage; Deserted at the Altar; Forget-Me-Not; The Vermilion Pencil; Night Life in Hollywood; The Village Blacksmith; **1923:** Three Who Paid; Souls for Sale; Mary of the Movies; St. Elmo; The Ghost Patrol; Purple Dawn; Human Wreckage; The Eternal Three; Gentle Julia; Slave of Desire; **1924:** Those Who Dance; Torment; Dynamite Smith; Sundown; The Silent Watcher; Tongues of Flame; **1925:** Woman on the Jury; A Son of His Father; Soul-Fire; The Lost World; New Brooms; Bulldog Courage; The King on Main Street; **1926:** Going Crooked; Lovey Mary; The Song and Dance Man; Young April; **1927:** Rubber Tires; Dress Parade; The American/The Flag Maker; A Harp in Hock; **1928:** The Matinee Idol; Sally of the Scandals; Anybody Here Seen Kelly?; **1929:** The Broadway Melody; The Hollywood Revue of 1929; The Girl in the Show; The Idle Rich; **1930:** Chasing Rainbows; See America Thirst; Good News; Conspiracy; They Learned About Women; **1931:** Morals for Women; **1936:** I Live Again; **1941:** Atlantic Ferry/Sons of the Sea; **1945:** Journey Together; **1951:** The Magic Box; No Highway in the Sky; **1953:** The Weak and the Wicked; **1954:** The Barefoot Contessa; Beau Brummell; **1955:** Touch and Go/The Light Touch; **1957:** The Story of Esther Costello; **1958:** Nowhere to Go; Next to No Time; **1959:** Too Young to Love; **1961:** Loss of Innocence/The Greengage Summer; The Roman Spring of Mrs. Stone; **1963:** The Wild Affair; Children of the Damned; **1966:** Promise Her Anything; **1967:** Battle Beneath the Earth; I'll Never Forget What's 'is Name; **1968:** Isadora; **1969:** On Her Majesty's Secret Service; **1971:** Sunday, Bloody Sunday; Catlow; **1974:** Vampyres; **1976:** Gulliver's Travels (voice); The Ritz; **1981:** Ragtime; Reds; Lady Chatterley's Lover; **1983:** The Hunger.

Select TV: **1974:** Mousey; **1980:** Edward and Mrs. Simpson (ms).

FRANK LOVEJOY

BORN: BRONX, NY, MARCH 28, 1914. DIED: OCTOBER 2, 1962.

A sternly humorless actor with a solid build and a name suggesting a gay porn star, Frank Lovejoy had acted on radio and on Broadway as far back as 1934's *Judgment Day*. It was not until 1948 that he came to Hollywood to appear in Universal's Yvonne DeCarlo western *Black Bart*. The following year he made much more of an impression, as one of the bigoted platoon members who cannot cope with having a black man among them, in the groundbreaking independent feature *Home of the Brave*. Warner Bros. put him under contract and drafted him back into the military for *Breakthrough* and *Force of Arms*, after which he found himself vying with Robert Young for the attentions of Joan Crawford in the soaper *Goodbye, My Fancy*. He was considered forceful enough to carry some of his own vehicles, including the self-explanatory *I Was a Communist for the FBI*, very much a product of the paranoid times; *Retreat, Hell!*, back in uniform, though this time in the Korean War, as an understanding Marine captain; and *The System*, as a bookie who sees his life fall apart after a client is killed. Over at RKO he was one of the victimized fishermen in Ida Lupino's best-remembered foray into directing, *The Hitch-Hiker*, then returned to Warners to appear in two of their popular 3-D offerings, *House of Wax*, as the heroic police inspector, and *The Charge at Feather River*, as a cavalry sergeant. After Warners, there were "B" leads in *Mad at the World*, as a detective; *Fingerman*, as an informant; the cult item

Shack Out on 101, as a government agent; and *Cole Younger, Gunfighter*, as the title character. He had mainly transferred his attention to television when he died of a heart attack in 1962, at age 48, while appearing in a New Jersey production of *The Best Man*, in the role he'd created on Broadway.

Screen: 1948: Black Bart; 1949: Home of the Brave; 1950: South Sea Sinner; In a Lonely Place; Three Secrets; Breakthrough; The Sound of Fury/Try and Get Me; 1951: Goodbye, My Fancy; I Was a Communist for the FBI; Force of Arms; Starlift; I'll See You in My Dreams; 1952: Retreat, Hell!; The Winning Team; 1953: The Hitch-Hiker; She's Back on Broadway; The System; House of Wax; The Charge at Feather River; 1954: Men of the Fighting Lady; Beachhead; 1955: Strategic Air Command; Mad at the World; Top of the World; The Americano; Fingerman; The Crooked Web; Shack Out on 101; 1956: Julie; 1957: Three Brave Men; 1958: Cole Younger, Gunfighter.

NY Stage: 1934: Judgment Day; 1937: Chalked Out; 1938: The Greatest Show on Earth; 1943: The Snark Was a Boojum; 1945: A Sound of Hunting; 1946: Woman Bites Dog; 1960: The Best Man.

Select TV: 1953: Second Meeting (sp); Out of the Night (sp); 1954: Search in the Night (sp); Baseball Blues (sp); Double Indemnity (sp); 1955: The Deceiving Eye (sp); The Caine Mutiny Court Martial (sp); 1956: Act of Decision (sp); The Whizzer (sp); Man Against Crime (series); Yellowbelly (sp); The Country Husband (sp); 1957: Sweet Charlie (sp); 1957–58: Meet McGraw (series); 1959: The Raider (sp); 1960: Shadow of a Pale Horse (sp); 1961: The Battle of the Paper (sp).

EDMUND LOWE

BORN: SAN JOSE, CA, MARCH 3, 1890.
DIED: APRIL 21, 1971.

Taking nearly a decade to find his break-through role, Edmund Lowe became a minor "name" during the transition from silence to sound, then stuck around long after he and the audience had mutually lost interest. A former schoolteacher, he left that profession to join a Los Angeles stock company, which led to movie work, beginning in 1915. For the next nine years he was just another of the era's slick-haired, mustachioed smoothies, eventually becoming one of the leading players at Fox Films, where his credits included *Silent Command*, *The Brass Bowl*, *Honor Among Men*, and *Marriage in Transit*. It was casting him against type, as the gruff, wisecracking Sergeant Quirt in *What Price Glory?*, sparring memorably with Victor McLaglen, that brought him to the peak of his fame. This was one of the biggest hits of the 1920s, so much so that McLaglen and Lowe were reteamed countless times, including two genuine sequels, *The Cock-Eyed World* and *Women of All Nations*, and such shameless variations as *Guilty as Hell* and *Under Pressure*. Lowe was also Warner Baxter's nemesis, Sgt. Mickey Dunn, in both the Oscar-winning *In Old Arizona* and *The Cisco Kid*; had the title role in *Chandu the Magician*; played the doctor carrying on with naughty Jean Harlow in *Dinner at Eight*; was sleuth Philo Vance in *The Garden Murder Case*; showed up as a pair of look-alikes in *The Great Impersonation*; and was the police captain who couldn't resist Mae West's bumps and grinds in *Every Day's a Holiday*. Many of his other assignments were programmers, and by the 1940s his career was really grinding down to uninspired fare, including an ill-advised final get together with McLaglen for *Call Out the Marines*. He seemed to disappear for a spell, then showed up later in a few unremarkable supporting parts.

Screen: 1915: The Wild Olive; 1917: The Spreading Dawn; 1918: The Reason Why; Vive La France; 1919: Eyes of Youth; Someone

Must Pay; 1920: The Woman Gives; Madonnas and Men; A Woman's Business; Someone in the House; The Devil; 1921: My Lady's Latchkey; 1922: Living Lies; Peacock Alley; 1923: The Silent Command; In the Palace of the King; The White Flower; Wife in Name Only; 1924: Honor Among Men; Barbara Frietchie; The Brass Bowl; Nellie the Beautiful Cloak Model; 1925: Soul Mates; The Winding Stair; Marriage in Transit; The Kiss Barrier; Greater Than a Crown; Ports of Call; East Lynne; The Fool; Champion of Lost Causes; East of Suez; 1926: Black Paradise; What Price Glory?; Siberia; The Palace of Pleasure; 1927: Iz Zat So?; Baloo; One Increasing Purpose; The Wizard; Publicity Madness; 1928: Happiness Ahead; Outcast; Dressed to Kill; 1929: The Cock-Eyed World; In Old Arizona; Making the Grade; Thru Different Eyes; This Thing Called Love; 1930: Good Intentions; The Painted Angel; Happy Days; Part Time Wife; Born Reckless; The Bad One; Men on Call; Scotland Yard; 1931: Women of All Nations; The Cisco Kid; Transatlantic; The Spider; Don't Bet on Women/More Than a Kiss; 1932: Attorney for the Defense; Guilty as Hell; Chandu the Magician; The Devil Is Driving; The Misleading Lady; 1933: Hot Pepper; Her Bodyguard; Dinner at Eight; I Love That Man; 1934: Let's Fall in Love; Gift of Gab; Bombay Mail; No More Women; 1935: Under Pressure; The Great Hotel Murder; Mr. Dynamite; The Best Man Wins; Thunder in the Night; King Solomon of Broadway; Black Sheep; The Great Impersonation; Grand Exit; 1936: Seven Sinners/Doomed Cargo; The Garden Murder Case; Mad Holiday; The Girl on the Front Page; 1937: Under Cover of Night; The Squeaker/Murder on Diamond Row; Espionage; 1938: Every Day's a Holiday; Secrets of a Nurse; Newsboys' Home; 1939: Our Neighbors — the Carters; The Witness Vanishes; 1940: Honeymoon Deferred; The Crooked Road; I Love You Again; Wolf of New York; Men Against the Sky; 1941: Flying Cadets; Double Date; 1942: Call Out the Marines; Klondike Fury; 1943: Murder in Times Square; Dangerous Blondes; 1944: Oh! What a Night; The Girl in the Case; 1945: Dillinger; The Enchanted Forest; The Strange Mr. Gregory; 1948: Good Sam; 1956: Around the World in Eighty Days; 1957: The Wings of Eagles; 1958: Plunderers of Painted Flats; The Last Hurrah; 1960: Heller in Pink Tights.

NY Stage: 1918: The Brat; The Walk-Offs; Roads of Destiny; 1919: The Son-Daughter; 1921: In the Night Watch; The Right to Strike; Trilby; 1922: Desert Sands; 1929: The Channel Road; 1930: Tonight or Never; 1945: The Ryan Girl

Select TV: 1949: Your Witness (series); 1951–53: Front Page Detective (series); 1957: Execution Night (sp).

MYRNA LOY

(MYRNA ADELE WILLIAMS) BORN: HELENA, MT, AUGUST 2, 1905. DIED: DECEMBER 14, 1993.

From exotic vamp to cosmopolitan wit to ideal wife/mom, Myra Loy tackled them all, but it was in comedy that she is most cherished. She became one of the infinite pleasures of the studio era, growing increasingly assured in her work until she was simply one of the great practitioners of the light comic touch. Moving to Los Angeles as a teen, she got a job dancing in the stage show at Grauman's Chinese Theatre before scoring a bit part in the movie *What Price Beauty?*, which, although filmed in 1925, was not released for another three years. In the interim she had tiny moments in such movies as *Ben-Hur*; *Don Juan*; *Ham and Eggs at the Front*, appearing throughout in blackface (!); *Across the Pacific*, portraying a native girl; the groundbreaking *The Jazz Singer*, as a chorus girl; and *Noah's Ark*.

During this period she had signed a contract with Warner Bros., and they gave her major roles in *Bitter Apples* and *Crimson City*, which was the first, but not the last, time she was cast as an Asian, no doubt because of her catlike eyes. There followed many roles like this, including playing an Indian in *The Black Watch*, a Mexican in *The Great Divide*, and an island native in *Isle of Escape*. After ending her stint with the studio, she began getting showier parts in some significant films, such as Will Rogers's leaden but popular version of *A Connecticut Yankee*, as temptress Morgan Le Faye, and two with Ronald Colman, *The Devil to Pay*, as the woman he sacrifices for Loretta Young, and *Arrowsmith*, as the plantation owner's daughter with whom he has a liaison.

It was at this point, 1932, that MGM decided to place her under contract, and in time this would prove to be her stepping stone to stardom. First they made her one of Marie Dressler's snooty stepchildren in *Emma*; Neil Hamilton's girlfriend in *The Wet Parade*; and Gilbert Roland's jealous partner in *The Woman in Room 13*. They also made sure she still had one more Asian part to play, as Boris Karloff's wicked daughter in the campy *The Mask of Fu Manchu*, a film that today's audiences either get a hoot out of or simply dismiss as horribly racist. Ironically two roles that she got on loan-out were more interesting than this whole batch, first over at Paramount, where she was a scream as the insatiably horny countess in the classic Maurice Chevalier musical *Love Me Tonight*, and then at RKO, where she was quite effective as the self-involved wife who doesn't understand poor Leslie Howard at all, in the stagebound but intelligent adaptation of the Broadway hit *The Animal Kingdom*.

Back at MGM she was seen in another intriguing adaptation of a stage play, *When Ladies Meet*, as a foolish author who sets her sights on married Frank Morgan, while *Night Flight*, successfully placed her alongside Clark Gable for the first time. By this point Loy should have felt that she'd risen to some higher position in the business, but Metro thought otherwise, not hesitating to cast her opposite real-life boxer Max Baer in *The Prizefighter and the Lady*, or to have her plunge into a bathtub full of rose petals for a silly Ramon Navarro melodrama, *The Barbarian*. However, an important turn of events came about because of 1934's *Manhattan Melodrama*, for it cast her opposite William Powell, and their scenes together had real snap. Because of it, the studio had the smart idea to team them again, and screen history was made. *The Thin Man* cast Loy as Nora, wife of sleuth Nick Charles (Powell), and not only was this the wittiest whodunit of its day but it also presented the two stars at the peak of their professionalism. Their effortless bantering, delivered with part mockery, part affection, was the blueprint for all others to follow, and they hit it off so well as a team that audiences continued to assume for years that they were man and wife off screen as well.

Before the studio came up with another *Thin Man* movie, they reteamed Loy with Powell on a more serious and less-satisfying level for *Evelyn Prentice*, in which she faced a murder rap. At Columbia she did Frank Capra's racetrack story, *Broadway Bill*, while Paramount gave her a chance to pair off with Cary Grant, although *Wings in the Dark* was not a sophisticated comedy but serious stuff about a blinded pilot. Back at MGM she was with Gable again for the marital drama *Wife vs. Secretary*, as the wife, though Jean Harlow actually gave her a run for her money on this occasion. She was with Powell again in the Academy Award-winning blockbuster *The Great Ziegfeld*, supposedly as Billie Burke, but playing it strictly as Myrna Loy. She then got Powell along with Spencer Tracy and Jean Harlow for a bright comedy, and the best of the non-*Thin Man* Loy-Powell films, *Libeled Lady*, in which she was the aloof heiress in question. There was the first of many sequels, *After the Thin Man*, which in no way shamed the

original, and then a notorious biographical flop with Gable, *Parnell*. With Powell she was in another comedy, *Double Wedding*, then did two in a row with Gable, the routine aviation drama-romance *Test Pilot*, and the better *Too Hot to Handle*, which wisely added some laughs to the adventure. There was another hit over at Fox, *The Rains Came*, in which she played the very unsympathetic rich bitch who sees the error of her ways after a combination earthquake and monsoon shakes up everyone's lives. A second sequel, *Another Thin Man*, was the last of the series to get critical appreciation, then she and Powell did *I Love You Again*, about amnesia, and *Love Crazy*, which showed definite signs of strain seeping into the fun. She spent most of World War II working for the Red Cross, her last three assignments for MGM being the last three, less-polished *Thin Man* movies, ending with *Song of the Thin Man*, in 1947.

She started off the postwar years with a bang, playing the devoted spouse of returning vet Fredric March in the 1946 Academy Award-winner for Best Picture, *The Best Years of Our Lives*, and she came to symbolize the warm and decent American wife that one could only hope was waiting back home. This was followed by two in a row with Cary Grant, this time with the right material. First was *The Bachelor and the Bobby-Soxer*, with Loy as a judge, and then *Mr. Blandings Builds His Dream House*, as the newly suburbanized wife with very definite ideas about paint colors. At Republic she did a horse story, *The Red Pony*, and then went to England for a soap opera, *That Dangerous Age*, which played in the U.S. under the fruity title *If This Be Sin*. There was a major mom role in the superficial but well-attended 1950 adaptation of the best-selling novel *Cheaper by the Dozen*, a part that she was asked to reprise in the follow-up, *Belles on Their Toes*. Leaving the screen again for a spell, she worked for UNESCO in Europe and then returned in *The Ambassador's Daughter*, where she ranked third in importance after Olivia de Havilland and John Forsythe.

Having passed the age of 50, she bowed out of star billing to play an alcoholic, which she did quite well, in *Lonelyhearts*, unhappily married to sarcastic editor Robert Ryan, and then again in *From the Terrace*, as Paul Newman's mom. In 1960 she did a fairly thankless part as Doris Day's aunt in the popular *Midnight Lace*, and then disappeared for another nine years, being coaxed back for a pretty worthless Jack Lemmon comedy, *The April Fools*, as Charles Boyer's wife. After that she spent a good deal of time in television movies before joining the all-star ensemble of the disaster epic *Airport 1975*, as one of the endangered passengers. It was nice to see her alongside fellow veteran Pat O'Brien (with whom she had appeared in *Consolation Marriage* back in 1931) in Burt Reynolds's *The End* (they were his parents), and her presence was especially gratifying in *Just Tell Me What You Want*, adding some spark to the indifferent proceedings, as Alan King's unappreciated secretary. Shortly afterwards she retired and wrote her autobiography, *Seeing and Believing*, published in 1987. There was a special Academy Award given shortly before her death, Loy being another shocking case of a special talent who was never so much as honored with a nomination by the Academy in all her years of making the movies a better place to go.

Screen: 1925: Sporting Life; Ben-Hur; Pretty Ladies; 1926: The Cave Man; The Gilded Highway; The Love Toy; Why Girls Go Back Home; So This Is Paris; Don Juan; Exquisite Sinner; The Third Degree; Across the Pacific; 1927: Finger Prints; When a Man Loves; Ham and Eggs at the Front; The Climbers; Bitter Apples; The Heart of Maryland; Simple Sis; The Jazz Singer; A Sailor's Sweetheart; The Girl From Chicago; If I Were Single; 1928: What Price Beauty? (filmed 1925); Beware of Married Men;

Turn Back the Hours; Crimson City; A Girl in Every Port; Heart of Maryland; Pay as You Enter; State Street Sadie; The Midnight Taxi; 1929: Noah's Ark; Fancy Baggage; The Desert Song; The Squall; The Great Divide; The Black Watch; Evidence; Hard-Boiled Rose; The Show of Shows; 1930: Cameo Kirby; Isle of Escape; Under a Texas Moon; Cock o' the Walk; Bride of the Regiment; The Bad Man; The Last of the Duanes; The Jazz Cinderella; The Truth About Youth; Renegades; Rogue of the Rio Grande; The Devil to Pay; 1931: The Naughty Flirt; Body and Soul; A Connecticut Yankee; Hush Money; Transatlantic; Skyline; Rebound; Consolation Marriage; Arrowsmith; 1932: Emma; The Wet Parade; Vanity Fair; New Morals for Old; The Woman in Room 13; Love Me Tonight; Thirteen Women; The Mask of Fu Manchu; The Animal Kingdom; 1933: Topaze; The Barbarian; The Prizefighter and the Lady; Scarlet River; When Ladies Meet; Penthouse; Night Flight; 1934: Men in White; Manhattan Melodrama; The Thin Man; Stamboul Quest; Evelyn Prentice; Broadway Bill; 1935: Wings in the Dark; Whipsaw; 1936: Wife vs. Secretary; Petticoat Fever; The Great Ziegfeld; To Mary — With Love; Libeled Lady; After the Thin Man; 1937: Parnell; Double Wedding; 1938: Man-Proof; Test Pilot; Too Hot to Handle; 1939: Lucky Night; The Rains Came; Another Thin Man; 1940: I Love You Again; Third Finger, Left Hand; 1941: Love Crazy; Shadow of the Thin Man; 1944: The Thin Man Goes Home; 1946: So Goes My Love; The Best Years of Our Lives; 1947: The Senator Was Indiscreet; The Bachelor and the Bobby-Soxer; Song of the Thin Man; 1948: Mr. Blandings Builds His Dream House; 1949: The Red Pony; If This Be Sin/That Dangerous Age; 1950: Cheaper by the Dozen; 1952: Belles on Their Toes; 1956: The Ambassador's Daughter; 1958: Lonelyhearts; 1960: From the Terrace; Midnight Lace; 1969: The April Fools; 1974: Airport 1975; 1978: The End; 1980: Just Tell Me What You Want.

Select TV: 1955: It Gives Me Great Pleasure (sp); 1957: Lady of the House (sp); Love Came Late (sp); No Second Helping (sp); 1959: Meet Me in St. Louis (sp); 1971: Death Takes a Holiday; Do Not Fold, Spindle or Mutilate; 1972: The Couple Takes a Wife; 1974: Indict and Convict; The Elevator; 1977: It Happened at Lakewood Manor/Ants; 1981: Summer Solstice.

BELA LUGOSI

(BELA FERENC DEZSO BLASKO) BORN: LUGOS, AUSTRIA-HUNGARY, OCTOBER 20, 1882. ED: BUDAPEST THEATRICAL ARTS ACADEMY. DIED: AUGUST 16, 1956.

The name Bela Lugosi is guaranteed to provoke a smile from even the most casual of film followers, but it is not always a smile of affection. There is often a feeling of condescension or derision towards the actor for his limitations and, particularly in the latter half of his career, his incredibly bad choice of films. Whatever his overall legacy, there is no denying that he has stamped the definitive image of vampires in general, and of Count Dracula specifically, on our consciousness for all time. He debuted on the Budapest stage in 1901 and became a major name there before turning to movies in 1915. When Communism overtook the country he moved to Germany in 1919, where he worked for another two years before making his home in America. Five years after his 1922 Broadway debut in The Red Poppy, he scored a resounding success playing the title role in the stage adaptation of Bram Stoker's Dracula. His thick accent was both seductive and menacing, but it was the reason Hollywood initially hesitated in asking Lugosi to repeat his role on film. When the original choice, Lon Chaney, passed

away, Universal and director Todd Browning decided to give Lugosi a try, and he came west to record Dracula on celluloid. The end result, a box-office smash, was instrumental in moving the studio into the horror genre, and made Lugosi a major motion picture name. Seen today, he is still the mesmerizing center of a fairly stage-bound and tame movie, causing generations to imitate his inimitable, hesitant introduction "I am...Drac...ula."

Right from the start Lugosi erred when he refused his follow-up assignment, Frankenstein, because he would not have any dialogue. He was, however, well utilized as the crazed scientist trying to find a mate for his gorilla in Murders in the Rue Morgue and (for United Artists) as a creepy plantation owner, with the memorable name Murder Legendre, who employs the undead in White Zombie. There was the lead in The Return of Chandu, playing radio's famous magician after having been his nemesis in the previous Chandu the Magician, and an unforgettable role as the hairy-faced Sayer of the Law in Paramount's eerie Island of Lost Souls. Then it was back to the home lot to pair off with Boris Karloff in The Black Cat, with Lugosi taking on one of his few restrained, normal roles, pretty much being the good guy. In contrast the two stars were put together again for The Raven, only this time it was Bela who got to be evil, surgically disfiguring the hapless Karloff. By their third teaming, The Invisible Ray, Lugosi was clearly a secondary character in the storyline. He was not asked to rise from the dead for Dracula's Daughter, but MGM dressed him up in similar garb for the bogus Mark of the Vampire. Not one to turn down work, he was busily employed at such poverty-row companies as Monogram and Imperial Distributors, appearing for the latter as twins in a ghastly thing called Murder by Television.

Universal still needed him for their horror output, and he came up with his second greatest screen creation, Igor, the vengeful criminal with the broken neck in Son of Frankenstein, probably the only time he stole the show from Karloff. He was asked to repeat the part in The Ghost of Frankenstein, but was no doubt eating crow when he agreed at last to play the monster in the 1943 follow-up, Frankenstein Meets the Wolf Man, looking very strange and physically inadequate in the famous make-up. Before that he appeared in one of his few "straight" films, Ninotchka, in a brief scene as the cold-hearted Commissar Razn; acted for the shoddiest company of them all, PRC, in Devil Bat, which had something to do with a deadly shaving cream; hit some kind of peak of camp as the half-simian scientist in The Ape Man; was pretty much wasted playing a Gypsy named Bela in another of Universal's most famous genre films, The Wolf Man; and was reduced to playing straight man for the East Side Kids in Spooks Run Wild (looking like Dracula again, although he was a menacing magician) and Ghosts on the Loose (as a Nazi). Unlike Karloff, who seemed to rise above such material, Lugosi seemed all too suited for it, looking as foolish as his surroundings. In 1943, Columbia summoned him for a decent chiller, The Return of the Vampire, which was as close to being Dracula as they could get without invoking a lawsuit from Universal, who still owned the rights to the character. Instead, Lugosi was Armand Tessla, playing only his second genuine bloodsucker in 12 years.

After sinking further with Return of the Ape Man, he supported the long-forgotten comedy team of Brown and Carney for both Zombies on Broadway and Genius at Work, being neither zombie nor genius, but a mad scientist and Lionel Atwill's servant, respectively. There was another chance to pair him off with comedians, in Abbott and Costello Meet Frankenstein, only this time the movie was a vastly superior entry in the comedy-horror genre, with Lugosi in his last dignified role, reprising Count

Dracula officially, one final time. Although the film was a hit, it did not revive interest in the actor, and the 1950s were his blackest period, with Lugosi suffering from financial difficulties and drug addiction. Two more cheesy comedies gave him work, *Bela Lugosi Meets a Brooklyn Gorilla*, hardly an honor to have your name featured in the title in this case, playing straight man to a grotesque pair of Martin and Lewis imitators, and the British *Old Mother Riley Meets the Vampire*, the last of Arthur Lucan's low-brow drag romps. Lugosi's involvement with hack filmmaker Edward D. Wood, Jr. became the stuff of Hollywood legend and later the subject of a feature film, this collaboration giving us the declining star in three horrible films: *Glen or Glenda*, as the on-screen narrator of this mind-boggling plea for tolerance for cross-dressers; *Bride of the Monster*, in his umpteenth mad scientist role, destroyed by a rubber octopus; and the immortal *Plan 9 From Outer Space*, reduced to a silent walk-on, flashing his Dracula cape, having died before the rest of the movie was shot. His role was finished by an obvious double, and the movie has contributed more than any other to making Lugosi something of a symbol of a once-heralded star hitting rock bottom. Martin Landau won an Oscar for playing him in this period in the excellent *Ed Wood*, hopefully restoring a bit of dignity to the tarnished Lugosi image.

Screen: 1917: Alarscobal Az Elet Kiralya; The Leopard; A Naszdal; Tavaszi Vihar; Az Ezredes/The Colonel; 1918: Casanova; Lulu '99; Kuzdelem a Letert; 1919: Sklaven Fremden Willens; 1920: Der Fluch der Menschen; The Head of Janus; Die Frau im Delphin; Die Todeskaraawane/Caravan of Death; Nat Pinkerton in Kampf; Lederstrumpf; Die Teufelsanbeter/The Devil Worshipers; 1921: Johann Hopkins III; Der Tanz auf dem Vulkan; 1922: The Last of the Mohicans; 1923: The Silent Command; 1924: The Rejected Woman; 1925: The Midnight Girl; Daughters Who Pay; 1928: How to Handle Women; The Veiled Woman; 1929: Prisoners; The Thirteenth Chair; Such Men Are Dangerous; 1930: Wild Company; Renegades; Viennese Nights; Oh for a Man; 1931: Dracula; Fifty Million Frenchmen; Women of All Nations; The Black Camel; Broadminded; 1932: Murders in the Rue Morgue; White Zombie; Chandu the Magician; 1933: The Death Kiss; Island of Lost Souls; Whispering Shadow (serial); International House; Night of Terror; The Devil's in Love; 1934: The Black Cat; Gift of Gab; The Return of Chandu; Chandu on the Magic Isle; The Mysterious Mr. Wong; 1935: The Best Man Wins; Mark of the Vampire; Murder by Television; The Raven; The Mystery of the Marie Celeste/Phantom Ship; 1936: The Invisible Ray; Shadow of Chinatown (serial); Postal Inspector; 1937: S.O.S. Coast Guard (serial); 1939: The Dark Eyes of London/The Human Monster; The Phantom Creeps (serial); The Gorilla; Son of Frankenstein; Ninotchka; 1940: The Saint's Double Trouble; Black Friday; You'll Find Out; The Devil Bat; 1941: The Invisible Ghost; The Black Cat; Spooks Run Wild; The Wolf Man; 1942: The Ghost of Frankenstein; Black Dragons; The Corpse Vanishes; Night Monster; Bowery at Midnight; 1943: Frankenstein Meets the Wolf Man; The Ape Man; Ghosts on the Loose; The Return of the Vampire; 1944: Voodoo Man; Return of the Ape Man; One Body Too Many; 1945: The Body Snatcher; Zombies on Broadway; 1946: Genius at Work; 1947: Scared to Death; 1948: Abbott and Costello Meet Frankenstein; 1952: Old Mother Riley Meets the Vampire/Vampire Over London/My Son the Vampire; Bela Lugosi Meets a Brooklyn Gorilla/The Boys From Brooklyn; 1953: Glen or Glenda; 1954: Bride of the Monster/Bride of the Atom; 1956: The Black Sleep; 1959: Plan 9 From Outer Space.

NY Stage: 1922: The Red Poppy; 1925: Arabesque; Open House; 1926: The Devil in the Cheese; 1927: Dracula; 1933: Murder at the Vanities.

PAUL LUKAS

(PÁL LUKÁCS) BORN: BUDAPEST, AUSTRIA-HUNGARY, MAY 26, 1887. ED: ACTORS' ACAD. OF HUNGARY. DIED: AUGUST 15, 1971.

A curiosity in the stardom department, Paul Lukas had a certain degree of dapper good looks and yet wasn't exactly leading-man handsome. He certainly wasn't a bad actor, yet there was something unexciting about him that made you look past whatever he was accomplishing, maybe in hopes of seeing someone else with real screen presence. Born on a train en route to Budapest, he made his professional stage debut in that city in 1916, starring in *Liliom*. The following year came his first movie, *Sphinx*, and he continued to appear in pictures in his native language until 1922 when he went to Vienna to play a part in *Eine Versunkene Welt*. Because Paramount head Adolph Zukor happened to catch him onstage in *Antonia*, Lukas was invited to come to Hollywood in 1928. For Paramount he did *Three Sinners*, while Goldwyn borrowed him for *Two Lovers*. Silents hid his heavy accent, but talkies were on their way, and Lukas suffered the indignity of having his dialogue dubbed by someone else in his first all-talking endeavor, *The Wolf of Wall Street*, where, like all of his American movies to date, he was a supporting player. For his home studio he continued to be one of those performers who usually got third billing below the main attractions, until they upped him to Ruth Chatterton's leading man in both *The Right to Love* and *Unfaithful*. Over at Universal he was one of the better things about the unfunny *Strictly Dishonorable*, as an over-sexed opera singer, and was the lawyer plotting to kill Nancy Carroll in *The Kiss Before the Mirror*. For the cheapie Majestic Pictures Corp. he was top billed in *Sing, Sinner, Sing*, as Leila Hyams's unscrupulous lover, then appeared in one of his few enduring films of the 1930s, *Little Women*, in a marvelous performance as Katharine Hepburn's older love interest, Professor Baer. Despite this peak, his impact on the movie industry was fairly unremarkable by this point, and he continued to appear in such Universal trifles as *By Candlelight*, *The Countess of Monte Cristo*, and *Affairs of a Gentleman*, top billed again, this time as a novelist-playboy.

Over at RKO he was Athos in one of the less well remembered versions of *The Three Musketeers*; seduced Ruth Chatterton in another of his "A" productions of this time, *Dodsworth*; then went off to England, in 1937, to find work there. Top among his output there was Alfred Hitchcock's classic *The Lady Vanishes*, in which he played a spy. Back in the States he was another bad egg, a U.S. Naval officer working for the SS, in Warner's *Confessions of a Nazi Spy*; returned for some more work overseas; then was straight man to Bob Hope in the comic-thriller *The Ghost Breakers*. A trip to Broadway provided his career with the shot-in-the-arm it needed, playing the honorable agent tracking down Nazis in Lillian Hellman's *Watch on the Rhine*. Warners bought the property and, since they had Bette Davis on board for box-office insurance, gave Lukas his stage role. A static but intelligent film, it preserved his fine, subtle work, earning him the Academy Award for Best Actor of 1943. This being wartime, Hollywood didn't quite know what else to do with a 50-year-old-plus, thickly accented actor, so he was a Nazi again in *Hostages*, and joined the Gestapo in *Address Unknown*, which marked the last time he would head the cast list. Instead he tried to drive Hedy Lamarr nuts in *Experiment Perilous* and was an unlikely cab driver in *Deadline at Dawn*.

During the early 1950s he was seen in two big productions, *Kim*, as a lama, and Disney's *20,000 Leagues Under the Sea*, shanghaied by Captain Nemo. Back on Broadway he got a chance to sing in Irving Berlin's *Call Me Madam*, but was replaced by George Sanders in the movie version. During the 1960s he could still be seen bringing his very serious presence to such movies as the boring remake of *The Four Horsemen of the Apocalypse*, in which he was another evil German, and *Scent of Mystery*, a flop adventure, notorious for being shot in "Smell-o-vision." He gave one of the few critically liked performances, as Dr. Dohmler, in the much-hated film of Fitzgerald's *Tender Is the Night*, and was once again a member of the medical profession, in the epic *55 Days at Peking*. In 1970 he retired to Spain and died the following year.

Screen: 1918: Sphynx; 1920: The Yellow Shadow; Little Fox; The Castle Without a Name/Castle Nameless; The Milliner; The Actress; Masamod; 1921: Telegram From New York; Love of the 18th Century; 1922: The Lady in Grey; Samson and Delilah; Lady Violette; Eine Versunkene Welt; 1923: The Glorious Life; A Girl's Way; Derumberkanuta Morgen; Az Egyhuszasos Lany; 1924: Egy Fiunak a Fele; 1928: Two Lovers; Three Sinners; Loves of an Actress; Hot News; Night Watch; The Woman From Moscow; Manhattan Cocktail; 1929: The Shopworn Angel; The Wolf of Wall Street; Illusion; Halfway to Heaven; 1930: Behind the Makeup; Slightly Scarlet; The Benson Murder Case; Young Eagles; The Devil's Holiday; Grumpy; Anybody's Woman; The Right to Love; 1931: Unfaithful; City Streets; Vice Squad; Women Love Once; Beloved Bachelor; Strictly Dishonorable; Working Girls; 1932: Tomorrow and Tomorrow; No One Man; Thunder Below; A Passport to Hell; Downstairs; 1933: Rockabye; Grand Slam; The Kiss Before the Mirror; Sing, Sinner, Sing; Captured!; Secret of the Blue Room; Little Women; By Candlelight; 1934: Glamour; The Countess of Monte Cristo; I Give My Love; Affairs of a Gentleman; The Fountain; Gift of Gab; 1935: Father Brown — Detective; The Casino Murder Case; Age of Indiscretion; The Three Musketeers; I Found Stella Parish; 1936: Dodsworth; Ladies in Love; 1937: Espionage; Dinner at the Ritz; Brief Ecstasy/Dangerous Secrets; Mutiny on the Elsinore; 1938: The Lady Vanishes; 1939: Confessions of a Nazi Spy; Captain Fury; Lady in Distress/A Window in London; 1940: The Ghost Breakers; Strange Cargo; 1941: Chinese Den/The Chinese Bungalow; The Monster and the Girl; They Dare Not Love; 1943: Watch on the Rhine; Hostages; 1944: Uncertain Glory; Address Unknown; Experiment Perilous; 1946: Deadline at Dawn; Temptation; 1947: Whispering City; 1948: Berlin Express; 1950: Kim; 1954: 20,000 Leagues Under the Sea; 1958: The Roots of Heaven; 1960: Scent of Mystery/Holiday in Spain; 1962: Tender Is the Night; The Four Horsemen of the Apocalypse; 1963: 55 Days at Peking; Fun in Acapulco; 1965: Lord Jim; 1968: Sol Madrid.

NY Stage: 1937: A Doll's House; 1941: Watch on the Rhine; 1950: Call Me Madam; 1952: Flight Into Egypt; 1955: The Wayward Saint.

Select TV: 1952: The Ringmaster (sp); Caprice (sp); Something to Celebrate (sp); 1955: The Thief (sp); 1959: Judgment at Nuremberg (sp); 1963: Four Kings (sp); 1970: The Challenge.

KEYE LUKE

BORN: CANTON, CHINA, JUNE 18, 1904.
RAISED IN SEATTLE, WA. ED: UNIV. OF WA.
DIED: JANUARY 12, 1991.

Employing Asian actors was never a top priority in Hollywood, but Keye Luke was one of the few to not only receive fairly steady work but to also achieve a pretty high level of name recognition. After his birth his parents returned to America where he was raised. Having studied design in college, he became a commercial

artist, and it was in this capacity that he came to Hollywood, working at RKO. While there he was asked to appear in some short subjects by a casting director desperate for English-speaking Asians. His feature debut came in 1934 in Greta Garbo's *The Painted Veil*, appearing as a doctor. The following year he was called on by Fox to play the role that made him famous, the appealingly naïve Lee Chan, the Number One Son of master sleuth Charlie Chan, played by the definitely un-Asian Warner Oland. Luke's debut entry, *Charlie Chan in Paris*, was the seventh in the series. During the late 1930s he was seen in eight Chan installments (in addition to playing Lee Chan in the Chan-inspired whodunit, *Mr. Moto's Gamble*), ending with *Charlie Chan at Monte Carlo*. Later down the line, substantial work no doubt hard to come by, he agreed to rejoin the series twice more in the late 1940s when they had gone over to Monogram. In the meantime, he was one of the authentic Asians supporting Caucasians Paul Muni and Luise Rainer in one of the big films of the day, *The Good Earth*, and was given star billing in the "B" *Phantom of Chinatown*, replacing Boris Karloff as Mr. Wong in this poorly received series.

Prior to World War II Luke was gainfully employed, playing the faithful assistant Kato in two Universal serials, *The Green Hornet* and *The Green Hornet Strikes Again*. There were other adventures for that company, *Adventures of Smilin' Jack* and *Lost City of the Jungle*, as well as work at MGM, where he was asked to join the medical team in *Dr. Gillespie's New Assistant* as Dr. Lee Wong How, a role he would reprise thrice more. If anybody had use for an Asian, Luke was usually at the top of the list, so he was a boxer in *Salute to the Marines*; another doctor in *Andy Hardy's Blonde Trouble*; and brought off playing Japanese in *Across the Pacific*, *Tokyo Rose*, and *First Yank in Tokyo*, among others. In 1958 he scored a hit in the Rodgers and Hammerstein musical *Flower Drum Song*, but was passed over in favor of Benson Fong for the film version. There was one final burst of glory, however, in the 1970s, when he was hired for the series *Kung Fu* to play David Carradine's blind spiritual adviser. There was also a last visit to familiar territory, supplying the voice of Charlie Chan in the Saturday morning children's series *The Amazing Chan and the Chan Clan*. His two best-known later film roles were in *Gremlins*, in which he sold the furry critter that multiplied into a destructive horde of monsters, and *Alice*, where he was a mysterious mystic supplying Mia Farrow with some magical potions.

Screen: 1934: The Painted Veil; 1935: Charlie Chan in Paris; Oil for the Lamps of China; Shanghai; Mad Love; Charlie Chan in Shanghai; Here's to Romance; Eight Bells; Murder in the Fleet; The Casino Murder Case; 1936: King of Burlesque; Anything Goes; Charlie Chan at the Circus; Charlie Chan at the Race Track; 1937: Charlie Chan on Broadway; The Good Earth; Charlie Chan at the Olympics; Charlie Chan at the Opera; 1938: Charlie Chan at Monte Carlo; International Settlement; Mr. Moto's Gamble; 1939: Disputed Passage; Barricade; North of Shanghai; Sued for Libel; 1940: Phantom of Chinatown; No, No, Nanette; Comrade X; The Green Hornet (serial); The Green Hornet Strikes Again (serial); 1941: Gang's All Here; Let's Go Collegiate; Bowery Blitzkrieg; Burma Convoy; No Hands on the Clock; Mr. and Mrs. North; Passage From Hong Kong; 1942: A Yank on the Burma Road; Invisible Agent; Somewhere I'll Find You; Mexican Spitfire's Elephant; North to the Klondike; Spy Ship; Across the Pacific; A Tragedy at Midnight; The Falcon's Brother; Journey for Margaret; Destination Unknown; Dr. Gillespie's New Assistant; 1943: Adventures of Smilin' Jack (serial); Dr. Gillespie's Criminal Case; Salute to the Marines; 1944: Andy Hardy's Blonde Trouble; Three Men in White; Between Two Women; 1945: First Yank in Tokyo; How Doooo

You Do?; Secret Agent X-9 (serial); **1946:** Tokyo Rose; Lost City of the Jungle; **1947:** Dark Delusion; **1948:** Sleep My Love; Waterfront at Midnight; The Feathered Serpent; **1949:** Sky Dragon; **1950:** Young Man With a Horn; **1953:** Fair Wind to Java; South Sea Woman; **1954:** The Bamboo Prison; World for Ransom; Hell's Half Acre; **1955:** Love Is a Many-Splendored Thing; **1956:** Around the World in Eighty Days; **1957:** Battle Hell/Yangtse Incident; **1968:** Nobody's Perfect; **1969:** The Chairman; **1970:** The Hawaiians; **1976:** Won Ton Ton, the Dog Who Saved Hollywood; **1978:** The Amsterdam Kill; **1979:** Just You and Me, Kid; **1984:** Gremlins; **1986:** A Fine Mess; **1988:** Dead Heat; **1989:** The Mighty Quinn; **1990:** Gremlins 2: The New Batch; Alice.

NY Stage: 1958: Flower Drum Song.

Select TV: 1953: The Traitor (sp); The Reign of Amelika Jo (sp); **1955:** Ring Once for Death (sp); **1956:** The Smuggler (sp); **1958:** In the Dark (sp); **1964–65:** Kentucky Jones (series); **1972:** Kung Fu; Anna and the King (series); **1972–74:** The Amazing Chan and the Chan Clan (series; voice); **1972–75:** Kung Fu (series); **1973:** The Cat Creature; **1974:** Judge Dee and the Monastery Murders; **1976:** Harry-O (series); **1981:** Fly Away Home; **1983:** Cocaine and Blue Eyes; **1985:** Blade in Hong Kong; **1986:** Kung Movie: The Movie; The Last Electric Knight; **1986–87:** Sidekicks (series).

JOHN LUND

BORN: ROCHESTER, NY, FEBRUARY 6, 1913.
DIED: MAY 9, 1992.

A decidedly square, stoic addition to Paramount's roster of stars during the postwar years, John Lund came to acting after working in New York in advertising. He made his professional debut in a pageant called *Railroads on Parade*, which played at the New York World's Fair in 1939. Two years later he ended up on Broadway in a production of *As You Like It*, and followed it with work on radio, both as an actor and writer. It was his performance in the 1945 play *The Hasty Heart* that got him noticed by Paramount, who gave him not one but two plumb roles, as both father and son, in the Olivia de Havilland soaper *To Each His Own*, in no way interfering with Ms. de Havilland's Oscar-winning emoting. From there he was blown off the screen by the hyper Betty Hutton in the Pearl White biopic *The Perils of Pauline*, and by both Jean Arthur and Marlene Dietrich in the excellent *A Foreign Affair*, playing a wiley G.I. in bomb-ravaged Berlin in the best of his screen assignments. He was atypically lively as a stunt man posing as a nerdy heir in *Miss Tatlock's Millions*, then sank with the rest of the cast in one of the most notoriously silly misfires of the late 1940s, *Bride of Vengeance*, in which treacherous Paulette Goddard marries him and then tries to poison him. This was followed by a weak but popular comedy based on the hit radio show *My Friend Irma*, but everybody came away talking about Martin and Lewis. The studio cast him adrift in a pair of sudsy dramas, *No Man of Her Own* and *Darling, How Could You!*, after which he went the expected route of all indistinctive actors, doing such standard western fare as *Bronco Buster*, *White Feather*, and *Dakota Incident*. Fittingly, he was called on to play one of drama's ultimate pills, George Kittredge, in *High Society*, the musical remake of *The Philadelphia Story*, and ended his movie career playing Sandra Dee's stuffy dad in the Universal fluff *If a Man Answers*.

Screen: 1946: To Each His Own; **1947:** The Perils of Pauline; Variety Girl; **1948:** A Foreign Affair; Night Has a Thousand Eyes; Miss Tatlock's Millions; **1949:** Bride of Vengeance; My Friend Irma; **1950:** No Man of Her Own; My Friend Irma Goes West;

Duchess of Idaho; **1951:** The Mating Season; Darling, How Could You!; **1952:** Steel Town; The Battle of Apache Pass; Bronco Buster; Just Across the Street; **1953:** The Woman They Almost Lynched; Latin Lovers; **1955:** Chief Crazy Horse; White Feather; Five Guns West; **1956:** Battle Stations; High Society; Dakota Incident; **1957:** Affair in Reno; **1961:** The Wackiest Ship in the Army; **1962:** If a Man Answers.

NY Stage: 1941: As You Like It; **1943:** Early to Bed; **1945:** The Hasty Heart; **1953:** An Evening with Will Shakespeare (ob).

WILLIAM LUNDIGAN

BORN: SYRACUSE, NY, JUNE 12, 1914.
DIED: DECEMBER 20, 1975.

Blank-looking William Lundigan was signed up by Universal Studios after some radio work and thrown into a whole slew of "B" pictures where his thrill-free personality fit right in. His first lead was in *That's My Story*, as a junior reporter; followed by *Freshman Year*, as a college boy; and *They Asked for It*, as a small town newspaper editor. When Universal had no further use for him he went over to Warners, where he was assigned to higher quality films but not in the leads, including several in support of Errol Flynn, *Dodge City*, *The Sea Hawk*, and *Santa Fe Trail*. After a while the studio figured he could carry some of their lesser fare, so he was given top billing in such cheapies as *The Case of the Black Parrot*, as a reporter solving a murder mystery, and *A Shot in the Dark*, as a reporter *helping* to solve a murder mystery. Next it was over to MGM where once again he bounced back from "A's" in support (*Salute to the Marines*) and "B" leads (*Sunday Punch*, as a prizefighter). As the 1940s came to a close, he was asked to join Fox, who did put him into a good film, *Pinky*, as the white doctor with whom light-skinned black Jeanne Crain falls in love. Finally getting leads in top-of-the-line releases, he was a music publisher in the June Haver musical *I'll Get By*; a doctor giving more time to his patients than to wife Dorothy McGuire in *Mother Didn't Tell Me*; a preacher who marries Susan Hayward in *I'd Climb the Highest Mountain*; and an officer pursued by islander Mitzi Gaynor in the featherbrained *Down Among the Sheltering Palms*. Clearly what appeal these films offered had little to do with the rigid and colorless Lundigan. Naturally he went to television, where he hosted the series *Climax*, among others. His final star part was in a low budget sci-fi adventure, *The Underwater City*.

Screen: 1937: Armored Car; Prescription for Romance; The Lady Fights Back; A Girl With Ideas; That's My Story; Westbound Limited; **1938:** State Police; Freshman Year; Reckless Living; Wives Under Suspicion; The Missing Guest; The Black Doll; The Crime of Doctor Hallett; Danger on the Air; The Jury's Secret; Letter of Introduction; Sinners in Paradise; **1939:** Three Smart Girls Grow Up; Dodge City; They Asked for It; The Forgotten Woman; The Old Maid; Legion of Lost Flyers; **1940:** The Fighting 69th; The Man Who Talked Too Much; Three Cheers for the Irish; Santa Fe Trail; East of the River; The Sea Hawk; **1941:** The Case of the Black Parrot; The Great Mr. Nobody; International Squadron; A Shot in the Dark; Sailors on Leave; Highway West; The Bugle Sounds; **1942:** The Courtship of Andy Hardy; Sunday Punch; Apache Trail; Northwest Rangers; Andy Hardy's Double Life; **1943:** Salute to the Marines; Dr. Gillespie's Criminal Case; Headin' for God's Country; **1945:** What Next, Corporal Hargrove?; **1947:** Dishonored Lady; The Fabulous Dorseys; **1948:** Inside Story; Mystery in Mexico; **1949:** State Department — File 649; Follow Me Quietly; Pinky; **1950:** Mother Didn't Tell Me; I'll Get By;

1951: The House on Telegraph Hill; I'd Climb the Highest Mountain; Love Nest; Elopement; 1953: Down Among the Sheltering Palms; Inferno; Serpent of the Nile; 1954: Riders to the Stars; Terror Ship/Dangerous Voyage; The White Orchid; 1962: The Underwater City; 1967: The Way West; 1968: Where Angels Go…Trouble Follows.

Select TV: 1953: A Man in the Kitchen (sp); The Bachelor (sp); 1954: Give the Guy a Break (sp); To Lift a Feather (sp); The Tryst (sp); 1954–58: Climax (series); Shower of Stars (series); 1955: The Indiscreet Mrs. Jarvis (sp); Total Recall (sp); Beyond (sp); 1958: K.O. Kitty (sp); No Time at All (sp); 1959–60: Men Into Space (series).

IDA LUPINO

BORN: LONDON, ENGLAND, FEBRUARY 4, 1914.
DIED: AUGUST 3, 1995.

Long at the table, waiting to dig in, once Ida Lupino was allowed her turn, she proved she could make a meal out of a juicy part, even at the risk of leaving teeth marks in the scenery. Nonetheless the actress with the husky voice and the moody, longing eyes made sure she was not to be taken lightly, even if too many of her movies were less than memorable. Perhaps sensing this, she decided to branch out and take command on the opposite side of the camera, a move that was a groundbreaking one as far as actresses were concerned. The daughter of English entertainer Stanley Lupino, she trained for a spell at RADA while making her movie debut, in 1933, in *Her First Affaire*, as a teen stuck on a famous novelist (George Curzon). There were a handful of other British films before she was invited by Paramount to test for the lead in their production of *Alice in Wonderland*. Although they vetoed her in favor of the more wholesome looking Charlotte Henry, they cast her opposite Buster Crabbe in *Search for Beauty*, with both playing Olympic swimmers. Although she was kept busy, there wasn't much worth mentioning about the material she was being handed, including *Ready for Love*, playing a spoiled girl in a small town; *Paris in Spring*, picked up on the Eiffel Tower by suicidal Tullio Carminati; and *Smart Girl*, top billed as an aspiring artist in love with law student Kent Taylor. It didn't seem like any great loss to Paramount to loan her elsewhere, so she appeared in *One Rainy Afternoon*, produced by Mary Pickford for UA, as a girl mistakenly kissed in a cinema by Francis Lederer; *Sea Devils*, for RKO, as the daughter of seaman Victor McLaglen; and *Let's Get Married*, a Columbia "B," in which she had to choose between politician Reginald Denny and weatherman Ralph Bellamy. After these she ended her Paramount contract with a hit comedy, *Artists and Models*, having little to do in support of top attraction Jack Benny.

In 1938 she wed actor Louis Hayward, a union that would last until 1945. There was a woman-in-peril role in the second of the Basil Rathbone Holmes films, *The Adventures of Sherlock Holmes*, then she was called back by Paramount for the part that changed everything, the selfish bitch who destroys blind artist Ronald Colman's painting in *The Light That Failed*. Right afterwards she went to Warners to gnaw at some scenery in her big mad scene in *They Drive by Night*, which so impressed that studio that she was signed to a contract. She started her official employment there on a high note, receiving billing *over* Humphrey Bogart for *High Sierra*, in the sort of role in which she excelled, a tough moll. She followed this with the best of the many versions of *The Sea Wolf*, stuck aboard a ship commanded by crazed Edward G. Robinson. Over at Columbia she and her husband teamed for the claustrophobic adaptation of the gothic

stage hit *Ladies in Retirement*, in which she played the housekeeper who takes charge, and, after continually turning down material on her home lot, she appeared in *Life Begins at 8:30* for Fox, as the crippled daughter of Monty Woolley.

Returning to Warners she landed the role of a lifetime, the pushy, deeply unsympathetic sister of Joan Leslie, who winds up alienating everyone around her in her single-minded effort to make sure her sibling succeeds in show business, in *The Hard Way*. It was a real tour de force, and, despite winning the New York Film Critics Award, she was not nominated for the hoped-for Oscar. This peak, alas, did not lead to a golden era of Lupino films. After a snappy jitterbug in *Thank Your Lucky Stars*, she did a mild romantic drama, *In Our Time*, with Paul Henreid; a flop comedy, *Pillow to Post*; and *Devotion* (held up for three years), which was supposed to tell the true story of the Bronte sisters (Lupino was Emily to Olivia de Havilland's Charlotte) but was just another slush-filled melodrama. Better was *Deep Valley*, in which she was a poor girl whose life is changed by a run-in with escaped con Dane Clark, but her stay at Warners came to a negligible end with *Escape Me Never*, a dire melodrama with Errol Flynn that spent two years on the shelf before receiving distribution in 1947. Having divorced Hayward, she married Columbia executive Collier Young, which may have helped her get a part in a decent western made for that studio, *Lust for Gold*.

In 1949, working for the independent Four Continents film company, she produced and co-wrote *Not Wanted*, about unwed motherhood. During director Elmer Clifton's illness she took over and got her first taste of directing, which pleased her tremendously. Soon after, she attained her first official directorial credit, with another cheapie, *Never Fear*, made for Eagle-Lion in 1950; sharing writing chores with her husband. As with all of her films, she was admired for her proficiency at the helm rather than any stellar talent or striking choice of material. Over at Universal she was saved from psycho Stephen McNally by Howard Duff in the melodrama *The Woman in Hiding*; within the year she divorced Young and wed Duff. She continued to rack up some further credits in the directorial field with *Outrage* (a look at sexual molestation, which she also co-wrote), *Hard, Fast and Beautiful* (about tennis, and featuring a cameo by herself), *The Bigamist* (the only time she gave herself a full-fledged role in one of her movies, as a wife not aware that she is sharing hubby Edmond O'Brien with Joan Fontaine), *The Hitchhiker* (perhaps the best known film she helmed, an over-heated melodrama that she co-wrote), and after a long break, *The Trouble With Angels* (the most financially successful of her efforts in this field).

Still holding on to her day job, she had a good role as a blind woman in *On Dangerous Ground*; co-starred again with Duff, in *Private Hell 36*, another "B" budget film that she co-wrote; treaded dangerously close to camp as the mean matron in *Women's Prison* (Duff was a doctor); was one of the less-venomous characters in a skewering of back-stabbing Hollywood, *The Big Knife*, as Jack Palance's wife; and was a "woman's news" reporter in the ensemble thriller *While the City Sleeps*, which was an offering from RKO on its wobbly last legs. (Duff was in it too, but they shared no scenes). Most of her later work was on TV, although she got good notices for playing Steve McQueen's mother in the 1972 theatrical release *Junior Bonner*. There were also roles in cheesy horror movies, *The Devil's Rain* and *The Food of the Gods* (battling giant bugs!); a strange cameo with former *They Drive by Night* co-star George Raft in the long-shelved *Deadhead Miles*; and a substantial assignment in a quickly disposed of film called *My Boys Are Good Boys*. She and Duff (they divorced in 1968) were also the stars of a TV series, *Mr. Adams and Eve*.

Screen: 1933: Her First Affaire; Money for Speed; High Finance;

Prince of Arcadia; The Ghost Camera; I Lived With You; **1934:** Search for Beauty; Come on Marines; Ready for Love; **1935:** Paris in Spring; Smart Girl; Peter Ibbetson; **1936:** Anything Goes; One Rainy Afternoon; Yours for the Asking; The Gay Desperado; **1937:** Sea Devils; Let's Get Married; Artists and Models; Fight for Your Lady; **1939:** The Lone Wolf Spy Hunt; The Lady and the Mob; The Adventures of Sherlock Holmes; The Light That Failed; **1940:** They Drive by Night; **1941:** High Sierra; The Sea Wolf; Out of the Fog; Ladies in Retirement; **1942:** Moontide; Life Begins at 8:30; The Hard Way; **1943:** Forever and a Day; Thank Your Lucky Stars; **1944:** Hollywood Canteen; In Our Time; **1945:** Pillow to Post; **1946:** Devotion (filmed 1943); The Man I Love; **1947:** Deep Valley; Escape Me Never; **1948:** Road House; **1949:** Lust for Gold; Woman in Hiding; **1951:** Hard, Fast and Beautiful (and dir.); On Dangerous Ground; **1952:** Beware, My Lovely; **1953:** Jennifer; The Bigamist (and dir.); **1954:** Private Hell 36 (and wr.); **1955:** Women's Prison; The Big Knife; **1956:** While the City Sleeps; Strange Intruder; **1969:** Backtrack; **1972:** Deadhead Miles (released 1982); Junior Bonner; **1975:** The Devil's Rain; **1976:** The Food of the Gods; **1978:** My Boys Are Good Boys (filmed 1972).

Select TV: 1954: Marriageable Male (sp); A Season to Love (sp); 1956: The Fearful Courage (sp); 1957–58: Mr. Adams and Eve (series); 1961: Image of a Doctor (sp); 1963: One Step Down (sp); 1972: Women in Chains; The Strangers in 7A; 1973: Female Artillery; I Love a Mystery; The Letters.

JIMMY LYDON

BORN: HARRINGTON PARK, NJ, MAY 30, 1923.

Gawky, skinny Jimmy Lydon made his mark as the hapless small town teen Henry Aldrich during the early 1940s, having come from New York theatre, where he'd made his debut, in 1937, in *Western Waters*. Two years later he came to Hollywood to appear as a good boy gone bad in *Back Door to Heaven*, eventually growing up to be Wallace Ford. RKO signed him to play Danny in *Little Men* and gave him the lead in *Tom Brown's Schooldays*, although neither of these was considered a definitive cinematic rendering of these famous books. In 1941 Paramount picked him to play the awkward but affable Aldrich for their "B" series of comedies, and Lydon, with his winning smile and infectious dopiness, was certainly a vast improvement over Jackie Cooper, who had done the part in two previous movies. Lydon began with *Henry Aldrich for President*, in 1941, and continued through eight more entries, ending with *Henry Aldrich's Little Secret*, in 1944. From there he dropped down to PRC cheapies like *The Town Went Wild* (with another former youth star, Freddie Bartholomew), and *When the Lights Go on Again*, but was lucky to land the role of the eldest son in Warners's prestigious and very popular adaptation of the nostalgic *Life With Father*. Columbia hired Lydon to play Skeezit in a "C" budget feature based on a comic strip, *Gasoline Alley*, which was followed by a sequel, *Corky of Gasoline Alley*, before the intended series was abandoned. There were tinier roles (by which point he was being billed as "James") in movies like *The Magnificent Yankee*, as an assistant to judge Louis Calhern, and *Island in the Sky*, before he finally decided to occupy his time in the production end of the business on television, serving as coordinating producer on *Wagon Train*, and associate producer on *77 Sunset Strip*, among others. He periodically returned to act in movies over the years in such films as the western *Death of a Gunfighter* and Disney's *Scandalous John*.

Screen: 1939: Back Door to Heaven; The Middleton Family at

the New York World's Fair; Two Thoroughbreds; **1940:** Tom Brown's Schooldays; Little Men; Bowery Boy; **1941:** Naval Academy; Henry Aldrich for President; **1942:** Cadets on Parade; The Mad Martindales; Henry and Dizzy; Henry Aldrich — Editor; Star Spangled Rhythm; **1943:** Henry Aldrich Gets Glamour; Henry Aldrich Swings It; Henry Aldrich Haunts a House; Aerial Gunner; **1944:** Henry Aldrich — Boy Scout; My Best Gal; Henry Aldrich Plays Cupid; Henry Aldrich's Little Secret; The Town Went Wild; When the Lights Go on Again; **1945:** Out of the Night/Strange Illusion; Twice Blessed; **1946:** Affairs of Geraldine; **1947:** Cynthia; Sweet Genevieve; Life With Father; **1948:** The Time of Your Life; Out of the Storm; Joan of Arc; An Old-Fashioned Girl; **1949:** Bad Boy; Miss Mink of 1949; Tuscon; **1950:** Tarnished; When Willie Comes Marching Home; Destination Big House; Hot Rod; September Affair; The Magnificent Yankee; **1951:** Gasoline Alley; Oh! Susanna; Corky of Gasoline Alley; **1953:** Island in the Sky; **1954:** The Desperado; **1955:** Rage at Dawn; **1956:** Battle Stations; **1957:** Chain of Evidence; **1960:** The Hypnotic Eye; I Passed for White; **1961:** The Last Time I Saw Archie; **1969:** Death of a Gunfighter; **1971:** Scandalous John; **1976:** Vigilante Force.

NY Stage: 1937: Western Waters; 1938: Sunup to Sundown; Sing Out the News; 1939: The Happiest Days.

Select TV: 1950–52: The First Hundred Years (series); 1954: Rocky Jones — Space Ranger (series); 1955: So This Is Hollywood (series); 1958: Love That Jill (series); 1975: Ellery Queen: Too Many Suspects; 1976: The New Daughters of Joshua Cabe; 1977: Peter Lundy and the Medicine Hat Stallion.

CAROL LYNLEY

(CAROLE ANN JONES) BORN: NEW YORK, NY, FEBRUARY 13, 1942.

A delicate-featured blonde who did all her best work before she reached 30, Carol Lynley began modeling as a teenager. This led to her Broadway debut in 1957, in *The Potting Shed*, for which she received a Theatre World Award. It was a *Life* magazine cover, however, that caught the attention of Walt Disney, who signed her to a contract in 1958. For him she made only one movie, *The Light in the Forest*, where she was highly appealing as a servant girl named Shenandoe who falls in love with James MacArthur. That same year, 1958, she made a splash on the New York stage playing the teenager who must face an unwanted pregnancy in *Blue Denim*. She was impressive enough to be asked to repeat her role in the 20th Century-Fox movie version, opposite Brandon De Wilde, and it was their performances that carried the slight, dated piece. Fox made her Fabian's hillbilly girlfriend in *Hound-Dog Man*; substituted her for Diane Varsi as Allison MacKenzie in the critically roasted follow-up, *Return to Peyton Place*; and made her one of three young women looking for romance in Madrid in *The Pleasure Seekers*, a revamping of *Three Coins in the Fountain*. She was a sweet ingénue in a minor Jack Lemmon comedy, *Under the Yum Yum Tree*, then got to play a dual role (mother and daughter) in the lengthy saga *The Cardinal*. For that same director, Otto Preminger, she was Keir Dullea's weird sibling in *Bunny Lake Is Missing*, then fell with a thud in the second, tackier (Jean) *Harlow* biography, not at all suited to play the screen's great platinum bombshell. By the end of the 1960s she was playing straight woman to Rowan and Martin in *The Maltese Bippy*; offering a sex change on Robert Walker's role in a thinly disguised re-do of *Strangers on a Train* called *Once You Kiss a Stranger*; and supporting Glen Campbell in *Norwood*. Things perked up a bit when she joined the starry cast of *The Poseidon Adventure*, as the ship's entertainer who sings (dubbed) "The Morning After." Despite the enormous success of that movie she mainly ended up on TV, while her rare ventures into theatrical features were confined to barely seen offerings like *The Cat and the Canary* and *Vigilante*.

Screen: 1958: The Light in the Forest; 1959: Blue Denim; Holiday for Lovers; Hound-Dog Man; 1961: Return to Peyton Place; The Last Sunset; 1963: The Stripper; Under the Yum Yum Tree; The Cardinal; 1964: Shock Treatment; The Pleasure Seekers; 1965: Harlow; Bunny Lake Is Missing; 1967: The Shuttered Room; 1968: Danger Route; 1969: The Maltese Bippy; Once You Kiss a Stranger; 1970: Norwood; 1972: Beware! The Blob; The Poseidon Adventure; 1973: Cotter; 1976: The Four Deuces; 1977: Bad Georgia Road; The Washington Affair/Out of Control (dtv); 1979: The Shape of Things to Come; 1982: The Cat and the Canary (filmed 1979); 1983: Vigilante; 1985: Balboa (dtv); 1987: Dark Tower (dtv); 1988: Blackout (dtv); 1990: Spirits (dtv); 1991: Howling IV: The Freaks (dtv); 1997: Neon Signs (dtv); 1998: Off the Menu: The Last Days of Chasen's; 1999: Drowning on Dry Land (dtv).

NY Stage: 1957: The Potting Shed; 1958: Blue Denim; 1960: Answered the Flute (ob); 1975: Absurd Person Singular; 1990: The Seagull: The Hamtons: 1990 (ob).

Select TV: 1956: Grow Up (sp); 1957: Junior Miss (sp); 1958: The Young and the Scared (sp); Rapunzel (sp); 1959: Deed of Mercy (sp); The Last Dance (sp); 1962: Whatever Happened to Miss Illinois (sp); 1965: The Fliers (sp); 1968: Shadow on the Land; The Smugglers; 1969: The Immortal; 1970: Weekend of Terror; 1971: The Cable Car Mystery; 1972: The Night Stalker; 1974: The Elevator; 1975: Death Stalk; 1976: Flood!; 1977: Fantasy Island; 1978: Having Babies II; The Cops and Robin; The Beasts Are in the Streets; 1984: In Possession; 1987: Best of Friends.

DIANA LYNN

(DOLORES LOEHR) BORN: LOS ANGELES, CA, OCTOBER 7, 1926. DIED: DECEMBER 18, 1971.

Initially noticed for her musical abilities, cute, tiny Diana Lynn showed a talent for comedy and became one of the nicer additions to the Paramount stable in the 1940s. As a child she was trained to be a concert pianist, joining the Los Angeles Junior Symphony Orchestra when she was only 11. Spotted while accompanying a friend during an audition, Lynn (who then called herself Dolly Loehr) was placed in the Goldwyn drama *They Shall Have Music*, filling the background as one of the talented child prodigies who make up Walter Brennan's music school. Similarly she showed up in Paramount's *There's Magic in Music*, billed as herself, as one of the many attendees of the National Music Camp at Interlocken, Michigan. She was given some lines in that one and was impressive enough to receive a contract from the studio, who changed her name and cast her as Rita Johnson's wisecracking sister in the hit comedy *The Major and the Minor*. She carried off the part with ease, resulting in her playing Jimmy Lydon's sweetheart in two Henry Aldrich films and winning the role for which she became best known, Betty Hutton's sassy sister in the raucous farce *The Miracle of Morgan's Creek*, commenting knowingly on the situation at hand and driving pop William Demarest to some extended pratfalls. Back with Hutton she got to display her musical talents again, as part of a sister quartet (Dorothy Lamour and Mimi Chandler were the others) in the sprightly *And the Angels Sing*. On a roll, Lynn was cast as the more sensible of the two girls (based on real life Emily Kimbrough)

who make a transatlantic trip in the tepid nostalgia piece *Our Hearts Were Young and Gay*, certainly proving herself more adept at this sort of contrived humor than her co-star, Gail Russell. This was followed by an Eddie Bracken vehicle, *Out of This World*, in which she was in charge of an all-girl orchestra, and then an inevitable reteaming with Russell, for *Our Hearts Were Growing Up*.

After finishing her contract she freelanced, showing up in a poor but popular Cary Grant romp, *Every Girl Should Be Married*, as Betsy Drake's best pal. Producer Hal Wallis wanted her to join the ensemble of the big-screen version of the radio success *My Friend Irma*, and since he distributed through Paramount, Lynn found herself back on her old lot for that film and its sequel, playing it straight while Marie Wilson and Jerry Lewis huffed and puffed for laughs. Next it was over to Universal for *Peggy*, as a Rose Bowl Queen wannabe, and the featherbrained *Bedtime for Bonzo*, proving to be as charming as ever in these quickly forgotten time-wasters. There were some westerns, including *Track of the Cat*, in which she was Tab Hunter's fiancée, and a return to familiar territory with *You're Never Too Young*, a Martin and Lewis remake of *The Major and the Minor*, with Lynn in the role once played by Ray Milland. After that she confined herself almost exclusively to the small screen, although there were was one obscure credit (with Milland), a potboiler called *Company of Killers*, shown in 1970, the year before she died following a stroke at the age of 45.

Screen: AS DOLLY LOEHR: 1939: They Shall Have Music; There's Magic in Music.

AS DIANA LYNN: 1942: The Major and the Minor; Star Spangled Rhythm; 1943: Henry Aldrich Gets Glamour: 1944: The Miracle of Morgan's Creek; And the Angels Sing; Henry Aldrich Plays Cupid; Our Hearts Were Young and Gay; 1945: Out of This World; Duffy's Tavern; 1946: Our Hearts Were Growing Up; The Bride Wore Boots; 1947: Easy Come, Easy Go; Variety Girl; 1948: Ruthless; Texas, Brooklyn and Heaven; Every Girl Should Be Married; 1949: My Friend Irma; 1950: Paid in Full; My Friend Irma Goes West; Rogues of Sherwood Forest; Peggy; 1951: Bedtime for Bonzo; The People Against O'Hara; 1953: Meet Me at the Fair; Plunder of the Sun; 1954: Track of the Cat; 1955: An Annapolis Story; You're Never Too Young; The Kentuckian; 1970: Company of Killers.

NY Stage: 1951: The Wild Duck; 1953: Horses in Midstream; 1963: Mary, Mary.

Select TV: 1950: Double Feature (sp); Down Bayou DuBac (sp); 1951: The Twinkle in Her Eye (sp); The Memoirs of Aimee Durant (sp); 1952: Marriage Is the Beginning (sp); National Honeymoon (sp); 1953: Best Seller (sp); 1954: The Blue Serge Suit (sp); Highway (sp); Borrowed Wife (sp); The Unlocked Door (sp); Good for You (sp); 1955: The Thief (sp); Love Letter (sp); Down From the Stairs (sp); Stage Door (sp); A Farewell to Arms (sp); The Seventh Veil (sp); 1956: Anything but Love (sp); Princess O'Rourke (sp); Forbidden Area (sp); The House That Jackson Built (sp); 1957: The Star Wagon (sp); A Sound of Different Drummers (sp); Junior Miss (sp); 1958: The Return of Ansel Gibbs (sp); Marriage of Strangers (sp); Boy on a Fence (sp); 1959: The Philadelphia Story (sp); 1961: The Mating Machine (sp).

JEFFREY LYNN

(RAGNAR GODFREY LIND) BORN: AUBURN, MA, FEBRUARY 16, 1909. ED: BATES COL. DIED: NOVEMBER 24, 1995.

The bulk of Jeffrey Lynn's movie career took place within the first four years he was on screen, debuting for Warners in 1938, following a stint as a schoolteacher and some acting in stock. For Warners he was Gemini in the astrology murder mystery *When Were You Born?*, and was promptly given the plumb role of the composer on whom the *Four Daughters* become infatuated, although most audiences seemed to keep their eyes on John Garfield. There were three sequels to this one, *Daughters Courageous*, *Four Wives*, and *Four Mothers*, plus another standout role, as the buddy of Cagney and Bogart, who ends up a lawyer, thereby staying out of trouble, in the gangster success *The Roaring Twenties*. As was usually the case, Lynn was overshadowed by the more dynamic personalities around him. This was evident in *All This, and Heaven Too*, in which he gave Bette Davis a second chance after imprisonment, and another with Cagney, the clichéd World War I epic *The Fighting 69th*. To compensate, he was given his own vehicles with *Law of the Tropics*, in which he played a rubber planter; *The Body Disappears*, about an invisibility formula; and *Underground*, with Lynn as the bad guy in this melodrama that had a somewhat higher budget than the other two. During World War II he joined Army Intelligence and was not seen again on screen until 1948, having slipped into support. There were scattered motion picture credits and a good deal of television work before he retired from the business in the late 1960s. He was last seen on the big screen playing a disgraced physician in the Frank Sinatra hit *Tony Rome*.

Screen: 1938: When Were You Born?; Cowboy From Brooklyn; Four Daughters; 1939: Yes, My Darling Daughter; Daughters Courageous; Espionage Agent; The Roaring Twenties; Four Wives; 1940: A Child Is Born; All This, and Heaven Too; The Fighting 69th; It All Came True; My Love Came Back; Money and the Woman; Flight From Destiny; 1941: The Body Disappears; Four Mothers; Law of the Tropics; Million Dollar Baby; Underground; 1948: Black Bart; For the Love of Mary; Whiplash; 1949: A Letter to Three Wives; Captain China; Strange Bargain; 1951: Home Town Story; Up Front; 1958: Lost Lagoon; 1960: Butterfield 8; 1967: Tony Rome.

NY Stage: 1935: A Slight Case of Murder; Stick-in-the-Mud; 1951: The Long Days; Lo and Behold!; 1961: A Call on Kuprin; 1966: Dinner at Eight.

Select TV: 1950: Miracle in the Rain (sp); 1951: Sweet Sorrow (sp); 1952: The Man I Marry (sp); Sleep No More (sp); Stone's Throw (sp); 1953: Thanks for a Lovely Evening (sp); The Accident (sp); My Son Jeep (series); 1954: High Man (sp); The Independent (sp); 1955–56: Star Stage (series); 1959: The Case of Julia Walton (sp); 1961: The Magic and the Loss (sp); The Spiral Staircase (sp); 1966–67: The Secret Storm (series).

SUE LYON
Born: Davenport, IA, July 10, 1946.

Having played the most controversial cinematic nymphet of them all, Sue Lyon remained a famous name despite a career that pretty much trickled away after that peak. A student of the Hollywood Professional School, she was chosen by director Stanley Kubrick to play the forthright blonde teen who gets James Mason's libido cooking overtime in the exceedingly fine, 1962 adaptation of Vladimir Nabokov's seemingly unfilmable novel, *Lolita*. Lyon was properly kittenish and, in the final scenes, made the believable change from girl to woman. Thanks to censorship concerns, a very intelligent movie became a hit, and Lyon was Hollywood's newest overnight sensation. She played a similar tease in *The Night of the Iguana*, flirting with defrocked preacher Richard Burton; was one of the *7 Women*, stranded in director John Ford's

final (panned) production, as a naïve missionary; appeared as one of the less-interesting Miami sinners, a spoiled rich girl who sets the plot in motion, in the Frank Sinatra noir success *Tony Rome*; and played the Southerner who captures con man Michael Sarrazin's fancy in *The Flim-Flam Man*. After this run of work she slowed down, showing up a few years later as the woman in daredevil George Hamilton's life in *Evel Knievel*, by which time it was pretty much decided that audiences had seen what she had to offer, which was much less than it appeared at first. There were a few more obscurities before she dropped out of sight altogether while only in her 30s.

Screen: 1962: Lolita; 1964: The Night of the Iguana; 1966: 7 Women; 1967: Tony Rome; The Flim-Flam Man; 1969: Four Rode Out; 1971: Evel Knievel; 1973: Tarots (nUSr); 1975: To Love, Perhaps to Die (nUSr); 1977: Crash!/Death Ride; End of the World; 1978: Towing/Who Stole My Wheels?; 1980: Alligator; 1984: Invisible Strangler/Astral Factor (filmed 1976).

Select TV: 1969: Arsenic and Old Lace (sp); 1970: But I Don't Want to Get Married; 1976: Smash-Up on Interstate 5; 1977: Don't Push — I'll Charge When I'm Ready (filmed 1969).

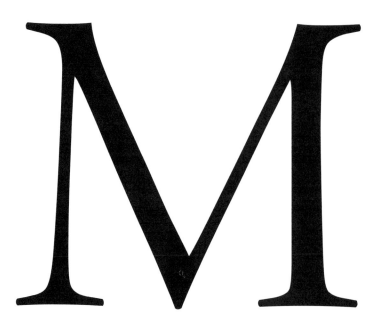

JAMES MacARTHUR

Born: Los Angeles, CA, December 8, 1937. Raised in Nyack, NY. ed: Harvard Univ.

With actress Helen Hayes and playwright Charles MacArthur as his adopted parents, it was only natural that James MacArthur would gravitate towards show business. He began appearing in summer stock as a child and on television, in small guest roles, as a teen. A segment of the anthology series *Climax*, called *Deal a Blow*, gave him a good role as a juvenile delinquent, and he was asked to repeat the part in 1957 when the piece was expanded for the big screen in what turned out to be director John Frankenheimer's debut in that medium, *The Young Stranger*. The following year Walt Disney gave him another shot at stardom, playing the young white lad raised by Indians in their version of the novel *The Light in the Forest*. MacArthur's work was accomplished enough for the studio to put him under contract, where they showcased him in three adventure movies: *Third Man on the Mountain*, in which he climbed up the Matterhorn; *Kidnapped*, the umpteenth big-screen version of the Robert Louis Stevenson tale; and, best of all, their excellent, enduring presentation of *Swiss Family Robinson*, in which he was the eldest son, Fritz. Heading elsewhere, he was one of *The Interns* in Columbia Pictures's popular medical soap opera ensemble; the eldest son in Henry Fonda's large backwoods brood in *Spencer's Mountain*; and Hayley Mills's romantic interest in *The Truth About Spring*. MacArthur may not have possessed his mom's greatness, but he was certainly more than competent, and a highly appealing actor at that.

After dropping back into support for *The Bedford Incident* and *Hang 'em High*, he had no qualms about taking a role on a television series. This turned out to be a wise decision, as the show, *Hawaii Five-O*, became one of the smash hit detective drama of the late 1960s and 1970s, MacArthur staying with it for 11 of its 12 years. There were some guest appearances after its run, but he soon decided he'd had enough of the actor's life and retired. In 1998 he popped up, out of the blue, to make an appearance in *Storm Chasers*, a television movie made for the Family Channel.

Screen: 1957: The Young Stranger; 1958: The Light in the Forest; 1959: Third Man on the Mountain; 1960: Kidnapped; Swiss Family Robinson; 1962: The Interns; 1963: Spencer's Mountain; Cry of Battle; 1965: The Truth About Spring; The Bedford Incident; Battle of the Bulge; 1966: Ride Beyond Vengeance; 1967: The Love-Ins; 1968: Hang 'em High; 1969: The Angry Breed.

NY Stage: 1960: Invitation to a March.

Select TV: 1955: Deal a Blow (sp); 1958: Tongues of Angels (sp); Young and Scared (sp); Ticket to Tahiti (sp); 1959: The Innocent Assassin (sp); 1960: Night of the Auk (sp); 1967: Willie and the Yank/Mosby's Marauders (sp); 1968: Lassiter; 1968–79: Hawaii Five-O; 1980: Alcatraz — The Whole Shocking Story; 1983: The Night the Bridge Fell Down (filmed 1979); 1998: Storm Chasers: Revenge of the Twister.

JEANETTE MacDONALD

Born: Philadelphia, PA, June 18, 1903. Died: January 14, 1965.

Back when audiences lined up to hear golden-throated sopranos trill like birds in glittering musicals, Jeanette MacDonald reigned. This blonde singer was not traditionally pretty, but she had a tangy way with a line and a fine sense of comic timing, and she was never as stuffy as her image might suggest. She took an interest in music at an early age and, like her older sister, Blossom (who later became known as Marie Blake and then Blossom Rock), journeyed to New York to find chorus work, debuting there in 1920, in *The Demi-Tasse Revue*. Eventually she was signed to a contract by the Shuberts, who gave her work in such other shows as *Yes, Yes, Yvette* and *Boom Boom*. With the arrival of talking pictures Hollywood was eager to import vocalists from the theater, and Paramount signed her up with the intention of placing her opposite Richard Dix. Instead Ernst Lubitsch requested her to team with Maurice Chevalier in the primitive but charming 1929 release *The Love Parade*, in which she was the Queen of Sylvania, who tries to bring this French lothario down to earth. She and Chevalier clicked so well that they would be brought together most felicitously at a later date. In the meantime she was co-starred with

Broadway's Dennis King in the studio's first all-Technicolor talkie, *The Vagabond King*, and got to introduce the immortal "Beyond the Blue Horizon" in *Monte Carlo*, which paired her with England's Jack Buchanan.

Paramount temporarily lost interest, so she wound up at UA for *The Lottery Bride*, and at Fox for some comedies before the studio called her back for that anticipated rematch with Chevalier, *One Hour With You*, half directed by George Cukor and completed by Lubitsch, with surprisingly happy results. Even better was Rouben Mamoulian's *Love Me Tonight*, where, as was often the case in such storylines, she pretended to be shocked by the brazen flirtations of her leading man (Chevalier, at his peak) while finding herself getting hot under the collar. Her comic flair was never more in evidence and she warbled beautifully such Rodgers and Hart standards as "Lover" and one of the greatest tunes ever written for a motion picture, "Isn't It Romantic?," which went on to become Paramount's unofficial theme song. Neither of these movies did spectacularly at the box office, but continued to find their supporters over the years, especially the latter, which is now considered one of the seminal musicals of its day.

MGM then came to MacDonald with the offer of a contract, and after a film project in England fell apart, she accepted. They first put her opposite star-on-the-wane Ramon Navarro in *The Cat and the Fiddle*, and then, bringing together the successful elements of the past, co-starred her with Chevalier, with Lubitsch at the helm, in *The Merry Widow*. Nice as it was, it didn't quite have the polish of the previous Chevalier-MacDonald outings, though it was still miles above many others of the genre produced up to that time. The studio's next project for her would send her soaring to the top of the popularity polls and point her towards permanent movie-musical immortality. *Naughty Marietta*, released in 1935, came from the Victor Herbert operetta, with MacDonald starring as a French princess (royalty, no doubt, suited her mock haughtiness) who escapes to the Colonies and falls for mercenary Nelson Eddy. Their banter together was playful and their duets sent fans of this kind of material into operetta heaven, most specifically the soaring "Ah, Sweet Mystery of Life." The movie was a smash and an Oscar nominee for Best Picture, leading both MGM and the public to the conclusion that MacDonald and Eddy were the next big thing. As a result they were quickly reunited for perhaps their most famous film together, *Rose-Marie*. The moment when they echoed their musical notes of devotion on "Indian Love Call" ("When I'm calling you-oo-oo-oo…") became one of the most indelible and heavily parodied sequences of 1930s cinema.

For a break from Eddy she was given Clark Cable in *San Francisco*, battling with him before the great earthquake finale, and belting out the unforgettable title anthem in a hokey but undeniably entertaining concoction that became one of the highest grossing movies made up to that time. Back with Eddy, there was another of their best films, *Maytime*, with MacDonald looking back on their doomed love affair, and making something memorable of this potentially hackneyed corn. This one gave them another signature duet with "Will You Remember (Sweetheart)?" There was another successful break from Eddy, with Allan Jones as her co-star, for *The Firefly*. Then came the last two of the Eddy films to really bring in the outstanding grosses, *The Girl of the Golden West*, and the Technicolor *Sweethearts*, which had them in modern dress tackling a really infuriating script about a bickering singing couple.

For another Eddy break she got Lew Ayres for *Broadway Serenade*, and then saw the fans of the MacDonald-Eddy team start to cool off with *New Moon*, which gave her yet another signature tune, "Lover Come Back to Me;" *Bitter Sweet*, an adaptation of Noel Coward's play, with which the author made very public his displeasure; and *I Married an Angel*, another bowdlerized version of a Broadway hit, that at least allowed them to sing Rodgers and Hart's "Spring Is Here." Between these she had done a remake of the ultra-icky *Smilin' Through*, appearing alongside the man she had wed in 1937, Gene Raymond. Since the Jeanette MacDonald the public had once embraced was no longer so beloved, MGM figured they would try her in something more comedic, but the result, *Cairo*, made next to no impact. During the war years she dabbled in professional opera, then was seen singing to the soldiers in Universal's all-star morale booster, *Follow the Boys*. She ended up back at MGM for one of those glossy Joe Pasternak items, *Three Daring Daughters*, where the "high point" had her and Jane Powell, among others, singing "The Dickey Bird Song." After that she was asked to share the screen with Claude Jarman, Jr. and Lassie in the sentimental *The Sun Comes Up*, where she sang briefly. There was an occasional cabaret engagement during the 1950s and then the realization that she had not gone completely out of favor when an album reteaming her with Eddy sold extremely well. By the time of her death in 1965, fan clubs celebrating the MacDonald-Eddy partnership had sprung up, and they continue to be among the most devoted and loyal of all such organizations.

Screen: 1929: The Love Parade; 1930: The Vagabond King; Monte Carlo; Let's Go Native; The Lottery Bride; Oh, for a Man; 1931: Don't Bet on Women; Annabelle's Affairs; 1932: One Hour With You; Love Me Tonight; 1934: The Cat and the Fiddle; The Merry Widow; 1935: Naughty Marietta; 1936: Rose-Marie; San Francisco; 1937: Maytime; The Firefly; 1938: The Girl of the Golden West; Sweethearts; 1939: Broadway Serenade; 1940: New Moon; Bitter Sweet; 1941: Smilin' Through; 1942: I Married an Angel; Cairo; 1944: Follow the Boys; 1948: Three Daring Daughters; 1949: The Sun Comes Up.

NY Stage: 1920: The Demi-Tasse Revue; 1922: A Fantastic Fricasee; 1923: The Magic Ring; 1925: Tip-Toes; 1927: Yes, Yes, Yvette; 1928: Sunny Days; Angela; 1929: Boom Boom.

SHIRLEY MacLAINE
(SHIRLEY MacLEAN BEATY)
BORN: RICHMOND, VA, APRIL 24, 1934.

The smart ones should have known that red-haired, beaming Shirley MacLaine was going to be around forever. Very much a star on her own terms, she couldn't really be compared to anyone who had come before her. She was alternately quirky and undeniably human; vulnerable and edgy. There were times when she couldn't be more original or assured in her work, while, on certain occasions, she slipped over the top, restraint be damned. She was already taking ballet lessons by the time her brother, Warren Beatty, was born in 1937, and she managed to land a chorus job in a 1950 New York revival of *Oklahoma!* For the next four years she got similar work, plus modeling and commercial spots on television. As understudy to Carol Haney in the original 1954 production of *The Pajama Game*, she became the New York Theater's most famous example of someone obtaining stardom in this Cinderella way, when she went on in Haney's place and found herself accepting an offer from Hollywood producer Hal Wallis as a result. She started off with a great director, Alfred Hitchcock, but in one of his weakest films, *The Trouble With Harry*, a black comedy in which she was one of the four principals trying to bury a body. For Wallis she backed up Dean Martin and Jerry Lewis in the splashy-but-empty *Artists and Models*, appearing in costume as a comic book bat lady; then she had the good fortune to be seen in the 1956 Oscar-winner for Best Picture and one of the monster hits of the decade, *Around the World in Eighty Days*, although she later looked back on her soft-spoken Indian princess role with embarrassment.

Back with Wallis she did very nicely in a pair of Shirley Booth films, one dramatic, *Hot Spell*, as her daughter, and one comedic, *The Matchmaker*, as the milliner matched with Anthony Perkins. She was already establishing her screen image of a gamine-like kook, and this was very much her character in *Some Came Running*, a hard-luck small town floozie in love with Frank Sinatra, impressing the industry enough that they gave her an Oscar nomination. Opposite David Niven she did a bright comedy, *Ask Any Girl*; took a supporting part to Anthony Franciosa in the theater-themed *Career*, where she got some showy scenes when she descended into alcoholism; and pretty much sank with the ship in the dull musical *Can-Can*, again appearing opposite Sinatra. That same year, 1960, she scored her highest marks yet, as the fragile elevator girl who nearly kills herself over married executive Fred MacMurray, in what turned out to be one of the screen's most perfect drama-comedies, *The Apartment*, her second movie to win the Academy Award for Best Picture. MacLaine herself got Oscar nomination number two, after which she finished off her commitment to Wallis with *All in a Night's Work*, which also found her getting into trouble for dallying with a businessman, in this case Dean Martin. There was a very bold role, as the unhappy schoolteacher who turns out to be a lesbian, in the strong but highly unpopular movie of *The Children's Hour*; then the flop *My Geisha*, produced by her husband, Steve Parker, in which Shirley buried herself under a ton of Asian make-up to land a part in a movie. There wasn't much of an audience for the tiresome two-character piece she did with Robert Mitchum, *Two for the Seesaw*, but they lined up for blocks to see her play a hard-bitten but sweet Parisian hooker in *Irma La Douce*, a movie that did itself damage by going on way too long. Nonetheless, it became one of her best-remembered parts and one for which she earned another Oscar nomination.

She delved into wacky territory with *What a Way to Go!*, the joke of which was that all of her husbands kept dying in bizarre ways and that they were played by major names. It was all done in a heavy-handed manner with MacLaine dolled up in various gaudy outfits and never once suggesting the light touch needed to make such humor work. Then she reached some sort of nadir with the grotesque *John Goldfarb, Please Come Home*, as a reporter masquerading as part of Peter Ustinov's Arabian harem. A neat caper film, *Gambit*, in which she spent a good deal of the opening portion of the story with her mouth shut, was followed by a multiepisode film, *Woman Times Seven*, which only went to prove that stretching herself to this degree wasn't such a good idea, at least not in material this poor. All of these were shaky box-office performers, and a similar response met one with much more going for it, *Sweet Charity*, an expensive musical imaginatively directed by Bob Fosse, with MacLaine at her best, as a well-meaning but dumb dancehall hostess who searches in vain for true love, finds it and then sees it slip away. Its unfortunate failure meant there was no reason she shouldn't take second billing to Clint Eastwood in one of his westerns, *Two Mules for Sister Sara*, in which she posed as a nun, which wasn't as silly as it sounded since she turned out to be a hooker in disguise.

After two dramas, *Desperate Characters*, in which she received some of her best notices, as an urban housewife watching her marriage fall to pieces, and the supernatural *The Possession of Joel Delaney*, didn't go over, she tried a television series that died

a quick death. At this point she discovered that things were much rosier on the cabaret circuit, eventually bringing her act to the Palace Theatre in New York. In 1977 she returned to movies on a high note, as the ex-ballerina locking horns with fellow dancer Anne Bancroft, in *The Turning Point*, earning another Oscar nomination in the process in a movie that actually managed to find a substantial audience, considering the rather specialized world it focused on. There was a difficult role in another prominent release, as a rich lady who finds herself turned on by mentally retarded Peter Sellers, in the satirical *Being There*, at one point masturbating in a discreetly filmed sequence. Two tales of adultery, *Loving Couples* and the much less repulsive *A Change of Seasons*, seemed to indicate that she was going to be stuck in sex comedies, but an eleventh-hour rescue, called *Terms of Endearment*, really placed her among the high-ranking ladies of the silver screen. As Aurora Greenaway, the infuriatingly self-righteous mother of Debra Winger, she was absolutely sensational in what was, like *The Apartment*, a masterpiece of humor blended effortlessly with pathos. The movie made a small fortune and became her third Best Picture Oscar-winner, while MacLaine found herself at last with the long-elusive Academy Award. Strangely, this was followed by a crass sequel, *Cannonball Run II*, and another extended period away from the movies.

When at last she came back, she began a surprisingly good run of work for an actress of her age (she was in her mid-50s). First was her role in the excellent British production *Madame Susatzka*, as a stubborn and sad music teacher turning a blind eye to the real world as her past crumbles around her. Perhaps having decided she had her trophy at last, there was no Oscar nod, despite this being another of her finest performances. Then *Steel Magnolias* found her at her bitchiest, trading insults with Olympia Dukakis, in this lucrative gathering of Southern women at a small-town beauty shop. As with many of her roles of this period, she allowed herself to look pretty worn, as she did sans wig at one point, in *Postcards From the Edge*, portraying a one-time movie star who is having drinking problems. This was a thinly disguised look at the life of Debbie Reynolds and daughter Carrie Fisher, who wrote the screenplay and the book on which it was based. There were more world-weary women in *Used People*, unlikely but not unacceptable as a Jewish New Yorker, and *Wrestling Ernest Hemingway*, very restrained in a supporting part in this look at lonely senior citizens in Southern Florida. Still getting leads, she was the former First Lady in *Guarding Tess*, bickering with secret service man Nicolas Cage; another wealthy woman in *Mrs. Winterbourne*; and, unwisely, Aurora Greenaway, reprising her Oscar-winning role, in *The Evening Star*, one sequel moviegoers adamantly refused to patronize.

Her one attempt at directing, *Bruno*, sat on the shelf before making an unheralded premiere on cable television and then being sold on videotape under the title *The Dress Code*. She served as producer on the Oscar-nominated documentary, *The Other Half of the Sky: A China Memoir*, chronicling her visit there; appeared in many variety specials (including the 1976 Emmy Award-winning *Gypsy in My Soul*); and authored several memoirs: *Don't Fall Off the Mountain* (1970), *You Can Get There From Here* (1975); *Out on a Limb* (1983), later appearing in a television adaptation; *Dancing in the Light* (1985); *It's All in the Playing* (1987), *Going Within: A Guide for Inner Transformation* (1989), *Dance While You Can* (1991), *My Lucky Stars* (1995), and *The Camino: A Journey of the Spirit* (2000). These have revealed her interest in reincarnation, which prompted many a tiresome joke about past lives from various standup comics and some good-natured kidding from MacLaine herself via a cameo in the Albert Brooks comedy *Defending Your Life*.

Screen: 1955: The Trouble With Harry; Artists and Models; 1956: Around the World in Eighty Days; 1958: Hot Spell; The Sheepman; The Matchmaker; Some Came Running; 1959: Ask Any Girl; Career; 1960: Can-Can; Ocean's Eleven; The Apartment; 1961: All in a Night's Work; Two Loves; The Children's Hour; 1962: My Geisha; Two for the Seesaw; 1963: Irma La Douce; 1964: What a Way to Go!; The Yellow Rolls-Royce; 1965: John Goldfarb, Please Come Home; 1966: Gambit; 1967: Woman Times Seven; 1968: The Bliss of Mrs. Blossom; 1969: Sweet Charity; 1970: Two Mules for Sister Sara; 1971: Desperate Characters; 1972: The Possession of Joel Delaney; 1977: The Turning Point; 1979: Being There; 1980: Loving Couples; A Change of Seasons; 1983: Terms of Endearment; 1984: Cannonball Run II; 1988: Madame Sousatzka; 1989: Steel Magnolias; 1990: Postcards From the Edge; Waiting for the Light; 1991: Defending Your Life; 1992: Used People; 1993: Wrestling Ernest Hemingway; 1994: Guarding Tess; 1996: Mrs. Winterbourne; The Evening Star; 1997: A Smile Like Yours; 1999: Get Bruce.

NY Stage: 1950: Oklahoma!; 1953: Me and Juliet; 1954: The Pajama Game; 1976: Shirley MacLaine at the Palace; 1984: Shirley MacLaine on Broadway.

Select TV: 1970: A World of Love (sp); 1971–72: Shirley's World (series); 1974: Shirley MacLaine: If They Could See Me Now (sp); 1976: Shirley MacLaine: Gypsy in My Soul (sp); 1977: The Shirley MacLaine Special: Where Do We Go From Here? (sp); 1979: Shirley MacLaine at the Lido (sp); 1980: Shirley MacLaine…Every Little Movement (sp); 1982: Shirley MacLaine: Illusions (sp); 1985: Shirley MacLaine (sp); 1987: Out on a Limb; 1995: The West Side Waltz; 1996: The Celluloid Closet; 1999: Joan of Arc; 2000: Bruno/The Dress Code (and dir.); 2001: These Old Broads; 2002: Hell on Heels: The Battle of Mary Kay; 2003: Salem Witch Trials.

BARTON MacLANE

BORN: COLUMBIA, SC, DECEMBER 25, 1902. ED: WESLEYAN UNIV. DIED: JANUARY 1, 1969.

Furrow-browed tough guy Barton MacLane always seem to be giving somebody a hard time, his mouth clamped tightly, his eyes squinty, as if he was in a constant state of threat. Following instruction at the American Academy of Dramatic Arts, he did stock work, then went to Broadway for several plays including *Rendezvous*, which he wrote. Paramount was the first studio to take an interest in him, but his brief employment there was fairly uninspired. It was Warner Bros. that established him as a fine heavy, as was evident from his work in *Black Fury*, as head of the police force that gave the striking workers a hard time; *Dr. Socrates*, as a gangster named Red Bastion; *Frisco Kid*, as a Barbary Coast troublemaker named Spider; *G Men*, as a mobster who marries Ann Dvorak and then shoots her; *Stranded*, as George Brent's racketeering nemesis; and *Bullets or Ballots*, as a criminal being duped by Edward G. Robinson. As was often the case with a stellar supporting player doing exemplary work, the studio would reward him on occasion with leading roles in "B" movies, including *Man of Iron*, where he was a mill foreman who loses the respect of his men once he is promoted; *Bengal Tiger*, as an animal trainer who winds up as cat food; and *Draegerman Courage*, in which he tried to improve inept mining conditions. There were also appearances opposite Glenda Farrell in the "Torchy Blane" films, as Detective Steve MacBride, her befuddled fellow investigator and fiancé. After

his contract with Warners expired, he could be seen all over the place, though in mostly lower-budgeted fare, like *Man of Courage*, *Song of Texas*, *The Underdog*, and Buster Crabbe's *Nabonga*. There were still cases when he was called on to strut his stuff in "A" fare, notably *The Maltese Falcon*, as the suspicious Lieutenant Dundy; *The Big Street*, as the selfish thug who cripples Lucille Ball; and *The Treasure of the Sierra Madre*, as the shady contractor who stiffs Humphrey Bogart for his pay. Westerns seemed to offer him the most employment in the 1950s, while the following decade found him in the recurring role of Gen. Peterson on the whimsical sitcom *I Dream of Jeannie*, which he was doing at the time of his death.

Screen: 1926: The Quarterback; 1929: The Cocoanuts; 1931: His Woman; 1933: Man of the Forest; Big Executive; To the Last Man; Tillie and Gus; The Torch Singer; Hell and High Water; The Thundering Herd; 1934: Lone Cowboy; The Last Round-Up; All of Me; 1935: The Case of the Curious Bride; Go Into Your Dance; G Men; Black Fury; Stranded; Page Miss Glory; The Case of the Lucky Legs; Dr. Socrates; I Found Stella Parish; Frisco Kid; Man of Iron; 1936: Ceiling Zero; The Walking Dead; Times Square Playboy; Bullets or Ballots; Jailbreak; Bengal Tiger; 1937: Smart Blonde; You Only Live Once; Wine, Women and Horses; God's Country and the Woman; San Quentin; Draegerman Courage; The Prince and the Pauper; Born Reckless; Ever Since Eve; Fly-Away Baby; The Adventurous Blonde; 1938: The Kid Comes Back; Blondes at Work; Torchy Gets Her Man; The Storm; Gold Is Where You Find It; You and Me; Prison Break; 1939: Stand Up and Fight; Big Town Czar; Torchy Blane in Chinatown; I Was a Convict; Mutiny in the Big House; Torchy Runs for Mayor; 1940: Men Without Souls; The Secret Seven; Gangs of Chicago; Melody Ranch; 1941: Come Live With Me; High Sierra; Western Union; Manpower; Barnacle Bill; Dr. Jekyll and Mr. Hyde; The Maltese Falcon; Wild Geese Calling; Hit the Road; 1942: Highways by Night; In This Our Life; All Through the Night; The Big Street; 1943: Men of Courage; A Gentle Gangster; Bombardier; Song of Texas; The Underdog; Crime Doctor's Strangest Case; 1944: Cry of the Werewolf; The Mummy's Ghost; Marine Raiders; Secret Command; Gentle Annie; Nabonga; 1945: The Spanish Main; Scared Stiff/Treasure of Fear; Tarzan and the Amazons; 1946: Santa Fe Uprising; San Quentin; Mysterious Intruder; 1947: Jungle Flight; Cheyenne; Tarzan and the Huntress; 1948: The Treasure of the Sierra Madre; Relentless; Unknown Island; The Dude Goes West; Silver River; The Walls of Jericho; Angel in Exile; 1949: Red Light; 1950: Kiss Tomorrow Goodbye; Rookie Fireman; The Bandit Queen; Let's Dance; 1951: Best of the Badmen; Drums in the Deep South; 1952: Bugles in the Afternoon; The Half-Breed; Thunderbirds; 1953: Sea of Lost Ships; Jack Slade; Captain Scarface; Kansas Pacific; Cow Country; 1954: Rails Into Laramie; The Glenn Miller Story; Jubilee Trail; Hell's Outpost; 1955: Last of the Desperadoes; The Silver Star; Treasure of Ruby Hills; Foxfire; Jail Busters; 1956: Backlash; Wetbacks; Jaguar; The Man Is Armed; Three Violent People; The Naked Gun; 1957: Sierra Stranger; Naked in the Sun; Hell's Crossroads; 1958: Girl in the Woods; The Geisha Boy; Frontier Gun; 1960: Gunfighters of Abilene; Noose for a Gunman; 1961: Pocketful of Miracles; 1964: Law of the Lawless; 1965: The Rounders; Town Tamer; 1968: Arizona Bushwhackers; Buckskin.

NY Stage: 1927: The Trial of Mary Dugan; 1928: Gods of the Lightning; 1929: Subway Express; 1931: Steel; 1932: The Tree; 1933: Rendezvous (and wr.); Hangman's Whip.

Select TV: 1960–62: The Outlaws (series); 1965–69: I Dream of Jeannie (series).

ALINE MacMAHON

BORN: MCKEESPORT, PA, MAY 3, 1899.
ED: BARNARD COL. DIED: OCTOBER 12, 1991.

With her unattractively accentuated cheek-bones, sad eyes, and flat manner of speech, Aline MacMahon was not a conventional star, although it was hoped that she could be sold as such in her early days. She proved to be a fine, sympathetic actress with a quick wit and tart tongue who then moved into character roles with ease as she became plumper and more motherly looking. Following work with a stock company in Yorkville, she came to Broadway in 1921, in *The Mirage*, and continued with a good deal of success through the next decade, with *Grand Street Follies* and *Artists and Models* among her credits. It was not her New York work, however, but her part in the West Coast premiere of George S. Kaufman's *Once in a Lifetime*, that won her an offer from Warner Bros. to join their company. She signed up in 1931 and immediately landed a good role, playing Edward G. Robinson's levelheaded secretary in *Five Star Final*, one of the year's Oscar nominees for Best Picture. It was not exactly a step up to support wheezy vaudeville comics Smith and Dale in *The Heart of New York*, so she went back to playing another loyal secretary (of Warren Williams) in *The Mouthpiece*, then was a fake countess in the slushy hit soap opera *One Way Passage*. Universal let her repeat her role in their 1932 movie version of *Once in a Lifetime*, as part of the vaudeville troupe that goes to Hollywood. For Warners she was cheated on by Robinson in *Silver Dollar*; chased after millionaire Guy Kibbee in *Gold Diggers of 1933*, where her comic flare was never more welcome; and got to play an old lady, Paul Muni's mom (though Muni was, in fact, four years her senior), in *The World Changes*.

Star billing came at last with the melodrama *Heat Lightning*, where she played a gas station attendant dismayed that the man she once loved has come back into her life, as a gangster (!). Continuing to play sad frumps, she was a shop owner named Bertha, who suffers after marrying no-good sailor Paul Kelly, in *Side Streets*; and then was the poor, dumped-on mother of a selfish family in *The Merry Frinks*, a mean-spirited concoction that was supposed to be a comedy. That one teamed her with Guy Kibbee, and they were back together again in the comedy-drama *Big Hearted Herbert*; the decidedly minor adaptation of Sinclair Lewis's classic novel *Babbitt*; *While the Patient Slept*, teamed to solve a murder; and *Mary Jane's Pa*, which ended her contract with Warners. After that she was the spinster aunt in MGM's *Ah, Wilderness!*; had a lead for that studio in *Kind Lady*, in which Basil Rathbone made her life hell; and, despite top-billing, took a back seat to newcomer Jimmy Lydon in *Back Door to Heaven*, as a schoolteacher. At this point she began to ease her way back into support with *Out of the Fog*, as Ida Lupino's unpleasant mom; and *Dragon Seed*, Oscar nominated as Katharine Hepburn's forlorn Chinese mother, trying her best to infuse this silly movie with some dignity. There was a larger role in *Tish*, teamed with Marjorie Main and ZaSu Pitts in this story of three spinsters who adopt a child, and *The Search* also gave her a substantial part, superbly playing the officer in charge of displaced children in postwar Germany. Despite such low points as *The Eddie Cantor Story*, playing his gushing Jewish mama, she was more than dependably good in such movies as *The Man from Laramie*, as a tough rancher; *I Could Go on Singing*, as Judy Garland's long-suffering assistant; and *All the Way Home*, as the comforting aunt, repeating her Broadway role.

Screen: 1931: Five Star Final; 1932: The Heart of New York; The Mouthpiece; Week-end Marriage; One Way Passage; Life Begins; Once in a Lifetime; Silver Dollar; 1933: The Life of Jimmy Dolan; Gold Diggers of 1933; Heroes for Sale; The World Changes; 1934: Heat Lightning; Side Streets; The Merry Frinks; Big-Hearted Herbert; Babbitt; 1935: While the Patient Slept; Mary Jane's Pa; I Live My Life; Ah, Wilderness!; Kind Lady; 1937: When You're in Love; 1939: Back Door to Heaven; 1941: Out of the Fog; 1942: The Lady Is Willing; Tish; 1943: Stage Door Canteen; Seeds of Freedom; 1944: Dragon Seed; Guest in the House; 1946: The Mighty McGurk; 1948: The Search; 1949: Roseanna McCoy; 1950: The Flame and the Arrow; 1953: The Eddie Cantor Story; 1955: The Man From Laramie; 1960: Cimarron; 1961: The Young Doctors; 1963: Diamond Head; I Could Go on Singing; All the Way Home.

NY Stage: 1921: The Mirage; The Madras House; 1922: The Green Ring; The Exciters; 1923: The Fine-Pretty World; 1924: Grand Street Follies; 1925: Artists and Models; 1926: Beyond the Horizon; 1927: Spread Eagle; Her First Affaire; 1928: Maya; 1929: Winter Bound; 1931: If Love Were All; 1940: Heavenly Express; 1942: The Eve of St. Mark; 1954: Confidential Clerk; 1955: A Day by the Sea; 1956: I Knock at the Door; Pictures in the Hallway (and 1971 Off Bdwy.); 1960: All the Way Home; 1966: The Alchemist; Yerma; 1967: The East Wind; Galileo; Walking to Waldheim; 1968: Tiger at the Gates; Cyrano de Bergerac; 1969: The Inner Journey; 1971: Mary Stuart; 1972: The Crucible; 1975: Trelawny of the Wells.

Select TV: 1952: The Town (sp); Morning's at Seven (sp); 1957: The Weston Strain (sp); 1958: The Desperate Age (sp); 1959: Medea (sp); 1965: Coriolanus (sp); 1972: Antigone (sp); For the Use of the Hall (sp).

FRED MacMURRAY

BORN: KANKAKEE, IL, AUGUST 30, 1908.
DIED: NOVEMBER 5, 1991.

Fred MacMurray never appeared to be putting much visible effort into whatever it was that made his screen persona work, which may have been part of his appeal. He was an accomplished light comedian, who just seemed to show up and get the job done without any frills, as well as a decent dramatic actor who, despite his nice-guy image, was always most effective when he was playing a man of few scruples. Originally a saxophonist, he played with several bands before joining Gus Arnheim as both musician and part-time vocalist. After this he became a member of another group, the Californian Collegians, who were featured in a Broadway revue called *Three's a Crowd*. This led to MacMurray appearing without them, as actor and saxophonist, in both *The Third Little Show* and *Roberta*. It was the latter that stirred up interest from the movie studios, and Paramount signed him to a contract in 1935 (earlier he had done some extra work in a handful of features). After loaning him to RKO for *Grand Old Girl*, they cast him opposite Claudette Colbert in *The Gilded Lily*, as a reporter, and the two clicked well enough that they would be teamed on six additional occasions over the years. Because of the Colbert picture, RKO asked for him again, this time for the excellent movie of the Pulitzer Prize-winning *Alice Adams*, as the nice young man whom Katharine Hepburn tries to impress. Back at Paramount he wound up with another leading lady whom he partnered with ease, Carole Lombard, in *Hands Across the Table*. He had an assured way with a flip line and a comforting cadence to his speaking voice that made him a relaxed fellow to be around. Not only that, but he never seemed to push his leading ladies out of the spotlight, which suited them just fine. With Colbert he was a bodyguard-turned-editor in the comedy *The Bride Comes Home*, then went Puritanical with somewhat less conviction for *Maid of Salem*, the story of the Salem witch hunts, before Arthur Miller made the same story glow in *The Crucible*. He was the city boy who invades hill country in the Technicolor yarn *The Trail of the Lonesome Pine*; teamed again with Lombard for *The Princess Comes Across*; and was a bandit who turns to law enforcement in *The Texas Rangers*.

As a musician (trumpeter, not saxophonist) in *Swing High, Swing Low* he got to play heavy drama, falling into disrepute when he and Lombard separated, in this remake of *The Dance of Life*; then he struck out with her on their fourth outing, the deadly dull *True Confessions*. Returning to glorious Technicolor, he was one of the *Men With Wings*, yet another of those flier flicks that didn't look much different from the rest, and then gave his best performance yet, as the no-good brother of Bing Crosby, in *Sing, You Sinners*, Crosby's sharpest vehicle of the 1930s. It was in lighter films that everybody seemed to appreciate him most though, so he did two of these with Madeleine Carroll, *Cafe Society* and *Honeymoon in Bali*, both of which fared better than a more serious one they knocked off together, *Virginia*, or a hash of farce and wartime espionage, *One Night in Lisbon*. In the meantime there was a nice role in the gentle, moving drama *Remember the Night*, as the lawyer who takes criminal Barbara Stanwyck home with him for the Christmas holidays. After that he hit a stagnant period with many a loan-out (*Little Old New York* at Fox, *The Lady Is Willing* for Columbia, *Dive Bomber!* at Warners) amid such uninspired fare on the home lot as the dud comedy *Take a Letter, Darling*, with Rosalind Russell, and *The Forest Rangers*, which one would be forgiven for confusing with some other MacMurray titles, *The Texas Rangers* or *Rangers of Fortune*, although this one actually had the distinction of introducing a hit song, "I've Got Spurs That Jingle Jangle Jingle." Colbert offered some relief with another comedic romance, *No Time for Love*, and there was a decent musical, *And the Angels Sing*, with MacMurray as a cocky bandleader who has his eye on sisters Dorothy Lamour and Betty Hutton. This was followed by the picture that turned out to be his cinematic peak, *Double Indemnity*, in which he played the sex-driven insurance investigator who thinks he is smarter than his cohort in crime, Barbara Stanwyck. Supposedly the part had been turned down by several other players, but MacMurray seized the chance and didn't mind cutting back on the sympathy in his portrayal of the duped loser. The movie was a solid critical and box-office hit and became one of the most famous of the dark noir dramas of the 1940s.

In the meantime he joined Colbert again for her farewell to Paramount, *Practically Yours*, and then ended his own employment there with a bizarre item, *Murder, He Says*, encountering a strange family of hillbillies in a none-too-subtle farce that has become a cult favorite for having the nerve to go that extra distance. Going over to Fox, he was in a time-travel musical that didn't fly, *Where Do We Go From Here?*; a biopic of flier Eddie Richenbacker, *Captain Eddie*; and a horse adventure, *Smoky*, which was the most successful of this batch. *Pardon My Past*, at Columbia, was notable in that he played a dual role, an affable ex-G.I. and a playboy with a gambling debt. Then he scored twice at the box office with Colbert in two innocuous comedies: *The Egg and I*, in which they were ex-city folk facing the turmoil of running a chicken farm, and *Family Honeymoon*, where MacMurray tried to charm Colbert's children after becoming their new daddy. This was followed by another lull, including such forgettable assignments as *Singapore*, with Ava Gardner; *Don't Trust Your Husband/An Innocent Affair*, with Madeleine Carroll again, long after the spark had been extinguished; *Never*

a Dull Moment, with Easterner Irene Dunne moving to a ranch to be near rodeo rider MacMurray (trying to repeat elements of *The Egg and I* formula); and *The Moonlighter*, with Stanwyck, for the third and least successful time. It was the role of a smirking jerk that got him temporarily out of the rut, playing to perfection the two-faced officer who sits back and lets Van Johnson look bad in *The Caine Mutiny*, one of the top-grossing movies of 1954. Then came secondary parts in some lush Fox offerings, *Woman's World* and *The Rains of Ranchipur*, followed by standard westerns like *The Far Horizons*, as Lewis to Charlton Heston's Clark in this fictionalized take on the two explorers, and *Good Day for a Hanging*, as a marshal trying to prove Robert Vaughn guilty of murder.

Unexpectedly, his movie career jumped into high gear when Walt Disney cast him as the doofy dad in the fantasy *The Shaggy Dog*, which became one of the big hits of 1959 and got that studio rolling on a profitable period of similar live-action comedies featuring high-concept gimmicks and enough slapstick to entice undemanding families. Walt Disney referred to MacMurray as his favorite actor, and MacMurray found steady and lucrative work as the star of six more Disney movies. *The Absent Minded Professor*, in which he invented a gravity-resistant substance, was certainly the best, while the period musical *The Happiest Millionaire* at least afforded him the opportunity to do some singing. Between these were a fairly lifeless family vacation to France, *Bon Voyage!*; the *Professor* sequel, *Son of Flubber*; and an icky and overlong tribute to the Boy Scouts, *Follow Me, Boys!* There was also one great final movie performance, outside the Disney lot, replacing the late Paul Douglas as the cool and smarmy corporate executive carrying on with elevator girl Shirley MacLaine in the superb, Oscar-winning *The Apartment*. As if this wasn't enough to keep him in the cash, he also wound up on an extremely successful television series, *My Three Sons*, starting in 1960 and continuing for over a decade. By the time the series had reached its later years, MacMurray had gotten a reputation for laziness, having his few scenes for each season filmed all at once, so he could take the rest of the year off. One year after the death of his first wife in 1953, he married actress June Haver, who had been his co-star in *Where Do We Go From Here?*

Screen: 1928: Girls Gone Wild; Tiger Rose; Glad Rag Doll; 1935: Grand Old Girl; The Gilded Lily; Car 99; Men Without Names; Alice Adams; Hands Across the Table; The Bride Comes Home; 1936: The Trail of the Lonesome Pine; Thirteen Hours by Air; The Princess Comes Across; The Texas Rangers; 1937: Maid of Salem; Champagne Waltz; Swing High, Swing Low; True Confession; Exclusive; 1938: Cocoanut Grove; Men With Wings; Sing, You Sinners; 1939: Cafe Society; Invitation to Happiness; Honeymoon in Bali; 1940: Remember the Night; Little Old New York; Too Many Husbands; Rangers of Fortune; 1941: Virginia; One Night in Lisbon; New York Town; Dive Bomber!; 1942: The Lady Is Willing; Take a Letter, Darling; The Forest Rangers; Star Spangled Rhythm; 1943: Flight for Freedom; Above Suspicion; No Time for Comedy; 1944: Standing Room Only; And the Angels Sing; Double Indemnity; Practically Yours; 1945: Murder; He Says; Where Do We Go From Here?; Captain Eddie; 1946: Pardon My Past; Smoky; 1947: Suddenly It's Spring; The Egg and I; Singapore; 1948: The Miracle of the Bells; On Our Merry Way; An Innocent Affair/Don't Trust Your Husband; Family Honeymoon; 1949: Father Was a Fullback; 1950: Borderline; Never a Dull Moment; 1951: A Millionaire for Christy; Callaway Went Thataway; 1952: Fair Wind to Java; 1953: The Moonlighter; 1954: The Caine Mutiny; Pushover; Woman's World; 1955: The Far Horizons; The Rains of Ranchipur; At Gunpoint; 1956: There's Always Tomorrow; 1957: Gun for a Coward; Quantez;

1958: Day of the Bad Man; Good Day for a Hanging; 1959: Face of a Fugitive; The Oregon Trail; The Shaggy Dog; 1960: The Apartment; 1961: The Absent Minded Professor; 1962: Bon Voyage!; 1963: Son of Flubber; 1964: Kisses for My President; 1966: Follow Me, Boys!; 1967: The Happiest Millionaire; 1973: Charley and the Angel; 1978: The Swarm.

NY Stage: 1930: Three's a Crowd; 1931: The Third Little Show; 1933: Roberta.

Select TV: 1955: Bachelor's Pride (sp); 1956: It's a Most Unusual Day (sp); 1957: False Witness (sp); 1958: One Is a Wanderer (sp); 1960–61: My Three Sons (series); 1974: The Chadwick Family; 1975: Beyond the Bermuda Triangle.

GORDON MacRAE

BORN: EAST ORANGE, NJ, MARCH 12, 1921.
DIED: JANUARY 24, 1986.

A fine baritone with a gentle, engaging personality, Gordon MacRae began singing on the radio while still a child, eventually turning to the stage, where he acted with a Long Island stock company. His voice won him work in a Broadway revue called Three to Make Ready and got him a recording contract. Warners, on the lookout for a fresh new vocalist, signed him up in 1948, starting him off with a serious "B" movie, The Big Punch. His first musical for them was Look for the Silver Lining, in which he portrayed (not very well) the first husband of entertainer Marilyn Miller, as interpreted by June Haver, while his second in this genre, The Daughter of Rosie O'Grady, also gave him the less-than-thrilling Ms. Haver to sing to. Much more pleasing as a co-star was Doris Day, whom he played opposite in Tea for Two, an adaptation of No, No, Nanette; The West Point Story, where they both played second fiddle to James Cagney; Starlift, both guesting; and in two charming nostalgia pieces, On Moonlight Bay, certainly the best of his Warners films, and its sequel, By the Light of the Silvery Moon.

A remake of The Desert Song was not what the 1953 public was looking for, so MacRae soon parted company with Warners, ending up in something even more obscure over at RKO, Three Sailors and a Girl, with Jane Powell. Good fortune did smile on him, however, as he was the one chosen to star in the long-awaited movie version of Rodgers and Hammerstein's Oklahoma!, proving to be a more than proficient Curly, beautifully singing such classic numbers as "Oh, What a Beautiful Mornin'" and the title tune. It became his best-known role, but the follow-up, Carousel, with the same songwriters and co-star, Shirley Jones, didn't duplicate the previous success, despite MacRae's commendable performance as the irresponsible carnival barker, Billy Bigelow. His heyday ended with a biopic, The Best Things in Life Are Free, in which he portrayed songwriter Buddy DeSylva, taking billing over Dan Dailey (as Ray Henderson) and Ernest Borgnine (as Lew Brown). Afterwards, he mainly sang in nightclubs and on TV. With wife (1941–67) Sheila MacRae he did a stage act and, after a long period, showed up in two movies, Zero to Sixty and The Pilot, both of which remained pretty much unseen. After a long struggle with booze he became an honorary chairman of the National Council on Alcoholism. His daughters Meredith and Heather MacRae also became actors.

Screen: 1948: The Big Punch; 1949: Look for the Silver Lining; 1950: Backfire; The Daughter of Rosie O'Grady; Return of the Frontiersmen; Tea for Two; The West Point Story; 1951: On Moonlight Bay; Starlift; 1952: About Face; 1953: By the Light of the Silvery Moon; The Desert Song; Three Sailors and a Girl; 1955: Oklahoma!; 1956: Carousel; The Best Things in Life Are

Free; 1978: Zero to Sixty; 1981: The Pilot/Danger in the Skies

NY Stage: 1943: Junior Miss; 1946: Three to Make Ready; 1967: I Do! I Do!

Select TV: 1955: Roberta (sp); 1956: The Gordon MacRae Show (series); 1956–57: Lux Video Theatre (series); 1957: One Sunday Afternoon (sp); Eileen (sp); 1958: Gift of the Magi (sp).

GEORGE MACREADY

BORN: PROVIDENCE, RI, AUGUST 29, 1909.
DIED: JULY 2, 1973.

A distrustful-looking character if ever there was one, George Macready had a superior, slightly effete air, a cold stare, and a calculated, insinuating way of speaking that made him seem like a minion of Satan. Onstage since his teens, he racked up a considerable amount of theater credits during the 1930s, including some Shakespeare and Victoria Regina. Columbia signed him to a contract in the early 1940s, and he went west to appear in the wartime drama Commandos Strike at Dawn, as a schoolteacher. For that same studio, Macready was a doctor controlled by hypnotist Rose Hobart in Soul of a Monster; was on the side of good, trying to expose the flawed judicial system, in The Man Who Dared; stooped so low as to murder a priest in The Walls Came Tumbling; shared the villainy honors with Henry Daniell in the popular Technicolor adventure The Bandit of Sherwood Forest; and certainly was more entertaining as the bad guy than Larry Parks was as the swashbuckling hero in The Swordsman. His roles in My Name Is Julia Ross, as the pillow-stabbing nutcase who holds Nina Foch prisoner, and in Gilda, as the possessive husband of Rita Hayworth, both suggested a possible gay side to his character, as did another of his most famous roles, the weasely cohort of Charles Laughton, in Paramount's superior thriller The Big Clock. For a change his home studio made him sympathetic in another Larry Parks romp, Gallant Blade, but otherwise it was back to the usual hisses in such fare as Fortunes of Captain Blood and Rogues of Sherwood Forest (this time as King John). It was nice to hear that delicious voice of his quoting Shakespeare in Julius Caesar (as Marullus), and he topped himself for sheer hatefulness as the very deranged General Mireau, who gets perverse pleasure in planning the execution of some French soldiers, in the powerful antiwar film Paths of Glory. In the 1960s he became well known to soap opera fans for his role as Martin Peyton on the TV version of Peyton Place. His final credits were in two horror movies, Count Yorga: Vampire and The Return of Count Yorga, both produced by his son, Michael.

Screen: 1942: Commandos Strike at Dawn; 1944: The Seventh Cross; The Story of Dr. Wassell; Wilson; Follow the Boys; Soul of a Monster; The Conspirators; The Missing Juror; 1945: Counter-Attack; Don Juan Quilligan; The Fighting Guardsman; The Monster and the Ape (serial); I Love a Mystery; A Song to Remember; My Name Is Julia Ross; 1946: The Man Who Dared; Gilda; The Walls Came Tumbling Down; The Return of Monte Cristo; The Bandit of Sherwood Forest; 1947: The Swordsman; Down to Earth; 1948: The Big Clock; The Black Arrow; Gallant Blade; Coroner Creek; Beyond Glory; 1949: Alias Nick Beal; Knock on Any Door; Johnny Allegro; The Doolins of Oklahoma; 1950: The Nevadan; A Lady Without a Passport; The Desert Hawk; Fortunes of Captain Blood; Rogues of Sherwood Forest; 1951: Tarzan's Peril; Detective Story; The Golden Horde; The Desert Fox; 1952: The Green Glove; 1953: Treasure of the Golden Condor; Julius Caesar; The Stranger Wore a Gun; The Golden Blade; 1954: Duffy of San Quentin; Vera Cruz; 1956: A Kiss Before Dying; Thunder Over Arizona;

1957: The Abductors; Gunfire at Indian Gap; Paths of Glory; **1958:** Plunderers of Painted Flats; The Alligator People; Jet Over the Atlantic; **1962:** Two Weeks in Another Town; Taras Bulba; **1964:** Seven Days in May; Dead Ringer; Where Love Has Gone; **1965:** The Great Race; The Human Duplicators; **1970:** Tora! Tora! Tora!; **1970:** County Yorga: Vampire (narrator); **1971:** The Return of Count Yorga.

NY Stage: 1926: The Scarlet Letter; The Trumpet Shall Sound; **1927:** Granite; Much Ado About Nothing; Martine; **1932:** The Passionate Pilgrim; Lucrece; School for Husbands; **1934:** Romeo and Juliet; **1935:** Victoria Regina; **1936:** Flesh Fields; Pomeroy's Past; **1937:** Merely Murder; **1938:** Save Me the Waltz; American Landscape; **1939:** The Brown Danube; Foreigners; **1940:** The Royal Family; **1954:** Saint Joan; **1958:** The Waltz of the Toreadors.

Select TV: 1952: Edge of the Law (sp); **1953:** The Island (sp); House for Sale (sp); **1955:** The Missing Men (sp); Louise (sp); The Conviction of Peter Shea (sp); The Bitter Choice (sp); Hung for a Sheep (sp); The Diamond as Big as the Ritz (sp); **1956:** The Night Goes On (sp); Panic (sp); The Film Maker (sp); **1957:** Flight From Tormendero (sp); **1960:** Thunder in the Night (sp); In the Presence of Mine Enemies (sp); The Three Musketeers (sp); **1961:** The Fifth Caller (sp); **1965–68:** Peyton Place (series); **1965:** Memorandum for a Spy (sp); **1966:** Fame Is the Name of the Game; **1969:** The Young Lawyers; Night Gallery; Daughter of the Mind.

GUY MADISON

(ROBERT OZELL MOSELY) BORN: BAKERSFIELD, CA, JANUARY 19, 1922. ED: BAKERSFIELD JR. COL. DIED: FEBRUARY 6, 1996.

Another stiff-jawed player who posed no threat to Hollywood's genuinely talented leading men, Guy Madison wasn't even looking for an acting job when he was spotted by a talent scout, while on shore leave from the Coast Guard during World War II. As a result, David O. Selznick gave him a brief scene, as a sailor, in his big home-front tearjerker *Since You Went Away*. Based expressly on his boyish, wavy-haired looks, he was given bigger roles, playing a postwar Marine hooking up with widow Dorothy McGuire in *Till the End of Time*, and the soldier Shirley Temple plans to marry in *Honeymoon*, in both cases performing with an amateurishness that was supposed to be compensated for by his handsome features. Finally getting out of uniform, he was a Texan-gone-East in *Texas, Brooklyn and Heaven*, then ended up on television as the star of *The Adventures of Wild Bill Hickok* (episodes of which were edited into several theatrical features as well). Because of the success of the series, it was decided that horseback was where Madison looked most at ease, and he was seen on the big screen in the 3-D hit *The Charge at Feather River*, rescuing Vera Miles and Helen Westcott from the Indians. He was also in *The Command*, as a doctor who ends up leading a wagon train; *The Last Frontier*, as a cavalry officer; and *Bullwhip*, as an innocent man saved from hanging by agreeing to marry Rhonda Fleming. Amid these were some sub-par 1950s entertainments like the heist yarn *5 Against the House*; the Jean Simmons soap opera *Hilda Crane*; and the combination dinosaur-cowboy cheapie *The Beast of Hollow Mountain*. Not unexpectedly, as he grew older and newer pinups rose from the ranks to take his place, he went to Europe for gladiator movies and other such fare that only true die-hard film fanatics would be able to name. Like many other stars of the past, he was last seen on theater screens making a cameo appearance in *Won Ton Ton, the Dog Who Saved Hollywood*. He was married (1949–54) to actress Gail Russell.

Screen (US releases only): 1944: Since You Went Away; **1946:** Till the End of Time; **1947:** Honeymoon; **1948:** Texas, Brooklyn and Heaven; **1949:** Massacre River; **1951:** Drums in the Deep South; **1952:** Red Snow; **1953:** The Charge at Feather River; Six Gun Decision; Border City Rustlers; Secret of Outlaw Flats; Two Gun Marshal; **1954:** The Command; **1955:** 5 Against the House; **1956:** The Last Frontier; On the Threshold of Space; Hilda Crane; The Beast of Hollow Mountain; Reprisal; **1957:** The Hard Man; **1958:** Bullwhip; **1960:** Jet Over the Atlantic; **1962:** Sword of the Conqueror; **1965:** Gunmen of the Rio Grande; **1966:** The Mystery of Thug Island; **1967:** Shatterhand; **1968:** Payment in Blood; **1976:** Won Ton Ton, the Dog Who Saved Hollywood.

Select TV: 1951–58: The Adventures of Wild Bill Hickok (series); **1955:** Passage to Yesterday (sp); **1956:** Sometimes It Happens (sp); **1957:** The Man Who Stole the Bible (sp); **1958:** Bold Loser (sp); **1959:** You Can't Win 'em All (sp); **1988:** Red River.

ANNA MAGNANI

BORN: ALEXANDRIA, EGYPT, MARCH 7, 1908. RAISED IN ROME. DIED: SEPTEMBER 26, 1973.

The volcanic earth mother of all Italian cinema, Anna Magnani was passionate, fearless, and exciting, with an underlying vulnerable streak running through most of the heroines she played. Despite a career spent principally on her native soil, she did manage to land some impressive roles in English-language features as well. There were acting lessons at the Corso Eleanora Duse, followed by singing jobs in clubs and work with stock companies. A meeting with film director Goffredo Alessandrini not only resulted in marriage (in 1933) but also allowed her entrance into the movie business, starting with a major role in the 1934 release *La Cieca di Sorrento*. It was on the stage that she began to make a name for herself, eventually returning to films in the 1940s, notably in *Teresa Venerdi/Doctor Beware*, as a music hall performer. The one that started the international acclaim was director Roberto Rossellini's stark *Open City*, often looked upon as the first significant movie to launch the Italian neorealism movement in cinema. Magnani herself seemed like the real thing, edgy and decidedly unglamorous, not the typical movie star, which made her a critics' favorite. Those of her follow-up features that played in America included *Angelina*, which won a prize at the Venice Film Festival, and *The Miracle*, in which she believed that the child she was pregnant with following a rape was the Messiah. The latter was helped to success by censorship problems in the U.S.

Playwright Tennessee Williams had become an admirer, and he fashioned *The Rose Tattoo* specifically for her, even though her English was not good enough for her to do it on Broadway as hoped (Maureen Stapleton played it). When producer Hal Wallis bought it to be filmed by Paramount, Magnani got her chance and scorched the screen as the Florida-based widow who wallows in self-pity, mourning her no-good husband until reawakened into life by lusty truck driver Burt Lancaster. The movie did very nicely at the box office and won her the Academy Award as Best Actress of 1955. For an American follow-up, she was Anthony Quinn's mail-order bride, who falls in love with his adopted son (Anthony Franciosa), in *Wild Is the Wind*, based on an Italian movie (*Furia*) that by-now-ex-husband Alessandrini had done. She and Quinn were a dynamic, volatile team and Magnani captured both the confusion of displacement, and the ache of a woman being commanded to bridle the spirit and passion that is her very essence. She got a second Oscar nomination for it, and then landed another terrific Williams role, in the adaptation of his *Orpheus Descending*, retitled *The Fugitive Kind*, as the small-town storekeeper desperately in love with drifter Marlon Brando. It was back to Italy for *…And the Wild, Wild Women*; *The Passionate Thief*, which featured Americans Ben Gazzara and Fred Clark but still couldn't work up any interest here; and *Mama Roma*, which did not hit U.S. shores until 1995 when the reviewers went wild for Magnani all over again. She made one more appearance in an American film, *The Secret of Santa Vittoria*, teamed again with Anthony Quinn, trying to hide wine from the Nazis, and a cameo, as herself, in *Fellini's Roma*, released shortly before her death in 1973.

Screen (US releases only): 1941: Doctor Beware; 1943: The Peddler and the Lady; 1944: Open City; 1946: Peddlin' in Society; 1947: Angelina; 1948: Scarred; 1950: Ways of Love; 1952: The Miracle; 1953: Belissima (It: 1951); The Golden Coach; 1955: The Rose Tattoo; 1957: Wild Is the Wind; 1958: Of Life and Love (It: 1953 as Siamo Donne); The Awakening (It: 1956); 1960: The Fugitive Kind; 1961: …And the Wild, Wild Women (It: 1959); 1967: Made in Italy; 1969: The Secret of Santa Vittoria; 1972: Fellini's Roma; 1995: Mama Roma (It: 1962).

MARJORIE MAIN

(MARY TOMLINSON) BORN: ACTON, IN,
FEBRUARY 24, 1890. DIED: APRIL 10, 1975.

This irresistible old buzzard with the challenging stare and a voice that squawked like a barnyard fowl, was the sort of character player who filled a room like a true star, and took a lot of the hot air out of it to boot, with her direct, ungenteel approach. The daughter of a minister, her decision to enter the acting field was not looked upon favorably by her family. She ended up on the Chautauqua Theatre Circuit, with various stock companies, and in vaudeville, before dropping out of the business temporarily when she married in 1921. Six years later she ended up on Broadway in the drama *Burlesque* and began appearing in films in 1932, mainly in teensy or unbilled roles. Back on the New York stage she was seen in *Music in the Air*, a part she repeated in the 1934 Fox movie version, and then had a more memorable case of the same when she was asked to play her Broadway role in the motion picture version of *Dead End*, creating a stunning impression as hoodlum Humphrey Bogart's world-weary slum mother who confronts her no good offspring with a crack across the mouth. Staying serious she was mom to Barbara Stanwyck in *Stella Dallas*; to Helen Mack in *King of the Newsboys*; and to Helen Parish in *Little Tough Guy*, among others. As one of those character players who always seemed older than she actually was, her mothering instincts often found her improbably cast, as in *Dark Command*, where she was Walter Pigeon's mother despite being only a year older than him in real life.

Main had done well repeating another stage role, in the MGM movie of *The Women*, and that studio thought she might be ideal as a comical foil to Wallace Beery, hoping to fill the hole left many years before by the late Marie Dressler. Signed by MGM, she and Beery sparred to good effect in *Wyoming*, where she was ninth billed, as a blacksmith named Mehitabel. They were reteamed, with Main upped to co-star status, for *Barnacle Bill*, the waterfront setting of which made it seem awfully close to Beery and Dressler's *Tugboat Annie*; *The Bugle Sounds*, which had a modern military backdrop; *Jackass Mail*, another comedic western; *Rationing*, which threw some topical wartime themes into the mix; *Bad Bascomb*, where little Margaret O'Brien was the principal attraction; and further down the line, *Big Jack*, in which they were fellow thieves in what turned out to be Beery's last film.

Audiences just loved seeing Main's name pop up in the credits, so in addition to her frequent supporting appearances, she was rewarded with larger roles as in *Tish*, as one of the spinsters (Aline MacMahon and ZaSu Pitts being the others) who adopt a baby girl; and the title role in *Gentle Annie*, heading a family of bank robbers. Though she was unforgettable on her home lot as the no-nonsense domestic in the classic *Meet Me in St. Louis*, and got to croak some lines in the title song of *The Harvey Girls*, her two best roles during the 1940s came elsewhere. Paramount's *Murder, He Says* found her at her most marvelously uninhibited, as the whip-wielding hillbilly lady in charge of a whacked-out family, while a similarly rural assignment at Universal, *The Egg and I*, gave her the role she would become most readily identified with, Ma Kettle. Teamed with the slow-drawling Percy Kilbride as Pa, Main was her usual brusk, sour-faced self, and earned a Best Supporting Actress Oscar nomination in the process. Universal was keen to cash in on this enterprise, so there were nine more Kettle pictures, all cheaply made, proudly low-brow, and profitable. After the last of them, *The Kettles on Old MacDonald's Farm*, in 1957, Main quietly retired.

Screen: 1931: A House Divided; 1932: Hot Saturday; 1933: Take a Chance; 1934: Crime Without Passion; Music in the Air; 1935: Naughty Marietta; 1937: Love in a Bungalow; Dead End; Stella Dallas; The Man Who Cried Wolf; The Wrong Road; The Shadow; Boy of the Streets; 1938: City Girl; Penitentiary; King of the Newsboys; Test Pilot; Prison Farm; Romance of the Limberlost; Little Tough Guy; Under the Big Top; Too Hot to Handle; Girls' School; There Goes My Heart; Three Comrades; 1939: Lucky Night; They Shall Have Music; The Angels Wash Their Faces; The Women; Another Thin Man; Two Thoroughbreds; 1940: I Take This Woman; Women Without Names; Dark Command; Turnabout; Susan and God; The Captain Is a Lady; Wyoming; 1941: The Wild Man of Borneo; The Trial of Mary Dugan; A Woman's Face; Barnacle Bill; The Shepherd of the Hills; Honky Tonk; The Bugle Sounds; 1942: We Were Dancing; The Affairs of Martha; Jackass Mail; Tish; Tennessee Johnson; 1943: Heaven Can Wait; Johnny Come Lately; 1944: Rationing; Gentle Annie; Meet Me in St. Louis; 1945: Murder He Says; 1946: The Harvey Girls; Bad Bascomb; Undercurrent; The Show-Off; 1947: The Egg and I; The Wistful Widow of Wagon Gap; 1948: Feudin', Fussin' and A-Fightin'; 1949: Ma and Pa Kettle; Big Jack; 1950: Ma and Pa Kettle Go to Town; Summer Stock; Mrs. O'Malley and Mr. Malone; 1951: Ma and Pa Kettle Back on the Farm; The Law and the Lady; Mr. Imperium; It's a Big Country; 1952: The Belle of New York; Ma and Pa Kettle at the Fair; 1953: Ma and Pa Kettle on Vacation; Fast Company; 1954: The Long, Long Trailer; Rose Marie; Ma and Pa Kettle at Home; Ricochet Romance; 1955: Ma and Pa Kettle at Waikiki; 1956: The Kettles in the Ozarks; Friendly Persuasion; 1957: The Kettles on Old MacDonald's Farm.

NY Stage: 1927: Burlesque; 1928: Salvation; 1930: Scarlet Sister Mary; 1931: Ebb Tide; 1932: Music in the Air; 1935: Jackson White; Dead End; 1936: The Women.

KARL MALDEN

(MLADEN SEKULOVICH) BORN: CHICAGO, IL,
MARCH 22, 1913. RAISED IN GARY, IN.
ED: GOODMAN THEATRE DRAMATIC SCHOOL.

With few frills, eccentricities, or special traits, bulbous-nosed Karl Malden was one of the cinema's most dependably good character actors, capable of projecting decency or villainy in a no-nonsense fashion. Having studied acting in Chicago, he journeyed to New York to seek work and wound up making his

Broadway debut in the original 1937 production of *Golden Boy*. Between other stage assignments he made one isolated movie appearance for RKO, in *They Knew What They Wanted*, as an uncouth party guest trying to kiss Carole Lombard, returned to New York, then joined the Army Air Force. His participation in the patriotic revue show *Winged Victory* brought him back to the movies when 20th Century-Fox filmed it, and he was signed to a contract by that studio. They didn't exactly spotlight him, although he was seen in some good movies like *Boomerang!*, as a detective helping Lee J. Cobb find out who killed a priest, and *The Gunfighter*, as a friendly bartender. In the meantime he had become a part of theater history playing Mitch in the original 1947 presentation of Tennessee Williams's groundbreaking Broadway drama *A Streetcar Named Desire*. He was asked to repeat his role in Warners's magnificent 1951 adaptation, which became as significant on screen as it had onstage. Portraying a simple but good-hearted man driven to the brink of disgust by the deluded Vivien Leigh, Malden was as satisfying as everyone else in the movie and received the Academy Award for Best Supporting Actor of the year.

Thanks to the Oscar the parts finally started getting bigger with the overheated *Ruby Gentry*, as Jennifer Jones's husband; *Take the High Ground*, as an army sergeant named Laverne (!); and *I Confess*, as the inspector investigating the murder in this minor Hitchcock entry. No doubt because it gave him a bona fide lead, he agreed to appear in a piece of 3-D silliness, *Phantom of the Rue Morgue*, hamming shamelessly as the mad scientist sicking his killer ape on his victims. Fortunately this was quickly forgotten by the release of *On the Waterfront*, which brought together the same star (Marlon Brando) and director (Elia Kazan) from *Streetcar*, creating another milestone in film, as gritty and realistic a social drama as had been seen up to that time. As the determined Father Barry, Malden created a characterization that was believable rather than the customary cinematic blueprint of the too-saintly-to-be-true man of the cloth, and got himself another Oscar nomination in the supporting category. Another lead, in another Tennessee Williams's creation, *Baby Doll*, as Carroll Baker's protective husband, gave him a good chance to emote, though this drama was not among that writer's more stellar efforts; as did his role in *Fear Strikes Out*, as the overbearing father of sensitive ballplayer Anthony Perkins, who drives the poor lad to a nervous breakdown. There was star billing in a combination aviation adventure-domestic drama, *Bombers B-52*, as an officer facing a change of employment and coping with daughter Natalie Wood's choice of boyfriends. Around this time he had enough clout to get himself a directorial credit, *Time Limit*, a courtroom drama starring Richard Widmark, that earned him some favorable critical reaction, though Malden never returned to this field again.

Back in front of the cameras he had some potent roles, playing the sleazy miner who tries to rape Maria Schell in *The Hanging Tree*, and the preacher whose pessimistic way of sermonizing depresses his congregation in Disney's nostalgic *Pollyanna*. A third one with (and directed by) Brando, *One-Eyed Jacks*, gave him another showy role that he carried off splendidly, the former outlaw who becomes a hypocritical man-of-the-law. Pretty much staying on a roll, he was Claudette Colbert's greedy husband in the glossy soaper *Parrish*; gave an excellent performance as the prison warden trying hard to understand individualistic inmate Burt Lancaster in *Birdman of Alcatraz*; and was ideally cast as the good-hearted Herbie in *Gypsy*, although the one song from the stage print that featured him, "Together, Wherever We Go," was cut from the final print. He was a down-on-his luck gambler in *The Cincinnati Kid*; one of the bad guys being tracked down by

Steve McQueen in *Nevada Smith*; a comic book villain in the deliberately silly Matt Helm romp *Murderers' Row*; a cutesy thief in *Hotel*; a con man hiding behind a series of disguises in Disney's *The Adventures of Bullwhip Griffin*; and about the only actor not obscured by George C. Scott's mighty force in the 1970 Oscar-winner *Patton*, as General Omar Bradley.

There was another starring role in a poor thriller, *Cat o' Nine Tails*, as a blind man helping to catch a killer, after which he signed up to do a TV series, *The Streets of San Francisco*, which made him a staple of that medium, as did the frequent American Express ads that featured him throughout the 1970s. Returning to cinemas, he wasn't particularly lucky with things like a pair of sequels that nobody was waiting for, *Beyond the Poseidon Adventure* and *The Sting II*, but fared better carrying two barely seen features, *Twilight Time*, reflecting his real Yugoslavian roots, as an old man suddenly stuck with his grandchildren, and *Billy Galvin*, as a construction worker discouraging his son from following in his footsteps. There was also one more bad-guy role, playing Barbra Streisand's molester dad, in *Nuts*, which also turned out to be his final big screen appearance. He served as president of the Academy of Motion Picture Arts and Sciences from 1989 and 1993. An interesting in-joke was the mention of Malden's real last name, Sekulovich, that pops up in throwaway dialogue in several of the movies he is featured in. In 1997 he published his autobiography, *When Do I Start?*

Screen: 1940: They Knew What They Wanted; 1944: Winged Victory; 1946: 13 Rue Madeleine; 1947: Boomerang!; Kiss of Death; 1950: The Gunfighter; Where the Sidewalk Ends; Halls of Montezuma; 1951: A Streetcar Named Desire; 1952: Diplomatic Courier; The Sellout; Operation Secret; Ruby Gentry; 1953: Take the High Ground; I Confess; 1954: Phantom of the Rue Morgue; On the Waterfront; 1956: Baby Doll; 1957: Fear Strikes Out; Bombers B-52; 1959: The Hanging Tree; 1960: Pollyanna; The Great Imposter; 1961: Parrish; One-Eyed Jacks; 1962: All Fall Down; Birdman of Alcatraz; Gypsy; 1963: How the West Was Won; Come Fly With Me; 1964: Dead Ringer; Cheyenne Autumn; 1965: The Cincinnati Kid; 1966: Nevada Smith; Murderers' Row; 1967: Hotel; Billion Dollar Brain; 1968: The Adventures of Bullwhip Griffin; Blue; Hot Millions; 1970: Patton; 1971: Cat o' Nine Tails; Wild Rovers; 1973: Summertime Killer; 1979: Beyond the Poseidon Adventure; Meteor; 1983: The Sting II; Twilight Time; 1986: Billy Galvin; 1987: Nuts.

NY Stage: 1937: Golden Boy; 1938: Missouri Legend; 1939: The Gentle People; Key Largo; 1940: Flight to the West; 1942: Uncle Harry; 1943: Counterattack; Sons and Soldiers; Winged Victory; 1945: The Assassin; 1946: Truckline Cafe; 1947: All My Sons; A Streetcar Named Desire; 1951: Peer Gynt; 1952: Desire Under the Elms; 1955: The Desperate Hours; 1957: The Egghead.

Select TV: 1972: The Streets of San Francisco; 1972–77: The Streets of San Francisco (series); 1977: Captains Courageous; 1980: Skag; Skag (series); 1981: Word of Honor; Miracle on Ice; 1984: With Intent to Kill; 1985: Alice in Wonderland; 1988: My Father, My Son; 1989: The Hijacking of the Achille Lauro; 1990: Call Me Anna; 1991: Absolute Strangers; 1992: Back to the Streets of San Francisco.

DOROTHY MALONE

(DOROTHY ELOISE MALONEY) BORN: CHICAGO, IL, JANUARY 30, 1925. RAISED IN DALLAS, TX. ED: SOUTHERN METHODIST UNIV.

Hers were among the most soulful eyes in the business, but Dorothy Malone didn't have to depend on just looks to create an impression. You could tell from her early performances that she was going to go a bit further than most starlets, and despite lapses into the sort of pulpy histrionics that many 1950s melodramas required, there was a lot of hard, solid work in an erratic output of films. It was while appearing in a college play that she was spotted by an RKO talent scout. For that studio she did bit parts but didn't rate a role with actual billing until Columbia put her in a "Boston Blackie" programmer, *One Mysterious Night*, in 1944. Signed by Warners, she had the "y" dropped from her last name and was listed as "Dorothy Malone" for the first time in 1945's *Too Young to Know*. The one that helped bring her some attention was the classic noir *The Big Sleep*, in which she had a memorable scene as a bespectacled bookstore clerk who willingly locks up shop in order to fiddle about with investigator Humphrey Bogart. She was given bigger roles in *One Sunday Afternoon*, in the part Olivia de Havilland had done in *The Strawberry Blonde*, and in two Joel McCrea westerns, *South of St. Louis* and *Colorado Territory*.

Leaving Warners, she found she wasn't exactly on the Hollywood "A" list and showed up over at Columbia as *The Killer That Stalked New York*, spreading a deadly disease in this well-done "B" thriller. She was also in the Realart western *The Bushwackers*, and in a batch for Allied Artists, including *Loophole* and *Security Risk*. There was another quickie, *The Fast and the Furious*, which was actually significant, being the very first production made by the company that eventually formulated into American International. Good sport that she was, she did straight-woman duty for Martin and Lewis on two occasions, *Scared Stiff* and *Artists and Models*; took on the acting challenge of falling in love with Liberace in the saccharine soaper *Sincerely Yours*; and was one of the ladies who did her duty for the U.S. Marines in the box-office hit *Battle Cry*. Between some more westerns, she got a chance to play a juicy soap opera vixen, the spoiled heiress determined to make Rock Hudson love her in the glossy Douglas Sirk trash *Written on the Wind*. The movie was a success with 1950s audiences who just loved this sort of thing, and there were nothing but raves for her no-holds-barred work that won her the Academy Award as Best Supporting Actress of 1956. From there she was the tormented first wife of Lon Chaney, horrified at the possibility of their son being deaf, in the decent biopic *Man of a Thousand Faces*; then she reteamed with Sirk and *Wind* co-stars Hudson and Robert Stack for the less popular *The Tarnished Angels*, giving herself to both men, while turning her back on Jack Carson's romantic overtures.

Staying in high melodrama she misstepped badly in the gloomy bio of alcoholic actress Diana Barrymore, *Too Much, Too Soon*, wallowing in drink. She then showed up in somewhat higher-budgeted westerns than most of those she'd done before, *Warlock*, swearing revenge on club-footed gunman Anthony Quinn, and *The Last Sunset*, which brought her back to Hudson's arms. In between she and Stack did the best of their films together, the tense *The Last Voyage*, in which Malone spent most of the movie trapped beneath some wreckage as an ocean liner sank beneath her. After playing one of the condescending adults in AIP's pea-brained but surprisingly popular *Beach Party*, she decided to boost her standing by turning her attention to television, playing Constance McKenzie (the role Lana Turner had done in the movie) in the nighttime serial version of *Peyton Place*, which ran successfully for several seasons. After that most of her employment came from the small screen with an occasional obscure movie credit along the way. Therefore most moviegoers were seeing her for the first time in years when she showed up as Sharon Stone's mysterious companion in the 1992 sensation *Basic Instinct*.

Screen: AS DOROTHY MALONEY: 1943: The Falcon and the Co-

eds; Gildersleeve on Broadway; Higher and Higher; 1944: Show Business; Step Lively; Seven Days Ashore; One Mysterious Night; Hollywood Canteen.

AS DOROTHY MALONE: 1945: Too Young to Know; 1946: Janie Gets Married; Night and Day; The Big Sleep; 1948: To the Victor; Two Guys From Texas; One Sunday Afternoon; 1949: Flaxy Martin; South of St. Louis; Colorado Territory; 1950: The Nevadan; Convicted; Mrs. O'Malley and Mr. Malone; The Killer That Stalked New York; 1951: Saddle Legion; 1952: The Bushwackers; 1953: Torpedo Alley; Scared Stiff; Law and Order; Jack Slade; 1954: Loophole; The Lone Gun; Pushover; Security Risk; Private Hell 36; The Fast and the Furious; Young at Heart; 1955: Five Guns West; Battle Cry; Tall Man Riding; Sincerely Yours; Artists and Models; At Gunpoint; 1956: Pillars of the Sky; Written on the Wind; Tension at Table Rock; 1957: Man of a Thousand Faces; Tip on a Dead Jockey; Quantez; The Tarnished Angels; 1958: Too Much, Too Soon; 1959: Warlock; 1960: The Last Voyage; 1961: The Last Sunset; 1963: Beach Party; 1964: Fate Is the Hunter; 1969: The Insatiables/Carnal Circuit (nUSr); 1975: The Man Who Would Not Die; Abduction; 1977: Golden Rendezvous/Nuclear Terror; 1979: Good Luck, Miss Wyckoff; Winter Kills; 1980: The Day Time Ended/Earth's Final Fury; 1983: The Being (filmed 1980); 1987: Rest in Pieces (dtv); 1992: Basic Instinct.

Select TV: 1953: Moorings (sp); 1954: Surprise Party (sp); Afraid to Live (sp); Our Son (sp); 1955: Mr. Onion (sp); Clown (sp); 1960: The Last Flight Out (sp); 1961: A Little White Lye (sp); Open Season (sp); 1964–68: Peyton Place (series); 1969: The Pigeon; 1976: The November Plan; Rich Man, Poor Man (ms); 1977: Little Ladies of the Night; Murder in Peyton Place; 1978: Katie: Portrait of a Centerfold; High Hopes (series); 1980: Condominium; 1982: Off Your Rocker (sp); 1984: He's Not Your Son!; 1985: Peyton Place: The Next Generation.

DAVID MANNERS

(RAUFF DE RYTHER DUAN ACKLOM)
BORN: HALIFAX, NOVA SCOTIA, CANADA,
APRIL 30, 1900. ED: UNIV. OF TORONTO.
DIED: DECEMBER 23, 1998.

In a brief, six-year period David Manners racked up a considerable list of credits before he realized that he was hardly the reason most people were going to the movies he was in. Despite a background in forestry, he decided to try acting as his life's profession and joined Basil Sydney's touring company in 1924. That same year came his Broadway debut, in *Dancing Mothers*, in support of Helen Hayes. When talkies came he was encouraged to try Hollywood, and a chance meeting with director James Whale landed him a part as one of the soldiers in the acclaimed antiwar drama *Journey's End*. Jumping from studio to studio, he was the Caliph in the pre-musical version of *Kismet*; Jonathan Harker (probably his best-known role) in the classic Universal version of *Dracula*; and a blind aviator inspired by evangelist Barbara Stanwyck in *The Miracle Woman*. He was George Arliss's business partner, helping him run a roadside gas station, in *The Millionaire*; a playboy pursued by Madge Evans in *The Greeks Had a Word for Them*; the drippy fiancé Katharine Hepburn turned away in *A Bill of Divorcement*; and the by-the-numbers love interest, upstaged by Boris Karloff, in both *The Mummy* and *The Black Cat*. He was also straight man to Eddie Cantor in the spoof *Roman Scandals*; a Greek warrior conquering Elissa Landi and her tribe of fighting women in the curious satire *The Warrior's Husband*; a murder suspect, top billed, in the Monogram cheapie *The Moonstone*;

and the title character in the pretty much forgotten movie of Dickens's unfinished novel, *The Mystery of Edwin Drood*. In 1936 he went into a period of retirement but resumed his New York stage career ten years later in the short-lived *Truckline Cafe*, which featured a young Marlon Brando in the supporting cast. He had a great success on Broadway and touring in a revival of *Lady Windermere's Fan*, only to retire from show business for good shortly thereafter.

Screen: **1930:** Journey's End; He Knew Women; Sweet Mama; Kismet; Mother's Cry; The Truth About Youth; The Right to Love; **1931:** Dracula; The Millionaire; The Last Flight; The Miracle Woman; The Ruling Voice; **1932:** The Greeks Had a Word for Them; Lady With a Past; Beauty and the Boss; Stranger in Town; Crooner; Man Wanted; A Bill of Divorcement; They Call It Sin; The Mummy; The Death Kiss; **1933:** From Hell to Heaven; The Warrior's Husband; The Girl in 419; The Devil's in Love; Torch Singer; Roman Scandals; **1934:** The Black Cat; The Luck of a Sailor; The Great Flirtation; The Moonstone; **1935:** The Perfect Clue; The Mystery of Edwin Drood; Jalna; **1936:** Hearts in Bondage; Lucky Fugitives; A Woman Rebels.

NY Stage: **1924:** Dancing Mothers; **1946:** Truckline Café; Hidden Horizon; **1947:** Lady Windermere's Fan.

JAYNE MANSFIELD

(VERA JANE PALMER) BORN: BRYN MAWR, PA, APRIL 19, 1933. DIED: JUNE 29, 1967.

More of a cinematic sight gag than a bona fide actress, Jayne Mansfield was at least aware that she was a caricature of an overly endowed woman and played the joke to the hilt. The bosomy, breathy blonde got her last name when she married, at 16 years of age, a man named Paul Mansfield. They both went to UCLA to study acting, but it was Jayne's curves that got her bits on television and in magazine photo spreads. She was signed to a contract by Warner Bros. who gave her two bit parts and then a more substantial one, as a mobster's moll, in *Illegal*, which starred Edward G. Robinson. On Broadway she played an outrageous sex-bomb in the hit *Will Success Spoil Rock Hunter?*, which gave 20th Century-Fox the idea of signing her up as a threat to the often temperamental and unpredictable Marilyn Monroe. For that studio she "ooed" and "ahhed" her way through a hodgepodge comedy-rock musical, *The Girl Can't Help It*, the most famous moment of which had her carrying two milk bottles in front of her breasts. She appeared in the more serious *The Wayward Bus*, not stretching all that much, being cast as a stripper in this weak adaptation of a John Steinbeck novel, and then the movie of *Rock Hunter*, which was silly, good-natured fun that didn't demand much more of her than undulations and squeals. After *Kiss Them for Me* proved that she was so lukewarm an attraction at the box office that even Cary Grant as her co-star couldn't get the crowds to show up, she went to Britain for the mild western spoof *The Sheriff of Fractured Jaw*, cast opposite Kenneth More.

She stayed on in England for a pair of thrillers, *The Challenge* and *Too Hot to Handle*, by which point it was clear that the Mansfield buzz had died down sooner than anyone thought possible. With her body-builder husband Mickey Hargitay (they had married shortly after her divorce from Mansfield, in 1958) she filmed the Italian-made *The Loves of Hercules*, which nobody bothered to ship to the States, then returned to the U.S. for the "B" bio *The George Raft Story*, as one of the fictional dames in his life. Other than the Europeans and some independent producers, nobody was all that interested in hiring someone who seemed like

a one-note attraction and whose fame was based more on the fan magazines than on any cinematic accomplishments. There was the movie business spoof *Panic Button*, which paired her with Maurice Chevalier; *Promises! Promises!*, which had nothing to do with the later Broadway musical but was, in fact, the first of her "nudie" films that gave adult grind-house audiences flashes of skin; *Las Vegas Hillbillys*, in which she shared the screen with another sexy babe who had become the butt of condescending jokes, Mamie Van Doren; *The Fat Spy*, an attempt to build a vehicle around tubby nightclub comic Jack E. Leonard; and others that seemed to have been made for very specialized, adults only venues. These included *Single Room Furnished* (produced and directed by Mansfield's new lover, Matteo Ottaviano/Matt Cimber) and *The Wild, Wild World of Jayne Mansfield* (featuring footage of her fatal car crash). Mansfield appeared in one final "A" Hollywood offering, *A Guide for the Married Man*, in a sequence with Terry-Thomas. Shortly after its release she became one of Hollywood's major casualties when she was decapitated in an automobile collision while driving from New Orleans. Her daughter is actress Mariska Hargitay, who had survived the accident while sleeping in the back seat of the car.

Screen: **1955:** Pete Kelly's Blues; Illegal; Hell on Frisco Bay; **1956:** Female Jungle; The Girl Can't Help It; **1957:** The Burglar; The Wayward Bus; Will Success Spoil Rock Hunter?; Kiss Them for Me; **1958:** The Sheriff of Fractured Jaw; **1960:** The Challenge; Too Hot to Handle/Playgirl After Dark (nUSr); The Loves of Hercules (nUSr); **1961:** The George Raft Story; **1962:** It Happened in Athens (nUSr); **1963:** Promises! Promises!; Homesick for St. Pauli (nUSr); **1964:** Panic Button (filmed 1961); Dog Eat Dog/When Strangers Meet; Primitive Love (nUSr); **1966:** The Fat Spy; Las Vegas Hillbillys; **1967:** A Guide for the Married Man; Spree; Single Room Furnished; **1968:** The Wild, Wild World of Jayne Mansfield.

NY Stage: **1955:** Will Success Spoil Rock Hunter?

Select TV: **1956:** The Bachelor (sp); **1957:** Holiday in Las Vegas (sp).

FREDRIC MARCH

(ERNEST FREDERICK MCINTYRE BICKEL) BORN: RACINE, WI, AUGUST 31, 1897. ED: UNIV. OF WI. DIED: APRIL 14, 1975.

An actor who clearly loved to act, Fredric March maintained a high and long-lasting level of fame built not so much on box-office figures but on the respect afforded him by an industry awed by his professionalism and the often fine results of his undertakings. He was guilty on more than one occasion of playing to the rafters, with actorish accents and mannerisms guaranteed to bring attention to himself, but it didn't matter as much as the diversity of what he attempted. Originally set on being a banker, he found himself, after college, looking for acting work instead. He got some modeling jobs as well as extra work in movies, those titles that have been verified being *The Devil*, *The Great Adventure*, and *Paying the Piper*. His Broadway debut came in 1920, in *Deburau*, and between New York assignments, he toured. It was his role spoofing John Barrymore, in the West Coast production of *The Royal Family*, that won him a contract with Paramount, who, like every other studio, was looking for rich stage voices now that talkies had arrived. They started him off in a small role opposite Ruth Chatterton, in *The Dummy*, then gave him more to do as a professor involved with Clara Bow in *The Wild Party*. *The Studio Murder Mystery* was notable because it was the first of several times he would appear on screen with his second wife (they had married in 1927), Florence Eldredge, while *Jealousy* proved just how sought after he was at the time, with March replacing Anthony Bushell by demand of star Jeanne Eagles, even though most of Bushell's footage had already been shot. He was with Chatterton again in *Sarah and Son*, as a lawyer; Bow in *True to the Navy*, as a sailor; and Nancy Carroll in *Laughter*, as a composer. His success as a movie star was solidified when he recreated his Barrymore spoof for the cameras in the retitled *The Royal Family of Broadway*, earning an Oscar nomination in the process. (He would reprise the role yet again, on television, in 1954).

The Oscar was his when he played fiction's most famous dual role in Paramount's 1932 version of *Dr. Jekyll and Mr. Hyde*, imaginatively directed by Rouben Mamoulian, with March throwing himself into both parts with lip-smacking abandon. Indeed his werewolf-like Mr. Hyde is almost a bit too grotesque for credibility's sake. In any event it was probably not a great idea to follow this up with another dual role (good brother/bad brother) in the inferior *Strangers in Love*, but he did get to play a drunk in *Merrily We Go to Hell*, the title of which made the movie sound more interesting than it was. He and everyone else became victims of the campy excesses of Cecil B. DeMille's kitsch classic *The Sign of the Cross*, and there was little he could do to rise above the relentless schmaltz of MGM's *Smilin' Through*, playing the lover of Norma Shearer in this highly popular attraction that managed to rate an Oscar nomination for Best Picture. There was the famous botched movie of Noel Coward's *Design for Living*, in which he shared Miriam Hopkins with Gary Cooper, and then one of his very best films of this period, *Death Takes a Holiday*, an atmospheric and haunting fantasy with March as the specter of Death taking on human form and falling in love.

Shortly after this his contract with Paramount ended, and he went over to 20th Century-Fox, just as they were on the verge of merging with Fox. The results were *The Affairs of Cellini*, a none-too-serious adventure with March as a cheeky womanizer, and the truncated but expertly done version of *Les Misérables*, with the actor as the relentlessly pursued Jean Valjean. Back at MGM he and Shearer were together again for the stagy and fairly stuffy *The Barretts of Wimpole Street*, with March as Robert Browning. For Goldwyn he was paired with that producer's famous "failed discovery," Anna Sten, in a version of Tolstoy's *Resurrection*, called *We Live Again*, and he and Garbo made a handsome pair of doomed lovers in MGM's prestigious *Anna Karenina*, just another example of how the actor could come off as somewhat stiff when doing costume drama. He was given the opportunity to play a blinded flier in *The Dark Angel*, failing to rise above the bathos in this second-rate Goldwyn soaper and not even bothering to attempt a British accent; seemed uncomfortable as Katharine Hepburn's tartan-wearing lover, the Earl of Bothwell, in *Mary of Scotland*; and then was asked to carry a popular but cumbersome costume epic for Warners, *Anthony Adverse*, which never obtained the greatness it strove for. As a freelancer he never had trouble finding work and ended up in one of his best films, *A Star Is Born*, for producer David O. Selznick. As the self-pitying alcoholic actor Norman Maine he gave one of his most memorable performances and ended up with another Oscar nomination in one of the definite inside-Hollywood movies (until the 1954 remake came along and pretty much trumped this version in every department). This was followed by another hit for the same producer, *Nothing Sacred*, with March displaying his comic timing to perfection, as the reporter exploiting Carole Lombard's bogus illness. It was wise to join DeMille again, for everything that director did turned to money, but March's overripe turn as pirate Jean Lafitte in the mediocre adventure *The Buccaneer* was not among his finest hours.

There was a lull in the importance of the material with *There Goes My Heart* and *Trade Winds*, so he and his wife found themselves only too happy to restart their theatrical careers, returning to New York for *Yr. Obedient Husband* in 1938. Back in the movies he got drunk again in *Susan and God*; opposed the Nazis in the intelligent *So Ends Our Night*; and had one of his gentlest roles in *One Foot in Heaven*, which looked at the life of a Methodist minister minus a lot of the expected saccharine such a topic promised. *I Married a Witch* was a delightful fantasy with March as both a Puritan and his modern day descendent, succumbing to sorceress Veronica Lake; *The Adventures of Mark Twain* found him convincingly cast as the famed author, though like most Hollywood interpretations of history, there was much fiction among the facts; and *Tomorrow, the World!* had him battling Nazis again, in this particular case his own adopted nephew, Skippy Homeier, in this unintentionally funny piece of dated wartime propaganda. These were followed in 1946 by a career peak, *The Best Years of Our Lives*, Goldwyn's lengthy but moving tribute to servicemen in the aftermath of World War II with March as the officer who must readjust to his relatively tedious bank job back home after experiencing glory overseas. For his subtle work he won his second Academy Award and could chalk up having participated in one of the highest grossing motion pictures of the entire decade. The film itself won the Oscar for Best Picture and remains one of the key motion pictures of its time. He and Eldredge then received equal roles for the first and only time on screen, in *Live Today for Tomorrow*, a story of euthanasia that fared so poorly that it received a second title, *An Act of Murder*, in a vain effort to re-sell it to an apathetic public. Likewise there was no support or enthusiasm for his interpretation of *Christopher Columbus*, the story of the explorer credited with founding America, which was made in England of all places!

Since Lee J. Cobb wasn't going to repeat his performance as Willy Loman in the movie of *Death of a Salesman*, March got the coveted part, with critical response ranging from raves to pans. This was, in fact, a surprisingly faithful, relentlessly uncommercial rendering of Arthur Miller's masterpiece and March fully captured the desperation of a man at the end of his rope, earning one final Oscar nomination in the process. This wasn't a box-office attraction, nor was *Man on a Tightrope*, about a circus troupe trying to escape from Communist-ruled Czechoslovakia, so he had no qualms about taking supporting roles in *Executive Suite*, refreshingly unsympathetic for a change, as a devious businessman; *The Bridges at Toko-Ri*, as the sensible admiral; *The Man in the Gray Flannel Suit*, off the mark as Gregory Peck's boss; and *Alexander the Great*, buried under a bushy beard, as that warrior's father, Phillip of Macedonia. Amid this bunch he held his own against Humphrey Bogart, playing the captive father in the tense hostage drama *The Desperate Hours*, accepting the part after Spencer Tracy balked at taking second billing.

Returning to the stage, he won a Tony for perhaps his most significant Broadway role, the self-centered patriarch, James Tyrone, in the original production of Eugene O'Neill's *Long Day's Journey Into Night*. Because of this, March was still able to secure some movie leads as well, with *Middle of the Night*, falling in love with much younger Kim Novak, a most unconvincing coupling; the superb *Inherit the Wind*, very theatrical as the bombastic, self-righteous religious lawyer based on William Jennings Bryant; and *The Young Doctor*, as the aging medico distrustful of new recruit Ben Gazzara. Approaching 70, he was still well-regarded enough to be chosen to essay some good roles in some top-line productions, such as *Seven Days in May*, as the worried President of the United States, facing a possible government takeover; *Hombre*, again outstanding as a louse; and, later on, with the highly specialized filmization of Eugene O'Neill's *The Iceman Cometh*, as Harry Hope. His name wasn't often included on the list of the immortal stars of the golden era, but one need only look back on the scope of his work to be very impressed by a decent percentage of what he left behind.

Screen: 1920: The Devil; The Great Adventure; Paying the Piper; 1929: The Dummy; The Wild Party; The Studio Murder Mystery; Paris Bound; Jealousy; Footlights and Fools; The Marriage Playground; 1930: Sarah and Son; Ladies Love Brutes; Paramount on Parade; True to the Navy; Manslaughter; Laughter; The Royal Family of Broadway; 1931: Honor Among Lovers; The Night Angel; My Sin; Dr. Jekyll and Mr. Hyde; 1932: Strangers in Love; Merrily We Go to Hell; Make Me a Star; Smilin' Through; The Sign of the Cross; 1933: Tonight Is Ours; The Eagle and the Hawk; Design for Living; 1934: All of Me; Death Takes a Holiday; Good Dame; The Affairs of Cellini; The Barretts of Wimpole Street; We Live Again; 1935: Les Misérables; Anna Karenina; The Dark Angel; 1936: Mary of Scotland; The Road to Glory; Anthony Adverse; 1937: A Star Is Born; Nothing Sacred; 1938: The Buccaneer; There Goes My Heart; Trade Winds; 1940: Susan and God; Victory; 1941: So Ends Our Night; One Foot in Heaven; Bedtime Story; 1942: I Married a Witch; 1944: The Adventures of Mark Twain; Tomorrow, the World!; 1946: The Best Years of Our Lives; 1948: Another Part of the Forest; Live Today for Tomorrow/An Act of Murder; 1949: Christopher Columbus; 1950: Titan: The Story of Michelangelo (narrator); 1951: Death of a Salesman; It's a Big Country; 1953: Man on a Tightrope; 1954: Executive Suite; 1955: The Bridges at Toko-Ri; The Desperate Hours; 1956: Alexander the Great; The Man in the Gray Flannel Suit; 1957: Albert Schweitzer (narrator); 1959: Middle of the Night; 1960: Inherit the Wind; 1961: The Young Doctors; 1963: The Condemned of Altona; 1964: Seven Days in May; 1967: Hombre; 1970: …tick…tick…tick…; 1973: The Iceman Cometh.

NY Stage: 1920: Deburau; 1921: Lei Aloha; 1922: The Lawbreaker; 1924: The Melody Man; 1925: Puppets; Harvest; 1926: The Half-Caste; 1926: The Devil in the Cheese; 1938: Yr. Obedient Husband; 1939: The American Way; 1941: Hope for a Harvest; 1942: The Skin of Our Teeth; 1944: A Bell for Adano; 1946: Years Ago; 1950: Now I Lay Me Down to Sleep; An Enemy of the People; 1951: The Autumn Garden; 1956: Long Day's Journey Into Night; 1961: Gideon.

Select TV: 1950: The Boor (sp); 1951: The Speech (sp); 1952: Ferry Crisis at Friday Point (sp); 1953: The Last Night of Don Juan (sp); 1954: The Royal Family (sp); A Christmas Carol (sp); 1956: Dodsworth (sp); 1958: The Winslow Boy (sp); 1959: Hamlet (sp).

MARGO

(María Marguerita Guadalupe Teresa Estela Bolado y Castilla) Born: Mexico City, Mexico, May 10, 1917. Died: July 17, 1985.

Thanks to one film, the exotic Margo wound up becoming better remembered than one would have thought, judging from her limitations. A professional dancer, she performed with Xavier Cugat's band, helping to popularize the rumba when the group came to America in the early 1930s. In 1934 she debuted on Broadway in *Sunday Nights at Nine*, the same year she was first seen on the big screen, playing the mistress Claude Rains believes he has killed, in the colorfully overheated *Crime Without Passion*. Naturally she was called on to appear in *Rumba*, Paramount's cash-in on the dance craze, then repeated her stage part of the gangster's sister who falls for Burgess Meredith in *Winterset*, a

somewhat pretentious and murky piece that received a degree of acclaim in its day. Then came the role that made her a part of motion picture lore, Maria, the unhappy resident of Shangri-La, in director Frank Capra's classic fantasy *Lost Horizon*. In one of the film's most famous scenes, Margo leaves the mountain paradise only to rapidly age and die in the snow. After a long absence that took her back to Broadway, she was seen (top billed) as a striptease dancer who finds an abandoned baby on Christmas Eve in Columbia's melodrama *Miracle on Main Street*. She also appeared in one of the lesser Val Lewton thrillers, *The Leopard Man*, and in the surprisingly popular wartime potboiler *Behind the Rising Sun*, wearing unconvincing Asian makeup to play a secretary who realizes that the man she loves has become a psychotic bent on world destruction, in this Japan-bashing propaganda piece that can only be taken as something of a joke by modern audiences. In 1945 she married actor Eddie Albert, and this resulted in one of Hollywood's most enduring marriages (lasting until her death in 1985). She was seen very little after their nuptials, showing up in the Oscar-winning *Viva Zapata!*, and making two appearances with Albert, in *I'll Cry Tomorrow* and *Where's the Action?* Her son is actor Edward Albert.

Screen: 1934: Crime Without Passion; 1935: Rumba; 1936: The Robin Hood of El Dorado; Winterset; 1937: Lost Horizon; 1940: Miracle on Main Street; 1943: The Leopard Man; Behind the Rising Sun; Gangway for Tomorrow; 1952: Viva Zapata!; 1955: I'll Cry Tomorrow; 1958: From Hell to Texas; 1962: Who's Got the Action?

NY Stage: 1934: Sunday Nights at Nine; 1935: Winterset; 1937: The Masque of Kings; 1938: Faust; 1939: The World We Make; 1941: Taynard Street; 1944: A Bell for Adano; 1950: ANTA Album.

Select TV: 1952: Enchanted Evening (sp); 1958: The Night the Phone Rang (sp); So Tender, So Profane (sp).

HUGH MARLOWE

(Hugh Herbert Hipple) Born: Philadelphia, PA, January 30, 1911. Died: May 2, 1982.

Usually called on to embody rationality and stoic uptightness, Hugh Marlowe had started his career as a radio announcer before turning to stage acting, receiving his training at the Pasadena Community Playhouse. In 1936 he made his motion picture debut, carrying a Pete Smith Specialty, "The Junior Diamond," then made two features for MGM, *Married Before Breakfast*, in a significant supporting part, as Florence Rice's fiancé, and, less importantly, *Between Two Women*, as a priest. With that he returned to the stage, appearing in such plays as *Kiss the Boys Goodbye* and *Lady in the Dark*. Because of the last he found himself back at Metro for a handful of supporting roles, including *Meet Me in St. Louis*, where he was seen, ever so briefly, dropping Lucille Bremer off from a date. Again, having gotten nowhere as a screen star, he hightailed it east, joining the Chicago company of *The Voice of the Turtle*, before making it back to New York, where he did three flops in a row, including an adaptation of *Laura*, in the Dana Andrews role. (His second wife, K.T. Stevens, to whom he was married from 1946 to 1968, was also in the cast.) In 1949 20th Century-Fox decided to sign him to a contract and at last Marlowe found himself being given some decent roles. He started off most impressively, as the New Englander who clashes with a pair of nuns in the charming *Come to the Stable*; played one of the Colonels under Gregory Peck's shaky command in the prestigious war film *Twelve O'Clock High*; and then had his best part, as Celeste Holm's playwright husband, in

All About Eve, although as perhaps the sanest character in that colorful bunch of theater types, his performance is probably the least remarked upon. Continuing at Fox, he was Patricia Neal's stiff boyfriend in the outstanding sci-fi offering *The Day the Earth Stood Still*; terrorized Susan Hayward in the western *Rawhide*; was given a Mohawk haircut by Cary Grant in *Monkey Business*; stole Jean Peters away from David Wayne in *Wait Till the Sun Shines, Nellie*; and was back with Hayward, as her viciously ungrateful husband, in *Garden of Evil*, in which he was trapped in a gold mine. Receiving top billing, he was the star of the sci-fi cheapie *Earth vs. the Flying Saucers*, and the reluctant hero of the "B" western *The Black Whip*. In later years he joined the cast of the daytime serial *Another World*, playing family patriarch Jim Matthews right up to his death.

Screen: 1937: Married Before Breakfast; Between Two Women; 1944: Marriage Is a Private Affair; Mrs. Parkington; Meet Me in St. Louis; 1949: Come to the Stable; Twelve O'Clock High; 1950: All About Eve; Night and the City; 1951: The Day the Earth Stood Still; Rawhide; Mr. Belvedere Rings the Bell; 1952: Monkey Business; Wait Till the Sun Shines, Nellie; Way of a Gaucho; Diplomatic Courier (narrator); Bugles in the Afternoon; 1953: The Stand at Apache River; 1954: Casanova's Big Night; Garden of Evil; 1955: Illegal; 1956: World Without End; Earth vs. the Flying Saucers; The Black Whip; 1960: Elmer Gantry; 1961: The Long Rope; 1962: Birdman of Alcatraz; Panic in Year Zero! (voice); 1963: 13 Frightened Girls; 1964: Seven Days in May; 1966: Castle of Evil; 1968: How to Steal the World (from TV); 1969: The Last Shot You Hear.

NY Stage: 1936: Arrest That Woman; 1938: Kiss the Boys Goodbye; 1940: Young Couple Wanted; 1941: The Land Is Bright; 1943: Lady in the Dark; 1947: It Takes Two; Laura; Duet for Two Hands; 1967: Deer Park (ob); Postcards (ob); 1968: Woman Is My Idea; 1974: All My Sons (ob).

Select TV: 1954: The Adventures of Ellery Queen (series); Her Kind of Honor (sp); 1955: Cross My Heart (sp); The Crime of Daphne Rutledge (sp); 1957: Who Is Picasso? (sp); 1958: Balance of Terror (sp); Bluebeard's Seventh Wife (sp); The 65th Floor (sp); 1963: The Third Side of the Coin (sp); 1970–82: Another World (series).

ALAN MARSHAL
Born: Sydney, Australia, January 20, 1909.
Died: July 9, 1961.

Suave second-lead Alan Marshal had the requisite dapper manner and moustache but still came off as something of a poor man's Ronald Colman, or perhaps a cut-rate David Niven. After a period with Fritz Leiber's Shakespearean Players, he came to New York where his work in *The Bishop Misbehaves* led to a contract with producer David O. Selznick. He was cast as a captain in the Technicolor saga *The Garden of Allah*, then went to MGM to play the murder victim in *After the Thin Man*. Staying there he did captain duty again in both *Conquest* and *Parnell*, looking so right in a uniform, no matter what the period. He was upped to top billing at RKO for *Invisible Enemy*, a cheapie that cast him as a playboy who dabbles in espionage. Since there was no great demand for Alan Marshal vehicles, however, he gladly went back to support for *The Adventures of Sherlock Holmes*, as Ida Lupino's fiancé; *The Hunchback of Notre Dame*, as Phoebus, the soldier killed by the jealous Cedric Hardwicke; and *Irene*, as the rich suitor whom Anna Neagle had no intention of ending up with as long as Ray Milland's billing was higher. As Dick, he was the least interesting of Ginger Rogers's three suitors

in the poor-but-popular *Tom, Dick and Harry*, while in *Lydia*, he was the man Merle Oberon foolishly waited to marry, ending up a spinster. Although he was cast as Irene Dunne's husband in one of the big hits of the war years, *The White Cliffs of Dover*, it was all her show, Marshal being disposed of early on in the story. It also happened to be the last film Marshal would make for 12 years, returning to play one of the superfluous males in *The Opposite Sex*. There were only two other film roles, playing the lover of Vincent Price's scheming wife in *House on Haunted Hill*, and the rancher whose much younger spouse, Tina Louise, is fooling around with Robert Ryan in *Day of the Outlaw*. He was performing in a Chicago revival of *Sextette*, opposite its author, Mae West, when he suffered a fatal heart attack.

Screen: 1936: The Garden of Allah; After the Thin Man; 1937: Night Must Fall; Conquest; Parnell; 1938: The Road to Reno; I Met My Love Again; Invisible Enemy; Dramatic School; 1939: The Adventures of Sherlock Holmes; Four Girls in White; Exile Express; The Hunchback of Notre Dame; 1940: Married and in Love; He Stayed for Breakfast; The Howards of Virginia; Irene; 1941: Lydia; Tom, Dick and Harry; 1944: Bride by Mistake; The White Cliffs of Dover; 1956: The Opposite Sex; 1959: House on Haunted Hill; Day of the Outlaw.

NY Stage: 1933: Foolscap; Going Gay; 1934: While Parents Sleep; Lady Jane; 1935: The Bishop Misbehaves; On Stage.

E.G. MARSHALL
Born: Owatonna, MN, June 18, 1910.
Ed: Univ. of MN. Died: August 24, 1998.

A character actor who never set out to steal center stage but proved a durable talent on the big and small screen through his mild-mannered, sensible presence, E.G. (he was adamant about keeping secret just what the initials stood for) Marshall started his stage career in 1933, five years before he made it to Broadway. Following WWII, Hollywood called on him for three of its docudramas of the period, *The House on 92nd Street* (as a morgue attendant), *13 Rue Madeleine*, and *Call Northside 777*. But he didn't really become a familiar figure until the 1950s when he played the lieutenant commander in *The Caine Mutiny*; a cop in *Pushover*; the governor in *Broken Lance*; the mild-mannered Juror Number Four in the classic *12 Angry Men*; the nervous bookkeeper in *The Bachelor Party*; and the prosecuting attorney trying to put Bradford Dillman and Dean Stockwell to death in *Compulsion*. Staying in the legal profession, he found small-screen stardom, winning a pair of Emmy Awards, playing veteran attorney Lawrence Preston on *The Defenders*, one of the most critically lauded drama series of the 1960s. In later years he returned to the movies, where he was seen as the frustrated husband who dumps Geraldine Page to start life anew in *Interiors*; the President of the United States who finds himself overpowered by aliens in *Superman II*; a cleanliness freak besieged by cockroaches in *Creepshow*; John Mitchell in *Nixon*; and the D.C. powerbroker whose wife is killed by Gene Hackman in *Absolute Power*.

Screen: 1945: The House on 92nd Street; 1946: 13 Rue Madeleine; 1947: Untamed Fury; Call Northside 777; 1952: Diplomatic Courier; 1954: Pushover; Broken Lance; The Bamboo Prison; The Caine Mutiny; The Silver Chalice; 1955: The Left Hand of God; 1956: The Scarlet Hour; The Mountain; 1957: 12 Angry Men; The Bachelor Party; Man of Fire; 1958: The Buccaneer; 1959: The Journey; Compulsion; Cash McCall; 1961: Town Without Pity; 1966: The Chase; 1969: The Bridge at Remagen; 1970: Tora! Tora! Tora!; 1971: The Pursuit of

Happiness; **1977:** Billy Jack Goes to Washington; **1978:** Interiors; **1981:** Superman II; **1982:** Creepshow; **1986:** My Chauffeur; Power; **1987:** La Gran Fiesta; **1989:** National Lampoon's Christmas Vacation; **1990:** Two Evil Eyes (The Black Cat); **1992:** Consenting Adults; **1993:** Russian Roulette (dtv); **1995:** Nixon; **1997:** Absolute Power.

NY Stage: **1938:** Prologue to Glory; The Big Blow; **1942:** Jason; The Skin of Our Teeth; The Petrified Forest (ob); **1944:** Jacobowsky and the Colonel; **1945:** Beggars Are Coming to Town; **1946:** Woman Bites Dog; The Iceman Cometh; **1948:** The Survivors; **1952:** The Gambler; **1953:** The Crucible; **1955:** Red Roses for Me; **1956:** Queen After Death; Waiting for Godot; **1959:** The Gang's All Here; **1967:** The Little Foxes; **1969:** Plaza Suite; **1973:** Nash at Nine; **1977:** The Gin Game; **1980:** John Gabriel Borkman; **1984:** Mass Appeal (ob); She Stoops to Conquer (ob).

Select TV: **1950:** The Dark Tower (sp); Kelly (sp); Mr. Mummery's Suspicion (sp); Valley Forge (sp); Macbeth (sp); My Granny Van (sp); The Touch of a Stranger (sp); Rip Van Winkle (sp); **1951:** The Great Escape (sp); Let Them Be Sea Captains (sp); Adventures of Hiram Holiday (sp); By-Line for Murder (sp); **1952:** Without Fear or Favor (sp); The Rugged Path (sp); The Monument (sp); The Vase (sp); Mr. Lazarus (sp); **1953:** The Oil Well (sp); Nemesis (sp); **1954:** Old Tosselfoot (sp); Middle of the Night (sp); Flight Report (sp); Yesterday's Magic (sp); **1955:** Yellow Jack (sp); Thunder in the House (sp); Donovan's Brain (sp); O Lonely Moon (sp); The Ox-Bow Incident (sp); **1956:** The Terrorists (sp); Keyhole (sp); O'Hoolihan and the Leprechaun (sp); The Little Foxes (sp); **1957:** The Duel (sp); The Out-of-Towners (sp); Clash by Night (sp); **1958:** Presence of the Enemy (sp); The Plot to Kill Stalin (sp); **1959:** A Quiet Game of Cards (sp); Man in Orbit (sp); Made in Japan (sp); The Indestructible Mr. Gore (sp); The Cherry Orchard (sp); **1960:** The Master Builder (sp); **1961:** The Night of the Storm (sp); **1961–65:** The Defenders (series); **1966:** The Poppy Is Also a Flower (also released theatrically); **1968:** A Case of Libel (sp); **1969:** This Town Will Never Be the Same (sp); The Littlest Angel (sp); **1969–73:** The Bold Ones: The New Doctors (series); **1970:** A Clear and Present Danger; **1971:** Vanished; The City; Ellery Queen: Don't Look Behind You; **1972:** Look Homeward Angel (sp); Pursuit; **1973:** Money to Burn; **1975:** The Abduction of Saint Anne; **1979:** Vampire; Disaster on the Coastliner; **1981:** The Phoenix; The Gangster Chronicles (series narrator); **1982:** Eleanor: First Lady of the World; **1983:** Kennedy (ms); Saigon: Year of the Cat; John Steinbeck's The Winter of Our Discontent; **1986:** Under Siege; **1987:** At Mother's Request; **1988:** Emma — Queen of the South Seas; **1989:** The Hijacking of the Achille Lauro; **1991:** Ironclads; **1993:** Stephen King's The Tommyknockers; **1994:** Oldest Living Confederate Widow Tells All; **1994–95:** Chicago Hope (series); **1997:** Miss Evers' Boys; The Defenders: Payback; **1998:** The Defenders: Choice of Evils.

HERBERT MARSHALL

BORN: LONDON, ENGLAND, MAY 23, 1890.
DIED: JANUARY 22, 1966.

Dry was the word for Herbert Marshall who possessed a certain world-weary elegance, his sleepy eyes and voice suggesting a trace of boredom with it all. He was best at playing unscrupulous men and cads, which meant it was very hard to warm up to him when he was supposed to be the hero. He went from theatrical business manager to acting, debuting in Brighton in 1911 and in London two years later. An injury during World War I caused his right leg to be amputated, a fact not well known to many moviegoers because it was hardly noticeable on screen, as long as he wasn't asked to do anything too physical. Returning to the stage, he became prominent enough to travel to America to appear in some Broadway plays, including These Charming People, in 1925. In England he did two silent films before he was asked by Paramount to journey overseas again, for the 1929 version of The Letter, as the lover who is pumped full of bullets. He didn't choose to stay in the U.S., returning to his home for Hitchcock's talkie debut, Murder, and a few others before Paramount coaxed him back again, for Secrets of a Secretary, as an English lord who falls in love with Claudette Colbert while engaged to her sister, and Blonde Venus, as Marlene Dietrich's drab chemist husband. These were followed by his best leading role on film — the raffish jewel thief dallying with both Miriam Hopkins and Kay Francis in Trouble in Paradise. Indeed it was a miracle that these three performers, who were not exactly peerless when it came to sparkling comedy, came off so appealingly, no doubt thanks to Ernst Lubitsch's impeccable direction. Now greatly in demand, Marshall was stuck in the jungle in DeMille's last flop before his long run of hits, Four Frightened People; went to MGM for Norma Shearer's Riptide, losing her to Robert Montgomery; and stayed there for one of the lesser Garbo vehicles, The Painted Veil, in a role not unlike the one he'd done with Dietrich, neglecting her for his scientific studies while she fooled around with another (George Brent).

For Universal he was in another bright comedy, The Good Fairy, as the stodgy, bearded professor loosened up by Margaret Sullivan, while back at Paramount he was a playwright loved by secretary Sylvia Sidney in Accent on Youth, and then suffered with starchy nobility while he lost Merle Oberon to blinded Fredric March in Goldwyn's The Dark Angel. He was certainly more enjoyable in the lighthearted surroundings of If You Could Only Cook, as a millionaire slumming as a butler, and in Mad About Music, pretending to be Deanna Durbin's dad, then he was in two properties that should have dwelt more on laughs: Zaza, where he was Colbert's admirer, and the deadly Angel, at his stuffiest, once again playing Dietrich's distracted husband. When it came time to remake The Letter, he went from playing the lover to the husband, though this piece was already starting to show its age. The same director (William Wyler) and leading lady (Bette Davis) teamed with him again for a much better property, The Little Foxes, in which he gave one of his best dramatic performances, as her sickly-but-determined husband. In between the Davis films he was a man you couldn't help but distrust, running a pacifist organization, in another for Hitchcock, Foreign Correspondent.

There was the blatantly uncommercial film of The Moon and Sixpence, with Marshall pretty much playing the author, Somerset Maugham, a part he did for real in 1946's The Razor's Edge, which, in contrast, turned out to be one of the big hits of the decade. He went from kindly and blind in The Enchanted Cottage to nasty in The Unseen; was preyed on for his fortune by wicked Joan Fontaine in Ivy, then was at his least sympathetic, playing the cold-hearted uncle in the 1949 version of The Secret Garden. By the early 1950s his involvement with top-of-the-line product was becoming a thing of the past as he ended up in the "B" crime drama The Underworld Story/The Whipped, as a tycoon whose daughter-in-law is murdered; some pulpy pirate adventures, Captain Black Jack and Anne of the Indies; Universal's first excursion into CinemaScope, The Black Shield of Falworth, the sort of costume picture he never seemed relaxed in; and a batch of sci-fi movies, Riders to the Stars, Gog, and his biggest hit in some time, The Fly, which he nevertheless spoke of with derision. The remainder of his career was spent in support, with Marshall not showing a great deal of interest in the material but no doubt asked to participate because the movies were either set or filmed in England. These included *Midnight Lace*, as Rex Harrison's business partner; *Five Weeks in a Balloon*, as the Prime Minister; *The List of Adrian Messenger*, in which he was an investigator; and *The Third Day*, where he played a sick man, looking ever bit as ill and tired himself in what turned out to be his final role. Among his wives (1929–40) was actress Edna Best. Their daughter, Sarah Marshall, also became an actress.

Screen: 1927: Mumsie; Dawn; 1929: The Letter; 1930: Murder; 1931: The Calendar/Bachelor's Folly; Michael and Mary; Secrets of a Secretary; 1932: The Faithful Heart; Blonde Venus; Trouble in Paradise; Evenings for Sale; 1933: The Solitaire Man; I Was a Spy; 1934: Four Frightened People; Riptide; Outcast Lady; The Painted Veil; 1935: The Good Fairy; The Flame Within; Accent on Youth; If You Could Only Cook; The Dark Angel; 1936: The Lady Consents; Till We Meet Again; Forgotten Faces; Girls' Dormitory; A Woman Rebels; Make Way for a Lady; 1937: Angel; Breakfast for Two; 1938: Mad About Music; Always Goodbye; Woman Against Woman; 1939: Zaza; 1940: The Letter; A Bill of Divorcement; Foreign Correspondent; 1941: Adventure in Washington; The Little Foxes; When Ladies Meet; Kathleen; 1942: The Moon and Sixpence; 1943: Flight for Freedom; Forever and a Day; Young Ideas; 1944: Andy Hardy's Blonde Trouble; 1945: The Enchanted Cottage; The Unseen; 1946: The Razor's Edge; Crack-Up; Duel in the Sun; 1947: Ivy; High Wall; 1949: The Secret Garden; 1950: The Underworld Story/The Whipped; Captain Blackjack; 1951: Anne of the Indies; 1952: Angel Face; 1954: Riders to the Stars; Gog; The Black Shield of Falworth; 1955: The Virgin Queen; 1956: Wicked as They Come; 1957: The Weapon; 1958: Stage Struck; The Fly; 1960: College Confidential; Midnight Lace; 1961: A Fever in the Blood; 1962: Five Weeks in a Balloon; 1963: The List of Adrian Messenger; The Caretakers; 1965: The Third Day.

NY Stage: 1922: The Voice From the Minaret; Fedora; 1925: These Charming People; 1928: The High Road; 1931: Tomorrow and Tomorrow; 1932: There's Always Juliet.

Select TV: 1950: Municipal Report (sp); 1951: An Inspector Calls (sp); 1952: The Unexpected (series); 1954: The Philadelphia Story (sp); 1955: The Browning Version (sp); 1956: Now, Voyager (sp); 1957: The Mystery of 13 (sp); 1958: Balance of Terror (sp).

DEAN MARTIN

(DINO PAUL CROCETTI) BORN: STEUBENVILLE, OH, JUNE 7, 1917. DIED: DECEMBER 25, 1995.

Because he seemed so lackadaisical about taking the whole show business thing too seriously, Dean Martin's value as an actor hasn't been given much deep consideration. By playing up the image of the smarmy crooner with too much booze in his system and a roving eye for fast ladies, he seemed to be thumbing his nose at those pretentious enough to believe that Hollywood wasn't supposed to be fun. It was exactly this jokey attitude that made audiences love him and value his sly sense of humor, which was put to good effect once he got Jerry Lewis out of the way. As a young man he had few aspirations beyond finding a place to sing, and this took him into the nightclub circuit, where he eventually met up with Lewis. They did some impromptu performances together and found that they clicked; the handsome, flip Italian crooner trading barbs with the scrawny, annoying man-child. In a short period of time they became all the rage and their no-holds-barred stage show the hottest ticket in town. Hal Wallis (who released through

Paramount) signed the team to a contract in 1949 and put them into the supporting cast of *My Friend Irma*, based on the popular radio show. It was clear that Martin and Lewis were the main reason for the hefty attendance figures, and a sequel, *My Friend Irma Goes West*, was immediately ordered. *At War With the Army*, made on the cheap for their studio but not for Wallis, was their first starring vehicle, and it firmly established them as box-office attractions. They were put into the sort of mildly amusing, paint-by-numbers comedies that many comedians before them had been making for years. The problem was that, despite Martin's top billing, these movies seemed to give Lewis the lion's share of the attention, with Dean shunted into the background, enacting disapproval towards his younger partner's childish antics and singing an occasional tune. If there was any consolation, he was at least finding solo success as a recording star, scoring a major hit with a number he introduced in *The Caddy*, "That's Amore," that would become one of his signature tunes.

As far as the scripts were concerned, he certainly couldn't have been too thrilled by *The Stooge*, a fairly bitter concoction in which he was an egotistical performer whose act thrives when Lewis joins him and goes down the tubes when they split. The suggestion that Martin was nothing without Lewis irked the performer, who was similarly disenchanted with his sidekick's hands-on approach to filmmaking. Martin was already becoming known as one of the most easy-going and easy-to-get-along-with people in the business, preferring a game of golf to any serious discussions about his work. The cash kept flowing in through a total of 16 Martin and Lewis movies released in a seven-year period, ending with *Hollywood or Bust* in 1956, by which time the duo had split, with Martin showing little concern or care about the demise of the act.

There should have been some concern, however, after his first solo venture, *Ten Thousand Bedrooms*, a musical with postcard glimpses of Rome and absolutely nothing else, turned out to be a major stinker. Wisely, he decided it wasn't necessary to carry the load and jumped at the chance to join the cast of *The Young Lions*, much to the horror of Montgomery Clift, who later relented since Martin's performance, as a Broadway performer who tries to avoid the draft out of sheer cowardice, turned out to be quite decent. The next film, *Some Came Running*, cast him as the lazy gambling pal of Frank Sinatra, and it showed a witty, light touch to his acting that had been pretty much ignored during the Lewis years. There was a third hit with *Rio Bravo*, with Martin impressively playing a drunk who is helped by John Wayne, in a fine western that continues to be hailed as one of the best of its era. He went back to support for *Who Was That Lady?*, stealing the show as Tony Curtis's cheeky pal, then solidified his membership with Sinatra's so-called "Rat Pack" by his involvement in the heist film *Ocean's Eleven*, which at least gave him a snappy song, "Ain't That a Kick in the Head?" By this point the Rat Pack was becoming one of the main attractions of the thriving Las Vegas nightclub scene, and Martin, along with Sinatra and Sammy Davis, Jr., ruled that town during the 1960s.

Making his second official musical since the Lewis split, he wound up in a winner, *Bells Are Ringing*, proving a pleasant leading man to the wonderful Judy Holliday, whose showcase it really was. There were some more Rat Pack movies: *Pepe*, making a cameo appearance along with his other cronies but inexplicably being treated like a surprise guest star and thereby receiving no billing; *Sergeant's 3*, which was a remake of *Gunga Din*, in cavalry uniforms; a lifeless western, *4 for Texas*; and best of the bunch, the musical *Robin and the 7 Hoods*, which included a sprightly number called "Style" with a trio consisting of Martin, Sinatra, and Bing Crosby. It was a pleasure to see Martin riff off of

Sinatra, even if the material never reached the heights one wished it would. Outside of the Sinatra fold there were lightweight comedies like *Who's Got the Action?*, which involved gambling, and the similarly titled *Who's Been Sleeping in My Bed?*, which involved television soap operas, as well as less-than-successful forays into drama with *Ada*, in which he made for a none-too-convincing gubernatorial candidate, and *Toys in the Attic*, with Martin oddly cast as the brother of Wendy Hiller and Geraldine Page, and taking a back seat to both. Most interesting of all was director Billy Wilder's brazen *Kiss Me, Stupid*, in which Martin was cast as a sex-crazed entertainer named Dino. Despite the hostile condemnation and outcry from the Legion of Decency that the movie received upon release in 1964, it has probably held up better than most of his films of that era, with Martin showing himself the ultimate good sport by allowing his onstage persona to be examined in so unflattering a light.

Returning to John Wayne and westerns, he scored as one of *The Sons of Katie Elder*, at one point sharing the screen with Dennis Hopper, a performer who couldn't be more contrary to the sort of show business Martin represented. A final one with Sinatra, *Marriage on the Rocks*, really got razzed by the press, marking the end of the Rat Pack gatherings, at least on the big screen. In 1965, while still in demand for movie work, Martin decided to accept a lucrative offer from NBC to do a weekly TV variety series, demanding as little rehearsal time as possible and letting home audiences experience a somewhat cleaner version of his laid-back nightclub act. *The Dean Martin Show* was denounced by critics as crass and unprofessional, but the viewers just loved it, and it made the singer that much bigger a star for the nine seasons it ran. Back in the movies he brought his leering style to a series of purposefully silly spy capers, playing bed-hopping secret agent Matt Helm, in *The Silencers* and *Murderers' Row*, both of which scored nicely at the box office, and *The Ambushers* and *The Wrecking Crew*, which performed less well, the quality of these pictures falling very quickly. Being a big fan of westerns, he kept at this genre with the lightweight *Texas Across the River*; the violent *Rough Night in Jericho*, in which he was cast against type as the villain; *5 Card Stud*, where he was a gambler battling shady preacher Robert Mitchum; and *Bandolero!*, in which he and James Stewart were unlikely outlaw brothers. He ended up in his greatest motion picture success ever when he was cast as the pilot in the all-star disaster epic *Airport*, one of the highest grossing films released up to that time, as well as an Oscar nominee for Best Picture.

Despite this high point it looked pretty certain that his movie career was coming to an end, the emergence of a more raw and real cinematic tone and approach to acting at odds with a performer whose "method" was no method at all. Some barely noticed westerns came and went; then he switched to the crime genre with *Mr. Ricco*, but his growing disinterest in putting too much effort into filmmaking was no longer compensated for by the box-office returns. He was content to swing his golf clubs and make a fortune crooning in Las Vegas, where he still continued to draw crowds well into the 1980s. There were occasional half-hearted TV specials and a surprise on-air reunion with Lewis on the latter's muscular dystrophy telethon in 1976, though a real reconciliation between the former partners had to wait another decade. Along with Sammy Davis, Jr. he returned to movies in a nonsensical supporting role, as a bogus priest, in the Burt Reynolds auto-race comedy, *The Cannonball Run*, which hoped to capture the spirit of the Rat Pack but didn't. Following the death of his son in a plane crash, Martin found performing less fulfilling and even backed out of a tour Sinatra and Davis had lined up with him. His final years were spent almost in seclusion,

while the revival of his recording of "That's Amore," via the film *Moonstruck*, reminded the customers of just what attracted them to his casual, devil-may-care style for years.

Screen: 1949: My Friend Irma; 1950: My Friend Irma Goes West; At War With the Army; 1951: That's My Boy; Sailor Beware; 1952: Jumping Jacks; Road to Bali; 1953: The Stooge; Scared Stiff; The Caddy; Money From Home; 1954: Living It Up; 3 Ring Circus; 1955: You're Never Too Young; Artists and Models; 1956: Pardners; Hollywood or Bust; 1957: Ten Thousand Bedrooms; 1958: The Young Lions; Some Came Running; 1959: Rio Bravo; Career; 1960: Who Was That Lady?; Bells Are Ringing; Ocean's Eleven; Pepe; 1961: All in a Night's Work; Ada; 1962: Sergeants 3; The Road to Hong Kong; Who's Got the Action?; 1963: Come Blow Your Horn; Toys in the Attic; Who's Been Sleeping in My Bed?; 4 for Texas; 1964: What a Way to Go!; Robin and the 7 Hoods; Kiss Me, Stupid; 1965: The Sons of Katie Elder; Marriage on the Rocks; 1966: The Silencers; Texas Across the River; Murderers' Row; 1967: Rough Night in Jericho; 1968: The Ambushers; Bandolero!; How to Save a Marriage (And Ruin Your Life); 5 Card Stud; 1969: The Wrecking Crew; 1970: Airport; 1971: Something Big; 1973: Showdown; 1975: Mr. Ricco; 1981: The Cannonball Run; 1984: Cannonball Run II.

Select TV: 1950–55: The Colgate Comedy Hour (series); 1957: The Dean Martin Show (sp); 1958: The Dean Martin Show (sp); 1959: The Dean Martin Show (sp); 1960: The Dean Martin Show (sp); 1965–74: The Dean Martin Show/The Dean Martin Comedy Hour (series); 1975: A Lucille Ball Special Starring Lucille Ball and Dean Martin (sp); Dean Martin's California Christmas (sp); 1976: Dean Martin's Red Hot Scandals of 1926 (sp); 1980: The Dean Martin Christmas Special (sp); 1981: Dean Martin's Christmas at Sea World (sp); 1983: Dean Martin in London (sp); 1985: Half-Nelson (series).

MARY MARTIN

BORN: WEATHERFORD, TX, DECEMBER 1, 1913.
DIED: NOVEMBER 3, 1990.

Hollywood really dropped the ball when it came to making Mary Martin one of its own. Here was a lady with a lovely singing voice, a warm personality, and talent to spare, who ended up in only a handful of films, making a lasting mark on the Broadway stage instead. Originally a dance instructor, she toured with her group, the Martinettes, without much success, so she went solo to try her luck in Hollywood. There she was hired to teach star Danielle Darrieux some dance steps for the film *The Rage of Paris*, and supposedly ended up with a bit in the film. Already becoming known for her singing voice, she dubbed the vocals of Margaret Sullavan on "Pack Up Your Troubles" in *The Shopworn Angel*, and Louise Hovick (Gypsy Rose Lee) on "Daughter of Mademoiselle" in *Battle of Broadway*, though there was no credit on either. There were some singing engagements that took her to New York and finally Broadway, where she brought down the house with her inimitable rendition of Cole Porter's "My Heart Belongs to Daddy" in *Leave It to Me*.

Because of this, Paramount signed her to a contract and made her Alan Jones's wife in the 1939 biopic *The Great Victor Herbert*. Much more satisfying was *Rhythm on the River*, where she proved to be just about the best screen partner (Bob Hope aside) that Bing Crosby ever had. They were reunited for *Birth of the Blues*, while in between she was seen with Jack Benny and Fred Allen in *Love Thy Neighbor*, and in the Scarlet O'Hara spoof, *Kiss the Boys Goodbye*. In light of the Crosby teamings, Paramount decided to try her alongside another crooner, Dick Powell, in

Star Spangled Rhythm, Happy Go Lucky, and *True to Life*, but despite this pleasant union, she and the studio were growing increasingly dissatisfied, and she went back East. There she became one of the legendary ladies of the musical theater, via her triumphs in *One Touch of Venus, South Pacific, Peter Pan*, and *The Sound of Music*, winning Tony Awards for the last three. Her son is actor Larry Hagman. In 1976 she published her autobiography, *My Heart Belongs*.

Screen: 1938: Battle of Broadway (voice); The Rage of Paris; The Shopworn Angel (voice); 1939: The Great Victor Herbert; 1940: Rhythm on the River; Love Thy Neighbor; 1941: Kiss the Boys Goodbye; Birth of the Blues; New York Town; 1942: Star Spangled Rhythm; 1943: Happy Go Lucky; True to Life; 1946: Night and Day; 1953: Main Street to Broadway.

NY Stage: 1938: Leave It to Me; 1943: One Touch of Venus; 1946: Lute Song; 1949: South Pacific; 1953: Kind Sir; 1954: Peter Pan; 1955: The Skin of Our Teeth; 1959: The Sound of Music; 1963: Jennie; 1966: I Do! I Do!; 1978: Do You Turn Somersaults?

Select TV: 1953: Ford Special (sp); 1955: Peter Pan (sp; and 1956, 1960); The Skin of Our Teeth (sp); 1956: Born Yesterday (sp); 1957: Annie Get Your Gun (sp); 1979: Valentine.

TONY MARTIN

(Alvin Morris) Born: San Francisco, CA, December 25, 1912. ed: St. Mary's Col.

Slick-haired vocalist Tony Martin had the type of sturdy-but-bland singing style that kept him employed in Hollywood musicals for a surprisingly lengthy period of time. A combination saxophonist and band vocalist, he came to movies in 1936, where he was seen as one of the sailors in *Follow the Fleet*. Then he went to Fox for a fairly substantial supporting role in a Jones Family comedy, *Back to Nature*, and popped up in the musicals *Pigskin Parade* and *Sing, Baby, Sing*, warbling "When Did You Leave Heaven?" in the latter and marrying (1937–40) the leading lady, Alice Faye. He was given his own vehicle with *Sing and Be Happy*, but wasn't colorful enough to carry the load, faring better with Faye on hand in both *You Can't Have Everything* and *Sally, Irene and Mary*; or playing straight man to Eddie Cantor in *Ali Baba Goes to Town*, and to the Ritz Brothers in both *Life Begins in College* and *Kentucky Moonshine*. There was an effort to toughen up his image with the prizefighting drama *Winner Take All*, but the studio dropped him afterwards. For MGM he sang "You Stepped Out of a Dream" in the top-heavy *Ziegfeld Girl*, and proved to be just about the dullest leading man ever dumped on the Marx Brothers, in *The Big Store*. In the late 1940s he got to play Pepe Le Moko, proving no threat to Charles Boyer, in the musical version of *Algiers*, now called *Casbah*. In 1948 he married Cyd Charisse, and that union would become one of Hollywood's most enduring marriages. He was called on to lend his increasingly stiff and unfashionable style of singing to MGM's *Easy to Love, Deep in My Heart* (singing "Lover Come Back to Me"), and *Hit the Deck*, before turning his attention to performing in nightclubs with his wife. In 1976 they penned a joint memoir, *The Two of Us*.

Screen: 1936: Follow the Fleet; Murder on the Bridle Path; The Farmer in the Dell; Sing, Baby, Sing; Back to Nature; Pigskin Parade; Poor Little Rich Girl; Banjo on My Knee; 1937: The Holy Terror; Sing and Be Happy; You Can't Have Everything; Life Begins in College; Ali Baba Goes to Town; 1938: Sally, Irene and Mary; Kentucky Moonshine; Thanks for Everything; Up the River; 1939: Winner Take All; 1940: Music in My Heart; 1941: Ziegfeld Girl; The Big Store; 1946: Till the Clouds Roll By; 1948:

Casbah; 1951: Two Tickets to Broadway; 1953: Easy to Love; Here Come the Girls; 1954: Deep in My Heart; 1955: Hit the Deck; 1956: Quincannon: Frontier Scout; 1957: Let's Be Happy; 1982: Dear Mr. Wonderful/Ruby's Dream (dtv).

Select TV: 1954–56: The Tony Martin Show (series).

LEE MARVIN

Born: New York, NY, February 19, 1924.
Died: August 29, 1987.

A splendid screen villain who later had a chance to prove himself an equally engaging star, lean, deep-voiced Lee Marvin had a cool, mocking air about him that made him ideal for both menace and heroism. A former Marine, he studied at the American Theater Wing under the G.I. Bill of Rights. In the late 1940s-early 1950s he was seen on both the New York stage and on television anthology programs. Around that same time he ended up in movies, including two directed by Henry Hathaway, *You're in the Navy Now/U.S.S. Teakettle*, as a member of Gary Cooper's crew, and *Diplomatic Courier*, as an MP. There was a bigger role, as one of the military ensemble in *Eight Iron Men*, but since the star was somebody by the name of Bonar Colleano, it wasn't exactly a front-rank item. He stayed either in military or western roles (or both, with *Seminole*, as a cavalry sergeant) until making a double breakthrough in 1953. First he essayed one of his most vicious roles, in the fine noir *The Big Heat*, where he entered the pantheon of all-time screen sadists when he tossed hot coffee in poor Gloria Grahame's face, and then added greatly to the revved-up motorcycle classic *The Wild One*, where he was the only other cast member able to draw some degree of attention away from Marlon Brando, playing the head of a rival gang of bikers who call themselves "the Beetles." There was another showy bad-guy part, teamed with Ernest Borgnine to give Spencer Tracy a hard time, in the spare and memorable *Bad Day at Black Rock*. This was followed by more creep and killer roles, in *A Life in the Balance*, as a religious nutcase murdering people he declares sinners; *Violent Saturday*, as a bank robber with a cold; and *I Died a Thousand Times*, doing henchman duty for criminal Jack Palance. Scattered among these were benign roles in *The Caine Mutiny*, as the ship's cook; *Not as a Stranger*, as Robert Mitchum's fellow medical student; and *Pete Kelly's Blues*, as a musician. He possessed the sort of charismatic scowl and suggestion of tension that made audiences look right past the leading man on occasion (say, Jack Webb, in the case of *Pete Kelly*) and focus on Marvin.

Shack Out on 101 found him cast as a beanery cook named Slob in a "B" movie that continued to find cult favor over the years, while he was handed some worthwhile material in *Attack*, where he was the butt-kissing colonel who refuses to notice what a detriment coward Eddie Albert is to his platoon. Marvin kept on proving his worth in things like *Raintree County*, giving one of this muddled epic's better performances, losing a footrace to Montgomery Clift and then becoming his friend over the course of the story. Next up he got star billing, after Brandon de Wilde, in *The Missouri Traveler*, as a stubborn landowner in this poorly done piece of rural nostalgia. Stardom came, as it often did to tough character actors, on the small screen, when he was cast as Lt. Frank Ballinger in the series *M Squad*, which settled in for a three-season run. When it was time to return to the big screen, it was in three John Wayne movies, his roles getting progressively larger. In *The Comancheros* he had a scene-stealing bit as a gun runner; in *The Man Who Shot Liberty Valance*, he excelled in another of his most famous nasty roles, as the bullying outlaw who torments James Stewart; and in *Donovan's Reef* he was treated almost as Wayne's equal, battling playfully with him in a pretty South Sea setting. The 1964 remake of *The Killers* finally gave him top billing, although this film was originally intended for television until deemed too violent, thereby getting some scattered theatrical bookings instead.

As part of the all-star ensemble he was a ballplayer who callously pawed at Vivien Leigh and got bonked with her shoe in *Ship of Fools*. Then the same year, he shot right to the top, playing a dual role in the hit comedy *Cat Ballou*. As Tim Strawn, the eerie villain with the steel nose, he was as effectively menacing as ever, but in the larger role of the eternally drunken, unkempt gunfighter Kid Shaleen, he revealed an unexpected comic side that was an absolute hoot to watch unfold. He won the Academy Award for Best Actor of 1965 and was, at long last, a bona fide movie star. His follow-up was a ripsnorting adventure, *The Professionals*, second billed to Burt Lancaster, with the two he-men portraying gunfighters hired to bring back kidnapped Claudia Cardinale from across the border. Next came one of the major action films of the decade, *The Dirty Dozen*, with Marvin as the nail-hard commander of a unit of misfits trained for a deadly mission against the Nazis. Because of its staggering success, he was now considered box-office material, though *Point Blank*, a violent and overbaked concoction in which he was a single-minded, emotionless gunman bent on revenge, was made for a more discriminate audience, and *Hell in the Pacific* was limited in its appeal by the very fact that Marvin and Toshiro Mifune were its only characters, nameless World War II adversaries on a deserted island. *Paint Your Wagon* gave him a role similar to his wiley drunk in *Cat Ballou*, only this time he got to sing, croaking his way through Lerner and Loewe's haunting "Wandrin' Star," among others. It did better business than the last two, although it was one of the costly musicals that were blamed for draining money away from the studios during the end of the 1960s. Another western, *Monte Walsh*, found him as a cowboy past his prime, and *Pocket Money* teamed him with Paul Newman with surprisingly lukewarm results.

Marvin kept his hard-assed persona going throughout the 1970s, but it was clear that he wasn't the guaranteed attraction producers had hoped for. He was a bad guy again, a mobster, in *Prime Cut*, only Gene Hackman's behavior was even worse, thereby making him the hero by default; and he wasn't exactly a commendable character in *The Spikes Gang* either, since his mission was to turn a group of teens into bank robbers. Marvin also found himself reunited with Ernest Borgnine in *The Emperor of the North Pole*, but this time they were stars and on-screen foes. As a break from all the action, he appeared in a film of Eugene O'Neill's *The Iceman Cometh*, meant for limited showings, in the part of Hickey, which everyone assumed Jason Robards would get to recreate on screen, though Marvin was certainly no slouch in this role. His bankability continued to decline through roles in the critically reviled racial melodrama *The Klansman*, as a Southern sheriff; the barely released *Shout at the Devil*, as a poacher waging war against the Germans during World War I; the minor western comedy *The Great Scout and Cathouse Thursday*; and a clichéd war film that nobody wanted to see, at least not in 1980, *The Big Red One*, this time as a commander of a squad of youthful soldiers. Indeed Marvin was better known to the public in the late 1970s for the lawsuit brought against him by his lady companion of six years, who hoped to get half of his earnings. The case was precedent setting, bringing the term "palimony" into the public consciousness. In any event his partner's claim was rejected, and she receive a small settlement. There was another insignificant actioner, *Death Hunt*, noticeable for teaming him with Charles Bronson, who had made his film

debut in the very same movie (*You're in the Navy Now*) that Marvin had. Marvin took a supporting villain role in *Gorky Park*, where he certainly showed up a very drab William Hurt as the hero, then wound up taking second billing to second-rate Chuck Norris in *The Delta Force*. Norris didn't seem to understand the lesson one could learn from Marvin, who proved that you could do a plethora of uninspired action films and still be one hell of a good actor.

Screen: 1951: U.S.S. Teakettle/You're in the Navy Now; Teresa; Hong Kong; 1952: Diplomatic Courier; We're Not Married!; The Duel at Silver Creek; Eight Iron Men; Hangman's Knot; 1953: Down Among the Sheltering Palms; Seminole; The Glory Brigade; The Stranger Wore a Gun; The Big Heat; Gun Fury; The Wild One; 1954: Gorilla at Large; The Caine Mutiny; The Raid; 1955: Bad Day at Black Rock; A Life in the Balance; Violent Saturday; Not as a Stranger; Pete Kelly's Blues; I Died a Thousand Times; Shack Out on 101; 1956: The Rack; Seven Men From Now; Pillars of the Sky; Attack; 1957: Raintree County; 1958: The Missouri Traveler; 1961: The Comancheros; 1962: The Man Who Shot Liberty Valance; 1963: Donovan's Reef; 1964: The Killers; 1965: Ship of Fools; Cat Ballou; 1966: The Professionals; 1967: The Dirty Dozen; Point Blank; 1968: Sergeant Ryker (from 1963 TV sp); Hell in the Pacific; 1969: Paint Your Wagon; 1970: Monte Walsh; 1972: Pocket Money; Prime Cut; 1973: Emperor of the North Pole; The Iceman Cometh; 1974: The Spikes Gang; The Klansman; 1976: Shout at the Devil; The Great Scout and Cathouse Thursday; 1979: Avalanche Express; 1980: The Big Red One; 1981: Death Hunt; 1983: Gorky Park; 1984: Canicule/Dog Day (dtv); 1986: The Delta Force.

NY Stage: 1949: Uniform of Flesh (ob); The Nineteenth Hole of Europe (ob); 1951: Billy Budd.

Select TV: 1953: Sound in the Night (sp); 1954: Open Season (sp); The Psychophonic Nurse (sp); The Day Before Atlanta (sp); Mr. Death and the Redheaded Woman (sp); 1955: The Martyr (sp); How Charlie Faust Won a Pennant for the Giants (sp); The Little Guy (sp); Shakedown Cruise (sp); Bail Out at 43,000 (sp); 1956: The Fool Killer (sp); 1957: The Doctors of Pawnee Kill (sp); Shadow of Evil (sp); 1957–60: M Squad (series); 1958: All I Survey (sp); 1959: A Fistful of Love (sp); A Man in Orbit (sp); The Last Reunion (sp); 1960: The American (sp); Don't You Remember? (sp); 1961: The Joke's on Me (sp); People Need People (sp); 1963: The Losers (sp); Epilogue (sp); The Case Against Paul Ryker (sp; theatrical release in 1968 as Sergeant Ryker); 1965: The Loving Cup (sp); 1985: The Dirty Dozen: The Next Mission.

MARX BROTHERS
BORN: NEW YORK, NY.
Chico
(LEONARD MARX). BORN: MARCH 22, 1887.
DIED: OCTOBER 11, 1961.
Harpo
(ADOLPH, LATER ARTHUR MARX). BORN: NOVEMBER 23, 1888. DIED: SEPTEMBER 28, 1964.
Groucho
(JULIUS MARX). BORN: OCTOBER 2, 1890.
DIED: AUGUST 19, 1977.
Zeppo
(HERBERT MARX). BORN: FEBRUARY 25, 1901.
DIED: NOVEMBER 30, 1979.

The screen's greatest anarchists, the Marx Brothers, knew no inhibitions and let their comic assault loose on everyone. Through puns, malapropisms, insults, slapstick, and a playful disregard for the normal and the serious, they created a world that was never to be equaled by any other comedy team. Alas, their motion picture output was small, and too much of it was hampered by studio conventions of the day that called for secondary love interests and storylines that were paid too much attention to by the screenwriters. They were pushed into show business by their mother and went through various unsuccessful vaudeville acts and routines (this included participation by another brother, Gummo/Milton, who bowed out long before their fame). Somewhere along the way their characters were born: Groucho, the leering wit with the grease-paint moustache and suggestively wiggling eyebrows; Chico, the confidence man with the pointy hat, tight coat, and Italian accent; and Harpo, mischievious, grinning, silent, and childlike, with a wig of curly hair and a coat full of any object, produced upon request. Youngest brother Zeppo would soon join up as the closest thing to a straight man, but he couldn't help but seem superfluous. After years on the road they finally scored in a musical comedy with some semblance of a plot, *I'll Say She Is*. It came to Broadway in 1924, and the brothers' wild antics made them the talk of the town. The following year they triumphed yet again, in *The Cocoanuts*, by which time there was talk of putting them in the movies. Once sound had arrived *The Cocoanuts* was filmed during the daytime in the typically clunky early talkie manner by Paramount at their Astoria studios, while the Brothers appeared at night in their third stage hit, *Animal Crackers*. That too was brought to the movies with only marginally more polish, looking like a photographed stage show, as was the case with so many movies of that early sound era. The important thing was that these films gave wider audiences a glimpse of the Marx madness, while the latter gave Groucho his signature song, "Hooray for Captain Spaulding."

It was time to move out to Hollywood proper, and the remaining three films under their Paramount contract were their most inspired creations. *Monkey Business* let them loose on an ocean liner, as a quartet of nameless stowaways, pretty much eschewing a plot until the last minute. *Horse Feathers* managed to get them into college, with Groucho as a professor; Zeppo, in perhaps his most substantial part, as Groucho's son (!); and Chico and Harpo, paired off as usual, as a team of scruffy dogcatchers. Their pinnacle came with *Duck Soup*, a truly ingenious and outlandish satire on politics and war set in the mythical kingdom of Fredonia. It included a magnificent mirror pantomime and some brilliantly off-the-wall musical numbers, all zippily directed by Leo McCarey in a breathlessly funny 70 minutes. This was, however, the first time Harpo was deprived of his customary harp solo, as was Chico of his spellbinding piano tricks. In fact the movie seemed to go out of its way to stick right to the laughs, bouncing merrily on its own crazy rhythm, which, in 1933, apparently turned out to be a mistake. It was their least popular movie at the time, the culmination of a steadily declining box office that, ironically, was in direct contrast to the ascending quality of their product.

Paramount felt there was no option but to bid them farewell. Fortunately producer Irving Thalberg, MGM's boy wonder, was a fan and signed them to a contract (minus Zeppo, who, sensing his uselessness, now worked as their agent) with the idea of softening them somewhat by having them help the plot along in the name of romance, assisting the secondary love interest. Things worked the first time out with *A Night at the Opera*, getting all the elements right, pitting the raucous team against the pretensions of the music world. Their greatest foil, straight-woman Margaret Dumont, who had appeared with them on Broadway and in three of their previous films, was back, and the brothers were given two supporting players that audiences actually could care about, Allan Jones and Kitty Carlisle. It also included perhaps their most famous setpiece, "the stateroom scene," with Groucho reluctantly

paying host to an onslaught of visitors in his tiny quarters aboard an ocean liner. The film was a hit as was the next, *A Day at the Races*, although Thalberg's sudden death prior to its completion took away some of the final polish and was instrumental in diminishing the Marxes' enthusiasm for concentrating on movies.

A break to go to RKO to shoot an adaptation of a stage hit they *hadn't* originated, *Room Service*, didn't jell, so it was back to the home lot for three fairly mechanical romps, each of which had moments of brilliance. *At the Circus* gave Groucho another of his best songs, "Lydia the Tattooed Lady;" *Go West* found some laughs in its prolonged train chase at the finale; and *The Big Store* at least had Dumont around for some requisite Groucho abuse. With that one, they ended their stay at MGM. As separate entities, Groucho was finding the greatest success starring on radio in the quiz show *You Bet Your Life*, while Chico had formed his own band. The trio was called back for two independent ventures, *A Night in Casablanca* and *Love Happy*, looking too old and disinterested for this sort of nonsense. The latter, in fact, was actually a star vehicle for Harpo, with smaller parts for Chico and Groucho. In the 1950s Groucho continued his emcee duties on television with even greater success, becoming more famous than ever. There was also one more Marx Brothers movie, albeit one in which they did not appear together, the absurd historical concoction *The Story of Mankind*, with Groucho as Peter Minuet, Chico as a monk counseling Christopher Columbus, and Harpo as Sir Isaac Newton. Groucho had also appeared, on his own, in such unimportant releases as *Copacabana*, where he played an agent trying to promote two Carmen Mirandas; *Double Dynamite*, which wasted both him and Frank Sinatra; *A Girl in Every Port*, in which he and William Bendix tried to hide a racehorse on a ship; and, later down the line, the screwy, drug-influenced *Skidoo*, in which he was a gangleader modestly called God.

In the late 1960s, with Chico and Harpo having passed away, Groucho suddenly found himself at the center of a fervid cult that had grown, championing the Marx Brothers as antiestablishment heroes and comic geniuses. As a result he was able to sell out a one-man show given at Carnegie Hall and to show up for a special Academy Award in 1973. In addition to his separate acting credits, Groucho also co-authored (with Norman Krasna) the script for a romantic comedy, *The King and the Chorus Girl*, in 1937. On television he appeared in an adaptation of a play he'd written, *Time for Elizabeth*, on *Bob Hope Presents the Chrysler Theatre*. His anecdotal memoirs were *Groucho and Me* (1959), *Memoirs of a Mangy Lover* (1964), and *The Groucho Letters* (1967); while Harpo penned *Harpo Speaks!* in 1961.

Screen: GROUCHO, HARPO, CHICO, AND ZEPPO: 1929: The Cocoanuts; 1930: Animal Crackers; 1931: Monkey Business; 1932: Horse Feathers; 1933: Duck Soup.

GROUCHO, CHICO, AND HARPO: 1935: A Night at the Opera; 1937: A Day at the Races; 1938: Room Service; 1939: At the Circus; 1940: Go West; 1941: The Big Store; 1946: A Night in Casablanca; 1949: Love Happy (and story by Harpo); 1957: The Story of Mankind.

GROUCHO: 1936: Yours for the Asking; 1947: Copacabana; 1950: Mr. Music; 1951: Double Dynamite; 1952: A Girl in Every Port; 1957: Will Success Spoil Rock Hunter?; 1968: Skidoo.

HARPO: 1925: Too Many Kisses; 1943: Stage Door Canteen.

NY Stage: 1924: I'll Say She Is; 1925: The Cocoanuts; 1928: Animal Crackers.

Select TV: HARPO, CHICO, AND GROUCHO: 1959: The Incredible Jewel Robbery (sp).

GROUCHO: 1950–61: You Bet Your Life (series); 1960: The Mikado (sp); 1962: The Holdout (sp); Tell It to Groucho (series); 1964: Time for Elizabeth (sp; and wr.).

CHICO: 1950: Papa Romani (sp); 1950–51: The College Bowl (series).

JAMES MASON

BORN: HUDDERSFIELD, YORKSHIRE, ENGLAND, MAY 15, 1909. ED: MARLBOROUGH, CAMBRIDGE. DIED: JULY 27, 1984.

Both matinee idol and great actor, James Mason was attractive, suave, and quietly powerful, with a melodious voice that could either soothe or menace. Since he was as adept at being a hero as he was playing a villain, it is not surprising that he became a box-office attraction in his native England, usually doing the latter. He took up drama in college, making his professional debut in *The Rascal*, in 1931, and his London bow two years later, in *Gallows Glorious*. It was while acting with the Gate Company in Dublin that he began appearing in low-budget films, "quota quickies" as they were official called in Britain, playing a newspaper reporter tracking down a killer in his first, *Late Extra*, in 1934. This didn't exactly catapult him to any enviable position in the British cinema, but at least he landed some leading roles, showing up as an investigator in *Troubled Waters*, and Tom Tulliver in an adaptation of *The Mill on the Floss*. There were also smaller parts in bigger budgeted films, *Fire Over England*, as a spy killed off early in the story, and *The Return of the Scarlet Pimpernel*, both from producer Alexander Korda. Mason himself received co-producer and co-writer credit, along with actress Pamela Kellino, for *I Met a Murderer*, with James as the unwitting killer and Kellino as the woman he meets while on the run. They became husband and wife (1941–64), and she, as Pamela Mason, dined out on his fame on the talk show circuits long after their divorce.

There was a higher profile lead in *This Man Is Dangerous*, as a private eye, and also in *Hatter's Castle*, a melodrama in which he was a doctor loved by Deborah Kerr. It was in melodrama that he became a star, for the Gainsborough Studio, first by being nasty to both wife Phyllis Calvert and mistress Margaret Lockwood, in *The Man in Grey*, and then by playing an evil Lord, who battles hero Stewart Granger in a duel, in a similar concoction called *Fanny by Gaslight*, also with Calvert. The latter, in fact, focused on Mason in its title change for the United States, *Man of Evil*. These were not the sort of heavy costume dramas that would stand the test of time, and Mason himself despised doing each and every one of them. However, in the 1940s, they seemed to be exactly what certain British audiences were eager to line up for and he wasn't so well off that there was any reason to refuse the money. Mean again, Mason was sadistic toward Calvert's sister, Dulcie Gray, in *They Were Sisters*, which also included the curious casting of wife Pamela playing his daughter. He then happily left Gainsborough behind to play the two roles that earned him the respect and international attention he had been searching for. First was *The Seventh Veil*, sternly making sure that his ward, Ann Todd, learned her piano lessons. It was a movie much admired in its day for its use of psychoanalysis to explain the heroine's unhappiness, earned an Academy Award for its screenplay, and did well not only in England but in the United States. Today it looks pretty much like a standard, mediocre soap opera, with Mason, though impressive, taking a backseat in screen time to his second-billed co-star. His status was further enhanced by something a little less slick, much more grim, and far more enduring, the excellent *Odd Man Out*, where he spent most the film dying from a bullet wound. It was this picture more than any other that placed Mason among the major names of British cinema and made him greatly in demand. He himself would look back on it as his proudest achievement.

Unlike many British stars, Mason not only preferred movies to theater but was also eager to go to Hollywood. Britain in fact wasn't too sorry to see him go, since he had no qualms about bad-mouthing the industry, and had soured his reputation when he refused to enlist during the war. He arrived in America without any prospect of work, prompting him to do a play, *Bathsheba*, that quickly flopped, further convincing him that he had next to no luck where the stage was concerned. Moving to California, he did an independent film for director Max Ophuls, *Caught*, turning down the role of the villain and opting for that of the poor doctor who tries to help Barbara Bel Geddes. It was a critical and financial failure. MGM gave him a small part, playing Flaubert at the beginning and close of *Madame Bovary*, after which Mason did bigger roles in a string of financial failures: *The Reckless Moment*, as a blackmailer; *East Side, West Side*, suffering through marital problems with Barbara Stanwyck; and *Pandora and the Flying Dutchman*, an odd, atmospheric fantasy that would later win its share of admirers. 20th Century-Fox did better by him, casting him as Field Marshal Rommel in *The Desert Fox* (which did well enough to rate a follow-up, *The Desert Rats*), and as a relentlessly cold-hearted spy in the icy *5 Fingers*.

There was another that he himself produced, Republic Pictures's *Lady Possessed*, which co-starred his wife, but it came and went without passing; as did another they penned, *Charade*, a trio of tales, made up of three dramas they'd done on television. Hollywood seemed to like him best as a bad guy, so he complied with the inferior remake of *The Prisoner of Zenda*, as Rupert of Hentzau; *Botany Bay*, as the sadistic captain in this poor-man's *Mutiny on the Bounty*; *The Story of Three Loves*, as a stern ballet impresario giving Moira Shearer a hard time, in the weakest episode of this three-part omnibus; and *Prince Valiant*, as the dreaded Black Knight. In between these he proved himself in some quality material, playing the tormented Brutus in MGM's prestigious, Oscar-nominated production of *Julius Caesar*, in many ways giving the film's best performance. There was no doubt that his contributions were worthwhile but he needed to knock one out of the park if he was going to really make his mark in the United States. Fortunately he got his chance when various others (including Cary Grant) turned down the 1954 remake of *A Star Is Born*. As the self-pitying alcoholic movie star who sees wife Judy Garland rise to the heights while he falls, he was magnificent, managing the miraculous feat of more than holding his own in what was clearly Garland's showcase. He received an Oscar nomination and capped the year with an even bigger money-maker, Disney's *20,000 Leagues Under the Sea*, looking just right as Jules Verne's half-mad Captain Nemo.

After these peaks, it was curious to see him playing Lucille Ball's guardian angel in a flabby comedy, *Forever, Darling*, but he tried to make up for it by producing his own vehicle, *Bigger Than Life*, tackling the role of a drug addict with much critical acclaim but no financial success whatsoever. There was a well-attended all-star soaper, *Island in the Sun*, where he murdered Michael Rennie because he thought he was fooling around with wife Patricia Owen, and then a pair of mediocre thrillers, *Cry Terror!*, where he was blackmailed into helping criminal Rod Steiger, and *The Decks Ran Red*, in which he was a captain confronting a mutiny. Dual box-office successes came in 1959. First he was relegated to supporting Cary Grant as the debonair villain in director Alfred Hitchcock's *North by Northwest*, but since this was one of the most enjoyable films ever, it hardly mattered. Then, taking billing *below* Arlene Dahl (!), he was back in Verne territory for an ideal Saturday matinee adventure, *Journey to the*

Center of the Earth, which turned out to be another of his best-remembered films of this period.

There were a pair of comedies that failed, *A Touch of Larceny* and *The Marriage-Go-Round*, followed by another of his pinnacles, the controversial adaptation of Nabokov's *Lolita*. As Humbert Humbert, he did an astonishing job of making his desires for 16-year-old Sue Lyon not only darkly funny but also deeply moving. It was, along with *A Star Is Born*, probably his finest hour on film. His own production, the pirate tale *Hero's Island*, was hardly a worthy follow-up, after which he slipped into support. He was certainly the most sympathetic character in the colossal spectacle *The Fall of the Roman Empire*, then had a brilliant few minutes tormenting Anne Bancroft about her husband's indiscretions in *The Pumpkin Eater*. There were the usual lengthy 1960s costumes pictures, including *Genghis Khan*, where he was made to look Chinese, complete with pigtail and false teeth; *Lord Jim*, in which he showed up late in the story, as a bowler-hatted buccaneer; *The Blue Max*, as a German general married to a much younger Ursula Andress; and the ghastly remake of *Mayerling* (though no one was blaming him), as Emperor Franz Joseph. Amid these he scored in a big way as Lynn Redgrave's much older suitor in one of the best British releases of the decade, *Georgy Girl*, once again making the character more sympathetic than expected and earning an Oscar nomination in the supporting category.

There were raves for his Trigorin in the 1968 adaptation of *The Seagull*, although this was meant for fairly restricted consumption, after which there was another of his producer credits for *Age of Consent*, which portrayed him as an artist seeking solitude in Australia, in a picture that wound up being seen by even fewer customers. There was consolation in the latter when he wound up meeting actress Clarissa Kaye (they wed in 1971 and remained so until his death). There came a career slump, where he began accepting work in all kinds of international productions, mainly to pay for the sizeable alimony his first wife had demanded. Among the few high points during this run of mostly unnecessary pictures were two American productions, *Child's Play*, as Robert Preston's professorial nemesis, and the tricky thriller *The Last of Sheila*, as a failing movie director invited on a murderous cruise. Despite the belief that all actors must eat, it was shocking to see him headlining such blatant trash as *Mandingo*, as a Southern bigot, cooling his feet on some hapless black boys. Amid this and all sorts of other disposable nonsense he was seen in a huge hit, *Heaven Can Wait*, at his most dapper in the role of the heavenly messenger, played by Claude Rains in the original, *Here Comes Mr. Jordan*. Also worth noting was *Murder by Decree*, with Mason as a fine Mr. Watson to Christopher Plummer's Sherlock Holmes, and *The Verdict*, in which he casually stole the film, as the lawyer who takes on attorney Paul Newman. For it he got another Oscar nomination and the last decent audience for one of his films. He kept on working up to his death of a heart attack in 1984, and it might be fair to say that despite too many poor choices, moviegoers hardly had a reason to gripe as long as he gave them 100 percent, which he almost always did. There was, in fact, another batch of rave notices for his final movie, *The Shooting Party*, a satire on class-consciousness, released posthumously. His 1981 autobiography was entitled *Before I Forget*.

Screen: 1935: Late Extra; 1936: Twice Branded; Troubled Waters; Prison Breaker; Blind Man's Bluff; The Secret of Stamboul; 1937: The High Command; The Mill on the Floss; Fire Over England; Catch as Catch Can; 1938: The Return of the Scarlet Pimpernel; 1939: I Met a Murderer (and co-wr.); 1941: This Man Is Dangerous/The Patient Vanishes; Hatter's Castle (US: 1948); 1942: The Night Has Eyes/Terror House; Alibi; Secret Mission;

Thunder Rock; 1943: The Bells Go Down; The Man in Grey; They Met in the Dark; 1944: Candelight in Algeria; Fanny by Gaslight/Man of Evil; Hotel Reserve; 1945: A Place of One's Own; They Were Sisters; The Seventh Veil; The Wicked Lady; 1947: Odd Man Out; The Upturned Glass; 1949: Caught; Madame Bovary; The Reckless Moment; East Side, West Side; 1950: One Way Street; 1951: Pandora and the Flying Dutchman; The Desert Fox; 1952: 5 Fingers; Lady Possessed (and co-prod.); The Prisoner of Zenda; Face to Face (The Secret Sharer); 1953: Charade (and co-wr.; prod.); The Desert Rats; Julius Caesar; The Story of Three Loves (The Jealous Lover); Botany Bay; The Man Between; 1954: Prince Valiant; A Star Is Born; 20,000 Leagues Under the Sea; 1956: Forever, Darling; Bigger Than Life (and prod.); 1957: Island in the Sun; 1958: Cry Terror!; The Decks Ran Red; 1959: North by Northwest; Journey to the Center of the Earth; 1960: A Touch of Larceny; The Trials of Oscar Wilde; The Marriage-Go-Round; 1962: Escape From Zahrain; Lolita; Hero's Island (and co-prod.); Tiara Tahiti; 1964: The Fall of the Roman Empire; Torpedo Bay (Fr: 1962); The Pumpkin Eater; 1965: Lord Jim; Genghis Khan; Les Pianos Mechaniques/The Player Pianos/The Uninhibited; 1966: The Blue Max; Georgy Girl; The Deadly Affair; 1967: Stranger in the House/Cop-Out; 1968: Duffy; Mayerling; The Sea Gull; 1969: Age of Consent (and prod.); 1970: Spring and Port Wine; 1971: Cold Sweat; 1972: The Yin and Yang of Mr. Go (dtv); Bad Man's River; Kill!/Kill! Kill!; Child's Play; 1973: The Last of Sheila; The Mackintosh Man; 1974: 11 Harrowhouse; The Marseille Contract/The Destructors; 1975: Mandingo; Inside Out/The Golden Heist; Autobiography of a Princess; La Citta Sconvolta/Kidnap Syndicate (US: 1981); Gente Di Rispetto/The Flower in His Mouth (nUSr); La Mano Sinistra Delle Legge/The Left Hand of the Law (nUSr); 1976: Paura in Citta/Hot Stuff/Street War; Voyage of the Damned; 1977: Cross of Iron; Homage to Chagall: The Colors of Love (narrator); 1978: Heaven Can Wait; The Boys From Brazil; The Water Babies; 1979: Murder by Decree; The Passage; Sidney Sheldon's Bloodline; 1980: ffolkes/North Sea Hijack; 1981: A Dangerous Summer/Flash Fire (dtv); 1982: Evil Under the Sun; The Verdict; 1983: Yellowbeard; 1985: The Assisi Underground; The Shooting Party.

NY Stage: 1947: Bathsheba; 1979: The Faith Healer.

Select TV: 1956: The James Mason Show (series); 1957: The Questioning Note (sp); The Thundering Wave (sp); 1958: No Boat for Four Months (sp); Not the Glory (sp); 1959: The Second Man (sp); A Sword for Marius (sp); 1960: The Hiding Place (sp); John Brown's Raid (sp); 1962: Rebecca (sp); 1966: Dare I Weep, Dare I Mourn (sp); 1968: The Legend of Silent Night (sp); 1973: Frankenstein: The True Story; 1974: Great Expectations; 1977: Jesus of Nazareth (ms); 1979: Salem's Lot; 1982: Ivanhoe; 1983: George Washington (ms); Alexandre; 1985: Dr. Fischer of Geneva; A.D. (ms).

ILONA MASSEY

(ILONA HAJMÁSSY) BORN: BUDAPEST, HUNGARY, JUNE 16, 1910. DIED: AUGUST 20, 1974.

A fairly minor (and very temporary) addition to MGM's musical stable, shapely blonde Ilona Massey started in the opera world of Vienna where she was also seen in two films, *Knox und die Lustigen Vagabunden* and *Der Himmel auf Erden*. Metro brought her to Hollywood in 1936 to give her the second female lead in *Rosalie*, as the woman in love with the man Eleanor Powell is supposed to marry. That film's male star, Nelson Eddy, was in the next, *Balalaika*, where Massey was upped to the co-star spot, as a cabaret singer pursued by Cossack Eddy. The response was so cool that MGM promptly dropped her. She married actor Alan Curtis in 1941 (they divorced a year later) and together they played Mister and Misses Fran Schubert in one of those clichéd composer biopic that were a staple in Hollywood's studio era, *New Wine*. Over at Universal she was a secret agent in love with transparent Jon Hall in *Invisible Agent*, and the daughter of the mad doctor in *Frankenstein Meets the Wolf Man*, neither of which she made, one assumes, for those who had followed her opera career. After the war there was another quickly forgotten reteaming with Eddy, *Northwest Outpost*; a Republic western with stoic Rod Cameron, *The Plunderers*; and the last official Marx Brothers comedy, *Love Happy*, where she had to compete with upcoming starlet Marilyn Monroe. Back in her native country she became an active participant in assisting Hungarian refugees, leaving show business behind in 1960.

Screen: 1935: Himmel auf Erden/Heaven on Earth (nUSr); Know und die Lustigen Vagabunden (nUSr); 1936: Rosalie; 1939: Balalaika; 1941: New Wine; International Lady; 1942: Invisible Agent; Frankenstein Meets the Wolf Man; 1946: Holiday in Mexico; The Gentleman Misbehaves; 1947: Northwest Outpost; 1948: The Plunderers; 1949: Love Happy; 1959: Jet Over the Atlantic.

NY Stage: 1943: Ziegfeld Follies of 1943.

Select TV: 1950: The Ambassadors (sp); The Shadow of a Man (sp); 1951: Purple and Fine Linen (sp); The Third Time (sp); The Sleeping Beauty (sp); 1952: Rendezvous (series); 1954–55: The Ilona Massey Show (series).

RAYMOND MASSEY

BORN: TORONTO, ONTARIO, CANADA, AUGUST 30, 1896. DIED: JULY 29, 1983.

That he was the screen's definitive Abraham Lincoln was enough to make Raymond Massey a part of cinema history. But his authoritative air, gaunt figure, slightly displeased, lopsided mouth, deep, measured voice, and piercing eyes would have made him a memorable addition to the motion picture field just the same. It was while serving with the Canadian military that he became interested in acting, performing in shows for the troops during World War I. Going to London he took up acting professionally, making his stage debut there in 1921, in a played called *In the Zone*. There were some British films that marked his introduction to the movies, including one in which he played Sherlock Holmes (*The Speckled Band*), made while he was a producer and actor at the Everyman Theatre. In 1931 he came to America for a version of *Hamlet*, and was asked to come west for a single Hollywood appearance, albeit in a notable film, *The Old Dark House*, as one of the visitors to the creepy manse in this cult favorite. Back in England he was made the nemesis of Leslie Howard in *The Scarlet Pimpernel*, then played the lead (and dual role) of John Cabal and his ancestor, in Britain's fascinating and visually influential look at the future, *Things to Come*, scripted by H.G. Wells. Summoned back to Hollywood, he played one of his most villainous roles, the scheming Black Michael, half brother to hero Ronald Colman, in the sterling 1937 adaptation of *The Prisoner of Zenda*; and then was only marginally more sympathetic as the unflappable island governor who takes the law to extremes while punishing native Jon Hall in *The Hurricane*.

It was on Broadway in 1938 that he first got a chance to play Lincoln, in Robert Sherwood's *Abe Lincoln in Illinois*, bearing a striking physical resemblance to the great orator and winning

raves for showing both the wit and weaknesses of the man. When RKO bought the property for filming, there was little doubt that Massey would recreate his role in the paired-down but nonetheless stirringly patriotic 1940 adaptation. There were no great fires lit at the box office, but it served its purpose in committing Massey's unforgettable portrait to celluloid, and he was rewarded with an Oscar nomination as well. That same year his interpretation of John Brown proved to be a highlight of Warners's Errol Flynn adventure, *Santa Fe Trail*, and, as with Lincoln, he would be called on to play the part in the future. During this time he hopped back over to England to participate in their stellar tribute to our Canadian allies, *49th Parallel/The Invaders*, in the important role of the AWOL soldier who subdues fleeing Nazi Eric Portman. Returning to Warner Bros., he joined the cast of the requisite anti-Nazi pieces, *Dangerously They Live* and *Desperate Journey*, and then, when Boris Karloff was tied up with touring in *Arsenic and Old Lace*, he was called on to play the demented, frozen-faced Jonathan Brewster in director Frank Capra's dandy version of that long-running Broadway farce. Considering the role was written with Karloff in mind, Massey proved to be a brilliant second choice, being both chilling and amusingly bizarre. He looked so very right in a general's uniform in a typical war film, *God Is My Co-Pilot*; supported Joan Crawford in one of her best, *Possessed*; and was part of the non-event that was *The Fountainhead*, as the newspaper tycoon who opposes Gary Cooper. Similarly, for RKO, he was in another famous property that didn't work at all on screen, *Mourning Becomes Electra*, as Rosalind Russell's father, killed off by his cheating spouse (Katina Paxinou). Goldwyn called on him to play the McCoy patriarch in one of the usually infallible producer's major flops, *Roseanna McCoy*, after which Warners gave him a larger role than usual in *Barricade*, as a sadistic mine owner who clashes with Dane Clark, in what was nothing more than a thinly disguised remake of *The Sea Wolf*, relocated to the Old West. Staying in that genre he challenged Randolph Scott to land ownership in *Sugarfoot*, but this being a Randolph Scott vehicle first, you knew whom to root for.

On TV he reprised *Abe Lincoln in Illinois* and showed up in *The Day Lincoln Was Shot*, while on Broadway he was revisiting another old friend, participating in the acclaimed *John Brown's Body*. Allied Artists gave Massey the opportunity to return to Brown yet again in *Seven Angry Men*, which marked one of the rare times he was given top billing on film, while he did some heavy duty scene chewing as another real-life character, bombastic stage actor Junius Booth, in *Prince of Players*. Between his military duties in *Battle Cry*, as a major, and *The Naked and the Dead*, as the impotent general who swears revenge on Cliff Robertson; there was another outstanding performance, as the cold-hearted father, who cannot understand the behavior of moody offspring James Dean, in *East of Eden*, their mutual lack of communication going on off screen as well. There weren't many significant movie roles being offered by the 1960s, though he was called on to show up ever so briefly as Lincoln in the all-star attraction *How the West Was Won*. Instead he found latter-day fame by dusting off Lionel Barrymore's old role of the gruff Dr. Gillespie in the popular TV series based on *Dr. Kildare*. He wrote the play *The Hanging Judge* (in 1952), which he did not appear in onstage but later did on television. His children include actors Daniel and Anna Massey, from his marriage (1929–39) to actress Adrianne Allen.

Screen: 1929: High Treason; 1931: The Speckled Band; 1932: The Face at the Window; The Old Dark House; 1934: The Scarlet Pimpernel; 1936: Things to Come; 1938: Fire Over England; Dreaming Lips; Under the Red Robe; The Prisoner of Zenda; The Hurricane; 1938: Drums/The Drum; Black

Limelight; **1940:** Abe Lincoln in Illinois; Santa Fe Trail; **1941:** Dangerously They Live; **1942:** 49th Parallel/The Invaders; Desperate Journey; Reap the Wild Wind; **1943:** Action in the North Atlantic; **1944:** Arsenic and Old Lace; The Woman in the Window; A Canterbury Tale (narrator); **1945:** God Is My Co-Pilot; Hotel Berlin; **1946:** Stairway to Heaven/A Matter of Life and Death; **1947:** Mourning Becomes Electra; Possessed; **1949:** The Fountainhead; Roseanna McCoy; **1950:** Chain Lightning; Barricade; Dallas; **1951:** Sugarfoot; Come Fill the Cup; David and Bathsheba; **1952:** Carson City; **1953:** The Desert Song; **1955:** Battle Cry; Seven Angry Men; East of Eden; Price of Players; **1957:** Omar Khayyam; **1958:** The Naked and the Dead; **1960:** The Great Impostor; **1961:** The Fiercest Heart; The Queen's Guards; **1963:** How the West Was Won; **1968:** Mackenna's Gold.

NY Stage: 1931: Hamlet; **1934:** The Shining Hour (and dir.); **1936:** Ethan Frome; **1938:** Abe Lincoln in Illinois; **1941:** The Doctor's Dilemma; **1942:** Candida; **1945:** Pygmalion; **1947:** How I Wonder; **1949:** The Father (and dir.); **1952:** John Brown's Body; **1958:** J.B.

Select TV: 1950: Laburnum Grove (sp); **1951:** Abe Lincoln in Illinois (sp); The Linden Tree (sp); **1954:** For These Services (sp); **1955:** Yellow Jack (sp); Bounty Court Martial (sp); The Late George Apley (sp); **1956:** The Hanging Judge (sp); The Day Lincoln Was Shot (sp); Adam's Son (sp); I Spy (series); **1957:** Mayerling (sp); A Matter of Life (sp); **1959:** Hitler's Secret (sp); **1960:** The Cruel Day (sp); **1961–66:** Dr. Kildare (series); **1962:** Two Counts of Murder (sp); **1967:** St. Joan (sp); **1971:** The President's Plane Is Missing; **1972:** All My Darling Daughters; **1973:** My Darling Daughters' Anniversary.

MARCELLO MASTROIANNI

BORN: FONTANA LIRI, ITALY, SEPTEMBER 28, 1923. ED: UNIV. OF ROME. DIED: DECEMBER 19, 1996.

The undisputed superstar of Italian cinema, Marcello Mastroianni's forte was playing none-too-innocent everymen who were victimized by the crazy world around them, something he did with such subtlety that it was often taken for granted just how good an actor he was. He was properly handsome and could be very suave, but there was a hangdog quality to his manner and a sadness in his eyes that made it appear as if he were carrying the weight of the world upon his back. When he was cast as a womanizer, there was often a touch of humor, cruelty, or sadness to the situation, thereby keeping him grounded and making audiences feel that he was someone they could commiserate with. It was while earning his keep in the accounting department at the Rome branch of Eagle-Lion films that he began taking acting classes. Director Luchino Visconti caught Mastroianni in one of his drama group's productions and offered him a place with his stage company. There were roles in Italian productions of *A Streetcar Named Desire* and *Death of a Salesman*, among others, leading to his motion picture debut in a 1947 version of *Les Misérables*, or *I Miserabili* in this case. During the early 1950s his movie roles grew in size, and he had his first success of any note with *Sensualita*, in which his wife cheated on him with his brother. It opened in Italy in 1952 and came to the U.S. in 1954, marking the first time Mastroianni was noticed here. The next two to find American distribution, *Too Bad She's Bad* and *The Miller's Beautiful Wife*, were significant because they found him acting opposite Sophia Loren, with whom he would team many times over the years. In the former they were cast as father and daughter. He had become a regular presence on the art house circuit, but the fever for Mastroianni really began in the States in

1960 with the release of the comedy *Big Deal on Madonna Street*, one of the movies that began the vogue for capers about colorful crooks. Then Fellini put him front and center in what would become one of the landmark events of Italian cinema, *La Dolce Vita*. Playing a character named Marcello, he observed the decadence of the shallow socialites of Rome in a movie that became a major crossover hit due, no doubt, to its "adult" content and the desire of more adventurous moviegoers to interpret the many unfathomable images and cryptic occurrences within.

More accessible was *Divorce — Italian Style*, a black comedy in which he tried to dispose of his dreary, mustachioed wife in order to marry his beautiful young cousin. Mastroianni found the right balance between deadpan humor and a mock degree of suffering, and he was so in favor at the time that his performance earned him an Oscar nomination, the first time a performer in a foreign-language production received that honor in the Best Actor category. This was followed by his other famous collaboration with Fellini, *8 1/2*, as the director's alter ego, an acclaimed filmmaker trying to develop his new movie while surrounded by the vultures of the press and the desirable women of his past. Again the press raved, and it became one of the milestones of expressionistic cinema for the very fervid fans, while the rest of the public found it as maddeningly opaque as *La Dolce Vita*. There was more acclaim for another more straightforward offering, *The Organizer*, about Italian labor unions, and then two that established him and Loren as the most famous team in Italian cinema, *Marriage — Italian Style*, in which he was very funny playing her philandering lover, anxious to move on to his next mistress, and the episodic *Yesterday, Today and Tomorrow*, which gave them both three roles to play, with Mastroianni as an exhausted husband helping her make babies to keep her out of jail; a writer picked up by a self-centered millionairess; and a call girl's increasingly frustrated client.

There was a great rush to play up his Casanova image opposite some of the sexy ladies of the 1960s, so he ended up with Virna Lisi in *Casanova 70*; Ursula Andress in the bizarre sci-fi offering *The Tenth Victim*, about legalized killing in the future; and Raquel Welch in *Shoot Loud, Louder...I Don't Understand*, which, if nothing else, was one of the dumbest titles of all time. Despite the fact that he had become an international superstar there was no great interest on his part to accept American offers. He cautiously entered the English language with a bit in the made-for-television *The Poppy Is Also a Flower*; ended up in Britain for *Diamonds for Breakfast*, where he was supposed to be Russian; and then joined Faye Dunaway in a love story directed by Vittorio de Sica, *A Place for Lovers*, which garnered some of the worst reviews of 1969. Back in Britain he played an Italian prince involved with the black residents of a London ghetto in the dreadful *Leo the Last*, and then reteamed with Loren for both *Sunflower* and *The Priest's Wife*, though there was less interest outside of Italy this time around. He and Giancarlo Giannini fought over Monica Vitti in *The Pizza Triangle*, a teaming that was of interest because, for a period in the 1970s, Giannini seemed to be taking over Mastroianni's place as Italy's leading attraction. There was a down period that included some films, *It Only Happens to Others* and *Liza*, with Catherine Deneuve, with whom he shared his life off screen, a relationship that produced a child, Chiara, who later became an actress. He had other motion picture failures during this time, *Rocco Papaleo*, with Lauren Hutton; director Roman Polanski's *What?*, playing an eccentric millionaire; and *Massacre in Rome*, as a priest, opposite Nazi Richard Burton. He and Loren were back in form for *A Special Day*, where it was fun seeing one of the cinema's latent heterosexuals pulling off playing a homosexual with conviction. The performance brought him another Oscar nomination. The brief vogue for Laura Antonelli found him cast opposite her in both *Wifemistress* and *The Divine Nymph*, then he ended up in another indulgence by Fellini, *City of Women*, although that director's avant-garde style was no longer the rage in 1981.

He actually did play Casanova in one of his more popular films around this time, *La Nuit de Varennes*; teamed up with Jack Lemmon in the lightweight comedy *Macaroni*; was a former dancer brought back for a reunion with Giulietta Masina (Fellini's wife) in *Ginger and Fred*; and became obsessed with a younger woman while at a health spa in *Dark Eyes*. By this point he had come to embody the world-weary lover of European cinema, and he got a third Oscar nod for the last film, creating a bit of ill will by bad-mouthing the Academy Award as an honor of no interest to him whatsoever. Needless to say, he didn't win. Now past retirement age, it was still common to see the aging star popping up in vehicles like *The Two Lives of Mattia Pascal* and *I Don't Want to Talk About It*, in which he fell in love with a dwarf, while also being cast against famous ladies past their prime, like Shirley MacLaine in *Used People*, which was his first major role in a genuine, U.S. production (scenes were shot in Brooklyn), and Julie Andrews in the barely distributed *A Fine Romance*. There was also a last teaming with Loren (reprising her strip scene from *Yesterday, Today and Tomorrow*) in the all-star *Ready to Wear*, and more films waiting on the back burner at the time of his death in 1996, including *Voyage to the Beginning of the World*, in which he played a filmmaker visiting various locations from his past. A three-hour remembrance/documentary, *Marcello Mastroianni: I Remember*, shot for Italian television, was shown theatrically in the United States in 1999.

Screen (US releases only): **1954:** Sensualita (It: 1952); **1956:** Too Bad She's Bad (It: 1954); **1957:** The Miller's Beautiful Wife (It: 1955); White Nights; **1958:** A Plea for Passion/The Bigamist (It: 1956); Lucky to Be a Woman; **1959:** The Most Wonderful Moment; The Tailor's Maid (It: 1957); Anatomy of Love; **1960:** Where the Hot Wind Blows (It: 1958); Big Deal on Madonna Street (It: 1958); **1961:** La Dolce Vita (It: 1960); La Notte (It: 1960); **1962:** Bell'Antonio (It: 1961); A Very Private Affair; Divorce — Italian Style (It: 1961); **1963:** Family Diary (It: 1962); 8 1/2; **1964:** Yesterday, Today and Tomorrow (It: 1963); The Organizer (It: 1963); Love on the Riviera (It: 1958); Marriage Italian-Style; **1965:** Casanova 70; Love à la Carte (It: 1960); The Tenth Victim; **1966:** Shoot Loud, Louder...I Don't Understand; **1967:** The Stranger; **1968:** The Man With the Balloons; Kiss the Other Sheik; Diamonds for Breakfast; **1969:** Ghosts — Italian Style; A Place for Lovers; **1970:** Leo the Last; Sunflower (It: 1969); The Pizza Triangle; **1971:** The Priest's Wife (It: 1970); It Only Happens to Others; **1972:** Fellini's Roma; **1973:** La Grand Bouffe; What?/Diary of Forbidden Dreams; Massacre in Rome; **1974:** Rocco Papaleo; **1975:** Down the Ancient Stairs; **1976:** Liza; Salut D'Ariste (Fr: 1974); The Sunday Woman; **1977:** We All Loved Each Other So Much (It. 1974); A Slightly Pregnant Man (Fr: 1973); A Special Day; **1978:** Oopsie Poopsie/Get Rita; **1979:** Wifemistress; The Divine Nymph (It: 1975); Stay as You Are; Todo Mondo; **1980:** Blood Feud/Revenge (It: 1979); **1981:** City of Women (It: 1980); La Pelle; Traffic Jam (It: 1978); **1982:** Beyond the Door/Beyond Obsession (dtv); **1983:** La Nuit de Varennes (It: 1982); **1984:** Gabriela (It: 1983); The Last Horror Film; **1985:** Henry IV; Allonsafan (It: 1974); Macaroni; **1986:** Ginger and Fred; **1987:** Dark Eyes; **1988:** The Two Lives of Mattia Pascal (It: 1985); **1991:** Everybody's Fine (It: 1990); **1992:** A Fine Romance; Intervista (It: 1987); Used People; **1993:** The Beekeeper (Ger: 1985); **1994:** I Don't Want to Talk About It; Ready to Wear; **1996:** Bye Bye Monkey (It: 1977); Three Lives and Only One Death;

1998: Pereira Declares; Voyage to the Beginning of the World.
Select TV: **1966:** The Poppy Is Also a Flower.

WALTER MATTHAU

(WALTER MATUSCHANSKAYASKY) BORN: NEW YORK, NY, OCTOBER 1, 1920. DIED: JULY 1, 2000.

The movies might have been content to let Walter Matthau earn his keep as a fine supporting player, specializing in heavies, but through a stroke of good fortune, audiences of the late 1960s were in the right frame of mind to embrace this stooped, disgruntled, rubbery-faced character actor as a star and the cinema was that much better for it. After serving with the Air Force during World War II, he studied acting at the Dramatic Workshop of the New York School for Social Research. He did much work in stock, a small role on Broadway in 1948's *Anne of the Thousand Days*, and the expected run of live television appearances. His reviews in the original Broadway production of *Will Success Spoil Rock Hunter?* were good enough that he got offers from Hollywood, and ended up being nasty right from the get go, taking a bullwhip to Burt Lancaster in *The Kentuckian*, and trading whisky to the Indians in the Kirk Douglas western *The Indian Fighter*. One he didn't wind up doing was *The Seven Year Itch*, though director Billy Wilder wanted him over Tom Ewell whom the Fox executives insisted on casting instead. Matthau remained serious for the time being, playing a reporter who stands by while Patricia Neal loses her cool in *A Face in the Crowd*; a racketeer in *Slaughter on Tenth Avenue*; a particularly bullying mobster who wants Elvis Presley to sing at his saloon in *King Creole*; and a doctor in *Voice in the Mirror*. He lightened up to play the ship's cook in a comedy, *Onionhead*, then, in a bizarre career footnote, directed himself in a "B" movie called *Gangster Story*, which, if nothing else, marked the first time he received top billing. Supporting Kirk Douglas again he was a lecher in *Strangers When We Meet*, then had his best role to date, as the drily cynical yet sympathetic sheriff, in Douglas's *Lonely Are the Brave*. There were raves for his comical turns in two movies that no one said much good about otherwise, *Who's Got the Action?*, in which he was a racketeer again, and *Ensign Pulver*, where he reprised William Powell's role of the level-headed ship's doctor in this sequel to *Mister Roberts*. There was a fun part as a faux CIA agent pretending to be Audrey Hepburn's ally in the light-hearted thriller *Charade*, and then a chance to really show his patented cynicism, egging the military to drop bombs on Russia in the nightmarish *Fail-Safe*.

Back on Broadway he won a Tony Award for *A Shot in the Dark* and, more significantly, for Neil Simon's smash hit comedy *The Odd Couple*. He was such a sensation in the latter that he became a hot property, and Billy Wilder, still eager to work with him, snatched him up for a juicy role in *The Fortune Cookie*, as the slithery lawyer who dreams up a scheme to get some hefty cash after brother-in-law Jack Lemmon is injured during a football game. Not only was the brilliant chemistry of these two actors first displayed to film audiences, but this part fully captured what Matthau did best, grumping his way through a character, with razor-sharp comic timing and a dead-pan cynicism that only made audiences love him all the more. He won a well-deserved Academy Award as Best Supporting Actor of 1966. It was time to make him into a full-fledged star. He had a winner with director Gene Kelly's clever look at would-be adulterers in *A Guide for the Married Man*, as a happily married husband who feels he must cheat on his spouse simply because it is expected of him. He then got to repeat his performance as everybody's favorite slob, sportswriter, and divorcé Oscar Madison, in the enormously popular 1968 film of *The Odd Couple*, once again partnered to perfection with Lemmon. There was a clumsy, stage-bound oddity with Anne Jackson, *The Secret Life of an American Wife*, which he spent most of shirtless, as an actor who is supposed to be a ladies' man, and the even more curious *Candy*, in which he showed up as a war-hungry general in this episodic star-filled sex comedy that was very much a product of the free-spirited late 1960s. He was perfect as one of fiction's great grouches, Horace Vandergelder, being hotly pursued for his money by Barbra Streisand (with whom he fought heatedly off screen) in the ultra-expensive but highly satisfying adaptation of the long-running musical *Hello, Dolly!*, released concurrently with one of his biggest moneymakers, the likeable *Cactus Flower*, again the object of desire, mooned over by both Ingrid Bergman and Goldie Hawn.

On a roll as one of the screen's foremost practitioners of comedy, he was a playboy after frumpy Elaine May's cash in *A New Leaf*, a troubled film that ended up fairly lopsided after much hacking and editing; and earned an Oscar nomination, under Lemmon's direction, for *Kotch*, playing an unjustly ignored old man who befriends a pregnant girl, cutting all the potential cutesiness out of the premise and making this old codger humorous, sympathetic and real. He offered up three different characterizations in another Neil Simon piece, *Plaza Suite*, as a long-married husband hoping to get the zing back in his life, a sleazy Hollywood executive hoping to score, and a beleaguered father of the bride; and found another fine partner in Carol Burnett in the semi-serious *Pete 'n' Tillie*, an examination of a mature relationship and the bumpy marriage that follows. That audiences preferred him in comedy was evident by the weak box-office returns on three crime thrillers: *Charley Varrick*, in which he played a bank robber who finds himself in hot water with gunman Joe Don Baker; *The Laughing Policeman*, as a San Francisco cop reluctantly teamed with Bruce Dern to find out who slaughtered a busload of citizens; and the best of the lot (and the most unfortunate failure of all of them), *The Taking of Pelham One Two Three*, a tense game of cat-and-mouse, in which he was a Transportation Authority official trying to bargain with thief Robert Shaw, who's holding a subway car hostage.

Dusting off *The Front Page*, Billy Wilder gave him another role he was born to play, conniving newspaper editor Walter Burns, once again tossing off barbs beautifully with Lemmon in the most faithful but least-liked film version of the famous play. He was then handed another golden opportunity by Neil Simon, *The Sunshine Boys*, where his relative youth (he was 54 years old) was covered up by his craggy features and prematurely aged demeanor. Cast opposite the real thing, George Burns, he brilliantly uncovered both the sadness and hilarity of this infuriating ex-vaudevillian, reliving past glories and dwelling only peripherally in the real world. He earned his third Oscar nomination. He had a huge box-office hit with *The Bad News Bears*, as a drunk who learns and teaches self esteem when he becomes baseball coach to a team of foul-mouthed kids, and another one that did very nicely, *House Calls*, in which he was surprisingly well-teamed with patrician Brit Glenda Jackson.

Around this time audiences began to lose interest, and despite his continually stellar work, there was poor attendance for the remake of *Little Miss Marker*, the one and only time he got a chance to appear in a world so ideal for him, that of author Damon Runyon; *First Monday in October*, in which he was a Chief Justice clashing with Jill Clayburgh; *Buddy Buddy*, where he had a final teaming with Wilder and Lemmon, albeit one that wasn't up to par; and *The Survivors*, which at least gave him a

chance to play off of Robin Williams. He had a major disaster with director Roman Polanski's misguided epic *Pirates*, as a grungy buccaneer; a secondary role as a nutcase in a dud Dan Aykroyd vehicle, *The Couch Trip*; and one that never saw the light of day in America, *Piccolo Diavolo/The Little Devil*, in which he supported hyperactive Italian comic Roberto Benignini. A serious Matthau showed up for a small bit as a senator discussing the Kennedy assassination in the all-star *JFK*, after which he was the only reason to sit through a live action version of *Dennis the Menace*, as crusty Mr. Wilson, enduring abuse from precocious Mason Gamble. At the end of that same year, 1993, he and Lemmon were back together again for a fairly obvious comedy, *Grumpy Old Men*, which mainly consisted of the two of them hurling insults at one another. To everyone's surprise it turned out to be a sizable success, which meant that audiences were still happy to have two pros around who were this reliable, even with weak material. After giving a very broad rendition of Albert Einstein in the romantic comedy *I.Q.*, there was a follow-up with Lemmon, *Grumpier Old Men*, and then something more interesting, a version of Truman Capote's *The Grass Harp*, directed by Matthau's son, Charles. In it he gave one of his most restrained performances, as the retired judge who joins some rebellious misfits in their tree house. Hoping to keep making a profit from their geriatric shenanigans, he was back with Lemmon for *Out to Sea* and, 30 years after the original, *The Odd Couple II*. One can almost excuse the bankrupt level of the ideas since it gave us the pleasure of watching Matthau at work. He was last seen as Meg Ryan's horny old dad in another film badly in need of his expertise, *Hanging Up*, released a few months before his death of a heart attack.

Screen: 1955: The Kentuckian; The Indian Fighter; 1956: Bigger Than Life; 1957: A Face in the Crowd; Slaughter on Tenth Avenue; 1958: Voice in the Mirror; King Creole; Ride a Crooked Trail; Onionhead; 1960: Gangster Story (and dir.); Strangers When We Meet; 1962: Lonely Are the Brave; Who's Got the Action?; 1963: Island of Love; Charade; 1964: Ensign Pulver; Fail-Safe; Goodbye Charlie; 1965: Mirage; 1966: The Fortune Cookie; 1967: A Guide for the Married Man; 1968: The Odd Couple; The Secret Life of an American Wife; Candy; 1969: Hello, Dolly!; Cactus Flower; 1971: A New Leaf; Kotch; Plaza Suite; 1972: Pete 'n' Tillie; 1973: Charley Varrick; The Laughing Policeman; 1974: The Taking of Pelham One Two Three; Earthquake (as **WALTER MATUSCHANSKAYASKY**); The Front Page; 1975: The Sunshine Boys; 1976: The Bad News Bears; 1978: Casey's Shadow; House Calls; California Suite; 1980: Little Miss Marker (and exec. prod.); Hopscotch; 1981: First Monday in October; Buddy Buddy; 1982: I Ought to Be in Pictures; 1983: The Survivors; 1985: Movers and Shakers; 1986: Pirates; 1988: The Couch Trip; Piccolo Diavolo/The Little Devil (nUSr); 1991: JFK; 1993: Dennis the Menace; Grumpy Old Men; 1994: I.Q.; 1995: Grumpier Old Men; 1996: The Grass Harp; I'm Not Rappaport; 1997: Out to Sea; 1998: The Odd Couple II; 2000: The Life and Times of Hank Greenberg; Hanging Up.

NY Stage: 1949: Anne of the Thousand Days; 1950: The Liar; 1951: Season in the Sun; Twilight Walk; 1952: Meeting You Again; One Bright Day; In Any Language; The Grey-Eyed People; 1953: The Ladies of the Corridor; 1954: The Burning Glass; 1955: The Wisteria Trees; Guys and Dolls; Will Success Spoil Rock Hunter?; 1958: Once More With Feeling; 1961: Once There Was a Russian; A Shot in the Dark; 1963: My Mother, My Father and Me; 1965: The Odd Couple.

Select TV: 1950: Shadow on the Heart (sp); 1952: The Basket Weaver (sp); Three Sundays (sp); 1953: Nightmare Number Three (sp); Nothing to Sneeze At (sp); The New Process (sp);

Othello (sp); Dry Run (sp); The Glorification of Al Toolum (sp); **1954:** Late Date (sp); Atomic Attack (sp); Flight Report (sp); **1955:** The Lost Weekend (sp); **1956:** The Big Vote (sp); **1957:** A Will to Live (sp); The Legacy (sp); The Trouble With Women (sp); **1958:** Code of the Corner (sp); **1960:** Juno and the Paycock (sp); The Rope Dancers (sp); My Heart's in the Highlands (sp); **1961:** Tallahassee 7000 (series); **1962:** Acres and Pains (sp); Big Deal in Laredo (sp); **1963:** The Takers (sp); **1964:** White Snow; Red Ice (sp); **1972:** Awake and Sing (sp); **1990:** The Incident; **1991:** Mrs. Lambert Remembers Love; **1992:** Against Her Will: An Incident in Baltimore; **1994:** Incident in a Small Town; **1998:** The Marriage Fool.

VICTOR MATURE

BORN: LOUISVILLE, KY, JANUARY 29, 1913.
DIED: AUGUST 4, 1999.

With his muscular frame, toothy smile, thick lips, and slick wave of hair, Victor Mature was apparently *somebody's* idea of the "ideal man" during the 1940s. At the time, this excused his wooden efforts at emoting, though, as far as most of today's audiences are concerned, it's hard to see even the physical attraction. It was while studying acting at the Pasadena Playhouse that he was signed to a long-term contract by producer Hal Roach. His official movie debut came in 1939, in a small role, as a gangster named Lefty, in the Joan Bennett film *The Housekeeper's Daughter*, but the one Roach really had him in mind for was the prehistoric epic *One Million B.C.*, which required him to battle big lizards and grunt at Carole Landis. This pretty much solidified his image as a man of brawn. After the adventure story *Captain Caution*, and RKO's weak rendering of *No, No, Nanette*, he went to Broadway and scored a hit opposite Gertrude Lawrence in the acclaimed musical *Lady in the Dark*. Because of this he got a contract with 20th Century-Fox, where, in his first assignment, he was accused of killing Ms. Landis in the popular thriller *I Wake Up Screaming*. That one starred Betty Grable, and he was placed alongside her again in two musicals, *Song of the Islands* and *Footlight Serenade* (though his dance number was cut from the final print in the latter). There was supposed to be another with Grable, *My Gal Sal*, but she was replaced by Rita Hayworth. In any event Mature didn't strike one as the first choice to convincingly play a songwriter, even in a typically fictionalized Hollywood biopic, in this case one about Paul Dresser. Taking time out for military service and another shot at Broadway (*Tars and Spars*), he returned to Fox and confounded the skeptics by giving a better-than-expected performance as the sickly Doc Holliday in one of the outstanding westerns of the decade, director John Ford's *My Darling Clementine*. He was once again accused of murder, in *Moss Rose*, then had *Kiss of Death* stolen from him by the far livelier Richard Widmark.

The studio let him go to Paramount for one with Betty Hutton, *Red, Hot and Blue*, again none too convincing in his on-screen occupation, that of a serious stage director; then that same company gave him the most suitable role of his career, temple-toppling strongman Samson, in their DeMille-directed box-office blockbuster of 1949, *Samson and Delilah*, a colorful slice of cheese with a stuntman filling in for Mature on the more arduous tasks. From this high point he went back to being Grable's leading man in *Wabash Avenue*, then was asked to play comedy in *Stella*, though he couldn't hold a candle to David Wayne's comic expertise in the same film. RKO felt he would look good in centurion garb and put him in the critically-panned adaptation of Shaw's *Androcles and the Lion*, as a Roman captain.

After appearing in one of the better Esther Williams vehicles, *Million Dollar Mermaid*, he had a trio of hit spectacles: *The Robe*, in which he portrayed a devout follower of Christ, and its sequel, *Demetrius and the Gladiators*, with Mature upped to the lead; as well as *The Egyptian*, where he actually seemed like a fountain of charisma next to the dreary Edmund Purdom.

His rugged facial features somehow allowed him to be more credibly cast as an Indian than most Caucasians, as he was in Universal's *Chief Crazy Horse*, after which he said goodbye to Fox with an above average crime film, *Violent Saturday*, as a small town dad who gets a chance to be a hero during a robbery. He quickly took a dive in a series of programmers and international adventures that gave him steady employment but meant little to moviegoers, including *Safari*, battling Mau Maus; *The Sharkfighters*; *China Doll*, purchasing an Asian bride; *Hannibal*, where he was, not surprisingly, upstaged by the elephants; and *The Tartars*, seeking revenge on barbaric Orson Welles. There was a mild comedy, *After the Fox*, in which he actually got some good reviews, amiably kidding himself as a vain, aging movie star; a weird appearance, playing someone called The Big Victor in the Monkees' starring film, *Head*; and then one last lead, as a gangster in a spoof that didn't make so much as a ripple, *Every Little Crook and Nanny*. He was pretty much retired when the producers of a 1984 television remake of *Samson and Delilah* came up with the idea of casting him as Samson's father, which, if nothing else, was a fitting way to bring closure to his show business career.

Screen: 1939: The Housekeeper's Daughter; **1940:** One Million B.C.; Captain Caution; No, No, Nanette; **1941:** I Wake Up Screaming; The Shanghai Gesture; **1942:** Song of the Islands; My Gal Sal; Footlight Serenade; Seven Days' Leave; **1946:** My Darling Clementine; **1947:** Moss Rose; Kiss of Death; **1948:** Fury at Furnace Creek; Cry of the City; **1949:** Red, Hot and Blue; Easy Living; Samson and Delilah; **1950:** Wabash Avenue; I'll Get By; Stella; Gambling House; **1952:** The Las Vegas Story; Androcles and the Lion; Something for the Birds; Million Dollar Mermaid; **1953:** The Glory Brigade; Affair With a Stranger; The Robe; Veils of Bagdad; **1954:** Dangerous Mission; Demetrius and the Gladiators; Betrayed; The Egyptian; **1955:** Chief Crazy Horse; Violent Saturday; The Last Frontier; **1956:** Safari; The Sharkfighters; **1957:** Zarak; Pickup Alley/Interpol; The Long Haul; **1958:** China Doll; Tank Force/No Time to Die; **1959:** Escort West; The Bandit of Zhobe; The Big Circus; Timbuktu; **1960:** Hannibal; The Tartars; **1966:** After the Fox; **1968:** Head; **1972:** Every Little Crook and Nanny; **1976:** Won Ton Ton, the Dog Who Saved Hollywood; **1979:** Firepower.
NY Stage: 1941: Lady in the Dark; **1944:** Tars and Spars.
Select TV: 1984: Samson and Delilah.

MARILYN MAXWELL

(MARVEL MARILYN MAXWELL) BORN: CLARINDA, IA, AUGUST 3, 1922. DIED: MARCH 20, 1972.

Half a musical comedy attraction, half a sexy blonde hired for window dressing, Marilyn Maxwell didn't really make any lasting impact as either, though it wasn't so much her fault as the lack of chances she had to shine. At 16 she became a vocalist for Amos Ascot and his band, moving from there up to Buddy Rogers's orchestra, then singing for Ted Weems. After taking some acting lessons with the Pasadena Playhouse she was signed by MGM, who didn't do much with her except give her background parts in *Stand by for Action* and *Presenting Lily Mars*, among others. More notable was her role as hospital social worker Ruth Edley, which she played in three *Dr. Kildare* entries. There was also straight-woman duty opposite Abbott and Costello in *Lost in a Harem* and Red Skelton in *The Show-Off*. Maxwell was finally given a chance to show her stuff, musically, when she played the vamp who gets Mickey Rooney drunk in *Summer Holiday*, singing "Weary Blues" to him. Around that time her contract expired, so she went elsewhere to play the nightclub singer Kirk Douglas dumps his wife for in the top-notch boxing drama *Champion*, and then found her niche in Christmas movie history when she got to introduce "Silver Bells," with Bob Hope, in *The Lemon Drop Kid*. Her career began to peter out in the late 1950s after playing a movie star in Jerry Lewis's *Rock-a-Bye Baby*, but Hope asked for her again for a secondary part in *Critic's Choice* (they had also done *Off Limits*, television gigs, and several military tours together), and she ended up in two of those faded-star westerns produced by A.C. Lyles in the 1960s, *Stage to Thunder Rock* and *Arizona Bushwhackers*.

Screen: 1942: Stand by for Action; 1943: Du Barry Was a Lady; Presenting Lily Mars; Thousands Cheer; Dr. Gillespie's Criminal Case; Salute to the Marines; Best Foot Forward; Swing Fever; Pilot # 5; 1944: Three Men in White; Lost in a Harem; Between Two Women; 1946: The Show-Off; 1947: High Barbaree; 1948: Summer Holiday; Race Street; 1949: Champion; 1950: Key to the City; Outside the Wall; 1951: The Lemon Drop Kid; New Mexico; 1953: Off Limits; East of Sumatra; Paris Model; 1955: New York Confidential; 1958: Rock-a-Bye Baby; 1963: Critic's Choice; 1964: Stage to Thunder Rock; The Lively Set; 1968: Arizona Bushwhackers; 1969: From Nashville With Music; 1970: The Phynx.

Select TV: 1953: Twinkle, Twinkle, Little Star (sp); 1954: Best Foot Forward (sp); 1955: Burlesque (sp); 1957: Snow Shoes (sp); 1961–62: Bus Stop (series); 1964: Have Girls Will Travel (sp); 1970: Wild Women.

VIRGINIA MAYO

(VIRGINIA CLARA JONES) BORN: ST. LOUIS, MO, NOVEMBER 30, 1920.

A leggy looker with big rosy cheeks and nearly crossed eyes, Virginia Mayo was that rare lady who made the successful leap from chorus girl-bit player to star. There was, at times, a glossy superficiality to her more benign characterizations, but under the right circumstances she could suggest tough, duplicitous women with a surprising edge. She appeared on Broadway in the cast of Eddie Cantor's *Banjo Eyes*, which resulted in her coming to Hollywood for a small role in *Jack London*, the star of which, Michael O'Shea, she later married, in 1947. There was work in an RKO cheapie, *Seven Days Ashore*, and, more significantly, in the debut movie of comedian Danny Kaye, *Up in Arms*, where she was one of the Goldwyn Girls. Goldwyn felt she was worth trying out as a full-fledged lead and he placed her opposite Bob Hope in one of his funniest farces, *The Princess and the Pirate*, where she looked luscious in Technicolor as royalty incognito, at one point slumming as a tavern singer (her vocals were dubbed). Because of her success in that, she was made one of Kaye's two leading ladies (Vera-Ellen was the other) in *Wonder Man*, playing a pretty sensational-looking librarian. She and Kaye clicked, so she was back with him for the weaker but equally popular *The Kid From Brooklyn*, which also featured Vera-Ellen, though this time she was Kaye's sister and therefore no competition for Mayo. As her reward for dressing up these glossy comedies so nicely, Goldwyn allowed Mayo to stretch, casting her as Dana Andrews's trampy wife, who has gotten tired of waiting for him to return from the war, in the 1946 Oscar winner for Best

Picture, *The Best Years of Our Lives*. She was extremely good in this role, but when she took on the challenge of playing a brassy broad who loosens up meek music professor Danny Kaye in *A Song Is Born*, a remake of *Ball of Fire*, she couldn't approach the heights Barbara Stanwyck had reached in the original. (Having been made a mere seven years before, too many moviegoers remembered just how much better overall the first one was.)

At this point she left Goldwyn and signed up with Warners, who made her *The Girl From Jones Beach*, a particularly idiotic comedy in which she was a schoolteacher who ends up modeling bathsuits; and *Flaxy Martin*, as a femme fatale who ensnares Zachary Scott. Her pinnacle at the studio came when she was cast as the sluttish wife of James Cagney in the sizzling *White Heat*, cheating on him with henchman Steve Cochran and eventually putting a bullet in his beloved old ma. There was a lesser one with Cagney, *The West Point Story*, and the studio offset her dramatic appearances by putting her in similar musical fluff, including *Painting the Clouds with Sunshine*, as a Vegas showgirl on the search for a wealthy husband; the dreadful *She's Working Her Way Through College*, a skewered reworking of *The Male Animal*, with Mayo as a burlesque queen hoping to get her degree; and *She's Back on Broadway*, where she was a fading Hollywood star retreating to the boards to reclaim her past glories. There were also costume pictures that didn't do much more than emphasize her beauty, like the bright Burt Lancaster romp *The Flame and the Arrow*, and the routine naval adventure *Captain Horatio Hornblower*. That she couldn't rise above bad material was evident in two of the silliest movies Warners produced during the 1950s, *King Richard and the Crusaders*, in which she was desired by a dark-skinned Rex Harrison while carrying on with knight Laurence Harvey, and *The Silver Chalice*, with Mayo at her most inept, as the wicked assistant to sorcerer Jack Palance. By the end of the 1950s she was no more than a routine leading lady to Alan Ladd in *The Big Land*, and to Clint Walker in *Fort Dobbs*; in between which a cardboard Cleopatra in the screwy all-star anthology *The Story of Mankind*. There wasn't much demand for her by the 1960s, so she ended up, as many before her, in some A.C. Lyles westerns. After that she would pop up in the credits of movies that didn't usually make their way outside of test-marketing engagements.

Screen: 1943: Jack London/The Adventures of Jack London; 1944: Seven Days Ashore; Up in Arms; The Princess and the Pirate; 1945: Wonder Man; 1946: The Kid From Brooklyn; The Best Years of Our Lives; 1947: The Secret Life of Walter Mitty; Out of the Blue; 1948: A Song Is Born; Smart Girls Don't Talk; 1949: The Girl From Jones Beach; Colorado Territory; Flaxy Martin; White Heat; Red Light; Always Leave Them Laughing; 1950: Backfire; The West Point Story; The Flame and the Arrow; 1951: Along the Great Divide; Painting the Clouds With Sunshine; Captain Horatio Hornblower; Starlift; 1952: She's Working Her Way Through College; The Iron Mistress; 1953: She's Back on Broadway; South Sea Woman; Devil's Canyon; 1954: King Richard and the Crusaders; The Silver Chalice; 1955: Pearl of the South Pacific; 1956: Great Day in the Morning; The Proud Ones; Congo Crossing; 1957: The Big Land; The Story of Mankind; The Tall Stranger; 1958: Fort Dobbs; 1959: Westbound; Jet Over the Atlantic; 1962: Revolt of the Mercenaries (Sp: 1960); 1965: Young Fury; 1966: Castle of Evil; 1967: Fort Utah; 1975: Fugitive Lovers/The Runaways; 1976: Won Ton Ton, the Dog Who Saved Hollywood; 1978: French Quarter; 1979: The Haunted; 1990: Evil Spirits (dtv); 1997: The Man Next Door (dtv).

NY Stage: 1941: Banjo Eyes.

Select TV: 1957: Execution Night (sp); 1959: Deathtrap (sp).

MIKE MAZURKI

(Mikhail Masuruski) Born: Tarnopol, Austria, December 25, 1909.
Died: December 9, 1990.

Built for maximum menace, Mike Mazurki was an ugly mug with an imposing figure and a harsh voice, an unforgettable presence who popped up in roles of all sizes (sometimes he seemed to be doing little more than literally filling up the background). A former professional wrestler, he has been reported as being glimpsed in various 1930s features, but his official movie career did not start until 1941 with a part in the campy *The Shanghai Gesture*. Thereafter he could be seen as a Japanese wrestler who takes on Robert Ryan in *Behind the Rising Sun*; the memorable Moose Malloy, who comes to private eye Dick Powell for assistance in *Murder, My Sweet*; the deadly Splitface, killing off the jurors who convicted him, in *Dick Tracy*; a dangerous carnival strongman in the cult favorite *Nightmare Alley*; and a wrestler who engages in one incredible grappling match with Stanislas Zbysko in the London-set noir *Night and the City*. He also played Don DeFore's homicidal brother, seeking revenge for his murder, in *Dark City*; one of George Raft's henchmen in the classic *Some Like It Hot*; a miner who causes Phil Silvers to detour in *It's a Mad Mad Mad Mad World*; a vulgar Mongolian warrior who makes Anne Bancroft submit to his desires in the trashy *7 Women*; and a bouncer named Mountain Ox, who battles with Roddy McDowall, in Disney's *The Adventures of Bullwhip Griffin*. Then, at long last, he had a leading role, as a fur trapper, in the cheap-o kiddie movie *Challenge to Be Free*, basically distributed to play at a few matinee showings. Fittingly he was last seen, fleetingly, in Warren Beatty's 1990 take on *Dick Tracy*.

Screen: 1934: Belle of the Nineties; 1935: Black Fury; 1941: The Shanghai Gesture; 1942: Gentleman Jim; That Other Woman; About Face; The McGuerins of Brooklyn; Dr. Renault's Secret; 1943: Taxi Mister; Mission to Moscow; Henry Aldrich Haunts a House; Behind the Rising Sun; Prairie Chickens; Thank Your Lucky Stars; Whistling in Brooklyn; Swing Fever; It Ain't Hay; Lost Angel; 1944: The Missing Juror; Summer Storm; The Canterville Ghost; The Thin Man Goes Home; The Princess and the Pirate; Shine On, Harvest Moon; Murder, My Sweet; 1945: Abbott and Costello in Hollywood; Dakota; Dick Tracy; The Horn Blows at Midnight; The Spanish Main; Nob Hill; 1946: The French Key; Live Wires; Mysterious Intruder; 1947: Sinbad the Sailor; I Walk Alone; Killer Dill; Nightmare Alley; Unconquered; 1948: Relentless; The Noose Hangs High; 1949: Come to the Stable; Neptune's Daughter; Abandoned; Rope of Sand; The Devil's Henchman; Samson and Delilah; 1950: Dark City; He's a Cockeyed Wonder; Night and the City; 1951: Pier 23; Criminal Lawyer; My Favorite Spy; Ten Tall Men; The Light Touch; 1954: The Egyptian; 1955: New York Confidential; New Orleans Uncensored; Davy Crockett — King of the Wild Frontier (from TV); Blood Alley; Kismet; 1956: Comanche; Man in the Vault; Around the World in Eighty Days; 1957: Hell Ship Mutiny; 1958: The Buccaneer; The Man Who Died Twice; 1959: Alias Jesse James; Some Like It Hot; 1960: The Facts of Life; 1961: The Errand Boy; Pocketful of Miracles; 1962: Swingin' Along/Double Trouble; Five Weeks in a Balloon; Zotz!; 1963: Donovan's Reef; 4 for Texas; It's a Mad Mad Mad Mad World; 1964: The Disorderly Orderly; Cheyenne Autumn; 1965: Requiem for a Gunfighter; 1966: 7 Women; 1967: The Adventures of Bullwhip Griffin; 1970: Which Way to the Front?; 1974: The Centerfold Girls; 1975: The Wild McCullochs; 1976: Challenge to Be Free (filmed 1972); Won Ton Ton, the Dog Who Saved Hollywood; 1978: One Man Jury; The Magic of Lassie; 1979: Gas Pump Girls; 1980: The Man With Bogart's Face/Sam Marlowe, Private Eye; 1981: Alligator; 1985: Doin' Time; 1987: Amazon Women on the Moon; 1990: Mob Boss (dtv); Dick Tracy.

NY Stage: 1960: Oh Kay!

Select TV: 1966–67: It's About Time (series); 1971: The Chicago Teddy Bears (series).

LON McCALLISTER

(Herbert Alonzo McCallister, Jr.)
Born: Los Angeles, CA, April 17, 1923.

Guileless, with cheeks that shone like apples polished on a plaid flannel shirt, Lon McCallister was the 1940s personification of the farm boy next door, a sweet kid with no pretensions who, after nearly 30 film bits, was suddenly deemed groomable for a stardom that was short-lived. As a teen he possessed a good enough singing voice to get him a job with a group called the Maxwell Choristers. As part of that choir he made his motion picture debut in the background of the 1936 version of *Romeo and Juliet*, becoming good friends with the director, George Cukor. For the next few years he was a strictly a bit film player and radio performer (when there was billing he was sometimes listed as Bud McCallister), until called on to play the boyish soldier, nicknamed California, who gets to recite lines with Katherine Cornell, playing herself, in the all-star morale booster *Stage Door Canteen*. That movie's producer, Sol Lesser, signed him to a contract, but since most of McCallister's assignments were on loan to 20th Century-Fox, it was understandably assumed by many that he was a regular at that studio. For them he participated in the big screen adapation of *Winged Victory*, as the fresh young recruit who's got a loving wife back home and a kid on the way, thereby sealing his fate when he takes his plane up for a test run; Walter Brennan's shy nephew in the Technicolor *Home in Indiana*, a role not unlike another he did with Brennan, *Scudda Hoo! Scudda Hay!*, in which he got a kick out of training mules, in a movie that wasn't really as bad as its ridiculous title suggested. For Lesser he was the farm hand suspicious of Edward G. Robinson in the melodrama *The Red House*, then partnered some growing child stars in *The Big Cat* (Peggy Ann Garner) and *The Story of Seabiscuit* (Shirley Temple). He finished his movie career in three Columbia programmers in the early 1950s and then retired from the business with no regrets, eventually switching his livelihood to real estate.

Screen: 1936: Romeo and Juliet; Let's Sing Again; 1937: Internes Can't Take Money; Souls at Sea; Stella Dallas; Make a Wish; 1938: The Adventures of Tom Sawyer; Judge Hardy's Children; Lord Jeff; That Certain Age; Little Tough Guys in Society; 1939: Spirit of Culver; Confessions of a Nazi Spy; The Angels Wash Their Faces; Babes in Arms; First Love; Joe and Ethel Turp Call on the President; 1940: High School; Susan and God; 1941: Henry Aldrich for President; 1942: Dangerously They Live; Always in My Heart; Spy Ship; Yankee Doodle Dandy; The Hard Way; Gentleman Jim; Quiet Please, Murder; Over My Dead Body; 1943: The Meanest Man in the World; Stage Door Canteen; 1944: Home in Indiana; Winged Victory; 1947: The Red House; Thunder in the Valley; 1948: Scudda Hoo! Scudda Hay!; 1949: The Big Cat; The Story of Seabiscuit; 1950: The Boy From Indiana; 1951: A Yank in Korea; 1952: Montana Territory; 1953: Combat Squad.

Select TV: 1950: The Wisteria Cottage (sp); Down Bayou DuBac (sp); 1951: Enemy Unknown (sp); 1953: My Daughter's Husband (sp); Operation Riviera (sp).

MERCEDES McCAMBRIDGE
(CARLOTTA MERCEDES AGNES McCAMBRIDGE)
BORN: JOLIET, IL, MARCH 17, 1918.

Tight-lipped Mercedes McCambridge, with her cold, demanding eyes, was a great supporting presence in the few movies she made, even if her delivery was a tad florid at times. The bulk of her early acting was done on radio prior to her going to Broadway, in 1945, to take a role in *A Place of Her Own*. Because of her stage work, she got the sort of satisfying movie debut role that few ever hope to get, the no-nonsense secretary and part-time lover of megalomaniac politician Broderick Crawford in the searing 1949 adaptation of the best-seller *All the King's Men*. She not only made a meal of the part but also won the Academy Award for Best Supporting Actress. With one of her co-stars from that film, John Ireland, she got a fairly substantial role in an overheated melodrama called *The Scarf*, playing a singing waitress named Cash and Carry Connie. Then she dallied in camp, as the butch cattle queen who opposes Joan Crawford, in the undeniably entertaining western *Johnny Guitar*, scorching the screen as one gun-toting female you'd be crazy to tangle with. There was another fine, Oscar nominated performance, as Rock Hudson's jealous sister, in *Giant*, after which she played Elizabeth Taylor's mom in the sensationalistic hit *Suddenly, Last Summer*, and George Hamilton's nasty, older wife in *Angel Baby*. There was little to remark on after that, except for her devastating, unbilled participation in the gargantuan box-office success of 1973, *The Exorcist*, as the vile, curse-spewing voice of the possessed Linda Blair, one of the most unforgettable examples of a performer making her mark without ever being seen or even billed. There were two memoirs, *The Two of Us* (1960) and *A Quality of Mercy* (1981).

Screen: 1949: All the King's Men; 1951: Inside Straight; Lightning Strikes Twice; The Scarf; 1954: Johnny Guitar; 1956: Giant; 1957: A Farewell to Arms; 1958: Touch of Evil; 1959: Suddenly, Last Summer; 1960: Cimarron; 1961: Angel Baby; 1965: Run Home Slow; 1969: Deadly Sanctuary/Marquis de Sade: Justine (nUSr); 99 Women/Island of Despair; 1973: The Exorcist (voice); 1974: Like a Crow on a June Bug/Sixteen; 1977: Thieves; 1979: The Concorde — Airport '79; 1983: Echoes.

NY Stage: 1945: A Place of Her Own; 1946: Woman Bites Dog; 1948: The Young and the Fair; 1963: Cages (ob); Who's Afraid of Virginia Woolf?; 1972: The Love Suicide at Schofield Barracks; 1991: Lost in Yonkers.

Select TV: 1950: The Voice of the Cricket (sp); The Lovely Menace (sp); 1952: Crossed and Double-Crossed (sp); 1953: Shadow of the Devil (sp); Fly With the Hawk (sp); 1955: Tender Is the Night (sp); 1956: A Public Figure (sp); Pretend You Belong to Me (sp); 1956–57: Wire Service (series); 1958: On the Brink (sp); 1966: The People Trip (sp); 1968: The Counterfeit Killer; 1972: Killer by Night; Two for the Money; 1973: The Girls of Huntington House; The President's Plane Is Missing; 1975: Who Is the Black Dahlia?; 1979: The Sacketts.

KEVIN McCARTHY
BORN: SEATTLE, WA, FEBRUARY 15, 1914.
ED: UNIV. OF MI.

Principally a man of the stage, Kevin McCarthy was never less than professional but hardly the stuff of which unforgettable actors are made. Trained at the Actors Studio, he made his Broadway debut in 1938, in *Abe Lincoln in Illinois*, and would stay exclusively on the boards for the next

decade or so, his only film appearance during this time being a brief bit as one of the fliers in Fox's adaptation of the patriotic hit *Winged Victory*. McCarthy finally made his big splash in the London production of Arthur Miller's landmark drama *Death of a Salesman*, playing the elder son, Biff, stifled by his inability to find his place in the world. Invited to repeat the part in the 1951 film version, he thereby made his "official" motion picture bow to great acclaim, earning a supporting actor Oscar nomination for his magnificent performance. In many ways he would never again dare exhibit so raw and riveting an emotional display. He continued in support, as the cattle baron's son accused of murder in *Stranger on Horseback*, and a bank robber in *Drive a Crooked Road*, among others. In a low-budget Pine-Thomas production, *Nightmare*, he had a star part, opposite Edward G. Robinson, as a jazz musician whose all-too-realistic visions suggest he may have committed murder. When at last he was given top billing, it was in a movie that was received quietly at the time but became his best-remembered work, the brilliant sci-fi paranoia thriller *Invasion of the Body Snatchers*. He was so memorably cast as the hero on the run from replicated earthlings that he would reprise the part in a gag appearance in the 1978 remake. After carrying the Fox cheapie *Diamond Safari*, it was back to secondary roles, where he was cast as figures of authority, cynics, windbags, or square-jawed villains. In *The Best Man* he was in top form, as Henry Fonda's campaign manager; *A Big Hand for a Little Lady*, cast him as one of the gamblers who takes on Joanne Woodward; and *Ace High*, was one of those 1960s spaghetti westerns with some American names thrown in for international appeal, with McCarthy as a desperado. Later he appeared in *Buffalo Bill and the Indians*, in bushy wig and moustache as a member of Paul Newman's colorful clique; *Hero at Large*, as a shady politician; *My Tutor*, as Matt Lattanzi's snobby dad; and *Innerspace*, as a scheming scientist who gets shrunk. His sister, author Marty McCarthy, was best known for writing *The Group*.

Screen: 1944: Winged Victory; 1951: Death of a Salesman; 1954: Drive a Crooked Road; The Gambler From Natchez; 1955: Stranger on Horseback; An Annapolis Story; 1956: Nightmare; Invasion of the Body Snatchers; 1958: Diamond Safari; 1961: The Misfits; 1963: 40 Pounds of Trouble; A Gathering of Eagles; The Prize; 1964: An Affair of the Skin; The Best Man; 1965: Mirage; 1966: A Big Hand for the Little Lady; The Three Sisters; 1967: Hotel; 1968: The Hell With Heroes; If He Hollers, Let Him Go!/Night Hunt; 1969: Ace High/Revenge at El Paso; 1972: Richard; Kansas City Bomber; 1975: Alien Thunder/Dan Candy's Law; Order to Kill; 1976: Buffalo Bill and the Indians, or Sitting Bull's History Lesson; 1978: Piranha; Invasion of the Body Snatchers; 1980: Hero at Large; Those Lips, Those Eyes; 1981: The Howling; 1983: My Tutor; Twilight Zone: The Movie; 1987: Hostage; Dark Tower (dtv); Innerspace; 1989: Fast Food; UHF; 1990: Love or Money; The Sleeping Car; 1991: Eve of Destruction; Ghoulies 3: Ghoulies Go to College (dtv); Final Approach; 1992: The Distinguished Gentleman; 1993: Matinee; 1994: Greedy; Judicial Consent (dtv); 1995: Just Cause; Steal Big, Steal Little; Mommy (dtv); 1998: Addams Family Reunion (dtv).

NY Stage: 1938: Abe Lincoln in Illinois; 1940: Flight to the West; 1942: Mexican Mural (ob); 1943: Winged Victory; 1946: Truckline Café; Joan of Lorraine; 1948: The Survivors; Bravo!; 1952: Anna Christie; 1953: Love's Labour's Lost; The Deep Blue Sea; 1954: The Seagull (ob); 1955: Red Roses for Me; 1958: The Day the Money Stopped; 1959: Two for the Seesaw; Marching Song (ob); 1960: Advise and Consent; 1962: Something About a Soldier; Brecht on Brecht (ob); 1964: The Three Sisters; 1967: A Warm Body; Cactus Flower; 1970: Happy Birthday, Wanda June (ob; and Bdwy.); 1972: The Children (ob); 1974: The Rapists (ob); 1975: Harry Outside (ob); 1976: Poor Murderer; 1984: Alone Together.

Select TV: 1950: Power Devil (sp); 1951: Hangman's House (sp); 1952: Sunk (sp); 1953: Double Jeopardy (sp); The King in Yellow (sp); 1954: Lucky Tommy Jordan (sp); Highway (sp); The Magnificent Lie (sp); Spring Reunion (sp); Satins and Spurs (sp); The Personal Touch (sp); 1955: Make Believe Mother (sp); 1956: The Secret Place (sp); 1957: Doctors of Pawnee Kill (sp); City in Flames (sp); The Last Singer (sp); The Medallion (sp); A Question of Survival (sp); 1959: Murder and Android (sp); 1961: Moment of Panic (sp); 1962: Two Black Kings (sp); Journey to Oblivion (sp); The First Day (sp); 1966: Crazier Than Cotton (sp); 1969: U.M.C.; The Survivors (series); 1972: A Great American Tragedy; Between Time and Timbuktu (sp); 1974: June Moon (sp); 1975: The Sea Gull (sp); 1977: Exo-Man; Mary Jane Harper Cried Last Night; 1980: Flamingo Road; Portrait of an Escort; 1981–82: Flamingo Road (series); 1982: Rosie: The Story of Rosemary Clooney; 1983: Amanda's (series); Making of a Male Model; 1984: Invitation to Hell; The Ratings Game; 1985: Deadly Intentions; The Midnight Hour; 1986: A Masterpiece of Murder; 1987: LBJ: The Early Years; Poor Little Rich Girl: The Barbara Hutton Story (ms); The Long Journey Home; 1988: Once Upon a Texas Train; 1989: Passion and Paradise; 1990: The Rose and the Jackal; 1991: Dead on the Money; 1991–92: Charlie Hoover (series); 1992: Duplicates; 1994: Roadracers; 1995: The Sister-in-Law; Liz: The Elizabeth Taylor Story; 1997: The Second Civil War; Elvis Meets Nixon.

DOUG McCLURE

BORN: GLENDALE, CA, MAY 11, 1935. ED: UCLA. DIED: FEBRUARY 5, 1995.

Grinning beneath a mess of blond hair, Doug McClure was a strapping man of action who made several forays into theatrical features but whose decidedly lightweight presence fared better on the small screen. Offers to do print ads and TV commercials eventually led to his big-screen bow for Fox, as a member of Robert Mitchum's destroyer crew, in the 1957 war drama The Enemy Below, after which he was back in the military, as a pilot in South Pacific. In 1960 he began to shift into higher gear with the high school drama Because They're Young, as one of the misunderstood teens; regular roles on two series, The Overland Trail and Checkmate; and an important part as Burt Lancaster's younger brother in the John Huston western The Unforgiven. He officially became a star when he was cast as Trampas (no longer the villain he was in the novel and movie adaptations) in the hit series based on The Virginian, which ran from 1962 to 1971. During this time Universal, the studio that produced the series, kept him busy on the big screen as well, giving him a good role as James Stewart's son-in-law in Shenandoah; in addition to casting him as James Darren's buddy in the racing flick The Lively Set; John Geste in the 1966 version of Beau Geste; and as the star of his own low-budget vehicles, The King's Pirate (in the role Errol Flynn had once played in Against All Flags), and the limp service comedy, Nobody's Perfect, both of which looked like they were made with the tube in mind. A TV movie staple in the 1970s, he was called back to the large screen for a quartet of cheesy British-made fantasies, the first three from Edgar Rice Burroughs stories: The Land That Time Forgot, finding dinosaurs in South America; At the Earth's Core, journeying to the center of the earth, with Peter Cushing; The People That Time Forgot, having been forgotten on that island from the earlier film; and Warlords of Atlantis. Also, on a similarly des-

perate entertainment level were the pricelessly stupid horror film Humanoids From the Deep, as a bad guy, and the Samurai ghost tale, The House Where Evil Dwells, where he ended up losing his head. His second wife was actress Barbara Luna.

Screen: 1957: The Enemy Below; 1958: South Pacific; 1959: Gidget; 1960: The Unforgiven; Because They're Young; 1964: The Lively Set; 1965: Shenandoah; 1966: Beau Geste; 1967: The King's Pirate; 1968: Nobody's Perfect; 1973: Hellhounds of Alaska/ Fight for Gold (dtv); 1974: What Changed Charley Farthing/The Bananas Boat; 1975: The Land That Time Forgot; 1976: At the Earth's Core; 1977: The People That Time Forgot; 1978: Warlords of Atlantis; 1980: Humanoids From the Deep; Firebird 2015 A.D. (dtv); 1982: The House Where Evil Dwells; 1984: Cannonball Run II; 1986: 52 Pick-Up; 1987: Omega Syndrome; 1988: Dark Before Dawn; Tapeheads; Prime Suspect (dtv); 1994: Maverick; 1995: Riders in the Storm (dtv).

NY Stage: 1980: The Roast.

Select TV: 1960: The Overland Trail (series); 1960–62: Checkmate (series); 1961: Street of Love (sp); 1962–71: The Virginian/The Men From Shiloh (series); 1967: The Longest Hundred Miles; 1971: Terror in the Sky; The Birdmen; The Death of Me Yet; 1972: Playmates; The Judge and Jake Wyler; 1972–73: Search (series); 1973: Shirts/Skins; Death Race; 1975: Satan's Triangle; 1975–76: Barbary Coast (series); 1977: Roots (ms); SST — Death Flight; 1978: Wild and Wooly; Strange Companions; 1979: The Rebels (ms); 1980: Nightside; 1985: Half Nelson; 1987–90: Out of This World (series); 1991: The Gambler Returns: The Luck of the Draw; 1992: Battling for Baby.

PATTY McCORMACK

BORN: BROOKLYN, NY, AUGUST 21, 1945.

Famous as one of filmdom's most horrific brats, Patty McCormack had been modeling since the age of four. This naturally led to acting, mostly on television (she was a regular on the series Mama), and a role in a "B" film, Two Gals and a Guy. Her rather short-lived stardom came when she was cast as the monstrous little girl who projects innocence on the outside while committing murder, in the 1954 Broadway hit The Bad Seed. Two years later she came to Hollywood to repeat her role in Warners's big-screen adaptation, although the censors required her to be done away with in a ludicrous, tacked-on ending, getting hit by a bolt of lightning! Despite its melodramatic excesses and badly overdone histrionics, the movie was a hit and earned young McCormack a supporting Oscar nomination, making her one of the youngest ever to be up for the trophy. To cash in on her success, Universal came up with a vehicle, Kathy O', which cast her as another brat, this time an incorrigible movie star, but it didn't suggest that she was going to be one of the cinema's lasting kiddie acts. That same year she showed up as one of the farm children who loses her parents and has to be given away to the neighbors in the sentimental All Mine to Give. In the 1960s she had no choice but to join in the cinematic "youth movement," thereby becoming one of The Explosive Generation, The Young Runaways, and The Young Animals, as well as singing the title song in The Mini-Skirt Mob. Apparently producers couldn't resist cashing in on her former fame as a celluloid hellraiser, an urge that lasted into the 1990s when she popped up in the direct-to-video thriller Mommy, as a killer mom.

Screen: 1951: Two Gals and a Guy; 1956: The Bad Seed; 1958: Kathy O'; All Mine to Give/The Day They Gave the Babies Away; 1960: The Snow Queen (voice); The Adventures of Huckleberry Finn; 1961: The Explosive Generation; 1962:

Jacktown; 1968: Maryjane; The Mini-Skirt Mob; The Young Runaways; The Young Animals/Born Wild; 1975: Bug; 1988: Saturday the 14th Strikes Back; 1995: Mommy (dtv); 1996: Mommy 2: Mommy's Day (dtv); 2000: The Silencing (dtv); 2001: Choosing Mathias (nUSr); The Medicine Show (nUSr); 2002: The Kids (dtv); Inhabited (nUSr).

NY Stage: 1953: Touchstone; 1954: The Bad Seed.

Select TV: 1953–56: Mama (series); 1954: I Remember, I Remember (sp); The Golden Box (sp); Somebody Special (sp); Jody and Me (sp); 1956: An Episode of Sparrows (sp); Alien Angel (sp); 1957: The Miracle Worker (sp); We Won't Be Any Trouble (sp); Child of Trouble (sp); Sing a Song (sp); The Clouded Image (sp); 1958: The Spell of the Tigress (sp); The Devil's Violin (sp); The Dungeon (sp); 1958–63: Young Dr. Malone (series); 1959: Peck's Bad Girl (series); Project Immortality (sp); Rachel's Summer (sp); Make Me Not a Witch (sp); 1966: Burning Bright (sp); 1970: The Best of Everything (series); 1979–80: The Ropers (series); 1983: Night Partners; 1984: Invitation to Hell; 1986: On Wings of Eagles (ms); 1999: Silent Predators; 2001: Robin Cook's Acceptable Risk.

JOEL McCREA

BORN: SOUTH PASADENA, CA, NOVEMBER 5, 1905. ED: POMONA UNIV. DIED: OCTOBER 20, 1990.

Not unlike Gary Cooper, Joel McCrea was tall, handsome, soft-spoken, and undeniably all-American. Though never a major box-office sensation like Cooper, he was the sort of low-keyed fellow movie audiences liked to have around, trustworthy and decent, an underrated light comedian, and one of the cinema's most convincing cowboys. From community theater productions he went into movies as an extra until elevated to a substantial role, in The Jazz Age, in 1929. He went over to MGM for a brief period, where his assignments included a secondary part in director Cecil B. DeMille's Dynamite, and then to Fox, where he was in Will Rogers's Lightnin'. In 1931 he became a contract player at RKO who cast him as a "regular feller" who ends up with socialite Dorothy Mackaill in Kept Husbands. The studio tried to picture him and Constance Bennett as a team, so they ended up in four films together, Born to Love, your standard soldier-presumed-dead-leaves-behind-pregnant-girlfriend melodrama; The Common Law, with McCrea as an American in Paris; Rockabye, which cast him as a playwright; and Bed of Roses, in which Bennett robbed McCrea, then loved him. There was also the kitschy Bird of Paradise, in which he fell for islander Dolores Del Rio; The Silver Cord (at MGM), notable for first teaming him with Frances Dee, who became his wife in 1933; and his best-remembered movie from this period, The Most Dangerous Game, in which he was hunted by crazed Leslie Banks. He was a dopey filling station attendant who ignores Ginger Rogers, opting for Marion Nixon instead, in Chance at Heaven, and the man pursuing The Richest Girl in the World, which was Miriam Hopkins posing as her own secretary. Ending his RKO stint, he stopped off at Paramount to play a kindly doctor in Private Worlds, and at Fox to continue his filmic medical practice, as Shirley Temple's dad, in Our Little Girl.

Goldwyn signed him to a contract, and he started off with three in a row with Hopkins: Barbary Coast, his honesty contrasting with Edward G. Robinson's unscrupulousness; Splendor, playing a rich boy who upsets his family by marrying a commoner; and his best film yet, These Three, in which he was linked with Merle Oberon but loved by Hopkins, resulting in a scandal at a girls' school. There was another big one for Goldwyn, Come

and Get It, about a logging family, in which Edward Arnold, Frances Farmer, and Walter Brennan were given all the showier scenes, and then he quietly kept his place again, while Bogart, Claire Trevor, and the Dead End Kids acted up a storm, in the outstanding film version of Dead End, where the character's handicap from the original play was, unfortunately, dispensed with. Over at Paramount McCrea created the role of Dr. Kildare in Internes Can't Take Money, but didn't stay with the property when it went over to MGM to become a successful series of low-budget dramas. He then did his first western, the popular but undistinguished Wells Fargo, helping to expand the famous delivery service while romancing his now-wife, Dee. There was another western that scored big at the box office, DeMille's Union Pacific, which marked the fourth time he'd been paired with Barbara Stanwyck (the others were Gambling Lady, Banjo on My Knee, and Internes...). He finished up his contract with Goldwyn with They Shall Have Music, which presented Jascha Heifetz and music as the salvation of slum kids. He and Ginger Rogers reunited to good effect in Primrose Path, in which he was a well-meaning guy who couldn't cope with her family's squalid background, and he was lucky to be given the lead in one of director Alfred Hitchcock's best films of the 1940s, Foreign Correspondent, as the crime reporter on the trail of an elusive Dutch diplomat.

Next up was a deal with Paramount, and it was during this period that his charm as a comedy player was best displayed, in director Preston Sturges's superb Sullivan's Travels, as the discontented movie director who takes to the road disguised as a hobo to see how the simple folk live. It segued from laughs to pathos effortlessly, but a follow-up for Sturges stuck pretty much to comedy, The Palm Beach Story, with McCrea squabbling with Claudette Colbert, but having the whole thing stolen from them both by Rudy Vallee of all people. A third for Sturges, the mostly serious The Great Moment, a period piece about the inventor of anesthesia, wasn't quite what anyone expected, and flopped in a big way. In between those he was back with Stanwyck for The Great Man's Lady, a very minor oil saga with major ambitions; accepted an offer from Columbia to appear with Jean Arthur in a tepid but popular wartime comedy, The More the Merrier; and stopped by Fox to play Hollywood's version of Buffalo Bill, where at least he didn't look as silly in long locks and goatee as one might have feared. For his Paramount finale the studio dusted off the one that had made Gary Cooper a star, The Virginian, principally because they could now do it in color.

McCrea was feeling mighty good on the range and pretty much made westerns his genre of choice from the late 1940s on. These included Ramrod, in which he tried to help Veronica Lake get back at villain Preston Foster; the low-keyed character study Four Faces West, with McCrea cast as a reluctant banker robber, opposite Dee as a nurse; Stars in My Crown, which was not so much an authentic western as a gentle rural piece about an upstanding preacher; and The Outriders, in which he participated in a wagon hijack, but unwillingly, this being Joel McCrea after all. He appeared in Frenchie, the ill-advised remake of Destry Rides Again, with his character no longer a youthful man of the law, as James Stewart was in the original; Cattle Drive, bringing bratty Dean Stockwell down to earth; Wichita, which became the basis of his later TV series, Wichita Town, though not with him playing Wyatt Earp as he did in the movie; Stranger on Horseback, as a gun-tottin' judge; The Oklahoman, as a doctor out West; Trooper Hook, which dealt with racism and partnered him with Stanwyck one last time; and The Gunfight at Dodge City, in which he portrayed a gambler-turned-sheriff. By the end of the 1950s these were pretty much dismissed as programmers, and McCrea, as many actors did when they spent so much time in the saddle, occasionally lapsed into dullness. There was one last career high point, however, when he was teamed with another old-timer who had become a western staple, Randolph Scott, for *Ride the High Country*, an intelligent and moving story that by rights should have been McCrea's swan song. Instead he came back for two that hardly showed up anywhere, *Cry Blood, Apache*, opposite son Jody, and *Mustang Country*. At the time of his death in 1990, his marriage to Dee had been one of the sturdiest and longest lasting in Hollywood history.

Screen: 1927: The Fair Co-Ed; The Enemy; 1928: Freedom of the Press; The Five O'Clock Girl; 1929: The Jazz Age; The Single Standard; So This Is College; Dynamite; 1930: The Silver Horde; Lightnin'; 1931: Once a Sinner; Kept Husbands; Born to Love; The Common Law; Girls About Town; 1932: Business and Pleasure; The Lost Squadron; Bird of Paradise; The Most Dangerous Game; Rockabye; The Sport Parade; 1933: The Silver Cord; Bed of Roses; Scarlet River; One Man's Journey; Chance at Heaven; 1934: Gambling Lady; Half a Sinner; The Richest Girl in the World; 1935: Private Worlds; Our Little Girl; Woman Wanted; Barbary Coast; Splendor; 1936: These Three; Two in a Crowd; Adventure in Manhattan; Come and Get It; Banjo on My Knee; 1937: Internes Can't Take Money; Woman Chases Man; Dead End; Wells Fargo; 1938: Three Blind Mice; Youth Takes a Fling; 1939: Union Pacific; They Shall Have Music; Espionage Agent; 1940: He Married His Wife; Primrose Path; Foreign Correspondent; 1941: Reaching for the Sun; Sullivan's Travels; 1942: The Great Man's Lady; The Palm Beach Story; 1943: The More the Merrier; 1944: Buffalo Bill; The Great Moment; 1945: The Unseen; 1946: The Virginian; 1947: Ramrod; 1948: Four Faces West; 1949: South of St. Louis; Colorado Territory; 1950: Stars in My Crown; The Outriders; Saddle Tramp; Frenchie; 1951: Cattle Drive; Hollywood Story; 1952: The San Francisco Story; Rough Shoot/Shoot First; 1953: Lone Hand; 1954: Border River; Black Horse Canyon; 1955: Stranger on Horseback; Wichita; 1956: The First Texan; 1957: The Oklahoman; Trooper Hook; Gunsight Ridge; The Tall Stranger; 1958: Cattle Empire; Fort Massacre; 1959: The Gunfight at Dodge City; 1961: Ride the High Country; 1970: Cry Blood, Apache/Machismo; 1974: The Great American Cowboy (narrator); 1976: Mustang Country; 1985: George Stevens: A Filmmaker's Journey; 1990: Preston Sturges: The Rise and Fall of an American Dreamer.

Select TV: 1959–60: Wichita Town (series); 1967: Winchester '73 (narrator).

HATTIE McDANIEL
Born: Wichita, KS, June 10, 1895.
Died: October 26, 1952.

Historically significant as the first black performer to win an Academy Award, Hattie McDaniel, nevertheless, was not granted the chance to benefit from this highest of industry honors and rise above playing anything more than domestics. It was as if she was aware of Hollywood's lowly opinion of her race and retaliated by becoming one of the cinema's great sassy observers of human foibles, grunting back at disrespect and stupidity with tart aplomb. After singing with Professor George Morrison's Colored Orchestra of Denver, she appeared in vaudeville and on radio (often said to be the first black woman to sing in that medium); and on the road with *Show Boat*. From there she went to Hollywood, making her debut in *The Golden West*, in 1932, cast as (surprise!) a servant. This

pretty much sealed her fate, though there were pleasant diversions of sorts along the way, starting with *Judge Priest*, one of the handful of times she got to show off her vocalizing talents, in this case with star Will Rogers. In *Alice Adams* she supplied the movie with its funniest scene, trying valiantly to serve dinner to Katharine Hepburn and her date Fred MacMurray in unbearable heat, and then had a real chance to sparkle, repeating her stage role in the 1936 version of *Show Boat*. Not only did she chirp in on "Can't Help Lovin' Dat Man," but also sang a great number written for the film, "Ah Still Suits Me," browbeating Paul Robeson for his laziness. The size of her assignments varied from film to film, as did the identity of her characters. Sometimes she was listed merely as "Black Woman," then, on occasion, conveniently, as Hattie, if at all. In the screwball classic *Nothing Sacred*, she was barely in it but had a priceless moment towards the beginning, exposing her delinquent husband, masquerading as a Sultan, as a fraud.

Her crowning moment, of course, came when she was cast as Vivien Leigh's "Mammy" in the motion picture event of 1939, *Gone With the Wind*. Despite the fact that she was basically doing servant duty again, she gave a strong performance, both humorous and moving, highlighted comically by the look of disbelief she gives the lying Scarlet (Leigh) from the back of a buckboard, and dramatically by her heartbreaking scene telling Melanie (Olivia de Havilland) of the misery the death of Scarlet's daughter has wrought. She won an extremely popular Academy Award for Best Supporting Actress and then went promptly back to playing maids and cooks. In the latter category she was the suffering mom who sees Bette Davis try to do evil to her son in *In This Our Life*, while in the World War II home-front epic *Since You Went Away*, she loyally stood by Claudette Colbert and her family in hard times. The all-star *Thank Your Lucky Stars* put her in a rousing production number, "Ice Cold Katie," and she sang the warm and lovely "Sooner or Later" in Disney's *Song of the South*. Radio didn't change her employment status, but it did alter her billing. As *Beulah*, she was undeniably a maid, but it was a starring role, one she was supposed to continue on television until illness forced her to relinquish the part (McDaniel ended up doing only two episodes) to another fine actress who'd similarly done more than her share of time in cinematic kitchens, Louise Beavers.

Screen: 1932: The Golden West; The Boiling Point; Blonde Venus; Hypnotized; Washington Masquerade; Are You Listening?; Impatient Maiden; Crooner; 1933: I'm No Angel; The Story of Temple Drake; Hello, Sister; 1934: Operator 13; King Kelly of the USA; Lost in the Stratosphere; Judge Priest; Babbitt; Little Men; Imitation of Life; Merry Wives of Reno; 1935: Music is Magic; Harmony Lane; Alice Adams; Traveling Saleslady; The Little Colonel; Another Face; China Seas; Murder by Television; We're Only Human; 1936: Gentle Julia; Next Time We Love; Show Boat; High Tension; Postal Inspector; The Singing Kid; Reunion; Libeled Lady; The First Baby; Hearts Divided; Star for a Night; The Bride Walks Out; Valiant Is the Word for Carrie; Can This Be Dixie?; 1937: Racing Lady; The Crime Nobody Saw; Saratoga; True Confession; 45 Fathers; Nothing Sacred; Over the Goal; The Wildcatter; Don't Tell the Wife; Merry-Go-Round of 1938; Quick Money; Sky Racket; Stella Dallas; 1938: Vivacious Lady; Battle of Broadway; The Shining Hour; The Mad Miss Manton; Carefree; The Shopworn Angel; 1939: Everybody's Baby; Zenobia; Gone With the Wind; 1940: Maryland; 1941: Affectionately Yours; The Great Lie; They Died With Their Boots On; 1942: The Male Animal; In This Our Life; George Washington Slept Here; 1943: Johnny Come Lately; Thank Your Lucky Stars; 1944: Since You Went Away; Janie; Three Is a Family; Hi, Beautiful; 1946: Janie Gets Married; Margie; Never

Say Goodbye; 1946: Song of the South; 1947: The Flame; 1948: Mickey; Family Honeymoon; 1949: The Big Wheel.
Select TV: 1952: Beulah (series).

RAY McDONALD

BORN: BOSTON, MA, JUNE 27, 1920.
DIED: FEBRUARY 20, 1959.

One of the unsung talents who brightened many an MGM musical, Ray McDonald was an exceptional dancer with a goofy charm, whom the studio just wasn't sure what to do with. With his sister Grace he began dancing in nightclubs at the age of ten. Eventually they both debuted on Broadway in the original 1937 production of *Babes in Arms*. It was an out-of-town engagement, in a show called *H'ya, Gentlemen*, that won him a contract with Metro in 1941. Oddly they debuted him in a non-musical part, in a programmer, *Down in San Diego*, in which he was able to display his comedic talents, as a teen helping to battle spies. He finally got a chance to cut loose on the dance floor in a sensational solo in the "Hoe-Down" number from the Rooney-Garland musical *Babes on Broadway*, and in a back-alley tap in *Born to Sing*, his only leading musical role for MGM. He was Mickey Rooney's doomed buddy in *Life Begins for Andy Hardy*, and Judy Garland's disgusted boyfriend in *Presenting Lily Mars*, before going off to join the war and the cast of the soldier-filled Broadway revue *Winged Victory*. When Fox decided to make a film of the last, McDonald was asked to do some footwork for the cameras but wasn't even given billing in the final print. Back at Metro he got to sing the title song in the all-star hit *Till the Clouds Roll By*, and had another chance to shine, dancing up a storm alongside Joan McCracken in the exciting "Pass That Peace Pipe" number from *Good News*. Dropped by the studio, he went to some poverty-row companies for *Shamrock Hill* and *There's a Girl in My Heart*, both of which paired him with Peggy Ryan. They became a team and then briefly (1953–57) husband and wife, prior to McDonald's untimely demise, accidentally choking on food in a Manhattan hotel room, though his death has been variously reported over the years as either a suicide or an accidental drug overdose.
Screen: 1941: Down in San Diego; Life Begins for Andy Hardy; Babes on Broadway; 1942: Born to Sing; 1943: Presenting Lily Mars; 1944: Winged Victory; 1947: Till the Clouds Roll By; Good News; 1949: Shamrock Hill; Flame of Youth; There's a Girl in My Heart; 1953: All Ashore.
NY Stage: 1937: Babes in Arms; 1943: Winged Victory; 1946: Park Avenue.

RODDY McDOWALL

(RODERICK ANDREW ANTHONY JUDE McDOWALL) BORN: LONDON, ENGLAND, SEPTEMBER 17, 1928. DIED: OCTOBER 3, 1998.

It's a rare child star that grows up to be as interesting to watch, if not more so, as an adult, but Roddy McDowall was such a case. Darling, sad eyed, and sensitive as a lad, he blossomed into a versatile, handsome performer with a penchant for playing snobs, eccentrics, and men of refinement, nicely punctuated by his gentle speaking voice. Both he and his sister Virginia were encouraged by their mom to try acting, and this led to Roddy's 1938 motion picture debut, in *Murder in the Family*, which also featured a youthful Glynis Johns. Altogether there were 15 British film appearances during this period, with titles like *Hey! Hey!*

USA!; Dirt; and Dead Man's Shoes, almost none of them of any consequence, although he did get to play the younger version of Emlyn Williams at the beginning of *You Will Remember*. McDowall's mother moved the children with her to America, where she hoped to get the film companies interested in her son. As chance would have it, 20th Century-Fox was looking for a boy, preferably English, for their prestigious production of *How Green Was My Valley*. (Before that one got started he had a brief scene aboard a ship with Walter Pigeon in the thriller *Man Hunt*.) The finished version of *Valley* turned out to be a masterful mood piece, meticulously directed by John Ford, about a family of Welsh coal miners. McDowall, as the youngest son, was astonishingly good, clearly one of the best child actors to be given a substantial role in an American production in quite some time. The surprise box-office success of the drama, along with its Academy Award for Best Picture of 1941, helped guarantee the young actor's position as a new star. Of course he would be called on to portray bigger stars as children, as he did in *Son of Fury* (Tyrone Power) and *The Keys of the Kingdom* (Gregory Peck), but the studio felt they could sell him in leading roles as well and gave him one in a quickie, *On the Sunny Side*, a bit of wartime propaganda in which he was a young lad sent to America to escape the blitz. Similarly he and some other moppets were safely escorted out of Germany by Monty Woolley in the enjoyable *The Pied Piper*, after which he scored in one of the most pleasing of all boy-and-his-horse pictures, *My Friend Flicka*.

As if it wasn't heartbreaking enough seeing McDowall get all teary eyed for an unwanted colt, MGM borrowed him for the film that featured his best-remembered role as an adolescent, *Lassie Come Home*. The story of a poor English boy who is crushed when his parents have to sell his beloved collie, this was the pinnacle of the studio's sharp eye for producing stellar family entertainment, with McDowall simply wonderful, acting alongside 11-year-old Elizabeth Taylor, who would become a lifelong friend. MGM kept him on to play Irene Dunne's snobby son in *The White Cliffs of Dover*, before he returned to Fox for an expected sequel, *Thunderhead — Son of Flicka*, and another with Woolley, *Molly and Me* (Gracie Fields was Molly). By the time he showed up for a Jane Powell musical at Metro, *Holiday in Mexico*, he was entering his lanky teenage years, and his contract with Fox had been dissolved. He got off to an intriguing start in his post-contract period by playing Malcolm in the weird Orson Welles production of *Macbeth*, which, if nothing else, was guaranteed to pop up in revival theaters for years to come. Then he signed with Monogram to star in a batch of immediately forgotten "B" movies, all of which listed him as an associate producer, making him one of the youngest performers to ever receive such a behind-the-scenes credit. These pictures included *Rocky*, another boy and his dog story; a quickie version of *Kidnapped*, portraying beleaguered hero David Balfour; *Tuna Clipper*, working on said vessel to pay off a debt; *Killer Shark*, which found him searching for his dad in Mexico; and *The Steel Fist*, playing a Russian.

Not unexpectedly he went over to television, where he began popping up in many live anthology shows and specials. More importantly he decided to study acting in New York, giving him a higher level of confidence as he entered adulthood. He was seen on Broadway in *No Time for Sergeants*, in the role Nick Adams would play in the movie; in *Compulsion*, in the part Dean Stockwell would do on film; and in the hit musical *Camelot*, in the role of Mordred (David Hemmings snagged that one on screen). He solidified his success as a stage actor when he won a Tony Award in 1960 for *The Fighting Cock*, shortly before picking up an Emmy Award for *Not Without Honor*.

After an eight-year absence he returned to the big screen in

1960 as one of *The Subterraneans*, but not one that had much to do with the characters in Jack Kerouac's original novel, and as a possible suspect in the Doris Day mystery *Midnight Lace*. He was also considered an important enough name that he was listed among the starry male cast of the D-Day epic *The Longest Day*, as a private. What really announced his return as a viable movie actor was *Cleopatra*, in which, as the ruthless Octavius, he pretty much commanded the screen in the second half of the lengthy movie, once Rex Harrison was killed off. There was no set pattern for the size of the roles he would accept after the success of *Cleopatra*, pretty much remaining in the background during the Hollywood exposé *Inside Daisy Clover*, as a studio secretary, but adding some spark to *The Third Day*, as George Peppard's petulant brother-in-law. In the all-star Biblical epic *The Greatest Story Ever Told*, he was just another apostle (Matthew), but had a significant role in Disney's *That Darn Cat!*, which displayed his knack for comedy. He was a CIA agent in *The Defector*, a movie starring another off-screen friend, Montgomery Clift; then landed one of his best roles ever, playing the brilliant, persuasive, and downright strange mentor of Tuesday Weld in the stinging satire *Lord Love a Duck*, which was destined for cult status only. It was worth noting that he got away with portraying a college student, despite the fact that he was only two years shy of 40. Continuing to show that he could play weirdoes with the best of them, he killed a woman with a pair of pruning sheers in the trashy *Shock Treatment*, and kept his mother's corpse for companionship in *It!*, which had nothing to do with the previous Clara Bow movie of the same name, but a great deal to do with *The Golem*. In a much more benign vein he carried the show playing a Boston butler, out of place in the Old West, in a lackluster Disney comedy, *The Adventures of Bullwhip Griffin*, and followed this with his most famous adult role, the simian Cornelius, who treats captured human Charlton Heston with decency, in the smash sci-fi hit *Planet of the Apes*. Although unrecognizable under John Chambers's unforgettable makeup design, he created an indelible impression and would return to the part on four more occasions (the best of which was *Escape From the Planet of the Apes*). He also appeared on a short-lived TV series version (though as a different character).

The nasty side of McDowall showed up in his roles in *The Loved One*, as an insensitive studio honcho who fires John Gielgud, and in the western *5 Card Stud*, as Katherine Justice's hot-headed, weaselly brother, gunned down by Robert Mitchum; while he played it hip as a music producer in the silly underwater comedy *Hello Down There*, a part not unlike the one he did in another stiff, *The Cool Ones*. Still looking youthful past the age of 40, he was a member of a parasitic rock band in *Angel, Angel, Down We Go*; was all but trimmed out of the musical *Bedknobs and Broomsticks*; and popped up as the ineffectual school principal in *Pretty Maids All in a Row*, most probably because it gave him a chance to act opposite another off-screen buddy, Rock Hudson (as did *Embryo*). He was one of the first to perish in the blockbuster *The Poseidon Adventure*, as a ship's waiter, and then had one of his last top-billed parts, as an occult researcher, in the well-liked but stodgy horror offering *Legend of Hell House*.

Ever busy, he was an annoying lawyer in *The Life and Times of Judge Roy Bean*; a supermarket manager, in an unbilled appearance in the white-trash car-chase epic *Dirty Mary Crazy Larry*; Barbra Streisand's gay personal assistant in *Funny Lady*, evoking derisive sneers from macho James Caan; and a Gypsy woman (!) in the lopsided farce *Rabbit Test*. Amid a lot of trash and many television assignments, he had a terrific part as a hammy horror movie TV host in *Fright Night*, a role he reprised in a little-seen sequel, and executive produced *Overboard*, a Goldie Hawn

comedy in which he gave himself a thankless butler role. In the 1990s he ended up in a lot of unworthy, direct-to-video fare, although there were parts in some respectable projects like *Last Summer in the Hamptons*, as a film preservation advocate, which he was in real life; *It's My Party*, as a gay friend of dying Eric Roberts (McDowall, who was gay, was often called on to play characters either openly or suggestively homosexual); and *The Grass Harp*, as a gossipy small-town barber. He directed *Tam Lin/The Devil's Widow*, which drew little praise, and published four volumes of his photography (*Double Exposure* and II, III, IV), which did, displaying the good taste that had been his trademark in even the lowest of projects.

Screen: 1938: Murder in the Family; I See Ice; John Halifax — Gentleman; Convict 99; Scruffy; Yellow Sands; Hey! Hey! USA; 1939: Poison Pen; The Outsider; Dead Man's Shoes; Just William; His Brother's Keeper; 1940: Saloon Bar; You Will Remember; 1941: This England; Man Hunt; How Green Was My Valley; Confirm or Deny; 1942: Son of Fury; On the Sunny Side; The Pied Piper; 1943: My Friend Flicka; Lassie Come Home; 1944: The White Cliffs of Dover; The Keys of the Kingdom; 1945: Thunderhead — Son of Flicka; Hangover Square (voice); Molly and Me; 1946: Holiday in Mexico; 1948: Rocky (and assoc. prod.); Kidnapped (and assoc. prod.); 1949: Tuna Clipper (and assoc. prod.); Black Midnight (and assoc. prod.); 1950: Killer Shark (and assoc. prod.); Everybody's Dancin'; Big Timber (and assoc. prod.); Macbeth (filmed 1948); 1952: The Steel Fist; 1960: The Subterraneans; Midnight Lace; 1962: The Longest Day; 1963: Cleopatra; 1964: Shock Treatment; 1965: The Greatest Story Ever Told; The Third Day; The Loved One; That Darn Cat!; Inside Daisy Clover; 1966: Lord Love a Duck; The Defector; 1967: The Adventures of Bullwhip Griffin; The Cool Ones; It!; 1968: Planet of the Apes; 5 Card Stud; 1969: Hello Down There; Midas Run; Angel, Angel, Down We Go/Cult of the Damned; 1971: Pretty Maids All in a Row; Escape From the Planet of the Apes; Bedknobs and Broomsticks; 1972: Conquest of the Planet of the Apes; The Poseidon Adventure; The Life and Times of Judge Roy Bean; 1973: The Legend of Hell House; Battle for the Planet of the Apes; Arnold; 1974: Dirty Mary Crazy Larry; 1975: Funny Lady; 1976: Mean Johnny Barrows; Embryo; 1977: Sixth and Main (nUSr); 1978: Rabbit Test; Laserblast; The Cat From Outer Space; 1979: Circle of Iron; Nutcracker Fantasy (voice); The Black Hole (voice); Scavenger Hunt; 1981: Charlie Chan and the Curse of the Dragon Queen; 1982: Evil Under the Sun; Class of 1984; 1985: Fright Night; 1986: GoBots: Battle of the Rock Lords (voice); 1987: Dead of Winter; Overboard (and exec. prod.); 1988: Doin' Time on Planet Earth; 1989: Fright Night II; Cutting Class; The Big Picture; 1990: Shakma; 1991: Going Under; The Naked Target (nUSr); 1992: Double Trouble; The Magical World of Chuck Jones; 1993: Angel 4: Undercover (dtv); 1994: Mirror Mirror 2: Raven Dance (dtv); 1995: The Color of Evening (dtv); Fatally Yours (dtv); Star Hunter (dtv); Last Summer in the Hamptons; 1996: It's My Party; The Grass Harp; 1997: Rudyard Kipling's The Second Jungle Book: Mowgli and Baloo; 1998: Something to Believe In (dtv); A Bug's Life (voice); 1999: Keepers of the Frame.

NY Stage: 1953: Misalliance; Escapade; 1955: The Doctor's Dilemma (ob); No Time for Sergeants; 1956: The Diary of a Scoundrel (ob); 1957: Good as Gold; Compulsion; 1958: A Handful of Fire; 1959: Look After Lulu; The Fighting Cock; 1960: Camelot; 1967: The Astrakhan Coat; 1997: A Christmas Carol.

Select TV: 1951: When We Were Married (sp); The Blues Street (sp); 1952: Phillip Goes Forth (sp); Salad Days (sp); It Pays to Advertise (sp); 1954: Buy Me Blue Ribbons (sp); My Client McDuff (sp); The Reality (sp); Emma (sp); 1956: The Good

Fairy (sp); In the Days of Our Youth (sp); Gwyneth (sp); **1957:** The Vicarious Years (sp); Talk You of Killing? (sp); A Night of Rain (sp); Rain in the Spring (sp); White-Headed Boy (sp); He's for Me (sp); **1958:** The Last of the Belles (sp); Heart of Darkness (sp); **1959:** Night of Betrayal (sp); Billy Budd (sp); **1960:** Tempest (sp); Our American Heritage: Not Without Honor (sp); **1961:** In a Garden (sp); The Power and the Glory (sp); **1964:** Wake Up Darling (sp); Mr. Biddle's Crime Wave (sp); The Wine-Dark Sea (sp); **1966:** The Fatal Mistake (sp); **1967:** Saint Joan (sp); **1969:** Night Gallery; **1971:** Terror in the Sky; A Taste of Evil; What's a Nice Girl Like You…?; **1973:** Miracle on 34th Street; **1974:** The Elevator; Planet of the Apes (series); **1976:** Flood; The Rhinemann Exchange (ms); **1977:** The Fantastic Journey (series); **1978:** The Thief of Bagdad; The Immigrants; The Martian Chronicles; **1979:** Hart to Hart; **1980:** The Memory of Eva Ryker; **1981:** The Million Dollar Face/Kiss of Gold; **1982:** Mae West; **1982–83:** Tales of the Gold Monkey (series); **1983:** This Girl for Hire; **1984:** The Zany Adventures of Robin Hood; **1985:** The Wind in the Willows (sp; voice); Hollywood Wives (ms); Alice in Wonderland; **1986:** Bridges to Cross (series); **1989:** Around the World in 80 Days (ms); **1990:** Carmilla; **1991:** Earth Angel; An Inconvenient Woman; Deadly Game; Sidney Sheldon's The Sands of Time; **1993:** Heads; **1994:** Hart to Hart: Home Is Where the Hart Is; **1995:** Of Unknown Origin/The Alien Within; **1996:** Dead Man's Island; Unlikely Angel; **1997:** Loss of Faith.

DARREN McGAVIN
Born: Spokane, WA, May 7, 1922.

A character player whose gruff exterior often hid an almost benign or likeable manner underneath, Darren McGavin studied acting at both the Neighborhood Playhouse and the Actors Studio. In 1945 he ended up at Columbia Studios, where he was asked to fill in the background on four films, after which he did *Fear*, at Monogram, then returned east for TV and stage work. On Broadway he was one of *My Three Convicts* and the title character in *The Rainmaker*, which was the one that reawakened Hollywood interest in him. As a result he showed his friendly side as a painter in Venice, in *Summertime*, and his evil side as a drug pusher in *The Man With the Golden Arm*; then was called on to be Jerry Lewis's first straight man after his split with Dean Martin, in *The Delicate Delinquent*, where his quiet ease was a welcome relief from the patented Lewis shtick. His old employer, Columbia, called on him to play an undercover cop in *The Case Against Brooklyn*, after which he was off to the small screen to make his mark playing the lead in the TV series version of *Mickey Spillane's Mike Hammer*. Television seemed to be his natural home, but he would return to the big screen on occasion, as in *Bullet for a Badman*, as the badman, jealous that Audie Murphy has married his ex-wife; *Mission Mars*, as one of the first men on the moon; *Mrs. Pollifax — Spy*, as a CIA agent going through some very mild escapades with Rosalind Russell; Disney's *Hot Lead and Cold Feet*, as an unscrupulous mayor; *A Christmas Story*, mugging shamelessly as the dad in this nostalgic holiday tale; and *Billy Madison*, as Adam Sandler's wealthy father. In 1973 he directed the horror film *Happy Mother's Day, Love George/Run, Stranger, Run*, shortly after participating in the cult TV series *The Night Stalker*, which brought him his most loyal following of all. He received an Emmy Award in 1990 for portraying Candice Bergen's dad on *Murphy Brown*.

Screen: **1945:** A Song to Remember; Kiss and Tell; She Wouldn't Say Yes; Counter-Attack; **1946:** Fear; **1951:** Queen for a Day; **1955:** Summertime; The Court-Martial of Billy Mitchell; The Man With the Golden Arm; **1957:** Beau James; The Delicate Delinquent; **1958:** The Case Against Brooklyn; **1964:** Bullet for a Badman; **1965:** The Great Sioux Massacre; Ride the High Wind/African Gold; **1968:** Mission Mars; **1971:** Mrs. Pollifax — Spy; **1973:** B Must Die; **1976:** No Deposit, No Return; **1977:** Airport '77; **1978:** Hot Lead and Cold Feet; Zero to Sixty; **1980:** Hangar 18/Invasion Force; **1981:** Firebird 2015 A.D. (dtv); **1983:** A Christmas Story; **1984:** The Natural; **1985:** Turk 182!; **1986:** Raw Deal; **1987:** From the Hip; **1988:** Dead Heat; **1990:** In the Name of Blood (nUSr); **1991:** Captain America (dtv); Blood and Concrete: A Love Story; **1992:** Happy Hell Night (dtv); **1995:** Billy Madison; **1996:** Still Waters Burn (dtv); **1998:** Small Time/ Waiting for the Man (dtv); Pros and Cons (dtv).

NY Stage: **1948:** The Old Lady Says No; **1949:** Death of a Salesman; Cock-a-Doodle-Doo (ob); **1953:** My 3 Angels; **1954:** The Rainmaker; **1956:** The Innkeepers; Lovers; **1957:** The Tunnel of Love; **1959:** Two for the Seesaw; **1961:** Blood, Sweat and Stanley Poole; **1964:** The King and I; **1966:** Dinner at Eight; **1985:** California Dog Fight (ob); **1987:** Bigfoot Stole My Wife (ob); **1989:** The Night Hank Williams Died (ob); **1993:** Greetings (ob).

Select TV: **1951–52:** Crime Photographer (series); **1952:** The Witness (sp); Recapture (sp); Better Than Walking (sp); **1953:** The Rainmaker (sp); **1954:** Blind Alley (sp); Fandango at War Bonnet (sp); **1955:** The Town That Refused to Die (sp); **1956:** Terror at My Heels (sp); Sunset Boulevard (sp); **1957:** The Original Miss Chase (sp); First Prize for Murder (sp); **1957–59:** Mickey Spillane's Mike Hammer (series); **1958:** The Fair-Haired Boy (sp); **1959–60:** Riverboat (series); **1962:** Marriage Marks the Spot (sp); **1964:** Parties to the Crime (sp); **1967:** The Outsider; **1968–69:** The Outsider (series); **1969:** The Challengers; **1970:** The Challenge; Berlin Affair; Tribes; **1971:** Banyon; The Death of Me Yet; **1972:** The Night Stalker; Something Evil; The Rookies; Say Goodbye, Maggie Cole; High Flying Spy; **1973:** The Night Strangler; The Six Million Dollar Man; **1974–75:** Kolchak: The Night Stalker (series); **1976:** Brink's: The Great Robbery; Law and Order; **1978:** The Users; **1979:** Ike (ms); Donovan's Kid; Love for Rent; **1980:** The Martian Chronicles (ms); Waikiki; **1984:** The Return of Marcus Welby, M.D.; **1983:** Small & Frye (series); **1984:** The Baron and the Kid; **1985:** My Wicked, Wicked Ways: The Legend of Errol Flynn; **1987:** Tales from the Hollywood Hills (A Table at Ciro's) (sp); **1988:** Inherit the Wind; The Diamond Trap; **1989:** Around the World in 80 Days (ms); **1990:** Child in the Night; By Dawn's Early Light; **1991:** Perfect Harmony; **1992:** Disaster in Time/Grand Tour; **1993:** The American Clock; **1994:** Danielle Steel's A Perfect Stranger; **1995:** Derby; Fudge-A-Mania.

CHARLES McGRAW
Born: New York, NY, May 10, 1914.
Raised in Akron, OH. Died: July 30, 1980.

His coarse voice and rough, unfriendly features made Charles McGraw perfect for adding some degree of grit to various gangster flicks and war movies. Although he was ideal supporting material, he was considered a strong enough player that he also made a brief stop along the way for some star parts. McGraw came to movies in 1942, having done some radio work, and made his debut in a small part in Fox's *The Undying Monster*, a werewolf thriller. He remained a supporting staple throughout the 1940s (in MGM's *Border Incident*, for example, he ran poor George Murphy over with a tractor) until RKO decided to showcase him in some of their programmers with more than acceptable results. The first of these was the 1949 release *The Threat*, in which he had a field day as a nasty escaped con who kidnaps a diverse group of people, including the cop who sent him up. Next up he switched sides to play the detective on the trail of William Talman and his gang of thieves in *Armored Car Robbery*, then fell into the shallow clutches of Joan Dixon, prompting him to commit robbery, in *Roadblock*. Finally he teamed with Marie Windsor to protect a gangster's widow in one of the most famous of all the "B" thrillers of the 1950s, *The Narrow Margin*. On the small screen he starred in the short-lived television versions of *The Falcon* and *Casablanca*, while appearing in a lot of military roles, in such movies as *One Minute to Zero*, *The Bridges at Toko-Ri*, and *Away All Boats*. There was also more detective work in *Slaughter on Tenth Avenue*, after which he was a disagreeable gladiator trainer in the epic *Spartacus*; a skeptical fisherman in *The Birds*; a police lieutenant in *It's a Mad Mad Mad Mad World*; and Scott Wilson's loser dad in *In Cold Blood*, among others. He died by bleeding to death after falling through a glass shower door.

Screen: 1942: The Undying Monster; 1943: The Moon Is Down; They Came to Blow Up America; The Mad Ghoul; Corvette K-225; Destroyer; 1944: The Imposter; The Seventh Cross; 1946: The Killers; 1947: The Big Fix; The Long Night; Brute Force; The Farmer's Daughter; The Gangster; Roses Are Red; T-Men; On the Old Spanish Trail; 1948: Hazard; The Hunted; Blood on the Moon; Berlin Express; 1949: Reign of Terror/The Black Book; Border Incident; Once More, My Darling; The Story of Molly X; Side Street; The Threat; Gun Crazy/Deadly Is the Female; 1950: Ma and Pa Kettle Go to Town; Armored Car Robbery; I Was a Shoplifter; 1951: Double Crossbones; His Kind of Woman; Roadblock; 1952: The Narrow Margin; One Minute to Zero; 1953: Thunder Over the Plains; War Paint; 1954: Loophole; The Bridges at Toko-Ri; 1956: Away All Boats; Toward the Unknown; The Cruel Tower; 1957: Joe Dakota; Joe Butterfly; Slaughter on Tenth Avenue; 1958: Saddle the Wind; The Defiant Ones; Twilight for the Gods; 1959: Man in the Net; The Wonderful Country; 1960: Spartacus; Cimarron; 1961: The Horizontal Lieutenant; 1963: The Birds; It's a Mad Mad Mad Mad World; 1967: The Busy Body; In Cold Blood; 1968: Hang 'em High; 1969: Pendulum; Tell Them Willie Boy Is Here; 1971: Johnny Got His Gun; 1972: Chandler; 1975: A Boy and His Dog; 1976: The Killer Inside Me; 1977: Twilight's Last Gleaming.

Select TV: 1953: The Cat With the Crimson Eyes (sp); 1954–55: The Falcon (series); 1955–56: Casablanca (series); 1956: Breakfast at Nancy's (sp); 1961: The Great Alberti (series); 1964: Once Upon a Savage Night (sp); 1965: Twixt the Cup and the Lip (sp); Nightmare in Chicago; 1971: O'Hara: U.S. Treasury: Operation Cobra; The Devil and Miss Sarah; 1971–72: The Smith Family (series); 1972: The Night Stalker; The Longest Night; 1973: Money to Burn; 1976: Perilous Voyage (filmed 1968).

DOROTHY McGUIRE

BORN: OMAHA, NE, JUNE 14, 1918.
DIED: SEPTEMBER 13, 2001.

Just about the nicest actress to come along in the wartime studio days, Dorothy McGuire was a delicate, pretty, and heartfelt performer. It wasn't feasible for her to be nasty or unsympathetic, so she became one of the cinema's pre-eminent figures of home-fire warmth and motherly love. In her native Omaha she joined the Community Playhouse as a teenager, appearing opposite fellow Omahan Henry Fonda, in *A Kiss for Cinderella*. While at school at Pine Manor in Wellesley,

Massachusetts, she auditioned for work in New York and ended up as an understudy in the original Broadway production of *Our Town*, eventually graduating to the lead. Stardom came when she was cast as *Claudia*, the childlike newlywed coping with her mother's illness. Producer David O. Selznick bought both the piece and McGuire's services with the intention of introducing her to movie audiences, but ended up selling both the property and McGuire to 20th Century-Fox. Fortunately Fox had no qualms about allowing an unknown to carry the film version of the Broadway hit, and she made one of the most sparkling debuts of the decade, cast opposite Robert Young (who, surprisingly, took second billing to the newcomer). The movie duplicated its stage success, and she followed it up with her first mother role, and one that would be among her most enduring, Katie Nolan, in the magnificent 1945 movie of *A Tree Grows in Brooklyn*. Although too young to have mothered her filmic offspring Peggy Ann Garner in real life, her portrayal was sincere and convincing, a splendid example of a physically small woman creating a strong impression.

She went to RKO to join Young again for *The Enchanted Cottage*, as a plain girl who falls for a man who is facially scared, a love story that reached for something special and missed. Better was one for Selznick (who, officially, still owned her contract), *The Spiral Staircase*, where she was at her most vulnerable, as a terrorized mute in this psychological thriller that scared the pants off of 1940s audiences, back when people accepted their shocks via suggestion. Selznick also made her a war widow who has no qualms about seeking comfort in Guy Madison in *Till the End of Time*, a movie that was always being unfavorably compared to the somewhat similar *The Best Years of Our Lives*. Back at Fox there was a sequel to *Claudia*, *Claudia and David*, about her having a baby, and then *Gentleman's Agreement*, which earned McGuire her sole Oscar nomination, no doubt because it was one of the rare times on screen that she got to display an unpleasant side (reacting unfavorably when Gregory Peck refuses to drop his ruse that he is Jewish around her snobby friends and family).

Between some returns to the stage, she was Burt Lancaster's love interest in *Mr. 880*, a movie that really belonged to Edmund Gwenn in the title role; part of the ensemble of the Korean War home-front drama *I Want You*, yet another film that was likened to *The Best Years*; a woman facing her mortality, in the sort of mind-numbing soap opera she usually avoided, *Invitation*; and one of the principals in another multi-character entertainment, *Three Coins in the Fountain*, allowing herself to cut loose after falling for Clifton Webb, in the best of the three storylines, in this enormously popular film whose chief virtue was its location filming in Rome. She took a back seat to much of the dramatics in a very good legal drama, *Trial*, as secretary to lawyer Glenn Ford, and then had one of her nicest mama roles, as the Quaker woman coping with the threat of the Civil War, in one of the outstanding films of the 1950s, *Friendly Persuasion*. This pretty much set the tone as she entered into her "mother" period, playing rural matriarch to Tommy Kirk and Kevin Corcoran in one of the most satisfying of all Disney films, *Old Yeller*. She was mother to some of Clifton Webb's children (he being a bigamist) in a flat comedy *The Remarkable Mr. Pennypacker*, then came her closest to playing a bitch, in the Universal vineyard melodrama *This Earth Is Mine*, after which she made adultery seem perfectly acceptable in one of the most famous soap operas of the late 1950s, *A Summer Place*.

Continuing to grace some of the major Hollywood productions of their day, she was pretty terrific as the turn-of-the-century mother who can't give husband Robert Preston what he wants sexually in *The Dark at the Top of the Stairs*, probably the finest of all the film adaptations of William Inge's plays; and came back to Disney for another of that company's top-notch offerings, *Swiss Family Robinson*, coming to terms with spending her life on a remote island. She was very laid back and sweet in a Disney musical, *Summer Magic*, and finally got to play the most famous mother of them all, Mary, in the star-studded epic about the life of Jesus, *The Greatest Story Ever Told*. Her last on-screen role was as a gentle grandma, in *Flight of the Doves*, while she was heard but not seen in the critically mauled adaptation of the best-seller *Jonathan Livingston Seagull*. From that point on she confined herself to television, with some live theater on the side. Whether her absence from the big screen was her decision or that of Hollywood, it was a loss nonetheless, since her presence could only be, as it always was, an asset. Her daughter, Topo Swope, was also an actress.

Screen: 1943: Claudia; 1945: A Tree Grows in Brooklyn; The Enchanted Cottage; 1946: The Spiral Staircase; Till the End of Time; Claudia and David; 1947: Gentleman's Agreement; 1950: Mother Didn't Tell Me; Mr. 880; 1951: I Want You; Callaway Went Thataway; 1952: Invitation; 1954: Make Haste to Live; Three Coins in the Fountain; 1955: Trial; 1956: Friendly Persuasion; 1957: Old Yeller; 1959: The Remarkable Mr. Pennypacker; This Earth Is Mine; A Summer Place; 1960: The Dark at the Top of the Stairs; Swiss Family Robinson; 1961: Susan Slade; 1963: Summer Magic; 1965: The Greatest Story Ever Told; 1971: Flight of the Doves; 1973: Jonathan Livingston Seagull (voice).

NY Stage: 1938: Our Town; 1939: Swingin' the Dream; 1940: Medicine Show; 1941: Kindy Lady; Claudia; 1951: Legend of Lovers; 1958: Winesburg, Ohio; 1976: The Night of the Iguana.

Select TV: 1951: Dark Victory (sp); 1954: A Garden in the Sea (sp); To Each His Own (sp); The Gioconda Smile (sp); The Philadelphia Story (sp); 1956: Pale Horse, Pale Rider (sp); 1972: She Waits; Another Part of the Forest (sp); 1975: The Runaways; 1976: Rich Man, Poor Man (ms); 1978: Little Women; 1979: The Incredible Journey of Dr. Meg Laurel; Little Women (series); 1983: Ghost Dancing; 1984: The Young and the Restless (series); 1985: Amos; Between the Darkness and the Dawn; 1986: American Geisha; 1988: I Never Sang for My Father (sp); 1990: Caroline?; The Last Best Year.

FRANK McHUGH

(Francis Curray McHugh)
Born: Homestead, PA, May 23, 1898.
Died: September 11, 1981.

At times it seemed next to impossible to find a Warner Bros. movie of the 1930s in which Frank McHugh did not appear. The reedy-voiced, wavy-haired actor with the round face and breathy way of laughing, with his indignant, drawn-out "ha...ha...ha"s, was usually seen as the loyal-but-dense sidekick, a shtick that could have its breaking point. His journey to the screen began by joining his parents' traveling troupe, which brought him to the Marguerite Bryant Players, the Sherman Kelly Stock Company, vaudeville, and finally Broadway, in 1925, in *The Fall Guy*. There was a supposed, unverified, silent movie credit (1926's *Mademoiselle Modiste*) and a 1928 short ("If Men Played Cards as Women Do"), before he was signed up in 1930 by Warners, a company he'd stay with for the next decade. He was first seen in a Joe E. Brown musical, *Top Speed*, and was seldom out of work thereafter. At United Artists he was one of the smart aleck reporters in *The Front Page* (appearing with real life friend Pat O'Brien), then, back on his home lot, he was a petty thief in *One Way Passage* (a part he was asked to repeat in the 1940 remake,

'*Til We Meet Again*) and sidekick to off-screen pal James Cagney (for the first of many times) in *The Crowd Roars*. He was drunk countless times for maximum (or minimum) comic effect, as in *Bright Lights* and *Union Depot*; was a ninny choreographer in *Footlight Parade* (with Cagney); made a less-than-scintillating team with the always-deadly Hugh Herbert in *Convention City*; and then was partnered with Allen Jenkins for comic relief in *Tomorrow at Seven*, the two actors playing a pair of dopey Chicago detectives. He was ideally cast as one of the Rude Mechanicals, Quince, in *A Midsummer Night's Dream*; was an ambulance driver eager for a plane crash in *Devil Dogs of the Air*; and got to play the brother of Cagney and O'Brien in *The Irish in Us*, which was all promise and no pay off.

The studio then handed him a gem of a leading role when they purchased one of the hottest Broadway comedies of the decade, *Three Men and a Horse*, which was filmed with a lot more fidelity than expected. McHugh was at the top of his form playing a mild-mannered greeting card writer with an uncanny knack for picking winning horses, who gets mixed up with a trio of fast-talking hoods. In a more serious vein he was the man Lola Lane wants to marry, initially, for his money, in *Four Daughters*, a role he would play in three sequels; starred in *He Couldn't Say No*, once again as a shy dolt, this time in love with Jane Wyman; and then did buddy duty to Cagney again, in *The Roaring Twenties*, *The Fighting 69th*, and *City for Conquest*. After his Warners contract came to an end he supported Bing Crosby in the Oscar-winning *Going My Way*, as a fellow priest; starred in a Universal quickie, *Little Miss Big*, a cutesy tale of a family that softens up bitchy old Fay Holden; and was seen in less-and-less important parts thereafter, showing up as a cook in *The Tougher They Come*; Marilyn Monroe's agent in *There's No Business Like Show Business*; and a waiter in *Career*.

Screen: 1930: Top Speed; College Lovers; The Dawn Patrol; Bright Lights; The Widow From Chicago; Going Wild; 1931: The Front Page; Millie; Kiss Me Again; Traveling Husbands; Up for Murder; Men of the Sky; Corsair; Bad Company; 1932: One Way Passage; Blessed Event; High Pressure; Union Depot; The Strange Love of Molly Louvain; Life Begins; The Dark Horse; The Crowd Roars; 1933: Parachute Jumper; Mystery of the Wax Museum; Grand Slam; Private Jones; The Telegraph Trail; Convention City; Lilly Turner; Footlight Parade; Professional Sweetheart; Hold Me Tight; The House on 56th Street; Elmer the Great; Son of a Sailor; Havana Widows; Tomorrow at Seven; Ex-Lady; 1934: Fashions of 1934; Heat Lightning; Smarty; Let's Be Ritzy; Merry Wives of Reno; Return of the Terror; Here Comes the Navy; Six Day Bike Rider; Happiness Ahead; 1935: Maybe It's Love; Gold Diggers of 1935; Devil Dogs of the Air; Page Miss Glory; The Irish in Us; A Midsummer Night's Dream; Stars Over Broadway; 1936: Moonlight Murder; Snowed Under; Freshman Love; Bullets or Ballots; Stage Struck; Three Men on a Horse; 1937: Ever Since Eve; Mr. Dodd Takes the Air; Marry the Girl; Submarine D-1; 1938: Swing Your Lady; He Couldn't Say No; Little Miss Thoroughbred; Boy Meets Girl; Valley of the Giants; Four Daughters; 1939: Dodge City; Wings of the Navy; Daughters Courageous; Dust Be My Destiny; The Roaring Twenties; On Your Toes; Indianapolis Speedway; Four Wives; 1940: Virginia City; The Fighting 69th; Till We Meet Again; I Love You Again; City for Conquest; 1941: Four Mothers; Back Street; Manpower; 1942: Her Cardboard Lover; All Through the Night; 1944: Going My Way; Marine Raiders; Bowery to Broadway; 1945: A Medal for Benny; State Fair; 1946: The Hoodlum Saint; Little Miss Big; The Runaround; 1947: Easy Come, Easy Go; Carnegie Hall; 1948: The Velvet Touch; 1949: Mighty Joe Young; Miss Grant Takes Richmond; 1950: Paid in

Full; The Tougher They Come; **1952:** My Son John; The Pace That Thrills; **1953:** It Happens Every Thursday; A Lion Is in the Streets; **1954:** There's No Business Like Show Business; **1958:** The Last Hurrah; **1959:** Say One for Me; Career; **1964:** A Tiger Walks; **1967:** Easy Come, Easy Go.

NY Stage: 1925: The Fall Guy; **1927:** Fog; Tenth Avenue; Excess Baggage; **1929:** Conflict; Show Girl; **1963:** A Funny Thing Happened on the Way to the Forum; **1967:** Finian's Rainbow.

Select TV: 1951: Mme. Modiste (sp); **1954:** The Muldoon Matter (sp); The Heart of a Clown (sp); The Happy Journey (sp); Two Little Minks (sp); **1955:** Miracle at Potter's Farm (sp); **1956:** The Silent Gun (sp); Doll Face (sp); The Man in the Black Robe (sp); **1957:** The Human Pattern (sp); Three Men on a Horse (sp); Fire and Ice (sp); **1958:** The Funny-Looking Kid (sp); **1959:** Apple of His Eye (sp); The Killers (sp); **1960:** Queen of the Orange Bowl (sp); Full Moon Over Brooklyn (sp); **1963:** Don't Shake the Family Tree (sp); **1964–65:** The Bing Crosby Show (series); **1968:** Way Down Cellar (sp).

VICTOR McLAGLEN

Born: Tunbridge Wells, Kent, England, December 10, 1886. Died: November 7, 1959.

Not unlike Wallace Beery and Broderick Crawford, pug-ugly, brutish Victor McLaglen was a character player with a leading man's Oscar to his credit. He seemed like the real thing, a hellraising ruffian with a soft side, dragged in from the corner pub to put a little gusto into some often less-than-inspired entertainments. His early days were restless ones, spent in the military, on farms, in the boxing ring, and in vaudeville. A chance encounter with a producer landed him a star part in *The Call of the Road*, the success of which suddenly made him a film star. As a result he played an actor tempted to murder his wife during a performance of *Othello* in *Carnival*; boxed in both *Corinthian Jack* and *The Gay Corinthian*, two films not related; and took to the sea for *A Sailor Tramp* and *Heartstrings*. The Americans were interested in casting him in a film with a title that seemed to sum up McLaglen himself, *The Beloved Brute*, so he took the role, playing an ex-con/wrestler, and stayed on in Hollywood. He was one of *The Unholy Three*, the Lon Chaney hit, in which he was cast as a mug who ends up getting killed by a gorilla (!); did some fisticuffs for director John Ford, who would become an important name in his career, in *The Fighting Heart*; and joined the Foreign Legion for the Ronald Colman version of *Beau Geste*. He was principally a supporting player by this point, but he crossed over into genuine stardom when he was cast as the sarcastic Captain Flagg, battling in best macho fashion with Edmund Lowe (as Sgt. Quint), in one of the biggest hits of the silent cinema, the anti-war piece *What Price Glory?* It was made for Fox, who promptly purchased McLaglen's contract from First National.

He continued to be a favorite of John Ford, who put him in *Hangman's House*, *Strong Boy*, and *The Black Watch*, the last being McLaglen's official talkie debut. His snapping, cockney accent was just what audiences would expect from him, so there was no trouble accepting him as a star with sound. Just to make sure, Fox put him and Lowe into a Flagg-Quint follow-up, *The Cockeyed World*, which proved to be further box-office gold despite being a typical, creaky early talkie. There was a third in the series, *Women of All Nations*, and then a fourth, *Hot Pepper*, made six years after the original entry, which proved to be one trip too many to a drying well. Before that, Paramount borrowed him so that he could be curiously paired with Marlene Dietrich in one

of her duller features, *Dishonored*, in which McLaglen was supposed to be a Russian who is bewitched and then deceived by her. Apparently this incongruous pairing was a match filmgoers liked, so the lovable lug was cast opposite such elegant ladies as Jeanette MacDonald in *Annabelle's Affairs*, with McLaglen as a bearded miner named Hefty Jack, who rescues and then marries her; and Elissa Landi in *Wicked*, the title of which referred to her, not McLaglen, who played her ex-boyfriend who helps her get her child back. After those he teamed with Lowe again, over at Paramount, for *Guilty as Hell*, which was not supposed to be an entry in the Flagg-Quint series, although their characters names, Mack and Kirk, made it close enough.

He finished his Fox contract, hopped over to England for a single picture, *Dick Turpin*, as the legendary highwayman, and then returned for the best thing he and John Ford had done yet, *The Lost Patrol*, a gripping drama about a British regiment being picked off one by one while trapped in the desert, with McLaglen as the sergeant. Back with Lowe he was a diver named Forty Fathoms in *No More Women*; a sand hog named Jumbo in *Under Pressure*; and a detective in *The Great Hotel Murder*. In between these he investigated a killing in *Murder at the Vanities*, and a robbery in *The Captain Hates the Sea*. Ford came through for him again, in a big way, casting him as the foolish, drunken Gypo Nolan, who sells his pal out for 20 pounds in *The Informer*. The movie was praised to the heavens (although it is now very much looked upon as an antique from its era), and McLaglen's bombastic turn wound up earning him the Academy Award for Best Actor of 1935, beating out the three leads of *Mutiny on the Bounty* (Laughton, Gable, and Tone). Of course the trophy elevated McLaglen's position in the industry, although the movie wasn't popular enough to indicate that his box-office status would change.

For cute effect he was teamed with two of the leading child stars of the 1930s, Freddie Bartholomew (*Professional Soldier*) and Shirley Temple (*Wee Willie Winkie*, which was another directed by Ford), then he came closer to holding his own than any of Mae West's leading men ever did, in *Klondike Annie*. He loved Claudette Colbert in *Under Two Flags*, though she preferred top-billed Ronald Colman; was about the only actor around who could carry a vehicle called *The Magnificent Brute*, as a steel worker; stooped to kidnapping in *Nancy Steele Is Missing!*; went to England again, to co-star with Gracie Field, in *We're Going to Be Rich*; and was a construction foreman who befriends Nelson Eddy in *Let Freedom Ring*. There was another career high, as one of the trio of fun-loving sergeants, in the rousing adventure tale *Gunga Din*, but, as always, he was one actor who couldn't seem to benefit from a step forward.

By the early 1940s he had slipped into programmer territory with *Diamond Frontier* and *Powder Town*. There wasn't a much brighter reception for another Lowe reunion, *Call Out the Marines*, but he did get to clown as a ruthless pirate in a Bob Hope hit *The Princess and the Pirate*. He found himself stuck with the likes of George Raft (*Whistle Stop*) and Jon Hall (*The Michigan Kid*), when the ever-loyal Ford rescued him, offering lusty supporting parts in three John Wayne westerns, *Fort Apache*, *She Wore a Yellow Ribbon*, and *Rio Grande*, playing the down-to-earth Sgt. Quincannon in the last two. Better yet, Ford put him in the rollicking, comical role of Maureen O'Hara's feisty father in *The Quiet Man*, earning McLaglen one last hurrah and an Oscar nomination in the supporting category. One of his last films, the programmer *The Abductors*, was directed by his son, Andrew McLaglen, whose latter works would include *McLintock!* and *Shenandoah*.

Screen: 1920: The Call of the Road; **1921:** Carnival; Corinthian

Jack; Prey of the Dragon; The Sport of Kings; 1922: The Glorious Adventure; A Romance of Old Bagdad; Little Brother of God; A Sailor Tramp; The Crimson Circle; 1923: The Romany; Heartstrings; M'Lord of the White Road; In the Blood; 1924: Women and Diamonds; The Gay Corinthian; The Passionate Adventure; The Beloved Brute; 1925: The Hunted Woman; Percy; The Unholy Three; Winds of Chance; The Fighting Heart; 1926: The Isle of Retribution; Men of Steel; Beau Geste; What Price Glory?; 1927: The Loves of Carmen; 1928: Mother Machree; A Girl in Every Port; Hangman's House; The River Pirate; 1929: Captain Lash; Strong Boy; The Black Watch; The Cock-Eyed World; Hot for Paris; 1930: Happy Days; On the Level; A Devil With Women; 1931: Dishonored; Not Exactly Gentlemen/Three Rogues; Women of All Nations; Annabelle's Affairs; Wicked; 1932: The Gay Caballero; The Devil's Lottery; While Paris Sleeps; Guilty as Hell; Rackety Rax; 1933: Hot Pepper; Laughing at Life; Dick Turpin; 1934: The Lost Patrol; No More Women; Wharf Angel; Murder at the Vanities; The Captain Hates the Sea; 1935: Under Pressure; The Great Hotel Murder; The Informer; 1936: Professional Soldier; Klondike Annie; Under Two Flags; The Magnificent Brute; 1937: Sea Devils; Nancy Steele Is Missing!; This Is My Affair; Wee Willie Winkie; 1938: Battle of Broadway; The Devil's Party; We're Going to Be Rich; 1939: Pacific Liner; Let Freedom Ring; Gunga Din; Captain Fury; Ex-Champ; Full Confession; Rio; The Big Guy; 1940: South of Pago Pago; Diamond Frontier; 1941: Broadway Limited; 1942: Call Out the Marines; Powder Town; China Girl; 1943: Forever and a Day; 1944: Tampico; The Princess and the Pirate; Roger Tuohy — Gangster; 1945: Rough, Tough and Ready; Love, Honor and Goodbye; 1946: Whistle Stop; 1947: Calendar Girl; The Michigan Kid; The Foxes of Harrow; 1948: Fort Apache; 1949: She Wore a Yellow Ribbon; 1950: Rio Grande; 1952: The Quiet Man; 1953: Fair Wind to Java; 1954: Prince Valiant; Trouble in the Glen; 1955: Many Rivers to Cross; City of Shadows; Lady Godiva; Bengazi; 1956: Around the World in Eighty Days; 1957: The Abductors; 1958: Sea Fury; Italiani sono Matti; Gli/The Italians Are Crazy (nUSr).

Select TV: 1952: Port of Call (sp); 1954: The Exposure of Michael O'Reilly (sp); 1955: Big Joe's Comin' Home (sp).

STEPHEN McNALLY

(HORACE VINCENT McNALLY) BORN: NEW YORK, NY, JULY 29, 1913. DIED: JUNE 4, 1994.

A strictly standard-rate performer, Stephen McNally went from juvenile work to portraying men of menace and burly confidence, usually in action fare or westerns. A former lawyer, he quit the profession to take up acting, ending up on Broadway in the early 1940s. In 1942 MGM signed him to a cotract under his real name, Horace McNally, which no doubt caused confusion for those expecting character player Horace McMahon to show up. Assignments included playing a reporter in *Keeper of the Flame*, and the company doctor in *Thirty Seconds Over Tokyo*. After his contract was up, he started fresh with a new name, Stephen, and made perhaps his greatest impact right off the bat, as the vile brute who rapes and is then murdered by Jane Wyman in *Johnny Belinda*. Universal decided it wanted to add him to their roster and had him join the Foreign Legion in *Rogues' Regiment*; cast him as a counselor trying to help some Brooklyn street kids in *City Across the River*; and put him on the right side of the law for the Burt Lancaster noir *Criss Cross*. He was teamed with the long-forgotten Marta Toren in Hollywood's first look at the Palestinian war, *Sword in the Desert*, and had another

of his best-remembered villain roles, as James Stewart's brother who steals the title rifle, in *Winchester '73*. The success of this made him a staple of Universal programmers of the 1950s, and he starred in such films as *Wyoming Mail*, as a postal inspector pretending to be a bank robber; *Apache Drums*, as a gambler; *The Lady Pays Off*, as a casino owner in this Linda Darnell stiff; and *The Black Castle*, as an eye-patch-wearing count, taking billing over the studio's former horror attractions Boris Karloff and Lon Chaney, Jr. After that he pretty much stayed on the range until he turned to television, where he was seen more frequently beginning in the 1960s.

Screen: AS HORACE McNALLY: 1942: Grand Central Murder; The War Against Mrs. Hadley; Eyes in the Night; For Me and My Gal; Dr. Gillespie's New Assistant; Keeper of the Flame; 1943: Air Raid Wardens; The Man From Down Under; 1944: An American Romance; Thirty Seconds Over Tokyo; 1945: Bewitched; Dangerous Partners; 1946: The Harvey Girls; Up Goes Maisie; Magnificent Doll.

AS STEPHEN McNALLY: 1948: Johnny Belinda; Rogues' Regiment; 1949: City Across the River; Criss Cross; The Lady Gambles; Sword in the Desert; Woman in Hiding; 1950: Winchester '73; No Way Out; Wyoming Mail; 1951: Air Cadet; Apache Drums; The Iron Man; The Raging Tide; The Lady Pays Off; 1952: Diplomatic Courier; The Duel at Silver Creek; The Black Castle; Battle Zone; 1953: Split Second; The Stand at Apache River; Devil's Canyon; 1954: Make Haste to Live; A Bullet Is Waiting; 1955: The Man From Bitter Ridge; Violent Saturday; 1956: Tribute to a Bad Man; 1957: Hell's Crossroads; 1958: The Fiend Who Walked the West; Johnny Rocco; Hell's Five Hours; 1959: Hell Bent for Leather; 1965: Requiem for a Gunfighter; 1968: Panic in the City; 1969: Once You Kiss a Stranger; 1972: Black Gunn; 1978: Hi-Riders; Kino, The Padre on Horseback/Mission to Glory.

NY Stage: AS HORACE McNALLY: 1940: Johnny Belinda; 1941: The Wookey.

Select TV: 1953: No Compromise (sp); 1954: Rabbit Foot (sp); The Big Man on Campus (sp); 1955: The Cool Ones (sp); Tiger at Noon (sp); The Verdict (sp); Foreign Wife (sp); 1956: Return to Nowhere (sp); 1957: Strange Disappearance (sp); 1958: Flight for Life (sp); 1959: Stampede at Bitter Creek (sp); 1960: The Mink Coat (sp); 1961–62: Target: The Corruptors (series); 1964: The Action of the Tiger (sp); 1969: The Lonely Profession; The Whole World Is Watching; 1971: Vanished; 1973: Call to Danger; 1974: Nakia ; 1975: The Lives of Jenny Dolan; 1976: Most Wanted.

MAGGIE McNAMARA

BORN: NEW YORK, NY, JUNE 18, 1928. DIED: FEBRUARY 18, 1978.

Few have started at such a peak only to fade so thoroughly away, leaving so little work behind them, as did Maggie McNamara. The pert and perky actress had done modeling as a teenager, which led to some *Life* magazine covers and her New York stage debut, in 1951, in *The King of Friday's Men*. It was while appearing in the Chicago production of the Broadway success *The Moon Is Blue* that Otto Preminger asked her to make her movie debut in the film version of that "controversial" play. Her sweet and enthusiastic performance as the young girl who makes much of the fact that she is a virgin, earned her an Oscar nomination. The movie, anemic and stagebound as it was, became a big hit, due to the outrage it caused when the production code office refused to give it their seal of approval because of the free use of the word "virgin," not to mention such other shockers as "seduce" and "mistress." Fox signed her to a contract, putting her in one hit, the Rome travelogue *Three Coins in the Fountain*, as the American girl in pursuit of Louis Jourdan, and one flop, *Prince of Players*, as the wife of Edwin Booth (Richard Burton). With that she backed away from movies and was far out of the public mind when she showed up on Broadway again, in *Step on a Crack*, in 1962, and then in another film for Preminger, *The Cardinal*. There was a brief marriage to director David Swift (*How to Succeed in Business*), and then she left show business altogether, finding work as a typist. She killed herself with an overdose of sleeping pills in 1978.

Screen: 1953: The Moon Is Blue; 1954: Three Coins in the Fountain; 1955: Prince of Players; 1963: The Cardinal.

NY Stage: 1951: The King of Friday's Men; 1962: Step on a Crack.

BUTTERFLY McQUEEN

(THELMA McQUEEN) BORN: TAMPA, FL, JANUARY 7, 1911. DIED: DECEMBER 22, 1995.

With her memorable name and a high-pitched voice so bizarre and cartoonish one might be inclined to believe it was all a big put on, Butterfly McQueen left a greater imprint on the film landscape than did more frequently employed actresses. Having studied dance, she became a member of the Venezuela Jones Negro Youth Group, where she received her nickname due to the fluttering nature of her arm movements. Her dancing took her to Broadway, where she was first seen in *Brown Sugar* in 1937. She went to Hollywood two years later to play a shop assistant in *The Women*, and then got the role that would make her famous for generations to come, the lazy, flighty slave Prissy in David O. Selznick's Oscar-winning classic *Gone With the Wind*. McQueen's full-bodied portrayal of a constantly yammering domestic, who inflates her value only to prove worthless when it comes to "birthin' babies," was undeniably funny but equally unnerving for many who felt that it was a negative and stereotypical interpretation of subservient blacks. Of course this became her stock role, appearing in similar parts in *Flame of the Barbary Coast*, *Mildred Pierce*, and another for Selznick, *Duel in the Sun*. After that it was on to television and then a long break from movies, taking various odd jobs while occasionally appearing on the stage. She returned to films, after more than a two-decade absence, playing herself in the all-star oddity *The Phynx*. This was followed by a cameo in the Moms Mabley vehicle *Amazing Grace*, and, further down the line, a very minor part in the Harrison Ford starrer *The Mosquito Coast*. She was given an Emmy Award in 1980 for her participation in the ABC Afterschool Special *The Seven Wishes of a Rich Kid*. She had once again been long out of the show business scene when the news came of her being accidentally burned to death while trying to light a stove.

Screen: 1939: The Women; Gone With the Wind; 1941: Affectionately Yours; 1943: I Dood It; Cabin in the Sky; 1945: Mildred Pierce; Flame of the Barbary Coast; 1946: Duel in the Sun; 1948: Killer Diller; 1970: The Phynx; 1974: Amazing Grace; 1986: The Mosquito Coast.

NY Stage: 1937: Brown Sugar; 1938: What a Life; 1939: Swining' the Dream; 1956: The World's My Oyster (ob); 1957: The School for Wives (ob); 1964: The Athenian Touch (ob); 1967: Curley McDimple (ob); 1969: Three Men on a Horse; Butterfly McQueen and Friends (ob); 1970: The Front Page.

Select TV: 1950: Give Us Our Dreams (sp); 1950–53: Beulah (series); 1959: The Green Pastures (sp); 1981: The Adventures of Huckleberry Finn; 1989: Polly.

STEVE McQUEEN

(TERRENCE STEVEN McQUEEN)
BORN: BEECH GROVE, IN, MARCH 24, 1930.
DIED: NOVEMBER 7, 1980.

Long before the word became overused, Steve McQueen epitomized "cool." His squinty-eyed, slightly simian features were that of a man more interested in hopping into a fast car than dealing with the problems of the human race. As far as he was concerned, he didn't have much to say but said a lot nonetheless, through his subtle poise, world-weariness, and direct honesty. It seemed fitting for his loner image that he came from a broken home, which made him something of a hellraiser as a youth. He went from a reform school into the Marines and then to New York, where he did all kinds of jobs until a chance meeting with acting coach Sanford Meisner got him work in a play and enrollment in the Neighborhood Playhouse. This was followed by further classes at the H-B Studios and at the Actors Studio, plus stage work in stock and rep. It was 1956 when things started to change. First he replaced Ben Gazarra in the Broadway hit *A Hatful of Rain*; did an uncredited bit as one of the street thugs in Paul Newman's sordid past in the Rocky Graziano biopic *Somebody Up There Likes Me*; and moved to Hollywood with his new wife, dancer Neile Adams. He got fourth billing in a quickly forgotten Allied Artist drama, *Never Love a Stranger*, followed by a low-budget chiller, *The Blob*, that was just another of the monster movies of the late 1950s, but one that became a cult favorite in later years due mainly to young McQueen's (billed here as "Steven") participation in it. The same year it was released, 1958, he became a TV star by way of the western series *Wanted: Dead or Alive*. Shortly after that came on the air, he showed up in his first starring film, *The Great St. Louis Bank Robbery*, a semi-documentary account of a real-life crime in which he was the definite standout among the amateurish and unknown supporting cast. This did not mean, however, that he was declared movie star material just yet, his next picture shunting him back into the supporting slot, as a jeep driver, in the Frank Sinatra war movie *Never So Few*, which was fortuitous in that it introduced McQueen to director John Sturges.

His big-screen break came in the next picture Sturges was lining up, a western remake of the Japanese art house sensation *Seven Samurai*, now retitled *The Magnificent Seven*. The movie, a decent moneymaker at the time, managed to stand on its own and actually built up its reputation with the passing years. As Yul Brynner's right-hand man, the third-billed McQueen displayed a mesmerizing star quality that made him stand out in a fairly decent cast, and was the only one of the title characters, along with Brynner, allowed to survive the carnage at the finale. MGM put him in *The Honeymoon Machine*, the sort of pinheaded 1960s fluff that was the antithesis of what McQueen would come to represent. He followed it with two war stories that brought him favorable notices but meager audiences, *Hell Is for Heroes*, at his most antisocial, as a moody private new to the company, and *The War Lover*, as a bomber pilot whose obsession with battle turns dangerous. His next movie, however, was a sizable hit and one of the finest films of the decade, *The Great Escape*, a superb ensemble piece about a real-life breakout from a prisoner of war camp, with McQueen at his rebel best, capping the lengthy drama with a memorable motorcycle chase. That one was followed by a teaming with Jackie Gleason that didn't jell, *Soldier in the Rain*, with McQueen overdoing the dumb yokel bit, as a supply sergeant, and thereby tripping up for the second time in comedy; and then a gritty, poignant drama-comedy with Natalie

Wood about an unwanted pregnancy, *Love With the Proper Stranger*, proving that under the right circumstances McQueen could play a romantic lead with ease. Bad dubbing worked against his playing a barroom singer in the rambling *Baby the Rain Must Fall*, and there wasn't much excitement to be had in *The Cincinnati Kid*, although this look at the world of high-stakes poker became another of his signature roles.

He was now considered quite a bankable name, and he excelled in the western *Nevada Smith*, playing the younger version of the character Alan Ladd had done in *The Carpetbaggers*, a man hell-bent on revenge. The poster image of a shirtless McQueen, dangling his arms from a rifle stretched across his shoulders, was the perfect summing up of the macho, swaggering persona the actor had created, and became better remembered than the movie itself. There followed the very expensive and very long *The Sand Pebbles*, with McQueen as a Navy man stationed in 1926 China, who befriends and then mercifully executes his protégé, Mako. This was just the right combination of tough bravado and sensitivity that he could make work so very well, and the movie's several Oscar nominations included one for McQueen. *The Thomas Crown Affair* was supposed to be a sharp and suspenseful caper movie, but got bogged down in a lot of fancy camera work and too much aimless cavorting with Faye Dunaway. It made money nonetheless and produced an Oscar-winning song, "The Windmills of Your Mind." *Bullitt* became the peak of his career, a mature San Francisco-based police thriller with a killer car chase sequence that the whole world turned up to see, and with that he solidified his position as one of the screen's great anti-heroes. Figuring it was time to lighten up a bit, he romped through the very pleasing *The Reivers*, as a hired hand on a series of adventures with Mitch Vogel and Rupert Crosse, no doubt the most assured of his comedic attempts, though he himself was displeased with his work in it. He then showed off his love for auto racing in *Le Mans*, concentrating too little on the dramatic aspect of the script and turning it into yet another example of how the thrills of the sport could never be fully captured on screen in order for the audience to share in the excitement.

Junior Bonner was just one of several rodeo-themed films that failed to get an audience in the early 1970s, but the mean-spirited *The Getaway*, in which he was an ex-con bank robber, was another one that the crowds lined up for. The latter marked the actor's first production for the newly formed First Artists (joining Paul Newman, Barbra Streisand, and Sidney Poitier as part of this much-publicized, star-studded quartet), and it turned out to be the only thing that company produced that would qualify as a moneymaker. It also introduced McQueen to his second wife (he and Adams split in 1971), actress Ali MacGraw. Their short-lived union (1973–78) was a particularly turbulent one, during which he basically demanded that she retire from the profession (as he had dictated Adams do as well).

Two more adventures kept him in wealth, *Papillon*, with McQueen once again involved in a real-life great escape, this one from Devil's Island, and *The Towering Inferno*, with the actor showing up well into the story, as a determined fire chief whose quick thinking helps save lives during the deadly blaze. In a prime example of squabbling over on-screen credit, he took billing *before* but *lower* than that of Paul Newman, the man under whom he once played a bit part. After that, he put his career on hold, cranking up his asking price until no one could afford to work with him. In an effort to show his range and destroy his brawn-over-brain image, he grew a bushy beard and tackled Ibsen, playing Dr. Stockmann in a film of *An Enemy of the People*. Nobody, including its distributor, Warner Bros., knew what to make of this sincere but unsuccessful endeavor, and, after some

test screenings, it was pretty much pulled and put into deep storage. By 1980 he was ready to come back to work and did so in a poor western, *Tom Horn*, which was the last gasp of First Artists, and then in an all too typical police thriller, *The Hunter*, which threw in an extensive car chase around Chicago in hopes of capturing some past glories. The enthusiasm for the actor seemed to have passed, but the public knew they had lost someone special when cancer claimed him later that year. An off-beat McQueen credit was his work as a stunt man on the 1976 drive-in flick *Dixie Dynamite*.

Screen: 1956: Somebody Up There Likes Me; 1958: Never Love a Stranger; The Blob (as STEVEN MCQUEEN); 1959: The Great St. Louis Bank Robbery; Never So Few; 1960: The Magnificent Seven; 1961: The Honeymoon Machine; 1962: Hell Is for Heroes; The War Lover; 1963: The Great Escape; Soldier in the Rain; Love With the Proper Stranger; 1965: Baby the Rain Must Fall; The Cincinnati Kid; 1966: Nevada Smith; The Sand Pebbles; 1968: The Thomas Crown Affair; Bullitt; 1969: The Reivers; 1971: Le Mans; On Any Sunday; 1972: Junior Bonner; The Getaway; 1973: Papillon; 1974: The Towering Inferno; 1978: An Enemy of the People (and exec. prod.); 1980: Tom Horn (and exec. prod.); The Hunter.

NY Stage: 1956: A Hatful of Rain.

Select TV: 1955: The Chivington Raid (sp); 1956: Bring Me a Dream (sp); 1957: The Defender (sp); 1958–61: Wanted: Dead or Alive (series).

PATRICIA MEDINA

BORN: LIVERPOOL, ENGLAND, JULY 19, 1919.

A wide-eyed, brunette beauty with a whole slew of swashbucklers and second-rate adventures to her credit, Patricia Medina debuted in her native country as a bit player, starting with 1937's *Dinner at the Ritz*. Her career stayed at this unremarkable level until 1944, when she was given a lead in the romantic comedy *Kiss the Bride Goodbye*, foolishly getting engaged to her pompous boss when she, in fact, loves another. By this time she had married (1941–52) actor Richard Greene, who appeared opposite her in *Don't Take It to Heart*, and she eventually accepted an offer to come to Hollywood, in 1946, with MGM putting her into the melodrama *The Secret Heart*, in support of Claudette Colbert. Her participation in a pair of hits, *The Foxes of Harrow* and *The Three Musketeers*, pretty much sealed her fate as a lady who looked great in period costumes. Therefore, after playing straight woman to a jackass in *Francis* and to — guess who? — in *Abbott and Costello in the Foreign Legion*, she was seen showing off sufficient cleavage in such lush nonsense for Columbia producer Sam Katzman as *The Lady and the Bandit*, in which she played the wife of highwayman Dick Turpin. There followed *The Magic Carpet*, in which she shared leading lady honors with Lucille Ball of all people; *Lady in the Iron Mask*, a sex change on the Dumas novel with Medina in a dual role; *Captain Pirate*, who was Louis Hayward, reprising Errol Flynn's old role of Captain Blood; *Siren of Bagdad*, which one assumes referred to Medina, as a deposed sultan's daughter; and *Pirates of Tripoli*, which, like the one before it, cast her opposite a very tired-looking Paul Henreid. Leaving this genre behind, she simply stooped lower, playing *The Buckskin Lady*; the heroine in a disposable horror movie, *The Beast of Hollow Mountain*; and the wicked queen in the as-awful-as-it-sounds fantasy *Snow White and the Three Stooges*. By the time the last was released she had married (1960) actor Joseph Cotten and would remain his wife until his death in 1994. The few movies she made after their union included two with Cotten, *Latitude Zero* and *The Timber Tramp*, neither of which received much distribution.

Screen: 1937: Dinner at the Ritz; 1938: Simply Terrific; Double or Quits; 1942: Spitfire/The First of Few; The Avengers/The Day Will Dawn; 1943: They Met in the Dark; 1944: Hotel Reserve; Kiss the Bride Goodbye; Don't Take It to Heart; 1945: Waltz Time; 1946: The Secret Heart; 1947: Moss Rose; The Foxes of Harrow; The Beginning or the End?; 1948: The Three Musketeers; 1949: O.K. Agostina/Children of Chance; The Fighting O'Flynn; Francis; 1950: Fortunes of Captain Blood; The Jackpot; Abbott and Costello in the Foreign Legion; 1951: Valentino; The Lady and the Bandit; The Magic Carpet; 1952: Aladdin and His Lamp; Lady in the Iron Mask; Captain Pirate; Desperate Search; 1953: Siren of Bagdad; Sangaree; Plunder of the Sun; Botany Bay; 1954: Phantom of the Rue Morgue; Drums of Tahiti; The Black Knight; 1955: Pirates of Tripoli; Duel on the Mississippi; Mr. Arkadin/Confidential Report; 1956: Uranium Boom; Stranger at My Door; Miami Expose; The Beast of Hollow Mountain; The Red Cloak; 1957: The Buckskin Lady; 1959: Missiles From Hell/Battle of the V1; 1959: Count Your Blessings; 1961: Snow White and the Three Stooges; 1968: The Killing of Sister George; 1969: Latitude Zero; 1973: The Timber Tramp.

NY Stage: 1962: Calculated Risk.

Select TV: 1953: Tangier Lady (sp); 1954: Imperfect Lady (sp); 1956: Alibi (sp); 1959: The Last Lesson (sp); Absalom, My Son (sp); 1960: The Night Juggler (sp); 1963: Man Without a Witness (sp).

DONALD MEEK

BORN: GLASGOW, SCOTLAND, JULY 14, 1880.
DIED: NOVEMBER 18, 1946.

A bald, worried little man whose name was all too fitting, Donald Meek, had begun his career in an Australian touring production of *Little Lord Fauntleroy*. He eventually found his way to America, where he acted with some stock companies before making his Broadway debut, in 1913, in *Going Up*. This was followed by much theatrical work dotted by a handful of film performances, including *Personal Maid*, where he played the father of Nancy Carroll, and *Love, Honor and Oh Baby*, in which he repeated his stage role (from *Oh, Promise Me*) as nosey musician Luther Bowen. Starting in 1934 he was suddenly all over the place, appearing in more than 30 features films in the next two years alone, not to mention starring in a series of short films, made for Warners, in which he appeared as Dr. Crabtree, helping investigate crimes with John Hamilton, as Inspector Carr. Among the many roles on which he would place his indelible stamp were the son scheming to get George Arliss's inheritance in *The Last Gentleman*; the tailor whom Victor McLaglen tries to get in trouble in *The Informer*; a blind man in *Peter Ibbetson*; the clerk invited to become part of the nonconformist family in *You Can't Take It With You*; and the whisky salesman who becomes best buddy to fellow-traveler and drunkard Thomas Mitchell in *Stagecoach*, arguably his most famous role. Other such parts were the prosecuting lawyer who challenges Henry Fonda in *Young Mr. Lincoln*; a studio head in *Hollywood Cavalcade*; a card sharp who pretends to be a minister in *My Little Chickadee*; a writer of western novels in *Blonde Inspiration*; and the judge who gets increasingly tipsy on mincemeat in the remake of *State Fair*.

Screen: 1923: Six Cylinder Love; 1929: The Hole in the Wall; 1930: The Love Kiss; 1931: The Girl Habit; Personal Maid; 1932: Wayward; 1933: College Coach; Ever in My Heart; Love, Honor and Oh Baby!; 1934: The Merry Widow; What Every Woman Knows; Hi, Nellie!; Murder at the Vanities; The Last Gentleman; The Mighty Barnum; The Captain Hates the Sea; Mrs. Wiggs of the Cabbage Patch; Bedside; The Defense Rests; 1935: Romance in Manhattan; The Whole Town's Talking; The Informer; Biography of a Bachelor Girl; The Return of Peter Grimm; Village Tale; Old Man Rhythm; Accent of Youth; Society Doctor; Baby Face Harrington; Barbary Coast; Captain Blood; Peter Ibbetson; China Seas; Happiness C.O.D.; Top Hat; The Gilded Lily; The Bride Comes Home; Mark of the Vampire; Kind Lady; She Couldn't Take It; 1936: Pennies From Heaven; Everybody's Old Man; Three Wise Guys; Love on the Run; Two in a Crowd; And So They Were Married; One Rainy Afternoon; Old Hutch; Three Married Men; 1937: Artists and Models; Maid of Salem; Double Wedding; Behind the Headlines; Make a Wish; You're a Sweetheart; Parnell; Three Legionnaires; The Toast of New York; Breakfast for Two; 1938: The Adventures of Tom Sawyer; Double Danger; Little Miss Broadway; You Can't Take It With You; Hold That Co-Ed; Having Wonderful Time; Goodbye Broadway; 1939: Hollywood Cavalcade; Jesse James; Stagecoach; Blondie Takes a Vacation; The Housekeeper's Daughter; Young Mr. Lincoln; Nick Carter — Master Detective; 1940: Dr. Ehrlich's Magic Bullet; The Man From Dakota; The Ghost Comes Home; Phantom Raiders; Third Finger, Left Hand; Turnabout; Star Dust; Hullabaloo; Sky Murder; The Return of Frank James; My Little Chickadee; Oh Johnny, How You Can Love; 1941: A Woman's Face; Come Live With Me; The Feminine Touch; Barnacle Bill; Wild Man of Borneo; Blonde Inspiration; Rise and Shine; Babes on Broadway; 1942: Keeper of the Flame; Seven Sweethearts; Tortilla Flat; The Omaha Trail; Maisie Gets Her Man; They Got Me Covered; 1943: Air Raid Wardens; DuBarry Was a Lady; Lost Angel; 1944: Two Girls and a Sailor; Maisie Goes to Reno; Rationing; Bathing Beauty; The Thin Man Goes Home; Barbary Coast Gent; 1945: State Fair; Colonel Effingham's Raid; 1946: Because of Him; Janie Gets Married; Affairs of Geraldine; 1947: The Fabulous Joe; Magic Town.

NY Stage: 1913: Going Up; 1919: Nothing But Love; 1920: The Hottentot; Little Old New York; 1921: Six Cylinder Love; 1923: Tweedles; The Potters; 1925: Easy Terms; 1926: Love 'em and Leave 'em; The Shelf; 1927: Spread Eagle; My Princess; The Ivory Door; 1928: Mr. Moneypenny; 1929: Jonesy; Broken Dishes; 1930: Oh, Promise Me; 1931: After Tomorrow; 1932: Take My Tip.

RALPH MEEKER

(RALPH RATHGEBER) BORN: MINNEAPOLIS, MN, NOVEMBER 21, 1920. ED: NORTHWESTERN UNIV. DIED: AUGUST 5, 1988.

Brazenly macho Ralph Meeker was primed for stardom but fell below that goal, due no doubt to his few genuinely memorable film assignments and a decidedly less-than-lovable personality. Following naval service during World War II, he began appearing on Broadway (including *Mister Roberts*, for which he received a Theatre World Award), eventually obtaining his big break when he took over from Marlon Brando in *A Streetcar Named Desire*, in 1949. It was a tough act to follow, but it piqued interest not just in Hollywood but overseas, resulting in a leading role in the Swiss-produced *Four in a Jeep*, as an M.P. in Vienna who aids housewife Viveca Lindfors. For MGM he played the sergeant who befriends timid John Ericson in *Teresa*, then had a demanding part in *Shadow in the Sky*, as a shell-shocked vet. He was a boxer in love with New Orleans dancer Leslie Caron in *Glory Alley*, and, less typically, on loan to Paramount, he was Betty Hutton's vaudeville partner-husband in the musical bio of Blossom Seeley, *Somebody Loves Me*. Back to Metro and more fitting material, he did *Code Two*, as an L.A. motorcycle cop; *Jeopardy*, at his most disagreeable, as an escaped killer who pretends to help distressed Barbara Stanwyck; and *The Naked Spur*, as an army deserter who hopes to share the reward for bringing Robert Ryan to justice. Only the last had any box-office success, and that one wasn't sold on Meeker's name, James Stewart being the real attraction. Despite his better efforts, Meeker was considered an also-ran, ideal for second features.

After that he returned to Broadway for his greatest theatrical triumph, playing the drifter who sets women's hearts aflutter, in the original production of William Inge's *Picnic*. Although he was not asked to repeat his role in the film version (William Holden did it), he did return to the movies to play what would become his signature part, the raspy-voiced, stone-hard private eye Mike Hammer, in *Kiss Me Deadly*, a blunt thriller that was championed with the passing of the years for its somewhat cruel and unsentimental streak, which included Meeker's interpretation of the Hammer role, considered by some Mickey Spillane aficionados to be the definitive one. After kidnapping Jane Russell in the trashy *The Fuzzy Pink Nightgown*, he was fortunate to be cast as one of the doomed soldiers in Stanley Kubrick's fine antiwar film *Paths of Glory*, cynically accepting his fate as he is sentenced to the firing squad. He stayed in a tough vein as he segued into supporting parts, playing Bugs Moran in *The St. Valentine's Day Massacre*; an army captain in the box-office smash *The Dirty Dozen*; and Tuesday Weld's moonshiner daddy in *I Walk the Line*. He ended up getting eaten by rats in *The Food of the Gods*, and killed off by aliens in *Without Warning*. In between these, he and his wife produced a story of teen criminals, *My Boys Are Good Boys*, but it received next to no distribution.

Screen: 1950: Four in a Jeep; 1951: Teresa; Shadow in the Sky; 1952: Glory Alley; Somebody Loves Me; 1953: Code Two; Jeopardy; The Naked Spur; 1955: Big House, U.S.A.; Desert Sands; Kiss Me Deadly; 1956: A Woman's Devotion; 1957: Run of the Arrow; The Fuzzy Pink Nightgown; Paths of Glory; 1961: Ada; Something Wild; 1963: Wall of Noise; 1967: The St. Valentine's Day Massacre; Gentle Giant; The Dirty Dozen; 1968: The Devil's Eight; The Detective; 1970: I Walk the Line; 1971: The Anderson Tapes; 1972: The Happiness Cage; 1975: Johnny Firecloud/Revenge of Johnny Firecloud; Brannigan; 1976: Love Comes Quietly (filmed 1973); The Food of the Gods; 1977: Hi-Riders; The Alpha Incident; 1978: My Boys Are Good Boys (and co-prod.); 1979: Winter Kills; 1980: Without Warning.

NY Stage: 1945: Strange Fruit; 1946: Cyrano de Bergerac; 1948: Mister Roberts; 1949: A Streetcar Named Desire; 1953: Picnic; 1958: Cloud 7; 1962: Something About a Soldier; 1964: After the Fall; But for Whom; Charlie; 1965: Mrs. Daly; 1971: The House of Blue Leaves (ob).

Select TV: 1951: A Sound of Hunting (sp); 1952: The Darkness Below (sp); 1955: Dominique (sp); 1956: Dino (sp); Of Missing Persons (sp); The Magic Horn (sp); The Guilty (sp); The Blue Wall (sp); 1957: Four Women in Black (sp); Deep Water (sp); 1958: Bluebeard's Seventh Wife (sp); 1958: Fifty Grand (sp); 1959: The Man Who Had No Friends (sp); The Sound of Murder (sp); Not for Hire (series); 1960: A Punt, a Pass and a Prayer (sp); 1961: Frank Clell's in Town (sp); 1963: Night Run to the West (sp); 1964: Three Persons (sp); Lost Flight; 1971: Hard Traveling (sp); The Reluctant Heroes; The Night Stalker; 1973: Birds of Prey; You'll Never See Me Again; The Police Story; 1974: Cry Panic; Night Games; The Girl on the Late, Late Show; 1975: The Dead Don't Die.

ADOLPHE MENJOU

(ADOLPH JEAN MENJOU) BORN: PITTSBURGH, PA, FEBRUARY 18, 1890. ED: CORNELL UNIV. DIED: OCTOBER 29, 1963.

Alternately dashing and wickedly sarcastic, Adolphe Menjou had a moustache that suggested a stage villain from the Victorian era, a dapper way with the ladies, and a bombastic brio that made it seem as if there was an exclamation point after his every line. He traveled to New York in 1913 with the intention of breaking into the movie business by hiring on as an extra. His first verified feature credit came in 1914, in *The Man Behind the Door*, in which he was seen as a circus ringmaster. There were few roles of any note during this era, save for *The Moth*, in which he was the neglectful husband of Norma Talmadge. It was not until after a break for military service that his career began to pick up steam, when he began getting roles in such high-profile productions as *The Faith Healer*, as a doctor; *The Sheik*, as the friend of hero Rudolph Valentino; Douglas Fairbanks's version of *The Three Musketeers*, as King Louis VIII; and *Clarence*, as an unscrupulous private secretary, supporting Wallace Reid. There was much hoopla over his being given the leading role in Charlie Chaplin's first foray into directing drama, *A Woman of Paris*, as a rich bounder having a sophisticated affair with Edna Purviance, but the film was, not unexpectedly, a financial failure. Nevertheless, it brought him much attention and Menjou settled in at Paramount as a major name for the remainder of the silent era, usually in films that required nobility or a smart wardrobe. These included parts in *Open All Night*, as a jealous husband; *The Fast Set*, as a playboy who lures married Betty Compson into his arms; *The Swan*, as a prince whose betrothed finds happiness elsewhere; *The King on Main Street*, as the title character, who ends up in Coney Island; *The Grand Duchess and the Waiter*, as a millionaire slumming as a servant in what was probably his biggest financial hit of this period; *A Social Celebrity*, as a barber pretending to be a French count; and *The Sorrows of Satan*, as a Prince who is probably the devil himself, the perfect Menjou role.

He was still at Paramount when the transition to talkies came, and his sound debut was in *Fashions in Love*, a comedy in which he was a pianist with an insatiable sexual appetite. This was followed by a big moneymaker, *Morocco*, in which he took a back seat to Marlene Dietrich and Gary Cooper, and then the movie that proved he was not only at ease in front of a microphone, but that he could discharge machine-gun-like patter with the best of them, *The Front Page*. As the lovably conniving newspaper editor Walter Burns, he received his first and only Oscar nomination. He would continue to fluctuate between lead, character star, and supporting player over the next decade or so. *Friends and Lovers* found him and Laurence Olivier battling over Lily Damita; *Morning Glory* cast him as the producer who gives Katharine Hepburn her big break; *A Farewell to Arms* was given a needed boost by his performance as Major Rinaldi; and *Little Miss Marker* made him Runyon's inimitable bookmaker, Sorrowful Jones, a rare case where a fellow performer was given substantial screen time in a Shirley Temple film.

Menjou recited some Shakespeare as the partner of *The Mighty Barnum*; really chewed at the scenery as a hyper, Russian stage director in *Gold Diggers of 1935*; was a washed-up, drunken actor with hints of John Barrymore about him in *Sing, Baby, Sing*; and played the fight manager of Harold Lloyd in *The Milky Way*. By the late 1930s he was one of the more in-demand players in Hollywood, even if he was occasionally stuck with little more to do than get excited over promoting Sonja Henie, as he did in her debut showcase at Fox, *One in a Million*. He had better pictures elsewhere with *A Star Is Born*, solid as the understanding studio producer Oliver Niles; *One Hundred Men and a Girl*, subdued as Deanna Durbin's unemployed trombone-playing dad; and *Stage Door*, in a part not unlike that in *Morning Glory*, once again cast as a Broadway producer giving Katharine Hepburn her big chance.

Top billed, he was another drunken actor in *Letter of Introduction*, and then played a movie producer in both the Technicolor hodgepodge *The Goldwyn Follies* and in *That's Right — You're Wrong*, grinning and bearing it while contending with the Ritz Brothers and Kay Kyser and His Band, respectively. The 1940 remake of *A Bill of Divorcement* saw him tackling Barrymore's old role to little acclaim, and he went directly for the rafters as a nutcase named Colonel Caraway in the screwball comedy *Road Show*. He joined Gloria Swanson for her ill-advised return to films, *Father Takes a Wife*; was at his most colorfully bombastic as the shady criminal lawyer in *Roxy Hart*; and was suavely self-righteous as Rita Hayworth's wealthy dad in *You Were Never Lovelier*. Things began to cool down as the material weakened with a Betty Grable musical, *Sweet Rosie O'Grady*, in which he was Robert Young's editor; *Step Lively*, the remake of *Room Service*, where he had the role Donald MacBride had done earlier, the flustered hotel manager; *Man Alive*, in which he played a magician named Kismet; and *Mr. District Attorney*, where he found himself in love with Marguerite Chapman.

There was a step up at last when he supported Tracy and Hepburn in one of their best films, *State of the Union*, in top form as a political wheeler-dealer. Alas, shortly after this he made his unfortunate mark on political history as one of the actors who had no qualms about naming names before the House Un-American Activities Committee. This, however, did nothing to keep him from working, as was the case for those supporting this heinous organization at the time. As a result, he was suspected of trying to kill Abraham Lincoln in *Tall Target*; was on the trail of a sex criminal in *The Sniper*; had a lively role as a French trapper in *Across the Wide Missouri*; and played one of the screen's great villains, the foolish and self-serving French general who allows his men to face a firing squad in *Paths of Glory*. He ended his career playing a crotchety old man in Disney's charming *Pollyanna*, then retired, three years before his death from hepatitis. There wasn't an obit that didn't fail to mention his reputation as one of filmdom's best-dressed men, a point he himself no doubt took pride in, having entitled his 1948 autobiography *It Took Nine Tailors*. His third wife was actress Verree Teasdale to whom he was wed from 1934 until his death.

Screen: 1915: The Man Behind the Door; 1916: A Parisian Romance; Nearly a King; The Habit of Happiness; The Price of Happiness; The Crucial Test; Manhattan Madness; The Reward of Patience; The Devil at His Elbow; The Kiss; The Scarlet Runner (serial); The Blue Envelope Mystery; 1917: The Valentine Girl; An Even Break; The Amazons; The Moth; 1920: What Happened to Rosa?; 1921: The Faith Healer; Courage; Through the Back Door; The Three Musketeers; Queenie; The Sheik; 1922: Arabian Love; Head Over Heels; Is Matrimony a Failure?; The Eternal Flame; The Fast Mail; Clarence; Pink Gods; Singed Wings; 1923: The World's Applause; Bella Donna; Rupert of Hentzau; A Woman of Paris; The Spanish Dancer; 1924: The Marriage Circle; Shadows of Paris; The Marriage Cheat; For Sale; Broadway After Dark; Broken Barriers; Sinners in Silk; Open All Night; The Fast Set; Forbidden Paradise; 1925: The Swan; A Kiss in the Dark; Are Parents People?; Lost — A Wife; The King of Main Street; 1926: The Grand Duchess and the Waiter; A Social Celebrity; Fascinating Youth; The Ace of Cads; The Sorrows of

Satan; 1927: Blonde or Brunette; Evening Clothes; Service for Ladies; A Gentleman of Paris; Serenade; 1928: A Night of Mystery; His Tiger Lady; His Private Life; 1929: Marquis Preferred; Fashions in Love; 1930: The Parisian (and Fr. version: Mon Gosse de Pere); L'Enigmatique Monsieur Parkes (Fr. version of Slightly Scarlet); Amor Audaz (Sp. version of Slightly Scarlet); Morocco; New Moon; 1931: Wir um Schalten auf Hollywood (Ger. version of The March of Time); Soyons Gai (Fr. version of Let Us Be Gay); The Easiest Way; The Front Page; Men Call It Love; The Great Lover; Friends and Lovers; 1932: Forbidden; Prestige; Bachelor's Affairs; Night Club Lady; Two White Arms; Blame the Woman/Diamond Cut Diamond; A Farewell to Arms; 1933: The Circus Queen Murder; Morning Glory; The Worst Woman in Paris?; Convention City; 1934: Easy to Love; The Trumpet Blows; Journal of a Crime; Little Miss Marker; The Great Flirtation; The Human Side; The Mighty Barnum; 1935: Gold Diggers of 1935; Broadway Gondolier; 1936: The Milky Way; Sing, Baby, Sing; Wives Never Know; One in a Million; 1937: A Star Is Born; Cafe Metropole; One Hundred Men and a Girl; Stage Door; 1938: The Goldwyn Follies; Letter of Introduction; Thanks for Everything; 1939: King of the Turf; Golden Boy; That's Right — You're Wrong; The Housekeeper's Daughter; 1940: A Bill of Divorcement; Turnabout; 1941: Road Show; Father Takes a Wife; 1942: Roxie Hart; Syncopation; You Were Never Lovelier; 1943: Hi Diddle Diddle; Sweet Rosie O'Grady; 1944: Step Lively; 1945: Man Alive; 1946: Heartbeat; The Bachelor's Daughters; 1947: I'll Be Yours; Mr. District Attorney; The Hucksters; 1948: State of the Union; 1949: My Dream Is Yours; Dancing in the Dark; 1950: To Please a Lady; 1951: The Tall Target; Across the Wide Missouri; 1952: The Sniper; 1953: Man on a Tightrope; 1955: Timberjack; 1956: The Ambassador's Daughter; Bundle of Joy; 1957: The Fuzzy Pink Nightgown; Paths of Glory; 1958: I Married a Woman; 1960: Pollyanna.

Select TV: 1953–54: My Favorite Story (series); 1958: Target (series).

MELINA MERCOURI
(Anna Amalia Mercouri)
Born: Athens, Greece, October 18, 1923.
Died: March 6, 1994.

This Greek comet was that country's most famous cinematic export, and she was all fire, high spirits, and throaty lustiness, for those who enjoyed that sort of thing. Born to a family of politicians, she eschewed that field (initially) to concentrate on theater, making her name in Greek versions of several American hits, including *A Streetcar Named Desire* and *The Seven Year Itch*. Director Michael Cacoyannis (who would later make his name with *Zorba the Greek*) launched her film career when he cast her as the lead in his first theatrical feature, *Stella*, in 1955. That film, along *He Who Must Die/Celui qui Doit Mourir*, about a Passion play, helped to get her noticed on the art-house circuit. The latter also introduced her to Jules Dassin, the man who would become her husband (in 1966) and most frequent director. Their next collaboration, *Where the Hot Wind Blows!*, teamed her with Yves Montand, and despite his presence plus that of Gina Lollobrigida and Marcello Mastroianni, it didn't make much impact. The one that did, however, *Never on Sunday*, was an unheralded item about a bombastic prostitute who lives by her own rules and regulations, while becoming the toast of the waterfront. The movie was highly entertaining, and Mercouri was a joy to behold, even though she was stuck playing most of her role opposite a colorless Dassin, who foolishly cast himself as the American who tries to tame and educate her. Helped by a best-selling title song, the picture was a major international hit, and Mercouri nabbed herself an Oscar nomination in 1960.

The Dassin-Mercouri team did a follow-up that received its share of both acclaim and condemnation, *Phaedra*, in which she carried on with stepson Anthony Perkins, after which she gave one of her best performances, in the multi-character *The Victors*, as George Peppard's temporary fling, a self-serving cynic who has left her principles behind in order to survive during the war. This was followed by the first Dassin-Mercouri English-language production, *Topkapi*, a snappy caper movie and the only other film she did that is as fondly remembered as *Never on Sunday*. The success of that one took her to Hollywood, where she fared badly in a crummy James Garner comedy, *A Man Could Get Killed*. Back to Dassin, they came up with *10:30p.m. Summer*, with Mercouri playing an alcoholic, but the critics' love affair with this husband and wife duo was cooling off, to say the least. Falling back on a surer thing, they took *Never on Sunday* to Broadway, turning it into a musical, *Illya Darling*, which achieved some degree of success. Between two more Hollywood misfires, *Gaily, Gaily*, with Mercouri as a madam, and *Once Is Not Enough*, in which she shared a bed with Alexis Smith, she and Dassin did *Promise at Dawn*, in which she was a Russian mom, and *The Rehearsal*, a criticism of the political situation in Greece that received next to no showings. (It was finally released in the U.S. in 2001, years after Mercouri's death). There was one more from this pair, *A Dream of Passion*, paralleling a production of *Medea* (with Mercouri) with the real-life tragedy of a woman (Ellen Burstyn) who has killed her children. Burstyn got the better notices, while many a critic remarked on the increasingly over-the-top nature of Mercouri's acting. Perhaps sensing a growing disinterest, she switched professions, going into politics at last, serving in parliament and as Minister of Cultural Affairs of Greece.

Screen (US releases only): 1958: The Gypsy and the Gentleman (UK: 1957); He Who Must Die (Fr: 1956); 1960: Where the Hot Wind Blows! (Fr: 1958); Never on Sunday; 1962: Phaedra; 1963: The Victors; 1964: Topkapi; 1966: A Man Could Get Killed; 10:30p.m. Summer; 1967: The Uninhibited/Les Pianos Mecaniques; 1969: Gaily, Gaily; 1970: Promise at Dawn; 1974: The Rehearsal (and prod.; US: 2001); 1975: Once Is Not Enough; 1977: Nasty Habits; 1978: A Dream of Passion.

NY Stage: 1967: Illya Darling; 1972: Lysistrata.

BURGESS MEREDITH

(OLIVER BURGESS MEREDITH)
BORN: CLEVELAND, OH, NOVEMBER 16, 1907.
ED: AMHERST COL. DIED: SEPTEMBER 9, 1997.

A versatile, magnetic talent, Burgess Meredith wasn't conventionally good looking, so Hollywood wasn't sure what to do with him as a young man. As he got older his fame actually increased, as did the rasp in his voice and his feisty, irascible nature, making him one of the industry's most colorful and quietly admired and cherished thespians. After college he became a member of Eva LaGallienne's Student Repertory Group, and made his New York theater debut with them in their 1930 production of *Romeo and Juliet*. Leaving the company, he scored a major success in the original 1935 production of Maxwell Anderson's *Winterset*, playing a young man trying to clear the name of his executed father. His performance was so acclaimed that when RKO decided to film the piece they actually asked Meredith to repeat his role. On screen the whole thing seemed a bit too stylized and pretentious for audiences to warm up to, but

despite the movie's box-office failure, it was clear that an exciting new presence had arrived. Putting him in *There Goes the Groom* wasn't the sort of thing to make him eager to stay in movies, so after playing a college kid called the Lippencott, in *Spring Madness*, he returned to Broadway for a third collaboration with Anderson (*High Tor* had come before this one), *The Star Wagon*. Hollywood did want him back, however, and MGM put him in support of Gable and Shearer as a rabble-rousing pacifist in *Idiot's Delight*, another notable stage work of its time that has not aged very well. This was followed by his best role of this period, the sensible and caring friend of retarded Lon Chaney, Jr., in the excellent 1939 film of *Of Mice and Men*. Although it was Chaney's performance that would become both imitated and singled out for admiration, it was Meredith who was the more impressive of the two, capturing the decency and quiet agony of this man. Not unlike *Winterset*, it was a prestige item that failed to find much support among moviegoers looking for something more commercial, but its critical acclaim was capped off by an Oscar nomination in the Best Picture category.

Meredith was fittingly cast as the intellectual among the prison inmates in *Castle on the Hudson*, then fought Fred Astaire for the favors of Paulette Goddard in one of the great dancer's weakest vehicles, *Second Chorus*, losing Goddard in the movie but winning her in real life. They married in 1944 and remained wed until 1949. Proving his worth in comedy, he was a nutty pianist in *That Uncertain Feeling*, and one of Ginger Rogers's suitors (easily the only one she should have bothered with in the first place) in the artificial *Tom, Dick and Harry*. During World War II he joined the Air Force and even directed two short films for them, "Welcome to Britain" (1943) and "Salute to France" (1944). Back from military duty he stayed in uniform for another of his quietly effective performances, as real-life war correspondent Ernie Pyle in *The Story of G.I. Joe*; then he wrote and produced a project for himself and Goddard, *Diary of a Chambermaid*, an honorable failure in which he cast himself as another odd bird, her flower-eating neighbor. There was another producing job by Meredith, *A Miracle Can Happen/On Our Merry Way*, in which he linked the three all-star tales together as a roving reporter, and then one he directed, *The Man on the Eiffel Tower*, in a small role as a knife grinder, taking a back seat to Charles Laughton and Franchot Tone. Following a small British film, *The Gay Adventure* (which was helped up for release for four years), he took an eight-year sabbatical from motion pictures and concentrated instead on both acting and directing for the stage, with some television on the side.

When he did return to movies, it was in unconvincing Asian makeup for Universal's undistinguished comedy *Joe Butterfly*, a project, no doubt, brought about by Meredith having replaced David Wayne as Sakini during the Broadway run of *The Teahouse of the August Moon*. After that it was another five-year break from theatrical films, with more emphasis on television and stage, including directing the 1960 musical *A Thurber Carnival*, for which he received a Tony Award. It was therefore something of a comeback when he showed up as an unhinged congressional witness in director Otto Preminger's *Advise and Consent*, reminding everyone just how good he could be with this scene-stealing bit. Preminger couldn't get enough of him and made him an old priest in *The Cardinal*; a naval commander sharing quarters with John Wayne in *In Harm's Way*; a self-righteous, bigoted Southern judge in *Hurry Sundown*; the prison warden in the screwy *Skidoo*; and even had him strip down for an unforgettable moment in *Such Good Friends*. In between these he was hired to play the top-hatted, quacking villain, the Penguin, on the smash hit TV series *Batman*, and created such a memorable impression that he became a star all over again to a whole generation of baby boomers, repeating the part in a quickie big-screen spin-off. Playing a volatile Indian in an Elvis Presley disaster, *Stay Away, Joe*, proved that he could sink with the ship, but he was a hoot as an crotchety old dirt-bag convict in *There Was a Crooked Man…*

Around this time he directed and wrote a film called *The Yin and Yang of Mr. Go*, which, after failing to get U.S. distribution, resurfaced briefly years later during the initial videocassette boom. As Karen Black's pathetic vaudevillian dad in 1975's *The Day of the Locust*, he was nothing less than brilliant and finally got himself an Oscar nomination, as he did the next year as Sylvester Stallone's tough fight trainer, Mickey, in the Academy Award-winning *Rocky*, a part he'd return to on three more occasions and another role that made him extremely well known to the new generation. There were leads in hardly-seen efforts like *The Great Bank Hoax* and *Oddball Hall*; a hammy bit as Anthony Hopkins's Jewish agent in *Magic*; anything-for-a-buck parts in nonsense like *The Sentinel*, as one of Christina Raines's hellish neighbors, *Clash of the Titans*, as Harry Hamlin's mentor, and *Santa Claus*, as a mystical spirit with a long white beard; the title role in Jean-Luc Godard's bizarrely self-indulgent *King Lear*; and a showy bit as Jack Lemmon's foul-mouthed old man in the hit *Grumpy Old Men*, and its sequel. There was also a directorial credit on an obscure 1984 film, *James Joyce's Women*. On TV he won an Emmy Award in 1977 for *Tail Gunner Joe*. In 1994 he published his memoirs, *So Far, So Good*.

Screen: 1936: Winterset; 1937: There Goes the Groom; 1938: Spring Madness; 1939: Idiot's Delight; Of Mice and Men; 1940: Castle on the Hudson; 1941: Second Chorus; San Francisco Docks; That Uncertain Feeling; The Forgotten Village (narrator); Tom, Dick and Harry; 1942: Street of Chance; 1945: The Story of G.I. Joe/Ernie Pyle's Story of G.I. Joe; A Walk in the Sun (narrator); 1946: Diary of a Chambermaid (and wr.; prod.); Magnificent Doll; 1947: Mine Own Executioner; 1948: On Our Merry Way/A Miracle Can Happen (and prod.); 1949: Jigsaw; The Man on the Eiffel Tower (and dir.); 1953: The Gay Adventure/Golden Arrow 1957: Joe Butterfly; 1962: Advise and Consent; 1963: The Cardinal; 1964: The Kidnappers/Man on the Run; 1965: In Harm's Way; 1966: The Crazy Quilt (narrator); Madame X; A Big Hand for the Little Lady; Batman; 1967: Hurry Sundown; 1968: The Torture Garden; Stay Away, Joe; Skidoo; 1969: Mackenna's Gold; Hard Contract; The Reivers (narrator); 1970: There Was a Crooked Man…; 1971: Clay Pigeon; The Yin & Yang of Mr. Go (and dir.; wr.; dtv); Such Good Friends; 1972: The Man; Beware! The Blob/Son of Blob; A Fan's Notes; 1974: Golden Needles; 1975: B Must Die; 92 in the Shade; The Day of the Locust; The Master Gunfighter (narrator); The Hindenburg; 1976: Burnt Offerings; Rocky; 1977: The Sentinel; Golden Rendezvous/Nuclear Terror; 1978: The Manitou; Foul Play; Magic; The Great Bank Hoax; 1979: Rocky II; 1980: When Time Ran Out…; Final Assignment; 1981: The Last Chase; Clash of the Titans; True Confessions; 1982: Rocky III; 1983: Twilight Zone: The Movie (narrator); 1985: Broken Rainbow (voice); Santa Claus; 1988: King Lear; Hot to Trot (voice); Full Moon in Blue Water; 1990: Oddball Hall; State of Grace; Rocky V; 1993: Grumpy Old Men; 1994: Camp Nowhere; Across the Moon (dtv); 1995: Tall Tale; Grumpier Old Men; 1996: Wild Bill: Hollywood Maverick.

NY Stage: 1930: Romeo and Juliet; The Green Cockatoo; Siegfried; 1931: People on the Hill; 1932: Liliom; Alice in Wonderland; 1933: Threepenny Opera; Little Ol' Boy; She Loves Me Not; 1934: Hipper's Holiday; 1935: Battleship Gertie; The Barretts of Wimpole Street; Flowers of the Forest; Winterset; 1937: High Tor; The Star Wagon; 1940: Liliom (revival); 1942:

Candida; 1946: The Playboy of the Western World; 1950: Happy as Larry (and dir.); 1951: The Little Blue Light; 1952: The Fourposter; 1953: The Remarkable Mr. Pennypacker; 1954: The Teahouse of the August Moon; 1956: Major Barbara; 1964: I Was Dancing.

Select TV: 1950: Our Town (sp); The Horse's Mouth (sp); I'm Still Alive (sp); 1952: Decision (sp); 1953–54: Excursion (series); 1954: Edison, the Man (sp); 1957: Haunted Harbor (sp); The Big Story (series); 1958: The Unfamiliar (sp); 1959: Ah, Wilderness!; 1961: Waiting for Godot (sp); 1962: Footnote to Fame (sp); 1963–65: Mr. Novak (series); 1964: The Square Peg (sp); 1971: Lock, Stock and Barrel; The Strange Monster of Strawberry Cove (sp); 1972: Getting Away from It All; Probe; 1972–73: Search (series); 1974–75: Korg: 70,000 B.C. (series narrator); 1977: Johnny, We Hardly Knew Ye; SST — Death Flight; Tail Gunner Joe; The Last Hurrah; 1978: Kate Bliss and the Ticker Tape Kid; The Return of Captain Nemo/The Amazing Captain Nemo; 1980–81: Those Amazing Animals (series); 1982–83: Gloria (series); 1984: Wet Gold; 1986: Outrage!; Mr. Corbett's Ghost (sp); 1991: The Night of the Hunter; 1992: Mastergate (sp).

UNA MERKEL
BORN: COVINGTON, KY, DECEMBER 10, 1903.
DIED: JANUARY 2, 1986.

Pretty enough to be a full-fledged star but usually relegated to secondary roles where she could often show up the leads without much effort, Una Merkel, with her squinty eyes and perky smile, was one of the peerless ladies when it came to the fine art of wisecracking. While studying acting (under Tyrone Power's mom), she earned a living modeling for *True Story* magazine before getting some extra work in films and landing a role on Broadway in *Montmartre*. This led to employment by D.W. Griffith as Lillian Gish's stand-in and a role in *The Fifth Horseman*, before she went back to the stage where her jobs included touring in the unappetizingly titled *Pigs*. When talkies came, Griffith was thoughtful enough to ask Merkel to take an actual job in front of the cameras, playing the doomed Ann Rutledge, in his 1930 production of *Abraham Lincoln*. From this she was upped to the lead in *The Eyes of the World*, as a simple mountain gal, and then started getting offers all over town. For MGM she was Robert Montgomery's jealous bride in *Private Lives*, while Fox made her the best pal of Janet Gaynor in the hit *Daddy Long Legs*, and Warners cast her as the secretary (the role later played by Lee Patrick) in the now-forgotten 1931 version of *The Maltese Falcon*. Columbia gave her top billing in a cheap mystery, *Secret Witness*, but she was made a mightier impact playing sidekick to Jean Harlow in *Red-Headed Woman*, and to Loretta Young in both *They Call It Sin* and *Midnight Mary*. Most significantly she was one of the tough chorines in Warners landmark musical, *42nd Street*, memorably joining Ginger Rogers for a portion of "Shuffle Off to Buffalo." By this point she was under contract to MGM, where she was almost always found in support or as part of an ensemble. These films included *The Merry Widow*, in which she was the Queen; *Evelyn Prentice*, where she added some needed humor to this serious soaper, as Myrna Loy's best friend; *Murder in the Fleet*, with Merkel as sailor Nat Pendleton's girl, Toots Timmons; and *Broadway Melody of 1936*, where she got to banter with Jack Benny, playing his secretary.

Her MGM contract came to an end in 1938, but that didn't slow her down. She delivered some welcome bite to the poor *True Confession*, as Carole Lombard's buddy; came back to MGM to play Lionel Barrymore's loyal housekeeper in the charming *On*

Borrowed Time; and then made cinematic history with her knock-down drag-out brawl with Marlene Dietrich in the western comedy-drama *Destry Rides Again*. At Universal she was asked to play second fiddle to Baby Sandy in *Sandy Gets Her Man*, and then to W.C. Fields in *The Bank Dick*, as his daughter. She participated in one of the big hits of 1941, *Road to Zanzibar*, one of the few times that Dorothy Lamour brought another lady along to share Bing and Bob, but that was it for a while as far as "A" product was concerned. Universal stuck her into some hour-long programmers, *Cracked Nuts* and *The Mad Doctor of Market Street*, and Monogram gave her *Sweethearts of the U.S.A.*; then she began to slip out of sight until the late 1940s. She was the patient wife of William Bendix in the slapsticky *Kill the Umpire*; took a different role than the one she'd essayed previously, playing Lana Turner's companion in the 1952 remake of *The Merry Widow*; showed up as a nun in *With a Song in My Heart*; was wooed by Arthur Hunnicutt in *The Kettles in the Ozarks*; and was Debbie Reynolds's rural mom in *The Mating Game*. Onstage she scored a hit playing the unhinged mother in *Summer and Smoke* (in La Jolla, California) and received a Tony Award for *The Ponder Heart*. When the former was finally committed to celluloid, in 1961, Merkel was asked to repeat her role and capped her career with raves and an Oscar nomination in the supporting category. There were three pictures for Disney and then an Elvis Presley vehicle before she and the movies parted company.

Screen: 1923: The White Rose; 1924: The Fifth Horseman; 1930: Abraham Lincoln; The Eyes of the World; The Bat Whispers; 1931: Command Performance; Don't Bet on Women; Six Cylinder Love; Daddy Long Legs; The Maltese Falcon; The Bargain; Wicked; Private Lives; The Secret Witness/Terror by Night; 1932: Red-Headed Woman; She Wanted a Millionaire; Impatient Maiden; Man Wanted; Huddle; They Call It Sin; Men Are Such Fools; 1933: The Secret of Madame Blanche; Whistling in the Dark; Clear All Wires; 42nd Street; Reunion in Vienna; Midnight Mary; Her First Mate; Beauty for Sale; Broadway to Hollywood; Bombshell; Day of Reckoning; The Women in His Life; 1934: This Side of Heaven; Murder in the Private Car; Paris Interlude; Bulldog Drummond Strikes Back; The Cat's Paw; Have a Heart; The Merry Widow; Evelyn Prentice; 1935: Biography of a Bachelor Girl; The Night Is Young; One New York Night; Baby Face Harrington; Murder in the Fleet; Broadway Melody of 1936; It's in the Air; 1936: Riffraff; Speed; We Went to College; Born to Dance; 1937: Don't Tell the Wife; The Good Old Soak; Saratoga; True Confession; 1938: Checkers; 1939: Four Girls in White; Some Like It Hot/Rhythm Romance; On Borrowed Time; Destry Rides Again; 1940: Comin' Round the Mountain; Sandy Gets Her Man; The Bank Dick; 1941: Double Date; Road to Zanzibar; Cracked Nuts; 1942: The Mad Doctor of Market Street; Twin Beds; 1943: This Is the Army; 1944: Sweethearts of the U.S.A.; 1947: It's a Joke, Son; 1948: The Man From Texas; The Bride Goes Wild; 1950: Kill the Umpire; My Blue Heaven; Emergency Wedding; 1951: Rich, Young and Pretty; A Millionaire for Christy; Golden Girl; 1952: With a Song in My Heart; The Merry Widow; 1953: I Love Melvin; 1955: The Kentuckian; 1956: The Kettles in the Ozarks; Bundle of Joy; 1957: The Fuzzy Pink Nightgown; The Girl Most Likely; 1959: The Mating Game; 1961: The Parent Trap; Summer and Smoke; 1963: Summer Magic; 1964: A Tiger Walks; 1966: Spinout.

NY Stage: 1922: Montmarte; 1925: The Poor Nut; Two by Two; Pigs; 1927: The Gossipy Sex; Coquette; 1929: Salt Water; 1943: Three's a Family; 1953: The Remarkable Mr. Pennypacker; 1956: The Ponder Heart; 1959: Take Me Along.

Select TV: 1952: My Wife Geraldine (sp); 1954: Two Little Minks (sp); 1955: Trucks Welcome (sp); 1957: The Greer Case

(sp); 1958: Aladdin (sp); Flint and Fire (sp).

ETHEL MERMAN

(ETHEL AGNES ZIMMERMAN) BORN: QUEENS, NY, JANUARY 16, 1908. DIED: FEBRUARY 15, 1984.

One didn't have a neutral opinion of Ethel Merman. The bombastic diva with the rangy, overpowering singing voice shook the rafters of Broadway theaters for some four decades, becoming one of its legendary names, but wasn't quite as welcome in movie houses where her style was a tad larger than life. A onetime stenographer, she took to singing in nightclubs and in vaudeville before taking a part in the 1930 production of the Gershwin musical *Girl Crazy*. Her ear-shattering rendition of "I Got Rhythm" became one of the musical theater's legendary moments, and she was immediately asked to drop in on an Ed Wynn musical being made for Paramount, *Follow the Leader*, where she sang "Satan's Holiday." She returned to the stage for a spell before being asked to lend support to Bing Crosby in *We're Not Dressing*, and to Eddie Cantor in both *Kid Millions* and *Strike Me Pink*. Between the last two, she scored a major triumph on Broadway in one of Cole Porter's most enduring shows, *Anything Goes*, where she introduced "You're the Top" and "I Get a Kick Out of You," among others. Paramount asked her to buddy up with Crosby again for the 1936 movie version, but aside from those two songs, little remained from the original piece. She went over to 20th Century-Fox to do some bickering (and ice skating!) with Cesar Romero in *Happy Landing*, and to sell some Irving Berlin numbers like "Pack Up Your Sins and Go to the Devil" in *Alexander's Ragtime Band*.

It was clear that Merman was nobody's idea of a Hollywood leading lady, so back she went again to New York for four more hits, *Du Barry Was a Lady*, *Panama Hattie*, *Something for the Boys*, and *Annie Get Your Gun*, none of which she was asked to repeat when the movies bought each of these properties (although she did a television version of the last in 1967, by which point she was far too old for the part of Annie Oakley). Aside from a guest bit in *Stage Door Canteen*, she was off the screen until 1953, when she was finally asked to preserve one of her stage triumphs on film, in this instance her Tony Award-winning turn as a Washington hostess-turned-ambassador, *Call Me Madam*, which she did for Fox. It was stagebound but captured everything good and bad about the performer, the good being her indomitable way of taking center stage, the bad her inability to give sincere and genuine attention to her fellow performers.

There was big, gaudy CinemaScope cornucopia of Irving Berlin numbers, *There's No Business Like Show Business*, where she went from the heights of the title tune to the depths of "A Sailor's Not a Sailor," which she did in seaman drag. There was one more Broadway event that placed her among the immortals of the musical stage, *Gypsy*, and one more case where she was passed over for the film adaptation in favor of someone who had proven herself as a movie star, in this instance Rosalind Russell. Instead she gamely allowed herself to be tossed around as Dorothy Provine's battle-ax mom in the super-comedy *It's a Mad Mad Mad Mad World*; played a madam in *The Art of Love*, a part originally written for Mae West; and did a memorable cameo as a shell-shocked soldier who thinks he's Ethel Merman in the wild spoof *Airplane!* Between these she continued to be celebrated as one of show business's true originals, allowing herself to drop occasionally into camp, as she did when she released a disco album of some of her greatest hits. Among her husbands was actor Ernest Borgnine, to whom she was wed for less than a year in 1964. She published her autobiography, *Merman*, in 1978.

Screen: 1930: Follow the Leader; 1934: We're Not Dressing; Kid Millions; 1935: Big Broadcast of 1936; 1936: Anything Goes; Strike Me Pink; 1938: Happy Landing; Alexander's Ragtime Band; Straight Place and Show; 1943: Stage Door Canteen; 1953: Call Me Madam; 1954: There's No Business Like Show Business; 1963: It's a Mad Mad Mad Mad World; 1965: The Art of Love; 1974: Journey Back to Oz (voice); 1976: Won Ton Ton, the Dog Who Saved Hollywood; 1980: Airplane!

NY Stage: 1930: Girl Crazy; 1931: George White's Scandals (11th Edition); 1932: Take a Chance; 1934: Anything Goes; 1936: Red, Hot and Blue; 1939: Stars in Your Eyes; Du Barry Was a Lady; 1940: Panama Hattie; 1943: Something for the Boys; 1946: Annie Get Your Gun; 1950: Call Me Madam; 1956: Happy Hunting; 1959: Gypsy; 1966: Annie Get Your Gun (revival); 1970: Hello, Dolly!

Select TV: 1954: Anything Goes (sp); Panama Hattie (sp); 1956: Reflected Glory (sp); Honest in the Rain (sp); 196: An Evening With Ethel Merman (sp); 1967: Annie Get Your Gun (sp); 1979: Rudolph and Frosty's Christmas in July (sp; voice).

DINA MERRILL

(NEDENIA HUTTON)
BORN: NEW YORK, NY, DECEMBER 9, 1928.
ED: GEORGE WASHINGTON UNIV.

It was no surprise that lovely Dina Merrill had an air of the elite about her, having been the daughter of millionaire stockbroker E.F. Hutton and socialite Marjorie Merriweather Post. She had worked as a fashion model in the mid-1940s while studying acting at both the American Academy of Dramatic Arts and the American Music and Dramatic Academy. After some stage and television roles, she made her motion picture debut in 1957, in *Desk Set*, as one of the information specialists working with Katharine Hepburn. She was straight woman to Jerry Lewis in the naval farce *Don't Give Up the Ship*, and looked nice enough in uniform that she was promoted from ensign to lieutenant for *Operation Petticoat*, one of the biggest box-office hits of 1959. Staying strictly in support, she helped run a sheep station in the Oscar-nominated *The Sundowners*; was cheated on by hubbie Laurence Harvey in *Butterfield 8*; was the distant wife, not the least bit interested in lawyer Burt Lancaster's problems, in *The Young Savages*; played Glenn Ford's girlfriend, seeking equal rights for women, in *The Courtship of Eddie's Father*; and attempted to bring some class to one of the more strained Bob Hope romps, *I'll Take Sweden*. In 1966 she married actor Cliff Robertson, to whom she would be wed for another 20 years. In the meantime she was given an actual lead in a barely seen concoction, *The Meal*, throwing a banquet so her friends can tear each other apart. She was the mother of groom Desi Arnaz, Jr., among the huge cast of *A Wedding*, and then, for the same director, Robert Altman, a movie studio secretary in *The Player*. By this point she appeared more interested in serving on the board of directors for various organizations, including, not surprisingly, E.F. Hutton.

Screen: 1957: Desk Set; 1958: A Nice Little Bank That Should Be Robbed; 1959: Don't Give Up the Ship; Catch Me If You Can (nUSr); Operation Petticoat; 1960: Butterfield 8; The Sundowners; 1961: Twenty Plus Two; The Young Savages; 1963: The Courtship of Eddie's Father; 1965: I'll Take Sweden; 1973: Running Wild; 1974: Throw Out the Anchor (nUSr); 1975: The Meal/Deadly Encounter; 1977: The Greatest; 1978: A Wedding; 1980: Just Tell Me What You Want; 1988: Caddyshack II; 1991: True Colors;

Twisted (dtv; filmed 1986); 1992: The Player; 1994: Suture; 1995: Point of Betrayal (dtv); 1996: Open Season; 1997: Milk & Money (dtv); 1998: Mighty Joe Young.

NY Stage: 1946: The Mermaids Singing; 1975: Angel Street; 1979: Are You Now or Have You Ever Been?; 1981: Suddenly, Last Summer (ob); 1983: On Your Toes; 1985: The Importance of Being Earnest (ob).

Select TV: 1955: A Place Full of Strangers (sp); 1956: The Center of the Maze (sp); 1958: One for All (sp); 1958: The Time of Your Life (sp); 1959: What Makes Sammy Run? (sp); The Fallen Idol (sp); 1960: Men in White (sp); 1961: Brandenburg Gate (sp); The Dispossessed (sp); 1962: Footnote to Fame (sp); The Court-Martial of Captain Wycliff (sp); 1963: The Candidate (sp); 1965: The Game (sp); 1968: The Sunshine Patriot; 1969: The Lonely Profession; Seven in Darkness; 1971: Mr. and Mrs. Bo Jo Jones; 1972: Family Flight; 1973: The Letters; 1976: Kingston: The Power Play; 1979: Roots: The Next Generations (ms); The Tenth Month; 1984: Hot Pursuit (series); Anna to the Infinite Power; 1989: Turn Back the Clock; 1990: Fear; 1993: Not in My Family; 1997: Something Borrowed, Something Blue; 1998: A Chance of Snow; 2001: The Glow; The Magnificent Ambersons.

GARY MERRILL

BORN: HARTFORD, CT, AUGUST 2, 1915.
ED: BOWDOIN COL., TRINITY COL.
DIED: MARCH 5, 1990.

A dark-browed actor with a dour demeanor and a decidedly unfriendly personality, Gary Merrill wasn't the type to outshine inferior material but kept himself employed for a fair amount of his career nonetheless. He made his professional bow in 1937 as part of a religious pageant and then went to Broadway that same year, replacing Jose Ferrer in *Brother Rat*. During World War II he joined the Air Force and participated in both of the big military revues of the time, *This Is the Army* and *Winged Victory*, making his motion picture debut in Fox's 1944 adaptation of the latter as a no-nonsense flight trainer. Following the war he landed one of the leads in Broadway's smash hit comedy *Born Yesterday* (the part William Holden would do in the movie) and this was instrumental in his getting a contract with 20th Century-Fox. They made him a colonel in the 1949 hit *Twelve O'Clock High*, and then gave him his best-remembered role, temperamental Bette Davis's director and lover in the classic *All About Eve*. One really believed he had the determination to take Davis in hand, and they continued their union off screen with a ten-year (1950–60) stormy marriage. There were also two more movie pairings for the couple, *Another Man's Poision*, a highly implausible meller made in Britiain, in which he pretended to be the husband she has just murdered; and *Phone Call From a Stranger*, in which Merrill was a plane crash survivor visiting the families of those who died.

Although he did participate in a worthy, Oscar-nominated war film, *Decision Before Dawn*, Merrill's movie assignments quickly slid into the routine, including playing a Confederate soldier out to steal from the Indians in *The Black Dakotas*; a small-town newspaperman in *The Missouri Traveler*; a pilot whose plane is in serious trouble in *Crash Landing*; and a flier who sleeps with his best buddy's wife and therefore must sacrifice his life in the final reel in a turgid soap made in England, *Bermuda Affair*. He took top-billing as a newly appointed captain facing corruption in *The Human Jungle*, an ensemble piece about a police precinct; was Tony Curtis's dad in *The Great Imposter*; landed on *Mysterious Island*, as one of the escaped soldiers in this Jules Verne fantasy; showed up as Lili Palmer's drab new husband in *The Pleasure of His Company*; battled a creature in an underwater lab in a worthless sci-fi entry, *Destination Inner Space*; played a terrorized subway passenger in *The Incident*; was slimy Pap in the musical version of *Huckleberry Finn*; and was equally down and dirty as a street derelict in *Thieves*. He made an unsuccessful bid for the Maine legislature in 1968. His autobiography, *Bette, Rita and the Rest of My Life*, was published in 1989.

Screen: 1944: Winged Victory; 1948: The Quiet One (narrator); 1949: Slattery's Hurricane; Twelve O'Clock High; 1950: Mother Didn't Tell Me; Where the Sidewalk Ends; All About Eve; 1951: The Frogmen; Decision Before Dawn; Another Man's Poison; 1952: The Girl in White; Night Without Sleep; Phone Call From a Stranger; 1953: A Blueprint for Murder; 1954: Witness to Murder; The Black Dakotas; The Human Jungle; 1956: Navy Wife; Bermuda Affair; 1958: Crash Landing; The Missouri Traveler; 1959: The Wonderful Country; 1960: The Savage Eye; 1961: The Great Imposter; Mysterious Island; The Pleasure of His Company; 1962: Hong Kong Farewell (nUSr); 1963: A Girl Named Tamiko; 1965: The Woman Who Wouldn't Die; 1966: Cast a Giant Shadow; Ride Beyond Vengeance; Destination Inner Space; Around the World Under the Sea; 1967: The Last Challenge; Clambake; 1968: The Incident; The Power; 1969: Amarsi Male (nUSr); 1974: Huckleberry Finn; 1977: Thieves.

NY Stage: 1937: Brother Rat; 1939: See My Lawyer; 1942: This Is the Army; 1943: Winged Victory; 1946: Born Yesterday; 1949: At War With the Army; 1959: The World of Carl Sandburg; 1962: Step on a Crack; 1980: Morning's at Seven.

Select TV: 1953: P.O.W. (sp); 1954: The Mask (series); The Great Chair (sp); 1954–55: Justice (series); 1957: Wedding Present (sp); If You Knew Elizabeth (sp); Hey Mac (sp); 1958: God Is My Judge (sp); The Starmaker (sp); 1959: A Quiet Game of Cards (sp); A Corner of the Garden (sp); The Best Way to Go (sp); 1960–61: Winston Churchill: The Valiant Years (series narrator); 1961: Money and the Minister (sp); 1963: The Machine That Played God (sp); 1964: The Reporter (series); 1965: The Highest Fall of All (sp); 1967: Hondo and the Apaches; 1969: Then Came Bronson; 1970: The Secret of the Sacred Forest (sp); 1971: Earth II; 1972: Young Dr. Kildare (series); 1973: Pueblo; 1979: The Seekers.

TOSHIRO MIFUNE

Born: Tsing-Tao, China, April 1, 1920.
Died: December 24, 1997.

Japanese cinema's premier superstar, the imposing Toshiro Mifune, was forever linked in movie lore with director Akira Kurosawa, who was instrumental in making him an international attraction. He was born in China to Japanese parents who returned to their country in time for Mifune to serve in the army during World War II. With virtually no acting experience, he was chosen to appear in a film, *Shin Baka Jidai/These Foolish Times*, in 1946. The following year he had a lead in *Genrei no Hate/Snow Trail*, and then played his first starring role, a crook suffering from tuberculosis, for the up-and-coming Kurosawa in *Yoidore Tenshi/Drunken Angel*. They joined forces again for *The Quiet Duel* and *Stray Dog*, but the one that put them on the map was *Rashomon*, in which Mifune was the bandit who rapes the wife of a nobleman. The gimmick was that the story was told from all three points of view, each showing a different take on the incident. Another director who was a frequent collaborator, Hiroshi Inagaki, gave Mifune the title role in *Samurai*, which played the U.S. in 1955 and won the Academy Award for Best Foreign-Language Film. It was dabbling in this same occupation that would bring Mifune and Kurosawa their greatest success, *Seven Samurai*,

released in its country of origin in 1954 and then in the states in 1956. Its story of a team of mercenaries hired to protect a village, was presented in a vivid, brutal fashion, and it became, arguably, the most famous Japanese film of all time and the inspiration for countless imitations, drawing the rapturous devotion of film students and directors for generations to come.

The Mifune-Kurosawa team was lavished with further praise for *Throne of Blood*, their take on *Macbeth*, and *The Hidden Fortress*, with Mifune as a feudal warlord meeting up with an escaped princess. The market was now clamoring for more Mifune, so some of the earlier films were dusted off for distribution in America and elsewhere. There was another seminal offering, *Yojimbo*, about a stoic stranger who comes between two feuding parties. This would serve as the basis for Clint Eastwood's first spaghetti western, *A Fistful of Dollars*, among others, and itself rated a sequel, *Sanjuro*. Mifune teamed one last time with Kurosawa, for *Red Beard*, as a doctor-turned-swordsman, after which he finally accepted an offer to appear in an American film. Since he was just part of a large ensemble in MGM's autorace epic *Grand Prix*, his contribution was hardly considered important, outside the fact that it helped to secure bookings in the East. In any case his voice was dubbed. A more significant American production for him, *Hell in the Pacific*, pitted him against Lee Marvin in a two-character piece in which they were wartime enemies unable to speak each other's language. Mifune's Japanese films, mainly those done with Inagaki, like *Daredevil in the Castle* and *Samurai Banners*, continued to pop up in the U.S., while Mifune was still asked to lend his name to such international films as *Red Sun*, a dreary western with Charles Bronson; the all-star *Midway*, as Admiral Yamamoto; the noisy farce *1941*, as a submarine commander trying to bomb California; and *The Challenge*, as one of two brothers fighting over a sword. TV audiences became familiar with him in the early 1980s when he played the title role in the extremely popular mini-series *Shogun*.

Screen (US releases only): 1952: Rashomon (Jp: 1950); 1955: Samurai (Jp: 1954); 1956: Seven Samurai (Jp: 1954); 1957: Throne of Blood; 1958: The Hidden Fortress; 1960: Drunken Angel (Jp: 1948); 1962: Yojimbo (Jp: 1961); 1963: Chusingura (Jp: 1962); Sanjuro (Jp: 1962); The Bad Sleep Well (Jp: 1960); High and Low; 1964: Stray Dog (Jp: 1949); 1965: Red Beard; Samurai Assassin; 1966: The Lost World of Sinbad (Jp: 1963); Grand Prix; 1967: I Live in Fear (Jp: 1955); The Sword of Doom/ Samurai Part 2 (Jp: 1955); Samurai Part 3 (Jp: 1956); 1968: The Secret Scrolls (Jp: 1957); The Secret Scrolls Part 2 (Jp: 1958); Whirlwind (Jp: 1964); Rebellion (Jp: 1967); Hell in the Pacific; 1969: Daredevil in the Castle (Jp: 1961); 1970: Samurai Banners (Jp: 1969); The Emperor and the General (Jp: 1967); Red Lion (Jp: 1969); Machibure; Band of Assassins (Jp: 1969); Zatoichi Meets Yojimbo; 1972: Red Sun; 1973: The Day the Sun Rose (Jp: 1967); The Militarists (Jp: 1970); 1974: The Ambitious (Jp: 1970); 1975: Paper Tiger; 1976: Midway; 1979: Winter Kills; 1941; 1980: Scandal (Jp: 1949); 1981: The Bushido Blade; Inchon; 1982: The Challenge; Love and Faith of Ogin (Jp: 1978); 1983: The Quiet Duel (Jp: 1949); 1992: Journey of Honor/ Shogun Mayeda; 1993: Shadow of the Wolf; 1995: Picture Bride.

Select TV: 1980: Shogun (ms).

VERA MILES

(Vera May Ralston) Born: Boise City, OK, August 23, 1929.

With a personality that could switch from cool to warm like the flick of a switch, Vera Miles made a career of being dependable rather than sensational. Most people do not think of her carrying films on her own, but rather lending her capable presence to a stronger leading man. A former model and beauty contest winner, she married Robert Miles with whom she traveled to Hollywood, both of them hoping to find employment. Her husband worked as a stunt man, while Vera ended up at RKO, putting in a fleeting appearance in the chorus in *Two Tickets to Broadway*, in 1951. Two years later she had a showier part in a popular 3-D film, Warners's *The Charge at Feather River*, as the girl captured by the Cheyennes who doesn't relish being rescued by the cavalry. There were "B" movie assignments with the racetrack drama *Pride of the Blue Grass*; the umpteenth Tarzan offering, *Tarzan's Hidden Jungle*, sharing the screen with Zippy the Chimp; *Wichita*, playing lady friend to Joel McCrea's Wyatt Earp; and *23 Paces to Baker Street*, helping blind writer Van Johnson to uncover a kidnapping. Her status moved up to a higher grade with *The Searchers*, although her scenes with Jeffrey Hunter were the least interesting in the film, and then she played an all-out bitch in *Autumn Leaves*, driving Cliff Robertson nuts by getting it on with his dad, Lorne Greene. Around this point Alfred Hitchcock came into the picture, hoping to make her his protégé. There were roles on his TV series and an impressive part in *The Wrong Man*, as the wife of Henry Fonda who ends up in a mental institution after her husband is arrested for a crime he didn't commit. Alas, the role Hitchcock had been grooming her for, the one that would demonstrate her true worth, in *Vertigo*, went to Kim Novak after Miles got pregnant.

Back to work, she turned Mayor Bob Hope's head in *Beau James*; stood by James Stewart through his many years as an agent in the lengthy *The FBI Story*; and proved that she was still pretty even with her head shaved in the turgid *5 Branded Women*. She returned once more to Hitchcock for her most famous screen role, the determined sister of slain Janet Leigh in *Psycho*, memorably finding Mrs. Bates in the fruit cellar in the stunning climax. Heading west she was the woman who causes John Wayne's ruin in *The Man Who Shot Liberty Valance*, and was very comfortably cast in three of Walt Disney's least successful features of the 1960s: *A Tiger Walks*; the Boy Scout weepie *Follow Me, Boys!*; and the underrated *Those Calloways*, playing wife to Brian Keith and mom to Brandon de Wilde, all of them hoping to save some wild geese. Staying friendly with wildlife she was mother to Clint Howard and his pet bear in *Gentle Giant* (Beth Brickell played the part when it became a TV series); then went back to John Wayne for both *The Green Berets*, where her part ended up on the cutting room floor, and for *Hellfighters*. Roughing it again she was a pioneer in another Disney flop, *The Wild Country*, and then actually got top billing at last for a minor western, *Molly and Lawless John*, sharing the title names with Sam Elliott, and going skinny-dipping at one point just to prove that this was now the 1970s. Her bad luck with Disney and the box office continued with *One Little Indian* and *The Castaway Cowboy*, although in both instances she got to work with James Garner. After a period away from theatrical features, she made the mistake of agreeing to appear in the woefully misguided sequel, *Psycho II*, reprising her role as Lila Crane. Most of her work in her later years, however, was on the small screen.

Screen: 1951: Two Tickets to Broadway; 1952: For Men Only/The Tall Lie; The Rose Bowl Story; 1953: The Charge at Feather River; So Big; 1954: Pride of the Blue Grass; 1955: Tarzan's Hidden Jungle; Wichita; 1956: 23 Paces to Baker Street; The Searchers; Autumn Leaves; The Wrong Man; 1957: Beau James; 1959: Web of Evidence/Beyond This Place; The FBI Story; 1960: A Touch of Larceny; 5 Branded Women; Psycho; 1961: Back Street; 1962: The Man Who Shot Liberty Valance; 1964: A Tiger Walks; 1965: Those Calloways; 1966: One of Our Spies Is Missing (from TV); Follow Me, Boys!; 1967: The Spirit Is Willing; Gentle Giant; 1968: Sergeant Ryker (from TV film); Kona Coast; 1969: It Takes All Kinds; Hellfighters; Mission Batangas; 1971: The Wild Country; 1972: Molly and Lawless John; 1973: One Little Indian; 1974: The Castaway Cowboy; 1977: Twilight's Last Gleaming; The Thoroughbreds/Run for the Roses; 1983: Psycho II; Brainwaves/Shadow of Death; 1984: The Initiation; 1985: Into the Night; 1995: Separate Lives.

Select TV: 1953: The Sail (sp); 1954: Walking John Stopped Here (sp); The Grey and Gold Dress (sp); The Tryst (sp); Championship Affair (sp); 1955: The House Where Time Stopped (sp); P.J. and the Lady (sp); Man on the Ledge; Inside Story (sp); Rookie of the Year (sp); 1956: The Great Lady (sp); The Letter (sp); 1957: The Taggart Light (sp); Panic Button (sp); 1958: Emergency Call (sp); 1959: Nora (sp); 1960: The Lawbreakers (sp); Incident at a Corner (sp); 1963: The Case Against Paul Ryker (later 1968 theatrical release); 1964: The Hanged Man; 1966: The People Trap (sp); 1971: In Search of America; Cannon; Owen Marshall: Counselor at Law/A Pattern of Morality; A Howling in the Woods; 1972: Jigsaw; A Great American Tragedy; 1973: Baffled!; Runaway!; 1974: Live Again, Die Again; The Underground Man; The Strange and Deadly Occurrence; 1976: McNaughton's Daughter; Judge Horton and the Scottsboro Boys; Smash-Up on Interstate 5; 1977: Fire!; 1978: And I Alone Survived; 1980: Roughnecks; 1981: Our Family Business; 1982: Rona Jaffe's Mazes and Monsters; 1983: Travis McGee; 1984: Helen Keller: The Miracle Continues; 1985: International Airport; 1989: The Hijacking of the Achille Lauro.

RAY MILLAND

(REGINALD ALFRED JOHN TRUSCOTT-JONES)
BORN: NEATH, GLAMORGANSHIRE, WALES,
JANUARY 3, 1905. ED: KING'S COL., LONDON.
DIED: MARCH 10, 1986.

He possessed one of the most relaxed personalities in movies, which kept most of his reviews on a level of respect rather than high praise, but that was perhaps the secret of Ray Milland's longevity in the business. There were gentlemen from the British Isles who were more forceful and those who were more debonair, but Milland seemed to have no pretensions about himself and kept his career at a fairly smooth meter, with some genuine high points along the way. Schooled in England, he entered show business as part of a dance team with Anna Neagle. This led to bits in British movies, first billed as "Spike Milland," of all things, and then as "Raymond" before settling on "Ray." By that time he had passed on a contract in Britain in favor of an offer in the States from MGM, who cast him as one of the illegitimate children in *The Bachelor Father*. After that the size of his roles fluctuated between significant, as the abdicated king of a mythical country in Will Rogers's *Ambassador Bill*, to miniscule, as a would-be suicide in *The Man Who Played God*. There was an important role, as the callous nephew who becomes the unwitting victim of Charles Laughton, in *Payment Deferred*, but Milland was no longer on the studio roster by the time it was released, and he returned to England for two minor pictures. Back in Hollywood he went to Paramount to play Carole Lombard's boyfriend in *Bolero*, and he was certainly more appealing than the film's star, George Raft. Also at that same studio, he was a British ninny trapped on a desert island with Lombard and Bing Crosby, among others, in the loony comedy *We're Not Dressing*, and impressed the front office enough that Paramount signed him to a contract. After supporting Burns and Allen in *Many Happy*

Returns, he got a chance to show his worth in light comedy with *The Gilded Lily*, as an incognito aristocrat who loves and leaves Claudette Colbert. The studio kept him away from the front lines, preferring that he remain a secondary player in such films as *Four Hours to Kill*, *The Glass Key*, and *The Big Broadcast of 1937*. When they did make him the leading man, it was to new-comer Dorothy Lamour in the silly film that got her into all those native roles, *The Jungle Princess*.

Over at Universal he was a decided asset to the first Deanna Durbin film, *Three Smart Girls*, as a wealthy banker who falls in love with Barbara Read, and then he came back to Paramount to carry on in Ronald Colman's footsteps in a "B" mystery, *Bulldog Drummond Escapes*, until he passed the role over to the much less interesting John Howard. Instead he did a pleasant screwball comedy with Jean Arthur, *Easy Living*, once again displaying a sure touch in this field, but this didn't mean he was allowed to pass on a Technicolor follow-up with Lamour, the pricelessly titled *Her Jungle Love*. At least she was a more promising leading lady then Olympe Bradna with whom Milland was stuck with in *Say It in French*, after which he somehow relinquished top billing to Isa Miranda for *Hotel Imperial*. All of this was forgiven by the 1939 version of *Beau Geste*, a superb rendering of the oft-filmed tale, with Milland as middle brother John, and the only one of the three (Gary Cooper and Robert Preston were the others) who could pass as having been raised in England.

Paramount sent him back to the U.K. for their version of the Terrence Rattigan stage hit, *French Without Tears*, which came out between loan-outs to Fox, where he was saddled with Sonia Henie in *Everything Happens at Night*, and to RKO, where he was back with former dance partner Anna Neagle for the lousy adaptation of the musical *Irene*, which tossed out most most of the stage numbers in favor of concentrating on the insipid plot. He appeared in a Technicolor adventure, *Untamed*; a fairly serious piece with Colbert, *Arise, My Love*, as a downed flier on the eve of World War II; a brighter teaming with her, *Skylark*, as her pre-occupied husband; and a big wartime hit, *I Wanted Wings* (although most of the attention was directed at luscious new-comer Veronica Lake). He was the hero of a Cecil B. DeMille blockbuster, *Reap the Wild Wind*, which featured Paulette Goddard with whom he was teamed in two others that didn't fly, *The Lady Has Plans* and *The Crystal Ball*. Before the last he had his best comedic chance to date, treading the lines of good taste as the military man who wonders why he's attracted to a little girl, who happens to be grown-up Ginger Rogers in disguise, in the delightful *The Major and the Minor*. He and Rogers were teamed for another popular one, *Lady in the Dark*, although it was another musical that didn't do justice to its acclaimed Broadway source, and then Milland carried one of the best ghost stories of the period, *The Uninvited*, well paired with Ruth Hussey, although Gail Russell was supposed to be the main attraction. Also good was *Ministry of Fear*, an intelligent thriller in which he went from a mental hospital right into the lap of the Nazis in war-torn London. Things were going well enough, but he leapt right up to the top when his *Major and the Minor* director, Billy Wilder, asked him to play the very difficult and unglamorous part of the alcoholic writer in *The Lost Weekend*. This became one of the landmark pictures of the 1940s, a grim and potent drama giving full and ugly attention to the dangers of drinking, with riveting work by Milland. Against all odds the movie was a smash hit, earning Academy Awards as Best Picture of 1945 and one for Milland as Best Actor.

Of course there was no place to go but down, and he did that dressed in silly period costumes for a Paulette Goddard showcase, *Kitty*; a Technicolor western, *California*, which despite the par-ticipation of Barbara Stanwyck seemed like a hundred others of that genre; and the affably dopey *Golden Earrings*, in which he wore just that while hiding out with Gypsy Marlene Dietrich. There was another fine one waiting around the corner, *The Big Clock*, a suspenseful noir, with Milland trying to clear himself of a murder Charles Laughton has committed, followed by a worth-less melodrama made in England, *So Evil My Love*. Back home he played it smooth and dangerous as a satanic mystery man trying to steer Thomas Mitchell down the path of wrong in *Alias Nick Beal*; went to Fox for a cute gimmick picture, *It Happens Every Spring*, inventing a chemical that repels baseballs from wood; and ended up out West again for one of his least favorite pictures, *Copper Canyon*, which forced him to work with Hedy Lamarr, with whom he did not get along at all. In *A Life of Her Own* MGM stuck him with Lana Turner, who was nowhere near as appealing as the scene-stealing cat that carried the whimsical *Rhubarb*, in which Milland was its guardian.

There were two minor alcoholism films, *Night Into Morning* and *Something to Live For* (Joan Fontaine was the drinker in the latter, which, like the former, drew unfavorable comparisons to *The Lost Weekend*); a real curiosity piece, *The Thief*, which had absolutely no dialogue and was therefore interesting for about ten minutes until the novelty wore off; and *Jamaica Run*, a thoroughly undistinguished finale to his Paramount contract. There was an upswing with a topnotch Hitchcock thriller, *Dial M for Murder*, with Milland at his oiliest, as a Londoner attempting to have wife Grace Kelly killed, and then his directorial debut, *A Man Alone*, a western in which he tried to expose a gang of bank robbers. Continuing behind the camera, he directed himself as a skipper hired to rescue Maureen O'Hara in *Lisbon*; as the title character in the British-made *The Safecracker*; and as a concerned father in *Panic in Year Zero*, the best liked of the batch, a decent sci-fi entry about the aftermath of a nuclear attack. This was a Roger Corman production, and he also put Milland in *The Premature Burial*, and one of the better of that budget-conscious director-producer's offerings of the 1960s, *X: The Man With the X-Ray Eyes*, in which Milland foolishly experimented with a formula that allowed him to see through objects, until there was no turning back.

Older and sans hairpiece, he received wide exposure as Ryan O'Neal's snobby dad in the phenomenally popular *Love Story*, but lowered himself as few actors of his stature ever did, playing a bigot whose head is grafted onto a black man's body in the horror movie jaw-dropper *The Thing With Two Heads*. He went on exuding dry (or was he merely bored?) menace or superiority in Disney's *Escape to Witch Mountain*, as a villainous millionaire; *The Last Tycoon*, portraying a lawyer; and *Oliver's Story*, repeating his *Love Story* part, to name a few of his more widely distributed titles of this period. He had published his autobiography, *Wide-Eyed in Babylon* (1976), the title of which suggested the sort of charm he once displayed in younger years when acting seemed to him more than just a paycheck.

Screen: AS SPIKE MILLAND: 1929: The Plaything.

AS RAYMOND MILLAND: 1929: The Informer; Piccadilly; The Flying Scotsman; The Lady From the Sea; 1930: Way for a Sailor; Passion Flower; 1931: The Bachelor Father; Son of India; Just a Gigolo; Strangers May Kiss; Bought; Ambassador Bill; Blonde Crazy; 1932: The Man Who Played God; But the Flesh Is Weak; Polly of the Circus; Payment Deferred; 1934: We're Not Dressing; Charlie Chan in London; The Mystery of Mr. X; Menace.

AS RAY MILLAND: 1933: Orders Is Orders; This Is the Life; 1934: Bolero; Many Happy Returns; 1935: One Hour Late; The Gilded Lily; Four Hours to Kill!; The Glass Key; Alias Mary Dow; 1936: Next Time We Love; The Return of Sophie Lang; The Big

Broadcast of 1937; The Jungle Princess; Three Smart Girls; **1937:** Bulldog Drummond Escapes; Wings Over Honolulu; Easy Living; Ebb Tide; Wise Girl; **1938:** Her Jungle Love; Men With Wings; Tropic Holiday; Say It in French; **1939:** Hotel Imperial; Beau Geste; Everything Happens at Night; French Without Tears; **1940:** Irene; The Doctor Takes a Wife; Untamed; Arise, My Love; **1941:** Skylark; I Wanted Wings; **1942:** The Lady Has Plans; Reap the Wild Wind; Are Husbands Necessary?; The Major and the Minor; Star Spangled Rhythm; **1943:** The Crystal Ball; Forever and a Day; **1944:** The Uninvited; Lady in the Dark; Till We Meet Again; Ministry of Fear; **1945:** The Lost Weekend; Kitty; **1946:** The Well-Groomed Bride; California; **1947:** The Imperfect Lady; The Trouble With Women; Variety Girl; Golden Earrings; **1948:** The Big Clock; Miss Tatlock's Millions; So Evil My Love; Sealed Verdict; **1949:** Alias Nick Beal; It Happens Every Spring; **1950:** A Woman of Distinction; Copper Canyon; A Life of Her Own; **1951:** Circle of Danger; Night Into Morning; Rhubarb; Close to My Heart; **1952:** Something to Live For; Bugles in the Afternoon; The Thief; **1953:** Jamaica Run; Let's Do It Again; **1954:** Dial M for Murder; **1955:** The Girl in the Red Velvet Swing; A Man Alone (and dir.); **1956:** Lisbon (and dir.; prod.); **1957:** Three Brave Men; The River's Edge; High Flight; **1958:** The Safecracker (and dir.); **1962:** The Premature Burial; Panic in Year Zero (and dir.); **1963:** X: The Man With the X-Ray Eyes; **1964:** Quick, Let's Get Married/The Confession; **1968:** Rose rosse per il Fuehrer/Red Roses for the Fuehrer/Code Name: Red Roses (nUSr); **1970:** Hostile Witness (and dir.); Company of Killers/The Hit Team; Love Story; **1972:** Embassy/Target: Embassy; The Thing With Two Heads; The Big Game; Frogs; **1973:** The House in Nightmare Park; Terror in the Wax Museum; The Student Connection/Witness to Murder (dtv); **1974:** Gold; **1975:** Escape From Witch Mountain; **1976:** The Swiss Conspiracy; Aces High; The Last Tycoon; **1977:** Slavers; Oil/The Billion Dollar Fire; The Uncanny; **1978:** La Ragazza in Pigiama Giallo/The Girl in the Yellow Pajamas (nUSr); Blackout; Oliver's Story; **1979:** The Attic; Game for Vultures; Battlestar: Galactica (from TV series); **1980:** Survival Run; **1986:** The Sea Serpent.
Select TV: 1953–55: Meet Mr. McNutley/The Ray Milland Show (series); **1956:** That's the Man (sp); Catch at Straws (sp); **1957:** Never Turn Back (sp); The Girl in the Grass (sp); Angel of Wrath (sp); **1958:** Battle for a Soul (sp); **1959:** A London Affair (sp); 1959–60: Markham (series); **1963:** The Silver Burro; **1969:** Daughter of the Mind; **1971:** River of Gold; Black Noon; **1975:** The Dead Don't Die; Ellery Queen: Too Many Suspects; **1976:** Rich Man, Poor Man (ms); Look What's Happened to Rosemary's Baby; Mayday at 40,000 Feet; **1977:** Seventh Avenue (ms); Testimony of Two Men; **1978:** Cruise Into Terror; **1979:** The Darker Side of Terror; **1980:** The Dream Merchants (ms); **1981:** Our Family Business; **1982:** The Royal Romance of Charles and Diana; **1983:** Starflight: The Plane That Couldn't Land; Cave-In; **1984:** Sherlock Holmes and the Masks of Death.

ANN MILLER
(JOHNNIE LUCILLE COLLIER)
BORN: HOUSTON, TX, APRIL 12, 1919.

There aren't many who would accuse Ann Miller of being a skilled thespian, since something about her glamorous air smacked of Hollywood phoniness, yet who can resist her vibrancy on the dance floor, with her machine gun-fast taps and breathtaking spins? The leggy brunette with the mile-wide smile learned to dance as a child, and that skill won her a talent contest at the Orpheum Theatre in Los Angeles. To cash in on

this, she sought movie work and ended up as an extra in *Anne of Green Gables* and *The Good Fairy*, and as an unbilled dancer in a chorus number in *The Devil on Horseback*. An engagement in San Francisco was seen by Lucille Ball, who helped get her a screen test at RKO. That studio made her just another dancer in *New Faces of 1937*, but gave her a moment in the spotlight in a number called "The Yankee Doodle Band," in *The Life of the Party*. Although she wasn't given much to do, it didn't hurt being cast as one of the acting hopefuls in *Stage Door*, since this was one of the major films of 1937. After that she was moved up the cast list for *Radio City Revels*, where her tapping was a welcome addition, and ended up in another big movie, *You Can't Take It With You*, the Best Picture Oscar winner of 1938, with Miller as the hopelessly second-rate, ballet-dancing daughter of the nutty, free-spirited family. Both she and Ball were wasted in a tame Marx Brothers offering, *Room Service*, so she felt quite justified in asking to be released from her contract so that she could go to New York to appear in *George White's Scandals*. Back at RKO her fiery numbers really put some zing into the mediocre adaptation of the stage hit *Too Many Girls*, particularly a snappy one with Desi Arnaz, with the questionable title "Spic 'n' Spanish." There was no doubt that her terpsichorean talents were impressive but the quality of her pictures was something else, and she ended up at the low-grade Republic Pictures for *Hit Parade of 1941* and *Melody Ranch*; traipsed over to Columbia for *Time Out for Rhythm* and *Go West, Young Lady*; and then went to Paramount for *True to the Army* and *Priorities on Parade*, finally getting top billing in the latter.

Columbia signed her to a contract with the intention of making sure she carried her own vehicles. These included two productions more memorable for their titles than their place in musical history, *Reveille With Beverly*, with Miller as a disc jockey, performing "Thumbs Up and V for Victory," and *What's Buzzin', Cousin?*, this time doing a war bond dance called "$18.75." She was teamed with fey and fidgety comedian Joe Besser for both *Hey Rookie* and *Eadie Was a Lady*; sang "Mr. Beebe" with Kay Kyser's Band in *Carolina Blues* (though she actually let Harold Nicholas dance the number); and reprised Claudette Colbert's old role in a musical remake of *It Happened One Night*, called *Eve Knew Her Apples*, in which she stuck expressly to singing with nary a tap to be heard. Marriage called, and she settled with Columbia over a film that she backed out of, *The Petty Girl*. (It was made, years later with Joan Caulfield). Fortunately the next studio that wanted her was the one that made the best musicals in town, MGM, and they started her in one of the big hits of 1948, *Easter Parade*. She had the secondary role of the bitchy ex-dance partner of Fred Astaire, and she was dynamite in her solo, "Shakin' the Blues Away," as well as in her elegant duets with Astaire. Although it was nice to be seen in higher quality material that would stand the test of time better than anything she'd done at Columbia, her leading-lady days were over, as MGM saw her expressly in supporting parts or in ensemble pieces. One of the latter was the delightful *On the Town*, where she rocked the house with her "Prehistoric Man" number, after which she was placed alongside Red Skelton for three films, *Watch the Birdie*, *Texas Carnival*, and *Lovely to Look At*, in the last singing "I'll Be Hard to Handle," while surrounded by a chorus of men in wolf masks.

She played another bitchy lady, in *Small Town Girl*, but swept stars Jane Powell and Farley Granger right under the rug with her amazing "I've Got to Hear That Beat" number, in which she tapped her way around a floor of disembodied musicians and their instruments. Best of all was *Kiss Me Kate*, where she did a sizzling "Why Can't You Behave?" solo and was given a terrific supporting trio in Bob Fosse, Tommy Rall, and Bobby Van for the "Tom, Dick and Harry" number. Alas from this height she had but one number (a flapper bit called "It") in *Deep in My Heart*; gave some bang to the finale of the routine *Hit the Deck*; and relinquished the musical program to June Allyson and Joan Collins, of all people, in *The Opposite Sex*. There was a very minor comedy, *The Great American Pastime*, after which she asked MGM to let her go. There were two more marriages, both to millionaires, which meant she was out of circulation for a while, seeing no financial need to work. After her divorces, she started showing up on television and then as one of the cast replacements in the long-running Broadway musical *Mame*. There was an unforgettable TV commercial for "Great American Soups," tapping away on top of a giant can; a TV presentation of *Dames at Sea*; a cameo as Art Carney's mistress in the all-star flop *Won Ton Ton, the Dog Who Saved Hollywood*; and a few clips in MGM's retrospective *That's Entertainment!* that made audiences fall in love with her all over again. There wasn't much the modern cinema could do with someone who belonged so exclusively to another era, but she had a smash hit run alongside another MGM alumnus, Mickey Rooney, in the Broadway revue *Sugar Babies*, with fans showing up to marvel at how she was able to keep the energy up after all those years. A mere 45 years after her last full-length, big screen acting role, she showed up to play a landlady for a couple of scenes in one of David Lynch's alienating weirdies, *Mulholland Dr.* In 1972 she published her autobiography, *Miller's High Life*.

Screen: 1934: Anne of Green Gables; 1935: The Good Fairy; 1936: The Devil on Horseback; 1937: New Faces of 1937; The Life of the Party; Stage Door; 1938: Radio City Revels; Having Wonderful Time; You Can't Take It With You; Room Service; Tarnished Angel; 1940: Too Many Girls; Hit Parade of 1941; Melody Ranch; 1941: Time Out for Rhythm; Go West, Young Lady; 1942: True to the Army; Priorities on Parade; 1943: Reveille With Beverly; What's Buzzin', Cousin?; 1944: Hey Rookie; Jam Session; Carolina Blues; 1945: Eadie Was a Lady; Eve Knew Her Apples; 1946: The Thrill of Brazil; 1948: Easter Parade; The Kissing Bandit; 1949: On the Town; 1950: Watch the Birdie; 1951: Texas Carnival; Two Tickets to Broadway; 1952: Lovely to Look At; 1953: Small Town Girl; Kiss Me Kate; 1954: Deep in My Heart; 1955: Hit the Deck; 1956: The Opposite Sex; The Great American Pastime; 1976: Won Ton Ton, the Dog Who Saved Hollywood; 1994: That's Entertainment! III; 2001: Mulholland Drive.

NY Stage: 1939: George White's Scandals; 1969: Mame; 1979: Sugar Babies.

Select TV: 1971: Dames at Sea (sp).

HAYLEY MILLS

BORN: LONDON, ENGLAND, APRIL 18, 1946.

As the British invasion swept the cinema in the 1960s, it seemed only natural that Walt Disney would hire his equivalent import, and thus the world came to know Hayley Mills. Blonde and eager, she had a guileless, breathy enthusiasm that seemed just right for the sort of family-friendly capers Disney put her through. Although she was ever so pleasant as she grew up, audiences continued to think of her almost exclusively through the work she did in her youth. Her father was one of England's top stars, John Mills, and it was in one of his movies, *Tiger Bay*, that she got started, playing an inquisitive slum girl who stumbles upon a murder and is abducted by killer Horst Buccholz. The raves were immediate for her natural and accomplished performance, and for the film itself, one of the most accessible of all the British new wave films.

As a result, Disney decided she was just what he was looking for to carry his remake of *Pollyanna*. Playing the little girl whose optimism changes those around her, she was perfect, keeping the potentially saccharine and insufferable qualities of this character in check and holding her own against one of the best casts ever assembled for a Disney picture. She made enough of an impact to received a special 1960 Academy Award, although the movie was not one of the studio's more popular features around that time. In contrast, *The Parent Trap* was a smash, offering two Hayleys for the price of one, as twins who meet at camp and conspire to bring their divorced parents back together. The conviction that you were watching two different characters was abetted greatly by special effects (and a double), but it was clear that Mills was the reason the audiences showed up for this weatherweight comedy. Returning to England, she did a film that was better than all her subsequent Disney offerings put together, *Whistle Down the Wind*, based on her mother, Mary Hayley Bell's, story. Hayley played the eldest of three children who think that escaped con Alan Bates is Jesus, again making her innocence believable and touching.

Back with Disney there were a pair of big adventure stories, *In Search of the Castaways*, going through earthquakes, floods, and fire to find her dad, and *The Moon-Spinners*, where she ended up at one point being terrorized on a windmill; a low-keyed musical, *Summer Magic*, where she proved no competition in this area for co-star Burl Ives; and another major hit, *That Darn Cat!*, in which she had the closest thing to an adult role of any film she made for that company. That same year, 1965, she ended her contract with the studio. During that time she was also allowed outside the Disney gates to play the young charge of nanny Deborah Kerr in Universal's disappointing adapation of the stage success *The Chalk Garden*, with dad on hand as a servant. Her first post-Disney credit was the romantic comedy *The Truth About Spring*, which also featured her father in the supporting cast, and he served as her director-producer on *Gypsy Girl/Sky West and Crooked*, which cast her as a simpleton, but nobody was particularly impressed. Instead the crowds turned out for something closer to Disney, *The Trouble With Angels*, with Hayley as a hellion at a convent school who changes her wicked ways under the watchful eye of Mother Superior Rosalind Russell.

That was it for American films for a while, and she resettled back in Britain for a fine, adult story, *The Family Way*, as a newlywed having trouble with husband Hywel Bennett and his parents, the dad being played by John Mills. It was directed by Roy Boulting, to whom she was later (1971–77) wed, despite his being 33 years her senior. There was a soaper about a girl losing her virginity while on vacation, *A Matter of Innocence/Pretty Polly*, and two more with Bennett, *Twisted Nerve* and *Endless Night*, all of which proved that interest in Mills as a movie star attraction had evaporated. There were some undistinguished British movies and several stage appearances in England, all of which pretty much kept her out of sight from American audiences until she showed up in a made-for-TV sequel, *Parent Trap II*, which did well enough to warrant a few more extensions of this tale. Her sister is actress Juliet Mills, with whom she and dad appeared in *The Last Straw*, which was finished in 1991 but never released. She received a Theatre World Award in 2000 for her New York stage debut in Noel Coward's *Suite in Two Keys*.

Screen: 1959: Tiger Bay; 1960: Pollyanna; 1961: The Parent Trap; Whistle Down the Wind; 1962: In Search of the Castaways; 1963: Summer Magic; 1964: The Chalk Garden; The Moon-Spinners; 1965: The Truth About Spring; That Darn Cat!; 1966: Gypsy Girl/Sky West and Crooked; The Trouble With Angels; The Daydreamer (voice); 1967: The Family Way; Africa — Texas

Style!; A Matter of Innocence/Pretty Polly; **1968:** Twisted Nerve; **1971:** Take a Girl Like You; **1972:** Endless Night; Mr. Forbush and the Penguins/Cry of the Penguins; **1975:** Deadly Strangers; Who Changed Charley Farthing?/The Bananas Boat; The Diamond Hunters/The Kingfisher Caper; **1988:** Appointment With Death; **1991:** The Last Straw (unreleased); **1994:** A Troll in Central Park (voice).

NY Stage: 2000: Suite in Two Keys (ob).

Select TV: 1982: The Flame Trees of Thika (ms); 1986: Parent Trap II; 1987: Good Morning, Miss Bliss (series); 1989: Parent Trap III; Parent Trap: Hawaiian Honeymoon; 1990: Back Home; After Midnight.

JOHN MILLS

(LEWIS ERNEST MILLS) BORN: FELIXSTOWE, SUFFOLK, ENGLAND, FEBRUARY 22, 1908.

Although he was never ranked among England's greatest thespians, John Mills had a career long enough and with enough popular successes that he never had to hang his head next to his more distinguished and versatile peers. He was at times rigidly militaristic, kindly, dull, workmanlike, and now and then superb. He followed his sister Annette into show business, first as a chorus boy, and then acting with a rep company in Singapore. Through his friendship with Noel Coward, he was recommended for the West End lead in a 1930 version of *Charley's Aunt*. After that and Coward's *Words and Music*, he made his film debut in 1932, playing a sailor in a Jessie Matthews vehicle *The Midshipmaid*. He began getting larger roles in cheap productions like *The River Wolves*, as an aspiring writer, and *A Political Party*, as the son of chimney sweep Leslie Fuller. He also landed the lead in one that was of a higher quality than these, *Forever England/Born for Glory*, as an illegitimate lad who becomes a naval hero. It would set the standard for the many Mills military roles to come. Because of this film, it was decided that he had proven himself worthy of carrying the load, as he did in *First Offence*, as a rich kid joining a gang of car thieves; *Tudor Rose*, as Guildford Dudley in this story of Lady Jane's brief reign on the throne of England; and *O.H.M.S.*, again in uniform, opposite American actor Wallace Ford.

It was in one of the major films of 1939, *Goodbye, Mr. Chips*, shot by MGM in England, that a large American audience really got to see Mills for the first time, although his participation, as a former student of Robert Donat's, wasn't exactly a standout part. With the coming of World War II it was rare to see him out of uniform, as he came to represent the British war effort on the big screen through *Cottage to Let/Bombsight Stolen*, as the bad guy, a German posing as an RAF pilot; *The Big Blockade*, again in flying gear, as the plane's navigator; Coward's *In Which We Serve*, as a sailor, in possibly the most lauded British movie of this period; and *Waterloo Road*, as a soldier who goes AWOL when he learns his wife is carrying on with Stewart Granger. He also appeared in *We Dive at Dawn*, maneuvering his ship through a minefield, and *The Way to the Stars*, becoming friends with fellow flier Michael Redgrave at a bomber station. The last was one of England's major hits during the war years, and he participated in another substantial moneymaker, *This Happy Breed*, living next door to the family whose story was followed over a 20-year period.

These put him in a solid box-office position on his home soil, while the next, *Great Expectations*, director David Lean's moody rendering of the classic Dickens novel, once again raised his profile elsewhere. Mills did a stalwart job, although he seemed colorless alongside such performers as Martita Hunt, Alec

Guinness, and Finlay Currie. Maintaining his high standing in England, he was in *The October Man*, suffering from amnesia as the title character in this suspense thriller; the biopic *Scott of the Antarctic*, about explorer Robert Scott's doomed race to the South Pool; and *The History of Mr. Polly*, doing his timid act as a draper's assistant who seeks a better life away from his nagging wife. Around this time he did a film made for RKO with an American director (Edward Dmytryk) and co-star (Martha Scott), *So Well Remembered*, about a newspaper editor fighting for better working condition in a factory town. He turned producer with the oddity *The Rocking Horse Winner*, playing a supporting role, as the groom who encourages John Howard Davies's obsessive behavior, but it failed, so he went back to barking orders, playing a submarine captain in *Morning Departure/Operation Disaster*.

By the early 1950s he had lost his box-office standing with *Mr. Denning Drives North* and *Above Us the Waves*, among others, so he segued into characters parts with *Hobson's Choice*, seeming a mite too long in the tooth to play the bootmaker whose marriage to Brenda de Banzie invokes the ire of her dad, Charles Laughton; *The End of the Affair*, as a detective in this unsuccessful first attempt to adapt Graham Greene's novel; and *War and Peace*, as a Russian with a cockney (!) accent, tramping through the snow with Henry Fonda. There was a comedy, *It's Great to Be Young*, as a schoolteacher whose students rally to his defense after he is canned; and an amusing cameo as a drunken carriage driver in the Oscar-winning *Around the World in Eighty Days* (he and Robert Morley were the only actors to appear in the 1989 TV remake as well). There was more war stuff with *Dunkirk*, trying to get his company through enemy lines; *Ice Cold in Alex/Desert Attack*, as a drunken captain evacuating two nurses from Tobruk, in a film that was hacked down considerably for American release; and *I Was Monty's Double*, as the officer who has to rescue impersonator Clifton James after sending him into enemy lines. He played another detective in *Tiger Bay*, which helped launch his daughter Hayley on her brief but successful period as a movie star, and then scored in one of his finest roles, the strict martinet butting heads with fellow officer Alec Guinness in *Tunes of Glory*. Disney called on him to play the dad in the 1960 version of *Swiss Family Robinson*, which turned out to be one of the financial and artistic peaks for that company.

Being overshadowed by Hayley during the early 1960s wasn't something he seemed to mind much, for he took supporting roles to her in *The Chalk Garden*, as a servant in the household at which she's come to stay; *The Truth About Spring*, as a con artist; *Gypsy Girl/Sky West and Crooked*, in this case serving as directed and producer; and, best of all, *The Family Way*, as Hywel Bennett's dad, whose fervid devotion to his dead friend raises some eyebrows. By this point it was not unexpected to see him popping up in all kinds of international offerings, and he led the all-star British cast of *The Wrong Box*, doing slapstick as a crotchety old crone; supported Hugh O'Brian in *Africa — Texas Style!*, which briefly became a TV series minus either actor; and played Field Marshal Haigh in the episodic musical *Oh! What a Lovely War*. There was a startling performance as a grotesque village idiot in *Ryan's Daughter*, speaking nary a word, and he evoked great audience sympathy amid the unwieldy running time. He went on to win the 1970 Academy Award as Best Supporting Actor. He was top billed for a children's film, *Run Wild, Run Free*, about a horse, and was also given a lead in *Dulcima*, as a country bumpkin exploited by a young girl. After that it was back to support for *Oklahoma Crude*, as Faye Dunaway's dad; *The Human Factor*; the much-despised remake of *The Big Sleep*, as a police inspector; the Oscar-winning *Gandhi*, as a Viceroy; and *Who's That Girl*, in support of Madonna. He was knighted in 1977 and published his autobiography, *Up in the Clouds,*

Gentlemen, Please, in 1981; with an illustrated follow-up, *Still Memories: An Autobiography in Photography*, released in 2000. His second wife, writer Mary Hayley Bell, whom he married in 1941, is the mother of Hayley, actress Juliet, and assistant director Jonathan Mills.

Screen: 1932: The Midshipmaid; 1933: Britannia of Billingsgate; The Ghost Camera; 1934: The River Wolves; A Political Party; Those Were the Days; The Lash; Blind Justice; Doctor's Orders; 1935: Royal Cavalcade/Regal Cavalcade; Forever England/Brown on Resolution/Born for Glory; Charing Cross Road; Car of Dreams; 1936: First Offence/Bad Blood; Tudor Rose/Nine Days a Queen; 1937: O.H.M.S./You're in the Army Now; 1938: The Green Cockatoo/Four Dark Hours; 1939: Goodbye, Mr. Chips; 1940: Old Bill and Son; 1941: Cottage to Let/Bombsight Stolen; The Black Sheep of Whitehall; 1942: The Young Mr. Pitt; The Big Blockade; In Which We Serve; 1943: We Dive at Dawn; 1944: This Happy Breed; Waterloo Road; 1945: The Way to the Stars; 1946: Great Expectations; 1947: So Well Remembered; The October Man; 1948: Scott of the Antarctic; 1949: The History of Mr. Polly; 1950: The Rocking Horse Winner (and prod.); Morning Departure/Operation Disaster; 1951: Mr. Denning Drives North; 1952: The Gentle Gunman; The Long Memory; 1953: Hobson's Choice; 1954: The Colditz Story; 1955: The End of the Affair; Above Us the Waves; Escapade; 1956: War and Peace; It's Great to Be Young; The Baby and the Battleship; Around the World in Eighty Days; 1957: Town on Trial; Vicious Circle/The Circle; 1958: Dunkirk; Ice Cold in Alex/Desert Attack; I Was Monty's Double; 1959: Tiger Bay; 1960: Season of Passion/Summer of the 17th Doll; Tunes of Glory; Swiss Family Robinson; 1961: The Singer Not the Song; 1962: Flame in the Streets; The Valiant; Tiara Tahiti; 1964: The Chalk Garden; 1965: The Truth About Spring; King Rat; Operation Crossbow/The Great Spy Mission; 1966: The Wrong Box; 1967: The Family Way; Chuka; Africa — Texas Style!; 1969: Oh! What a Lovely War; Run Wild, Run Free; Lady Hamilton Zwischen Smach und Liebe/Emma Hamilton (nUSr); La Morte non ha Sesso/A Black Veil for Lisa (nUSr); 1970: Adam's Woman (nUSr); Ryan's Daughter; 1972: Dulcima; Young Winston; 1973: Lady Caroline Lamb; Oklahoma Crude; 1975: The Human Factor; 1976: Trial by Combat/Dirty Knights Work; 1978: The Devil's Advocate; The Big Sleep; 1979: The Thirty-Nine Steps; Zulu Dawn; 1982: Gandhi; 1983: Sahara; 1987: Who's That Girl; 1988: When the Wind Blows (voice); 1991: The Last Straw (unreleased); 1993: Deadly Advice (nUSr); 1996: Hamlet; 1997: Gentlemen Don't Eat Poets/The Grotesque; Bean.

NY Stage: 1987: Pygmalion.

Select TV: 1967: Dundee and the Culhane (series); 1974: The Zoo Gang (series); 1978: Dr. Strange; Quatermass; 1979: Quatermass (series); 1984: The Masks of Death; A Woman of Substance (ms); 1985: Murder with Mirrors; 1986: Hold the Dream; 1989: Around the World in 80 Days; The Lady and the Highwayman; Ending Up; A Tale of Two Cities; 1992: Night of the Fox; Harnessing Peacocks (sp); 1993: Frankenstein; The Big Freeze; 1994: Martin Chuzzlewit; 1998: Cats (sp); 2001: The Gentleman Thief.

MARTIN MILNER
Born: Detroit, MI, December 28, 1927.
Raised in CA. ed: USC.

Boyishly comforting, Martin Milner's real claim to show business fame came on the small screen, in a somewhat brasher characterization than those he was known to play

in the movies. As a teenager he auditioned for and won the role of John Day, the second eldest red-headed son of William Powell and Irene Dunne, in the hugely successful 1947 film of *Life With Father*. Recovery from polio put things on hold for a bit, but when he returned it was decided that he could add a certain likable innocence to the high testosterone in all those war movies, and starting with his performance as a private in *Sands of Iwo Jima*, he was seen in *Halls of Montezuma*, *Operation Pacific*, *Battle Zone*, *Francis in the Navy*, and *The Long Gray Line*, among others. He was one of Burt Lancaster's brothers in *Gunfight at the O.K. Corral*, after which Lancaster tried to pin a dope rap on him in *Sweet Smell of Success*, with Milner as the jazz musician who has the audacity to fall in love with Lancaster's sister. He continued his nice guy bit, as an aspiring stage writer, waiting patiently for Natalie Wood to notice him, in *Marjorie Morningstar*; comforting Dorothy Malone by showing off his thinning hairline in the silly soap bio *Too Much, Too Soon*; and taking up too much of the unnecessary romantic subplot in *Compulsion*. He turned out to be less than lovable in the gimmicky horror movie *13 Ghosts*; put on a loin cloth for the spectacularly stupid *The Private Lives of Adam and Eve*; and then became a part of early 1960s television history when he tooled around the country with George Maharis in the hit series *Route 66*, which made more famous than ever. After that ended he returned to movies to try to take some of the smarm out of *Valley of the Dolls*, marrying self-destructive Patty Duke, then found himself in another popular TV show, *Adam-12*, this time riding around in a cop car. From that point on all of his salary came from toiling on the small screen.

Screen: 1947: Life With Father; 1948: The Wreck of the Hesperus; 1949: Sands of Iwo Jima; 1950: Louisa; Our Very Own; 1951: Halls of Montezuma; Fighting Coast Guard; I Want You; Operation Pacific; 1952: Battle Zone; Belles on Their Toes; The Captive City; Last of the Comanches; My Wife's Best Friend; Springfield Rifle; 1953: Destination Gobi; 1955: Francis in the Navy; The Long Gray Line; Mister Roberts; Pete Kelly's Blues; 1956: On the Threshold of Space; Screaming Eagles; Pillars of the Sky; 1957: Gunfight at the O.K. Corral; Man Afraid; Sweet Smell of Success; 1958: Marjorie Morningstar; Too Much, Too Soon; 1959: Compulsion; 1960: Sex Kittens Go to College; 13 Ghosts; The Private Lives of Adam and Eve; 1965: Zebra in the Kitchen; 1967: Valley of the Dolls; 1968: Three Guns for Texas; 1969: Ski Fever.

Select TV: 1954: Rim of Violence (sp); 1954–55: The Stu Erwin Show (series); 1955: Mr. Schoolmarm (sp); 1957–58: The Life of Riley (series); 1958: Debut (sp); 1959: Chain of Command (sp); 1960–64: Route 66 (series); 1965: The War and Eric Kurtz (sp); Starr: First Baseman (sp); 1966: When Hell Froze (sp); 1968: Land's End (sp); 1968–75: Adam-12 (series); 1972: Emergency; 1973: Runaway!; 1974: Hurricane; 1975–76: Swiss Family Robinson (series); 1977: SST: Death Flight; 1978: Flood!; Black Beauty (ms); Little Mo; 1979: Crisis in Mid-air; The Last Convertible (ms); The Seekers (ms); 1981: The Ordeal of Bill Carney; 1990: Nashville Beat.

YVETTE MIMIEUX
Born: Hollywood, CA, January 8, 1939.

Almost ethereally beautiful, Yvette Mimieux had a wispy, somewhat spacey quality about her in her early roles, a manner that did not suggest a strong screen presence outside of her looks. Although she grew a bit more self-assured as she aged, hers was never a talent of maximum proportions. Born and raised in

Hollywood, she won a beauty contest that inevitably led to modeling and then a contract with MGM in 1959. She started in one of those junky movies produced by Albert Zugsmith, *Platinum High School*, then appeared in one of the best remembered of all science fiction films, *The Time Machine*, where she was required to be a doe-like simpleton from the future, Weena of the passive Eloi. In the trend-setting beach frolic *Where the Boys Are*, she was involved in one of its more serious subplots, as the airheaded college girl on break who winds up getting raped, then went down with the ship in the disastrous remake of *The Four Horsemen of the Apocalypse*, as a student in Paris. She was completely out of her league taking on the difficult part of Olivia de Havilland's mildly retarded daughter in *Light in the Piazza*; played the title role in "The Dancing Princess" segment of the Cinerama family film *The Wonderful World of the Brothers Grimm*; and was Charlton Heston's sister, who bounces from James Darren to George Chakiris, in the lush soap opera *Diamond Head*.

There was a step in the right direction, playing Dean Martin's childlike bride in *Toys in the Attic*, but MGM sent her on her way with a fairly blah melodrama, *Joy in the Morning*, all wishy-washy as a young newlywed having problems with hubby Richard Chamberlain. Disney made her straight woman to a bunch of chimps in one of their mildest comedies, *Monkeys, Go Home!*, then she helped participate in one of those heist movies that were prevalent in the 1960s, *The Caper of the Golden Bulls*, which was set in Pamplona, Spain. It seemed as if she was added to certain movies just to be a decorative presence, as in *Dark of the Sun*, a standard action adventure; *Skyjacked*, a cheesy airline melodrama, in which she was a helpful stewardess; and *The Neptune Disaster*, where she was part of a submarine rescue team. In between these she appeared in a surprisingly successful but vapid sex-romp, *Three in the Attic*, as one of the women getting her sexual revenge on womanizing Christopher Jones, and in one of the least-seen movies of its day, *The Picasso Summer*, a strange tale about a couple (Albert Finney was the co-star) seeking out their artistic hero. By the early 1970s she was becoming a staple of made-for-television movies, eventually contributing to the writing on two of them, *Hit Lady* and *Obsessive Love*. She did take an occasional trip back to the big screen, as in the drive-in favorite *Jackson County Jail*, as a victimized inmate who escapes, and Disney's poorly received attempt to enter the big-budget sci-fi arena, *The Black Hole*. One of her husbands was director Stanley Donen, to whom she was wed in 1972.

Screen: 1960: Platinum High School; The Time Machine; Where the Boys Are; 1962: Light in the Piazza; The Four Horsemen of the Apocalypse; The Wonderful World of the Brothers Grimm; 1963: Diamond Head; Toys in the Attic; 1964: Looking for Love; 1965: Joy in the Morning; The Reward; 1967: Monkeys, Go Home!; The Caper of the Golden Bulls; 1968: Dark of the Sun/The Mercenaries; Three in the Attic; 1969: The Picasso Summer; 1971: The Delta Factor; 1972: Skyjacked; 1973: The Neptune Factor; 1975: Journey Into Fear; 1976: Jackson County Jail; 1979: The Black Hole; 1983: Mystique/ Circle of Power.

Select TV: 1960: The Clown (sp); 1967: Desperate Hours (sp); 1970–71: The Most Deadly Game (series); 1971: Death Takes a Holiday; Black Noon; 1974: Hit Lady (and wr.); 1975: The Legend of Valentino; 1977: Ransom for Alice!; Snowbeast; 1978: Outside Chance; Devil Dog: The Hound of Hell; 1979: Disaster on the Coastliner; 1982: Forbidden Love; 1983: Night Partners; 1984: Obsessive Love (and co-wr.; prod.); 1985: Berrenger's (series); 1986: The Fifth Missile; 1990: Perry Mason: The Case of the Desperate Deception; 1992: Jackie Collins' Lady Boss.

SAL MINEO

(Salvatore Mineo, Jr.) Born: Bronx, NY, January 10, 1939. Died: February 12, 1976.

As the "sensitive" street kid of the movies, Sal Mineo was one of the major heartthrobs of the late 1950s and an actor of considerable emotional depth, whose career pretty much trickled off before he had even reached 30. Growing up as a delinquent youth in the Bronx, his mother encouraged him to get involved in dramatics, which led to his being cast in a teeny role in the original 1951 Broadway production of *The Rose Tattoo*. Within that same year he ended up in the cast of *The King and I*, as the young prince. After a break he made his motion picture debut, portraying Tony Curtis at a younger age in Universal's version of the Brink's Robbery, *Six Bridges to Cross*. This was followed by an appearance as one of the cadets under Charlton Heston's supervision in *The Private War of Major Benson*, and then the one that made him a star, *Rebel Without a Cause*, as the emotionally distressed mistfit teen Plato, who worships James Dean. Mineo, who was himself gay, did not hold back on emphasizing this lad's homosexual inclinations and, as a result, was quite unlike most angst-ridden youths in films of that time. He earned an Oscar nomination in the supporting category, which was where he stayed for *Crime in the Streets*, as a fellow thug of John Cassavetes; and *Giant*, as a Mexican boy who ends up getting killed in the war. He was becoming a hot name in the fan magazines, so he was made the lead in another juvenile delinquent story, *Dino*, which he had already done on TV, playing a kid released from reform school who is befriended by social worker Brian Keith. Clearly an edgy and watchable screen presence, he moved over to Columbia to carry *The Young Don't Cry*, as a confused youngster helping escaped con James Whitmore.

Since his dark ethnicity made him seemingly ideal for all kinds of roles, Disney cast him as an Indian, *Tonka*, who befriends a horse; then he took on what was basically his only flat-out comedic role, in the Fox farce *A Private's Affair*, in which he and his buddies participated in a television variety offering. Hoping for a real dramatic feast, he played his idol in *The Gene Krupa Story*, and was critically roasted for his portrayal of the hyper, drug-addicted drummer. Acclaim came again for *Exodus*, with Mineo earning another Oscar nomination, for playing the bitter Jewish boy who joins an Israeli terrorist group; his big, somewhat overwrought scene being his painful reminiscence about being raped while in the prison camps. Staying in support, he trekked through the desert with Yul Brynner in the flop *Escape From Zahrain*, then was another sensitive Indian, in the all-star western *Cheyenne Autumn*, the cast of which consisted of such other "Native Americans" as Dolores Del Rio and Ricardo Montalban. Clearly aiming for something away from the Hollywood mainstream, he was an obsessed busboy, emphasizing his "manhood" in a pair of tight white chinos, tormenting Juliet Prowse in the New York-set sleazefest *Who Killed Teddy Bear?*, a down-and-dirty thriller that became a cult favorite in later years. In 1969 he received some attention for directing an Off Broadway production of the gay-themed prison drama *Fortune and Men's Eyes*, but Hollywood wasn't giving him much to do, beyond playing a balloonist in the disaster epic *Krakatoa: East of Java*, and a simian who was killed off early on in *Escape From the Planet of the Apes*. It was while returning from a rehearsal for the play *P.S. Your Cat Is Dead* that he was stabbed to death in front of his apartment in West Hollywood. Mineo's killer was not identified until several years after his murder.

Screen: 1955: Six Bridges to Cross; The Private War of Major

Benson; Rebel Without a Cause; **1956:** Crime in the Streets; Somebody Up There Likes Me; Giant; Rock, Pretty Baby; **1957:** Dino; The Young Don't Cry; **1958:** Tonka/A Horse Named Comanche; **1959:** A Private's Affair; The Gene Krupa Story; **1960:** Exodus; **1962:** Escape From Zahrain; The Longest Day; **1964:** Cheyenne Autumn; **1965:** The Greatest Story Ever Told; Who Killed Teddy Bear?; **1969:** 80 Steps to Jonah; Krakatoa: East of Java/Volcano; **1971:** Escape From the Planet of the Apes.

NY Stage: AS SALVATORE MINEO: **1951:** The Rose Tattoo; Dinosaur Wharf; The King and I.

AS SAL MINEO: **1962:** Something About a Soldier.

Select TV: **1955:** The Trees (sp); **1956:** Dino (sp); The Dream (sp); **1956:** The Magic Horn (sp); **1957:** Drummer Man (sp); Barefoot Soldier (sp); **1958:** Aladdin (sp); **1961:** Cry Vengeance (sp); **1966:** The Dangerous Days of Kiowa Jones; **1967:** A Song Called Revenge (sp); Stranger on the Run; **1969:** The Challengers; **1971:** In Search of America; **1972:** The Family Rico; How to Steal an Airplane/Only One Day Left Before Tomorrow (filmed 1968).

CARMEN MIRANDA

(MARIA DO CARMO MIRANDA DA CUHNA)
BORN: LISBON, PORTUGAL, FEBRUARY 9, 1909.
RAISED IN BRAZIL. DIED: AUGUST 5, 1955.

A limited act if ever there was one, Carmen Miranda, the "Lady with the Tutti-Frutti Hat," could nonetheless always be depended upon to raise a smile from wartime audiences, especially in the tired musicals she usually participated in, where her eccentric energy was like a burst of adrenalin. In Brazil, where she grew up, she became a nightclub singer, which led to her own radio show and appearances in four motion pictures produced in that country. She was popular enough for America to take interest, and she was hired to appear on Broadway in *Streets of Paris*, creating a stir cavorting through what would become one of her signature numbers, "South American Way." 20th Century-Fox had her film the song for insertion into the 1940 Betty Grable musical *Down Argentine Way*, and she became an immediate audience favorite. Excited by her reception, Fox signed her to a contract where she was called on to rattle off her lines in fractured English, wear something outrageous on her head, and wiggle her eyebrows in broad fashion as she sang a specialty song or two in the middle of *That Night in Rio* ("Chica Chica Boom Chic" and "I Yi Yi Yi Yi — I Like You Very Much"), *Week-end in Havana* ("The Nango"), and *The Gang's All Here* (reaching some sort of summit of camp with "The Lady With the Tutti-Frutti Hat" with its unforgettable phallic bananas). The studio gave her top billing at last in *Greenwich Village*, although she shared the screen with Don Ameche, William Bendix, and Vivian Blane, and then again for *Something for the Boys*, which basically dismantled the Cole Porter original on which it was based, though they retained the plot, about Miranda receiving radio signals in her dental fillings!

After the uninspired box-office performance of those, she found herself taking billing *below* Ms. Blaine for *Doll Face* and *If I'm Lucky*, an indication that the less of Miranda there was, the safer the studio felt. In any case her heyday with that company was over, so she did an independent production opposite Groucho Marx, *Copacabana*, requiring her to masquerade as a mysterious nightclub chanteuse. Next she went over to MGM for *A Date With Judy*, principally on hand for the sight gag of her dancing with oafish Wallace Beery, and *Nancy Goes to Rio*, suggesting that her material hadn't varied too much over the years, as

she was given a song called "Cha Bomm Pa Pa." She was thrown into one of the Martin and Lewis comedies, *Scared Stiff*, to perform three songs, now being treated as something of a nostalgia act. Two years later she was dead of a heart attack at age 46. If nothing else she left behind an indelible, still-mimicked image, which is more than can be said for many an entertainer with longer-lasting careers and credits of infinitely higher quality. In 1994 a documentary appeared, *Carmen Miranda: Bananas Is My Business*.

Screen: **1933:** A Voz do Carnaval (nUSr); **1935:** Alo, Alo, Brasil (nUSr); Estudantes (nUSr); **1936:** Alo, Alo, Carnval (nUSr); **1938:** Banana da Terra (nUSr); **1940:** Down Argentine Way; **1941:** That Night in Rio; Week-end in Havana; **1942:** Springtime in the Rockies; **1943:** The Gang's All Here; **1944:** Four Jills and a Jeep; Greenwich Village; Something for the Boys; **1945:** Doll Face; **1946:** If I'm Lucky; **1947:** Copacabana; **1948:** A Date With Judy; **1950:** Nancy Goes to Rio; **1953:** Scared Stiff.

NY Stage: **1939:** Streets of Paris; **1941:** Sons o' Fun.

CAMERON MITCHELL

(CAMERON MIZELL) BORN: DALLASTOWN, PA, NOVEMBER 4, 1918. DIED: JULY 6, 1994.

With so many credits to his name it's a wonder Cameron Mitchell found time to sleep. Early on he was a solid actor, but seeing some of the tired trash he stooped to appearing in later on, one can only assume he was getting in those 40 winks while the cameras were rolling. He came to New York in the late 1930s to become an actor, and it was via Alfred Lunt that he got his break, making his Broadway debut in 1939, in *Jeremiah*. After serving with the Air Corp during World War II, he ended up in Hollywood, where MGM utilized his rugged looks in several small military roles, in *What Next, Corporal Hargrove?*, and *They Were Expendable*, among others. Columbia gave him a leading role in a "B" movie, *Leather Gloves*, about a boxer and the effect he has on the inhabitants of a small town, and then he returned to Broadway for his greatest stage success, playing Happy in the landmark drama *Death of a Salesman*, winning a Theatre World Award. Fortunately he was asked to repeat his role in the excellent 1951 film version, for it revitalized Hollywood's interest in him. In starring roles he carried *Smuggler's Gold*, as a deep-sea diver, and the color sci-fi adventure, *Flight to Mars*, as an astronaut, before joining the 20th Century-Fox roster for a spell. There he was at his most vicious, as the bandit terrorizing the snowbound cast of *The Outcasts of Poker Flat*; played Marius in a forgotten rendering of *Les Misérables*; charmed Lauren Bacall as a millionaire incognito in the 1953 smash hit comedy *How to Marry a Millionaire*; supplied the voice of the unseen Jesus in *The Robe*; suffered from a brain tumor in the "B" western *Powder River*; was one of Gary Cooper's unsavory partners, trying to attack Susan Hayward, in *Garden of Evil*; married Dana Wynter in *The View From Pompey's Head*; and swaggered with brio as Jigger in the Rodgers and Hammerstein musical *Carousel*. Away from that studio he was gunned down by a jealous James Cagney in *Love Me or Leave Me*, and threw himself wholeheartedly into playing real-life boxer Barney Ross, battling drug addiction in a noble effort, *Monkey on My Back*. With the blink of an eye he was deep into programmer territory with *Inside the Mafia*, *Pier 5 Havana*, and *Three Came to Kill*, all made for an independent company called Premium.

By the 1960s he was one of the many American performers who found themselves getting steady employment in European product, including spectacles like *Fury of the Vikings* and *Caesar the Conqueror*, and horror films like *Monster of the Wax Museum* and *Isle of the Doomed/Maneater of Hydra*. He had a role in a good film among all this, *Hombre*, as a sheriff, as well as television employment on a western series, *The High Chaparral*, and a chance to chew a little scenery in a drive-in offering, *Rebel Rousers*, as an Establishment square encountering a pack of bikers. There was also a worthwhile western, *Ride in the Whirlwind*, in which he and Jack Nicholson were cowboys inadvertently caught up in a feud, but after playing the festival circuit nobody bothered to distribute it to cinemas. Television kept him extremely busy during the 1970s, but his big-screen offerings just got cheesier and cheesier with *The Klansman*, *The Toolbox Murders*, and *Without Warning*, to name but a few of the higher profile ones. There was a chance to make some deliberate laughs, broadly playing a gang boss, in the 1982 comedy *My Favorite Year*, but then it was back to anything-for-a-paycheck fare like *Night Train to Terror*, *The Tomb*, and *Mutant War*, looking like a man determined to die working.

Screen: 1945: What Next, Corporal Hargrove?; They Were Expendable; The Hidden Eye; 1946: The Mighty McGurk; 1947: High Barbaree; Cass Timberlane; 1948: Tenth Avenue Angel; Homecoming; Adventures of Gallant Bess; Leather Gloves; Command Decision; 1951: Smuggler's Gold; Man in the Saddle; Death of a Salesman; Flight to Mars; 1952: Japanese War Bride; Okinawa; The Sellout; The Outcasts of Poker Flat; Pony Soldier; Les Misérables; 1953: Man on a Tightrope; How to Marry a Millionaire; Powder River; The Robe (voice); 1954: Hell and High Water; Gorilla at Large; Garden of Evil; Desiree; 1955: Strange Lady in Town; Love Me or Leave Me; House of Bamboo; The Tall Men; The View From Pompey's Head; 1956: Carousel; Tension at Table Rock; 1957: The Day They Gave the Babies Away/All Mine to Give; Monkey on My Back; No Down Payment; Escapade in Japan; 1959: Pier 5 Havana; Inside the Mafia; Face of Fire; 1960: Three Came to Kill; As the Sea Rages; The Unstoppable Man (nUSr); 1961: Erik the Conqueror/Fury of the Vikings (nUSr); 1962: Attack of the Normans/Conquest of the Normans (nUSr); 1963: Caesar the Conqueror; The Last of the Vikings; Dulcinea (nUSr); 1964: Minnesota Clay (nUSr); Dog Eat Dog/When Strangers Meet (nUSr); Killer's Canyon/Last Gun (nUSr); 1965: The Black Duke; Blood and Black Lace; 1966: Nightmare in Wax/Crimes in the Wax Museum; 1967: Hombre; Ride in the Whirlwind; Autopsy of a Ghost (nUSr); The Treasure of Makuba; 1968: Knives of the Avenger (nUSr); Island of the Doomed/Maneater of Hydra; 1970: Rebel Rousers; 1972: Buck and the Preacher; Slaughter; The Big Game; 1974: The Midnight Man; The Klansman; Medusa (nUSr); 1975: The Taste of the Savage/Eye for an Eye; Political Asylum (nUSr); 1977: Viva Knievel!; Haunts; Slavers (nUSr); 1978: The Toolbox Murders; The Swarm; Texas Detour; Enforcer From Death Row/Ninja Nightmare (dtv); 1980: Silent Scream; Without Warning; Supersonic Man; 1981: Texas Lightning; The Demon (dtv); Screamers/The Fish Men; Frankenstein Island; 1982: Cataclysm (dtv); Kill Squad; Raw Force; My Favorite Year; It's Called Murder, Baby (dtv); 1983: The Guns and the Fury (dtv); Terror on Tape (dtv); 1984: Killpoint; Go for the Gold (dtv); 1985: Night Train to Terror/Shiver; Prince Jack; 1986: Low Blow; The Tomb; Mission: Kill (dtv); Blood Link; 1987: Nightforce (dtv); The Messenger; The Offspring/From a Whisper to a Scream; Hollywood Cop (dtv); Deadly Prey (dtv); A Rage to Kill (dtv); 1988: Space Mutiny (dtv); Swift Justice (dtv); Memorial Valley Massacre (dtv); Killers (dtv); 1989: Codname: Vengeance (dtv); No Justice; Easy Kill (dtv); Cult People (dtv); 1990: Action U.S.A. (dtv); Crossing the Line (dtv);

Demon Cop (dtv); Terror in Beverly Hills (dtv); 1993: Trapped Alive (dtv); 1995: Jack-O (dtv).

NY Stage: 1939: Jeremiah; 1940: The Taming of the Shrew; 1941: The Trojan Women; 1949: Death of a Salesman; 1950: Southern Exposure; 1970: Les Blancs; 1978: The November People.

Select TV: 1952: The Kirby's (sp); Prison Doctor (sp); 1953: Kill That Story! (sp); 1955: The Ox-Bow Incident (sp); Man on the Ledge (sp); 1956: The Prowler (sp); The Bounty Hunter (sp); Command (sp); 1958: Brotherhood of the Bell (sp); The Bromley Touch (sp); Dog in a Bush Tunnel (sp); 1960: Omaha Beach: Plus 15 (sp); Meeting at Appalachia (sp); 1960–62: The Beachcomber (series); 1967–71: The High Chaparral (series); 1970: The Andersonville Trial (sp); 1971: Thief; The Reluctant Heroes; 1972: Cutter; The Delphi Bureau; The Rookies; 1973: The Stranger; 1974: Hitchhike!; The Hanged Man; The Girl on the Late, Late Show; 1975: Swiss Family Robinson; 1975–76: Swiss Family Robinson (series); 1976: The Quest; Flood!; 1977: The Hostage Heart; Testimony of Two Men (ms); 1978: Return to Fantasy Island; The Bastard; Black Beauty (ms); How the West Was Won (ms); 1979: Hanging by a Thread; 1980: Wild Times; Turnover Smith; OHMS; 1983: Kenny Rogers as The Gambler Part II: The Adventure Continues; 1986: Dream West (ms).

THOMAS MITCHELL

BORN: ELIZABETH, NJ, JULY 11, 1892.
DIED: DECEMBER 17, 1962.

During the height of the studio era, Thomas Mitchell was right up there near the very top of the list of most-in-demand character actors. Undeniably Irish, the stocky, beady-eyed performer had a bit of puffed-up bluster about him that he had a tendency to overdo on occasion, but he was always worth a look, sometimes performing gloriously. Originally a reporter for his hometown paper, he turned his attention to acting, making his Broadway debut with the Ben Greet Players in *The Tempest*. While making his name as a stage performer, he began dabbling in playwrighting with three titles produced for the New York stage: *Glory Hallelujah* (1926; the only one in which he did not appear), *Little Accident* (1928; the basis for the Gary Cooper film *Casanova Brown*), and *Cloudy With Showers* (1931). There was one silent film assignment during this period, but he did not go to Hollywood for keeps until 1936 when he played a supporting part in *Craig's Wife*, as a family friend driven to murder by his philandering spouse. This was done at Columbia, where he also did *Theodora Goes Wild*, as the editor who serializes Irene Dunne's risqué novel, and his first for director Frank Capra, *Lost Horizon*, as the robust fugitive who finds the hidden sanctuary of Shangri-La very much to his liking. That same year he excelled as the son who must separate his aging parents in *Make Way for Tomorrow*, and as the very sensible doctor who has to deliver a baby in the midst of *The Hurricane*, his first job for another director who would make good use of him, John Ford. His work in the latter earned him a 1937 Oscar nomination in the supporting category.

He'd already begun to establish himself as one of the top supporting players in the business, and the year 1939 would solidify this position, as he was seen in five of the most highly regarded pictures of that year. First, he was back with Ford again, giving a showy, magnificent performance as the alcoholic doctor who depletes poor Donald Meek of his liquor samples in the landmark western character study *Stagecoach*. Again he was asked to deliver a baby under difficult circumstances, only this time it was his own self-induced stupor that provided the hindrance. In *Only Angels Have Wings* he was Cary Grant's sidekick, then took to nipping at the bottle again, as a reporter, helping Jean Arthur give support to James Stewart in *Mr. Smith Goes to Washington*. Of course his mostly widely seen role was as Vivien Leigh's Irish dad in *Gone With the Wind*, slowly losing his mind after the devastation of the Civil War, after which he was King of the Beggars, Cloppin, in the screen's best version of *The Hunchback of Notre Dame*. To cap off this peak year he won the Academy Award for Best Supporting Actor for *Stagecoach*.

1940 was equally impressive in that Mitchell was elevated into some leading roles for *Swiss Family Robinson*, top billed as the dad of the marooned brood in this lesser rendering of the famous tale, and *Angels Over Broadway*, drunk again but trying to do good by saving suicidal John Qualen's life, in a real feast of a role that he took full advantage of. Although John Wayne got first billing, it was really Mitchell who took center stage in another for Ford, *The Long Voyage Home*, arguably his finest two hours on film, as the swaggering sailor who lives heart and soul for the sea for he knows no other life. Warners gave him the starring role in a quickie, *Flight From Destiny*, as a college professor who decides to do something good when he finds out he hasn't long to live, then he turned mean for *Moontide*, blackmailing Jean Gabin until fate intervenes. There was the title role in *The Immortal Sergeant*, although Henry Fonda got top billing, and then another lead of sorts, playing Pat Garrett to Jack Buetel's Billy the Kid in the sensationalistic western *The Outlaw*, which ran into trouble because of the problems the censors had with Jane Russell's cleavage.

He did his dependable sidekick bit in the exciting pirate yarn *The Black Swan* and in the Clark Gable-Greer Garson romance *Adventure*; tried to drive Merle Oberon nuts in *Dark Waters*; portrayed secretary Joseph Tumulty in Fox's long-winded prestige item *Wilson*, and writer Ned Buntline in *Buffalo Bill*; and then had to suffer valiantly after all five of his boys are killed in the war in the true story *The Sullivans*. In the late 1940s he did his most famous part for Frank Capra, the undependable but well-meaning Uncle Billy who causes James Stewart's awful night of desperation by losing an important bank deposit in *It's a Wonderful Life*. Along with *Gone With the Wind*, it became the film for which he would become best remembered by future generations. There was another important, sizable role, in Paramount's interesting supernatural tale *Alias Nick Beal*, in which he was tempted by satanic Ray Milland, and participation in another of the key entries in the western genre, *High Noon*, as the town official who tries to persuade Gary Cooper to leave for the benefit of the community. Between assignments on television, where he not only had regular roles on three series but won a 1952 Emmy Award for his body of work that year, he returned to the screen on occasion, ending his career back under Capra's guidance, and playing a likable lush once again, in *Pocketful of Miracles*. Along with Sidney Buchman, he received writer credit on the 1934 Paramount film *All of Me*.

Screen: 1923: Six Cylinder Love; 1936: Craig's Wife; Adventure in Manhattan; Theodora Goes Wild; 1937: When You're in Love; Man of the People; Lost Horizon; I Promise to Pay; Make Way for Tomorrow; The Hurricane; 1938: Love, Honor and Behave; Trade Winds; 1939: Stagecoach; Only Angels Have Wings; Mr. Smith Goes to Washington; Gone With the Wind; The Hunchback of Notre Dame; 1940: Swiss Family Robinson; Three Cheers for the Irish; Our Town; The Long Voyage Home; Angels Over Broadway; 1941: Flight From Destiny; Out of the Fog; 1942: Joan of Paris; Song of the Islands; Moontide; This Above All; Tales of Manhattan; The Black Swan; 1943: The Immortal Sergeant; The Outlaw; Bataan; Flesh and Fantasy; 1944: The Sullivans; Buffalo Bill; Wilson; Dark Waters; 1945: The Keys of the Kingdom; Within These Walls; Captain Eddie; Adventure;

1946: Three Wise Fools; The Dark Mirror; It's a Wonderful Life; 1947: High Barbaree; The Romance of Rosy Ridge; 1948: Silver River; 1949: Alias Nick Beal; The Big Wheel; 1951: Journey Into Light; 1952: High Noon; 1954: Secret of the Incas; Destry; 1956: While the City Sleeps; 1958: Handle With Care; 1959: Too Young to Love; 1961: By Love Possessed; Pocketful of Miracles.

NY Stage: 1916: Under Sentence; 1917: Nju; 1918: Crops and Croppers; Redemption; 1919: Dark Rosaleen; 1920: Not So Long Ago; 1921: The Playboy of the Western World; Kiki; 1926: The Wisdom Tooth; 1927: Blood Money; Nightstick; 1928: Little Accident (and wr.; dir.); 1931: Cloudy With Showers (and wr.; dir.); 1932: Riddle Me This!; Clear All Wires!; Honeymoon; 1935: Fly Away Home; Stick-in-the-Mud; 1947: An Inspector Calls; 1949: The Biggest Thief in Town; 1950: Death of a Salesman; 1953: Hazel Flagg; 1960: Cut of the Axe.

Select TV: 1951: Ah, Wilderness! (sp); The Long View (sp); The Skin of Our Teeth (sp); 1952: The Farmer's Hotel (sp); The Chase (sp); Promotion (sp); The Fascinating Stranger (sp); The Square Peg (sp); The Country Lawyer (sp); Mr. Nothing (sp); A Time of Innocence (sp); 1953: Country Editor (sp); Of Time and the River (sp); 1954: The Gentle Deception (sp); The Good of His Soul (sp); The Rise and Fall of Silas Lepham (sp); Afraid to Live (sp); Shadow of Truth (sp); 1954–55: Mayor of the Town (series); 1955: Freight (sp); The Unforgivable (sp); The Adventures of Huckleberry Finn (sp); The Man Who Was Dead (sp); Miracle on 34th Street (sp); 1956: The Ballad of Mender McClure (sp); Try Me for Size (sp); It Started With Eve (sp); 1957: O. Henry Playhouse (series); Miller's Millions (sp); 1958: The Nightingale (sp); The Velvet Trap (sp); Natchez (sp); 1958–59: Glencannon (series); 1959: Ladybug (sp); 1960: The Secret of Freedom (sp); The Right Man (sp); 1961: The Joke and the Valley (sp).

ROBERT MITCHUM
BORN: BRIDGEPORT, CT, AUGUST 6, 1917.
DIED: JULY 1, 1997.

His career encompassed more than 50 years of stardom, but of all the actors to achieve his level of fame, few had as many undistinguished films as did Robert Mitchum. This gave him the reputation of a workman-like performer who took what was given to him, did his job, and often did it well. It also contributed to the image of a cynic who rather lazily walked through some of the more routine assignments. The man with the ultra-cool demeanor and the droopy eyelids had done a variety of odd jobs that took him to California where he worked as a professional boxer, aircraft factory employee, and shoe clerk. Through his sister, a nightclub singer, he got an agent who found him work as a studio writer, but he quickly left that behind to offer himself up for extra work. He was first seen playing one of the bad guys in a Hopalong Cassidy western, *Hoppy Serves a Writ*, in 1943, and that year astute filmgoers could spot him in no less than 18 other features, including another Hoppy film, *Bar 20*, this time on the side of good; *The Human Comedy*, as one of the soldiers on leave who flirt with Donna Reed and her friends; and *Beyond the Last Frontier*, as a spy who turns heroic for the climax. Over at Monogram there was a bigger role than usual, in *When Strangers Marry*, and he was showing enough promise that RKO signed him to a contract where they started him off supporting one of the less memorable comedy teams of the era, Brown and Carney, in the western musical *The Girl Rush*. His first official starring role came with another in the guns 'n' saddle genre, *Nevada*, as a cowpoke accused of murder, after which he had trouble realizing Barbara Hale wasn't a boy in *West of the Pecos*.

Mitchum's breakthrough came in 1945 with the United Artists release *The Story of G.I. Joe/Ernie Pyle's Story of G.I. Joe*, and his performance as a tough but understanding captain, whose company's campaign from North Africa to Italy is covered by correspondent Burgess Meredith, represented everything he would do best, with that touch of compassion under the world weariness. He received his only Oscar nomination, in the supporting category.

Back at RKO he began receiving better treatment in pictures with more generous budgets, starting with *Till the End of Time*, playing a former soldier suffering from a head injury; one of 1947's Oscar nominees for Best Picture, *Crossfire*, as assured as any of its many outstanding performances, playing a soldier who helps get the goods on bigoted murderer Robert Ryan; *Out of the Past*, perhaps the prime Mitchum noir film of the period, dangerously falling for femme fatale Jane Greer; and *Rachel and the Stranger*, portraying an Indian scout who comes between married couple Loretta Young and William Holden, even singing some tunes in the process. Meanwhile MGM had borrowed him for two failures, *Undercurrent*, with Katharine Hepburn, and *Desire Me*, with Greer Garson, two women he did not complement on screen. In 1948, after another well-liked western, *Blood on the Moon*, in which he was a hired gun for villain Robert Preston who turns against his boss, he became the center of scandal when he was arrested for possession of marijuana, a charge that stood out in the days before this sort of thing became common among the Hollywood folk. It allowed his studio to play up his image as a dangerous "rebel," and it only served to enhance his reputation for future generations.

Perhaps consciously, the "nice" side of Mitchum was on hand for the color Republic western *The Red Pony*, as the handyman who helps young Peter Miles, and RKO's sweet Christmas love story, *Holiday Affair*, where he romanced Janet Leigh. He followed these with *Where Danger Lives*, helping to introduce the quickly forgotten Howard Hughes discovery, Faith Domergue; *My Forbidden Past*, ensnared by temptress Ava Gardner; and *His Kind of Woman* and *Macao*, two attempts by Hughes to make Mitchum and Jane Russell a hot new team (unfortunately the pair of them together produced very little empathy among audiences). *The Lusty Men* wasn't as hot as the title promised, it being about rodeos, and *Second Chance* was notable only because it was shot in 3-D. These were the kinds of routine melodramas that helped to kill off RKO, and indeed Mitchum severed his ties with them in 1954, after a comedy with Jean Simmons, *She Couldn't Say No*.

Things improved for him with Fox's *River of No Return*, which, despite being superficial CinemaScope nonsense, was high profile stuff because Marilyn Monroe was in it; a popular soap opera, *Not as a Stranger*, though he was a shade on the dull side as a medical student; and, most notably, *The Night of the Hunter*, excelling in one of his most famous roles, as the murderous preacher with "love" and "hate" tattooed on his fingers. This was far from hot box office at the time, but its uncompromising sense of unrest promised it a huge cult following while proving that there was a deeply unsympathetic side to Mitchum that could be used to great effect. He went tongue-in-cheek for *Bandido*, as an American adventurer south of the border, then did two good ones for 20th Century-Fox, *Heaven Knows, Mr. Allison*, at his most appealing, as the stranded soldier who respectfully falls in love with nun Deborah Kerr (they had the only roles of any substantial size), and *The Enemy Below*, as the captain of a destroyer trying to sink Curt Jurgens's German sub. At Columbia Jack Lemmon stole the attention from him and Rita Hayworth in *Fire Down Below*, and then Mitchum co-wrote and did some songs

for one that cast his son Jim as his brother (!), *Thunder Road*, a tedious moonshining tale that inexplicably became a drive-in favorite over the years. As the 1960s came, he reigned over a troubled family in a fairly successful soaper, *Home From the Hills*, again at his least likable; participated in one of the rare Cary Grant flops of the time, *The Grass Is Greener*; and then gave one of his best performances, playing with surprising conviction an Australian sheepherder, in one of that year's Oscar nominees for Best Picture, *The Sundowners*. There was another comedy nobody wanted to see, *The Last Time I Saw Archie*, then his other great sadistic part, in *Cape Fear*, terrorizing Gregory Peck and his family.

He had one of the bigger roles in the all-star smash *The Longest Day*, about the D-Day invasion, and did another movie in which he and his leading lady were pretty much the only major characters on hand, *Two for the Seesaw*, with Shirley MacLaine, only this affair between two lonely people hadn't a single thing to distinguish it from a dozen better movies like it. Also with MacLaine, he was one of her millionaire husbands in the overdressed and undernourished comedy *What a Way to Go!*, making love to her at one point in a giant champagne glass, and then carried a whole batch of vehicles that caused barely a ripple, *Rampage*, a love triangle set in the jungle; *Man in the Middle*, a British-made courtroom drama in which he defended officer Keenan Wynn on a murder charge; and *Mister Moses*, leading some Africans to their homeland. Someone had the great idea of teaming him with John Wayne for *El Dorado*, which stood out during this weak period, before he dipped into another string of routine fare, *Villa Rides!*, as a pilot captured by Yul Brynner; *Anzio*, as a war correspondent covering the famous invasion; *Young Billy Young*, as a sheriff based on Wyatt Earp; and a less serious western, *The Good Guys and the Bad Guys*, as a marshal past his prime.

He was cast as Sarah Miles's sad schoolteacher husband in one of the big pictures of 1970, *Ryan's Daughter*, successfully making the transition into the newer, more "realistic" style of cinema that had come to fruition with the fall of the production code. His box office continued to be shaky at best, but filmmakers still hired him for the weary grit that they felt he possessed. Therefore there were critical plaudits from some circles but sparse audiences for *The Friends of Eddie Coyle*, with Mitchum as a small-time crook in this bleak glimpse of the Boston criminal underworld; *The Yakuza*, which blended Japanese rituals with gangsters; and *Farewell, My Lovely*, in which he played the greatest of all cynical private eyes, Philip Marlowe, a character well-suited to his persona. After the total wipeout of two more thrillers, *The Amsterdam Kill*, and the disastrous remake of *The Big Sleep*, again as Marlowe, it was time to admit that supporting roles were his future. Not that this meant he would be appearing in strictly high-grade stuff, as proven by the dopey kangaroo comedy *Matilda*; *Breakthrough*, which teamed him with an equally tired Richard Burton; and the Canadian *Agency*, among others, each barely finding distribution. There was an "A" production, *That Championship Season*, with Mitchum as a basketball coach holding an uncomfortable reunion with his star players, but it failed to repeat its stage success. The one that did give him a final starring role in the limelight was a production for television, *The Winds of War*, the ultra-expensive and much-watched mini-series about World War II. Then it was back to the movies, serving as a last minute replacement for Burt Lancaster in *Maria's Lovers* and for John Huston in *Mr. North*. A small part in a Bill Murray comedy, *Scrooged*, was one of the few to be seen by a substantial audience, the antithesis of *Dead Man*, a black and white western that marked one last visit to this genre. When he died he was spoken of as one of the movies' most admired professionals and enduring stars, certainly evoking warmer memories for his own contributions than for the quality of so many of his films. In addition to Jim Mitchum, his son Christopher is also an actor.

Screen: 1943: Hoppy Serves a Writ; Follow the Band; The Human Comedy; The Leather Burners; Border Patrol; Colt Comrades; Bar 20; We've Never Been Licked; Doughboys in Ireland; Corvette K-225; Aerial Gunner; Lone Star Trail; The Dancing Masters; False Colors; Riders of the Deadline; Minesweeper; Beyond the Last Frontier; Cry Havoc; Gung Ho!; 1944: Johnny Doesn't Live Here Anymore; Mr. Winkle Goes to War; When Strangers Marry; Thirty Seconds Over Tokyo; Girl Rush; Nevada; 1945: West of the Pecos; The Story of G.I. Joe; 1946: Till the End of Time; Undercurrent; The Locket; 1947: Pursued; Crossfire; Desire Me; Out of the Past; 1948: Rachel and the Stranger; Blood on the Sun; 1949: The Red Pony; The Big Steal; Holiday Affair; 1950: Where Danger Lives; 1951: My Forbidden Past; His Kind of Woman; The Racket; 1952: Macao; One Minute to Zero; The Lusty Men; Angel Face; 1953: White Witch Doctor; Second Chance; 1954: She Couldn't Say No; River of No Return; Track of the Cat; 1955: Not as a Stranger; The Night of the Hunter; Man With the Gun; 1956: Foreign Intrigue; Bandido; 1957: Heaven Knows, Mr. Allison; The Enemy Below; Fire Down Below; 1958: Thunder Road (and co-wr.); The Hunters; 1959: The Angry Hills; The Wonderful Country; 1960: Night Fighters/A Terrible Beauty; Home From the Hill; The Grass Is Greener; The Sundowners; 1961: The Last Time I Saw Archie; 1962: Cape Fear; The Longest Day; Two for the Seesaw; 1963: The List of Adrian Messenger; Rampage; 1964: Man in the Middle; What a Way to Go!; 1965: Mister Moses; 1967: The Way West; El Dorado; 1968: 5 Card Stud; Villa Rides!; Anzio; Secret Ceremony; 1969: Young Billy Young; The Good Guys and the Bad Guys; 1970: Ryan's Daughter; 1971: Going Home; 1972: The Wrath of God; 1973: The Friends of Eddie Coyle; 1975: The Yakuza; Farewell, My Lovely; 1976: Midway; The Last Tycoon; 1977: The Amsterdam Kill; 1978: The Big Sleep; Matilda; 1979: Breakthrough/Sergeant Steiner; 1980: Agency/Mind Games; Nightkill; 1982: That Championship Season; 1984: The Ambassador; 1985: Maria's Lovers; 1988: Mr. North; Scrooged; 1990: Presumed Dangerous/Believed Violent (nUSr); 1991: Midnight Ride (dtv); Cape Fear; 1992: The Seven Deadly Sins (nUSr); 1993: Woman of Desire (dtv); Tombstone (narrator); 1995: Backfire! (dtv); Wild Bill: Hollywood Maverick; Pakten: Waiting for Sunset (nUSr); 1996: Dead Man; 1997: James Dean: Race With Destiny (dtv).

Select TV: 1982: One Shoe Makes It Murder; 1983: The Winds of War (ms); A Killer in the Family; 1985: The Hearst-Davies Affair; Reunion at Fairborough; North and South (ms); Promises to Keep; 1986: Thompson's Last Run; 1988–89: War and Remembrance (ms); 1989: Brotherhood of the Rose; Jake Spanner: Private Eye; 1990: A Family for Joe; A Family for Joe (series); 1992–94: African Skies (series).

MARILYN MONROE
(NORMA JEANE MORTENSON)
BORN: LOS ANGELES, CA, JUNE 1, 1926.
DIED: AUGUST 5, 1962.

There has probably been more written about Marilyn Monroe than any other movie star in the history of cinema. She represented, and continues to embody, everything that is good and bad, glamorous and phony, beautiful and tacky about Hollywood and its product. Her breathy voice and exaggerated sexuality, mixed with a bubble-headed innocence, has been endlessly mimicked by others but few came close to capturing the vulnerable little girl buried under the platinum hair and temptress's wiggle, the one everybody wound up feeling so protective of long after it was too late and tragedy had swallowed her up. Her origins as an illegitimate child raised by foster parents and growing up in a dead-end life have been well documented. She was already married and divorced before she was 20, during which time she worked in a factory and began doing part-time work as a photographer's model. These photos began circulating through Hollywood, and both producer Howard Hughes and 20th Century-Fox showed interest. The latter signed her to a contract, put her into a teensy role in a Lon McCallister film, *Scudda Hoo! Scudda Hay!*, and then promptly chopped her out of the final print (save for an extreme long shot in which she is seen from the back in a canoe). Therefore her first role in which she could actually be seen was in a "B," *Dangerous Years*, showing up as a waitress. Unimpressed, the studio dropped her but would come calling again soon enough.

In the meantime Columbia co-starred her with Adele Jergens as *Ladies of the Chorus*, a nothing "B" movie, in which she looked stunning as a burlesque performer, and the last official Marx Brothers movie, *Love Happy*, bumping and grinding in front of Groucho, resulting in the expected innuendos. By the late 1940s she was a recognizable face and body in fan magazines but little more. Further notoriety came with her famous nude calendar pinup that became the most widely circulated and reproduced celebrity skin photo of its day. After more chorus work in *A Ticket to Tomahawk*, she got two important roles in two of the best films of 1950: *The Asphalt Jungle*, curling up suggestively on a couch as Louis Calhern's mistress, and *All About Eve*, a delight as the relentlessly stupid and talentless protégé of George Sanders. The charisma was there, but the acting abilities were still in doubt. Therefore she stayed as mere decoration for *The Fireball*, a movie made to cash in on the Roller Derby craze, with Mickey Rooney; *As Young as You Feel*, as a secretary; *Love Nest*, as a sexy tenant in William Lundigan's apartment building; and *Clash by Night*, as Keith Andes's anxious bride. Her participation in these made them the sort of otherwise forgettable movies that people would seek out in later years, following her fame. Around this time 20th Century-Fox was convinced that they could finally do something with her, that a major movie star was waiting to be born. They almost put an end to that dream with *Don't Bother to Knock*, giving her the absolutely impossible role of a mentally unbalanced baby sitter, a part she wrestled and lost with on every level. That one was crowded with enough other characters that the blame didn't fall squarely on her, and she continued to be part of the ensemble in *We're Not Married*, paired with nebbishy David Wayne for the first time; *O. Henry's Full House*, as a street-walker in the "Cop and the Anthem" segment, with Charles Laughton; and *Monkey Business*, notable mainly because she got to share the screen with Cary Grant.

Her fortunes changed at last with *Niagara*, where she sizzled as the sultry bitch who tries to kill husband Joseph Cotten and winds up dead herself at the famous honeymoon site. Although Cotten was the real star, it was sold on Monroe's name and image, and there was no doubt the crowds showed up because of her. The excitement carried over to the musical *Gentlemen Prefer Blondes*, in which she was teamed memorably with Jane Russell, causing an avalanche of breast-related double entendres and giving Monroe one of her seminal moments on film, steamily undulating to "Diamonds Are a Girl's Best Friend." She was now one of the most talked-about personalities of the decade, and these two hits were followed by another major smash, *How to Marry a Millionaire*, billed *after* Betty Grable but *before* Lauren Bacall, as the money-hungry ditz who has trouble seeing without her glasses. Again she ended up with mild-mannered David

Wayne, letting the scrawny guys of the world realize some sort of fantasy. Even a piece of rubbish like *River of No Return*, a backwoods adventure tale with Robert Mitchum and some particularly bad rear-projection photography, could get by on her participation in it, and she was a great asset at the turnstiles to the over-stuffed musical tribute to Irving Berlin, *There's No Business Like Show Business*, where her suggestive renditions of "Heat Wave" and "Lazy" were highlights or missteps, according to who was doing the reporting. That same year, 1954, saw her highly publicized but brief marriage to baseball legend Joe DiMaggio. To cap all this off there was another monster hit that really showed her comical abilities off to great advantage, *The Seven Year Itch*, in which she was the nameless Girl Upstairs, innocently turning on horny neighbor Tom Ewell, and bringing off this potentially coy part as only she could. It also gave her another of her endlessly reproduced film moments, standing on a subway grate as a blast of air blew her skirt up around her panties.

Now at the peak of her fame and powers, she turned down a fluffy musical, *How to Be Very, Very Popular*. She knew damn well that she was Fox's most valuable asset and used every opportunity she could to back away from certain film projects in order to make demands for greater control over her material and salary. In this particular instance she packed up and moved to New York to study her craft at the famed Actors Studio. Under the tutelage of Lee Strasberg she was determined to prove that there was substance behind the body and came back to Hollywood with a vengeance, reaping raves for her work as the sad, hopelessly second-rate saloon singer in the broad adaptation of the William Inge stage success *Bus Stop*. It was another moneymaker for her, although seen today there is evidence of her trying just a mite too hard for the Oscar nomination that did not materialize. Nonetheless it made even better, future actresses realize that they would forever have to compete with Monroe's indelible stamp on the part.

There was another headline-making marriage, in 1956, this time to playwright Arthur Miller. (She and DiMaggio had dissolved their union within a year). Next up was her own production, made in England for Warner Bros., *The Prince and the Showgirl*, notable for its incongruous teaming of Monroe and Laurence Olivier, though the nightmare it became trying to film it seemed hardly worth the mild results, with Olivier, who also directed, not hiding his disdain for his co-star. Staying away from Fox, she did the one that would become her greatest and best-loved film, the pricelessly funny *Some Like It Hot*. Entering the story late, she still managed to justify her top billing, playing another small-talent entertainer with the sweet disposition of a child, Sugar Kane, who falls hopelessly in love with bespectacled Tony Curtis, in one of the most quoted seduction scenes in movie history. The film's triumph seemed to wash over the fact that she was becoming increasingly difficult to work with, causing endless delays, with stories of her irrational and selfish behavior becoming as legendary as the movie itself. There was also little effort made to hide the fact that she was depending on pills and alcohol to fight off depression, while her need to consult her on-set drama coach, Paula Strasberg, on her every line reading drove most of her directors and co-workers to exasperation.

Back at Fox she did a dull musical, *Let's Make Love*, where her typically sensuous rendition of the title tune was one of the few highpoints. It was yet another production that turned into an unnecessary headache due to Monroe's lack of cooperation. As her marriage to Miller was collapsing, he wrote a screenplay with her in mind, the result being *The Misfits*, one of the great "almost" movies of all time, and one that Monroe did with great

reluctance. As an aimless divorcee hooking up with a batch of horse wranglers, she definitely showed that she'd come a long way from her days as a looker with not much to offer in the acting department. There was a moody melancholia to the whole thing, one that is only further enhanced when seen to day, knowing that it would turn out to be not only co-star Clark Gable's last film but Monroe's as well. While shooting *Something's Got to Give*, a Fox remake of the marital comedy *My Favorite Wife*, with Dean Martin, she began missing work, pushing the once patient studio to the limit. They ultimately had no choice but to fire her. Footage from the unfinished film later popped up in the 1963 documentary *Marilyn*, and decades later more of it resurfaced, showing her to be miscalculating the tone of the piece altogether. After her dismissal from the film, she bottomed out, wallowing in depression, and finally ending it all in Hollywood's most publicized suicide, taking an overdose of barbiturates. Speculation continued for decades on whether or not she took her own life, stories of her recently ended relationship with President John F. Kennedy cited as the reason for a possible cover-up or conspiracy. It only added fuel to a legend that would not cease to grow. After a while it seemed as if not a week went by without a new biography on Monroe, and her image continued to fix itself in the mind of anyone even vaguely interested in movies, as the gorgeous blonde who found that success at the top of the Hollywood heap was not enough.

Screen: 1947: Dangerous Years; 1948: Scudda-Hoo! Scudda Hay!; Ladies of the Chorus; 1949: Love Happy; 1950: A Ticket to Tomahawk; The Asphalt Jungle; All About Eve; The Fireball; Right Cross; 1951: Home Town Story; As Young as You Feel; Love Nest; Let's Make It Legal; 1952: Clash by Night; Don't Bother to Knock; We're Not Married!; O. Henry's Full House; Monkey Business; 1953: Niagara; Gentlemen Prefer Blondes; How to Marry a Millionaire; 1954: River of No Return; There's No Business Like Show Business; 1955: The Seven Year Itch; 1956: Bus Stop; 1957: The Prince and the Showgirl; 1959: Some Like It Hot; 1960: Let's Make Love; 1961: The Misfits.

RICARDO MONTALBAN

BORN: MEXICO CITY, MEXICO, NOVEMBER 25, 1920.

There was no finer example of Hollywood's persona of the suave "Latin lover" than Ricardo Montalban. His voice was richly seductive, his manner most winning, the talent more than evident, and he offered enough of a spark to stick around longer than expected and keep his name on the tongues of future generations. His first trip to Hollywood while a teenager was to learn English, and although there was interest in him from the studios, he instead followed his brother, actor Carlos Montalban, to New York, which led to him being cast in a handful of plays. After that it was back to Mexico where he became a performer in several films made there, starting with *El Verdugo de Sevilla*, in 1942. By 1944 he had met and married Loretta Young's sister Georgiana, which of course got him further attention in Hollywood circles. MGM signed him to a contract and put him in an Esther Williams film, *Fiesta*, where the definite highlight was his flamenco dance with Cyd Charisse. Similarly the two stole scenes again with their footwork in *On an Island With You* and *The Kissing Bandit*, in the latter instance being joined by Ann Miller. In 1949 he was not only reteamed with Williams in *Neptune's Daughter*, but also got to sing the Oscar-winning "Baby It's Cold Outside," as a polo player trying to woo the swimming camp. This was all light-hearted fare, so the studio figured they'd let him stretch and did so by making him one of the soldiers in their fine Oscar-nominated war film *Battleground* and, better yet, casting him as a Mexican agent who poses as an illegal migrant worker in order to uncover criminal activities in *Border Incident*, in many ways his most satisfying film work. He became a boxer for *Right Cross*; romanced Jane Powell in *Two Weeks With Love*; and then went west, as an outlaw in *Mark of the Renegade* (for Universal) and as an Indian in *Across the Wide Missouri*. MGM was testing his patience with *Sombrero*, where his was just one of the multiple plots in this drama set in a Mexican village, and especially with *Latin Lovers*, one of those deadly Lana Turner soaps of the 1950s. The studio decided not to bother renewing his contract after the latter.

He went to Columbia and Fox, respectively, for the kinds of costume programmers made in abundance during that era, *The Saracen Blade* and the Italian-produced *Queen of Babylon*. He received a career boost when he displayed his range by playing a Japanese kabuki performer in the one of the big hits of 1957, *Sayonara*, and by singing on Broadway as the co-star of the Lena Horne musical *Jamaica*. Starting in the 1960s, he began to establish himself as a character actor of note, as a gangster in *Let No Man Write My Epitaph*; an Italian officer in *Hemingway's Adventures of a Young Man*; an Indian in *Cheyenne Autumn*; a priest in *The Singing Nun*; an arrogant movie star who tries to seduce Shirley MacLaine in *Sweet Charity*; and the circus owner who aides simians on the run Roddy McDowall and Kim Hunter in *Escape From the Planet of the Apes*. In 1977, in a stroke of good fortune, he was cast as the mysterious host of a vacation spot called *Fantasy Island*, first in a television movie and then in a series that ran from 1978 to 1984, making him a star all over again. This led to villain roles in *Star Trek: The Wrath of Khan*, reprising a part he'd done on the television series in the 1960s, and the spoof *The Naked Gun: From the Files of Police Squad!* In 1978 he earned an Emmy Award for his appearance on *How the West Was Won, Part II*. With Bob Thomas he wrote his memories, *Reflections: A Life in Two Words*, published in 1980.

Screen: 1942: El Verdugo de Sevilla; 1943: La Razon de la Culpa; Cinco Fueron Escogidos; 1943: Santa; La Fuga; Fantasia Ranchera; 1944: Cadetes de la Naval; La Hora de la Verdad; Nosotros; 1945: Pepita Jimenez; 1947: Fantasia Rachera; Fiesta; 1948: On an Island With You; The Kissing Bandit; 1949: Neptune's Daughter; Battleground; Border Incident; 1950: Mystery Street; Right Cross; Two Weeks With Love; 1951: Mark of the Renegade; Across the Wide Missouri; 1952: My Man and I; 1953: Sombrero; Latin Lovers; 1954: The Saracen Blade; 1955: A Life in the Balance; 1956: Sombra Verde/Untouched; Three for Jamie Dawn; Queen of Babylon; 1957: Sayonara; 1960: Let No Man Write My Epitaph; 1961: The Black Buccaneer/Rage of the Buccaneers/Pirate Warrior; Desert Warrior (Sp: 1956); 1962: The Reluctant Saint; Hemingway's Adventures of a Young Man; 1963: Love Is a Ball; 1964: Cheyenne Autumn; 1966: The Money Trap; Madame X; The Singing Nun; 1968: Sol Madrid; Blue; 1969: Sweet Charity; 1971: The Deserter; Escape From the Planet of the Apes; 1972: Conquest of the Planet of the Apes; 1973: The Train Robbers; 1976: Won Ton Ton, the Dog Who Saved Hollywood; Joe Panther; 1980: Kino, the Padre on Horseback/Mission to Glory (dtv; filmed 1977); 1982: Star Trek: The Wrath of Khan; 1983: Cannonball Run II; 1988: The Naked Gun: From the Files of Police Squad!; 2002: Spy Kids 2: The Island of Lost Dreams.

NY Stage: 1955: Seventh Heaven; 1957: Jamaica; 1973: Don Juan in Hell.

Select TV: 1955: Cardboard Casanova (sp); 1956: Esteban's Legacy (sp); Broken Arrow (sp); Rhubarb in Apartment 7-8 (sp); Operation Cicero (sp); 1957: Child of Trouble (sp); 1959: Target

for Three (sp); 1960: Jeff McCleod: The Last Reb (sp); Rashomon (sp); 1961: Auld Acquaintance (sp); 1963: The Glass Palace (sp); Epilogue (sp); 1964: The Fantasticks (sp); 1965: In Any Language (sp); 1966: Alice Through the Looking Glass (sp); 1967: The Longest Hundred Miles; To Sleep, Perchance to Dream (sp); 1969: Black Water Gold; The Pigeon; 1970: The Aquarians; 1971: Sarge: The Badge or the Cross; The Face of Fear; The Desperate Mission; 1972: Fireball Forward; 1974: Wonder Woman; The Mark of Zorro; 1976: McNaughton's Daughter; 1977: Fantasy Island; Captains Courageous; 1978: How the West Was Won; Part II; Return to Fantasy Island; 1978–84: Fantasy Island (series); 1985–87: Dynasty II: The Colbys (series); 1994: Heaven Help Us (series).

YVES MONTAND

(Ivo Livi) Born: Monsummano, Italy, October 13, 1921. Raised in France. Died: November 9, 1991.

In France he was one of the top attractions of the postwar era, and, like so many others who made their mark in Europe, he was soon in great demand the world over. There was a certain dry cynicism that made him a solid presence, but it didn't exactly translate well into English, and he was just as often a bore. For someone so frequently branded with a reputation as a hot-blooded Frenchman, he was actually born in Italy, although he left there when he was a child, moving with his family to Marseilles. When he was just 18 he began earning money by singing in nightclubs and cinemas, eventually making his way up to classier establishments, and eventually becoming the lover of singer Edith Piaf. His film debut came in 1946, in a film she was appearing in, *Etoile sans Lumiere*, and he was also seen as a prize-fighter in *L'Idole*. Warner Bros. was impressed enough to sign him to a contract, but he backed out of it. By the early 1950s he was gaining quite a reputation for his singing engagements and did some warbling in the movies *Souvenirs Perdus/Lost Property* and *Paris Chante Toujors*. In 1951 he married actress Simone Signoret, to whom he would remain wed until her death in 1985.

Film stardom came in 1953 with *Le Salaire de la Peur/The Wages of Fear*, a thriller about a group of men transporting a dangerous shipment of nitroglycerine. It became a worldwide success (it came to the U.S. in 1955) and one of the most acclaimed French productions to date. Of the films he made in the immediate years following this triumph, one with Signoret, the French version of *The Crucible*, retitled *Witches of Salem*, and an Italian one with Gina Lollobrigida and Marcello Mastroianni, *Where the Hot Wind Blows!*, were those to receive the widest release elsewhere. By the end of the 1950s he was well enough known, not only in the world of cinema but on the concert circuit, for Hollywood to beckon a second time. This time he agreed, albeit reluctantly, because his English was so poor. For Fox he played a millionaire incognito romancing Marilyn Monroe in *Let's Make Love*, and both his accent and charisma remained impenetrable to most American audiences. Still struggling, he was strangely cast as Lee Remick's seducer in the Southern-set *Sanctuary*; Ingrid Bergman's neglected husband in *Goodbye Again*; and Shirley MacLaine's deceived hubby in the comedy *My Geisha*. It was back to France for a mystery with Signoret, *The Sleeping Car Murder*, and a political thriller, *The War Is Over*, both of which confirmed the consensus that he fared best on home turf.

In between these he was seen in the all-star productions *Is Paris Burning?*, as a sergeant, and the racecar hit *Grand Prix*, as Eva Marie Saint's lover who is killed on the track. There was a romance with Annie Girardot and Candice Bergen, *Live for Life*, and then one of his career peaks, *Z*, another political thriller, this one about an assassination plot, directed by Costa-Gavras. This was one of the most talked-about films of 1969, becoming only the second foreign-language film to ever be nominated for an Oscar for Best Picture (*Grand Illusion*, 31 years earlier, had been the first). It wound up winning in the official Foreign-Language Film category and, more impressively, was a crossover hit, bringing in customers unaccustomed to seeing movies with subtitles. Montand teamed with Costa-Gavras twice more in the early 1970s, for *The Confession*, as Communist leader Arthur London, on trial for treason, and *State of Siege*, once again involving political assassination. Although they drew heavy critical support, the audiences were less entranced this time out. In between Montand did one last American film, *On a Clear Day You Can See Forever*, uncomfortably paired with Barbra Streisand, although he did get to sing the title song.

Despite his high profile as a leading figure of the French cinema, there were several of his films that were not transported to America. Those that were shipped this way included *Tout va Bien*, because Jane Fonda was his co-star; *César and Rosalie*, a love triangle with Romy Schneider and Sami Frey; *Vincent, Francois, Paul and the Others*, about a group of male friends unwinding on the weekend; and *Clair de Femme*, another teaming with Costa-Gavras, but one that found them attempting a romance, albeit a downbeat one. Director Claude Berri gave him a final pair of triumphs with a two-part story, *Jean de Florette* and its follow-up, *Manon of the Spring*. He had the deeply unsympathetic role of a scheming farmer who sets out to destroy Gerard Depardieu. Three years after Signoret's death, Montand's girlfriend gave birth to his only child. In 1992 his autobiography, *You See, I Haven't Forgotten*, was published.

Screen (US releases only): 1954: The Red Inn (narrator); 1955: The Wages of Fear (Fr: 1953); 1957: The Wide Blue Road (US: 2001); 1958: Premier May; Witches of Salem; 1959: Heroes and Sinners/The Heroes Are Tired (Fr: 1955); 1960: Where the Hot Wind Blows! (Fr: 1959); Let's Make Love; 1961: Sanctuary; Goodbye Again; 1962: My Geisha; 1966: The Sleeping Car Murders; Is Paris Burning?; Grand Prix; 1967: The War Is Over/La Guerre est Finie; Live for Life; 1969: The Devil by the Tail; Z; 1970: On a Clear Day You Can See Forever; The Confession; 1972: Cesar and Rosalie; 1973: Tout va Bien; State of Siege; 1975: Delusions of Grandeur (Fr: 1971); 1976: Vincent, Francois, Paul and the Others; 1977: Lovers Like Us/The Savage (Fr: 1975); 1980: Clair de Femme; The Case Against Ferro/Police Python 357 (Fr: 1976); 1983: Choice of Arms (Fr: 1981); 1987: Jean de Florette; Manon of the Spring.

NY Stage: 1959: An Evening With Yves Montand (and dir.); 1961: An Evening With Yves Montand (and dir.).

MARIA MONTEZ

(MARIA AFRICA ANTONIA GARCIA VIDAL DE SANTO SILAS) BORN: BARAHONA, DOMINICAN REPUBLIC, JUNE 6, 1918. DIED: SEPTEMBER 7, 1951.

Her name became synonymous with the exotic Technicolor nonsense cranked out by Universal Pictures during the 1940s, which made Maria Montez one of the reigning figures of cinematic camp. Her accent was thick, her acting a joke, and even her greatest admirers had to admit that Maria Montez couldn't manage much else beyond striking semi-alluring poses while clad in some kind of silly looking sarong or headdress. She traveled to Europe as a teenager,

where she acted with a theater troupe, and then came to America where she took up modeling. This led to a contract in 1941 with Universal, for whom she debuted in a bit part in *Lucky Devils*. Later that same year she was upped to fourth billing for a "B" western, *Boss of Bullion City*, and then became the female center of attention in the tropical island opus *South of Tahiti*, tempting shipwrecked Brian Donlvey. The one that made her name was *Arabian Nights*, the studio's first full Technicolor feature, where, as Scheherazade, she raised one's opinion of co-star Jon Hall's acting. It was a hit and won its share of admirers over the years, kitsch fanciers who overlooked the turgidness of this endeavor. They also found places in their hearts for *White Savage*, the *Arabian Nights* sequel; *Cobra Woman*, which gave fans two Marias for the price of one (as twins); and *Ali Baba and the Forty Thieves* and *Sudan*, both of which co-starred her male equal, Turhan Bey. There was a musical, *Bowery to Broadway*, where her dance number was mostly done by a double; a tale of intrigue and Nazis, *Tangier*; and a western, *Pirates of Monterey*, which brought her association with Universal to an end in 1947. There was a flop, *The Wicked City*, co-starring husband Jean-Pierre Aumont (they had married in 1943), and some foreign films prior to her death of a heart attack at 33.

Screen: 1941: Lucky Devils; The Invisible Woman; Boss of Bullion City; That Night in Rio; Raiders of the Desert; Moonlight in Hawaii; South of Tahiti; 1942: Bombay Clipper; The Mystery of Marie Roget; Arabian Nights; 1943: White Savage/White Captive; 1944: Ali Baba and the Forty Thieves; Cobra Woman; Follow the Boys; Gypsy Wildcat; Bowery to Broadway; 1945: Sudan; 1946: Tangier; 1947: The Exile; Pirates of Monterey; 1948: Siren of Atlantis; 1949: Portrait d'un Assassin (nUSr); 1950: The Wicked City; Sensuality; The Pirate's Revenge/Revenge of the Pirates; 1953: The Thief of Venice (filmed 1950).

GEORGE MONTGOMERY

(GEORGE MONTGOMERY LETZ) BORN: BRADY, MT, AUGUST 29, 1916. ED: UNIV. OF MT. DIED: DECEMBER 12, 2000.

There wasn't much to distinguish George Montgomery from all the other tall and rugged movie males of his era, except for the fact that he always sounded as if he was talking through clenched teeth. Curiously, his school days found him studying interior decorating while dabbling in heavyweight boxing on the side. He went to Los Angeles to find employment doing the former, but wound up being hired as an extra for the Gene Autry western, *The Singing Vagabond*, in 1935. He continued at this while doing double duty as a stunt man, using his real name. In 1940 20th Century-Fox took an interest in him, signing him to a contract, redubbing him George Montgomery and casting him as the second lead in *The Cisco Kid and the Lady*. Upped to the lead, opposite Carole Landis, in *Cadet Girl*, he was officially given the seal of approval by the fan magazines, and the studio decided they'd picked a winner. He was the stoic leading man for Ginger Rogers in *Roxie Hart*, and for Betty Grable in *Coney Island*; and got top billing for *Ten Gentlemen From West Point*, as the hick who enters the famed military academy, and for *Bomber's Moon*, where he and Kent Taylor escaped from a prison camp.

1943 marked not only his entrance into the Army for real but also his much-publicized marriage to singer Dinah Shore (they divorced in 1960). After the war he was back at Fox for another standard musical, *Three Little Girls in Blue*; played the least impressive of the screen's several Philip Marlowes of the 1940s in

The Brasher Doubloon; and ended his stint there in two westerns with the equally nondescript Rod Cameron, *Belle Starr's Daughter* and *Dakota Lil*. After *Davy Crockett — Indian Scout*, in which he played not the legendary backwoodsman, but his cousin, he went to Columbia for more westerns and adventures of the "B" variety, this obviously being his niche. His films for Columbia included *Cripple Creek*, in which he was a government agent posing as an outlaw; *The Pathfinder*, from James Fenimore Cooper's tale and not officially a western though it featured Montgomery in buckskins; *Jack McCall — Desperado*, with the actor as a Southerner in the Union army; *Fort Ti*, which stood out from this batch (literally) because it was in 3-D; and *Masterson of Kansas*, in which Montgomery played Bat.

The offerings kept shrinking further in prestige, and after Columbia he was at Allied Artists for *Canyon River* and *New Day at Sundown*; United Artists for *Huk*, which referred to a group of marauding Phillipinos, and *Toughest Gun in Tombstone*; and Republic (on its last legs) for *Pawnee*. This naturally led to much of the same fare on the small screen, where he starred in the series *Cimarron City* for a brief period. After a cheap reprise of *King Solomon's Mines*, now called *Watusi*, he signed with Warners to direct-produce-write and star in a pair of quickies, *The Steel Claw*, as a Marine who loses a hand, and *Samar*, about a penal colony fighting Spanish colonization. These were followed by similar, even more poorly attended Renaissance man assignments for Commonwealth United, *From Hell to Borneo* and *Guerrillas in Pink Lace*; some foreign-made cheapies; a "topical" 1960s drug film, *Hallucination Generation*; and spokesman duty for Johnson Floor Wax.

Screen: AS GEORGE LETZ: **1935:** The Singing Vagabond; **1937:** Springtime in the Rockies; **1938:** Gold Mine in the Sky; The Lone Ranger (serial; aka feature: Hi-Yo Silver; 1940); Billy the Kid Returns; Come on Rangers; The Old Barn Dance; Under Western Stars; Army Girl; Pals of the Saddle; Santa Fe Stampede; Shine On, Harvest Moon; Hawk of the Wilderness (serial); **1939:** Rough Riders Round-Up; Wall Street Cowboy; Frontier Pony Express; The Mysterious Miss X; I Was a Convict; Southward Ho!; Men on Conquest; The Night Riders; S.O.S. Tidal Wave; The Cisco Kid and the Ladies; Wyoming Outlaw; New Frontier; In Old Monterey; The Arizona Kid; Saga of Death Valley; South of the Border.

AS GEORGE MONTGOMERY: **1940:** Jennie; Star Dust; Young People; Charter Pilot; **1941:** The Cowboy and the Blonde; Accent on Love; Riders of the Purple Sage; Last of the Duanes; Cadet Girl; **1942:** Roxie Hart; Orchestra Wives; Ten Gentlemen From West Point; China Girl; **1943:** Coney Island; Bomber's Moon; **1946:** Three Little Girls in Blue; **1947:** The Brasher Doubloon; **1948:** Lulu Belle; The Girl From Manhattan; Belle Starr's Daughter; **1950:** Dakota Lil; Davy Crockett — Indian Scout; The Iroquois Trail; **1951:** The Sword of Monte Cristo; The Texas Rangers; **1952:** Indian Uprising; Cripple Creek; The Pathfinder; **1953:** Jack McCall — Desperado; Fort Ti; Gun Belt; **1954:** The Battle of Rogue River; The Lone Gun; Masterson of Kansas; **1955:** Seminole Uprising; Robber's Roost; **1956:** Huk; Canyon River; **1957:** Last of the Badmen; New Day at Sundown; Gun Duel in Durango; Street of Sinners; Pawnee; Black Patch; **1958:** Man From God's Country; Toughest Gun in Tombstone; Badman's Country; **1959:** Watusi; King of the Wild Stallions; **1961:** The Steel Claw (and dir.; prod.; co-wr.); **1962:** Samar (and dir.; prod.; co-wr.); **1964:** From Hell to Borneo (and dir.; prod.; wr.); Guerillas in Pink Lace (and dir.; prod.; wr.); **1965:** Battle of the Bulge; **1967:** Bomb at 10:10; Outlaw of Red River/Django the Condemned (nUSr); Hallucination Generation; Hostile Guns; **1968:** Warkill; **1969:** Strangers at Sunrise; **1970:** Satan's

Harvest (and dir.); Ride the Tiger (and dir.; nUSr); **1972:** The Daredevil; **1986:** Dikij Veter/Wild Wind (nUSr).

Select TV: **1955:** The Traveling Salesman (sp); **1956:** Claire (sp); **1957:** The Quiet Stranger (sp); Thousand Dollar Gun (sp); **1958–59:** Cimarron City (series); **1984:** Children's Island (sp).

ROBERT MONTGOMERY

(HENRY MONTGOMERY, JR.) BORN: BEACON, NY, MAY 21, 1904. DIED: SEPTEMBER 27, 1981.

A staple of MGM's studio heyday, Robert Montgomery spent the earlier part of his career looking dapper in a tux, cracking wise, and romancing some of the top leading ladies of the time. Further down the line he dedied he wanted to prove himself capable of worthier things and adopted a more stoic, serious, tough-guy persona, which only went to emphasize that aloof, unsympathetic streak he often possessed. He had originally gone to New York City to make his name as a writer, but ended up acting instead, eventually joining a rep company in Rochester before heading back to Manhattan and a handful of appearances on Broadway. One of them, *Possession*, got him a screen test that impressed MGM, who signed him to a contract in 1929, debuting him among the ensemble of the comedy *So This Is College*, as a football player. His first notable part was in *Untamed*, as Joan Crawford's boyfriend, and then he was teamed with Norma Shearer for the first of several occasions, in one of her hits of the day, *Their Own Desire*. He stood by and watched her marriage collapse while quipping dryly in *The Divorcee*, and similarly downed a lot of drinks while she made up her mind about Neil Hamilton, in *Strangers May Kiss*. In between he played second fiddle to Buster Keaton in *Free and Easy*; had a standout role as a wimpy inmate-turned-stoolie in the Oscar-nominated prison drama *The Big House*; was back with Crawford in one of her "flapper" films, *Our Blushing Brides*; and played the student in love with artists' model Greta Garbo, in one of her lesser vehicles, *Inspiration*. He was finally considered worthy of being Shearer's equal for the fairly faithful but nonetheless uninspired 1931 screen version of Noel Coward's stage favorite, *Private Lives*, and for *Riptide*, as a playboy who tempts her away from Herbert Marshall. Before the latter he was allowed to carry *But the Flesh Is Weak*, as an impoverished playboy living off rich women in London, but went back to taking second billing for *Letty Lynton*, with Crawford again; *Faithless*, with Tallulah Bankhead; *When Ladies Meet*, waiting patiently for Ann Harding to wise up to how much he means to her; and *Another Language*, where one was rooting for John Beal, not Montgomery, to get Helen Hayes in the final reel.

That he was still not making any great strides as a solo attraction was evident though, from *Night Flight*, in which he was part of an all-star cast but billed fifth; *Forsaking All Others*, in which he took a secondary role to Clark Gable; and another batch where the women were the selling point: *Vanessa: Her Love Story*, with Helen Hayes; *Biography of a Bachelor Girl*, with Ann Harding; *No More Ladies*, with Joan Crawford, and *Petticoat Fever*, with Myrna Loy. The studio did give him center stage for *Hide-Out*, where he was right on the mark as a combination Manhattan bon vivant-racketeer, softened by his stay in the country; and *Piccadilly Jim*, which allowed him to do what he did best, excel at light comedy, in this case playing a cartoonist in London. Then it was back to Joan Crawford yet again, in a remake of one that Shearer had done, *The Last of Mrs. Cheyney*, in his umpteenth cheeky playboy role. It was this feeling of running in place that made him ask MGM to purchase the Broadway thriller *Night Must Fall*, as a vehicle for him. As the Irish hired hand who happens to be toting around in his hatbox the head of the woman he has killed, he suggested the right degree of charm with the hint of a screw or two coming unhinged, earning raves and an Oscar nomination for this stagebound piece. Its success did not guarantee great changes and after being lent out to Warners, for *Ever Since Eve*, his home studio reteamed him with his *Night Must Fall* co-star, Rosalind Russell, in *Live, Love and Learn* and *Fast and Loose*, to remind people that they could do comedy as well.

He was in a noble effort about the cure for malaria, *Yellow Jack*, as the platoon commander whose men are suffering from the disease; one of Janet Gaynor's last leads, *Three Loves Has Nancy*; and *Earl of Chicago*, as a gangster inheriting a British title. But none of these did much to convince him that he shouldn't be looking for work elsewhere. Perhaps to placate him Metro let him play crazy again, trying to bump off Ingrid Bergman, in *Rage of Heaven*. That same year, 1941, he teamed nicely with Carole Lombard in director Alfred Hitchcock's fairly forgettable attempt at sophisticated comedy, *Mr. and Mrs. Smith*, then reached another high plateau, over at Columbia, as the saxophone-playing boxer who accidentally ends up in heaven, in *Here Comes Mr. Jordan*. This was one of the best fantasies of its day, a whopping hit, and one that earned Montgomery another Oscar nomination for his wry comical turn. By this point his interests were stretching elsewhere to include presidency of the Screen Actors Guild and military service during World War II. He went from ambulance driver to the U.S. Navy, rising to the rank of lieutenant commander and receiving the Bronze Star in the process.

When he came home to MGM he stayed in military uniform to play the rather stoic torpedo boat commander in *They Were Expendable*, a war movie that really worked when it was focusing on the human element. It was also a pivotal credit in Montomgery's career because he stepped in as director when John Ford took sick during the production. Finding this field very much to his liking, he was eager to do more and got his wish with *Lady in the Lake*, which had the neat gimmick of being seen entirely through detective Philip Marlowe's (Montgomery) eyes. It was his farewell to MGM, but he continued behind the camera, though less successfully, with *Ride the Pink Horse*, at his grimmest in this moody noir; *Once More, My Darling*, in which he played a movie star on whom Ann Blyth has a crush; and *Eye Witness*, a British production in which he was an attorney in London. Sensing that his career on the big screen was reaching an impasse, he decided to concentrate on television, finding great success, serving as host, sometime director, and occasional star of the long-running anthology series *Robert Montgomery Presents*. During the 1950s he also served as television consultant to President Dwight Eisenhower. He returned to Broadway as the director of *The Big Two* (1947), *The Desperate Hours* (1955, for which he won a Tony Award), and *Calculated Risk* (1962). There was also one more directorial credit on the big screen, *The Gallant Hours*, which starred his lifelong friend James Cagney. Around this time he passed the acting baton on to his daughter Elizabeth, who found her fame on the small screen, as the star of the sitcom *Bewitched*.

Screen: 1929: So This Is College; Three Live Ghosts; The Single Standard; Untamed; 1930: Their Own Desire; Free and Easy; The Divorcee; Sins of the Children/The Richest Man in the World; The Big House; Our Blushing Brides; Love in the Rough; War Nurse; 1931: Inspiration; The Easiest Way; Strangers May Kiss; Shipmates; The Man in Possession; Private Lives; 1932: Lovers Courageous; But the Flesh Is Weak; Letty Lynton; Blondie of the Follies; Faithless; 1933: Hell Below; Made on Broadway; When Ladies Meet; Another Language; Night Flight; 1934: Fugitive Lovers; Riptide; The Mystery of Mr. X; Hide-Out; Forsaking All Others; 1935: Vanessa: Her Love Story; Biography of a Bachelor Girl; No More Ladies; 1936: Petticoat Fever; Trouble for Two; Piccadilly Jim; 1937: The Last of Mrs. Cheyney; Night Must Fall; Ever Since Eve; Live, Love and Learn; 1938: The First Hundred Years; Yellow Jack; Three Loves Has Nancy; 1939: Fast and Loose; 1940: Earl of Chicago; Haunted Honeymoon/Busman's Honeymoon; 1941: Mr. and Mrs. Smith; Rage of Heaven; Here Comes Mr. Jordan; Unfinished Business; 1945: They Were Expendable; 1946: Lady in the Lake (and dir.); 1947: Ride the Pink Horse (and dir.); 1948: The Saxon Charm; The Secret Land (voice); June Bride; 1949: Once More, My Darling (and dir.); 1950: Eye Witness/Your Witness (and dir.); 1960: The Gallant Hours (narrator; and dir.).

NY Stage: 1921: The Mask and the Face; 1924: Dawn; 1925: The Complex; The Carolinian; 1926: Bad Habits of 1926; 1928: The High Hatters; Possession.

Select TV: 1950–57: Lucky Strike Theater/Robert Montgomery Presents (series).

GRACE MOORE

(MARY WILLIE GRACE MOORE)
BORN: SLABTOWN, TN, DECEMBER 5, 1901.
DIED: JANUARY 26, 1947.

Back in another time when women with trained voices rated film vehicles, Grace Moore was an opera singer who managed to make the rare crossover from her field to become a movie attraction, albeit a temporary one. Having studied voice in her native Tennessee, she sang in Washington and then in New York, where she was featured in some of Irving Berlin's *Music Box Revue*s. Her 1928 debut at the Metropolitan Opera in *La Bohème* followed, and two years later she had a contract with MGM. The result was a flop, *A Lady's Morals*, a biopic of Jenny Lind, opposite Wallace Beery as P.T. Barnum, and the somewhat better attended *New Moon*, which paired her with Lawrence Tibbett and allowed her to sing "Lover Come Back to Me." Hollywood was sufficiently unimpressed, so she went back to Broadway and had a hit with *The Du Barry*, making the movies reconsider their opinion of her drawing power. Columbia got her and put her into *One Night of Love*, as an aspiring singer who falls in love with her temperamental voice teach (Tulio Carmanati) while trilling her way from Italian cafes to the Met. Somehow this feather-light concoction filled cinemas in large numbers, making opera more accessible to moviegoers in a way that it hadn't before. It also earned Moore a surprise Oscar nomination and made her a darling of the critics, though seen today it is difficult to fathom what exactly made her performance and the picture worthy of this degree of praise. The studio followed this with *Love Me Forever*, with Leo Carrillo; *The King Steps Out*, with Franchot Tone, which was actually more in the style of operetta rather than straight opera; *When You're in Love*, with Cary Grant, in which she was supposed to be an Australian and even sang "Minnie the Moocher" at one point, as a way of letting her hair down; and *I'll Take Romance*, in which she was kidnapped by Melvyn Douglas. The law of diminishing returns was to be expected, and she'd gained a reputation for being difficult on the set, causing her and Columbia to part company. There was one more movie, *Louise*, made in France, after which she returned to the stage. She published her autobiography, *You're Only Human Once*, in 1946, the year before her death in a plane crash in Copenhagen. In 1953 Kathryn Grayson played her in an all-too typical, superficial biopic, *So This Is Love*.

Screen: 1930: A Lady's Morals; New Moon; 1934: One Night of Love; 1935: Love Me Forever; 1936: The King Steps Out; 1937: When You're in Love; I'll Take Romance; 1939: Louise.

NY Stage: 1920: Hitchy Koo; 1922: Above the Clouds; 1923: Music Box Revue; 1924: Music Box Revue; 1932: The Du Barry.

ROGER MOORE

BORN: LONDON, ENGLAND, OCTOBER 14, 1927.
ED: RADA.

The cinema had pretty much proclaimed the suavely handsome Roger Moore a light-weight addition to the medium when, late in his career, he stepped into the hottest series in movie history and became the bona fide movie star he was supposed to have become two decades before. Dropping out of school, he took an apprentice position at a cartoon studio before he was convinced that his good looks could get him extra work in movies. As a result he found such employment in notable British productions like *Caesar and Cleopatra* and *Perfect Strangers/Vacation From Marriage*. This encouraged him to enroll at the Royal Academy of Dramatic Arts to learn his craft and hopefully make a living at it. Following service in the British Army, he acted on radio and in rep, with some modeling assignments on the side. In London's West End he was seen as part of the crew in *Mister Roberts* and as one of the stars of *The Little Hut*, then decided to try his luck in New York. There he racked up a number of television credits and made his Broadway bow in a 1953 one-nighter, *A Pin to See the Peepshow*, and then returned to London where he accepted an offer from MGM. For them he debuted as a tennis player who has his eye on Elizabeth Taylor in *The Last Time I Saw Paris*, then moved up to playing King Henry II, lover of Lana Turner, in one of those opulent and empty-headed costume pictures of the 1950s, *Diane*. Leaving MGM, he gave television another shot, knocking off one season in the title role of *Ivanhoe* before accepting a contract with Warners. They put him in two forgettable romantic dramas, *The Miracle*, as the Duke of Wellington's nephew, and *The Sins of Rachel Cade*, as an American in the RAF; and a "B" western, *Gold of the Seven Saints*.

Television finally found him a role that brought him some genuine attention, debonair adventurer Simon Templar in the British series version of *The Saint*, reprising the character George Sanders had played several times on the big screen. The program aired first in syndication before being picked up by NBC in 1967. Moore not only directed some episodes but also had part ownership in the series through Bamore Ltd., making him a wealthy man. Through that company he made two flop theatrical features, *Crossplot* and *The Man Who Haunted Himself*, which once again seemed to indicate that he was not cut out for film stardom. That theory changed when he was selected to replace Sean Connery as the screen's most famous man of adventure, James Bond. He debuted in the role in 1973's *Live and Let Die*, and its tremendous success assured the nervous producers that the vast audience for this series had accepted him in the part. There followed *The Man With the Golden Gun*; *The Spy Who Loved Me*, the biggest hit of his Bonds; *Moonraker*; *For Your Eyes Only*, perhaps the best of the Moore offerings; *Octopussy*, which was released the same year that Connery returned to the part in a rival Bond production, thereby drawing the inevitable comparisons that were not in Moore's favor to say the least; and *A View to a Kill*. Moore brought a lighter, self-parodying quality to the role that certain Bond purists never appreciated, and by 1985 he

had grown weary of the part, handing it over to the more serious Timothy Dalton. During his lucrative run as Secret Agent 007 he tried his devil-may-care approach on such other cheeky adventure films as *Escape From Athena*; *ffolkes*, as a counterterrorist who enjoys needlepoint; and *The Sea Wolves*, bantering with David Niven, whom he had long ago supported in *The King's Thief*. There was next to no interest in these from the public, indicating that it was strictly the Bond name they were going to see. In later years Moore was seen very infrequently, popping up as the villain in *The Quest*, with Jean-Claude Van Damme, to name one of the higher profile jobs. For Paramount's 1997 big screen adaptation of *The Saint* he supplied a vocal cameo.

Screen: 1945: Vacation From Marriage/Perfect Strangers; Caesar and Cleopatra; 1946: Gaiety George; Piccadilly Incident; 1949: Paper Orchid; The Gay Lady/Trottie True; 1954: The Last Time I Saw Paris; 1955: Interrupted Melody; The King's Thief; Diane; 1959: The Miracle; 1961: The Sins of Rachel Cade; Gold of the Seven Saints; The Rape of the Sabines/Romulus and the Sabines; 1962: No Man's Land/Un Branco di Vigliacchi (nUSr); 1969: Crossplot; 1970: The Man Who Haunted Himself; 1973: Live and Let Die; 1974: Gold; The Man With the Golden Gun; 1975: That Lucky Touch; 1976: Shout at the Devil; Street People; 1977: The Spy Who Loved Me; 1978: The Wild Geese; 1979: Escape to Athena; Moonraker; 1980: ffolkes/North Sea Hijack; 1981: Sunday Lovers; The Sea Wolves; For Your Eyes Only; The Cannonball Run; 1983: Octopussy; Curse of the Pink Panther; 1984: The Naked Face; 1985: A View to a Kill; 1988: The Magic Snowman (voice); 1990: Bullseye! (dtv); 1991: Fire, Ice and Dynamite (dtv); 1992: Bed and Breakfast (filmed 1989); 1996: The Quest; 1997: The Saint (voice); 1998: Spice World; 2001: The Enemy (nUSr).

NY Stage: 1953: A Pin to See the Peepshow.

Select TV: 1956: A Murder Is Announced (sp); This Happy Breed (sp); 1957: The Taggar Light (sp); The Remarkable Mr. Jerome (sp); 1957–58: Ivanhoe (series); 1959–60: The Alaskans (series); 1960–61: Maverick (series); 1963–69: The Saint (series); 1971–72: The Persuaders (series); 1976: Sherlock Holmes in New York; 1995: The Man Who Wouldn't Die (and co-prod.); 1999: D.R.E.A.M. Team; The Dream Team (series).

TERRY MOORE

(HELEN LUELLA KOFORD)
BORN: LOS ANGELES, CA, JANUARY 7, 1929.

Apparently the pouty and petite Terry Moore had trouble finding the right screen persona, judging from the four different stage names she sported. The daughter of actress Luella Bickmore, she was modeling as a child before acting on radio and with the Pasadena Playhouse. She made her motion picture debut in 1940 at 20th Century-Fox, billed under her real name, way down the cast list of *Maryland*. After awhile she tried the name Judy Ford, appearing in three films with this billing, including *Gaslight*, in which she was the younger version of the character played by Ingrid Bergman. It was then back to Helen Koford before PRC made her Jan Ford for her first significant role, in the teen hot-rod melodrama, *The Devil on Wheels*. She finally settled on Terry Moore for her leading role in the Columbia comedy *The Return of October*, wherein she thought her uncle was reincarnated as a horse. Possessing a down to earth quality that made her seem comfortable with animals, she went to RKO for her most famous role, the proud and protective owner of the giant gorilla in the fantasy *Mighty Joe Young*, after which she appeared opposite a dancing squirrel in *The Great Rupert*, for filmmaker George Pal. After performing girlfriend duty for Mickey Rooney (*He's a Cockeyed Wonder*) and Robert Cummings (*The Barefoot Mailman*), she got a plum dramatic role, as the young boarder whose shapeliness drives Burt Lancaster wild in *Come Back, Little Sheba*, earning an Oscar nomination, though she was certainly overshadowed in the acting department not only by Lancaster but by the great Shirley Booth. From there she went over to 20th Century-Fox for one of director Elia Kazan's lesser efforts, *Man on a Tightrope*, as Fredric March's wayward daughter; donned a bathing suit to swim *Beneath the 12-Mile Reef*; and played Tyrone Power's love interest in the CinemaScope adventure *King of the Khyber Rifles*. None of these proved her to be much more than a decorative presence, nor did they indicate that there was much justification for that Oscar nod.

She slipped down into support for *Daddy Long Legs*, as Leslie Caron's roommate, and for *Peyton Place*, where she was pretty much lost among the vast cast, as the heroine's friend, Betty Anderson. Elsewhere she was the waitress in the cult "B" *Shack Out on 101*, and was back doing standard girlfriend stuff for Audie Murphy in *Cast a Long Shadow*. She foundered in the sensationalistic happenings of *Platinum High School*, and in *Why Must I Die?*, as a singer accused of murder, in this tale that clearly hoped to repeat the success of the similar *I Want to Live*. Youth was on her side, so she came off looking like one of the kids in three of those A.C. Lyles westerns of the 1960s that specialized in hiring aging performers past their bankable prime, *Black Spurs*, *Town Tamer*, and *Waco*. There were the expected junk movies, followed by a brief return to the spotlight in 1984, when she received a settlement from the Howard Hughes estate, having claimed to be briefly wed to the reclusive billionaire (as indicated in her book *Beauty and the Billionaire*), and with her centerfold spread in *Playboy*, presumably done to prove that a woman could still look desirable in her 50s. There was an odd credit, *Beverly Hills Brats*, a flat, poorly distributed comedy that she also co-produced and co-wrote, and a fleeting cameo in the remake of *Mighty Joe Young*.

Screen: AS HELEN KOFORD: 1940: Maryland; 1944: Sweet and Low Down; Since You Went Away; 1945: Son of Lassie; 1946: Shadowed; 1948: Summer Holiday.

AS JUDY FORD: 1942: My Gal Sal; A-Haunting We Will Go; True to Life; 1944: Gaslight.

AS JAN FORD: 1947: The Devil on Wheels.

AS TERRY MOORE: The Return of October; 1949: Mighty Joe Young; 1950: The Great Rupert; He's a Cockeyed Wonder; Gambling House; 1951: Two of a Kind; Sunny Side of the Street; The Barefoot Mailman; 1952: Come Back, Little Sheba; 1953: Man on a Tightrope; Beneath the 12-Mile Reef; King of the Khyber Rifles; 1955: Daddy Long Legs; Shack Out on 101; Postmark for Danger/Portrait of Alison; 1956: Between Heaven and Hell; 1957: Bernardine; Peyton Place; 1959: A Private's Affair; Cast a Long Shadow; 1960: Platinum High School; Why Must I Die?; 1965: Black Spurs; Town Tamer; City of Fear; 1966: Waco; 1968: A Man Called Dagger; 1972: The Daredevil; 1978: Death Dimension/The Kill Factor; 1982: Double Exposure; 1985: Hellhole; 1986: W.A.R.: Women Against Rape/Death Blow (dtv); 1989: American Boyfriends (dtv); Beverly Hills Brats (and co-wr.; prod.); Father's Day (dtv); Going Overboard (dtv); 1998: Second Chances (dtv); Mighty Joe Young; 1999: Final Voyage (dtv); 2000: Stagefest (dtv).

Select TV: 1953: It Happened in a Pawn Shop (sp); 1955: Scandal at Peppernut (sp); 1956: The Moneymaker (sp); The Shadow Outside (sp); 1957: The Clouded Image (sp); 1958: The Man Who Asked for a Funeral (sp); 1962–63: Empire (series); 1965: The Highest Fall of All (sp); 1970: Quarantined; 1976: Smash-Up on Interstate 5; 1989: Jake Spanner: Private Eye;

1991: Marilyn and Me.

VICTOR MOORE

BORN: HAMMONTON, NJ, FEBRUARY 24, 1876.
DIED: JULY 23, 1962.

Victor Moore spoke like a man at the end of his rope, with a quavering whine that suggested he might explode or burst into tears at any minute. And it is that voice that stays most clearly in the minds of those who remember this pudgy, balding comical performer with either fondness or disdain. He was a vaudevillian who started his stage career in the mid-1890s and continued on the boards (mainly in an act with his wife, Emma Littlefield) for another two decades before making his motion picture bow in the starring role of *Chimmie Fadden*, which fared well enough to rate a sequel. There was also a soaper called *The Clown*, which was of interest because it served as the basis for the later, better known *The Champ*. After three years of an unremarkable film career, Moore went back to the stage, eventually making his way to Broadway, where he lent dependable support in such musicals as *Oh Kay!* and *Funny Face*, the latter with Fred and Adele Astaire. In between these assignments he did a series of short subjects and then came to Paramount to team with Helen Kane in two moldy musicals of the early 1930s, *Dangerous Nan McGrew* and *Heads Up*. Broadway called again, and he returned to a series of hits, starting with the Gershwins' *Of Thee I Sing*, as the dumbfounded vice-presidential candidate Throttlebottom; its sequel, *Let 'em Eat Cake*; Cole Porter's classic *Anything Goes*, as Public Enemy #13, Moonface Martin; another for Porter, *Leave It to Me!*; and *Louisiana Purchase*. In between these he was at Universal for two minor offerings, *Romance in the Rain*, as a magazine publisher, and the all-star *Gift of Gab*, then did the sidekick bit usually reserved for Edward Everett Horton in one of the best of the Astaire-Rogers vehicles, *Swing Time*, nicely teamed with Helen Broderick.

RKO kept him around for a pair of top-billed roles opposite Broderick, in *We're on the Jury*, playing a character named Pudgy Beaver, and *Meet the Missus*, bumbling (of course) in and out of trouble while in Atlantic City. For a break in the routine he went over to Paramount for what turned out to be his most fulfilling serious role, the senior citizen who must face being separated from wife Beulah Bondi, in the sensitive *Make Way for Tomorrow*. After that it was back to Broderick and RKO, albeit in support, for the musicals *She's Got Everything* and *Radio City Revels*. After his stage triumph in *Louisiana Purchase*, Paramount signed him up for their 1941 film version, but most of Irving Berlin's songs were disposed of on the way to the screen and the result was little more than a second rate Bob Hope comedy. That company kept him on for some other films, including *Star Spangled Rhythm*, as the gateman at Paramount Pictures who pretends to be the head of the studio to impress a bunch of soldiers; *Riding High*, as Dorothy Lamour's dad; and *Duffy's Tavern*, as part of the storyline of this all-star revue. At MGM he participated in an annoying skit with Edward Arnold called "Pay the Two Dollars" in *Ziegfeld Follies*; had a fun moment singing in a barbershop quartet with Jack Benny, Fred Allen, and Don Ameche in *It's in the Bag*; and teamed with Lamour again for one of the segments of the unsuccessful multi-story film *On Our Merry Way*. There was a brief return to Broadway for a revival of *On Borrowed Time*, and a television version of *Louisiana Purchase* before he came back to movies to play the justice of the peace who causes the furor that sets the plot in motion in *We're Not Married!*, and to help Marilyn Monroe get her toe unstuck from the tub tap in *The Seven Year Itch*.

Screen: 1915: Chimmie Fadden; Chimmie Fadden Out West; Snobs; 1916: The Race; The Best Man; The Clown; 1917: Oh! U-Boat; Faint Heart and Fair Lady; 1918: Bungalowing; Moving; 1925: The Man Who Found Himself; 1930: Dangerous Nan McGrew; Heads Up; 1934: Romance in the Rain; Gift of Gab; 1936: Swing Time; Gold Diggers of 1937; 1937: We're on the Jury; Make Way for Tomorrow; Meet the Missus; The Life of the Party; She's Got Everything; 1938: This Marriage Business; Radio City Revels; 1941: Louisiana Purchase; 1942: Star Spangled Rhythm; 1943: The Heat's On; Riding High; True to Life; 1944: Carolina Blues; 1945: It's in the Bag!; Duffy's Tavern; 1946: Ziegfeld Follies; 1947: It Happened on 5th Avenue; 1948: A Miracle Can Happen/On Our Merry Way; 1949: A Kiss in the Dark; 1952: We're Not Married!; 1955: The Seven Year Itch.

NY Stage: 1906: Forty-Five Minutes from Broadway; 1907: The Talk of New York; 1911: The Happiest Night of His Life; 1925: Easy Come, Easy Go; 1926: Oh Kay!; 1927: Allez-Oop!; Funny Face; 1928: Hold Everything; 1929: Me for You; Heads Up; 1930: Prince Charming; 1931: She Lived Next to the Firehouse; 1932: Of Thee I Sing; 1933: Let 'em Eat Cake; 1934: Anything Goes; 1938: Leave It to Me!; 1940: Louisiana Purchase; 1942: Keep 'em Laughing; 1945: Hollywood Pinafore; 1946: Nellie Bly; 1953: On Borrowed Time; 1957: Carousel.

Select TV: 1951: Louisiana Purchase (sp); 1953: A Time for Heroes (sp); 1955: Stage Door (sp).

AGNES MOOREHEAD

BORN: CLINTON, MA, DECEMBER 6, 1906.
ED: UNIV. OF WI, AADA. DIED: APRIL 30, 1974.

Biddies, crones, grandes dames, intimidating moms, and spinster aunts; if the role called for someone with the air of a disapproving school marm, Agnes Moorehead fit the bill. An intelligent, accomplished actress, she was often an effortless scene stealer, though on more than one occasion she went a little too far to make an impression, lapsing into mugging, maybe as a way of compensating for weak material, maybe because it was better to be remembered than woven into the background. While still young, she performed with the St. Louis Municipal Opera Co., then returned to theater after a spell of teaching English, making her Broadway debut in 1929, in Scarlet Pages. During the 1930s she was heard frequently on the radio and even toured in vaudeville before joining Orson Welles's Mercury Theater. Under his direction she made her 1941 movie debut, as the mother of Citizen Kane, in one brief sequence, supporting the decision that her son be taken away to live in wealth. Staying with Welles, she played the spinster aunt whose composure begins to slowly unravel in The Magnificent Ambersons, a brilliant performance that established her as a character player of the highest caliber and earned her her first Oscar nomination. After one more for Welles, Journey Into Fear, she and Eugene Pallette made a charmingly offbeat couple in the Damon Runyon drama The Big Street, after which she was signed to a contract by MGM. For them she was just as implausible trying to be Chinese as the rest of the cast of Dragon Seed, and sported an unconvincing French accent for Mrs. Parkington, which nonetheless copped her a second Oscar nod. For Selznick she was the pretentious friend of Claudette Colbert, who gets on that lady's bad side, in the homefront soap Since You Went Away; was Fredric March's spinster sister with a viable reason to hate Nazi nephew Skippy Homeier in the silly Tomorrow, the World!, for UA; then went back to MGM to play a humorless farm wife in Our Vines Have Tender Grapes, and another spinster, romanced by Frank Morgan, in Summer

Holiday, the charming musical version of O'Neill's Ah, Wilderness! For producer Walter Wanger she acted under a ton of old-age makeup to play a centenarian in The Lost Moment, which was Hollywood's version of the unfilmable Henry James novel The Aspern Papers.

At Warners she nabbed two outstanding parts, the murderous bitch in Dark Passage, making one of the movies' great dramatic exits through a plate glass window, and the no-nonsense aunt of Jane Wyman in Johnny Belinda, resulting in Oscar mention number three. She continued to hop around from studio to studio, playing the mother of James Stewart (although he was only two years younger than she; not the last time such a case would occur) in The Stratton Story; giving a very understated performance as the understanding warden in the best of all the women-in-prison pictures, Caged; going off the deep end as the emotionally distraught mom of suicidal Richard Basehart in Fourteen Hours; and staring down a group of gleeful musicians at one point in Show Boat, as the crabby Parthy. She was back with Wyman in three of that leading lady's popular soaps of the 1950s, The Blue Veil, as one of her wealthy employers; Magnificent Obsession, as her nurse; and All That Heaven Allows, as a socially conscious country-club lady. Getting silly she was John Wayne's nagging Asian mama in the opulently stupid The Conqueror, and Jerry Lewis's overbearing maw in Pardners; followed by more and more moms in Raintree County (Montgomery Clift); The True Story of Jesse James (Robert Wagner); and How the West Was Won (Debbie Reynolds).

There was at least a single starring role, even if it was in an old-fashioned horror movie, in The Bat, as a mystery writer experiencing creaking doors at an old mansion. Back with Jerry Lewis she was a devious department store owner in Who's Minding the Store?, then had a wild role as a dirt trash housekeeper in Hush…Hush, Sweet Charlotte, overacting with such brio that it brought her one final Oscar nomination. Around that time she took on the television role that would make her famous to a whole new generation, Endora, the grand witch mother of Elizabeth Montgomery in the hit sitcom Bewitched, which she did for eight seasons. Also on the tube she was awarded with an Emmy for guesting on The Wild Wild West. On radio she made a lasting impression as the star of one of the most famous presentations in that medium, Sorry, Wrong Number, as the bed-ridden lady who overhears her own murder being plotted.

Screen: 1941: Citizen Kane; 1942: The Magnificent Ambersons; Journey Into Fear; The Big Street; 1943: The Youngest Profession; Government Girl; 1944: Jane Eyre; Dragon Seed; Since You Went Away; The Seventh Cross; Mrs. Parkington; Tomorrow, the World!; 1945: Keep Your Powder Dry; Our Vines Have Tender Grapes; Her Highness and the Bellboy; 1947: Dark Passage; The Lost Moment; 1948: Summer Holiday; The Woman in White; Stations West; Johnny Belinda; 1949: The Stratton Story; The Great Sinner; Without Honor; 1950: Caged; 1951: Captain Blackjack; Fourteen Hours; Show Boat; The Blue Veil; The Adventures of Captain Fabian; 1952: The Blazing Forest; 1953: The Story of Three Loves (The Jealous Lover); Scandal at Scourie; Main Street to Broadway; Those Redheads From Seattle; 1954: Magnificent Obsession; 1955: Untamed; The Left Hand of God; 1956: All That Heaven Allows; Meet Me in Las Vegas; The Conqueror; The Revolt of Mamie Stover; The Swan; Pardners; The Opposite Sex; 1957: Raintree County; The True Story of Jesse James; Jeanne Eagles; The Story of Mankind; 1959: Night of the Quarter Moon; Tempest; The Bat; 1960: Pollyanna; 1961: Twenty Plus Two; Bachelor in Paradise; 1962: Jessica; 1963: How the West Was Won; Who's Minding the Store?; 1964: Hush…Hush, Sweet Charlotte; 1966: The Singing Nun; 1971:

What's the Matter With Helen?; 1972: Dear Dead Delilah; 1973: Charlotte's Web (voice).

NY Stage: 1929: Scarlet Papers; 1951: Don Juan in Hell; 1962: Lord Pengo; 1973: Don Juan in Hell (revival); Gigi.

Select TV: 1953: Lullaby (sp); 1955: Roberta (sp); 1956: Teacher (sp); 1957: The Life You Save (sp); A Tale of Two Cities (sp); 1958: Rapunzel (sp); The Dungeon (sp); 1960: Trial by Fury (sp); 1964–72: Bewitched (series); 1966: Alice Through the Looking Glass (sp); 1969: The Ballad of Andy Crocker; 1971: Marriage: Year One; The Strange Monster of Strawberry Cove; Suddenly Single; 1972: Rolling Man; Night of Terror; Frankenstein: The True Story; 1974: Rex Harrison Presents Stories of Love (sp).

POLLY MORAN

(Pauline Theresa Moran) Born: Chicago, IL, June 28, 1883. Died: January 25, 1952.

Shapeless, rambunctious Polly Moran lived to make people laugh, subtlety be damned, and made her biggest impact during a brief period when she and the more enduring Marie Dressler were an unofficial team. A vaudevillian at 15, she eventually signed up with Mack Sennett for some two-reelers, the best known of which featured her as a western character, Sheriff Nell, which she had originally done onstage. There followed some more shorts at National Film Corporation of America and cbc Film Corp., but she never achieved the heights of popularity of many of the other silent film comedians and decided to return to vaudeville. Her movie career was revived in 1927 when MGM decided to team her with Dressler in the comedy *The Callahans and the Murphys* (Moran was Mrs. Murphy), which drew the wrath of the Irish for its unflattering stereotypes and became a box-office failure. Moran, however, became a regular supporting presence at the studio in such features as Lon Chaney's *London After Midnight* and Garbo's *The Divine Woman*. There was something about Moran and Dressler's pairing that had delighted the executives despite their initial lack of public interest, and they were back together again for *Bringing Up Father*, in 1928, and for one sequence of the all-star omnibus *The Hollywood Revue of 1929*. After lending support in *Chasing Rainbows*, the women finally scored their audience hit as the leads of *Caught Short*, in 1930, followed by their two biggest moneymakers, *Reducing* and *Politics*, the appeal of which is singularly absent to modern sensibilities. With *Prosperity* the novelty of these fleshy women knocking about had worn out its welcome, and Moran left MGM. There was a blatant attempt by Republic Pictures to duplicate the Dressler-Moran teaming by putting the latter alongside the marvelous Alison Skipworth in *Two Wise Maids* and *Ladies in Distress*, but the team didn't catch on. Moran went into semi-retirement, popping up on occasion for character roles, such as the housekeeper who takes to the witness stand in *Adam's Rib*, and the mother of Gloria De Haven in *The Yellow Cab Man*.

Screen (shorts): 1914: Ambrose's Little Hatchet; 1915: Their Social Splash; A Favorite Fool; He Painted Her; The Hunt; A Rascal of Wolfish Ways or A Polished Villain; Hogan Out West; A Hash House Fraud; Those College Girls/His Better Half; 1916: The Village Blacksmith; A Bath House Blunder; By Stork Alone; His Wild Oats; Madcap Ambrose; Vampire Ambrose; Love Will Conquer; Because He Loved Her; Safety First Ambrose; By Stork Delivery; 1917: Her Fame and Shame; Cactus Nell; Taming Target Center; His Naughty Thought; Sheriff Nell; She Needed a Doctor; His Uncle Dudley; Roping Her Romeo; The Pullman Bride; 1918: Sheriff Nell's Tussle; The Battle Royal; Saucy Madeline; Two Tough Tenderfeet; She Loved Him Plenty; 1928:

Movie Chatterbox; 1929: Dangerous Females; 1930: The Rounder; Crazy House; 1931: Jackie Cooper's Christmas; The Stolen Jools; 1936: Oh Duchess; 1938: Sailor Maid; 1949: Prize Maid.

Screen (features): 1921: Skirts; Two Weeks with Pay; The Affairs of Anatol; 1923: Luck; 1926: The Scarlet Letter; 1927: The Callahans and the Murphys; The Enemy; The Thirteenth Hour; Buttons; London After Midnight; 1928: The Divine Woman; Rose-Marie; Detectives; Bringing Up Father; A Little Bit of Fluff; Telling the World; While the City Sleeps; Beyond the Sierras; Shadows of the Night; Show People; Honeymoon; 1929: Speedway; China Bound; The Hollywood Revue of 1929; The Unholy Night; So This Is College; Hot for Paris; 1930: Chasing Rainbows; The Girl Said No; Caught Short; Those Three French Girls; Way Out West; Way for a Sailor; Remote Control; Paid; 1931: Reducing; Guilty Hands; It's a Wise Child; Politics; 1932: The Passionate Plumber; Prosperity; 1933: Alice in Wonderland; 1934: Down to Their Last Yacht; Hollywood Party; 1937: Two Wise Maids; 1938: Ladies in Distress; Red River Range; 1939: Ambush; 1940: Meet the Missus; Tom Brown's Schooldays; 1941: Petticoat Politics; 1949: Red Light; Adam's Rib; 1950: The Yellow Cab Man.

KENNETH MORE

Born: Gerrards Cross, Buckinghamshire, England, September 20, 1914. Died: July 12, 1982.

One of Britain's favorite actors during the 1950s, Kenneth More, through no discernible tricks or showy techniques, slid comfortably between lighthearted comedy and straightforward drama, be he a suave lover, a smirking clown, or a stoic man of iron will hiding an inner torment. A rare actor who could lay claim to having been a professional fur-trapper, he did just that in Canada before returning to England to do stagehand and understudy work at London's Windmill Theatre. There were bit roles in movies, starting in 1935, and then legit theater in Newcastle. The war interrupted his acting pursuits, but he resumed them in London, in 1946, with *And No Birds Sing*, and on television. Beginning with *School for Secrets/Secret Flight*, in 1946, there were several small movie assignments, followed by a successful return to the boards with *The Way Things Go*, in 1950. Because of that, his movie roles got somewhat larger with *The Clouded Yellow*, as a Secret Service man; *Brandy for the Parson*, as a brandy smuggler; and *The Yellow Balloon*, as the dad of a wronged boy. There were also supporting parts in two films that featured Hollywood stars working in England, *No Highway in the Sky* (James Stewart) and *Never Let Me Go* (Clark Gable), which meant these were among More's more highly visible jobs in the U.S. market during the early 1950s.

A second West End hit, *The Deep Blue Sea*, gave his career a major boost and was instrumental in his being cast in the comedy that finally put him on top, *Genevieve*, an adorable concoction about two couples participating in a motor race (Genevieve was More's car). It was one of the key British comedies of its day, winning that country's equivalent of the Oscar and giving More a chance to show just how good he could be at this sort of playful lark. He managed to follow it with another big offering of the mid-1950s, *Doctor in the House*, a bright romp that went on to spawn a whole slew of less sophisticated sequels, none of which featured More. There was also the film adaptation of *The Deep Blue Sea*, which won him further raves as the lover of miserably unhappy Vivien Leigh, despite the fact that the general consensus was that the piece did not work on the big screen. Nonetheless he was on a roll and landed two of his best-remembered parts, as the butler who takes charge after a shipwreck in *The Admirable Crichton/Paradise Lagoon*, and Officer Lightoller in *A Night to Remember*, a compact and gripping re-creation of the sinking of the Titanic that was unanimously rated as far superior to the 1953 Hollywood version and became one of the more frequently viewed British films with the passing years. America sent him Jayne Mansfield to play alongside of in a lukewarm western spoof, *The Sheriff of Fractured Jaw*, and Lauren Bacall for the adventure tale *North West Frontier/Flame Over India*. In between these he was in the remake of *The 39 Steps*, which was acceptable for those unfamiliar with the Hitchcock original. Bigger than any of these was 1960s *Sink the Bismarck!*, with More at his most convincingly militaristic, tracking the famed German battleship in what turned out to be one of the most popular British films to play in America during this time.

The 1960s had arrived and the British new-wave cinema with it, and perhaps More was thought of as being part of the old guard, for his box-office appeal in his native land began to slow down with his roles in *Man in the Moon*; *The Greengage Summer/Loss of Innocence*, as a thief on the run who attracts teenager Susannah York; and most disappointing for him, *The Comedy Man*, as a second-rate performer. Turning 50, he went back to the theater where his credits included a musical version of *Crichton*, now called *Our Man Crichton*, and then to television where he scored a major success as one of the stars of the most acclaimed British mini-series of its day, *The Forsyte Saga*. Movies now offered him character parts, and he was a drunk in *Dark of the Sun/The Mercenaries*; the Kaiser in the all-star curio *Oh! What a Lovely War*; the Ghost of Christmas Present in the musical *Scrooge*, singing "I Like Life" with Albert Finney; and Lord Chamberlain in another revision of a familiar tale told in song, *The Slipper and the Rose*, which was a variation on *Cinderella*. The rest of his film career consisted of a few insignificant offerings, including a barely seen Disney release, *Unidentified Flying Oddball*, in which he played King Arthur. The Kenneth More Theatre opened in Ilford, Essex, in 1974. He wrote three memoirs, *Happy Go Lucky* (1959), *Kindly Leave the Stage* (1965), and *More or Less* (1978).

Screen: 1935: Look Up and Laugh; 1936: Carry on London; Windmill Revels; 1946: School for Secrets/Secret Flight; 1948: Scott of the Antarctic; 1949: Man on the Run; Now Barabbas Was a Robber; Stop Press Girl; 1950: Morning Departure/Operation Disaster; Chance of a Lifetime; The Clouded Yellow; 1951: The Franchise Affair; No Highway in the Sky; Appointment With Venus/Island Rescue; 1952: Brandy for the Parson; The Yellow Balloon; 1953: Never Let Me Go; Genevieve; Our Girl Friday/The Adventures of Sadie; 1954: Doctor in the House; 1955: The Man Who Loved Redheads (narrator); Raising a Riot; The Deep Blue Sea; 1956: Reach for the Sky; 1957: The Admirable Crichton/Paradise Lagoon; 1958: A Night to Remember; The Sheriff of Fractured Jaw; Next to No Time!; 1959: The 39 Steps; Flame Over India/Northwest Frontier; 1960: Sink the Bismarck!; Man in the Moon; 1961: Loss of Innocence/The Greengage Summer; 1962: Some People; We Joined the Navy; The Longest Day; 1963: The Comedy Man; 1968: Dark of the Sun/The Mercenaries; 1969: Fraulein Doktor; Oh! What a Lovely War; Battle of Britain; 1970: Scrooge; 1976: The Slipper and the Rose; 1977: Where Time Began (nUSr); 1978: Leopard in the Snow; 1979: Unidentified Flying Oddball/The Spaceman and King Arthur.

Select TV: 1963: Talking Sport (sp); 1967: The White Rabbit (ms); 1967–68: The Forsyte Saga (series); 1974: Father Brown (series); 1978: An Englishman's Castle; 1981: A Tale of Two Cities.

JEANNE MOREAU

BORN: PARIS, FRANCE, JANUARY 23, 1928.
ED: PARIS CONSERVATORY OF DRAMA.

In the postwar era there was probably no other French import who induced such rapturous critical praise as Jeanne Moreau. Her trademark downcast mouth and the hauntingly suggestive gaze of her eyes made her the reigning queen of that smoldering, European sensuality that made the art house circuits light up in those days. Upon graduating from acting school she immediate found success onstage, which led to her film debut in 1949, in *Dernier Amour*, in support of Annabella. She was steadily employed during the 1950s in such movies as *Docteur Schweitzer*; *Touchez Pas au Grisbi*; *Secrets d'Alcove/The Bed*, with Richard Todd; and *Les Hommes en Blanc*. But it was not until late in the decade that the Americans began importing her movies, starting with *Julietta*, in which she played the fiancée of Jean Marais. It had played in France in 1953 but did not find a home in the U.S. until four years later. The one that really got Moreau-fever percolating in the world market was director Louis Malle's *The Lovers*, where she was an unfulfilled wife who finds solace with other men. There followed her first notable international effort, *5 Branded Women*, as one of the crew-cut Yugoslavian ladies who become resistance fighters. The film was a bore, but it didn't matter because she was creating a further stir with some others that were making their way across the Atlantic, *Frantic/Elevator to the Gallows*, a thriller also made with Malle, with Moreau once again playing an unfaithful wife, and *Les Liaisons Dangereuses*, which set the classic tale of sexual destruction in the modern era.

Moreau had three more major assignments, *Moderator Cantabile*, this time acting opposite the biggest French male star of the period, Jean-Paul Belmondo; *La Notte*, again projecting disillusionment with her marriage, her husband being Marcello Mastroianni, in this moody drama that received high praise because it was directed by another critic's fave, Michelangelo Antonioni; and perhaps her best-loved movie of this time, *Jules and Jim*, at her most disarming, as the factious girl bouncing back and forth between best friends Henri Serre and Oskar Werner. Everywhere one turned there was Moreau in roles of varying sizes: in a reteaming with Belmondo, *Banana Peel*; in her first genuine American film, the episodic *The Victors*, very effective as a terrified war widow seeking comfort from soldier Eli Wallach; and in three for Orson Welles, *The Trial*, *Falstaff*, and *The Immortal Story*. She appeared in the all-star *The Yellow Rolls-Royce*, cheating on husband Rex Harrison; made her one try at the adventure market in *The Train*, helping Burt Lancaster escape from the Nazis; and had the inevitable pairing with the other big French lady of the 1960s, Brigitte Bardot, in *Viva Maria!*, which promised far more than it delivered.

A pair of movies for director Tony Richardson, *Mademoiselle*, in which she was a teacher/pyromaniac, and *The Sailor from Gibraltar*, where she played an oversexed woman searching for her lover, were declared pretentious, but she did score another hit with the Francois Truffaut thriller *The Bride Wore Black*, taking revenge on the men who killed her husband. There was a big British flop, *Great Catherine*, from the Shaw play, and then her first movie in a long time to not make it outside France, *Le corps de Diane*. She was Lee Marvin's love interest in the western *Monte Walsh*, but since most of her next batch never made it to the U.S., it seemed as if she'd been away for quite some time when she showed up as an ex-con bedding Gerard Depardieu and Patrick Dewaere in the art house hit *Going Places*.

In Hollywood she was once again part of an all-star cast, in *The Last Tycoon*, as a fading actress, then showed a whole new side of her talents, directing, writing, and starring in *Lumiere*, again as a movie star. By this point she was beginning to display a lived-in look and an increasingly eccentric manner that only made her more fascinating, to some. She took on another directorial-writing job, *L'Adolescente*, though this time staying exclusively behind the scenes in this tale of a young girl developing a crush on an older man. Little was heard of her during the 1980s except for *Querelle*, a bizarre piece of homoerotica in which she played a bar owner-singer, so it was not until she had a supporting role in the 1991 hit *La Femme Nikita*, that she was once again highly visible on this side of the Atlantic. That one seemed to help in revitalizing interest in her, and she made for a colorful presence as a nun in *Map of the Human Heart*; the flamboyant family friend who tries to dissuade betrothed Lena Headey from going through with her marriage in *The Summer House*; an author examining her relationships, past and present, in *The Proprietor*; and Clare Danes's loving grandma, a Holocaust survivor, in *I Love You, I Love You Not*. Her husbands included director William Friedkin to whom she was wed from 1977 to 1980.

Screen (US releases only): 1957: Julietta (Fr: 1953); 1959: The Lovers; 1960: 5 Branded Women; 1961: Frantic/Elevator to the Gallows (Fr: 1958); La Notte; Les Liaisons Dangereuses (Fr: 1959); 1963: The Trial; Jules and Jim; The Victors; 1964: Bay of Angels (Fr: 1963); Moderator Cantabile (Fr: 1960); The Yellow Rolls-Royce; 1965: Banana Peel (Fr: 1963); The Train; Eva (Fr: 1962); Diary of a Chambermaid; Viva Maria!; 1966: Mademoiselle; 1967: Falstaff/Chimes at Midnight; The Sailor From Gibraltar; 1968: The Bride Wore Black; Great Catherine; The Oldest Profession; 1969: The Immortal Story; The Fire Within (Fr: 1963); 1970: Monte Walsh; Alex in Wonderland; 1974: Le Petit Théâtre de Jean Renoir (Fr: 1971); Going Places; 1976: French Provincial (Fr: 1974); The Last Tycoon; Lumiere (and dir.; wr.); 1977: Mr. Klein; 1981: Your Ticket Is No Longer Valid; Joanna Francesca (Fr: 1973); 1982: The Trout; 1983: Querelle; The Wizard of Babylon; 1984: Heat of Desire; 1988: Calling the Shots; 1991: La Femme Nikita; Until the End of the World; 1992: The Lover (narrator); Alberto Express (Fr: 1990); 1993: Map of the Human Heart; The Summer House/The Clothes in the Wardrobe; 1995: The Old Lady Who Walked in the Sea (Fr: 1993); 1996: The Proprietor; 1997: I Love You, I Love You Not; 1998: Ever After.

RITA MORENO

(ROSITA DOLORES ALVERIO) BORN: HUMACAO, PUERTO RICO, DECEMBER 11, 1931. RAISED IN NEW YORK, NY.

An erratic career with some juicy high points and a fiery nature that was rarely exploited to the fullest degree, would not naturally lead you to think that Rita Moreno was one of only two performers to win the four top entertainment awards in competition: Oscar, Tony, Emmy, and Grammy. This was an achievement she was quick to point out, albeit innacurately, claiming it as exclusively hers, overlooking the fact that Helen Hayes was the first to accomplish this feat. Unlike Hayes she became a familiar motion picture "name" without ever actually having had a single film built expressly around her. She studied dance since childhood but made her theatrical debut in a dramatic part (billed as Rosita Moreno) in the 1945 Broadway production of *Skydrift*. Five years later she made her first movie, an independent quickie, *So Young, So Bad*, as a juvenile delinquent who commits

suicide after a sadistic matron cuts off her hair. Moving up to bigger budgets, MGM hired her play a Tahitian island girl in *Pagan Love Song*, since they figured her ethnicity qualified her to play a variety of nationalities. She was called on for UA's "B" movie, *The Ring*, since this was a rare film of the time to focus on Mexican-Americans, in this case a story involving the prizefighting biz, while her participation in the classic musical *Singin' in the Rain* was confined to a few peripheral moments as a starlet. There were the expected Indian parts, in *The Yellow Tomahawk*, as a squaw named Honey Bear, and in *Seven Cities of Gold*; after which she landed the important role of Yul Brynner's mistress, Tuptim, who suffers because she loves another, in *The King and I*, which gave her, her greatest exposure to date. This did little for her, however, as her next assignment was a cheap rendering of *The Deerslayer*, after which she seemed to be stepping backwards, appearing in another juvenile delinquent drama, *This Rebel Breed*, cast as a pregnant teen, despite the fact that Moreno was on the brink of turning 30.

Her place in movie history was assured when she was chosen over Broadway original Chita Rivera to play Anita in the 1961 film version of *West Side Story*. Despite her vocals being dubbed (as they were in *The King and I*) she was a thrilling presence, exuberantly dancing to "America" and dramatically doing the strongest work in the film, earning an Academy Award as Best Supporting Actress. Alas, there wasn't much anyone wanted to do with a Puerto Rican actress, Oscar or not, so she wound up in two Warners programmers, *Samar* and *Cry Battle*, before heading to Broadway for *The Sign in Sidney Brustein's Window*. She resurfaced on the big screen as Marlon Brando's kidnapping accomplice in *The Night of the Following Day*, one of that actor's many disasters of the period; played a stripper in *Marlowe*; and then had a startling bit, performing fellatio on Jack Nicholson at the end of *Carnal Knowledge*.

In 1971 she became a cast member of the children's educational program *The Electric Company*, and it was for her work on a recorded version of this series that she earned her Grammy. The Tony Award came in 1975 for her wild rendering of no-talent bathhouse entertainer Googie Gomez in the farce *The Ritz*. She repeated the part in the 1976 movie version, proving to be one of the better things about this flat transfer. Later, an often over-enthusiastic and extremely well-preserved Moreno was seen on screen as a low-class Philadelphian in *Happy Birthday, Gemini*, a shrill adaptation of a long-running Broadway comedy, *Gemini*; Jack Weston's undeniably Italian wife in *The Four Seasons*; Darnell Martin's hyper mom in *I Like It Like That*; a dance instructor in *Angus*; and Carl Reiner's stuck-up wife in *Slums of Beverly Hills*. She and Ben Gazzara did manage to secure leading roles in *Blue Moon*, a very minor production about an aging couple, but she was better known around that time for appearing as a nun in the controversial cable series *Oz*. Her Emmy Awards came for guesting on *The Muppet Show* (1977) and on *The Rockford Files* (1978).

Screen: AS ROSITA MORENO: 1950: So Young, So Bad.

AS RITA MORENO: The Toast of New Orleans; Pagan Love Song; 1952: The Fabulous Senorita; The Ring; Singin' in the Rain; Cattle Town; 1953: Ma and Pa Kettle on Vacation; Latin Lovers; Fort Vengeance; El Alamein; 1954: Jivaro; The Yellow Tomahawk; Garden of Evil; 1955: Untamed; 1956: Seven Cities of Gold; The Lieutenant Wore Skirts; The King and I; The Vagabond King; 1957: The Deerslayer; 1960: This Rebel Breed; 1961: Summer and Smoke; West Side Story; 1963: Cry of Battle; 1969: The Night of the Following Day; Popi; Marlowe; 1971: Carnal Knowledge; 1976: The Ritz; 1978: The Boss's Son; 1980: Happy Birthday, Gemini; 1981: The Four Seasons; 1991: Age Isn't Everything/Life in the Food Chain (dtv); 1993: Italian Movie (dtv); 1994: I Like It Like That; Carmen Miranda: Bananas Is My Business; 1995:

Angus; **1998:** Slums of Beverly Hills; **1999:** Carlo's Wake (dtv); **2000:** Blue Moon; **2001:** Piñero.

NY Stage: AS ROSITA MORENO: **1945:** Skydrift.

AS RITA MORENO: **1964:** The Sign in Sidney Brustein's Window; **1970:** Gantry; Last of the Red Hot Lovers; **1974:** The National Health; **1975:** The Ritz; **1981:** Wally's Cafe; **1985:** The Odd Couple.

Select TV: **1952:** Saint and Senorita (sp); **1953:** The Cat With the Crimson Eyes (sp); **1954:** Wonderful Day for a Wedding (sp); **1956:** Broken Arrow (sp); **1957:** The Daughter of Mata Hari (sp); **1959:** The Stone (sp); **1960:** Alas Babylon (sp); El Bandito (sp); **1970–76:** The Electric Company (series); **1979:** Anatomy of a Seduction; **1981:** Evita Peron; **1982:** Portrait of a Showgirl; Working (sp); **1982–83:** 9 to 5 (series); **1989–90:** B.L. Stryker (series); **1991:** Top of the Heap (series); **1994–95:** The Cosby Mysteries (series); **1995:** The Wharf Rat; **1997–2003:** Oz (series); **1998:** The Spree; **1999:** Resurrection; The Rockford Files: If It Bleeds…It Leads; **2002:** American Family (series).

DENNIS MORGAN

(STANLEY MORNER) BORN: PRENTICE, WI, DECEMBER 30, 1909. DIED: SEPTEMBER 7, 1994.

A fixture at Warners during the 1940s, friendly-faced Dennis Morgan was a singer foremost but wasn't groomed to stay exclusively in the musical genre, proving himself a pleasant addition to light comedies, straight drama, westerns, and even war movies. A one-time radio announcer, he did some acting with stock companies and even dabbled in opera before making his movie debut in 1936 (under his real name) in *I Conquer the Sea!*, starring as a whaling harpoonist, of all things, in a cheapie made for a company called Academy Pictures Distributing. After that he did bits and supporting parts (sometimes as Stanley Morner, sometimes as Richard Stanley, if billed at all), including *Navy Blue and Gold*, as a lieutenant; *Piccadilly Jim*, as a band singer; and, most curiously, *The Great Ziegfeld*, standing before the spectacular revolving staircase, mouthing "A Pretty Girl Is Like a Melody" while Allan Jones sang the vocals. His two most significant roles during this period were in *Song of the City* and *Mama Steps Out*, in the latter appearing as a vocalist pursued by Betty Furness. In 1939 he was signed by Warner Bros., who promptly changed his name to Dennis Morgan and decided to groom him for bigger things by featuring him as the lead in some "B's" like *Waterfront*, in which he was a longshoreman; *No Place to Go*, with Morgan letting his crotchety dad move in with him; and *Tear Gas Squad*, which allowed him to sing "When Irish Eyes Are Smiling" *and* join the police force. Between these leads he was seen in more lavish fare like *The Fighting 69th*, as part of the very Irish cast of this James Cagney vehicle, and, most important of all, *Kitty Foyle*, borrowed by RKO to play the man whom Ginger Rogers marries only to find unhappiness.

That movie's success was instrumental in raising Morgan's status, so Warners pushed him into "A" assignments with *Affectionately Yours*, a flop comedy with Merle Oberon; *Captains of the Clouds*, in which he received second billing to Cagney; another important one, *In This Our Life*, where he played the husband Bette Davis callously plucks away from sister Olivia de Havilland; and *The Hard Way*, in which he really clicked playing an entertainer, paired off with Jack Carson. It was time to start fully utilizing the singing Morgan, and so he was part of the story line that connected all the guest stars together in *Thank Your Lucky Stars*, warbling Frank Loesser's catchy "I'm Ridin' for a Fall," among others. He appeared in *The Desert Song*, the creaky operetta updated to include Nazis, and in *Shine On, Harvest*

Moon, playing the co-writer of that song, Jack Norworth. His next films, the standard war picture *God Is My Co-Pilot*, in which he portrayed real-life Flying Tigers hero Col. Robert Lee Scott, and the slight comedy with the cheerful title, *Christmas in Connecticut*, where he played a war hero entertained by Barbara Stanwyck, fared better at the box office.

In the postwar era, Warners definitely decided to concentrate on Morgan the vocalist, and they put him into a whole pile of musicals that, unfortunately, had plots between the songs, such as *The Time, the Place and the Girl*, which gave him a pleasant song, "A Gal in Calico;" *My Wild Irish Rose*, where he played Chauncey Olcott, composer of the title tune and others Irish ditties like it that were, after all, the sort of things Morgan put across best; *Two Guys from Texas*, in which he and Carson had a cute number called "I Wanna Be a Movie Cowboy;" and *It's a Great Feeling*, which had both him and Carson playing themselves in an all-star tour of the Warners backlot. The 1950s arrived, and his drawing power wasn't sufficient enough for the studio to keep him around after such forgettable items as *Painting the Clouds With Sunshine* and *Cattle Town*. After leaving them he did some programmers and a short-lived TV series, *21 Beacon Street*, before retiring to devote his interest to the American Cancer Society. Like many stars long absent from the movie scene, he was called back to make a guest appearance in the negligible spoof *Won Ton Ton, the Dog Who Saved Hollywood*, appearing near the start of the film as a tour guide.

Screen: AS STANLEY MORNER: **1936:** I Conquer the Sea!; Suzy; The Great Ziegfeld; Piccadilly Jim; Old Hutch; **1937:** Song of the City; Mama Steps Out; Navy Blue and Gold.

AS RICHARD STANLEY: **1938:** Men With Wings; King of Alcatraz; **1939:** Illegal Traffic; Persons in Hiding.

AS DENNIS MORGAN: **1939:** Waterfront; The Return of Dr. X; No Place to Go; **1940:** The Fighting 69th; Three Cheers for the Irish; Tear Gas Squad; Flight Angels; River's End; Kitty Foyle; **1941:** Affectionately Yours; Bad Men of Missouri; Kisses for Breakfast; **1942:** Captains of the Clouds; In This Our Life; Wings of the Eagle; The Hard Way; **1943:** Thank Your Lucky Stars; The Desert Song; **1944:** The Very Thought of You; Hollywood Canteen; Shine On, Harvest Moon; **1945:** God Is My Co-Pilot; Christmas in Connecticut; **1946:** One More Tomorrow; Two Guys from Milwaukee; The Time, the Place and the Girl; **1947:** Cheyenne; My Wild Irish Rose; Always Together; **1948:** To the Victor; Two Guys From Texas; One Sunday Afternoon; **1949:** It's a Great Feeling; The Lady Takes a Sailor; **1950:** Perfect Strangers; Pretty Baby; **1951:** Raton Pass; Painting the Clouds With Sunshine; **1952:** This Woman Is Dangerous; Cattle Town; **1955:** Pearl of the South Pacific; The Gun That Won the West; **1956:** Uranium Boom; **1968:** Rogue's Gallery; **1976:** Won Ton Ton, the Dog Who Saved Hollywood.

Select TV: **1953:** Atomic Love (sp); **1954:** Open Season (sp); **1955:** Not Captain Material (sp); Celebrity (sp); Stage Door (sp); **1959:** 21 Beacon Street (series); **1963:** The Old Man and the City (sp).

FRANK MORGAN

(FRANCIS PHILIP WUPPERMAN) BORN: NEW YORK, NY, JUNE 1, 1890. DIED: SEPTEMBER 18, 1949.

For those who know him only as the Wizard of Oz, it should be pointed out that that particular role was just one of many in a successful two-decade career in which Frank Morgan was among the foremost character actors in Hollywood. Although he could do drama, comedy was his forte, and he had his own brand of patented shtick that he raised to some kind of high art, jabbering his lines as if caught in a lie, mumbling little asides to reassure himself and often punctuating them with a titter of laughter and the tag "uh…yes." The younger brother of actor Ralph Morgan, he knocked about in odd jobs that even included a stint as a cowboy before he entered vaudeville. This led to legit work and his Broadway bow in 1914, in *A Woman Killed With Kindness*, some tours, and then his motion picture debut in 1915, in *The Suspect*. There were 12 more feature films over the next four years before he went back to the theater, where his credits included *Seventh Heaven* and *Gentlemen Prefer Blondes*, with some movies on the side like *The Man Who Found Himself*, which featured brother Ralph. Because of his success as the ditzy king in Broadway's *Rosalie*, he was signed to a contract by Paramount, who presented him in his talkie debut, *Queen High*, in 1930, starring alongside another brilliant practitioner in the art of comic stammering, Charlie Ruggles, the two playing bickering garter manufacturers. There was another important role, in *Laughter*, as the well-meaning but dull millionaire husband of unfaithful Nancy Carroll, after which the contract was ended when he went back to Broadway to appear with Fred Astaire in *The Band Wagon*.

Returning to Hollywood, he was at his most uncharacteristically serious as the husband on trial for murdering Gloria Stuart in *The Kiss Before the Mirror*, and played a thinly disguised version of New York mayor Jimmy Walker in the Rodgers and Hart musical *Hallelujah, I'm a Bum* before joining the roster at MGM, in 1933, remaining under contract with that company until his death 16 years later. They made him a drunk in *The Nuisance*, and then gave him one of his best straight roles, as the philandering publisher who strings along both Ann Harding and Myrna Loy in the very sophisticated *When Ladies Meet*. He starred as a vaudevillian in the interminable *Broadway to Hollywood* and showed just how likable he could be, even as a no-gooder, playing Jean Harlow's selfish dad in *Bombshell*. Fox borrowed him to play the birdbrained Duke of Florence in *Affairs of Cellini*, which was just about the peak of the fumbling-bumbling Morgan style (he'd done the role on Broadway in 1923 when the piece was called *The Firebrand*), and he ended up earning an Oscar nomination in the Best Actor category. RKO gave him top billing for *By Your Leave*, as a businessman facing a midlife crisis, while his home lot followed suit, moving him up to the top of the cast list for *The Perfect Gentleman*, as a money-squandering major who decides to mend his careless ways, and for *Beg, Borrow or Steal*, as a con artist pretending to be an aristocrat for his daughter's benefit. It was, however, with his supporting work, playing varying buffoons, affable flirts, and men of weak will, that he impressed most, including parts in Universal's *The Good Fairy*; *Naughty Marietta*, as the governor; *Saratoga*; and *Rosalie*, repeating his Broadway role. In *Port of Seven Seas* he was the older man who winds up marrying the woman of his dreams, Maureen O'Sullivan, knowing she doesn't love him, and then he finished off the decade in the role (or roles) that would give him movie immortality, *The Wizard of Oz*, replacing a stubborn W.C. Fields, who couldn't come to terms with MGM.

As the 1940s began, there were still plenty of worthy parts to come, starting with *The Shop Around the Corner*, in which he was outstanding as the storeowner tormented by his wife's indiscretions. Ever busy, he supported Fred Astaire in *Broadway Melody of 1940*; James Stewart and Margaret Sullavan in the ultra-serious anti-Nazi piece *The Mortal Storm*, as a professor; and Clark Gable in *Boom Town*. As a lead he was a downtrodden pet shop owner, who faces all sorts of bad luck, in *The Ghost Comes Home*; a washed-up vaudevillian trying to break into radio in *Hullabaloo*; a do-gooder falsely accused of murder in *Washington Melodrama*;

and a con man trying to pass himself off as *The Wild Man of Borneo*. Metro handed him a real showcase in their otherwise wobbly adaptation of John Steinbeck's *Tortilla Flat*. As a simple, dog-loving peasant, Morgan, hidden behind a bushy gray beard, gave a restrained and beautiful performance, and was just about the only cast member to make an acceptable crack at a Spanish accent. The great acclaim for this most beloved of character actors was further solidified by an Oscar nomination in the supporting category. That was followed by another of his finest, most-subdued performances, as the old telegraph operator who hides his pain in drink in *The Human Comedy*, after which he was Irene Dunne's dad in a big hit, *The White Cliffs of Dover*; Fred Astaire's fellow con in *Yolanda and the Thief*; and proved that he was one of the few performers who could hold his own next to the cinema's most famous canine in *Courage of Lassie*. There was no other actor more suited to play the drunken uncle, who constantly disappoints devoted Agnes Moorehead, as he did in *Summer Holiday*, the charming musical remake of *Ah, Wilderness!*, and he kept right on working, busier than ever, playing the king in *The Three Musketeers*, James Stewart's devoted buddy in *The Stratton Story*, a gambler in *Any Number Can Play*, and a fire chief in *Key to the City*. He'd just started playing Buffalo Bill in *Annie Get Your Gun* when he died of a heart attack. Louis Calhern replaced him in the film, but his absence in the movie industry left an unfillable void.

Screen: AS FRANCIS WUPPERMAN: 1916: The Suspect.

AS FRANK MORGAN: 1916: The Daring of Diana; 1917: Light Darkness; A Modern Cinderella; That Girl Philippa; Who's Your Neighbor?; A Child of the Wild; Baby Mine; Raffles; the Amateur Cracksman; 1918: The Knife; At the Mercy of Men; 1919: Gray Towers Mystery; The Golden Shower; 1924: Manhandled; Born Rich; 1925: The Man Who Found Himself; The Crowded Hour; Scarlet Saint; 1927: Love's Greatest Mistake; 1930: Queen High; Dangerous Nan McGrew; Fast and Loose; Laughter; 1932: Secrets of the French Police; The Half-Naked Truth; 1933: The Billion Dollar Scandal; Hallelujah, I'm a Bum; Luxury Liner; The Kiss Before the Mirror; Reunion in Vienna; The Nuisance; When Ladies Meet; Best of Enemies; Broadway to Hollywood; Bombshell; 1934: The Cat and the Fiddle; Success at Any Price; Sisters Under the Skin; Affairs of Cellini; A Lost Lady; There's Always Tomorrow; The Mighty Barnum; By Your Leave; 1935: The Good Fairy; Enchanted April; Naughty Marietta; Escapade; I Live My Life; The Perfect Gentleman; 1936: The Great Ziegfeld; The Dancing Pirate; Trouble for Two; Piccadilly Jim; Dimples; 1937: The Last of Mrs. Cheyney; The Emperor's Candlesticks; Saratoga; Rosalie; Beg, Borrow or Steal; 1938: Paradise for Three; Port of Seven Seas; The Crowd Roars; Sweethearts; 1939: Broadway Serenade; The Wizard of Oz; Henry Goes Arizona; Balalaika; 1940: Broadway Melody of 1940; The Shop Around the Corner; The Mortal Storm; Hullabaloo; The Ghost Comes Home; Boom Town; 1941: Keeping Company; Washington Melodrama; The Wild Man of Borneo; Honky Tonk; The Vanishing Virginian; 1942: Tortilla Flat; White Cargo; 1943: The Human Comedy; A Stranger in Town; Thousands Cheer; 1944: The White Cliffs of Dover; Casanova Brown; 1945: Yolanda and the Thief; 1946: Courage of Lassie; Lady Luck; The Cockeyed Miracle; The Great Morgan; 1947: Green Dolphin Street; 1948: Summer Holiday; The Three Musketeers; 1949: The Stratton Story; Any Number Can Play; The Great Sinner; 1950: Key to the City.

NY Stage: 1914: A Woman Killed With Kindness; Mr. Wu; 1915: Under Fire; Under Sentence; 1918: Rock-a-Bye Baby; 1919: My Lady Friends; 1920: Her Family Tree; 1921: The White Villa; The Triumph of X; The Dream Maker; 1922: Seventh Heaven; 1923:

The Lullaby; The Firebrand; 1926: A Weak Woman; Gentlemen Prefer Blondes; 1927: Puppets of Passion; Hearts Are Trumps; Tenth Avenue; 1928: Rosalie; 1929: Among the Married; The Amorous Antic; 1930: Topaez; 1931: The Band Wagon; 1932: Hey Nonny Nonny!

HARRY MORGAN

(HARRY BRATSBURG) BORN: DETROIT, MI, APRIL 10, 1915. ED: UNIV. OF CHICAGO.

So dependable he was often taken for granted, Harry Morgan (formerly Henry Morgan — he graciously changed it in the late 1950s to avoid confusion with the radio-TV celebrity of the same name) seemed to be around forever in films and on television, hardly ever taking center stage but quietly lending support with his somewhat sour-faced expression and disgruntled voice. Opting for acting over a life as a salesman, he ended up in a production of *The Petrified Forest*, in Mt. Kisco, NY, that starred Frances Farmer, who got him involved with the Group Theatre. He was featured in their landmark production of *Golden Boy*, which led to a contract with 20th Century-Fox in 1942. They cast him in a whole slew of secondary parts, notably as Henry Fonda's silent riding partner in the most majestic of westerns, *The Ox-Bow Incident*. After Fox he could be seen as Charles Laughton's nasty little bodyguard in *The Big Clock*; Edward G. Robinson's neighbor in *All My Sons*; the town cripple in *Madame Bovary*; an ex-fighter in *Dark City*, which prophetically faced him off with future TV co-star Jack Webb; a man accused of kidnapping a black girl in *The Well* (a key role); Audrey Totter's second husband, who accuses nanny Jane Wyman of kidnapping, in *The Blue Veil*; and the town banker in *High Noon*. In 1954 he did the loyal pal part to perfection, tickling the ivories as Chummy McGregor in one of the big movies of the year, *The Glenn Miller Story*, and started his run as one of the most ubiquitous of television regulars with the first of his 11 series, *December Bride*. When he wasn't seen on TV he was back at the movies, presiding over the court in *Inherit the Wind*; sitting around a campfire portraying General Grant in the all-star *How the West Was Won*; taunting John Wayne in *The Shooting*; or lending his affably crabby presence to Disney comedies like *The Barefoot Executive* and *Charley and the Angel*. On TV he filled Ben Alexander's old shoes in the 1967 revival of *Dragnet*, playing Officer Bill Gannon, a role he would reprise in the 1987 Dan Aykroyd motion picture spoof, and found perhaps his greatest small-screen fame as the deadpan Colonel Potter on the long-running *M*A*S*H*, for which he won an Emmy in 1980.

Screen: AS HENRY MORGAN: 1942: The Loves of Edgar Allan Poe; The Omaha Trail; To the Shores of Tripoli; Orchestra Wives; Crash Dive; A-Haunting We Will Go; 1943: Crash Dive; The Ox-Bow Incident; Happy Land; 1944: Wing and a Prayer; Roger Touhy — Gangster; The Eve of St. Mark; Gentle Annie; 1945: A Bell for Adano; State Fair; 1946: It Shouldn't Happen to a Dog; Dragonwyck; Johnny Comes Flying Home; Somewhere in the Night; From This Day Forward; 1947: The Gangster; 1948: Race Street; The Big Clock; The Saxon Charm; All My Sons; Yellow Sky; Moonrise; 1949: Red Light; Down to the Sea in Ships; Strange Bargain; Holiday Affair; Madame Bovary; 1950: Outside the Wall; The Showdown; Dark City; 1951: Appointment with Danger; The Blue Veil; Belle le Grand; When I Grow Up; The Well; The Highwayman; Scandal Sheet; 1952: My Six Convicts; Big Jim McLain (narrator); Boots Malone; Bend of the River; High Noon; What Price Glory?; Apache War Smoke; Stop, You're Killing Me; Toughest Man in Arizona; 1953: Thunder Bay; Torch

Song; Arena; Champ for a Day; 1954: The Glenn Miller Story; The Forty-Niners; About Mrs. Leslie; Prisoner of War; 1955: The Far Country; Not as a Stranger; Strategic Air Command; 1956: The Bottom of the Bottle; Backlash; Star in the Dust; The Teahouse of the August Moon; 1957: Under Fire.

AS HARRY MORGAN: 1959: It Started With a Kiss; 1960: The Mountain Road; Inherit the Wind; Cimarron; 1963: How the West Was Won; 1965: John Goldfarb, Please Come Home; 1966: Frankie and Johnny; What Did You Do in the War, Daddy?; 1967: The Flim-Flam Man; 1969: Support Your Local Sheriff!; 1970: Viva Max!; 1971: The Barefoot Executive; Scandalous John; Support Your Local Gunfighter; 1972: Snowball Express; 1973: Charley and the Angel; 1975: The Apple Dumpling Gang; 1976: The Shootist; 1978: The Cat From Outer Space; 1979: The Apple Dumpling Gang Rides Again; 1986: The Flight of the Dragon (voice; dtv); 1987: Dragnet; 1996: Wild Bill: Hollywood Maverick; 1998: Family Plan (dtv); 1999: Crosswalk (nUSr).

NY Stage: AS HARRY BRATSBURG: 1937: Golden Boy; 1939: The Gentle People; My Heart's in the Highlands; Thunder Rock; 1940: Night Music; Heavenly Express; 1941: The Night Before Christmas; Hello Out There.

Select TV: 1954–59: December Bride (series); 1960–62: Pete and Gladys (series); 1963–64: The Richard Boone Show (series); 1965–65: Kentucky Jones (series); 1967–70: Dragnet (series); 1969: Dragnet; 1970: But I Don't Want to Get Married; 1971: The Feminist and the Fuzz; Ellery Queen: Don't Look Behind You; 1971–72: The D.A. (series); 1972: Hec Ramsey: The Century Turns; 1972–74: Hec Ramsey (series); 1974: Sidekicks; 1975: The Last Day (narrator); 1975–83: M*A*S*H (series); 1977: The Magnificent Magical Magnet of Santa Mesa; Exo-Man; 1978: Maneaters Are Loose!; Murder at the Mardi Gras; Kate Bliss and the Ticker Tape Kid; The Bastard; 1979: Backstairs at the White House (ms); Roots: The Next Generations (ms); The Wild Wild West Revisited; You Can't Take It With You (sp); Better Late Than Never; 1980: Roughnecks; Scout's Honor; More Wild Wild West; 1981: Rivkin: Bounty Hunter; 1983: Agatha Christie's Sparkling Cyanide; 1983–74: AfterM*A*S*H (series); 1986: Blacke's Magic (series); 1987: You Can't Take It With You (series); 1989: The Incident; 1992: Against Her Will: An Incident in Baltimore; 1994: Incident in a Small Town.

PATRICIA MORISON

(EILEEN PATRICIA MORISON) BORN: NEW YORK, NY, MARCH 19, 1914.

With her blazingly wide eyes, pale skin, and raven hair, Patricia Morison cut a striking figure in her decade-long period of Hollywood employment but seldom carried any project of note, having to wait until she returned to Broadway to achieve her greatest fame. Daughter of a part-time playwright-actor, William Morison (a.k.a. Norman Rainey), she studied at the Neighborhood Playhouse, then made her Broadway bow in *Growing Pains*, in 1933. Five years later her performance in *The Two Bouquets* caught the eye of a Paramount talent scout, and she was signed up by that studio, who gave her a showy role, as a social climber, in a "B" film, *Persons in Hiding*. Despite being giving the lead in one of the company's more lavish 1940 releases, the Technicolor romance-adventure *Untamed*, with Ray Milland, she was, for the most part, relegated to their less-prestigious fare, including *The Roundup* and *A Night in New Orleans*. After being shunted into a supporting role in some Dorothy Lamour hokum, *Beyond the Blue Horizon*, she went elsewhere, but things didn't improve. The "A" films, like *The*

Song of Bernadette and *Without Love*, hardly spotlighted her, while there was little to be said for the "B's" like *Hitler's Madman*, with Morison as a valiant Czech villager; a Monogram musical, *Silver Skates*; and *Tarzan and the Huntress*, where she got Johnny Weissmuller's dander up because she was out to trap some critters for a zoo. The Sherlock Holmes entry *Dressed to Kill* gave her a chance to drip venom as the villainess, but her role as Victor Mature's wife in *Kiss of Death* was completely edited out of the final print. Luckily the New York theater had a plump part waiting for her, and she found her niche in musical history, playing actress Lilli Vanessi and her stage alter-ego, *The Taming of the Shrew's* Kate, in *Kiss Me Kate*, where she got to introduce Cole Porter's "So in Love," among others. Though she showed up as George Sand in the Franz Liszt biopic *Song Without End*, she stuck almost exclusively to stage and television in her later years, finding the fulfillment she never got from her employment in the movies.

Screen: 1939: Persons in Hiding; I'm From Missouri; The Magnificent Fraud; 1940: Rangers of Fortune; Untamed; 1941: The Roundup; Romance of the Rio Grande; One Night in Lisbon; 1942: Night in New Orleans; Beyond the Blue Horizon; Are Husbands Necessary?; 1943: Silver Skates; The Song of Bernadette; Where Are Your Children?; Hitler's Madman; Calling Dr. Death; The Fallen Sparrow; 1945: Lady on a Train; Without Love; 1946: Danger Woman; Dressed to Kill; 1947: Tarzan and the Huntress; Song of the Thin Man; Queen of the Amazons; 1948: Sofia; The Return of Wildfire; The Prince of Thieves; 1960: Song Without End; 1976: Won Ton Ton, the Dog Who Saved Hollywood.

NY Stage: 1933: Growing Pains; 1938: The Two Bouquets; 1944: Allah Be Praised!; 1948: Kiss Me Kate; 1954: The King and I; 1965: Kiss Me Kate (revival).

Select TV: 1950: Rio Rita (sp); 1951: Light Up the Sky (sp); 1952: The Cases of Eddie Drake (series); 1953: The Man in the Box (sp); The Ladies on His Mind (sp); 1956: Dream (sp); The Trophy (sp); 1958: Kiss Me Kate (sp); 1963: The Secrets of Stella Crozier (sp); 1985: Mirrors.

ROBERT MORLEY

Born: Semley, Wiltshire, England, May 25, 1908. ed: RADA. Died: June 3, 1992.

You could always count on Robert Morley to bring any movie, good or bad, to a higher plane, with his blubbery air of superiority and disdain, courtesy of his witty line readings or the mere raising of his bushy brows. Following his schooling, he acted with several theater groups, notably Sir Frank Benson's Company, and even formed his own troupe with fellow actor Peter Bull. In 1936 he had his first West End successes, playing Oscar Wilde in a play of that name, and Higgins in *Pygmalion*. Because of these, MGM chose him to portray the hopelessly clumsy and ultimately pathetic King Louis XVI in their lavish 1938 production of *Marie Antoinette*. Morley's impersonation of this foolish, child-like man was certainly memorable, and he earned his one and only Oscar nomination, in the supporting category. He did not, however, have any great desire to stay in Hollywood and would not film there again until 1963.

Back in England he starred as songwriter Leslie Stuart in *You Will Remember*, and then really established his versatility, by convincingly playing the elderly Andrew Undershaft in one of the cream of the British crop of movies of the 1940s, *Major Barbara*. He remained pretty much a supporting player, notably in *The Young Mr. Pitt*, as Robert Donat's nemesis, although he was called

on to carry the show as one of *The Ghosts of Berkeley Square*, a mild fantasy with Felix Alymer as the other spirit. *The African Queen* was his first American-financed production since *Marie Antoinette* and therefore afforded him his widest U.S. exposure in some time, in his small but pivotal role as Katharine Hepburn's missionary brother, who is slain early on in the film. That was followed by leads in *Curtain Up*, as a theatrical producer, in this comedy pairing him with the marvelous Margaret Rutherford; *The Final Test*, as a playwright and cricket fancier worshipped by a young boy; and *The Story of Gilbert and Sullivan*, as the famed librettist, the more acerbic W.S. Gilbert. Some more American productions filming in Europe required his services, so he played pomposity to good effect in the cult item *Beat the Devil*, leading a gang of motley crooks and supposedly writing some of his own dialogue; went nuts as George III in *Beau Brummell*; was back on the throne of France (as Louis XI) for *Quentin Duward*; appeared at David Niven's men's club in *Around the World in Eight Days* (he would also show up in the television remake); and was a buffoonish traveler in *The Journey*, lending support to Yul Brynner and Deborah Kerr.

Opposite Michael Redgrave, he was seen in one of the lesser offerings from the esteemed Ealing Studios, *Law and Disorder*, as a judge, and then got to recreate his Oscar Wilde in the movie of that name, which premiered in 1960, the same year as the more lavish and better-liked *The Trials of Oscar Wilde* with Peter Finch, although Morley's style was better suited to the part. After appearing in one of those Italian-made spectacles of the early 1960s, *Joseph and His Brethren* (as Potiphar), he began popping up in all sorts of international productions, usually, he claimed, for some quick cash. These included *The Young One*, playing the dad of pop singer Cliff Richard (they reteamed later for *Finders Keepers*); *The Road to Hong Kong*, camping it up as a mad scientist; *Murder at the Gallop*, reuniting with Margaret Rutherford; the critically lambasted remake of *The Old Dark House*; his return to Hollywood, *Take Her, She's Mine*, trying vainly to breathe some life into this lame James Stewart comedy; *Genghis Khan*, clearly giving credence to that claim of doing it for the big bucks, sporting a ponytail as the Emperor of China; *Topkapi*, as the mastermind behind the robbery; the slapstick hit *Those Magnificent Men in Their Flying Machines*, backing the big airplane race, as Sarah Miles's father; *A Study in Terror*, portraying Mycroft Holmes, though hardly under inspired circumstances; *The Alphabet Murders*, teaming with Tony Randall's Hercule Poirot; *The Loved One*, as an expatriate in this black Hollywood satire; *Hotel Paradiso*, grotesquely playing to the rafters in this labored door slamming farce; *Way Way Out*, looking stranded in one of Jerry Lewis's worst; and *Hot Millions*, playing a computer expert.

He had, by this time, become one of Britain's treasures, and as he grew jowlier and grumpier, he continued to add his unmistakable finesse and petulant scowl to *Cromwell*, as the Duke of Manchester; *Theater of Blood*, going gloriously into camp overdrive as a prissy drama critic forced to eat his own puppies; and *Who Is Killing the Great Chefs of Europe?*, stealing the show as a brittle magazine editor, the closest thing to a lead role in some time. He dabbled in playwrighting over the years, his best-known work being *Edward, My Son*, written in collaboration with Noel Langley, first performed in 1948, and filmed by MGM the following year. (Morley appeared in a television version of the play, in 1955). His autobiography, published in 1966, was entitled *Robert Morley: Responsible Gentleman*. Morley's son (from his marriage to Joan Buckmaster, daughter of actress Gladys Cooper) is writer Sheridan Morley.

Screen: 1938: Marie Antoinette; 1941: You Will Remember;

Major Barbara; **1942:** This Was Paris; The Big Blockade; The Foreman Went to France; The Young Mr. Pitt; **1945:** I Live in Grosvenor Square/A Yank in London; **1948:** The Ghosts of Berkeley Square; **1949:** The Small Black Room/Hour of Glory; **1951:** Outcast of the Islands; The African Queen; **1952:** Curtain Up; **1953:** The Final Test; The Story of Gilbert and Sullivan/The Great Gilbert and Sullivan; Melba; **1954:** Beat the Devil; The Good Die Young; The Rainbow Jacket; Beau Brummell; **1955:** Quentin Durward; **1956:** Loser Takes All; Around the World in Eighty Days; **1958:** Law and Disorder; The Sheriff of Fractured Jaw; **1959:** The Journey; The Doctor's Dilemma; Libel; **1960:** The Battle of the Sexes; Oscar Wilde; Joseph and His Brethren; **1961:** The Young Ones; **1962:** Go to Blazes; The Road to Hong Kong; The Boys; **1963:** Nine Hours to Rama; Murder at the Gallop; Ladies Who Do; The Old Dark House; Take Her, She's Mine; **1964:** Hot Enough for June/Agent 8 3/4; Of Human Bondage; Topkapi; **1965:** Genghis Khan; Those Magnificent Men in Their Flying Machines or How I Flew from London to Paris in 25 Hours 11 Minutes; The Loved One; Life at the Top; A Study in Terror; **1966:** The Alphabet Murders; Hotel Paradiso; Tendre Voyou/Tender Scoundrel (nUSr); Finders Keepers; **1967:** The Trygon Factor; Woman Times Seven; **1968:** Hot Millions; **1969:** Some Girls Do; Sinful Davey; **1970:** Twinky/Lola; Cromwell; Doctor in Trouble; Song of Norway; **1971:** When Eight Bells Toll; **1973:** Theater of Blood; **1976:** Hugo the Hippo (voice); The Blue Bird; **1978:** Who Is Killing the Great Chefs of Europe?; **1979:** Scavenger Hunt; **1980:** The Human Factor; Oh, Heavenly Dog!; **1981:** The Great Muppet Caper; Loophole; **1983:** High Road to China; **1985:** Second Time Lucky (nUSr); **1987:** The Wind (dtv); The Trouble With Spies; **1988:** Little Dorrit; **1990:** Istanbul (dtv).
NY Stage: 1936: Oscar Wilde.
Select TV: 1955: Edward, My Son (sp); 1959: Misalliance (sp); Oliver Twist (sp); 1960: Heaven Can Wait (sp); 1961: If the Crown Fits (series); 1962: The Big Day (sp); 1963: Our Man in Moscow (sp); 1969: Charge! (series); 1974: Great Expectations; 1982: The Old Men at the Zoo (ms); The Deadly Game; 1985: Alice in Wonderland (sp); 1988–89: War and Remembrance (ms); 1989: Around the World in 80 Days (ms); The Lady and the Highwayman.

CHESTER MORRIS

(JOHN CHESTER MORRIS)
BORN: NEW YORK, NY, FEBRUARY 16, 1901.
DIED: SEPTEMBER 11, 1970.

So perfect for the cops and robbers genre of 1930s movies, Chester Morris was a game player of these types, and with his full, rounded chin, flat nose, and furrowed brow, really looked the part of a street-bred tough mug. The son of stage actors William Morris and Etta Hawkins, he began acting as a teen, making his movie bow in 1917, in *An Amateur Orphan*, and then, the following year, on Broadway, in *The Copperhead*. In between the legit stage and a vaudeville act with his family, he was seen in a smattering of silent movies but didn't really become a star until he wowed the theater critics with the 1927 Broadway melodrama *Crime*. Because of it, he was asked to make his talkie debut in the highly successful gangster melodrama *Alibi*, in which he was the hardened criminal searching for someone to cover his tracks after a robbery turns to murder. Both the film and Morris received Oscar nominations, and his career as one of the big new stars of the sound era was launched. Seen today the movie is one of the most dated and awkward of all early talkies and Morris's mediocre performance stands out only when compared to the wretched one

given by co-star Regis Toomey.

Warners put him in the film version of one of his stage plays, *Fast Life*, after which he was seen in two of the major MGM offerings of 1930, both of which were up for Oscars in the Best Picture category for 1929–30: *The Divorcee*, where he was the husband Norma Shearer drives away through jealousy, and *The Big House*, the top prison epic of the era, with Morris, in his favorite role, as a tough inmate who sees the error of his ways. He was one of the rare performers of the day who didn't stay tied to one studio too long, and so he hopped from Paramount (*The Miracle Man*, as a crook on the run) to Universal (*King for a Night*, as a boxer) and back to MGM (*Red-Headed Woman*, as the boss driven wild with desire by Jean Harlow). Morris got to play a bad guy, albeit one who actually turns out to be good, a fed undercover to trap Joseph Calleia, in *Public Hero No. 1*, and was one of the bank robbers softened up by their interaction with a baby in the earlier, less-known, but far superior version of *Three Godfathers*. These were among the better regarded of his pictures during the mid-late 1930s, which more typically included such programmer quickies as *They Met in a Taxi*, he being the cabbie who meets Fay Wray; *I Promise to Pay*, with Morris in debt to loan shark Leo Carrillo; and *Frankie and Johnny*, in which he looked curious in high hat and waistcoat. Others were *Blind Alley*, where he was the escaped killer analyzed by psychologist Ralph Bellamy, a plot later revised for *The Dark Past*; *Smashing the Rackets*, in which he was a New York district attorney, a character clearly based on Thomas E. Dewey; *Sky Giant*, with Morris fighting Richard Dix for Joan Fontaine's attentions; and *Five Came Back*, one of the better remembered of the plane-crash survivor adventures.

It was now a matter of who was interested in banking on the next Morris melodrama, and after a stint for Republic with *Wagons Westward* and *The Girl From God's Country*, Columbia hired him for a 61-minute opus called *Meet Boston Blackie*, in which he was a former crook-turned-crimefighter. Released in 1941, it clicked well enough that the studio decided to turn it into a series. Morris kept his increasingly grim visage submerged in 13 more entries, three of which, *The Chance of a Lifetime*, *One Mysterious Night*, and *The Phantom Thief*, were the only ones that did not include Blackie's name in the title. As the 1950s arrived, Morris focused his attention on the small screen and the stage, where he was seen on Broadway in *The Fifth Season* and *Advise and Consent*, among others. During his run as Captain Queeg in *The Caine Mutiny Court-Martial*, at the Bucks County Playhouse, he ended his own life with an overdose of pills.
Screen: 1917: An Amateur Orphan; 1918: The Beloved Traitor; 1923: Loyal Lives; 1925: The Road to Yesterday; 1929: Alibi; Fast Life; Woman Trap; The Show of Shows; 1930: Playing Around; She Couldn't Say No; Second Choice; The Case of Sergeant Grischa; The Divorcee; The Big House; The Bat Whispers; 1931: Corsair; 1932: The Miracle Man; Cock of the Air; Sinners in the Sun; Red-Headed Woman; Breach of Promise; 1933: Infernal Machine; Blondie Johnson; Tomorrow at Seven; Golden Harvest; King for a Night; 1934: Embarrassing Moments; Let's Talk It Over; Gift of Gab; The Gay Bride; 1935: Princess O'Hara; I've Been Around; Public Hero No.1; Society Doctor; Pursuit; 1936: Moonlight Murder; Three Godfathers; Frankie and Johnny; Counterfeit; They Met in a Taxi; 1937: The Devil's Playground; I Promise to Pay; Flight From Glory; 1938: Law of the Underworld; Sky Giant; Smashing the Rackets; 1939: Pacific Liner; Blind Alley; Five Came Back; Thunder Afloat; 1940: The Marines Fly High; Wagons Westward; The Girl From God's Country; 1941: No Hands on the Clock; Meet Boston Blackie; Confessions of Boston Blackie; 1942: Alias Boston Blackie; Boston Blackie Goes to Hollywood; Canal Zone; I Live on

Danger; Wrecking Crew; **1943:** Tornado; The Chance of a Lifetime; Aerial Gunner; After Midnight With Boston Blackie; High Explosive; **1944:** Gambler's Choice; Secret Command; One Mysterious Night; Double Exposure; **1945:** Boston Blackie Booked on Suspicion; Rough, Tough and Ready; Boston Blackie's Rendezvous; **1946:** One Way to Love; Boston Blackie and the Law; A Close Call for Boston Blackie; The Phantom Thief; **1947:** Blind Spot; **1948:** Boston Blackie's Chinese Adventure; Trapped by Boston Blackie; **1955:** Unchained; **1956:** The She-Creature; **1970:** The Great White Hope.

NY Stage: **1918:** The Copperhead; **1919:** Thunder; **1921:** The Mountain Man; **1922:** The Exciters; **1923:** Extra; **1926:** The Home Toners; Yellow; **1927:** Crime; **1928:** Whispering Friends; Fast Life; **1954:** The Fifth Season; **1957:** The Girl of the Golden West (ob); **1958:** Blue Denim; **1960:** Advise and Consent; **1966:** The Subject Was Roses.

Select TV: **1951:** Act of God Notwithstanding (sp); **1952:** Billy Budd (sp); Welcome Home Lefty (sp); **1953:** Final Edition (sp); **1954:** Jack Sparling (sp); Death and Life of Larry Benson (sp); **1955:** Blow Up at Cortland (sp); **1956:** The Arena (sp); Time Lock (sp); **1957:** Child of Trouble (sp); Men of Prey (sp); **1959:** Whisper of Evil (sp); Morning's at Seven (sp); **1960:** Diagnosis: Unknown (series); **1961:** A String of Beads (sp); **1964:** Knight's Gambit (sp); **1965:** The Fliers (sp).

WAYNE MORRIS

(BERT DE WAYNE MORRIS) BORN: LOS ANGELES, CA, FEBRUARY 17, 1914. ED: LOS ANGELES CITY COL. DIED: SEPTEMBER 14, 1959.

A Warners regular during the prewar era, Wayne Morris was tall and blond, with a slow-drawling way with a line that could be engaging but more often was just a step up from dull. A student of the Pasadena Playhouse, he was one of the lucky ones, spotted by a Warner Bros. talent scout after a few stage appearances there and signed to a contract in 1936. He was used as a small-part actor, convincingly taking to the ice as a player named Jumbo Mullins, in *King of Hockey*, to name but one of his assignments, before his breakthrough, as the affable bellhop who is promoted by Edward G. Robinson into becoming a champion prizefighter, in *Kid Galahad*. Shamelessly the studio did a quick cash-in with Morris (this time top billed) playing a cowboy who takes to the ring, in the 60-minute cheapie *The Kid Comes Back*. Now officially a star, he was given two other plumb roles by the company, a land baron challenged by villain Charles Bickford, in *Valley of the Giants*, a Technicolor adventure, and one of a trio of cadets (the others being Ronald Reagan and Eddie Albert) in *Brother Rat*, an amusing romp. This was followed by an unsuccessful sequel, *Brother Rat and a Baby*; another boxing film, *The Kid From Kokomo*, in which he was a feller who was pretty convinced he was the son of Whistler's Mother; and the cheesy vampire flick *The Return of Doctor X*, in which he played a reporter.

Paramount borrowed him for *The Quarterback* and the hit aviation drama *I Wanted Wings*, then he was back to Warner Bros. for the haunted-house comedy *The Smiling Ghost*, by which point whatever it was that Morris had to offer was no longer much to speak of. He called a halt to his movie career to sign up with the Navy Air Corps, where he became one of Hollywood's more distinguished servicemen, receiving several medals and being promoted to the rank of lieutenant commander. He was, in fact, off the screen a full six years, perhaps longer than any other "name" actor who served. After the war he turned up in adaptations of two famous stage hits, *The Voice of the Turtle*, more

appropriately placed in support, here as Eve Arden's boyfriend, and *The Time of Your Life*, pleasant but unremarkable as James Cagney's bar buddy. He was outlaw Cole Younger in 1949's *The Younger Brothers*, which was something of a promotion, having played the lesser role of Bob Younger in 1941's *Bad Men of Missouri*; then ended his contract for Warners by supporting Gary Cooper in the flying epic *Task Force*. It was not surprising that he went directly to the "B" unit of Columbia for *The Tougher They Come* and *The Big Gusher*, as well as grinding out mostly westerns for the second-line companies, Monogram, Realart, and Allied Artists. This undistinguished run of assignments was interrupted by one class picture, *Paths of Glory*, in which he was ideally cast as the foolish, cowardly officer who winds up being placed in charge of the firing squad. He was fairly busy on television, making various guest appearances and acting on several dramatic anthology series, when he collapsed and died of a heart attack at the age of 45.

Screen: **1936:** China Clipper; King of Hockey; Polo Joe; Here Comes Carter; **1937:** Smart Blonde; Once a Doctor; Land Beyond the Law; Kid Galahad; Submarine D-1; **1938:** Love, Honor and Behave; The Kid Comes Back; Men Are Such Fools; Valley of the Giants; Brother Rat; **1939:** The Kid From Kokomo; The Return of Doctor X; **1940:** Brother Rat and a Baby; Double Alibi; An Angel From Texas; Flight Angels; Ladies Must Live; The Quarterback; Gambling on the High Seas; **1941:** Three Sons of o' Guns; I Wanted Wings; Bad Men of Missouri; The Smiling Ghost; **1947:** Deep Valley; The Voice of the Turtle/One for the Book; **1948:** The Big Punch; The Time of Your Life; **1949:** A Kiss in the Dark; John Loves Mary; The Younger Brothers; The House Across the Street; Task Force; **1950:** Johnny One-Eye; The Tougher They Come; Stage to Tucson; **1951:** Sierra Passage; The Big Gusher; Yellow Fin; **1952:** The Bushwhackers; Desert Pursuit; Arctic Flight; **1953:** The Fighting Lawman; The Marksman; Star of Texas; **1954:** The Master Plan; Riding Shotgun; The Desperado; Two Guns and a Badge; Port of Hell; **1955:** Lord of the Jungle; The Green Buddha; Cross Channel; Lonesome Trail; **1956:** The Dynamiters/The Gelignite Gang; **1957:** Paths of Glory; Plunder Road; **1959:** The Crooked Sky; **1961:** Buffalo Gun (filmed 1958).

NY Stage: **1957:** The Cave Dwellers.

Select TV: **1955:** The Mink Doll (sp); **1956:** The Clay Pigeon (sp).

VIC MORROW

BORN: BRONX, NY, FEBRUARY 14, 1932. ED: FL STATE COL. DIED: JULY 23, 1982.

A slate-hard actor who couldn't help but look mean, even when he was playing relatively benign characters, Vic Morrow had done *A Streetcar Named Desire* in stock before he got his big film break, being cast as the cheap hoodlum in the 1955 classic *Blackboard Jungle*. His petulant, dangerous, and always angry student, who has it in for teacher Glenn Ford, was unforgettable and led to immediate typecasting as bad guys, in *Tribute to a Bad Man*, giving James Cagney a hard time; *King Creole*, swaying Elvis Presley into the criminal world; *Hell's Five Hours*, holding hostages at a missile depot; and *Portrait of a Mobster*, playing the leading role of real-life Dutch Schultz. Television took him away from this temporarily, although it made sure he was still a tough guy, starring as platoon sergeant Chip Saunders in the series *Combat*, which ran for five years during the 1960s. That pretty much made him a television regular; though he did take a break during this time to put together a very personal big-screen project, directing, co-writing, and co-producing a 1966 version of the Jean Genet play *Deathwatch*, which he'd starred in Off Broadway in 1958. His other stints behind the camera, the western *A Man Called Sledge* and *The Evictors*, also went pretty much unnoticed. Between television movies he was seen as the sheriff determined to nab *Dirty Mary Crazy Larry*, and the hotheaded Little League coach who cruelly berates son Brandon Cruz in *The Bad News Bears*. Sadly his final role made him one of the movies' most tragic figures. Signed to play a bigot who winds up repenting for his sins in *Twilight Zone: The Movie*, he and two child actors were killed during the filming of a helicopter stunt. His daughter is actress Jennifer Jason Leigh.

Screen: 1955: Blackboard Jungle; It's a Dog's Life (voice); 1956: Tribute to a Bad Man; 1957: Men in War; 1958: God's Little Acre; King Creole; Hell's Five Hours; 1960: Cimarron; 1961: Portrait of a Mobster; Posse From Hell; 1969: Target: Harry/How to Make It; 1974: The Take; Dirty Mary Crazy Larry; 1975: The Babysitter/Wanted: Babysitter/The Raw Edge; 1976: The Bad News Bears; Treasure of Matecumbe; 1977: Funeral for an Assassin; 1978: Message From Space; 1979: The Evictors (and dir.); 1980: Humanoids From the Deep; 1981: Great White; 1983: 1990: The Bronx Warriors; Twilight Zone: The Movie.

NY Stage: 1958: Deathwatch (ob).

Select TV: 1962–67: Combat (series); 1971: A Step Out of Line; Travis Logan, D.A.; River of Mystery; 1972: The Glass House; The Weekend Nun; 1973: The Police Story; Tom Sawyer; 1974: Nightmare; The California Kid; 1975: Death Stalk; The Night That Panicked America; Captains and the Kings (ms); 1977: Roots (ms); The Man With the Power; The Hostage Heart; The Ghost of Cypress Swamp (sp); Curse of the Black Widow; 1978: Wild and Wooly; 1979: Stone; The Last Convertible (ms); The Seekers; 1980: B.A.D. Cats (series).

ROBERT MORSE
BORN: NEWTON, MA, MAY 18, 1931.

With his eternal boyishness, wicked gap-toothed smile, and plucky enthusiasm, Robert Morse seemed poised to take the entertainment business by storm, much in the manner of Mickey Rooney. His opportunities turned out to be infinitely less in number but with at least one towering peak along the way. After serving in the Navy he followed his brother to New York to seek acting jobs, ending up on television in a soap, *The Secret Storm*, and on radio's *True Confessions*. In 1955 he made his Broadway debut, as the naïve clerk Barnaby in the hit comedy *The Matchmaker*, being the only cast member to repeat his role in the film version three years later. There wasn't, however, any great demand for him by movie producers for the time being, so he returned to the theater for three triumphs in a row: *Say Darling* (for which he received a Theatre World Award), *Take Me Along*, and, most significantly, *How to Succeed in Business Without Really Trying*. In the last-named he gave one of the classic performances of the musical stage, as the ingratiating corporate climber J. Pierpont Finch, earning a Tony Award.

Hollywood begged for him to come back and cast him as a song and dance man in *The Cardinal*; stuck him in two coy and crummy MGM sex romps, *Honeymoon Hotel* and *Quick Before It Melts*; and made him the deadpan British observer of the weird funeral folk in *The Loved One*. The last was pretty much dismissed in its day but grew in reputation over the years as a rare black comedy that clicked. On the other hand Morse had the misfortune of appearing in one of the all-time worst attempts to

mix the macabre with the humorous, *Oh Dad, Poor Dad, Mama's Hung You in the Closet and I'm Feeling So Sad*, in a grotesque turn, as Rosalind Russell's pampered and seemingly retarded son. In 1967 the long-overdue film of *How to Succeed...* arrived, capturing to perfection Morse's original, bizarre, and utterly charming work for future generations to cherish. It became the role of a lifetime, although the film did much less business than some of the more expensive movie musicals of the day. That same year he had another of his more successful forays into cinema with *A Guide for the Married Man*, wittily giving an attentive Walter Matthau the most deliriously misguided advice on how to cheat on one's spouse. Sporting a moustache, he was a would-be embezzler fumbling through the bedroom shenanigans of *Where Were You When the Lights Went Out?*, at one point amusingly comparing teeth gaps with Terry-Thomas.

After starring in the oddball singing sitcom *That's Life!* and in a lighthearted Disney item, *The Boatniks*, he returned to the theater to do his take on Jack Lemmon's *Some Like It Hot* role in the musical re-do, *Sugar*. This was followed by years in touring shows, some uninspired television assignments, voice work, and two quickly forgotten movies, *Hunk* and *The Emperor's New Clothes*. There was one final theatrical peak, with his uncanny impersonation of Truman Capote in *Tru*, a part for which he earned his second Tony Award. He later repeated it on television, winning an Emmy.

Screen: 1956: The Proud and the Profane; 1958: The Matchmaker; 1963: The Cardinal; 1964: Honeymoon Hotel; Quick Before It Melts; 1965: The Loved One; 1967: Oh Dad, Poor Dad, Mama's Hung You in the Closet and I'm Feeling So Sad; How to Succeed in Business Without Really Trying; A Guide for the Married Man; 1968: Where Were You When the Lights Went Out?; 1970: The Boatniks; 1987: Hunk; The Emperor's New Clothes.

NY Stage: 1955: The Matchmaker; 1958: Say Darling; 1959: Take Me Along; 1961: How to Succeed in Business Without Really Trying; 1972: Sugar; 1976: So Long 174th Street; 1989: Tru.

Select TV: 1954: The Secret Storm (series); 1955: Man on Spikes (sp); 1958: Rain in the Morning (sp); 1959: Thieves' Carnival (sp); 1960: The Velvet Glove (sp); 1968–69: That's Life (series); 1978: The Stingiest Man in Town (voice; sp); 1979: Jack Frost (sp; voice); 1983–74: Monchichis (series; voice); 1984: Calendar Girl Murders; 1986–88: Pound Puppies (series; voice); 1992: Tru (sp); 1993: Wild Palms (ms); 1995: Here Come the Munsters; 2000: City of Angels (series).

ZERO MOSTEL
(SAMUEL JOEL MOSTEL) BORN: BROOKLYN, NY, FEBRUARY 28, 1915. DIED: SEPTEMBER 8, 1977.

Zero Mostel was a man of the theater first and foremost, but his bombastic, bug-eyed presence could not help but be felt on the big screen as well, even if the number of worthy celluloid assignments added up to much less than they should have. Originally set on becoming an artist, he began performing in nightclubs to supplement his meager income and wound up as part of a Broadway revue called *Keep 'em Laughing*. This, along with a stint at the Paramount Theater, got him noticed by an MGM talent scout, and he ended up with a dual role in the screen version of *Du Barry Was a Lady*, though much of his footage ended up on the cutting room floor. It was a bad omen, and his outspoken politics were instrumental in the studio not bothering to find him further work.

He went back to New York for some plays before returning for another try at the movies, notably in *Panic in the Streets*, in which he and Jack Palance were the criminals unwittingly spreading a plague through New Orleans. Shortly afterwards he became one of those unfortunate performers whose previous political beliefs got them unjustly blacklisted during the McCarthy witchhunts. Mostel therefore left Hollywood behind once again, turning to the safer and more open-minded Broadway Theater. It was in the 1958 Off Broadway production of *Ulysses in Nighttown* that he finally got his due, earning rave notices and an Obie Award. This was followed by the quirky *Rhinoceros*, in which he enacted a man turning into the title character, and the comedic pinnacle of his career, *A Funny Thing Happened on the Way to the Forum*, where he played the scheming slave Pseudolos. Both won him Tony Awards; the next one made him a theater legend.

Tony number three came for *Fiddler on the Roof*, with Mostel both humorous and moving as the wearied milkman Tevye, who faces life's misfortunes while trying in vain to hold onto traditions. The show became one of the longest running musicals in Broadway history, and it became Mostel's signature role, although he was not asked to repeat it in the 1971 movie version. (Topol, who had done the part in London, was chosen instead). Mostel was, however, asked to reprise his other great role, in the 1966 movie of *A Funny Thing Happened on the Way to the Forum*, which retained the laughs and Mostel's masterfully funny timing though not enough of the songs. It was up to director-writer Mel Brooks to give him the one movie role that would rank among his greatest triumphs, the lascivious, desperate, and overbearing Max Bialystock, who comes up with a wild plot to make money from a flop play called *Springtime for Hitler*, in the hilarious *The Producers*. Despite a mild box-office response outside the major cities, it became one of the most revered and quoted of all comedies with the passing of the years.

There was a western spoof that got few bookings, *The Great Bank Robbery*, and then one that showed his more serious side, *The Angel Levine*, where he was uncharacteristically subdued, as an old Jewish tailor visited by heavenly Harry Belafonte, in this tepid allegory. Other projects, like *Marco*, as Kublai Khan; *Foreplay*, in which he was the President of the United States, forced to bed his wife on TV; and *Mastermind*, a Charlie Chan send-up that spent eight years on the shelf, all came and went, as did the film of *Rhinoceros*, which had trouble translating what was suggested onstage into reality on film. There was one final role that worked splendidly, mainly because it was so close to home, the blacklisted entertainer who is ruined by McCarthyism, in *The Front*. He died from cardiac arrest shortly after reprising Tevye on Broadway. His son is actor Josh Mostel, who appeared in such movies as *Jesus Christ Superstar*, *Radio Days*, and *City Slickers*.

Screen: 1943: Du Barry Was a Lady; 1950: Panic in the Streets; The Enforcer; 1951: The Guy Who Came Back; Sirocco; Mr. Belvedere Rings the Bell; The Model and the Marriage Broker; 1966: A Funny Thing Happened on the Way to the Forum; 1968: The Producers; Great Catherine; 1969: The Great Bank Robbery; 1970: The Angel Levine; 1972: The Hot Rock; 1974: Marco; Rhinoceros; 1975: Foreplay/The President's Women; 1976: The Front; Journey Into Fear; Hollywood on Trial; 1977: Mastermind (filmed 1969); Once Upon a Scoundrel (filmed 1973); 1978: Watership Down (voice); 1979: Red, White and Zero; Best Boy;

NY Stage: 1942: Café Crown; Keep 'em Laughing; Top-Notchers; 1945: Concert Varieties; 1946: Beggar's Holiday; 1952: Flight Into Egypt; 1954: A Stone for Danny Fisher (ob); 1955: Lunatics and Lovers; 1956: The Good Woman of Setzuan (ob); 1957: Good as Gold; 1958: Ulysses in Nighttown (ob); 1961: Rhinoceros; 1962: A Funny Thing Happened on the Way to the

Forum; 1964: Fiddler on the Roof; 1974: Ulysses in Nighttown (revival); 1976: Fiddler on the Roof (revival).

Select TV: 1959: Zero Mostel (sp); The World of Sholom Aleichem (sp); 1961: Waiting for Godot (sp); 1967: Zero Hour (sp); 1978: The Little Drummer Boy (sp; voice).

ALAN MOWBRAY

BORN: LONDON, ENGLAND, AUGUST 18, 1896.
DIED: MARCH 25, 1969.

He always seemed stuffy and aloof, so Hollywood took these traits and used Alan Mowbray time and again to play the windy Englishman. Following some stage work in his native country, he came to New York in 1923, where he carried on his theatrical career, which included appearing in a play he himself wrote and directed, *Dinner Is Served*. In 1931 he was asked to Hollywood, where he played George Washington in *Alexander Hamilton* and then again, briefly, in *The Phantom President*; the cad killed by Lionel Barrymore in *Guilty Hands*; the majordomo in Eddie Cantor's spoof *Roman Scandals*; Inspector Lestrade in *A Study in Scarlet*; and the British officer Miriam Hopkins unwisely loves in *Becky Sharp*, the first Technicolor release. In the late 1930s he entered a prime period, perfecting his pompous act in *In Person*, *She Couldn't Take It*, and *Hollywood Hotel*, in each case playing a vain actor of limited talent. After these he was a difficult movie director in *Stand In*; the former school chum of William Powell's in *My Man Godfrey*; and the acerbic butler, Wilkins, in *Topper*, perhaps his best-remembered role. He was Patsy Kelly's love interest, with the intriguing name of Pennypacker E. Pennpacker, in *There Goes My Heart*; leered at Rita Hayworth in *Music in My Heart*; teamed with Eric Blore in the poor film version of *The Boys From Syracuse*; got top billing, as a producer, in *Curtain Call*, and in the less popular follow-up, *Footlight Fever*; and played it straight, as the snobby husband of Vivien Leigh, distressed to learn that she's carrying on with Laurence Olivier, in *That Hamilton Woman*. In the midst of a great deal of programmer fodder like *The Devil With Hitler* (as Lucifer come to Earth to confront Der Führer), *The Phantom of 42nd Street*, *Sunbonnet Sue*, and *The Main Street Kid*, he was back in servitude again, in *His Butler's Sister*; reprised Washington again for *Where Do We Go from Here?*; was a deformed mystic in the epic *Captain From Castile*; and had an interesting bit as a drunken actor, being razzed by the townsfolk, in the famous western *My Darling Clementine*. The 1950s found him landing most of his jobs on television, including a starring role on the show *Colonel Humphrey J. Flack*, finally popping up in a few "A" pictures again, including two of 1956's most honored, *The King and I*, as the British Ambassador, and *Around the World in Eighty Days*, as a consul.

Screen: 1931: God's Gift to Women; The Man in Possession; Guilty Hands; Alexander Hamilton; Honor of the Family; Leftover Ladies; 1932: Silent Witness; Nice Women; Lovers Courageous; The World and the Flesh; Man About Town; Winner Take All; Jewel Robbery; Two Against the World; The Man Called Back; Sherlock Holmes; Hotel Continental; The Phantom President; The Man From Yesterday; 1933: Peg o' My Heart; A Study in Scarlet; Voltaire; Berkeley Square; The Midnight Club; The World Changes; Roman Scandals; Our Betters; Her Secret; 1934: Long Lost Father; Where Sinners Meet; The Girl From Missouri; Charlie Chan in London; The House of Rothschild; Cheaters; Little Man, What Now?; One More River; Embarrassing Moments; 1935: Night Life of the Gods; Lady Tubbs; Becky Sharp; The Gay Deception; In Person; She

Couldn't Take It; **1936:** Rose-Marie; Rainbow on the River; Muss 'em Up; Ladies in Love; Mary of Scotland; Desire; Give Us This Night; The Case Against Mrs. Ames; Fatal Lady; My Man Godfrey; **1937:** Four Days' Wonder; As Good as Married; Topper; Vogues of 1938; Stand-In; On Such a Night; Music for Madame; On the Avenue; The King and the Chorus Girl; Marry the Girl; Hollywood Hotel; **1938:** Merrily We Live; There Goes My Heart; Topper Takes a Trip; **1939:** Never Say Die; The Llano Kid; Way Down South; **1940:** Music in My Heart; Curtain Call; The Villain Still Pursued Her; Scatterbrain; The Boys From Syracuse; The Quarterback; **1941:** That Hamilton Woman; That Uncertain Feeling; Footlight Fever; The Cowboy and the Blonde; Moon Over Her Shoulder; I Wake Up Screaming; Ice-Capades; The Perfect Snob; **1942:** The Mad Martindales; Panama Hattie; A Yank at Eton; We Were Dancing; Isle of Missing Men; Yokel Boy; The Devil With Hitler; The Powers Girl; **1943:** Slightly Dangerous; His Butler's Sister; So This Is Washington; Holy Matrimony; Stage Door Canteen; **1944:** The Doughgirls; My Gal Loves Music; Ever Since Venus; **1945:** The Phantom of 42nd Street; Bring on the Girls; Men in Her Diary; Sunbonnet Sue; Earl Carroll Vanities; Tell It to a Star; Where Do We Go From Here?; **1946:** Terror by Night; My Darling Clementine; Idea Girl; **1947:** Lured; Merton of the Movies; The Pilgrim Lady; Captain From Castile; **1948:** The Prince of Thieves; The Main Street Kid; My Dear Secretary; Don't Trust Your Husband/An Innocent Affair; Every Girl Should Be Married; **1949:** You're My Everything; Abbott and Costello Meet the Killer Boris Karloff; The Lovable Cheat; The Lone Wolf and His Lady; **1950:** The Jackpot; Wagon Master; **1951:** The Lady and the Bandit; Crosswinds; **1952:** Just Across the Street; Androcles and the Lion; Blackbeard the Pirate; **1954:** Ma and Pa Kettle at Home; The Steel Cage; **1955:** The King's Thief; **1956:** The King and I; The Man Who Knew Too Much; Around the World in Eighty Days; **1961:** A Majority of One.

NY Stage: 1926: The Sport of Kings; 1928: These Modern Women; 1929: Dinner Is Served (and dir.; wr.); The Amorous Antic; 1930: The Apple Cart; 1963: Enter Laughing.

Select TV: 1950: Small Town Story (sp); 1951: Agent From Scotland Yard (sp); 1952: Annual Honeymoon (sp); 1953: Colonel Humphrey J. Flack (sp); 1953–54, 1958–59: Colonel Humphrey Flack/The Fabulous Fraud/Colonel Flack (series); 1954–55: The Mickey Rooney Show (series); 1955: The House Always Wins (sp); Alias Mr. Hepp (sp); 1956: No Limit (sp); A Long Way From Texas (sp); The Best in Mystery (series); 1958: A Contest of Ladies (sp); 1960–61: Dante (series).

PAUL MUNI

(MUNI WEISENFREUND) BORN: LEMBERG, AUSTRIA-HUNGARY, SEPTEMBER 22, 1895. RAISED IN NEW YORK, NY. DIED: AUGUST 25, 1967.

In his heyday Paul Muni was hailed as the master thespian *par excellence* of the Warner Bros. lot, adept at accents and disguises, whose versatility allowed him to slip into the most intellectual of roles after playing an everyman or a hoodlum. Today there are times when the work seems much less impressive, with more than a touch of theatricality entering the mix, though he can still be mighty entertaining to watch, if only because he took on a wider gamut of types than most actors of his day ever dared. Born into a theatrical family, he came to America while still very young, settling in New York. Starting in 1918 he became a member of a Yiddish stock company and then the Jewish Art Theatre. He went to London in 1924 for some theater work and then made his long-delayed American English-speaking stage debut, in 1926, when he replaced Edward G. Robinson in the Broadway production of *We Americans*. The next year a role in *Four Walls* brought him much attention, and, as a result, he was signed to a contract by Fox Studios. His success was instantaneous, as his debut, *The Valiant*, in which he was a murderer about to be executed who hopes his mother does not find out about his unsavory doings, earned him an Oscar nomination. His follow-up, *Seven Faces*, gave him a chance to play seven different parts, which was instrumental in bringing him a reputation for versatility.

Instead of continuing at Fox he bailed out of the deal and returned to Broadway for *Counselor-at-Law*, a role John Barrymore would play in the film version. (Muni, however, would repise it on live-television in 1948). From this he got an offer from United Artists to play a ruthless mobster, patterned after Al Capone, in *Scarface*. Along with *Little Caesar* and *The Public Enemy*, it was championed as one of the landmarks in the gangster genre, while Muni was hailed as a true motion picture star. Although *Caesar* and *Enemy* are hindered by the clunkiness found in many early talkies, the star turns by Edward G. Robinson and James Cagney respectively, give them a fire that is still effective today. Muni, on the other hand, seems to be trying too hard to suggest a combination of brutality and mental unbalance, his performance being one of the major factors that has made *Scarface* the least potent of these three works. Warners snatched him up with great plans for his future, starting him at the top with *I Am a Fugitive From a Chain Gang*, one of the finest and most enduring of studio's "social problem" pictures. Muni was a wronged man sentenced to hard labor for a crime he didn't commit, who then makes something of his life after escaping from prison. Both Muni and the picture were in the running for Oscars. He got to age in *The World Changes*, rising from farmer to millionaire inventor of the refrigerated freight-car; gave the closest thing he would ever give to a lighthearted performance, in *Hi, Nellie!*, a flop about an editor demoted to columnist; was desired by Bette Davis in *Bordertown*, as a Mexican lawyer; and tackled the injustice of the coal industry in *Black Fury*.

It was prophetic that he was seen browsing through a copy of a book on Louis Pasteur in the film *Dr. Socrates*, for that was indeed his next role and the one that pegged him as some kind of specialist in the thinking man's biopic. *The Story of Louis Pasteur* approached its subject matter with surprising taste and intelligence while remaining thoroughly entertaining. Muni, as the dedicated French doctor, won endless praise for his restraint, winning the Academy Award as Best Actor of 1936. This was followed by a pair of dual triumphs in two of the critical favorites of 1937, both of which turned into surprise box-office hits. First was MGM's *The Good Earth*, where he, with shaved head and a modicum of makeup, was the dignified Chinese farmer in Pearl Buck's sweeping tale. Then, donning a bushy beard and spectacles, he earned another Oscar nod for playing a famous Frenchman, in *The Life of Emile Zola*, the highlight of which was his impassioned defense of persecuted Captain Alfred Dreyfuss, though this subplot suffered from the omission of the anti-Semitism that was behind the whole thing to begin with. *Zola* received the Academy Award for Best Picture of 1937.

Less popular was *Juarez*, in which he was the very stern and stoic Mexican advocate for democracy, submerging himself into the part perhaps deeper than he had ever gone. The failure of this and *We Are Not Alone*, in which he was a British doctor during World War I, caused Muni and Warners to part company. It looked like as good a time as any to return to the stage, which he did, winning praise for *Key Largo*. Back at the movies his prestige was slowly evaporating with his roles in *Hudson's Bay*, as a French fur trapper; a routine war film, *Commandos Strike at Dawn*; and even with one that brought in large audiences, *A Song to Remember*, with Muni hamming it up in bushy wig and mutton-chops as Chopin's mentor, Joseph Elsner. Since his next two films, *Angel on My Shoulder* and the Italian-made *Stranger on the Prowl*, were low profile items, it seemed as if he'd been out of the public eye for some time when he had another stage success, in 1955, with *Inherit the Wind*, winning a Tony Award playing a character based on Clarence Darrow. The acclaim for that one resulted in one more leading role back in front of the cameras, the old Jewish doctor practicing in the slums of Brooklyn, in *The Last Angry Man*. Despite its lack of wide appeal it was nice to see Muni throwing himself into a juicy part like the old days, and as a finale to his screen career it was more than honorable, earning him another Oscar nomination. Shortly afterward his failing eyesight caused him to back out of the limelight. Upon his death in 1967 he did not necessarily leave behind the lasting legacy his position in the 1930s suggested he would. Instead his work had brought him more than enough accolades in his lifetime, that being the period, after all, when it counted most to Muni himself.

Screen: 1929: The Valiant; Seven Faces; 1932: Scarface; I Am a Fugitive From a Chain Gang; 1933: The World Changes; 1934: Hi, Nellie!; 1935: Bordertown; Black Fury; Dr. Socrates; 1936: The Story of Louis Pasteur; 1937: The Good Earth; The Woman I Loved; The Life of Emile Zola; 1939: Juarez; We Are Not Alone; 1940: Hudson's Bay; 1942: Commandos Strike at Dawn; 1943: Stage Door Canteen; 1945: A Song to Remember; Counter-Attack; 1946: Angel on My Shoulder; 1953: Stranger on the Prowl; 1959: The Last Angry Man.

NY Stage: 1926: We Americans; 1927: Four Walls; 1930: This One Man; 1931: Rock Me Julie; Counselor-at-Law; 1939: Key Largo; 1942: Yesterday's Magic; 1946: A Flag Is Born; 1949: They Knew What They Wanted; 1955: Inherit the Wind.

Select TV: 1948: Counselor-at-Law (sp); The Valiant (sp); 1953: The People vs. Johnston (sp); 1956: A Letter From the Queen (sp); 1958: Last Clear Chance (sp).

JULES MUNSHIN

BORN: NEW YORK, NY, FEBRUARY 22, 1915.
DIED: FEBRUARY 19, 1970.

A decidedly unsubtle combination singer-comedian, who had a chance to shine briefly in MGM's musical heyday, long-faced Jules Munshin had done comedy in various Catskill resorts and in vaudeville before performing with George Olsen's Band. In 1946 he scored a major success on Broadway as part of the revue *Call Me Mister*, which resulted in a contract with Metro. He made his debut for them doing a bit of shtick as a disgruntled waiter in *Easter Parade*, followed by *Take Me Out to the Ballgame*, in which he was part of an athletic trio rounded out by Gene Kelly and Frank Sinatra. Their big number, "O'Brien to Ryan to Goldberg" was there to pretty much point out Munshin's Jewish heritage. The best thing about this lesser addition to the studio's musical output was that the same three male leads were reunited for the far superior *On the Town*, where this time Munshin got to join in the infectious "New York, New York" number, shot on location, and in the title song, while also being mistaken for the ancestor of the original Neanderthal man. After that success, he returned to the stage and then went to France to star in *Monte Carlo Baby*, which only surfaced in most markets later down the line because a pre-stardom Audrey Hepburn was in the cast. Back with MGM he dueted with Dean Martin in one

of the few bearable moments from *Ten Thousand Bedrooms*, and cavorted disarmingly with Peter Lorre and Joseph Bullof through the Cole Porter song "Siberia," as one of the disgraced Russians, in *Silk Stockings*. Following some more Broadway runs, he was last seen on the big screen in one of the more obscure Disney movies of the 1960s, *Monkeys, Go Home!* He had just played the Mayor in a Broadway revival of *The Front Page* and was starting rehearsals for an Off Broadway play called *Duet for Solo Voice* when he suffered a fatal heart attack.

Screen: 1948: Easter Parade; 1949: Take Me Out to the Ball Game; That Midnight Kiss; On the Town; 1954: Monte Carlo Baby; 1957: Ten Thousand Bedrooms; Silk Stockings; 1964: Wild and Wonderful; 1967: Monkeys, Go Home!

NY Stage: 1943: The Army Play by Play; Pack Up Your Troubles; 1946: Call Me Mister; 1950: Bless You All; 1952: Mrs. McThing; 1960: The Good Soup; 1961: Show Girl; The Gay Life; 1965: Oklahoma!; 1966: Barefoot in the Park; 1970: The Front Page.

Select TV: 1957: Sing a Song (sp); 1968: Kiss Me Kate (sp).

AUDIE MURPHY

BORN: KINGSTON, TX, JUNE 20, 1924.
DIED: MAY 28, 1971.

Leave it to Hollywood to take World War II's most decorated soldier and turn him into a movie star. Boyish, personable, but never considered enough of an accomplished actor to excel at anything other than standard western fare, Audie Murphy had grown up poor, the child of sharecroppers. His 28 citations during the war included the Congressional Medal of Honor, which made him a media sensation with a future open to all sorts of possibilities. Paramount invited him to do a small role, as a fellow cadet of Alan Ladd's, in the 1948 release *Beyond Glory*, and he certainly looked nice enough up on the big screen to be given the pivotal role of a juvenile delinquent sent to a reform ranch in Allied Artists's *Bad Boy*. The same year, 1949, he published his best-selling account of his war exploits, *To Hell and Back*, and married actress Wanda Hendrix, a union that lasted but a year.

Now a part of the Hollywood scene, he began his lengthy stint as a cowboy attraction under contract to Universal, with *Sierra*, which was distinguished only by the fact that he and Ms. Hendrix managed to chalk up this single film credit together in the course of their short marital pairing. More notable were some of his assignments outside the usual saddle sagas, starting with the good 1951 film version of the classic novel *The Red Badge of Courage*, where, ironically, he was cast as a cowardly soldier who flees from battle. It only made sense that Murphy himself appear in the 1955 filmization of *To Hell and Back*, which told the whole tale in standard Hollywood war movie fashion and was, most fittingly, his biggest box-office success. Among the westerns, *Destry* was of interest because it was a re-do of the more fondly remembered *Destry Rides Again*, with Murphy in James Stewart's old role, while *Walk the Proud Land* had him playing a real life character, Indian agent John Philips Clum, and *The Guns of Fort Petticoat* (made at Columbia) at least had the gimmick of having him lead a gang of women in fighting against the Indians. For a change of venue, Universal made him a boxer in *World in My Corner*; a photographer facing off with a Japanese wheeler-dealer, played by Burgess Meredith, in *Joe Butterfly*; and the bad guy brother of James Stewart in *Night Passage*.

After these he played the title role in United Artists's adaptation of Graham Greene's *The Quiet American*, which dropped most of the politics in favor of a mystery plot. Murphy's work was judged adequate and nothing more. He was more interesting as the angry brother of Burt Lancaster in a higher-profile western for director John Huston, *The Unforgiven*, but then it was back to Universal for less and less distinguished horse pictures, including *Seven Ways From Sundown*, which was only worth mentioning because the title was the name of the character he played (!). After Universal he continued these horse operas elsewhere, ending this string of programmers, albeit temporarily, at Columbia, in 1967, with *40 Guns to Apache Pass*, as a Cavalry officer who takes on Cochise. The next year he declared bankruptcy, prompting him to produce one more vehicle, *A Time for Dying*, in which he played Jesse James. Bookings were few. He was killed in a private plane crash in 1971, and, because his war heroics always outshone his film career, it was only fitting that he was buried in Arlington National Cemetery.

Screen: 1948: Beyond Glory; Texas, Brooklyn and Heaven; 1949: Bad Boy; 1950: Sierra; The Kid From Texas; Kansas Raiders; 1951: The Red Badge of Courage; The Cimarron Kid; 1952: The Duel at Silver Creek; 1953: Gunsmoke; Column South; Tumbleweed; 1954: Ride Clear of Diablo; Drums Across the River; Destry; 1955: To Hell and Back; 1956: World in My Corner; Walk the Proud Land; 1957: The Guns of Fort Petticoat; Joe Butterfly; Night Passage; 1958: The Quiet American; Ride a Crooked Trail; The Gun Runners; 1959: No Name on the Bullet; The Wild and the Innocent; Cast a Long Shadow; 1960: Hell Bent for Leather; The Unforgiven; Seven Ways From Sundown; 1961: Posse From Hell; Battle of Bloody Beach; 1962: Six Black Horses; 1963: Showdown; War Is Hell (narrator); Gunfight at Comanche Creek; 1964: The Quick Gun; Bullet for a Badman; Apache Rifles; 1965: Arizona Raiders; Gunpoint; 1966: Trunk to Cairo; The Texican; 1967: 40 Guns to Apache Pass; 1971: A Time for Dying (and prod.)

Select TV: 1955: Incident (sp); 1960: The Man (sp); 1961: Whispering Smith (series).

GEORGE MURPHY
BORN: NEW HAVEN, CT, JULY 4, 1902.
ED: YALE UNIV. DIED: MAY 3, 1992.

Considerably more pleasing a performer to spend time with than a certain *other* actor who rose to the top in politics, George Murphy had his dedication and inoffensiveness to pull him through, not being any great threat to those more talented in the dramatic, comedic, and dancing departments. Moving to New York to find work in the stock market, he met up with Julie Johnson and hit upon the idea of forming a dance team. The duo, who wed in 1926, performed in clubs and eventually in the London production of the hit musical *Good News*. Back in New York they did two shows as a team before Murphy went solo, for *Of Thee I Sing* and *Roberta*, which were instrumental in his being signed to a movie contract by producer Samuel Goldwyn. The result was a sole assignment, *Kid Millions*, in which he was upstaged by star Eddie Cantor. From there he went to Columbia for a quartet of undistinguished films before signing up with MGM in 1937. They didn't do all that much more for him at first, although they let him dance with Eleanor Powell and Buddy Ebsen in the extravaganza *Broadway Melody of 1938*. He went over to Universal to pair off with Alice Faye for *You're a Sweetheart*, and to Fox for *Little Miss Broadway*, which meant he had to back off while Shirley Temple, Jimmy Durante, and Edna Mae Oliver took center stage. Back at MGM there were better assignments with *Broadway Melody of 1940*, in which he had a glorious moment dancing with Fred Astaire to Cole Porter's

"Please Don't Monkey With Broadway;" *Two Girls on Broadway*, a remake of *The Broadway Melody*, which gave him the central role as the hoofer loved by both Lana Turner and Joan Blondell; and *Little Nellie Kelly*, in which he played the nice guy who marries Judy Garland.

RKO asked him to pursue Lucille Ball in *A Girl, a Guy, and a Gob*, and take the same course of action with Ginger Rogers, in *Tom, Dick and Harry*, both of which, if nothing else, showed he could be affable in the comedy department. After that they tried to showcase a tougher Murphy image by mixing music and gangsters in *The Mayor of 44th Street*. Returning to MGM, he watched newcomer Gene Kelly dance off with Judy Garland in *For Me and My Gal*, then got a chance to show his serious side again in one of the big war movies of the 1940s, *Bataan*. Alongside that other future Republican, Ronald Reagan, he was in *the* box-office blockbuster of 1943, *This Is the Army*, singing "My Sweetie;" then was back on the cinematic Great White Way again, playing a producer, in both *Broadway Rhythm* and *Step Lively*, in the latter making a poor replacement for Groucho Marx who'd done the role earlier in *Room Service*.

Coming full circle he was back in support of Eddie Cantor in *Show Business*, though this time the comedian (who also produced) gave Murphy more to do, including singing "It Had to Be You." It seemed as if Murphy was fated to be the nice guy who took a back seat to others and did so for *Cynthia*, with Elizabeth Taylor, and in two sentimental Margaret O'Brien vehicles, *Tenth Avenue Angel* and *The Big City*. Metro did ask him to participate in one of the best of all war films of the 1940s, *Battleground*, and in a superior adventure, *Border Incident*, as an FBI agent trying to stop illegal Mexican workers from being killed. In both he looked considerably older and was no doubt on the verge of going the character player route, had he not decided to call it quits, not only with Metro but with movies altogether, signing off with a programmer, *Talk About a Stranger*, in 1952

He had already shown his blossoming interest in politics by this point, having been instrumental in organizing Hollywood's Republican Committee and serving as president of the Screen Actors Guild. Though he was finished with acting, MGM kept him under salary to act as a kind of promoter of the industry, which included hosting the series MGM *Parade*. From there he served as chairman of the National Republican Committee and finally stepped into the political spotlight in a big way when he was elected Senator in 1965, representing California as a member of Congress until 1970. That same year he published his autobiography, *Say...Didn't You Used to Be George Murphy?*

Screen: 1934: Kid Millions; Jealousy; 1935: I'll Love You Always; After the Dance; Public Menace; 1936: Woman Trap; 1937: Top of the Town; Women Men Marry; London by Night; Broadway Melody of 1938; You're a Sweetheart; 1938: Little Miss Broadway; Letter of Introduction; Hold That Co-Ed; 1939: Risky Business; 1940: Broadway Melody of 1940; Two Girls on Broadway; Public Deb No. 1; Little Nellie Kelly; 1941: A Girl, a Guy, and a Gob; Tom, Dick and Harry; Ringside Maisie; Rise and Shine; 1942: The Mayor of 44th Street; For Me and My Gal; The Navy Comes Through; The Powers Girls; 1943: Bataan; This Is the Army; 1944: Step Lively; Broadway Rhythm; Show Business; 1945: Having Wonderful Crime; 1946: Up Goes Maisie; 1947: The Arnelo Affair; Cynthia; 1948: Tenth Avenue Angel; The Big City; 1949: Border Incident; Battleground; 1951: No Questions Asked; It's a Big Country; 1952: Walk East on Beacon; Talk About a Stranger.

NY Stage: 1929: Hold Everything; 1931: Shoot the Works; Of Thee I Sing; 1933: Roberta.

Select TV: 1955–56: MGM Parade (series).

DON MURRAY

BORN: HOLLYWOOD, CA, JULY 31, 1929.
ED: AADA.

In the late 1950s, nice looking, understated Don Murray came to prominence as the average guy who just happened to have some anxieties underneath his seemingly calm surface. He was a child of fringe show business people, his mother having been a Ziegfeld girl and his father a dance director at Fox. He took up acting and made his Broadway bow, while still a teen, in a bit role in *The Insect Comedy*, in 1948. Soldiering was something he did not want to do in real life and refused enlistment into the Korean War, registering as a conscientious objector. His career impetus may have been slowed down by this stance somewhat, for it was not until he did *The Skin of Our Teeth*, years later in New York, that things finally got up and running. Fox decided to test him for the key role of the manic rodeo star who relentlessly pursues singer Marilyn Monroe in *Bus Stop*. He won the part and an Oscar nomination for Best Supporting Actor, although the obnoxious behavior of the character was something he seemed unable to find the charm in, despite his better efforts to make him boyishly likable. The year of the movie's release, 1956, he wed one of his co-stars from the film, Hope Lange, and they remained a couple until 1961.

The good roles kept coming in the meantime with *The Bachelor Party*, where Murray was an angst-ridden businessman trying to find the meaning of his routine life during a night of revelry, and *A Hatful of Rain*, in which he did perhaps his most outstanding work, as the seemingly stable husband of Eva Marie Saint who is trying to keep his drug addiction hidden from her and his stern dad. He was an innocent on the run in the western *From Hell to Texas*; the rancher who loses his sense of human decency in *These Thousand Hills*; and an Irish-American med student in *Shake Hands With the Devil*, holding his own against James Cagney. Expanding his interests and hoping to make movies that expressed his concerns about society, he wrote (as Don Deer) and co-produced *The Hoodlum Priest*, a somber, well-done account of the real-life Jesuit priest Charles Dismas Clark and his efforts to help a young street kid. There was one last career high point, with *Advise and Consent*, as the young married senator whose homosexual past is brought out in the open for blackmail purposes, in the best of all director Otto Preminger's films.

He then took part in another religious-slanted biopic steeped in good intentions, *One Man's Way* (this time he played Reverend Norman Vincent Peale), which did not repeat the critical success of his earlier clerical role. After biding his time with some routine westerns, *Kid Rodelo* and the remake of *The Plainsman*, as well as a goofy Hammer adventure, *The Viking Queen*, he stepped behind the camera as director for another religious story, *The Cross and the Switchblade*, which covered similar ground as *The Hoodlum Priest* but, again, minus the praise. There was also a lack of interest in the other efforts he worked on behind the scenes, *Childish Things/Confessions of Tom Harris*, a story of a prizefighter that he wrote and appeared in; and *Damien*, another biographical look at a priest, on which he served as director and writer only. During the 1970s a majority of his acting was done on the small screen (there was also a Broadway appearance in *Same Time, Next Year*, with ex-wife Hope Lange), but he began popping up in some major theatrical films in the 1980s, including *Endless Love*, as Brooke Shields's free-spirited dad who disapproves of her boyfriend, and *Peggy Sue Got Married*, as Kathleen Turner's father. There was also a regular role on the nighttime soap *Knots Landing*.

Screen: 1956: Bus Stop; 1957: The Bachelor Party; A Hatful of Rain; 1958: From Hell to Texas; 1959: These Thousand Hills; Shake Hands With the Devil; 1960: One Foot in Hell; 1961: The Hoodlum Priest (and prod., wr. AS DON DEER); 1962: Advise and Consent; Escape From East Berlin; 1964: One Man's Way; 1965: Baby the Rain Must Fall; 1966: Kid Rodelo; The Plainsman; 1967: Sweet Love Bitter; The Viking Queen; 1969: Childish Things/Confessions of Tom Harris (and co-wr.; prod.); 1971: Happy Birthday, Wanda June; 1972: Conquest of the Planet of the Apes; 1973: Cotter; 1976: Deadly Hero; 1981: Endless Love; 1983: I Am the Cheese; 1986: Radioactive Dreams; Peggy Sue Got Married; Scorpion (dtv); 1987: Made in Heaven; 1990: Ghosts Can't Do It; 2001: Island Prey (nUSr).

NY Stage: 1948: The Insect Play; 1951: The Rose Tattoo; 1955: The Skin of Our Teeth; 1956: The Hot Corner; 1973: Smith (ob); 1976: The Norman Conquests; 1977: Same Time, Next Year.

Select TV: 1950: The Taming of the Shrew (sp); 1952: Mr. Lazarus (sp); 1955: The Skin of Our Teeth (sp); A Man Is 10 Feet Tall (sp); 1956: Moment of Courage (sp); 1957: For I Have Loved Strangers (sp); 1958: The Hasty Heart (sp); 1959: Billy Budd (sp); Winterset (sp); 1960: Alas; Babylon (sp); 1964: Made in America (series); 1967: The Borgia Stick; 1968–69: The Outcasts (series); 1969: Daughter of the Mind; 1970: The Intruders; 1972: Justin Morgan Had a Horse (sp); 1974: The Girl on the Late, Late Show; The Sex Symbol; 1975: A Girl Named Sooner; 1977: How the West Was Won (ms); 1978: Rainbow; 1979: Crisis in Mid-Air; 1979–81: Knots Landing (series); 1980: If Things Were Different; The Boy Who Drank Too Much; Fugitive Family; 1981: Return of the Rebels; 1983: Thursday's Child; Branagan and Mapes; Quarterback Princess; 1984: License to Kill; A Touch of Scandal; 1986: Something in Common; 1987: Stillwatch; The Stepford Children; Mistress; 1989: Brand New Life (series); My father Can't Be Crazy, Can He? (sp); 1991: Sons and Daughters (series); 1996: Hearts Adrift.

GEORGE NADER

BORN: LOS ANGELES, CA, OCTOBER 19, 1921.
ED: OCCIDENTAL COL. DIED: FEBRUARY 4, 2002.

Nobody, least of all George Nader himself, was fooled into thinking that this was an actor who had any special qualities to offer outside of his uncomplicated good looks. A member of the Pasadena Playhouse, he launched his movie career in 1949 as the lead in an obscure Swedish-British-American production called *Memory of Love*. Journeying to Hollywood, he became a minor player in such movies as *Phone Call From a Stranger*, as a pilot, and *Two Tickets to Broadway*, as a techie. He was then elevated to the more important roles in "B's," such as *Monsoon*, falling in love with both Ursula Theiss and her sister, and *Miss Robin Crusoe*, which required him to be washed up on the beach in order to keep Amanda Blake company on her deserted island. His fairly negligible résumé reached some kind of Nader nadir with *Robot Monster*, a cheesy sci-fi which later became a jaw-dropping favorite of aficionados of 1950s camp. Rescue of sorts came when Universal decided they might want to promote him as rugged new star. They made him part of the ensemble of *Six Bridges to Cross*, as a Boston cop in this story of the famous Brink's robbery, and *Away All Boats*, second billed as a Navy man fighting the Japanese, a pretty standard WWII actioner that was one of the studio's bigger hits of 1956. In addition, he was featured in such silliness as *Lady Godiva*, as nudist Maureen O'Hara's Saxon hubbie, and *Congo Crossing*, surveying both the landscape *and* Virginia Mayo. He started to branch out into more serious efforts with *Man Afraid*, as a priest who fears revenge from the father whose son he killed in self-defense; *Flood Tide*, trying to reach out to an unhinged adolescent; and *Appointment With a Shadow*, as a reporter trying to overcome alcoholism. These projects seemed to bode well for the future. Instead he went over to TV, including a stint as Ellery Queen, and then resumed his movie career in Germany, appearing as secret agent Jerry Cotton in several adventures clearly patterned after the James Bond films. Few of these efforts were much heard of outside of Europe.

Screen: 1949: Memory of Love; 1950: Rustlers on Horseback; 1951: The Prowler; Two Tickets to Broadway; Overland Telegraph; Take Care of My Little Girl; 1952: Phone Call From a Stranger; 1953: Monsoon; Down Among the Sheltering Palms; Robot Monster; Sins of Jezebel; 1954: Miss Robin Crusoe; Carnival Story; Four Guns to the Border; 1955: Six Bridges to Cross; The Second Greatest Sex; Lady Godiva; 1956: Away All Boats; Congo Crossing; The Unguarded Moment; Four Girls in Town; 1957: Man Afraid; Joe Butterfly; 1958: Flood Tide; Appointment With a Shadow; The Female Animal; Nowhere to Go; 1963: The Secret Mark of D'Artagnan; 1965: The Human Duplicators; Die Rechnung — Eiskalt Serviret (nUSr); Tread Softly/Operation Hurricane (nUSr); Mordnacht in Manhattan (nUSr); Um null uhr schanppt die Falle zu (nUSr); 1967: Der Morderclub von Brooklyn (nUSr); The Million Eyes of Sumuru; House of 1,000 Dolls; 1968: Radhapura — Endstation der Verdammten (nUSr); Der Tod im Roten Jaguar (nUSr); Dynamit in gruner Seide/Death and Diamonds (nUSr); 1969: Todeschusse am Broadway/Deadly Shots on Broadway (nUSr); 1973: Beyond Atlantis.

Select TV: 1953: The Lady Wears a Star (sp); Appointment With Death (sp); 1954: Account Closed (sp); His Brother's Girl (sp); 1956: The Glass Web (sp); 1957: One Way Street (sp); 1958–59: The Adventures of Ellery Queen/Ellery Queen (series); 1959–60: Man and the Challenge (series); 1961–62: Shannon (series); 1974: Nakia.

CONRAD NAGEL

BORN: KEOKUK, IA, MARCH 16, 1896.
DIED: FEBRUARY 24, 1970.

Despite the fact that his film career took in a wide scope — the height of the silent era, the transition to sound, and the Hollywood studio heyday — stoically blond Conrad Nagle, with the penetrating stare, remains one of the less distinctive or fondly remembered stars of yore. After receiving a degree from the School of Oratory, he joined the Princess Stock Company in Des Moines then went to New York where he made his stage debut as a cast replacement in *The Natural Law*. Following several more theatrical assignments, he was asked to play Laurie in the 1919 version of *Little Women*, which had the distinction of actually being filmed at Louisa May Alcott's home. Returning to the theater, he became involved with Actors' Equity, which would, in time, lead to his participation in the formation of the Screen Actors Guild. Meanwhile, Paramount signed him to a contract following the favorable impression he'd made in *The Fighting Chance*, in 1920. There he found his stardom on the rise because of a pair of movies under the direction of Cecil B. DeMille: *Fool's Paradise*, which required him to play a man who is accidentally blinded; and *Saturday Night*, as a millionaire's son who marries laundress Leatrice Joy. More melodrama followed with *Singed Wings*, in which he and Adolphe Menjou both craved Bebe Daniels; *Bella Donna*, where he was nearly poisoned by Pola Negri; and *Lawful Larceny*, in which he cheated on his wife. Goldwyn took him on for four films, including *Three Weeks*, as Aileen Pringle's lover, before he signed up with MGM in 1924.

He stayed with MGM for four years, playing a Kentucky bumpkin in *Sun Up*; the man in love with Marion Davies's look-alike sister in *Lights of Old Broadway*; an alcoholic in *Dance Madness*; a soldier stationed in Germany in *Tin Hats*; and the hero in Lon Chaney's lost thriller *London After Midnight*. It was then over to Warners for *The Girl From Chicago* and *Tenderloin*, in both cases playing gangsters, and *The Michigan Kid*, as a gambler. He had no trouble getting used to talkies as was proven by his first production with partial sound, *Caught in the Fog*, a thriller set on a houseboat. He kept popping up all over the place, at that point probably at the peak of his popularity. He lost Kay Johnson to Charles Bickford in *Dynamite*; defended Greta Garbo, accused of murdering her husband, in *The Kiss*; was Lillian Gish's royal tutor in *One Romantic Night*; and pined for Norma Shearer, who wed another, in *The Divorcee*. In *Redemption* he was cast opposite Eleanor Boardman, with whom he'd done many a film in the pre-sound era, and in an Oscar nominee for Best Picture, *East Lynne*, he was the rich but boring husband who drives Ann Harding into Clive Brook's arms. During all this he served as vice president of the Motion Picture Academy of Arts and Sciences, working his way up to president in 1932. The organization's failure to keep the unions from overtaking Hollywood was blamed on Nagel, who found himself pretty much blacklisted by the mid-1930s, as proven by the cheap quality of films he was being offered. These include four movies as FBI agent Alan O'Connor, starting with *Yellow Cargo*, in 1936, and one he directed but did not appear in, *Love Takes Flight*. In time he became a frequent voice on radio and was seen in various series in the early days of television, before returning to character work including *All That Heaven Allows*, as the white-haired gent courting Jane Wyman, and *Stranger in My Arms*, as the henpecked husband of Mary Astor.

Screen: 1918: Little Women; 1919: The Lion and the Mouse; The Red Head; 1920: The Fighting Chance; Midsummer Madness; Unseen Forces; 1921: What Every Woman Knows; Sacred and Profane Love; The Lost Romance; Fool's Paradise; 1922: Saturday Night; Hate; The Ordeal; Nice People; The Impossible Mrs. Bellew; Singed Wings; 1923: Grumpy; Bella Donna; Lawful Larceny; The Rendezvous; 1924: Name the Man; Three Weeks; The Rejected Woman; Tess of the D'Urbervilles; Sinners in Silk; Married Flirts; The Snob; 1925: Excuse Me; Cheaper to Marry; Pretty Ladies; Sun Up; Lights of Old Broadway; So This Is Marriage?; The Only Thing; 1926: Memory Lane; Dance Madness; Exquisite Sinner; The Waning Sex; There You Are!; Tin Hats; 1927: Heaven on Earth; Slightly Used; Quality Street; The Girl From Chicago; London After Midnight; If I Were Single; 1928: Tenderloin; Glorious Betsy; Diamond Handcuffs; The Michigan Kid; The Mysterious Lady; The Crimson City; State Street Sadie; The Terror (narrator); Caught in the Fog; Red Wine;

1929: The Redeeming Sin; The Idle Rich; Kid Gloves; The Hollywood Revue of 1929; The Thirteenth Chair; The Kiss; The Sacred Flame; Dynamite; 1930: The Second Wife; One Romantic Night; The Divorcee; The Ship From Shanghai; Redemption; Numbered Men; A Lady Surrenders; Today; Du Barry — Woman of Passion; Free Love; 1931: East Lynne; Bad Sister; The Right of Way; Three Who Loved; The Reckless Hour; Son of India; Pagan Lady; Hell Divers; 1932: The Man Called Back; Kongo; Divorce in the Family; Fast Life; 1933: Constant Woman; Ann Vickers; 1934: The Marines Are Coming; Dangerous Corner; 1935: One Hour Late; Death Flies East; One New York Night; 1936: Ball at Savoy/With Pleasure Madame; The Girl From Mandalay; Yellow Cargo; Wedding Present; 1937: Navy Spy; The Gold Racket; Bank Alarm; 1940: The Mad Empress; One Million B.C.; I Want a Divorce; 1945: They Shall Have Faith/Forever Yours; The Adventures of Rusty; 1948: The Vicious Circle; 1948: Stage Struck; 1955: All That Heaven Allows; 1957: Hidden Fear; 1959: A Stranger in My Arms; The Man Who Understood Women.

NY Stage: 1915: The Natural Law; Experience; 1916: The Man Who Came Back; 1918: Forever After; 1933: The First Apple; 1943: The Skin of Our Teeth; 1945: Tomorrow the World; 1946: State of the Union; 1948: Goodbye, My Fancy; 1951: Music in the Air; 1953: Be Your Age; 1957: Four Winds; 1962: Captains and the Kings.

Select TV: 1949–50: The Silver Theatre (series); 1950: The First Show of 1950 (series); 1949–52: Celebrity Time (series); 1951: A Star Is Born (series); 1953–54: Broadway to Hollywood — Headline Clues (series); 1955: The Answer (sp). Conrad Nagel Theater (series); Hollywood Prevue (series); 1956: The Wonderful Gift (sp); 1957: The Duel (sp); The Weston Strain (sp); 1961: The Dispossessed. (sp)

J. CARROLL NAISH

(JOSEPH PATRICK CARROLL NAISH)
BORN: NEW YORK, NY, JANUARY 21, 1900.
DIED: JANUARY 24, 1973.

His ability to play characters of different nationalities was so impressive you were never quite sure just what J. Carroll Naish's real background was. It so happened he was Irish, but he portrayed just about everything but that, from Italians to Indians to Mexicans, often with great relish but sometimes with a deadly earnest, self-conscious manner that was a bit forced and somewhat hackneyed. After having served in the military during World War I, he made his way to California where he did various jobs including stunt and extra work on many films, few of which have been authenticated or verified. He acted with a road company and then went to Broadway for a play that got him summoned back to Hollywood. This time he was given some actual acting roles, starting with *Scotland Yard*, in which he was a plastic surgeon. It being the early 1930s he was frequently seen playing gangsters, in *Beast of the City*, *The Mouthpiece*, and *Afraid to Talk*, among others, while also showing up as Loretta Young's Chinese father in *The Hatchet Man*; a sleazy lawyer in *No Other Woman*; Leon Trotsky in *British Agent*; Ginger Rogers's killer in *Upper World*; the Grand Vizier in the 1935 action hit *The Lives of a Bengal Lancer*; one of the pirates in *Captain Blood*; and a bandit called Three-Fingered Jack in *The Robin Hood of El Dorado*. At this point, he was not a well-known character player to the general public but was much admired in the business for his ability to jump into such a wide range of roles — big and small, smarmy or pathetic — without hesitation.

As with many supporting players, "B" movies were instrumental in expanding the size of his roles. This was especially true at Paramount where he was *King of Alcatraz*, as an escaped gangster who smuggles himself aboard a ship dressed as an old lady; ruled *Island of Lost Men*, as a gunrunner; and received top billing in *Illegal Traffic*, in which he ran a shady operation that helped criminals escape the police. At his most weasely, he was the legionnaire who ratted on Gary Cooper in *Beau Geste*, but then had a sympathetic role, as the former matador who ends up a street vagrant, in *Blood and Sand*. With the coming of World War II he was, of course, Japanese in both *Behind the Rising Sun*, where he was about the only cast member to at least make an attempt at an accent, and in *Dragon Seed*; a Nazi in *Waterfront*; and the Italian prisoner captured by Humphrey Bogart and his squad in *Sahara*. The last was a taut action film with a collection of solid characterizations of which Naish, in one of his less interesting performances, was singled out for an Oscar nomination. He got a second nod from the Academy in 1945 for his somewhat coy work as the gentle Mexican peasant who accepts his slain son's honor in *A Medal for Benny*. Horror fans saw him as the hunchback assistant to Boris Karloff in the pastiche *House of Frankenstein* and as the title role in *The Monster Maker*, while he scored a lead in the crime film *Enter Arsene Lupin*, as the detective out to trap Charles Korvin. Still proving hard to peg, he was Sitting Bull in the musical *Annie Get Your Gun* (and then again, four years later, in the straightforward account *Sitting Bull*), General Phil Sheridan in *Rio Grande*; the Mafia leader Gene Kelly takes revenge on in *Black Hand*; and Santa Ana, the Mexican general who led the slaughter at the Alamo, in *The Lost Command*. During the 1950s he began concentrating less on films so he could spend some time on the small screen. He starred in the series *Life With Luigi* (which he'd done on radio as well) and *The New Adventures of Charlie Chan*, among others.

Screen: 1930: Scotland Yard; Good Intentions; Cheer Up and Smile; Double Cross Roads; 1931: The Royal Bed; Homicide Squad; Gun Smoke; Ladies of the Big House; Tonight of Never; Kick In; 1932: Beast of the City; Two Seconds; Tiger Shark; The Hatchet Man; The Kid From Spain; The Conquerors; The Mouthpiece; Weekend Marriage; Big City Blues; Crooner; The Famous Ferguson Case; No Living Witness; Afraid to Talk; 1933: Central Airport; Captured!; Frisco Jenny; The Mad Game; The Devil's in Love; Ann Vickers; The Past of Mary Holmes; No Other Woman; Elmer the Great; Infernal Machine; Arizona to Broadway; The Whirlwind; Silent Men; The Last Trail; The World Gone Mad; The Avenger; Notorious But Nice; The Big Chance; Mystery Squadron (serial); 1934: The President Vanishes; British Agent; Marie Galante; Upperworld; Murder in Trinidad; One Is Guilty; The Hell Cat; Sleepers East; Return of the Terror; Bachelor of Arts; Girl in Danger; The Defense Rests; Hell in the Heavens; What's Your Racket?; 1935: The Lives of a Bengal Lancer; The Crusades; Black Fury; Captain Blood; Front Page Woman; Special Agent; Under the Pampas Moon; Little Big Shot; Behind Green Lights; Confidential; 1936: The Charge of the Light Brigade; The Leathernecks Have Landed; Special Investigator; Anthony Adverse; Ramona; Absolute Quiet; Crack-Up; Two in the Dark; The Robin Hood of El Dorado; We Who Are About to Die; Exclusive Story; The Return of Jimmy Valentine; Charlie Chan at the Circus; Moonlight Murder; 1937: Night Club Scandal; Think Fast, Mr. Moto; Song of the City; Border Cafe; Hideaway; Bulldog Drummond Comes Back; Thunder Trail; Sea Racketeers; 1938: Daughter of Shanghai; Her Jungle Love; King of Alcatraz; Tip-Off Girls; Illegal Traffic; Bulldog Drummond in Africa; Hunted Men; Prison Farm; 1939: Beau Geste; King of Chinatown; Persons in Hiding; Hotel Imperial; Island of Lost Men; Undercover Doctor; 1940: Typhoon; Queen of the Mob; Down Argentine Way; Golden

Gloves; A Night at Earl Carroll's; 1941: Blood and Sand; The Corsican Brothers; Birth of the Blues; That Night in Rio; Accent on Love; Forced Landing; Mr. Dynamite; 1942: Tales of Manhattan; The Pied Piper; Dr. Renault's Secret; The Man in the Trunk; Dr. Broadway; Gentleman at Heart; Sunday Punch; Jackass Mail; 1943: Sahara; Behind the Rising Sun; Gung Ho!; Good Morning Judge; Batman (serial); Harrigan's Kid; Calling Dr. Death; 1944: Voice in the Wind; House of Frankenstein; Dragon Seed; The Whistler; Enter Arsene Lupin; Two-Man Submarine; Jungle Woman; Monster Maker; Waterfront; 1945: The Southerner; A Medal for Benny; Strange Confession; Getting Gertie's Garter; 1946: Humoresque; The Beast With Five Fingers; Bad Bascomb; 1947: The Fugitive; Carnival in Costa Rica; 1948: The Kissing Bandit; Joan of Arc; 1949: That Midnight Kiss; Canadian Pacific; 1950: The Toast of New Orleans; Please Believe Me; Annie Get Your Gun; The Black Hand; Rio Grande; 1951: Across the Wide Missouri; Bannerline; Mark of the Renegade; 1952: Clash by Night; The Denver and Rio Grande; Ride the Man Down; Woman of the North Country; 1953: Beneath the 12-Mile Reef; Fighter Attack; 1954: Sitting Bull; Saskatchewan; 1955: Violent Saturday; Hit the Deck; New York Confidential; Rage at Dawn; The Last Command; Desert Sands; 1956: Rebel in Town; Yaqui Drums; 1957: This Could Be the Night; The Young Don't Cry; 1961: Force of Impulse; 1971: Dracula vs. Frankenstein/Blood of Frankenstein.

NY Stage: 1929: The Broken Chain; 1955: A View From the Bridge; A Memory of Two Mondays.

Select TV: 1952: Life With Luigi (series); 1953: Wedding Day (sp); 1954: A Medal for Benny (sp); 1955: Wild Call (sp); 1956: The Mysterious Cargo (sp); Key Largo (sp); 1958: Hiawatha (sp); My Father the Fool (sp); The New Adventures of Charlie Chan (series); 1960–61: Guestward Ho! (series); 1964: The Hanged Man; 1968: For Love or $$$. (sp); 1969: Cutter's Trail.

ALAN NAPIER

(ALAN NAPIER-CLAVERING) BORN: HARBORNE, BIRMINGHAM, ENGLAND, JANUARY 7, 1903. ED: RADA. DIED: AUGUST 8, 1988.

Bean-pole thin expatriate Alan Napier was usually on hand to look very distinguished, sometimes even threatening, and often just to let you know that something was most specifically set in England. Overall it was not a career in which he spent very much time taking center stage, his roles usually being of an extremely secondary nature. His London stage debut came in 1924, in *Dandy Dick*, and he soon became a staple of the English theater, often playing characters much older than himself. During this period he was occasionally called on for a film assignment, notably *The Four Just Men*, in which he was the villain plotting to stop all passage through the Suez Canal. In 1939 he came to America for a lead in a Broadway play, *Lady in Waiting*, and for the small role of a prison chaplain in a Paul Muni movie, *We Are Not Alone*. Hollywood had found a new Englishman to add to its growing Anglo stable, which already included Nigel Bruce, Cedric Hardwicke, and C. Aubrey Smith, among others. Napier was seen as a coal miner in *The Invisible Man Returns*; a postman in *The House of the Seven Gables*; the chief engineer in *The Hairy Ape*; a pro-Nazi in *Action in Arabia*; a restaurant owner abducted by schoolboys in *A Yank at Eton*; Geraldine Fitzgerald's unhappy estranged husband in *Three Strangers*; the Earl of Warwick in *Joan of Arc*; Captain Kidd in *Double Crossbones*; and the added role of a friar in Orson Welles's production of *Macbeth*. Amid all this, he actually got a sizable part, in Paramount's hit psychological thriller *The Uninvited*, which allowed him the rare opportunity to the get the girl, in this case Ruth Hussey, at the movie's climax. His films continued to run the gamut of the extreme high of *Johnny Belinda* (as the defense attorney) to the lows of menacing the Bowery Boys in *Master Minds*; from spouting Shakespeare in *Julius Caesar* to ruling *The Mole People*. Sometimes it seemed as if he was doing little more than filling in the background, as in *Young Bess*, *The Court Jester*, or *My Fair Lady*. His last role of any significance also turned out to be the one for which he would be most fondly remembered: the ever loyal, ever calm butler Alfred on the highly popular camp series *Batman*, which he repeated in the 1966 theatrical spin-off.

Screen: 1930: Caste; 1931: Stamboul; 1932: In a Monastery Garden; 1933: Loyalties; 1936: Wings Over Africa; 1937: For Valour; The Wife of General Ling; 1939: The Four Just Men/The Secret Four; We Are Not Alone; 1940: The Invisible Man Returns; The House of the Seven Gables; 1941: Confirm or Deny; 1942: Eagle Squadron; A Yank at Eton; The Cat People; Random Harvest; We Were Dancing; 1943: Assignment in Brittany; The Song of Bernadette; Madame Curie; Appointment in Berlin; Lost Angel; Lassie Come Home; 1944: The Uninvited; The Hairy Ape; Action in Arabia; Mademoiselle Fifi; Ministry of Fear; Dark Waters; Thirty Seconds Over Tokyo; 1945: Isle of the Dead; Hangover Square; 1946: Three Strangers; House of Horrors; A Scandal in Paris; The Strange Woman; 1947: Sinbad the Sailor; High Conquest; Ivy; Fiesta; Driftwood; Unconquered; Forever Amber; Adventure Island; The Lone Wolf in London; Lured; 1948: Joan of Arc; Macbeth; Johnny Belinda; My Own True Love; Hills of Home; 1949: Criss Cross; Tarzan's Magic Fountain; A Connecticut Yankee in King Arthur's Court; Manhandled; The Red Danube; Master Minds; Challenge to Lassie; 1950: Double Crossbones; Tripoli; 1951: Tarzan's Peril; The Great Caruso; The Highwayman; The Blue Veil; Across the Wide Missouri; The Strange Door; 1952: Big Jim McLain; 1953: Young Bess; Julius Caesar; 1954: Desiree; 1955: Moonfleet; 1956: The Court Jester; Miami Expose; The Mole People; 1957: Until They Sail; 1959: Island of Lost Women; Journey to the Center of the Earth; 1961: Wild in the Country; 1962: Tender Is the Night; The Premature Burial; 1963: The Sword in the Stone (voice); 1964: My Fair Lady; Marnie; 36 Hours; 1965: Signpost to Murder; The Loved One; 1966: Batman.

NY Stage: 1940: Lady in Waiting; 1952: Gertie; 1953: Coriolanus (ob); 1956: Too Late the Phalarope.

Select TV: 1956: Operation Cicero (sp); 1962–63: Don't Call Me Charlie (series); 1966–68: Batman (series); 1973: Crime Club; 1974: QBVII (ms); 1978: The Bastard; Centennial (ms); 1981: The Monkey Mission.

MILDRED NATWICK

BORN: BALTIMORE, MD, JUNE 19, 1905.
ED: BENNETT COL. DIED: OCTOBER 25, 1994.

It was hard not to crack a smile when this warm, witty, sharp-featured character player with the quavering voice would appear on screen. Mildred Natwick, who was peerless at comedy yet heartbreakingly good in serious roles, was as assured a character actress as there ever was. Unfortunately, she didn't do feature film work as often as one would have wished. Having studied drama in college, she unsuccessfully sought work in New York and ended up, instead, in Washington, DC as part of a children's theater company that included Henry Fonda. He invited her to join the University Players, which, in turn, brought her to Broadway at last, with *Carry Nation*, in 1932. Natwick

spent the rest of the decade in theater until she was asked by director John Ford to join the ensemble of his *The Long Voyage Home*, in a brief but memorable bit as a lady of the waterfront. Back on Broadway she scored one of her greatest triumphs as Madame Arcati in *Blithe Spirit* (a part she would later play on television), which resulted in further interest from the movies. On the big screen, she was an asset to *Yolanda and the Thief*, as Lucille Bremer's fluttery aunt; *A Woman's Vengeance*, as a nurse; and the Frank Sinatra flop *The Kissing Bandit*. John Ford called on her again, to play the dying mother whose baby is taken care of by *3 Godfathers* and to portray the wife of George O'Brien, being escorted safely out of Indian Territory by John Wayne, in *She Wore a Yellow Ribbon*.

She got her best Ford assignment yet, and gave one of her most memorable performances, as the Widow Tillane — who gives Wayne her property to spite money hungry Victor McLaglen — in *The Quiet Man*, everybody's favorite look at the Ireland that never was but should have been, and one of the big attractions of 1952. Three years later she landed a part that was about as close to a movie lead as she was ever going to get, the New England spinster who, along with Edmund Gwenn, John Forsythe, and Shirley MacLaine, thinks that she is responsible for the dead body in Hitchcock's *The Trouble With Harry*. It was Natwick, more than any of the other cast members, who made one forget just how feeble the whole thing was. This was followed by a movie high point, as the campy sorceress Griselda in *The Court Jester*, where she became a part of comedy history swapping the memorable "pellet with the poison" dialogue with Danny Kaye. Returning to Broadway, she was so good in the Neil Simon smash *Barefoot in the Park* that she was asked to repeat the role in the 1967 movie version. Playing Jane Fonda's widowed mom, who is romanced by Charles Boyer, Natwick earned her sole Oscar nomination. This revitalized interest in her for all kinds of spinster and biddy parts, so she was one of the vacationers in *If It's Tuesday, This Must Be Belgium*; paired off with Helen Hayes on the small screen as one of *The Snoop Sisters*, for which she won an Emmy; showed up as Burt Reynolds's dotty mom in the musical *At Long Last Love*, though no one bothered to give her a song; and sagely offered advice to a forlorn Michelle Pfeiffer in *Dangerous Liaisons*.

Screen: 1940: The Long Voyage Home; 1945: The Enchanted Cottage; Yolanda and the Thief; 1947: The Late George Apley; A Woman's Vengeance; 1948: The Kissing Bandit; 3 Godfathers; 1949: She Wore a Yellow Ribbon; 1950: Cheaper by the Dozen; 1952: Against All Flags; The Quiet Man; 1955: The Trouble With Harry; 1956: The Court Jester; Teen-age Rebel; 1957: Tammy and the Bachelor; 1967: Barefoot in the Park; 1969: If It's Tuesday, This Must Be Belgium; The Maltese Bippy; Trilogy; 1974: Daisy Miller; 1975: At Long Last Love; 1982: Kiss Me Goodbye; 1988: Dangerous Liaisons.

NY Stage: 1932: Carry Nation; 1933: Amourette; Spring in Autumn; 1934: The Wind and the Rain; The Distaff Side; 1935: Night in the House; 1936: End of Summer; Love From a Stranger; 1937: Candida (and revivals in 1942 and 1946); The Star-Wagon; 1938: Missouri Legend; 1939: Stars in Your Eyes; Christmas Eve; 1941: The Lady Who Came to Stay; Blithe Spirit; 1946: Playboy of the Western World; 1952: The Grass Harp; 1954: Coriolanus (ob); 1957: The Waltz of the Toreadors; 1958: The Day the Money Stopped; The Firstborn; 1960: The Good Soup; Critic's Choice; 1963: Barefoot in the Park; 1969: Our Town; 1970: Landscape (ob); 1971: 70 Girls 70; 1979: Bedroom Farce.

Select TV: 1950: The Horizontal Man (sp); The Feast (sp); My Granny Van (sp); 1951: One Pair of Hands (sp); Mr. Pratt and the Triple Horror Bill (sp); The Skin of Our Teeth (sp); 1952: The

Grass Harp (sp); **1953:** The Marmalade Scandal (sp); The Bartlett Desk (sp); The Happy Rest (sp); **1954:** Tom O'Shanter (sp); The Almighty Dollar (sp); Mr. Simmons (sp); A Garden by the Sea (sp); **1955:** Uncle Ed and Circumstances (sp); Christopher Bean (sp); **1956:** Blithe Spirit (sp); Always Welcome (sp); Eloise (sp); **1957:** The Big Heist (sp); **1959:** Waltz of the Toreadors (sp); **1961:** The Power and the Glory (sp); **1962:** Arsenic and Old Lace (sp); **1971:** Do Not Fold, Spindle or Mutilate; **1972:** The House Without a Christmas Tree (sp); The Female Instinct/The Snoop Sisters; **1973:** Money to Burn; A Thanksgiving Treasure (sp); **1973–74:** The Snoop Sisters (series); **1975:** The Easter Promise (sp); **1976:** Addie and the King of Hearts (sp); **1979:** Little Women (series); You Can't Take It With You (sp); **1982:** Maid in America; **1987:** Deadly Deception.

ANNA NEAGLE

(FLORENCE MARJORIE ROBERTSON)
BORN: LONDON, ENGLAND, OCTOBER 20, 1904.
DIED: JUNE 3, 1986.

A very important name in the annals of British film history but less so in America, Anna Neagle started as a chorus dancer, working her way up to a co-starring part with Jack Buchanan in the West End musical *Stand Up and Sing*, in 1931. Producer-director Herbert Wilcox signed her to a movie contract that same year and later became her husband (1943–77); with rare exceptions, he was also her constant director. There was a film in support of Buchanan, *Goodnight Vienna*, and then a starring role in the first movie of *Bitter Sweet*, which failed. The picture that made her a star in her native country, *Nell Gwynn*, cast her as the real-life actress who caused some commotion in England when she became mistress to King Charles II (Cedric Hardwicke). This was followed by the role that would make her that much more famous in the rest of the world, Queen Victoria in *Victoria the Great*, and its immediate sequel, *Sixty Glorious Years/Queen of Destiny*. Because of these, RKO asked Neagle and Wilcox to come to Hollywood in hopes of finding a niche for her there. Their first assignment for her, *Nurse Edith Cavell* was a timely account of that lady's noble efforts during World War I, after which she was placed in three musicals of which only *Irene*, despite having most of its original stage songs removed, was somewhat popular. After the others, *No, No, Nanette* and *Sunny*, failed it was clear that Neagle and her mentor should hightail it back to Britain. There she pleased the public with the aviation drama *They Flew Alone*, as real-life flier Amy Johnson; *I Live in Grosvenor Square/A Yank in London*, which kept her in touch with America since Dean Jagger played one of her suitors; *Piccadilly Incident*, in which the war separated her from husband Michael Wilding; *Spring in Park Lane*, where she had suspicions about footman Wilding but fell for him just the same; *Odette*, the biopic of the famed British agent who defied the Nazis and ended up in a concentration camp; and *The Lady With a Lamp*, playing the legendary "angel of mercy" Florence Nightingale. Her popularity fell off during the 1950s, so she gave producing a whirl, with three vehicles for singer Frankie Vaughan, *These Dangerous Years*, *Wonderful Things*, and *The Heart of a Man*, none of which succeeded. After that her work was confined to the stage. She was made a Dame in 1969.

Screen: 1930: School for Scandal; Should a Doctor Tell?; **1931:** The Chinese Bungalow; **1932:** Goodnight Vienna/Magic Night; **1933:** The Flag Lieutenant; The Little Damozel; Bitter Sweet; **1934:** The Queen's Affair/Runaway Queen; Nell Gwynn; **1935:** Peg of Old Drury; **1936:** Limelight/Backstage; The Three Maxims/The Show Goes On; **1937:** London Melody/Girls in the Street; Victoria the Great; **1938:** Sixty Glorious Years/ Queen of Destiny; **1939:** Nurse Edith Cavell; **1940:** Irene; No, No, Nanette; **1941:** Sunny; **1942:** They Flew Alone/Wings and the Woman; **1943:** Forever and a Day; The Yellow Canary; **1945:** I Live in Grosvenor Square/A Yank in London; **1946:** Piccadilly Incident; **1947:** The Courtneys of Curzon Street; **1948:** Spring in Park Lane; **1949:** Maytime in Mayfair; Elizabeth of Ladymead; **1950:** Odette; **1951:** The Lady With a Lamp; **1952:** Derby Day/Four Against Fate; **1954:** Lilacs in the Spring/Let's Make Up; **1955:** King's Rhapsody; **1956:** My Teenage Daughter/Teenage Bad Girl; **1957:** No Time for Tears; **1958:** The Man Who Wouldn't Talk; **1959:** The Lady Is a Square.

PATRICIA NEAL

(PATSY LOUISE NEAL) BORN: PACKARD, KY, JANUARY 20, 1926. RAISED IN KNOXVILLE, TN. ED: NORTHWESTERN UNIV.

Hollywood was only too happy to take Patricia Neal into its fold. She was attractive, with a voice that was alternately sexy and comforting, and she could act too. The fact that she was even better at her craft than anybody initially seemed to be aware of didn't mean that the studios went out of their way to find outstanding showcases for her. In time, this superb actress did get her chance to shine. One of her teachers at college started a summer theater in Eaglesmere, PA, and it was there that she got her start, eventually seeking employment in New York. She was hired as an understudy for *The Voice of the Turtle*, eventually stepping into the footlights there and in the Chicago production of the hit comedy. This got her the lead back in New York in *Another Part of the Forest*, the prequel to *The Little Foxes*, as the younger version of Regina. It also brought her a Tony Award at the very first ceremony for Broadway's highest honor. Warner Bros. signed her to a contract, starting her off as Ronald Reagan's fiancée in *John Loves Mary*, a comedy that did not duplicate its stage success, and the failed version of Ayn Rand's cult novel *The Fountainhead*, as the columnist who becomes Gary Cooper's lover. This plot point spilled over into real life, as Neal became the most famous and serious of the actor's many extramarital affairs. Before she and Coop reteamed for another uninspired effort, *Bright Leaf*, she landed a good role, as the nurse who trades barbs with the wounded soldiers in *The Hasty Heart* — the first movie during this early part of her movie career that really allowed her to shine. *Three Secrets* was a soap opera about as trio of women wondering which of their sons has survived a plane crash, and *The Breaking Point* let her sizzle with cynicism as the whore involved with John Garfield in this successful re-thinking of *To Have and Have Not*.

Operation Pacific was a fairly tedious war movie, although she paired off with co-star John Wayne quite well (as they would again, 14 years later in *In Harm's Way*). After that she and Warners parted company and Neal went to Fox to play the mother who befriends alien Michael Rennie in *The Day the Earth Stood Still*. She may have found the whole thing quite funny while she was making it, but the end result was one of the best sci-fi movies of its day. There was no doubt that she brought strength and brains to everything she did, but Hollywood had little interest in anyone who hadn't proven themselves a sure thing at the box office. Therefore, she found herself being cast in very minor films at this point in her career, including *Diplomatic Courier*, as a communist agent, and *Something for the Birds*, as a bird activist, which allowed her to act opposite Edmund Gwenn, although her real leading man, alas, was Victor Mature. She sought work in Europe and wound up settling in England after she married author Roald

Dahl there in 1953. She did not stay in the U.K. for long, luckily, returning to Broadway where her acclaimed work in a revival of *The Children's Hour*, and as a cast replacement in *Cat on a Hot Tin Roof*, made Hollywood wonder if they had let go of something special. Warners hired her for her only late 1950s film, *A Face in the Crowd*, which offered up Neal at her best, as the reporter who loses her cool after she realizes she's been taken in by megalomaniac country music star Andy Griffith. There were indications that her days as a leading lady were over, however, when she was given what was clearly a supporting part in *Breakfast at Tiffany's*. But, as the rich New Yorker, code named "2-E," who keeps George Peppard around for sex, she made a meal of the role.

Full appreciation came with *Hud*; her performance, as the weary ranch housekeeper who has given up on men, was, in its own subtle, unforgettable way, one of the screen's finest. Tossing sexual innuendos back and forth with Paul Newman, while trying to resist his raw magnetism, found a great actress at her peak and she won the Academy Award as Best Actress of 1963. This pretty much wiped away the memory of a British thriller, *Psyche 59*, with Neal as a blind woman, and one in which her entire role was left on the cutting-room floor, *The Third Secret*. During the filming of *7 Women* she suffered a series of strokes and for a time it seemed as if there was little hope of recovery (Anne Bancroft replaced her). Her comeback from the illness was much publicized and she capped her triumph with another excellent performance as a woman beaten but undefeated by the world, in *The Subject Was Roses*, which earned her another Oscar nomination. Back in England, her husband wrote *The Night Digger* for her, about a spinster attracted to a young man on the run from the police, which was followed by an unsuccessful horror movie, *Happy Mother's Day, Love George/Run, Stranger, Run*. She settled into television, where the story of her own stroke was dramatized (*The Patricia Neal Story*) with Glenda Jackson playing her. On the big screen, she was wed to James Mason in the trashy *The Passage*; was barely glimpsed at all as Fred Astaire's wife in *Ghost Story*; and had another starring role, as the old maid whose interest in an Asian offends sister Shelley Winters, in a gloomy independent drama, *An Unremarkable Life*. After another long break she showed up in the Robert Altman ensemble *Cookie's Fortune*, as a dotty old Southern lady whose suicide sets the plot in motion. She and Dahl divorced in 1983. In 1988 she published her memoirs, *As I Am* (co-authored with Richard DeNeut).

Screen: 1949: John Loves Mary; The Fountainhead; It's a Great Feeling; The Hasty Heart; 1950: Bright Leaf; The Breaking Point; Three Secrets; 1951: Operation Pacific; Raton Pass; The Day the Earth Stood Still; Week-End With Father; 1952: Diplomatic Courier; Washington Story; Something for the Birds; 1954: Stranger From Venus/Immediate Disaster; La Tua Donna/Your Woman; 1957: A Face in the Crowd; 1961: Breakfast at Tiffany's; 1963: Hud; 1964: Psyche '59; 1965: In Harm's Way; 1968: The Subject Was Roses; 1971: The Night Digger; 1973: Baxter; Happy Mother's Day, Love George/Run, Stranger, Run; 1974: B Must Die; 1978: Widow's Nest (nUSr); 1979: The Passage; 1981: Ghost Story; 1989: An Unremarkable Life; 1999: Cookie's Fortune.

NY Stage: 1946: The Voice of the Turtle; Another Part of the Forest; 1952: The Children's Hour; 1953: The Scarecrow (ob); School for Scandal (ob); 1955: A Roomful of Roses; 1958: Cat on a Hot Tin Roof; 1959: The Miracle Worker.

Select TV: 1954: Spring Reunion (sp); A Handful of Diamonds (sp); 1957: The Playroom (sp); 1958: The Gentleman from Seventh Avenue (sp); 1960: The Stronger (sp); 1961: The Magic and the Loss (sp); 1962: That's Where the Town's Going (sp); 1971: The Homecoming: A Christmas Story; 1974: Things in Their Season; 1975: Eric; 1977: Tail Gunner Joe; 1978: A Love

Affair: The Eleanor and Lou Gehrig Story; The Bastard; **1979:** All Quiet on the Western Front; **1984:** Shattered Vows; Love Leads the Way; Glitter; **1990:** Caroline?; **1993:** A Mother's Right: The Elizabeth Morgan Story; Heidi.

POLA NEGRI

(APOLLONIA CHALUPIEC) BORN: YANOWA, POLAND, DECEMBER 31, 1894. RAISED IN WARSAW. DIED: AUGUST 1, 1987.

An exotically haunted-looking lady of the silent era, whose image far outlived her actual work, Pola Negri debuted as a dancer with the Russian Imperial Theatre in St. Petersburg. In time she became a legit actress, first appearing on the stage in Warsaw in 1913 and then making her motion picture bow the following year, in *Niewolnica Zmyslow*, which she herself wrote. Under her real name, she maintained a successful career in her native country but was persuaded to expand her fortunes by going to Germany in 1917, and changing her name to Pola Negri. There she was directed by the up-and-coming Ernst Lubitsch in *The Eyes of the Mummy*, *Gypsy Blood/Carmen* and, most notably, *Madame DuBarry*. It was the last, released in the U.S. as *Passion*, that prompted Hollywood to take notice of her. For the time being, she stayed on in Germany to make a few more successful movies, including *One Arabian Night* and *The Red Peacock*, before arriving in Hollywood under contract to Paramount in 1923. Her first in the U.S. was *Bella Donna*, in which she was a bad wife cheating on her husband with an Egyptian sheik, a silly premise that successfully emphasized the exotic screen image the studio hoped to cultivate. There followed in rapid succession *The Spanish Dancer*, which was supposed to have been a Valentino vehicle; *Shadow of Paris*, in which she played an Apache girl; the comedy *Forbidden Paradise*, which was the first Lubitsch film made in Hollywood; *A Woman of the World*, as a glamorous lady in love with mid-westerner Holmes Herbert; and *The Crown of Lies*, as an actress asked to impersonate royalty. It was clear that there was more interest in her in the fan magazines, which covered her supposed exploits, like cavorting through town with a pet tiger on a leash.

Still, the studio prevailed and the results yielded her two most highly regarded films: *Hotel Imperial*, as a maid who finds herself in the middle of a conflict between the Austrians and the Russians (years later this plot became better known when re-used for *Five Graves to Cairo*); and *Barbed Wire*, as a French girl who finds trouble when she defies prejudice and falls in love with German prisoner Clive Brook. From these heights she began to slide downward with *The Woman on Trial*; *The Secret Hour*, as a mail-order bride in the first screen adaptation of *They Knew What They Wanted*; and her last for Paramount, *The Woman From Moscow*, a gloomy tale of forbidden love between a princess and a revolutionary. She returned to Europe where she did one film in England, *The Woman He Scorned*, and then made her official talkie debut, for RKO, in 1932 with *A Woman Commands*, a poorly received melodrama which only emphasized her heavy accent and the public's lack of interest in her. With that, it was back to Germany where her career resumed with a modicum of public interest, starting with *Moskau-Shanghai*. Since she was Jewish and working under the Hitler regime, it wasn't long before she bounced right back to America. For United Artists she played Adolphe Menjou's wife in the screwball comedy *Hi Diddle Diddle* and then retired for over 20 years before doing a pivotal role as an enigmatic lady in the Disney adventure *The Moon-Spinners*, where, for nostalgia's sake, she was seen leading a leopard about on a leash.

Screen (US releases only): 1918: Gypsy Blood; The Yellow Ticket; The Eyes of the Mummy; 1919: Passion/Madame DuBarry; 1920: Camille/The Red Peacock; 1921: Mad Love; The Wildcat; 1923: Montmarte; Hollywood; Bella Donna; The Cheat; The Spanish Dancer; 1924: Shadows of Paris; Men; Lily of the Dust; Forbidden Paradise; 1925: East of Suez; The Charmer; Flower of Night; A Woman of the World; 1926: The Crown of Lies; Good and Naughty; 1927: Hotel Imperial; Barbed Wire; The Woman on Trial; 1928: Three Sinners; The Secret Hour; Loves of an Actress; The Woman From Moscow; 1929: The Woman He Scorned/The Way of Lost Souls; 1932: A Woman Commands; 1943: Hi Diddle Diddle; 1964: The Moon-Spinners.

GENE NELSON

(Eugene Leander Berg) Born: Seattle, WA, March 24, 1920. Died: September 16, 1996.

A terrific dancer with a most appealing nature about him, Gene Nelson had to be content to fill a secondary slot in movie musical history and then, when that genre started trickling out of fashion, to find a career elsewhere, behind the cameras. As a youngster he not only studied dance but became an expert ice skater as well, which led to his participating in Sonia Henie's *Hollywood Ice Revue*, and *It Happens on Ice*, in New York. Joining the Army led to his film debut in *This Is the Army*, and after the war he did some parts at Fox (including one in the musical *I Wonder Who's Kissing Her Now*, and one in the 1947 Best Picture Oscar winner, *Gentleman's Agreement*, intervening when his buddy starts a fight with John Garfield) before he ended up as part of a Broadway stage revue, *Lend an Ear*, which earned him a Theatre World Award. On the basis of that triumph, Warners signed him up in 1950. This was hardly a golden period for the musical genre at this particular studio, but Nelson never failed to be a bright spot, starting with a typical turn-of-the-century June Haver vehicle, *The Daughter of Rosie O'Grady*. He actually got to be the lead, opposite Doris Day, in *Lullaby of Broadway*, and then was placed next to Virginia Mayo in *Painting the Clouds With Sunshine*, *She's Working Her Way Through College*, and *She's Back on Broadway*, all of which were badly in need of his energy. There was a straight, non-singing, non-dancing part in *Crime Wave*, just to prove he could handle that sort of thing, and then he won the role of his career, the affable cowhand Will Parker, in the 1955 film version of Rodgers and Hammerstein's classic *Oklahoma!*, which included his rousing rendition of "Everything's Up to Date in Kansas City." This was pretty much his peak. He followed this with some "B" films before he decided to take a crack at directing with a horror film for Fox, *Hand of Death*, which opened up a new arena for him. He was assigned to helm mostly quickie 1960s musicals, his résumé consisting of *Hootenanny Hoot* (1963), Elvis Presley's *Kissin' Cousins* (1964; which he also wrote); *Your Cheatin' Heart*, a biopic of country singer Hank Williams and Nelson's most commendable work behind the camera; another Elvis romp, *Harum Scarum* (1965), *The Cool Ones* (also writer), *The Perils of Pauline* (1967), and the television movies *Wake Me When It's Over* (1969; also producer) and *The Letter* (1973), which he co-directed with Paul Krasny. In 1971 he returned to Broadway to triumph in the acclaimed Stephen Sondheim musical *Follies*.

Screen: 1943: This Is the Army; 1947: I Wonder Who's Kissing Her Now; Gentleman's Agreement; 1948: Apartment for Peggy; The Walls of Jericho; 1950: The Daughter of Rosie O'Grady; The West Point Story; Tea for Two; 1951: Lullaby of Broadway; Starlift; Painting the Clouds With Sunshine; 1952: She's Working

Her Way Through College; 1953: Three Sailors and a Girl; She's Back on Broadway; 1954: Crime Wave; So This Is Paris; 1955: Oklahoma!; The Atomic Man/Timeslip; Dial 999/The Way Out; 1961: The Purple Hills; 1962: 20,000 Eyes; 1963: Thunder Island; 1981: S.O.B.

NY Stage: 1948: Lend an Ear; 1958: Oklahoma!; 1971: Follies; 1974: Good News.

Select TV: 1954: Lend an Ear (sp); 1955: Tryout (sp); The Missing Men (sp); Broadway (sp); A Kiss for Santa (sp); 1956: Fiddlin' Man (sp); 1957: A Man's Game (sp); 1958: The Woman of High Hollow (sp); 1960: Shangri-La (sp); 1972: Family Flight; 1973: A Brand New Life.

LOIS NETTLETON

Born: Oak Park, IL, August 6, 1929.

Yet another of those fine actresses, often taken for granted, who was stuck too many times in second-hand material, Lois Nettleton often rose above it all but never rose high enough to get to the top. She studied at Chicago's Goodman Theatre and in New York at the Actors' Studio, before receiving her break when she was cast in the 1949 Broadway drama *The Biggest Thief in Town*. More theater followed including some Shakespeare at Stratford, CT, with Katharine Hepburn, and a part in the television version of *Meet Me in St. Louis*. She was glimpsed fleetingly in the aptly named *A Face in the Crowd*, and finally made her official motion picture debut in 1962, in *Period of Adjustment*, playing Anthony Franciosa's less-than-bright wife. Two more films for MGM followed: *Come Fly With Me*, as the most appealing of the three stewardesses looking for romance — the others being Dolores Hart and Pamela Tiffin — and a very tame western romance, *Mail Order Bride*, in the title role, as the gentle widow brought to marry hellraiser Keir Dullea. None of these did the trick in making her an attraction, so she wound up, not surprisingly, as a regular player on the small screen. While toiling there she still managed to add some film credits to her résumé, including the talky sci-fi curio *Bamboo Saucer*, as a Russian scientist; two mild western spoofs, *The Good Guys and the Bad Guys*, and *Dirty Dingus Magee*, as a libidinous schoolmarm; *The Honkers*, as James Coburn's fed-up, ex-wife who has gone on to a better man; and *The Best Little Whorehouse in Texas*, in a heavily truncated role, as a waitress once involved with sheriff Burt Reynolds. In each case you felt she was giving the best she could under the circumstances. On television she won Emmy Awards for the special *The American Woman: Portraits in Courage* (1977) and the religious program *Insight* (1983).

Screen: 1957: A Face in the Crowd; 1962: Period of Adjustment; 1963: Come Fly With Me; 1964: Mail Order Bride; 1968: Bamboo Saucer/Collision Course; 1969: The Good Guys and the Bad Guys; 1970: Dirty Dingus Magee; 1971: The Sidelong Glances of a Pigeon Kicker/Pigeons; 1972: The Honkers; 1975: The Man in the Glass Booth; 1976: Echoes of a Summer; 1980: Soggy Bottom USA; 1981: Deadly Blessing; 1982: Butterfly; The Best Little Whorehouse in Texas; 1994: Mirror Mirror 2: Raven Dance (dtv); The Feminine Touch (nUSr).

NY Stage: 1949: The Biggest Thief in Town; 1951: Darkness at Noon; 1956: Cat on a Hot Tin Roof; 1959: God and Kate Murphy; Silent Night, Lonely Night; 1966: The Wayward Stork; 1973: A Streetcar Named Desire; 1976: They Knew What They Wanted (ob); 1979: Strangers

Select TV: 1954–55: The Brighter Day (series); 1956: Rendezvous (sp); An Incident of Love (sp); 1958: Accused of Murder (sp);

1959: Meet Me in St. Louis (sp); Seed of Guilt (sp); 1960: Woman in White (sp); Duet for Two Hands (sp); Emmanuel (sp); 1962: The Shadowed Affair (sp); 1966: Heartbreak House (sp); 1967: Valley of Mystery; 1967–68: Accidental Family (series); 1969: Any Second Now; 1970: Weekend of Terror; 1971: The Forgotten Man; Terror in the Sky; 1972: Women in Chains; 1974: The Last Bride of Salem (sp); 1975: Fear on Trial; 1977: All That Glitters (series); The American Woman: Portraits in Courage; (sp) Washington: Behind Closed Doors (ms); 1980: Tourist; 1985: Brass; 1986: Manhunt for Claude Dallas; 1987: You Can't Take It With You (series); 1988–89: In the Heat of the Night (series); 1996: The Good Doctor: The Paul Fleiss Story; 1996–98: General Hospital (series).

ANTHONY NEWLEY

Born: London, England, September 24, 1931.
Died: April 14, 1999.

British Renaissance man Anthony Newley possessed a highly theatrical style of show business bravado that impressed one as either boldly original or unappetizingly mannered. Working as a copyboy in postwar London, he was spotted by film director Geoffrey de Barkus who auditioned him for the lead in the serial Dusty Bates. Newley got the part and became the British film industry's all-purpose young cockney of the late 1940s and early 1950s. During this time he had standout assignments in Vice Versa, wherein he switched personalities with dad Roger Livesey, and David Lean's superb rendering of Oliver Twist, in a memorable performance as the Artful Dodger. After entering his 20s, his career did not take off as hoped and he was generally shunted to smaller parts, such as in Top of the Form, as a student; The Cockleshell Heroes, as one of the soldiers under Jose Ferrer's command; and Fire Down Below, as a Hispanic waiter. Meanwhile he did a stage revue, Cranks, which did nicely in London but less so when it came to New York. Back in movies, he was upped to some leads, in Idle on Parade, as a rock n' roller drafted into the Army, which gave him a hit song with "I've Waited So Long," and Jazzboat, in which he fell in with a gang of crooks. After all this work he was still just a minor figure on the British entertainment scene but that was about to change when he took matters into his own hands and came up with a theatrical piece made to showcase his versatility. Stop the World — I Want to Get Off was an oddity set in a circus tent — an allegory told in music and pantomime about a selfish man, Littlechap, who lets love slip by. Newley directed and, along with Leslie Bricusse, wrote both the book and songs, including "What Kind of Fool Am I?" which became his signature tune. Despite qualms about its pretensions, it was a smash both in London and New York and made Newley, at long last, into an international star.

This resulted in a feature film, The Small World of Sammy Lee, based on a BBC play he'd done called Sammy, in which he received excellent notices as a small-time loser who works as an emcee at a strip joint. There was a second stage success, which he also directed, The Roar of the Greasepaint — The Smell of the Crowd, which gave him another big song with "Who Can I Turn To?" By now he was a popular recording artist and a frequent variety show guest on TV, but was curiously passed over for the quickly made 1966 film of Stop the World, in favor of newcomer Tony Tanner. Instead he sang in the 1967 family musical Doctor Dolittle (Bricusse did the script and songs), as the affable buddy of Rex Harrison, in what would turn out to be his best-known movie role. He then played an Englishman in New York who falls for Sandy Dennis, not knowing she hasn't long to live, in Sweet

November, a terrible romantic comedy that put an end to his being giving the leads in any other such things. He then decided to chuck all sense of reason by directing himself in a bizarre, self-written, self-indulgent jaw-dropper called Can Hieronymus Merkin Ever Forget Mercy Humppe and Find True Happiness?, which was a combination of naughty sex and music hall-style vulgarity, centering on his character's infatuation with young girls. At one point Newley appeared butt-naked while his then-wife (1963–70) Joan Collins sang a song, a sequence that gave one an idea of his aspirations as a filmmaker. As director-only he did an anti-Vietnam story, Summertree; directed and wrote another West End musical with Bricusse, The Good Old Bad Old Days, which did not transfer to New York; worked with Bricusse to write the songs for the film Willy Wonka and the Chocolate Factory (earning an Oscar nomination in the process); went solo as composer for the flop Mr. Quilp; and then pretty much made his living as a Las Vegas act until showing up in a tacky children's movie, The Garbage Pail Kids, based on a series of bubble gum cards. He and Bricusse also supplied the lyrics for the memorable title song from the 1964 James Bond adventure Goldfinger, and wrote songs for the 1976 television version of Peter Pan.

Screen: 1946: Dusty Bates (serial); 1947: Little Ballerina; 1948: Vice Versa; Oliver Twist (US: 1951); The Guinea Pig/The Outsider; Vote for Huggett; 1949: Don't Ever Leave Me; A Boy, a Girl and a Bike; Golden Salamander; 1950: Madeleine; Highly Dangerous; 1952: Those People Next Door; Top of the Form; 1954: Up to His Neck; 1955: Blue Peter/Navy Heroes; Above Us the Waves; 1956: The Cockleshell Heroes; Port Afrique; Last Man to Hang; X the Unknown; The Battle of the River Plate/Pursuit of the Graf Spee; The Last Man to Hang; 1957: The Good Companions; Fire Down Below; High Flight; 1958: How to Murder a Rich Uncle; No Time to Die/Tank Force; The Man Inside; 1959: The Lady Is a Square; The Bandit of Zhobe; Idle on Parade; The Heart of a Man; In the Nick; Jazzboat; Killers of Kilimanjaro; 1960: Let's Get Married; 1963: The Small World of Sammy Lee; 1967: Doctor Dolittle; 1968: Sweet November (and co-song); 1969: Can Hieronymus Merkin Ever Forget Mercy Humppe and Find True Happiness? (and dir.; wr.; prod.; co-songs); 1975: Mr. Quilp/The Old Curiosity Shop (and songs); 1976: It Seemed Like a Good Idea at the Time; 1987: The Garbage Pail Kids Movie.

NY Stage: 1956: Cranks; 1962: Stop the World — I Want to Get Off (and dir.; co-wr.; co-songs); 1965: The Roar of the Greasepaint — The Smell of the Crowd (and dir.; co-wr.; co-songs); 1974: Anthony Newley-Henry Mancini.

Select TV: 1958: Sammy (sp); 1960: The Strange World of Gurney Glade (sp); 1966: Lucy in London (sp); 1971: The Anthony Newley Show (sp); 1980: Animal Talk (sp); 1983: Malibu; 1985: Alice in Wonderland; Blade in Hong Kong; 1986: Outrage!; Stagecoach; 1988: Limited Partners/It's About Money (sp); 1990: Coins in a Fountain; Polly Comin' Home; 1992: Boris and Natasha.

NANETTE NEWMAN

Born: Northampton, England, May 29, 1934.

This liltingly lovely British actress, in whose company it was always a pleasure to spend some time, made her screen debut in 1945, in a short film, "Here We Come Agathering," followed by her television bow six years later. Her early years mainly consisted of undistin-guished supporting parts until her fortunes changed when actor Bryan Forbes, whom she had married in 1954, turned his attention to writing and then directing. From that point on he became an instrumental presence in her career. Therefore, she was seen in the Forbes-scripted *League of Gentlemen* and the 1964 remake of *Of Human Bondage*, where she was a relief from Kim Novak and Laurence Harvey, playing the nice girl who waits patiently for Dr. Harvey to come around. Under her husband's direction she popped up at the end of *The L-Shaped Room*, as the girl who comes to rent the room as Leslie Caron moves on; in *Séance on a Wet Afternoon*, most effective as the distraught mother who doesn't realize she's seeking help from the very people who've kidnapped her daughter; and then, most delightfully, as Michael Caine's incredibly air-headed love interest in the rambunctious farce *The Wrong Box*. Less successfully, she and Caine were together for the dreary caper film *Deadfall*, after which she was just as lost as the rest of the starry cast in *The Madwoman of Chaillot*, as Katharine Hepburn's niece. After providing some decoration to the fantasy *Captain Nemo and the Underwater City*, Forbes gave her a real showcase as the paraplegic who is loved by Malcolm McDowell in *The Raging Moon*, but this wasn't much more than a second-rate soap opera that evoked very little public interest. She began to focus less on acting and more on her family and in writing, eventually publishing several children's books and some on cooking as well. In between this, her spouse coaxed her back to play one of *The Stepford Wives* and the grown-up version of Elizabeth Taylor in the sequel *International Velvet*.

Screen: 1953: Personal Affair; 1960: The League of Gentlemen; Faces in the Dark; 1961: Call Me Genius/The Rebel; Pit of Darkness; House of Mystery; Dangerous Afternoon; The Painted Smile; 1962: Twice Around the Daffodils; 1963: The Wrong Arm of the Law; The L-Shaped Room; 1964: Seance on a Wet Afternoon; Of Human Bondage; 1966: The Wrong Box; 1967: The Whisperers; 1968: Deadfall; 1969: The Madwoman of Chaillot; Oh! What a Lovely War; 1970: Captain Nemo and the Underwater City; 1971: Long Ago Tomorrow/The Raging Moon; 1972: The Love Ban; 1975: The Stepford Wives; Man at the Top; 1978: International Velvet; 1986: Restless Natives; 1993: Mystery of Edwin Drood (nUSr).

Select TV: 1962: Raiders of the Spanish Main; 1969: Journey Into Darkness; 1981: Jessie; Stay With Me Till Morning (series); 1982: Let There Be Love (series); 1987: Late Expectations (series); 1990: The Endless Game.

PAUL NEWMAN

Born: Cleveland, OH, January 26, 1925.
ed: Kenyon Col., Yale School of Drama.

His world-famous blue eyes would have been enough to give him gainful employment before the cameras. However, Paul Newman not only had talent but, as time would verify, was one of the very best actors the cinema would ever see. Because of this, and a knack for choosing mostly quality material, his reign as a top-of-the-line star carried him for more than 40 years. He came to be one of the truly dependable names, easily slipping from glossy 1950s studio productions to the rebellious new cinema of the late 1960s. His sardonic, slightly wary "battle with the world at large" manner made him a watchable everyman, albeit one who just happened to be aging better than most of the general public. There was intelligence in everything he did, though he couldn't help but embellish so much of it with that sexy swagger he possessed. In time he became the most masterfully subtle of all actors, able to say with a glance what lesser thespians couldn't put across with three pages of monologue. It was while attending college under the G.I. bill that he began to

find acting to his liking, which led to work with several stock companies and further study at the Yale School of Drama. Along with thousands of other hopefuls, he came to New York in the late 1940s-early 1950s, hoping to find jobs either on the stage or in the myriad of live TV dramas that were all over the small screen at the time. He began to pop up quite frequently in the latter, before getting his stage break, playing the small-town friend of Ralph Meeker in the Broadway hit *Picnic*. There were stirrings among the theater community about a great-looking guy who could act, and he earned a Theatre World Award for the role and acceptance into the prestigious Actors Studio. (He did not, however, get to repeat his part in Columbia's 1955 film version of *Picnic*; Cliff Robertson played it).

Warner Bros., on the other hand, was keen to have Newman and signed him to a contract in 1954. Few of the screen's immortals ever started off as badly as he did, playing the plastic young hero who makes *The Silver Chalice* for the Last Supper. It was one of the silliest of all the Biblical epics of the 1950s and Newman's wooden performance suggested nothing of his capabilities. The film became more famous later on when he took out an ad in the trades, apologizing for its existence, during the week of its TV premiere. MGM borrowed him for the well-meaning but weak military courtroom drama, *The Rack*, and for the first production that allowed him to really strut his stuff, *Somebody Up There Likes Me*, playing real-life hood-turned-boxer Rocky Graziano with a thick-accented intensity and charm to spare. Secondary billing in the soaps *The Helen Morgan Story*, which he particularly hated doing, and the better *Until They Sail*, suggested that he was biding his time. Things really began to cook when he was cast as the drifter who gets spinster Joanne Woodward all fired up, in a well-done Southern melodrama based on Faulkner, *The Long Hot Summer*. He and Woodward had crossed paths previously in the New York acting world (she'd been an understudy in *Picnic*) and they became one of Hollywood's great off-screen duos when they wed in 1958. That same year Newman was in a smash hit, *Cat on a Hot Tin Roof*, stumbling around on his crutch with a constant drink in his hand; he and the other cast members threw themselves into it was such gusto that it almost made you forget how diluted the original play had become in its transfer to the big screen. It brought him the first of many Oscar nominations.

He was a brooding Billy the Kid in the lop-sided *The Left-Handed Gun*, which would, in time find, its share of admirers; and then he and Woodward wound up in *Rally 'Round the Flag Boys!*, which marked the first time he stumbled trying to play comedy. He brought his intelligence to *The Young Philadelphians*, a saga about an ambitious law student, and to something that would have been pure suds otherwise, *From the Terrace*, which again featured Woodward, although they were a couple at odds in this one. Mixing heroism with intensity, he carried the lengthy *Exodus*, helping his fellow Jews escape the British and find their way to Palestine, in this admirable attempt to film Leon Uris's masterful novel. By now he was one of the biggest names in the business, a position that was only enhanced when he found a whole batch of new admirers with *The Hustler*. This was a bleaker, less glossy entertainment than he was used to appearing in and one of the most praised films of 1961. As pool shark Fast Eddie Felson, he was the perfect anti-hero — cocky, sexy, and cynical. It became one of his defining roles, earning him Oscar nomination number two. Having played the gigolo lover of Geraldine Page in *Sweet Bird of Youth* on Broadway, he was the natural choice to film it, though whatever made it work on the boards was mostly absent on the Technicolor widescreen. More interesting was another with Woodward, *Paris Blues*, a story of two jazz musicians and their women, and despite the presence of two other very talented people, Sidney Poitier and Diahann Carroll, it was an inexplicable failure. *Hud*, however, proved to be Newman at his summit, a brilliant and harsh look at an irresponsible young man whose seemingly good-natured cavorting hides a rotted soul. Again he managed to show the charming nature within the danger but not at the expense of laying bare the repulsive side of the man. He found himself in another box-office hit in another career-defining part with another nod from Oscar.

This he followed with lighter fare, *A New Kind of Love*, the sort of silly 1960s comedy that one couldn't imagine him and Woodward going to see let alone consenting to be in; *The Prize*, a poor man's Hitchcock romp; and the heavy-handed farce *What a Way to Go!*, in an eccentric turn as a French painter. Newman himself liked his work in *The Outrage*, heavily made up and accented as a Mexican bandit, but his bold attempt to expand his range just didn't click. At least he got the real Hitchcock for the thriller *Torn Curtain*, proving an adept hero on the run despite animosity on the set with the master filmmaker, after which he was perfect as a modern-day private eye in *Harper*. In 1967 he reached another career peak, first with *Hombre*, an underrated western in which he was a half-breed facing prejudice from his fellow passengers on a stagecoach; and then in perhaps his ultimate outsider role, *Cool Hand Luke*, the chain gang member who brags his way into the admiration of his fellow convicts. The latter marked another date with Oscar but he once again came home empty-handed. Sitting in an enviable position to do pretty much whatever he pleased, he chose to direct and produce a vehicle for Woodward, *Rachel, Rachel*, to glowing reviews and an Oscar nomination — the film ended up as one of the final contenders for Best Picture of 1968. *Winning*, which featured a typical love story with Woodward, was made to express his growing infatuation with auto racing, while *Butch Cassidy and the Sundance Kid* was a glorious romp, a western done in a seemingly off-the-cuff style, about a pair of ne'er-do-well bank robbers. It matched him in full box-office splendor with Robert Redford and became one of the gargantuan box-office hits of all time. By this point he was becoming well known as one of the industry's most outspoken liberals and hoped to sum up his views on film with *WUSA*, but it turned out to be one of his biggest failures.

Sometimes a Great Notion brought him back behind the cameras after he sacked original director Richard Colla, and then he directed another one to showcase his wife, *The Effect of Gamma Rays on Man-in-the-Moon Marigolds*, only this time the grim reality of the piece wasn't something the customers wanted to see. Around this time he got involved in a grand production plan for some of the biggest names in the industry to form their own company, the others being Steve McQueen, Sidney Poitier, and Barbra Streisand; the result was First Artists. However, Newman's maiden venture for the company, *Pocket Money*, was one of his lesser offerings, although it was intriguing to see him playing someone who didn't have much going on upstairs. On the other hand, he showed up in two of the grand entertainments of the 1970s: *The Sting*, in which he reunited with Redford in a film about a pair of Chicago con men, a lark that wound up being his biggest hit ever and the 1973 Academy Award-winner for Best Picture; and *The Towering Inferno*, which paired him with another great male co-star, Steve McQueen, who possessed a similar anti-hero film persona. Newman went west for some character work, playing the ornery hanging judge in *The Life and Times of Judge Roy Bean* (his second and last First Artists film), and the long-haired showman-fraud in *Buffalo Bill and the Indians, or Sitting Bull's History Lesson*. Much more to the general public's taste was the purposefully vulgar *Slap Shot*, with Newman as an aging hockey player, a role he counted among his favorites. After disastrous slip-ups with the pretentious *Quintet* and the cheesy disaster epic *When Time Ran Out...*, he had another run of good fortune with the controversial *Fort Apache — The Bronx*, as a sympathetic cop fighting corruption in a bleak urban neighborhood, and two that were high on good intentions but low on excitement, *Absence of Malice*, as a decent man libeled by the press, and *The Verdict*, as an alcoholic lawyer getting his final shot at glory. The last two brought him Oscar nominations.

Overstepping his bounds, he served as star, director, co-writer and producer on *Harry and Son*, a flabby story of a strained father and son relationship that died the death. Figuring honor was long overdue, the Motion Picture Academy gave him a special Oscar at its 1985 Awards ceremony but Newman wasn't about to rest on his laurels yet, coming back with a bang reprising *The Hustler*'s Fast Eddie Felson in *The Color of Money*. This was a rare justification of doing a sequel to a good movie and having Tom Cruise in it helped immensely it at the box office. Newman's brilliantly low-keyed work, playing a man who rises above the con world he himself has created, won him his long-awaited Academy Award for Best Actor. There were directorial credits with *The Shadow Box* (for TV) and *The Glass Menagerie*, and his own acting just kept getting better and better with an unexpectedly flamboyant performance as politician Earl Long in *Blaze*, and a quiet one as Joanne's distant but loving husband in *Mr. and Mrs. Bridge*. After taking his first out-and-out supporting role and coming up with his best stab at comedy, in *The Hudsucker Proxy*, as a corporate bigwig, he stepped into the sort of part that caps the career of a great star, with *Nobody's Fool*. In this film, he played a loner who has failed through most of his life but nonetheless stands out in his small town as a sort of life force via his individuality. This made for Oscar nomination number eight and the promise of further great things to come, although a follow-up, *Twilight*, a modern day L.A. noir, under the same director, Robert Benton, proved a disappointment. There was little to get excited over with *Message in a Bottle*, as Kevin Costner's dad, or the tired caper film, *Where the Money Is*, as an old thief roped into one last job, but he was splendid dabbling in evil, playing a Depression era gangland boss who must deliver vengeance on his favored adopted son (Tom Hanks), in *Road to Perdition*, in an Oscar-nominated performance. There was a Jean Hersholt Humanitarian Award bestowed upon him by the Academy in 1994, recognizing his many efforts in this area including the Hole-in-the-Wall-Gang Camp for terminally ill children, and the proceeds he has donated from his best-selling Newman's Own food products.

Screen: 1954: The Silver Chalice; 1956: The Rack; Somebody Up There Likes Me; 1957: The Helen Morgan Story; Until They Sail; 1958: The Long Hot Summer; The Left-Handed Gun; Cat on a Hot Tin Roof; Rally 'Round the Flag, Boys!; 1959: The Young Philadelphians; 1960: Exodus; From the Terrace; 1961: The Hustler; Paris Blues; 1962: Hemingway's Adventures of a Young Man; Sweet Bird of Youth; 1963: Hud; A New Kind of Love; The Prize; 1964: What a Way to Go!; The Outrage; 1965: Lady L; 1966: Torn Curtain; Harper; 1967: Hombre; Cool Hand Luke; 1968: The Secret War of Harry Frigg; 1969: Winning; Butch Cassidy and the Sundance Kid; 1970: King: A Filmed Record...Montgomery to Memphis; WUSA; 1971: Sometimes a Great Notion/Never Give an Inch (and dir.; co-exec. prod.); 1972: Pocket Money; The Life and Times of Judge Roy Bean; 1973: The Mackintosh Man; The Sting; 1974: The Towering Inferno; 1975: The Drowning Pool; 1976: Buffalo Bill and the Indians, or Sitting Bull's History Lesson; Silent Movie; 1977: Slap Shot; 1979: Quintet; 1980: When Time Ran Out...; 1981: Fort Apache — The Bronx; Absence of Malice; 1982: The Verdict;

1984: Harry and Son (and dir.; co-wr.; prod.); 1986: The Color of Money; 1988: Hello Actors Studio; 1989: Fat Man and Little Boy; Blaze; 1990: Mr. and Mrs. Bridge; 1994: The Hudsucker Proxy; Nobody's Fool; 1998: Twilight; 1999: Message in a Bottle; 2000: Where the Money Is; 2002: Road to Perdition.

NY Stage: 1953: Picnic; 1955: The Desperate Hours; 1959: Sweet Bird of Youth; 1964: Baby Want a Kiss; 2002: Our Town.

Select TV: 1953: The Bells of Damon (sp); One for the Road (sp); 1954: Party Night (sp); Guilty Is the Stranger (sp); Knife in the Dark (sp); 1955: Five in Judgment (sp); Bridge of the Devil (sp); The Death of Billy the Kid (sp); Our Town (sp); The Battler (sp); 1956: The Army Game (sp); The Five Fathers of Pepi (sp); Bang the Drum Slowly (sp); The Rag Jungle (sp); 1958: The 80 Yard Run (sp).

JULIE NEWMAR

(JULIA CHARLENE NEWMEYER)
BORN: LOS ANGELES, CA, AUGUST 16, 1933.

Tall and sultry Julie Newmar remained looking fine for years, which meant the depth of her assignments pretty much stayed on the level of looks over substance. Trained as a dancer, she debuted with the Los Angeles Opera Company at age 15, then pursued work in this capacity in Hollywood. She showed up in a Bing Crosby musical, *Just for You*; some costume epics; *The Band Wagon*, glimpsed in "The Girl Hunt" ballet; and then was one of the kidnapped beauties in the 1954 hit *Seven Brides for Seven Brothers*, which would be her best known credit from this period. She then went to Broadway to dance in *Silk Stockings* and to gyrate provocatively as Stupefyin' Jones in *Li'l Abner*. After this she got her first non-musical part, in the comedy *The Marriage-Go-Round*, winning the Tony Award for playing a Swedish bombshell looking for a man to impregnate her. She got to repeat her parts in the film versions of both *Li'l Abner* and *The Marriage-Go-Round*, in the latter playing opposite James Mason, although it did not duplicate its stage success. Television made her a robot for the sitcom *My Living Doll* and gave her immortality as the best Catwoman of them all, on the camp classic *Batman*. Back on the big screen, she was an Indian in *Mackenna's Gold*, and a sexy werewolf in Rowan and Martin's *The Maltese Bippy*. After that she was seen sporadically in regional theater and on television until she began popping up in junky exploitation titles of the 1980s, including *Streetwalkin'*, as a character named Queen Bee; *Nudity Required*, in which she did indeed strip down; and *Ghosts Can't Do It*, as an angel. She became one of the few performers to actually have her name featured in a film title, with the drag queen comedy *To Wong Foo — Thanks for Everything — Julie Newmar*, appearing as herself at the climax.

Screen: 1952: Just for You; 1953: Slaves of Babylon; The Band Wagon; Serpent of the Nile; 1954: Seven Brides for Seven Brothers; 1959: The Rookie; Li'l Abner; 1960: The Marriage-Go-Round; 1963: For Love or Money; 1969: Mackenna's Gold; The Maltese Bippy; 1970: Up Your Teddy Bear/Mother; 1975: Dieci Bianchi Uccisi da un Piccolo Indiano/Blood River (nUSr); 1983: Hysterical; 1984: Streetwalkin'; Love Scenes/Ecstasy; 1985: Evils of the Night (dtv); 1987: Deep Space (dtv); Dance Academy (dtv); 1988: Nudity Required (dtv); 1989: Cyber-C.H.I.C./Robo-Chic (dtv); 1990: Ghosts Can't Do It; 1994: Oblivion; 1995: To Wong Foo — Thanks for Everything — Julie Newmar; 1996: Oblivion 2: Backlash (dtv); 1999: If… Dog… Rabbit (dtv).

NY Stage: 1955: Silk Stockings; 1956: Li'l Abner; 1959: The Marriage-Go-Round; 1961: Once There Was a Russian.

Select TV: 1964–65: My Living Doll (series); 1970: McCloud: Who Killed Miss U.S.A.?/Portrait of a Dead Girl; 1971: The Feminist and the Fuzz; 1972: A Very Missing Person; 1977: Terraces.

ROBERT NEWTON

BORN: SHAFTSBURY, DORSET, ENGLAND, JUNE 1, 1905. DIED: MARCH 25, 1956.

British star/character player Robert Newton had a mad glint in his eyes and a full-throttle style that ensured he wouldn't fade into the background. A professional actor from the time he appeared with the Birmingham Rep at age 15, he was a fairly consistent presence on the London theater scene before shifting his focus to films in the late 1930s. He was a stoolie in *The Green Cockatoo/Four Dark Hours*; the controller clashing with Charles Laughton in *Vessel of Wrath/The Beachcomber* (he was upped to the lead for the inferior 1954 remake); and Laughton's nemesis again in Hitchcock's *Jamaica Inn*. He was brilliant as Bill Walker, the bully reformed by Wendy Hiller, in *Major Barbara*; was Diana Wynyard's cousin in the earlier version of *Gaslight/Angel Street*; was at his most restrained playing the dad in the popular adaptation of Noel Coward's *This Happy Breed*, seeing his London family through grief and happiness over a 20-year period; gave Shakespeare a go as the Ancient Pistol in *Henry V*; and painted James Mason in *Odd Man Out*. He took the lead as the doctor who schemes to murder his unfaithful wife's lover in *Obsession/The Hidden Room*, and was scarily on the mark as the brutish Bill Sykes in the moody adaptation of *Oliver Twist*. When Disney decided to remake *Treasure Island* in England it seemed inconceivable to cast anyone but Newton as Long John Silver, and it is his interpretation that stands above the rest, solidly implanting "arr-rr-r-r" in the piratical lexicon. (Newton did, in fact, repeat the role, in the Australian *Long John Silver/Return to Treasure Island*, and on a short-lived syndicated television series). After playing the headmaster in *Tom Brown's School Days*, he went to Hollywood where he seemed enable to shake the Long John mannerisms playing a rowdy private (named Bill Sykes!) in *Soldiers Three*. He was, not surprisingly, over the top as *Blackbeard the Pirate*; fanatically chased Michael Rennie while playing Javert in the 1952 version of *Les Miserables*; appeared as one of the Christians in the failed translation of Shaw's *Androcles and the Lion*; and faced possible disaster as one of the imperiled plane passengers in *The High and the Mighty*. Sadly, he died of a heart attack shortly after completing the role of Inspector Fix in the movie that would bring him his largest audience, the 1956 Academy Award-winner *Around the World in Eighty Days*.

Screen: 1932: Reunion; 1937: Fire Over England; Dark Journey; Farewell Again/Troopship; The Squeaker/Murder on Diamond Row; The Green Cockatoo/Four Dark Hours; 1938: Vessel of Wrath/The Beachcomber; Yellow Sands; 1939: Poison Pen; Dead Men Are Dangerous; Jamaica Inn; Hell's Cargo/Dangerous Cargo; 1940: 21 Days/21 Days Together; Bulldog Sees It Through; Busman's Honeymoon/Haunted Honeymoon; Gaslight/Angel Street; 1941: Major Barbara; Hatter's Castle (US: 1948); They Flew Alone/Wings and the Woman; 1944: This Happy Breed; Henry V (US: 1946); 1945: Night Boat to Dublin; 1946: Odd Man Out; 1947: Temptation Harbour; 1948: Snowbound; Oliver Twist; Kiss the Blood Off My Hands; 1949: Obsession/The Hidden Room; 1950: Treasure Island; Waterfront; 1951: Tom Brown's Schooldays; Soldiers Three; 1952: Blackbeard the Pirate; Les Miserables; 1953: Androcles and the Lion; The Desert Rats; 1954: Long John Silver; The High and the Mighty; The Beachcomber; 1956: Around the World in Eighty Days.

Select TV: 1955: Under the Black Flag (sp); The Adventures of Long John Silver (series).

NICHOLAS BROTHERS
Fayard
BORN: MOBILE, AL, OCTOBER 20, 1914.
Harold
BORN: PHILADELPHIA, PA, MARCH 27, 1921.
DIED: JULY 3, 2000.

There was probably no better proof of Hollywood's misuse of black talent during its studio era than the Nicholas Brothers. The exuberant, gravity defying splits, leaps, glides, and taps of these amazing dancers today draw gasps and applause from a more enlightened audience, but their skin color kept them in the specialty number category, denying them the chance to fill out full-bodied roles. The sons of vaudeville performers, they taught themselves to dance and made enough of a hit in nightclubs to be asked on radio's *The Horn and Hardart Kiddie Hour*. They became a sensation at New York's Cotton Club and this led to their film debut in an all-black short subject, "Pie Pie Blackbird," in 1932, the same year they popped up during the big production number, "I Want to Be a Minstrel Man," in the Eddie Cantor film *Kid Millions*. Between other black films they went mainstream on Broadway as part of the 1936 edition of *Ziegfeld Follies* and in the original production of *Babes in Arms*. Because of the latter, 20th Century-Fox hired them to juice up some of their musicals and they did so on six occasions, including *Sun Valley Serenade*, in which they and Dorothy Dandridge cavorted to the chart-topper "Chattanooga Choo-Choo," and *Stormy Weather*, performing "Jumpin' Jive," in which they did their eye-popping splits as they descended a staircase, in perhaps the most amazing and best remembered of all their routines. Harold married Dandridge in 1942 (they divorced in 1951) and appeared solo in *Reckless Age* and *Carolina Blues*. The brothers were back together on Broadway in *St. Louis Woman* and for a dynamite teaming with Gene Kelly, in the "Be a Clown" dance in MGM's *The Pirate*. After years of appearing in nightclubs and on television it was this last number, featured in the 1974 compilation documentary *That's Entertainment!*, that was instrumental in revitalizing interest in the duo after the civil rights era had changed the entertainment industry for the better. Harold was asked to participate in some films on his own, notably in *Tap*, as one of the many veteran black hoofers, while Fayard received a Tony Award as one of the choreographers on the New York stage revue *Black and Blue* in 1939.

Screen (features): NICHOLAS BROTHERS: **1933:** Kid Millions; **1935:** Big Broadcast of 1936; **1937:** Calling All Stars; **1940:** Down Argentine Way; Tin Pan Alley; **1941:** The Great American Broadcast; Sun Valley Serenade; **1942:** Orchestra Wives; **1943:** Stormy Weather; **1948:** The Pirate; **1952:** El Mensaje de la Muerte (nUSr); **1956:** Bonjour Kathrin (nUSr).
FAYARD: **1970:** The Liberation of L.B. Jones; **2002:** Night at the Golden Eagle.
HAROLD: **1933:** The Emperor Jones; **1944:** Reckless Age; Carolina Blues; **1963:** Empire de la Nuit (nUSr); **1974:** Uptown Saturday Night; **1976:** Disco 9000/Fass Black; **1989:** Tap; **1991:** The Five Heartbeats; **1995:** Funny Bones.
NY Stage: **1936:** Ziegfeld Follies; **1937:** Babes in Arms; **1946:** St. Louis Woman.

LESLIE NIELSEN
BORN: REGINA, SASKATCHEWAN, CANADA, FEBRUARY 11, 1926.

In one of the more unexpected "second acts" in show business history, Leslie Nielsen became "funny." This rather serious, neutral-looking actor who graced movie and TV screens for years without provoking much comment one way or the other, finally developed an identifiable personality. The nephew of actor Jean Hersholt, he started on a Calgary radio station as an announcer and disc jockey, and even attended a school run by future *Bonanza* star Lorne Greene with the intention of making a career out of it. Instead he ended up in New York, studying acting at the Neighborhood Playhouse while starting to compile one of the longest résumés of television guest and anthology appearances in that medium's history. In 1956 he was hired to do some films for MGM, debuting as the nosy reporter in the suspense thriller *Ransom*, and showing up as one of the unnecessary men in *The Opposite Sex*. He then became a small part of science-fiction history, playing the stoic commander who lands on *Forbidden Planet*, which became one of the seminal and enduring adventures in the sci-fi genre, although Nielsen's participation wasn't much remarked upon at the time. There was a lead role in a "B" film, *Hot Summer Night*, as a reporter who tangles with a bunch of hoods, and then half of the title role in *Tammy and the Bachelor*, which marked his last legit romantic lead he would have on the big screen. Television claimed him for regular roles as Disney's *Swamp Fox* and for short-lived stints on *The New Breed* and *Peyton Place*. Back in the movies he showed up as a mogul in Paramount's *Harlow*; a wimpy legionnaire in the remake of *Beau Geste*; George Custer in the re-do of *The Plainsman*; and straight man to Don Knotts in *The Reluctant Astronaut*.

By the 1970s he was pretty much an all-purpose actor who was sometimes a guest star, sometimes a secondary lead in TV films, or a supporting player in theatrical releases, such as in *The Poseidon Adventure*, as the captain of the ill-fated ship, killed off by the offending tidal wave; *Viva Knievel!*, as a drug lord using daredevil Evel Knievel for his dastardly plot; and *City on Fire*, as the mayor of the smoldering metropolis in one of his occasional projects filmed in his native country. Fortunately the makers of the disaster spoof *Airplane!* were looking for the kind of customarily serious performers who would populate the real thing, and hired Nielsen to play a doctor with an aversion to being called "Shirley." His deadpan comic timing was a revelation and he was hired by the same team behind that hit film for a series, *Police Squad!* which ran very briefly but developed a cult following. In the meantime, he buried Ted Danson alive in the anthology thriller *Creepshow* and had one of his last serious parts, as the abusive john killed by hooker Barbra Streisand in *Nuts*. Nielsen dusted off the straight-faced idiot Lieutenant Frank Dreben character from *Police Squad!* for the theatrical spin-off, *The Naked Gun*, and scored another winner in a rare case of a flop series leading to a financially successful feature film. From that point on he became associated almost exclusively with spoofs and shamelessly silly comedies. There were two more *Naked Gun* farces; a juvenile *Exorcist* parody, *Repossessed*; an appearance as a department store Santa Claus in *All I Want for Christmas*; the Mel Brooks flop *Dracula: Dead and Loving It*, in which he made no impression whatsoever kidding the Count; the espionage send-up *Spy Hard*; a dreadful live-action reprise of the animated *Mr. Magoo*, which required him to appear bald-headed; and a spoof of *The Fugitive*, called *Wrongfully Accused*, which had him on the run from another aging star, Richard Crenna. He published the autobiography *The Naked Truth* (1993) and the humor books *Leslie Nielsen's Stupid Little Golf Book* (1995) and *Leslie Nielsen's Bad Golf My Way* (1996).

Screen: **1956:** Ransom; Forbidden Planet; The Vagabond King; The Opposite Sex; **1957:** Hot Summer Night; Tammy and the Bachelor; **1958:** The Sheepman; **1964:** Night Train to Paris; **1965:** Harlow; **1966:** Beau Geste; The Plainsman; **1967:** Gunfight in Abilene; The Reluctant Astronaut; Rosie!; **1968:** Counterpoint;

Dayton's Devils; **1969:** How to Commit Marriage; Change of Mind; Four Rode Out; **1971:** The Resurrection of Zachary Wheeler; **1972:** The Poseidon Adventure; **1973:** And Millions Will Die; **1976:** Project: Kill; **1977:** Day of the Animals/Something Is Out There; Viva Knievel!; Sixth and Main; The Amsterdam Kill; **1979:** City on Fire; Riel (dtv); **1980:** Airplane!; Prom Night; **1981:** The Creature Wasn't Nice/Spaceship; **1982:** Foxfire Light (dtv); Wrong Is Right; Creepshow; **1985:** The Homefront (narrator); **1986:** The Patriot; Soul Man; **1987:** Home Is Where the Hart Is; Nightstick (dtv); Nuts; **1988:** Dangerous Curves; The Naked Gun: From the Files of Police Squad!; **1990:** Repossessed; **1991:** The Naked Gun 2 1/2: The Smell of Fear; All I Want for Christmas; **1993:** Surf Ninjas; **1994:** Digger (dtv); SPQR: 2000 and a Half Years (nUSr); Naked Gun 33 1/3: The Final Insult; **1995:** Dracula: Dead and Loving It; **1996:** Spy Hard; **1997:** Mr. Magoo; **1998:** Wrongfully Accused; **1999:** Family Plan (dtv); **2001:** Camouflage (dtv); Kevin of the North (dtv); **2002:** 2001: A Space Travesty (dtv); Men With Brooms.

Select TV: 1950: The Survivors (sp); Never Murder Your Grandfather (sp); The Luck of Guldeford (sp); Home for Christmas (sp); The Last Cruise (sp); The Philadelphia Story (sp); **1951:** The Magic Wire (sp); Lover's Leap (sp); Flame-Out (sp); October Story (sp); **1952:** Crown of Shadows (sp); 20,000 Leagues Under the Sea (sp); Appointment to Mars (sp); A Kiss for Cinderella (sp); **1953:** Another Chance (sp); The Rumor (sp); Candle in a Bottle (sp); A Story to Whisper (sp); **1954:** Dark Possession (sp); Castles in Spain (sp); A Guest at the Embassy (sp); **1958:** The Right Hand Man (sp); **1959:** The Velvet Alley (sp); Nora (sp); **1959–61:** Swamp Fox (ms); **1960:** Journal of Hope (sp); **1961–62:** The New Breed (series); **1963:** One Step Down (sp); **1964:** See How They Run; **1965:** Black Cloak/Dark Intruder; **1966:** When Hell Froze (sp); Death of a Salesman (sp); **1968:** Shadow Over Elveron; Hawaii Five-O; Companions in Nightmare; **1969:** Trial Run; Deadlock; **1969–70:** The Bold Ones: The Law Enforcers (series); **1970:** Night Slaves; Bracken's World (series); The Aquarians; Hauser's Memory; **1971:** Incident in San Francisco; They Call It Murder; **1973:** Snatched; The Letters; **1974:** Can Ellen Be Saved?; **1976:** Brink's: The Great Robbery; **1977: 1978:** Little Mo; **1979:** Institute for Revenge; Backstairs at the White House (ms); The Return of Charlie Chan/Happiness is a Warm Clue; **1980:** OHMS; **1982:** Police Squad! (series); **1983:** The Night the Bridge Fell Down; Cave-In!; **1984:** Shaping Up (series); **1985:** Reckless Disregard; Blade in Hong Kong; **1987:** Fatal Confession: A Father Dowling Mystery; **1991:** Chance of a Lifetime; **1995:** Rent-a-Kid; Mr. Willoughby's Christmas Tree (sp); **1996:** Harvey; **1998:** Safety Patrol; **2000:** Santa Who?; **2000–2002:** N.Y.U.K. (series); **2001:** Lieography (series).

DAVID NIVEN

(JAMES DAVID GRAHAM NIVEN) BORN: LONDON, ENGLAND, MARCH 1, 1909. DIED: JULY 29, 1983.

Of all the actors who projected that dry, urbane, upper-class British sense of style, audiences felt most comfortable with David Niven. He wasn't stage trained and therefore did not represent an elitism or snobbery towards films that might have scared the common folk away. Nor was his sophistication too aloof or impenetrable. Whether in war films, costume dramas, or the genre in which he most excelled, comedy, he seemed like a regular fellow who just happened to have an accent that made him talk better than most of the other blokes around.

Initially a military man, he was a member of the Highland Light Infantry until that ran its course and he began to travel, ending up in Los Angeles where he sought extra work in motion pictures. He was supposedly involved in such movies as *Cleopatra* and *Mutiny on the Bounty*, though he was first visible in *Without Regret*, as Elissa Landi's brother. He was in *Barbary Coast*, as a sailor (his first movie under his contract to Samuel Goldwyn), and *Rose-Marie*, as one of the fellows interested in Jeanette MacDonald. In 1936 Fox figured they could risk him as the lead in a "B" production and he turned out to be well-suited to play millionaire Bertie Wooster in *Thank You, Jeeves*, opposite Arthur Treacher. Suddenly the assignments grew in importance, with *Dodsworth*, as a shipboard gigolo, and *The Charge of the Light Brigade*, as a young captain who dies in battle. Thanks to this last one especially, he began popping up pretty regularly whenever a suave-looking Englishman was needed, as in *Bluebeard's Eighth Honeymoon*, as Claudette Colbert's friend; *Four Men and a Prayer*, going to India to avenge father C. Aubrey Smith's death; the remake of *The Dawn Patrol*, as Errol Flynn's pal; and Goldwyn's *Wuthering Heights*, as a very wimpy Edgar Linton (a role he was not at all keen to play) in one of the major releases of 1939, and an Oscar nominee for Best Picture. In the meantime, Fox had given him another lead, in *Dinner at the Ritz*, a British production, in which he romanced Annabella on the Riviera. RKO then hired him for the one that was instrumental in proving his worth as a light comedian par excellence, *Bachelor Mother*, as the rich playboy in love with salesgirl Ginger Rogers. Goldwyn put him in support of Gary Cooper in a grim war film, *The Real Glory*, and then gave him top billing in a role that had done wonders for Ronald Colman, *Raffles*, as a gentleman thief, with Niven adapting it to fit his own personality quite nicely.

After this he joined the British Army, staying in England where he managed to participate in two patriotic war films, *The First of the Few* and *The Way Ahead*. Following military service he did one more film in Britain, which turned out to be his best to date, *A Matter of Life and Death/Stairway to Heaven*, one of the most imaginative of all the Powell-Pressburger films. Niven, in a strong and sympathetic performance, was an RAF pilot who visits the afterlife to argue his case for why he should be allowed to live. In the meantime, he was obligated to finish his contract to Goldwyn so went back to California. He did one good one for that producer, *The Bishop's Wife*, a charming Christmas-themed fantasy that allowed him to act opposite Cary Grant, as well as a flop, *Enchantment*, aging during the two stories, the first of which had him romancing Theresa Wright. On loan he did *Magnificent Doll*, playing an unlikely Aaron Burr to Ginger Rogers's Dolly Madison; *The Perfect Marriage* with Loretta Young; and *The Other Love*, with Barbara Stanwyck. He then returned to England for two costume pictures both of which failed, *Bonnie Prince Charlie* and *The Elusive Pimpernel*, a remake of the property that had starred Leslie Howard, revised as a musical only to have all the songs cut from the release print. This was not a peak period for him as he did a pair of forgettable, sound-alike comedies *A Kiss in the Dark* and *A Kiss for Corliss*, and was demoted to playing second lead to Mario Lanza in *The Toast of New Orleans*. In uniform he tried to bring some dignity to the lowbrow *Soldiers Three*, as their commander, and attempted to rescue some cows in the light-hearted *Appointment with Venus*, which was made back in England. Things brightened considerably with a hit movie that wasn't very good but reminded people just how nice it was to have Niven around in such cases, *The Moon Is Blue*, a decidedly stage-bound piece in which he tried to have his way with virgin Maggie McNamara; there was no doubt that he was the best thing in it. He bided his time with

The Love Lottery, in which he was won by Anne Vernon; *The King's Thief*, reduced to playing second fiddle to Ann Blyth and Edmund Purdom; and *The Birds and the Bees*, likewise given billing *after* Mitzi Gaynor and George Gobel, not an enviable position to be in.

As luck would have it, he was chosen by producer Mike Todd to carry his lavish epic *Around the World in Eighty Days*, and was more than delighted to play Jules Verne's regimented hero Phileas Fogg, the punctual, stoic Englishman who loosens up on his global voyage. Though looked upon today as more of a travelogue than a great adventure, this turned out to be one of the most heavily attended attractions of its day, the 1956 Academy Award-winner for Best Picture, and probably Niven's most famous film credit. After that one he displayed his comic finesse again, in *The Little Hut*, showing up co-stars Ava Gardner and Stewart Granger; *Oh, Men! Oh, Women!*, which brought him back again to Ginger Rogers; and the unnecessary remake of *My Man Godfrey*, doing what he could under the misguided circumstances, in the old William Powell role. He took a break for drama, in both cases with Deborah Kerr. The first, *Bonjour Tristesse*, in which he was a cad responsible for driving her to suicide, was declared a flat-out disaster in its day, though admirers attempted to elevate its status in later years. The other, *Separate Tables*, was one of the most prestigious films of 1958. Niven, holding back admirably on his cheeky savoir faire, was quite good as the bogus Army major who has blemished his reputation by molesting women in the cinema. His efforts landed him the Academy Award for Best Actor. Again he chose to follow a career peak with comedy and got to shine opposite Shirley MacLaine in *Ask Any Girl*; tried his best to inject some life into the anti-television *Happy Anniversary*; and really scored as the drama critic trying to cope with moving to the suburbs in one of the best Doris Day films, *Please Don't Eat the Daisies*. It didn't hurt at all to be involved in one of the big war movies of the day, *The Guns of Navarone*, as a demolitions expert. After this, he did some European fare, *The Best of Enemies* and *Guns of Darkness* among them, before returning to spectacle territory with *55 Days at Peking*, a depiction of the events surrounding the Chinese Boxer Rebellion of 1900, with Niven quietly effective as the troubled British ambassador. Still, audiences liked him best in comedy and he had a major hit with *The Pink Panther*, as a jewel thief, although the movie was stolen from him and the rest of the cast by Peter Sellers as Inspector Clouseau. He then played a con man in the *Bedtime Story*, bringing out a lighter side of Marlon Brando, who absolutely adored working with him.

Still being given leads, he jumped aboard the espionage bandwagon of the 1960s for *Where the Spies Are*, as Dr. Jason Love; sunk with the ship in a curiosity called *The Extraordinary Seaman*, as a dead naval commander; romped through one of the prime "groovy" artifacts of the era, *Casino Royale*, at last playing James Bond (author Ian Fleming had always envisioned his super-spy in the person of Niven); re-united with Kerr for a tacky birth control farce, *Prudence and the Pill*; and was very out of place as an average suburban dad in the surprisingly popular *The Impossible Years*, the last two being shining examples of the coyly leering material being produced in lieu of the production code being abandoned. Things were not so rosy and it was clear that the actor would accept just about anything to keep working. There was *The Brain*, an international comedy about a train heist that went nowhere, after which he reached some kind of nadir with *The Statue*, the central prop of which was a nude sculpture of Niven with an enormous penis. *King, Queen, Knave* barely surfaced outside of Europe; *Old Dracula* was a juvenile vampire spoof that seemed made for undemanding drive-in patrons; and

Paper Tiger, an old-man-and-impressionable-youngster tale, seemed to prove that he had set out to do a movie that absolutely *nobody* wanted to see. His visibility rose with a pair of Disney comedies, *No Deposit, No Return* and *Candleshoe*, in between which he did a smart teaming with Maggie Smith, spoofing Nick and Nora Charles in what would be his last genuine moneymaker, *Murder by Death*. He was one of the few passengers who was not a murder suspect in *Death on the Nile*; reteamed with his old *Guns of Navarone* co-star, Gregory Peck, for the lukewarm adventure *The Sea Wolves*; added the missing spark to a flat Burt Reynolds caper *Rough Cut*; and wound up reprising his own jewel thief role in two wrongheaded sequels, *The Trail of the Pink Panther* and *The Curse of the Pink Panther*, made *after* Peter Sellers had passed away. Niven himself died shortly before the release of the last (his failing voice was dubbed by impressionist Rich Little). It was unlikely that many of these movies kept his reputation intact, but his image as a witty raconteur was greatly enhanced by two of the most popular and well-regarded of all Hollywood memoirs, *The Moon's a Balloon* (1972) and *Bring on the Empty Horses* (1975), which revealed an actor who never failed to find the fun amid all the hard work and phoniness of the industry. He also published a novel, *Go Slowly, Come Back Quickly* (1981).

Screen: 1934: Cleopatra; 1935: Mutiny on the Bounty; Without Regret; Barbary Coast; A Feather in Her Hat; Splendor; 1936: Rose-Marie; Palm Springs; Thank You, Jeeves; Dodsworth; The Charge of the Light Brigade; Beloved Enemy; 1937: We Have Our Moments; The Prisoner of Zenda; Dinner at the Ritz; 1938: Bluebeard's Eighth Wife; Four Men and a Prayer; Three Blind Mice; The Dawn Patrol; 1939: Wuthering Heights; Bachelor Mother; Eternally Yours; The Real Glory; 1940: Raffles; 1942: The First of Few/Spitfire; 1944: The Way Ahead/The Immortal Battalion; 1946: A Matter of Life and Death/Stairway to Heaven; Magnificent Doll; The Perfect Marriage; 1947: The Other Love; The Bishop's Wife; 1948: Bonnie Prince Charlie; Enchantment; 1949: A Kiss in the Dark; A Kiss for Corliss; 1950: The Toast of New Orleans; The Elusive Pimpernel/The Fighting Pimpernel; 1951: Happy Go Lovely; Soldiers Three; The Lady Says No; Appointment With Venus/Island Rescue; 1953: The Moon Is Blue; 1954: The Love Lottery; Happy Ever After/Tonight's the Night; 1955: Carrington VC/Court Martial; The King's Thief; 1956: The Birds and the Bees; Around the World in Eighty Days; 1957: The Silken Affair; The Little Hut; Oh, Men! Oh, Women!; My Man Godfrey; 1958: Bonjour Tristesse; Separate Tables; 1959: Ask Any Girl; Happy Anniversary; 1960: Please Don't Eat the Daisies; 1961: The Guns of Navarone; The Best of Enemies; 1962: The Captive City/The Conquered City; The Road to Hong Kong; Guns of Darkness; 1963: 55 Days at Peking; 1964: The Pink Panther; Bedtime Story; 1965: Lady L; 1966: Where the Spies Are; 1967: Eye of the Devil; Casino Royale; 1968: Prudence and the Pill; The Impossible Years; 1969: The Extraordinary Seaman; Before Winter Comes; The Brain; 1971: The Statue; 1972: King, Queen, Knave; 1975: Old Dracula/Vampira; Paper Tiger; 1976: No Deposit, No Return; Murder by Death; 1978: Candleshoe; Death on the Nile; 1979: Escape to Athena; A Nightingale Sang in Berkeley Square/The Big Scam; 1980: Rough Cut; 1981: The Sea Wolves; 1982: The Trail of the Pink Panther; 1983: Better Late Than Never; The Curse of the Pink Panther.

Select TV: 1951: Not a Chance (sp); 1952: The Sheffield Story (sp); 1952–56: Four Star Playhouse (series); 1957–58: Alcoa Theatre (series); 1958: The Fatal Charm (sp); Taps for Jeffrey (sp); 1958: Decision by Terror (sp); 1959: The David Niven Show (series); 1964–65: The Rogues (series); 1974: The Canterville Ghost (sp); 1976: David Niven's World (series); 1979: A Man Called Intrepid.

LLOYD NOLAN

BORN: SAN FRANCISCO, CA, AUGUST 11, 1902.
ED: STANFORD UNIV. DIED: SEPTEMBER 27, 1985.

Lloyd Nolan brought a lot of good common sense with him to his often-forgettable films and that was his strong point. You felt safe in his hands for here was a fellow who didn't put up with nonsense and could offer comfort to those less well adjusted than he. In a less benign mode, he was the sort of actor who downplayed villainy for maximum impact, knowing that less show could offer far more menace. Having done theater in college he acted in vaudeville before joining the Pasadena Playhouse. His Broadway debut came in 1929, in *Cape Cod Follies*, and he became a star four years later in a production of *One Sunday Afternoon*. This brought him a screen test and a part in Paramount's *Stolen Harmony*, a George Raft vehicle. Bad guy roles in *Counterfeit*, as the fake money manufacturer, and *The Texas Rangers*, as the "Polka Dot" bandit, confirmed that he might be a worthwhile investment, so Paramount signed him to a contract in 1936. Still playing up his bad side, he managed to stand out above the stars in *Internes Can't Take Money*, as a bookie; *Exclusive*, as a racketeer who buys a newspaper business in order to exact revenge; *Ebb Tide*, as an American who has cracked up and gone native, declaring himself an island god, hardly a part well-suited for him; *Wells Fargo*, robbing hero Joel McCrea in this popular western; and Mae West's *Every Day's a Holiday*, as an oily politician. As his reward for all his hard work, he was upped to "B" leads for *Hunted Men*, though still on the side of evil, again as a racketeer; *Prison Farm*, as a murderer who tricks Shirley Ross into marrying him; *King of Alcatraz*, as a radio operator out to stop escaped con J. Carroll Naish; *Ambush*, as a truck driver who falls in with a gang of thieves; and *Undercover Doctor*, as an FBI agent.

Leaving Paramount for Fox he was still considered "B" material as he starred as the mysterious man who confesses to a murder in *The Man Who Wouldn't Talk*, and then played the title sleuth in *Michael Shayne: Private Detective*. The latter went over well enough that he played Shayne on six more occasions with *Sleepers West*; *Dressed to Kill*, in which the victims were all bumped off while costumed for a play; *Blue, White and Perfect*, which involved diamond smuggling; *The Man Who Wouldn't Die*; *Just Off Broadway*; and *Time to Kill*, a tale of counterfeiting derived from a Raymond Chandler story. Back at Paramount, he was a more comical gangster than usual in *Buy Me That Town*; went to war for two hits, MGM's *Bataan* and Paramount's *Guadalcanal Diary*; and took top billing as an ex-ballplayer trying to restore his reputation in *It Happened in Flatbush*. He gave a beautiful performance as the friendly cop who comes to love tenement mom Dorothy McGuire in *A Tree Grows in Brooklyn*, and was in another standout film of the era, *The House on 92nd Street*, in charge of the investigation of a spy ring, before playing a bad guy again in the engrossing noir *Lady in the Lake*. He pretty much reprised his FBI role from *92nd Street* in the similarly documentary-style *The Street With No Name*; bullied Bob Hope in the Damon Runyon tale *The Lemon Drop Kid*; then went to TV to play *Martin Kane — Private Eye*, which sounded suspiciously like Michael Shayne. Onstage he scored a major triumph as the unstable Captain Queeg in *The Caine Mutiny Court-Martial* and, although he didn't get to repeat the part in the 1954 motion picture, he did it on television the following year, winning an Emmy Award. The year 1957 was a cinema high point — first with *A Hatful of Rain*, at his very best, as the stern dad who is shattered to discover that his son is a drug addict; and then with the blockbuster *Peyton Place*, as the level-headed town

doctor, in his own quietly controlled way giving the standout performance in this uneven soap opera. He was murdered by Anthony Quinn in *Portrait in Black*; was the sensible customs inspector in *Airport*; and was a regular on the hit series *Julia*, as a grumpy physician. Pretty much a television staple by the 1970s, he did return to the movies for one last good role, as the bickering husband of Maureen O'Sullivan in Woody Allen's *Hannah and Her Sisters*, released shortly after his death.

Screen: 1935: Stolen Harmony; G Men; Atlantic Adventure; She Couldn't Take It; One Way Ticket; 1936: Lady of Secrets; Big Brown Eyes; You May Be Next; Devil's Squadron; Counterfeit; The Texas Rangers; Fifteen Maiden Lane; 1937: Internes Can't Take Money; King of Gamblers; Exclusive; Ebb Tide; Wells Fargo; Every Day's a Holiday; 1938: Dangerous to Know; Tip-Off Girls; Hunted Men; Prison Farm; King of Alcatraz; 1939: St. Louis Blues; Ambush; Undercover Doctor; The Magnificent Fraud; 1940: The Man Who Wouldn't Talk; The House Across the Bay; Johnny Apollo; Gangs of Chicago; The Man I Married; Pier 13; The Golden Fleecing; Michael Shayne — Private Detective; Charter Pilot; Behind the News; 1941: Sleepers West; Mr. Dynamite; Dressed to Kill; Buy Me That Town; Blues in the Night; Steel Against the Sky; Blue, White and Perfect; 1942: It Happened in Flatbush; Apache Trail; Just Off Broadway; Manila Calling; Time to Kill; The Man Who Wouldn't Die; 1943: Bataan; Guadalcanal Diary; 1945: A Tree Grows in Brooklyn; Circumstantial Evidence; Captain Eddie; The House on 92nd Street; 1946: Somewhere in the Night; Two Smart People; Lady in the Lake; 1947: Wild Harvest; 1948: Green Grass of Wyoming; The Street With No Name; 1949: Bad Boy; The Sun Comes Up; Easy Living; 1951: The Lemon Drop Kid; 1953: Island in the Sky; Crazylegs; 1956: The Last Hunt; Santiago; Toward the Unknown; 1957: Abandon Ship!/Seven Waves Away; A Hatful of Rain; Peyton Place; 1960: Portrait in Black; Girl of the Night; 1961: Susan Slade; 1962: We Joined the Navy; 1963: The Girl Hunters; 1964: Circus World; 1965: Never Too Late; 1966: An American Dream; 1967: The Double Man; 1968: Ice Station Zebra; 1970: Airport; 1974: Earthquake; 1978: The Private Files of J. Edgar Hoover; My Boys Are Good Boys; 1980: Galyon (dtv); 1984: Prince Jack; 1986: Hannah and Her Sisters.

NY Stage: 1929: Cape Cod Follies; 1930: Sweet Stranger; 1931: Reunion in Vienna; 1932: Americana; 1933: One Sunday Afternoon; 1934: Ragged Army; Gentlewoman; 1953: The Caine Mutiny Court-Martial; 1960: One More River.

Select TV: 1950: The Barker (sp); 1951–52: Martin Kane — Private Eye (series); 1955: Sailor on Horseback (sp); The Caine Mutiny Court-Martial (sp); 1957: Galvanized Yankee (sp); 1958–59: Special Agent 7 (series); 1959: Ah, Wilderness! (sp); Six Guns for Donegan (sp); 1960: The Seventh Miracle (sp); 1961: Call to Danger (sp); 1962: Special Assignment (sp); 1963: Two Faces of Treason (sp); The Case Against Paul Ryker (theatrical in 1968 as Sgt. Ryker); 1964: Mr. Biddle's Crime Wave (sp); 1967: Wings of Fire; 1968–71: Julia (series); 1973: Isn't It Shocking?; 1975: The Abduction of Saint Anne; The Sky's the Limit; 1976: The November Plan; 1977: Flight to Holocaust; Fire!; 1979: Valentine; 1984: It Came Upon the Midnight Clear.

MABEL NORMAND

BORN: STATEN ISLAND, NY, NOVEMBER 9, 1892.
DIED: FEBRUARY 23, 1930.

In a field that belonged almost exclusively to men, Mabel Normand was the one female silent movie comic who garnered a devoted following. Alas, like a bad pre-talkie melodrama, it all ended quickly and tragically. As a teenager she modeled, ending up on the cover of the *Saturday Evening Post*, which led to doing extra work in movies as early as 1910. It was while appearing in short subjects for Biograph Studios that she met Mack Sennett, who was eager to form his own company. The two became an item off screen and, when he established Keystone Company in 1912, she went with him, in time becoming prolific enough to occasionally find her name in the title. Her real fame came when Sennett paired her with corpulent comedian Roscoe "Fatty" Arbuckle in a 1913 short called "The Water Picnic." The teaming clicked and the pair did dozens more of these frantic comedies over a three-year period. During this time she was considered important enough to be cast in Hollywood's first full-length comedy, *Tillie's Punctured Romance*, which gave her a chance to work with both Charlie Chaplin and Marie Dressler. By 1916 Normand had become a big enough star that she decided to become her own producer (she had already directed or co-directed some of her films but never took on-screen credit), setting up the Mabel Normand Feature Film Company. Unfortunately, she got off to a bad start since the organization's maiden vehicle, *Mickey*, took two years to find a distributor. At that point she left Sennett to do feature films for Samuel Goldwyn, starting with *Dodging a Million* in 1918. Thanks to Goldwyn, *Mickey* was at last distributed and proved to be a great success, which helped erase the less-than-ecstatic response to her foray into drama, *Joan of Plattsburg*.

She followed *Mickey* with *Peck's Bad Girl*, in which she foiled a gang of crooks; *A Perfect 36*, rising from boardinghouse employee to salesgirl; *The Jinx*, as a hapless circus worker; and *The Slim Princess*. In each, the audiences loved this petite lady's sense of knockabout fun, combined with a touch of Chaplinesque pathos — the lowly girl who endures duress but makes good in the end. After *What Happened to Rosa*, which had her pretending to be a Spanish seductress, she returned to Sennett for *Oh Mabel Behave!*, which was hastily thrown together from previous material, and, more prestigiously, *Molly O'*, which was to be her big reunion with the filmmaker who had made her name in the first place. During its financially lucrative run, Normand's name landed in the papers because of her peripheral involvement in the scandal behind the murder of director William Desmond Taylor — she visited him on the night of his death. This caused no repercussion to her film career but the involvement of her chauffeur in the shooting of actress Edna Purviance's lover did takes its toll on Normand's popularity, as all kinds of stories about the actress's drug abuse were unleashed. Her final Sennett feature, *The Extra Girl*, still presented her at her most likable but there was a distinct drop in attendance. She decided to try stage work and when that didn't pan out returned to Hollywood, where she did some shorts for Hal Roach that made next to no impact. After marrying actor Lew Cody in 1926 she retired from the public eye and died of tuberculosis at the age of 37, one of Hollywood's first sad examples of a promising career cut short far too early. In 1974 Bernadette Peters played her in the short-lived Broadway musical *Mack & Mabel*.

Screen (shorts): 1910: The Indiscretions of Betty; Wilful Peggy; Over the Garden Wall; 1911: Betty Becomes a Maid; The Subduing of Mrs. Nag; When a Man's Married His Troubles Begin; Piccioala; The Troublesome Secretaries; The Changing of Silas Warner; The Diving Girl; How Betty Won the School; His Mother; The Baron; The Revenue Man and the Girl; The Squaw's Love; The Making of a Man; Her Awakening; The Unveiling; Italian Blood; The Inventor's Secret; Their First Divorce Case; Through His Wife's Picture; A Victim of Circumstances; Saved from Himself; Why He Gave Up; 1912:

The Engagement Ring; The Brave Hunter; The Furs; Help! Help!; The Interrupted Elopement; A Dash Thru the Clouds; The Fickle Spaniard; Helen's Marriage; Hot Stuff; Katchem Kate; Oh Those Eyes; Tomboy Bessie; The Tourists; The Tragedy of a Dress Suit; What the Doctor Ordered; The Water Nymph; The New Neighbor; Pedro's Dilemma; Stolen Glory; The Ambitious Butler; The Flirting Husband; The Grocery Clerk's Romance; Cohen at Coney Island; At It Again; Mabel's Lovers; The Deacon's Trouble; A Temperamental Husband; The Rivals; Mr. Fix-It; A Desperate Lover; Brown's Seance; A Family Mix-Up; A Midnight Elopement; Mabel's Adventures; The Duel; Mabel's Stratagem; 1913: Mabel's Dad; The Cure That Failed; The Mistaken Masher; The Deacon Outwitted; Just Brown's Luck; The Battle of Who Run; Heinze's Resurrection; Mabel's Heroes; The Professor's Daughter; Red-Hot Romance; A Tangled Affair; The Sleuths at the Floral Parade; The Rural Third Degree; A Strong Revenge; Foiling Fickle Father; A Doctored Affair; The Rube and the Baron; Those Good Old Days; Father's Choice; The Ragtime Band; At 12 O' Clock; Her New Boy; A Little Hero; Mabel's Awful Mistake; Hubby's Job; The Foreman of the Jury; Barney Oldfield's Race for Life; The Hansom Driver; The Speed Queen; The Waiters' Picnic; For the Love of Mabel; The Telltale Light; A Noise from the Deep; Love and Courage; Professor Bean's Removal; The Riot; Baby Day; Mabel's New Hero; The Gypsy Queen; Mabel's Dramatic Career; The Faithful Taxicab; The Bowling Match; Speed Kings; Love Sickness at Sea; A Muddy Romance; Cohen Saves the Day; The Gusher; Zuzu the Band Leader; The Champion; Fatty's Flirtation; 1914: A Misplaced Foot; Mabel's Stormy Love Affair; Won in a Closet; Mabel's Bare Escape; Mabel's Strange Predicament; Love and Gasoline; Mack At It Again; Mabel at the Wheel; Caught in a Cabaret; Mabel's Nerve; The Alarm; The Fatal Market; Her Friend the Bandit; Mabel's Busy Day; Mabel's Married Life; Mabel's New Job; Those Country Kids; Mabel's Latest Prank;' Mabel's Blunder; Hello Mabel!; Gentlemen of Nerve; Lovers' Post Office; His Trysting Place; How Heroes Are Made; Fatty's Jonah Day; Fatty's Wine Party; The Sea Nymphs; Getting Acquainted; 1915: Mabel and Fatty's Washing Day; Mabel and Fatty's Single Life; Fatty and Mabel at the San Diego Exposition; Mabel, Fatty and the Law; Fatty and Mabel's Married Life; That Little Band of Gold; Wished on Mabel; Mabel and Fatty Viewing the World's Fair at San Francisco; Their Social Splash; Mabel's Willful Way; Mabel Lost and Won; The Little Teacher; My Valet; Stolen Magic; 1916: Fatty and Mabel Adrift; He Did and He Didn't; The Bright Lights; 1918: Stake Uncle Sam to Play Your Hand; 1926: The Raggedy Rose; The Nickel Hopper; One Hour Married; Anything Once; 1927: Should Men Walk Home?

Screen (features): 1912: Neighbors; 1914: Tillie's Punctured Romance; 1918: Dodging a Million; The Floor Below; Joan of Plattsburg; The Venus Model; Back to the Woods; Mickey; Peck's Bad Girl; A Perfect 36; 1919: Sis Hopkins; The Pest; When Doctors Disagree; Upstairs; The Jinx; 1920: Pinto; The Slim Princess; 1921: What Happened to Rosa; Oh Mabel Behave!; Molly O'; 1922: Head Over Heels; 1923: Susanna; The Extra Girl.

SHEREE NORTH

(DAWN BETHEL) BORN: HOLLYWOOD, CA, JANUARY 17, 1933.

Fox's CinemaScope blonde of the late 1950s, Sheree North wound up hanging in there a lot longer than anyone expected, and grew into a more interesting presence as she shed the gloss and experience toughened her up. A dancer from the age of ten, she worked in clubs in Los Angeles and Las Vegas, eventually making her way to Broadway in *Hazel Flagg*. She and her show-stopping number, "You're Gonna Dance With Me, Willie," were among the few things retained when it transferred to the movies as the Martin and Lewis vehicle, *Living It Up*. In 1955 20th Century-Fox figured they might be able to spin her into a new star, so they signed her up and placed her next to the soon-to-depart Betty Grable for a weak semi-musical, *How to Be Very, Very Popular*, where North had her moment in the spotlight performing "Shake, Rattle and Roll." She then enlisted while hubby Tom Ewell stayed a civilian in the comedy *The Lieutenant Wore Skirts*; stole the show dancing to "Birth of the Blues" in the biopic *The Best Things in Life Are Free*; was Tony Randall's loyal suburban housewife in the ensemble drama *No Down Payment*; and played second fiddle to flash-in-the-pan Christine Carere, as her press agent, in *Mardi Gras*. After that, she stuck expressly to theater and television before returning to the big screen in 1966 in the monster flick *Destination Inner Space*, and then, more significantly, in a character role as "the other woman" in the police thriller *Madigan*. She was soon a fairly regular presence, doing a very impressive job of playing blowsy ladies past their prime in such movies as *The Gypsy Moths*, as Gene Hackman's stripper girlfriend; *Lawman*, as your standard good-hearted whore; *The Organization*, as the head of a drug ring; *Charley Varrick*, as a photographer making a phony passport for Walter Matthau; *The Shootist*, as John Wayne's ex-lover; *Rabbit Test*, impregnating Billy Crystal; and *Maniac Cop*, as a crippled policewoman.

Screen: 1951: Excuse My Dust; 1953: Here Come the Girls; 1954: Living It Up; 1955: How to Be Very, Very Popular; The Lieutenant Wore Skirts; 1956: The Best Things in Life Are Free; 1957: The Way to the Gold; No Down Payment; 1958: In Love and War; Mardi Gras; 1966: Destination Inner Space; 1968: Madigan; 1969: The Trouble With Girls (and How to Get Into It); The Gypsy Moths; 1971: Lawman; The Organization; 1973: Charley Varrick; 1974: The Outfit; 1975: Breakout; 1976: Survival (filmed 1969); The Shootist; 1977: Telefon; 1978: Rabbit Test; 1979: Only Once in a Lifetime; 1988: Maniac Cop; 1991: Cold Dog Soup (dtv); Defenseless; 2000: Dying to Get Rich/Susan's Plan (dtv).

NY Stage: 1953: Hazel Flagg; 1962: I Can Get It for You Wholesale; 1985: California Dog Fight (ob).

Select TV: 1954: Lend an Ear (sp); Anything Goes (sp); 1957: Topaz (sp); 1965: The Crime (sp); 1967: Code Name: Heraclitus (sp); 1969: Then Came Bronson; 1971: Vanished; 1972: Rolling Man; 1973: Trouble Comes to Town; Snatched; Maneater; Key West; 1974: Winter Kill; 1975: A Shadow in the Streets; Big Eddie (series); 1976: Most Wanted; 1977: The Night They Took Miss Beautiful; 1978: A Real American Hero; 1979: Amateur Night at the Dixie Bar and Grill; Women in White; Portrait of a Stripper; 1980: Marilyn: The Untold Story; 1980–81: I'm a Big Girl Now (series); 1983: Legs; Bay City Blues (series); 1984: Scorned and Swindled; 1989: Jake Spanner: Private Eye; 1991: Dead on the Money.

KIM NOVAK

(MARILYN PAULINE NOVAK) BORN: CHICAGO, IL, FEBRUARY 13, 1933.

There was an unmistakable star quality about Kim Novak that made her stand out above the dozens of other cinematic platinum blondes. At the same time she somehow managed to be utterly vacuous, leaving great big gaping voids in the middle of many of her films. Having modeled in Chicago, she journeyed west to see where her looks might take

her and ended up in a teensy part in a 1954 Jane Russell movie for RKO, *The French Line*. The folks at Columbia were impressed enough to give her the star buildup. She started with the noir-like *Pushover*, wherein she conned Fred MacMurray into murdering her lover, much as Barbara Stanywck had done to him in *Double Indemnity*, only the difference between the two actresses was inestimable. After dallying with Jack Lemmon in *Phffft* and playing a nightclub singer involved with a bunch of petty crooks in a poor caper film, *5 Against the House*, she got her big chance when she was assigned the pivotal role of the small-town beauty who is seduced by drifter William Holden in *Picnic*. This was a monumental bit of miscasting, with the glossily manufactured Novak in no way suggesting a naïve gal from the Midwestern sticks, in an otherwise acceptable film of the William Inge play. It went on to be one of 1955's biggest hits, as did *The Man with the Golden Arm*, where she played the nice girl in the life of drug addict Frank Sinatra. Continuing her run of good luck she was in a third success, *The Eddy Duchin Story*, as the first wife of Tyrone Power.

It was becoming clear that the public was responding to her. There was even decent attendance for the first film she carried on her own, *Jeanne Eagles*, a dreadful biopic of the late actress, which only emphasized Novak's inability to bring conviction to a part and her habit of going down with the ship. Fortunately Sinatra and Rita Hayworth were around to take the emphasis off of her in the musical *Pal Joey*, where she gyrated most uncomfortably through Rodgers and Hart's "That Terrific Rainbow," her vocals dubbed by Trudy Irwin. It took a pair of teamings with James Stewart to finally utilize her breathy, almost unnatural voice and otherworldly blank stare to good effect. Alfred Hitchcock's *Vertigo* allowed her to play Stewart's distant object of obsession and then, later in the plot, a woman who might be her look-alike. Her hesitancy as an actress and her undeniably stunning looks were perfect in creating a certain air of vulnerability and mystery about the character in what would be hailed, in time, as one of that director's masterpieces. More popular in its day was *Bell Book and Candle*, in which Novak played a Greenwich Village witch who captures Stewart through magic, but must face the fact that she's not supposed to fall for a mortal. The spacey Novak qualities suggested someone not of this earth and the performance clicked.

After that she fell in love with more older men — Fredric March in *Middle of the Night* and Kirk Douglas in *Strangers When We Meet* — before paling beside the more adept farceurs James Garner and Tony Randall in the MGM comedy *Boys' Night Out*. Miraculously she got billing *over* Jack Lemmon for *The Notorious Landlady*, at one point sporting an atrocious cockney accent, in this mild comedy-mystery that marked the end of her relationship with Columbia. There was a disastrous remake of *Of Human Bondage*, grimly playing the selfish waitress who destroys Laurence Harvey, and then *Kiss Me, Stupid*, director Billy Wilder's often pricelessly funny sex comedy that ran into censorship problems. Novak, as a waitress-whore named Polly the Pistol, was either being very daring or intent on irritating audiences more than usual — she played the entire part with an affected head cold. *The Amorous Adventures of Molly Flanders*, a strained and garish female *Tom Jones* rip-off, which introduced her to a new husband (1965–66), Richard Johnson; and *The Legend of Lylah Clare*, in a dual role as a dead actress and her look-alike, were the sort of horrors to stop dead the careers of better actresses, so Novak found herself quickly fading from the spotlight. Amid some television movies, she showed up in theaters in the anthology *Tales That Witness Madness*; in a supporting part in *The White Buffalo*, one of the least popular of all the Charles Bronson movies of the 1970s; *Just a Gigolo*, a problematic production which was notable only for marking the last on-screen appearance of Marlene Dietrich; *The Mirror Crack'd*, in which she sparred bitchily with Elizabeth Taylor, evoking warm notices from critics who'd forgotten how much they'd roasted her work in the past; and *Liebestraum*, spending most of the film suffering and looking terrible while laying in a hospital bed. Prior to that, she spent a season as a regular on the nighttime soap opera *Falcon Crest*, which was really the kind of glossy thing she looked most at home in.

Screen: 1954: The French Line; Pushover; Phffft; 1955: Son of Sinbad; 5 Against the House; Picnic; The Man with the Golden Arm; 1956: The Eddy Duchin Story; 1957: Jeanne Eagles; Pal Joey; 1958: Vertigo; Bell Book and Candle; 1959: Middle of the Night; 1960: Strangers When We Meet; Pepe; 1962: Boys' Night Out; The Notorious Landlady; 1964: Of Human Bondage; Kiss Me, Stupid; 1965: The Amorous Adventures of Moll Flanders; 1968: The Legend of Lylah Clare; 1969: The Great Bank Robbery; 1973: Tales That Witness Madness; 1977: The White Buffalo; 1980: The Mirror Crack'd; 1981: Just a Gigolo (UK: 1979); 1990: The Children; 1991: Liebestraum.

Select TV: 1973: Third Girl From the Left; 1975: Satan's Triangle; 1983: Malibu; 1986–87: Falcon Crest (series).

RAMON NOVARRO

(RAMON GIL SAMANIEGOS) BORN: DURANGO, MEXICO, FEBRUARY 6, 1899. DIED: OCTOBER 31, 1968.

One of the major stars of the silent era, Ramon Novarro was supposed to be another Rudolph Valentino but his screen image was much less exotic, more accessible, and occasionally charming. An undeniably handsome man, with bright eyes and a lovely smile, he took to both drama and lighter fare with ease. As he grew out of his looks and had to deal with microphones, something in his magnetism began to evaporate, leading to one of the longest and, ultimately, saddest declines in movie history. His family came to Los Angeles in 1914 and he found work as a singing waiter. While landing extra work in films, he danced in vaudeville with the Marion Morgan troupe and this led to a specialty number in a Mack Sennett comedy, *A Small Town Idol*. His big break came when director Rex Ingram selected him to play the villain, Rupert of Hentzau, in the 1922 version of the oft-filmed *The Prisoner of Zenda*. This landed him a contract with Ingram, who planned to build him into a star. Casting him opposite Ingram's wife, Alice Terry, resulted in three films that did the trick: *Where the Rainbow Ends*, a tale of forbidden love between a native and a missionary's daughter; *Scaramouche*, in the title role; and *The Arab*, which once again had him in love with a white woman. Around this time Metro-Goldwyn-Mayer was coming into being and Novarro's contract was sold to that company. He became a street criminal in *The Red Lily* and a cadet in *The Midshipman*, which actually featured footage shot at the Annapolis Naval Academy. Film immortality came when he was selected to play the title role in *Ben-Hur*, the biggest and most expensive motion picture made in Hollywood up to that time. He made for a most ingratiating hero and, since the movie was the hoped-for smash for the company, rose to the very top of the profession.

There were two films set in Spain, the soppy *Lovers?*, and the adventure *The Road to Romance*, after which he was at his sweetest in the title role of *The Student Prince in Old Heidelberg*, falling for tavern maid Norma Shearer. He was a nice sailor in *Across to Singapore*, which was followed by two less popular productions, *Forbidden Hours* and *The Flying Fleet*, another Navy

story. Because of the poor box-office showing of these two films, the studio figured it might be beneficial to let him sing "Pagan Love Song" in some sequences of the otherwise silent *The Pagan* (he spent most of the movie in nothing but a sarong), and then let him warble in an all-talkie, *Devil May-Care*. Since audiences could now hear that he had a Spanish accent, he was Spanish for *In Gay Madrid* and *Call of the Flesh* (he also directed the Spanish version of the latter and co-directed the French version), but it was clear that his popularity had waned. *Son of India* was the sort of interracial romance he was supposed to have grown out of years before, after which he had one final success with *Mata Hari* ("What's the matter, Mata?"), probably not due to Novarro but because it featured Greta Garbo. He was an absolute disaster pretending to be Chinese for *The Son-Daughter*, remade *The Arab* as *The Barbarian*, and then played a composer opposite the more popular Jeanette MacDonald in *The Cat and the Fiddle*. He was an Indian in the quickly forgotten adaptation of the Pulitzer Prize-winning *Laughing Boy*, and did one last musical, *The Night is Young*, an icky operetta that died the death at the box office and really put an end to his Hollywood career as a star attraction. After stage work in London, he directed, wrote, and produced a Spanish-language film, *Contra la Corriente*, then went over to Republic Pictures for two films, *The Sheik Steps Out* and *A Desperate Adventure*, which did nothing to reinstate him. As a result, he went to the foreign-language market for the French *La Comedie de Bonheur* and the Mexican *La Virgen que Forjo Una Patria*, before returning to Hollywood, paunchier and grayer, as a character player in such movies as *We Were Strangers* and *Crisis*. There was a break of ten years after which director George Cukor gave him a job as the villain in *Heller in Pink Tights*, which marked his final appearance infront of the cameras. All but the most nostalgic had pretty much forgotten about Novarro when his lurid murder on Halloween night put him back in the news — he was beaten to death in his home by a pair of street hustlers set on robbing him.

Screen: AS RAMON SAMANIEGOS: 1917: Joan the Woman; The Little American; The Hostage; 1919: The Goat; 1921: A Small Town Idol; 1922: Mr. Barnes of New York.

AS RAMON NOVARRO: 1922: The Prisoner of Zenda; Trifling Women; 1923: Where the Pavement Ends; Scaramouche; 1924: The Arab; Thy Name is Woman; The Red Lily; 1925: A Lover's Oath (filmed 1922); The Midshipman; Ben-Hur; 1927: Lovers?; The Road to Romance; The Student Prince in Old Heidelberg; 1928: Across to Singapore; A Certain Young Man; Forbidden Hours; 1929: The Flying Fleet; The Pagan; Devil May-Care; 1930: In Gay Madrid; Call of the Flesh; 1931: Daybreak; Son of India; 1932: Mata Hari; Huddle; The Son-Daughter; 1933: The Barbarian; 1934: The Cat and the Fiddle; Laughing Boy; 1935: The Night Is Young; 1937: The Sheik Steps Out; 1938: A Desperate Adventure; 1940: La Comedie du Bonheur (nUSr); 1942: La Virgen que Forjo una Patria/The Saint That Forged a Country (nUSr); 1949: We Were Strangers; The Big Steal; 1950: The Outriders; Crisis; 1960: Heller in Pink Tights.

Select TV: 1958: Elfego — Lawyman or Gunman(sp); Law and Order Inc. (sp).

O

JACK OAKIE

(Lewis Delaney Offield) Born: Sedalia, MO, November 12, 1903. Died: January 23, 1978.

Pudgy-faced comedian Jack Oakie was one of Paramount's resident players during the early 1930s, where his goofy yokels often had a habit of overstaying their welcome. With pretty much next to no show business experience, he came to New York seeking work and ended up dancing in the choruses of *Little Nellie Kelly* and *Artists and Models*. As luck would have it, director Wesley Ruggles caught him in the Rodgers and Hart musical *Peggy-Ann* and asked him to play a small part for him in the film *Finders Keepers*, which earned him a contract with Paramount in 1928. Supporting Clara Bow, he was a sailor named Searchlight Doyle, in *The Fleet's In*, a property the studio would return to on several occasions, and a characterization so successful that Oakie was asked to reprise it in 1930's *Sea Legs*. After supporting Bow again in *The Wild Party*, and Fredric March in *The Dummy*, he got the lead in *Fast Company*, as a small time baseball fan who rises to the big league — a story that became better known when it was filmed a few years later as *Elmer the Great*. Now a star, he was a stowaway in love with Ginger Rogers in *The Sap From Syracuse*; a prizefighter who becomes a polo player to impress the snobs in *The Social Lion*; and a cab driver marooned on an island with Jeanette MacDonald in *Let's Go Native*, one of the many variations of the play *The Admirable Crichton*. Remaining dumb but affable, he was an insurance salesman taken in by gangsters in *The Gang Buster*, and a naïve songwriter, wide-eyed in the big bad city, in *June Moon*. After that he reached some kind of comic peak as the salesman visiting the screwball country of Klopstokia in *Million Dollar Legs*, a strong contender for the funniest film of its day.

He was one of Gary Cooper's soldier buddies in *If I Had a Million*, and went over to Universal for the mild screen adaptation of the Kaufman and Hart stage hit *Once in a Lifetime*, as a vaudevillian who accidentally takes Hollywood by storm. He played Jack Haley's fellow songwriter in *Sitting Pretty*; was Tweedledum next to Roscoe Karns's Tweedledee in *Alice in Wonderland*; and then became a staple of those campus comedy-

musicals that Paramount made a killing on during the 1930s, including *College Humor*, *College Rhythm*, and *Collegiate*. By this time he was starting to segue into the sidekick position as he did for *The Call of the Wild*, with Clark Gable, and *The Texas Rangers*, with Fred MacMurray. In 1936 he signed up with RKO where he played an egotistical movie detective who takes on a real case in *Super Sleuth*, and Lucille Ball's overbearing press agent in *The Affairs of Annabel*, a comedy that did well enough to rate an immediate sequel, *Annabel Takes a Tour*, released within the same year. Soon afterwards he switched over to Fox but not before he scored a bull's-eye with his dazzlingly funny send-up of Benito Mussolini in Charlie Chaplin's *The Great Dictator*, which earned him an Oscar nomination in the supporting category. At Fox he was asked to lend often stale comic support to some glossy musicals, such as *The Great American Broadcast*, *Song of the Islands*, and *Hello, Frisco, Hello*, before moving on to even lesser fare at Universal. He jumped back to Fox to play a vaudevillian named Bozo, the loyal buddy of alcoholic Dan Dailey in *When My Baby Smiles at Me*, a role he would repeat on television years later, under the property's original title, *Burlesque*. After a period away he returned to do a few brief character roles including *Around the World in Eighty Days*, as a ship's captain, and *Lover Come Back*, as a randy business executive. He did some scattered television appearances after that but chose not to return to movies, having become enormously wealthy over the years and therefore having no need to work strictly for cash.

Screen: 1923: His Children's Children; Big Brother; 1924: His Darker Self; Classmate; 1928: Finders Keepers; Road House; The Fleet's In; Someone to Love; 1929: Sin Town; Chinatown Nights; The Wild Party; Close Harmony; The Dummy; The Man I Love; Fast Company; Street Girl; Hard to Get; Sweetie; 1930: Paramount on Parade; Hit the Deck; The Social Lion; Let's Go Native; The Sap From Syracuse; Sea Legs; 1931: The Gang Buster; June Moon; Dude Ranch; Touchdown; 1932: Dancers in the Dark; Sky Bride; Make Me a Star; Million Dollar Legs; Madison Square Garden; If I Had a Million; Once in a Lifetime; Uptown New York; 1933: From Hell to Heaven; Sailor Be Good; The Eagle and the Hawk; College Humor; Too Much Harmony; Sitting Pretty; Alice in Wonderland; 1934: Looking for Trouble; Murder at the Vanities; Shoot the Works; College Rhythm; 1935:

The Call of the Wild; King of Burlesque; 1936: Colleen; The Big Broadcast of 1936; Florida Special; The Texas Rangers; That Girl From Paris; Collegiate; 1937: Champagne Waltz; Super Sleuth; The Toast of New York; Fight for Your Lady; Hitting a New High; 1938: Radio City Revels; The Affairs of Annabel; Annabel Takes a Tour; Thanks for Everything; 1940: Young People; The Great Dictator; Tin Pan Alley; Little Men; 1941: Rise and Shine; The Great American Broadcast; Navy Blues; 1942: Song of the Islands; Iceland; 1943: Hello, Frisco, Hello; Wintertime; Something to Shout About; 1944: It Happened Tomorrow; The Merry Monahans; Sweet and Low Down; Bowery to Broadway; 1945: That's the Spirit; On Stage Everybody; 1946: She Wrote the Book; 1948: Northwest Stampede; When My Baby Smiles at Me; 1949: Thieves' Highway; 1950: Last of the Buccaneers; 1951: Tomahawk; 1956: Around the World in Eighty Days; 1959: The Wonderful Country; 1960: The Rat Race; 1961: Lover Come Back.

NY Stage: 1924: Little Nellie Kelly; 1925: Artists and Models; 1926: Peggy Ann.

Select TV: 1955: Burlesque (sp); 1958: The Award Winner (sp).

SIMON OAKLAND

BORN: NEW YORK, NY, AUGUST 28, 1922.
DIED: AUGUST 29, 1983.

This smirking character actor with the growling voice cut such an imposing figure as a man of authority that it was odd to think that, of all things, he started off as a violinist. When that didn't work out he studied acting with the American Theatre Wing and made his Broadway debut in 1948 in *The Skipper Next to God*. He appeared in several plays after that before making his film bow in 1958, as a police chief in *The Brothers Karamazov*. Over the next decade or so he chalked up some impressive performances on his résumé with *I Want to Live!*, as the journalist covering Susan Hayward's trip to the gas chamber; *Psycho*, as the psychiatrist who shows up at the end to explain the whole grizzly affair; *West Side Story*, as the bigoted New York City cop Lieutenant Shrank, perhaps his most enduring role; *Ready for the People*, top billed, as a district attorney, in what was actually a failed TV pilot that ended up in movie theaters; *The Sand Pebbles*, at his most effective, as the bullying sailor who makes life hell for Mako; *Tony Rome*, as the Miami millionaire who hires Frank Sinatra to investigate his daughter's odd behavior; and *Bullitt*, as the police captain who assigns Steve McQueen to guard a key witness. In the 1970s he made the small screen his home, popping up on a regular basis in four different series including the cult favorite *Kolchak: The Night Stalker*, as Darren McGavin's editor, and *Ba Ba Black Sheep*, in which he played a general.

Screen: 1958: The Brothers Karamazov; I Want to Live!; 1960: Who Was That Lady?; The Rise and Fall of Legs Diamond; Psycho; Murder, Inc.; 1961: West Side Story; 1962: Hemingway's Adventures of a Young Man; Follow That Dream; Third of a Man; 1963: Wall of Noise; 1964: The Raiders; Ready for the People (from tv); 1965: The Satan Bug; 1966: The Plainsman; The Sand Pebbles; 1967: Tony Rome; 1968: Chubasco; Bullitt; 1970: On a Clear Day You Can See Forever; 1971: The Hunting Party; Scandalous John; 1972: Chato's Land; 1973: Emperor of the North Pole; Happy Mother's Day, Love George/Run, Stranger, Run.

NY Stage: AS SI OAKLAND: 1948: The Skipper Next to God; Light Up the Sky; 1949: Caesar and Cleopatra; 1952: The Shrike; 1954: Sands of the Negev; 1955: Men in White.

AS SIMON OAKLAND: 1956: The Great Sebastians; 1957: Inherit the Wind; 1958: The Trial of Dmitri Karamazov; 1963: Five Evenings; Have I Got a Girl for You!; 1969: Angela; 1971: Twigs; 1977: The Shadow Box.

Select TV: 1965: Who Has Seen the Wind?; 1971: The Cable Car Murder; 1972: The Night Stalker; 1973: The Night Strangler; Toma; Key West; 1973–74: Toma (series); 1974–75: Kolchak: The Night Stalker (series); 1977–78: Ba Ba Black Sheep (series); 1977: Young Joe: The Forgotten Kennedy; 1978: Evening in Byzantium; 1978–79: David Cassidy — Man Undercover (series).

MERLE OBERON

(ESTELLE MERLE O'BRIEN THOMPSON)
BORN: CALCUTTA, INDIA, FEBRUARY 19, 1911.
DIED: NOVEMBER 23, 1979.

With skin that looked as smooth as porcelain, Merle Oberon was indeed one of the most distinctively beautiful of all stars, but her appeal pretty much ended there. She carried herself like royalty and thereby kept a wall between herself and the audience, her acting style being rather haughty and more than a shade dull. She came from a background cloaked in mystery but it seems that she was born to a British father and Indian mother in India, not Tasmania, as was stated for years in studio bios. Stories also claim that she would pass her mother off as her servant for fear of embarrassment. In any case, she came to England in the late 1920s and sought work in show business under the unlikely name of Queenie O'Brien. While doing extra work she was spotted by producer-director Alexander Korda, who was instantly taken with her and changed her name to Merle Oberon. He cast her as the mousy secretary with whom Roland Young falls in love in *Wedding Rehearsal*, and, more importantly, the tragic Anne Boleyn in *The Private Life of Henry VIII*, which was the biggest British import in the U.S. up to that time. After playing Charles Boyer's Japanese wife in *The Battle* and one of the ladies wooed by the aging Douglas Fairbanks in *The Private Life of Don Juan*, she showed up in another important costume picture that was prominently distributed in America, *The Scarlet Pimpernel*, where she was at her most aloof, as Leslie Howard's wife. Hollywood was eager to get her and she accepted an offer from 20th Century-Fox to play one of the women in the life of look-alike Maurice Chevaliers in *Folies-Bergère*, which marked the great French singer's farewell to America for a while. Goldwyn signed Oberon to a contract in 1935 and she started off well, receiving an Oscar nomination for *The Dark Angel*, playing the wife who is distressed when she thinks lover Fredric March is dead, marries Herbert Marshall on the rebound, and then must face the fact that March is very much alive and blind. The nomination was bestowed upon her, no doubt, because she spent nearly the entire film either shedding tears or on the verge of it. From this relentlessly puerile soap opera, she ended up in what was probably the best of all her films, *These Three*, the deliberately distorted adaptation of *The Children's Hour*, as the schoolteacher who realizes best friend Miriam Hopkins covets Merle's man, Joel McCrea. After *Beloved Enemy*, a romantic drama set against the Irish Rebellion of 1921, she went back to England where her car accident caused the abandonment of what would become the most famous unfinished movie of its day, *I Claudius*.

Instead she did a pair of comedies, both given a spark of prestige by being shot in Technicolor: *Over the Moon*, with Rex Harrison and *The Divorce of Lady X*, with Laurence Olivier. She then returned to America and to Goldwyn for a fun comedy with Gary Cooper, *The Cowboy and the Lady*, and the movie with which her name is synonymous, *Wuthering Heights*. This was one of 1939's most prestigious offerings, although nothing she did could keep this insufferable character from being anything but a ninny and a bore. The box-office results were average rather than spectacular but the film trumped *Gone With the Wind* for the New York Film Critics' Award and it remained much revered in certain circles for decades to come. She was at the height of her standing in Hollywood but left Goldwyn and went back to England yet again, finally marrying Korda in 1939 (they divorced in 1945). Their stay there produced one piece of blatant propaganda, *The Lion Has Wings*, after which they decided it was safer to steer clear of the war by staying in America. Warners signed Oberon up for two movies, *Till We Meet Again*, the remake of the dated soaper *One Way Passage*; and a romantic triangle, *Affectionately Yours*; neither film did much business so she was promptly let go. Freelancing she did a Lubitsch comedy, *That Uncertain Feeling*, her comic timing paling next to the likes of Burgess Meredith and Melvyn Douglas, and then made one last one for her husband, *Lydia*, which required her to look back on the loves of her life. Its lack of success meant that what little interest movie audiences had in her had waned. As a result she got top billing but was not the center of attention of *The Lodger*, with Laird Cregar stealing the show as a character based on Jack the Ripper, nor of the surprisingly well-attended biopic *A Song to Remember*, where Cornel Wilde as Chopin was the main attraction; though Oberon, playing George Sand, did look great in slacks.

In 1945 she married cameraman Lucien Ballard (they divorced in 1949), and during their union he lit and photographed her in *This Love of Ours*, *Temptation*, *Night Song*, and *Berlin Express*. She descended into Universal costume nonsense with *A Night in Paradise*, fell for blind pianist Dana Andrews in *Night Song*, and helped fight the Nazis in *Berlin Express*, none of which pretended to be anything more than standard product churned out to keep some people employed. Therefore it was time to hightail it back to Europe yet again, meaning it was some time before most Americans saw her back on the big screen, playing Josephine to Marlon Brando's Napoleon in the stodgy *Desiree*, although Jean Simmons had the main female role. Over the next several years Oberon made sporadic appearances, in each case eliciting comment on how regally lovely she looked: *The Price of Fear*, as Lex Barker's lover; *The Oscar*, as an actress past her prime; and *Hotel*, as a duchess. There was one last leading role, as an older lady involved with a much younger man, in *Interval*, a self-produced, downbeat disaster of no appeal whatsoever, although things did end up happily in real life with Oberon marrying her co-star, Robert Wolders.

Screen: 1929: The Three Passions; 1930: A Warm Corner; Alf's Button; 1931: Fascination; Never Trouble Trouble; 1932: Ebb Tide; Aren't We All?; Service for Ladies; For the Love of Mike; Wedding Rehearsal; Men of Tomorrow; 1933: Strange Evidence; The Private Life of Henry VIII; 1934: The Battle/Thunder in the East; The Broken Melody; The Private Life of Don Juan; 1935: The Scarlet Pimpernel; Folies Bergère; The Dark Angel; 1936: These Three; Beloved Enemy; 1938: The Divorce of Lady X; The Cowboy and the Lady; 1939: Wuthering Heights; The Lion Has Wings; 1940: Over the Moon (filmed 1937); Till We Meet Again; 1941: That Uncertain Feeling; Affectionately Yours; Lydia; 1943: Forever and a Day; Stage Door Canteen; First Comes Courage; 1944: The Lodger; Dark Waters; 1945: A Song to Remember; This Love of Ours; 1946: A Night in Paradise; Temptation; 1947: Night Song; 1948: Berlin Express; 1951: Pardon My French; 1952: Dans la vie tout s'rrange (nUSr); 1953: Affair in Monte Carlo/24 Hours in a Woman's Life; 1954: Todo es Possible en Granada/All Is Possible in Granada (nUSr); Desiree; Deep in My Heart; 1956: The Price of Fear; 1963: Of Love and Desire; 1966: The Oscar;

1967: Hotel; 1973: Interval.

Select TV: 1953: Sound Off My Love (sp); Allison Ltd. (sp); The Journey (sp); 1954: The Man Who Came to Dinner (sp); 1955: Second Night (sp); Cavalcade (sp); The Frightened Woman (sp); 1957: I Will Not Die (sp); Assignment Foreign Legion (series).

HUGH O'BRIAN

(Hugh Krampke) Born: Rochester, NY, April 19, 1925. Raised in Chicago, IL. ed: Univ. of Cincinnati.

One of those ingratiating men of machismo and action who owed his fame more to television than to the big screen, Hugh O'Brian had been a Marine before he ended up in Southern California where he dabbled in theater. This led to live television work but when the jobs ran out he became a part-time salesman which led him to meeting agent Milo Frank who, in turn, introduced him to Ida Lupino who gave him a part in a film she directed called *Young Lovers*. Universal took a look at his beefy handsomeness and decided he might be an attractive addition to their supporting players and signed him to a contract in 1951. He was mainly given roles in westerns including *Cave of Outlaws*, *The Raiders*, *The Cimarron Kid*, and *Seminole*, as an Indian. However, in more offbeat assignments, he was a crooked politician in a Dan Dailey musical, *Meet Me at the Fair*, and the last-minute substitute for Bud Abbott in *Fireman, Save My Child*, which started as an Abbott and Costello comedy until the latter fell ill. After leaving the studio he took some jobs at Fox (he was one of Spencer Tracy's unloved sons in *Broken Lance*, and a songwriter who hooks up with Mitzi Gaynor in *There's No Business Like Show Business*) then found stardom on the small screen playing the famed lawman in *The Legend of Wyatt Earp*, which ran for six years. During the series's run he got himself top billing for two westerns: *The Brass Legend*, in which he had a memorable showdown with villain Raymond Burr, and *The Fiend Who Walked the West*, as the ex-con out to stop psychopath Robert Evans in this re-thinking of *Kiss of Death*. After *Earp* ended he turned into a very likable leading man in a lot of minor movies. He was Pamela Tiffin's love interest in *Come Fly With Me*; one of the men in the life of Lana Turner in *Love Has Many Faces*; an acceptable hero in the unnecessary remake of *Ten Little Indians*; a tough sergeant in *Ambush Bay*, which brought him back, cinematically at least, to the Marines; and an American lassoing wild animals in *Africa — Texas Style!*, which later became a TV series without him (Chuck Connors played the part). He did return to television for some films and a short-lived series, *Search*, making less frequent trips back to theatrical films including *The Shootist*, as one of the gunslingers out to kill John Wayne, and *Twins*, as Arnold Schwarzenegger's athletic dad.

Screen: 1950: The Young Lovers/Never Fear; D.O.A.; The Return of Jesse James; Rocketship XM; Beyond the Purple Hills; Never Fear; 1951: Vengeance Valley; Fighting Coast Guard; On the Loose; Buckaroo Sheriff of Texas; Little Big Horn; Cave of Outlaws; The Cimarron Kid; 1952: Red Ball Express; The Battle at Apache Pass; Sally and Saint Anne; Son of Ali Baba; The Raiders; The Lawless Breed; 1953: Meet Me at the Fair; Seminole; The Man From the Alamo; The Stand at Apache River; Back to God's Country; 1954: Fireman, Save My Child; Saskatchewan; Drum's Across the River; Broken Lance; There's No Business Like Show Business; 1955: White Feather; The Twinkle in God's Eye; 1956: The Brass Legend; 1958: The Fiend Who Walked the West; 1959: Alias Jesse James; 1963: Come Fly With Me; 1965: Love Has Many Faces; In Harm's Way; 1966: Ten Little Indians; Ambush

Bay; Il Segreto del Vestito Rosso/Assassination in Rome; 1967: Africa — Texas Style!; 1969: Strategy of Terror; 1975: Killer Force; 1976: The Shootist; 1979: Game of Death; 1988: Doin' Time on Planet Earth; Twins.

Select TV: 1951: Going Home (sp); 1952: Shifting Sands (sp); 1955: The Engagement Ring (sp); A Light in France (sp); 1955–61: The Life and Legend of Wyatt Earp (series); 1956: Tall Dark Stranger (sp); 1957: Ringside Seat (sp); Invitation to a Gunfighter (sp); 1958: Reunion (sp); 1959: Chain of Command (sp); 1960: Graduation Dress (sp); 1961: Wingless Victory (sp); Feathertop (sp); 1962: Spellbound (sp); 1964: Runaway (sp); 1967: Dial M for Murder (sp); 1968: A Punt, a Pass and a Prayer (sp); 1970: Wild Women; 1971: Harpy; 1972: Probe; 1972–73: Search (series); 1975: Murder on Flight 502; 1977: Benny & Barney: Las Vegas Undercover; Fantasy Island; Murder at the World Series; 1978: Cruise Into Terror; Greatest Heroes of the Bible (ms); 1979: The Seekers; 1990: Gunsmoke: The Last Apache; 1991: The Gambler Returns: Luck of the Draw; 1994: Wyatt Earp: Return to Tombstone.

EDMOND O'BRIEN

BORN: NEW YORK, NY, SEPTEMBER 10, 1915.
DIED: MAY 9, 1985.

His face was usually fixed in a troubled squint, while his voice had a tone that suggested someone bringing bad news. Edmond O'Brien seemed pretty serious about his craft and left behind a nice fat résumé that ranged from character heavies and sidekicks to leads and support. Sometimes he did his job magnificently, though every so often he merely blended in with the background. He earned a scholarship to the Neighborhood Playhouse School of the Theatre, after which he did summer stock before debuting on Broadway in 1936, in *Daughters of Atreus*. Joining Orson Welles's Mercury Theatre, he did some radio and stage work with them including *Julius Caesar*, in which he played Marc Antony. RKO signed him to a contract and he launched his official movie career most impressively, as the love-struck poet Gringoire in the definitive screen rendering of *The Hunchback of Notre Dame*. In time, it would be odd to look back on this slim and pleasant-looking lad and realize the stockier, coarser person he would soon grow into was the same Edmond O'Brien. In the meantime, the studio made him the "guy" trying to win Lucille Ball in *A Girl, a Guy, and a Gob*; a member of the *Parachute Battalion*; and paired him nicely with Eve Arden, as news reporters, in the quickly forgotten *Obliging Young Lady*. He then joined the Air Force. While there he showed up on Broadway in the all-soldier revue *Winged Victory* and therefore got to be in 20th Century-Fox's film version of the same, in one of the principle roles, a down-to-earth native of Brooklyn, a point frequently mentioned in the dialogue. Following the war, he hooked up with Universal, which gave him some significant secondary parts, in *The Killers*, as the insurance investigator who links Burt Lancaster to the crooks; *Another Part of the Forest*, as the unscrupulous Ben Hubbard in this prequel to *The Little Foxes*, following Charles Dingle in the role; and *A Double Life*, as a press agent. Over at Warners, he was the cop who went undercover to trap James Cagney in the classic *White Heat*, giving a deeply dislikable performance that made you root for the bad guy. There was also a starring role, as an attorney posing as Vincent Price's bodyguard, in *The Web*, after which he wound up in one of the most memorable of all "B" pictures of the day, *D.O.A.*, as the hapless fellow who tries to figure out who has poisoned him. Remaining star material for awhile, he played a

telephone repairman who gets roped into a wiretapping scheme in *711 Ocean Drive*; a cop avenging his fellow officer's death in *Between Midnight and Dawn*; a lawyer turned gunman in the western *Warpath*; an innocent motorist taken hostage by escaped killer William Tallman in *The Hitch-Hiker*; an ex-criminal who loses his memory in *Man in the Dark*, which was shot in 3-D in an effort to enhance its humdrum storyline; and *Shield for Murder*, as a corrupt cop in a "B" noir made interesting because Howard W. Koch allowed O'Brien to share the directorial chores.

He was one of the less impressive performers in the 1953 version of *Julius Caesar*, playing Casca, and then he picked up an Academy Award for Best Supporting Actor of 1954, no doubt for adding a bit of juice to the fairly lifeless *The Barefoot Contessa*, as a nervous press agent. Turning nasty, he was a Prohibition-era mobster in *Pete Kelly's Blues*; then went to England to play the lead in an acceptable rendering of *1984*, which, unfortunately, went through a change of ending for its American release. Taking to the courtroom, he was a military lawyer in *The Rack* and then a district attorney who feels his client might actually be guilty in *The World Was His Jury*. In between, he was a gangster in that cockamamie combination of rock 'n' roll music and comedy, *The Girl Can't Help It*, one of those movies that inexplicably developed a cult following in later years, and then, sticking to the musical genre, was Tommy Sands's manager in *Sing, Boy, Sing*. In a heroic mode, he was a crewmember who helped save Dorothy Malone from the sinking ship in *The Last Voyage*, after which he made his full-fledged directorial debut (also co-producing) with a mean little thriller, *Man Trap*. Among the fine ensemble of *The Man Who Shot Liberty Valance*, he was the newspaper editor who gets beaten up by Lee Marvin; put on a general's uniform for the all-star spectacle *The Longest Day*; and got himself another Oscar nomination, for *Seven Days in May*, as the senator who remains loyal to the worried President (Fredric March). He was a ship's captain in *The Great Impostor*, which was notable in that it was written by his brother, Liam O'Brien; played the real life Charles E. Dederich, who founded the famed drug rehab center, in *Synanon*; was the general in charge of shrinking the team of scientists in the famous sci-fi adventure *Fantastic Voyage*; did his comical bad guy routine in a Don Knotts stiff, *The Love God?*; and was almost unrecognizable as a bearded geezer in the violent and controversial *The Wild Bunch*. His health failing, he cut back on his work load and was last seen as a mobster in an obscure Richard Harris flop, *99 and 44/100% Dead*. He retired shortly afterward, being diagnosed with Alzheimer's disease. Another previous credit, a horror film called *Dream No Evil*, surfaced in 1975. He was married to actresses Nancy Kelly (1941–42), who appeared with him in *Parachute Batallion*, and Olga San Juan (1948–67), who did a bit in O'Brien's 1960 film *The Third Voice*.

Screen: 1939: The Hunchback of Notre Dame; 1941: A Girl, a Guy, and a Gob; Obliging Young Lady; Parachute Battalion; 1942: Powder Town; 1943: The Amazing Mrs. Holliday; 1944: Winged Victory; 1946: The Killers; 1947: The Web; A Double Life; 1948: Another Part of the Forest; An Act of Murder; For the Love of Mary; Fighter Squadron; 1949: White Heat; 1950: D.O.A.; Backfire; 711 Ocean Drive; The Admiral Was a Lady; Between Midnight and Dawn; The Redhead and the Cowboy; 1951: Warpath; Two of a Kind; Silver City; 1952: The Greatest Show on Earth; The Denver and Rio Grande; The Turning Point; 1953: The Hitch-Hiker; Julius Caesar; Cow Country; Man in the Dark; China Venture; The Bigamist; 1954: The Shanghai Story; The Barefoot Contessa; Shield for Murder (and co-dir.); 1955: Pete Kelly's Blues; 1956: 1984; A Cry in the Night; D-Day, the Sixth of June; The Rack; The Girl Can't Help It; 1957: The Big Land; Stopover Tokyo; 1958: The World Was His Jury; Sing, Boy,

Sing; 1959: Up Periscope; 1960: The Last Voyage; The Third Voice; 1961: The Great Impostor; 1962: Bird Man of Alcatraz; Moon Pilot; The Man Who Shot Liberty Valance; The Longest Day; 1964: Seven Days in May; Rio Conchos; The Climbers/The Ambitious Ones (Fr: 1959); 1965: Sylvia; Synanon; 1966: Fantastic Voyage; 1967: Peau d'espion/To Commit a Murder (nUSr); The Viscount; 1969: The Love God?; The Wild Bunch; 1972: They Only Kill Their Masters; 1974: Lucky Luciano; 99 44/100% Dead; 1975: Dream No Evil/Now I Lay Me Down to Die (filmed 1971).

NY Stage: 1936: Daughters of Atreus; 1937: Julius Caesar; The Star-Wagon; 1939: Henry IV; 1940: Leave Her to Heaven; Romeo and Juliet; 1943: Winged Victory; 1952: I've Got Sixpence.

Select TV: 1951: Ice Bound (sp); A Matter of Life (sp); 1953: Ricochet (sp); To Any Soldier (sp); Lineman's Luck (sp); 1954: Charlie C Company (sp); The Net Draws Tight (sp); 1955: Dark Stranger (sp); The Heart's a Forgotten Hotel (sp); End of Flight (sp); 1956: A Ticket for Thaddeus (sp); 1957: Tower Room 14-A (sp); To Have and Have Not (sp); The Comedian (sp); 1958: The Male Animal (sp); The Town That Slept With the Lights On (sp); Coney Island Winter (sp); 1959: The Blue Men (sp); 1960: Johnny Midnight (series); 1961: Killer in the House (sp); 1962–63: Sam Benedict (series); 1964: The Hanged Man; 1965: Gallagher (sp); The Long Hot Summer (series); The Further Adventures of Gallagher (sp); 1967: The Doomsday Flight; The Outsider; 1968: Flesh and Blood (sp); 1970: The Intruders; 1971: River of Mystery; What's a Nice Girl Like You?; 1972: Jigsaw; 1973: Isn't It Shocking?

MARGARET O'BRIEN

(ANGELA MAXINE O'BRIEN)
BORN: LOS ANGELES, CA, JANUARY 15, 1937.

During World War II, the whole world fell in love with child star Margaret O'Brien. She had doleful, wanting eyes, a downcast mouth, and a most genteel way of enunci-ating a line. A lot her emoting may have been mechanical and pre-programmed, but it didn't seem to matter because you couldn't help but take a shine to her determination to please. MGM was looking for some youngsters for the Mickey Rooney-Judy Garland musical *Babes on Broadway* and spotted the child in some print ads she had done. O'Brien (unbilled but referred to in the film as Maxine), wound up in the movie in a priceless bit, in which she auditions for James Gleason pleading "Don't send my brother to the chair!" The studio was convinced they'd discovered someone with great possibilities and gave her the role of the mis-placed war orphan who wins her way into soldier Robert Young's heart in *Journey for Margaret*. The film's success proved the studio correct, but in the meantime O'Brien was given only very small parts in such movies as *Dr. Gillespie's Criminal Case* and *Madame Curie*. Her first official vehicle was *Lost Angel*, playing a young genius who is loosened up and humanized by reporter James Craig. Then 20th Century-Fox borrowed her to play Adele in an important production, *Jane Eyre*, but her phony French accent was the one detriment in this otherwise fine film. Back at MGM, she had a come-and-go British accent as the young owner of the castle in *The Canterville Ghost*, once again charming Robert Young as a man in uniform. This was followed by her best-loved film, *Meet Me in St. Louis*, in which she played Tootie, the iras-cible, youngest daughter of the Smith family, nearly drawing attention away from top-billed Judy Garland, especially in the movie's memorable Halloween sequence. The Academy of Motion Picture Arts and Sciences awarded her a special "juvenile"

Oscar at the 1944 ceremony.

Now an official box-office draw, she was a farm girl learning about life in a gentle bit of Americana, *Our Vines Have Tender Grapes*, and then enchanted galumphing Wallace Beery in the western *Bad Bascomb*. The formula was set to have Margaret turn on the charm in order to win over the skeptical adults, and shed some tears whenever possible, for maximum heartbreak, as she did in the soap operas *Tenth Avenue Angel*, in which she befriended ex-con George Murphy, and *The Big City*, as an orphan raised by cop Murphy, cantor Danny Thomas, and priest Robert Preston. By this time, she was starting to grow out of her precocious stage and this manipulative plotting was wearing thin. The "older" Margaret, therefore, showed up as Beth in the 1949 version of *Little Women*, and as Mary Lennox in *The Secret Garden*, both of which only proved that as she aged her acting limitations were becoming painfully obvious. These two produc-tions also marked her farewell to MGM and Margaret bid her breeding ground goodbye at age 12. As with all growing child stars, there was much made of her first screen kiss, but when she got it, from Allen Martin, Jr., in Columbia's *Her First Romance*, nobody really seemed too concerned. After going overseas to do an Italian movie, she returned to U.S. films, playing a bright-eyed teenager in a horse picture, *Glory*, but the public apparently couldn't accept Margaret O'Brien with a bosom and it passed pretty much unnoticed. Aside from lingering in the background of the western *Heller in Pink Tights*, there was little heard from her once she had passed the age of 20. There were some summer stock jobs and an occasional TV guest shot (including one on former co-star Robert Young's series *Marcus Welby, M.D.*), plus a handful of films that pretty much skipped playing in theaters altogether.

Screen: 1941: Babes on Broadway; 1942: Journey for Margaret; 1943: Dr. Gillespie's Criminal Case; Thousands Cheer; Lost Angel; Madame Curie; 1944: Jane Eyre; The Canterville Ghost; Music for Millions; Meet Me in St. Louis; 1945: Our Vines Have Tender Grapes; 1946: Bad Bascomb; Three Wise Fools; 1947: The Unfinished Dance; 1948: Tenth Avenue Angel; The Big City; 1949: Little Women; The Secret Garden; 1951: Her First Romance; 1954: Agente S3S Operazione Uranio (nUSr); 1956: Glory; 1960: Heller in Pink Tights; 1972: Annabelle Lee (nUSr); Diabolic Wedding (nUSr); 1981: Amy; 1996: Sunset After Dark (dtv); 1998: Hollywood Mortuary (dtv); Off the Menu: The Last Days of Chasen's.

Select TV: 1951: The Lovely Margaret (sp); 1953: The White Gown (sp); A Breath of Air (sp); 1954: Daughter of Mine (sp); 1955: South of the Sun (sp); Midsummer (sp); 1957: Winter in April (sp); The Mystery of Thirteen (sp); Come to Me (sp); The Young Years (sp); The Little Minister (sp); 1958: Trial by Slander (sp); 1959: The Second Happiest Day (sp); Big Doc's Girl (sp); 1962: The Betrayal (sp); 1964: The Turncoat (sp); 1968: Split Second to an Epitaph; 1977: Testimony of Two Men (ms).

PAT O'BRIEN

(WILLIAM JOSEPH PATRICK O'BRIEN, JR.)
BORN: MILWAUKEE, WI, NOVEMBER 11, 1899.
ED: MARQUETTE UNIV. DIED: OCTOBER 15, 1983

Hollywood's walking embodiment of Ireland, Pat O'Brien was a fine actor who could spit out wisecracks and snappy repartee with the best of them, but wasn't someone who could usually carry a movie without a solid co-star. Although his list of films was of an admirable length, there were too many that were promptly forgotten after viewing and, indeed, what one remembers best about his contribution to the cinema is how marvelously he bantered on screen with real-life buddy James Cagney. He was a high school classmate of Spencer Tracy's and together the pair enlisted in the Navy. After his discharge, O'Brien attended Marquette University where he had his first taste of the theater, starring in a production of *Charley's Aunt*. Moving to New York, he got work as a chorus boy in the 1923 musical *Adrienne*, then took acting classes at Sargent's School of Drama where Tracy was once again a fellow student. O'Brien returned to Broadway in 1925, in *A Man's Man*, and pretty much stayed on the boards for the next five years, capped by his success in *The Up and Up*. This earned him an offer from producer Howard Hughes to play reporter Hildy Johnson in the movie of the stage smash *The Front Page*, which O'Brien eagerly accepted. The film turned out to be a pretty good adaptation of the classic comedy and one of the bigger hits of the year, starting off the young actor with a bang. There was no contract attached to this so he freelanced with *The Strange Case of Clara Deane*, as Wynne Gibson's criminal husband; *Virtue*, as a cab driver who falls for Carole Lombard, not knowing she was once a prostitute; *Consolation Marriage*, as a reporter who agrees to an "open" marriage with Irene Dunne; *Air Mail*, as a womanizing pilot; *Laughter in Hell*, as an engineer who ends up on a chain gang after killing his wife and her lover; and *American Madness*, as a bank teller, in this social drama from director Frank Capra. The last was about the only distinguished offering in the bunch.

Therefore he had no reason to refuse a contract offer from Warner Bros., entering into the period of his career for which he would be best remembered. They started him off opposite the delightful Joan Blondell with *I've Got Your Number*, but what really clicked was a teaming with James Cagney in the otherwise fairly routine *Here Comes the Navy*. O'Brien was his superior officer, chastising Cagney for his devil-may-care attitude, and they zinged insults back and forth with the dexterity of a couple of tennis pros. The studio knew it had struck some kind of gold and reunited them for the weak aerial drama *Devil Dogs of the Air*; *Ceiling Zero*, as mail fliers; *The Irish in Us*, a disappointing mix of family blarney and fisticuffs, in which their real-life pal Frank McHugh played their third brother; *Boy Meets Girl*, in which they were breathlessly funny as a pair of fast-talking Hollywood screenwriters; *The Fighting 69th*, with O'Brien as real-life World War I hero Father Duffy; and *Torrid Zone*, a none-too-serious tale set in a South American banana plantation with O'Brien as its egotistical boss. The most famous of the lot was 1938's *Angels With Dirty Faces*, in which they were New York street kids who grow up to take separate paths of good and evil, with O'Brien becoming a priest and Cagney ending up a hood. Something about O'Brien as the soft-spoken man of the cloth, praying for his friend who is sentenced to die in the electric chair, struck the right chord and it became, perhaps, the defining role of his career. Minus Cagney, he again found a fine foil in Blondell in *Back in Circulation* and *Off the Record*; took to the boxing ring for *The Personality Kid*; gave Humphrey Bogart a hard time as a cop in *The Great O'Malley*; and played talent scout to Dick Powell in both *Twenty Million Sweethearts* and *The Cowboy From Brooklyn*.

There was another career high point when he played Notre Dame's *Knute Rockne — All-American*, and forever became everyone's cinematic ideal of how a football coach is supposed to behave. That same year, 1940, he was a reporter in the soap opera *'Til We Meet Again*, and the warden of Sing Sing prison in *Castle on the Hudson*; then ended his contract with Warners. Back to freelancing, he did a lot of war-themed flag wavers like *Two Yanks in Trinidad*, *Flight Lieutenant*, and *The Navy Comes Through*, and took a backseat to Deanna Durbin in *His Butler's Sister*, as the ser-

vant of the title. He also took billing under the inferior George Raft for *Broadway*, based on the hit play of yore. RKO dug out some additional biographical stories of Irish Americans for O'Brien to play, so he wound up as combination football-coach-and-soldier Frank Cavanaugh in *The Iron Major* and *Fighting Father Dunne*, which was a pseudo *Boys Town* tale. There was the oddball allegory *The Boy With Green Hair*, and then another pairing with Raft, *A Dangerous Profession*, that only proved that both actors were no longer much of an attraction for late 1940s audiences. Nevertheless, O'Brien stayed in the top slot for some "B" programmers, such as *Johnny One-Eye*, which did not refer to him but a precocious mutt, and *Criminal Lawyer*. He had better luck supporting longtime friend Spencer Tracy in both *The People Against O'Hara* and *The Last Hurrah*, and doing his bit as a tough Chicago cop in the classic comedy *Some Like It Hot*. Subsequent appearances were mainly on television, although he showed up in a 1960s western, *Town Tamer*; and did a cameo with Dead End Kids' alumnus Huntz Hall and Leo Gorcey in the curio *The Phynx*. After another absence, he returned to theatrical features to play Burt Reynolds's dad in *The End* and a lawyer in *Ragtime*, which also featured Cagney, although they shared no scenes together. In 1964 he published his autobiography, *The Wind at My Back*.

Screen: 1931: The Front Page; Flying High; Honor Among Lovers; Personal Maid; Consolation Marriage; 1932: Final Edition; Hell's House; The Strange Case of Clara Deane; Scandal for Sale; American Madness; Hollywood Speaks; Virtue; Air Mail; 1933: Destination Unknown; The World Gone Mad; Bureau of Missing Persons; Bombshell; Laughter in Hell; Flaming Gold; College Coach; 1934: I've Got Your Number; Gambling Lady; Twenty Million Sweethearts; Here Comes the Navy; The Personality Kid; I Sell Anything; Flirtation Walk; 1935: Devil Dogs of the Air; In Caliente; Oil for the Lamps of China; Page Miss Glory; The Irish in Us; Stars Over Broadway; Ceiling Zero; 1936: I Married a Doctor; Public Enemy's Wife; China Clipper; 1937: The Great O'Malley; Slim; San Quentin; Back in Circulation; Submarine D-1; 1938: Women Are Like That; The Cowboy From Brooklyn; Boy Meets Girl; Garden of the Moon; Angels With Dirty Faces; 1939: Off the Record; The Kid From Kokomo; Indianapolis Speedway; The Night of Nights; 1940: The Fighting 69th; Slightly Honorable; Castle on the Hudson; 'Til We Meet Again; Torrid Zone; Flowing Gold; Escape to Glory; Knute Rockne — All-American; 1942: Two Yanks in Trinidad; Flight Lieutenant; Broadway; The Navy Comes Through; 1943: Bombardier; The Iron Major; His Butler's Sister; 1944: Secret Command; Marine Raiders; 1945: Having Wonderful Crime; Man Alive; 1946: Perilous Holiday; Crack-Up; 1947: Riffraff; 1948: Fighting Father Dunne; The Boy with Green Hair; 1949: A Dangerous Profession; 1950: Johnny One-Eye; The Fireball; 1951: The People Against O'Hara; Criminal Lawyer; 1952: Okinawa; 1954: Jubilee Trail; Ring of Fear; 1955: Inside Detroit; 1957: Kill Me Tomorrow; 1958: The Last Hurrah; 1959: Some Like It Hot; 1965: Town Tamer; 1970: The Phynx; 1978: Billy Jack Goes to Washington; The End; 1981: Ragtime.

NY Stage: 1923: Adrienne; 1925: A Man's Man; 1926: You Can't Win (AS W. J. P. O'BRIEN); Henry — Behave; Gertie; Broadway; 1930: This Man's Town; The Up and Up; Overture; 1957: Miss Lonelyhearts.

Select TV: 1951: The Irish Drifter (sp); Tin Badge (sp); 1952: A Man's World (sp); The Face of Autumn (sp); 1953: One for the Road (sp); Second Sight (sp); 1954: The Chase (sp); 1955: Newspaper Man (sp); Dinner at Eight (sp); 1956: Who's Calling (sp); Thirty-Year Man (sp); Exit Laughing (sp); 1957: Strange Query (sp); Invitation to a Gunfighter (sp); 1958: The

Brotherhood of the Bell (sp); **1959:** I Captured the King of Leprechauns (sp); **1960–61:** Harrigan and Son (series); **1963:** Thunder in a Forgotten Town (sp); **1964:** Threatening Eye (sp); The Jack is High (sp); **1965:** The Crime (sp); **1969:** The Over the Hill Gang; **1972:** Welcome Home, Johnny Bristol; The Adventures of Nick Carter; **1975:** The Sky's the Limit; **1976:** Kiss Me, Kill Me; **1980:** Scout's Honor.

VIRGINIA O'BRIEN

BORN: LOS ANGELES, CA, APRIL 18, 1919.
DIED: JANUARY 23, 2001.

A marvelous "novelty act" among the many treasures of the MGM musical, Virginia O'Brien's shtick required her to sing a song in a monotone with a deadpan expression on her face. There was also a pleasing comical talent inherent in her work, but the studio didn't see much reason to push her beyond the supporting cast. The niece of movie director Lloyd Bacon, she made her professional debut as part of a Los Angeles production of the revue *Meet the People*, claiming later that she developed her frozen-faced style during the run simply out of sheer stage fright. In any event, she was a riot and lucked out because MGM studio boss Louis B. Mayer happened to have caught her act and immediately signed her to a contract. Before her movie career was launched, she went to Broadway for *Keep Off the Grass*, a revue that also featured Ray Bolger. For MGM she debuted in *Hullabaloo*; participated in the "Sing While You Sell" number in the Marx Brothers' *The Big Store*; played herself in *Ringside Maisie*; and sang "Your Words and My Music" in the fairly dry *Lady Be Good*. Likewise, she added some zing to *Panama Hattie*, chiming in on "Let's Be Buddies," and to another unfaithful adaptation of a Broadway musical hit, *DuBarry Was a Lady*, singing "Salome" and joining the principles in the finale, "Friendship." Still in support, she stole the show as a welder doing "Say That We're Sweethearts Again" in the film of *Meet the People*, and sat upon a carousel horse while she wailed "Bring on Those Wonderful Men" in the all-star revue *Ziegfeld Follies*. *The Harvey Girls* offered her perhaps her best opportunity, not only chirping "The Wild Wild West" while making a horseshoe, but joining Judy Garland and (a dubbed) Cyd Charisse for the gentle "It's a Great Big World" number. After supporting Red Skelton in *Merton of the Movies*, as a Hollywood stuntwoman, she ended her stay at MGM. Aside from tiny roles in *Francis in the Navy* and Disney's *Gus*, both of which, curiously, involved mules, she confined her subsequent entertaining to an occasional revue show. Her first husband (1942–55) was actor Kirk Alyn, best known for playing the first screen Superman.

Screen: 1940: Hullabaloo; Sky Murder; **1941:** The Big Store; Ringside Maisie; Lady Be Good; **1942:** Ship Ahoy; Panama Hattie; **1943:** DuBarry Was a Lady; Thousands Cheer; **1944:** Two Girls and a Sailor; Meet the People; **1946:** Ziegfeld Follies; The Harvey Girls; The Show-Off; **1947:** The Great Morgan; Till the Clouds Roll By; Merton of the Movies; **1955:** Francis in the Navy; **1976:** Gus.

NY Stage: 1940: Keep Off the Grass.

ARTHUR O'CONNELL

BORN: NEW YORK, NY, MARCH 29, 1908.
DIED: MAY 18, 1981.

Success was a long time coming for character actor Arthur O'Connell; he was knocking around the business some 20 years before things finally clicked. Having done vaudeville, stock, and stage work as far away as London, he had first shown up in movies as early as 1938, playing a student in *Freshman Year*, for Universal. For the next ten years he pretty much stayed in low gear, appearing as reporters in both *Citizen Kane* and *State of the Union*, to name two of his better-known projects. Everything changed when he was cast as the hapless Howard Bevans, who is pretty much shamed into marrying the spinster schoolteacher in the 1953 Broadway hit *Picnic*. He repeated the role in the popular 1955 film adaptation, earning an Oscar nomination and becoming heavily in demand. He was Don Murray's common sense buddy in *Bus Stop*; a kindly office manager in love with Judy Holliday's secretary in *The Solid Gold Cadillac*; a colonel in the military ensemble comedy *Operation Mad Ball*; a cowardly con man in *Man of the West*; an alcoholic teacher in *Voice in the Mirror*; James Stewart's legal assistant, who also has a thing for nipping at the sauce, in *Anatomy of a Murder*, a performance that earned him a second Oscar nomination; a prison warden in *The Great Impostor*; the dad of Ann-Margret's fiancé in *Pocketful of Miracles*; a corrupt politician lectured to by a look-alike sea serpent in the fantasy *7 Faces of Dr. Lao*; the backwoods pa of one of the dual Elvises in *Kissin' Cousins*; a music publisher in *Your Cheatin' Heart*; the newspaper tycoon who sponsors *The Great Race*; a colonel who helps to miniaturize the team of scientists in *Fantastic Voyage*; Don Knotts's dad in *The Reluctant Astronaut*; and a priest in *The Poseidon Adventure*. Alzheimer's disease forced him to retire in the mid-1970s.

Screen: 1938: Freshman Year; Murder in Soho/Murder in the Night; **1940:** Dr. Kildare Goes Home; The Leather Pushers; And One Was Beautiful; The Golden Fleecing; Two Girls on Broadway; **1941:** Lucky Devils; Citizen Kane; **1942:** Man From Headquarters; Fingers at the Window; Law of the Jungle; Shepherd of the Ozarks; Blondie's Blessed Event; Yokel Boy; **1944:** It Happened Tomorrow; **1948:** One Touch of Venus; Open Secret; State of the Union; The Naked City; Homecoming; The Countess of Monte Cristo; Force of Evil; **1950:** Love That Brute; **1951:** The Whistle at Eaton Falls; **1955:** Picnic; **1956:** The Solid Gold Cadillac; The Man in the Gray Flannel Suit; The Proud Ones; Bus Stop; **1957:** The Monte Carlo Story; Operation Mad Ball; April Love; The Violators; **1958:** Voice in the Mirror; Man of the West; **1959:** Gidget; Anatomy of a Murder; Hound-Dog Man; Operation Petticoat; **1960:** Cimarron; **1961:** The Great Impostor; Misty; A Thunder of Drums; Pocketful of Miracles; **1962:** Follow That Dream; **1964:** Kissin' Cousins; 7 Faces of Dr. Lao; Your Cheatin' Heart; **1965:** Nightmare in the Sun; The Third Day; The Monkey's Uncle; The Great Race; **1966:** Ride Beyond Vengeance; The Silencers; Birds Do It; Fantastic Voyage; **1967:** A Covenant With Death; The Reluctant Astronaut; **1968:** The Power; If He Hollers, Let Him Go!; **1970:** The Last Valley; Suppose They Gave a War and Nobody Came/War Games; Do Not Throw Cushions Into the Ring (nUSr); There Was a Crooked Man...; **1972:** Ben; The Poseidon Adventure; They Only Kill Their Masters; **1973:** Wicked, Wicked; **1974:** Huckleberry Finn; **1975:** The Hiding Place.

NY Stage: 1943: The Army Play-by-Play; **1949:** How Long Till Summer; **1952:** Anna Christie; Golden Boy; **1953:** Picnic; **1954:** Lunatics and Lovers; **1958:** Comes a Day; **1970:** Remote Asylum.

Select TV: 1950: Summer Had Better Be Good (sp); **1953–54:** Mr. Peepers (series); **1954:** All Our Yesterdays (sp); Mr. Simmons (sp); Knight in a Business Suit (sp); **1955:** A Terrible Day (sp); The Outsiders (sp); **1967–68:** The Second Hundred Years (series); **1969:** Seven in Darkness; **1971:** A Taste of Evil; **1974:** Shootout in a One-Dog Town.

DONALD O'CONNOR

BORN: CHICAGO, IL, AUGUST 28, 1925.

Being at Universal Studios was both a blessing and a curse for the energetic, highly talented Donald O'Connor. On one hand, it put him at the center of attention as their number one male musical star (Deanna Durbin held the distaff position), yet because they were not known for producing the finest material in the genre, little of what he did there seemed worthy of his abilities. Instead, he wound up making his most lasting imprint on the cinematic landscape playing straight man to a jackass, and by co-starring in the one musical that reigned over all the rest, which was made, not surprisingly, elsewhere, at MGM. Born to the business, his parents were circus performers (calling themselves The Nelson Comiques), and he joined the family in their vaudeville act when he was a baby, eventually working his way up to stealing the show with his singing and tap dancing routines. It was while performing in California that he and his brothers, Jack and Billy, were asked to do a guest bit in a Warner Bros. musical pastiche called *Melody for Two*, only to find themselves sliced out of the final print. The boys returned to the stage and were participating in a benefit at the Ambassador Hotel when a Paramount talent scout asked Donald to test for the role of the kid brother of Bing Crosby and Fred MacMurray in *Sing, You Sinners*. O'Connor got the part and was an instant hit, more than holding his own against his co-stars. In addition to being asked to play the younger versions of MacMurray and Gary Cooper in *Men With Wings* and *Beaut Geste*, respectively, he was given a few important roles in such movies as *Sons of the Legion*, helping to clear dad Lynne Overman's name; *Tom Sawyer — Detective*, in the title role; and *Boy Trouble*, as a ruffian who moves in with Charlie Ruggles and Mary Boland, a movie that did well enough to spin off a sequel, *Night Work*. Having entered his awkward teen years, the studio felt they'd done all they could with him and let him go.

After another stint of touring with his family, he was signed up by Universal in 1941 and stayed with that studio for the next 14 years. For his first three assignments he was seen in secondary roles in three Andrews Sisters programmers: *What's Cookin'?*, *Private Buckaroo*, and *Give Out, Sisters*, in each case partnered with gawky-but-charming teen dancer Peggy Ryan. The two youngsters had an infectious enthusiasm when they hit the floor together, so the studio immediately put them together again for *Get Hep to Love*, where warbling youngster Gloria Jean was the official lead, and *When Johnny Comes Marching Home Again*, an Allan Jones vehicle. O'Connor was back with Jean for *It Comes Up Love* and then teamed with Susannah Foster for *Top Man*, only this time he was promoted to leading man. These were all pretty anemic offerings, with the spirited O'Connor kicking up a storm in the middle of it all, trying gamely to inject some energy into the proceedings. It was a relief when he was put back alongside Peggy Ryan, this time as the stars of *Chip Off the Old Block*, followed by the vaudeville story *The Merry Monahans*, with Ryan as his sister and Jack Oakie as his drunken dad. There was a break while he joined the U.S. Army Air Force Special Services and then he was back one last time with Ryan, for *Patrick the Great*. It seemed like a good idea to team him with Deanna Durbin, as the studio did for *Something in the Wind*, but his role was secondary to hers, suggesting that Universal did not see the romantic possibilities in these two.

In 1949 the studio put together a property from a book by David Stern, about a young lieutenant who becomes the friend and confidant of a talking mule (voice by Chill Wills). The resulting film, *Francis*, though it hadn't many more laughs than your standard service comedy, managed to arouse the interest of the general public because of its silly gimmick, becoming the surprise smash of the year, and giving a great boost to O'Connor's standing with Universal. In between a few more fluffy musical comedies — *The Milkman*, which teamed him with Jimmy Durante; *Curtain Call at Cactus Creek*, as the stage manager of a tatty touring show out West; and the tepid pirate spoof *Double Crossbones* — he returned to Francis five more times, going to the races and West Point among various destinations, finally ending with *Francis in the Navy*, in 1955. This left the final installment in the series, *Francis in the Haunted House*, for Mickey Rooney to do.

Fortunately, some other studios had far more interesting material for O'Connor, starting — first and foremost — with MGM and *Singin' in the Rain*, where he kept up with co-star Gene Kelly every step of the way in this joyous spoof of Hollywood's transition from silence to sound. O'Connor reached the summit of his career, performing one of the classic show-stopping numbers of all time with "Make 'em Laugh," his gravity-defying somersaults off the walls continuing to draw gasps of astonishment from gleeful audiences to this day. That studio also put him and Debbie Reynolds in the very pleasant *I Love Melvin*, while Fox gave him a good role as Ethel Merman's secretary in *Call Me Madam*, which included a duet with her on Irving Berlin's classic counterpoint song, "You're Just in Love," and a number not in the original show, added expressly for O'Connor, "What Do I Care for Love?," in which he pranced through a room filled with balloons. On a more garish note, he was Merman's son in the everything-but-the-kitchen-sink salute to Berlin, *There's No Business Like Show Business*, cavorting through "Lazy" with Marilyn Monroe, and coming off relatively well despite having to sing "Alexander's Ragtime Band" with a Scottish accent.

Finally free of Universal, he went over to Paramount to join Bing Crosby and Mitzi Gaynor for the fairly poor re-do of *Anything Goes*, and then was chosen to play the great silent movie comedian in *The Buster Keaton Story*, where his impressive physical re-creations of Keaton's routines were the only thing that really worked in this all-too-typical, highly fabricated biopic. By this point, he had already segued easily into TV, winning an Emmy Award for his work on *Colgate Comedy Hour* in 1953. That medium, as well as Las Vegas and other club venues, were instrumental in keeping his name before the general public from then on. Since the movie musical was starting to fade into history, film producers would only call on him on rare occasions, as they did for *Cry for Happy*, as Glenn Ford's fellow-sailor; *The Wonders of Aladdin*, as a fairly long-in-the-tooth Aladdin in this international mishmash made in Tunisia; *That Funny Feeling*, which brought him back to Universal, to play the business partner of Bobby Darin; *Ragtime*, his one good latter-day film, as an old-time entertainer, singing "I Could Love a Million Girls;" *Toys*, as Robin Williams's father, expiring early in the story; and *Out to Sea*, seen dancing, albeit briefly, as a cruise ship host, and adding a momentary feeling of good cheer to the proceedings.

Screen: 1938: Sing, You Sinners; Sons of the Legion; Men With Wings; Tom Sawyer — Detective; 1939: Unmarried; Death of a Champion; Boy Trouble; Night Work; Million Dollar Legs; Beau Geste; On Your Toes; 1942: What's Cookin'?; Private Buckaroo; Get Hep to Love; Give Out, Sisters; When Johnny Comes Marching Home; 1943: It Comes Up Love; Mister Big; Top Man; 1944: This is the Life; Chip Off the Old Block; Follow the Boys; Bowery to Broadway; The Merry Monahans; 1945: Patrick the Great; 1947: Something in the Wind; 1948: Are You With It?; Feudin', Fussin' and A-Fightin'; 1949: Yes Sir, That's My Baby; Francis; 1950: The Milkman; Curtain Call at Cactus Creek; 1951:

Double Crossbones; Francis Goes to the Races; 1952: Singin' in the Rain; Francis Goes to West Point; 1953: Call Me Madam; I Love Melvin; Walking My Baby Back Home; Francis Covers the Big Town; 1954: Francis Joins the WACs; There's No Business Like Show Business; 1955: Francis in the Navy; 1956: Anything Goes; 1957: The Buster Keaton Story; 1961: Cry for Happy; The Wonders of Aladdin; 1965: That Funny Feeling; 1974: That's Entertainment!; 1981: Ragtime; 1982: Pandemonium; 1986: A Time to Remember; 1992: Toys; 1996: Father Frost (dtv); 1997: Out to Sea.

NY Stage: 1981: Bring Back Birdie; 1983: Show Boat.

Select TV: 1950–54: Colgate Comedy Hour (series co-host); 1954–55: The Donald O'Connor Show (series); 1957: The Jet-Propelled Couch (sp); 1958: The Red Mill (sp); 1966: Brilliant Benjamin Boggs (sp); Olympus 7-0000; 1968: The Donald O'Connor Show (series); 1983: Alice in Wonderland (sp); 1985: Alice in Wonderland (sp); 1994: Bandit's Silver Angel.

UNA O'CONNOR

(AGNES TERESA McGLADE)
BORN: BELFAST, IRELAND, OCTOBER 23, 1880.
DIED: FEBRUARY 4, 1959.

First and foremost you remember her scream. Una O'Connor was a scrawny, bird-like biddy with wide eyes and a nervous nature, adept at playing jittery skeptics and curmudgeonly crones on the verge of hysteria. Her theatrical debut came in 1911, appearing in *The Showing of Blanco Posnet* for the Abbey Theatre. She traveled with the play to Broadway and then bounced back and forth between the London and New York stage. Her performance as the cockney maid in Noel Coward's *Cavalcade*, in London, caught the attention of Hollywood and she was asked to repeat the part in the 1933 Oscar-winning film version. That same year she did the first of her two great screamer roles, which found her a place in the hearts of horror aficionados, in *The Invisible Man*, as the nosy innkeeper's wife, freaking out while transparent Claude Rains unwrapped his bandages. Two years later came her other assignment of the same nature, as Minnie the high-strung housekeeper, in *Bride of Frankenstein*, trying to convince the locals that the Monster is still alive. Between her seemingly endless list of domestics (from *Chained* to *Rose-Marie* to *Little Lord Fauntleroy* to *The Canterville Ghost*) she had a very serious role, as the grieving mother of the slain Wallace Ford in *The Informer*. Another of her best-remembered roles found her yet again in servitude, this time in the employ of Maid Marian (Olivia de Havilland), and becoming the unexpected object of flirtation thanks to merry man Herbert Mundin, in the classic *The Adventures of Robin Hood*. She did variations on this part in two other Errol Flynn swashbucklers, *The Sea Hawk* and *The Adventures of Don Juan*, stopping off in between to play the very unpleasant, domineering mother of Charles Laughton in *This Land Is Mine*, blowing the whistle on saboteur Kent Smith; and Richard Haydn's cranky mom in *Cluny Brown*, where she earned a plethora of the movie's laughs simply by clearing her throat. After a long absence from the big screen she showed up for an important courtroom scene, as the hard-of-hearing maid of the murder victim, in *Witness for the Prosecution*, repeating her stage role.

Screen: 1929: Dark Red Roses; 1930: Murder!; Timbuctoo; To Oblige a Lady; 1933: Cavalcade; Pleasure Cruise; Mary Stevens M.D.; The Invisible Man; 1934: Orient Express; The Poor Rich; All Men Are Enemies; Stingaree; The Barretts of Wimpole Street; Chained; 1935: David Copperfield; Father Brown — Detective; Bride of Frankenstein; The Informer; Thunder in the Night; The

Perfect Gentleman; 1936: Little Lord Fauntleroy; Rose-Marie; Suzy; Lloyds of London; The Plough and the Stars; 1937: Personal Property; Call It a Day; 1938: Return of the Frog; The Adventures of Robin Hood; 1939: We Are Not Alone; His Brother's Keeper; All Women Have Secrets; 1940: It All Came True; Lillian Russell; The Sea Hawk; He Stayed for Breakfast; 1941: Kisses for Breakfast; The Strawberry Blonde; Her First Beau; Three Girls About Town; 1942: Always in My Heart; Random Harvest; My Favorite Spy; 1943: This Land Is Mine; Forever and a Day; Holy Matrimony; Government Girl; 1944: The Canterville Ghost; My Pal Wolf; 1945: Christmas in Connecticut; The Bells of St. Mary's; 1946: Cluny Brown; Of Human Bondage; The Return of Monte Cristo; Child of Divorce; 1947: Unexpected Guest; Ivy; Lost Honeymoon; Banjo; The Corpse Came C.O.D.; 1948: Fighting Father Dunne; The Adventures of Don Juan; 1957: Witness for the Prosecution.

NY Stage: 1911: The Showing of Blanco Posnet; The Well of Saints; 1924: The Fake; 1926: Autumn Fire; 1945: The Ryan Girl; 1948: The Linden Tree; 1949: The Shop at Sly Corner; 1950: The Enchanted; 1954: The Starcross Story; Witness for the Prosecution.

Select TV: 1949: Mrs. Moonlight (sp); 1950: The Walking Stick (sp); Little Women (sp); 1951: At Mrs. Beam's (sp); 1952: The Vintage Years (sp); Prologue to Glory (sp); 1954: Night Must Fall (sp); The Shop at Sly Corner (sp).

MAUREEN O'HARA

(MAUREEN FITZSIMMONS) BORN: MILLWALL, IRELAND, AUGUST 17, 1920.

If Pat O'Brien was the male equivalent of the Hollywood Irish, then Maureen O'Hara represented the distaff side, her accent often creeping through to betray her origins. She was one of the most stunningly lovely of all stars, with bright eyes, high cheekbones, and her famous mane of red hair so suitable for Technicolor. There was poise and class in her but earth and fire as well and she became, in time, one of those ladies whom everybody seemed to like having around. She projected good common sense and a warm stability, wiping out the memory of so much of the twaddle she'd made her name in. While still young she acted on Dublin radio, which led to her to joining the Abbey Theatre at age 14. There were minor roles, using her real name, in the films *Kicking the Moon Around* and *My Irish Molly*, after which she was signed to a contract by producer Eric Pommer and actor Charles Laughton, who had formed their own independent production company. Their primary motive was to have her co-star opposite Laughton in the last movie Alfred Hitchcock would direct in England for awhile, *Jamaica Inn*. It was not greeted as one of the Master's finer hours though O'Hara did, in fact, make for a most engaging heroine in distress. The film also insured that she would play Esmeralda in RKO's 1939 adaptation of *The Hunchback of Notre Dame*, at the request of Laughton, who was to star. Beautiful and deeply sympathetic in the role, she was an instant success and RKO took over her contract. In her follow-up assignment, she couldn't help but come up short reprising Katharine Hepburn's star-making role in the remake of *A Bill of Divorcement*, and wasn't all that convincing as a nightclub dancer in *Dance, Girl, Dance*, although she did get a chance to deliver the blatantly anti-male speech at the end that would make the movie a favorite of feminists in later years.

Director John Ford stepped in and signed her up to play the female member of the Welsh siblings in 20th Century-Fox's prestigious *How Green Was My Valley*. This was another giant step forward in making her into a major star, the film being a hit with audiences as well as the Academy Award-winner for Best Picture of 1941. Thanks to this one, Fox took over part of her contract, making her a key player at two studios. For Fox she decorated the military flag-wavers, *To the Shores of Tripoli* and *The Immortal Sergeant*, and was Tyrone Power's love interest in her first foray into color, the swashbuckling adventure *The Black Swan*. This particular film was great fun but paved the way for a genre she would get stuck in with diminishing results over the years. RKO put her into two anti-Nazi films, the more humanistic *This Land Is Mine*, as a schoolteacher secretly loved by Laughton, and a thriller with John Garfield, *The Fallen Sparrow*, in which she was used as a deadly pawn by the enemy. Fox made her the woman in the life of *Buffalo Bill* (Joel McCrea), and then she had two costume hits, *The Spanish Main*, which was notable as RKO's first Technicolor offering in years, and *Sinbad the Sailor*, who was Douglas Fairbanks, Jr. with tongue planted firmly in cheek. There was a blatant soaper, *Sentimental Journey*, in which she and John Payne adopt a child because they can't have one of their own, and then the best of all her Fox assignments, *Miracle on 34th Street*, as the all-too-practical mom of Natalie Wood, who tries to teach the child not to believe in Santa Claus. An Oscar nominee for Best Picture, it would only grow in stature over the years to become a treasured Christmas classic and one of those movies that O'Hara was very grateful to be associated with. *The Foxes of Harrow* was a cumbersome epic of the old South, with O'Hara supposedly playing a French girl, and Rex Harrison as the man she marries and snipes at endlessly. After this she was a mother again, a role she would come to fit into so comfortably over the years, in *Sitting Pretty*, the cute comedy that introduced Clifton Webb as sardonic wit Lynn Belvedere. After a trip to England to do *Britannia Mews*, she came back to Hollywood to finish off both her contracts, with *A Woman's Secret* for RKO, and *Father Was a Fullback* for Fox.

As the 1950s began, she entered something of a low point in her career with a lot of junky programmers at Universal but with salvation coming intermittently in the person of John Ford. Universal put her in *Bagdad*, which gave her a chance to sing, displaying an acceptable set of pipes; *Flame of Araby*, as your standard red-headed Arab princess; *Against All Flags*, with Errol Flynn, whom she was bound to cross paths with someday; and *Lady Godiva*, which was notable more for what it didn't reveal than what it did. At Paramount she showed up in a routine adventure, *Tripoli*, which was notable only because it was directed by her second husband (1941–52) Will Price. Ford cast her as the estranged wife of soldier John Wayne in *Rio Grande*, and the two clicked so well together that there was an encore for *The Quiet Man*. This, of course, was the O'Hara that most moviegoers remember best: the feisty colleen, the wind blowing through her hair, as she resists and then gives in to the wooing of Wayne, in what turned out to be perhaps the most magical of all of Ford's films. She was then the faithful wife in two clunky Ford biopics, *The Long Gray Line*, which was Tyrone Power playing West Point athletic instructor Marty Maher, and *The Wings of Eagles*, which was Wayne as flier and Hollywood writer Frank Wead. After showing up as the woman who tries to assist reluctant spy Alec Guinness in *Our Man in Havana*, the more matronly but no less attractive O'Hara showed up as the mother of scheming twins, played by Hayley Mills, in Disney's very uninspired but very popular *The Parent Trap*. This movie, along with *Mr. Hobbs Takes a Vacation* and *Spencer's Mountain*, cemented her image as one of the ultimate cinematic mother figures, warm and wise. Back in a western mode, she had the central role of the mother who is

taking her dead son to be buried in *The Deadly Companions*, and romped with Wayne in the comedic *McLintock!*, which was a kind of variation of *The Quiet Man*. This movie was not only a profitable film in its time but became one of the most steadily viewed on the small screen for years to come, chalking up high ratings through countless prime time airings. O'Hara also portrayed a stubborn widow in *The Rare Breed*, attracting the interest of both James Stewart and Brian Keith, two actors with whom she had played off of very nicely before. Nobody was much interested in a domestic comedy she did with Jackie Gleason, *How Do I Love Thee?*, and there was a distinct secondary feel to her part as Wayne's estranged wife in *Big Jake*, which marked their fifth and final pairing. With that she retired to St. Croix with her third husband, former Brigadier General Charles Blair, but was happily coaxed out of retirement in 1991 to play John Candy's outspoken Irish mom in the innocuous comedy *Only the Lonely*. She seemed to have hardly aged at all and made one lament the years gone by without her.

Screen: 1938: Kicking the Moon Around; My Irish Molly/Little Miss Molly; 1939: Jamaica Inn; The Hunchback of Notre Dame; 1940: A Bill of Divorcement; Dance, Girl, Dance; 1941: They Met in Argentina; How Green Was My Valley; 1942: To the Shores of Tripoli; Ten Gentlemen From West Point; The Black Swan; 1943: The Immortal Sergeant; This Land Is Mine; The Fallen Sparrow; 1944: Buffalo Bill; 1945: The Spanish Main; 1946: Sentimental Journey; Do You Love Me?; 1947: Sinbad the Sailor; The Homestretch; Miracle on 34th Street; The Foxes of Harrow; 1948: Sitting Pretty; 1949: Britannia Mews; A Woman's Secret; Father Was a Fullback; Bagdad; 1950: Comanche Territory; Tripoli; Rio Grande; 1951: Flame of Araby; 1952: At Sword's Point; The Quiet Man; Kangaroo; Against All Flags; The Redhead From Wyoming; 1953: War Arrow; 1954: Malaga/Fire Over Africa; 1955: The Long Gray Line; The Magnificent Matador; Lady Godiva; 1956: Lisbon; Everything But the Truth; 1957: The Wings of Eagles; 1960: Our Man in Havana; 1961: The Parent Trap; The Deadly Companions; 1962: Mr. Hobbs Takes a Vacation; 1963: Spencer's Mountain; McLintock!; 1965: The Battle of the Villa Fiorita; 1966: The Rare Breed; 1970: How Do I Love Thee?; 1971: Big Jake; 1991: Only the Lonely.
NY Stage: 1960: Christine.
Select TV: 1960: Mrs. Miniver (sp); The Scarlet Pimpernel (sp); 1962: Spellbound (sp); 1963: A Cry of Angels (sp); 1973: The Red Pony; 1995: The Christmas Box; 1998: Cab to Canada; 2000: The Last Dance.

DAN O'HERLIHY
BORN: WEXFORD, IRELAND, MAY 1, 1919.
ED: NATIONAL UNIV. OF IRELAND.

A low-keyed Irish actor who crossed over into American product but — despite an occasional juicy role — pretty much hovered under the wide-recognition radar, Dan O'Herlihy had studied architecture in college. This led to him becoming a set designer for the Abbey Theatre where he found his interest shifting to acting. He made his British film bow in the 1947 hit *Odd Man Out*, as one of the men who robs the mill at the beginning of the story, and then, a year later, was invited to America where he was a thoroughly undistinguished Alan Breck, opposite Roddy McDowall's David Balfour, in the Monogram version of *Kidnapped*. That same year saw him play MacDuff in Orson Welles's odd but effective filming of *Macbeth*. However, the movies envisioned him more as a man of action than of the classics and he was put into such films as *At Sword's*

Point, as Aramis in this sequel of sorts to *The Three Musketeers*; *Sword of Venus*, a touring show version of *The Count of Monte Cristo*, as Danglars; and a pair of Tony Curtis swashbucklers, *The Black Shield of Falworth* and *The Purple Mask*. In between these, director Luis Bunuel handed him a one-man tour de force with his highly compelling take on *Adventures of Robinson Crusoe*, with O'Herlihy asked to carry a good portion of the movie on his own, battling loneliness and managing against the odds to maintain a somewhat civilized existence on a deserted tropical island. The actor wound up with a surprise Oscar nomination when the film was released in the U.S. in 1954 and it became the crowning achievement of his career. This did not, however, change his star status and he pretty much stayed a supporting figure with *Home Before Dark*, as the unfeeling husband of unstable Jean Simmons; *Imitation of Life*, as the stage director and eventual lover of Lana Turner; *A Terrible Beauty/The Night Fighters*, as a club-footed IRA leader; *The Cabinet of Caligari*, an ill-advised remake of the German classic, in this instance taking the lead, as Glynis John's crazed tormentor; *Fail-Safe*, in the pivotal role of the air force pilot who experiences prophetic bullfighting nightmares; *Waterloo*, as Marshal Ney; *MacArthur*, as President Franklin Roosevelt; *The Last Starfighter*, unrecognizable under heavy makeup, as an alien fighter pilot; and *Robocop*, as a corporate CEO in this violent sci-fi hit.

Screen: 1947: Odd Man Out; Hungry Hill; 1948: Kidnapped; Macbeth; Larceny; 1950: The Iroquois Trail; 1951: The Desert Fox; Soldiers Three; The Highwayman; The Blue Veil; 1952: At Sword's Point; Actors and Sin; Operation Secret; Invasion U.S.A.; 1953: Sword of Venus; 1954: Robinson Crusoe/Adventures of Robinson Crusoe; Bengal Brigade; The Black Shield of Falworth; 1955: The Purple Mask; The Virgin Queen; 1956: City After Midnight/That Woman Opposite; 1958: Home Before Dark; 1959: Imitation of Life; The Young Land; 1960: A Terrible Beauty/The Night Fighters; One Foot in Hell; 1961: King of the Roaring '20s — The Story of Arnold Rothstein; 1962: The Cabinet of Caligari; 1964: Fail-Safe; 1968: How to Steal the World (from TV); 1969: 100 Rifles; The Big Cube; 1970: Waterloo; 1972: The Carey Treatment; 1974: The Tamarind Seed; 1977: MacArthur; 1983: Halloween III: Season of the Witch; 1984: The Last Starfighter; 1986: The Whoopee Boys; 1987: Robocop; The Dead; 1990: Robocop 2.

NY Stage: 1949: The Ivy Green.

Select TV: 1953: Trapped (sp); The Wine of St. Albans (sp); 1954: The White Steed (sp); 1955: Love Letter (sp); No Stone Unturned (sp); The Seventh Veil (sp); Christmas Guest (sp); 1957: The Blackwell Story (sp); The Duel (sp); Fire and Ice (sp); 1959: Robbie and His Mary (sp); 1960: To the Sounds of Trumpets (sp); 1961: Bury Me Twice (sp); 1963–64: The Travels of Jaimie McPheeters (series); 1964: The Shattered Glass (sp); 1966: The Long Hot Summer (series); 1972: The People; 1974: QBVII (ms); 1975: Jeannie: Lady Randolph Churchill (ms); 1976: Banjo Hackett: Roamin' Free; 1977: Good Against Evil; Deadly Game; 1979: A Man Called Sloane (series); 1981: Death Ray 2000; Artemis 81; 1984: The Whiz Kids (series); Nancy Aster (sp); 1986: Dark Mansions; 1993: Love, Cheat and Steal; 1998: The Rat Pack.

DENNIS O'KEEFE

(Edward Vance Flanagan)
Born: Fort Madison, IA, March 29, 1908.
ed: USC. Died: August 31, 1968.

Second-string star Dennis O'Keefe was in the business for so many years, piling up so many assignments, that he wound up with more credits under his original stage name of "Bud Flanagan" than under the one he'd become better known by. A one-time vaudevillian, he entered movies as a bit player and extra starting in 1931, and would continue in that capacity for the next seven years, appearing in more than one hundred films (!) without actually being billed. Things changed in 1938 when he wound up at MGM, where he was cast as a boxer called The Kanarsy Kid, who tangles with outlaw Wallace Beery, in *The Bad Man of Brimstone*. O'Keefe was almost exclusively thought of as second-feature material and most of his films were as such. He showed a capability in both drama and comedy but lacked that extra spark that distinguishes an unforgettable actor from a serviceable one. Among his leads during his heyday were in *I'm Nobody's Sweetheart Now*, a romantic comedy with Helen Parrish; two versions of *Mr. District Attorney*, made only six years apart for audiences with short memories; *Her Adventurous Night*, as the dad of troubled teen Scotty Beckett; *Up in Mabel's Room*, as the dopey husband trying to retrieve a piece of incriminating lingerie; *Getting Gertie's Gartie*, which was a virtual replay of *Mabel*, this time with a piece of jewelry; *Abroad With Two Yanks*, fighting William Bendix for Helen Walker's attentions; *Brewster's Millions*, the fourth and best of the many versions of the old farce about the guy who must spend $1 million in a brief period of time in order to inherit more; *T-Men*, one of those documentary-type noirs of the period, about counterfeiters; and *The Great Dan Patch*, as the owner of the title racehorse. During the 1950s he directed one of his own movies, *Angela*, about an ex-GI who gets involved with a shady lady in Italy; and also had his own TV series, *The Dennis O'Keefe Show*, which ran a season.

Screen: AS BUD FLANAGAN: 1931: Cimarron; Reaching for the Moon; 1932: Crooner; Two Against the World; Cabin in the Cotton; Night After Night; Central Park; Scarface; Hat Check Girl; Big City Blues; The Man From Yesterday; I Am a Fugitive From a Chain Gang; A Bill of Divorcement; Merrily We Go to Hell; 1933: Hello Everybody!; Girl Missing; From Hell to Heaven; The Eagle and the Hawk; Gold Diggers of 1933; Too Much Harmony; I'm No Angel; Duck Soup; The House on 56th Street; Lady Killer; Torch Singer; Broadway Thru a Keyhole; Blood Money; 1934: Upperworld; Wonder Bar; Jimmy the Gent; Smarty; Registered Nurse; Fog Over Frisco; Man With Two Faces; Madame DuBarry; Lady By Choice; College Rhythm; Transatlantic Merry-Go-Round; Imitation of Life; The Meanest Gal in Town; The Red Rider (serial); Death on the Diamond; Desirable; The Girl From Missouri; He Was Her Man; Coming Out Party; Broadway Bill; 1935: Devil Dogs of the Air; Rumba; Gold Diggers of 1935; Mississippi; Let 'em Have It; Top Hat; Doubting Thomas; The Daring Young Man; Every Night at Eight; Anna Karenina; Personal Maid's Secret; It's in the Air; Shipmates Forever; Broadway Hostess; Dante's Inferno; Burning Gold; The Man Who Broke the Bank at Monte Carlo; Mary Burns — Fugitive; Biography of a Bachelor Girl; 1936: The Singing Kid; Anything Goes; Hats Off; Love Before Breakfast; Mr. Deeds Goes to Town; 13 Hours by Air; And So They Were Married; Nobody's Fool; Sworn Enemy; Rhythm on the Range; Yours for the Asking; Libeled Lady; Theodora Goes Wild; The Accusing Finger; Born to Dance; The Plainsman; San Francisco; Great Guy; Till We Meet Again; Three Smart Girls; The Last Outlaw; Piccadilly Jim; 1937: Married Before Breakfast; Top of the Town; When's Your Birthday?; Parole Racket; Swing High, Swing Low; Captains Courageous; A Star Is Born; Riding on the Air; Girl From Scotland Yard; Easy Living; Saratoga; The Firefly; Blazing Barriers; The Great Gambini; One Mile From Heaven; The Big City; The Lady Escapes; A Yank at Oxford; 1938: Vivacious Lady.

as Dennis O'Keefe: 1938: Bad Man of Brimstone; Hold That Kiss; The Chaser; Vacation From Love; **1939:** Burn 'em Up O'Connor; The Kid From Texas; That's Right — You're Wrong; **1940:** La Conga Nights; Alias the Deacon; Pop Always Pays; I'm Nobody's Sweetheart Now; Girl From Havana; Arise, My Love; You'll Find Out; **1941:** Mr. District Attorney; Bowery Boy; Topper Returns; Broadway Limited; Lady Scarface; Week-End for Three; **1942:** The Affairs of Jimmy Valentine; Moonlight Masquerade; **1943:** Hangmen Also Die; Tahiti Honey; Good Morning Judge; The Leopard Man; Hi Diddle Diddle; **1944:** The Fighting Seabees; Up in Mabel's Room; The Story of Dr. Wassell; Aboard With Two Yanks; Sensations of 1945; **1945:** Earl Carroll's Vanities; Brewster's Millions; The Affairs of Susan; Getting Gertie's Garter; Doll Face; **1946:** Her Adventurous Night; **1947:** Mr. District Attorney; Dishonored Lady; T-Men; **1948:** Raw Deal; Walk a Crooked Mile; Siren of Atlantis; **1949:** Cover Up; The Great Dan Patch; Abandoned; **1950:** The Eagle and the Hawk; Woman on the Run; The Company She Keeps; **1951:** Follow the Sun; Passage West; **1952:** One Big Affair; Everything I Have is Yours; **1953:** The Lady Wants Mink; The Fake; The Diamond Wizard; **1954:** Drums of Tahiti; **1955:** Angela (and dir.); Las Vegas Shakedown; Chicago Syndicate; Inside Detroit; **1957:** Dragoon Wells Massacre; Sail Into Danger; Lady of Vengeance; **1958:** Graft and Corruption; **1961:** All Hands on Deck; **1963:** The Naked Flame.

NY Stage: 1963: Never Too Late; **1964:** Never Live Over a Pretzel Factory.

Select TV: 1951: Route Nineteen (sp); **1953:** A Time for Heroes (sp); **1955:** Yellow Jack (sp); The Human Jungle (sp); **1956:** It's Always Sunday (sp); Five Minutes to Live (sp); **1957:** The Traveling Corpse (sp); Suspicion (series); **1959–60:** The Dennis O'Keefe Show (series).

WARNER OLAND

(Jonah Werner Ohlund)
Born: Umea, Sweden, October 3, 1880.
Died: August 5, 1938.

The one and only Charlie Chan, Warner Oland — who never resorted to makeup to play the famous Asian sleuth — fully took charge of the character and presented a man of gentility and cunning. The writing in these films may suggest a simplification of a race but little of the fault can rest with Oland, who did his job with total conviction. When he was 13 his family moved to America, settling in Connecticut. His first professional acting job was in *The Christian*, starring Sarah Bernhardt, after which he either appeared in or produced several plays over the next 14 years. His first motion picture is hard to verify, some sources crediting him with appearing as early as *Jewels of the Madonna* in 1909, while others indicate *Sin*, in 1915, as his debut. In any event the first time he really registered on screen was in 1917, when he played villains in two serials: *Patria*, in which he was first seen portraying an Asian, and the Pearl White starrer, *The Fatal Ring*. Throughout the silent era he established himself as one of the most hiss-able bad guys in the business and he certainly wasn't all that likable in his most famous 1920s credit, as the stubborn cantor father of Al Jolson in the semi-talkie milestone *The Jazz Singer* (he also had the distinction of appearing in *Don Juan*, the first feature with synchronized music). Before his signature role arrived, he stayed on the side of evil as one of fiction's other famous Asian characters, *The Mysterious Dr. Fu Manchu*, which he first did in 1929 and then reprised on two other occasions (including a cameo in *Paramount on Parade*). In 1931 Fox chose

him to portray Earl Derr Biggers's intrepid Honolulu police investigator in *Charlie Chan Carries On*, and one of the classic pairings of actor and role took place.

Oland would play Chan in 15 more films in the series, only one of which, *Black Camel*, did not feature the character's name in the title. Since the original author passed on in 1933, the producers figured there was no need to stick to the novels any more and began creating their own Chan adventures, in most cases sending him to various locales which were usually spelled out in the titles. In 1935's *Charlie Chan in Paris*, Keye Luke was introduced as the loyal but often bumbling Number One Son, Lee, giving Oland a perfect foil for some witty observations and wisecracks. While the series was keeping Oland more than busy, he still accepted other work as well, retreating back to his no-good ways again as the general who hijacks the *Shanghai Express* and rapes Anna May Wong in the bargain; getting stranded in the stupefying *The Son-Daughter*, as the nefarious Sea Crab, who ends up strangled by Helen Hayes with his own pony-tail; and taking a pivotal role in *Werewolf of London*, as the doctor whose interest in the cure for Henry Hull's lycanthropy is not what it seems. In the midst of a messy divorce and coping with his increasingly failing health, Oland walked off of what was to be *Charlie Chan at Ringside* and was suspended by the studio. Returning to Sweden he contracted pneumonia and died. The Chan film was rewritten as *Mr. Moto's Gamble*, to accommodate Peter Lorre in *his* Asian detective role. Eventually Sidney Toler took over the role of Chan with 1938's *Charlie Chan in Honolulu*. Oland was credited with writing the English translation of the play *The Stranger*, which appeared on Broadway in 1913.

Screen: 1915: Sin; The Unfaithful Wife; **1916:** The Eternal Question/The Eternal Sappho; The Serpent; Destruction; The Fool's Revenge; The Reapers; The Rise of Susan; **1917:** Patria (serial); The Fatal Ring (serial); The Cigarette Girl; **1918:** The Mysterious Client; Convict 993; The Naulahka; The Yellow Ticket; **1919:** The Lightning Raider (serial); Witness for the Defense; The Avalanche; Mandarin's Gold; Twin Pawns; The Mad Talon; Roaring Oaks; **1920:** The Third Eye; The Phantom Foe (serial); **1921:** The Yellow Arm (serial); Hurricane Hutch; **1922:** East Is West; The Pride of Palomar; **1923:** His Children's Children; **1924:** Curlytop; One Night in Rome; So This Is Marriage; The Fighting American; The Throwback; **1925:** Flower of Night; Don Q — Son of Zorro; The Winding Stair; Riders of the Purple Sage; Infatuation; **1926:** Tell It to the Marines; Don Juan; The Marriage Clause; The Mystery Club; Twinkletoes; Man of the Forest; **1927:** A Million Bid; The Jazz Singer; Sailor Izzy Murphy; When a Man Loves; Good Time Charley; Old San Francisco; What Happened to Father; **1928:** The Scarlet Lady; Wheel of Chance; Stand and Deliver; Dream of Love; Tong War; **1929:** Chinatown Nights; The Studio Murder Mystery; The Mysterious Dr. Fu Manchu; The Mighty; The Faker; **1930:** The Vagabond King; Dangerous Paradise; Paramount on Parade; The Return of Dr. Fu Manchu; **1931:** Drums of Jeopardy; Dishonored; Charlie Chan Carries On; Black Camel; Daughter of the Dragon; The Big Gamble; **1932:** Shanghai Express; Charlie Chan's Chance; Passport to Hell; The Son-Daughter; **1933:** Charlie Chan's Greatest Case; Before Dawn; As Husbands Go; **1934:** Mandalay; Bulldog Drummond Strikes Back; Charlie Chan's Courage; Charlie Chan in London; The Painted Veil; **1935:** Charlie Chan in Paris; Charlie Chan in Egypt; Werewolf of London; Shanghai; Charlie Chan in Shanghai; **1936:** Charlie Chan's Secret; Charlie Chan at the Circus; Charlie Chan at the Race Track; Charlie Chan at the Opera; **1937:** Charlie Chan at the Olympics; Charlie Chan on Broadway; Charlie Chan at Monte Carlo.

NY Stage: 1902: The Eternal City; **1905:** The Prodigal Son;

1907: The Master Builder; A Doll's House; 1909: The Vampire; 1911: The Price; 1912: The Father.

EDNA MAY OLIVER

(EDNA MAY NUTTER) BORN: MALDEN, MA, NOVEMBER 9, 1883. DIED: NOVEMBER 9, 1942.

Almost always indelicately referred to as "horse-faced," this scene-stealing lady was one of the treasures of moviegoing in the 1930, usually playing toughened old spinsters who wouldn't stand for a jot of nonsense, raising an eyebrow and making a disapproving sniff with her nose. There was no doubt who was in charge when Edna May Oliver was around. At first a light-opera singer, she turned legit in 1911, making her Broadway bow five years later in a play called *The Master*. There were several other New York theatrical appearances to come, concluding in 1927 with her most famous, playing Parthy in the original production of the groundbreaking musical *Show Boat*. In the meantime, she had started showing up in movies including some Richard Dix vehicles, *Icebound* and *Let's Get Married*. With the arrival of sound she was signed to a contract by RKO, who felt she might make a good foil for the comedy team of Wheeler and Woolsey, assigning her roles in three of their films, *Half Shot at Sunrise*, *Cracked Nuts*, and *Hold 'em Jail*. In between, she was the meddlesome pioneer woman in *Cimarron*, and got top billing in *Laugh and Get Rich*, playing the owner of a boardinghouse who must suffer through a marriage to shiftless Hugh Herbert. Oliver's tangy deliver was such a delight that the studio kept her busy in starring roles for a spell with *Fanny Foley Herself*, a soap opera about a vaudevillian and her daughters; *Ladies of the Jury*, as a society matron who takes charge of a murder case when she ends up on the jury; and best of all, *Penguin Pool Murder*, where, as schoolteacher and part-time sleuth Hildegarde Withers, she was memorably teamed with James Gleason. This one went over well enough that they were called back together for two sequels, *Murder on the Blackboard* and *Murder on a Honeymoon*.

She seemed the only possible choice to play Aunt March in the definitive screen version of *Little Women*, and likewise was the first face that came to mind looking at the Tenniel drawings of the Red Queen in *Alice in Wonderland*, which she did for Paramount. Universal came up with the intriguing teaming of Oliver and fussy Edward Everett Horton for the comedy *The Poor Rich*, after which she played another character of classic literature, Aunt Betsey, in David Copperfield, a standout in a movie rich with fine character actors. In *A Tale of Two Cities* she was Miss Pross, who dies at the hand of wicked Blanche Yurka in a knock-down drag-out fight, and filled yet another part which seemed to have her name stamped all over it, the Nurse, in *Romeo and Juliet*. She bitched at Frank Morgan as the queen of the mythical country in *Rosalie*, after which it was refreshing to see her grumbling at cutesy Shirley Temple in *Little Miss Broadway*, though you knew damn well that Shirley would melt Edna's frosty reserve and triumph in the end. With so much good work behind her, it was about time to recognize her accomplishments, and she received a well-deserved Oscar nomination for her unforgettable performance as the feisty old pioneer who puts up a brave stand against the Indians in John Ford's colorful *Drums Along the Mohawk*. Still going strong, she was the cranky talent agent who is charmed by Fred Astaire and Ginger Rogers in *The Story of Vernon and Irene Castle*, and had another career high point, as the snooty aunt of Laurence Olivier, in *Pride and Prejudice*. Her final role was that of Merle Oberon's spirited old grandmother in *Lydia*, released the year before Oliver passed away on her 59th birthday, leaving a hard-to-fill void in the cinematic crones' hall of fame.

Screen: 1923: Wife in Name Only; Three O'Clock in the Morning; 1924: Restless Wives; Icebound; Manhattan; 1925: Lovers in Quarantine; The Lady Who Lied; The Lucky Devil; 1926: The American Venus; Let's Get Married; 1929: The Saturday Night Kid; 1930: Half Shot at Sunrise; 1931: Cimarron; Laugh and Get Rich; Forbidden Adventure/Newly Rich; Cracked Nuts; Fanny Foley Herself; 1932: Ladies of the Jury; The Conquerors; Hold 'em Jail; Penguin Pool Murder; 1933: Meet the Baron; The Great Jasper; It's Great to Be Alive; Ann Vickers; Only Yesterday; Little Women; Alice in Wonderland; 1934: The Poor Rich; The Last Gentleman; Murder on the Blackboard; We're Rich Again; 1935: David Copperfield; Murder on a Honeymoon; No More Ladies; A Tale of Two Cities; 1936: Romeo and Juliet; 1937: Parnell; My Dear Miss Aldrich; Rosalie; 1938: Paradise for Three; Little Miss Broadway; 1939: Second Fiddle; Nurse Edith Cavell; The Story of Vernon and Irene Castle; Drums Along the Mohawk; 1940: Pride and Prejudice; 1941: Lydia.

NY Stage: 1916: The Master; Oh Boy; 1919: The Rose of China; 1920: My Golden Girl; The Half-Moon; 1921: Wait 'Til We're Married; Her Salary Man; 1922: The Rubicon; Wild Oats Lane; 1923: Icebound; 1924: In His Arms; 1925: Isabel; Cradle Snatchers; 1927: Show Boat.

LAURENCE OLIVIER

BORN: DORKING, SURREY, ENGLAND, MAY 22, 1907. DIED: JULY 11, 1989.

So striking were the talents of this British legend that his name would become synonymous with great acting. Laurence Olivier was one of the towering figures of the London stage, perhaps its most acclaimed practitioner of Shakespeare, and the first director of England's National Theatre Company. He did not, as was the case of so many titans of the English theatre, look down on films, and built a most impressive body of work in that medium, resulting in ten Academy Award nominations for acting, one mention for directing, and two honorary Oscars. A master of accents, makeup, and disguise, he would often bury himself inside a character to mesmerizing effect, but also possessed a singular grace and simplicity when just looking and sounding like himself. With someone as prone to taking risks as he was, there were, inevitably, missteps and flights into the grotesque. It was all part of an eagerness not to repeat himself or bore the audience. In the long run, you couldn't help but remain in awe. It was only appropriate that his first stage experience at school found him doing Shakespeare, in *The Taming of the Shrew*, cast as Katharine. He studied for the profession at Elsie Fogerty's Central School of Speech Training and Dramatic Art in London and, while there, made his West End debut, in 1924, in a small part in *Byron*. After that he joined a touring company, Lena Ashwell Players, and then became a member of the Birmingham Rep, which brought him back to the London stage. Through such West End plays as *Harold* and *Journey's End*, he began to be noticed and even crossed the Atlantic at this point, to make his Broadway bow, in 1929, in a failure, *Murder on the Second Floor*. Back home, he landed in a nice big hit, playing the second lead in *Private Lives*, which also brought him back to New York in support of Noel Coward and Gertrude Lawrence. In the meantime, he married his other co-star, Jill Esmond, in 1930, the same year he was first seen in a motion picture, *The Temporary Widow*, a comedy-mystery made in Germany.

His early excursions into film were not encouraging, with a 38-

minute long-quota quickie, *Too Many Crooks*, as a playboy, and the higher budgeted *Potiphar's Wife*, as a chauffeur. He even made two pictures in Hollywood during this time, under contract to RKO: *Friends and Lovers*, as an army lieutenant who falls in love with his superior officer's wife (Elissa Landi), and *Westward Passage*, as a struggling writer married to Ann Harding. In between there was a loan-out to Fox for *The Yellow Ticket*, also with Landi. He looked and sounded good but none of these offered anything he could really shine in, so the impact he made was close to nil. Nor was there much comment made about one he did in England that was supposed to be the start of Gloria Swanson's new career there, *Perfect Understanding*, or a comedy with Gertrude Lawrence, *No Funny Business*. To add insult to injury, MGM asked him to play opposite Greta Garbo in *Queen Christina* and then sent him packing after two weeks, replacing him with John Gilbert. There was also his first and least remembered film encounter with Shakespeare, *As You Like It*, starring as Orlando to Elisabeth Bergner's Rosalind.

It hardly mattered that he hadn't taken the film world by storm; he won much applause for alternating Romeo and Mercutio in *Romeo and Juliet* in London, and then debuted with the Old Vic in *Hamlet*, which was the real beginning of his ascent into the theatrical stratosphere. Still figuring there was something to be achieved by crossing over into films, he signed up with the prestigious Alexander Korda in 1937. His first picture for Korda, *Fire Over England*, was also the first time he really clicked on screen, helped no doubt by the sparks he was creating in his love scenes with leading lady Vivien Leigh. They were also paired in *21 Days*, which was not released until they both had their smash hits in America in 1939. By that time they were one of the acting world's most famous couples, marrying in 1940. After a string of Shakespearean triumphs for the Old Vic including *Macbeth*, *Henry V*, and *Othello* (as Iago), he accepted another offer from Hollywood, this time to star as Heathcliffe in Samuel Goldwyn's very important production of *Wuthering Heights*. It was hailed as one of the great romances of its day and managed the astounding feat of snatching away the New York Film Critics' award from Leigh's film, *Gone With the Wind*. Despite the fact that Olivier failed to rise above the overwhelming melodrama of it all, he became the newest rage and earned his first Oscar nomination.

His immediate follow-ups were infinitely better. First, in director Alfred Hitchcock's U.S. debut, he was a marvelously brooding Max DeWinter in the Academy Award-winner for Best Picture of 1940, *Rebecca*; and then he was the charmingly snobbish Darcy in MGM's extremely good rendering of Jane Austen's *Pride and Prejudice*, matching well with Greer Garson, although he later had nothing but negative criticism for her work. The former was the more popular of the two and brought him a second Oscar nomination. Staying in classy properties, Olivier, Leigh, and Korda did an American-made production that was supposed to solidify the alliance between the U.S. and the U.K., *That Hamilton Woman*, with Olivier looking very stern sporting wig and eye patch as Lord Nelson. It was all very stiff and stuffy but got the best plug of all when Winston Churchill proclaimed it his favorite film of all time. Returning to England, he was seen in another popular and far better piece of propaganda, *49th Parallel/The Invaders*, in a short bit as a French Canadian trapper, boisterously playing the part to the hilt and thereby staying in one's memory, just as he'd hoped. He then threw himself into his own ambitious morale booster, a film of *Henry V*, in which he not only acted, but directed, produced, and adapted the text. It was a startlingly imaginative offering, with his own glorious performance creating fire at the center and it became an absolute sensation in Britain when it opened in 1944. Two years later it was

equally cherished by the American press, earning Olivier an Oscar mention for his acting and a special award from the Academy. It was also instrumental in convincing the skeptics who hadn't cared for previous forays into Shakespeare that the Bard could indeed succeed on screen. Olivier was not one to rest on his laurels and decided he would put his *Hamlet* on celluloid as well (he was the star, director, and producer). As dark and gloomy as *Henry V* was full of color and pageantry, it was an even bigger hit with the general public. To add to the acclaim, the 1948 release became the first British production to be given the Academy Award for Best Picture. Since Olivier wound up with his own Oscar for his performance, he entered the record books as the first actor in Academy history to direct himself in his award-winning role. With a third nomination in the directing category, he had reached some kind of artistic summit. A further sign of his high standing was his being knighted during the film's production, at the time the youngest actor to be given this honor.

Back with the Old Vic he did *School for Scandal*, *Richard III*, and directed his wife in *A Streetcar Named Desire*, which was instrumental in her getting to do the film version. Olivier's movie career at this point consisted of a well-regarded cameo as a cockney police officer in the all-star celebration of the creation of motion pictures, *The Magic Box*; his often overlooked, achingly sad portrayal of the restaurant owner whose life is ruined by his passion for Jennifer Jones in the surprisingly bleak *Carrie*; and *The Beggar's Opera*, which gave him a chance to sing on screen. A third Shakespeare project as director-producer-actor (and adapter), *Richard III*, was less assured but was given a full-blooded lift by Olivier's masterful portrayal of the evil king. Its box office in America was pretty much killed off because it was shown simultaneously on television, but he was Oscar nominated just the same. Hoping to grab a somewhat broader audience, he directed himself alongside the last actress one would have expected to see pairing off with the Great Olivier, Marilyn Monroe, in *The Prince and the Showgirl*; it was very mild fluff and, despite the initial hype, not particularly popular. Kirk Douglas and Burt Lancaster had the great idea of casting him as General Burgoyne in their adaptation of Shaw's *The Devil's Disciple* and despite Olivier's unhappiness with the whole affair, he proved once again how mesmerizing he could be in a handful of scenes, downplaying against his co-stars' bravado to great effect. As the 1950s came to a close, he scored another major theatrical triumph in both London and New York as the egotistical, second-rate music hall star Archie Rice in *The Entertainer*. He also found television as a viable showcase for his talents, winning an Emmy Award for *The Moon and Sixpence* in 1959.

His crumbling marriage to Leigh came to an end in 1960, the same year he married Joan Plowright. She played his daughter in *The Entertainer* onstage and then again when it was successfully expanded into a feature film, for which Olivier copped yet another Oscar nomination, in 1960. That same year, he participated in the best of all the costume spectacles of that era, *Spartacus*, richly authoritative as the manipulative, sexually ambiguous Roman emperor. Between two movie roles in which he pretty much looked and sounded like his off-screen self — *Term of Trial*, as a spineless schoolteacher, and *Bunny Lake Is Missing*, as a police inspector — he took the reigns of the newly established and very important National Theatre Company, which had begun in 1963. There he did the title role in *Othello*, which was pretty much filmed intact for cinema release. It was one of the last times it was acceptable for a white performer to wear black face on screen, for no one would deny Olivier the chance to tackle yet another of the Bard's significant creations. Boldly adapting black mannerisms and body language it was a controversial performance, alternately electrifying and grotesque, once again proving that when it came to a challenge there were few as fearless as he. The film wasn't much seen outside of select venues but he and several others of the cast were nominated by the Academy.

Once he passed the 60-year-old mark, the possibility of leading film roles was becoming less of a reality. Those star parts he did manage to secure were *Dance of Death*, again adapted from a National Theatre production, but one so specialized and limited in appeal that it did not play in America until 1979, a full decade after its British release; and his last three Oscar-nominated roles: *Sleuth*, brilliantly going one-on-one with Michael Caine in this tricky and well-scripted piece; *Marathon Man*, creepily effective as the blade-wielding Nazi who tortures Dustin Hoffman in the dentist chair; and the otherwise silly *The Boys From Brazil*, this time on the side of good, searching for Nazi Gregory Peck. Of a more secondary nature were his roles as the kindly con man who befriends the young lovers in *A Little Romance* and vampire hunter Dr. Van Helsing in the 1979 version of *Dracula*. Television, by this point, was offering him classier assignments and he collected four more Emmys, for *Long Day's Journey Into Night*, which he'd done onstage; *Love Among the Ruins*, which paired him with Katharine Hepburn; *Brideshead Revisited*, one of the most highly regarded mini-series of its day; and *King Lear*. There were, alas, plenty of embarrassments at the movies, though, with Olivier shamelessly hamming it up for the cash in *The Betsy*, as a horny auto tycoon; *The Jazz Singer*, as Neil Diamond's disapproving cantor papa; *Clash of the Titans*, as Zeus, of course; and *Inchon*, looking like a wax-works version of General MacArthur. Cameos in *The Bounty* and *Wild Geese II*, as well as a silent appearance in one of director Derek Jarman's monstrosities, *War Requiem*, brought the curtain down on his career on a minor note, but in no way diminished his remarkable standing as an inspirational actor. He directed but did not appear in the Broadway plays *Venus Observed* (1952), *The Tumbler* (1960), and *Filumena* (1980). In 1970 he became the first actor to be bestowed with the title of Lord. There were two publications: his memoir, *Confessions of an Actor* (1982), and *On Acting* (1986).

Screen: 1930: The Temporary Widow; Too Many Crooks; 1931: Potiphar's Wife/Her Strange Desire (US: 1932); Friends and Lovers; The Yellow Ticket; 1932: Westward Passage; 1933: Perfect Understanding; No Funny Business (US: 1934); 1935: Moscow Nights/I Stand Condemned (US: 1936); 1936: As You Like It; Q Planes/Clouds Over Europe (US: 1939); 1937: Fire Over England; 1938: The Divorce of Lady X; 1939: Wuthering Heights; 1940: Conquest of the Air; 21 Days/21 Days Together (filmed 1937); Rebecca; Pride and Prejudice; 1941: That Hamilton Woman/Lady Hamilton; 49th Parallel/The Invaders (US: 1942); 1943: The Demi-Paradise/Adventure for Two; 1944: This Happy Breed (narrator); Henry V (and dir.; prod.; text. editor; US: 1946); 1948: Hamlet (and dir.; prod.); 1951: The Magic Box (US: 1952); 1952: Carrie; 1953: A Queen Is Crowned (narrator); The Beggar's Opera; 1955: Richard III (and dir.; prod.; adapt.; US: 1956); 1957: The Prince and the Showgirl (and dir.; prod.); 1959: The Devil's Disciple; 1960: Spartacus; The Entertainer; 1962: Term of Trial (US: 1963); 1965: Bunny Lake Is Missing; Othello; 1966: Khartoum; 1968: Romeo and Juliet (narrator); The Shoes of the Fisherman; 1969: The Dance of Death (US: 1979); Oh! What a Lovely War; Battle of Britain; 1970: Three Sisters (and dir.; US: 1974); 1971: Nicholas and Alexandra; 1972: Lady Caroline Lamb (US: 1973); Sleuth; 1974: The Rehearsal (nUSr); 1976: Marathon Man; The Seven-Per-Cent Solution; 1977: A Bridge Too Far; 1978: The Gentleman Tramp (narrator); The Betsy; The Boys From Brazil; 1979: A Little Romance; Dracula; 1980: The Jazz Singer; 1981: Clash of the Titans; 1982: Inchon;

1984: The Bounty; The Jigsaw Man; 1985: Wild Geese II; 1989: War Requiem.

NY Stage: 1929: Murder on the Second Floor; 1931: Private Lives; 1933: The Green Bay Tree; 1939: No Time for Comedy; 1940: Romeo and Juliet; 1946: Henry IV (Parts 1 and 2); Oedipus; The Critic; Uncle Vanya; 1951: Caesar and Cleopatra; Antony and Cleopatra; 1958: The Entertainer; 1960: Becket.

Select TV: 1958: John Gabriel Borkman (sp); 1959: The Moon and Sixpence (sp); 1961: The Power and the Glory (sp); 1963: Uncle Vanya (sp); 1969: Male of the Species (sp; narrator); 1970: David Copperfield (sp; also released theatrically); 1973: Long Day's Journey Into Night (sp); The World at War (series narrator); 1974: The Merchant of Venice (sp); 1975: Love Among the Ruins; 1976: The Collection (sp; and prod.); Cat on a Hot Tin Roof; Hindle Wakes (sp.; and dir.; prod.); 1977: Jesus of Nazareth (ms); Come Back, Little Sheba (and prod.); 1978: Daphne Laureola (and prod.); Saturday Sunday Monday (sp); 1981: Brideshead Revisited (ms; US: 1982); A Voyage Round My Father (sp); 1983: King Lear (sp); Mr. Halpern and Mr. Johnson (sp); Wagner (ms; also released theatrically); A Talent for Murder; 1984: The Ebony Tower; The Last Days of Pompeii (ms); 1986: Peter the Great (ms); 1986: Lost Empires (ms).

OLE OLSEN

(JOHN SIGVARD OLSEN) BORN: WABASH, IN, NOVEMBER 6, 1892. DIED: JANUARY 26, 1963.

& CHIC JOHNSON

(HAROLD OGDEN JOHNSON) BORN: CHICAGO, IL, MARCH 5, 1891. DIED: FEBRUARY 28, 1962.

Pure baggy-pants vaudevillians, Olsen and Johnson were the kind of anything-for-a-laugh comics who were a great hit in live theater but never quite repeated their fame on the big screen. Olsen was a violinist who started up a group of nightclub musicians. Johnson eventually joined them as a pianist and comedy became an increasingly important part of the act. Olsen and Johnson separated from the rest of the band to go on the vaudeville circuit and they became headliners. When talking pictures arrived Warner Bros. decided to give them a try, resulting in three pictures, *Oh, Sailor Behave!*, which included a number they composed called "The Laughing Song;" *50 Million Frenchmen*, which had nothing to recommend it since it disposed of all the Cole Porter songs that had made it a hit on Broadway; and *Gold Dust Gertie*, which was only of passing interest because Olsen wore a mustache for the first and last time. Olsen was a bit of a washout as a movie presence and Johnson's main shtick was an annoying, high-pitched laugh, so, having accomplished little, they went back to their more appreciative live audiences, developing a touring revue they eventually called *Hellzapoppin'*. This show came to Broadway in 1938 and turned out to be the crowning achievement of the duo's career, an unprecedented smash hit, a wild free-for-all mix of comedy and music that seemed to change on a nightly basis. In 1941 Universal tried to make a movie of it, with something resembling a story line. Despite the fact that so theatrical an entertainment was never going to survive a film adaptation, per se, there were moments of bizarre and sometimes sublime inspiration. Continuing in this deliberately silly vein were the team's Universal follow-ups, *Crazy House*, set in Hollywood and often considered the high point of their celluloid ventures, and *Ghost Catchers*, the requisite haunted house romp. After the failure of *See Our Lawyer*, they went back to the revue format, trying to recapture the fun of *Hellzapoppin'* both onstage, in *Laughing Room Only*, and on television, where they starred in the short-lived *Fireball Fun for All*.

Screen: 1930: Oh, Sailor Behave!; 1931: Fifty Million Frenchmen; Gold Dust Gertie; 1936: Country Gentlemen; 1937: All Over Town; 1941: Hellzapoppin'; 1943: Crazy House; 1944: Ghost Catchers; 1945: See My Lawyer.
NY Stage: 1933: Take a Chance; 1938: Hellzapoppin' (and wr.); 1941: Sons o' Fun (and wr.); 1945: Laffing Room Only (and wr.); 1950: Pardon Our French (and wr.).
Select TV: 1949: Fireball Fun for All (series).

NANCY OLSON

BORN: MILWAUKEE, WI, JULY 14, 1928.
ED: UNIV. OF WI, UCLA.

Wholesomely blonde and apple-cheeked, Nancy Olson was something of a half-sister in looks to her contemporary, Barbara Bel Geddes, but had talent and charm all her own. The work came quickly at the beginning but, over time, the jobs were much too infrequent and she achieved little prominence beyond her first decade or so in front of the camera. Fresh out of college she was engaged to play one of Randolph Scott's two leading ladies (Jane Wyatt was the other) in the Fox western *Canadian Pacific*, then was put under contract over at Paramount. That studio gave her no less than three assignments with William Holden, starting with the best thing she would ever do and one of the towering achievements in film history, *Sunset Blvd.* She played script girl Betty Schaeffer, the light of decency in this stinging and still brilliant look at Hollywood, reluctantly falling in love with failing writer Holden and earning an Oscar nomination in the process. There followed *Union Station*, as a railway passenger helping Holden solve a kidnapping, and *Submarine Command*, as his wife back home. In between, she was one of Bing Crosby's nicest leading ladies in *Mr. Music*, and stopped by Warners for a remake of *A Farewell to Arms*, retitled *Force of Arms*, set in Korea and co-starring, no surprise, William Holden. Now part of that studio, she was John Wayne's lover in one of his weakest films, *Big Jim McLain*; showed up late in the story as Steve Forrest's artist girlfriend in *So Big*; and was part of the hit ensemble drama *Battle Cry*. In time, Disney seemed to be the right place for Olson and she was the servant who befriends Hayley Mills in *Pollyanna*; Fred MacMurray's increasingly frustrated fiancée in one of the company's major successes of the 1960s, *The Absent Minded Professor*, a part she repeated in the sequel *Son of Flubber*; and sensible wives in both the serious pro-Indian drama *Smith!* (Glenn Ford), and the slapstick-ridden *Snowball Express* (Dean Jones). In later years she showed up as the mother of Linda Blair in the disaster sequel *Airport 1975*, and as Michael Ontkean's mom in *Making Love*. Her first husband (1950–57) was lyricist Alan Jay Lerner; her second Capital Records chairman Alan W. Livingston.
Screen: 1949: Canadian Pacific; 1950: Sunset Blvd.; Union Station; Mr. Music; 1951: Force of Arms; Submarine Command; 1952: Big Jim McLain; 1953: So Big; 1954: The Boy From Oklahoma; 1955: Battle Cry; 1960: Pollyanna; 1961: The Absent Minded Professor; 1963: Son of Flubber; 1969: Smith!; 1972: Snowball Express; 1974: Airport 1975; 1982: Making Love; 1997: Flubber.
NY Stage: 1957: The Tunnel of Love; 1960: Send Me No Flowers; 1962: Mary, Mary.
Select TV: 1954: The Teacher (sp); For the Love of Kitty (sp); The Royal Family (sp); 1955: The Women (sp); 1956: High Tor (sp); 1958: Second Chance (sp); 1961: Family Outing (sp); 1977: Kingston: Confidential (series); 1984: Paper Dolls (series).

PATRICK O'NEAL

BORN: OCALA, FL, SEPTEMBER 26, 1927.
ED: UNIV. OF FL. DIED: SEPTEMBER 9, 1994.

Inescapably uninviting in manner and look, prematurely gray Patrick O'Neal was a fairly distant movie presence who hadn't the spark for stardom but carved a minor niche as a dryly smarmy character player with a droning, world-weary voice. Trained at the Actors Studio and the Neighborhood Playhouse, he began appearing in live television in the early 1950s before he took a break for duty in the U.S. Air Force. He made his motion picture bow as the colorless hero of a 3-D Vincent Price thriller *The Mad Magician*; showed up as Tony Curtis's rival in *The Black Shield of Falworth*; then returned to television where he starred in a one-season offering, *Dick and the Duchess*, among others. Stardom of sorts arrived when he played the disgraced reverend in the original Broadway production of Tennessee Williams's *The Night of the Iguana* (Richard Burton did the part in the film version) and then appeared Off Broadway in *The Ginger Man*. The latter meant enough to him that it became the name of his own restaurant, which he opened in Manhattan in 1963. By the time of these theatrical triumphs he'd resumed his movie career where his credits included *From the Terrace*, as the psychiatrist Joanne Woodward is dallying with on the side; *In Harm's Way*, as an opportunistic navy man; *Alvarez Kelly*, as a Union army officer; *Chamber of Horrors*, in a starring role, as a crazed, one-handed psycho seeking revenge in this cheapjack thriller sold with the gimmick of a "horror horn" that signaled when something bloody was about to happen; *A Fine Madness*, as a psychiatrist; *Matchless*, another lead in another cheesy feature, as a journalist chased by spies because he has a ring that turns him invisible; *Where Were You When the Lights Went Out?*, as Doris Day's philandering husband; *The Secret Life of an American Wife*, as Anne Jackson's disinterested spouse; *The Way We Were*, as a Hollywood director; and *The Stepford Wives*, as the slimy leader of a dangerous male chauvinist organization. After that it was mostly television, including commercial voice-overs, though he did return to the movies on a few occasions including *Alice*, in a brief flashback as Mia Farrow's father; *For the Boys*, as a Hollywood honcho; and the hit action film *Under Siege*, as the ship's captain. Over the years he had expanded his restaurant holdings to include a co-ownership of an establishment in Beverly Hills with actor Carroll O'Connor. There was also a directorial credit on an obscure film called *Circle Back*.
Screen: 1954: The Mad Magician; The Black Shield of Falworth; 1960: From the Terrace; 1961: A Matter of Morals; 1963: The Cardinal; 1965: In Harm's Way; King Rat; 1966: Alvarez Kelly; A Fine Madness; Chamber of Horrors; 1967: Matchless; 1968: Assignment to Kill; Where Were You When the Lights Went Out?; The Secret Life of an American Wife; 1969: Stiletto; Castle Keep; 1970: The Kremlin Letter; El Condor; 1971: Corky; 1973: Silent Night, Bloody Night; The Way We Were; 1975: The Stepford Wives; 1985: The Stuff; 1987: Like Father, Like Son; 1989: New York Stories; 1990: Q&A; Alice; 1991: The Diary of the Hurdy Gurdy Man (nUSr); For the Boys; 1992: Under Siege.
NY Stage: 1954: Oh, Men! Oh, Women!; 1958: Lulu; 1961: A Far Country; The Night of the Iguana; 1963: The Ginger Man; 1982: Children of Darkness.
Select TV: 1954: The Road to Tara (sp); Dear Little Fool (sp); Sue Ellen (sp); 1954–55: Portia Faces Life (series); 1955: Do It Yourself (sp); 1956: The Piper of St. James (sp); 1957–58: Dick and the Duchess (series); 1958: Today Is Ours (series); 1960: Diagnosis: Unknown (series); 1961: The Magic and the Loss (sp);

1965: The Loving Cup (sp); 1968: Companions in Nightmare; 1972: Cool Million; 1974: To Kill a King; 1975: Crossfire; 1976: The Killer Who Wouldn't Die; Twin Detectives; Arthur Hailey's The Moneychangers (ms); 1977: The Deadliest Season; Sharon: Portrait of a Mistress; The Last Hurrah; 1978: To Kill a Cop; Like Mom, Like Me; 1978–79: Kaz (series); 1980: Make Me an Offer; 1982: Fantasies; 1983–84: Emerald Point N.A.S. (series); 1984: Sprague; 1985: Perry Mason Returns; 1988: Maigret; 1993: Perry Mason: The Case of the Skin-Deep Scandal.

MAUREEN O'SULLIVAN

BORN: BOYLE, COUNTY ROSCOMMON, IRELAND, MAY 17, 1911. DIED: JUNE 23, 1998.

It was no mean feat to become best known for scampering around in jungle pictures and yet somehow retain one's dignity, but that's just what Maureen O'Sullivan accomplished. She took it one step further by earning her place as one of the most charming and lovely of all 1930s screen ingénues. Spotted at a horse show by director Frank Borzage, she was invited to come to Hollywood and test for a role in his film Song o' My Heart. She got the part and ended up under contract to Fox, where the most notable of her credits during this brief period were the futuristic musical Just Imagine, which purported to show us what life in 1980 New York would be like, and Will Rogers's clunky but popular A Connecticut Yankee, as King Arthur's daughter, Princess Alisande. In 1932 she signed a contract with MGM and was promptly given the role that would make her name, Jane Parker, the aristocrat who ends up falling for jungle boy Johnny Weissmuller, in Tarzan the Ape Man. This was just a lot of malarkey, but the two leads seemed so right for their roles (not yet toned down in their sensuality by the censors) that the whole thing clicked, turning it into a profitable hit. Unlike Weissmuller, O'Sullivan had capabilities to expand into other assignments and did not get pigeonholed exclusively into this part. The studio let her play Charles Laughton's daughter, who doesn't realize her dad has committed murder to better her life, in Payment Deferred; and Robert Young's fiancée in both Strange Interlude and Tugboat Annie.

When the Weissmuller follow-up, Tarzan and His Mate, the best and most bizarre of the series entries, proved just as successful as the first, it was clear that MGM was going to keep making these things until the audiences grew weary or the stars outgrew their loincloths. Meanwhile, O'Sullivan was happily earning her keep in some of the company's top productions including the delightful The Thin Man, as the heroine around whom all the criminal activities take place; the stodgy The Barretts of Wimpole Street, defying tyrannical dad Charles Laughton by loving sea captain Ralph Forbes, and if nothing else, looking attractive in period costume; David Copperfield, in perhaps her best remembered non-Jane role of the period, as the delicate Dora, and pulling off a big death scene in the bargain; Anna Karenina, as Kitty, who ends up marrying a man she can't stand; The Bishop Misbehaves, masterminding a plan to rob Reginald Owen; The Devil-Doll, as the estranged daughter of prison escapee Lionel Barrymore; A Day at the Races, as Allan Jones's love interest and one of the few genuinely unobtrusive heroines to appear in a Marx Brothers comedy; A Yank at Oxford, playing the very proper Englishwoman with whom Robert Taylor falls in love, in this production that was shot on location and featured O'Sullivan's former schoolmate, Vivien Leigh, among the cast; and Port of Seven Seas, as the French fishmonger's daughter, the role later made famous by Leslie Caron in Fanny.

During this period she and Weissmuller had settled down in tree-house bliss in Tarzan Escapes, and added Johnny Sheffield to their family as "Boy" in Tarzan Finds a Son, both of which represented slicker, more wholesome views of jungle life than their predecessors, with O'Sullivan's once skimpy costume redesigned to please the puritans. The 1940s began on another high note with O'Sullivan as one of Greer Garson's ninny sisters in Pride and Prejudice. After this she knocked off two more Tarzan epics before the studio temporarily put an end to their involvement in the never-ending adventures in 1942, with Tarzan's New York Adventure, in which Jane was taken out of her jungle outfit and put back into street clothing. This also put an end to O'Sullivan's contract at MGM and she decided to take temporary retirement to raise the several children she had or was then having with director John Farrow, whom she had married in 1936. For him she did his best-regarded work, The Big Clock, as Ray Milland's wife, and the more typical Where Danger Lives. There were a few more forgettable films including Mission Over Korea and Bonzo Goes to College, which must have seemed like a step backwards since it required her once again to act opposite an ape; as well as one of the best Randolph Scott westerns of the 1950s, The Tall T, as a newlywed held for ransom by outlaw Richard Boone. In 1962 she made her Broadway debut as the elderly mom who suddenly finds herself expecting a baby in Never Too Late, and repeated the role in the far less popular 1965 movie version. The previous year her husband had passed away and her daughter, Mia Farrow, was on her way to her own stardom when she was cast in the series Peyton Place. O'Sullivan returned to the movies for an odd joke appearance with Weissmuller in The Phynx, repeating their "Tarzan-Jane" dialogue. Then, after a lengthy period during which she mainly focused on theatre, she had one of her best roles ever, as Farrow's alcoholic, former-actress mom in Hannah and Her Sisters, which reawakened interest in her and led to a smattering of other movie and television roles.

Screen: 1930: Song o' My Heart; So This Is London; Just Imagine; Princess and the Plumber; 1931: A Connecticut Yankee; Skyline; 1932: Tarzan the Ape Man; The Silver Lining; The Big Shot; Strange Interlude; Skyscraper Souls; Payment Deferred; Okay America!; Fast Companions/Information Kid; 1933: Robber's Roost; The Cohens and Kellys in Trouble; Tugboat Annie; Stage Mother; 1934: Tarzan and His Mate; The Thin Man; The Barretts of Wimpole Street; Hideout; 1935: West Point of the Air; David Copperfield; Cardinal Richilieu; The Flame Within; Anna Karenina; Woman Wanted; The Bishop Misbehaves; 1936: Tarzan Escapes; The Voice of Bugle Ann; The Devil-Doll; 1937: A Day at the Races; Between Two Women; The Emperor's Candlesticks; My Dear Miss Aldrich; 1938: A Yank at Oxford; Hold That Kiss; Port of Seven Seas; The Crowd Roars; Spring Madness; 1939: Let Us Live; Tarzan Finds a Son; 1940: Pride and Prejudice; Sporting Blood; 1941: Tarzan's Secret Treasure; Maisie Was a Lady; 1942: Tarzan's New York Adventure; 1948: The Big Clock; 1950: Where Danger Lives; 1952: Bonzo Goes to College; 1953: All I Desire; Mission Over Korea; 1954: Duffy of San Quentin; The Steel Cage; 1957: The Tall T; 1958: Wild Heritage; 1965: Never Too Late; 1970: The Phynx; 1985: Too Scared to Scream; 1986: Hannah and Her Sisters; Peggy Sue Got Married; 1987: Stranded.

NY Stage: 1962: Never Too Late; 1966: The Subject Was Roses; 1967: Keep It in the Family; 1970: The Front Page; Charley's Aunt; 1973: No Sex Please — We're British; 1980: Morning's at Seven.

Select TV: 1952: The Lucky Coin (sp); 1953: Parents' Week-End (sp); The Trestle (sp); Message in a Bottle (sp); 1954: Daughter of Mine (sp); 1956: The Blessed Midnight (sp); Michael and Mary (sp); 1957: End of Innocence (sp); 1964: Today (series); 1972: The Crooked Hearts; 1976: The Great Houdini; 1989: Good Ole

Boy/The River Pirates (sp); **1991**: With Murder in Mind; **1992**: The Habitation of Dragons; **1994**: Hart to Hart: Home is Where the Hart Is.

PETER O'TOOLE

BORN: CONNEMARA, COUNTY GALWAY, IRELAND, AUGUST 2, 1932. RAISED IN LEEDS, ENGLAND. ED: RADA.

Unlike most of his contemporaries of the 1960s British invasion, Peter O'Toole made his impact not in gritty black-and-white kitchen-sink dramas but in Technicolored, international extravaganzas with big budgets, and costumed pageantry. He was thin, tall, beautifully blond-haired, and larger than life, commanding the screen with an intense, often galvanizing mania and booming manner of speech that was mostly enthralling and sometimes deliciously hammy. In later years, after an excessive lifestyle of boozing, his appearance was shockingly dissipated, his focus sometimes less concentrated, and his choice of material often negligible, though the star power still hung on. When he was just a year old his family moved to Leeds, England, where he studied to be a journalist. When theater drew him away from writing, he appeared in some rep plays and then attended RADA, which led to acting with the Bristol Old Vic. In 1956 he made his London stage bow in a production of *Major Barbara*, billed as "Peter Shirley," and then drew some attention with his performances in *Waiting for Godot* and in the title role of *Hamlet*. After a tour of *The Holiday*, where he met Sian Phillips, who became his wife in 1958, he got his big break when he was cast as a cockney soldier in *The Long the Short and the Tall*, which won him raves. Around this point he started his movie career with a Disney production shot in England, *Kidnapped*, in which he had a memorable scene challenging Peter Finch on the bagpipes. After that he was a member of the Scots Guard, who inadvertently helps Aldo Ray plan his heist, in *The Day They Robbed the Bank of England*, and had a strange part as a mountie in an Anthony Quinn French-Italian-British Eskimo saga *The Savage Innocents*, in which his voice was dubbed by another actor.

Back onstage he won more favorable attention in *The Merchant of Venice* and *The Taming of the Shrew*, then got his chance at major movie stardom when Albert Finney decided not to accept the leading role in David Lean's lavish production on the life of *Lawrence of Arabia*. Treated pretty much as a newcomer, few actors ever came into the public consciousness on such a torrent of acclaim and prestige. As the enigmatic military man who becomes a god of sorts to the Arab people, he was a spellbinding combination of charisma and torment. The film was one of the principal blockbusters of the 1960s, earning the Academy Award for Best Picture of 1962 and continues to be hailed as one of the most hypnotic and influential of all great movies. O'Toole became one of the most discussed names of the day and received the first of his many Oscar nominations. Staying historical, he was the bombastic King Henry II, feuding with and loving the more laid-back Richard Burton as Archbishop *Becket*. Their duel of ideals made this one thinking-man's costume picture that clicked both critically and with the public. O'Toole, in arguably his finest performance, earned another Oscar nod. In the off-the-wall, Woody Allen-scripted farce *What's New, Pussycat?*, he was a sex magnet searching for fidelity and, despite awful reviews, it was another moneymaker. There were also good attendance figures for the episodic *The Bible*, in which he showed up in the story of Sodom and Gomorrah, as three angels, and, to a lesser degree, *How to Steal a Million*, charmingly partnered with Audrey Hepburn in

this Parisian-set caper movie. *The Night of the Generals* ended his run of box-office luck, with his curiously blank performance as a murderous Nazi adding to the negativity. There also wasn't much to be said of the 1968 version of Shaw's *Great Catherine*, which he himself was behind the creation of, via his new production company, Keep Films, formed with producer Jules Buck.

Rescue came with a reprise of his Henry II character, in *The Lion in Winter*, magnificently taking this force of nature to an older but no less volatile point in his life. Brilliantly matched with Katharine Hepburn, the two created a sensation in what was basically a series of disjointed, acting set pieces, and he wound up with his third unsuccessful bid for the Oscar. The fourth came with the musical remake of *Goodbye, Mr. Chips*, singing his own songs and quietly underplaying the difficult role of a socially inept and dull man awakened by love. Little about this production worked beyond O'Toole (and a brief appearance by his wife, from whom he was divorced in 1979). Despite his own favorable notices, it was a major box-office flop, setting off a long and bleak period for him at the movies. His clout began to fall with *Brotherly Love/Country Dance*, a comedy with Susannah York that dealt with everybody's favorite topic of incest; *Murphy's War*, a decent World War II adventure in which he was an Irishman valiantly fighting a one-man battle with the Nazis; and *Man of La Mancha*, this time with his vocals dubbed, in a disastrous attempt to put the highly theatrical Broadway hit on film. Under different, non-musical circumstances, he might have made an ideal Don Quixote. That same year, 1972, he recovered somewhat with *The Ruling Class*, throwing himself whole hog into the role of an aristocrat who is lapsing into murder and madness. There was another Oscar nomination for this one, but it was a weird, overlong, and often shrill film — strictly one for the cult crowd. After both *Rosebud*, in which he was a mercenary trying to rescue some kidnapped women, and *Man Friday*, a revisionist take on Robinson Crusoe, received savage reviews and died painful deaths, he found himself in a batch of movies that were simply ignored altogether, *Foxtrot*, *Power Play*, and *Zulu Dawn*.

Appearing as Tiberius in the pseudo-pornographic *Caligula* seemed to indicate that he had bottomed out but there were two glimmers of light ahead. In *The Stunt Man* he rose to the occasion splendidly, as a hypnotically self-involved movie director; and then he parodied his own wrecked state, playing a boozy movie star who gets his chance to shine during a live 1950s television appearance, in the bright comedy *My Favorite Year*. Both reminded audiences of just how exciting he could be given good material; he chalked up Oscar nominations six and seven, still failing to bring home the trophy and thereby tying the record (with buddy Richard Burton) for the performer with the most mentions minus a win. His profile ascended sufficiently at this point to restore his once-illustrious name, but he almost immediately returned to junk, with *Supergirl*, as heroine Helen Slater's mentor; the lead role in *Creator*, as a scientist trying to clone human beings; and *High Spirits*, as a nobleman scheming to get tourists to his castle. One can only hope that he was rewarded with sizable paychecks. There was a high-class production amid these, the 1987 Oscar-winner *The Last Emperor*, in which he played an English tutor and literally stood out among the mostly Asian cast members. Slipping up again, he did several films that either stayed in Europe or went straight to video including *Wings of Fame* and *The Rainbow Thief*, the latter reuniting him with his *Lawrence* co-star, Omar Sharif. He was still seen on a few occasions in more mainstream fare like *King Ralph*, playing straight man to John Goodman; *Fairy Tale: A True Story*, as Arthur Conan Doyle; and *Phantoms*, a horror movie as bad as any he had done. There was a 1992 autobiography, *Loitering With Intent: The Child*, and its 1997 follow-up *Loitering With Intent: The Apprentice*, both of which suggested the summing up of a career fans continued to hope might catch fire again.

Screen: 1960: Kidnapped; The Savage Innocents; The Day They Robbed the Bank of England; 1962: Lawrence of Arabia; 1964: Becket; 1965: Lord Jim; What's New, Pussycat?; The Sandpiper (voice); 1966: The Bible; How to Steal a Million; 1967: The Night of the Generals; Casino Royale; 1968: Great Catherine; The Lion in Winter; 1969: Goodbye, Mr. Chips; 1970: Brotherly Love/Country Dance; 1971: Murphy's War; 1972: Under Milk Wood; The Ruling Class; Man of La Mancha; 1975: Rosebud; Man Friday; 1976: Foxtrot/The Far Side of Paradise (nUSr); 1978: Power Play (dtv); 1980: Caligula (filmed 1977); Zulu Dawn; The Stunt Man; 1982: My Favorite Year; 1984: Supergirl; 1985: Creator; 1986: Club Paradise; 1987: The Last Emperor; 1988: High Spirits; 1990: Wings of Fame (dtv); On a Moonlit Night (nUSr); 1990: The Nutcracker Prince (voice); The Rainbow Thief (dtv); 1991: Isabelle Eberhardt (nUSr); King Ralph; 1992: Rebecca's Daughters (nUSr); 1993: The Seventh Coin; 1997: Fairy Tale: A True Story; 1998: Phantoms; 1999: The Manor (nUSr); Molokai: The Story of Father Damien (dtv); 2002: Global Heresy (dtv); The Final Curtain (nUSr).

NY Stage: 1987: Pygmalion.

Select TV: 1968: Present Laughter (sp); 1976: Rogue Male; 1980: Strumpet City (series); 1981: Masada (ms; theatrical as The Antagonists); 1983: Svengali; Pygmalion (sp); 1984: Kim; 1987: The Dark Angel/Uncle Silas (sp; US: 1991); 1990: Crossing to Freedom/The Pied Piper; 1992: Civvies; 1994: Heaven & Hell: North & South Book II (ms); 1995: Heavy Weather (ms); 1996: Gulliver's Travels; 1998: Coming Home; 1999: Joan of Arc; Jeffrey Bernard Is Unwell (sp; and dir.; prod.).

OUR GANG

Wally Albright
(WALTON ALBRIGHT, JR.): BORN: BURBANK, CA, SEPTEMBER 3, 1925. DIED: AUGUST 7, 1999.

Matthew "Stymie" Beard
BORN: LOS ANGELES, CA, JANUARY 1, 1925. DIED: JANUARY 8, 1981.

Scotty Beckett
BORN: OAKLAND, CA, OCTOBER 4, 1929. DIED: MAY 10, 1968.

Tommy "Butch" Bond
BORN: DALLAS, TX, SEPTEMBER 16, 1926.

Janet Burston
BORN, CA, JANUARY 11, 1935. DIED: MARCH 3, 1998.

Peggy Cartwright
BORN: VANCOUVER, BC, CANADA, NOVEMBER 14, 1912. DIED: JUNE 13, 2001.

Norman "Chubby" Chaney
BORN: BALTIMORE, MD, JANUARY 18, 1918. DIED: MAY 29, 1936.

Joe Cobb
BORN: SHAWNEE, OK, NOVEMBER 7, 1917. DIED: MAY 21, 2002.

Jackie Condon
(JOHN MICHAEL CONDON): BORN: LOS ANGELES, CA, MARCH 25, 1918. DIED: OCTOBER 13, 1977.

Mickey Daniels
(RICHARD DANIELS, JR.): BORN: ROCK SPRINGS, WY, OCTOBER 11, 1914. DIED: AUGUST 20, 1970.

Jean Darling
(DOROTHY JEAN LeVAKE): BORN: SANTA MONICA, CA, AUGUST 23, 1922.

Dorothy "Echo" DeBorba
BORN: LOS ANGELES, CA, MARCH 28, 1925.

Johnny Downs
BORN: BROOKLYN, NY, OCTOBER 10, 1913. DIED: JUNE 6, 1994.

Darla Hood
BORN: LEEDEY, OK, NOVEMBER 8, 1931. DIED: JUNE 13, 1979.

Allen "Farina" Hoskins
BORN: BOSTON, MA, AUGUST 9, 1920. DIED: JULY 26, 1980.

Bobby "Wheezer" Hutchins
BORN: TACOMA, WA, MARCH 29, 1925. DIED: MARCH 17, 1945.

Mary Ann Jackson
BORN: LOS ANGELES, CA, JANUARY 14, 1923.

Darwood "Waldo" Kaye
(DARWOOD KENNETH SMITH): BORN: FORT COLLINS, CO, SEPTEMBER 8, 1929. DIED: MAY 15, 2002.

Leonard "Woim" Kibrick
BORN: MINNEAPOLIS, MN, SEPTEMBER 6, 1924. DIED: JANUARY 4, 1993.

Mary Kornman
IDAHO FALLS, ID, DECEMBER 27, 1915. DIED: JUNE 1, 1973.

Billy "Froggy" Laughlin
BORN: SAN GABRIEL, CA, JULY 5, 1932. DIED: OCTOBER 31, 1948.

Eugene "Porky" Lee
(GORDON EUGENE LEE): BORN: FT. WORTH, TX, OCTOBER 25, 1933.

Kendall "Breezy Brisbane" McComas
BORN: HOLTON, KS, OCTOBER 29, 1916. DIED: OCTOBER 15, 1981.

George "Spanky" McFarland
BORN: DALLAS, TX, OCTOBER 2, 1928. DIED: JUNE 30, 1993.

Dickie Moore
(JOHN RICHARD MOORE, JR.): BORN: LOS ANGELES, CA, SEPTEMBER 12, 1925.

Ernest "Sunshine Sammy" Morrison
(FREDERICK ERNEST MORRISON): BORN: NEW ORLEANS, LA, DECEMBER 20, 1912. DIED: JULY 24, 1989.

Carl "Alfalfa" Switzer
BORN: PARIS, IL, AUGUST 7, 1927. DIED: JANUARY 21, 1959.

Billie "Buckwheat" Thomas
(WILLIAM HENRY THOMAS, JR.): BORN: LOS ANGELES, CA, MARCH 12, 1931. DIED: OCTOBER 10, 1980.

Producer Hal Roach's inspired series of comedic shorts, focusing on the hi-jinks of a group of diverse and rambunctious children, became one of the joys of moviegoing for more than 20 years and stood the test of time beautifully when the films became favorites of subsequent generations in their countless television revivals. Known variously as the "Our Gang Comedies" or "Hal Roach's Rascals" and then, in its television years, as "The Little Rascals," the series began in 1922 with the two-reeler "Our Gang" starring Ernie "Sunshine Sammy" Morrison (the first of several African-American stars of the group; he later joined another series, "East Side Kids"), Jackie Condon, and Peggy Cartwright. Over the years, various kids would be added and dropped, but the first batch to make any impact consisted of Morrison and Condon; excitable Allen "Farina" Hoskins, who went on to appear in more of these shorts than any of the other kids; freckle-faced Mickey Daniels, who pretty much became the centerpiece of the early shorts; Jackie Davis; Mary Kornman; and the requisite over-weight member, Joe Cobb. Of the many kids who were added to the mix in the first couple of years, Johnny Down seemed to catch on most successfully. The trick to what made these comedies work was not only their keenly orchestrated slapstick, but the naturalism with which the youngsters played their scenes together. These were situations people could relate to, with the children coming up with inventive ways to have fun or earn some money, and what resulted was given a wild spin via their humor. There were occasional examples of crudeness and unfortunate lapses into racial quips at the expense of the African-American children. It should be remembered, however, that this series represented a rare case — in a fairly racist and segregated society — in which blacks and whites were seen interacting with one another as equals. The quality of the series (which was released through Pathe up until 1928's "The Smile Wins") lagged by the end of the 1920s, but the Gang received a fresh infusion of life when sound arrived (the first talking Our Gang comedy was "Small Talk" in 1929).

During this transition, sour-faced Mary Ann Jackson and blonde-haired Jean Darling became the female leads, with pint-sized Bobby "Wheezer" Hutchins as the adorable "little guy" of the group, and the mournful, circle-eyed Pete the Pup added for good measure. The "fat kid" role was passed on to Norman "Chubby" Chaney and the series found a genuine star in Jackie Cooper (see separate entry), who first showed up in "Shivering Shakespeare" in 1930. He would go on to become a major box-office attraction the following year with his work in the non-Rascal features Skippy and The Champ. The early 1930s were perhaps the golden period of the Our Gang shorts, with their combination of laugh-out-loud hilarity, pathos, and humanity, as well as moments approaching the surreal in such shorts as "Bear Shooters," "Pups Is Pups," "Teacher's Pet" (with June Marlowe as the charming schoolteacher Miss Crabtree), "School's Out," "Love Business," "Helping Grandma," "Big Ears" and "Dogs Is Dogs." Dorothy "Echo" Deborba was brought along for added girl appeal and the bald-headed, derby-wearing Matthew "Stymie" Beard, with his sassy delivery and impish smile, turned out to be, arguably, the most beloved member in the series's history. Kendall "Breezy Brisbane" McComas showed up to carry some entries but it was the arrival of George "Spanky" McFarland in 1932 (he even rated his own self-titled vehicle that year) that gave the Rascals their most famous and enduring performer. Chubby cheeked, with a floppy golfer's hat and an irresistible pouting face, he became the bona fide star of the two-reelers during the remainder of the 1930s, and would stay with the series even as it entered its down phase at MGM in the early 1940s.

The "Spanky era" also brought forth affable Dickie Moore; tough guy Tommy "Butch" Bond; curly-haired Wally Albright; possibly the cutest of all the children, Scotty Beckett, with his oversized sweater and crooked cap; freckled meanie Leonard "Woim" Kilbrick; the initially androgynous Billie "Buckwheat" Thomas, who went from knee-length pullover and ribbons in his hair to regular boy's clothing and afro; the button-cute, befuddled Eugene "Porky" Lee; the perky Darla Hood; bespectacled and prissy Darwood "Waldo" Kaye; and Spanky's best partner, the squeaky-voiced Carl "Alfalfa" Switzer, whose trademark was a spike of hair atop his head, pointing straight upward. The series was on such a roll during this period that it earned its place in Oscar history when the Gang received the Academy Award for Best Short Subject in 1936 for "Bored of Education." There was also a single feature, General Spanky, which was set during the Civil War, but it was neither good nor very popular and there was no further call for another. The Spanky-Alfalfa-Buckwheat-Porky-Darla series came to an unofficial end in 1938 (with "Hide and Seek"), after which they were no longer produced by Hal Roach, but directly by Roach's distributor, MGM. The series had been reduced to one reel as far back as the Oscar-winning "Bored of Education" and it was decided to keep them at this length. Although the Rascals continued for another six years, these shorts were an increasingly mechanical lot and would not be revered or revived with the official Roach output in the passing years. The two notable additions during this time were Mickey Gubitoski, or Bobby "Mickey" Blake, who, in time, would grow up to become Robert Blake (see separate entry), and the bespectacled Billy "Froggy" Laughlin with his grotesquely guttural, scratchy voice. It all came to an end with "Tale of a Dog" in 1945 (although their penultimate effort, "Dancing Romeo," was actu-ally released two weeks later) with Buckwheat, Froggy, Mickey, and Janet Burston as the stars. There had been 221 titles, more than any other film series.

Screen (shorts): 1922: Our Gang; Fire Fighters; Young Sherlocks; One Terrible Day; A Quiet Street; Saturday Morning; 1923: The Big Show; The Cobbler; The Champeen; Boys to Board; A Pleasant Journey; Giants vs. Yanks; Back Stage; Dogs of War; Lodge Night; July Days; No Noise; Stage Fright; Derby Day; Sunday Calm; 1924: Tire Trouble; Big Business; The Buccaneers; Seein' Things; Commencement Day; Cradle Robbers; Jublio Jr.; It's a Bear; High Society; The Sun Down Limited; Every Man for Himself; Fast Company; The Mysterious Mystery!; 1925: The Big Town; Circus Fever; Dog Days; The Love Bug; Ask Grandma; Shootin' Injuns; Official Officers; Mary — Queen of Tots; Boys Will Be Joys; Your Own Back Yard; Better Movies; One Wild Ride; 1926: Good Cheer; Buried Treasure; Monkey Business; Baby Clothes; Uncle Tom's Uncle; Thundering Fleas; Shivering Spooks; The Fourth Alarm; War Feathers; Telling Whoppers; 1927: Bring Home the Turkey; Seeing the World; Ten Years Old; Love My Dog; Tired Business Men; Baby Brother; The Glorious Fourth; Olympic Games; Chicken Feed; Yale vs. Harvard (first for MGM); The Old Wallop; Heebee Jeebees; Dog Heaven; 1928: Playin' Hooky; Spook Spoofin'; Rainy Days; The Smile Wins; Edison, Marconi & Co.; Barnum & Ringling Inc.; Fair and Muddy; Crazy House; Growing Pains; Old Gray Hoss; School Begins; The Spanking Age; 1929: Election Day; Noisy Noises; The Holy Terror; Wiggle Your Ears; Fast Freight; Small Talk; Little Mother; Railroadin'; Lazy Days; Boxing Gloves; Cat, Dog & Co.; Bouncing Babies; Saturday's Lesson; Moan & Groan Inc.; 1930: Shivering Shakespeare; The First Seven Years; When the Wind Blows; Bear Shooters; A Tough Winter; Pups Is Pups; Teacher's Pet; School's Out; 1931: Helping Grandma; Love Business; Little Daddy; Bargain Day; Fly My Kite; Big Ears; Shiver My Timbers; Dogs Is Dogs; 1932: Readin' and Writin'; Free Eats; Spanky; Choo-Choo!; The Pooch; Hook and Ladder; Free Wheelin'; Birthday Blues; A Lad an' a Lamp; 1933: Fish Hooky; Forgotten Babies; The Kid from Borneo; Mush and Milk; Bedtime Worries; Wild Poses; 1934: Hi-Neighbor!; For Pete's Sake!; The First Round-Up; Honky Donkey; Mike Fright; Washee Ironee; Mama's Little Pirate; Shrimps for a Day; 1935: Anniversary Trouble; Beginner's Luck; Teacher's Beau; Sprucin' Up; Little Papa; Little Sinner; Our Gang Follies of 1936; 1936: The Pinch Singer; Divot Diggers; The Lucky Corner; Second Childhood; Arbor Day; Bored of Education; Two Too Young; Pay as You Exit; Spooky Hooky; 1937: Reunion in Rhythm; Glove Taps; Hearts Are Trumps; Three Smart Boys; Rushin' Ballet; Roamin' Holiday; Night 'n' Gales; Fishy Tales; Framing Youth; The Pigskin Palooka; Mail and Female; Our Gang Follies of 1938; 1938: Canned Fishing; Bear Facts; Three Men in a Tub; Came the Brawn; Feed 'em and Weep; The Awful Tooth; Hide and Shriek; The Little Ranger; Party Fever; Aladdin's Lantern; Men in Fright; Football Romeo; Practical Jokers; 1939: Alfalfa's Aunt; Tiny Troubles; Duel Personalities; Clown Princes; Cousin Wibur; Joy Scouts; Dog Daze; Auto Antics; Captain Spanky's Show Boat; Dad for a Day; Time for Our Lessons; 1940: Alfalfa's Double; The Big Premiere; All About Hash; The New Pupil; Bubbling Troubles; Goin' Fishin'; Good Bad Boys; Waldo's Last Stand; Kiddie Kure; 1941: Fightin' Fools; Baby Blues; Ye Ole Minstrels; 1-2-3 Go!; Robot Wrecks; Helping Hands; Come Back, Miss Pipps; Wedding Worries; 1942: Melodies Old and New; Going to Press; Don't Lie; Surprised Parties; Doin' Their Bit; Rover's Big Chance; Might Lak a Goat; Unexpected Riches; 1943: Benjamin Franklin Jr.; Family Troubles; Calling All Kids; Farm Hands; Election

Daze; Little Miss Pinkerton; Three Smart Guys; 1944: Radio Bugs; Dancing Romeo; Tale of a Dog.

Screen (features): OUR GANG: 1937: General Spanky.

WALLY ALBRIGHT: 1929: The Case of Lena Smith; Thunder; Wonder of Women; The Single Standard; The Trespasser; 1931: Salvation Nell; Sob Sister; The Prodigal; Law of the Sea; East Lynne; 1932: The Silver Lining; Thirteen Women; The Conquerors; End of the Trail; 1933: Zoo in Budapest; Mr. Skitch; The Wrecker; Ann Vickers; 1934: The Count of Monte Cristo; Kid Millions; As the Earth Turns; 1935: Waterfront Lady; Black Fury; O'Shaughnessy's Boy; 1936: The Cowboy Star; 1937: Old Louisiana; Maid of Salem; The Woman I Love; What Price Vengeance?; Captains Courageous; It Happened in Hollywood; Roll Along Cowboy; 1938: Sons of the Legion; King of the Sierras; 1939: Mexicali Rose; 1940: The Grapes of Wrath; Johnny Apollo; 1941: Public Enemies; 1942: Junior Army; A Yank at Eton; 1953: The Wild One.

MATTHEW "STYMIE" BEARD: 1927: Uncle Tom's Cabin; My Best Girl; 1929: Hallelujah; Show Boat; Hearts in Dixie; 1930: Mamba; 1934: Kid Millions; 1935: Captain Blood; 1936: Rainbow on the River; 1937: Penrod and Sam; Slave Ship; 1938: Jezebel; Kentucky; Two Gun Man From Harlem; Beloved Brat; 1939: Way Down South; The Great Man Votes; Swanee River; 1940: Broken Strings; The Return of Jesse James; 1941: Belle Starr; 1943: Stormy Weather; 1944: Show Business; 1945: Fallen Angel; 1947: Dead Reckoning; 1974: Truck Turner; 1976: Disco 9000/Fass Black; 1978: The Buddy Holly Story; 1980: Pray TV.

SCOTTY BECKETT: 1933: Gallant Lady; I Am Suzanne; 1934: Stand Up and Cheer; Babes in Toyland; Sailor Made Widow; Whom the Gods Destroy; George White's Scandals; 1935: Dante's Inferno; Pursuit; I Dream Too Much; 1936: Anthony Adverse; The Charge of the Light Brigade; Old Hutch; The Case Against Mrs. Ames; 1937: Life Begins With Love; Conquest; Wells Fargo; A Doctor's Diary; It Happened in Hollywood; Bad Man From Brimstone; 1938: Marie Antoinette; Listen, Darling; You're Only Young Twice; The Devil's Party; Four's a Crowd; 1939: The Flying Irishman; Mickey the Kid; Our Neighbors the Carters; The Escape; Love Affair; Days of Jesse James; Blind Alley; 1940: Street of Memories; Gold Rush Maisie; My Favorite Wife; The Bluebird; My Son, My Son; 1941: Aloma of the South Seas; Father's Son; The Vanishing Virginian; 1942: Kings Row; Between Us Girls; It Happened in Flatbush; 1943: Heaven Can Wait; Good Luck Mr. Yates; The Boy From Stalingrad; The Youngest Profession; 1944: Ali Baba and the Forty Thieves; The Climax; 1945: Junior Miss; Circumstantial Evidence; 1946: The Jolson Story; My Reputation; White Tie and Tails; Her Adventurous Night; 1947: Cynthia; Dangerous Years; 1948: Michael O'Halloran; A Date With Judy; 1949: Battleground; 1950: Nancy Goes to Rio; The Happy Years; Louisa; 1951: Gasoline Alley; Corky of Gasoline Alley; 1953: Hot News; 1956: Three for Jamie Dawn; 1957: The Oklahomans.

TOMMY "BUTCH" BOND: 1934: Kid Millions; 1936: The Return of Jimmy Valentine; Libeled Lady; Counterfeit; 1937: Married Before Breakfast; Rosalie; Hideaway; 1938: Blockheads; City Streets; 1939: Five Little Peppers and How They Grew; 1940: Five Little Peppers at Home; Five Little Peppers in Trouble; Out West With the Peppers; A Little Bit of Heaven; 1941: New York Town; Adventure in Washington; 1943: This Land Is Mine; 1944: Man From Frisco; 1946: The Beautiful Cheat; 1947: Gas House Kids Go West; Gas House Kids in Hollywood; 1948: Big Town Scandal; Adventures of Superman (ms); 1949: Battleground; Tokyo Joe; Any Number Can Play; 1950: Hot Rod; Atom Man vs. Superman (ms); 1951: Call Me Mister; Bedtime for Bonzo.

JANET BURSTON: 1941: Blondie Goes Latin; 1942: Blondie Goes to College; 1947: Ginger.

PEGGY CARTWRIGHT: 1920: Love; The Third Generation; 1922: Penrod; Afraid to Fight; 1923: Robin Hood Jr.; 1924: A Lady of Quality; The Iron Horse; 1932: Goodnight Vienna.

JOE COBB: 1924: Girl Shy; 1941: Where Did You Get That Girl?; Tuxedo Junction; 1944: Meet Me in St. Louis.

JACKIE CONDON: 1922: Penrod; Doctor Jack; 1924: Girl Shy.

MICKEY DANIELS: 1922: Doctor Jack; 1923: Safety Last; 1924: Girl Shy; 1933: Constant Woman; This Day and Age; 1934: It Happened One Night; Broadway Bill; This Side of Heaven; 1935: Social Error; Roaring Roads; Magnificent Obsession; 1936: The Great Ziegfeld; Early to Bed; Three Men on a Horse; 1937: Mr. Dodd Takes the Air; 1940: Li'l Abner; 1941: Miss Polly; 1945: The Mask of Dijon.

JEAN DARLING: 1933: Only Yesterday; 1934: Jane Eyre; Babes in Toyland; 1953: The I Don't Care Girl.

JOHNNY DOWNS: 1928: The Trail of '98; 1934: Babes in Toyland; 1935: College Scandal; Coronado; So Red the Rose; The Virginia Judge; 1936: The First Baby; Everybody's Old Man; The Arizona Raiders; College Holiday; Pigskin Parade; 1937: Blonde Trouble; Turn Off the Moon; Clarence; Thrill of a Lifetime; 1938: Hold That Co-Ed; Algiers; Swing, Sister, Swing; Hunted Men; 1939: Parents on Trial; Hawaiian Nights; Laugh It Off; Bad Boy; First Offenders; 1940: I Can't Give You Anything But Love, Baby; A Child Is Born; Slightly Tempted; Sing Dance Plenty Hot; Melody and Moonlight; 1941: Honeymoon for Three; Red Head; Adam Had Four Sons; Sing Another Chorus; Moonlight in Hawaii; All-American Co-Ed; 1942: Freckles Comes Home; The Mad Monster; Behind the Eight Ball; 1943: Harvest Melody; Adventures of the Flying Cadets (serial); Campus Rhythm; 1944: What a Man!; Twilight on the Prairie; Trocadero; 1945: Forever Yours; Rhapsody in Blue; 1946: The Kid From Brooklyn; 1949: Square Dance Jubilee; 1950: Hills of Oklahoma; 1953: Column South; The Girls of Pleasure Island; Call Me Madam; Cruisin' Down the River; Here Come the Girls.

DARLA HOOD: 1936: The Bohemian Girl; Neighborhood House; 1939: The Ice Follies of 1939; 1942: Born to Sing; 1943: Happy Land; 1957: Calypso Heat Wave; 1959: The Bat.

ALLEN "FARINA" HOSKINS: 1932: You Said a Mouthful; 1933: The Mayor of Hell; The Life of Jimmy Dolan; 1935: Reckless.

MARY ANN JACKSON: 1931: Laughing Sinners; 1941: Her First Beau; 1950: Ma and Pa Kettle Go to Town.

DARWOOD WALDO KAYE: 1940: Heroes of the Saddle; 1943: Best Foot Forward; 1946: My Reputation.

LEONARD "WOIM" KIBRICK: 1934: Lone Cowboy; Kid Millions; 1935: Under Pressure; 1936: Poor Little Rich Girl; Dimples; 1937: The Great O'Malley; Love Is News; 1938: Love Is a Headache; 1939: Fisherman's Wharf; Rose of Washington Square; Jesse James; It's a Wonderful World; 1942: Roxie Hart.

MARY KORNMAN: 1931: Are These Our Children?; 1933: College Humor; Bondage; Neighbors' Wives; Flying Down to Rio; 1934: The Quitter; Madame DuBarry; Strictly Dynamite; Picture Brides; 1935: Roaring Roads; The Desert Trail; Queen of the Jungle; Adventurous Knights; Smokey Smith; 1936: The Calling of Dan Matthews; 1937: Youth on Parole; Swing It Professor; 1938: King of the Newsboys; I Am a Criminal; 1940: On the Spot.

KENDALL "BREEZY BRISBANE" McCOMAS: 1931: Daddy Long Legs; The Spider; 1933: Man's Castle; 1934: Chained.

GEORGE "SPANKY" McFARLAND: 1933: Day of Reckoning; 1934: Kentucky Kernels; Miss Fane's Baby is Stolen; 1935: Here Comes the Band; O'Shaughnessy's Boy; 1936: The Trail of the Lonesome Pine; 1938: Peck's Bad Boy With the Circus; 1943: Johnny Doughboy; I Escaped From the Gestapo; 1944: The

Cowboy and the Senorita; The Woman in the Window; 1986: The Aurora Encounter (dtv).

DICKIE MOORE: 1927: The Beloved Rogue; 1928: Object Alimony; 1929: Madame X; 1930: The Three Sisters; Sons of the Gods; Let Us Be Gay; The Matrimonial Bed; Passion Flower; Lawful Larceny; 1931: Aloha; Seed; Three Who Loved; Confessions of a Co-Ed; The Star Witness; The Squaw Man; Husband's Holiday; Manhattan Parade; 1932: Union Depot; The Expert; Disorderly Conduct; So Big; Million Dollar Legs; Winner Take All; Deception; Blonde Venus; Racing Strain; No Greater Love; Fireman, Save My Child; The Devil Is Driving; 1933: Oliver Twist; Gabriel Over the White House; Man's Castle; Cradle Song; The Wolf Dog; Obey the Law; 1934: Gallant Lady; Upperworld; In Love With Life; Fifteen Wives; The Human Side; This Side of Heaven; 1935: Tomorrow's Youth; Little Men; Without Children; Peter Ibbetson; The World Accuses; Swellhead; So Red the Rose; Timothy's Quest; 1936: The Little Red School House; The Story of Louis Pasteur; 1937: The Life of Emile Zola; The Bride Wore Red; Madame X; 1938: Love, Honor and Behave; The Gladiator; My Bill; The Arkansas Traveler; 1939: The Under-Pup; Hidden Power; 1940: A Dispatch From Reuters; 1941: Sergeant York; The Great Mr. Nobody; 1942: The Adventures of Martin Eden; Miss Annie Rooney; 1943: Jive Junction; The Song of Bernadette; Heaven Can Wait; Happy Land; 1944: The Eve of St. Mark; Youth Runs Wild; Sweet and Lowdown; 1947: Out of the Past; Dangerous Years; 1948: Behind Locked Doors; 16 Fathoms Deep; 1949: Bad Boy; Tuna Clipper; 1950: Killer Shark; Cody of the Pony Express; 1952: The Member of the Wedding; Eight Iron Men.

ERNEST "SUNSHINE SAMMY" MORRISON: 1916: Soul of a Child; 1918: Out West; 1918: Dolly Does Her Bit; Winning Grandma; Dolly's Vacation; Milady o' the Beanstalk; 1919: The Little Diplomat; Peggy Does Her Darnedest; 1920: Get Out and Get Under; 20 Haunted Spooks; Number Please?; 1922: Penrod; 1940: Gang War/Crime Street; I Can't Give You Anything But Love, Baby; Boys of the City; That Gang of Mine; Fugitive From a Prison Camp; 1941: Pride of the Bowery; Flying Wild; Bowery Blitzkrieg; Spooks Run Wild; Mr. Wise Guy; In This Our Life; Let's Get Tough!; Smart Alecks; 'Neath Brooklyn Bridge; 1943: Kid Dynamite; The Ape Man; Hit Parade of 1943; Clancy Street Boys; Ghosts on the Loose; 1944: Follow the Leader; Greenwich Village; 1976: Jim, the World's Greatest.

CARL "ALFALFA" SWITZER: 1936: Easy to Take; Kelly the Second; Too Many Parents; 1937: Pick a Star; Wild and Woolly; 1938: Scandal Street; 1939: The Ice Follies of 1939; 1940: I Love You Again; Barnyard Follies; 1941: Reg'lar Fellers; 1942: There's One Born Every Minute; My Favorite Blonde; Henry and Dizzy; The War Against Mrs. Hadley; Mrs. Wiggs of the Cabbage Patch; Johnny Doughboy; 1943: Dixie; The Human Comedy; Shantytown; 1944: Together Again; Rosie the Riveter; Going My Way; The Great Mike; 1945: She Wouldn't Say Yes; Man Alive; 1946: Gas House Kids; Courage of Lassie; It's a Wonderful Life; 1947: Gas House Kids Go West; Gas House Kids in Hollywood; 1948: On Our Merry Way; State of the Union; Big Town Scandal; 1949: A Letter to Three Wives; 1950: Redwood Forest Trail; House by the River; 1951: Cause for Alarm!; Here Comes the Groom; Two Dollar Bettor; 1952: I Dream of Jeannie; Pat and Mike; The WAC from Walla Walla; 1953: Island in the Sky; 1954: The High and the Mighty; Track of the Cat; This Is My Love; 1955: Not as a Stranger; 1956: Between Heaven and Hell; Dig That Uranium; The Ten Commandments; 1957: Motorcycle Gang; 1958: The Defiant Ones.

BILLIE "BUCKWHEAT" THOMAS: 1942: Mokey; Whistling in Dixie; 1943: Honeymoon Lodge; 1945: Colorado Pioneers.

MARIA OUSPENSKAYA

BORN: TULA, RUSSIA, JULY 29, 1876. ED: WARSAW CONSERVATORY, ADASHEFF'S SCHOOL OF DRAMA. DIED: DECEMBER 3, 1949.

With only 20 American movie credits to her name, the teensy, deadly serious, and often creepily mysterious Maria Ouspenskaya was an unforgettable addition to the Hollywood scene. A member of Stanislavsky's famed Moscow Art Theatre, she came with them to America in 1923 and stayed on to open an acting school, while continuing to perform in the theater. In 1929 she began the Maria Ouspenskaya School of Dramatic Art in both New York and Hollywood, thereby making a name for herself among the acting community before she finally accepted an offer to appear in an American motion picture. The role of the bitchy baroness, who doesn't want Ruth Chatterton to marry her son, was one she had done in the Broadway version of *Dodsworth*, and she made such an impression in this extremely brief part that she earned an Oscar nomination. Three years later she was in the running again for one of her most famous roles, the wise and kindly grandmother of Charles Boyer, in the hit romantic drama *Love Affair*. After that, she was the first on call for wizened old crones in movies such as *The Rains Came*, as the rigid Maharanee; *Waterloo Bridge*, again none too lovable, as the stern ballet teacher; *Dr. Erlich's Magic Bullet*, helping Edward G. Robinson to finance his experiments to cure syphilis; *The Mortal Storm*, as James Stewart's mother; *Kings Row*, as Robert Cummings's grandmother; *The Wolf Man*, as Maleva the Gypsy, another signature part and one which she repeated, in *Frankenstein Meets the Wolf Man*; and *The Shanghai Gesture*, as a mute. The assignments started getting less prestigious with RKO's *Tarzan and the Amazons*, and she was already starting to slow down at the time of her tragic death, falling asleep while smoking a cigarette and perishing in the subsequent fire.

Screen: 1915: Sverchok Na Pechi/The Cricket on the Hearth; 1916: Nichtozhniye/Worthless; 1917: Belated Flowers/Dr. Toporkov; 1919: Zazhivo Pogrebennii/Buried Alive; 1923: Khveska/Hospital Guard Khveska; 1929: Tanka the Innkeeper and Her Father; 1936: Dodsworth; 1937: Conquest; 1939: Love Affair; The Rains Came; Judge Hardy and Son; 1940: Beyond Tomorrow; Waterloo Bridge; Dr. Ehrlich's Magic Bullet; The Mortal Storm; Dance, Girl, Dance; The Man I Married; 1941: The Wolf Man; The Shanghai Gesture; 1942: Kings Row; The Mystery of Marie Roget; 1943: Frankenstein Meets the Wolf Man; 1945: Tarzan and the Amazons; 1946: I've Always Loved You; 1947: Wyoming; 1949: A Kiss in the Dark.

NY Stage: 1923: Tsar Fyodor Ivanovitch; 1924: The Saint; 1925: The Jest; 1926: The Witch; 1927: The Taming of the Shrew; 1930: The Three Sisters; 1931: The Passing Present; 1934: Dodsworth; 1935: Abide With Me; 1936: Daughters of Atreus; 1943: Outrageous Fortune.

LYNNE OVERMAN

BORN: MARYVILLE, MO, SEPTEMBER 19, 1887. ED: UNIV. OF MO. DIED: FEBRUARY 19, 1943.

A staple of the Paramount stock company for close to ten years, Lynne Overman was one of the period's premier wisecrackers and sardonic sidekicks. Leaving behind careers as a jockey and a minstrel, he began legit acting in 1907 and made his Broadway debut nine years later, in *Fair and Warmer*. After a break to serve in the Navy, he shuttled back and forth between the London and New York stage until Paramount signed him to a contract in 1934. Although he started off in *Midnight*, a Universal film for which he was loaned out, he was seldom seen in pictures thereafter other than those from his home studio. These films included *Little Miss Marker*, as Adolphe Menjou's buddy, Regret; *She Loves Me Not*, as a press agent; *Men Without Names*, as a government agent helping Fred MacMurray trap some gangsters; *Collegiate*, as a character called Sour-Puss; *Poppy*, as a corrupt lawyer who hopes to discredit W. C. Fields and marry a rich countess; *Wild Money*, as a reporter vying with Edward Everett Horton for the attention of Louise Campbell; *Hotel Haywire*, as the dentist falsely accused of cheating on wife Mary Carlisle; *Death of a Champion*, top billed as a "human encyclopedia," involved in a murder at a dog show; *Typhoon*, as a submarine skipper who shanghais Robert Preston; *North West Mounted Police*, as a Scottish scout; *Caught in the Draft*, as Bob Hope's agent who is drafted into the army along with his cowardly client; and *Star Spangled Rhythm*, sharing the sketch "If Men Played Cards as Men Do" with Fred MacMurray, Franchot Tone, and Ray Milland. He died of a heart attack at the age of 55.

Screen: 1928: Perfect Crime; 1934: Midnight; Little Miss Marker; The Great Flirtation; Broadway Bill; She Loves Me Not; You Belong to Me; 1935: Enter Madame!; Rumba; Paris in Spring; Men Without Names; Two for Tonight; Collegiate; 1936: Poppy; Yours for the Asking; Three Married Men; The Jungle Princess; 1937: Blonde Trouble; Partners in Crime; Nobody's Baby; Don't Tell the Wife; Murder Goes to College; Wild Money; Hotel Haywire; Night Club Scandal; True Confession; 1938: The Big Broadcast of 1938; Her Jungle Love; Hunted Men; Spawn of the North; Sons of the Legion; Men With Wings; Ride a Crooked Mile; 1939: Persons in Hiding; Death of a Champion; Union Pacific; 1940: Edison, the Man; Typhoon; Safari; North West Mounted Police; 1941: Aloma of the South Seas; Caught in the Draft; New York Town; There's Magic in Music; 1942: Roxie Hart; Reap the Wild Wind; The Forest Rangers; Silver Queen; Star Spangled Rhythm; 1943: Dixie; The Desert Song.

NY Stage: 1919: Come-On Charlie; 1920: Honey Girl; 1921: Just Married; 1927: The Gossipy Sex; People Don't Do Such Things; 1928: Sunny Days; 1929: Button Button; 1930: Dancing Partner; 1931: Company's Coming; 1932: Hot-Cha!; The Budget.

REGINALD OWEN

(JOHN REGINALD OWEN) BORN: WHEATHAMPSTEAD, HERTFORDSHIRE, ENGLAND, AUGUST 5, 1887. ED: TREE'S ACAD. OF DRAMATIC ARTS, LONDON. DIED: NOVEMBER 5, 1972.

One of those undeniably British character players who seemed to be around everywhere you looked, Reginald Owen had a theatre career dating back to his London debut in 1905, in *The Tempest*. Two decades later he came to America to appear onstage, first in Chicago and then on Broadway in *The Carolinian*. U.S. movie audiences first saw him as Jeanne Eagles's husband in Paramount's 1929 version of *The Letter*. He was Robert Montgomery's unsympathetic brother in *The Man in Possession*; Dr. Watson to Clive Brook's interpretation of *Sherlock Holmes*, and then Holmes himself in the ultra-cheap version of *A Study in Scarlet*; King Louis XV in both *Voltaire* and *Madame DuBarry*; the Prince whom Greta Garbo is none too excited about marrying in *Queen Christina*; and the man who comes to Leslie Howard's rescue by offering him employment in *Of Human Bondage*. In 1935 MGM placed him

under contract and he would remain in their employ for the next 18 years. Aside from scoring the leading role of Scrooge in one of the less satisfying versions of Dickens's *A Christmas Carol*, he was an ever-present face (though his countenance was less distinctive than many other ubiquitous character players) in scores of movies including *A Tale of Two Cities*, as the lawyer, Stryver; *Anna Karenina*, as Garbo's no-good brother; the 1936 Best Picture-winner, *The Great Ziegfeld*, as that man's business manager; *The Bride Wore Red*, as an Italian admiral; *Rosalie*, as the chancellor; *Kidnapped*, as the captain who snatches up Freddie Bartholomew; *Everybody Sing*, as the head of a family of screwballs; the Oscar-winning *Mrs. Miniver*, as the air-raid warden; *Woman of the Year*, as a lawyer; *Above Suspicion*, as a Nazi; *The Canterville Ghost*, as Charles Laughton's hateful father; *National Velvet*, as a farmer; *Cluny Brown*, as Jennifer Jones's employer; *Green Dolphin Street*, as a sea captain; and *The Secret Garden*, as the groundskeeper who helps bring the title location alive again. On one of his loan-outs, to Paramount, he was asked to reprise Louis XV, albeit in a lighter vein, for Bob Hope's *Monsieur Beaucaire*. Still going strong in his senior years, Disney fans saw him as the eccentric Admiral Boom in *Mary Poppins* and as a general in *Bedknobs and Broomsticks*.

Screen: 1916: Sally in Our Alley; 1923: Phroso; 1929: The Letter; 1931: Platinum Blonde; The Man in Possession; 1932: A Woman Commands; Lovers Courageous; Sherlock Holmes; The Man Called Back; Downstairs; 1933: Robber's Roost; The Big Brain; Double Harness; A Study in Scarlet (and co-wr.); The Narrow Corner; Voltaire; Robbers' Roost; Queen Christina; 1934: Nana; Stingaree; Of Human Bondage; The Human Side; The House of Rothschild; The Countess of Monte Cristo; Here Is My Heart; Fashions of 1934; Mandalay; Madame DuBarry; Where Sinners Meet; Music in the Air; 1935: Enchanted April; Anna Karenina; The Bishop Misbehaves; Escapade; A Tale of Two Cities; The Good Fairy; The Call of the Wild; 1936: Petticoat Fever; Rose-Marie; Yours for the Asking; Adventure in Manhattan; The Girl on the Front Page; Love on the Run; Trouble for Two; The Great Ziegfeld; 1937: Conquest; Rosalie; The Bride Wore Red; Madame X; Personal Property; Dangerous Number; 1938: Kidnapped; The Girl Downstairs; Everybody Sing; Paradise for Three; A Christmas Carol; Three Loves Has Nancy; Vacation From Love; 1939: Fast and Loose; Hotel Imperial; Bridal Suite; The Real Glory; Remember?; Bad Little Angel; 1940: Hullabaloo; The Earl of Chicago; Florian; The Ghost Comes Home; 1941: Free and Easy; Blonde Inspiration; Tarzan's Secret Treasure; A Woman's Face; They Met in Bombay; Lady Be Good; Charley's Aunt; 1942: Random Harvest; We Were Dancing; I Married an Angel; Pierre of the Plains; Somewhere I'll Find You; Cairo; White Cargo; Reunion in France; Woman of the Year; Mrs. Miniver; 1943: Assignment in Britanny; Madame Curie; Three Hearts for Julia; Above Suspicion; Forever and a Day; Salute to the Marines; 1944: The Canterville Ghost; 1945: National Velvet; Captain Kidd; She Went to the Races; The Valley of Decision; The Sailor Takes a Wife; Kitty; 1946: Monsieur Beaucaire; Diary of a Chambermaid; Cluny Brown; Piccadilly Incident; 1947: Thunder in the Valley; The Imperfect Lady; Green Dolphin Street; If Winter Comes; 1948: The Pirate; Julia Misbehaves; Hills of Home; The Three Musketeers; 1949: The Secret Garden; Challenge to Lassie; 1950: Kim; Grounds for Marriage; The Miniver Story; 1953: The Great Diamond Robbery; 1954: Red Garters; 1958: Darby's Rangers; 1962: Five Weeks in a Balloon; 1963: Tammy and the Doctor; The Thrill of It All; 1964: Voice of the Hurricane; Mary Poppins; 1967: Rosie!; 1971: Bedknobs and Broomsticks.

NY Stage: 1925: The Carolinian; 1926: Little Eyolf; The Importance of Being Earnest; The Play's the Thing; 1927: Skin Deep; The Marquise; 1928: The Three Musketeers; 1929:

Candle-Light; **1930:** Out of a Blue Sky; Petticoat Influence; **1932:** Through the Years; Child of Manhattan; **1950:** Affairs of State; **1972:** A Funny Thing Happened on the Way to the Forum.

Select TV: **1959:** The Dream (sp); A Diamond Is a Boy's Best Friend (sp).

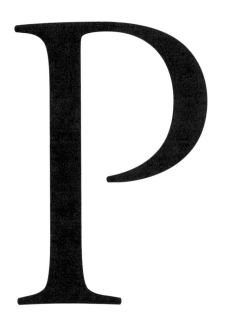

P

GERALDINE PAGE

Born: Kirksville, MO, November 22, 1924.
ed: Goodman Theatre School.
Died: June 13, 1987.

Spinsters, unstable or vulnerable ladies, and persons hanging on by an emotional thread — Geraldine Page cornered the market in these types and became one of the most acclaimed actresses of her generation. If there was a habit of pouring on the weird tics a bit, it could be chalked up to her refusal to play it safe and easy. Despite the fact that most people considered her a figure of the stage, she had a pretty damn good run of luck in the movies with some extremely worthy parts and eight Oscar nominations for her efforts. After studying acting at the Goodman Theatre School in Chicago, she performed in stock and in *Out of the Night*, an obscure 1947 movie produced by the Moody Bible Institute, the distribution history of which is unclear. Once in New York, she did the expected early live TV guest shots while studying with Uta Hagen. Her big break came in 1952 when she won the lead role of the shy Southern spinster Alma Winemiller in Tennessee Williams's *Summer and Smoke*, which made her the next big thing in the world of Off Broadway. She made her Broadway debut the following year in *Mid-Summer*, receiving a Theatre World Award for her work. Hollywood got wind of her favorable notices and gave her a nothing role in *Taxi* and, more significantly, the female lead in the John Wayne hit *Hondo*, as the gentle pioneer woman with whom he falls in love. The credits inaccurately announced "introducing Geraldine Page" and, perhaps as a way of welcoming her to the movies, she received a supporting Oscar nomination for her thoroughly professional but rather unremarkable performance.

In any event, the welcome did not include any other jobs, so she went back east and did, among others, *The Rainmaker* and *Sweet Bird of Youth*, the latter allowing her to play another juicy Williams heroine — a drugged-up, fading movie star. Eight years had passed without another motion picture credit but suddenly the film industry was interested all over again and she got to repeat her two big Williams stage roles on film. It was only fitting that both Paramount's *Summer and Smoke* and MGM's *Sweet*

Bird of Youth earned her two more Oscar nominations, as Page was among the better things about two fairly weak adaptations. One of her co-stars in the latter, Rip Torn, became her husband in 1963 and remained so until her death. Staying spinsterish, she was Dean Martin's annoyingly possessive sister in *Toys in the Attic* and then had a showcase as a postmistress (in movie terms this meant spinster) having a fling with Glenn Ford while in Manhattan in the innocuous *Dear Heart*. Of these, the only one to have any degree of box-office success was *Sweet Bird*, a fact no doubt contributed more to co-star Paul Newman than to Page.

Between trips back to the theater, she and Torn were Peter Kastner's overbearing parents in the anything-goes comedy *You're a Big Boy Now*, and the Academy must've been crazy about her because this cartoonish performance got her Oscar nod number four. On TV she won an Emmy Award as the kindly aunt in the adaptation of Truman Capote's *A Christmas Memory* (it was later added to a theatrical compilation called *Trilogy*) and she dueted with Gladys Cooper on the song "There Are Those" in the Disney musical *The Happiest Millionaire*, playing John Davidson's snobby mom. Back in a lead, she was the evil lady whom Ruth Gordon hopes to expose as a murderer in an enjoyable bit of the macabre, *What Ever Happened to Aunt Alice?*, and won a second Emmy Award for *The Thanksgiving Visitor*, once again playing the same character she'd done so splendidly in *A Christmas Memory*. She was then a weird schoolmistress in a disturbing Clint Eastwood flop *The Beguiled*; Cliff Robertson's mom (she was actually only one year older than he was) in *J. W. Coop*; Carol Burnett's flamboyant matchmaking friend in *Pete 'n' Tillie* (Oscar nominated); an evangelist in *The Day of the Locust*, fitting right into to this collection of Los Angeles grotesques; and an unorthodox nun in *Nasty Habits*, which also found Torn among the cast.

There was another triumphant lead, as the hopelessly neurotic mother, a woman seeking perfection as her life crumbles around her, in Woody Allen's first foray into out-and-out drama, *Interiors*. This resulted in her sixth mention from Oscar, after which she seemed to segue back into supporting roles including *Honky Tonk Freeway*, as another comical nun; *I'm Dancing as Fast as I Can*, as a cancer patient; *The Pope of Greenwich Village*, in a wonderfully showy, Oscar-nominated role as the tough, bitter mom of a murdered cop; *The Bride*, in a worthless servitude part; and *White Nights*, playing it relatively normal as Mikhail Baryshnikov's agent. Fortunately there was one more golden starring role to be had, the lonely old lady who takes off to visit her childhood home in Horton Foote's *The Trip to Bountiful*. This was Page at her absolute peak — full of life and sensitivity, as a gentle-hearted, emotional woman facing her mortality; it was only fitting that this was the one that finally earned her the Academy Award. There was nothing special about her follow-up assignments in two barely seen productions, *My Little Girl* and *Native Son*, so it was not surprising that she found solace back in New York for an abbreviated run on Broadway as Madame Arcati in a revival of *Blithe Spirit*. When she failed to show up for a matinee performance, it was discovered that she had suffered a heart attack and died at her Manhattan home.

Screen: 1947: Out of the Night; 1953: Taxi; Hondo; 1961: Summer and Smoke; 1962: Sweet Bird of Youth; 1963: Toys in the Attic; 1964: Dear Heart; 1966: The Three Sisters; You're a Big Boy Now; 1967: La Chica del Lunes/Monday's Child (nUSr); The Happiest Millionaire; 1969: What Ever Happened to Aunt Alice?; Trilogy (incl. A Christmas Memory from TV); 1971: The Beguiled; 1972: J. W. Coop; Pete 'n' Tillie; 1973: Happy as the Grass Was Green/Hazel's People; 1975: The Day of the Locust; 1977: Nasty Habits; The Rescuers (voice); 1978: Interiors; 1981: Harry's War; Honky Tonk Freeway; 1982: I'm Dancing as Fast as I Can; 1984: The Pope of Greenwich Village; 1985: The Bride; Flanagan/Walls of Glass; White Nights; The Trip to Bountiful; 1986: My Little Girl; Native Son.

NY Stage: 1952: Yerma (ob); Summer and Smoke (ob); 1953: Mid-Summer; 1954: The Immoralist; The Rainmaker; 1956: The Innkeepers; 1957: Separate Tables; 1959: Sweet Bird of Youth; 1963: Strange Interlude; 1964: The Three Sisters; P.S. I Love You; 1966: The Great Indoors; 1967: Black Comedy/White Lies; 1969: Angela; 1973: Look Away (ob); 1974: Absurd Person Singular; 1977: Creditors (ob); The Stronger (ob); Miss Julie (ob); 1980: Clothes for a Summer Hotel; Mixed Couples; 1982: Agnes of God; 1983: The Inheritors (ob); 1984: Paradise Lost (ob); Ghosts (ob); 1985: The Madwoman of Chaillot (ob); Clarence (ob); Vivat! Vivat! Regina (ob); A Lie of the Mind (ob); 1986: The Circle (ob); 1987: Blithe Spirit.

Select TV: 1952: The Shadowy Third (sp); 1954: Miss Look-alike (sp); 1955: The Turn of the Screw (sp); Shoot It Again (sp); The Hill Wife (sp); 1957: Fire and Ice (sp); Portrait of a Murderer (sp); 1958: No Hiding Place (sp); Old Man (sp); 1959: People Kill People (sp); 1966: Barefoot in Athens (sp); A Christmas Memory (sp); 1968: The Thanksgiving Visitor (sp); 1971: Monterrat (sp); 1972: Look Homeward Angel (sp); 1974: Live Again, Die Again; 1977: Something for Joey; 1982: The Blue and the Gray (ms); 1984: The Parade; The Dollmaker; 1985: The Adventures of Huckleberry Finn; 1986: Nazi Hunter: The Beate Klarsfeld Story.

DEBRA PAGET

(DEBRALEE GRIFFIN) BORN: DENVER, CO, AUGUST 19, 1933.

An all-purpose ingénue who was very prominent at 20th Century-Fox during the early 1950s, Debra Paget wound up being better remembered for her nice looks than a memorable legacy of work. She was offered a contract with that studio when she was just 15 years old and was promptly assigned to the cast of the crime drama *Cry of the City*. Attention first came in 1950 when she played the delicate Indian girl whom scout James Stewart weds and loses to violence in the popular and

important western *Broken Arrow*. It was one of the earliest movies to examine the abuse of Native Americans, though Paget couldn't have looked less authentically Indian if she tried. Because of the acclaim this film rightly received, the size of her roles increased, with *Anne of the Indies*, as Louis Jourdan's wife, who is kidnapped by lady pirate Jean Peters, and the most unnecessary remake of *Bird of Paradise*, as a Polynesian lovely dallying with Jourdan yet again. She was Cosette in the 1952 version of *Les Misérables* and a fictionalized singer-dancer who marries Robert Wagner in the John Philip Sousa bio *The Stars and Stripes Forever*. Apparently finding her most at ease in costume pictures and period adventures, the studio put her into *Prince Valiant*, again opposite Wagner, though Janet Leigh filled the chief female role; the kitschy *Princess of the Nile*, leading her people against evil Michael Rennie, while doing some exotic dancing on the side; *The Gambler From Natchez*, as a curvaceous river girl with her eye on Dale Robertson; and *White Feather*, back in the wigwam, as a Native American named Appearing Day, who falls in love with surveyor Wagner. There were large audiences for *Love Me Tender*, because Elvis Presley was making his film debut in it, and over at Paramount, Cecil B. DeMille's super-spectacle *The Ten Commandments*, in which she shared the secondary love interest storyline with John Derek. Fritz Lang took her to Germany to appear as an Indian dancer in both *The Tiger of Eschnapur* and *The Indian Tomb*, which were spliced together for their American release, becoming *Journey to the Lost City*. Her career ended with roles in two Vincent Price thrillers for AIP, *Tales of Terror* and *The Haunted Palace*, after which she married an oil tycoon and retired from the business in 1964.

Screen: 1948: Cry of the City; 1949: It Happens Every Spring; Mother Is a Freshman; House of Strangers; 1950: Broken Arrow; 1951: Fourteen Hours; Bird of Paradise; Anne of the Indies; 1952: Belles on Their Toes; Les Miserables; The Stars and Stripes Forever; 1954: Prince Valiant; Demetrius and the Gladiators; Princess of the Nile; The Gambler From Natchez; 1955: White Feather; Seven Angry Men; 1956: The Last Hunt; Love Me Tender; The Ten Commandments; 1957: The River's Edge; Omar Khayyam; 1958: From the Earth to the Moon; 1959: Journey to the Lost City (The Tiger Eschnapur/The Indian Tomb); 1960: Why Must I Die?; The Highwaymen; Cleopatra's Daughter; 1961: The Most Dangerous Man Alive; 1962: Tales of Terror; I Masnaderieri (nUSr); 1964: The Haunted Palace.

Select TV: 1956: Gun in His Hand (sp); The Man Who Lost His Head (sp).

JANIS PAIGE

(DONNA MAE TJADEN) BORN: TACOMA, WA, SEPTEMBER 16, 1922.

A brassy, colorful showgirl type, Janis Page seemed game to take charge of the musical genre though her chances to shine in anything above the ordinary were few. After an attempt to sing opera didn't pan out, she moved with her mother to Los Angeles where she earned her keep working at the Hollywood Canteen. She got a chance to perform there, was spotted by a Metro talent scout, and signed to a contract where she was given only one assignment, *Bathing Beauty*, then dropped. Warners scooped her up and started her off, appropriately enough, in a small part in *Hollywood Canteen*. After a straight role, as the nice girl who loves tormented Paul Henreid, in the remake of *Of Human Bondage*, and a singing one, as a gangster's moll in *Her Kind of Man*, the studio added her to their musical stable where she was a decided plus to *Two Guys From*

Milwaukee; *The Time, the Place and the Girl*; *One Sunday Afternoon*, as the strawberry blonde; and *Romance on the High Seas*, where the real star was newcomer Doris Day. She was just right for playing Wild West floozies, as she did in *Cheyenne* and *The Younger Brothers*, but the studio wasn't sufficiently impressed and dropped her in 1950. Since nothing interesting was going on in her movie career, she wisely turned to the theater and scored a major triumph in the Broadway musical hit *The Pajama Game*. When every principal member of the stage cast *but* Paige was asked to do the film version (Doris Day got her part) there was compensation when she wound up nearly stealing the show in MGM's *Silk Stockings*, as a saucy movie star, especially in the "Stereophonic Sound" duet with Fred Astaire. Her comic expertise was on hand in *Please Don't Eat the Daisies* (again backing up Day) and *Bachelor in Paradise*, among others, and she appeared as prostitutes in both *The Caretakers* and *Welcome to Hard Times*, before her larger-than-life persona was retired by the oncoming realism of late 1960s cinema. After that she showed up almost exclusively on television or onstage.

Screen: 1944: Bathing Beauty; Hollywood Canteen; 1946: Of Human Bondage; Her Kind of Man; Two Guys From Milwaukee; The Time, the Place and the Girl; 1947: Love and Learn; Cheyenne; 1948: Always Together; Winter Meeting; Wallflower; Romance on the High Seas; One Sunday Afternoon; 1949: The Younger Brothers; The House Across the Street; 1950: This Side of the Law; 1951: Mr. Universe; Fugitive Lady; Two Gals and a Guy; 1957: Silk Stockings; 1960: Please Don't Eat the Daisies; 1961: Bachelor in Paradise; 1963: Follow the Boys; The Caretakers; 1967: Welcome to Hard Times; 1994: Natural Causes (dtv).

NY Stage: 1951: Remains to Be Seen; 1954: The Pajama Game; 1963: Here's Love; 1968: Mame; 1984: Alone Together.

Select TV: 1955–56: It's Always Jan (series); 1957: The Latch Key (sp); 1958: Roberta (sp); 1959: Chez Rouge (sp); 1962: Blues for a Hanging (sp); 1963: Last of the Private Eyes (sp); 1969: Roberta (sp); 1975: The Turning Point of Jim Malloy; 1976: The Return of Joe Forrester/Cop on the Beat; Lanigan's Rabbi; 1977: Lanigan's Rabbi (series); 1980: Valentine Magic on Love Island; Angel on My Shoulder; 1981: Bret Maverick; 1983: The Other Woman; Gun Shy (series); Baby Makes Five (series); 1985–86: Trapper John M.D. (series); 1987: Capitol (series); 1989: General Hospital (series); 1990–93: Santa Barbara (series)

JACK PALANCE

(VOLADIMIR PALAHNUIK)
BORN: LATTIMER, PA, FEBRUARY 18, 1919.
ED: UNIV. OF NC, STANFORD UNIV.

Definitely not a pretty face, Jack Palance couldn't help but become one of Hollywood's fiercest villains, with his harsh, breathy voice, flattened nose, and reconstructed, war-scared features. That this sometimes riveting, but just as often hammy, player branched out on several occasions into leads and stuck around long enough to become something of an icon was the real surprise. His war injuries came in a flight-training accident during his World War II stint in the Air Force. After his discharge he meant to study journalism but fell into theatrics instead. He landed his first Broadway role almost instantly, playing a Russian guard in *The Big Two*, in 1947. He was asked to understudy Anthony Quinn in the tour of *A Streetcar Named Desire*, which led to his taking over for Brando back on Broadway for a brief period. That play's director, Elia Kazan, liked him enough to cast him in his gripping film thriller *Panic in the Streets*. Billed as

Walter Palance, he made a most forceful debut as the desperate killer who, along with sidekick Zero Mostel, unwittingly begins spreading a deadly virus throughout New Orleans. Following his role as one of the Marines in Fox's well-attended *Halls of Montezuma*, he returned to Broadway where he received a Theatre World Award for his work in *Darkness at Noon*. Hollywood wanted him back as soon as possible and he scored two home runs in a row, earning back-to-back Oscar nominations, for playing the scorned actor who marries and then plots to dispose of Joan Crawford in *Sudden Fear*, and, better yet, the cold-blooded hired gun in the classic western, *Shane*, leaving his mark as one of the most loathsome of all movie bad guys. Despite his unconventional looks, the success of these films dictated that he could now be upped to leads. He was a convincing-looking Apache Indian in *Arrowhead*; a man suspected of being Jack the Ripper in *Man in the Attic*; and Attila the Hun in *The Sign of the Pagan*, in each case emphasizing his menacing side. After his ludicrous work as the wicked magician in the epic *The Silver Chalice*, he pulled out all the stops as the manic movie star on the edge in the film version of the stage hit *The Big Knife*. Foolishly, he then tried to follow in Bogart's footsteps, playing a gunman on the run in *I Died a Thousand Times*, a remake of *High Sierra*. His fine work as the lieutenant, who suffers because of the incompetence around him, in the gritty war film *Attack*, further proved that, even as the hero, he was not a sympathetic presence. Around the same time, he won an Emmy Award for playing one of his most famous roles — the pathetic, washed-up prizefighter in Rod Serling's *Requiem for a Heavyweight*.

He played Anthony Perkins's absent dad (one assumes Tony's character's good looks came from his mother's side of the family) in the western *The Lonely Man*, and twins in *The House of Numbers*, but neither signaled that there was much interest in him as a headliner where the box office was concerned. Not surprisingly, he went to Europe where he did come international offerings like *The Mongols*, as Genghis Khan's kid, and *Barabbas*, snarling to the hilt as a vicious gladiator. It seemed as if he'd been away from American productions for quite some time when he showed up as the Mexican villain, who turns out to be not so bad after all, in the hit action film *The Professionals*. The high profile status of this piece did not mean he was going to cease heading in whatever direction he could to find work, however. During the late 1960s and early 1970s, his name was found on all kinds of blink-and-you-miss-them international efforts, horror thrillers, westerns, adventures, and whatnots — few of which made so much as a dent in the U.S. market. Among the better known, but not necessarily high quality, productions were *They Came to Rob Las Vegas*, as the cop on the trail of the thieves; *Che!*, a career low point, as Fidel Castro; *Monte Walsh*, teamed up with Lee Marvin as a pair of over-the-hill cowboys; *The Horsemen*, which had the relentlessly un-commercial premise of a sport involving a decapitated calf's head; and *Oklahoma Crude*, as a wicked land developer. There was no telling where he'd pop up, be it in something called *Cocaine Cowboys*; the campy thriller *Alone in the Dark*, as an escaped mental patient; or hosting the series *Ripley's Believe It or Not* (with daughter Holly Palance).

A role as an eccentric artist in the art house hit *Bagdad Café*, and as one of the villains in the youth western *Young Guns*, seemed to revitalize mainstream interest in him, so he did more bad-guy work in two popular 1989 releases, *Batman* and *Tango and Cash*. A lighter side of his menace and machismo was on hand in the Billy Crystal comedy *City Slickers*. He played Curly, a no-nonsense cowhand, and this was a classic example of a flippant comedian getting even bigger laughs by playing off a straight man adept at projecting stony common sense. Palance wound up winning the Academy Award for Best Supporting Actor of 1991 and the choice seemed worthwhile when, in one of the more bizarre acceptance speeches in Oscar history, the 70-year-old plus actor dropped to the stage and did one-armed push-ups to show his appreciation. For his follow-ups he played straight man to Chevy Chase in *Cops and Robbersons*, and did a variation on his award-winning role in *City Slickers II: The Legend of Curly's Gold*, Curly having died off the first time around.

Screen: AS WALTER (JACK) PALANCE: 1950: Panic in the City; Halls of Montezuma.

AS JACK PALANCE: 1952: Sudden Fear; 1953: Shane; Second Chance; Flight to Tangier; Arrowhead; 1954: Man in the Attic; Sign of the Pagan; The Silver Chalice; 1955: Kiss of Fire; The Big Knife; I Died a Thousand Times; 1956: Attack; 1957: The Lonely Man; House of Numbers; 1958: The Man Inside; 1959: Ten Seconds to Hell; Beyond All Limits; 1960: Austerlitz/The Battle of Austerlitz; The Barbarians (nUSr); 1961: The Last Judgment (nUSr); The Mongols; 1962: Sword of the Conqueror; Warriors Five; Barabbas; 1963: Night Train to Milan/Il Criminale (nUSr); 1964: Contempt; 1965: Once a Thief; 1966: The Professionals; 1967: Kill a Dragon; 1968: Torture Garden; 1969: A Bullet for Rommel (nUSr); Deadly Sanctuary/Marquis de Sade: Justine; They Came to Rob Las Vegas; The Desperados; Che!; Legion of the Damned/Battle of the Commandos; 1970: The Mercenary/A Professional Gun (filmed 1968); The McMasters; Monte Walsh; 1971: The Horsemen; 1972: Si Puo Fare...Amigo/It Can Be Done Amigo/The Big and the Bad (nUSr); Chato's Land; Companeros; 1973: Brothers Blue (nUSr); Oklahoma Crude; 1974: Craze; Te Deum/Con Men/Sting of the West (nUSr); 1976: The Four Deuces; The Cop in Blue Jeans (dtv); Cry of the Wolf/Great Adventure; Erotic Eva/Black Cobra (nUSr); 1977: Mister Scarface/The Big Boss; Welcome to Blood City (nUSr); 1978: God's Gun/A Bullet from God; One Man Jury; 1979: Dead on Arrival/The One Man Jury; The Shape of Things to Come; The Sensuous Nurse/I Will, If You Will (filmed 1976); Cocaine Cowboys; 1980: Bloody Avenger (dtv); Without Warning; Safari Express (filmed 1976); Unknown Powers (dtv); Angels' Brigade/Seven From Heaven (filmed 1978); Hawk the Slayer; 1982: Alone in the Dark; 1984: Portrait of a Hitman/Jimbuck/The Last Contract (filmed 1977); 1985: George Stevens: A Filmmaker's Journey; 1988: Gor; Bagdad Cafe; Young Guns; 1989: Outlaw of Gor (dtv); Batman; Tango and Cash; 1990: Solar Crisis (dtv); 1991: City Slickers; 1993: Cyborg II (dtv); 1994: Cops and Robbersons; City Slickers II: The Legend of Curly's Gold; The Swan Princess (voice); 1998: Marco Polo/The Incredible Adventures of Marco Polo (dtv); 1999: Treasure Island (dtv); 2001: Prancer Returns (dtv).

NY Stage: AS WALTER PALANCE: 1947: The Big Two; 1948: A Temporary Island (ob); The Vigil; 1949: A Streetcar Named Desire; 1951: Darkness at Noon.

Select TV: 1950: The Man Who Couldn't Remember (sp); 1951: The King in Yellow (sp); 1952: Little Man Big World (sp); 1953: The Kiss-Off (sp); The Brandenburg Gate (sp); 1956: Requiem for a Heavyweight (sp); 1957: The Last Tycoon (sp); The Death of Manolete (sp); 1963–64: The Greatest Show on Earth (series); 1966: Alice Through the Looking Glass (sp); 1968: Dr. Jekyll & Mr. Hyde (sp); 1973: Dracula; 1974: The Godchild; 1975: The Hatfields and the McCoys; 1975–76: Bronk (series); 1979: The Last Ride of the Dalton Gang; 1980: The Ivory Ape; The Golden Moment: An Olympic Love Story; 1981: Evil Stalks This House; 1982–86: Ripley's Believe It or Not (series); 1992: Keep the Change; 1995: Buffalo Girls; 1997: I'll Be Home for Christmas; Ebeneezer; 1999: Sarah Plain and Tall: Winter's End;

2002: Living With the Dead.

EUGENE PALLETTE

BORN: WINFIELD, KS, JULY 8, 1889.
DIED: SEPTEMBER 3, 1954.

Rotund, dark-browed Eugene Pallette had the froggiest voice in the business, a guttural rasp that usually barked out impatient commands at all the fools intent on driving him mad. The son of actors, he himself joined a theatrical touring company while he was a teen. Starting somewhere between 1910 and 1912, he began doing extra work, making his earliest credits hard to document, not to mention it being difficult to distinguish which were short-subjects and which were feature length. In any case, he did a whole slew of one-reelers prior to appearing in the two most famous full-length attractions of this period, *The Birth of a Nation*, as a Union soldier, and *Intolerance*, as the heroic Prosper Latour. Among his more notable silent movie credits were *Terror Island*, as the villain in this Harry Houdini offering; the Douglas Fairbanks version of *The Three Musketeers*, as Aramis; and *Chicago*, as Phyllis Haver's lover who winds up dead. He was also around for the very first all-talking feature, the otherwise thoroughly undistinguished *Light of New York*, becoming, as time passed, virtually the only cast member recognizable to future generations. With the coming of sound, he signed a contract with Paramount, showing up in such early talking hits as *The Love Parade*, as the minister of war, and *The Virginian*. He also played the inept Sergeant Heath in the first of the Philo Vance murder mysteries, *The Canary Murder Case*, opposite William Powell as the suave sleuth. He was asked to repeat the part on five other occasions, in *The Green Murder Case*, *The Benson Murder Case*, *Paramount on Parade*, *The Kennel Murder Case*, and, finally, *The Dragon Murder Case*, in 1934, by which point the series had moved over to Warner Bros. with Warren William in the lead.

Other notable roles found him playing the King in the 1931 version of *Huckleberry Finn*; a stagecoach driver in *Wild Girl*; a gambler on board the *Shanghai Express*; and the husband of unfaithful Bette Davis in *Bordertown*. In 1936 he topped all his previous roles with his hilarious portrayal of the millionaire, outspokenly exasperated by nutty wife Alice Brady, in the screwball gem *My Man Godfrey*. This began a "golden" period of work for Pallette which included *Topper*, as a house detective; a reteaming with Brady, in *One Hundred Men and a Girl*; his unforgettable Friar Tuck in the classic *The Adventures of Robin Hood*; *Mr. Smith Goes to Washington*, as one of Edward Arnold's political toadies; the Deanna Durbin charmer *First Love*, as the down-to-earth millionaire who finally tells off his pretentious family; *The Mask of Zorro*, as Father Felipe; and *The Lady Eve*, as Henry Fonda's hot-tempered dad. Also alongside Fonda he was a college trustee in *The Male Animal*, and then, playing one of his less gruff characters, romanced Agnes Moorehead in the Damon Runyon tale *The Big Street*. Ever the dad, he was father to Paulette Goddard in *The Forest Rangers*, Gene Tierney in *Heaven Can Wait*, and Jeanne Crain in *In the Meantime Darling*, not to mention doing straight-man duties for Abbott and Costello in *It Ain't Hay*. By the late 1940s he was working principally at the poverty row companies. It was later revealed that he had been blacklisted by the major studios because of his fascist politics and outspoken racism. Apparently his harsh on-screen persona wasn't exactly masking a lovable codger underneath.

Screen: 1915: The Birth of a Nation; 1916: Intolerance; Hell-to-Pay Austin; Gretchen the Greenhorn; Children in the House; Going Straight; Sunshine Dad; 1917: The Lonesome Chap; The

Winning of Sally Temple; Heir of the Ages; Ghost House; The Bond Between; The Marcellini Millions; World Apart; Each to His Kind; **1918:** A Man's Man; His Robe of Honor; Madam Who; Tarzan of the Apes; Viviette; The Turn of the Card; Breakers Ahead; No Man's Land; **1919:** Be a Little Sport; The Amateur Adventuress; Fair and Warmer; Words and Music By...; **1920:** Terror Island; Alias Jimmy Valentine; Parlor, Bedroom and Bath; **1921:** The Three Musketeers; Fine Feathers; **1922:** Without Compromise; Two Kinds of Women; **1923:** Hell's Hole; A Man's Man; To the Last Man; North of Hudson Bay; **1924:** The Wolf Man; The Cyclone Rider; The Galloping Fish; Wandering Husbands; **1925:** The Light of Western Stars; Ranger of the Big Pines; Without Mercy; **1926:** Mantrap; Desert Valley; Rocking Moon; Whispering Smith; The Fighting Edge; The Volga Boatman; Whispering Canyon; **1927:** Chicago; Moulders of Men; **1928:** Out of the Ruins; The Goodbye Kiss; The Red Mark; Lights of New York; His Private Life; **1929:** The Canary Murder Case; The Greene Murder Case; The Studio Murder Mystery; The Love Parade; The Virginian; Pointed Heels; The Dummy; The Kibitzer; **1930:** The Benson Murder Case; Playboy of Paris; Paramount on Parade; Slightly Scarlet; Sea Legs; Let's Go Native; Follow Thru; The Sea God; The Border Legion; Men Are Like That; The Santa Fe Trail; **1931:** Fighting Caravans; It Pays to Advertise; The Adventures of Huckleberry Finn; Girls About Town; Dude Ranch; Gun Smoke; **1932:** Shanghai Express; Strangers of the Evening; Wild Girl; Dancers in the Dark; Tom Brown of Culver; Thunder Below; The Half Naked Truth; The Night Mayor; **1933:** Hell Below; The Kennel Murder Case; From Headquarters; Mr. Skitch; Shanghai Madness; Made on Broadway; Storm at Daybreak; **1934:** Friends of Mr. Sweeney; Caravan; One Exciting Adventure; Cross Country Cruise; Strictly Dynamite; I've Got Your Number; The Dragon Murder Case; **1935:** Bordertown; Steamboat Round the Bend; All the King's Horses; Baby Face Harrington; Black Sheep; **1936:** The Golden Arrow; Stowaway; Easy to Take; My Man Godfrey; The Luckiest Girl in the World; The Ghost Goes West; **1937:** The Crime Nobody Saw; One Hundred Men and a Girl; Clarence; She Had to Eat; Topper; **1938:** There Goes My Heart; The Adventures of Robin Hood; **1939:** Wife, Husband and Friend; First Love; Mr. Smith Goes to Washington; **1940:** Sandy Is a Lady; Young Tom Edison; He Stayed for Breakfast; It's a Date; A Little Bit of Heaven; The Mark of Zorro; **1941:** Unfinished Business; Ride, Kelly, Ride; World Premiere; The Bride Came C.O.D.; The Lady Eve; Appointment for Love; Swamp Water; **1942:** Almost Married; The Male Animal; Are Husbands Necessary?; Tales of Manhattan; The Big Street; Lady in a Jam; The Forest Rangers; Silver Queen; **1943:** It Ain't Hay; The Gang's All Here; The Kansan; Slightly Dangerous; Heaven Can Wait; **1944:** Pin Up Girl; In the Meantime Darling; Heavenly Days; Step Lively; Sensations of 1945; The Laramie Trail; Lake Placid Serenade; **1945:** The Cheaters; **1946:** Suspense; In Old Sacramento.

LILLI PALMER

(LILLIE MARIE PEISER) BORN: POSEN, GERMANY, MAY 24, 1914. DIED: JANUARY 27, 1986.

Unlike many European imports who ended up in English-language films, Lilli Palmer had not only the requisite beauty but offered grace, intelligence, genuine depth, and, most significantly, warmth. She studied drama in Berlin and Darmstadt before fleeing to Paris when the Nazis came to power. While performing there in cabarets, she attracted the interest of

some folks in the British film industry and this resulted in her co-starring as a Russian opposite Esmond Knight in *Crime Unlimited*. Because of this, she was signed to a contract by Gaumont-British in 1935. There she played one of the car thieves in *First Offence/Bad Blood*; leading lady to "Street Singer" Arthur Tracy in *Command Performance*; and a baroness assisting burglar Tom Walls in *Crackerjack/The Man with a Hundred Faces*. As the 1940s arrived she went to the stage, scoring a success in *No Time for Comedy*, before returning to the movies to play one of the ghosts visiting Michael Redgrave in *Thunder Rock*. In 1943 she married Rex Harrison and appeared with him in *The Rake's Progress/Notorious Gentleman*, as the wife who nearly offs herself when her caddish spouse begins carrying on with another. Warner Bros. offered her a contract at the same time Harrison was accepting one with Fox, so she made her American debut, in 1946, as an Italian, in *Cloak and Dagger*, one of those many tales of wartime intrigue being made in that era, this one starring Gary Cooper. She followed that film with *Body and Soul* (for UA), as the classy lady in the life of boxer John Garfield; *My Girl Tisa*, as an immigrant; and MGM's *No Minor Vices*, a poor comedy in which she was torn between dull husband Dana Andrews and artist Louis Jourdan.

She and Harrison went back to the theater and had a Broadway hit with *Bell Book and Candle*. Because of that, they ended up in the movie version of *The Fourposter*, an examination of a marriage through the passing years, but one that was decidedly cool box-office material since the Harrisons were the only two characters in the whole film. The pair divorced in 1957, by which time Palmer was in Germany making films, including a version of *Anastasia*, called *Is Anna Anderson Anastasia?*, and the remake of *Madchen in Uniform*, as the teacher whose female pupil falls in love with her. Hollywood was suddenly interested again and she made a very favorable impression on three occasions: *But Not for Me*, really putting some spark into this comedy, as Clark Gable's ex-wife; *The Pleasure of His Company*, as Fred Astaire's ex; and, best of all, *The Counterfeit Traitor*, as a spy who becomes William Holden's lover with tragic results. From that point on she was globetrotting, making movies in all corners of the world. Since some of them were American or English-language international productions she was seen on U.S. screens from time to time. These occasions included *Operation Crossbow*, as a Dutch partisan; *The Amorous Adventures of Moll Flanders*, seeming to be above such rubbish, as a madam; the spy flicks *Sebastian* and *High Commissioner/Nobody Runs Forever*; *Oedipus the King*, as Jocasta; *de Sade* as Madame de Montreuil; *The Boys From Brazil*, as Laurence Olivier's wife; and *The Holocroft Covenant*, as Michael Caine's mother. She was married to actor Carlos Thompson (with whom she starred in *Between Time and Eternity*) from 1957.

Screen (UK and US releases only): 1935: Crime Unlimited; **1936:** First Offence/Bad Blood; Wolf's Clothing; Secret Agent; **1937:** Good Morning Boys; The Great Barrier/Silent Barriers; Sunset in Vienna/Suicide Legion; Command Performance; **1938:** Crackerjack/The Man with a Hundred Faces; **1939:** A Girl Must Live; Blind Folly; **1940:** The Door With Seven Locks/Chamber of Horrors; **1942:** Thunder Rock; **1943:** The Gentle Sex; **1944:** English Without Tears; **1945:** The Rake's Progress/Notorious Gentleman; **1946:** Beware of Pity; Cloak and Dagger; **1947:** Body and Soul; **1948:** My Girl Tisa; No Minor Vices; **1950:** The Wicked City; **1951:** The Long Dark Hall; **1952:** The Fourposter; **1953:** Main Street to Broadway; **1959:** The Glass Tower; But Not for Me; **1960:** Between Time and Eternity; Conspiracy of Hearts; **1961:** The Pleasure of His Company; Modigliani of Montparnasse (filmed 1957); **1962:** The Counterfeit Traitor;

1963: The Miracle of the White Stallions; 1964: Of Wayward Love; 1965: The Amorous Adventures of Moll Flanders; Operation Crossbow/The Great Spy Mission; And So to Bed (filmed 1963); 1966: Madchen in Uniform (filmed 1958); 1967: Jack of Diamonds; 1968: Sebastian; Oedipus the King; The High Commissioner/Nobody Runs Forever; 1969: Hard Contract; de Sade; 1971: The House That Screamed; Murders in the Rue Morgue; 1972: What the Peeper Saw/Night Child; 1978: The Boys From Brazil; 1985: The Holcroft Covenant.

NY Stage: 1949: My Name is Aquilon; Caesar and Cleopatra; 1950: Bell Book and Candle; 1952: Venus Observed; 1953: The Love of Four Colonels.

Select TV: 1951: The Lilli Palmer Show (series); 1952: Three Hours Between Planes (sp); 1953: The Main Possession (sp); 1955–56: Lilli Palmer Theatre (series); 1956: The Taming of the Shrew (sp); 1967: The Diary of Anne Frank (sp); 1970: Hauser's Memory; 1975: The Zoo Gang (ms); 1986: Peter the Great (ms).

FRANKLIN PANGBORN

BORN: NEWARK, NJ, JANUARY 23, 1893.
DIED: JULY 20, 1958.

It's hard to think of a role in which Franklin Pangborn didn't have at least one moment where he put his hands on his hips, pinched his droopy puss, and stewed with prissy disapproval over someone who'd got under his skin. The movies' great effete fussbudget had been a member of Alla Nazimova's stage company before debuting in support of Beatrice Lillie in the 1926 film *Exit Smiling*, sporting what would become a typical Pangborn name, Cecil Lovelace. Although he actually managed a lead during this early period, in *My Friend From India*, he seemed like just another hard-working player until he really began to hit his stride in 1933, when he played flustered hotel managers in both *Flying Down to Rio* and *International House*, in which he was ripe for some W. C. Fields put-downs. He was never away from work long, popping up to do his patented shtick in such movies as *Cockeyed Cavaliers*, as the town crier; *Mr. Deeds Goes to Town*, as a tailor; *My Man Godfrey*, as the emcee of the scavenger hunt; *Three Smart Girls*, as a jeweler; *Stage Door*, as Adolphe Menjou's butler; *Dr. Rhythm*, in one of his most unforgettable assignments, as the store clerk who twists tongues with Beatrice Lillie doing her famous "damask dinner napkins" routine; *Hotel Haywire*, as a brush salesman; *The Bank Dick*, as bank examiner J. Pinkerton Snoopington; and another with Fields, *Never Give a Sucker an Even Break*, pretty much playing himself. Showing up as the exasperated radio announcer in *Christmas in July* meant that he had been welcomed into director-writer Preston Sturges's stable of peerless character players, so he minced for Sturges in *Sullivan's Travels*, as a studio employee; *The Palm Beach Story*, as a landlord; and as the frantic emcee in *Hail the Conquering Hero*, among others. He was last seen as a marquis in the Marie Antoinette sequence of the all-star disaster *The Story of Mankind*.

Screen: 1926: Exit Smiling; 1927: The Cradle Snatchers; Fingerprints; Getting Gertie's Garter; The Girl in the Pullman; My Friend From India; The Night Bride; The Rejuvenation of Aunt Mary; 1928: Blonde for a Night; The Rush Hour; On Trial; 1929: The Sap; Lady of the Pavements; 1930: A Lady Surrenders; Cheer Up and Smile; Not So Dumb; Her Man; 1931: A Woman of Experience; 1932: A Fool's Advice/Meet the Mayor; Stepping Sisters; The Half Naked Truth; Midnight Patrol; 1933: International House; Design for Living; Professional Sweetheart; Headline Shooters; Sweepings; Bed of Roses; The Important Witness; Only Yesterday; Flying Down to Rio; 1934: Manhattan Love Songs; Young and Beautiful; Strictly Dynamite; Unknown Blonde; Many Happy Returns; King Kelly of the U.S.A.; Cockeyed Cavaliers; Imitation of Life; College Rhythm; That's Gratitude; Tomorrow's Youth; 1935: The Headline Woman; $1,000 a Minute; Eight Bells; She Couldn't Take It; She Married Her Boss; 1936: Mr. Deeds Goes to Town; Three Smart Girls; The Luckiest Girl in the World; Don't Gamble With Love; My Man Godfrey; To Mary — With Love; The Mandarin Mystery; Hats Off; Tango; Doughnuts and Society; 1937: Step Lively, Jeeves; I'll Take Romance; They Wanted to Marry; The Lady Escapes; She Had to Eat; Swing High, Swing Low; It Happened in Hollywood; Danger — Love at Work; High Hat; Turn Off the Moon; Easy Living; It's All Yours; When Love Is Young; A Star Is Born; Love on Toast; Rich Relations; She Married an Artist; Dangerous Holiday; She's Dangerous; Hotel Haywire; All Over Town; We Have Our Moments; The Life of the Party; Stage Door; Living on Love; 1938: Thrill of a Lifetime; Vivacious Lady; Rebecca of Sunnybrook Farm; Three Blind Mice; Always Goodbye; Joy of Living; Just Around the Corner; Carefree; Bluebeard's Eighth Wife; Dr. Rhythm; Mad About Music; Four's a Crowd; The Girl Downstairs; 1939: Topper Takes a Trip; Broadway Serenade; 5th Ave. Girl; 1940: Turnabout; The Villain Still Pursued Her; Public Deb. No. 1; Christmas in July; Hit Parade of 1941; The Bank Dick; Spring Parade; 1941: Where Did You Get That Girl?; A Girl, a Guy, and a Gob; Flame of New Orleans; Bachelor Daddy; Obliging Young Lady; Tillie the Toiler; Never Give a Sucker an Even Break; Week-End for Three; Mr. District Attorney in the Carter Case; 1942: Sullivan's Travels; George Washington Slept Here; Strictly in the Groove; Moonlight Masquerade; The Palm Beach Story; Now, Voyager; What's Cookin'?; Call Out the Marines; 1943: Two Weeks to Live; Stage Door Canteen; Reveille With Beverly; Holy Matrimony; Crazy House; Honeymoon Lodge; Never a Dull Moment; His Butler's Sister; 1944: Hail the Conquering Hero; My Best Gal; The Great Moment; The Reckless Age; Allergic to Love; 1945: The Horn Blows at Midnight; Hollywood and Vine; See My Lawyer; You Came Along; Tell It to a Star; 1946: Lover Come Back; Two Guys From Milwaukee; 1947: Calendar Girl; I'll Be Yours; Mad Wednesday/The Sin of Harold Diddlebock; 1948: Romance on the High Seas; 1949: My Dream Is Yours; Down Memory Lane; 1950: Her Wonderful Lie/Addio Mimi; 1957: Oh, Men! Oh, Women!; The Story of Mankind.

NY Stage: 1911: The Triumph of an Empress; The Lily and the Prince; Camille; 1913: Joseph and His Brethren; 1924: Parasites.

IRENE PAPAS

BORN: CHILIMODION, GREECE, MARCH 9, 1926.
ed: ROYAL DRAMA SCHOOL OF ATHENS.

A towering international actress who seemed to wear the mask of Greek tragedy on her face, Irene Papas had, oddly enough, started in show business as a musical variety show performer. She came to movies in 1950 with the Greek film *The Lost Angels*. Papas continued to make a name for herself in her native country and then in some Italian productions, before she was asked to come to the U.S. to play in the western *Tribute to a Bad Man*, where she was refreshingly out of the ordinary as James Cagney's love interest. She went back to Greece to portray both *Antigone* and *Electra*, in between which she assisted Gregory Peck and Anthony Quinn in fighting the Nazis in one of the big hits of 1961, *The Guns of Navarone*. It was with Quinn that she once again made an impact on American audiences, in *Zorba the Greek*, as the widow Alan Bates courts, leading to tragedy. Now established as a strong presence, she was called on to strut her stuff, playing a variety of nationalities in all kinds of global productions. In English she was in a Mafia drama, *The Brotherhood*; played Catherine of Aragon in *Anne of the Thousand Days*; partnered with Quinn again in *A Dream of Kings*, which looked at the Greek community in Chicago; was Helen of Troy in the grimly un-commercial *The Trojan Women*; and was one of the international cast of suspects in the trashy thriller *Bloodline*. In her native tongue, she showed up as Clytemnestra in *Iphigenia*, which reunited her with *Zorba* director Michael Cacoyannis. After an extended period away from English-language releases she was the obvious choice when a Greek woman of some years was needed to play the mother of Christian Bale in *Captain Corelli's Mandolin*.

Screen (US releases only): 1953: Man From Cairo; 1954: Theodora — Slave Empress; 1956: Tribute to a Bad Man; 1959: Attila (It: 1954); 1960: The Unfaithfuls (filmed 1953); 1961: The Guns of Navarone; 1962: Electra; 1964: The Moon Spinners; Zorba the Greek; 1968: We Still Kill the Old Way; The Desperate Ones; The Brotherhood; 1969: A Dream of Kings; Z; Anne of the Thousand Days; 1971: The Trojan Women; 1975: Bambina; 1976: Blood Wedding; 1977: Mohammad — Messenger of God; Iphigenia; 1979: Sidney Sheldon's Bloodline; 1980: Eboli; 1981: Lion of the Desert; 1984: Erendira; 1985: Into the Night; The Assisi Underground; 1987: Sweet Country; 1988: High Season; 1991: Island; 2001: Captain Corelli's Mandolin.

NY Stage: 1967: That Summer — That Fall; Iphigenia in Aulis; 1973: Medea; 1980: The Bacchae.

Select TV: 1975: Moses — The Lawgiver (ms; and 1976 theatrical as Moses); 1994: Jacob; 1997: The Odyssey.

CECILIA PARKER

BORN: FORT WILLIAM, ONTARIO, CANADA, APRIL 26, 1905. RAISED IN ENGLAND. DIED: JULY 25, 1993.

First, foremost, and forever Andy Hardy's sister, Cecilia Parker was building up a steady, albeit unremarkable, career in movies when she stepped into a highly successful series that put her name on the map. Growing up in England, she originally intended to make opera her vocation, but when her family moved to Los Angeles, she ended up doing extra work in films. Fox signed her to a contract in 1931 but did little with her. Instead she appeared in some "B" westerns including *Tombstone Canyon*, with Ken Maynard; *Rainbow Ranch*, with Rex Bell; and *Riders of Destiny*, with John Wayne. Things changed when she went to MGM, where she was Greta Garbo's sister in *The Painted Veil*, and, more significantly, Eric Linden's girlfriend in *Ah, Wilderness!* The latter film also featured Lionel Barrymore and Spring Byington, as Linden's parents and Mickey Rooney as his little brother. The Barrymore-Byington-Rooney combination was kept in mind when the studio concocted a warm family drama-comedy entitled *A Family Affair*, about the small-town Hardy clan, with Parker added as Rooney's sister, Marion (playing a 19-year-old but in actuality past 30). Linden (with whom Parker had done three more films at Grand National, *In His Steps*, *Girl Loves Boy*, and *Sweetheart of the Navy*) was back as her love interest and the whole thing clicked with audiences, starting the successful Andy Hardy series. Although Barrymore and Byington found themselves replaced by Lewis Stone and Fay Holden, Parker and Rooney were retained for the follow-up, *You're Only Young Once*. Although Parker was given her share of attention in some of the first offerings, it was clear that the character was far too stuck-up

to cultivate much interest or sympathy and, besides, most audiences showed up to see Rooney anyway. Parker was missing for the two 1941 entries, due to pregnancy, and then retired from acting after *Andy Hardy's Double Life*, in 1942. She was coaxed back once more, for the ill-fated *Andy Hardy Comes Home*, in 1958, and then disappeared once again from the business, this time for keeps.

Screen: 1930: A Lady's Morals; The Unholy Three; 1931: Women of All Nations; Frankenstein; Young as You Feel; 1932: The Rainbow Trail; Mystery Ranch; The Lost Special; The Gay Caballero; Jungle Mystery; Tombstone Canyon; 1933: Unknown Valley; Rainbow Ranch; The Fugitive; Riders of Destiny; Damaged Lives; Secret Sinners; Trail Drive; 1934: Gun Justice; The Man Trailer; Lost Jungle (serial); I Hate Women; The Painted Veil; Honor of the Range; Here Is My Heart; High School Girl; 1935: Enter Madame; Ah, Wilderness!; Naughty Marietta; Three Live Ghosts; 1936: The Mine With the Iron Door; Below the Deadline; Old Hutch; In His Steps; 1937: Girl Loves Boy; A Family Affair; Hollywood Cowboy; Ride Along Cowboy; Sweetheart of the Navy; You're Only Young Once; 1938: Judge Hardy's Children; Love Finds Andy Hardy; Out West With the Hardys; 1939: Burn 'Em Up O'Connor; The Hardys Ride High; Andy Hardy Gets Spring Fever; Judge Hardy and Son; 1940: Andy Hardy Meets Debutante; 1941: Gambling Daughters; 1942: The Courtship of Andy Hardy; Grand Central Murder; Seven Sweethearts; Andy Hardy's Double Life; 1958: Andy Hardy Comes Home.

ELEANOR PARKER

BORN: CEDARVILLE, OH, JUNE 26, 1922.

Red headed and cat-eyed, Eleanor Parker was quite ravishing to behold but she wanted to prove herself an actress as well. She got her wish and became one of the more happily employed ladies of the 1950s, landing some juicy roles. Despite some good work, she often over-reached her capabilities and was guilty of flaring the nostrils and quivering the lip for minimum impact. She began acting in Cleveland in her teens and then moved to Southern California where she joined the Pasadena Playhouse. While there she was offered a contract with Warners and signed with that company, only to wind up having her footage deleted from the final print of *They Died With Their Boots On*. Instead she wound up in some short subjects and then in some "B" melodramas including *Buses Roar* and *The Mysterious Doctor*, about a headless ghost. There was an "A" assignment, as Walter Huston's very proper daughter in the pro-Russian *Mission to Moscow*, and this was her door into higher profile, if not top-notch, material starting with *Between Two Worlds*, the updated remake of *Outward Bound*, as the regretful near-suicide who is given a second chance at life, and *The Very Thought of You*, as Dennis Morgan's war bride. There was a distinct step up when she was cast as another soldier's wife, in *Pride of the Marines*, trying to cope with husband John Garfield having been blinded in battle. She then stumbled badly, trying to tackle Bette Davis's old role of the bitchy British waitress in the remake of *Of Human Bondage*; and landing in two of Errol Flynn's flops of the period, *Never Say Goodbye* and *Escape Me Never*. There was a hit with the faithful translation of the Broadway smash *The Voice of the Turtle*, as the actress wooed by soldier Ronald Reagan, but those two lacked a certain degree of color, so Eve Arden easily stole the whole show from both of them. It was supposed to be impressive that Parker was playing a dual role in the gothic melodrama *The Woman in White*, but she was rather passively dull as the heroine and merely bad as her deranged look-alike, an escapee from the nuthouse. She then got her best chance when she was cast as the naïve thing who gets toughened while serving time in prison in the surprisingly stark and effective *Caged*. This was just about the summit of the cherished women in prison genre and she wound up with an Oscar nomination for what was probably her best work. Her contract with Warners now ended, she foolishly went to Columbia, to play one of the women in the life of *Valentino*, as artificial as the rest of the cast in this classic bit of hokum, and then wisely went to Paramount to chew into the part of Kirk Douglas's wife, who is treated with scorn by him because of her abortion, in *Detective Story*. She wound up receiving her second Oscar nomination in the Best Actress category, despite the fact that this was pretty much a supporting part.

MGM invited her to join their stable and she started off well, cheekily playing the jealous actress who spars with Stewart Granger in the swashbuckler *Scaramouche*. She then played the concerned wife of Robert Taylor in the true-life military drama about the man chosen to drop the first atomic bomb, *Above and Beyond*; and had a better role, as the woman who turns out to be a Confederate agent, helping John Forsythe and his men break from prison in *Escape from Fort Bravo*. Paramount borrowed her to play the newly imported bride who hates living the plantation life in *The Naked Jungle*, though her battling with Charlton Heston was of secondary interest to the famous ant attack climax. Back at MGM she was off by a mile as the hillbilly tomboy in the comedic western *Many Rivers to Cross*, and then did some mighty noble suffering in *Interrupted Melody*, as real-life opera singer Marjorie Lawrence, whose only reason for having her story told on film was because she battled polio. This was, perhaps, the epitome of the ham-fisted, glossily artificial soap operas of the 1950s, but Parker, nonetheless, scored her third Oscar nomination for it. Hamming again she was the self-pitying cripple married to Frank Sinatra in *The Man in the Golden Arm*, which gave her a second major hit in a row. There was another popular one with Sinatra, *A Hole in the Head*, but before that, she made a game attempt at playing a woman with a split personality in *Lizzie*, a property that fared badly because it was on the market the same year Joanne Woodward got an Oscar for a similar role in *Three Faces of Eve*. She wasn't particularly sympathetic as Robert Mitchum's neglected wife in *Home From the Hill*, nor was there much to be said about being asked to reprise Lana Turner's old role in the much-hated sequel *Return to Peyton Place*. In support, she appeared in the part by which most audiences know her best, the snooty baroness who assumes she's going to marry Christopher Plummer in the 1965 Oscar-winner *The Sound of Music*; got mired in the lamentable *The Oscar*, as the agent who makes the mistake of "discovering" arrogant Stephen Boyd; and went into some heavy emoting as the unhinged wife who goes out the window in *An American Dream*. She was a feline fancier whom nephew Michael Sarrazin tries to kill in *Eye of the Cat*, which had the then-novel distinction of having alternate footage added for its initial television showing. As the 1970s arrived, TV became her principal means of employment, though she did resurface to play a murdered tycoon's widow in the quickly forgotten *Sunburn*.

Screen: 1942: The Big Shot (voice); Buses Roar; 1943: The Mysterious Doctor; Mission to Moscow; 1944: Between Two Worlds; Crime by Night; The Last Ride; The Very Thought of You; Hollywood Canteen; 1945: Pride of the Marines; 1946: Of Human Bondage; Never Say Goodbye; 1947: Escape Me Never (filmed 1945); Always Together; The Voice of the Turtle/One for the Books; 1948: The Woman in White; 1949: It's a Great Feeling; 1950: Chain Lightning; Caged; Three Secrets; 1951: Valentino; A Millionaire for Christy; Detective Story; 1952: Scaramouche; Above and Beyond; 1953: Escape from Fort Bravo; 1954: The Naked Jungle; Valley of the Kings; 1955: Many Rivers to Cross; Interrupted Melody; The Man With the Golden Arm; 1956: The King and Four Queens; 1957: Lizzie; The Seventh Sin; 1959: A Hole in the Head; 1960: Home From the Hill; 1961: Return to Peyton Place; 1962: Madison Avenue; 1964: Panic Button; 1965: The Sound of Music; 1966: The Oscar; An American Dream; 1967: Warning Shot; The Tiger and the Pussycat; 1968: How to Steal the World (from TV); 1969: Eye of the Cat; 1979: Sunburn.

Select TV: 1963: Seven Miles of Bad Road (sp); 1964: Knight's Gambit (sp); 1969: Hans Brinker (sp); 1969–70: Bracken's World (series); 1971: Maybe I'll Come Home in the Spring; Vanished; 1972: Home for the Holidays; 1973: The Great American Beauty Contest; 1977: Fantasy Island; 1978: The Bastard; 1979: She's Dressed to Kill; 1980: Once Upon a Spy; 1981: Madame X; 1991: Dead on the Money.

FESS PARKER

BORN: FORT WORTH, TX, AUGUST 16, 1925.
ED: UNIV. OF TX, USC.

So unalterably rural and homespun was this shy, stoic, and affable performer that it seems unimaginable to find Fess Parker anywhere but on the frontier or the backwoods — and that's pretty much where his career kept him. After serving in the navy, he went into a national touring company of *Mister Roberts*. This led to his debut in the Universal western *Untamed Frontier*, in 1952. He supported Gary Cooper in *Springfield Rifle* and Randolph Scott in *Thunder Over the Plains*, but he was basically a fresh face when Walt Disney chose him to play the legendary Indian fighter Davy Crocket for a three-part installment of his weekly TV series. The trilogy captured the fancy of half the youngsters in America, making coonskin caps the rage and Parker a star. There was so much interest in the character that Disney was able to stitch together the episodes and release them into theaters, as *Davy Crocket: King of the Wild Frontier*. Following another run of episodes called *The Legends of Davy Crocket*, the company edited them into another feature as well, *Davy Crocket and the River Pirates*, with a modicum of success. By this time, Parker had shown up as one of the soldiers in the hit *Battle Cry*, for Warners, but since his contract was with Disney he did four in a row for that studio, with *The Great Locomotive Chase*, as real-life Civil War raider James J. Andrews, a part that could be construed as villainous, depending on which side you were rooting for; *Westward Ho The Wagons!*, leading a wagon party that consisted of some of the Mouseketeers; *Old Yeller*, getting second billing but only showing up briefly at the beginning and end as Tommy Kirk's wizened dad; and *The Light in the Forest*, befriending James MacArthur. Admittedly, there was a stoic sameness to what he did and after co-starring parts in *The Hangman*, as the town sheriff; *The Jayhawkers*, seeking revenge on Jeff Chandler for killing his wife; and *Hell Is for Heroes*, as the no-nonsense sergeant in charge, it wasn't long before he retreated back to the small screen, putting another coonskin-hatted American hero on his résumé with the weekly series *Daniel Boone*. During its run he did one theatrical feature, Fox's remake of the horse saga *Smoky*. He retired from the business in the 1970s to become an hotelier.

Screen: 1952: Untamed Frontier; No Room for the Groom; Springfield Rifle; 1953: Thunder Over the Plains; Island in the

Sky; The Kid From Left Field; Take Me to Town; **1954:**
Dragonfly Squadron; Them!; The Bounty Hunter; **1955:** Davy
Crocket: King of the Wild Frontier (from TV); Battle Cry; **1956:**
The Great Locomotive Chase; Davy Crocket and the River
Pirates (from TV); Westward Ho the Wagons!; **1957:** Old Yeller;
1958: The Light in the Forest; **1959:** The Hangman; Alias Jesse
James; The Jayhawkers; **1962:** Hell Is for Heroes; **1966:** Smoky.
Select TV: 1955: Davy Crocket (ms); The Legends of Davy
Crocket (ms); **1958:** Turn Left at Mount Everest (sp); The Hasty
Hanging (sp); **1960:** Aftermath (sp); **1961:** Ambush at Wagon
Gap (sp); The Secret Mission (sp); **1962–63:** Mr. Smith Goes to
Washington (series); **1964–70:** Daniel Boone (series); **1972:**
Climb an Angry Mountain.

LARRY PARKS

(SAMUEL KLAUSMAN LAWRENCE PARKS)
BORN: OLATHE, KS, DECEMBER 13, 1914.
RAISED IN JOLIET, IL. ED: UNIV. OF IL.
DIED: APRIL 13, 1975.

Columbia Picture's fairly unremarkable
stock player of the 1940s, Larry Parks racked
up more than 40 credits at the studio, toiling mostly in programmers, but it was his big break in one of their "A"
productions that kept him from almost certain cinematic obscurity. Working with an amateur drama group convinced him that
he could be an actor, so he took off for New York where he
worked as an usher at the Radio City Music Hall while looking
for jobs in the theater. In time he joined with the Group Theatre,
making friends with John Garfield who suggested he seek work
in Hollywood. Parks tested for a role in *Here Comes Mr. Jordan*
and, although he didn't get the job, wound up with a Columbia
contract. Starting off with *Mystery Ship* in 1941, he found himself
employed in an endless stream of "B" productions including *The
Boogie Man Will Get You*, buying a rundown inn, not realizing
that Boris Karloff is conducting scientific experiments on the
premises; *Hello Annapolis*, as a naval cadet; *Is Everybody Happy?*,
as a pianist-turned-trumpeter; *The Black Parachute*, masquerading as a Nazi to get behind enemy lines; *Sergeant Mike*,
one for the kids, about a soldier training pooches for combat; and
She's a Sweetheart, a western about the Younger Brothers, which
was in color, at least. For his pains he landed the role of Al Jolson
in the studio's lavish biopic of the immortal entertainer, *The
Jolson Story*. Since Jolson himself supplied the singing voice it was
up to Parks to merely mime his mannerism, which he did well
enough to earn an Oscar nomination. Despite the fact that this
bio glossed over the harsher side of the singer and went so far as
to exclude any mention of ex-wife Ruby Keeler, as per her wishes,
it was amazingly popular — enough so to warrant a sequel, *Jolson
Sings Again*, which was also a smash. This one covered the far less
interesting later stage of the performer's life and included an
almost unbearably coy moment in which Parks, playing Jolson,
meets Parks playing Larry Parks. In between the Jolson stories the
actor had done another musical, *Down to Earth*, the clunky
"sequel" to the movie he didn't get cast in, way back when, *Here
Comes Mr. Jordan*. He also showed up as a most unlikely swashbuckler in both *The Gallant Blade* and *The Swordsman*,
supposedly passing for French and Scottish, respectively.
Ultimately, he became one of the casualties of the Communist
witch-hunts in the early 1950s, refusing to name names and being
blacklisted as a result. He and wife Betty Garrett (whom he'd
married in 1944) found work in Europe and on the stage, before
Parks returned to American films to play a colleague of
Montgomery Clift's in *Freud*. During this period of inactivity he

had taken up a second career as a building contractor and that
wound up being his principle means of support. He had been
long out of sight when he died of a heart attack in 1975.
Screen: 1941: Mystery Ship; Harmon of Michigan; Three Girls
About Town; You Belong to Me; Sing for Your Supper; **1942:**
North of the Rockies; Canal Zone; Alias Boston Blackie; The
Boogie Man Will Get You; Blondie Goes to College; Harvard,
Here I Come; A Man's World; Hello Annapolis; Flight
Lieutenant; They All Kissed the Bride; Atlantic Convoy;
Submarine Raider; You Were Never Lovelier; **1943:** Redhead from
Manhattan; Power of the Press; Is Everybody Happy?; Reveille
With Beverly; Destroyer; First Comes Courage; The Deerslayer;
The Racket Man; **1944:** Hey Rookie; Stars on Parade; The Black
Parachute; She's a Sweetheart; **1945:** Sergeant Mike; Counter-
Attack; **1946:** Renegades; The Jolson Story; **1947:** Her Husband's
Affairs; Down to Earth; The Swordsman; **1948:** The Gallant
Blade; **1949:** Jolson Sings Again; **1950:** Emergency Wedding;
1952: Love Is Better Than Ever; **1958:** Cross-Up/Tiger by the Tail
(UK: 1955); **1962:** Freud.
NY Stage: 1937: Golden Boy; **1938:** All the Living; **1939:** My
Heart's in the Highlands; **1957:** Tunnel of Love; **1958:** Bells Are
Ringing; **1960:** Beg, Borrow or Steal; **1963:** Love and Kisses.
Select TV: 1954: The Happiest Day (sp); Wedding March (sp);
1955: A Smattering of Bliss (sp); **1957:** The Penlands and the
Poodle (sp).

GAIL PATRICK

(MARGARET LAVELLE FITZPATRICK) BORN:
BIRMINGHAM, AL, JUNE 20, 1911. ED: HOWARD
COL., UNIV. OF AL. DIED: JULY 6, 1980.

Remembered best for her glamorously
haughty roles, Gail Patrick had the looks to
be a star but excelled at being less-than-lov-
able, so a featured player she remained. She fully intended to
make law her life, but on a whim decided to try out for a
Paramount talent search; the company was looking for someone
to play "the Panther Woman" in *Island of Lost Souls*. Although she
didn't get the part, she was one of the finalists and was given a
contract with the studio, starting off with a bit as a secretary in
the final segment of *If I Had a Million*. Eventually the studio
promoted her to larger roles in *Death Takes a Holiday*, as one of
the houseguests who encounters mysterious Fredric March;
Murder at the Vanities, as a murder victim; and *Mississippi*, as the
Southern belle who is just too damn icy to end up with hero Bing
Crosby. There were substantial parts in "B's" like *The Preview
Murder Mystery*, as an actress whose life is in danger; *Wanderer of
the Wasteland*, as the fiancée of innocent man on the run Dean
Jagger; and *Two Fisted*, hiring Lee Tracy and Roscoe Karns to
serve as her butlers to scare off her estranged husband. However,
her best chance came when she was on loan to Universal where
she was a joy as the coolly acerbic sister of Carole Lombard in the
comedy classic *My Man Godfrey*, bitchily slinging off her lines
with expertise. Back at Paramount she was one of the leads in a
Jack Benny vehicle, *Artists and Models*, but otherwise it was
mainly "B's" as usual, with *King of Alcatraz*, as a nurse, and
Dangerous to Know, in her customary socialite mode. It was up to
another studio again, RKO, to better utilize her and they did so, in
Stage Door; where she was the most aloof of the aspiring actresses
in this juicily scripted drama-comedy. Leaving Paramount in
1939, she continued her reign of tart bitchery in *My Favorite Wife*,
as Cary Grant's new bride; *Love Crazy*; and *We Were Dancing*,
before trailing off into employment at various "B" studios by the
late 1940s. Leaving acting in 1948, she and her third husband,

Cornwall Jackson, later found behind-the-scenes success as the producers of the long-running courtroom series *Perry Mason*.

Screen: 1932: If I Had a Million; 1933: The Mysterious Rider; The Phantom Broadcast; Murders in the Zoo; Mama Loves Papa; To the Last Man; Cradle Song; 1934: Death Takes a Holiday; Murder at the Vanities; Wagon Wheels; The Crime of Helen Stanley; Take the Stand; One Hour Late; 1935: Rumba; Mississippi; Doubting Thomas; No More Ladies; Smart Girl; The Big Broadcast of 1936; Wanderer of the Wasteland; The Lone Wolf Returns; Two Fisted; 1936: Two in the Dark; The Preview Murder Mystery; Early to Bed; My Man Godfrey; Murder With Pictures; White Hunter; 1937: John Meade's Woman; Her Husband Lies; Artists and Models; Stage Door; 1938: Mad About Music; Dangerous to Know; Wives Under Suspicion; King of Alcatraz; 1939: Disbarred; Man of Conquest; Grand Jury Secrets; Reno; 1940: My Favorite Wife; The Doctor Takes a Wife; Gallant Sons; 1941: Love Crazy; Kathleen; 1942: Tales of Manhattan; Quiet Please, Murder; We Were Dancing; 1943: Hit Parade of 1943; Women in Bondage; 1944: Up in Mabel's Room; 1945: Brewster's Millions; Twice Blessed; 1946: The Madonna's Secret; Rendezvous With Annie; Claudia and David; The Plainsman and the Lady; 1947: Calendar Girl; King of the Wild Horses; 1948: The Inside Story.

ELIZABETH PATTERSON

(MARY ELIZABETH PATTERSON)
BORN: SAVANNAH, TN, NOVEMBER 22, 1874.
ED: MARTIN COL., COLUMBIA INST.
DIED: JANUARY 31, 1966.

A spinsterish old crone who looked tiny enough to pick up with one hand but who possessed the spunk that dared you to try it, Elizabeth Patterson studied drama in Chicago before joining the touring companies of Ben Greet and Stuart Walker. The latter took her to Broadway where she kept busy, but with an interruption in 1926 to make two silent films, *The Boy Friend* and *The Return of Peter Grimm*. With the arrival of sound she found herself in almost constant demand, making approximately 100 films over the next 30 years. She was seen as a German baroness in *The Smiling Lieutenant*; the head of the orphanage in the 1931 version of *Daddy Long Legs*; Katharine Hepburn's aunt in *A Bill of Divorcement*; one of the knitting aunties in *Love Me Tonight*; Mickey Rooney's mom in *Hide-Out*; the maid who's proposed to by her employee in *Her Master's Voice*, repeating her stage role; Janet Gaynor's mother in *Small Town Girl*; in a rare top-billed role, as the crabby old ranch owner who softens up after she takes in some runaway kids, in two versions of *Timothy's Quest*; the beloved mother of Bing Crosby, Fred MacMurray, and Donald O'Connor in *Sing, You Sinners*, which was one of her finest hours on film; Heather Angel's cranky Aunt Blanche in three *Bulldog Drummond* capers; Fred MacMurray's rural aunt who shows Barbara Stanwyck a simpler life in *Remember the Night*; the victim in question in the "B" whodunit *Who Killed Aunt Maggie?*; the important role of the long-suffering wife of dirt-poor Charley Grapewin in the oddball movie of the Broadway smash *Tobacco Road*; the landlady running a boardinghouse of misfits in *The Shocking Miss Pilgrim*; and Barry Fitzgerald's housekeeper in *Welcome Stranger*. As luck would have it, she got the best role of her career when she was nearing 75, as the old lady who helps to fight off the lynch mob in MGM's potent indictment of racism, *Intruder in the Dust*. Shortly after that one ended up in the recurring role of babysitter Mrs. Trumbull on the hit series *I Love Lucy*, which would keep her face familiar to audiences for generations to come.

Screen: 1926: The Boy Friend; The Return of Peter Grimm; 1929: South Sea Rose; Words and Music; 1930: The Cat Creeps; The Big Party; The Lone Star Ranger; Harmony at Home; 1931: Tarnished Lady; The Smiling Lieutenant; Daddy Long Legs; Heaven on Earth; Penrod and Sam; Husband's Holiday; 1932: The Expert; Play Girl; So Big; New Morals for Old; Miss Pinkerton; Love Me Tonight; Life Begins; Guilty as Hell; A Bill of Divorcement; Man Wanted; Two Against the World; The Conquerors; They Call It Sin; Breach of Promise; No Man of Her Own; 1933: They Just Had to Get Married; The Infernal Machine; Golden Harvest; The Story of Temple Drake; Hold Your Man; Ever in My Heart; Doctor Bull; Secret of the Blue Room; Dinner at Eight; 1934: Hideout; 1935: Chasing Yesterday; So Red the Rose; Men Without Names; 1936: Her Master's Voice; Small Town Girl; Timothy's Quest; Three Cheers for Love; The Return of Sophie Lang; Old Hutch; Go West, Young Man; 1937: High, Wide and Handsome; Hold 'em Navy; Night Club Scandal; Night of Mystery; 1938: Scandal Street; Bluebeard's Eighth Wife; Bulldog Drummond's Peril; Sing, You Sinners; Sons of the Legion; 1939: The Story of Alexander Graham Bell; Bulldog Drummond's Secret Police; Bulldog Drummond's Bride; Bad Little Angel; The Cat and the Canary; Our Leading Citizen; 1940: Remember the Night; Adventure in Diamonds; Anne of Windy Poplars; Earthbound; Who Killed Aunt Maggie?; 1941: Michael Shayne — Private Detective; Tobacco Road; Kiss the Boys Goodbye; The Vanishing Virginian; Belle Starr; 1942: Lucky Legs; Her Cardboard Lover; Almost Married; My Sister Eileen; I Married a Witch; Beyond the Blue Horizon; 1943: The Sky's the Limit; 1944: Follow the Boys; Hail the Conquering Hero; Together Again; 1945: Lady on a Train; Colonel Effingham's Raid; 1946: I've Always Loved You; The Secret Heart; 1947: The Shocking Miss Pilgrim; Welcome Stranger; Out of the Blue; 1948: Miss Tatlock's Millions; 1949: Song of Surrender; Intruder in the Dust; Little Women; 1950: Bright Leaf; 1951: Katie Did It; 1952: The Washington Story; 1955: Las Vegas Shakedown; 1957: Pal Joey; 1959: The Oregon Trail; 1960: Tall Story.

NY Stage: 1913: Everyman; 1917: The Family Exit; In the Zone; 1918: Jonathan Makes a Wish; 1919: A Night in Avignon; 1920: The Piper; 1921: Intimate Strangers; 1922: Why Not?; 1923: Magnolia; 1924: Gypsy Jim; Lazybones; 1925: The Book of Charm; 1926: A Puppet Play; 1922: Spellbound; Paradise; 1928: Carry On; Rope; Box Seats; 1929: The Marriage Bed; Man's Estate; 1930: Solid South; 1933: Her Master's Voice; 1934: Spring Freshet.

Select TV: 1950: Our Town (sp); 1953: The Marriage Fix (sp); 1953–56: I Love Lucy (series); 1954: Vote of Confidence (sp); 1955: The Adventures of Huckleberry Finn (sp); 1956: The Day the Trains Stopped Running (sp); 1957: Mr. and Mrs. McAdam (sp); Cross Heirs (sp); 1958: Portrait of a Murderer (sp); 1960: Tomorrow (sp).

KATINA PAXINOU

(KATINA CONSTANTOPOULOUS) BORN: PIRAEUS, ATHENS, GREECE, DECEMBER 17, 1900.
ED: CONSERVATORY OF GENEVA, SWITZERLAND.
DIED: FEBRUARY 22, 1973.

A major figure of the Greek stage but little known or remembered by anyone but Oscar trivia fans, Katina Paxinou was a founder, with husband Alexis Minotis, of the National Greek Theatre, where she did the expected run of classic roles like *Mother Courage* and *Electra*. She came to New York in 1942 to play the lead in *Hedda Gabler* and this production was instrumental in her being selected by director Sam Wood to play the tough and overpowering Spanish guerilla leader Pilar in the lavish and much-touted 1943 adaptation of Ernest Hemingway's *For Whom the Bell Tolls*. The film was a smash hit and Paxinou was everything the role required in fire and spirit, pretty much dominating the proceedings and ending up winning the Academy Award for Best Supporting Actress. There wasn't much Hollywood could think of to do with a middle-aged, none-too-glamorous actress with a thick accent, so she ended up as a Czech underground fighter in *Hostages*; Rosalind Russell's scheming mother in the disastrous attempt to put *Mourning Becomes Electra* on film, giving a bombastic performance more suitable for a Greek amphitheatre; and an Italian with the curious name of Mona Zeppo Costanza in the costumer *Prince of Foxes*. Later down the line, there was a notable role as a Sicilian widow in director Luchino Visconti's epic-length *Rocco and His Brothers*, but her subsequent work was mostly done back on the boards.

Screen: 1930: Electra; 1943: For Whom the Bell Tolls; Hostages; 1945: Confidential Agent; 1947: Mourning Becomes Electra; The Inheritance/Uncle Silas; 1949: Prince of Foxes; 1955: Mr. Arkadin/Confidential Report; 1959: The Miracle; 1960: Rocco and His Brothers/Savage Run; 1968: Zita (nUSr); 1970: A Savage Summer (nUSr).

NY Stage: 1930: Electra; 1942: Hedda Gabler; 1944: Sophie; 1951: The House of Bernarda Alba; 1952: Electra; Oedipus Tyrannus; 1961: The Garden of Sweets.

JOHN PAYNE

Born: Roanoke, VA, May 23, 1912.
ed: Columbia Univ. Died: December 6, 1989.

When you think of 20th Century-Fox in the 1940s it is hard to exclude John Payne from the mix, although this blandly serviceable actor was just about at the bottom of the rung as far as electrifying screen personalities were concerned. Having studied voice at Juilliard he did some singing and radio work before going west to seek employment in films. As "John Howard Payne" he landed a supporting role in a very prestigious Samuel Goldwyn production, *Dodsworth*. This was followed by his first leading role, as a press agent scheming against and falling in love with Mae Clarke, in the Grand National musical *Hats Off*; a "B" assignment at Fox, *Fair Warning*, as a swimming instructor; and an indie released through Paramount, *Love on Toast*, as a soda jerk entered in a soup contest. There was very little to suggest any special qualities from these assignments but Fox saw potential and signed him to a contact in 1940. He started off as leading man to the equally unexceptional Linda Darnell in *Star Dust*, a movie that was easily stolen by Roland Young. He was then teamed with Jack Oakie to play songwriters in *Tin Pan Alley*, a minor black and white musical that turned out to be a success because it paired the popular Alice Faye and the up-and-coming Betty Grable in the leads. It also marked the start of Payne's association with that studio's interchangeable musicals, although he wasn't exactly called on to be the center of attention in any of them. Those he plodded through consisted of *The Great American Broadcast*, with Faye and Oakie; *Sun Valley Serenade*, with Sonia Henie; *Week-end in Havana*, with Faye and Carmen Miranda; *Iceland*, with Henie; *Springtime in the Rockies*, with Grable and Miranda; *Footlight Serenade*, with Grable; *Hello, Frisco, Hello*, with Grable and June Haver; and *Wake Up and Dream*, with Haver.

In between, he was given more serious fare with *Remember the Day*, as Claudette Colbert's lost love; the hit war film *To the Shores of Tripoli*, as a cocky young marine squaring off with veteran non-com Randolph Scott, a premise done before and since with far more compelling stars; *Sentimental Journey*, as a Broadway producer who must relate to his adopted child after wife Maureen O'Hara dies; and *The Razor's Edge*, at his dullest as the man Gene Tierney opts for over Tyrone Power. His contract with Fox ended on a high note, however, with *Miracle on 34th Street*, as the lawyer who winds up defending Santa Claus in court, certainly his best and most enduring film. He went over to Paramount's second-feature Pine-Thomas unit where his credits included *Captain China*; *The Eagle and the Hawk*; *Tripoli*, back in the Marines but circa 1805; *Crosswinds*; and *The Vanquished*, as a Confederate officer returning home after the war. In between these he ended up in some well-regarded noir thrillers of the 1950s with *Kansas City Confidential*, as an ex-con who must prove his innocence after he is named chief suspect in a robbery; *99 River Street*, in one of his more effective performances, as an ex-pug accused of killing his faithless wife; and *Slightly Scarlet*, helping to fight big-city corruption. The was a welcome, uncharacteristic change when he went completely nasty to play a ruthless politician in one he himself produced, *The Boss*, but after the duds *Bailout at 43,000* and the filmed-in-Copenhagen *Hidden Fear*, he turned to television for the series *Restless Gun*. Payne seemed to have been long out of the public consciousness when he and former co-star Alice Faye were reunited for a revival of the stage musical *Good News*. He toured with the production but dropped out of it during previews, before it officially opened on Broadway. He first wife (1937–43) was actress Anne Shirley and his second (1944–50), Gloria De Haven.

Screen: 1936: Dodsworth; Hats Off; 1937: Fair Warning; Love on Toast; 1938: College Swing; Garden of the Moon; 1939: Wings of the Navy; Bad Lands; Indianapolis Speedway; Kid Nightingale; 1940: Star Dust; Maryland; The Great Profile; King of the Lumberjacks; Tear Gas Squad; Tin Pan Alley; 1941: The Great American Broadcast; Week-end in Havana; Remember the Day; Sun Valley Serenade; 1942: To the Shores of Tripoli; Iceland; Springtime in the Rockies; Footlight Serenade; 1943: Hello, Frisco, Hello; 1945: The Dolly Sisters; 1946: Sentimental Journey; The Razor's Edge; Wake Up and Dream; 1947: Miracle on 34th Street; 1948: Larceny; The Saxon Charm; 1949: El Paso; The Crooked Way; Captain China; 1950: The Eagle and the Hawk; Tripoli; 1951: Passage West; Crosswinds; 1952: Caribbean; The Blazing Forest; Kansas City Confidential; 1953: Raiders of the Seven Seas; The Vanquished; 99 River Street; 1954: Rails Into Laramie; Silver Lode; 1955: Santa Fe Passage; Hell's Island; The Road to Denver; Tennessee's Partner; 1956: Slightly Scarlet; Rebel in Town; Hold Back the Night; The Boss (and prod.); 1957: Bailout at 43,000; Hidden Fear; 1968: They Ran for Their Lives; 1970: The Savage Wild.

NY Stage: 1935: At Home Abroad; 1974: Good News.

Select TV: 1951: The Name is Bellingham (sp); Exit (sp); 1954: The Philadelphia Story (sp); 1955: Lash of Fear (sp); Alice in Wonderland (sp); 1956: Deadline (sp); 1957–59: Restless Gun (series; and exec. prod.); 1962: The Little Hours (sp).

GREGORY PECK

(Eldred Gregory Peck) Born: La Jolla, CA, April 5, 1916. ed: San Diego St. Col., Berkeley Col.

This most impossibly handsome of actors was the true definition of an enduring star. Gregory Peck was a tower of integrity, playing men challenging an imperfect world with more than a dash of common sense and a great deal of nobility and strength. Generations of audiences loved and trusted him even though he could lapse into a stoicism that only emphasized a limited range. It didn't matter. He had only to open his mouth and speak with that deep, beautifully modulated voice and you were under his spell. It was no surprise that it was that voice that got him attention in school, where a public speaking course brought to mind the possibility of acting. This he took up at Berkeley College where he played Starbuck in *Moby Dick*, a piece that would arise again in his lifetime. Moving to New York in 1939, he worked as a barker at the World's Fair and as a tour guide at Radio City/Rockefeller Center. Accepted into the Neighborhood Playhouse, he dabbled in modeling before joining the Barter Theatre in Abingdon, VA, and appeared with various other stock companies. His Broadway debut came in 1942 in *The Morning Star* and, after two more short-lived plays, he accepted an offer from writer-producer Casey Robinson to appear along with a bunch of other unknowns in the film *Days of Glory*. As the leader of a band of Soviet guerillas, his star power was evident from the word go but this piece was too low-keyed for wide acceptance. Hollywood was very interested, however, and 20th Century-Fox snatched him up and put him into a lavish and overlong story of a missionary in China, *The Keys of the Kingdom*. He was required to age from 20 to 80 and, as a result, wound up with his first Oscar nomination and stardom.

Freelancing successfully, he was in great demand and got involved in some of the big ones of the day: MGM's *The Valley of Decision*, a typical soap saga in which he was the wealthy son attracted to Irish servant Greer Garson; Selznick's *Spellbound*, as a troubled amnesiac in this decent Hitchcock drama which allowed him to romance Ingrid Bergman; MGM's *The Yearling*, as the kind-hearted paw to youngin' Claude Jarman, Jr., in one of the best-made and best-loved family films of its day, with Peck giving a solid performance that earned him another Oscar nod; and the ultimate Selznick production of the 1940s, *Duel in the Sun*, in a game attempt to play a rotter, raping Jennifer Jones and shooting brother Joseph Cotten, in this classic example of an overheated melodrama lighting box-office fires. Back playing a nice guy, he was an author passing himself off as a Jew in *Gentleman's Agreement*, director Elia Kazan's well-intentioned dissection of anti-Semitism, a film looked upon by modern audiences as very mild dramatic fare but one that did much good in its day. Peck was once again up for an Oscar and the film, a big hit, won the Academy Award for Best Picture of 1947. There was a dreary reunion with Hitchcock for the courtroom drama *The Paradine Case*, and a good western, *Yellow Sky*, which found him playing a bank robber, albeit one who's not really such a bad guy. MGM's *The Great Sinner* put him opposite Ava Gardner (he would later call her his favorite co-star) but audiences stayed away. He capped the 1940s with his best work to date, playing the martinet who starts to crack under the strain of battle in *Twelve O'Clock High*, which gave him Oscar mention number four.

Sporting a moustache he was *The Gunfighter*, as an aging, hired gun trying to put his past behind him — an admirable western that brought Peck some of his best notices, while another in that genre, *Only the Valiant*, he would look back upon as the low point of his career. After looking nice in period naval duds for the made-in-Britain *Captain Horatio Hornblower*, he did a pair of sizable box-office hits with Susan Hayward, *David and Bathsheba*, a character driven Biblical spectacle in which he did a lot of soul searching as the King who covets another's wife, and *The Snows of Kilimanjaro*, which added Ava Gardner to the mix, with Peck a somewhat glamorized version of Ernest Hemingway's alter-ego. In 1953 came *Roman Holiday*, his first real foray into comedy —

a genuinely magical romance that worked beyond all expectations — with Audrey Hepburn as the princess to whom Peck's sardonic American reporter loses his heart. After a period when his popularity seemed on the wane, with two that were made in England, *Man with a Million* and *The Purple Plain*, he bounced back with another success, *The Man in the Grey Flannel Suit*, sympathetic as the Madison Avenue executive/suburbanite haunted by his wartime past. There was, and continues to be, controversy over his casting as Ahab in *Moby Dick*, but it was, in fact, a risk that paid off with Peck often mesmerizing in an atypical turn as the nutty and fearsome captain in this underrated attempt to film the un-filmable.

Another romantic comedy, *Designing Woman*, with Lauren Bacall, didn't click at all but he excelled as a man of integrity in a fine western, *The Big Country*, as the city slicker who comes between warring ranchers. *Port Chop Hill* was an anti-war film with a Korean War setting, one that emphasized gritty action over characterization; *Beloved Infidel* found him blatantly miscast as F. Scott Fitzgerald; and the surprisingly well-attended *On the Beach* was a stark look at the end of the world, though the multiple romantic interludes between Peck and Ava Gardner somewhat diluted the power of this indictment against nuclear war. Continuing his relative good luck into the 1960s, he commanded the military unit that was ordered to blow up *The Guns of Navarone*, one of the most popular adventure movies of its day, helped a great deal by the star power on hand; and then he and his family were terrorized by sleazy Robert Mitchum in a tense and moody melodrama, *Cape Fear*. This was followed by the summit of his career, *To Kill a Mockingbird*, a beautiful rendering of Harper Lee's Pulitzer Prize-winning novel with Peck magnificent as the gentle lawyer who gives equal attention to his motherless children and to a hopeless court case. This was one of the finest examples of great acting through understatement and Peck was awarded the Academy Award as Best Actor of 1962, one of the most applauded choices in this category. Although he was very much in his element as a decent military psychiatrist in *Captain Newman, M.D.*, he was curiously cast as a Spaniard in the flop war film *Behold a Pale Horse*. More regrettably, a pair of thrillers didn't fare so well either: *Mirage*, as a scientist wondering what happened while his memory was gone, and the delightful, tongue-in-cheek *Arabesque*, as a professor racing through England with Sophia Loren. That Peck's reign as a leading attraction was hitting a rut was not helped by the fairly boring output of movies with which he ended the 1960s, including the muddled political thriller *The Chairman*; the overblown western *Mackenna's Gold*; and *Marooned*, in which he kept Americans at ease while a trio of astronauts were stranded up above. There was absolutely no interest in the depressing *I Walk the Line*, as a sheriff made a fool by Tuesday Weld and her hillbilly clan; or the westerns *Shoot-Out*, which teamed with a little girl (Dawn Lyn), and *Billy Two-Hats*, which gave him Desi Arnaz, Jr. as his Indian co-hort. After those he served as producer on *The Trial of the Catonsville Nine* and *The Dove*, neither of which brought in more than specialized audiences.

Rescue came with a horror movie of all things, *The Omen*, a fairly creepy and ultra-violent tale of an American ambassador whose child turns out to be the spawn of Satan. Peck gave this whole thing enough credibility to make it work, scoring a major box-office success. From that he was asked to play *MacArthur*, the controversial World War II general, in a long-winded biopic that nevertheless contained one of his best later-career performances, and Nazi Josef Mengele in *The Boys From Brazil*, his most blatantly villainous role and one in which he seemed almost totally ill at ease. By the 1980s it seemed only natural that he would finally accept offers from television and it was there that he played the role one would have thought he'd have gotten around to years before, Abraham Lincoln, in the mini-series *The Blue and the Grey*. He could easily have rested on his laurels but instead showed up in his first non-starring role in a motion picture, *Amazing Grace and Chuck*, playing the president of the United States, after which he had the title role in *Old Gringo*, replacing an ailing Burt Lancaster, as writer Ambrose Bierce. There was one last good part, as the aging company president in *Other People's Money*, once again embodying decency as he challenged corporate sleazeball Danny DeVito for the control of his business. It was hard to think of any other still-active star from Hollywood's past that could have brought so much good will with him to the part. Nostalgically he took on smaller roles in two remakes of his earlier triumphs, a lawyer in the 1991 version of *Cape Fear*, and Father Mapple in the 1998 television re-do of *Moby Dick*. In 1989 he received the American Film Institute Life Achievement Award. His children from his second marriage, Tony and Cecelia Peck, have also acted.

Screen: 1944: Days of Glory; 1945: The Keys of the Kingdom; The Valley of Decision; Spellbound; 1946: The Yearling; Duel in the Sun; 1947: The Macomber Affair; Gentleman's Agreement; The Paradine Case; 1948: Yellow Sky; 1949: The Great Sinner; Twelve O'Clock High; 1950: The Gunfighter; 1951: Only the Valiant; Captain Horatio Hornblower; David and Bathsheba; 1952: The World in His Arms; The Snows of Kilimanjaro; 1953: Roman Holiday; 1954: Night People; Man With a Million/The Million Pound Note; The Purple Plain; 1956: The Man in the Grey Flannel Suit; Moby Dick; 1957: Designing Woman; 1958: The Big Country; The Bravados; 1959: Pork Chop Hill; Beloved Infidel; On the Beach; 1961: The Guns of Navarone; 1962: Cape Fear; To Kill a Mockingbird; 1963: How the West Was Won; Captain Newman, M.D.; 1964: Behold a Pale Horse; 1965: Mirage; 1966: Arabesque; 1969: The Stalking Moon; Mackenna's Gold; The Chairman; Marooned; 1970: I Walk the Line; 1971: Shoot Out; 1974: Billy Two Hats/The Lady and the Outlaw; 1976: The Omen; 1977: MacArthur; 1978: The Boys From Brazil; 1981: The Sea Wolves; 1987: Amazing Grace and Chuck; 1989: Old Gringo; 1991: Other People's Money; Cape Fear; 1996: Wild Bill: Hollywood Maverick.

NY Stage: 1942: The Morning Star; The Willow and I; 1943: Sons and Soldiers; 1991: The Will Rogers Follies (voice).

Select TV: 1982: The Blue and the Grey (ms); 1983: The Scarlet and the Black; 1993: The Portrait (and exec. prod.); 1998: Moby Dick.

GEORGE PEPPARD
BORN: DETROIT, MI, OCTOBER 1, 1928.
ED: CARNEGIE MELLON. DIED: MAY 8, 1994.

Given his blue-eyed, blond-haired good looks, you'd have thought that George Peppard could have gotten away with being another handsome pile of wood but he happened to be a fine actor, one who attained his brief period in the spotlight until the "A" material dried up. Having studied drama in school, he made his legit theater debut in 1949 with the Pittsburgh Playhouse, followed by a stint with the Oregon Shakespeare Festival. Heading for New York, he ended up on some television dramas and on Broadway in *The Girls of Summer*. Along with two of its cast members, Arthur Storch and Pat Hingle, he was hired for the film version of the controversial novel/play *End as a Man*, now called *The Strange One*, playing one of the cadets who can't tolerate Ben Gazzara's bullying abuse.

From there it was back to television and another play, *The Pleasure of His Company*, which sparked further interest from Hollywood. Paired up with Harry Guardino, he was a member of the battalion trying to take *Pork Chop Hill*, and then, under a contract he had signed with MGM, played the neglected son of land baron Robert Mitchum in the glossy drama *Home From the Hill*, easily giving the best performance in the film. There were nothing but pans for *The Subterraneans*, a supposedly bold look at the beatnik life, but he was marvelous playing the kept writer who tries to break through to free spirit Audrey Hepburn in Paramount's *Breakfast at Tiffany's*. Surrounded by eccentrics, he proved that he could bring attention to himself via quiet nuances. He finished off his MGM contract in the all-star *How the West Was Won*, where he was called on to carry the bulk of the second half of this lengthy epic, proving himself a very able hero.

There was another ensemble piece, *The Victors*, a disturbing, often-brilliant look at the life of some soldiers *off* the battlefields during World War II. In his segment, Peppard, the most sardonic member of the company, has a brief fling with enterprising Melina Mercouri, who turns out to be even more cynical that he is. Bigger than all of these, money-wise, was *The Carpetbaggers*, an enjoyable piece of trash and flash from the best-selling Harold Robbins novel, with Peppard as the impossibly arrogant, cold-blooded protagonist who climbs to the top of the Hollywood scene. The cast included Elizabeth Ashley, to whom he was later married (1966–70). There was another wartime ensemble, *Operation Crossbow*; then a flat drama about amnesia, *The Third Day*; after which he was arrogant as hell again for the lavish aviation epic *The Blue Max*, looking convincingly German. He then went over to Universal for a string of films that cooled off his standing, starting with *Tobruk*, a war epic with Rock Hudson; *Rough Night in Jericho*, a violent western with Dean Martin; *P.J.*, which showed him to good effect as the jaded private eye type; *What's So Bad About Feeling Good?*, a dumb comedy about a toucan spreading a happiness virus; *One More Train to Rob*, a jokey western; and *The Groundstar Conspiracy*, a confusing thriller. That same studio signed him up for a detective series, *Banacek*, which had a two-year run. In the 1980s he came back to weekly television again when Universal cast him in *The A Team*, which helped revitalize a flagging career and became just about the only hit project he participated in during the latter part of his career. In between television work he was seen on the big screen in the flop apocalyptic adventure *Damnation Alley* and in a Roger Corman sci-fi cheapie, *Battle Beyond the Stars*, to name two of his theatrical ventures that got somewhat better distribution than the others. There was also one he directed himself in, *Five Days From Home*, about an escaped con trying to reach his sickly son; it was barely shown anywhere. One could hardly blame him for often somewhat looking bored during these later, less sunny years.

Screen: 1957: The Strange One; 1959: Pork Chop Hill; 1960: Home From the Hill; The Subterraneans; 1961: Breakfast at Tiffany's; 1963: How the West Was Won; The Victors; 1964: The Carpetbaggers; 1965: Operation Crossbow; The Third Day; 1966: The Blue Max; 1967: Tobruk; Rough Night in Jericho; 1968: P.J.; What's So Bad About Feeling Good?; 1969: House of Cards; Pendulum; 1970: The Executioner; A Canon for Cordoba; 1971: One More Train to Rob; 1972: The Groundstar Conspiracy; 1974: Newman's Law; 1977: Damnation Alley; 1978: Five Days From Home (and dir.; prod.); 1979: An Almost Perfect Affair; From Hell to Victory (dtv); Your Ticket Is No Longer Valid (dtv); 1980: Battle Beyond the Stars; 1982: Target Eagle (dtv); 1984: Treasure of the Yankee Zephyr/Race to the Yankee Zephyr (filmed 1981); 1990: Silence Like Glass; 1992: The Tigress (dtv).

NY Stage: 1956: Girls of Summer; 1958: The Pleasure of His

Company.

Select TV: 1956: Flying Object at Three O'Clock High (sp); 1957: A Walk in the Forest (sp); The Big Buildup (sp); Aftermath (sp); 1958: End of the Rope (sp); 1960: Incident at a Corner (sp); 1964: Little Moon of Alban (sp); The Game with Glass Pieces (sp); 1972: The Bravos; Banacek: Detour to Nowhere; 1972–74: Banacek (series); 1975: One of Our Own; Guilty or Innocent: The Sam Sheppard Case; 1975–76: Doctors' Hospital (series); 1979: Crisis in Mid-Air; Torn Between Two Lovers; 1983–87: The A Team (series); 1988: Man Against the Mob; 1989: Man Against the Mob: The Chinatown Murders; 1990: Night of the Fox.

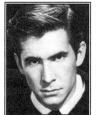

ANTHONY PERKINS
BORN: NEW YORK, NY, APRIL 4, 1932.
ED: ROLLINS COL. DIED: SEPTEMBER 12, 1992.

Few stars get to create such an impression in a single role that they not only become a part of movie history but of American folklore itself. Such was the case with rail thin, shy, and handsome Anthony Perkins, who segued over the course of his career from gulping, sensitive juveniles to playing the ultimate screen mental case and then on to a whole barrage of stuttering, quivering whackos, to the point where one couldn't tell whether this was acting or self-parody. His father was stage and screen actor Osgood Perkins, but he died when Tony was all of five years old so his son remembered little of him. To overcome his shyness, his mother encouraged him to take up acting and he joined the Battlesboro Summer Theatre in Vermont, making his debut at age 16. He continued in summer stock while attending Rollins College in Florida. While there, he decided to try out for a role he had already done in the play *Years Ago*, which was being turned into a movie called *The Actress*, to be directed by George Cukor for MGM. As luck would have it, he got the role of Jean Simmons's boyfriend and, although he immediately proved himself a most ingratiating screen presence, there were no other offers forthcoming. Undaunted, he went to New York to find work there and got his big break when he followed John Kerr in the role of the sensitive student accused of being gay in *Tea and Sympathy*. This led to his being cast as the son of Quakers Gary Cooper and Dorothy McGuire in one of the best films of 1956, *Friendly Persuasion*. As the gentle pacifist farm lad who is distressed when he is forced to enlist and then kill in battle, he was exceptional, earning an Oscar nomination in the supporting category and being treated like a newcomer by those who had somehow forgotten about *The Actress*.

Paramount signed him up to a contract and gave him the demanding part of mentally tormented baseball player Jim Piersall, who cracks under the pressure of his domineering dad, in *Fear Strikes Out*, and he proved that he had what it took to carry a film, though this was hardly the sort of subject that late 1950s audiences wanted to patronize in large numbers. Nonetheless he was proclaimed one of the most exciting new discoveries of his day and, to further expand his appeal, he started recording songs, winding up with a minor hit with "Moonlight Swim." This helped give him the nice-guy-next-door image Hollywood hoped to cultivate. To that end, he was the son who resents his estranged outlaw dad Jack Palance in *The Lonely Man*, and the naïve young sheriff who receives assistance on how to carry out his duties from older and wiser Henry Fonda in *The Tin Star*. His likability took the smarminess out of his carrying on with stepmom Sophia Loren in *Desire Under the Elms*, and he was ideal as girl-shy clerk Cornelius Hackl in the period piece *The Matchmaker*, a few years before the world knew it better as

Hello, Dolly!. There wasn't much he could do as the adventurer who falls in love with wood nymph Audrey Hepburn in the disastrous film version of *Green Mansions*, although he did get to sing the title song. However, he was very good as the new dad who must cope with the possibility of euthanasia as his family faces the effects of radiation poisoning in one of the major releases of 1959, *On the Beach*. His lankiness made him suitable to portray a basketball player in the very mild comedy *Tall Story*, after which he got the role that would change his life forever, not to mention the course of motion pictures. He was an inspired choice to play Norman Bates in director Alfred Hitchcock's *Psycho*, seemingly sweet and vulnerable on the outside but with a dementia in his eyes that hinted at the insanity within. The director went on record as being shocked that Perkins did not even rate a nomination from the Academy, and it is indeed one of that organization's more glaring omissions. The movie was a smash hit, a brilliantly unsettling exercise in terror that continues to frighten audiences and influence filmmakers to this day. It brought the horror genre to a whole new level that would often challenge the bounds of good taste, and Perkins became forever identified with the role, mostly to the detriment of his career. Before the film opened, he had returned to Broadway to star in the musical *Greenwillow*, which failed on its initial run but developed a cult following over the years. His involvement in that work was instrumental in keeping him away from the *Psycho* set when its most famous sequence, the shower murder, was actually shot. A stand-in had to be used.

Now more greatly in demand than ever, he chose to refuse all of Hollywood's immediate offers and go to Europe instead, a move that might have been personally fulfilling but knocked him right off of the "A" list. He was a sensitive law student smitten with older woman Ingrid Bergman in *Goodbye Again*, which may have been the first indication that he was taking the shambling, awkward man-boy act a bit too far; fooled around with his stepmother again, in this case Melina Mercouri, in *Phaedra*; played Sophia Loren's scheming husband in *Five Miles to Midnight*; seemed an acceptable choice to embody the puzzled Josef K in Orson Welles's maddening adaptation of Kafka's *The Trial*; and starred as a reluctant spy in *Ravishing Idiot*, opposite Brigitte Bardot. Since these did not result in the hoped-for acclaim, he returned to America where he did *The Fool Killer*, playing another oddball, one who befriends a young boy (Edward Albert), in a period drama almost completely neglected in its day, though it wound up with its share of supporters. He appeared on Broadway in one of Neil Simon's more superficial comedies, *The Star-Spangled Girl*, and on television in the quirky musical *Evening Primrose*, which was guaranteed a devout following for decades to come because Stephen Sondheim wrote the songs. There was another foray into wacko territory with *Pretty Poison*, in this case hooking up with Tuesday Weld, whose behavior turns out to be more dangerous than his. This one failed too despite some favorable notices, but in time it was recognized as one of the more underrated, disturbing films of the 1960s, though neither of the stars thought much of it. After that he showed up in supporting roles in *Catch-22*, as the nervous Chaplain Tapman in this hit-or-miss adaptation of one of the best-liked novels of the 1960s; *WUSA*, as a welfare worker; and *The Life and Times of Judge Roy Bean*, as a priest in the Wild West.

In 1970 he directed himself Off Broadway in the controversial *Steambath*, and got all the best notices as the neurotic homosexual producer in *Play It As It Lays*. By this time, there were certain tics and mannerisms creeping into his work that some interpreted as genius and others took as annoying tricks designed to nab attention. Off screen he was known for being moody and derisive of his profession. It was also common knowledge that he was gay, so it came as a surprise to many when he married photographer Berrie Berenson in 1973. That same year he and Sondheim teamed to write the clever script for the murder mystery *The Last of Sheila*, after which Perkins showed up in his first hit movie in 14 years, *Murder on the Orient Express*, as victim Richard Widmark's valet and therefore one of the suspects. Gay again, he was the bitchy photographer who tries to bed Diana Ross in *Mahogany*; replaced Anthony Hopkins on Broadway in the long-running *Equus*; then was haunted by Geraldine Chaplin's reappearance in his life in *Remember My Name*, another one made for select audiences. Going for something much more commercial, he was one of the space crew in Disney's *The Black Hole*, a lackluster attempt to cash in on *Star Wars*. He then decided it was time to drag Norman Bates out for a new generation in a sorry sequel, *Psycho II*, which did well enough to rate two more follow-ups, *Psycho III*, which Perkins directed, and *Psycho IV*, which was made for cable television. In between, he was outrageous as a creepy street preacher in director Ken Russell's fearless *Crimes of Passion*, his best film in some time, though like so many others he did, *not* for all tastes, and then directed a black comedy, *Lucky Stiff*, which got little attention. The same could be said for most of his later jobs, including a Jekyll-Hyde story with a touch of Jack the Ripper, *Edge of Sanity*, and *A Demon in My View*, which went straight to video. There was something sad about seeing a once-stellar talent such as Perkins mug around in such nonsense, but there didn't seem to be any rescue or relief in sight when it was announced that he had succumbed to complications from AIDS at the age of 60. His son, Osgood Perkins, became an actor, appearing in such movies as *Six Degrees of Separation* and *Legally Blonde*. Perkins's widow was among the passengers aboard the airliner that was deliberately flown into the north tower of the World Trade Center by terrorists on September 11, 2001.

Screen: 1953: The Actress; 1956: Friendly Persuasion; 1957: Fear Strikes Out; The Lonely Man; The Tin Star; 1958: Desire Under the Elms; This Angry Age; The Matchmaker; 1959: Green Mansions; On the Beach; 1960: Tall Story; Psycho; 1961: Goodbye Again; 1962: Phaedra; 1963: The Trial; Five Miles to Midnight; 1964: Two Are Guilty; Ravishing Idiot; 1965: The Fool Killer/Violent Journey; 1966: Is Paris Burning?; 1968: The Champagne Murders; Pretty Poison; 1970: Catch-22; WUSA; 1971: Someone Behind the Door; 1972: Ten Days Wonder; Play It As It Lays; The Life and Times of Judge Roy Bean; 1974: Lovin' Molly; Murder on the Orient Express; 1975: Mahogany; 1978: Remember My Name; 1979: Winter Kills; The Black Hole; 1980: Twice a Woman; ffolkes/North Sea Hijack; Double Negative (dtv); 1983: Psycho II; 1984: Crimes of Passion; 1986: Psycho III (and dir.); 1988: Destroyer/Shadow of Death; 1989: Edge of Sanity; 1990: The Naked Target (nUSr); 1992: A Demon in My View (dtv).

NY Stage: 1955: Tea and Sympathy; 1957: Look Homeward Angel; 1960: Greenwillow; 1962: Harold; 1966: The Star-Spangled Girl; 1970: Steambath (ob; and dir.); 1975: Equus; 1979: Romantic Comedy.

Select TV: 1954: The Missing Years (sp); The Fugitive (sp); 1955: Mr. Blue Ocean (sp); 1956: Home Is the Hero (sp); The Silent Gun (sp); Winter Dreams (sp); Joey (sp); 1966: Evening Primrose (sp); 1970: How Awful About Allan; 1978: First You Cry; Les Miserables; 1983: The Sins of Dorian Gray; For the Term of His Natural Life; 1984: The Glory Boys; 1987: Napoleon & Josephine: A Love Story; 1990: Daughter of Darkness; I'm Dangerous Tonight; Ghost Writer; Psycho IV: The Beginning; 1992: In the Deep Woods.

MILLIE PERKINS

BORN: PASSAIC, NJ, MAY 12, 1938.

A frail thing who hardly showed the characteristics necessary to be a survivor in her initial appearances, Millie Perkins hung on and kept her hand in for decades, playing timorous ladies well into middle age and beyond. A magazine model, she was one of the many hopefuls who tried out for the lead in director George Stevens's prestigious 1959 film version of the Broadway hit *The Diary of Ann Frank* for 20th Century-Fox. She got the role amid much fanfare and press and, although she gave it her best shot, Perkins was a tad too glamorous in looks and inexperienced in the acting department to hold her own against the other, more adept cast members. Nonetheless the movie's success and her brief marriage (1960–64) to actor Dean Stockwell assured her a place in the Hollywood spotlight. A role in an Elvis Presley vehicle, *Wild in the Country*, and as the principal female in *Ensign Pulver*, did little to enhance her position. However, her moody, enigmatic performance as the determined woman, who hires Warren Oates to take her into the desert, in the spottily booked western *The Shooting* showed much promise. There were roles in other indie products like *Wild in the Streets* and *Cockfighter*, but little was heard from her until she began showing up in the 1980s as ineffectual moms in *At Close Range* (Sean Penn's) and *Wall Street* (Charlie Sheen's). This was a type she continued on television (in a series about her one-time co-star, *Elvis*), direct-to-video titles, and in major features like *The Chamber*, weeping over the children who were killed by bigoted Gene Hackman.

Screen: 1959: The Diary of Anne Frank; 1961: Wild in the Country; 1963: Dulcinea; 1964: Ensign Pulver; 1966: The Shooting; 1967: Ride in the Whirlwind; 1968: Wild in the Streets; 1974: Cockfighters/Born to Kill; 1975: Lady Cocoa; 1976: The Witch Who Came From the Sea; 1983: Table for Five; 1985: George Stevens: A Filmmaker's Journey; 1986: At Close Range; Jake Speed; 1987: Slam Dance; Wall Street; 1988: Two Moon Junction; 1991: Pistol: The Birth of a Legend; 1993: Necronomicon (dtv); 1995: Bodily Harm (dtv); 1996: The Chamber; 2001: A Woman's a Helluva Thing (nUSr).

Select TV: 1961: Street of Love (sp); 1981: A Gun in the House; The Trouble With Grandpa; 1982: Love in the Present Tense; 1983: The Haunting Passion; 198384: Knots Landing (series); 1984: License to Kill; Anatomy of an Illness; Shattered Vows; 1985: A.D. (ms); The Other Lover; 1986: Penalty Phase; The Thanksgiving Promise; 1987: Strange Voices; 1988: Broken Angel; 1990: Elvis (series); Call Me Anna; 1993: Murder of Innocence; 1994: Midnight Run for Your Life; 1996: Harvest of Fire; The Summer of Ben Tyler; 1998: Any Day Now (series).

BROCK PETERS

(GEORGE FISHER) BORN: NEW YORK, NY, JULY 2, 1927. ED: CCNY.

An often unsung performer who managed to land himself some pretty impressive roles in an era when most black actors could not depend on anything even vaguely resembling steady employment, Brock Peters got his first professional job while a teen in a touring production of *Porgy and Bess* in 1943. Following college, the deep-voiced actor did a few more stage roles prior to his motion picture debut in the 1954 adaptation of *Carmen Jones*, in which he was Harry Belafonte's sergeant. It was another five years before he was back on screen, for the same director, Otto Preminger, this time in the movie of *Porgy and Bess* and upped to the important role of the villainous Crown, making a solid impression. In the early 1960s he entered the most impressive phase of his career, starting with his fine portrayal of Tom Robinson, the innocent man accused of rape, in one of the outstanding movies of the decade, *To Kill a Mockingbird*. This was followed by two films in which he was discreetly gay, *The L-Shaped Room*, as Leslie Caron's next-door neighbor who pines for Tom Bell; and *The Pawnbroker*, as the sinister hood who uses Rod Steiger's establishment to launder money. He was the token black in Charlton Heston's regiment in *Major Dundee*, and likewise among the ensemble on the besieged subway car in the lukewarm *The Incident*. Returning to uniform, he had the central role of the Union soldier who faces prejudice when he returns to the South in *The McMasters*, a movie that was actually distributed to theatres with both an upbeat and a downbeat ending, and then got star billing in the specialized movie version of the musical *Lost in the Stars*, playing Reverend Kumalo, a role he'd done on Broadway in 1972. In later years he kept up his reputation for reliability, even in the thankless role of Admiral Cartwright, which he did in two *Star Trek* films. There was also an all-black version of *The Importance of Being Earnest*, in which he played Dr. Chausible, but only the most astute moviegoers caught that one. He also received producer credit on the films *Gone Are the Days* (1963) and *Five on the Black Hand Side* (1973).

Screen: 1954: Carmen Jones; 1959: Porgy and Bess; 1962: To Kill a Mockingbird; 1963: Heavens Above!; The L-Shaped Room; 1965: The Pawnbroker; Major Dundee; 1968: The Incident; Daring Game; P.J.; 1969: Ace High; 1970: The McMasters; 1971: Jack Johnson (narrator); 1972: Black Girl; 1973: Slaughter's Big Rip-Off; Soylent Green; 1974: Lost in the Stars; 1975: Framed; 1976: Two Minute Warning; 1986: Star Trek IV: The Voyage Home; 1991: The Importance of Being Earnest; Alligator II (dtv); Star Trek VI: The Undiscovered Country; 1996: Ghosts of Mississippi; 1998: Park Day (nUSr); 2000: The Last Place on Earth (nUSr); 2001: No Prom for Cindy (voice; dtv).

NY Stage: 1943: Porgy and Bess; 1944: Anna Lucasta; 1956: Mister Johnson; 1961: King of the Dark Chamber; Kwamina; 1966: The Caucasian Chalk Circle; 1972: Lost in the Stars.

Select TV: 1960: The Snows of Kilimanjaro (sp); 1972: Welcome Home, Johnny Bristol; 1977: Seventh Avenue (ms); SST: Death Flight; 1978: Black Beauty (ms); 1979: The Incredible Journey of Dr. Meg Laurel; Roots: The Next Generations (ms); 1981: The Adventures of Huckleberry Finn; 1982–85: The Young and the Restless (series); 1983: Agatha Christie's A Caribbean Mystery; 1988: Broken Angel/Best Intentions; To Heal a Nation; 1989: Polly!; 1990: The Big One: The Great Los Angeles Earthquake; 1992: Highway Heartbreaker; The Secret; You Must Remember This; 1994: Cosmic Slop; 1995: The Element of Truth; 1995–98: Star Trek: Deep Space Nine (series); 1996: Le Baron (ms).

JEAN PETERS

(ELIZABETH JEAN PETERS) BORN: CANTON, OH, OCTOBER 15, 1926. ED: UNIV. OF MI, OH ST. DIED: OCTOBER 13, 2000.

She had the requisite pretty face to get into the movies and enough ability to stick around for nine years, but Jean Peters was, frankly, never the standout attraction in any of her movies. A Miss Ohio State contest winner, she ended up in Hollywood where 20th Century-Fox was impressed enough to sign her to a contract. She would stay exclusively with that studio except for a single loan-out. They started her off as a determined peasant girl

in love with Tyrone Power in the grand and very popular Technicolor epic *Captain From Castile* and never left her wanting for work after that. In quick succession she showed up in *Deep Waters*, as a welfare worker looking after troubled Dean Stockwell; *Love That Brute*, as the recreation director romanced by racketeer Paul Douglas; *Anne of the Indies*, top-billed as a lady pirate; *Viva Zapata!*, as Brando's woman in perhaps the most critically admired of all the films she appeared in; *Wait 'Till the Sun Shines, Nellie*, as Nellie, the restless wife of David Wayne who longs for a life outside their small town; *Niagara*, as the one sympathetic character in the piece, kidnapped by Joseph Cotten; *Pickup on South Street*, as the agent whose purse Richard Widmark lifts; *A Blueprint for Murder*, in one of her femme fatale roles, accused of poisoning her stepchild; *Vicki*, as a waitress who is murdered, reprising Carol Landis's part in this remake of *I Wake Up Screaming*; the popular Rome travelogue *Three Coins in the Fountain*, taming womanizer Rosanno Brazzi; and her last for Fox, *A Man Called Peter*, as the devoted wife of minister Richard Todd. She took her one break from Fox when she played the squaw in the life of Burt Lancaster in United Artists's *Apache*, in 1954. The girlfriend of millionaire Howard Hughes, she retired when they married in 1957. After their divorce in 1971, she popped up on television in *Winesburg, Ohio* but there were no further movie offers.

Screen: 1947: Captain From Castile; 1948: Deep Waters; 1949: It Happens Every Spring; 1950: Love That Brute; 1951: Take Care of My Little Girl; As Young as You Feel; Anne of the Indies; 1952: Viva Zapata!; Wait Till the Sun Shines, Nellie; Lure of the Wilderness; O. Henry's Full House; 1953: Niagara; Pickup on South Street; A Blueprint for Murder; Vicki; 1954: Three Coins in the Fountain; Apache; Broken Lance; 1955: A Man Called Peter.

Select TV: 1973: Winesburg, Ohio (sp); 1976: Arthur Hailey's The Moneychangers (ms); 1981: Peter and Paul.

SUSAN PETERS

(SUZANNE CARNAHAN)
BORN: SPOKANE, WA, JULY 3, 1921.
RAISED IN OR AND LOS ANGELES, CA.
DIED: OCTOBER 24, 1952.

One of Hollywood's saddest victims of fate, Susan Peters had started her career as one of the luckier young hopefuls, landing a small role in director George Cukor's *Susan and God* shortly after high school graduation. After that she studied at Max Reinhardt's School of Dramatic Arts and, during a showcase production, was spotted by a Warners talent scout. Signed to that studio in 1940, she was featured in several films, few of which gave her much to do. MGM, however, felt she had possibilities and added her to the company roster in 1942, starting her off in *Tish*, playing the wife of Richard Quine, whom she married the following year. By that time, she'd played Stephen McNally's wife in *Dr. Gillespie's New Assistant* and had been assigned to the pivotal role of the fiancée of amnesiac Ronald Colman in *Random Harvest*. The latter was one of the year's big movies and, for her acceptable but hardly noteworthy performance, she earned an Oscar nomination in the supporting category. From this she was rushed into three leads, *Assignment at Brittany*, opposite Jean-Pierre Aumont; the comedy *Young Ideas*, in which she was top-billed *over* Mary Astor and Herbert Marshall, playing a meddlesome college girl trying to break up their marriage; and the controversial *Song of Russia*, as a pianist who falls for Robert Taylor. On New Year's Day of 1945, tragedy struck on a hunting trip with her husband, when her gun accidentally discharged, the bullet lodging itself in her spine. Left paralyzed from the waist down, Peters faced an uncertain future in the business. MGM tried to come up with scripts for her but she found them too treacly and ended her contract. She divorced Quine in 1948, the same year she made her final movie, for Columbia, *Sign of the Ram*, playing an abrasive invalid who nearly destroys her family. It failed and she found work in regional theater and then on television, where she started a series, *Miss Susan*, as a wheelchair-bound lawyer. She died shortly after ending the series, having lost the desire to go on. In 1989 ex-husband Quine, who had since become a film director, took his own life by shooting himself.

Screen: AS SUZANNE CARNAHAN: 1940: Susan and God; Money and the Woman; Santa Fe Trail; 1941: The Strawberry Blonde; Meet John Doe; Here Comes Happiness.

AS SUSAN PETERS: 1941: Scattergood Pulls the Strings; Three Sons O'Guns; 1942: The Big Shot; Tish; Andy Hardy's Double Trouble; Dr. Gillespie's New Assistant; Random Harvest; 1943: Young Ideas; Assignment in Brittany; Song of Russia; 1945: Keep Your Powder Dry; 1948: Sign of the Ram.

Select TV: 1951: Miss Susan (series).

SLIM PICKENS

(LOUIS BERT LINDLEY, JR.) BORN: KINGSBERG, CA, JUNE 29, 1919. DIED: DECEMBER 8, 1983.

It was that voice, that whiny twang, that seemed to come from way down deep in the soil of white-trash Hicksville USA, that made Slim Pickens so very right for the movie western. A former clown on the rodeo circuit (where he got his memorable stage name), he was fairly well-known in that world when he decided to try his hand as an actor, debuting in the cast of the 1950 Errol Flynn western *Rocky Mountain*. From there he became a staple at Republic Pictures, where he showed up in several "B's," usually playing characters named Slim Pickens. He segued into higher budgeted fare with director John Ford's *The Sun Shines Bright*, as a backwoodsman, and became an even more familiar presence once the 1960s arrived, making an indelible impression as the loathsome deputy who torments Marlon Brando in *One-Eyed Jacks*. However, his cinematic peak came in a non-western, though his character was a cowboy through-and-through, in *Dr. Strangelove or: How I Learned to Stop Worrying and Love the Bomb*. As the outspoken redneck Major "King" Kong, his raw and real persona was never better utilized and his surreal bomb-riding sequence became one of the great moments in movie history. He was called on to pilot the vehicle of the title in the 1966 remake of *Stagecoach* (following in the boot-steps of Andy Devine) and had another hilarious role as Harvey Korman's henchman who leads the soundstage brawl at the climax of the classic cowboy spoof *Blazing Saddles*. He showed up in no fewer than three different television series toward the end of his life, and even got top billing, running *Pink Motel*, a trashy sex comedy with Phyllis Diller. He retired after surgery to remove a brain tumor left him unable to work.

Screen: 1950: Rocky Mountain; 1952: Colorado Sundown; The Last Musketeer; Old Oklahoma Plains; Border Saddlemates; Thunderbirds; South Pacific Trail; The Story of Will Rogers; 1953: Old Overland Trail; Iron Mountain Trail; Down Laredo Way; Shadows of Tombstone; Red River Shore; The Sun Shines Bright; 1954: The Boy From Oklahoma; Phantom Stallion; The Outcast; 1955: The Last Command; Santa Fe Passage; 1956: Stranger at My Door; When Gangland Strikes; The Great Locomotive Chase; Gun Brothers; 1957: Gunsight Ridge; 1958:

Tonka; The Sheepman; 1959: Escort West; 1960: Chartroose Caboose; 1961: One-Eyed Jacks; A Thunder of Drums; 1963: Savage Sam; 1964: Dr. Strangelove or: How I Learned to Stop Worrying and Love the Bomb; 1965: Major Dundee; In Harm's Way; Up From the Beach; The Glory Guys; 1966: An Eye for an Eye/Talion; Stagecoach; 1967: The Flim Flam Man; Rough Night in Jericho; 1968: Will Penny; Never a Dull Moment; Skidoo; 1969: Eighty Steps to Jonah; 1970: Operation Snafu/Situation Normal All Fouled Up; The Ballad of Cable Hogue; Savage Season; 1971: The Deserter; 1972: The Cowboys; J.C./Iron Horsemen; The Honkers; The Getaway; 1973: Pat Garrett and Billy the Kid; 1974: Blazing Saddles; Bootleggers; Ginger in the Morning; 1975: Legend of Earl Durand; Rancho Deluxe; Poor Pretty Eddie; The Apple Dumpling Gang; White Line Fever; 1976: Pony Express Rider; Hawmps; 1977: Mr. Billion; The White Buffalo; 1978: Wishbone Cutter/The Shadow of Chikara/Shadow Mountain; The Swarm; Smokey and the Good Time Outlaw; 1979: The Sweet Creek Country War; Beyond the Poseidon Adventure; 1941; The Black Hole (voice); 1980: Tome Horn; Spirit of the Wind; Honeysuckle Rose; Christmas Mountain (dtv); 1981: The Howling; 1982: Pink Motel.

Select TV: 1961–62: The Outlaws (series); 1963: Bristle Face (sp); 1967: Custer (series); 1971: Sam Hill: Who Killed the Mysterious Mr. Foster?; The Desperate Mission; The Devil and Miss Sarah; 1972: Rolling Man; 1973: Hitched; 1974: Twice in a Lifetime; The Gun and the Pulpit; 1975: Babe; 1976: Banjo Hackett: Roamin' Free; 1979: The Sacketts; B.J. and the Bear (series); Undercover with the KKK; 1980: Swan Song; 1981: This House Possessed; Charlie and the Great Balloon Race; Nashville Grab; 1981–82: Nashville Palace (series); 1981–83: Hee-Haw (series); 1982: Filthy Rich (series).

MARY PICKFORD

(GLADYS SMITH) BORN: TORONTO, ONTARIO, CANADA, APRIL 8, 1893. DIED: MAY 29, 1979.

Certainly the most popular female star of the silent cinema, Mary Pickford was very much a product of a bygone era, when someone could be labeled "America's Sweetheart" without cynicism or irony. If there was an irony, it was the fact that behind the feisty and lovable ladies, orphans, and curly-locked heroines she played on the screen was a shrewd businesswoman. This was fortunate as far as her future income was concerned because she was an outstanding example of a performer whose charm pretty much disappeared with the advent of sound. A child performer at the age of five, she acted with stock and touring companies in such plays as *Uncle Tom's Cabin* and *The Fatal Wedding*, billed under her real name. She came to Broadway in 1907 to appear in *The Warrens of Virginia* and took this property around the country for two years, at the end of which she was hired by D. W. Griffith to appear in a short called "Pippa Passes." Between 1909 and 1912 she would appear in over 125 short subjects, her first starring role being "The Violin Maker of Cremona," which co-starred Owen Moore, who became her first husband (1909–1915). "The Little Teacher" is often credited as the film that started her on the road to success and she was in demand enough at this point that she was able to accept a more lucrative offer from Independent Motion Picture Co. in 1910. This stint didn't last but a year by which time she returned, bigger than ever, to Biograph. She stayed there until she decided she wanted to return to the stage and ended her contract with them, coming back to Broadway in 1912 to great fanfare in *A Good Little Devil*. It was an unprecedented move for a major film star in that era to leave the world of movies, even temporarily, to do theater.

Adolph Zukor's Famous Players paid her to reprise *A Good Little Devil* on film in 1913, and although it did not duplicate its stage success, she was given a contract for that company where she did score a sizable hit the next year with *Tess of the Storm Country*. Despite the fact that she was now 20, audiences had no trouble accepting her as a sweet young girl with a head full of golden curls; she would continue this masquerade for years to come. What her fans liked best was to see her as the poor put-upon thing, smiling through it all, who triumphs over great adversity by the end. This was why there was little surprise that her roles for Famous Players at this time included *Cinderella* and *Nell Gwynn* (in *Mistress Nell*). She was the biggest star for the company when they merged with Jesse Lasky's Company (it eventually became Paramount) and her hits at the time included *Poor Little Rich Girl*; *Rebecca of Sunnybrook Farm*; and *The Little Princess*, all of which were dusted off in some form or another two decades later for Shirley Temple; *The Little American*, a romantic triangle directed by Cecil B. DeMille that even threw in the sinking of the Lusitania for good measure; *Stella Maris*, which allowed her not only to play the dear crippled girl but the homely old crone who cares for her, a display of versatility that won her further devotees; the unforgettably titled *Amarilly of Clothes Line Alley*; and *Captain Kidd Jr.* The year 1919 saw the end of her contract with Zukor and found her romantically involved with just about the hottest actor around, Douglas Fairbanks. After signing up to do three pictures for First National, of which *Daddy Long Legs* was the biggest hit, she and Fairbanks, together with Charlie Chaplin and director D. W. Griffith, established United Artists in order to distribute their own product, a milestone event in motion picture history. Another milestone, as far as the fans were concerned, was the marriage of Pickford and Fairbanks in 1920; it made them the most famous acting couple of their day.

Pickford's first production under the United Artists banner was a prime choice, *Pollyana*, as the relentlessly optimistic 12-year-old (she was now 27) whose bright outlook changes the sourpusses around her. This became one of the defining properties of her career and the same could be said of *Little Lord Fauntleroy*, in which she pulled off playing the title character as well as his mother, Dearest. This was an example of Pickford diving into potentially sticky waters and emerging triumphant; the whole point of the boy being teased for his sissified clothes and manner was diluted by having an older woman playing him. Not wanting to tamper with the box-office sales, she dusted off one of her early hits, *Tess of the Storm Country*, and the crowds showed up all over again. Wanting to take a risk and deciding it was time to grow up, she hired director Ernst Lubitsch to guide her through *Rosita*, in which she was cast as a dancing girl in love with a nobleman. The making of the movie was a nightmare, the public response softer than expected, and Pickford hated the finished product. Giving in to the desire that she play younger again, she compromised by playing an 18-year-old in *Dorothy Vernon of Haddon Hall*, a lavish costume epic set in the court of Queen Elizabeth I (a movie which she is said to have directed portions of). She then went back to more juvenile territory, portraying a street kid in *Little Annie Rooney*, after which she was the protector of a group of orphans stuck in an alligator swamp in *Sparrows*. Since she was supposed to be the eldest of these youngins, it could be theorized that she was at least becoming a motherly figure, in spirit. Her silent career ended with a bright comedy, *My Best Girl*, which really showed the lighter direction her career should have gone at this point. It also paired her with Buddy Rogers, who would later become her off-screen partner as well.

Choosing *Coquette* as her first venture into sound was considered a wise move at the time. It was United Artists's first sound feature and a popular one, despite the fact that it was just as creaky and static as most melodramas of the day. Pickford gesticulated wildly as a Southern girl whose miserable dad ruins her romantic life and she wound up getting an Academy Award. Seen today, it is fairly safe to say that her performance is a strong contender for the worst to ever receive the coveted Best Actress Oscar. This was followed by the long-awaited screen teaming of Pickford and Douglas Fairbanks, in *The Taming of the Shrew*, a truncated version of the Shakespeare play that pleased no one and only emphasized the fact that both stars had rather unattractive speaking voices. Of course the curious showed up, though in later years it was branded with a reputation as a spectacular failure. Two years passed before she filmed again, this time opting for a musical, *Kiki*, in another misguided performance, as a French chorus girl. It was clear that the girlish magic that had captivated everyone for years was now coming across as faintly grotesque and the movie flopped, as did her last, *Secrets*, a melodrama with Leslie Howard. She officially retired from movie acting in 1933 and, two years later, she and Fairbanks ended their evaporating marriage. In 1937 she married former co-star Buddy Rogers and the two settled into a happy relationship at the famed Beverly Hills estate Pickfair. To keep busy Pickford did some writing and guested on radio. In 1936 she was appointed vice president of United Artists and stayed as an owner of the corporation until she and Chaplin were bought out in 1953. She also received credit as producer on *One Rainy Afternoon* (1936), *The Gay Desperado* (1936), and *Sleep My Love* (1948). Long out of the spotlight, the public had its first glimpse of her in some time when she was seen on film accepting her special Academy Award at the 1976 ceremony. Her movies were little circulated by that time and she was a vague name from the past to most viewers who probably wouldn't have been able to tap into her old-fashioned charms anyway. In 1956 she published her memoir, *Sunshine and Shadow*. Her brother Jack Pickford (1896–1933) was also a star of some note during the silent era.

Screen (features): 1913: Caprice; In a Bishop's Carriage; 1914: Heart's Adrift; Tess of the Storm Country; A Good Little Devil; Such a Little Queen; The Eagle's Mate; 1915: Behind the Scenes; Fanchon the Cricket; Cinderella; Mistress Nell; The Dawn of a Tomorrow; Little Pal; Rags; The Girl from Yesterday; 1916: Poor Little Peppina; Madame Butterfly; The Foundling; The Eternal Grind; Hulda from Holland; Less Than the Dust (also exec. prod.); 1917: Pride of the Clan; Poor Little Rich Girl (and exec. prod.); Romance of the Redwoods (and exec. prod.); The Little American (and exec. prod.); Rebecca of Sunnybrook Farm (and exec. prod.); The Little Princess (and exec. prod.); 1918: Stella Maris (and exec. prod.); Amarilly of Clothes Line Alley (and exec. prod.); Johanna Enlists; M'liss (and exec. prod.); How Could You Jean? (and exec. prod.); 1919: Captain Kidd Jr. (and exec. prod.); Daddy Long Legs (and prod.); The Hoodlum (and exec. prod.); Heart o' the Hills (and exec. prod.); 1920: Pollyanna (and exec. prod.); Suds (and exec. prod.); 1921: The Love Light (and prod.); Through the Back Door (and prod.); Little Lord Fauntleroy (and prod.); 1922: Tess of the Storm Country (and prod.); 1923: Rosita (and prod.); Hollywood; 1924: Dorothy Vernon of Haddon Hall (and prod.); 1925: Little Annie Rooney (and prod.); 1926: Sparrows (and prod.); 1927: My Best Girl (and prod.); The Gaucho; 1929: Coquette; The Taming of the Shrew; 1931: Kiki; 1933: Secrets.

NY Stage: 1907: The Warrens of Virginia; 1913: A Good Little Devil.

WALTER PIDGEON
BORN: EAST ST. JOHN, NEW BRUNSWICK,
CANADA, SEPTEMBER 23, 1897.
ED: NEW ENGLAND CONSERVATORY OF MUSIC.
DIED: SEPTEMBER 25, 1984.

Fatherly in nature, Walter Pidgeon didn't exactly take the cinema by storm with his deep, sonorous voice and muted personality, but he racked up a long and fairly illustrious list of credits, making him an enduring, dependable participant throughout the changing eras of Hollywood. He made his stage debut in a production of Shaw's *You Never Can Tell*, after which he teamed up with Elsie Janis as a singing duo, touring in vaudeville. He made his Broadway debut in *The Puzzles of 1925*, which got him a small role as a reporter in the Paramount film *Mannequin* the following year. Freelancing, he wound up in all kinds of movies that did nothing to establish him in any way. Nevertheless, First National signed him to a contract at the dawn of the talkies, since he had all that singing experience behind him. They put him in four paired-down versions of some old stage operettas, *Bride of the Regiment*, *Viennese Nights*, *Sweet Kitty Bellairs*, and *Kiss Me Again*, but they were nothing more than further dubious contributions to the static musical genre of the time. After a few more supporting parts, he returned to New York where he did four plays including *The Night of January 16th* and *There's Wisdom in Women*. From these he received some movie offers, signing a contract with producer Walter Wanger who gave him two assignments, *Big Brown Eyes* and *Fatal Lady*, and then dropped him. His less-than-inspired film career then continued over at Universal for a spell, until salvation came from MGM who signed him up in 1937. They started him off in what turned out to be his first really popular movie, *Saratoga*, although he had the role of the rich guy who clearly was never going to win Jean Harlow over Clark Gable. Similar things happen to him in *Girl of the Golden West*, as a sheriff in love with Jeanette MacDonald (of course Nelson Eddy got her), and *Too Hot to Handle*, as a newsreel journalist keen on Myrna Loy (Gable won again). He was, however, deemed worthy of winning Mary Astor in *Listen, Darling*, but then the real stars of the film were Judy Garland and Freddie Bartholomew anyway.

He got to play the lead in *Nick Carter — Master Detective*, a part he revived again in *Phantom Raiders* and *Sky Murder*, and then was borrowed by 20th Century-Fox for two of his best roles, the assassin on the run after he tries to kill Hitler, in *Man Hunt*, and the priest who gently romances Maureen O'Hara in *How Green Was My Valley*, showing how the low-keyed Pidgeon style cold be put to excellent use, in this Academy Award-winner for Best Picture. Meanwhile, back on the home lot, something magical happened when he was cast alongside Greer Garson in a gooey melodrama about orphans, *Blossoms in the Dust*. Something about them seemed to register with 1940s audiences, be it their levelheaded reaction to adversity or the impression of a really good marriage at work. In any case, the studio put them together again for *Mrs. Miniver* and it became one of the smash hits of the war years. Americans went crazy over this glossy portrait of the British homefront and how its citizens maintained their spirit as the Nazis crept into their backyards. The movie won the Academy Award for Best Picture of 1942, making it the second year in a row that Pidgeon was involved in the big prize winner. Pidgeon, for his warm, pipe-smoking reserve, received a nomination and was in the running the following year as well, playing Garson's dedicated husband and fellow-scientist in *Madame Curie*, which was surprisingly straightforward as 1940s biopics went and, even more surprisingly, another box-office hit.

The Garson-Pidgeon combo continued its financial winning streak with the ponderous *Mrs. Parkington*, in which Pidgeon played Garson's flamboyant millionaire hubby, and then, trying something different, with the comedy *Julia Misbehaves*, which was pretty poor stuff. In between, Pidgeon had a mature romance with Ginger Rogers in the entertaining *Week-end at the Waldorf* and was a patient dad to eager youngster Jane Powell in the musical *Holiday in Mexico*, though most of the songs belonged to Ms. Powell.

He was the Major General in MGM's all-male, intellectual war film, *Command Decision*; was asked to share Garson with top-billed Errol Flynn and Robert Young for *That Forsyte Woman*; and then he and Greer were roped into the bad idea of bringing back the Minivers for *The Miniver Story*, which was actually shot in England this time. There was an attempt at a new series, following in the footsteps of Ronald Colman, among others, with *Calling Bulldog Drummond*, but its impact was nil and there was no demand for any others. The dad years were fast upon him and he did such duty in *Million Dollar Mermaid* (Esther Williams), *The Last Time I Saw Paris* (Elizabeth Taylor), *Hit the Deck* (Jane Powell again), and *The Rack* (Paul Newman); while he was the perfect executive type in both *The Bad and the Beautiful*, as a studio head, and *Executive Suite*, as one of the corporate bigwigs vying for the top spot. A last teaming with Garson, *Scandal at Scourie*, received the thumbs-down from critics and viewers, while a big-budget sci-fi adventure, *Forbidden Planet* — in a role inspired by Shakespeare's Prospero — turned out to be one of the best-loved films of the genre and gave him a kind of lasting fame to its fans. In that same area, he was Admiral Nelson in the big-screen version of *Voyage to the Bottom of the Sea*, and was at his best as the Senate majority leader in the all-star *Advise and Consent*. The last time large audiences saw him on the big screen was in *Funny Girl*, in a fairly small role as impresario Florenz Ziegfeld. There also were lesser assignments in such movies as *Skyjacked*, as a senator; *The Neptune Factor*, as a scientist; and *Harry in Your Pocket*, as an old-time pickpocket. After a guest bit in Mae West's camp classic *Sextette*, he retired from acting in 1978.

Screen: 1926: Mannequin; The Outsider; Miss Nobody; Old Loves and New; Marriage License; 1927: Heart of Salome; The Gorilla; The Girl from Rio/Sumuru; The Thirteenth Juror; 1928: The Gateway of the Moon; Woman Wise; Turn Back the Hours; Clothes Make the Woman; Melody of Love; 1929: Her Private Life; A Most Immoral Lady; 1930: Bride of the Regiment; Sweet Kitty Bellairs; Show Girl in Hollywood; The Gorilla; Going Wild; Viennese Nights; 1931: Kiss Me Again; The Hot Heiress; 1932: Rockabye; 1933: The Kiss Before the Mirror; 1934: Journal of a Crime; 1936: Big Brown Eyes; Fatal Lady; She's Dangerous; 1937: Girl Overboard; As Good as Married; A Girl with Ideas; Saratoga; My Dear Miss Aldrich; 1938: Man-Proof; The Girl of the Golden West; The Shopworn Angel; Too Hot to Handle; Listen, Darling; 1939: Society Lawyer; 6,000 Enemies; Stronger Than Desire; Nick Carter — Master Detective; 1940: It's a Date; Dark Command; The House Across the Bay; Phantom Raiders; Sky Murder; Flight Command; 1941: Man Hunt; Blossoms in the Dust; How Green Was My Valley; Design for Scandal; 1942: Mrs. Miniver; White Cargo; 1943: Madame Curie; The Youngest Profession; 1944: Mrs. Parkington; 1945: Week-end at the Waldorf; 1946: Holiday in Mexico; The Secret Heart; 1947: If Winter Comes; Cass Timberlane; 1948: Command Decision; Julia Misbehaves; 1949: The Red Danube; That Forsyte Woman; 1950: The Miniver Story; 1951: Soldiers Three; Calling Bulldog Drummond; The Unknown Man; Quo Vadis (narrator); 1952: The Sellout; Million Dollar Mermaid; The Bad and the Beautiful; 1953: Scandal at Scourie; Dream Wife; 1954: Executive

Suite; Men of the Fighting Lady; The Last Time I Saw Paris; Deep in My Heart; **1955:** The Glass Slipper (narrator); Hit the Deck; **1956:** Forbidden Planet; The Rack; These Wilder Years; **1961:** Voyage to the Bottom of the Sea; **1962:** Big Red; Advise and Consent; The Two Colonels; **1963:** The Shortest Day; **1967:** Warning Shot; **1968:** Funny Girl; **1969:** Rascal (narrator); The Vatican Affair; **1972:** Skyjacked; **1973:** The Neptune Factor; Harry in Your Pocket; **1974:** Yellow Headed Summer; **1976:** Won Ton Ton, the Dog Who Saved Hollywood; Two Minute Warning; **1978:** Sextette.

NY Stage: 1925: Puzzles of 1925; **1934:** No More Ladies; **1935:** Something Gay; There's Wisdom in Women; Night of January 16th; **1956:** The Happiest Millionaire; **1959:** Take Me Along; **1966:** Dinner at Eight.

Select TV: 1959: Meet Me in St. Louis (sp); **1965:** Cinderella (sp); **1967:** How I Spent My Summer Vacation/Deadly Roulette; Cosa Nostra: Arch Enemy of the FBI; **1970:** The House on Green Apple Road; The Mask of Sheba; **1972:** The Screaming Woman; **1974:** Live Again, Die Again; The Girl on the Late, Late Show; **1975:** You Lie So Deep My Love; Murder on Flight 502; **1976:** The Lindbergh Kidnapping Case.

ZASU PITTS

Born: Parsons, KS, January 3, 1898.
Died: June 7, 1963.

Frail, nervous, sad-faced ZaSu (pronounced Zay-Soo) Pitts had hoped to show the world that she could be a fine dramatic actress and pretty much did so, at least for a while, during the silent era. But her fluttery nature and expressive hands, not to mention her very name, were just flat-out funny so, when sound came and audiences could hear her quavering voice as well, she made a living as one of the most distinctive of all character comediennes. While still in her teens, she journeyed to Hollywood to seek employment and landed some extra work and stunt jobs with producer Al Christie. She started getting small parts at various studios, including roles in two Mary Pickford films, *Rebecca of Sunnybrook Farm* and *How Could You Jean?*, and then was upped to star billing in 1919, for director King Vidor, in *Better Times*, a gentle drama-comedy about a plain-Jane who pretends to be in love with a famous baseball player. In a similar vein, she starred in *Seeing It Through, Bright Skies, The Heart of Twenty,* and *Patsy,* which required her to pass herself off as a man. The second and third of these teamed her with Tom Gallery whom she married in 1920 (and divorced 12 years later). She stayed dramatic for *West of the Water Tower* and *Triumph,* among others, and then was given the crowning role of her silent film career, in director Erich von Stroheim's ambitious *Greed,* in which she performed beautifully as the wife whose selfish and petty money-hoarding leads to her demise. Continuing to gain critical raves, she was a suffragette in *Wages for Wives*; a kidnapper in *Mannequin*; Wallace Beery's girlfriend in *Casey at the Bat*; and the neglected wife of Emil Jannings in *Sins of the Fathers.* Declaring that she was his favorite actress, von Stroheim hired her again for *The Wedding March,* where she was moving as the crippled heiress whom von Stroheim himself is forced to marry. The project was unwieldy enough to require a second part to the story, *The Honeymoon,* but only European audiences were allowed to see it, albeit in a truncated form. Similarly, only the Europeans got to see her play Lew Ayres's mom in *All Quiet on the Western Front*; it was decided that she came across as too comical in the part and was replaced in the sound version by Beryl Mercer. This occurrence pretty much signaled the end of her serious acting years and

so, to comical effect, she was romantically pursued by James Gleason in *Oh Yeah!,* and played the complaining maid in *No, No, Nanette,* a part she would repeat in the 1940 version as well.

Paramount cast ZaSu and Leon Errol as the leads in *Finn and Hattie,* a pair of America low-lifes on vacation in Paris, and then Universal teamed her with the equally sad-looking Slim Summerville for *Unexpected Father.* The studio liked the combination enough to pair them up again for *They Just Had to Get Married; Out All Night; Her First Mate; Love, Honor and Oh Baby!;* and *Love Birds,* while RKO also borrowed them for *Their Big Moment.* Around the same time, producer Hal Roach saw ZaSu as a perfect foil for the pretty Thelma Todd and made them a kind of female Laurel and Hardy for 17 short subjects, starting with "Let's Do Things" in 1931 and ending with "One Track Minds" two years later. Pitts quit the series and was replaced by Patsy Kelly. Also during this period of broad comedy, Erich von Stroheim came looking for her one last time for his final directorial effort, *Hello, Sister,* where she played a lonely woman who loses James Dunn to her best friend. It was another of the temperamental director's aborted, tampered-with efforts and an utter box-office and critical failure, sending Pitts right back into comedy. Therefore she was El Brendel's fed-up fiancée in *The Meanest Gal in Town*; a hammy actress in *Sign It and Like It*; Will Rogers's wife in *Mr. Skitch*; and spinster Tabitha Hazy, who finds an unlikely suitor in W. C. Fields in the best scene in *Mrs. Wiggs of the Cabbage Patch.* The high point of her comedic career came in 1935 when she played the Widow Judson, who attracts the attention of proper British butler Charles Laughton, in the charming *Ruggles of Red Gap,* one of the big hits of the year. RKO hired her to take over the role of the amateur sleuth Hildegarde Withers, previously played by Edna May Oliver, in the "B's" *The Plot Thickens* and *Forty Naughty Girls,* after which she traveled to England to star in a pair of minor comedies, *Wanted* and *Merry Comes to Town.* As the 1940s arrived, she continued to ply her trade playing spinsters and domestics but in increasingly less-prestigious fare, such as *Mexican Spitfire's Baby* (as Miss Pepper, a role she repeated in *Mexican Spitfire at Sea*), and *Meet the Mob.* There were also late reteamings with Slim Summerville in *Niagara Falls* and *Miss Polly.* She had a good role as one of the old biddies in MGM's *Tish* and then left the movies for a bit to do some stage work. She returned in a pair of hits, *Life With Father,* as Irene Dunne's fluttery cousin Cora, and *Francis,* as a lieutenant (a role she returned to in *Francis Joins the WACs*), but then began cutting down on her movie roles considerably. She was last seen as Doris Day's nervous maid in *The Thrill of It All,* and the police station switchboard operator in *It's a Mad Mad Mad Mad World,* both released posthumously.

Screen (shorts): 1917: Tillie of the Nine Lives; He Had 'em Buffaloed; Canning the Cannibal King; The Battling Bellboy; O-My the Tent-Mover; Behind the Map; Why They Left Home; His Fatal Beauty; Uneasy Money; We Have the Papers; Desert Dilemma; Behind the Footlights; **1928:** Sunlight; **1931:** Let's Do Things; Catch as Catch Can; The Pajama Party; War Mamas; **1932:** Seal Skins; On the Loose; Red Noses; Strictly Unreliable; The Old Bull; Show Business; Alum and Eve; The Soilers; **1933:** Sneak Easily; Asleep in the Feet; Maids a la Mode; Bargain of the Century; One Track Minds.

Screen (features): 1917: The Little Princess; **1918:** A Modern Musketeer; How Could You, Jean?; Talk of the Town; A Society Sensation; A Lady's Name; **1919:** As the Sun Went Down; Better Times; Men, Women and Money; The Other Half; Poor Relations; **1920:** Seeing It Through; Bright Skies; Heart of Twenty; **1921:** Patsy; **1922:** Is Matrimony a Failure?; For the Defense; Youth to Youth; A Daughter of Luxury; **1923:** Poor

Men's Wives; The Girl Who Came Back; Souls for Sale; Mary of the Movies; Three Wise Fools; Hollywood; Tea — With a Kick; 1924: West of the Water Tower; Daughters of Today; Triumph; The Goldfish; Changing Husbands; Wine of Youth; The Fast Set; Secrets of the Night; Legend of Hollywood; 1925: Greed; The Great Divide; The Re-Creation of Brian Kent; Pretty Ladies; Old Shoes; A Woman's Faith; The Business of Love; Lazybones; Thunder Mountain; Wages for Wives; The Great Love; 1926: Mannequin; What Happened to Jones; Monte Carlo; Early to Wed; Her Big Night; Sunny Side Up; Risky Business; 1927: Casey at the Bat; 1928: Wife Savers; Buck Privates; 13 Washington Square; Sins of the Fathers; The Wedding March; The Honeymoon (nUSr); 1929: The Dummy; The Squall; Twin Beds; The Argyle Case; Oh Yeah!; This Thing Called Love; Her Private Life; Paris; The Locked Door; 1930: No, No, Nanette; Honey; All Quiet on the Western Front (European version only); The Devil's Holiday; Little Accident; Monte Carlo; The Squealer; War Nurse; Sin Takes a Holiday; The Lottery Bride; Free Love; River's End; Passion Flower; 1931: Finn and Hattie; Bad Sister; Beyond Victory; Seed; A Woman of Experience; The Guardsman; The Big Gamble; Their Mad Moment; Penrod and Sam; The Secret Witness; 1932: Broken Lullaby/The Man I Killed; Unexpected Father; Steady Company; Shopworn; The Trial of Vivienne Ware; Strangers of the Evening; Westward Passage; Is My Face Red; Destry Rides Again; Make Me a Star; Roar of the Dragon; The Crooked Circle; Back Street; Blondie of the Follies; Vanishing Frontier; Madison Square Garden; Once in a Lifetime; 1933: They Just Had to Get Married; Out All Night; Hello, Sister; Professional Sweetheart; Her First Mate; Aggie Appleby — Make of Men; Meet the Baron; Love, Honor and Oh Baby!; Mr. Skitch; 1934: The Meanest Gal in Town; Sing and Like It; Two Alone; Love Birds; Three on a Honeymoon; Private Scandal; Dames; Their Big Moment; Mrs. Wiggs of the Cabbage Patch; The Gay Bride; 1935: Ruggles of Red Gap; Spring Tonic; She Gets Her Man; Hot Tip; Going Highbrow; The Affair of Susan; 1936: 13 Hours by Air; Mad Holiday; The Plot Thickens; 1937: Sing Me a Love Song; Wanted; Merry Comes to Town; Forty Naughty Girls; 52nd Street; 1939: The Lady's From Kentucky; Mickey the Kid; Naughty But Nice; Nurse Edith Cavell; Eternally Yours; 1940: It All Came True; No, No, Nanette; 1941: Broadway Limited; Mexican Spitfire's Baby; Niagara Falls; Weekend for Three; Miss Polly; Uncle Joe; The Bashful Bachelor; 1942: Meet the Mob; Mexican Spitfire at Sea; Tish; 1943: Let's Face It; 1946: Breakfast in Hollywood; The Perfect Marriage; 1947: Like With Father; 1949: Francis; 1952: The Denver and Rio Grande; 1954: Francis Joins the WACs; 1957: This Could Be the Night; 1961: Teen-Age Millionaire; 1963: The Thrill of It All; It's a Mad Mad Mad Mad World.

NY Stage: 1944: Ramshackle Inn; 1953: The Bat.

Select TV: 1954: Pardon My Aunt (sp), The Happy Touch (sp), The Man Who Came to Dinner (sp); 1955: The Silent Partner (sp); 1956: Mr. Belvedere (sp); 1956–60: Oh Susanna!/The Gale Storm Show (series).

DONALD PLEASENCE

BORN: WORKSOP, NOTTINGHAMSHIRE, ENGLAND, OCTOBER 5, 1919. DIED: FEBRUARY 2, 1995.

Throughout an astoundingly large and often obscure group of films, Donald Pleasence played a wide range of characters in a variety of genres and yet most audiences cannot help but think of him as one of film's foremost weirdos, suitable for films with a touch of the macabre. Perhaps it was his odd gaze

or his meditative speaking voice that pegged him as a member of the cuckoo bin but he pretty much became a staple in horror and the fantastic, playing doctors and scientists who, if not completely "out there," often seemed to be. While employed as a railway stationmaster, he sought work in theater and eventually became a stage manager at a theatrical company on Channel Island. He made his acting debut there in 1939; three years later he was seen on the London stage for the first time, in a production of Twelfth Night. After spending part of World War II as a prisoner of war, he returned to the theater in such plays as Vicious Circle and Right Side Up, and joined Vivien Leigh and Laurence Olivier in their tour of Caesar and Cleopatra and Antony and Cleopatra, which marked his first appearance on Broadway, in 1951. Back in London, he won notice for Hobson's Choice and Ebb Tide (which he wrote), resulting in some film offers, making his motion picture bow in 1954, in the farce Orders are Orders. This was followed by various other supporting roles, including The Beachcomber, as an Indian; The Black Tent, as an Arab; the remake of A Tale of Two Cities, as the two-faced Barsad; and Look Back in Anger, as the barrow-market official. True fame came when he caused a stir playing the tramp in the controversial Harold Pinter drama The Caretaker, which was first seen in London in 1960 and then brought to America the following year. There was a film made of the piece in 1964, with the actor (along with Alan Bates and Robert Shaw) repeating his role (and serving as one of the producers). It was not meant for wide consumption and even had the misfortune of having its name changed to The Guest in the U.S., so as not to be confused with the Polly Bergen melodrama The Caretakers. In the early 1960s Pleasence considerably increased his film assignments, including his earliest forays into the horror field, with Circus of Horrors, as its drunken owner, who's done in by a bear, and Mania/The Flesh and the Fiends, as the notorious real-life grave robber, William Hare, both films becoming well regarded among genre fans.

After additional small roles, as a Parliament member in No Love for Johnnie, and as a Dutch policeman in Lisa/The Inspector, he had the first significant part in a major American production, as the pathetic forger who realizes he is losing his eyesight, in the masterful adventure The Great Escape. This, along with his part as the devious scientist in the miniaturizing sci-fi hit Fantastic Voyage, became one of his two best-known roles as far as 1960s mainstream audiences were concerned. However, his two juiciest leads during this period were in a pair of films that cemented his reputation as a masterful interpreter of men-on-the-egde, Dr. Crippen, as the timid real-life wife murderer who made British headlines 50 years earlier, and the cult-favorite Cul-de-Sac, as the pathetic, cross-dressing husband who is terrorized by a pair of hoods. Now a standard presence on the big screen, he was one of the Nazis in The Night of the Generals; appeared fleetingly but memorably as the scar-faced, cat-stroking Blofeld in the James Bond adventure You Only Live Twice; was at his over-the-top peak as the nutso backwoods preacher in Will Penny; played one of the unscrupulous businessmen trying to destroy Paris in the all-star flop The Madwoman of Chaillot; and was the evil gun trader in the pro-Indian western Soldier Blue. His bald head came in handy for the pretentious futuristic fable THX-1138, since everyone was supposed to be sans hair, after which he was the wicked Uncle Ebenezer in the umpteenth version of Kidnapped, and the stupid baron in the creepy update of The Pied Piper. Roles in the anthology horror stories Tales That Witness Madness and From Beyond the Grave (which also featured his daughter, Angela) were instrumental in many associating him with this genre. There were other such assignments, in The Mutations, as a wacko scientist combining people with plants; *Land of the Minotaur*, as the priest opposing evil Peter Cushing; *The Devil Within Her*, as the doctor who delivers the spawn of Satan; and *The Uncanny*, as a character unsubtly called De'Ath. In between these he was showed up in somewhat more main-stream fare, playing a Hollywood hack in *The Last Tycoon*; a doctor in *Oh, God!*; and Heinrich Himmler in *The Eagle Has Landed*, to name some of his more widely released credits. In 1978 he appeared as the prophetically grim and determined psychiatrist Dr. Loomis in the effective chiller *Halloween*, and since this became a good-sized hit it pretty much made him famous all over again, allowing him to reprise the character countless times right up to the end; his last appearance in the role, in *Halloween: The Curse of Michael Myers*, being released posthumously. During those assignments he worked exhaustively, grinding out dozens of credits that often went straight to video or never showed up in the U.S. at all. Among those that did see the light of day were the Frank Langella version of *Dracula*, as Dr. Seward; *Escape from New York*, as the captured American president; *Alone in the Dark*, as a pot-smoking psychiatrist; *Hanna's War*, as a captain; the 1989 version of *Ten Little Indians*, as the Judge; and the Woody Allen comedy *Shadows and Fog*, as a doctor.

Screen: 1954: Orders Are Orders; 1955: The Beachcomber; Value for Money; 1956: 1984; Decision Against Time/The Man in the Sky; The Black Tent; 1957: Stowaway Girl; All at Sea/Barnacle Bill; 1958: Heart of a Child; A Tale of Two Cities; The Man Inside; 1959: The Two-Headed Spy; Look Back in Anger; 1960: Killers of Kilimanjaro; The Battle of the Sexes; Circus of Horrors; Hell Is a City; The Wind Cannot Read; Sons and Lovers; Mania/The Flesh and the Fiends; Suspect; The Big Day; A Story of David; 1961: No Love for Johnnie; The Risk; The Shakedown; The Hands of Orlac; Spare the Rod; What a Carve Up!/Home Sweet Homicide; 1962: Lisa/The Inspector; 1963: The Great Escape; 1964: Dr. Crippen; The Guest/The Caretaker; 1965: The Greatest Story Ever Told; The Hallelujah Trail; 1966: Fantastic Voyage; 1967: Cul-De-Sac; Matchless; Eye of the Devil; The Night of the Generals; You Only Live Twice; 1968: Will Penny; 1969: The Madwoman of Chaillot; Arthur, Arthur; 1970: Outback; 1971: Soldier Blue; Kidnapped; THX 1138; 1972: The Jerusalem File; The Pied Piper; Deathline/Raw Meat; Wedding White; 1973: Innocent Bystanders; Watch Out, We're Mad (nUSr); From Beyond the Grave; Malachi's Cove (nUSr); The Mutations; The Rainbow Gang; Tales That Witness Madness; 1974: Barry McKenzie Holds His Own; The Black Windmill; La Loba y Paloma (nUSr); 1975: Escape to Witch Mountain; Hearts of the West; Journey Into Fear; 1976: The Devil Within Her; Dirty Knights' Work/Trial by Combat; Land of the Minotaur/The Devil's Men; The Passover Plot; The Last Tycoon; 1977: Blood Relatives; The Eagle Has Landed; Night Creature/Devil Cat; Oh, God!; Tomorrow Never Comes; The Uncanny; Telefon; 1978: The Angry Man/Jigsaw (nUSr); L'Ordre et la Securite du Monde (nUSr); Power Play; Sgt. Pepper's Lonely Hearts Club Band; Halloween; 1979: Good Luck, Miss Wyckoff; Dracula; Jaguar Lives!; 1980: The Monster Club; The Puma Man (dtv); 1981: Escape from New York; Halloween II; 1982: Alone in the Dark; 1983: The Devonsville Terror; Nothing Underneath (nUSr); Where is Parsifal?; 1984: Treasure of the Yankee Zephyr; A Breed Apart; Frankenstein's Great Aunt Tillie (dtv); Terror in the Aisles; 1985: Warrior of the Lost World; The Ambassador; Dario Argento's World of Horror (nUSr); Creepers; To Kill a Stranger (nUSr); Treasure of the Amazon; Operation 'Nam (dtv); 1986: Into the Darkness (dtv); Nosferatu in Venice; 1987: Django Strikes Again (nUSr); Off Balance/Phantom of Death (dtv); Specters/Spettri (dtv); Prince of Darkness; Double Target;

Warrior Queen (dtv); Animali Metropolitani (nUSr); 1988: Angel Hill/Last Platoon; The Commander (nUSr); Casablanca Express (dtv); Hanna's War; The House of Usher (dtv); Paganini Horror (nUSr); Ground Zero; Halloween 4: The Return of Michael Myers; 1989: River of Death; Halloween 5: The Revenge of Michael Myers; Ten Little Indians; 1990: Buried Alive; American Tiger (dtv); Donne Armate/Women in Arms (nUSr); 1991: L'avvoltoio puo Attendere (nUSr); Billions (dtv); 1992: Dien Bien Phu (nUSr); Shadows and Fog; 1993: The Big Freeze (nUSr); Femme Fatale; The Advocate/Hour of the Pig; 1995: Halloween: The Curse of Michael Myers; Safe Haven (nUSr); 1997: Fatal Frames (dtv).

NY Stage: 1951: Caesar and Cleopatra; Antony and Cleopatra; 1961: The Caretaker; 1964: Poor Bitos; 1968: The Man in the Glass Booth; 1972: Wise Child.

Select TV: 1955–58: The Adventures of Robin Hood (series); 1967: The Diary of Anne Frank (sp); 1973: Dr. Jekyll and Mr. Hyde (sp); 1975: The Count of Monte Cristo; 1977: Jesus of Nazareth (ms); Goldenrod; 1978: The Dark Secret of Harvest Home (voice); The Defection of Simas Kudirka; The Bastard; Centennial (ms); 1979: Gold of the Amazon Women; Better Late Than Never; All Quiet on the Western Front; The French Atlantic Affair (ms); 1982: Computerside; Witness for the Prosecution; 1984: Master of the Game; The Black Arrow; The Barchester Chronicles (ms); 1985: The Corsican Brothers; Mansfield Park (ms); 1987: Basements/The Room (sp); 1988: The Great Escape II: The Untold Story.

SUZANNE PLESHETTE

BORN: NEW YORK, NY, JANUARY 31, 1937.
ED: SYRACUSE UNIV.

Husky-voiced, dark-haired Suzanne Pleshette was a sexy and smart presence when she came upon the movie scene in the late 1950s-early 1960s, but she spent a decade shuffling back and forth between high melodrama and more benign roles in Disney films, getting far better reviews than most of the pictures themselves. By the 1970s she decided that television was more to her liking and pretty much hung her hat there from that point on. A student of the Neighborhood Playhouse, she made her Broadway debut in a tiny part in the 1957 drama *Compulsion*, which was followed by guest spots on television shows, such as *Have Gun Will Travel*. Soon afterward, Jerry Lewis chose her to be his leading lady in *The Geisha Boy*, but that didn't lead to any further films so she went back to stage and television. She returned to movies in 1962 as the star of Warners's lush soap opera *Rome Adventure*, dallying with the older Rosanno Brazzi but winding up with Troy Donahue. After pursuing Tony Curtis in the light-hearted *40 Pounds of Trouble*, and having her eyes pecked out in most enduring film, *The Birds*, she was back with Donahue in the western *A Distant Trumpet* and the soap *Youngblood Hawke*, marrying the actor ever so briefly that same year, 1964. She got her own showcase with *A Rage to Live*, as a promiscuous lady searching desperately for happiness, but it was just another slick pile of trash, so she found herself acting very wholesome (with encouraging box-office results), as the likable heroine of three Disney comedies, *The Ugly Dachshund*, *The Adventures of Bullwhip Griffin*, and *Blackbeard's Ghost*, and as Steve McQueen's love interest in the western *Nevada Smith*. After playing the tour guide in the ensemble comedy/travelogue *If It's Tuesday, This Must Be Belgium*, and a rough and tumble westerner in *Support Your Local Gunfighter*, she settled in for a successful six-year run as Bob Newhart's wife on *The Bob Newhart Show*, followed by countless telefilms.

Screen: 1958: The Geisha Boy; 1962: Rome Adventure; 1963: 40 Pounds of Trouble; The Birds; Wall of Noise; 1964: A Distant Trumpet; Fate Is the Hunter; Youngblood Hawke; 1965: A Rage to Live; 1966: The Ugly Dachshund; Nevada Smith; Mister Buddwing; 1967: The Adventures of Bullwhip Griffin; 1968: Blackbeard's Ghost; The Power; 1969: How to Make It/Target Harry; If It's Tuesday, This Must Be Belgium; 1970: Suppose They Gave a War and Nobody Came; 1971: Support Your Local Gunfighter; 1976: The Shaggy D.A.; 1979: Hot Stuff; 1980: Oh, God! Book II; 1998: Off the Menu: The Last Days of Chasen's.

NY Stage: 1957: Compulsion; 1958: The Cold Wind and the Warm; 1959: The Golden Fleecing; 1960: The Miracle Worker; 1982: Special Occasions.

Select TV: 1960: The House of Bernarda Alba (sp); 1961: Love is a Lion's Roar (sp); 1962: Days of Glory (sp); The Contenders (sp); 1963: Corridor 400 (sp); 1966: After the Lions — Jackals (sp); 1967: Wings of Fire; 1968: Flesh and Blood (sp); 1970: Along Came a Spider; Hunters Are for Killing; 1971: River of Gold; In Broad Daylight; 1972–78: The Bob Newhart Show (series); 1975: The Legend of Valentino; 1976: Law and Order; Richie Brockelman: Private Eye; 1978: Kate Bliss and the Ticker Tape Kid; 1979: Flesh & Blood; 1980: If Things Were Different; 1981: The Star Maker; 1982: Fantasies; Help Wanted — Male; 1983: Dixie: Changing Habits; One Cooks, the Other Doesn't; 1984: For Love or Money; Suzanne Pleshette Is Maggie Briggs (series); 1985: Kojak: The Belarus File; 1986: Bridges to Cross (series); 1987: A Stranger Waits; 1988: Alone in the Neon Jungle; 1989: Nightingales (series); 1990: Leona Helmsley: The Queen of Mean; 1992: Battling for Baby; 1993: A Twist of the Knife; 1994–95: The Boys Are Back (series).

CHRISTOPHER PLUMMER

(ARTHUR CHRISTOPHER ORME PLUMMER)
BORN: TORONTO, ONTARIO, CANADA,
DECEMBER 13, 1927. RAISED IN MONTREAL.

In the theater, Christopher Plummer rose up through the ranks to become one of the most praised thespians of his generation, while on screen he was held in lesser esteem, missing out on full-fledged stardom. Film saw him being both commanding and intense, sometimes clearly bored with his job, and often over-wrought or out of his element, but the high points made rich use of his talents. He started out as a member of Ottawa's Canadian Repertory Theatre before moving over to the Bermuda Rep and finally making it to Broadway in 1954, in The Starcross Story. The following season he received a Theatre World Award for The Dark Is Light Enough, and became a name attraction after playing the Earl of Warwick in The Lark, and via his many roles with the Shakespeare Festivals in both Connecticut and Ontario. As a result, there were two Hollywood offers — Stage Struck, as the playwright infatuated with Susan Strasberg in this mediocre retread of Morning Glory, and in the leading role as a boozing conservationist in Wind Across the Everglades — but neither made a ripple. He went back to the stage, playing a wealth of classical roles from Hamlet to Richard III to King Henry II with the Shakespeare Festivals, while scoring another Broadway hit in 1958 with J. B. During this time, he also gained a reputation as one of the classier thespians on television, on many occasions acting for Hallmark Hall of Fame in such works as Little Moon of Alban, Captain Brassbound's Conversion, and Cyrano de Bergerac. His movie career resumed in 1964 with his unapologetically hammy portrayal of the dangerously mad emperor in the ultra-lavish epic

The Fall of the Roman Empire. Then came the film he balked at doing, only to find it become the one audiences would forever remember him for, The Sound of Music, as the stern Captain von Trapp, whose heart is melted by governess Julie Andrews. It became the highest-grossing musical of them all, one of the best-loved motion pictures of all time, and the Academy Award-winner for Best Picture, but Plummer was unhappy with the finished product, principally because his own vocals were dubbed (by Bill Lee) despite promises to the contrary.

Because of that movie's tremendous success, there were several attempts to present Plummer as an intellectual star attraction and each one of them went bust at the turnstiles, even among the small audiences some of them were intended for. These included Triple Cross, as real-life World War II spy Eddie Chapman; a stagy Oedipus the King, committing both incest and fratricide in every-body's idea of a feel-good night out at the cinema; Lock Up Your Daughters, a grotesque attempt at period farce, as Lord Foppington; The Royal Hunt of the Sun, the best-liked of this batch and Plummer's own favorite of his movie assignments, as Incan king Atahuallpa (he had played the other lead, Pizzaro, on the stage); and the very expensive international spectacular Waterloo, as Lord Wellington. Having put the movie-star trip behind him, he was back on Broadway winning a Tony Award for the musical Cyrano. His subsequent movie career would consist of many jobs agreed on for quick cash but there were some highs along the way that helped keep him in the public eye. In 1975 he was in the hit sequel The Return of the Pink Panther, reprising David Niven's old role as the debonair thief, and had good fun playing author Rudyard Kipling in the adventure epic The Man Who Would Be King. He was an excellent choice to play a some-what more humane version of Sherlock Holmes in Murder by Decree, squaring off with Jack the Ripper; and then was suavely unpleasant trying to charm the leading ladies in Hanover Street, Somewhere in Time, and Eyewitness. He had an arrogant, dis-trustful side to him that made him ideal for villainy as he showed in the send-up of Dragnet; Star Trek VI: The Undiscovered Country, in heavy makeup as General Chang; and Twelve Monkeys, as Brad Pitt's shady dad. He was almost unrecognizable as a homeless man, coarsely referred to as Shitty, in Where the Heart Is, and was in good form as the police inspector trying to get to the bottom of the mystery in Dolores Claiborne. One of his very best roles came after he'd turned 70, in The Insider, where he was properly self-satisfied as newsman Mike Wallace, but he fol-lowed this with a negligible credit, appearing as Dr. Van Helsing in the teen-geared Dracula 2000. Bouncing back in the right direction, he appeared in his second Oscar-winner for Best Picture, A Beautiful Mind, very serious as the shrink who diag-noses Russell Crowe's schizophrenia, and in the remake of Nicholas Nickleby as the heartless Uncle Ralph. His second Tony came for portraying (John) Barrymore, while on television he earned Emmys for the mini-series The Moneychangers and, in 1994, for narrating a Madeline animated special.

Screen: 1958: Stage Struck; Wind Across the Everglades; 1964: The Fall of the Roman Empire; 1965: The Sound of Music; Inside Daisy Clover; 1967: The Night of the Generals; Triple Cross; 1968: Oedipus the King; Nobody Runs Forever/The High Commissioner; 1969: Battle of Britain; The Royal Hunt of the Sun; Lock Up Your Daughters; 1970: Waterloo; 1973: The Pyx; 1975: Conduct Unbecoming; The Spiral Staircase; The Return of the Pink Panther; The Man Who Would Be King; 1977: The Day That Shook the World; Aces High; The Assignment (dtv); 1978: International Velvet; 1979: Murder by Decree; Starcrash; The Silent Partner; Hanover Street; Arthur Miller on Home Ground; 1980: Somewhere in Time; 1981: Being Different (narrator);

Eyewitness; The Disappearance (filmed 1977); **1982:** The Amateur; **1984:** Ordeal by Innocence; Dreamscape; **1985:** Lily in Love; **1986:** The Boy in Blue; The Boss' Wife; An American Tail (voice); **1987:** Dragnet; **1988:** I Love N.Y. (dtv); Light Years (voice); Souvenir (dtv); Nosferatu in Venice (dtv); Shadow Dancing (dtv); **1989:** Mindfield (dtv); Kingsgate (nUSr); **1990:** Where the Heart Is; Red-Blooded American Girl (dtv); **1991:** Firehead; Don't Tell Mom the Babysitter's Dead; Money (nUSr); Star Trek VI: The Undiscovered Country; **1992:** Rock-a-Doodle (voice); Malcolm X; **1993:** Impolite (nUSr); **1994:** Wolf; Crackerjack (dtv); **1995:** Dolores Claiborne; Twelve Monkeys; **1998:** Secret Agenda/Hidden Agenda (dtv); Madeline: Lost in Paris (dtv; narrator); Clown at Midnight (dtv); Blackheart (dtv); **1999:** The Insider; **2000:** The Dinosaur Hunter (nUSr); Dracula 2000; **2001:** Full Disclosure (dtv); A Beautiful Mind; **2002:** Lucky Break; Ararat; Nicholas Nickleby.

NY Stage: **1954:** The Starcross Story; Home Is the Hero; **1955:** The Dark Is Light Enough; The Lark; **1956:** Night of the Auk; **1958:** J.B.; **1963:** The Resistible Rise of Arturo Ui; **1965:** The Royal Hunt of the Sun; **1973:** Cyrano; The Good Doctor; **1978:** Drinks Before Dinner; **1982:** Othello; **1988:** Macbeth; **1994:** No Man's Land; **1997:** Barrymore.

Select TV: **1951:** Othello (sp); **1953:** The Gathering Night (sp); Dark Victory (sp); **1955:** The King's Bounty (sp); Cyrano de Bergerac (sp); **1956:** Even the Weariest River (sp); Oedipus Rex (sp); **1957:** The Prince and the Pauper (sp); **1958:** Little Moon of Alban (sp); The Lady's Not for Burning (sp); Johnny Belinda (sp); **1959:** The Philadelphia Story (sp); A Doll's House (sp); **1960:** Captain Brassbound's Conversion (sp); **1961:** Time Remembered (sp); The Prisoner of Zenda (sp); **1961–62:** Playdate (series); **1962:** Cyrano de Bergerac (sp); Macbeth (sp); **1964:** Hamlet (sp); **1971:** Don Juan in Hell (sp); **1974:** After the Fall (sp); **1976:** Arthur Hailey's The Moneychangers (ms); **1977:** Jesus of Nazareth (ms); **1980:** Desperate Voyage; The Shadow Box; **1981:** When the Circus Came to Town; Dial M for Murder; **1982:** Little Gloria…Happy at Last; **1983:** The Scarlet and the Black; The Thorn Birds (ms); Prototype; **1986:** Crossings (ms); Spearfield's Daughter (ms); The Velveteen Rabbit (sp; voice); **1987:** A Hazard of Hearts; **1990:** A Ghost in Monte Carlo; Counterstrike (series); **1991:** Young Catherine; The First Circle; A Marriage: Georgia O'Keeffe and Alfred Stieglitz (sp); **1992:** Danielle Steel's Secrets; Sidney Sheldon's A Stranger in the Mirror; Liar's Edge; **1995:** Kurt Vonnegut's Harrison Bergeron; **1996:** We the Jury; Conspiracy of Fear; Skeletons; **1997:** The Arrow; **1998:** Winchell; **2000:** Nuremberg; Possessed; American Tragedy; **2001:** On Golden Pond (sp); Night and Day; **2002:** Agent of Influence.

SIDNEY POITIER

Born: Miami, FL, February 20, 1927.
Raised on Cat Island, Bahamas.

By the late 1940s the time had come for the entertainment industry's outlook on the Black American to change and there was no better man to lead the way than Sidney Poitier. Almost single-handedly he awakened a movie-going world steeped in prejudice to the realization that his race could be smart, complex, good-looking, and have the same problems and triumphs as the next fellow, regardless of color. That he was also one of the most affable personalities in movies was as instrumental to his success as the fact that he was, quite simply, a superb actor. Raised on his parent's tomato plantation in the Bahamas, he returned to America as a teen and did odd jobs

before serving in the army as a physiotherapist. After the war, he moved to New York and once again found himself aimlessly seeking work. He decided to apply to the American Negro Theatre, which rejected him because of his West Indian accent. After working to improve his voice, he was accepted by the company, taught acting and then graduated to roles in several of their productions. He made his professional debut in 1946, in the all-black Broadway production of *Lysistrata*, which promptly closed after four performances. There was a touring company of *Anna Lucasta*; a part in an Army Signal Corps documentary, *From Whom Cometh My Help*, which marked his first "unofficial" film work; and then a test with 20th Century-Fox for their anti-racism drama *No Way Out*. Poitier got the part of the dedicated doctor who is accused of accidentally killing the brother of bigot Richard Widmark and wound up giving the best performance in this rather overheated melodrama.

This being the early 1950s, good parts for blacks were hard to come by, so he went to England to play a minister in a worthy adaptation of Alan Paton's novel *Cry the Beloved Country*, then returned home to act among the non-basketball cast members of *Go, Man, Go*, which was the Hollywood-ized story of the real-life Harlem Globetrotters. His next step to success came when he was cast as the very cool and controlled student, enduring novice teacher Glenn Ford's suspicions, in the 1955 landmark juvenile-delinquent scorcher *Blackboard Jungle*. He was thoroughly convincing as a teenager, despite being nearly 30 years old. That same year on television, he was the dockworker fighting the racketeers in the *Philco Playhouse* presentation, *A Man Is Ten Feet Tall*, which was redone with Poitier for the big screen as *Edge of the City*, a fine drama that suffered from unfair comparisons to *On the Waterfront*. There was another commendable project with *Something of Value*, in which he was a South African turned bitter by racism. It was a movie good enough that almost wiped away the memory of *Band of Angels*, a trashy Civil War soaper and the only time Poitier stooped to portraying a slave.

Official, full-fledged stardom came with *The Defiant Ones*, a much-touted message picture with Poitier and Tony Curtis as a pair of battling convicts literally changed together as they escape the sheriff's posse. The road from bigotry to understanding was predestined but well done nonetheless. The picture became a surprise box-office hit, garnered several Oscar nominations, including one for Best Picture, and, more significantly, one for Poitier, making him the first black male in the running for the award. Because he was now a "name," with a major hit on his hands, he was snatched up for the long-awaited film version of *Porgy and Bess*, despite the fact that he did not want to be in it and couldn't sing (Robert McFarren dubbed his vocals). The movie, under Otto Preminger's rather leaden direction, was indifferently received and, years later, withdrawn from circulation by a very unhappy Gershwin estate, making it one of the great long-unavailable curios of the musical genre. Poitier's performance was acceptable under the circumstances. The year 1959 marked his return to the New York stage in the ground-breaking *A Raisin in the Sun*, the first Broadway play written by a black woman, Lorraine Hansberry. As the well-meaning son, who faces opposition in his many efforts to find a better life for himself and his family, he won raves. Repeating the role in the faithful 1961 film version for Columbia, he gave what was perhaps his finest performance, intense and heartfelt to the nth degree, but the movie was not the widespread hit it should have been. Prior to that, he dealt with racism in the army in *All the Young Men* and teamed nicely with Paul Newman as a jazz musician in *Paris Blues*, where he was also given an equal-opportunity romantic interest in Diahann Carroll. The latter film emphasized how

Poitier's character had fled to Paris to escape bigotry in the United States. Since it was the height of the civil rights movement, there were still plenty of motion pictures back home that needed him to stress the point that Hollywood was dealing with the issue; hence the hokey *Pressure Point*, where he was a psychiatrist enduring racial slurs from unhinged patient Bobby Darin.

The next milestone to come along involved a small and gentle film, *Lilies of the Field*, about a G.I. conned into helping some German nuns build a chapel in the desert. It was, in its own unpretentious way, one of the nicest movies of the decade, and became not only the sleeper hit of 1963, but one of that year's Oscar nominees in the Best Picture category. Although it didn't offer any staggering acting challenges, there was no doubt that the movie owed most of its success to the great charm and empathy Poitier brought to it. This time he won the Academy Award, becoming the first black performer to take home the trophy for a leading role. (It would be 38 years before this happened again, when the 2001 Best Actress and Actor awards went to Halle Berry and Denzel Washington; fittingly the same evening Poitier was bestowed with an honorary Oscar) Oddly, Poitier followed up this triumph by playing a Moorish villain in the unsuccessful Viking picture *The Long Ships*, which reteamed him with his first co-star, Richard Widmark. The two were somewhat better served by the doomsday submarine thriller *The Bedford Incident*, after which Poitier had another of his most likable roles, in *A Patch of Blue*, befriending an abused blind woman but unable to keep himself from losing a bit of his heart to her, albeit in a most chaste manner. Heroic as ever, he tried to save Anne Bancroft from suicide in *The Slender Thread*, a prolonged telephone conversation that didn't make for very compelling cinema; and then teamed with James Garner for a poorly done western, *Duel at Diablo*, again laying to rest traditions in a genre formerly dominated by whites.

His glory year came in 1967, with three smash hits and three signature roles. First up was *To Sir, With Love*, as the teacher who takes a bunch of unruly British teens in hand and turns them into presentable ladies and gentlemen. Refreshingly, Poitier's color was not in question, though it was certainly crucial to *In the Heat of the Night*, in which he was a brilliant detective from the north who clashes with white-trash sheriff Rod Steiger. Third and most profitable was *Guess Who's Coming to Dinner*, where he hoped to marry a white girl, causing a heavy discussion among the various principals in this well-scripted but stage-bound piece. The fact that audiences were rooting for him all the way was indicative of the advances he helped to bring about over the previous decade or so. He wound up being voted the number one box-office attraction in America. Surprisingly, he didn't get an Oscar nomination for any of these despite the fact that he was at his most magnificent in *In the Heat of the Night*, that year's Academy Award-winner for Best Picture.

A mild romance, *For Love of Ivy*, followed this peak, and then the box-office clout quickly eroded with *The Lost Man*, an updating of *Odd Man Out*, which featured future wife Joanna Shimkus (they wed in 1976); and with *They Call Me MISTER Tibbs!* and *The Organization*, two routine sequels to *In the Heat of the Night*. As the 1970s arrived, black actors were, blessedly, becoming more common and Poitier teamed with another who had traveled much of the road simultaneously with him, Harry Belafonte, for a jokey western, *Buck and the Preacher*. It was only notable in that it marked Poitier's first excursion behind the camera as director. He continued to act and direct with the lightweight love story *A Warm December*, and then in three sassy comedies with Bill Cosby for First Artists (the company Poitier helped form with Barbra Streisand, Paul Newman, and Steve

McQueen): *Uptown Saturday Night*, which was the best of the lot; *Let's Do It Again*, which earned the most money; and 1977's *A Piece of the Action*, which marked the last time he would appear on screen for more than a decade. Having decided he was more at ease directing, he turned out one massive hit, the Gene Wilder-Richard Pryor romp *Stir Crazy*, in 1980, and then three flops, *Hanky Panky* (1982), *Fast Forward* (1985), and *Ghost Dad* (1990), in each case proving that he was perhaps wise to leave this field to someone else. He did return to acting in 1988, with surprisingly little fanfare, as a cop in *Shoot to Kill*, after which he was an FBI agent in both *Little Nikita* and *The Jackal*, with a stop in between to play a computer hacker in *Sneakers*. None of them seemed particularly taxing on his talents but it was ever so nice to have someone of his stature back in the running. There was also some television work, which included playing Thurgood Marshall in the acclaimed *Separate But Equal*, and reprising Mr. Thackeray in the ill advised sequel, *To Sir, With Love II*. In 1992 he received the American Film Institute Life Achievement Award. His autobiography, *This Life*, was published in 1980; with a follow-up, *The Measure of a Man: A Spiritual Autobiography*, in 1999. On Broadway he directed the short-lived 1968 comedy *Carry Me Back to Morningside Heights*.

Screen: 1949: From Whence Cometh Help; 1950: No Way Out; 1951: Cry the Beloved Country; 1952: Red Ball Express; 1954: Go, Man, Go!; 1955: Blackboard Jungle; 1956: Good-Bye, My Lady; 1957: Edge of the City; Something of Value; Band of Angels; 1958: The Mark of the Hawk/Shaka Lulu/Accused; The Defiant Ones; Virgin Island; 1959: Porgy and Bess; 1960: All the Young Men; 1961: Paris Blues; A Raisin in the Sun; 1962: Pressure Point; 1963: Lilies of the Field; 1964: The Long Ships; 1965: The Greatest Story Ever Told; The Bedford Incident; A Patch of Blue; The Slender Thread; 1966: Duel at Diablo; 1967: To Sir, With Love; In the Heat of the Night; Guess Who's Coming to Dinner; 1968: For Love of Ivy (and story); 1969: The Lost Man; 1970: King: A Filmed Record…Montgomery to Memphis (narrator); They Call Me MISTER Tibbs!; 1971: The Organization; 1972: Brother John; Buck and the Preacher (and dir.); 1973: A Warm December (and dir.); 1974: Uptown Saturday Night (and dir.); 1975: The Wilby Conspiracy; Let's Do It Again (and dir.); 1977: A Piece of the Action (and dir.); 1988: Shoot to Kill; Little Nikita; 1992: Sneakers; 1995: Wild Bill: Hollywood Maverick; 1997: The Jackal.

NY Stage: 1946: Lysistrata; 1948: Anna Lucasta; 1959: A Raisin in the Sun.

Select TV: 1952: Parole Chief (sp); 1955: Fascinating Stranger (sp); A Man is Ten Feet Tall (sp); 1991: Separate But Equal; 1995: Children of the Dust/A Good Day to Die; 1996: To Sir, With Love II; 1997: Mandela and deKlerk; 1998: David and Lisa; 1999: Free of Eden (and exec. prod.); The Simple Life of Noah Dearborn; 2001: The Last Brickmaker in America.

DICK POWELL

BORN: MOUNTAIN VIEW, AR, NOVEMBER 14, 1904. ED: LITTLE ROCK COL. DIED: JANUARY 3, 1963.

Warner Brothers's crooner-in-residence during its musical heyday of the 1930s, Dick Powell glowed with a kind of gosh-and-golly ebullience that wasn't to be taken all that seriously. He sang nicely, was affable, and, when the tide started to turn, was smart enough to redefine his image, proving himself as a serious actor of some merit and then branching out farther yet by going behind the scenes as a director. Not surprisingly, he started off as a vocalist for various bands before becoming the emcee at a theater in Pittsburgh. It was there that he was spotted by a Warners talent scout and asked to audition for the title role in a movie called, appropriately, *The Crooner*. Instead of getting that part, he ended up playing a radio singer whom columnist Lee Tracy just loves picking on in the breezy comedy *Blessed Event*. After two minor parts (including one on loan to Fox), he was put into the cast of what was to become the hottest and most influential musical of 1933, *42nd Street*. As the juvenile who sings "Young and Healthy" and romances the endearingly second-rate Ruby Keeler, he did his job proficiently and was immediately cast in similar roles in two follow-ups, *Footlight Parade* and *Gold Diggers of 1933*. By the end of 1933, he was one of the studio's biggest stars and was allowed to separate from Ms. Keeler for *College Coach*, which placed him on the football field; the clunky *Wonder Bar*, where he managed to pinch Dolores Del Rio away from top-billed Al Jolson at the climax; and *Twenty Million Sweethearts*, as a singing waiter who becomes a radio sensation. There was a demand for more Powell-Keeler pairings, however, so they were soon back together again, most profitably, for *Dames*, in which he introduced one of the era's most enduring songs, "I Only Have Eyes for You;" and the flat-footed West Point romance *Flirtation Walk*, which was popular enough in its day to manage the amazing feat of earning an Oscar nomination for Best Picture.

There was another big one with *Gold Diggers of 1935*, although even the fans were probably starting to notice that things were pretty turgid outside of the Harry Warren-Al Dubin songs and Busby Berkeley's brilliant staging of the numbers. Powell was allowed to do one that wasn't a musical, *Page Miss Glory*, as a stunt pilot in love with chambermaid Marion Davies; and then proved that he could succeed elsewhere, on loan to Fox, with *Thanks a Million*, which had him running for governor while singing along with his campaign speeches. There was controversy over his being cast in Warners's all-star version of *A Midsummer Night's Dream* but, if far from a trained Shakespearean, he was quite acceptable as a very lively Lysander. He and Keeler called it quits after *Broadway Gondolier* and *Colleen*, the latter featuring Joan Blondell, whom he married in 1936. It must have been a relief for Powell to sever his ties with Keeler, for she had pretty much retained the same awkward, tentative lack of experience, while he had proven himself a very relaxed and able practitioner of song and comedy. There was one last *Gold Diggers* film (of 1937), wherein he sang the catchy "With Plenty of Money and You;" another loan-out to Fox, for the popular *On the Avenue*; which let him introduce another standard, Irving Berlin's "I've Got My Love to Keep Me Warm;" and two that are remembered, if at all, for the classic songs they gave the world, *Hollywood Hotel* ("Hooray for Hollywood") and *Going Places* ("Jeepers Creepers"), though it was Louis Armstrong who got to put his stamp on the latter. The whole routine was becoming numbingly familiar and he was anxious to go elsewhere once his contract ended in 1939. Signing up with Paramount, he got off to a terrific start with one of the snappiest of the Preston Sturges comedies, *Christmas in July*, in which he thinks he's won a coffee contest. This was followed by two with Blondell, *I Want a Divorce* (they got one in real-life in 1945), and *Model Wife*, the latter made for Universal. Also at the latter studio he took star billing alongside Abbott and Costello for *In the Navy*, before the studio realized they didn't need a "name" to help bolster the comedy duo's future vehicles.

At Paramount, he and Mary Martin made a pleasant team on three occasions: *Star Spangled Rhythm* (singing "Hit the Road to Dreamland"), *Happy Go Lucky*, and *True to Life*; before Powell decided his career wasn't going in a much different direction than it had taken at Warners. He found solace doing a fantasy, *It*

Happened Tomorrow, which had the intriguing premise of a man receiving the daily newspaper a day in advance, and then really broke the mold when RKO allowed him to play ultra-tough private eye Philip Marlowe in *Murder, My Sweet*. This one pretty much set the standard for the genre, with its moody photography and punchy voice-over narration, though Powell's good work was no match for Bogart in the same role in *The Big Sleep*. There were more noirs, including two for Columbia: *Johnny O'Clock*, as a gambler in hot water, and *To the Ends of the Earth*, which involved dope smuggling; and one in which he played a mountie, *Mrs. Mike*, which signaled that he was beginning to slip into second features. He married June Allyson in 1945 and they did two unremarkable films together in 1950, *The Reformer and the Redhead* and *Right Cross*. Things got better with the thriller *The Tall Target*, in which he raced against time to stop an attempted assassination of Abraham Lincoln aboard a moving train; the mild whimsy *You Never Can Tell*, having great fun playing the reincarnation of a dog; and *The Bad and the Beautiful*, at his best as a cynical screenwriter married to Gloria Grahame. That same year he jumped eagerly into television, producing, hosting, and starring in *Four Star Playhouse*, *Dick Powell's Zane Grey Theater*, and *The Dick Powell Show*, resulting in a special posthumous Emmy Award in 1963. Prior to that, he ended his movie career in front of the camera with the very slight romantic comedy *Susan Slept Here*, co-starring Debbie Reynolds, and then went into directing with *Split Second* (1953); *The Conqueror* (1956), an unfortunate bit of camp with John Wayne as Genghis Kahn; *You Can't Run Away From It* (1956), starring his wife, in this awkward semi-musical remake of *It Happened One Night*; *The Enemy Below* (1957), a taut wartime thriller that was the best of the bunch; and *The Hunters* (1958).

Screen: 1932: Big City Blues (voice); Blessed Event; Too Busy to Work; 1933: The King's Vacation; 42nd Street; Gold Diggers of 1933; Footlight Parade; College Coach; Convention City; 1934: Wonder Bar; Twenty Million Sweethearts; Dames; Happiness Ahead; Flirtation Walk; 1935: Gold Diggers of 1935; Page Miss Glory; Broadway Gondolier; Shipmates Forever; Thanks a Million; A Midsummer Night's Dream; 1936: Colleen; Hearts Divided; Stage Struck; Gold Diggers of 1937; 1937: On the Avenue; The Singing Marine; Varsity Show; Hollywood Hotel; 1938: Cowboy from Brooklyn; Hard to Get; Going Places; 1939: Naughty But Nice; 1940: Christmas in July; I Want a Divorce; 1941: In the Navy; Model Wife; 1942: Star Spangled Rhythm; 1943: Happy Go Lucky; True to Life; Riding High; 1944: Meet the People; It Happened Tomorrow; Murder, My Sweet; 1945: Cornered; 1947: Johnny O'Clock; 1948: To the Ends of the Earth; Station West; Pitfall; Rogue's Regiment; 1949: Mrs. Mike; 1950: The Reformer and the Redhead; Right Cross; 1951: The Tall Target; Cry Danger; You Never Can Tell; 1952: The Bad and the Beautiful; 1954: Susan Slept Here.

Select TV: 1952–56: Four Star Playhouse (series; and prod.); 1956–61: Dick Powell's Zane Grey Theater (series; and prod.); 1961–63: The Dick Powell Show (series; and prod.).

ELEANOR POWELL

BORN: SPRINGFIELD, MA, NOVEMBER 21, 1912.
DIED: FEBRUARY 11, 1982.

When it came to tap dancing, Eleanor Powell was simply dynamite, the movies' reigning practitioner of this form of terpsichorean movement. It was the exhausting spins and rapid-fire click of her heels, presented with a smile ever so broad and sunny, that endeared her to audiences who knew better than to expect much *off* the dance floor. As a child, she performed in nightclubs in Atlantic City and, at age 16, got her big break when she was asked by songwriter Gus Edwards to dance at the Ritz Grill. Some Broadway shows followed, including *Follow Through*, and an edition of the *George White Scandals*, after which she went to Fox to do her thing in a movie called *George White's 1935 Scandals*. She then returned to New York for one last stage show, *At Home Abroad*, then was signed up by MGM in 1935. Her success there was instantaneous, with the all-star *Broadway Melody of 1936*, the highlights of which included Powell strutting her stuff to the tune "I've Got a Feelin' You're Foolin'" (a sequence that won the first Oscar for Dance Direction) and a rooftop bit with Buddy Ebsen, while the low points had her impersonating a French music-hall star. There were more great tap numbers in *Born to Dance*, with "Swingin' the Jinx Away," performed before an onstage battleship; *Broadway Melody of 1938*, this time joined by George Murphy, for "I'm Feeling Like a Million;" *Rosalie*, with its mammoth staging of the title song, featuring Powell dancing on a series of drums; and *Honolulu*, tapping while jumping rope to the title number. The box office had cooled down by the last one so, to perk things up, she got Fred Astaire as her partner in *Broadway Melody of 1940*, where their tap duel, done on a reflecting floor, to Cole Porter's "Begin the Beguine," was, in many ways, her finest moment on film. Though her "Fascinatin' Rhythm" was clearly the high point of *Lady Be Good*, there was an increasing feeling that Powell wasn't much of a varied act. Like other one-trick ponies Sonia Henie and Esther Williams, she could not be depended upon to carry the plot portions of her films in the acting department, thereby hampering her future in front of the cameras. After *I Dood It*, in which the highpoint had Powell tapping her way through a succession of lariats, she temporarily retired in 1943 to marry Glenn Ford, and the studio wasn't all that sorry to see her go. Aside from two guest appearances, she pretty much confined her dancing thereafter to nightclubs and Vegas. She and Ford divorced in 1959 and, after finding religion, Powell became an Ordained Minister of the Unity Church.

Screen: 1935: George White's 1935 Scandals; Broadway Melody of 1936; 1936: Born to Dance; 1937: Broadway Melody of 1938; Rosalie; 1939: Honolulu; 1940: Broadway Melody of 1940; 1941: Lady Be Good; 1942: Ship Ahoy; 1943: I Dood It; Thousands Cheer; 1944: Sensations of 1945; 1950: The Duchess of Idaho.

NY Stage: 1928: The Opportunists; 1929: Follow Thru; 1930: Fine and Dandy; 1931: George White's Scandals; 1932: Hot Cha!; George White's Music Hall Varieties; 1935: At Home Abroad.

JANE POWELL

(SUZANNE LORRAINE BURCE)
BORN: PORTLAND, OR, APRIL 1, 1928.

The cheeriest of cinematic sopranos, Jane Powell very much belonged to a bygone era, when rosy-cheeked nice girls with birdlike voices were in vogue. The fact that she seldom wound up in top-of-the-line productions didn't seem to bode well for her status in the future but, looking back on her films, the thing that works best about most of them is Powell herself, wholesome but never cloying, ambitiously giving it the best she had to offer. Already a remarkably good singer at the age of six, she wound up a star on a local radio station, which resulted in an offer to come to Hollywood to sing on a program called *Stars Over Hollywood*. That got her regular work on *The Edgar Bergen-Charlie McCarthy Show* and an eventual contract with MGM. First they loaned her out to United Artists for two movies,

starting with a forgettable item called *Song of the Open Road*, which also featured Bergen and McCarthy. She played herself, using the new name Hollywood had bestowed upon her. Her MGM term began in 1946, playing Walter Pidgeon's daughter in *Holiday in Mexico*, with Powell developing a crush on pianist Jose Iturbi much to the dismay of young Roddy McDowall. She sang "Ave Maria," among other songs, and this over-long, ponderous concoction did quite nicely at the box office. This was a Joe Pasternak production and it was, alas, this producer and not the far superior Arthur Freed, who wound up supervising most of Powell's films. After playing the offspring of one of the studio's previous soprano superstars, Jeanette MacDonald, in *Three Daring Daughters*, she had another big hit with *A Date With Judy*, in which she cast aside gulping Scotty Beckett in order to swoon over Robert Stack, and introduced one of her best-known numbers, "It's a Most Unusual Day."

The formula of the sweet young teen who sings while losing her heart to older men was carried through in *Nancy Goes to Rio* (Barry Sullivan), a remake of Deanna Durbin's *It's a Date*; and *Two Weeks with Love* (Ricardo Montalban), her own personal favorite and a cut above most of the others. Fortunately the routine was interrupted when she was asked to replace pregnant June Allyson in *Royal Wedding*, a Freed production that was easily her best film so far. Teamed with Fred Astaire, as his sister and dancing partner, she had another hit vocal with "Too Late Now," and brought down the house cutting up with him to "How Could You Believe Me When I Said I Love You When You Know I've Been a Liar All My Life?" She went back to Pasternak and the same old Powell stuff for *Rich, Young and Pretty*, discovering that her "deceased" mother (Danielle Darrieux) is very much alive and performing in Parisian nightclubs, and *Small Town Girl*, which was stolen from her by supporting cast members Bobby Van and Ann Miller. Another high point came with another property away from Pasternak, *Seven Brides for Seven Brothers* — her biggest hit and best-loved musical — playing the new wife of Howard Keel who brings a touch of civilization to this ruffian and his siblings. The film was well enough liked in its day to wind up with an Oscar nomination in the Best Picture category. There was *Athena*, a tepid spoof of health fanaticism, and then *Hit the Deck*, which brought her contract to a close, pretty much ending up where she started, as Walter Pidgeon's daughter. Over at RKO, she did *The Girl Most Likely*, a musical remake that didn't improve much on its source, *Tom, Dick & Harry*. It was one of that studio's last offerings, being dumped on the market by Universal, which had taken over the distribution of many of their final releases. Things came to a sorry end with *Enchanted Island*, in which she was very uncomfortably cast as a native girl. In between these two she'd attempted to go strictly dramatic with *The Female Animal*, a soap opera in which she was saddled with Hedy Lamarr as her co-star. There were no further offers and, since musicals were supposedly going out of fashion in the late 1950s, she sought work elsewhere, doing several television appearances, touring shows (including a production of *Seven Brides for Seven Brothers*, with Keel), and ending up on Broadway at last in 1974, following one-time co-star Debbie Reynolds in *Irene*. In 1988 she married her fifth husband, former child-star Dickie Moore, the same year she published her autobiography, *The Girl Next Door...and How She Grew*. A few television films and Off Broadway stage appearances followed.

Screen: 1944: Song of the Open Road; 1945: Delightfully Dangerous; 1946: Holiday in Mexico; 1948: Three Daring Daughters; A Date With Judy; Luxury Liner; 1950: Nancy Goes to Rio; Two Weeks With Love; 1951: Royal Wedding; Rich, Young and Pretty; 1953: Small Town Girl; Three Sailors and a

Girl; **1954:** Seven Brides for Seven Brothers; Athena; Deep in My Heart; **1955:** Hit the Deck; **1957:** The Girl Most Likely; The Female Animal; **1958:** Enchanted Island; **1985:** Marie; **1999:** Picture This (dtv).

NY Stage: 1974: Irene; **1996:** After-Play (ob); **2000:** Avow (ob).

Select TV: 1957: Ruggles of Red Gap (sp); Encounter on a Second Class Coach (sp); Hurricane (sp); Cupid Wore a Badge (sp); **1958:** Music in the Night (sp); Fix a Frame for Mourning (sp); The Lady Takes a Stand (sp); **1959:** Meet Me in St. Louis (sp); **1961:** Feathertop (sp); **1962:** View from the Eiffel Tower (sp); **1972:** Wheeler and Murdoch; **1972:** The Letters; **1976:** Mayday at 40,000 Feet; **1985–86:** Loving (series); **2000:** The Sandy Bottom Orchestra; Perfect Murder, Perfect Town.

WILLIAM POWELL

BORN: PITTSBURGH, PA, JULY 29, 1892.
DIED: MARCH 5, 1984.

Dapper, gentle of speech, and ever-so-assured, William Powell made it all seem so easy. With pencil moustache and slick-backed hair, he resembled a gentleman from a turn-of-the-century barber shop quartet and, although there was something comfortably old-fashioned about his grace and good breeding, there was a wicked wit to his delivery that, to this day, makes him one of the smartest and most watchable practitioners of sophisticated comedy. Against his family's wishes he went to New York to study acting at the American Academy of Dramatic Art. Following graduation in 1912 came a few rough years of poverty, some Broadway bit parts, and much work in stock. Success came, at last, with the 1920 Broadway production of *Spanish Love*, which brought him raves and an offer from director Albert Parker to play the assistant of evil Professor Moriarty in the John Barrymore film of *Sherlock Holmes*, which he did sans moustache and billed as William H. Powell. This set the tone for his roles in silent movies, being cast as a slithery cad or outright villain, as he was in *When Knighthood Was in Flower*, as the King of France; *Under the Red Robe*, as the Duc D'Orleans; and *Dangerous Money*, as a greedy, impoverished prince. The latter starred Bebe Daniels and he was asked to play second lead to her on several other occasions. In the meantime, he was the scheming Italian count who marries Lilian Gish in *Romola*, looking unintentionally amusing in a pageboy wig but earning a Paramount contract as a result. That studio allowed him to play nice for a change in *Faint Perfume*, as leading man to Seena Owen, but then it was back to the moustache twirling. He dumped wife Florence Vidor in *Sea Horses*; tried to abduct helpless Shirley Mason in the western *Desert Gold*; and had a showy role as a slimy thief in one of the big films of 1926, *Beau Geste*. Bespectacled, he was George Wilson, the gas station operator who shoots the title character in the first movie version of *The Great Gatsby*. He was also a gangster in *New York*; a frizzy-haired Spaniard and nemesis of cross-dressing Bebe Daniels in *Senorita*; Gary Cooper's rival in *Nevada*; and a sword-wielding bad guy in *She's a Shiek*, getting away with cavorting about in Arabian garb and goatee because he wasn't yet the William Powell moviegoers grew to love.

There was a big step up with *The Last Command*, although he was still not exactly lovable, as the movie director who taunts former Russian nobleman Emil Jannings. As he played it, the character suggested some complexity, and, since this was one of the first movies to be in the running for a Best Picture Oscar, it was a good one to have on his résumé. For the time being, he remained a practitioner of villainy but his career was about to

take a turn for the better with the advent of sound. He starred as a man in hiding in Paramount's first all-talking feature, *Interference*, and audiences were pleasantly surprised to find out that his voice was not so much sinister as relaxed and comforting. The studio immediately cast him as cagey and smooth detective Philo Vance in the murder mystery *The Canary Murder Case*, making him at last an official star attraction. There was another Vance offering, *The Greene Murder Case*, and a melodrama, *Behind the Make-Up*, which not only had him being dislikable again, but marked the first of several pairings with Kay Francis. With Francis he had a hit, *Street of Chance*, playing a gambler who is ruining his family, following by his third Vance mystery, *The Benson Murder Case*. He then went back to Francis for *For the Defense*, playing a famous criminal lawyer who misbehaves for her sake. There were back-to-back 1931 films featuring Carole Lombard, *Man of the World* and *Ladies' Man*, neither of which allowed them to flex their comic muscles. They did, however, marry that same year but were divorced within two years, remaining good friends nonetheless. In the meantime, Powell accepted a more lucrative offer from Warner Brothers, where he was back with Francis for *Jewel Robbery*; did one last Vance, *The Kennel Murder Case*; was cast alongside Joan Blondell, a promising teaming unfulfilled, in *Lawyer Man*; didn't jell with Bette Davis in *Fashions of 1934*; and had his biggest hit with Francis in the soggy *One-Way Passage*, loving her aboard an ocean liner, although he is bound for prison and she had a fatal disease. Powell had the capabilities of rising above this sludge but Francis did not; it is his work that keeps the many melodramas he did during this period from being completely disposable.

Lucky for Powell, Warners wasn't impressed enough with him to keep his contract going. This allowed him to accept an offer from MGM, thereby bringing forth the golden era of his career. Things started off splendidly with the engrossing *Manhattan Melodrama*, growing up to be governor while childhood buddy Clark Gable goes bad. Best of all, Myrna Loy was his leading lady and their chemistry together was instantaneous and inspired. Someone had the great idea to put Powell and Loy together again and did so, albeit in a lighter vein, with *The Thin Man*, a high point of film comedy. Powell was the casual private sleuth Nick Charles, drinking to excess and playfully trading insults with his socialite wife Nora. Added to this was a spunky terrier named Asta and a mystery plot that was quite secondary to the fun; it all came together beautifully. Both the film and Powell were up for Oscars and this very popular movie convinced much of the paying public that this was exactly how married couples should behave. Powell and Loy were back for a third one in a row, *Evelyn Prentice*, which was an undistinguished legal drama. After that, Powell went over to RKO, first to pair off with Ginger Rogers in *Star of Midnight*, which, not coincidentally, had him doing his own private investigating, and then, most pleasingly, with Jean Arthur in *The Ex-Mrs. Bradford*, which, not wanting to steer too far from a good thing, had them playing amateur sleuths. In between these two, Powell was the star of *The Great Ziegfeld*, a three-hour colossus about the legendary showman that didn't require him to be much more than his dapper and charming self. It was one of the most heavily promoted and attended motion pictures of the decade and it won the Academy Award for Best Picture of 1936. Universal then borrowed him for what would be a peak in the screwball comedy genre, *My Man Godfrey*, with Powell taking the title role of the practical butler to flighty heiress Carole Lombard. His calm reserve was masterful amid the mayhem and it brought him a second Oscar nomination. Back on his home lot, he continued to prove that he was just about the best light comedy player in Hollywood with the worthy sequel

After the Thin Man, and with *Libeled Lady*, another smartly scripted one, which not only had him locking horns with Loy but gave him a second leading lady to click with, Jean Harlow. By this point, he and Harlow were an item off screen (they had previously appeared together in *Reckless*) and he was devastated by her premature death in 1937. Back in melodrama, he did the remake of *The Last of Mrs. Cheyney*, badly matched with Joan Crawford, and *The Emperor's Candlesticks*, a lighthearted costume picture in which he was a spy.

Following the discouraging box-office returns of the last two, it was back to Loy for *Double Wedding*, in which he was a bohemian artist; *Another Thin Man*; *I Love You Again*, as an amnesiac; the clunky *Love Crazy*, which had Powell dressing as an old biddy at one point; and *Shadow of the Thin Man*. After two with the inferior Hedy Lamarr, *Crossroads* and *The Heavenly Body*, the studio requested two more Nick and Nora capers, *The Thin Man Goes Home* and *Song of the Thin Man*, but the old spark was starting to sputter, marking the end of this much loved series. Warner Bros. borrowed him for the long-awaited movie version of the (then) longest-running show in Broadway history, *Life With Father*. Powell was a brilliant choice to play the irascible, demanding, and completely human patriarch, presiding over his well-to-do family in turn-of-the-century New York. It was perhaps his finest hour before the cameras but he wound up losing the Oscar to longtime friend Ronald Colman. The movie was a smash hit and there were also raves for his character work as the incredibly dense politician in *The Senator Was Indiscreet*, but that one was pretty much treated like a second feature. Still on break from the home lot, he wound up in the very silly fantasy *Mr. Peabody and the Mermaid*, released through Universal, and then went to 20th Century-Fox for *Dancing in the Dark*, as a washed-up actor who tries to make a star of Betsy Drake. To finish up his contract at MGM, he was one of the many stars in the multi-episode *It's a Big Country*, being "talked at" by James Whitmore on a train; and *The Girl Who Had Everything*, a tiresome remake of *A Free Soul*, in which he had his last starring part, in Lionel Barrymore's old role, as the lawyer who comes to the rescue of his spoiled daughter. His final appearances were in two of the most popular movies of the 1950s: *How to Marry a Millionaire*, as the very classy older man Lauren Bacall plans on marrying before she opts for the younger but less interesting Cameron Mitchell, and *Mister Roberts*, as the delightfully sardonic ship's doctor. With that he happily retired to Palm Springs with his third wife, actress Diana Lewis, whom he had married in 1940. There he remained in quiet seclusion for nearly 30 years, until his death in 1984 at age 91. It is intriguing to speculate on the kinds of parts he might have played as the movies got farther away from the style of his era, but since he had more than proven himself and earned a niche as one of the great names of the studio era, it was great to see him go out on top.

Screen: 1922: Sherlock Holmes; When Knighthood Was in Flower; Outcast; 1923: The Bright Shawl; Under the Red Robe; 1924: Dangerous Money; Romola; 1925: Too Many Kisses; Faint Perfume; My Lady's Lips; The Beautiful City; 1926: White Mice; Sea Horses; Desert Gold; The Runaway; Aloma of the South Seas; Beau Geste; Tin Gods; The Great Gatsby; 1927: New York; Love's Greatest Mistake; Senorita; Special Delivery; Time to Love; Paid to Love; Nevada; She's a Sheik; 1928: The Last Command; Beau Sabreur; Feel My Pulse; Partners in Crime; The Dragnet; The Vanishing Pioneer; Forgotten Faces; Interference; 1929: The Canary Murder Case; The Four Feathers; Charming Sinners; The Greene Murder Case; Pointed Heels; 1930: Behind the Make-Up; Street of Chance; The Benson Murder Case; Paramount on Parade; Shadow of the Law; For the Defense; 1931:

Man of the World; Ladies' Man; The Road to Singapore; 1932: High Pressure; Jewel Robbery; One Way Passage; Lawyer Man; 1933: Private Detective 62; Double Harness; The Kennel Murder Case; 1934: Fashions of 1934; The Key; Manhattan Melodrama; The Thin Man; Evelyn Prentice; 1935: Star of Midnight; Reckless; Escapade; Rendezvous; 1936: The Great Ziegfeld; The Ex-Mrs. Bradford; My Man Godfrey; Libeled Lady; After the Thin Man; 1937: The Last of Mrs. Cheyney; The Emperor's Candlesticks; Double Wedding; 1938: The Baroness and the Butler; 1939: Another Thin Man; 1940: I Love You Again; Love Crazy; 1941: Shadow of the Thin Man; 1942: Crossroads; 1943: The Youngest Profession; The Heavenly Body; 1944: The Thin Man Goes Home; 1946: Ziegfeld Follies; The Hoodlum Saint; 1947: Song of the Thin Man; Life With Father; The Senator Was Indiscreet; 1948: Mr. Peabody and the Mermaid; 1949: Take One False Step; Dancing in the Dark; 1951: It's a Big Country; 1952: The Treasure of Lost Canyon; 1953: The Girl Who Had Everything; How to Marry a Millionaire; 1955: Mister Roberts.

NY Stage: 1912: The Ne'er Do Well; 1916: The King; The Judge of Zalamea; 1917: Going Up; 1922: Spanish Love; The Woman Who Laughed.

TYRONE POWER

(TYRONE EDMUND POWER, JR.)
BORN: CINCINNATI, OH, MAY 5, 1913.
DIED: NOVEMBER 15, 1958.

It is not surprising that somebody as "movie-star handsome" as Tyrone Power was a cinematic attraction for so long, even if his talents were forever in question. Audiences warmed up to him not only because of his looks but because, despite them, he seemed so accessible, sincere, and average. On occasion he came through with a fine performance but he was not dependable in this department, lapsing into woodenness more often than one cares to remember. Officially he was Tyrone Power, Jr., being the son of an actor who carved his niche more in theater than on film. Having done some acting with a Chicago Shakespearean troupe, the younger Power traveled to Hollywood with his dad in the early 1930s and found work on radio. While there, his father died during filming of *The Miracle Man*, a prophetic event, but Power stayed on, getting small bits in two cadet movies, *Tom Brown of Culver* and *Flirtation Walk*. Getting nowhere, he decided to give Broadway a try and it was his performance in *St. Joan*, with Katharine Cornell, that attracted the attention of the Fox studios. They signed him to a contract in 1936 and cast him in secondary roles in *Girls' Dormitory* and *Ladies in Love*, in which he romanced Loretta Young. Feeling he had proven himself, the studio gave him the central role (though he was fourth billed) in the historical drama *Lloyd's of London*, back when the movies had a knack for creating good fiction out of something as seemingly unexciting as the creation of an insurance company. The film was a hit and Power was officially placed on the Fox "A" list as a star attraction. There was the comedy *Love is News*, playing a reporter, again opposite Loretta Young, which did well enough not only for the two stars to be immediately reunited for *Cafe Metropole* and *Second Honeymoon*, but for Power to remake the property 11 years later, as *That Wonderful Urge*. In 1938 he had starring roles in three of the year's top films. The first and second were musical-dramas with Alice Faye and Power's real-life friend Don Ameche, and both productions received Oscar nominations for Best Picture: *In Old Chicago*, as the son of the lady whose cow supposedly started the big blaze, and *Alexander's Ragtime Band*, which was wall-to-wall Irving Berlin songs, though as the bandleader Power wasn't asked to do any of the warbling. The third was a loan-out to MGM for the ultra-lavish *Marie Antoinette*, as the Count who loves Norma Shearer, a part that was quite secondary to hers and just the sort of costume role that would make his detractors look back on him as a stiff.

Back on the home lot he was torn between Loretta Young and Annabella in *Suez*, ending up with the former after the latter nobly sacrifices herself during the big sandstorm sequence. In real life, it was Annabella who won out, becoming his wife in 1939 and remaining so for the following nine years. On a roll, he showed up in glorious Technicolor in *Jesse James*, a top-notch western, despite the fact that you couldn't help but think that the real outlaw was nowhere near as pleasant a fellow as Power, and *The Rains Came*, where he was none-too-convincing as an Indian doctor who falls for snobby Myrna Loy in this mediocre soaper highlighted by its special effects. He was the equivalent of gambler Nicky Arnstein in *Rose of Washington Square*, since this was a thinly disguised look at the life of Fanny Brice, but wasn't, despite being at a box-office peak, considered above being cast in his *second* Sonia Henie ice skating vehicle, *Second Fiddle* (the first had been *Thin Ice*, in 1937). There was an effort to harden his pretty-boy image by making him a criminal in *Johnny Apollo*, but he was much more at home re-creating two Douglas Fairbanks, Jr. roles to great financial returns, the highly entertaining *The Mark of Zorro*, as the fop Don Diego who moonlights as the masked swordsman, and the much weaker *Blood and Sand*, as the arrogant toreador who dabbles with Rita Hayworth and Linda Darnell when not hanging out with the bulls. Having proved himself a very capable swashbuckler, he returned to that field with *The Black Swan*, which turned out to be one of the very best adventures in the pirate genre. He then churned out the requisite wartime fare with *A Yank in the RAF*, with Betty Grable; *This Above All*, a decent romantic drama with Joan Fontaine; and *Crash Dive*, a submarine epic, with Anne Baxter thrown for an unnecessary sideline romance. After that one, he left the movies to serve in the Marine Corps, thereby disappearing from the big screen for three years. He returned with a bang in the very popular rendering of W. Somerset Maugham's *The Razor's Edge*, though he hardly suggested the complexities of the character, a man searching for the meaning of his existence after suffering through the war. Better was *Nightmare Alley*, in which he played an unscrupulous carnival barker who ends up an alcoholic. It was a welcome change of pace and today is one of his most highly regarded films though, at the time, it fared badly at the box office.

That was quickly compensated for by the Technicolor extravaganza *Captain From Castile*, as a fugitive nobleman who joins Cortez as he begins his conquest of Mexico; and the stodgy, made-in-England *The Black Rose*, both of which found sizable audiences. In between there was *The Luck of the Irish*, in which Cecil Kellaway stole the show as a Leprechaun in this gimmicky comedy, which was guaranteed future annual television showings on St. Patrick's Day. The early 1950s represented a bleak dropping off in material and popularity, with clinkers such as the self-explanatory *American Guerilla in the Philippines*; *I'll Never Forget You*, the unnecessary remake of *Berkeley Square*, in the Leslie Howard role; and *King of the Khyber Rifles*, as a half-caste British army captain, which would seem to indicate an actor of greater range than he was capable of displaying. There was a somewhat better public response to *The Mississippi Gambler*, which he made at Universal, though it was no less routine than the others. He found some satisfaction returning to Broadway for *John Brown's Body*, an unusual, staged reading. Suddenly his career took an upswing with two Columbia biopics, *The Long Gray Line*,

affecting an Irish accent and aging over the decades as West Point's athletic trainer, Marty Maher, in one of director John Ford's duller efforts, though Power considered it his favorite of his performances; and the better *The Eddy Duchin Story*, as the famed pianist, up to his ears in the melodramatic misfortunes that these kinds of stories wallowed in. Going over to England to act onstage in *The Devil's Disciple*, he wound up in an engrossing drama about a captain who must play God in order to save the lives of some lifeboat passengers in *Abandon Ship!*, and ended his long run at Fox as one of the too-old-for-their-roles stars of *The Sun Also Rises*. There was a tricky part as the man accused of murder in *Witness for the Prosecution*, and he wound up giving his best performance, cunning and charming, in his best movie. Alas, what future highs he had to offer could only be speculated upon, as he died of a heart attack on the set of *Solomon and Sheba* during a dueling scene. He was replaced by Yul Brynner. His second wife (1949–55) was actress Linda Christian. Two of his children, Taryn and Tyrone, Jr. (the latter born *after* his dad's death), later showed up in some film roles.

Screen: 1932: Tom Brown of Culver; 1934: Flirtation Walk; 1935: Northern Frontier; 1936: Girls' Dormitory; Ladies in Love; Lloyd's of London; 1937: Love Is News; Cafe Metropole; Thin Ice; Second Honeymoon; In Old Chicago; 1938: Alexander's Ragtime Band; Marie Antoinette; Suez; 1939: Jesse James; The Rains Came; Rose of Washington Square; Second Fiddle; Day-Time Wife; 1940: Johnny Apollo; Brigham Young; The Mark of Zorro; 1941: Blood and Sand; A Yank in the RAF; 1942: Son of Fury; This Above All; The Black Swan; 1943: Crash Dive; 1946: The Razor's Edge; 1947: Nightmare Alley; Captain From Castile; 1948: The Luck of the Irish; That Wonderful Urge; 1949: Prince of Foxes; 1950: The Black Rose; American Guerilla in the Philippines; 1951: Rawhide; I'll Never Forget You/The House in the Square; 1952: Diplomatic Courier; Pony Soldier; 1953: The Mississippi Gambler; King of the Khyber Rifles; 1955: Untamed; The Long Gray Line; 1956: The Eddy Duchin Story; 1957: Abandon Ship!/Seven Waves Away; The Sun Also Rises; Witness for the Prosecution.

NY Stage: 1935: Romance; Flowers of the Forest; Romeo and Juliet; 1936: Saint Joan; 1953: John Brown's Body; 1955: The Dark is Light Enough; 1958: Back to Methuselah.

Select TV: 1956: Miss Julie (sp).

PAULA PRENTISS

(Paula Ragusa) Born: San Antonio, TX, March 4, 1939. ed: Northwestern Univ.

An instant success, fresh out of college, Paula Prentiss had statuesque beauty and a natural ability at comedy that made her one of the better additions to movies in the early 1960s. The material was seldom up to par and at times she did have a tendency to overplay the neurotic kooks, but there were sparks of inspiration in much of what she did. While studying at Northwestern she met and married (in 1960) fellow aspiring thespian Richard Benjamin. An MGM talent scout took Prentiss west to Hollywood while Benjamin spent most of the 1960s onstage. Prentiss was cast as the "nice" college girl — the one who prefers marriage to sex — on vacation in studio-bound Fort Lauderdale in *Where the Boys Are*, and she proved to be one of the better things about this popular but feeble comedy. Since her leading man in that movie, Jim Hutton, clicked with her so nicely they were immediately reteamed by MGM in three other ultra-light romps: *The Honeymoon Machine*; *Bachelor in Paradise*, in support of Bob Hope; and *The Horizontal Lieutenant*. Universal borrowed her for *Man's Favorite Sport?*, which was, alas, director Howard Hawks on a bad day, while for UA, she was a nervous conquest of smarmy pianist Peter Sellers in *The World of Henry Orient*, and a nut case whom Peter O'Toole tries to get into bed in *What's New, Pussycat?*. In 1967–68 she and husband Benjamin did a well-regarded but short-lived TV series, *He and She*, and both showed up in *Catch-22*, where Prentiss boldly entered the post-code era by doing full-frontal nudity. After an Elliott Gould disaster, *Move*, and an overwrought sequence in *Last of the Red Hot Loves*, she did some serious supporting roles in *The Parallax View* and *The Stepford Wives*, as well as some telefilms. After securing the lead as a lady cop in an unsuccessful adaptation of the Joseph Wambaugh novel *The Black Marble*; appearing with Benjamin in a cheesy horror spoof, *Saturday the 14th*; and playing an over-sexed wife in the last and least Billy Wilder film, *Buddy Buddy*, she retired for more than a decade. She returned in 1996 in an unbilled cameo as a nurse in the film *Mrs. Winterbourne*, which was directed by her husband.

Screen: 1960: Where the Boys Are; 1961: The Honeymoon Machine; Bachelor in Paradise; 1962: The Horizontal Lieutenant; 1963: Follow the Boys; 1964: Man's Favorite Sport?; The World of Henry Orient; Looking for Love; 1965: In Harm's Way; What's New, Pussycat?; 1970: Catch-22; Move; 1971: Born to Win; 1972: Last of the Red Hot Lovers; 1974: Crazy Joe; The Parallax View; 1975: The Stepford Wives; 1980: The Black Marble; 1981: Saturday the 14th; Buddy Buddy; 1996: Mrs. Winterbourne.

NY Stage: 1963: As You Like It; 1969: Arf; The Great Airplane Snatch; 1975: The Norman Conquests; 1998: Power Plays (ob).

Select TV: 1967–68: He and She (series); 1972: The Couple Takes a Wife; 1977: Having Babies II; 1978: No Room to Run; 1979: Friendships, Secrets and Lies; 1980: The Top of the Hill; 1983: Packin' It In; M.A.D.D.: Mothers Against Drunk Drivers.

ELVIS PRESLEY

BORN: TUPELO, MS, JANUARY 8, 1935.
DIED: AUGUST 16, 1977.

In the world of rock 'n' roll Elvis Presley was and is "The King," a performer held in such high esteem that one only has to speak of him by his first name for instant recognition. Despite the fact that he is about the only singer in this field of music to become a full-time movie actor, that very same name often provokes condescending guffaws when it comes to assessing his acting talents and his often inane choice of cinematic material. It was while working as a truck driver in Memphis that others discovered that he had a knack for singing and he was signed up by the local record label, Sun, and then by Colonel Tom Parker, who became his notoriously demanding agent and promoter. From there he went to the larger RCA label and scored a number one smash hit with "Heartbreak Hotel." With his gyrating hips and uninhibited display of sexuality, Presley was like a burst of energy to the mid-1950s music industry, a centrifugal force that helped usher in the era of rock 'n' roll. He became a teen idol of the first order and Hollywood was so eager to have him that several of the major studios offered contracts, with Presley signing with no less than three of them: 20th Century-Fox, Paramount (via producer Hal Wallis), and MGM. Fox launched him (third billed) in the western *Love Me Tender*, in which his very modern persona was curiously out of place in the period. Nonetheless, there was a smoldering presence and the movie made a quick and tidy profit. Paramount gave him top billing for *Loving You*, which included the chart hit "(Let Me Be Your) Teddy Bear," while MGM's *Jailhouse Rock*, with its dynamite

title tune, solidified the image of the hurt bad boy, which many of his fans came to cherish. *King Creole* was his peak, with Elvis playing a tough kid who gets his break as a singer only to become involved with the New Orleans gangster world. It was the closest he would come to giving a sincere, accomplished performance and the film itself was tautly directed by one of the few genuine pros under which the singer would work, Michael Curtiz, but it did not rank among his biggest box-office hits. Right afterward he was drafted into the army depriving fans of any celluloid endeavors during 1959.

When he returned in 1960, with *G.I. Blues*, it was clear that this was a softer, safer Elvis, which left several of his admirers less than happy. His dramatic turn as a half-breed facing prejudice, in *Flaming Star*, was a noble effort in a serious western, well directed by Don Siegel. No doubt because Presley sang only twice and had no female lead of his own, the box office was weak, so he returned to more candy-coated fare with *Blue Hawaii*, one of his most popular features, which included perhaps the prettiest song he ever recorded, "I Can't Help Falling in Love With You," and then with a misguided remake of *Kid Galahad*, which meant he got to take his shirt off a lot, since he was playing a prizefighter. After more serious Elvis in *Wild in the Country*, scripted by Clifford Odets of all people, and *Follow That Dream*, in which he helped some orphans, the sillier Presley was back with *Girls! Girls! Girls!*, which featured another of his signature songs, "Return to Sender," and *Fun in Acapulco*, where the cheesiness of the productions was becoming evident. The singer was clearly matted into the Mexican locales and the score included such stiffs as "There's No Room to Rhumba in a Sportscar." By this point, the performer was famous for pretty much walking through the proceedings, knocking 'em off quick and cheap for an easy buck. However, he did have to stay on his toes for *Viva Las Vegas*, since it featured a director, George Sidney, who actually had a talent for making musicals, and a co-star, Ann-Margret, who was given her share of time in the spotlight. The end result was probably the most spirited and enjoyable of the Presley offerings, not to mention a box-office peak from which there would be nowhere to go but down.

Although Presley was still a best-selling recording artist, by the mid-1960s he was facing competition from the Beatles and a newer form of rock music. Oddly, he didn't change a thing when it came to the sort of brainless movies he was becoming accustomed to and they now seemed more square than ever to young audiences who had experienced a whole 'nother way of looking at pop figures on film, with *A Hard Day's Night*. There were twin Presleys in the hillbilly romp *Kissin' Cousins*; a rare case of a teaming with a major star of the past, Barbara Stanwyck, in *Roustabout*; a sorry dramatization of *Frankie and Johnny*; ditsy titles, such as *Tickle Me*, *Clambake*, and *Stay Away, Joe*; a return to the islands for *Paradise — Hawaiian Style*, in which he introduced the immortal "Queenie Waheenee's Papayan Surprise;" and interchangeable race car stories, *Spinout* and *Speedway*. There has been much debate among aficionados as to which was the Presley nadir, with the crass Indian reservation comedy *Stay Away, Joe* a strong contender for the bottom spot. He was no longer guaranteed to make the top ten with his singles and made a smart return to his roots with a 1968 TV special that presented him performing in concert without frills, for the most part. He was back at the top of the charts with the songs "In the Ghetto" and "Suspicious Minds" but the moviegoing public wasn't buying the more down-to-earth Elvis as a former outlaw in *Charro!*, or as a ghetto doctor in *Change of Habit*, which co-starred Mary Tyler Moore as a nun. Luckily, he found that he could pack 'em in big time in Las Vegas, and suddenly the image of the white jump-suited, paunchy rocker with the humongous sideburns became stuck in everyone's minds as the lasting image of Presley. There were a pair of concert documentaries, *Elvis — That's the Way It Is* and *Elvis on Tour*, that were regarded as the first Presley movie credits in years not be embarrassed about, after which he seemed content to earn his millions in the fabled gambling capitol. His premature death from a heart attack, in 1977 at age 42, suddenly made him famous all over again; his image grew to legendary proportions as he became an unparalleled cult figure to some and the unfortunate butt of jokes to those who couldn't cope with the tackiness of such celebratory items as Elvis lamps, figurines, and bedroom slippers. Presley's famed Memphis home, Graceland, became a popular tourist destination. His former wife (1967–73) Priscilla Presley later became an actress, appearing opposite Leslie Nielsen in the *Naked Gun* comedies, while his daughter, Lisa Marie, married and quickly split from actor Nicolas Cage in 2002.

Screen: 1956: Love Me Tender; 1957: Loving You; Jailhouse Rock; 1958: King Creole; 1960: G.I. Blues; Flaming Star; 1961: Wild in the Country; Blue Hawaii; 1962: Follow That Dream; Kid Galahad; Girls! Girls! Girls!; 1963: It Happened at the World's Fair; Fun in Acapulco; 1964: Kissin' Cousins; Viva Las Vegas; Roustabout; 1965: Girl Happy; Tickle Me; Harum Scarem; 1966: Frankie and Johnny; Paradise — Hawaiian Style; Spinout; 1967: Easy Come, Easy Go; Double Trouble; Clambake; 1968: Stay Away, Joe; Speedway; Live a Little, Love a Little; 1969: Charro!; The Trouble With Girls (and How to Get Into It); Change of Habit; 1970: Elvis: That's the Way It Is; 1972: Elvis on Tour.

Select TV: 1968: Elvis (sp).

ROBERT PRESTON

(ROBERT PRESTON MESERVEY)
BORN: NEWTON HIGHLANDS, MA, JUNE 8, 1918.
DIED: MARCH 21, 1987.

Few actors have come so alive in life's ever-so important "second act" as Robert Preston. For years he was a serviceable, virile-voiced presence in "B" movies and melodramas, cast as standard good guys, sarcastic cads, or outright villains. It was hardly a career to cause much comment until he decided to flex his muscles onstage, landing the role of a lifetime, which seemed to bring out a wealth of untapped colors and characteristics. His journey to the movies was swift. He joined the Pasadena Playhouse where he did a production of *Idiot's Delight* that was seen by a Paramount talent scout. Signed to a contract in 1938, the actor was cast as one of the heroes in a "B" movie starring J. Carroll Naish, *King of Alcatraz*, and stayed in that secondary unit for *Illegal Traffic* and *Disbarred*, until rescue came with two of the big films of 1939: *Beau Geste*, as the youngest of the brothers, Digby, and *Union Pacific*, as the bad guy. The latter was directed by Cecil B. DeMille and, despite the fact that Preston was singularly unimpressed with the famous director, he worked with him again, in the ultra-silly Technicolor epic *North West Mounted Police*, in which he was murdered after deserting his post, and *Reap the Wild Wind*, taking a bullet from evil brother Raymond Massey. Both were hefty money-earners. In between them, he was stuck in one of those Dorothy Lamour jungle things, *Moon Over Burma*, as an alcoholic plantation worker sobered up by her love; had his eye on Mary Martin in *New York Town*, many years before they scored a success together in the theater; and fell right back into "B's" again with *Night of January 16th*, a murder-mystery based on a play by Ayn Rand; *Pacific Blackout*, an espionage tale that also played in

some venues as *Midnight Angel*; and *Night Plane From Chungking*, a variation on *Shanghai Express*. On a somewhat higher note, he was the affable detective in a good noir, *This Gun for Hire*, although fellow cast members Alan Ladd, Veronica Lake, and Laird Cregar got most of the attention; and was one of the soldiers in a popular but routine wartime adventure, *Wake Island*.

After a stint in the Air Force, he was back at the studio, now billed *below* Alan Ladd, for *Wild Harvest*, as his rival; and then was borrowed by UA to play the cowardly and doomed husband of Joan Bennett in *The Macomber Affair*, the first time he felt satisfied with his work on screen. After effortlessly playing a pair of western bad guys in *Blood on the Moon* and *Whispering Smith*, again opposite Ladd, he managed to get out of his contract with Paramount in 1948, though not without a bit of a struggle. It did not, initially, seem as if he'd made a smart move, since the late 1940s-early 1950s brought him nothing but one uninspired movie after another, ranging from the oil melodrama *Tulsa*, with Susan Hayward, to *The Lady Gambles*, with Barbara Stanwyck; *My Outlaw Brother*, with Mickey Rooney; and *Cloudburst*, made in England. With no place to go but up at this point, he figured he would try his hand at the theater. He was Jose Ferrer's replacement in *Twentieth Century*, followed by several other productions that, if nothing else, at least gave him credentials in the legit New York stage. The tide turned magnificently when he was cast as the lovable charlatan Harold Hill in the 1957 musical *The Music Man*. It became a smash hit and Preston was suddenly hailed as the most exciting addition to the American Musical Theatre to come down the pike in a long time. He won the Tony Award, and his renditions of such showstoppers as "Trouble" and "76 Trombones," became legendary. When Warner Bros. bought the rights to the show he was not considered a sure thing for the lead, so he was only too happy to sign a contract with them and do another film first, just to remind them of his abilities in front of the camera. The excellent adaptation of William Inge's *The Dark at the Top of the Stairs* turned out to showcase Preston at his best, as a philandering, fed-up husband. What's more, it had a midwestern, period setting not unlike the one Harold Hill had dwelt in and so *The Music Man* movie was his, resulting in one of the most faithful and enjoyable motion picture adaptations of a hit Broadway show in years. It earned an Oscar nomination for Best Picture and captured, for future generations, one of the most dynamic matings of actor and role.

This was followed by a failure from the same director of *Music Man*, Morton Da Costa — a comedy called *Island of Love*, in which Preston was again cast as a con artist — and then another fine slice of Americana, *All the Way Home*, in which he was seen only in the first half of the film, as the dad who leaves behind a grieving family to cope with his unexpected death. After that he decided he was having a lot more fun doing live theater and became very much at home on the Broadway stage. His work there included the original production of *The Lion in Winter*; a musical reunion with Mary Martin in the two-character *I Do! I Do!*, winning his second Tony Award; and the cult favorite *Mack and Mabel*, as motion picture pioneer Mack Sennett. Back in the movies, there were worthwhile parts as Steve McQueen's dad in *Junior Bonner*; a lead as the increasingly evil teacher in *Child's Play*; a brief supporting part — singing "Loving You" to Lucille Ball and soon-after dying — in *Mame*; and a funny bit as the foul-mouthed football-team owner in *Semi-Tough*. The down-and-dirty Preston was very much in evidence, stealing scenes right and left, as a quack Hollywood physician in the rude satire *S.O.B.* and that movie's director, Blake Edwards, gave him one last glorious role, as the charming and unapologetically gay cabaret performer in *Victor/Victoria*. He was never more charismatically in charge and his achingly funny Oscar-nominated performance made one realize that for the bulk of his movie career Hollywood had never even bothered to let him play comedy. There was one last movie role, as the alien mentor of *The Last Starfighter*, an adventure aimed principally at children, followed by several television movies, prior to his death from cancer in 1987. His wife (from 1940) was actress Catherine Craig.

Screen: 1938: King of Alcatraz; Illegal Traffic; 1939: Disbarred; Union Pacific; Beau Geste; 1940: Typhoon; North West Mounted Police; Moon Over Burma; 1941: The Lady From Cheyenne; Parachute Battalion; New York Town; Night of January 16th; Pacific Blackout/Midnight Angel; 1942: Reap the Wild Wind; This Gun for Hire; Wake Island; Star Spangled Rhythm; 1943: Night Plane from Chungking; 1947: Wild Harvest; The Macomber Affair; Variety Girl; 1948: The Big City; Blood on the Moon; Whispering Smith; 1949: Tulsa; The Lady Gambles; 1950: The Sundowners; 1951: My Outlaw Brother; When I Grow Up; Best of the Bad Men; 1952: Face to Face; Cloudburst; 1955: The Last Frontier; 1960: The Dark at the Top of the Stairs; 1962: The Music Man; 1963: How the West Was Won; Island of Love; All the Way Home; 1972: Junior Bonner; Child's Play; 1974: Mame; 1977: Semi-Tough; 1981: S.O.B.; 1982: Victor/Victoria; 1984: The Last Starfighter.

NY Stage: 1951: Twentieth Century; 1952: The Male Animal; 1953: Men of Distinction; 1954: His and Hers; The Magic and the Loss; The Tender Trap; 1955: Janus; 1957: The Hidden River; The Music Man; 1963: Too True to Be Good; Nobody Loves an Albatross; 1964: Ben Franklin in Paris; 1966: The Lion in Winter; I Do! I Do!; 1974: Mack and Mabel; 1977: Sly Fox.

Select TV: 1951: Blockade (sp); The Old Lady Shows Her Medals (sp); Man Against Crime (series); The Nymph and the Lamp (sp); 1952: Kelly (sp); The Juggler (sp); The Promise (sp); Happily But Not Forever (sp); Anywhere U.S.A. (series); 1953: Hope for a Harvest (sp); 1954: The End of Paul Dane (sp); 1955: The Bogey Man (sp); It Gives Me Pleasure (sp); Drop on the Devil (sp); 1956: Child of the Regiment (sp); Missouri Legend (sp); Made in Heaven (sp); 1957: The Animal Kingdom (sp); The Trial of Lizzie Borden (sp); 1959: The Bells of St. Mary's (sp); 1960: Years Ago (sp); 1975: My Father's House; 1979: The Chisholms (ms); 1979–80: The Chisholms (series); 1980: The Man That Corrupted Hadleyburg (sp); 1982: Rehearsal for Murder; 1983: September Gun; 1984: Finnegan Begin Again; 1986: Outrage!

VINCENT PRICE

(VINCENT LEONARD PRICE, JR.) BORN: ST. LOUIS, MO, MAY 27, 1911. ED: YALE, UNIV. OF LONDON. DIED: OCTOBER 25, 1993.

There was a great theatrical flair to most of what Vincent Price did, which kept him very entertaining as an actor but also meant he was seldom as threatening as he was supposed to be. As an outright villain he could be disagreeable and duplicitous, rather like a spoiled child who has caused a great a deal of trouble because he hasn't gotten his way. Despite his imposing figure and height he seemed effete (it was well known that despite his marriages, Price was gay) and weak enough for the hero to overpower him with a single punch. His great fame came via horror movies, when the genre didn't depend so much on gore, and he was a classy, albeit sometimes hammy, addition to it, with his magnificent speaking voice and menacing leer. Originally he hoped to become an artist but, following college, dabbled in some dramatic work at the Riverdale School in New York. While in

London to further his education, he auditioned for a production of *Chicago* with the Gate Theatre and won the role, which convinced him to put art aside. This was followed by a production of *Victoria Regina*, in which he was Prince Albert, and he so impressed everyone in the part that when the decision was made to bring the piece to New York in 1935, with Helen Hayes in the lead, Price was asked to repeat his performance. Following some stock work, he accepted an offer from Universal Studios. The company put him into a light comedy with Constance Bennett, *Service de Luxe*, in the hopes that it could sell him to the public as a suave, mustachioed Ronald Colman-type matinee idol. Since this wasn't quite the reaction he got, he next played the pathetic Duke of Clarence in *Tower of London*, supporting Basil Rathbone and Boris Karloff among others, and then did very nicely following in Claude Rains's footprints in *The Invisible Man Returns*, which brought attention to his rich voice. In 1940 he signed up with 20th Century-Fox, which cast him in the small but pivotal role of Mormon founder Joseph Smith in *Brigham Young*; King Charles II in *Hudson's Bay*, being one of the few actors to look quite comfortable in a ringlet wig and ruffled sleeves; the Imperial French prosecutor who challenges Jennifer Jones in *The Song of Bernadette*, a marvelously rigid and commanding performance; secretary of the treasury William Gibbs McAdoo, who became son-in-law to President (Woodrow) *Wilson*; and, best of all, the weak-willed playboy fiancé of Gene Tierney in *Laura*, at one point getting slugged by the more rugged Dana Andrews.

Some of these were among the studio's most prestigious offerings of the period, as were *The Keys of the Kingdom*, in which he had a small part as a pompous monsignor, and *Leave Her to Heaven*, as Tierney's spurned fiancé, hoping to pin her death on Jeanne Crain. As a reward for his good work he was given the lead in a "B," *Shock*, as a sinister psychiatrist trying to do away with Lynn Bari; and then got to marry Tierney in the popular but tedious *Dragonwyck*, although he was still a bad guy. After his contract expired he took his villainy elsewhere, playing an arrogant magician who ends up murdered by Henry Fonda in *The Long Night*; the corrupt politician Boss Tweed in *Up in Central Park*, which was notable because he ended up marrying its costume designer, Mary Grant; and Richelieu in MGM's lavish 1948 version of *The Three Musketeers*, although the censors didn't allow him to be a Cardinal this time out. There was a break from the routine when he actually was allowed to be funny, playing a vain soap company executive in *Champagne for Caesar*, after which he had one of his favorite roles, as real-life James Addison Reavis, who tried to swindle the United States, in *The Baron of Arizona*, made for the cheapie Lippert company. Light-hearted again, he portrayed a second-rate movie actor in *His Kind of Woman*, opposite Jane Russell, and this got him a follow-up assignment with her, *The Las Vegas Story*. His fortunes were soon about to change. Warner Bros. decided to remake their 1933 thriller *Mystery of the Wax Museum* under the title *House of Wax*, the first studio-made production in the trendy new 3-D process, and Price was cast as the sculptor who has an evil technique for making his wax figures so lifelike. The movie, a good deal of hokey fun, was a tremendous financial success and would forever be the best remembered and most revived movie done in this ultimately annoying and limited gimmick. It was the unofficial launching of the actor as a horror star but after another 3-D opus, *The Mad Magician*, he did a little of everything, including the costume romp *Son of Sinbad*, as Omar Khayyam; a Mario Lanza vehicle, *Serenade*; *The Ten Commandments*, as a wicked slave driver killed off by Anne Baxter; and the all-star *The Story of Mankind*, as the Devil, though referred to here as Mr. Scratch.

There was another popular horror movie, *The Fly*, although he had a secondary role, as David Hedison's brother. His career as a star in this field really took off after this, with two of producer-director William Castle's gimmick films: *House on Haunted Hill*, which found him trying to scare his guests to death, using devices such as a skeleton on wires, one that was reproduced in select theater engagements; and *The Tingler*, as a scientist studying fear. The latter had a vibrating contraption wired to select moviegoers' seats for a "tingly" effect. There was a reprisal of a hoary old stage play, *The Bat*, and a crummy sequel, *The Return of the Fly*, in which he was upped to the lead. His career was set for the next decade or so. Roger Corman decided to use Price for a series of classy-looking horror movies using Edgar Allan Poe as the very loose basis of many of them. The first of these was *House of Usher*, and it not only did quite nicely, but even got some support from the critics. After a stop at Jules Verne for *Master of the World*, Price went way, way over the top for *Pit and the Pendulum*, as a betrayed husband driven to madness; did a Poe three-parter with *Tales of Terror*, offering the stories "Morella," "The Black Cat," and "The Case of M. Valdemar;" participated in a tongue-in-cheek version of *The Raven*, as a magician battling with Boris Karloff; found himself possessed by an evil ancestor in *The Haunted Palace*, which really derived more from H. P. Lovecraft than Poe; went over to England for *The Masque of the Red Death*, which was perhaps the best-liked of the lot; and ended the Poe-Corman cycle with *The Tomb of Ligeia*, wearing a pair of groovy sunglasses while haunted by his dead wife.

Elsewhere, he was gainfully employed, rescuing Chinese girls from white slavers in *Confessions of an Opium Eater*; and doing a trio of Hawthorne stories in *Twice-Told Tales*, the last being "The House of the Seven Gables" which he'd already done as a feature for Fox in 1940, though this time he was the villain rather than his brother. AIP also cast him in another fun-fest with fellow horror thesps Karloff, Peter Lorre, and Basil Rathbone, *The Comedy of Terrors*; made him *The Last Man on Earth*, battling zombies in this Italian co-production; and then allowed things to get pretty damn silly with *Dr. Goldfoot and the Bikini Machine*, which somehow rated an Italian follow-up, *Dr. Goldfoot and the Girl Bombs*; bad movies better known for their titles than their content.

In between lesser efforts, such as *The Oblong Box* and *Madhouse*, he had three of his very best vehicles, all of which were made in England: *The Conqueror Worm/Witchfinder General*, a creepy historical piece about the witch-hunt hysteria, in which he was surprisingly restrained as the diabolically self-serving Matthew Hopkins; *The Abominable Dr. Phibes*, an inventive and cheeky tale of revenge in which he did away with the doctors who let his wife die on the operating table by using the Biblical plagues as his inspiration; and *Theatre of Blood*, perhaps the finest of all his films, utilizing a similar theme of vengeance, but this time casting him all too perfectly as an over-the-top actor killing off the critics who'd given him bad reviews. This was pretty much the summing up of his career and with the box office cooling down, he took it easy from that point on, basically showing up in guest spots or limited supporting roles. Indeed two attempts to pair him with other stars of the genre, *The Monster Club* (John Carradine and Donald Pleasence) and *The House of the Long Shadows* (Peter Cushing, Christopher Lee, and Carradine), were barely released, indicating that his time in the spotlight had passed. Audiences saw him doing various television ads and hosting the PBS *Mystery* anthology, and heard him voicing the villain rat in Disney's *The Great Mouse Detective* and reading a poem during Michael Jackson's famous "Thriller" music video. There was a surprise "normal" production, *The Whales of August*, where he showed up as a Russian emigré who drops by on Ann

Sothern, and a touching role as the scientist who creates *Edward Scissorhands* only to die before the boy is finished. By that point he had become something of a treasured figure, not only in the annals of horror but in the field of show business itself, having left behind a reputation as one of the sweetest and most gentlemanly of all performers. His third wife (1974–1991) was actress Coral Browne, whom he had electrocuted under a hairdryer in *Theatre of Blood*. He authored the autobiographical *I Know What I Like* (1959) and *The Book of Joe*, about his dog.

Screen: 1938: Service de Luxe; 1939: The Private Lives of Elizabeth and Essex; Tower of London; 1940: The Invisible Man Returns; Green Hell; The House of the Seven Gables; Brigham Young; 1941: Hudson's Bay; 1943: The Song of Bernadette; 1944: The Eve of St. Mark; Wilson; Laura; The Keys of the Kingdom; 1945: A Royal Scandal; Leave Her to Heaven; 1946: Shock; Dragonwyck; 1947: The Web; Moss Rose; The Long Night; 1948: Up in Central Park; Abbott and Costello Meet Frankenstein (voice); Rogues' Regiment; The Three Musketeers; 1949: The Bribe; Bagdad; 1950: Champagne for Caesar; The Baron of Arizona; Curtain Call at Cactus Creek; 1951: His Kind of Woman; Adventures of Captain Fabian; Pictura: Adventure in Art; 1952: The Las Vegas Story; 1953: House of Wax; 1954: Dangerous Mission; Casanova's Big Night; The Mad Magician; 1955: Son of Sinbad; 1956: Serenade; While the City Sleeps; The Vagabond King (narrator); The Ten Commandments; 1957: The Story of Mankind; 1958: The Fly; House on Haunted Hill; 1959: The Big Circus; Return of the Fly; The Tingler; The Bat; 1960: House of Usher/The Fall of the House of Usher; 1961: Master of the World; Pit and the Pendulum; Naked Terror (narrator); 1962: Convicts 4; Tales of Terror; Confessions of an Opium Eater; Nefertite Regina del Nilo/Queen of the Nile (nUSr); Tower of London; 1963: The Raven; Diary of a Madman; Beach Party; Rage of the Buccaneers/The Black Buccaneer; The Haunted Palace; Twice-Told Tales; The Comedy of Terrors; 1964: The Last Man on Earth; The Masque of the Red Death; 1965: The Tomb of Ligeia; Taboos of the World (narrator); War-Gods of the Deep/City Under the Sea; Dr. Goldfoot and the Bikini Machine; 1966: Dr. Goldfoot and the Girl Bombs; 1967: The Jackals; House of a Thousand Dolls; 1968: The Conqueror Worm/Witchfinder General; More Dead Than Alive; 1969: The Trouble With Girls (and How to Get Into It); The Oblong Box; Spirits of the Dead (voice); 1970: Scream and Scream Again; Cry of the Banshee; 1971: The Abominable Dr. Phibes; 1972: Dr. Phibes Rises Again; 1973: Theatre of Blood; 1974: Madhouse; Percy's Progress/It's Not the Size That Counts (US: 1978); 1975: Journey Into Fear (US: dtc); 1979: Scavenger Hunt; 1980: Days of Fury (narrator); 1981: The Monster Club; 1983: House of the Long Shadows; 1984: Bloodbath at the House of Death (dtv); 1986: The Great Mouse Detective (voice); 1987: The Offspring/From a Whisper to a Scream; The Whales of August; 1988: Dead Heat; 1990: Edward Scissorhands; 1995: Arabian Knight (voice).

NY Stage: 1935: Victoria Regina; 1937: The Lady Has a Heart; 1938: The Shoemaker's Holiday; Heartbreak House; Outward Bound; 1941: Angel Street; 1953: Richard III; 1954: Black-Eyed Susan; 1968: Darling of the Day; 1978: Diversions and Delights.

Select TV: 1950–52: Pantomime Quiz (series); 1951: The Promise (sp); 1952: The Game of Chess (sp); Monsieur Beaucaire (sp); Dream Job (sp); 1953: Sheila (sp); Bullet for a Stranger (sp); 1956: The Ballad of Mender McClure (sp); Sister (sp); One Thousand Eyes (sp); Forbidden Area (sp); 1957: The Blue Hotel (sp); High Barrier (sp); The Clouded Image (sp); The Iron Rose (sp); Lone Woman (sp); 1958: Angel in the Air (sp); Angel Street (sp); E.S.P. (series); 1960: The Chevy Mystery Show (series); The Three Musketeers (sp); Shame the Devil (sp); 1969: The Heiress (sp);

1971: Here Comes Peter Cottontail (sp; voice); What's a Nice Girl Like You...?; 1979: Time Express (series); 1981–89: Mystery (series host); 1982: Rudigore (sp); Faerie Tale Theatre: Snow White (sp); 1985–86: The 13 Ghosts of Scooby-Doo (series; voice); 1991: Backtrack/Catchfire; 1993: The Heart of Justice.

DOROTHY PROVINE

BORN: DEADWOOD, SD, JANUARY 20, 1937.
ED: UNIV. OF WA.

An ingratiating blonde, Dorothy Provine's fame came from playing a snappy television flapper, though on the big screen she came across as much more of a sweet and demure sort of gal. She was not long out of college when she began landing guest spots on the small screen in various series. Warners took an interest in her, hiring her to be a regular on the one-season program The Alaskans, and then making her famous by casting her as singer Pinky Pinkham in The Roaring Twenties, which ran only a single season more than her other show had. By the time of the latter, she had already essayed the lead in a negligible AIP quickie, The Bonnie Parker Story, which in no way shook the screen as Faye Dunaway's interpretation would a decade later, and had the distinction of being The 30 Foot Bride of Candy Rock, a juvenile feature that marked Lou Costello's only non-Bud Abbott feature and his farewell to the screen. After her television shows, she wound up in some popular comedies starting with It's a Mad Mad Mad Mad World, as Milton Berle's wife and the only principle character who is not engulfed by greed; Good Neighbor Sam, as Jack Lemmon's ever-patient wife, who allows him to pose as husband to Romy Schneider; The Great Race, in a small part as a racy saloon singer; and That Darn Cat!, as Hayley Mills's older sister. There was another fun romp, Who's Minding the Mint?, as the loyal girlfriend of treasury employee Jim Hutton, helping him participate in the heist. Clearly she was becoming one of the nicer additions to this kind of colorful, brightly played 1960s lark. However, following her contribution to another Disney offering, Never a Dull Moment, she married British director Robert Day, retired from the scene, and was basically never heard from again.

Screen: 1958: The Bonnie Parker Story; Live Fast, Die Young; 1959: Riot in Juvenile Prison; The 30 Foot Bride of Candy Rock; 1963: Wall of Noise; It's a Mad Mad Mad Mad World; 1964: Good Neighbor Sam; 1965: The Great Race; That Darn Cat!; 1966: Kiss the Girls and Make Them Die; One Spy Too Many (from TV); 1967: Who's Minding the Mint?; 1968: Never a Dull Moment.

Select TV: 1959–60: The Alaskans (series); 1960–62: The Roaring Twenties (series); 1968: The Sound of Anger.

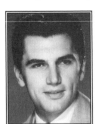

EDMUND PURDOM

BORN: WELWYN GARDEN CITY, HERTFORDSHIRE, ENGLAND, DECEMBER 19, 1924.
ED: ST. IGNATIUS COL.

Hollywood has tried to make stars out of all sorts of non-starters and Edmund Purdom was one of the major failures of the 1950s. After doing rep work in Northampton and Kettering, he went to London where his credits included Romeo and Juliet. He came to Broadway as part of the company of the Olivier-Leigh presentations of Antony and Cleopatra and Caesar and Cleopatra, and then went to California where he appeared on screen as Officer Lightoller in Titanic, and as one of James Mason's servants in Julius Caesar. When Mario Lanza got temperamental over doing

The Student Prince, MGM came up with the terrible idea of hiring Purdom for the part and using Lanza's pre-recorded vocals. This resulted in a leading man who could neither sing nor act, but that didn't stop Fox from borrowing him to play the title role in The Egyptian, one of the dreariest of the many Biblical epics of the day. Most of the blame for this was placed on Purdom, but it was fairly popular, nonetheless. The same could not be said for Athena, in which he was a boring attorney romancing Jane Powell; The Prodigal, in which he actually managed to seem like the better actor when playing opposite Lana Turner; or The King's Thief, which at least had David Niven in the cast to provide some relief. After this period, he returned to Europe where he began popping up in those costume pictures that were in abundance in the early 1960s, including The Cossacks, Herod the Great, and The Loves of Salammbo. Making Italy his home, he continued to show up from time to time in productions made there or elsewhere in Europe, including Frankenstein's Castle of Freaks; Night Child, one of the many Exorcist rip-offs of the 1970s; Pieces, as a college professor creating a human jigsaw puzzle; Don't Open 'Til Christmas, about a Santa Claus killer, which he also directed; and After the Fall of New York, as the president of the United States, in a violent tale of the future.

Screen (US releases only): 1953: Titanic; Julius Caesar; 1954: The Student Prince; The Egyptian; Athena; 1955: The Prodigal; The King's Thief; 1956: Stranger Intruder; 1960: The Cossacks; Trapped in Tangiers (filmed 1957); Herod the Great; 1962: The Loves of Salammbo; Malaga/Moment of Danger; White Slave Ship; 1963: Suleiman the Conqueror; Last of the Vikings; Lafayette; The Comedy Man; 1965: The Yellow Rolls-Royce; 1966: Contest Girl/The Beauty Jungle; 1975: Frankenstein's Castle of Freaks; Evil Fingers; 1976: Night Child; 1977: Mister Scarface/Big Boss; 1983: Ator the Fighting Eagle (dtv); Pieces; 1984: Don't Open 'Til Christmas (and dir.); 1985: The Assisi Underground; After the Fall of New York; 1990: Endless Descent/The Gift (dtv).

NY Stage: 1951: Caesar and Cleopatra; Antony and Cleopatra; 1956: Child of Fortune.

Select TV: 1957: The Sword of Freedom (series); 1980: Sophia Loren: Her Own Story; 1983: The Scarlet and the Black (ms); The Winds of War (ms).

EDNA PURVIANCE

(OLGA EDNA PURVIANCE)
BORN: PARADISE VALLEY, NV, OCTOBER 21, 1895.
DIED: JANUARY 13, 1958.

Charlie Chaplin's unpretentious and charming leading lady for most of his best comedies, Edna Purviance had worked as a secretary in San Francisco when she was recommended to the comedian, who was looking for someone with whom he could click on screen without being overshadowed. She started off with the short "A Night Out" in 1915, playing a married lady at the hotel where a drunken Chaplin is running rampant. From that point until 1923, she was to appear in every one of his vehicles accept for his solo outing, "One A.M." These included the title role in his spoof of "Carmen" and participating in his best period, for the Mutual Film Company, where she was a Gypsy girl in "The Vagabond;" a wealthy lass dubbed Miss Moneybags in "The Count;" the shop owner's daughter in "The Pawnshop;" a young acting hopeful who disguises herself as a man at one point in "Behind the Screen;" a mission worker in "Easy Street;" and a fellow foreigner new to New York in "The Immigrant." She stayed with Chaplin as he moved into longer movies, such as The

Pilgrim and *The Kid*. It was finally decided that she would be given her own dramatic vehicle directed and written by Chaplin, who was not to appear except for a cameo. The resulting film, *A Woman of Paris*, wasn't bad, just unremarkable, and public interest was small to say the least. At that point the comedian decided to feature other leading ladies in his new comedies and refused to distribute *A Woman of the Sea*, which Purviance had made under the direction of Josef von Sternberg. With that she retired from acting. Despite his uncharitable treatment of the von Sternberg film, the great comic generously kept Purviance on the payroll for the remainder of her life and even asked her to do extra work in two of his later movies.

Screen (shorts): 1915: A Night Out; The Champion; In the Park; A Jitney Elopement; The Tramp; By the Sea; Work; A Woman; The Bank; Carmen; A Night in the Show; Shanghaied; 1916: Police; The Fireman; The Floorwalker; The Vagabond; The Count; The Pawnshop; The Rink; Behind the Screen; 1917: Easy Street; The Cure; The Immigrant; The Adventurer; 1918: Triple Trouble; A Dog's Life; The Bond; Shoulder Arms; 1919: Sunnyside; A Day's Pleasure; 1921: The Idle Class; 1922: Pay Day.

Screen (features): 1921: The Kid; 1923: The Pilgrim; A Woman of Paris; 1926: A Woman of the Sea/The Seagull (nUSr); The Education of a Prince (nUSr); 1946: Monsieur Verdoux; 1952: Limelight.

Q

ANTHONY QUAYLE

(John Anthony Quayle) Born: Ainsdale, England, September 7, 1913. ed: RADA. Died: October 20, 1989.

A fine, distinguished, often undervalued performer, Anthony Quayle's preference for the stage was evident, but he was to pop up from time to time on the big screen over the course of five decades. Though he never achieved stardom there, he gained a reputation as a class "A" character player. Following drama courses, he did some music hall stints before making his legit debut in 1931, in *Robin Hood*. The following year he became a member of the Old Vic Company and then enlisted in the Royal Artillery, where he rose to the rank of major. After the war he took up directing with a production of *Crime and Punishment*, and then joined the Shakespeare Memorial Theatre (later Royal Shakespeare Theatre) as both actor and director. During a stage career that would include such American credits as *Galileo* and *Sleuth*, he was seen on the big screen in such movies as *Pygmalion*, fixing Wendy Hiller's hair; Laurence Olivier's Oscar-winning *Hamlet*, as Marcellus; *The Wrong Man*, as Henry Fonda's attorney; *Woman in a Dressing Gown*, in a rare starring role, as the husband who makes the mistake of dumping his wife for another woman; *Ice Cold in Alex/Desert Attack*, suspected of being a German spy; *The Guns of Navarone*, heading the team of military saboteurs in this blockbuster action hit; the Academy Award-winner for Best Picture of 1962, *Lawrence of Arabia*, as Colonel Harry Brighton, and, as always, looking absolutely authentic in uniform; *H.M.S. Defiant/Damn the Defiant!*, as the crewman who attempts to lead a mutiny aginst stern Dirk Bogarde; *A Study in Terror*, as a police surgeon involved in the Jack the Ripper case; *Anne of the Thousand Days*, as the doomed Cardinal Woolsey, a quietly moving performance that earned him his sole Oscar nomination; Woody Allen's *Everything You Always Wanted to Know About Sex*, as the monarch who puts wife Lynn Redgrave in a chastity belt; and *The Eagle Has Landed*, as a Nazi. He was given an Emmy Award for his role in the tv mini-series *QBVII*. Knighted in 1985, he was also the author of two novels, *Eight Hours from England* (1945) and *On Such a Night* (1947).

Screen: 1938: Pygmalion; 1948: Hamlet; Saraband for Dead Lovers/Saraband; 1955: Oh…Rosalinda!!; 1956: Pursuit of the Graf Spee/The Battle of the River Plate; The Wrong Man; 1957: Woman in a Dressing Gown; No Time for Tears; 1958: The Man Who Wouldn't Talk; Ice Cold in Alex/Desert Attack; 1959: Tarzan's Greatest Adventure; A Touch of Hell/Serious Charge; 1960: The Challenge; 1961: The Guns of Navarone; 1962: Damn the Defiant!/HMS Defiant; Lawrence of Arabia; 1964: The Fall of the Roman Empire; 1965: Operation Crossbow/The Great Spy Mission; 1966: East of Sudan; A Study in Terror; 1967: Misunderstood/Incompreso (nUSr); 1968: Mackenna's Gold; 1969: Before Winter Comes; Anne of the Thousand Days; 1972: Everything You Always Wanted to Know About Sex But Were Afraid to Ask; 1973: The Nelson Affair/Bequest to the Nation; 1974: The Tamarind Seed; 1977: The Eagle Has Landed; 1978: The Chosen/Holocaust 2000; 1979: Murder by Decree; 1988: The Legend of the Holy Drinker (nUSr); Buster; 1989: Magdalene (dtv); King of the Wind (dtv).

NY Stage: 1936: The Country Wife; 1956: Tamburline the Great; 1958: The Firstborn (and dir.); 1967: Galileo; 1968: Halfway Up a Tree; 1970: Sleuth; 1978: Do You Turn Somersaults?

Select TV: 1955: The Merry Wives of Windsor (sp); 1956: The Barretts of Wimpole Street (sp); 1961: The Rose Affair (sp); 1966: Barefoot in Athens (sp); The Poppy Is Also a Flower (also theatrical release); 1968: A Case of Libel (sp); 1969: Destiny of a Spy; 1971: Strange Report (series); The Six Wives of Henry VIII (ms; narrator); 1973: The Evil Touch (series host); Jarrett; 1974: QBVII (ms); Great Expectations; 1975: Moses the Lawgiver (ms; and theatrical 1976 as Moses); 1976: 21 Hours at Munich; 1978: Ice Age (sp); 1979: Henry IV Part 1 (sp); Henry V Part 2 (sp); 1981: Masada (ms); Dial M for Murder; The Manions of America; 1984: Lace; The Last Days of Pompeii (ms); The Testament of John (sp); 1985: The Heart of the Dragon (series narrator); The Key to Rebecca (sp); 1988: The Bourne Identity; 1989: Confessional; 1990: The Endless Game.

ANTHONY QUINN

(ANTONIO RUDOLFO OAXACA QUINN) BORN:
CHIHUAHUA, MEXICO, APRIL 21, 1915. RAISED IN
LOS ANGELES, CA. DIED: JUNE 3, 2001.

For years moviegoers felt the smoldering presence of Anthony Quinn ready to burst through into something bigger and better, as he essayed all kinds of quickie supporting parts and villainous bits. Perhaps it was racism that made it so hard for Hollywood's first and, to date, only male superstar from Mexico, to make it to the top. When he did reach leading man status, it became a challenge to find the right vehicles in which to showcase him, resulting in a lot of worthless endeavors. The best of him was very good indeed but more than once he felt the need to go for the rafters as if he was trying to guarantee that he would never be forgotten. His family moved to Los Angeles when he was a boy and it was there that he did some theater, including a production of *Hay Fever*, that got him some attention, resulting in a small part as a prisoner in a Universal "B" film, *Parole*, in 1936. In a very short time he would become the best-known name in the cast. Because of his ethnic looks he was often cast as Indians and the first such case was in the Cecil B. DeMille epic *The Plainsman*, which earned him a contract with Paramount. On the "A" side, he was a Hawaiian in Bing Crosby's *Waikiki Wedding*; a Panamanian putting the moves on Carole Lombard in *Swing High, Swing Low*; a captain fighting in the Spanish Civil War in *Last Train from Madrid*, a significant role though his billing hardly indicated it; a French pirate in *The Buccaneer*; and a bad guy in *Union Pacific*. The last two were also directed by DeMille, who became his father-in-law in 1938, when Quinn married his daughter, Katharine. Up to this point, he was mostly hired to be very threatening and oily. So, hoping to find something different elsewhere, he got out of his contract.

Over at Warners he was a dancer in *City for Conquest*; Chief Crazy Horse in their fictionalized look at General Custer, *They Died With Their Boots On*; and a tough gangster, and therefore the straight man, in the light-hearted Edward G. Robinson romp *Larceny, Inc*. Fox cast him as the best buddy of matador Tyrone Power in *Blood and Sand*; a pirate in the grand adventure *The Black Swan*; the brooding and uncooperative Mexican who faces a lynch mob in *The Ox-Bow Incident*, certainly one of the finest films he ever appeared in; and Chief Yellow Hand in another piece of Hollywood fiction, *Buffalo Bill*. Over at RKO he went Asian for a significant role as a guerilla leader in *China Sky*, which was at least an attempt to create a sympathetic portrayal of the Chinese, but it took Allied Artists to come up with his first genuine, top-billed starring role, in *Black Gold*, playing opposite his real-life wife, as an American Indian befriending a Chinese orphan. It suggested that he could carry a film but was treated as nothing more than the modest release it was. Fed up with the lack of progress in his Hollywood status, he decided to try the theater and his performance as Stanley Kowolski in the touring company and later New York City Center revival of *A Streetcar Named Desire* did a great deal to give him credibility and respect in the acting world. When he returned to movies he started off strong, with *The Brave Bulls*, one of the movies' better depictions of the controversial subject of bullfighting, as Mel Ferrer's savy manager; and *Viva Zapata!*, in which he more than held his own against Marlon Brando, playing the brother of the famed Mexican revolutionary. For the latter and, perhaps, as a reward for hanging on so long, he was given the Academy Award for Best Supporting Actor of 1952.

Initially this honor changed things very little, for he followed it by playing the nemesis of Errol Flynn in a standard swashbuckler *Against All Flags*; of Rock Hudson in *Seminole*; and of Robert Taylor in *Ride, Vaquero!*, the only difference from his early days being that these were now in color and his billing was higher. Figuring he had nothing to lose, he accepted an offer from Carlo Ponti and Dino DeLaurentiis for three Italian films: two lavish-but-cardboard epics, *Ulysses*, in support of Kirk Douglas, and *Atilla*, which featured a pre-famous Sophia Loren; and one gem, *La Strada*. This last turned out to be one of the great foreign movies of its day, and, indeed, of all time, with Quinn first rate as the brutish and stupid circus strongman who destroys the happiness of simple waif Giulietta Masina and others. It won the Oscar for Best Foreign Language Film of 1956, the same year Quinn took home his second trophy in the supporting category as a very colorful Paul Gaugin in *Lust for Life*, certainly one of the briefest roles to earn the award. He had already been getting leads in America, although hardly in anything that was "box office." These included a lesser bullfighting film, *The Magnificent Matador*, this time in the ring himself; *The Wild Party*, going full-hog as a footballer-turned-hood; and *Man From Del Rio*, a well-meaning western that used his Mexican heritage as a statement against prejudice. After another foreign production, *The Hunchback of Notre Dame*, which was unanimously considered inferior to the earlier versions, he reached another of his peaks, as the lusty, domineering Italian immigrant whose wife is carrying on with his adopted son in a well done melodrama, *Wild Is the Wind*, which got him an Oscar nod in the lead category.

He was then given a chance to direct, via his father-in-law, who was the executive producer of the 1958 remake of *The Buccaneer*, though the end results in no way suggested any need to continue in this field. This was no loss since he was now full-fledged star material, as he showed with the soap operas *Hot Spell*, married to Shirley Booth; *Black Orchid*, romancing mobster's widow Sophia Loren; and *Portrait in Black*, foolishly helping Lana Turner to kill her husband. These were fairly standard items of their time while *The Savage Innocents* was a rather curious multilingual thing in which he was an Eskimo, apparently determined to cover every possible ethnic type that he'd missed putting on his résumé. The early 1960s was his prime period as a big, international name and he was part of two of Columbia Pictures's mightiest spectacles, *The Guns of Navarone*, as a Greek resistance fighter helping Gregory Peck and his team to sabotage the title weapons, while promising to kill Peck after the mission; and *Lawrence of Arabia*, dynamic as the Arab chief who joins forces with Peter O'Toole. In a quieter, black-and-white mode he was very touching as the pathetic and dim-witted fighter at the end of his rope in *Requiem for a Heavyweight*, which was meant for smaller audiences, having already received great acclaim on television with Jack Palance in the lead. He and Peck were reteamed with much less success for *Behold a Pale Horse*, and nobody was too keen to see Ingrid Bergman take revenge on him in *The Visit*, a critically panned version of a much-admired play. However, there was nothing but high praise for his rousing portrayal of *Zorba the Greek*, taking impressionable Alan Bates under his wing and teaching him to enjoy life for all its worth. This turned out to be one of the sleeper hits of 1964, earning Oscar nominations for Best Picture and one for Quinn as well. It would become his signature role — the one that captured his power as a major screen presence when he was on the mark.

Alas, nothing seemed to go right after that. A string of dull vehicles threatened to topple him from the heights he had reached, including *The 25th Hour*, as a Romanian peasant searching for his wife; *The Happening*, playing a kidnapped mobster, in a movie that became better known for its hit title song; *Guns for San Sebastian*, as a heroic Mexican bandit; the incoherent *The Magus*, as a magician; and the ambitious but dry *The Shoes of the Fisherman*, rising from peasant to pope. There was more interest in the comedic *The Secret of Santa Vittoria*, as a volatile Italian hiding wine from the Nazis; and *Across 110th Street*, a violent crime tale set in Harlem in which he was a persistent cop handling justice in his own manner. He persevered into the 1970s and beyond with further flops like *A Walk in the Spring Rain*, a love story reuniting him with Ingrid Bergman; *Flap*, as a pathetic Indian; *The Don Is Dead*, one of the many cash-ins on *The Godfather*; *Mohammad: Messenger of God*; the ghastly *The Greek Tycoon*, as a thinly disguised version of Aristotle Onassis (he later played the real thing on television); and *Lion of the Desert*, an expensive Libyan-British co-production and the sort of epic that nobody wanted to see in 1981. It was time to try something safe, so he returned to the stage in the revival of the musical version of *Zorba* (Hershel Bernardi had done it originally) and it was the first time in years that his name proved to be a lure to customers. There was a resurgence of sorts in the early 1990s with Quinn being cast in some major Hollywood productions like *Revenge*, taking just that out on young wife Madeleine Stowe and her lover Kevin Costner; *Jungle Fever*, as John Turturro's morose Italian dad; *Only the Lonely*, trying to romance Maureen O'Hara (his one time leading lady in *The Magnificent Matador*); and *A Walk in the Clouds*, still a life force though now playing a grandpa. It made one marvel, to look back on the 60 years he had been at work through good and bad, having nothing left to prove yet still seemingly eager to prove it. His marriage to DeMille ended in 1965. He published two autobiographies, *The Original Sin* (1972) and *One Man Tango* (1995).

Screen: 1936: Parole; Night Waitress; Sworn Enemy; The Plainsman; 1937: Partners in Crime; Swing High, Swing Low; Waikiki Wedding; The Last Train From Madrid; Daughter of Shanghai; 1938: The Buccaneer; Dangerous to Know; Tip-Off Girls; Hunted Man; Bulldog Drummond in Africa; King of Alcatraz; 1939: King of Chinatown; Union Pacific; Island of Lost Men; Television Spy; 1940: Emergency Squad; Road to Singapore; Parole Fixer; The Ghost Breakers; City for Conquest; Texas Rangers Ride Again; 1941: Blood and Sand; Thieves Fall Out; Knockout; Bullets for O'Hara; The Perfect Snob; They Died With Their Boots On; 1942: Larceny, Inc.; Road to Morocco; The Black Swan; 1943: The Ox-Bow Incident; Guadalcanal Diary; 1944: Buffalo Bill; Ladies of Washington; Roger Touhy — Gangster; Irish Eyes Are Smiling; 1945: Where Do We Go from Here?; China Sky; Back to Bataan; 1946: California; 1947: Sinbad the Sailor; The Imperfect Lady; Black Gold; Tycoon; 1951: The Brave Bulls; Mask of the Avenger; 1952: Viva Zapata!; The World in His Arms; The Brigand; Against All Flags; 1953: Seminole; Ride, Vaquero!; East of Sumatra; Blowing Wild; City Beneath the Sea; 1954: The Long Wait; Cavalleria Rusticana/Fatal Desire (nUSr); 1955: Ulysses; Attila (US: 1958); The Magnificent Matador; The Naked Street; Seven Cities of Gold; 1956: Donne Probite/Angels of Darkness (It: 1953); Lust for Life; Man From Del Rio; The Wild Party; La Strada; 1957: The River's Edge; The Ride Back; The Hunchback of Notre Dame; Wild Is the Wind; 1958: Hot Spell; Black Orchid; 1959: Last Train From Gun Hill; Warlock; 1960: Heller in Pink Tights; Portrait in Black; The Savage Innocents; 1961: The Guns of Navarone; 1962: Barabbas; Lawrence of Arabia; Requiem for a Heavyweight; 1964: Behold a Pale Horse; The Visit; Zorba the Greek; 1965: Marco the Magnificent; A High Wind in Jamaica; 1966: Lost Command; 1967: The 25th Hour; The Happening; The Rover; 1968: Guns for San Sebastian; The Magus; The Shoes

of the Fisherman; 1969: The Secret of Santa Vittoria; A Dream of Kings; 1970: A Walk in the Spring Rain; R.P.M.; Flap; 1972: Across 110th Street (and exec. prod.); 1973: Deaf Smith and Johnny Ears; The Don Is Dead; 1974: The Destructors/The Marseille Contract; 1976: Tigers Don't Cry/Target of the Assassin (nUSr); 1977: Mohammad; Messenger of God/The Message; 1978: The Inheritance/Eredita Ferramonti (It: 1976); The Greek Tycoon; The Children of Sanchez (dtv); Caravanas; 1979: The Passage; 1981: Lion of the Desert; The Con Artists/The Switch (It: 1977); High Risk; The Salamander (dtv); 1982: Regina (dtv); 1983: Valentina/1919 (nUSr); 1988: A Man of Passion (dtv); Stradivari (nUSr); 1990: Revenge; Ghosts Can't Do It; 1991: A Star for Two (nUSr); Only the Lonely; Jungle Fever; Mobsters; 1993: Last Action Hero; 1995: A Walk in the Clouds; 1996: Somebody to Love; Il Sindaco/The Mayor (nUSr); Seven Servants (nUSr); 1999: Oriundi (nUSr); 2002: Avenging Angelo (nUSr).

NY Stage: 1947: The Gentleman From Athens; 1950: A Streetcar Named Desire; Born in Texas; 1960: Becket; 1962: Tchin-Tchin; 1983: Zorba.

Select TV: 1951: The House of Dust (sp); Dark Fleece (sp); 1954: The Long Trail (sp); 1955: Bandit's Hideout (sp); 1971: The City; 1971–72: The Man and the City (series); 1977: Jesus of Nazareth (ms); 1987: Treasure Island in Outer Space (It: ms); 1988: Onassis: The Richest Man in the World; 1990: The Old Man and the Sea; 1994: This Can't Be Love; Hercules and the Amazon Women; Hercules and the Lost Kingdom; Hercules and the Circle of Fire; Hercules in the Underworld; Hercules in the Maze of the Minotaur; 1996: Gotti; 1999: Carmino de Santiago (ms).

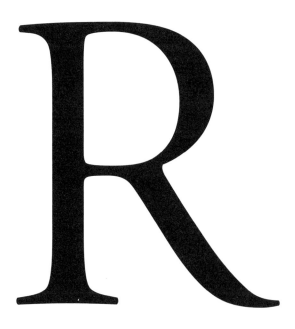

R

GEORGE RAFT

(George Ranft) Born: New York, NY,
September 26, 1895. Died: November 24, 1980.

Often heaped into the same group as
Bogart, Cagney, and Robinson when it came
to defining the movie gangster image of the
1930s, George Raft certainly had the creden-
tials, having actually rubbed elbows with the real thing in his
early days as he rose to stardom. Unlike the others, however, he
had no range or complexity and, with only his evil sneer and
rude, stoic manner to fall back on, it was an act that wore thin
over time. Once his youth was gone, the sense of danger he
exuded became monotonous and his deadlier vehicles were made
only drearier by his presence. He went from prizefighter to
dancer, eventually partnering Elsie Pilcer, with whom he was seen
in some Broadway shows. Around this time he made friends with
such underworld figures as Owney Madden, who helped get him
a job at Texas Guinan's nightclub. Guinan, in turn, got Raft into
the movies as part of the cast of her vehicle *Queen of the Night
Clubs*, which led to other bits including *Taxi!*, where he had a
quick moment on the dance floor, sharing the same scene with
James Cagney. The one that made him a name was *Scarface*, in
which, as second in command to mobster Paul Muni, he cleverly
made an impression via his incessant habit of flipping a coin and
catching it. This slick move became his trademark and the part
won him a contract with Paramount in 1932. They started him
off with *Madame Racketeer* and *Night After Night*, films stolen
from him by Alison Skipworth and Mae West, respectively. He
was a star attraction in *The Undercover Man*, in which he played
a good guy; a taxi driver trying to put his past behind him in *The
Pick-Up*; and then was purposefully dislikable as an ex-con in *All
of Me*, taking billing after Fredric March and Miriam Hopkins.
Better known was the film he did on loan to United Artists, *The
Bowery*, an enjoyably crude glimpse at turn-of-the-century New
York, in which he played Steve Brody, the fellow who supposedly
jumped off the Brooklyn Bridge as a stunt.

Raft dusted off his dancing skills for *Bolero*, which whipped up
enough interest that it actually rated a sequel, *Rumba*; was cast as
an Asian for *Limehouse Blues*; investigated Ray Milland's murder

in *The Glass Key*, a story that became better known in its 1942 version; and was a bandleader in *Every Night at Eight*, a film better
remembered for featuring the hit song "I'm in the Mood for
Love" than for Raft's performance.

It was becoming clear that Raft was not only ho-hum as a
box-office attraction but had great trouble evoking sympathy
when he wasn't asked to be an out-and-out rat. Fortunately, he
had Gary Cooper to carry him through *Souls at Sea*, and
Henry Fonda for *Spawn of the North*, but on his own, in *The
Lady's From Kentucky*, he was a bust and Paramount was none
too sorry to end his contract in 1939. It was only natural that
Warner Bros., the unofficial home of the gangster genre, took
him on. He fared better than in the past, placed alongside
Cagney for *Each Dawn I Die*, a good prison melodrama;
Bogart in *Invisible Stripes*, in which he tried to keep impressionable younger brother William Holden away from a life of
crime; Bogart again for *They Drive by Night*, a well-done story
of sibling truckers involved in murder that was probably the
best thing Raft did around this time; and Robinson in
Manpower, with the two playing electrical linemen battling
over Marlene Dietrich.

While at Warner Bros., Raft made some strange choices,
turning down such projects as *The Maltese Falcon* and
Casablanca, which was foolish on his part when one considers the
quality of their screenplays, but ultimately a lucky thing for
Bogart and the movie-going public in general. He was soon
dropped by the studio and went over to Universal to do some
dancing again, first in their adaptation of the stage play
Broadway, in a script that was revised so that Raft actually played
himself; and then for their all-star contribution to the war effort,
Follow the Boys, which was the poorest of these efforts, no doubt
because it depended on Raft to carry the plot. Over at 20th
Century-Fox, he actually had something resembling a hit with
Nob Hill, a thoroughly undistinguished mixture of melodrama
and music featuring Joan Bennett. After that came some pretty
bleak times.

Raft hung in there for years, always with star billing but in one
routine vehicle after another starting with *Johnny Angel* (not to be
confused with the later *Johnny Allegro*) and on through *Mr. Ace*,
which reteamed him with Sylvia Sidney, his co-star nearly a

decade before in *You and Me*; *Christmas Eve*, which proved he was the last mug anyone wanted hanging around for the holidays; *Intrigue*, leaving behind his smuggler's life and helping to feed Chinese orphans; *Red Light*, a quasi-religious melodrama; *Outpost in Morocco*, as an aging foreign legionnaire; and then a few made in Europe, including *Lucky Nick Cain*; *I'll Get You* (which shouldn't be confused with *I'll Get You for This*, the British title for *Lucky Nick*); and *The Man from Cairo*. In most of these films he seemed to be standing around like a cigar-store Indian, counting the minutes to pay day. Back in America, he took second-billing to some other stars who were no longer in their prime: Ginger Rogers (*Black Widow*), Robert Taylor (*Rogue Cop*), and Edward G. Robinson (*Bullet for Joey*), then landed a supporting role that was better than anything else he'd done, playing gangster Spats Columbo, on the trail of musicians Jack Lemmon and Tony Curtis, in the comedy classic *Some Like It Hot*. After that, Raft was called on for guest spots in such films as *The Ladies' Man*, which required him at one point to ballroom dance with Jerry Lewis; *Casino Royale*, still flipping that coin before expiring; and *Sextette*, which, for nostalgia's sake, found him alongside Mae West once again. There was even a biography, *The George Raft Story* (1961), which starred Ray Danton and would seem to indicate that Raft's life off screen was more interesting than anything he had to offer in front of the cameras.

Screen: 1929: Queen of the Night Clubs; 1931: Quick Millions; Goldie; Hush Money; Palmy Days; 1932: Taxi; Scarface; Dancers in the Dark; Night World; Love Is a Racket; Madame Racketeer; Night After Night; If I Had a Million; The Undercover Man; 1933: Pick-Up; Midnight Club; The Bowery; 1934: All of Me; Bolero; The Trumpet Blows; Limehouse Blues; 1935: Rumba; Stolen Harmony; The Glass Key; Every Night at Eight; She Couldn't Take It; 1936: It Had to Happen; Yours for the Asking; 1937: Souls at Sea; 1938: You and Me; Spawn of the North; 1939: The Lady's From Kentucky; Each Dawn I Die; I Stole a Million; Invisible Stripes; 1940: The House Across the Bay; They Drive By Night; 1941: Manpower; 1942: Broadway; 1943: Background to Danger; Stage Door Canteen; 1944: Follow the Boys; 1945: Nob Hill; Johnny Angel; 1946: Whistle Stop; Mr. Ace; Nocturne; 1947: Christmas Eve; Intrigue; 1948: Race Street; 1949: Outpost in Morocco; Johnny Allegro; Red Light; A Dangerous Profession; Let's Go to Paris/We Will All Go to Paris; 1951: Lucky Nick Cain/I'll Get You for This; 1952: Loan Shark; I'll Get You/Escape Route; 1953: Man from Cairo; 1954: Black Widow; Rogue Cop; 1955: A Bullet for Joey; 1956: Around the World in Eighty Days; 1959: Some Like It Hot; Jet Over the Atlantic; 1960: Ocean's Eleven; 1961: The Ladies Man; Two Guys Abroad (nUSr); 1964: For Those Who Think Young; The Patsy; 1965: Rififi in Paris/The Upper Hand; 1967: Casino Royale; Five Golden Dragons; 1968: Skidoo; 1969: The Great Sex War/Make Love Not War (nUSr); 1972: Hammersmith Is Out; Deadhead Miles; 1978: Sextette; 1980: The Man With Bogart's Face.

NY Stage: 1925: The City Chap; Gay Paree; 1926: No Foolin'.

Select TV: 1953: I Am the Law (series).

LUISE RAINER
BORN: VIENNA, AUSTRIA, JANUARY 12, 1910.

The first performer to bring home back-to-back Academy Awards, lovely, delicate Luise Rainer was also instrumental in creating the legend of the Oscar jinx. Aside from her award-winning performances, little of what she did was of much consequence or interest and, after disappearing from the scene, she became more the answer to a trivia question than a

legend. Stage trained by Max Reinhardt, she worked in theatre in both Vienna and London and was seen in two movies in her native country, *Sehnsucht 202* and *Heut' Kommt's Drauf an*, during that time. The critics raved, and MGM sought her out, signing her to a contract in 1935. In her first assignment she replaced Myrna Loy in *Escapade*, playing opposite William Powell for what would be the first of three screen pairings. No one was overly enthusiastic about her or the film, but Powell was impressed enough with her that he may have suggested she be cast as performer Anna Held in MGM's much ballyhooed musical bio of 1936, *The Great Ziegfeld*. Hers was pretty much a supporting part with one big acting moment, offering Powell best wishes on his new marriage through a veil of tears. This was the first of her Oscar-winners, though she was clearly more impressive in the second, uttering very few lines but vividly conveying the strength of the wearied Chinese peasant woman O-Lan in *The Good Earth*. Perhaps it was the startling contrast to Anna Held that provoked the Academy to honor her two years in a row. Nevertheless she would later remark that nothing worse could have happened to her and, indeed, few thespians could ever have lived up to such acclaim and hype.

She was the Russian wife of Spencer Tracy, facing deportation in *Big City* and then had a chance to lighten up with a tongue-in-cheek espionage outing with Powell, *The Emperor's Candlesticks*. Things began to unravel when she was cast as a Southerner in *The Toy Wife* and then had her role cut down considerably in another biopic, *The Great Waltz*, as the suffering wife of Johann Strauss. After the failure of *Dramatic School*, she and MGM gladly parted company. Her marriage (1937–40) to playwright Clifford Odets took up most of her attention, to a point where she later felt she had not appreciated her time spent in Hollywood nor the accolades she had received there. After the divorce and an unsuccessful play on Broadway, *A Kiss for Cinderella*, she returned to the movies in 1943, appearing for Paramount in *Hostages*, just one of many wartime efforts about underground fighters and Nazis; it, as well as her return to pictures, went pretty much unnoticed. After that, her sporadic acting appearances were curious to say the least, including an appearance for controversial director Leni Riefenstahl in *Tiefland* (released in 1954, though her footage was shot over a decade earlier); stage work in London and Boston; roles on early television including *Rosalind*; and guest appearances on such unlikely series as *Combat* and, even more curiously, *The Love Boat*. Quite unexpectedly, she showed up at the Academy Award ceremony in 1998 to celebrate the gathering of several of the past Oscar winners. There was also a return to the cinema in *The Gambler*, which took some time getting picked up for American distribution, despite the curiosity appeal of her supporting role.

Screen: 1932: Sehnsucht 202/Yearning 202 (nUSr); 1933: Heut Kommt's Drauf an (nUSr); 1935: Escapade; 1936: The Great Ziegfeld; 1937: The Good Earth; Big City; The Emperor's Candlesticks; 1938: The Toy Wife; The Great Waltz; Dramatic School; 1943: Hostages; 1954: Tiefland (filmed 1942–45); 1999: The Gambler.

NY Stage: 1942: A Kiss for Cinderella; 1950: The Lady From the Sea.

Select TV: 1950: Rosalind (sp); 1952: Love Came Late (sp); 1953: Bouquet for Caroline (sp); 1954: Torment (sp); 1988: A Dancer (Swiss).

ELLA RAINES
(ELLA WALLACE RAUBES) BORN: SNOQUALMIE FALLS, WA, AUGUST 6, 1921. ED: UNIV. OF WA. DIED: MAY 30, 1988.

Best known for her tenure at Universal in the 1940s, pretty but tough-looking Ella Raines studied drama in college then set out for New York. Instead of stage work, she found herself under exclusive contract with director Howard Hawks and actor-producer Charles Boyer. The former put her into *Corvette K-225*, a naval drama in which she was part of the requisite love interest subplot, as Randolph Scott's gal. MGM borrowed her for its nursing salute, *Cry Havoc*, and at Paramount she was very lucky to land the role as Eddie Bracken's girlfriend in what would turn out to be her best movie, director Preston Sturges's smart satire *Hail the Conquering Hero*. She got herself a prime starring role, as the secretary who does some investigating to save boss Alan Curtis's neck, in *Phantom Lady* (she later reprised the part on television) and because of it Universal bought her contract from Hawks and Boyer. There, she was the beauty for whom Charles Laughton murders his wife in the intriguing melodrama *The Suspect*; then took a similar turn in *The Strange Affair of Uncle Harry*, causing George Sanders to try to murder his spinster sister. Dan Duryea took a fancy to her in *White Tie and Tails*, after which she was good as Whit Bissel's demanding wife, whose need for a fur coat lands him in the pen, in *Brute Force*. This, like her role in *The Senator Was Indiscreet*, as the reporter who publishes William Powell's diary and gets him in hot water, was not a showcase for her, suggesting that Hollywood saw her as nothing more than back-up for bigger stars. When her career was reduced to Republic cheapies like *Fighting Coast Guard* and *Ride the Man Down*, she figured she'd try her hand at television, where she not only starred in her own series, *Janet Dean: Registered Nurse*, but also wrote some of the episodes. In the late 1950s, she retired and moved back to her home state.

Screen: 1943: Corvette K-225; Cry Havoc; 1944: Phantom Lady; Hail the Conquering Hero; Tall in the Saddle; Enter Arsène Lupin; The Suspect; 1945: The Strange Affair of Uncle Harry; 1946: The Runaround; White Tie and Tails; 1947: Time Out of Mind; The Web; Brute Force; The Senator Was Indiscreet; 1949: The Walking Hills; Impact; A Dangerous Profession; 1950: The Second Face; Singing Guns; 1951: Fighting Coast Guard; 1952: Ride the Man Down; 1956: The Man in the Road.

NY Stage: 1955: The Wisteria Trees.

Select TV: 1950: The Phantom Lady (sp); You Can't Take It With You (sp); 1954: Janet Dean: Registered Nurse (series; and co-wr.).

CLAUDE RAINS

(WILLIAM CLAUDE RAINS)
BORN: LONDON, ENGLAND, NOVEMBER 10, 1889.
DIED: MAY 30, 1967.

A simply splendid example of a character actor who was so admired, so good, and so instrumental to the success of many a film that he was a star in his own right, Claude Rains cultivated his own share of followers who continue to be devotees in the decades after his passing. He could play decent fellows to be sure, but it seemed a shame to waste those snooty vocal cadences exclusively on nice men when he was such a snidely confident, richly persuasive villain, and it is perhaps in this latter mode that audiences think of him most fondly. He had started as a child vocalist on the London stage in 1899, in a production of *Nell of Old Drury*. After years of behind-the-scenes work, he made his official acting bow in 1911, in *The Gods of the Mountain*, then joined the Granville-Barker company as general manager, coming to America in 1915 with their production of *Androcles and the Lion*. For the next 15 years he became a name in the English theatre while also teaching drama at RADA There was also a small part in

a film in 1920, *Build Thy House*, which has often been left off his résumé. In 1926, he returned to Broadway in *The Constant Nymph* and became a star there in such plays as *Volpone* and *The Man Who Reclaimed His Head*. There were offers from Hollywood and the role he accepted became one of the most curious introductions to a famous actor in movie history: *The Invisible Man*. It would become one of his signature roles, despite the fact that he was glimpsed but briefly at the end. Since this was just about the peak of the Universal "horror" output of the time it brought full attention to his floridly distinctive voice, and the studios were eager to utilize him, front and center. Such was the case in *Crime Without Passion*, a bizarrely over-the-top melodrama by Hecht and MacArthur that let him go at full throttle as a lawyer who must cover his tracks after a murder. His cinematic career was off with a bang and Universal asked him to recreate his stage role in *The Man Who Reclaimed His Head*, where he was once again driven to murder. He then played the dope-addict choirmaster in *The Mystery of Edwin Drood*, a character chosen to be the murderer (naturally) by the screenwriters, since this was adapted from Charles Dickens's unfinished novel.

In 1936, he signed up with Warner Bros. and it was there that he experienced his peak years, starting with *Anthony Adverse*, stealing the film hands-down as the nasty Italian nobleman who kills Louis Hayward. He showed up as Napoleon in the Dick Powell musical *Hearts Divided*; was mean again, as the Earl of Hertford, in a grand rendering of *The Prince and the Pauper*; and then had the lead as the opportunistic Southern lawyer in the once-potent *They Won't Forget*, a melodrama about mob violence that brought out the ham-fisted worst in him. He was part of the peerless ensemble of one of the most enduring of all 1930s romps, *The Adventures of Robin Hood*, one of the rare times when he was out-sneered in the villainy department, in this case by Basil Rathbone; then had two of his nice roles, *White Banners*, as the inventor-dad who hires wise Fay Bainter to act as maid in his household; and *Four Daughters*, as the musician-father of the title characters. The latter did so well that he and most of the principles were asked back for three sequels: *Daughters Courageous*, *Four Wives*, and *Four Mothers*. In the meantime, Columbia borrowed him to play the senator who starts off as James Stewart's role model and ends up embodying every ethically bankrupt politician, in *Mr. Smith Goes to Washington*. This fine portrait of a good man gone bad earned him his first Oscar nomination. With a goatee, he was the oily ambassador in *The Sea Hawk*, in this case allowing Henry Daniell the lion's share of the hisses; and then had another of his most famous roles, over at Columbia, with the hit fantasy *Here Comes Mr. Jordan*, imperious as ever as the heaven-sent messenger who assists freshly deceased boxer Robert Montgomery in getting a new body. Meanwhile, he was borrowed by Universal for another of their high-grade horror films, *The Wolf Man*, as Lon Chaney, Jr.'s dad, horrified to discover that his son has been cursed.

Still on a roll, he came back to Warner Bros., where he was downright creepy as the domineering father of Betty Field in *Kings Row*; sympathetic and level-headed as the psychiatrist who saves Bette Davis from wallowing in self-pity in *Now, Voyager*; and simply brilliant as the cynical Captain Louis Renault, the "poor corrupt official" in the best-loved of all the wartime romances, *Casablanca*. The last earned him Oscar nomination number two, and while this provided a terrific opportunity for the industry to reward him for his stellar track record if nothing else, Charles Coburn took home the prize instead. Undaunted, he was back in the running again in 1944, for playing *Mr. Skeffington*, the used husband of opportunistic Bette Davis. The Skeffington part came after a go at the title role in the remake of

The Phantom of the Opera, which in no way erased memories of Lon Chaney in the original. Another important star turn came when he returned home to England for the first time in years, giving a commanding and often magnificent performance opposite Vivien Leigh in the very expensive rendering of Shaw's *Caesar and Cleopatra*, which actually managed to find a respectable audience who were not intimidated by Bernard Shaw's intelligent and thought-provoking dialogue. There was another triumph, as the weak and mother-dominated agent who marries Ingrid Bergman, in *Notorious*, managing to find a sympathetic side to this bad guy and earning his final Oscar nomination. He then did the flip side of *Mr. Jordan*, coming to Earth from the other direction in *Angel on My Shoulder*, and despite the fact that Rains was probably most people's cinematic ideal to embody Satan, it was inferior to the former. The next year, when Columbia actually decided to reprise the Mr. Jordan character in the musical *Down to Earth*, Rains passed, and the role went to Roland Culver instead.

Back with Davis at Warner Bros., he was her jealous composer husband in *Deception*, a film that suggested their glory days were in the past. Rains ended his contract there by starring as a radio writer who kills and then dramatizes the crime in *The Unsuspected*. Suddenly he was no longer in demand for top-grade fare as he went to Paramount for the undistinguished melodramas *Rope of Sands* and *Song of Surrender*; slipped further down the ladder going over to RKO to support Faith Domergue, in *Where Danger Lives*, as the rich husband she plots to dispose of, and then as a Nazi menacing Dana Andrews in *Sealed Cargo*. It was time to see what employment was being offered back on his home ground, so he returned to England again for *The Man Who Watched the Trains Go By*, playing a clerk who commits murder and loses his mind as a result. In 1950, Rains successfully returned to Broadway to star in *Darkness at Noon*, but was pretty much neglected by Hollywood until 1959, when he was asked to play Rock Hudson's granddad in the soap opera *This Earth Is Mine*. There was a role as the professor in a kiddie matinee favorite, *The Lost World*, acting opposite rear-projected dinosaurs; and then he showed up in one of the most distinguished of all 1960s productions, *Lawrence of Arabia*, crisply playing the head of the British Intelligence. There was one last substantial role, as the senior lawyer who serves as the inspiration to Richard Chamberlain in *Twilight of Honor*, followed by a tiny part as Herod in the all-star *The Greatest Story Ever Told*, made two years before he died after an intestinal hemorrhage. It is a testament to his work that he is spoken of more fondly than many of the "name" headliners from whom he casually stole scenes.

Screen: 1920: Build Thy House; 1933: The Invisible Man; 1934: Crime Without Passion; The Man Who Reclaimed His Head; 1935: The Clairvoyant; The Mystery of Edwin Drood; The Last Outpost; 1936: Anthony Adverse; Hearts Divided; Stolen Holiday; 1937: The Prince and the Pauper; They Won't Forget; 1938: Gold Is Where You Find It; The Adventures of Robin Hood; White Banners; Four Daughters; 1939: They Made Me a Criminal; Juarez; Daughters Courageous; Mr. Smith Goes to Washington; Four Wives; 1940: Saturday's Children; The Sea Hawk; The Lady With Red Hair; 1941: Four Mothers; Here Comes Mr. Jordan; The Wolf Man; 1942: Kings Row; Moontide; Now, Voyager; 1943: Casablanca; Forever and a Day; Phantom of the Opera; 1944: Passage to Marseille; Mr. Skeffington; 1945: Caesar and Cleopatra; This Love of Ours; 1946: Strange Holiday (filmed 1942) Notorious; Angel on My Shoulder; Deception; 1947: The Unsuspected; 1949: The Passionate Friends/One Woman's Story; Rope of Sand; Song of Surrender; 1950: The White Tower; Where Danger Lives; 1951: Sealed Cargo; 1953: The Paris Express/The Man Who Watched the Trains Go By; 1956:

Lisbon; 1959: This Earth Is Mine; 1960: The Lost World; 1961: Battle of the Worlds; 1962: Lawrence of Arabia; 1963: Twilight of Honor; 1965: The Greatest Story Ever Told.

NY Stage: 1926: The Constant Nymph; 1927: Lally; Out of the Sea; 1929: The Camel Through the Needle's Eye; Karl and Anna; The Game of Love and Death; 1930: The Apple Cart; 1931: He; 1932: The Moon in the Yellow River; Too True to Be Good; The Man Who Reclaimed His Head; The Good Earth; 1933: American Dream; 1934: They Shall Not Die; 1951: Darkness at Noon; 1954: The Confidential Clerk; 1956: Night of the Auk.

Select TV: 1953: The Man Who Liked Dickens (sp); The Archer Case (sp); 1956: A Night to Remember (sp); President (sp); Antigone (sp); 1957: On Borrowed Time (sp); The Pied Piper (sp); 1959: Judgment at Nuremberg (sp); Once Upon a Christmas Tree (sp); 1963: Something About Lee Wiley (sp); The Takers (sp); 1965: Cops and Robbers (sp).

JESSIE RALPH

(JESSICA RALPH CHAMBERS) BORN: GLOUCESTER, MA, NOVEMBER 5, 1864. DIED: MAY 30, 1944.

Doughy, singularly unlovely Jessie Ralph was a welcome sight during the 1930s, when she looked so right in costume pieces as wizened or outspoken old ladies and crotchety biddies. During her 20-some years in the theatre she had done some silent features, but it was not until her Broadway work in *Child of Manhattan* and *The Good Earth* that she was asked to come to Hollywood, where she eventually repeated both parts on film. She also was seen as Richard Bennett's deceitful housekeeper Zoe in *Nana*; Nurse Peggotty in *David Copperfield*; the stuffy Mrs. Fisher, melted by her trip to Italy in *Enchanted April*; Mme. Magloire in *Les Misérables*; Kay Francis's traveling companion in *I Found Stella Parish*; a charwoman in *Metropolitan*; Jack Holt's wealthy mother, who is evacuated from her home during the great earthquake, in *San Francisco*; Myrna Loy's great-aunt in *After the Thin Man*; Maureen O'Sullivan's mom in *Port of Seven Seas*; Greta Garbo's loyal maid Nanine in *Camille*; the poverty-stricken apple seller helped by Freddie Bartholomew in *Little Lord Fauntleroy*; the fairy who sends Shirley Temple off to seek *The Blue Bird*; and W.C. Field's crabby mother-in-law in *The Bank Dick*. Following her role in *They Met in Bombay*, a leg amputation caused her to retire.

Screen: 1915: Mary's Lamb; 1916: New York; 1921: Such a Little Queen; 1933: Elmer the Great; Cocktail Hour; Child of Manhattan; Ann Carver's Profession; 1934: Coming-Out Party; One Night of Love; Evelyn Prentice; Nana; We Live Again; Murder at the Vanities; The Affairs of Cellini; 1935: David Copperfield; Enchanted April; Les Misérables; Paris in Spring; Vanessa: Her Love Story; I Live My Life; Jalna; Metropolitan; I Found Stella Parish; Captain Blood; 1936: Bunker Bean; The Garden Murder Case; The Unguarded Hour; San Francisco; After the Thin Man; Little Lord Fauntleroy; Yellow Dust; Walking on Air; 1937: The Good Earth; Camille; Double Wedding; The Last of Mrs. Cheyney; 1938: Love Is a Headache; Port of Seven Seas; Hold That Kiss; 1939: St. Louis Blues; Cafe Society; Four Girls in White; The Kid from Texas; Mickey the Kid; Drums Along the Mohawk; 1940: The Blue Bird; Star Dust; The Girl from Avenue A; I Can't Give You Anything But Love, Baby; The Bank Dick; I Want a Divorce; 1941: The Lady from Cheyenne; They Met in Bombay.

NY Stage: 1906: The Kreutzer Sonata; 1907: The Straight Road; 1909: Such a Little Queen; 1911: The Price; 1912: A Rich Man's Son; 1913: The Escape; After Five; 1914: Help Wanted; 1915: The

Revolt; **1916:** His Bridal Night; Rich Man, Poor Man; **1918:** Once Upon a Time; A Prince There Was; **1922:** Malvalocca; **1923:** Romeo and Juliet; Pelleas and Melisande; **1925:** The Depths; Man With a Load of Mischief; The Taming of the Shrew; **1926:** The Virgin; The Shelf; **1927:** The Road to Rome; **1929:** Paolo and Francesca; **1930:** Twelfth Night; **1932:** Child of Manhattan; The Good Earth.

VERA (HRUBA) RALSTON

(Vera Helena Hruba) Born: Prague, Czechoslovakia, July 12, 1921. Died: February 9, 2003.

When you're considered the poor man's Sonja Henie, it's safe to say that your place in movie history won't be taken too seriously — and such was the fate of Vera (Hruba) Ralston. She had been runner-up to Henie in the 1936 Olympic skating championships, and when 20th Century-Fox signed Henie, Republic Pictures figured they would cash in on Ralston, first by giving her specialties in *Ice-Capades* and *Ice-Capades Revue* under her real name, and then (as Vera Hruba Ralston) in her own starring musicals, *Lake Placid Serenade* and *Murder in the Music Hall*. Unlike Ms. Henie, Ralston and her mentor, studio boss Herbert J. Yates, had dreams of her succeeding as a dramatic attraction too, so by 1946, she was presented strictly minus the blades with her name finally shortened to Vera Ralston. For the next 12, thickly-accented years she never left the Republic lot, where she was seen in such westerns as *The Plainsman and the Lady*, the former referring to William Elliott; *Wyoming*; *The Fighting Kentuckian*, perhaps her best known credit because it starred John Wayne (they had earlier paired up for *Dakota*); *Belle Le Grande*, in which she was a gambler; and *Gunfire at Indian Gap*. There were also such adventures as *Angel on the Amazon*, and *Fair Wind to Java*, with Ralston as the native love interest of Fred MacMurray; not to mention melodramas like *Accused of Murder*, in which she was a nightclub singer. It all came to an end with *The Man Who Died Twice*, in a role as a widow trying to find out why her husband was killed in an explosion. With that she retired. It's safe to say that most moviegoers were hardly thrilled by her, but at least she found herself a husband when she and Yates married in 1952, a union that lasted until his death in 1966.

Screen: as Vera Hruba: **1941:** Ice-Capades; **1942:** Ice-Capades Revue.

as Vera Hruba Ralston: **1944:** The Lady and the Monster; Storm Over Lisbon; Lake Placid Serenade; **1945:** Dakota; **1946:** Murder in the Music Hall.

as Vera Ralston: **1946:** The Plainsman and the Lady; **1947:** The Flame; Wyoming; **1948:** I, Jane Doe; Angel on the Amazon; **1949:** The Fighting Kentuckian; **1950:** Surrender; **1951:** Belle Le Grande; The Wild Blue Yonder; **1952:** Hoodlum Empire; **1953:** Fair Wind to Java; A Perilous Journey; **1954:** Jubilee Trail; **1955:** Timberjack; **1956:** Accused of Murder; **1957:** Spoilers of the Forest; Gunfire at Indian Gap; **1958:** The Notorious Mr. Monks; The Man Who Died Twice.

MARJORIE RAMBEAU

Born: San Francisco, CA, July 15, 1889. Died: July 7, 1970.

Marjorie Rambeau had been a leading lady on the stage and screen for many years when she established her film-role forte in the early 1930s, as the saucy but worn-out woman who'd seen better days. In an unusual career start she first hit the stage as a young girl, singing and playing the banjo for goldminers in the Pacific Northwest. When she was older, she toured up and down the Pacific coast in various plays before finally showing up on Broadway in 1913, in *Kick-In*, a play written by her then-husband (1912–1917) Willard Mack. In 1916, she made her film debut, and appeared in six features before returning to Broadway, where she ultimately earned a reputation for her hard drinking and difficult temperament. When the talkies came, she made a vivid impression as the waterfront floozy murdered by Marie Dressler in one of the biggest hits of 1930, *Min and Bill*. The tone was set for her on-screen type and she was Wallace Beery's cheeky gal, Mame, in *Hell Divers*; an alcoholic sludge in *Man's Castle*; Joan Crawford's fellow show girl in *Laughing Sinners*; another boozer in *A Modern Hero*; and a former opera singer down in the dumps in *Leftover Ladies*. She took top billing as an ex-actress running a boarding house in the "B" *Dizzy Dames*; and unwisely tried to follow in the departed Dressler's footsteps in *Tugboat Annie Sails Again*, which partnered her with Alan Hale. There was a terrific showcase for Rambeau as the trampy mother of Ginger Rogers, who sees her daughter move on to a better life, in *Primrose Path*, a role for which she received an Oscar nomination. After playing wacko evangelist Sister Bessie to the hilt in the watered-down but nevertheless still bizarre version of *Tobacco Road*, she took to the sauce again, to sing "I Dreamt I Dwelt in Marble Halls," in *Salome, Where She Danced*. In the late 1940s, an injury in a car accident severely hindered her ability to walk, and for the rest of her career she was often seen with a cane or merely sitting down to disguise her condition. Of her last batch of movies, the definite highlight found her playing Joan Crawford's tough-talking former-actress mother in *Torch Song*, a performance good enough to land her another supporting Oscar nomination. After playing another old trouper, in a brief bit in *Man of a Thousand Faces*, she left the movies and settled in Palm Springs.

Screen: **1917:** The Dazzling Miss Davison; Motherhood; The Greater Woman; The Debt; The Mirror; Mary Moreland; **1919:** The Common Cause; **1920:** The Fortune Teller; **1926:** Syncopating Sue; **1930:** Her Man; Min and Bill; **1931:** Inspiration; The Easiest Way; A Tailor-Made Man; Strangers May Kiss; The Secret Six; Laughing Sinners; Son of India; Silence; Leftover Ladies; Hell Divers; **1933:** Strictly Personal; The Warrior's Husband; Man's Castle; **1934:** Palooka; A Modern Hero; Grand Canary; Ready for Love; **1935:** Under Pressure; Dizzy Dames; **1937:** First Lady; **1938:** Merrily We Live; Woman Against Woman; **1939:** Sudden Money; The Rains Came; Laugh It Off; Heaven With a Barbed Wire Fence; **1940:** Santa Fe Marshal; Primrose Path; 20 Mule Team; Tugboat Annie Sails Again; East of the River; **1941:** Tobacco Road; Three Sons O' Guns; **1942:** Broadway; **1943:** In Old Oklahoma; **1944:** Oh What a Night!; Army Wives; **1945:** Salome, Where She Danced; **1948:** The Walls of Jericho; **1949:** The Lucky Stiff; Any Number Can Play; Abandoned/Abandoned Woman; **1953:** Forever Female; Torch Song; Bad for Each Other; **1955:** A Man Called Peter; The View from Pompey's Head; **1956:** Slander; **1957:** Man of a Thousand Faces.

NY Stage: **1913:** Kick In; **1914:** So Much For So Much; **1915:** Sadie Love; **1916:** Cheating Cheaters; **1917:** Eyes of Youth; **1918:** Where Poppies Bloom; **1919:** The Fortune Teller; The Unknown Woman; **1920:** The Sign On the Door; **1921:** Daddy's Gone A-Hunting; **1922:** The Goldfish; **1923:** As You Like It; **1924:** The Road Together; **1925:** The Valley of Content; Antonia; **1926:** The Night Duel.

Select TV: **1953:** Atomic Love (sp); **1955:** The Blue Ribbon (sp); **1956:** Prologue to Glory (sp); That Evil Woman (sp).

TONY RANDALL

(LEONARD ROSENBERG) BORN: TULSA, OK,
FEBRUARY 26, 1920. ED: NORTHWESTERN UNIV.

An often brilliant practitioner of light
comedy, Tony Randall's early screen persona
was that of a lovable, articulate schlub with
a hangdog look on his face, his manner
hilariously luckless, whether he won the girl or not.
Television gave him his signature role and he became everybody's idea of
the actor-as-intellectual: fastidious, slightly snobby, and seemingly superior to much of the material he played. Arriving in
New York in the early 1940s, he joined the prestigious
Neighborhood Playhouse and began getting work on radio,
including a recurring part on *I Love a Mystery*. After spending
four years in the Army Signal Corps, he returned to radio before
touring with Katharine Cornell in *The Barretts of Wimpole
Street*. With her he made his Broadway bow, in 1948, in
Antony and Cleopatra, and continued to do some theatre and
live television before finally receiving his first brush with
fame, playing Harvey Weskit, the fellow teacher of Wally
Cox, in the situation comedy *Mr. Peepers*. Back on Broadway,
he scored his biggest hit there as the cynical reporter E.K.
Hornbeck in the original production of *Inherit the Wind*,
which resulted in a contract with 20th Century-Fox. They
started him off in support, as a patient who is in love with
analyst David Niven's fiancée, in *Oh, Men! Oh, Women!*, and
then he was promptly promoted to his first lead, playing a
Madison Avenue exec in the cartoonish satire *Will Success
Spoil Rock Hunter?* He followed this with his only genuinely
serious o n - s c r e e n role, as Sheree North's alcoholic, philandering suburban husband in the ensemble drama *No Down
Payment*, but he was so good at producing laughs that
Hollywood never really bothered to tap into this side of him
again. He went to MGM on loan for the fairly dreadful *The
Mating Game*, falling for farmer's daughter Debbie Reynolds,
and then really hit it big as the hapless suitor of Doris Day
in one of the smash hits of 1959, *Pillow Talk*. He said goodbye to Fox, playing Yves Montand's public relations man in
one of those unfortunate movies that became a nightmare to
shoot because of Marilyn Monroe's participation in it, *Let's
Make Love*, and then tried in vain to give some life to MGM's
disastrous 1960 version of *The Adventures of Huckleberry Finn*,
as the phony King. Universal was so pleased with the Day-
Hudson-Randall combination that they reteamed the trio,
once delightfully, in *Lover Come Back*, and once drably, in
Send Me No Flowers. In between, Randall did two of the
many silly comedies Universal was famous for in the early
1960s: *The Brass Bottle*, finding genie Burl Ives within the titular object, and *Fluffy*, which was the name of a benign lion.

Randall's own favorite screen appearance was in the superior
fantasy *7 Faces of Dr. Lao*, playing the central role of the mysterious Chinese magician as well as a myriad of mythical beings
including Medusa, Pan, and Merlin, all under William Tuttle's
startlingly good, Academy Award-winning makeup. He was then
the first American to play Agatha Christie's Hercule Poirot in
The Alphabet Murders, which was hardly a serious enterprise in
tone; went spy spoofing in *Bang, Bang, You're Dead*; and ended
up living below the sea in the campy *Hello Down There*, which
somehow brought together marine biology, rock 'n' roll, and
Merv Griffin. It seemed as good a time as any to return to television in a weekly series, and Randall wound up in the part he
was born to play: fussbudget Felix Unger in *The Odd Couple*, the
small screen adaptation of Neil Simon's play (he had done the

part onstage in Chicago and in Las Vegas). The show clicked,
earning him an Emmy Award in 1975, and he remained firmly
associated with the character and his self-righteous mannerisms.
From that point on he became a fixture of the small screen,
although he was called back to the movies on a few occasions. He
was one of the technicians controlling the body during inter-
course in a segment of Woody Allen's *Everything You Always
Wanted to Know About Sex*; was on the lookout for hidden cash
in the flop comedy *Scavenger Hunt*; showed up as Cloris
Leachman's foul-mouthed butler in *Foolin' Around*; played himself, subbing for the kidnapped Jerry Lewis, in *The King of
Comedy*; and was a judge in the noir send-up *Fatal Instinct*. There
was another series, *Love, Sidney*, spun off from a telefilm in which
Randall's character was clearly gay, an aspect timidly dropped
during its weekly run. Reaching the age when most actors take it
easy or retire, he put up his own money to start the National
Actors Theatre, a repertory theatre group in New York that officially commenced in 1991. The controversial company often
featured Randall in its productions, sometimes in roles for which
he was blatantly unsuitable (in *Three Men on a Horse* and *The
Government Inspector* he defiantly played characters much younger
than himself); some nostalgic (a reprise of *Inherit the Wind*, this
time playing the Henry Drummond character, filling in for an
ailing George C. Scott); and once, ideal (*The Sunshine Boys*
reteamed him with former *Odd Couple* co-star Jack Klugman).

Screen: 1957: Oh, Men! Oh, Women!; Will Success Spoil Rock
Hunter?; No Down Payment; 1959: The Mating Game; Pillow
Talk; 1960: The Adventures of Huckleberry Finn; Let's Make
Love; 1961: Lover Come Back; 1962: Boys' Night Out; 1963:
Island of Love; 1964: The Brass Bottle; 7 Faces of Dr. Lao; Send
Me No Flowers; 1965: Fluffy; 1966: The Alphabet Murders;
Bang, Bang, You're Dead!/Our Man in Marakesh; 1969: Hello
Down There; 1972: Everything You Always Wanted to Know
About Sex But Were Afraid to Ask; 1979: Scavenger Hunt; 1980:
Foolin' Around; 1983: The King of Comedy; 1986: My Little
Pony (voice); 1989: It Had to Be You; 1990: That's Adequate!;
Gremlins 2: The New Batch (voice); 1993: Fatal Instinct; 2003:
Down With Love.

NY Stage: AS ANTHONY RANDALL: 1941: The Circle of Chalk;
1948: Antony and Cleopatra; To Tell the Truth; 1950: Caesar
and Cleopatra.

AS TONY RANDALL: 1955: Inherit the Wind; 1958: Oh Captain!;
1966: UTBU; 1989: M. Butterfly; 1992: A Little Hotel on the
Side; 1993: Three Men on a Horse; 1994: The Government
Inspector; 1995: The School for Scandal; 1996: Inherit the Wind
(revival); 1997: The Sunshine Boys; 2002: The Resistible Rise of
Arturo Ui (ob).

Select TV: 1950–52: One Man's Family (series); 1952–55: Mr.
Peepers (series); 1953: A Little Something in Reserve (sp); The
Badger Game (sp); In Albert's Room (sp); When Lovely
Woman (sp); 1954: The Huntress (sp); Nightmare in Algiers
(sp); The Beautiful Wife (sp); 1955: One Mummy Too Many
(sp); 1956: Man on a Tiger (sp); 1957: The Hollywood
Complex (sp); The Playroom (sp); 1959: Coogan's Reward (sp);
Martin's Folly (sp); The Second Happiest Day (sp); Hello
Charlie (sp); 1960: The Secret of Freedom (sp); So Help Me
Aphrodite (sp); Strictly Solo (sp); 1962: Arsenic and Old Lace
(sp); 1969: The Littlest Angel (sp); 1970–75: The Odd Couple
(series); 1976–78: The Tony Randall Show (series); 1978: Kate
Bliss and the Ticker Tape Kid; 1981: Sidney Shorr: A Girl's Best
Friend; 1981–83: Love, Sidney (series); 1984: Off Sides/Pigs vs.
Freaks (filmed 1980); 1985: Hitler's SS: Portrait in Evil; 1986:
Sunday Drive; 1988: Save the Dog!; 1989: The Man in the
Brown Suit; 1993: The Odd Couple: Together Again.

BASIL RATHBONE

(PHILIP ST. JOHN BASIL RATHBONE) BORN:
JOHANNESBURG, SOUTH AFRICA, JUNE 13, 1892.
ED: REPTON COL. DIED: JULY 21, 1967.

It was no small feat for Basil Rathbone to wind up as the reigning champion in not one but two cinematic categories: best all-around villain and definitive Sherlock Holmes. Suave, imperious, and grandly self-satisfied, he didn't need to ham for results because his precise, confident delivery of a line could stop one cold, making him ideal when it came to essaying men at their blackest and the world's greatest cerebral detective at his craftiest. Born to a well-to-do British mining engineer father, he was educated in England after which he joined an acting company run by his cousin, Sir Frank Benson, in 1911. With them he toured the U.S. then went to London in 1914 for his West End debut in *The Sin of David*. Following military duty with the Liverpool Scottish Regiment, he acted both at Stratford-Upon-Avon and in London, during which time he made his film debut, in 1921, in *Innocent*, followed shortly afterward by *The Fruitful Vine*; in each case he played a rotter. Once again extending his talents across the Atlantic, he did two plays on Broadway, *The Czarina* and *The Swan*, which were instrumental in Rathbone doing his first American film, *Trouping with Ellen*, in which he played an aristocrat in love with a chorus girl. There was a substantial role as the leader of a gang of jewel thieves in the Mae Murray starrer *The Masked Bride*, but he was more frequently employed at this point on the stage, including the play *Judas*, which he also wrote. Because of his fine speaking voice, he was hired by MGM at the dawn of the talkies to play opposite Norma Shearer in a stage-bound bit of sophistication called *The Last of Mrs. Cheyney* and, since this was a major hit, he landed himself a contract with that studio. They did not, however, have much use for him, casting him as Philo Vance in a creaky whodunit, *The Bishop Murder Case*, although William Powell had already established himself in the part over at Paramount. After a few loan-outs, he went back to Broadway and then to England for some films, but little on his motion picture résumé at this point was worth noting.

The turning point came in 1935, when MGM asked him to play Mr. Murdstone in their class "A" production of *David Copperfield*. Rathbone made such a vivid and chilling impression as the sadistic ogre who becomes Freddie Bartholomew's stepfather, that he became one of the hottest talents in the industry. Hopping from one prestige production to the next, these were the richest years of his movie life, starting with *Anna Karenina*, as the husband Greta Garbo neglects for Fredric March; then on to *A Tale of Two Cities*, as the wicked Marquis St. Evremonde, who gets his comeuppance after callously running a peasant over with his carriage; then *The Last Days of Pompeii*, as Pontius Pilate; and *Captain Blood*, as the French pirate Levasseur, dueling so memorably with Errol Flynn that Rathbone would be remembered as one of the movies' foremost sword fighters. On a roll, he got his sole chance on screen to spout Shakespeare, as Tybalt in *Romeo and Juliet*, and it was such a pleasure to hear him do so that he earned his first Oscar nomination in the newly established supporting category. He desired, in vain, Marlene Dietrich in *The Garden of Allah*, and Loretta Young, in *Private Number*; then got killed off by Kay Francis for trying to put the moves on her daughter in *Confession*. Nasty even in relatively light-hearted circumstances, he was the Russian who tortured Claudette Colbert and Charles Boyer in *Tovarich*, then played perhaps his most famous and enduring bad guy role, Sir Guy of Gisborne, the nemesis of the poor in *The Adventures of Robin Hood*, in which

his staircase duel with Errol Flynn became one of the most mimicked of all movie battles. That same year he dropped all the villainy and went tongue-in-cheek to play the decrepit, witty Louis XI in *If I Were King*. Virtually unrecognizable in both appearance and voice, it was a brilliant tour de force and by rights he should have won the Oscar for which he was nominated.

In 1939, Rathbone found himself stepping into the horror genre for the first time with *Son of Frankenstein*, in a sympathetic role as the offspring of the mad doctor, and since Universal treated *Tower of London* as something not unlike a thriller, it might be said that he essayed another of their great monsters, playing the scheming, hunchbacked Richard III. That same year he took on another role that, although it was hardly a warm character, was a change of pace from outright meanness, that of Sherlock Holmes in 20th Century-Fox's production of *The Hound of the Baskervilles*. Rathbone actually took second billing to Richard Greene, since his character drops out of sight for a lengthy portion of the storyline, but there is no question as to who walked off with the picture. The film did quite nicely and Rathbone was so on the mark as the brainy and arrogant detective that he was immediately asked to reprise the role (opposite Nigel Bruce as Watson) in *The Adventures of Sherlock Holmes*, this time as the official star. Reaching another peak with a sword, he was Captain Pasquale, crossing blades with Tyrone Power in *The Mark of Zorro*, and then took the title role in *The Mad Doctor*, a "B" item that has earned its share of followers over the years. World War II had started, so it was no surprise that he was called on to play a Nazi in *Above Suspicion*, but more curious that Universal was interested in reviving Holmes with a modern slant, thereby allowing the duo to battle the Nazis, a proposal Rathbone and Bruce accepted. They appeared in 12 more entries and, despite the cheesiness of transplanting these 19th century icons to the present day, this became one of the best-loved series of mysteries in movie history. Starting with *Sherlock Holmes and the Voice of Terror* in 1942, and ending with the budget in an obvious state of decline with *Dressed to Kill*, in 1946, Rathbone left an indelible mark on the character, though he himself was only too happy to leave it (at least temporarily) behind.

Also during the Holmes years he was the repulsive nobleman who gets a suit of armor hurled at him by Joan Fontaine in *Frenchman's Creek*, a stodgy costume picture where his colorful presence was never more welcome; taught Ginger Rogers how to pick pockets in *Heartbeat*; and then returned to the theatre where he triumphantly played the cold-hearted Doctor Sloper in *The Heiress*. He also returned to Holmes, first on television, and then on Broadway in 1953, though the latter did not run very long. Back in the movies he played it straight while Bob Hope got the laughs in *Casanova's Big Night*, and did likewise in *The Court Jester*, which gave him his last great sword fight, albeit a comic one, with Danny Kaye. Top billed, he was another mad scientist in a low-budget production called *The Black Sleep*, which pretty much sealed his fate for the remainder of his movie career. Aside from a supporting bit as a banker (mean, of course) in a prestigious John Ford production, *The Last Hurrah*, his last decade found him in an increasingly sad state of employment, winding up in AIP junk and tacky horror offerings, the titles of which seemed to trumpet their level of inanity: *Queen of Blood*, which he filmed concurrently with *Voyage to the Prehistoric Planet*; *The Ghost in the Invisible Bikini*; and *Hillbillys in a Haunted House*, which cast him alongside two other actors badly in need of new agents, Lon Chaney, Jr. and John Carradine. In addition to these, he dusted off an old role for the Italian-made *Pontius Pilate*, and teamed up with thriller icons Boris Karloff and Vincent Price for *The Comedy of Terrors*, an experience that left him cold. In time, these titles faded into obscurity and the Rathbone reputation only grew in stature thanks to repeated viewings of the very best work of his vintage years. In 1962 he published his autobiography, *In and Out of Character*.

Screen: 1921: Innocent; The Fruitful Vine; 1923: The School for Scandal; 1924: Trouping with Ellen; 1925: The Masked Bride; 1926: The Great Deception; 1929: The Last of Mrs. Cheyney; Barnum Was Right; 1930: The Bishop Murder Case; A Notorious Affair; The Lady of Scandal; This Mad World; The Flirting Widow; A Lady Surrenders; Sin Takes a Holiday; 1932: A Woman Commands; 1933: After the Ball; One Precious Year; Loyalties; 1935: David Copperfield; Anna Karenina; The Last Days of Pompeii; A Feather in Her Hat; A Tale of Two Cities; Captain Blood; Kind Lady; 1936: Private Number; Romeo and Juliet; The Garden of Allah; 1937: Love from a Stranger/A Night of Terror; Confession; Tovarich; Make a Wish; 1938: The Adventures of Marco Polo; The Adventures of Robin Hood; If I Were King; The Dawn Patrol; 1939: Son of Frankenstein; The Hound of the Baskervilles; The Adventures of Sherlock Holmes; The Sun Never Sets; Rio; Tower of London; 1940: Rhythm on the River; The Mask of Zorro; 1941: The Mad Doctor; The Black Cat; Paris Calling; International Lady; 1942: Fingers at the Window; Crossroads; Sherlock Holmes and the Voice of Terror; Sherlock Holmes and the Secret Weapon; 1943: Sherlock Holmes in Washington; Sherlock Holmes Faces Death; Crazy House; Above Suspicion; 1944: Frenchman's Creek; Bathing Beauty; Sherlock Holmes and the Spider Woman; The Scarlet Claw; The Pearl of Death; 1945: The House of Fear; Pursuit to Algiers; The Woman in Green; 1946: Terror by Night; Dressed to Kill; Heartbeat; 1949: The Adventures of Ichabod and Mr. Toad (voice); 1954: Casanova's Big Night; 1955: We're No Angels; 1956: The Court Jester; The Black Sleep; 1958: The Last Hurrah; 1962: Pontius Pilate; The Magic Sword; Tales of Terror; Two Before Zero (narrator); 1963: The Comedy of Terrors; 1965: Voyage to the Prehistoric Planet; 1966: Queen of Blood/Planet of Blood; Ghost in the Invisible Bikini; 1967: Hillbillys in a Haunted House; Autopsy of a Ghost (nUSr).

NY Stage: 1922: The Czarina; 1923: The Swan; 1924: The Assumption of Hannele; 1925: The Grand Duchess and the Waiter; 1926: Port o' London; The Captive; 1927: Love is Like That; Julius Caesar; The Command to Love; 1929: Judas (and wr.); 1930: A Kiss of Importance; 1931: Heat Wave; 1932: The Devil Passes; 1933: Romeo and Juliet; 1946: Obsession; 1947: The Heiress; 1950: Julius Caesar; The Gioconda Smile; 1952: Jane; 1953: Sherlock Holmes; 1957: Hide and Seek; 1959: J.B.

Select TV: 1950: Queen of Spades (sp); Sherlock Holmes (sp); 1951: Dr. Jekyll and Mr. Hyde (sp); 1952: Masquerade (sp); Your Lucky Clue (series); 1953: Criminal at Large (sp); The Firebrand (sp); The Adventure of the Black Baronet (sp); 1954: The House of Gair (sp); A Christmas Carol (sp); 1955: The Selfish Giant (sp); 1956: The Stingiest Man in Town (sp); 1957: The Lark (sp); Soldier in Love (sp); Huck Finn (sp); 1958: Hans Brinker (sp); Aladdin (sp); 1961: Victoria Regina (sp); 1966: The Pirates of Flounder Bay (sp); 1967: Soldier in Love (sp).

ALDO RAY

(Aldo DaRe) Born: Pen Argyl, PA, September 25, 1926. Raised in Crockett, CA. ed: Univ. of CA/Berkeley. Died: March 27, 1991.

Because he looked like a jar-headed non-com who'd just put his platoon through basic training, gargle-voiced Aldo Ray became the movies' ideal soldier for the 1950s. Fittingly he had served in the U.S. Navy (as a frogman) prior to playing football in college. The latter experience won him a part in the gridiron film *Saturday's Hero*, but he temporarily backed away from movies to serve as constable in his hometown. Director George Cukor was interested in hiring him and gave him two terrific roles, first as Judy Holliday's husband in the bittersweet *The Marrying Kind*, and then an out-and-out comical one, as the dim-witted boxer in the Tracy-Hepburn hit *Pat and Mike*. His cinematic stint in the military started with a role as the marine who heats up the tropics with Rita Hayworth in *Miss Sadie Thompson*. He solidified this image with the box-office smash *Battle Cry*, as a Marine private; the bowdlerized filmization of *The Naked and the Dead*, as a near-psychotic officer who takes out his shattered love life on his men; followed by the fairly minor efforts *Three Stripes in the Sun* and *Men in War*. He showed up as the brawny member of the trio of cons in *We're No Angels*, very ill at ease in this cutesy comedy; and carried on with Tina Louise in the popular but poor rendering of the steamy best-seller *God's Little Acre*. By the early 1960s, the offers had begun to lose their level of prestige and he went to England for *The Day They Robbed the Bank of England*, masterminding a heist behind Peter O'Toole's back; and *Johnny Nobody*, in the title role of an amnesiac who murders an atheist. It was then off to Australia for *Siege of Pinchgut/Four Desperate Men*; to Italy for *Musketeers of the Sea*; and then on to the independent circuit for *Nightmare in the Sun*, playing a corrupt sheriff in a movie directed by the fading star of Ray's first film, John Derek.

In the mid-1960s, a chunkier Ray re-emerged in mainstream fair, starting with Paramount's overheated Carol Baker-vehicle *Sylvia*, and continuing with the jerky spoof *What Did You Do in the War, Daddy?*, which found him back in uniform, as a sergeant; the heist caper *Dead Heat on a Merry-Go-Round*, as one of James Coburn's fellow-thieves; and *The Green Berets*, supporting John Wayne in this controversial Vietnam flick, again as a sergeant. There was a top-billed part as a cop taking on a bunch of hippies in a deadly AIP drive-in epic, *Riot on Sunset Strip*, which set the direction for another downward career slide in the 1970s. Among his assignments during this period were *The Centerfold Girls*, as a rapist; *Angel Unchained*, once again battling hippies, as a redneck sheriff; *Stud Brown*; *Haunts*, back behind a sheriff's badge; *Psychic Killer*, as a police detective; the cameo-ridden *Won Ton Ton, the Dog Who Saved Hollywood*, trying to rape Madeline Kahn; and all kinds of fly-by-night cheapies. Things bottomed out when he appeared (fully clothed) as part of the storyline of a hard-core porn film called *Sweet Savage*, which led to his expulsion from the Screen Actors Guild in 1986 for having accepted work in non-union productions. There were a few other titles that presumably put food on the table, like *Frankenstein's Great Aunt Tillie*, as a Transylvanian burgomaster; *Biohazard*, fighting a lizard from outer space; and *Prison Ship/Star Slammer*, as a sadistic guard, prior to his death from throat cancer. One of his wives (1954–56) was actress Jeff Donnell. His son, Eric DaRe also became an actor.

Screen: 1950: Saturday's Hero; My True Story; 1952: The Marrying Kind; Pat and Mike; 1953: Let's Do It Again; Miss Sadie Thompson; 1955: We're No Angels; Battle Cry; Three Stripes in the Sun; 1956: Nightfall; 1957: Men in War; 1958: The Naked and the Dead; God's Little Acre; 1960: Four Desperate Men/Siege of Pinchgut; The Day They Robbed the Bank of England; Musketeers of the Sea; 1961: Johnny Nobody; 1964: Nightmare in the Sun; 1965: Sylvia; 1966: What Did You Do in the War, Daddy?; Dead Heat on the Merry-Go-Round; 1967: Welcome to Hard Times; Riot on Sunset Strip; Kill a Dragon; The Violent Ones; 1968: The Power; The Green Berets; 1969: Suicide Commando; 1970: Angel Unchained; 1972: And Hope to Die;

1973: Tom/The Bad Bunch; 1974: Dynamite Brothers/Stud Brown; The Centerfold Girls; 1975: Seven Alone; The Man Who Would Not Die; Gone With the West; Psychic Killer; 1976: Inside Out; Won Ton Ton, the Dog Who Saved Hollywood; The Haunted; 1977: Haunts/The Veil; Kino, the Padre on Horseback/Mission to Glory (dtv); Sky Dove (dtc); 1978: Death Dimension/Freeze Bomb/Black Eliminator/Black Samurai; The Lucifer Complex (dtv); Bog; 1979: The Glove; Sweet Savage; Don't Go Near the Park/Nightstalker (dtc); 1980: Human Experiments; 1982: The Great Skycopter Rescue (dtv); Boxoffice; Dark Sanity/Straitjacket (dtv); The Secret of NIMH (voice); 1983: Mongrel (dtv); Frankenstein's Great Aunt Tillie (dtv); 1984: Vultures in Paradise/Flesh and Bullets (dtv); To Kill a Stranger (dtv); The Executioner Part II; 1985: Biohazard; Evils of the Night; 1986: Terror on Alcatraz (dtv); 1987: Hollywood Cop (dtv); The Sicilian; 1988: Star Slammer/Prison Ship; 1989: Swift Justice/Hateman (dtv); Blood Red; 1990: Shock 'em Dead (dtv); Shooters (dtv).

Select TV: 1958: K.O. Kitty (sp); 1963: Lollipop Louie (sp); 1964: Have Girls — Will Travel (sp); 1968: The Deep End (sp); 1969: Deadlock; 1972–73: The Houndcats (series; voice); 1975: Promise Him Anything…; 1979: Women in White.

MARTHA RAYE

(MARGARET THERESA YVONNE REED)
BORN: BUTTE, MT, AUGUST 27, 1916.
DIED: OCTOBER 19, 1994.

Martha Raye's mouth was her fortune and she opened it time and again in a big way: bellowing, cackling, and mugging to a point of exhaustion, seldom heeding the adage that less is more. Apparently that's just the way her fans liked it. Born to a pair of vaudevillians, she went onstage as a child and continued to sing and perform comedy into her teens, first in vaudeville, then as part of a revue entitled Calling All Stars, and finally as a solo act in nightclubs. She was spotted during an engagement at Hollywood's Trocadero club by director Norman Taurog, who immediately hired her to support Bing Crosby in Rhythm on the Range. Paired principally with Bob Burns, she made sure she left her mark, playing to the rafters and scoring a hit with the song "Mr. Paganini." Paramount was thrilled and signed her to a contract, making her part of the ensembles in both The Big Broadcast of 1936 and The Big Broadcast of 1938, in which she was indelicately tossed about by a bunch of deckhands in her big number. Hoping to cash in on her first screen assignment, they put her in two other Crosby vehicles, Waikiki Wedding and Double or Nothing, singing the strip-spoof "It's On, It's Off." They also gave her top-billing for Hideaway Girl, although co-stars Shirley Ross and Robert Cummings had just as much to do, if not more, and for Mountain Music, a profitable release due to audiences who no doubt were thrilled by the none-too-subtle possibilities of casting Raye as a hillbilly. There were also Jack Benny comedies (College Holiday, Artists & Models) and three with Bob Hope (College Swing, Give Me a Sailor, and Never Say Die). It was during the second of these that the studio stopped hammering home her gawky and noisy nature and tried to sell her as a leading lady, going so far as to have her win a legs contest against Betty Grable of all people.

After matching mouths with Joe E. Brown in $1,000 a Touchdown, and playing The Farmer's Daughter, she was dumped by Paramount and picked up by Universal. They started her off in the 1940 screen version of the Broadway hit The Boys from Syracuse, but since they saw fit to dispose of most of what had worked in the theatre it was not a triumph. After supporting

Abbott and Costello in Keep 'em Flying, as twins, and Olsen and Johnson in Hellzapoppin', where she chased after Mischa Auer like a puma closing in on a gazelle, she was off the Universal lot for a brief spell at 20th Century-Fox. There Raye, Carole Landis, Kay Francis, and Mitzi Mayfair recreated, in Hollywood fashion, their real-life USO tour of North Africa in Four Jills in a Jeep. Then she was back making faces with Joe E. Brown again in Pin-Up Girl, only this time she was taking billing below Betty Grable. This was followed by her finest hour on film, playing the obnoxious wife whom murderer Charlie Chaplin tries in vain to bump off, in Monsieur Verdoux, where her hamminess added much life to the slow and talky black comedy. After that she was off the big screen for 16 years, doing nightclub work, television, and summer stock before returning in a relatively subdued manner in the Doris Day musical Billy Rose's Jumbo, waiting for Jimmy Durante to finally break down and marry her.

During the Vietnam War, she resumed her task of entertaining the troops (which led to her receiving the Jean Hersholt Humanitarian Award in 1969), then showed up on Broadway as one of the replacements in Hello, Dolly! The over-the-top Martha was seen briefly in the cameo-filled The Phynx, and as a witch in the garish children's musical Pufnstuf. Following replacement stints on the television series McMillan and Alice, and a role as one of the endangered passengers in a goofy disaster film, The Concorde: Airport '79, she was out of view for some years due to declining health (she eventually had a leg amputated). In the final years of her life she made the news because of her marriage (number seven) to a much younger man and her lawsuit against the creators of Bette Midler's For the Boys, claiming they had stolen ideas from her own life.

Screen: 1936: Rhythm on the Range; The Big Broadcast of 1937; College Holiday; 1937: Hideaway Girl; Waikiki Wedding; Mountain Music; Double or Nothing; Artists & Models; 1938: The Big Broadcast of 1938; College Swing; Give Me a Sailor; Tropic Holiday; 1939: Never Say Die; $1,000 a Touchdown; 1940: The Farmer's Daughter; The Boys from Syracuse; 1941: Navy Blues; Keep 'Em Flying; Hellzapoppin'; 1944: Four Jills and a Jeep; Pin-Up Girl; 1947: Monsieur Verdoux; 1962: Billy Rose's Jumbo; 1970: The Phynx; Pufnstuf; 1979: The Concorde: Airport '79.

NY Stage: 1940: Hold Onto Your Hats; 1967: Hello, Dolly!; 1971: No, No, Nanette.

Select TV: 1950: Anything Goes (sp); 1954–56: All-Star Revue/The Martha Raye Show (series); 1970–72: The Bugaloos (series); 1976–77: McMillan (series); 1979: The Gossip Columnist; 1981: Pippin (sp); 1982–84: Alice (series); 1985: Alice in Wonderland (sp).

GENE RAYMOND

(RAYMOND GUION) BORN: NEW YORK, NY,
AUGUST 13, 1908. DIED: MAY 3, 1998.

If the highly unexceptional Gene Raymond had any identifying characteristic, it was his starkly blond hair. It gave him a pretty-boy look, though that image was promptly negated by his tough New York accent. To fans of the gossip magazines, he was probably better known as Mr. Jeanette MacDonald. A child actor, he attended New York's Professional Children's School, making his Broadway debut in 1920, at the age of 11, in The Piper. For the next ten years he worked there in such productions as The Potters, Cradle Snatchers, Jonesy, and Young Sinners; the last was crucial in earning him a contract with Paramount in 1931. They started him off in a Nancy Carroll vehicle, Personal Maid, in which she played the domestic who falls in love with Raymond, as the son of the household. Since this was not one of that lady's hits, Raymond did not make much of an impact, but he was kept busy nonetheless. He was a condemned man made wealthy in the weakest sequence of *If I Had a Million*; the cuckolded husband in MGM's popular *Red Dust*; the animal lover who falls for Loretta Young in the much admired *Zoo in Budapest*; a pilot who finds himself thoroughly upstaged by Astaire and Rogers in their first pairing, *Flying Down to Rio*; and the vocalist on "All I Do is Dream of You" in *Sadie McKee*. RKO cast him opposite Ann Sothern in a minor musical, *Hooray for Love*, and seeing the possibilities of a profitable pairing teamed them on four more occasions, *Walking on Air*, *The Smartest Girl in Town*, *There Goes My Girl*, and *She's Got Everything*, only to be proven wrong where the box office was concerned. Raymond's real-life partner was found in Jeanette MacDonald, whom he married in 1937 and remained wed to until her death in 1965. Needless to say, her screen career far eclipsed his and they appeared in the same movie only once, the 1941 remake of the moldy old soap opera *Smilin' Through*. For Eagle-Lion Studios he directed, co-scripted, and starred in light-hearted mystery, *Million Dollar Weekend*, made strictly to fill out the low-half of double bills. Eventually theatre and television took up most of Raymond's acting time until he returned to the cinema in character roles, including *The Best Man*, as Cliff Robertson's brother.

Screen: 1931: Personal Maid; Ladies of the Big House; 1932: If I Had a Million; The Night of June 13th; Forgotten Commandments; Red Dust; 1933: Ex-Lady; Zoo in Budapest; Ann Carver's Profession; Brief Moment; Flying Down to Rio; The House on 56th Street; I Am Suzanne!; 1934: Coming Out Party; Transatlantic Merry-Go-Round; Sadie McKee; 1935: The Woman in Red; Behold My Wife; Hooray for Love; Transient Lady; Seven Keys to Baldpate; 1936: Love on a Bet; The Bride Walks Out; Walking on Air; The Smartest Girl in Town; That Girl from Paris; 1937: There Goes My Girl; The Life of the Party; 1938: She's Got Everything; Stolen Heaven; 1940: Cross-Country Romance; 1941: Mr. and Mrs. Smith; Smilin' Through; 1946: The Locket; 1948: Assigned to Danger; Sofia; Million Dollar Weekend (and dir.; co-wr.); 1955: Hit the Deck; 1957: Plunder Road; 1964: The Best Man; I'd Rather Be Rich; 1970: Five Bloody Graves (narrator).

NY Stage: AS RAYMOND GUION: 1920: The Piper; 1921: Eyvind of the Hills; 1922: Why Not; 1923: The Potters; 1925: Cradle Snatchers; 1927: Take My Advice; 1928: Mirrors; Sherlock Holmes; Say When; The War Song; 1929: Jonesy; Young Sinners. AS GENE RAYMOND: 1957: A Shadow of My Enemy.

Select TV: 1950: The Pharmacist's Mate (sp); 1952: The American Leonardo (sp); The Letter (sp); This Thing Called Love (sp); 1953: The Girl That I Married (sp); 1953–55: Fireside Theatre (series); 1954: Dawn at Damascus (sp); 1955: Dear Diane (sp); 1956: TV Readers Digest (series); Skylark (sp); Heart of a Husband (sp); Hollywood Summer Theatre (series); The Wisp End (sp); 1959: Big Doc's Girl (sp); 1961: The Shame of Paula Marsten (sp); The Haven (sp); 1964: The Hanged Man; 1970: Paris 7000 (series).

RONALD REAGAN

BORN: TAMPICO, IL, FEBRUARY 6, 1911.
ED: EUREKA COL.

Were presidential elections based on acting talent, it is doubtful Ronald Reagan would have gotten anywhere near the White House. This lumpy-haired, thoroughly unremarkable performer was a regular addition to the Warner Bros. stock company for 15 years, landing an occasional prestigious part among a lot of second-rate roles. During this period he dabbled in union-related politics and, in time, this captured his interest far and above acting. The man who had once been a mere blip on the motion-picture scene eventually rose to the highest office in the land, for the most part without the support of the industry to which he once belonged.

It was during college that Reagan first ran for office (he was elected president of the student body), but his post-school interests lay in radio and he became a sports announcer on WOC in Davenport, Iowa. In time the station became a part of NBC and went national, making his a well-known voice of the airwaves during the mid-1930s. It also got him a screen test with Warner Bros., who signed him to a contract in 1937, casting him, without much imagination, as a radio announcer in *Love Is On the Air*. After doing more of the same in *Hollywood Hotel*, they gave him the leads in two "B's," *Sergeant Murphy*, which was the name of the horse Reagan's character smuggles into England to win the Grand National, and *Accidents Will Happen*, as an insurance investigator. On a higher level was the pleasing military comedy, *Brother Rat*, adapted from the stage hit, in which he, Wayne Morris, and Eddie Albert were academy roommates. It was safe to say that few of the laughs were his doing. Back in "B's," he did *Secret Service of the Air*, and its sequels *Code of the Secret Service*, *Smashing the Money Ring*, and *Murder in the Air*, playing an agent named Lieutenant "Brass" Bancroft, while also supporting Bette Davis in one of her biggest soaps, *Dark Victory*, as an irresponsible party friend, referred to by Geraldine Fitzgerald's character as a "parasite."

There was a 1940 sequel to his own film, *Brother Rat and a Baby* (that same year, he married one of his co-stars from the film, Jane Wyman), and a follow-up to one he hadn't done, *Angels With Dirty Faces*, called *The Angels Wash Their Faces*, in which he made a pallid substitute for James Cagney. It was also in 1940 that he played one of his defining screen roles, real-life Notre Dame halfback George Gipp, in *Knute Rockne — All American*. The part provided him with a solid image among football fans throughout the land as well as a nickname — "The Gipper" — that the press would return to time and again in the future when the campaign spirit called for it. This was not, however, a lead role, so he remained in programmers like *Tugboat Annie Sails Again* (romantically paired with Wyman), and *Nine Lives Are Not Enough*, until another impressive part landed in his lap in one of the studio's big films of 1942, *Kings Row*. As Robert Cummings's small town friend, who winds up with his legs needlessly amputated, his oft-praised performance was acceptable, no more. The famous scene where he wakes up, comprehends the awful act that has disfigured him, and shouts "Where's the rest of me?" was another cinematic moment that stayed with him, providing the title for his 1965 autobiography. Joining the army air corps in 1942 kept him off the screen for a spell, although he was allowed a break to participate in the storyline of the morale booster *This is the Army*, as George Murphy's son!

After the war, Reagan was back at Warner Bros., appearing in one of the famous "dogs" of the era, *That Hagen Girl*, in which he was suspected of being the father of illegitimate Shirley Temple, and then the fairly faithful rendering of the stage smash *The Voice of the Turtle*, as the soldier who falls for Eleanor Parker. He was back in uniform in a similar stage-adapted piece, *John Loves Mary*, though one not as well received, and then did a grimly unappealing piece, *Night Unto Night*, in which he was a dying scientist romancing Viveca Lindfors. Much better was one he made for the studio over in England, *The Hasty Heart*, as a wounded vet who befriends terminally ill Richard Todd while in a military hospital. It was, perhaps, his strongest performance. During this time, he had also become one of the officers of the Screen Actors Guild. He was elected president of that organization in 1947, serving for five consecutive terms. Meanwhile, back at his day job, he was an attorney battling the Ku Klux Klan in *Storm Warning*, and epileptic ballplayer Grover Cleveland Alexander in the biopic *The Winning Team*, which was a curio in that it often seemed more like a Doris Day musical than a sports film.

By this point he had been going on fruitless loan-outs to Paramount for such disposable programmers as *The Last Outpost*, *Tropic Zone*, and *Hong Kong*, hardly proving a draw in such turgid circumstances. He had also gone to Universal for the notorious *Bedtime for Bonzo*, which had him cavorting with a chimpanzee. This rather mild and more tedious-than-embarrassing comedy was later used for anti-Reagan ammunition during his political years. Reagan had, by this time, divorced Wyman in 1948, marrying actress Nancy Davis in 1952. He had also become a fixture on the small screen, hosting *General Electric Theatre* and becoming something of a traveling spokesman for them, addressing the workers in the GE plants around the country. Back at the movies, RKO put him opposite Barbara Stanwyck for *Cattle Queen of Montana*, which was just another western, and then Columbia hired him and Davis for *Hellcats of the Navy*, not the camp classic liberals would later peg it to be, but a minor navy adventure that only went to show just how uncharismatic these two performers could be. Reagan was back at the helm of the Screen Actors Guild yet again in 1959 and three years later made his famous switch from liberal to conservative, supporting one-time cinematic daddy George Murphy in his campaign for the California senate. After one last film, *The Killers*, in which he played his first bona-fide villain, he abandoned acting to concentrate on the political scene.

In 1966, he was elected governor of California, a position he held until 1974. He had had his eye on the White House for years and, no doubt aided by an American public that got a kick out of the idea of a former movie star running the country, was elected in 1980, taking office on January 20, 1981, and then again, four years later after winning his bid for a second term. As a result, the 1980s became a dark decade for the liberal faction of the country to whom Reagan, the oldest man to be sworn into office, seemed woefully out of touch with on such issues as equal rights, abortion, and AIDS. Two of Reagan's children, Ronald Reagan, Jr. and Patti Davis, dabbled in acting, he in the film *Soul Man* and she in the syndicated soap *Rituals*.

Screen: 1937: Love Is on the Air; Hollywood Hotel; 1938: Swing Your Lady; Sergeant Murphy; Accidents Will Happen; Cowboy from Brooklyn; Boy Meets Girl; Brother Rat; Going Places; Girls on Probation; 1939: Dark Victory; Secret Service of the Air; Code of the Secret Service; Naughty But Nice; Hell's Kitchen; Angels Wash Their Faces; Smashing the Money Ring; 1940: Brother Rat and a Baby; An Angel from Texas; Murder in the Air; Knute Rockne — All-American; Tugboat Annie Sails Again; Santa Fe Trail; 1941: The Bad Man; Million Dollar Baby; Nine Lives Are Not Enough; International Squadron; 1942: Kings Row; Juke Girl; Desperate Journey; 1943: This Is the Army; 1947: Stallion Road; That Hagen Girl; The Voice of the Turtle/One for the Books; 1949: John Loves Mary; Night Unto Night; The Girl from Jones Beach; It's a Great Feeling; The Hasty Heart; 1950: Louisa; 1951: Storm Warning; The Last Outpost; Bedtime for Bonzo; Hong Kong; 1952: She's Working Her Way Through College; The Winning Team; 1953: Tropic Zone; Law and Order; 1954: Prisoner of War; Cattle Queen of Montana; 1955:

Tennessee's Partner; 1957: Hellcats of the Navy; 1961: The Young Doctors (narrator); 1964: The Killers.

Select TV: 1950: The Disappearance of Mrs. Gordon (sp); 1952: The Priceless Gift (sp); 1953: First Born (sp); A Job for Jimmy Valentine (sp); Message in a Bottle (sp); And Suddenly You Knew (sp); 1953–54: The Orchid Award (series); 1954: The Jungle Trap (sp); The Edge of Battle (sp); Beneath These Waters (sp); 1954–62: General Electric Theatre (series); 1965–66: Death Valley Days (series).

MICHAEL REDGRAVE

BORN: BRISTOL, ENGLAND, MARCH 20, 1908. ED: CAMBRIDGE. DIED: MARCH 21, 1985.

One of the great names of the British theatre, Michael Redgrave was also a leading figure in that country's cinema for two decades. Although it is hard to equate most of what is available to us on screen with greatness, he is certainly a performer of much polish, grace, and thought. He was the son of actors (his father Roy Redgrave had appeared in silent films in Australia), but he almost did not continue the family tradition, opting initially for a career teaching modern languages. After interest in that field ran its course, he joined the Liverpool Rep, debuting for them in *Counselor-at-Law* in 1934. In London he established himself as a member of the Old Vic and became a star through such plays as *The Country Wife* and *As You Like It*. As a result he was signed to a contract by the Gainsborough film company and started off most winningly, in Alfred Hitchcock's *The Lady Vanishes*, proving himself an acceptable cinematic hero. There followed a soap opera, *Stolen Life*, as an Alps explorer, and *A Window in London*, a melodrama with a tricky twist, after which he ended up in some of the major English movies of the war years. These were *The Stars Look Down*, as a coal miner who hopes to improve the deplorable working conditions in his town; *Kipps*, as a draper's assistant who inherits a fortune, taken from the H.G. Wells novel (the author was featured in a prologue but it was chopped prior to release); *Thunder Rock*, as the loner who takes a job tending a lighthouse until spirits convince him to rejoin the world; *The Way to the Stars*, a flag-waving morale booster about the RAF and one of the major hits in Britain at that time; and *The Captive Heart*, as a Czech POW pretending to be a dead British officer. In the last he acted opposite Rachel Kempson, whom he had married in 1935. Following the war (he had a short stint in the navy), he played one of his most famous and enduring roles, the ventriloquist who is slowly going nuts because he's possessed by his dummy, in the supernatural anthology *Dead of Night*.

At this time he accepted two offers from Hollywood, neither of which turned out to be very popular, although the first brought him respectable notices and his sole Oscar nomination. This was the troubled production of *Mourning Becomes Electra*, playing Rosalind Russell's doomed weakling brother, in a movie that was sliced down to various lengths from its original 175-minute running time, though it pleased next to no one in any form. In any case Redgrave's performance was just as overwrought as everyone else's in the cast. The other was a Fritz Lang thriller, *Secret Beyond the Door*, a pseudo-*Suspicion* melodrama that Redgrave went on record as hating. Back in England he wound up with two of his best film roles, as the disliked schoolmaster who sees his life falling apart in *The Browning Version*, and the crafty Jack in the charming adaptation of *The Importance of Being Earnest*, which would, over the years, become perhaps his best-known motion picture part, as far as American audiences were concerned. His leading man era came to a close with the thriller *The Night My Number Came Up*, as a man foreseeing disaster for the plane on which he is a passenger; *The Dam Busters*, as the inventor of the mines used to combat the Nazis; the melodramatic *Time Without Pity*, as an alcoholic who must save his son who has been condemned to die; and *The Quiet American*, as a cynical journalist in Saigon. Becoming a character player, he was seen in supporting and guest roles in such movies as *1984*, as the cool underground member who turns out to be the enemy; *Shake Hands with the Devil*, as an IRA general; *The Wreck of the Mary Deare*, as a lawyer; *The Innocents*, hiring Deborah Kerr to take care of the creepy household; *The Loneliness of the Long Distance Runner*, top billed but clearly in support as the prison warden; *The Hill*, as a drunken doctor; the musical remake of *Goodbye, Mr. Chips*, as the headmaster; and *Nicholas and Alexandra*, as the czar's foreign affairs minister Sazonov. There was some further stage work and television but, by the mid-to-late 1970s, his failing health caused him to retire. He fathered three children, Vanessa, Corin and Lynn, all of whom became actors, and remained married to Kempson to the end, although it was disclosed after his death that he had been homosexual. He was the author of two memoirs: *Mask or Face* (1958) and *In My Mind's Eye* (1983). He was knighted in 1959.

Screen: 1938: The Lady Vanishes; Climbing High; 1939: Stolen Life; A Window in London/Lady in Distress; The Stars Look Down; 1941: Kipps; Atlantic Ferry/Sons of the Sea; Jeannie; 1942: Thunder Rock; The Big Blockade; 1945: The Way to the Stars/Johnny in the Clouds; Dead of Night; 1946: The Years Between; The Captive Heart; 1947: The Man Within/The Smugglers; Fame Is the Spur; Mourning Becomes Electra; 1948: Secret Beyond the Door; 1951: The Browning Version; The Magic Box; 1952: The Importance of Being Earnest; 1954: The Green Scarf; The Sea Shall Not Have Them; 1955: The Night My Number Came Up; The Dam Busters; Mr. Arkadin/Confidential Report; Oh…Rosalinda!!; 1956: 1984; 1957: Time Without Pity; The Happy Road; 1958: The Quiet American; Law and Disorder; Behind the Mask; 1959: Shake Hands With the Devil; The Wreck of the Mary Deare; 1961: No My Darling Daughter; The Innocents; 1962: The Loneliness of the Long Distance Runner; 1965: Young Cassidy; The Hill; The Heroes of Telemark; 1967: The 25th Hour; 1968: Assignment K; 1969: Oh! What a Lovely War; Battle of Britain; Goodbye, Mr. Chips; 1970: Goodbye Gemini; 1971: The Go-Between; Nicholas and Alexandra; 1972: Connecting Rooms (filmed 1970).

NY Stage: 1948: Macbeth; 1955: Tiger at the Gates; 1956: The Sleeping Prince (and dir.); 1961: The Complaisant Lover.

Select TV: 1952: My Brother Henry (sp); 1953: The Bear (sp); 1955: She Stoops to Conquer (sp); 1957: Ruggles of Red Gap (sp); 1963: Hedda Gabler (sp); 1964: The Great War (series narrator); 1966: The Canterville Ghost (sp); 1967: Uncle Vanya (sp); Alice in Wonderland (sp); 1968: Heidi (sp); The Tempest (sp); Mr. Dickens of London (sp); 1970: David Copperfield (theatrical in UK); Hamlet (sp); 1971: Don Juan in Hell (sp); 1973: Dr. Jekyll and Mr. Hyde.

DONNA REED

(DONNA BELLE MULLENGER) BORN: DENISON, IA, JANUARY 27, 1921. ED: LOS ANGELES CITY COL. DIED: JANUARY 14, 1986.

Perhaps it was her very niceness that caused Donna Reed to be underrated in her profession. She was one of MGM's principal wartime ingenues and as those types go she was one of the most pleasing of the bunch: warm, pretty without seeming to be studio manufactured, wholesome without being too sticky. When called on to emote she could more than hold her own. In high school she was a beauty contest winner and, when she moved to California to attend college, was voted Campus Queen, which got her picture circulated to the right people in the entertainment business. As a result she was tested and signed by MGM in 1941 and they immediately put her into *The Get-Away*, a "B" opposite Robert Sterling, where she was billed as "Donna Adams." That was also her name in *Babes on Broadway*, but the studio didn't care for the sound of it and decided on "Reed" when she showed up as a secretary in *Shadow of the Thin Man*. They made her a wallflower who gets the hots for Mickey Rooney in *The Courtship of Andy Hardy*; the secondary love interest in the Wallace Beery-Marjorie Main vehicle *The Bugle Sounds*; the stepmom that Robert Blake doesn't care for in *Mokey*; and the girlfriend of a nutcase in both *Calling Dr. Gillespie* and *Dr. Gillespie's Criminal Case*. She was also lucky to be featured in the cast of one of the studio's finest offerings of the 1940s, *The Human Comedy*, as Mickey Rooney's sister Bess, and in a sizable wartime hit, *See Here, Private Hargrove*, as Robert Walker's girlfriend. Her best chance on her home lot came with John Ford's exceptional war film, *They Were Expendable*, where she stood out amid the mostly male cast as the army nurse involved with soldier John Wayne.

Frank Capra then borrowed her for *It's a Wonderful Life*, and she was terrific as the small town girl who becomes the anchor of restless James Stewart's life. Years later, this movie would become so beloved that it would rank as her most identifiable film role. It did not at the time, however, encourage MGM to renew her option and, after her spectacular ascent to redemption, climbing up the rocks to reach the convent in *Green Dolphin Street*, she was dropped. At Paramount she teamed with Alan Ladd for *Beyond Glory* and *Chicago Deadline*, was a likable love interest for Dean Martin in *The Caddy*, and was in love with John Wayne again, in the sentimental *Trouble Along the Way*, for Warners. In the meantime she had signed with Columbia, where she gave support to exploited athlete John Derek in *Saturday's Hero*, and was his fellow-reporter in *Scandal Sheet*. The Columbia period became worthwhile when she got the against-type role of the prostitute who falls for G.I. Montgomery Clift in *From Here to Eternity*. It was as assured a performance as any in the film and she won the Academy Award for Best Supporting Actress of 1953. This didn't mean that her subsequent Columbia assignments rose above the routine, with such titles as the western *They Rode West* or the jungle programmer *Beyond Mombasa*. However she did get to strut her stuff as the distressed mom of a kidnapped child, back at her alma mater, MGM, in *Ransom*, and provided wifely comfort to Steve Allen in the well-attended Universal biopic *The Benny Goodman Story*. In partnership with her second husband, Tony Owen, she put together a television series, *The Donna Reed Show*, which ran for eight years and did a lot to solidify her uncomplicated nice-lady image. After years out of the spotlight in semi-retirement she returned to television to replace Barbara Bel Geddes on the prime time soap opera *Dallas* for a single season, before she succumbed to cancer of the pancreas.

Screen: AS DONNA ADAMS: 1941: The Get-Away; Babes on Broadway.

AS DONNA REED: 1941: Shadow of the Thin Man; The Bugle Sounds; 1942: Calling Dr. Gillespie; The Courtship of Andy Hardy; Mokey; Eyes in the Night; Apache Trail; 1943: The Human Comedy; Dr. Gillespie's Criminal Case; Thousands Cheer; The Man From Down Under; 1944: See Here, Private Hargrove; Mrs. Parkington; Gentle Annie; 1945: The Picture of Dorian Gray; They Were Expendable; 1946: Faithful in My Fashion; It's a Wonderful Life; 1947: Green Dolphin Street; 1948: Beyond Glory; 1949:

Chicago Deadline; **1951:** Saturday's Hero; **1952:** Scandal Sheet; Hangman's Knot; **1953:** Trouble Along the Way; Raiders of the Seven Seas; The Caddy; From Here to Eternity; Gun Fury; **1954:** Three Hours to Kill; They Rode West; The Last Time I Saw Paris; **1955:** The Far Horizons; The Benny Goodman Story; **1956:** Ransom; Backlash; **1957:** Beyond Mombasa; **1958:** The Whole Truth; **1960:** Pepe; **1974:** The Yellow Headed Summer.

Select TV: **1954:** Portrait of Lydia (sp); **1957:** Flight from Tormendero (sp); The Other Side of the Curtain (sp); **1958–66:** The Donna Reed Show (series); **1979:** The Best Place to Be; **1983:** Deadly Lessons; **1984–85:** Dallas (series).

STEVE REEVES

BORN: GLASGOW, MT, JANUARY 21, 1926.
DIED: MAY 1, 2000.

So muscular was Steve Reeves that his name became synonymous with the sort of over-the-top bodybuilding star known for pecs over talent. During the early years of his career, he worked his way up through the customary progression of titles in this sort of competition: Mr. Pacific, Mr. America, Mr. World, and finally the coveted Mr. Universe. Because of his fame, Hollywood came looking for him to fill out the background in MGM's health-craze musical *Athena*, while notorious amateur filmmaker Ed Wood actually gave him an acting role, as a cop, in *Jail Bait*. It was up to Italy to turn him into an actual movie star and they did just that with *Hercules*, a fairly cheesy affair but one that proved so popular it paved the way for years worth of Italian sword-and-sandal epics with busty babes and sometimes bustier men. Although there would be endless Hercules pictures produced, Reeves did only the immediate follow-up, *Hercules Unchained*, which, like the first, was distributed in America by Warner Bros. Instead he varied things a bit, playing Philippides in *Giant of Marathon*; the hero of the remake of *The Thief of Baghdad*; *Morgan the Pirate*; Romulus in *Duel of the Titans*, opposite another iron pumper, Gordon Scott, as Remus; Aeneas in *The Trojan War*; the son of Spartacus in *The Slave*; and *Sandokan the Great*, which took place, atypically for him, in 19th century North Africa. These were all fairly juvenile efforts made to please the Saturday-matinee crowd and, perhaps, select gay circles that relished this combination of kitsch and beefcake. In a final effort to change his image, he did a western, *A Long Ride from Hell*, but it didn't convince American filmmakers that they'd been missing out on much and he soon retired, returning to the States to operate a ranch.

Screen: **1954:** Athena; Jail Bait/Hidden Face; **1958:** Hercules; **1959:** Goliath and the Barbarians; **1960:** Giant of Marathon; The Last Days of Pompeii; Hercules Unchained; **1961:** The White Warrior/The White Devil; The Thief of Baghdad; Morgan the Pirate; **1962:** The Trojan War; **1963:** Duel of the Titans/Romulus and Remus; The Slave/Son of Spartacus; The Last Glory of Troy/The Avenger; The Shortest Day (nUSr); **1965:** Sandokan the Great; Sandokan and the Pirates of Malaya; **1970:** A Long Ride from Hell (and co-wr.).

NY Stage: **1953:** Kismet; **1955:** The Vamp.

CARL REINER

BORN: BRONX, NY, MARCH 20, 1922.

Personable, bright-voiced Carl Reiner seemed to have tried his hand at a little of everything: writing, directing; performing in television, on screen, for the stage, and even for recordings — not to mention knocking off a book or two. Despite varying degrees of success at each, he became one of the esteemed names in the field of comedy. He had acted with a small theatre group prior to enlisting in the army during World War II, where he was one of the entertainers in the special services unit alongside fellow-performer Howard Morris. This led to a part in a G.I. revue, *Call Me Mister*, followed by two others of a similar format, and a role on an early television series, *The Fashion Story*. Max Leibman, the producer of one of Reiner's revue shows, *Alive and Kicking*, hired him to appear on his new variety series, *Your Show of Shows*, which made him one of the most familiar faces of early 1950s television. By the end of the decade Reiner began getting acting offers for films and showed up as lawyers in *Happy Anniversary* and *The Gazebo*, both fairly ordinary parts. In the meantime he really scored on television as the creator and writer of *The Dick Van Dyke Show*, where he also played the egotistical television star Alan Brady. Back in movies he was Gidget's dad in *Gidget Goes Hawaiian*, an air traffic controller in *It's a Mad Mad Mad Mad World*, and then had his best movie part, as the hapless husband besieged by Alan Arkin and his submarine crew, in one of the top comedies of the decade, *The Russians Are Coming! The Russians Are Coming!*. In 1967, he successfully started his motion picture directorial career with the adaptation of his own autobiographical novel *Enter Laughing*. Aside from cameos in some of his directorial efforts, Reiner was seen from time to time in other directors' movies, including *The End*, as a health-conscious doctor; *Slums of Beverly Hills*, as Alan Arkin's intimidating brother; and the remake of *Ocean's Eleven*, as an old-time thief helping to rob some Las Vegas casinos.

Reiner received Emmy Awards for acting in *Caesar's Hour* two years running (1956, 1957); as writer of *The Dick Van Dyke Show* on three separate occasions (1962, 1963, 1964); for producing the Van Dyke series (1965, 1966); for co-writing *The Sid Caesar-Imogene Coca-Carl Reiner-Howard Morris Special*, in 1967; and for guesting on the series *Mad About You* in 1995. In addition to the many television series on which he appeared, he also served as creator-producer-and writer on the 1970s sitcom *The New Dick Van Dyke Show*. Together with fellow *Your Show of Shows* alumni Mel Brooks he created and appeared on the comedy album *The 2,000 Year Old Man*, which became one of the best-known records in that field, spawning a television special as well as some sequels over the years. In the theatre he was the director and writer of the farce *Something Different*, which ran on Broadway for a very brief period in 1967. Although he did not act in any of son Rob Reiner's directorial efforts, he did play a doctor in the film *The Spirit of 76*, helmed by his other son, Lucas. His full list of movies credits as a director are: *Enter Laughing* (1967; also prod., wr.), *The Comic* (1969; also prod., wr.; and appeared as a slimy agent), *Where's Poppa?* (1970), *Oh, God!* (1977; and in a bit recreating *The Picture of Dorian Gray*), *The One and Only* (1978), *The Jerk* (1979; and showed up cross-eyed as a victim of a pair of trendy glasses), *Dead Men Don't Wear Plaid* (1982; and wr.; and as a Nazi villain); *The Man with Two Brains* (1983; and wr.), *All of Me* (1984), *Summer Rental* (1985), *Summer School* (1987; and as a departing teacher), *Bert Rigby, You're a Fool* (1989; and wr.), *Sibling Rivalry* (1990), *Fatal Instinct* (1993; and as a judge), and *That Old Feeling* (1997).

Screen: **1959:** Happy Anniversary; The Gazebo; **1961:** Gidget Goes Hawaiian; **1963:** The Thrill of It All (and wr.); It's a Mad Mad Mad Mad World; **1965:** The Art of Love (and wr.); **1966:** Don't Worry, We'll Think of a Title; The Russians Are Coming! The Russians Are Coming!; **1967:** A Guide for the Married Man; **1969:** The Comic (and dir.; prod. wr.); Generation; **1977:** Oh, God! (and dir.); **1978:** The End; **1979:** The Jerk (and dir.; wr.);

1982: Dead Men Don't Wear Plaid (and dir.; co-wr.); 1987: Summer School; In the Mood (voice); 1990: The Spirit of 76; 1993: Fatal Instinct (and dir.); 1998: Slums of Beverly Hills; 2000: The Adventures of Rocky and Bullwinkle; 2001: Ocean's Eleven; The Majestic (voice).

NY Stage: 1946: Call Me Mister; 1948: Inside U.S.A.; 1950: Alive and Kicking.

Select TV: 1948–49: The Fashion Story (series); 1949: The Fifty-Fourth Street Revue (series); 1950: Eddie Condon's Floor Show (series); 1950–54: Your Show of Shows (series); 1954: Droodles (series); 1954–57: Caesar's Hour (series); 1958: Sid Caesar Invites You (series); 1958–59: Keep Talking (series); 1960–61: Take a Good Look (series); 1961–66: The Dick Van Dyke Show (series; and creator; wr.; prod.); 1963: The Art Linkletter Show (series); 1964–65: The Celebrity Game (series); 1967: The Sid Caesar-Imogene Coca-Carl Reiner-Howard Morris Special (sp); 1975: Medical Story; 1976: Good Heavens (series; and exec. prod.); 1981: Skokie; 1983: Faerie Tale Theatre: Pinocchio (sp); 1991: Sunday Best (series); 1995: The Right to Remain Silent; 1998: Hercules (series; voice).

LEE REMICK

BORN: BOSTON, MA, DECEMBER 14, 1935.
DIED: JULY 2, 1991.

Right from the start Lee Remick seemed to have something special, for she was both pretty in a completely natural way and an incredibly good actress without showy technique or tricks. Like most actresses, she was more in demand by movie makers when she was younger, which meant that television would get the best of her in later years. She had been a dance student for many years when a chance acquaintance with playwrights Mary Orr and Reginald Denham got her an acting role in their 1953 play Be Your Age. Despite its quick closing she landed an agent who got her plenty of work on television including a segment of Robert Montgomery Presents called All Expenses Paid. This was seen by director Elia Kazan who was looking for someone to play a Southern baton twirler named Betty Lou in A Face in the Crowd. Remick got the part and made enough of an impression to win the role of Anthony Franciosa's sexed-up wife in The Long Hot Summer, holding her own against the likes of Paul Newman, Joanne Woodward, and Orson Welles. A third prestige item, Anatomy of a Murder, really made her name and she was outstanding as Ben Gazzara's sluttish wife, who seems to be less concerned about having been raped than she's supposed to be. Next up she was the young widow who falls for TVA rep Montgomery Clift in Wild River, a decent movie that didn't fare very well at the box office, though she always spoke of the part as being her favorite. Southern again, she was involved in the mucked-up movie version of Faulkner's Sanctuary and then was a stalked bank teller in a mediocre thriller Experiment in Terror. That movie's director, Blake Edwards, gave her a better part when he chose her to play the nice girl who ends up a hopeless alcoholic in the shattering screen adaptation of the television drama Days of Wine and Roses. She was nothing short of superb, but in a competitive year at the Oscars she had to make due with a nomination, the only one she'd ever receive.

She wanted to prove that she had the right touch for comedy, but since The Wheeler Dealers and The Hallelujah Trail were both stinkers nothing was proven except that she was above such material. In between she played the loving wife of ex-con Steve McQueen in Baby the Rain Must Fall, which was all acting-over-content, and then went to Broadway for a successful thriller, Wait

Until Dark, though Audrey Hepburn got to play the part when it was made into a film. Remaining in the thriller mode she returned to movies for one of her best, No Way to Treat a Lady, paired off with George Segal, although it was really Rod Steiger's show. She seemed wasted as Frank Sinatra's wife in The Detective, and then moved to England where she did a pair of comedies with Richard Attenborough, the sophisticated A Severed Head, and the game adaptation of Joe Orton's classic stage comedy Loot, as the crafty nurse. There was also the very dry movie version of Edward Albee's A Delicate Balance, as Katharine Hepburn's daughter, around which time her run of television roles seemed to start. When she did show up back at the movies it was as the poor mother tormented by her devil offspring in the horror hit The Omen, followed by a derivative psychological thriller, The Medusa Touch, as Richard Burton's shrink. There was one last starring role on the big screen, in the Merchant-Ivory presentation of The Europeans, as an American baroness, after which she was a difficult piano instructor in The Competition, and Jack Lemmon's ex in Tribute. Outside of the little-seen Australian drama Emma's War, there were no more film roles for the next 11 years of her life, which ended much too soon when she succumbed to cancer of the liver.

Screen: 1957: A Face in the Crowd; 1958: The Long Hot Summer; 1959: These Thousand Hills; Anatomy of a Murder; 1960: Wild River; 1961: Sanctuary; 1962: Experiment in Terror; Days of Wine and Roses; 1963: The Running Man; The Wheeler Dealers; 1965: Baby the Rain Must Fall; The Hallelujah Trail; 1968: No Way to Treat a Lady; The Detective; 1969: Hard Contract; 1971: A Severed Head; Sometimes a Great Notion/ Never Give an Inch; 1972: Loot; 1973: The Hunted/Touch Me Not (dtc); A Delicate Balance; 1975: Hennessy; 1976: The Omen; 1977: Telethon; 1978: The Medusa Touch; 1979: The Europeans; 1980: The Competition; Tribute; 1988: Emma's War.

NY Stage: 1953: Be Your Age; 1964: Anyone Can Whistle; 1966: Wait Until Dark.

Select TV: 1953: Double in Ivory (sp); 1954: My Little Girl (sp); Death and Life of Larry Benson (sp); 1955: Man Lost (sp); 1956: All Expenses Paid (sp); The Landlady's Daughter (sp); 1957: The Last Tycoon (sp); Circle of Fear (sp); 1958: Last Clear Chance (sp); 1960: The Tempest (sp); 1962: The Farmer's Daughter (sp); 1967: Damn Yankees (sp); 1972: The Man Who Came to Dinner (sp); Summer and Smoke (sp); Of Men and Women (sp); 1973: And No One Could Save Her; The Blue Knight; 1974: QBVII (ms); 1975: Hustling; A Girl Named Sooner; Jennie: Lady Randolph Churchill (sp); 1977: The Ambassadors (sp); 1978: Breaking Up; Arthur Hailey's Wheels (ms); 1979: Torn Between Two Lovers; Ike (ms); 1980: Haywire; The Women's Room; 1982: The Letter; 1983: Faerie Tale Theatre: The Snow Queen (sp); The Gift of Love: A Christmas Story; 1984: A Good Sport; Mistral's Daughter (ms); Rearview Mirror; I Do! I Do! (sp); 1985: Toughlove; Follies in Concert (sp); 1986: Of Pure Blood; Eleanor: In Her Own Words (sp); 1987: Nutcracker: Money, Madness and Murder; The Vision; 1988: Jesse; 1989: Bridge to Silence; Around the World in 80 Days (ms); Dark Holiday.

MICHAEL RENNIE

BORN: BRADFORD, YORKSHIRE, ENGLAND,
AUGUST 25, 1909. ED: LEYS COL.
DIED: JUNE 10, 1971.

Tall, smoothly handsome Michael Rennie possessed a fine, authoritative speaking voice that could, at times, make him seem like a bit of a stick. The fact that Hollywood pictured him mainly in stodgy costume films was no help, so it was in a sci-fi role that he won the most attention. While working as a salesman in London, he began appearing in bits in movies around 1935. In time he was actually winning leads, in *The Tower of Terror*, rescuing Movita from a nutty lighthouse keeper, and *The Big Blockade*, as an RAF pilot. Following his war service he starred in *I'll Be Your Sweetheart*, as a publisher trying to establish copyright laws; and *White Cradle Inn*, as Madeleine Carroll's philandering husband, among others. He showed up as King Edward in 20th Century-Fox's *The Black Rose*, which was shot in England, and wound up under contract to that studio. There he played his best role, the intelligent, peace-seeking alien Klatu, in what turned out to be one of the most literate and enduring of all 1950s sci-fi films, *The Day the Earth Stood Still*. Fox also gave him a chance to play Jean Valjean in one of the lesser versions of *Les Misérables*, then made him Jeffrey Hunter's superior officer in *Sailor of the King*; the disciple Peter in the CinemaScope hit *The Robe*; Tyrone Power's commanding officer in *King of the Khyber Rifles*; Bernadotte in *Desiree*; Father Junipero Serra, the man who founded California's early missions, in *Seven Cities of Gold*; Ginger Rogers's new husband in *Teenage Rebel*; a drifter murdered by James Mason in the popular soaper *Island in the Sun*; and one of the adventurers discovering prehistoric life in the dopey remake of *The Lost World*. In 1963, he repeated his stage role as the conceited actor in *Mary, Mary* but, apart from *Hotel*, as Merle Oberon's shady husband, and *The Devil's Brigade*, as a general, the remainder of his film career consisted of many barely-seen international efforts. On television he reprised Orson Welles's famous role of Harry Lime in a one-season adaptation of *The Third Man*.

Screen: 1936: The Man Who Could Work Miracles; Gypsy; Secret Agent; 1937: Gangway; The Squeaker/Murder on Diamond Row; Bank Holiday/Three on a Week-End; 1938: The Divorce of Lady X; 1939: This Man in Paris; 1941: This Man Is Dangerous/The Patient Vanishes; Turned Out Nice Again; Pimpernel Smith/Mister V; Dangerous Moonlight/Suicide Squadron; Ships with Wings; 1942: The Tower of Terror; The Big Blockade; 1945: I'll Be Your Sweetheart; The Wicked Lady; Caesar and Cleopatra; 1947: The Root of All Evil; White Cradle Inn/High Fury; 1948: Idol of Paris; Uneasy Terms; 1949: The Golden Madonna; 1950: Trio; The Black Rose; Miss Pilgrim's Progress; The Body Said No!; 1951: I'll Never Forget You/The House in the Square; The Thirteenth Letter; The Day the Earth Stood Still; The Desert Fox (narrator); 1952: Phone Call from a Stranger; 5 Fingers; Les Misérables; 1953: The Desert Rats (narrator); Sailor of the King/Single Handed; ; The Robe; King of the Khyber Rifles; Titanic (narrator); Dangerous Crossing; 1954: Demetrius and the Gladiators; Princess of the Nile; Desiree; 1955: Mambo; Soldier of Fortune; Seven Cities of Gold; The Rains of Ranchipur; 1956: Teenage Rebel; 1957: Island in the Sun; Omar Khayyam; 1958: Battle of the VI/Missle from Hell; 1959: Third Man on the Mountain; 1960: The Lost World; 1963: Mary, Mary; 1966: Ride Beyond Vengeance; Cyborg 2087; 1967: Hotel; 1968: The Power; Commando Attack; The Young, the Evil and the Savage; Death on the Run (nUSr); The Battle of El Alamein; The Devil's Brigade; 1969: Subterfuge; 1970: Assignment Terror/Dracula vs. Frankenstein; Surabaya Conspiracy.

NY Stage: 1961: Mary, Mary.

Select TV: 1955: Dr. Jekyll and Mr. Hyde (sp); 1957: Strange Sanctuary (sp); Circle of the Day (sp); The Mystery of the Red Room (sp); 1958: The Connoisseur (sp); 1959–60: The Third Man (series); 1960: The Scarlet Pimpernel (sp); 1963: The Invincible Mr. Disraeli (sp); 1965: Rapture at 240 (sp); 1967: Blind Man's Bluff (sp).

ANNE REVERE

BORN: NEW YORK, NY, JUNE 25, 1903.
ED: WELLESLEY COL. DIED: DECEMBER 18, 1990.

A real no-nonsense, iron-jawed lady of tremendous presence, Anne Revere came off not unlike a strong-willed pioneer woman of the past, with an indomitable sense of spirit and resillience. After nearly a decade in stock and rep she debuted on Broadway in 1931 in *The Great Barrington*. Two years later she proved so successful in the play *The Double Door* that Paramount asked her to repeat her role as the tormented sister in the film version. Not a single other movie offer followed, however, so she returned to New York where she starred in Lillian Hellman's groundbreaking lesbianism drama *The Children's Hour*. In 1940, RKO asked her back to Hollywood to play the wife of escaped con Paul Guilfoyle in *One Crowded Night* and she stayed there for the next 11 years, where she became everyone's ideal of the levelheaded mom. This was underscored by her Oscar-nominated work as Jennifer Jones's practical mother in *The Song of Bernadette*, a variation of which she would play in *National Velvet*, where she saw daughter Elizabeth Taylor become infatuated with winning the derby, but made sure that she and everyone in the family kept a firm grip on reality. For the latter role she was given the Academy Award for Best Supporting Actress of 1945. There was another nomination, for playing Gregory Peck's sickly but supportive ma, in the 1947 Oscar-winner for Best Picture, *Gentleman's Agreement*. Elsewhere she was mother to John Garfield in *Body and Soul* and Montgomery Clift in *A Place in the Sun*, to name but two. Shortly after the latter, she refused to testify before the House Un-American Activities Committee, resigned from the Screen Actors Guild, and was blacklisted in Hollywood. Fortunately there was stage work available and she returned to Broadway, winning a Tony Award in 1960 for *Toys in the Attic*. There were some television roles as well, but she was not seen on the big screen again until 1970 when Otto Preminger asked her to play a small part in *Tell Me That You Love Me, Junie Moon*.

Screen: 1934: The Double Door; 1940: One Crowded Night; The Howards of Virginia; 1941: Men of Boys Town; Remember the Day; The Devil Commands; Design for Scandal; H.M. Pulham Esq.; The Flame of New Orleans; 1942: The Gay Sisters; Are Husbands Necessary?; The Falcon Takes Over; Meet the Stewarts; Star Spangled Rhythm; 1943: The Song of Bernadette; Shantytown; Old Acquaintance; The Meanest Man in the World; 1944: Standing Room Only; Rainbow Island; The Keys of the Kingdom; Sunday Dinner for a Soldier; The Thin Man Goes Home; 1945: National Velvet; Don Juan Quilligan; Fallen Angel; 1946: Dragonwyck; 1947: The Shocking Miss Pilgrim; Forever Amber; Body and Soul; Gentleman's Agreement; Carnival in Costa Rica; 1948: Secret Beyond the Door; Scudda Hoo! Scudda Hay!; Deep Waters; 1949: You're My Everything; 1951: The Great Missouri Raid; A Place in the Sun; 1970: Tell Me That You Love Me, Junie Moon; Macho Callahan; 1976: Birch Interval.

NY Stage: 1931: The Great Barrington; Lady With a Lamp; 1932: Wild Waves; 1933: The Double Door; 1934: The Children's Hour; 1937: As You Like It; 1939: The Three Sisters; 1951: Four Twelves are 48; 1958: Cue for Passion; 1959: Jolly's Progress; 1960: Toys in the Attic; 1966: Night of the Dance.

Select TV: 1960: The House of Bernarda Alba (sp); 1961: Four by Tennessee Williams (sp); 1965: The Trojan Women (sp); 1970–71: Search for Tomorrow (series); 1972: Two for the Money; 1976: Ryan's Hope (series).

DEBBIE REYNOLDS

(MARY FRANCES REYNOLDS)
BORN: EL PASO, TX, APRIL 1, 1932.

Just about the perkiest of 1950s personalities, Debbie Reynolds was forever in there pitching a fast ball, aiming to please, singing exuberantly, strutting her stuff, emoting up a storm, and wanting very much to make an impression. She certainly did just that and for a lot longer than many might have predicted, despite the fact that there were better vocalists, more adept comediennes, and stronger actresses. While in high school she was voted Miss Burbank, which resulted in interest from Warner Bros., who gave her a walk-on as one of Betty Lynn's friends in *June Bride*, and a bigger role as June Haver's sister in *The Daughter of Rosie O'Grady*, then promptly dropped her. MGM decided to give her a whirl and gave her some show stopping numbers in two musicals, in both paired up with Carlton Carpenter. The first, *Three Little Words*, required her to play singer Helen Kane, which meant she mouthed "I Wanna Be Loved By You" while the real Kane did the "boop-boopie-doo" vocals. She was better utilized in *Two Weeks With Love*, as Jane Powell's younger sister, memorably doing a lightning fast rendition of "Abba-Dabba Honeymoon." She was then the lucky ingenue chosen to play leading lady to Gene Kelly in what turned out to be the pinnacle of the MGM movie musicals, *Singin' in the Rain*. For the role, she had to pretend she was dubbing vocals for Jean Hagen and to keep up with Kelly and Donald O'Connor in one of the most charming of all musical sequences, "Good Morning." As her reward, she and O'Connor were together for the lighter *I Love Melvin*, which required her to be tossed about, at one point, dressed as a football. She then did the weak adaptation of the Max Shulman stories, *The Affairs of Dobie Gillis*, and the better *Give a Girl a Break*, where, at one point, she danced backwards among a sea of balloons with Bob Fosse.

On loan to RKO, she was the younger girl in love with much older Dick Powell in the slight but popular *Susan Slept Here*, then returned for two lesser songfests with Jane Powell, *Athena* and *Hit the Deck*, in love with Vic Damone and Russ Tamblyn, respectively. She was appropriately perky as a starlet in a stage-bound Frank Sinatra comedy, *The Tender Trap*, and then got to prove that she could carry a straight drama with *The Catered Affair*, as the daughter of poor tenement dwellers Bette Davis and Ernest Borgnine. With her new husband (1955–59), singer Eddie Fisher, she did an uninspired RKO musical, *Bundle of Joy*, a remake of *Bachelor Mother*, which was very much a dated product of its time. She then went over to Universal for a cutesy thing about a poor Southern girl who sets straight the messed up lives of the rich. The film was *Tammy and the Bachelor*, but is often simply called "Tammy," since her rendition of that song was such a major hit. Back on her home lot she was another rural gal in a tiresome farce nearly salvaged by Tony Randall, *The Mating Game*, and was paired with Glenn Ford in two comedies that did decent business, *It Started With a Kiss*, as a spunky dancer, and the better *The Gazebo*, where her sordid past became the stuff of blackmail. Over at 20th Century-Fox she did a gooey religious-themed musical, *Say One for Me*, which at least allowed her to appear with Bing Crosby, and then wound up in a good drama-comedy over at Paramount, *The Rat Race*, as a down-on-her luck dancer struggling to stay afloat in Manhattan. She participated in the worst sequence of the all-star *Pepe*, drunkenly cavorting to "Tequila" with Cantinflas; wasn't all that appealing as the young lady who becomes overly obsessed with dad Fred Astaire in *The Pleasure of His Company*; but aged with a fair amount of convic-

tion in the all-star, Oscar-nominated epic *How the West Was Won*, as the only character to be around from the opening episode to the finale.

After doing a family comedy of dangerous sugar content, *My Six Loves*, as an actress adopting some kids, she landed the title role in the adaptation of the long-running Broadway hit *Mary, Mary*, where she seemed to be overcompensating for very weak material. This was followed by another film taken from a Broadway success, *The Unsinkable Molly Brown*, where she was a bundle of energy as the lady who goes from poverty to riches. Despite having dropped a lot of the songs on the way from stage to screen, it made a hefty profit and earned her an Oscar nomination, making it one of her greatest triumphs. It was also one of the last movie musicals to resemble those of the glory days of MGM. The horrid *Goodbye Charlie*, wherein she was the reincarnation of a slain gangster, was one of her career low points as indeed it was for all its participants, but the ultra-sentimental *The Singing Nun* became one of her most identifiable roles, despite a mild critical and audience response at the time. Better and more popular was the ensemble *Divorce American Style*, bickering with hubby Dick Van Dyke in a tartly scripted satire on urban marriage. After the failure of *How Sweet It Was*, she opted for weekly television with *The Debbie Reynolds Show*, which wasn't around for very long. She gave a good performance in a "horror" offering, *What's the Matter With Helen?*, as a mom running a talent school in depression era Hollywood, then scored a major personal success on Broadway with the 1974 revival of the musical *Irene*.

Over the next 20 years she was content to do nightclub work and a smattering of TV, while concentrating on opening her movie memorabilia museum in Las Vegas, a long-cherished project that had little success. Her type had seemingly gone out of style, but actor-director Albert Brooks came up with a suitable use of her, casting her as his sweet but critical *Mother*, which allowed her to give perhaps her finest performance in a complex part. Back in the public eye, she followed that by playing the small-town mom puzzled to hear that son Kevin Kline is gay in the 1997 hit *In & Out*. After that it was mostly voice-over work and more nightclub performing. She published her autobiography, *Debbie: My Life*, in 1988. Her daughter is actress-writer Carrie Fisher, who wrote a television movie, *These Old Broads*, for her.

Screen: 1948: June Bride; 1950: The Daughter of Rosie O'Grady; Three Little Words; Two Weeks With Love; 1951: Mr. Imperium; 1952: Singin' in the Rain; Skirts Ahoy!; 1953: I Love Melvin; The Affairs of Dobie Gillis; Give a Girl a Break; 1954: Susan Slept Here; Athena; 1955: Hit the Deck; The Tender Trap; 1956: The Catered Affair; Bundle of Joy; Meet Me in Las Vegas; 1957: Tammy and the Bachelor; 1958: This Happy Feeling; 1959: The Mating Game; Say One for Me; It Started With a Kiss; The Gazebo; 1960: The Rat Race; Pepe; 1961: The Pleasure of His Company; The Second Time Around; 1963: How the West Was Won; My Six Loves; Mary, Mary; 1964: The Unsinkable Molly Brown; Goodbye Charlie; 1966: The Singing Nun; 1967: Divorce American Style; 1968: How Sweet It Is; 1971: What's the Matter With Helen?; 1973: Charlotte's Web (voice); 1974: That's Entertainment!; 1992: The Bodyguard; 1993: Heaven and Earth; 1994: That's Entertainment! III; 1996: Mother; 1997: Wedding Bell Blues; In & Out; 1998: Kiki's Delivery Service (voice; dtv); Fear and Loathing in Las Vegas (voice); Zack and Reba (dtv); Rudolph the Red-Nosed Reindeer (voice); 1999: Keepers of the Frame; 2000: Rugrats in Paris: The Movie (voice).

NY Stage: 1974: Irene; 1976: Debbie; 1982: Woman of the Year.

Select TV: 1969–70: The Debbie Reynolds Show (series); 1981: Aloha Paradise (series); 1987: Sadie and Son; 1989: Perry Mason: The Case of the Musical Murder; 1992: Battling for Baby; 1998:

Halloweentown; The Christmas Wish; **1999:** A Gift of Love: The Daniel Huffman Story; **2000:** Virtual Mom; **2001:** These Old Broads; Halloweentown II.

MARJORIE REYNOLDS

(MARJORIE GOODSPEED) BORN: BUHL, ID, AUGUST 12, 1917. DIED: FEBRUARY 1, 1997.

From child actress of the silents to 1930s programmer ingenue to Paramount contractee to familiar television face of the 1950s, Marjorie Reynolds had experience on her side, rather than any great distinction. After a few film bits as a youngster, she took time off for school and then returned in 1933 as "Marjorie Moore" for her first stop at Paramount. There she appeared in *College Humor* and *Big Broadcast of 1936*, and starred in the independent cheapie *Wine, Women and Song*, which had her going from the convent to the wicked stage. Having married production manager-writer Jack Reynolds, she changed her name to Marjorie Reynolds in 1937 and became the heroine of such low-budget offerings as *Tex Rides With the Boy Scouts*, which was not a gay porno movie as the title suggested but a vehicle for cowboy star Tex Ritter; *Black Bandit*, who was Bob Baker playing a dual role; *Rebellious Daughters*, in which she was blackmailed over some compromising photos; and three of Boris Karloff's "Mr. Wong" mysteries: *Mr. Wong in Chinatown, The Fatal Hour*, and *Doomed to Die*, as reporter Bobby Logan. Paramount decided they could make something "A" list out of her and started her off with a bang in *Holiday Inn*, where she got to dance with Fred Astaire and to "sort-of" help introduce "White Christmas" with Bing Crosby (her vocals were dubbed). She was also with Crosby in *Dixie*; looked pretty in costume garb in Bob Hope's *Monsieur Beaucaire*; and got another good opportunity, trying to help Ray Milland clear his name, in director Fritz Lang's fine wartime thriller *Ministry of Fear*. Over at United Artists, she was part of the dizzy romp *Up in Mabel's Room*, and played Lou Costello's fellow-spirit in Universal's *The Time of Their Lives*, which was another of her better assignments. She was falling back into programmers by the early 1950s when she was asked to play William Bendix's wife Peg in the second television version of *The Life of Riley*, which brought her a good degree of attention for five seasons.

Screen: AS MARJORIE GOODSPEED: **1923:** Scaramouche; The Broken Wing; **1924:** Revelation.

AS MARJORIE MOORE: **1933:** Wine, Women and Song; **1935:** The Big Broadcast of 1936; **1936:** Collegiate; College Holiday.

AS MARJORIE REYNOLDS: **1937:** Murder in Greeenwich Village; Tex Rides With the Boy Scouts; **1938:** Black Bandit; Man's Country; Delinquent Parents; Guilty Trails; Western Trails; Overland Express; Rebellious Daughters; Six-Shootin' Sheriff; **1939:** Streets of New York; Racketeers of the Range; Mr. Wong in Chinatown; Mystery Plane; The Phantom Stage; Stunt Pilot; Danger Flight; Timber Stampede; Sky Patrol; **1940:** The Fatal Hour; Midnight Limited; Doomed to Die; Chasing Trouble; Enemy Agent; Up in the Air; **1941:** Secret Evidence; Robin Hood of the Pecos; Dude Cowboy; Cyclone on Horseback; The Great Swindle; Tillie the Toiler; Top Sergeant Mulligan; Law of the Timber; **1942:** Holiday Inn; Star Spangled Rhythm; **1943:** Dixie; **1944:** Ministry of Fear; Up in Mabel's Room; Three Is a Family; **1945:** Bring on the Girls; Duffy's Tavern; **1946:** Monsieur Beaucaire; Meet Me on Broadway; The Time of Their Lives; **1947:** Heaven Only Knows; **1948:** Bad Men of Tombstone; **1949:** That Midnight Kiss; **1950:** The Great Jewel Robbery; Customs Agent; Rookie Fireman; **1951:** The Home Town Story; His Kind of Woman; **1952:** Models Inc.; No Holds Barred; **1955:** Mobs

Inc.; **1959:** Juke Box Rhythm; **1964:** The Silent Witness.

Select TV: **1951:** A Case of Marriage (sp); **1952:** Luckiest Guy in the World (sp); **1953–58:** The Life of Riley (series); **1962:** The Cake Baker (sp).

RALPH RICHARDSON

BORN: CHELTENHAM, ENGLAND, DECEMBER 19, 1902. DIED: OCTOBER 10, 1983.

He was ranked in the upper echelons of the British theatre along with Olivier, Gielgud, and Redgrave, but Ralph Richardson was not a fancier of the cinema. Nonetheless he seemed to be all over movie screens for decades, sometimes making a considerable impression while at others coming off as a bit of a stuffed shirt. He started with a Brighton rep company before moving over to Birmingham rep, with whom he came to London for his debut there, in 1926, in *The Farmer's Wife*. In 1930, he became a member of the esteemed Old Vic where his roles ranged from Caliban to Bottom to Henry V. The movies made offers and he was first seen as a vicar in a Boris Karloff thriller, *The Ghoul*, in 1933. He played the lead in *The Return of Bulldog Drummond*, though Americans had already accepted Ronald Colman in this part, before producer Alexander Korda signed him to a contract. Korda started him out with two good movies written by H.G. Wells: *Things to Come*, as a warlord, and *The Man Who Could Work Miracles*, as a colonel. He then got another star part, in *South Riding*, as the squire who falls for the local headmistress. By this time, American audiences had seen him on Broadway in *Romeo and Juliet* (as Mercutio) and in his first real hit movie here, *The Citadel*, showing up as one of Robert Donat's colleagues. More memorably he was the wry Major Hammond of the Yard in *Q Planes*, investigating the disappearance of test bombers, and the blinded military officer, Durrance, in the best-remembered big screen version of *The Four Feathers*.

After World War II, Richardson became one of the leading figures behind and in front of the scenes at the Old Vic, where his triumphs included *Uncle Vanya* and *Cyrano de Bergerac*. Back in movies, he was Vivien Leigh's husband in the lesser version of *Anna Karenina*, and then landed perhaps the most rewarding role of his motion picture career, as the adulterous butler who ends up involved in the accidental death of his wife, in *The Fallen Idol*, a finely crafted combination character study-suspense story that won England's BFA best picture award for 1948. The next year he finally went to Hollywood for what turned out to be another of his best roles: the cruel and unloving Dr. Sloper in the masterful rendering of *The Heiress*, a part that earned him a supporting Oscar mention. Returning home he was heralded for playing the aircraft manufacturer in the rather staid *Breaking the Sound Barrier*; was a parson in a sad Christmas tale, *The Holly and the Ivy*; and had his sole Shakespearean screen role, as Buckingham, in Laurence Olivier's *Richard III*. After *Smiley*, as the kindly vicar, he became one of those grand men of the English acting world who consented to appear in all kinds of international productions, the best known of which were *Oscar Wilde*, as Sir Edward Carson; *Exodus*, as a British general overseeing the unrest in Israel; the blockbuster epic *Doctor Zhivago*, as Omar Sharif's adopted father; *The Wrong Box*, where he was very funny as a senile old coot everyone is trying to get rid of; *The Bed Sitting Room*, mutating into the title object in one of his stranger assignments; *Tales from the Crypt*, as the crypt-keeper; *O Lucky Man!*, in a dual role; *Rollerball*, as a futuristic librarian; *Dragonslayer*, as an old sorcerer; *Time Bandits*, as, presumably, God; and

Greystoke: The Legend of Tarzan Lord of the Apes, as Tarzan's doddering old granddad, a role that earned him a posthumous Oscar nomination. During this run of films his best latter-day part came with *Long Day's Journey Into Night*, in which he was at the top of his game as the self-centered father who watches his family fall apart around him. He was knighted in 1947.

Screen: 1933: The Ghoul; Friday the Thirteenth; 1934: The Return of Bulldog Drummond; Java Head; The King of Paris; 1935: Bulldog Jack/Alias Bulldog Drummond; 1936: Things to Come; The Man Who Could Work Miracles; 1937: Thunder in the City; 1938: South Riding; The Divorce of Lady X; The Citadel; 1939: Q Planes/Clouds Over Europe; The Four Feathers; The Lion Has Wings; On the Night of the Fire/The Fugitive; 1942: The Day Will Dawn/The Avengers; The Silver Fleet; 1943: The Volunteer; 1946: School for Secrets/Secret Flight; 1948: Anna Karenina; The Fallen Idol; 1949: The Heiress; 1951: Outcast of the Islands; Home at Seven/Murder on Monday (and dir.); 1952: Breaking the Sound Barrier; The Holly and the Ivy; 1955: Richard III; 1956: Smiley; A Passionate Stranger/A Novel Affair; 1960: Our Man in Havana; Oscar Wilde; Exodus; 1962: Long Day's Journey Into Night; The 300 Spartans; 1964: Woman of Straw; 1965: Doctor Zhivago; 1966: Chimes at Midnight (narrator); The Wrong Box; Khartoum; 1969: Oh! What a Lovely War; Battle of Britain; The Looking Glass War; Midas Run; The Bed Sitting Room; 1971: Eagle in a Cage; 1972: Who Slew Auntie Roo; Tales from the Crypt; Alice's Adventures in Wonderland; 1973: Lady Caroline Lamb; O Lucky Man!; A Doll's House; 1975: Rollerball; 1978: Watership Down (voice); 1981: Dragonslayer; Time Bandits; 1984: Greystoke: The Legend of Tarzan Lord of the Apes; Give My Regards to Broad Street; 1985: Invitation to the Wedding (nUSr).

NY Stage: 1935: Romeo and Juliet; 1946: Henry IV Part 1; Henry IV Part 2; Uncle Vanya; Oedipus; The Critic; 1957: Waltz of the Toreadors; 1963: The School for Scandal; 1970: Home; 1976: No Man's Land.

Select TV: 1963: Hedda Gabler (sp); 1967: Blanding's Castle (series); 1969: Twelfth Night (sp); 1970: David Copperfield (theatrical in UK); 1971: She Stoops to Conquer (sp); Home (sp); 1973: Upon This Rock; 1974: Frankenstein: The True Story; 1977: Jesus of Nazareth (ms); The Man in the Iron Mask; 1979: Charlie Muffin; 1982: Witness for the Prosecution; 1983: Wagner.

DON RICKLES

BORN: NEW YORK, NY, MAY 8, 1926. ED: AADA.

Long before stand-up comedy got downright nasty, Don Rickles was about as abrasive and insulting as that field had to offer. Trouble was, this sort of thing couldn't sustain a half-hour television series, let alone a full-length feature, so the Rickles who showed up on screen was a milder version of the one audiences loved being barbecued by. Originally he was just another actor getting work on live television and in features, starting with *Run Silent, Run Deep*, where he was part of Clark Gable's submarine crew, and as a bad guy in *The Rat Race*, trying to lead Debbie Reynolds into a life of prostitution. To supplement his meager income, he put together a comedy act for the clubs that went nowhere until he started letting the hecklers have it back with some stinging barbs. In time he was getting booked on the talk shows and became a favorite guest during the 1960s, where he could liven up many an otherwise routine affair. Films saw him playing a carny sharpie in *X: The Man with the X-Ray Eyes*, and one of the adult dim-wits in

four of the AIP "beach" movies, starting with *Pajama Party*, in which he was an alien. There were failed attempts at weekly television series, a supporting bit as a card dealer in *Where It's At*, and a larger one, as a member of Clint Eastwood's platoon of thieves in *Kelly's Heroes*. In time he found steadier employment as a Vegas regular with occasional guest shots on the small screen. Therefore it had been a while since most folks had thought of seeing him in the movie houses when he played Robert Loggia's henchman in the vampire comedy *Innocent Blood*, literally falling apart after becoming a bloodsucker. Afterward, he had a worthless role as Robert De Niro's lackey in *Casino*, and a better one as the wise-cracking voice of Mr. Potato-Head in *Toy Story* and its sequel.

Screen: 1958: Run Silent, Run Deep; 1959: The Rabbit Trap; 1960: The Rat Race; 1963: X: The Man With the X-Ray Eyes; 1964: Pajama Party; Muscle Beach Party; Bikini Beach; 1965: Beach Blanket Bingo; 1967: Enter Laughing; 1968: The Money Jungle; 1969: Where It's At; 1970: Kelly's Heroes; 1989: Keaton's Cop; 1992: Innocent Blood; 1995: Casino; Toy Story (voice); 1998: Off the Menu: The Last Days of Chasen's; Dennis the Menace Strikes Again (dtv); Quest for Camelot (voice); Dirty Work; 1999: Toy Story 2 (voice).

Select TV: 1955: A Note of Fear (sp); 1956: The Listener (sp); 1968–69: The Don Rickles Show (series); 1970: The Many Sides of Don Rickles (sp); 1971–72: The Don Rickles Show (series); 1972: Don Rickles: Alive and Kicking (sp); 1976–78: C.P.O. Sharkey (series); 1980: For the Love of It; 1984: Foul-Ups Bleeps and Blunders (series); 1988: The Don Rickles Special (sp); 1993: Daddy Dearest (series).

THELMA RITTER

BORN: BROOKLYN, NY, FEBRUARY 14, 1905. ED: AADA. DIED: FEBRUARY 5, 1969.

The dry-witted, stinging, Brooklynese delivery of Thelma Ritter made her one of the best supporting players in the history of movies. For more than 20 years her name in the opening credits guaranteed a smile of recognition, not to mention frequent salvation of some otherwise dreary offerings. Onstage since childhood, she acted in stock before making her Broadway debut in 1926, in *The Shelf*. Work was less than plentiful for Ritter and her husband, Joseph Moran, so the latter switched interests to advertising, eventually becoming president of the firm of Young & Rubican. This allowed his wife to retire and raise their children, while taking occasional jobs on radio. Director George Seaton offered her a small part in the Christmas classic-to-be *Miracle on 34th Street* and her scene-stealing moment as a mom impressed that Santa Claus has sent her from Macy's to a rival department store earned her a contract with 20th Century-Fox. Between playing a gossip in *A Letter to Three Wives* and a maid in *Father Was a Fullback*, she showed her serious side as a concerned ghetto mom in Universal's well-intentioned look a juvenile delinquency, *City Across the River*. If these weren't proof enough that she had something very special to offer, her role as Bette Davis's sassy dresser in *All About Eve* clinched it, with Ritter making a meal out of one of the best scripts ever written. It brought her her first Oscar nomination and she would be in the running so frequently over the next 12 years that she would earn the dubious distinction of earning the most nominations in the supporting category without a win.

Her other Oscar mentions came for playing John Lund's displaced, outspoken mother, who poses as his cook, in *The Mating Season*, a central role despite getting *fourth* billing and in many ways the best screen showcase she would ever get; the nurse of crippled Susan Hayward in *With a Song in My Heart*, probably the least distinctive of her nominated parts; a pathetic informer, who winds up getting whacked, in *Pickup on South Street*, easily the best thing in the movie; Doris Day's comically soused cleaning lady in the box-office smash *Pillow Talk*; and Burt Lancaster's loving mom in *Bird Man of Alcatraz*. Amid these she was also superb as James Stewart's sardonic nurse in *Rear Window*, which, along with *Eve*, would probably become her most memorable and enduring role. Almost getting star billing, she was Monty Woolley's daughter-in-law in the forgettable *As Young as You Feel*, and the marriage broker who sways Jeanne Crain from a married man to Scott Brady in *The Model and the Marriage Broker*. In smaller parts she was a character based on but not referred to as Molly Brown in *Titanic*; Fred Astaire's sardonic (of course!) secretary in *Daddy Long Legs*; Edward G. Robinson's wife in *A Hole in the Head*; and a divorcee in the sad and moody *The Misfits*. Her services were never more needed in the 1960s when she ended up in one limp comedy after another including *For Love or Money*; *A New Kind of Love*; *Move Over, Darling*; and *What's So Bad About Feeling Good?* There was a more serious Ritter in *The Incident*, as one of the passengers held hostage aboard a subway, and a trip to Broadway for *New Girl in Town*, a musical version of *Anna Christie*, for which she did get to bring home an award at last, the Tony. On television she won great acclaim for playing a Bronx mother in Paddy Chayefsky's *The Catered Affair*, but her old *Eve* co-star Bette Davis got the part when it was filmed for the big screen by MGM.

Screen: 1947: Miracle on 34th Street; 1949: A Letter to Three Wives; City Across the River; Father Was a Fullback; 1950: Perfect Strangers; All About Eve; I'll Get By; 1951: The Mating Season; As Young as You Feel; The Model and the Marriage Broker; 1952: With a Song in My Heart; 1953: Titanic; The Farmer Takes a Wife; Pickup on South Street; 1954: Rear Window; 1955: Daddy Long Legs; Lucy Gallant; 1956: The Proud and Profane; 1959: A Hole in the Head; Pillow Talk; 1961: The Misfits; The Second Time Around; 1962: Bird Man of Alcatraz; 1963: How the West Was Won; For Love or Money; A New Kind of Love; Move Over, Darling; 1965: Boeing-Boeing; 1968: The Incident; What's So Bad About Feeling Good?

NY Stage: 1926: The Shelf; 1931: In Times Square; 1957: New Girl in Town; 1966: UTBU.

Select TV: 1953: The Laughmaker (sp); 1955: The Ghost Writer (sp); The Show-Off (sp); The Catered Affair (sp); The Late Christopher Bean (sp); 1957: The Human Pattern (sp); 1960: Sarah's Laughter (sp).

RITZ BROTHERS

BORN: NEWARK, NJ. RAISED IN BROOKLYN, NY.
Al: BORN: AUGUST 27, 1901.
DIED: DECEMBER 22, 1965.
Jimmy : BORN: OCTOBER 5, 1904.
DIED: NOVEMBER 17, 1985.
Harry: BORN: MAY 22, 1907.
DIED: MARCH 29, 1986.

The Brothers Ritz aimed low, all but inducing themselves into states of apoplexy in their pop-eyed mugging. It worked for some, and sent shudders down the spines of others. If they had a plus side it was that they usually worked some song and dance into their shtick. However, their biggest flaw, outside of their over-dependency on facial tics, was a lack of distinguishable characteristics — one Ritz didn't seem all that much different than another. They began separate dalliances in vaudeville in the early 1920s before their fourth brother, George, became their agent and suggested they become a team — which they did, making their professional bow as such in 1925, in Coney Island. Becoming successful draws in vaudeville, they were asked by impresario Earl Carroll to do some routines in his 1925 production *The Florida Girl*, followed by some revue shows. As a result they did a two-reeler for Educational Pictures, called "Hotel Anchovy," and this served as their screen test for 20th Century-Fox, who figured they could use them as comic relief in some of their musicals. Their first such assignment was in *Sing, Baby, Sing*, which starred Alice Faye, as did *On the Avenue* and *You Can't Have Everything*, the latter featuring a typical Ritz moment of sophistication, a song tributing long underwear. In between, they got on roller skates in *One in a Million*, then went to Goldwyn for his ragtag review *The Goldwyn Follies*, where their big set piece was the number "Serenade to a Fish." All of these did quite nicely at the box office, so their home studio gave them more to do in *Kentucky Moonshine*, as fake hillbillies, and *Straight Place and Show*, a racetrack farce. Their best chance came when the studio did a semi-musical, tongue-in-cheek version of *The Three Musketeers*, with Don Ameche as D'Artagnan, and the brothers pretending to be the title characters. They were starred in a moldy comical thriller, *The Gorilla*, which caused them to balk at the material they were being given and walk out on their contracts. After all was settled, they did one more movie for Fox, *Pack Up Your Troubles*, and then went elsewhere, just as interest was beginning to wane.

Universal snatched them up and plunked them opposite the Andrews Sisters in *Argentine Nights*, in addition to starring them in three other "B" films, including the inevitable western romp, *Hi'Ya, Chum*, and a gangster spoof, *Never a Dull Moment*, which signaled the end of the Ritzes as movie stars. They retreated to the nightclub circuit and then found themselves doing guest spots on television when that new medium arrived. They were still plugging away at their decidedly unsubtle act when brother Al suffered a heart attack and died in 1965. The remaining Ritzes, Harry and Jimmy, had their admirers and they were dragged out to do some goofing around in *Blazing Stewardesses* and *Won Ton Ton, the Dog Who Saved Hollywood*, as cleaning women (!), while longtime fan Mel Brooks hired Harry for a bit in a tailor shop in that director's homage to old-time humor, *Silent Movie*.

Screen (features): AL, JIMMY, AND HARRY: 1936: Sing, Baby, Sing; 1937: One in a Million; On the Avenue; You Can't Have Everything; Life Begins in College; 1938: The Goldwyn Follies; Kentucky Moonshine; Straight Place and Show; 1939: The Three Musketeers; The Gorilla; Pack Up Your Troubles; 1940: Argentine Nights; 1942: Behind the Eight Ball; 1943: Hi'Ya Chum; Never a Dull Moment.

HARRY AND JIMMY: 1975: Blazing Stewardesses; Won Ton Ton, the Dog Who Saved Hollywood.

HARRY: 1976: Silent Movie.

NY Stage: 1925: The Florida Girl; 1931: Everybody's Welcome; 1932: Earl Carroll Vanities; 1934: Casino Varieties; Continental Varieties.

JASON ROBARDS

(JASON NELSON ROBARDS, JR.) BORN: CHICAGO, IL, JULY 26, 1922. DIED: DECEMBER 26, 2000.

Not your conventional matinee-idol type, Jason Robards had a long, hang-dog look to his face and possessed of a strong, resonant voice that could be used magnificently to play defeated, troubled men, or persons of cunning or villainy. He was so good at what he did that people came to accept him as a "movie star," or rather a leading "character player," which allowed him to fluctuate back and forth between carrying an occasional movie, leading the supporting cast, or merely popping up in others expressly for the money. His father, Jason Robards (Sr.), was an actor with a long history in the theatre and more than 100 movie credits to his name. His parents divorced when he was five years old and young Jason spent the bulk of his time living with dad around the film business, which might explain why he had no attraction at first to following in the old man's footsteps. After naval duty during World War II, he changed his mind and attended the American Academy of Dramatic Arts, after which he made his professional debut in Rehoboth Beach, Delaware, in 1947, as Jason Robards, Jr. Later that same year he was first seen on the Broadway stage in bit parts, including that of the rear end of the cow in a Children's World Theatre production of *Jack and the Beanstalk*. A meeting with director Jose Quintero changed his fortunes, and under his guidance Robards showed up in two plays by Eugene O'Neill, a revival of *The Iceman Cometh*, as Hickey, and the original production of *Long Day's Journey Into Night*, as James, Jr. The critics were in awe and Robards was, very quickly, hailed as the supreme interpreter of the author's work, winning an Obie for the former and a Theatre World Award for the latter. Further acclaim came with *The Disenchanted*, which won him a Tony Award. By this time, he had accepted an offer to appear in a movie, MGM's *The Journey*, as a wounded Russian refugee, more than holding his own against established film names Yul Brynner and Deborah Kerr.

He was unlucky with his two follow-up pictures, *By Love Possessed*, as Lana Turner's impotent husband, and the critically hated rendering of F. Scott Fitzgerald's *Tender is the Night*, as the psychiatrist who makes the mistake of marrying wealthy Jennifer Jones. However, he was the sole member of the original cast to repeat his part in the 1962 motion picture adaptation of *Long Day's Journey Into Night*. Although meant for the art houses, this was the film that really established him as movie material and showed Hollywood just how strong he could be on the big screen. There were more raves for his work as George S. Kaufman in otherwise poorly reviewed bio of Moss Hart, *Act One*, and then another stage triumph in *A Thousand Clowns*. He lucked out again when the time came to make the movie, and the cinematic interpretation of the piece remains one of the sharpest of all 1960s motion picture comedies. The role of nonconformist Murray Burns, which marvelously utilized Robards's trenchant sense of sardonic humor, was one of his cinematic peaks. The film itself was up for a Best Picture Oscar, but Robards was, amazingly, not even in the running for the best actor trophy. There was a fluffy sex comedy from a Broadway show he *hadn't* done, *Any Wednesday*, with Jane Fonda as his mistress, then supporting work in two superior ensembles, *A Big Hand for the Little Lady*, as a gambler, and *Divorce American Style*, as Jean Simmons's ex. He slipped up badly with his broad interpretation of Al Capone in *The St. Valentine's Day Massacre*; captured the seediness of a cheeky burlesque entertainer in the enjoyable *The Night They Raided Minsky's*; was Vanessa Redgrave's wealthy lover, Paris Singer, in the outstanding biopic *Isadora*; and looked uncomfortable in the boring spaghetti western *Once Upon a Time in the West*, in which he and Henry Fonda suffered the further indignity of being billed *below* Claudia Cardinale. He remained in that genre with far better results, playing the grubby prospector destroyed by the changing of the old West, in one of director Sam Peckinpah's best films, *The Ballad of Cable Hogue*.

Nobody was raving about the love story *Fools*, in which he was

a horror movie actor shacking up with much younger Katharine Ross, and the reaction was downright hostile to his Brutus in the 1971 version of *Julius Caesar*. With these, not to mention his disinterested work as General Short in the Pearl Harbor epic *Tora! Tora! Tora!*; the slumming he seemed to be doing in the horror opus *Murders in the Rue Morgue*; and the would-be cult film *A Boy and His Dog*, it was little wonder he retreated back to O'Neill onstage, winning greater prestige reviving *Long Day's Journey* (this time as the father), and playing the older version of James Tyrone, Jr. in *A Moon for the Misbegotten*. Fortunately the movies were not done with him and he was given a pair of literate scripts that required him to play some real-life men, *Washington Post*-editor Ben Bradley in *All the President's Men*, and author Dashiell Hammett in *Julia*. These were not flashy parts, but they showed just how brilliant he could be through subtlety and nuance. He wound up with back-to-back Academy Awards for Best Supporting Actor, the only actor to date to do so in that particular category. (As if to emphasize the distance he wished to maintain from Hollywood, he did not show up for the ceremony on either occasion). There were villain parts in the dull *Comes a Horseman*, trying to snatch Jane Fonda's land; and the ultra-silly *Hurricane*, as Mia Farrow's disapproving father; and then another great biographical part, in *Melvin and Howard*, in which he was creepily effective as the injured Howard Hughes. This one got him a third Oscar nomination. In star parts he was a member of the team hoping to *Raise the Titanic!*; Marsha Mason's con-man dad in a weak Neil Simon comedy, *Max Dugan Returns*; and the small-town librarian battling evil in *Something Wicked This Way Comes*, a big-budget, Disney-backed adaptation of Ray Bradbury's novel that pleased no one except the author.

Robards had, by this time, become one of the most admirer performers of his age, and was constantly employed either on the small screen, including *Inherit the Wind*, for which he won an Emmy Award as attorney Henry Drummond; in the theatre, where he returned to *Long Day's Journey* a third time; or in motion pictures. The latter allowed him to play a country grandpa in *Square Dance*; a roaring drunk in *Bright Lights, Big City* (Robards's own drinking problems over the years had been well known); Diane Keaton's lawyer in *The Good Mother*; and a determined cop in the Bill Murray comedy *Quick Change*. There was an indescribably bizarre leading role in the teen comedy *Dream a Little Dream*, which required him to swap bodies with Corey Feldman and to sing the title song (earlier in his career he had done something called *Mr. Sycamore*, which required him to turn into a tree!); and then some worthwhile supporting roles in *Parenthood*, as Steve Martin's wearied and unloving dad; *The Adventures of Huck Finn*, adding some spice to this fair adaptation, as the King; and *Philadelphia*, as the bigoted senior law partner who fires Tom Hanks when he discovers he has AIDS. Slowing down, there were mere cameos in such movies as *Little Big League*, *Crimson Tide*, *Beloved*, and *Enemy of the State* (he didn't bother to take billing in the last three). Amid these he two more meaty roles, as the repulsive, incestuous father of Michelle Pfeiffer and Jessica Lange in the badly botched rendering of the Pulitzer Prize-winning novel *A Thousand Acres*, and as the dying millionaire in the ensemble piece *Magnolia*, playing the entire part while lying down and doing so with the sort of conviction that suggested that the actual end was near. About a year after its release he did indeed pass away, having suffered from cancer. His second marriage (1961–69) had been to actress Lauren Bacall. Their son, Sam, also became an actor. Robards was, early on, often billed as Jason Robards, Jr. In so much as he surpassed his father in terms of stature, many sources now refer to the elder as Jason Robards, Sr. so as not to confuse.

Screen: AS JASON ROBARDS, JR.: 1959: The Journey; 1961: By Love Possessed; Tender Is the Night; 1962: Long Day's Journey Into Night.

AS JASON ROBARDS: 1963: Act One; 1965: A Thousand Clowns; 1966: Any Wednesday; A Big Hand for the Little Lady; 1967: Divorce American Style; The St. Valentine's Day Massacre; Hour of the Gun; 1968: The Night They Raided Minsky's; Isadora; 1969: Once Upon a Time in the West; 1970: The Ballad of Cable Hogue; Operation Snafu/Situation Normal All Fouled Up; Tora! Tora! Tora!; Fools; 1971: Julius Caesar; Johnny Got His Gun; Murders in the Rue Morgue; 1972: The War Between Men and Women; 1973: Pat Garrett and Billy the Kid; The Execution/The Spy Who Never Was; 1975: A Boy and His Dog; Mr. Sycamore; 1976: All the President's Men; 1977: Julia; 1978: Comes a Horseman; 1979: Hurricane; 1980: Raise the Titanic!; Caboblanco; Melvin and Howard; 1981: The Legend of the Lone Ranger; 1982: Burden of Dreams; 1983: Max Dugan Returns; Something Wicked This Way Comes; 1987: Square Dance; 1988: Bright Lights, Big City; The Good Mother; 1989: Dream a Little Dream; Parenthood; 1990: Quick Change; 1991: Reunion; 1992: Storyville; 1993: The Adventures of Huck Finn; The Trial; Philadelphia; 1994: The Paper; Little Big League; 1995: Crimson Tide; 1997: A Thousand Acres; 1998: Heartwood (dtv); The Real Macaw (nUSr); Beloved; Enemy of the State; 1999: Magnolia.

NY Stage: 1947: Jack and the Beanstalk; 1953: American Gothic; 1956: The Iceman Cometh; 1956: Long Day's Journey Into Night; 1958: The Disenchanted; 1960: Toys in the Attic; 1961: Big Fish, Little Fish; 1962: A Thousand Clowns; 1964: After the Fall; But for Whom Charlie; Hughie; 1965: The Devils; 1968: We Bombed in New Haven; 1972: The Country Girl; 1973: A Moon For the Misbegotten; 1976: Long Day's Journey Into Night (revival; also dir.); 1977: A Touch of the Poet; 1979: O'Neill and Carlotta; 1983: You Can't Take it With You; 1985: The Iceman Cometh (revival); 1987: A Month of Sundays; 1988: Long Day's Journey Into Night (revival); Ah, Wilderness!; 1989: Love Letters (and Bdwy); 1991: Park Your Car in Harvard Yard; 1994: No Man's Land; 1995: Moonlight (ob); Molly Sweeney (ob).

Select TV: 1955: A Picture in the Paper (sp); The Incredible World of Horace Ford (sp); The Death of Billy the Kid (sp); The Outsiders (sp); 1956: Even the Weariest River (sp); Proud Passage (sp); 1957: Nobody's Town (sp); The Big Build-Up (sp); 24 Hours to Dawn (sp); 1959: For Whom the Bell Tolls (sp); People Kill People Sometimes (sp); Billy Budd (sp); A Doll's House (sp); 1960: The Iceman Cometh (sp); 1962: That's Where the Town's Going (sp); 1963: One Day in the Life of Ivan Denisovich (sp); 1964: Abe Lincoln in Illinois (sp); 1966: Shipwrecked (sp); Noon Wine (sp); 1967: The Belle of 14th Street (sp); 1972: The House Without a Christmas Tree (sp); 1973: Old Faithful (sp); The Thanksgiving Treasure (sp); 1974: The Country Girl (sp); 1975: The Easter Promise (sp); A Moon for the Misbegotten (sp); 1976: Addie and the King of Hearts (sp); 1977: Washington: Behind Closed Doors (ms); 1978: A Christmas to Remember; 1980: Haywire; FDR: The Last Year; 1982: Hughie (sp); 1983: The Day After; 1984: Sakharov; You Can't Take It With You (sp); 1985: The Long Hot Summer; The Atlanta Child Murders; 1986: Johnny Bull; The Last Frontier; 1987: Laguna Heat; Norman Rockwell's Breaking Home Ties; 1988: Inherit the Wind; The Christmas Wife; 1991: The Perfect Tribute; Chernobyl: The Final Warning; An Inconvenient Woman; Black Rainbow; Mark Twain & Me; 1993: Heidi; 1994: The Enemy Within; 1995: My Antonia; Journey; 2000: Going Home.

RACHEL ROBERTS

BORN: LLANELLY, CARMARTHENSHIRE, WALES, SEPTEMBER 20, 1927. ED: UNIV. OF WALES, RADA. DIED: NOVEMBER 27, 1980.

Not blessed with the glamour usually associated with stardom, Rachel Roberts went for the grit and came up with a smattering of interesting movie parts before the pain she was so good at portraying on screen turned out to be the real thing. Starting out with the Shakespeare Memorial Theatre in Stratford-on-Avon, she then made her London debut, in 1953, in The Buccaneer. In the 1950s, while acting with the Old Vic, she began popping up in fairly unimportant roles in such movies as Valley of Song and The Good Companions, and then landed a fine part in one of the wealth of gritty angry-young-man films of the 1960s, Saturday Night and Sunday Morning, in which she was outstanding as Albert Finney's pregnant mistress. Staying in the same mode of blowsy women in bad relationships, she went through the pain of dallying with Richard Harris in This Sporting Life, her world-weary work good enough to earn her an Oscar nomination. Just prior to that she married (1962–71) Rex Harrison and it was with him that she did one of her few movies during that period, A Flea in Her Ear, a flop rendering of a Geroges Feydeau farce. With Finney again she did the scarcely seen Alpha Beta; experienced Hollywood trash in a big way playing one of the Doctors' Wives; and found herself in her two biggest hits with Murder on the Orient Express, as Wendy Hiller's traveling companion; and Foul Play, as one of the villains in this Goldie Hawn comedy. There were good roles in Picnic at Hanging Rock, as the teacher whose students mysteriously disappear, and Yanks, as Lisa Eichhorn's dying mum. She moved to California in the mid-1970s, taking a role on the short-lived series The Tony Randall Show. It was while there that she took her own life, poisoning herself in the backyard of her home, having suffered from mental illness, severe depression, and chronic alcoholism for many years. Her final credits, the theatrical film Charlie Chan and the Curse of the Dragon Queen, and the television movie The Wall, were both released posthumously.

Screen: 1953: The Weak and the Wicked; Valley of Song; The Limping Man; 1954: The Crowded Day; 1957: The Good Companions; 1960: Our Man in Havana; Saturday Night and Sunday Morning; 1961: Girls on Approval; 1963: This Sporting Life; 1968: A Flea in Her Ear; 1969: The Reckoning/A Matter of Honor; 1971: Wild Rovers; Doctors' Wives; 1973: The Belstone Fox; O Lucky Man!; Alpha Beta; 1974: Murder on the Orient Express; 1977: Picnic at Hanging Rock; 1978: Foul Play; 1979: Yanks; When a Stranger Calls; 1981: Charlie Chan and the Curse of the Dragon Queen.

NY Stage: 1973: The Visit; Chemin de Fer; 1975: Habeas Corpus; 1979: Once a Catholic.

Select TV: 1966: Blithe Spirit (sp); 1969: The Destiny of a Spy 1972: Baffled!; 1974: Great Expectations; 1976–78: The Tony Randall Show (series); 1977: A Circle of Children; 1979: 3 By Cheever: The Sorrows of Gin (sp); The Old Crowd (sp); 1980: The Hostage Tower; 1982: The Wall.

CLIFF ROBERTSON

BORN: LA JOLLA, CA, SEPTEMBER 9, 1925. ED: ANTIOCH COL.

Good enough to win an Oscar but not outstanding enough to overcome the frequently mediocre material he was involved in, Cliff Robertson was personable and forceful when he needed to be, a commendable working's man's actor, hardly the sort to garner guaranteed raves, hardly the sort to offend. He entered the acting field after military service, joining a touring company production of *Three Men on a Horse* in 1947. Going to New York to seek employment, he did some live television dramas before landing a part in *The Wisteria Trees* on Broadway in 1955. Joshua Logan was the author of *Trees*, so Robertson was fresh in that man's mind when Logan was assigned to direct the film version of *Picnic*. He got cast as the fiancé of Kim Novak, who loses her to best friend William Holden, and his was one of several good performances in what turned out to be one of the most popular movies of 1955. The studio that released it, Columbia, put Robertson under contract, and let him shine in his immediate follow-up role, playing Joan Crawford's mentally unhinged younger lover in *Autumn Leaves*, helping the piece to rise above the expected soap opera level. Back on Broadway, he won great acclaim and a Theatre World Award for playing the young drifter in *Orpheus Descending*, but was passed over in favor of Marlon Brando when it was adapted for the movies as *The Fugitive Kind*. Instead he did some slight assignments, the Jane Powell musical *The Girl Most Likely*, as one of her three fiancés; and the beach frolic *Gidget*, which, although popular, seemed somewhat beneath him. There was also a major role as an officer in *The Naked and the Dead*; his performance being one of the better things about this muddled adaptation that hardly pleased readers of Norman Mailer's groundbreaking war novel. Columbia finally gave him top billing in *Battle of the Coral Sea*, but this was a very minor war drama, with Robertson as a submarine captain escaping from the Japanese.

He was hardly considered important enough at this point to carry a film on his name alone, so he took a foreign job in *As the Sea Rages*; a secondary part to Dean Martin and Shirley MacLaine in *All in a Night's Work*; swung from a trapeze with Esther Williams in *The Big Show*; and did an icky Debbie Reynolds comedy, *My Six Loves*, as a preacher. Between these he did a tough melodrama, *Underworld USA*, which found certain favor over the years because it was directed by overrated cult figure Sam Fuller, and was the main focus in a popular ensemble piece, *The Interns*, sacrificing his medical career to perform an abortion on his lover, Suzy Parker. There was much press on the fact that President Kennedy personally selected him to portray him as a young sailor in the war epic *PT-109* and, although it would often be mentioned on Robertson's list of notable films, it didn't fair well at the box office. There was a cutesy romantic comedy, *Sunday in New York*, as Jane Fonda's overly protective brother, and then, opposite her dad, Henry, he was a determined presidential candidate in the splendid 1964 film version of Gore Vidal's Broadway triumph *The Best Man*, giving one of his best performances in what might very well have been his best film. Since it didn't do the business it deserved, Robertson went back to soap operas like *Love Has Many Faces*, in which he was a cad cheating on rich wife Lana Turner, and took a secondary part in *The Honey Pot*, as an actor hired to help Rex Harrison deceive his mistresses. Therefore he was hardly on a winning streak when he wound up with two financial successes in 1968, *The Devil's Brigade*, the blatant rip-off of *The Dirty Dozen*, and *Charly*, an expansion of a television drama, *The Two Worlds of Charlie Gordon*, that he'd originally done back in 1961. Having secured the movie rights, he gave himself a meaty role as the mentally challenged baker's assistant who temporarily becomes a genius via a break-through operation before reverting back to his previous state. It was a solid performance in a decent film, that turned into a career high when he won the Academy Award for Best Actor of 1968 against some fairly stiff competition.

Now considered a possible money attraction, Robertson had a string of starring roles in box-office failures: *Too Late the Hero*, a war film on which he clashed off screen with co-star Michael Caine; the critically acclaimed *J.W. Coop*, the story of a drifter who aspires to rodeo stardom, which he himself directed and wrote; *The Great Northfield Minnesota Raid*, a bleak look at the James Brothers, with Robertson as Jesse; *Ace Eli and Rodger of the Skies*, which only became notable in later years because Steven Spielberg helped write it; and *Man on a Swing*, a police thriller with Joel Grey. Faring somewhat better was an atmospheric chiller, *Obsession*, in which he married Geneviève Bujold because she resembled his dead wife. By the late 1970s he had become basically a television name, and then entered a period of industry blacklisting after exposing the unscrupulous financial dealings of studio head David Begelman. He did return to theatrical features in the 1980s, playing Jacqueline Bisset's cold-hearted husband in *Class*; a steely executive in the sci-fi offering *Brainstorm*; and, best of all, *Playboy* tycoon Hugh Hefner in director Bob Fosse's chilling dissection of fame, *Star 80*. After that it was a combination of television (including a role on the nightly soap *Falcon Crest*), voice-overs for AT&T commercials, and an occasional movie part, including *Malone*, as the villain plotting world domination; *Wild Hearts Can't Be Broken*, as a traveling showman in the Buffalo Bill vein; *Escape from L.A.*, this time as a fictitious President of the United States; and the hugely popular comic book come to life, *Spider-Man*, as Tobey Maguire's doomed uncle. On television he won an Emmy Award for the 1965 episode "The Game" from the anthology series *Bob Hope Presents the Chrysler Theatre*. He was married from 1966 to 1989 to actress Dina Merrill.

Screen: 1955: Picnic; 1956: Autumn Leaves; 1957: The Girl Most Likely; 1958: The Naked and the Dead; 1959: Gidget; Battle of the Coral Sea; 1960: As the Sea Rages; 1961: All in a Night's Work; Underworld USA; The Big Show; 1962: The Interns; 1963: My Six Loves; PT-109; 1964: Sunday in New York; The Best Man; 633 Squadron; 1965: Love Has Many Faces; Masquerade; Up From the Beach; 1967: The Honey Pot; 1968: The Devil's Brigade; Charly; 1970: Too Late the Hero; 1972: J.W. Coop (and dir.; wr.); The Great Northfield Minnesota Raid; 1973: Ace Eli and Rodger of the Skies; 1974: Man of a Swing; 1975: Three Days of the Condor; Out of Season; 1976: Midway; Shoot; Obsession; 1977: Fraternity Row (narrator); 1978: Dominique/Dominique Is Dead; 1979: The Pilot/Danger in the Skies (and dir.); 1983: Class; Brainstorm; Star 80; 1985: Shaker Run; 1987: Malone; 1991: Wild Hearts Can't Be Broken; 1992: Wind; 1994: Renaissance Man; 1995: Pakten/Waiting for Sunset (nUSr); 1996: Escape From L.A.; 1997: Race/Melting Pot (dtv); 1998: Assignment Berlin (nUSr); 2000: Mach 2 (dtv); Family Tree; 2001: Frightmare/Paranoid (dtv); 2002: Falcon Down (dtv); Spider-Man; The 13th Child: The Legend of the Jersey Devil (and co-wr.).

NY Stage: 1953: Late Love; 1955: The Wisteria Trees; 1957: Orpheus Descending; 1990: Love Letters.

Select TV: 1954: The Use of Dignity (sp); 1956: A Fair Shake (sp); 1958: Natchez (sp); The Days of Wine and Roses (sp); 1959: Goodbye Johnny (sp); The Hard Road (sp); Shadow of Evil (sp); 1960: The Cruel Day (sp); The Man Who Knew Tomorrow (sp); 1961: The Two Worlds of Charlie Gordon (sp); The Small Elephants (sp); Man on a Mountaintop (sp); 1962: Saturday's Children (sp); 1965: The Game (sp); 1967: Verdict for Terror; 1968: The Sunshine Patriot; 1973: The Man Without a Country; 1974: A Tree Grows in Brooklyn; 1975: My Father's House; 1976: Return to Earth; 1977: Washington: Behind Closed Doors (ms); 1978: Overboard; 1982: Two of a Kind; 1983–84: Falcon Crest (series); **1985:** The Key to Rebecca; **1986:** Dreams of Gold: The Mel Fisher Story; **1987:** Ford: The Man and the Machine; **1990:** Dead Reckoning; **1995:** Judith Krantz's Dazzle.

DALE ROBERTSON

(DAYLE ROBERTSON) BORN: HARRAH, OK, JULY 14, 1923. ED: OK MILITARY ACAD.

Like many before, during, and since his years as a leading man, Dale Robertson got the he-man push, but didn't show enough sparkle to make the grade, and therefore wound up a dependable, stoic attraction of programmer westerns. A one-time boxer, football player, and soldier, he was looking for work in California when somebody suggested he try the movies. He was first seen doing bit parts in films like *Flamingo Road*, as a cop, and *The Girl from Jones Beach*, as a lifeguard, before 20th Century-Fox signed him up to play Jesse James, supporting Randolph Scott, in *Fighting Man of the Plains*. This was followed by another with Scott, *Caribou Trail*, after which he tried in vain to woo Betty Grable away from higher billed Dan Dailey in *Call Me Mister*, and stood by college girlfriend Jeanne Crain in *Take Care of My Little Girl*. He was top billed as a Napoleonic era lawyer in a quickly forgotten action picture, *Lydia Bailey*, and as the widower who starts life anew in *Return of the Texan*. He was back with Grable for *The Farmer Takes a Wife*, made during her waning years as a box-office star, with Robertson no match for Henry Fonda in the original version. Suddenly the assignments were getting shorter and cheaper, including *The Silver Whip*, swearing vengeance on bandit John Kellogg, and *The Gambler from Natchez*, swearing vengeance on those who killed his dad. His days with Fox now over, he went elsewhere, befriending the title character in *Sitting Bull*, holding off the Indians in *Dakota Incident*, and going from gunman to judge in *Law of the Lawless*. By this time he had become a staple of the small screen western, where he starred in the hit series *Tales of Wells Fargo*, and later hosted *Death Valley Days*.

Screen: **1948:** The Boy With Green Hair; **1949:** The Girl from Jones Beach; Flamingo Road; Fighting Man of the Plains; **1950:** Caribou Trail; Two Flags West; **1951:** Call Me Mister; Take Care of My Little Girl; Golden Girl; **1952:** Lydia Bailey; Return of the Texan; The Outcasts of Poker Flat; O. Henry's Full House; **1953:** The Silver Whip; The Farmer Takes a Wife; City of Bad Men; Devil's Canyon; **1954:** The Gambler from Natchez; Sitting Bull; **1955:** Top of the World; Son of Sinbad; **1956:** High Terrace; A Day of Fury; Dakota Incident; **1957:** Hell Canyon Outlaws; **1958:** Fast and Sexy; **1964:** Law of the Lawless; Blood on the Arrow; Coast of Skeletons; **1965:** The Man From Button Willow (voice); **1966:** One Eyed Soldiers.

Select TV: **1956:** The Face (sp); A Tale of Wells Fargo (sp); **1957:** The Still Trumpet (sp); **1957–62:** Tales of Wells Fargo (series); **1966–68:** The Iron Horse (series); **1968–72:** Death Valley Days (series); **1974:** Melvin Purvis: G-Man; **1975:** The Kansas City Massacre; **1979:** The Last Ride of the Dalton Gang; **1981:** Dynasty (series); **1987–88:** J.J. Starbuck (series).

PAUL ROBESON

BORN: PRINCETON, NJ, APRIL 9, 1898. ED: RUTGERS UNIV., COLUMBIA UNIV. LAW SCH. DIED: JANUARY 23, 1976.

His became one of the legendary names of the 20th century but Paul Robeson's fame was due more to his achievements as a singer and an activist than his brief and choppy career in cinema. At Rutgers he had been not only an exceptional student, but a leading athlete as well. Initially he chose to pursue a career in law but during his studies began dabbling in theatrics, a field that he realized would offer a black man greater opportunities during the 1920s. He sang and acted in both America and Britain, notably in Eugene O'Neill's *The Emperor Jones*, and in the 1932 revival of *Show Boat*. There had been two inconsequential movie roles but his first of note was in the 1932 movie version of *The Emperor Jones*, which brought him great acclaim though it did not fare as well at the box office as it had onstage. The film was a rare case of a black performer carrying a Hollywood production, but it did not open any further doors in that town for Robeson or for any other black actors at the time.

He received his next offer for a lead from the British, *Sanders of the River*. He hated the finished product, in which he was an African chief befriending British commissioner Leslie Banks, and returned to Hollywood to reprise his stage role as Joe in Universal 1936 rendering of *Show Boat*. Although it was a secondary part, he made a lasting impact, singing "Ol' Man River" as well as a delightful duet with Hattie McDaniel, "Ah Still Suits Me." Determined not to play stereotypical and demeaning roles, he returned to England for *Song of Freedom*, as a singer who is heir to an African dynasty; *Jericho Jackson*, as a deserter who becomes a Bedouin chief; *King Solomon's Mines*, leading the expedition through Africa; and *The Proud Valley*, as a miner. The last was one of the few roles he was pleased with, but he was disgusted by his segment in the multi-part *Tales of Manhattan*, in which he and Ethel Waters were simpleton farmers, and never made another movie. In 1943, Robeson triumphed on Broadway as *Othello*, but ran into trouble for his outspoken criticism of racism in America, citing fairer treatment of blacks in the Soviet Union. Not surprisingly he became one of the most tragic victims of the blacklisting period of the 1950s, and his career never fully recovered. It was not until a few years before his death of a stroke, in 1976, that the industry began to put aside the politics and appreciate the artist once again.

Screen: **1925:** Body and Soul; **1930:** Borderline; **1932:** The Emperor Jones; **1935:** Sanders of the River; **1936:** Show Boat; Song of Freedom; **1937:** Big Fella; King Solomon's Mines; Jericho/Dark Sands; **1940:** The Proud Valley; **1942:** Tales of Manhattan; Native Land (narrator).

NY Stage: **1921:** Simon the Cyrenian; **1922:** Taboo; **1924:** The Emperor Jones; All God's Chillun Got Wings; **1926:** Black Boy; **1928:** Porgy; **1932:** Show Boat; **1939:** John Henry; **1943:** Othello.

EDWARD G. ROBINSON

(EMANUEL GOLDENBERG) BORN: BUCHAREST, ROMANIA, DECEMBER 12, 1893. RAISED IN NY. ED: AADA. DIED: JANUARY 26, 1973.

By sheer force and talent, Edward G. Robinson got Hollywood producers and audiences alike to overlook the fact that his was not a pretty puss and became a bona-fide star, one of the classic players of his era. Pug-faced, with a snarling, snapping delivery, he could walk on screen and dominate it fully, despite his tiny, squat frame. His became one of the half-dozen or so most mimicked voices and it is still hard to imagine him saying a line without putting the pointed "see?" at the end of each sentence. Although he was best remembered for tough guys and gangsters, he also played his share of milquetoasts and decent men. Despite some unfortunate lapses into scenery chewing, he was often magnificent and, indeed, has been pointed to more than anyone else as the most shameful example of a great actor who was never once nominated for an Oscar.

Joining his family in New York City at age nine, he became interested in dramatics while in school and made his professional bow in 1913, in Binghamton, New York, in a production of *Paid in Full*. This was followed by rep work, a tour of *Kismet* in Canada, and, finally, Broadway in 1915, in *Under Fire*, where he was billed as E.G. Robinson. He was a fixture there for the next 14 years and, between successes in *Banco* and *The Racket*, he had jobs in two silent films, *Arms and the Woman*, and *The Bright Shawl*. But it was his stage performance in *The Racket* that made Hollywood come calling for real and he was cast as a criminal called The Fox in a melodrama made by Paramount at Astoria Studios, *The Hole in the Wall*. There was more crime stuff at Universal with *Night Ride*, after which he overdid the Italian accent for *A Lady to Love*, an early version of *They Knew What They Wanted*. Universal kept him on the shady side of justice for *Outside the Law*, and cast him as an unlikely Asian in *East Is West*, before he did indeed go west, to Hollywood, for the movie that changed his life.

Little Caesar was, at first glance, just another gangster melodrama but, due in no small way to Robinson's dynamic interpretation of the two-bit hood who rises ruthlessly to the top of the game, it stood out from the pack and became one of the biggest movies of 1930. It is often pointed to as the most influential film of its genre and credited as the impetus for the onslaught of gritty, urban, machine-gun dramas, both good and bad, that would define a part of Hollywood's and, more specifically, Warner Bros. Studios's, image in that era. Robinson became a star and a contract player at Warners, who made him a gambler in *Smart Money*, notable mainly because it placed Robinson opposite a then relatively unknown James Cagney for the first and only time on screen together. Riding high, Robinson got to shine as a fast-talking newspaper editor in *Five Star Final*, which helped wipe away the awful taste of him slipping back into Asian makeup for *The Hatchet Man*, and his performance in *Two Seconds*, where his climactic courtroom speech reached Kabuki-like proportions of silliness. With moustache, he was a crippled fisherman in *Tiger Shark*, and played real-life miner-senator H.A.W. Tabor in *Silver Dollar*; lightened up for the gangster spoof *The Little Giant*; and had the misfortune of linking up with Kay Francis for *I Loved a Woman*. Things were becoming fairly routine at his home lot, so it was no surprise that he accepted offers elsewhere and wound up more satisfied with the results of Columbia's *The Whole Town's Talking*, a once highly-regarded but flaccid concoction, in which he played two roles, a shy clerk and the notorious gangster for whom he is mistaken, in one of director John Ford's mercifully rare forays into humor, and Goldwyn's *Barbary Coast*, as an ambitious saloon keeper, which was pretty much a gangster role but one set in the 1850s, thereby allowing him to wear an earring.

Back at Warner Bros., he was one of the good guys in *Bullets or Ballots*, which marked the first time he shared the screen with the up-and-coming Humphrey Bogart; and then a boxing manager who can't help but tangle with hoods in a good one, *Kid Galahad*, which not only featured Bogart again, but teamed Robinson most effectively with Bette Davis. There was another spoof of criminals, *A Slight Case of Larceny*, a vast improvement over his previous venture into this territory, after which he tangled with Bogart again in the uncomfortably titled *The Amazing Dr. Clitterhouse*, and then tackled a topical subject in *Confessions of a Nazi Spy*, the first Hollywood film to take a look at the growing danger, albeit in a fairly standard manner. He followed this with another picture on a subject the movies weren't quick to speak up on, syphilis, with

the biopic *Dr. Ehrlich's Magic Bullet*. The screenwriters were careful to create an intelligent entertainment on the discovery of the cure for the affliction, while avoiding explicit use of the word; the end result was Robinson's favorite of all his roles. Going for laughs again, he went from criminal to monk in *Brother Orchid*; did another biopic, *A Dispatch from Reuters*, another of his personal favorites; and really lit up the screen as the vicious sea captain in *The Sea Wolf*, the best of the many adaptations of the Jack London tale, though it could hardly be called a faithful rendering. *Manpower* had him sparring over Marlene Dietrich with George Raft, a co-star he over-powered with very little effort, while *Larceny, Inc.* was another of his gangland comedies that clicked, at one point allowing him to dress as Santa Claus. As the failed attorney who tries to impress his former classmates at a reunion, he clearly stole the episodic *Tales of Manhattan*, but was starting to lose some ground with such wartime offerings as *Tampico* and *Mr. Winkle Goes to War*.

His career was thankfully jump-started with a secondary but important role in *Double Indemnity*, as Fred MacMurray's friend and fellow insurance investigator, who tries to solve the murder plot within. It was Robinson at his finest but he had become so dependably good by that point that the performance was taken for granted by many, and there was no Oscar nomination for him among the many that the film received. For director Fritz Lang, he was a good man destroyed by his lust for Joan Bennett in *The Woman in the Window*, a formula that worked so well that they repeated it with even better results in the excellent *Scarlet Street*, a film that also reflected his real-life interest in painting. He was Margaret O'Brien's firm but loving farmer dad in a pleasant bit of Americana, *Our Vines Have Tender Grapes*, and another Nazi hunter in *The Stranger*, looking for evil Orson Welles in small town America. There was a bad man lurking underneath his deceptively simple exterior in *The Red House* (produced for his own Film Guild Corporation company), as there was in the decent adaptation of Arthur Miller's *All My Sons*, in which he was a munitions manufacturer with a dirty secret. Now taking billing *below* Bogart, he was gloriously mean as the gangster who holds the cast hostage in *Key Largo*, then played a ruthless banker who has corrupted his sons in *House of Strangers*, which turned out to be his last important assignment for a spell.

Still a star, he began falling off into second features and programmers with such films as the two-part *Actors and Sin*, as a washed-up thespian in the serious segment; *Big Leaguer*, as the manager of the New York Giants; *The Glass Web*, which was a crime story involving television; *The Violent Men*, which cast him with Barbara Stanwyck, both of them having seen better days; and *A Bullet for Joey*, again teamed with a very tired George Raft. Now officially a "character-star," he showed up looking more than a bit out of place as the trouble-making overseer Dathan in *The Ten Commandments*, which was one of the most popular movies of the 1950s, and as Frank Sinatra's older and wiser brother in another hit, *A Hole in the Head*. There was a heist movie, *Seven Thieves*, which would be followed later in the 1960s by more of the same with *Grand Slam*, *Mad Checkmate/It's Your Move*, *Operation St. Peter's*, and *Never a Dull Moment*. The fact that he was reduced to traveling to Europe to seek employment in any sort of picture merely meant that he was anxious to act. Hollywood gave him work in *Pepe*, one of the guest stars who actually had a substantial role, playing himself, but as a producer, and he was back in that profession for *My Geisha*, then switched over to director for *Two Weeks in Another Town*. He was a decided asset to most of these films and certainly was the best thing about the poorly done, *Rashomon*-inspired western, *The Outrage*, as a con man narrating the story within. There was top billing for the

British-made *A Boy Ten Feet Tall/Sammy Going South*, though his role was clearly a supporting one; a dual role in *The Prize*; and little more than expanded cameos, as a corporate tycoon in *Good Neighbor Sam*; as a mob boss, unbilled and killed off early, in *Robin and the 7 Hoods*; and as secretary of the interior Carl Shurz in the epic *Cheyenne Autumn*. Perhaps his best role during this period was as the gambler Steve McQueen challenges in *The Cincinnati Kid*, playing with cool efficiency against one of the great stars of *his* time. He died in 1973, before the distribution of his last film, *Soylent Green*, a dull sci-fi story where his presence was never more welcome or needed. That same year, the Academy finally decided to give him a special Oscar, a long overdue recognition for a man who gave 100 percent to the profession he clearly loved. His autobiography, also published that year, was entitled *All My Yesterdays*.

Screen: 1916: Arms and the Woman; 1923: The Bright Shawl; 1929: The Hole in the Wall; 1930: Night Ride; A Lady to Love; Outside the Law; East Is West; The Widow From Chicago; Little Caesar; 1931: Smart Money; Five Star Final; 1932: The Hatchet Man; Two Seconds; Tiger Shark; Silver Dollar; 1933: The Little Giant; I Loved a Woman; 1934: Dark Hazard; The Man With Two Faces; 1935: The Whole Town's Talking; Barbary Coast; 1936: Bullets or Ballots; 1937: Thunder in the City; Kid Galahad; The Last Gangster; 1938: A Slight Case of Murder; The Amazing Dr. Clitterhouse; I Am the Law; 1939: Confessions of a Nazi Spy; Blackmail; 1940: Dr. Ehrlich's Magic Bullet; Brother Orchid; A Dispatch From Reuters; 1941: The Sea Wolf; Manpower; Unholy Partners; 1942: Larceny, Inc.; Tales of Manhattan; 1943: Destroyer; Flesh and Fantasy; 1944: Tampico; Mr. Winkle Goes to War; Double Indemnity; The Woman in the Window; 1945: Our Vines Have Tender Grapes; Journey Together; 1946: Scarlet Street; The Stranger; 1947: The Red House; 1948: All My Sons; Key Largo; Night Has a Thousand Eyes; 1949: House of Strangers; It's a Great Feeling; 1950: Operation X/My Daughter Joy; 1952: Actors and Sin; 1953: Big Leaguer; Vice Squad; The Glass Web; 1954: Black Tuesday; 1955: The Violent Men; Tight Spot; A Bullet for Joey; Illegal; 1956: Hell on Frisco Bay; Nightmare; The Ten Commandments; 1959: A Hole in the Head; 1960: Seven Thieves; Pepe; 1961: My Geisha; 1962: Two Weeks in Another Town; 1963: A Boy Ten Feet Tall/Sammy Going South; The Prize; 1964: Good Neighbor Sam; Robin and the 7 Hoods; The Outrage; Cheyenne Autumn; 1965: The Cincinnati Kid; 1967: Peking Blonde/The Blonde From Peking; 1968: Grand Slam; The Biggest Bundle of Them All; Un Scacco Tutto Matto/Mad Checkmate/It's Your Move (nUSr); Operazione San Pietro/Operation St. Peter's (nUSr); Never a Dull Moment; 1969: Mackenna's Gold; 1970: Song of Norway; 1973: Neither By Day Nor Night; Soylent Green.

NY Stage: 1915: Under Fire; 1916: Under Sentence; 1917: The Pawn; 1918: The Little Teacher; 1919: First Is Last; Night Lodging; 1920: Poldekin; Samson and Delilah; 1921: The Idle Inn; 1922: The Deluge; Banco; 1923: Peer Gynt; The Adding Machine; Launzi; A Royal Fandango; 1924: The Firebrand; 1925: Androcles and the Lion; 1926: The Goat Song; The Chief Thing; Henry Behave; Juarez and Maximilian; Ned McCobb's Daughter; 1927: The Brothers Karamazov; Right You Are If You Think You Are; The Racket; 1928: A Man With Red Hair; 1929: Kibitzer; 1930: Mr. Samuel; 1956: Middle of The Night.

Select TV: 1953: Witness for the Prosecution (sp); 1954: Epitaph for a Spy (sp); 1955: ...And Son (sp); A Set of Values (sp); 1958: Shadows Tremble (sp); 1959: A Good Name (sp); Loyalty (sp); 1960: The Devil and Daniel Webster (sp); 1961: The Drop-Out (sp); 1965: Who Has Seen the Wind? (sp); 1969: U.M.C.; 1970: The Old Man Who Cried Wolf; 1971: U.S.A. (sp).

FLORA ROBSON

BORN: SOUTH SHIELDS, DURHAM, ENGLAND, MARCH 28, 1902. ED: RADA. DIED: JULY 7, 1984.

Stalwart British actress Flora Robson seemed to effortlessly inject equal doses of dignity and life into countless international films throughout a career that spanned more than a half-century. Her London stage bow came in 1921, in *Will Shakespeare*, and she distinguished herself there and in rep, receiving film offers after her West End triumph in *Desire Under the Elms*. In motion pictures, she had supporting parts as a mom in *Dance, Pretty Lady*, and as Anne Grey's best friend in *One Precious Year*, but continued to find more favor on the stage, where her credits included *The Anatomist, Measure for Measure*, and *Macbeth*. Her regal presence was utilized on film in *Catherine the Great*, as the Dowager Czarina; and *Fire Over England*, as Elizabeth I, after which she went to Hollywood to play the housekeeper in *Wuthering Heights*. She fared well enough in that one to stick around to play George Raft's long-suffering mother in *Invisible Stripes*; Queen Elizabeth I again, in *The Sea Hawk*; Sterling Hayden's mom in *Bahama Passage*; and the mulatto servant in *Saratoga Trunk*, appearing so unlike herself that she earned an Oscar nomination.

Returning to England, she was a spinster, one of the *2,000 Women* in a French internment camp; led the cast of a tepid bit of patriotic good will, *Great Day*, preparing her town for a visit from Eleanor Roosevelt; was the scowling maid Ftatateeta in the expensive *Caesar and Cleopatra*; and played a nun who displays an unexpected knack for horticulture in the moody *Black Narcissus*. She was part of the ensemble of *Holiday Camp*, again as a spinster; was wicked as a vengeful countess in *Saraband for Dead Lovers*; and was ideally cast as the Nurse in the 1954 film of *Romeo and Juliet*. Continued stage work kept her among the most quietly admired of British thespians, including roles in *Ladies in Retirement, The Innocents*, and *The Aspern Papers*. Entering her elderly years, 1960s moviegoers saw her as the disagreeable Chinese Empress in *55 Days at Peking*; Rod Taylor's mum in *Young Cassidy*; and a kidnapped missionary in the silly *7 Women*. By the early 1970s, her drawn looks and sharp features led to a string of horror film roles with *The Shuttered Room, Eye of the Devil*, and *The Beast in the Cellar*, in which she had an actual leading role, as a woman who hides her deranged brother in the basement. She was created a Dame of the British Empire in 1960.

Screen: 1931: A Gentleman of Paris; 1932: Dance, Pretty Lady; 1933: One Precious Year; 1934: Catherine the Great; 1937: Fire Over England; Farewell Again/Troopship; 1939: Poison Pen; Wuthering Heights; We Are Not Alone; The Lion Has Wings; Invisible Stripes; 1940: The Sea Hawk; 1942: Bahama Passage; 1944: 2,000 Women; 1945: Saratoga Trunk; Great Day; Caesar and Cleopatra; 1946: The Years Between; 1947: Black Narcissus; Frieda; 1948: Holiday Camp; Good Time Girl; Saraband for Dead Lovers; 1953: The Tall Headlines; Malta Story; 1954: Romeo and Juliet; 1957: High Tide at Noon; No Time for Tears; 1958: The Gypsy and the Gentleman; Innocent Sinners; 1963: 55 Days at Peking; Murder at the Gallop; 1964: Guns at Batasi; 1965: Young Cassidy; Those Magnificent Men in Their Flying Machines or How I Flew From London to Paris in 25 Hours 11 Minutes; A King's Story (voice); 1966: 7 Women; 1967: The Shuttered Room/Blood Island; Eye of the Devil; 1970: Fragment of Fear; 1971: The Beast in the Cellar; 1972: The Beloved; Alice's Adventures in Wonderland; 1979: Dominique; 1981: Clash of the Titans.

NY Stage: 1940: Ladies in Retirement; 1941: Anne of England;

1942: The Damask Cheek; 1948: Macbeth; 1950: Black Chiffon.
Select TV: 1978: Les Misérables; 1979: A Man Called Intrepid;
1980: Gaugin the Savage; A Tale of Two Cities.

MAY ROBSON

(MARY JEANETTE ROBISON)
BORN: MELBOURNE, AUSTRALIA, APRIL 19, 1858.
DIED: OCTOBER 20, 1942.

Most audiences didn't take note of her until
she was past 70, by which time, short, stout,
pinch-faced May Robson was making a
killing in Hollywood playing prickly old ladies with a habit of letting their tongues wag without apologies. At the age of 16 she had
married and moved to America, but found herself in need of a
profession when her husband died young. She took up acting in
New York, making her stage debut in 1884, in *The Hoop of Gold*.
Her theatrical credits during the 19th century are difficult to
trace or verify, but it is known that she acted for a period with the
Empire Theatre Company and scored a major success in 1907
with *The Rejuvenation of Aunt Mary*, a property in which she
would appear intermittently over the years. There were some
early silent films, starting with *How Molly Made Good*, in 1915,
but her official movie career did not commence until 1926. Her
roles at this time included a tough nightclub hostess in *The Angel
of Broadway*, and the lead in a movie version of *The Rejuvenation
of Aunt Mary*, in 1927. When sound arrived, she starred as strong-
willed eccentric in *Mother's Millions*, and scored two other
significant parts, as the senior citizen disgusted with her old age
home in the final segment of *If I Had a Million*, and, in the best
role of her career, as the vagrant apple seller turned into a socialite
by her cronies to impress her daughter in *Lady for a Day*. This was
a charming Frank Capra concoction and she was perfect in both
the comedic and sentimental moments, earning an Oscar nomination as Best Actress. Although she was well into her 70s, more
leading roles followed: as a drunk adopted for publicity's sake by
Carole Lombard in *Lady by Choice*, a plot and title shamelessly
suggesting her previous triumph; *You Can't Buy Everything*, once
again as a rich eccentric; *Grand Old Girl*, as a high school principal who challenges a gambling operation; *Strangers All*, as a
widowed mom of four; and the unforgettably titled *Granny Get
Your Gun*, as a sharpshooter, once again taking on evil gamblers.
In support, her many roles included the cigar-chomping hotel
owner in *Reunion in Vienna*; Joan Crawford's dislikable mom in
Letty Lynton; the Queen of Hearts in the all-star *Alice in
Wonderland*; Fredric March's mother in *Anna Karenina*; Bobby
Breen's granny in the hit musical *Rainbow on the River*; Janet
Gaynor's supportive grandma in *A Star Is Born*; Aunt Polly in
Selznick's Technicolor version of *The Adventures of Tom Sawyer*;
the kindly Aunt Etta in *Four Daughters*, a role she repeated in its
three sequels; Katharine Hepburn's startled aunt, who confronts
Cary Grant about his crossdressing, in *Bringing Up Baby*; and an
espionage agent in *Joan of Paris*. No doubt she would have con-
tinued at this furious pace had she not died at age 83.
Screen: 1915: How Molly Made Good; 1916: A Night Out; 1926:
Pals in Paradise; 1927: A Harp in Hock; Rubber Tires; The Angel
of Broadway; The King of Kings; Chicago; Turkish Delight; The
Rejuvenation of Aunt Mary; 1928: The Blue Danube; 1931:
Mother's Millions/The She-Wolf; 1932: Letty Lynton; Strange
Interlude; Little Orphan Annie; If I Had a Million; Red-Headed
Woman; 1933: Reunion in Vienna; Dinner at Eight; Broadway to
Hollywood; Solitaire Man; Dancing Lady; Beauty for Sale; One
Man's Journey; Alice in Wonderland; Lady for a Day; Men Must
Fight; The White Sister; 1934: Straight Is the Way; You Can't Buy

Everything; Lady by Choice; 1935: Mills of the Gods; Grand Old
Girl; Vanessa: Her Love Story; Three Kids and a Queen; Strangers
All; Anna Karenina; Reckless; Age of Indiscretion; 1936: The
Captain's Kid; Wife vs. Secretary; Rainbow on the River; 1937: A
Star Is Born; Woman in Distress; The Perfect Specimen; 1938: The
Texans; Bringing Up Baby; The Adventures of Tom Sawyer; Four
Daughters; 1939: Yes, My Darling Daughter; The Kid From
Kokomo; Daughters Courageous; That's Right — You're Wrong;
Nurse Edith Cavell; Four Wives; They Made Me a Criminal; 1940:
Texas Rangers Ride Again; Irene; Granny Get Your Gun; 1941:
Four Mothers; Playmates; Million Dollar Baby; 1942: Joan of Paris.
NY Stage: 1899: Lord and Lady Algy; Make Way for the Ladies;
1900: Self and Lady; Lady Huntworth's Experiment; 1901: Are
You a Mason?; The Messenger Boy; 1902: The Billionaire; 1903:
Dorothy of Haddon Hall; 1904: It Happened in Nordland; 1905:
Cousin Billy; 1906: The Mountain Climber; 1907: The
Rejuvenation of Aunt Mary; 1911: The Three Lights (and wr.);
1926: Two Orphans.

CHARLES "BUDDY" ROGERS

BORN: OLATHE, KS, AUGUST 13, 1904.
ED: UNIV. OF KS. DIED: APRIL 21, 1999.

As one of the movies' classic "Boy Next
Door" types, perhaps it was fated that
Buddy Rogers would marry Mary Pickford,
the woman dubbed "America's Sweetheart."
But by the time they were wed, his days as a sweetly smiling college lad were over and he was content to rest on the laurels of his
brief days in the sun. With no previous training, he was picked
to join Paramount's School of Acting and the studio quickly cast
him as W.C. Fields's son in *So's Your Old Man*. He then appeared
in *Fascinating Youth*, alongside some other young hopefuls, of
whom only Thelma Todd was ever heard from again. His breakthrough year was 1927, when he teamed charmingly with
Pickford in *My Best Girl*, and then was chosen to play one of the
callow youths who experience the horrors of war in the aviation
blockbuster *Wings*. The film starred Clara Bow, but Rogers and
Richard Arlen were the real center of attention, and it was their
believable (and surprisingly physical) on-screen friendship that
made the whole thing work. It won the very first Academy Award
for Best Picture, made a fortune, and became one of the enduring
classics of the silent era. Suddenly a "name," Rogers had the first
of what would become his signature "gosh-gee-whiz" collegiate
roles, with *Varsity*, after which he was in the first adaptation of
one of Broadway's longest running and most quickly dated plays,
Abie's Irish Rose. It marked the first of five films with Nancy
Carroll and this pairing continued into the sound era with *Close
Harmony*, which cast him as a bandleader; *The River of Romance*;
Illusion; and *Follow Thru*, from the Broadway hit, which
included the song "Button Up Your Overcoat."

Rogers took to the trapeze in *Half-Way to Heaven*; did another
aviation drama, *Young Eagles*, the unofficial and soon forgotten
sequel to *Wings*; and was back crooning in *Safety in Numbers*, as
a sweet young millionaire who falls in love with one of the girls
assigned to "protect" him, Kathryn Crawford (and ultimately
choosing her over Carole Lombard). *Heads Up* found him as a
singing member of the Coast Guard; *Along Came Youth* stranded
him in London; and *This Reckless Age* cast him as a spoiled kid
who sees the error of his ways when Dad faces financial ruin.
Paramount bid him good-bye with *Take a Chance*, from another
Broadway musical, and if nothing else it allowed him to sing "It's
Only a Paper Moon." Seeing his popularity waning, he went to
England to make a few movies. When he returned to the States,

Pickford had finally received her divorce from Douglas Fairbanks, allowing her to marry Rogers in 1937 (they remained wed up to her death in 1979). Between grade "B" assignments at Monogram (*Double Trouble*) and PRC (*House of Errors*), Rogers took on Donald Woods's old role as Lupe Velez's husband for three entries in the *Mexican Spitfire* series for RKO. During this period he continued to entertain with his band, often wowing audiences with his talent for playing several instruments, and took up producing films with for his wife's company, United Artists: *Little Iodine* (1946), *Sleep My Love* (1946), and *Stork Bites Man* (1948). By the late 1950s, he had retired happily to be with his family at Pickfair, occasionally coaxed to do television guest spots, including one on the series *Petticoat Junction*, in which he reunited with *Wings* co-star Richard Arlen.

Screen: 1926: So's Your Old Man; Fascinating Youth; More Pay — Less Work; 1927: Wings; My Best Girl; Get Your Man; 1928: Varsity; Someone to Love; Red Lips; 1929: Abie's Irish Rose; Close Harmony; River of Romance; Perfect Day; Illusion; Halfway to Heaven; 1930: Young Eagles; Heads Up; Paramount on Parade; Safety in Numbers; Follow Thru; Along Came Youth; 1931: Lawyer's Secret; Road to Reno; Working Girls; 1932: This Reckless Age; 1933: Best of Enemies; Take a Chance; 1935: Old Man Rhythm; 1936: Dance Band; 1937: Week-End Millionaire/Once in a Million; This Way Please; 1938: Let's Make a Night of It; 1941: Golden Hoofs; Double Trouble; Mexican Spitfire's Baby; Sing for Your Supper; 1942: Mexican Spitfire at Sea; House of Errors; Mexican Spitfire Sees a Ghost; 1943: That Nasty Nuisance; 1948: Don't Trust Your Husband/An Innocent Affair; 1957: The Parson and the Outlaw.

Select TV: 1951: Cavalcade of Bands (series).

GINGER ROGERS

(VIRGINIA KATHERINE MCMATH)
BORN: INDEPENDENCE, MO, JULY 16, 1911.
DIED: APRIL 25, 1995.

Because she was half of the greatest dance team in movie history, Ginger Rogers is considered one of the screen immortals. How high in esteem she would've been held without Fred Astaire is open to debate. For the most part, she could be winning while cracking wise in comedy, though there were occasional instances when she was rather coy and shrill. As a dramatic actress she was competent but limited. Very much a part of the studio era, she did not mature gracefully with the passage of time and by the 1960s seemed to be a luminary stuck in the past, held back from competing in the more realistic mode of acting by glamour and artifice.

She started dancing as a youngster, making her first notable stage appearance with Eddie Foy in Fort Worth, Texas, where she had moved with her sister and her divorced mother. With Mom's guidance she continued in vaudeville, eventually leading an act called "Ginger and Her Redheads," and then "Ginger and Pepper," the latter being her first husband. Heading for New York, she got a job singing with the Paul Ash Orchestra and then a part on Broadway, in *Top Speed*, in 1929. Based on that, Paramount hired her to play opposite Charles Ruggles in the comedy *Young Man of Manhattan*, where she immortalized the expression "cigarette me, big boy," proving an instant success. Following her stage appearance in *Girl Crazy*, Paramount signed Rogers to a contract and kept Ruggles nearby in both *Queen High* and *Honor Among Lovers*, while other supporting parts saw her playing off of Jack Oakie (*The Sap From Syracuse*) and Ed Wynn (*Follow the Leader*). Leaving Paramount, she drifted around from here to there with two Joe E. Brown comedies, *The Tenderfoot* and *You Said a Mouthful*, to name but two of her assignments. She was working but she wasn't exactly distinguishing herself from others of her type.

Her first leap into the annals of movie musical history came when she was cast as one of the sassy, leggy chorines in Warner Bros.'s groundbreaking *42nd Street*. As Anytime Annie, she did her part in the famous "Shuffle Off to Buffalo" number, knocked off some tart one-liners, and certainly showed more talent than the movie's star, Ruby Keeler. The studio asked her back for their follow-up, *Gold Diggers of 1933*, this time letting her sing "We're in the Money" in pig latin. RKO signed her to a contract in 1933, but she took some roles elsewhere before her term with them began, including Universal's *Don't Bet on Love*, as a manicurist opposite Lew Ayres, who became her husband (1934–41). As luck would have it, Rogers arrived at RKO just as the studio was looking for somebody who could play comedy *and* dance, to be paired off with stage star Fred Astaire in supporting roles in the studio's musical extravaganza *Flying Down to Rio*. Their big moment came in the "Carioca" number and no one in the audience was watching the top-billed stars, Dolores Del Rio and Gene Raymond, by the movie's end. The studio was eager to team the dancing duo again but, unlike Astaire, Rogers insisted on doing other work between her musical assignments. These would include *Chance at Heaven*, putting up with Joel McCrea's nonsense until he realized she was the girl for him; *Upper World* (over at Warner Bros.), as a chorus girl who winds up shot by J. Carroll Naish; *Twenty Million Sweethearts* (also at WB) as a radio performer; *Romance in Manhattan*, as a chorus girl in love with immigrant Francis Lederer; and *Star of Midnight*, nicely paired with William Powell in one of his pseudo-*Thin Man* outings.

With Astaire she was *The Gay Divorcee*, in their first star pairing, and it was clear that there was magic at work. This one pretty much set the tone, with Rogers edgy and hard to crack, resisting Astaire's advances until he literally swept her off her feet. The box-office returns thrilled RKO, who gave the duo second and third billing to Irene Dunne in *Roberta*, another hit, followed by their signature film, *Top Hat*. Again Rogers was snooty and petulant, glamorous and lovely, fluttering about in her famous feather dress in the classic "Cheek to Cheek" number. She and Astaire were becoming icons of the depression era, giving audiences a fantasy of elegance. They sparkled again in *Follow the Fleet*, where their "Let's Face the Music and Dance" sequence was another of the many masterpieces they created; *Swing Time*, which included the delightful "Pick Yourself Up" duet to name but one of its many highpoints; and *Shall We Dance*, which included a climax of Astaire dancing with a chorus of girls wearing Ginger masks. Both stars requested a temporary break and Rogers wound up with a winner in *Stage Door*, giving one of her very best performances, as the hopeful actress who has it in for aspiring thespian Katharine Hepburn, until she discovers she's not as tough as she pretends to be. There was a enjoyable one with James Stewart, *Vivacious Lady*, which showed just how on the mark her comedic timing could be, as did *Bachelor Mother*, where she played a shopgirl who ends up with an abandoned child, matched most enjoyably with David Niven. On the other hand she seemed positively bored throughout *5th Ave. Girl*, as a jobless Manhattanite who ends up living in millionaire Walter Connolly's mansion. The last two Astaire-Rogers musicals of the 1930s — *Carefree*, in which she was put under analysis and for once was chasing *him*, and *The Story of Vernon and Irene Castle*, where she got to do some major emoting when he dies at the climax — were a slight change from the formula, but the profits were weakening and both stars were eager to move on.

Rogers needn't have worried. She was entering her peak as a solo box-office attraction, starting with *Primrose Path*, effective as a girl from the slums trying to rise above her station, and *Kitty Foyle*, ably playing another shopgirl, one who marries money only to learn that she really loves the man she left behind. She played the part with confidence and, although there was nothing particularly remarkable about the performance, the success of the film proved that she could carry this sort of soap opera with the best of them. She won the Academy Award as Best Actress of 1940. Not wanting to leave comedy behind, she did *Lucky Partners* with Ronald Colman, which did not live up to expectations, and *Tom, Dick and Harry*, which found her at her most unbearably coy, as a woman being courted by three different men. Better was one in which she stretched, *Roxie Hart*, playing a cynical brunette tramp facing a murder rap, and another she did on loan to Paramount, *The Major and the Minor*, requiring her to impersonate a child, which she did quite amusingly and with some degree of conviction. There was one with Cary Grant, *Once Upon a Honeymoon*, a comedy-drama involving Nazis that seemed to trivialize the issues at hand and simply didn't gel; *Tender Comrades*, a simplified look at the women on the homefront that later gained a bad reputation for its nod to communism; and Paramount's lavish but bowderlized adaptation of *Lady in the Dark*, in which she struggled with the role of the magazine editor who seeks analysis because of her personal problems. The last did very nicely at the box office, as did *I'll Be Seeing You*, where she gave a good performance as a parolee who falls in love while on a break from the pen; and *Weekend at the Waldorf*, a revision of *Grand Hotel*, in which she was paired off with Walter Pidgeon. She clearly had been one of the leading female attractions of the war years, but after these peaks her popularity began to slide.

She stumbled badly with *Heartbeat*, playing a female Oliver Twist to Basil Rathbone's Fagin, and with *Magnificent Doll*, which purported to tell the story of Dolly Madison. It was therefore wise of her to jump at the chance to work with Astaire again when Judy Garland took ill during *The Barkleys of Broadway*. It included a reprise of one of their RKO standards, "They Can't Take That Away From Me," and proved a great boost to her career. As a result she did Warner Bros.'s indictment of the KKK, *Storm Warning*; played an attorney married to hick Jack Carson in *The Groom Wore Spurs*; was part of Fox's episodic *We're Not Married!*, opposite Fred Allen; misstepped with Cary Grant once again, in *Monkey Business*, this time aping the manners of a child without finesse; spoofed silent movies as a faded star cashing in on her past in *Dreamboat*; and played an actress who begins to realize that she must step aside for the younger Pat Crowley in *Forever Female*. The last was probably the most enjoyable film she did during the 1950s and she got some of her best notices playing a gangster's moll in *Tight Spot*. Back at RKO she did one of the last productions of that studio, *The First Travelling Saleslady*, an extremely mild western comedy, and participated in one of the "misunderstood youth" pictures of the era, *Teenage Rebel*, trying to win back the love of unhappy daughter Betty Lou Keim. At 20th Century-Fox she appeared in her last major league film, *Oh, Men! Oh, Women!*, back on the psychiatrist couch, complaining about inattentive husband Dan Dailey. There were two half-hearted projects in the 1960s, the hardly-seen *Quick, Let's Get Married*, and the cheaper of the two *Harlow* bio films, in which she played Carol Lynley's mom. There was a latter day triumph when she became the first lady to take over from Carol Channing in the smash Broadway musical *Hello, Dolly!*, but after that she was content to rest on her laurels except for an occasional nightclub appearance. Her fourth husband (1953–57) was actor Jacques Bergerac, who appeared in support of her in the British *Beautiful*

Stranger/Twist of Fate. She published her autobiography, *Ginger: My Story*, in 1991. The following year she was a recipient of the Kennedy Center Honors, only to face the indignity of having Astaire removed from the accompanying film clips at the insistence of his misguided widow, a petty act that would have been insulting to any of his former co-stars, let alone the one with whom his name remains forever linked.

Screen: 1930: Young Man of Manhattan; The Sap From Syracuse; Queen High; Follow the Leader; 1931: Honor Among Lovers; The Tip Off; Suicide Fleet; 1932: Carnival Boat; The Tenderfoot; The Thirteenth Guest; Hat Check Girl; You Said a Mouthful; 1933: 42nd Street; Broadway Bad; Gold Diggers of 1933; Professional Sweetheart; A Shriek in the Night; Don't Bet on Love; Sitting Pretty; Flying Down to Rio; Chance at Heaven; Rafter Romance; 1934: Finishing School; Change of Heart; Twenty Million Sweethearts; Upperworld; The Gay Divorcee; Romance in Manhattan; 1935: Roberta; Star of Midnight; Top Hat; In Person; 1936: Follow the Fleet; Swing Time; 1937: Shall We Dance; Stage Door; 1938: Having Wonderful Time; Vivacious Lady; Carefree; 1939: The Story of Vernon and Irene Castle; Bachelor Mother; 5th Ave. Girl; 1940: The Primrose Path; Lucky Partners; Kitty Foyle; 1941: Tom, Dick and Harry; 1942: Tales of Manhattan; The Major and the Minor; Once Upon a Honeymoon; 1943: Tender Comrade; 1944: Lady in the Dark; I'll Be Seeing You; 1945: Weekend at the Waldorf; 1946: Heartbeat; Magnificent Doll; 1947: It Had to Be You; 1949: The Barkleys of Broadway; 1950: Perfect Strangers; 1951: Storm Warning; The Groom Wore Spurs; 1952: We're Not Married!; Monkey Business; Dreamboat; 1953: Forever Female; 1954: Black Widow; Beautiful Stranger/Twist of Fate; 1955: Tight Spot; 1956: The First Travelling Saleslady; Teenage Rebel; 1957: Oh, Men! Oh, Women!; 1965: Quick, Let's Get Married/The Confession; Harlow; 1985: George Stevens: A Filmmaker's Journey.

NY Stage: 1929: Top Speed; 1930: Girl Crazy; 1951: Love and Let Love; 1965: Hello, Dolly!

Select TV: 1954: Tonight at 8:30 (sp); 1960: Never Too Late (sp); 1965: Cinderella (sp); 1966: Terror Island (sp).

ROY ROGERS

(LEONARD FRANKLIN SLYE) BORN: CINCINNATI, OH, NOVEMBER 5, 1911. DIED: JULY 6, 1998.

Of that once-dominant, curious type known as the "singing cowboy," Roy Rogers was the most beloved, most popular, and certainly the most enduring. Dubbed "the King of the Cowboys," the ultra-wholesome, squinty-eyed, nice-looking feller was a favorite among young fans of the western, who didn't seem to mind that this do-gooder usually took care of the bad guys with a minimal amount of gunplay and violence. Moving to California in the late 1920s, he became a fruit picker, doing some guitar playing and singing on the side. He sang on the radio with a group called Tom Murray's Hollywood Hillbillies and eventually assembled another, more popular group, The Sons of the Pioneers. The Pioneers began popping up in shorts and features with Rogers using either his real name or "Dick Weston," though he was not usually billed separately. In 1938, Republic Pictures was looking for someone to replace a demanding Gene Autry, whose success had led him to request a substantial pay increase. The studio auditioned and cast Rogers, giving him his stage name and launching him with *Under Western Stars*, as a Congressman who goes to Washington to save a dust bowl region. The movie was a hit and Rogers was immediately given one follow-up vehicle after another, including *Billy the Kid Returns*, not as the famous outlaw but a look-alike; *Wall Street Cowboy*, an oddity set in the modern era; the biopics *Young Buffalo Bill* and *Young Bill Hickok*; and *The Border Legion*, from a popular Zane Grey story. He had, by this time, found a comfortable sidekick in crusty old codger George "Gabby" Hayes and the two appeared in support of John Wayne, Walter Pigeon, and Claire Trevor in one of the studio's more lavish forays into the genre, *Dark Command*. There was, of course, a co-star far more important to Rogers's success and that was his golden Palomino, initially called Golden Cloud, but soon dubbed Trigger.

By 1943, he had been voted the top western movie star in America and would keep that position until he decided to move from the big screen to the small one. In the meantime he was *Robin Hood of the Pecos* and then *Jesse James at Bay*, which marked the last of his movies to favor action over music. In one of his rare excursions outside the Republic gates, he guested in the all-star *Hollywood Canteen*, where he introduced Cole Porter's hit "Don't Fence Me In." That same year, 1944, he was given Dale Evans (b. Frances Octavia Smith in Uvalde, TX, on October 31, 1912) as his leading lady for *The Cowboy and the Senorita*, and they clicked so well that she quickly became as much a part of these films as Gabby and Trigger. In 1947, a year after the death of Rogers's first wife, he and Evans became man and wife, becoming nearly inseparable on screen and off. With a few exceptions, all of Evans's assignments for Republic were to be in Rogers's movies. Not unexpectedly there was a quicky called *Don't Fence Me In*, and one that really put Trigger in the center of the story, *My Pal Trigger*, which not only was considered one of his best films by fans but would remain Rogers's favorite as well. Following *Pals of the Golden West* in 1951, he began *The Roy Rogers Show* on NBC television. The series ran until 1957, making Rogers as popular as ever. There were two comedic roles with Bob Hope, in *Son of Paleface* and *Alias Jesse James*, after which he kept to personal appearances with only one isolated return to movies in the 1970s, in the barely distributed *Mackintosh and T.J.* By then most youngsters knew his name for the fast food franchise he had started in partnership with the Marriott Corporation. He and Evans published their autobiography, *Happy Trails*, in 1979, named, of course, for their classic theme song. Rogers died of heart failure in 1998, while Evans passed away on February 7, 2001.

Screen: AS LEONARD SLYE OR DICK WESTON: **1935:** Way Up Thar; The Old Homestead; Gallant Defender; **1936:** The Big Show; Rhythm on the Range; The Mysterious Avenger; California Mail; Song of the Saddle; The Old Corral; **1937:** The Old Wyoming Trail; Wild Horse Rodeo; **1938:** The Old Barn Dance.
AS ROY ROGERS: **1938:** Under Western Stars; Billy the Kid Returns; Come on Rangers; Shine On, Harvest Moon; **1939:** Rough Riders' Round-Up; Frontier Pony Express; Southward Ho!; In Old Caliente; Wall Street Cowboy; The Arizona Kid; Jeepers Creepers; Saga of Death Valley; Days of Jesse James; **1940:** Young Buffalo Bill; Dark Command; The Carson City Kid; The Ranger and the Lady; Colorado; Young Bill Hickok; The Border Legion; **1941:** Robin Hood of the Pecos; Arkansas Judge; In Old Cheyenne; Sheriff of Tombstone; Nevada City; Bad Man of Deadwood; Jesse James at Bay; Red River Valley; **1942:** Man from Cheyenne; South of Santa Fe; Sunset on the Desert; Romance on the Range; Sons of the Pioneers; Sunset Serenade; Heart of the Golden West; Ridin' Down the Canyon; **1943:** Idaho; King of the Cowboys; Song of Texas; Silver Spurs; The Man From Music Mountain; Hands Across the Border; **1944:** The Cowboy and the Senorita; The Yellow Rose of Texas; Song of Nevada; San Fernando Valley; Lights of Old Santa Fe; Brazil; Lake Placid Serenade; Hollywood Canteen; **1945:** Utah; Bells of Rosarita; The Man from Oklahoma; Sunset in El Dorado; Don't Fence Me In; Along the Navajo Trail; **1946:** Song of Arizona; Rainbow Over Texas; My Pal Trigger; Under Nevada Skies; Roll On, Texas Moon; Home in Oklahoma; Out California Way; Heldorado; **1947:** Apache Rose; Hit Parade of 1947; Bells of San Angelo; Springtime in the Sierras; On the Old Spanish Trail; **1948:** The Gay Ranchero; Under California Stars; Eyes of Texas; Melody Time; Night Time in Nevada; Grand Canyon Trail; The Far Frontier; **1949:** Susanna Pass; Down Dakota Way; The Golden Stallion; **1950:** Bells of Coronado; Twlight in the Sierras; Trigger Jr.; Sunset in the West; North of the Great Divide; Trail of Robin Hood; **1951:** Spoilers of the Plains; Heart of the Rockies; In Old Amarillo; South of Caliente; Pals of the Golden West; **1952:** Son of Paleface; **1959:** Alias Jesse James; **1975:** Mackintosh and T.J.
Select TV: 1951–57: The Roy Rogers Show (series; and exec. prod.).

WILL ROGERS

BORN: OOLOGAH, INDIAN TERRITORY (LATER OK), NOVEMBER 4, 1879.
DIED: AUGUST 15, 1935.

It was only fitting that a fellow who claimed to have never met a man he didn't like was among the most beloved of show business entertainers. In his heyday, Will Rogers was viewed with great affection as a common man who made wry commentary on all aspects of American life in a lighthearted, folksy manner. A big hit onstage and radio, he transferred his aw-shucks delivery to the big screen most lucratively. With the passage of time, there is little to recommend about these rather clunky comedies and Rogers, though certainly affable, made no effort towards giving a seamless performance and the "hems" and "haws" sometimes make for painful viewing.

Growing up in Claremore, Oklahoma, he took an interest in roping and lariat tricks and it was while working aboard a ship that he ended up in South Africa and joined a Wild West Show there. He brought his lasso prowess to similar productions in the States, making his New York debut in 1905, at Madison Square Garden. Moving over to vaudeville, he enhanced his lariat tricks with commentary and storytelling, and this brought him an offer to appear in a Broadway musical, *The Wall Street Girl*, in 1912. Following appearances in other musicals, he joined Florenz Ziegfeld's *Midnight Frolic*, as well as that man's *Follies* of 1917 and 1918, where he really established his persona as the head-scratching, gum-chewing, friendly cowboy who made dry and perceptive, but never vicious, witticisms about daily events and politics. Samuel Goldwyn signed him to a contract in 1918, starting him off in *Laughing Bill Hyde*, shot in Fort Lee, New Jersey. It did nicely despite the fact that Rogers's strong point was clearly words. Among his other Goldwyn comedies were *Jubilo*, a favorite of Rogers's, based on a *Saturday Evening Post* story; *Water Water Everywhere*, turning a tough saloon into a soda fountain; and *Doubling for Romeo*, a Hollywood spoof. Elsewhere he did a version of Washington Irving's *The Headless Horseman*, and then a series of two-reel parodies for Hal Roach, including "Uncensored Movies," "Jes Passin' Through," "Gee Whiz, Genevieve," "The Cake Eater," "A Truthful Liar," "Big Moments From Little Pictures," and "Two Wagons — Both Covered." Outside of pictures he became a popular traveling lecturer and newspaper columnist, but it was not until sound arrived that his motion picture career finally took a big leap forward.

Encouraged by his continuing box-office pull onstage, 20th Century-Fox cast him as a rich Oklahoman who travels to

Europe in *They Had to See Paris*, something of a variation on *Dodsworth*, with Rogers as the simple man stuck with a pretentious wife eager to find a place in society. Despite its early talkie dullness, it did well enough for Fox to keep him aboard. There was the obvious follow-up, *So This Is London*, and an adaptation of *Lightnin'*, which had run for a record number of performances on Broadway back in 1918. The crowds flocked to his take on *A Connecticut Yankee*, although this premise was handled far better years later by Bing Crosby. Rogers was hardly what anybody would call "an actor" and his impatience with multiple takes was evident on the screen, as he could often be heard hesitating and stumbling over lines, which also caused clumsy pauses from his fellow performers.

The successful Rogers formula continued with *Ambassador Bill*, again playing the good ol' boy abroad, this time in a mythical country; *Business and Pleasure*, traveling from the Midwest to the Middle East; *Down to Earth*, the sequel to *They Had to See Paris*; and *Too Busy to Work*, a remake of *Jubilo*. For a change he was given an equally important Fox talent, Janet Gaynor, as his co-star, for *State Fair*, and it is probably the best and most enduring of his movies, a simple, homespun story about a family attending the title event. For John Ford he did some ultra-laid back rural pieces, *Doctor Bull* and *Judge Priest*, small town medicine and law respectively, and although these movies were very well liked in their day, their charms seem singularly elusive with the passing of time. Remaining in the small-town mode, he was a banker involved with horses in *David Harum*, and, in *Handy Andy*, was once again in opposition to his social-climbing wife, in this case Peggy Wood, with whom he had co-starred in *Almost a Husband*, way back in 1919. He kept the studio happy, cranking 'em out fast and furious, doing *The County Chairman*, which Fox had been hoping he'd do since they first put him under contract; *Doubting Thomas*, in which wife Billie Burke had acting ambitions; *Steam Boat 'Round the Bend*, another one directed by John Ford; and *In Old Kentucky*, in which he did some dance steps with Bill Robinson. The last two were released posthumously and were both very profitable, the country wanting to embrace the last of this greatly admired man who had perished in an airplane crash with famed aviator Wiley Post. The Rogers spirit of good will and generosity lived on by way of a charity established in his name, its continuing presence in movie theatres across the country giving most future generations their only contact with the legendary figure. In 1953, there was an innocuous movie bio, *The Will Rogers Story*, with his son, Will, Jr., portraying his dad, and, in 1991, a Broadway musical, *The Will Rogers Follies*, with Keith Carradine originating the lead role.

Screen (features): 1918: Laughing Bill Hyde; 1919: Almost a Husband; Jubilo; 1920: Water Water Everywhere; Jes' Call Me Jim; The Strange Boarder; Honest Hutch; Cupid the Cowpuncher; Guile of Women; 1921: Boys Will Be Boys; An Unwilling Hero; Doubling for Romeo; A Poor Relation; 1922: One Glorious Day; The Headless Horseman; 1923: Hollywood; 1927: Tip Toes; A Texas Steer; 1929: They Had to See Paris; 1930: Happy Days; So This Is London; Lightnin'; 1931: A Connecticut Yankee; Young As You Feel; Ambassador Bill; 1932: Business and Pleasure; Down to Earth; Too Busy to Work; 1933: State Fair; Doctor Bull; Mr. Skitch; 1934: David Harum; Handy Andy; Judge Priest; 1935: The County Chairman; Life Begins at 40; Doubting Thomas; Steamboat 'Round the Bend; In Old Kentucky.

NY Stage: 1912: The Wall Street Girl; 1915: Hands Up; Town Topics; Midnight Frolic; 1917: Ziegfeld Follies of 1917; 1918: Ziegfeld Follies of 1918; 1921: Ziegfeld Midnight Frolic of 1921; 1922: Ziegfeld Follies of 1922; 1925: Ziegfeld Follies of 1925;

1928: Three Cheers.

GILBERT ROLAND

(Luis Antonio Damaso de Alonso)
Born: Chihuahua, Mexico, December 11, 1905. Died: May 15, 1994.

Saddled with the stereotype of the "Latin lover," Gilbert Roland had to wait some years before he was appreciated for his acting ability, but since he aged better than most stars, it wasn't such a bad deal. Originally intent on becoming a bullfighter, he changed his mind after his family moved to the States, eventually traveling to Hollywood to become an actor. His good looks got him a bit in First National's *The Lady Who Lied*, and he promptly had his name changed to Gilbert Roland for his second credit, *The Plastic Age*, combining the names of two actors he admired, John Gilbert and Ruth Roland. Linked off camera with Norma Talmadge, they soon became an on-screen couple as well with *Camille* (in which Roland played Armand, the role later done by Robert Taylor in the better known 1936 version); *The Dove*; *The Woman Disputed*, in which he was an Austrian officer; and *New York Nights*. Unlike Talmadge, his career was not hurt by the coming of sound, and he proved a great asset to some productions, appearing in the Spanish versions of such movies as *Men of the North* and *The Men in Her Life*. His parts, however, were suddenly smaller or in less significant properties and he showed up challenging Buster Keaton to a duel in *The Passionate Plumber*; playing a heroic D.A. in the Mayfair cheapie *No Living Witness*; being whipped by Clara Bow in *Call Her Savage*; doing the requisite gigolo duty for Mae West in *She Done Him Wrong*; and complying with more of the same for Constance Bennett in *Our Betters*. Bennett would become his sometime off-screen lover and they finally married in 1940, divorcing five years later.

In the meantime Roland was racking up too many minor credits, though he did get occasional "A" work, as in Paramount's trashy look at the Spanish Civil War, *Last Train from Madrid*, as one of the men panting over Dorothy Lamour; *Juarez*, as the traitorous Colonel Lopez; and, in a similar sounding part, Captain Lopez in *The Sea Hawk*. Not surprisingly, he was asked by Monogram to play the Cisco Kid, becoming the fourth actor to do so (Duncan Reynaldo had just preceded him), starting with *The Gay Cavalier* in 1946, and ending with a sixth entry, *King of the Bandits*, in 1947. A sense of legitimacy was attained when he was cast as a Cuban laborer by director John Huston in *We Were Strangers*, making many realize that Roland was better than most of the material he'd been handed over the years. Because of this he was back in higher profile pieces like *Crisis* with Cary Grant; *Ten Tall Men*, a cheeky Burt Lancaster romp; *Bullfighter and the Lady*, getting a chance to cinematically fulfill his once-intended professional dream in this much-admired look at the sport; *The Bad and the Beautiful*, revisiting his "Latin lover" image by seducing Gloria Grahame in this award-laden Hollywood story; *The Miracle of Our Lady of Fatima*, an earnest religious tale supposedly based on a true incident and of one of his favorite films; and two wet ones, *Beneath the Twelve-Mile Reef* and *Underwater!*, the latter famous for holding its premiere 20 feet below the surface in Silver Springs, Florida. In a nasty mode he was a killer in *The Midnight Story*; took to the highwire over Niagara Falls (albeit with rear projection) in *The Big Circus*; and played an Indian alongside some other Hispanic actors in John Ford's *Cheyenne Autumn*. Still going strong into his 70s, he popped up in the Bahamas for *Islands in the Stream*, and out west in *Barbarosa*, before bowing out quietly for retirement.

Screen: AS LUIS DE ALONSO: 1925: The Lady Who Lied.
AS GILBERT ROLAND: 1925: The Plastic Age; The Midshipman; 1926: The Campus Flirt; The Blonde Saint; 1927: Camille; Rose of the Golden West; The Love Mart; The Dove; 1928: The Woman Disputed; 1929: New York Nights; 1930: Men of the North; Monsieur Le Fox (nUSr; Sp. version of Men of the North); 1931: Resurreccion (nUSr; Sp. version of Resurrection); Hombres en Mi Vida (nUSr; Sp. version of The Men in Her Life); 1932: The Passionate Plumber; No Living Witness; Life Begins; A Parisian Romance; Call Her Savage; The Woman in Room 13; 1933: She Done Him Wrong; Tarnished Youth/ Gigolettes of Paris; Our Betters; Una Viuda Romantica/The Romantic Widow (nUSr); Yom Tu y Ella/I, Thou and She (nUSr); After Tonight; 1934: Elinor Norton; 1935: Mystery Woman; Ladies Love Danger; Julieta Compra un Hijo/Juliet Buys a Baby (nUSr); 1937: Midnight Taxi; Thunder Trail; Last Train from Madrid; 1938: Gateway; 1939: Juarez; La Vida Bohemia (nUSr); 1940: The Sea Hawk; Gambling on the High Seas; Isle of Destiny; Rangers of Fortune; 1941: Angels With Broken Wings; My Life With Caroline; 1942: Isle of Missing Men; Enemy Agents Meet Ellery Queen; 1944: The Desert Hawk (serial); 1945: Captain Kidd; 1946: The Gay Cavalier; La Rebellion de Los Fantamas (nUSr); South of Monterey; Beauty and the Bandit; 1947: Riding the California Trail; High Conquest; The Other Love; Pirates of Monterey; Robin Hood of Monterey; King of the Bandits; 1948: The Dude Goes West; 1949: We Were Strangers; Malaya; 1950: The Torch; Crisis; The Furies; 1951: Ten Tall Men; Bullfighter and the Lady; Mark of the Renegade; 1952: My Six Convicts; Glory Alley; The Miracle of Our Lady of Fatima; Apache War Smoke; The Bad and the Beautiful; 1953: Beneath the Twelve-Mile Reef; The Diamond Queen; Thunder Bay; 1954: The French Line; 1955: Underwater!; The Racers; That Lady; The Treasure of Pancho Villa; 1956: Bandido; Around the World in Eighty Days; Three Violent People; 1957: The Midnight Story; 1958: The Last of the Fast Guns; 1959: The Wild and the Innocent; The Big Circus; 1960: Guns of the Timberland; 1962: Samar; 1964: Cheyenne Autumn; 1965: The Reward; 1967: Catch Me If You Can (nUSr); 1968: Every Man for Himself/The Ruthless Four; Any Gun Can Play/Go Kill and Come Back; 1969: Between God, the Devil and a Winchester; 1971: The Christian Licorice Store; 1972: Johnny Hamlet (filmed 1969); 1973: Running Wild; 1975: The Pacific Connection (nUSr); 1977: Islands in the Stream; The Black Pearl; 1981: Caboblanco; 1982: Barbarosa.

Select TV: 1954: The Arden Woodsman (sp); 1957: Invitation to a Gunfighter (sp); Rich Man, Poor Man (sp); 1959: Border Justice (sp); 1960: El Bandido (sp); Adios el Cuchillo (sp); 1966: The Poppy Is Also a Flower; 1973: Incident on a Dark Street; 1974: The Mark of Zorro; 1975: The Deadly Tower (narrator); 1979: The Sacketts.

RUTH ROMAN

BORN: BOSTON, MA, DECEMBER 23, 1923.
DIED: SEPTEMBER 9, 1999.

A somewhat icy beauty who showed increasingly interesting talents as she got older, Ruth Roman was the daughter of a circus barker and continued the show biz tradition by attending the Bishop Lee Dramatic School. After work with the New England Rep Company, among others, she made her film debut with a bit part in *Stage Door Canteen*, and continued in this capacity for a some time until she was given the title role in 20th Century-Fox's *Belle Starr's Daughter*, joining a band of outlaws to avenge Mom's death. Better assignments were around the corner, as she was given key roles in two top 1949 releases: *The Window*, as one of the killers who wants young witness Bobby Driscoll out of the way, and *Champion*, as the wife left behind by ambitious boxer Kirk Douglas. Warner Bros. signed her to a contract with stardom in mind, but she took a back seat to Milton Berle in *Always Leave Them Laughing*, and to Bette Davis in the overcooked *Beyond the Forest*. She also provided romantic duties in a pair of westerns, the Randolph Scott hit *Colt .45*, and one of Gary Cooper's weakest, *Dallas*. In the thriller genre she was an actress fearing that Richard Todd might bump her off in *Lightning Strikes Twice*, and made little impact in one of Alfred Hitchcock's best, *Strangers on a Train*, as Farley Granger's concerned girlfriend. After Warner Bros., she wished for Dorothy McGuire's demise in the soapy *Invitation*; did one of James Stewart's "A" westerns, *The Far Country*; and a lot of programmers, of which the standouts were *Rebel in Town*, as the distraught mom of a murdered boy, and *Joe Macbeth*, an oddity updating the Shakespeare tragedy to the gangster world. In her maturing years she seemed game for some complex material, but instead was used in horrors and drive-in fare, including *The Baby*, as a whacked-out mom who keeps her grown son in diapers; *The Killing Kind*, as John Savage's unfortunate lawyer; and *Echoes*, as the mom of tormented art student Richard Alfieri. Her nonacting claim to fame was being one of the survivors of the sinking of the *Andrea Doria*.

Screen: 1943: Stage Door Canteen; 1944: Ladies Courageous; Since You Went Away; Harmony Trail/White Stallion; Storm Over Lisbon; 1945: Jungle Queen (serial); The Affairs of Susan; See My Lawyer; You Came Along; Incendiary Blonde; She Gets Her Man; 1946: Gilda; Without Reservations; 1948: The Big Clock; Night Has a Thousand Eyes; Good Sam; Belle Starr's Daughter; 1949: The Window; Champion; Beyond the Forest; Always Leave Them Laughing; 1950: Barricade; Colt .45; Three Secrets; Dallas; 1951: Lightning Strikes Twice; Strangers on a Train; Starlift; Tomorrow Is Another Day; 1952: Invitation; Mara Maru; Young Man With Ideas; 1953: Blowing Wild; 1954: Tanganyika; Down Three Dark Streets; The Shanghai Story; 1955: The Far Country; 1956: The Bottom of the Bottle; Joe Macbeth; Great Day in the Morning; Rebel in Town; 1957: Five Steps to Danger; 1958: Bitter Victory; 1959: Desert Desperados/ The Sinner; 1961: Look in Any Window; Milagro a los Cobardes/Miracle of the Cowards (nUSr); 1965: Love Has Many Faces; 1973: The Baby; 1974: The Killing Kind; A Knife for the Ladies/Silent Sentence; Impulse; Dead of Night/Deathdream; 1976: Day of the Animals; 1983: Echoes.

Select TV: 1951: Mme. Fifi (sp); 1954: The Chase (sp); 1955: Darkness at Noon (sp); 1956: Panic (sp); 1959: The Philadelphia Story (sp); 1963: The Candidate (sp); 1965–66: The Long Hot Summer (series); 1970: The Old Man Who Cried Wolf; 1971: Incident in San Francisco; 1973: Go Ask Alice; 1974: Punch and Jody; 1979: The Sacketts; 1980: Willow B: Women in Prison; 1986: Knots Landing (series).

CESAR ROMERO

BORN: NEW YORK, NY, FEBRUARY 15, 1907.
DIED: JANUARY 1, 1994.

The "Latin from Manhattan," Cesar Romero was never without his moustache and seldom without a job, filling roles of varying sizes here and there for some 60 years, earning a reputation for dependability; no more, no less. Early on he formed a dance team with Janette Hackett, and they entertained in various New York nightclubs, eventually ending up in the 1928 Broadway revue *Lady Do*. An ailment caused Romero to seek a career outside of dancing and he began to show up on the legit stage, touring in *Strictly Dishonorable* and doing *Dinner at Eight* in New York. His film debut came in 1933, with a bit part in a quickie mystery called *The Shadow Laughs*, after which he popped up in the cast of one of the big movies of 1934, *The Thin Man*, as the smarmy younger husband of Maureen O'Sullivan's mom. There was something unsavory in his toothy smile, so he was seen trying to hit on Margaret Sullavan in *The Good Fairy* and, because of his ethnic looks, was cast as all kinds of foreigners, playing Indians in *Clive of India* and *Wee Willie Winkie*; a Spaniard in one Dietrich's dullest, *The Devil Is a Woman*; and a German in *Rendezvous*, to name a few. In the late 1930s, 20th Century-Fox added him to their payroll, giving him top billing in the "B" *Dangerously Yours*, as a detective pretending to be a jewel thief; then putting him on ice skates alongside Ethel Merman (!) in *Happy Landing*. Now a staple of that studio, he was usually cast in second leads, playing singing teacher to Loretta Young in *Wife, Husband and Friend*; an Indian servant in one of the better Shirley Temple vehicles, *The Little Princess*; and Warner Baxter's henchman in *Return of the Cisco Kid*. That last movie inspired Fox to do a series of "B" productions based on the popular character, upping Romero to the lead, starting with *The Cisco Kid and the Lady*, and taking him through five more entries, ending with *Ride on Vaquero* in 1941.

Not forgetting that Romero had started in the profession as a dancer, Fox put him in the Alice Faye musical *The Great American Broadcast*, and he was featured in a plethora of their glossy wartime offerings, *Week-end in Havana*, *Orchestra Wives*, *Springtime in the Rockies*, and *Coney Island*. There was a break from films while he served in the Coast Guard during World War II, and when he returned he landed the key role of Cortez in one of the big Technicolor hits of 1947, *Captain From Castile*, cutting an imposing figure. After a curious assignment over at MGM, playing an Englishman in *Julia Misbehaves*, he ended his employment at Fox playing Betty Grable's philandering lover in *The Beautiful Blonde From Bashful Bend*, and a gangster in the Paul Douglas comedy *Love That Brute*. Taking another lead, he was a heel who stole from June Havoc and tossed her to the police in *Once a Thief*; then did villain duty in the hit western *Vera Cruz*. By the early 1960s, the gray-haired but still dapper actor showed up as a criminal wanting a piece of the action in *Ocean's Eleven*; playing Bobby Darin's dad in *If a Man Answers*; and as Connie Stevens's crazed magician father in *Two on a Guillotine*. On television he created such an indelible impression as the maniacal Joker on the *Batman* television series (and in a theatrical film spin-off) that he suddenly became extremely well known to a whole new generation of fans. In the 1970s, he became a staple of some of Disney's lesser known gimmick comedies, like *The Computer Wore Tennis Shoes* and *The Strongest Man in the World*, while also appearing in such curios as *The Spectre of Edgar Allan Poe*, as an asylum head, and *Lust in the Dust*, as a padre. A frequent escort to social affairs of many of cinema's famous ladies, he was constantly referred to as Hollywood's most "eligible bachelor," a coy way of evading any discussion of his homosexuality.

Screen: 1933: The Shadow Laughs; 1934: The Thin Man; Cheating Cheaters; British Agent; 1935: The Good Fairy; Strange Wives; Clive of India; Cardinal Richelieu; Hold 'Em Yale; The Devil Is a Woman; Diamond Jim; Metropolitan; Rendezvous; Show Them No Mercy; 1936: Love Before Breakfast; Nobody's Fool; Public Enemy's Wife; Fifteen Maiden Lane; She's Dangerous; 1937: Armored Car; Wee Willie Winkie; Dangerously Yours; 1938: Happy Landing; My Lucky Star;

Always Goodbye; Five of a Kind; 1939: Wife, Husband and Friend; The Little Princess; Return of the Cisco Kid; Charlie Chan at Treasure Island; Frontier Marshal; The Cisco Kid and the Lady; 1940: Viva Cisco Kid; Lucky Cisco Kid; He Married His Wife; The Gay Caballero; 1941: Tall, Dark and Handsome; Romance of the Rio Grande; Ride on Vaquero; The Great American Broadcast; Dance Hall; Week-end in Havana; 1942: A Gentleman at Heart; Tales of Manhattan; Orchestra Wives; Springtime in the Rockies; 1943: Coney Island; Wintertime; 1947: Captain From Castile; Carnival in Costa Rica; 1948: Deep Waters; That Lady in Ermine; Julia Misbehaves; 1949: The Beautiful Blonde From Bashful Bend; 1950: Love That Brute; Once a Thief; 1951: Happy Go Lovely; FBI Girl; The Lost Continent; 1952: Scotland Yard Inspector; The Jungle; 1953: Prisoners of the Casbah; Shadow Man/Street of Shadows; 1954: Vera Cruz; 1955: The Americano; The Racers; 1956: The Sword of Granada; Around the World in Eighty Days; The Leather Saint; 1957: The Story of Mankind; 1958: Villa!; 1960: Ocean's Eleven; Pepe; 1961: 7 Women From Hell; 1962: If a Man Answers; 1963: We Shall Return; Donovan's Reef; The Castillian; 1964: A House Is Not a Home; 1965: Two on a Guillotine; Sergeant Deadhead; Marriage on the Rocks; 1966: Batman; 1968: Hot Millions; Skidoo; 1969: A Talent for Loving; Crooks and Coronets; Midas Run; 1970: The Computer Wore Tennis Shoes; Latitude Zero; Madigan's Millions; 1972: Soul Soldier/The Red White and Black; Now You See Him, Now You Don't; 1973: The Proud and the Damned; 1974: The Spectre of Edgar Allan Poe; 1975: The Strongest Man in the World; Timber Tramps (filmed 1973); 1977: Kino, the Padre on Horseback/Mission to Glory (dtc); 1979: Monster; 1984: Lust in the Dust; 1988: Mortuary Academy; 1989: Judgment Day (dtv); 1990: Simple Justice (dtv); Preston Sturges: The Rise and Fall of an American Dreamer; 1994: Carmen Miranda: Bananas Is My Business.

NY Stage: 1927: Lady Do; 1929: The Street Singer; 1932: Dinner at Eight.

Select TV: 1951: The Big Hello (sp); 1952: Tango (sp); A Letter From Home (sp); 1953–54: Chevrolet Showroom (series); 1954: The Long Goodbye (sp); 1954–55: Passport to Danger (series); 1955: Situation Wanted (sp); 1957: Old Spanish Custom (sp); Mrs. Snyder (sp); 1958: Birthday Present (sp); 1959–61: Take a Good Look (series); 1961: The Battle of the Paper Bullets (sp); 1977: Don't Push — I'll Charge When I'm Ready (filmed 1969); 1985–87: Falcon Crest (series).

MICKEY ROONEY

(JOSEPH YULE, JR.) BORN: BROOKLYN, NY, SEPTEMBER 23, 1920.

Almost a walking, talking history of show business, Mickey Rooney, with his roller-coaster career, was perhaps the most fascinating of all actors, running the gamut from box-office highs to made-for-the money lows, starting as a cocky little kid and ending up an elderly statesmen of the movie's golden era, albeit one full of incomprehensible shticks and mannerisms. A pint-sized bundle of energy, he was one of the liveliest additions to motion pictures and just as often one of the most undisciplined hams ever to hit the footlights. Folks have loved him and hated him in equal doses; Marlon Brando declared him the best actor in films, which was high praise indeed. In truth, whatever his appeal, it is impossible to imagine the entertainment field without him. Born to a pair of vaudevillians, he was not yet two when he was participating in their act and it was Mom who took him to Hollywood when the parents split, finding him work in children's stage revues. This led to a role as a midget (with a moustache!) in a 20th Century-Fox two-reeler called "Not to Be Trusted," and then another midget role, in a feature, *Orchids and Ermine*, in 1927. Producer Larry Darmour of F.B.O. Studios was impressed by the tyke and made him the star of a series of two-reelers derived from a popular comic strip about an irrepressible kid named Mickey Maguire. That became Rooney's off-screen name as well for the run of the series, which was released between August 1927 (starting with "Mickey's Circus," the only time he was billed as "Mickey Yule") and March 1934 (ending with "Mickey's Medicine Man"), with distribution passing over the years from F.B.O. to Radio Pictures to Columbia. Although he was 14 by the time the shorts were abandoned, his tiny stature allowed him to convincingly play younger, as it would for so much of his career.

He resumed work in features in 1932, but for copyright reasons it was decided that he could not continue to use the name of Mickey Maguire. So it was, while playing an orphan kid in Universal's *Fast Companions*, that someone came up with "Rooney" as an option. Now an all-purpose child actor, he played the king of a mythical country in the Tom Mix-vehicle *My Pal the King*; a dancing vaudevillian who grows up to be Eddie Quillan in *Broadway to Hollywood*; young John Boles in *Beloved*; and young Clark Gable in *Manhattan Melodrama*. The last one showed just how effortlessly he could make an impression in a brief period of time and MGM put him under contract. His work during the early years of his contract ranged from *Chained*, where he was glimpsed briefly playing in a swimming pool, to *Hide-Out*, where he stole scenes as Maureen O'Sullivan's rambunctious kid brother. The studio loaned him out frequently; to Columbia, where he played Ann Sothern's sibling in *Blind Date*; to Fox, where he was a small-town boy named Freckles in *The Country Chairman*; and, most importantly, to Warner Bros. for their lavish rendering of *A Midsummer Night's Dream*. Rooney had appeared in the famous Hollywood Bowl stage production directed by Max Reinhardt, and his no-holds barred interpretation of Puck is among the most unforgettably bizarre and maddening performances ever put on film. It made him more famous than ever, but MGM still wasn't sure exactly what to do with him. They gave him the fairly thankless role of the younger brother in *Ah, Wilderness!*, then loaned him to David Selznick for *Little Lord Fauntleroy*, which marked the first time he'd play tough opposite the more delicate Freddie Bartholomew, in this case as a boot black with a heavily emphasized Brooklyn accent, who remains Freddie's loyal friend when the latter moves to England.

MGM decided that this pairing really clicked and put the two of them alongside a third child star, Jackie Cooper, in *The Devil Is a Sissy*, a gimmick that worked beautifully in this story of an aristocratic lad who becomes the unlikely pal of some street kids. Then, in one of the top productions of 1937, *Captains Courageous*, Rooney, very much in support of Bartholomew, appeared as the cabin boy who takes some of the pomp out of stuck-up rich kid Freddie. In both cases he was excellent and the critics were beginning to rave. He was, in fact, so in demand that Fox borrowed him to play the cabin boy torn between his loyalty to guilt ridden Warner Baxter and unrepentant Wallace Beery in the stark adventure *Slave Ship*, which Rooney pulled off with his usual professionalism. Not surprisingly, considering his tiny frame, he was called on to play a jockey, first at Warner Bros., in *Down the Stretch*, and then back on the home lot in *Thoroughbreds Don't Cry*, which was significant because it marked the first of several teamings with Judy Garland, whose more restrained persona perfectly complimented his often undis-

ciplined exuberance. There was another fairly minor entry in 1937, but it would be a milestone in his career: *A Family Affair*, a pleasant drama-comedy about the small-town Hardy family, presided over by judge Lionel Barrymore and mom Spring Byington. This picture did so nicely at the box office that there was a demand for another, resulting in *You're Only Young Once*, with Lewis Stone and Fay Holden now playing the parents. The second batch of healthy financial returns encouraged MGM to start a low-budget series of pictures. The original intent was to focus on each family member (Cecilia Parker was sister Marian; Sara Haden spinster Aunt Milly) but there was no doubt that Rooney, as the anxious, hyperactive, girl-crazy teenager, Andy Hardy, was pulling the lion's share of audience attention his way. Most of the films required Andy to be led astray in his single-minded pursuit of the opposite sex, only to see the error of his ways, per a stern but loving lecture by level-headed Dad. It wasn't surprising that after *Judge Hardy's Children*, the fourth entry was entitled *Love Finds Andy Hardy*, and the series, from that point on, would become known as the "Andy Hardy" films. Sweet, overly idealized, and pretty much interchangeable, they presented a comforting portrait of small-town America that seemed suited for the times and were fondly remembered by fans for years, Rooney becoming a lasting image of what every parent wished their teen could be like.

Now officially a box-office "name," Rooney kept at the Hardy films while staying very busy on other projects. These included another with Bartholomew, *Lord Jeff*, again bringing the British brat down to earth (with an Irish accent, no less); *Stablemates*, which paired him quite well with lovable lug Wallace Beery, in this variation on the latter's influential *The Champ*; and *Boys Town*, one of the big melodramas of the era, with Rooney as the incorrigible, stogie-smoking punk who does a turnabout for the better through the guidance of Father Flanagan, as played by Spencer Tracy. It was another of Mickey's most famous roles, but it brought out his worst excesses, with maudlin crying jags and too much effort put into "big moments" for your viewing pleasure. Nonetheless MGM knew they had a hot property on their hands and put a corncob pipe in his mouth for *The Adventures of Huckleberry Finn*, one of the better versions of the much-adapted novel; cast him as a bumbling *Young Tom Edison*, which was more a boys' adventure story rather than an examination of the greatest of all inventors; and partnered him with Garland again for a lively and corny musical, *Babes in Arms*, in which he danced with gusto, did impersonations, and behaved like a comet in flight. For his efforts he got an Oscar nomination, which really proved that he was playing among the big boys now.

In addition to some Hardy films in which she appeared, Rooney did three more musicals with Garland, *Strike Up the Band*; *Babes on Broadway*, in which the pair had a charming moment introducing the hit song "How About You;" and the best of the bunch, *Girl Crazy*, with Mickey as an irresponsible playboy set straight during his stay at a dude ranch, with a batch of great Gershwin tunes on hand. These films, with their youthful spirits and "let's put on a show" enthusiasm became a part of movie folklore in their own endearingly hokey way. Like the Hardy films they presented a gentle, mythical view of adolescence, but one that everybody at the time liked to believe was possible. *Men of Boys Town*, allowed for some more Rooney tears, although this time he let Darryl Hickman steal scenes away from him; while *A Yank at Eton* was another variation of the bad-boy-turned-good formula and a tired one at that, of interest only because Freddie Bartholomew, who had once received billing *over* Rooney, was now clearly supporting him. Reaching a peak, Rooney played the young telegraph messenger experiencing life on the homefront in the superb *The Human Comedy*, giving a controlled performance that was in many ways his best, and again ending up in the running for an Oscar.

Before going off to war he did another of his best movies, *National Velvet*, again proving that a toned-down Rooney was certainly a good thing. Upon his return MGM decided on another Andy Hardy entry, *Love Laughs at Andy Hardy*, but its weak grosses, along with the fact that Rooney, short or not, was outgrowing this sort of thing, convinced them to lay the series to rest. A tougher Mickey took to the boxing ring for *Killer McCoy*, then graduated to the role of the older brother in *Summer Holiday*, a well-done musical remake of *Ah, Wilderness!* and an unfortunate box-office failure. In a disastrous career move he played lyricist Lorenz Hart in the studio's lavish and cliche-ridden bio of Rodgers and Hart, *Words and Music*, and overacted shamelessly to a point where his histrionics became legendary in the annals of camp. He and MGM parted company soon afterward.

As the 1940s came to a close he began working in mostly lower budgeted programmers, a clear indication of the loss of his box-office appeal. A tiresome auto race picture, *The Big Wheel*, in which he was a cocky driver hoping to follow in his late father's tracks, didn't steer too far from the "redemption of Mickey" formula Metro had put him through, but *Quicksand*, in which he was an auto-mechanic-turned-criminal was an attempt to try something different. *My Outlaw Brother*, found him South of the Border, searching for bad sibling Robert Stack; *The Strip* allowed him to show off his prowess at the drums, as a musician involved with hoods; *All Ashore* was a Columbia musical directed by former co-star Richard Quine, who would call on his services again; *A Slight Case of Larceny* found him at his most obnoxious, as an opportunistic gas station owner; *The Atomic Kid*, a poorly done "message" comedy from his own production company, cast him as the hapless victim of an A-bomb blast that makes him radioactive; while another self-produced piece, *The Twinkle in God's Eye*, was an icky effort in which he was a parson out West. What rescued Rooney at this point was his character work, as a soldier convinced by Bob Hope to take up boxing, in the service comedy *Off Limits*, and as the helicopter pilot who goes down for the count with buddy William Holden in *The Bridges at Toko-Ri*. These made the industry realize that it was wrong to write him off, as did his Oscar-nominated work in *The Bold and the Brave*. This was Rooney at his best, brimming over with an infectious spirit and swaggering brio, as a GI who, in his big scene, indulges in a frantic crap game during a bombing raid, risking the money he's saved to open his restaurant. There was a gangster quickie, *Baby Face Nelson*, which won its share of admirers over the years, but it seemed sad to see him taking over from a fed-up Donald O'Connor in the last of Universal's Talking Mule comedies, *Francis in the Haunted House*, or reprising his most famous part in *Andy Hardy Comes Home*, which was too bland to even be considered camp.

In the late 1950s he tried too hard to make an impression playing a psychotic, reprising Preston Foster's old role in a stagy remake of *The Last Mile*, and then got involved with classic junk producer Albert Zugsmith, playing a crook in *The Big Operator*; a concerned dad in *Platinum High School*; and, most grievously, the Devil himself in *The Private Lives of Adam and Eve*, the blame for this last horror landing more than a little on Rooney's own shoulders, in so much as he took credit as co-director. There was a good movie, *Breakfast at Tiffany's*, in which his gooney Japanese impersonation was its one drawback, after which he was at his best, as the sad, loyal trainer of washed-up pug Anthony Quinn in *Requiem for a Heavyweight*. Teaming up with Buddy Hackett made no impact the first time out, in the juvenile gimmick

comedy *Everything's Ducky*, but they clicked when reunited for the all-star hit *It's a Mad Mad Mad Mad World*, in which they spent most of the time trying to pilot an out-of-control airplane.

Like many stars seeking employment and possible tax breaks in the 1960s, Rooney went the European route with stops at Yugoslavia for *Secret Invasion*, Beirut for *Twenty-Four Hours to Kill*, and Italy for *Devil in Love*. Perhaps he traveled because back home he was offered nothing better than a Beach Party epic, *How to Stuff a Wild Bikini*; a lifeless whimsy, *The Extraordinary Seaman*; and director Otto Preminger's off-the-wall, star-studded drug comedy *Skidoo*, in which he was relatively restrained compared to all the chaos around him, as a jailed informer. There was a nice part as a cross-eyed silent movie comedian who remains a close friend to fading star Dick Van Dyke in the underrated *The Comic*, but once the 1970s arrived it became harder to keep track of Rooney's career as he began showing up in all kinds of little-seen efforts, like the Nixon satire *Richard*, as his guardian angel; a Mafia spoof, *The Godmothers*, for which he not only wrote the script but the music as well; and *B.J. Lang Presents*, a bizarro trash item in which he was crazed Hollywood makeup artist torturing Luana Anders. On the plus side he pretty funny as a vain, aging actor hiring Michael Caine to ghost his memoirs in *Pulp*, and did a bit of singing in a fun Disney fantasy *Pete's Dragon*, as Helen Reddy's boozy dad. By the time he appeared as one of the hosts in MGM's *That's Entertainment!*, audiences were a bit shocked at his aged appearance, as if it reminded them that even Andy Hardy could not escape the passing of time. The 1970s ended on a high note when he made his Broadway debut in the burlesque musical *Sugar Babies*, bringing in the crowds as he hadn't in years and reaping all kinds of praise as a man who had become something of a show business institution. The same year, 1979, he played an older variation of his role from *National Velvet*, a grizzled horse-trainer, in *The Black Stallion*, and he was so totally on the mark in this lovely film that he received a fourth Oscar nomination.

On television he had a flop series, *One of the Boys* (his third to fail), then played a retarded man in the telefilm *Bill*, which earned him an Emmy Award. It was the greatest acclaim he'd received from the television world since 1957, when he had scored as a ruthlessly abusive comic in the *Playhouse 90* production of *The Comedian*. (The latter's director, John Frankenheimer, would later echo Brando's praise by calling Rooney the best actor he had ever worked with). After this period of renewed interest subsided, he pretty much went back to the anything-for-a-buck Mickey, the better-known of the credits consisting of *Erik the Viking*, a Monty Pythonesque spoof in which he was Tim Robbins's grandfather; *My Heroes Have Always Been Cowboys*, as a doddering senior citizen friend of Ben Johnson's; and *Babe: Pig in the City*, as a drunken old circus clown. Among his more questionable assignments were such direct-to-video or never-to-be-seen-in-America oddities as *Silent Night, Deadly Night 5: The Toy Maker*, a warped version of Pinocchio in which he created a robot son; *The Milky Life*, in which he showed up wearing a diaper; and *The Legend of O.B. Taggart*, a western for which he received screenplay credit. For Canadian television he played Father Flanagan, the founder of Boys Town, in *Brothers' Destiny*, but little mention was made of this nostalgic bit of casting.

He also wrote two memoirs, *i.e.* (1965) and *Life Is Too Short* (1991), and the novel *The Search for Sonny Skies* (1994) about a former chid star. In 1951, he directed but did not appear in *My True Story*, a "B" melodrama made for Columbia and starring Helen Walker; and produced the 1956 Republic Sabu film *Jaguar*. Gossip-wise he was famous for having been married eight times, his first wife (1942–43) being actress Ava Gardner; his third (1949–51) actress Martha Vickers; his fourth (1952–59) actress Elaine Davis, who took billing as "Mrs. Mickey Rooney" in *The Atomic Kid*. Dad Joe Yule popped up in small parts in several of his offspring's movies; Mickey's son Tim Rooney acted in such movies as *Village of the Giants* and *Riot on Sunset Strip*; while Teddy Rooney played Mickey's son in *Andy Hardy Comes Home*. At the 1982 Academy Award ceremony he was awarded an Honorary Academy Award and, despite his controversial position in the industry, there would be few who would deny that he was one of its most tireless workers. Even to some of his detractors his name cannot help but evoke a nostalgic smile and some degree of respect.

Screen (shorts): AS MICKEY MAGUIRE: 1927: Mickey's Circus; Mickey's Pals; Mickey's Battle; Mickey's Eleven; 1928: Mickey's Parade; Mickey in School; Mickey's Nine; Mickey's Little Eva; Mickey's Wild West; Mickey in Love; Mickey's Triumph; Mickey's Babies; Mickey's Movies; Mickey's Rivals; Mickey the Detective; Mickey's Athletes; Mickey's Big Game Hunt; 1929: Mickey's Great Idea; Mickey's Explorers; Mickey's Menagerie; Mickey's Last Chance; Mickey's Brown Derby; Mickey's Northwest Mounted; Mickey's Initiation; Mickey's Midnight Follies; Mickey's Surprise; Mickey's Mixup; Mickey's Big Moment; 1930: Mickey's Champs; Mickey's Strategy; Mickey's Mastermind; Mickey's Luck; Mickey's Whirlwind; Mickey's Warriors; Mickey the Romeo; Mickey's Merry Men; Mickey's Winners; Mickey's Musketeers; Mickey's Bargain; 1931: Mickey's Stampede; Mickey's Crusaders; Mickey's Rebellion; Mickey's Diplomacy; Mickey's Wildcats; Mickey's Thrill Hunters; Mickey's Helping Hand; Mickey's Sideline; 1932: Mickey's Travels; Mickey's Holiday; Mickey's Golden Rule; Mickey's Busy Day; Mickey's Charity; Mickey's Big Business; 1933: Mickey's Ape Man.

AS MICKEY ROONEY: 1933: Mickey's Race; Mickey's Big Broadcast; Mickey's Disguises; Mickey's Touchdown; Mickey's Tent Show; Mickey's Covered Wagon; 1934: Mickey's Minstrels; Mickey's Rescue; Mickey's Medicine Man; 1936: Pirate Party on Catalina Island; 1940: Rodeo Dough; 1941: Cavalcade of the Academy Awards; Meet the Stars No. 4; 1948: Rough But Hopeful; 1952: Screen Snapshots #205; 1953: Mickey Rooney — Then and Now; 1957: Playtime in Hollywood; 1958: Glamorous Hollywood.

Screen (features): AS JOE YULE, JR.: 1927: Orchids and Ermine.

AS MICKEY MAGUIRE: 1932: The Beast of the City; Sin's Pay Day; High Speed; Officer 13.

AS MICKEY ROONEY: 1932: Fast Companions; My Pal the King; 1933: The Big Cage; The Life of Jimmy Dolan; The Big Chance; Broadway to Hollywood; The Chief; The World Changes; 1934: Beloved; I Like It That Way; Love Birds; The Lost Jungle (serial); Manhattan Melodrama; Half a Sinner; Blind Date; Death on the Diamond; Chained; Hide-Out; 1935: The County Chairman; The Healer; Reckless; A Midsummer Night's Dream; Ah, Wilderness!; Riff-Raff; 1936: Little Lord Fauntleroy; The Devil Is a Sissy; Down the Stretch; 1937: Captains Courageous; Slave Ship; A Family Affair; Hoosier Schoolboy; Live, Love and Learn; Thoroughbreds Don't Cry; You're Only Young Once; 1938: Love Is a Headache; Judge Hardy's Children; Hold That Kiss; Lord Jeff; Love Finds Andy Hardy; Boys Town; Stablemates; Out West With the Hardys; 1939: The Adventures of Huckleberry Finn; The Hardys Ride High; Andy Hardy Gets Spring Fever; Babes in Arms; Judge Hardy and Son; 1940: Young Tom Edison; Andy Hardy Meets Debutante; Strike Up the Band; 1941: Andy Hardy's Private Secretary; Men of Boys Town; Life Begins for Andy Hardy; Babes on Broadway; 1942: The Courtship of Andy Hardy; A Yank at Eton; Andy Hardy's Double Life; 1943: The

Human Comedy; Girl Crazy; Thousands Cheer; 1944: Andy Hardy's Blonde Trouble; 1945: National Velvet; 1946: Love Laughs at Andy Hardy; 1947: Killer McCoy; 1948: Summer Holiday; Words and Music; 1949: The Big Wheel; 1950: Quicksand; He's a Cockeyed Wonder; The Fireball; 1951: My Outlaw Brother; The Strip; 1952: Sound Off; 1953: All Ashore; Off Limits; A Slight Case of Larceny; 1954: Drive a Crooked Road; The Atomic Kid (and prod.); The Bridges at Toko-Ri; 1955: The Twinkle in God's Eye (and prod.; co-song wr.); 1956: Francis in the Haunted House; The Bold and the Brave; Magnificent Roughnecks; 1957: Operation Mad Ball; Baby Face Nelson; 1958: Andy Hardy Comes Home (and prod.; co-songs); A Nice Little Bank That Should Be Robbed; 1959: The Last Mile; The Big Operator; 1960: Platinum High School/Trouble at 16; The Private Lives of Adam and Eve (and co-dir.); 1961: King of the Roaring 20's — The Story of Arnold Rothstein; Breakfast at Tiffany's; Everything's Ducky; 1962: Requiem for a Heavyweight; 1963: It's a Mad Mad Mad Mad World; 1964: The Secret Invasion; 1965: How to Stuff a Wild Bikini; Twenty-four Hours to Kill; 1966: Ambush Bay; 1968: The Devil in Love; Skidoo; 1969: The Extraorindary Seaman; The Comic; 80 Steps to Jonah; 1970: The Cockeyed Cowboys of Calico County; Hollywood Blue; 1971: B.J. Lang Presents/The Manipulator; 1972: Richard; Pulp; 1973: The Godmothers (and wr.; co-music); 1974: Ace of Hearts/Juego sucio en Panama (nUSr); Thunder County/Swamp Fever/Cell Block Girls; That's Entertainment!; Journey Back to Oz (voice; filmed 1963); 1975: Bon Baisers de Hong Kong/From Hong Kong With Love (nUSr); Rachel's Man (nUSr); 1976: Find the Lady; 1977: The Domino Principle; Pete's Dragon; 1978: The Magic of Lassie; 1979: The Black Stallion; 1980: Arabian Adventure; 1981: The Fox and the Hound (voice); 1983: The Emperor of Peru/Odyssey of the Pacific; 1985: The Care Bears Movie (voice); 1986: Lightning, the White Stallion; 1989: Eric the Viking; 1991: My Heroes Have Always Been Cowboys; 1992: Silent Night, Deadly Night 5: The Toy Maker (dtv); La Vida Lactea/The Milky Life (nUSr); Sweet Justice (dtv); Maximum Force (dtv); Little Nemo: Adventures in Slumberland (voice); The Legend of Wolf Mountain; 1994: Outlaws: The Legend of O.B. Taggart (and wr.; nUSr); That's Entertainment! III; Revenge of the Red Baron (dtv); Radio Star (nUSr); Making Waves (nUSr); 1997: Boys Will Be Boys (dtv); Killing Midnight (dtv); Animals (dtv); 1998: Michael Kael in Katango (nUSr); Sinbad: The Battle of the Dark Knights (nUSr); Babe: Pig in the City; Internet Love (nUSr); The Face on the Barroom Floor (nUSr); 2001: The First of May; 2002: Topa Topa Bluffs (dtv).

NY Stage: 1979: Sugar Babies; 1992: The Will Rogers Follies; 1998: The Wizard of Oz.

Select TV: 1952: Saturday's Children (sp); 1954–55: Hey, Mulligan/The Mickey Rooney Show (series); 1957: The Lady Was a Flop (sp); The Comedian (sp); Mr. Broadway (sp); Pinocchio (sp); 1958: Eddie (sp); 1960: The Mickey Rooney Show (sp); The Money Driver (sp); 1961: Who Killed Julie Greer? (sp); Somebody's Waiting (sp); 1963: Five Six, Pickup Sticks (sp); The Hunt (sp); 1964: The Seven Little Foys (sp); 1964–65: Mickey (series); 1965: Kicks (sp); 1970: Santa Claus Is Coming to Town (sp; voice); 1972: Evil Roy Slade; 1973: NBC Follies (series); 1974: The Year Without Santa Claus (sp; voice); 1979: Donovan's Kid; Rudolph and Frosty's Christmas in July (sp; voice); 1980: My Kidnapper, My Lover; 1981: Leave 'em Laughing; Bill; Senior Trip; 1982: One of the Boys (series); 1983: Bill: On His Own; 1984: It Came Upon the Midnight Clear; 1986: The Return of Mickey Spillane's Mike Hammer; Little Spies; There Must Be a Pony; 1988: Bluegrass; 1990: The Adventures of the Black Stallion (series); 1991: The Gambler

Returns: The Luck of the Draw; **1995:** Brothers' Destiny/The Road Home; **2000:** Phantom of the Megaplex; **2001:** Lady and the Tramp II (voice).

SHIRLEY ROSS

(BERNICE GAUNT) BORN: OMAHA, NE, JANUARY 7, 1909. ED: UCLA. DIED: MARCH 9, 1975.

Pretty much around to smile, sing a tune, look pretty, and not upstage the leading man, Shirley Ross started out as a vocalist with the Gus Arnheim band. While appearing with the group at the Beverly Wilshire Hotel, she got a contract with MGM, who gave her bits in *Bombshell* and *Hollywood Party*; larger parts in *Calm Yourself* (as Ralph Morgan's younger wife) and *San Francisco*, then dropped her. Paramount took her on and this period of employment turned out to be the high point of her film career, starting off with one of the leads in one of the studio's popular potpourri musicals, *The Big Broadcast of 1937*, as a radio announcer taunting tenor Frank Forest. This was followed by the title role in *Hideaway Girl*, as a mysterious woman who catches Robert Cummings's fancy; two with Bing Crosby, *Waikiki Wedding*, as Miss Pineapple, and *Paris Honeymooon*, where she lost him to the annoying Franciska Gaal; and three with Bob Hope. The first of these, *The Big Broadcast of 1938*, gave her a moment of musical comedy immortality of sorts, since she dueted with Hope on the first hearing of what ultimately became his signature song, the Oscar-winning "Thanks for the Memory." This gentle sequence proved so popular that they ended up in a movie by that name, introducing another hit, "Two Sleepy People." Their third together, *Some Like It Hot*, was very minor stuff and Ross's last for the studio. During the 1940s she was seen starring in two "B" musicals over at Republic, *Sailors on Leave* and *A Song for Miss Julie*, and then retired to concentrate on her family. Apart from some scattered television work, she pretty much faded from the scene.

Screen: 1933: Bombshell; **1934:** Hollywood Party; Manhattan Melodrama; The Girl From Missouri; The Merry Widow; **1935:** Age of Indiscretion; Calm Yourself; **1936:** San Francisco; Devil's Squadron; The Big Broadcast of 1937; **1937:** Hideaway Girl; Waikiki Wedding; Blossoms on Broadway; **1938:** Prison Farm; The Big Broadcast of 1938; Thanks for the Memory; **1939:** Paris Honeymoon; Cafe Society; Some Like It Hot/Rhythm Romance; Unexpected Father; **1941:** Sailors on Leave; Kisses for Breakfast; **1945:** A Song for Miss Julie.

Select TV: 1955: Technique (sp).

CHARLES RUGGLES

BORN: LOS ANGELES, CA, FEBRUARY 8, 1886. DIED: DECEMBER 23, 1970.

One of the sparkling reasons that Paramount stood above all other studios when it came to comedy in the 1930s, Charles Ruggles was a short, mousey-voiced character whose speciality was stuttering, henpecked husbands. He made his acting debut with a stock company in San Francisco in 1905, then toured with the Oliver Morosco troupe, up and down the West Coast. A year after his short-lived 1914 Broadway debut, in *Help Wanted*, he did three films. They all were released by his future employer, Paramount, but none did much to convince him or the movies that they were a needed match. He returned to the theatre, where his better-known properties included *White Collars*, *Queen High* (which he repeated on screen

in 1930), and the Rodgers and Hart musical *Spring Is Here*. The last got him his official Paramount contract and he made his talkie debut for them playing a drunken newsman in *Gentlemen of the Press*, in support of Walter Huston. Again with Huston he was seen in *The Lady Lies*, which also featured Claudette Colbert. He popped up with her again in *Young Man of Manhattan*, although his principle scenes were with newcomer Ginger Rogers. Continuing the daisy chain of assignments he was back with Rogers for *Honor Among Lovers*, but not before being borrowed by Columbia to take on the cross-dressing title role in the less-well-remembered version of the famed stage farce *Charley's Aunt*. His home studio rewarded him for his stellar work with a lead in *The Girl Habit*, as a skirt-chasing millionaire, but it made much less impact then his droll supporting turns in a trio of Maurice Chevalier hits, *The Smiling Lieutenant*, as a married man with the hots for Claudette Colbert; *One Hour With You*, hitting on Jeanette MacDonald; and *Love Me Tonight*, as the Vicomte who has failed to pay his tailoring bill.

He was a hoot as the timid, clumsy clerk who gets revenge on his intolerant employee in a segment of *If I Had a Million*, teamed so perfectly with the chattery, nagging Mary Boland that Paramount saw great future opportunities in their pairing. They would, in fact, link up for another 14 films, the best known of which were *Six of a Kind*, in which they spent a reckless vacation with Burns and Allen, and the marvelous *Ruggles of Red Gap*, in which Ruggles was Egbert Floud, the vulgar westerner who wins gentleman's gentleman Charles Laughton in a poker game. As stars Ruggles and Boland headed such small programmer comedies as *People Will Talk*, *Night Work*, *Wives Never Know*, and *Boy Trouble*. In addition to these, Ruggles showed up battling memorably with Edward Everett Horton over Kay Francis in *Trouble in Paradise*; having tea as the March Hare in *Alice in Wonderland*; as gangster Moonface Martin in the truncated adaptation of *Anything Goes*; and in a quite serious part, as Frances Farmer's journalist father, in *Exclusive*. Borrowed on occasion, he ended up in RKO's comedic masterpiece *Bringing Up Baby*, eccentrically demonstrating his leopard calls as flaky big game hunter Horace Applegate. After ending his alliance with Paramount in 1940, he freelanced and his more notable productions included *No Time for Comedy*, as the cuckolded husband of Genevieve Tobin; and two back at Paramount: *Our Hearts Were Young and Gay*, as actor Otis Skinner, and *A Stolen Life*, supporting Bette Davis's dual roles. Opting for television and theatre, he disappeared from movie screens completely during the 1950s but returned (to Paramount, naturally) for the comedies *All in a Night's Work* and *The Pleasure of His Company*, in the latter repeating his Tony Award-winning role as the dryly lovable grandpa. Staying in the granddad mode he showed up in Disney's *The Parent Trap* and Paramount's *Papa's Delicate Condition*, remaining a low-keyed but always professional and welcome presence in some other mild comedies of the 1960s before cancer claimed him at 84.

Screen: 1915: Peer Gynt; The Majesty of the Law; The Reform Candidate; **1923:** The Heart Raider; **1929:** Gentlemen of the Press; The Lady Lies; The Battle of Paris; **1930:** Roadhouse Nights; Young Man of Manhattan; Queen High; Her Wedding Night; Charley's Aunt; **1931:** The Smiling Lieutenant; Honor Among Lovers; The Girl Habit; Beloved Bachelor; Husband's Holiday; **1932:** This Reckless Age; One Hour With You; This Is the Night; Make Me a Star; Love Me Tonight; 70,000 Witnesses; The Night of June 13; Trouble in Paradise; Evenings for Sale; If I Had a Million; Madame Butterfly; **1933:** Murders in the Zoo; Terror Aboard; Melody Cruise; Mama Loves Papa; Goodbye Love; Girl Without a Room; Alice in Wonderland; **1934:** Six of a Kind; Melody in Spring; Murder in the Private Car; Friends of

Mr. Sweeney; The Pursuit of Happiness; 1935: Ruggles of Red Gap; People Will Talk; No More Ladies; The Big Broadcast of 1936; 1936: Anything Goes; Early to Bed; Hearts Divided; Wives Never Know; Yours for the Asking; Mind Your Own Business; 1937: Turn Off the Moon; Exclusive; 1938: Bringing Up Baby; Breaking the Ice; Service De Luxe; His Exciting Night; 1939: Boy Trouble; Sudden Money; Invitation to Happiness; Night Work; Balalaika; 1940: The Farmer's Daughter; Opened by Mistake; Maryland; Public Deb No. 1; No Time for Comedy; The Invisible Woman; 1941: Honeymoon for Three; Model Wife; The Parson of Panamint; Go West, Young Lady; The Perfect Snob; 1942: Friendly Enemies; 1943: Fixie Dugan; 1944: Our Hearts Were Young and Gay; The Doughboys; Three Is a Family; 1945: Bedside Manner; Incendiary Blonde; 1946: A Stolen Life; Gallant Journey; The Perfect Marriage; My Brother Talks to Horses; 1947: It Happened on 5th Avenue; Ramrod; 1948: Give My Regards to Broadway; 1949: The Lovable Cheat; Look for the Silver Lining; 1961: All in a Night's Work; The Pleasure of His Company; The Parent Trap; 1963: Son of Flubber; Papa's Delicate Condition; 1964: I'd Rather Be Rich; 1966: The Ugly Dachshund; Follow Me, Boys!

NY Stage: 1914: Help Wanted; 1915: Rolling Stones; 1917: Canary Cottage; 1918: The Passing Show of 1918; 1919: Tumble In; The Girl in the Limousine; 1920: Ladies' Night; 1921: The Demi-Virgin; 1923: Battling Butler; 1925: White Collars; 1926: Queen High; 1928: Rainbow; 1929: Spring Is Here; 1943: Try and Get It; 1958: The Pleasure of His Company; 1962: The Captain and the Kings; 1964: Roar Like a Dove.

Select TV: 1949–52: The Ruggles/The Charlie Ruggles Show (series); 1953: The Consul (sp); 1954–55: The World of Mr. Sweeney (series); 1956: The Luck of Amos Currie (sp); 1957: Crisis in Coroma (sp); 1958: The Male Animal (sp); A Delicate Affair (sp); 1959: Once Upon a Christmas Tree (sp); The Bells of St. Mary's (sp); 1961: Happiest Day (sp); 1967: Carousel (sp).

JANICE RULE

BORN: NORWOOD, OH, AUGUST 15, 1931.

Seldom recognized despite years of dependable support, Janice Rule had started as a dancer but switched to straight acting after breaking her ankle during the Broadway run of Miss Liberty. Warner Bros. signed her up to support Joan Crawford in Goodbye, My Fancy, and to carry part of the storyline that connected the all-star guest appearances in Starlift. MGM took her on after that for Holiday for Sinners, a Mardi Gras melodrama, and Rogue's March, where she was Peter Lawford's love interest. Her break came back on Broadway in Picnic, playing the pretty Midwesterner who stops drifter Ralph Meeker in his tracks. Her performance resulted in lots of television work, but Columbia opted to give her role to Kim Novak in the movie version of Picnic. Just to rub it in Columbia did cast her in Bell Book and Candle, where she was required to lose James Stewart to Ms. Novak. In between guest appearances, telefilms, and stage work, she could be seen on the big screen choosing sensitive Jeffrey Hunter over his brother Fred MacMurray in Gun for a Coward; playing the man-hating beatnik in The Subterraneans; taking a divided interest in both George Segal and Yul Brynner in Invitation to a Gunfighter; escaping from fiancé Richard Widmark in Alvarez Kelly; attempting an Irish brogue in Welcome to Hard Times; being rescued by secret agent Dean Martin in The Ambusher; taunting ex-lover Burt Lancaster in The Swimmer, in one of her best-ever performances; and joining the bed-hopping trash of Doctor's Wives. In later years, the older Rule could be seen

as the weird lady painting the swimming pool in 3 Women, and as the mother of a pair of bicyclists in American Flyers. She was married (1969–79) to actor Ben Gazzara.

Screen: 1951: Goodbye, My Fancy; Starlift; 1952: Holiday for Sinners; Rogue's March; 1956: A Woman's Devotion; 1957: Gun for a Coward; 1958: Bell Book and Candle; 1960: The Subterraneans; 1964: Invitation to a Gunfighter; 1966: The Chase; Alvarez Kelly; 1967: Welcome to Hard Times; 1968: The Ambushers; The Swimmer; 1971: Doctors' Wives; Gumshoe; 1973: Kid Blue; 1977: 3 Women; 1982: Missing; 1984: Rainy Day Friends/L.A. Bad; 1985: American Flyers.

NY Stage: 1949: Miss Liberty; 1950: Great to Be Alive; 1953: Picnic; 1954: The Flowering Peach; 1955: The Carefree Tree; 1958: The Night Circus; 1961: The Happiest Girl in the World; 1971: The Homecoming.

Select TV: 1954: The Brownstone (sp); Home Again, Home Again (sp); 1955: The Bride Cried (sp); 1957: The Life You Save (sp); 1957: Four Women in Black (sp); 1958: Angel in the Air (sp); The Last of the Belles (sp); 1959: Train for Tecumseh (sp); 1960: The Snows of Kilimanjaro (sp); Journey to the Day (sp); 1962: Tonight in Samarkand (sp); The Love of Claire Ambler (sp); 1968: Shadow on the Land (sp); 1969: Trial Run (sp); 1971: The Devil and Miss Sarah; 1978: The Word (ms).

SIG RUMANN

BORN: HAMBURG, GERMANY, OCTOBER 11, 1884. ED: ILMENAN COL. DIED: FEBRUARY 14, 1967.

Hollywood's ideal embodiment of the blustering, overbearing German, Sig Rumann had acted in stock in his native country before serving in World War I. He came to the U.S. in 1924, where he joined the Irving Place Theatre, which presented foreign-language plays, until he was asked to appear in the 1929 Broadway production of The Channel Road. There was a single movie appearance during this time, in The Royal Box, and a notable stage role, as the businessman in Grand Hotel, the part Wallace Beery would play in the noted movie version. 20th Century-Fox put Rumann under contract in 1934 and started him off in The World Moves On, as a baron running a cotton business. Playing villainously, he was a saboteur in Marie Galante; the domineering father who keeps Anna Sten away from Gary Cooper in The Wedding Night; and the arrogant opera impresario who gets his comeuppance courtesy of the Marx Brothers in A Night at the Opera. This last bit of casting proved so magical a teaming that he was back with the Brothers two years later, playing a frustrated surgeon, for a brief sequence in A Day at the Races, and then again, in 1946, for A Night in Casablanca, as an ex-Nazi in hiding. He participated in two of the best-remembered comedies of the 1930s, Nothing Sacred, as the doctor who exposes fraud Carole Lombard (he repeated the part in the 1954 Martin and Lewis remake, Living It Up) and Ninotchka, as one of the Russian fuctionaries who is seduced by capitalism. Of course, as America entered World War II, he was called on to join the cinematic branch of the SS, which he did in Confessions of a Nazi Spy, So Ends Our Night, Desperate Journey, and The Hitler Gang, as von Hindenburg. Best of all, he was the hilariously egotistical Gestapo chief in To Be or Not to Be, whose repeated line "So they call me 'Concentration Camp' Ehrhardt" became the most famous catchphrase from the film. Director Billy Wilder took advantage of his comedic talents, casting him as doctors in both A Foreign Affair and The Fortune Cookie, and, best of all, in one of his other enduring roles, the two-faced concentration camp guard Schultz in the classic Stalag 17. Originally billed as

Siegfried Rumann, he was also billed on occasion as Sig Ruman.
Screen: 1929: The Royal Box; 1934: The World Moves On; Marie Galante; Servants' Entrance; 1935: Under Pressure; The Wedding Night; The Farmer Takes a Wife; A Night at the Opera; East of Java; Spring Tonic; 1936: The Princess Comes Across; The Bold Caballero; 1937: On the Avenue; Maytime; Midnight Taxi; Think Fast, Mr. Moto; This Is My Affair; A Day at the Races; The Great Hospital Mystery; Thin Ice; Love Under Fire; Lancer Spy; Seventh Heaven; Heidi; Nothing Sacred; Thank You, Mr. Moto; 1938: Paradise for Three; The Saint in New York; I'll Give a Million; Suez; Girls on Probation; The Great Waltz; 1939: Honolulu; Never Say Die; Confessions of a Nazi Spy; Only Angels Have Wings; Ninotchka; Remember?; 1940: Dr. Ehrlich's Magic Bullet; Outside the 3-Mile Limit; I Was an Adventuress; Four Sons; Bitter Sweet; Comrade X; Victory; 1941: So Ends Our Night; That Uncertain Feeling; The Man Who Lost Himself; The Wagons Roll at Night; Love Crazy; Shining Victory; This Woman Is Mine; World Premiere; 1942: To Be or Not to Be; Remember Pearl Harbor; Crossroads; We Were Dancing; Enemy Agents Meet Ellery Queen; Desperate Journey; Berlin Correspondent; China Girl; 1943: Tarzan Triumphs; They Came to Blow Up America; Sweet Rosie O'Grady; Government Girl; The Song of Bernadette; 1944: It Happened Tomorrow; The Hitler Gang; Summer Storm; House of Frankenstein; 1945: The Dolly Sisters; A Royal Scandal; The Men in Her Diary; She Went to the Races; 1946: A Night in Casablanca; Faithful in My Fashion; Night and Day; 1947: Mother Wore Tights; 1948: If You Knew Susie; The Emperor Waltz; Give My Regards to Broadway; 1949: Border Incident; 1950: Father Is a Bachelor; 1951: On the Riviera; 1952: The World in His Arms; O. Henry's Full House; 1953: Ma and Pa Kettle on Vacation; Stalag 17; Houdini; 1954: The Glenn Miller Story; Living It Up; White Christmas; 3 Ring Circus; 1955: Carolina Cannonball; Many Rivers to Cross; Spy Chasers; 1957: The Wings of Eagles; 1961: The Errand Boy; 1964: Robin and the 7 Hoods; 36 Hours; 1966: The Fortune Cookie; Way…Way Out; Last of the Secret Agents?
NY Stage: 1929: The Channel Road; Half Gods; 1939: Grand Hotel; 1933: Alien Corn; Eight Bells; 1942: Lilly of the Valley; 1961: Once There Was a Russian.
Select TV: 1952: Life With Luigi (series).

BARBARA RUSH

BORN: DENVER, CO, JANUARY 4, 1927.
ED: UNIV. OF CA.

Another of the movies' lovely ladies who was originally chalked up as mere programmer window-dressing, but hung in there on perseverance and talent, Barbara Rush had been acting since she was a child, with her first appearance at a Santa Barbara theatre. The abilities she displayed while acting in college earned her a scholarship to the Pasadena Playhouse. From there she went to Hollywood where Paramount stuck her into the supporting cast of *Molly*, adapted from the popular radio-television show *The Goldbergs*; made her second lead to Corinne Calvet in the "B" adventure *Quebec*; required her to look pretty while the Earth faced extinction in *When Worlds Collide*; and gave her a decent part in the western *Flaming Feather*, as the woman whose life was saved by shady Victor Jory and thereby feels obligated to marry him. Universal snatched her up next for an acceptable sci-fi outing, *It Came From Outer Space*, as Richard Carlson's fiancée; two programmers with Rock Hudson, *Taza — Son of Cochise* and *Captain Lightfoot*; and a role as Jane Wyman's step-daughter in one of the studio's big soap operas of the 1950s, *Magnificent*

Obsession. It took 20th Century-Fox to start giving her some meaty parts with *Bigger Than Life*, trying to cope with husband James Mason's drug addiction; *No Down Payment*, as the wife of Pat Hingle, who doesn't want to involve herself in neighborhood integration, appearing on screen with ex-husband (1950–55) Jeffrey Hunter; and *The Young Lions*, as Dean Martin's love interest. She was the socialite Paul Newman is denied marriage to in *The Young Philadelphians*; the wife cheated on by Kirk Douglas in *Strangers When We Meet*; was attractively partnered with Frank Sinatra for both *Come Blow Your Horn* and *Robin and the 7 Hoods*; and got another good part from Fox in *Hombre*, as Fredric March's snobbish younger wife. Though she would be seen sporadically on the big screen after that (playing moms to the likes of Bruce Jenner in *Can't Stop the Music* and Daryl Hannah in *Summer Lovers*), she became more firmly associated with television movies from the late 1960s on.
Screen: 1950: Molly; 1951: The First Legion; Quebec; When Worlds Collide; Flaming Feather; 1953: It Came From Outer Space; Prince of Pirates; 1954: Taza — Son of Cochise; Magnificent Obsession; The Black Shield of Falworth; 1955: Captain Lightfoot; Kiss of Fire; 1956: World in My Corner; Bigger Than Life; Flight to Hong Kong; 1957: Oh, Men! Oh, Women!; No Down Payment; 1958: The Young Lions; Harry Black and the Tiger; 1959: The Young Philadelphians; 1960: The Bramble Bush; Strangers When We Meet; 1963: Come Blow Your Horn; 1964: Robin and the 7 Hoods; 1967: Hombre; 1969: Strategy of Terror; 1972: The Man; 1974: Superdad; 1980: Can't Stop the Music; 1982: Summer Lovers.
NY Stage: 1984: A Woman of Independent Means.
Select TV: 1954: Gavin's Darling (sp); 1955: Shadow of a Doubt (sp); The Amazing Mrs. Holliday (sp); 1956: Night Song (sp); 1957: The Troublemakers (sp); 1958: The Connoisseur (sp); 1960: Alas Babylon (sp); 1961: Notorious (sp); 1962: A Very Special Girl (sp); 1962–63: Saints and Sinners (series); 1965: In Darkness Waiting (sp); 1966: Storm Crossing (sp); 1968–69: Peyton Place (series); 1971: Suddenly Single; 1972: Cutter; The Eyes of Charles Sand; Moon of the Wolf; 1973: Crime Club; 1973–74: The New Dick Van Dyke Show (series); 1975: The Last Day; 1979: Death on the Freeway; The Seekers; 1980: Flamingo Road; 1981–82: Flamingo Road (series); 1983: The Night the Bridge Fell Down (filmed 1980); Between Friends; 1990: Web of Deceit; 1992–94: All My Children (series); 1995: Widow's Kiss.

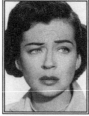

GAIL RUSSELL

BORN: CHICAGO, IL, SEPTEMBER 23, 1924.
DIED: AUGUST 26, 1961.

A true causality of Hollywood, Gail Russell possessed big, sad, haunted eyes but not a great deal of acting talent. She was groomed for stardom, felt uncomfortable about the whole thing, sought solace in drink, and was dead before the age of 40. Without an iota of acting lessons or experience, she was tested by Paramount while still in high school and signed to a contract in 1943. They launched her in a small role in a "B," *Henry Aldrich Gets Glamour*, and then gave her a plum lead, as the strange young girl linked to the supernatural happenings in *The Uninvited*. Although clearly untrained, she had the right degree of oddness to get by on this particular occasion and, since this was one of the most highly regarded of cinema ghost stories, it made her a star. As a follow-up she and Diana Lynn played sisters on vacation in Paris in a mediocre period comedy *Our Hearts Were Young and Gay*, in which Russell's work showed a marked improvement. Both of these movies rated sequels (*The Unseen* and *Our Hearts Were Growing Up*, respectively) between which Russell was made leading lady to Alan Ladd in one of his hits, *Salty O'Rourke*, although the chemistry between Ladd and Stanley Clements was more interesting. She did one of her better-known roles on loan, as the Quaker girl who tames John Wayne, in a well-done anti-violence piece, *Angel and the Badman*, then returned to Paramount to unconvincingly play a femme fatale in another Ladd film, *Calcutta*. Wayne took her back again for *Wake of the Red Witch*, but after two Paramount programmers, *Captain China* and *The Lawless*, the studio dropped her. There was a brief (1949–54) marriage to actor Guy Madison and then a descent into alcoholism, which led to her ending up in a sanitarium on more than one occasion. She recovered sufficiently to return to the screen in 1955 with *Seven Men from Now*, a Randolph Scott western, and *The Tattered Dress*, in which she got to do some heavy emoting as a lying witness. Her final film was *The Silent Call*, a doggie story released in 1961. That same year, she was found dead in her apartment and despite the autopsy crediting "natural causes," it was clear that alcohol had prompted her early demise.

Screen: 1943: Henry Aldrich Gets Glamour; **1944:** The Uninvited; Lady in the Dark; Our Hearts Were Young and Gay; **1945:** The Unseen; Salty O'Rourke; Duffy's Tavern; **1946:** Our Hearts Were Growing Up; The Bachelor's Daughters; **1947:** Angel and the Badman; Calcutta; Variety Girl; **1948:** Night Has a Thousand Eyes; Moonrise; Wake of the Red Witch; **1949:** Song of India; El Paso; The Great Dan Patch; Captain China; **1950:** The Lawless; **1951:** Air Cadet; **1956:** Seven Men From Now; **1957:** The Tattered Dress; **1958:** No Place to Land; **1961:** The Silent Call.

HAROLD RUSSELL

BORN: NORTH SYDNEY, NOVA SCOTIA, CANADA, JANUARY 14, 1914. RAISED IN CAMBRIDGE, MA. DIED: JANUARY 29, 2002.

With a single movie credit to his name and one of the most inspiring of all life stories, Harold Russell became one of the most famous of all Oscar-winners. During World War II, he joined the paratroopers and, in 1944, while serving as an instructor at Camp MacKall, North Carolina, he suffered a life-changing accident. A charge of dynamite he was holding unexpectedly went off, resulting in the amputation of both hands three inches above the wrist. He was fitted with a pair of prosthetic devices in which hooks took the place of his hands and went through a period of psychological and physical recovery he would later recount in his first autobiography, *Victory in My Hands*, which he co-wrote with Victor Rosen and published in 1949. (A follow-up book, *The Best Years of My Life*, came out in 1981). In hopes of offering support to soldiers in similar circumstances, he made a short film about his experiences and it was this two-reeler, "Diary of a Sergeant," that caught the attention of producer Samuel Goldwyn and director William Wyler. Wyler cast Russell as the amputee who must face coming home to his small town parents and loyal girl-friend, in his epic look at the aftermath of World War II, *The Best Years of Our Lives*. The movie was a box-office smash and among its many prizes was Russell's Academy Award for Best Supporting Actor of 1946. In an unprecedented feat, he was also given a special Oscar that same year "for bringing hope and courage to his fellow veterans through his performance." With no immediate plans to continue an acting career, he turned his attention toward the rehabilitation of handicapped vets. In addition to lecturing and touring hospitals, he served with such organizations as the American Veterans of World War II, the World Veterans

Federation, and the President's Committee on Employment of the Handicapped. He returned to the screen unheralded in 1980 to play one of the handicapped bar denizens who befriends embittered cripple John Savage in *Inside Moves*, bringing his movie total up to two. Even less noted was his appearance in a 1997 direct-to-video feature, *Dogtown*.

Screen: 1946: The Best Years of Our Lives; **1980:** Inside Moves; **1997:** Dogtown (dtv).

JANE RUSSELL

(ERNESTINE JANE GERALDINE RUSSELL)
BORN: BEMIDJI, MN, JUNE 21, 1921.

Sulky Jane Russell shot to stardom because of her ample chest measurement and she was the first to admit that her physical appearance kept her famous more than anything akin to solid acting talent. She had a way of spitting out a barb or an insult that suggested possibilities, but it was difficult to warm up to her icy stoicism and she was just one of many actresses whose movie star glow dimmed with age. While modeling, she took some acting courses — including classes at Max Reinhardt's Theatrical Workshop — but it wasn't her cirriculum that attracted the attention of producer Howard Hughes. He cast her as the sultry sagebrush vixen Rio in *The Outlaw*, a look at the Billy the Kid legend that ran into major difficulties with the censors. Originally released in a limited run in 1943, its wide distribution was stalled when various theatre circuits refused it, citing some suggestive dialogue, an air of sexuality, and the emphasis on Russell's bosom. Cuts were made, with a token showing in 1946, and finally a wider release in 1950. During all this time the publicity made Russell one of the hottest sex symbols of the day and the movie, despite a chilly critical reception, had audiences lining up at whatever venues would dare to play it. Under contract to Hughes, she was loaned out to United Artists for *Young Widow*, a routine soap opera designed to provide a glimpse of the actress for those who were *Outlaw*-deprived, and, more agreeably, to Paramount for *The Paleface*, as the brusquely butch Calamity Jane, hilariously teamed with cowardly Bob Hope in one of his best and most profitable features. When Hughes began to wield great power at RKO, Russell became a staple of that studio's 1950s melodramas during what turned out to be its final years of existence.

She started off her RKO contract with *His Kind of Woman*, as a bar singer biding her time in Mexico and falling for gambler Robert Mitchum. The pairing of the sleepy-eyed, sardonic Mitchum with the similarly cynical Russell clicked and they were asked to reprise their chemistry in *Macao*, which duplicated the formula with less success. In the meantime she was leered at by Groucho Marx in *Double Dynamite*; proved a less-than-thrilling combination with Victor Mature in *The Las Vegas Story*; and played another famous lady of the West — Belle Starr — in *Montana Belle*, which had been shot for Republic but bought for distribution by RKO. On loan she found greater box-office success with the inevitable Paramount sequel, *Son of Paleface*, and then the Fox musical *Gentlemen Prefer Blondes*. The teaming of the snippy, world-wise Russell with the bubble-headed but delectable Marilyn Monroe worked like a charm and their duet of "Two Little Girls from Little Rock" became a classic, while Russell's solo, "Ain't There Anyone Here for Love?," in which she was surrounded by a gymnasium full of self-involved muscle men, was camp at its most delirious. Back at RKO she did the 3-D musical *The French Line*, as a Texan in Paris, and the scuba-drama *Underwater!*, which hoped to provide more of Jane in a bikini thanks to the splendor of Super-Scope.

Ending her contract with Hughes, she went to 20th Century-Fox to team with Clark Gable for a numbingly routine but popular western, *The Tall Men*; did a sequel, *Gentlemen Marry Brunettes*, minus Monroe, which only proved who the real lure was in the first film; and helped produced the disastrous farce *The Fuzzy Pink Nightgown*, appearing in a blonde wig as a movie star who falls for her kidnapper, Ralph Meeker. From there she earned her keep singing in nightclubs, coming back to movies on occasion for such "B" features as *Born Losers*, a film that gained some attention in later reissues for its introduction of Tom Laughlin as Billy Jack. Television audiences in the 1970s knew her best for doing some brassiere commercials, a gig that didn't indicate a hell of a lot of progress.

Screen: 1943: The Outlaw; 1946: Young Widow; 1948: The Paleface; 1951: His Kind of Woman; Double Dynamite; 1952: The Las Vegas Story; Macao; Montana Belle; Son of Paleface; Road to Bali; 1953: Gentlemen Prefer Blondes; 1954: The French Line; 1955: Underwater!; Foxfire; The Tall Men; Gentlemen Marry Brunettes; 1956: Hot Blood; The Revolt of Mamie Stover; 1957: The Fuzzy Pink Nightgown; 1964: Fate Is the Hunter; 1966: Johnny Reno; Waco; 1967: Born Losers; 1970: Darker Than Amber.

NY Stage: 1971: Company.

Select TV: 1958: MacCready's Woman (sp); 1959: Ballad for a Badman (sp); 1984: The Yellow Rose (series).

ROSALIND RUSSELL

BORN: WATERBURY, CT, JUNE 4, 1907.
ED: AADA. DIED: NOVEMBER 28, 1976.

There was a rock-solid determination to Rosalind Russell that kept her going through both good and bad times, the sort of no-nonsense, indefatigable strength that made audiences embrace her for decades. She was a peerless banterer in the realm of comedy, could zing an acerbic quip with the best of them, and, when letting down her guard, could project a certain warmth, though she was somehow less cherished for doing out-and-out drama. Her presence was never less than that of a star, but as she grew older her larger-than-life qualities almost made her seem too big for certain roles. Shortly after graduating from the American Academy of Dramatic Arts, she joined a stock company in Saranac Lake, NY, then returned to Manhattan to make her Broadway debut, in 1930, in *The Garrick Gaieties*. Following more stage work she was simultaneously signed by Universal and MGM, opting for the latter. Her debut came in 1934, as the client who tries to steal William Powell from Myrna Loy, in *Evelyn Prentice*. It was a fairly theatrical performance that didn't lead to anything more than a string of supporting roles: as Joan Crawford's friend in *Forsaking All Others*, and as the Countess whom Ramon Novarro does not wish to marry in *The Night Is Young*. Promoted to second leads, she was Alison Skipworth's secretary in *The Casino Murder Case*, then took on some colorless roles as women who didn't wind up with the leading man, in *Reckless*, where Franchot Tone cast her off for Jean Harlow then commited suicide, and *China Seas*, where Clark Gable planned to wed her until Harlow sets him straight. Similarly, she was the prim woman in Ronald Colman's life in Fox's *Under Two Flags*, only this time she lucked out when her rival, Claudette Colbert, bit the dust. It was a series of roles for which Russell was badly miscast. A loan to Columbia proved to be a great boost for her, with *Craig's Wife*, as John Boles's wife, whose

obsession with propriety and a well kept home alienate everyone around her.

Back at her home lot, the studio rewarded Russell's new-found success by putting her in one of their major productions of 1937, *Night Must Fall*, in which she played the personal assistant to Dame May Whitty, a rigid woman who is not taken in by the charms of dangerous Robert Montgomery. She followed this with a comedy, also with Montgomery, *Live, Love and Learn*, as a socialite marrying an impoverished artist who suddenly becomes famous. Warners borrowed her for another comedy, *Four's a Crowd*, but MGM kept her serious for *The Citadel*, a popular look at an idealistic doctor, filmed in England. In it, Russell was a schoolmistress in a Welsh mining town who ends up married to Robert Donat. This was followed by her peak assignment at the studio, *The Women*, where she had the showiest role in this deliciously scripted ensemble, as the gossipy bitch Sylvia Fowler. She made a meal of it, and won raves. If *The Women* established Russell's reputation as one of the foremost ladies of comedy, she pretty much snatched the crown with her next picture. Columbia's *His Girl Friday* was a tricky gender switch on *The Front Page*, with Russell as the fast-talking reporter Hildy Johnson, who thinks she's happy to unload the profession for prize drip Ralph Bellamy though ex-husband Cary Grant knows better. This was Russell at her most masterful and assured, with her and Grant swatting lines back and forth like a pair of tennis pros. It came to be regarded as one of the high points in screen comedy and is one of her two great signature roles.

She stayed with comedy for *Hired Wife*, with Brian Aherne; *No Time for Comedy*, with James Stewart (a pairing that did not fulfill its promise); *This Thing Called Love*, in which she married Melvyn Douglas only to inform him that she wants to remain celibate for three months, at least in terms acceptable for 1941; *The Feminine Touch*, getting jealous when she thinks Don Ameche is cheating on her with Kay Francis; *They Met in Bombay*, now upped to Clark Gable's leading lady; and *Design for Scandal*, cast as a judge (she would be back on the bench in 1949 for *Tell it to Judge*, a comedy with Robert Cummings). In 1941, she married agent Frederick Brisson. He persuaded her to end her alliance with MGM, but her first assignment elsewhere, a limp teaming with Fred MacMurray at Paramount, *Take a Letter, Darling*, suggested that maybe she'd made a mistake. This was compensated for by a delightful comedy at Columbia, *My Sister Eileen*, in which she was again near perfect as the witty and self-effacing sibling of man-magnet Janet Blair. Its success was further enhanced by Russell's first Oscar nomination. Taking to the air, she played a thinly disguised version of Amelia Earhart (Earhart's widower sold the story on the condition that his wife's name not be mentioned) in the aviation romance *Flight for Freedom*; played another real-life lady, Louise Randall Pierson, an early advocate of women's lib, in *Roughly Speaking*; and then got RKO to back a long-cherished project, *Sister Kenny*, about the nurse who found a treatment for infantile paralysis only to receive years of opposition from the medical board. The last lost a great deal of money for the studio, being the rare biopic that didn't dwell on its subject's love life, but Russell's was an effective performance, aging from idealistic angel of mercy to a more embittered but still determined old woman. She followed this with one she wasn't too keen to make, *Mourning Becomes Electra*, which wound up even deeper in red ink then the last one. This was one of Russell's more misguided performances, florid and self-righteously angry, creating little sympathy or understanding for what should have been a compelling central figure. This suicidally non-commercial attempt to bring Eugene O'Neill's endless saga to the screen was seen by most audiences, if at all, with approximately one hour of footage cleaved from its original 175-minute length. Despite the failure of both of these productions, Russell wound up with back-to-back Oscar nominations.

Her husband served as the producer on *The Velvet Touch*, with Russell as an actress who commits murder, but it was another case of a promising career slipping away and, after the failure of two comedies, *A Woman of Distinction*, and *Never Wave at a WAC*, Russell decided to return to Broadway. She never made a better decision, for her dual triumphs in the musical *Wonderful Town* (in which she reprised her role of Ruth Sherwood from *My Sister Eileen*, winning a Tony Award) and the comedy *Auntie Mame* made her the toast of the Great White Way. Between them she came back to Hollywood to do a commendable job as the spinster who begs Arthur O'Connell to marry her in *Picnic*, and then was allowed to reprise her stage role in the 1958 movie of *Auntie Mame*. A box-office smash, it captured Russell's great performance as the eccentric life-loving Mame Dennis, another part with which her name would be synonymous, not to mention bringing her a fourth Oscar nomination.

The 1960s found her back in leading roles, although she was sharply criticized for her miscasting as a Jewish widow in *A Majority of One*, and proved a flat out embarrassment as the domineering mom in *Oh Dad, Poor Dad, Mama's Hung You in the Closet and I'm Feeling So Sad*, certainly one of the worst movies of the decade. She was quite good as another monster mother, in the 1962 adaptation of the much-revered stage musical, *Gypsy*, though resentment rising from Ethel Merman being passed over for the part, colored the critical assessment of Russell's performance for years to come. There was a popular comedy *The Trouble With Angels*, in which she was a very regal Mother Superior, and one last lead in a tame caper she herself scripted (as "C.A. McKnight"), *Mrs. Pollifax — Spy*. There was another behind the scenes credit, supplying the story for the 1956 Esther Williams drama *The Unguarded Moment*. Her posthumously published autobiography, *Life Is a Banquet* (the title was a reference to her famous line from *Auntie Mame*) looked back on a varied but nonetheless fulfilling career.

Screen: 1934: Evelyn Prentice; The President Vanishes; Forsaking All Others; 1935: The Night Is Young; West Point of the Air; The Casino Murder Case; Reckless; China Seas; Rendezvous; 1936: It Had to Happen; Under Two Flags; Trouble for Two; Craig's Wife; 1937: Night Must Fall; Live, Love and Learn; 1938: Man-Proof; Four's a Crowd; The Citadel; 1939: Fast and Loose; The Women; 1940: His Girl Friday; Hired Wife; No Time for Comedy; 1941: This Thing Called Love; They Met in Bombay; The Feminine Touch; Design for Scandal; 1942: Take a Letter, Darling; My Sister Eileen; 1943: Flight for Freedom; What a Woman!; 1945: Roughly Speaking; She Wouldn't Say Yes; 1946: Sister Kenny; 1947: The Guilt of Janet Ames; Mourning Becomes Electra; 1948: The Velvet Touch; 1949: Tell It to the Judge; 1950: A Woman of Distinction; 1952: Never Wave at a WAC; 1955: The Girl Rush; Picnic; 1958: Auntie Mame; 1961: A Majority of One; 1962: Five Finger Exercise; Gypsy; 1966: The Trouble With Angels; 1967: Oh Dad, Poor Dad, Mama's Hung You in the Closet and I'm Feeling So Sad; Rosie!; 1968: Where Angels Go…Trouble Follows; 1971: Mrs. Pollifax — Spy (and wr.)

NY Stage: 1930: The Garrick Gaieties; The Second Man; 1931: Company's Coming; 1953: Wonderful Town; 1956: Auntie Mame.

Select TV: 1956: The Night Goes On (sp); 1958: Wonderful Town (sp); 1972: The Crooked Hearts.

ANN RUTHERFORD

(MARY CECILIA RAMONE) BORN: VANCOUVER, BRITISH COLUMBIA, CANADA, NOVEMBER 2, 1920.

Best remembered for her role as Polly Benedict, Andy Hardy's steady gal, Ann Rutherford (who, from certain angles resembled a junior Rosalind Russell) was all over the MGM lot for a number of years, playing pretty teens and ingenues with a slightly stuck-up air about them. Born to show business parents, she was moved from San Francisco to Los Angeles where she began acting in stock and on radio before signing a contract with Mascot Pictures, which later became Republic. In 1935, they started her off in a serial, *The Fighting Marine*, and kept her around to play leading lady to both Gene Autry and John Wayne, before MGM put her on its payroll two years later. Following some small roles, she was selected to play Polly in the second installment in the Hardy series, *You're Only Young Once*, replacing Margaret Marquis who had done the role originally in *A Family Affair*. Since Andy (Mickey Rooney) was always eyeing any girl who passed his way, Rutherford was often in a snit, folding her arms and scolding him for his behavior. Following 12 consecutive appearances (out of 16 entries), she bailed out in 1942, after *Andy Hardy's Double Life*. During that time she had also played the Ghost of Christmas Past in *A Christmas Carol*; Vivien Leigh's younger sister Careen O'Hara in *Gone With the Wind*; Lydia Bennet, the sister who runs off with Mr. Wickham (Edward Ashley) in *Pride and Prejudice*; and Red Skelton's leading lady in *Whistling in the Dark* and its two sequels. After finishing off her contract with MGM, she returned to Republic for two quickies, was seen into two Technicolor hits, *The Secret Life of Walter Mitty*, as Danny Kaye's shallow fiancée, and *Adventures of Don Juan*, then began popping up on television. She skipped the 1958 Andy Hardy reunion movie but showed up back at her old studio in 1972 for a bit as Tom Ewell's wife in the murder mystery *They Only Kill Their Masters*. She was married to producer William Dozier (best known for the *Batman* series) from 1953 until his death in 1991.

Screen: 1935: The Fighting Marines (serial); Waterfront Lady; Melody Trail; The Singing Vagabond; 1936: The Lawless Nineties; Doughnuts and Society; The Harvester; Comin' Round the Mountain; Down to the Sea; The Oregon Trail; The Lonely Trail; 1937: The Bride Wore Red; Public Cowboy No. One; The Devil Is Driving; Espionage; Live, Love and Learn; You're Only Young Once; 1938: Of Human Hearts; Judge Hardy's Children; Love Finds Andy Hardy; A Christmas Carol; Dramatic School; Out West With the Hardys; 1939: Four Girls in White; The Hardys Ride High; Andy Hardy Gets Spring Fever; These Glamour Girls; Dancing Co-Ed; Judge Hardy and Son; Gone With the Wind; 1940: Pride and Prejudice; Andy Hardy Meets Debutante; Wyoming; The Ghost Comes Home; Keeping Company; 1941: Andy Hardy's Private Secretary; Washington Melodrama; Whistling in the Dark; Life Begins for Andy Hardy; Badlands of Dakota; 1942: The Courtship of Andy Hardy; This Time for Keeps; Orchestra Wives; Whistling in Dixie; Andy Hardy's Double Life; 1943: Whistling in Brooklyn; Happy Land; 1944: Bermuda Mystery; 1945: Two O'Clock Courage; Bedside Manner; 1946: Murder in the Music Hall; The Madonna's Secret; Inside Job; 1947: The Secret Life of Walter Mitty; 1948: Adventures of Don Juan; 1950: Operation Haylift; 1972: They Only Kill Their Masters; 1976: Won Ton Ton, the Dog Who Saved Hollywood.

Select TV: 1951: Unfinished Business (sp); 1952: The Cavorting Statue (sp); 1957: Success (sp); 1958: The Male Animal (sp).

MARGARET RUTHERFORD

BORN: LONDON, ENGLAND, MAY 11, 1892.
DIED: MAY 22, 1972.

Old age was certainly kind to Margaret Rutherford, who didn't really become a movie star until she was past 50. Short, jolly, and rotund, with the jowls of a bloodhound, she never failed to lift the spirits, often being the one thing audiences remembered from her more disappointing assignments. Initially a teacher, she joined the Old Vic School and made her theatrical bow for them in 1925, in a pantomime, *Little Jack Horner*. With a few theatre credits behind her, she made her motion picture debut in 1936, in *Dusty Ermine*, an adventure film that also went under the name *Hideout in the Alps*. Others followed, including the thriller *Talk of the Devil*, which paired her with director Carol Reed for the first time, and *Believed Married*, in which she already looked elderly enough to pass as a grandmother. Much of this work went without mention but her fortunes changed after a series of memorable roles on the London stage in such productions as *Spring Meeting*, *The Importance of Being Earnest*, and *Blithe Spirit*, all of which she would repeat on film. The movie of *Spring Meeting* arrived in 1941, and Rutherford stole the notices as the horseplaying Aunt Bijou. British audiences had grown very fond of her in a few short years and, although she would pop up in dramatic fare like *Yellow Canary* and *The Demi-Paradise*, she was shown to her best advantage in such comedies as *English Without Tears*, a wartime romance in which she was an advocate for bird rights. *Blithe Spirit* was filmed under the direction of Carol Reed for release in England in 1945; it opened in America the following year and for the first time Rutherford gained appreciation across the ocean. Her performance as the delightfully batty medium Madame Arcati would become one of her most cherished roles.

By the late 1940s, Ealing Studios had begun its brief but much revered period of distinctive comedies and Rutherford showed up in one of the best, *Passport to Pimlico*, as a pixilated history professor. She also lent a helping hand elsewhere in some less inspired fare such as *Miranda*, attending to mermaid Glynis Johns (and repeating the part in the sequel *Mad About Men*), and *The Happiest Days of Your Life*, as one of the heads of St. Swithin's girls school, acting opposite another British treasure, Alistair Sim. The long-awaited movie of *The Importance of Being Earnest* debuted in 1952 and it preserved most of the pleasures of this classic play along with Rutherford as the definitive befuddled nurse maid Miss Prism (U.S. audiences had gotten a chance to see her in this work on Broadway a few years earlier, albeit as Lady Brackell). As a star attraction she was an amateur playwright in *Curtain Up*; a fan of writer Richard Hearne, who pursuades him to recover a secret whisky formula, in *Miss Robin Hood*; and a religious fanatic involved with racing in *Aunt Clara*. These did not receive much distribution outside her native land and were not favorably commented upon outside of Rutherford's contributions to them. Back in support she was an usherette in *The Smallest Show on Earth*; Ian Carmichael's aunt in *I'm All Right Jack*; and Danny Kaye's aunt in *On the Double*. MGM then decided to make a movie featuring Agatha Christie's great amateur sleuth Miss Marple and, although Rutherford wasn't quite what the author had envisioned, she turned *Murder, She Said* into a surprise hit and one of the more enjoyable mysteries of its period. Four more Miss Marples of decreasing value followed and it became the role for which she was probably best known. Her partner in investigation was character actor Stringer Davis, whom she had married in 1954. She showed up in the all-star ensemble

The V.I.P.s, as an impoverished countess on her way to Florida, and although it was hardly a significant highpoint in her career, she gave this overly dry and somber movie a needed lift and was therefore given an Academy Award for Best Supporting Actress. After being made a Dame of the British Empire in 1966, she appeared in three more films including *Chimes at Midnight*, as Mistress Quickly, a rare serious role. Her autobiography was published the year she passed away, in 1972.

Screen: 1936: Dusty Ermine/Hideout in the Alps; Talk of the Devil; 1937: Beauty and the Barge; Catch as Catch Can; Missing Believed Married; 1940: Quiet Wedding; 1941: Spring Meeting; 1943: The Yellow Canary; The Demi-Paradise/Adventure for Two; 1944: English Without Tears/Her Man Gilbey; 1945: Blithe Spirit; 1947: Meet Me at Dawn; While the Sun Shines; 1948: Miranda; 1949: Passport to Pimlico; 1950: The Happiest Days of Your Life; Her Favorite Husband/The Taming of Dorothy; 1951: The Magic Box; 1952: Curtain Up; Castle in the Air; The Importance of Being Earnest; Miss Robin Hood; 1953: Innocents in Paris; Trouble in Store; 1954: The Runaway Bus; Mad About Men; Aunt Clara; 1955: An Alligator Named Daisy; 1957: The Smallest Show on Earth; Just My Luck; 1959: I'm All Right, Jack; 1961: On the Double; Murder, She Said; 1963: The Mouse on the Moon; Murder at the Gallop; The V.I.P.s; 1964: Murder Most Foul; 1965: Murder Ahoy; 1966: The Alphabet Murders; Chimes at Midnight/Falstaff; 1967: A Countess From Hong Kong; The Wacky World of Mother Goose (voice); 1969: Arabella.

NY Stage: 1947: The Importance of Being Earnest; 1960: Farewell Farewell Eugene.

PEGGY RYAN

(MARGARET O'RENE RYAN)
BORN: LONG BEACH, CA, AUGUST 28, 1924.

On occasion, Hollywood has actually overlooked sex appeal in favor of talent, which was fortunate for the very plain-looking but enthusiastic and highly likable Peggy Ryan, a terrific dancer and a staple at Universal Studios in the 1940s. A member of her parents' dance act by the age of four, she had popped up in a 1930 short, "The Wedding of Jack and Jill," and then enrolled in the Hollywood Professional School. George Murphy saw her at a benefit and recommended her to Universal for a duet with him in the 1937 film *Top of the Town*. She followed this with some non-musical assignments including one as a starving youngster in *The Grapes of Wrath*, but for the most part she was treated as a newcomer following her success in the touring revue *Meet the People*. This got her a contract with the studio that had debuted her, Universal, and they put her next to Donald O'Connor, in support of the Andrews Sisters, in *What's Cookin'?* When the hotstepping moves of these exuberant youngsters got such a tremendous public response, Universal decided they could make some cash pairing O'Connor and Ryan on an on-going basis and did just that with *Private Buckaroo*; *Get Hep to Love*; *Give Out, Sisters*; *When Johnny Comes Marching Home*; *Mister Big*; *Top Man*; *Chip Off the Old Block*; *Follow the Boys*; *This Is the Life*; *The Merry Monahans* (the first time they shared the top billing spots); *Bowery to Broadway*; and *Patrick the Great*. It was hard for even their biggest fans to endure or distinguish the plots of most of these, but the dancing of Ryan and O'Connor was magical. Following World War II, her services were no longer required by Universal and she ended up dancing in three low-budget musicals, on television, and in nightclubs with the underrated Ray McDonald, who briefly became her husband (1953–57). In 1958, she married emcee-columnist Eddie Sherman and settled down to live in Hawaii. It was this relocation that brought her back into the public eye, when she was hired to play Jack Lord's secretary Jenny for the long-running cop show *Hawaii Five-O*, which she did while teaching dance on the side.

Screen: 1937: Top of the Town; Women Men Marry; 1939: She Married a Cop; The Flying Irishman; 1940: The Grapes of Wrath; Sailor's Lady; 1942: What's Cookin'?; Miss Annie Rooney; Private Buckaroo; Get Hep to Love; Give Out, Sisters; Girls Town; When Johnny Comes Marching Home; 1943: Mister Big; Top Man; 1944: Chip Off the Bold Block; Follow the Boys; This Is the Life; The Merry Monahans; Bowery to Broadway; Babes on Swing Street; 1945: That's the Spirit; Patrick the Great; Here Come the Co-Eds; On Stage Everybody!; Men in Her Diary; 1949: Shamrock Hill; There's a Girl in My Heart; 1953: All Ashore.

NY Stage: 1940: Meet the People.

Select TV: 1969–76: Hawaii Five-O (series); 1980: Pleasure Palace.

ROBERT RYAN

BORN: CHICAGO, IL, NOVEMBER 11, 1909.
ED: LOYOLA UNIV., DARTMOUTH COL.
DIED: JULY 11, 1973.

A fine, serious actor who seemed above all the frills and nonsense of Hollywood fakery, Robert Ryan became a star without ever really being a dependable money maker or adhering to the heroism expected of a leading man. He comfortably segued between men of integrity and steely-eyed bastards, often dropping into second leads and support but always holding his own. In college he went from boxing to journalism then, following school, modeling to acting, joining the Max Reinhardt Theatrical Workshop in California. This led to a role in a musical, *Too Many Husbands*, which got him a contract with Paramount. They launched him in a supporting part in a gangster "B," *Queen of the Mob*, but after a few other incidental assignments, he was off the payroll and back on the stage, scoring a hit on Broadway with Clifford Odets's *Clash by Night*. As a result, RKO invited him to come work for them and they started started him off in a standard war movie, *Bombardier*, marking the first of many times that Ryan would look so at ease in a uniform. He was also in military duds as a friend of Fred Astaire's in *The Sky's the Limit*, then got to remind people that he had experience in the ring, taking on Mike Mazurki for a bizarre combination boxing-wrestling match in the pulpy hit *Behind the Rising Sun*. In the ensemble piece *Gangway for Tomorrow*, he was a racecar driver working on an assembly line during the war; then was personally requested by star Ginger Rogers to play her husband who is killed in battle in the shamelessly sentimental *Tender Comrade*. He squabbled with superior officer Pat O'Brien in *Marine Raiders* in 1944, before becoming a marine for real.

When he returned from military service he was still under the employ of RKO who kept him uniform, making him a Coast Guard tortured by his war experiences in the melodrama *The Woman on the Beach*, and a bigoted G.I. who murders Jewish Sam Levene in *Crossfire*. The latter was one of the studio's best dramatic efforts of the late 1940s and a surprisingly profitable message picture that wound up satisfying just about everyone. Ryan, in the first of his mean roles, wound up with his sole Oscar nomination, in the supporting category. Now hovering between star and second lead, he got second billing to Merle Oberon in the espionage thriller *Berlin Express*, and to Randolph Scott in *Return of the Bad Men* (not to be confused with Ryan's later film

Best of the Bad Men), here playing a much nastier version of the Sundance Kid than the one made famous in the 1960s by Robert Redford. MGM borrowed him to play a crippled vet who wants to get even with Van Heflin in *Act of Violence*, after which he was back on the RKO lot for his best role there, broken-down prizefighter Stoker Thompson, in director Robert Wise's *The Set-Up*, a succinct and potent look at the corrupt world of boxing, which not only showed this actor in all his glory but was one of the best movies on this subject ever made. He continued in the sort of melodramas the studio churned out during the early 1950s including *I Married a Communist* (one of the earliest anti-Red propaganda films); *The Racket*, as a mobster; *On Dangerous Ground*, as a sadistic, bitter cop; *Clash by Night*, a weak rendering of the triangle drama he'd done onstage, this time upped to one of the leads; and *Beware My Lovely*, as a whacko handyman who terrorizes Ida Lupino. He then parted company with RKO, having been an asset to them for years.

Over at MGM he was nasty again, in one of the best James Stewart westerns of the 1950s, *The Naked Spur*; was left for dead by scheming wife Rhonda Fleming in the 3-D *Inferno*; made a nice pairing with Shirley Booth in *About Mrs. Leslie*, a romance for adults; and played perhaps his most famous bad guy role, the main townie trying to kill off snooping visitor Spencer Tracy, in *Bad Day at Black Rock*. Dropping back over at RKO, he was in two of the duds that helped bring that place to a close, *Escape to Burma* and *Back from Eternity*; was Clark Gable's rival for Jane Russell in the surprisingly popular 20th Century-Fox western *The Tall Men*; put on fatigues again as the commander of a lost platoon in the well-liked *Men in War*; was out of his element as poor white trash farmer Ty Ty Walden in the flat-footed rendering of the risqué novel *God's Little Acre*; stole scenes as the cynical newspaper editor in *Lonelyhearts*; was a bad guy up against an even badder Burl Ives in *Day of the Outlaw*; and was bigoted again, in the "message" robbery film *Odds Against Tomorrow*, reluctantly joining forces with Harry Belafonte. After a flop Alaskan epic, *Ice Palace*, he looked out of place as John the Baptist in *King of Kings*, but was right at home playing a general in one of the larger roles in the all-star smash *The Longest Day*. He reached another of his peaks, playing the loathsome Claggart in Peter Ustinov's very good adaptation of *Billy Budd*; was part of Burt Lancaster's band of rescuers in a enjoyable action film *The Professionals*; showed up in two of the major macho endeavors of the late 1960s, *The Dirty Dozen*, as a colonel, and *The Wild Bunch*, excellent as William Holden's former outlaw buddy who is now on the side of the law. He deserved better than his roles in such productions as *The Love Machine*, *Pancho Villa*, and *Executive Action*, and got it with the limited-run film of *The Iceman Cometh*, receiving praise right up to the end, having died of cancer the year (1973) it premiered.

Screen: 1940: Queen of the Mob; Golden Gloves; North West Mounted Police; Texas Rangers Ride Again; 1941: The Feminine Touch; 1943: Bombardier; The Sky's the Limit; Behind the Rising Sun; The Iron Major; Gangway for Tomorrow; Tender Comrade; 1944: Marine Raiders; 1947: Trail Street; The Woman on the Beach; Crossfire; 1948: Berlin Express; Return of the Badmen; The Boy With Green Hair; Act of Violence; 1949: Caught; The Set-Up; I Married a Communist/The Woman on Pier 13; 1950: The Secret Fury; Born to Be Bad; 1951: Best of the Badmen; Flying Leathernecks; Hard, Fast and Beautiful; The Racket; 1952: On Dangerous Ground; Clash by Night; Beware My Lovely; Horizons West; 1953: The Naked Spur; City Beneath the Sea; Inferno; 1954: Alaska Seas; About Mrs. Leslie; Her 12 Men; 1955: Bad Day at Black Rock; Escape to Burma; House of Bamboo; The Tall Men; 1956: The Proud Ones; Back From Eternity; 1957:

Men in War; **1958:** God's Little Acre; Lonelyhearts; **1959:** Day of the Outlaw; Odds Against Tomorrow; **1960:** Ice Palace; **1961:** The Canadians; King of Kings; **1962:** The Longest Day; Billy Budd; **1964:** The Inheritance (narrator); **1965:** The Crooked Road; Battle of the Bulge; **1966:** The Dirty Game/The Secret Agents; The Professionals; **1967:** The Busy Body; The Dirty Dozen; Hour of the Gun; **1968:** Custer of the West; A Minute to Pray, a Second to Die/Outlaw Gun; Anzio; **1969:** The Wild Bunch; **1970:** Captain Nemo and the Underwater City; **1971:** Lawman; The Love Machine; **1972:** And Hope to Die; **1973:** Lolly Madonna XXX; The Iceman Cometh; Executive Action; **1974:** The Outfit.

NY Stage: 1941: Clash by Night; **1954:** Coriolanus; **1962:** Mr. President; **1969:** The Front Page; **1971:** Long Day's Journey Into Night.

Select TV: 1955: Lincoln's Doctor's Bag (sp); **1957:** On Edge(sp); The Crowd Pleaser (sp); Hidden Witness (sp); **1958:** The Seventh Letter (sp); The Giant Step (sp); The Perfectionist (sp); The Great Gatsby (sp); **1960:** The Snows of Kilimanjaro (sp); **1963:** Are There Any More Out There Like You? (sp); **1966:** Guilty or Not Guilty (sp); **1970:** The Front Page (sp); **1973:** The Man Without a Country.

S

SABU
(SABU DASTAGIR)
BORN: KARAPUR, MYSORE, INDIA,
JANUARY 27, 1924. DIED: DECEMBER 2, 1963.

Excitable, long-haired, and seldom seen in shirt or shoes, Sabu was the exotic nature boy of pulp adventure cinema, the son of an elephant driver who inherited the family "business" when he was nine. He was discovered by a British film crew, on location in India shooting footage for an adaptation of a Rudyard Kipling tale to be titled *Elephant Boy*. Sabu became the title character and the obviously natural way in which he related to the beasts was instrumental in the movie's success. He was placed under contract by Alexander Korda who put him in *Drums*, and then gave him the two roles he would become most famous for, the title character in *The Thief of Bagdad*, where his exploits with the gigantic Djinni (Rex Ingram) were this elaborate fantasy's highlights; and Mowgli in *The Jungle Book*, a role unthinkable to cast anyone else in. Hollywood was eager to grab him while he still had some novelty appeal and Universal signed him to a contract in 1942. He did three of their turgid Technicolor extravaganzas, all starring Jon Hall and Maria Montez: *Arabian Nights*, *White Savage*, and *Cobra Woman*, adding a needed lift to each. After serving in the U.S. Air Force during World War II, he ended up in some fairly cheesy adventure movies like *Man-Eater of Kumaon*, and *Savage Drums*, although he did get involved in one classy production, *Black Narcissus*, as a general, receiving high billing for a relatively small role. He did some European productions in the 1950s, including *Hello, Elephant*; and was famous enough to have his name appear in the title of *Sabu and the Magic Ring*, a film pieced together from some television pilots. The passing of the years proved that little had changed, as he was still seen, in his last two roles, cavorting among the wild creatures of *Rampage* and Disney's *A Tiger Walks*, the latter released posthumously, following his death from a heart attack.

Screen: 1937: Elephant Boy; 1938: Drums/The Drum; 1940: The Thief of Bagdad; 1942: The Jungle Book; Arabian Nights; 1943: White Savage; Cobra Woman; 1946: Tangier; 1947: Black Narcissus; 1948: Man-Eater of Kumaon; The End of the River; 1949: Song of India; 1951: Savage Drums; 1952: Hello, Elephant; 1954: Jungle Hell/The Treasure of the Bengal; 1955: The Black Panther; 1956: Jaguar; 1957: Sabu and the Magic Ring; 1959: Mistress of the World (nUSr); 1963: Rampage; 1964: A Tiger Walks.

EVA MARIE SAINT
BORN: NEWARK, NJ, JULY 4, 1924.
ED: BOWLING GREEN ST. UNIV.

In a career of too few movies, Eva Marie Saint still managed to be one of the brightest lights of her era, a lady who was incredibly talented without being showy and ethereally lovely without arrogantly drawing attention to her good looks. While studying drama in college she worked at NBC, which led to her professional debut on the radio in the mid-1940s. On television she joined the cast of the nighttime serial *One Man's Family* and, after some live dramas there, went to Broadway to appear in *The Trip to Bountiful*, opposite Lillian Gish. Her fine notices (she won a Theatre World Award) in that production brought her to the attention of director Elia Kazan who wanted a newcomer to play the nice Jersey girl who falls in love with tough lug Marlon Brando in *On the Waterfront*. She got the part and her sense of the character's decency and confusion were beautifully conveyed, her romantic awakening to Brando among the best moments in a motion picture strewn start to finish with greatness. It became one of the groundbreaking dramas of the cinema and everyone involved would forever look back on it with pride, including Saint who won the Academy Award for Best Supporting Actress of 1954 for her portrayal.

Surprisingly, at this point, she chose to return to television, most notably in the musical of *Our Town*, before showing up back in cinemas as Bob Hope's leading lady in *That Certain Feeling*. Perhaps it was her intention to show that she could play comedy, but, since this was not one of the comedian's funnier movies, little was proven. She then appeared in MGM's lavish, muddled Civil War epic *Raintree County*, playing the girl Montgomery Clift should have married instead of the unstable Elizabeth Taylor. That same year, 1957, there was nothing but praise for her magnificent performance as the frightened wife who watches husband Don Murray fall apart from drug addiction in *A Hatful of Rain*, one of the best urban dramas of the 1950s. Saint reached another career pinnacle with *North by Northwest*, playing the frosty blonde who seduces man-on-the-run Cary Grant. The film turned out to be not only one of the most highly attended movies of 1959, but also the most entertaining motion picture Alfred Hitchcock ever directed. After playing the caring nurse who becomes personally involved in looking after Jewish refugee Jill Haworth in *Exodus*, Saint stretched her acting skills and played a neurotic woman in *All Fall Down*, a drama that reached and missed, finding no audience interest. Adapting a German accent, she was another nurse, one who reluctantly participates in a plot to trick spy James Garner, in *36 Hours*, a far more worthy project than the more widely attended *The Sandpiper*, where she once again took a backseat to Elizabeth Taylor.

In 1966, Saint starred in two more big box-office winners, *The Russians Are Coming! The Russians Are Coming!*, where she played Carl Reiner's sensible wife in undoubtedly one of the decade's most enjoyable comedies; and *Grand Prix*, as Yves Montand's lover, giving this long-winded racecar melodrama its heart. *Loving*, a highly contemporary 1970s look at a failing marriage, proved that Saint had moved effortlessly with the changing cinema; though another stale Bob Hope vehicle, *Cancel My Reservation*, turned out to be very much a thing of the past. After some stage work, she concentrated almost exclusively on television, eventually winning an Emmy Award for the telefilm, *People Like Us*. In 1986 she was back on the big screen, after a 14-year absence, to portray Jackie Gleason's estranged wife, who finally liberates herself from his selfish behavior, in *Nothing in Common*. It was such a pleasure to have her back that one couldn't help but feel the loss when there was no follow-up performance and would not be one for yet another decade. When she did return it was in one that found no American distributor, *Mariette in Ecstasy*, and in *I Dreamed of Africa*, where much of her role as Kim Basinger's mom ended up on the cutting room floor.

Screen: 1954: On the Waterfront; 1956: That Certain Feeling; 1957: Raintree County; A Hatful of Rain; 1959: North by Northwest; 1960: Exodus; 1961: All Fall Down; 1964: 36 Hours; 1965: The Sandpiper; 1966: The Russians Are Coming! The Russians Are Coming!; Grand Prix; 1969: The Stalking Moon; 1970: Loving; 1972: Cancel My Reservation; 1986: Nothing in Common; 1996: Mariette in Ecstasy (nUSr); 2000: I Dreamed of Africa.

NY Stage: 1953: The Trip to Bountiful; 1972: The Lincoln Mask; 1983: Duet for One (ob).

Select TV: 1949: June Moon (sp); 1950–52: One Man's Family (series); 1953: Wish on the Moon (sp); End of the Honeymoon (sp); O for 37 (sp); 1954: The Old Maid (sp); The Joker (sp); Middle of the Night (sp); Mr. Death and the Redheaded Woman (sp); 1955: Yellow Jack (sp); Our Town (sp); 1964: Her School for Bachelors (sp); Carol for Another Christmas (sp); 1976: The Machans; 1978: A Christmas to Remember; 1979: When Hell Was in Session; 1980: The Curse of King Tut's Tomb; 1981: The Best Little Girl in the World; Splendor in the Grass; 1983: Malibu; Jane Doe; 1984: Love Leads the Way; Fatal Vision; 1986: The Last Days of Patton; A Year in the Life; 1987: Norman Rockwell's Breaking Home Ties; 1987–88: Moonlighting (series); 1988: I'll Be Home for Christmas; 1990: Voyage of Terror: The Achille Lauro Affair; People Like Us; 1991: Danielle Steel's Palomino; 1993: Kiss of a Killer; 1995: My Antonia; 1996: Titanic; After Jimmy; 1997: Time to Say Goodbye; 1999: Jackie's Back!; 2000: Papa's Angels.

S.Z. SAKALL
(EUGENE GERO SZAKALL)
BORN: BUDAPEST, HUNGARY, FEBRUARY 2, 1884.
DIED: FEBRUARY 12, 1955.

The portly fellow with the fluttery jowls and skittish nerves ("nyah! nyah! nyah!"), S.Z. Sakall was such an endearing presence that he earned the fitting nickname, "Cuddles," and it was by this description that audiences came to identify him, although it was not a billing he used professionally. He took up acting as a teenager and gave himself the stage name of "Szoeke Szakall," which translated into "Blond Beard," thereby describing his appearance at the time. He performed in two Hungarian films in 1916, and followed these with a stint with the Royal Orpheum of Budapest, before going to Vienna to act in a play that he wrote, *String Quartet*. He then traveled to Berlin for a performance of another of his works, *Albert VIII*, and it was there that his reputation was made as both stage actor and writer, bringing him film offers, not only from Germany but also back in his native country and in Austria. To escape the oncoming menace of Nazism, the actor accepted an offer to do a movie in Great Britain, *The Lilac Domino*, which marked his first English-language role, and then wisely used his familial connection to producer Joe Pasternak to get a job in Hollywood, arriving there in 1939 to appear in a Deanna Durbin film, *It's a Date*, billed now as "S.Z. Sakall." In no time his fractured English, spoken in his pinched, nasal voice, and his cheek-slapping shtick to express distress, made him one of the joyous scene-stealers of 1940s films. There was another Durbin film, *Spring Parade*, encouraging her romance with Robert Cummings; a part as one of the professors in the delightful *Ball of Fire*; and a sequence playing a gullible investor conned by James Cagney into hearing the title song of *Yankee Doodle Dandy*, made at Warner Bros. where Sakall was put under contract.

At Warners he was pretty much lost among the outstanding cast of *Casablanca*, playing the headwaiter at Rick's cafe; did his stock "kindly papa" character in *Shine On, Harvest Moon*; pretended to be Barbara Stanwyck's uncle in order to bring some authentic atmosphere to her ruse in *Christmas in Connecticut*; and provided some needed color to the tedium of the Errol Flynn western *San Antonio*. In the meantime other studios still wanted him — he was the town butcher in MGM's lovely *The Human Comedy*; Sonja Henie's uncle in Fox's *Wintertime*; Uncle Latsie (Hungarian at last!) in Fox's bland hit bio *The Dolly Sisters*; and a music teacher in MGM's *Cynthia*. Back at Warners he became a staple of the many unremarkable Technicolor musicals the studio had to offer in the late 1940s, providing the sort of broad comedic relief these films needed to keep audiences from drifting off during the inanities of the plot. Some of these included *Cinderella Jones*; *Two Guys from Milwaukee*; *The Time, the Place and the Girl*; *April Showers*; *Romance on the High Seas* (Doris Day's debut, with Sakall in yet another "uncle" role.); and *Look for the Silver Lining*. Borrowed again by MGM, he had one of his best roles, as the temperamental shop keeper whose precious Stradivarius is sabotage by Buster Keaton, in *In the Good Old Summertime*. There were three more musicals with Doris Day and then he went back over to MGM where his assignments included a bit in the episode film *It's a Big Country*, as a bigoted Hungarian immigrant. He published his autobiography, *The Story of Cuddles: My Life Under the Emperor Franz Joseph, Adolf Hitler and the Warner Brothers*, in 1954, and it was a rare instance of an actor who mostly praised the town and industry that provoked vitriol in so many others.

Screen (US releases only): 1940: It's a Date; Florian; My Love Came Back; Spring Parade; 1941: The Man Who Lost Himself; That Night in Rio; The Devil and Miss Jones; Ball of Fire; 1942: Broadway; Yankee Doodle Dandy; Seven Sweethearts; Casablanca; 1943: Thank Your Lucky Stars; The Human Comedy; Wintertime; 1944: Shine On, Harvest Moon; Hollywood Canteen; 1945: Wonder Man; Christmas in Connecticut; The Dolly Sisters; San Antonio; 1946: Cinderella Jones; Two Guys from Milwaukee; Never Say Goodbye; The Time, the Place and the Girl; 1947: Cynthia; 1948: April Showers; Romance on the High Seas; Embraceable You; Whiplash; 1949: My Dream Is Yours; In the Good Old Summertime; Look for the Silver Lining; Oh, You Beautiful Doll; 1950: Montana; The Daughter of Rosie O'Grady; Tea for Two; 1951: Lullaby of Broadway; Sugarfoot; Painting the Clouds with Sunshine; It's a Big Country; 1953: Small Town Girl; 1954: The Student Prince.
Select TV: 1954: Yours for a Dream (sp).

GEORGE SANDERS

BORN: ST. PETERSBURG, RUSSIA, JULY 3, 1906.
ED: BRIGHTON COL. DIED: APRIL 25, 1972.

Imperious, suave, and dryly self-satisfied, George Sanders was one of the screen's most treasured cynics, maintaining great poise while committing murder, cheating on women, and looking down on the whole world, often with cigarette in hand, his magnificent voice making music of even the very worst dialogue. He was born to British parents in Russia, the family returning to home ground once the Revolution began. Sanders intended to enter the textile industry but took up acting after that didn't pan out, making his London stage bow in a play called *Ballyhoo*. This led to his motion picture debut, in 1936, in *Find the Lady*, followed by a few other British films, the best known of which was the fantasy *The Man Who Could Work Miracles*, as a mythical god. 20th Century-Fox was looking for someone to play Madeleine Carroll's gambler husband in *Lloyd's of London* and Sanders fit the bill, so they signed him up to a contract as well. He was given work in such "A" productions as *Love Is News*, where he played a count, and *Slave Ship*, as a rebellious crew member named Lefty. At the same time he secured leading parts in lesser-known films like *Lancer Spy*, where he portrayed a German officer, and *International Settlement*, as a gunrunner. Dolores De Rio, whose star was on the wane, was his leading lady in both. It was RKO that helped make him a "name" in the business, when they cast him as Leslie Charteris's sophisticated crime fighter, Simon Templar, in the 1939 release *The Saint Strikes Back*, taking over the role from Louis Hayward. Sanders fit the part so well that he played it four more times, ending with *The Saint in Palm Springs*, in 1941, before Hayward finally decided to return to the part.

Otherwise he was establishing himself as a villain par excellence with *Confessions of a Nazi Spy* and *Nurse Edith Cavell*, playing shifty Germans in both; *The House of Seven Gables*, sending his brother (Vincent Price) to jail; *The Son of Monte Cristo*, as the evil Count Gurko; *Son of Fury*, treating nephew Tyrone Power like dirt; and *Manhunt*, as another Nazi. Alfred Hitchcock had utilized him to good effect in both the Oscar-winning *Rebecca*, as the dead woman's cousin, and *Foreign Correspondent*, as a reporter, though in neither case as the bad guy. No doubt not wanting to stay exclusively in supporting roles, he agreed to do a whole different detective series for RKO, starting with *The Gay Falcon*, the title of which was no reflection on the fellow's sexual preference. Instead the character was only a

slight variation on *The Saint*, close enough for Leslie Chateris to sue. Sanders did three more "Falcon" entries, ending with *The Falcon's Brother*, which was truth in advertising, in so much as his on-screen brother was played by his real-life sibling, the sound-alike Tom Conway. The plot conveniently had Sanders die so Conway could take over the series. For United Artists Sanders was actually given a grade "A" showcase of his own with *The Moon and Sixpence*, a surprisingly somber adaptation of Somerset Maugham, playing a painter based on Paul Gaugin, in this talk-fest that had zero commercial appeal. After pirate duty in *The Black Swan*, buried under a bushy red beard, and a renewal of his cinematic SS membership in *This Land Is Mine*, in which he foolishly collaborated with the Germans and ended up taking his own life in regret, he was on the side of the law for *They Came to Blow Up America* and *The Lodger*, in the latter trying to protect Merle Oberon from "pseudo-Jack the Ripper" Laird Cregar. His finest chance yet came when he played the ultra-cynical Lord Henry Wooton in MGM's magnificent 1945 screen version of *The Picture of Dorian Gray*, stealing scenes with aplomb in what was one of the great pairings of actor and role.

Universal gave him the lead in *The Strange Affair of Uncle Harry*, wher his character intended to kill his meddling spinster sister (Geraldine Fitzgerald), but ended up murdering his other sibling instead; while UA starred him as thief-turned-police in the costumer *A Scandal in Paris*, and as a womanizer in *The Private Affairs of Bel Ami*, though neither film showed any great audience interest in Sanders vehicles. Instead he was proving himself a great asset in support with *The Ghost and Mrs. Muir*, losing Gene Tierney to spirit Rex Harrison; *Forever Amber*, in wig and frills as Charles II; and *Samson and Delilah*, as the villainous Saran of Gaza. The last two were among the most popular movies of the late 1940s, despite the first being incredibly boring and the latter ranking among the silliest of director Cecil B. DeMille's kitschy spectacles. Then came his signature role, the acidic, self-confident drama critic Addison DeWitt in *All About Eve*, which gave him a superb script to sink his teeth into and of which he made a glorious feast, being the only cast member of this much honored film to earn an Academy Award. There was another hit with *Ivanhoe*, again as the bad guy, and he kept popping up in period things throughout the 1950s like *King Richard and the Crusaders*, *The King's Thief*, and *Solomon and Sheba*, although he often looked uncomfortable in these performances, as if he was having trouble withholding his contempt for such nonsense.

He did get to play the Lichtenburg general, for whom Ethel Merman temporarily stops throwing attention on herself, in the musical *Call Me Madam*; tried to drive Barbara Stanwyck nuts after she accuses him of homicide in *Witness to Murder*; and turned on the charm on then-wife (1949–57) Zsa Zsa Gabor in *Death of a Scoundrel* (which also featured brother Tom Conway). Amid a whole slew of international credits he received top billing for *Bluebeard's Ten Honeymoons*, as the wife-killing Landru, and the fine sci-fi thriller *Village of the Damned*, as one of the fathers whose child is born during an alien takeover. During the 1960s he could be seen in the Disney adventure *In Search of the Castaways*; playing straight man to Peter Sellers's Inspector Clouseau in *A Shot in the Dark*; supporting Sonny and Cher in their one film vehicle, *Good Times*; providing the voice of the wicked tiger Shere Khan in *The Jungle Book*, probably his most widely-seen credit during this period; and appearing in drag in the spy melodrama *The Kremlin Letters*. He claimed to work strictly for the money and never failed to express his revulsion and disinterest towards the profession he seemed so good at. Therefore it wasn't much of a surprise when he took his own life in 1972, giving boredom as the reason. He had published his autobiography, *Memoirs of a*

Professional Cad, in 1960.

Screen: 1936: Find the Lady; Strange Cargo; The Man Who Could Work Miracles; Dishonour Bright; Lloyd's of London; 1937: Love Is News; Slave Ship; The Lady Escapes; Lancer Spy; 1938: International Settlement; Four Men and a Prayer; 1939: Mr. Moto's Last Warning; The Outsider (filmed 1936); The Saint Strikes Back; The Saint in London; So This Is London; Confessions of a Nazi Spy; Nurse Edith Cavell; Allegheny Uprising; 1940: The Saint's Double Trouble; Rebecca; Green Hell; The House of the Seven Gables; The Saint Takes Over; Foreign Correspondent; Bitter Sweet; The Son of Monte Cristo; 1941: Rage of Heaven; The Saint in Palm Springs; Manhunt; The Gay Falcon; A Date With the Falcon; Sundown; 1942: Son of Fury; The Falcon Takes Over; Her Cardboard Lover; Tales of Manhattan; The Falcon's Brother; The Black Swan; Quiet Please, Murder; 1943: The Moon and Sixpence; This Land Is Mine; They Came to Blow Up America; Appointment in Berlin; Paris After Dark; 1944: Action in Arabia; The Lodger; Summer Storm; 1945: The Picture of Dorian Gray; Hangover Square; The Strange Affair of Uncle Harry; 1946: A Scandal in Paris; The Strange Woman; 1947: The Private Affairs of Bel Ami; The Ghost and Mrs. Muir; Lured; Forever Amber; 1949: The Fan; Samson and Delilah; 1950: All About Eve; 1951: I Can Get It for You Wholesale; The Light Touch; 1952: Captain Blackjack (filmed 1950); Ivanhoe; Assignment Paris; 1953: Voyage to Italy/Strangers; Call Me Madam; 1954: Witness to Murder; King Richard and the Crusaders; 1955: Jupiter's Darling; Moonfleet; The Scarlet Coat; The King's Thief; 1956: Never Say Goodbye; While the City Sleeps; That Certain Feeling; Death of a Scoundrel; 1957: The Seventh Sin; 1958: The Whole Truth; From the Earth to the Moon; 1959: That Kind of Woman; Solomon and Sheba; 1960: The Last Voyage; A Touch of Larceny; Bluebeard's Ten Honeymoons; Village of the Damned; 1961: The Rebel/Call Me Genius; Trouble in the Sky/Cone of Silence; Five Golden Hours; Le Rendezvous (nUSr); 1962: Operation Snatch; In Search of the Castaways; 1963: Cairo; The Cracksman (nUSr); 1964: F.B.I. Operazione Baalbeck (nUSr); Dark Purpose; A Shot in the Dark; The Golden Head (nUSr); 1965: Ecco (narrator); World by Night (narrator); The Amorous Adventures of Moll Flanders; 1966: The Quiller Memorandum; 1967: Trunk in Cairo; Warning Shot; Good Times; The Jungle Book (voice); 1968: One Step to Hell; 1969: The Candy Man; Seven Secrets of Sumuru/Future Woman (nUSr); The Best House in London; 1970: The Kremlin Letter; 1971: Night of the Assassins (nUSr); The Body Stealers/Thin Air; 1972: Doomwatch; Endless Night; 1973: Psychomania.

Select TV: 1955: Laura (sp); 1956: Dream (sp); Bitter Waters (sp); The Charlatan (sp); 1957: The Man Who Inherited Everything (sp); George Sanders Mystery Theatre (series); 1958: Night of the Stranger (sp); 1961: The Small Elephants (sp); 1968: Laura (sp).

TELLY SAVALAS

(ARISTOTLE SAVALAS) BORN: GARDEN CITY, NY, JANUARY 21, 1924. DIED: JANUARY 22, 1994.

So tough he could border on being a parody of himself, chrome-domed Telly Savalas was, however, a scorchingly good actor in the right circumstances and one who seemed to relish his stardom when television brought wide-spread attention to him late in life. Through a relative he got a job as a writer for the U.S. Department of State Information Service, which led to a position as senior director with the ABC news department during the mid-1950s. While teaching adult education classes, he went on an audition for a role in a television anthology drama and got the part. Actor-producer Burt Lancaster, impressed by his TV work, made him a police lieutenant in the 1961 drama *The Young Savages*, and he and that film's director, John Frankenheimer, cast Savalas the following year as Lancaster's fellow-inmate, who latches on to Burt's interest in birds, in *Birdman of Alcatraz*, an unheralded performance that snagged him an Oscar nomination. He had arrived and soon became a familiar face on 1960s movie screens with *The Man From the Diner's Club*, as the villain in Danny Kaye's last vehicle; *Battle of the Bulge*, as a black marketeering soldier; *The Greatest Story Ever Told*, as Pontius Pilate; *The Slender Thread*, helping Sidney Poitier run a crisis center; the 1966 remake of *Beau Geste*, in its only worthy performance, as wicked Sergeant Dagineau; *The Dirty Dozen*, as one of the most colorful members of the motley crew in this massive box-office hit; *The Scalphunters*, another standout performance, as the nasty leader of a gang of thieves; *The Assassination Bureau*, as the effete bad guy in this cheeky romp; *Crooks and Coronets*, a barely seen caper comedy, but in the lead, as a gangster; *On Her Majesty's Secret Service*, as James Bond nemesis Ernst Blofeld; and *Kelly's Heroes*, back in the military, as a sergeant helping Clint Eastwood pull off a heist. A television movie, *The Marcus-Nelson Murders*, found him playing no-nonsense NY detective Theo Kojak so impressively that CBS spun a series off of it, *Kojak*, which made him a star to those who weren't familiar with him at that point (he won an Emmy Award for the role in 1974). He continued in movies during this period, though mostly of a rather cheap variety, including *House of Exorcism* and *Crime Boss*. In later years he reprised the lollipop-sucking Kojak for some telefilms and a subsequent series, and even popped up in two *Dirty Dozen* sequels for the tube, although his character had died in the original movie. In 1977 he directed, wrote, produced, and starred in *Beyond Reason*, playing a psychiatrist having an affair with a patient, but after sitting on the shelf for years, it ended up going directly to cable outlets and video shelves.

Screen: 1961: The Young Savages; Mad Dog Coll; 1962: Birdman of Alcatraz; Cape Fear; The Interns; 1963: Love Is a Ball; The Man From the Diner's Club; Johnny Cool; 1964: The New Interns; 1965: John Goldfarb, Please Come Home; The Greatest Story Ever Told; Battle of the Bulge; Genghis Khan; The Slender Thread; 1966: Beau Geste; 1967: The Dirty Dozen; The Karate Killers (from TV); 1968: Sol Madrid; The Scalphunters; Buona Sera, Mrs. Campbell; 1969: The Assassination Bureau; Mackenna's Gold; Crooks and Coronets/Sophie's Place; On Her Majesty's Secret Service; 1970: Land Raiders; Kelly's Heroes; 1971: Pretty Maids All in a Row; Clay Pigeon; A Town Called Hell; 1972: The Killer Is on the Phone/Scenes from a Murder (dtv); 1973: The Family/Violent City (filmed 1970); 1974: Horror Express; A Reason to Live, A Reason to Die; Sonny and Jed/Bandera Bandits; 1975: Pancho Villa (filmed 1972); Redneck; Killer Force; 1976: Inside Out; House of Exorcism/Lisa and the Devil; Crime Boss; 1977: Beyond Reason (and dir.; wr.; dtv); 1978: Capricorn One; 1979: Beyond the Poseidon Adventure; Escape to Athena; The Muppet Movie; 1980: The Border/Border Cop/The Blood Barrier (dtv); 1982: Fake-Out/Nevada Heat (dtv); Silent Rebellion (dtv); 1984: Cannonball Run II; 1986: GoBots: Battle of the Rock Lords (voice); 1988: Faceless (nUSr); 1993: Mind Twister (dtv); 1995: Backfire (dtv).

Select TV: 1959: House of Cards (sp); 1960: Engineer of Death (sp); Operation North Star (sp); 1961: Acapulco (series); Three Soldiers (sp); 1962: The Hands of Danofria(sp); 1964: The Action of the Tiger(sp); 1971: Mongo's Back in Town; 1972: Visions; 1973: The Marcus-Nelson Murders; She Cried Murder!; 1973–78: Kojak (series); 1980: Alcatraz: The Whole Shocking Story; 1981: Hellinger's Law; 1985: Kojak: The Belarus File; The

Cartier Affair; Alice in Wonderland; 1987: Kojak: The Price of Justice; The Dirty Dozen: The Deadly Mission; 1988: The Dirty Dozen: The Fatal Mission; 1989: The Hollywood Detective; 1989–90: Kojak (series).

JOHN SAXON

(CARMEN ORRICO) BORN: BROOKLYN, NY, AUGUST 5, 1935.

With a face that suggested a deeper level of moods than was usually revealed, John Saxon went from hunky leading man in 1950s soaps to weekly television shows to a stream of drive-in/video junk that even a devoted fan would have trouble keeping track of. A photo of Saxon modeling a swimsuit got him an agent but he opted to study in New York, making his film debut as a teenager, standing in the background in Central Park during the beginning of It Should Happen to You, in 1954. Universal Studios put him under contract and trained him before casting him in its juvenile delinquent drama Running Wild. His official star launch came with The Unguarded Moment, as a seemingly shy student who happens to be assaulting unsuspecting women on the side, and with Rock, Pretty Baby, as a moody high-schooler who wants to be a successful guitarist. The latter rated a sequel, Summer Love, and although there was no reason to chase Saxon off the lot, there wasn't any reason to start dusting the mantle for trophy space either, due to his annoying tendency to ape Brando's angst. He continued as Sandra Dee's love interest in The Restless Years; the fairly popular Lana Turner soaper Portrait in Black; and (over at MGM) The Reluctant Debutante. His somewhat ethnic looks allowed him to play a Puerto Rican ex-con in Cry Tough, and an Indian who desires half-breed Audrey Hepburn in The Unforgiven, after which he was a dangerous soldier in the independent quickie War Hunt, and back doing boyfriend duty in the hit Mr. Hobbs Takes a Vacation. At Universal he was a villainous Mexican in The Appaloosa, opposite Brando; a sheriff in Death of a Gunfighter; and the Mexican-American Robert Duvall wants killed in Joe Kidd. There was also a TV series for Universal, The Bold Ones, which aired just about the time he started dabbling in oddities like Planet of Blood, setting the tone for so much of his later career. He was lucky enough to participate in one of the big hits of 1973, Enter the Dragon, which really started the craze for Kung Fu movies, and among the better known features he was seen in during his latter years were The Electric Horseman, as the corporate bad guy; and A Nightmare on Elm Street, as the police lieutenant investigating the murders in a small town. In 1988 he directed a direct-to-video item, Death House, about prisoners who become zombies, reflecting the sort of movie he'd become most closely associated with at that point.

Screen: 1954: It Should Happen to You; 1955: Running Wild; 1956: The Unguarded Moment; Rock, Pretty Baby; 1958: Summer Love; The Restless Years; The Reluctant Debutante; This Happy Feeling; 1959: Cry Tough; The Big Fisherman; 1960: Portrait in Black; The Unforgiven; The Plunderers; 1961: Posse From Hell; 1962: War Hunt; Mr. Hobbs Takes a Vacation; Agostino; 1963: The Girl Who Knew Too Much/The Evil Eye; The Cardinal; 1965: The Cavern; Blood Beast From Outer Space/Night Caller From Outer Space; The Ravagers; 1966: The Appaloosa; Queen of Blood/Planet of Blood; 1968: For Singles Only; I Came I Saw I Shot (nUSr); 1969: Death of a Gunfighter; 1970: Company of Killers/The Hit Team; 1972: Joe Kidd; 1973: Enter the Dragon; Mr. Kingstreet's War/Heroes Die Hard; 1974: Black Christmas; 1975: Family Killer/Mafia War; Mitchell; 1976:

Cross Shot (nUSr); Napoli Violenta/Death Dealers (nUSr); Mark Colpisce Ancora/A Special Cop in Action (nUSr); 1977: Strange Shadows in an Empty Room; Moonshine County Express; The Swiss Conspiracy; 1978: The Bees; Shalimar/Deadly Thief; 1979: Fast Company; The Glove; The Electric Horseman; 1980: Running Scared (dtv); Beyond Evil; Battle Beyond the Stars; 1981: Blood Beach; 1982: Scorpion With Two Tails (dtv); Wrong Is Right; Cannibals in the Street/Invasion of the Flesh Hunters/Cannibal Apocalypse; 1983: Desire (dtv); The Big Score; 1984: A Nightmare on Elm Street; 1985: Fever Pitch; 1986: Hands of Steel; 1987: A Nightmare on Elm Street 3: Dream Warriors; Unsane/Tenebrae (filmed 1983); 1988: Death House (and dir.; dtv); Nightmare Beach/Welcome to Spring Break (dtv); 1989: Criminal Act/Tunnels (dtv); My Mom's a Werewolf; 1990: Aftershock (dtv); The Final Alliance (dtv); Blood Salvage; The Last Samurai (dtv); Crossing the Line (dtv); The Arrival (dtv); 1991: Payoff (dtv); Deadly Conspiracy/Frame Up II: The Cover-Up; 1992: Maximum Force (dtv); Hellmaster (dtv); Animal Instincts (dtv); 1993: Blackmail (dtv); The Baby Doll Murders (dtv); No Escape, No Return (dtv); 1994: Beverly Hills Cop III; Killing Obsession (dtv); Wes Craven's New Nightmare; 1995: Jonathan of the Bears (nUSr); The Killers Within (dtv); 1996: From Dusk Till Dawn; 1997: Lancelot: Guardian of Time (dtv); 1998: Joseph's Gift (dtv); Criminal Minds (dtv); 1999: The Party Crashers (nUSr); 2001: Living in Fear (dtv); Night Class/Seduced by a Thief (nUSr); 2002: Outta Time; The Road Home (dtv).

Select TV: 1961: Cat in the Cradle (sp); 1962: A Time to Die (sp); 1966: After the Lion — Jackals (sp); 1967: The Doomsday Flight; Winchester '73; 1968: Istanbul Express; 1969–72: The Bold Ones: The Doctors (series); 1970: The Intruders; 1973: Planet Earth; 1974: Strange New World; 1975: Can Ellen Be Saved?; 1976: Snatched; Raid on Entebbe; 79 Park Avenue; 1980: Golden Gate; 1982: Brothers-in-Law; 1983: Prisoners of the Lost Universe; 1984: Half Slave, Half Free; 1986–87: Falcon Crest (series); 1991: Blackmail; 1995: Liz: The Elizabeth Taylor Story.

MARIA SCHELL

(MARGARETE SCHELL) BORN: VIENNA, AUSTRIA, JANUARY 5, 1926.

Capable of a delicate sincerity, Maria Schell seemed ready to become something of a latter-day Ingrid Bergman, but her moment in the star spotlight was brief and, in no time, she was more readily identified as Maximilian Schell's older sister. Billed as "Gritli Schell" she made her motion picture debut in the 1941 Swiss film, Steinbruch/Quarry, and continued in various German and Swiss productions throughout the 1940s and into the early 1950s. She made her English-language debut in Britain's all-star salute to the invention of motion pictures, The Magic Box, as the tragic first-wife of Robert Donat, and stayed over there to play the Austrian lover of Trevor Howard in The Heart of the Matter, and the Belgian girl who falls in love with and then betrays enemy Marius Goring in the downbeat So Little Time. It was her work in the Austrian The Last Bridge, as a doctor captured by Yugoslavian partisans, and the French Gervaise, from the Emile Zola tale, that sparked interest from Hollywood. She started off well there, playing Grushenka in MGM's colorful rendering of The Brothers Karamazov, and was fine as the blind Swiss girl who falls for doctor Gary Cooper in the western, The Hanging Tree. After doing Bergman's part in the television version of For Whom the Bell Tolls, she was back out west with less pleasing results, in MGM's ill-fated re-make of Cimarron, then went to England to play the woman who falls in love with sex-offender Stuart Whitman in *The Mark*. Despite the acclaim for this movie, she chose to retire for a spell. She returned in the late 1960s but much of her work was now in Europe and only the more astute American moviegoers took note of her in *The Odessa File*, which also featured brother Max; *Voyage of the Damned*, as one of the doomed Jews aboard the ship; *Superman*, as a Krypton elder; and *Nineteen Nineteen*, as a one-time patient of Sigmund Freud.

Screen (US releases only): 1952: The Magic Box; 1955: The Heart of the Matter; Angelika; 1957: The Last Bridge (Eur: 1954); Gervaise (Fr: 1955); 1958: Dreaming Lips (Ger: 1952); The Brothers Karamazov; 1959: The Hanging Tree; The Sins of Rose Bernd (Ger: 1957); 1960: As the Sea Rages; Cimarron; 1961: The Mark; 1969: 99 Women; The Devil by the Tail; 1972: Night of the Blood Monster; 1974: The Odessa File; 1976: Folies Bourgeoises/The Twist; Voyage of the Damned; 1978: Superman; 1981: Just a Gigolo; 1983: La Passante (dtv); 1986: Nineteen Nineteen.

Select TV: 1958: World From a Sealed-Off Box (sp); 1959: For Whom the Bell Tolls (sp); 1960: Ninotchka (sp); 1968: Heidi (sp); 1979: Christmas Lilies of the Field; 1980: The Martian Chronicles (ms); 1982: Inside the Third Reich; 1984: Samson and Delilah.

MAXIMILIAN SCHELL

BORN: VIENNA, AUSTRIA, DECEMBER 8, 1930. RAISED IN SWITZERLAND.

A formidable international star who made a towering initial impact in America, the strongly persuasive Maximilian Schell didn't choose the easy path of fame, attaching his name to a lot of blatantly uncommercial projects, always capable of pulling off fine work if anyone cared to see it. His father was playwright Ferdinand Hoffman Schell, his mother actress Margarethe Noe, and his older sister Maria Schell, who had been acting in movies since 1941. The family had moved to Switzerland as the Nazis began their reign of terror and it was there that Maximilian began acting in theatre. His film debut came in 1955, in a German motion picture, *Kinder Mutter und ein General/Children, Mother and the General*, playing an officer, and this was followed by seven more made in Europe. He was asked to come to America in 1958, for a Broadway play, *Interlock*, and to portray Marlon Brando's ill-tempered commanding officer, who ends up disfigured, in the 20th Century-Fox epic *The Young Lions*, where he managed to create a distinct impression. This was followed by the 1959 television drama *Judgment at Nuremberg*, featured on the anthology series *Playhouse 90*, where he was so good playing the fiery defense attorney that he was the only one of the principles asked to repeat his performance in the lengthened 1961 movie adaptation. Again, on the big screen, he was nothing short of electrifying as the counselor whose determination to place the blame for the Holocaust on anyone else but his clients brings morality into question. In a movie filled with outstanding acting, Schell won an Academy Award for Best Actor for 1961. Alas, he followed it with a trio of failures: the bowdlerized filmization of the Broadway success *Five Finger Exercise*, as the tutor whom older Rosalind Russell falls for; *The Reluctant Saint*, as a Franciscan priest (one of his own favorite roles); and the pretentious *The Condemned of Altona*, as the guilt-wracked son who stood trial at Nuremberg.

Loosening up, he appeared in a highly enjoyable caper film, *Topkapi*, which was the last time for a while that his name would be associated with something that actually had a commercial run. Despite his better efforts there was little or no commercial interest in *Return From the Ashes*, as murderous, philandering chess player; director Sidney Lumet's critically well-liked but

trivial spy thriller *The Deadly Affair*, in a small role as an agent bedding James Mason's wife; or *Counterpoint*, as a Nazi clashing with conductor Charlton Heston. Looking for approval and money he did a big-budget action film, albeit a poor one, *Krakatoa — East of Java*, as a captain transporting a boat load of convicts; and then started dabbling behind the camera, producing *The Castle*, playing the role of K from the Kafka novel of that name. Aiming for something a bit more commercial he wrote, directed, produced, and played a supporting role in *First Love*, and then did the same chores for the much-praised *The Pedestrian*, which wound up with an Oscar nomination for Best Foreign Language Film. In the meantime there were Nazis, ex-Nazis, and variations of such to be played, and he did this in the thriller *The Odessa File*, as a concentration camp butcher in hiding; *The Man in the Glass Booth*, as a Jew accused of being a war criminal, a fiery tour de force performance that ran the gamut from riveting to out-of-control in a movie for very specialized audiences, but one that earned him an Oscar nomination; *Cross of Iron*; and the all-star *A Bridge Too Far*, his first commercial success since *Topkapi*. Back as director-writer-producer-supporting actor he did *End of the Game*, as a veteran police inspector teaming up with Jon Voight to trap crooked businessman Robert Shaw, but it was barely distributed by 20th Century-Fox. For that same studio he appeared in the surprisingly popular *Julia*, showing up but briefly to pass information to Jane Fonda, but playing the part so keenly and proficiently that he rated another Oscar nomination.

Sloppy melodramas that paired him with younger women, *Players* (Ali MacGraw) and *Together?* (Jacqueline Bisset), were not exactly career high points and, although he was given top billing in Disney's expensive sci-fi adventure *The Black Hole*, it proved to be a pale attempt to cash in on the *Star Wars* craze, with Schell as your basic mad scientist in space. Choosing to not appear on screen in one of his own productions he directed and wrote *Tales From the Vienna Woods*, and then took on the challenging assignment of building a documentary around his former *Nuremberg* co-star, Marlene Dietrich. He wound up with perhaps his most successful and best known work as director-writer, *Marlene*, in which he interviewed the cranky star who spoke openly of her career but refused to have her face shown on screen. *The Chosen*, in which he was Barry Miller's Zionist father, gave him his best part in an American movie in years and he played the title role in one of the most widely viewed TV mini series of the 1980s, *Peter the Great*. He was the eccentric millionaire supposedly turning rare animals into gourmet food in the comedy *The Freshman*, which allowed him to interact briefly once again with his first American co-star, Marlon Brando; came to the aid of some lost youngsters in the Disney adventure *A Far Off Place*; played wearied immigrant poppas in both *Little Odessa* and *Telling Lies in America*; had familial problems in the end-of-the-world epic, *Deep Impact*; and showed up as an evil cardinal in league with some blood suckers in *Vampires*. He returned once more to a familiar property, *Judgment at Nuremberg*, now re-written for the stage, and with Schell taking over the part of the judge his younger character had defended.

Screen: 1955: Kinder Mutter und ein General/The Children, Mother and the General (nUSr); 1956: Der 20 Juli/The Plot to Assassinate Hitler (nUSr); Reifende Jugend/Ripening Youth (nUSr); Ein Madchen aus Flandern (nUSr); Ein Herz Kehrt Heim (nUSr); 1957: Taxichauffeur Bantz (nUSr); Die Letzten Werden die Ersten Sein (nUSr); 1958: The Young Lions; Ein Wunderbaren Sommer (nUSr); 1961: Judgment at Nuremberg; 1962: Five Finger Exercise; The Reluctant Saint; 1963: The

Condemned of Altona; 1964: Topkapi; 1965: Return From the Ashes; 1967: The Deadly Affair; 1968: The Desperate Ones; Counterpoint; 1969: Krakatoa — East of Java; The Castle (and prod.); Simon Bolivar (nUSr); 1970: First Love (and dir.; wr.; prod.); 1971: Trotta (and wr.; nUSr); 1972: Pope Joan; Paulina 1880 (nUSr); 1974: The Pedestrian (and dir.; wr.; prod.); The Odessa File; 1975: The Man in the Glass Booth; 1976: St. Ives; 1977: The Day That Shook the World/Assassination!; Cross of Iron; A Bridge Too Far; Julia; 1979: Players; Avalanche Express; The Black Hole; 1981: Together?/I Love You, I Love You Not (filmed 1979); 1982: The Chosen; Les Iles (nUSr); 1985: Man Under Suspicion/Morgen in Alabama; The Assissi Underground; 1986: Marlene (and dir.; wr.; prod.); 1989: The Rose Garden; 1990: The Freshman; 1992: Labyrinth (nUSr); 1993: Justice (nUSr); A Far Off Place; 1996: Little Odessa; The Vampyre Wars (nUSr); 1997: The Eighteenth Angel (nUSr); Telling Lies in America; 1998: Deep Impact; John Carpenter's Vampires; 1999: On the Wings of Love (nUSr); 2000: I Love You Baby (nUSr); Just Messing About/Fisimatenten (nUSr); Left Luggage (filmed 1998); 2002: Mein Schwester Maria (and dir.; co-wr.; nUSr); Festival in Cannes.

NY Stage: 1958: Interlock; 1969: A Patriot For Me; 2001: Judgement At Nuremberg.

Select TV: 1959: Judgment at Nuremberg (sp); 1960: The Three Musketeers (sp); 1968: Heidi (sp); 1980: The Diary of Anne Frank; 1982: The Phantom of the Opera; 1986: Peter the Great (ms); 1991: Young Catherine; 1992: Miss Rose White; Stalin; 1993: Candles in the Dark (and dir.); 1994: Abraham; 1996: The Thorn Birds: The Missing Years; 1999: Joan of Arc; 2000: Song of the Lark.

JOSEPH SCHILDKRAUT

BORN: VIENNA, AUSTRIA, MARCH 22, 1895.
ED: AADA. DIED: JANUARY 21, 1964.

Thin, pale-featured Joseph Schildkraut started as a leading man in his own country and in silent features. When it came to talkies, his accent made him perfect for character villains, though his two best remembered roles found him on the side of good. The son of actor Rudolph Schildkraut, he studied under Albert Basserman, came to America with his dad in 1910, and eventually enrolled in the American Academy of Dramatic Arts in New York. Back in Europe he acted with Max Reinhardt's company, then settled in the U.S. for good in 1920. He made his American movie debut, in 1922, playing Lillian Gish's lover, Chevalier de Vaudry, in *Orphans of the Storm*, and, between other stage assignments, was upped to star billing for such films as *The Road to Yesterday*, which had two plots running concurrently, ending in a train wreck; *Young April*, in a dual role, as father and son; and the first film version of *Show Boat*, as Ravenel. He had already started slipping into villainy, having played Judas in the 1927 version of *The King of Kings*, and a repulsive hunchback who marries poor Leatrice Joy in *The Blue Danube*. By 1934 the die was cast as he played Herod in *Cleopatra*; Wallace Beery's nemesis General Pascal in *Viva Villa*, killing Henry B. Walthall and ending up pinned to the ground to bake in the sun for his crimes; a deceptively accommodating and solicitous flesh trader in *Slave Ship*, giving a wildly off-beat performance; and the effete, power-mad Duc d'Orleans in *Marie Antoinette*, almost unrecognizable beneath the drag-like make-up.

In contrast, he was sympathetic and moving as the wrongly imprisoned Captain Dreyfuss in *The Life of Emile Zola* and won the Academy Award for Best Supporting Actor of 1937. Resuming his villainous roles, he played the ambitious Fouquet in *The Man in the Iron Mask*; a thief in *Mr. Moto Takes a Vacation*; the caddish shop employee who is cuckolding his boss (Frank Morgan) in *The Shop Around the Corner*; a courtier who engages in some sword play with Bob Hope in *Monsieur Beaucaire*; and a corrupt senator in *Gallant Legion*. After the last he was mostly busy on television and in theatre, having one final triumph in the latter, playing the father and sole survivor of the family hiding in an attic from the Nazis in *The Diary of Anne Frank*. He repeated his role in the acclaimed 1959 movie version of the play and, in his own understated way, gave the best performance in the film. By the time his last movie, *The Greatest Story Ever Told*, debuted, he'd been dead for more than a year, having filmed his role of Nicodemus shortly before succumbing to a heart attack. He published his autobiography, *My Father and I*, in 1959.

Screen: 1920: Der Roman der Motesse Orth (nUSr); 1922: Orphans of the Storm; 1923: The Song of Love; 1925: The Road to Yesterday; 1926: Young April; Meet the Prince; Shipwrecked; 1927: His Dog; The King of Kings; The Heart Thief; The Forbidden Woman; 1928: Tenth Avenue; The Blue Danube; 1929: Show Boat; Mississippi Gambler; 1930: Night Ride; Cock o' the Walk; Die Sehnsucht jeder Frau/A Lady to Love (nUSr); 1931: Venetian Nights/Carnival (nUSr); 1932: The Blue Danube; 1934: Cleopatra; Viva Villa; Sisters Under the Skin; 1935: The Crusades; 1936: The Garden of Allah; 1937: Souls at Sea; Slave Ship; The Life of Emile Zola; Lancer Spy; Lady Behave; 1938: Suez; The Baroness and the Butler; Marie Antoinette; 1939: The Man in the Iron Mask; Idiot's Delight; Lady of the Tropics; The Three Musketeers; Mr. Moto Takes Vacation; The Rains Came; Pack Up Your Troubles; 1940: Rangers of Fortune; The Shop Around the Corner; Phantom Raiders; Meet the Wildcat; 1941: The Parson of Panamint; 1945: Flame of the Barbary Coast; The Cheaters; 1946: Monsieur Beaucaire; The Plainsman and the Lady; 1947: Northwest Outpost; 1948: Gallant Legion; Old Los Angeles; 1959: The Diary of Anne Frank; 1961: King of the Roaring 20's — The Story of Arnold Rothstein; 1965: The Greatest Story Ever Told.

NY Stage: 1921: Pagans; 1923: Peer Gynt; 1924: The Firebrand; 1931: Anatol; 1932: Liliom; Dear Jane; 1935: Tomorrow's Holiday (and prod.); 1941: Clash By Night; 1942: Uncle Harry; 1944: The Cherry Orchard; 1951: The Green Bay Tree; 1953: Love's Labour's Lost; 1955: The Diary Of Anne Frank.

Select TV: 1950: Uncle Harry (sp); Six Characters in Search of an Author (sp); 1951: Appearances and Reality (sp); 1952: The Professor (sp); 1953: Point of Honor (sp); The Last Night of Don Juan (sp); Hamlet (sp); 1953–54: Joseph Schildkraut Presents (series); 1955: The Hammer and the Sword (sp).

ROMY SCHNEIDER

(ROSEMAIRE MAGDALENA ALBACH-RETTY)
BORN: VIENNA, AUSTRIA, SEPTEMBER 23, 1938.
RAISED IN GERMANY. DIED: MAY 29, 1982.

Unlike most European beauties who were imported for American productions of the 1960s, Romy Schneider was not only attractive but actually had vitality and charm in place of the usual aloofness associated with these ladies. The child of actors Wolf Albach-Retty and Magda Schneider, she made her movie debut playing her mom's daughter in *Wenn der Weisse Flieder Wieder Bluht*, in 1953, which set her career rolling. She played Queen Victoria in *The Story of Vickie*, and continued her rise to stardom in Germany in various costume romances and musicals, notably *Sissi*, as Princess Elizabeth of Austria, a film popular enough to rate two sequels (they were combined into a single feature, *Forever My Love*, for wider release in 1962). By that time, the international market was calling for her services and she started off playing a nympho in Orson Welles's cryptic, made-in-Paris take on *The Trial*; then did two epics for Columbia, *The Victors*, as the violinist who captures George Hamilton's heart with her innocence, until he realizes she is whoring on the side; and *The Cardinal*, getting the hots for a priest-in-training, played by Tom Tryon. From these films she went on to two highly commercial comedies (probably the two movies that Americans know her best for): *Good Neighbor Sam*, where she pretended to be married to Jack Lemmon, and *What's New, Pussycat?*, where she tried to get Peter O'Toole to stop having sex with every woman he sees. She went back to the European market in the late 1960s where her assignments ranged from disposable efforts like *My Son, My Lover*; *The Hero/Bloomfield*; *The Assassination of Trotsky*; and *The Sensuous Assassin*, to more significant efforts that kept her a major part of the (mostly) French film scene, including *Cesar and Rosalie*, as a woman shared between two men, played by Yves Montand and Sami Frey; *Ludwig*, reprising her Empress Elizabeth role; and the grim *Clair de Femme*, as a woman emotionally damaged by her daughter's death in an auto accident. She was busy right up to the time she died of a heart attack at the age of 43.

Screen (US releases only): 1958: The Story of Vickie (Ger: 1954); 1959: Mon Petit; Scampolo; 1961: Purple Noon; 1962: Boccaccio '70; 1963: The Trial; The Victors; The Cardinal; 1964: Good Neighbor Sam; 1965: What's New, Pussycat?; 1966: Maedchen in Uniform (Ger: 1958); 10:30 p.m. Summer; 1967: Triple Cross; 1969: Otley; 1970: My Son, My Lover; The Swimming Pool; The Things of Life; 1972: The Hero/Bloomfield; The Assassination of Trotsky; Cesar and Rosalie; 1973: Ludwig; 1974: Loving in the Rain; Le Trio Infernal; 1975: The Sensuous Assassin (Fr: 1970); The French Way/Love at the Top; 1976: The Old Gun/Vengeance One by One; Dirty Hands; 1977: That Most Important Thing: Love (Fr: 1975); 1978: Mado; A Woman at Her Window; 1979: Sidney Sheldon's Bloodline; A Simple Story; 1980: Clair de Femme; Group Portrait with Lady; 1982: Garde a Vue/Under Suspicion; Deathwatch (Eur: 1980); 1983: La Passante.

GEORGE C. SCOTT

(GEORGE CAMPBELL SCOTT) BORN: WISE, VA, OCTOBER 18, 1927. RAISED IN DETROIT, MI. ED: UNIV. OF MO. DIED: SEPTEMBER 22, 1999.

It was immediately evident upon his arrival in movies that George C. Scott was one of the most dynamic, uncompromising new talents to hit the screens in years. With his pointedly unattractive features and gravelly voice, he was destined for character support but, in time, his edgy, domineering presence was simply too powerful to keep him from leading roles. Although the energy was usually there, to a point where he sometimes stooped to some uncalled for hamming, he was not lucky when it came to vehicles and it was often hard to remember just how good he could be in light of the poor material. Having been a Marine he went to college on the G.I. Bill of Rights, but switched from journalism to acting during his stay there. This was followed by stock work in Detroit after which he journeyed to New York to seek employment, nabbing the lead in the New York Shakespeare Festival production of *Richard III*, in 1957. The acclaim was unanimous, winning him a Theatre World Award among other honors, and within the same season he appeared in *As You Like It* and

Children of Darkness. In the latter he co-starred with Colleen Dewhurst who became his third wife (1960–65) and fourth as well (they remarried, 1967–72). Because of this run of strong performances Hollywood sought him out and, after a colorful part as a manic preacher in the Gary Cooper western *The Hanging Tree*, he created his first great impression on film, as the cagey lawyer who goes head-to-head with James Stewart, in one of the big movies of 1959, *Anatomy of a Murder*. He received his first Oscar nomination (in the supporting category) and promptly got another one for his next movie, *The Hustler*, in which he was nothing less than brilliant playing the cool, smarmy promoter. This also marked the first time he would cause trouble where awards were concern, being the first actor to go on record as refusing his nomination.

His first leading role was in director John Huston's muddled all-star failure, *The List of Adrian Messenger*, as a Scotland Yard inspector, after which he showed that he could play comedy with the best of them in *Dr. Strangelove or: How I Learned to Stop Worrying and Love the Bomb*, unforgettable as the dense and gung-ho Pentagon general Buck Turgison, mugging to perfection in what was one of the seminal movies of the 1960s. Around that time he did a well-liked television series, *East Side, West Side*, and appeared in the best of the three sequences in *The Yellow Rolls-Royce*, as a swaggering gangster who loses his mistress (Shirley MacLaine) to another man (Alain Deloin). Similarly he was one of the better things about the episodic and meandering epic *The Bible*, bringing some fire to the latter part of the movie as Abraham; and had great fun playing a wiley con man in *The Flim Flam Man*, both films giving audiences the impression that Scott was much older than he actually was. He showed up in the challenging *Petula*, a movie far too complex and unnerving for wide acceptance but one that gave him a great opportunity, playing the unhappy, disillusioned doctor who gets hooked on a woman (Julie Christie) more troubled than himself. He compensated on Broadway by appearing in a highly commercial piece, Neil Simon's *Plaza Suite*, playing three different roles. By this point he was undoubtedly a star but leapt unexpectedly into the superstar category with *Patton*, getting the part after several other names turned it down. It was an old-fashioned bio film on an epic scale, but what made it soar above so many others was Scott's electrifying turn as the foul-mouthed, egotistical force of nature, General George Patton, creating admiration and awe for one of World War II's major players at a time when the U.S. was in a very anti-war mood. It became one of the biggest hits of 1970 and racked up seven Academy Awards, including one for Best Picture and, more interestingly, for Scott as Best Actor. Prior to the ceremony, he had gone on record as saying he would turn the trophy down if he won and the Academy stood by its choice nonetheless, making him the first actor to ignore the honor altogether. And the snubb only helped to make him that much better known.

After the controversy he essayed one of his more charming roles, as the loony lawyer who thinks he is Sherlock Holmes, in the sadly neglected *They Might Be Giants*, and then was back in a surprise hit, *The Hospital*, a disturbing, jet black comedy in which he was the frustrated, impotent surgeon questioning both his profession and his life. It put him in the running for another Oscar but, perhaps figuring it was unlikely he'd win a second year in a row, he kept quiet about the award, which went to Gene Hackman anyway. There was marginal public interest in a downbeat cop drama, *The New Centurions*, but his directorial debut, *Rage*, as a dad driven to just that after his son is infected with poisonous gas, was coolly received. Similarly he got the thumbs down for *Oklahoma Crude*, as a grizzled boozer out to help Faye Dunaway strike oil; *Bank Shot*, a laughless comedy caper in which he heisted an entire bank; and *The Savage Is Loose*, another film that he directed, its only distinction being that Scott also financed and distributed it independently, in an effort to prove that filmmakers had no use for interference from the major studios, a point that severely backfired as this unpleasant story of incest had no success whatsoever. There was more audience interest in the highly publicized *The Day of the Dolphin*, which nonetheless was considered a disappointment by fans of the novel; and *The Hindenburg*, an all-star look at the voyage of the ill-fated zeppelin, in which he played a sympathetic Nazi. Lost among these films was the low-keyed *Islands in the Stream*, in which he played a thinly disguised version of Ernest Hemingway, proving to be the perfect choice to embody the author, and *Movie Movie*, in which he cheekily portrayed both a fight manager and a stage director in this good-natured, two-part spoof of double features.

The writing was on the wall for Scott where his potential as a leading box-office name was concerned after the poor response to *Hardcore*, a sordid and phoney movie about a pious dad searching the porno world to find his runaway daughter; *The Changeling*, a tame ghost story filmed in Canada; and *The Formula*, which presented the intriguing pairing of Scott and the one other actor who had also turned down an Oscar, Marlon Brando. Scott, in the lead role, clearly came away the winner, although this thriller was so uninspired that most critics merely took the time to make cruel comments on how fat both performers had become. Although he was top billed he was quickly written out of the plot of *Taps*, which, ironically, turned out to be the first real hit he'd done in some time.

Not surprisingly, he turned towards television at this stage of his career, where his roles included Fagin, Scrooge, Mussolini, and finally Patton again in the sequel *The Last Days of Patton*. This medium seemed to keep him a star, as did his occasional trips back to the stage where he was seen giving his all in such works as *Death of a Salesman*, *Present Laughter*, and *On Borrowed Time*, all of which he directed as well (he also directed but did not appear in *All God's Chillun' Got Wings*, in 1975, and *Design for Living*, in 1984). The movies, by contrast, held little value for Scott, with such bombs as *Firestarter*, a strong contender for the worst of the many bad Steven King adaptations, with Scott as a murderous, pony-tailed child molester; *The Exorcist III*, a disastrous horror film which had little to do with the original 1973 blockbuster; and *Angus*, as the grandpa of the overweight hero of this teen comedy. It wasn't surprising that there was a touch of detached weariness to his work in these films. There was, nevertheless, still great admiration for Scott, with the Emmy Award committee bestowing the second of their trophies upon him (the first had been for *The Price*) in 1998 for the remake of *12 Angry Men*, in the part that Lee J. Cobb had done on screen. There was no report on whether he ever picked up either of these honors, though he made no indication that he disapproved of this particular award. In 1972 he married Trish Van Devere, who had appeared with him in *The Last Run*; and would also show up alongside him in *The Day of the Dolphin*, *The Savage Is Loose*; *Movie Movie*; and *The Changeling*. One of his children is actor Campbell Scott, from his first marriage to Dewhurst.

Screen: 1959: The Hanging Tree; Anatomy of a Murder; 1961: The Hustler; 1963: The List of Adrian Messenger; 1964: Dr. Strangelove or: How I Learned to Stop Worrying and Love the Bomb; The Yellow Rolls-Royce; 1966: The Bible; Not With My Wife You Don't!; 1967: The Flim-Flam Man; 1968: Petulia; 1970: Patton; 1971: They Might Be Giants; The Last Run; The Hospital; 1972: The New Centurions; Rage (and dir.); 1973: Oklahoma Crude; The Day of the Dolphin; 1974: Bank Shot;

The Savage Is Loose (and dir.; prod.); 1975: The Hindenburg; 1977: Islands in the Stream; 1978: Crossed Swords/The Prince and the Pauper; Movie Movie; 1979: Hardcore; 1980: The Changeling; The Formula; 1981: Taps; 1984: Firestarter; 1990: The Exorcist III; The Rescuers Down Under (voice); 1993: Malice; 1995: Angus; 1999: Gloria.

NY Stage: 1957: Richard III (ob); 1958: As You Like It (ob); Children of Darkness (ob); Comes A Day; 1959: The Andersonville Trial; 1960: The Wall; 1962: General Seeger (and dir.); The Merchant of Venice; 1963: Desire Under The Elms (ob); 1967: The Little Foxes; 1968: Plaza Suite; 1973: Uncle Vanya; 1975: Death of a Salesman (and dir.); 1976: Sly Fox; 1980: Tricks of the Trade; 1982: Present Laughter (and dir.); 1986: The Boys in Autumn; 1991: On Borrowed Time (and dir.); 1993: Wrong Turn at Lungfish (ob); 1996: Inherit the Wind.

Select TV: 1958: A Tale of Two Cities (sp); The Outcasts of Poker Flat (sp); We Haven't Seen Her Lately (sp); The Empty Chair (sp); 1959: Trap for a Stranger (sp); Target for Three (sp); Winterset (sp); 1960: Don Juan in Hell (sp); 1961: The Power and the Glory (sp); 1963–64: East Side, West Side (series); 1965: A Time for Killing (sp); 1967: The Crucible (sp); 1971: The Price (sp); Jane Eyre (sp); 1972: The Trouble with People (sp); 1975: Fear on Trial; 1976: Beauty and the Beast (sp); 1982: Oliver Twist; 1983: China Rose; 1984: A Christmas Carol; 1985: Mussolini: The Untold Story (ms); 1986: Choices; The Last Days of Patton; Murders in the Rue Morgue; 1987: Pals; 1987–88: Mr. President (series); 1989: The Ryan White Story; 1990: Descending Angel; 1991: Finding the Way Home; 1993: Curacao/Deadly Currents; 1994: Traps (series); The Whipping Boy/Prince Brat and the Whipping Boy; In the Heat of the Night: A Matter of Justice; 1995: Tyson; 1996: Family Rescue; Titanic; 1997: Country Justice/Family Rescue; 12 Angry Men; 1999: Rocky Marciano; Inherit the Wind.

LIZABETH SCOTT

(Emma Matzo) Born: Scranton, PA, September 29, 1922.

She had the look: blonde and sulky, with dark brows, and the husky voice that made her a great femme fatale for the noir genre, but Lizabeth Scott wasn't long for Hollywood and, after a decade or so of work, she pretty much did a vanishing act. After some summer stock in Lake Ariel, NY, she went to Manhattan to study drama and did some modeling. A chance meeting with producer Hal B. Wallis brought her to Hollywood and he signed her to contract around the time he was departing Warners to go to Paramount. Given the p.r. tag of "The Threat," she was unveiled in 1945 in the soaper *You Came Along*, as the treasury department official who marries G.I. Robert Cummings, only to lose him to leukemia. This was not the sort of drama that best suited her and she fared better in *The Strange Love of Martha Ivers*, battling Barbara Stanwyck over Van Heflin. A loan-out to Columbia gave her her best and best-remembered role, in *Dead Reckoning*, playing the shady dame who hooks up with Humphrey Bogart, trying to find out who murdered his friend. She was an acceptable fill-in for Lauren Bacall and returned to her home lot to appear in some minor efforts of this hard-boiled genre: *Desert Fury*, as a woman who desires gambler-on-the-run John Hodiak; *I Walk Alone*, playing a nightclub singer whose ex, Burt Lancaster, returns from prison; and *Dark City*, once again trilling in the clubs, while involved with Charlton Heston, in his Hollywood debut. Similarly she was borrowed by various outside companies for such melodramas as *Two of a Kind* and *The Racket*, which were more suitable for her persona than a western she did with Alan Ladd, *Red Mountain*, or the Martin and Lewis comedy, *Scared Stiff*. She finished off her contract to Wallis by taking a back seat to Elvis Presley in *Loving You*, as a publicist who turns him into a singing sensation. Apart from some television she disappeared from the show business scene until she showed up in the 1972 noir homage *Pulp*, giving an intriguingly weird performance as a woman married into royalty. There was little comment made about her return, however, and afterwards she once again dropped out of sight.

Screen: 1945: You Came Along; 1946: The Strange Love of Martha Ivers; 1947: Dead Reckoning; Desert Fury; Variety Girl; 1948: Pitfall; I Walk Alone; 1949: Too Late for Tears; Easy Living; 1950: Paid in Full; Dark City; The Company She Keeps; 1951: Two of a Kind; The Racket; Red Mountain; 1952: Stolen Face; 1953: Scared Stiff; Bad for Each Other; 1954: Silver Lode; 1957: The Weapon; Loving You; 1972: Pulp.

NY Stage: AS ELIZABETH SCOTT: 1942: The Skin Of Our Teeth.

Select TV: 1955: I'll Always Love You Natalie (sp); 1956: Overnight Haul (sp).

MARTHA SCOTT

BORN: JAMESPORT, MO, SEPTEMBER 22, 1914.
ED: UNIV. OF MI.

When she arrived in Hollywood in the early 1940s, Martha Scott was touted as one of the great new finds and the star-making machine went into overtime. Problem was she was simply a fine actress, but never one who possessed any uniquely defining traits, or colorful idiosyncrasies that would have allowed her to reach the top and stay there. A veteran of several stock companies, she came to New York where she became a regular on the radio. She became an overnight star when she was cast as Emily in the original 1938 production of one of the theatre's most enduring plays, Thornton Wilder's *Our Town*. Two years later Scott made her motion picture debut by repeating the part in the film version, independently produced by Sol Lesser for distribution by United Artists. Although the stylization of the piece didn't transfer particularly well to the big screen, the movie was successful and she was quiet lovely in the role, earning an Oscar nomination. She quickly followed it with *The Howards of Virginia*, one of the cinema's many unsuccessful attempts to capture the Revolutionary War on film and a rare Cary Grant money-loser of that era. To cash in on her success in *Our Town*, she got her own showcase, *Cheers for Miss Bishop*, a sentimental look at an old maid schoolteacher. In it her character aged over several years, a feat she repeated in the better *One Foot in Heaven*, this time as the wife of minister Fredric March.

With no studio to tie her down, she returned to the stage, but the few movie roles she played in the 1940s, including the comedy *Hi Diddle Diddle*, and the western, *War of the Wildcats*, added little prestige to her position in the industry. Over in England, however, she did get to eschew her usual niceness to play a malicious woman in *So Well Remembered*, henpecking husband John Mills. In the mid-to late 1950s she turned to more motherly roles in some major films, including *The Desperate Hours*, where she and her family were held hostage by Humphrey Bogart and his gang; and the two mightiest of the Biblical epics of the day, *The Ten Commandments* and *Ben-Hur*, contracting leprosy in the latter, as Charlton Heston's mother. After that her film appearances were sporadic to say the least, including roles in *The Turning Point*, and the little-seen *Doin' Time on Planet Earth*. In addition to acting she was also a theatrical producer of such

plays as *The Time of Your Life* and *First Monday in October*.

Screen: 1940: Our Town; The Howards of Virginia; 1941: Cheers for Miss Bishop; They Dare Not Love; One Foot in Heaven; 1943: Stage Door Canteen; Hi Diddle Diddle; War of the Wildcats/In Old Oklahoma; 1947: So Well Remembered; 1949: Strange Bargain; 1951: When I Grow Up; 1955: The Desperate Hours; 1956: The Ten Commandments; 1957: Sayonara; Eighteen and Anxious; 1959: Ben-Hur; 1973: Charlotte's Web (voice); 1974: Airport 1975; 1977: The Turning Point; 1988: Doin' Time on Planet Earth.

NY Stage: 1938: Our Town; 1939: Foreigners; 1942: The Willow and I; 1944: Soldier's Wife; 1945: The Voice of the Turtle; 1947: It Takes Two; 1950: Design for a Stained Glass Window; 1951: The Number; 1952: The Male Animal; 1953: The Remarkable Mr. Pennypacker; 1958: Cloud 7; 1960: A Distant Bell; The Tumbler; The 49th Cousin; 1965: The Subject Was Roses; 1975: The Skin of Our Teeth; 1991: The Crucible.

Select TV: 1951: The Choir Rehearsal (sp); 1956: Footlight Frenzy (sp); 1957: Backwoods Cinderella (sp); 1959: Rachel's Summer (sp); 1972: The Devil's Daughter; 1974: Thursday's Game; 1975: The Abduction of St. Anne; The Bionic Woman; Medical Story; 1976: The Bionic Woman (series); 1978: The Word (ms); 1979; 1985: Dallas (series); 1979: Charleston; 1980: Beulah Land (ms); Father Figure; 1980–81: Secrets of Midland Heights (series); 1983: Summer Girl; Adam; 1985–86: General Hospital (series); 1986: Adam: His Song Continues; 1989: Love and Betrayal; 1990: Daughter of the Streets.

RANDOLPH SCOTT

(RANDOLPH CRANE) BORN: ORANGE COUNTY, VA, JANUARY 23, 1898. ED: UNIV. OF NC.
DIED: MARCH 2, 1987.

Like many a performer whose acting limitations made them suitable for quiet, stoic men of the west, Randolph Scott hemmed and hawed his way through various genres in his younger years until it was clear that riding the range taxed his wooden thesping the least. From the late 1940s until his retirement he did his cinematic chores strictly on horseback and that was how he came to be best remembered. Following school, a chance encounter with mogul Howard Hughes got him some extra work in a handful of movies after which he went to the Pasadena Playhouse to study his craft. During this period he was cast as a rube in the big city in a cheapie film entitled *Women Men Marry*, and was signed to a contract by Paramount after being spotted onstage in *The Broken Wing*. They started him off as second leads in *The Sky Bride* and *Hot Saturday*, in the latter battling Cary Grant for Nancy Carroll (despite both men marrying on several occasions, their off-screen relationship was cause for much speculation over the years); and starred him in a pair of low-budget westerns, *Wild Horse Mesa* and *Heritage of the Desert*. For a while it appeared that the saddle would claim him at this early stage of his career, until RKO asked him to play the ex-football player who inherits a dress shop in the musical *Roberta*. Clearly he was no threat to drawing attention from co-stars Fred Astaire and Ginger Rogers, so he showed up alongside them again for *Follow the Fleet*. In between these he did the spectacularly silly *She*, as the hero entranced by age-defying Helen Gahagan, and, back at Paramount, *So Red the Rose*, a Civil War romance that was a major failure for that company. Borrowed by United Artists he was cast in one of his best-known roles of the 1930s, Hawkeye in *The Last of the Mohicans*; then, back at Paramount, was a suitable sounding board for Mae West's quips in *Go West, Young Man*.

After playing Irene Dunne's love interest in another musical, *High, Wide and Handsome*, and carrying a large-scale western, *The Texans*, his contract expired. 20th Century-Fox pictured him as a very tall leading man for Shirley Temple in *Rebecca of Sunnybrook Farm* and *Susannah of the Mounties*; and let him play marshals in both *Jesse James* and *Frontier Marshal*, the latter, in fact, being Wyatt Earp. Back in second leads he was featured in two big 1940 releases, *Virginia City*, teamed with Errol Flynn; and the funny *My Favorite Wife*, where Irene Dunne had the none-too-difficult task of choosing between him or Cary Grant. There was a typical but popular wartime drama, *To the Shores of Tripoli*, where he was cast as a drill sergeant; after which he was John Wayne's rival in both *The Spoilers* (featuring one of the screen's great knock-down fights) and *Pittsburgh*. He fought the war, movie-wise, in *Gung Ho*, about a real-life Marine attack on Makin Island; *Bombardier*, in which he and Pat O'Brien did some fighting over Anne Shirley as well; and the awkwardly titled but well-liked *Corvette K-225*, as a Canadian naval officer.

Since he was winning little favor in such films as the uninspired adventure *Captain Kidd*, where he played the hero, and the dreary family drama *Christmas Eve*, the lure of the West became very strong indeed. He'd reached the age of 50, hadn't grown more exciting with the passing years, and decided that this genre was where fans appreciated him best. Among the better-received of these films were *Trail Street*, which found him playing Bat Masterson; *Colt .45*, a story of a gun salesman out to track down his stolen rifles, which was his most popular offering from this period; *The Stranger Wore a Gun*, which was made in 3-D; *A Lawless Street*, which gave him an intriguing leading lady in Angela Lansbury; *The Tall T*, which, of the many he made for director Budd Boetticher, developed something of a cult following; and *Buchanan Rides Alone*, which was more tongue-in-cheek than the rest. His last movie, *Ride the High Country*, was probably the best of all his westerns. Teamed with another celluloid cowboy, Joel McCrea, and teetering on the side of no-good for once, Scott was at his most appealing, making for a grand farewell. He retired soon afterwards, one of the wealthiest men in the business.

Screen: 1928: Sharp Shooters; 1929: The Black Watch; The Far Call; The Virginian; Dynamite; 1931: The Women Men Marry; 1932: Sky Bride; Hot Saturday; A Successful Calamity; Wild Horse Mesa; Heritage of the Desert; 1933: Hello Everybody; Murders in the Zoo; Supernatural; Cocktail Hour; Man of the Forest; Sunset Pass; To the Last Man; Broken Dreams; The Thundering Herd; 1934: The Last Round-Up; Wagon Wheels; 1935: Home on the Range; Village Tale; Rocky Mountain Mystery; Roberta; She; So Red the Rose; 1936: Follow the Fleet; And Sudden Death; The Last of the Mohicans; Go West, Young Man; 1937: High, Wide and Handsome; 1938: Rebecca of Sunnybrook Farm; The Texans; The Road to Reno; 1939: Jesse James; Susannah of the Mounties; Frontier Marshal; Coast Guard; 20,000 Men a Year; 1940: Virginia City; My Favorite Wife; When the Daltons Rode; 1941: Western Union; Belle Starr; 1942: Paris Calling; To the Shores of Tripoli; The Spoilers; Pittsburgh; 1943: The Desperadoes; Bombardier; Corvette K-225; 1944: Gung Ho; Follow the Boys; 1945: Belle of the Yukon; China Sky; Captain Kidd; 1946: Abilene Town; Badman's Territory; Home, Sweet Homicide; 1947: Trail Street; Gunfighters; Christmas Eve; 1948: Albuquerque; Coroner Creek; Return of the Badmen; 1949: The Walking Hills; The Doolins of Oklahoma; Canadian Pacific; Fighting Man of the Planes; 1950: The Nevadan; Colt .45; The Cariboo Trail; 1951: Sugarfoot; Santa Fe; Fort Worth; Man in the Saddle; Starlift; 1952: Carson City; The Man Behind the Gun; Hangman's Knot; 1953: The

Stranger Wore a Gun; Thunder Over the Plains; 1954: Riding Shotgun; The Bounty Hunter; 1955: Ten Wanted Men; Rage at Dawn; Tall Man Riding; A Lawless Street; 1956: Seven Men From Now; 7th Cavalry; 1957: The Tall T; Shoot-Out at Medicine Bend; Decision at Sundown; 1958: Buchanan Rides Alone; 1959: Ride Lonesome; Westbound; 1960: Comanche Station; 1962: Ride the High Country.

ZACHARY SCOTT

BORN: AUSTIN, TX, FEBRUARY 24, 1914.
DIED: OCTOBER 3, 1965.

A specialist in duplicitous, spineless sort of bad men, Zachary Scott, with his weak features and pencil moustache, was seen at his best in the mid-to-late 1940s. He dropped out of college to become a seaman and eventually wound up in England, where he joined the English Repertory Company and did theater in Bath. Back in America he worked with the Westport County Playhouse before going to Broadway where his success in *Those Endearing Young Charms* won him a contract with Warner Bros. They started him out with an important role in a mediocre noir, *The Mask of Dimitrios*, as the villain pursued by Peter Lorre and Sidney Greenstreet. They then loaned him out for a rare sympathetic part and his best lead, in *The Southerner*, playing a determined sharecropper in this absorbing drama directed by Jean Renoir. Back at Warners he played his best remembered cad role, as the fellow shot in the opening scene of *Mildred Pierce*, and teamed with that film's star, Joan Crawford, to good effect years later in *Flamingo Road*, as a politically ambitious deputy. In between he replaced Humphrey Bogart as the author who falls for Alexis Smith in the romantic triangle *Stallion Road*; was cheated on by Ann Sheridan in *The Unfaithful*; and taken in by femme fatale Virginia Mayo in *Flaxy Martin*. Out west he stole Randolph Scott's guns in *Colt .45*, and, after leaving Warners, was the bad guy in Fox's *The Secret of Convict Lake*, making off with some stolen cash from Ethel Barrymore's village of women. His usefulness in "A" features apparently having been exhausted, he started popping up in various "B" features and British productions in between television assignments and stage work. In the early 1960s, there was a leading role in one of the lesser movies from director Luis Bunuel, *The Young One*, in which he played a racist who takes advantage of a young girl. He was last seen suavely sneering while Jerry Lewis made strange faces in *It's Only Money*.

Screen: 1944: The Mask of Dimitrios; Hollywood Canteen; 1945: The Southerner; Mildred Pierce; Danger Signal; 1946: Her Kind of Man; 1947: The Unfaithful; Stallion Road; Cass Timberlane; 1948: Ruthless; Whiplash; 1949: South of St. Louis; Flaxy Martin; Flamingo Road; One Last Fling; 1950: Guilty Bystander; Colt .45; Shadow on the Wall; Born to Be Bad; Pretty Baby; 1951: Lightning Strikes Twice; The Secret of Convict Lake; Let's Make It Legal; 1952: Wings of Danger; 1953: Appointment in Honduras; 1955: Treasure of Ruby Hills; Shotgun; Flame of the Islands; 1956: Bandido; 1957: The Counterfeit Plan; Man in the Shadow/Violent Stranger; 1960: Natchez Trace; 1961: The Young One; 1962: It's Only Money.

NY Stage: 1941: Circle of Chalk; Ah, Wilderness!; 1942: The Damask Cheek; 1943: The Rock; Those Endearing Young Charms; 1956: The King and I; 1959: Requiem for a Nun; 1963: A Rainy Day in Newark.

Select TV: 1950: The Big Sleep (sp); The Valiant (sp); 1953: King Coffin (sp); 1954: Pearl-Handled Guns (sp); Break in the Mirror (sp); The Grand Tour (sp); 1955: It Gives Me Great Pleasure (sp);

The Drifter (sp); 1956: Point of Honor (sp); Flight Into Danger (sp); 1960: The Scarlet Pimpernel (sp); 1961: Jane Eyre (sp); 1962: Big Deal in Laredo (sp); The Expendables.

JEAN SEBERG

BORN: MARSHALLTOWN, IA, NOVEMBER 13, 1938.
DIED: SEPTEMBER 8, 1979.

A curious enigma, Jean Seberg was an American actress who never got much praise for her work on her home turf but became something of a favorite in foreign fare. Her troubled personal life gave her a vulnerable image which no doubt helped her develop a cult with some, while her appeal still remains a mystery to others. At age 17 the minimally trained actress was chosen after a much-publicized search to play the lead in director Otto Preminger's film of Bernard Shaw's *Saint Joan* and it became one of the most famously panned debuts in film history. A follow-up with Preminger, *Bonjour Tristesse*, wasn't much more encouraging, but she did come off nicely as the scientist's daughter who falls for Peter Sellers in the friendly farce *The Mouse That Roared*, which, like the other two films, was released by Columbia, for whom she was under contract. Her reputation was made, however, when she was chosen by director Jean-Luc Godard to appear opposite Jean-Paul Belmondo in *Breathless*. This, of course, became one of the groundbreaking events of the cinema with its free-form style of jump cuts and restless camera, and Seberg would be forever held in high esteem by students of pretentious college film courses for decades to come. There were further foreign films, including *In the French Style*, with Stanley Baker; another teaming with Belmondo, *Backfire*; and *Birds in Peru*, directed by Romain Gary, who was her husband from 1963 to 1970. She was back in the U.S. for *Lilith*, as a mental patient who catches doctor Warren Beatty's fancy; *A Fine Madness*, as Sean Connery's fling; *Paint Your Wagon*, as a mail order bride in this expensive musical (her one song was dubbed); and, most notably, the box-office blockbuster *Airport*, as Burt Lancaster's mistress. After that, her stock fell with such undistinguished films as *The French Conspiracy*; *Kill!, Kill!, Kill!* (directed by her now ex-husband Gary), and *The Corruption of Chris Miller*. In 1979 she was found dead in her car, having overdosed on barbiturates. 11 years later Gary killed himself as well.

Screen: 1957: Saint Joan; 1958: Bonjour Tristesse; 1959: The Mouse That Roared; 1960: Let No Man Right My Epitaph; 1961: Breathless/A Bout de Soufflé (Fr: 1959); The Five Day Lover; Les Grandees Personas/A Taste of Love/Time Out for Love (nUSr); La Recreation/Playtime (nUSr); 1962: Congo Vivo/Eruption (nUSr); 1963: In the French Style; 1964: Lilith; Les Plus Belles Escroqueries du Monde/World's Most Beautiful Swindlers (nUSr); 1965: Echappment Libre/Backfire (Fr: 1964); Un Milliard dans le Billiard/Diamonds Are Brittle (nUSr); 1966: Moment to Moment; A Fine Madness; La Ligne de Demarcation/Line of Demarcation (nUSr); 1967: Estouffade a la Caraibe/The Looters (nUSr); La Route de Corinthe/The Road to Corinth (nUSr); 1968: Birds in Peru; 1969: Pendulum; Paint Your Wagon; 1970: Airport; Macho Callahan; 1971: Dead of Summer; Questa Specie d'Amore/This Kind of Love (nUSr); 1973: The French Conspiracy; Camorra (nUSr); 1974: Kill/Kill! Kill! Kill! (Fr: 1972); 1975: The Corruption of Chris Miller/Behind the Shutters (Sp: 1973); 1974: La Hautes Solitudes (nUSr); Bianchi Cavalli d'Agoto/White Horses of Summer (nUSr); 1975: Le Grand Delire (nUSr); 1977: The Wild Duck.

Select TV: 1973: Mousey.

PETER SELLERS

(RICHARD HENRY SELLERS)
BORN: SOUTHSEA, ENGLAND, SEPTEMBER 8, 1925.
DIED: JULY 24, 1980.

To many he was the epitome of the actor who only came to life when buried deep within a role; the more eccentric the better. Peter Sellers was a fairly average-looking guy off screen but his chameleon-like knack for creating hilariously odd characters with a variety of accents and quirks was simply phenomenal, making him one of those special performers who was and still is cherished, despite the often poor quality of his films. While serving in the RAF during World War II, he performed in a revue called *The Gang Show*. Following the war he told jokes at a seedy London theater called the Windmill and worked on radio where he teamed up with Harry Secombe, Spike Milligan, and Michael Bentine to become The Goons. Their irreverent style of humor and their hit program, *The Goon Show*, made them famous throughout England. Sellers, along with Secombe and Milligan, debuted on screen in 1951, in *Penny Points to Paradise*, for the first time playing someone older than himself, a colonel in this particular instance. The remaining Goon, Bentine (who eventually quit the group), came along for *Down Among the Z Men*, but neither of these films transferred the Goon's irreverent brand of humor to motion pictures with much success. Sellers did have the good fortune to join the cast of *The Ladykillers*, one of the pinnacles of British comedy, as the Teddy Boy member of Alec Guinness's gang of would-be thieves. As the Goons were trickling out as a team, Sellers found himself in demand for colorful character parts, including *The Smallest Show on Earth*, cast as a drunken projectionist, and his first Hollywood-financed credit, *tom thumb*, in which he and Terry-Thomas added some needed life to this coy concoction, as a pair of cartoonish villains. They reteamed up again for their own starring comedy, *Carlton-Browne of the F.O./Man in a Cocked Hat*, a spoof of foreign diplomacy, after which came the movie that shot Sellers to the top of his field, *The Mouse That Roared*, playing three roles delightfully, including one in drag, in this amusing farce about the world's tiniest country declaring war on the United States. Columbia Pictures distributed the film in America, which meant it got seen outside the usual art house venues customarily reserved for British product.

This film, along with *I'm All Right, Jack*, in which he convincingly played an elderly, pig-headed union rep and stole every scene he was in, made him the king of British comedy just as the 1960s arrived. He was a Scotsman contemplating murder in *The Battle of the Sexes*; dragged out his devastating Indian impersonation for *The Millionairess*, an otherwise tired comedy that at least allowed him to act opposite Sophia Loren; directed himself to mediocre notices in *Mr. Topaz/I Like Money*, the umpteenth version of the Pagnol comedy; got some of his best reviews to date as the librarian who tries to seduce Mai Zetterling in *Only Two Can Play*; stumbled badly as a selfish old philanderer in a flat-footed farced, *Waltz of the Toreadors*; masterminded a robbery in the amusing *The Wrong Arm of the Law*; and played a clergyman in the satirical *Heavens Above!* There was also an important supporting role as the mysterious Claire Quilty in the controversial 1962 adaptation of *Lolita*, and his combination of wry comedy and neuroses presented the actor at his most brilliant.

Much in demand, he achieved the sort of peak year in 1964 that most actors could only dream of. First he pulled off another triple-play, his most famous multi-character tour de force, in director Stanley Kubrick's lacerating and influential black comedy about military destruction, *Dr. Strangelove or: How I*

Learned to Stop Worrying and Love the Bomb. As the bald, ineffectual President of the United States, the level-headed Air Force officer, and the creepy, wheelchair-bound ex-Nazi of the title role, he was so wickedly on the mark that it seemed a shame that an injury kept him from also taking the role that Slim Pickens played — the bomb-riding major. The movie was a surprise hit and Sellers's still talked-about work received an Oscar nomination. Continuing his run of good fortune, he took second billing to David Niven in *The Pink Panther*, but made the movie exclusively his own with his sidesplitting characterization of the hopelessly stupid French detective Jacques Clouseau. Before the year was out he was called back to play the part again in the even better *A Shot in the Dark*, making this his most famous and best-loved of all his characterizations, one that would be instrumental in resurrecting his career later on. In the meantime he took a supporting part (with star billing) as the egotistical, womanizing pianist in *The World of Henry Orient*, for once being upstaged, in this case by teenagers Merrie Spaeth and Tippy Walker. He was also due to play the desperate songwriter in Billy Wilder's farce, *Kiss Me, Stupid*, but his busy schedule caught up with him and he suffered a heart attack, relinquishing the role to Ray Walston.

Back in action he donned a page-boy wig and a thick German accent to chew the scenery as a sexually frustrated psychiatrist in *What's New, Pussycat?*, an undisciplined farce that somehow became a blockbuster smash. He went back to crime for *After the Fox*, a teaming with writer Neil Simon that didn't click; had a priceless cameo as a cat-crazy doctor in *The Wrong Box*; and played it straight as one of the James Bond-imitators in *Casino Royale*, another out-of-control 1960s artifact that unsuspecting fans of the real 007 series showed up for. There was little to note about *The Bobo*, except that it co-starred him with then-wife (1963–68) Britt Ekland. There were a few inspired moments in the plotless *The Party*, in which he combined his Indian characterization with that of Clouseau, and he had fun with his last hit for a while, *I Love You, Alice B. Toklas*, as the conservative fellow who drops out of society to join the hippie movement. Around that same time he turned down playing Fagin in the big-screen adaptation of *Oliver!*, while Alan Arkin took over his signature role for the horrid *Inspector Clouseau*, which proved that audiences would only accept Sellers in the part. Sellers himself had by this point developed a reputation for being insecure and difficult to work with. His industry standing wasn't helped by the string of failures that knocked him way off the "A" list, including the subversively nutty *The Magic Christian*, as a rich eccentric, teamed up with Ringo Starr; the weirdly unsettling *Hoffman*, where he blackmailed Sinead Cusack into his bed; *There's a Girl in My Soup*, a disappointing pairing with Goldie Hawn, which actually generated some degree of interest, due to Hawn's participation; *Where Does It Hurt?*, a tasteless medical spoof; *The Optimists*, perhaps the most unfortunate of the flops, featuring Sellers as a busker who befriends some children; and *Undercovers Heroes*, which again gave him a gallery of characters to play, but this time in the most wretched of circumstances.

There had also been some films that skipped wide distribution altogether, including *The Blockhouse*, one of his few attempts to play it completely straight, as a teacher trapped in an underground bunker. There was no reason at this stage of his career to turn down director Blake Edwards's offer to revitalized Clouseau for *The Return of the Pink Panther*. It proved to be an eleventh hour boost to both their careers and Sellers was hailed as a genius all over again, embraced by a new generation, eager to see what other tricks he still had left in his bag. Alas, there weren't many more. To play it safe there were two more moneymaking Clouseau films, both of which showed an increasing loss of dis-

cipline and restraint. In between these films, he scored as a Charlie Chan-like sleuth in *Murder by Death*, his second and much better Neil Simon script. He also did two awful comical renderings of famous properties, *The Prisoner of Zenda*, doing three roles, and *The Fiendish Plot of Dr. Fu Manchu*, playing both the nefarious villain and Scotland Yard inspector Nayland Smith. Before the latter, he realized a long-cherished dream to play the simple-minded gardener who becomes advisor to the President in the low-keyed satire *Being There*. At his most restrained, he was not only very funny but enormously moving and received yet another Oscar nomination, a final reward for his faith in the project. A few months after this, and shortly before the release of *Fu Manchu*, he succumbed to a heart attack. There was a crass attempt to further exploit him, via outtakes patched into *The Trail of the Pink Panther*, but it did little to harm his legacy. Further unsuccessful attempts to resurrect the series without Sellers only emphasized just how irreplaceable he was. His fourth wife was actress Lynne Frederick (from 1977).

Screen: 1951: Penny Points to Paradise; 1952: Down Among the Z Men; 1954: Beat the Devil (voice); Orders Are Orders; Our Girl Friday/The Adventures of Sadie (voice); Fire Over Africa/Malaga (voice); 1955: John and Julie; The Ladykillers; 1956: The Man Who Never Was (voice); 1957: The Smallest Show on Earth; The Naked Truth/Your Past Is Showing; 1958: Up the Creek; tom thumb; 1959: Carlton-Browne of the F.O./Man in a Cocked Hat; The Mouse That Roared; I'm All Right, Jack; The Battle of the Sexes; 1960: Two-Way Stretch; Never Let Go; The Millionairess; 1961: Mr. Topaze/I Like Money (and dir.); 1962: Only Two Can Play; Waltz of the Toreadors; The Road to Hong Kong; Lolita; The Wrong Arm of the Law; The Dock Brief/Trial and Error; 1963: Heavens Above!; 1964: Dr. Strangelove or: How I Learned to Stop Worrying and Love the Bomb; The Pink Panther; A Shot in the Dark; The World of Henry Orient; 1965: What's New, Pussycat?; 1966: After the Fox; The Wrong Box; 1967: Woman Times Seven; Casino Royale; The Bobo; 1968: The Party; I Love You, Alice B. Toklas; 1969: The Magic Christian; 1970: Hoffman; A Day at the Beach (nUSr); There's a Girl in My Soup; 1972: Where Does It Hurt?; Alice's Adventures in Wonderland; 1973: The Optimists; The Blockhouse; Soft Beds, Hard Battles/Undercovers Hero (US: 1975); Ghost in the Noonday Sun (dtv); 1974: The Great McGonagall (dtv); 1975: The Return of the Pink Panther; 1976: Murder by Death; The Pink Panther Strikes Again; 1978: Revenge of the Pink Panther; 1979: The Prisoner of Zenda; Being There; 1980: The Fiendish Plot of Dr. Fu Manchu.

Select TV: 1956: A Show Called Fred (series); Son of Fred (series); Idiot Weekly; Price 2d (series); 1964: Carol for Another Christmas (sp); 1967: Alice in Wonderland (sp); 1968: The Goon Show (sp); 1972: The Last Goon Show (sp).

OMAR SHARIF

(MICHAEL SHALHOUB)
BORN: ALEXANDRIA, EGYPT, APRIL 10, 1932.
ED: VICTORIA COL., CAIRO.

The impact Egypt's first (and, to date, only) international star, Omar Sharif, made in his debut English-language film was so great that it was deemed he be touted as an exotic new movie star. He possessed a certain darkly romantic air but his range was limited, and the bad material he mostly did only emphasized his dull side. Born into wealth, of Lebanese and Syrian parents, he grew up speaking French but learned Arabic when an acquaintance offered him a leading role in the film *The Blazing Sun*, where he was billed Omar el Cherif. The leading lady, Faten Hamama, became his wife (1955–66) and she was his co-star in several other Egyptian movies until he was chosen by director David Lean to play Sherif Ali Ibn El Karish in the massive, highly publicized production of *Lawrence of Arabia*. His entrance in the storyline, appearing on horseback as if from a mirage in an extended long-shot, was one of the most famous and hypnotic ever captured on film, and he proved a magnetic on-screen partner for star Peter O'Toole. Sharif earned an Oscar nomination in the supporting category and became a star. He quickly became associated with the international spectacles of the 1960s, although the first three he did as follow-ups to *Lawrence* all lost money: *Marco the Magnificent* (not released in the U.S. until 1966), where Sharif played a sheik opposite leading man Horst Buchholz; *The Fall of the Roman Empire*, which paired him with Sophia Loren for the first time, though her character preferred Stephen Boyd; and the most disastrous of the lot, *Genghis Khan*, which starred Sharif in the title role. There was also the all-star episode film, *The Yellow Rolls-Royce*, in which he and Ingrid Bergman had a taste of romance while battling the Nazis, and *Behold a Pale Horse*, a flop war film headlined by Gregory Peck and Anthony Quinn, with Sharif supporting them, as a priest. Lean called on him again and directed him in the hit that he would be forever identified with — *Doctor Zhivago*. It became one of the highest grossing motion pictures in history, and the recipient of multiple awards and honors, although it was the surrounding cast that made the difference, not Sharif who was utterly unremarkable in the title role.

From that high he was back with O'Toole, this time playing a Nazi, in *The Night of the Generals*, and then with Loren in a botched attempt at an adult fairy tale, *More Than a Miracle*. There was a third movie smash that made him an indelible part of the decade, *Funny Girl*. Cast as Nicky Arnstein, the charming but undependable gambler husband of Fanny Brice, Sharif pretty much took a back seat to co-star Barbra Streisand, although he did chirp in briefly on one song. Then came a string of disasters that helped killed whatever appeal he had, *Mackenna's Gold*, which only proved that he had an unsympathetic side that made him a believable bad guy; *The Appointment*, a dreary love story with Anouk Aimee; *Mayerling*, an equally numbing movie with Catherine Deneuve; *Che!*, a horrendous biopic of the Cuban revolutionary that was perhaps the lowest point of his star years; *The Last Valley*, an anti-war tale set during the Thirty Years War; and *The Horsemen*, which featured the always hot box-office subject of buzkashi tournaments. Letting his hair turn gray, he showed up in another less-than-exciting romance, *The Tamarind Seed*, opposite Julie Andrews; reprised Nicky Arnstein for a few minutes in *Funny Lady*; and then slipped into support for two of the biggest bombs of the late 1970s — *Ashanti*, where he played a prince, and *Bloodline*, where he was suspected of trying to murder Audrey Hepburn. No longer expected to carry a movie he, nonetheless, continued his bad luck of appearing in films that sent audiences running the other way, including *The Baltimore Bullet*, in which he challenged James Coburn in a billiards showdown; *Green Ice*, as a villain in this barely distributed Ryan O'Neal vehicle; and the spoof *Top Secret!*, at one point getting crushed in an auto compactor. There were many foreign jobs that went nowhere outside the territories in which they were made, and some television, but Sharif was no doubt better known in his later years for his syndicated bridge column that ran in select newspapers. He wrote a book on the subject, *Omar Sharif's Life in Bridge*, as well as an autobiography, *The Eternal Male*. After a long period away from mainstream movies he showed up supporting Antonio Banderas in *The 13th Warrior*, an adventure tale with supernatural overtones.

Screen (US releases only): 1962: Lawrence of Arabia; **1964:** The Fall of the Roman Empire; Behold a Pale Horse; The Yellow Rolls-Royce; **1965:** Genghis Khan; Doctor Zhivago; **1966:** Marco the Magnificent (filmed 1964); **1967:** The Night of the Generals; More Than a Miracle; **1968:** Funny Girl; Mayerling; **1969:** Mackenna's Gold; The Appointment; Che!; **1971:** The Last Valley; The Horsemen; **1972:** The Burglars; **1974:** The Mysterious Island of Captain Nemo; The Tamarind Seed; Juggernaut; **1975:** Funny Lady; **1976:** Crime and Passion/Ace Up My Sleeve; The Pink Panther Strikes Again; **1977:** The Right to Love (filmed 1972); **1979:** Ashanti; Sidney Sheldon's Bloodline; **1980:** The Baltimore Bullet; Oh, Heavenly Dog!; **1981:** Green Ice; **1984:** Top Secret!; **1990:** Mountains of the Moon; The Rainbow Thief (dtv); **1992:** Beyond Justice (dtv); **1999:** The 13th Warrior. **Select TV: 1966:** The Poppy Is Also a Flower (and theatrical); **1980:** S-H-E; Pleasure Palace; **1984:** The Far Pavillions (ms); **1986:** Peter the Great (ms); Harem; Anastasia: The Mystery of Anna; **1988:** Grand Larceny; **1991:** Memories of Midnight (ms); **1992:** Mrs. 'arris Goes to Paris; **1994:** Lie Down with Lions; **1996:** Gulliver's Travels.

MICKEY SHAUGHNESSY

(JOSEPH SHAUGHNESSY) BORN: NEW YORK, NY, AUGUST 5, 1920. DIED: JULY 23, 1985.

Although lunks, mugs, and brawny men of slow thought were Mickey Shaughnessy's specialty, he often brought out their benign side, usually going for comical effect. In fact he had been doing stand-up comedy in nightclubs after a stretch in the military and it was during one of his engagements that he was signed to a contract by Columbia. They quite appropriately cast him as Aldo Ray's brother in *The Marrying Kind*, and then put him in cavalry duds as one of the unfortunate besieged soldiers in *Last of the Comanches*, which was far from the last time he'd been seen in uniform or out west. He was the affable supply sergeant Leva in *From Here to Eternity*; journeyed to Mars in the hokey George Pal space adventure *Conquest of Space*; and was Gregory Peck's idiotic bodyguard with a knack for sleeping with his eyes open in *Designing Woman*. He reached what was perhaps his peak year in 1957, playing the murdered long shore boss in *Slaughter on Tenth Avenue*; Elvis Presley's loyal buddy Hunk in *Jailhouse Rock*; and, probably his most famous role, the foul-mouthed Farragut Jones whose cuss-words are bleeped on the soundtrack in the otherwise forgettable service comedy *Don't Go Near the Water*. For further laughs he was a bouncer named Jumbo McCall in *The Sheepman*; supported Jerry Lewis in *Don't Give Up the Ship*; played a drunken hotel porter in *North to Alaska*; and showed up as The Duke, alongside Tony Randall, in the otherwise terrible 1960 version of *The Adventures of Huckleberry Finn*. In addition to some Albert Zugsmith eye-rollers like *College Confidential*, as the evil town's magistrate-grocer, and *Sex Kittens Go to College*, he was a suitable Runyonesque lug, appearing as Glenn Ford's chauffeur, in *Pocketful of Miracles*; a deputy in the all-star *How the West Was Won*; and a police sergeant in the whorehouse drama *A House is Not a Home*. He ended his movie career going for some broad laughs in a pair of Disney comedies, *Never a Dull Moment*, and *The Boatniks*. When the film work stopped coming in, he went back to playing the comedy club circuit.

Screen: 1952: The Marrying Kind; Last of the Comanches; **1953:** From Here to Eternity; **1955:** Conquest of Space; **1956:** The Burglar; **1957:** Slaughter on Tenth Avenue; Designing Woman; Jailhouse Rock; Until They Sail; Don't Go Near the Water; **1958:**

A Nice Little Bank That Should Be Robbed; The Sheepman; Gunman's Walk; 1959: Edge of Eternity; The Hangman; Don't Give Up the Ship; 1960: Sex Kittens Go to College; College Confidential; The Adventures of Huckleberry Finn; North to Alaska; 1961: King of the Roaring 20's — The Story of Arnold Rothstein; Dondi; Pocketful of Miracles; 1963: How the West Was Won; 1964: A House Is Not a Home; A Global Affair; 1968: Never a Dull Moment; 1970: The Boatniks; 1986: Hellfire/Primal Scream.

NY Stage: 1965: Kelly.

Select TV: 1967: A Boy Called Nuthin' (sp); 1969: My Dog the Thief (sp); 1971: The Chicago Teddy Bears (series).

ROBERT SHAW

BORN: WESTHOUGHTON, LANCASHIRE, ENGLAND, AUGUST 9, 1927. RAISED IN SCOTLAND AND CORNWALL, ENGLAND. ED: RADA. DIED: AUGUST 27, 1978.

A bullish, imposing British player who also happened to have a poet's heart, Robert Shaw managed to maintain dual careers as both actor and writer only to die prematurely, after having reached full-fledged, worldwide stardom in the former profession. His first professional job was with the Shakespeare Memorial Theatre in Stratford-upon-Avon and this led to his West End theater debut, in 1951, supporting Alec Guinness in Hamlet. That same year he had a bit in one of Guinness's films, The Lavender Hill Mob, as a chemist. While becoming a noted Shakespearean actor on the London stage, he continued to show up in some films, including the much-admired 1954 war drama The Dam Busters, as a flier, and A Hill in Korea, as a corporal; and even carried his own short-lived series on British television, The Buccaneers. Shortly after this he presented his first play, Off the Mainland, to poor notices, but fared better with his debut novel, The Hiding Place (1959), which he himself later adapted for British television, and which showed up in distorted versions on Playhouse 90, and in the Guinness film, Situation Hopeless — But Not Serious. Returning to theatre, he scored a major triumph as part of the cast of the military drama The Long and the Short and the Tall, and this was followed by further stage successes with The Changeling and The Caretaker, the latter marking his Broadway debut, in 1961. Consequently offered more substantial film work, he starred in the adaptation of The Caretaker, which played in the U.S. under the name of The Guest; assumed a virtually silent role as the blond-haired, barrel-chested assassin in the James Bond smash From Here to Eternity, indulging in a particularly nasty fight with Sean Connery in a train compartment; and secured the starring role in The Luck of Ginger Coffey, where he splendidly essayed his version of the angry young man, as did many of the best British actors in the 1960s. Opposite him was actress Mary Ure whom he had married in 1963 (she died in 1975).

Entering the 1960s spectacle market, he was a Nazi tank commander in Battle of the Bulge, and the flamboyant General in a curious U.S.-Spanish production of Custer of the West, again playing opposite his wife. Between these he made a tremendous impact as the bellowing, intimidating King Henry VIII in A Man for All Seasons, implying a sexual swagger unlike any other actor who'd done the role previously on film. Shaw earned an Oscar nomination in the supporting category, while the film itself won the Academy Award as Best Picture of 1966. For a spell his film choices were less commercial, including a pretty straightforward filmization of Harold Pinter's The Birthday Party, as the mysterious lodger; the ambitious The Royal Hunt of the Sun, as Pizarro;

Figures in a Landscape, principally a two-character piece, with Malcolm McDowell, as fugitives on the run; and The Hireling, as the chauffeur who falls for unstable aristocrat Sarah Miles. He was, however, seen by millions as the racketeer fleeced by Paul Newman and Robert Redford in the lighthearted The Sting, his second credit to walk off with an Oscar for Best Picture. This was followed by a tense cat-and-mouse subway thriller, The Taking of Pelham One Two Three, where he gave one of his best performances, as the enigmatic thief; and then Jaws, in a full-throttle, colorful turn, as the crusty shark hunter, making one of the gorier, more unforgettable exits in film history. This became one of the highest grossing movies of all time and, thanks to its success, Shaw became very famous. As a result, he was given top-billing for the old-fashioned Swashbuckler; the complex terrorist thriller Black Sunday; and the soggy adventure The Deep, where he played a toned-down version of his Jaws role. Better than these but less popular was his return to villainy, in Robin and Marian, as the blustering Sheriff of Nottingham. He starred in two second-rate action films, Force 10 from Navarone and Avalanche Express, then suffered a fatal heart attack prior to the distribution of both. Since the latter film was not quite finished much of Shaw's voice wound up being over-dubbed by another actor. His most famous literary work was The Man in the Glass Booth, which first surfaced as a novel, then as a play and film (with Maximilian Schell), though Shaw asked that his name be removed from the credits of the last. His other novels were The Sun Doctor (1962), The Flag (1964), and A Card from Morocco (1969).

Screen: 1954: The Dam Busters; 1956: Doublecross; A Hill in Korea/Hell in Korea; 1958: Sea Fury; 1959: Libel; 1962: The Valiant; 1963: Tomorrow at Ten; The Cracksman; The Caretaker/The Guest; 1964: From Russia With Love; The Luck of Ginger Coffey; 1965: Battle of the Bulge; 1966: A Man for All Seasons; 1968: Custer of the West; The Birthday Party; 1969: Battle of Britain; The Royal Hunt of the Sun; 1971: Figures in a Landscape; A Town Called Bastard/A Town Called Hell; 1972: Reflection of Fear; Young Winston; 1973: The Hireling; The Sting; 1974: The Taking of Pelham One Two Three; 1975: Diamonds; Jaws; 1976: End of the Game/Getting Away With Murder; Robin and Marian; Swashbuckler; 1977: Black Sunday; The Deep; 1978: Force 10 From Navarone; 1979: Avalanche Express.

NY Stage: 1961: The Caretaker; 1964: The Physicists; 1970: Gantry; 1971: Old Times; 1974: The Dance Of Death.

Select TV: 1957–58: The Buccaneer (series: UK); 1964: Hamlet (sp); Carol for Another Christmas (sp); 1968: Luther (sp).

DICK SHAWN

(RICHARD SCHULEFAND) BORN: BUFFALO, NY, DECEMBER 1, 1923. ED: UNIV. OF BUFFALO, UNIV. OF MIAMI. DIED: APRIL 17, 1987.

A comical performer who, unlike so many others, made more of an impression the more he mugged, Dick Shawn started his career as a nightclub comedian. This led to performing his routines on television throughout the 1950s and providing warm-up for Betty Hutton at the Palace in New York. During the late 1950s, there was an isolated movie assignment, where, playing himself, he sang the title song in the musical The Opposite Sex. He was called back for a filmic follow-up in 1960, when he played straight man to Ernie Kovacs and others in a very mild service farce, Wake Me When It's Over. After securing top-billing as a bumbling genie in the juvenile The Wizard of Baghdad, he stole scenes as Ethel Merman's hopped-up lifeguard son in the all-star hit It's a Mad Mad Mad Mad World. Going back to the service for another comedy, *What Did You Do in the War, Daddy?*, wasn't a great idea, nor was there much to be said for another feeble offering, *Penelope*, with Shawn cast as the analyst in love with patient Natalie Wood. He even managed to top these stinkers with *Way...Way Out*, at his least appealing, as a Russian cosmonaut, in this most terrible of all bad Jerry Lewis films. He was gloriously off-the-wall, however, as a hippie named LSD, who, in turn, gets to do his zonked-out interpretation of Adolph Hitler, in the Mel Brooks classic *The Producers*, making this the role he'd be best remembered for. For most of the early 1970s he did television guest star work or reprised his stage act. Later down the line there were a smattering of movie comedies, few of which had much of a theatrical life except for *Love at First Bite*, as a police lieutenant; *Angel*, a none-too serious look at the wackos inhabiting Hollywood Boulevard, with Shawn playing a flamboyant transvestite; and *Maid to Order*, as Ally Sheedy's rich employer. By the time this last film was released he had died, having suffered a heart attack in the middle of his stage routine, the audience at first believing that his collapse was part of the act.

Screen: 1956: The Opposite Sex; 1960: Wake Me When It's Over; The Wizard of Baghdad; 1963: It's a Mad Mad Mad Mad World; 1965: A Very Special Favor; 1966: Way...Way Out; Penelope; What Did You Do in the War, Daddy?; 1968: The Producers; 1969: The Happy Ending; 1977: Looking Up; 1979: Love at First Bite; 1983: Goodbye, Cruel World; Young Warriors; 1984: Angel; The Secret Diary of Sigmund Freud; 1985: Beer (dtv); 1986: Water; The Check Is in the Mail; The Perils of P.K.; 1987: Maid to Order; 1988: Rented Lips.

NY Stage: 1948: For Heaven's Sake Mother; 1953: Betty Hutton and Her All-Star International Show; 1962: The Egg; 1964: A Funny Thing Happened on the Way to the Forum; 1965: Peterpat; Fade Out — Fade In; 1968: I'm Solomon; 1970: Steambath; 1975: A Musical Jubilee; 1976: The World of Sholem Aleichem (ob).

Select TV: 1954: Sunday in Town (sp); 1971: Evil Roy Slade; 1974: The Year Without Santa (sp; voice); 1978: Mary (series); 1979: Fast Friends; 1984: Faerie Tale Theatre: The Emperor's New Clothes (sp); 1985: Hail to the Chief (series).

NORMA SHEARER

(EDITH NORMA SHEARER) BORN: MONTREAL, CANADA, AUGUST 10, 1902. DIED: JUNE 12, 1983.

At the dawn of the talkies Norma Shearer was at the top of her profession, a box-office attraction and the queen of the MGM lot, a position she would hold throughout the 1930s as she attempted to expand her range. To most moviegoers she was a genteel lady with a certain air of sophistication and a penchant for bringing forth an ocean of tears. Audiences seemed to appreciate her more than the critics, but she was better at her craft than most suggested, despite the fact that the sort of hankie-clutching melodramas she specialized in were very much a product of their time and of little interest to later generations. She learned the piano at a young age and made her living performing at nickelodeons. When this led nowhere she and her sister sought extra work in films, and Norma first began showing up on screen in 1920, in bits in such movies as *The Flapper* and *Way Down East*. This led to some larger parts, in *The Stealers*, among others, and the lead in *The Man Who Paid*. Most of her work had been made in New York or elsewhere up to this point, so it was not until she signed a contract with Louis B. Mayer, in 1923, that she went to Hollywood. Mayer launched her as a debutante in *Pleasure Mad*, then saw her stardom rise via several

loan-outs, including *The Wolf Man* (which was *not* a tale of lycanthropy) with John Gilbert; and *Empty Hands*, where she played a character stranded on a desert island with Jack Holt. She came back to Metro for *Broken Barriers*, portraying a flapper who saves James Kirkwood from a miserable marriage, and, more importantly, *He Who Gets Slapped*, a circus melodrama that boasted Lon Chaney, John Gilbert, and the distinction of being the first official Metro-Goldwyn-Mayer release. It was well-known by this point that Mayer's right-hand man, Irving Thalberg, was crazy about Shearer and he was instrumental in making her one of Hollywood's biggest names.

She played dual roles, a rich girl and a bad girl from the wrong side of the tracks in *Lady of the Night*; a passenger who plants herself in a train wreck victim's apartment in *A Slave of Fashion*, a premise very similar to Cornell Woolrich's *I Married a Dead Man*; a girl who transforms herself from plain-Jane to beauty in *His Secretary*; a criminal lawyer in *The Waning Sex*; a cabaret hostess in *After Midnight*; Ramon Novarro's love interest in a tuneless but pleasing romance, *The Student Prince in Old Heidelberg*, directed by Ernst Lubitsch; and, a temptress in *Lady of Chance*, where she spoke on screen for the first time. Her voice was quite acceptable for the new talking cinema and, since she was doing just fine on the popularity polls and had married Thalberg in 1927, there was no chance she was going any place but up. Her transition to sound came with *The Trial of Mary Dugan* (which was particularly significant because it was also MGM's premier non-musical all-talkie) and *The Last of Mrs. Cheyney*, properties that failed to disguise their stage origins. However, since movie audiences weren't expecting much more in 1929, both films were highly popular. Likewise the crowds turned out for the clunky, all-star *The Hollywood Revue of 1929*, in which she and John Gilbert gave fairly unimpressive renderings of the balcony scene from *Romeo and Juliet*, a script she'd be given a second chance at further down the line. She had an affair with Robert Montgomery in *Their Own Desire*, and then was loved by him after she left husband Chester Morris in *The Divorcee*. These were the sort of ultra-glamorous, suffering women-of-wealth roles that audiences ate up. She competed against herself for the Oscar for both performances and won for the latter.

The hits continued with *Let Us Be Gay*, which put her alongside the equally popular Marie Dressler; *Strangers May Kiss*, as a free-spirit cavorting through Europe after boyfriend Neil Hamilton walks out on her; *A Free Soul*, a hokey gangster story that ended in a big trial scene, allowing her and Lionel Barrymore, portraying her lawyer and dad, to pull out all the scene-stealing stops. The latter film boasted the added box-office power of Leslie Howard and the fast-rising Clark Gable, and earned Shearer another Oscar nomination. She and Montgomery showed a lighter side in the faithful but arch screen adaptation of Noel Coward's stage hit *Private Lives*, and she pretty much hit a wall with the misguided attempt to bring Eugene O'Neill's *Strange Interlude* to the screen. No matter, this was quickly followed by another weepy that had audiences lining up, *Smilin' Through*, an oft-filmed bit of romantic that allowed her to play both Leslie Howard's dead fiancée and the fiancée's niece. It was the sort of soap opera that became nearly unwatchable with the passing of the years, although at the time it rated an Oscar nomination as the year's Best Picture. Similarly, there was little that dated well in *The Barretts of Wimpole Street*, in which she portrayed the sickly, father-dominated Elizabeth Barrett, receiving a fourth Oscar mention, in 1934. There had been no Shearer film in 1933, and she skipped 1935 and 1937 as well, a move that hoped to give her films a certain level of prestige and anticipation, a ploy which did, in fact, work.

Although she and Leslie Howard were obviously far too old for their parts, they led the cast in the studio's lavish version of *Romeo and Juliet*, a risky venture for Shearer to attempt, but something she actually pulled off to a certain degree, successfully holding her own against the more experienced Howard. Since both the film and Shearer received Oscar nods, little was made of the fact that it had trouble earning back its cost. The same was also true with the studio's big 1938 release, *Marie Antoinette*, where, dressed to the nines, Shearer looked every inch a lady of royalty. She also threw herself into the part 100 percent, resulting in her best performance, as this tragic heroine, a victim of circumstance in this telling of the story. While the film was being prepared, Thalberg died at the age of 39. His premature demise was one of the decade's most mourned events, not just for the studio, which he had helped build into Hollywood's most highly regarded company, but also for the grief-stricken Shearer, who supposedly never got over the loss. Fortunately, she stayed afloat for a while with *Idiot's Delight*, a fairly muddled comedy-drama in which she played a fake countess with a blonde wig and a thick accent, and *The Women*, certainly the most satisfying of all her forays into comedy, despite her somewhat limited role, as the woman uncertain of whether she's being cheated on by her (unseen, off screen) husband. She ended her contract with a topical drama, *Escape*, helping to get Nazimov out of a concentration camp, and two slight comedies that failed, *We Were Dancing*, supposedly adapted from Noel Coward, and *Her Cardboard Lover*, which referred to Robert Taylor. She had worked exclusively for MGM since 1924. Like Garbo, she chose to close-up shop entirely, retiring for good in 1942, rather than sticking around for a likely, more public decline. Unlike Garbo, her almost-total retreat from the public eye did not provoke an enduring, legendary image and she was much less known to modern day audiences when she passed away in 1983. Her brother, Douglas Shearer (1899–1971), was in charge of Metro's sound department, his name popping up on every one of the studio's releases during its heyday.

Screen: 1920: The Flapper; The Restless Sex; Way Down East; The Stealers; 1921: The Sign on the Door; 1922: The Leather Pushers (serial); The Man Who Paid; The Bootleggers; Channing of the Northwest; 1923: A Clouded Name; Man and Wife; The Devil's Partner; Pleasure Mad; The Wanters; Lucretia Lombard; 1924: The Trail of the Law; The Wolf Man; Blue Water; Broadway After Dark; Broken Barriers; Married Flirts; Empty Hands; The Snob; He Who Gets Slapped; 1925: Excuse Me; Lady of the Night; Waking Up the Town; A Slave of Fashion; Pretty Ladies; The Tower of Lies; His Secretary; 1926: The Devil's Circus; The Waning Sex; Upstage; 1927: The Demi-Bride; After Midnight; The Student Prince in Old Heidelberg; 1928: The Latest from Paris; The Actress; Lady of Chance; 1929: The Trial of Mary Dugan; The Last of Mrs. Cheyney; The Hollywood Revue of 1929; 1930: Their Own Desire; Let Us Be Gay; The Divorcee; 1931: Strangers May Kiss; A Free Soul; Private Lives; 1932: Strange Interlude; Smilin' Through; 1934: Riptide; The Barretts of Wimpole Street; 1936: Romeo and Juliet; 1938: Marie Antoinette; 1939: Idiot's Delight; The Women; 1940: Escape; 1942: We Were Dancing; Her Cardboard Lover.

ANN SHERIDAN

(CLARA LOU SHERIDAN) BORN: DENTON, TX, FEBRUARY 21, 1915. DIED: JANUARY 21, 1967.

The combination of Ann Sheridan's come-hither look and her deep, suggestive voice was enough to get her christened the "Oomph" girl by Hollywood publicists but, fortunately, she had more irons in the fire than that limited moniker suggested. Somewhat underappreciated for the part she played in making Warner Bros.'s heyday what it was, she was not only sexy but could put real snap into delivering a line. That she was acerbic without ever losing a glimmer of the warmth and reassurance she always possessed, made her a particularly special treat. While attending college in Texas she submitted her photo to Paramount's 1933 "Search for Beauty" contest and won. As a result they gave her a fleeting role in a movie by that name and signed her to a contract in 1934. Under her real name she did walk-ons and extra work in more than a dozen films before graduating to something more substantial in *Behold My Wife*, as a stenographer driven to suicide. This also marked the first time she was billed as Ann Sheridan. Alas, it was soon back to unbilled bits, in such movies as *Mississippi* and *The Crusades*, before the studio ended her contract. Warners rescued her just when the future was looking bleak and signed her up in 1936, giving her a supporting part in a James Melton musical, *Sing Me a Love Song*. Although she could be seen in some above-the-line material like *Black Legion*, as the wife of doomed Dick Foran, and *San Quentin*, as a nightclub singer drawn to bad guy Humphrey Bogart, she was mainly thought of by the studio as a "B" attraction, given leads in such things as *She Loved a Fireman*, as a manicurist in love with hose-toting Dick Foran; *The Patient in Room 18*, as Patric Knowles's girlfriend-nurse; and *Broadway Musketeers*, joining forces with fellow orphans (and second-string Warners attractions), Margaret Lindsay and Marie Wilson.

The turning point came when she was paired off with James Cagney in one of the biggest films of 1938, *Angels With Dirty Faces*, as his childhood friend, who grows up to become a social worker. It had been clear all along that she had something great to offer and here was sufficient proof, as she more than held her own against the dynamic Cagney. Suddenly there was no hesitation in inviting her to be a part of the company's "A" unit. As a result, she played one of the ladies who turned John Garfield bad in *They Made Me a Criminal*; the saloon gal in the popular Errol Flynn western *Dodge City*; and the nice girl in the life of con Garfield in *Castle on the Hudson*. There was also *Angels Wash Their Faces*, which sounded like a sequel to the first *Angels* movie, though she played an altogether different character, a woman crusading against City Hall corruption. Her career really took off in 1940 when she played a singer helping Humphrey Bogart start a nightclub in *It All Came True*, and teamed up with Cagney in *Torrid Zone*, in which he memorably extolled her "14 carat oomph," and then again in *City for Conquest*. Best of all was another with Bogart, *They Drive by Night*, with Sheridan as one of the screen's sassiest hash slingers, though she didn't hook up with Bogart, but instead landed top-billed George Raft. She was the secretary secretly pining for ladies' man George Brent in *Honeymoon for Three*, and actually nabbed him for real off screen for a very brief marriage (1942–43). There were good roles in two of the studios' major prestige items of the early 1940s, *The Man Who Came to Dinner*, as the dishy actress, a showier part than that of higher-billed Bette Davis, and *Kings Row*, where Sheridan gave one of her best performances, as the slum girl who marries tragic hero Ronald Reagan.

She had the title role in the poorly received *Juke Girl*, which, despite sounding like a musical set in a soda shop, was about crop-pickers; proved a charming straight woman to Jack Benny in *George Washington Slept Here*, though most of the laugh-lines the character had in the play were given to Benny; had a show-stopping number, "Love Isn't Born, It's Made," in the all-star extravaganza *Thank Your Lucky Stars*; and played performer Nora Bayes in one of those biopics that were flooding the screens in the 1940s, *Shine On, Harvest Moon*. Two comedies she did, *The Doughgirls*, and *One More Tomorrow*, had better casts than end results, after which she had a hit soap/noir, *Nora Prentiss*, as the singer who sees poor Kent

Smith ruin his life for her sake; and a flat-out soap, *The Unfaithful*, loosely remade from *The Letter*. Leaving Warners in 1948, she teamed with Gary Cooper in one of his weaker films, *Good Sam*, then had a whopping hit over at Fox as a no-nonsense military woman who drives Cary Grant around France in *I Was a Male War Bride*, a gimmick comedy given its luster by the two leads. A follow-up comedy for the same studio, *Stella*, did not duplicate its success, no doubt because this one starred Victor Mature instead of Grant. With decreasing budgets, Sheridan did four films for Universal, including *Take Me to Town*, for the last time showing up as a nightclub singer. After that, the purse strings tightened even more, for RKO's *Appointment in Honduras*, and the well-liked *Come Next Spring*, for Republic Pictures. It was certainly nice having her in *The Opposite Sex*, the pointless remake of *The Women*, but, after bottoming out with *Woman and the Hunter*, she decided to do walk away from the cameras to do some regional theatre instead. During the 1960s she appeared for a brief period as a regular on the daytime serial, *Another World*, and then in primetime, on *Pistols and Petticoats*. Sadly, she died during the run of the latter, leaving too many of her career peaks in the distant past, perhaps one reason she was spoken of too seldom when it came to hailing the great screen ladies of yesterday.

Screen: AS CLARA LOU SHERIDAN: 1934: Beauty for Sale; Bolero; The Lemon Drop Kid; One Hour Late; Ready for Love; Ladies Should Listen; Shoot the Works; Mrs. Wiggs of the Cabbage Patch; You Belong to Me; Come on Marines; Kiss and Make Up; The Notorious Sophie Lang; College Rhythm; Murder at the Vanities; Wagon Wheels; Limehouse Blues; 1935: Rumba; Enter Madame; Home on the Range.

AS ANN SHERIDAN: Behold My Wife; Car 99; Rocky Mountain Mystery; Mississippi; The Glass Key; The Crusades; Red Blood Courage; Fighting Youth; 1936: Black Legion; 1937: The Great O'Malley; San Quentin; Wine, Women and Horses; The Footloose Heiress; Alcatraz Island; 1938: She Loved a Fireman; Little Miss Thoroughbred; Cowboy from Brooklyn; The Patient in Room 18; Mystery House; Broadway Musketeers; Letter of Introduction; Angels With Dirty Faces; 1939: They Made Me a Criminal; Dodge City; Naughty But Nice; Winter Carnival; Indianapolis Speedway; The Angels Wash Their Faces; 1940: Castle on the Hudson; It All Came True; Torrid Zone; They Drive by Night; City for Conquest; 1941: Honeymoon for Three; Navy Blues; The Man Who Came to Dinner; 1942: Kings Row; Juke Girl; Wings for the Eagle; George Washington Slept Here; 1943: Edge of Darkness; Thank Your Lucky Stars; 1944: Shine On, Harvest Moon; The Doughgirls; 1946: One More Tomorrow; 1947: Nora Prentiss; The Unfaithful; 1948: The Treasure of the Sierra Madre; Silver River; Good Sam; 1949: I Was a Male War Bride; 1950: Stella; Woman on the Run; 1952: Steel Town; Just Across the Street; 1953: Take Me to Town; Appointment in Honduras; 1956: Come Next Spring; The Opposite Sex; 1957: Woman and the Hunter/ Triangle on Safari.

Select TV: 1953: Malaya Incident (sp); The Lovely Day (sp); The Prize (sp); 1956: Hunted (sp); 1957: The Hard Way (sp); Without Incident (sp); 1958: The Dark Cloud (sp); The Time of Your Life (sp); 1960: The Imposter (sp); 1964–65: Another World (series); 1966–67: Pistols and Petticoats (series).

ANNE SHIRLEY

(DAWN EVELEEN PARIS) BORN: NEW YORK, NY, APRIL 17, 1918. DIED: JULY 4, 1993.

Specializing in sweet girls and dewey-eyed innocents, Anne Shirley was in pictures almost as soon as she could walk, made the change to grown-up ingénue with success,

and then retired from the profession before she'd even reached the age of 30. Billed as "Dawn O'Day," she made her professional bow, in 1922, in *The Hidden Woman*. Throughout silent movies she was steadily employed, including a series of shorts, starting with "Alice's Mysterious Mystery," in 1926. Audiences watched her grow up right into the talkies and when RKO decided to make her the lead in their 1934 production of *Anne of Green Gables*, they did a curious thing, getting rid of her stage name and re-christening her after the character in the film, Anne Shirley. The movie established her as a charming "new" star and the studio put her under contract. For her follow-ups she played the title roles in *Chatterbox*, as an aspiring actress who fails at her goal; and *M'Liss*, as a mountain gal wooed by schoolmaster John Beal. Goldwyn borrowed her for the 1937 version of *Stella Dallas*, and this eternally silly soap opera turned out to be her career peak, earning her an Oscar nomination in the supporting category, playing the ungrateful daughter for whom mom Barbara Stanwyck sacrifices all. Back on the home lot she ended up in prison in *Condemned Women*, though she was still an innocent, taking the rap for her lover; did another noted homespun piece, *Mother Carey's Chickens*; was an exploited worker in the intriguingly titled *Boy Slaves*; and was back playing the character who gave her her stage name, in *Anne of Windy Poplars*, which did not duplicate the earlier movie's success. She was not asked to carry such films as *Four Jacks and a Jill*, as the Jill, a band singer; *All That Money Can Buy*; or *Murder, My Sweet*, which was just as well, because she was upstaged by more interesting performers in each of them. She'd been married (1937–43) to actor John Payne but when she moved on to husband number two (1945–48), producer Adrian Scott, she put her career on hold. She finally found happiness with her third marriage, to screenwriter Charles Lederer, which lasted from 1949 until his death in 1976. By that time her movie career was a distant memory.

Screen: AS DAWN O'DAY: 1922: The Hidden Woman; Moonshine Valley; 1923: The Spanish Dancer; The Rustle of Silk; 1924: The Fast Set; The Man Who Fights Alone; 1925: Riders of the Purple Sage; 1927: The Callahans and the Murphys; Night Life; 1928: Mother Knows Best; Sins of the Fathers; 1929: Four Devils; 1930: City Girl; Liliom; 1931: Rich Man's Folly; Gun Smoke; 1932: Young America; So Big; The Purchase Price; Three on Match; Emma; Rasputin and the Empress; 1933: The Life of Jimmy Dolan; 1934: Finishing School; The Key; This Side of Heaven; School for Girls.

AS ANNE SHIRLEY: Anne of Green Gables; 1935: Steamboat 'Round the Bend; Chasing Yesterday; 1936: Chatterbox; M'Liss; Make Way for a Lady; 1937: Too Many Wives; Meet the Missus; Stella Dallas; 1938: Condemned Women; Law of the Underworld; Mother Carey's Chickens; A Man to Remember; Girls' School; 1939: Boy Slaves; Sorority House; Career; 1940: Vigil in the Night; Saturday's Children; Anne of Windy Poplars; 1941: West Point Widow; Unexpected Uncle; All That Money Can Buy/The Devil and Daniel Webster; 1942: Four Jacks and a Jill; The Mayor of 44th Street; The Powers Girl; 1943: Lady Bodyguard; Bombardier; Government Girl; 1944: Man from Frisco; Music in Manhattan; Murder, My Sweet.

SYLVIA SIDNEY

(SOPHIA KOSOW) BORN: BRONX, NY, AUGUST 8, 1910. DIED: JULY 1, 1999.

Her big beautiful eyes always seemed on the verge of tears and that was the image of Sylvia Sidney that most of us retain from her heyday: small, vulnerable, and suffering.

There was a tough streak in her too and, as her career in movies dried up, she kept plugging away, finally returning to the cinema as feisty old lady who had "survivor" stamped all over her. Trained at the Theatre Guild School, she was a teenager when she made her professional stage bow, in 1926, in *The Challenge of Youth*, in Washington D.C. The following year she made her Broadway bow, in *The Squall*, and then got a lead role, in *Crime*. During this time she was first seen on the big screen, glimpsed as herself, in *Broadway Nights*, then joined a stock company in Denver. By this point the movies wanted to see if her talents could transfer to celluloid, so Fox offered her a key supporting role in the court-room thriller *Thru Different Eyes*, requiring her to emote to the heavens as she told the true circumstances that led to the murder in question. Neither she nor the studio was satisfied with the end results, so she went back to the stage where she had a major Broadway success in *Bad Girl*. This time Paramount made overtures and she accepted the role of the good girl whose boyfriend, Gary Cooper, gets roped into a world of crime, in *City Streets*. They certainly made an interesting pair, his towering height contrasted against her elfin size, and Sidney, more at ease in the world of gangsters than he was, became a star. There were striking similarities between her next two films, *Confessions of a Co-Ed*, and *An American Tragedy*, because she was unmarried and impregnated by Phillips Holmes in both. In the latter, in the role Shelley Winters would later do in the remake *A Place in the Sun*, she got all the best notices for what turned out to be one of the studio's most famous box-office failures of the early 1930s.

Goldwyn borrowed her for the adaptation of Elmer Rice's acclaimed play *Street Scene*, and, by keeping it stage-bound, actually wound up with one of the more interesting experimental pictures of the time, a slice of tenement life, with Sidney at her very best as the girl who has ambitions to rise above it all. It was financially another bust, however, so she returned to Paramount for the overheated melodrama *Ladies of the Big House*, one of the earliest examples of that favorite genre, the women-in-prison flick, and then paired off with Fredric March for a tepid look at a disintegrating marriage, *Merrily We Go to Hell*. Because there was a slight Asian quality to her features, she had the title role in *Madame Butterfly*, which Paramount decided to film *without* the songs; then she was back in familiar territory, playing another Theodore Dreiser heroine left pregnant, in *Jennie Gerhardt*. For a relief, the studio let her play comedy with *30 Day Princess*, as an actress posing as royalty, opposite Cary Grant; and *Accent on Youth*, as the secretary loved by boss Herbert Marshall. After that she signed a contract with producer Walter Wanger (who distributed through Paramount) and had one of her most famous roles, in *Mary Burns — Fugitive*, as the cafe owner whose infatuation with Alan Baxter sends her plunging into a life of crime. In glorious Technicolor she was the backwoods girl whom Fred MacMurray tries to educate in *The Trail of the Lonesome Pine*; took a break by going to England to work with Hitchcock in *Sabotage*; then did two films with director Fritz Lang: *You Only Live Once*, where she once again fell into a life of crime, and *Fury*, watching innocent boyfriend Spencer Tracy face mob violence. Despite their honorable intentions, both films showed Lang and Sidney at their most melodramatic.

Fortunately Goldwyn came calling once again to cast her as the heroine in a bleak view of city life, in this case *Dead End*, from Sidney Kingsley's hit play. She was outstanding as the concerned, slum-raised sister of ruffian Billy Halop and this was her best film since her last for Goldwyn and, indeed, probably the best film she would ever appear in. She went back to Wanger for *You and Me*, which co-starred George Raft, and did

another look at slum life, *One Third of a Nation*, after which she bought out her contract and returned east for some stage work. Three movies back in Hollywood reminded audiences that she was still around: the circus melodrama *The Wagons Roll at Night*, with Bogart; *Blood on the Sun*, as a Eurasian, opposite James Cagney; and *The Searching Wind*, as a journalist discussing the issues of war with Robert Young in what turned out to be the sort of heavy fare audiences didn't care to see. A reunion with Raft, *Mr. Ace*; the inferior 1952 version of *Les Misérables*, as Fantine; a well-liked caper film, *Violent Saturday*, dropping down the cast list, as a librarian; and, finally, a "B" film, *Behind the High Wall*, finished her career in films for some time. Between 1956 and 1973 she concentrated exclusively on theatre and occasional television parts. When she showed up playing Joanne Woodward's tough-talking Manhattan mother in *Summer Wishes, Winter Dreams*, many were surprised at how weathered she was by the years. She was also splendid in the part and finally got the Oscar nomination she'd never before received. She continued to show up playing crotchety, crinkle-faced, butt-puffing old broads on television and in movies, the latter including *Used People*, nicely paired with Jessica Tandy, as a long-time friend; and two fantasies, *Beetlejuice*, checking people into the afterlife; and *Mars Attacks!*, as Lukas Haas's grandmother, who helps save the world from hostile aliens. She was married (1935–36) to publisher Bennett Cerf and then later (1938–47) to actor Luther Adler.

Screen: 1927: Broadway Nights; 1929: Thru Different Eyes; 1931: City Streets; Confessions of a Co-Ed; An American Tragedy; Street Scene; Ladies of the Big House; 1932: The Miracle Man; Merrily We Go to Hell; Make Me a Star; Madame Butterfly; 1933: Pick-Up; Jennie Gerhardt; 1934: Good Dame; Thirty Day Princess; 1935: Behold My Wife; Accent on Youth; Mary Burns — Fugitive; 1936: The Trail of the Lonesome Pine; Fury; 1937: Sabotage/A Woman Alone; You Only Live Once; Dead End; 1938: You and Me; 1939: One Third of a Nation; 1941: The Wagons Roll at Night; 1945: Blood on the Sun; 1946: The Searching Wind; Mr. Ace; 1947: Love from a Stranger; 1952: Les Misérables; 1955: Violent Saturday; 1956: Behind the High Wall; 1973: Summer Wishes, Winter Dreams; 1976: God Told Me To/Demon; 1977: I Never Promised You a Rose Garden; 1978: Damien: Omen II; 1982: Hammett; 1983: Corrupt/Copkiller; 1988: Beetlejuice; 1992: Used People; 1996: Mars Attacks!

NY Stage: 1927: The Squall; Crime; 1928: Mirrors; The Breaks; Gods of the Lightning; 1929: Nice Women; Cross Roads; 1930: Many a Slip; Bad Girl; 1937: To Quito And Back; 1939: The Gentle People; 1953: The Fourposter; 1956: A Very Special Baby; 1958: Auntie Mame; 1963: Enter Laughing; 1964: Riverside Drive (Damn You Scarlett O'Hara/All My Pretty Little Ones)(ob); 1967: Barefoot in The Park; 1976: Me Jack, You Jill; 1977: Vieux Carre.

Select TV: 1952: Experiment (sp); Time to Go (sp); The Letter (sp); 1953: Dark Victory (sp); Kind Lady (sp); Angel Street (sp); 1954: Catch My Boy on Sunday (sp); 1955: Reception (sp); The Heart's a Forgotten Hotel (sp); Man on the Ledge (sp); 1957: Helen Morgan (sp); Circle of Fear (sp); 1958: The Gentleman from Seventh Avenue (sp); 1960: The Committeeman (sp); 1963: In the Last Place (sp); 1971: Do Not Fold, Spindle or Mutilate; 1975: The Secret Night Caller; Winner Take All; 1976: Death at Love House; 1977: Raid on Entebbe; Snowbeast; 1978: Siege; 1980: The Gossip Columnist; FDR: The Last Year; The Shadow Box; 1981: A Small Killing; 1982: Having It All; 1984: Come Along With Me; 1985: Finnegan Begin Again; An Early Frost; 1987: Pals; 1990: Andre's Mother (sp); The Witching of Ben Wagner (sp); 1998–99: Fantasy Island (series).

SIMONE SIGNORET

(SIMONE KAMINKER) BORN: WIESBADEN, GERMANY, MARCH 25, 1921. RAISED IN PARIS. DIED: SEPTEMBER 30, 1985.

As the earth mother of French cinema, Simone Signoret exuded a combination of sexuality, longing, and cynicism that made her one of the most respected and interesting actresses to come out of Europe in the postwar era. Like her Italian counterpart, Anna Magnani, she dabbled on occasion in English-language features with some success and also allowed herself to look like hell as she aged, which made her that much more real and fascinating. While acting in Paris with a fringe theater group, she began getting bits in films, starting with *Le Prince Charmant*, in 1942. Two years later she married director Yves Allegret, who gave her significant roles in his movies *La Boite aux Reves* and *Les Demons de l'Aube/Dawn Devils*. Her performance in the 1945 film *Macadam* was one of the first to gain her attention outside France and because of it she was offered a role in a British thriller, *Against the Wind*, but it didn't rate a follow-up, prompting her to return home. Her husband cast her as a prostitute in *Dedee d'Anvers/Dedee*, and as a temptress who marries and ruins the life of Bernard Blier in *Maneges*. She divorced Allegret after this film and married singer-actor Yves Montand in 1951, a union that lasted until her death. The year prior, she had made an unheralded American debut, in a Cornel Wilde romance filmed in Switzerland, *Four Days Leave*. She then did a run of French films that really helped make her name: *La Ronde*, in the opening and closing scenes, as a whore; *Casque d'Or/Golden Marie*, again as a lady of the night; *Therese Raquin*, having a doomed love affair with Raf Vallone; and, most notably, *Diabolique*, plotting the murder of lover Paul Meurisse in one of the most influential thrillers of the postwar period. Because Hollywood was afraid to tackle it at the time, there was also the French adaptation of Arthur Miller's classic play, *The Crucile*. Renamed *The Witches of Salem*, Signoret teamed with husband Montand in this tale of the Salem witch trials, that was, no doubt, hoping for a more sensational box-office response than it got.

Back in England she appeared as the neglected mistress of selfish Laurence Harvey in *Room at the Top*, in the part by which most filmgoers outside of France identify her. This was one of the best and most popular of the "angry young man" movies that were helping to establish Britain as a towering force in motion pictures during this time. Signoret was simply heartbreaking in her portrayal, earning some of the best notices of her career and winning an Academy Award for Best Actress of 1959. Despite Hollywood's offers, she returned to French filmmaking and then to England for a gloomy drama with Laurence Olivier, *Term of Trial*, as his nagging wife. When she finally agreed to do some American movies, she created another memorable portrait of a sad lady grasping at a final love, in *Ship of Fools*, as the drug-addicted countess carrying on with captain Oskar Werner. It earned her another Oscar nomination and was followed with three more English-language features: *The Deadly Affair*, as a Holocaust survivor and wife of a slain agent; *Games*, as the strange woman who carves her way into the lives of young couple James Caan and Katharine Ross; and *The Sea Gull*, as Arkadina. Despite encouraging reviews she decided it was time to go back to France once again and there she remained. From then onward only select Signoret films were imported to America. These included *The Confession*, with Montand, one of the political thrillers that helped make director Costa-Gavras's name; *Madame Rosa*, where Signoret, now paunchy and worn, graduated from playing hookers to madam in this poignant tale that won the Oscar for Best Foreign Language Film of 1978; *I Sent a Letter to My Love*, with Signoret inadvertently falling for her paralyzed brother via anonymous correspondence; and *L'Adolescent*, directed by Jeanne Moreau. She published her memorably titled autobiography, *Nostalgia Isn't What It Used to Be*, in 1976.

Screen (US releases only): 1946: Macadam; 1949: Dedee/Dedee D'Anvers; 1950: The Cheat/Maneges; Four Days Leave; 1951: La Ronde; 1955: Diabolique; 1958: The Witches of Salem; 1959: Room at the Top; 1963: Term of Trial; 1964: Today We Live/The Day and the Hour/Le Jour et l'Heure; Sweet and Sour; 1965: Ship of Fools; Love a la Carte/Adua e le Compagne (Fr: 1960); 1966: The Sleeping Car Murders; Is Paris Burning?; 1967: The Deadly Affair; Games; 1968: The Sea Gull; 1970: The Confession; 1974: The Widow Couderc (Fr: 1971); 1975: Le Chat/The Cat; 1977: Death in the Garden (Fr: 1956); 1978: Madame Rosa; 1980: The Case Against Ferro/Police Python 357; 1981: I Sent a Letter to My Love; 1982: L'Adolescent/The Adolescent; 1983: L'etoile du Nord/The North Star.

HENRY SILVA

BORN: BROOKLYN, NY, SEPTEMBER 15, 1928.

The frozen threat of death imprinted on Henry Silva's tightened countenance made him one of the screen's genuinely unpleasant villains, a look he maintained well into his old age, as he traveled from mainstream productions to foreign items to direct-to-video fare. A member of the Group Theatre and the Actors Studio, he was first seen on screen as a Mexican in *Viva Zapata!*, prior to making his impact as the creepy drug dealer in the original 1955 stage production of *A Hatful of Rain*, a role he reenacted on screen two years later with total conviction. Hollywood realized it had found an ideal bad guy with an indeterminate ethnicity (he was, in fact, of Puerto Rican parentage) and as such he was seen as the murderous outlaw named Chink in *The Tall T*; the Indian out to destroy bird-girl Audrey Hepburn in *Green Mansions*; Jerry Lewis's wicked stepbrother in *Cinderfella*; a member of Frank Sinatra's gang of casino thieves in *Ocean's Eleven*; an Asian assassin who indulges in a memorable altercation with Sinatra in *The Manchurian Candidate*; and the Indian Chief Mountain Hawk in *Sergeant's 3*, the remake of *Gunga Din*, in a role that was the equivalent of the one Eduardo Ciannelli played in the original. He was given his own starring roles, as a Sicilian gangster in *Johnny Cool*; and, less auspiciously, in *The Return of Mr. Moto*, an ill-advised attempt to revive the Asian sleuth, and *Hail, Mafia*, again as a hit man. By the end of the 1960s he was beginning to dabble in European cinema, though he would return somewhat prominently to American features in the 1980s, terrorizing Burt Reynolds in *Sharky's Machine*, Chuck Norris in *Code of Silence*, Steven Seagal in *Above the Law*, and Warren Beatty in *Dick Tracy*, in the latter hiding his none-too-pretty face under piles of makeup to portray a hood named Influence. In his 70s he was still up to no good, playing the head of a low-rent crime family, in *Ghost Dog: The Way of the Samurai*.

Screen: 1952: Viva Zapata!; 1956: Crowded Paradise; 1957: A Hatful of Rain; The Tall T; 1958: The Law and Jake Wade; The Bravados; Ride a Crooked Trail; 1959: Green Mansions; The Jayhawkers; 1960: Ocean's Eleven; Cinderfella; 1962: Sergeant's 3; The Manchurian Candidate; 1963: A Gathering of Eagles; Johnny Cool; 1964: The Secret Invasion; 1965: The Reward; The Return of Mr. Moto; 1966: The Plainsman; 1967: The Hills Run Red; Matchless; Hail, Mafia; Assassination (nUSr); 1968: Never a Dull Moment; Quella carogna dell'Ispettore Sterling/Frame Up (nUSr); **1969:** Probabilitia Zero (nUSr); **1971:** The Animals; **1972:** Man and Boy; The Falling Man (nUSr); L'insolent/The Killer (nUSr); Les Hommes (nUSr); **1973:** The Italian Connection/Manhunt in Milan; Il Boss/Wipeout (nUSr); Zinksarge fur die Goldjungen/Battle of the Godfathers (nUSr); Cry of a Prostitute; **1975:** L'uomo della Strada fa Giustizia/The Manhunt (nUSr); White Fang to the Rescue (nUSr); **1976:** Shoot; Il Trucido e lo Sbirro/Tough Cop (nUSr); Poliziotti Violenti/Crimebusters (dtv); **1977:** Fox Bat (nUSr); Napoli Spara/Weapons of Death (nUSr); **1978:** Almost Human/The Kidnap of Mary Lou (It: 1974); **1979:** Love and Bullets; Buck Rogers in the 25th Century; **1980:** Alligator; Virus (dtv); **1981:** Thirst; Sharky's Machine; **1982:** Wrong Is Right; Megaforce; Trapped/Baker County USA (dtv); **1983:** Chained Heat; La Marginal/Outsider (nUSr); Violent Breed (dtv); **1984:** Cannonball Run II; **1985:** Escape from the Bronx; Lust in the Dust; Code of Silence; **1986:** Allan Quatermain and the Lost City of Gold; Amazon Women on the Moon; **1988:** Above the Love; Bulletproof; Trained to Kill (dtv); **1989:** White Cobra Express (nUSr); Cy-Warrior (nUSr); **1990:** Critical Action (nUSr); Dick Tracy; L'Ultima Partita/Opponent/Last Match (nUSr); **1991:** Fists of Steel (dtv); The Colombian Connection (dtv); **1992:** South Beach (dtv); **1993:** The Harvest; **1994:** Possessed by the Night (dtv); The Silence of the Hams (dtv); **1995:** Fatal Choice (dtv); Drifting School (nUSr); **1996:** The Prince (dtv); Mad Dog Time/Trigger Happy; **1997:** The End of Violence; **1999:** Unconditional Love; **2000:** Ghost Dog: The Way of the Samurai; **2001:** Ocean's Eleven.

NY Stage: 1953: Camino Real; 1955: A Hatful of Rain.

Select TV: 1955: Darkness at Noon (sp); 1957: Don't Touch Me (sp); 1971: Black Noon; 1973: Drive Hard, Drive Fast (filmed 1969); 1977: Contract on Cherry Street; 1983: Happy; 1992: Three Days to Kill; 1997: Batman: Gotham Knights (series; voice); 1999: Justice.

PHIL SILVERS

(PHILIP SILVERSMITH) BORN: BROOKLYN, NY, MAY 11, 1912. DIED: NOVEMBER 1, 1985.

A performer with two distinct personas, Phil Silvers was one comedian who got funnier with age. In his early days he was a jabbering chump, often playing best pal to the leading man, his frantic shtick punctuated by the buffoonish twitches of a man unaware of his own idiotic behavior. During the 1950s, as he allowed audiences to see his balding pate, he got sassier and more wizened, embodying the insincere, fast-talking con man. He was suddenly in charge and everything seemed to click. A child singer, he joined the Guy Edwards Revue at age 13 and, once he grew out of that, toured in vaudeville as part of a comedy act. He became a burlesque comic for Minsky's, telling jokes between strip routines until he was hired to both act and write material for the Broadway musical *Yokel Boy.* That show earned him a contract with MGM, who did nothing with him and allowed him to go over to Republic to make his movie debut, in *Hit Parade of 1941,* which was little more than the cinematic equivalent of a radio show. Metro gave him a specialty moment in *Lady Be Good,* but for the most part they were content to loan him out, to RKO for *Tom, Dick and Harry,* where he really tried one's patience as an obnoxious ice cream man; to Republic for *Ice-Capades*; and to Warners for *You're in the Army Now,* where he mugged along with Jimmy Durante. 20th Century-Fox invited him to join the company and he provided some tired comic

"relief" to the dumb plots of some Betty Grable musicals, including *Coney Island* and *Billy Rose's Diamond Horseshoe.* Columbia gave him his first memorable film assignment, as sidekick to Gene Kelly, in the lavish and very popular musical *Cover Girl,* where he got a chance to shine, singing and dancing with Kelly and Rita Hayworth in the snappy "Make Way for Tomorrow" number.

After a few more look-alike Fox assignments, Silvers went back to Broadway where he scored a major success with the musical *High Button Shoes,* causing MGM to call him back to pair him with Kelly again for *Summer Stock,* the low point of which had the two performers clad in hillbilly garb, yowling through the song "Heavenly Music." It was then back to Broadway for another smash, *Top Banana,* a revue that really marked the beginning of the sharper, less oafish Silvers. He not only won the Tony Award but started being treated as a star rather than the leading man's best buddy. After a quickly filmed presentation of *Top Banana,* he went to television where his career soared up through the ranks, thanks to the weekly series *You'll Never Get Rich,* where he played the irascible military smooth-talker Sergeant Ernie Bilko. This character, for which Silvers won two Emmy Awards, became such a classic edition to the small screen that the show would often be referred to in the future simply as *Sgt. Bilko.* Returning to the movies in the 1960s, he played another oily character, in the all-star *It's a Mad Mad Mad Mad World,* getting a lion's share of the laughs as the greediest of the money-hunting characters. Shedding his glasses for the first time in years, he was the opportunistic whorehouse owner Marcus Lycus in *A Funny Thing Happened on the Way to the Forum,* a piece he fit into so well that he took the lead role of the slave Pseudolus in the 1972 Broadway revival, winning another Tony Award. Prior to that there was a terrible Foreign Legion spoof, *Follow That Camel,* and a fairly straightforward role, as one of the vets returning to ex-lover Gina Lolobrigida, in *Buena Sera, Mrs. Campbell.* In the 1970s he confined himself to television guest work, occasionally appearing in weak big-screen comedies like *The Chicken Chronicles, The Cheap Detective,* and *The Happy Hooker Goes Hollywood,* looking less than healthy (due to a stroke) and probably eager to be elsewhere. He published his autobiography *This Laugh Is on Me,* in 1973.

Screen: 1940: Hit Parade of 1941; **1941:** The Penalty; Tom, Dick and Harry; Lady Be Good; Ice-Capades; The Wild Man of Borneo; You're in the Army Now; **1942:** Roxie Hart; My Gal Sal; Footlight Serenade; Just Off Broadway; All Through the Night; Tales of Manhattan (restored print only); **1943:** Coney Island; A Lady Takes a Chance; **1944:** Cover Girl; Four Jills and a Jeep; Take It or Leave It; Something for the Boys; **1945:** Billy Rose's Diamond Horseshoe; A Thousand and One Nights; Don Juan Quilligan; **1946:** If I'm Lucky; **1950:** Summer Stock; **1954:** Top Banana; Lucky Me; **1962:** 40 Pounds of Trouble; **1963:** It's a Mad Mad Mad Mad World; **1966:** A Funny Thing Happened on the Way to the Forum; **1967:** A Guide for the Married Man; Follow That Camel; **1968:** Buona Sera, Mrs. Campbell; **1970:** The Boatniks; **1975:** The Strongest Man in the World; **1976:** Won Ton Ton, the Dog Who Saved Hollywood; **1977:** The Chicken Chronicles; **1978:** The Cheap Detective; **1979:** Racquet; There Goes the Bride; **1980:** The Happy Hooker Goes Hollywood.

NY Stage: 1939: Yokel Boy; 1947: High Button Shoes; 1951: Top Banana; 1960: Do Re Mi; 1971: How the Other Half Loves; 1972: A Funny Thing Happened on the Way to the Forum.

Select TV: 1948–49: The Arrow Show (series); 1955–59: You'll Never Get Rich/The Phil Silvers Show (series); 1959: The Ballad of Louie the Louse (sp); 1960: The Slowest Gun in the West (sp); 1963–64: The New Phil Silvers Show (series); 1967: Damn Yankees (sp); 1977: The New Love Boat; The Night They Took

Miss Beautiful; **1979:** Goldie and the Boxer.

ALASTAIR SIM

BORN: EDINBURGH, SCOTLAND, OCTOBER 9, 1900. DIED: AUGUST 19, 1976.

Ghoulishly sad-eyed Alastair Sim, whose teeth seemed to bulge forth from his mouth, was one of England's comical treasures, his stardom rising as he reached his 50s. Originally a teacher, he dabbled in amateur theatrics on the side, making his professional London bow in a 1930 production of *Othello*. Following a run of stage work, he made his film debut in 1935, in a "quota quickie" called *Riverside Murder*, and found himself in demand as a supporting player in similar fare, including *Late Extra* and *Clothes and the Woman*, in both as a servant; and *Gangway*, as a detective, in the first of several films with Jessie Matthews. He was a genie in *Alf's Button Afloat*, and Sergeant Bingham, investigating a murder with *Inspector Hornleigh*, a role that he would repeat in two sequels. These roles were important since they raised his stature in the industry and, after reprising his stage role as a secret agent in *Cottage to Let*, he achieved top billing, as a professor, in *Let the People Sing*, and stole the notices, once again playing a detective, in *Green for Danger*. He entered his peak years starting with *Hue and Cry*, a charming Ealing comedy in which he played an author who gets mixed up with some juvenile crime-fighters. There followed Hitchcock's *Stage Struck*, as Jane Wyman's sleuthing dad; *The Happiest Days of Your Life*, as a befuddled headmaster, opposite Margaret Rutherford, both working overtime to compensate for this weak farce; *Laughter in Paradise*, hilarious as a novelist willing to commit a crime to win some money; *A Christmas Carol*, the definitive version of the Dickens classic and the film that most audiences know him best for; and his well-remembered dual roles as the headmistress (just the thought of someone as blatantly unattractive as Sim in drag was good for some laughs) and her unsavory brother in *The Belles of St. Trinian's*. He finished out the 1950s playing a headmaster, once again, in *School for Scoundrels*, and supporting Sophia Loren in *The Millionairess*. After a long absence he showed up briefly as a doddering bishop in *The Ruling Class*, and took top billing in a little-seen Disney film shot in England, *The Littlest Horse Thieves*.

Screen: 1935: Riverside Murder; The Case of Gabriel Perry; A Fire Has Been Arranged; The Private Secretary; Troubled Waters; Late Extra; **1936:** Wedding Group/Wrath of Jealousy; The Big Noise; Man in the Mirror; Keep Your Seats Please; The Mysterious Mr. Davis/My Partner; Mr. Davis; **1937:** Strange Experiment; Clothes and the Woman; Gangway; The Squeaker/Murder in Diamond Row; A Romance in Flanders; Melody and Romance; **1938:** Sailing Along; The Terror; Alf's Button Afloat; This Man Is News; **1939:** Climbing High; Inspector Hornleigh; This Man in Paris; Inspector Hornleigh on Holiday; **1940:** Law and Disorder; **1941:** Inspector Hornleigh Goes to It; Cottage to Let/Bombsight Stolen; **1942:** Let the People Sing; **1944:** Waterloo Road; **1946:** Green for Danger; **1947:** Hue and Cry; Captain Boycott; **1948:** London Belongs to Me/Dulcimer Street; **1950:** The Happiest Days of Your Life; Stage Fright; **1951:** Laughter in Paradise; Lady Godiva Rides Again; A Christmas Carol/Scrooge; **1952:** Folly to Be Wise; **1953:** Innocents in Paris; **1954:** An Inspector Calls; The Belles of St. Trinian's; **1955:** Escapade; Geordie/Wee Geordie; **1956:** The Green Man; **1957:** Blue Murder at St. Trinian's; **1959:** The Doctor's Dilemma; Left, Right and Center; **1960:** School for Scoundrels; The Millionairess; **1961:** The Anatomist; **1972:** The Ruling Class; **1975:** Royal Flash; **1976:** The Littlest Horse Thieves/Escape from the Dark.

Select TV: 1967: Misleading Cases (series); **1972:** Cold Comfort Farm (sp); **1976:** Rogue Male.

JEAN SIMMONS

BORN: LONDON, ENGLAND, JANUARY 31, 1929.

She was one of England's most effervescent talents of the postwar era and, like Deborah Kerr and Audrey Hepburn, the latter with whom she shared some of the same delicate traits and mannerisms, she was embraced by America during the 1950s, where she became an accomplished and cherished addition to stateside cinema. As a youngster she learned acting at the Ada Foster School which opened the way to movie roles, starting in 1944 when she played Margaret Lockwood's sister in *Give Us the Moon*. After essaying another sister role (Patricia Medina's) in *Kiss the Bride Goodbye*, she showed up as a singer in *The Way to the Stars*, and as a handmaiden somewhere in the background of the big-budgeted *Caesar and Cleopatra*. In 1946, she was signed to a contract by J. Arthur Rank, who cast her in one of the most prestigious British films of the decade, *Great Expectations*, where she made a vivid impression as the snooty younger version of Estella. That one was not only a success in England but also one of the highest profile British motion pictures to play in the U.S. in the late 1940s, as were *Black Narcissus*, in which she was done up in dark make-up to play an Indian girl, and, most significantly, Laurence Olivier's brooding version of *Hamlet*. As the tragic Ophelia, Simmons suggested years of experience and wound up with an Oscar nomination for Best Supporting Actress of 1948. Staying in her native land for a spell, she became a box-office attraction via *The Blue Lagoon*, in which she and Donald Houston grew from shipwrecked children to lovers; *Adam and Evelyne*, paired opposite Stewart Granger, who became her husband in 1950; *So Long at the Fair*, in which she searched for her missing brother; *The Clouded Yellow*, a muddled chase film in which she was a moody, troubled girl assisted by Trevor Howard; and a segment of the Maugham omnibus, *Trio*. Since her husband signed a contract with MGM, she came to Hollywood with him. Unfortunately, Rank had sold her contract and she had the rotten luck of ending up at the slowly disintegrating RKO.

Things started off badly with the troubled and much-panned version of *Androcles and the Lion*, in which she played opposite stoic Victor Mature, who was also her leading man in *Affair with a Stranger*. Over at MGM, with her husband, she was well cast as Elizabeth I in the costume drama *Young Bess*, skillfully suggesting the growing strength of this formidable lady in her early days, and sparkled in the title role of *The Actress*, Ruth Gordon's autobiographical tale of a determined young stage hopeful growing up in New England. In it, Simmons played the daughter of Teresa Wright, to whom she actually bore some slight resemblance. It was one of Simmons's best films but an unfortunate flop. She compensated for its failure by appearing in the biggest box-office hit of 1953, *The Robe*, in which she looked beautiful, if nothing else. The film was somewhat better than another expensive load of costume hokum, *The Egyptian*, in which she simply blended in with the rest of the large cast, as a girl who dies for her religious convictions. However, she was front and center for *Desiree*, opposite Marlon Brando as Napoleon, a dreary teaming that was made up for by *Guys and Dolls*, in which she seemed to be having great fun singing and dancing as the Salvation Army lady, Sister Sarah, who falls for Brando's charming gambler, Skye Masterson. It was a great success and she got her own vehicles as a result: *Hilda Crane*, which was very much a 20th Century-Fox soap opera of the 1950s, except for Simmons's independent character, and *This Could Be the Night*, a mild comedy about a school teacher involved with a gangster (shades of *Guys and Dolls*). She and Granger went home to do *Footsteps in the Fog*; while she and Paul Newman made an attractive team in the forgettable soap, *Until They Sail*. After that, she won hero Gregory Peck from the much less interesting Carroll Baker in the epic western, *The Big Country*. There was another Simmons showcase, *Home Before Dark*, where she played a woman recovering from a nervous breakdown but, despite her expected excellent notices, there was no audience rush to see her.

Because of Rock Hudson's participation, there was some interest in the vintner family saga *This Earth Is Mine*, after which she appeared in two of the best movies of 1960: *Elmer Gantry*, in which she was terrific as the dedicated evangelist seduced by charlatan Burt Lancaster, and *Spartacus*, in which she was touching and comforting as the slave girl loved by Kirk Douglas. Simmons was at her peak as an actress in *Gantry* and the man who directed her to this performance, Richard Brooks, became her husband that year, after she divorced Granger. A comedy with Cary Grant and Deborah Kerr, *The Grass Is Greener*, was not the hoped for hit and, although there was no audience for *All the Way Home*, this proved to be another acting peak for Simmons, in an emotional tour de force as a small-town wife and mom who must cope with the unexpected death of her beloved husband (Robert Preston). She took over the role of Laurence Harvey's wife in *Life at the Top*, a sequel to *Room at the Top* (Heather Sears had originally done the part); and then she showed up late in the storyline to pretty much steal the show, as the bored, blonde Manhattanite on a scavenger hunt in *Mister Buddwing*. There was a bright comedy, *Divorce American Style*, with Dick Van Dyke, and then her husband (they would divorce in 1977) wrote and directed a vehicle for her, *The Happy Ending*, in which she was a woman facing a mid-life crisis. There was nothing particularly exceptional about the film, but it seemed to be the right time to honor Simmons and her career, so she got an Oscar nomination for it, her first and only in the leading category. She did the older woman-younger man bit in a British film, *Say Hello to Yesterday*, which marked her farewell as a motion picture lead. From that point on she mainly did television. The few theatrical films she did were so low profile that it seemed like she'd been off the screen forever when she finally showed up as one of the unhappy ladies in Ellen Burstyn's quilting circle in *How to Make an American Quilt*, looking frailer but no less appealing than she had always been. On television she won an Emmy Award for the mini series *The Thorn Birds*.

Screen: 1944: Give Us the Moon; Mr. Emmanuel; Kiss the Bride Goodbye; Meet Sexton Blake; 1945: Caesar and Cleopatra; The Way to the Stars; 1946: Great Expectations (US: 1947); 1947: Hungry Hill; Black Narcissus; Uncle Silas/The Inheritance; The Woman in the Hall; 1948: Hamlet; 1949: The Blue Lagoon; Adam and Evelyne; 1950: So Long at the Fair; Cage of Gold; Trio; The Clouded Yellow; 1952: Androcles and the Lion; Angel Face; 1953: Young Bess; Affair With a Stranger; The Actress; The Robe; 1954: She Couldn't Say No; A Bullet Is Waiting; The Egyptian; Desiree; 1955: Footsteps in the Fog; Guys and Dolls; 1956: Hilda Crane; 1957: This Could Be the Night; Until They Sail; 1958: The Big Country; Home Before Dark; 1959: This Earth Is Mine; 1960: Elmer Gantry; Spartacus; 1961: The Grass Is Greener; 1963: All the Way Home; 1965: Life at the Top; 1966: Mister Buddwing; 1967: Rough Night in Jericho; Divorce American Style; 1969: The Happy Ending; 1971: Say Hello to Yesterday;

1975: Mr. Sycamore; 1978: Dominique; 1988: Going Undercover/The Yellow Pages (filmed 1985); The Dawning; 1995: How to Make an American Quilt; 2001: Final Fantasy: The Spirits Within (voice).

Select TV: 1966: Crazier Than Cotton (sp); 1967: The Lady Is My Wife (sp); Soldier in Love (sp); 1968: Heidi; 1975: The Easter Promise; 1978: The Dain Curse (ms); 1979: Beggarman, Thief; 1981: Golden Gate; Jacqueline Susann's Valley of the Dolls; A Small Killing; 1983: The Thorn Birds (ms); 1985: Midas Valley; 1986: North and South Book II (ms); 1987: Perry Mason: The Case of the Lost Love; 1988: A Friendship in Vienna (narrator); Inherit the Wind; 1989: Great Expectations; 1990: Sense and Sensibility (sp); Laker Girls; People Like Us; 1991: Dark Shadows (series); 1995: Daisies in December; 1998: Barbara Taylor Bradford's Her Own Rules.

FRANK SINATRA

(FRANCIS ALBERT SINATRA) BORN: HOBOKEN, NJ, DECEMBER 12, 1915. DIED: MAY 14, 1998.

There are a select few allowed into the Pantheon of the Show Business Gods, those who not only excelled at their craft but helped define and influence generations to come, those towering figures about whom the word "legendary" can be applied without risk of an argument. Frank Sinatra certainly received that level as far as vocalizing was concerned, earning such generous nicknames as "The Chairman of the Board" and "The Voice," for the way in which he took a song, wrapped his soul around it, and sold it with a heartfelt grace that seemed so easy. Because of the iconic position he reached in the music and recording world, his status as an actor and, indeed as a movie star, were often taken for granted, as if his critics were not willing to concede that he could do two things well. He was, in fact, an exceptionally good actor, despite reports of his impatience with the whole technique of filmmaking. A joyful addition to musicals, a sly light comedian, and an often powerhouse dramatic player, he also made that profession seem like the easiest thing in the world to do. He had taken an interest in singing quite early on, entering amateur contests while a teen and eventually touring with the Major Bowes Amateur Hour. Returning to the East Coast, he sang on some local radio stations in New York, almost never for any salary and, since that was getting him nowhere, took a job as a regular performer-host at a roadhouse called the Rustic Cabin, in Englewood, New Jersey. It was there that he was seen by trumpeter Harry James, who was looking for a vocalist to front his new band. Sinatra joined up and it was with them that he made his first record, "From the Bottom of My Heart," in 1939. When Sinatra saw his chance to move up a notch further with the better-known Tommy Dorsey Orchestra, he jumped at the chance and soon found his voice becoming one of the most recognizable in the country. The group was invited to do some guest movie appearances and Sinatra was first seen on screen in a very minor Paramount production called *Las Vegas Nights*, singing "I'll Never Smile Again." He felt it was time to go solo and did so with unprecedented success, his sold-out engagements at New York's Paramount Theatre during 1942–43 becoming the stuff of show business myth, his soft crooning causing millions of young women to scream in adoration.

RKO figured it was time to cash in on him as a star and put him in *Higher and Higher*, giving him third billing after Michele Morgan and Jack Haley, though it was clear that audiences showed up for the skinny Italian with the wavy hair. This was followed by a weak re-do of *Room Service*, called *Step Lively*, with

Sinatra in the part done earlier by Frank Albertson, and he might have been stuck floundering in this studio's less-than-stellar stabs at the genre had MGM not borrowed him for one of their super productions of 1945, *Anchors Aweigh*. They thought enough of him to give him billing *over* their own attractions, Gene Kelly and Kathryn Grayson, and he and Kelly made a delightful team, with Sinatra cast as the bashful, virginal sailor trying to learn how to please the ladies from his more experienced buddy. The movie was a smash, Sinatra got a hit song out of the deal, "I Fall in Love Too Easily," and better yet, was able to switch his contract to Metro. Before he left RKO he did a short film on the subject of tolerance, "The House I Live In," and it gave him an important degree of respect, earning him a special Academy Award. Meanwhile, MGM gave him the finale spot, singing "Ol' Man River," in their all-star tribute to Jerome Kern, *Till the Clouds Roll By*; after which he did two with Grayson, *It Happened in Brooklyn*, which wasn't considered major enough to shoot in color, but did give him a nice number shot on location on the Brooklyn Bridge; and the garish and silly *The Kissing Bandit*, which was certainly one of the low points of his cinematic career. Fortunately Kelly came calling again, first for *Take Me Out to the Ball Game*, and then, more importantly, *On the Town*, with the two back in sailor duds again, this time white instead of blue. Despite dropping most of the songs from the Broadway original, this was a sparkling entertainment in its own right, one of the peaks of the MGM musical heyday, and one that presented Sinatra at his happiest and most appealing.

Unwisely, he left the studio and, as the early 1950s arrived, he suddenly found himself in a less assured position than he'd been in years, as his records (Columbia severed ties after a decade in business together) began to lose money and an attempt at a weekly television series proved a disappointment. When he married actress Ava Gardner in 1951 their over-publicized union kept him in the public eye more than anything that he was doing career-wise. A blessing from heaven arrived when director Fred Zinnemann nixed the initial casting of Eli Wallach as the doomed Private Maggio in the much-hyped screen version of James Jones's best seller *From Here to Eternity*. Sinatra got the role instead and not only saved his career but also turned in a startlingly good performance, as the puny but tough soldier who stands up to brutish stockade sergeant Ernest Borgnine and pays for it with his life. He won the Academy Award for Best Supporting Actor of 1953 and found himself right back on top again. To coincide with the sweet rebirth of his acting career, Capitol Records signed him to a contract, where the combination of arranger Nelson Riddle with Sinatra's maturing voice proved to be perfectly in sync. Thus began the phase of his recording career that produced a string of albums that showed his brilliance as a singer and would continue to represent the very best of pop music for decades to come. Meanwhile, he did an admirable job playing a nasty mug out to assassinate the President in the low-budget *Suddenly*, and reprised John Garfield's old role in *Young at Heart*, a remake of *Four Daughters*, in which he was a disillusioned music arranger. Although he and co-star Doris Day only duetted briefly, he got a hit record out of the title song. He had no qualms about taking a backseat to Robert Mitchum in the medical soap, *Not as a Stranger*; launched his screen image as the cool lady-killer in the glossy *The Tender Trap*; had to be content with the secondary part of Nathan Detroit in the colorful adaptation of *Guys and Dolls*, after Goldwyn favored Marlon Brando for the lead over him; and then capped a string of notable 1955 releases with *The Man with the Golden Arm*, giving a riveting performance as a junkie, resulting in another Oscar nomination.

In *High Society*, the musical remake of *The Philadelphia Story*,

he played James Stewart's old role, which meant that he got to pair up with the idol of his youth, Bing Crosby, for one of the most joyous duets in the history of the genre, "Well, Did You Evah?" He then misstepped badly in an effort to play a peasant in *The Pride and the Passion*, sporting a silly set of bangs and a ridiculous Spanish accent. Thanks to the added casting of Cary Grant and Sophia Loren it was a moneymaker nonetheless. His box-office standing was hot, his records were selling by the millions, and he was becoming the star attraction of America's gambling resort Las Vegas, which helped solidify the image of the saloon singer crooning to the masses and proving that even tough guys could be sensitive. In time his friendship with fellow entertainers Dean Martin and Sammy Davis, Jr. also boosted him to a revered position as the "king of cool," casually boozing, cracking wise, and bedding any broad he cared to in a manner many came to find arrogant and misogynistic. On screen he played nightclub performer Joe E. Lewis in *The Joker Is Wild*, introducing the Oscar-winning song, "All the Way;" was perfectly cast as the love-'em and leave-'em anti-hero of *Pal Joey* (the character changed from dancer to singer for his benefit), featuring a catalog of Rodger and Hart songs that were among the best he ever did; and was a vet returning to his small town in *Some Came Running*. This film marked his first with Dean Martin, with whom he clicked beautifully, and boasted a bevy of Oscar-nominated performances by several cast members, which did not include Sinatra who, in truth, effortlessly acted them all under the table. A lighthearted Frank Capra story, *A Hole in the Head*, gave him another Oscar-winning standard, "High Hopes," and was much more appealing than the heavy war film *Never So Few*. Back to musicals, something went seriously wrong with *Can-Can*, a tedious affair, which, if nothing else, allotted for his haunting rendition of Cole Porter's "It's All Right with Me."

Ocean's Eleven, a none-too-exciting heist story set in Vegas, was the first of the so-called "Rat Pack" flicks, which meant it featured Frank Sinatra, Dean Martin, Sammy Davis, Jr., Joey Bishop, and some other late-night cronies. They were back in various increments for *Sergeants 3*, a cavalry revision of *Gunga Din*; *4 for Texas*, a tired western; and the best of the lot, *Robin and the 7 Hoods*, a full-fledged musical. It gave Sinatra, Crosby, and Martin a chance to harmonize on the snappy "Style," as well as introducing one of Sinatra's best numbers ever, "My Kind of Town." Between these larks he matched the cranky Spencer Tracy scene for scene in *The Devil at 4 O'Clock*, and took on the strangest, most challenging film of his career, director John Frankenheimer's cryptic and fascinating *The Manchurian Candidate*, as a once-brainwashed soldier who must stop a political assassination. He was miscast as Tony Bill's playboy older brother in *Come Blow Your Horn*, in so much as the film's characters were based on playwright Neil Simon and his brother and he, therefore, should have been younger and Jewish. He surprised everyone by choosing to direct himself in the anti-war film, *None But the Brave*, a curious decision since his desire for single takes was well known by this point, making him the last person one could imagine going through the tedium of directing. In any event, the film got points for more than what it set out to accomplish, rather than for what it achieved. Far more satisfying was the exciting World War II escape story, *Von Ryan's Express*, which kept his box-office popularity afloat. However, a smarmy sex comedy with Dean Martin and Deborah Kerr, *Marriage on the Rocks*; a dud heist film, *Assault on a Queen*; and the confused, British-made *The Naked Runner* injured his standing. He was once again a prominent name in the gossip columns, however, for marrying (1966–68) actress Mia Farrow when he was 50 years old and she was 21.

Audiences loved the idea of Sinatra as a cool private eye, which is what he played to perfection in the Miami-set *Tony Rome*, and also showed up for the more serious and controversial *The Detective*, in which he enacted a man wracked with guilt over executing the wrong man for a homosexual murder, proving those who thought his recent work was slacking dead wrong; he still had the goods. This film seemed to suggest that he could adapt easily to the post-production code era of the late 1960s but, after cheekily mugging in a western spoof, *Dirty Dingus Magee*, he concentrated on nightclub engagements before his much-publicized retirement. Fortunately this self-imposed exile did not last very long and he was soon back filling arenas and concert halls, his voice rustier with age but his delivery more poignant with the additional years. Unlike most of his contemporaries, he was held in higher esteem than ever before and, even more surprisingly, was accepted by younger fans as well. There was a one-shot return to films in the leading role of *The First Deadly Sin*, again as a tough cop with a moral side, but audience attendance was low. Instead, he got himself back on the charts in the middle of the rock era with his rendition of "Theme from New York, New York" and remained the center of controversy every time he tussled with a rude photographer or an inquisitive reporter. Dozens of articles and books poured forth from all over about his holier-than-thou manner, his supposed ties with the Mob, and his unapologetic way of running life on his own terms. Not surprisingly, there was less coverage of his endless charity work or mention of the inimitable class he still managed to project under his world-weary, brusque exterior. The Motion Picture Academy did, however, honor him with the Jean Hersholt Humanitarian Award in 1970. When he died in 1998, the press and public responded as if an era had passed, that a giant had disappeared, the likes of which we would never experience again.

Screen: 1941: Las Vegas Nights; 1942: Ship Ahoy; 1943: Reveille with Beverly; Higher and Higher; 1944: Step Lively; 1945: Anchors Aweigh; 1947: Till the Clouds Roll By; It Happened in Brooklyn; 1948: The Miracle of the Bells; The Kissing Bandit; 1949: Take Me Out to the Ball Game; On the Town; 1951: Double Dynamite; 1952: Meet Danny Wilson; 1953: From Here to Eternity; 1954: Suddenly; 1955: Young at Heart; Not as a Stranger; The Tender Trap; Guys and Dolls; The Man with the Golden Arm; 1956: Meet Me in Las Vegas; Johnny Concho; High Society; Around the World in Eighty Days; 1957: The Pride and the Passion; The Joker Is Wild; Pal Joey; 1958: Kings Go Forth; Some Came Running; 1959: A Hole in the Head; Never So Few; 1960: Can-Can; Ocean's Eleven; Pepe; 1961: The Devil at 4 O'Clock; 1962: Sergeants 3; The Road to Hong Kong; The Manchurian Candidate; 1963: Come Blow Your Horn; The List of Adrian Messenger; 4 for Texas; 1964: Robin and the 7 Hoods; 1965: None But the Brave (and dir.; prod.); Von Ryan's Express; Marriage on the Rocks; 1966: Cast a Giant Shadow; The Oscar; Assault on a Queen; 1967: The Naked Runner; Tony Rome; 1968: The Detective; Lady in Cement; 1970: Dirty Dingus Magee; 1974: That's Entertainment!; 1980: The First Deadly Sin; 1984: Cannonball Run II; 1990: Listen Up: The Lives of Quincy Jones.

Select TV: 1950–52: The Frank Sinatra Show (series); 1953: Anything Goes (sp); 1955: Our Town (sp); 1957–58: The Frank Sinatra Show (series); 1959: Timex Special: The Frank Sinatra Show (sp); Timex Special: An Afternoon with Frank Sinatra (sp); 1960: Frank Sinatra: Here's to the Ladies! (sp); Timex Special: Welcome Back Elvis (sp); 1965: Frank Sinatra: An American Original (sp); Frank Sinatra: A Man and His Music (sp); 1966: Frank Sinatra: A Man and His Music II (sp); 1967: Frank Sinatra: A Man and His Music +Ella+Jobim (sp); 1968: Francis Albert Sinatra Does His Thing (sp); 1969: Sinatra (sp); 1973: Ol' Blue

Eyes is Back (sp); 1974: Sinatra: The Main Event (sp); 1976: John Denver and Friend (sp); 1977: Frank Sinatra and Friends (sp); Contract on Cherry Street; 1978: Dean Martin Celebrity Roast: Frank Sinatra (sp); 1980: Sinatra: The First 40 years (sp); 1981: Sinatra: The Man and His Music (sp); 1982: Sinatra: Concert for the Americas (sp); 1989: Frank, Liza and Sammy: The Ultimate Event (sp).

PENNY SINGLETON

(Mariana Dorothy McNulty)
Born: Philadelphia, PA, September 15, 1908.
ed: Columbia Univ.

It wasn't even her natural hair color, but Penny Singleton embodied the part of comic strip heroine Blondie Bumstead and, therefore, was thought of as being "blonde" to millions of Americans who figured that she was born into the role and did nothing else. A chorus girl, she'd danced in the original 1927 Broadway production of *Good News* and then showed up in the film version three years later, under the name "Dorothy McNulty." She kept this billing for a while, until 1938 when she changed it to "Penny Singleton" to play the lead in a Republic Pictures "B" musical, *Outside of Paradise*, as the co-owner of a castle in Ireland, visited by bandleader Phil Regan. Warner Bros. utilized her as a secondary player in such movies as *Mr. Chump* and *Secrets of an Actress*, until Columbia decided to shoot a quickie film based on Chic Young's popular comic strip about a sweet blonde housewife and her hyper husband, Dagwood Bumstead. Singleton dyed her hair and got the part in the 1938 release, entitled *Blondie*, an innocuous and utterly forgettable 68 minute comedy that proved popular enough for the studio to turn it into a series, with the first follow-up, *Blondie Meets the Boss*, appearing the following year. These were domestic comedies appealing to the lowest common denominator, with the perky Singleton easier to take than her squeaky-voiced male counterpart, Arthur Lake, as Dagwood. After the first 12 entries Columbia cautiously took "Blondie" out of the title for the two that were distributed in 1943, *It's a Great Life* and *Footlight Glamour*, with the intention of dumping the series altogether. Public outcry was great enough that production resumed and the Bumsteads remained on screen until 1950 with *Beware of Blondie*, bringing the final total of "Blondie" films to 28. Latter day audiences mostly identify her as the voice of the space age mom in the animated series, *The Jetsons*.

Screen: AS Dorothy McNulty: 1930: Good News; Love in the Rough; 1936: After the Thin Man; 1937: Vogues of 1938; Sea Racketeers.

AS Penny Singleton: 1938: Outside of Paradise; Swing Your Lady; Men Are Such Fools; Boy Meets Girl; Mr. Chump; The Mad Miss Manton; Garden of the Moon; Secrets of an Actress; Hard to Get; Blondie; Racket Busters; 1939: Blondie Meets the Boss; Blondie Takes a Vacation; Blondie Brings Up Baby; 1940: Blondie on a Budget; Blondie Has Servant Trouble; Blondie Plays Cupid; 1941: Blondie Goes Latin; Blondie in Society; Go West, Young Lady; 1942: Blondie Goes to College; Blondie's Blessed Event; Blondie for Victory; 1943: It's a Great Life; Footlight Glamour; 1945: Leave It to Blondie; 1946: Life With Blondie; Young Widow; Blondie's Lucky Day; Blondie Knows Best; 1947: Blondie's Big Moment; Blondie's Holiday; Blondie in the Dough; Blondie's Anniversary; 1948: Blondie's Reward; Blondie's Secret; 1949: Blondie's Big Deal; Blondie Hits the Jackpot; 1950: Blondie's Hero; Beware of Blondie; 1964: The Best Man; 1990: Jetsons: The Movie (voice).

NY Stage: AS Dorothy McNulty: 1926: The Great

Temptations; **1927:** Good News; **1932:** Hey Nonnynonny!; Walk a Little Faster;
AS PENNY SINGLETON: **1972:** No, No, Nanette.
Select TV: **1950:** Cause for Suspicion (sp); **1962–67, 1969–76, 1979–83:** The Jetsons (series; voice).

LILIA SKALA

BORN: VIENNA, AUSTRIA, NOVEMBER 28, 1896.
ED: UNIV. OF DRESDEN.
DIED: DECEMBER 18, 1994.

A real inspiration to not hang one's career up too early, Lilia Skala had been a theater and film actress in her native country for many years before fleeing to America just as Hitler took power. Coming to the United States, she ended up in some Broadway productions, including *Call Me Madam*, as the Grand Duchess, a part she repeated in the film version. Despite several television appearances during the 1950s, the acting offers were not plentiful enough to keep her financially solvent, so, by the early 1960s, she began doing odd jobs to make ends meet, ending up busing restaurant tables. Past the age of retirement, she was cast as the gentle but demanding Mother Superior, who insists that Sidney Poitier build a chapel for herself and the other German-speaking nuns in her parish, in *Lilies of the Field*. Suddenly the world was aware of this fine actress and she earned a supporting Oscar nomination and garnered offers for work. She ended up aboard the *Ship of Fools*; in a coy Doris Day spy spoof, *Caprice*; and as an authoritative doctor helping out mental patient Cliff Robertson in *Charly*. After a stint on the daytime serial *Search for Tomorrow* and a few television movies, she was back on theater screens as one of the lonely patrons of *Roseland*. Still not content to call it quits, she continued to show up sporadically, playing a Grandmother in *Heartland*; Jennifer Beals's dance mentor in the 1983 hit *Flashdance*; a therapist in *House of Games*; and a psychic in *Men of Respect*, a modern rethinking of *Macbeth*.
Screen: **1931:** Purpur und Waschblau/Purple and True Blue; **1936:** Madchenpensionat; Blumen aus Nizza/Flowers from Nice; **1937:** Die Unentschuldigte Stunde/The Unexcused Hour; **1953:** Call Me Madam; **1963:** Lilies of the Field; **1965:** Ship of Fools; **1967:** Caprice; **1968:** Charly; **1976:** Deadly Hero; **1977:** Roseland; **1980:** Heartland; **1982:** The End of August; **1983:** Flashdance; Testament; **1987:** House of Games; **1991:** Men of Respect.
NY Stage: **1941:** Letters to Lucerne; **1950:** With a Silk Thread; Call Me Madam; **1969:** Zelda; **1970:** 40 Carats; **1974:** Medea and Jason; **1981:** The Survivor.
Select TV: **1949:** Three-Cornered Moon (sp); **1952:** Claudia: The Story of a Marriage (series); **1954:** Woman With a Past (sp); **1955:** The King's Bounty (sp); **1957:** The Last Act (sp); **1962:** The Love of Claire Ambler (sp); **1965:** Who Has Seen the Wind? (sp); **1967:** Ironside; **1968:** Split Second to an Epitaph; The Sunshine Patriot; **1969–70:** Search for Tomorrow (series); **1972:** Probe; **1974:** The Guiding Light (series); **1976:** Eleanor and Franklin; **1979:** Sooner or Later.

RED SKELTON

(RICHARD BERNARD SKELTON)
BORN: VINCENNES, IN, JULY 18, 1913.
DIED: SEPTEMBER 17, 1997.

Always a baggy pants clown at heart, Red Skelton fidgeted and mugged, puffed out his cheeks and crossed his eyes, shook his mop of red hair into a wild disarray, and did just about anything for a laugh. As a child he performed in medicine and minstrel shows before entering burlesque. There he teamed up with Edna Stillwell for a comedic act and eventually married her. They toured vaudeville and, while engaged at New York's Paramount Theatre, Skelton was asked to enact some of his routines, including his dunking donut bit and "Guzzler's Gin," on Rudy Vallee's radio show, and he soon became a name in that medium. RKO asked to him to add some comical spark to a weak adaptation of the Broadway hit *Having a Wonderful Time*, where he played a camp counselor named Itchy, after which he and his wife wrote and produced a stage revue for themselves called *Paris in Swing*. A few short subjects were created to bring further attention to the comedian but it was his hosting of President Roosevelt's March of Dimes ceremonies that was instrumental in getting him a test with MGM. The studio signed him to a contract in 1940 and promptly put him into a serious movie, *Flight Command*, supporting Robert Taylor, and in the role of a dopey hospital orderly in two *Dr. Kildare* outings. After being used in a dreary musical, *Lady Be Good*, he got his own vehicle, *Whistling in the Dark*, a cornball combination of thrills and supposed laughs, in which he was a hammy radio actor trying to save his competing girlfriends from danger. It proved popular enough to rate a pair of sequels, *Whistling in Dixie*, and *Whistling in Brooklyn*. In the meantime, the studio liked the idea of plunking him in the middle of their musicals and did so with *Ship Ahoy*, where he was paired with Virginia O'Brien; and two clunky adaptations of Cole Porter stage hits, *Panama Hattie*, and *DuBarry Was a Lady*, the latter marking the first time the public got to see his striking red hair in Technicolor.

During this time Skelton had become enormously successful on radio, so MGM was more than glad to have him around. *I Dood It* was notable only because it boasted Vincente Minnelli as its director, while *Bathing Beauty* was the first that he did with Esther Williams. In the all-star omnibus *Ziegfeld Follies*, he was given a chance to preserve his "Guzzler's Gin" routine on film, playing an advertising picth-man getting drunk on his own product, then did two so-so remakes of properties that had been around for sometime, *The Show-Off*, and *Metron of the Movies*. Columbia borrowed him for *The Fuller Brush Man*, a film that turned out, ironically, to be a bigger hit than anything on his home lot. Soon afterwards he made a stale Civil War spoof, *A Southern Yankee*, and helped introduce the Oscar-winning song, "Baby, It's Cold Outside," in *Neptune's Daughter*. Toning down his shtick a notch, he paired up with Fred Astaire to play tunesmiths Bert Kalmar and Harry Ruby in one of the more enjoyable composer biopics, *Three Little Words*, then did another out-and-out musical, *Excuse My Dust*, a period piece about the horseless carriage. He provided some frenetic comedy relief for Howard Keel in *Texas Carnival* and *Lovely to Look At*, then tried to show his serious side in two insignificant films, *The Clown*, a re-do of *The Champ*, with Skelton portraying a drunk, and *Half a Hero*, as a magazine writer in suburbia. By this point he had begun his weekly television variety series, *The Red Skelton Show*, which would go on to become one of the longest-running programs in the history of that medium (it brought him three Emmy Awards). There was little reason to keep doing theatrical films when the small screen was proving so lucrative and by the 1960s he confined himself to cameos in *Ocean's Eleven*, as himself, and *Those Magnificent Men in Their Flying Machines*, pantomiming the history of flight. After his show went off the air in the early 1970s, he performed his act in nightclubs and in Las Vegas until changing tastes told him it was time to wipe off the greasepaint and call it a day.
Screen: **1938:** Having Wonderful Time; **1940:** Flight Command;

1941: The People vs. Dr. Kildare; Lady Be Good; Whistling in the Dark; Dr. Kildare's Wedding Day; 1942: Ship Ahoy; Maisie Gets Her Man; Panama Hattie; Whistling in Dixie; 1943: DuBarry Was a Lady; I Dood It; Whistling in Brooklyn; Thousands Cheer; 1944: Bathing Beauty; 1946: Ziegfeld Follies; The Show-Off; 1947: Merton of the Movies; 1948: The Fuller Brush Man; A Southern Yankee; 1949: Neptune's Daughter; 1950: The Yellow Cab Man; The Fuller Brush Girl; Three Little Words; Duchess of Idaho; Watch the Birdie; 1951: Excuse My Dust; Texas Carnival; 1952: Lovely to Look At; 1953: The Clown; Half a Hero; The Great Diamond Robbery; 1954: Susan Slept Here; 1956: Around the World in Eighty Days; 1957: Public Pigeon No. 1; 1960: Ocean's Eleven; 1965: Those Magnificent Men in Their Flying Machines or How I Flew From London to Paris in 25 Hours 11 Minutes.

Select TV: 1951–71: The Red Skelton Show (series); 1956: The Big Slide (sp); 1960: The Man in the Funny Suit (sp).

ALISON SKIPWORTH

(ALISON MARY ELLIOTT MARGARET GROOM)
BORN: LONDON, ENGLAND, JULY 25, 1863.
DIED: JULY 5, 1952.

Wittily sardonic, cartoonishly misshapen and gloriously adept at the fine art of comedy, Alison Skipworth was one of the many gems on Paramount's talent roster in the early 1930s, a woman who usually played nobody's fool. She held her own against the likes of Mae West and Bette Davis and was, hands down, the best foil W.C. Fields ever had. In her younger years she worked as a model before making her 1894 London stage debut in *The Gaiety Girl*. A year later she was first seen on Broadway in the operetta *An Artist's Model*, and decided to make New York her home, appearing there in several shows, including *39 East*. She repeated her role in the 1920 film version, which also marked her first excursion into motion pictures. There was one other silent film credit but, for the most part, she confined her acting interests to the theater throughout the 1920s, her most notable credits being *The Torch Bearers* and *The Swan*. Once talking pictures were firmly established, MGM summoned her to appear in an adaptation of Somerset Maugham's *The Circle*, retitled *Strictly Unconventional*, and, despite its box-office failure, this started her official movie career rolling, at the age of 67. For Samuel Goldwyn she was a rich lady duped by the charming Ronald Colman in *Raffles*, and was another woman of wealth, albeit a dead one, in Warners's stagy rendering of the supernatural theater hit, *Outward Bound*. There seemed to be no lack of offers from various studios and producers, and the one she accept was a long-term contract with Paramount, in 1932, after pleasing them with her performance as Nancy Carroll's impoverished Countess mom in *Night Angel*.

For her follow-up she played Carole Lombard's mother in *Sinners in the Sun*, and then had no problem stealing the show from George Raft while playing the title role of *Madame Racketeer*, which pretty much set the standard for the lovable, "con artist" type that audiences would associate with her. It was Raft who asked for her again, for *Night After Night*, and this time she got to swap dialogue with Mae West in that great lady's very first film. From that peak she went even higher, being cast alongside W.C. Fields for one of the best segments of the episodic *If I Had a Million*, helping him run roadhogs off the highways. They were an inspired team and would come together again most memorably for *Tillie and Gus*, as the Winterbottoms, as cheeky a pair of con artists to ever grace the screen. The two also showed up in the latter half of *Six of a Kind*, the other four being two other magical couples, George Burns and Gracie Allen, and

Charlie Ruggles and Mary Boland. In the meantime, Skipworth was mean to Marlene Dietrich in *Song of Songs*; portrayed royalty gone bankrupt in *A Lady's Profession*, playing a character most amusingly named Lady Beulah Bonnell of Twicket on Topping; was up to her con tricks, trying to get some cash from Stuart Erwin in *He Learned About Women*; and was a good choice to play the Duchess in the star-filled costume party, *Alice in Wonderland*. Elsewhere she reprised her *Torch Bearers* role in a quickly forgotten adaptation, retitled *Doubting Thomas*; had one priceless scene as Miriam Hopkins's disagreeable employer in the first official Technicolor film, *Becky Sharp*; waited on selfish Bette Davis in *Dangerous*; and was the equivalent of the Sidney Greenstreet role in *Satan Met a Lady*, later remade, and vastly improved upon, as *The Maltese Falcon*. After Paramount, she did a few more films, including top-billed parts for Republic that paired her with Polly Moran, in *Two Wise Maids*, as a schoolteacher nicknamed "Old Lady Ironsides," and *Ladies in Distress*, where she played a small-town mayor opposing a gang of racketeers. Following the latter, she returned to the theater before retiring in 1942.

Screen: 1920: 39 East; 1921: Handcuffs or Kisses; 1930: Strictly Unconventional; Raffles; DuBarry — Woman of Passion; Outward Bound; Oh for a Man!; 1931: The Virtuous Husband; Night Angel; The Road to Singapore; Devotion; Tonight or Never; 1932: High Pressure; Unexpected Father; Sinners in the Sun; Madame Racketeer; Night After Night; If I Had a Million; 1933: Tonight is Ours; A Lady's Profession; He Learned About Women; Midnight Club; Song of Songs; Tillie and Gus; Alice in Wonderland; 1934: Coming Out Party; Six of a Kind; Wharf Angel; Shoot the Works; The Notorious Sophie Lang; Here Is My Heart; The Captain Hates the Sea; 1935: The Casino Murder Case; Doubting Thomas; The Devil Is a Woman; Becky Sharp; The Girl from Tenth Avenue; Shanghai; Dangerous; Hitch-Hike Lady; 1936: Stolen Holiday; The Princess Comes Across; Satan Met a Lady; Two in a Crowd; The Gorgeous Hussy; White Hunter; 1937: Two Wise Maids; 1938: King of the Newsboys; Wide Open Faces; Ladies in Distress.

NY Stage: 1895: An Artist's Model; 1900: The Interrupted Honeymoon; The Man of Forty; 1901: The Way of the World; 1903: The Princess and the Butterfly; The Frisky Mrs. Johnson; Captain Dieppe; 1904: Man's Proposes; 1906: Cymbeline; 1908: The Prisoner Of Zenda; 1910: Suzanne; 1913: The Old Firm; The Marriage Game; 1916: Major Pendennis; 1917: L'Elevation; 1918: The Woman on the Index; Betty at Bay; 1919: 39 East; 1921: Lilies of the Field; 1922: The Torch Bearers; 1923: The Swan; 1925: The Enchanted April; The Grand Duchess and the Waiter; 1926: Port O'London; Ashes of Love; Buy Buy Baby; New York Exchange; 1927: Julie; Garden Of Eden; Spellbound; Los Angeles; 1928: Mrs. Dane's Defense; Say When; Angela; 1929: Cafe de Danse; Button Button; A Prime for Lovers; 1930: Marseilles; 1938: Thirty Days Hath September; 1939: When We Were Married; 1941: First Stop To Heaven.

WALTER SLEZAK

BORN: VIENNA, AUSTRIA, MAY 3, 1902.
ED: UNIV. OF VIENNA. DIED: APRIL 21, 1983.

A character actor who could never be accused of blending into the background, Walter Slezak was very distinctly upfront with his corpulent figure, bushy hair and mustache, shifty eyes, and high-pitched, sneering voice. He was a magnificently oily bad guy but also possessed a jolly, Old Country warmth, qualities that were put to better use in the theater, as were his relatively unknown talents as a singer. He had in fact been sired by a noted opera star, Leo Slezak, but initially chose a career in banking. It wasn't long before he changed his mind and began acting onstage and in films, starting with *Sodom and Gomorrah*, in 1921. By 1932, he had added more than 20 German films to his résumé and had even dropped by America, in 1930, to appear on the Broadway stage in a play called *Meet My Sister*. Wisely anticipating the oncoming trouble in Europe, he returned to New York for *Music in the Air*, and chose to stay there. He remained in American theater for the next decade until World War II broke out and Hollywood, in need of menacing Germans, came calling, with RKO casting him as the unctuous baron/Nazi agent who persuades a reluctant Ginger Rogers to marry him, in *Once Upon a Honeymoon*, a curiously unsatisfying blend of comedy and drama. Nonetheless, Slezak proved himself a most forceful screen presence and was back for two more anti-Nazi pieces for the studio, in both cases sporting a handicap to emphasize the character's moral perversity, *This Land Is Mine*, with a fake arm, and *The Fallen Sparrow*, with a limp. He joined the ensemble for director Alfred Hitchcock's unforgettable *Lifeboat*, as the German who seems to have the upper hand, believing he is rowing the other characters to their doom, in what is probably his most famous screen role.

Very much in demand, he was the harassed hotel manager in *Step Lively*; went to Goldwyn for *The Princess and the Pirate*, as the pompous governor who invites Bob Hope to join him in a bath; played the wealthy Russian who builds an opera house for Yvonne De Carlo in *Salome, Where She Danced*; battled heroic Paul Henreid in the Technicolor pirate film *The Spanish Main*; and was sinister in a similar setting, playing a barber aboard Douglas Fairbanks, Jr.'s ship in *Sinbad the Sailor*. No doubt at home in piratical territory, he was the fellow Judy Garland was set to marry in the MGM musical *The Pirate*, thereby playing the title character. He was then called on to play straight man to some comedians and did so most memorably in *The Inspector General*, as the unscrupulous traveling con artist who exploits Danny Kaye, after which he was cast opposite Red Skelton in *The Yellow Cab Man*, and Bud and Lou in *Abbott and Costello in the Foreign Legion*. Perhaps it was playing opposite a monkey *and* Ronald Reagan, in *Bedtime for Bonzo*, or the fact that he was cast in yet another musical, *Call Me Madam*, and again not asked to sing, that made him return to Broadway, first for *My 3 Angels* (a role he later did on TV), and then, at last, a musical, *Fanny*. The latter turned out to be a great personal triumph for him, winning him a Tony Award. Back in the movies, he was the keeper of Rock Hudson's Italian villa in *Come September*, and got top billing as the main crook in Disney's remake of *Emil and the Detectives*. By the early 1970s he had retired and ended his own life a decade later following a series of illnesses. His daughter, Erika, became one of the long-running daytime serial players via her role on *One Life to Live*. In 1962, he published his autobiography, *What Time's the Next Swan?*

Screen (US releases only): 1942: Once Upon a Honeymoon; 1943: This Land Is Mine; The Fallen Sparrow; 1944: Lifeboat; Till We Meet Again; Step Lively; The Princess and the Pirate; 1945: Salome, Where She Danced; The Spanish Main; Cornered; 1947: Sinbad the Sailor; Born to Kill; Riffraff; 1948: The Pirate; 1949: The Inspector General; 1950: The Yellow Cab Man; Spy Hunt; Abbott and Costello in the Foreign Legion; 1951: Bedtime for Bonzo; People Will Talk; 1953: Call Me Madam; Confidentially Connie; White Witch Doctor; 1954: The Steel Cage; 1957: Ten Thousand Bedrooms; 1959: The Miracle; 1961: Come September; 1962: The Wonderful World of the Brothers Grimm; 1964: Wonderful Life/Swingers' Paradise; Emil and the

Detectives; 1965: A Very Special Favor; 24 Hours to Kill; 1966: Copelius; 1967: The Caper of the Golden Bulls; 1971: Black Beauty; Treasure Island; 1976: The Mysterious House of Dr. Copelius (filmed 1972).

NY Stage: 1930: Meet My Sister; 1932: Music In The Air; 1934: Ode To Liberty; 1936: May Wine; 1938: I Married an Angel; 1941: The Trojan Women; Little Dark House; 1953: My 3 Angels; 1954: Fanny; 1957: The First Gentleman; 1958: The Gazebo.

Select TV: 1951: Collector's Item (sp); Dr. Anonymous (sp); The Innocence of Pastor Muller (sp); 1954: Papa Is All (sp); 1956: The Good Fairy (sp); Portrait of a Citizen (sp); This Is Show Business (series); 1957: The Best Wine (sp); Pinocchio (sp); 1958: The Gentleman from Seventh Avenue (sp); Beaver Patrol (sp); The Public Prosecutor (sp); 1959: The Slightly Fallen Angel (sp); My Three Angels (sp); 1960–61: The Sunday Mystery Hour (series); 1963: A Cry of Angels (sp); 1968: Legend of Robin Hood (sp); Heidi (sp).

EVERETT SLOANE

BORN: NEW YORK, NY, OCTOBER 1, 1909. ED: UNIV. OF PA. DIED: AUGUST 6, 1965.

Small in stature, with hawk-like features and a direct manner, Everett Sloane was doing college dramatics when a chance meeting with the owner of Philadelphia's Hedgerow Theatre encouraged him to quit school and act full-time. Although there were some New York stage credits, including *Boy Meets Girl*, his principle employment came from radio where he was best known for playing Sammy on *The Goldbergs* for many years. During that time he met Orson Welles, who invited Sloane to join him in Hollywood for his much heralded project *Citizen Kane*, where he was cast as Bernstein, the one friend of Kane's who stays loyal as that man's power and ego increase. Aging believably from opportunistic youth to wizened old man, he was just as good as the rest of this stellar cast and would be remembered for this part above all others. He returned to radio and theater after that, although Welles would utilize him again, most brilliantly in *Lady from Shanghai*, as the wealthy, crippled, and jealous husband of Rita Hayworth, memorably addressing her as "lover" with venom in his voice. The rest of Hollywood finally caught on to him and he was seen as Marlon Brando's doctor in *The Men*; the head of Murder, Inc. in *The Enforcer*; the district attorney who sides with Jane Wyman when she's accused of kidnapping, in *The Blue Veil*; Tony Curtis's foster dad in *The Prince Who Was a Thief*, a costume adventure and a genre he looked particularly out-of-place in; and a slithery Hollywood agent in *The Big Knife*. For his hard work he was rewarded with a pair of terrific roles, as the ruthless corporate executive in the intelligent *Patterns* (which he'd done on television), and as Paul Newman's fight manager in one of the better biopics, *Somebody Up There Likes Me*. Director Vincente Minnelli cast him in two prestigious MGM projects, *Lust for Life*, as the doctor who aides Van Gogh in his final days; and *Home from the Hill*, as Luana Patten's dad. By the 1960s Sloane was reduced to supporting Lana Turner, in *By Love Possessed*, and Jerry Lewis in both *The Patsy* and *The Disorderly Orderly*. Distressed at the realization that he was going blind, he took his own life, as his own father had done decades earlier.

Screen: 1941: Citizen Kane; 1942: Journey Into Fear; 1948: Lady From Shanghai; 1949: Prince of Foxes; 1950: The Men; 1951: Bird of Paradise; The Enforcer; Sirocco; The Prince Who Was a Thief; The Blue Veil; The Desert Fox; 1952: The Sellout; Way of a Gaucho; 1955: The Big Knife; 1956: Patterns; Somebody Up There Likes Me; Lust for Life; 1958: Marjorie Morningstar; The Gun

Runners; 1960: Home From the Hill; 1961: By Love Possessed; 1962: Brushfire!; 1963: The Man From the Diner's Club; 1964: The Patsy; Ready for the People; The Disorderly Orderly.

NY Stage: 1929: Playing With Love; 1935: Boy Meets Girl; 1941: A Bell For Adano; 1947: How I Wonder; 1953: Room Service; 1954: Black-Eyed Susan.

Select TV: 1950: Vincent Van Gogh (sp); Semmelweis (sp); 1951: Perspective (sp); 1953: Mark of Caine (sp); A Breath of Air (sp); Flowers From a Stranger (sp); Man Versus Town (sp); 1954: The Secret Self (sp); 1955: Patterns (sp); The Silent Woman (sp); The Emperor Jones (sp); The King's Bounty (sp); 1956: High Tor (sp); Noon on Doomsday (sp); President (sp); Flying Object at Three O'Clock (sp); Rachel (sp); Massacre at Sand Creek (sp); 1957: Night Drive (sp); Exclusive (sp); The Customs of the Country (sp); Official Detective (series); Success! (sp); 1958: Man on a Rack (sp); 1958: The Strong Man (sp); 1959: Hitler's Secret (sp); The Sounds of Eden (sp); 1960: Alas Babylon (sp); 1961: The Million Dollar Incident (sp); The Dick Tracy Show (series; voice); 1962: The Wall Between (sp); The Problem in Cell 13 (sp).

ALEXIS SMITH

(MARGARET ALEXIS FITZSIMMONS SMITH) BORN: PENTICTON, BRITISH COLUMBIA, CANADA, JUNE 8, 1921. RAISED IN LOS ANGELES, CA. ED: LOS ANGELES CITY COL. DIED: JUNE 9, 1993.

Maturity was the best thing to happen to Alexis Smith, who started out as a rather glossy and superficial addition to the Warners roster in the 1940s, then began showing increasing signs of depth with each passing year. She grew up in Los Angeles, where she attended Hollywood High School, and landed her first professional job, performing ballet at the Hollywood Bowl when she was 13. It was while acting in a college production of *The Night of January 16th* that she was spotted by some talent agents who offered her a contract with Warner Bros. in 1940. They started her off as window dressing in a few films before allowing her to play the female lead in the "B" mystery-comedy, *The Smiling Ghost* and in a Technicolor Errol Flynn vehicle, *Dive Bomber!*, which was significant for her only because the supporting cast featured Craig Stevens. Stevens would be cast as her leading man in *Steel Against the Sky*, and the pair married in 1944, staying man and wife until Smith's death. She was lucky to get into another, better Flynn film, *Gentleman Jim*, then got her first major challenge, in *The Constant Nymph*, a curious bit of casting because the character was supposed to be much older than she actually was. In any case she was deeply unsympathetic as the wealthy lady who can't abide husband Charles Boyer's devotion to free spirited Joan Fontaine. Comedy-wise, she took a backseat to Eve Arden in *The Doughgirls*, and to Jack Benny and the rest of the cast in *The Horn Blows at Midnight*, in which she played an angel. There were unsympathetic parts in two of Humphrey Bogart's misfires, *Conflict* and *The Two Mrs. Carrolls*, in both cases being the reason Bogie plotted to dispose of his wife, though, frankly, she hardly seemed worth the trouble. Going the biopic route, she did the loyal wife/girlfriend bit in *The Adventures of Mark Twain*, *Rhapsody in Blue*, and *Night and Day*, at her most facile in the last, as the wife of composer Cole Porter.

There was another film with Flynn, the poor *San Antonio*; a badly received remake of Of *Human Bondage*, in which she starred as the writer, the part originally played by Kay Johnson in the better 1934 version; and an equally un-called for re-do of *The Animal Kingdom*, retitled *One More Tomorrow*, with Smith starring in the Myrna Loy role. She did a horse picture with Ronald Reagan, *Stallion Road*; got top billing in *The Woman in White*,

though Eleanor Parker had the more challenging role; and was the mom on the verge of divorce in a softened version of Moss Hart's play *The Decision of Christopher Blake*. She was cast as the unhappy wife of Zachary Scott in both *Whiplash* and *One Last Fling*, then finished her Warners contract almost exactly where she started, opposite Errol Flynn, in *Montana*, which did not duplicate the box-office successes of their earlier teamings. Universal threw her some parts, including a juicy one as a narcotics cop infiltrating a gang of drug traffickers, in *Undercover Girl*. Over at Paramount she was merely "the other woman" in Bing Crosby's *Here Comes the Groom*, where Jane Wyman was clearly the more appealing choice. A British picture, *The Sleeping Tiger*, allowed her to go nuts for the climax, then she was back in bio-wife mode for *The Eternal Sea*, in which she portrayed Admiral John Hopkins's distaff half, and *Beau James*, as New York City mayor Jimmy Walker's misses. There was definite progress in her work and it showed, particularly in her performance as the married woman who gets the hots for Paul Newman in *The Young Philadelphians*. Afterwards, she concentrated on theater and finally made it to Broadway in a big way, winning a Tony Award for the acclaimed Stephen Sondheim musical, *Follies*. Returning to the movies in 1975, she did an eye-opening lesbian scene with Melina Mercouri in *Once Is Not Enough*, and played a wealthy horse owner in the Walter Matthau vehicle *Casey's Shadow*. Clearly she had become a more relaxed and interesting presence than she'd been in her glamour years, but her appearances were few. In *Tough Guys*, she was romanced by ex-con Burt Lancaster, and was seen fleetingly as a New York socialite in *The Age of Innocence*, released posthumously.

Screen: 1940: The Lady With Red Hair; She Couldn't Say No; 1941: Flight From Destiny; The Great Mr. Nobody; Passage From Hong Kong; Three Sons o'Guns; Singapore Woman; Affectionately Yours; The Smiling Ghost; Dive Bomber!; Steel Against the Sky; 1942: Gentleman Jim; 1943: The Constant Nymph; Thank Your Lucky Stars; 1944: The Adventures of Mark Twain; The Doughgirls; Hollywood Canteen; 1945: The Horn Blows at Midnight; Conflict; Rhapsody in Blue; San Antonio; 1946: One More Tomorrow; Of Human Bondage; Night and Day; 1947: Stallion Road; The Two Mrs. Carrolls; 1948: Always Together; The Woman in White; The Decision of Christopher Blake; Whiplash; 1949: South of St. Louis; One Last Fling; Any Number Can Play; 1950: Montana; Wyoming Mail; Undercover Girl; 1951: Here Comes the Groom; Cave of the Outlaws; 1952: The Turning Point; 1953: Split Second; 1954: The Sleeping Tiger; 1955: The Eternal Sea; 1957: Beau James; 1958: This Happy Feeling; 1959: The Young Philadelphians; 1975: Once Is Not Enough; 1977: The Little Girl Who Lives Down the Lane; 1978: Casey's Shadow; 1982: La Truitte/The Trout; 1986: Tough Guys; 1993: The Age of Innocence.

NY Stage: 1971: Follies; 1973: The Women; 1975: Summer Brave; 1978: Platinum.

Select TV: 1955: The Back of Beyond (sp); To Kill a Man (sp); 1956: September Affair (sp); The Gay Sisters (sp); 1958: I Shot a Prowler (sp); 1959: The Last Autumn (sp); 1984, 1990: Dallas (series); 1985: A Death in California; 1986: Dress Gray; 1988: Hothouse (series); Marcus Welby M.D.: A Holiday Affair.

C. AUBREY SMITH

(CHARLES AUBREY SMITH) BORN: LONDON, ENGLAND, JULY 21, 1863. ED: CAMBRIDGE. DIED: DECEMBER 20, 1948.

Was there anyone as unmistakably British or as eternally old as C. Aubrey Smith? This long-faced, bushy-browed thespian came to embody Hollywood's idea of the old guard resilience of the Empire, first hiring him at the ripe old age of 68. A one-time member of the national cricket team, he began acting onstage in 1893 and then came to Broadway three years later. His film debut was in an American production, *Builder of Bridges*, in 1915, and he continued to do movies between stage assignments, though mainly in England, during the silent era. At the start of the 1930s he traveled to Hollywood where MGM asked him to repeat his stage part in their 1931 adaptation of *The Bachelor Father*, in which he played a lonely old aristocrat who seeks out his three illegitimate children. They also had him play Leslie Howard's dad in *Never the Twain Shall Meet*; a doctor in *Son of India*; Robert Montgomery's old man in *The Man in Possession*; and Maureen O'Sullivan's father, James Parker, who goes searching for the elephant's graveyard, in *Tarzan the Ape Man*, the popular adventure that led to the long-running series. The rest of the film industry wanted to utilize this actor who could so marvelously evoke the spirit of England with the simple puff of a pipe. His career quickly sprouted and he became one of the most ubiquitous of all character players over the next two decades. Paramount, perhaps figuring that French and British roles were interchangeable, cast him as the wealthy Duke d'Artelines and allowed him to join in the song "The Son of a Gun Is Nothing But a Tailor," in the magical musical *Love Me Tonight*, and also made him the corrupt chairman of Kay Francis's perfume company in *Trouble in Paradise*. Over at RKO he had a most winning role, as the old actor who is charmed by young stage hopeful Katharine Hepburn, in *Morning Glory*. At MGM he played Franchot Tone's snobbish dad in *Bombshell*; Greta Garbo's servant in *Queen Christina*; and then wen to Fox to portray the Duke of Wellington in the successful historical piece *The House of Rothschild*.

There were some leads along the way, notably the 1934 version of the famed horror tale *The Monkey's Paw*, as the old codger who brings the destructive item into a young couple's household, and the Majestic Pictures's "B" picture, *Curtain at Eight*, as a kindly detective. However, it was in support that he was best remembered and he continued to appear in some of the major pictures of their day, including *Cleopatra*, as a Roman general; *The Gilded Lily*, as Ray Milland's father; *The Lives of a Bengal Lancer*, as the British major who sagely gives orders in Colonial India (exactly the sort of role that one immediately equates Smith with); *The Crusades*, as a hermit; *Little Lord Fauntleroy*, in perhaps his finest hour on film, as Freddie Bartholomew's disagreeable grandfather who begins to soften up because of the young lad's kindness; *The Garden of Allah*, as a priest; *Romeo and Juliet*, as Lord Capulet; *Wee Willie Winkie*, which put him back in uniform, in India; *The Prisoner of Zenda*, as Colonel Zapt; *The Hurricane*, as the island priest whose praying proves ineffectual against the raging winds; and *Kidnapped*, as the Duke of Argyle. He returned to England to reprise his Duke of Wellington role for *Sixty Glorious Years*, and for the 1939 version of *The Four Feathers*, as the doddering General Burroughs. Despite the fact that he was losing his hearing and approaching 80, there was no let up on work back in Hollywood. He was murdered in *Another Thin Man*; died in the jungles after a plane crash in *Five Came Back*; reprised Henry Stephenson's role of the family doctor in the remake of *A Bill of Divorce*; had a small part as a colonel visiting Manderlay in the Oscar-winning *Rebecca*; was Robert Taylor's father in the remake of *Waterloo Bridge*; had another fairly large role, as the wealthy fellow who returns as a ghost to guide a pair of lovers, in *Beyond Tomorrow*; and was seen fleetingly, as a bishop in the 1941 version of *Dr. Jekyll & Mr. Hyde*. Having been officially knighted in 1944, "Sir" C. Aubrey Smith chose to finish off his career in his adapted homeland of America (with the exception of his penulti-

mate credit, *An Ideal Husband*), where his later parts included the title role in Republic's *Scotland Yard Inspector*; a character who gets bumped off in the classic murder mystery, *And Then There Were None*; and Mr. Lawrence in the 1949 remake of *Little Women*, which was released posthumously.

Screen: 1915: Builder of Bridges; John Glayde's Honor; 1916: Jaffrey; The Witching Hour; 1918: Red Pottage; 1920: The Face at the Window; Castles in Spain; The Shuttle of Life; 1922: Flames of Passion; The Bohemian Girl; 1923: The Temptation of Carlton Earle; 1924: The Unwanted; The Rejected Woman; 1930: The Perfect Alibi/Birds of Prey; Such Is the Law; 1931: Contraband Love; Trader Horn; The Bachelor Father; Dancing Partner; Never the Twain Shall Meet; Just a Gigolo; The Man in Possession; Guilty Hands; Daybreak; Son of India; Surrender; Phantom of Paris; 1932: Polly of the Circus; Tarzan the Ape Man; But the Flesh Is Weak; Love Me Tonight; No More Orchids; Trouble in Paradise; The Monkey's Paw; 1933: They Just Had to Get Married; The Barbarian; Adorable; Luxury Liner; Secrets; Morning Glory; Bombshell; Queen Christina; 1934: The House of Rothschild; Bulldog Drummond Strikes Back; One More River; The Scarlet Empress; Cleopatra; We Live Again; Caravan; Curtain at Eight; The Firebird; Gambling Lady; 1935: The Gilded Lily; The Right to Live; Clive of India; The Crusades; The Lives of a Bengal Lancer; The Florentine Dagger; China Seas; Jalna; Transatlantic Tunnel/The Tunnel; 1936: Little Lord Fauntleroy; The Garden of Allah; Romeo and Juliet; Lloyd's of London; 1937: Wee Willie Winkie; The Prisoner of Zenda; The Hurricane; Thoroughbreds Don't Cry; 1938: Four Men and a Prayer; Sixty Glorious Years/Queen of Destiny; Kidnapped; 1939: East Side of Heaven; The Sun Never Sets; The Under-Pup; The Four Feathers; Five Came Back; Eternally Yours; Another Thin Man; Balalaika; 1940: A Bill of Divorcement; City of Chance; Beyond Tomorrow; Rebecca; Waterloo Bridge; A Little Bit of Heaven; 1941: Maisie Was a Lady; Free and Easy; Dr. Jekyll & Mr. Hyde; 1943: Forever and a Day; Two Tickets to London; Madame Currie; Flesh and Fantasy; 1944: The White Cliffs of Dover; Secrets of Scotland Yard; The Adventures of Mark Twain; Sensations of 1945; 1945: They Shall Have Faith/Forever Yours; Scotland Yard Investigator; And Then There Were None; 1946: Rendezvous with Annie; Cluny Brown; 1947: High Conquest; Unconquered; 1948: An Ideal Husband; 1949: Little Women.

NY Stage: 1896: The Notorious Mrs. Ebbsmith; 1903: The Light That Failed; 1904: Hamlet; 1907: The Morals of Marcus; 1911: The Runaway; 1914: The Legend of Leonora; Evidence; The Lie; 1923: Mary, Mary, Quite Contrary; 1926: The Constant Wife; 1928: The Bachelor Father; 1941: Spring Again.

KENT SMITH

(FRANK KENT SMITH) BORN: NEW YORK, NY, MARCH 19, 1907. ED: HARVARD UNIV. DIED: APRIL 23, 1985.

Because his method was soft, cerebral, and unobtrusive, it would be safe to say that Kent Smith was not a name that caused ripples of excitement at its mere mention. He'd acted with the University Players, Maryland Theatre in Baltimore and with a Washington D.C. children's theater, before his professional break in the play *Blind Window*, which opened and closed in Baltimore in 1929. Three years later he arrived on Broadway for *Men Must Fight*; had notable success in a supporting part in *Dodsworth*; joined Catherine Cornell's group; and did a sole film appearance, in MGM's *The Garden Murder Case*, as Virginia Bruce's lover. After several other Broadway and regional credits, he was offered a contract by RKO who introduced him in two low-budgeted entries that wound up being surprise hits: *Cat People*, in which he played the husband of the mysterious half-feline Simone Simon; and *Hitler's Children*, a trashy anti-Nazi opus. Prior to joining the Air Force, he was one of the few American-born stars of the all-star British salute *Forever and a Day*; defiantly fought the Nazis in *This Land Is Mine*; and helped link *The Curse of the Cat People* with its predecessor, as a worried dad whose daughter is speaking with a ghost. Following the war he was in another popular, low-key thriller of the day, *The Spiral Staircase*, as the doctor attracted to mute Dorothy McGuire, and then, staying in the medical profession, went over to Warner Bros. for one of his best roles, as the physician who destroys his life for the love of thoughtless Ann Sheridan in *Nora Prentiss*. During the 1950s he became a familiar face on television and, after a period away from movies of doing mostly theater, he returned to the cinema as a grayer and older character actor in *Sayonara* and *Imitation General*, in both instances as a general. Continuing his run of silver-haired authority figures, he played a doctor in the soap opera, *Susan Slade*; the Secretary of the Air Force in Disney's *Moon Pilot*; a general in *The Balcony*; the Secretary of War in *A Distant Trumpet*; and a newspaper editor in *Death of a Gunfighter*. He also created some confusion by appearing in both *Games* and *The Games*. On television he was a regular on the nighttime soap *Petyon Place* and was called on, for nostalgia's sake, to be in *The Cat Creature*, another feline thriller.

Screen: 1936: The Garden Murder Case; 1942: Cat People; Hitler's Children; 1943: Forever and a Day; This Land Is Mine; 1944: Three Russian Girls; Youth Runs Wild; The Curse of the Cat People; 1946: The Spiral Staircase; 1947: Magic Town; The Voice of the Turtle; Nora Prentiss; 1948: Design for Death (narrator); 1949: My Foolish Heart; The Fountainhead; 1950: The Damned Don't Cry; This Side of the Law; 1952: Paula; 1956: Comanche; 1957: Sayonara; 1958: Imitation General; The Badlanders; Party Girl; The Mugger; 1959: This Earth Is Mine; 1960: Strangers When We Meet; 1961: Susan Slade; 1962: Moon Pilot; 1963: The Balcony; 1964: A Distant Trumpet; The Young Lovers; 1966: The Trouble With Angels; 1967: A Covenant With Death; Games; 1968: Kona Coast; The Money Jungle; 1969: Death of a Gunfighter; Assignment to Kill; 1970: The Games; 1972: Pete 'n' Tillie; 1973: Lost Horizon; Maurie; 1978: The Companion (filmed 1972).

NY Stage: 1932: Men Must Fight; 1933: Heat Lightning; Spring in Autumn; The Drums Begin; 1934: Dodsworth; 1936: Seen But Not Heard; 1937: Candida; The Star Wagon; 1938: How to Get Tough About It; 1939: Jeremiah; Christmas Eve; 1940: International Incident; Old Acquaintance; 1947: The Story of Mary Surratt; Antony and Cleopatra; 1950: The Wisteria Trees; Burning Bright; 1951: The Autumn Garden; Richard II; The Wild Duck; 1953: Charley's Aunt; 1954: What Every Woman Knows; 1955: Bus Stop; 1956: Saint Joan.

Select TV: 1950: The End Is Known (sp); 1951: Wayward Season (sp); 1952: Waterfront Boss (sp); The Sound of Waves Breaking (sp); The Jungle (sp); 1953–54: The Philip Morris Playhouse (series); 1954: King Richard II (sp); 1955: Dark Victory (sp); 1957: Slow Assassination (sp); Success! (sp); 1958: Last Town Car (sp); The Cause (sp); 1961: The Golden Acres (sp); 1964–67: Peyton Place (series); 1967–68: The Invaders (series); 1970: How Awful About Allan; 1971: The Last Child; 1972: The Night Stalker; Probe; Another Part of the Forest (sp); The Crooked Hearts; The Judge and Jake Wyler; The Snoop Sisters/Female Instinct; 1973: The Affair; The Cat Creature; 1974: Murder or Mercy; The Disappearance of Flight 412; 1976–77: Once an Eagle (ms).

ELKE SOMMER

(ELKE SCHLETZ) BORN: BERLIN, GERMANY, NOVEMBER 5, 1940.

Possessing just the right amount of none-too-serious sex appeal that the international market craved in the 1960s, Elke Sommer became a familiar face in commercial entertainments until age became her enemy. While at college, studying to be a diplomatic interpreter, somebody decided that her body held more lucrative possibilities than her verbal skills and she became a model, which eventually led to her 1958 debut, in the German film *Das Totenschiff*. This was followed by a whole slew of international films, German and otherwise, including the British *Why Bother to Knock?* American audiences first glimpsed her towards the end of the lengthy *The Victors*, as George Hamilton's girlfriend, who had been assaulted by the Russians, and, in a larger role, as a Swedish government official helping Paul Newman find Edward G. Robinson in *The Prize*. She got her best part, as the innocent girl who keeps winding up under arrest, in the funniest of all the Inspector Clouseau films, *A Shot in the Dark*, which was followed by the sort of frenetic comedies that gave the era a bad name, *The Art of Love*, as a suicidal girl who falls in love with Dick Van Dyke, and *Boy, Did I Get a Wrong Number!*, as an actress tired of taking bubble baths. In a more serious vein she was Glenn Ford's rich wife in *The Money Trap*, and Stephen Boyd's girl in *The Oscar*, which was funnier than most of her intended comedies. There was an amusing attempt to turn Bulldog Drummond into James Bond with *Deadlier Than the Male*, as a sexy assassin; the ghastly *The Wicked Dreams of Paula Schultz*, in which she pole vaulted over the Berlin wall while interacting with the cast principals from the TV series *Hogan's Heroes*; and the poorest of the Matt Helm romps, *The Wrecking Crew*. By the 1970s she was appearing in such horrors as England's penis transplant comedy, *Percy*, and *House of Exorcism*, in which she was terrorized in a creepy mansion by Telly Savalas and others. In her middle age, and afterwards, American audiences saw her mainly on television, if at all.

Screen (US releases only): 1963: The Victors; The Prize; 1964: Love the Italian Way (It: 1960); A Shot in the Dark; 1965: The Art of Love; Bambole/The Dolls; Why Bother to Knock? (UK: 1961); 1966: The Money Trap; The Oscar; Boy, Did I Get a Wrong Number!; 1967: The Venetian Affair; The Corrupt Ones; Deadlier Than the Male; 1968: The Wicked Dreams of Paula Schultz; The Invincible Six; 1969: The Wrecking Crew; They Came to Rob Las Vegas; 1971: Percy; Zeppelin; 1972: Baron Blood; 1975: Ten Little Indians; Carry on Behind (dtv); 1976: House of Exorcism/Lisa and the Devil; 1977: The Swiss Conspiracy; 1978: The Astral Factor/ Invisible Strangler; It's Not the Size That Counts/Percy's Progress (UK: 1975); 1979: The Treasure Seekers (dtv); The Prisoner of Zenda; The Double McGuffin; A Nightingale Sang in Berkeley Square/The Big Scam (dtv); 1985: Lily in Love; 1992: Severed Ties (dtv).

Select TV: 1972: Probe; 1979: Stunt Seven; 1980: The Top of the Hill; 1982: Inside the Third Reich (ms); 1985: Jenny's War; 1986: Peter the Great (ms) Anastasia: The Mystery of Anna; 1987: Adventures Beyond Belief.

GALE SONDERGAARD

(EDITH HOLM SONDERGAARD) BORN: LITCHFIELD, MN, FEBRUARY 15, 1899. ED: UNIV. OF MN. DIED: AUGUST 14, 1985.

Gale Sondergaard's characteristic sinister sneer made her one of the screen's most formidable bad women yet also lended an exotic touch to her no good creations. There was no telling how many more tasty roles she might have compiled onto an already rich list of credits had she not be one of the most noteworthy of all of filmdom's blacklist victims. Her dramatic studies at school led to a job with the John Kellard Shakespeare Touring Company, followed by work with various other stock groups. She came to New York in 1928 and got a part in the Theatre Guild's production of *Faust*, which featured Herbert J. Biberman. Two years later they married and, when Biberman was put under contract to direct and write films for Columbia Pictures, Sondergaard moved west with him, though with no acting offers or prospects of her own on the horizon. She auditioned for Mervyn LeRoy for a role in Warners's lavish costume epic, *Anthony Adverse*, and got the part. As the villainous housekeeper who conspires with the even more unctuous Claude Rains, she wound up making Academy Award history, becoming the very first winner in the newly establish Best Supporting Actress category, for what was, in reality, a rather ordinary performance. No matter, it made her a hot property and she wound up far surpassing her husband's career, which mostly consisted of scripting programmers. Following her prize-winning role, she played one of the hysterical citizens in *Maid of Salem*, and wound up with most of her part on the cutting room floor. She then appeared in the Oscar-winning Best Picture of 1937, *The Life of Emile Zola*, as the wife of falsely accused Joseph Schildkraut, probably her most sympathetic role ever.

Although she could be found in perfectly benign roles, as an aging French actress who teaches drama in *Dramatic School*, for instance, Hollywood liked her sense of icy mystery and cast her as a thief who corrupts Freddie Bartholomew in *Lord Jeff*; the cold Empress Eugenie in *Juarez*; and a spooky housekeeper in the Bob Hope comedy, *The Cat and the Canary*. In 1940, she had two contrasting roles, as Tylette the Cat, in the fantasy film *The Blue Bird*, in which she gave a perfectly ridiculous performance; and the Eurasian wife of the man murdered by Bette Davis in *The Letter*, in which she provided the necessary aura of doom. She was on the side of the Nazis, of course, in Bob Hope's *My Favorite Blonde*, and in the more serious *Appointment in Berlin*. After World War II she played one of her best-known roles, the title character in *The Spider Woman*. As the nemesis of Basil Rathbone's Sherlock Holmes her character and performance got such a favorable reception that Universal figured she could carry a "B" sequel without him. The resulting film, *The Spider Woman Strikes Back*, wasn't among the classier assignments of her career, any more than *A Night in Paradise* was, in which she played a wicked sorceress. In contrast she did get a good part in a grade "A" production, *Anna and the King of Siam*, receiving an Oscar nomination for her dignified work as Lady Thiang, the neglected "head wife" of egotistical ruler Rex Harrison. She was straight woman to Abbott and Costello in *The Time of Their Lives*, as a mysterious housekeeper, and to Crosby and Hope in *Road to Rio*, hypnotizing Dorothy Lamour to do her bidding. A few years later, her movie career was brought to a halt when she stood by her husband, whose stance against the House Un-American Activities got him blacklisted and labeled as one of the "Hollywood Ten." During this period of inactivity she developed and toured in a one-woman stage show before coming back to the cinema under her husband's direction, in *Slaves*, in 1969. Biberman passed away two years later and Sondergaard continued acting until her retirement (this time by choice) in the early 1980s.

Screen: 1936: Anthony Adverse; 1937: Maid of Salem; Seventh Heaven; The Life of Emile Zola; 1938: Lord Jeff; Dramatic School; 1939: Never Say Die; Juarez; The Cat and the Canary;

The Llano Kid; 1940: The Blue Bird; The Mark of Zorro; The Letter; 1941: The Black Cat; Paris Calling; 1942: My Favorite Blonde; Enemy Agents Meet Ellery Queen; 1943: A Night to Remember; Appointment in Berlin; Isle of Forgotten Sins; Crazy House; The Strange Death of Adolf Hitler; 1944: The Spider Woman; Follow the Boys; Christmas Holiday; The Invisible Man's Revenge; Gypsy Wildcat; The Climax; Enter Arsene Lupin; 1946: The Spider Woman Strikes Back; A Night in Paradise; Anna and the King of Siam; The Time of Their Lives; 1947: Pirates of Monterey; Road to Rio; 1949: East Side, West Side; 1969: Slaves; 1976: Hollywood Horror High/The Comeback/Savage Intruder (filmed 1968); Pleasantville; The Return of a Man Called Horse; Hollywood on Trial; 1983: Echoes (filmed 1980).

NY Stage: 1928: Faust; Major Barbara; Strange Interlude; 1929: Karl and Anna; Red Rust; 1933: American Dream; Doctor Monica; 1934: Invitation to a Murder; 1940: Cue for Passion; 1965: The Woman; 1967: Kicking The Castle Down; 1977: John Gabriel Boorkman; 1980: Goodbye, Fidel.

Select TV: 1970: The Best of Everything (series); 1973: The Cat Creature; 1976: Ryan's Hope (series); 1978: Centennial (ms).

ANN SOTHERN

(HARRIET ARLENE LAKE) BORN: VALLEY CITY, ND, JANUARY 22, 1909. ED: UNIV. OF WA. DIED: MARCH 15, 2001.

Because she was mainly relegated to "B" pictures in her golden days, there is a tendency to think that the studios under-appreciated Ann Sothern. It is hard to think, however, that she ever went completely unnoticed since she was not one to dissipate under the spotlight, often delivering wisecracks and a splash of color to pretty much anything that she appeared in. She spent her youth traveling with her mother, who was a concert singer. At the dawn of the talkies, her mother gave vocal lessons in Hollywood and Sothern was able to score some bit parts in films under her real name, including *The Show of Shows*, in a sister act sequence with sibling Marion Byron. Getting nowhere in the movies, she decided to try Broadway and ended up as the lead in *America's Sweetheart*, then toured in Gershwin's *Of Thee I Sing*. At this point Columbia decided to put her under contract, changed her name to "Ann Sothern," and starred her opposite Edmund Lowe in *Let's Fall in Love*, as a sideshow performer being groomed for legit stardom. Since the studio was doing little beyond putting her in "B" fare, she had no qualms about being loaned out elsewhere for some musicals: Goldwyn's *Kid Millions*, with Eddie Cantor; 20th Century-Fox's *Folies Bergère*, with Maurice Chevalier; and RKO's *Hooray for Love*, with Gene Raymond. Back on her home lot she carried another musical, *The Girl Friend*, which was notable because it paired her with actor Roger Pryor who became her first husband (1936–42). After *Don't Gamble With Love*, Columbia dropped her and she went to RKO who decided to make a team of Sothern and Gene Raymond and put them in *Walking on Air*, *The Smartest Girl in Town*, *There Goes My Girl*, and *She's Got Everything*, despite the fact that Sothern bore no love for her co-star.

In Walter Wanger's production for United Artists, *Trade Winds*, she was cast in her secondary role as Fredric March's wisecracking secretary and it was this film that did the trick for her. When all was said and done, it was Sothern that everyone was talking about and MGM consequently hired her for the title role of *Maisie*, in 1939. Playing the part of a brash vaudevillian stranded in a small town, she was very much in her element and the studio was so thrilled by the response that they went ahead with plans to make her character the star of a continuing series. There were eight more entries in all, taking Sothern up to *Undercover Maisie*, in 1947. During this period MGM also put her in some other comedies, including *Fast and Furious*, a light-hearted mystery in the style of the "Thin Man" movies, with Franchot Tone as her partner; *Dulcy*, in which she played a flake, reprising a role previously done by both Constance Talmadge and Marion Davies; and the memorably titled *Joe and Ethel Turp Call on the President*, with William Gargan as Joe. There were also some fairly lumbering musicals, like *Lady Be Good*, which was only notable in that she introduced the Academy Award-winning song "The Last Time I Saw Paris," and *Panama Hattie*, in which she took over Ethel Merman's role, though few numbers were retained from the Broadway original, "I've Still Got My Health" and "Let's Be Buddies" being exceptions. There was also an occasional chance to show her worth as a serious actress, most specifically in *Cry Havoc*, the studio's salute to wartime nurses, in which she played a former waitress who volunteers. MGM engaged her to sing "Where's That Rainbow?" in the Rodgers and Hart biopic *Words and Music*, and to play Jane Powell's mom in the old-fashioned *Nancy Goes to Rio*, but her stand-out film at this time was Fox's *A Letter to Three Wives*, in which she played a writer married to a younger man (Kirk Douglas).

The movies seemed to have little use for her during the 1950s, save for the murder mystery *The Blue Gardenia*, in which she supported Anne Baxter. She went to television, where she had a hit with the sitcom *Private Secretary*, and then *The Ann Sothern Show*. When she returned to motion pictures in 1964, in *The Best Man*, she was certainly heftier, but as watchable as ever, stealing scenes as an overbearing Washington hostess. This apparently helped remind producers of her abilities because she was soon making herself heard in supporting roles in *Lady in a Cage*, as a low-life allowing Olivia de Haviland to be tormented; *Sylvia*, as a drunk; and *Chubasco*, as a madam. In the 1970s she actually wound up with top billing in an intriguing psychological thriller, *The Killing Kind*, as a blowsy mama driving her smothered son, John Savage, to murder. This was followed by some other drive-in fare, like *Crazy Mama*, as Cloris Leachman's partner in crime, and *The Manitou*, about an killer Indian midget. On television she was asked to participate in the remake of *A Letter to Three Wives*, this time playing the mother of the character Linda Darnell had played in the original; then returned to the big screen for one last moment of triumph, as the neighbor courted by Vincent Price, in *The Whales of August*. Supporting the very fragile-looking team of Bette Davis and Lilian Gish, she provided the energy to this somber piece, as she had done countless times in the past, and finally got herself an Oscar nomination in tribute to her long career. Her second husband was actor Robert Sterling (1943–49) who had appeared with her in *Ringside Maisie*. Their daughter, Tisha Sterling, was also an actress.

Screen: AS HARRIET LAKE: 1927: Broadway Nights; 1929: Hearts in Exile; The Show of Shows; 1930: Hold Everything; Whoopee; Doughboys.

AS ANN SOTHERN: 1933: Let's Fall in Love; Broadway Thru a Keyhole; 1934: Melody in Spring; The Party's Over; The Hell-Cat; Blind Date; Kid Millions; 1935: Folies Bergère; Eight Bells; Hooray for Love; The Girl Friend; Grand Exit; 1936: You May Be Next; Hell-Ship Morgan; Don't Gamble with Love; My American Wife; Walking on Air; The Smartest Girl in Town; 1937: Dangerous Number; Fifty Roads to Town; There Goes My Girl; Super Sleuth; Danger — Love at Work; There Goes the Groom; 1938: She's Got Everything; Trade Winds; 1939: Maisie; Hotel for Women; Fast and Furious; Joe and Ethel Turp Call on the President; 1940: Congo Maisie; Brother Orchid; Gold Rush Maisie; Dulcy; 1941: Maisie Was a Lady; Ringside Maisie; Lady Be Good; 1942: Maisie Gets Her Man; Panama Hattie; 1943: Three Hearts for Julia; Swing Shift Maisie; Thousands Cheer; Cry Havoc; 1944: Maisie Goes to Reno; 1946: Up Goes Maisie; 1947: Undercover Maisie; 1948: April Showers; Words and Music; 1949: A Letter to Three Wives; The Judge Steps Out; 1950: Shadow on the Wall; Nancy Goes to Rio; 1953: The Blue Gardenia; 1964: The Best Man; Lady in a Cage; 1965: Sylvia; 1968: Chubasco; 1973: The Killing Kind; 1974: Golden Needles; 1975: Crazy Mama; 1978: The Manitou; 1980: The Little Dragons; 1987: The Whales of August.

NY Stage: AS HARRIETTE LAKE: 1930: Smiles; 1931: America's Sweetheart; Everybody's Welcome.

AS ANN SOTHERN: 1951: Faithfully Yours.

Select TV: 1952: Lady With a Will (sp); Let George Do It (sp); 1953–57: Private Secretary (series); 1957: With No Regrets (sp); Holiday in Las Vegas (sp); 1958–61: The Ann Sothern Show (series); 1965–66: My Mother the Car (series; voice); 1967: The Outsider; 1971: Congratulations It's a Boy!; A Death of Innocence; 1972: The Weekend Nun; 1973: The Great Man's Whiskers; 1976: Captains and the Kings (ms); 1985: A Letter to Three Wives.

NED SPARKS

(EDWARD ARTHUR SPARKMAN) BORN: GUELPH, ONTARIO, CANADA, NOVEMBER 19, 1883. DIED: APRIL 3, 1957.

If audiences didn't know the name of this gaunt, grouchy-looking actor they certainly knew his voice, best described as a monotonous whine of curmudgeonly disapproval, which became one of the most imitated in the business. Ned Sparks started out in Alaska, of all places (supposedly drawn there by the gold rush), singing southern tunes before he became a comedian on the vaudeville circuit. He switched to legit theater and then moved to Hollywood in 1915, where he was first seen on film in *Little Miss Brown*. Needless to say, without his voice his impact was minimal. It wasn't until talking pictures developed that audiences really began to take note of him in such films as *Nothing But the Truth*, in which he repeated his part from the stage; and *Street Girl*, cast as a jazz musician. From that point on the cigar-chomping sour puss could be seen putting some zing into such movies as *Corsair*, as a weasely bootlegger; *Gold Diggers of 1933*, as a Broadway producer; *Lady for a Day*, as Warren Williams's flunky, ironically named Happy McGuire; *Alice in Wonderland*, as the Caterpillar; *Going Hollywood*, as a movie director; *Hi, Nellie!*, as a reporter; *Servants' Entrance*, as the memorably named Hjalmar Gnu, a comic strip creator with writer's block; *Imitation of Life*, in one of his most likable roles, as the vagrant who becomes Claudette Colbert's business manager; *Down to Their Last Yacht*, as an inept captain; *Collegiate*, sharing the screen with the similarly sardonic Lynne Overman; *The Bride Walks Out*, making a perfect team with Helen Broderick; *Hawaii Calls*, in one of his larger roles, as a songwriter befriending cutesy Bobby Breen; and *The Star Maker*, as Bing Crosby's publicist. When the 1940s arrived he cut back his appearances considerably and, after appearing as James Stewart's sidekick in *Magic Town*, he retired.

Screen: 1915: Little Miss Brown; 1919: A Virtuous Vamp; The Social Pirate; Temperamental Wife; 1920: In Search of a Sinner; Nothing But the Truth; The Perfect Woman; Good References; 1922: A Wide Open Town; The Bond Boy; 1924: The Law Forbids; 1925: Bright Lights; His Supreme Moment; Faint

Perfume; The Boomerang; Seven Keys to Baldpate; The Only Thing; Soul Mates; 1926: The Hidden Way; Mike; Love's Blindness; The Auction Block; Oh What a Night; Money Talks; When the Wife's Away; 1927: Alias the Lone Wolf; The Secret Studio; Alias the Deacon; The Small Bachelor; 1928: The Magnificent Flirt; On to Reno; The Big Noise; 1929: Nothing But the Truth; The Canary Murder Case; Strange Cargo; Street Girl; 1930: Love Comes Along; The Fall Guy; Double Cross Roads; The Devil's Holiday; Conspiracy; Leathernecking; 1931: Iron Man; The Secret Call; Corsair; Kept Husbands; 1932: The Miracle Man; Big City Blues; Blessed Event; The Crusader; 1933: 42nd Street; Gold Diggers of 1933; Too Much Harmony; Lady for a Day; Going Hollywood; Secrets; Alice in Wonderland; 1934: Hi, Nellie!; Servants' Entrance; Private Scandal; Marie Galante; Imitation of Life; Sing and Like It; Down to Their Last Yacht; 1935: Sweet Adeline; Sweet Music; George White's 1935 Scandals; Collegiate; 1936: The Bride Walks Out; One in a Million; Two's Company; 1937: Wake Up and Live; This Way Please; 1938: Hawaii Calls; 1939: The Star Maker; 1941: For Beauty's Sake; 1943: Stage Door Canteen; 1947: Magic Town.

NY Stage: AS NED A. SPARKS: 1912: Little Miss Brown; 1914: The Charm of Isabel; Sylvia Runs Away; A Perfect Lady; The Show Shop; 1916: Nothing But the Truth; 1920: My Golden Girl; Jim Jam Jems; 1921: The All-Star Idlers of 1921.

ROBERT STACK

BORN: LOS ANGELES, CA, JANUARY 13, 1919.
ED: USC.

Who could have predicted that the pleasant, nice-looking, and somewhat stoic fellow who was called on to kiss one of America's darlings would still be around six decades later, when more tantalizing talents would have come and gone? Robert Stack had endurance to spare and became a genuine star, an award-winning thespian, and the sort of authoritative guy that one could trust. Raised in wealth, he was well traveled, a polo player, and a skeet champion when he decided to give acting a whirl, joining the Henry Duffy College of the Theatre. Spotted by a talent scout from Universal, he was given a plum assignment with which to make his motion picture bow, giving teenage singing sensation Deanna Durbin her first on-screen smooch in First Love, a charming Cinderella-like tale. This cinematic event produced headlines and made him instantly famous in the fan magazines. Signed to a contract by the studio, he was promptly lent out to MGM, to play Frank Morgan's Nazi son, in The Mortal Storm, then came back to romance Durbin again in Nice Girl?, and Deanna-wannabe Gloria Jean in A Little Bit of Heaven. He was given top billing for the western Badlands of Dakota, in which he snatched Ann Rutherford away from brother Broderick Crawford, as well as for Universal's big war movie of 1942, Eagle Squadron, in which he played a Yank pilot who romances English girl Diana Barrymore. He was in military attire again, to play the soldier enamored with Carole Lombard, in the classic black comedy To Be or Not to Be, then put on a uniform for real when he joined the Navy. When he returned he was back in familiar territory, boyishly romancing young Jane Powell, in A Date With Judy, then showed unexpected spirit as a brash athlete in the Bing Crosby vehicle, Mr. Music. Playing nasty, he was the unlikely sibling of Mickey Rooney in My Outlaw Brother; was an arrogant American dabbling in the bloody and controversial sport in the acclaimed Bullfighter and the Lady; and was then involved in a movie milestone of sorts when he starred in a cheesy jungle adventure, Bwana Devil, which happened to be the first feature

shot and exhibited in 3-D and thereby a box-office hit.

This meant that he was assigned to some other routine adventures, including the westerns War Paint and Conquest of Cochise, and the aviation success The High and the Mighty, in which he played the captain who gets understandably nervous when his plane loses an engine. Nobody was too keen on such Stack offerings as House of Bamboo or Good Morning, Miss Dove, but he did some of his best work in the showy role of the selfish, drunken playboy who marries Lauren Bacall in the ultra-glossy soap opera, Written on the Wind, made for his old stomping ground, Universal. Superficial and well attended by fans, it earned Stack an Oscar nomination in the supporting category and helped revitalize his career. Hoping to cash in on this moneymaker, Universal put Stack back with two of his co-stars from that film, Dorothy Malone and Rock Hudson, for The Tarnished Angels, but nobody was fooled the second time around. John Paul Jones proved that he was one of the last actors you wanted to see in a ponytail but he and Malone did another one that worked, The Last Voyage, an exciting tale about a sinking ocean liner. Before that was released, Stack agreed to play real-life treasury agent Eliot Ness in what was to become one of the hottest and most famous crime dramas in television history, The Untouchables. It became his defining role and won him an Emmy Award. Following its run he worked in foreign films before settling back for more television work. He returned to movies showing a lighter, less uptight style, first in the overblown slapstick comedy 1941, as a general, and, more memorably, the smash hit parody Airplane!, as a clueless ex-flyer. He settled in for a long run as the host of the docu-series Unsolved Mysteries, while his latter-day movie credits included Uncommon Valor, as the father of a soldier missing in action, and Joe Versus the Volcano, as a doctor. In 1980 he published his autobiography, Straight Shooting.

Screen: 1939: First Love; 1940: The Mortal Storm; A Little Bit of Heaven; 1941: Nice Girl?; Badlands of Dakota; 1942: To Be or Not to Be; Eagle Squadron; Men of Texas; 1948: A Date With Judy; Miss Tatlock's Millions; Fighter Squadron; 1950: Mr. Music; 1951: My Outlaw Brother; Bullfighter and the Lady; 1952: Bwana Devil; 1953: War Paint; Conquest of Cochise; Sabre Jet; 1954: The High and the Mighty; The Iron Glove; 1955: House of Bamboo; Good Morning, Miss Dove; 1956: Great Day in the Morning; Written on the Wind; 1957: The Tarnished Angels; 1958: The Gift of Love; 1959: John Paul Jones; 1960: The Last Voyage; 1963: The Caretakers; 1966: Is Paris Burning?; 1967: The Corrupt Ones/The Peking Medallion; Le Soleil de Voyous/Action Man (nUSr); 1970: Story of a Woman; 1978: Un Second Souffle/A Second Wind (nUSr); 1979: 1941; 1980: Airplane!; 1983: Uncommon Valor; 1985: My Kingdom for … (nUSr); 1986: Big Trouble; The Transformers (voice); 1988: Plain Clothes; Dangerous Curves; Caddyshack II; 1990: Joe Versus the Volcano; 1996: Wild Bill: Hollywood Maverick; Beavis and Butthead Do America (voice); 1998: BASEketball; 1999: Mumford; 2001: Killer Bud (dtv); Recess: School's Out (voice).

Select TV: 1951: Inside Story (sp); Route 19 (sp); 1952: Thirty Days (sp); 1953: Storm Warnings (sp); Ever Since the Day (sp); 1954: Indirect Approach (sp); 1955: Laura (sp); 1956: The Lord Don't Play Favorites (sp); 1957: Panic Button (sp); 1959: The Untouchables/The Scarface Mob (sp); 1959–63: The Untouchables (series); 1964: The Command (sp); 1965: Memorandum for a Spy/Asylum for a Spy (sp); 1968: Laura (sp); 1968–71: The Name of the Game (series); 1974: The Strange and Deadly Occurrence; 1975: Adventures of the Queen; Murder on Flight 502; 1976: Most Wanted; 1976–77: Most Wanted (series); 1979: Undercover With the KKK (narrator); 1981–82: Strike Force (series); 1984: George Washington (ms); 1985: Midas

Valley; Hollywood Wives (ms); **1987**: Perry Mason: The Case of the Sinister Spirit; Falcon Crest (series); **1988–97**: Unsolved Mysteries (series); **1991**: The Return of Eliot Ness; **1992**: Final Appeal: From the Files of Unsolved Mysteries (series); **1998**: Hercules (series; voice); **1999**: Sealed With a Kiss.

TERENCE STAMP

BORN: LONDON, ENGLAND, JULY 22, 1939.

Possessing a pair of the most piercing, mesmerizing eyes in the business, it was clear that Terence Stamp would make some sort of impact on the cinema and so he did, on his own terms. Unlike some of his peers who reached stardom in the 1960s, Stamp didn't seem to be aiming to please and, instead, chose a wide range of odd, non-commercial products if he chose to work at all. Years later he re-emerged, grayer but still striking and still the same damn good actor he'd been all along. He was a struggling stage thespian when Peter Ustinov chose him to play the title role in his film version of *Billy Budd*. Stamp was hypnotically enigmatic as the young seaman who unleashes a fury in the wicked and repressed Robert Ryan, earning an Oscar nomination (in the supporting category, despite having the title role) and becoming one of the big names in British films in one fell swoop. After playing a bad schoolboy in *Term of Trial*, he went to Broadway to take on the title role in *Alfie*, but lost the part to Michael Caine when it was made into a highly successful film. For his consolation he played *The Collector*, the sad and mentally unbalanced fellow who kidnaps Samantha Eggar in the hope that he can force her to love him. He was brilliant and surprisingly sympathetic in this difficult part, and the film was one of the most rewarding and disturbing of the decade. It seemed strange to follow this triumph with a role as an effete boy-toy in the wretched spy spoof *Modesty Blaise*, but he had the satisfaction of coming off as the best of the leads in the failed adaptation of *Far from the Madding Crowd*, as the sergeant who loves and leaves Julie Christie. There was a much-publicized disaster, *Blue*, as an American raised by Mexicans, and then the controversial *Teorema*, in which he played another enigmatic fellow, sleeping with all the members of an Italian household. Delving into the fantastic, he was Toby Dammit in Fellini's segment of *Spirits of the Dead*, and then a man waking out of a 30-year coma in *The Mind of Mr. Soames*. With this eclectic body of work behind him, he dropped out of the scene for a spell, spending most of his time studying spiritualism in India.

When audiences saw him next it was in the opening scenes of the blockbuster fantasy *Superman*, as the evil General Zod, a role that was expanded for the 1981 sequel. He did some European flops, including *Together?*, with Jacqueline Bisset, and *Monster Island*, based on a Jules Verne story, but then scored back on home turf with *The Hit*, playing a mob informer. He was suddenly invited to enter the world of big-budget commercial Hollywood filmmaking and did so with *Legal Eagles*; *Wall Street*, in which he was in his element as Michael Douglas's rich and ruthless nemesis; *Young Guns*; and *Alien Nation*, where he was buried under a lot of bizarre makeup, as were many of the cast members. He was a crisply elegant villain in each film and these performances helped re-establish his career. Still proving that he liked to take risks, he played a deadpan transsexual, parading about in gaudy frocks as one of a trio of traveling drag performers in the Australian hit, *The Adventures of Priscilla Queen of the Desert*, his presence never more of an asset to weak material. He again returned to the world of independent productions, with some dead-on-arrival films that seemed designed to chase audi-

ences from theatres, including *Bliss*, as a sex therapist helping troubled Craig Sheffer; and *Love Walked In*, as a rich man from whom Denis Leary tries to extort money. In contrast, he ended up in one of the big commercial properties of the decade, *Star Wars Episode I: The Phantom Menace*, in a fleeting role as a member of a space council. Linking himself to his cinematic past he reprised his *Poor Cow* character in the L.A.-based *The Limey*, where he did little but walk around scowling. He wrote his autobiography, *Coming Attractions*, in 1988.

Screen: **1962**: Billy Budd; **1963**: Term of Trial; **1965**: The Collector; **1966**: Modesty Blaise; **1967**: Far from the Madding Crowd; **1968**: Poor Cow; Blue; **1969**: Teorema; Spirits of the Dead/Histories Extraordinaires; **1970**: The Mind of Mr. Soames; **1971**: Un Stagione all'inferno/Season in Hell (nUSr); **1975**: Hu-Man (nUSr); **1976**: Strip-tease/Insanity (dtv); **1978**: Superman; **1979**: Meetings With Remarkable Men; The Divine Nymph (filmed 1976); **1981**: Together?/I Love You, I Love You Not; Superman II; Monster Island (dtv); Vatican Conspiracy (dtv); **1985**: The Hit; The Company of Wolves; Link; **1986**: Legal Eagles; Skin/Hud (nUSr); **1987**: The Sicilian; Wall Street; **1988**: Young Guns; Alien Nation; **1990**: Genuine Risk; **1991**: Beltenbros/Prince of Shadows (nUSr); **1993**: The Real McCoy; **1994**: The Adventures of Priscilla — Queen of the Desert; **1995**: Mind Bender/Uri Geller (nUSr); **1997**: Limited Edition/Tire a part (nUSr); Bliss; **1998**: Love Walked In; **1999**: Star Wars Episode 1: The Phantom Menace; Bowfinger; The Limey; **2000**: Red Planet; **2001**: Revelation (nUSr); **2002**: My Wife Is an Actress; Full Frontal; The Kiss (nUSr).

NY Stage: **1964**: Alfie.

Select TV: **1978**: The Thief of Baghdad; **1986**: The Alamut Ambush/Deadly Recruits; Cold War Killers; **1997–98**: The Hunger (series); **1999**: Kiss the Sky.

LIONEL STANDER

BORN: NEW YORK, NY, JANUARY 11, 1908.
DIED: NOVEMBER 30, 1994.

His voice was as harsh and lacerating as his personality and Lionel Stander was greatly appreciated by lovers of the caustic and unsentimental for most every appearance he bestowed upon movies, be they good or bad. He started on the New York stage in 1928, in *The Final Balance*, and had made enough of a name for himself by the early 1930s that he did some short subjects with Shemp Howard and was eventually asked to do a feature film at Paramount's Astoria studios, *The Scoundrel*. He was soon in Hollywood, under contract to Columbia, although he bounced around from studio to studio, playing all kinds of tough mugs, including gangster Butch Gonzola in *We're in the Money*; sardonic press agent Cornelius Cobb in the brilliant *Mr. Deeds Goes to Town*; Edward Arnold's right-hand man in *Meet Nero Wolfe*; and his most famous role, as Libby, the acerbic studio publicist who has no qualms about telling Fredric March how much he loathes him, in *A Star is Born*. During the 1940s most of his assignments were of a less-than prestigious nature, including *Tahiti Honey* and *Gentleman Joe Palooka*, although he did show up in such "A" product as *Guadalcanal Diary*, as a sergeant called Butch; *Call Northside 777*; and the Danny Kaye feature, *The Kid from Brooklyn*, as Spider Schultz, the exact same role he'd done opposite Harold Lloyd in the earlier version, *The Milky Way*. A victim of the McCarthy witch hunts, he left the business for a period, finding work as a Wall Street broker before returning in the 1960s, as a hood in *The Loved One*, and, most memorably, a mobster terrorizing Donald

Pleasence in *Cul-de-Sac*. He then spent a great deal of time making movies in Italy until America coaxed him back to spread his crotchety charms in such movies as *New York, New York*; *1941*; *Cookie*; and *The Last Good Time*. In the meantime, he became a very familiar face on television as Max, the chauffeur, in the series *Hart to Hart* and its later telefilm reunions.

Screen: 1935: The Scoundrel; Page Miss Glory; The Gay Deception; We're in the Money; Hooray for Love; I Live My Life; If You Could Only Cook; 1936: The Music Goes Round; Mr. Deeds Goes to Town; Meet Nero Wolfe; More Than a Secretary; The Milky Way; Soak the Rich; They Met in a Taxi; 1937: The League of Frightened Men; A Star Is Born; The Last Gangster; 1938: No Time to Marry; Professor Beware; The Crowd Roars; 1939: Ice Follies of 1939; What a Life!; 1941: The Bride Wore Crutches; 1943: Guadalcanal Diary; Tahiti Honey; Hangmen Also Die; 1945: The Big Show-Off; A Boy, a Girl, and a Dog; 1946: Specter of the Rose; In Old Sacramento; The Kid from Brooklyn; Gentleman Joe Palooka; 1947: The Sin of Harold Diddlebock/Mad Wednesday; 1948: Texas, Brooklyn and Heaven; Call Northside 777; Unfaithfully Yours; Trouble Makers; 1951: Two Gals and a Guy; St. Denny the Dip; 1963: The Moving Finger; 1965: The Loved One; 1966: Promise Her Anything; Cul-de-Sac; 1967: Vrata Raja/Gates to Paradise (nUSr); Al Di la Della Legge/Beyond the Law (nUSr); 1968: A Dandy in Aspic; Sette Vole Sette/Seven Times Seven (nUSr); 1969: Once Upon a Time in the West; H25 (nUSr); Zenabel (nUSr); Boot Hill; Giacomo Casanova: Childhood and Adolescence (nUSr); 1970: Mir Hat es Immer Spass Gemacht/The Naughty Cheerleader (nUSr); 1971: Stanza 17-17 (nUSr); The Gang That Couldn't Shoot Straight; 1972: Treasure Island; The Adventures of Pinocchio (nUSr); Te Deum/Father Jackleg (nUSr); Don Camillo e l Giovani d'Oggi (nUSr); Pulp; Tutti Fratelli Nel West/Miss Dynamite/Where the Bullets Fly (nUSr); Piazza Pulita/1931: Once Upon a Time in New York (nUSr); Siamo Tutti in Liberta Provvisoria (nUSr); Milano Calibro 9/Caliber 9 (nUSr); 1973: La Mano Nera? Prima della Mafia; Piu della Mafia/The Black Hand (nUSr); Crescete e Moltiplicatevi (nUSr); Innocenza e Turbamento/Innocence and Desire (nUSr); Mordi e Fuggi/Dirty Weekend (nUSr); Partirono Preti Tornarono Curati/Hallelujah to Vera Cruz (nUSr); 1975: The Sensuous Sicilian/The Sensual Man; La Novizia (nUSr); Giubbe Rosse/Red Coat; The Senator Likes Women; The Black Bird; 1976: San Pasquale Baylonne protettore delle donne/Sex for Sale (nUSr); Ah si? ... e io lo dico a Zorro/Who's Afraid of Zorro? (nUSr); 1977: The Cassandra Crossing; New York, New York; 1978: Matilda; Cyclone (dtv); 1979: Between Miracles; 1941; 1982: The Squeeze/The Big Rip-Off (filmed 1979); 1986: The Transformers (voice); 1989: Wicked Stepmother; Cookie; 1991: Joey Takes a Cab; 1994: The Last Good Time.

NY Stage: 1928: The Final Balance; Singing Jailbirds; 1929: SS Glencairn; Red Dust; 1930: With Privileges; 1931: The House Beautiful; 1933: Little Ol' Boy; The Drums Begin; 1934: The Wooden Slipper; Bride of Torozko; 1939: Summer Night; 1941: Banjo Eyes; 1952: Pal Joey; 1961: The Conquering Hero; The Policemen; 1963: The Resistible Rise of Arturo Ui; 1964: Luther.

Select TV: 1979–84: Hart to Hart (series).

KIM STANLEY

(PATRICIA KIMBERLY REID) BORN: TULAROSA, NM, FEBRUARY 11, 1925. ED: UNIV. OF NM. DIED: AUGUST 20, 2001.

There is so little of Kim Stanley on film that it has only added to the mystery of this superb, intense, and apparently troubled actress, who became one of the most admired performers of her

day before dropping from the scene. She was a student of the Actors Studio, where she trained under Elia Kazan and Lee Strasberg. She made her Broadway bow in 1949, in *Monserrat*; won the Theatre World Award for *The Chase*; and achieved great acclaim for her work in the original productions of two notable William Inge plays, *Picnic* and *Bus Stop*, losing her roles in the film versions to Susan Strasberg and Marilyn Monroe, respectively. Instead, she became one of the most prominent names during television's live anthology drama period of the 1950s in productions ranging from *The Scarlet Letter* to *Clash by Night*. Columbia finally offered her a leading role, in *The Goddess*, and she played the part of the selfish Hollywood star who craves love but cannot give it brilliantly. The film was critically acclaimed but a box-office failure and there was no immediate follow-up. Nor did she even get credit for her most famous film, narrating *To Kill a Mockingbird*, as the grown-up Scout. Back on television, she won an Emmy Award for guesting on *Ben Casey*. In England, she gave another stunning performance, as the very disturbed psychic who forces her wimpy husband, Richard Attenborough, into helping her kidnap a child, in the haunting *Séance on a Wet Afternoon*. Again Stanley won raves, especially for her chillingly convincing breakdown at the movie's climax, and received an Oscar nomination. The nomination prompted no great demand for her services, however, and she eventually bowed out of the acting scene by the late 1960s, having suffered a genuine nervous collapse. Retiring from the public eye, she chose to teach acting at the College of Santa Fe. In 1982 Jessica Lange coaxed her back to the big screen, to play her mother, in *Frances*, the story of tormented actress Frances Farmer. Everyone was so glad to have Stanley back that, despite her often-shrill performance, she wound up with another Oscar nomination, and a follow-up part, as Pancho Barnes, in *The Right Stuff*. After winning another Emmy, for playing Big Momma in *Cat on a Hot Tin Roof*, opposite Lange again, she once again disappeared.

Screen: 1958: The Goddess; 1962: To Kill a Mockingbird (narrator); 1964: Séance on a Wet Afternoon; 1966: The Three Sisters; 1982: Frances; 1983: The Right Stuff.

NY Stage: 1949: St. Joan; Montserrat; 1951: The House Of Bernarda Alba; 1952: The Chase; 1953: Picnic; 1954: The Traveling Lady; 1955: Bus Stop; 1957: A Clearing in the Woods; 1958: A Touch of the Poet; 1959: Cheri; 1961: A Far Country; 1963: Natural Affection; 1964: The Three Sisters.

Select TV: 1951: The Anniversary (sp); 1952: The Witness (sp); 1953: A Young Lady of Property (sp); The Strong Women (sp); 1954: The Brownstone (sp); The Scarlet Letter (sp); 1955: The Witing Place (sp); 1956: Flight (sp); Conspiracy of Hearts (sp); Joey (sp); Death Is a Spanish Dancer (sp); In the Days of Our Youth (sp); 1957: The Traveling Lady (sp); Clash by Night (sp); 1960: Tomorrow (sp); 1968: Flesh and Blood (sp); 1969: U.M.C.; 1970: Dragon Country (sp); 1971: I Can't Imagine Tomorrow (sp); 1985: Cat on a Hot Tin Roof (sp).

BARBARA STANWYCK

(RUBY STEVENS) BORN: BROOKLYN, NY, JULY 16, 1907. DIED: JANUARY 20, 1990.

There was no mistaking that Barbara Stanwyck was every inch a star, it being pretty close to impossible for someone else to draw focus from her anytime she was on screen. She was one of the toughest of all the great ladies of the cinema; she could level somebody with a simple sneer. But she was also graciously warm, heartbreaking when hurt, and sexier than anyone gave her credit for being. Like many of the women who plied their trade in melodrama, she had a tendency to go too heavy on the histrionics, with a clutched hand to the hair for emphasis, and there were certainly a lot of forgettable titles on her tally sheet. Despite these faults, no one ever thought any less of her and her co-stars were almost unanimous in praise of her professionalism and grace. While earning her keep as a secretary, she auditioned for a chorus girl job at a New York's Strand Theatre Roof nightclub. This was followed by other club jobs and finally legit chorus work in Broadway's *George White's Scandals of 1923.* Changing her name because it sounded more like a burlesque dancer than an actress, she became Barbara Stanwyck when asked to do a serious role in *The Noose*, in 1926. This led to her being cast in, ironically, *Burlesque* as the performer who watches her husband's fall from fame, and it made her famous on the theatrical scene, that and the fact that she became the wife of noted stage thespian Frank Fay, in 1928. Stanwyck had already done background work on a film, *Broadway Nights*, as a dancer, but her official motion picture debut was in *The Locked Door*, made in New York, as a secretary implicated in murder. It failed so she went west with her husband in hopes of having better luck there. Director Frank Capra gave her the lead, as a goodtime gal who marries wealthy Ralph Graves, in *Ladies of Leisure* and Columbia was impressed enough to put her under contract.

The studio solidified her image as a thick-skinned doll though most of the titles she starred in have long faded into obscurity, including *Ten Cents a Dance*, in which she played a dance hall hostess; *The Miracle Woman*, a somewhat muddled look at the world of phony evangelism that was banned in Britain and became one of Capra's rare box-office flops; *Forbidden*, in which she went from prim librarian to murderess; and *The Bitter Tea of General Yen*, a fascinating tale about the forbidden love between a missionary's wife and an Asian. This was, no doubt, Stanwyk's best-known film from this era, yet another failure for Capra, this being his most atypical work. The film was also significant in the annals of exhibition history because it was the attraction that opened the Radio City Music Hall. During this time Stanwyck's services were called on elsewhere, most frequently by Warner Bros., where she was first seen in *Night Nurse*, as a valiant angel of mercy trying to save some sickly kids from their drunken mother, working for the first time with director William A. Wellman, who would later call her his favorite actress. Also, for Warners, she did *So Big*, a compact version of Edna Ferber's sprawling, Pulitzer Prize-winning novel; *The Purchase Price*, in which she, once again, played a nightclub entertainer; *Ladies They Talk About*, as a granite-hard dame who ends up behind bars; *Baby Face*, one of the most eye-opening of all pre-Code dramas, about a woman who works her way up from lowly honky tonk bar maid to society lady, man by man, with no apologies; and *Gambling Lady*, not to be confused with her later vehicle, *The Lady Gambles*. After her Columbia deal expired, she had several diverse freelance assignments, including *Annie Oakley*, with Stanwyck an ideal choice to play history's most famous woman sharpshooter in this somewhat leaden, highly fictionalized bio; *The Bride Walks Out*, an entry in the screwball comedy genre of the era, as a model who wants to return to work when she and husband Gene Raymond can't make ends meet; *His Brother's Wife*, a curious mixture of romance and jungle melodrama which marked her first of three with Robert Taylor; director John Ford's troubled production of *The Plough and the Stars*, in which she worked alongside members of Dublin's Abbey Theatre; *Internes Can't Take Money*, the first Dr. Kildare movie, as a patient; and *This Is My Affair*, again starring opposite Taylor. She and Fay were officially divorced in 1937 and Taylor became her new husband two years later.

The turning point that helped put her among the top female stars of the day came with Samuel Goldwyn's 1937 remake of *Stella Dallas*. Stanwyck played the lowbrow lady who devotes her life to her daughter's happiness as she becomes increasingly vulgar, much to the grown kid's dismay. She did what she could with this frustratingly silly story and it was just the sort of thing audiences wanted in that era, bringing her much acclaim and an Oscar nomination. To follow it up she made two films with Herbert Marshall: the comical *Breakfast for Two*, and the soapy *Always Goodbye*; then a screwball comedy with Henry Fonda, *The Mad Miss Manton*, in which she played a socialite who stumbles upon a dead body. A big hit with the western epic *Union Pacific* brought her into her peak years, this being followed by *Golden Boy*, as the woman who falls for boxer William Holden in this somewhat softened version of the classic Clifford Odets play. There was the gentle and underrated *Remember the Night*, as a shop-lifter being shown the simple life by Fred MacMurray before she must do her time in jail; *The Lady Eve*, giving one of her most brilliant performances, as the cunning con artist who dupes naïve Henry Fonda; *Meet John Doe*, as an opportunistic reporter who sets up and then falls in love with rube Gary Cooper, in the best of her films with Frank Capra; *Ball of Fire*, one of the great comedies of its day, earning Stanwyck an Oscar nomination for her most sizzling performance, as the jive-talking stripper on the lam, who is melted by timid professor Gary Cooper; *Lady of Burlesque*, again playing a stripper and adding some juice to an otherwise second-rate affair; and *The Great Man's Lady*, an epic that allowed her to age to 100 years old, albeit with some rather unconvincing makeup.

The Stanwyck summit came with *Double Indemnity*, director Billy Wilder's tart and gripping noir that set the standard for all such genre pictures that followed. Stanwyck, with platinum blonde hair, was never more potent, as the flirtatious wife who cons Fred MacMurray into helping dispose of her husband with fatal results for all. Selfishness was never so seductive and she was nominated for a third Academy Award but amazingly did not win, the world being so much in love with Ingrid Bergman at the time. On a milder note she went to Warners for *Christmas in Connecticut*, a soft comedy that became a holiday perennial because of its evocative title; *My Reputation*, a very 1940s-type soap opera about a widower whose friendship with George Brent causes ugly gossip; and *The Two Mrs. Carrolls*, a misguided teaming with Humphrey Bogart in which she suspected him of trying to murder her. Paramount put her in a silly comedy, *The Bride Wore Boots*; a juicy melodrama, *The Strange Love of Martha Ivers*, where she and Kurt Douglas misbehaved as a ruthless couple while Van Heflin stood by, waiting for them to devour one another; the popular *California*, a by-the-numbers Technicolor western with Ray Milland; and, most notably, *Sorry, Wrong Number*, which put too much padding on Lucille Fletcher's classic radio play but brought Stanwyck a fourth Oscar nomination, as the selfish, bed-ridden lady who suspects that she's about to be murdered. The studio also made sure they further exploited her naughty side in *The File on Thelma Jordan*, where she tread into familiar *Double Indemnity* territory, using Wendell Corey to murder a rich aunt, and *The Furies*, in which her character behaved so abominably that she tossed a pair of scissors into Judith Anderson's eye.

The 1950s saw her constantly at work but with a tapering off in importance where most of the projects were concerned. There were reteamings with former co-stars in scripts that seemed like pale attempts to reprise the past, including *To Please a Lady*, with Clark Gable; *Blowing Wild*, with Gary Cooper; *The Moonlighter* and *There's Always Tomorrow*, with Fred MacMurray; plus a long-delayed pairing with James Cagney, in *These Wilder Years*, which almost seemed like a "B" movie despite their presence. There were some decent programmers that put her in peril, like *Jeopardy*, in which she tried to save husband Barry Sullivan from drowning while being terrorized by Ralph Meeker; and *Witness to Murder*, in which she tattled on killer George Sanders, thereby flirting with danger. There were also some big budget attractions like *Titanic*, in which she bickered with husband Clifton Webb until the great ship went down, and *Executive Suite*, her classiest film of this period, but one in which she gave the weakest performance among a stellar cast, scene chewing shamelessly as the ex-mistress of the late company president. There was a poor rendering of another Clifford Odets work, *Clash by Night*, in which she married drab Paul Douglas while being attracted to pushy Robert Ryan; and some westerns, a genre she always looked at home in, including *Cattle Queen of Montana*; *The Violent Men*, in which she let crippled husband Edward G. Robinson go up in flames; and *Trooper Hook*, her last of several with Joel McCrea. Going over to television she won an Emmy for the anthology series *The Barbara Stanwyck Show* and then another for *The Big Valley*. She returned to the movies in 1962, playing a lesbian madame in *Walk on the Wild Side*, which was something of a bold move when it became more publicly known after her death that she herself was gay. Perhaps to keep her name fresh with the younger public, she did *Roustabout*, supporting Elvis Presley, then reteamed with ex-husband Robert Taylor (they'd divorced in 1951) in *The Night Walker*, one of producer William Castle's rare thrillers to dispense with any gimmicks. Sticking exclusively to television in her later years, she won another Emmy, for the mini series *The Thorn Birds*. She received the American Film Institute Life Achievement Award (1987) while the motion picture industry gave her a special Oscar (1982) to rectify the shameful omission of one of the most admired of all actresses having never been given her due in this department.

Screen: 1927: Broadway Nights; 1929: The Locked Door; Mexicali Rose; 1930: Ladies of Leisure; 1931: Illicit; Ten Cents a Dance; Night Nurse; The Miracle Woman; 1932: Forbidden; Shopworn; So Big; The Purchase Price; 1933: The Bitter Tea of General Yen; Ladies They Talk About; Baby Face; Ever in My Heart; 1934: Gambling Lady; A Lost Lady; 1935: The Secret Bride; The Woman in Red; Red Salute; Annie Oakley; 1936: A Message to Garcia; The Bride Walks Out; His Brother's Wife; Banjo on My Knee; The Plough and the Stars; 1937: Internes Can't Take Money; This Is My Affair; Stella Dallas; Breakfast for Two; 1938: Always Goodbye; The Mad Miss Manton; 1939: Union Pacific; Golden Boy; 1940: Remember the Night; 1941: The Lady Eve; Meet John Doe; Young Belong to Me; Ball of Fire; 1942: The Great Man's Lady; The Gay Sisters; 1943: Lady of Burlesque; Flesh and Fantasy; 1944: Double Indemnity; Hollywood Canteen; 1945: Christmas in Connecticut; 1946: My Reputation; The Bride Wore Boots; The Strange Love of Martha Ivers; California; 1947: The Two Mrs. Carrolls; The Other Love; Cry Wolf; Variety Girl; 1948: B.F.'s Daughter; Sorry, Wrong Number; 1949: The Lady Gambles; East Side, West Side; 1950: Thelma Jordan/The File on Thelma Jordan; No Man of Her Own; The Furies; To Please a Lady; 1951: The Man With a Cloak; 1952: Clash by Night; 1953: Jeopardy; Titanic; All I Desire; The Moonlighter; Blowing Wild; 1954: Witness to Murder; Executive Suite; Cattle Queen of Montana; 1955: The Violent Men; Escape From Burma; 1956: There's Always Tomorrow; The Maverick Queen; These Wilder Years; 1957: Crime of Passion; Trooper Hook; Forty Guns; 1962: Walk on the Wild Side; 1964: Roustabout; 1965: The Night Walker.

NY Stage: AS RUBY STEVENS: 1923: George White's Scandals of

1923; Artists and Models; 1924: Keep Kool; 1925: Gay Paree.
AS BARBARA STANWYCK: 1926: The Noose; 1927: Burlesque; 1929: Vaudeville (at the Palace); 1933: Tattle Tales.
Select TV: 1956: Sudden Silence (sp); 1958: The Freighter (sp); Three Years Dark (sp); Trail to Nowhere (sp); 1959: Hang the Heart High (sp); Lone Woman (sp); 1960–61: The Barbara Stanwyck Show (series); 1961: Star Witness (sp); 1962: Special Assignment (sp); 1965–69: The Big Valley (series); 1970: The House That Wouldn't Die; 1971: A Taste of Evil; 1973: The Letters; 1983: The Thorn Birds (ms); 1985–86: The Colbys (series).

MAUREEN STAPLETON
(LOIS MAUREEN STAPLETON) BORN: TROY, NY, JUNE 21, 1925.

Arguably one of the half dozen finest actresses to make her name in the postwar era, Maureen Stapleton, who came across as too matronly for her years, just didn't fit the mold of what Hollywood wanted and, therefore, went through years of sporadic activity before the cameras. Time rectified things and her unglamorous persona was suddenly just right for playing sweet and troubled characters in their autumn years, making her an invaluable player to the film scene. She studied at the Herbert Berghof studio, helped create a stock company called the Greenbush Summer Theatre, and did stage work in Mount Kisco, NY. Returning to Manhattan, she did some insignificant stage parts before she was chosen to play the Italian heroine of Tennessee Williams's *The Rose Tattoo*, winning both a Theatre World and Tony Award for the role. This made her one of the most admired performers in the theater and her reputation soared via her additional work in *27 Wagons Full of Cotton*, revivals of *The Crucible* and *The Sea Gull*, plus another of Williams's works, *Orpheus Descending*. She was soon landing roles on television and was finally invited to do a movie, playing the sad correspondent who winds up using the gullible Montgomery Clift in *Lonelyhearts*, stealing every scene she was in and ending up with a supporting-actress Oscar nomination in the process. She also appeared in *The Fugitive Kind*, the movie version of *Orpheus Descending*, although she was demoted from the lead to the less significant role of the artist. There were two more movies from stage hits, *A View from the Bridge*, a French-produced version of Arthur Miller's mighty play, as Raf Vallone's neglected wife, and *Bye Bye Birdie*, singing "Kids" while playing the overbearing mom of Dick Van Dyke, who was a mere six months younger than her in real life.

On television she won an Emmy for the special *Among the Paths to Eden*, and then did some serious emoting as the distressed wife, who knows husband Van Heflin is going to blow up the plane, in the blockbuster hit *Airport*, earning another supporting Oscar nod in the process. She did get a chance to repeat one of her theater roles, in the movie version of *Plaza Suite* (onstage she'd done all three parts, for the movie Barbara Harris and Lee Grant shared them with her), the wife trying to re-ignite the spark in her tired marriage, the film's best segment. Onstage she got another Tony, as the alcoholic actress in *The Gingerbread Lady*, and was a breath of fresh air in director Woody Allen's ultra-artsy *Interiors*, playing the down-to-earth new wife of E.G. Marshall, earning Oscar nomination number three. She was Lauren Bacall's protective secretary in *The Fan*; lowered herself to appear with kid star Gary Coleman in *On the Right Track*, as a bag lady; and was outstanding as outspoken radical Emma Goldman in the epic *Reds*, which at last brought her an Academy Award.

Having left the stage behind, she was more available for filming than ever before and played a lowbrow role as Michael Keaton's crude mother in *Johnny Dangerously*; sparkled as a senior citizen whose life is made better by alien visitors in the popular *Cocoon*; turned up as a shady realtor in *The Money Pit*; and played Meryl Streep's therapist in *Heartburn*. In a nice, later-life occurrence, she got an actual starring role, as the owner of a dying Catskills resort, in *Sweet Lorraine*, after which she had another show-stopping assignment, as Barbra Streisand's teary, distraught mother in *Nuts*. There was little reason for the sequel *Cocoon: The Return*, nor was she given much to play in the ensemble comedy *Passed Away*, as Jack Warden's widow, or *Addicted to Love*, as Matthew Broderick's grandmother, although no one in their right mind would complain about having her on hand in such undernourished films. In 1995 she published her memoirs, *A Hell of a Life*.

Screen: 1958: Lonelyhearts; 1960: The Fugitive Kind; 1962: A View From the Bridge; 1963: Bye Bye Birdie; 1969: Trilogy (from TV); 1970: Airport; 1971: Plaza Suite; Summer of '42 (voice); 1978: Interiors; 1979: Lost and Found; The Runner Stumbles; 1981: The Fan; On the Right Track; Reds; 1984: Johnny Dangerously; 1985: The Cosmic Eye (voice); Cocoon; 1986: The Money Pit; Heartburn; 1987: Sweet Lorraine; Made in Heaven; Nuts; 1988: Doin' Time on Planet Earth; Cocoon: The Return; Hello, Actors Studio; 1992: Passed Away; 1994: Trading Mom; 1995: The Last Good Time; 1997: Addicted to Love; 1998: Wilbur Falls/Dead Silence (dtv).

NY Stage: 1946: The Playboy of the Western World; 1947: Antony and Cleopatra; 1949: Detective Story; 1950: The Bird Cage; 1951: The Rose Tattoo; 1953: The Emperor's Clothes; The Crucible; 1954: The Sea Gull; 1955: 27 Wagons Full of Cotton; 1956: Orpheus Descending; 1958: The Cold Wind and the Warm; 1960: Toys in the Attic; 1965: The Glass Menagerie; 1966: The Rose Tattoo (Revival); 1968: Plaza Suite; 1970: Norman, Is That You?; The Gingerbread Lady; 1972: The Country Girl; The Secret Affairs of Mildred Wild; 1975: The Glass Menagerie; 1978: The Gin Game; 1981: The Little Foxes.

Select TV: 1952: What Happened? (series); Carrie Marr (sp); 1953: The Accident (sp); 1954: The Mother (sp); 1955: Incident in July (sp); 1956: Rachel (sp); 1958: All the King's Men (sp); 1959: For Whom the Bell Tolls (sp); 1960: Tessie Malfitano (sp); 1961: Four by Tennessee Williams (sp); 1962: The Betrayal (sp); 1966: Save Me a Place at Forest Lawn (sp); 1967: Among the Paths to Eden (sp); 1974: Tell Me Where It Hurts; 1975: Queen of the Stardust Ballroom; 1976: Cat on a Hot Tin Roof; 1977: The Gathering; 1979: Letters from Frank; The Gathering Part II; 1981: The Electric Grandmother; 1982: Little Gloria…Happy at Last; 1983: Alice in Wonderland; 1984: Family Secrets; Sentimental Journey; 1985: Private Sessions; 1988: The Thorns (series); Liberace: Behind the Music; 1992: Last Wish; Miss Rose White.

TOMMY STEELE

(THOMAS HICKS) BORN: LONDON, ENGLAND, DECEMBER 17, 1936.

With a mile-wide smile that seemed to expose the biggest set of teeth in the business, the exuberant Tommy Steele started off in the world of rock 'n' roll, until he had to concede that it was the old fashioned quality of musical comedy that was really in his blood and pointed his career in a different direction. His first professional job was as a singing bellhop on ocean liners, followed by a stint with a skiffle trio that included future *Oliver!* composer Lionel Bart. He ended up

singing solo in London coffee houses where he was discovered by entrepeneur John Kennedy, who guided Steele to a top 20 hit, "Rock With the Caveman." For a brief period he became one of England hottest pop idols, selling millions of records to the youngsters and making girls go wild at concerts. He was well-known enough for his starring film debut to be called *The Tommy Steele Story*, though it was re-christened *Rock Around the World* for distribution elsewhere. This was followed by *The Duke Wore Jeans*, in which he played dual roles; *Tommy the Toreador*, as a seaman who fills in for a jailed matador; and *It's All Happening*, as a talent scout entertaining orphans. By the time the last film played in the U.S., as *The Dream Maker*, his period as both a recording star and a cinema attraction had passed. Wisely, he saught legit work as an actor, appearing in *She Stoops to Conquer*, at the Old Vic, and then, in 1963, took the lead in a London musical, *Half a Sixpence*, based on the H.G. Wells novel *Kipps*. It did so well there that Steele was hailed as terrific addition to the musical stage and invited to repeat his triumph in New York.

Since the Hollywood studios were hopping on the musical bandwagon that looked so inviting in the wake of *The Sound of Music*'s box-office smash, Steele got involved in three of the less expensive ones produced in the late 1960s. In the very last production presided over by Walt Disney himself, *The Happiness Millionaire*, he was the Irish butler employed by a rich Philadelphia family, but this was too adult for that company's usual kiddie audience, not to mention over-long and under-plotted. There was an adaptation of *Half a Sixpence*, shot in England but helmed by an American adept at musicals, George Sidney; but the dire reviews kept audiences away. Best of the lot was *Finian's Rainbow*, a fantasy derived from the Burton Lane-E.Y. Harburg stage property of 20 years back, with Steele as a particularly manic leprechaun, pursuing a stolen pot of gold. He sang and danced to the enchanting "When I'm Not Near the Girl I Love," and achieved the goal of anyone working in this genre, getting to share the screen with Fred Astaire. Since the era of the big family musical was fast passing, he opted to do a straight period adventure as his next assignment, *Where's Jack*, but its failure marked the end of Steele as an international name. Afterwards he stuck almost exclusively to the London stage with occasional television appearances in his homeland. In 1983 he published a novel, *The Final Run*.

Screen: 1957: Kill Me Tomorrow; The Tommy Steele Story/Rock Around the World; 1958: The Duke Wore Jeans; 1959: Tommy the Toreador; 1960: Light Up the Sky/Skywatch; 1963: It's All Happening/The Dream Maker; 1967: The Happiest Millionaire; 1968: Half a Sixpence; Finian's Rainbow; 1969: Where's Jack.

NY Stage: 1965: Half a Sixpence.

Select TV: 1969: Twelfth Night (sp); 1974: My Life, My Song (sp); 1978: The Yeomen of the Guard (sp); 1979: Quincy's Quest (sp).

ROD STEIGER

BORN: WESTHAMPTON, NY, APRIL 14, 1925. DIED: JULY 9, 2002.

Burly and seething with intensity, Rod Steiger was damned if people were going to leave the movie theatre forgetting which part he'd played. His measured jumps from quiet, mannered speech to bellowing outbursts were fun to anticipate and he quickly became a memorable and exciting presence. He was also a tough cookie to harness and he chalked up enough over-wrought lapses in judgment to hurt the reputation of an actor who had more than once reached greatness. Born to show business parents, he decided to study acting on the G.I. Bill, after having served in the Navy in World War II. During the late 1940s he became one of the multitude of famous names to learn his craft at the Actors Studio, which led to him showing up numerous times on live television in the golden era of anthology series. One of those dramas, Paddy Chayefsky's *Marty*, made him a desirable property, the most appetizing and important offer coming from director Elia Kazan, who wanted him to play Marlon Brando's brother in *On the Waterfront*. This was Steiger's second movie (he'd shown up in MGM's *Teresa* in 1951, as John Ericson's therapist) and, like everyone else in the cast, he would become a part of motion picture history because of his involvement in it. As Charlie, the second-rate hoodlum who lowers himself to pulling a gun on his own kin, he was properly pathetic and received a well-deserved Oscar nomination in the supporting category. From that point on the work kept coming at a rapid clip, and Steiger played a bullying movie mogul in *The Big Knife*, which promptly warned audiences of much future scene-chewing to come; the menacing farmhand Jud in *Oklahoma!*, where he was unfortunately deprived of his solo, "Lonely Room;" the under-handed attorney in *The Court-Martial of Billy Mitchell*; a thug with the deceptive name of Pinky in *Jubal*; and a no-good boxing promoter in *The Harder They Fall*, more than holding his own against Humphrey Bogart.

These films helped establish him as one of the mightiest character actors of the 1950s and his success was such that it made sense that the studios would push him up to leading roles. To that end, he joined the Sioux Indians when he could not cope with the South's defeat in *Run of the Arrow*; played a farmer whose wife, Diana Dors, tries to kill him in *The Unholy Wife*, a movie he especially hated; went to England for *Across the Bridge*, based on a Graham Greene story; and shook the rafters as *Al Capone*, a so-so biopic of the most famous gangster of them all. It was back to letting others carry the load with *Seven Thieves*, one of the many colorful caper films to populate the 1960s; *The Mark*, an acclaimed British-made drama about a child-molester, with Steiger as Stuart Whitman's helpful psychiatrist; and *The Longest Day*, in which he was just one of many names in this grandiose depiction of D-Day. That at least kept his name before the public, which was more than could be said for the various foreign productions that occupied his time during the early 1960s, including *The World in My Pocket* (Germany) and *Time of Indifference* (Italy). It would, therefore, not be unjust to say that 1965 was his comeback year. He started off with a towering performance in *The Pawnbroker*, at his most restrained and effective, as a Holocaust survivor who has deadened himself to the repercussions of human contact. Helped by outstanding reviews and, no doubt, by it being the first major American motion picture to feature nudity, it was a success, making it a high watermark in Steiger's career, probably his finest achievement, earning him an Oscar nomination. He was also seen in a cult-worthy performance, as the mother-dominated mortician Mr. Joyboy, in the dark satire *The Loved One*, and as Julie Christie's slithery suitor in one of the monster hits of the year, *Doctor Zhivago*.

These films helped return him to the "A" list and guaranteed that he land a plum role, as the bigoted Southern sheriff who comes to respect black detective Sidney Poitier, in director Norman Jewison's *In the Heat of the Night*. This was another of the most important films of the era, a literate cop thriller that was also a subtle statement on racism, and Steiger added great levels of depth to a potentially clichéd character. The film took the Oscar for Best Picture of 1967 and Steiger was awarded the Academy Award for Best Actor. With the success of this film, he officially showed his potential to be a box-office "name" and it would take years before it was evident that the moody and portly character actor didn't really have any clout in that area. Because of *In the Heat*, a cheesy Italian comedy he'd done

before it, *The Girl and the General*, suddenly surfaced, but his official follow-up quickly erased the bad taste that one left. He displayed his versatility magnificently in *No Way to Treat a Lady*, once again mother-dominated, as a deranged actor who uses all kinds of disguises to charm and then kill women. There was a touch of black comedy to both the film and his performance, thereby making his extremes both fun to watch and acceptable in the context. After this peak, his career began to go wrong almost immediately with *The Sergeant*, a monumentally depressing drama about a homosexual Army sergeant with a fixation on a handsome private (John Philip Law), just the sort of thing nobody wanted to see, which was also the case with the pretentious *The Illustrated Man*, in which Steiger's body was tattooed from head to toe. This film featured his second wife, Claire Bloom, as did *Three Into Two Won't Go*; both were released in 1969, the year they divorced after ten years of marriage. Overseas again, he was Napoleon in an expensive money-loser, *Waterloo*; teamed with James Coburn in a spaghetti western killed off by its dreadful title, *Duck, You Sucker*; and continued his bad luck with two international biopics, *Lucky Luciano* and *The Last Days of Mussolini*, though if anyone had to play the volatile Italian dictator, Steiger was the one to do it.

His American projects fared no better since there was no possible interest in quirky projects like *Happy Birthday, Wanda June*, from a Kurt Vonnegut play, or another movie with a horrid title, *Lolly Madonna XXX*, about feudin' hillbillies. Going for more traditional fare, he went belly up in England with *Hennessy*, in which he tried to blow up Parliament to avenge his family's death, and then did an acceptable imitation of the great comedian in *W.C. Field and Me*, which was too old fashioned for 1976 audiences to care. Supporting Sylvester Stallone, he was the Head of the Senate Investigations Committee in *F.I.S.T.*, and had his first box-office hit in some time with the ultra-silly *The Amityville Horror*, as the priest who tries to chase the demons away. Amid all the rubbish he kept churning out during the 1980s and beyond, he was a Nazi colonel in *The Lucky Star*, a film that fared better in its native Canada; a lawman in an underrated western, *Cattle Annie and Little Britches*; Robby Benson's rabbi father in *The Chosen*, a gentle performance that ranked among his best; and seemed to be having fun playing a crazed, self-appointed executioner in the tongue-in-cheek *Guilty as Charged*. These were the exceptions in a career that was badly crippled by such assignments as *Breakthrough*, as a World War II general; *Lion of the Desert*, again jutting forth his chin as Mussolini; *The Naked Face*, from a Sidney Sheldon novel; *The Kindred*, as a nutty scientist trying to raise a cat from the dead; the none-too-serious *American Gothic*, as a crazed backwoods killer; *The January Man*, as the curse-spewing mayor of New York; the deadly film of Carson McCuller's *The Ballad of the Sad Cafe*, as a fiery preacher; *The Specialist*, sporting an inept Spanish accent, as the villain in this Sylvester Stallone vehicle; *Carpool*, reducing to supporting the talentless Tom Arnold; and *Truth or Consequences N.M.*, munching a good deal of scenery, as a mob boss. In higher grade, "A" product, he was squashed by a Martian in *Mars Attacks!*, which was at least *supposed* to be funny, and played judges in both *Crazy in Alabama* and *The Hurricane*, the latter a reunion with his *In the Heat of the Night* director, Norman Jewison. By this point there seemed to be a certain whacked-out energy to his thesping, causing one to either relish his no-holds barred approach or lament his lack of discipline.

Screen: 1951: Teresa; 1954: On the Waterfront; 1955: The Big Knife; Oklahoma!; The Court-Martial of Billy Mitchell; 1956: Jubal; The Harder They Fall; Back from Eternity; 1957: Run of the Arrow; The Unholy Wife; Across the Bridge; 1958: Cry Terror!; 1959: Al Capone; 1960: Seven Thieves; 1961: The Mark; The World in My Pocket/On Friday at Eleven; 1962: 13 West Street; Convicts 4; The Longest Day; 1963: Hands Across the City; 1965:

Time of Indifference; The Pawnbroker; The Loved One; Doctor Zhivago; 1967: In the Heat of the Night; 1968: E venne un Uomo/And There Came a Man (filmed 1965; nUSr); The Girl and the General (filmed 1965); No Way to Treat a Lady; The Sergeant; 1969: The Illustrated Man; Three Into Two Won't Go; 1970: Waterloo; 1971: Happy Birthday, Wanda June; 1972: Duck, You Sucker!/A Fistful of Dynamite; The Heroes; 1973: Lolly Madonna XXX/Lolly Madonna War; 1974: The Last Days of Mussolini/The Last Four Days; 1975: Lucky Luciano; Hennessy; 1976: W.C. Fields and Me; 1977: Portrait of a Hitman/Jim Buck/The Last Contract; 1978: Dirty Hands (Fr: 1975); F.I.S.T.; 1979: Love and Bullets; Breakthrough/Sergeant Steiner; The Amityville Horror; 1980: Klondike Fever; The Lucky Star; 1981: Wolf Lake/The Honor Guard (filmed 1978); Lion of the Desert; Cattle Annie and Little Britches; 1982: The Chosen; The Magic Mountain; 1984: The Naked Face; 1987: The Kindred; Catch the Heat; 1988: American Gothic; Hello, Actors Studio; 1989: The January Man; That Summer of White Roses (dtv); Exiles (nUSr); Try This One on for Size (nUSr); 1991: Men of Respect; The Ballad of the Sad Cafe; 1992: Guilty as Charged; The Player; 1993: Kölcsönkapott idö (nUSr); The Neighbor (dtv); 1994: Black Water/Tennessee Nights (nUSr); The Last Tattoo (dtv); The Specialist; 1995: Seven Sundays (nUSr); Captain Nuke and the Bomber Boys/Demolition Day (dtv); 1996: Carpool; Mars Attacks!; 1997: The Real Thing/Livers Ain't Cheap (dtv); Shiloh; The Kid (dtv); Truth or Consequences, N.M.; 1998: Animals (dtv); Incognito; Body and Soul (dtv); Off the Menu: The Last Days of Chasen's; Modern Vampires (dtv); Legacy (dtv); 1999: Shiloh 2: Shiloh Season; Cypress Edge (dtv); Crazy in Alabama; End of Days; The Hurricane; 2000: Flying Dutchman/Frozen in Fear (dtv); 2001: Lightmaker (dtv); 2002: Hollywood Sign (dtv); A Month of Sundays (dtv); 2003: Poolhall Junkies.

NY Stage: 1949: Stevedore; 1950: An Enemy of the People; 1951: Night Music; 1952: Seagulls Over Sorrento; 1959: Rashomon; 1962: Moby Dick.

Select TV: 1952: Raymond Schindler: Case One (sp); The Inn (sp); 1953: My Brother's Keeper (sp); Marty (sp); The Dutch Schultz Story (sp); Other People's Houses (sp); 1954: Smokescreen (sp); The Man Most Likely (sp); 1955: Yellow Jack (sp); Anatomy of Fear (sp); 1956: Markheim (sp); 1957: The Lonely Wizard (sp); 1958: A Town Has Turned to Dust (sp); 1960: The Book of Silence (sp); 1964: A Slow Fade to Black (sp); 1966: Death of a Salesman (sp); 1977: Jesus of Nazareth (ms); 1983: Cook and Peary: The Race to the Pole; 1984: The Glory Boys; 1985: Hollywood Wives (ms); 1986: Sword of Gideon; 1988: Desperado: Avalanche at Devil's Ridge; 1989: Passion and Paradise; 1991: In the Line of Duty: Manhunt in the Dakotas/Midnight Murders; 1992: Sinatra; 1993: Armistead Maupin's Tales of the City (ms); 1995: Tom Clancy's OP Center; In Pursuit of Honor; Choices of the Heart: The Margaret Sanger Story; Columbo: Strange Bedfellows; Out There; 1996: Dalva; EZ Streets (series); 1998: Alexandria Hotel; 2001: The Last Producer.

JAN STERLING

(JANE STERLING ADRIANCE)
BORN: NEW YORK, NY, APRIL 3, 1923.

Other actresses had the fame and money but Jan Sterling had the critics on her side, being one of the outstanding cinematic ladies of the 1950s, one who could, in a flash, be abrasive or vulnerable, delicate or tough. A child of wealth, she was sent to England to studying acting at the Fay Compton School and then came back to America to make her Broadway debut, at

15, in *Bachelor Born*, billed as Jane Sterling. She switched to "Jan" in 1945, for *The Rugged Path*, and earned such positive reviews that the sad-eyed blonde was asked to join the cast of one of Warners's big prestige films of 1948, *Johnny Belinda*, where she fit right in among the experienced movie pros, as the white trash girlfriend of rapist Stephen McNally. In 1950 she married actor Paul Douglas, then showed up as an inmate named Smoochie in *Caged*, a raw women's prison drama. Staying bad, she was a moll in both *Union Station*, where she helped Lyle Bettger carry out a kidnapping, and *Appointment with Danger*. She then got a lead, and the best part of her career, in director Billy Wilder's scorching dissection of the press, *Ace in the Hole*, as the bored, selfish wife of a hapless man trapped in a mineshaft. Despite the film's major box-office failure, this upped her standing somewhat as far as the industry was concerned and she was given further leading roles, in the gentler *Rhubarb*, which was stolen by the title cat; *Flesh and Fury*, as a bitch out to exploit deaf-mute fighter Tony Curtis; and *Sky Full of Moon*, as a sassy Vegas doll who falls for rube Carlton Carpenter. She added juice to the ensemble pieces *Split Second*, as one of the hostages of a group of escaped cons; *The Human Jungle*, about life at a police station; and, most notably, *The High and the Mighty*, as a world-wearied lady aboard the troubled plane, a performance that earned her an Oscar nomination in the supporting category.

Over at Allied Artists she got boosted back up to the star spot, her first, in fact, with top-billing, for *Return from the Sea*, but this was a very minor league romance from a company then struggling to enter the majors. Over at Universal she supported Joan Crawford in the overheated *Female on the Beach*, as a shady real-estate agent with her eye on Jeff Chandler; and backed-up Hedy Lamar in the hokey *The Female Animal*, as a one-time actress. Between these she had a good one, *The Harder They Fall*, playing splendidly off of Humphrey Bogart, as his wife; and landed back in the slammer, as a forger, in *Women's Prison*. She went to England to play the lady who offers a ray of hope for Edmond O'Brien in the first, ambitious film adaptation of George Orwell's *1984*, and then offered sympathetic support, as the wife of longshoreman Mickey Shaughnessy, in *Slaughter on Tenth Avenue*. It was not an encouraging sign that she showed up among the eclectic cast of *High School Confidential*, one of producer Albert Zugsmith's rubbishy 1950s melodramas, and this indeed marked the end of the line for Sterling as far as steady film work was concerend. Douglas died in 1959 and she began making television and the stage her preferred line of business. She was asked to participate in one of the earliest of the "teen-beach" romps, *Love in a Goldfish Bowl*, after which she was not seen again on the big screen for another seven years, when she played one of the terrorized subway passengers in a failed thriller, *The Incident*. She portrayed unhappy wives in two trashy films, *The Angry Breed* and *The Minx*, and the stagnant state of her career may have prompted her to move to England, where she spent most of her time living with actor Sam Wanamaker. In 1981 she appeared, seemingly out of the blue, as Walter Matthau's wife in *First Monday in October*, but it was an insignificant part, suggesting nothing of her previous triumphs.

Screen: 1948: Johnny Belinda; 1950: The Skipper Surprised His Wife; Mystery Street; Caged; Union Station; 1951: Appointment With Danger; The Mating Season; Ace in the Hole/The Big Carnival; Rhubarb; 1952: Flesh and Fury; Sky Full of Moon; 1953: Split Second; The Vanquished; Pony Express; 1954: Alaska Seas; The High and the Mighty; Return from the Sea; The Human Jungle; 1955: Women's Prison; Female on the Beach; Man with a Gun; 1956: The Harder They Fall; 1984; 1957: Slaughter on Tenth Avenue; 1958: The Female Animal; High

School Confidential; Kathy O'; 1961: Love in a Goldfish Bowl; 1968: The Incident; 1969: The Angry Breed; The Minx; 1976: Sammy Somebody; 1981: First Monday in October.

NY Stage: AS JANE STERLING: 1938: Bachelor Born; 1939: When We Are Married; 1940: Grey Farm; 1941: Panama Hattie; 1943: This Rock; 1944: Over 21.

AS JAN STERLING: 1945: The Rugged Path; Dunnigan's Daughter; 1946: This Too Shall Pass; Present Laughter; 1949: Two Blind Mice; Born Yesterday; 1957: Small War On Murray Hill; 1962: The Perfect Set-Up; 1963: Once for the Asking; 1965: Friday Night; 1970: The Front Page; 1974: Come Back, Little Sheba; 1978: The November People.

Select TV: 1954: Book Overdue (sp); 1955: Ferry to Fox Island (sp); A Note of Fear (sp); Desert Story (sp); 1956: The Unfaithful (sp); Hawk's Head (sp); She Married Her Boss (sp); Requiem for a Heavyweight (sp); 1957: The Great Lie (sp); Clipper Ship (sp); 1958: Run, Joe, Run (sp); 1960: Chinese Finale (sp); At Your Service (sp); 1961: You're in the Picture (series); 1962: In Close Pursuit (sp); 1964: Made in America (series); 1969–70: The Guiding Light (series); 1976: Having Babies; 1979: Backstairs at the White House (ms); 1980: My Kidnapper, My Love; 1982: Dangerous Company.

CONNIE STEVENS
(CONCETTA ANN INGOLIA)
BORN: BROOKLYN, NY, AUGUST 8, 1938.

Bright and eager to please, but never really taken all that seriously, Connie Stevens was sweet and sexy in a very fluffy sort of way. Having won several talent contests, she trained at the Hollywood Professional School, showed up in a TV commercial, and toured as part of a girl group called the Three Debs. After roles in some typical late 1950s troubled teen fare, both sporting priceless titles, *Young and Dangerous* and *Eighteen and Anxious*, she was chosen by Jerry Lewis to be his leading lady in *Rock-a-Bye Baby*, and she went down easy enough with audiences to signal that she was on her way. There was a stop-off into more teen delinquency for *The Party Crashers*, and then a hit television series, *Hawaiian Eye*, in which she played singer-photographer Cricket Blake. This made her one of those ubiquitous fan magazine faces of the era, and she was soon back in movies as the youngin' in love with Troy Donahue in *Parrish*, after which she had the title role, opposite Troy again, in *Susan Slade*, in which she shamed her mother by having a child out of wedlock. Both were very typical of the glossy soap operas of the early 1960s, the former more popular than the latter. Presumably because Warners wanted to keep promoting Connie and Troy as a great screen team, they were back again for the lighter *Palm Springs Weekend*, although Stevens, in fact, was linked romantically in the storyline with Robert Conrad. She then stumbled through *Never Too Late*, as Maureen O'Sullivan's daughter, who's appalled to find out she's going to have a baby sister; *Two on a Guillotine*, a flat thriller, as the daughter of nutty magician Cesar Romero; and the worst of all Jerry Lewis movies, *Way…Way Out*, with the pair of them playing the world's least likely astronauts. Television seemed like the natural escape, so she stuck around there for most of her career, although she would be summoned back to the movies occasionally, atypically as a singer in a gangster thriller directed by Robert Aldrich, *The Grissom Gang*; and an attempt to put in her bid for the action crowd, *Scorchy*, as a narc. Not surprisingly, she showed up for nostalgia's sake in two intentionally campy movies, *Grease 2*, as a high school teacher, and in *Back to the Beach*, as Tommy Hinckley's very well pre-

served mom. In 1961 she had a top ten hit with the song, "Sixteen Reasons" and won a Theatre World Award for her Broadway debut in *The Star-Spangled Girl*. Confounding the skeptics, she directed, wrote, and produced a documentary on Vietnam, *A Healing*, in 1997. Her first husband (1963–66) was actor James Stacy; her second (1967–69) singer Eddie Fisher; her daughters are actresses Joely Fisher and Tricia Leigh Fisher; her brother was actor John Megna (1952–95), best known for playing Dill in *To Kill a Mockingbird*.

Screen: 1957: Eighteen and Anxious; Young and Dangerous; 1958: Dragstrip Riot; Rock-a-Bye Baby; The Party Crashers; 1961: Parrish; Susan Slade; 1963: Palm Springs Weekend; 1965: Two on a Guillotine; Never Too Late; 1966: Way…Way Out; 1971: The Grissom Gang; 1976: Scorchy; 1978: Sgt. Pepper's Lonely Hearts Club Band; 1982: Grease 2; 1987: Back to the Beach; 1988: Tapeheads; 1996: Love Is All There Is; 1997: James Dean: Race With Destiny/James Dean: Live Fast, Die Young (dtv); 2001: Returning Mickey Stern (dtv).

NY Stage: 1966: The Star-Spangled Girl.

Select TV: 1959–63: Hawaiian Eye (series); 1964: Wendy and Me (series); 1969: The Littlest Angel (sp); 1970: Mister Jericho; 1971: Kraft Music Hall Presents The Des O'Connor Show (series); 1972: Call Her Mom; Playmates; Every Man Needs One; 1974: The Sex Symbol; 1979: Love's Savage Fury; 1980: Scruples (ms); Murder Can Hurt You; 1981: Side Show; 1988: Bring Me the Head of Dobie Gillis; 1988–89: Starting from Scratch (series); 2001: Becoming Dick; 2002: Titus (series).

INGER STEVENS
(INGER STENSLAND)
BORN: STOCKHOLM, SWEDEN, OCTOBER 18, 1934.
DIED: APRIL 30, 1970.

A wistfully lovely blonde with a hard edge under her smooth surface, Inger Stevens was a troubled lady whose bumpy path led to yet another of Hollywood's unhappy endings. She came to the United States when she was 13, learned English to a point where her accent was completely undetectable, and then ran off to New York to find work in show business. While dancing at the Latin Quarter she took acting classes with Lee Strasberg that led to some live television guest work and a contract with Fox that went nowhere. Instead, she auditioned for and won the role of Bing Crosby's younger ex-wife in the MGM drama, *Man on Fire*, battling with him over custody of their son. Although the film had little success she quickly moved into three other assignments: *Cry Terror!*, again playing opposite a much older co-star, James Mason, this time stressing over their kidnapped child; *The Buccaneer*, as one of the ladies in love with pirate Yul Brynner; and *The World, the Flesh, and the Devil*, as the last woman on earth. There were no raves but she had presence, though not enough to suggest that she be withheld from working on television, which is what she did for the time being, doing more guest spots and finally her own series, *The Farmer's Daughter*, in which she reprised the role Loretta Young had done on screen. It made her famous enough for the scandals rags to make much of her marriage to a black musician at a time when this sort of thing was frowned upon by the stubbornly narrow minded. After her show's cancellation she returned to feature films, working extensively and, as previously, paired off with actors much older than herself, playing Walter Matthau's loving spouse in *A Guide for the Married Man*; the neglected wife of detective Richard Widmark in *Madigan*; a lady barber romanced by Dean Martin in *5 Card Stud*; and a widow attracted to Anthony Quinn in *A Dream of*

Kings. She had shown increasing assurance over the years but she cut her promising future short when she took an overdose of sleeping pills in 1970.

Screen: 1957: Man on Fire; 1958: Cry Terror!; The Buccaneer; 1959: The World, the Flesh, and the Devil; 1964: The New Interns; 1967: A Guide for the Married Man; A Time for Killing; 1968: Firecreek; Madigan; 5 Card Stud; Hang 'em High; 1969: House of Cards; A Dream of Kings.

NY Stage: 1956: Debut; 1960: Roman Candle; 1964: Mary, Mary.

Select TV: 1954: Sue Ellen (sp); Strangers in Hiding (sp); 1955: The Conviction of Peter Shea (sp); 1959: Diary of a Nurse (sp); The Indestructible Mr. Gore (sp); 1961: The Prisoner of Zenda (sp); 1962: Price of Tomatoes (sp); 1963: The Last of the Big Spenders (sp); 1963–66: The Farmer's Daughter (series); 1967: The Borgia Stick; 1970: Run, Simon, Run; The Mask of Sheba.

MARK STEVENS

(RICHARD STEVENS) BORN: CLEVELAND, OH, DECEMBER 13, 1915. DIED: SEPTEMBER 15, 1994.

As were many before him and many since, Mark Stevens was groomed for movie stardom only to find that his sort of passive screen presence fared better in the less demanding medium of television. In Canada he had studied painting at the Sir George Williams School of Fine Arts only to drift into radio, ending up as an announcer and station manager at WJW in Akron, Ohio. He journeyed to Hollywood where was signed by Warners who placed him in the background of several features, including the war films *Destination Tokyo* and *Objective, Burma!*, where he looked properly rugged and military. His official billing at this time was "Stephen Richards," although he was not credited on most of these assignments. Fox decided to polish him up and introduce him like a newcomer, re-naming him "Mark Stevens," and making him one of the inmates in a "B" prison melodrama, *Within These Walls.* They bumped him up to the lead in a good noir, *The Dark Corner,* in which he played the sort of cool private eye that one expected to find in these kinds of movies, though he lacked the color and edge of Humphrey Bogart, or even Bob Montgomery for that matter. Fox made him one of those faceless composers of those many biopic musicals of the day, *I Wonder Who's Kissing Her Now,* as Joe Howard, the fellow who gave the world, "Hello, My Baby;" starred him as a fed in *The Street of No Name,* one of the trendy docu-dramas of the late 1940s; and let him play Olivia de Havilland's loyal and forgettable husband in an important film, *The Snake Pit.* His contract soon ended and, when the 1950s arrived, he found himself on the tube as *Martin Kane: Private Eye,* and heading the cast of *Big Town,* eventually producing the latter through his own company. He ended up back on the big screen directing himself in five programmers before trickling out of the public eye.

Screen: AS STEPHEN RICHARDS: 1943: Destination Tokyo; 1944: Passage to Marseille; The Doughgirls; Hollywood Canteen; 1945: Objective, Burma!; Pride of the Marines; God Is My Co-Pilot.

AS MARK STEVENS: Within These Walls; 1946: From This Day Forward; The Dark Corner; 1947: I Wonder Who's Kissing Her Now; 1948: The Street With No Name; The Snake Pit; 1949: Sand; Oh, You Beautiful Doll; Dancing in the Dark; 1950: Please Believe Me; Between Midnight and Dawn; 1951: Target Unknown; Katie Did It; Little Egypt; Reunion in Reno; 1952: Mutiny; 1953: The Big Frame/The Lost Hours; Torpedo Alley; Jack Slade; 1954: Cry Vengeance (and dir.); 1956: Timetable (and dir.); 1957: Gunsight Ridge; 1958: Gun Fever (and dir.); Gunsmoke in Tucson; 1960: September Storm; 1964: Escape

from Hell Island (and dir.); Fate Is the Hunter; Frozen Alive; 1965: Sunscorched (and dir.; co-wr.); 1966: Vayas con Dios; Gringo!/Go With God Gringo! (nUSr); 1969: Espana otra Vez (nUSr); 1970: La Lola Dien Que no Vive Sola (nUSr); 1971: Es Usted mi Padre? (nUSr); 1972: La Furia del Hombre Lobo/Fury of the Wolfman (nUSr).

Select TV: 1952: Birth of a Hero (sp); 1953: This Is My Heart (sp); Confession (sp); 1953–54: Martin Kane: Private Eye (series); 1954–56: Big Town (series; and prod.); 1956: Washington Incident (sp); 1957: A Reasonable Doubt (sp).

STELLA STEVENS

(ESTELLE EGGLESTON) BORN: YAZOO CITY, MS, OCTOBER 1, 1936. ED: MEMPHIS ST. UNIV.

In the 1960s, Stella Stevens was on the right track. She was a great looking lady for whom the critics were always rooting. Decorative and winsomely sweet, she clearly showed a talent for comedy and for something a little grittier when given the chance. As she aged she inevitably went over to television, which was certainly a better direction than the direct-to-video route she took later on. She did some modeling and a *Playboy* spread before going to Hollywood, where she was signed to a contract by 20th Century-Fox. They debuted her in the chorus of a Bing Crosby film, *Say One for Me,* and then let Paramount have her. There she at least got a chance to make something of an impression, as the cartoonish Appassionata Von Climax in the musical, *Li'l Abner,* a droll and purposefully artifical-looking adaptation of the stage success. They then gave her two good dramatic assignments, first as the title role in *Man-Trap,* as Jeffrey Hunter's alcoholic nympho wife, and *Too Late Blues,* as a sad jazz singer who falls into prostitution, one of the early, interesting efforts by director John Cassavetes before he spun way out of control. For some reason the next natural step seemed to be to pair her off with Elvis Presley, as they did in one of his mediocre efforts, *Girls! Girls! Girls!,* and then with Jerry Lewis in *The Nutty Professor,* as the college student he is smitten with. The latter turned out to be the better deal since this was Lewis's best film and Stevens registered more charm than one might have expected in what was, after all, supposed to be Jerry's showcase. She then went over to MGM for a pair of comedies with Glenn Ford: the gentle *The Courtship of Eddie's Father,* as his dim-bulb love interest, and the dopey *Advance to the Rear,* as a prostitute.

In Britain she sank with an awful comedy, *The Secret of My Success;* added some pluck to the first of the Matt Helm films, *The Silencers,* where a good deal of the comedy came from her clumsiness; paired up with Glenn Ford again, this time for a dreary South-of-the-border drama, *Rage;* played a tough and free-thinking nun in *Where Angels Go ... Trouble Follows;* and did one of those weak sex comedies that were trickling away by the end of the 1960s, *How to Save a Marriage (And Ruin Your Life).* There was another good role, as a whore, in one of director Sam Peckinpah's best, *The Ballad of Cable Hogue,* but she then got stuck in another Mexican stinker, *A Town Called Hell,* before being singled out for praise among the cast of the poor feminist comedy, *Stand Up and Be Counted.* It was nice to see her in a big hit, *The Poseidon Adventure,* as the former tart married to cop Ernest Borgnine, but she was starting to become more closely associated with television by the mid-1970s. Things were not all that promising back at the movies where she married a corpse in a deadly black comedy, *Arnold;* dealt drugs in the blaxploitation flick *Cleopatra Jones and the Casino of Gold;* had little to do in the nostalgic *Nickelodeon;* and played a Gypsy in a rubbishy horror thing called *The Maintou*. It would have been nice to think that her fortunes would have changed somewhere along the line, but when she showed up as the butch prison warden in a Linda Blair howler called *Chained Heat*, the writing was on the wall. Much like her son, actor Andrew Stevens, she became a staple of the lowest form of video fodder, including several with her offspring like the aptly titled *Down the Drain*, *The Terror Within II*, *Illicit Dreams* (which Andrew also directed), and *Body Chemistry III & IV*, not to mention those not in support of her son, including *Mom*, as a aging hooker; and *The Granny*, as a zombie senior citizen. She directed a documentary, *The American Heroine*, and *The Ranch*, a comedy starring her son.

Screen: 1959: Say One for Me; The Blue Angel; Li'l Abner; 1961: Man-Trap; 1962: Too Late Blues; Girls! Girls! Girls!; 1963: The Nutty Professor; The Courtship of Eddie's Father; 1964: Advance to the Rear; 1965: Synanon; The Secret of My Success; 1966: The Silencers; Rage; 1968: Where Angels Go…Trouble Follows; How to Save a Marriage (And Ruin Your Life); Sol Madrid; 1969: The Mad Room; 1970: The Ballad of Cable Hogue; 1971: A Town Called Hell/A Town Called Bastard; 1972: Slaughter; Stand Up and Be Counted; The Poseidon Adventure; 1973: Arnold; 1975: Cleopatra Jones and the Casino of Gold; 1976: Las Vegas Lady; Nickelodeon; 1978: The Manitou; 1981: Wacko; 1983: Chained Heat; 1986: The Longshot; Monster in the Closet (filmed 1983); 1990: Mom (dtv); Down the Drain (dtv); Last Call (dtv); The Terror Within II (dtv); Exiled in America (dtv); 1992: The Nutty Nut (dtv); South Beach (dtv); 1993: Eye of the Stranger (dtv); Little Devils: The Birth (dtv); 1994: Molly and Gina (dtv); Point of Seduction: Body Chemistry III (dtv); Illicit Dreams (dtv); Hard Drive (dtv); 1995: Star Hunter (dtv); The Granny (dtv); Invisible Mom (dtv); Body Chemistry IV: Full Exposure (dtv); 1996: Virtual Combat (dtv); 1997: Bikini Hotel (dtv); 2001: The Long Ride Home (dtv); 2002: Jim Brown: All-American.

Select TV: 1960: Operation Dress (sp); 1961: The Great Alberti (sp); 1971: In Broad Daylight; 1972: Climb an Angry Mountain; 1973: Linda; 1974: The Day the Earth Moved; Honky Tonk; 1975: The New Original Wonder Woman; 1976: Kiss Me, Kill Me; Wanted: The Sundance Woman; 1977: Charlie Cobb: Nice Night for a Hanging; Murder in Peyton Place; The Night They Took Miss Beautiful; 1978: Cruise Into Terror; The Jordan Chance; 1979: Friendship, Secrets and Lies; Hart to Hart; The French Atlantic Affair (ms); 1980: Make Me an Offer; Children of Divorce; 1981: Twirl; 1981–82: Flamingo Road (series); 1983: Women of San Quentin; 1984: Amazons; No Man's Land; 1986: A Masterpiece of Murder; 1987: Tales from the Hollywood Hills: A Table at Ciro's (sp); Fatal Confession: A Father Dowling Mystery; 1988: Man Against the Mob; 1989: Jake Spanner: Private Eye; 1989–90: Santa Barbara (series); 1994: National Lampoon's Attack of the 5 Ft. 2 Women; 1996: General Hospital (series); Subliminal Seduction; In Cold Blood; 1997: The Christmas List; The Dukes of Hazard: Reunion!; 2000: By Dawn's Early Light; 2001: Strip Mall (series).

JAMES STEWART
BORN: INDIANA, PA, MAY 20, 1908.
ED: PRINCETON UNIV. DIED: JULY 2, 1997.

Very possibly the best-loved motion picture star of all, James Stewart got on everybody's good side. If you liked comedies, he could screwball with the best of them; for fans of the horse-opera he came to personify the American West, right up there alongside John Wayne; in drama he was one of the first actors to allow himself to display tears and vulnerability, like a

real man would. Audiences felt good when he loped onto the screen, beanpole thin, with that shy, gulping manner and the hesitant drawl that became one of the most-mimicked of all voices. Through several generations he stayed firmly and thoroughly a star, simply because he always was a magnificent actor. If some didn't notice the scope of his talents, it was because he was so self-effacing about it, which was why audiences liked him all along. He'd gone to school to study architecture, but met up with Joshua Logan who coaxed him into joining Cape Cod's summer stock group, the University Players. Henry Fonda was one member of the group and would remain one of Stewart's life-long friends. One of the plays that Stewart appeared in, *Carry Nation*, was deemed good enough to transfer to Broadway, and the star went with it, debuting there in 1932. It quickly closed, but Stewart wound up in a hit, *Goodbye Again*, by the end of the same year. Six more productions followed, by which time he'd stirred up enough interest from Hollywood that he screen-tested with MGM and was signed to a contract in 1935. They introduced him in a Spencer Tracy film, *The Murder Man*, in which he was an eager news reporter named Shorty, and then gave him the crucial role of Jeanette MacDonald's fugitive brother, the one whom mountie Nelson Eddy is looking for, in *Rose-Marie*.

He was loaned out to Universal for *Next Time We Love*, because Margaret Sullavan, an alumnus of the University Players, specifically asked for him, making this his largest role yet. Returning to his home base, he found himself back in secondary leads for *Wife vs. Secretary*, as Jean Harlow's neglected boyfriend, and *The Gorgeous Hussy*, as one of Joan Crawford's cast-aside suitors, but got top-billing, for the first time, in *Speed*, a "B" picture about auto racing, and helped introduce the Cole Porter hit "Easy to Love," in *Born to Dance*, one of the year's big moneymakers. 20th Century-Fox borrowed him only to miscast him, as Parisian sewer worker Chico, in the unwanted remake of *Seventh Heaven*. After this misstep, things started improving for him back at Metro, with *Navy Blue and Gold*, adding a welcome bit of neuroses to the role of the naval cadet haunted by his father's past record; *Of Human Hearts*, challenging his parson dad Walter Huston at every opportunity and being scolded by Abraham Lincoln for neglecting his maw, Beulah Bondi; RKO's *Vivacious Lady*, his first real success in comedy, as the straight-laced professor who marries showgirl Ginger Roger; and *The Shopworn Angel*, similarly playing a rube who hooks up with a wordly lady, in this instance, Margaret Sullavan, again. His next loan-out proved to be his biggest break yet, playing the nice guy who falls in love with Jean Arthur and takes a shine to her unconventional clan in director Frank Capra's *You Can't Take It With You*. This was one of the big comedies of its day and it ended up winning the Academy Award for Best Picture of 1938, though it is the least regarded of the three Stewart did with this director. Before they teamed again he did Selznick's *Made for Each Other*, getting one chance only to star with one of the most admired ladies in the field of comedy, Carole Lombard, and ending up, ironically, in a melodrama.

MGM put him on skates for *The Ice Follies of 1939*, one of the low points of his employment there, proving that he was in no position yet to refuse assignments; then teamed him with Claudette Colbert for a bright comedy, *It's a Wonderful World*, which would often be unjustly forgotten because of the similarity of its title with a later film of Stewart's. Back with Capra and Columbia, he soared right up to the very top with *Mr. Smith Goes to Washington*, a sharply written political satire-drama about corruption in the nation's capital, with Stewart in what would become one of his defining roles, the idealistic young senator who wins over the cynics with his optimism. It made him some sort of moralistic hero for the cause of the common man and his senate filibuster scene became one of the most famous in movie history. The film, one of the bonafide classics of 1930s Hollywood, brought Stewart his first Oscar nomination. Things kept going swimmingly as he played another good man confronting corruption, in *Destry Rides Again*, a jokey Universal western that ended up fairly serious by the finale. He then did the third and best of his four teamings with Sullavan, *The Shop Around the Corner*, one of the loveliest of all motion picture romances, with Stewart playing the clerk who, at first, doesn't realize that the woman he is battling with is his cherished pen pal. Fourth up for this duo was the much more serious *The Mortal Storm*, a strong drama about the growing Nazi menace, after which Stewart did the "rube and the sophisticate" bit yet again, for Warners's *No Time for Comedy*, with much less success than one would have hoped for from a pairing with Rosalind Russell. It didn't matter, however, because that was followed by *The Philadelphia Story*, which became just about everyone's ideal of the sophisticated comedy, MGM-style. Stewart, who was third-billed, was as assured as ever, playing the reporter who temporarily loses his heart to socialite Katharine Hepburn, and he won the Academy Award for Best Actor of 1940.

This triumph caused most to overlook two failures, *Come Live with Me*, as a writer facing deportation, and *Pot o'Gold*, Stewart's own personal choice for his worst picture, as well as one lousy moneymaker, *Ziegfeld Follies*, which put him in the same movie as Judy Garland, but foolishly paired him off with Lana Turner instead. He took a break from films to join the Air Force, where he became an officer of the highest merit and one of the most distinguished men in the acting profession to serve during World War II. When he returned to Hollywood, with five years having passed since his last screen appearance, he and Capra got together for a project for the latter's newly established independent company, Liberty Films. The end result was Stewart's favorite of his films and, in time, most of the World's, too. *It's a Wonderful Life* was a beautifully done combination of Americana and fantasy, with Stewart as a small-town guy, tired of his decent and uneventful life, who is given a chance to see how those around him would have fared had he never lived. In an effort to make it seem like a newly discovered gem, folks from future generations would write it off as a failure on its initial run, though it was, in fact, a respectable box-office performer in its time and one of the five nominees for the 1946 Best Picture Oscar. Stewart himself was in the running for the trophy for the third time. Although *Magic Town* didn't click, he did very nicely with one of Fox's best late 1940s docu-dramas, *Call Northside 777*, as a reporter trying to spring innocent Richard Conte from prison. With his hair grayed to look older, he did his first film for director Alfred Hitchcock, *Rope*, an experimental piece shot in continuous takes, and something that wouldn't get its due for years to come. Rather than go to that one, audiences went in big numbers to a numbingly familiar biopic, MGM's *The Stratton Story*, in which he was a ballplayer who comes back to the game after losing a leg in hunting accident. That he made so hackneyed a script palatable was a sterling example of the conviction he brought to all his material.

After a disappointing pairing with Spencer Tracy, in *Malaya*, he went over to Universal to do a western for director Anthony Mann, *Winchester '73*, and that film did so well that the two would team up frequently during the 1950s, mostly in this genre. There was another western, for Fox, *Broken Arrow*, one of the first to treat Native Americans with respect, and, just to emphasize the film's noble intentions, Stewart was given a romance with an Indian woman, although the impact was diluted by the fact that she was played by Caucasian Debra Paget. Having taken over the role of Elwood P. Dowd during *Harvey*'s Broadway run, he was guaranteed of getting the part in the 1950 movie version. This turned out to be another of his greatest roles — the gentle drunk whose visions of a giant white rabbit make him the sort of nutcase everyone aspires to be. It brought him his fourth Oscar nod and remains one of Hollywood's most induring whimsies. In England he did a good thriller, *No Highway in the Sky*, about an airplane in trouble while in flight, playing the part of the absent-minded scientist with a lot more humor than one might have expected in such circumstances. He then wound up in the cast of another Best Picture Oscar winner, *The Greatest Show on Earth*, doing the whole part disguised in clown make-up, which was essential in so much as his character was on the run from the police. It was a most unusual credit on his résumé and, with the passing years, when this colorful blockbuster began to be looked on with disdain by more cynical generations, Stewart was about the only element spared any razzing. The westerns kept coming in the meantime, with Stewart scoring further hits with *Bend of the River*; *The Naked Spur*, the best of the lot, a tense tale in which he was a bounty hunter out to get Robert Ryan; *The Far Country*; and *The Man from Laramie*. There was a massive moneymaker with another biopic, *The Glenn Miller Story*, which rose above the usual clichés with its wonderful music; and then *Strategic Air Command*, a tiresome Air Force flick that also did quite nicely.

His western box-office success cooled down somewhat with *Night Passage*, and there was little audience turn-out for *The Spirit of St. Louis*, a well-done account of Charles Lindbergh's famous solo flight that almost made one forget how old Stewart looked in a part he would have been ideal for, 20 years earlier. No doubt the peaks of this period were three films for Hitchcock: *Rear Window*, a splendid execution of a gimmick, in which everything was shot on one big set and seen from Stewart's apartment, where he was a wheelchair-bound peeping tom; *The Man Who Knew Too Much*, a superior remake of the same director's 1934 film, with Stewart and Doris Day trying to locate their kidnapped son; and *Vertigo*, a tale of obsession which resulted in one of the actor's most mature and haunting performances, as a tormented man in love with aloof Kim Novak and her "look-alike." The last film fared poorest at the time, but came to be considered one of the most influential and brilliant of all films. That same year, 1958, Stewart and Novak were back together for a whimsical look at witchcraft, in *Bell Book and Candle*, after which he was a lawyer taking on an unsavory case in one of the big "adult" movies of its day, *Anatomy of a Murder*. He was marvelous locking horns with rival attorney George C. Scott and this performance brought him his fifth and final Oscar mention. There were few other actors one would want to journey down an extensive history of the Federal Bureau of Investigations with, but Stewart guided his audiences engagingly through *The F.B.I. Story*, after which he was in two movies for director John Ford: *Two Rode Together*, which pretty much faded into obscurity, despite his excellent, unsentimental work as a mercenary, and the better *The Man Who Shot Liberty Valance*, again playing a decent man trying to stand up to evil, in one of the great director's most-highly regarded, later-day works. It is worth noting that Stewart was considered important enough to rate billing *above* John Wayne, quite an achievement, in so much as Wayne was at his box-office peak during this period.

Mr. Hobbs Takes a Vacation was a funny family comedy, often unfairly grouped with the two duds that followed, *Take Her, She's Mine* and *Dear Brigitte*. In between he was a trapper who marries Carroll Baker in the lengthy, star-filled epic *How the West Was Won*, and had his last big financial success, in 1965, as the war-hating patriarch in *Shenandoah*. After a decent plane-crash drama, *The Flight of the Phoenix*, he did some westerns, including two with Fonda, *Firecreek*, and the comical *The Cheyenne Social Club*, but the two stars were now in their 60s and audiences were starting to look elsewhere for newer faces. Stewart's last starring role, as a glass-eyed ex-con, in *Fools' Parade*, passed by with barely any notice, so he chose to do television, starring in two series, neither of which caught on. The movies coaxed him back to do a supporting role, in John Wayne's last movie, *The Shootist*, as his doctor, and it should have been, in a perfect world, Stewart's last film, considering the lack of undistinguished fare he went out on. There was the dopey disaster melodrama *Airport '77*, as a millionaire; the dated *The Magic of Lassie*, in which he even got to sing while playing a folksy old grandpa; the much-hated remake of *The Big Sleep*, as the old coot who hires Philip Marlowe; the basically unreleased *A Tale of Africa*; and *An American Tail: Fievel Goes West*, which only required his voice. In his later years he published a book of poems and then went into seclusion after his beloved wife Gloria died. He was presented with the Kennedy Center Honors, the American Film Institute Film Achievement Award, the Presidential Medal of Freedom, and a special Academy Award in 1984. These were testaments not only to his unsurpassable contributions to the motion picture field, but because he struck so many moviegoers as the sort of human being that the world could use more of.

Screen: 1935: The Murder Man; 1936: Rose-Marie; Next Time We Love; Wife vs. Secretary; Small Town Girl; Speed; The Gorgeous Hussy; Born to Dance; After the Thin Man; 1937: Seventh Heaven; The Last Gangster; Navy Blue and Gold; 1938: Of Human Hearts; Vivacious Lady; The Shopworn Angel; You Can't Take It With You; 1939: Made for Each Other; The Ice Follies of 1939; It's a Wonderful World; Mr. Smith Goes to Washington; Destry Rides Again; 1940: The Shop Around the Corner; The Mortal Storm; No Time for Comedy; The Philadelphia Story; 1941: Come Live With Me; Pot o' Gold; Ziegfeld Girl; 1946: It's a Wonderful Life; 1947: Magic Town; 1948: Call Northside 777; On Our Merry Way/A Miracle Can Happen; Rope; You Gotta Stay Happy; 1949: The Stratton Story; Malaya; 1950: Winchester '73; Broken Arrow; The Jackpot; Harvey; 1951: No Highway in the Sky; 1952: The Greatest Show on Earth; Bend of the River; Carbine Williams; 1953: The Naked Spur; Thunder Bay; 1954: The Glenn Miller Story; Rear Window; 1955: The Far Country; Strategic Air Command; The Man From Laramie; 1956: The Man Who Knew Too Much; 1957: The Spirit of St. Louis; Night Passage; 1958: Vertigo; Bell Book and Candle; 1959: Anatomy of a Murder; The FBI Story; 1960: The Mountain Road; 1961: Two Rode Together; X-15 (narrator); 1962: The Man Who Shot Liberty Valance; Mr. Hobbs Takes a Vacation; 1963: How the West Was Won; Take Her, She's Mine; 1964: Cheyenne Autumn; 1965: Dear Brigitte; Shenandoah; The Flight of the Phoenix; 1966: The Rare Breed; 1968: Firecreek; Bandolero!; 1970: The Cheyenne Social Club; 1971: Fools' Parade; 1974: That's Entertainment!; 1976: The Shootist; 1977: Airport '77; 1978: The Big Sleep; The Magic of Lassie; 1981: A Tale of Africa/Afurika Monogatari; 1991: An American Tail: Fievel Goes West (voice).

NY Stage: 1932: Carry Nation; Goodbye Again; 1933: Spring in Autumn; All Good Americans; 1934: Yellow Jack; Divided by Three; Page Miss Glory; 1935: A Journey by Night; 1947: Harvey; 1970: Harvey (revival).

Select TV: 1955: The Windmill (sp); 1957: The Town Is Past (sp);

The Trail to Christmas (sp); 1959: Cindy's Fella (sp); 1962: Flashing Spikes (sp); 1971–72: The Jimmy Stewart Show (series); 1972: Harvey (sp); 1973: Hawkins on Murder; 1973–74: Hawkins (series); 1981: Mr. Kruger's Christmas (sp); 1983: Right of Way; 1986: North and South, Book II (ms).

PAUL STEWART

(PAUL STERNBERG) BORN: NEW YORK, NY, MARCH 13, 1908. DIED: FEBRUARY 17, 1986.

Another of the many fine performers whose motion picture career was launched via their involvement with Orson Welles, the dark-browed, graying Paul Stewart had started in radio, where he was heard on hundreds of broadcasts during the 1930s. With a few Broadway credits to his name, he joined Welles's Mercury Players in 1938, serving as both performer and producer of their radio program, *Mercury Theatre on the Air*. When Welles came to Hollywood to give the world *Citizen Kane*, Stewart was among the cast, photographed in a sinister manner, as Raymond, the servant who offers some insight into the cryptic "Rosebud," near the end of the film. Of course producers couldn't help but look at Stewart's dark countenance and see him as a villain, casting him as Cary Grant's ex-partner who tries to steer him wrong in *Mr. Lucky*, and the killer who tries to dispose of witness Bobby Driscoll in the taut "B"-classic *The Window*, which was probably the best screen role he would ever have. After that he was seen as the group medical officer in *Twelve O'Clock High*; the fight manager abandoned by arrogant Kirk Douglas in *Champion*; a sports writer telling *The Joe Louis Story*; a mob boss befriended by undercover agent Dennis O'Keefe in *Chicago Syndicate*; a gang leader in the future-cult film *Kiss Me Deadly*; the owner of the title establishment, who hires Elvis Presley to bring in the crowds, in *King Creole*; the administrator at a school for mentally retarded children in *A Child Is Waiting*; a journalist reporting on the executions of the killers in *In Cold Blood*; Florenz Ziegfeld in *W.C. Fields and Me*; and, still looking properly threatening, a mob Godfather in *Revenge of the Pink Panther*. Starting in the mid-1950s he also began working behind the cameras directing television episodes.

Screen: 1941: Citizen Kane; 1942: Johnny Eager; 1943: Government Girl; Mr. Lucky; 1948: Berlin Express (narrator); 1949: The Window; Illegal Entry; Easy Living; Champion; Twelve O'Clock High; 1950: Walk Softly, Stranger; Edge of Doom; 1951: Appointment With Danger; 1952: Carbine Williams; Deadline U.S.A.; Loan Shark; We're Not Married!; The Bad and the Beautiful; 1953: The Juggler; The Joe Louis Story; 1954: Prisoner of War; Deep in My Heart; 1955: Chicago Syndicate; Kiss Me Deadly; Hell on Frisco Bay; The Cobweb; 1956: The Wild Party; 1957: Top Secret Affair; 1958: King Creole; 1959: Flor de Mayo/Beyond All Limits (nUSr); 1963: A Child Is Waiting; 1965: The Greatest Story Ever Told; 1967: In Cold Blood; 1969: How to Commit Marriage; Jigsaw; 1972: Los Fabulosos de Trinidad/ Fabulous Trinity (nUSr); 1974: F for Fake; 1975: The Day of the Locust; Murph the Surf/Live a Little, Steal a Lot; 1976: W.C. Fields and Me; 1977: Opening Night; 1978: Revenge of the Pink Panther; 1981: S.O.B.; Nobody's Perfekt; 1982: Tempest.

NY Stage: 1931: Two Seconds; 1932: East Of Broadway; Bulls Bears And Asses; 1938: Wine Of Choice; 1941: Native Son; 1950: Mister Roberts.

Select TV: 1950: Over 21 (sp); 1955: Top Secret (series); 1956: Confession (sp); 1958: The First Star (sp); 1959: Deadline (series);

1964: A Case of Armed Robbery (sp); 1966–67: The Man Who Never Was (series); 1970: Carter's Army; 1971: City Beneath the Sea; 1978: The Dain Curse.

JILL ST. JOHN

(JILL OPPENHEIM) BORN: LOS ANGELES, CA, AUGUST 19, 1940.

A small and shapely redhead who grew from "nice girl" into a more blatant sex kitten during the loosening of the motion picture code, Jill St. John had been in the business since she was a child, acting on the radio soap serial *One Man's Family*, under her real name. She continued to work in that medium until she went to college, during which time she got a film offer from Universal, being treated as pretty much of a newcomer when she showed up as one of the girls in love with John Saxon in a pea-brained teen romance, *Summer Love*, in 1957. Fox made her offspring to Clifton Webb in two comedies, *The Remarkable Mr. Pennypacker* and *Holiday for Lovers*, in the latter somebody's idea of an accomplished sculptress, after which she was seen trekking through the Amazon looking for dinosaurs in the hokey Irwin Allen remake of *The Lost World*. There was a attempt to move up to higher quality fare with *The Roman Spring of Mrs. Stone* and an adaptation of Fitzgerald's *Tender is the Night*, but since the critical reception was so negative for both, St. John found herself back in more suitable territory, doing the sort of broad commercial comedies that were very much a part of the 1960s, including *Come Blow Your Horn*, paired with swinging bachelor Frank Sinatra; the Jerry Lewis romp *Who's Minding the Store?*, as the rich girl posing as an elevator operator; and *Eight on a Lam*, where she was simply dreadful as a golddigger hitting on Bob Hope. More serious were *The Liquidator*, a spy saga with Rod Taylor; the unintentionally funny *The Oscar*, as Stephen Boyd's stripper girlfriend; and *Banning*, appearing as a lady after golfer opposite Robert Wagner, someone she would catch up with later on in real-life. Looking totally ill at ease in period costumes, she reprised Maureen O'Hara's role in *The King's Pirate*, a cheap remake of *Against All Flags*, and then did two of her more popular films, *Tony Rome*, terrific as a smart-alecky Miami Beach divorcée, and *Diamonds Are Forever*, as Bond-girl Tiffany Case. By the mid-1970s she was predominantly a television name, although she showed up on the big screen as the warden in a trashy women's prison picture, *The Concrete Jungle*. Little was heard of her in later years outside of becoming the new Mrs. Robert Wagner, in 1990. Earlier, she had been married (1967–69) to singer Jack Jones.

Screen: 1957: Thunder in the East; 1958: Summer Love; 1959: The Remarkable Mr. Pennypacker; Holiday for Lovers; 1960: The Lost World; 1961: The Roman Spring of Mrs. Stone; 1962: Tender Is the Night; 1963: Who's Been Sleeping in My Bed?; Come Blow Your Horn; Who's Minding the Store?; 1964: Honeymoon Hotel; 1966: The Liquidator; The Oscar; 1967: Banning; Eight on the Lam; Tony Rome; The King's Pirate; 1971: Diamonds Are Forever; 1972: Sitting Target; 1982: The Concrete Jungle; The Act/Bless 'em All (dtv); 1992: The Player; 1998: Something to Believe In (dtv); 2001: The Calling (dtv); 2002: The Trip (dtv).

Select TV: 1957: Junior Miss (sp); 1963: The House Next Door (sp); 1965: Russian Roulette (sp); 1966: Fame Is the Name of the Game; 1967: How I Spent My Summer Vacation; 1969: The Spy Killer; 1970: Foreign Exchange; 1976: Brenda Starr; 1977:

Telethon; 1979: Hart to Hart; 1982: Rooster; 1983–84: Emerald Point N.A.S. (series); 1989: Around the World in 80 Days (ms); 1995: Out There.

DEAN STOCKWELL

(ROBERT DEAN STOCKWELL)
BORN: HOLLYWOOD, CA, MARCH 5, 1935.

There were three successful chapters in the career of Dean Stockwell, as he went from child actor to young adult leading man and, finally, to character player, resurfacing triumphantly just when skeptics assumed he had nothing left to offer. He was, in fact, extremely good in all three of these phases, as much at ease amid the MGM studio gloss as he was in off-the-wall drive-in fare and esoteric art house offerings. His parents were both entertainers, his father's claim-to-fame being that he was the singing voice of Prince Charming in Disney's *Snow White and the 7 Dwarfs*. Dean and his younger brother, Guy, were both swept into the business, making their professional debuts on Broadway, in 1943, in *The Innocent Voyage*. Although Guy did not return to acting until his adult years (he was perhaps best known as the star of Universal's 1966 remake of *Beau Geste*), Dean was spotted by an MGM talent scout and brought to Hollywood for a screen test. He was put under contract and launched with a small part, as Gregory Peck's son, in *The Valley of Decision* in 1945. Later that same year he had the more important role of Kathryn Grayson's nephew, who runs away in hopes of joining the Navy, in the hit musical *Anchors Aweigh*, at one point being sung to sleep by Frank Sinatra. Rather than fritter him away on nothing parts, the studio saw him as a potential star and allowed him to carry the first half of the epic tale *The Green Years*, playing a Scottish lad who grows up to be Tom Drake, and then let him reprise Jackie Coogan's old role in *The Mighty McGurk*, which was pretty much a re-do of *The Champ*, going so far as to feature Wallace Beery himself in the title role. He had little to do as Nick Charles, Jr. in *Song of the Thin Man*, the last of the famous detective series, but was fortunate to be borrowed by Fox for the 1947 Oscar-winner *Gentleman's Agreement*, again as Peck's son, this time facing anti-Semitism when dad poses as a Jew, giving a mature and heartfelt performance as a very hurt and confused child.

Although he wasn't considered an actual box-office draw, the offers kept on coming simply because he was one of the least-mannered child actors around. RKO starred him as *The Boy with Green Hair*, an odd bit of pretentious whimsy, making a statement against war, while his home studio cast him as the bed-ridden Colin in *The Secret Garden*, opposite a rapidly growing Margaret O'Brien. It was clear that of the two, Stockwell was maturing more impressively as an actor. After supporting Joel McCrea in *Stars in My Crown*, Stockwell was moved up to the frontlines for two major releases, the delightfully nostalgic *The Happy Years*, splendidly playing a defiant prep school lad who makes friends in spite of himself in perhaps his most satisfying performance during this period, and *Kim*, in the title role, and certainly the best thing about this flat rendering of the famous Kipling story. Having reached the ripe old age of 15, he was no longer wanted at MGM, so he went over to Universal to do a western, *Cattle Drive*, then dropped out of sight for five years, returning in some television anthology dramas. Back on the big screen he poured on the James Dean-angst as Fred MacMurray's hell-raising brother in *Gun for a Coward*, and did *The Careless Years*, one of the many glossy teen dramas that populated the screens in the late 1950s. What saved him at this point, and gave him a ton of credibility as he made the uncomfortable transition to adulthood, was being cast as one of the homosexual murderers in Broadway's *Compulsion*, a drama based on the real-life Leopold and Loeb case of the 1920s. Stockwell was so good in the role that he was retained for the film version and revealed an even more layered talent than he had shown as a kid, with his brooding and creepy performance as the arrogant killer. This was followed by two other good roles in two more important films: *Sons and Lovers*, as the rebellious coal miner's son, and *Long Day's Journey Into Night*, as the consumptive Edward, more than holding his own against the likes of Katharine Hepburn and Jason Robards. Selective of his roles at this point, he chose to do a French-British romance, *Rapture*, and then donned hippie hair as a guru in *Psych-Out*, one of the drug-influenced AIP cheapies of the late 1960s that can only be looked upon today as camp.

Frizzy-haired with mustache, he showed up in some crummy horror films, *The Dunwich Horror*, and the memorably titled *The Werewolf of Washington* (his father also had a small part), as well as the requisite motorcycle epic, *The Loners*, in which he played a half-breed. By the mid-1970s his interest in the business had waned and he was suddenly nowhere in sight, having dropped out to become a real estate broker. In the 1980s, he began to resurface in mainstream work like *Wrong Is Right*, as a government official, and his own property, *Human Highway*, an anti-nuke film that he co-wrote and co-directed with musician Neil Young. His fine performance as Harry Dean Stanton's level headed brother in *Paris, Texas* really helped herald his return and suddenly Stockwell was someone people wanted to work with again. He showed up as the corrupt doctor in the sci-fi flop *Dune*; had one of his more unforgettable gigs, wearing make-up and miming to the song, "In Dreams," in the cult classic *Blue Velvet*; was one of the bad guys in Eddie Murphy's hit sequel *Beverly Hills Cop II*; and played a macho Marine officer in *Gardens of Stone*. He really hit the bull's-eye with his pricelessly funny performance as a gangster terrified of jealous wife Mercedes Ruehl in *Married to the Mob*, for which he earned an Oscar nomination in the supporting category. Shortly afterwards he landed the role of Scott Bakula's other-worldly counselor-guardian in the television series *Quantum Leap*, which became a favorite among sci-fi aficionados. It was just as well that he took to television, because in the 1990s the movie assignments got cheesier, resulting in a lot of direct-to-video titles, although he did get a chance to shine in *The Player*, partnered with Richard E. Grant, trying to hustle a script to Tim Robbins. Among his other high-budgeted assignments were *McHale's Navy*, as the excitable Captain Binghamton; *Air Force One*, as President Harrison Ford's defense secretary; and *John Grisham's The Rainmaker*, as a judge. He was briefly married (1960–62) to actress Millie Perkins.

Screen: 1945: The Valley of Decision; Abbott and Costello in Hollywood; Anchors Aweigh; 1946: The Green Years; Home, Sweet Homicide; The Mighty McGurk; 1947: Song of the Thin Man; The Romance of Rosy Ridge; The Arnelo Affair; Gentleman's Agreement; 1948: Deep Waters; The Boy with Green Hair; 1949: Down to the Sea in Ships; The Secret Garden; 1950: Stars in My Crown; The Happy Years; Kim; 1951: Cattle Drive; 1957: Gun for a Coward; The Careless Years; 1959: Compulsion; 1960: Sons and Lovers; 1962: Long Day's Journey Into Night; 1965: Rapture; 1968: Psych-Out; 1970: The Dunwich Horror; 1971: The Last Movie; 1972: The Loners; 1973: The Werewolf of Washington; 1975: Win, Place or Steal/The Big Payoff/Another Day at the Races; The Pacific Connection; 1976: Won Ton Ton, the Dog Who Saved Hollywood; Tracks; 1982: Wrong Is Right; Human Highway (and co-dir.; co-wr.); 1983:

Alsino and the Condor; 1984: Paris, Texas; Dune; 1985: To Kill a Stranger (dtv); The Legend of Billie Jean; To Live and Die in L.A.; Papa Was a Preacher (dtv); 1986: Blue Velvet; 1987: Gardens of Stone; Beverly Hills Cop II; Banzai Runner (dtv); 1988: The Blue Iguana; The Time Guardian; Tucker: The Man and His Dream; Married to the Mob; Palais Royale/Smokescreen (dtv); Jorge; um Brasileiro/The Long Haul (nUSr); 1989: Stickfighter (filmed 1975; dtv); Buying Time (dtv); Limit Up; 1990: Sandino (nUSr); 1992: Friends and Enemies (dtv); The Player; 1994: Chasers; 1995: Naked Souls (dtv); 1996: Mr. Wrong; Midnight Blue (dtv); 1997: The Last Resort (dtv); McHale's Navy; Living in Peril (dtv); Air Force One; John Grisham's The Rainmaker; 1998: Sinbad: The Battle of the Dark Knights (nUSr); 1999: Restraining Order (dtv); The Venice Project (nUSr); Water Damage (dtv); Rites of Passage (dtv); 2000: In Pursuit (dtv); The Flunky (nUSr); 2001: The Quickie (nUSr); Interno (nUSr); 2002: CQ; Face to Face (dtv); 2003: Buffalo Soldiers.

NY Stage: 1943: The Innocent Voyage; 1957: Compulsion.

Select TV; 1956: Innocent Witness (sp); Class of '58 (sp); 1957: Fight the Whole World (sp); 1958: God Is My Judge (sp); 1959: The Family Man (sp); Made in Japan (sp); The Killers (sp); 1961: The Joke and the Valley (sp); 1964: Their Own Executioners (sp); 1971: Paper Man; The Failing of Raymond; 1972: The Adventures of Nick Carter; 1976: The Return of Joe Forrester/Cop on the Beat; 1977: A Killing Affair; 1981: Born to Be Sold; 1987: Kenny Rogers as The Gambler Part III: The Legend Continues; 1989–93: Quantum Leap (series); 1991: Son of the Morning Star; Backtrack; 1992: Shame; Fatal Memories; 1993: Bonanza: The Return; 1994: In the Line of Duty: The Price of Vengeance; Vanishing Son II (dtv); Justice in a Small Town; The Innocent; Madonna: Innocence Lost; 1995: Deadline for Murder: From the Files of Edna Buchanan; The Langoliers; 1996: Unabomber: The True Story; Twilight Man; 1997: The Shadow Men; Closer to Danger; The Tony Danza Show (series); Popular Science (series); 1998: It's True (series); 1999: What Katy Did; 2000: They Nest.

LEWIS STONE
(LOUIS SHEPHERD STONE)
BORN: WORCESTER, MA, NOVEMBER 15, 1879.
DIED: SEPTEMBER 12, 1953.

It was hard to imagine MGM without Lewis Stone who, during the studio's blossoming years at the dawn of talkies into the early 1950s, came to represent some kind of dependable spirit of no-nonsense acting. The long-faced, gray-since-youth thespian had served in the Spanish-American War under Major Walter Reed, whom he would later portray on film, in *Yellow Jack*, in 1938. After that he became part of a stock company that toured Canada with a play called *Side-Tacked*, and eventually made it to Broadway in *The Bowery After Dark*. Following some more tours and a triumphant return to New York in *The Bird of Paradise*, in 1912, he was signed to do a film for Essany, *The Man Who Found Out*. He continued to fluctuate between movie and stage for a while until the former won out, as interest in him as a motion picture lead increased. Therefore, he became an under-cover spy in *Inside the Lines*; both a Mountie and his prey in *The River's End* (and then appeared soon afterwards in Mountie uniform for *Nomads of the North*, *The Golden Snare* and *The White Mouse*); a womanizing pianist in *The Concert*; and a British earl gone bad in *Pilgrims of the Night*. There was even a film that he had written the story for, *Man's Desire*, in which he ran a lumber camp. MGM hired him to play the coveted dual leading roles in their 1922 production of *The Prisoner of Zenda*, and although he seemed rather aged for the part(s), its success was instrumental in making him that much more famous to the movie-going public. Thereafter, he was lured by bad women — Estelle Taylor, in *A Fool There Was*, and Leatrice Joy, in *You Can't Fool Your Wife*; was the Marquis de la Tour in the 1923 rendering of *Scaramouche*, a property he'd return to in 1952, albeit in a smaller role; and led a team of adventurers into *The Lost World*, one of the pioneering movies in the field of special effects.

The last was made for First National for whom he was under contract and he stayed with them for *The Talker*, battling his wife over women's rights; *Too Much Money*, as a millionaire suddenly bankrupt; *An Affair of the Follies*, as another man of wealth, falling for mechanic's wife Billie Dove; *The Prince of Headwaiters*, in the title role; and *The Private Life of Helen of Troy*, as the King of Troy. Over at Paramount he did *The Patriot*, and, although Emil Jannings had the juicier part of the crazed Russian Czar, it was Stone who had the title role, as the prime minister who tries to destroy the ruler to save his country. Stone got the best of the reviews, wound up with his one and only Oscar nomination, and accepted an offer, in 1929, from long-time admirer Louis B. Mayer to come work at Metro, staying under contract to that company for the remainder of his life. He started off in a Greta Garbo vehicle, *A Woman of Affairs*, as her father, and this would be the first of six with the star, making him the actor with whom she worked the most. Continuing in some of the studio's big releases during the early sound era, he was Norma Shearer's lawyer in *The Trial of Mary Dugan*; Ruth Chatterton's husband in *Madame X*; Robert Montgomery's father in *Their Own Desire*; the warden in *The Big House*; Garbo's older lover in *Romance*; and Helen Hayes's rich lover, who turns out to be a thief, in *The Sin of Madelon Claudet*. He was now a star name who was not expected to carry the load and, to that degree, he was in a most enviable position. He solidified his standing as one of the studio's formidable talents in the next two with Garbo: *Mata Hari*, as her cold and callous superior, and best of all *Grand Hotel*, in which he was memorable as the world-wearied, birth-marked Dr. Otternschlag, who caps the movie with its famous line, "Grand Hotel...people come, people go...nothing ever happens."

With requisite goatee, he was a Southerner with a drinking problem in *The Wet Parade*; an archeologist kept from his sons because of a *Divorce in the Family*; and the invincible Scotland Yard inspector Nayland Smith, battling evil Asian Boris Karloff in the kitschy *The Mask of Fu Manchu*. Stone himself went mildly Asian for *The Son-Daughter*, saddled with the name of Dr. Dong Tong; was the department store owner facing Depression hardships in *Looking Forward*, paired with MGM's other grand old man, Lionel Barrymore; and did his last and best with Garbo, *Queen Christina*, as her counselor. He took something of a back seat to some of the more colorful characters in *Treasure Island*, as Captain Smollett; *David Copperfield*, as Mr. Wickfield; and *China Seas*, as a disgraced sea captain, but was in top form as the eloquent outlaw in the 1936 version of *Three Godfathers*, as the learned member of this band of second-rate bank robbers. Although he'd get interesting offers elsewhere, notably Universal's *The Man Who Cried Wolf*, where he was an actor confessing to murders in order to cover up his guilt over the one he is really planning, it was his home lot that gave him the part which made him a part of movie lore, Judge James K. Hardy. Lionel Barrymore, who had originated the character in *A Family Affair*, was forced, due to physical constrictions, to abandon this part in the second of the Hardy family series, *You're Only Young Once*. Stone was hired as his

replacement and made the role completely his own, becoming a whole generation's idea of the wizened and lecturing old dad, with a word of wisdom on every subject. It was evident that Mickey Rooney was the real star of the series, but Stone held on to his top billing for most of the run, which ended, for him, with *Love Laughs at Andy Hardy*, in 1946. He kept quite busy after that series had run its course, from *State of the Union*, as Angela Lansbury's tycoon dad, to *Stars in My Crown*, as a small-town doctor, to the 1952 version of *The Prisoner of Zenda*, as a cardinal. The year after the last was released, he died of a heart attack while chasing some vandals off his property.

Screen: 1915: The Man Who Found Out; 1916: Honor's Altar; The Havoc; According to the Code; 1918: Inside the Lines; The Man of Bronze; 1919: Man's Desire (and co-wr.); 1920: The River's End; Milestones; Held by the Enemy; Nomads of the North; 1921: The Concert; Beau Revel; Don't Neglect Your Wife; The Child Thou Gavest Me; Pilgrims of the Night; The White Mouse; 1922: The Rosary; The Prisoner of Zenda; A Fool There Was; Trifling Women; 1923: The Dangerous Age; The World's Applause; You Can't Fool Your Wife; Scaramouche; 1924: Cytherea; Why Men Leave Home; The Stranger; Inez From Hollywood; Husbands and Lovers; 1925: The Lost World; Cheaper to Marry; Confessions of a Queen; The Talker; The Lady Who Lied; Fine Clothes; What Fools Men; 1926: Too Much Money; The Girl From Montmartre; Old Loves and New; Don Juan's Three Nights; Midnight Lovers; The Blonde Saint; 1927: An Affair of the Follies; The Notorious Lady; The Prince of Headwaiters; Lonesome Ladies; The Private Life of Helen of Troy; 1928: The Foreign Legion; The Patriot; Freedom of the Press; A Woman of Affairs; 1929: The Trial of Mary Dugan; Wild Orchids; Madame X; Wonder of Women; Their Own Desire; 1930: The Big House; Strictly Unconventional; Romance; The Office Wife; Passion Flower; 1931: Inspiration; Father's Son; My Past; The Secret Six; Always Goodbye; The Bargain; The Sin of Madelon Claudet; Strictly Dishonorable; The Phantom of Paris; Mata Hari; 1932: Grand Hotel; The Wet Parade; Letty Lynton; Night Court; New Morals for Old; Red-Headed Woman; Unashamed; Divorce in the Family; The Mask of Fu Manchu; The Son-Daughter; 1933: Men Must Fight; The White Sister; Looking Forward; Bureau of Missing Persons; Queen Christina; 1934: You Can't Buy Everything; The Mystery of Mr. X; The Girl From Missouri; Treasure Island; 1935: David Copperfield; Vanessa — Her Love Story; West Point of the Air; Public Hero No. 1; China Seas; Woman Wanted; Shipmates Forever; 1936: Three Godfathers; The Unguarded Hour; Small Town Girl; Sworn Enemy; Suzy; Don't Turn 'em Loose; 1937: Outcast; The Thirteenth Chair; The Man Who Cried Wolf; You're Only Young Once; 1938: Bad Man of Brimstone; Judge Hardy's Children; Stolen Heaven; Yellow Jack; Love Finds Andy Hardy; The Chaser; Out West With the Hardys; 1939: The Ice Follies of 1939; The Hardys Ride High; Andy Hardy Gets Spring Fever; Joe and Ethel Turp Call on the President; Judge Hardy and Son; 1940: Andy Hardy Meets Debutante; Sporting Blood; 1941: Andy Hardy's Private Secretary; Life Begins for Andy Hardy; The Bugle Sounds; 1942: The Courtship of Andy Hardy; Andy Hardy's Double Life; 1944: Andy Hardy's Blonde Trouble; 1946: The Hoodlum Saint; Three Wise Fools; Love Laughs at Andy Hardy; 1948: State of the Union; 1949: The Sun Comes Up; Any Number Can Play; 1950: Key to the City; Stars in My Crown; Grounds for Marriage; 1951: Night Into Morning; Angels in the Outfield; Bannerline; It's a Big Country; The Unknown Man; 1952: Just This Once; Talk About a Stranger; Scaramouche; The Prisoner of Zenda; 1953: All the Brothers Were Valiant.

NY Stage: The Bowery After Dark; **1912:** Bird of Paradise; **1913:** The Misleading Lady; **1915:** Inside The Lines; **1916:** Bunny; **1917:** The Brat; **1918:** Nancy Lee; Where Poppies Bloom.

SUSAN STRASBERG

BORN: NEW YORK, NY, MAY 22, 1938.
DIED: JANUARY 21, 1999.

With her father, Lee Strasberg, being the esteemed guru of the Actors Studio, Susan Strasberg had much to live up to when she entered the profession, and impress she did, initially, although her career lost its course along the way. Following some modeling jobs, she went legit and made her New York stage debut Off Broadway, in *Maya*, in 1953. After this came television appearances and then her dazzling Broadway bow, in 1955, as the star of *The Diary of Anne Frank*, winning a Theatre World Award in the process. By the time it was running she had already filmed her first two movies, *The Cobweb*, and *Picnic*, stealing scenes as Kim Novak's tomboyish little sister. At first all seemed fine, but her performance in the 1957 remake of *Morning Glory*, now dubbed *Stage Struck*, as an ambitious New York actress, showed that she couldn't come close to the winning qualities Katharine Hepburn had displayed in the original. When the 1960s arrived she took off for Europe, where she showed up in the Yugoslav-Italian concentration camp drama *Kapo*, and romanced Dirk Bogarde in the British war film *McGuire, Go Home!/The High Bright Sun*. Back in America she had a rocky marriage to actor Christopher Jones (with whom she appeared in *Chubasco*), dabbled in the drug scene, and ended up in two prime AIP drive-in youth flicks of the day: *The Trip*, having little to do as Peter Fonda's estranged wife, and *Psych-Out*, taking on the lead role, as a deaf runaway who ends up freaking out in San Francisco's Haight-Ashbury district. Next came the television movie scene, though she would return to theatrical features when called on, her questionable choices doing nothing to reestablish her, including *The Legend of Hillbilly John*, as a witch; *The Manitou*, in which she grew an evil creature on her back; *Bloody Birthday*, as a teacher; and *The Delta Force*, as a plane passenger taken hostage. She published two memoirs, *Bittersweet* (1980), and *Marilyn and Me: Sisters, Rivals and Friends* (1992).

Screen: **1955:** The Cobweb; Picnic; **1957:** Stage Struck; **1960:** Kapo; **1961:** Scream of Fear/Taste of Fear; **1962:** The Shortest Day; Hemingway's Adventures of a Young Man; **1964:** Disorder; **1965:** McGuire, Go Home!/The High Bright Sun; **1967:** The Trip; **1968:** The Name of the Game Is Kill; Psych-Out; Chubasco; The Brotherhood; **1969:** Sweet Hunters/Jailbird; **1972:** So Evil, My Sister/The Sibling/Psycho Sisters; **1973:** And Millions Will Die; The Legend of Hillbilly John/Who Fears the Devil; **1976:** Sammy Somebody; **1977:** Rollercoaster; **1978:** The Manitou; **1979:** In Praise of Older Women; **1981:** Sweet 16; Bloody Birthday; **1983:** The Returning/Witch Doctor (dtv); **1986:** The Delta Force; **1988:** Prime Suspect (dtv); **1989:** The Runnin' Kind; **1990:** Schweitzer/The Light in the Jungle (dtv); **1992:** The Cherry Orchard (nUSr).

NY Stage: **1953:** Maya (ob); **1955:** The Diary of Anne Frank; **1957:** Time Remembered; **1958:** The Shadow of the Gunman; **1963:** The Lady of the Camelias.

Select TV: **1953:** Catch a Falling Star (sp); **1954:** Romeo and Juliet (sp); The Marriage (series); **1955:** Mr. Blue Ocean (sp); **1958:** Debut (sp); **1959:** The Cherry Orchard (sp); **1963:** Four Kings (sp); **1967:** Cosa Nostra: Arch Enemy of the FBI; **1969:** A Matter of Humanities/Marcus Welby, M.D.; **1970:** Hauser's

Memory; **1971:** Mr. and Mrs. Bo Jo Jones; **1973:** Toma; Frankenstein; **1973–74:** Toma (series); **1977:** SST: Death Flight; **1978:** The Immigrants; **1979:** Beggarman, Thief; **1982:** Mazes and Monsters.

ROBERT STRAUSS

BORN: NEW YORK, NY, NOVEMBER 8, 1913.
DIED: FEBRUARY 20, 1975.

Dark-browed and lowbrow, Robert Strauss was an uninhibited, sometimes welcome, growling supporting player, whose spotty career received a great kick via Broadway. A one-time salesman, he made his New York stage bow, in 1937, as part of the cast of *Having Wonderful Time*. There was a sole early film appearance, playing a grocer in a semi-documentary about civil rights, *Native Land*, in 1942. After the war he was back to the theater with Mae West's *Catherine Was Great*, *Detective Story*, and, most importantly, *Stalag 17*, where he won raves as the prison camp cut-up, Stosh. Because of its success, Paramount signed him to a contract and made him a prime comic foil for the team of Martin and Lewis on three occasions: *Sailor Beware*, *Jumping Jacks*, and *Money From Home*. Of course what the studio really had in mind was for Strauss to repeat his stage role in the 1953 film version of *Stalag 17*, which, as directed and adapted by Billy Wilder, turned out to surpass the original. Strauss, still billed as "Stosh," but officially referred to on screen as "Animal," once again made a splash, partnered for maximum comic effect with Harvey Lembeck, and he earned an Oscar nomination in the supporting category. Needless to say, this made him perfect for further military offerings and he was seen in uniform in *Attack*, *The Bridges at Toko-Ri*, *Wake Me When It's Over*, and *The Last Time I Saw Archie*. Strauss, who usually looked as if he'd forgotten to shave on the way to work, could always be relied upon to bring some coarse laughs to such films as *The Seven Year Itch*, as the building super; *Li'l Abner*, as dirty mountain hillbilly named Romeo Scragg; and *The Thrill of It All*, where he showed up to clean the soap bubbles out of Doris Day's swimming pool. Elvis Presley used him for support in *Girls! Girls! Girls!*, as a club owner, and *Frankie and Johnny*, as Anthony Eisley's henchman; and Jerry Lewis had him back for *The Family Jewels*, as a pool hall proprietor. In one of his larger roles, he was the opportunistic buddy who exploits Mickey Rooney's exposure to radiation in a very bad comedy with an anti-nuke message, *The Atomic Kid*. Toward the end of his career he wound up with two strange credits, appearing as a movie producer in *Movie Star American Style or LSD I Hate You!*, a drug comedy set in a rest home and advertised as being shot in "LSD color," and taking the lead in a Danish exploitation film made for the grind-house crowd, which went under the name of *Dagmar's Hot Pants, Inc.* in America.

Screen: **1942:** Native Land; **1950:** The Sleeping City; **1951:** Sailor Beware; **1952:** The Redhead from Wyoming; Jumping Jacks; **1953:** Stalag 17; Money from Home; Here Come the Girls; **1954:** Act of Love; The Atomic Kid; The Bridges at Toko-Ri; **1955:** The Seven Year Itch; The Man with the Golden Arm; **1956:** Attack; **1958:** Frontier Gun; I, Mobster; **1959:** Li'l Abner; 4-D Man; Inside the Mafia; **1960:** Wake Me When It's Over; September Storm; **1961:** The Last Time I Saw Archie; Dondi; The George Raft Story; Twenty Plus Two; **1962:** Girls! Girls! Girls!; **1963:** The Wheeler Dealers; The Thrill of It All; **1964:** Stage to Thunder Rock; **1965:** Harlow; That Funny Feeling; The Family Jewels; **1966:** Frankie and Johnny; **1967:** Movie Star — American Style or LSD I Hate You!; **1968:** Fort Utah; **1972:** Dagmar's Hot Pants, Inc.

NY Stage: 1937: Having Wonderful Time; 1944: Catherine Was Great; 1946: Nellie Bly; 1949: Detective Story; 1950: Twentieth Century; 1951: Stalag 17; 1958: Portofino.
Select TV: 1960: So Help Me, Aphrodite (sp); 1965–66: Mona McCluskey (series).

RAY STRICKYLN

(LEWIS RAYMOND STRICKLIN, JR.)
BORN: HOUSTON, TX, OCTOBER 8, 1928.
DIED: MAY 14, 2002.

The rollercoaster career of Ray Stricklyn began with drama classes at New York's Irvine Studio, regional theatre, and small bits on live television in the early 1950s. He landed an important role in a short-lived play, The Climate of Eden, which earned him a Theatre World Award, and then one of the leads in an Off Broadway revival of The Grass Harp. This led to more regional theater jobs and a quick scene, as a shell-shocked soldier, in the film The Proud and Profane. He traveled to Hollywood to see what work he could find in the movies and got a few more small roles, including Crime in the Streets, as a hood, and Somebody Up There Likes Me, as a GI pal of Paul Newman's. Things finally began to look up when he was cast as Debbie Reynolds's brother in The Catered Affair, and then as one of the survivors of an Indian massacre in The Last Wagon. He wound up with a good part, as Gary Cooper's alcoholic son, in Ten North Frederick, and got a contract with Fox. They made him one of Clifton Webb's many kids in a poor comedy, The Remarkable Mr. Pennypacker; a member of Claude Rains's expedition in the negligible remake of The Lost World; and the title role in a "B," western Young Jesse James. He did some of his best work as a nasty thug terrorizing one-armed sheriff Jeff Chandler in The Plunderers, but things pretty much ground to a halt by the early 1960s. Despite occasional parts on television and theater work, he gravitated into the publicity end of the business for a lengthy period until he won great acclaim for a revival of Tennessee Williams's Vieux Carre, and then playing Williams himself, in a one-man show he conceived, Confessions of a Nightingale. In 1999 he published his autobiography, Angels & Demons, speaking openly of his homosexuality and alcoholism.

Screen: 1956: The Proud and Profane; Crime in the Streets; Somebody Up There Likes Me; The Catered Affair; The Last Wagon; 1958: The Return of Dracula; Ten North Frederick; 1959: The Remarkable Mr. Pennypacker; The Big Fisherman; 1960: Young Jesse James; The Lost World; The Plunderers; 1965: Arizona Raiders; 1968: Track of Thunder; 1976: La Illegal (nUSr); 1977: Dogpound Shuffle; 1985: Write to Kill (nUSr).

NY Stage: 1952: The Climate of Eden; 1953: The Grass Harp; 1986: Confessions of a Nightingale (and co-wr.; ob).

Select TV: 1956: Front Page Father (sp); 1957: For Better, For Worse (sp); 1970: The Andersonville Trial (sp); 1984: Jealousy; 1986: North & South Book II (ms); 1992: Danielle Steel's Secrets; 1993: Hart to Hart Returns; 1991–92: Days of Our Lives (series).

WOODY STRODE

BORN: LOS ANGELES, CA, JULY 28, 1914.
ED: UCLA. DIED: DECEMBER 31, 1994.

Tall, head-shaven, muscular Woody Strode was mainly relegated to the usual roles afforded black actors in his day, until his dignified way with a line and striking stature were finally put to some good use. A college footballer,

he played professionally with the Cleveland Rams and the Calgary Stampeders, with some wrestling thrown in for good measure. He made his movie debut in 1941, playing a tribal policeman in the African adventure Sundown, and then appeared sporadically in bits throughout the next two decades, usually playing natives in such things as the Bomba opuses, The Lion Hunters and Bomba and the African Treasure, and the Bowery Boys quickie Jungle Gents. His bigger budgeted assignments included Demetrius and the Gladiators, as a gladiator, and The Ten Commandments, as the King of Ethiopia. In 1960 he hit his prime, first as the crewman who helps rescue Dorothy Malone in the exciting race-against-the-clock thriller The Last Voyage; then in the title role of director John Ford's flawed-but-interesting Sergeant Rutledge, as a cavalry soldier accused of murder and rape; and, finally, in the brief but crucial role he became best remembered for, Drabba, the slave who fights Kirk Douglas in the arena for the pleasure of Laurence Olivier and company, in the mighty epic Spartacus. He was always most effective as a man of few words and continued to make an impression in such films as Two Rode Together, as a villainous Comanche; Genghis Khan, as part of the very un-Asian cast; 7 Women, fighting to the death with fellow Mongolian Mike Mazurki; and one of his best, The Professionals, as a member of the title mercenaries in this popular western. Never one to be seen seated at a desk, he continued in westerns and action adventures of increasing cheapness, last showing up ever so briefly in the flip western The Quick and the Dead, released after his death. He published his autobiography, Goal Dust (written with Sam Young), in 1990.

Screen: 1941: Sundown; 1942: Star Spangled Rhythm; 1943: No Time for Love; 1951: Bride of the Gorilla; The Lion Hunters; 1952: Caribbean; Bomba and the African Treasure; 1953: City Beneath the Sea; 1954: Jungle Gents; The Gambler from Natchez; Demetrius and the Gladiators; 1955: Son of Sinbad; 1956: The Ten Commandments; 1958: Tarzan's Fight for Life; The Buccaneer; 1959: Pork Chop Hill; 1960: The Last Voyage; Sergeant Rutledge; Spartacus; 1961: The Sins of Rachel Cade; Two Rode Together; 1962: The Man Who Shot Liberty Valance; 1963: Tarzan's Three Challenges; 1965: Genghis Khan; 1966: 7 Women; The Professionals; 1968: Black Jesus; Shalako; 1969: Boot Hill; Che!; Once Upon a Time in the West; 1970: The Unholy Four; 1971: The Last Rebel; The Deserter; 1972: Black Rodeo (narrator); The Ravengers; 1973: King Gun/The Gatling Gun; The Italian Connection/Manhunt; 1975: Loaded Guns/Stick 'em Up, Darlings (dtv); We Are No Angels (nUSr); 1976: Winterhawk; Keoma/The Violent Breed (nUSr); 1977: Oil/The Billion Dollar File; Kingdom of the Spiders; 1979: Ravagers; Jaguar Lives!; 1980: Cuba Crossing/Assignment: Kill Castro (nUSr); 1983: Vigilante; The Final Executioner; The Black Stallion Returns; The Violent Breed (dtv); 1984: Jungle Warriors; The Cotton Club; 1985: Scream/The Outing (dtv); Angor: Cambodian Express (dtv); Lust in the Dust; 1989: Bronx Executioner (dtv); 1992: Storyville; 1993: Posse; 1995: The Quick and the Dead.

Select TV: 1970: Breakout; 1973: Key West; 1986: On Fire; 1987: A Gathering of Old Men.

GLORIA STUART

BORN: SANTA MONICA, CA, JULY 4, 1910.
ED: UNIV. OF CA/BERKELEY.

Few performers ever had so unexpected a comeback as did Gloria Stuart, long after most movie fans had closed the book on her film career. In college she acted with the

Berkeley Players then moved over to the prestigious Pasadena Playhouse, where her performance in a production of *The Seagull* earned her a contract with Universal Pictures. She soon became one of the hardest working ingénues in 1930s films, starting off on loan to Warners, for *Street of Women*, telling her father's mistress, Kay Francis, to dump dad and leave. Though few producers thought of her as more than decoration, she did wind up in two of Universal's most enduring entries in the horror field, the tongue-in-cheek *The Old Dark House*, terrorized by Boris Karloff and others, and *The Invisible Man*, as the distressed girlfriend of the transparent Claude Rains. These were both directed by James Whale, who used her again in one of his less-known works, *The Kiss Before the Mirror*, as Paul Lukas's bored and bitchy adulterous wife. None-too-satisfied with most of her home lot assignments, she was only too pleased to go elsewhere, ending up in some box-office hits like the Eddie Cantor spoof *Roman Scandals*; the James Cagney-Pat O'Brien offering *Here Comes the Navy*, as the sister O'Brien wants to keep far from Cagney; and *Gold Diggers of 1935*, where she had the misfortune of being engaged to Hugh Herbert. Fox took her on in the latter-half of the decade where, amid several "B's," her better known films were *The Prisoner of Shark Island*, as the properly distraught wife of wrongly incarcerated Warner Baxter; two of Shirley Temple's vehicles, *Poor Little Rich Girl* and *Rebecca of Sunnbrook Farm*; and the Ritz Brothers's version of *The Three Musketeers*, as Queen Anne. Having married writer Arthur Sheekman in 1934, she eventually turned away from show business to concentrate on her home life, later becoming an artist. In the mid 1970s she returned quietly to acting, doing mainly television films, though she did show up in some features films, including *My Favorite Year*, briefly sharing the dance floor with Peter O'Toole. Less quietly she was cast as the centenarian who remembers the fateful voyage of *Titanic*, which became the highest-grossing movie of all time and the Academy Award-winner for Best Picture of 1997. Suddenly the focus of much attention, Stuart was acclaimed for her touching portrayal and ended up with an Oscar nomination at 87, the oldest performer to be so honored. This led to a few inconsequential roles on television and in theatrical features. Her 1999 autobiography was entitled *I Just Kept Hoping*.

Screen: **1932:** Street of Women; The Old Dark House; The All American; Air Mail; **1933:** Laughter in Hell; Roman Scandals; The Kiss Before the Mirror; Private Jones; The Girl in 419; It's Great to Be Alive; The Invisible Man; Secret of the Blue Room; Sweepings; **1934:** Beloved; I Like It That Way; I'll Tell the World; Here Comes the Navy; The Love Captive; Gift of Gab; **1935:** Maybe It's Love; Gold Diggers of 1935; Laddie; Professional Soldier; **1936:** The Prisoner of Shark Island; Poor Little Rich Girl; 36 Hours to Kill; The Girl on the Front Page; Wanted: Jane Turner; The Crime of Dr. Forbes; **1937:** The Lady Escapes; Girl Overboard; Life Begins in College; **1938:** Rebecca of Sunnybrook Farm; Change of Heart; Island in the Sky; Keep Smiling; Time Out for Murder; The Lady Objects; **1939:** The Three Musketeers; It Could Happen to You; Winner Take All; **1943:** Here Comes Elmer; **1944:** The Whistler; Enemy of Women; **1946:** She Wrote the Book; **1982:** My Favorite Year; **1984:** Mass Appeal; **1986:** Wildcats; **1997:** Titanic; **1999:** The Love Letter; **2001:** The Million Dollar Hotel.

Select TV: **1975:** Adventures of the Queen; The Legend of Lizzie Borden; **1976:** Flood!; **1977:** In the Glitter Palace; **1978:** The Two Worlds of Jennie Logan; **1979:** The Best Place to Be; The Incredible Journey of Dr. Meg Laurel; **1981:** The Violation of Sarah McDavid; Shootdown; **1989:** She Knows Too Much; **2000:** My Mother the Spy; **2001:** Murder, She Wrote: The Last Free Man.

MARGARET SULLAVAN
BORN: NORFOLK, VA, MAY 16, 1911.
DIED: JANUARY 1, 1960.

The abbreviated film career of Margaret Sullivan was partially a reflection on her own disinterest in Hollywood rather than on her talents, which were rarely in question. She was, quite simply, one of the best actresses the movies had the privilege to present during the 1930s, offering a warmly human personality and an ability to bring some dignity to even the soapiest of plots. She was but a teen when she traveled to Boston to study acting at E.E. Clive's Copley Dramatic School. This led to her joining the University Players, which performed on Cape Cod and included future superstars Henry Fonda and James Stewart among the company. From her work in a touring production of *Strictly Dishonorable*, she got an offer to come to Broadway and made her debut there in *A Modern Virgin*, in 1931, the same year she and Fonda married (they were divorced the following year). After that she popped up in the replacement cast during the Broadway run of *Dinner at Eight*, where she was spotted by director John M. Stahl, who offered her the lead in a Universal melodrama, *Only Yesterday*. In it, she was left pregnant by soldier John Boles, resulting in the inevitable hardships through the passing years. Both the public and the studio were pleased at how effortlessly she managed to bring some credibility to the slushy proceedings and she was signed to a contract. There followed the intriguingly titled *Little Man, What Now?*, about German unemployment following World War I, and a charming comedy, *The Good Fairy*, in which she captured the heart of stuffy Herbert Marshall on screen, and the film's director, William Wyler, off (they were together somewhat longer than Sullivan and Fonda, marrying in 1934 and divorcing in 1936).

Paramount borrowed her for its flop Civil War drama, *So Red the Rose*, and, with better results, a teaming with her-ex husband, Fonda, *The Moon's Our Home*. In between she did her first and least of four with James Stewart, *Next Time We Love*, then returned to New York to triumph in *Stage Door*, in 1936. The next year came husband number three, agent Leland Hayward (their union would last until 1947). Back in movies, she signed with MGM and got off to a promising start with the ponderous but popular *Three Comrades*, dying gallantly and being loved by Robert Taylor, Franchot Tone, and Robert Young. It earned her her sole Oscar nomination. There was a better rematch with Stewart, the remake of *The Shopworn Angel*, as a selfish actress who comes to realize that she is quite happy that a bumpkin soldier is infatuated with her, after which they were back again for the peak of her movie career, *The Shop Around the Corner*. As the shopgirl who doesn't realize her hated fellow-employee Stewart is her mysterious pen-pal, she was never more effervescent or touching, helping to turn this Ernst Lubitsch concoction into one of the best loved films of its day. As icing on the cake, she and Stewart did a potent anti-Nazi film that same year, *The Mortal Storm*. Staying on that topic Sullivan did *So Ends Our Night*, for United Artists, as a Jew fleeing Germany, and returned to Universal for the best-liked version of the Fannie Hearst weepy *Back Street*, as Charles Boyer's kept woman, once again adding immeasurable grace and conviction to this hoary old tale of adultery. After playing a nurse in *Cry Havoc*, she left the movies for quite a spell, having a major Broadway hit with *The Voice of the Turtle*. She was not asked to do the film of it (Eleanor Parker played her role) but finished off her career with a quickly forgotten soap for Columbia, *No Sad Songs for Me*, as a woman dying of cancer. Stage performances continued to earn her praise, with *Sabrina Fair* and *The Deep Blue Sea*, among others. The sparkle she conveyed in her work helped to cover the unhappiness of her personal life, which included a hearing problem that rendered her nearly deaf by the time she took her own life, with an overdose of sleeping pills, at the age of 48.

Screen: 1933: Only Yesterday; 1934: Little Man, What Now?; 1935: The Good Fairy; So Red the Rose; 1936: Next Time We Love; The Moon's Our Home; 1938: Three Comrades; The Shopworn Angel; The Shining Hour; 1940: The Shop Around the Corner; The Mortal Storm; 1941: So Ends Our Night; Back Street; Appointment for Love; 1943: Cry Havoc; 1950: No Sad Songs for Me.

NY Stage: 1931: A Modern Virgin; If Love Were All; 1932: Happy Landing; Chrysalis; 1933: Bad Manners; Dinner at Eight; 1936: Stage Door; 1943: The Voice of the Turtle; 1952: The Deep Blue Sea; 1953: Sabrina Fair; 1955: Janus.

Select TV: 1948: The Storm (sp); 1949: The Twelve Pound Look (sp); 1951: Touchstone (sp); Still Life (sp); The Nymph and the Lamp (sp); 1954: State of the Union (sp).

BARRY SULLIVAN

(PATRICK BARRY SULLIVAN) BORN: NEW YORK, NY, AUGUST 29, 1912. ED: TEMPLE UNIV. DIED: JUNE 6, 1994.

He of the tall, manly, reliable mode, Barry Sullivan's no-frills style could be a relief from a fellow actor's more melodramatic thesping one moment, while his lack of sizzle could render him close to invisible on other occasions. Following college dramatics, he did stock work and made his Broadway debut, in 1936, in *I Want a Policeman*. After a few other theater engagements he was signed up by Paramount, who put him in a Claire Trevor vehicle, *The Woman of the Town*, which wound up being distributed by UA. He was seen in some hits, playing a doctor in *Lady in the Dark*, and Loretta Young's callous fiancé in *And Now Tomorrow*, then went over to Monogram to play the selfish lover of skater Belita in a curious combination of noir and ice, *Suspense*. Allied Artists gave him top-billing as *The Gangster*, playing a man driven to crime by his rotten environment, Sullivan proved he had the stuff to carry a film, if not a major one. Back at Paramount he was jealous husband Tom Buchanan in that studio's ambitious but unsuccessful 1949 attempt to film *The Great Gatsby*. MGM decided they'd take a crack at him and he became an all purpose addition to the studio roster during the early 1950s. He played it straight amid the musical numbers in *Nancy Goes to Rio*, with Jane Powell and *Skirts Ahoy!*, with Esther Williams; was an escaped Confederate soldier riding with Joel McCrea in *The Outriders*; proved hardly the ideal choice for frothy romantic comedy in *Grounds for Marriage*; was the rich Mike courting Jane Wyman in *Three Guys Named Mike*; and ended up in his best film during this period, *The Bad and the Beautiful*, as the director manipulated by domineering mogul Kirk Douglas.

Over at RKO he did one of his personal favorites, *Payment on Demand*, a very minor Bette Davis offering in which he was the straying husband she wants to divorce. He then became one of those folks asked to carry the myriad of "B" attractions that filled the bottom half of double bills during the 1950s, including *No Questions Asked*, as an insurance investigator threatened by the mob; *Jeopardy*, a decent quickie, in which he spent most of the movie pinned under a pylon while the rising tide crashed about him; *China Venture*, as a naval officer who kidnaps a Japanese admiral; *Wolf Larsen*, playing the wacko sea captain in this umpteenth version of *The Sea Wolf*; and *Playgirl*, which was not the skin magazine but Colleen Miller. He was asked to stand by

stoically while the better-paid leading ladies emoted to the heavens in *Queen Bee*, with Joan Crawford; *Julie*, with Doris Day; and *Another Time, Another Place*, with Lana Turner. Not suprisingly, he was very much at home in westerns by this point, including *Dragoon Wells Massacre*, guiding a group of travelers across the plains after an Indian attack, and *Seven Ways from Sundown*, as the nasty villain in this Audie Murphy vehicle. By the 1960s and 1970s he had fallen into the position of long-time pseudo-star hired for dependable support, easily shifting from television to features, hardly asking for much more than a steady income to keep the wolf from the door. He was therefore seen in *A Gathering of Eagles*, where he got to play an alcoholic Air Force commander; the cheesier of the rival *Harlow* biopics, as Ginger Rogers's disreputable husband; *An American Dream*, as a no-nonsense cop; the corny disaster hit *Earthquake*, as a doctor; and *Oh, God!*, seen briefly, as a priest. There was also a little-seen thriller called *The Washington Affair*, which gave him top billing, as a corrupt businessman out to destroy Tom Selleck. It was a remake of *Intimacy*, an even more obscure movie Sullivan had done earlier for the same director.

Screen: 1943: The Woman of the Town; High Explosive; 1944: Lady in the Dark; And Now Tomorrow; Rainbow Island; 1945: Getting Gertie's Garter; Duffy's Tavern; 1946: Suspense; 1947: Framed; The Gangster; 1948: Smart Woman; 1949: Bad Men of Tombstone; The Great Gatsby; Any Number Can Play; Tension; 1950: Nancy Goes to Rio; A Life of Her Own; The Outriders; Grounds for Marriage; 1951: Mr. Imperium; Three Guys Named Mike; Inside Straight; Payment on Demand; No Questions Asked; Cause for Alarm!; The Unknown Man; 1952: Skirts Ahoy!; The Bad and the Beautiful; 1953: Jeopardy; Cry of the Hunted; China Venture; 1954: Playgirl; The Miami Story; Loophole; Her 12 Men; 1955: Strategic Air Command; Queen Bee; Texas Lady; 1956: The Maverick Queen; Julie; 1957: The Way to the Gold; Dragoon Wells Massacre; Forty Guns; 1958: Wolf Larsen; Another Time, Another Place; 1960: Seven Ways from Sundown; The Purple Gang; 1962: Light in the Piazza; 1963: A Gathering of Eagles; 1964: Pyro; Stage to Thunder Rock; Man in the Middle; 1965: My Blood Runs Cold; Harlow; Planet of the Vampires/Demon Planet; 1966: Intimacy; An American Dream; 1968: Buckskin; How to Steal the World (from TV); The Silent Treatment; 1969: Tell Them Willie Boy Is Here; It Takes All Kinds (nUSr); 1970: Shark! (filmed 1967); 1972: The Candidate (voice); 1973: Pat Garrett and Billy the Kid (in re-edited version only); 1974: Earthquake; 1975: The Human Factor; Take a Hard Ride; 1976: Survival; Grand Jury; Napoli Violenta/Violent Protection (nUSr); 1977: Oh, God!; The Washington Affair; 1978: French Quarter; Caravans.

NY Stage: 1936: I Want a Policeman; St. Helena; 1938: All That Glitters; Eye on the Sparrow; 1962: Johnny 2x4; 1954: The Caine Mutiny Court-Martial; 1956: Too Late The Phalarope.

Select TV: 1953: As the Flame Dies (sp); 1954: The Fugitives (sp); 1955: It Might Happen Tomorrow (sp); The Merry Widow (sp); The Caine Mutiny Court-Martial (sp); 1956: A Bell for Adano (sp); Career (sp); 1957: Snow Shoes (sp); One Way Passage (sp); Ain't No Time for Glory (sp); 1957–58: Harbourmaster/Adventure at Scott Island (series); 1958: Tide of Corruption (sp); Nightmare at Ground Zero (sp); This Day in Fear (sp); 1959: Bill Bailey, Won't You Please Come Home (sp); A Quiet Game of Cards (sp); The Hard Road (sp); Dark December (sp); My Three Angels (sp); 1960: City in Bondage (sp); Operation Northstar (sp); 1960–62: The Tall Man (series); 1962: The World's Greatest Robbery (sp); 1965: The Last Clear Chance (sp); 1966: The Poppy Is Also a Flower (also theatrical); 1966–67: The Road West (series); 1967: Johnny Belinda (sp); 1969: The Experiment (sp); This Town Will Never Be the Same (sp); Night Gallery; The Immortal; 1970: The House on Green Apple Road; 1971: The Price (sp); Yuma; Cannon; 1972: Kung Fu; Another Part of the Forest (sp); 1973: The Magician; Savage; Letters from Three Lovers; 1974: Hurricane; 1976: Collision Course: Truman vs. MacArthur (sp); Once an Eagle (ms); 1976–77: Rich Man, Poor Man Book II (ms); 1978: The Bastard (ms); The Immigrants; No Reason to Run; 1979: Backstairs at the White House (ms); 1980: Casino.

CLINTON SUNDBERG

BORN: APPLETON, MN, DECEMBER 7, 1903.
ED: HAMLINE UNIV. DIED: DECEMBER 14, 1987.

A droop-faced, scratchy-voiced character player who was a staple at MGM during the late 1940s and early 1950s, Clinton Sundberg had spent several years as a teacher of English literature until he decided he'd prefer to give acting a shot. After stock work in New England, he made his Broadway debut in 1933, in Nine Pine Street. Over the next decade he became associated with such notable stage comedies as Boy Meets Girl, Room Service, and Arsenic and Old Lace, but was not invited to Hollywood until after supporting Spencer Tracy in his return to the boards, The Rugged Path. Metro started him out in 1946, playing Robert Taylor's Washington co-hort in Undercurrent. His usually lighthearted presence was perfect for filling out the background in many a film, musicals in particular, and he was seen as a haberdashery clerk in Love Laughs at Andy Hardy; a disrespectful butler in Living in a Big Way; a college professor in Good News; a shoe clerk trying to give Mickey Rooney some stature in Words and Music; a more serious role than usual, as an air force major in the military drama Command Decision; a friendly bartender ready to lend an ear in Easter Parade; Van Johnson's fellow shop clerk, performing with a mild Scandinavian accent in, In the Good Old Summertime; a theatrical producer worried about his bickering stars in The Barkleys of Broadway; a Wild West Show promoter to whom Betty Hutton sings "Doin' What Comes Natur'ly" in Annie Get Your Gun; and the mission organist smitten with Vera-Ellen in The Belle of New York. He returned to Broadway to play it straight in the 1955 hit The Diary of Anne Frank, but his movie roles thereafter were few. The astute listener could hear his familiar voice in the animated film Arabian Knight, released eight years (!) after his death.

Screen: 1946: Undercurrent; The Mighty McGurk; Love Laughs at Andy Hardy; 1947: Living in a Big Way; Song of Love; Song of the Thin Man; Desire Me; Undercover Maisie; The Hucksters; Good News; 1948: The Kissing Bandit; Good Sam; The Bride Goes Wild; Easter Parade; Mr. Peabody and the Mermaid; A Date With Judy; Words and Music; Command Decision; 1949: Big Jack; In the Good Old Summertime; The Barkleys of Broadway; 1950: Annie Get Your Gun; Key to the City; Father Is a Bachelor; Duchess of Idaho; The Toast of New Orleans; Two Weeks With Love; Mrs. O'Malley and Mr. Malone; 1951: On the Riviera; The Fat Man; As Young as You Feel; 1952: The Belle of New York; 1953: The Girl Next Door; Main Street to Broadway; Sweethearts on Parade; The Caddy; 1956: The Birds and the Bees; 1961: Bachelor in Paradise; 1962: The Wonderful World of the Brothers Grimm; 1963: How the West Was Won; 1967: Hotel; 1995: Arabian Knight (voice).

NY Stage: 1933: Nine Pine Street; 1936: I Want a Policeman; 1941: Arsenic and Old Lace; 1945: The Rugged Path; 1955: The Diary of Anne Frank; 1958: The Man in the Dog Suit; 1961: Midgie Purvis; 1964: Mary, Mary.

Select TV: 1968: Shadow Over Elveron.

GRADY SUTTON

BORN: CHATTANOOGA, TN, APRIL 5, 1906.
DIED: SEPTEMBER 17, 1995.

One of the screen's great twerps, a stocky, Southern-accented, pop-eyed mass of nelly nerves and persnickety blundering, Grady Sutton was the sort of performer whose roles usually came in quick but memorable flashes. A connection with director William A. Seiter got him extra work in one of that man's films, The Mad Whirl, in 1924, and he continued to do bits, garnering little attention until he finally started to get billing in the early 1930s. A two-realer he did with W.C. Fields, "The Pharmacist," proved that his doltishness made him an ideal foil for the great comedian, who used him brilliantly in Man on the Flying Trapeze, as his shiftless, mother-dominated brother-in-law, and in the role for which most people remember him best, Una Merkel's dopey fiancé, Og Oggilby, in The Bank Dick. Apart from these there was another Fields film, You Can't Cheat an Honest Man, as a carnival employee, and a whole slew of others, including Alice Adams, as Katharine Hepburn's hopelessly loutish date; Stage Door, seen working in a butcher shop; My Man Godfrey, as the idiot heir Carole Lombard plans to marry to spite William Powell; Turn Off the Moon, as Charlie Ruggles's nephew, with the memorable name Truelove Spencer; Valiant Is the Word for Carrie, in which Arline Judge married him after losing John Howard; The Lady Takes a Chance, wooing Jean Arthur; and Anchors Aweigh, showing up for a date with Kathryn Grayson only to be chased away by Gene Kelly and Frank Sinatra. In later years he was given work in his friend George Cukor's A Star Is Born, as a Hollywood columnist, and My Fair Lady, showing up both at the Ascot racetrack and at the embassy ball, though whether he was supposed to be the same character was not made clear. Elsewhere he could be spotted in I Love You, Alice B. Toklas, as an undertaker; Myra Breckinridge, playing poker with John Huston; and his last, Rock 'n' Roll High School, as the president of the school board.

Screen (features): 1925: The Mad Whirl; The Freshman; 1926: Skinner's Dress Suit; The Boy Friend; 1928: The Sophomore; 1929: Tanned Legs; 1930: Bigger and Better; Wild Company; Let's Go Native; Hit the Deck; 1932: Movie Crazy; This Reckless Age; The Age of Consent; Hot Saturday; Pack Up Your Troubles; 1933: The Story of Temple Drake; College Humor; Ace of Aces; Sweetheart of Sigma Chi; Only Yesterday; 1934: Bachelor Bait; Gridiron Flash; 1935: Stone of Silver Creek; Laddie; Alice Adams; Man on the Flying Trapeze; Dr. Socrates; 1936: Palm Springs; King of the Royal Mounted; She's Dangerous; Valiant Is the Word for Carrie; Pigskin Parade; My Man Godfrey; 1937: Waikiki Wedding; Stage Door; We Have Our Moments; Dangerous Holiday; Love Takes Flight; Turn Off the Moon; Behind the Mike; Two Minutes to Play; 1938: Vivacious Lady; Having Wonderful Time; Alexander's Ragtime Band; Joy of Living; Hard to Get; Three Loves Has Nancy; The Mad Miss Manton; 1939: You Can't Cheat an Honest Man; It's a Wonderful World; In Name Only; Naughty But Nice; Blondie Meets the Boss; They Made Her a Spy; The Angels Wash Their Faces; Three Sons; Three Smart Girls Grow Up; The Flying Irishman; 1940: Anne of Windy Poplars; Lucky Partners; Sky Murder; Torrid Zone; Too Many Girls; The Bank Dick; City of Chance; We Who Are Young; Millionaire Playboy; He Stayed for Breakfast; Millionaires in Prison; 1941: Blondie in Society; Doctors Don't Tell; Father Takes a Wife; You Belong to Me; Three Girls About Town; She Knew All the Answers; Flying Blind; Bedtime Story; 1942: Whispering Ghosts; Four Jacks and a Jill; The Affairs of

Martha; The Bashful Bachelor; Somewhere I'll Find You; 1943: The More the Merrier; A Lady Takes a Chance; What a Woman!; 1944: The Great Moment; Johnny Doesn't Live Here Anymore; Week-End Pass; Nine Girls; Allergic to Love; Goin' to Town; Since You Went Away; Hi, Beautiful; Casanova Brown; Guest Wife; 1945: Grissly's Millions; A Royal Scandal; Three's a Crowd; On Stage Everybody; Her Lucky Night; Captain Eddie; The Stork Club; She Went to the Races; A Bell for Adano; Anchors Aweigh; Pillow to Post; Song of the Prairie; Sing Your Way Home; Brewster's Millions; 1946: Ziegfeld Follies; The Fabulous Suzanne; My Dog Shep; Holiday in Mexico; Hit the Hay; It's Great to Be Young; Nobody Lives Forever; Idea Girl; The Plainsman and the Lady; The Magnificent Rogue; Partners in Time; The Show Off; Susie Steps Out; Dragonwyck; Two Sisters from Boston; No Leave, No Love; 1947: Dead Reckoning; Beat the Band; Philo Vance's Gamble; Love and Learn; My Wild Irish Rose; 1948: Always Together; Romance on the High Seas; Jiggs and Maggie in Court; Last of the Wild Horses; My Dear Secretary; 1949: Grand Canyon; Air Hostess; 1954: Living It Up; A Star Is Born; White Christmas; 1962: Madison Avenue; The Chapman Report; Billy Rose's Jumbo; 1963: Come Blow Your Horn; 4 for Texas; 1964: My Fair Lady; 1965: Tickle Me; 1966: The Chase; The Bounty Killer; Paradise Hawaiian Style; 1968: I Love You, Alice B. Toklas; 1969: The Great Bank Robbery; 1970: Suppose They Gave a War and Nobody Came; Myra Breckinridge; Dirty Dingus Magee; 1971: Support Your Local Gunfighter; 1979: Rock 'n' Roll High School.

Select TV: 1966–67: The Pruitts of Southampton (series); 1968: Something for a Lonely Man.

GLORIA SWANSON

(Gloria Josephine May Swenson)
Born: Chicago, IL, March 27, 1898.
Died: April 4, 1983.

Although she was principally a silent film star (and one of the reigning queens of that era), Gloria Swanson's place in film history has much to do with a single role she played long after the movies had learned to talk. Minus sound, she worked the audience with those bewitching eyes and the sort of grand gestures expected in those days. Later, she developed a haughtier and more imperious quality, one which kept her very much on a lofty plane of respect for the remainder of her life. While a teenager she found extra work at Essanay Studios and received her first billing, in a 1915 short with the unwieldy title, "The Fable of Elvira and Farina and the Meal Ticket." She did some two-reelers that starred Wallace Beery doing his drag act, "Sweedie," and the two married in 1916. They divorced three years later, by which time she was working in Hollywood for Mack Sennett. She did not, however, fancy herself a knockabout comedy star and, therefore, accepted an offer to go elsewhere, to Triangle Studios, where she was made the star of several dramatic features, including Her Decision, ambitiously marrying her boss for cash; You Can't Believe Everything, re-evaluating her life after saving a man from drowning; and Wife or Country, as a German spy. These didn't do much for her but they caught the attention of director Cecil B. DeMille, who wanted her to work for him over at Paramount. Together they did a series of melodramas and comedies there that made her into one of the biggest stars of the day, starting with Don't Change Your Husband, in which she dumped her first spouse only to find out that her new one is a philanderer. Continuing with DeMille, she did For Better or Worse; Male and Female, one of the many cinematic adaptations of The

Admirable Crichton, in which she was shipwrecked and, during a bizarre fantasy sequence, fed to the lions; Why Change Your Wife?, so named to cash in on the first one, this time co-starring with Bebe Daniels as her rival; Something to Think About, in which she was widowed and unhappily remarried to a cripple; and The Affairs of Anatol, betrayed by husband Wallace Reid, but forgiving him nonetheless. After DeMille she went over to work for director Sam Wood and their teamings included Beyond the Rocks!, a solid box-office teaming with Rudolph Valentino, in which he wooed her after saving her life in a mountain climbing accident; and Bluebeard's Eighth Wife, playing the latest spouse to the much-married Huntley Gordon. Going east to Paramount's Astoria lot, she next paired up with director Allan Dwan and was now at her peak of popularity. Together they presented her as a Parisian musical hall entertainer in Zaza; a cheated-on wife in A Society Scandal; a clerk who becomes a flirtatious flapper in Manhandled; the lover of Foreign Legionnaire Ben Lyon in The Wages of Virtue; and a waitress who decides to become an actress to woo back boyfriend Lawrence Gray in The Untamed Lady. United Artists made her the tempting offer of serving as producer on her own films, so she went there, in 1927, and formed her own company with then-lover Joseph Kennedy. The first film, The Loves of Sunya, found her gazing into a crystal ball to see how her love affairs would end up, but it wasn't well liked. She made up for it with Sadie Thompson, playing a great floozy role and doing it with such gusto and conviction that she earned an Oscar nomination in the process. Alas, it is one of those movies that survive with pieces missing, in this case most of the climax. There was bad luck with the next, Queen Kelly, an ambitious production that ran into problems when she fired extravagant director Erich von Stroheim. The film was never completed as intended and would not screen in anything akin to a finished print in the United States until many decades later, when it was hailed as a fascinating curio that might have been something greater.

Not intimidated by sound as many of her contemporaries were, Swanson made the transition with ease with The Trespasser, in which her marriage was destroyed by her heartless father-in-law. For it, she received a second Oscar nomination, scored a hit, and seemed to be on her way to a successful career in sound films. Unfortunately, the failure of her next film, What a Widow!, a comedy that reteamed her with Allan Dwan, put an end to her alliance with Kennedy, and she went back to being just an actress for hire with Indiscreet. There was one more Swanson production, the British-made Perfect Understanding, with Laurence Olivier, but when it flopped UA was only too happy to send her on her way. She went to Fox to play an opera diva in Music in the Air, which was only notable because Billy Wilder worked on the script. Her film career having temporarily ended, she did some stage work, eventually coming back, for reasons best known to herself, for a worthless RKO comedy, Father Takes a Wife, in 1941. When she returned to motion pictures again, in 1950, it was for a very worthy one indeed, Sunset Blvd., Wilder's baroque and brilliant film, about a silent film star trying to regain her past glory and dragging down struggling writer William Holden as she sinks into madness. As deluded, secluded Norma Desmond, she essayed one of the most unforgettable of all screen characters, bordering dangerously on camp but always showing the pitiable woman beneath the raging ego. She earned a third Oscar nomination and would continue to reap kudos and fame from this movie for the remainder of her life. There were, however, three more movies that did nothing to enhance her reputation: the farce Three for Bedroom C; the Italian satire Nero's Mistress; and Airport 1975, in which she played herself. There were occasional stage roles and, despite the paucity of work, she made sure she stayed enough in the public conscience that no one ever dare confuse her with the role she had made exclusively her own. In 1980 she published her autobiography, *Swanson on Swanson*.

Screen (features): 1918: Society for Sale; Her Decision; You Can't Believe Everything; Every Woman's Husband; Shifting Sands; Station Content; Secret Code; Wife or Country; 1919: Don't Change Your Husband; For Better For Worse; Male and Female; 1920: Why Change Your Wife?; Something to Think About; 1921: The Great Moment; The Affairs of Anatol; Under the Lash; Don't Tell Everything; 1922: Her Husband's Trademark; Beyond the Rocks!; Her Gilded Cage; The Impossible Mrs. Bellew; 1923: My American Wife; Prodigal Daughter; Hollywood; Bluebeard's Eighth Wife; Zaza; 1924: The Humming Bird; A Society Scandal; Manhandled; Her Love Story; The Wages of Virtue; 1925: Madame Sans-Gene; The Coast of Folly; Stage Struck; 1926: Untamed Lady; Fine Manners; 1927: The Loves of Sunya; 1928: Sadie Thompson; Queen Kelly; 1929: The Trespasser; 1930: What a Widow!; 1931: Indiscreet; Tonight or Never; 1933: Perfect Understanding; 1934: Music in the Air; 1941: Father Takes a Wife; 1950: Sunset Blvd.; 1952: Three for Bedroom C; 1956: Nero's Mistress/Nero's Weekend; 1974: Airport 1975.

NY Stage: 1945: A Goose for the Gander; 1947: Bathsheba; 1950: Twentieth Century; 1951: Nina; 1971: Butterflies Are Free.

Select TV: 1953: The Pattern (sp); 1954: The Gloria Swanson Show/Crown Theatre with Gloria Swanson (series); 1964: Who Is Jennifer? (sp); 1974: The Killer Bees.

RUSS TAMBLYN

BORN: LOS ANGELES, CA, DECEMBER 30, 1934.

His boundless energy forever ingrained him in the minds of musical fans who cherished his athletic contributions to the genre, though Russ Tamblyn was, in fact, never taught to dance. He had started out as a child actor on radio (his dad, Eddie Tamblyn, had been a minor movie player in the 1930s) and appeared with a Los Angeles theater group before making his movie debut (as Rusty Tamblyn) in 1948, in RKO's *The Boy With Green Hair*, as a student. After playing the young John Dall in the cult noir *Gun Crazy*, and starring as a troubled kid in a badly dated juvenile delinquent- baseball film, *The Kid from Brooklyn*, he ended up at MGM, making a solid impression as Elizabeth Taylor's sassy younger brother in one of the big hits of 1950, *Father of the Bride*. Staying on the lot he did the sequel, *Father's Little Dividend*, went through basic training in *Take the High Ground*, and then made his first leap into movie musical history, as the youngest of the Pontapee siblings in one of the true favorites of the era, *Seven Brides for Seven Brothers*, stunning audiences with his exuberant jumps while using an axe during the famous barn-raising scene. The studio gave him a lesser follow-up, *Hit the Deck*, as Debbie Reynolds's Navy love interest, as well as secondary parts in some westerns. This meant it was up to another company, Allied Artists, to showcase him in his first top-billed vehicle, *The Young Guns*, as a gunfighter's son trying to live down dad's past; a tale told with an adolescent crowd in mind. He then went over to Fox to play nice guy Norman Page in the blockbuster soap opera *Peyton Place*, and his sincere but unspectacular performance actually earned him an Oscar nomination in the supporting actor category. His reward back on the home lot was one of producer Albert Zugsmith's awful teen movies, *High School Confidential*, as the new kid in town; *tom thumb*, a corny kids film that required him to act alone prior to being matted into the action; and the remake of *Cimarron*, as a gunslinger named The Cherokee Kid. Cast alongside some of the best dancers in the business, he not only held his own in the magnificent, Oscar-winning film version of *West Side Story*, but made the part of Jets gang leader Riff the high point of his career.

There was one more chance to dance, playing the woodsman who gets to whirl with Yvette Mimieux, during one segment of the multi-story, Cinerama production of *The Wonderful World of the Brothers*, and then he was a non-believer in the paranormal, wisecracking his way through *The Haunting*. Going backwards in time to the days of the Vikings, he was Richard Widmark's bounding sidekick in Columbia's very unsuccessful costume adventure, *The Long Ships*, which essentially marked the end of his involvement in big budget items. Instead, he ended up overseas in a Spanish western, *Son of a Gunfighter*, which sounded suspiciously like an earlier films of his, and a Japanese monster movie called *War of the Gargantuas*, which would gain some kind of bemused following among lovers of the unintentionally hilarious. The Hollywood that was interested in him by the late 1960s consisted of producers who dabbled in drive-in fare, so he ended up falling in with a band of men-haters in *The Female Bunch*; forcing LSD on former *West Side Story* co-star Richard Beymer, in *Free Grass*; playing a swastika-wearing biker-whacko terrorizing college girls in *Satan's Sadists*; and participating in one of those movies pieced together over the years from various unrelated shoots, *Dracula vs. Frankenstein*. He dropped out of the scene for a long stretch, though he would suddenly appear out of the blue on occasion in movies like the bizarre anti-nuke comedy, *Human Highway*, in which he ran a filling station. In the midst of some direct-to-video items, he had a brief resurgence when he was cast on the self-proclaimed cult television series *Twin Peaks*, reminding everyone that he was still around and available. It didn't do much for him except send him back to the same cheapjack genre stuff he was doing before.

Screen: AS RUSTY TAMBLYN: 1948: The Boy With Green Hair; 1949: Gun Crazy/Deadly Is the Female; Reign of Terror/The Black Book; The Kid from Cleveland; Samson and Delilah; 1950: Captain Carey, USA; Father of the Bride; The Vicious Years; 1951: As Young as You Feel; Father's Little Dividend.

AS RUSS TAMBLYN: 1952: The Winning Team; Retreat, Hell!; 1953: Take the High Ground; 1954: Seven Brides for Seven Brothers; Deep in My Heart; 1955: Hit the Deck; Many Rivers to Cross; 1956: The Fastest Gun Alive; The Last Hunt; The Young Guns; 1957: Peyton Place; Don't Go Near the Water; 1958: High School Confidential; tom thumb; 1960: Cimarron; 1961: West

Side Story; **1962**: The Wonderful World of the Brothers Grimm; **1963**: How the West Was Won; Follow the Boys; The Haunting; **1964**: The Long Ships; **1966**: Son of a Gunfighter; War of the Gargantuas; **1969**: The Female Bunch; Free Grass/Scream Free; Satan's Sadists; **1971**: The Last Movie; Dracula vs. Frankenstein; **1975**: Win, Place or Steal/Another Day at the Races; **1976**: Black Heat/The Murder Gang; **1982**: Human Highway; **1987**: Cyclone; Commando Squad; **1989**: Necromancer (dtv); B.O.R.N. (dtv); Blood Screams (dtv); The Phantom Empire (dtv); Desert Steel (dtv); **1990**: Aftershock (dtv); **1991**: Wizards of the Demon Sword (dtv); **1993**: Little Devils: The Birth (dtv); **1994**: Cabin Boy; **1995**: Attack of the 60 Ft. Centerfold (dtv); Starstruck (nUSr); Rebellious (nUSr); **1996**: Invisible Mom (dtv); **1996**: Johnny Mysto: Boy Wizard (dtv); **1997**: Little Miss Magic; Invisible Dad (dtv); Ghost Dog/My Magic Dog (dtv).

Select TV: **1990–91**: Twin Peaks (series); **1992**: Running Mates; **1999**: Inherit the Wind; Days of Our Lives (series).

AKIM TAMIROFF

BORN: TIFLIS, RUSSIA, OCTOBER 29, 1899.
DIED: SEPTEMBER 17, 1972.

Bombastic, smarmy, and edgy, with a marvelously fractured accent, Akim Tamiroff was not one to creep quietly in front of the lens, gobbling scenes with great (and sometimes unapologetically hammy) effect. A student of the Moscow Art Theatre, he traveled with that company to America in 1923, doing a series of plays in New York and eventually joining the Theatre Guild. He settled down in the U.S. for good, traveling to Hollywood in the early 1930s to seek film work and making his big-screen bow, in 1933, doing a series of unbilled bits in various films. Any producer looking for a thick accent to suggest a foreign locale was quick to hire Tamiroff and he was seen as an Italian in *Murder in the Private Car*; a Mexican in *Go Into Your Dance*; and an Indian in *The Lives of a Bengal Lancer*, to name but a few. In 1936 his status among character players ascended when he pulled off playing the insidious Chinese warlord in the Gary Cooper adventure *The General Died at Dawn*, the title referring to his demise. Although his make-up was no more convincing than most attempts to turn Caucasians into Asians, his performance was surprisingly subtle and frequently mesmerizing, earning him an Oscar nomination in the first year the supporting category was established. Paramount, who distributed the film, put him under contract and actually made him a temporary star of some "B" unit offerings, with *King of Gamblers*, in the title role, as a gangster in love with Claire Trevor; *The Great Gambini*, as a clairvoyant who offers his services to the police; *Dangerous to Know*, as a hood torn between Gail Patrick and Anna May Wong; *Ride a Crooked Mile*, as a Cossack-turned-cattle rustler; *The Magnificent Fraud*, as an actor hired to impersonate an assassinated South American president; and the remake of Emil Jannings's *The Way of All Flesh*, as a bank cashier ruined by a bad woman.

Audiences got a great kick out of this squat, singularly unhandsome actor's colorful thesping and, after this brief period of playing leads, he continued to be happily employed in secondary characters parts. These included his sharp work as the political boss who puts bum Brian Donlevy into office in *The Great McGinty*; his scene-chewing as the snarling villain in *The Corsican Brothers*; his affable interpretation of a lazy paisano in *Tortilla Flat*; and one of his smarmier parts, as the Egyptian innkeeper who opens his lodgings to Rommel and his Nazis, in *Five Graves to Cairo*. In 1943 he gave probably his finest performance, as the vulgar, duplicitous Spanish partisan leader whose position is usurped by Katina Paxinou, in one of the big ones of the decade, *For Whom the Bell Tolls*. This was quintessential Tamiroff, weak-willed yet commanding, and he was once again in the running for an Oscar in the supporting category. This did not, however, keep him on a roll and he was soon ending up with inferior assignments, including *Dragon Seed*, as one of the Chinamen poisoned by Katharine Hepburn; the unfaithful 1944 version of *The Bridge of San Luis Rey*, as Lynn Bari's uncle; *A Scandal in Paris*, as partner to thief George Sanders; and *My Girl Tisa*, as Lili Palmer's dad. In the late 1950s he benefited from working with Orson Welles, on *Mr. Arkadin*, as a derelict, and, more significantly *Touch of Evil*, as the slovenly Mexican crime boss whom Welles murders. By this point he was involved in more increasingly international productions and foreign films, while his American assignments included *Ocean's Eleven*, as the mastermind behind the heist; *Romanoff and Juliet*, as a Russian ambassador; *Topkapi*, where he had a "thing" for the equally portly Peter Ustinov; and *Lt. Robin Crusoe, USN*, as an island chief. Late in his career he actually got a starring role, albeit an incredibly embarrassing one, as *The Vulture*, showing up with his head perched upon a prop bird body, proving there was nothing certain performers wouldn't do to keep working. He was married to actress Tamara Shayne.

Screen: **1933**: The Barbarian; Clear All Wires!; Gabriel Over the White House; The Devil's in Love; Storm at Daybreak; Professional Sweetheart; Queen Christina; Murder in the Private Car; **1934**: Fugitive Lovers; The Merry Widow (and French version: La Veuve Joyeuse); Now and Forever; Sadie McKee; Chained; Lady by Choice; The Great Flirtation; Here Is My Heart; Whom the Gods Destroy; The Scarlet Empress; The Captain Hates the Sea; Wonder Bar; **1935**: The Winning Ticket; The Lives of a Bengal Lancer; Black Fury; Naughty Marietta; China Seas; The Big Broadcast of 1936; Rumba; Paris in Spring; The Gay Deception; Go Into Your Dance; Two Fisted; The Last Outpost; Reckless; Ladies Love Danger; **1936**: Woman Trap; Desire; Anthony Adverse; The General Died at Dawn; The Story of Louis Pasteur; The Jungle Princess; **1937**: King of Gamblers; The Great Gambini; High, Wide and Handsome; The Soldier and the Lady; Her Husband Lies; This Way Please; **1938**: Dangerous to Know; Ride a Crooked Mile; Spawn of the North; The Buccaneer; **1939**: Paris Honeymoon; The Magnificent Fraud; King of Chinatown; Disputed Passage; Union Pacific; Honeymoon in Bali; **1940**: The Great McGinty; The Way of All Flesh; North West Mounted Police; Texas Rangers Ride Again; Untamed; **1941**: The Corsican Brothers; New York Town; **1942**: Tortilla Flat; **1943**: His Butler's Sister; Five Graves to Cairo; For Whom the Bell Tolls; **1944**: The Miracle of Morgan's Creek; Dragon Seed; The Bridge of San Luis Rey; Can't Help Singing; **1946**: Pardon My Past; A Scandal in Paris; **1947**: The Gangster; Fiesta; **1948**: My Girl Tisa; Relentless; **1949**: Black Magic; Outpost in Morocco; **1953**: Desert Legion; You Know What Sailors Are; **1954**: They Who Dare; Cartouche; **1955**: Mr. Arkadin/Confidential Report; The Black Forest; The Widow/La Vedova (Fr: 1954); **1956**: The Black Sleep; Anastasia; **1957**: Battle Hell/Yangtse Incident; **1958**: Touch of Evil; Me and the Colonel; **1959**: Desert Desperadoes/The Sinner (It: 1955); **1960**: Ocean's Eleven; **1961**: Romanoff and Juliet; Seduction of the South/The Italian Brigands (nUSr); The Last Judgment (nUSr); Tartar Invasion (nUSr); La Moglie di Mio Marito (nUSr); **1962**: The Reluctant Saint; A Queen for Caesar (nUSr); **1963**: With Fire and Sword (filmed 1961); The Trial; The Black Tulip (nUSr); The Bacchantes (filmed 1961); **1964**: Panic Button; Bambole/The Dolls; Spuit Elf (nUSr); Topkapi; **1965**: Marco the Magnificent;

Chimes at Midnight/Falstaff; Lord Jim; Crime on a Summer Morning (nUSr); The Liquidator; Marie-Chantal: Doctor Kha (nUSr); 1966: Alphaville; After the Fox; Hotel Paradiso; Lt. Robin Crusoe, USN; Adultery Italian Style (nUSr); 1967: The Vulture; Un Gangster venuto da Brooklyn (nUSr); A Rose for Everyone; 1968: Great Catherine; O tutto o Nicente/Either All or None (nUSr); 1969: The Great Train Robbery; 1970: Sabra (nUSr); The Girl Who Couldn't Say No.

NY Stage: 1923: Tsar Fyodor Ivanovitch; Brothers Karamazov; Mistress of the Inn; In the Claws of Life; Enough Stupidity in Every Wise Man; 1924: The Death of Pazukhin; 1940: The Life Line; 1959: Rashomon.

Select TV: 1952: Trouble on Pier 12 (sp); 1955: Broadway (sp); The Chocolate Soldier (sp); 1956: One Forty-Two (sp); 1957: The Miracle Worker (sp); 1960: Thunder in the Night (sp); 1962: View from the Eiffel Tower (sp); 1969: Then Came Bronson.

JESSICA TANDY

BORN: LONDON, ENGLAND, JUNE 7, 1909.
DIED: SEPTEMBER 11, 1994.

There was no doubt that the tiny and dignified Jessica Tandy was one of the great names of the English-speaking theater for five decades, but her place in movie history during most of those years was relatively unexceptional. It was not until she was past the age of 70 that she became one of the most familiar senior thespians of the screen and could, at last, be considered a bonafide movie star. She studied her craft at the Ben Greet Academy of Acting and made her professional debut in London at age 16. Five years later she came to New York for her first appearance there, in The Matriarch, then returned to her native land, making her motion picture bow, in 1932, in The Indiscretions of Eve, where she had a song and dance bit, playing a cockney maid. That same year she married actor Jack Hawkins and they remained together for the next ten years, while Tandy established herself as a major name on the London stage. With the outbreak of World War II, she relocated to America and married Hume Cronyn in 1942, forming not only one of the longest-lasting marriages in show business history but one of the great acting partnerships as well. Since Cronyn was heading to Hollywood for work, Tandy came with him and they did their first of many screen teamings, in 1944's The Seventh Cross, in which they were a couple helping concentration camp escapee Spencer Tracy. In The Valley of Decision, she was the woman Gregory Peck weds, much to the displeasure of Greer Garson; in The Green Years, she had the bizarre task of portraying Cronyn's daughter; and she was wasted playing maids in two stodgy costume pieces of their day, Dragonwyck and Forever Amber. If Hollywood wasn't going to do right by her, there was always the theater and she went to Broadway to play the most important stage role of her career, Blanche Du Bois, in the original 1947 production of Tennessee Williams's ground- breaking drama A Streetcar Named Desire, winning a Tony Award for her performance. She was the only one of the four New York stage principles passed over for the 1951 film adaptation.

In the theater she continued to hold her position as one of Broadway's reigning stars, winning great acclaim for such works as The Fourposter, Five Finger Exercise, and A Delicate Balance, to name but a few. During this period she would accept an occasional movie offer, such as The Desert Fox, as the wife of Field Marshal Rommel (James Mason); Disney's

The Light in the Forest, as the mother of James MacArthur; Hitchcock's The Birds, as the standoffish mom of Rod Taylor; and Butley, her first British movie in years, as a school board member who battles with Alan Bates. In 1981 she and Cronyn were featured in a movie together for the first time in nearly 40 years, a noisy multi-character comedy, Honky Tony Freeway, then appeared briefly in a far better picture, The World According to Garp, as Glenn Close's disapproving parents. They were then given actual leads in two fantasies, Cocoon, as a pair of Florida seniors who are among those rejuvenated by aliens, and Batteries Not Included, as a New York couple who are assisted by teeny Martians in an effort to save their apartment building from developers. Because of these films, Cronyn and Tandy had become very prominent in the minds of casting agents and this was instrumental in Tandy landing the best part of her cinematic career, in Driving Miss Daisy. As the aloof, fussy and self-centered Southern aristocrat who comes to realize that her black chauffeur (Morgan Freeman) is indeed the closest friend she has ever had, she was as good as anyone would expect this magnificent actress to be. At 80, she became the oldest acting recipient of the Academy Award, and this very genteel movie not only made an unexpected fortune, but won the Oscar for Best Picture of 1989. This was followed by a supporting Oscar nod, as the spirited old lady who tells her tale to Kathy Bates, in Fried Green Tomatoes, and she kept right on going with Used People, as Shirley MacLaine's cranky mom, and Nobody's Fool, as Paul Newman's landlady-former teacher, released after her death from ovarian cancer. On television, she won an Emmy Award for repeating her Tony Award-winning Broadway role in Foxfire. Her second Tony was won for The Gin Game.

Screen: 1932: The Indiscretions of Eve; 1938: Murder in the Family; 1944: The Seventh Cross; Blonde Fever; 1945: The Valley of Decision; 1946: The Green Years; Dragonwyck; 1947: Forever Amber; 1948: A Woman's Vengeance; 1950: September Affair; 1951: The Desert Fox; 1958: The Light in the Forest; 1962: Hemingway's Adventures of a Young Man; 1963: The Birds; 1974: Butley; 1981: Honky Tonk Freeway; 1982: The World According to Garp; Still of the Night; Best Friends; 1984: The Bostonians; 1985: Cocoon; 1987: Batteries Not Included; 1988: The House on Carroll Street; Cocoon: The Return; 1989: Driving Miss Daisy; 1991: Fried Green Tomatoes; 1992: Used People; 1994: Camilla; Nobody's Fool.

NY Stage: 1930: The Matriarch; The Last Enemy; 1938: Time and the Conways; 1939: The White Steed; 1940: Geneva; Jupiter Laughs; 1941: Anne of England; 1942: Yesterday's Magic; 1947: A Streetcar Named Desire; 1950: Hilda Crane; 1951: The Fourposter; 1955: The Honeys; Day by the Sea; 1958: The Man in the Dog Suit; 1959: Triple Play; Five Finger Exercise; 1964: The Physicists; 1966: A Delicate Balance; 1970: Camino Real; 1971: Home; All Over; 1972: Samuel Beckett Festival (Happy Days; Not I) (ob); 1974: Noel Coward in Two Keys; 1977: The Gin Game; 1981: Rose; 1982: Foxfire; 1983: The Glass Menagerie; 1985: Salonika (ob); 1986: The Petition.

Select TV: 1948: Portrait of a Madonna (sp); 1950: Hedda Gabler (sp); 1951: Icebound (sp); Hangman's House (sp); 1954: The Marriage (series); 1955: Christmas 'Til Closing (sp); 1956: The Great Adventure (sp); The School Mistress (sp); The Confidence Man (sp); A Murder Is Announced (sp); 1957: The Five Dollar Bill (sp); Clothes Make the Man (sp); Little Miss Bedford (sp); 1959: The Fallen Idol (sp); The Moon and Sixpence (sp); 1981: The Gin Game (sp); 1987: Foxfire; 1991: The Story Lady; 1994: To Dance With the White Dog.

DON TAYLOR

BORN: FREEPORT, PA, DECEMBER 13, 1920.
ED: PENN ST. UNIV. DIED: DECEMBER 29, 1998.

A very average screen presence of a mildly engaging manner, Don Taylor did his job in this department for close to 20 years before he decided there were greener pastures behind the lens. A chance meeting with writers Julius and Philip Epstein encouraged him to try acting, and he got a contract at MGM who used him in bits parts, mostly playing soldiers, in films like *The Human Comedy* and *Swing Shift Maisie*. He became a real participant in the war when he joined the Air Force during World War II, appearing in the famous military stage production of *Winged Victory*. In Hollywood he repeated his part in the film version, as a most enthusiastic recruit who breaks down when he realizes his eye problems will keep him from being a flyer, and then went to Universal to partner Barry Fitzgerald in one of the best and most influential noir films of the late 1940s, *The Naked City*, as a New York City investigator trying to uncover the killer of a young woman. Back at MGM he was in uniform again for a major war film, *Battleground*, and then played the role for which he is probably best known, the fiancé of Elizabeth Taylor, in one of the top moneymakers of 1950, *Father of the Bride*, which didn't require him to be much more than innocuous. Although he did take featured roles in quality films, such as *The Blue Veil*, as the kindly eye doctor who comes to Jane Wyman's aide; *Stalag 17*, as the lieutenant William Holden must smuggle out of the camp, and *I'll Cry Tomorrow*, as a soldier who marries Susan Hayward while on a bender, there were also plenty of programmers, like *Men of Sherwood* Forest, as an unlikely Robin Hood, and *Love Slaves of the Amazon*, the sort of "B" fodder that was never going to please anyone with *that* title. One of his best roles was one of his last, as the sanctimonious sergeant whose religious principles are questioned by Wendell Corey in *The Bold and the Brave*, an interesting World War II character study.

Having directed an episode of *Alfred Hitchcock Presents*, he saw a more interesting and lucrative future in this field and made his theatrical debut in this capacity, in 1961, with the silly Mickey Rooney-Buddy Hackett comedy, *Everything's Ducky*, about a talking bird. Although he would do most of his directing on television, there were ten more theatrical assignments of which *Escape from the Planet of the Apes* (1971) and the musical version of *Tom Sawyer* (1973) were the best. The others were *Ride the Wild Surf* (1964), *Jack of Diamonds* (1967), *The Five Man Army* (1969), *Echoes of a Summer* (1976), *The Great Scout and Cathouse Thursday* (1976), *The Island of Dr. Moreau* (1977), *Damien: Omen II* (1978), and *The Final Countdown* (1980). Among the television movies he directed were *Heat of Anger* (1972), *The Gift* (1979), *Listen to Your Heart* (1982) and *My Wicked, Wicked Ways: The Legend of Errol Flynn* (also writer; 1985). He was married (from 1964) to British actress Hazel Court.

Screen: 1943: Girl Crazy; The Human Comedy; Thousands Cheer; Swing Shift Maisie; Salute to the Marines; 1944: Winged Victory; 1947: Song of the Thin Man; 1948: The Naked City; For the Love of Mary; 1949: Battleground; Ambush; 1950: Father of the Bride; 1951: Flying Leathernecks; Target Unknown; Father's Little Dividend; Submarine Command; The Blue Veil; 1952: Japanese War Bride; 1953: The Girls of Pleasure Island; Destination Gobi; Stalag 17; 1954: Johnny Dark; Men of Sherwood Forest; 1955: I'll Cry Tomorrow; 1956: The Bold and the Brave; Ride the High Iron; 1957: Love Slaves of the Amazon; 1962: The Savage Guns.

NY Stage: 1943: Winged Victory; 1954: Fragile Fox.

Select TV: 1954: The Taming of the Shrew (sp); Decision at Sea (sp); Presento (sp); 1955: Penny Serenade (sp); Three Months to Remember (sp); The Careless Cadet (sp); 1956: The Teacher and Hector Hodge (sp); Only Yesterday (sp); Innocent Bystander (sp); 1958: Home Again (sp); All I Survey (sp); 1961: The Silent Sentry.

ELIZABETH TAYLOR

BORN: LONDON, ENGLAND, FEBRUARY 27, 1932.

If press attention is the measure of what makes someone a star, then Elizabeth Taylor is the greatest of them all. From childhood onward, her life was on display for all to see, and it was a fascinating one, full of husbands, illnesses, career highs and lows, with a camera pointed in her face documenting every move. Because of this she is known by the whole world, and because she was so beautiful and glamorous, she came to epitomize the Hollywood high-life. Her acting has, therefore, become second nature to most people, which is just as well, because she has been, for the most part, merely competent, sometimes inadequate, and now and then above average, with occasional instances when she rose most brilliantly to become something special. When World War II arrived she was taken from London to Hollywood, where her mother thought that her child's pretty looks might get her work in the movies. Her hunch was correct and an acquaintance got Elizabeth seen by some people at Universal, who cast her next to Alfalfa Switzer in the supporting cast of a 1942 "B" comedy, *There's One Born Every Minute*, which is only remembered today, if at all, because of it being her debut. Much higher in stature was Taylor's second feature, done over at MGM, *Lassie Come Home*, in which she was the nice rich girl whose dad puts the lovable collie in their kennel. Photographed in glorious Technicolor, she had stunning violet eyes and raven-black hair and the studio knew they were on to something, signing her to a contract. First they loaned her to Fox, where she was seen in *Jane Eyre*, as young Jane's sickly friend who succumbs, and then she came back to the home lot alongside *Lassie* co-star (and lifelong friend) Roddy McDowall for a bit in *The White Cliffs of Dover*. It was time to give her the star treatment and she got her first lead, as the young horse-enthusiast, Velvet Brown, in one of the best family films of its era, *National Velvet*, giving an effervescent and heart-felt performance of great charm that would surpass most of her later, grown-up work.

Growing older and increasing lovely, she was given her own title-role vehicle, *Cynthia*, a sticky and very minor thing about an ailing teen that did little for her, after which she benefited by being in some very popular movies including *Life with Father* (on loan to Warners), as the cousin who comes to visit; *A Date with Judy*, as Jane Powell's sister; and the Technicolor remake of *Little Women*, as Amy. Her first official "adult" role was opposite another Taylor, Robert, in *Conspirator*, but it received less attention than what would be the first of many weddings, to hotelier Nicky Hilton, in 1949. She returned to work in one of the nicest movies of the era, *Father of the Bride*, in which she was the daughter of Spencer Tracy and Joan Bennett, alternately thrilled and reluctant to take the vows to yet another Taylor, Don. She gained some credibility when she was chosen by director George Stevens to co-star in his artistic remake of *An American Tragedy*, now re-christened *A Place in the Sun*. As the aristocratic girl who is frightened by her passion for lower class Montgomery Clift, she was assured and convincing enough to hold her own against one of the best actors of them all. Unlike so many before and since, she'd made the transition from child star to adult with nary a hitch. However, back home at Metro she was in a bit of a rut where roles were concerned, and it seemed that there wasn't much use for her beyond her looks in the highly popular *Ivanhoe*, as Rebecca, or *Beau Brummell*, appearing quite dazzling in some lush and frilly costumes. In between she did some soap operas like *The Girl Who Had Everything*, a semi-remake of Norma Shearer's *A Free Soul*, in which she etched a deeply unsympathetic characterization of a rich girl who gets the hots for gangster Fernando Lamas, and *The Last Time I Saw Paris*, which was supposed to be an updating of F. Scott Fitzgerald's *Babylon Revisited*. Around this time was marriage number two (1952–57), to Michael Wilding, the only of her show business husbands opposite whom she would never act.

George Stevens rescued her again when he cast her as the Eastern girl who adapts to the ways of Texas in *Giant*, one of the finest films of the decade and a towering box-office success. It was also one of her strongest and subtlest performances, certainly more accomplished than the next four, all of which would bring her Oscar nominations. The first came for *Raintree County*, a rambling Civil War tale, the plot of which allowed her to slowly go crazy, thereby securing her some degree of critical attention, even if she did the role with more gusto than conviction. Next up was the somewhat diluted version of Tennessee Williams's Broadway triumph *Cat on a Hot Tin Roof*. Though her work paled next to that of her co-stars Paul Newman and Burl Ives, she gave it a good shot and the sight of her slinking about in her slip while trying to turn on her disinterred husband was an unforgettable image of late-1950s cinema. There was another, lesser Williams adaptation, *Suddenly, Last Summer*, in which she again lost her grip on reality, this time because she saw her gay cousin getting devoured by a pack of hungry island boys. Finally, she was a hardened, high class Manhattan prostitute who thinks she's found an escape from her loveless existence in *Butterfield 8*. Like those before it, this was a huge hit with the public, despite being more than a bit dull, and Taylor's performance was better than her own later assessment of it would indicate. She did, in fact, nab the Academy Award for the role, although it was a shared opinion that her near-fatal illness at the time was instrumental in her receiving the trophy rather than her acting. The film also saw her performing opposite her fourth husband (1959–64), singer Eddie Fisher, with whom she had caused a scandal when the fan magazines accused her of stealing him from Debbie Reynolds.

Fisher was soon out of the picture anyway, because the entire civilized world became aware that Taylor was carrying on big-time with Richard Burton, one of her leading men in the most over-publicized movie of the early 1960s, *Cleopatra*. This film became legendary for the money 20th Century-Fox poured into, the constant delays and production problems, giving it a soiled reputation for decades to come. It was, in truth, more intelligent than most grandiose costume pictures and the most highly attended film released in 1963. This did not negate the fact that the movie nearly bankrupted its studio, and that Taylor, looking ridiculously ravishing in one outrageous costume after another, suggested the sexuality of the character but hardly the greatness that made her so strong a ruler. She and Burton were now inseparable to a point where they would become the media's pet couple of the decade, and it would be hard to imagine that even their biggest admirers did not get royally sick of them after a while. Together they did two soap operas: *The V.I.P.s*, a multi-character tale of people stranded at a London airport, theirs being perhaps the least interesting of the storylines; and *The Sandpiper*, a turgid tale of adultery in which Taylor made for a fairly unconvincing free-spirited beach dweller. Then came the movie that made the whole union worthwhile, *Who's Afraid of Virginia Woolf?* Initially fans of Edward Albee's groundbreaking play were horrified at the choice of Taylor to play the slatternly, hard-drinking, middle-aged professor's wife but all reservations were put to rest with her stunning and often brilliant performance, the actress digging deeply into this overbearing yet emotionally fragile character in a way she hadn't done before or would ever do again. It was the very apex of her career and this time there was no quibbling about bestowing her with an Academy Award.

There was an ideal follow-up for her and Burton, *The Taming of the Shrew*, in which she didn't do badly by Shakespeare, as the feisty hellcat, though it was clear who was the better actor in the family. Alas, this would be the last movie she did that would in any way resemble a success, critically or financially. Although her position as the queen of all tabloid movie stars remained unchallenged, she began an unfortunate series of bad career choices that would damage the ground she had gained with *Virginia Woolf*. First was one she had hoped to do with Clift, *Reflections in a Golden Eye*, but ended up making with Marlon Brando. As the adulterous Army wife she was at her most shrill and there was even less to like with *The Comedians*, struggling with a German accent as Peter Ustinov's unfaithful spouse in this long-winded adaptation of the Graham Greene novel; *Dr. Faustus*, appearing briefly as Helen of Troy; and *Boom*, all box-office flops with Burton. The last, an adaptation of a Tennessee Williams failure, *The Milk Train Doesn't Stop Here Anymore*, was a particular turn-off for the folks who lapped up all the weekly gossip on Taylor, a gathering of grotesques with Taylor too young to play the petulant and unpleasant millionairess. Nor did anybody care to sit through two forays into kinky themes, *Secret Ceremony*, with Taylor as a former prostitute kidnapped by nympho Mia Farrow; and *X, Y & Zee*, in which she slept with Susannah York to get back at philandering hubby Michael Caine. Continuing the descent, there was the two-character disaster *The Only Game in Town*, as a showgirl carrying on with Warren Beatty; and the last two of her theatrical features with Burton, the barely seen *Under Milk Wood*, and *Hammersmith Is Out*, as a waitress. For added measure she and Richard also scored zero on a two-part television movie, *Divorce His/Divorce Hers*. Their real-life divorce, in 1974, was, of course, headline making, but their brief remarriage, in 1976, was yawn-inducing to a public that was beginning to wonder what all the fuss was about. Meanwhile, Taylor's cinematic bad luck did not let up, with the expensive Russian-made remake of *The Blue Bird*, which got murdered by the press and then disappeared, nor with *A Little Night Music*, in which she was given the chance to sing the musical's biggest number, "Send in the Clowns," with her own wispy, ineffectual voice, a moment which didn't exactly rescue the fading song and dance genre.

Badly in need of a career boost, she got it when she chose to make her long-delayed stage debut with *The Little Foxes*. It was a Broadway sensation and one last acting hurrah that gave her the sort of respect she was hoping for. A follow-up, *Private Lives*, for her own short-lived theater company, reunited her with Burton, but it nearly erased all the good notices she'd gotten the first time out. There were more headlines when she became wife (1978–82) to Virginia Senator John Warner, jokes about her excessive weight gain, and the inevitable crash and burn as she checked herself into rehab for drug and alcohol problems. Television was her salvation in the 1980s where she did some films like *Malice in Wonderland*, as gossip columnist Louella Parsons; *There Must Be a Pony*, as a fading star; and *Sweet Bird of Youth*, ditto. Her movie career had dried up to a point where *Young Toscanini* was not only greeted with laughs during its European engagements but kept from U.S. distribution altogether. There was money coming in from the sales of her own perfume, White Diamonds, but she chose something more important to commit herself to in the late 1980s. Following the death of friend Rock Hudson from AIDS, she co-founded the American Foundation for AIDS Research in 1985, raising millions to fight this horrible epidemic. Her dedicated efforts brought her the Jean Hersholt Humanitarian Award in 1993, the same year she received the American Film Institute Life Achievement Award. Despite her recent track record, including a clumsy guest spot in *The Flintstones*, the honor seemed fully justified for a lady who did, after all, keep audiences spellbound with the sort of unforgettable presence that better actors couldn't even hope to exude.

Screen: 1942: There's One Born Every Minute; 1943: Lassie Come Home; 1944: Jane Eyre; The White Cliffs of Dover; 1945: National Velvet; 1946: Courage of Lassie; 1947: Cynthia; Life With Father; 1948: A Date With Judy; Julia Misbehaves; 1949: Little Women; Conspirator; 1950: The Big Hangover; Father of the Bride; 1951: Father's Little Dividend; A Place in the Sun; Callaway Went Thataway; 1952: Love Is Better Than Ever; Ivanhoe; 1953: The Girl Who Had Everything; 1954: Rhapsody; Elephant Walk; Beau Brummell; The Last Time I Saw Paris; 1956: Giant; 1957: Raintree County; 1958: Cat on a Hot Tin Roof; 1959: Suddenly, Last Summer; 1960: Scent of Mystery; Butterfield 8; 1963: Cleopatra; The V.I.P.s; 1965: The Sandpiper; 1966: Who's Afraid of Virginia Woolf?; 1967: The Taming of the Shrew; Doctor Faustus; Reflections in a Golden Eye; The Comedians; 1968: Boom; Secret Ceremony; 1970: The Only Game in Town; 1972: X, Y & Zee/Zee & Co.; Under Milk Wood; Hammersmith Is Out; 1973: Night Watch; Ash Wednesday; 1974: That's Entertainment!; 1975: The Driver's Seat (filmed 1973); 1976: The Blue Bird; 1977: A Little Night Music; 1979: Winter Kills; 1980: The Mirror Crack'd; 1981: Genocide (narrator); 1988: Young Toscanini (nUSr); 1994: The Flintstones.

NY Stage: 1981: The Little Foxes; 1983: Private Lives.

Select TV: 1973: Divorce His, Divorce Hers; 1976: Victory at Entebbe; 1978: Return Engagement; 1983: Between Friends; 1985: Malice in Wonderland; North & South (ms); 1986: There Must Be a Pony; 1987: Poker Alice; 1988: Who Gets the Friends?; 1989: Sweet Bird of Youth; 2001: These Old Broads.

ROBERT TAYLOR
(SPANGLER ARLINGTON BRUGH)
BORN: FILEY, NE, AUGUST 5, 1911. ED: DOANE COL., POMONA COL. DIED: JUNE 8, 1969.

In the 1930s there seemed to be few stars more strikingly handsome than Robert Taylor, whose friendly smile suggested a more open personality, but who maintained a stoic reserve instead. The public swooned and made him into a top attraction, a staple of MGM's film factory for nearly 25 years. Over time he grew a moustache and established a somewhat more rugged image, but he never really loosened up and that was just part of the trouble. He was a formidable hero of little-to-no range, solid, well mannered, and professional, but never all that compelling. He attended Pomona College where he studied drama, and it was while appearing in their production of *Journey's End* that he was offered a contract with MGM. The studio signed him up in 1934 and promptly loaned him to Fox, where he was the love interest of Mary Carlisle, who was playing Will Rogers's daughter, in *Handy Andy*. Back at MGM, his star potential was tested in some "B" movies, *Times Square Lady*, as a nightclub manager, and *Murder in the Fleet*, as a naval lieutenant. The fan response was

encouraging enough for the studio to give Taylor one of the leads in an important musical, *Broadway Melody of 1936*, where he even got to introduce a hit tune, "I've Got a Feeling You're Fooling," though no one would accuse him of being a singer. Then Universal borrowed him for one of the big soaps of the era, *Magnificent Obsession*, as the selfish wastrel who accidentally blinds Irene Dunne and then becomes a doctor to make it up to her. These two movies helped push him right up to the top of the "wanted" list, and he followed them playing another self-involved sharpie, in *Small Town Girl*, falling for Janet Gaynor, and then another doctor, one involved in a bumpy romance with Barbara Stanwyck, in *His Brother's Wife*. Off screen, he and Stanwyck became an item and they married in 1939. They would remained wed until 1952, although it was latter cited by more than one source that both showed more than a passing interest in members of their own sex.

Continuing on a roll, he was a spirited sailor infatuated with Joan Crawford in the costume romance *The Gorgeous Hussy*, and then came under a slew of criticism for his inferior emoting opposite Greta Garbo in her best known melodrama, *Camille*. From there he returned to Stanwyck (on screen) for another pairing, in Fox's *This Is My Affair*, as a secret agent for President McKinley; and was pretty much doing what he'd done before in *Broadway Melody of 1938*, although his character had a different name in this chapter. He was the arrogant American schooling over in England for *A Yank at Oxford*; was one of Margaret Sullavan's men in *Three Comrades*, where his popularity, not his superior talent, dictated that he win her from Franchot Tone and Robert Young; did some boxing to prove that he had a macho side, in *The Crowd Roars*; and went west for *Stand Up and Fight*, which was not to be confused with his later World War II effort, *Stand by for Action*. There were few sparks between him and Hedy Lamarr in *Lady of the Tropics*, and he wasn't much of a comedian as evidenced by *Remember?*, in which he and Greer Garson drink a potion that allows them to forget who they are and fall in love again. He then did one of those wonderful soap operas of the era that owe little to real life and everything to studio gloss and proficiency, *Waterloo Bridge*, as a soldier remembering his doomed romance with street walker Vivien Leigh. There was another hit with the Technicolor *Billy the Kid*, offering a colorless interpretation of the famous outlaw, and then a crime drama, *Johnny Eager*, which was stolen from him and Lana Turner, hands down, by Van Heflin. Of course, he was called on for war propaganda, which meant he was in *Flight Command*, and the better-than-average *Bataan*, before he joined the Navy for real.

When he returned from service, he attempted to stretch, playing the neurotic and dangerous husband of Katharine Hepburn, in *Undercurrent*, which only went to prove that he could be unsympathetic if he wanted to be, though this wasn't the ideal circumstance in which to prove it. Things were slipping box office-wise with *The Bribe*, in which he gave a flat reading of the sort of noirish role Bogart excelled at, and *Conspirator*, again playing a villain, a Commie out to kill wife Elizabeth Taylor, who was certainly more believable as a Brit than he was. There were also no high attendance figures for *Devil's Doorway*, which was a shame for it contained some of his more admirable work, as an Indian returning from fighting in the Civil War who is treated like dirt once he tries to claim land for his own. What rescued his box-office standing was MGM's ultra-expensive remake of *Quo Vadis?*, and, although he was strictly wooden as the Roman centurion who ends up loving Christian Deborah Kerr, this was so popular that it was instrumental in bringing on the whole wave of Biblical spectacles so prevalent in the 1950s and early 1960s. It was pretty mediocre stuff but got an Oscar nomination for Best Picture, as did the livelier *Ivanhoe*, a standard knights-in-shining-armor tale that definitely suggested adventure films were the way for Taylor to go. There was a bio film, *Above and Beyond*, as the pilot who dropped the first A-bomb, once again suggesting none of the complexities that might have made this person an interesting film subject in the first place; *All the Brothers Were Valiant*, a routine whaling adventure with Stewart Granger; and *Knights of the Round Table*, which was just what its title suggested. He went to Egypt for *Valley of the Kings*, did some knock-about comedy with Eleanor Parker in *Many Rivers to Cross*, and made the best of his sword and armor epics, *Quentin Durward*, which had more humor than the others and a terrific battle in a bell tower for its climax.

In 1956 20th Century-Fox borrowed him for a by-the-numbers war film, *D-Day, the Sixth of June*, marking the first time he'd worked away from MGM since the same studio had asked for him for *This is My Affair*, back in 1937. The box-office returns on the melodrama *Tip on a Dead Jockey* and the westerns *Saddle the Wind* and *The Law and Jake Wade*, suggested that interest in the actor was trickling away. There was later-day cult interest in the lurid crime tale *Party Girl*, but at the time it was just another genre film and marked the end of his relationship with Metro. After a western for Paramount, *The Hangman*, he decided to do a television series and was enough of a star that his name was officially part of the title, *The Detectives Starring Robert Taylor* (later, his second wife, Ursula Thiess, joined the cast). Back on the big screen, he starred in some programmers like *The House of the Seven Hawks*; worked for Disney in one of their drearier, more serious films, *The Miracle of the White Stallions*; returned to MGM for a "B" western, *Cattle King*; and even co-starred with ex-wife Barbara Stanwyck to prove that there were no hard feelings, in a William Castle thriller, *The Night Walker*. His career ended in a most undistinguished manner, doing a bunch of European pictures of no marketable U.S. value, including *Savage Pampas* and *The Day the Hot Line Got Hot*, as well as a telefilm *Return of the Gunfighter*. It therefore must have at least been a boost to his ego for his character in *Where Angels Go...Trouble Follows* to be swooned over by a batch of teenage girls.

Screen: 1934: Handy Andy; There's Always Tomorrow; Wicked Woman; 1935: Society Doctor; West Point of the Air; Times Square Lady; Murder in the Fleet; Broadway Melody of 1936; Magnificent Obsession; 1936: Small Town Girl; Private Number; His Brother's Wife; The Gorgeous Hussy; 1937: Camille; Personal Property; This Is My Affair; Broadway Melody of 1938; 1938: A Yank at Oxford; Three Comrades; The Crowd Roars; 1939: Stand Up and Fight; Lucky Night; Lady of the Tropics; Remember?; 1940: Waterloo Bridge; Escape; Flight Command; 1941: Billy the Kid; When Ladies Meet; 1942: Johnny Eager; Her Cardboard Lover; Stand by for Action; 1943: The Youngest Profession; Bataan; Song of Russia; 1944: The Fighting Lady (narrator); 1946: Undercurrent; 1947: High Wall; 1948: The Secret Land (narrator); 1949: The Bribe; Ambush; Conspirator; 1950: Devil's Doorway; 1951: Quo Vadis?; Westward the Women; 1952: Ivanhoe; Above and Beyond; 1953: I Love Melvin; Ride, Vaquero!; All the Brothers Were Valiant; Knight of the Round Table; 1954: Valley of the Kings; Rogue Cop; 1955: Many Rivers to Cross; Quentin Durward; 1956: The Last Hunt; D-Day, the Sixth of June; The Power and the Prize; 1957: Tip on a Dead Jockey; 1958: Saddle the Wind; The Law and Jake Wade; Party Girl; 1959: The Hangman; The House of the Seven Hawks; 1960: Killers of Kilimanjaro; 1963: The Miracle of the White Stallions; Cattle King; 1964: A House Is Not a Home; 1965: The Night Walker; 1966: Johnny Tiger; Savage Pampas; Hondo and the

Apaches (nUSr); 1967: The Glass Sphinx (nUSr); 1968: Where Angels Go...Trouble Follows; The Day the Hot Line Got Hot.
Select TV: 1959–62: The Detectives Starring Robert Taylor (series); 1966–68: Death Valley Days (series host).

ROD TAYLOR
BORN: SYDNEY, AUSTRALIA, JANUARY 11, 1929.
ED: EAST SYDNEY FINE ARTS COL.

A handsome, affable leading man who lent his quietly engaging personality to a number of commercial productions from the 1960s before he took the expected programmer-action movie route, Rod Taylor had initially set out to study art. Instead, he decided to take acting classes at Sydney's Independent Theatre School. This got him a stage role in a production of *Misalliance*, bits in two Australian films, and a bigger part, as a blind man, in *Long John Silver*. He traveled to Hollywood and was engaged by 20th Century-Fox to give support to Bette Davis in *The Virgin Queen*, which encouraged him to seek further work in America. In addition to the smaller roles he received, there were important ones in the Allied Artist sci-fi thriller *World Without End*, in which he played one of the astronauts who travel into the future, and *The Catered Affair*, as the fellow Debbie Reynolds is engaged to marry. He was greatly helped by getting cast in some major late-1950s releases, including *Giant*, in which he played a British baron; *Raintree County*, as a Southerner; and *Separate Tables*, one of the less interesting of the multiple stories, paired off with Audrey Dalton. During this time he'd been under contract to MGM and, after playing a guy out to woo Shirley MacLaine in *Ask Any Girl*, they let him carry George Pal's imaginative production of H.G. Wells's *The Time Machine*. He proved to be a marvelous intellectual hero and, although this movie was mainly appreciated for its Oscar-winning special effects, it became a favorite over the years and is probably the first credit that comes to mind when Taylor's name is mentioned.

Since he wasn't immediately offered any big assignments as a follow-up, he went to Europe to do some films and then returned for Alfred Hitchcock's *The Birds*, in which he tried to protect his family and girlfriend Tippi Hedren from the feathery onslaught. Then he teamed with Rock Hudson for a military drama, *A Gathering of Eagles*; admitted to being Australian for the first time in years, as part of the popular ensemble *The V.I.P.s*; was at his most pleasing romancing Jane Fonda in the tepid *Sunday in New York*; and was good as a complex villain, a German doctor working for the Nazis to get information out of James Garner, in *36 Hours*. Director John Ford's less mainstream piece, *Young Cassidy* (the story of writer Sean O'Casey), proved that Taylor had the ability to tackle something more challenging if someone would give him the chance. Retuning to familiar ground, he teamed with Doris Day in two of her fluffiest films, *Do Not Disturb* and *The Glass Bottom Boat*; and headed the cast of a glossy but minor multi-character melodrama, *Hotel*, which was adapted from a major bestseller. He then began his run of adventure offerings that helped diffuse what little draw he had: *The Liquidator*, one of the many spy/espionage offerings of the era; *Chuka*, a western he himself produced; *Dark of the Sun*, the most successful of this bunch, starring Taylor as a mercenary rescuing refugees from the Congo; and the British *Nobody Runs Forever/The High Commissioner*, a Cold War thriller without the thrills. He played the older lover of Daria Halprin in one of the major disasters of 1970, *Zabriskie Point*, and then figured it was time to start taking whatever work he could get, including television appearances. His post-stardom theatrical ventures included supporting John Wayne in *The Train Robbers*; playing the villain in a Richard Harris movie that nobody wanted to see, *The Deadly Trackers*; and taking the title role in the cheesy remake of *Trader Horn*. Fans were required to stick to the small screen if they wanted to see him in material that didn't require a map to hunt down, and, among many telefilms, he had a regular role on the nighttime soap *Falcon Crest*. Later he popped up in cinemas as a television executive in the satire, *Open Season*, and returned to his native land for a dud comedy, *Welcome to Woop Woop*, as a crazy old coot in charge of a ratty Outback shantytown.

Screen: AS RODNEY TAYLOR: 1951: The Stewart Expedition; 1954: King of the Corral Sea; Long John Silver.

AS ROD TAYLOR: 1955: The Virgin Queen; Hell on Frisco Bay.

AS RODNEY TAYLOR: Top Gun; 1956: The Rack; World Without End; The Catered Affair; Giant; 1957: Raintree County; 1958: Step Down to Terror; Separate Tables; 1959: Ask Any Girl; 1960: The Time Machine; Queen of the Amazons/Colossus and the Amazon Queen; 1961: One Hundred and One Dalmatians (voice); 1962: Seven Seas to Calais; 1963: The Birds; A Gathering of Eagles; The V.I.P.s; 1964: Sunday in New York; Fate Is the Hunter; 36 Hours; 1965: Young Cassidy; Do Not Disturb; 1966: The Glass Bottom Boat; The Liquidator; 1967: Hotel; Chuka (and prod.); 1968: Dark of the Sun/The Mercenaries; The Hell With Heroes; Nobody Runs Forever/The High Commissioner; 1970: Zabriskie Point; 1971: The Man Who Had Power Over Women; Darker Than Amber; 1973: The Train Robbers; The Deadly Trackers; Trader Horn; 1975: The Heroes (filmed 1972); 1976: Blondy/Vortex (nUSr); 1978: Hell River/Partisani (filmed 1974); 1979: The Treasure Seekers (dtv); The Picture Show Man (Aus 1977); 1983: A Time to Die (filmed 1979); On the Run; 1985: Marbella (dtv); Mask of Murder/The Investigator (nUSr); 1995: Point of Betrayal (nUSr); 1996: Open Season; 1998: Welcome to Woop Woop.

Select TV: 1955: The Browning Version (sp); Killer Whale (sp); The Last Day on Earth (sp); 1957: The Young Years (sp); 1958: Verdict of Three (sp); The Great Gatsby (sp); The Long March (sp); 1959: The Raider (sp); Misalliance (sp); 1960: Capital Gains (sp); Early to Die (sp); Thunder in the Night (sp); 1960–61: Hong Kong (series); 1962: The Ordeal of Dr. Shannon (sp); 1971: Powder Keg; Bearcats (series); 1972: Family Flight; 1975: A Matter of Wife … and Death; 1976: The Oregon Trail; 1977: The Oregon Trail (series); 1980: Cry of the Innocent; 1981: Hellinger's Law; Jacqueline Bouvier Kennedy; 1982: Charles and Diana: A Royal Love Story; 1983–84: Masquerade (series); 1986: Outlaws; 1986–87: Outlaws (series); 1988–90: Falcon Crest (series); 1991: Danielle Steel's Palomino; 1992: Grass Roots; 1998: The Warlord: Battle for the Galaxy.

SHIRLEY TEMPLE

BORN: SANTA MONICA, CA, APRIL 23, 1928.

Her name became synonymous with the term "child star" and there haven't been any cinematic moppets who've even come close to achieving the sort of popularity and historical impact Shirley Temple had on the country. She was curly-haired, chubby-cheeked, bursting with energy and an eagerness to please. She was also precocious to the point of nausea, over-emphasizing every goody-goody line, pouring on each inflection of cheer and wringing forth every tear in a manner that had nothing whatsoever to do with real acting. Her career in movies began before she was even five years old, when her mother brought her around the studios, determined to find the child work. Educational Pictures hired her to appear in

a series of shorts called "Baby Burlesks," which had kids spoofing notable movies and stars of the times. Among the titles were "War Babies," "Pie Covered Wagon," "Kid 'n Hollywood," and "Dora's Dunkin' Donuts." In the middle of these shorts, she made her feature debut in an independent cheapie, *Red Haired Alibi*, playing the daughter of wealthy New Yorker Grant Withers, and this was followed by other supporting parts, which presented her just another kid actor. What made the difference was her being cast as James Dunn's daughter in the Fox musical *Stand Up and Cheer*, since it required her to sell a number on her own, a song called "Baby Take a Bow." The response was enthusiastic enough for the studio to put her under contract, but before they gave her anything more substantial to do, she went over to Paramount to play the title role in the adaptation of Damon Runyon's *Little Miss Marker*, where she was part of a prime ensemble, including Adolphe Menjou and Charles Bickford. The fact that this turned out to be the best movie she would ever do makes one wonder want kind of career she might have had under the superior supervision of that studio.

Eager to cash in on a good thing, Fox entitled her official studio follow-up *Baby Take a Bow* and cast her alongside Dunn again, after which she had an additional film at Paramount, *Now and Forever*, which had the added plus of Gary Cooper and Carole Lombard as the headlining stars. With Dunn once more, as well as fellow-moppet Jane Withers, she did *Bright Eyes*, which was notable because it featured Temple performing the song that would become her cutesy signature number, "On the Good Ship Lollipop," which, incidentally, was not sung on a ship but an airplane. Now officially a star (she'd received a special Oscar already, in 1934), she carried *The Little Colonel*, set during the post-Civil War South, and remembered chiefly because it was the first time that she danced with the marvelous Bill Robinson. This sequence was such a treat, in fact, that she would not only reteam for similar terpsichorean moments with Robinson, but with other grown-ups, including Buddy Ebsen, in *Captain January*, and Arthur Treacher, in *The Little Princess*. In the meantime, the Temple formula was being established, with The Precious One, usually orphaned or single-parented, playing cupid or bringing happiness to all the needy adults around her. Not content to better the lives of the common folk, she went right to the top on occasion, charming the likes of Abraham Lincoln, in *The Littlest Rebel*, and Queen Victoria, in *The Little Princess*. Fortunately, there were times when the emphasis marginally shifted to her co-stars, as with Alice Faye and Jack Hayley in *Poor Little Rich Girl*, where they played a pair of vaudevillians; or Victor McLaglen, who was able to dilute some of Temple's high sugar content in *Wee Willie Winkie*. She was a godsend to her studio, raking in big bucks at a time when they needed it and she was soon one of the most famous names in America. Fox bought some expected properties for her, like *Heidi*, and utilized familiar titles, such as *Rebecca of Sunybrook Farm*, which had nothing whatsoever to do with Kate Douglas Wiggin's story but involved the world of radio instead. Whenever possible, Temple sang, offering her bubbly, self-conscious renditions of such hits as "Animal Crackers (in My Soup)" in *Curly Top*, and "You've Got to S-M-I-L-E" in *Stowaway*.

Since her emoting and singing were an even match, the relief came with her dancing and she held her own with George Murphy in *Little Miss Broadway*, and up against Robinson, once again, in *Just Around the Corner*. Fox thought highly enough of Temple to photograph her in Technicolor for both *The Little Princess* and *The Blue Bird*. While the former was typical of what the fans had come to expect, and ended up being one of her more enjoyable offerings, the latter was a heavy-handed disaster and proved instrumental in bringing her relationship with the com-

pany to a close. After *Young People*, the 12-year-old went over to MGM where she did *Kathleen*, and then *Miss Annie Rooney*, for UA. Both failed so it was wise of her to take supporting roles in two popular David O. Selznick productions, *Since You Went Away*, as one of Claudet Colbert's daughters holding forth the home-front, and *I'll Be Seeing You*, as Ginger Rogers's cousin, which turned out to be one of her more noble acting efforts. As an apple-cheeked teen she was simply a bigger version of what she'd been as a child, only now it was evident that she lacked the real talent it took to endure as an adult performer. Temple vehicles like *Kiss and Tell* and *That Hagen Girl* brought poor notices and scant attendance. When she shared the screen with more accomplished adults, her films fared much better, as was the case with *The Bachelor and the Bobby-Soxer*, in which she played a high schooler with a crush on Cary Grant, and *Fort Apache*, as Henry Fonda's sister, saddled with the unforgettably ghastly name of Philadelphia Thursday. It all came to an end with the requisite girl-and-her-horse film, *The Story of Seabiscuit*, in which she dared to attempt an Irish accent while acting opposite the real thing, Barry Fitzgerald, and *A Kiss for Corliss*, in which she mooned over a bemused David Niven. By the time of these 1949 releases, she had married and divorced actor John Agar with whom she'd appeared with in *Fort Apache*. There was a television anthology show for kids and then her retirement. In 1969, as Shirley Temple Black, she became a U.N. Representative and, later, Ambassador to Ghana and then Czechoslovakia. All of this good will duty seemed to please people the world over who liked having her around and were no doubt aware that there was no longer any place in show business for the little girl who did the unthinkable by growing up. In 1988 she published her autobiography, most appropriately entitled *Child Star*.

Screen (features): 1932: Red Haired Alibi; 1933: To the Last Man; Out All Night; 1934: Carolina; Mandalay; Stand Up and Cheer; Now I'll Tell; Change of Heart; Little Miss Marker; Baby Take a Bow; Now and Forever; Bright Eyes; 1935: The Little Colonel; Our Little Girl; Curly Top; The Littlest Rebel; 1936: Captain January; Poor Little Rich Girl; Dimples; Stowaway; 1937: Wee Willie Winkie; Heidi; Ali Baba Goes to Town; 1938: Rebecca of Sunnybrook Farm; Little Miss Broadway; Just Around the Corner; 1939: The Little Princess; Susannah of the Mounties; 1940: The Blue Bird; Young People; 1941: Kathleen; 1942: Miss Annie Rooney; 1944: Since You Went Away; I'll Be Seeing You; 1945: Kiss and Tell; 1947: The Bachelor and the Bobby-Soxer; Honeymoon; That Hagen Girl; 1948: Fort Apache; 1949: Mr. Belvedere Goes to College; Adventure in Baltimore; The Story of Seabiscuit; A Kiss for Corliss.

Select TV: 1958–61: Shirley Temple's Storybook/Shirley Temple Theatre (series).

TERRY-THOMAS

(THOMAS TERRY HOAR STEVENS)
BORN: LONDON, ENGLAND, JULY 14, 1911.
DIED: JANUARY 8, 1990.

With his gapped-tooth grin and handle-bar mustache, Terry-Thomas *looked* funny, so it was only fitting that he play comedy as he did to a tee, embodying the fussy, hissing British ninny to such perfection that he gained ample crossover appeal in the U.S. market. He started as a film extra in the 1930s, some of his verified credits being *It's Love Again* and *Rhythm Racketeer*. While doing this he was also earning a living as a cabaret emcee. Following World War II, he got a role in the stage revue *Piccadilly Hayride*, which got him on the radio and then on television,

where he starred in his own show, *How Do You View?* Discounting all the false starts and bit roles, his first official movie wasn't until 1956, when he joined the cast of a military farce, *Private's Progress*, a major hit in the United Kingdom that ensured him further offers. The Boulting Brothers snatched him up for a pair of comedies that pitted him against Ian Carmichael: *Brothers-in-Law*, with T-T as his legal client, and *Lucky Jim*, in which he played the snooty son of professor Hugh Griffith, who was, in fact, a year younger than T-T. He did four films with Peter Sellers: the wickedly funny *The Naked Truth/Your Past is Showing*, both being blackmailed by a scandal magazine; *tom thumb*, in which they were the liveliest aspect of this Hollywood-financed kiddie film, as a pair of insipid baddies; *Carlton-Browne of the F.O./Man in a Cocked Hat*, in which he played an inept diplomat; and *I'm All Right, Jack*, one of the most popular comedies from Britain at the time, featuring T-T as a factory manager. Among these he also starred in *Too Many Crooks*, in which he refused to pay his wife's ransom when she's kidnapped by bungling criminals, and *Make Mine Mink*, where he gathered a bunch of old ladies together for a heist. The Terry-Thomas persona of the often-caddish nitwit with the upper crust accent was firmly established and America was interested in taking a crack at him.

He started off in the U.S. with a leaden farce for Fox, *Bachelor Flat*, as a horny Englishman who has women problems in sunny California; then returned to the U.K. for *Operation Snatch*, a World War II comedy set in Gibraltar; *Kill or Cure*, which found him among the elderly, at a nursing home; and the brightest of these, *The Mouse on the Moon*, a film that showed him at his most comically unctuous, as a secret agent. For America he did two Cinerama offerings, *The Wonderful World of the Brothers Grimm*, as a spineless knight, and the smash hit *It's a Mad Mad Mad Mad World*, where he memorably bickered with Milton Berle in this all-star pursuit for hidden cash. In a similar slapstick vein, he played the hissable bad guy Sir Percy Ware-Armitage in a grand aviation romp, *Those Magnificent Men in Their Flying Machines*, the role that most Americans probably know him best for and one that he played variations on in the unofficial follow-up, *Blast off!* (aka *Those Fantastic Flying Fools*) and in a sequel of sorts, called *Monte Caro or Bust* (aka *Those Daring Young Men in Their Jaunty Jalopies*), starring as Sir Percy's look-alike brother. He was a decided asset supporting Jack Lemmon in *How to Murder Your Wife*, as his loyal valet; Tony Randall in *Bang, Bang, You're Dead!*, as an Arab villain; Jerry Lewis in the London-made *Don't Raise the Bridge, Lower the River*, as his accomplice in crime; and Doris Day in *Where Were You When the Lights Went Out?*, as a naughty film director, all of which only went to show that he was not getting the cream of the crop as far as Hollywood scripts were concerned. Nor was he any luckier traveling to Italy for the rotten spy spoof, *Kiss the Girls and Make Them Die*, or *Arabella*, which required him to play four different roles. Returning to Britain as the international dominance of that era cooled down, he was seen in *The Abominable Dr. Phibes*, where Vincent Price literally drained the blood out of him; *Vault of Horror*, where he was done in by wife Glynis Johns; and then in another U.S. production, *The Last Remake of Beau Geste*, in a thankless part, as a prison governor. These were done between some further Italian assignments and trashy revisions of *Tom Jones* and *The Hound of the Baskervilles*. In late 1970s he was forced to retire, having suffered for years from Parkinson's disease.

Screen: 1936: It's Love Again; Rhythm in the Air; This'll Make You Whistle; 1937: Rhythm Racketeer; 1939: Climbing High (voice); Flying Fifty Five; 1940: For Freedom; Under Your Hat; 1947: The Brass Monkey; 1948: A Date With a Dream; 1949: Helter Skelter; Melody Club; 1956: Private's Progress; The Green

Man; 1957: Brothers-in-Law; Lucky Jim; The Naked Truth/Your Past Is Showing; Happy Is the Bride; Blue Murder at St. Trinian's; 1958: tom thumb; Too Many Crooks; 1959: Carlton-Browne of the F.O./Man in a Cocked Hat; I'm All Right, Jack; 1960: School for Scoundrels; Make Mine Mink; 1961: His and Hers; A Matter of WHO; Bachelor Flat; 1962: Operation Snatch; Kill or Cure; The Wonderful World of the Brothers Grimm; 1963: The Mouse on the Moon; It's a Mad Mad Mad Mad World; 1964: Strange Bedfellows; The Wild Affair; 1965: Those Magnificent Men in Their Flying Machines or How I Flew From London to Paris in 25 Hours 11 Minutes; How to Murder Your Wife; You Must Be Joking!; 1966: Bang, Bang, You're Dead!/Our Man in Marrakesh; Munster, Go Home!; The Sandwich Man; The Daydreamer (voice); La Grande Vadrouille/Don't Look Now — We're Being Shot At (nUSr); Kiss the Girls and Make Them Die; 1967: The Perils of Pauline; Top Crack (nUSr); Blast Off!/Those Fantastic Flying Fools/Rocket to the Moon; The Karate Killers (from TV); Arabella; 1968: Danger: Diabolik; How Sweet It Is!; Don't Raise the Bridge, Lower the River; Uno Scacco tutto matto/Mad Checkmate (nUSr); Where Were You When the Lights Went Out?; 1969: 2,000 Years Later; Sette Volte Sette/Seven Times Seven (nUSr); Monte Carlo or Bust/Those Daring Young Men in Their Jaunty Jalopies; Una su 13/Twelve Plus One (nUSr); Arthur! Arthur! (nUSr); 1970: Le Mur de l'Atlantique/Atlantic Wall (nUSr); 1971: The Abominable Dr. Phibes; 1972: Dr. Phibes Rises Again; The Heroes; 1973: The Vault of Horror; Colpo Grosso…Grossissimo…Anzi Probabile (nUSr); Robin Hood (voice); 1974: Who Stole the Shah's Jewels? (nUSr); 1976: Spanish Fly; Side by Side (nUSr); The Bawdy Adventures of Tom Jones; 1977: The Last Remake of Beau Geste; 1978: The Hound of the Baskervilles; 1980: Febbre a 40!/Happy Birthday, Harry; 1981: The Cherry Picker (dtv; filmed 1972).

Select TV: 1951: How Do You View? (series); 1956: Friday Night With Terry-Thomas (series); Strictly T-T (series); 1960: Lord Arthur Savile's Crime (sp); 1965: Everybody's Got a System (sp); 1967: I Love a Mystery; 1967–68: The Old Campaigner (series).

PHYLLIS THAXTER

BORN: PORTLAND, ME, NOVEMBER 20, 1921.

A gentle lady who cornered the market on playing "nice" women and loving wives without the usual expected dollop of saccharine, Phyllis Thaxter came from a show biz related family, her mother having been a member of the Ben Greet Players. Thaxter, while still a teenager, joined a stock company in her home state and then in Montreal. From there she journeyed to New York where she made her Broadway bow, in 1939, in What a Life!, and then got lucky when she was chosen to understudy Dorothy McGuire in Claudia. While McGuire went to Hollywood, Thaxter toured with the part and, during the San Francisco run, was screen-tested and eventually signed by MGM. They started her off in the ultimate home-front wife role, being sweet and concerned over husband Van Johnson as he went off to spend Thirty Seconds Over Tokyo. She did supporting parts in big films like Week-end at the Waldorf and The Sea of Grass, in which she played the daughter of Spencer Tracy and Katharine Hepburn. She had her own "B" vehicle, Bewitched, which allowed her to portray a woman with a split personality, though her "evil" side was undermined by having her voiced dubbed by Audrey Totter (!). She was certainly the more appealing prospect for leading man Gene Kelly, when contrasted with Marie McDonald, in Living in a Big Way, after which she did the soap route, as Margaret O'Brien's mom in one of the

studio's long-on-the-shelf flops, Tenth Avenue Angel. After MGM, there were more loyal wife parts in Jim Thorpe — All-American, with Burt Lancaster; Come Fill the Cup, with Gig Young; and Springfield Rifle, with Gary Cooper. Considering all the goodness she exuded it was a bit of a surprise to find her as one of the inmates in Women's Prison, though her character's manslaughter charge came about because of a car accident. Her marriage to James Aubrey, the misguided corporate executive who was instrumental in selling off most of MGM studios and thereby destroying so much of its legacy, meant she worked only sporadically in later years, although there were two worthwhile parts, in The World of Henry Orient, as Merrie Spaeth's kindly mom, and Superman, as his earthly adopted mother. Her daughter is actress Skye Aubrey.

Screen: 1944: Thirty Seconds Over Tokyo; 1945: Bewitched; Week-end at the Waldorf; 1947: The Sea of Grass; Living in a Big Way; 1948: Sign of the Ram; Tenth Avenue Angel; Blood on the Moon; 1949: Act of Violence; 1950: No Man of Her Own; The Breaking Point; 1951: Fort Worth; Jim Thorpe — All-American; Come Fill the Cup; 1952: She's Working Her Way Through College; Springfield Rifle; Operation Secret; 1955: Women's Prison; 1957: Man Afraid; 1964: The World of Henry Orient; 1978: Superman.

NY Stage: 1939: What a Life!; 1940: There Shall Be No Night; 1941: Claudia; 1948: Sundown Beach; 1961: Take Her, She's Mine.

Select TV: 1953: Miracle in the Rain (sp); Tin Wedding (sp); 1954: Atomic Attack (sp); 1955: Penny Serenade (sp); Man Out of the Rain (sp); The Hayfield (sp); 1956: Dara (sp); Mr. Cinderella (sp); 1959: Frederick (sp); The House of Truth (sp); 1961: Bury Me Twice (sp); 1964: The Threatening Eye (sp); 1971: Incident in San Francisco; 1972: The Longest Night; 1976–77: Once an Eagle (ms); 1985: Three Sovereigns for Sarah.

ERNEST THESIGER

BORN: LONDON, ENGLAND, JANUARY 15, 1879.
ED: MARLBOROUGH COL.
DIED: JANUARY 14, 1961.

Eccentric, effete, and unforgettable, Ernest Thesiger, with his knife-sharp features, evil eyes, and pretentiously precise diction, was the sort of character player who could always put on a good show, even in the tiniest part. After abandoning a career as an artist, he made his London stage debut, in 1909, in Colonel Smith. While continuing with his theatrics in such classics as Peter Pan and Macbeth, he made his 1916 film bow, in a short, "The Real Thing a Last," a Shakespeare spoof, and would return to movies off and on during the silent era. In 1932 he made his first Broadway appearance, in The Devil Passes, and that same year was invited by friend James Whale to do a role in his film, The Old Dark House. It turned out to be an inspired bit of casting and the flamboyantly gay Thesiger's campy turn as Horace Femm, one of the weirdest members of that household of loons and creeps, suggested the combination of fright and underlying fun that was a staple of Whale's work. Three years later, Thesiger would top that role in another Whale film, Bride of Frankenstein, where his inspired performance as the insidious Dr. Pretorious would instill him deep in the hearts of horror aficionados for generations. With his wild hair and slithery menace, he was as frightening and memorable as The Monster himself. The actor was, however, more at home in his native country than Hollywood and most of his remaining work was done there. Among his other roles were the devious servant murdered by Boris Karloff in The Ghoul; the crazed killer in They Drive by Night; the Duke of Berri in Henry V; the boy king's self-satisfied tutor, Theodotus, in Caesar and

Cleopatra; an undertaker, a most suitable profession for this cadaverous character player, in *A Christmas Carol*; the Emperor Tiberius in the CineamScope hit *The Robe*; and four in support of Alec Guinness: *Last Holiday*, as the doctor who holds the key to Guinness's illness; *The Man in the White Suit*, as an imperious mill owner; *Father Brown*, as a doddering old curator; and most memorably, *The Horse's Mouth*, as the crotchety old millionaire taunted by Guinness's bohemian artist.

Screen: 1918: Nelson; The Life Story of David Lloyd George; 1919: A Little Bit of Fluff; 1921: The Adventures of Mr. Pickwick; The Bachelor Club; 1929: Weekend Wives; 1930: The Vagabond Queen; 1932: The Old Dark House; 1933: Heart Song/The Only Girl; The Ghoul; 1934: My Heart Is Calling You; The Night of the Party; 1935: Bride of Frankenstein; 1936: The Man Who Could Work Miracles; 1938: The Ware Case; They Drive by Night; Lightning Conductor; 1943: The Lamp Still Burns; My Learned Friend; 1944: Don't Take It to Heart; Henry V (US: 1946); 1945: A Place of One's Own; Caesar and Cleopatra; 1946: Beware of Pity; 1947: The Man Within/The Smugglers; Jassy; Ghosts of Berkeley Square; 1948: The Winslow Boy; Portrait from Life/The Girl in the Painting; The Bad Lord Byron; Quartet; The Brass Monkey/Lucky Mascot; 1950: Last Holiday; 1951: The Man in the White Suit; Laughter in Paradise; A Christmas Carol/Scrooge; The Magic Box; The Woman's Angle; 1953: Thought to Kill; Meet Mr. Lucifer; The Robe; 1954: Man with a Million/The Million Pound Note; The Detective/Father Brown; Make Me an Offer; 1955: Value for Money; An Alligator Named Daisy; Quentin Durward; Who Done It?; 1956: Three Men in a Boat; 1957: Doctor at Large; 1958: The Truth About Women; The Horse's Mouth; 1960: Battle of the Sexes; Sons and Lovers; 1961: The Roman Spring of Mrs. Stone.

NY Stage: 1932: The Devil Passes; 1934: The Sleeping Clergyman; 1937: Madame Bovary; 1950: As You Like It; 1957: The Country Wife.

DANNY THOMAS

(Amos Jacobs) Born: Deerfield, MI, January 6, 1912. Died: February 6, 1991.

A radio and nightclub entertainer who found television infinitely more in tune with his affable but very average talents, Danny Thomas had started out as a singer on a Detroit radio station. In time he became an emcee and comic in select nightclubs, which awakened some interest in him from Hollywood. He was signed up to do two films at MGM, both with child star Margaret O'Brien, *The Unfinished Dance*, in which he played her guardian, and *The Big City*, as one of the three men who adopt her, a Jewish cantor. Those performances did little to get moviegoers excited about him, so he went over to Fox to support Betty Grable in *Call Me Mister*, where he was given a specialty number entitled "Lament to the Pots and Pans." It was then on to Warner Bros., who put him in *I'll See You in My Dreams*, one of the multitude of composer biopics that were in vogue during the 1940s and early 1950s. This particular one found him playing Gus Kahn and it was the closest thing he ever had to a movie hit. Next up was a most curious attempt to resurrect *The Jazz Singer* for a new generation, with Thomas as the cantor's son (cast as a Jew again, despite his Catholic upbringing) who answers the call of show business. It was unashamedly old fashioned and, like all of his films, seemed to emphasize a schmaltzy personality. Already seen guesting on the small screen, he found a perfect vehicle there, pretty much a variation of his own life, playing a nightclub performer trying to balance show business

with his family life, in *Make Room for Daddy/The Danny Thomas Show*. It became an 11-season hit, brought him an Emmy Award in 1954, and firmly established him as a major name of that medium (where he also became a producer of such shows as *Gomer Pyle, USMC* and *The Mod Squad*). He published his autobiography, *Make Room for Danny*, in 1990. His daughter, Marlo, became known for her own series, *That Girl*, while his son, Tony, was a producer of television and films (*Dead Poets Society*).

Screen: 1947: The Unfinished Dance; 1948: The Big City; 1951: Call Me Mister; I'll See You in My Dreams; 1953: The Jazz Singer; 1964: Looking for Love; 1966: Don't Worry, We'll Think of a Title; 1974: Journey Back to Oz (voice; filmed 1964).

Select TV: 1950–52: All Star Revue (series); 1953–64: Make Room for Daddy/The Danny Thomas Show (series); 1967: Guys 'n' Geishas (sp); 1967–68: The Danny Thomas Hour (series); 1970–71: Make Room for Granddaddy (series); 1976–77: The Practice (series); 1978: Three on a Date; 1980–81: I'm a Big Girl Now (series); 1986–87: One Big Family (series); 1988: Side by Side.

MARSHALL THOMPSON

(James Marshall Thompson) Born: Peoria, IL, November 27, 1925. Died: May 18, 1992.

From gulping juvenile to programmer leading man to a very minor form of television stardom, Marshall Thompson wasn't expected to do much more than his job and did so unassumingly, professionally. It is not surprising, considering his mild demeanor, that he originally intended to be a priest, but a religious play he penned got him interested in dramatics instead. While at college, he was tested and signed by Universal to appear opposite Gloria Jean in *Reckless Age*. MGM liked what they saw and put him under contract. There, he was a tall, feckless innocent in movies like *They Were Expendable*, in which he played an ensign; and *The Clock*, as the boyfriend who can't get a word in edgewise. Eventually he got a lead in *Gallant Bess*, a minor horsey picture in which he was a soldier who befriended and trained a four-legger. Attempting to put some grit into his image, the studio let him play an unhinged mental hospital escapee holding some bar patrons hostage in *Dial 1119*, and the would-be assassin of Abraham Lincoln in *The Tall Target*. After that film MGM dropped him and he went the "B" route with *The Basketball Fix*, as a corrupted athlete; *Cult of the Cobra*, as a G.I. being pursued by vengeful Faith Domergue; *Lure of the Swamp*, as a tour guide tangling with thieves; and some sci-fi thrillers, *Fiend Without a Face*, about invisible brains; and the better *It! The Terror from Beyond Space*, about an alien stalking the crew of a space vehicle. There was an unfortunate pro-Vietnam War film, *A Yank in Viet-Nam*, directed and co-produced by himself, and then a children's picture he helped write, *Clarence, the Cross-Eyed Lion*, that did well enough to inspire a series, *Daktari*, in which Thompson had a three year run as a kindly veterinarian working in Africa.

Screen: 1944: Reckless Age; The Purple Heart; Blonde Fever; 1945: The Valley of Decision; The Clock; Twice Blessed; They Were Expendable; 1946: Bad Bascomb; The Show-Off; The Cockeyed Miracle; Gallant Bess; The Secret Heart; 1947: The Romance of Rosy Ridge; 1948: Homecoming; B.F.'s Daughter; Words and Music; Command Decision; 1949: Roseanna McCoy; Battleground; 1950: Devil's Doorway; Stars in My Crown (narrator); Mystery Street; Dial 1119; 1951: The Tall Target; The Basketball Fix; 1952: My Six Convicts; The Rose Bowl Story; 1953: The Caddy; 1954: Port of Hell; 1955: Battle Taxi; Cult of the

Cobra; Crashout; To Hell and Back; Good Morning, Miss Dove; **1957:** East of Kilimanjaro; Lure of the Swamp; **1958:** Fiend Without a Face; It! The Terror from Beyond Space; The Secret Man; **1959:** First Man Into Space; **1961:** Flight of the Lost Balloon; **1962:** No Man Is an Island; **1964:** A Yank in Viet-Nam (and dir.; co-prod.); **1965:** Clarence, the Cross-Eyed Lion (and co-wr.); Zebra in the Kitchen; **1966:** Around the World Under the Sea; To the Shores of Hell (nUSr); **1971:** George! (and co-wr.; prod.); **1977:** The Turning Point; **1982:** White Dog; **1984:** Bog! (filmed 1978).

NY Stage: 1953: A Girl Can Tell.

Select TV: 1952: Visit from a Stranger (sp); **1953:** Life of the Party (sp); **1955:** The Rack (sp); Stranger in the Desert (sp); **1956:** Command (sp); The House of Seven Gables (sp); **1957:** Young Man from Kentucky (sp); The Blackwell Story (sp); Moment of Decision (sp); The Fall of the House of Usher (sp); **1960:** The World of Giants (series); **1960–61:** Angel (series); **1966–69:** Daktari (series); **1969–71:** Jambo (series); **1973:** George (series); **1978:** Cruise Into Terror; Centennial (ms); **1986:** Dallas: The Early Years.

THREE STOOGES

Moe Howard

(Moses Horwitz) Born: Brooklyn, NY, June 19, 1897. Died: May 4, 1975.

Larry Fine

(Louis Feinberg) Born: Philadelphia, PA, October 5, 1902. Died: January 24, 1975.

Curly Howard

(Jerome Lester Horwitz) Born: Brooklyn, NY, October 22, 1903. Died: January 18, 1952.

Shemp Howard

(Samuel Horwitz) Born: Brooklyn, NY, March 17, 1895. Died: November 23, 1955.

Joe Besser

Born: St. Louis, MO, August 12, 1907. Died: March 1, 1988.

Curly Joe DeRita

(Joseph Wardell) Born: Philadelphia, PA, July 12, 1909. Died: July 3, 1993.

Ted Healy

(Charles Ernest Lee Nash) Born: Kaufman, TX, October 1, 1896. Died: December 21, 1937.

Gloriously lowbrow, the Three Stooges outlasted many of their more critically approved of contemporaries to become favorites of multiple generations of fans who recognized the dexterity behind their precisely orchestrated slapstick. Face slaps, pulled hair, noses yanked by pliers — there was nothing too outrageous for the trio, who dominated the short-subject market for an impressive 25 years. The original vaudeville pairing consisted of brothers Moe and Shemp Howard, who teamed with Ted Healey to play his "stooges" at Brooklyn's Prospect Theatre, in 1922. Three years later, Larry Fine joined the group, and the billing became "Ted Healy and His Three Stooges." When Shemp left the group in 1932, the youngest Howard brother, Curly, replaced him, ushering in the most perfect of the team's many groupings. Moe was the leader; cranky and sour-faced, with a tendency to inflict violence on his co-horts, most mem-

orably with a two-fingered eye poke. Larry was the hapless patsy, his wild hair just ready for tugging. Curly was the most inspired member of them all, a one-man cyclone of fidgets, fits, dog barks, high-pitched whines, curious hand flaps to indicate disapproval, and manic floor-spins. His laugh, consisting of a self-satisfied "nyuk-nyuk-nyuk," became one of the most imitated of all comedic trademarks. Once the Stooges decided to separate from Healy, the latter did some feature appearances, usually as snide sidekicks, until his early death. Meanwhile, the trio was signed by Columbia Pictures for their series of sometimes classic knock-about short subjects. They started with an odd one, "Woman Haters" in 1934, told entirely in rhyme, continued through to their Oscar-nominated "Men in Black," and kept their shtick going until Curly left the team due to illness, in 1947.

Shemp, in the meantime, played supporting roles to the likes of Abbott and Costello and W.C. Fields, as well as appearing in his own two-reelers. He replaced his ailing brother, starting with "Fright Night" (1947), and continuing through "Commotion on the Ocean," which was released after his death. The series never again reached the dizzying heights of fun once Curly departed since Shemp's manic persona, with its trademark "heebeebee" gasps, had none of his younger sibling's sweetly engaging quality. During Shemp's period of employment, the team entered the 3-D craze with two of their offerings, "Spooks" and "Pardon My Backfire," and did a feature for United Artists, *Gold Raiders*. With Columbia still interested in grinding out two-reelers after Shemp's passing, the team hired Joe Besser, who'd done his share of short subjects for the studio, and he brought his patented shtick of sissified nervous nics to the increasingly uninspired material. By the time he called it quits in 1959 the older shorts had been getting a tremendous response from a whole new generation of children via television broadcasts. This encouraged Columbia to find yet another third man for the group, coming up with rotund Joe DeRita, who had actually done a handful of two-reelers for the studio years before. This time the Stooges actually starred in some features, made expressly for the Saturday matinee trade, starting with the sci-fi spoof, *Have Rocket, Will Travel*, and ending with the western satire, *The Outlaws Is Coming!*, in 1965. They continued to do guest spots and personal appearance tours until deteriorating health and old age brought on retirement. By that time the original Curly shorts, complete with all the slapstick "violence" that had been getting snipped away via censorship on television, were being played at midnight shows to the fervent appreciation of eager Stooge followers everywhere. Long after their deaths, Moe, Larry, and Curly remain among the most iconic and recognizable figures of the golden age of the Hollywood studio era. And how many motion picture personalities could lay claim to having Christmas tree ornaments designed in their image?

Screen (shorts; all with Moe and Larry): Curly, Ted Healy: **1933:** Nertsery Rhymes; Beer and Pretzels; Hello Pop!; Plane Nuts; Hollywood on Parade; Screen Snapshots; **1934:** The Big Idea. Curly: Woman Haters; Punch Drunks; Men in Black; Three Little Pigskins; **1935:** Horses' Collars; Restless Knights; Screen Snapshots #6; Pop Goes the Easel; Uncivil Warriors; Pardon My Scotch; Hoi Polloi; Three Little Beers; **1936:** Ants in the Pantry; Movie Maniacs; Half-Shot Shooters; Disorder in the Court; A Pain in the Pullman; False Alarms; Whoops, I'm an Indian; Slippery Silks; **1937:** Grips, Grunts and Groans; Dizzy Doctors; Three Dumb Clucks; Back to the Woods; Goofs and Saddles; Cash and Carry; Playing the Ponies; The Sitter-Downers; **1938:** Termites of 1938; Tassels in the Air; Flat Foot Stooges; Healthy,

Wealthy and Dumb; Violent Is the Word for Curly; Three Missing Links; Mutts to You; **1939:** Three Little Sew and Sews; We Want Our Mummy; A-Ducking They Did Go; Screen Snapshots #9; Yes, We Have No Bonanza; Saved By the Belle; Calling All Curs; Oily to Bed, Oily to Rise; Three Sappy People; **1940:** You Nazty Spy; Rockin' Through the Rockies; A-Plumbing We Will Go; Nutty But Nice; How High Is Up?; From Nurse to Worse; No Census, No Feeling; Cookoo Cavaliers; Boobs in Arms; **1941:** So Long, Mr. Chumps; Dutiful But Dumb; All the World's a Stooge; I'll Never Heil Again; An Ache in Every Stake; In the Sweet Pie and Pie; Some More of Somoa; **1942:** Loco Boy Makes Good; Cactus Makes Perfect; What's the Matador; Matri-Phony; Three Smart Saps; Even as I.O.U.; Sock-a-Bye Baby; **1943:** They Stooge to Conga; Dizzy Detectives; Spook Louder; Back from the Front; Three Little Twirps; Higher Than a Kite; I Can Hardly Wait; Dizzy Pilots; Phony Express; A Gem of a Jam; **1944:** Crash Goes the Hash; Busy Buddies; The Yokes on Me; Idle Roomers; Gents Without Cents; No Dough, Boys; **1945:** Three Pests in a Mess; Booby Dupes; Idiots Deluxe; If a Body Meets a Body; Micro-Phonies; **1946:** Beer Barrel Polecats; A Bird in the Head; Uncivil Warbirds; Three Troubeldoers; Monkey Businessmen; Three Loan Wolves; G.I. Wanna Go Home; Rhythm and Weep; Three Little Pirates; **1947:** Half-Wits' Holiday.

SHEMP: Fright Night; Out West; Hold That Lion (w/cameo by **CURLY**); Brideless Groom; Sing a Song of Six Pants; All Gummed Up; **1948:** Shivering Sherlocks; Pardon My Clutch; Squareheads of the Round Table; Fiddlers Three; Hot Scots; Heavenly Daze; I'm a Monkey's Uncle; Mummy's Dummies; A Crime on Their Hands; **1949:** The Ghost Talks; Who Done It?; Hocus Pocus; Fuelin' Around; Malice in the Palace; Vagabond Loafers; Dunked in the Deep; **1950:** Punchy Cowpunchers; Hugs and Mugs; Dopey Dicks; Love at First Bite; Self-Made Maids; Three Hams on Rye; Studio Stoops; Slaphappy Sleuths; A Snitch in Time; **1951:** Three Arabian Nuts; Baby Sitters' Jitters; Don't Throw That Knife; Scrambled Brains; Merry Mavericks; The Tooth Will Out; Hula-La-La; The Pest Man Wins; **1952:** A Missed Fortune; Listen, Judge; Corny Casanovas; He Cooked His Goose; Gents in a Jam; Three Dark Horses; Cuckoo on a Choo Choo; **1953:** Up in Daisy's Penthouse; Booty and the Beast; Loose Loot; Tricky Dicks; Spooks; Pardon My Backfire; Rip, Sew and Stitch; Bubble Trouble; Goof on the Roof; **1954:** Income Tax Sappy; Musty Musketeers; Pals and Gals; Knutzy Knights; Shot in the Frontier; Scotched in Scotland; **1955:** Fling in the Ring; Of Cash and Hash; Gypped in the Penthouse; Bedlam in Paradise; Stone Age Romeos; Wham Bam Slam; Hot Ice; Blunder Boys; **1956:** Husbands Beware; Creeps; Flagpole Jitters; For Crimin' Out Loud; Rumpus in a Harem; Hot Stuff; Scheming Schemers; Commotion on the Ocean.

JOE BESSER: 1957: Hoofs and Goofs; Muscle Up a Little Closer; A Merry Mix-Up; Space Ship Sappy; Guns A-Poppin'; Horsing Around; Rusty Romeos; Outer Space Jitters; **1958:** Quiz Whizz; Fifi Blows Her Top; Pies and Guys; Sweet and Hot; Flying Saucer Daffy; Oil's Well That Ends Well; **1959:** Triple Crossed; Sappy Bullfighters.

Screen (features): MOE, LARRY, SHEMP, TED HEALY: 1930: Soup to Nuts.

MOE, LARRY, CURLY, TED HEALY: 1933: Turn Back the Clock; Meet the Baron; Dancing Lady; Myrt and Marge; **1934:** Fugitive Lovers; Hollywood Party.

MOE, LARRY, CURLY: The Captain Hates the Sea; **1938:** Start Cheering; **1941:** Time Out for Rhythm; **1942:** My Sister Eileen; **1945:** Rockin' in the Rockies; **1946:** Swing Parade of 1946.

MOE, LARRY, SHEMP: 1951: Gold Raiders.

MOE, LARRY, CURLY JOE: 1959: Have Rocket, Will Travel; **1961:** Snow White and the Three Stooges; **1962:** The Three Stooges Meet Hercules; The Three Stooges in Orbit; **1963:** The Three Stooges Go Around the World in a Daze; It's a Mad Mad Mad Mad World; 4 for Texas; **1965:** The Outlaws Is Coming!

MOE: 1958: Space Master X-7; **1966:** Don't Worry, We'll Think of a Title; **1973:** Doctor Death: Seeker of Souls

SHEMP: 1935: Convention Girl; **1937:** Hollywood Round-Up; Headin' East; **1940:** Millionaires in Prison; The Leatherpushers; The Bank Dick; Give Us Wings; **1941:** Six Lessons from Madame La Zonga; Buck Privates; Meet the Chump; Mr. Dynamite; Too Many Blondes; In the Navy; Tight Shoes; San Antonio Rose; Hit the Road; Hold That Ghost; Hellzapoppin'; The Invisible Woman; **1942:** Butch Minds the Baby; Mississippi Gambler; The Strange Case of Dr. Rx; Private Buckeroo; Pittsburgh; Arabian Nights; **1942:** How's About It?; It Ain't Hay; Keep 'Em Slugging; Crazy House; Strictly in the Groove; **1944:** Three of a Kind; Moonlight and Cactus; The Strange Affair; Crazy Knights; **1945:** Trouble Chasers; **1946:** The Gentleman Misbehaves; One Exciting Week; Dangerous Business; Blondie Knows Best.

SHEMP, JOE BESSER: 1949: Africa Screams.

JOE BESSER: 1940: Hot Steel; **1944:** Hey Rookie!; **1945:** Eadie Was a Lady; **1946:** Talk About a Lady; **1948:** Feudin,' Fussin' and a-Fightin'; **1950:** Woman in Hiding; Joe Palooka Meets Humphrey; Outside the Wall; The Desert Hawk; **1953:** I, the Jury; Sins of Jezebel; **1955:** Abbott and Costello Meet the Keystone Kops; Headline Hunters; **1956:** Two Gun Lady; **1959:** The Plunderers of Painted Flats; Say One for Me; The Rookie; The Story on Page One; **1960:** Let's Make Love; **1961:** The Silent Call; The Errand Boy; **1962:** The Hand of Death; **1968:** With Six You Get Eggroll; **1969:** The Comeback; **1970:** Which Way to the Front?

JOE DERITA: 1944: The Doughgirls; **1945:** The Sailor Takes a Wife; **1946:** People Are Funny; **1948:** Coroner Creek; **1958:** The Bravados.

TED HEALY: 1933: Stage Mother; Bombshell; **1934:** Lazy River; Operator 13; Paris Interlude; Death on a Diamond; The Band Plays On; **1935:** The Winning Ticket; The Casino Murder Case; Reckless; Murder in the Fleet; Mad Love; Here Comes the Band; It's in the Air; **1936:** Speed; San Francisco; Sing, Baby, Sing; The Longest Night; Mad Holiday; **1937:** Man of the People; Good Old Soak; Varsity Show; **1938:** Love Is a Headache; Hollywood Hotel.

NY Stage: TED HEALY, SHEMP: 1927: A Night In Spain.

TED HEALY, MOE, LARRY, SHEMP: 1929: A Night In Venice; **MOE, LARRY, CURLY: 1939:** George White Scandals of 1939.

JOE BESSER: 1932: The Passing Show of 1932; **1941:** Sons O' Fun; **1946:** If The Shoe Fits.

Select TV: MOE. LARRY, CURLY JOE: 1965: The New Three Stooges (series).

JOE BESSER: 1952: The Abbott and Costello Show (series); **1962–65:** The New Joey Bishop Show (series); **1969:** The Monk.

LAWRENCE TIBBETT

BORN: BAKERSFIELD, CA, NOVEMBER 16, 1896.
DIED: JULY 15, 1960.

A fine baritone, Lawrence Tibbett became the first opera singer to officially cross over to movie stardom, if only for a fleeting few years. Interested in a career in opera, he started by singing in movie theatres before going to New York to study under Frank La Forge. In 1923 he made his debut with the Metropolitan Opera with *Boris Godunov*, and then leapt to stardom with *Falstaff*, becoming one of the company's major attractions, carrying such productions as *Peter Ibbetson* and *The*

King's Henchman. When talking pictures arrived, MGM eagerly signed him to a contract and put him in their Technicolor production of *The Rogue Song*, which, just to show mainstream audiences that this was not a stuffy affair, included Laurel and Hardy in the cast. The film, which required him at one point to sing enthusiastically while being whipped, was a major box-office hit, with Tibbett winning a sufficient degree of praise to end up with an Oscar nomination. Despite all its prestige at the time, the studio let the movie slip through the cracks over the years and it became one of the most famous "lost" films of the early sound era. There were three immediate follow-ups, with *New Moon*, *The Prodigal*, and *Cuban Love Song*, but each one did increasingly less business than the last. He and the studio parted company only a year after they'd linked up, prompting him to return to the stage until called back to Hollywood by Fox, who decided to give him a second try with *Metropolitan* and *Under Your Spell*, which only went to show that his real home was at the Met. He continued to have star status there until 1950 when he played his last role for them in *Khovantchina*.

Screen: 1930: The Rogue Song; New Moon; 1931: The Prodigal; Cuban Love Song; 1935: Metropolitan; 1936: Under Your Spell.

NY Stage: 1923: King Lear; 1947: The Miracle in the Mountains; 1950: The Barrier; 1951: Anta Album; 1956: Fanny.

GENE TIERNEY
BORN: BROOKLYN, NY, NOVEMBER 20, 1920.
DIED: NOVEMBER 6, 1991.

During the 1940s Gene Tierney was 20th Century-Fox's leading light in the looks department. As an actress she was usually less than memorable, though inoffensively so and her career was helped greatly, in part, by her winding up in some of the studio's top products of the day. If the role required that she be lovely and desirable or pleasantly attentive, she fit the bill just fine. A chance meeting with director Anatole Litvak got her an offer from Warner Bros. but she opted to take a role on Broadway, in *Mrs. O'Brien Entertains*, in 1938. This led to a more prominent part in the original stage production of *The Male Animal*, which brought further Hollywood overtures, with Tierney finally settling for Fox. They debuted her as the newspaperwoman in love with outlaw Henry Fonda in their Technicolor western, *The Return of Frank James*, which meant they intended her for "A" products. These included the sanitized screen version of the long-running stage hit *Tobacco Road*, in which she sluttishly writhed about as the "white trash" Ellie May, in just one of the film's many bizarrely off-putting performances. After this she was given the title role in *Belle Starr*, although Randolph Scott got billing above her, indicating that the studio wasn't quite ready to trust her to carry a movie on her own name. These films were followed by attempts to make Tierney an exotic temptress, with her playing a Eurasian in UA's *The Shanghai Gesture*; a Polynesian, Dorothy Lamour-type in *Son of Fury*; and the *China Girl*, none of which helped bring her the credibility and respect she sought. Fortunately, she ended up in something lighter, with Ernst Lubitsch's charming *Heaven Can Wait*, though it hardly seemed fair that she received billing *over* Don Ameche, whose showcase this was. Then came the role for which she became best known, the mysterious woman whose portrait entrances detective Dana Andrews, in the classic noir, *Laura*. The part required her to make her entrance well into the story after already being presumed dead, but her air of otherworldliness

came more from the premise than anything she might have done to suggest it.

From there she went into another acclaimed offering, *A Bell for Adano*, though someone had the dumb idea of slapping a blonde wig on her. She then showed that being wicked and neurotic was the sort of thing she should have been doing all along when she really sank her teeth into the lead role in *Leave Her to Heaven*. As the insanely jealous wife of Cornel Wilde, she made for a most entertaining femme fatale, at one point sitting eerily still while poor Daryl Hickman drowned in front of her, and wound up with an Oscar nomination. It was an enormous box-office hit as well, as were the next two films, *Dragonwyck*, a rather dry and talky gothic thriller, and *The Razor's Edge*, in which she was the self-centered rich girl desired by Tyrone Power, in this ineffectual rendering of the brilliant Somerset Maugham novel. This was followed by the most appealing of all her performances, in *The Ghost and Mrs. Muir*, an enduring fantasy in which she fell for dead sea captain Rex Harrison. She then did several of the noirs that were popular in the postwar period, playing a shoplifter in *Whirlpool*; taking a backseat to the colorful cast of *Night and the City*, as Richard Widmark's concerned girlfriend; and helping Dana Andrews clear her dad of murder in *Where the Sidewalk Ends*, a reunion with her co-star and director (Otto Preminger) of *Laura* that also featured a quickie appearance by her then-husband (1941–52), designer Oleg Cassini.

Paramount borrowed her to play a lady of wealth who marries lower class John Lund in the bright comedy *The Mating Season*, which was stolen from her and everyone else by Thelma Ritter, and then she went back to Fox to play it straight opposite Danny Kaye in one of his lesser vehicles, *On the Riviera*. She finished off her contract unmemorably with *Way of a Gaucho*, again as a society woman, falling in love with Rory Calhoun. MGM made her the tragic Puritan who tosses herself off the Mayflower in *Plymouth Adventure*, and she played the Russian wife of Clark Gable in *Never Let Me Go*. Back at Fox she was the Pharaoh's sister in *The Egyptian*, which proved that she was being moved down the cast list, and a nurse in wartime China in *The Left Hand of God*, supporting Humphrey Bogart. During the late 1950s she dropped out of sight and it was later revealed that she had suffered a nervous breakdown from which she was recuperating. In 1962, Preminger brought her back to the screen with a small part as a Washington hostess in the all-star *Advise and Consent*. This led to secondary roles in *Toys in the Attic* and *The Pleasure Seekers*, which were done to remind folks that she was still available if they were interested. Having remarried into great wealth it was not necessary that she work and she was only employed twice more, both times in television presentations.

Screen: 1940: The Return of Frank James; Hudson's Bay; 1941: Tobacco Road; Belle Starr; Sundown; The Shanghai Gesture; 1942: Son of Fury; Rings on Her Fingers; Thunder Birds; China Girl; 1943: Heaven Can Wait; 1944: Laura; 1945: A Bell for Adano; Leave Her to Heaven; 1946: Dragonwyck; The Razor's Edge; 1947: The Ghost and Mrs. Muir; 1948: The Iron Curtain; That Wonderful Urge; 1949: Whirlpool; 1950: Night and the City; Where the Sidewalk Ends; 1951: The Mating Season; On the Riviera; The Secret of Convict Lake; Close to My Heart; 1952: Way of a Gaucho; Plymouth Adventure; 1953: Never Let Me Go; 1954: Personal Affair; Black Widow; The Egyptian; 1955: The Left Hand of God; 1962: Advise and Consent; 1963: Toys in the Attic; 1964: The Pleasure Seekers.

NY Stage: 1938: Mrs. O'Brien Entertains; 1939: Ring Two; 1940: The Male Animal.
Select TV: 1960: Journey to a Wedding (sp); 1969: Daughter of the Mind; 1980: Scruples (ms).

LAWRENCE TIERNEY

BORN: BROOKLYN, NY, MARCH 15, 1919. ED: MANHATTAN COL. DIED: FEBRUARY 26, 2002.

There were few noir stars as authentically tough as Lawrence Tierney and that, not his stoic acting and immobile expression, made him a cult favorite. Though his off-screen misbehavior and multiple arrests cut his career short in his heyday, this sort of contempt for propriety elevated him to legendary status in the eyes of later fans and filmmakers. The older brother of actor Scott Brady, he excelled initially at track sports before giving a shot at the stage, winning a role on Broadway in *A Man's House*, in 1943. RKO signed him up and placed him in the supporting cast of the thriller *The Ghost Ship*, as a lieutenant who meets an ugly fate. After similar secondary parts, he got his chance at a lead, over at Monogram, with their taut biopic *Dillinger*, where he really came across as the mean son of a bitch one would imagine the real gangster to have been. RKO eventually cashed in on his success with *The Devil Thumbs a Ride*, in which he played a murderous hitchhiker; *Born to Kill*, perhaps the definitive Tierney vehicle, about an unbalanced killer who somehow seduces both Claire Trevor and her sister; and *Bodyguard*, where he was tough, but on the side of the law this time, and framed for murder. He stayed in this mode as the movies got shorter and cheaper with *The Hoodlum* and *Kill or Be Killed*, but, by the mid-1950s, his reputation as a hellraiser had gotten him arrested so frequently that Hollywood could no longer put up with him. As a result he wound up taking odd jobs outside the industry while accepting an occasional motion picture offer that ranged from the Spanish-made *Custer of the West*, as Gerneral Phil Sheridan, to *Exorcism at Midnight*, as a doctor, to *Arthur*, as Jill Eikenberry's iron-fisted dad. Old age seemed to have enhanced his brutishness and the husky-voiced, bald-domed Tierney was suddenly starting to regain the interest of the younger Hollywood. He appeared as Ryan O'Neal's unscrupulous dad in *Tough Guys Don't Dance*; a police detective in *The Runestone*; and the mastermind behind a group of thieves in *Reservoir Dogs*. That he was yet again arrested during the production of the last only went to prove that he had no intention of changing the lifestyle that made him who he was.
Screen: 1943: The Ghost Ship; Government Girl; Sing Your Worries Away; Gildersleeve on Broadway; 1944: Youth Runs Wild; The Falcon Out West; Seven Days Ashore; 1945: Sing Your Way Home; Mama Loves Papa; Dillinger; Those Endearing Young Charms; Back to Bataan; 1946: San Quentin; Badman's Territory; Step by Step; 1947: The Devil Thumbs a Ride; Born to Kill; 1948: Bodyguard; 1950: Kill or Be Killed; Shakedown; 1951: The Hoodlum; Best of the Badmen; 1952: The Bushwhackers; The Greatest Show on Earth; 1954: The Steel Cage; 1956: Singing in the Dark; Female Jungle; 1963: A Child Is Waiting; 1968: Custer of the West; 1971: Such Good Friends; 1973: Exorcism at Midnight/Naked Evil; 1975: The Abduction; 1977: Andy Warhol's Bad; 1978: The Kirilan Witness; 1979: Never Pick Up a Stranger/Blood Rage (dtv); 1980: Gloria; 1981: Arthur; The Prowler/Rosemary's Killer; 1982: Midnight; 1984: Nothing Lasts Forever; 1985: Prizzi's Honor; Silver Bullet; 1986: Murphy's Law; 1987: From a Whisper to a Scream/The Offspring; Tough Guys Don't Dance; 1988: The Naked Gun: From the Files of Police Squad!; 1989: The Horror Show; 1990: Why Me?; 1991: Wizards of the Demon Sword (dtv); City of Hope; 1992: The Runestone; Reservoir Dogs; 1993: The Death Merchant (dtv); Eddie Presley (dtv); 1994: Junior; 1995: Starstruck (nUSr); 1996: 2 Days in the Valley; 1997: Portrait in Red/Dark Red (dtv); American Hero (nUSr); 1998: Southie (dtv); Armageddon; Evicted (nUSr).
NY Stage: 1943: A Man's House.
Select TV: 1984: Terrible Joe Moran; 1990: Dillinger; 1993: Casualties of Love: The Long Island Lolita Story; 1994: A Kiss Goodnight.

PAMELA TIFFIN

(PAMELA WONSO) BORN: OKLAHOMA CITY, OK, OCTOBER 13, 1942. ED: HUNTER COL.

A 1960s-style Hollywood ingénue with a knack for playing "dumb" girls, Pamela Tiffin had been a fashion model as a teen until she decided to study acting with Stella Adler. She started off in two major 1961 releases, *Summer and Smoke*, as the simple girl Laurence Harvey opts for over Geraldine Page, and what turned out to be her best film, *One, Two, Three*, as the vapid boss's daughter who marries commie Horst Buccholz, much to the horror of James Cagney. Next up she repeated Jeanne Crain's part in the remake of *State Fair*, singing the big hit from the earlier version, "It Might as Well Be Spring," though her vocals, like Ms. Crain's, were dubbed. She fit right in to the fluffy comedies of the 1960s with *Come Fly with Me*, as a stewardess on the look-out for a husband; *The Pleasure Seekers*, this time following in the footsteps of Maggie McNamara in this variation on *Three Coins in the Fountain*; and *For Those Who Think Young*, one of those beach frolics that populated the screens at the time. In Italy she co-starred with Marcello Mastroianni in a misfire, *Kiss the Other Shiek*, and decided soon afterwards to live there. Although she returned to Hollywood for *Harper*, as Lauren Bacall's daughter, and *Viva Max!*, in which she was held hostage at the Alamo, she continued to work mainly for Italian productions, many of which never reached American shores. This, and her limited range, no doubt contributed to her falling off the radar screens of even the most ardent followers of film. Eventually she dropped out of the business altogether.
Screen: 1961: Summer and Smoke; One, Two, Three; 1962: State Fair; 1963: Come Fly With Me; 1964: The Pleasure Seekers; For Those Who Think Young; The Lively Set; 1965: The Hallelujah Trail; 1966: An Almost Perfect Crime (nUSr); Harper; 1968: Kiss the Other Shiek (filmed 1965); Kiss Me with Kisses (nUSr); I Protagonisti/The Protagonist (nUSr); 1969: L'Arcangelo/The Archangel (nUSr); Viva Max!; 1971: The Viking Who Came from the South (nUSr); Cose di Cosa Nostra/Gang War; 1972: Deaf Smith and Johnny Ears; 1973: La Signora e State Violentata/The Lady Has Been Raped (nUSr); 1975: Evil Fingers/The Fifth Cord (filmed 1971).

GEORGE TOBIAS

BORN: NEW YORK, NY, JULY 14, 1901. DIED: FEBRUARY 27, 1980.

As much an expected presence in Warner Bros. films of the 1940s as any of the studio's stable of stars, dopey-faced, luggish George Tobias was often on hand for quick comic relief, playing sidekicks, mildly threatening villains, or broad ethnic types. He made his New York theatrical debut in 1920, in *The Mob*, then first came to Broadway four years later in *What*

Price Glory? He spent an additional 15 years onstage before Hollywood tested him and put him into the supporting cast of MGM's *Maisie*. Within the year Warners signed him up and kept him extremely busy. He had a serious part, as a South American revolutionary, in *Torrid Zone*, with James Cagney; was Cagney's cornerman, Pinky, in *City for Conquest*; snarled as the unscrupulous and jealous African mine owner in *South of Suez*, and actually got top-billing, playing a bum who shows up at his ex-lover's doorstep, in the "B" comedy *Calling All Husbands*. He supported Cagney several more times, including *The Strawberry Blonde*, as his small-town buddy, and *Yankee Doodle Dandy*, as a Broadway producer. He was the requisite comic relief for war movies like *Air Force*, a chauffeur in *Mission to Moscow*, and, when Warners was through with him, he freelanced, including a spell over at RKO, where he had one of his best roles, as Robert Ryan's unsavory fight manager, in *The Set-Up*. In 1957 he repeated his Broadway role of the Russian commissar in *Silk Stockings*, having played a completely different part in the original 1939 film version, *Ninotchka*. He found latter-day fame as the calm neighbor with the frantic wife in the series *Bewitched* a part he pretty much played a blatant copy of, opposite his series co-star, Alice Pearce, in *The Glass Bottom Boat*.

Screen: 1939: Maisie; They All Came Out; Balalaika; Ninotchka; The Hunchback of Notre Dame; 1940: Music in My Heart; Saturday's Children; Torrid Zone; The Man Who Talked Too Much; River's End; They Drive by Night; Calling All Husbands; City for Conquest; South of Suez; East of the River; 1941: The Strawberry Blonde; The Bride Came C.O.D.; Affectionately Yours; You're in the Army Now; Sergeant York; Out of the Fog; 1942: Wings for the Eagle; My Sister Eileen; Yankee Doodle Dandy; Juke Girl; Captains of the Clouds; 1943: Mission to Moscow; Thank Your Lucky Stars; This Is the Army; Air Force; 1944: Make Your Own Bed; The Mask of Dimitrios; Passage to Marseille; Between Two Worlds; 1945: Mildred Pierce; Objective, Burma!; 1946: Her Kind of Man; Nobody Lives Forever; Gallant Bess; 1947: My Wild Irish Rose; Sinbad the Sailor; 1948: The Adventures of Casanova; 1949: The Judge Steps Out; Everybody Does It; The Set-Up; 1950: Southside 1-1000; 1951: Rawhide; Mark of the Renegade; The Magic Carpet; Ten Tall Men; 1952: Desert Pursuit; 1954: The Glenn Miller Story; 1955: The Seven Little Foys; 1957: The Tattered Dress; Silk Stockings; 1958: Marjorie Morningstar; 1963: A New Kind of Love; 1964: Bullet for a Badman; 1965: Nightmare in the Sun; 1966: The Glass Bottom Boat; 1970: The Phynx.

NY Stage: 1920: The Mob; 1924: What Price Glory?; 1928: The Grey Fox; 1929: S.S. Glencairn; Fiesta; 1934: Sailors of Cattaro; 1935: Black Pit; Paths of Glory; Hell Freezes Over; 1936: Star Spangled; The Emperor Jones; You Can't Take It With You; 1938: Good Hunting; 1952: Stalag 17; 1955: Silk Stockings.

Select TV: 1958: The Enemy Within (sp); 1959–61: Adventures in Paradise; 1964–72: Bewitched (series).

ANN TODD

BORN: HARTFORD, ENGLAND, JANUARY 24, 1909. DIED: MAY 6, 1993.

The beautiful British lady with the stony glare, Ann Todd became an international star after nearly 15 years in front of movie cameras. Following some stage work, she was engaged to appear in films, starting with *Keepers of Youth*, in which she played a school teacher on whom Garry Marsh sets a lecherous eye. The following year she was given the star treatment with *The Water Gipsies*, as the waterfront dweller who has her portrait painted by wealthy Ian Hunter. She remained a minor figure of British cinema in such films as *The Return of Bulldog Drummond*, as the sleuth's kidnapped wife, and the classic sci-fi epic *Things to Come*. It was her stage work during World War II, in *Lottie Dundass*, that helped boost her reputation and led to her being cast in the role that brought her lasting fame, the pianist tormented and driven to therapy by her harsh, crippled guardian, James Mason, in *The Seventh Veil*. Despite it being little more than a very glossy English soap opera, this became one of the gigantic hits among British films of the 1940s and spread its reach across the Atlantic where it earned an Oscar for its screenplay. Todd herself went to Hollywood for a one shot deal that sounded promising but turned out to be a major disappointment, *The Paradine Case*, a courtroom mystery ponderously directed by Alfred Hitchcock, of all people. Back to Britain she went, doing another dreary one, this time with Hollywood's Ray Milland, *So Evil My Love*, before marrying director David Lean in 1949 (they divorced in 1957). For Lean she did three films, *One Woman's Story/The Passionate Friends*, in which she was married to Claude Rains and pined for lover Trevor Howard; *Madeline*, a costume melodrama about a Scottish murderess; and *Breaking the Sound Barrier*, as the daughter of aircraft manufacturer Ralph Richardson. After the last she began dividing her time equally between film, stage, and television before going behind the cameras in the 1960s to make travel documentaries. Her 1980 autobiography was entitled *The Eighth Veil*.

Screen: 1931: Keepers of Youth; The Ghost Train; These Charming People; 1932: The Water Gipsies; 1934: The Return of Bulldog Drummond; 1936: Things to Come; 1937: Action for Slander; The Squeaker/Murder on Diamond Row; South Riding; 1939: Poision Pen; 1941: Danny Boy; Ships with Wings; 1945: Vacation from Marriage/Perfect Strangers; The Seventh Veil; 1946: Gaiety George/Showtime; Daybreak; 1947: The Paradine Case; 1948: So Evil My Love; 1949: The Passionate Friends/One Woman's Story; 1950: Madeline; 1952: Breaking the Sound Barrier; 1954: The Green Scarf; 1957: Time Without Pity; 1961: Taste of Fear/Scream of Fear; 1963: Son of Captain Blood; 1965: Ninety Degrees in the Shade; 1971: The Fiend/Beware My Bethren; 1980: The Human Factor.

NY Stage: 1957: Four Winds.

Select TV: 1955: Edward, My Son (sp); 1958: Letter from Cairo (sp); Not the Glory (sp); 1959: The Grey Nurse Said Nothing (sp); 1960: The Snows of Kilimanjaro (sp).

RICHARD TODD

(RICHARD ANDREW PALETHORPE-TODD) BORN: DUBLIN, IRELAND, JUNE 11, 1919.

A rigidly handsome addition to the British cinema who made occasional forays into Hollywood productions, Richard Todd started out with a performance good enough to keep him going over some pretty unremarkable years. In 1939 he helped create the Dundee Rep, but his theater work was interrupted while he served in the war. He returned to that company following military service and because of his work with them was given a screen test, which resulted in his 1948 film debut, in *For Them That Trespasses*. The next year he won the plum role of Lachie, the Scottish soldier who realizes that he has only a short time to live, in *The Hasty Heart*. Both sympathetic and bullheaded, he was exceptional in a well done if stage-bound piece, given added interest in the U.S. by the casting of Ronald Reagan and Patricia Neal in the other central roles. Todd earned an Oscar nomination and followed it with the role of the accused killer in Hitchcock's made-in-Britain thriller *Stage Fright*. For Warners, he finally went to the U.S., for *Lightning Strikes Twice*, playing a man suspected of having murdered his wife and then returned home for a dual role in *Flesh and Blood* (Warners distributed this film as well). Disney thought him ideal swashbuckler material and put him in *The Story of Robin Hood and His Merrie Men*, *The Sword and the Rose*, and *Rob Roy, the Highland Rogue*, while Fox gave him a mawkish but popular religious biopic, *A Man Called Peter*, the Man being Peter Marshall, who became the U.S. Senate chaplain, and then *The Virgin Queen*, in which he played Sir Walter Raleigh. He had a major hit in his native land with the war film *The Dam Busters*, but saw his career dry up with some minor things like *The Yangtse Incident* and *The Naked Earth*. By the 1960s he had drifted into programmers like *The Boys*, in which he played a barrister, and *Coast of Skeletons*, an atmospheric title for a tame adventure. He did show up back in America, after a long period away, for one of those wild attempts to dramatize the hippie movement of the late 1960s, *The Love-Ins*, as a professor who drops out. Most subsequent efforts received few bookings. He published two volumes of memoirs in the 1980s.

Screen: 1948: For Them That Trespass; 1949: The Hasty Heart; The Interrupted Journey; 1950: Stage Fright; Portrait of Clare; 1951: Lightning Strikes Twice; Flesh and Blood; 1952: The Story of Robin Hood and His Merrie Men; 24 Hours in a Woman's Life/Affair in Monte Carlo; The Venetian Bird/The Assassin; 1953: The Sword and the Rose; Rob Roy, the Highland Rogue; 1954: Les Secrets of d'Alcove/The Bed; 1955: A Man Called Peter; The Virgin Queen; The Dam Busters; 1956: D-Day, the Sixth of June; Marie Antoinette; 1957: The Yangtse Incident/Battle Hell; Saint Joan; Chase a Crooked Shadow; 1958: The Naked Earth; Intent to Kill; 1959: Danger Within/Breakout; 1960: Never Let Go; 1961: The Long and the Short and the Tall/Jungle Fighters; Why Bother to Knock? (and prod.); The Hellions; 1962: The Longest Day; Crime Does Not Pay; The Boys; 1963: The Very Edge; 1964: Coast of Skeletons/Death Drums Along the River/ Sanders (nUSr); 1965: The Battle of the Villa Fiorita; Operation Crossbow; 1967: The Love-Ins; 1968: Subterfuge; 1970: Dorian Gray; 1972: Asylum; 1977: Number One of the Secret Service (nUSr); 1978: The Big Sleep; 1979: The Sky Is Falling (nUSr); Home Before Midnight; 1982: House of the Long Shadows.

Select TV: 1953: Wuthering Heights (sp); 1974: The Next Scream You Hear/Not Guilty!; 1976: Dominic/Boy Dominic (series); 1985: Jenny's War; The Last Place on Earth (ms); 1988: Murder One; 1991: Sherlock Holmes and the Incident at Victoria Falls.

THELMA TODD

BORN: LAWRENCE, MA, JULY 29, 1905.
DIED: DECEMBER 16, 1935.

A bright and lovely blonde who, in her very brief but busy career, made her name in comedies, both long and short, Thelma Todd had been a teacher before winning the Miss Massachusetts beauty contest. This prompted Paramount to sign her up for their Astoria acting school and, along with its 15 other graduates, debuted her in the 1926 feature, *Fascinating Youth*. This was followed by standard leading lady parts in *Nevada*, with Gary Cooper, and *The Gay Defender*, with Richard Dix, before the studio dropped her. While taking roles in features like *Seven Footprints to Satan*, in the lead; *Follow Thru*, as a golfer, and *Corsair* (billed one time only as "Alison Lloyd," in an effort to give her a fresh start), she sharpened her comedic skills at the Hal Roach Studios, playing opposite the likes of Laurel and Hardy and Charlie Chase. Playing it straight, she did two Marx Brothers

gems, *Monkey Business*, as a shipboard moll, and her best known feature role, the "College Widow," who dabbles with all four of the brothers, in *Horse Feathers*. In the meantime, Roach had decided to launch a sort of "female Laurel and Hardy," teaming Todd with fluttery ZaSu Pitts. The two women did 17 two-reel comedies, starting with "Let's Do Things," in 1931, and ending with "One Track Minds," in 1933. This series of comedies never became a critical favorite and pretty much passed into obscurity in later years. When Pitts took off for greener pastures, she was replaced by the raucous, wisecracking Patsy Kelly. Kelly and Todd would do another 21 entries, from "Beauty and the Bus," in 1933, to "All-American Toothache," in 1936. The last was released posthumously as the beautiful Todd became another of the movie capital's mysterious tragedies, having been found dead in her garage of carbon monoxide poisoning. Presumed a suicide, it was not discovered until decades later that a gangster lover had been responsible for her untimely demise.

Screen (shorts): 1929: Look Out Below; Snappy Sneezer; Crazy Feet; Stepping Out; Unaccustomed as We Are; Hurdy Gurdy; Hotter Than Hot; Shy Boy; 1930: The Head Guy; The Real McCoy; Whispering Whoopee; Another Fine Mess; All Teed Up; Dollar Dizzy; Looser Than Loose; High Cs; The Fighting Parson; The Shrimp; The King; 1931: Catch as Catch Can; Love Fever; Let's Do Things; Voice of Hollywood No. 13; Chickens Come Home; Rough Seas; The Pip from Pittsburgh; The Pajama Party; War Mamas; On the Loose; 1932: The Nickel Nurser; Seal Skins; Cauliflower Alley; Strictly Unreliable; Red Noses; Alum and Eve; The Old Bull; Show Business; Sneak Easily; The Soilers; 1933: Maids a la Mode; One Track Minds; Asleep in the Fleet; Bargain of the Century; Air Fright; Beauty and the Bus; Backs to Nature; 1934: Maid in Hollywood; Babes in the Goods; Three Chumps Ahead; Opened by Mistake; Bum Voyage; Soup and Fish; I'll Be Suing You; One Horse Farmers; Done in Oil; 1935: The Tin Man; Treasure Blues; Slightly Static; Twin Triplets; Top Flat; Sing, Sister, Sing; The Misses Stooge; Hot Money; 1936: All-American Toothache.

Screen (features): 1926: Fascinating Youth; The Popular Sin; God Gave Me Twenty Cents; 1927: Rubber Heels; Fireman, Save My Child; Nevada; The Gay Defender; The Shield of Honor; 1928: The Noose; Vamping Venus; Heart to Heart; The Crash; The Haunted House; Naughty Baby; 1929: Seven Footprints to Satan; Trial Marriage; The House of Horror; Careers; Her Private Life; The Bachelor Girl; 1930: Follow Thru; Her Man; Command Performance; 1931: Aloha; Swanee River; The Hot Heiress; No Limit; Broad-Minded; Monkey Business; The Maltese Falcon; Corsair (AS ALISON LLOYD); 1932: This Is the Night; Speak Easily; Horse Feathers; Klondike; Big Timer; Deception; Call Her Savage; 1933: Air Hostess; The Devil's Brother; Cheating Blondes; Mary Stevens M.D.; Counsellor-at-Law; Sitting Pretty; Son of a Sailor; You Made Me Love You; 1934: Palooka; Hips, Hips, Hooray!; Bottoms Up; The Poor Rich; Cockeyed Cavaliers; Take the Stand; Lightning Strikes Twice; 1935: After the Dance; Two for Tonight; 1936: The Bohemian Girl.

SIDNEY TOLER

BORN: WARRENSBURG, MO, APRIL 28, 1874.
ED: UNIV. OF KS. DIED: FEBRUARY 12, 1947.

Apart from the controversial casting of a non-Asian in the role of super sleuth Charlie Chan, the tall Missouri-born Caucasian Sidney Toler was also saddled with the unenviable task of following in the footsteps of the superior Warner Oland. He was already in his 50s when he became one of the many stage actors called on to give films a new voice when talkies arrived, playing an Englishman in the Ruth Chatterton version of the oft-filmed *Madame X*, in 1929. During the 1930s he was seen as a detective in *Blonde Venus*; a cop out to get revenge on Warren William in *Upper World*; a wrestling manager laid-up in the hospital in *Registered Nurse*; an undertaker out to swindle the Indians in *Massacre*; a crooked warden in *The Daring Young Man*; and Daniel Webster in *The Gorgeous Hussy*, to name but a few. His busy but unremarkable position in film history suddenly changed when Fox needed someone to replace Warner Oland, who had died suddenly while battling with the studio over his latest Charlie Chan assignment. Toler was brought in for *Charlie Chan in Honolulu* in 1938, and despite his rather dull interpretation of the character, got the vote of approval from audiences, and, therefore, from the head office. Fox put him through another 11 Chan adventures, with Victor Sen Yung brought in to partner him as Jimmy Chan, Number Two Son, filling the spot vacated by Number One Son, Keye Luke. By the time the studio decided to call it quits in 1942, with *Castle in the Desert*, it seemed as if the Chan series had run its course. Monogram, knowing that these pictures had been getting cheaper and cheaper over the years anyway, decided to pick up where Fox had left off, hiring Toler for *Charlie Chan in the Secret Service*, in 1944. Three years later Toler died after finishing *The Trap* and was replaced by Roland Winters, who kept the Chan cases going until interest was no longer strong enough to warrant their continuation. Toler was also responsible for writing the plays *Golden Days* (which he also directed; 1921), *The Exile* (1923), *Bye Bye, Barbara* (1924), and *Ritzy* (also director; 1930).

Screen: 1929: Madame X; 1931: Strictly Dishonorable; White Shoulders; 1932: Strangers in Love; Is My Face Red?; Radio Patrol; Speak Easily; Blondie of the Follies; Blonde Venus; The Phantom President; Tom Brown of Culver; 1933: He Learned About Women; King of the Jungle; Billion Dollar Scandal; The Narrow Corner; The Way to Love; The World Changes; 1934: Dark Hazard; Massacre; Spitfire; The Trumpet Blows; Here Comes the Groom; Operator 13; Registered Nurse; Upperworld; 1935: The Daring Young Man; Call of the Wild; Orchids to You; Champagne for Breakfast; Romance in Manhattan; This Is the Life; 1936: Three Godfathers; Give Us This Night; The Longest Night; The Gorgeous Hussy; Our Relations; 1937: That Certain Woman; Double Wedding; 1938: Gold Is Where You Find It; Wide Open Faces; One Wild Night; Charlie Chan in Honolulu; Up the River; Mysterious Rider; If I Were King; 1939: King of Chinatown; Disbarred; Heritage of the Desert; The Kid from Kokomo; Charlie Chan in Reno; Charlie Chan at Treasure Island; Law of the Pampas; Charlie Chan in City of Darkness; 1940: Charlie Chan in Panama; Charlie Chan's Murder Cruise; Chan Charlie at the Wax Museum; Murder Over New York; 1941: Dead Men Tell; Charlie Chan in Rio; 1942: Castle in the Desert; 1943: A Night to Remember; Adventures of Smilin' Jack (serial); White Savage; Isle of Forgotten Sins; 1944: Charlie Chan in the Secret Service; The Chinese Cat; Black Magic; 1945: The Jade Mask; The Scarlet Clue; It's in the Bag; The Shanghai Cobra; Red Dragon; 1946: Dark Alibi; Shadows Over Chinatown; Dangerous Money; 1947: The Trap.

NY Stage: 1903: The Office Boy; 1918: Someone in the House; 1919: On the Hiring Line; 1920: Sophie; Foot-Loose; Poldekin; Deburau; 1921: Kiki; 1922: Forty-Niners; 1923: Laugh, Clown, Laugh; 1925: The Dove; Canary Dutch; 1927: Tommy; 1929: Mrs. Bumpstead-Leigh; It's A Wise Child.

DAVID TOMLINSON

BORN: HENLEY-ON-THAMES, OXFORSHIRE, ENGLAND, MAY 7, 1917. DIED: JUNE 24, 2000.

A plump-cheeked British character actor who excelled at the "silly-ass" Englishman stereotype, David Tomlinson made his professional stage bow in 1935. Five years later he made his motion picture debut, in support of Margaret Lockwood, in *Quiet Wedding*. His movie career was interrupted for Air Force service and then resumed in 1945 with, appropriately, an Air Force epic, *The Way to the Stars*. Roles began to increase in size with *School for Secrets*, as a man killed trying to perfect radar; *Master of Bankdam*, as the spoiled son of an industrial family; *Love in Waiting*, as a shy restaurant manager involved with waitress Peggy Evans; and *The Chiltern Hundreds*, as an unsuccessful political candidate. During the 1950s he became one of the more familiar faces in British cinema, with *Calling Bulldog Drummond*, appropriately cast as Algy; *Castle in the Air*, as an impoverished Earl trying to sell-off his home; *All for Mary*, as a man who wins the love of the innkeeper's daughter; and *Up the Creek*, as a naval lieutenant commanding a cruiser full of misfits. Since very few of these films were imported to America, only the most astute of U.S. moviegoers were all that familiar with him when he played Lord Fellamar, the lecherous ninny with designs on Susannah York, in the international, Oscar-winning hit *Tom Jones*. In 1964, he was given a real plum part, playing the distracted dad who finds redemption with the help of magical Julie Andrews in *Mary Poppins*, the sparkling Disney musical that became such a phenomenal moneymaker that Tomlinson suddenly found a certain cinematic immortality for having been a part of it. Because of this film's success, Disney also made him the snarling villain in the surprisingly popular *The Love Bug*, and allowed him to romp with Angela Lansbury in another lavish musical, *Bedknobs and Broomsticks*, which brought many unfavorable comparisons to the much superior *Mary Poppins*. After these there were a few unremarkable movies and roles, including *Dominique*, as a lawyer, and *The Fiendish Plot of Dr. Fu Manchu*, as Sir Roger Avery, before he retired from the scene.

Screen: 1940: Quiet Wedding; Garrison Follies; 1941: Pimpernel Smith; Name Rank and Number; My Wife's Family; 1945: The Way to the Stars; 1946: School for Secrets/Secret Flight; Journey Together; Fame is the Spur; The Adventuress/I See a Dark Stranger; 1947: Master of Bankdam; 1948: Easy Money; Broken Journey; Warning to Wantons; Love in Waiting; Sleeping Car to Trieste; Miranda; Here Come the Huggetts; My Brother's Keeper; 1949: Helter Skelter; Vote for Huggett; Landfall; Marry Me; The Chiltern Hundreds/The Amazing Mr. Beecham; 1950: So Long at the Fair; The Wooden Horse; 1951: The Magic Box; Hotel Sahara; Calling Bulldog Drummond; 1952: Made in Heaven; Castle in the Air; 1953: Is Your Honeymoon Really Necessary?; 1955: All for Mary; 1956: Three Men in a Boat; 1957: Carry on Admiral/The Ship Was Loaded; 1958: Up the Creek; Further Up the Creek; 1960: Follow That Horse!; 1963: Tom Jones; 1964: Mary Poppins; 1965: The Truth About Spring; War Gods of the Deep/City Under the Sea; 1966: The Liquidator; 1969: The Love Bug; 1971: Bedknobs and Broomsticks; 1975: Bon Baisers de Hong Kong/From Hong Kong With Love (nUSr); 1977: Wombling Free; 1978: Dominique; Water Babies; 1980: The Fiendish Plot of Dr. Fu Manchu.

FRANCHOT TONE

(STANISLAUS PASCAL FRANCHOT TONE)
BORN: NIAGARA FALLS, NY, FEBRUARY 27, 1905.
ED: CORNELL UNIV. DIED: SEPTEMBER 18, 1968.

The devil-may-care charm of Franchot Tone was never more evident than in the 1930s, when it was acceptable to see leading men strutting around in tuxedos, playfully inebriated, and spinning off a suggestive line of banter in an effort to woo the ladies. He was one of the smoothest of actors when it came to playing it light and carefree but he longed for roles of meatier dramatic weight. In truth, he was never quite as assured or memorable when he got into heavier histrionics. He went from Buffalo's McGarry players to New York's New Playwright Company, which he joined in 1928. The following year he became a member of the Theatre Guild and soon was helping to form the Group Theatre. While acting on Broadway in the evenings, he filmed *The Wiser Sex* in the daytime, portraying the doomed cousin of attorney Melvyn Douglas. It was his stage role in *Success Story* that brought him an offer from MGM. He began his tenure with that company in 1933, with *Gabriel Over the White House*, playing presidential secretary to Walter Huston, followed by *Today We Live*, as Joan Crawford's brother. This marked the first time he and Crawford would appear together and they found enough to enjoy about one another after work hours to become man and wife in 1935, a union that would last for four years. Again with Crawford, he was a playboy love struck by her brusque charms, in *Dancing Lady*, a role he'd pretty much done opposite Jean Harlow in *Bombshell*, and, in both cases, losing them to others with better billing. Wealthy again, he was the son of Crawford's employer in *Sadie McKee*, in which he watched her marry rich alcoholic Edward Arnold, after he treats her cruelly. On loan with Fox, he played both a New Orleans cotton king and his offspring in *The World Moves On*, and then came back to Metro for top-billing in a "B" film, *Straight Is the Way*, as a Jewish ex-con determined not to fall back into his evil ways.

Things really started cooking when he found himself in three of 1935's major releases, starting with *The Lives of a Bengal Lancer*, at his quipping, self-satisfied best, sparring cheekily with fellow soldier Gary Cooper. It was Tone's personal favorite among his roles and a grand adventure that brought in the customers in huge numbers. Even better was *Mutiny on the Bounty*, where he was given a role (not in the other versions) of equal importance to Clark Gable and Charles Laughton, since neither of those parts could be completely defined as heroes where the head office was concerned. He was something akin to Gable's conscience, the officer disgusted with Laughton's monstrous behavior, who nevertheless stays loyal to England. It brought him his only Oscar nomination while the movie itself took the Academy Award for Best Picture. Further dwelling within Oscar's aura, he was architect who loves selfish Bette Davis in her Academy Award-winning performance in *Dangerous*. Between these he was the rich guy enamored with a performer again (in this case Harlow) in *Reckless*; an inventor who hooks up with Harlow in *Suzy*, spending a good deal of time off screen when he is believed dead; and did *No More Ladies*, with new bride Crawford, though he lost her once again on screen, this time to Robert Montgomery. He got her at last in *The Gorgeous Hussy*, a dry but popular costume romance, but since Gable was the other man in *Love on the Run*, there was no doubt who Crawford would clinch at the end of that one. Going for social significance but ending up with high melodrama, Tone was a naïf seduced by firearms while serving in the military in *They Gave Him a Gun*;

then did one last film with Crawford, *The Bride Wore Red*, in which he played an Italian postal clerk of all things, and again triumphed over Crawford's other suitor, in this instance Robert Young. He then settled in for light fare with *Man-Proof*, a disappointing teaming with Myrna Loy; *Love Is a Headache*, as a columnist in love with stage star Gladys George; and *Three Loves Has Nancy*, ending up no better than doofy Grady Sutton, since love number two, Robert Montgomery, won leading lady Janet Gaynor. Tone did a comical mystery, *Fast and Furious*, before parting with MGM in 1939.

During the 1940s, he was still doing leads but was clearly losing his standing as a major player. Over at Universal he was thrice the older man whom Deanna Durbin swoons for, in *Nice Girl?*, *His Butler's Sister*, and *Because of Him*, the difference being that in the first her affections weren't reciprocated because she was considered too young, whereas the second and third time out she won him over. At Paramount, he ended up in a good World War II adventure, *Five Graves to Cairo*, as a soldier confronting Erich von Stroheim; played the man left on the outside yet again in *True to Life*, losing Mary Martin to Dick Powell; and realized wife Veronica Lake was a spy in *The Hour Before the Dawn*, an adaptation of a Somerset Maugham novel. At Universal he got to play a shady character in *Phantom Lady*, then found himself opposite the studio's pseudo-Durbin, Susannah Foster, in *That Night with You*. After confusing moviegoers by following *Lost Honeymoon* with *Honeymoon*, he was clearly relegated to supporting material in *Every Girl Should Be Married*, with Cary Grant, as Betsy Drake's flirty boss. He became a programmer player with *Jigsaw* and *The Man on the Eiffel Tower*, both of which featured his second wife (1941–48), Jean Wallace, and then supported Bing Crosby in *Here Comes the Groom*, still getting rejected by the leading lady, in this case Jane Wyman. A theatrical endeavor with *Uncle Vanya* caused him to co-direct, produce, and star in a filmed version, but it hardly received any distribution. There was an important assignment, playing the sickly President, in the all-star *Advise and Consent*, then lesser parts in *In Harm's Way*, *Mickey One*, and *The High Commissioner*, and a continuing role on the popular doctor series *Ben Casey*. His other wives were actresses Barbara Payton (1951–52), with whom he was involved in a headline-making brawl during the 1950s, and Dolores Dorn (1956–59).

Screen: 1932: The Wiser Sex; 1933: Gabriel Over the White House; Today We Live; Midnight Mary; The Stranger's Return; Stage Mother; Bombshell; Dancing Lady; 1934: Moulin Rouge; Sadie McKee; The World Moves On; Straight Is the Way; The Girl From Missouri; Gentlemen Are Born; 1935: The Lives of a Bengal Lancer; One New York Night; Reckless; Mutiny on the Bounty; No More Ladies; Dangerous; 1936: Exclusive Story; The Unguarded Hour; The King Steps Out; Suzy; The Gorgeous Hussy; Love on the Run; 1937: Quality Street; They Gave Him a Gun; Between Two Women; The Bride Wore Red; 1938: Man-Proof; Love Is a Headache; Three Comrades; Three Loves Has Nancy; The Girl Downstairs; 1939: Fast and Furious; 1940: Trail of the Vigilantes; 1941: Nice Girl?; She Knew All the Answers; This Woman Is Mine; 1942: The Wife Takes a Flyer; Star Spangled Rhythm; 1943: Pilot #5; Five Graves to Cairo; True to Life; His Butler's Sister; 1944: The Hour Before the Dawn; Phantom Lady; Dark Waters; 1945: That Night With You; 1946: Because of Him; 1947: Lost Honeymoon; Honeymoon; Her Husband's Affairs; 1948: I Love Trouble; Every Girl Should Be Married; 1949: Jigsaw; The Man on the Eiffel Tower; Without Honor; 1951: Here Comes the Groom; 1958: Uncle Vanya (and co-dir.; prod.); 1962: Advise and Consent; 1964: La Bonne Soupe/Careless Love (nUSr); 1965: In Harm's Way; Mickey One; 1968: The High Commissioner/Nobody Runs Forever.

NY Stage: 1927: The Belt; Centuries; 1928: The International; The Age of Innocence; 1929: Uncle Vanya; Red Dust; Cross Roads; Meteor; 1930: Hotel Universe; Pagan Lady; 1931; 1931: Green Grow the Lilacs; The House of Connelly; 1932: Night Over Taos; A Thousand Summers; Success Story; 1939: The Gentle People; 1940: The Fifth Column; 1945: Hope for the Best; 1953: Oh, Men! Oh, Women!; 1955: The Time of Your Life; 1956: Uncle Vanya; 1957: A Moon for the Misbegotten; 1961: Mandingo; 1963: Strange Interlude; Bicycle Ride to Nevada; 1964: The Dirty Old Man; 1967: Beyond Desire.

Select TV: 1950: Murder at the Stork Club (sp); Walk the Dark Streets (sp); 1953: One Summer's Rain (sp); 1954: 12 Angry Men (sp); The Fifth Wheel (sp); 1955: Too Old for Dolls (sp); The Guardsman (sp); Red Gulch (sp); The Sound and the Fury (sp); 1956: Steinmetz (sp); Even the Weariest River (sp); Survival (sp); The Little Foxes (sp); 1957: Bend in the Road (sp); The Thundering Wave (sp); 1958: Trial by Slander (sp); Ticket to Tahiti (sp); The Thundering Wave (sp); The Crazy Hunter (sp); The Time of Your Life (sp); 1959: A Quiet Game of Cards (sp); Body and Soul (sp); Hidden Image (sp); 1960: The Shape of the River (sp); 1962: The Betrayal (sp); 1964: See How They Run; 1965–66: Ben Casey (series); 1968: Shadow Over Elveron.

MEL TORME

BORN: CHICAGO, IL, SEPTEMBER 13, 1925.
DIED: JUNE 5, 1999.

A major figure in the world of pop and jazz vocalizing, Mel Torme was also ambitious enough to make an occasional foray into the world of acting, with a few respectable credits as a result. As a child he sang with Chicago bands and performed on the radio as both vocalist and actor. At 16 he auditioned for the Harry James band with a song he'd written, "Lament for Love," selling the tune but not his own services. Instead, he went to California and joined a band comedian Chico Marx put together for an extremely short period of time, serving as singer, drummer, and arranger. RKO hired him to fill out the cast of its 1944 musical, *Higher and Higher*, but it was Frank Sinatra who got the attention in that one. There were other musicals, including *Pardon My Rhythm* and *Let's Go Steady*, where he was backed by his own group, the Mel-Tones. By the postwar years he'd become something of a bobby-soxer sensation with his soothing tones, earning the nickname "The Velvet Fog" (which he detested), and singing "Lucky in Love" in MGM's Technicolor college romp *Good News*. During the 1950s, he became a familiar face of television, earning great praise and an Emmy nomination for playing Mickey Rooney's put-upon brother in the *Playhouse 90* presentation of *The Comedian*. With this success, he tried some serious acting on the screen but wound up in three nonsensical potboilers produced by Albert Zugsmith: *Girls Town*, *The Big Operator*, and *The Private Lives of Adam and Eve*. In the more interesting *Walk Like a Dragon*, he was oddly cast as a gunslinger among a principally Asian cast. He had by this time switched his interest over to jazz music and, by the 1970s, had become one of the most admired artists in the field of jazz singing. Among his other accomplishments were a Grammy Award for the album, *An Evening with George Shearer and Mel Torme* in 1982, and composing the holiday standard "The Christmas Song." He wrote television scripts for *Run for Your Life* and *The Virginian*; the novel, *Wynner* (1978); the book, *The Other Side of the Rainbow* (1970), about his experiences as musical advisor on *The Judy Garland Show*; and the autobiography *It Wasn't All Velvet* (1988).

Screen: 1944: Higher and Higher; Pardon My Rhythm; Ghost

Catchers; 1945: Let's Go Steady; Junior Miss; Janie Gets Married; 1947: Good News; 1948: Words and Music; 1950: Duchess of Idaho; 1958: The Fearmakers; 1959: Girls Town; The Big Operator; 1960: Walk Like a Dragon; The Private Lives of Adam and Eve; 1964: The Patsy; 1966: A Man Called Adam; 1975: Land of No Return/Snowman; 1989: Daffy Duck's Quackbusters (voice); 1991: The Naked Gun 2 1/2: The Smell of Fear.

Select TV: 1951: TV's Top Tunes (series); 1951–52: The Mel Torme Show (series); 1953: Summertime USA (series); 1957: The Comedian (sp); 1971: It Was a Very Good Year (series); 1982: Pray TV.

RIP TORN

(ELMORE RUAL TORN, JR.) BORN: TEMPLE, TX, FEBRUARY 6, 1931. ED: UNIV. OF TX.

A richly talented actor, Rip Torn was always too busy doing his job to worry about whether he was considered star material or not. He wound up with a long and varied list of theatre, film, and television credits, going from handsome but unsympathetic young lead to gruff character player, the latter hardly resembling the younger Torn at all. While at the Dallas Institute of Performing Arts, he apprenticed at the Knox Street Players before joining the Army. In 1955 he went to New York to look for work and ended up understudying Alex Nicol, playing the character of Brick during the original run of *Cat on a Hot Tin Roof*, eventually making his Broadway bow in the role. That play's director, Elia Kazan, also gave him his first film break, giving him a bit in the controversial *Baby Doll*. Between live television assignments the actor showed up on screen as a prison camp survivor who breaks down on the witness stand in *Time Limit*, and one of the soldiers in Gregory Peck's platoon in *Pork Chop Hill*. He won a Theatre World Award for his work in *Chaparral*, and made a splash on Broadway, playing vengeful Tom Finley, Jr., in *Sweet Bird of Youth*, eventually switching to the lead once Paul Newman left the cast. Summoned to Hollywood, he was impressive as the tormented Judas in MGM's lavish remake of *King of Kings*, and then repeated his original stage role as Tom, Jr. in the disappointing film of *Sweet Bird*. In 1963 he married that film's star, Geraldine Page (he had originally been married, 1955–61, to actress Ann Wedgeworth). Dredging up his nasty side, he was a gambler in *The Cincinnati Kid*; a sadistic war-happy sergeant in *Beach Red*; and a Mafia kingpin in *Sol Madrid*. Nor were he and Page all that lovable in the black comedy *You're a Big Boy Now*, as Peter Kastner's overbearing, over-the-top parents.

Going the independent route, Torn starred as a hippie biker in *Beyond the Law*, one of the oddities directed by author Norman Mailer (and not to be confused with Torn's 1992 direct-to-video release of the same name), and a psychiatrist taping his sex fantasies in *Coming Apart*, a title that seemed to be some kind of joke, considering his name. Somewhat higher in profile was the ambitious attempt to film *Tropic of Cancer*, which gave him a real showcase, as the sexually indulgent Henry Miller, in this X-rated Paramount release. This was perhaps his prime screen role alongside a low-budget drama, *Payday*, in which he played a small time country singer spending his life on the road. He was a professor investigating alien David Bowie in the maddening *The Man Who Fell to Earth*, and a moody farmer in *Heartland*, but then started showing up in more commercial fare. These included *Nasty Habits*, as a priest, in a film that also featured his wife; *The Seduction of Joe Tynan*, as a randy politician; *Jinxed*, as Bette Midler's abusive husband; *A Stranger Is Watching*, in something akin to a lead, as a vagrant who kidnaps Kate Mulgrew; and

Summer Rental, as a crusty old beach dweller. In between these he did his usual professional job, playing a dirt-poor Florida farmer, in *Cross Creek*, and, since he'd never gotten an Oscar nomination before, he received a token one for this. There was a droll bit as Albert Brooks's heavenly lawyer in *Defending Your Life*, showing a sense of humor he'd not often had a chance to display. As a result, he did a comedic television series, *The Larry Sanders Show* and won a much-deserved Emmy Award for it, starring as Garry Shandling's down-to-earth producer. He had not stopped making pictures in the meantime, starring as Walt Whitman in *Beautiful Dreamers*, and a feisty property owner fighting the government in *Where the Rivers Flow North*. He also kept on doing supporting work in such films as *Canadian Bacon*, as a gung-ho general; *How to Make an American Quilt*, as a straying husband; the blockbuster hit *Men in Black*, as the head of an organization of alien hunters; very minor roles in two very good films, *The Insider*, as a public relations advisor, and *Wonder Boys*, as a pompous writer; plus *Freddy Got Fingered*, where he faced the indignity of taking direction from a talentless television comedian, Tom Green. In 1988 he directed the disastrous Whoopi Goldberg vehicle *The Telephone*. His cousin is actress Sissy Spacek.

Screen: 1956: Baby Doll; 1957: A Face in the Crowd; Time Limit; 1959: Pork Chop Hill; 1961: King of Kings; 1962: Hero's Island; Sweet Bird of Youth; 1963: Critic's Choice; 1965: The Cincinnati Kid; 1966: One Spy Too Many (from TV); You're a Big Boy Now; 1967: Beach Red; 1968: Beyond the Law; Sol Madrid; 1969: Coming Apart; 1970: Tropic of Cancer; Maidstone; 1972: Slaughter; One P.M.; 1973: Payday; Cotter; 1974: Crazy Joe; 1976: Birch Interval; The Man Who Fell to Earth; 1977: Nasty Habits; 1978: Coma; The Private Files of J. Edgar Hoover; 1979: The Seduction of Joe Tynan; 1980: Heartland; One-Trick Pony; First Family; 1982: A Stranger Is Watching; The Beastmaster; Jinxed; Scarab; Airplane II: The Sequel; 1983: Cross Creek; 1984: Misunderstood; Flashpoint; Songwriter; City Heat; 1985: Summer Rental; Beer; 1987: Extreme Prejudice; Nadine; 1989: Hit List; Cold Feet; 1990: Silence Like Glass; 1991: Defending Your Life; 1992: Hard Promises; Beautiful Dreamers; Dolly Dearest (dtv); Beyond the Law/Fixing the Shadow (dtv); 1993: Robocop 3; 1994: Where the Rivers Flow North; 1995: For Better or Worse; Canadian Bacon; How to Make an American Quilt; 1996: Down Periscope; Death Falls (dtv); 1997: Trial and Error; Hercules (voice); Men in Black; The Mouse; 1998: Senseless; 1999: The Insider; 2000: Wonder Boys; 2001: Freddy Got Fingered; 2002: Men in Black II; Rolling Kansas (nUSr).

NY Stage: 1956: Cat on a Hot Tin Roof; 1958: Chaparral (ob); 1959: Sweet Bird of Youth; 1961: Daughter of Silence; 1963: Desire Under the Elms (ob); Strange Interlude; 1964: Blues for Mr. Charlie; 1966: The Kitchen (ob); The Country Girl; 1967: The Deer Park (ob); 1968: The Cuban Thing; 1969: Dream of a Blacklisted Actor; 1971: The Dance of Death; 1974: Barbary Shore (ob); 1975: The Glass Menagerie; 1977: Creditors (ob; and dir.); 1979: Seduced (ob); 1980: Mixed Couples; 1982: The Man and the Fly (ob); 1993: Anna Christie; 1998: The Young Man From Atlanta.

Select TV: 1956: Murder of a Sandflea (sp); Wetback Run (sp); 1957: The Little Bullfighter (sp); The Killer Instinct (sp); 1958: The Charm (sp); Eddie (sp); Bomber's Moon (sp); Johnny Belinda (sp); 1959: Murder and the Android (sp); Face of a Hero (sp); The Tunnel (sp); 1961: Twenty-Four Hours in a Woman's Life (sp); 1971: Monserrat (sp); 1972: A Marriage Proposal (sp); 1973: The President's Plane Is Missing; 1975: Attack on Terror: The FBI vs. the Ku Klux Klan; 1976: Song of Myself (sp); 1978: Betrayal; Steel Cowboy; 1979: A Shining Season; Blind Ambition

(ms); 1980: Rape and Marriage: The Rideout Case; Sophia Loren: Her Own Story; 1982: The Blue and the Gray (ms); 1984: When She Says No; 1985: The Execution; The Atlanta Child Murders; Cat on a Hot Tin Roof (sp); 1986: Dream West (ms); Manhunt for Claude Dallas; 1987: J. Edgar Hoover; Laguna Heat; The King of Love; Destination: America; 1988: April Morning; 1989: Sweet Bird of Youth; 1990: None So Blind; By Dawn's Early Light; Pair of Aces; 1991: Columbo: Death Hits the Jackpot; 1991: Another Pair of Aces: Three of a Kind; My Son Johnny; 1992: T-Bone and Wesel; A Mother's Right: The Elizabeth Morgan Story; Dead Ahead: The Exxon Valdez Disaster; 1992–98: The Larry Sanders Show (series); 1994: Heaven & Hell: North & South Book III (ms); Heart of a Child; 1995: Letter to My Killer; She Stood Alone: The Tailhook Scandal; 1996: The Almost Perfect Bank Robbery; 1997–98: Ghost Stories (series narrator); 1998: Seasons of Love; 1999: Balloon Farm; Passing Glory; The Almost Perfect Bank Robbery; 2000: A Vision of Murder: The Story of Danielle.

AUDREY TOTTER

BORN: JOLIET, IL, DECEMBER 20, 1918.

One of the great hard-edged dames of the noir genre, Audrey Totter sparkled during the postwar era, maintaining a comfortable level of fame without the burdens of full-fledged superstardom. While a teen she did stock theater and this led to her Chicago theater debut, in 1938, in *The Copperhead*, opposite Ian Keith, whose rep company she joined. A tour with them in *My Sister Eileen* brought her to New York, where she became one of the busiest of all radio actresses. MGM signed her up in 1944 and immediately gave her an unsavory part, as the floozy who makes her dough by rolling servicemen, in *Main Street After Dark*. Contrasting roles in *The Postman Always Rings Twice*, as John Garfield's pickup, and *The Cockeyed Miracle*, as the likable ingénue, convinced the studio of her talents, and Robert Montgomery, making his directorial debut, grabbed her for the stylish and unique *Lady in the Lake*. Totter wound up with a tour de force role and gave perhaps the finest performance of her career, having to act most of the movie directly facing the camera, since the story's gimmick was that it was told entirely from Montgomery's point of view. This was followed by *High Wall*, in which she played a prison psychiatrist trying to breakthrough to crazed Robert Taylor; *Any Number Can Play*, in which she cast her eye on brother-in-law Clark Gable; and *Tension*, in a prime Totter bitch role, as mousey Richard Basehart's unrepentant, cheating wife. There were worthy loan-outs to Univeral in *The Saxon Charm*, in which she played a nightclub singer; Paramount's *Alias Nick Beal*, in which she tempted politician Thomas Mitchell; and, in another of her best parts, RKO's *The Set-Up*, starring as boxer Robert Ryan's concerned wife. During the 1950s, she dropped into support, as in *The Blue Veil*, in which she was a seemingly nice mom who turns on nanny Jane Wyman and accuses her of stealing her child, and then found herself in cheaper fare like the 3-D offering *Man in the Dark*; *Women's Prison*, which was as campy as its title promised; and *Jet Attack*, a particularly bad programmer about the Korean War. Having happily married in 1952, she became less and less interested in film work, instead concentrating mostly on television, where she eventually accepted a regular role on the popular 1970s series *Medical Center*, as Nurse Wilcox.

Screen: 1944: Main Street After Dark; 1945: Bewitched (voice); Dangerous Partners; Her Highness and the Bellboy; The Sailor Takes a Wife; Adventure; The Hidden Eye; 1946: The Secret

Heart (voice); Ziegfeld Follies (voice); The Postman Always Rings Twice; The Cockeyed Miracle; Lady in the Lake; **1947:** The Beginning or the End; The Unsuspected; High Wall; **1948:** The Saxon Charm; **1949:** The Set-Up; Alias Nick Beal; Any Number Can Play; Tension; **1950:** Under the Gun; **1951:** The Blue Veil; FBI Girl; **1952:** The Sellout; Assignment — Paris; My Pal Gus; **1953:** The Woman They Almost Lynched; Man in the Dark; Cruising' Down the River; Mission Over Korea; Champ for a Day; **1954:** Massacre Canyon; **1955:** Women's Prison; A Bullet for Joey; The Vanishing American; **1957:** Ghost Diver; **1958:** Jet Attack; Man or Gun; **1964:** The Carpetbaggers; **1965:** Harlow; **1968:** Chubasco; **1979:** The Apple Dumpling Gang Rides Again.
Select TV: **1953:** Ever Since the Day (sp); **1954:** Meet McGraw (sp); **1955:** One Man Missing (sp); **1956:** One Life (sp); **1958–59:** Cimarron City (series); **1960:** Mystery at Malibu (sp); **1961:** My Darling Judge (sp); **1962–63:** Our Man Higgins (series); **1967:** The Outsider; **1969:** U.M.C.; **1972–76:** Medical Center (series); **1978:** The Nativity; **1980:** The Great Cash Giveaway; **1984:** City Killer.

LEE TRACY

(WILLIAM LEE TRACY) BORN: ATLANTA, GA, APRIL 14, 1898. ED: UNION COL., SCHENECTADY. DIED: OCTOBER 18, 1968.

Arguably the early talkies' number one practitioner of the fine art of rapid-fire banter and saucy put downs, Lee Tracy carried the smart-ass routine too far into his personal life and suffered for it. A one-time U.S. treasury agent, he entered show business as a vaudevillian then went legit, eventually making his Broadway bow in *The Show-Off*, in 1924. His performances in *Broadway* and, especially, *The Front Page*, where he created the role of reporter Hildy Johnson, made him famous. Hollywood, excited over his mile-a-minute delivery, eagerly snatched him up once sound arrived, with Fox casting him as a vaudevillian, opposite Mae Clarke, in *Big Time*, and as Charles Farrell's unscrupulous friend in *Liliom*. Signing a contract with Warner Bros. he was a standout as the persistent reporter, lightening up the atmosphere of the horror film *Doctor X*, then got the quintessential Lee Tracy role, in *Blessed Event*, as the Walter Winchell-like columnist who doesn't care whose life he wrecks in pursuit of a good story. He was a state representative and descendent of Button Gwinnett in *Washington Merry-Go-Round*, then signed a contract MGM, where he breathed some life and humor into the rather gloomy John Barrymore storyline of *Dinner at Eight*, as his agent, and into the mediocre *Bombshell*, as Jean Harlow's p.r. man. Next up, he was scheduled to play the reporter who covers Wallace Beery's exploits in *Viva Villa*, but, while on location in Mexico, Tracy, who was by this point a known hellraiser and heavy drinker, caused an uproar when he urinated on a public parade from his hotel balcony. Promptly fired by Metro, he began dropping down the Hollywood "A" list, ending up at RKO, where he played the leads in second features like *Criminal Lawyer* and *Fixer Dugan*. Having given up the movies for stage by the late 1940s, he scored a major success on Broadway playing the ailing U.S. president in *The Best Man*, a role he repeated on the big screen with his usual expertise, earning an Oscar nomination in the supporting category. He had the curious distinction of appearing in two movies (1934, 1945) for Universal that were both entitled *I'll Tell the World*, but otherwise unrelated in content, the first being a comedy about a reporter trailing a Grand Duke, while the second was a distorted adaptation of Nathanael West's *Miss Lonelyhearts*.

Screen: **1929:** Big Time; **1930:** Born Reckless; Liliom; She Got What She Wanted; **1932:** The Strange Love of Molly Louvain; Love Is a Racket; Doctor X; Blessed Event; Washington Merry-Go-Round; Night Mayor; The Half-Naked Truth; **1933:** Clear All Wires; Private Jones; The Nuisance; Dinner at Eight; Turn Back the Clock; Bombshell; Advice to the Lovelorn; **1934:** I'll Tell the World; You Belong to Me; The Lemon Drop Kid; **1935:** Carnival; Two Fisted; **1936:** Sutter's Gold; Wanted — Jane Turner; **1937:** Criminal Lawyer; Behind the Headlines; **1938:** Crashing Hollywood; **1939:** Fixer Dugan; The Spellbinder; **1940:** Millionaires in Prison; **1942:** The Payoff; **1943:** Power of the Press; **1945:** Betrayal from the East; I'll Tell the World; **1947:** High Tide; **1964:** The Best Man.
NY Stage: **1924:** The Show-Off; **1925:** The Book of Charm; **1926:** Glory Hallelujah; The Wisdom Tooth; Broadway; **1928:** The Front Page; **1930:** Oh, Promise Me; **1931:** Louder Please!; **1935:** Bright Star; **1940:** Every Man For Himself; **1949:** The Traitor; Metropole; **1950:** Mr. Barry's Etchings; The Show-Off (revival); **1951:** Idiot's Delight; **1960:** The Best Man; **1965:** Minor Miracle.
Select TV: **1950:** The Traitor (sp); **1951:** Light Up the Sky (sp); **1951–52:** The Amazing Mr. Malone (series); **1952–53:** Martin Kane: Private Eye (series); **1956:** Good Old Charlie Fay (sp); **1959:** New York Confidential (series).

SPENCER TRACY

BORN: MILWAUKEE, WI, APRIL 5, 1900. ED: RIPON COL. DIED: JUNE 10, 1967.

For 37 years Spencer Tracy towered as one of film's greatest stars and, as far as the public was concerned, he earned that position partly because he never seemed to behave like one. Although he could be cantankerous, demanding, and difficult on the set, what the world saw in the finished product was a stocky, average-looking guy who projected decency, strength, and intelligence. There weren't usually any frills or trappings to his performance (indeed, he didn't even like wearing makeup), which made him so very accessible. For an industry steeped in phoniness, he seemed to rise above all the nonsense and sell a straight and honest bill of goods. It was while in college, as a pre-med student, that he discovered his enthusiasm for acting, having excelled on the debating team. In New York he was accepted into the Sergeant's School to study acting (Pat O'Brien was a fellow-student) and made his Broadway debut, in 1922, playing a robot in *R.U.R.*, for the Theatre Guild. He acted with some stock companies between appearing in some other New York plays, most of which had short runs. Finally, he found himself in a solid hit, *The Last Mile*, in which his dynamic turn as hot-headed convict Mears made him the most talked about actor on the theater scene. Director John Ford, having caught the show, was looking for someone to carry a prison movie he was making for Fox called *Up the River*. The film, an odd mix of comedy and drama, also featured Humphrey Bogart, marking the only time these very independent legends would act opposite one another. Fox enthusiastically offered Tracy a contract and, in 1931, he headed west to start his very lucrative stay in Hollywood, beginning with *Quick Millions*, which quickly established him as a riveting screen presence, playing a trucker who moves up to the big time world of racketeering before his inevitable downfall.

His Fox years did not include a great deal of memorable material but there was little to fault in Tracy's contributions. During this period the highlights included *Goldie*, because it marked the first time he played opposite Jean Harlow, with whom he clicked beautifully; *20,000 Years in Sing-Sing*, made on loan to Warners to replace an uncooperative James Cagney, giving him his only pairing with Bette Davis; *The Power and the Prize*, which received great praise for its off-beat manner of telling the story, with Tracy at his own funeral, reviewing his life and how he became a powerful railroad baron; *Man's Castle*, as a Depression-era vagrant trying to rise above his station; and his last for the studio, *Dante's Inferno*, which imaginatively paralleled a carny barker's rise to power against an eye-popping re-creation of hell, a sequence that kept the film well-known with the passing years. Tracy had already become temperamental and hard to handle, refusing work and walking off certain unsatisfactory pictures, ending up at one point arrested for drunkenness while filming *It's a Small World*. Fox fired him but he was too good to go too long without work and MGM eagerly grabbed him once he was available (they'd earlier borrowed him for *The Show-Off*), placing him under contract in 1935, a union that would last for 20 years. They started him with the short but effective *The Murder Man*, as a smart-ass reporter, then put him with Harlow in *Riffraff*, and opposite Myrna Loy in *Whispaw*. The three of them, combined with William Powell, made something golden together with *Libeled Lady*, one of the top screwball comedies of the period. Since this was a high-wattage cast, Tracy, a leading man but not quite yet a box-office headliner in his own right, had to accept fourth billing. Prior to that one he did director Fritz Lang's well-intended anti-mob violence piece, *Fury*, featuring one of Tracy's rare miscalculated trips over the top, and *San Francisco*, which made him secondary to stars Clark Gable and Jeanette MacDonald, but showed that he could push others right off the screen with very little effort. As Gable's wizened buddy who becomes a priest, he received the first of nine Oscar nominations. MGM realized that they had made a wise investment, for Tracy was now not just a leading man but also a major star.

They quickly bestowed upon him as juicy a role as he could hope for, the life-loving Portuguese fisherman Manuel, in their sterling 1937 adaptation of Rudyard Kipling's *Captains Courageous*. Robustly directed by Victor Fleming, this was one of the studio's standout productions of the decade and, despite an accent that never quite sounded authentic, Tracy was superb, clearly having the time of his life in what he always considered his favorite role. He won the Academy Award for Best Actor of the year. He teamed surprisingly well with Joan Crawford for *Mannequin*; was very much at home with Gable and Loy in *Test Pilot*, then jumped into one of the most famous of all his roles, playing the level-headed Father Flanagan in *Boys Town*. This was an entertaining but very syrupy concoction and Tracy's direct and unsentimental approach to the project helped keep it on firm ground. For it he received a second Academy Award, becoming the first male performer to be given back-to-back Oscars. As a follow-up he did his first of only two trips off the Metro lot during his stay there, returning in both cases to his old stomping ground, Fox. First up, in 1939, was a very well done adventure tale, *Stanley and Livingstone*, or at least Hollywood's version of the famous story, with Tracy as Henry M. Stanley, the journalist who travels through Africa to find Cedric Hardwicke's Livingstone.

Back at Metro, he got involved in a troubled production, *I Take This Woman*, which gave him an unworthy co-star in Hedy Lamarr, but then appeared in Technicolor for one of the greatest outdoor adventures of the era, *Northwest Passage*, leading his rangers through some gorgeous scenery to battle bloodthirsty Indians. There was the workman-like biopic *Edison, the Man*, which was a semi-sequel, being the second installment in a two-picture salute to the great inventor, the first having been *Young Tom Edison*, with Mickey Rooney. Nonetheless the two films combined couldn't begin to cover the scope of this man's achieve-

ments. He then did his last with Gable, *Boom Town*, Tracy having become so popular and important in his own right that he would no longer abide taking second billing to anyone. Starting with the unnecessary but acceptable sequel, *Men of Boys Town*, he was to remain at the head of the cast list from then on.

He did not seem at ease in the uneven remake of *Dr. Jekyll and Mr. Hyde* (of course using far less makeup than Fredric March had in the earlier version), but found himself opposite his true cinematic equal when he played sports writer Sam Craig to Katharine Hepburn, as columnist Tess Harper, in *Woman of the Year*. This was a smart, adult battle of the sexes and few performers have so instantly or so thoroughly clicked as did these two great actors, with a spark of knowing innuendo to their banter and a respect and admiration that simply leapt off the screen. In real life they became Hollywood's most famous unmarried couple (Tracy was married, with two children, since 1928 and would never divorce) and teamed on screen another eight times, adding much to motion pictures over the next three decades. In the meantime, he and Lamarr were none-too-convincing Spaniards in *Tortilla Flat*; after which he and Hepburn got more serious for *Keeper of the Flame*, which dealt with fascism, proving that they were always better suited to something with a lighter touch. *A Guy Named Joe*, in which Tracy was a dead pilot returned to earth to do a good deed, was one of the biggest hits of the war era, though he gave too much of the movie (not to mention Irene Dunne) over to Van Johnson. *The Seventh Cross* found him escaping a concentration camp and required him to do the first half hour of the film with nary a word of dialogue. Surprisingly, considering his success in films, he returned to Broadway to do one last play, *The Rugged Path*, encouraged to do so by Hepburn. On screen they did *Without Love*, which was probably their most trivial teaming, and *The Sea of Grass*, which was definitely their weakest, a soggy family saga set in New Mexico. There was another soap opera, *Cass Timberlane*, which did not have the benefit of Hepburn but gave Tracy a lackluster but more box-office friendly co-star in Lana Turner; *Edward, My Son*, which he did in England, playing one of his rare unsympathetic roles, as a man who destroys everyone in his path to provide for his selfish (unseen) son; and *Malaya*, a teaming with James Stewart that came up short to say the least.

Between these, he and Hepburn were marvelous as a politician and his supportive wife in director Frank Capra's thoughtful *State of the Union*, and then reached the pinnacle of their pairings together, with director George Cukor's witty and hilarious *Adam's Rib*. Playing a married team of lawyers, who must face off during a murder trial, they were never more assured in their playing, feasting on a razor-sharp screenplay by Garson Kanin and Ruth Gordon. This was not only a box-office hit but one of the most enduring of all comedies of its era. Likewise, Tracy ended up in another much-loved film, *Father of the Bride*, in which he faced frustrations and heartbreak as daughter Elizabeth Taylor gets wed. He played the role with such insight and comedic know-how that he was up for his fourth Oscar nomination. This success assured the expected sequel, *Father's Little Dividend*, after which there was another rematch with Hepburn-Cukor-Kanin-Gordon with *Pat and Mike*, which actually managed to be almost as good as *Adam's Rib*. Sadly, there was little public interest in *The Actress*, a gentle piece of nostalgia, based on Gordon's memoirs of growing up in New England, and, after bringing the pilgrims to America for the Thanksgiving perennial *Plymouth Adventure*, Tracy did his second loan-out to Fox, in 1954 for *Broken Lance*, giving a mighty performance as the feisty head of an unhappy family of ranchers. He ended his relationship with MGM on a high note, in *Bad Day at Black Rock*, in which he showed just how commanding he could be by playing the part in a very controlled manner, starring as a mysterious one-armed fellow who shows up in a desert hellhole and battles the vicious locals. It brought him another Oscar nomination. He and Hepburn did their contribution to the Cinemascope era with the bright *Desk Set*, and then Tracy went very artsy for Warners's ambitious filming of *The Old Man and the Sea*. Essentially a one-man tour de force, it was obvious why he would be drawn to the part, though it turned out to be a very difficult shoot, with mixed results and, in the end, a major financial failure. For compensation, he was given another Oscar nod. In a more comfortable mode he did *The Last Hurrah* for John Ford, the director who'd guided him through his first film job, portraying a wiley old politician coming to the end of his days.

As the 1960s began, Tracy had, by this point, become legendary for his crabby on-set behavior and his impatience with multiple takes. Off screen he battled with the bottle and was not in the best of health. Aside from director Mervyn LeRoy's *The Devil at 4 O'Clock*, which teamed him for maximum impact with Frank Sinatra, all of his final movies were directed by Stanley Kramer, one of the few directors who could control the actor and didn't put up with his complaints. They got off to a magnificent start with *Inherit the Wind*, with the plump and sweaty Tracy throwing himself full-throttle into the role of the lawyer who defends the teaching of evolution. He received his seventh Oscar mention for what was probably the most thrilling and emotionally galvanizing performance of his career. As the judge who presides over the war criminal trials in *Judgment at Nuremberg*, he was authoritatively brilliant, resulting in yet another go at the Oscar, while he pretty much stayed outside the physical horseplay in the all-star *It's a Mad Mad Mad Mad World*, as a police officer keeping his eye on the greedy events at hand, giving credibility to the slapstick proceedings in what turned out to be a box-office smash. Even more popular was *Guess Who's Coming to Dinner*, his farewell, in which he and Hepburn had to deal with their daughter's decision to marry Sidney Poitier. Tracy was as watchable as ever in this very old fashioned entertainment with a liberal 1960s message and wound up with his ninth Oscar nomination (a record at the time), posthumously, having died only days after shooting his final scenes. It was clear that he was one of the old-time stars who glided with ease into the new cinema of the day and had indeed been at home through all of the cinema's many changes — the sign of a truly great star. He never had to bend to the media-pandering, glamorous images associated with such luminaries. Instead, he let his talent speak for himself and carry him straight to the top.

Screen: 1930: Up the River; 1931: Quick Millions; Six-Cylinder Love; Goldie; 1932: She Wanted a Millionaire; Sky Devils; Disorderly Conduct; Young America; Society Girl; Painted Woman; Me and My Gal; 20,000 Years in Sing Sing; 1933: Face in the Sky; Shanghai Madness; The Power and the Glory; The Mad Game; Man's Castle; 1934: Looking for Trouble; The Show-Off; Bottoms Up; Now I'll Tell; Marie Galante; 1935: It's a Small World; The Murder Man; Dante's Inferno; Whipsaw; 1936: Riffraff; Fury; San Francisco; Libeled Lady; 1937: They Gave Him a Gun; Captains Courageous; Big City; 1938: Mannequin; Test Pilot; Boys Town; 1939: Stanley and Livingstone; 1940: I Take This Woman; Young Tom Edison; Northwest Passage; Edison, the Man; Boom Town; 1941: Men of Boys Town; Dr. Jekyll and Mr. Hyde; 1942: Woman of the Year; Tortilla Flat; Keeper of the Flame; 1943: A Guy Named Joe; 1944: The Seventh Cross; Thirty Seconds Over Tokyo; 1945: Without Love; 1947: The Sea of Grass; Cass Timberlane; 1948: State of the Union; 1949: Edward, My Son; Adam's Rib; Malaya; 1950: Father of the Bride; 1951: Father's Little Dividend; The People Against O'Hara; 1952: Pat and Mike; Plymouth Adventure; 1953: The Actress; 1954: Broken Lance; 1955: Bad Day at Black Rock; 1956: The Mountain; 1957: Desk Set; 1958: The Old Man and the Sea; The Last Hurrah; 1960: Inherit the Wind; 1961: The Devil at 4 O'Clock; Judgment at Nuremberg; 1963: How the West Was Won (narrator); It's a Mad Mad Mad Mad World; 1967: Guess Who's Coming to Dinner.

NY Stage: 1922: R.U.R.; 1923: A Royal Fandango; 1926: Yellow; 1927: The Baby Cyclone; 1929: Conflict; Nigger Rich; Dread; 1930: The Last Mile; 1945: The Rugged Path.

BILL TRAVERS

(WILLIAM LINDON-TRAVERS) BORN: NEWCASTLE-UPON-TYNE, ENGLAND, JANUARY 3, 1922. DIED: MARCH 29, 1994.

Strapping, cleft-chinned Bill Travers was tailor-made for physical roles, before becoming best known in his later years for his family-friendly critter movies. The younger brother of actress Linden Travers, he served in the military before acting with a rep company and then making his way to the London stage. He made his film debut in 1950, unbilled, in *The Wooden Horse*. For several years he remained very much a supporting or minor player in such films as *Mantrap/Man in Hiding*, as Lois Maxwell's new husband, and the Lawrence Harvey version of *Romeo and Juliet*, as Benvolio. He got his first big star role with *Wee Geordie/Geordie*, a cute tale of a burly Scotsman who ends up hammer throwing at the Olympics. Because of it he got upped to important roles in two British-made MGM films, *Bhowani Junction*, as a half-caste railway boss loved by Ava Gardner, and the failed update of *The Barretts of Wimpole Street*, as poet Robert Browning, the part Fredric March had done in the earlier version. In 1957 he and actress Virginia McKenna (b. London, June 7, 1931) were cast as a couple who inherit a run-down cinema in *The Smallest Show on Earth*, and they fell in love off screen as well, marrying that year and remaining so until Travers's death. In the meantime they portrayed lovers in the melodrama *Passionate Summer*, while Travers was the hero in a superior monster tale, *Gorgo*, about a captured sea creature whose vengeful mother destroys London; and played a doomed cavalry officer in a muddled American western, *Duel at Diablo*. In 1966 he and McKenna were together again in an extremely appealing wildlife adventure *Born Free*, as the real-life Addamson couple who raised a lion cub as a pet. It became one of the best-loved and best-known movies of this sort, a world-wide hit, and was responsible for the Travers family developing their own off-screen interest in animal preservation. This was reflected in three of their later films, all of which Travers helped write: *Ring of Bright Water* (about an otter); *An Elephant Called Slowly* (released here for television); and *Christian the Lion*, also directed by Travers, detailing their exploits while filming *Born Free*. They did not, however, appear in the official *Born Free* sequel, *Living Free*, handing over their roles to Nigel Davenport and Susan Hampshire.

Screen: 1950: The Wooden Horse; Trio; 1951: The Browning Version; 1952: The Story of Robin Hood and His Merrie Men; Hindle Wakes/Holiday Weekend; It Started in Paradise; Outpost in Malaya/The Planter's Wife; 1953: Mantrap/Man in Hiding; Shadow Man/Street of Shadows; The Genie; Undercover Agent/Counterspy; The Square Ring; 1954: Romeo and Juliet; 1955: Footsteps in the Fog; Wee Geordie/Geordie; 1956: Bhowani Junction; 1957: The Barretts of Wimpole Street; The Seventh Sin; The Smallest Show on Earth; 1958: Passionate Summer; 1959:

The Bridal Path; **1961:** Gorgo; Two Living, One Dead; The Green Helmet; Invasion Quartet; **1966:** Born Free; Duel at Diablo; **1968:** A Midsummer Night's Dream (TV in US); **1969:** Ring of Bright Water (and co-wr.); An Elephant Called Slowly (and co-wr.; prod.; TV in US); **1970:** Rum Runners/Boulevard du Rhum; **1973:** The Belstone Fox; **1976:** Christian the Lion/The Lion at World's End (and dir.; prod.; wr.).

NY Stage: 1961: A Cook For Mr. General; **1964:** Abraham Cochrane.

Select TV: 1957: A Cook for Mr. General (sp); **1960:** Born a Giant (sp); **1963:** Lorna Doone (ms); **1968:** The Admirable Crichton (sp); **1979:** Bloody Ivory; **1984:** The First Olympics: Athens; 1896.

HENRY TRAVERS

(TRAVERS JOHN HEAGERTY) BORN: BERWICK-ON-TWEED, NORTHUMBERLAND, ENGLAND, MARCH 5, 1874. DIED: OCTOBER 18, 1965.

A warm, grandfatherly character player, Henry Travers, with his tweedy, English countryside manner, eyebrows as bushy as a terrier's, and crackly voice, was in theater nearly 40 years before launching his movie career. He'd started out with the O'Grady Stock Company, which toured England, and, during his long run with them, did an occasional play in London. In 1917 he decided to move to America and ended up in New York making his Broadway debut, in 1919, in *The Faithful*, for the newly formed Theatre Guild. He became one of that group's most dependable players and, over the next several years, was seen in such works as *Liliom*, *Arms and the Man*, *Pygmalion*, and *Volpone*. It was while appearing in *Reunion in Vienna* that he was approached by MGM to not only repeat his role in their proposed film version, but to sign a contract with the studio as well. Just to show how late in the game he was starting his cinematic career, he wound up playing father to Frank Morgan, an actor who didn't exactly photograph as a strapping youth. Next up, he was more convincingly cast as dad to Robert Montgomery in *Another Language*, then spent most of his contract on loan-out, including roles in two classic tales of the supernatural, Universal's *The Invisible Man*, as Claude Rains's former employer and Gloria Stuart's dad; and *Death Takes a Holiday*, as a baron confronted by Fredric March. Most of his succeeding roles were extremely minor but he stood out in *Seven Keys to Baldpate*, as Peters, the inn's hermit; *Pursuit*, as a nosey paperhanger who tries to collect a reward on kidnapped Scotty Beckett; and *Too Many Parents*, as the well-liked janitor at a boy's military school.

In 1936 he returned to Broadway for what would turn out to be his greatest triumph there, playing free-spirited Martin Vanderhoff in the prize-winning *You Can't Take It With You*. Although Lionel Barrymore got the role in the film version, Travers was summoned back to the movies as a result, signing a new contract with Warners. They made him dad to *The Sisters*; the prison librarian, inevitably named Pop, in *You Can't Get Away with Murder*; and doctors in two 1939 hits, *Dark Victory* and *Dodge City*. He traded his stethoscope for a reverend's collar in Fox's soapy epic *The Rains Came* and for a judge's robe for MGM's *Remember?*; then showed up as Ginger Rogers's gramps in RKO's *Primrose Path*, and Joan Leslie's farmer dad in *High Sierra*. Continuing in some of the top features of the 1940s, he was one of the lovable old professors in the ace comedy *Ball of Fire*; the kindly gardener, a welcome presence on the wartime England homefront, in *Mrs. Miniver*, which brought his only Oscar nomination; *Random Harvest*, as yet another doctor; *Shadow of a Doubt*, as Teresa Wright's small-town dad; and *Dragon Seed*,

looking even less Asian than most of the cast while playing Agnes Moorhead's husband. Among these supporting roles, he got something akin to a lead, in *The Moon Is Down*, as the mayor of a Norwegian town who stands up to the Nazis and suffers for it, a character he reprised to some degree in the *None Shall Escape*, though this time he was a priest. Getting mean for once he was the Scrooge-like landlord who causes problems for priest Bing Crosby in the enormously popular *The Bells of St. Mary's*; played straight man to Abbott and Costello in one of their best films, *The Naughty Nineties*, as a riverboat captain; and popped up briefly as a storekeeper in *The Yearling*. His role as James Stewart's slightly befuddled but kindly guardian angel Clarence, in *It's a Wonderful Life*, was prime Travers and the part that would bring him lasting screen immortality. Following some much smaller parts he quietly retired.

Screen: 1933: Reunion in Vienna; Another Language; My Weakness; The Invisible Man; **1934:** Death Takes a Holiday; Born to Be Bad; The Party's Over; Ready for Love; **1935:** Maybe It's Love; After Office Hours; Four Hours to Kill; Escapade; Seven Keys to Baldpate; Pursuit; Captain Hurricane; **1936:** Too Many Parents; **1938:** The Sisters; **1939:** You Can't Get Away With Murder; Dark Victory; Stanley and Livingstone; On Borrowed Time; Dodge City; The Rains Came; Remember?; **1940:** The Primrose Path; Edison, the Man; Anne of Windy Poplars; Wyoming; **1941:** High Sierra; The Bad Man; A Girl, a Guy, and a Gob; I'll Wait for You; Ball of Fire; **1942:** Mrs. Miniver; Pierre of the Plains; Random Harvest; **1943:** Shadow of a Doubt; The Moon Is Down; Madame Curie; **1944:** None Shall Escape; Dragon Seed; The Very Thought of You; **1945:** Thrill of a Romance; The Naughty Nineties; The Bells of St. Mary's; **1946:** Gallant Journey; The Yearling; It's a Wonderful Life; **1948:** The Flame; Beyond Glory; **1949:** The Girl from Jones Beach.

NY Stage: 1917: The Pipes of Pan; **1918:** A Pair of Petticoats; The Betrothal; **1919:** The Faithful; **1920:** The Power of Darkness; Jane Clegg; Treasure; Heartbreak House; **1921:** Liliom; Cloister; **1922:** He Who Gets Slapped; From Morn To Midnight; R.U.R.; **1923:** Windows; The Failures; Saint Joan; **1925:** Caesar and Cleopatra; Arms and The Man; **1926:** The Chief Thing; At Mrs. Beam's; Pygmalion; **1927:** The Brothers Karamazov; Right You Are — If You Think You Are; The Doctor's Dilemma; **1928:** Marco Millions; Volpone; **1929:** The Camel Through the Needle's Eye; **1930:** A Month in the Country; **1931:** Getting Married; Reunion in Vienna; **1932:** The Good Earth; **1936:** You Can't Take It With You.

ARTHUR TREACHER

BORN: BRIGHTON, ENGLAND, JULY 23, 1894. DIED: DECEMBER 14, 1975.

Long of face and tall of body, with crisp diction and a snobby air of disdain about him, Arthur Treacher became pigeon-holed as Hollywood idea of the perfect English butler and so the image stuck. Following military service during World War I, he took up acting in England before moving to the United States in 1926, where he made his Broadway bow in *The Great Temptations*. While appearing onstage he made his first film, *The Battle of Paris* (shot in Astoria, NY) and then came to Hollywood in 1934. There he did his first butler stint, in *Fashions of 1934*, after which he was the Donkeyman in *David Copperfield*; an agitator in *Cardinal Richelieu*; a sleep-inducing colonel in *The Daring Young Man*; Ninny's Tomb in Warners delightful rendering of *A Midsummer Night's Dream*; Alison Skipworth's flunky, on the trail of a valuable jeweled horn, in *Satan Met a*

Lady; and pin-headed Sir Evelyn Oakleigh in *Anything Goes*, just of a sampling of the sort of parts he did when he wasn't carrying a serving tray or answering a doorbell. In 1936 he was cast as the savviest of all butlers in 20th Century-Fox's "B" film *Thank You, Jeeves*, receiving top-billing as the manservant and brainpower behind David Niven as irresponsible playboy Bertie Wooster. This film did nicely enough to rate a sequel, *Step Lively, Jeeves*, which helped establish Treacher as the one to beat when playing the gentleman's gentleman. Fox kept him around to play mostly variations of the same kind of part, although he did have a nice moment dancing with Shirley Temple in *The Little Princess*. During the 1950s he turned his attention to theater and television and only came back to films once, to play the ruffled Constable in Disney's *Mary Poppins*. He became a familiar face afterwards as Merv Griffin's dryly acerbic talk show sidekick and kept his name alive years after his death, having leased it to a popular fast food fish and chips restaurant chain.

Screen: 1929: The Battle of Paris; 1934: Fashions of 1934; Desirable; Gambling Lady; The Key; Riptide; Madame Du Barry; The Captain Hates the Sea; Here Comes the Groom; Hollywood Party; Forsaking All Others; 1935: Bordertown; The Woman in Red; Orchids to You; Magnificent Obsession; The Nitwits; Going Highbrow; No More Ladies; David Copperfield; Cardinal Richilieu; I Live My Life; Personal Maid's Secret; Bright Lights; Curly Top; Go Into Your Dance; Remember Last Night?; Let's Live Tonight; The Daring Young Man; Splendor; Hitch-Hike Lady; A Midsummer Night's Dream; 1936: Mister Cinderella; Stowaway; The Case Against Mrs. Ames; Hearts Divided; Satan Met a Lady; Under Your Spell; Anything Goes; Thank You, Jeeves; 1937: Heidi; Step Lively, Jeeves; You Can't Have Everything; Thin Ice; She Had to Eat; 1938: Mad About Music; My Lucky Star; Always in Trouble; Up the River; 1939: Bridal Suite; Barricade; The Little Princess; 1940: Irene; Brother Rat and a Baby; 1942: Star-Spangled Rhythm; 1943: The Amazing Mrs. Holliday; Forever and a Day; 1944: Chip Off the Old Block; In Society; 1945: National Velvet; Swing Out, Sister; Delightfully Dangerous; That's the Spirit; 1947: Slave Girl; Fun on a Weekend; 1948: The Countess of Monte Cristo; 1949: That Midnight Kiss; 1950: Love That Brute; 1964: Mary Poppins.

NY Stage: 1926: The Great Temptations; 1928: The Madcap; The Silent House; 1931: Colonel Satan; Wonder Bar; The School for Scandal; The Cat and the Fiddle; 1940: Panama Hattie; 1943: Ziegfeld Follies; 1949: Caesar and Cleopatra; 1950: Getting Married; 1958: Back to Methuselah; 1959: The Fighting Cock.

Select TV: 1950: Uncle Dynamite (sp); 1951: A Christmas Carol (sp); 1952: The Room Next Door (sp); It's a Small World (sp); 1953: Mr. Pettengill Here (sp); 1954: Tom O'Shanter (sp); Alice in Wonderland (sp); 1956: Down You Go (series); 1960: The Enchanted (sp); 1961: You're in the Picture (series); 1965–72: The Merv Griffin Show (series).

CLAIRE TREVOR

(Claire Wemlinger) Born: New York, NY, March 8, 1908. ed: AADA. Died: April 8, 2000.

Unlike most stars, Claire Trevor did not have great distinction to her features, which turned out to be a blessing. Instead of being sold on her looks, people hired her to act and this she did very well indeed, carving out a niche in supporting parts in "A" films and leads in programmers, usually playing tough ladies who weren't as hard as they thought they were. She started acting with stock companies in Ann Arbor, Michigan, and Southampton, New York, between which she filmed some shorts

for Vitagraph in Astoria, NY. Her Broadway bow was in *Whistling in the Dark*, in 1932, followed by *The Party's Over*, and it was during the run of the latter that Fox offered her a contract. They launched her in two George O'Brien westerns, *Life in the Raw* and *The Last Trail*, then made her a reporter opposite Spencer Tracy in *The Mad Game*. Next up were three with James Dunn: *Jimmy and Sally*; *Hold That Girl*, in which she played a reporter again, and, this being the early 1930s, tossed off one-liners with the sort of sass that made that era famous for characters like this; and *Baby Take a Bow*, in which Shirley Temple was added to the mix. Fox saw her as a "B" star and so she carried such things as *Elinor Norton*, as a woman married to the insanely jealous Hugh Williams; *Black Sheep*, as a shipboard dancer; *Star for a Night*, as a chorus girl trying to hide her life from her blind mother Jane Darwell; *Career Woman*, as an honest lawyer teamed with a flamboyant one, Michael Whalen; and *One Mile from Heaven*, which brought up the intriguing possibility of a black woman giving birth to a white child, with Trevor as a reporter investigating the matter. When she did get into higher-budgeted productions it meant playing secondary roles, as she did in *To Mary — With Love*, supporting Myrna Loy, and the best-known of her Fox films, *Dante's Inferno*, as Spencer Tracy's worried wife.

Her big chance came off the lot, when Goldwyn borrowed her to play Humphrey Bogart's ex-girlfriend for *Dead End*. In a terrific cast she was the only one to receive an Oscar nomination, for her show-stopping scene when Bogie realizes that she is now a prostitute, and a sickly one to boot. Her contract at Fox ended with *Walking Down Broadway*, in 1938, and she went to Warners to play opposite Bogart again, in *The Amazing Dr. Clitterhouse*, and to portray a saloon girl in the Old West, in *Valley of the Giants*, both of which were a step up from the budgets she was accustomed to back at Fox. She returned to that studio at that point to play second fiddle to the Dionne Quintuplets in *Five of a Kind*, which did not indicate much faith in that Oscar nomination. However, director John Ford invited her to go west and, fortunately, she accepted, because the film was *Stagecoach*, and it helped bring more prestige to that genre than any other western of its day. Trevor was solid as the toughened floozy, driven out of town, who falls for heroic gunslinger John Wayne, and this would be the role that would most readily bring her name to mind with the passing of the years.

Not surprisingly, she and Wayne were put into two follow-ups, *Allegeny Uprising*, a Revolutionary war tale, and *Dark Command*, a fictionalized account of Quantrill's Raiders. She was fought over by William Holden and Glenn Ford in Columbia's "A" budget *Texas*, which must have been flattering for her because, for once, the leading lady was nearly a decade older than both of her leading men. However, at MGM, she was shunted into a secondary role in *Honky Tonk*, supporting the inferior Lana Turner. She was slipping back into second-features when she got into one of the major noir thrillers of the day, RKO's *Murder, My Sweet*, playing a shady, two-timing dame. It was clear that this was the genre she was born to be a part of. She remained a bad girl for *Johnny Angel*; went legit for Pat O'Brien, playing his fiancée, in *Crack-Up*; then essayed another great hard-edged doll role, in *Born to Kill*, getting very friendly with her sister's new husband, killer Lawrence Tierney. For all her hard and often under-appreciated work, she finally got her industry seal of approval, winning an Academy Award for her splendid work as Edward G. Robinson's broken-down, alcoholic moll in *Key Largo*. In the movie's most famous scene Trevor did a lousy rendition of "Moanin' Low," in hopes that Robinson would let her have the drink she so desperately craves. Now pretty much a supporting character player, she was an actress accused of the murder

Rosalind Russell committed in *The Velvet Touch*; Brian Donlvey's comical secretary in *The Lucky Stiff*; Sally Forrest's ambitious mom in *Hard, Fast and Beautiful*; and an aging beauty aboard the troubled plane in *The High and the Mighty*. For the last she received another Oscar nomination, though she herself thought little of the film. She continued to appear sporadically, an ever welcome presence, in such movies as *Marjorie Morningstar*, as Natalie Wood's mother; *Two Weeks in a Another Town*, as Edward G. Robinson's nagging wife; *How to Murder Your Wife*, similarly shrewish to Eddie Mayehoff; and then, after a long absence, as Sally Field's quipping mother in *Kiss Me Goodbye*. On television she won an Emmy for *Dodsworth*.

Screen: 1933: Life in the Raw; The Last Trail; The Mad Game; Jimmy and Sally; 1934: Hold That Girl; Wild Gold; Baby Take a Bow; Elinor Norton; 1935: Spring Tonic; Black Sheep; Dante's Inferno; Navy Wife; My Marriage; 1936: The Song and Dance Man; Human Cargo; To Mary — With Love; Star for a Night; 15 Maiden Lane; Career Woman; 1937: Time Out for Romance; King of Gamblers; One Mile from Heaven; Dead End; Second Honeymoon; Big Town Girl; 1938: Walking Down Broadway; The Amazing Dr. Clitterhouse; Valley of the Giants; Five of a Kind; 1939: Stagecoach; I Stole a Million; Allegheny Uprising; 1940: Dark Command; 1941: Texas; Honky Tonk; 1942: The Adventures of Martin Eden; Crossroads; Street of Chance; 1943: The Desperadoes; Good Luck, Mr. Yates; The Woman of the Town; 1944: Murder, My Sweet; 1945: Johnny Angel; 1946: Crack-Up; The Bachelor's Daughters; 1947: Born to Kill; 1948: Raw Deal; Key Largo; The Velvet Touch; The Babe Ruth Story; 1949: The Lucky Stiff; 1950: Borderline; 1951: Best of the Bad Men; Hard, Fast and Beautiful; 1952: Hoodlum Empire; My Man and I; Stop, You're Killing Me; 1953: The Stranger Wore a Gun; 1954: The High and the Mighty; 1955: Man Without a Star; Lucy Gallant; 1956: The Mountain; 1958: Marjorie Morningstar; 1962: Two Weeks in Another Town; 1963: The Stripper; 1965: How to Murder Your Wife; 1967: The Cape Town Affair; 1982: Kiss Me Goodbye.

NY Stage: 1932: Whistling in the Dark; 1933: The Party's Over; 1947: The Big Two.

Select TV: 1953: Alias Nora Hall (sp); 1954: Foggy Night (sp); 1955: No Sad Songs for Me (sp); 1956: Foolproof (sp), If You Knew Elizabeth (sp), Dodsworth (sp); 1959: Happy Hill (sp); 1960: The Revolt of Judge Lloyd (sp); 1987: Norman Rockwell's Breaking Home Ties.

TOM TRYON

BORN: HARTFORD, CT, JANUARY 14, 1926.
ED: YALE UNIV. DIED: SEPTEMBER 4, 1991.

Leaving behind a movie career that found him involved with some major endeavors, though his own contributions seldom rated much favorable mention, stoically square-jawed Tom Tryon turned to the typewriter and became a best-selling author. Initially hoping to be an artist, he went from scene painting to acting while working at the Cape Playhouse on Cape Cod. From there he studied at the Neighborhood Playhouse, which led to him joining Jose Ferrer's rep company, appearing in *Cyrano de Bergerac* and *Richard III*. Paramount and Hal Wallis signed him to a joint contract and he was introduced in a murder triangle that went bust, *The Scarlet Hour*. He fared better as one of the *Three Violent People*, as Charlton Heston's embittered one-armed brother, and in *I Married a Monster from Outer Space*, a well-done sci-fi offering with a dime-store title, that required him to be zombie-like as the husband possessed by aliens.

Alternating between commitments to Disney and Fox, he did a mini series, *Tales of Texas John Slaughter*, and a mild tale of monkeys and astronauts, *Moon Pilot*, for the former; and the Biblical epic, *The Story of Ruth*, and an unsuccessful war film, *Marines, Let's Go!*, for the latter. His most important screen chance to score came when director Otto Preminger selected him to carry the lengthy religious epic *The Cardinal*. The result of the hellish shoot was hardly worth the trouble, for Tryon just didn't have the stuff to standout above better actors like Burgess Meredith and John Huston, and wound up with some fairly chilly notices. He was last seen on the big screen starring in *Color Me Dead*, a remake of *D.O.A.*, as a poisoned man seeking his killer. Sitting down to write himself a script, he wound up changing it to a novel and published the supernatural thriller *The Other*, which became a bestseller in 1971. He adapted and executive produced a fairly well-received film version the following year and then left movie making behind for the more lucrative and fulfilling world of fiction writing, which included the novels *Lady* and *Crowned Heads*, the latter consisting of four bizarre tales of Hollywood careers gone sour.

Screen: 1956: The Scarlet Hour; Screaming Eagles; Three Violent People; 1957: The Unholy Wife; 1958: I Married a Monster from Outer Space; 1960: The Story of Ruth; 1961: Marines, Let's Go!; 1962: Moon Pilot; The Longest Day; 1963: The Cardinal; 1965: In Harm's Way; The Glory Guys; 1969: Color Me Dead.

NY Stage: 1952: Wish You Were Here; 1953: Cyrano de Bergerac; Richard III.

Select TV: 1956: Not What She Pretended (sp); The Fall of the House of Usher (sp); 1957: Young Man from Kentucky (sp); Charley's Aunt (sp); Wuthering Heights (sp); 1958: Nobody Will Ever Know (sp); Strange Witness (sp); 1958–61: Tales of Texas John Slaughter (ms); 1965: Mr. Governess (sp); 1967: Winchester '73; Wipeout (sp).

FORREST TUCKER

BORN: PLAINFIELD, IN, FEBRUARY 12, 1919.
ED: GEORGE WASHINGTON UNIV.
DIED: OCTOBER 25, 1986.

One of those lucky actors who essentially stumbled into show business and never had to look back, Forrest Tucker gave Hollywood a try in the early 1940s, figuring correctly that his acceptable looks might land him some small roles. Within a year he found himself carrying a PCR quickie, *Emergency Landing*, and then under contract to Columbia, who made him part of their "B" stock company. After returning from the war, the budgets did not increase but his roles did, including *Dangerous Business*, in which he played an attorney, and *Renegades*, as one of Larry Parks's outlaw brothers. The last set the direction for most of his upcoming roles and he became a familiar western performer in such programmers as *Adventures in Silverado*, as a hooded highwayman; *The Last Bandit*, as Bill Elliott's no-good brother; *The Nevadan*, being dogged by marshal Randolph Scott; *California Passage*, as a saloon owner fighting buddy Jim Davis for Adele Mara; and *Warpath*, as one of the men who killed Edmond O'Brien's fiancee. In between these he bullied Gregory Peck over his hunting dog in *The Yearling*, and had a good role as one of the Marines who clashes with sergeant John Wayne in the hit *Sands of Iwo Jima*. During the 1950s, for a change of pace, he went overseas to England where he was an American romancing Scottish Margaret Lockwood in *Trouble in the Glen*, and carried some sci-fi films, *Cosmic Monster*, *The Crawling Eye*, and *The*

Abominable Snowman of the Himalayas. Back in America, he had the pivotal but brief role as the Southerner who makes Rosalind Russell a very rich widow in *Auntie Mame*, and then became well known to television viewers for the spoof sitcom *F Troop*. In later years he was principally a television actor, though he did return to play the villain in *Chisum*, opposite former co-star John Wayne, and to do a lead in the little-seen *The Wild McCullochs*, as a Texas millionaire.

Screen: 1940: The Westerner; 1941: Emergency Landing; New Wine; Honolulu Lu; Canal Zone; 1942: Tramp, Tramp, Tramp; Shut My Big Mouth; Parachute Nurse; The Spirit of Stanford; Keeper of the Flame; Boston Blackie Goes Hollywood; My Sister Eileen; Submarine Raider; Counter Espionage; 1946: The Man Who Dared; Talk About a Lady; Renegades; Dangerous Business; Never Say Goodbye; The Yearling; 1947: Gunfighters; 1948: Adventures in Silverado; The Plunderers; Coroner Creek; Two Guys from Texas; 1949: The Big Cat; Brimstone; The Last Bandit; Sands of Iwo Jima; Hellfire; 1950: The Nevadan; Rock Island Trail; California Passage; 1951: Fighting Coast Guard; Oh! Susanna; Crosswinds; The Wild Blue Yonder; Flaming Feather; Warpath; 1952: Montana Belle; Hoodlum Empire; Bugles in the Afternoon; Hurricane Smith; Ride the Man Down; 1953: Pony Express; San Antone; Flight Nurse; 1954: Jubilee Trail; Laughing Anne; Trouble in the Glen; 1955: Break in the Circle; Rage at Dawn; Finger Man; The Vanishing American; Night Freight; Paris Follies of 1956/Fresh from Paris; 1956: Stagecoach to Fury; Three Violent People; 1957: The Quiet Gun; The Deerslayer; The Abominable Snowman of the Himalayas; 1958: Girl in the Woods; The Cosmic Monster/The Strange World of Planet X; The Crawling Eye/The Trollenberg Terror; Auntie Mame; Gunsmoke in Tucson; Fort Massacre; 1959: Counterplot; 1966: Don't Worry, We'll Think of a Title; 1968: The Night They Raided Minsky's; 1970: Barquero; Chisum; 1972: Cancel My Reservation; 1975: The Wild McCullochs; 1977: Final Chapter — Walking Tall; The Wackiest Wagon Train in the West (dtv); 1984: A Rare Breed (filmed 1981); 1986: Thunder Run; 1987: Outtakes.

NY Stage: 1964: Fair Game For Lovers.

Select TV: 1950: The Hoosier School-Master (sp); 1954: Blizzard-Bound (sp); 1955–56: Crunch and Des (series); 1956: Rebuke Me Not (sp); 1957: Member in Good Standing (sp); The Quiet Stranger (sp); The Softest Music (sp); 1958: The Cold Touch (sp); 1965–67: F Troop (series); 1967: A Boy Called Nuthin' (sp); 1971: Alias Smith and Jones; 1972: Welcome Home, Johnny Bristol; Footsteps; 1973: Jarrett; Dusty's Trail (series); 1975: The Ghost Busters (series); 1976–77: Once an Eagle (ms); 1977: The Incredible Rocky Mountain Race; 1978: Black Beauty (ms); A Real American Hero; 1979: The Rebels; 1981: The Adventures of Huckleberry Finn; 1982–83: Filthy Rich (series); 1983: Blood Feud; 1986: Timestalkers.

SONNY TUFTS

(BOWEN CHARLTON TUFTS III) BORN: BOSTON, MA, JULY 16, 1911. ED: YALE UNIV. DIED: JUNE 4, 1970.

Big, blond, and missing that special something that separates the real talents from those shuffling unmemorably and innocuously through their careers, Sonny Tufts had not intended to be an actor at first, hoping to be either a bandleader or opera singer. Instead he sang standards, both in revues and in supper clubs, before traveling to Hollywood to take a screen test. Paramount liked what they saw and cast him as the Marine private in love with nurse Paulette Goddard in one of the studio's biggest patri-

otic offerings of 1943, *So Proudly We Hail!* The studio pictured him in lighter roles and gave him one of the twin Betty Huttons at the fade out of *Here Comes the Waves*; cashed in on his first role with the shamelessly titled *I Love a Soldier*, opposite Goddard again; slapped the name of Pug Prentice on him in their nostalgic *Miss Susie Slagle's*; and had him lose Olivia de Havilland to Ray Milland in *The Well-Groomed Bride*. In a more serious vein, he was one of the bad guys in the remake of *The Virginian*, and flew mail in *Blaze of Noon*, as a character that couldn't help but provoke unintentional laughs from latter-day audiences, in so much as he was named Ronald McDonald. His Paramount contract ended with one of Betty Hutton's least popular movies, *Cross My Heart*, and, by the early 1950s, he was landing in some trouble off screen, including an arrest for drunkenness. By that point few of the major studios had much interest in his services. Instead, he ended up in such independents as *The Gift Horse*, and the pricelessly stupid *Cat Women of the Moon*, as an astronaut who lands on a planet of telepathic babes. Amid these "B" assignments he did show up in a big hit, as the man Tom Ewell is jealous of, in *The Seven Year Itch*, but it did not revitalize his career. He spent most of the remainder of the 1960s on television, where his name became something of a cruel punchline for comedians, a fact not helped by Tufts concluding his career in a picture called *Cottonpickin' Chickenpickers*.

Screen: 1939: Ambush; 1943: So Proudly We Hail!; Government Girl; 1944: Here Come the Waves; In the Meantime, Darling; I Love a Soldier; 1945: Bring on the Girls; Duffy's Tavern; Miss Susie Slagle's; 1946: Swell Guy; The Virginian; The Well-Groomed Bride; Cross My Heart; 1947: Variety Girl; Blaze of Noon; Easy Come, Easy Go; 1948: The Untamed Breed; 1949: The Crooked Way; Easy Living; 1952: The Gift Horse/Glory at Sea; 1953: No Escape; Run for the Hills; 1954: Cat Women of the Moon/Rocket to the Moon; Serpent Island; 1955: The Seven Year Itch; 1956: Come Next Spring; 1957: The Parson and the Outlaw; 1965: Town Tamer; 1967: Cottonpickin' Chickenpickers.

NY Stage: 1938: Who's Who; 1939: Sing for Your Supper.

Select TV: 1956: A Tale of Two Citizens (sp); 1964: Have Girls — Will Travel (sp); 1968: Land's End (sp).

LANA TURNER

(JULIA JEAN MILDRED FRANCES TURNER) BORN: WALLACE, ID, FEBRUARY 8, 1921. RAISED IN CA. DIED: JUNE 29, 1995.

Manufactured for our viewing pleasure, Lana Turner was a bonafide movie star, her face and name splashed across fan magazines until she became synonymous with the kind of superficial glitz that was in abundance during the studio era. Although she remained in the public eye for many decades, she was remembered more for her persona rather than her talent, being one of the few stars that hardly seemed much more advanced in her acting abilities at the end of her career than she'd been at the beginning. Despite the legends, she was *not* discovered sipping a Coke at Schwab's Drugstore, but at some other, less famous establishment in Los Angeles, after she and her mother had moved there in the mid-1930s. The man who had noticed just how beautiful and sexy Turner already looked at the age of 15 was *Hollywood Reporter* publisher Billy Wilkerson, and he got her signed with a talent agency who in turn got her a bit in *A Star is Born* and a test with director Mervyn LeRoy. As a result, she was cast as the very alluring teen who becomes the murder victim in *They Won't Forget*. Her initial appearance on screen, sauntering provocatively around town in a tight sweater, caused an immediate and favorable reaction, prompting the press machines to start working overtime. MGM signed her to a contract in 1938 and cast her as the spoiled girl who catches Mickey Rooney's eye in *Love Finds Andy Hardy*; one of the attendees of *Dramatic School*; a flirt who gets Lew Ayres's libido kicking in *Calling Dr. Kildare*; and the title role in *Dancing Co-Ed*, which featured bandleader Artie Shaw who became the first (1940–41) of seven husbands.

MGM decided to elevate her into the big time with their starry extravaganza, *Ziegfeld Girl*, giving her plenty of melodramatic moments, as the show biz hopeful who crashes and burns, but this hokum only stressed how far she had to go even to come within miles of co-stars Judy Garland and James Stewart. Undeterred, the studio kept her in top-of-the-line productions, casting her the decent lady who falls under the charms of Clark Gable in *Honky Tonk*. This did quite well and prompted further pairings of the two, though this was, by default, the best of them. In the meantime, she was cast not as the bad girl, as expected, but the refined one, in the mediocre remake of *Dr. Jekyll and Mr. Hyde*; got to go bonkers as Robert Taylor's moll in *Johnny Eager*; and was back with Gable for *Somewhere I'll Find You*, as Hollywood's idea of a war correspondent. Following a leave of absence to have a baby, she returned with a comedic triangle, *Marriage Is a Private Affair*, and a woman-in-the-military flag waver, *Keep Your Powder Dry*, both of which were pretty much sold on her name, though the box-office returns weren't anything special. No matter, for she followed them with six big money-makers in a row, starting with the all-star, *Week-end at the Waldorf*, a semi-remake of *Grand Hotel*, with Turner taking over the Joan Crawford role. Biggest of the bunch was *The Postman Always Rings Twice*, in which she played a dangerous femme fatale who convinces John Garfield to murder her husband. This famous noir has always suffered in comparison to the similar and better *Double Indemnity*, as does Turner when stacked up against Barbara Stanwyck. Despite this, at the time it brought her some of her best reviews. The hits continued with *Green Dolphin Street*, a rambling epic of old New Zealand with an earthquake thrown in to liven things up; *Cass Timberlane*, a forgettable soap opera in which she was a social inferior married to once-respected judge Spencer Tracy; *Homecoming*, another film with Gable, as the nurse who woos him away from wife Anne Baxter while they're stitching up the wounded on the battlefront; and *The Three Musketeers*, in which she unfairly commanded top-billing, as Milday de Winter, since she was one of the weaker aspect of a generally colorful film.

With the coming of the 1950s, she was directed by George Cukor in the melodrama *A Life of Her Own*, though all the attention went to supporting player Ann Dvorak; then did a pair of musicals, although she couldn't sing a note: *Mr. Imperium*, an attempt to cash in on Ezio Pinza's success onstage in *South Pacific*, which flopped; and the remake of *The Merry Widow*, which actually did passable business. The high point during this period was undoubtedly director Vincente Minnelli's engrossing look at the movie industry, *The Bad and the Beautiful*, where, as the difficult, alcoholic movie star battling with self-involved Kirk Douglas, Turner gave the closest thing she would ever give to a good performance. Afterward, she went right back to the sort of superficial gloss she'd been doing before with *Latin Lovers*, which brought her back to director Mervyn LeRoy to no avail; *The Flame and the Flesh*, a hopeless love triangle set in Italy; *Betrayed*, the last and least of her teamings with Gable; *The Prodigal*, a classic bit of 1950s kitsch, in which she played the High Priestess of Love, acting against a performer even more limited then herself, Edmund Purdom, and making her dramatic exit by

falling into a pit of flames; and her last for the studio, *Diane*, set in 16th century France and proving for once and for all that she knew how to wear gorgeous costumes. Elsewhere she paired off with John Wayne for Warners's *The Sea Chase*, and with Richard Burton for *The Rains of Ranchipur*, Fox's ill-advised remake of *The Rains Came*. Around this time she wrapped up marriage number four (1953–57) to actor Lex Barker. Rescue came when she landed the lead in *Peyton Place*, the much-anticipated film of what had become the hottest bestseller of all time. As small-town mom Constance MacKenzie, trying to hide the secret of her daughter's illegitimacy, she was the same old Lana but, since this was a gigantic success and the Academy went overboard showering Oscar nominations upon this banal offering, Turner got one as well.

Its financial success was further enhanced by Turner's involvement in one of Hollywood's most famous and shocking scandals, when her teenage daughter stabbed her mother's latest lover, gangster Johnny Stompanato, who had abused mom one time too many. Over the years there would be many theories on just what had happened that night and who was really responsible for the crime, adding a certain juice and mystery to the Turner name. In the meantime, she kept churning out the soap operas with *Another Time, Another Place*, opposite a very young Sean Connery; and then producer Ross Hunter's ultimate Universal gloss job of the era, *Imitation of Life*, an inferior re-do of the earlier Claudette Colbert film, with the character changed from business woman to actress for Turner, which therefore made it a stretch to play. There was also some interest in the somewhat more enjoyable *Portrait in Black*, in which she planned her husband's murder with lover Anthony Quinn, and marginal interest in two mild comedies, *Bachelor in Paradise*, with Bob Hope, and *Who's Got the Action?*, with Dean Martin. Fans, however, weren't showing up for such passé melodramas as *By Love Possessed*, as an unhappily married drunk; *Love Has Many Faces*, where she ended up getting gored by a bull; or the umpteenth remake of *Madame X*, which she certainly threw herself into whole hog, as the unfaithful mother doomed to suffer for her sins. By the time the last one was released, in 1966, Turner's style of arch emoting and this kind of slick hokum was really falling out of favor with contemporary critics who were looking towards actors with less concern for their appearance. Not surprisingly, she turned to television, but her series, *The Survivors*, made a fast exit. Four times she returned to theatrical features: *The Big Cube*, ending up in the nut house after accidentally taking LSD; *Persecution*, as Ralph Bates's domineering, cat-crazy mama; *Bittersweet Love*, confessing to an affair with the father of her son-in-law; and *Witches Brew*, as a veteran spell caster. Only the most slavishly devoted caught up with any of these during their aborted runs. She did show up briefly on the popular nighttime serial *Falcon Crest*, which was the only really appropriate outlet in existence by the 1980s for the sort of superficial dramatics that had been her specialty.

Screen: 1937: A Star Is Born; They Won't Forget; Topper; The Great Garrick; **1938:** The Adventures of Marco Polo; Four's a Crowd; Love Finds Andy Hardy; Rich Man, Poor Girl; Dramatic School; **1939:** Calling Dr. Kildare; These Glamour Girls; Dancing Co-Ed; **1940:** Two Girls on Broadway; We Who Are Young; **1941:** Ziegfeld Girl; Dr. Jekyll and Mr. Hyde; Honky Tonk; **1942:** Johnny Eager; Somewhere I'll Find You; **1943:** The Youngest Profession; Slightly Dangerous; Du Barry Was a Lady; **1944:** Marriage Is a Private Affair; **1945:** Keep Your Powder Dry; Week-end at the Waldorf; **1946:** The Postman Always Rings Twice; **1947:** Green Dolphin Street; Cass Timberlane; **1948:** Homecoming; The Three Musketeers; **1950:** A Life of Her

Own; **1951:** Mr. Imperium; **1952:** The Merry Widow; The Bad and the Beautiful; **1953:** Latin Lovers; **1954:** The Flame and the Flesh; Betrayed; **1955:** The Prodigal; The Sea Chase; Diane; The Rains of Ranchipur; **1957:** Peyton Place; **1958:** The Lady Takes a Flyer; Another Time, Another Place; **1959:** Imitation of Life; **1960:** Portrait in Black; **1961:** By Love Possessed; Bachelor in Paradise; **1962:** Who's Got the Action?; **1965:** Love Has Many Faces; **1966:** Madame X; **1969:** The Big Cube; **1975:** Persecution; **1976:** Bittersweet Love; **1985:** Witches' Brew (filmed 1978).

Select TV: **1969–70:** The Survivors (series); **1982–83:** Falcon Crest (series).

BEN TURPIN

(BERNARD TURPIN) BORN: NEW ORLEANS, LA, SEPTEMBER 17, 1869. RAISED IN NEW YORK, NY. DIED: JULY 1, 1940.

Back when one's physical impairment could be used for comedy, Ben Turpin got a lot of laughs because his pixilated expression was emphasized by his crossed-eyes, a trait that kept him famous long after other silent movie comedians had passed into obscurity. It was speculated that his affliction came from damage done to his optic nerve while throwing himself about in vaudeville. In any case, his knockabout act proved most appealing to the Essany company and he signed with them as early as 1907, doing one-reelers (most of which cannot be verified as there are no records of their existence). Taking a break to return to the theatre, he was soon back at Essany, though not as a star, instead supporting Wallace Beery in his "Sweedie" shorts; Bronco Billy Anderson in his "Snakeville" series; and Charlie Chaplin in the two-reelers "His New Job" and "A Night Out." Going over to Mutual, Turpin was partnered with Paddy McGuire for some films and then with Rube Miller in such titles as "Doctoring a Leak" and "He Died and He Didn't." Real stardom came at last when the king of comedy producers, Mack Sennett, signed him up in 1917. Turpin became famous for his send-ups of current hit films, including "Three Foolish Weeks" and "The Reel Virginian," as well as starring in the features *A Small Town Idol*, about a nobody who goes west and becomes a movie star, and *The Shriek of Araby*, a spoof of the Rudolph Valentino craze. By the time of the talkie era, Turpin, who was demanding, eccentric, and never easy to work with, had gone into semi-retirement. When he did show up in talking films it was in small parts, including the delightfully surreal *Million Dollar Legs*, as a mysterious black-clad spy, and two tributes to the silent film era, *Keystone Hotel* and *Hollywood Cavalcade*.

Screen (shorts): **1909:** Ben Gets a Duck and Is Ducked; Midnight Disturbance; Mr. Flip; **1914:** Sweedie and the Lord; Sweedie and the Double Exposure; Sweedie's Skate; Sweedie Springs a Surprise; The Fickleness of Sweedie; Sweedie Learns to Swim; She Landed a Big One; Sweedie and the Troublemaker; Sweedie at the Fair; Madame Double X; Golf Champion Chick Evans Links with Sweedie; **1915:** Sweedie's Suicide; Sweedie and Her Dog; Two Hearts That Beat as Ten; Sweedie's Hopeless Love; Sweedie Goes to College; Love and Trouble; Sweedie Learns to Ride; Sweedie's Hero; Clubman's Wager; Curiosity; A Coat Tale; Others Started But Sophie Finished; Sophie and the Fakir; A Quiet Little Game; The Merry Models; Snakeville's Hen Medic; Snakeville's Champion; Snakeville's Debutantes; Snakeville's Twins; It Happened in Snakeville; How Slippery Slim Saw the Show; Two Bold Bad Men; The Undertaker's Wife; A Bunch of

Matches; The Bell-Hop; Versus Sledge Hammers; Too Much Turkey; His New Job; A Night Out; The Champion; A Christmas Revenge; A Burlesque of Carmen; **1916:** A Safe Proposition; Some Bravery; A Waiting Game; Taking the Count; When Papa Died; National Nuts; Nailing on the Lid; Just for a Kid; Lost and Found; Bungling Bill's Dress Suit; His Blowout; The Delinquent Bridegrooms; The Iron Mitt; Hired and Fired; A Deep Sea Liar; For Ten Thousand Bucks; Some Liars; The Stolen Booking; Doctoring a Leak; Poultry a la Mode; Ducking a Discord; He Did and He Didn't; Picture Pirates; Shot in the Fracas; Jealous Jolts; The Wicked City; **1917:** A Circus Cyclone; Masked Mirth; Bucking the Tiger; Caught in the End; Frightened Flirts; His Bogus Boast; A Studio Stampede; The Musical Marvel; The Butcher's Nightmare; When Ben Bolted; A Bedroom Blunder; Cactus Nell; Sole Mates; Lost — A Cook; The Pawnbroker's Heart; Oriental Love; A Clever Dummy; Roping Her Romeo; Are Waitresses Safe?; Taming Target Center; **1918:** She Loved Him Plenty; Sheriff Nell's Tussle; Saucy Madeline; The Battle Royal; Love Loops the Loop; Two Tough Tenderfeet; Whose Little Wife Are You?; Hide and Seek Detectives; **1919:** Cupid's Day Off; No Mother to Guide Him; When Love Is Blind; Salome vs. Shenandoah; The Dentist; A Lady's Tailor; East Lynne with Variations; Sleuths; Uncle Tom Without a Cabin; **1920:** The Star Boarder; The Quack Doctor; You Wouldn't Believe It; **1921:** Love's Outcast; Love and Doughnuts; **1922:** Bright Eyes; Step Forward; Home-Made Movies; **1923:** Where's My Wandering Boy Tonight?; Pitfalls of a Big City; Asleep at the Switch; The Daredevil; **1924:** Romeo and Juliet; Ten Dollars or Ten Days; Three Foolish Weeks; Yukon Jake; The Hollywood Kid; The Reel Virginian; **1925:** The Marriage Circus; The Wild Goose Chaser; Raspberry Romance; **1926:** A Blonde's Revenge; The Prodigal Bridegroom; When a Man's a Prince; A Hollywood Hero; A Harem Knight; **1927:** Love's Languid Lure; Broke in China; Daddy Boy; The Jolly Jilter; The Pride of Pikeville; The Bull Fighter; **1928:** The Eyes Have It; **1931:** Our Wife; **1933:** Hollywood on Parade; Techno-Crazy; **1935:** Bring 'em Back a Lie.

Screen (features): **1919:** Yankee Doodle in Berlin; **1920:** Down on the Farm; Married Life; **1921:** Home Talent; A Small Town Idol; **1923:** The Shriek of Araby; Hollywood; **1925:** Hogan's Alley; **1926:** Steel Preferred; **1927:** The College Hero; **1928:** A Woman's Way; The Wife's Relations; **1929:** The Show of Shows; The Love Parade; **1930:** Swing High; **1931:** Cracked Nuts; Ambassador Bill; **1932:** Hypnotized; Million Dollar Legs; Make Me a Star; **1934:** Law of the Wild (serial); **1935:** Keystone Hotel; **1939:** Hollywood Cavalcade; **1940:** Saps at Sea.

RITA TUSHINGHAM

BORN: LIVERPOOL, ENGLAND, MARCH 14, 1940.

Waif-like, skinny, doe-eyed, and undeniably original, Rita Tushingham became one of the iconic figures of the dominant British cinema of the 1960s, but could not carry her status into the next decade. While a teenager, she joined a rep company in her home town of Liverpool and it was during this period that she answered an ad in a show business trade looking for a newcomer to star in the film version of the successful play, *A Taste of Honey*. Selected by director Tony Richardson to carry the load, she played the part of the lonely, ungainly girl, impregnated by a black sailor, who must escape her overbearing mother, as though it were written expressly for her. It became one of the key films in the era of gritty black and white working class dramas from England and Tushingham became an instant star. Her stardom was further enhanced by three other good films: *The Leather Boys*, in which she married motorcycle mechanic Colin Campbell but has trouble coping with his lifestyle; *Girl with Green Eyes*, as an immature young lady carrying on an affair with much older Peter Finch; and the hilarious *The Knack and How to Get It*, as the girl looking for a real romance while being hit on by sleazy Ray Brooks. Of course, these didn't make a tenth of what the grandiose epic *Doctor Zhivago* made, though her principal function in that film was to appear at the opening and the finale to hear the story of her parents, told by Alec Guinness. Soon afterwards her career started to slip with *The Trap*, in which she was stuck in Canada with Oliver Reed; *Smashing Time*, a goony, semimusical look at Mod London with Lynn Redgrave; *The Guru*, in which she played a hippie going to India; and the messy satire *The Bed-Sitting Room*, where she floundered about in a ruined England following a nuclear war. After that she kept busy onstage, while her films of the 1970s and 1980s were no longer imported to America as eagerly as they'd been before. Among those few that did cross the Atlantic were *The Housekeeper*, in which she had the title role, and *An Awfully Big Adventure*, where she had a brief bit, as the heroine's aunt.

Screen: 1961: A Taste of Honey; 1963: A Place to Go; The Leather Boys; 1964: Girl With Green Eyes; 1965: The Knack and How to Get It; Doctor Zhivago; 1966: The Trap; 1967: Smashing Time; 1968: Diamonds for Breakfast; 1969: The Guru; The Bed-Sitting Room; 1972: Straight on Till Morning/Dressed for Death; The Case of Laura C.; Where Do You Go from Here?; 1974: Instant Coffee; 1975: Rachel's Man; The Human Factor; Ragazzo di Borgata/Slow Boy (nUSr); 1977: Gran Bolito/Black Journal (nUSr); Pane, Burro e Marmelata/Bread, Butter and Marmelade (nUSr); 1978: Mysteries; 1982: Spaghetti House; 1984: A Dream to Believe/Flying; 1986: The Housekeeper/Judgment in Stone; 1988: Resurrected; Hard Days, Hard Nights; 1991: Paper Marriage; 1992: Rapture of Deceit; 1993: Desert Lynch; 1995: An Awfully Big Adventure; 1996: The Boy from Mercury; 1997: Under the Skin; 1999: Swing; 2001: Out of Depth.

Select TV: 1973: Situation/Slaughter Day; Little Red Riding Hood (sp); 1974: No Strings (series); 1976: The Search for Green Eyes; 1988: Bread (series); 1998: Spending Nights with Joan; 1990: Sunday Pursuit.

U

MIYOSHI UMEKI
BORN: OTARU, HOKKAIDO, JAPAN, APRIL 3, 1929.

The winsomely pretty, gentle-mannered Miyoshi Umeki became the first Asian performer to be bestowed with an Academy Award, but ended up with very few show business credits to her name despite this. She had been a radio and nightclub singer since she was a teenager and came to New York in the 1950s in hopes of expanding her audience. Arthur Godfrey put her on his television series for a spell and then her big break came when director Joshua Logan went looking for someone to play Red Buttons's tragic war bride in his film of the best-selling James Michener novel *Sayonara*. As the sweet wife who is so dismayed at the prejudice she encounters that she is willing to disfigure herself for her husband, Umeki proved that she could act. For her relatively small part she ended up with the Academy Award for Best Supporting Actress of 1957. For her follow-up she was given one of the key roles and star billing in the Rodgers and Hammerstein Broadway musical *Flower Drum Song*, as a mail order bride newly arrived in San Francisco. The same year that she repeated her part in the 1961 film version (taking a back seat to Nancy Kwan, who now received top billing), she was one of the geishas in *Cry for Happy*, a mild Glenn Ford comedy. Staying very much in support, she did two more movies and then let several years lapse before audiences saw her playing Mrs. Livingston, the kindly housekeeper to Bill Bixby and Brandon Cruz, on the television series version of *The Courtship of Eddie's Father*. (In the film, the part had been played by a Caucasian actress, Roberta Sherwood). After its cancellation, Umeki disappeared from the show business scene altogether. When a gathering of past Oscar-winners took place at the 1997 Academy Awards ceremony, she could not be located.

Screen: 1957: Sayonara; 1961: Cry for Happy; Flower Drum Song; 1962: The Horizontal Lieutenant; 1963: A Girl Named Tamiko.
NY Stage: 1958: Flower Drum Song.
Select TV: 1955: Arthur Godfrey and His Friends (series); 1962: The Teahouse of the August Moon (sp); 1969–72: The Courtship of Eddie's Father (series).

PETER USTINOV
BORN: LONDON, ENGLAND, APRIL 16, 1921.

The marvelously adept Peter Ustinov quickly established himself as the sort of show business personality who was at home doing just about anything. In addition to acting he directed, wrote novels, and authored plays, indulging in the serious and the comedic with equal fervor, though it is in drolly amusing, larger-than-life roles that audiences seemed to love him best. Born to Russian parents who had immigrated to London, he began studying acting while a teenager, making his professional bow in 1938, in a rep company production of *The Wood Demon*. There was a short film, "Hullo, Fame," and a semi-documentary, *Mein Kampf — My Crimes*, before he appeared in some full-length fictional motion pictures. In *The Goose Steps Out* and *One of Our Aircraft Is Missing*, he played German and Dutch characters respectively, thereby displaying, right off the bat, his penchant for accents. He had already penned some plays and got co-screenwriting credit for *The Way Ahead*, which he also acted in; then directed, wrote, and produced (but did not appear in), *School for Secrets/Secret Flight*, a war film, and *Vice Versa*, a comical fantasy in which a father and son switch personalities. Next up he shared credit as director with Michael Anderson on *Private Angelo*, in which Ustinov played an Italian soldier who wants nothing more than to stop fighting. Although it was notable that he'd done all of these films before he was even 30, none of them were greeted with more than a passing nod and hardly made him the "boy" genius that Orson Welles had been proclaimed under similar circumstances.

Ustinov was, in fact, pretty much an unknown name outside of England when he made his first international splash, with MGM's lavish spectacle, *Quo Vadis?* Following Charles Laughton's lead when that actor had played Nero on screen, Ustinov chewed acres of scenery and camped it up to the nth degree, adding a good deal of fun to the long-winded and generally mediocre proceedings, earning himself an Oscar nomination in the supporting category. He followed it with three more Hollywood productions, *Beau Brummell*, again stealing the show, as the Prince of

Wales; *The Egyptian*, a movie he particularly hated making, as Edmund Purdom's eye-patch-wearing servant; and *We're No Angels*, a would-be comedy about a trio of escaped cons, playing opposite Humphrey Bogart and Aldo Ray. Going foreign he did *Lola Montes*, the much-butchered Max Ophuls flop, in which he played a ringmaster. This was followed by three Italian co-productions that didn't travel overseas. Therefore it was his own play, *Romanoff and Juliet*, which he also acted in, in both New York and London, that kept his name before the general public during the late 1950s. Returning to spectacles, he ended up in one of the best — *Spartacus*, in which he wittily played the wily, selfish slave dealer who ends up making a heroic gesture in spite of himself. It was a massive hit and Ustinov won the Academy Award for Best Supporting Actor of 1960. That same year he was equally good as the Australian slacker who helps sheepherder Robert Mitchum and his family in another popular film, *The Sundowners*. Less well-received was the 1961 film version of *Romanoff and Juliet*, a very mild satire on Russian-U.S. relations, which looked just like another Universal comedy of the 1960s, what with Sandra Dee and John Gavin in the cast.

After this he reached his high-water mark as film director-writer-star with *Billy Budd*, magnificently dramatizing Herman Melville's novel for the screen and superbly playing the good-hearted but troubled captain who must deal with the enigmatic title character. Also terrific was his hilarious performance as the somewhat reluctant participant in the big heist in *Topkapi*, sweating and twitching to perfection, and getting himself a second Academy Award. Then came some slumps with the ultra-stupid *John Goldfarb, Please Come Home*, mugging without shame as a pea-brained Arabian king; and his own project, *Lady L*, in which he showed up for an extended cameo as a bumbling prince in this leaden, over-dressed farce. Top-billed he was *Blackbeard's Ghost*, a popular Disney comedy aimed expressly at the kids; was Elizabeth Taylor's cuckolded husband in the all-star disappointment *The Comedians*; and then paired off beautifully with Maggie Smith for the charming romantic comedy *Hot Millions*, which he helped script with Ira Wallach, earning an Oscar nomination in the writing department. Next up he was a bumbling Mexican general trying to recapture the Alamo in *Viva Max!*, a comedy that didn't do much with its intriguing premise; then had another failure as director-actor with *Hammersmith Is Out!*, a black comedy with the Burtons; and gave a spirited reading as the voice of the spoiled Prince John in Disney's all-animal version of *Robin Hood*. For that studio he scampered about through two of their least successful offerings of the 1970s, *One of Our Dinosaurs Is Missing*, as a Chinese investigator, and *Treasure of Matecumbe*, as a medicine man, in between which he showed up as the only surviving elder in the futuristic sci-fi adventure *Logan's Run*, living in the ruins of the Capitol Building with a bunch of cats. There was a success of sorts when he took over the part of Belgian sleuth Hercule Poirot in the stylish who-dunit *Death on the Nile*, a role he would repeat first on screen, in *Evil Under the Sun*; several times on television, and then back in theatres for *Appointment with Death*, by which point interest had evaporated completely.

Prior to and during the Poirot period he kept showing up in all sorts of half-hearted and barely seen international productions, such as the incoherent *Purple Taxi*, which included Fred Astaire among the cast; *Ahsanti*, a major bomb about slave trading; and an unnecessary remake of *The Thief of Baghdad*, as the Caliph. Figuring (inaccurately) that audiences had some interest in seeing him play famous detectives of literature, he was cast in *Charlie Chan and the Curse of the Dragon Queen*. However, this was 1981 and moviegoers no longer had much tolerance for non-Asians

playing such roles in heavy makeup and the film was heavily criticized as such. Returning to the director-producer-writer-star mold he did a long-cherished pet project, *Memed My Hawk*, as a wicked dictator clashing with rebellious Simon Dutton. There was next to no interest in it from critics or audiences and it quickly disappeared wherever it screened. After so many disappointments and cockeyed projects, it was nice to see Ustinov show up playing a straightforward part in a good, mainstream Hollywood presentation, *Lorenzo's Oil*, as one of the doctors who attempts to help distraught parents Susan Sarandon and Nick Nolte cure their stricken child. Less welcome were *Stiff Upper Lips*, a dud spoof of the Merchant Ivory costume pictures, and *The Bachelor*, as Chris O'Donnell's wealthy grandfather. On television he won Emmy Awards for *Life of Samuel Johnson*, *Barefoot in Athens*, and *A Storm in Summer*. His other credits as playwright include *Photo Finish*, *Life in My Hands*, *The Unknown Soldier and His Wife*, *Half Way Up the Tree*, and *Beethoven's Tenth*. His many books include the short story collection *Add a Dash of Pity* (1962), *The Wit of Peter Ustinov* (1969), *Ustinov at Large* (1993), and the memoir *Dear Me* (1977). He was knighted in 1990.

Screen: 1940: Mein Kampf — My Crimes/After Mein Kampf; 1942: The Goose Steps Out; One of Our Aircraft Is Missing; Let the People Sing; 1944: The Way Ahead/Immortal Batallion (and co-wr.); 1945: The True Glory; 1949: Private Angelo (and co-dir.; wr.; prod.); 1950: Odette; 1951: Hotel Sahara; The Magic Box; Quo Vadis?; 1954: Beau Brummell; The Egyptian; 1955: We're No Angels; Lola Montez; 1957: I Girovaghi/The Wanderers (nUSr); Un Angel Paso sobre Brooklyn/An Angel Passed Over Brooklyn/The Man Who Wagged His Tail (nUSr); 1958: Les Espions/The Spies (nUSr); 1960: Spartacus; The Sundowners; 1961: Romanoff and Juliet (and dir.; wr.; prod.); 1962: Billy Budd (and dir.; co-wr.; prod.); 1963: Alleman/Everyman (narrator); Women of the World (narrator); 1964: Topkapi; 1965: John Goldfarb, Please Come Home; Lady L (and dir.; wr.); 1967: The Comedians; 1968: Blackbeard's Ghost; Hot Millions (and co-wr.); 1969: Viva Max!; 1972: Hammersmith Is Out! (and dir.); 1973: Robin Hood (voice); 1975: One of Our Dinosaurs Is Missing; 1976: Logan's Run; Treasure of Matecumbe; 1977: Un Taxi Mauve/Purple Taxi (US: 1980); The Last Remake of Beau Geste; 1978: Doppio Delitto/Double Murders (nUSr); The Mouse and His Child (voice); Death on the Nile; Metamorphoses/Winds of Change (narrator; nUSr); 1979: Ashanti; Nous Maigrirons Ensemble/We'll Grow Thin Together (nUSr); Players; Tarka the Otter (narrator); 1981: Charlie Chan and the Curse of the Dragon Queen; The Great Muppet Caper; 1982: Grendel Grendel Grendel (voice); Evil Under the Sun; 1984: Memed My Hawk (and dir.; wr.; US: 1986); 1988: Appointment With Death; 1989: The French Revolution (nUSr); 1990: C'era un Castello con 40 Cani/There Was a Castle With 40 Dogs (nUSr); 1992: Lorenzo's Oil; 1995: The Phoenix and the Magic Carpet (nUSr); 1999: Stiff Upper Lips; The Bachelor.

NY Stage: 1957: Romanoff and Juliet (and wr.); 1963: Photo Finish (and wr.; co-dir.); 1974: Who's Who In Hell (and wr.); 1984: Beethoven's Tenth (and wr.).

Select TV: 1957: Life of Samuel Johnson (sp); 1958: Moment of Truth (sp); The Empty Chair (sp); 1966: Barefoot in Athens (sp); 1969: Babar the Elephant (sp; voice); 1970: A Storm in Summer (sp); 1971: Gideon (sp); The American Revolution 1770–1783: A Conversation With Lord North (sp); 1973: The Last King in America (sp); 1977: Jesus of Nazareth (ms); 1978: The Thief of Baghdad; 1979: Einstein's Universe (sp; narrator); 1981: Dr. Snuggles (series; voice); Omni: The New Frontier (series); 1985: Thirteen for Dinner; 1986: Dead Man's Folly; Murder in Three Acts; Peter Ustinov's Russia: A Personal History (sp; and co-wr.);

1988: The Secret Identity of Jack the Ripper (sp); 1989: Around the World in 80 Days (ms); 1990: Peter Ustinov in China (sp); 1993: Inside the Vatican (ms; and co-wr.); 1994: Celebrating Haydn with Peter Ustinov (sp); 1995: The Old Curiosity Shop (sp); An Evening with Sir Peter Ustinov (sp); 1998: Planet Ustinov (series); 1999: Alice in Wonderland; Animal Farm (voice); On the Trail of Mark Twain (ms); 2001: Victoria & Albert; 2003: Salem Witch Trials.

V

RUDOLPH VALENTINO

(Rodolfo Alfonzo Raffaelo Pierre Filibert
Guglielmi di Valentina d'Antonguolla)
Born: Castellaneta, Italy, May 6, 1895.
Died: August 23, 1926.

His is one of the iconic names of cinema,
even to those who never dared to watch a
silent film. There was something so definitive about Rudolph
Valentino as the ultimate nostril flaring, chest-baring, silent
screen love idol that his image managed to burn magnetically,
decades after his untimely demise. When he was 18 he came to
New York where he eventually worked as a dancer at clubs and in
dance halls, while also dabbling in some petty criminal activities,
which got him jailed on more than one occasion. His terpsichorean skills led to some stage musicals on the road, before he
went to Los Angeles in hopes of breaking into the movies, which
turned out to be an easier prospect than expected, given his
smashing looks and bedroom eyes. He made his debut, in 1917,
doing extra work (there is debate over exactly what films he
appeared in during this early period). He then showed up as a
dancer in *Alimony*; was given a bigger role, as an Italian count, in
A Married Virgin; then was upped to leading man (billed as
Rudolpho de Valentina at this point) in *A Society Sensation*, as the
rich lad who falls for poor girl Carmel Myers. All of this happened within the course of a single year. Staying on at Universal,
there was a follow-up with Myers, *All Night*, and one with Mae
Murray, *Delicious Little Devil*. He continued to be gainfully
employed, sometimes in big parts, sometimes in supporting bits,
appearing in such films as *The Big Little Person*, where, this being
the pre-talkie era, he could pass as an Irishman; *Out of Luck*, as a
bad guy; *Eyes of Youth*, in which he romanced Clara Kimball
Young for shady reasons; *Passion's Playground*, as Norman Kerry's
brother; and *The Wonderful Chance*, as a mobster. In 1921, his fortunes changed when Metro chose him to play a pivotal role in
their lavish adaptation of *The Four Horsemen of the Apocalypse*, as
the layabout son who turns into a war hero. His tempestuous
tango sequence became one of the most talked about scenes in
films to date and the movie was a tremendous success, one of the
top grossing motion pictures of the decade.

Valentino was, overnight, the hottest thing in movies and he
followed this up with *Camille*, opposite Nazimova, which featured sets by Natasha Rambova, who became his wife and agent
of sorts. Despite their union it was pretty well known in
Hollywood that the couple indulged in affairs with both sexes. It
was during the production of *The Conquering Power* that he made
salary demands and, when Metro refused to meet them, he signed
up with Paramount. They put him into the ideal Valentino property, *The Sheik*, where the sight of him in his Arabian headpiece,
seducing Agnes Ayres in his poshly decorated tent, became such
a famous and lasting screen image that it was parodied for years
to come by people who had never even seen the film. This film
made him more popular than ever and he followed it with the
adventure *Moran of the Lady Letty*; *Beyond the Rocks*, where he
romanced married Gloria Swanson; and another of his big ones,
Blood and Sand, as the cocky matador seduced by temptress Nita
Naldi. Nobody was about to send any acting awards in
Valentino's direction, but there was no doubting the impact he
made on screen through his mere presence. At his wife's instance
he did *The Young Rajah*, which was too kitschy even for the fans;
Monsieur Beaucaire, a lighthearted romp that did well; and
another failure, *Cobra*, which, despite its title, was set in an
antique shop. With that he went over to United Artists for a pair
of adventures, *The Eagle*, and a safe bet, *Son of the Sheik*. The success of both indicated that he was back on track. The same year
of the latter's release, 1926, he died suddenly from peritonitis
caused by a perforated ulcer. His New York City funeral, attended
by a multitude of weeping fans, became the stuff of legend only
further adding to the Valentino mystique.

Screen: **1917:** Patria; **1918:** Alimony; A Society Sensation; All
Night; **1919:** Delicious Little Devil; A Rogue's Romance; The
Home-Breaker; Virtuous Sinners; The Big Little Person; Nobody
Home/Out of Luck; Eyes of Youth; **1920:** A Married
Virgin/Frivolous Wives (filmed 1918); An Adventuress/Isle of
Love; The Cheater; Passion's Playground; Once to Every Woman;
Stolen Moments; The Wonderful Chance; **1921:** The Four
Horsemen of the Apocalypse; Uncharted Seas; Camille; The
Conquering Power; The Sheik; **1922:** Moran of the Lady Letty;
Beyond the Rocks; Blood and Sand; The Young Rajah; **1924:**
Monsieur Beaucaire; A Sainted Devil; **1925:** Cobra; The Eagle;

1926: Son of the Sheik.

RUDY VALLEE

(HUBERT PRIOR VALLEE) BORN: ISLAND POND,
VT, JULY 28, 1901. ED: UNIV. OF ME, YALE.
DIED: JULY 3, 1986.

It's hard to believe that Rudy Vallee once
had the ladies screaming in adoration as
Sinatra and the Beatles would in later years,
but this very square, wavy haired crooner with the quavery vocals
was indeed a 1920s singing sensation. It was the very dated quality
of his persona that he later parlayed into a fairly successful career
as a comedic character actor. He sang with bands before forming
his own group, the Connecticut Yankees (in addition to vocalizing, he also played the saxophone), and with them he became a
big hit in nightclubs and on radio, notably with what would
become his signature song, "I'm Just a Vagabond Lover." This was
shortened to *The Vagabond Lover* for his feature debut, which was
just another primitive talkie, with Vallee looking very uncomfortable infront of a camera lens, his every scene being stolen by
the never-more-welcome Marie Dressler. He continued to show
up in many RKO shorts, such as "Campus Sweethearts," "Rudy
Vallee Melodies," etc., while guesting in the all-star extravaganzas
Glorifying the American Girl, and *International House*. He kept his
career going on radio while being cast in minor musicals like
Golddiggers in Paris, one of those Warner Bros. concoctions given
a lift by Busby Berkeley's clever staging, and *Time Out for
Rhythm*, a tired Columbia cornucopia that threw in everything
from Ann Miller to the Three Stooges.

In 1942 director-writer Preston Sturges had the smart idea to
utilize the increasingly old-fashioned Vallee mannerisms to comical effect in *The Palm Beach Story*, where he was achingly funny
as Mary Astor's nerdy, bespectacled brother. This opened up a
whole new career for him as a supporting player and, in addition
to some other Sturges films, he was seen to good effect in *The
Bachelor and the Bobby Soxer*, as Cary Grant's rival for Myrna Loy,
and *I Remember Mama*, in a completely serious role, as a doctor.
In 1961 his by-then-dormant career got another temporary jolt of
energy when he played the corporate executive windbag, Jasper
Bigley, in the Broadway musical smash *How to Succeed in Business
Without Really Trying*, a part he recreated to perfection in the
delightful 1967 film version of the show. For his follow-up he was
placed opposite another singer, albeit one with whole different
approach to his craft, Elvis Presley, in *Live a Little, Love a Little*.
There were also guest spots in two of the odder offerings of the
1970s, *The Phynx*, and *Won Ton Ton, the Dog Who Saved
Hollywood*, both of which gathered up an eclectic mix of past stars
that were no longer of much interest to modern audiences. He
wrote three memoirs: *Vagabond Dreams Come True* (1930), *My
Time Is Your Time* (1962) and *Let the Chips Fall* (1975). His second
wife (1943–45) was actress Jane Greer.

Screen: 1929: The Vagabond Lover; Glorifying the American
Girl; 1933: International House; George White's Scandals; 1935:
Sweet Music; 1938: Gold Diggers of Paris; 1939: Second Fiddle;
1941: Too Many Blondes; Time Out for Rhythm; 1942: The Palm
Beach Story; 1943: Happy Go Lucky; 1945: It's in the Bag; Man
Alive; 1946: People Are Funny; The Fabulous Suzanne; 1947: The
Sin of Harold Diddlebock/Mad Wednesday; The Bachelor and
the Bobby-Soxer; 1948: I Remember Mama; So This Is New
York; Unfaithfully Yours; My Dear Secretary; 1949: Mother Is a
Freshman; The Beautiful Blonde from Bashful Bend; Father Was
a Fullback; 1950: The Admiral Was a Lady; 1954: Ricochet
Romance; 1955: Gentlemen Marry Brunettes; 1957: The Helen

Morgan Story; 1967: How to Succeed in Business Without Really
Trying; 1968: Live a Little, Love a Little; The Night They Raided
Minsky's (narrator); 1970: The Phynx; 1975: Sunburst/Slashed
Dreams; 1976: Won Ton Ton, the Dog Who Saved Hollywood.
NY Stage: 1929: Vaudeville at The Palace; 1931: George White's
Scandals; 1935: George White's Scandals of 1935; 1939: The
Man in Possession; 1961: How to Succeed in Business Without
Really Trying.
Select TV: 1956: Jenny Kissed Me (sp); 1958: The Battle for
Wednesday Night (sp); Hansel and Gretel (sp); 1964–65: On
Broadway Tonight (series).

RAF VALLONE

BORN: TROPEA, CALABRIA, ITALY,
FEBRUARY 17, 1916. ED: UNIV. OF TURIN.
DIED: OCTOBER 31, 2002.

Burly, earthy Raf Vallone was a late-starting
Italian performer whose craggy features and
strong persona were eventually utilized to
potent effect in various productions outside his native land. A
former reporter, a chance meeting with director Giuseppe De
Santis got him a role as a sergeant in *Bitter Rice*, one of the most
notable of the Italian neo-realist dramas of the late 1940s. This led
to a lead in *No Peace Among the Olives*, as a shepherd, and he
became a major name in his country during the 1950s, though
only a handful of his releases crossed the pond, including *Anna*,
in which he was reunited with his *Bitter Rice* co-star, Silvana
Mangano; *Rome — 11 O'clock*, about a real life tragedy in which
several innocent girls were killed; and *The Adulteress/Therese
Raquin*, as Simone Signoret's lover. It was not until the early
1960s that he entered the American consciousness, appearing in
two films with Sophia Loren — *Two Women*, in which he
appeared for a brief sequence as a truck driver, and *El Cid*, as
Charlton Heston's nemesis. He then starred in the coveted role of
the Brooklyn dockworker who is destroyed by his desires for his
niece in director Sidney Lumet's adaptation of Arthur Miller's
powerful play, *A View from the Bridge*. Thereafter, he became a
familiar presence in various English-language features, including
The Cardinal, as a man of the cloth; *Harlow*, as Carroll Baker's
unpleasant stepfather; *Nevada Smith*, as a monk; *The Italian Job*,
as a Mafia boss; *Cannon for Cordoba*, as the latter part of the title,
a Mexican general; *Rosebud*, as Isabelle Huppert's father; *The
Other Side of Midnight*, getting major exposure in this trashy hit
from a bestseller, as Marie-France Pisier's Greek millionaire husband; *An Almost Perfect Affair*, as the spouse Monica Vitti cheats
on; and *The Godfather Part III*, in which he was back in Cardinal
red. He married actress Elena Varzi in 1952, and she appeared
with him in some of his early films.

Screen (US releases only): 1950: Bitter Rice (It: 1948); 1953:
Anna; Rome — 11 O'Clock; 1955: Le Avventure di Mandrin/
Don Juan's Night of Love (It: 1951); 1957: Passionate Summer;
1959: The Adulteress/Therese Raquin (It: 1953); No Escape; The
Sins of Rose Bernd (Ger: 1956); Guendalina (It: 1957); 1961: Two
Women; El Cid; 1962: A View From the Bridge; Phaedra; 1963:
The Cardinal; 1964: The Secret Invasion; 1965: Harlow; 1966:
Nevada Smith; Kiss the Girls and Make Them Die; 1968: The
Desperate Ones; 1969: The Italian Job; 1970: The Kremlin Letter;
Cannon for Cordoba; 1971: A Gunfight; 1973: Summertime
Killer; 1974: Terror in 2-A/Girl in Room 2-A; 1975: Rosebud; The
Human Factor; That Lucky Touch; 1977: The Other Side of
Midnight; 1978: The Greek Tycoon; 1979: An Almost Perfect
Affair; Arthur Miller on Home Ground; 1981: Lion of the Desert;
1983: A Time to Die; 1990: The Godfather Part III.

Select TV: 1973: Honor Thy Father; Catholics; 1983: The Scarlet and the Black; 1985: Christopher Columbus; 1991: The First Circle; A Season of Giants.

BOBBY VAN

(ROBERT STEIN) BORN: NEW YORK, NY, DECEMBER 6, 1928. DIED: JULY 31, 1980.

An exuberantly gawky, ever-smiling dancer with something of a passing resemblance to a young Ray Bolger, it was Bobby Van's bad luck to come along just when his sort of showcase was riding off into the sunset. He made his professional debut at 14, performing in the Catskills, and then went on to nightclubs and a spot in the Broadway revue *Alive and Kicking*. MGM signed him to a contract in 1952, putting him in a specialty number, as himself, in the Esther Williams vehicle *Skirts Ahoy!*, and, in support of Mario Lanza, in *Because You're Mine*. Giving him the star treatment, they handed him the title role in a black and white semi-musical, *The Affairs of Dobie Gillis*, as the nebbishy, girl-struck high schooler of Max Shulman's stories; allowed him to dance up a storm as Gremio, in what turned out to be the stand-out film of his career, *Kiss Me Kate*; and gave him his best chance of all in the Jane Powell vehicle, *Small Town Girl*, where he stopped the show with his amazing and exhaustingly energetic hop through town. He followed this with the lead in a Broadway revival of *On Your Toes* (in Bolger's old role) but, just when things seemed to be taking off, his momentum stopped. He returned to nightclubs and television, did a 1960s monster movie, *The Navy vs. the Night Monsters*, triumphed again, on Broadway, in a revival of *No, No, Nanette*, and then proved to be the only cast member at ease in the notorious flop musical remake of *Lost Horizon*, in a reworking of the role Edward Everett Horton had done the first time out. After that he became a staple on game shows, giving many the mistaken impression that he had little to offer outside of the unctuously insincere smiles that most men in that dubious line of work have to offer. He was married to actress Elaine Joyce from 1968 to his premature death from brain cancer.

Screen: 1952: Skirts Ahoy!; Because You're Mine; 1953: Small Town Girl; The Affairs of Dobie Gillis; Kiss Me Kate; 1966: The Navy vs. the Night Monsters; 1972: The Doomsday Machine; 1973: Lost Horizon.

NY Stage: 1950: Alive and Kicking; 1954: On Your Toes; 1971: No, No, Nanette; 1975: Dr. Jazz.

Select TV: 1964–65: Mickey (series); 1969: Lost Flight; 1975: Showoffs (series); 1976: The Fun Factory (series); 1977: Bunco; 1979: Make Me Laugh (series); 1980: The Hustler of Muscle Beach.

LEE VAN CLEEF

BORN: SOMERVILLE, NJ, JANUARY 9, 1925. DIED: DECEMBER 14, 1989.

A gaunt, viciously squinty-eyed character player in American westerns for more than a decade, Lee Van Cleef went to Italy to appear in some of the best remembered films of the spaghetti western genre and found himself a star. After spending time in the Navy, he worked as an accountant before joining a small theater group. He then went west to Hollywood, where he found himself immediately typecast in the horse opera genre, starting off in one of the biggest and most famous of them all, *High Noon*, as one of the killers menacingly awaiting the train. After that, Van Cleef was seldom out of the saddle with such credits as *The Nebraskan*, a 3-D offering, as a

psychotic killer-deserter; *The Desperado*, as a pair of twins; *Tribute to a Bad Man*, as a cattle rustler; and *The Lonely Man*, as a character who reminds Jack Palace of his outlaw past. Outside this area, he was seen as a womanizing bank robber in *Kansas City Confidential*; a homosexual hoodlum in the tense noir *The Big Combo*; and an earthling in cahoots with the aliens in the campy sci-fi offering *It Conquered the World*. There was little to complain about since the work was pretty steady but, unexpectedly, he became a star of the genre he had paid his dues in, when he went to Italy in the mid-1960s to make a pair of westerns for director Sergio Leone. The resulting films, the deadly dull *For a Few Dollars More*, and the much better *The Good, the Bad, and the Ugly*, had him paired off against the equally sun-baked and taciturn Clint Eastwood, with few exchanges made between the two actors, outside of an occasional glare, before guns went blazing. Van Cleef, mustachioed, gray haired, and lean, was an especially vicious villain in the latter, and suddenly he was getting his own European-made vehicles like *Death Rides a Horse*, in which he was teamed with John Philip Law to seek vengeance on those who'd wronged him; and *Sabata*, as a gambler-turned-bounty hunter, a film popular enough to warrant two sequels. Back home, there were similar American outings like *El Condor*, as a con man teamed with Jim Brown, and *Barquero*, as a barge operator who crosses villain Warren Oates, but none of these brought Van Cleef half the success that Eastwood got from his participation in the Leone films. As he grew older he continued in action-related fare, which seemed increasingly low profile, and headlined a television series, *The Master*, a martial arts offering.

Screen: 1952: High Noon; Untamed Frontier; Kansas City Confidential; The Lawless Breed; 1953: Arena; The Bandits of Corsica; Tumbleweed; The Beast from 20,000 Fathoms; Vice Squad; The Nebraskan; Private Eyes; White Lightning; Jack Slade; 1954: Arrow in the Dust; Gypsy Colt; Dawn at Socorro; Prince of the Nile; The Desperado; The Yellow Tomahawk; Rails Into Laramie; 1955: The Big Combo; Ten Wanted Men; I Cover the Underworld; Man Without a Star; The Naked Street; The Road to Denver; The Vanishing American; A Man Alone; Treasure of Ruby Hills; 1956: The Conqueror; Tribute to a Bad Man; Red Sundown; Pardners; Accused of Murder; It Conquered the World; The Quiet Gun; 1957: Gunfight at the O.K. Corral; Last Stagecoach West; The Lonely Man; Joe Dakota; Gun Battle in Monterey; The Badge of Marshal Brennan; The Tin Star; Raiders of Old California; China Gate; 1958: The Bravados; Day of the Bad Man; Machete; The Young Lions; 1959: Ride Lonesome; Guns, Girls and Gangsters; 1961: Posse from Hell; 1962: The Man Who Shot Liberty Valance; 1963: How the West Was Won; 1966: For a Few Dollars More; 1967: The Good, the Bad, and the Ugly; 1968: The Big Gundown; Beyond the Law (nUSr); Commandos/ Sullivan's Marauders (nUSr); 1969: Death Rides a Horse; Day of Anger; 1970: Barquero; El Condor; Sabata; 1971: Captain Apache; 1972: The Magnificent Seven Ride!; Return of Sabata; 1973: The Grand Duel/Storm Rider (dtv); 1975: Bad Man River (It: 1972); Power Kill; Take a Hard Ride; 1976: The Stranger and the Gunfighter/Blood Money; Mean Frank and Crazy Tony/Escape from Death Row (It: 1973); 1977: Kid Vengeance; The Perfect Killer/Satanic Mechanic (dtv); 1978: Diamante Lobo/God's Gun; 1980: The Octagon; 1981: Escape from New York; 1982: The Squeeze/The Big Rip-off (It: 1978); 1985: Jungle Raiders; 1986: Codename: Wild Geese; Armed Response; 1988: The Commander (nUSr); 1989: Speed Zone; 1990: Thieves of Fortune (dtv).

Select TV: 1954: Four Things He'd Do (sp); Duel at the O.K. Corral (sp); 1956: Deadline (sp); 1957: The Blue Hotel (sp); 1977:

Nowhere to Hide/Fatal Chase (dtv); **1979**: The Hard Way; **1984**: The Master (series).

MAMIE VAN DOREN

(JOAN LUCILLE OLANDER) BORN: ROWENA, SD, FEBRUARY 6, 1931.

There are those who have great affection, albeit of a definitely campy nature, for the bosomy, platinum blonde Mamie Van Doren, whose name was linked to some of the cheesier Hollywood fare of the late 1950s and early 1960s. A one-time secretary for a law firm, she took up singing, joined the Ted Fio Rita orchestra, and eventually headed to Hollywood where she did some bit parts under her real name. Universal decided to give her a shot and signed her up in 1953, changed her name, and cast her as the femme fatale who has a thing for seducing football players in *All American*, a Tony Curtis vehicle. They kept her mainly in support, though she did have the female lead in *Running Wild*, as auto thief Jan Merlin's sultry babe. Director Howard W. Koch took advantage of her growing fame and put her into *Untamed Youth*, where she fit right into the women-in-prison genre, and *Born Reckless*, as a rodeo rider, neither of which indicated that anyone was out to take her too seriously. In the meantime, junk producer Albert Zugsmith saw her as ideal for his incredibly silly combinations of youth exploitation players, fringe celebrities, and fading stars in such atrocities as *High School Confidential*, where she had the hots for nephew Russ Tamblyn; *The Beat Generation*, in which she was nearly raped by Ray Danton; *Girls Town*, where she was sent up the river again; *The Private Lives of Adam and Eve*, as Eve, in this jaw-droppingly awful parable, co-directed by Mickey Rooney; and the immortal *Sex Kittens Go to College*, as a stripper who becomes the head of a college science department. Since these movies did nothing more than prove that she had little to offer beyond her rather plastic looks, there was no place to go but down and she ended up in a nudie, *3 Nuts in Search of a Bolt*, and in some other films better remembered for the titles than their content, *Voyage to the Planet of the Prehistoric Women* and *Las Vegas Hillbillys*. After a long absence, she popped up in a straight-to-video item, *Free Ride*; one that failed to find American distribution, *The Vegas Connection*; and an "R" rated teen flick, *Slackers*, in which the now 70-year-old Van Doren stayed true to her trashy image by displaying some skin.

Screen: AS JOAN OLANDER: **1950**: Jet Pilot (released 1957); **1951**: His Kind of Woman; Two Tickets to Broadway; Footlight Varieties.
AS MAMIE VAN DOREN: **1953**: All American; Forbidden; **1954**: Yankee Pasha; Francis Joins the WACs; **1955**: Ain't Misbehavin'; The Second Greatest Sex; Running Wild; **1956**: Star in the Dust; **1957**: Untamed Youth; The Girl in Black Stockings; **1958**: High School Confidential; Teacher's Pet; **1959**: Born Reckless; The Beat Generation/This Rebel Age; Guns, Girls and Gangsters; Girls Town/Innocent and the Damned; The Big Operator; Le bellissime gambe di Sabrina/ The Beautiful Legs of Sabrina (nUSr); **1960**: Vice Raid; College Confidential; Sex Kittens Go to College/The Beauty and the Robot; The Private Lives of Adam and Eve; **1964**: The Sheriff Was a Lady; 3 Nuts in Search of a Bolt; The Candidate; **1966**: The Navy vs. the Night Monsters; Las Vegas Hillbillys; **1968**: Voyage to the Planet of the Prehistoric Women; You've Got to Be Smart; **1971**: The Arizona Kid; **1986**: Free Ride (dtv); **1999**: The Vegas Connection (nUSr); **2002**: Slackers.

DICK VAN DYKE

BORN: WEST PLAINS, MO, DECEMBER 13, 1925. RAISED IN DANVILLE, IL.

During the 1960s Dick Van Dyke was one of the brightest talents in both movies and on television, a versatile fellow who was eager to do it all — clowning, singing, dancing, with some serious emoting on the side. He seemed fashioned for a show business of an earlier time, so it was a battle to find the right property to make proper use of him, and by the time the 1970s arrived, his heyday was already behind him. It was while running an ad agency in Illinois that he teamed up with Phil Erickson to create a nightclub act called the Merry Mutes, in which the two men mimed to records. After that, Van Dyke hosted some local talk shows in Atlanta and New Orleans, before moving to New York where he became host of *CBS Cartoon Theatre*. He was soon a very prolific face on television, showing up on several programs, including yet another one he hosted, *Laugh Line*. There was a flop Broadway show, *The Boys Against the Girls*, which got him a Theatre World Award, and this was soon followed by a major hit, *Bye Bye Birdie*, for which he won raves and a Tony Award. He then made what turned out to be a very wise choice, accepting an offer to star in his own weekly sitcom, created by writer-performer Carl Reiner. The result, *The Dick Van Dyke Show*, became one of the classic series of the medium and it made him a household name, earning him three Emmy Awards in the process. Since he was now extremely famous, Columbia Pictures had no qualms about letting him repeat his Broadway role, as the mother-dominated songwriter, in their exuberant 1963 film version of *Bye Bye Birdie*, and he proved to be a delightful screen presence. His stardom was solidified by his equal billing with the other very famous and more established names in a heavy-handed black comedy, *What a Way to Go!*, as the first of Shirley MacLaine's many doomed husbands.

Walt Disney then chose him to partner Julie Andrews in what turned out to be the crowning live-action achievement of that studio, *Mary Poppins*. As Bert, the friendly chimney sweep-sidewalk artist, Van Dyke was so amiable that few cared about his thoroughly unconvincing cockney accent, and this musical fantasy deservedly became one of the most popular films of all time. For the same studio he fared less well with the castaway spoof *Lt. Robin Crusoe, USN*, although his name carried it to success, but he did score in a sharp comedy for adults, *Divorce American Style*, breaking up with Debbie Reynolds and pursuing Jean Simmons on the re-bound. Hoping to copy the success of *Mary Poppins*, the producers of the James Bond films built a big family musical around him based on the book *Chitty Chitty Bang Bang* and, despite some high points, including a snappy dance number called "Me Ol' Bamboo," it wound up losing a great deal of money. An ideal showcase followed with *The Comic*, a poignant and probing look at the rise and fall of a fictionalized silent movie comedian. It was directed and scripted by Carl Reiner with loving care, and clearly gave Van Dyke the sort of tour de force opportunity that he deserved, but it was dumped by its distributor, Columbia Pictures, and made little impact. There was more public interest in the scathing anti-smoking comedy *Cold Turkey*, in which he played a small-town priest, but rather than continue with movies he tried another series with Reiner, *The New Dick Van Dyke Show*. From that point on he pretty much stayed on the small screen, where he searched for years for another show that audiences would enjoy seeing him in, earning an Emmy for the variety offering *Van Dyke and Company*, and one for the children's special, *The Wrong Way Kid*. Theatrically, he stumbled badly in a serious film, *The Runner Stumbles*, as a priest accused of murdering the young nun he secretly loved, and briefly appeared behind much make-up to play the D.A. in *Dick Tracy*. He finally got his second, long-running television show with *Diagnosis Murder*, which featured his son Barry among the cast. His brother, Jerry, had appeared as his sibling on *The Dick Van Dyke Show* and would continue to act in his more talented brother's shadow for years to come.

Screen: 1963: Bye Bye Birdie; 1964: What a Way to Go!; Mary Poppins; 1965: The Art of Love; 1966: Lt. Robin Crusoe, USN; 1967: Divorce American Style; Fitzwilly; 1968: Never a Dull Moment; Chitty Chitty Bang Bang; 1969: The Comic; Some Kind of a Nut; 1971: Cold Turkey; 1979: The Runner Stumbles; 1990: Dick Tracy.

NY Stage: 1959: The Boys Against the Girls; 1960: Bye Bye Birdie; 1980: The Music Man.

Select TV: 1955–56: The Morning Show (series); 1956: CBS Cartoon Theatre (series); 1958: The Chevy Showroom Starring Andy Williams (series); 1958–59: Mother's Day (series); Pantomime Quiz (series); 1959: Laugh Line (series); Trap for a Stranger (sp); 1961–66: The Dick Van Dyke Show (series); 1967: The Dick Van Dyke Special (sp); 1968: Dick Van Dyke and the Other Woman: Mary Tyler Moore (sp); 1971: The First Nine Months Are the Hardest (sp); Dick Van Dyke Meets Bill Cosby (sp); 1971–74: The New Dick Van Dyke Show (series); 1974: The Morning After; Julie & Dick in Covent Garden (sp); 1975: The Confessions of Dick Van Dyke (sp); 1976: Van Dyke and Company (series); 1977: The Carol Burnett Show (series); 1982: Drop Out Father; The Country Girl (sp); 1983: Found Money; 1984: The Wrong Way Kid (sp); 1985: Breakfast With Les and Bess (sp); 1986: Arthur Hailey's Strong Medicine; 1987: Ghost of a Chance; 1988: The Van Dyke Show (series); 1991: Daughters of Privilege; 1992: Diagnosis Murder; The House on Sycamore Street; 1993: A Twist of the Knife; 1993–2001: Diagnosis Murder (series; and exec. prod.); 2002: A Town Without Pity; Without Warning.

JO VAN FLEET
BORN: OAKLAND, CA, DECEMBER 30, 1914.
ED: COL. OF THE PACIFIC. DIED: JUNE 10, 1996.

Despite a late start in films and only a dozen movies to her credit, Jo Van Fleet proved to be a memorable, versatile character actress, one who was determined to leave the audience impressed by her efforts. She studied acting under Sanford Meisner at the Neighborhood Playhouse and made her Broadway debut, in 1946, in a production of *The Winter's Tale*. She won a Tony Award for her role in *The Trip to Bountiful*, and then was invited by director Elia Kazan, for whom she'd acted onstage in *Flight Into Egypt* and *Camino Real*, to make her long overdue motion picture bow, in his production of *East of Eden*. As the long-absent mother of James Dean, she was mesmerizing in her portrayal of this strong-willed, cold-hearted lady who has left her family to run a brothel, and she won an Academy Award for Best Supporting Actress of 1955. That same year she also scored in two other major releases, *I'll Cry Tomorrow*, as Susan Hayward's determined mother, and *The Rose Tattoo*, as Anna Magnani's nemesis. These established her as a formidable film player and she ripped into such subsequent parts as Kirk Douglas's alcoholic mistress in *Gunfight at O.K. Corral*, and *Wild River*, where she convincingly portrayed a feisty 80-year-old Southern matriarch who doesn't want to give up her land to the TVA. After another absence, she

again passed effortlessly for playing much older women, first with her stunning one-scene performance as Paul Newman's dying mama in *Cool Hand Luke*, and then her broad comedic role as Peter Sellers's overbearing Jewish mother in *I Love You, Alice B. Toklas*. She was last seen on screen as one of the weird apartment owners in *The Tenant*, and then sporadically on television after that.

Screen: 1955: East of Eden; I'll Cry Tomorrow; The Rose Tattoo; 1956: The King and Four Queens; 1957: Gunfight at the O.K. Corral; 1958: This Angry Age; 1960: Wild River; 1967: Cool Hand Luke; 1968: I Love You, Alice B. Toklas; 1969: 80 Steps to Jonah; 1971: The Gang That Couldn't Shoot Straight; 1976: The Tenant.

NY Stage: 1946: The Winter's Tale; 1947: The Whole World Over; 1949: The Closing Door; 1950: King Lear; 1952: Flight Into Egypt; 1953: Camino Real; The Trip to Bountiful; 1957: Look Homeward Angel; 1960: Rosemary; The Alligators; 1962: Oh Dad, Poor Dad, Mama's Hung You In The Closet and I'm Feelin' So Sad (ob); 1965: The Glass Menagerie.

Select TV: 1952: The Thin Air (sp); 1954: Morning Star (sp); 1955: Joe's Boy (sp); Concerning Death (sp); Assassin (sp); Heidi (sp); 1958: The Crazy Hunter (sp); 1959: 30 Pieces of Silver (sp); The Human Comedy (sp); Disaster (sp); 1960: Volpone (sp); 1961: Four by Tennessee Williams (sp); The Night of the Storm (sp); 1964: Satan's Waitin' (sp); The World I Want to Know (sp); 1965: Cinderella (sp); 1967: Verdict for Terror (sp); 1972: The Family Rico; 1973: Satan's School for Girls; 1974: Paradise Lost (sp); 1980: Power; 1986: Seize the Day.

DIANE VARSI
BORN: SAN MATEO, CA, FEBRUARY 23, 1938.
DIED: NOVEMBER 19, 1992.

Perhaps fame was not what Diane Varsi was looking for when she entered the acting profession, but she got it right from the get go, before promptly turning her back on the whole maddening business. Prior to coming to Hollywood she had already married twice, worked in various jobs, done some singing, and played drums in a band. After taking some acting classes with actor Jeff Corey, she did a screen test for 20th Century-Fox, who was looking for a fresh newcomer to fill the important role of Allison MacKenzie in their big-screen adaptation of the red-hot bestseller, *Peyton Place*. As the sweet, small-town girl awakening to her sexual feelings and finding out about her own illegitimacy, she was competent and more often then not, fairly colorless. But, since the Academy went wild throwing nominations every which way at this very tame rendering of the much more enjoyable novel, Varsi found herself in the running in the supporting category. She did not get the award but she suddenly found herself hyped as a major new star. Fox cast her as Gary Cooper's rebellious daughter, who suffers a miscarriage, in *Ten North Frederick*, and then as the college girl who can't break through to depraved Dean Stockwell in *Compulsion*. She could hardly compete with the more accomplished performers in each of these movies and, fed up with the whole picture business, walked out on her contract and retired to Vermont. Years later she resumed acting, notably in the hit *Wild in the Streets*, as the spaced out former child star Sally LeRoy, but jobs were sporadic and she disappeared again after a small role in *I Never Promised You a Rose Garden*, in 1977.

Screen: 1957: Peyton Place; 1958: Ten North Frederick; From Hell to Texas; 1959: Compulsion; 1967: Sweet Love Bitter; 1968: Roseanna (nUSr); Wild in the Streets; Killers Three; 1970: Bloody Mama; 1971: Johnny Got His Gun; 1977: I Never

Promised You a Rose Garden.
Select TV: 1959: The Dingaling Girl (sp); **1972:** The People.

ROBERT VAUGHN
BORN: NEW YORK, NY, NOVEMBER 22, 1932.
RAISED IN MINNEAPOLIS, MN.
ED: UNIV. OF MN, LA ST. COL.

A serious, above-average thespian, Robert Vaughn found his peak of fame when he was cast in a hit television series and then spent the remainder of his career pretty much taking whatever assignments came his way. His questionable choices of work frequently caused audiences to forget his acting capabilities. The son of actors, he got his own start while still a youngster, acting on radio during the 1940s. As he got older he did some sports reporting and then moved with his mother to Los Angeles, where his interest in performing was rejuvenated while attending college. A production of *End as a Man* got him a contract with Hecht-Lancaster but nothing came of it. Instead, he wound up in DeMille's mighty *The Ten Commandments*, somewhere among the multitudes, as a spear-carrier, and in Republic's "B" version of the Jesse James saga, *Hell's Crossroads*, as the famous outlaw's slayer, Bob Ford. For Columbia he headed a juvenile delinquent cheapie called *No Time to be Young*, and then went over to AIP for its goofy *Teenage Caveman*, in the title role. This was the sort of movie that would rear its ugly head once he became famous. It didn't matter much though because, within a year, he landed a terrific, showy part, as Paul Newman's screwed-up, alcoholic buddy, who ends up losing an arm and being accused of murder in *The Young Philadelphians*. His fine performance brought him an Oscar nomination for Best Supporting Actor. After that he stood out from the pack as the suave gunslinger in *The Magnificent Seven*, but stayed firmly in support as the nasty son of the circus clan in *The Big Show*, and as a regular on television's *The Lieutenant*. It was that medium that boosted his fortunes when MGM decided to cash in on the spy craze created by the James Bond films with a weekly series called *The Man from U.N.C.L.E.* As debonair super agent Napoleon Solo, Vaughn became one of the most familiar names on mid-1960s television, and the series was popular enough to have some of its episodes stitched together for release in cinemas, starting with *To Trap a Spy* in 1966 and ending with *How to Steal the World* in 1968.

Following the demise of the series, Vaughn went back to support for one of the biggest hits of 1968, *Bullitt*, as the assistant D.A. intent of nagging cop Steve McQueen. It was a reminder that the actor could project a steely side and, often, an unsympathetic, oily one as well. He was a major in a tired war movie, *The Bridge at Remagen*; Casca in the heavily panned 1971 film of *Julius Caesar*; and the surgeon who brings Terence Stamp to life in a genteel sci-fi drama *The Mind of Mr. Soames*. There was a syndicated series, *The Protectors*, and a role as one of the casualties of *The Towering Inferno*, before he ended up having some success on the small screen with a pair of politically-based mini series, *Washington: Behind Closed Doors*, for which he won an Emmy, and *Backstairs at the White House*, in which he played Woodrow Wilson. He began to dabble in the supremely silly with *Demon Seed*, as the voice of the computer that rapes Julie Christie; *Brass Target*, as an evil colonel out to kill General Patton; the barely released *Good Luck, Miss Wyckoff*, as a doctor; the Canadian *Starship Invasions*, as a UFO expert; the purposefully funny *Battle*

Beyond the Stars, the joke of which had him pretty much dusting off his *Magnificent Seven* character; and *S.O.B.*, as the ruthless studio head who likes wearing women's lingerie. He continued his glaring villainy in *Superman III* and *Black Moon Rising*, before falling into the bottomless pit of straight-to-video limbo. Those that actually made it to theatres, though barely, included *Transylvania Twist*, as a comic vampire; *That's Adequate*, as Adolf Hitler; and three made for the MTV crowd, *Joe's Apartment*, *BASEketball*, and *Pootie Tang*. He also made several guest appearances on the television adaptation of *The Magnificent Seven*. In 1972, he authored *Only Victims: A Study of Show Business Blacklisting*.

Screen: 1956: The Ten Commandments; **1957:** Hell's Crossroads; No Time to Be Young; **1958:** Teenage Caveman; Unwed Mother; **1959:** Good Day for a Hanging; The Young Philadelphians; **1960:** The Magnificent Seven; **1961:** The Big Show; **1963:** The Caretakers; **1966:** To Trap a Spy (from TV); The Spy with My Face (from TV); The Glass Bottom Boat; One Spy Too Many (from TV); One of Our Spies Is Missing (from TV); **1967:** The Venetian Affair; The Karate Killers (from TV); The Spy in the Green Hat (from TV); The Helicopter Spies (from TV); **1968:** How to Steal the World (from TV): Bullitt; **1969:** If It's Tuesday, This Must Be Belgium; The Bridge at Remagen; **1970:** The Mind of Mr. Soames; **1971:** Julius Caesar; The Statue; Clay Pigeon; **1974:** The Towering Inferno; **1975:** Wanted: Babysitter (nUSr); **1977:** Demon Seed (voice); **1978:** Starship Invasions; Brass Target; **1979:** Good Luck, Miss Wyckoff; **1980:** Hangar 18; Battle Beyond the Stars; Virus (nUSr); **1981:** S.O.B.; Sweet Dirty Tony/Cuba Crossing; **1983:** Superman III; **1984:** Atraco en la Jungla (nUSr); **1986:** Black Moon Rising; The Delta Force; **1987:** Hour of the Assassin (dtv); Nightstick (dtv); Brutal Glory/Kid McCoy (dtv); Killing Birds (dtv); **1988:** Captive Rage/Fair Trade (dtv); Renegade/They Call Me Renegade (nUSr); **1989:** The Emissary (dtv); Skeleton Coast (dtv); C.H.U.D. II: Bud the C.H.U.D. (dtv); Transylvania Twist; Buried Alive (dtv); River of Death; **1990:** Nobody's Perfect (dtv); That's Adequate!; Blind Vision (dtv); **1991:** Going Under; **1993:** Little Devils/Witch Academy (dtv); **1994:** Dust to Dust (dtv); **1996:** Joe's Apartment; Menno's Mind (dtv); Visions (nUSr); **1997:** Vulcan (nUSr); The Sender (dtv); Motel Blue (dtv); Milk and Money (dtv); An American Affair (dtv); **1998:** McCinsey's Island (nUSr); BASEketball; **2000:** Cottonmouth (dtv); **2001:** Pootie Tang; **2002:** Happy Hour (dtv); **2003:** Hoodlum & Son (dtv).

NY Stage: 2003: The Exonerated.

Select TV: 1959: Made in Japan (sp); **1960:** The Last Flight (sp); **1963–64:** The Lieutenant (series); **1964–68:** The Man from U.N.C.L.E. (series); **1972:** The Woman Hunter; **1972–74:** The Protectors (series); **1976:** Kiss Me, Kill Me; Captains and the Kings (ms); **1977:** Washington: Behind Closed Doors (ms); **1978:** Centennial (ms); The Islander; **1979:** The Rebels (ms); Backstairs at the White House (ms); Mirror, Mirror; The Lucifer Complex; **1980:** Doctor Franken; The Gossip Columnist; City in Fear; **1982:** Fantasies; The Day the Bubble Burst; A Question of Honor; The Blue and the Gray (ms); Inside the Third Reich; **1983:** The Return of the Man from U.N.C.L.E.; Intimate Agony; **1983–84:** Emerald Point N.A.S. (series); **1985:** International Airport; Evergreen (ms); Private Sessions; **1986:** Murrow; Prince of Bel Air; **1986–87:** The A Team (series); **1987:** Desperado; **1988–89:** Reaching for the Sky (series narrator); **1990:** Perry Mason: The Case of the Defiant Daughter; Dark Avenger; **1992:** Tracks of Glory; **1993:** Danger Theatre (series host); **1995:** Dancing in the Dark; As the World Turns (series); Escape to Witch Mountain; **1998:** Virtual Obsession.

CONRAD VEIDT

(Hans Conrad Weidt) Born: Potsdam, Germany, January 22, 1893.
Died: April 3, 1943.

A major figure in German silent cinema, Conrad Veidt had a slightly sinister, commanding air about him that made him ideal for roles of a florid and baroque nature. A student of Max Reinhardt, he did theater in Berlin before making his first motion picture appearance, in a 1917 film called *Der Spion/The Spy*. That same year he made an important connection when director Richard Oswald asked him to star in *Das Tagebuch einer Verlorenen/Diary of a Lost Girl*, as a doctor destroyed by a bad woman. They became frequent collaborators on some of the country's most provocative movies of the day, including *Die Prostitution*; *Anders als die andern*, which approached the subject of homosexuality (Veidt was himself gay) in a surprisingly open manner for its day; and *Kurfurstendamm*, in which he played the Devil. In between these, there were notable roles like Phileas Fogg in a version of *Around the World in Eighty Days*, Frederic Chopin in *Nocturno der Liebe*; dual characters suggested by Dr. Jekyll and Mr. Hyde in *Der Januskopf/The Two-Faced Man*; Lord Nelson in *Lady Hamilton*; and Cesare Borgia in *Lucrezia Borgia*. He also took the time to direct himself in both *Wahnsinn/Madness* and *Die Nacht auf Goldenhall/The Night at Goldenhall*. The most famous of all his films during this period, however, was the dazzling horror-fantasy *The Cabinet of Dr. Caligari*, in which he played the killer somnambulist Cesare in one of the most original, influential, and striking movies to come out of silent cinema. During the 1920s he continued to be one of Germany's busiest actors with *Hands of Orlac*, as the pianist given the hands of a killer; *The Brothers Schellenberg*, in another dual role, as rich siblings, one benevolent and one irresponsible; and *The Student of Prague*, a variation on the Faust theme.

He'd become famous enough for Hollywood to make him offers and he went there to play Louis XI in *The Beloved Rogue*, and then did three for Universal: *A Man's Past* and *The Last Performance*, which were quickly forgotten; and *The Man Who Laughs*, in which was as creepily effective as he was in his most memorable work back home, playing a man whose face has been disfigured into a permanent smile. Since none of these made money, he returned to Germany to make his sound debut in *Das Land Ohne Feruen/Terra Senza donne/Bride 68*, in 1929, and kept at it for another three years until the Nazi regime forced him to seek work elsewhere. He went to England to make *Rome Express*, but came back home for *Wilhelm Tell* and *Jew Suss*, a journey that nearly proved catastrophic when the Nazis tried to keep him there under the pretense that he was ill, until the authorities at Gaumont British, for whom he was now under contract, intervened. He settled in England for such movies as *The Passing of the Third Floor Back*, as a mysterious stranger, and *Dark Journey*, as Vivien Leigh's lover and nemesis. His involvement in the lavish fantasy *The Thief of Bagdad*, as the evil Grand Vizier, brought him back to Hollywood since part of the movie was shot there. Because the American film industry was now looking for men like Veidt to portray nasty Nazis, he stayed on to terrorize Norma Shearer in *Escape*, Red Skelton in *Whistling in the Dark*, and Humphrey Bogart in *All Through the Night*. Also with Bogart he was featured in the Oscar-winning *Casablanca*, as the imperious Major Strasser, who is shot by the hero at the airport in the movie's climax. There was one more Nazi role after that, in *Above Suspicion*, released after he had died of a heart attack while golfing.

Screen (select silents): 1917: Der Spion/The Spy; 1918: Tagebuch einer Verlorenen/Diary of a Lost Girl; Henriette Jacoby; Nocturno der Liebe; Opium; 1919: Around the World in Eighty Days; Peer Gynt; Anders als die Andern/Different from the Others; Die Prostitution; Prinz Kuckuck/Prince Cuckoo; Wahnsinn/Madness (and dir.); Satanas; The Cabinet of Dr. Caligari; 1920: Patience; Der Januskopf/The Two-Faced Man; Die Nacht auf Goldenhall/The Night at Goldenhall (and dir.); Kurfurstendamm; Manolescus Memoiren/Memories of Manolescu; Der Gangin die Nacht/The Dark Road; Christian Wahnschaffe; 1921: Lady Hamilton; The Indian Tomb/Above the Law; 1922: Lucrezia Borgia; 1923: Paganini; Wilhelm Tell; 1924: Karlos and Elizabeth; Waxworks; Hands of Orlac; 1925: Ingmar's Inheritance; 1926: Die Gieger von Florenz/Impetuous Youth; The Brothers Schellenberg/The Two Brothers; Der Student von Pragg/The Student of Prague/The Man Who Cheated Life; 1927: The Beloved Rogue; A Man's Past; 1928: The Man Who Laughs; 1929: The Last Performance; **(sound films):** Das Land Ohne Freuen/Terra senza donne/Bride 68; 1930: The Last Company/Thirteen Men and a Girl; Die Grosse Sehnsucht/The Great Passion; 1931: Cape Forlorn; Der Mann der den Mord Beging/The Man Who Committed Murder; Die Nacht der Entscheidung/The Night of Decision; The Congress Dances; Die andere Seite/Journey's End; Rasputin; 1932: Die Schwarze Husar/The Black Husar; F.P.I. Doesn't Answer; Ich und die Kaiserin; Rome Express; The Wandering Jew; 1933: I Was a Spy; 1934: Wilhelm Tell/The Legend of William Tell; Jew Suss/Power; Bella Donna; 1935: The Passing of the Third Floor Back; 1936: King of the Damned; 1937: Under the Red Robe; Dark Journey; 1938: Tempete sur l'Asie/Storm Over Asia; Le Joureur d'Eches/The Chess Player; 1939: The Spy in Black; 1940: Escape; Contraband; The Thief of Bagdad; 1941: A Woman's Face; Whistling in the Dark; The Men in Her Life; 1942: Nazi Agent; All Through the Night; 1943: Casablanca; Above Suspicion.

LUPE VELEZ

(Maria Guadalupe Vélez de Villalobos) Born: San Luis Potosi, Mexico, July 18, 1908.
Died: December 14, 1944.

A pint-size bundle of dynamic energy, Lupe Velez, with her hyper mannerisms and fractured English, was a source of gleeful, lowbrow chuckles for some and just too much for others to endure. Though convent-educated, she quickly left that life behind and took up dancing at age 15. She set her sights on Hollywood and journeyed there to find work, ending up in a stage show, *Music Box Revue*, where she was seen by producer Hal Roach. Roach put her in two shorts, including "Sailors, Beware!" with Laurel and Hardy, and Douglas Fairbanks, having got wind of her vitality, cast her as his leading lady in the 1927 adventure *The Gaucho*, in which she made an immediate impression as a hot-blooded mountain girl. Audiences first got to hear her less-than-perfect English in *Lady of the Pavements*, a Pygmalion-like story in which she was a cabaret dancer passing as a woman of high society, after which she caught Gary Cooper's eye on screen in *Wolf Song*, as well as off, where they became one of the most talked about romantic pairings in Hollywood. Velez bounced about from studio to studio, showing up at Universal for *The Storm*, as a French-Canadian girl snowbound with William "Stage" Boyd, and *Resurrection*, from the Leo Tolstoy novel; Paramount for *The Broken Wing*, as a Mexican villager who falls for aviator Melvyn Douglas; and several MGM films, including DeMille's remake of *The Squaw Man*, and the Lawrence Tibbett musical, *Cuban Love Song*. These were all dramas, but RKO used her for laughs, to good effect, in *The Half-Naked Truth*, as a carny dancer exploited by sharpy Lee Tracy.

In 1933, she married the screen's Tarzan, Johnny Weissmuller, and they made for one of the movie capital's most publicized and stormy unions, one that would come close to divorce time and again, until they finally called it quits for real in 1938. In the meantime, she appeared as the *Hot Pepper*, in the last of the waning Victor McLaglen/Edmund Lowe teamings; battled with Laurel and Hardy during the all-star *Hollywood Party*; and played opposite Jimmy Durante in both *Palooka*, in which she boiled the blood of boxer Stuart Erwin, and *Strictly Dynamite*, as Durante's temperamental radio partner. She went to England to do some pictures and, when she returned, RKO hired her for a raucously pea-brained comedy called *The Girl from Mexico*. In it she played, as if in a state of apoplexy, an entertainer named Carmelita Fuentes, who takes Manhattan by storm and winds up snaring ad-man Donald Woods in the process. Comic Leon Errol was there as Woods's Uncle Matt and the end result pleased the studio to a point where they decided there was a potential series to be made from this disposable little item. Later that same year, in 1939, they officially launched the series under the name *Mexican Spitfire*, with Velez and Woods now married, and Errol kept on to do his brand of fidgety shtick. The movie made a healthy profit and the title became the perfect description of its star, who would be forever remembered for these quickly made, proudly unsophisticated comedies. There were six more entries, ending with *Mexican Spitfire's Blessed Event*, which actually involved a baby ocelot, not her own offspring. In 1944 she returned to her native Mexico for one last movie, *Nana*, and then took an overdose of sleeping pills later that year, despondent over her latest unsuccessful love affair.

Screen: 1927: The Gaucho; 1928: Stand and Deliver; 1929: Lady of the Pavements; Tiger Rose; The Wolf Song; Where East Is East; 1930: The Storm; Hell Harbor; East Is West (and Spanish version: Oriente es Occidente); 1931: Resurrection; The Squaw Man; Cuban Love Song; 1932: Hombres en mi vida (Spanish version of Men in Her Life); The Broken Wing; Kongo; The Half-Naked Truth; Hot Pepper; Mr. Broadway; 1934: Laughing Boy; Palooka; Hollywood Party; Strictly Dynamite; 1936: The Morals of Marcus; Gypsy Melody; 1937: High Flyers; 1938: Mad About Money/He Loved an Actress/Stardust; La Zandunga (nUSr); 1939: The Girl from Mexico; Mexican Spitfire; 1940: Mexican Spitfire Out West; 1941: Six Lessons from Madame La Zonga; Mexican Spitfire's Baby; Playmates; Honolulu Lu; 1942: Mexican Spitfire at Sea; Mexican Spitfire Sees a Ghost; Mexican Spitfire's Elephant; 1943: Ladies' Day; Mexican Spitfire's Blessed Event; Redhead from Manhattan; 1944: Nana.

NY Stage: 1932: Hot-Cha!; 1933: Strike Me Pink; 1936: Transatlantic Rhythm; 1938: You Never Know.

VERA-ELLEN
(VERA-ELLEN WESTMYER ROHE)
BORN: CINCINNATI, OH, FEBRUARY 16, 1920.
DIED: AUGUST 30, 1981.

Her career was little more than a decade long, but Vera-Ellen was a most pleasant addition to the movie musical during that period. Sweet, agile, and petite, with a tiny waist that seemed to be no more three inches in circumference, she was a terrific dancer and a sprightly turn or two on the dance floor was all audiences ever expected, since her acting was severely limited and her vocals were always done by others. A dancer since childhood,

she eventually taught the craft before joining Major Bowe's Amateur Hour's touring show, during the late 1930s. This led to work as a Rockette at the Radio City Music Hall, nightclub entertaining, and finally Broadway chorus work in such shows as the first Lerner and Loewe credit, *Very Warm for May*, and Ethel Merman's *Panama Hattie*. She was given a larger part in *A Connecticut Yankee*, and was signed to a contract by Samuel Goldwyn's company as a result. They started her off in a Danny Kaye vehicle, *Wonder Man*, where she and Kaye dance to the "Bali Boogie," and she mimed "So in Love" while June Hutton did the vocalizing. Playing it safe, this hit was followed by another with Kaye, *The Kid from Brooklyn*, and then a loan-out to Fox, *Three Little Girls in Blue*, where she danced on a gigantic organ to the tune of "You Make Me Feel So Young." Since Goldwyn had nothing else for her to do, her contract was cancelled, and she went over to MGM to partner Gene Kelly in a sizzling rendition of "Slaughter on Tenth Avenue," supplying the definite highlight of the tepid Rodgers and Hart biopic, *Words and Music*. After that triumphant credit, it was not exactly a step up to play the ingénue in *Love Happy*, even if it did feature the Marx Brothers, since the comedians looked old and tired in what was their last, cheaply made, vehicle.

Fortunately, MGM had the good sense to see that she could fit in quite nicely to their stable of musical stars and put her under contract in 1949. She started on a high note, playing "Miss Turnstiles," in one of the studio's top attractions, *On the Town*, and once again came off as a very appealing personality, as long as you didn't analyze her acting attempts too closely. Having proved that she was a marvelous partner for Gene Kelly, MGM decided to try her out with Fred Astaire in *Three Little Words*, and she matched him brilliantly. They were teamed again for *The Belle of New York*, a charming turn-of-the-century romance that gave Vera-Ellen her best opportunity, though it was a tad too whimsical for audiences and therefore not a hit. Two she did on loan-out, however, did very nicely, starting with *Call Me Madam*, at Fox, where one had to forgive her atrocious attempt at a foreign accent, since she got to dance with Donald O'Connor. She then appeared in one of Paramount's all-time box-office champs, *White Christmas*, back with Danny Kaye, but very much in support. There was one last musical, *Let's Be Happy*, made in England, which had been the locale of a previous one in 1951, *Happy Go Lovely*, but, in the end, there was no indication of why she had bothered to make either trip. In the meantime, she married a millionaire and this meant that there was no fiscal reason for her to keep working. She retired in the late 1950s and kept almost completely out of the public eye for the rest of her life.

Screen: 1945: Wonder Man; 1946: The Kid from Brooklyn; Three Little Girls in Blue; 1947: Carnival in Costa Rica; 1948: Words and Music; 1949: Love Happy; On the Town; 1950: Three Little Words; 1951: Happy Go Lovely; 1952: The Belle of New York; 1953: Call Me Madam; Big Leaguer; 1954: White Christmas; 1956: Let's Be Happy.

NY Stage: 1939: Very Warm For May; 1940: Higher and Higher; Panama Hattie; 1942: By Jupiter; 1943: A Connecticut Yankee.

Select TV: 1957: The Man Across the Hall (sp).

GWEN VERDON
BORN: CULVER CITY, CA, JANUARY 13, 1925.
DIED: OCTOBER 18, 2000.

Although she undulated her way through several Hollywood musicals, it took Broadway to appreciate and correctly utilize the talents of Gwen Verdon. Her father was an electrician at MGM and she was taught dancing by Marge Champion's dad. While still young, she was dancing at such locales as the Shrine Auditorium (she is said to have participated in a ballet sequence in the Grace Moore musical *The King Steps Out* at this point in her life) and eventually linked up with choreographer-dancer Jack Cole. With him she performed in nightclubs and then in some Broadway shows he worked on, including *Alive and Kicking*. Heading back to California, she did mostly uncredited work, even when given a solo or specialty spot, on such pictures as *On the Riviera*; *David and Bathsheba*, as a slave girl; and *The Farmer Takes a Wife*, dancing with pie plates on her feet. A scene-stealing supporting part in Broadway's *Can-Can* made her the talk of the town and she got herself a Tony Award for it. She followed that with *Damn Yankees*, earning another Tony, and became a star. That show's choreographer, Bob Fosse, had found the perfect interpreter of his technique and they married in 1960 (they separated in 1970 but never officially divorced). There were two more Tonys, for *New Girl in Town* and *Redhead*, and, in a rare instance of good common sense, Warner Bros. actually let her repeat her role as the comical temptress Lola in their 1958 film of *Damn Yankees*, which was brightly directed by Stanley Donen and allowed her to duet with Fosse himself in the "Who's Got the Pain?" number. She scored her biggest Broadway hit in 1966, in *Sweet Charity*, but Shirley MacLaine got the part in the film. Verdon did return to movies, dancing briefly, in *The Cotton Club*, and, as she got older and more frail, played a senior citizen in *Cocoon*, doing a quick few steps with Don Ameche, and Diane Keaton's dying aunt in *Marvin's Room*.

Screen: 1936: The King Steps Out; 1951: On the Riviera; David and Bathsheba; 1952: Dreamboat; The Merry Widow; 1953: The Mississippi Gambler; Meet Me After the Show; The I Don't Care Girl; The Farmer Takes a Wife; 1955: Gentlemen Marry Brunettes; 1958: Damn Yankees; 1984: The Cotton Club; 1985: Cocoon; 1987: Nadine; 1988: Cocoon: The Return; 1990: Alice; 1996: Marvin's Room; 1999: Walking Across Egypt (dtv).

NY Stage: 1948: Magdalena; 1950: Alive and Kicking; 1953: Can-Can; 1955: Damn Yankees; 1957: New Girl in Town; 1959: Redhead; 1966: Sweet Charity; 1972: Children! Children!; 1975: Chicago.

Select TV: 1954: Native Dancer (sp); 1970: Foul (sp); 1983: Legs; 1984: The Jerk Too; 1994: Oldest Living Confederate Widow Tells All; 1996: In Cold Blood; 1998: Best Friends for Life; 2000: The Dress Code/Bruno.

MARTHA VICKERS

(MARTHA MacVICAR) BORN: ANN ARBOR, MI, MAY 28, 1925. DIED: NOVEMBER 2, 1971.

After a false start, Martha Vickers got a new name and a second chance to make a temporary splash. However, her assignments got pallid and she became better known for being one of Mickey Rooney's many wives. A former model, she was signed to a movie contract by David O. Selznick, who didn't use her at all, so it was up to Universal to "introduce" her to the movie-going public, as a corpse, in *Frankenstein Meets the Wolf Man*, in 1943. After a few more unremarkable roles she went to RKO to do bigger parts in *Marine Raiders* and *The Falcon in Mexico*, and then was sent on her way. Warner Bros. was next to give her a try and they gave her the star push, rearranging her surname to "Vickers." They re-launched her spectacularly in *The Big Sleep*, in which she was pretty unforgettable as Lauren Bacall's trampy, fun-loving sister, who gets involved in blackmail and drapes herself flirtatiously into detective Humphrey Bogart's

arms on their first meeting. It was the high point of her movie career and the one role that would keep her face alive for years to come. For her follow-up she got to sing "A Gal in Calico" with Dennis Morgan and Jack Carson in *The Time, the Place and the Girl*; was a rich benefactor of songwriters Carson and Robert Hutton in a poor comedy, *Love and Learn*; and a millionaire's daughter in *That Way with Women*, a remake of *The Millionaire* that nobody really asked for. With that, Warners dropped her and she briefly married (1948) publicist and future producer A.C. Lyles , before linking up with Rooney in 1949, a union that lasted until 1951. After that there were a handful of "B" pictures, including *The Big Bluff*, as a rich woman whose scheming husband is horrified to find out that she isn't going to die as he thought. By the 1960s, she had dropped out of sight, and died when she was only 46 years old.

Screen: AS MARTHA MacVICAR: 1943: Frankenstein Meets the Wolf Man; Hi'Ya, Sailor; Top Man; Captive Wild Woman; 1944: The Mummy's Ghost; This Is the Life; Marine Raiders; The Falcon in Mexico.

AS MARTHA VICKERS: 1946: The Big Sleep; The Time, the Place and the Girl; The Man I Love; 1947: Love and Learn; That Way With Women; 1948: Ruthless; 1949: Alimony; Bad Boy; Daughter of the West; 1955: The Big Bluff; 1957: The Burglar; 1959: Four Fast Guns.

Select TV: 1954: That Other Sunlight (sp); The Last 30 Minutes (sp); Night Visitor (sp); 1955: The Indiscreet Mr. Jarvis (sp).

ERICH VON STROHEIM

(ERICH OSWALD STROHEIM) BORN: VIENNA, AUSTRIA-HUNGARY, SEPTEMBER 22, 1885. DIED: MAY 12, 1957.

Erich von Stroheim was a true original, an actor whose advancing age, balding head, and arrogant manner were in no way deterrents to him playing a "ladies' man." His stock in trade was the caddish seducer, done up in uniform and monocle, giving rich and willing women the eye. The publicity department eventually came up with a suitable name, "The Man You Love to Hate." As a director he became one of the most undisciplined and extravagant in the field, causing all kinds of budget overruns in an effort to put his often dazzling, often decadent vision on screen. Much of his early life remains a mystery, but he did emigrate to the United States in 1906, where he did some reporting and writing for newspapers and magazines before taking up acting. He traveled to Los Angeles where he received extra work, the first credit often cited as the 1914 Lillian Gish vehicle, *Captain Macklin*. Continuing to act, he also became a member of D.W. Griffith's company, doing some behind the scenes jobs as well. Supposedly, he did tiny bits in the director's two most famous pictures, *The Birth of a Nation* and *Intolerance*, but it was director-actor John Emerson who started giving him substantial parts, in films like *His Picture in the Papers* and *The Social Secretary*. Universal gave him his big break with the 1919 World War I melodrama *The Heart of Humanity*, in which he was so loathsome that he tossed a crying baby out of a window at one point. He wasted no time convincing the studio to allow him to direct as well as act, starting with a script he had written, *Blind Husbands*, in which his character causes jealousy when he pities a neglected wife. It was a critically liked film and made Universal some cash, so everybody was pleased, particularly von Stroheim who was now considered a director of merit. He followed this success with *The Devil's Passkey*, a film that he helmed but did not appeared in.

Next up was the first of his two most famous directorial efforts in which he himself also starred. In *Foolish Wives*, he charmed ladies out of their money, broke their hearts, and was finally slain and literally thrown in a sewer as punishment for his callous behavior. This was also the first instance in which von Stroheim let one of his productions get out of hand, resulting in Universal taking his lengthier version away from him and trimming it to a more watchable two hours. He never made it through *The Merry-Go-Round*, being initially replaced as star by Norman Kerry and then as director by Rupert Julian. More bad luck happened over at MGM when they took *Greed* from him and hacked it down from his unreasonably proposed length of eight hours to something closer to two and a half. The end result was the most impressive of his films, even in this truncated form but it remained a jinxed failure to many. Continuing this pattern he was fired from *The Merry Widow*, for which he'd served as director and writer, then went over to Paramount for *The Wedding March*. This time he destroyed Fay Wray's heart, as the prince who chooses instead to marry timid ZaSu Pitts for her money. Again, what was left on screen was silent filmmaking at its most engrossing, but it was only half of what von Stroheim intended, its latter half being distributed only in Europe, as *The Honeymoon*, and then subsequently lost over the years. One final silent as director, *Queen Kelly*, fared even worse, with the entire production being shut down by its star and producer, Gloria Swanson, before it was finished. Years later it would be revived with still photos and title cards filling in the gaps, once again showing great unfulfilled promise.

As talkies arrived there was still interest in him von Stroheim an actor, so he played a ventriloquist who flips out in *The Great Gabbo*; a butler who is really a German spy in *Three Faces East*; and a novelist who lives with and loves Greta Garbo in *As You Desire Me*, where they made an ideal team, though this was hardly one of her better films. Fox gave him one last chance as a director, on a film called *Walking Down Broadway*, but it was yet another unfinished work and most of it was re-filmed by Alfred Werker before it finally showed up under the name *Hello, Sister!* After two cheaper films and temporary behind-the-scenes employment at MGM, he went to Europe where he acted in several French films, the most famous being *Grand Illusion*, in which he played the German prison camp commander who takes a humane interest in his designated enemy Pierre Fresnay. Since this was the most acclaimed foreign film of its day, and the first in another language to ever receive an Oscar nomination for Best Picture, it was clearly another feather in von Stroheim's cap. Because war was cooking in Europe, Hollywood was interested in having him return to play some Nazis, which he did in *So Ends Our Night*; director Billy Wilder's *Five Graves to Cairo*, as Field Marshal Rommel; and *The North Star*. His status weakened, however, when he began working at Republic on such programmers as *The Lady and the Monster* and *Scotland Yard Inspector*. He returned to France again, where he stayed for the remainder of his life, except for one important excursion back to Hollywood for the movie most people would best remember him for, *Sunset Blvd.* As Gloria Swanson's faithful butler, Max, who turns out to have been her ex-husband, he was creepy, sad, and properly haunting, earning an Oscar nomination in the supporting category. His remaining films were all foreign-language productions, none of which received distribution in the United States.

Screen: 1915: Captain Macklin; Ghosts; The Birth of a Nation; 1916: His Picture in the Papers; The Social Secretary; Macbeth; The Flying Torpedo; Intolerance (and asst. dir.); Less Than the Dust; 1917: Panthea; In Again, Out Again; Reaching for the Moon; Sylvia of the Secret Service; Draft 258; 1918: The Unbeliever; Hearts of the World; The Hun Within; 1919: The

Heart of Humanity; 1919: Blind Husbands (and dir.; wr.); 1921: Foolish Wives (and dir.; wr.); 1928: The Wedding March (and dir.; wr.; second half released in Europe as The Honeymoon); 1929: The Great Gabbo; 1930: Three Faces East; 1931: Friends and Lovers; 1932: The Lost Squadron; As You Desire Me; 1934: Crimson Romance; Fugitive Road; 1935: The Crime of Dr. Crespi; 1937: Marthe Richard (nUSr); Grand Illusion; Mademoiselle Docteur; L'Alibi (nUSr); 1938: Les Pirates de Rail (nUSr); L'Affaire Lafarge (nUSr); Les Disparus de St. Agil/Boys' School; Ultimatum; Gibraltar; 1939: Derriere la Façade/Rue de Montmartre (nUSr); Macao Enfer de Jeu/Gambling Hell; Rappel Immediat/Immediate Call; Le Monde Tremblera/The World Will Shake (nUSr); Pieges/Personal Column; 1940: Tempete sur Paris/Thunder Over Paris; Menaces/Threats (nUSr); Paris — New York; I Was an Adventuress; 1941: So Ends Our Night; 1943: Five Graves to Cairo; The North Star; 1944: The Lady and the Monster; Storm Over Lisbon; 1945: The Great Flammarion; Scotland Yard Investigator; 1946: The Mask of Dijon; La Foire aux Chimeres/The Devil and the Angel (nUSr); On ne Meurt pas Comme Ca!/One Does Not Die That Way (nUSr); 1947: La Danse de Mort (and co-wr.; nUSr); 1948: La Signal Rouge (nUSr); 1949: Portrait du'un Assassin/Portrait of an Assassin (nUSr); 1950: Sunset Blvd.; 1952: Alarune/Unnatural (nUSr); 1953: Minuit …Quai deBercy/Midnight … Quai de Bercy (nUSr); 1954: L'Envers du Paradis/The Other Side of Paradise (nUSr); Alerte au Sud/Alert in the South (nUSr); 1955: Napoleon; Seire Moire/The Infiltrator (nUSr); La Madone des Sleepings (nUSr).

MAX VON SYDOW

(CARL ADOLF VON SYDOW) BORN: LUND, SKÅNE, SWEDEN, APRIL 10, 1929. ED: CATHEDRAL SCHOOL OF LUND, ROYAL ACAD. OF STOCKHOLM.

Of all the performers who came to fame interpreting the works of Ingmar Bergman, gaunt, deep-voiced Max von Sydow, an actor who could command the screen through the subtlest of gestures, had the best luck in crossing over into American productions. He studied acting at the Royal Academy of Stockholm and, while there, made his film debut, in a tiny part, in *Bara en Mor/Only a Mother*, in 1949. During the early 1950s he concentrated mainly onstage acting, appearing at the Norrkoping-Linkoping Municipal Theatre, the Municipal Theatre of Halsingborg, and the Municipal Theatre of Malmo. It was at Malmo that he met director Ingmar Bergman who invited him to carry his upcoming production, *The Seventh Seal*. This film was instrumental in making Bergman's worldwide reputation and, when released in the U.S. in 1958, became the most talked about import of its day. Von Sydow, properly melancholy and brooding, was the disillusioned knight who literally confronts Death in a symbolic game of chess. Now officially a member of Bergman's stock company, he did smaller roles for him in *Wild Strawberries* and *Brink of Life*, before moving back to the leads in *The Magician*; *The Virgin Spring*, one of the director's best and an Oscar-winner for Best Foreign Language Film, with Von Sydow as the father who avenges his daughter's rape; *Through a Glass Darkly*, another Oscar-winner, in which he watched helplessly as wife Harriet Andersson lost her mind; and *Winter Light*, as a fisherman confronting the nuclear age. The acclaim was such that Hollywood started making offers and von Sydow made his English-language debut in director George Steven's massive and expensive *The Greatest Story Ever Told*, where he was a most persuasive and dignified Jesus.

He stuck around for some further American productions, with a western, *The Reward*, and *The Quiller Memorandum*, a spy film that made little impression. However, he did get to carry one of the more popular movies of 1966, *Hawaii*. Despite receiving second billed to Julie Andrews it was actually Von Sydow's show from start to finish, though the character was too pig-headed for most people to care. Returning to Bergman, he did *Hour of the Wolf*, as an artist worried that he has lost his talent, and *The Passion of Anna*, giving one of his best performances, as the emotionally deadened loner who attracts two very needy women, Liv Ullman and Bibi Andersson. He continued in international productions, like the confusing spy thriller *The Kremlin Letter*; *Night Visitor*, as a prisoner avenging those who put him away; and *The Touch*, which was Bergman's first English-language film and a major critical and financial flop. He teamed again with Ullman for director Jan Troell's *The Emigrants* and this was unusually successful for a foreign-language film, so much so that it received an Oscar nomination in the Best Picture category and rated a sequel, *The New Land*. In 1973, he got the widest exposure of his career when he played the elderly priest who tries to remove the devil from Linda Blair in the phenomenally popular horror movie *The Exorcist*. At this point he figured he had a good deal going, as long as he could make vehicles in Europe and take supporting roles in American productions, thereby keeping his reputation as a consummate actor of serious intent intact and remaining financially solvent at the same time.

He took the lead in the 1974 film version of Hesse's unfilmmable novel *Steppenwolf*, and then leant his expertise to such U.S. movies as *Three Days of the Condor*, as the mysterious agent out to murder Robert Redford; *Voyage of the Damned*, as the tormented captain of the doomed ship; *Brass Target*, in which he was intent on killing General Patton; the worthless 1979 remake of *Hurricane*, as the island doctor, in the role Thomas Mitchell had done the first time out; and *Flash Gordon*, playing it tongue-in-cheek all the way as the nefarious Emperor Ming, and looking startlingly like Charles Middleton from the original 1930s serial. Back in Sweden he led a dangerous balloon expedition to the North Pole in *The Flight of the Eagle*, and ended up in one his very best films, *Pelle the Conqueror*, a downbeat but moving story of a dirt poor and ignorant widower trying to raise his young son while working as a stablehand in 19th century Denmark. Good as he was, the whole film was stolen from him, hands down, by 12-year-old Pelle Hvenegaard as the title character. Nonetheless, von Sydow ended up with his first ever Oscar nomination, while the film itself took the Academy Award for Best Foreign Language Film of 1988. In America he played a batch of doctors, in *Dreamscape*; *Dune*, where he was one of the few not to sink with the ship in this sci-fi disaster; *Duet for One*, which reteamed him with Julie Andrews; and *Awakenings*, the only one of these to have any wide commercial appeal. Woody Allen gave him a juicy role as Barbara Hershey's cantankerous, complaining artist love in *Hannah and Her Sisters*, but his showcase assignments usually came from across the sea, including *Father*, in which he was suspected of being a Nazi by his daughter; *The Best Intentions*, portraying Bergman's grandfather in this autobiographical piece, co-scripted by the retired director; *The Silent Touch*, as a composer coaxed out of retirement; and *Hamsun*, as a writer blinded to the reality of Nazi Germany. Back in America, among his larger roles there, he was the embodiment of Satan, driving a small town to madness, in *Needful Things*; Robin Williams's weird guide to the Underworld in *What Dreams May Come*; a shrewd lawyer fighting for an Asian man accused of murder in *Snow Falling on Cedars*; and the creator of a futuristic law enforcement agency in *Minority Report*. Von Sydow made his directorial debut, in 1988, with *Katinka*, but no one distributed it in the U.S.

Screen (US releases only): 1958: The Seventh Seal (Swe: 1957); 1959: Wild Strawberries (Swe: 1957); The Magician (Swe: 1958); 1960: Brink of Life (Swe: 1958); 1960: The Virgin Spring; 1962: Through a Glass Darkly (Swe: 1961); 1963: Winter Light (Swe: 1962); 1965: The Greatest Story Ever Told; The Reward; 1966: Hawaii; The Quiller Memorandum; 1968: Hour of the Wolf; Shame; 1970: The Passion of Anna (Swe: 1969); The Kremlin Letter; 1971: The Night Visitor; The Touch; 1972: The Emigrants (Swe: 1971); 1973: Embassy (UK: 1972); The New Land (Swe: 1972); The Excorcist; 1974: Steppenwolf; 1975: The Apple War (Swe: 1971); Three Days of the Condor; 1976: The Ultimate Warrior; Voyage of the Damned; 1977: Exorcist II: The Heretic; March or Die; Other Side of Paradise/Foxtrot (filmed 1975); 1978: Brass Target; 1979: A Look at Liv; Hurricane; 1980: Flash Gordon; 1981: Illustrious Corpses (It: 1976); Victory; 1982: Deathwatch; She Dances Alone (voice); Conan the Barbarian; 1983: The Flight of the Eagle; Strange Brew; Never Say Never Again; 1984: Dreamscape; Dune; 1985: George Stevens: A Filmmaker's Journey; Codename: Emerald; 1986: Hannah and Her Sisters; Duet for One; 1987: The Wolf at the Door; 1988: Pelle the Conqueror; 1990: Awakenings; 1991: A Kiss Before Dying; Until the End of the World; 1992: Zentropa (narrator); The Best Intentions; The Ox; Father; The Bachelor/Dr. Grassler; 1993: The Silent Touch; Needful Things; 1995: Judge Dredd; 1997: Jerusalem; Hamsun; 1998: What Dreams May Come; 1999: Private Confessions; Snow Falling on Cedars; 2002: Minority Report; Intacto.

NY Stage: 1977: The Night of the Tribades; 1981: Duet For One.

Select TV: 1964: Sweden: Fire and Ice (sp); 1967: The Diary of Anne Frank (sp); 1984: Samson and Delilah; Kojak: The Belarus File; 1985: The Last Place on Earth (sp); Christopher Columbus (ms); 1987: Quo Vadis; 1989: Red King, White Knight; 1990: Hiroshima: Out of the Ashes; 1993: Grandfather's Journey; 1994: Radetzky March; 1995: Citizen X; 1997: Hostile Waters; Solomon; 2000: Nuremberg.

W

ROBERT WAGNER

BORN: DETROIT, MI, FEBRUARY 10, 1930.
RAISED IN LOS ANGELES, CA.

There was little to suggest in the early years of Robert Wagner's career that he'd still be at it half a century later. A nice-looking, personable fellow, he was never the sort to earn critical kudos but his smooth, unthreatening nature seemed to relax folks, especially the undemanding audience that made television their prime source of entertainment. His family moved to Los Angeles when he was a youngster and he ended up rubbing elbows with the stars by caddying at the Bel Air Country Club. Following school, he decided to offer himself up to the casting offices and this resulted in a bit in MGM's boys school romp *The Happy Years*, which got him a casting agent who, in turn, wrangled him a contract with 20th Century-Fox in 1950. That studio launched him in a pair of routine military dramas, *Halls of Montezuma* (Marines) and *The Frogmen* (Navy), in both instances supporting Richard Widmark. He did, however, manage to impress with his small role as the young, shell-shocked soldier to whom Susan Hayward sings, in the best scene in the hit biopic, *With a Song in My Heart*. In *Stars and Stripes Forever*, he was the fictionalized inventor of the sousaphone; was back in uniform again for the weak remake of *What Price Glory?*; managed to survive the sinking of *Titanic*; and finally got top billing, playing a Greek sponge diver, in a dreary adventure, *Beneath the 12-Mile Reef*. He played the title role in the juvenile costume epic *Prince Valiant*, sporting a silly page boy wig and taking billing *below* the villain, James Mason, and got his best opportunity at Fox with *Broken Lance*, as the cherished son of domineering cattle baron Spencer Tracy. He was borrowed by United Artists for his meatiest role, playing, with the right amount of psychotic self-righteousness, the crazed killer in a fine rendering of Ira Levin's first novel, *A Kiss Before Dying*, and then was unconvincingly cast as Tracy's greedy younger brother in Paramount's *The Mountain*.

Back at Fox, the studio allowed him to play up his bad side, as these other companies had done, in a minor western, *The True Story of Jesse James*, in which he interpreted the famed outlaw as

an alienated teen, after which he supported Bing Crosby in a contrived musical drama, *Say One for Me*. He married Natalie Wood in 1957 and they did their one and only theatrical feature together, *All the Fine Young Cannibals*, which was pretty much drummed out of town by the critics. Wagner was supposed to be a Paul Newman or Steve McQueen-type character, brooding and sexually charismatic, an act he hadn't the chops to pull off. After this misstep, he pretty much became something of an all-purpose player, who neither greatly enhanced nor detracted from the films that he participated in. Finding time to fight various cinematic battles he was in *The War Lover*, as McQueen's co-pilot, and the all-star *The Longest Day*; and played straight man to Ernie Kovacs in *Sail a Crooked Ship*, and to Peter Sellers in the popular *The Pink Panther*, in which he was a jewel thief. As he grew older (though he aged spectacularly well), he displayed a bit of the smarmy bon vivant and this was evident in his performances in *Harper*, as a pilot and possible murder suspect; *Banning*, as an arrogant golf pro; *The Biggest Bundle of them All*, in which he plotted a heist; and *Winning*, as Paul Newman's racecar rival, who ends up bedding his wife, Joanne Woodward. In 1968 he started a reasonably successful series, *It Takes a Thief* and began to settle very comfortably into the world of television. He did show up occasionally in cinemas, getting burned to death in *The Towering Inferno*; trying to destroy the title vehicle in *The Concorde — Airport '79*; playing a Hollywood producer in *Dragon: The Bruce Lee Story*; and standing by with an amusingly stoic manner as Mike Myers's chief henchman in three *Austin Powers* comedies. In 1979 he launched another weekly series, *Hart to Hart* and this property continued on long after cancellation in a series of telefilms. Although he and Natalie Wood had divorced in 1962, they remarried in 1972 and remained wed until Wood's tragic death in 1981. In 1990, Wagner married actress Jill St. John and the two showed up, playing themselves, in the star-studded *The Player*.

Screen: 1950: The Happy Years; Halls of Montezuma; 1951: The Frogmen; Let's Make It Legal; 1952: With a Song in My Heart; What Price Glory?; Stars and Stripes Forever; 1953: Titanic; The Silver Whip; Beneath the 12-Mile Reef; 1954: Prince Valiant; Broken Lance; 1955: White Feather; 1956: A Kiss Before Dying; The Mountain; Between Heaven and Hell; 1957: The True Story of Jesse James; Stopover Tokyo; **1958:** The Hunters; Mardi Gras; In Love and War; **1959:** Say One for Me; **1960:** All the Fine Young Cannibals; **1962:** Sail a Crooked Ship; The Longest Day; The War Lover; **1963:** The Condemned of Altona; **1964:** The Pink Panther; **1966:** Harper; **1967:** Banning; **1968:** Don't Just Stand There; The Biggest Bundle of them All; **1969:** Winning; **1974:** The Towering Inferno; **1976:** Midway; **1979:** The Concorde — Airport '79; **1983:** Curse of the Pink Panther; I Am the Cheese; **1991:** Delirious; **1992:** The Player; **1993:** Dragon: The Bruce Lee Story; **1997:** Overdrive (nUSr); Austin Powers: International Man of Mystery; **1998:** Wild Things; Off the Menu: The Last Days of Chasen's: Something to Believe In (dtv); **1999:** Dill Scallion; No Vacancy (nUSr); Austin Powers: The Spy Who Shagged Me; Love and Fear (nUSr); Crazy in Alabama; The Kidnapping of Chris Burden (nUSr); Play It to the Bone; **2000:** Forever Fabulous (nUSr); **2001:** Sol Goode (nUSr); Jungle Juice (nUSr); **2002:** Nancy & Frank (nUSr); Austin Powers in Goldmember; **2003:** Hollywood Homicide.

Select TV: 1955: The Ox-Bow Incident (sp); **1956:** Gun in His Hand (sp); **1966:** The Enemy on the Beach (sp); Runaway Boy (sp); **1967:** How I Spent My Summer Vacation; **1968–70:** It Takes a Thief (series); **1971:** City Beneath the Sea; The Cable Car Murder/Crosscurrent; **1972:** Killer by Night; Madame Sin (and exec. prod.); Colditz (series); The Streets of San Francisco; **1973:** The Affair; **1975:** The Abduction of Saint Anne; Switch; **1975–78:** Switch (series); Death at Love House; Cat on a Hot Tin Roof; **1978:** Pearl (ms); The Critical List; **1979:** Hart to Hart; **1979–84:** Hart to Hart (series); **1984:** To Catch a King; **1985:** Lime Street (series; and exec. prod.); **1986:** There Must Be a Pony (and exec. prod.); **1987:** Love Among Thieves; **1988:** Windmills of the Gods; Indiscreet; **1989:** Around the World in 80 Days (ms); **1991:** This Gun for Hire; False Arrest; **1992:** Danielle Steel's Jewels; The Trials of Rosie O'Neill (series); **1993:** Deep Trouble; Hart to Hart Returns; **1994:** Parallel Lives; Hart to Hart: Home Is Where the Hart Is; Heaven & Hell: North and South Book III (ms); Hart to Hart: Crimes of the Hart; Hart to Hart: Old Friends Never Die; **1995:** Hart to Hart: Secrets of the Hart; Dancing in the Dark; Hart to Hart: Two Harts in Three-Quarters Time; **1996:** Hart to Hart: Till Death Do Us Hart; Hart to Hart: Harts in High Season; **1999:** Fatal Error; **2000:** Rockets Red Glare; Becoming Dick; **2001:** The Retrievers; **2002:** Hour of Stars (series host).

RAYMOND WALBURN

Born: Plymouth, IN, September 9, 1887.
Died: July 26, 1969.

One of the screen's great blithering fuddy-duddies, Raymond Walburn made his professional theater debut in Oakland, in 1907, and, nine years later, first appeared on the Broadway stage, in *Cordelia Blossom*. This was followed by his first motion picture experience, in 1916, with the serial, *The Scarlet Runner*. He returned to the stage, made a brief detour to Hollywood in 1929, for *The Laughing Lady*, was back on Broadway for a spell, and then pretty much made the movies his permanent place of employment for 20 years, starting in 1934. He was the phony racetrack gambler in both *Broadway Bill* and its remake *Riding High*; the hateful Danglars, who sends Robert Donat to prison in *The Count of Monte Cristo*; a hard-drinking politician in *Thanks a Million*; the butler of newly-rich Gary Cooper in *Mr. Deeds Goes to Town*; Irene Dunne's charlatan dad in *High, Wide and Handsome*; and ZaSu Pitts's tycoon husband in *Eternally Yours*. He fit in perfectly with director-writer Preston Sturges's stock company and did, perhaps, his two most famous roles for him, in *Christmas in July*, as the jittery coffee company

owner, and *Hail the Conquering Hero*, as the corrupt mayor, at his blustering best. During the 1940s he shared part of the title roles with Lee Tracy in the RKO quickie, *Millionaires in Prison*; played *The Man in the Trunk*, a ghost out to find his killer; and then went over to Monogram for *Henry the Rainmaker*, a no-budget comedy that the studio saw as a potential series. Walburn followed it with four more entries as small town hero Henry Latham (*Leave It to Henry*; *Father Makes Good*; *Father's Wild Game*; *Father Takes the Air*). He ended his career back on Broadway, in 1965, in, *A Very Rich Woman*.

Screen: 1916: The Scarlet Runner (serial); The Tarantula; **1929:** The Laughing Lady; **1934:** The Count of Monte Cristo; Broadway Bill; Lady by Choice; The Great Flirtation; Jealousy; The Defense Rests; **1935:** Mills of the Gods; Thanks a Million; It's a Small World; She Married Her Boss; Society Doctor; Death Flies East; I'll Love You Always; Welcome Home; Redheads on Parade; **1936:** The Lone Wolf Returns; The Great Ziegfeld; They Met in a Taxi; The King Steps Out; Craig's Wife; Mr. Deeds Goes to Town; Absolute Quiet; Three Wise Guys; Mr. Cinderella; Born to Dance; **1937:** High, Wide and Handsome; Breezing Home; Thin Ice; Murder in Greenwich Village; Let's Get Married; It Can't Last Forever; Broadway Melody of 1938; **1938:** The Battle of Broadway; Sweethearts; Professor Beware; Gateway; Start Cheering; **1939:** The Under-Pup; Let Freedom Ring; It Could Happen to You; Heaven With a Barbed-Wire Fence; Eternally Yours; **1940:** Flowing Gold; Third Finger, Left Hand; Dark Command; Christmas in July; San Francisco Docks; Millionaires in Prison; **1941:** Confirm or Deny; Kiss the Boys Goodbye; Rise and Shine; Louisiana Purchase; Bachelor Daddy; Puddin' Head; **1942:** The Man in the Trunk; **1943:** Lady Bodyguard; Let's Face It; Dixie; The Desperadoes; Dixie Dugan; **1944:** Heavenly Days; And the Angels Sing; Music in Manhattan; Hail the Conquering Hero; **1945:** I'll Tell the World; The Cheaters; Honeymoon Ahead; **1946:** Breakfast in Hollywood; Rendezvous With Annie; The Plainsman and the Lady; Lover Come Back; The Affairs of Geraldine; The Sin of Harold Diddlebock/Mad Wednesday; **1948:** State of the Union; **1949:** Henry the Rainmaker; Leave It to Henry; Red, Hot and Blue; **1950:** Riding High; Key to the City; Father Makes Good; Short Grass; Father's Wild Game; **1951:** Excuse My Dust; Father Takes the Air; Golden Girl; **1953:** She Couldn't Say No; **1955:** The Spoilers.

NY Stage: 1916: Cordelia Blossom; **1922:** Manhattan; The Awful Truth; **1924:** The Show-Off; **1926:** If I Was Rich; **1927:** Sinner; The Triumphant Bachelor; Take My Advice; **1928:** The Great Necker; **1929:** On Call; Zeppelin; Freddy; **1930:** Three Little Girls; **1931:** The House Beautiful; **1932:** Bridal Wise; The Budget; Tell Her the Truth; The Show-Off (and dir.; revival); **1933:** Man Bites Dog; The Pursuit of Happiness; **1946:** Park Avenue; **1962:** A Funny Thing Happened on the Way to the Forum; **1965:** A Very Rich Woman.

Select TV: 1954: Christmas in July (sp); **1958:** Be My Guest (sp).

CLINT WALKER

(Norman Eugene Walker) Born: Hartford, IL, May 30, 1927.

At 6' 6" Clint Walker was impossible to miss, which was just as well because, beyond that height, there wasn't a hell of a lot to get excited over about this relentlessly wooden actor, whose principal fame came from television westerns. He'd bummed around in all sorts of jobs before ending up as a guard at the Sands Hotel in Las Vegas. From there he went to Hollywood where he became a nightclub bouncer and this led to film work, first playing Tarzan (billed as "Jett Norman") in a Bowery Boys cheapie, *Jungle Gents*, and then as a Sardinian captain in *The Ten Commandments*. By the time the latter movie opened he had already been hired by Warner Bros. to carry their weekly western series *Cheyenne*. As silent drifter Cheyenne Bodie, he became a major star of the small screen since the show had a very healthy eight season run. During its stay he did some big-screen westerns, *Fort Dobbs* and *Yellowstone Kelly*, which meant it was just Walker under a different name than the one he had on television. After the show's demise, he tried comedy, as Doris Day's millionaire suitor, in *Send Me No Flowers*; received Frank Sinatra's undemanding direction in *None But the Brave*; and did a pair of animal films, the acceptable *Maya*, about an elephant, and the cheesy *Night of the Grizzly*. He had his most memorable screen role as the towering Samson Posey, one of the violent soldiers recruited by Lee Marvin to be *The Dirty Dozen*; followed by the lighthearted westerns, *Sam Whiskey* and *The Great Bank Robbery*. Walker returned to television for a flop series, *Kodiak*, and could occasionally be spotted on the big screen in low-profile movies like *Baker's Hawk*, in which he came to the rescue of hermit Burl Ives; *The White Buffalo*, supporting former *Dirty Dozen* co-star Charles Bronson in one of the latter's biggest flops; and *Hysterical*, ending up a zombie in this sole screen vehicle for an unfunny team of television comedians, the Hudson Brothers.

Screen: AS JETT NORMAN: 1954: Jungle Gents.

AS CLINT WALKER: 1956: The Ten Commandments; 1958: Fort Dobbs; 1959: Yellowstone Kelly; 1961: Gold of the Seven Saints; 1964: Send Me No Flowers; 1965: None But the Brave; 1966: Maya; Night of the Grizzly; 1967: The Dirty Dozen; 1969: Sam Whiskey; More Dead Than Alive; The Great Bank Robbery; 1970: The Phynx; 1972: Pancho Villa; 1976: Baker's Hawk; 1977: Deadly Harvest; The White Buffalo; 1983: Hysterical; 1985: The Serpent Warriors; 1998: Small Soldiers (voice).

Select TV: 1955–62: Cheyenne (series); 1964: Portrait of an Unknown Man (sp); 1971: Yuma; 1972: Hardcase; The Bounty Man; 1974: Scream of the Wolf; Killdozer; Kodiak (series); 1977: Snowbeast; 1978–79: Centennial (ms); 1979: Mysterious Island of Beautiful Women; 1991: The Gambler Returns: Luck of the Draw.

ROBERT WALKER

BORN: SALT LAKE CITY, UT, OCTOBER 13, 1918.
DIED: AUGUST 27, 1951.

On screen he was soft-spoken with an open, friendly face, adept at playing gulping soldiers and all-around vulnerable nice guys. This was a testament to Robert Walker's talents as an actor, since this facade masked the off-screen reality of a severely tormented man who was driven to heavy drinking and eventual self-destruction. He studied at the American Academy of Dramatic Arts where he met and married Jennifer Jones (1939–45) who was his co-star in a production of *The Barretts of Wimpole Street*. Together they journeyed west to Hollywood to seek work and Walker ended up doing bits in three 1939 releases, starting with United Artists's *Winter Carnival*, and an independent cheapie, *I'll Sell My Life*, for a company called Select Attractions. When nothing else came up, the couple returned east, where Walker did some radio, including a regular role on the series *Myrt and Marge*. While there Jones was signed to a contract by powerful producer David O. Selznick and, although he was instrumental in getting Walker hooked up with MGM, he eventually wooed Jones away from her husband, an event from which many said Walker never recovered. In 1943,

MGM put Walker in uniform to play the doomed young sailor in a popular war film, *Bataan*. Believing that he epitomized every homefront mother's idea of the son they sent away to battle, the studio gave him the star push with their adaptation of Marion Hargrove's best-selling memoirs, *See Here, Private Hargrove*. This instantly forgettable service comedy wasn't all that different from a hundred others made before or since, but since Walker was so likeable in the lead it made a small fortune and put the young actor in the bright young star category.

He stayed in the military for three more of the biggest hits of their day, *Since You Went Away*, as an affable corporal, appearing for the only time on the big screen opposite Jones and parting with her memorably at a railway station when he is sent back to duty; *Thirty Seconds Over Tokyo*; and, best of all, *The Clock*, a simple and lovely wartime romance set in Manhattan, with Judy Garland as the girl he meets and weds while on leave. Between two pairings with the sugary sweet June Allyson, *Her Highness and the Bellboy*, and *The Sailor Takes a Wife* (again marrying while on leave), he did the inevitable sequel to the one that had made him a star, *What Next, Corporal Hargrove?*, which was much broader than the first. There was little he could do with the customary composer-bio clichés adherent in *Till the Clouds Roll By*, where he was supposed to be Jerome Kern, but it was intriguing to see him being nasty, as he was in *The Sea of Grass*, as offspring to Katharine Hepburn and Spencer Tracy. Next he pined for Hepburn in *Song of Love*, where he was Johannes Brahms, playing you-know-what to put the kids to sleep, and then went to Universal for their lifeless adaptation of the Broadway hit *One Touch of Venus*, which tossed out most of the original score as was the strange habit of the time. He seemed to be stuck in neutral with things like *The Skipper Surprised His Wife*, which was easy to confuse with an earlier title of his, *The Sailor Takes a Wife*, but he once again seemed comfortable in a part that required him to misbehave, playing Burt Lancaster's adopted kin, in *Vengeance Valley*. Director Alfred Hitchcock then gave him the role of a lifetime, the smooth, homicidal homosexual who ensnares Farley Granger in his deadly plans in *Strangers on a Train*. Walker received the best notices of his career and seemed about to advance to a whole new level of authority as an actor. However, while filming his next picture, the hysterical anti-Red piece *My Son John*, he died of respiratory failure, following a heavy drinking bout, having by that point gained a reputation as one of Hollywood's most unhappy alcoholics. The picture was finished using outtakes from *Strangers*. His look-alike son, Robert, Jr., became an actor, starring in such movies as *Ensign Pulver* and *Young Billy Young*.

Screen: 1939: Winter Carnival; These Glamour Girls; Dancing Co-Ed; 1941: I'll Sell My Life; 1943: Bataan; Madame Curie; 1944: See Here, Private Hargrove; Since You Went Away; Thirty Seconds Over Tokyo; 1945: The Clock; Her Highness and the Bellboy; What Next, Corporal Hargrove?; The Sailor Takes a Wife; 1947: Till the Clouds Roll By; The Sea of Grass; The Beginning or the End; Song of Love; 1948: One Touch of Venus; 1950: Please Believe Me; The Skipper Surprised His Wife; 1951: Vengeance Valley; Strangers on a Train; 1952: My Son John.

JEAN WALLACE

(JEAN WALASEK) BORN: CHICAGO, IL, OCTOBER 12, 1923. DIED: FEBRUARY 14, 1990.

An attractive blonde who spent her early years in the shadow of one celebrity husband and then became the exclusive co-star of her second better-known spouse, Jean Wallace had started in movies as a chorus girl, in *Louisana Purchase* and *Ziegfeld Girl*. The same year that both of those were released, 1941, she married actor Franchot Tone which at least raised her profile within the industry. She continued to dabble sporadically in features, working her way up to "A"-product like *Blaze of Noon* and *When My Baby Smiles at Me*, in the latter as the showgirl who hopes to snatch Dan Dailey away from Betty Grable. Tone got her the leading lady role in a small-scale crime film with an anti-racist theme, *Jigsaw*, but by the time it and another they did together, *The Man in the Eiffel Tower*, were distributed in 1949, the couple had divorced. In 1951 she married actor Cornel Wilde and they co-starred in a top-notch noir thriller, *The Big Combo*, with Wallace outstanding as the lady who throws her allegiance from cop Wilde to bad guy Richard Conte; and in a programmer, *Star of India*, where she was improbably cast as a 17th century Dutch secret agent sent to retrieve the stolen title jewel. Together they formed their own production company, Theodora Productions, and launched their series of collaborations with *Storm Fear*, a thriller in which Wallace loved criminal Wilde but was married to his weakling brother Dan Duryea. Wallace would work only in movies directed by her husband for the remainder of her career, an arrangement that, if nothing else, showed her up as the better actor. She was his love interest in both the racecar drama *The Devil's Hairpin*, and one set in the world Venezuelan oil fields, *Maracaibo*; a somewhat elderly Guinevere to his similarly long-in-the-tooth Lancelot in *The Sword of Lancelot*; wife to his soldier in *Beach Red*; and the mom trying to save her family from an annihilating virus in *No Blade of Grass*, which Wilde directed but did not appear in. She missed out on his best directorial effort, *The Naked Prey*, since it did not call for a substantial female role. The couple divorced in 1983.

Screen: 1941: Louisana Purchase; Ziegfeld Girl; 1944: You Can't Ration Love; 1946: It Shouldn't Happen to a Dog; 1947: Blaze of Noon; 1948: When My Baby Smiles at Me; 1949: Jigsaw/Gun Moll; The Man on the Eiffel Tower; 1950: The Good Humor Man; Native Son; 1954: Star of India; 1955: The Big Combo; Storm Fear; 1957: The Devil's Hairpin; 1958: Maracaibo; 1963: The Sword of Lancelot/Lancelot and Guinevere; 1967: Beach Red; 1970: No Blade of Grass.

Select TV: 1952: So Help Me (sp); 1965: The Blond Dog (sp).

ELI WALLACH
BORN: BROOKLYN, NY, DECEMBER 7, 1915.
ED: UNIV. OF TX, CCNY.

Once he got his relatively late start in movies, it was only fitting that Eli Wallach became one of the more ubiquitous character players, for he was, in his own unpretentious way, the sterling example of the consummate actor. There was barely a role he could not fit with ease, whether it required him to be smarmy, warm-hearted, humorous, devious, world-weary, or wise. Following college the raspy-voiced Wallach studied acting at the Neighborhood Playhouse, where he had received a scholarship, and then later with Lee Strasberg at the Actors Studio. After a break to serve in the Army during World War II, he made his Broadway debut, in 1945, in *Skydrift*. He did a stint with Eva La Gallienne's American Repertory Theatre and appeared in an Equity Library Theatre production of *This Property Is Condemned*, which was not only his first experience with the work of Tennessee Williams, but the play that introduced him to Anne Jackson. They wed in 1948, becoming one of show business's longest running marriages, as well as frequent co-stars over the years. It was in another drama by

Williams that Wallach got his big break, playing the Italian truck driver in the original 1951 production of *The Rose Tattoo*, for which he received a Theatre World Award. This brought interest from Columbia Pictures, who offered him the role of Maggio in *From Here to Eternity*, but Wallach declined and Frank Sinatra got the part. Instead, he wound up back onstage in a Williams flop, *Camino Real*, and then finally made his motion picture debut in another script by that same author, *Baby Doll*. This turned out to be one of the more controversial films of the 1950s, which was a great plus to Wallach, who was exceptional as the oversexed Sicilian set on curling up with Karl Malden's child bride, Carroll Baker.

Wallach took a rare starring role in his follow-up movie, playing a psychotic and single-minded killer named Dancer, in director Don Siegel's crisp "B" thriller, *The Lineup*. He stayed villainous to portray the snarling Mexican bandit in the hit western, *The Magnificent Seven* and then, keeping that numeral in mind, impersonated a crippled baron in order to help rob a Monte Carlo casino in *Seven Thieves*. As the ex-pilot helping Clark Gable rope stallions in *The Misfits*, he turned out to be the sole principal from that doomed cast to survive the decade. Turning bad again, he was George Peppard's gunfighter nemesis in the latter half of the lengthy *How the West Was Won*, then displayed his gentler side, as the sergeant who finds himself comforting a frightened French war widow, Jeanne Moreau, in director-writer Carl Foreman's underrated anti-war film *The Victors*. To show his versatility with accents and his comfort in playing a range of nationalities, he took all kinds of parts in all kinds of films, good and bad, playing a lecherous South American dictator in the coy farce *Kisses for My President*; Pola Negri's Greek henchman in Disney's lightweight adventure, *The Moon-Spinners*; and Far Easterners in both *Genghis Khan* and *Lord Jim*. He was adept at making a part colorful without lapsing into the grotesquerie of camp. Having fun, he was the bamboozled art collector in *How to Steal a Million* (replacing George C. Scott, who was dismissed from the project) and then was outrageously devious as Clint Eastwood's grubby partner in crime in *The Good, the Bad, and the Ugly*. Since this was the peak of the spaghetti western genre, it became one of Wallach's best-remembered roles, and even got him his own vehicle in this genre, *Ace High*. In the meantime, he did get to recreate one of the parts he'd done onstage, the sexually frustrated mailman who decides to kidnap a woman for companionship, in the goofily eccentric comedy *The Tiger Makes Out*, marking his first on-screen appearance with Jackson, which was followed by their second, lesser one, *How to Save a Marriage (And Ruin Your Life)*, with Wallach as the cheating husband and his misses playing his mistress.

Having, by the 1970s, established himself as a very familiar movie name and face, he kept his plate full, showing up as the father of a junkie in *The People Next Door*; cameoing as a deli clerk in a scene with Jackson in *The Angel Levine*; playing the lawyer of semi-innocent George Kennedy in *Zigzag*; appearing as a Mafia don in *Crazy Joe*; and backing up Jackson, as a monsignor in the Watergate satire *Nasty Habits*. Wallach was also a beach dweller in the damp thriller *The Deep*; a New York detective investigating supernatural occurrences in the unpleasant *The Sentinel*; a rabbi in *Girlfriends*; and dual roles, a crooked fight promoter and a backstage doorman, in the double-feature send-up *Movie Movie*. Outside of these mainstream credits, he was not averse to accepting all kinds of questionable roles in foreign-made productions, which also meant that certain samples of his work never showed up on American shores. Wallach also never strayed far from the stage and kept at it long after many others his age had retired or resigned themselves to working exclusively before a camera. Late in life he had a personal theater triumph in *Cafe Crown*, and, during that period, was seen on film in one of his larger latter-day parts, as the father of a champion javelin thrower in the little-seen *Sam's Son*. The older, but no less marvelous Wallach could also be seen as the hilarious, sight-impaired gunman in *Tough Guys* (replacing Adolph Caesar, who died during production); the doctor trying to determine Barbra Streisand's mental state in *Nuts*; another Mafia don, this one succumbing to a poisoned cannoli, in a tepid sequel, *The Godfather Part III*; a wealthy backer in the Hollywood comedy *Mistress*; a dying veteran in the multi-character *Article 99*; and a rabbi in *Keeping the Faith*. In 1999 he and his wife were back onstage in *Remembering Tennessee Williams* to celebrate the playwright who had brought them together and was instrumental in bringing Wallach his fame. On television he received an Emmy Award for the special *The Poppy Is Also a Flower*, which later received theatrical play as a feature film.

Screen: 1956: Baby Doll; 1958: The Lineup; 1960: Seven Thieves; The Magnificent Seven; 1961: The Misfits; 1962: Hemingway's Adventures of a Young Man; 1963: How the West Was Won; The Victors; Act One; 1964: The Moon-Spinners; Kisses for My President; 1965: Lord Jim; Genghis Khan; 1966: How to Steal a Million; 1967: The Tiger Makes Out; The Good, the Bad, and the Ugly; 1968: How to Save a Marriage (And Ruin Your Life); A Lovely Way to Die; 1969: Mackenna's Gold; The Brain; Ace High; 1970: Zigzag; The Angel Levine; The People Next Door; The Adventures of Gerard (nUSr); 1971: Romance of a Horsethief; 1973: Cinderella Liberty; 1974: Crazy Joe; Viva la Muerte … tua!/Companeros/Don't Turn the Other Cheek; 1975: L'Chaim — To Life! (narrator); Samurai/El Blanco/Shoot First (nUSr); Attenti al Buffone!/Eye of the Cat (nUSr); 1976: Stateline Motel/Last Chance; E Tanta Pura/Too Much Fear (nUSr); 1977: The Sentinel; Nasty Habits; The Domino Principle; The Deep; 1978: Girlfriends; Squadra Antimafia/Little Italy (nUSr); Movie Movie; 1979: Circle of Iron; Firepower; Winter Kills; 1980: The Hunter; 1983: The Salamander; 1984: Sam's Son; 1985: Sanford Meisner — The Theatre's Best Kept Secret; 1986: Tough Guys; 1987: Nuts; 1988: Hello, Actors Studio; 1989: Funny; 1990: The Two Jakes; The Godfather Part III; 1991: Terezin Diary (narrator); 1992: Article 99; Mistress; Night and the City; 1994: Honey Sweet Love (nUSr); 1996: Two Much; The Associate; 2000: Uninvited (nUSr); Keeping the Faith.

NY Stage: 1945: Skydrift; 1946: King Henry VIII; What Every Woman Knows; Androcles and the Lion; 1947: Yellow Jack; Alice in Wonderland/Through the Looking Glass; Antony and Cleopatra; 1949: Mister Roberts; 1950: The Lady From the Sea; 1951: The Rose Tattoo; 1953: Camino Real; Scarecrow (ob); 1954: Mademoiselle Colombe; 1955: The Teahouse of the August Moon; 1956: Major Barbara; 1958: The Chairs (ob); The Cold Wind and the Warm; 1961: Rhinoceros; 1963: The Tiger/The Typists (ob); 1964: Luv; 1968: Staircase; 1972: Promenade All!; 1973: The Waltz of the Toreadors; 1974: Saturday, Sunday, Monday; 1978: The Diary of Anne Frank (ob); 1979: Every Good Boy Deserves Favor (ob); 1982: Twice Around the Park; 1984: The Nest of the Wood Grouse (ob); 1988: Cafe Crown (ob; and Bdwy 1989); 1992: The Price; 1993: In Persons (ob); 1994: The Flowering Peach; 1997: Visiting Mr. Green (ob); 1999: Remembering Tennessee Williams (ob); 2001: Down the Garden Path (ob).

Select TV: 1949: The Beautiful Bequest (sp); 1952: Stan the Killer (sp); 1953: The Baby (sp); 1954: The Brownstone (sp); 1955: Shadow of the Champ (sp); Mr. Blue Ocean (sp); 1956: Fragile Affair (sp); 1957: The Lark (sp); The Man Who Wasn't Himself (sp); 1958: The Plot to Kill Stalin (sp); My Father the Fool (sp); 1959: For Whom the Bell Tolls (sp); I Don Quixote (sp); 1960:

The Margaret Bourke-White Story (sp); Birthright (sp); Lullaby (sp); Hope Is the Thing With Feathers (sp); 1966: The Poppy Is Also a Flower (and theatrical); 1967: Dear Friends (sp); 1971: Paradise Lost (sp); The Typists (sp); 1973: A Cold Night's Death/The Chill Factor; 1974: Indict and Convict; 1976: Twenty Shades of Pink (sp); 1977: Seventh Avenue (ms); 1978: Harold Robbins' The Pirate (ms); 1980: Fugitive Family; 1981: The Pride of Jesse Hallam; Skokie; 1982: The Wall; The Executioner's Song; 1984: Anatomy of an Illness; 1985: Embassy; Our Family Honor; Murder: By Reason of Insanity; Christopher Columbus (ms); 1985–86: Our Family Honor (series); 1986: Rocket to the Moon (sp); Something in Common; 1987: The Impossible Spy; 1989: A Matter of Conscience (sp); 1991: Vendetta: Secrets of a Mafia Bride; 1992: Legacy of Lies; Teamster Boss: The Jackie Presser Story; 1993: Vendetta 2: The New Mafia; 1998: Naked City: Justice With a Bullet; 2000: Bookfair Murders; 2002: Monday Night Mayhem.

RAY WALSTON

BORN: NEW ORLEANS, LA, DECEMBER 2, 1914.
DIED: JANUARY 1, 2001.

An impish character player who was a highly adept presence once he made his long overdue arrival on the film scene, Ray Walston had started out in the printing business until employment in Houston brought him in contact with a local theater group. From there it was on to the Cleveland Playhouse and then New York for his Broadway debut, playing Osric in a 1945 production of *Hamlet*. Among other stage credits, he appeared in *Kiss Them for Me*, in Connecticut, though in a role different from the one he'd do in the 1957 movie version, and in *South Pacific*, in the London production, as enterprising seaman Luther Billis, a part he'd be asked to repeat in the 1958 film. In the meantime, he made his big splash as the crafty Mr. Applegate (a pseudonym for the Devil) in the hit musical, *Damn Yankees*. Fortunately, he was invited to preserve his sly performance on film and this would prove to be Walston's signature role. Further establishing himself in movies, he was a washed-up pianist in *Say One for Me*; one of the sleazy executives borrowing Jack Lemmon's key to *The Apartment*; a college professor in *Tall Story*; and a department store official in the Jerry Lewis vehicle *Who's Minding the Store?* He signed up to do a situation comedy that he came to despise, *My Favorite Martian*, during the run of which he landed his best movie part (replacing an ailing Peter Sellers), as the frustrated amateur songwriter, who gives his loving wife over to sleazy Dean Martin and ends up bedding hooker Kim Novak, in director Billy Wilder's much-hated but often brilliantly funny examination of the sexes, *Kiss Me, Stupid*. He donned drag to stalk Doris Day in *Caprice*; was a scruffy prospector (with no songs) in the musical *Paint Your Wagon*; found himself right at home as one of the Depression era con men in the Oscar-winning *The Sting*; squinted and snarled as Poopdeck Pappy in the oddball live-action version of *Popeye*; represented the grown-up faction, as a flustered school teacher, in *Fast Times at Ridgemont High* (a part he repeated in the short-lived TV series); and did some shtick as a blind news vendor in *Johnny Dangerously*. Amid such junk as *Private School*, *Paramedics*, and *Ski Patrol*, he had a rare big screen dramatic role, playing the crotchety old farm hand Candy, in the 1992 version of *Of Mice and Men*, then got asked to join the cast of the series *Picket Fences*, which brought him a 1995 Emmy Award for playing the wizened small-town Judge Henry Bone.

Screen: 1957: Kiss Them for Me; 1958: Damn Yankees; South

Pacific; 1959: Say One for Me; 1960: The Apartment; Portrait in Black; Tall Story; 1962: Convicts 4; 1963: Who's Minding the Store?; Wives and Lovers; 1964: Kiss Me, Stupid; 1967: Caprice; 1969: Paint Your Wagon; 1973: The Sting; 1976: Silver Streak; 1977: The Happy Hooker Goes to Washington; 1980: Popeye; 1981: Galaxy of Terror; 1982: Fast Times at Ridgemont High; 1983: O'Hara's Wife; Private School; 1984: Johnny Dangerously; 1986: Rad; 1987: From the Hip; O.C. and Stiggs; 1988: Blood Relations (dtv); Paramedics; Saturday the 14th Strikes Back; 1989: A Man of Passion (dtv); 1990: Ski Patrol; Blood Salvage; 1991: Popcorn; 1992: The Player; Of Mice and Men; 1996: House Arrest; 1999: My Favorite Martian; 2001: Early Bird Special (dtv).

NY Stage: 1945: Hamlet; 1946: The Front Page; 1948: The Survivors; Summer and Smoke; 1949: Richard III; Mrs. Gibbon's Boys; The Rat Race; 1953: Me and Juliet; 1954: House of Flowers; 1955: Damn Yankees; 1958: Who Was That Lady I Saw You With?; 1966: Agatha Sue I Love You.

Select TV: 1950: Uncle Harry (sp); 1954: The Hero (sp); 1957: There Shall Be No Night (sp); 1958: Shadows Tremble (sp); 1959: The Killers (sp); 1960: Uncle Harry (sp); 1963–66: My Favorite Martian (series); 1978: Institute for Revenge; 1982: The Kid with the Broken Halo; The Fall of the House of Usher; 1983: This Girl for Hire; 1984: The Jerk Too; For Love or Money; 1985: Amos; Silver Spoons (series); 1986: Ask Max; Fast Times (series); 1988: Crash Course; Red River; 1989: Class Cruise; I Know My First Name Is Steven; 1990: Angel of Death; 1991: Pink Lightning; One Special Victory; 1992–96: Picket Fences (series); 1994: Stephen King's The Stand (ms); 1996: Project ALF; 1997: Tricks; The Westing Game/Get a Clue; 1998: Addams Family Reunion; 1999: Swing Vote.

HENRY B. WALTHALL

(HENRY BRAZEALE WALTHALL) BORN: SHELBY CITY, AL, MARCH 16, 1878. DIED: JUNE 17, 1936.

His place in motion picture history rests firmly in the fact that he had the principal male lead in America's first important feature, *The Birth of a Nation*, but Henry B. Walthall's career would stretch another two decades beyond that landmark production. Having given up a career in law, he took up acting, which led to Broadway and then to movies, starting in 1909 when he became a member of D.W. Griffith's Biography film company. For Griffith he appeared in the famed director's first feature, *Judith of Bethulia*, and then the most significant motion picture of its day, *The Birth of a Nation*, as the Confederate "Little Colonel," and, ostensibly, the hero, though it is hard to cheer him today, as he leads the Ku Klux Klan to victory. After the Griffith triumph, the actor played Edgar Allen Poe in *The Raven*; the Lone Wolf in *False Faces*; Roger Pryne in *The Scarlet Letter* (a role he repeated in the 1934 sound version as well); an ex-con rehabilitated by a painter in *Parted Curtains*; a priest in *The Road to Mandalay*; and Richard Arlen's father in the first Oscar-winner for Best Picture, *Wings*. Fittingly he was around for Griffith's first talkie, *Abraham Lincoln*, as Colonel Marshall, and had, by this point, become a hard-working character actor of a certain dignity. He was the kidnapped scientist in *Chandu the Magician*; a zoo keeper in *Central Park*; a paralytic who blinks his eyes to communicate in *Me and My Gal*; an old actor in *42nd Street*; a judge driven to suicide in *Headline Shooter*; a small-town doctor in *A Girl of the Limberlost*; an alcoholic aided by Lee Tracy in *The Lemon Drop Kid*; the Mexican rebel called The Christ-Fool in *Viva Villa!*; the conscientious owner of the amusement attraction known as *Dante's Inferno*; the long-imprisoned Dr. Manette in *A Tale of Two Cities*; and the dying

scientist who creates the shrinking process in *The Devil-Doll*.

Screen (features): 1913: Judith of Bethulia; 1914: Home Sweet Home; The Avenging Conscience; Classmates; Lord Chumley; The Odalisque; The Mountain Rat; The Gangsters of New York; The Floor Above; 1915: The Birth of a Nation; Ghosts; Beulah; The Circular Path; The Raven; 1916: The Misleading Lady; The Strange Case of Mary Page (serial); The Spider and the Fly; The Sting of Victory; Pillars of Society; The Birth of a Man; The Truant Soul; 1917: The Little Shoes; The Saint's Adventure; Burning the Candle; 1918: His Robe of Honor; False Faces; Humdrum Brown; With Hoops of Steel; The Great Love; And a Still Small Voice; 1919: The Boomerang; The Long Lane's Turning; Modern Husbands; False Faces; The Long Arm of Mannister; 1920: A Splendid Hazard; The Confession; Parted Curtains; 1921: The Flower of the North; 1922: The Ableminded Lady; One Clear Call; The Kick Back; The Long Chance; The Marriage Chance; 1923: The Face on the Barroom Floor; Gimme; The Unknown Purple; Boy of Mine; 1924: Single Wives; The Bowery Bishop; 1925: The Golden Bed; The Woman on the Jury; On the Threshold; The Girl Who Wouldn't Work; Kit Carson Over the Great Divide; Kentucky Pride; Dollar Down; Simon the Jester; The Plastic Age; 1926: Three Faces East; The Barrier; The Unknown Soldier; The Scarlet Letter; The Road to Mandalay; Everybody's Acting; 1927: Fighting Love; The Enchanted Island; Wings; The Rose of Kildare; A Light in the Window; London After Midnight; 1928: Love Me and the World Is Mine; Freedom of the Press; 1929: Stark Mad; Speakeasy; The Bridge of San Luis Rey; The Jazz Age; Black Magic; From Headquarters; River of Romance; The Trespasser; In Old California; Phantom in the House; Blaze o' Glory; 1930: Tol'able David; Temple Tower; Abraham Lincoln; The Love Trader; 1931: Is There Justice?; Anybody's Blonde; 1932: Hotel Continental; Police Court; Strange Interlude; Alias Mary Smith; Chandu the Magician; Klondike; Cabin in the Cotton; Ride Him, Cowboy; Central Park; Me and My Gal; Self Defense; 1933: The Wolf Dog (serial); 42nd Street; Flaming Signal; The Whispering Shadow (serial); Somewhere in Sonora; Laughing at Life; Headline Shooter; Her Forgotten Past; Murder in the Museum; The Sin of Nora Moran; 1934: Viva Villa!; Men in White; Dark Hazard; Murder in the Museum; City Park; Judge Priest; A Girl of the Limberlost; The Lemon Drop Kid; The Scarlet Letter; Love Time; Bachelor of Arts; 1935: Helldorado; Dante's Inferno; A Tale of Two Cities; 1936: The Garden Murder Case; The Mine With the Iron Door; Hearts in Bondage; The Last Outlaw; The Devil-Doll; China Clipper.

NY Stage: 1906: The Great Divide; Pippa Passes; 1918: The Awakening.

SAM WANAMAKER

(SAMUEL WATENMAKER) BORN: CHICAGO, IL, JUNE 14, 1919. ED: DRAKE UNIV. DIED: DECEMBER 18, 1993.

A tight-lipped, serious actor who registered on screen far less than his stage reputation would lead one to believe, Sam Wanamaker was a blacklist victim of the Communist witchhunts who found solace and employment in England, where he embarked on his dream project. He'd trained for the stage at Chicago's Goodman Theatre, then did stock work before making his Broadway debut, in 1942, in *Cafe Crown*. In 1948 he was invited to make his motion picture bow in the ultra-patriotic *My Girl Tisa*, as Lili Palmer's immigrant love interest. Before he could make a follow-up, trouble began brewing over his political stance. Anticipating problems, he took off for England in 1949 where he starred in three films, *Give Us This Day*, acting for blacklisted director Edward Dmytryk; *Mr. Denning Drives North*, as a lawyer who comes to realize that his fiancée's father might be guilty of murder; and *The Secret*, as an unscrupulous American in the U.K. who finds himself involved in murder and diamond smuggling. Despite his relocation, he was still denied steady movie work, so he concentrated on the British stage as both actor and director. In 1957 he was made director of the New Shakespeare Cultural Center in Liverpool and, in 1959, joined the Shakespeare Memorial Theatre Company at Stratford-upon-Avon. By this point he'd become obsessed with the notion of raising money to build a replica of the Globe Theatre, approximately on its original London site, on the south bank of the Thames. He return to movie acting under the guidance of fellow expatriate and blacklist victim Joseph Losey, in *The Concrete Jungle/The Criminal*, helping Stanley Baker in a racetrack robbery, and returned to American films with *Taras Bulba*. Over the years he showed up as Stewart Whitman's flying partner in *Those Magnificent Men in Their Flying Machines*; a secret agent out to retrieve a bomb in the bomb *The Day the Fish Came Out*; Goldie Hawn's father in *Private Benjamin*; the head of a Mafia family in *Raw Deal*; Diane Keaton's boss in *Baby Boom* (a role he repeated on television when it became a short-lived series); and, in an ironic twist, a lawyer encouraging Robert De Niro to supply names during the McCarthy era in *Guilty by Suspicion*. He had established the Shakespeare Globe Trust in 1971 to get the re-creation of the theater underway. Although he did not live to see the completion of the project, he was present at its groundbreaking ceremony. Among his credits as director are four undistinguished theatrical features, *The File of the Golden Goose* (1969), *The Executioner* (1970), *Catlow* (1971), and *Sinbad and the Eye of the Tiger* (1977). His daughter is actress Zoë Wanamaker.

Screen: 1948: My Girl Tisa; 1949: Give Us This Day/Salt to the Devil; 1951: Mr. Denning Drives North; 1955: The Secret; 1959: The Battle of the Sexes (narrator); 1960: The Criminal/The Concrete Jungle; 1962: Taras Bulba; 1964: Man in the Middle; 1965: Those Magnificent Men in Their Flying Machines; The Spy Who Came in from the Cold; 1967: The Day the Fish Came Out; Warning Shot; 1968: Danger Route; 1975: The Sellout/The Set-Up; The Spiral Staircase; 1976: Voyage of the Damned; 1977: Billy Jack Goes to Washington; 1978: Death on the Nile; 1979: From Hell to Victory; 1980: Private Benjamin; The Competition; 1984: Irreconcilable Differences; 1985: The Aviator; 1986: Raw Deal; 1987: Superman IV: The Quest for Peace; Baby Boom; 1988: Judgment in Berlin; 1989: Secret Ingredient/Cognac (dtv); 1991: Guilty by Suspicion; Pure Luck; 1992: City of Joy.

NY Stage: 1942: Cafe Crown; 1943: Counterattack; 1946: This Too Shall Pass; Joan of Lorraine; 1948: Goodbye, My Fancy (and dir.); 1950: Arms and the Man; 1961: A Far Country.

Select TV: 1972: Arturo Ui (sp); 1973: Mousey; 1974: The Law; 1978: Holocaust (ms); 1979: A Deadly Game/Charlie Muffin; 1981: Winston Churchill: The Wilderness Years (ms); Our Family Business; 1982: I Was a Male Order Bride; 1984: Heartsounds; The Ghost Writer; 1985: Berrenger's (series); Deceptions; Embassy; 1987: Sadie and Son; The Two Mrs. Grenvilles; 1988–89: Baby Boom (series); 1989: The Shell Seekers; 1990: Running Against Time; Always Remember I Love You; 1993: Wild Justice; Killer Rules; Bloodlines: Murder in the Family.

JACK WARDEN

(JACK WARDEN LEBZELTER) BORN: NEWARK, NJ, SEPTEMBER 18, 1920.

If Jack Warden seemed like the kind of stalwart player who'd been around forever, it was because his career in movies stretched over half a century, during which time he became the ideal for filmmakers who were looking for gruff, often under-educated fellows, who spoke their mind, often wisely, just as often not. Fittingly, he'd been a boxer, tugboat sailor, and bouncer, during which he also served in the Navy and then as a paratrooper. In Dallas he joined the Margo Jones Theatre Company and acted with them from 1947 to 1951. He sought work in film and television, ending up playing several service men in such pictures as *The Frogmen*, *You're in the Navy Now/U.S.S. Teakettle*, and the Oscar-winning *From Here to Eternity*. Meanwhile, he'd made his New York stage bow Off Broadway in a revival of *Golden Boy*, in 1952, followed by his first Broadway production, *Lullaby*, in 1954. Television audiences were growing used to his face from various live dramas and through his weekly role as the coach on the sitcom *Mr. Peepers*. Three 1957 releases upped his status as a character player, starting with *Edge of the City*, as the troublemaking dock boss; *12 Angry Men*, as the loud-mouth juror more interested in getting to a baseball game then discussing the trial; and *The Bachelor Party*, as Don Murray's blow-hard friend who won't admit how lonely he really is. The movies put him back in the military for *Darby's Rangers*; *Run Silent, Run Deep*, and *Wake Me When It's Over*, between which he was the mentally retarded Ben in Fox's game attempt to film the unfilmmable, *The Sound and the Fury*. He was the Boston doctor out of place in Hawaii in *Donovan's Reef*, and a brutal sergeant in the whittled-down 1964 version of *The Thin Red Line*. Also in uniform, he got to carry his own series, *The Wackiest Ship in the Army*, as a character not in the original Jack Lemmon film on which it was based.

Back in films he was getting more sizable roles, as one of the funeral attendees in *Bye Bye Braverman*; Michael Douglas's pro-war dad in *Summertree*; a World War II general in a flop comedy *Welcome to the Club*; and the sheriff in pursuit of Gregory Peck in *Billy Two Hats*. Suddenly on a roll, he wound up in some of the top releases of the 1970s, playing Richard Dreyfuss's cab driver dad in *The Apprenticeship of Duddy Kravitz*; showing his comic skills as Lee Grant's cheating husband in the hit *Shampoo*, earning his first Oscar nomination; joining the fine ensemble of *All the President's Men*, as Washington Post editor Harry Rosenfeld; going doctoring in the Agatha Christie whodunnit *Death on the Nile*; receiving another Oscar mention, as the football manager who is befuddled by Warren Beatty's return to earth in *Heaven Can Wait*, doing a highly commendable job of reprising James Gleason's old role in this remake of *Here Comes Mr. Jordan*; flaking out as a judge in *…And Justice for All*; and making it to the Oval Office, playing the President of the United States, who gets advice from half-wit Peter Sellers in *Being There*. As the star of a mild comedy *Used Cars*, he got to play a dual role, as rival car dealing brothers; then played Ryan O'Neal's foul-mouthed garment manufacturing dad in *So Fine*; Paul Newman's loyal fellow lawyer in *The Verdict*; and the pawnbroker targeted for a heist in *Crackers*. Proving that he'd stoop to anything just to work, he was John Ritter's arrogant store owner dad in *Problem Child*, which required him to do some mooning at one point; the corpse at the center of *Passed Away*; a bed-ridden toy executive in *Toys*; and the manager of a baseball team whose star player was a flatulent chimpanzee, in *Ed*. Better suited, he was Alan King's ill-fated brother in *Night and the City*; a Broadway agent in *Bullets Over Broadway*; Peter Gallagher's godfather in *While You Were Sleeping*; and Warren Beatty's long-time political aide in *Bulworth*. On television, he won an Emmy Award for *Brian's Song*. All in all, an impressive output from an impressive performer.

Screen: 1951: The Frogmen; The Man with My Face; U.S.S. Teakettle/You're in the Navy Now; 1952: Red Ball Express; 1953: From Here to Eternity; 1957: Edge of the City; 12 Angry Men; The Bachelor Party; 1958: Darby's Rangers; Run Silent, Run Deep; 1959: The Sound and the Fury; That Kind of Woman; 1960: Wake Me When It's Over; 1962: Escape from Zahrain; 1963: Donovan's Reef; 1964: The Thin Red Line; 1966: Blindfold; 1968: Bye Bye Braverman; 1971: The Sporting Club; Summertree; Welcome to the Club; Who Is Harry Kellerman and Why Is He Saying Those Terrible Things About Me?; 1973: The Man Who Loved Cat Dancing; Billy Two Hats; 1974: The Apprenticeship of Duddy Kravitz; 1975: Shampoo; 1976: All the President's Men; 1977: The White Buffalo; 1978: Heaven Can Wait; Death on the Nile; 1979: Dreamer; The Champ; Beyond the Poseidon Adventure; ...And Justice for All; Being There; 1980: Used Cars; 1981: The Great Muppet Caper; Chu Chu and the Philly Flash; Carbon Copy; So Fine; 1982: The Verdict; 1984: Crackers; 1985: The Aviator; 1986: The Cosmic Eye (voice); 1987: September; 1988: The Presidio; 1990: Everybody Wins; Problem Child; 1991: Problem Child 2; 1992: Passed Away; Night and the City; Toys; 1993: Guilty as Sin; 1994: Bullets Over Broadway; 1995: While You Were Sleeping; Mighty Aphrodite; Things to Do in Denver When You're Dead; 1996: Ed; 1997: The Island on Bird Street (nUSr); 1998: Chairman of the Board; Bulworth; Dirty Work; 1999: A Dog of Flanders; 2000: The Replacements.

NY Stage: 1952: Golden Boy; 1954: Lullaby; Sing Me No Lullaby (ob); 1955: A View From the Bridge; 1956: A Very Special Baby; 1958: The Body Beautiful; 1963: Cages; 1969: The Man In The Glass Booth; 1978: Stages.

Select TV: 1950: Ann Rutledge (sp); 1953: Snookie (sp); The Promise (sp); Dream House (sp); 1953–55: Mr. Peepers (series); 1954: Native Dancer (sp); Dr. Rainwater Goes A-Courtin' (sp); Class of '58 (sp); 1955: Norby (series); Shadow of the Champ (sp); The Petrified Forest (sp); The Mechanical Heart (sp); 1956: Tragedy in a Temporary Town (sp); 1957: The Lark (sp); 1959: The Blue Men (sp); 1961: The Asphalt Jungle (series); 1964: The Watchman (sp); 1965: Gallegher (sp); 1965–66: The Wackiest Ship in the Army (series); 1967: Gallegher Goes West (sp); 1967–69: N.Y.P.D. (series); 1971: Brian's Song; The Face of Fear; What's a Nice Girl Like You...?; 1972: Man on a String; Lieutenant Schuster's Wife; 1974: The Godchild; Remember When; A Memory of Two Mondays (sp); 1975: Journey from Darkness; They Only Come Out at Night; 1976: Jigsaw John (series); 1977: Raid on Entebbe; 1979: Topper; 1979–80: The Bad News Bears (series); 1980: A Private Battle; 1983: Hobson's Choice; 1984: Helen Keller: The Miracle Continues; 1984–86: Crazy Like a Fox (series); 1985: Robert Kennedy and His Times (ms); A.D. (ms); Alice in Wonderland; 1987: Hoover vs. the Kennedys: The Second Civil War; Still Crazy Like a Fox; The Three Kings; 1988: Dead Solid Perfect; 1989: Knight & Daye (series); 1990: Judgment; 1995: Problem Child 3: Junior in Love.

H.B. WARNER

(HENRY BYRON WARNER) BORN: LONDON, ENGLAND, OCTOBER 26, 1876. ED: UNIV. COL. OF LONDON. DIED: DECEMBER 21, 1958.

Before he excelled as a busy and versatile character player in talkies, the gaunt, distinguished looking H.B. Warner was a star of early 20th century theater and then silent features, racking up nearly 150 movie appearances in a 43 year span. Originally intent on a medical career, he switched to acting, coming to America in 1905, where he toured and did Broadway, often opposite Eleanor Robson. In 1914 he brought his stage success of *The Ghost Breaker* to film, thereby launching his motion picture career. He was a married diplomat loved by dance hall girl Gloria Swanson in *Zaza*; lost wife Alma Rubens to her lover in *Is Love Everything?*; portrayed a vet who winds up a hotel porter in *Sorrell and Son* (a role he'd repeat in the 1934 sound remake); and had the title role in the western *Whispering Smith*. Despite being over 50 years old at the time, Cecil B. DeMille cast him as Jesus in his 1927 epic *The King of Kings*, which became his best-remembered role of the silent era. Warner made his talking picture bow as the cuckolded husband of Emma Hamilton (Corrinne Griffith) in *The Divine Lady*, and barely took a rest for the next 15 years or so. He was the host of the afterlife in *Liliom*; one of George Arliss's prisoners in *Green Goddess*; a man driven to suicide by Edward G. Robinson's nosey newspaper in *Five Star Final*; and an Asian in the ultra-silly *The Son-Daughter*, although Warner was more credible at pulling this sort of thing off than most Caucasians, being asked to do it again on a few occasions. As Inspector Fife of Scotland Yard, he assisted Warner Oland in *Charlie Chan's Chance*; threw daughter Sylvia Sidney out of the house upon discovering that she is carrying Edward Arnold's child, in *Jennie Gerhardt*; and showed up as the teacher, Gabelle, in MGM's teaming epic, *A Tale of Two Cities*.

Director Frank Capra took a liking to the actor and put him in four of his biggest hits, one after the other, starting with *Mr. Deeds Goes to Town*, where he was the judge presiding over Gary Cooper's sanity hearing; then moving on to Shangri-La, where he was the wise and kindly Tibetan priest Chang in *Lost Horizon*, a performance good enough to bring him his one and only Oscar nomination, in the supporting category. Also for Capra he was the business partner driven to ruin, and then death, by Edward Arnold in *You Can't Take It With You*, a mordantly serious character not in the original play, and the Senate majority leader in *Mr. Smith Goes to Washington*. Between these he played Colonel Nielson of Scotland Yard in four of the "Bulldog Drummond" films, supporting John Howard. Also, showing his knack for getting cast as all types and races, he was Chinese again in *The Adventures of Marco Polo*, introducing Gary Cooper to the wonders of spaghetti; an Indian in both *The Garden Murder Case* and *The Rains Came*; and a Polynesian island chief in some Maria Montez foolishness, *South of Tahiti*. After a busy year in 1941, in which he was a judge in *All That Money Can Buy/The Devil and Daniel Webster*; an invalid in *Topper Returns*, and the top-billed star of a poverty row "Z," in *City of Missing Girls*, his workload began to simmer down. Capra called him back again for a standout role, as the druggist who turns into a crazed old drunk in James Stewart's nightmare world, in the classic *It's a Wonderful Life*, and then he proved a good sport, allowing himself to be referred to as one of the "waxworks," playing bridge with one-time co-star Gloria Swanson, in *Sunset Blvd.* There was one last film for Capra, *Here Comes the Groom*, and also one for De Mille, who gave him a tiny part, as Amminadab, in his remake of *The Ten Commandments*.

Screen: 1914: The Ghost Breaker; Your Ghost and Mine; Lost Paradise; 1915: The Beggar of Cawnpore; The Raiders; 1916: The Vagabond Prince; The Market of Vain Desire; The House of a Thousand Candles; Shell 43; A Wife's Sacrifice; 1917: The Danger Trail; The Seventh Sin; God's Man; 1919: The Man Who Turned White; A Fugitive from Matrimony; For a Woman's Honor; The Pagan God; Gray Wolf's Ghost; Maruja; 1920:

Haunting Shadows; Uncharted Channels; Dice of Destiny; The White Dove; One Hour Before Dawn; Felix O'Day; 1921: Below the Deadline; When We Were Twenty-One; 1923: Zaza; 1924: Is Love Everything?; 1926: Silence; Whispering Smith; 1927: The King of Kings; French Dressing; Sorrell and Son; 1928: Conquest; The Romance of a Rogue; The Naughty Duchess; Man-Made Woman; 1929: The Doctor's Secret; The Divine Lady; The Trial of Mary Dugan; The Gamblers; The Show of Shows; The Argyle Case; Stark Mad; Tiger Rose; Wedding Rings; 1930: Liliom; Green Goddess; The Second Floor Mystery; On Your Back; The Princess and the Plumber; The Furies; Wild Company; 1931: Woman of Experience; Expensive Women; Five Star Final; The Reckless Hour; The Prodigal; 1932: A Woman Commands; The Menace; The Son-Daughter; The Phantom of Crestwood; Tom Brown of Culver; Charlie Chan's Chance; The Crusader; Cross-Examination; Unholy Love; 1933: Jennie Gerhardt; Christopher Bean; Supernatural; Justice Takes a Holiday; 1934: Behold My Wife; Grand Canary; Sorrell and Son; Night Alarm; In Old Santa Fe; 1935: Born to Gamble; A Tale of Two Cities; 1936: Moonlight Murder; The Garden Murder Case; The Blackmailer; Mr. Deeds Goes to Town; Rose of the Rancho; Along Came Love; 1937: Torpedoed!/Our Fighting Navy; Victoria the Great; Lost Horizon; 1938: The Toy Wife; The Adventures of Marco Polo; Bulldog Drummond in Africa; You Can't Take It With You; The Girl of the Golden West; Kidnapped; Army Girl; 1939: Arrest Bulldog Drummond!; The Rains Came; Bulldog Drummond's Secret Police; The Gracie Allen Murder Case; Bulldog Drummond's Bride; Nurse Edith Cavell; Mr. Smith Goes to Washington; Let Freedom Ring; 1940: New Moon; 1941: All That Money Can Buy/The Devil and Daniel Webster; Topper Returns; The Corsican Brothers; City of Missing Girls; South of Tahiti; Ellery Queen and the Perfect Crime; 1942: Crossroads; A Yank in Libya; Boss of Big Town; 1943: Hitler's Children; Women in Bondage; 1944: Faces in the Fog; Action in Arabia; Enemy of Women; 1945: Captain Tugboat Annie; Rogues' Gallery; 1946: Gentleman Joe Palooka; Strange Impersonation; It's a Wonderful Life; 1947: Driftwood; The High Wall; 1948: Prince of Thieves; 1949: Hellfire; The Judge Steps Out; El Paso; 1950: Sunset Blvd.; 1951: The First Legion; Here Comes the Groom; Journey Into Light; Savage Drums; 1956: The Ten Commandments; 1957: Darby's Rangers.

NY Stage: 1908: The Battle; 1910: Alias Jimmy Valentine; 1913: Blackbirds; The Ghost Breaker; 1918: Out There; Sleeping Partners; 1921: Danger; 1923: You and I; 1924: Silence.

RUTH WARRICK
BORN: ST. LOUIS, MO, JUNE 29, 1915.
ED: UNIV. OF MO.

An actress whose fame rests on the two roles that bracketed an otherwise fairly unremarkable career, Ruth Warrick started in show business as a radio singer. In 1941 Orson Welles hired her to play Charles Foster Kane's very proper first wife, Emily, the President's niece, in the classic Citizen Kane. Her participation in this most highly revered of all great movies included the famous dinner table sequence in which her disintegrating marriage to Welles is deftly portrayed in a series of quick conversations and camera swipes. She remained at that film's releasing studio, RKO, to star to no avail in Obliging Young Lady, in which she basically "kidnapped" a child so the girl's parents will reunite; Journey Into Fear, as Joseph Cotten's wife; Petticoat Larceny, as the aunt of kidnapped Joan Carroll; The Iron Major, as the devoted spouse of All-American Pat O'Brien; and

China Sky, as an American doctor in worn-torn China. Elsewhere she was loved by a pair of Douglas Fairbanks Jrs. in The Corsican Brothers; played the missus of artist Ray Bellamy in Guest in the House; the home-front wife of Edward G. Robinson in Mr. Winkle Goes to War; Bobby Driscoll's disapproving mom in one of the best of all Disney films, Song of the South; the stuck-up wife of horse owner Dennis O'Keefe in The Great Dan Patch; one of the three wives suspected of adultery in Three Husbands; and Betty Hutton's sympathetic sister-in-law in Let's Dance. She segued over to television where she appeared on the soaps As the World Turns, Peyton Place, and in Joan Bennett's old role in the short-lived small-screen adaptation of Father of the Bride. There were a smattering of movie character parts and then, just when it seemed like her best years were behind her, she landed the role that would make her a major name in the world of daytime dramas, Phoebe Tyler, in All My Children, a part she played well past retirement age. Appropriately, she called her 1980 autobiography The Confessions of Phoebe Tyler.

Screen: 1941: Citizen Kane; The Corsican Brothers; 1942: Obliging Young Lady; Journey Into Fear; 1943: Forever and a Day; Petticoat Larceny; The Iron Major; 1944: Secret Command; Mr. Winkle Goes to War; Guest in the House; 1945: China Sky; 1946: Perilous Holiday; Song of the South; Swell Guy; 1947: Driftwood; Daisy Kenyon; 1948: Arch of Triumph; 1949: The Great Dan Patch; Make Believe Ballroom; 1950: Three Husbands; Second Chance; Beauty on Parade; Let's Dance; One Too Many; 1954: Roogie's Bump; 1966: Ride Beyond Vengeance; 1969: The Great Bank Robbery; 1983: Deathmask/Unknown; The Returning/Witch Doctor.

NY Stage: 1957: Miss Lonelyhearts; 1959: Single Man at a Party; 1960: Take Me Along; 1973: Irene.

Select TV: 1956–60: As the World Turns (series); 1961–62: Father of the Bride (series); 1965–67: Peyton Place (series); 1970–: All My Children (series); 1985: Peyton Place: The Next Generation.

ETHEL WATERS
BORN: CHESTER, PA, OCTOBER 31, 1896.
DIED: SEPTEMBER 1, 1977.

Faced not only with the customary Hollywood barrier of race, but a definite lack of glamour, it is all the more remarkable that Ethel Waters got more than one chance to sparkle on screen. The shapeless singer with the loving smile, grew up dirt poor, working at various menial jobs before landing her first professional stint, as a nightclub performer called "Sweet Mama Stringbean." There was much feeling and warmth in her interpretation of the blues and by the late 1920s she become a genuine star, appearing on Broadway in such shows as Africana, Lew Leslie's Blackbirds of 1930, and As Thousands Cheer. Hollywood invited her to sing some numbers (including "Am I Blue") in one of those graceless early talkies, On With the Show, which had the one distinction of being the first color musical. Back on Broadway, she had a major success, starring in Cabin in the Sky, and this brought her some more movie work starting with Tales of Manhattan, which put her and Paul Robeson in a rather demeaning segment of the multi-storyline; Cairo, reduced to playing Jeanette MacDonald's maid; and, thankfully, the movie version of Cabin in the Sky. As the optimistic Petunia Jackson, she put her special brand of magic on "Taking a Chance on Love" and a new song, "Happiness Is Just a Thing Called Joe," which showed her at her best, optimistic and inviting. Skipping ahead a few years, she returned to the movies to receive an Oscar nomination for playing Jeanne Crain's granny in *Pinky*, and then scored onstage again, this time without music, as the sensible and loving housekeeper in *The Member of the Wedding*. Wisely, she was retained for the film version and this would become the Waters part that most people would hold dearest to their hearts. Her television work included the series *Beulah* and a production of *The Sound and the Fury*, as Dilsey, a role she would repeat on screen. She wrote two memoirs, *His Eye Is on the Sparrow* (1953) and *To Me It's Wonderful* (1972).

Screen: 1929: On With the Show; 1934: Gift of Gab; 1942: Tales of Manhattan; Cairo; 1943: Cabin in the Sky; Stage Door Canteen; 1949: Pinky; 1952: The Member of the Wedding; 1959: The Sound and the Fury.

NY Stage: 1927: Africana; 1930: Lew Leslie's Blackbirds of 1930; 1931: Rhapsody in Black; 1933: As Thousands Cheer; At Home Abroad; 1939: Mamba's Daughters; 1940: Cabin in the Sky; 1943: Laugh Time; 1945: Blue Holiday; 1950: The Member of the Wedding; 1953: At Home With Ethel Waters.

Select TV: 1950–52: Beulah (series); 1955: Speaking to Hannah (sp); The Sound and the Fury (sp); 1957: Sing for Me (sp).

LUCILE WATSON

BORN: QUEBEC, CANADA, MAY 27, 1879. ED: AADA. DIED: JUNE 24, 1962.

Great at playing patrician moms with a bit of high falutin' self-satisfaction, Lucile Watson studied at the American Academy of Dramatic Arts, followed by a lengthy career on the Broadway stage, beginning at the turn of the century. During this time there was a sole film credit, *The Girl With Green Eyes*, adapted from a play she had done. When she was 55, she was hired by MGM to return to motion pictures, making her talking picture debut as La Comtesse in the Helen Hayes vehicle, *What Ever Woman Knows*. Although she remained on Hollywood's list of prime character actresses, she never left the stage very far behind, returning for several triumphs, notably *Pride and Prejudice* and *Watch on the Rhine*. In the meantime, movie-wise, she was the loyal housekeeper of Deanna Durbin and her sisters in the Universal hit *Three Smart Girls*, and did a run of mom roles, including *Sweethearts*, as Jeanette MacDonald's mother; *Made for Each Other*, as a truly insufferable and self-righteous meddler, disapproving of her son James Stewart's marriage to Carole Lombard; *The Women*, dispensing advice to daughter Norma Shearer; and *Waterloo Bridge*, casting aside Vivien Leigh, who is in love with her offspring, Robert Taylor. Warner Bros. asked her to repeat her *Watch on the Rhine* role and her performance, as Bette Davis's widowed Washington mom, brought her an Oscar nomination in the supporting category. She continued playing matriarchal roles with *My Reputation*, with Barbara Stanwyck; *Song of the South*, as the kindly and understanding grandmother of lonely Bobby Driscoll; and *The Razor's Edge*, with Gene Tierney, among others; was the brittle Aunt March in the 1949 remake of *Little Women*; an Austrian princess in *The Emperor Waltz*; and a real pain in the ass as Betty Hutton's unreasonable mother-in-law in *Let's Dance*. Her first husband was actor Rockcliffe Fellowes.

Screen: 1916: The Girl With Green Eyes; 1934: What Every Woman Knows; 1935: The Bishop Misbehaves; 1936: A Woman Rebels; The Garden of Allah; Three Smart Girls; 1938: The Young in Heart; Sweethearts; 1939: Made for Each Other; The Women; 1940: Florian; Waterloo Bridge; 1941: Mr. and Mrs. Smith; The Great Lie; Rage in Heaven; Footsteps in the Dark; Model Wife; 1943: Watch on the Rhine; 1944: Uncertain Glory;

Till We Meet Again; The Thin Man Goes Home; 1946: My Reputation; Tomorrow Is Forever; Never Say Goodbye; The Razor's Edge; Song of the South; 1947: Ivy; 1948: The Emperor Waltz; Julia Misbehaves; That Wonderful Urge; 1949: Little Women; Everybody Does It; 1950: Let's Dance; Harriet Craig; 1951: My Forbidden Past.

NY Stage: 1902: Hearts Aflame; The Girl With Green Eyes; 1903: Glad of It; 1904: The Dictator; 1907: Captain Jinks of the Horse Marines; The Lemonade Boy; Her Sister; 1909: The City; 1912: Just to Get Married; The Truth Wagon; The Point of View; 1913: The Bridal Path; 1914: Under Cover; 1915: Mr. Myd's Mystery; The Eternal Magdalene; 1916: The Fear Market; His Bridal Night; 1917: Losing Eloise; 1918: The Fountain of Youth; A Marriage of Convenience; 1919: Moonlight and Honeysuckle; 1920: Respect for Riches; The Unwritten Chapter; Heartbreak House; 1921: The White Villa; March Hares; Everybody; 1922: The Nest; Fools Errant; 1923: You and I; 1923: The Far Cry; 1926: Ghosts; The Importance of Being Earnest; Mozart; 1927: Off-Key; Love Is Like That; 1930: That's the Woman; 1934: No More Ladies; Post Road; 1935: Pride and Prejudice; 1936: Prelude to Exile; 1937: Yes, My Darling Daughter; 1939: Dear Octopus; 1941: Watch on the Rhine; 1943: The Family; 1950: Ring Round the Moon; 1953: The Bat; Late Love.

Select TV: 1948: The Old Lady Shows Her Medals (sp); 1950: The Chair (sp); 1951: The Case of the Calico Dog (sp); The Partnership (sp); 1952: Years of Grace (sp); 1954: A Favor for a Friend (sp).

DAVID WAYNE

(WAYNE DAVID MCKEEHAN) BORN: TRAVERSE CITY, MI, JANUARY 30, 1914. ED: WESTERN MI COL. DIED: FEBRUARY 9, 1995.

Although he was more often cast as a secondary player than as a lead, David Wayne could easily push many a star aside with his sharp comic timing, knowing wit, and spurts of nervous energy. A one-time statistician, he took up acting in the mid-1930s with the Cleveland Shakespeare Company, which led to his Broadway bow, in 1938, in *Escape This Night*. Although comfortably employed, he made little impact over the next nine years until he was cast as Leprechaun Og in the Burton Lane-E.Y. Harburg hit musical fantasy, *Finian's Rainbow*. Wayne got to introduce "When I'm Not Near the Girl I Love," received a Theatre World Award, and wound up with the very first Tony Award ever given in the supporting category. Thinking Irish, producer David O. Selznick hired him to play Joseph Cotten's cabbie friend in his haunting *Portrait of Jennie*, which came out shortly after Wayne scored another smash on Broadway, playing Ensign Pulver in the original 1948 production of *Mister Roberts*. He went to MGM where he made quite an impression in *Adam's Rib*, as Katharine Hepburn's fidgety and effete friend, a role that allowed him to sing a Cole Porter song, "Amanda." 20th Century-Fox was interested in adding him to their roster of stars and he first appeared for them to good effect in *Stella*, where he stole the notices, as the worried nephew who decides to bury then unearth the body of his dead uncle. He was then called on to support Betty Grable in one of her weakest films, *My Blue Heaven*, when in fact he himself should have been getting showcased in his own musical. Instead, it was up to Universal to give him his first movie lead, as the sardonic infantry soldier Joe, partnered with Tom Ewell, as Willie, in the comedy *Up Front*, a pleasant adaptation of the famed comic strip. Meanwhile, over at Columbia, a more serious side of Wayne could be seen in the uncalled for remake of the German classic *M*, in which he made a game attempt to follow in the footsteps of Peter Lorre, playing a child killer.

Back at Fox he was the nice guy pianist who helped and then married singer Susan Froman (Susan Hayward) in the highly popular biopic *With a Song in My Heart*, and was seen in two all-star episode films, *We're Not Married!*, and *O. Henry's Full House*, in both cases in the sequences featuring Marilyn Monroe, the latter being an interpretation of "The Cop and the Anthem." The studio gave Wayne his own vehicles at last with *Wait Till the Sun Shines, Nellie*, a piece of sentimental Americana about a beleaguered barber in a small town, and *Tonight We Sing*, getting some of his rare bad reviews as he struggled to come-up with a convincing accent while playing Russian impresario Sol Hurok. *Down Among the Sheltering Palms* at least allowed him to sing, and he was paired very nicely with Monroe again for *How to Marry a Millionaire*, where he appealed to her because, like her, he wore glasses. MGM didn't let him repeat another of his Tony Award-winning stage successes when they filmed *The Teahouse of the August Moon* (Wayne did do it later, on television), but instead cast him as Frank Sinatra's envious married buddy in *The Tender Trap*. He had his best dramatic part back at Fox, as unhinged Joanne Woodward's none-too-sympathetic husband, in *The Three Faces of Eve*; was wasted as Jerry Lewis's Dean Martin replacement in *The Sad Sack*; and went serious again for *The Last Angry Man*, as a TV producer who wants to do a profile on slum doctor Paul Muni. Gone from cinemas for most of the 1960s, he returned, looking much older, to play a scientist trying to stop a deadly virus in the literate sci-fi thriller *The Andromeda Strain* (oddly, the character had the very same name, Charles Dutton, as one Wayne played that same year on the short-lived television series *The Good Life*), then did a great deal of TV, including regular work on two series, *Ellery Queen* and *House Calls*. At the movies he had fun playing the swishy journalist in the 1974 version of *The Front Page*; was one of the livelier things about the musical *Huckleberry Finn*, as the Duke; and showed up as the World's Oldest Train Conductor in the farcical *Finders Keepers*.

Screen: 1948: Portrait of Jennie; 1949: Adam's Rib; 1950: The Reformer and the Redhead; Stella; My Blue Heaven; 1951: Up Front; M; As Young as You Feel; 1952: With a Song in My Heart; Wait Till the Sun Shines, Nellie; We're Not Married!; O. Henry's Full House; 1953: Tonight We Sing; Down Among the Sheltering Palms; The I Don't Care Girl; How to Marry a Millionaire; 1954: Hell and High Water; 1955: The Tender Trap; 1956: The Naked Hills; 1957: The Three Faces of Eve; The Sad Sack; 1959: The Last Angry Man; 1961: The Big Gamble; 1971: The Andromeda Strain; The African Elephant (narrator); 1974: Huckleberry Finn; The Front Page; 1975: The Apple Dumpling Gang; 1979: The Prize Fighter; 1984: Finders Keepers; 1987: The Survivalist (dtv).

NY Stage: 1938: Escape This Night; Dance Night; 1940: The Scene of the Crime; 1943: The Merry Widow; 1944: Peepshow; 1946: Park Avenue; 1947: Finian's Rainbow; 1948: Mister Roberts; 1953: The Teahouse of the August Moon; 1956: The Ponder Heart; The Loud Red Patrick (and prod.); 1958: Say Darling; 1960: Send Me No Flowers; 1962: Venus at Large; 1963: Too True to Be Good; 1964: After the Fall; Marco Millions; But for Whom Charlie; Incident at Vichy; 1965: The Yearling; 1966: Show Boat; 1968: The Happy Time.

Select TV: 1950: The Dreams of Jasper Hornby (sp); 1955: Norby (series); Darkness at Noon (sp); 1956: Morning's at Seven (sp); 1957: Ruggles of Red Gap (sp); Junior Miss (sp); The Jet-Propelled Couch (sp); 1959: Strawberry Blonde (sp); 1960: The Devil and Daniel Webster (sp); 1962: The White Lie (sp); The Teahouse of the August Moon (sp); 1966: Lamp at Midnight

(sp); Holloway's Daughter (sp); 1967: Dear Friends (sp); 1969: Arsenic and Old Lace (sp); 1970: The Boy Who Stole the Elephants; 1971–72: The Good Life (series); 1972: The Catcher; 1974: The Return of the Big Cat; The FBI Story: The FBI vs. Alvin Karpis — Public Enemy Number One; 1975: Ellery Queen/Too Many Suspects; 1975–76: The Adventures of Ellery Queen (series); 1977: In the Glitter Palace; Tubby the Tuba (sp; voice); Once an Eagle (ms); 1978: Black Beauty (ms); Loose Change (ms); Murder at the Mardi Gras; Dallas (series); It's a Bird! It's a Plane! It's Superman! (sp); The Gift of Love; 1979: The Girls in the Office; An American Christmas Carol; 1979–82: House Calls (series); 1987: Poker Alice.

JOHN WAYNE

(MARION MICHAEL MORRISON)
BORN: WINTERSET, IA, MAY 26, 1907. RAISED IN SOUTHERN CA. ED: USC. DIED: JUNE 11, 1979.

John Wayne's place in American motion picture history is inestimable. Few stars maintained their box-office standing for as long a period as he did, giving his fans the sort of rugged heroics that made them feel like they were watching someone truly in charge. He was physically imposing, impatient with nonsense and fools, fit for action, a crusader for decency and patriotism. He was also gentlemanly and shy towards the ladies with a lot more going on behind his frequently squinting eyes than his detractors maintained, giving shadings of complexity to certain roles when called on to do so. His name became a part of folklore, serving as an icon for the American West and Hollywood's idea of a one-man fighting army in times of war. As attitudes changed, the liberal factions looked down upon him for his right wing politics, bullheadedness, and misogynistic machismo, but Wayne could almost give a damn what others felt about him, which only made him that much more admirable. There were few actors, be they more versed or better trained in their craft, that could muster up a fraction of the power he brought simply by walking on screen. It was while attending USC on a football scholarship that he did part-time work at Fox, moving props, doing occasional stunt work and a bit part here and there. He made friends with director John Ford who, along with fellow footballer Ward Bond, became one of his most important relationships, off screen and on. Ford, however, was an "A" director at the time and would not call on Wayne for a picture until more than a decade later. Instead, following some small parts, Wayne was chosen to carry an expensive western for director Raoul Walsh, *The Big Trail*, about a wagon train venturing into the wide open spaces of America. The movie was shot in a rare widescreen process, which turned out to be a hindrance since few theatres could actually show it. As a result, it became one of the louder flops of 1930 and Wayne didn't quite become the star the movie was supposed to have made him. Awkward as he was at times, there were also clear hints of a handsome, charming presence who simply needed to relax and be himself.

He went over to Columbia for a thoroughly unproductive period that ended in him getting on studio chief Harry Cohn's bad side. During this time there were some Mascot cheapies and then another contract, with Warners, who mainly used him in grade "C" westerns. Just to show that he was going absolutely nowhere, another low-grade company, Monogram, called on his services, turning him into a singing cowboy (with a dubbed voice!) for *Riders of Destiny*. Wayne hated this genre and let it be known, so the studio dropped the vocalizing and let him concentrate on pure action. He was beginning to develop a following in the rural markets, but that didn't mean much to the major studios or audiences interested in first run features. With *Westward Ho*, in 1935, he went over to yet another poverty row company, Republic, but it was here that his popularity began to rise, in material that was not all that different from what he'd been getting before, but satisfied the masses nonetheless. These assignments included *Overland Stage Raiders*, released in 1938, in which he was first teamed with Ray Corrigan and Max Terhune as "the Three Mesquiteers," for a series of adventures that Wayne came to loathe. It was all up to John Ford to come to Wayne's rescue and so he did, offering something that was miles above the standard fare, a character driven film that didn't sacrifice the action fans would expect. The movie, *Stagecoach*, released in 1939, was a box-office smash and Wayne, as the gentle gunman known as The Ringo Kid, was suddenly noticed by those who hadn't given him the time of day before. Republic, realizing they had a hot property on their hands, kept him under contract well into the 1950s, thrilled to be profiting from the major studios that were bidding for his services. Never a man to take it easy, Wayne hopped from one project to the next as his status rose higher and higher. First, he was teamed with his *Stagecoach* co-star, Claire Trevor, in both *Allegheny Uprising* and *Dark Command*, before returning to Ford for another masterfully crafted character piece, *The Long Voyage Home*, where he was sympathetic and likable as a sailor named Swede, despite his less than successful attempts at a Swedish accent.

Universal paired him with Marlene Dietrich on three occasions, with diminishing results, starting with *Seven Sinners*; the remake of *The Spoilers*, in which he brawled memorably with Randolph Scott; and *Pittsburgh*. The teaming of the shambling man of action with the European glamour queen worked, as it seemed to off screen, as they became lovers for a brief period, as Wayne's first marriage was falling apart. Republic kept him in standard stuff, although now the budgets were somewhat higher, since Wayne was the one bona fide star on the lot. These included *Lady for a Night*, with Joan Blondell; *In Old California*, which was not to be confused with *In Old Oklahoma*; the first of Wayne's World War II epics, *Flying Tigers*; and *Flame of the Barbary Coast*, which was capped off by a mini version of the San Francisco earthquake. Over at Paramount he got to be seen in color in the gentle *The Shepherd of the Hills*, as a mountain man, and DeMille's *Reap the Wild Wind*, playing something akin to a villain and getting punished for it by a killer giant squid; while Metro hired him to pair off with Joan Crawford, of all people, in *Reunion in France*, where he showed up late in the tale as an flier trying to escape from the Nazis. It was up to Ford once again to provide him with superior material, as he did with *They Were Expendable*, a war story, but one that concentrated on the interaction between the people involved on a human level, with a particularly lovely and believable romance between Wayne and nurse Donna Reed. It was a hit, as were most of these, and erased from most people's minds the fact that Wayne had not bothered to offer himself up for actual military service. He'd become big enough by the post war period that he was able to serve as his own producer for the first time, with *Angel and the Badman*, a nice western tale with an anti-violence message but not one of his more popular vehicles.

He did, however, enter a fairly lucrative period in the late 1940s, starting with *Fort Apache*, for Ford; director Howard Hawks's *Red River*, a complex tale of a cattle drive in which he clashed with surrogate son Montgomery Clift, with Wayne at his most stubbornly fascinating, winning raves for this massive money maker; the remake of *3 Godfathers*, which was inferior to the lesser known 1936 version; *Wake of the Red Witch*, a Republic

adventure that, if nothing else, brought him the name of his production company, Batjac; Ford's *She Wore a Yellow Ribbon*, excelling in a character part, as an aging cavalry officer, one he would often cite as his personal favorite among his roles; and *Sand of Iwo Jima*, marvelous as a tough-as-nails Marine sergeant, relentlessly drilling his men for action. This was one fellow you didn't want to disobey and you knew, in the end, that his hard tactics were all for the good of his company. Wayne earned an Oscar nomination and, after a long, hard climb, could safely declare that he was at the very top of the industry. There was a third Ford cavalry film, *Rio Grande* (as the same character he played in *Fort Apache*, Kirby York, only with an "e" added to his last name), which gave him his first teaming with his best leading lady, Maureen O'Hara, with Wayne as a career officer, challenging her over the love of their son, Claude Jarman, Jr. After that, he signed a contract with Warners, and although the cash kept coming in, there was little to be said for many of the properties he did for this studio, including the clichéd submarine drama *Operation Pacific*; the trite anti-red clunkers *Big Jim McLain* and *Blood Alley*; the sentimental football weepy *Trouble Along the Way*; and a misconceived pairing with Lana Turner, *The Sea Chase*. Fortunately, he talked Republic into hiring John Ford so the director could dramatize his love for Ireland in *The Quiet Man*. As the prizefighter who hopes to settle down in the rolling hills of Erin and court colleen Maureen O'Hara, Wayne had one of his best loved roles in a film lush with atmosphere, spirit, and subtlety. Everything about it clicked and it was, hands down, the best thing he did at Republic, one of the high points of his career, and, to many, including certain non-Wayne movie fans, the best motion picture in which he would ever appear.

Meanwhile, back at Warners, he shot *Hondo* in 3-D, romancing pioneer woman Geraldine Page; and had another solid success with *The High and the Mighty*, his first in widescreen, and the forerunner of the "disaster" film. Due to legal technicalities both movies would drop out of sight for decades, with the former finally being unearthed after Wayne's death, but the latter remaining in limbo as of the arrival of the new millennium. In addition to these assignments, he had also committed to doing some projects for RKO, but these included two of the worst of his career: *Jet Pilot*, which mogul Howard Hughes tinkered with so much that the movie, started in 1950, did not surface in theatres until 1957, and *The Conqueror*, with Wayne ludicrously miscast as Genghis Khan in a badly misconceived adventure that would attain some sort of camp status in years to come. On a far less funny level the latter film achieved notoriety because a large percentage of the participants involved would die of cancer, a fact blamed on the use of contaminated soil, the location of the production being shot in a region used for atomic bomb testing. In the meantime, Wayne was more at home with another Ford film, *The Searchers*, a rambling tale of an angry man obsessed, but one in which Wayne was at his most mesmerizing, determined to rescue Natalie Wood from the hated Comanches. Like *Red River* he was not afraid to be dangerously dislikable in his single-mindedness and he was that much more interesting as a result. Its great reviews and profitability helped wipe away the failures of *The Wings of Eagles*, a biopic of aviator-writer Frank Wead, that took him too far away from what the fans expected; *Legend of the Lost*, a poor treasure hunt tale with Sophia Loren; and another bit of bizarre miscasting, with Wayne playing Ambassador Townsend Harris, in *The Barbarian and the Geisha*, working under director John Huston, whom he despised.

There was another pinnacle with Hawks's *Rio Bravo*, made with the right balance of action and humor, in which he was a sheriff being helped by a group of misfits to fight off the villains. Surprisingly disappointing was *The Horse Soldiers*, which seemed like a sure thing, what with Ford at the helm and William Holden as a co-star. Neither actor had reason to worry much since they each took away $750,000 for their efforts, among the highest star salaries paid up to that time. This was followed by the most personal project of Wayne's career, *The Alamo*, which he partially financed himself and directed, wanting to pay tribute to the Texas heroes who had given their lives in one of the country's most legendary battles. The movie, in which he starred as Davy Crockett, wound up costing a whopping $12 million and, despite a respectable degree of public interest, didn't make Wayne a dime. It got a token Oscar nomination for Best Picture, but was far less than the definitive telling of this great saga that it should have been. More fun was *North to Alaska*, which was a comedic adventure, an assured balance between action and good-natured male high jinks, a tone that he would try to achieve with less success in the plotless *Hatari!*, which found him chasing wild animals for zoos; his last with Ford, the weak *Donovan's Reef*; and *McLintock!*, a variation on *The Quiet Man*, once again paired with O'Hara. In between he was fine as a westerner realizing that the changing world is passing him by in *The Man Who Shot Liberty Valance*, the first time in years that he'd taken second billing, his co-star being James Stewart. There were smaller roles in the all-star productions *The Longest Day*, really taking charge during his scenes, as a no-nonsense lieutenant colonel, in this grand depiction of the D-Day invasion; the episodic *How the West Was Won*, as General Sherman, in Ford's sequence about the Civil War; and, most strangely, *The Greatest Story Ever Told*, glimpsed ever so briefly as a centurion overseeing the crucifixion of Christ. Shortly after filming an overlong World War II saga, *In Harm's Way*, he had a much-publicized battle with cancer, which he managed to lick.

He returned with another enjoyable western, *The Sons of Katie Elder*, and a lively variation on *Rio Bravo*, this one called *El Dorado*, pairing him with Robert Mitchum. He then made his statement *in favor of* the Vietnam War with *The Green Berets* (also serving as director), and this became the movie that really put him on the bad side of the left-wing critics and the newer generation of Hollywood players. It was trashed for being a simple-minded rendering of a controversial conflict, but it still brought in the customers. In contrast, there was nothing but praise from all parties for *True Grit*, in which he was a one-eyed, pot-bellied drunken sheriff, Rooster Cogburn, who snaps to in order to help a young girl get revenge on the men who murdered her father. Audiences turned up in big numbers, making this a personal triumph for Wayne, who was at his very best in a showy and hugely enjoyable performance. He won the Academy Award for Best Actor of 1969, which was one of the most applauded choices that organization ever made. Everything after that was almost an anti-climax. There were more familiar westerns, including *The Undefeated*; a last one with Hawks, *Rio Lobo*; and *The Cowboys*, which at least had the gimmick of Wayne being in charge of a bunch of youngsters. Trying for something different he did two cop movies, a genre he had stayed away from in the past, with *McQ* and *Brannigan*, the latter utilizing the old "fish out of water" premise by placing him in London, but he was starting to look and act tired. Nor was it the most inspired idea to revive his recent great role in *Rooster Cogburn*, though it did allow him to co-star with another living legend, Katharine Hepburn. Someone of Wayne's stature deserved to have a fitting climax to his career and he got it with *The Shootist*, playing a dying gunfighter whose reputation will not let him rest. The box office had fallen off by this point and he was about to lose his

second battle with cancer. After his death, many modern day critics had decided that his sort of Hollywood had pretty much vanished anyway but he turned out to be one of the best-represented of all the old time names once the video industry hit. After a while even those who'd scoffed at him had to look at the scope of his work and be mightily impressed by an individual who remained true to his ideals. His son, Patrick Wayne, also became an actor.

Screen: 1928: Mother Machree; Hangman's House; 1929: Salute; Words and Music (AS DUKE MORRISON); 1930: Men Without Women; Rough Romance; Cheer Up and Smile; The Big Trail; 1931: Girls Demand Excitement; Three Girls Lost; Men Are Like That; Range Feud; Maker of Men; 1932: Haunted Gold; Shadow of the Eagle (serial); Hurricane Express (serial); Texas Cyclone; Lady and Gent; Two-Fisted Law; Ride Him, Cowboy; The Big Stampede; 1933: The Telegraph Trail; Central Airport; His Private Secretary; Somewhere in Sonora; Life of Jimmy Dolan; The Three Musketeers (serial; also released as feature Desert Command); Baby Face; The Man from Monterey; Riders of Destiny; Sagebrush Trail; 1934: West of the Divide; Lucky Texan; Blue Steel; The Man from Utah; Randy Rides Alone; The Star Packer; The Trail Beyond; 'Neath Arizona Skies; 1935: Lawless Frontier; Texas Terror; Rainbow Valley; Paradise Canyon; The Dawn Rider; Westward Ho; Desert Trail; New Frontier; Lawless Range; 1936: The Lawless Nineties; King of the Pecos; The Oregon Trail; Winds of the Wasteland; The Sea Spoilers; The Lonely Trail; Conflict; 1937: California Straight Ahead; I Cover the War; Idol of the Crowds; Adventure's End; 1938: Born to the West/Hell Town; Pals of the Saddle; Overland Stage Raiders; Santa Fe Stampede; Red River Range; 1939: Stagecoach; The Night Riders; Three Texas Steers; Wyoming Outlaw; New Frontier/Frontier Horizon; Allegheny Uprising; 1940: Dark Command; Three Faces West; The Long Voyage Home; Seven Sinners; 1941: A Man Betrayed; Lady from Louisiana; The Shepherd of the Hills; Lady for a Night; 1942: Reap the Wild Wind; The Spoilers; In Old California; Flying Tigers; Reunion in France; Pittsburgh; 1943: Lady Takes a Chance; In Old Oklahoma/War of the Wildcats; 1944: The Fighting Seabees; Tall in the Saddle; 1945: Flame of the Barbary Coast; Back to Bataan; Dakota; They Were Expendable; 1946: Without Reservations; 1947: Angel and the Badman (and prod.); Tycoon; 1948: Fort Apache; Red River; 3 Godfathers; Wake of the Red Witch; 1949: She Wore a Yellow Ribbon; The Fighting Kentuckian (and prod.); Sands of Iwo Jima; 1950: Rio Grande; 1951: Operation Pacific; Flying Leathernecks; 1952: The Quiet Man; Big Jim McLain; 1953: Trouble Along the Way; Island in the Sky; Hondo; 1954: The High and the Mighty; 1955: The Sea Chase; Blood Alley; 1956: The Conqueror; The Searchers; 1957: The Wings of Eagles; Jet Pilot (filmed 1950); Legend of the Lost; 1958: I Married a Woman; The Barbarian and the Geisha; 1959: Rio Bravo; The Horse Soldiers; 1960: The Alamo (and dir.; prod.); North to Alaska; 1961: The Comancheros; 1962: The Man Who Shot Liberty Valance; Hatari!; The Longest Day; 1963: How the West Was Won; Donovan's Reef; McLintock!; 1964: Circus World; 1965: The Greatest Story Ever Told; In Harm's Way; The Sons of Katie Elder; 1966: Cast a Giant Shadow; 1967: The War Wagon; El Dorado; 1968: The Green Berets (and co-dir.); Hellfighters; 1969: True Grit; The Undefeated; 1970: Chisum; Rio Lobo; 1971: Big Jake; 1972: The Cowboys; Cancel My Reservation; 1973: The Train Robbers; Cahill: U.S. Marshal; 1974: McQ; 1975: Brannigan; Rooster Cogburn; 1976: The Shootist.

Select TV: 1955: Rookie of the Year (sp); 1970: Swing Out, Sweet Land (sp); 1971: Directed by John Ford (sp).

DENNIS WEAVER

BORN: JOPLIN, MO, JUNE 4, 1924.
ED: UNIV. OF OK.

Though he did a fair amount of motion picture work, it was television that made lean and ingratiating Dennis Weaver into a star, where he kept audiences at ease, usually as a comfortable kind of rural everyman. A track star in college, he missed going to the Olympics, so decided to give acting a try, studying with the Actors Studio before showing up in the replacement cast of Broadway's *Come Back, Little Sheba*. Helped by Shelley Winters, he wound up under contract with Universal Pictures who debuted him way down the cast list of a Robert Ryan western, *Horizons West*. For the most part he remained in western gear in such offerings as *The Man from the Alamo*, *War Arrow*, and *Chief Crazy Horse*. Elsewhere he was a police captain in the big-screen version of *Dragnet*; an intelligence officer in *The Bridges at Toko-Ri*; a heroic handyman in love with Jean Wallace in *Storm Fear*; and John Brown, Jr. in *Seven Angry Men*. In 1955 he was cast as James Arness's limping, twangy-voiced deputy Chester Goode on the smash hit western television series, *Gunsmoke* and became an overnight star. He stayed with the long-running show for nine seasons, winning an Emmy Award in 1959, and doing an occasional movie role on the side, notably *Touch of Evil*, in an unexpectedly off-the-wall performance as a hyper motel manager, and *The Gallant Hours*, as James Cagney's military aide. He was uncharacteristically villainous as Bibi Andersson's bigoted, unfeeling husband in *Duel at Diablo*; mugged along with the rest of the principals, as an astronaut, in a dire comedy, *Way…Way Out*, and had a rare movie lead, as an Everglades warden whose family owns a benign bear in *Gentle Giant*, which led to the weekly series, retitled *Gentle Ben*. He followed this with a more popular series, *McCloud*, as a sheriff transported to the streets of New York. From that point on he was almost exclusively a television actor, doing many telefilms, the best remembered of which was the Steven Spielberg-directed *Duel*, in which Weaver was terrorized by a determined trucker.

Screen: 1952: Horizons West; The Raiders/Riders of Vengeance; 1953: The Lawless Breed; The Redhead from Wyoming; Mississippi Gambler; Law and Order; Column South; It Happens Every Thursday; The Man from the Alamo; The Golden Blade; The Nebraskan; War Arrow; 1954: Dangerous Mission; Dragnet; 1955: Ten Wanted Men; The Bridges at Toko-Ri; Seven Angry Men; Chief Crazy Horse; 1956: Storm Fear; 1958: Touch of Evil; 1960: The Gallant Hours; 1966: Duel at Diablo; Way…Way Out; 1967: Gentle Giant; 1970: A Man Called Sledge; 1971: What's the Matter With Helen?; 1988: Walking After Midnight (nUSr); 1995: Two Bit & Pepper (dtv); 1998: Escape from Wildcat Canyon (dtv); 2000: Submerged (dtv).

NY Stage: 1950: Come Back, Little Sheba; 1951: Out West of Eighth.

Select TV: 1955–64: Gunsmoke (series); 1958: Dungeon (sp); 1964–65: Kentucky Jones (series); 1966: Showdown with the Sundance Kid (sp); 1967–69: Gentle Ben (series); 1968: Mission Batangas; 1970: McCloud: Who Killed Miss U.S.A.?/Portrait of a Dead Girl; 1970–76: McCloud (series); 1971: The Fogotten Man; Duel; 1972: Rolling Man; 1973: Female Artillery; The Great Man's Whiskers; Terror on the Beach; 1977: Intimate Strangers; 1978: The Islander; Pearl (ms); Ishi: The Last of His Tribe; 1978–79: Centennial (ms); 1979: The Ordeal of Patty Hearst; Stone; 1980: Amber Waves; The Ordeal of Dr. Mudd; 1981: The Day the Loving Stopped; 1982: Don't Go to Sleep; 1983: Cocaine:

One Man's Seduction; 1983–84: Emerald Point N.A.S. (series); 1985: Going for the Gold: The Bill Johnson Story; 1986: A Winner Never Quits; The Best Christmas Pageant Ever (sp); 1987: Bluffing It; 1987–88: Buck James (series); 1988: Disaster at Silo 7; 1989: The Return of Sam McCloud (and prod.); 1992: Mastergate (sp); Lonesome Dove: The Series (series); 1994: Greyhounds; 1997: Stolen Women Captured Hearts; Seduction in a Small Town; 2000: The Virginian; High Noon.

CLIFTON WEBB

(WEBB PARMALLEE HOLLENBECK)
BORN: INDIANAPOLIS, IN, NOVEMBER 19, 1891.
DIED: OCTOBER 13, 1966.

Everybody's favorite prissy snob, Clifton Webb was dapper, dryly critical of others, and oh so pleased with himself, which was exactly what audiences loved about him. He was usually raising his nose, looking down with superiority at some other, less confident character, and tossing off a witty bon mot or insult with the sting of a wasp. It was not a greatly varied act but it was all too much fun to wish it otherwise. Though it was not evident in anything he did in his film career, Webb had, in fact, started out in the world of musicals, first by singing opera in Boston and then forming a nightclub act with Bonnie Glass. As a singer-dancer he became a star of the Broadway stage in such shows as *See America First*, *Sunny*, *Treasure Girl*, and *As Thousands Cheer*, in which he got to sing the Irving Berlin classic "Easter Parade." During this period he made four silent features, starting with *Polly With a Past*, in 1920, and was about to re-start his movie career in the 1930s, as a dancer in the Fred Astaire mode, but nothing ever came of it. Instead he returned to the theater where his credits included the original New York production of Noel Coward's *Blithe Spirit*, which revitalized the movie industry's interest in Webb when he brought the production to Los Angeles. He was hired by director Otto Preminger to play the snooty writer, Waldo Lydecker, who obsesses over Gene Tierney, in *Laura*, and he was effortlessly the best thing about this talky noir, earning an Oscar nomination in the supporting category and a contract with 20th Century-Fox. He remained exclusively with that studio for the rest of his career. Following his first hit he did a lesser-known but superior noir, *The Dark Corner*, as a cold-blooded art gallery proprietor who sets up private eye Mark Stevens to take the fall for a murder rap; and then salvaged the fairly dreary adaptation of Somerset Maugham's masterful novel *The Razor's Edge*, where he was absolutely perfect as the unapologetically stuck-up Elliott Templeton, a performance that brought him a second supporting-actor Oscar nomination.

He was upped to the starring role, though billed *below* Robert Young and Maureen O'Hara, in the delightful *Sitting Pretty*, this time using his patented snooty character in a comedic storyline. In this particular instance he was Mr. Belvedere, a self-proclaimed genius, who winds up playing babysitter in a small town and causing an uproar when he writes a book exposing the shortcomings of the locals. The audiences ate it up and Webb was once again in the running for an Oscar, this time in the lead category. It was followed by a pair of all too typical sequels, *Mr. Belvedere Goes to College*, where he, of course, got to show the faculty just how much smarter he was than they, and then, a few years later, *Mr. Belvedere Rings the Bell*, which had him trying to improve the conditions in an old folks' home, suggesting a definite softening of the once-acerbic and self-involved character. His very effete nature and the aversion to children he'd portrayed previously, made him seem miscast as the mighty patriarch of a large brood in *Cheaper by the Dozen*, but this superficial adaptation of the beloved bestseller was another box-office winner. There was a fantasy, *For Heaven's Sake*, where he was a tart-tongued angel; *Dreamboat*, in which he had fun playing a conceited old silent movie star who thinks he has left his past life behind by taking up teaching; *Stars and Stripes Together*, where it seemed hard to take him seriously behind that beard and spectacles, as John Philip Sousa; and *Titanic*, an acceptable recreation of the famous sinking that sufficed until better versions of the story came along. His romance with Dorothy McGuire was probably the most agreeable of the multiple storylines in the tiresome but enormously successful Rome travelogue *Three Coins in the Fountain*, after which he journeyed to England for the straightforward espionage tale *The Man Who Never Was*, portraying a British (he always seemed to have hailed from that country anyway) naval officer who outwits the Nazis. He was back in the family mode for *The Remarkable Mr. Pennypacker*, a particularly crummy comedy about a bigamist, and *Holiday for Lovers*, as an overbearing psychiatrist worried about his grown daughter's attraction to men. After a short absence he showed up looking considerably older in *Satan Never Sleeps*, as a priest in war-torn China, taking a secondary role to top-billed William Holden.

Screen: 1920: Polly With a Past; 1924: Let No Man Put Asunder; 1925: New Toys; The Heart of a Siren; 1944: Laura; 1946: The Dark Corner; The Razor's Edge; 1948: Sitting Pretty; 1949: Mr. Belvedere Goes to College; 1950: Cheaper by the Dozen; For Heaven's Sake; 1951: Mr. Belvedere Rings the Bell; Elopement; 1952: Dreamboat; Stars and Stripes Forever; 1953: Titanic; Mister Scoutmaster; 1954: Three Coins in the Fountain; Woman's World; 1956: The Man Who Never Was; 1957: Boy on a Dolphin; 1959: The Remarkable Mr. Pennypacker; Holiday for Lovers; 1962: Satan Never Sleeps.

NY Stage: 1913: The Purple Road; 1914: Dancing Around; 1915: Ned Wayburn's Town Topics; 1916: See America First; 1917: Love O'Mike; 1918: Listen Lester; 1920: As You Were; 1923: Jack and Jill; Meet the Wife; 1924: Parasites; 1925: Sunny; 1928: She's My Baby; Treasure Girl; 1929: The Little Show; 1930: Three's a Crowd; 1932: Flying Colors; 1933: As Thousands Cheer; 1936: And Stars Remain; 1938: You Never Know; 1939: The Importance of Being Earnest; 1941: Blithe Spirit; 1946: Present Laughter.

JACK WEBB

(JOHN RANDOLPH WEBB) BORN: SANTA MONICA, CA, APRIL 2, 1920. DIED: DECEMBER 23, 1982.

A jack-of-all-trades, with a clipped, monotonous, self-important voice, Jack Webb had, not surprisingly, begun his career on radio where, despite the overly serious manner that mimics would rib for decades to come, he hosted a comedy show. Following his success in that medium as the star of *Pat Novak, Private Eye*, he began doing supporting work in films, notably in *The Men*, as one of the paraplegics who attempts to jolly Marlon Brando out of his depression; *Sunset Blvd.*, uncharacteristically ebullient, as the affable assistant director engaged to Nancy Olson; and *Appointment With Danger*, which also featured Harry Morgan, with whom he would co-star in later years. By this point he had created *Dragnet* on radio and it ran there for seven years before repeating its tremendous success on television. Webb's no-nonsense performance as Sergeant Joe Friday, not to mention the program's deeply earnest voice-over narration, catchphrases ("Just the facts, ma'am"), and urgent music score, made it one the medium's best-remembered, most influential, and spoofable cop shows. Webb transferred the

characters over to the large screen in 1954, adding color, and, despite the fact that it played like a hundred other uninspired cop films, it was a box-office success. He went on to direct, produce (for his own Mark VII Productions), and star in the features *Pete Kelly's Blues*, a tale of musicians and gangsters in Prohibition-era Kansas that was probably the most enjoyable of his directorial efforts; *The D.I.*, as a hard-ass drill instructor; *-30-*, as a newspaper reporter; and *The Last Time I Saw Archie*, which was his one shot at comedy and the only one of these in which he gave the lead to someone else, that someone being Robert Mitchum. No doubt discourged by declining box-office returns of each, he returned to where he was more at home, on the small screen, including a *Dragnet* reprise in the late 1960s, with Harry Morgan replacing Ben Alexander as Webb's investigative partner. In addition to those series that he himself appeared in, he also produced/executive produced such programs as *77 Sunset Strip*, *Adam 12*, *Emergency*, and *Mobile One*, directing episodes of most of them as well. His first wife (1945–53) was actress Julie London.

Screen: 1948: He Walked by Night; Hollow Triumph; 1949: Sword in the Desert; 1950: Halls of Montezuma; The Men; Dark City; Sunset Blvd.; 1951: Appointment With Danger; U.S.S. Teakettle/You're in the Navy Now; 1954: Dragnet (and dir.); 1955: Pete Kelly's Blues (and dir.; prod.); 1957: The D.I. (and dir.; prod.); 1959: -30- (and dir.; prod.); 1961: The Last Time I Saw Archie (and dir.; prod.).

Select TV: 1952–59: Dragnet (series; and dir.; prod.); 1962–63: General Electric True (series host); 1967–70: Dragnet (series; and dir.; prod.; co-wr.); 1973: Escape (series; narrator).

ROBERT WEBBER

BORN: SANTA ANA, CA, OCTOBER 14, 1924. DIED: MAY 17, 1989.

A ubiquitous character actor for some four decades on screens both big and small, the passively indistinctive features of Robert Webber were somehow quite suitable for his many performances as unsavory or weak men. Following service with the Marines during World War II, he acted in stock before making his Broadway debut, in 1948, in *Two Blind Mice*. Two years later he was first seen on motion picture screens, playing a member of the real-life Tri-State Gang in Warners's *Highway 301*, though he principally made his living during this period on TV, doing various anthology dramas or guest spots. Back in the movies he was the glib ad man, Juror Number 12, in the classic *12 Angry Men*, and managed to land a pair of star parts, playing a Marine saving a nun and bunch of school girls, in *The Nun and the Sergeant*, and an amnesia victim in the British-made thriller, *Hysteria*. He was more at home doing supporting parts however, and he showed up as Joanne Woodward's lover in *The Stripper*, (repeating his stage role from *A Loss of Roses*); an oily private school patron in *The Sandpiper*; torturing Julie Harris in *Harper*; killing Cyd Charisse in *The Silencers*; playing one of Lee Marvin's superior officers in the hit *The Dirty Dozen*; and giving Ryan O'Neal a hard time as a migrant farm boss in *The Big Bounce*. There was another lead, in a cheapie French-Italian thriller, *Hired Killer*, in the title role, and three in a row for director Blake Edwards: *Revenge of the Pink Panther*, as a French assassin; *10*, as Dudley Moore's gay songwriting partner; and *S.O.B.*, as a nervous publicist with a weak bladder. His final motion picture role was as the prosecuting attorney trying to prove that Barbra Streisand is *Nuts*.

Screen: 1950: Highway 301; 1957: 12 Angry Men; 1962: The Nun and the Sergeant; 1963: The Stripper; 1965: Hysteria; The Sandpiper; The Third Day; 1966: Hired Killer (US: 1968); Dead

Heat on a Merry-Go-Round; Harper; The Silencers; 1967: The Dirty Dozen; Don't Make Waves; 1968: Manon 70 (nUSr); 1969: The Big Bounce; 1970: The Great White Hope; 1971: $; 1973: Piedone a Hong Kong/Flatfoot in Hong Kong (nUSr); 1974: Bring Me the Head of Alfredo Garcia; 1976: Midway; 1977: Passi di Morte Perduti Nel Buio/Death Steps in the Dark (nUSr); Madame Claude/The French Woman (nUSr); Squadra Antifurto/Hit Squad (nUSr); 1977: L'imprecateur/The Accuser (nUSr); The Choirboys; 1978: Casey's Shadow; Revenge of the Pink Panther; 1979: Courage Fyuons/Courage...Let's Run! (nUSr); 10; Gardenia (nUSr); Tous Vedettes/All Stars (nUSr); 1980: Private Benjamin; 1981: Sunday Lovers; S.O.B.; 1982: The Final Option/Who Dares Wins; Wrong Is Right; 1985: Wild Geese II; 1987: Nuts.

NY Stage: 1948: Two Blind Mice; 1949: Goodbye, My Fancy; 1951: The Royal Family; 1955: No Time For Sergeants; 1957: Orpheus Descending; Fair Game; 1959: A Loss of Roses; 1960: Period of Adjustment.

Select TV: 1950: Welcome Home (sp); 1952: There Was a Crooked Man (sp); 1953: Three Steps to Heaven (sp); 1957: All Those Beautiful Girls (sp); 1963: The Candidate (sp); 1970: The Movie Murderer; Hauser's Memory; 1971: Thief; 1972: Cutter; 1973: Hawkins on Murder/Death and the Maiden; Double Indemnity; 1974: Murder or Mercy; 1975: Death Stalk; 1977: Harold Robbins' 79 Park Avenue (ms); 1978: The Young Runaways; 1979: The Streets of L.A.; 1980: Tenspeed and Brownshoe; 1981: The Two Lives of Carol Letner; 1982: Not Just Another Affair; Don't Go to Sleep; 1983: Starflight: The Plane That Couldn't Land/ Starflight One; Shooting Stars; 1984: Getting Physical; Cover-Up; No Man's Land; 1985: Half Nelson; In Like Flynn; 1986: Assassin; 1987: The Ladies; 1988: Something Is Out There.

VIRGINIA WEIDLER

BORN: EAGLE ROCK, CA, MARCH 21, 1927.
DIED: JULY 1, 1968.

First a minor league child performer and then a second-tier teen star for MGM, agreeable, tomboyish Virginia Weidler made her acting debut as a four-year-old in a small part in *Surrender*, in 1931. After playing Constance Bennett's niece in *After Today*, she was cast as one of Pauline Lord's shantytown children in *Mrs. Wiggs of the Cabbage Patch*, which earned her a contract with Paramount. They made her the star of *Girl of the Ozarks*, as an undisciplined mountain youngin' looking after her ailing maw, but since the public response was so mild, she was put back into support, playing a puritan child in *Maid of Salem*, and the little girl who accidentally starts the fire on the ship in *Souls at Sea*. Her role as the precocious ranch hand's daughter, who attaches herself to Mickey Rooney in *Out West with the Hardys*, spotlighted her comic abilities, so an enthusiastic MGM put her under contract, in 1938. She showed up in one of the studio's big offerings for 1939, *The Women*, as Norma Shearer's daughter; partnered Rooney again, as his clever little sister, in *Young Tom Edison*; and then had the role of a lifetime, as Dinah Lord, Katharine Hepburn's sassy sibling, in one of the smoothest of all screen comedies, *The Philadelphia Story*. The last became her best-known role and MGM did make some half-hearted efforts to cash in on her success in that film. She made for a pleasant song-and-dance partner to the always-engaging Ray McDonald in *Born to Sing*; was Ann Rutherford's kid sister in a pair of forgettable comedies, *Keeping Company* and *This Time for Keeps*; had her own solo showcase, playing a star-crazy autograph

hunter, in *The Youngest Profession*; and then was essentially upstaged by various other cast members in the Technicolor musical *Best Foot Forward*. Following its release, she and MGM parted company. She eventually ended up in a short-lived Broadway play, *The Rich Full Life*, before marrying and turning her back on show business for good, leaving the profession at the ripe old age of 18.

Screen: 1931: Surrender; 1933: After Tonight; 1934: Mrs. Wiggs of the Cabbage Patch; 1935: Laddie; Freckles; The Big Broadcast of 1936; Peter Ibbetson; 1936: Timothy's Quest; Girl of the Ozarks; The Big Broadcast of 1937; 1937: Maid of Salem; The Outcasts of Poker Flat; Souls at Sea; 1938: Scandal Street; Love Is a Headache; Mother Carey's Chickens; Men with Wings; Too Hot to Handle; Out West With the Hardys; 1939: The Great Man Votes; The Under-Pup; Fixer Dugan; The Rookie Cop; The Women; Outside These Walls; The Lone Wolf Spy Hunt; Bad Little Angel; Henry Goes Arizona; 1940: Young Tom Edison; All This, and Heaven Too; Gold Rush Maisie; The Philadelphia Story; Keeping Company; 1941: I'll Wait for You; Barnacle Bill; Babes on Broadway; 1942: This Time for Keeps; Born to Sing; The Affairs of Martha; 1943: The Youngest Profession; Best Foot Forward.

NY Stage: 1945: The Rich Full Life.

JOHNNY WEISSMULLER

(PETER JONAS WEISSMULLER) BORN: FREIDORF, AUSTRIA-HUNGARY, JUNE 2, 1904. RAISED IN CHICAGO, IL. ED: UNIV. OF CHICAGO. DIED: JANUARY 20, 1984.

Of all the dozens of fit young men who were called on to play Edgar Rice Burroughs's vine-grappling hero of the jungle, Tarzan, the one who stood above the rest and stayed firmest in moviegoer's minds as the definitive interpreter of the part was Johnny Weissmuller. This was not, of course, any compliment to his acting abilities, since they were, to be charitable, almost non-existent. It was his physical prowess, his near-innocent way of speaking, and his lack of glamour and polish that made him seem genuinely at home among the chimps and other wildlife. A swimmer since childhood, his prowess at the sport was already well known by the time he entered college. He swam in both the 1924 and 1928 Olympics, winning a then-record five gold medals. Further accolades followed and he cashed in on his fame by appearing in water shows across the country, and by doing a bit as a Greek Adonis in the early Paramount talkie *Glorifying the American Girl*. When MGM decided to film two of the Burroughs Tarzan stories, they went looking for someone who fit the bill and found it in Weissmuller. They launched him with great fanfare in *Tarzan the Ape Man*, where he ogled Maureen O'Sullivan, swung from the trees, cavorted with monkeys, battled ferocious pygmies, wore a most revealing loin cloth, and perfected the most startling, unmistakable call of the wild in cinema history. The movie, as creaky as it all seems today, was a tremendous success, giving the studio great satisfaction in knowing that they already had a follow-up planned. The "sequel," *Tarzan and His Mate*, was just as popular and, by general consensus, would come to be considered the best entry in the series. Alternately thrilling, bizarre, campy, and sexy, it featured rampaging elephants, boulder-tossing gorillas, Weissmuller riding a rhino, and a nude swimming scene by O'Sullivan that was excised from later reissues. To further prove that Weissmuller had "arrived" in Hollywood, he married one of the industry's most volatile performers, Lupe Velez, in 1933, resulting in a turbulent six-year marriage.

In the meantime, MGM kept him wet and wild for *Tarzan Escapes*, which wound up having much of its footage refilmed after proving too violent for test audiences; *Tarzan Finds a Son!*, which introduced Johnny Sheffield as Boy; *Tarzan's Secret Treasure*, and *Tarzan's New York Adventure*, which gave him the Brooklyn Bridge to swing on for a change. Unlike his co-star, O'Sullivan, nobody in the front office gave the slightest thought to Weissmuller taking any other roles outside of Tarzan, and when MGM decided to drop the series they got rid of their star swimmer as well. RKO snatched him up and he continued there in six more adventures, beginning with *Tarzan Triumphs* in 1943, until it was agreed that the actor was getting a bit long in the tooth for the part. Over at Paramount he teamed with another former Tarzan, Buster Crabbe, for *Swamp Fire*, marking the only time on screen that Weissmuller did not star as either the Lord of the Apes or his next creation, Jungle Jim. The latter was the brainchild of Columbia producer Sam Katzman, who purchased the rights to the comic strip character, believing there was still some money to be made from Weissmuller by keeping him in the jungle, but putting his shirt on to hide his expanding waistline. The Jungle Jim films were cheap, uninspired, and strictly for indiscriminating youngsters, with Weissmuller as awkward and ill at ease as ever when it came to reading lines. The studio sold the property off to television before the film series ended, so the actor actually wound up playing a character called Johnny Weissmuller for the last three entries, in order to avoid any legal complications. After the show's cancellation, he retired to concentrate on running a swimming pool company, finally returning to the big screen 15 years later for a priceless cameo appearance, doing his "Me, Tarzan — You, Jane" shtick with O'Sullivan in one of the stranger films of 1970, *The Phynx*. Similarly, he also popped up in another movie sprinkled with guest spots by actors no longer in demand, *Won Ton Ton, the Dog Who Saved Hollywood*, playing a studio stagehand. He published his autobiography, *Water, World and Weissmuller*, in 1967.

Screen: 1929: Glorifying the American Girl; 1932: Tarzan the Ape Man; 1934: Tarzan and His Mate; 1936: Tarzan Escapes; 1939: Tarzan Finds a Son!; 1941: Tarzan's Secret Treasure; 1942: Tarzan's New York Adventure; 1943: Tarzan Triumphs; Stage Door Canteen; Tarzan's Desert Mystery; 1945: Tarzan and the Amazons; 1946: Tarzan and the Leopard Woman; Swamp Fire; 1947: Tarzan and the Huntress; 1948: Tarzan and the Mermaids; Jungle Jim; 1949: The Lost Tribe; 1950: Captive Girl; Mark of the Gorilla; Pygmy Island; 1951: Fury of the Congo; Jungle Manhunt; 1952: Jungle Jim in the Forbidden Land; Voodoo Tiger; 1953: Savage Mutiny; Valley of the Headhunters; Killer Ape; 1954: Jungle Man-Eaters; Cannibal Attack; 1955: Jungle Moon Men; Devil Goddess; 1970: The Phynx; 1976: Won Ton Ton, the Dog Who Saved Hollywood.

Select TV: 1955: Jungle Jim (series).

TUESDAY WELD

(SUSAN WELD) BORN: NEW YORK, NY, AUGUST 27, 1943.

A doe-eyed, beautiful blonde who was already projecting a kittenish sexuality in her teens, Tuesday Weld set out to prove that she was a lot more serious than her silly name suggested and did, in time, win her share of critical admirers. The weekday name derived from "Tu-Tu," a childish variation of her real name, Susan. As a young girl, she was already doing modeling jobs and moved up from print ads to television

commercials, before she got her chance to act, when she was cast in the lead role in one of those cheaply produced, brain-dead teen films of the late 1950s, *Rock, Rock, Rock!*, where her vocals were dubbed by Connie Francis. 20th Century-Fox put her under contract in 1958, starting her out as the flirtatious youngster Comfort Goodpasture in the frenetic comedy *Rally 'Round the Flag, Boys!* Despite that movie's relative box-office success, the studio let her go elsewhere to do her thing, which included a stint on a popular television series, *The Many Loves of Dobie Gillis*, as Thalia Menninger, Dwayne Hickman's pretentious love interest. She had a sentimental part as the crippled daughter of Danny Kaye in *The Five Pennies*; was the collegiate ingénue in a Bing Crosby vehicle, *High Time*; and wound up in two of director Albert Zugsmith's notorious films, more famous for their titles than their content, *Sex Kittens Go to College*, and *The Private Lives of Adam and Eve*, both of which suggested Weld was nothing more than a lovely but vacuous cipher. Fox put her to work in three films, *Return to Peyton Place*, a critically-reviled sequel in which she took over the role Hope Lange had done in the original; an Elvis Presley drama, *Wild in the Country*, as his dirt-trash cousin; and a noisy Terry-Thomas comedy, *Bachelor Flat*. She fared better as another misbehaving young lady, in *Soldier in the Rain*, sharing scenes with Jackie Gleason and Steve McQueen, though this wasn't much of a film either, despite the presence of those two talented men.

She was back with McQueen for the overrated *The Cincinnati Kid*, as the girlfriend he chucks aside for a fling with Ann-Margaret, and got roped into one of those horrible smut-comedies that gave the 1960s a bad name, *I'll Take Sweden*, as the daughter Bob Hope wants to protect from the libido of Frankie Avalon. It was the next couple of movies that brought her praise at last, though they were all the sort of properties that were fated for cult status rather than commercial success in their day. First was the black comedy *Lord Love a Duck*, in which she wittily portrayed a Southern California college girl who has her every wish and whim taken care of by a whacked-out Roddy McDowall. Then she went dangerous, as the unhinged girl who seduces Anthony Perkins into helping her kill her mother, in *Pretty Poison*, a portrait in self-righteous evil that was certainly among her most memorable work, although Weld herself disliked the film. Similarly, she tangled sheriff Gregory Peck in her web in *I Walk the Line*, as a hillbilly moonshiner's self-serving daughter. Steering away from the mainstream, she did one of director Henry Jaglom's very personal offerings, designed to test the patience of the average moviegoer, *A Safe Place*, as a young woman who can't cope with the real world, and teamed with Perkins again, for *Play It As It Lays*, as an actress recovering from a nervous breakdown, drifting through her meaningless life. After a spell off the big screen, she triumphantly returned as Diane Keaton's self-indulgent, pill-popping sister in *Looking for Mr. Goodbar*, earning an Oscar nomination in the supporting category. This resulted in wife roles in the grim *Who'll Stop the Rain*, as Michael Moriarty's partner; the botched satire *Serial*, wed to Martin Mull; *Thief*, trying to better her life with criminal James Caan; and *Author! Author!*, as Al Pacino's selfish companion. She had a showy part as a nympho moll in *Once Upon a Time in America*, and a silly one as the divorced mom for whom son Charlie Schlatter kidnaps Elvis Presley (David Keith) in *Heartbreak Hotel*. Disappearing again for a few years, she returned looking rather blowsy, as Robert Duvall's troubled wife, in *Falling Down*, and as Keanu Reeve's mother in *Feeling Minnesota*. Yet another several years went by before she showed up providing some of the better moments of the multi-character *Chelsea Walls*, as Kris Kristofferson's wife. She was married for a brief time (1980–85) to comedian Dudley Moore.

Screen: 1956: Rock, Rock, Rock!; The Wrong Man; 1958: Rally 'Round the Flag, Boys!; 1959: The Five Pennies; 1960: Because They're Young; High Time; Sex Kittens Go to College; The Private Lives of Adam and Eve; 1961: Return to Peyton Place; Wild in the Country; Bachelor Flat; 1963: Soldier in the Rain; 1965: I'll Take Sweden; The Cincinnati Kid; 1966: Lord Love a Duck; 1968: Pretty Poison; 1970: I Walk the Line; 1971: A Safe Place; 1972: Play It as It Lays; 1977: Looking for Mr. Goodbar; 1978: Who'll Stop the Rain?; 1980: Serial; 1981: Thief; 1982: Author! Author!; 1984: Once Upon a Time in America; 1988: Heartbreak Hotel; 1993: Falling Down; 1996: Feeling Minnesota; 2001: Investigating Sex; 2002: Chelsea Walls.

NY Stage: 1957: The Dark at the Top of the Stairs.

Select TV: 1959–60: The Many Loves of Dobie Gillis (series); 1967: The Crucible (sp); 1974: Reflections of Murder; 1976: F. Scott Fitzgerald in Hollywood; 1978: A Question of Guilt; 1980: Mother and Daughter: The Loving War; 1981: Madame X; 1982: The Rainmaker (sp); 1983: The Winter of Our Discontent; 1984: Scorned and Swindled; 1986: Circle of Violence; Something in Common.

ORSON WELLES

(George Orson Welles) Born: Kenosha, WI, May 6, 1915. Died: October 10, 1985.

The word "genius" has been bandied about throughout show business with reckless abandon but, if indeed a list of the half-dozen or so of those to qualify must be drawn up, then certainly Orson Welles fits the bill. His achievements came fast and frequently, as he always seemed to be dabbling in something, either as an actor, narrator, writer, director, or producer, sometimes working in all these areas on the same project. In movies, he started out at the summit, starring in and creating the film most often cited as the greatest of them all — Citizen Kane — and that alone might have been all he needed to accomplish. Instead, he kept on creating and looking for the financial means with which he *could* create. As a result, his was a rag-tag career of questionable choices punctuated by heights of magnificence. Through it all he was never less than one of the most entertaining people to ever set foot before a camera. That he was ambitious was evident early on, since he was already acting, adapting, and directing plays in grade school. A journey to Ireland brought him an offer to act with the Dublin Gate Theatre when he was all of 15 years old. His capabilities as a performer were already becoming known in theater circles and Katharine Cornell hired him to join her in a touring production of The Barretts of Wimpole Street, back in the states. In 1934 he made his debut on radio, a medium that was crucial in bringing him fame; directed his first movie, a short called "Hearts of Age;" and first acted on Broadway, playing Tybalt, in a production of Romeo and Juliet. He joined the WPA's Federal Theatre in 1936, winning great acclaim for his staging of an all-black Macbeth, and of the controversial pro-labor musical, The Cradle Will Rock. On radio he did the voice of Lamont Cranston in a highly popular drama The Shadow, and founded his own Theatre Company, Mercury, which presented works both for the New York stage and on the airwaves.

The first thing to give him legendary status was an accident of sorts, when his 1938 Halloween Eve radio presentation of the H.G. Wells's story "The War of the Worlds" was mistaken for a real Martian invasion by the more gullible listeners. This would remain one of the most famous broadcasts in the history of that

medium and Welles relished his role as charlatan and troublemaker. Hollywood was eager for this "boy wonder" to come make a film and RKO signed him to a contract others would have envied, one that essentially allowed him free reign over a project of his own choosing, a decision the studio would come to regret, though it benefited the future of moviemaking for all time. Welles, producing under his Mercury Theatre banner, served as director and co-writer (with Herman Mankewicz) on a thinly disguised look at the life of newspaper tycoon William Randolph Hearst. The result, Citizen Kane, was unlike anything the motion picture medium had seen up to that time, a bold and cinematically innovative look at the life of a megalomaniac billionaire as seen through the reminiscences of friends and acquaintances. As was much documented over the years, the Hearst press did its best to try to kill the film and, despite enormous critical acclaim, it did not play well outside the larger cities, losing money for its studio. Although Welles and Mankewicz would share an Academy Award for their script, the film lost out in all other categories, including Best Picture and Welles as Best Actor. Of course time would rectify all of that, as Citizen Kane came to be looked upon by every future filmmaker and true film aficionado with awe and reverence. How nice, therefore, that it is one of the movies that lives up to every bit of its hype and beyond, including Welles's own performance, going from opportunistic young lad to decrepit old man with total conviction in a virtuoso turn.

RKO, less enchanted by their prize employee than before, nevertheless let him try again, and his follow-up, an adaptation of Booth Tarkington's Pulitzer Prize-winning The Magnificent Ambersons, was equally superb, even without Welles appearing on screen, since he chose to stay behind the scenes for this sad and haunting story of the death of a more genteel era. Though Welles wound up with his second Oscar nominee in a row for Best Picture, it became the first of his aborted works, being tampered with and cut by the unhappy studio once its maker had gone to South America to work on It's All True, a documentary that would remain unfinished. After that he supervised (uncredited) and co-wrote (with actor, friend, and frequent collaborator, Joseph Cotten) a confused tale of intrigue, Journey Into Fear, also adding a much-needed jolt of life to the film, playing a Turkish police colonel, and then showed just how good an actor he could be under someone else's guidance, in Jane Eyre, moodily brilliant as Rochester. At Universal he sawed Marlene Dietrich in half for a segment of Follow the Boys, which was notable only because it displayed his life-long interest in magic; then he mugged his way through a very soapy melodrama, Tomorrow Is Forever, which was the weakest thing he'd done up to that point and, of course, the most financially successful. He finished his stay at RKO directing and starring in The Stranger, probably the most conventional and accessible of all his works, about an ex-Nazi living incognito in small-town America. In the meantime, his marriage (1943–47) to the great beauty of the era, Rita Hayworth, gave him more attention in the general public's eye than any of these films and, right after their divorce, they teamed at Columbia for The Lady from Shanghai, with Welles adding his masterful touch to this puzzling but always dazzling noir. Inevitably, it was one of the less popular movies that Hayworth made for the studio.

Seeking support from whomever would have him, Welles filmed a version of Macbeth, which he'd done onstage in Salt Lake City, at Republic Studios, using sets left over from another film. Welles's imaginary touches were evident throughout, but since it was yet another box-office flop, he figured it was time to hightail it out of Hollywood and see what kind of work he could get in Europe. In England he stole the show playing Harry Lime in the complex thriller *The Third Man*, casting an indelible presence over the proceedings even when he wasn't on screen, in what would become the most famous of all his acting roles not directed by himself. For money's sake he did some made-in-Europe spectacles for Fox: *Prince of Foxes* and *The Black Rose*, and put that cash towards finishing his three-years-in-the-making version of *Othello*. When finally released in limited engagements, it turned out to be one of the most stunning of all movie adaptations of Shakespeare, but, once again, would have to wait for the passing of the years to get its due. There were guest appearances in various foreign productions, including *Royal Affairs in Versailles*, in which he was miscast as Ben Franklin, a role he'd do later on as well; and *Napoleon*, as the governor of St. Helena. Both of these films were done, presumably, to finance *Confidential Report /Mr. Arkadin*, which stuck too close to the *Citizen Kane* formula to win him much praise at the time. Finished in 1955, it would not show up in America until 1962, at which time it received little notice. Thanks to Charlton Heston there was another chance to direct in Hollywood. Having been offered the role of the sleazy, corrupt police officer in *Touch of Evil*, Heston suggested to Universal that Welles direct and write the movie as well. It was a brilliant decision for this was yet another devastating original, atmospheric and nightmarish, with Welles giving one of his grandest, most unforgettable performances, as the obese, decadent man of the law, huffing and puffing towards his downfall. Of course it died the death and Welles never again directed an American movie.

He did stick around to act in some major releases for 20th Century-Fox: *The Long Hot Summer*, as the sweaty Southern patriarch; *The Roots of Heaven*, as a television broadcaster who gets shot in the ass while on safari; and, best of all, *Compulsion*, where he reminded people just how effective an actor he was, under-playing the Darrow-like lawyer, defending a pair of child-murderers. It was then back to Europe where he did everything from *David and Goliath*, directing his own scenes as King Saul, minus on-screen credit, to the glossy soap *The V.I.P.s*, as a flamboyant and vulgar filmmaker. He himself directed and appeared in *The Trial*, which was Welles at his most audience-unfriendly, a gloomy and maddening adaptation of Kafka, and the more pleasing *Chimes at Midnight*, a combination of Shakespeare works, in which Welles, now monstrously overweight, was Falstaff. Neither got much play outside a very select art house circuit, and his next, *The Immortal Story*, wound up having its premiere on French television. In the meantime, he appeared as a Swedish ambassador in the all-star bore *Is Paris Burning?*; had a good scene as Cardinal Woolsey in the Oscar-winning *A Man for All Seasons*; and showed up briefly as one of the bad guys in *Casino Royale*, sitting around like royalty, belly bulging forth like a Buddha, cheekily puffing a cigar, performing magic, and barely hiding the fact that he was doing it for the cash. This did, in fact, become the latter-day image that most people would have of Welles, mainly from his frequent talk show appearances, little realizing the major talent hidden behind the bravado and the mischievous twinkle in his eye.

By the 1970s there was no telling where he might pop up, be it in such curious, often unreleased foreign fare as *The Thirteen Chairs* and *Malpertius*, to strange independent films, like *The Sailor from Gibraltar* and *A Safe Place*. Of the more high profile offerings, he was General Dreedle in *Catch-22*; Louis XVIII in the major money-loser *Waterloo*, and a Cuban industrialist in *Voyage of the Damned*. Between these he wrote (under the name O.W. Jeeves) a quickly forgotten version of *Treasure Island*, in which he bombastically played Long John Silver, and directed his last, and probably worst, film, *F for Fake*, a omnibus on magic

and frauds, bringing a quiet end to what had started out as the most promising directorial career of them all. Over the years there were countless aborted projects, most notably *Don Quixote* and *The Other Side of the Wind*, left unfinished because of lack of financing or, perhaps, waning interest on Welles's part. To keep paying the bills he did many voice-overs (ranging from a series of wine commercials to a Bugs Bunny documentary) and could be seen on screen in *The Muppet Movie*, a rare box-office hit to have him among the cast; *Butterfly*, a camp attempt to make a star of Pia Zadora; and *Someone to Love*, as himself. When he died in 1985, it was only the beginning of the regret for what "might have been." Looking back at what he did manage to accomplish, his status only rose higher and higher. For sheer audacity and imagination, for his ability to make almost ever frame interesting, he was, in a way, the greatest of all directors. And being that he was no slouch at writing and acting, it wasn't such a bad legacy to leave behind at all.

Screen: 1940: Swiss Family Robinson (narrator); 1941: Citizen Kane (and dir.; co-wr.; prod.); 1942: The Magnificent Ambersons (narrator; and dir.; wr.; prod.); Journey Into Fear (and co-wr.; prod.); 1944: Jane Eyre (and uncredited prod.); Follow the Boys; 1946: Tomorrow Is Forever; The Stranger (and dir.; and uncredited co-wr.); Duel in the Sun (narrator); 1948: The Lady From Shanghai (and dir.; wr.; prod.); Macbeth (and dir.; wr.; prod.); 1949: Black Magic (and uncredited co-dir.); The Third Man (and uncredited co-wr.; US: 1950); Prince of Foxes; 1950: The Black Rose; 1952: Othello (and dir.; wr.; prod.; US: 1955); Trent's Last Case; 1953: The Little World of Don Camillo (narrator of English-language version; It: 1951); Man, Beast and Virtue (nUSr); 1954: Royal Affairs in Versailles (US: 1957); Napoleon; Trouble in the Glen; 1955: Three Cases of Murder; Mr. Arkadin/Confidential Report (and dir.; wr.; prod.; US: 1962); 1956: Moby Dick; 1958: Man in the Shadow; Touch of Evil (and dir.; wr.); The Vikings (narrator); South Seas Adventure (narrator); The Long Hot Summer; The Roots of Heaven; 1959: High Journey (narrator); Compulsion; Ferry to Hong Kong (US: 1961); 1960: Austerlitz (dtv); David and Goliath (and uncredited co-dir.; US: 1961); Crack in the Mirror; 1961: Lafayette (US: 1963); I Tartari/The Tartars (US: 1962); King of Kings (narrator); 1962: The Trial (and dir.; wr.); Laviamoci il Cervello/RoGoPaG (dtv); 1963: The V.I.P.s; 1964: The Finest Hours (narrator); 1965: Marco the Magnificent (US: 1966); 1966: Is Paris Burning?; Chimes at Midnight/Falstaff (US: 1967); A Man for All Seasons; 1967: Casino Royale; The Sailor from Gibraltar; A King's Story (narrator); 1968: I'll Never Forget What's 'is Name; The Immortal Story (and dir.; wr.; US: 1969); Oedipus the King; The Last Roman/Fight for Rome (dtv); 1969: House of Cards; Barbed Wire (narrator; nUSr); Tepepa ... Viva la Revolution (nUSr); The Southern Star; Twelve Plus One (and uncredited wr.; dtv); Kaumpf um Rom II: Der Verrat (nUSr); 1970: Start the Revolution Without Me; The Kremlin Letter; Catch-22; Battle of Neretva (US: 1971); 1971: Waterloo; A Safe Place; 1972: Malpertius (nUSr); Ten Days Wonder; Get to Know Your Rabbit; Treasure Island (and co-wr.; AS O.W. JEEVES); Necromancy/The Witching/Rosemary's Disciples; 1974: F for Fake (and dir.; co-wr.; US: 1977); 1975: Bugs Bunny Superstar (narrator); Ten Little Indians/And Then There Were None (voice); 1976: Voyage of the Damned; 1977: The Challenge...A Tribute to Modern Art (narrator); 1978: Hot Tomorrows (voice); 1979: The Late Great Planet Earth (and uncredited co-wr.); The Double McGuffin (narrator; dtv); Filming Othello; The Muppet Movie; 1980: The Secret of Nikole Tesla (nUSr); 1981: The Man Who Saw Tomorrow; History of the World Part 1 (narrator); Genocide (narrator); 1982: Butterfly; 1983: Hot Money (dtv);

1984: In Our Hands; Slapstick of Another Kind (voice); Where Is Parsifal? (dtv); 1985: Almonds and Raisins (narrator); 1986: The Transformers (voice); 1988: Someone to Love (filmed 1985).

NY Stage: 1934: Romeo and Juliet; 1935: Panic; 1936: Horse Eats Hat (and co-wr.; dir.); Ten Million Ghosts; 1937: The Tragical History of Doctor Faustus (and dir.; set des.); Julius Caesar (and dir.; adapt.); 1938: Heartbreak House (and dir.; prod.); Danton's Death (and dir.; adapt.); 1941: Native Son (and dir.); 1946: Around the World in Eighty Days (and dir.; wr.; prod.); 1956: King Lear (and dir.; adapt.).

Select TV: 1953: King Lear (sp); 1955: Orson Welles' Sketch Book (BBC series); 1956: Twentieth Century (sp); The Fountain of Youth (sp; and dir.; wr.; designer); 1970: Upon This Rock (sp); 1971: The Silent Years (series host); 1972: The Man Who Came to Dinner (sp); 1973–74: Orson Welles' Great Mysteries (BBC series host); 1977: It Happened One Christmas; 1978: A Woman Called Moses (narrator); 1980: The Orson Welles Story/With Orson Welles: Stories from a Life in Film (sp); Shogun (narrator; ms); 1985: Scene of the Crime (series host).

OSKAR WERNER

(OSKAR JOSEPH SCHLIESSMAYER)
BORN: VIENNA, AUSTRIA, NOVEMBER 13, 1922.
DIED: OCTOBER 23, 1984.

Deeply sensitive in looks and manner, the blond-haired, sad-eyed Oskar Werner was a tremendous attraction in his native country, making it only natural that he should be summoned for an occasional English-language assignment. He began acting as a teenager, studying under Helmuth Krauss, and did a walk-on in the 1938 film Geld Fallt von Himmel. His stint with the German Army ended with him deserting, after which he made a name for himself at Vienna's Burgtheater. During that time he returned to motion pictures, starting with Angel With the Trumpet, which played in the U.S. in 1951. That same year Fox asked him to portray the German soldier who is willing to spy for the Americans in Decision Before Dawn, and his humanization of this character made it a fascinating tale to watch. It won him much acclaim and, although the movie ended up snagging an Oscar nomination for Best Picture, it fell into unjustified obscurity with the passing years. Nor did Werner's contract with Fox work out. Instead, he returned to Europe for more stage, including a much-admired Hamlet, in 1955, and such movies as Lola Montes and The Life and Loves of Mozart. He was, therefore, almost treated like a newcomer when he scored a great success as Jules, part of a love triangle shared with Jeanne Moreau and Henri Serre in Jules and Jim, one of the most critically lauded and universally appealing French films to be released in the 1960s. As a result, he was invited back to America to play the wearied ship's doctor, who has a touching and very real fling with passenger Simone Signoret, in Ship of Fools. Theirs were the standout performances of a fine ensemble and Werner earned an Oscar nomination. For his follow-up vehicles, he was the disillusioned book destroyer in the underrated adaptation of the futuristic allegory Fahrenheit 451; an orchestra conductor having an extra-marital fling in the old-fashioned Interlude; and a priest in the long-winded The Shoes of the Fisherman. After a lengthy absence he and Faye Dunaway played a couple on board a doomed ocean liner returning to Nazi shores in Voyage of the Damned, which was uncomfortably close in premise to the superior Ship of Fools. He became a virtual recluse following its release.

Screen (US releases only): 1951: Angel With the Trumpet; Erotica; Decision Before Dawn; Wonder Boy/The Wonder Kid;

1955: Lola Montes; 1956: The Last Ten Days; 1959: The Life and Loves of Mozart (Austria: 1955); 1962: Jules and Jim; 1965: Ship of Fools; The Spy Who Came in From the Cold; 1966: Fahrenheit 451; 1968: Interlude; The Shoes of the Fisherman; 1976: Voyage of the Damned.

MAE WEST

BORN: BROOKLYN, NY, AUGUST 17, 1892.
DIED: NOVEMBER 22, 1980.

There was one and only one Mae West, which is, of course, the highest tribute one can pay to all the truly great film stars. Wiggling along in glittery gay-1890s attire, with an occasional faux gesture of touching-up her hair, she sized up her men with no question of what was behind her thoughts, and then let go with a suggestive zinger or two. It was all a great big put-on, sending up sex with the sort of exaggerated zeal of a drag queen. Depression era audiences loved her and her racy, though never tasteless, material helped liven things up considerably, to a point where many credit her with bringing on firmer restrictions in the production code. As a child performer she made her dancing debut at the Royal Theatre in Brooklyn, then acted with some stock companies. At 15 she began performing in vaudeville and made her legit Broadway bow, in 1911, in a revue called A La Broadway. There was a short-lived act with her sister and then she moved up to the lead in a musical comedy with Ed Wynn, Sometime, which opened in 1918. In it she brought much attention to herself by introducing the shimmy dance. West continued to be a success in vaudeville but was looking for something to raise her status in the legit theater world. Under the name "Jane Mast" she wrote a play for herself, guaranteed to infuriate the censors, and named it Sex, just to make sure it wouldn't slip by unnoticed. The police raids it prompted brought West the sort of notoriety she had hoped for and this was topped by the scandal of her next writing credit, The Drag, in which she did not appear, the play dealing openly with the subject of male homosexuality.

Despite their fame and box-office success both plays were trashed by the critics, so West came up with one more likely to please, Diamond Lil, which became her biggest hit by far. On the basis of this and another called The Constant Sinner, Paramount Pictures made her an offer to support George Raft in Night After Night. She arrived in Hollywood, promptly went to work rewriting her part, and walked off with the film. Her opening scene included one of her most famous exchanges, as a hat-check girl complimented her on her jewelry with the comment, "Goodness, what beautiful diamonds," to which West replied, "Goodness had nothing to do with it, dearie." Paramount was most eager to sign her to a contract and to showcase her in her own vehicles, so she accepted their offer on the condition that they let her adapt Diamond Lil into a film. Retitled She Done Him Wrong, it became one of the most popular movies of 1933, and is often credited with helping pull its studio out of a desperate financial slump. West was very much in charge as entertainer Lady Lou, who lures Rescue Mission volunteer Cary Grant into her snare, uttering her most famous line of all, "Come up some time and see me." It set the pattern for all West films, with every man falling at her feet and the great lady providing all the juice to what was fairly standard material apart from her. No one could accuse her of acting; she merely sashayed around the set, waiting to speak her lines with little interest in the existence of the other actors. There were no complaints. As long as she put her hand on her hip, strutted her stuff, and kept the double entendres flying, everybody was happy.

I'm No Angel didn't veer too far from the previous film, going so far as to include Cary Grant again, but it was a better movie overall and no doubt the most enjoyable of the West vehicles. In it she tamed some lions, commanded her maid, Beulah, to "Peel me a grape," and was given up-front credit for the screenplay. The box office kept clicking for *Belle of the Nineties* and *Goin' to Town*, but the Hays Office started to intervene, which meant she was asked to tone down a lot of what made her so much fun in the first place. *Klondike Annie* gave her perhaps her most suitable co-star in brutish Victor McLaglen, but the interest in her had already begun to taper off. She herself remained gloriously entertaining but the material was obviously compromised and growing weaker. After *Every Day's a Holiday*, she and Paramount went their separate ways. Universal had the inspired idea to team her with W.C. Fields in *My Little Chickadee*, and although both their names appeared on the screenplay credit, it was in truth West who did the bulk of the writing. The two great stars did not get along and, although this remains a very famous movie on both their résumés, it was nowheres near as good as it might have been. Columbia hired her next, but she regretted signing on for *The Heat's On* almost immediately, for aside from her participation it didn't look any different than a hundred other assembly line musical comedies of the 1940s.

By this point, West had become one of the most famous women in the world but she was in her 50s and Hollywood wasn't sure what to do with her. She figured it was time to return to the theater and did a play, *Catherine Was Great*, that she'd been trying to get made as a film, and reprised *Diamond Lil* on Broadway. Careful to keep herself well preserved despite her advancing years, she kept her name before the public by doing an outrageous nightclub act in Las Vegas and other venues, in which she was frequently surrounded by scantily clad muscle men. On television she played herself on *Mr. Ed*; did a memorable rendition of "Baby, It's Cold Outside" with Rock Hudson at the Academy Awards; and guested on *The Red Skeleton Show*. Rather than resting on her laurels, she began touring another of her plays, *Sextette*, and then accepted an offer to return to movies in the ghastly rendering of the Gore Vidal novel *Myra Breckinridge*, where she was its only saving grace. Just when everyone assumed that this was her swan song, a misguided film of *Sextette* showed up, and was instantly proclaimed one of the most jaw dropping of all camp classics. In the storyline the now 80-years-plus West, in a sadly deteriorating state and moving about as if on automatic pilot, was still fawned over by a gaggle of leading men, which was a frightening sight to see. She was quickly forgiven for this and, in a strange way, its very existence somehow made perfect sense in this woman's very ballsy career, which set its own rules and followed its own single-minded course. West never did have her foot very much in reality (as was painfully obvious in her 1959 autobiography, *Goodness Had Nothing to Do With It*) and it is doubtful we'd have wanted her any other way.

Screen: 1932: Night After Night; 1933: She Done Him Wrong; I'm No Angel (and wr.); 1934: Belle of the Nineties (and wr.); 1935: Goin' to Town (and wr.); 1936: Klondike Annie (and wr.); Go West, Young Man (and wr.); 1938: Every Day's a Holiday (and wr.); 1940: My Little Chickadee (and co-wr.); 1943: The Heat's On; 1970: Myra Breckinridge; 1978: Sextette.

NY Stage: 1911: A La Broadway; Vera Violetta; 1912: A Winsome Widow; 1918: Sometime; 1921: The Mimic World of 1921; 1926: Sex (and wr.; AS JANE MAST); 1927: The Wicked Age (and wr.; AS JANE MAST); 1928: Diamond Lil (and wr.); 1931: The Constant Sinner (and wr.); 1944: Catherine was Great (and wr.); 1947: Come On Up; 1949: Diamond Lil (and wr.; revival); 1951:

Diamond Lil (and wr.; revival).

JACK WESTON

(JACK WEINSTEIN) BORN: CLEVELAND, OH, AUGUST 21, 1924. DIED: MAY 3, 1996.

Adept at playing sweaty, fidgety, insecure fellows, mostly in a comical vein, Jack Weston had started acting at the Cleveland Playhouse. After a break for military service he returned to the stage, toured with the USO then went to New York where he joined the American Theatre Wing. He made his Broadway debut in *Season in the Sun*, in 1950, and after some more stage work, became a very familiar face guesting on television. He then segued over to films, playing stage managers in both *Stage Struck* and *Imitation of Life*, after which he was put to much better use in *Please Don't Eat the Daisies*, as the cab driver who also happens to be a playwright, hitting just the right comedic notes as he would so often. Following some unsuccessful television series of his own, he became an in-demand movie character player, portraying a drunken signalman in *The Honeymoon Machine*; a butler out to kill Jerry Lewis in *It's Only Money*; a basketball coach taking his team on vacation in *Palm Springs Weekend*; Don Knotts's buddy in *The Incredible Mr. Limpet*, much of which required him to act opposite a cartoon fish; a card player uncharitably named Pig in *The Cincinnati Kid*; one of the smarmy thugs out to torment sightless Audrey Hepburn in *Wait Until Dark*; Ingrid Bergman's graceless date in *Cactus Flower*; and an undercover detective in *Fuzz*, which required him to dress as a nun at one point. Returning to Broadway, he played a garbage man hiding out in a gay bathhouse in *The Ritz*, and, when it was filmed in 1976, he got to repeat his role, making this his sole big screen lead, though the movie did not repeat its success in the new medium. Well-teamed with his *Ritz* co-star Rita Moreno, he was a dentist who pays for his obsession with his Mercedes in the hit *The Four Seasons* (a role he repeated on the sort-lived series version); after which he was Tom Selleck's mechanic sidekick in *High Road to China*; a wearied talent agent with a pair of talentless clients in *Ishtar*; the owner of a Catskills resort in the surprise success *Dirty Dancing*; and an evil toy manufacturer in a juvenile sci-fi entry, *Short Circuit 2*.

Screen: 1958: Stage Struck; I Want to Live!; 1959: Imitation of Life; 1960: Please Don't Eat the Daisies; 1961: All in a Night's Work; The Honeymoon Machine; 1962: It's Only Money; 1963: Palm Springs Weekend; 1964: The Incredible Mr. Limpet; 1965: Mirage; The Cincinnati Kid; 1967: Wait Until Dark; 1968: The Thomas Crown Affair; 1969: The April Fools; Cactus Flower; 1971: A New Leaf; 1972: Fuzz; 1973: Marco; 1976: Gator; The Ritz; 1979: Cuba; 1980: Can't Stop the Music; 1981: The Four Seasons; 1983: High Road to China; 1986: The Longshot; Rad; 1987: Ishtar; Dirty Dancing; 1988: Short Circuit 2.

NY Stage: 1950: Season in the Sun; 1952: South Pacific; 1956: Bells Are Ringing; 1975: The Ritz; 1976: California Suite; 1978: Cheaters; 1979: Break a Leg; 1980: One Night Stand; 1981: The Floating Light Bulb; 1985: The Baker's Wife (ob); 1989: Measure For Measure (ob); The Tenth Man.

Select TV: 1953–54: Rod Brown of the Rocket Rangers (series); 1955: Stage Door (sp); 1958: Harvey (sp); 1960–61: My Sister Eileen (series); 1961–62: The Hathaways (series); 1966: Fame Is the Name of the Game; 1968: The Counterfeit Killer; Now You See It, Now You Don't; 1973: I Love a Mystery (filmed 1967); Deliver Us From Evil; 1977: Harold Robbins' 79 Park Avenue (ms); 1984: The Four Seasons (series); 1986: If Tomorrow Comes (ms).

BERT WHEELER
(Albert Jerome Wheeler) Born: Paterson, NJ, April 7, 1895. Died: January 18, 1968.
& ROBERT WOOLSEY
Born: Oakland, CA, August 14, 1889. Died: October 31, 1938.

None too subtle or original in their efforts to get laughs, Wheeler and Woolsey had their fling with fame, but their comedies were seldom revived or remembered with the passing years. Wheeler, with the whiny voice and child-like mannerisms, had been a star in vaudeville and the Ziegfeld Follies, prior to teaming with the lesser-known Woolsey, whose cigar chomping and way of delivering a one-liner bore an uncomfortable resemblance to George Burns. Ziegfeld paired them as the comic relief for his Broadway musical *Rio Rita*, which was so popular that RKO-Radio bought the property and the duo for a movie version. Released in 1929, it was one of the many ponderous, unimaginatively filmed songfests of the early talkie era, but the studio's first major hit nonetheless. Delighted with Wheeler and Woolsey, RKO put them under contract. Their immediate follow-ups, *The Cuckoos* and *Dixiana*, were also creaky comedies with music, but they were finally allowed their own official vehicle with *Half Shot at Sunrise*, a World War I spoof. They cavorted through such obvious and coyly titled quickies as *Caught Plastered*, which found them renovating a drug store, and *Diplomaniacs*, which hoped to join the ranks of such off-the-wall political satires as *Duck Soup* and *Million Dollar Legs*, but simply succeeded in being very weird rather than funny. Between these they carried the comedy again in another moldy rendering of a stage hit, *Girl Crazy*. They reached some sort of peak in 1934 with the costume romp *Cockeyed Cavaliers*, probably the most enjoyable of their films, and *Kentucky Kernels*, which gave them Little Rascal Spanky McFarland as a foil. The last had a genuinely accomplished director, George Stevens, at the helm, as did *The Nitwits*, a murder mystery farce, but after that one the interest in these two clowns began to slacken rather quickly. By the time they had slipped into such tired vehicles as *On Again Off Again* and *High Flyers*, Woolsey was suffering from kidney disease. After his death in 1938, his partner continued solo in a few films but fared better back on the stage, where his assignments included taking over the role of Elwood P. Dowd in the long running Broadway hit, *Harvey*.

Screen: Wheeler and Woolsey: **1929:** Rio Rita; **1930:** The Cuckoos; Dixiana; Half Shot at Sunrise; Hook, Line and Sinker; **1931:** Cracked Nuts; Caught Plastered; Peach O'Reno; **1932:** Girl Crazy; Hold 'Em Jail; **1933:** So This Is Africa; Diplomaniacs; **1934:** Hips Hips Hooray; Cockeyed Cavaliers; Kentucky Kernels; **1935:** The Nitwits; The Rainmakers; **1936:** Silly Billies; Mummy's Boys; **1937:** On Again, Off Again; High Flyers.
Wheeler: 1931: Too Many Cooks; **1939:** Cowboy Quarterback; **1941:** Las Vegas Nights.
Woolsey: 1931: Everything's Rosie.
NY Stage: Wheeler and Woolsey: **1927:** Rio Rita; **1931:** Scandals.
Wheeler: 1923: Ziegfeld Follies of 1923; **1942:** New Priorities of 1943; **1943:** Laugh Time; **1946:** Harvey; **1949:** All for Love; **1952:** Three Wishes of Jamie; **1959:** The Gang's All Here.
Woolsey: 1919: Nothing But Love; **1921:** The Right Girl; The All-Star Idlers of 1921; **1922:** The Blue Kitten; The Lady in Ermine; **1923:** Poppy; **1925:** Mayflowers; **1926:** Honest Liars; **1927:** My Princess.
Select TV: Wheeler: **1950:** Rio Rita (sp); **1955–56:** Brave Eagle (series).

JESSE WHITE
(Jesse Marc Weidenfeld) Born: Buffalo, NY, January 4, 1918. Died: January 9, 1997.

Snapping sourly and blustering with all the delicacy of a carnival barker was Jesse White's specialty, an act that was best showcased in comedy. He had, in fact, done stand-up comedy in nightclubs before giving the legit stage a try, making his Broadway debut, in 1943, in *Sons and Soldiers*. The following year he won raves playing the crude sanitarium orderly, Wilson, who shows his soft side by romancing the hero's nephew, in *Harvey*, which became one of the longest running shows in theater history. This got him teensy roles in two major 1947 films, *Kiss of Death*, as a cabbie, and *Gentleman's Agreement*, as an elevator operator, seen with his back to the camera. When Universal decided to film *Harvey*, in 1950, he, along with Josphine Hull, were the only original cast members asked to repeat their roles, which White did effectively enough to be asked to do it yet again, in the 1970 Broadway revival and a 1972 television adaptation. His success in the part opened the door to White becoming a movie and television regular. On screen he could be seen playing a district attorney in *Bedtime for Bonzo*; Stanley the waiter in the 1951 film of *Death of a Salesman*; Victor Mature's carny sidekick in *Million Dollar Mermaid*; Gary Merrill's police partner in *Witness to Murder*; and one of the plane crash survivors in *Back from Eternity*. The older he got the less serious he was called on to be and used his knack for barnstorming for laughs in *Country Music Holiday*, as a fast-talking agent; the Jerry Lewis vehicle *It's Only Money*, as a detective; *It's a Mad Mad Mad Mad World*, as a tower control radio operator; and two empty-headed AIP romps, *Pajama Party* and *The Ghost in the Invisible Bikini*, as a con man named J. Sinister Hulk. The role that really put his face in the public eye, however, came on television, playing the lonely repairman in a series of Maytag wash machine commercials that ran from 1967 to 1989. During this period he had an interesting role as Miles Chapin's overbearing Borscht belt comedian father in *Bless the Beasts and Children*.

Screen: **1947:** Kiss of Death; Gentleman's Agreement; **1948:** Texas, Brooklyn and Heaven; **1950:** Harvey; **1951:** Death of a Salesman; Katie Did It; Bedtime for Bonzo; Francis Goes to the Races; Callaway Went That Away; **1952:** The Girl in White; Million Dollar Mermaid; **1953:** Gunsmoke; Forever Female; Champ for a Day; **1954:** Hell's Half Acre; Witness to Murder; **1955:** Not as a Stranger; The Girl Rush; **1956:** The Come On; The Bad Seed; Back from Eternity; He Laughed Last; **1957:** Designing Woman; Johnny Trouble; God Is My Partner; **1958:** Country Music Holiday; Marjorie Morningstar; **1960:** The Rise and Fall of Legs Diamond; The Big Night; Three Blondes in His Life; **1961:** The Tomboy and the Champ; A Fever in the Blood; On the Double; The Right Approach; **1962:** Sail a Crooked Ship; It's Only Money; **1963:** The Yellow Canary; It's a Mad Mad Mad Mad World; **1964:** Pajama Party; A House Is Not a Home; Looking for Love; **1965:** Dear Brigitte; **1966:** The Ghost in the Invisible Bikini; **1967:** The Spirit Is Willing; The Reluctant Astronaut; **1970:** Togetherness; **1971:** Bless the Beasts and Children; **1973:** The Brothers O'Toole; **1975:** Return to Campus; **1976:** Las Vegas Lady; Nashville Girl; Won Ton Ton, the Dog Who Saved Hollywood; **1977:** New Girl in Town; **1978:** The Cat from Outer Space; **1986:** Monster in the Closet (filmed 1983); **1993:** Matinee.
NY Stage: **1943:** Sons and Soldiers; My Dear Public; **1944:** Mrs. Kimball Presents; Helen Goes To Troy; Harvey; **1948:** Born Yesterday; Red Gloves; **1965:** Kelly; Kiss Me Kate; **1969:** The

Front Page; **1970:** Harvey (revival).
Select TV: 1953–57: Private Secretary (series); **1955–57:** The Danny Thomas Show (series); **1956:** The Hefferan Family (sp); **1960–61:** The Ann Sothern Show (series); **1970:** George M! (sp); **1972:** Harvey (sp); Of Thee I Sing (sp).

STUART WHITMAN
BORN: SAN FRANCISCO, CA, FEBRUARY 1, 1926.

Bushy-browed and cleft-chinned, with a wearied face that always looked lived in, even at a younger age, Stuart Whitman rose from unbilled bits to star player but lost what capabilities and drive he possessed once the "A" work dried up. As did many a leading man who specialized in macho roles, he began outside the realm of show business, in boxing. In college he took up dramatics, eventually learning his craft under Michael Chekhov and with a theater group actor Arthur Kennedy had thrown together. He made his motion picture debut, in 1951, doing walk-ons in what would become perhaps the two best-known sci-fi movies released that year, *When Worlds Collide* and *The Day the Earth Stood Still*. From there he hopped from one studio to the next, showing up as a sergeant in *The Veils of Baghdad*; a man on the beach in *Interrupted Melody*; a cavalry lieutenant in *Seven Men from Now*; and a lab technician in *Crime of Passion*, to name but a few. His leap into more important roles came when Warner Bros. cast him as Johnny in *Johnny Trouble*, playing a college freshman Ethel Barrymore suspects might be the grandson she has never known. 20th Century-Fox saw star possibilities and signed him to a contract in 1958, launching him as Diane Varsi's musician lover in the Gary Cooper soap opera, *Ten North Frederick*. Next up he was a bad influence on Fabian in *Hound-Dog Man*, got hanged in the western, *These Thousand Hills*, and loved and left Joanne Woodward in Hollywood's strange attempt to film Faulkner's *The Sound and the Fury*. Finally obtaining top-billing, he was a singer caught up in crime in *Murder, Inc.*, where he was clearly out-shone by Peter Falk, and then donned Biblical garb to replace Stephen Boyd in *The Story of Ruth*, which was one of the less exciting offerings in this once-popular genre.

Now officially a star, though hardly a major attraction, he was in a minor western, *The Fiercest Heart*, and a major one, the entertaining *The Comancheros*, which did good business, not because of Whitman, but because John Wayne was the star. As good luck would have it, he got handed another role scheduled for someone else (Richard Burton) in *The Mark*. This film was a subtle and sad examination of a man released from prison following accusations of child molestation. Whitman gave it his best shot and captured the feel of someone shrinking back from the eyes of the world, earning an Oscar nomination in the process. He was one of the many star names in the World War II epic *The Longest Day*; pretended to be nuts in the trashy *Shock Treatment*; and then took a back seat to villains Richard Boone and Edmond O'Brien in *Rio Conchos*. As an aw-shucks Texas flier he had his biggest hit at the Fox studio with what turned out to be his farewell for them, *Those Magnificent Men in Their Flying Machines*. After the failure of a bleak survival-in-the-desert tale, *Sands of the Kalahari* (this time replacing George Peppard) and the lurid filming of the Norman Mailer best-seller *An American Dream*, he decided to try television and struggled through a season of a lavish western series, *Cimarron Strip*. After that his career in theatrical features never recovered although he would keep cranking out title after title. He seemed increasingly bored throughout his involvement in such drive-in gems as *Captain Apache*; the killer rabbit movie *Night of the Lepus*; the cannibal sickie *Tender Flesh*; the cult favorite *Crazy Mama*, as a

sheriff who joins Cloris Leachman in her life of crime; and the cheesy cash-in on the Jim Jones suicide tragedy, *Guyana: Cult of the Damned*, with Whitman's character called Rev. Jim Johnson for reasons left unexplained. Nearly all of his later titles were strictly direct-to-video if they saw the light of day at all.

Screen: 1951: When Worlds Collide; The Day the Earth Stood Still; **1952:** Barbed Wire; One Minute to Zero; **1953:** All American; Appointment in Honduras; Walking My Baby Back Home; All I Desire; The Veils of Bagdad; **1954:** Passion; Silver Lode; Prisoner of War; Rhapsody; Brigadoon; Rhapsody; **1955:** King of the Carnival (serial); Interrupted Melody; Diane; **1956:** Seven Men from Now; **1957:** Crime of Passion; War Drums; Johnny Trouble; Hell Bound; The Girl in Black Stockings; Bombers B-52; **1958:** Darby's Rangers; Ten North Frederick; China Doll; The Decks Ran Red; **1959:** Hound-Dog Man; These Thousand Hills; The Sound and the Fury; **1960:** Murder, Inc.; The Story of Ruth; **1961:** The Fiercest Heart; The Comancheros; Francis of Assisi; The Mark; **1962:** Convicts 4; The Longest Day; **1963:** The Day and the Hour; **1964:** Rio Conchos; Signpost to Murder; Shock Treatment; **1965:** Those Magnificent Men in Their Flying Machines or How I Flew from London to Paris in 25 Hours 11 Minutes; Sands of the Kalahari; **1966:** An American Dream; **1969:** Sweet Hunters (nUSr); **1970:** The Invincible Six/The Heroes; The Last Escape; **1971:** Captain Apache; **1972:** Night of the Lepus; Run, Cougar, Run; **1974:** Welcome to Arrow Beach/Tender Flesh; **1975:** Crazy Mama; Call Him Mr. Shatter/Shatter; **1976:** Las Vegas Lady; Mean Johnny Barrows; **1977:** Oil/The Billion Dollar Fire; Strange Shadows in an Empty Room/Blazing Magnums; The White Buffalo; Eaten Alive/Death Trap; Thoroughbreds/Run for the Roses; Ruby; Maniac/Assault on Paradise/Ransom; **1979:** Delta Fox; Treasure Seekers/Contraband (nUSr); Woman from the Torrid Land (nUSr); **1980:** Guyana: Cult of the Damned; Hostages! (nUSr); Cuba Crossing/Sweet Dirty Tony/Assignment: Kill Castro/The Mercenaries; **1981:** Demonoid: Messenger of Death; The Monster Club (dtv); When I Am King (nUSr); **1982:** Butterfly; Horror Safari/Invaders of the Lost Gold (nUSr); **1984:** Vultures in Paradise/Vultures (dtv); **1985:** Treasure of the Amazon (dtv) Deadly Invader (dtv); First Strike (dtv); **1988:** Moving Target (dtv); **1989:** Reactor/Deadly Reactor (dtv); **1990:** Omega Cop (dtv); Mob Boss (dtv); **1991:** Heaven and Earth (narrator); **1992:** Smooth Talker (dtv); **1993:** Sandman (nUSr); Lightning in a Bottle (nUSr); Private Wars (dtv); **1994:** The Color of Evening (nUSr); Improper Conduct (dtv); Trial by Jury; **1995:** Land of Milk and Honey (nUSr); **1998:** Second Chances (dtv).

Select TV: 1956: Desert Encounter (sp); **1957:** Encounter on a Second-Class Coach (sp); **1963:** A Killing Sundial (sp); **1966:** The People Trap (sp); **1967–68:** Cimarron Strip (series); **1970:** The Man Who Wanted to Live Forever; **1971:** City Beneath the Sea; Revenge; **1972:** The High Flying Spy; The Woman Hunter; **1973:** The Man Who Died Twice; Curse of the Cat Creature; **1978:** Go West, Young Girl; Harold Robbins' The Pirate; **1979:** The Last Convertible (ms); The Seekers; Women in White; **1980:** Condominium; **1985:** Beverly Hills Cowgirl Blues; **1987:** Stillwatch; **1988:** Hemingway (ms); Once Upon a Texas Train; **1995:** Wounded Heart; **2000:** The President's Man.

JAMES WHITMORE
BORN: WHITE PLAINS, NY, OCTOBER 1, 1921.
RAISED IN BUFFALO, NY. ED: YALE UNIV.

A stocky fellow whose gruff, direct style was always bringing up comparisons (usually favorable, thank goodness) to Spencer Tracy, James Whitmore was very much his own man and proved it time and again, becoming one of those reliable character players who was just as well known as many a star name. During World War II he served with the Marines and got his first taste of acting when he did a USO tour of *The Milky Way*. Following a stint with the Petersboro Players in New Hampshire, he came to New York to study with the American Theatre Wing, then got a role as a sergeant in the original Broadway production of *Command Decision*, earning a Tony and Theatre World Award for his performance. MGM gave the part in the film version to Van Johnson, but Whitmore received some compensation when Columbia hired him to play Glenn Ford's Treasury Department partner in *The Undercover Man*, in 1949. The next year MGM decided they could use him as a much more down-to-earth kind of sergeant, in what turned out to be one of the better war films of the era, *Battleground*. Whitmore, looking permanently caked with the dirt and grit of combat, was a standout in a fine cast and earned an Oscar nomination in the supporting category. Metro put him under contract, letting him play another sidekick part, in *The Asphalt Jungle*, and then gave him leading roles in two films, the interesting fantasy *The Next Voice You Hear…*, in which his life was changed when God begins speaking on the radio, and the comedic murder mystery *Mrs. O'Malley and Mr. Malone*, which placed him opposite Marjorie Main, in what was intended to be the first of a series that never materialized due to a tepid public response. Back in support, he was Mario Lanza's sergeant in *Because You're Mine*; a derelict in *All the Brothers Were Valiant*; Fernando Lamas's partner in crime in *The Girl Who Had Everything*; straight man to Red Skelton in *The Great Diamond Robbery*; and, best of all, a dumb thug in *Kiss Me Kate*, where he and Keenan Wynn shared the spotlight for a delightful duet, performing Cole Porter's "Brush Up Your Shakespeare."

After leaving Metro, he was a state trooper in a good sci-fi thriller, *Them!*, tracking giant ants in Los Angeles; another sergeant, in the highly popular ensemble *Battle Cry*; Gloria Graham's grizzled dad in *Oklahoma!*, buried under old man makeup; the standard best buddy role in a standard-but-successful biopic, *The Eddy Duchin Story*; the convict enlisting Sal Mineo's assistance in *The Young Don't Cry*; and a weird investigator in *Who Was That Lady?* Another lead came his way in a heartfelt movie, *Black Like Me*, adapted from the best-seller about a man who chemically darkened his skin to experience prejudice first hand. Whitmore didn't look particularly convincing passing as an African American, but this Allied Artist release deserved points for effort. Going for laughs he was the dim-witted captain in *Waterhole # 3*, then disappeared under monkey make-up as the assembly president in the smash hit, *Planet of the Apes*. The actor had returned on occasion to the theater since going to Hollywood and received some of his most enthusiastic notices for a one-man show, *Will Rogers' USA* (which was taped for TV), leading to an even more acclaimed solo venture (in D.C.), *Give 'Em Hell, Harry!*, playing Harry S. Truman. The latter was videotaped and then transferred to film for a token theatrical showing, and, since outstanding male roles were apparently in short supply in 1975, Whitmore, for his full-throttle interpretation of the 33rd President, wound up with an unexpected Oscar nomination. Because of it, he earned his place in Oscar trivia history as the only nominated performer to not share the screen with a single other actor. This did not, however, prompt a wealth of follow-up movie offers and he returned to the screen only sporadically over the next two decades, playing a patient judge in *Nuts*, and an old convict who loses his sense of purpose when finally released back into the outside world in *The Shawshank Redemption*. In between he starred with Jose Ferrer in a little-seen cheapie, *Old Explorers*. He was married (1972–79) to actress Audra Lindley. His son from his first marriage, James Whitmore, Jr., became an actor before turning to television directing.

Screen: 1949: The Undercover Man; Battleground; 1950: Please Believe Me; The Asphalt Jungle; The Outriders; The Next Voice You Hear…; Mrs. O'Malley and Mr. Malone; 1951: It's a Big Country; Across the Wide Missouri; The Red Badge of Courage (narrator); Shadow in the Sky; 1952: Because You're Mine; Above and Beyond; 1953: Kiss Me Kate; The Girl Who Had Everything; All the Brothers Were Valiant; The Great Diamond Robbery; 1954: The Command; Them!; 1955: Battle Cry; The McConnell Story; The Last Frontier; Oklahoma!; 1956: The Eddy Duchin Story; Crime in the Streets; 1957: The Young Don't Cry; 1958: The Deep Six; The Restless Years; 1959: Face of Fire; 1960: Who Was That Lady?; 1964: Black Like Me; 1967: Chuka; Waterhole # 3; 1968: Nobody's Perfect; Planet of the Apes; Madigan; 1969: The Split; Guns of the Magnificent Seven; 1970: Tora! Tora! Tora!; 1972: Chato's Land; 1973: The Harrad Experiment; La Polizia incrimina la legge assolve/High Crime/Calling Crime Command (nUSr); 1974: Where the Red Fern Grows; Il Venditore di Palloncini/The Balloon Vendor/The Last Circus Show (nUSr); 1975: Give 'Em Hell, Harry!; 1977: The Serpent's Egg; 1978: Bully; 1980: The First Deadly Sin; 1986: The Adventures of Mark Twain (voice); 1987: Nuts; 1990: Old Explorers; 1994: The Shawshank Redemption; 1996: Wild Bill: Hollywood Maverick; 1997: The Relic; 2000: Here's to Life! (dtv); 2001: The Majestic.

NY Stage: 1947: Command Decision; 1958: Winesburg, Ohio; 1964: A Case of Libel; 1970: Inquest; 1974: Will Rogers' USA; 1977: Bully; 1982: Almost an Eagle; 1983: Elba (ob); 1990: About Time (ob); Handy Dandy (ob).

Select TV: 1954: For Value Received (sp); 1956: The Blonde Mink (sp); This Business of Murder (sp); The Velvet Trap (sp); Profile in Courage (sp); 1957: Fear Has Many Faces (sp); Nothing to Lose (sp); Deep Water (sp); Galvanized Yankee (sp); 1958: Free Week-End (sp); 1959: Dark December (sp); The Sounds of Eden (sp); 1960–61: The Law and Mr. Jones (series); 1961: The Witch Next Door (sp); 1962: Focus (sp); Big Day for Ascrambler (sp); 1963: The Long Long Life of Edward Smalley (sp); 1964: Rumble on the Docks (sp); The Tenderfoot; 1969: My Friend Tony (series); 1970: The Challenge; 1971: If Tomorrow Comes; 1972: Will Rogers' USA (sp); 1972–73: Temperature's Rising (series); 1974: The Canterville Ghost (sp); 1975: I Will Fight No More Forever; 1978: The Word (ms); 1980: Rage; Mark I Love You; The Golden Honeymoon (sp); 1984: Celebrity (ms); 1986: All My Sons (sp); 1988: Favorite Son (ms); 1989: Glory! Glory!; 1990: Sky High; 1999: Swing Vote; 2001: Ring of Endless Light.

DAME MAY WHITTY

BORN: LIVERPOOL, ENGLAND, JUNE 19, 1865.
DIED: MAY 29, 1948.

It was only fitting that this tiny, very regal old lady be billed with the title bestowed upon her by the Order of the British Empire (in 1918), since Dame May Whitty brought such class and dignity to Hollywood during her decade-plus career there. Onstage in the city of her birth from age 16, she made her London theatrical bow, in 1882, in *Boccacio*. 13 years later she first came to America as part of a tour with Sir Henry Irving and his theatrical company. She remained principally a star of the stage, though there was a smattering of film assignments during the silent era. In 1935 she played the part of the selfish old lady who is charmed by a maniacal killer in the London production of Emlyn Williams's *Night Must Fall* (opposite Williams himself) and made such a hit that she brought it to Broadway the following year. In 1937 MGM invited Whitty to recreate her role in the film adaptation, which she did marvelously, sniping at her employees and wallowing in self-pity until she gets her comeuppance from deranged Robert Montgomery. It brought her an Oscar nomination in the supporting category and a contract with the studio. Before she officially settled into the world of Hollywood moviemaking, she returned to England for one of her best-remembered roles, old Miss Froy, who somehow disappears on a moving train, in director Alfred Hitchcock's suspenseful *The Lady Vanishes*. Also for that director she played Joan Fontaine's mother in *Suspicion*, then returned to MGM to receive another Oscar nomination, for *Mrs. Miniver*, as the distinguished grandmother whose main interest is in the annual flower competition. Opposite her real-life husband Ben Webster, she was the old lady who temporarily befriends the lost pooch in *Lassie Come Home*; then played the nosey neighbor in *Gaslight*; the scheming mother of crazed George Macready in *My Name Is Julia Ross*; the Mother Superior who lives atop a seaside mountain in *Green Dolphin Street*; and Terry Moore's aunt in *The Return of October*, released the year of her death, 1948.

Screen: 1914: Enoch Arden; 1915: The Little Minister; 1920: Colonel Newcome, the Perfect Gentleman; 1937: Night Must Fall; Conquest; The Thirteenth Chair; 1938: I Met My Love Again; The Lady Vanishes; 1940: Raffles; Return to Yesterday; A Bill of Divorcement; 1941: One Night in Lisbon; Suspicion; 1942: Mrs. Miniver; Thunder Birds; 1943: The Constant Nymph; Flesh and Fantasy; Lassie Come Home; Madame Curie; Stage Door Canteen; Forever and a Day; Slightly Dangerous; Crash Dive; 1944: The White Cliffs of Dover; Gaslight; 1945: My Name Is Julia Ross; 1946: Devotion; 1947: This Time for Keeps; Green Dolphin Street; If Winter Comes; 1948: Sign of the Ram; The Return of October.

NY Stage: 1908: Irene Wycherly; 1932: There's Always Juliet; 1936: Night Must Fall; 1937: Yr. Obedient Husband; 1940: Romeo and Juliet; 1941: The Trojan Women; 1945: Therese.

MARY WICKES

(MARY ISABELLE WICKENHAUSER) BORN: ST. LOUIS, MO, JUNE 13, 1910. ED: WASHINGTON UNIV. DIED: OCTOBER 22, 1995.

A gangly, hatchet-faced lady who administered a welcome touch of vinegar in her many roles as maids, secretaries, spinsters, and nuns, Mary Wickes made her theatrical debut at the Berkshire Playhouse in Stockbridge, Massachusetts. Starting with *The Farmer Takes a Wife*, in 1934, she became a familiar face on Broadway, culminating in her role as Nurse Preen, who receives a good deal of Monty Wooley's verbal abuse, in *The Man Who Came to Dinner*. An offer to repeat her part in the 1941 Warner Bros. film brought her to movies (she would play the part again years later on television) and from that point on she was almost always called on to provide some laughs with her tart, snappish delivery and her sardonic glare, which could cut someone down to size as easily as any insult. She was self-involved Gladys Cooper's nurse in *Now, Voyager*; acerbic domestics in *June Bride* and *I'll See You in My Dreams*, to name but two; pretty much took up where Marjorie Main left off, as the housekeeper in both *On Moonlight Bay* and *By the Light of the Silvery Moon*, Warners's attempts at cozy musical nostalgia in the tradition of *Meet Me in St. Louis*; and was back looking after things as the

innkeeper in Paramount's holiday perennial *White Christmas*. By this point she was becoming a noted character player on the small screen as well, most notably as Liz O'Neal, Danny Thomas's publicist in *The Danny Thomas Show*. Back on the big screen she was one of the pick-a-little talk-a-little gossips in *The Music Man*; Eddie Mayehoff's secretary in *How to Murder Your Wife*; and one of the more amusing nuns in both *The Trouble with Angels* and its sequel, *Where Angels Go...Trouble Follows*. Though she stuck mostly to television during the 1970s and 1980s, she got a sudden spurt of film roles in the 1990s, playing Meryl Streep's grandmother in *Postcards from the Edge*; sour-faced Sister Mary Lazarus in *Sister Act* and its sequel; and, fittingly, crotchety Aunt March in the 1994 remake of *Little Women*.

Screen: 1941: The Man Who Came to Dinner; 1942: The Mayor of 44th Street; Private Buckaroo; Now, Voyager; Who Done It?; Blondie's Blessed Event; 1943: Rhythm of the Islands; Happy Land; My Kingdom for a Cook; How's About It?; Higher and Higher; 1948: The Decision of Christopher Blake; June Bride; 1949: Anna Lucasta; 1950: The Petty Girl; 1951: On Moonlight Bay; I'll See You in My Dreams; 1952: The Will Rogers Story; Young Man With Ideas; Bloodhounds of Broadway; 1953: By the Light of the Silvery Moon; The Actress; Half a Hero; 1954: Destry; Ma and Pa Kettle at Home; White Christmas; 1955: Good Morning, Miss Dove; 1956: Dance With Me Henry; 1957: Don't Go Near the Water; 1958: The Proud Rebel; 1959: It Happened to Jane; 1960: Cimarron; 1961: One Hundred and One Dalmatians (voice); The Sins of Rachel Cade; 1962: The Music Man; 1964: Fate Is the Hunter; Dear Heart; 1965: How to Murder Your Wife; 1966: The Trouble With Angels; 1967: The Spirit Is Willing; 1968: Where Angels Go...Trouble Follows; 1972: Napoleon and Samantha; Snowball Express; 1980: Touched by Love; 1990: Postcards from the Edge; 1992: Sister Act; 1993: Sister Act 2: Back in the Habit; 1994: Little Women; 1996: The Hunchback of Notre Dame (voice).

NY Stage: 1934: The Farmer Takes a Wife; 1935: One Good Year; 1936: Spring Dance; Stage Door; Swing Your Lady; 1937: Hitch Your Wagon!; Father Malachy's Miracle; 1938: Danton's Death; 1939: Stars in Your Eyes; The Man Who Came To Dinner; 1941: George Washington Slept Here; 1944: Jackpot; Dark Hammock; 1945: Hollywood Pinafore; 1946: Apple of His Eye; Park Avenue; 1948: Town House; 1979: Oklahoma!

Select TV: 1948: Catbird Seat (sp); Goodbye Miss Lizzie (sp); 1949: Mary Poppins (sp); Dark Hammock (sp); 1949–50: Inside USA with Chevrolet (series); 1950: The Peter Lind Hayes Show (series); 1953: Bonino (series); 1954–55: The Halls of Ivy (series); 1956–57: The Danny Thomas Show; 1959–61: Dennis the Menace (series); 1961–62: Mrs. G. Goes to College/The Gertrude Berg Show (series); 1963–64: Temple Houston (series); 1968–71: Julia (series); 1969: The Monk; 1972: The Man Who Came to Dinner (sp); 1973–75: Sigmund and the Sea Monsters (series); 1975–76: Doc (series); 1979: Willa; 1985: The Canterville Ghost (sp); 1986: The Christmas Gift; 1987: Fatal Confession: A Father Dowling Mystery; Almost Partners; 1989–91: Father Dowling Mysteries (series); 1995: Life With Louie (series; voice).

RICHARD WIDMARK

BORN: SUNRISE, MN, DECEMBER 26, 1914. ED: LAKE FOREST UNIV.

A sense of danger and a quick fuse temper gave Richard Widmark his edge, making him one of those rare stars who could show both his good and bad side in the same role with ease. Many remember him for his more demonic, maniacal performances, but he was, in fact, always more interesting to watch on a subtler level. Originally a pre-law student at college, he became so involved in dramatics that it completely consumed him. He eventually journeyed to New York to look for work and got a job on a radio program called *Aunt Jenny's Real Life Stories*, which was followed by regular employment in that medium. In 1943 he made his Broadway debut, in *Kiss and Tell*, and his good notices in that play brought him several other stage roles. It was, however, his radio work that got him an audition for director Henry Hathaway, who was looking for somebody new and unique to play the cackling villain Tommy Udo in the Fox noir, *Kiss of Death*. Widmark made sure he was remembered, playing the part with a self-satisfied sneer and a distinctive giggle whenever he was about to do something particularly sadistic, most notably the unforgettable moment in which he pushes Mildred Dunnock down a flight of stairs in her wheelchair. Widmark got an Oscar nomination in the supporting category for what can't help but come across today as a rather mannered, gimmicky performance. 20th Century-Fox was very excited by the possibility of a new star and put him under contract. For the time being he stayed wicked in secondary parts for *The Street with No Name*, as a thug with an inhaler; *Road House*, framing and torturing Cornel Wilde; and *Yellow Sky*, a superior western in which he was a mean bank robber named Dude.

Fox gave him his first top-billed role with *Down to the Sea in Ships*, a whaling drama, after which he had a run of major releases in 1950 that solidified his standing as a significant talent in the industry. *Night and the City* was an outstanding noir set in London, with Widmark superb as a pathetic schemer who gets his comeuppance; *Panic in the Streets* was one of the best of the studio's "realism" dramas, shot on location in New Orleans, and centering on his efforts to track down a pair of plague carriers; *No Way Out* found him going way over the top, as a racist bastard who is determined to kill physician Sidney Poitier, in a movie that was much praised in its day for its statement on bigotry; and *Halls of Montezuma* was standard World War II stuff but one that was very popular with the masses. He was next seen battling against: raging forest fires, in *Red Skies of Montana*; Marilyn Monroe's inept emoting, in *Don't Bother to Knock*; and light comedy, something he never quite felt at home at, in *My Pal Gus*. Somewhat on the wrong side of the law he was a pickpocket in a weak thriller, *Pickup on South Street*, and endured acting opposite one of studio head Darryl Zanuck's "discoveries," Bella Darvi, for *Hell and High Water*. To finish off his contract with Fox he took secondary roles to Gary Cooper in *Garden of Evil*, at his most sarcastic as an adventurer, and to Spencer Tracy in *Broken Lance*, as his neglected, bitter son. He was one of the better things about the star-filled mental hospital melodrama *The Cobweb*, as a psychiatrist; went out west again for two poor films, *Backlash* and *Run for the Sun*, and then for a better one, made back at Fox, *The Last Wagon*, in which he played a despised outsider who takes control of the survivors of an Indian massacre. Stretching his acting capabilities, he was in over his head as the Dauphin in *Saint Joan*, after which he presented the first film under his own banner, Heath Productions, *Time Limit*, a military courtroom drama. In that company's marginally more popular second feature, *The Trap*, Widmark starred as a lawyer trying to bring criminal Lee J. Cobb to justice against insurmountable odds. In between, he was at sea in another comedy that didn't click, *The Tunnel of Love*, with Doris Day; and took billing *above* Henry Fonda for the western allegory *Warlock*, though Fonda had the better role.

Widmark had become one of those front rank stars who got steady work, was something akin to a household name, and yet didn't really have much drawing power at the box office. Still he was considered a potent enough name to have on board for John Wayne's expensive production of *The Alamo*, playing a testy Jim Bowie and clashing with Wayne on the set. Another of his own productions, *The Secret Ways*, was notable only in that his wife, Jean Hazelwood, wrote it, after which he joined the cast of what was perhaps his best film, *Judgment at Nuremberg*, in which he played the very angry prosecuting attorney, just one of the many spot-on performances in the film. There were two of director John Ford's later-day failures, *Two Rode Together*, where he and Shirley Jones participated in a rather intrusive romantic subplot, and *Cheyenne Autumn*, taking the principal role in this lengthy epic, as a cavalry officer reluctant to pursue a tribe of displaced Indians. There were two that reunited him with Sidney Poitier, *The Long Ships*, where he looked very out-of-place in this Viking adventure, and *The Bedford Incident*, in which he was more at home in this interesting anti-war drama, as a ship's commander, facing a Cold War crisis. Paired off with William Holden, he was a one-eyed Confederate officer in a forgettable western, *Alvarez Kelly*; and, similarly, was seen alongside some other aging stars who were coming to the end of their heydays, Robert Mitchum and Kirk Douglas, in *The Way West*. A police thriller, *Madigan*, offered him a good opportunity and, despite the fact that he died in the end, was revived for a short-lived television series. *Death of a Gunfighter* was significant because his interracial romance with Lena Horne was done casually (and because it was the first movie to receive the famous "Allen Smithee" credit, when director Bob Totten asked to have his name removed). He did the first-ever two part telemovie, *Vanished*, then returned to the big screen for a personal favorite, *When the Legends Die*, as an aging rodeo star. Going into supporting mode, he was the character who was killed off in the all-star whodunit, *Murder on the Orient Express*; played snarling bad guys in *Coma*, *Hanky Panky*, and *Against All Odds*; and was last seen acting on the big screen in *True Colors*, as a politician. Despite the decreasing size of his roles, he still possessed enough star quality to make his presence felt in each of these films.

Screen: 1947: Kiss of Death; 1948: The Street With No Name; Road House; Yellow Sky; 1949: Down to the Sea in Ships; Slattery's Hurricane; 1950: Night and the City; Panic in the Streets; No Way Out; Halls of Montezuma; 1951: The Frogmen; 1952: Red Skies of Montana; Don't Bother to Knock; O. Henry's Full House; My Pal Gus; 1953: Destination Gobi; Pickup on South Street; Take the High Ground; 1954: Hell and High Water; Garden of Evil; Broken Lance; 1955: A Prize of Gold; The Cobweb; 1956: Backlash; The Last Wagon; Run for the Sun; 1957: Saint Joan; Time Limit (and prod.); 1958: The Law and Jake Wade; The Tunnel of Love; 1959: The Trap; Warlock; 1960: The Alamo; 1961: The Secret Ways (and prod.); Two Rode Together; Judgment at Nuremberg; 1963: How the West Was Won; 1964: The Long Ships; Flight from Ashiya; Cheyenne Autumn; 1965: The Bedford Incident; 1966: Alvarez Kelly; 1967: The Way West; 1968: Madigan; 1969: Death of a Gunfighter; A Talent for Loving; 1970: The Moonshine War; 1972: When the Legends Die; 1974: Murder on the Orient Express; 1976: To the Devil a Daughter; The Sell-Out; 1977: Twilight's Last Gleaming; The Domino Principle; Rollercoaster; 1978: Coma; The Swarm; 1979: Bear Island; 1981: National Lampoon Goest to the Movies (dtv); 1982: Hanky Panky; 1983: The Final Option/Who Dares Wins; 1984: Against All Odds; 1991: True Colors; 1996: Wild Bill: Hollywood Maverick.

NY Stage: 1943: Kiss and Tell; Get Away Old Man; 1944: Trio; 1945: Kiss Them for Me; Dunnigan's Daughter.

Select TV: 1971: Vanished; 1972–73: Madigan (series); 1973: Brock's Last Case; 1975: Benjamin Franklin: The Rebel (sp); The

Last Day; **1979:** Mr. Horn; **1980:** All God's Children; **1981:** A Whale for the Killing; **1985:** Blackout; **1987:** A Gathering of Old Men; **1988:** Once Upon a Texas Train; **1989:** Cold Sassy Tree.

HENRY WILCOXON

BORN: DOMINICA, BRITISH WEST INDIES, SEPTEMBER 8, 1905. DIED: MARCH 6, 1984.

A stern-faced, classically featured actor, whose famed rested in his alliance with director Cecil B. DeMille, Henry Wilcoxon had been a member of England's Birmingham Reperatory Company. This led to London stage work and a handful of British movies in the early 1930s, starting with *The Perfect Lady*, as a Canadian loved by leading lady Moira Lynd. It was while appearing onstage in *The Barretts of Wimpole Street* that he was spotted by a talent agent from Paramount, who was looking for a replacement for Fredric March, who had bailed out of DeMille's lavish production of *Cleopatra*. Wilcoxon made a suitably romantic Marc Antony and looked more plausible than most actors in a Roman toga. This sublimely kitschy epic was followed by an even more spectacular one for DeMille, *The Crusades*, with Wilcoxon as Richard the Lionheart, allotted sufficient time to romance Loretta Young between battles. Perhaps it was his scowling countenance that kept him from becoming a true star attraction at Paramount, because he got the remainder of his leading roles over at the less prestigious Republic Pictures, carrying *The President's Mystery*, as a lawyer who fakes his own death; *Prison Nurse*, in jail for a mercy killing; and *Woman Doctor*, straying because wife Frieda Inescort is spending too much time at the hospital. In support, he was the British major captured by the evil Magua in *The Last of the Mohicans*; the Captain of the Watch in the witty *If I Were King*; and the Vicar in the Oscar-winning *Mrs. Miniver*. Following a lengthy break to serve in the U.S. Navy during World War II, he was employed again by DeMille in both *Unconquered* and *Samson and Delilah*, in the latter taking over some behind-the-scenes production responsibilities though receiving no on-screen credit. That oversight was compensated for when he was credited as associate producer on the Oscar-winning *The Greatest Show on Earth*, in which he was also cast as the detective on the trail of fugitive James Stewart, and on *The Ten Commandments*. He was upped to producer on the remake of *The Buccaneer*, before taking a break from acting altogether. In later years he was seen in various character parts, including *Man in the Wilderness*, as an old Indian, and *Caddyshack*, as a priest who makes the mistake of golfing during an electrical storm.

Screen: **1931:** The Perfect Lady; **1932:** Self-Made Lady; The Flying Squad; **1933:** Taxi to Paradise; Lord of the Manor; **1934:** Princess Charming; Cleopatra; **1935:** The Crusades; **1936:** The Last of the Mohicans; A Woman Alone/Two Who Dared; The President's Mystery; **1937:** Dark Sands/Jericho; Souls at Sea; **1938:** Keep Smiling; Prison Nurse; Mysterious Mr. Moto; Five of a Kind; Arizona Wildcat; If I Were King; **1939:** Woman Doctor; Chasing Danger; Tarzan Finds a Son; **1940:** Free, Blonde and 21; The Crooked Road; Earthbound; Mystery Sea Raider; **1941:** Scotland; That Hamilton Woman; The Lone Wolf Takes a Chance; The Corsican Brothers; South of Tahiti; **1942:** Mrs. Miniver; The Man Who Wouldn't Die; Johnny Doughboy; **1947:** The Dragnet; Unconquered; **1949:** A Connecticut Yankee in King Arthur's Court; Samson and Delilah; **1950:** The Miniver Story; **1952:** The Greatest Show on Earth (and assoc. prod.); Scaramouche; **1956:** The Ten Commandments (and assoc. prod.); **1965:** The War Lord; **1967:** The Doomsday Machine; **1968:** The

Private Navy of Sgt. O'Farrell; **1971:** Man in the Wilderness; **1975:** Against a Crooked Sky; **1976:** Won Ton Ton, the Dog Who Saved Hollywood; Pony Express Rider; **1978:** F.I.S.T.; **1980:** Caddyshack; The Man With Bogart's Face/Sam Marlowe, Private Eye; **1981:** Sweet Sixteen.

NY Stage: **1948:** The Vigil.

Select TV: **1971:** Sarge: The Badge or the Cross; **1974:** Log of the Black Pearl; The Tribe/Cro-Magnon; **1978:** When Every Day Was the Fourth of July; **1979:** The Two Worlds of Jenny Logan; **1980:** Enola Gay: The Man, the Mission, the Atomic Bomb.

CORNEL WILDE

(CORNELIUS WILDE) BORN: NEW YORK, NY, OCTOBER 13, 1915. ED: COLUMBIA UNIV. DIED: OCTOBER 16, 1989.

It is questionable that anyone might have looked upon Cornel Wilde as the chief virtue of any of the films in which he was involved. As movie star material goes, his looks were far from stunning, while his acting was minimally acceptable at best. Perhaps realizing this, he shifted his latter-day interest over to directing, with further mixed results. He began his acting career with a stock company in Saugerties, New York, and, shortly afterwards, landed his first job on Broadway, in *Moon Over Mulberry Street*, in 1935. While playing Tybalt in support of Laurence Olivier's Romeo, he was engaged to do four films at Warners Bros., one of which was the Humphrey Bogart classic *High Sierra*, where he was seen as a hotel clerk. Warners wasn't interested but Fox was, and they put him under contract in 1941, starting him off as the love interest of Lynn Bari in a cheapie, *The Perfect Snob*. He remained at Fox to support Monty Woolley in *Life Begins at Eight-Thirty*, and to play leading man to Sonia Henie in *Wintertime*, but landed the role that made him famous over at Columbia. *A Song to Remember* was a lavish biopic of Fredric Chopin, one that was no less silly or fabricated than any other Hollywood examination of a famous composer, but a film that made a ton of money nonetheless. Wilde looked good in period costumes, but there was certainly nothing in his routine performance to suggest why he wound up with an Oscar nomination. His follow-up, the none-too-serious swashbuckler *A Thousand and One Nights*, in which he played Aladdin, was something he seemed more at home in, as was the popular *The Bandit of Sherwood Forest*, cast as Robin Hood's offspring, where he got to show off his real-life prowess at fencing. Between these was in another hit, back home at Fox, *Leave Her to Heaven*, prompting a jealous rage from unhinged Gene Tierney.

There was a glossy musical, *Centennial Summer*, as a Frenchman; the dreary costumer *Forever Amber*, where the lackluster combination of Wilde and Linda Darnell was enough to put anyone to sleep; a comedy with Ginger Rogers, *It Had to Be You*; the noir *Road House*, upstaged by Richard Widmark; and *Shockproof*, where he co-starred opposite his first wife (1937–51), Patricia Knight. His contract now officially finished, he swashbuckled again, at RKO, in *At Sword's Point*; was back at Fox for another less-than-sparkling pairing with Darnell, *Two Flags West*; and then appeared for Paramount in the biggest box-office success of his career, *The Greatest Show on Earth*, credibly cast as the arrogant trapeze artist who winds up crippling himself in a fall. It won the Best Picture Oscar for 1952, but didn't do a thing for Wilde's industry status, since he ended up in nothing more than some tired adventure pictures with titles like *California Conquest* and *Treasure of the Golden Condor*. There were two with his second wife (1951–83), Jean Wallace, *Star of India*, and the top-notch noir *The Big Combo*, as a cop after mobster Richard Conte. He was back with Wallace again for *Storm Fear*, which was strictly routine fare, with Wilde as an escaped con, only this time he served as director and producer as well. Compelled to continue with this new sideline interest he also starred in and directed *The Devil's Hairpin*, a story about autoracing; *Maracaibo*; which involved Venezuelan fire-fighters; *Lancelot and Guinevere*, in which he played a long-in-the-tooth Lancelot; *Beach Red*, set in World War II; and *Shark's Treasure*. The standout of his directorial efforts was, no doubt, *The Naked Prey*, a tense adventure in which he spent most of the movie clad only in a loincloth, on the run from tormenting natives. He directed but did not appear in the futuristic allegory *No Blade of Grass* and was an actor only in such movies as the Grand Canyon thriller *Edge of Eternity*; the Dick Van Dyke vehicle *The Comic*; and *The Fifth Musketeer*, as an aged D'Artagnan.

Screen: 1940: The Lady With Red Hair; 1941: Kisses for Breakfast; High Sierra; Knockout/Right to the Heart; The Perfect Snob; 1942: Manila Calling; Life Begins at Eight-Thirty; 1943: Wintertime; 1945: A Song to Remember; A Thousand and One Nights; Leave Her to Heaven; 1946: The Bandit of Sherwood Forest; Centennial Summer; 1947: The Homestretch; Forever Amber; It Had to Be You; 1948: The Walls of Jericho; Road House; 1949: Shockproof; 1950: Four Days Leave/Swiss Tour; Two Flags West; 1952: At Sword's Point (filmed 1949); The Greatest Show on Earth; California Conquest; Operation Secret; 1953: Treasure of the Golden Condor; Main Street to Broadway; Saadia; 1954: Star of India; Woman's World; Passion; 1955: The Big Combo; The Scarlet Coat; Storm Fear (and dir.; prod.); 1956: Hot Blood; 1957: Beyond Mombasa; Omar Khayyam; The Devil's Hairpin (and dir.; wr.; prod.); 1958: Maracaibo (and dir.; prod.); 1959: Edge of Eternity; 1962: Constantine and the Cross; 1963: The Sword of Lancelot/Lancelot and Guinevere (and dir.; prod.); 1966: The Naked Prey (and dir.; prod.); 1967: Beach Red (and dir.; wr.; prod.); 1969: The Comic; 1970: No Blade of Grass (voice; and dir.; prod.); 1975: Shark's Treasure (and dir.; wr.; prod.); 1978: The Norsemen; 1979: The Fifth Musketeer.

NY Stage: 1933: They All Came to Moscow; 1935: Moon Over Mullberry Street; 1937: Having Wonderful Time; 1939: Pastoral; White Plume; 1940: Romeo and Juliet.

Select TV: 1955: The Blond Dog (sp); 1961: The Great Alberti (sp); 1964: Doesn't Anyone Know Who I Am? (sp); 1972: Gargoyles.

MICHAEL WILDING

BORN: WESTCLIFFE-ON-SEA, ESSEX, ENGLAND, JULY 23, 1912. ED: CHRIST COL., HORSHAM. DIED: JULY 8, 1979.

An erudite, handsome, low-keyed British performer who dabbled for a spell in Hollywood with less-than-sterling results, Michael Wilding had been a commercial artist before taking up acting. He made his London stage debut in *Chase the Ace*, in 1933, then did rep work in the provinces. That same year he'd done some extra jobs on film and remained an inconsequential movie figure while continuing to do theatre, notably in *Victoria Regina* and *Tonight at 8:30*. In 1940 he received two film parts of some size, playing one of the titular roles in a mild comedy, *Sailors Three/Three Cockeyed Sailors*, and the juvenile lead in *Spring Meeting*. He was Michael Redgrave's best friend in *Kipps*, an author in *Dear Octopus/The Randolph Family*, and the butler loved by Penelope Ward in *English Without Tears*. He finally became a star and a box-office attraction in the late 1940s,

starring in such motion pictures as *An Ideal Husband*, as the cynical Lord Goring; *Spring in Park Lane*, as a nobleman turned footman; and *Maytime in Mayfair*, as a dress shop proprietor. For Alfred Hitchcock he did one of that director's weakest, *Under Capricorn*, and the better *Stage Fright*, as the detective on the case. His official American debut came at MGM in 1951, as a stylish jewel thief, opposite Greer Garson, in *The Law and the Lady*, another version of the oft-filmed *The Last of Mrs. Cheyney*. He was then the blind pianist who softens Joan Crawford's abusive nature in *Torch Song*, where he really seemed to evaporate next to so strong a presence as Crawford; the epileptic Pharaoh in the dreary *The Egyptian*; a too-old prince to Leslie Caron's Cinderella in a misguided revision of the fairy tale, *The Glass Slipper*; and a Revolutionary War major in *The Scarlet Coat*. After these he quietly he slipped into support, playing Gary Cooper's business partner in *The Naked Edge*, and one of Nancy Kwan's clients in *The World of Suzie Wong*, among others, but to many he was best remembered for being one of Elizabeth Taylor's many husbands (1952–57). He was married to actress Margaret Leighton, from 1963 until her death in 1976.

Screen: 1933: Bitter Sweet; Heads We Go/The Charming Detective; 1935: Late Extra; 1936: Wedding Group/Wrath of Jealousy; 1939: There Ain't No Justice!; 1940: Tilly of Bloomsbury; Convoy; Sailors Don't Care; Sailors Three/Three Cockeyed Sailors; Spring Meeting; 1941: The Farmer's Wife; Kipps; Cottage to Let/Bombsight Stolen; Ships With Wings; 1942: Secret Mission; The Big Blockade; In Which We Serve; 1943: Underground Guerillas/Undercover; Dear Octopus/The Randolph Family; 1944: English Without Tears/ Her Man Gilbey; 1946: Carnival; Piccailly Incident; 1947: The Courtneys of Curzon Street/The Courtney Affair; An Ideal Husband; 1948: Spring in Park Lane; 1949: Maytime in Mayfair; Under Capricorn; 1950: Stage Fright; Into the Blue/Man in the Dinghy (and prod.); 1951: The Lady With a Lamp; The Law and the Lady; 1952: Derby Day/Four Against Fate; Trent's Last Case; 1953: Torch Song; 1954: The Egyptian; 1955: The Glass Slipper; The Scarlet Coat; 1957: Zarak; 1958: Hello, London; 1959: Danger Within/Breakout; 1960: The World of Suzie Wong; 1961: The Naked Edge; The Best of Enemies; 1962: A Girl Named Tamiko; 1968: The Sweet Ride; 1969: Code Name: Red Roses; 1970: Waterloo; 1973: Lady Caroline Lamb.

NY Stage: 1964: Mary, Mary.

Select TV: 1955: Cavalcade (sp); 1956: Stranger in the Night (sp); 1958: Verdict of Three (sp); 1959: The Case of the Two Sisters (sp); Dark as the Night (sp); 1966: The Fatal Mistake (sp); 1973: Frankenstein: The True Story.

WARREN WILLIAM

(WARREN WILLIAM KRECH)
BORN: AITKIN, MN, DECEMBER 2, 1894. ED: AADA. DIED: SEPTEMBER 24, 1948.

Looking like a curious cross between Basil Rathbone and Mischa Auer, Warren William was a prime addition to the Warner Bros. roster in the early 1930s, usually playing suave rotters, snapping off colorful dialogue with great assurance and authority. Following military service during World War II, he studied acting at the American Academy of Dramatic Art. While doing stock and New York theatre, he did a few silent films, including a Pearl White serial called *Plunder*, all under his real name. He dropped the "Krech" and replaced it with his middle name, starting in 1924 with the play *The Wonderful Visit*, and became a very prominent name on Broadway during the late

1920s. When sound pictures arrived, the deep, sophisticated tone of his voice was thought ideal for the microphone and Warner Brothers signed him to a contract in 1931, launching him almost simultaneously in two melodramas, *Expensive Women*, as the composer in love with Dolores Costello, and *Honor of the Family*, as a Hungarian captain driving temptress Bebe Daniels away from his wealthy father. The standard William characterization of the caddish womanizer was set with *Beauty and the Boss*, in which he was a wealthy, misogynistic banker with a habit of bedding his secretaries. During 1932 he rose to top-billing with *The Mouthpiece*, as a flamboyant lawyer who falls in with a bunch of gangsters, a showcase that captured the actor at his best. From there he moved on to *The Dark Horse*, trying to get dimwit candidate Guy Kibbee elected; *Skyscraper Souls* (for MGM), as the owner of the world's tallest building; *Employees' Entrance*, where he was just smashing as an unapologetically ruthless department store manager; *The Mind Reader*, as a con man pretending to be clairvoyant; and *Gold Diggers of 1933*, as a millionaire who falls for showgirl Joan Blondell.

It was actually at Columbia that William got his best-remembered film and role from this era, playing Damon Runyon's Dave the Dude in one of director Frank Capra's charming comedies, *Lady for a Day*. Similarly, another of his more famous roles came between Warners assignments, over at Paramount, playing a very regal and persuasive Julius Caesar in DeMille's colorful look at the conquests of *Cleopatra*. Back over at Warners he was Kay Francis's unfaithful husband in *Dr. Monica*, and Joan Blondell's bickering one in the insufferable *Smarty*, before someone thought of him as William Powell's replacement for the Philo Vance detective series with *The Dragon Murder Case*. This presented another side of William, a sophisticated fighter of crime, and to this end he was infallible lawyer Perry Mason in *The Case of the Howling Dog*, making him the first actor to play this part on screen, which he would do again for the next three installments of the series. He was also the private investigator out to trap Melvyn Douglas in *Arsene Lupin Returns*; a variation of Sam Spade (called Ted Shane) in *Satan Met a Lady*, a wretched earlier version of *The Maltese Falcon*; and, again, Philo Vance, though given more comedic opportunities this time out, in *The Gracie Allen Murder Case*. Before the last was released, he was summoned by Columbia to take over the role of Michael Laynard from Francis Lederer in the studio's series of *Lone Wolf* escapades, involving a one-time jewel-thief who dabbles in crime fighting. This part seemed to fit William best of all and he wound up playing the character nine times, beginning with *The Lone Wolf Spy Hunt*, in 1939, and ending with *One Dangerous Night*, in 1943. In between these he showed up in such "A" features as *The Man in the Iron Mask*, as an aging D'Artagnan, and *Lillian Russell*, as one of Alice Faye's admirers. He had dipped into PRC and Monogram cheapies by the time of his death from bone cancer.

Screen: AS WARREN KRECH: 1920: The Town That Forgot God; 1923: Plunder (serial).

AS WARREN WILLIAM: 1927: Twelve Miles Out; 1931: Expensive Women; Honor of the Family; 1932: Under 18; The Woman From Monte Carlo; Beauty and the Boss; The Mouthpiece; The Dark Horse; Skyscraper Souls; Three on a Match; The Match King; 1933: Employees' Entrance; The Mind Reader; Gold Diggers of 1933; Lady for a Day; Goodbye Again; 1934: Bedside; Smarty; Dr. Monica; Upperworld; The Dragon Murder Case; Cleopatra; The Case of the Howling Dog; The Secret Bride; Imitation of Life; 1935: Living on Velvet; The Case of the Curious Bride; Don't Bet on Blondes; The Case of the Lucky Legs; 1936: Stage Struck; The Widow from Monte Carlo; Times Square

Playboy; The Case of the Velvet Claws; Satan Met a Lady; Go West, Young Man; 1937: The Firefly; Outcast; Madame X; Midnight Madonna; 1938: Wives Under Suspicion; Arsene Lupin Returns; The First Hundred Years; 1939: The Lone Wolf Spy Hunt; The Gracie Allen Murder Case; The Man in the Iron Mask; Day-Time Wife; 1940: The Lone Wolf Meets a Lady; Lillian Russell; Trail of the Vigilantes; Arizona; The Lone Wolf Strikes; 1941: Wild Geese Calling; The Lone Wolf Takes a Chance; The Lone Wolf Keeps a Date; The Wolf Man; Secrets of the Lone Wolf; 1942: Wild Bill Hickok Rides; Counter Espionage; 1943: Passport to Suez; One Dangerous Night; 1945: Out of the Night/Strange Illusion; 1946: Fear; 1947: The Private Affairs of Bel Ami.

NY Stage: AS WARREN KRECH: 1920: Mrs. Jimmie Thompson; 1921: John Hawthorne; We Girls.

AS WARREN WILLIAM: 1924: The Wonderful Visit; Expressing Willie; 1925: Nocturne; The Blue Peter; Rosmersholm; Twelve Miles Out; 1926: Easter One Day More; Fanny; 1927: Paradise; 1928: Veils; The Golden Age; Sign of the Leopard; 1929: Let Us Be Gay; Week-End; 1930: Out of a Blue Sky; The Vikings; Stepdaughters of War; The Vinegar Tree.

ESTHER WILLIAMS

BORN: LOS ANGELES, CA, AUGUST 8, 1922.
ED: USC.

Because she did something that no one else did to attain their place in movie history, Esther Williams is one of the best-remembered and most unique performers of them all. Rather than act, which seemed to be a bit of a challenge for her, she swam and did so in high MGM style, in a series of gloriously kitschy water ballets, the likes of which had never been seen before or since. A first-rate swimmer since childhood, she won several local prizes with the intention of entering the 1940 Olympics, which were cancelled due to World War II. Instead, she was invited by Bill Rose to join his San Francisco Aquacade, where she wound up in the pool with the movies' other famed swimmer, Johnny Weissmuller. MGM spotted her and offered her a contract in 1941, though not initially with the intention of having her glide through water, but to act (!), in *Somewhere I'll Find You*, in the role that wound up going to Lana Turner anyway. Instead she found herself giving Mickey Rooney an underwater kiss in *Andy Hardy's Double Life*. For her official Technicolor debut, she took a secondary part to Red Skelton but had the title role in *Bathing Beauty*. There was one simple swim at the outset, followed by an inane plot and then a flashy climax staged by John Murray Anderson to the strains of "Blue Danube Waltz," as Esther coaxed spurts of water to shoot in the air to the beat of the music. The audience response was good and she returned in a big hit, *Thrill of a Romance*, with Van Johnson, who would be her co-star on three later occasions. There was a dramatic role, as William Powell's love interest in *The Hoodlum Saint*, which brought her little mention, and then *Fiesta*, which had her fighting bulls in an effort to prove that she could do a dumb movie *without* a pool. The fans wanted water though, so the studio gave her pinheaded plots and handsome leading men for her to spurn the advances of, punctuated, thankfully, by a plunge or two. *On an Island With You*, let her do some synchronized swimming while playing a movie star in Hawaii; *Take Me Out to the Ball Game*, found her at her most disagreeable, as the owner of a turn-of-the-century ball team; *Neptune's Daughter*, allowed her to help introduce a classic, Oscar-winning song, "Baby, It's Cold Outside;" *Duchess of Idaho*, offered the sight of her and Van Johnson dancing while holding a potato between their heads; *Pagan Love Song*, placed her in front of some spectacular Tahitian scenery; *Texas Carnival*, had her swimming in Howard Keel's dreams; and *Skirts Ahoy!*, gave her a pair of children to cavort with.

She reached her box-office heights with *Million Dollar Mermaid*, a glossy biography of 1920s swimming star Annette Kellerman. Despite the fact that the film resembled real-life about as much as most Hollywood biopics, it was probably her most entertaining movie and featured the most dazzling of her ballets, a spectacle of orange smoke and trapeze moves staged for maximum impact by Busy Berkeley. *Dangerous When Wet*, another of her better-written vehicles, had her swimming the English channel and romping with the animated Tom and Jerry, while *Easy to Wed*, set in Cypress Gardens, had little if anything going for it, so the producers decided to end it with a wild, water-ski extravaganza that included Williams plunging to the sea from a hovering helicopter. Her heyday came to an end with *Jupiter's Darling*, a goofy musical set in Ancient Rome that had her swimming with living statues. The whole thing was outrageous enough to be more enjoyable than most of her efforts, which were usually in danger of putting the spectators to sleep when they strayed to far from a pool or a song cue. After MGM she did some straight roles, including *The Unguarded Moment*, as a teacher presumably attacked by a student, and *The Big Show*, a circus tale which did see her get wet briefly. In addition to these there were some nightclub engagements and aquatic shows, both live and on television. There was a successful line of Esther Williams bathing suits; a marriage to her *Dangerous When Wet* co-star Fernando Lamas, which lasted from 1967 until his death in 1982; and an autobiography, *Million Dollar Mermaid*, published in 1999. By that time her name became the sort to always raise a smile at its mention. From some, it may have been meant derisively, but even they couldn't help but hold a little bit of fondness for the Cinema's First Lady of Swim.

Screen: 1942: Andy Hardy's Double Life; 1943: A Guy Named Joe; 1944: Bathing Beauty; 1945: Thrill of a Romance; 1946: Ziegfeld Follies; The Hoodlum Saint; Easy to Wed; 1947: Fiesta; This Time for Keeps; 1948: On an Island With You; 1949: Take Me Out to the Ball Game; Neptune's Daughter; 1950: Duchess of Idaho; Pagan Love Song; 1951: Texas Carnival; Callaway Went Thataway; 1952: Skirts Ahoy!; Million Dollar Mermaid; 1953: Dangerous When Wet; Easy to Love; 1955: Jupiter's Darling; 1956: The Unguarded Moment; 1958: Raw Wind in Eden; 1961: The Big Show; La Fuente Magica/The Magic Fountain (nUSr); 1994: That's Entertainment! III.

Select TV: 1957: The Armed Venus (sp); 1960: Esther Williams in Cypress Gardens (sp).

JOHN WILLIAMS

BORN: CHALFONT, BUCKINGHAMSHIRE, ENGLAND, APRIL 15, 1903. DIED: MAY 5, 1983.

A marvelously dry Englishman who could say volumes with the simple raising of an eyebrow, John Williams made his stage debut at age 13, playing John in a London production of *Peter Pan*. He continued steadily in British theater until 1924 when he made a sidetrip to New York to appear in the play *The Fake*. Fluctuating between London and New York, he was seen in the latter during the 1930s in such productions as *Dodsworth* and *No Time for Comedy*. He returned to England to serve in the RAF during World War II and was seen in a few British movies of the 1940s, including *The Goose Steps Out* and

The Foreman Went to France. He entered the Hollywood scene when Alfred Hitchcock cast him as a barrister in *The Paradine Case*, and from that point on mainly made his living in American films. Williams had his banner year in 1954 when he repeated his Broadway role as the intrepid inspector in Hitchcock's version of *Dial M for Murder* (and would repeat it yet again, in 1958, on TV's *Hallmark Hall of Fame*), and then showed warmth and common sense as Audrey Hepburn's chauffeur dad in one of the loveliest of all romantic comedies, *Sabrina*. He was on the trail of suspected cat burglar Cary Grant in his third for Hitchcock, *To Catch a Thief*, and returned to the old Bailey, assisting Charles Laughton, in *Witness for the Prosecution*. In between he had a good role, as one of the oily businessman trying to oust a meddling Judy Holliday from the board of directors, in *The Solid Gold Cadillac*; and could be found coming to the aid of some terrorized women in *Kind Lady* (Ethel Barrymore) and *Midnight Lace* (Doris Day). In time he was utilizing his unflappable reserve as straight man for Jerry Lewis, in *Visit to a Small Planet*; Marty Allen and Steve Rossi, in *Last of the Secret Agents?*; and Elvis Presley, in *Double Trouble*, to all of which he brought a needed bit of class. On television he became a familiar face pitching a classical record package, a spot that ran for more than a decade and kept playing even after (!) his death.

Screen: 1941: The Goose Steps Out; The Foreman Went to France/Somewhere in France; 1947: A Woman's Vengeance; The Paradine Case; 149: Blue Scar; The Dancing Years; 1950: Kind Lady; 1951: The Lady and the Bandit; 1953: Thunder in the East; 1954: Dial M for Murder; The Student Prince; Sabrina; 1955: To Catch a Thief; 1956: D-Day, the Sixth of June; The Solid Gold Cadillac; 1957: Will Success Spoil Rock Hunter?; Island in the Sun; Witness for the Prosecution; 1959: The Young Philadelphians; 1960: Midnight Lace; Visit to a Small Planet; 1965: Harlow; Dear Brigitte; 1966: Last of the Secret Agents?; 1967: Double Trouble; 1968: The Secret War of Harry Frigg; A Flea in Her Ear; 1976: No Deposit, No Return; 1978: Hot Lead, Cold Feet.

NY Stage: 1924: The Fake; 1926: The Ghost Train; 1927: Mixed Doubles; 1928: The High Road; 1930: One Two Three; 1933: Ten Minute Alibi; 1934: Dodsworth; 1936: Call It A Day; 1937: Barchester Towers; 1939: No Time For Comedy; 1941: Claudia; 1946: Pygmalion; 1948: Anne of the Thousand Days; 1949: The Velvet Glove; 1952: Venus Observed; Dial M For Murder; 1955: The Dark Is Light Enough; 1961: Ross; 1964: The Chinese Prime Minister; 1970: Hay Fever.

Select TV: 1959: Dossier (sp); 1958: Dial M for Murder (sp); 1963: Pygmalion; 1964–65: The Rogues (series); 1972: The Hound of the Baskervilles.

CHILL WILLS

BORN: SEAGOVILLE, TX, JULY 18, 1903. DIED: DECEMBER 15, 1978.

A shaggy-haired, folksy feller who was pure Texas, Chill Wills was the sort of character player who added considerable dollops of color to the western genre and any other terrain he managed to visit. First an amateur singer in medicine and minstrels shows, he later became part of a professional group in Burkeburnett, Texas. After that he acted in stock companies, but continued to sing in clubs with his friends in an act called Chill Wills and His Avalon Boys. It was as part of this group that he made his motion picture bow, in 1934, singing around a campfire in *It's a Gift*, followed by some crooning in a Hop-Along Cassidy western, *Bar 20 Rides Again*. Eventually he went solo as an actor, appearing as George O'Brien's saddle sidekick, Whopper Hatch, on several occasions and rising from mere programmer fare to an occasional "A" such as MGM's *Boom Town*, where he was the deputy sheriff. For that studio he was Robert Walker's drill sergeant in *See Here, Private Hargrove*; the wagon driver, Mr. Neely, in the classic *Meet Me in St. Louis*; the fiancé of Judy Garland, who's relieved when she declines to be his bride, in *The Harvey Girls*; and one of the backwoods neighbors in *The Yearling*. His greatest movie fame came most curiously, through a role that made extensive use of his raspy, homespun speech pattern, when he was asked to dub the voice of the talking mule that becomes Donald O'Connor's buddy and confidant in *Francis*. This minor Universal comedy became one of the biggest money-makers of 1949 and Wills was called back to supply the sardonic jackass's observations for five of the six sequels (Paul Frees replaced him in the last), including *Francis Joins the WACs*, where he was also allowed to appear on screen as well, as a General. For the same studio he actually got a lead, in the low-brow comedy western *Ricochet Romance*, where he was paired with the equally indelicate Marjorie Main in hopes of pleasing the "Ma & Pa Kettle" crowd. From that point on, it was rare not to see him in western gear, which he wore in two of the biggest productions in which he was involved, *Giant*, where he was the lovable Uncle Bawley, and *The Alamo*, as the hell-raising Beekeeper. The latter earned him his one and only Oscar nomination and he made history by becoming the first performer to campaign ruthlessly in the industry trades, a factor which, no doubt, was instrumental in his *not* winning. In 1965 he played wealthy and unscrupulous rancher Jim Ed Love in *The Rounders*, a role he repeated the following year in the short-lived television version.

Screen: 1934: It's a Gift; 1935: Bar 20 Rides Again; 1936: Call of the Prairie; Anything Goes; 1937: Hideaway Girl; Nobody's Baby; Way Out West; 1938: Lawless Valley; 1939: Arizona Legion; Sorority House; Racketeers of the Range; Timber Stampede; Allegheny Uprising; Trouble in Sundown; 1940: Boom Town; Sky Murder; The Westerner; Wyoming; Tugboat Annie Sails Again; 1941: Western Union; The Bad Man; Billy the Kid; Belle Starr; Honky Tonk; The Bugle Sounds; 1942: Tarzan's New York Adventure; Rationing; Her Carboard Lover; Apache Trail; The Omaha Trail; Stand By for Action; 1943: Best Foot Forward; A Stranger in Town; 1944: See Here, Private Hargrove; Barbary Coast Gent; Sunday Dinner for a Soldier; I'll Be Seeing You; Meet Me in St. Louis; 1945: Leave Her to Heaven; What Next, Corporal Hargrove?; 1946: The Harvey Girls; Gallant Bess; The Yearling; 1947: Heartaches; High Barbaree; 1948: That Wonderful Urge; The Sainted Sisters; Family Honeymoon; The Saxon Charm; Raw Deal; Northwest Stampede; Loaded Pistols; 1949: Tulsa; Red Canyon; Francis (voice); 1950: Rio Grande; Rock Island Trail; High Lonesome; Stella; The Sundowners; 1951: Oh! Susanna; Cattle Drive; The Sea Hornet; Francis Goes to the Races (voice); 1952: Bronco Buster; Ride the Man Down; Francis Goes to West Point (voice); 1953: Small Town Girl; The City That Never Sleeps; The Man from the Alamo; Francis Covers the Big Town (voice); Tumbleweed; 1954: Francis Joins the WACs; Ricochet Romance; 1955: Hell's Outpost; Timberjack; Francis in the Navy (voice); 1956: Giant; Kentucky Rifle; Santiago; Gun for a Coward; 1957: Gun Glory; 1958: From Hell to Texas; 1959: The Sad Horse; 1960: The Alamo; 1961: Gold of the Seven Saints; Where the Boys Are; The Deadly Companions; The Little Shepherd of Kingdom Come; 1963: Young Guns of Texas; The Wheeler Dealers; McLintock!; The Cardinal; 1965: The Rounders; 1966: Fireball 500; 1970: The Liberation of L.B. Jones; 1971: The Steagle; 1973: Pat Garrett and Billy the Kid; Guns of a Stranger; 1977: Mr. Billion; Poco.

Select TV: 1960: Tomorrow (sp); 1961–62: Frontier Circus (series); 1966–67: The Rounders (series); 1969: The Over the Hill Gang; 1970: The Over the Hill Gang Rides Again; 1978: Stubby Pringle's Christmas (sp).

MARIE WILSON

(KATHERINE WHITE) BORN: ANAHEIM, CA, AUGUST 19, 1916. DIED: NOVEMBER 23, 1972.

Sporting ultra-blonde locks, great big eyes, a generous mouth, and a breathily high-pitched voice, Marie Wilson made a career out of playing mostly pea-brained but good-natured women, an act she made a killing with on radio and, to a lesser degree, television. Shortly after her family moved to Hollywood, she was spotted by talent scouts for Warner Bros. who put her under contract while she was still a teen. In the meantime she was seen as Mary Quite Contrary in Laurel and Hardy's *Babes in Toyland*, before Warners first utilized her, in *Stars Over Broadway*. For that studio she was Warren Williams's flighty secretary in *Satan Met a Lady*; a bass player at a nightclub in *Melody for Two*; a soldier's wife involved in murder in *The Invisible Menace*; a carny stripper in *Public Wedding*; Carole Lombard's ditsy maid in *Fools for Scandal*; and had a standout role as the studio employee whose baby becomes a movie star in the fast-paced *Boy Meets Girl*. She remained, for the most part, a "B" player, with *Broadway Musketeers*, forming a trio of grown-up orphans with Margaret Lindsay and Ann Sheridan; *Cowboy Quarterback*, as Bert Wheeler's backwoods girlfriend; and *Sweepstakes Winner*, as a clueless waitress making good on a prize racehorse. Soon afterwards, she left Warners and remained in mostly second-string stuff during the 1940s, including *Harvard, Here I Come* and *You Can't Ration Love*. In 1947 she accepted an offer to portray another dim blonde, this time on the radio, and became a major name at last, as *My Friend Irma* (Peterson), a good-hearted but clueless legal secretary. There were two popular spin-off movies for Paramount, *My Friend Irma*, and *My Friend Irma Goes West*, both bolstered by the addition of the red hot comedy team of Dean Martin and Jerry Lewis, and a television version as well. Her bubble-headed shtick, by this point, annoyed as many people as it entertained. After the series left the air she could be seen as Marie Antoinette in *The Story of Mankind*, and as James Stewart's irritating houseguest in *Mr. Hobbs Takes a Vacation*.

Screen: 1934: Babes in Toyland; Down to Their Last Yacht; 1935: The Girl Friend; Stars Over Broadway; Miss Pacific Fleet; Broadway Hostess; Ladies Crave Excitement; 1936: Colleen; The Big Noise; Satan Met a Lady; China Clipper; King of Hockey; 1937: Melody for Two; The Great Garrick; Public Wedding; 1938: The Invisible Menace; Fools for Scandal; Boy Meets Girl; Broadway Musketeers; 1939: Cowboy Quarterback; Sweepstakes Winner; Waterfront; Should Husbands Work?; 1941: Rookies on Parade; Virginia; Flying Blind; 1942: Harvard, Here I Come; Broadway; She's in the Army; 1944: Shine On, Harvest Moon; Music for Millions; You Can't Ration Love; 1946: No Leave, No Love; Young Widow; 1947: The Private Affairs of Bel Ami; Linda Be Good; The Fabulous Joe; 1949: My Friend Irma; 1950: My Friend Irma Goes West; 1952: A Girl in Every Port; Never Wave at a WAC; 1953: Marry Me Again; 1957: The Story of Mankind; 1962: Mr. Hobbs Takes a Vacation.

Select TV: 1952–54: My Friend Irma (series); 1970: Where's Huddles? (series; voice).

MARIE WINDSOR

(EMILY MARIE BERTELSEN) BORN: MARYSVALE, UT, DECEMBER 11, 1919. ED: BRIGHAM YOUNG UNIV. DIED: DECEMBER 10, 2000.

Those lips! Those eyes! In the postwar years there were bad women and femme fatales aplenty, and Marie Windsor, with the sultry lids and dangerously full lips that promised a million temptations was one of the very best. Winner of various beauty contests in her native state, including Miss Utah, she studied acting afterwards, first at college and then with Marie Ouspenskaya. In Hollywood she started out in an ultra-low budget musical for Hal Roach, *All-American Co-Ed*, in 1941, and remained mostly in "B" programmers in nothing parts during the next two years. Disillusioned, she opted for some theater and radio work, finally returning to movies under contract to MGM in 1947, where she was given some small parts, including *Song of the Thin Man*, as a gun moll, and *The Three Musketeers*, as Angela Lansbury's disloyal lady-in-waiting. Her first decent chance came with *Force of Evil*, in which she put the moves on hero John Garfield, but since this was not a major hit in its day the studio saw no great reason to keep her around. Instead, she got her first lead at United Artists, in *Outpost in Morocco*, where she was saddled with an aging George Raft as her co-star. Republic snatched her up and finally did something right with her, making her the second female lead in John Wayne's *The Fighting Kentuckian*, where she paid dearly for trying to cheat the French settlers of their land. She was clearly more engaging than the higher-billed Vera Hruba Ralston, so the studio followed this with a star part in *Hellfire*, as a wicked, lying vixen named Doll Brown. It was clearly a programmer, but it gave her an opportunity to really run with a part, one that became, in fact her all-time favorite.

Next up was *The Showdown*, where she was another lady of questionable morals, a saloonkeeper joining a cattle drive. At Universal she reprised the Una Merkel part in a remake of *Destry Rides Again*, called *Frenchie*; was a lady buccaneer at Columbia in *Hurricane Island*; a dance hall babe known as *Dakota Lil*, for Fox; the destructive bitch trying to tear an interracial marriage apart in *Japanese War Bride*; and the no-nonsense gambler running the town in *Outlaw Women*. None of these were high-profile fare, but since she got to strut her stuff it hardly mattered and this she did marvelously in *The Narrow Margin*, one of the tightest little second features of the early 1950s. As the gangster's moll, being protected from extermination by Charles MacGraw, she made for one tough dame. Back at Republic she was another nasty bundle of goods in *City That Never Sleeps*, betraying and therefore being killed by lover William Talman. After bottoming out in the cheese-classic *Cat Women of the Moon* and playing straight woman to a declining Abbott and Costello in *Abbott and Costello Meet the Mummy*, she scored big with *The Killing*, perhaps her most treacherous role, as the cheating wife of criminal Elijah Cook, Jr., who betrays him and ends up no better off than the rest of the unsavory cast. Since this was directed by Stanley Kubrick, it became Windsors most revived performance and one that is justifiably acclaimed to this day. Still she stayed in mostly second-rate fare and remained a reliable presence as she got older and the parts got smaller, with the latter-day Windsor showing up mostly in westerns, including *The Good Guys and the Bad Guys*, *Support Your Local Gunfighter*, and *Cahill U.S. Marshal*. She was last seen running a Hollywood Book shop in the dirt-cheap *Commando Squad*.

Screen: 1941: All-American Co-Ed; 1942: The Big Street; Smart Alecks; Eyes in the Night; 1943: Chatterbox; Three Hearts for

Julia; Pilot No. 5; 1947: Song of the Thin Man; The Hucksters; The Romance of Rosy Ridge; The Unfinished Dance; 1948: On an Island With You; The Three Musketeers; Force of Evil; 1949: The Beautiful Blonde From Bashful Bend; Outpost in Morocco; The Fighting Kentuckian; Hellfire; 1950: Dakota Lil; The Showdown; Double Deal; Frenchie; 1951: Little Big Horn; Two Dollar Bettor; Hurricane Island; 1952: Japanese War Bride; The Sniper; The Narrow Margin; Outlaw Women; The Jungle; 1953: The Tall Texan; City That Never Sleeps; Trouble Along the Way; The Eddie Cantor Story; So This Is Love; 1954: Cat Women of the Moon/Rocket to the Moon; Hell's Half Acre; The Bounty Hunter; Silver Star; 1955: Abbott and Costello Meet the Mummy; No Man's Lady; Swamp Women; 1956: Two Gun Woman; The Killing; 1957: The Unholy Wife; The Girl in Black Stockings; The Story of Mankind; The Parson and the Outlaw; 1958: Day of the Bad Man; Island Women; 1962: Paradise Alley; 1963: Critic's Choice; The Day Mars Invaded Earth; 1964: Mail Order Bride; Bedtime Story; 1966: Chamber of Horrors; 1969: The Good Guys and the Bad Guys; 1971: Support Your Local Gunfighter; One More Train to Rob; 1973: Cahill — U.S. Marshal; 1974: The Outfit; 1975: Hearts of the West; 1977: Freaky Friday; 1983: Lovely But Deadly; 1987: Commando Squad.

Select TV: 1954: For Value Received (sp); Live a Little (sp); 1955: Time Is Just a Place (sp); Tom and Jerry (sp); 1957: Hour of Glass (sp); 1959: The Salted Mine (sp); 1960: Johnny Come Lately (sp); 1970: Wild Women; 1974: Manhunter; 1979: Salem's Lot; 1985: J.O.E. and the Colonel; 1988: Supercarrier (series).

CHARLES WINNINGER

BORN: ATHENS, WI, MAY 26, 1884. DIED: JANUARY 27, 1969.

A cherubic, white-haired gentleman who often portrayed blustery dads, Charles Winninger had a terrible habit of overplaying his hand, pouring on the sentiment at times, miscalculating his intentions, and remaining far less likable or versatile than he seemed to think he was. Born into a family of vaudevillians, the Winninger Family Concert Company, he was soon joining them onstage before going legit in stock, then coming to Broadway in 1910. He did a few short films and, over the next 15 years, four silent features, but remained principally a stage actor, including roles in some George M. Cohan musicals and Ziegfeld revues. In 1927 he became a part of Broadway history when he created the role of Cap'n Andy in the original production of Jerome Kern and Oscar Hammerstein II's groundbreaking musical *Show Boat*, which was instrumental in reawakening Hollywood's interest in Winninger. He made his talkie debut, in 1930, in *Soup to Nuts*, and was soon afterwards seen as Bette Davis's wealthy dad in *Bad Sister*; the folksy family doctor in *Children of Dreams*; a photographer in *The Sin of Madelon Claudet*; the physician who helps Barbara Stanwyck become a *Night Nurse*; Laura La Plante's protective old man in *God's Gift to Women*; and the family patriarch charmed by Colleen Moore in *Social Register*. In 1936 he got to preserve his Cap'n Andy in the second screen version of *Show Boat*, but his weepy emoting was hardly one of its highlights. Now established as one of the movies' foremost roly-poly character men, he had the key role of the estranged poppa whom Deanna Durbin and her sisters hope to reunite with their mom (Nella Walker) in *Three Smart Girls*, one of the highest grossing pictures of 1936, and not one that has stood the test of time particularly well. In his dotty fool mode he was the doctor who told Carole Lombard she was going to die in

Nothing Sacred and a Manhattan millionaire agog over Mae West in *Every Day's a Holiday*, sporting the screwy name of Von Regible Van Pelter Van Doon III. In *Babes in Arms*, he was Mickey Rooney's self-pitying vaudevillian dad; the town drunk who gets appointed sheriff as a joke in *Destry Rides Again*; and a vaudevillian once again, in one of the lesser Bing Crosby vehicles, *If I Had My Way*. He was simply too obnoxious for words as the selfish father who makes Judy Garland's life miserable in *Little Nellie Kelly*, and, since MGM didn't see otherwise, he was again Garland's old man, in her poorest film, *Ziegfeld Girl*. Durbin got to play his offspring again, in two sequels, *Three Smart Girls Grow Up* and *Hers to Hold*, and he was head of the family that went to the *State Fair*, the character thankfully relegated to support, unlike it had been in the Will Rogers version. He did, however, get to follow in Rogers's footsteps once more, this time with top-billing, in director John Ford's personal favorite of his films, *The Sun Shines Bright*, a remake of *Judge Priest*, which made little impact at the time of its release. Winninger was last seen, if at all, most fittingly as St. Nick, in a cheapie that was barely distributed during the 1960s, *The Miracle of Santa's White Reindeer*.

Screen: 1916: A September Mourning; 1924: Pied Piper Malone; 1926: The Canadian; Summer Bachelors; 1930: Soup to Nuts; 1931: Flying High; The Bad Sister; The Sin of Madelon Claudet; Fighting Caravans; Children of Dreams; Night Nurse; God's Gift to Women; Gun Smoke; Husband's Holiday; 1934: Social Register; 1936: Show Boat; White Fang; Three Smart Girls; 1937: Woman Chases Man; Cafe Metropole; The Go-Getter; You're a Sweetheart; Nothing Sacred; You Can't Have Everything; Every Day's a Holiday; 1938: Hard to Get; Goodbye Broadway; 1939: Destry Rides Again; Three Smart Girls Grow Up; Babes in Arms; Barricade; 1940: Beyond Tomorrow; If I Had My Way; My Love Came Back; Little Nellie Kelly; 1941: The Get-Away; Ziegfeld Girl; My Life With Caroline; Pot o'Gold; 1942: Friendly Enemies; 1943: Coney Island; A Lady Takes a Chance; Hers to Hold; Flesh and Fantasy; 1944: Sunday Dinner for a Soldier; Broadway Rhythm; Belle of the Yukon; 1945: State Fair; She Wouldn't Say Yes; 1946: Lover Come Back; 1947: Living in a Big Way; Something in the Wind; 1948: The Inside Story; Give My Regards to Broadway; 1950: Father Is a Bachelor; 1953: The Sun Shines Bright; Torpedo Alley; Champ for a Day; A Perilous Journey; 1955: Las Vegas Shakedown; 1960: Raymie; 1963: The Miracle of Santa's White Reindeer.

NY Stage: 1910: The Yankee Girl; 1912: The Wall Street Girl; 1916: The Cohan Revue of 1916; 1918: The Cohan Revue of 1918; 1919: The Passing Show of 1919; 1920: Ziegfeld Follies; 1921: The Broadway Whirl; 1923: The Good Old Days; 1925: No, No, Nanette; 1926: Oh, Please!; 1927: Yes, Yes, Yvette; Show Boat; 1932: Through the Years; Show Boat (revival); 1934: Revenge With Music; 1951: Music In The Air.

Select TV: 1950: Call Me Mister (sp); 1954: The Whale on the Beach (sp); The Philadelphia Story (sp); 1955: His Maiden Voyage (sp); 1956: The Charles Farrell Show (series).

JONATHAN WINTERS

BORN: DAYTON, OH, NOVEMBER 11, 1925.
ED: KENYON COL.

An inspired comic with an uncanny knack for off-the-cuff improvisation, Jonathan Winters's style was tough to capture in the linear storytelling of motion pictures. In fact, the best of Winters was so good that anything below par seemed to be an awful waste of his talents, which was the best way to describe too much of his film career. He had been a disc jockey in his native city before coming to New York to appear in nightclubs and then on television guest spots, where he became a particular favorite on the *Tonight* show. He had his own short-lived variety show but seemed to fare better showing up for bits on other people's programs. In 1963 he made a most impressive big screen debut in the slapstick extravaganza *It's a Mad Mad Mad Mad World*, where his hapless trucker, who holds a grudge against slimy Phil Silvers, was a standout among the incredible cast of comedians. This was followed by two other good ones, the dark cult favorite *The Loved One*, in a dual role, as a pair of brothers carrying on a rivalry in the funeral business, and *The Russians Are Coming! The Russians Are Coming!*, in which he was delightful as Brian Keith's excitable deputy. Then the good fortune ran out, starting with a pointless cameo as a horny professor in *Penelope*; a similarly tacked-on part, as the late dad in question, in the ghastly adaptation of *Oh Dad, Poor Dad, Mama's Hung You in the Closet and I'm Feeling So Sad*; some desperate comic relief for a sub-par Bob Hope in *Eight on the Lam*; and a disappointing role as a Southern general, opposite Peter Ustinov, in a very mild farce, *Viva Max!* There had been two more variety series, some garbage bag commercials, and eventual treatment for manic-depression and alcoholism. He returned to the public eye, supporting fellow-ad-lib expert Robin Williams, who always cited Winters as his idol, in *Mork and Mindy*, and later down the line won an Emmy for a flop series, *Davis Rules*. Later movie roles seemed to indicate that producers still had no idea what to do with him, judging from *Moon Over Parador*, where he played a CIA man; *The Flintstones*, as a grizzled caveman; *The Shadow*, as a Police Commissioner; and *The Adventures of Rocky and Bullwinkle*, in which he had three different roles, none of which suggested in the slightest just how funny he could be. He published a collection of stories, *Winters Tales: Stories and Observations for the Unusual*, in 1987, and *Hang Ups*, a photo essay of his paintings, the following year.

Screen: 1961: Alakazam the Great (voice); 1963: It's a Mad Mad Mad Mad World; 1965: The Loved One; 1966: The Russians Are Coming! The Russians Are Coming!; Penelope; 1967: Oh Dad, Poor Dad, Mama's Hung You in the Closet and I'm Feeling So Sad; Eight on the Lam; 1969: Viva Max!; 1979: The Fish That Saved Pittsburgh; 1986: Say Yes; 1987: The Longshot; 1988: Moon Over Parador; 1994: The Flintstones; The Shadow; 1995: Arabian Knight (voice); 2000: The Adventures of Rocky and Bullwinkle.

NY Stage: 1954: John Murray Anderson's Almanac.

Select TV: 1955: And Here's the Show (series); 1956: NBC Comedy Hour (series); 1956–57: The Jonathan Winters Show (series); 1958: Masquerade Party (series); 1960: Babes in Toyland (sp); 1964–66: Linus the Lionhearted (series; voice); 1965–67: The Andy Williams Show (series); 1967–69: The Jonathan Winters Show (series); 1968: Now You See It, Now You Don't; 1970–71: The Andy Williams Show (series); Hot Dog (series); 1972–74: The Wacky World of Jonathan Winters (series); 1980: More Wild Wild West; 1981–82: Mork and Mindy (series); 1983–84: Hee-Haw (series); 1985: Alice in Wonderland; 1987: Jonathan Winters: On the Ledge (sp); 1988–89: The Completely Mental Misadventures of Ed Grimley (series; voice); 1990: Gravedale High (series; voice); 1991–92: Davis Rules (series); 1992: Fish Police (series; voice).

SHELLEY WINTERS

(SHIRLEY SCHRIFT) BORN: EAST ST. LOUIS, IL,
AUGUST 18, 1922. RAISED IN BROOKLYN, NY.
ED: WAYNE UNIV.

If there were any complaints to be made about Shelley Winters, it was her tendency to claw at a role in a big, big way, but who would be so foolish as to wish her to tone it down? She was a brassy, exciting screen presence, most at home playing vulgar women who were outspoken, pathetic, sadly screwed up, or just plain funny. After laboring in bits and extra work, she broke through into the frontlines and became a star and stayed a star, even when she was regularly relegated to the supporting position. Long before she became the earthy, overweight lady a whole generation pictured her as, she was svelte, sexy, and vampish, and started her career by modeling for the Ladies Garment Workers Union. For them she appeared in the hit revue *Pins and Needles*, and then, thanks to her role in *Rosalinda*, received an offer to come work for Columbia Pictures. Rather than give her real parts, they pretty much shoved her into the background, usually minus any upfront billing, in such movies as *What a Woman!*, and *Cover Girl*. As "Shelley Winter" she had a substantial part in a cheap-o UA adaptation of *Knickerbocker Holiday*, but then the assignments shrunk in size again until George Cukor chose her for the pivotal part of the waitress who gets Ronald Colman excited, not realizing he is a dangerous nutcase, in *A Double Life*. This made her perfect to play loose women, women on the wrong side of the law, doomed women, and women given the heave-ho by the men they love. She was Dan Duryea's moll, pining for an already-taken John Payne, in *The Gangster*; more molls in *Larceny* and *Johnny Stool Pigeon*; Myrtle, the garage mechanic's pitiable wife, struck down by a hit-and-run driver, in the 1949 version of *The Great Gatsby*; and William Powell's mistress, who ends up dead, in *Take One False Step*.

Universal finally gave her a starring role, in *South Sea Sinner*, a steamy melodrama that cast her as an island cabaret singer, being fought over by two decidedly uninteresting men, Macdonald Carey and Luther Adler. Staying in that mode, she was *Frenchie*, unwisely treading where Marlene Dietrich had gone, in this un-called for remake of *Destry Rides Again*; and a dancehall girl who snags hero James Stewart at the finale of *Winchester '73*, a popular western. She then wound up with a real prize role, over at Paramount, in their prestige production for 1951, *A Place in the Sun*. As the sad, whining factory girl who gets in the way of Montgomery Clift's path to success by getting pregnant, she managed to make this potentially annoying creature sympathetic and earned an Oscar nomination in the lead category. Released that same year were *He Ran All the Way*, playing yet another factory worker, one held hostage by John Garfield, in his final movie; *Behave Yourself!*, where she over-did it as Farley Granger's complaining wife; and *Meet Danny Wilson*, which found her nightclub singing yet again, though, in this instance it meant she got to duet on "A Good Man Is Hard to Find" with Frank Sinatra. There was very little box-office interest in such Universal programmers as *Untamed Frontier*, with Joseph Cotten, in which she played a waitress out west, or *Playgirl*, as Collen Miller's meddlesome sister, but she was widely seen in MGM's ensemble drama, *Executive Suite*, as Paul Douglas's mistress, and in the last Alan Ladd adventure to bring in a substantial audience, *Saskatchewan*, as a saloon gal on the run from the law. In Europe, she did *Mambo* with Vittorio Gassman, released shortly after her marriage to him (1952–54), and then got another great "victim" part, in director Charles Laughton's genuinely disturbing *The*

Night of the Hunter, as the foolish widow who invites psychotic preacher Robert Mitchum into her bed, thereby ending up at the bottom of a lake with her throat cut, in one of the more unforgettable and horrifying images of 1950s cinema.

In support, she was the German woman who backs out of marrying a Jew in *I Am a Camera*; and a sluttish actress who ends up dead in *The Big Knife*; then took over Ida Lupino's old part in another remake that nobody requested, *I Died a Thousand Times*, based on *High Sierra*. Going to Broadway she had a hit with *A Hatful of Rain*, married (1957–60) one of its leading men, Anthony Franciosa, but did not get to repeat her role in the movie version (Eva Marie Saint did it). Instead, she was the unreasonable Mrs. Van Daan, who selfishly makes being hidden in an attic away from the Nazis into her own personal dilemma, in *The Diary of Anne Frank*. Although it was hardly the standout performance in the ensemble, it seemed fitting to bestow Winters with an Oscar by this point, so she got one for it, in the supporting category. She got to rip into *Let No Man Write My Epitaph*, as the mother of slum youth James Darren, a territory she returned to for *The Young Savages*.

There was another pathetic lady, one attracted to an uncaring younger man, Ray Danton, in *The Chapman Report*, but prior to that she landed the role of a lifetime, playing the self-deluded, pitiable Charlotte Haze in *Lolita*, making her both grotesque and sad in her attempts to appear sexy to boarder and eventual spouse James Mason, who only has designs on her teenage daughter, Sue Lyon. Surprisingly she was not even in the running for an Oscar but, over the years, it became one of her most celebrated performances. It took a couple of whorehouses to put her back at the top of the cast list, as she was in both *The Balcony*, an artsy attempt to film the Jean Genet play, and the more blatantly trashy *A House Is Not a Home*, both of which failed whatever audiences they were looking for. For compensation she got another great part, in *A Patch of Blue*, in which she was positively frightening as one of cinema's true monster mothers, having blinded daughter Elizabeth Hartman in a drunken rage and atoning for it not one bit, a truly memorable portrayal of slovenly selfishness. It brought her a second Oscar for Best Supporting Actress.

Now entering her plump, matronly years, there was a run of good roles, with *Harper*, as a one-time movie actress; *Alfie*, taking the wind out of Michael Caine's sails, as a predatory American who beds him and then dumps him when she decides he's too old; *Enter Laughing*, as Rene Santoni's nervous, low-class Jewish mama; *The Scalphunters*, in comical high gear, as Telly Savalas's blowsy, lazy woman; and *Wild in the Streets*, as the mother of rock singer-President Christopher Jones, ending up in a prison camp and then finding solace in hallucinogenics. She was clearly having a good time in the kinky *Bloody Mama*, as the overbearing gang-leader Ma Barker; and did some lip-smacking emoting in a pair of "horror" tales, *What's the Matter With Helen?*, slowly cracking up in 1930s Hollywood after her son is jailed for murder, and *Whoever Slew Auntie Roo?*, a ludicrous re-thinking of Hansel and Gretel, as an unstable lady perceived as a witch by a pair of troublesome youngsters. There was a gigantic box-office success with *The Poseidon Adventure*, with Winters verging on the outrageous, as a hefty mama who happens to be a champion swimmer, a part that brought her another Oscar nomination. She was entering that stage where she went anywhere and everywhere for work, resulting in a lot of unseen films and questionable credits. Among those worth noting were *Cleopatra Jones*, in which she slugged it out with agent Tamara Dobson to campy effect, as a drug-lord named Mommy; the underrated *Next Stop, Greenwich Village*, as another overbearing Jewish mother, distressed to see son Lenny Baker moving into the big bad city; the Disney musical *Pete's Dragon*, as dirt-bag hillbilly intent on kidnapping the young hero; *King of the Gypsies*, as a weepy Gypsy mama; *The Magician of Lublin*, treating the cinematic world to a glimpse of her breasts; the chaotic satire *S.O.B.*, as a venal Hollywood agent with an interesting in bedding young women; the Chuck Norris adventure *The Delta Force*, as a hijacking victim; *Purple People Eater*, a cheesy kid's picture derived from an old pop record, in which she played a senior citizen facing eviction; the gloomy *An Unremarkable Life*, in a leading role, as Patricia Neal's interfering, insufferable sister; *Stepping Out*, as a sassy dance school pianist; and *Heavy*, as the mother of overweight Pruitt Taylor Vince. On television she won an Emmy Award for the drama *Two Is the Number*. There were two autobiographies, *Shelley, Also Known as Shirley* (1981) and *Shelley II: The Middle of My Century* (1989), both of which were said to play fast and loose with the facts and pour on the high drama for maximum impact, which seemed so fitting, given her personality. A play she had written in 1959, *Gestations of a Weather Man*, received some token workshops and performances over the years.

Screen: 1943: What a Woman!; 1944: Sailor's Holiday; She's a Soldier Too; Knickerbocker Holiday; Cover Girl; Together Again; 1945: Tonight and Every Night; A Thousand and One Nights; Dancing in Manhattan; Escape in the Fog; 1946: Two Smart People; 1947: Living in a Big Way; New Orleans; Killer McCoy; The Gangster; A Double Life; 1948: Red River; Larceny; Cry of the City; 1949: The Great Gatsby; Take One False Step; Johnny Stool Pigeon; 1950: South Sea Sinner; Winchester '73; Frenchie; 1951: A Place in the Sun; He Ran All the Way; Behave Yourself!; The Raging Tide; 1952: Phone Call From a Stranger; Meet Danny Wilson; Untamed Frontier; My Man and I; 1954: Executive Suite; Tennessee Champ; Saskatchewan; Playgirl; 1955: Mambo; The Night of the Hunter; I Am a Camera; The Big Knife; I Died a Thousand Times; The Treasure of Pancho Villa; 1956: Cash on Delivery/To Dorothy a Son (UK: 1954); 1959: The Diary of Anne Frank; Odds Against Tomorrow; 1960: Let No Man Write My Epitaph; 1961: The Young Savages; 1962: Lolita; The Chapman Report; 1963: The Balcony; Wives and Lovers; 1964: A House Is Not a Home; 1965: The Greatest Story Ever Told; A Patch of Blue; 1966: A Time of Indifference (It: 1964); Harper; Alfie; 1967: Enter Laughing; 1968: The Scalphunters; Wild in the Streets; Buona Sera, Mrs. Campbell; 1969: The Mad Room; Arthur! Arthur! (nUSr); 1970: How Do I Love Thee?; Bloody Mama; Flap; 1971: What's the Matter With Helen?; Whoever Slew Auntie Roo?; 1972: The Poseidon Adventure; 1973: Blume in Love; Cleopatra Jones; 1975: Poor Pretty Eddie/Redneck County; Diamonds; That Lucky Touch; 1976: Something to Hide/Shattered (UK: 1973); Next Stop, Greenwich Village; Journey Into Fear; The Tenant; 1977: Mimi Bluette: Fiore del Mio Giardino (nUSr); Gran Bolito/Black Journal (nUSr); The Three Sisters (taped in 1966); Tentacles; Un Borghese Piccolo Piccolo/A Very Little Man (nUSr); Pete's Dragon; 1978: King of the Gypsies; 1979: City on Fire; The Visitor; The Magician of Lublin; 1981: Looping (nUSr); S.O.B.; 1983: Fanny Hill (nUSr); 1984: Ellie; Over the Brooklyn Bridge; 1985: Déjà vu; Witchfire (and exec. prod.; dtv); 1986: The Delta Force; Very Close Quarters (dtv); 1987: Marilyn Monroe: Beyond the Legend; 1988: Hello Actors Studio; Purple People Eater; 1989: An Unremarkable Life; 1991: Superstar: The Life and Times of Andy Warhol; Touch of a Stranger (dtv); Stepping Out; 1993: The Pickle; 1994: The Silence of the Hams (dtv); 1995: Backfire (dtv); Jury Duty; Raging Angels (dtv); 1996: Heavy; The Portrait of a Lady; 1999: La Bomba (nUSr).

NY Stage: 1939: Pins and Needles; 1941: The Night Before Christmas; Meet The People; 1942: Rosalinda; 1947: Oklahoma!; 1955: A Hatful of Rain; 1956: Girls of Summer; 1962: The Night of the Iguana; 1963: Cages (ob); 1966: Under The Weather; 1970: Minnie's Boys; 1973: The Effect of Gamma Rays on Man-in-the-Moon Marigolds (ob).

Select TV: 1954: Mantrap (sp); Sorry, Wrong Number (sp); 1955: The Women (sp); 1957: A Double Life (sp); Inspired Alibi (sp); Smarty (sp); Beyond This Place (sp); Polka (sp); 1962: The Cake Baker (sp); The Way from Darkness (sp); 1964: Two Is the Number (sp); 1965: Back to Back (sp); 1971: Revenge; A Death of Innocence; 1972: The Adventures of Nick Carter; 1973: The Devil's Daughter; 1974: Big Rose: Double Trouble; The Sex Symbol; 1976: Frosty's Winter Wonderland (sp; voice); 1978: The Initiation of Sarah; 1979: Elvis; The French Atlantic Affair (ms); Rudolph and Frosty's Christmas in July (sp; voice); 1985: Alice in Wonderland; 1992: Weep No More My Lady; 1995: Mrs. Munck; 1999: Gideon.

ESTELLE WINWOOD

(ESTELLE GOODWIN) BORN: KENT, ENGLAND, JANUARY 24, 1883. DIED: JUNE 20, 1984.

An unforgettable, chicken-necked, wobble-voiced old crone, Estelle Winwood had been around the world of show business for decades before most audiences came to know her in her 70s, when she made her mark in a smattering of parts, as frail but defiantly crabby biddies. Trained at the Liverpool Repertory Company, she made her professional debut at age 16 on the eve of the turn of the century. In 1916 she first acted on the American stage and remained there principally, though she would return to England from time to time. It was in her native country that she signed on for her first movie, *The Night Angel*, in 1931, only to find herself edited from the finished print. Two years later she made her film debut proper in *The House of Trent*, a quota quickie, and then returned to the States where she did her sole U.S. movie during this period, *Quality Street*, as one of Katharine Hepburn's nosey neighbors. Nearly two decades had passed before she found herself back in front of the cameras, playing a version of the Fairy Godmother to Leslie Caron's Cinderella in MGM's *The Glass Slipper*. Realizing they had uncovered a truly eccentric presence, producers began finding small roles for her, which Winwood made count with every frame, including *The Swan*, as Grace Kelly's dotty aunt; *23 Paces to Baker Street*, as a barmaid; *This Happy Feeling*, as a flakey housekeeper in this Debbie Reynolds comedy; *The Misfits*, as a persistent church lady taking up a collection in a bar; *The Magic Sword*, appropriately cast as a witch; *The Notorious Landlady*, providing a daft climax as her wheelchair went rolling down the English coast; and *Camelot*, as Vanessa Redgrave's attendant. No doubt her best-known part was in a movie she herself thought little of, Mel Brooks's quotable comedy *The Producers*, offering her body to money-hungry Zero Mostel and uttering the phrase "Hold Me! Touch Me!" as only she could. She was last seen playing Elsa Lanchester's wheelchair-bound nurse in the spoof *Murder by Death*, and lived to the ripe old age of 101.

Screen: 1933: The House of Trent; 1937: Quality Street; 1955: The Glass Slipper; 1956: The Swan; 23 Paces to Baker Street; 1958: This Happy Feeling; Alive and Kicking; 1959: Darby O'Gill and the Little People; 1960: Sergeant Rutledge; 1961: The Misfits; 1962: The Magic Sword; The Notorious Landlady; The Cabinet of Caligari; 1964: Dead Ringer; 1967: Games; Camelot; 1968: The Producers; 1969: Jenny; 1976: Murder by Death.

NY Stage: 1916: Hush; 1917: A Successful Calamity; Why

Marry?; 1918: A Little Journey; 1919: Moliere; Too Many Husbands; 1921: The Tyranny of Love; The Circle; 1922: Madame Pierre; Go Easy Mabel; The Red Poppy; 1923: Anything Might Happen; Spring Cleaning; 1925: The Buccaneer; 1926: A Weak Woman; The Chief Thing; Beau-Strings; Head or Tail; 1927: Trelawney of the Wells; Fallen Angels; 1928: We Never Learn; The Furies; 1930: Scarlet Sister Mary; 1931: The Admirable Crichton; 1934: The Distaff Side; 1935: Eden End; 1936: I Want a Policeman!; 1938: The Merry Wives of Windsor (and prod.); Good Hunting; 1939: The Importance of Being Earnest; When We Are Married; 1940: Ladies in Retirement; 1944: Ten Little Indians; 1946: Lady Windermere's Fan; 1949: The Madwoman of Chaillot; 1950: Mrs. Warren's Profession; 1952: Mr. Pickwick; 1956: Speaking of Murder; 1959: Lute Song; 1966: Nathan Weinstein: Mystic, Connecticut.

Select TV: 1950: Masque (sp); 1952: Outward Bound (sp); 1953: Criminal at Large (sp); Miss Mabel (sp); 1954: Birthright (sp); A Bargain With God (sp); The Bat (sp); 1954: The Promise (sp); Tonight at 8:30 (sp); 1956: Adam and Evening (sp); 1957: The Conversation Table (sp); 1958: The Woman at High Hollow (sp); 1966: The People Trap (sp); 1969: Appalachian Autumn (sp).

JOSEPH WISEMAN

Born: Montreal, Quebec, Canada, May 15, 1918. ed: CCNY.

Although he preferred to think of himself as a man of the theatre, Joseph Wiseman also ended up in some fairly interesting movie projects as well, where his technique ranged from manically out-of-control to a more preferable quiet repose. Having made his Broadway debut, in 1938, among the vast cast of *Abe Lincoln in Illinois*, it was more than a decade before he made some kind of theatrical impact, with his hyper characterization of an arrested thief who causes havoc at a police station, in *Detective Story*. Following a role as a unionist in *With These Hands*, a quickie film made for the International Ladies Garment Workers Union, he was called on to repeat his stage part in Paramount's 1951 movie of *Detective Story*, where director William Wyler failed to tone down his shrill emoting, resulting in a singularly grotesque turn. Typed as a villain, he was an eager revolutionary in *Viva Zapata!*; Michael Rennie's fellow-convict in one of the remakes of *Les Misérables*; a racketeer in *Champ for a Day*; and had roles in two of the silliest of the 1950s Biblical spectacles, *The Silver Chalice*, as a rabble rouser and *The Prodigal*, as a con man. He was absolutely brilliant in his small but important role as the trouble-making preacher man in *The Unforgiven*, and showed up towards the end of the first James Bond epic, *Dr. No*, giving a certain grace and menace to the title character. It became perhaps the motion picture role most readily connected to his name, despite his relatively meager amount of on-screen time. In a similarly laid-back manner, he was the very gentlemanly Louis Minsky in *The Night They Raided Minsky's*, and, in another of his finest performances, Richard Dreyfus's aloof uncle, the only one who seems to be onto his nephew's selfish get-rich-quick schemes, in *The Apprenticeship of Duddy Kravitz*. In lesser projects he could be seen as Mafia men in *Stiletto* and *The Valachi Papers*; following in Orson Welles's footsteps, playing the Turkish police chief, in the little-seen remake of *Journey Into Fear*; and showing up as an automobile tycoon in the trashy *The Besty*.

Screen: 1950: With These Hands; 1951: Detective Story; 1952: Les Misérables; Viva Zapata!; 1953: Champ for a Day; 1954: The Silver Chalice; 1955: Melba (narrator); The Prodigal; 1957: The Garment Jungle; Three Brave Men; 1960: The Unforgiven; 1962:

The Happy Thieves; 1963: Dr. No; 1968: Bye Bye Braverman; The Night They Raided Minsky's; 1969: Stiletto; 1971: Lawman; 1972: The Valachi Papers; 1974: The Apprenticeship of Duddy Kravitz; 1975: Journey Into Fear; 1977: Homage to Chagall (narrator); 1978: The Betsy; 1979: Buck Rogers in the 25th Century (from tv); Jaguar Lives!

NY Stage: 1938: Abe Lincoln In Illinois; 1940: Journey to Jerusalem; 1941: Candle in the Wind; 1943: The Barber Has Two Sons; The Three Sisters; 1944: Storm Operation; 1946: Joan of Lorraine; 1947: Antony and Cleopatra; 1949: Detective Story; That Lady; 1950: King Lear; 1952: Golden Boy; 1955: The Lark; 1957: The Duchess of Malfi; 1964: Marco Millions; After the Fall; Incident At Vichy; 1969: In the Matter of J. Robert Oppenheimer; 1971: The Last Analysis; 1972: Enemies; 1976: Zalmen Or The Madness of God; 1978: The Lesson; 1986: Largo Desolato; 1989: The Tenth Man; 1994: Unfinished Stories; Slavs!: Thinking About the Longstanding Problems of Virtue and Happiness; 2001: Judgment at Nuremberg.

Select TV: 1954: Arrowsmith (sp); Death Takes a Holiday (sp); 1955: Billy Budd (sp); Darkness at Noon (sp); 1959: Lepke (sp); 1964: Carol for Another Christmas (sp); 1967: The Outsider; 1970: The Mask of Sheba; 1972: Pursuit; 1974: QBVII (ms); Men of the Dragon; 1975: Zalmen: Or the Madness of God (sp); 1977: Murder at the World Series; 1981: Masada (ms); 1983: Rage of Angels; 1984: Ghost Writer; 1986: Seize the Day; Crime Story (series); 1988: Lady Mobster.

JANE WITHERS

Born: Atlanta, GA, April 12, 1926.

As if 20th Century-Fox didn't have enough cash pouring in from moppet superstar Shirley Temple, they added the feistier Jane Withers to the payroll for those who wanted a kid act with a little less saccharine. Apparently a wizard at performing before she was five years old, she was soon doing impersonations and songs on local stages and on radio, where she ended up with her own show. Heading to Hollywood, she did a bit part in Fox's *Handle With Care*, in 1932, which brought her to the attention of director David Butler who needed a hellion to go one-on-one with Temple in *Bright Eyes*. Withers, as an uproariously spoiled brat, essentially stole the show and Fox decided to showcase her in her own vehicles, starting with *Ginger*, in which she played a street-wise slum kid opposite minor child luminary Jackie Searl. Unlike the Temple films, these pictures were kept closer to a "B" budget, with running times averaging a little over an hour. There followed such titles as *Paddy O'Day*, which required her to speak with an Irish accent; *Gentle Julia*, not in the title role, since her fans didn't want her gentle; *Little Miss Nobody*, in which she raised hell at a foundling home; the aptly named *The Holy Terror*, as a Naval mascot; and *Keep Smiling*, at one point sending up cutesy boy singer Bobby Breen. Getting her first screen kiss, in *Boy Friend*, from George Ernest, meant she was growing up, while assigning her to support the Ritz Brothers in *Pack Up Your Troubles* and Gene Autry in *Shooting High*, meant she was losing her solo box-office clout. In 1941 Withers herself (using the pseudonym "Jerrie Walters") supplied the storyline for *Small Town Deb*, having a sibling rivalry with snooty Cobina Wright, Jr., but it wasn't a hit so she left Fox the next year. Having married a millionaire in 1947, she had no reason to work but did return to acting nine years later to play a lively, vulgar Texas lady of wealth in the classic epic *Giant*. Although there were only two other movie appearances (including *Captain Newman, M.D.*, where she played a nurse), she did several television roles and, in that medium, played the character latter-day audiences would best remember her for — Josephine the Plumber, on a long-running series of Comet sink cleanser ads.

Screen: 1932: Handle With Care; 1933: Zoo in Budapest; 1934: It's a Gift; Imitation of Life; Bright Eyes; 1935: Ginger; The Good Fairy; The Farmer Takes a Wife; This Is the Life; Paddy O'Day; 1936: Gentle Julia; Little Miss Nobody; Pepper; Can This Be Dixie?; 1937: The Holy Terror; Angel's Holiday; Wild and Woolly; 45 Fathers; Checkers; 1938: Rascals; Keep Smiling; Always in Trouble; The Arizona Wildcat; 1939: Boy Friend; Pack Up Your Troubles; Chicken Wagon Family; 1940: Shooting High; High School; Youth Will Be Served; Girl from Avenue A; 1941: Golden Hoofs; A Very Young Lady; Her First Beau; Small Town Deb; 1942: Young America; Johnny Doughboy; The Mad Martindales; 1943: The North Star; 1944: My Best Gal; Faces in the Fog; 1946: Affairs of Geraldine; 1947: Danger Street; 1956: Giant; 1961: The Right Approach; 1963: Captain Newman, M.D.

Select TV: 1959: The Pink Burro (sp); 1975: All Together Now; 1999–2001: Mickey Mouse Works (series; voice); 2001: Hunchback of Notre Dame II (voice).

ANNA MAY WONG

(WONG LIU TSONG) BORN: LOS ANGELES, CA, JANUARY 3, 1905. DIED: FEBRUARY 2, 1961.

Although her roles seldom rose above the stereotype of the exotic Eastern ladies of mystery, Anna May Wong found her place in the Hollywood history books simply by being the first Asian American actress to find something akin to stardom at a time when there were few such possibilities for non-Caucasians. As a youngster she found work as a bit player, starting with the 1919 Nazimova film, *The Red Lantern*. Two years later she received billing as the wife of Lon Chaney in *Bits of Life*, then showed up in the first un-official Technicolor film, *The Toll of the Sea*, where she drowned herself. Remaining in secondary parts, she was Tiger Lily in *Peter Pan*; more suitably cast as Chaney's daughter in *Mr. Wu*; and one of the Chinese people being given a hard time by villain Warner Oland in *Old San Francisco*. Knowing she had little chance for advancement in America, she moved temporarily to Europe, in 1928, and found herself readily employed both onstage and screen, principally in England where she starred in the film *The Flame of Love*, as a Russian dancer. Her Broadway role in *On the Spot* revitalized Hollywood interest in her, so she returned there in 1931 to play the evil daughter of Fu Manchu, played by Oland, in *Daughter of the Dragon*, then stabbed to death that same actor in her best-known movie, *Shanghai Express*, in which she was clearly in support of Marlene Dietrich. After some further British film roles, she appeared for Paramount in *Limehouse Blues*, jealously in love with an unconvincing Chinese-American George Raft; and then had top-billing in four "B" pictures: *Daughter of Shangai*, in which she tried to destroy the smugglers who killed her father; *Dangerous to Know* (adapted from *On the Spot*), as mistress to gangster Akim Tamiroff; *King of Chinatown*, in a most interesting role, as a doctor hoping to form a Red Cross unit, and whose kindness inspires Tamiroff to go straight; and *Island of Lost Men*, in which she tried to clear her father's name. In each of the last three of these films, it is worth noting that the none-too-creative writers gave her "Ling" as a last name. Of course, World War II erased her from her position of prominence and she ended up working for the poverty row company PRC Studios. In the 1950s she was seen mostly on television and returned to features after a

long absence, in support of Lana Turner in *Portrait in Black*, which was released shortly before her death.

Screen: 1919: The Red Lantern; 1920: Dinty; 1921: The First Born; Shame; Bits of Life; 1922: The Toll of the Sea; 1923: Thundering Dawn; Drifting; 1924: The 40th Door (serial); Lilies of the Field; The Thief of Bagdad; The Alaskan; Peter Pan; 1925: Forty Winks; 1926: Fifth Avenue; A Trip to Chinatown; The Desert's Toll; The Dragon Horse/The Silk Bouquet; 1927: Driven from Home; Mr. Wu; Old San Francisco; The Chinese Parrot; Streets of Shanghai; The Devil Dancer; 1928: The Crimson City; Chinatown Charlie; Across to Singapore; Song (nUSr); 1929: The City Butterfly (nUSr); Piccadilly; 1930: Elstree Calling; The Flame of Love; 1931: Daughter of the Dragon; 1932: Shanghai Express; 1933: A Study in Scarlet; 1934: Tiger Bay; Chu Chin Chow; Java Head; Limehouse Blues; 1937: Daughter of Shanghai; 1938: Dangerous to Know; When Were You Born?; 1939: King of Chinatown; Island of Lost Men; 1941: Ellery Queen's Penthouse Mystery; 1942: Bombs Over Burma; Lady from Chungking; 1949: Impact; 1960: The Savage Innocents; Portrait in Black.

NY Stage: 1930: On the Spot.

Select TV: 1951: The Gallery of Madame Liu-Tsong (series); 1956: The Letter (sp); The Chinese Game (sp); 1959: The Voodoo Factor (sp).

NATALIE WOOD

(NATASHA GURDIN) BORN: SAN FRANCISCO, CA, JULY 20, 1938. DIED: NOVEMBER 29, 1981.

Natalie Wood was such a curious paradox. Her persona, that of the high school cheerleader who was everybody's friend, rounded out with a dash of the bad girl eager to sow her oats, could evoke acres of good wishes from many a moviegoer, not to mention her industry peers, few of whom had anything bad to say about her. Her actually legacy as an actress is less of a sure thing. In a career cut far too short, there were certainly a number of admirable performances but enough miscalculations strewn along the way to suggest less than met the eye. When she was all of five years old, her mother schemed to have her interact with Hollywood director Irving Pichel, who was on location in their town to shoot *Happy Land*. Pichel was so enchanted by the child that he gave her a fleeting bit in the film, as a youngster dropping her ice cream cone. Sure that her offspring had a career in movies, Natalie's mom upped the family and relocated to Los Angeles, where she used their minor connection to the director to secure further work. Renamed "Natalie Wood," the child very quickly began getting parts, starting over at RKO where she was Orson Welles's adopted kid, a grieving war orphan, in a popular soaper, *Tomorrow is Forever*. At Fox she did the most famous role of her childhood years, Susan Walker, the youngster who very firmly does *not* believe in Santa Claus until Edmund Gwenn convinces her otherwise, in the instant classic *Miracle on 34th Street*. She clearly registered a cut above the standard kiddy thespian and had she given up acting before adulthood her work in that picture would still have given her some sort of cinematic immortality. It did not, however, make her a star attraction at the time, as she pretty much stuck to playing the children or little sisters of leading players. Among her assignments were playing the daughters of Gene Tierney, in *The Ghost and Mrs. Muir*; Celeste Holm, in *Chicken Every Sunday*; Walter Brennan, in *The Green Promise*; Fred MacMurray, in *Father Was a Fullback* and *Never a Dull Moment*; Jane Wyatt, in *Our Very Own*; Margaret Sullavan, in *No Sad Songs for Me*; James Stewart, in *The Jackpot*; Joan Blondell, in *The Blue Veil*; Bing

Crosby, in *Just for You*; and Bette Davis, in *The Star*.

Her leap up to another level of fame came with *Rebel Without a Cause*, one of the seminal films of the 1950s. In it, she starred as the very angry high schooler who finds romance with equally troubled James Dean. Her very dedicated performance was proof enough that she had graduated from mere kid to serious actress and it brought her an Oscar nomination in the supporting category and further work from its studio, Warner Bros. It was followed by another important role, in director John Ford's complex western *The Searchers*, as the white girl kidnapped and raised by the Indians. She was required to be petulant and uncooperative, characteristics she often had no trouble projecting, despite her personality being quite the opposite. A quartet of Warners vehicles, including *The Burning Hills* and *The Girl He Left Behind*, did absolutely nothing for her career but she did carry a big, much-hyped film, *Marjorie Morningstar*, based on the smash best-seller by Herman Wouk. As an ambitious Jewish girl trying to make it as an actress, she was game but far from galvanizing, and it was only too fitting that her character ultimately discovered that she wasn't as accomplished a thespian as she had thought all along. She struggled with a French accent for *Kings Go Forth*, as the object of desire of both Frank Sinatra and Tony Curtis; then did two glossy soaps, *Cash McCall*, and *All the Fine Young Cannibals*, the latter of which had the distinction of being her sole big-screen appearance opposite Robert Wagner to whom she was married twice (1957–63; and then again from 1972 until her death). In 1961 she soared to the top with two of the major releases of the year. In *West Side Story*, she landed the coveted role of Maria, the Hispanic Juliet whose love for her Caucasian Romeo, Richard Beymer, causes dissension between their warring gangs. Despite her singing voice being dubbed, she created a strong enough impression that few complained about the casting. The film won the Academy Award for Best Picture of the year, was acclaimed as one of the screen's finest musicals, earned a fortune, and became her best loved role. She herself was up for the Oscar trophy for *Splendor in the Grass*, ambitiously portraying a small town girl whose love for Warren Beatty eventually leads to a nervous breakdown. It, too, was popular and another feather in her cap.

There was a second musical, *Gypsy*, this time singing for herself, though none too impressively, as the girl who grew up to be the most famous stripper of them all, Gypsy Rose Lee. This was followed by perhaps her best work, in *Love With the Proper Stranger*, as the working class girl who wants very badly for Steve McQueen to make the right decision about their relationship when she discovers she is pregnant. It brought her a third Oscar nomination. She followed it with a pair of comedies both featuring Tony Curtis: *Sex and the Single Girl*, which, like her broad performance, was all too typical of its era, and the far more enjoyable *The Great Race*, in period costume, as a feminist reporter. She then stumbled badly with *Inside Daisy Clover*, as an ordinary young lady from the sticks who becomes an overnight star, an action in no way believable in light of her amateurish performance. Even worse was *This Property Is Condemned*, as a Southern girl trying to escape her trashy past. Finally, *Penelope* displayed a very shrill comedic technique on her part, with Wood as a supposedly kooky thief. After a three-year absence she returned to the cinema with a bang in *Bob & Carol & Ted & Alice*, playing a character who wants to do some extra-marital swinging, with the cooperation of husband Robert Culp. This smart satire brought her a lot of press for making the transition to the freer cinema of the late 1960s and it became one of the highest grossing films of the decade. Oddly she did not follow it up immediately, thereby losing what position in the industry she had regained.

Instead, during the 1970s, she mainly stuck to television, doing remakes of *Cat on a Hot Tin Roof* and *From Here to Eternity*, neither of which managed to erase memories of the earlier versions. On the big screen there was an end-of-the-world disaster, *Meteor*, and a smarmy sex comedy, *The Last Married Couple in America*, that wasted an opportunity to play off of George Segal. While making the sci-fi drama *Brainstorm*, she drowned under mysterious circumstances off Catalina Island, causing the film to be completed with a double. The shock this tragic demise sent through the industry confirmed that Wood was a much beloved figure. Her daughter is actress Natasha Gregson Wagner.

Screen: AS NATASHA GURDIN: 1943: Happy Land.

AS NATALIE WOOD: 1946: Tomorrow Is Forever; The Bride Wore Boots; 1947: Miracle on 34th Street; The Ghost and Mrs. Muir; Driftwood; 1948: Scudda Hoo! Scudda Hay!; Chicken Every Sunday; 1949: The Green Promise; Father Was a Fullback; 1950: Our Very Own; No Sad Songs for Me; The Jackpot; Never a Dull Moment; 1951: Dear Brat; The Blue Veil; 1952: Just for You; The Rose Bowl Story; The Star; 1954: The Silver Chalice; 1955: One Desire; Rebel Without a Cause; 1956: The Searchers; The Burning Hills; A Cry in the Night; The Girl He Left Behind; 1957: Bombers B-52; 1958: Marjorie Morningstar; Kings Go Forth; 1959: Cash McCall; 1960: All the Fine Young Cannibals; 1961: Splendor in the Grass; West Side Story; 1962: Gypsy; 1963: Love With the Proper Stranger; 1964: Sex and the Single Girl; 1965: The Great Race; Inside Daisy Clover; 1966: This Property Is Condemned; Penelope; 1969: Bob & Carol & Ted & Alice; 1972: The Candidate; 1975: Peeper; 1976: James Dean: The First American Teenager; 1979: Meteor; 1980: The Last Married Couple in America; Willie and Phil; 1983: Brainstorm.

Select TV: 1952: Playmates (sp); 1953–54: Pride of the Family/ The Paul Hartman Show (series); 1954: The Plot Against Miss Pomeroy (sp); I'm a Fool (sp); 1955: The Wild Bunch (sp); Too Old for Dolls (sp); Heidi (sp); Miracle at Potter's Farm (sp); Feathertop (sp); 1958: Girl on the Subway (sp); 1973: The Affair; 1976: Cat on a Hot Tin Roof; 1979: From Here to Eternity (ms); The Cracker Factory; Hart to Hart (AS NATASHA GURDIN); 1980: The Memory of Eva Ryker.

JOANNE WOODWARD

BORN: THOMASVILLE, GA, FEBRUARY 27, 1930. ED: LSU.

Rather than making her endure the customary Hollywood sex appeal build up, producers seemed to be aware right off the bat that Joanne Woodward was a lady who could act and allowed her to do so. Intelligent, determined, engagingly unique, with a heartbreaking crackle to her voice, she got an impressive number of opportunities to shine, making her one of the outstanding actresses of her generation. As luck would have it she married one of the top stars in the business, which brought her much public attention and fame without having the burden of being a box-office attraction herself. Having acted while in college, she went north to study in New York at two of its most prestigious training grounds, the Neighborhood Playhouse and the Actors' Studio. There were some live television appearances and a job as an understudy in the Broadway hit *Picnic*, which featured Paul Newman among its cast members. After that it was back to the small screen, where her role in a *Ford Star Playhouse* presentation of *Interlude* brought her to the attention of Fox executive Buddy Adler, who put her under contract in 1955. The studio did not utilize her immediately and, instead, loaned her out to Columbia for the western *Count Three and Pray*, where she was cast as a hillbilly hellraiser (with a butch haircut) who eventually makes herself more lady-like, and then to United Artists for *A Kiss Before Dying*, a fine adaptation of the Ira Levin novel, in which she was the poor college girl whose pregnancy drives psycho Robert Wagner to murder. Fox finally launched their new employee with a bang, allowing her to play a painfully shy woman suffering from a split personality, in *The Three Faces of Eve*. The movie was basically a series of therapy sessions with Dr. Lee J. Cobb, but Woodward made the transition from meek lamb to flirtatious bad girl quite convincing and earned raves. It brought her the Academy Award for Best Actress of 1957. A few weeks prior to the Oscar ceremony she and Newman wed.

Rather than follow-up this triumph with another vehicle, she did an ensemble piece, *No Down Payment*, as a trampy suburban housewife; and then her first theatrical feature with Newman, *The Long Hot Summer*, as a frigid woman melted by his wastrel charms. They were one show business couple who acted off of one another beautifully, though their choice of material was not always inspired. This was certainly the case with *Rally 'Round the Flag, Boys!*, a frenetic comedy in which they both seemed properly embarrassed. She was Yul Brynner's bastard child in Hollywood's interpretation of Faulkner's unfilmmable *The Sound and the Fury*; did a bit of over-emoting as a trashy Southern drunk in *The Fugitive Kind*, in support of Marlon Brando and Anna Magnani; and was the shrew who drives Newman into Ina Balin's arms in *From the Terrace*, a lush and over-long soap opera that was reasonably popular in its day. A fourth with Newman, *Paris Blues*, was much less attended but probably their smoothest teaming so far, a low-keyed romance set in the world of jazz. She finally did get a project sold on her name, an adaptation of William Inge's *A Loss of Roses*, that, for box-office insurance, was renamed *The Stripper*, which made it sound a lot more lurid than it was, for there was never an instance when this classiest of actresses would ever lend her name to a project that was in anyway genuinely beneath her talents. After her Fox tenure, she went to Warner Brothers for two unusual offerings that deserved to do better: *A Fine Madness*, enduring husband Sean Connery's philandering and off-the-wall behavior; and the lighthearted western *A Big Hand for a Little Lady*, as a gentle pioneer filling in for ailing spouse Henry Fonda in a big stakes poker game.

With Newman behind the camera, she got herself a real tour de force showcase with *Rachel, Rachel*, a sad and all too truthful tale of a drab, small-town teacher whose loveless existence she hopes to put an end to when a former schoolmate (James Olsen) returns to town. Her stunningly good performance was self-reflective and touching without every lapsing into self pity and she earned an Oscar nomination, received the finest reviews of her career, and found herself in a surprise moneymaker to boot. More ordinary, but equally popular, was *Winning*, a racing tale that reflected Newman's love of the track, but another teaming, in *WUSA*, in which she appeared as a world-wearied hooker, found little interest from the general public. Sadly, the refreshingly quirky *They Might Be Giants* had little success either, with Woodward as a frumpy psychiatrist named Dr. Watson, who blossoms while treating a nutcase (George C. Scott), who believes himself to be Sherlock Holmes. She and Scott made for a most engaging pair and it ranked among her finest performances. Another Newman-directed vehicle, *The Effect of Gamma Rays on Man-in-the-Moon Marigolds*, found her excelling as a coarse, eccentric, and destructive single mother, in a movie as unrelentingly honest and sad in its own way as *Rachel, Rachel* had been, though its unruly and off-putting title may have contributed in some way to why the customers failed to show. No luckier in finding an audience was another worthy character study, *Summer Wishes, Winter*

Dreams, with Woodward, again, simply marvelous as a New York wife and mother trying to cope with a life that refuses to be easy. The latter at least brought her attention from her peers, bringing her another Oscar mention.

She was very much in support of her husband in *The Drowning Pool*, as an ex-girlfriend, after which she got tired of waiting for good parts in motion pictures and began making herself a familiar face on television, where she was treated with more respect. Among the many projects she did in that medium, there were two that brought her Emmy Awards: *See How She Runs*, and *Do You Remember Love?* Between these she could be seen on the big screen as Burt Reynolds's estranged wife in *The End*, and then, once again, as a former love interest of Newman's, in his failed effort as director-star-producer-writer, *Harry and Son*. Figuring it was time for Newman to coach her through another meaty role, the husband-and-wife duo teamed to record her stage performance of Amanda Wingfield in *The Glass Menagerie*. It was a purposefully stageband movie, released by a very minor distributor, but a fine documentation of Woodward giving another of her impressive performances. In 1990 she and Newman finally acted side-by-side again in roles of equal size and importance with *Mr. and Mrs. Bridge*, where she was quite moving and pitiable as a well-to-do wife and mother who doesn't realize she is being suffocated by her regimented lifestyle. It brought her a fourth Oscar nomination. Overall, television audiences continued to have the better opportunities to experience her still luminous capabilities, in such films as *Blind Spot* (which she produced) and *Breathing Lessons*, though she did get some nice moments to shine back on the big screen, as the mother of dying Tom Hanks in *Philadelphia*, which at least was widely seen. On television she also won another Emmy as co-producer of the 1990 special, *The Legacy of the Group Theatre*. Also in that medium she directed episodes of the series *Family* and the *American Playhouse Presentation* of *Come Along With Me* (1981).

Screen: **1955:** Count Three and Pray; **1956:** A Kiss Before Dying; **1957:** The Three Faces of Eve; No Down Payment; **1958:** The Long Hot Summer; Rally 'Round the Flag, Boys!; **1959:** The Sound and the Fury; The Fugitive Kind; **1960:** From the Terrace; **1961:** Paris Blues; **1963:** The Stripper; A New Kind of Love; **1964:** Signpost to Murder; **1966:** A Fine Madness; A Big Hand for the Little Lady; **1968:** Rachel, Rachel; **1969:** Winning; **1970:** King: A Filmed Record…Montgomery to Memphis; WUSA; **1971:** They Might Be Giants; **1972:** The Effect of Gamma Rays on Man-in-the-Moon Marigolds; **1973:** Summer Wishes, Winter Dreams; **1975:** The Drowning Pool; **1978:** The End; **1984:** Harry and Son; **1987:** The Glass Menagerie; **1990:** Mr. and Mrs. Bridge; **1993:** The Age of Innocence (narrator); Philadelphia; **2000:** My Knees Were Jumping: Remembering the Kindertransports (narrator).

NY Stage: **1953:** Picnic; **1954:** The Lovers; **1964:** Baby Want a Kiss; **1981:** Candida.

Select TV: **1952:** Penny (sp); **1953:** Young Lady of Property (sp); The Young and the Fair (sp); **1954:** The Dancers (sp); Stir Mugs (sp); Unequal Contest (sp); Interlude (sp); Five Star Final (sp); Segment (sp); Welcome Home (sp); Homecoming (sp); **1955:** Dark Stranger (sp); Cynara (sp); Full Circle (sp); The Late George Apley (sp); White Gloves (sp); The Eleven O'Clock Flight (sp); **1956:** Prologue to Glory; Family Protection (sp); Watch the Sunset (sp); Starfish (sp); The Girl in Chapter One (sp); A Man's World (sp); **1958:** The 80 Yard Run (sp); **1971:** All the Way Home (sp); **1977:** Sybil; Come Back, Little Sheba; **1978:** See How She Runs; A Christmas to Remember; **1979:** Streets of L.A.; **1980:** The Shadow Box; **1981:** Crisis at Central High; **1984:** Passions; **1985:** Do You Remember Love?; **1993:** Foreign Affairs; Blind Spot (and prod.); **1994:** Breathing Lessons.

MONTY WOOLLEY

(EDGAR MONTILLION WOOLLEY) BORN: NEW YORK, NY, AUGUST 17, 1888. ED: HARVARD, YALE. DIED: MAY 6, 1963.

Before Clifton Webb arrived on the scene, the bearded, cultured, and enjoyably snobby Monty Woolley personified the movies' idea of the discreetly gay, mannered, know-it-all, whose tongue cut like a razor those for whom he felt a superior disdain. Born into a comfortable lifestyle, he was schooled at both Harvard and Yale, ending up at the latter as an assistant professor of drama where he befriended songwriter Cole Porter. In the early 1930s he became a Broadway director of such shows as *The Second Little Show*, *America's Sweetheart*, and *Jubilee*, and one of the great wits and socialites of Manhattan's theater scene. Hollywood was pretty sure he'd make a colorful addition to the character player roster and he arrived there in 1936, eventually playing an art dealer in MGM's *Live, Love and Learn*, and one of Carol Lombard's doctors in Selznick's *Nothing Sacred*. Remaining in fairly unspectacular parts for the time being, he was the governor in *The Girl of the Golden West*; a frustrated backer in *Everybody Sing*; Margaret Sullavan's physician in *Three Comrades*; a psychiatrist in *Young Dr. Kildare*; and a judge in *Midnight*. In 1939 the playwriting team of Kaufman and Hart needed someone properly acerbic to embody their interpretation of bitchy drama critic Alexander Woolcott (here called "Sheridan Whiteside") and found the perfect actor in Woolley, who made *The Man Who Came to Dinner* the role of his career. Warners engaged him to repeat the part on film, making him a motion picture star. Despite giving higher billing to contractees Bette Davis and Ann Sheridan, it was really Woolley's show all the way, as he spat out insults and put downs from his wheelchair, aiming them at lackeys and suck-ups with equal venom. It would have been, in truth, a much less memorable experience without him.

Because of the movie's success, Fox put him into his own vehicles, starting with *The Pied Piper*, which was not much more than a variation on Whiteside, but a more pleasing motion picture overall. Woolley was a crusty old English gent (no accent needed, in so much as the American born performer always sounded as if he were from the U.K.), who reluctantly agrees to aide some wartime children, including Roddy McDowall and Peggy Ann Garner. They, in turn, to no one's surprise melted his heart. Woolley made it all acceptable and perfect entertainment for the home-front audiences, earning an Oscar nomination in the process. The studio then cast him as a washed-up thespian in *Life Begins at Eight-Thirty*, which allowed him, at one point, to hit the booze and don a shabby Santa Claus costume, as was fitting for the movies' most famous white-bearded actor. In *Holy Matrimony*, he was a crabby old painter who arrives in England in the guise of his late valet, a comedy that gave him an opportunity to pair up with Britain's beloved Gracie Fields, a duet that paid off nicely enough for an encore, *Molly and Me*, two years later. In between, he was the grumpy boarder whom Claudette Colbert and family take in during the war years in the epic hit *Since You Went Away*, a role that brought him an another Oscar mention, this time in the supporting category. Despite his advancing years he was called on to play his younger self in the silly Cole Porter biopic *Night and Day*, where his rendition of "Miss Otis Regrets" was one of the film's better moments. He returned to Fox in 1951 to star in a mild comedy, *As Young as You Feel*, as a senior executive forced to retire. After a non-descript appearance in *Kismet* (the Middle Eastern setting required beards, after all) and some television, including a reprise of *The Man*

Who Came to Dinner, he retired to Florida.

Screen: 1936: Ladies in Love; 1937: Live, Love and Learn; Nothing Sacred; 1938: Arsene Lupin Returns; The Girl of the Golden West; Everybody Sing; Three Comrades; Lord Jeff; Artists and Models Abroad; Young Dr. Kildare; Vacation from Love; 1939: Never Say Die; Midnight; Zaza; Man About Town; Honeymoon in Bali; Dancing Co-Ed; 1941: The Man Who Came to Dinner; 1942: The Pied Piper; Life Begins at Eight-Thirty; 1943: Holy Matrimony; 1944: Since You Went Away; Irish Eyes Are Smiling; 1945: Molly and Me; 1946: Night and Day; 1947: The Bishop's Wife; 1948: Miss Tatlock's Millions; 1951: As Young as You Feel; 1955: Kismet.

NY Stage: 1936: On Your Toes; 1938: Knights of Song; 1939: The Man Who Came To Dinner.

Select TV: 1954: The Man Who Came to Dinner (sp); The Christmas Story Hour (sp); 1956: Eloise (sp).

FAY WRAY

BORN: CARDSTON, ALBERTA, CANADA, SEPTEMBER 15, 1907. RAISED IN AZ, UT, SO. CA.

Alluringly pretty, undeniably appealing, and clearly talented, Fay Wray effortlessly made the transition from silence to sound and became one of the busiest ladies of that shaky period in movie history. Her lasting immortality, however, all came down to a rendezvous with a big ape and the fact that, unlike her male co-stars in that classic film, her name made one giggle because it rhymed. Having come from a family that migrated here and there, she ended up in Hollywood, where she was spotted in a high school play and was signed to appear in a short called "Gasoline Love," in 1923. For some reason, she was envisioned as the perfect western heroine and wound up in several horse operas, including *Wild Horse Stampede* and *Lazy Lighting*. Her big chance to advance beyond this genre came when Erich von Stroheim chose her to play his love interest in one of his ambitious directorial efforts, *The Wedding March*. As the poor innocent girl who falls in love with a self-indulgent prince (von Stroheim) who romances her and then dumps her to marry for money, Wray was heartbreakingly good. Only the first half of the intended, four hour work wound up being completed and shown in America (the remainder of it showed up in Europe, as *The Honeymoon*) but it was a critical triumph for the actress nonetheless. Because of it she ended up under contract to Paramount, who paired her with Gary Cooper in *Legion of the Condemned*, an aviation drama that attempted to repeat the success of *Wings* but didn't. Nor did she and Cooper fare any better in *The First Kiss* and *The Texan*, despite the studio's better efforts to sell them as *the* romantic duo of the day.

Wray continued to look attractive as the lady within the male-dominated storylines of several pictures with Richard Arlen: *The Four Feathers*, as the wife who believes he is a coward; the hit *Thunderbolt*, as the moll of gangster George Bancroft; *The Border Legion*, and *The Conquering Horde*, both taking her back to western territory; and *The Sea God*, in which she was rescued from cannibals. Wray then freelanced at various studios, doing Columbia's expensive Frank Capra adventure *Dirigible*, as the patient wife of flyer Ralph Graves; Goldwyn's *The Unholy Garden*, as the girl who captures the heart of thief Ronald Colman; and two Technicolor horror movies for Warners, in both of which she screamed as Lionel Atwill menaced, *Doctor X*, and *Mystery of the Wax Museum*. She went over to RKO where she and Joel McCrea were on the run from deranged Leslie Banks in the screen's best adaptation of *The Most Dangerous Game*, which was produced by Merian C. Cooper and directed by Ernest B. Schoedsack. Both of these men reteamed for an even more ambitious project in which Wray would encounter thrills and chills she'd never before imagined. The resulting adventure, *King Kong*, became, of course, one of the genuine classics of cinema, a rip-roaring, outrageous combination of state-of-the-art special effects, action, and surprising emotion. Wray screamed and screamed in wide-eyed terror, as anyone would expect of a person who is being lusted after by a gorilla the size of an apartment building. The movie, a smash in its day, continued to find loyal audiences from generation to generation, making the actress very famous, even to those who never realized this was just one of her many movie credits.

Of course, nothing would bring her to these heights again, but she still stayed quite active throughout the 1930s with *Ann Carver's Profession*, as a lawyer in a quickly forgotten drama notable because it was written by Robert Riskin, who would become important in her life; *One Sunday Afternoon*, as the small town girl dentist Gary Cooper pines for in this very weak bit of nostalgia; *The Bowery*, as a poor girl being fought over by Wallace Beery and George Raft, in one of the most enjoyably uncouth of all the pre-Code movies of the era; *The Countess of Monte Cristo*, as a bit player pretending to be the title character; *Viva Villa!*, as the doomed object of Wallace Beery's lust; and *Affairs of Cellini*, as the girl who wins philandering duke Frank Morgan. In 1935 she went over to England to do a handful of films, including *Bulldog Jack* and *The Clairvoyant*, then returned to mostly "B" work in Hollywood, in a batch of Columbia cheapies, the titles of which left little to the imagination: *They Met in a Taxi*, *It Happened in Hollywood*, and *Murder in Greenwich Village*. In 1942 she married Riskin, marking her second marriage to a writer, having been wed to John Monk Saunders from 1928 to 1939. Wray retired to concentrate on her new marriage and remained so occupied until returning to movies in 1953 with the Fox adventure *Treasure of the Golden Condor*, two years before Riskin passed away. As a fairly non-descript character actress, she supported Joan Crawford in *Queen Bee* and Alan Ladd in *Hell on Frisco Bay*, then appeared to represent the older generation in some films geared towards the teenage market: *Rock, Pretty Baby*; *Summer Love*; and *Dragstrip Riot*. After a third marriage, she retired once again though she did pop up in a secondary role in a Henry Fonda telefilm, *Gideon's Trumpet*, and was always available for tributes to that mighty gorilla, who took her to the observation deck of the Empire State Building the hard way. In 1989 she published her autobiography, *On the Other Hand*.

Screen: 1925: The Coast Patrol; A Cinch for the Gander; 1926: Wild Horse Stampede; Lazy Lightning; Don't Shoot; The Man in the Saddle; 1927: Loco Luck; A One Man Game; Spurs and Saddles; 1928: The Wedding March; Legion of the Condemned; The Streets of Sin; The First Kiss; The Honeymoon (nUSr); 1929: The Four Feathers; Pointed Heels; Thunderbolt; 1930: Behind the Make-Up; The Border Legion; Captain Thunder; Paramount on Parade; The Sea God; The Texan; 1931: The Finger Points; The Conquering Horde; Three Rogues/Not Exactly Gentlemen; Dirigible; The Lawyer's Secret; The Unholy Garden; 1932: Stowaway; Doctor X; The Most Dangerous Game; 1933: The Vampire Bat; Mystery of the Wax Museum; King Kong; Below the Sea; Ann Carver's Profession; The Woman I Stole; The Big Brain; One Sunday Afternoon; Shanghai Madness; The Bowery; Master of Men; 1934: Madame Spy; Once to Every Woman; The Countess of Monte Cristo; Viva Villa!; Affairs of Cellini; Black Moon; The Richest Girl in the World; Cheating Cheaters; Woman in the Dark; 1935: Bulldog Jack/Alias Bulldog Drummond; Come Out of the Pantry; Mills of the Gods; White Lies; The Clairvoyant; 1936: Roaming Lady; When Knights Were Bold; They Met in a Taxi; 1937: It Happened in Hollywood/Once a Hero; Murder in Greenwich Village; 1938: The Jury's Secret; 1939: Smashing the Spy Ring; Navy Secrets; 1940: Wildcat Bus; 1941: Adam Had Four Sons; Melody for Three; 1942: Not a Ladies' Man; 1953: Treasure of the Golden Condor; Small Town Girl; 1955: The Cobweb; Queen Bee; Hell on Frisco Bay; 1956: Rock, Pretty Baby; 1957: Crime of Passion; Tammy and the Bachelor; 1958: Summer Love; Dragstrip Riot; 1998: Off the Menu: The Last Days of Chasen's.

NY Stage: 1931: Nikki; Mr. Big; 1941: Golden Wings.

Select TV: 1953–54: The Pride of the Family (series); 1955: My Son Is Gone (sp); 1956: It's Always Sunday (sp); Times Like These (sp); Exit Laughing (sp); 1957: The Iron Horse (sp); 1958: Eddie (sp); 1959: The Second Happiest Day (sp); 1961: Money and the Minister (sp); 1980: Gideon's Trumpet.

TERESA WRIGHT

(MURIEL TERESA WRIGHT) BORN: NEW YORK, NY, OCTOBER 27, 1918.

Certainly one of the outstanding additions to the movie scene during the 1940s, Teresa Wright was adept at her craft from the word "go," playing ladies who were larger in spirit than her small stature suggested. Her sad eyes and the aching vulnerability in her voice made her ideal for enduring any hardship the screenwriters threw her way. As the years passed she dropped in and out of sight, with only a smattering of big-screen roles in her senior years, suggesting the waste of the fine character player she'd become. Having excelled in her school plays, she joined the Wharf Theatre in Provincetown, Massachusetts for two summers, before seeking jobs in New York. She auditioned to understudy Martha Scott in the original Broadway production of *Our Town*, playing a smaller role until the time came to take over the star spot when Scott was summoned to Hollywood. After touring with the show, she won a role in the original cast of *Life with Father*, which went on to become the longest running non-musical in Broadway history. Its tremendous success brought a lot of attention to Wright and it was during the show's run that producer Samuel Goldwyn's talent scouts spotted her, signing her to a contract with the intention of launching her as a bright new discovery in the prestigious 1941 film adaptation of Lillian Hellman's *The Little Foxes*. In so much as her role, as the kindly daughter of the unscrupulous Regina, was greatly built up from the play, it was a relief that she was worthy of the shifted emphasis, holding her own against Bette Davis at her most venomous. To assure Goldwyn that she'd been a good investment, she earned an Oscar nomination.

All of Hollywood was eager to utilize her and MGM purchased her services for their much-trumpeted tribute to the British homefront, *Mrs. Miniver*. She was the very charming young lady who marries the Miniver son, Richard Ney, only to become one of the causalities of the war. All of this played very effectively in 1942 and this film became a major box-office smash and the recipient of a batch of Oscars, including Best Picture and one for Wright in the supporting category, despite an uncertain attempt at a British accent. As if this wasn't enough acclaim, she was also up for the trophy in the lead category, playing the supportive wife of Yankee great Lou Gehrig (Gary Cooper) in the equally popular *The Pride of the Yankees*, reacting to the news of her husband's impending death with much dignity and love. With three Oscar mentions for her first three films, Wright was on top of the world and managed to stay there when Universal and Alfred Hitchcock borrowed her to play the small-town heroine who slowly becomes disillusioned with the realization that her bon vivant uncle, Joseph Cotten, is a killer on the run, in the excellent *Shadow of a Doubt*. Back with Cooper she continued her run of moneymakers with *Casanova Brown*, a very lackluster comedy, in which he kidnapped the baby she put up for adoption. Wright then joined the ensemble of the most widely attended movie of the immediate postwar era, *The Best Years of Our Lives*. As the perky daughter of returning vet Fredric March, she showed a greater level of depth than the part suggested, especially in her romance with troubled Dana Andrews; the end result was one of her finest performances. In addition to its tremendous financial success, the movie became Wright's second Academy Award-winning film for Best Picture. From there she did a Warners western, *Pursued*, a dark tale of a woman who marries the man who killed her brother with the intention of revenge. It was written by Niven Busch, whom she had married in 1942.

Two mild comedies for Paramount, *The Imperfect Lady* and *The Trouble with Women*, indicated that she was losing ground, as did her last for Goldwyn, *Enchantment*, which did not have the importance of her previous offerings for the company. There was another one penned by her husband, *The Capture*, which had certain similarities to their earlier collaboration, in so much as the plot involved Lew Ayres marrying Wright after killing her husband. It failed and the couple divorced in 1952. Wright did have a good part in the meantime, in *The Men*, as the wife who must cope with the physical and psychological trauma suffered by her paralyzed war vet husband, Marlon Brando, in his movie debut. She took a backseat to Ray Milland and Joan Fontaine as a pair of drinkers, in *Something to Live For*, and then to Spencer Tracy and Jean Simmons in the lovely, nostalgic *The Actress*. Playing Simmons's mom, she certainly bore a strong physical resemblance to that actress but seemed a tad too young in the part. Paramount gave her an important leading role in their adaptation of the red-hot bestseller *The Search for Bridey Murphy*, a supposedly true story that was later discredited. Playing a woman under hypnosis, who reveals a split personality as an Irish peasant, gave her a chance to strut her stuff, but the movie did not repeat the success of the property on which it was based. After playing the mom who is far too concerned over daughter Sandra Dee's virginity in the teen-oriented *The Restless Years*, she turned to television and stage. Among the movie roles she chose to accept over the next four decades were Simmons's mom, again, in *The Happy Ending*; one of the lonely customers at the New York dance club *Roseland*; Diane Keaton's mother in *The Good Mother*; and Matt Damon's landlady in *John Grisham's The Rainmaker*.

Screen: 1941: The Little Foxes; 1942: Mrs. Miniver; The Pride of the Yankees; 1943: Shadow of a Doubt; 1944: Casanova Brown; 1946: The Best Years of Our Lives; 1947: Pursued; The Imperfect Lady; The Trouble with Women (filmed 1945); 1948: Enchantment; 1950: The Capture; The Men; 1952: Something to Live For; California Conquest; The Steel Trap; 1953: The Actress; Count the Hours; 1954: Track of the Cat; 1956: The Search for Bridey Murphy; 1957: Escapade in Japan; 1958: The Restless Years; 1969: Hail, Hero!; The Happy Ending; 1977: Roseland; 1980: Somewhere in Time; 1988: The Good Mother; 1997: John Grisham's The Rainmaker.

NY Stage: 1938: Our Town; 1939: Life With Father; 1957: The Dark at the Top of the Stairs; 1968: I Never Sang For My Father; 1969: Who's Happy Now? (ob); 1975: Death of a Salesman; Ah, Wilderness!; 1980: Morning's at Seven; 1991: On Borrowed Time.

Select TV: 1952: The Sound of Waves Breaking (sp); Dress in the Window (sp); Alicia (sp); 1954: The Happiest Day (sp); The End of Paul Dane (sp); 1955: The Good Sisters (sp); Love Is Eternal (sp); Red Gulch (sp); Lady in the Wind (sp); The Devil's Disciple (sp); Miracle on 34th Street (sp); 1956: Number Five Checked Out (sp); Once to Every Woman (sp); The Lonely Ones (sp); The Faithful Heart (sp); Child of the Regiment (sp); 1957: The Miracle Worker (sp); Sister Louise Goes to Town (sp); Edge of Innocence (sp); 1959: Trap of the Stranger (sp); The Hours Before Dawn (sp); 1960: The Margaret Bourke-White Story (sp); 1961: Intermezzo (sp); 1962: The Big Laugh (sp); 1967: Desperate Hours (sp); 1969: Appalachian Autumn (sp); 1972: Crawlspace; 1974: The Elevator; 1975: Flood!; 1980: The Golden Honeymoon (sp); 1983: Bill: On His Own; 1990: Perry Mason: The Case of the Paris Paradox; 1991: Lethal Innocence; The Fig Tree (sp).

JANE WYATT

BORN: CAMPGAW, NJ, AUGUST 12, 1911.

A warmly inviting lady with a gentle, cultured voice, Jane Wyatt never became a real star in the more than 25 films she made prior to her television career, so it was up to the latter medium to give her the part most folks most readily identify her with. Having done understudy work, she made her Broadway debut, in 1931, in *Give Me Yesterday*. Following some more, less-than-popular theater assignments she was given a contract by Universal for whom she debuted in 1934, as Diana Wynyard's sister, in *One More River*. Next up she did the studio's uninspired version of *Great Expectations*, as Estella, and then had her own vehicle, *The Luckiest Girl in the World*, proving to dad Edward Arnold that she can live in Manhattan on a meager savings. It did not bring her any sort of fame, but her next assignment turned out to be her best-known film, Columbia's lavish and haunting *Lost Horizon*, in which she was lovely as the denizen of Shangri-La who is instrumental in coaxing outsider Ronald Colman into staying on and forsaking the real world. Instead of cashing in on that movie's success, she went back to the stage and lost some momentum where the studios were concerned. On returning to Hollywood, much of her work was in "B" programmers, like *Girl from God's Country*, *Weekend for Three*, and *Army Surgeon*. There were, however, some "A"-line productions, including *None But the Lonely Heart*, as one of the bright spots in Cary Grant's slum life; *Gentleman's Agreement*; as Dorothy McGuire's bigoted sister; *Boomerang!*, as the understanding wife of attorney Dana Andrews; *Task Force*, as Gary Cooper's loyal spouse; and *Our Very Own*, as the mom who must comfort daughter Ann Blyth when the latter finds out she's been adopted. She stretched her acting capabilities by playing a murderous socialite in *The Man Who Cheated Himself*, but folks liked her best when she was being sweet, as proven by her role as the all-American 1950s mom in the long-running sitcom *Father Knows Best*. It brought her three Emmy Awards and became her signature part. She did not do a great deal outside of television after it went off the air, though she did show up in cinemas as Maureen O'Sullivan's friend in *Never Too Late*, and as Leonard Nimoy's pointy-eared mom in *Star Trek IV: The Voyage Home*, repeating a role she'd done earlier on the sci-fi series.

Screen: 1934: One More River; Great Expectations; 1936: We're Only Human; The Luckiest Girl in the World; 1937: Lost Horizon; 1940: Girl from God's Country; 1941: Hurricane Smith/Double Identity; Weekend for Three; Kisses for Breakfast; 1942: The Navy Comes Through; Army Surgeon; 1943: Buckskin Frontier; The Kansan; 1944: None But the Lonely Heart; 1946:

Strange Conquest; The Bachelor's Daughters; **1947:** Boomerang!; Gentleman's Agreement; **1948:** Pitfall; No Minor Vices; **1949:** Bad Boy; Canadian Pacific; Task Force; **1950:** House by the River; My Blue Heaven; Our Very Own; The Man Who Cheated Himself; **1951:** Criminal Lawyer; **1957:** Interlude; **1961:** Two Little Bears; **1965:** Never Too Late; **1976:** Treasure of Matecumbe; **1986:** Star Trek IV: The Voyage Home.

NY Stage: 1931: Give Me Yesterday; **1932:** The Fatal Alibi; Dinner at Eight; The Mad Hopes; **1933:** Evensong; Conquest; For Services Rendered; **1934:** The Joyous Season; Lost Horizons; **1935:** The Bishop Misbehaves; **1938:** Save Me the Waltz; **1940:** Night Music; Quiet Please!; **1945:** Hope for the Best; **1951:** The Autumn Garden.

Select TV: 1950: Kitty Foyle (sp); **1952:** Lovers and Friends (sp); A Southern Lady (sp); Protect Her Honor (sp); **1953:** The Walsh Girls (sp); To Love and to Cherish (sp); **1954–60:** Father Knows Best (series); **1955:** Daisy Daisy (sp); **1958:** The Laughing Willow (sp); **1961:** The Wingless Victory (sp); **1964:** See How They Run; **1966:** When Hell Froze (sp); **1968:** My Father and My Mother (sp); **1970:** Weekend of Terror; **1971:** Neighbors (sp); **1973:** You'll Never See Me Again; Tom Sawyer; **1975:** Katherine; **1976:** Amelia Earhart; **1977:** The Father Knows Best Reunion (sp); Father Knows Best: Home for Christmas (sp); **1978:** Superdome; A Love Affair: The Eleanor and Lou Gehrig Story; The Nativity; The Millionaire; **1982:** Missing Children: A Mother's Story; **1989:** Amityville 4: The Evil Escapes; **1995:** Simisola.

JANE WYMAN
(Sarah Jane Fulks) Born: St. Joseph, MO, January 4, 1914.

The versatility of Jane Wyman was evident right there on her face, one that, with wide, searching eyes and its seemingly passive immobility, could suggest a stern, thick-skinned lady and then, in a blink, a warm and vulnerable one. She was good at playing either type and, once she got past all the years of waiting and slogging it out in bits and "B's," proved to be right up there with the best of the golden era's suffering heroines. She had trained as a dancer while a youngster, but couldn't break into that side of the business when she first made the rounds. Instead, she ended up as a radio singer before returning to dance, joining the Le Roy Prinz troupe. Without billing, she showed up in several films in the chorus, ranging from Goldwyn's *The Kid from Spain* to several at Paramount, including *Rumba* and *Anything Goes*, though whether she is visible in any of these is questionable. Taking the last name of her first husband, whom she'd divorce when still in her teens, she became "Jane Wyman" and went for some screen tests. Warner Bros. put her under contract and she first showed up from them as a chorus girl auditioning for Dick Powell in *Stage Struck*. Between doing similar parts in other Warners musicals, she got billing in a "B," *Smart Blonde*, a "Torchy Blane" mystery in which she was a hat check girl at Addison Richards's nightclub. She was a secretary who helps guide the radio career of crooner Kenny Baker in *Mr. Dodds Takes the Air*, and then got top billing in an hour-long quickie, *Public Wedding*, in which she and William Hopper got married inside of a fake amusement park whale. The studio decided they liked her in their second-string programmers and she did such titles as *He Couldn't Say No*, "he" being a wimpy Frank McHugh, who forfeited Wyman for Diana Lewis; *Private Detective*, in the title role, although she gladly gave up the sleuthing profession for marriage in the end, this being the 1930s; *Torchy Plays With Dynamite*, this time upped to playing Torchy

herself when Glenda Farrell went elsewhere; and *Kid Nightingale*, as the girlfriend of boxer John Payne.

While doing these films, she appeared as the blonde chasing after cadet Ronald Reagan in a bright comedy, *Brother Rat*, catching him in real life and marrying him in 1940 (they divorced in 1948). As a result, they were reteamed for the sequel, *Brother Rat and a Baby*; *An Angel from Texas*, as a team of married promoters; and *Tugboat Annie Sails Again*, supporting Marjorie Rambeau, who was given the thankless task of taking over the title role from the late, great Marie Dressler. The studio still had no intention of bettering Wyman's lot, but kept her busy with *Flight Angels*, as a stewardess; *My Love Came Back*, in which she and Olivia de Havilland took violin lessons; *Bad Men of Missouri*, a western she particularly hated doing; *You're in the Army Now*, a dopey slapstick comedy notable because her kiss with Regis Toomey made the record books for length; and *The Body Disappears*, in which she, as did some of the other cast members, turned invisible. Up to the higher budget bracket, she was the daughter of parolee Edward G. Robinson in a fun comedy, *Larceny, Inc.*, where she found herself in love with luggage salesman Jack Carson. With Carson she was also in *Princess O'Rourke*, as Olivia de Havilland's best buddy; *The Doughgirls*, as the pin-headed member of a man hungry quartet; the all-star *Hollywood Canteen*, as herself; and *Make York Own Bed*, a flop comedy which she and Carson carried, as a pair of detectives posing as domestics. As was often the case when contractees found themselves stagnating on their home lot, it took two loan-outs to bring her into the stars' circle. For Paramount she was Ray Milland's level headed girlfriend, coping valiantly with his drinking problem, in the 1945 Oscar-winner, *The Lost Weekend*, while at MGM she was Claude Jarman, Jr.'s stern swamp-country maw in the classic boy-and-his-deer drama *The Yearling*, a part that brought her an Oscar nomination.

Warners, in the meantime, was at least allowing her to show off her vocal abilities in the Cole Porter biopic *Night and Day*, but after a quickly forgotten western, *Cheyenne*, the studio suddenly realized it was time to give her the respect she so obviously deserved. What they gave her was the lead role in one of the most challenging of all their productions of the 1940s, *Johnny Belinda*. In it she played Belinda, a scruffy, sad, and simple deaf mute who is raped, gives birth and then murders the child's father. It was a beautifully executed and tasteful rendering of difficult material, and went on to become one of the highest grossing movies of the year. Wyman was deeply moving, having to convey her trauma, confusion, and loving nature without a single word of dialogue. She won a well-deserved Academy Award, one of those happy times when a performer's crowning achievement is the one the Academy recognizes. Curiously, her follow-up movies were a pair of tired comedies: *A Kiss in the Dark*, which wasted an opportunity to play off of David Niven, and *The Lady Takes a Sailor*, in which the sailor was Dennis Morgan. More interesting were *Stage Fright*, in which she played the drab heroine of this much maligned but quite acceptable Hitchcock melodrama, and *The Glass Menagerie*, a bowdlerized version of the Tennessee Williams masterpiece, although her own interpretation of Laura was quite lovely indeed. For Paramount she teamed with Bing Crosby in one of his money-making vehicles, *Here Comes the Groom*, the highlight of which was their duet of the Oscar-winning "In the Cool, Cool, Cool of the Evening," resulting in an immediate follow-up teaming, *Just for You*. In between these she did a decent soap opera at RKO, *The Blue Veil*, as a nanny who gave up her own happiness to take care of others' children. Allowing her to age and suffer in a tight-lipped manner over a course of 30 years, the film gave audiences the cry they sought and brought Wyman another Oscar nomination.

There was a very typical biopic wife role in *The Story of Will Rogers*, where the famed humorist was played by his real-life son; and a pair of remakes, *Let's Do It Again*, which was *The Awful Truth* with music, and *So Big*, an epic tale of Texas, though not epic enough to be shot in color. It marked the official end of her Warners contract. At Universal she had a big fat box-office hit with another remake, *Magnificent Obsession*, as the woman accidentally blinded by selfish Rock Hudson. Wyman played the part with stoic dignity and got Oscar nomination number four. To satisfy a public clamoring for more of the same, she and Hudson did a follow-up, *All That Heaven Allows*, in which their age difference was emphasized. Both were the sort of glossy melodramas that screamed "1950s!" and were not the kind of movies to pass the scrutiny of a later, more cynical era, though some schoalrs tried to make a cock-eyed, subversive auteur out of the director responsible for both, Douglas Sirk. More pleasant was a soap that Wyman did back at Warners, *Miracle in the Rain*, as a lonely secretary who loses her grip on life when she loses Van Johnson to the war. Surprisingly, she chose to do television at this point, hosting her own anthology series and essentially putting an end to her position as a star attraction. She returned to the screen to play Clifton Webb's wife in *Holiday for Lovers*, and then in two for Disney, the very good *Pollyanna*, top-billed as Hayley Mills loveless aunt, and the dreary *Bon Voyage!*, as Fred MacMurray's spouse. Her theatrical motion picture career ended with a lame Bob Hope comedy, *How to Commit Marriage*, but there was one final triumphant act when she ended up heading the cast of a popular prime time soap, *Falcon Crest*. During its run her ex-husband, Ronald Reagan, had made it to the White House, but since Wyman had long before surpassed him in achievements, it would be safe to conclude that she had no regrets.

Screen: AS SARAH JANE FULKS: **1932:** The Kid from Spain; **1933:** Elmer the Great; **1934:** All the King's Horses; College Rhythm; **1935:** Rumba; Stolen Harmony; **1936:** King of Burlesque; Polo Joe; My Man Godfrey; Here Comes Carter; Bengal Tiger; Anything Goes. AS JANE WYMAN: Stage Struck; Cain and Mabel; Gold Diggers of 1937; **1937:** Smart Blonde; The King and the Chorus Girl; Ready, Willing and Able; Slim; The Singing Marine; Mr. Dodd Takes the Air; Public Wedding; **1938:** The Spy Ring; Fools for Scandal; He Couldn't Say No; Wide Open Faces; The Crowd Roars; Brother Rat; **1939:** Tail Spin; Private Detective; The Kid from Kokomo; Torchy Plays With Dynamite; Kid Nightingale; **1940:** Brother Rat and a Baby; An Angel from Texas; Flight Angels; My Love Came Back; Tugboat Annie Sails Again; Gambling on the High Seas; **1941:** Honeymoon for Three; Bad Men of Missouri; You're in the Army Now; The Body Disappears; **1942:** Larceny, Inc.; My Favorite Spy; Footlight Serenade; **1943:** Princess O'Rourke; **1944:** Make Your Own Bed; Crime by Night; The Doughgirls; Hollywood Canteen; **1945:** The Lost Weekend; **1946:** One More Tomorrow; Night and Day; The Yearling; **1947:** Cheyenne; Magic Town; **1948:** Johnny Belinda; **1949:** A Kiss in the Dark; The Lady Takes a Sailor; It's a Great Feeling; **1950:** Stage Fright; The Glass Menagerie; **1951:** Three Guys Named Mike; Here Comes the Groom; The Blue Veil; Starlift; **1952:** Just for You; The Story of Will Rogers; **1953:** Let's Do It Again; So Big; **1954:** Magnificent Obsession; **1955:** All That Heaven Allows; Lucy Gallant; **1956:** Miracle in the Rain; **1959:** Holiday for Lovers; **1960:** Pollyanna; **1962:** Bon Voyage!; **1969:** How to Commit Marriage; **1996:** Will Bill: Hollywood Maverick; **1998:** Off the Menu: The Last Days of Chasen's.

Select TV: **1955:** Amelia (sp); **1955–58:** Jane Wyman Presents the Fireside Theatre/Jane Wyman Theatre (series; and prod.); **1956:** Sound of Thunder (sp); **1957:** Summer Playhouse (series); **1959:** A Deadly Guest (sp); **1961:** Labor of Love (sp); **1971:** The Failing of Raymond; **1979:** The Incredible Journey of Dr. Meg Laurel; **1981–90:** Falcon Crest (series).

ED WYNN

(ISAIAH EDWIN LEOPOLD) BORN: PHILADELPHIA, PA, NOVEMBER 9, 1886. DIED: JUNE 19, 1966.

Happily billing himself as "the Perfect Fool," Ed Wynn was one of those comedians who flourished in nearly every avenue of entertainment, but whose fluttery, over-the-top mannerisms, giggly self-consciousness, and lisping, simple-minded shtick often came across as singularly grotesque and grating on the big screen. Starting in 1902, he traveled the country in a variety of vaudeville acts, including one with Hilda Keenan who became his first wife. In 1910 he made his legit New York debut in *The Deacon and the Lady*, then, three years later, made it to the Palace in an act called "The King's Jester." This was successful enough that he went on to the Ziegfeld Follies, in 1914 and 1915. He was becoming one of the most popular acts in the revue-musical field, even writing some of the productions in which he appeared, including *Ed Wynn's Carnival* and *The Perfect Fool*. As was the case with many New York stage performers of the 1920s, he was invited by Paramount Pictures to do a film at their Astoria Studios, the result of which was *Rubber Heels*, in which he was a detective on the trail of some jewel thieves. Wynn was not comfortable in the new medium and did not film again until sound had arrived, with Paramount buying the rights to his Broadway vehicle *Manhattan Mary*, and re-christening it *Follow the Leader*. Now audiences could hear his bellowing, nervous nitwit routines in their full volume, but there was more promise for a future in movies for his co-star, Ginger Rogers, than for the jittery comic. He did not do a follow-up vehicle until he'd made a splash on radio, playing Texaco's wacky fire chief, therefore prompting MGM to star him in a wretched comedy called *The Chief*. Not surprisingly he decided to stick with what was working, continuing to thrive on the airwaves and on the New York stage.

He brought his comedy to television in its early stages, with *The Ed Wynn Show*, earning two Emmy Awards in the process. A second phase of his career began through the help of his son Keenan Wynn, who was, by the 1950s, one of the busiest character players in Hollywood. The elder Wynn joined his offspring in the cast of the Universal drama *The Great Man*, and on television in the acclaimed *Playhouse 90* presentation of *Requiem for a Heavyweight*, showing a welcome restraint when playing it serious. This paved the way for character work in both the small and big screen, the latter finding him in two major late 1950s releases, *Marjorie Morningstar*, as Natalie Wood's beloved but vulgar uncle, and *The Diary of Anne Frank*, as the kindly Mr. Dussell, who shares the attic space with the Frank family. The latter was the sort of somber drama that made all its participants look good and, as was often the case when a performer known for one kind of genre ventures into another with competence, the Motion Picture Academy applauded Wynn with an Oscar nomination in the supporting category. From that point on he mainly restricted himself to family-type entertainment, including *Cinderfella*, as Jerry Lewis's dotty fairy godfather; and *Dear Brigitte*, as an old sea captain. Most everything else was done for the Disney studio, starting with *The Absent Minded Professor*, in which he reprised his fire chief character in a sequence with Keenan; continuing through *Babes in Toyland*, at his most infuriating as the befuddled toymaker; reaching a peak with

Mary Poppins, memorably floating in the air because his character couldn't stop laughing; and ending with the fantasy film, *The Gnome-Mobile*, in which he played the ancient gnome king, released the year after his death.

Screen: 1927: Rubber Heels; 1930: Follow the Leader; 1933: The Chief; 1943: Stage Door Canteen; 1951: Alice in Wonderland (voice); 1956: The Great Man; 1958: Marjorie Morningstar; 1959: The Diary of Anne Frank; 1960: Cinderfella; 1961: The Absent Minded Professor; Babes in Toyland; 1963: Son of Flubber; 1964: The Patsy; Mary Poppins; 1965: The Greatest Story Ever Told; Dear Brigitte; Those Calloways; That Darn Cat!; 1966: The Daydreamer (voice); 1967: The Gnome-Mobile.

NY Stage: 1910: The Deacon and The Lady; 1914: Ziegfeld Follies of 1914; 1915: Ziegfeld Follies of 1915; 1916: The Passing Show of 1916; 1917: Doing Our Bit; 1918: Over the Top; Sometime; 1919: Shubert Gaieties of 1919; 1920: Ed Wynn's Carnival (and wr.); 1921: The All-Star Idlers of 1921; The Perfect Fool (and wr.; songs); 1924: The Grab Bag (and wr.; prod.; songs); 1927: Manhattan Mary; 1930: Simple Simon (and wr.); 1931: The Laugh Parade (and wr.; prod.); 1937: Hooray for What!; 1940: Boys and Girls Together (and dir.; wr.; prod.); 1942: Laugh, Town, Laugh! (and wr.; prod.).

Select TV: 1949–50: The Ed Wynn Show (series); 1950–52: All Star Revue (series); 1956: Requiem for a Heavyweight (sp); 1957: The Great American Hoax (sp); On Borrowed Time (sp); 1958–59: The Ed Wynn Show (series); 1959: Meet Me in St. Louis (sp); Miracle at the Opera (sp); Miracle on 34th Street (sp); 1960: The Greatest Man Alive (sp); The Man in the Funny Suit (sp); 1964: For the Love of Willadean; Treasure in the Haunted House.

KEENAN WYNN

(Francis Xavier Aloysius Keenan Wynn)
Born: New York, NY, July 27, 1916.
Died: October 14, 1986.

Being the offspring of one of the more famous comedic performers of his day, Keenan Wynn wisely chose to enter show business as a serious actor, hoping to avoid comparisons with dad Ed Wynn, whose forte was blatant silliness. The younger Wynn had no trouble getting work, becoming one of the most steadily employed of all character players, fitting comfortably into nearly any kind of film, playing affable sidekicks, shifty schemers, con men, simpletons, sad sacks, and villains, both benign and deadly, with a sort of off-the-cuff brio that was sometimes broad but always easier to take than his old man's hard-sell approach. Show business was all around him, with not only his dad, but his mom and grandfather having also been stage actors. Keenan joined the profession, first by doing stunt work for Joan Crawford (!) in MGM's *Chained*, then by appearing with the Lakewood Players in Maine, with some radio work thrown in for good measure. In 1935 he made his Broadway debut in *Remember the Day*, which was followed by several other plays, including *Two for the Show* and *Johnny on the Spot*. An audition for MGM brought him a contract in 1942, and he was launched with the teensiest of roles, playing a sergeant in a Clark Gable-Lana Turner drama *Somewhere I'll Find You*, and a theatrical agent in *For Me and My Gal*. After playing a gangster in *Lost Angel*, he got his first notable supporting role, as Robert Walker's fellow-soldier in the hit *See Here, Private Hargrove*, a part he reprised in the sequel, *What Next, Private Hargrove?* With his work in these, as well as his drunk routine in *The Clock*, and his comedic pairings with Lucile Ball in both *Without Love* and *Easy to Wed* (playing the role Spencer Tracy

had done in the original version *Libeled Lady*), Wynn had clearly arrived as one of the studio's best second tier players.

MGM preferred the actor in a lighter vein, so they gave him a comical spot in the all-star *Ziegfeld Follies*, in which he lot his cool while trying to place a telephone call; *No Leave, No Love*, a D.O.A. musical-comedy in which he and Van Johnson were Marines in New York; *The Cockeyed Miracle*, as a ghost, making him the dad of Frank Morgan; *The Three Musketeers*, as Planchet; and, best of all *The Hucksters*, where he really hit the bull's-eye playing a second-rate and much-hated comedian. The studio also kept him on the sidelines in such musical fare as *Neptune's Daughter*, *Three Little Words*, and *The Belle of New York*; though he did get to play a dual role, American and British cousins, in *Royal Wedding*, and was allowed to warble a bit in *Annie Get Your Gun*, as a promoter, joining the principals in the show-stopping "There's No Business Like Show Business." In his shining moment in this genre, he and James Whitmore, as a pair of two-bit hoods, did a hilarious rendition of Cole Porter's "Brush Up Your Shakespeare" in the delightful adaptation of *Kiss Me Kate*. In a more serious mode, he helped Howard Keel find his lost kids in *Desperate Search*; stole the notices as a washed up boxer in *Holiday for Sinners*; and sported a deadly hook for a hand in the Civil War "B" *The Marauders*. Having ended his contract with MGM in 1955, his workload didn't let up in the least. In the "B" cult favorite *Shack Out on 101*, he was the owner of the title dive in question; *The Man in the Grey Flannel Suit* featured him as Gregory Peck's fellow soldier in the flashback sequences; in *Johnny Concho*, he was a parson who helps Frank Sinatra dispose of the bad guys; and *The Great Man*, in which he was a nasty media promoter, was notable because it also featured his dad. That same year, 1956, the two Wynns both scored in the famed *Playhouse 90* premiere, *Requiem for a Heavyweight*.

There was no let up on the desire to utilize Wynn, so he played one of Jane Russell's kidnappers in *The Fuzzy Pink Nightgown*; a Hollywood manager in *The Perfect Furlough*; the villain in Disney's *The Absent Minded Professor*, sharing the screen with dad again, in a sequence near the climax; an old sailor in *The Americanization of Emily*; and in one of his briefer but best-remembered roles, the no-nonsense Colonel "Bat" Guano, skeptical of "pre-verts" and reluctant to break into a Coca-Cola machine, in *Dr. Strangelove*. With a shaved-head (and his increasingly bushy moustache) he was Tony Curtis's loyal sidekick in the epic comedy *The Great Race*; and played the snarly bad-guy in the remake of *Stagecoach*. He was an informer who assists Lee Marvin in the ultra-cynical *Point Blank*; a grizzled old driver in John Wayne's *The War Wagon*; the bigoted politician who winds up turning black in the musical *Finian's Rainbow*; and the sheriff in the spaghetti western *Once Upon a Time in the West*. Starting in the 1970s and leading into the 1980s, he became one of those actors who was determined to pick up a paycheck and had no qualms about where he did his filming or what the work entailed, resulting in a lot of foreign titles and cheap-jack items whose release status is anybody's guess. Among the more high-profile assignments were *Cancel My Reservation* and *The Devil's Rain*, in both instances portraying a sheriff; Disney's *Herbie Rides Again*, reprising his *Absent Minded Professor* villain; the all-star *Nashville*, giving a touching performance as Shelley Duvall's uncle, waiting for his beloved wife to pass away; and *Best Friends*, as Burt Reynolds's dad. The same year that he appeared in *Black Moon Rising* and *Hyper Sapien*, he passed away, which was about the only thing that could interrupt his seemingly non-stop schedule. His autobiography was entitled, appropriately enough, *Ed Wynn's Son* (1959). He is the father of writer Tracy Keenan Wynn.

Screen: 1942: Somewhere I'll Find You; For Me and My Gal; Northwest Rangers; 1943: Lost Angel; 1944: See Here, Private Hargrove; Since You Went Away; Marriage Is a Private Affair; 1945: Without Love; The Clock; Between Two Women; Weekend at the Waldorf; What Next, Corporal Hargrove?; 1946: Ziegfeld Follies; Easy to Wed; The Thrill of Brazil; No Leave, No Love; The Cockeyed Miracle; 1947: The Hucksters; Song of the Thin Man; 1948: B.F.'s Daughter; The Three Musketeers; My Dear Secretary; 1949: Neptune's Daughter; That Midnight Kiss; 1950: Love That Brute; Annie Get Your Gun; Three Little Words; 1951: Royal Wedding; Angels in the Outfield; Kind Lady; Texas Carnival; It's a Big Country; 1952: Phone Call From a Stranger; The Belle of New York; Skirts Ahoy!; Fearless Fagan; Sky Full of Moon; Desperate Search; Holiday for Sinners; 1953: Battle Circus; Code Two; All the Brothers Were Valiant; Kiss Me Kate; 1954: The Long, Long Trailer; Men of the Fighting Lady; Tennessee Champ; 1955: The Marauders; The Glass Slipper; Running Wild; Shack Out on 101; 1956: The Man in the Gray Flannel Suit; Johnny Concho; The Naked Hills; 1957: The Great Man; Don't Go Near the Water; Joe Butterfly; The Fuzzy Pink Nightgown; 1958: The Deep Six; A Time to Love and a Time to Die; The Perfect Furlough; 1959: A Hole in the Head; That Kind of Woman; 1960: The Crowded Sky; 1961: The Absent Minded Professor; King of the Roaring 20's — The Story of Arnold Rothstein; 1962: Il Re di Poggioreale/Black City (nUSr); 1963: Pattern for Plunder/The Bay of Saint Michel/Operation Mermaid; Son of Flubber; 1964: Dr. Strangelove or: How I Learned to Stop Worrying and Love the Bomb; Man in the Middle; Honeymoon Hotel; Stage to Thunder Rock; The Patsy; Bikini Beach; The Americanization of Emily; Nightmare in the Sun; 1965: The Great Race; 1966: Promise Her Anything; Stagecoach; Around the World Under the Sea; Night of the Grizzly; 1967: Warning Shot; Run Like a Thief; Welcome to Hard Times; The War Wagon; 1968: Finian's Rainbow; Blood Holiday; Frame Up (nUSr); 1969: Mackenna's Gold; Smith!; The Monitors; Once Upon a Time in the West; Viva Max!; 80 Steps to Jonah; 1970: Loving; 1971: Pretty Maids All in a Row; The Animals/The Desperados; L'Uomo Dagli Occhi di Ghiaccio/The Man with Icy Eyes (nUSr); B.J. Presents/The Manipulator; 1972: Wild in the Sky/Black Jack; Cancel My Reservation; Spara, Gringo, Spara/Shoot, Gringo, Shoot/Longest Hunt (nUSr); The Mechanic; Snowball Express; 1973: Night Train to Terror (nUSr); 1974: Herbie Rides Again; The Internecine Project; 1975: The Legend of Earl Durrand; Nashville; The Man Who Would Not Die; A Woman for All Men; The Devil's Rain; Panhandle Caliber 38 (filmed 1972); 1976: He Is My Brother; High Velocity; The Killer Inside Me; The Shaggy D.A.; 1977: Orca; Kino, the Padre on Horseback/Mission to Glory (dtv); 1978: Coach; Piranha; Laserblast; Parts: The Clonus Horror; 1979: Hollywood Knight/Hard Knocks (filmed 1977); The Thoroughbreds/The Treasure Seekers/Jamaican Gold (dtv); Monster/The Toxic Horror (dtv); The Dark; Sunburn; The Glove; Touch of the Sun/No Secrets (dtv); 1980: Just Tell Me What You Want; 1982: The Last Unicorn (voice); Best Friends; 1983: Hysterical; Wavelength; 1985: Prime Risk; 1986: Black Moon Rising; Hyper Sapien.

NY Stage: 1935: Remember the Day; 1936: Black Widow; 1937: Hitch Your Wagon; 1938: The Star-Wagon; 1939: One for the Money; 1940: Two for the Show; 1941: The More the Merrier; 1942: Johnny on the Spot; Strip for Action.

Select TV: 1955: The Rack (sp); Broadway (sp); Like Father, Like Son (sp); Lash of Fear (sp); A Midsummer Daydream (sp); 1956: Circle of Guilt (sp); Twentieth Century (sp); Requiem for a Heavyweight (sp); The Ballad of Jubal Pickett (sp); 1957: The Last Tycoon (sp); Cab Driver (sp); The Gentle Deceiver (sp); The

Troublemakers (sp); 1958: No Time at All (sp); 1959: Afternoon of the Beast (sp); The Ledge (sp); 1959–60: Troubleshooters (series); 1960: The Man in the Funny Suit (sp); Don't Look Down (sp); 1961: The Joke and the Valley (sp); The Power and the Glory (sp); You're in the Picture (series); 1962: Seeds of April (sp); 1963: The Losers (sp); 1964: Runaway (sp); Charlie: He Couldn't Kill a Fly (sp); 1969: The Young Lawyers; 1970: The House on Greenapple Road; Santa Claus Is Coming to Town (sp; voice); 1971: Asssault on the Wayne; Cannon; Terror in the Sky; 1972: Assignment: Munich; 1973: Hijack!; 1974: Hit Lady; 1975: Target Risk; Jeremiah of Jacob's Neck (sp); 1976: The Lindbergh Kidnapping Case; The Quest; The Longest Drive; 1977: Sex and the Married Woman; 1978: The Bastard; 1979: The Billion Dollar Threat; 1979–80: Dallas (series); 1980: Mom, the Wolfman, and Me; 1981: The Monkey Mission; 1982: A Piano for Mrs. Cimino; The Capture of Grizzly Adams; 1983: The Return of the Man from U.N.C.L.E.; 1984–85: Call to Glory (series); 1985: Mirrors; Code of Vengeance; 1986: The Last Precinct (series).

DANA WYNTER

(DAGMAR SPENCER-MARCUS) BORN: LONDON, ENGLAND, JUNE 8, 1930. ED: NO. LONDON COLLEGIATE, RHODES UNIV. OF SO. AFRICA.

Though it suggested a certain pretension to pronounce her first name as "Donna," the elegant Dana Wynter, was surprisingly accessible when it came to her choice of screen projects. The daughter of a well-to-do surgeon, she spent part of her upbringing in South Africa where she initially planned to follow in dad's footsteps until the stage proved more appealing. Returning to England, she began acting under the name Dagmar Wynter, where she was strictly a minor supporting player in movies that included two Hollywood productions made overseas, *The Crimson Pirate* and *Knights of the Round Table*. At the suggestion of director Lewis Milestone, she dumped her exotic name and opted for "Dana" as she started appearing in various live television productions, including a remake of *Laura*, and in a short-lived Broadway show, *Black-Eyed Susan*. Fox put her under contact, making her Richard Egan's former lover in *The View from Pompey's Head*; the girl in the lives of soldiers Robert Taylor and Richard Todd in *D-Day, the Sixth of June*; and the German woman who must choose between fiancé Helmut Dantine and soldier Mel Ferrer in *Fraulein*. Ironically, all of these major productions were quickly forgotten while a low-budget sci-fi thriller she did, *Invasion of the Body Snatchers*, came to be considered, over time, one of the most highly-regarded, most literate and chilling of all films of that genre, and the movie that kept her name alive years after she'd faded from the scene. In the meantime, she participated in an underrated drama of apartheid, *Something of Value*; an interesting examination of the IRA, *Shake Hands with the Devil*; a hit war film, *Sink the Bismarck!*; a light Danny Kaye vehicle, *On the Double*; and the quixotic thriller, *The List of Adrian Messenger*. Television then took up most of her time, though she did appear as Burt Lancaster's unsympathetic wife in the blockbuster *Airport*. As work became more and more scarce, she turned to freelance journalism.

Screen: AS DAGMAR WYNTER: 1951: White Corridors; Lady Godiva Rides Again; 1952: The Woman's Angle; It Started in Paradise; The Crimson Pirate; 1953: Colonel March Investigates; Knights of the Round Table.

AS DANA WYNTER: 1955: The View from Pompey's Head; 1956: Invasion of the Body Snatchers; D-Day, the Sixth of June; 1957: Something of Value; 1958: Fraulein; In Love and War; 1959:

Shake Hands With the Devil; **1960:** Sink the Bismarck!; **1961:** On the Double; **1963:** The List of Adrian Messenger; **1968:** If He Hollers, Let Him Go!/Dead Right; **1970:** Airport; **1973:** Santee; **1975:** Le Sauvage/Lovers Like Us/Call Me Savage.

NY Stage: **1954:** Black-Eyed Susan.

Select TV: **1954:** The Man with the Gun (sp); **1955:** It Might Happen Tomorrow (sp); Laura (sp); **1957:** Winter Dreams (sp); **1958:** The Violent Heart (sp); **1959:** The Wings of the Dove (sp); **1962:** The Great Anatole (sp); **1963:** The Fifth Passenger (sp); **1965:** That Time in Havana (sp); The Crime (sp); **1966–67:** The Man Who Never Was (series); **1968:** Companions in Nightmare; **1969:** Any Second Now; **1971:** Owen Marshall: Counselor at Law/A Pattern of Morality; **1973:** The Connection; **1974:** The Questor Tapes; **1975:** The Lives of Jenny Dolan; **1978–82:** Bracken (series); **1979:** Backstairs at the White House (ms); **1980:** M Station: Hawaii; **1984:** The Royal Romance of Charles and Diana; **1993:** The Return of Ironside.

DIANA WYNYARD

(DOROTHY COX) BORN: LONDON, ENGLAND, JANUARY 16, 1906. DIED: MAY 13, 1964.

Giving Hollywood the sort of blue-blooded high style it desired for certain films of the 1930s, Diana Wynyard had a mild degree of success though her work has had a less-than-endearing effect of latter-day audiences. She started on the London stage with a bit in *The Grand Duchess*, in 1925, then joined William Armstrong's Liverpool theatrical company before returning to the West End for the hits *Sorry You've Been Troubled* and *The Old Bachelor*. In 1932 she came to Broadway to appear in *The Devil Passes*, which brought her a contract with MGM who made her the Princess in support of the Barrymores in *Rasputin and the Empress*. Her second film, made for Fox, was the surprisingly popular *Cavalcade*, the story of a British family over a course of 30 years. It won the Academy Award for Best Picture of 1932–33 and Wynyard, as the supposedly admirable matriarch, received an Oscar nomination. The acclaim both her performance and the movie received in their day is singularly elusive by today's standards. Back at MGM she did an anti-war film, *Men Must Fight*, and a romance with John Barrymore, *Reunion in Vienna*. After a few more unpopular loan-outs, she journeyed back to England to do theatre. Returning to movies she was the tormented wife in the earlier, better-regarded version of *Gaslight*; starred opposite her *Cavalcade* husband, Clive Brook, in *Freedom Radio*; played the wife of John Gielgud's Disraeli in *The Prime Minister*, and appeared in a film for her then-husband (1943–47), director Carol Reed, *Kipps*. She was Lady Chiltern in the first version of Oscar Wilde's *An Ideal Husband*; the mum of John Howard Davies in *Tom Brown's Schooldays*, and, in what must have seemed like a bit of an insult, was cast as the mother (!) of James Mason, who was but two years her junior, in the American box-office hit *Island in the Sun*. During all of these she continued to work most fruitfully in the theatre.

Screen: **1932:** Rasputin and the Empress; **1933:** Cavalcade; Men Must Fight; Reunion in Vienna; **1934:** Where Sinners Meet; Let's Try Again; One More River; **1939:** On the Night of the Fire/The Fugitive; **1940:** Gaslight/Angel Street; **1941:** Freedom Radio/A Voice in the Night; The Prime Minister; Kipps; **1947:** An Ideal Husband; **1951:** Tom Brown's Schooldays; **1956:** The Feminine Touch/The Gentle Touch; **1957:** Island in the Sun.

NY Stage: **1932:** The Devil Passes; **1958:** Cue For Passion; **1959:** Heartbreak House.

Select TV: **1957:** Mayerling (sp); **1959:** The Second Man (sp).

Y

SUSANNAH YORK

(Susannah Yolande Fletcher)
Born: London, England, January 9, 1941.
Raised in Scotland. ed: RADA.

Without being promoted with her own vehicles, Susannah York became one of the few leading ladies during the male-dominated British invasion of the 1960s to become a star. She had a bright, warm personality and began to get credit for her range as time went on though, in fact, she was always very good at what she did. It wasn't long after schooling that she got work, both in theater and on television, leading to her motion picture debut in a very prestigious production, *Tunes of Glory*, as Alec Guinness's daughter. The property that brought her more attention, however, was *The Greengage Summer/Loss of Innocence*, where she fell for an older man, Kenneth More. This resulted in a supporting assignment in an American film, *Freud*, in a key role as a neurotic, sexually repressed patient of Montgomery Clift's. The next step was to become famous in the international market and she accomplished this with *Tom Jones*, the movie sensation of 1963, in which her felicitous portrayal of Albert Finney's ladylove seemed as fresh as almost everything else about this delicious Oscar-winning comedy. The offers came pouring in but they didn't seem to be among the cream of the crop, judging from the dreary *The 7th Dawn*, with William Holden, or the lame romance-thriller *Kaleidoscope*, with Warren Beatty. In between was an acceptable plane-crash drama, *Sands of the Kalahari*, and, after this batch, another high point, *A Man for All Seasons*, in which she starred in her second Academy Award wining film for Best Picture, marvelous as Paul Scofield's very devoted and level-headed daughter. There were no benefits, however, from her appearances in a spy thriller *Sebastian*; a caper film, *Duffy*; the lurid lesbian drama, *The Killing of Sister George*, where Coral Browne had an intimate encounter with one of her breasts; or *Lock Up Your Daughters!*, which was an example of the many bad period romps that *Tom Jones* spawned.

She was in two all-star British productions, *Oh! What a Lovely War* and *Battle of Britain*, which were indications of her status at that time rather than good roles. She wound up much better off in an American film, *They Shoot Horses, Don't They?* In the showy role of a platinum blonde wanna-be starlet, who cracks up in the middle of a dance marathon, she was an outstanding addition to a fine ensemble of players, earning an Oscar nomination in the supporting category. As the 1970s arrived she stayed busy but became increasingly unlucky when it came to ending up in projects that had much staying power or interest beyond certain select audiences. She was the sister Peter O'Toole desired in *Brotherly Love/Country Dance*; the car-hop wife of Rod Steiger in *Happy Birthday, Wanda June*; the lover of both Michael Caine and Elizabeth Taylor in *X, Y & Zee/Zee and Company*; a troubled author in a cryptic and pretentious Robert Altman drama, *Images*, her only true cinematic showcase; one of *The Maids*, an American Film Theatre presentation meant for limited customers; and an Army widow in the all-star *Conduct Unbecoming*. There was a mighty box-office success with *Superman*, but few took note of her fleeting role as the title character's mom. It was back to the curios with *The Shout*, where her life is invaded by stranger Alan Bates; *The Silent Partner*, a decent thriller, with Elliot Gould; *The Awakening*, a moldy mummy tale; and *Falling in Love Again*, as Gould's sensible wife. Stage then claimed her and, since she was now in her 40s, when she did return to movies it was as a supporting player, in *A Summer Story* and *Diamond's Edge/Just Ask for Diamond*, which were among the last of her features to actually receive some sort of theatrical distribution.

Screen: 1960: Tunes of Glory; There Was a Crooked Man; 1961: Loss of Innocence/The Greengage Summer; 1962: Freud; 1963: Tom Jones; 1964: The 7th Dawn; 1965: Sands of the Kalahari; 1966: Kaleidoscope; A Man for All Seasons; 1968: Sebastian; Duffy; The Killing of Sister George; 1969: Lock Up Your Daughters!; Oh! What a Lovely War; Battle of Britain; They Shoot Horses, Don't They?; 1970: Brotherly Love/Country Dance; 1971: Happy Birthday, Wanda June; 1972: X, Y & Zee/Zee and Company; Images; 1974: Gold; 1975: The Maids; Conduct Unbecoming; That Lucky Touch; 1976: Sky Riders; 1977: Eliza Fraser/Rollicking Adventures of Eliza Fraser (nUSr); 1978: Long Shot (nUSr); The Shout; Superman; 1979: The Silent Partner; 1980: The Awakening; Falling in Love Again; 1981: Superman II; Alice (dtv); 1981: Loophole/Break In; 1983: Yellowbeard; 1987: Prettykill; Superman IV: The Quest for Peace (voice); Bluebeard, Bluebeard (nUSr); **1988:** Land of Faraway; A Summer Story; American Roulette (dtv); Just Ask for Diamond/Diamond's Edge; **1989:** A Handful of Time (nUSr); Melancholia (nUSr); **1990:** Fate (dtv); **1993:** Pretty Princess (nUSr); The Higher Mortals (nUSr); **1997:** Loop (nUSr); Diana & Me (nUSr); **2002:** Visitors (nUSr).

NY Stage: 1981: Hedda Gabler; 1984: The Human Voice.

Select TV: 1966: The Fall of the House of Usher (sp); 1971: Jane Eyre; 1979: Prime Regent (ms); The Golden Gate Murders; 1982: We'll Meet Again (series); 1984: A Christmas Carol; 1985: Star Quality; 1989: The Man from the Pru; After the War (ms); 1991: Devices and Desires (ms); 1991–92: Trainer (series); 1992: Illusions; 1997: Dark Blue Perfume; 1998: So This Is Romance?; 2000: St. Patrick: The Irish Legend.

ALAN YOUNG

BORN: NORTH SHIELDS, TYNE-AND-WEAR, ENGLAND, NOVEMBER 19, 1919. RAISED IN VANCOUVER, CANADA.

Perhaps too gentle in manner to succeed on the big screen, the boyishly pleasant Alan Young ventured on occasion into theatrical features but found television to be his bread and butter. Having achieved a small degree of fame in Canadian radio, he decided to try his luck in that field in America, where he moved in 1944. While performing on the airwaves, 20th Century-Fox put him in college in supporting roles in both *Margie* and *Mr. Belvedere Goes to College.* Real fame came with early television, where he landed his own variety series, *The Alan Young Show,* which brought him raves and an Emmy Award. Because of its success, he got his own motion picture vehicle, the memorably titled *Aaron Slick From Punkin Crick,* a slice of musical corn in which he was the yokel who saves Dinah Shore from city slicker Robert Merrill. This was followed by his most significant screen role, as the kindly tailor who becomes a hero to the persecuted Christians in *Androcles and the Lion,* which was part Bernard Shaw and part RKO spectacle, Howard Hughes-style. The uneasy mix resulted in a major box-office and critical failure, though Young came away with all the best notices. After playing Jane Russell's love interest in *Gentleman Marry Brunettes,* and showing up as Rod Taylor's friend, as well as his future descendent, in the sci-fi classic *The Time Machine,* it was back to television. There he found the role that would give him lasting fame, the good-natured architect with the talking horse, in *Mister Ed,* which was pretty much a small-screen version of the Francis the Talking Mule movies. At the end of the 1960s, Young chucked the spotlight to devote his time to the Christian Scientist religion. When he did return to acting it was mainly in family fare, which included supplying the voice of Scrooge McDuck in the short *Mickey's Christmas Carol,* the series *DuckTales,* and its spin-off feature.

Screen: 1946: Margie; 1949: Chicken Every Sunday; Mr. Belvedere Goes to College; 1952: Aaron Slick From Punkin Crick; 1963: Androcles and the Lion; 1955: Gentlemen Marry Brunettes; 1958: tom thumb; 1960: The Time Machine; 1976: Baker's Hawk; 1978: The Cat From Outer Space; 1980: Scruffy (dtv; voice); 1986: The Great Mouse Detective (voice); 1990: DuckTales: The Movie: Treasure of the Lost Lamp (voice); 1994: Beverly Hills Cop III; 2002: The Time Machine.

NY Stage: 1967: The Girl in The Freudian Slip.

Select TV: 1950–53: The Alan Young Show (series); 1954: Saturday Night Revue (series); 1961–65: Mister Ed (series); 1981–86: Spider Man and His Amazing Friends (series; voice); 1984–90: The Smurfs (series; voice); 1987–92: DuckTales (series; voice); **1988:** Coming of Age (series); **1991:** Earth Angel; **1994:** Hart to Hart: Home Is Where the Hart Is; **1994–96:** The Ren & Stimpy Show (series; voice); **2001:** House of Mouse (series; voice).

GIG YOUNG

(BYRON ELLSWORTH BARR)
BORN: ST. CLOUD, MN, NOVEMBER 4, 1913.
DIED: OCTOBER 19, 1978.

Easy to take and suavely pleasing in looks, Gig Young was often best when he was asked to put a cheeky spin on a line, showing a fine flair for light comedy. When he was given a part with some meat to it, he could also display some impressive acting chops. When not, he had a tendency to simply blend into the woodwork. He was one of the many noted alumnae of the prestigious Pasadena Playhouse and it was while performing there that he was seen by a Warners talent scout. Under his real name, they started him out as a pilot in the Errol Flynn vehicle *Dive Bomber!,* and mainly kept him in some kind of uniform for his miniscule (and unbilled) parts in such features as *They Died With Their Boots On, Sergeant York,* and *Captains of the Clouds.* There was, however, another actor going under the name of "Byron Barr" and, once it looked as if the newer Barr was ready to be groomed for bigger things, it was necessary to find a different name. In one of the more curious bits of film trivia, the actor first received billing as "Gig Young" while playing a character by that very name in the 1942 Barbara Stanwyck soaper, *The Gay Sisters.* There followed small parts in the popular *Air Force,* and in the Bette Davis drama *Old Acquaintance,* in which he courted her daughter, after which he joined the Coast Guard. He returned to Warners in 1947, having made little noise previously, and made just as little impact with a pair of quickly forgotten melodramas, *Escape Me Never,* and *The Woman in White,* in which he was particularly wooden as the hero of this gothic nonsense. Freelancing, he ended up in a pair of hits, MGM's *The Three Musketeers,* as a Porthos, and Republic's *Wake of the Red Witch,* but all eyes were on Gene Kelly in the former and John Wayne in the latter.

Columbia put him under contract and although he ended up in a decent western, *Lust for Gold,* he was passed over for the lead in *The Loves of Carmen,* in favor of Glenn Ford, instead ending up biding his time in a lightweight comedy, *Tell It to the Judge,* supporting Rosalind Russell. He refused to continue at the studio and was suspended. In 1950 RKO gave him his first official lead, *Hunt the Man Down,* a "B" variation on *Call Northside 777,* in which he tried to clear an innocent man 12 years after his conviction. He ended up as a Nazi, of all things, in Universal's *Target Unknown,* and then returned to Warner Bros. with good reason, having been offered a solid part in *Come Fill the Cup,* as the spoiled, rich alcoholic whom James Cagney tries to reform. Finally getting a chance to show his value as a serious actor, Young was first rate, earning a supporting Oscar nomination in the process. Alas, in a case of life imitating art, the bottle would later take its toll on the performer for real. In the meantime, MGM was the next to offer him a contract and gave him top billing in *Holiday for Sinners,* as a New Orleans physician questioning his decision to help the destitute. There was a comedy, *You for Me,* which was unusual in that he actually got the girl, Jane Greer, at the end, something that wasn't the norm for him in most situations; was Elizabeth Taylor's drab boyfriend, whom she dumps for criminal Fernando Lamas, in *The Girl Who Had Everything,* a remake of *A Free Soul*; and did one of the many 3-D pictures of the time, *Arena,* as a rodeo star. He wound up faring better at Republic, in *The City That Never Sleeps,* as a fed-up cop who nearly succumbs to his darker instincts. After that he figured it was time to pack up and go elsewhere and headed for Broadway where he scored a hit in *Oh, Men! Oh, Women!* Back in movies, he was the nice guy who shows up at the household of Doris Day and her sisters in *Young at Heart*, and played the older man dating the hostage-held Mary Murphy in the tense *The Desperate Hours*.

He then slipped into his series of suitor roles, losing Katharine Hepburn in *Desk Set*, Doris Day in *Teacher's Pet*, and Shirley MacLaine in *Ask Any Girl*. He was a drunk again in *Teacher's Pet*, this time playing it for laughs and getting another Oscar nomination. Returning to drama, he was on trial for murder in *The Story on Page One*; was very funny as Cary Grant's financial adviser, who's mistaken for Grant's gay lover, in the hit *That Touch of Mink*; was a poor choice to take over Edward G. Robinson's role in the remake of *Kid Galahad*, as fight manager to Elvis Presley; and got the girl again, Sophia Loren, in a critically roasted thriller, *Five Miles to Midnight*. He also ended up with Shirley Jones in *A Ticklish Affair*, but somehow taking the lead in this fluffy comedy, rather than doing his requisite secondary part, made him seem that much less interesting. After a stint on television, as one of the rotating stars of *The Rogues*, he returned to movies in a thriller, *The Shuttered Room*, and then in a far more impressive movie, *They Shoot Horses, Don't They?* As the ultra-cynical emcee of a spirit-killing dance marathon, Young never made a false move, confounding the skeptics (including co-star Jane Fonda who initially balked at his casting) who thought he hadn't the weight to carry off such a part. He won the Academy Award for Best Supporting Actor of 1969. For his reward, he got top-billing in the ensemble comedy *Lovers and Other Strangers*, carrying on an extra-marital affair with a teary Anne Jackson. Immersed in dramatic fare, he played a nasty gay villain in *Bring Me the Head of Alfredo Garcia*; James Caan's smarmy boss in *The Killer Elite*; and a drunken passenger aboard *The Hindenburg*, though he seemed to have tongue firmly in cheek, especially in the latter. The sly smile he was famous for apparently hid a world of demons judging from his sordid death, shooting himself after having killed his fifth wife. Among those to whom he'd been previously wed (1956–63) was actress Elizabeth Montgomery.

Screen: AS BYRON BARR: 1941: Dive Bomber!; They Died With Their Boots On; One Foot in Heaven; Sergeant York; 1942: Captains of the Clouds; The Male Animal.

AS GIG YOUNG: The Gay Sisters; 1943: Air Force; Old Acquaintance; 1947: Escape Me Never; 1948: The Woman in White; The Three Musketeers; 1949: Wake of the Red Witch; Lust for Gold; Tell It to the Judge; 1950: Hunt the Man Down; 1951: Target Unknown; Only the Valiant; Slaughter Trail; Come Fill the Cup; Too Young to Kiss; 1952: Holiday for Sinners; You for Me; 1953: The Girl Who Had Everything; The City That Never Sleeps; Arena; Torch Song; 1954: Young at Heart; 1955: The Desperate Hours; 1957: Desk Set; 1958: Teacher's Pet; The Tunnel of Love; 1959: Ask Any Girl; The Story on Page One; 1962: That Touch of Mink; Kid Galahad; 1963: Five Miles to Midnight; For Love or Money; A Ticklish Affair; 1964: Strange Bedfellows; 1967: The Shuttered Room/Blood Island; 1969: They Shoot Horses, Don't They?; 1970: Lovers and Other Strangers; 1974: Bring Me the Head of Alfredo Garcia; 1975: A Black Ribbon for Deborah/Deborah (nUSr); Michele (nUSr); The Killer Elite; The Hindenburg; 1978: Game of Death.

NY Stage: 1953: Oh, Men! Oh, Women!; 1956: The Teahouse of the August Moon; 1960: Under the Yum-Yum Tree; 1967: There's a Girl in My Soup.

Select TV: 1950: Lady With Ideas (sp); 1953: The Sunday Punch (sp); Part of the Game (sp); 1954: Tonight at 8:30 (sp); 1956: Sauce for the Goose (sp); 1958: A Dead Ringer (sp); 1959: The

Philadelphia Story (sp); 1961: The Spiral Staircase (sp); 1963: The End of the World (sp); 1964–65: The Rogues (series); 1968: Companions in Nightmare; 1971: The Neon Ceiling; 1974: The Great Ice Rip-Off; 1975: The Turning Point of Jim Malloy; 1976: Sherlock Holmes in New York; Gibbsville (series); 1977: Spectre.

LORETTA YOUNG

(GRETCHEN MICHAELA YOUNG) BORN: SALT LAKE CITY, UT, JANUARY 6, 1913. RAISED IN LOS ANGELES, CA. DIED: AUGUST 12, 2000.

For two decades Loretta Young represented the ever-busy Hollywood star, rising from a sparkling, wide-eyed ingénue to a major leading lady. In the right role, be it comedic or melodramatic, she was an efficient player. Her lady-like gentility, however, meant that there was little opportunity to see her stretch and there was a sense of reserve to her acting that kept her from getting down and dirty. Her motion picture beginnings seemed relatively painless, compared to the trek many took to the big time. She and her three sisters were dragged to the studios to be hired as bit players, Loretta making her screen bow in *Sirens of the Sea*, when she was all of four years old. After a few more inconsequential appearances as a child, there was a break from filming until she became a teen at which point she was chosen to be the ingénue in Lon Chaney's *Laugh, Clown, Laugh*, as the circus performer he pines for in vain. Warner Bros. signed her to a contract in 1928 and she made her talkie debut shortly afterwards, in support of Myrna Loy in the Gypsy drama, *The Squall*. She was the star of a minor underworld drama, *The Girl in the Glass Cage*, which referred to her tending a movie box office, and paired off with Douglas Fairbanks, Jr. for *The Careless Age*, which did well enough to encourage the studio to put them together again for *The Fast Life*, *The Forward Pass*, *Loose Ankles*, and later down the line, *I Like Your Nerve*. In 1930 she made a romantic comedy in which she and Grant Withers found romance through the personal columns, *The Second Floor Mystery*, and they enjoyed each other's company enough to get married in real life, a union that was dissolved within a year, during which time they also showed up on screen in the aptly titled *Too Young to Marry*. During this time among the better-remembered pictures in which Young took part were *The Man from Blankley's*, a box-office hit with John Barrymore; *The Devil to Pay*, for Goldwyn, in which she won the heart of cad Ronald Colman; and *Taxi!*, as the nice girl who marries volatile James Cagney.

Director Frank Capra, on the brink of becoming Columbia's top director, borrowed her to play a reporter who nearly loses Robert Williams to Jean Harlow in a bright comedy, *Platinum Blonde*; after which it was a step down to don some faux Asian makeup for *The Hatchet Man*, marrying Edward G. Robinson and getting involved in a tong war. Also for her home studio she was *Play Girl*, nearly brought down in her quest for success by her husband's gambling addiction; a convicted killer (albeit one who killed a guy who deserved to die) brought to a maternity ward to give birth in the ensemble *Life Begins*; was fought over by David Manners, Louis Calhern and George Brent in *They Call It Sin*; and gave into the wolfish wiles of Warren William in *Employees' Entrance*. It was interesting to note that around the time the last was released she had only just turned 20 years old and yet had some 37 movies to her credit. She was, in a way, a genuine motion picture star and a bright addition to Warners, but she was not exactly a money-making draw, nor were many of the movies she showed up in remembered for much longer than the time they spent in general release. In typical fashion she wound up enjoying two loan-outs more than anything she was being offered on the home lot, with Fox's *Zoo at Budapest*, escaping from an orphanage, in this unusual drama that actually made a statement against the unethical treatment of animals; and MGM's *Midnight Mary*, as a convicted murderess looking back on how her life went wrong, and one of the rare instances when Young played a tough babe, doing so with total conviction. When she clicked with Spencer Tracy in Fox's *Man's Castle*, Zanuck was only too happy to take her away from Warners to his 20th Century Pictures, an offer she gratefully accepted.

She started off for them in a hit, *House of Rothschild*, though she was fairly nondescript in the ingénue role; wound up being out of her league in a part intended for Jean Harlow, playing an unwed mother out to trap Cary Grant, in *Born to Be Bad*; led a cast of noble nurses in *The White Parade*, one of the year's Oscar nominees for Best Picture; did two films in support of Ronald Colman, *Bulldog Drummond Strikes Back* and *Clive of India*; and was added to the mix in the highly distorted adaptation of *The Call of the Wild*. At Paramount she was merely decoration in one of DeMille's outrageous blockbusters, *The Crusades*, then returned to Zanuck whose company was joined by Fox to become 20th Century-Fox, where Young's first assignment under that banner was *Private Number*, the one about the servant girl who captures the heart of the son of the house, in this case, Robert Taylor. There were three light comedies with Tyrone Power, *Ladies in Love*, *Love Is News*, and *Second Honeymoon*, and then the more serious *Suez*. Amid these there were the sound-alike *Wife, Doctor and Nurse* and *Wife, Husband and Friend*, the confusion compounded by having Warner Baxter in both, though the first was meant to be serious, the latter intended to be funny. There was the popular Technicolor horseracing picture, *Kentucky*, remembered, if at all, in later years for Walter Brennan's Oscar-winning supporting role; and the biopic *The Story of Alexander Graham Bell*, as his wife. The latter film sent her packing from Fox, since she was not allowed to play the character accurately as the deaf-mute she really was. Instead, in a compromise to the nervous studio, she played the part as a deaf woman who spoke. Young decided she would freelance but soon accepted a contract with Columbia, who put her into some comedies: *The Doctor Takes a Wife*, with Ray Milland; *He Stayed for Breakfast*, a reversal of *Ninotchka*, with that film's star, Melvyn Douglas; *A Bedtime Time*, as an actress who doesn't want to star in husband Fredric March's next play; and *A Night to Remember*, investigating a murder with Brian Aherne; all of which showed her to better advantage than *The Men in Her Life*, in which she was miscast as a prima ballerina.

From Columbia she went over to Paramount where she co-starred in two movies with Alan Ladd: *China*, a World War II propaganda film, in which she helped him battle the evil Japanese; and the very well-attended sudser *And Now Tomorrow*, in which she relapsed into deafness while falling for her doctor. In between, Universal made her the executive officer in charge of the Women's Auxiliary Ferrying Squadron in *Ladies Courageous*, one of the requisite "women at war" dramas necessary to boost home-front morale. Then she did a pleasant western comedy with Gary Cooper, *Along Came Jones*, and Orson Welles's most commercially conscious of all his directorial accomplishments, *The Stranger*, as a small-town wife who realizes that she's married to a Nazi. Selznick had banked on Ingrid Bergman accepting *The Farmer's Daughter*, a cutesy story of a Swedish housemaid who ends up running for congress, but when she passed, Young got the part. Despite her uncertain accent and an overall coyness to the proceedings, it was a very popular picture, resulting in Young's first Oscar nomination. The story goes that all the press and pre-hype indicated that Rosalind Russell would clinch the trophy for *Mourning Becomes Electra*, but, in the end, it was Young who won, no doubt in tribute to the longevity of her career. That same year,

1947, she had the title role in the more satisfying *The Bishop's Wife*, finding herself attracted to guardian angel Cary Grant, then played a bondswoman in *Rachel and the Stranger*. She returned to Fox for *Come to the Stable*, very nicely underplaying a nun determined to build a childrens hospital, and receiving a second Oscar nomination in the process. After that she went back to what were basically programmers, including the thriller *Cause for Alarm!*, trying to intercept an incriminating letter; *Because of You*, as a parolee cheating on husband Jeff Chandler; and, finally, a low-keyed comedy about a small-town newspaper, *It Happens Every Thursday*. She was only too happy to go to television at this point and had an amazingly successful run with the anthology series *The Loretta Young Show*, winning three Emmy Awards for it. After a long retirement she came back to do two television movies, invoking warm notices, being a name from the past who had out-lived most of her peers. She published her (mostly ghosted) autobiography, *The Things I Had to Learn*, in 1961.

Screen: AS GRETCHEN YOUNG: 1919: Sirens of the Sea; The Only Way; 1921: White and Unmarried; The Sheik.

AS LORETTA YOUNG: 1927: Naughty But Nice; 1928: Her Wild Oat; Whip Woman; Laugh, Clown, Laugh; The Magnificent Flirt; The Head Man; Scarlet Seas; 1929: The Squall; The Girl in the Glass Cage; The Careless Age; The Fast Life; The Show of Shows; The Forward Pass; 1930: Loose Ankles; Show Girl in Hollywood; The Second Floor Mystery; The Man from Blankley's; Road to Paradise; Kismet; The Devil to Pay; The Truth About Youth; 1931: Beau Ideal; The Right of Way; Three Girls Lost; Too Young to Marry; Big Business Girl; I Like Your Nerve; Platinum Blonde; The Ruling Voice; 1932: Taxi!; The Hatchet Man; Play Girl; Weekend Marriage; Life Begins; They Call It Sin; 1933: Employees' Entrance; Grand Slam; Zoo in Budapest; The Life of Jimmy Dolan; Midnight Mary; Heroes for Sale; The Devil's in Love; She Had to Say Yes; Man's Castle; 1934: House of Rothschild; Bulldog Drummond Strikes Back; Born to Be Bad; Caravan; The White Parade; 1935: Clive of India; The Call of the Wild; Shanghai; The Crusades; 1936: The Unguarded Hour; Private Number; Ramona; Ladies in Love; 1937: Love Is News; Cafe Metropole; Love Under Fire; Wife, Doctor and Nurse; Second Honeymoon; 1938: Four Men and a Prayer; Three Blind Mice; Suez; Kentucky; 1939: The Story of Alexander Graham Bell; Wife, Husband and Friend; Eternally Yours; 1940: The Doctor Takes a Wife; He Stayed for Breakfast; 1941: The Lady From Cheyenne; The Men in Her Life; A Bedtime Story; 1943: A Night to Remember; China; 1944: Ladies Courageous; And Now Tomorrow; 1945: Along Came Jones; 1946: The Stranger; The Perfect Marriage; 1947: The Farmer's Daughter; The Bishop's Wife; 1948: Rachel and the Stranger; The Accused; 1949: Mother Is a Freshman; Come to the Stable; 1950: Key to the City; 1951: Cause for Alarm!; Half Angel; 1952: Paula; Because of You; 1953: It Happens Every Thursday.

Select TV: 1953–61: A Letter to Loretta/The Loretta Young Show (series); 1962–63: The New Loretta Young Show (series); 1986: Christmas Eve; 1989: Lady in the Corner.

ROBERT YOUNG

BORN: CHICAGO, IL, FEBRUARY 22, 1907.
RAISED IN SEATTLE, WA AND LOS ANGELES, CA.
DIED: JULY 21, 1998.

While amassing a large list of movie credits, Robert Young, with his bright speaking voice and trustworthy persona, became the sort of inoffensive, dependable leading man who got to carry an occasional picture without ever becoming a box-office attraction, which was just fine by him. While acting at the famed Pasadena Playhouse, he took odd jobs, including some extra work in films, though his credits here have never been documented. It was while touring in a play called *The Ship* that he was signed by an agent who got him a screen test at MGM. The studio put him under contract in 1931 and immediately shipped him over to Fox, for *The Black Camel*, as one of the suspects in this Charlie Chan mystery. Back at MGM he got to play Helen Hayes's grown-up son in *The Sin of Madelon Claudet*, a creaky melodrama to be sure, but one that earned Hayes her Oscar, therefore making it a notable movie for Young to have been involved in. Pretty soon it seemed that wherever you looked Young was to be found, including *The Wet Parade*, as a crusader against alcohol (Young himself would battle the bottle in later years); *New Morals for Old*, top billed for the first time, as a wallpaper designer who wants to be a true artist; *Strange Interlude*, as Norma Shearer's lover, who dies in a plane crash; Goldwyn's *The Kid From Spain*, playing straight man to Eddie Cantor, but benefiting from appearing in this box-office success nonetheless; *Today We Live*, no match for Gary Cooper when it came to Joan Crawford making the choice between her suitors; *Tugboat Annie*, hardly causing a ripple, what with Marie Dressler and Wallace Beery in full swing; RKO's *Spitfire*, impregnating mountain girl Katharine Hepburn; and the prestigious *House of Rothschild*, where he and Loretta Young were the serviceable young lovers.

He did a baseball "B," *Death on the Diamond*, and a higher-grade football drama, *The Band Plays On*; changed his tawdry ways by denouncing communism in *Red Salute*; was one of the society drunks involved in a loopy murder mystery in *Remember Last Night?*; and went over to Paramount to lose Claudette Colbert to Fred MacMurray (they were, after all, under contract and he was the visiting outsider) in *The Bride Comes Home*. Just to confuse matters, afterwards he was shortly seen in RKO's *The Bride Walks Out*, with Barbara Stanwyck, and MGM's *The Bride Wore Red*, with Joan Crawford. Between these, he went to England to be directed by Hitchcock in *Secret Agent*, where he more than held his own against John Gielgud and Peter Lorre; then returned to the states to be charmed by Shirley Temple (he was an actor who was very much at ease with children) in *Stowaway*; and to be rejected by Colbert, again, in Paramount's *I Met Him in Paris*. Back at MGM he was the irresponsible West Point cadet in *Navy Blue and Gold*, convincing as a jerk who changes his self-serving ways in time for the good of the team; did some costume pictures, *The Emperor's Candlesticks*, and *The Toy Wife*; and shared the title roles with Robert Taylor and Franchot Tone in the popular *Three Comrades*, in which he was in love with Margaret Sullavan, but dropped out of the running for her affections once he was conveniently killed. Always good looking in slick-backed hair and fancy clothes, he was a millionaire in love with his secretary, Ruth Hussey, in the "B" picture, *Rich Man, Poor Girl*; played a dual role in the Eleanor Powell musical *Honolulu*, though he hardly suggested much difference between the two characters; and paired with Ann Sothern for *Maisie*, which turned out to be a surprise hit, though he was not called back for any of the sequels.

Despite the fact that he was considered the sort of unimportant contractee to support a horse in *Florian*, and to play a patient of Lew Ayres's in the series entry *Dr. Kildare's Crisis*, he was included in two of MGM's top pictures of 1940: *Northwest Passage*, a rousing adventure in which he was Spencer Tracy's second in command, and *The Mortal Storm*, in which he turned to Nazism much to the horror of girlfriend Margaret Sullavan. At Fox he did a big western, *Western Union*; was songwriting partner to Ann Sothern in a dull musical, *Lady Be Good*; and took second billing

despite the fact that he was the whole show in the long-winded *H.M. Pulham, Esq.*, as a Bostonian who allows himself a bit of fun in his stuffy life, thanks to Hedy Lamarr. (She would later speak of him as her favorite co-star). Still dipping into the "B" unit, he was *Joe Smith, American*, a bit of wartime propaganda, as a munitions worker; teamed with Jeanette MacDonald in *Cairo*, a combination of comedy-music-and spy stuff; and appeared in one of his best-loved movies, *Journey for Margaret*, allowing Margaret O'Brien to steal the show, but doing so most gallantly, as a war correspondent in England. Fox borrowed him to outstanding effect in *Claudia*, a nice movie about a newly married couple that also introduced Dorothy McGuire to the screen; and less so in *Sweet Rosie O'Grady*, which was just another Betty Grable musical, albeit a highly attended one. Finishing off his MGM contract he was back with O'Brien for an offbeat fantasy, *The Canterville Ghost*, once again proving to be a hero with whom audiences felt very much at ease. RKO reteamed him with McGuire with lesser results in *The Enchanted Cottage*, as misfits who fall in love; as did Fox for a sequel, *Claudia and David*. In between, he filmed Lillian Hellman's political statement, *The Searching Wind*, for Paramount, playing a U.S. Ambassador in pre-World War II Europe.

RKO called on his services for three films in a row. The first, *Lady Luck*, was a mild comedy about gambling, with Barbara Hale; but the others offered fine opportunities. The juicy *They Won't Believe Me* gave him what was certainly the nastiest role of his career, playing a callous philanderer who causes tragedy for the three women he is deceiving; while the Oscar-nominated *Crossfire*, an intelligent drama in which he was a police captain, coolly interrogating anti-Semitic Robert Ryan on the murder of Sam Levene, showed him at his most concentrated, making his own quiet impression amid the showier roles. The two films offered perhaps the finest performances of Young's career. The following year found him in another moneymaker, *Sitting Pretty*, drolly playing straight man to acerbic Clifton Webb, but he began to hit bumps after that. He was back with a now-grown-up Shirley Temple in *Adventure in Baltimore*; looked a bit long in the tooth to be the "young" architect in love with married Greer Garson in *That Forsyte Woman*, the wobbly attempt to film *The Forsyte Saga*; reteamed with past co-star Joan Crawford for *Goodbye, My Fancy*; and took a supporting role to Charlton Heston for a minor Paramount adventure *The Secret of the Incas*. Shortly after that film he decided to turn his successful radio show, *Father Knows Best*, into a television program, which he did with phenomenal results, guaranteeing that he would never be seen on a motion picture screen again. The series brought him two Emmy Awards, a pile of cash and a place in the family sitcom hall of fame. By the time he returned for another series, *Marcus Welby, M.D.* in 1969 (it brought him another Emmy Award), his days as a movie star were so far behind him a whole generation of admirers hadn't a clue about his long and productive stint as one of the less-heralded but busier figures from Hollywood's hallowed studio era.

Screen: 1931: The Black Camel; The Sin of Madelon Claudet; Guilty Generation; Hell Divers; 1932: The Wet Parade; New Morals for Old; Unashamed; Strange Interlude; The Kid From Spain; 1933: Today We Live; Men Must Fight; Hell Below; Tugboat Annie; Saturday's Millions; The Right to Romance; 1934: Carolina; Spitfire; House of Rothschild; Lazy River; Cardboard City; Hollywood Party; Paris Interlude; Whom the Gods Destroy; Death on the Diamond; The Band Plays On; 1935: West Point of the Air; Vagabond Lady; Calm Yourself; Red Salute; Remember Last Night?; The Bride Comes Home; 1936: Secret Agent; It's Love Again; Three Wise Guys; The Bride Walks

Out; Sworn Enemy; The Longest Night; Stowaway; **1937:** Dangerous Number; I Met Him in Paris; Married Before Breakfast; The Emperor's Candlesticks; The Bride Wore Red; Navy Blue and Gold; **1938:** Paradise for Three; Josette; The Toy Wife; Three Comrades; Rich Man, Poor Girl; The Shining Hour; **1939:** Honolulu; Bridal Suite; Maisie; Miracles for Sale; **1940:** Florian; Northwest Passage; The Mortal Storm; Sporting Blood; Dr. Kildare's Crisis; **1941:** Western Union; The Trial of Mary Dugan; Lady Be Good; Married Bachelor; H.M. Pulham, Esq.; **1942:** Joe Smith: American; Cairo; Journey for Margaret; **1943:** Slightly Dangerous; Claudia; Sweet Rosie O'Grady; **1944:** The Canterville Ghost; **1945:** The Enchanted Cottage; Those Endearing Young Charms; **1946:** The Searching Wind; Claudia and David; Lady Luck; **1947:** They Won't Believe Me; Crossfire; **1948:** Relentless; Sitting Pretty; **1949:** Adventure in Baltimore; Bride for Sale; That Forsyte Woman; And Baby Makes Three; **1951:** Goodbye, My Fancy; The Second Woman; **1952:** The Half-Breed; **1954:** The Secret of the Incas.

Select TV: 1954: Keep It in the Family (sp); 1954–60: Father Knows Best (series); 1961–62: Window on Main Street (series); 1965: The Admiral (sp); 1966: Holloway's Daughters (sp); 1969: Marcus Welby M.D./A Matter of Humanities; 1969–76: Marcus Welby M.D. (series); 1971: Vanished; 1972: All My Darling Daughters; 1973: My Darling Daughters' Anniversary; 1977: Father Knows Best Reunion (sp); Father Knows Best: Home for Christmas (sp); 1978: Little Women; 1979: Little Women (series); 1984: The Return of Marcus Welby M.D.; 1987: Conspiracy of Love; Mercy or Murder?; 1988: Marcus Welby M.D.: A Holiday Affair.

ROLAND YOUNG

BORN: LONDON, ENGLAND, NOVEMBER 11, 1887.
ED: SHERBORNE COL., LONDON UNIV., RADA.
DIED: JUNE 5, 1953.

There is no scale to measure the amount of pleasure Roland Young brought to Hollywood comedies of the 1930s and 1940s. This short, balding Englishman with the abbreviated but bushy moustache was a genius at understated humor. With his pursed-lipped delivery, nervous stammer, and murmurs of confusion, he could raise more laughs with a mere quizzical "hmmmn" than some actors could with an entire monologue. Having studied drama at the Royal Academy of Dramatic Arts, he made his London stage debut, in 1908, in *Find the Woman*, then came to Broadway four years later to appear in *Hindle Wakes* (he became a U.S. citizen in 1918). Following service in World War I, he acted with the Theatre Guild and in three plays written specifically for him by Clare Kummer: *Good Gracious Annabelle!*, *A Successful Calamity*, and *Rollo's Wild Oat*. Kummer's daughter, Marjorie, appeared in the last and she became Young's wife in 1921 (they divorced in 1940). He made his motion picture debut in 1922, ideally cast as Dr. Watson to John Barrymore's *Sherlock Holmes*, and then showed up as a character named Houidini Hart in crime melodrama called *Grit*. However, rather than continuing in pictures, he returned to the stage and didn't shoot another film until the sound era arrived. With that he was signed to a contract by MGM, in 1929, and they launched him in a mystery thriller, *The Unholy Night*, as a nobleman. This was followed by such films as DeMille's weird *Madam Satan*, in which he parachuted from a burning blimp into the Central Park Zoo for the climax; *New Moon*, as Grace Moore's Russian papa; and the quickly forgotten remake of *The Squaw Man*. Borrowed by Fox, he repeated his stage role of the tycoon battling for control of a mine in what

was now retitled *Annabelle's Affairs* (Annabelle was Jeanette MacDonald), then he returned to MGM to play the drama critic opposite the Lunts in their only movie vehicle, *The Guardsman*.

When his MGM contract ran out he was fortunate to be asked to grace some of Paramount's polished comical offerings of the day, including *One Hour with You*, cuckolded by wife Genevieve Tobin, who is fooling around with Maurice Chevalier; *This Is the Night*, in which he hired Lily Damita to pose as his misses in order to continue his fling with married Thelma Todd; *A Lady's Profession*, as a Brit running a speakeasy in America, with the delightful Alison Skipworth as his sister; *His Double Life*, top billed, as the shy artist posing as his own valet in order to marry widow Lillian Gish; and, best of all, *Ruggles of Red Gap*, as part of a peerless ensemble in one of the truly delightful comedies of its day, playing the Earl of Burnstead who loses his manservant, Charles Laughton, in a poker game to coarse millionaire Charlie Ruggles. He returned to MGM to perfectly embody the slithery Uriah Heep in the all-star rendition of *David Copperfield*, showing how his spinelessness could be used for villainous effect, after which he had no trouble stealing scenes from Kay Francis in one of her Warners weepies, *Give Me Your Heart*. He returned to his homeland for one of his very best roles, in the imaginative *The Man Who Could Work Miracles*, an H.G. Wells-scripted fantasy in which he was a meek clerk given the power to perform astonishing feats. While there he also did *King Solomon's Mines* (with monocle), supplying comic relief, and the Jessie Matthews vehicle, *Sailing Along*. Returning to the U.S., producer Hal Roach gave him the part for which he would become best remembered, the title role in *Topper*. This gimmicky whimsy about a pair of carefree ghosts (Constance Bennett and Cary Grant), who help a stuffy banker break out of his shell, gave Young a prime showcase in which to display his ace comic timing, since he was often required to do some carefully orchestrated solo physical comedy while his co-stars remained invisible. He received his only Oscar nomination, but in the supporting category, which was odd in so much as he not only had the title role, but clearly had the biggest part in the film.

The success of the movie prompted a follow-up, *Topper Takes a Trip* (minus Cary Grant, alas), and, since he and Billie Burke paired off so nicely as the Toppers, they were together again in *The Young in Heart*, heading a family of con artists, with Young as a fake colonel referred to as "Sahib." In support, he was a college professor in *Here I Am a Stranger*; an actor who retires into wealth in *The Night of Nights*; a talent scout in *Star Dust*; a millionaire suffering financial woes in the aborted filmization of *No, No, Nanette*; and Katharine Hepburn's sardonic Uncle Willie in *The Philadelphia Story*, in which he was especially funny suffering a "morning after" hangover. He was back in the leading slot, one last time, for another sequel, *Topper Returns*, a farcical murder mystery that didn't have much connection to the original film. He nearly married Marlene Dietrich, of all people, in *The Flame of New Orleans*; appeared as a friend of Garbo's in her last movie, *Two-Faced Woman*; and then had a serious sequence in the omnibus *Forever and a Day*, in which he and Gladys Cooper react to the death of their son during the war. There was a final hurrah, being part of the excellent ensemble in one of the most accomplished of all murder mysteries, *And Then There Were None*, as the policeman; the most likable of all the victims, and one who nearly made it to the end of the picture alive. It was something of a change of pace seeing him play a strangler in *The Great Lover*, but since this was a Bob Hope comedy it wasn't to be taken all that seriously. Taking a backseat to Fred Astaire and Betty Hutton in *Let's Dance*, he then played a con man posing as a clergyman in the cheaply made *St. Benny the Dip*, and ended his career on a low note with a European-made programmer *The Man from Tangier*, released in 1953, the year of his death.

Screen: 1922: Sherlock Holmes; 1924: Grit; 1929: The Unholy Night; Her Private Life; 1930: The Bishop Murder Case; Wise Girls; Madam Satan; New Moon; 1931: Don't Bet on Women; The Prodigal; Annabelle's Affairs; The Squaw Man; The Guardsman; Pagan Lady; 1932: A Woman Commands; Lovers Courageous; One Hour With You. This Is the Night; Street of Women; 1933: Wedding Rehearsal; They Just Had to Get Married; A Lady's Profession; Pleasure Cruise; Blind Adventure; His Double Life; 1934: Here Is My Heart; 1935: David Copperfield; Ruggles of Red Gap; 1936: The Unguarded Hour; One Rainy Afternoon; Give Me Your Heart; The Man Who Could Work Miracles; 1937: Gypsy; Call It a Day; King Solomon's Mines; Topper; Ali Baba Goes to Town; 1938: Sailing Along; The Young in Heart; 1939: Topper Takes a Trip; Yes, My Darling Daughter; The Night of Nights; Here I Am a Stranger; 1940: He Married His Wife; Irene; Star Dust; Private Affairs; Dulcy; The Philadelphia Story; No, No, Nanette; 1941: Topper Returns; The Flame of New Orleans; Two-Faced Woman; 1942: The Lady Has Plans; They All Kissed the Bride; Tales of Manhattan; 1943: Forever and a Day; 1944: Standing Room Only; 1945: And Then There Were None; 1948: You Gotta Stay Happy; Bond Street; 1949: The Great Lover; 1950: Let's Dance; 1951: St. Benny the Dip; 1953: The Man from Tangier.

NY Stage: 1912: Hindle Wakes; 1915: John Gabriel Borkman; 1916: The Sea Gull; Literature; 1916: Good Gracious Annabelle!; 1917: A Successful Calamity; The Rescuing Angel; The Gipsy Trail; 1918: A Trench Fantasy; The Big Scene; A Doll's House; 1919: Luck in Pawn; Buddies; 1920: Scrambled Wives; Rollo's Wild Oat; 1922: Madame Pierre; The '49ers; 1923: Anything Might Happen; The Devil's Disciple; 1924: Beggar on Horseback; Hedda Gabler; 1925: The Tale of the Wolf; The Last of Mrs. Cheyney; 1928: The Queen's Husband; 1933: Her Master's Voice; 1935: The Distant Shore; A Touch of Brimstone; 1938: Spring Thaw; 1943: Ask My Friend Sandy; Another Love Story.

Select TV: 1949: All's Fear (sp); 1951: Mr. Mummery's Suspicion (sp); 1963: Uncle Fred Flits By (sp).

Z

EFREM ZIMBALIST, JR.
BORN: NEW YORK, NY, NOVEMBER 30, 1918.

Strictly of the serviceable-but-unexciting school of acting, Efrem Zimbalist, Jr. kept his very un-Hollywood name no doubt in honor of his dad, who was a quite renowned concert violinist, while his show business roots also extended to his mother, Alma Gluck, an opera singer. A Neighborhood Playhouse drama student, he made his New York stage bow, in 1945, in *The Rugged Path*, followed by work with the American Repertory Theatre. He dabbled in producing as well; did a key part in the Fox film *House of Strangers*, turning brother Richard Conte into the police; and then worked with his dad at the Curtis Institute of Music for a spell. He returned to acting officially in 1954 and, following his Broadway role in *Fallen Angels*, was put under contract to Warner Bros. On the big screen he was the pilot in love with young Natalie Wood in *Bombers B-52*; a union officer in the trashy Civil War drama *Band of Angels*; and one of the drivers carting dangerous explosives in *Violent Road*, an Americanization of *The Wages of Fear*. Fame came, not unexpectedly, on the small screen, playing the cool private eye Stuart Bailey on the hit series, *77 Sunset Strip*. During its six-season run Warners gave him theatrical work as part of the ensembles of *The Crowded Sky* and *The Chapman Report*, as well as the starring role in a low-grade political drama *A Fever in the Blood*, as an honest judge. There was another lead, in a worthless Lana Turner soap, *By Love Possessed*, jumping into bed with her because her impotent husband can't do the job. As a movie star he was strictly low-wattage but it didn't matter. Shortly after *77 Sunset Strip* went off the air, he was back in another successful series, *The FBI*, as Inspector Lewis Erskine, and that drama settled in for a nine-year run. He returned to movies to play Audrey Hepburn's absent husband in the thriller *Wait Until Dark*, one of the passengers in *Airport 1975*, and a comical government official in the spoof *Hot Shots!* His latter-day voice work included playing the butler Alfred for the *Batman* animated series. His daughter, actress Stephanie Zimablist, was best known for the series *Remington Steele*.

Screen: 1949: House of Strangers; 1957: Bombers B-52; Band of Angels; 1958: The Deep Six; Violent Road; Girl on the Run; Too Much, Too Sun; Home Before Dark; 1960: The Crowded Sky; 1961: A Fever in the Blood; By Love Possessed; 1962: The Chapman Report; 1965: The Reward; Harlow; 1967: Wait Until Dark; 1974: Airport 1975; 1983: The Avenging/Two Against the Wind (dtv); 1989: Elmira (nUSr); 1991: Hot Shots!; 1993: Batman: Mask of the Phantasm (voice).

NY Stage: 1945: The Rugged Path; 1946: Henry VIII; What Every Woman Knows; Androcles and the Lion; 1947: Yellow Jack; 1948: Hedda Gabler; 1956: Fallen Angels.

Select TV: 1954–55: Concerning Miss Marlowe (series); 1956: The Film Maker (sp); Stover at Sublimity (sp); 1957: Execution Night (sp); 1958–64: 77 Sunset Strip (series); 1965–74: The FBI (series); 1975: Who Is the Black Dahlia?; 1978: A Family Upside Down; Terror Out of the Sky; 1979: The Best Place to Be; The Gathering Part II; 1980: Scruples (ms); 1982: Family in Blue; Beyond Witch Mountain; 1983: Baby Sister; Shooting Stars; 1986: Hotel (series); 1990: Zorro (series); 1992–98: Batman: The Animated Series (series; voice); 1993: Trade Winds (ms); 1998: Cab to Canada; 2001: The First Day.

GEORGE ZUCCO
BORN: MANCHESTER, ENGLAND, JANUARY 11, 1886. ED: RADA. DIED: MAY 28, 1960.

Where "A" level material was concerned, George Zucco was a finely tuned character player, but, relegated a peg or two to programmers and poverty row quickies, he was a star. The latter earned him a cult status of sorts, for his gallery of evil-eyed wackos, and often caused one to underrate the talents of a man who was, in fact, very adept and professional at his job. It was during a move to work in Canada that he began acting, touring with a stock company before making his official stage bow in Saskatchewan, in 1908, for *What Happened to Jones?* There followed vaudeville in the United States, military service for England during World War I, and courses at RADA, after which he became a busy performer on the London stage. In 1931, he made his motion picture bow, in Britain, playing the title role in *Dreyfus*, the unjustly imprisoned real-life Jewish captain accused of treason. Following a run on Broadway in *Victoria Regina*, he accepted an offer from MGM, who gave him the role of a psychologist in the popular 1936 sequel, *After the Thin Man*. Also for Metro, he played lawyers in both *Sinner Take All* and *Parnell*; the count who sets up Joan Crawford as a phony society lady in *The Bride Wore Red*; a secret service man in *The Firefly*; a sanitarium doctor taking care of Margaret Sullavan in *Three Comrades*; and a low-life thief using Freddie Bartholomew to help him steal in *Lord Jeff*. In 1939 he made for a fine Moriarty in the second of Basil Rathbone's Holmes entries, *The Adventures of Sherlock Holmes*; stole a deadly death ray in the thriller *Arrest Bulldog Drummond*; and fit in very nicely into the gallery of harsh faces in the towering remake of *The Hunchback of Notre Dame*, playing the prosecutor out to destroy poor Maureen O'Hara.

His appearance as the evil high priest, who revives the gauzed menace to do his bidding, in Universal's 1940 sequel, *The Mummy's Hand*, is usually credited as the beginning of his ascent into the pantheon of the horror genre. Despite the fact that he was killed off in the climax, he returned twice more for a pair of follow-ups, *The Mummy's Tomb* and *The Mummy's Ghost*. Although he could still be seen throughout the decade in top-of-the-line material like *The Black Swan*, as the unscrupulous Jamaican governor; *Week-end at the Waldorf*, as a potentate visiting the establishment; *Captain from Castile*, betraying Tyrone Power; and *The Barkleys of Broadway*, as a judge, he was given more substantial roles in the cheaper stuff. These included *The Monster and the Girl*, in which he placed the brain of an unjustly executed man into a gorilla for the sake of revenge; *Dr. Renault's Secret*, in which he stayed in simian territory, turning a gorilla into J. Carroll Naish; *The Mad Ghoul*, turning David Bruce into a zombie to rob graves; *The Black Raven*, dictating murder at a mysterious inn; *Dead Men Walk*, playing both the dead man doing the walking as well as his twin brother; *Voodoo Man*, sending unsuspecting motorists into Bela Lugosi's clutches, though it should have appeared suspicious that someone as well-spoken as Zucco was running a gas station; *The Flying Serpent*, ordering a cheesy looking winged puppet to do his deadly deeds; and *Who Killed "Doc" Robbin?* which, unlike the others, was in color and supposed to be funny on purpose. He stopped acting in 1951, nine years before his death, because of an unspecified illness that caused him to finish his days in a sanitarium.

Screen: 1931: Dreyfus/The Dreyfus Case; 1932: There Goes the Bride; The Man from Toronto; The Midshipman; 1933: The Good Companions; The Roof; 1934: Autumn Crocus; What Happened Then?; What's in a Name?; Something Always Happens; 1935: It's a Bet; 1936: After the Thin Man; Sinner Take All; The Man Who Could Work Miracles; 1937: Parnell; The Firefly; Saratoga; London by Night; Madame X; The Bride Wore Red; Conquest; Rosalie; Souls at Sea; 1938: Arsene Lupin Returns; Marie Antoinette; Lord Jeff; Fast Company; Vacation from Love; Three Comrades; Suez; Charlie Chan in Honolulu; 1939: Arrest Bulldog Drummond; The Magnificent Fraud; The Cat and the Canary; Captain Fury; The Adventures of Sherlock Holmes; Here I Am a Stranger; The Hunchback of Notre Dame; 1940: New Moon; The Mummy's Hand; Dark Streets of Cairo; Arise, My Love; 1941: The Monster and the Girl; Topper Returns; International Lady; A Woman's Face; Ellery Queen and the Murder Ring; 1942: My Favorite Blonde; Half-Way to Shanghai; The Mad Monster; The Black Swan; Dr. Renault's Secret; The Mummy's Tomb; 1943: The Mad Ghoul; The Black Raven; Dead Men Walk; Sherlock Holmes in Washington; Holy Matrimony; Never a Dull Moment; 1944: House of Frankenstein; The Seventh Cross; Shadows in the Night; The Mummy's Ghost; Voodoo Man; 1945: Hold That Blonde; Midnight Manhunt/One

Exciting Night; Sudan; Having Wonderful Crime; Confidential Agent; Fog Island; Week-end at the Waldorf; 1946: The Flying Serpent; 1947: Scared to Death; Desire Me; Captain From Castile; Moss Rose; Where There's Life; The Imperfect Lady; Lured; 1948: Tarzan and the Mermaids; Who Killed Doc Robbin?; Secret Service Investigator; Joan of Arc; The Pirate; 1949: Madame Bovary; The Secret Garden; The Barkleys of Broadway; 1950: Let's Dance; Harbor of Missing Men; 1951: David and Bathsheba; The First Legion; Flame of Stamboul.

NY Stage: 1929: Journey's End; 1935: Victoria Regina.

BIBLIOGRAPHY

Arntz, James and Thomas S. Wilson. *Julie Andrews*. Chicago: Contemporary
  Books, 1995.
Baer, D. Richard. *The Film Buff's Checklist of Motion Pictures (1912–1979)*.
  Hollywood, CA: Hollywood Film Archive, 1979.
Baltake, Joe. *The Films of Jack Lemmon*. Secaucus, NJ: Citadel Press, 1977.
Bawden, James. "Gail Patrick." *Films in Review* (May 1981): 286–294.
———. "Janet Leigh" *Films in Review* (Jan. 1979), 114.
Beaver, Jim. "John Carradine: A Venerable Eccentric." *Films in Review* (Oct.
  1979): 449–466.
Bergman, Ronald. *The United Artists Story*. New York: Crown, 1986.
Bigwood, James. "Alan Napier." *Films in Review* (Feb. 1979): 89–104.
Billman, Larry. *Fred Astaire: A Bio-Bibliography*. Westport, CT: Greenwood Press,
  1997.
Blum, Daniel. *Screen World*. Vols. 1–15, 1950–1964.
Bodeen, DeWitt. "Alice Brady: Wasn't the Aimless Malaprop She Played So Well."
  Films in Review (Nov. 1966): 555–573.
———. "Charles Farrell." *Films in Review* (Oct. 1976): 449–468.
———. "Florence Bates: Was as Valiant as a "Character Woman" as She Was
  in Actual Life." *Films in Review* (Dec. 1966): 641–654.
———. "Lewis Stone." *Films in Review* (March 1981): 138–155.
———. "Marjorie Rambeau." *Films in Review* (March 1978): 129–142.
———. "Neil Hamilton." *Films in Review* (March 1982): 147–161.
———. "Ricardo Cortez." *Films in Review* (June–July 1984): 322–335.
———. "Richard Arlen." *Films in Review* (June–July 1979): 337–353.
———. "Sessue Hayakawa: First International Japanese Film Star." *Films in
  Review* (April 1976): 193
———. "ZaSu Pitts." *Films in Review* (June–July 1980): 321–342.
Bojarski, Richard and Kenneth Beals. *The Films of Boris Karloff*. Secaucus, NJ:
  Citadel Press, 1974.
Bookbinder, Robert. *The Films of Bing Crosby*. Secaucus, NJ: Citadel Press, 1977.
Bowers, Ronald. "Gale Sondergaard: A Story of Survival." *Films in Review*
  (Aug.–Sept. 1978): 385–397.
Bragg, Melvyn. *Richard Burton: A Life*. New York: Warner Books, 1988.
Brooks, Tim. *The Complete Directory to Prime Time TV Stars, 1946–Present*.
  New York: Ballantine Books, 1987.
Brooks, Tim and Earle Marsh. *The Complete Directory to Prime Time Network and
  Cable TV Shows, 1946–Present* Sixth Edition. New York: Ballantine Books, 1995.
Brown, Barry. "Henry Travers, 1874–1965." *Films in Review* (June–July 1974):
  337–349.
Buckley, Michael. "Arthur Kennedy." *Films in Review* (Dec. 1988): 578–587, (Jan.

1989): 14–23.
———. "Dean Stockwell: An Interview." (Jan. 1985): 34–43.
———. "Gig Young: Were Life Simpler Than It Is He'd Have Fared Better."
  Films in Review (Feb. 1971): 66–84.
———. "Gloria Grahame." *Films in Review* (Dec. 1989): 578–588 (Jan.–Feb.
  1990), 2–15.
———. "Eileen Heckart." *Films in Review* (Feb. 1988): 80–90.
———. "Roddy McDowall." *Films in Review* (Sept. 1988): 386–397 (Oct.
  1988), 458–471.
———. "Tony Randall: An Interview." *Films in Review* (Feb. 1986): 66–77.
Callow, Simon. *Charles Laughton: A Difficult Actor*. New York: Fromm
  International Publishing Corporation, 1987.
Carlyle, John. "Lon McCallister: Imaged Youthful American Innocence in the Era
  of World War II." *Films in Review* (Aug.–Sept. 1972): 405–415.
Chic, Brian M. "Henry Daniell." *Films in Review* (Jan. 1983): 15–24.
Collura, Joe. "Sterling Holloway." *Films in Review* (June 1991): 172–181.
Connor, Jim. *Ann Miller: Tops in Taps: An Authorized Pictorial History*. New York:
  Franklin Watts, 1981.
Curtis, James. *Between Flops: A Biography of Preston Sturges*. New York: Limelight
  Editions, 1982.
Davis, Crit. "Joseph Schildkraut: Inherited His Belief That Acting Is More Than
  a Profession." *Films in Review* (Feb. 1973): 71–91.
DeCarl, Lennard. "Alexis Smith: Beauty and Rectitude Are Sometimes
  Indifferently Rewarded." *Films in Review* (June–July, 1970): 355–367.
Deschner, Donald. *The Complete Films of Spencer Tracy*. Secaucus, NJ: Citadel
  Press, 1993.
———. *The Films of Cary Grant*. Secaucus, NJ: Citadel Press, 1973.
Dewey, Donald. *James Stewart: A Biography*. Atlanta: Turner Publishing, 1996.
Dickens, Homer. *The Complete Films of James Cagney*. New York: Carol
  Publishing, 1989.
———. *The Films of Barbara Stanwyck*. Secaucus, NJ: Citadel Press, 1984.
———. *The Films of Gary Cooper* . Secaucus, NJ: Citadel Press, 1970.
Dooley, Roger B. "Jane Wyatt: Brought Good Manners to Some Inconsequential
  Films." *Films in Review* (Jan. 1972): 28–40.
Eames, John Douglas. *The MGM Story*. New York: Crown Publishers, 1979.
———. *The Paramount Story*. New York: Crown Publishers, 1985.
Erlewine, Michael et al. *The VideoHound & All-Movie Guide Stargazer*. Detroit:
  Visible Ink Press, 1996.
Fetrow, Alan G. *Feature Films, 1940–1949: A United States Filmography*. Jefferson,
  NC: McFarland & Company, Inc., 1994.

————. *Feature Films, 1950–1959: A United States Filmography*. Jefferson, NC: McFarland & Company, Inc., 1998.

Fields, Ronald J. *W.C. Fields: A Life on Film*. New York: St. Martin's Press, 1984.

Finstad, Suzanne. *Natasha: The Biography of Natalie Wood*. New York: Three Rivers Press, 2001.

Fishgall, Gary. *Against Type: The Biography of Burt Lancaster*. New York: Holiday House, 1995.

Fitzgerald, Michael G. *Universal Pictures: A Panoramic History in Words, Pictures, and Filmographies*. Westport, CT: Arlington House, 1977.

Fordin, Hugh. *The World of Entertainment!: Hollywood's Greatest Musicals*. Garden City, NY: Doubleday and Company, Inc., 1975.

Foster, Allan. *The Movie Traveler: A Film Fan's Guide to the UK and Ireland*. Edinburgh: Polygon, 2000.

Fricke, John. *Judy Garland: World's Greatest Entertainer*. New York: Henry Holt & Company, 1992.

Furmanek, Bob and Ron Palumbo. *Abbott and Costello in Hollywood*. New York: Perigee Books, 1991.

Godfrey, Lionel. *Paul Newman: Superstar*. New York: St. Martin's Press, 1978.

Halliwell, Leslie. *Mountain of Dreams: The Golden Years of Paramount Pictures*. New York: Stonehill Publishing Co., 1976.

Hanson, Patricia King. *The American Film Institute Catalog of Motion Pictures Produced in the United States: Feature Films, 1931–1940*. Berkeley: University of California Press, 1993.

Hardy, Phil. *The Encyclopedia of Horror Movies*. New York: Harper & Row, 1986.

————. *The Encyclopedia of Western Movies*. Minneapolis: Woodbury Press, 1984.

————. *The Overlook Film Encyclopedia: The Gangster Film*. Woodstock, NY: Overlook Press, 1998.

Harris, Robert A. and Michael S. Lasky. *The Films of Alfred Hitchcock*. Secaucus, NJ: Citadel Press, 1976.

Harvey, Stephen. *Directed by Vincente Minnelli*. New York: Harper & Row, 1989.

Hicks, Jimmie. "Charles Coburn." *Films in Review* (May 1987): 258–279.

Hirschhorn, Clive. *The Columbia Story*. New York: Crown, 1989.

————. *The Hollywood Musical*. New York: Crown, 1983.

————. *The Universal Story*. New York: Crown, 1983.

————. *The Warner Bros. Story*. New York: Crown, 1979.

Hofstede, David. *Audrey Hepburn: A Bio-Bibliography*. Westport, CT: Greenwood Press, 1994.

Holland, Larry Lee. "Adolphe Menjou." *Films in Review* (Oct. 1983): 463–473.

————. "Conrad Nagel, 1897–1970: A Forgotten Founder of the Academy of Motion Picture Arts and Sciences." *Films in Review* (May 1979): 265–282.

————. "Warner Oland." *Films in Review* (June–July 1985): 354–361.

————. "William Haines." *Films in Review* (March 1984): 165–172.

Hope, Bob and Bob Thomas. *The Road to Hollywood: My Forty-Year Love Affair with the Movies*. Garden City, NY: Doubleday & Co., Inc., 1977.

Howard, James. *The Complete Films of Orson Welles*. Secaucus, NJ: Citadel Press, 1991.

Hurley, Joseph. "Jessica Tandy and Hume Cronyn." *Films in Review* (Oct. 1983): 450–462.

Jewell, Richard B. and Vernon Harbin. *The RKO Story*. New York: Arlington House, 1982.

Juran, Robert A. *Old Familiar Faces: The Great Character Actors and Actresses of Hollywood's Golden Era*. Sarasota, FL: Movie Memories Publishing, 1995.

Karney, Robin. *The Hollywood Who's Who: The Actors and Directors in Today's Hollywood*. New York: Continuum, 1993.

Kass, Judith M. *The Films of Montgomery Clift*. Secaucus, NJ: Citadel Press, 1979.

Kline, Jim. *The Complete Films of Buster Keaton*. Secaucus, NJ: Citadel Press, 1993.

Leaming, Barbara. *Marilyn Monroe*. New York: Three Rivers Press, 1998.

Leibfred, Philip. "Anna May Wong." *Films in Review* (March 1987): 146–152.

Lenburg, Jeff et al. *The Three Stooges Scrapbook*. Secaucus, NJ: 1982.

Levy, Shawn. *King of Comedy: The Life and Art of Jerry Lewis*. New York: St. Martin's Press, 1996.

Lewis, Kevin. "Charles "Buddy" Rogers: America's Boyfriend." *Films in Review* (Dec. 1987): 578–590.

Lundquist, Gunnar. "Nils Asther: The International Star." *Films in Review* (Aug.–Sept. 1978): 385–403.

Maltin, Leonard. *Leonard Maltin's Movie & Video Guide*. 2000 Edition. New York: Signet, 1999.

————. *Leonard Maltin's Movie Encyclopedia*. New York: Plume, 1995.

————. *Movie Comedy Teams*. New York: New American Library, 1985.

————. *Our Gang: The Life and Times of the Little Rascals*. New York: Crown Publishers, 1977.

Mank, Gregory. "Colin Clive, 1900–1937." *Films in Review* (May 1980): 257–268.

————. "Lionel Atwill, 1885–1946." *Films in Review* (Mar. 1977): 129–144.

Manso, Peter. *Brando: The Biography*. New York: Hyperion, 1994.

Mantle, Burns and Garrison P. Sherwood. *The Best Plays of 1899–1909*. Philadelphia: Blakiston Company, 1944.

————. *The Best Plays of 1909–1919*. New York: Dodd, Mead and Company, 1933.

Marill, Alvin H. *The Complete Films of Edward G. Robinson*. Secaucus, NJ: Citadel Press, 1990.

————. "Eli Wallach" *Films in Review* (Aug–Sept. 1982): 400–413.

————. "Jack Hawkins, 1910–1973." *Films in Review* (Jan. 1976): 5–24.

————. "Mickey Rooney." *Films in Review* (June–July, 1982): 334–352.

————. *Movies Made for Television: The Telefeature and the Mini-Series, 1964–1984*. New York: Zoetrope, 1984.

Martin, Len D. *The Allied Artists Checklist: The Feature Films and Short Subjects, 1947–1978*. Jefferson, NC: McFarland & Company, 1993.

McCabe, John and Al Kilgore. *Laurel & Hardy*. Richard Feiner and Company, 1975.

McCarty, John. *The Complete Films of John Huston*. Secaucus, NJ: Citadel Press, 1987.

McClelland, Doug. "Barbara Hale." *Films in Review* (May 1979): 290–296.

McDonald, Gerald D. et al. *The Films of Charlie Chaplin*. New York: Bonanza Books, 1965.

McGee, Mark Thomas. *Fast and Furious: The Story of American International Pictures*. Jefferson, NC: McFarland & Company, 1984.

McGilligan, Patrick. *Cagney: The Actor as Auteur*. San Diego: A.S. Barnes & Company, Inc., 1982.

McNeil, Alex. *Total Television*. 4th Edition. New York: Penguin Books, 1996.

Michael, Paul. *The Great American Movie Book*. Englewood Cliffs, NJ: Prentice-Hall Inc., 1980.

————. *Movie Greats: The Players, Directors, Producers*. New York: Garland Books, 1969.

Monush, Barry. *International Television & Video Almanac*. 41st Edition. New York, 1996.

The New York Times Directory of the Theatre. New York: Arno Press/Quadrangle, 1972.

Newquist, Roy. *Conversations With Joan Crawford*. New York: Berkley Books, 1980.

Nolan, Jack Edmund. "Vera Miles." *Films in Review* (May 1973): 281–291.

Nollen, Scott Allen. *Boris Karloff: A Critical Account of His Screen, Stage, Radio, Television, and Recording Work*. Jefferson, NC: McFarland & Company, Inc., 1991.

Parish, James Robert. *Actors' Television Credits, 1950–1972*. Metuchen, NJ: Scarecrow Press, 1973.

————. *Hollywood Character Actors*. Carlstadt, NJ: Rainbow Books, 1979.

————. *Hollywood Players: The Thirties*. New Rochelle, NY: Arlington House, 1976.

————. *The Paramount Pretties*. New Rochelle, NY: Castle Books, 1972.

Parish, James Robert and Ronald L. Bowers. *The Golden Era: The MGM Stock Company*. New York: Bonanza, 1972.

Parish, James Robert and Lennard DeCarl. *Hollywood Players: The Forties*. New Rochelle, NY: Arlington House, 1976.

Parish, James Robert and William T. Leonard. *The Funsters*. New Rochelle, NY: Arlington House, 1979.

Parish, James R. and Michael R. Pitts. "Lon Chaney, Jr., 1906–1973." *Films in Review* (Nov. 1973): 529–548.

Parish, James Robert and Don E. Stanke. *The Glamour Girls*. New Rochelle, NY: Arlington House, 1975.

Perry, Danny. *Cult Movies: The Classics, the Sleepers, the Weird, and the Wonderful*. New York: Dell, 1981.

———. *Cult Movies 2: Fifty More of the Classics, the Sleepers, the Weird, and the Wonderful*. New York: Dell, 1983.

———. *Cult Movies 3: Fifty More of the Classics, the Sleepers, the Weird, and the Wonderful*. New York: Dell, 1988.

Perry, George. *Forever Ealing: A Celebration of the Great British Film Studio*. London: Pavilion, 1981.

Peters, Neal and David Smith. *Ann-Margret: A Photo Extravaganza and Memoir*. New York: Delilah Books, 1981.

Phillips, Gene D. *Stanley Kubrick: A Film Odyssey*. New York: Popular Library, 1975.

Pickard, Roy. "Lee J. Cobb." *Films in Review* (Nov. 1977): 525–537.

———. *The Oscar Stars: From A-Z*. London: Headline, 1996.

Quinlan, David. *British Sound Films: The Studio Years, 1928–1959*. Totowa, NJ: Barnes & Noble Books, 1985.

———. *The Film Lover's Companion: An A to Z Guide to 2,000 Stars and the Movies They Made*. Secaucus, NJ: Citadel Press, Carol Publishing Group, 1997.

———. *Quinlan's Illustrated Directory of Film Comedy Actors*. New York: Henry Holt and Company, 1992.

Quirk, Lawrence J. *The Complete Films of Ingrid Bergman*. New York: Carol Publishing, 1991.

———. *The Complete Films of William Powell*. Secaucus, NJ: Citadel Press, 1986.

———. *The Films of Fredric March*. New York: Citadel Press, 1971.

———. *The Films of Lauren Bacall*. Secaucus, NJ: Citadel Press, 1986.

———. *The Films of Ronald Colman*. Secaucus, NJ: Citadel Press, 1977.

———. *The Films of William Holden*. Secaucus, NJ: Citadel Press, 1973.

Ricci, Mark et al. *The Complete Films of John Wayne*. Secaucus, NJ: Citadel Press, 1983.

Ringgold, Gene. *The Films of Rita Hayworth: The Legend and Career of a Love Goddess*. Secaucus, NJ: Citadel Press, 1974.

Ringgold, Gene and DeWitt Bodeen. *Chevalier: The Films and Career of Maurice Chevalier* . Secaucus, NJ: Citadel Press, 1973.

Ringgold, Gene and Clifford McCarty. *The Films of Frank Sinatra*. Secaucus, NJ: Citadel Press, 1971.

Roberts, Florian. "Elsa Lanchester." *Films in Review* (Aug.–Sept. 1976): 385–404.

Roberts, Randy and James S. Olson. *John Wayne: American*. New York: Free Press, 1995.

Rooney, Mickey. *Life Is Too Short*. New York: Ballantine Books, 1991.

Sackett, Susan. *Hollywood Sings!: An Inside Look at Sixty Years of Academy Award Nominated Songs*. New York: Billboard Books, 1995.

Schickel, Richard. *Harold Lloyd: The Shape of Laughter*. Boston: New York Graphic Society, 1974.

Server, Lee. "Gloria Stuart." *Films in Review* (Feb. 1988): 66–75.

Shipman, David. *The Great Movie Stars: The International Years*. New York: St. Martin's Press Inc., 1972.

———. *The Great Movie Stars 1: The Golden Years*. Boston: Little, Brown and Company, 1989.

———. *The Great Movie Stars 2: The International Years*. Boston: Little, Brown and Company, 1989.

St. Charnez, Casey. *The Complete Films of Steve McQueen*. Secaucus, NJ: Citadel, 1992.

Stine, Whitney and Bette Davis. *Bette Davis: Mother Goddam*. New York: Berkley Books, 1974.

Stricklyn, Ray. *Angels & Demons: One Actor's Hollywood Journey*. Los Angeles: Belle Publishing, 1999.

Thomas, Tony. *The Films of Gene Kelly: Song and Dance Man*. Secaucus, NJ: Citadel Press, 1974.

Thomas, Tony and Aubrey Solomon. *The Films of 20th Century-Fox*. Secaucus, NJ: Citadel Press, 1985.

Thompson, Howard. *The New York Times Guide to Movies on TV*. Chicago: Quadrangle Books, 1970.

Tuska, John. *The Complete Films of Mae West*. Secaucus, NJ: Citadel Press, 1992.

Vermilye, Jerry. *The Complete Films of Audrey Hepburn*. Secaucus, NJ: Citadel, 1996.

———. *The Complete Films of Laurence Olivier*. Secaucus, NJ: Citadel Press, 1992.

Von Gunden, Kenneth. *Alec Guinness: The Films*. Jefferson, NC: McFarland & Company, 1987.

Walker, Alexander. *Fatal Charm: The Life of Rex Harrison*. New York: St. Martin's Press, 1992.

Walker, John. *Halliwell's Filmgoer's & Video Viewer's Companion*. New York: Harper Collins, 1995.

Weldon, Michael. *The Psychotronic Encyclopedia of Film*. New York: Ballantine Books, 1983.

———. *The Psychotronic Video Guide*. New York: St. Martin's Griffin, 1996.

Wiley, Mason and Damien Bona. *Inside Oscar: The Unofficial History of the Academy Awards*. 10th Anniversary Edition. New York: Ballantine Books, 1996.

Williams, Lucy Chase. *The Complete Films of Vincent Price*. Secaucus, NJ: Citadel Press, 1995.

Willis, John. *Screen World*. Volumes 16–53. New York: Crown/Applause Books.

Winecoff, Charles. *Split Image: The Life of Anthony Perkins*. New York: Dutton, 1996.

Zimmerman, Paul D. and Burt Goldblatt. *The Marx Brothers at the Movies*. New York: Signet, 1968.